The Cambridge Guide to American Theatre

This new and updated encyclopedic *Guide,* with over 2,700 cross-referenced entries, covers all aspects of the American theatre from its earliest history to the present. Entries include people, venues, and companies scattered through the United States, plays and musicals, and theatrical phenomena. Additionally, there are some 100 topical entries covering theatre in major U.S. cities and such disparate subjects as Asian American theatre, Chicano theatre, censorship, Filipino American theatre, one-person performances, performance art, and puppetry. Major popular forms are represented in entries such as "circus," "burlesque," "vaudeville," and "tent shows," and it provides a strong emphasis on contemporary theatre while retaining its unique historical perspective. Highly illustrated, the *Guide* is supplemented with a thorough historical survey as Introduction, a Bibliography of major sources published since the compilation of the first edition, and a unique and valued Biographical Index covering over 3,200 individuals mentioned in the text. This new edition includes hundreds of new and updated entries, making it the most up-to-date guide to American theatre available.

Emeritus Professor of Theatre and English at Brown University, Providence, Rhode Island (where he also held the Asa Messer distinguished chair), Don B. Wilmeth has received career achievement awards from the Association for Theatre in Higher Education, the American Society for Theatre Research (for whom he served as president), the New England Theatre Conference, and the Theatre Library Association. He is Dean Emeritus of the College of Fellows of the American Theatre. In addition to two editions of this book, he is the author, editor, or coeditor of fourteen other books, including the award-winning *George Frederick Cooke: Machiavel of the Stage* and the three-volume *Cambridge History of American Theatre* (coedited with Christopher Bigsby). He was an advisory editor for the *Cambridge Guide to Theatre,* contributed one of three sections to *Theatre in the Colonies and United States, 1750–1915: A Documentary History* (Cambridge), and has edited volumes of plays, written for dozens of reference works and essay collections, and served as a frequent consultant to documentary film projects. He has been editor of two book series: Cambridge Studies in American Theatre and Drama and the Palgrave Studies in Theatre and Performance History. He is also a stage director and actor. Currently residing in Keene, New Hampshire, he holds a courtesy appointment at Keene State College.

The Cambridge Guide to American Theatre

SECOND HARDCOVER EDITION

Edited by

DON B. WILMETH
Brown University

Assistant to the Editor

LEONARD JACOBS

CAMBRIDGE
UNIVERSITY PRESS

CAMBRIDGE UNIVERSITY PRESS
Cambridge, New York, Melbourne, Madrid, Cape Town, Singapore,
São Paulo, Delhi

Cambridge University Press
The Edinburgh Building, Cambridge CB2 8RU, UK

Published in the United States of America
by Cambridge University Press, New York

www.cambridge.org
Information on this title: www.cambridge.org/9780521835381

First published 2007

Printed in the United Kingdom at the University Press, Cambridge

A catalogue record for this publication is available from the British Library.

ISBN 978-0-521-83538-1 hardback

Contents

Preface   *page* vii

Acknowledgments   xi

List of contributors   xiii

List of entries deleted from the paperback edition (1996)   xiv

List of topical entries   xv

Note to the reader   xvi

Introduction   1

Alphabetical entries   47

Bibliography of select books since 1995 on the
     American theatre   709

Biographical index   721

Preface

This new edition of the *Cambridge Guide to American Theatre* focuses more than previous editions on the contemporary scene while retaining its original historical perspective. Original contributors are credited for information up to 1992; all but a few updates since have been the responsibility of the editor of this present version, unless otherwise indicated by a second (or, in some instances, a third) set of initials. A few entries have been replaced with entirely new ones; in these instances the initials are of the new author. A majority of entries have undergone some fine-tuning. In order to accommodate updates, corrections, and especially new entries, it has been necessary to delete some fifty entries, conflate or trim many others, and reshape a few. Completely deleted entries are listed elsewhere in the front matter. Illustrations have been limited as well, with an emphasis on earlier images (more contemporary photographs are readily available elsewhere) and unusual theatrical ventures; a balance has been sought in iconography, in most instances providing theatrical insight (rather than "civilian" portraits). Sources no longer appear at the end of entries (though biographical resources are sometimes given within an entry), again for space reasons. Near the end there is provided a Bibliography of useful published sources since 1995, organized into several categories. A source of limited value – if at all – when the first edition was undertaken in 1990 is the Internet. Today, it is virtually impossible not to "Google" a name or theatre company, even though data found via this avenue must always be corroborated. Uniquely, the *Guide* concludes with a Biographical Index that provides dates (when available) and major occupations (keyed to entries in the text) for a majority of individuals mentioned but without their own entries. Users of earlier editions have been most laudatory about this feature of the *Guide*.

This *Guide* has been designed to offer scholars, students, and general readers a comprehensive view of the history and present practice of the theatre in the United States. We hope it will be a useful reference source for concise, carefully selected, and authoritative information on a broad spectrum of topics relating to American theatre from its earliest history to the present (our cutoff date for most substantive data has been

11 June 2006, the day of the Tony Award presentation for the 2005–6 season), beginning with a detailed Introduction. Death dates and a few key updates have been inserted as late as production of the volume would allow (early June 2007). There has been a conscious effort to be sensitive to not only contemporary theatre but to theatre outside of New York City. In addition, although a one-volume format necessarily limits the contents (and has dictated the inclusion of a large number of relatively brief entries), there has been a concerted effort to cover American theatre in the broadest possible terms; indeed, the original goal in 1993, in part, was to help redefine, through the variegated coverage of the *Guide,* just what American theatre *is;* this edition continues this aim, albeit lines must invariably be drawn. Nevertheless, we have included numerous topics that often fall outside of what was once considered theatre – such as circus, magic, vaudeville, burlesque, and folk festivals. There are entries not only on these popular forms but also on numerous marginalized and minority groups and artists, including gay/lesbian, African American, Asian American, Filipino American, and Nuyorican theatre, among others. (In this edition the decision has been made not to hyphenate such terms.) A modest amount of attention is given to performance art, especially those artists who tend toward more theatrical presentations. Although in all these instances the coverage has by necessity often been slighter than wished, we nevertheless believe users of the *Guide* will find many categories covered that have too frequently been omitted from similar reference works, including other one-volume references compiled since our first efforts.

We have also included overviews on several major cities – Atlanta, Boston, Philadelphia, Los Angeles, Seattle, San Francisco, Chicago, Minneapolis, and Washington, DC – that have both an active past and present history of theatre. We are grateful to several of the original authors for help in updating several of these entries, and to Michael B. Dixon for assistance with Minneapolis. (New York's theatrical history permeates the volume as a whole.) In addition, we have tried to include major companies (and in some cases venues) throughout the country, thus truly providing national coverage. With cross-listings some geographical locales can be constructed by the user.

Moreover, we have included a highly select number of entries on certain specific plays and musicals; these do not provide detailed plot synopses or textual analyses (since this is not a guide to drama as literature), but rather give brief stage histories, touch on themes, and offer just enough information on plot or structure to lead the user to the next step – which, in most instances, will be to read the actual script. Users should note that, unless indicated otherwise, the dates given for plays refer to first performances. We have avoided the truly obscure titles and productions by both choice and necessity (space), although to some users there will be apparent obscurities.

On the assumption that there are more guides to film than to the stage, actors whose careers primarily have been on the screen have been omitted (with some obvious exceptions); for artists who have extensive media careers as well as stage ones, the latter has been highlighted. Although the names of many foreign theatre artists can be found scattered through the *Guide,* only those who have settled in the United States, are of seminal importance, and/or spent a large portion of their career working on U.S. stages have their own entries. If one wishes to trace the activities of an individual who is mentioned in the text but does not have a major entry, it is often possible to do so via this volume's Biographical Index (compiled by the editor). This index is quite exhaustive, although some minor figures have been omitted, as has one major one – William Shakespeare, who is cited so often that listing him would add pages to the index. Note that every reasonable effort has been made, including personal contact by either the editor or the assistant to the editor, Leonard Jacobs, to locate dates for those names included in this index, but in some instances this has been difficult or impossible. We would welcome for future editions any missing dates provided by users of this *Guide.*

Original entries in the 1993 edition were written by more than eighty contributors, whose initials appear beneath their original assignments. In some cases, as indicated above, the result of extensive collaborations, two sets of initials appear. (A list of contributors is provide in the front matter of this volume, matching initials against names.) Major entries updated by the original author have initials followed by an asterisk (*). Contributors are ultimately responsible for the reliability of their individual entries (up to updates, the responsibility of the editor), although the original editors attempted to verify any questionable fact. A sizable number of corrections have been made in this edition, thanks in part to careful users of the *Guide.* We are extraordinarily grateful for the excellent work of our original army of scholars, researchers, and writers, without which this *Guide* would not have been possible. We have tried, within the limitations of a reference work and the contraints of our general style, to allow original and new contributors to speak with their own voices and, when appropriate, to express their own points of view. Indeed, on occasion more than one contributor has dealt with overlapping subjects, and thus several points of view are represented – a situation that we consider an asset rather than a liability.

Our original contributors carefully chose details and emphases to highlight the importance of each entry's inclusion. Attributions for all quotations, although not always included in the *Guide,* were indeed supplied by the contributors, thus making it possible for us to verify their accuracy when necessary. The editor of this edition has followed the same formula.

The most difficult stage in the evolution of a reference work of this sort is, of course, the selection of individual entries. The various lists of deletions and additions for its two hardback and single paperback editions went through many phases, with input from numerous individuals. This job was no easier for this edition than it was for the first. Ultimately, however, the current editor is responsible for all choices, and contributors and advisors cannot be held accountable for some obvious oversight. Such discoveries are unavoidable, for a one-volume guide can only be selective, and editors admittedly often divulge their own predilections and biases – certainly true in my case – despite a concerted effort for balance and objective coverage of essentials. What is most regretted is the necessary exclusion once more of a sizable number of worthy candidates, especially theatre academics and writers. In this edition, however, 340 new entries have been added, again from a much longer list of possibilities.

We have tried to make the *Guide* accessible in many ways. In addition to the aforementioned Biographical Index, there is a list of Topical Entries at the beginning of the *Guide,* intended to direct readers to more comprehensive entries of interest. One may begin on the macro level by reading the Introduction (in part or in whole), then move on to a subtopic within the history (e.g., musical theatre), and end up checking entries for specific plays, companies, and venues cross-referenced in that entry. Alternatively, starting at the micro level, an entry for a specific individual or play might lead to entries on certain cities or performance categories. Cross-referencing, shown in small capitals, is extensive but not exhaustive; topics are cross-referenced when they can in some obvious way enlighten a specific entry. Entries are listed alphabetically, on a word-by-word basis. (We have used the spelling "theatre" throughout, except where it appears as Theater in a proper name – often slippery to determine.)

This *Guide* was originally a spin-off from the *Cambridge Guide to Theatre* edited by Martin Banham, to whom we remain indebted; users of this *Guide* will find that source invaluable as a supplement to this one. Other similar references of value are listed in the Bibliography.

Acknowledgments

The editor and contributors are indebted to too many librarians, archivists, and other individuals to enumerate here; however, without their expertise this volume would have been impossible. The editor is especially grateful for the untiring efforts of Leonard Jacobs, who served as his assistant, vetting new entries, writing numerous key new ones, and in general serving as a sounding board from the beginning. Similarly, Tice L. Miller, coeditor of the first edition, friend, and colleague, contributed in numerous ways whenever needed, including the writing of new entries and updating of many of his original ones. Specifically, for the present edition I am also grateful for special assistance and advice to the following (among others unintentionally omitted): Arnold Aronson (who updated a number of crucial topical entries), Eric Bentley, Sarah Brown, Kate Burton, Drew Campbell (a new contributor who updated several entries on design and technical theatre), Marvin Carlson (author of updates on theory), David Carlyon, Philip Carrubba, Tom Connolly, Ramona Curry, William W. Demastes, Richard Dietrich, Michael Bigelow Dixon, Liz Engelman, Oskar Eustis, Caitlin Fitzwater, Brenda Foley, Evelina Fernandez, Ann Haugo, Nancy Hereford, Jorge Huerta (contributor to entries on Chicano and Latino theatre), Jeffrey Eric Jenkins (current editor of the *Best Plays* series and always eager to be of assistance), C. Lee Jenner (my source without equal for current programs), Odai Johnson, William Davies King, the late Warren Kliewer, Joseph Kissane, Michèle LaRue, Esther Kim Lee, Robert Leonard, Martha LoMonaco, Felicia H. Londré, Ashley Lucas, Adrienne Macki, Jay Malacher, Laurence Maslon, Jeffrey Mason, Cary Mazer, the late Arthur Miller, Tim Miller, Heather Nathans, Bobbi Owens (costume authority par excellence and an unselfish and eager contributor to this edition), Ralph B. Peña, Carol Petersen, Edwin Quist, Amy Richard, Michael Ritchie, Annalisa Rosmarin, John Rouse, Robert Schanke, Rebecca Schneider (helpful with performance-art entries), Jimmy Seacat, Laurence Senelick (who updated several topical entries), James Shearwood, Raven Snook, Julie Strandberg, Curt Tofteland, Paula Vogel, Ronald Wainscott, Julia Walker, Wesley Williams, and William S. Yellow Robe Jr.

It would be a great slight if I did recognize here those contributors who have died during the evolution of the *Guide*. These were great experts and close friends, each irreplaceable: Alec Baron, John Degen, Errol G. Hill, James Kotsilibas-Davis, Stephen Langley, Nellie McCaslin, Richard Moody, M. Elizabeth Osborn, and Louis Sheaffer.

At Cambridge University Press, Sarah Stanton served as initiator and early advisor to the initial project; throughout the process she has always been available for advice and counsel. In the reference department in the U.K., Caroline Bundy supported the idea of a paperback edition following the official first edition, and efficiently and enthusiastically encouraged that effort from its inception. Just prior to her retirement she endorsed this new edition. The present edition then passed to the capable hands of Victoria L. Cooper and Rebecca Jones. With Michael Gnat we were fortunate to have a superb production editor for this hardback edition, not only perspicacious but truly eagle-eyed and thankfully knowledgeable about the theatre as well; his suggestions have made this a better and more accessible *Guide,* and we were lucky that he could both copy-edit and typeset the new edition. Finally, we are very much in the debt of all those before us who contributed to the study of American theatre history, and especially to those responsible for the important standard theatre references that enabled the present volume. (Some of these individuals are included in the Bibliography for this edition, and others appear in the first editions.)

Contributors

Note: † = deceased; • = new contributor to this edition.

AA	Arnold Aronson	GSA	Gordon A. Armstrong	NK	Nicolás Kanellos
AB	Alec Baron†	GW	George Woodyard	NMcC	Nellie McCaslin†
AC	Andrew (Drew) Campbell•	HFP	Hilary F. Poole	NP	Naima Prevots
AEG	A. E. Green	JA	James Aikens	NS	Nahma Sandrow
AF	Angelika Festa	JD	John Degen†	PAD	Peter A. Davis
AH	Ann Haugo•	JDM	Jeffrey D. Mason	PCK	Philip C. Kolin
AHS	Arthur H. Saxon	JDo	Jill Dolan	PT	Peter Thomson
AR	Amy Richard•	JER	Joel E. Rubin	RAH	Roger A. Hall
AS	Alisa Solomon	JH	Jorge Huerta•	RAS	Robert A. Schanke
BBW	Barry B. Witham	JHo	John Houchin•	RE	Ronald Engle
BCM	Brenda C. Murphy	JK-D	James Kotsilibas-Davis†	REK	Richard E. Kramer
BF	Brenda Foley•	JLB	John L. Bracewell	RG	Randy Gener•
BM	Bogdan Mischiu	KF	Kathy Fletcher	RHW	Ronald H. Wainscott
BMcC	Bruce A. McConachie	KME	Kathryn Marguerite Ervin	RJ	Ricky Jay
BMcN	Brooks McNamara	KN	Kent Neely	RKB	Rosemarie K. Bank
BO	Bobbi Owen	LAB	Larry Brown	RM	Richard Moody†
CI	Christopher Innes	LDC	Larry D. Clark	RP	Richard Poole•
CLJ	C. Lee Jenner	LF	Lisa Fusillo	RS	Rebecca Schneider•
DanB	Dan Bacalzo•	LJ	Leonard Jacobs•	RW	Ron West
DB	David Bradby	LM	Laurence Maslon	SF	Scott Fosdick
DBW	Don B. Wilmeth	LS	Laurence Senelick	SG	Spencer Golub
DC	David Carlyon•	LSh	Louis Sheaffer†	SL	Stephen Langley†
DJW	Daniel J. Watermeier	MB	Misha Berson	SMA	Stephen M. Archer
DM	Dorothy Mandel	MBan	Martin Banham	STC	Scott T. Cummings•
DMcD	Douglas McDermott	MBD	Michael B. Dixon•	SW	Stanley Weintraub
EGH	Errol G. Hill†	MC	Marvin Carlson	TC	Thomas Connolly
EH	Erin Hurley	MCH	Mary C. Henderson	TH-S	Tori Haring-Smith
EK	Eileen Kearney	MEO	M. Elizabeth Osborn†	TL	Thomas Leabhart
ER	Elizabeth Ramirez	MF	Mark Fearnow	TLM	Tice L. Miller
FB	Frances Bzowski†	MK	Margaret M. Knapp	TP	Thomas Postlewait
FH	Foster Hirsch	MR	Maarten Reilingh	WD	Weldon Durham
FHL	Felicia H. Londré	MS	Maxine S. Seller	WJM	Walter J. Meserve
GD	Geraldine Duclow	MSL	Martha S. LoMonaco•		
GL	George Latshaw†	MvW	Manon van de Water•		

Entries Deleted from the Paperback Edition (1996)

academic theatre
Albertson, Jack
Allen, Jay Presson
Amen Corner, The
American Theatre Company
Angelou, Maya
At the Foot of the Mountain
Autumn Garden, The
Babe, Thomas
Bacall, Lauren
Balsam, Martin
Barton, Lucy
Bates, Kathy
Bel Geddes, Barbara
Bovasso, Julie
Broadway Alliance, The
Capalbo, Carmen
Chelsea Theatre Center
D.C. Black Repertory Theatre
Downing, Robert
Dukes, David
d'Usseau, Arnaud
Futz
Gerard, Rolf
Heifner, Jack
Hogan's Goat

Holy Ghosts
I Never Sang for My Father
Iron Clad Agreement
Journey of the Fifth Horse
Kalem, T. E.
Kanin, Fay
Kroll, Jack
Langfelder, Dulcinea
Lanier, Sidney
Lee, Franne
Loose Ends
Manhattan Punch Line
Noonan, John Ford
Pawley, Thomas D., III
Purdy, James
Porter, Stephen
Rahman, Aishah
Road Company, The
Servant in the House, The
Stavis, Barrie
Turner, Darwin
Voelpel, Fred
Weiner, Bernard
White, Edgar
Wilson, Edwin
Woodward, Charles, Jr.

Topical Entries

African American theatre
agents
AIDS in the American theatre
alternative theatre
animal impersonation
animals as performers
architecture, theatre
Asian American theatre
Atlanta
awards, theatrical
borscht belt
Boston
Brecht in the American theatre
burlesque show
caricature/caricaturists
censorship
Chautauqua and Lyceum
Chekhov on the American stage
Chicago
Chicano theatre
children's theatre
circus in America
clubs, theatrical
collective theatre groups
community theatre/
    Little Theatre movement
costume
criticism
Cuban American theatre
dance in the American theatre
documentary theatre
dramatic theory
economics
ethnic theatre
female/male impersonation

feminist theatre
Filipino American theatre
fires
folk and festival performance
frontier theatre
gay and lesbian theatre
Gilbert and Sullivan in America
Gypsy Robe
Hispanic theatre
Ibsen on the American Stage
industrial drama movement
international stars and
    companies
Los Angeles
magic in the United States
medicine shows
mime/pantomime
Minneapolis–St. Paul
minstrel show
musical theatre
Native Americans portrayed
    onstage
Native American ritual/theatre
New Vaudeville
New York City theatres
nightclubs
nudity
Nuyorican theatre
Off-Broadway
Off-Off Broadway
one-person peformances
outdoor drama
pageants/pageantry
participatory theatre
performance art

periodicals/serials
Philadelphia
photographers
playbill/program
pornographic theatre
puppetry in the U.S.
resident nonprofit professional
    theatre
revue
San Francisco
scenic design
Seattle
Shakespeare on the American
    stage
Shakespearean festivals
Shaw and the American theatre
showboats
societies and associations,
    theatrical
sound in the American theatre
stage lighting
stock companies
summer stock
support services
Syndicate, Theatrical
tent show
Toby
toy theatre, or juvenile drama
training, actor
unions
vaudeville
Washington, DC
Wild West exhibition
Yankee theatre
Yiddish theatre

Note to the Reader

Entries are listed alphabetically on a word-by-word basis, ignoring hyphens and apostrophes. Thus "Arch Street Theatre" appears before "architecture"; "de Mille" before "DeBar."

Names beginning with "Mc" have been ordered as though spelled "Mac," "St." has been alphabetized as "Saint."

Those parts of a person's name that are or were not commonly used are placed in parentheses: e.g., Boothe (Luce), Clare. Where people adopted different names, the alternative names appear in square brackets after the more familiar one: e.g., Astaire [né Austerlitz], Fred.

Cross-referencing, shown in small capitals, is extensive but not exhaustive; topics are cross-referenced when they can in some obvious way enlighten a specific entry. Initial articles in play titles are not included in cross-references: e.g., *The* CRUCIBLE is found under the letter C.

"Theatre" has been spelled as such unless a proper name is given as Theater (e.g., Guthrie Theater). Careful attention has been paid to such distinctions.

Introduction: Survey from the beginning to the present

1. To the Civil War

The early history of the American theatre is largely one of the transference of European traditions, primarily those of provincial England, and a gradual development toward self-identity, which did not reach its full potential until after WWI. Early settlers in the colonies, many representing the same antitheatre element that existed in England, through the exigencies of the times diverted their energies into other and more complex channels than entertainment. As actors in the real-life drama of survival in hostile surroundings, colonists, with some notable exceptions, reflected Benjamin Franklin's attitude: "After the first cares for the necessities of life are over, we shall come to think of the embellishments."

The earliest records of theatre in the New World were not English in origin at all; indeed, the initial dramatic performances were the NATIVE AMERICAN RITUALS performed by Indians of the North and South. Early in the 16th century the Spanish discovered Aztec performances in Mexico that blended song, dance, comic byplay, and animal imitations; warlike tribes in the U.S. Northeast, though less inclined to organized theatricals, had variegated revels; and tribes in the Pacific Northwest created elaborate stage effects for dramatizations of tribal mythology. More complex theatre, however, is tenuously documented as having occurred in Spanish as early as 1538 in the Southwest and Mexico and by 1606 in French, in what is now Canada.

With the establishment of the first settlement (Jamestown, VA, 1607) in what would become the U.S., two traditions were quickly established among the English-speaking residents. The southern colonies, especially the Royalist colony of Virginia, were more congenial to the theatre; Puritan New England and Quaker-dominated Pennsylvania were vehemently against this frivolous pastime, although William Penn's efforts were inevitably overturned by regal veto, the king and his court being strong supporters of the theatre in England. Nonetheless, in various colonies between 1700 and 1716 laws were passed against the theatre with some effect. In Massachusetts, Increase Mather expressed the typical Puritan attitude when he wrote in 1687 that "there is much discourse of beginning Stage-Plays in New England. The last year Promiscuous Dancing was openly practised." Despite such outcries, there were local amateur theatricals from an early date. A nonextant piece called *Ye Bare and Ye Cubb,* the first recorded play in English presented in the colonies, was written by one William Darby of Accomac Country, VA, and performed in 1665 by Darby, Cornelius Wilkinson, and Philip Howard in Cowles Tavern, though this is the last recorded performance in Virginia until 1702. In 1687 a BOSTON innkeeper named John Wing attempted to outfit a room in his establishment for theatrical use, but to no avail: Attitudes like Mather's and the protests of Judge Samuel Sewall ended the brief experiment. There is evidence, however, that three years later a Harvard College student, Benjamin Colman, wrote the first play (*Gustavus Vasa*) by an American to be acted in the colonies. In Virginia students at William and Mary College offered in 1702 the recitation of a "pastoral colloquy" before the governor. Other colloquies of this sort were offered at other institutions of higher learning. Between 1699 and 1702 a Richard Hunter petitioned for permission to produce plays in New York, then a town of 4,436 people; it was granted, but no more is known. On 6 May 1709, however, the Governor's Council in New York forbade "play acting and prize fighting," with no rationale provided.

Early evidence of professional efforts is scattered and imprecise. The British vagabond player Anthony (Tony) Aston is generally credited as the first professional actor in America; in 1703, in his early 20s, he acted in "Charles Town," SC, writing that he "turn'd *Player* and *Poet,* and wrote one Play on the Subject of the Country." He then claims to have gone to New York. His play is unknown, and in 1704 he returned to London. In 1715, the first known play written and published in America appeared. Written by Governor Robert Hunter of New York, *Androboros* is a satire on the citizens of that city and the New York Senate. There is no record of performance.

For the next 35 years theatrical activity was sporadic. In 1716, in Williamsburg, VA, the most advanced town in the colonies to promote theatre, William Levingston, who ran a dancing school, built a theatre that was operated by his indentured servants William and Mary Stagg until Levingston's death in 1729. In 1724 a makeshift playhouse (The New Booth) was built in the Society Hill section of PHILADELPHIA for "roap dancing" and the traditional clown pieces called Pickleherring. The 1730s marks the advancement of Charleston as a theatrical center and the erection of a theatre in DOCK ST. in 1736. During the same period there was limited activity in New York: In 1730 an amateur production of *Romeo and Juliet* was presented, the first SHAKESPEARE ON THE AMERICAN STAGE; in 1732 a space above a commercial establishment was turned into a playing space; and in 1735 at "The New Theatre" (a converted warehouse in Pearl St.) a season of recent English plays, including *The Beaux' Stratagem,* was presented.

A sustained record of professional theatre in Philadelphia, which quickly became America's theatrical center until about 1825, dates from 1749 and is associated with the activities of the first professional company known in the colonies under WALTER MURRAY AND THOMAS KEAN, about whom we know virtually nothing. In August they performed in Plumstead's Warehouse, converted for use as a playhouse; by February they were performing in New York in a converted building in Nassau St. In October 1751 they opened a new, crudely built wooden playhouse in Williamsburg, played in Maryland the following year as The Virginia Company of Comedians, and then drifted into obscurity. They had, however, as historian Hugh F. Rankin indicates, acted "as an advance agent for those to follow, whetting the appetite of the colonials for the drama and upon occasion wearing down religious and moralistic opposition."

The next chapter in the history of theatre in America is the story of one company, The London Company of Comedians (renamed in 1763 The AMERICAN COMPANY of Comedians), and their total dominance of the theatrical scene for 50 years, beginning in 1752 under the leadership of LEWIS HALLAM SR. and continuing from 1758 under DAVID DOUGLASS, who married Hallam's widow. The Hallam Company, sent to America on speculation by Lewis's eldest brother, William, who remained in London, arrived in Williamsburg with a completely professional company of 12 adults and 3 children, a complete repertoire of plays, and basic scenery and costumes. Operating on a sharing system, the company began their first season at Kean's old playhouse on 16 September with *The Merchant of Venice;* in July 1754 they moved to New York, carrying with them a letter of endorsement from Governor Dinwiddie to the governor of New York. Until October 1754 they played in New York, Philadelphia, Annapolis, and Charleston, spending the next three years in Jamaica, where Lewis Hallam died in 1755. Douglass, an erstwhile actor and printer, brought the company back to New York in 1758, and within six years had added "American" to their name. Despite continued opposition from all quarters (Puritan, Quaker, Lutheran, Presbyterian, Baptist), Douglass, with LEWIS HALLAM JR. as leading man, took his company up and down the East Coast, building new theatres or revamping old buildings, and introducing significant new British plays to the public. In the early 1760s Douglass even attempted an invasion of New England, first in Newport, RI, in 1761, and the next year in Providence – both stops a challenge to his ingenuity. In order to avoid criticism, he apparently advertised his plays as "moral dialogues," and in Providence he called his makeshift playhouse a "schoolhouse." Literally drummed out of town, Douglass returned to New York, where he opened the temporary Chapel of Beekman Street Theatre in 1761, followed in 1766 and 1767 by the construction of two more important and permanent theatres.

The first permanent theatre on the American continent, the SOUTHWARK THEATRE (1766), which stood until 1912, also was the scene for the first professionally produced play by a native author: Thomas Godfrey's *The Prince of Parthia,* a heroic tragedy in blank verse set in Parthia near the beginning of the Christian era – and thus in no way American in subject matter – premiered on 24 April 1767. It was sheer chance that this play earned its historic position, for a play called *The Disappointment* by Thomas Forrest was to receive that honor but was abruptly withdrawn because it contained "personal reflections unfit for the stage." Douglass's second major venture, the JOHN STREET THEATRE, opened 7 December 1767, predominating among NEW YORK CITY THEATRES for 30 years.

On 20 October 1774 the Continental Congress forbade all extravagance and dissipation, including stage entertainments; Douglass and his company returned to the West Indies the following year. Other than military theatricals, theatre ceased during the hostilities, though plays – many little more than political satire in dialogue form and the majority unperformed – were written during the period, including those by MERCY OTIS WARREN, HUGH HENRY BRACKENRIDGE, and ROBERT MUNFORD. Also written were anonymous pieces such as *The Blockheads,* inspired by the performance in Boston of General John Burgoyne's farce *The Blockade of Boston,* as well as John Leacock's *The Fall of British Tyranny* (both 1776). The real activity, however, took place among the military on both sides. In 1775 the John Street was renamed the Theatre Royal and presented a long series of dramatic productions performed by the British military, until their evacuations in 1783. The same was true in other major cities, such as Boston, where a theatre was organized in Faneuil Hall during 1775–7, and Philadelphia, where a Captain Delancey and Captain John André, later involved with Benedict Arnold, were leaders of a theatrical group under General William Howe. Despite edicts to the contrary, the Continental Army also performed: At Valley Forge, for example, Washington's troops presented Addison's *Cato* in 1778.

After the Revolution, in 1782, professionals began to return. Lewis Hallam Jr. brought back the Old American Company from Jamaica in 1784, picking up where they had left off in 1774. Along with JOHN HENRY, they were the major actors of the day, joined soon by THOMAS WIGNELL. On 16 April 1787 the reinstated company offered the first professional production of a native American comedy on an American subject: ROYALL TYLER's *The CONTRAST,* which, among other firsts, introduced Jonathan the stage YANKEE, the prototype of many subsequent Yankees and the first native type to be developed. With the elimination of all repression, Philadelphia was stimulated as a theatre center due to the efforts of Wignell and Alexander Reinagle, a musician, who in 1794 opened the superior CHESTNUT STREET THEATRE with a new group of actors. After this period of reestablishment, the 1790s became a decade of rapid expansion. Wignell erected theatres in Baltimore (1794) and Washington (1800); in 1792 JOHN HODGKINSON joined the Old American Company; with the repealing of restrictive laws in New England, Boston and Providence became important centers, especially with the opening of Boston's FEDERAL STREET THEATRE in 1794, followed two years later by the Haymarket; and other scattered activity spread theatre throughout the young country, including French-speaking theatres in Charleston (1794) and in New Orleans (1791, though not part of the U.S. until 1803). In 1798 New York kept pace with Philadelphia with the opening of the PARK (New) THEATRE, where WILLIAM DUNLAP, whose drama *The Father* had been performed at the John Street in 1789, initially became a partner of Lewis Hallam Jr. and John Hodgkinson but ultimately assumed the management, recording a career of ups and downs, ending in bankruptcy in 1805. After a brief period of management by actor THOMAS ABTHORPE COOPER, STEPHEN PRICE, America's first professional manager, took control in 1809 and, by encouraging star appearances, beginning with GEORGE FREDERICK COOKE in 1810, helped undermine the stock system. Actors such as Cooper and JOHN HOWARD PAYNE (remembered primarily as a playwright) exploited the starring possibilities, and – after the uncertainties of the War of 1812 – a steady flow of actors from England appeared, including in the 1820s Edmund Kean, JUNIUS BRUTUS BOOTH, WILLIAM B. WOOD, WILLIAM WARREN SR., TYRONE POWER, LAURA KEENE, Charles Kean, and JOHN BROUGHAM, to mention only a few.

More significant than foreign imports of stars and plays was the slow Americanization of the theatre, which accelerated during the first half of the 19th century. Native-born stars began to emerge in the 1820s, beginning with EDWIN FORREST, America's first great actor and the first native-born performer to create excitement abroad. In his footsteps came Augustus A. Addams, MCKEAN BUCHANAN, John R. Scott, J. Hudson Kirby, and, most significant, JOHN MCCULLOUGH, E. L. DAVENPORT, and JAMES MURDOCH (and, toward the end of this period, great actors like EDWIN BOOTH and JOSEPH

JEFFERSON III). Among the actresses of the period, none received more acclaim than Forrest's contemporary CHARLOTTE CUSHMAN, who by midcentury was the dominating tragic actress on the American stage and an international star. Other actresses of note during the first half of the century include MARY ANN DUFF, JOSEPHINE CLIFTON, CLARA FISHER, MAGGIE MITCHELL, LOTTA CRABTREE, ADAH ISAACS MENKEN, and ANNA CORA MOWATT, remembered today for her play FASHION (1845), the most significant native comedy of manners of its time. Its central character is Trueman, another Yankee in the tradition of *The Contrast*'s Jonathan; such roles were the speciality of numerous significant American comic actors, including JAMES H. HACKETT, GEORGE HANDEL HILL, DANFORTH MARBLE, and Joshua Silsbee (as well as the later JOHN E. OWENS and DENMAN THOMPSON).

Parallel with the emergence of American-born actors is the growth of native plays and native characters. As a result of a playwriting contest sponsored first in 1828 by Forrest for "the best tragedy, in five acts, of which the hero, or principal character shall be an original of the country," 200 plays were submitted overall and nine prizes awarded; four plays were retained in his repertoire. The first winner, JOHN AUGUSTUS STONE's METAMORA, which harkens back to Major Robert Roger's 1766 play *Ponteach* and other early dramatic efforts to write plays about the noble red man, became the most durable of the dozens of Indian plays written and performed for the next half-century (see NATIVE AMERICANS RITUAL/THEATRE). Stone was one of a number of notable playwrights of the period from Philadelphia; others included JAMES NELSON BARKER, ROBERT MONTGOMERY BIRD, RICHARD PENN SMITH, MORDECAI MANUEL NOAH, ROBERT T. CONRAD, and SAMUEL WOODWORTH.

In addition to the Indian and the Yankee, a minor native character was the stage Negro, first appearing in John Murdock's *The Triumphs of Love* (1795) and culminating in the many versions of UNCLE TOM'S CABIN beginning in 1852. Related to the dramatic development of African American characters is the phenomenal popularity of the blackface MINSTREL SHOW stimulated by THOMAS D. RICE in the late 1820s. Two additional types emerged before the Civil War: the tough city lad, Mose the fire b'hoy, as depicted in BENJAMIN BAKER's *A GLANCE AT NEW YORK* (1848); and the stouthearted frontiersman, beginning with Colonel Nimrod Wildfire in JAMES K. PAULDING's *The LION OF THE WEST* (1831). In addition to the development of native types, American drama up to midcentury was dominated by the burlesques and dramas of immigrant playwright-actors like John Brougham and DION BOUCICAULT. Advancements in writing techniques were made by GEORGE HENRY BOKER, arguably the period's best writer of romantic drama in the English-speaking world, in particular his FRANCESCA DA RIMINI (1855), though Bird's romantic plays as performed by Forrest were more popular.

As the U.S. expanded its territory, enterprising theatre entrepreneurs took small companies into the Ohio and Mississippi Valley, beginning in 1815 when SAMUEL DRAKE went from Albany, NY, into FRONTIER settlements in Kentucky, Ohio, and Tennessee. JAMES H. CALDWELL established a first-rate English-speaking theatre in New Orleans by 1819. The names NOAH LUDLOW and SOL SMITH were familiar ones along the rivers and in the wild; combining forces they established the first real theatre in St. Louis in 1835. CHICAGO's first theatre dates from 1847. During the same period William Chapman was operating his Mississippi Floating Theatre (see SHOWBOATS). By midcentury, thanks to the gold rush, theatre came to California. The first theatrical performance by professional actors was given in SAN FRANCISCO in 1850, and by 1862 the SALT LAKE THEATRE (UT) was established. The star system was unequivocally aided by this westward expansion, for Western managers paid higher salaries than in the East to attract the best talent available.

By 1800 a definite shift of influence from Philadelphia to New York had begun. Philadelphia's population in 1820 was 63,802, New York's 123,706; by 1840 it was 93,655 to 312,710, and by midcentury New York boasted almost half a million people. The Chestnut Street Theatre, managed by William Warren and William B. Wood, began to lose dominance in Philadelphia in 1811, followed in 1828 by the ARCH STREET THEATRE and the WALNUT STREET THEATRE (renovated from a CIRCUS to a theatre in 1811). Philadelphia could not support three major theatres, and in 1828–9 all three went bankrupt. The country was rapidly changing, with a growing urban lower-class audience on the rise, significant emigrations on the horizon, an active revolt against English domination of the stage in motion, and a major civil war around the corner. Gradually playwrights were able to gain a living writing plays, encouraged by the copyright law of 1856. The number and quality of playhouses increased, gas STAGE LIGHTING was introduced in 1816, native SCENIC DESIGNers were gaining recognition, and greater realism – given impetus by the 1846 presentation of Charles Kean's *King John* – was sought. The Lafayette Theatre, built in New York in 1826, boasted of border lights and equipment for aquatic and equestrian drama (see ANIMALS AS PERFORMERS). The second Park opened in 1821 with a capacity of 2,500, topped by the 3,500 of the first BOWERY THEATRE in 1826. The CHATHAM GARDEN THEATRE opened in 1825; what became BARNUM'S AMERICAN MUSEUM began operation in 1841, as did the famous BOSTON MUSEUM, which operated a most successful

stock company for almost 50 years beginning in 1843; the
ASTOR PLACE OPERA HOUSE opened in 1847; Brougham's
Lyceum in 1850. Some of the more successful managements
up to midcentury fought the growing trends of stars and long
runs: for example, WILLIAM MITCHELL at the Olympic Theatre in New York during 1839–50. WILLIAM E. BURTON, who
leased Palmo's Opera House in 1848 and opened it as BUR-
TON'S CHAMBERS STREET THEATRE, followed suit, dominating as the fashionable New York theatre until the emergence
of the WALLACK'S stock company beginning in 1853.

By the Civil War the American theatre had undeniably
established a strong, individualistic mainstream tradition,
relatively free of foreign influence, despite strong impulses
from new European migrations to America. After a brief curtailment of growth, the American theatre would experience
a great period of prosperity following the War Between the
States, lasting until about 1915.   DBW

2. The Civil War to the First World War

The Civil War only disrupted theatrical activities in the East,
and by early 1862 the theatres in New York, Boston, and Philadelphia were open and thriving. Such patriotic pieces as
CHARLES GAYLER's *Bull Run; or, the Sacking of Fairfax Courthouse*
(1861) appeared in New York at the New Bowery Theatre
three weeks after the actual battle. Into the 1880s Wallack's
continued as the leading New York playhouse, offering a
steady diet of old and new British comedies with a superb
acting company that included MME. ELIZABETH PONISI, ROSE
COGHLAN, HENRY J. MONTAGUE, and CHARLES COGHLAN.
William Warren remained a fixture at the Boston Museum
until his retirement in 1883, offering a wide range of comic
roles, classic as well as contemporary. MRS. JOHN DREW managed a talented company at the Arch Street Theatre in Philadelphia during 1861–92, establishing the careers of her son,
John Drew, and her daughter, Georgina Drew Barrymore (see
DREW–BARRYMORE).

At the beginning of the decade, Edwin Forrest and Charlotte Cushman reigned as the leading tragedians in America,
although Forrest's position was being challenged by EDWIN
BOOTH, the son of English-born tragedian J. B. Booth. Young
Booth had served his apprenticeship in California (1852–6)
and returned east in 1856 to establish himself as a star. Success the following year in Boston and New York made him an
actor to watch. In the fall of 1862 he played in New York at
the same time as Forrest, inviting comparison with the older
actor. Cultivated theatre patrons had long abandoned Forrest and found Booth's quiet, unassuming, intellectual, and

refined style more suitable for their ideal of a "temple of the arts." Booth's slight but handsome physique (dark hair and eyes) made him the ideal late Victorian tragedian, much as Forrest's muscular physique had attracted patrons 30 years earlier. Critic Nym Crinkle (ANDREW C. WHEELER) thought Booth's Hamlet resembled a 19th-century gentleman more than a 16th-century courtier. Although his most famous role was Hamlet – which he played for 100 performances at the Winter Garden Theatre during the 1864–5 season – he excelled in other roles requiring intellectual rather than emotional or physical force: Iago, Richard II, Shylock, Cardinal Richelieu (in Bulwer-Lytton's play), and Bertuccio in Tom Taylor's *The Fool's Revenge*. Booth departed from tradition in building his own theatre (BOOTH'S, 1869) with neither a raked and grooved stage, an apron, nor proscenium doors. A better actor than manager, he succumbed to the financial panic of 1873 and lost the theatre through bankruptcy. Considered by historians as America's finest actor, Booth spent the last two decades of his life successfully touring as a star.

Booth was not the only actor challenging theatrical traditions: MATILDA HERON became an overnight success in 1857 with her portrayal of Marguerite Gautier in Dumas's *The Lady of the Camellias* (called *Camille* in New York), exhibiting a style of acting marked by excessive emotional display and a seeming lack of technique and control. For the next half-century, the style attracted such actresses as LUCILLE WESTERN, CLARA MORRIS, and MRS. LESLIE CARTER. JOSEPH JEFFERSON III also broke with the traditional school in the 1860s with his portrayal of RIP VAN WINKLE in Boucicault's dramatization. After presenting it in London (1865) for 170 performances, Jefferson brought it to New York in 1866 and, in the title role, established himself as the leading comedian of his age, as Booth was the leading tragedian. Jefferson endowed Rip with charm, humor, and pathos: His quiet, even casual, style seemed free of all staginess, with nothing forced or unnatural. In 1874 FRANK MAYO idealized the frontiersman in FRANK H. MURDOCH's drama *DAVY CROCKETT*; like Jefferson, Mayo underplayed the emotional points and offered a style of acting that seemed natural to his audiences.

Dramatic tastes changed significantly in the 1860s: The historical costume dramas of Stone, Bird, Knowles, and Bulwer-Lytton began to go out of fashion; more popular were melodramas that offered adventure, romance, and obligatory sensational events. In AUGUSTIN DALY's most successful melodramas, suspense and novel disasters abound: a man tied to railroad tracks facing an approaching train (*UNDER THE GASLIGHT*, 1867); the heroine stranded on a steamship about to explode (*A Flash of Lightning*, 1868); or the rescue of a man bound to a log entering a sawmill (*The Red Scarf,* 1868). These dramas had broad emotional appeal and played to a large popular audience.

The excitement over *Camille* and the new French drama resulted in numerous adaptations. There was good reason for these French plays achieving instant popularity: They dealt with contemporary events and discussed subjects formerly considered taboo (adultery, for example). DION BOUCICAULT made a profession out of Anglicizing French plays; Augustin Daly was responsible in part or whole for 44 adaptations of French drama, in addition to borrowing others from the German and English theatres. Although the Dramatic Copyright Law of 1856 improved the playwright's legal rights, it was not until the International Copyright Agreement was accepted by the U.S. in 1891 that managers found it as profitable to produce native plays as foreign ones.

American social comedies and dramas in the 1870s reflected the important topics of the day: stock speculation, social climbing, the winning of the West, divorce, and the family – and, in a romantic way, the Civil War. Daly's big hit of 1875, *The Big Bonanza,* poked fun at those who naively attempted to make a "killing" on Wall St. BRONSON HOWARD offered a more serious treatment of the subject in *The BANK-ER'S DAUGHTER* (1878), and in *Young Mrs. Winthrop* (1883) he touched upon the subjects of money, social status, and divorce. In *The HENRIETTA* (1887) Howard suggested that the country's obsession with making money was leading to moral decline. (This theme was explored by DAVID BELASCO and HENRY C. DEMILLE in *Men and Women* [1890], and exploited by CLYDE FITCH in *The Climbers* [1901]; a better play of the genre, LANGDON MITCHELL's *The NEW YORK IDEA* [1906], sat-irizes divorce and social customs among the wealthy.) Histo-rians have regarded Bronson Howard as the first professional playwright in America because he successfully made a living from his plays. His biggest hit, *SHENANDOAH* (1889), used the Civil War as a background for an essentially romantic plot, as did WILLIAM GILLETTE's spy stories *Held by the Enemy* (1886) and *SECRET SERVICE* (1896), Belasco's *The Heart of Maryland* (1895), and Fitch's *Barbara Frietchie* (1899).

The frontier and the winning of the West provided count-less plots and characters, including Davy Crockett and the American cowboy. Daly used the West as the setting for his *HORIZON* (1871), as did BRET HARTE for *Two Men of Sandy Bar* (1876), JOAQUIN MILLER for *The DANITES in the Sierras* (1887), BARTLEY CAMPBELL for *My PARTNER* (1879), AUGUSTUS THO-MAS for *Arizona* (1899), and Belasco for *The GIRL OF THE GOLDEN WEST* (1905). WILLIAM VAUGHN MOODY's *The GREAT DIVIDE* (1906) contrasts the East and the West in what some histori-ans regard as the first modern American play.

In the final years of the 19th century a more realistic treatment of subject began to replace or alter melodrama. Playwrights rejected long-held conventions dearly loved by audiences – including romantic plots, spine-chilling rescues, and happy endings – in favor of a truthful depiction of life. The farce-comedies of EDWARD HARRIGAN in the 1870s and '80s offered a theatrical but authentic portrait of life among the recent immigrants in New York; WILLIAM DEAN HOWELLS called Harrigan the American Goldoni, and championed his plays. In the 1890s, the increased interest in IBSEN offended traditionalists like WILLIAM WINTER and JOHN RANKEN TOWSE, but the new drama was defended by critics Howells, HAMLIN GARLAND, and JAMES G. HUNEKER. JAMES A. HERNE's MARGARET FLEMING (1890) presented a realistic portrait of the consequences of a husband's infidelity and avoided a happy ending. His more conventional SHORE ACRES (1892) maintained the externals of realism but returned in character and plot to sentimental melodrama, and was similar in style to Denman Thompson's The OLD HOMESTEAD (1886). Augustus Thomas also combined the trappings of realism and local color in Alabama (1891), Arizona (1899), The WITCHING HOUR (1907), and The COPPERHEAD (1918). More important are EDWARD SHELDON's SALVATION NELL (1908), The NIGGER (1909), and The Boss (1911), which deal with social problems in a realistic framework.

The public's demand for popular entertainment was insatiable. ADAH ISAACS MENKEN's Mazeppa (1861) thrilled the masculine element of the audience as she gave the illusion of riding nude on the back of a wild horse. The BLACK CROOK (1866) created a vogue for elaborate musical spectacle, owing much of its success to a Parisian ballet troupe of 100 "beautiful girls" in flesh-colored tights. LYDIA THOMPSON's "British Blondes" Burlesque Company from London drew crowded houses in New York for seven months (1868–9) (see BURLESQUE). French companies presented the new opéra bouffe of Jacques Offenbach to New York audiences in the late 1860s, and MAURICE GRAU formed a company in the 1870s to present French operettas and French stars. EVANGELINE (1874) offered an American version of opéra bouffe; written by Edward E. Rice and J. C. Goodwin, it featured a scantily clad female chorus, elaborate scenery, and comedian NAT GOODWIN. The success of the KIRALFY brothers' AROUND THE WORLD IN EIGHTY DAYS (1875) set the standard for large-scale spectacular theatre for the next two decades. The comic operettas of GILBERT AND SULLIVAN found an audience in this country after the huge success of HMS Pinafore in 1878–9. CHARLES HOYT's "musical trifle," A TRIP TO CHINATOWN (1890), offered songs, dances, and risqué comedy in addition to a thin plot and ran for 650 performances. A decade later, an English import, *FLORODORA* (1900), survived for 505 performances and made famous its sextette of chorus girls. FLORENZ ZIEGFELD inaugurated his *Follies* REVUE in 1907, featuring beautiful girls, elaborate costumes and sets, and leading comedians; over the years he discovered such talents as FANNY BRICE, W. C. FIELDS, EDDIE CANTOR, and BERT WILLIAMS.

Operetta continued its hold on American MUSICAL THE-ATRE into the 1920s. VICTOR HERBERT gained success with European-styled pieces and is regarded as America's first important composer of operetta. The proper setting for oper-etta remained in Central Europe, with Franz Lehar's memo-rable *The MERRY WIDOW* (1907) and with operettas by RUDOLF FRIML and SIGMUND ROMBERG.

Specialists such as LOTTA CRABTREE charmed New York City audiences during 1867–91 with her singing, dancing, and banjo playing. A master of the quick costume change, she played both Little Nell and the Marchioness in John Brougham's dramatic version of *The Old Curiosity Shop,* as well as six roles in *The Little Detective.* GEORGE L. FOX drew packed houses to the Olympic Theatre (1868) with the pantoMIME *Humpty Dumpty,* which he was to perform for 1,268 times in New York alone. EDDIE FOY gained fame in the 1890s by clowning in such musical pieces as *Sinbad the Sailor* (1891) and *Ali Baba* (1892). TONY PASTOR presented the top speciality acts at his VAUDEVILLE theatres in the 1870s and '80s, includ-ing the Four Cohans, LILLIAN RUSSELL, and the WEBER AND FIELDS comedy duo. GEORGE M. COHAN would move from vaudeville to the musical stage, establishing himself as a star in 1904–5 in his own *LITTLE JOHNNY JONES.* Lillian Russell became a leading star on the American musical stage. Weber and Fields opened their own Music Hall in 1896, which for seven years was regarded as one of Broadway's brightest attractions. The future of the speciality acts in the 20th cen-tury, however, lay with B. F. KEITH and EDWARD F. ALBEE, businessmen who introduced continuous vaudeville and organized the industry into a giant national circuit, gaining a near monopoly over it.

Economics and public taste after the Civil War dictated a change in the theatrical order. Although Wallack and Burton had been strong managers, the most powerful force in the theatre had been the actor as star. Realism and the demand for artistic unity made the rise of the modern director inevit-able. During the 1869–70 season, Augustin Daly leased the FIFTH AVENUE THEATRE and began developing his own com-pany. He hired actors by type rather than by lines of business; often cast plays without regard to tradition, lines of business, or possession of parts; rehearsed each play with careful atten-tion to interpretation, blocking, costuming, and scenery; and, while he opposed the star system, developed a succession of

stars including AGNES ETHEL, FANNY DAVENPORT, CLARA
MORRIS, and ADA REHAN. At his own DALY'S THEATRE in the
1880s, he featured a quartet of actors including John Drew,
Ada Rehan, MRS. G. H. GILBERT, and JAMES LEWIS. Known as
the home of light comedy in New York, Daly's displaced Wallack's as the most fashionable playhouse in the city. In 1884
he toured his company to London – the first American to do
so – and later to Paris and Germany. Four years later he produced *The Taming of the Shrew* at Stratford-upon-Avon in the
Shakespeare Memorial Theatre. Historians consider him the
first American régisseur in the style of the Duke of Saxe-
Meiningen.

A. M. PALMER tightly controlled every aspect of his productions at the UNION SQUARE THEATRE (1872–83), the MADI-
SON SQUARE THEATRE (1884–91), and Wallack's old theatre
(renamed Palmer's, 1888–96). Whereas Daly's Theatre was
known as the home of comedy, Palmer's featured "polite
melodrama," which he mounted with taste and care. With
the assistance of A. R. CAZAURAN, Palmer built a strong company by hiring established actors such as Agnes Ethel, Clara
Morris, KATE CLAXTON, ROSE EYTINGE, Charles R. Thorne Jr.,
and JAMES O'NEILL. His most popular successes included
Kate Claxton in *The Two Orphans* (1874); RICHARD MANSFIELD
in *A Parisian Romance* (1883); and premieres of Clyde Fitch's
Beau Brummell (1890) and Augustus Thomas's *Alabama* (1891).

STEELE MACKAYE also saw himself as an all-powerful manager who shaped every aspect of his productions. He designed
the elevator stage at the Madison Square Theatre (1880),
which allowed for an entire setting to be shifted in 40 seconds. He also built the LYCEUM THEATRE (1884–5) and taught
the Delsarte system of expression. In 1887 he directed his
own *Paul Kauvar,* which demonstrated his skill in handling
crowd scenes in the Meiningen manner; but MacKaye
remains a controversial figure in the American theatre
because he failed to finish most of his projects.

Through staging, lighting, and scenery, David Belasco
attempted to create the illusion of real life. He served as stage
manager of the Madison Square and Lyceum theatres in the
1880s, after which he turned to producing in 1895. Also a successful playwright, Belasco excelled in writing sentimental
melodramas, which he tailored for specific stars and interpolated with enough contemporary thought to make them
seem modern. He starred MRS. LESLIE CARTER in *Zaza* (1899);
BLANCHE BATES in *MADAME BUTTERFLY* (1900); Bates and
GEORGE ARLISS in *Sweet Kitty Bellairs* (1903); DAVID WARFIELD
in *The Return of Peter Grimm* (1911); and a replica of a Childs
restaurant in *The Governor's Lady* (1912). Belasco used publicity
to make stars out of his actors and is credited by some historians with being the most successful of American régisseurs;

but while he involved himself directly in producing theatre, his business methods were little different from other commercial producers.

By the mid-1870s the resident STOCK COMPANY and repertory system had become unprofitable to maintain and were rapidly being replaced by "combination companies." A play would open in New York, run until attendance lagged, then be transported in its entirety – actors, sets, properties – from city to city. The number of such "combination" companies steadily increased until the NEW YORK DRAMATIC MIRROR reported nearly 100 companies on the road during the 1876–7 season. MacKaye's HAZEL KIRKE (1880) was sent out in three road companies while still running in New York. Interest in local plays, companies, and actors was replaced by interest in touring attractions. Theatrical trade papers in New York, such as *Dramatic News* (1875) and *Dramatic Mirror* (1879), were established to cater to this interest.

Touring in America promised financial rewards for INTERNATIONAL STARS and native actors alike. Adelaide Ristori made the first of several American tours in 1866, acting in Italian except for her last visit in 1884–5. The English actress Adelaide Neilson made her first of two American appearances in 1872. Tommaso Salvini made his American debut in 1873 and returned four more times, playing with American actors in bilingual performances. HENRY E. ABBEY brought Sarah Bernhardt to the U.S. in 1880 for her first tour of seven months, which covered 50 cities and 156 performances. In 1883 Abbey also brought Henry Irving, Ellen Terry, and the Lyceum Company for the first of several visits; Irving's carefully mounted productions set a new standard for the American stage. Eleonora Duse imported her natural style of acting to New York for the first of four visits in 1893, and, on her last international tour in 1924, died in Pittsburgh.

All major American stars toured. After the loss of his theatre in 1873, Edwin Booth spent the last two decades of his life touring in Shakespearean and pseudoromantic plays, including two seasons (1887–9) with LAWRENCE BARRETT. JOHN McCULLOUGH, an actor in the Forrest tradition, gave up management of the CALIFORNIA THEATRE (1875) to tour for the next nine seasons. Of the new generation of actors, Richard Mansfield toured in such eccentric parts as Baron Chevrial in *A Parisian Romance* (1883) and in the title roles in PRINCE KARL (1886), *Dr. Jekyll and Mr. Hyde* (1887), *Richard III* (1889), *Beau Brummel* (1890), and *Cyrano de Bergerac* (1898). Mansfield introduced the plays of SHAW to an American audience as Bluntschli in *Arms and the Man* (1894) and later as Dick Dudgeon in *The Devil's Disciple* (1897). OTIS SKINNER had learned his trade in Booth's and Daly's companies and scrambled to play roles such as Hajj in *KISMET* (1911), which would best showcase his talents. E. H. SOTHERN made a hit with Edward Rose's romantic drama *The Prisoner of Zenda* (1895), and later acted Shakespeare together with his second wife, JULIA MARLOWE. The public's loss of interest in the traditional repertory and the demand for new plays left Mansfield and his generation scrambling to find suitable vehicles in which to star.

Establishing herself in the 1880s as a star in light comedy and melodrama, MRS. MINNIE MADDERN FISKE adjusted better to the demands of the new drama. She encouraged the production of IBSEN ON THE AMERICAN STAGE by acting Nora in *A Doll's House* (1894), the title role in *Hedda Gabler* (1903), Rebecca West in *Rosmersholm* (1907), and Mrs. Alving in *Ghosts* (1927). She also created the title character in Edward Sheldon's *Salvation Nell* (1908). Probably more effective in comedy, Mrs. Fiske was praised for her psychological truthfulness and simplicity of effects. Critics associated her in style with Duse. She and her husband, HARRISON GREY FISKE, leased the MANHATTAN THEATRE in 1903 and established an acting company, allowing them to remain independent of the Theatrical SYNDICATE.

ARNOLD DALY, like Mansfield, brought Shaw's plays before an American public. In 1903 he directed and starred in the American premiere of *Candida*, which ran for 133 performances. In 1904–5 he organized a company that produced *You Never Can Tell, The Man of Destiny, How He Lied to Her Husband*, a revival of *Candida*, and *Mrs Warren's Profession;* the last was considered an immoral play and led to Daly's arrest (see CENSORSHIP). Although acquitted, he soon lost the zeal for dramatic reform and reverted to performing in standard works.

The growing power of the businessman in the American theatre can be evidenced in the 1890s with the demise of Palmer's and Daly's companies, and the rise of the Frohman brothers as New York's leading producers. DANIEL FROHMAN had assumed control of the Lyceum Theatre from Steele MacKaye in 1885 and established a stock company and acting school, which lasted from 1887 until 1902. His company included such stellar performers as E. H. Sothern, VIRGINIA HARNED, Mary Mannering, WILLIAM FAVERSHAM, HENRIETTA CROSMAN, HENRY MILLER, GEORGIA CAYVAN, Herbert Kelcey, and JAMES H. HACKETT. He minimized risks and maximized profits by producing bright new plays by established writers, including Belasco and DeMille's *The Charity Ball* (1889); Henry Arthur Jones's *The Dancing Girl* (1891); Pinero's *Trelawny of the Wells* (1898); and Fitch's *The Moth and the Flame* (1898). CHARLES FROHMAN established two companies at Proctor's in 1890 to produce and tour new plays. In 1893 he built the EMPIRE THEATRE, which quickly gained the reputation of being a "star factory." He hired John Drew from Daly's company in 1892 and added William Gillette to his stable of stars, including MAUDE ADAMS, Ethel Barrymore, and HENRY E. DIXEY. His numerous hits include Belasco and FRANKLIN FYLES's *The Girl I Left Behind Me* (1893); JAMES M. BARRIE's *The Little Minister* (1897) and *Peter Pan* (1905), both starring Maude Adams; and William Gillette's SHERLOCK HOLMES (1899).

Charles Frohman is best known for organizing in 1896 a theatrical trust comprising three partnerships: Frohman and Al Hayman; the booking firm of MARC KLAW and ABRAHAM L. ERLANGER; and Philadelphia theatre owners S. F. Nixon and J. Fred Zimmerman. Called the SYNDICATE, this trust gained a monopoly over the American theatre by controlling bookings, theatre buildings, and talent. In 1896 they either operated or directly controlled 33 first-class houses from coast to coast, and by 1903 had extended their holdings to 70. At the height of their power, they had exclusive rights to book over 700 theatres. The canceling of engagements, double bookings, broken contracts, and general disorganization that characterized theatre of the 1880s were eliminated. For 15 years Frohman and the Syndicate tightly controlled the American theatre and ran it on "big business" principles. They judged a play's worth solely on its ability to generate a profit. The SHUBERTS' (Lee, Sam, and Jacob J.) "Independent Movement" in 1900 challenged the position of the Syndicate: They also gained control over theatres from coast to coast; offered attractive bookings to independent managers; and began producing their own shows. Fierce competition between the two groups resulted in an oversupply of attractions and theatres; cities built separate theatres for Syndicate and Independent productions. ECONOMIC disaster was averted by an agreement between the two parties in 1914. Charles Frohman went down in the *Lusitania* in 1915, and afterward the Syndicate declined in power. The SHUBERT ORGANIZATION remained a vital force in the 20th-century American theatre.

Critics WALTER PRICHARD EATON, NORMAN HAPGOOD, BRANDER MATTHEWS, John Ranken Towse, and William Winter denounced the Syndicate's purely commercial policy in the early 1900s and envisaged a national theatre supported by either public or private funds. Interest in the idea grew with the *Arena* publishing the symposium "A National Art Theatre for America" in 1904. Four years later HEINRICH CONRIED announced plans for such a company in New York, and despite his death the following year, money was raised and the NEW THEATRE opened under WINTHROP AMES's direction on 6 November 1909 with Julia Marlowe and E. H. Sothern in *Antony and Cleopatra*. The lack of a well-trained company and the New Theatre's poor acoustics contributed to its demise in 1911, although the project may have been doomed from the start: 20th-century theatre problems could not be solved with 19th-century solutions. This attempt to create an art theatre did express dissatisfaction with the triteness of the American stage, an attitude reinforced through visits in the 1910s by such foreign companies as the Irish Players of the Abbey Theatre (1911), MAX REINHARDT's company in *Sumurun* at the Casino Theatre (1912), Granville Barker's productions at Wallack's Theatre for the New Stage Society of New York (1915), and Jacques Copeau's Vieux-Colombier Company at the Old Garrick Theatre (1917). These companies demonstrated that theatre could be more than manufactured entertainment for mass tastes and could touch the human mind and spirit in an important way. WILLIAM A. BRADY, a commercial producer, presented Edward Sheldon's *The Boss* (1911) and Shaw's *Major Barbara* (1915). Amateur theatre groups were organized throughout the country, inspired by artists such as Maurice Browne of the Chicago Little Theatre (1912). In New York, the WASHINGTON SQUARE PLAYERS (1914), led by LAWRENCE LANGNER and Edward Goodman, produced the plays of Ibsen, CHEKHOV, and Shaw, as well as important new works by American writers. In 1916 the PROVINCETOWN PLAYERS presented *Bound East for Cardiff*, the first O'NEILL play to be staged. The same year, in Detroit, SHELDON CHENEY founded *THEATRE ARTS*, a magazine dedicated to the art of the theatre. In 1919, members of the recently defunct Washington Square Players founded the THEATRE GUILD, the first U.S. professional art theatre. Led by Lawrence Langner, PHILIP MOELLER, THERESA HELBURN, and others, the Guild became an important theatre offering professional productions of plays not normally seen in the commercial theatre.   TLM

3. The First World War to the 1960s

After WWI, ACTORS' EQUITY demanded improved working conditions in the theatre and pushed for unionization of the acting profession; this resulted in an actors' strike in 1919. Stagehands had first organized themselves into a UNION in 1886, and later had affiliated with the American Federation of Labor (1894). After several unsuccessful attempts, performers formed Actors' Equity in 1913. Producers, including GEORGE M. COHAN and the SHUBERTS, fought the union and were joined by many actors who considered themselves artists not laborers; but on 6 August 1919, Equity went out on strike, demanding official recognition and a closed shop for legitimate performers. They were supported by the stagehands and musicians, as well as by the AFL. The Theatre Guild met Equity's terms immediately, but all other producers resisted, and their plays closed. On 6 September, the producers capitulated and signed contracts that stipulated minimum contracts, improved rehearsal conditions, higher pay, and better working conditions.

In 1920 the PROVINCETOWN PLAYERS brought EUGENE O'NEILL's first full-length play, BEYOND THE HORIZON, to Broadway, where it ran for 111 performances and won a Pulitzer Prize. Critics GEORGE JEAN NATHAN and Ludwig Lewisohn touted play and author as important new forces in the American theatre. O'Neill followed with *The* EMPEROR JONES (1920), an expressionistic drama that featured CHARLES GILPIN and the scenery of CLEON THROCKMORTON, and ANNA CHRISTIE (1921), starring PAULINE LORD. Working quickly, within three years he had added *The Straw* (1921) and *The First Man* (1922), dominating the American theatre of the 1920s as no playwright had in previous decades.

Popular successes in the 1920s include AVERY HOPWOOD and MARY ROBERTS RINEHART's *The* BAT (1920), which ran over two years, and Anne Nichols's ABIE'S IRISH ROSE (1922), which received scathing reviews but survived for 2,327 performances. Hopwood made a fortune writing such risqué fluff as *The* GOLD DIGGERS (1919) and *The Demi-Virgin* (1921). The ZIEGFELD *Follies* began to look dated in the 1920s, but gaining in popularity were all-Negro revues, such as NOBLE SISSLE and EUBIE BLAKE's SHUFFLE ALONG (1921), and *Blackbirds* (1928), a compendium of songs and dances that made a star of hoofer BILL "BOJANGLES" ROBINSON. Musical comedy survived because of pretty chorus girls and memorable songs by VINCENT YOUMANS, GEORGE GERSHWIN, COLE PORTER, and RICHARD RODGERS, and such superb performers as W. C. FIELDS, AL JOLSON, ED WYNN, FANNY BRICE, BERT WILLIAMS, WILL ROGERS, BERT LAHR, and JIMMY DURANTE. GEORGE AND IRA GERSHWIN created a new jazz style with hits such as *Lady, Be Good!* (1924), *Tip-Toes* (1925), and *Funny Face* (1927). The MARX BROS. clowned in such vehicles as *The* COCOANUTS (1925) by GEORGE S. KAUFMAN and IRVING BERLIN, and ANIMAL CRACKERS (1928) by Kaufman, MORRIE RYSKIND, and others, after which they took their buffoonery to Hollywood.

Operetta remained popular, with long runs for Rudolf Friml's ROSE-MARIE (1924) and Sigmund Romberg's *The* STUDENT PRINCE (1924) and *The* DESERT SONG (1926). SHOW BOAT (1928), by JEROME KERN and OSCAR HAMMERSTEIN II, broke new ground by drawing on American musical traditions and by better integrating the book, music, songs, and dances; JOSEPH URBAN designed the show, adding to his reputation for creating opulent sets for opera, theatre, and the *Ziegfeld Follies.*

Although the New Theatre had failed to create a more artistic American stage in the early 1910s, efforts continued into the 1920s. ARTHUR HOPKINS, ROBERT EDMOND JONES, and John Barrymore (see DREW-BARRYMORE) combined forces in 1920 to present Shakespeare's *Richard III,* and two years later to revive *Hamlet* in a somewhat untraditional interpretation by Barrymore. The production ran 101 performances, and Barrymore repeated his success in London (1925). In 1923, the MOSCOW ART THEATRE's acting company visited New York. Critics pretended not to notice that the company performed in Russian as they praised its ensemble training. Although the Stanislavsky system of acting was not unknown in the U.S., demonstration of the MAT work to New York audiences had lasting impact. Two members of the company, RICHARD BOLESLAVSKI and MARIA OUSPENSKAYA, remained in America to teach in the AMERICAN LABORATORY THEATRE. In 1925 WALTER HAMPDEN moved his own company (founded 1918) into the Colonial (later the Hampden) Theatre and for five years offered Shakespeare, Ibsen, Rostand, and other less commercial playwrights. EVA LE GALLIENNE leased the 50-year-old Fourteenth Street Theatre in 1926, gathered together a company of veterans and newcomers, and opened with Chekhov's *The Three Sisters;* few critics showed interest, but Le Gallienne kept her CIVIC REPERTORY THEATRE intact for six years, presenting 34 plays, most of which would have been fiscally impossible on Broadway.

Under the guidance of LAWRENCE LANGNER, the Theatre Guild emerged in the 1920s as America's most artistic producing organization. The company – which at one time included ALFRED LUNT AND LYNN FONTANNE, DUDLEY DIGGES, Helen Westley, LEE SIMONSON, and PHILIP MOELLER – presented a number of important world premieres, including Shaw's *Heartbreak House* (1920) and ELMER RICE's expressionistic *The ADDING MACHINE* (1923). In 1925 they opened their own Guild Theatre with a production of Shaw's *Caesar and Cleopatra.* During 1920–30 the Guild offered 67 different productions, 15 the work of American playwrights.

American comedy became more worldly in the 1920s with George S. Kaufman, replacing its penchant for folksy, romantic, and sentimental nonsense with witty and irreverant stabs at native society and culture. Kaufman and MARC CONNELLY's *DULCY* (1921) elevated Lynn Fontanne to stardom and was the first of their collaborations, which included *To the Ladies* (1922), *Merton of the Movies* (1922), and *BEGGAR ON HORSEBACK* (1924), the last an expressionistic satire on American business. Kaufman collaborated successfully with other writers, including EDNA FERBER and MOSS HART; Connelly enjoyed his greatest triumph with his solo *The GREEN PASTURES* (1930), which played for 640 performances. GEORGE KELLY attracted attention in 1922 with *The Torchbearers,* a satire on the Little Theatre movement (see COMMUNITY THEATRE), before writing his highly popular comedy *The SHOW-OFF* two years later and his Pulitzer Prize–winning *CRAIG'S WIFE* in 1925. PHILIP BARRY and S. N. BEHRMAN wrote fashionable comedies with wit and style, albeit a streak of sentimentality. Behrman's *The Second Man* (1927) featured Alfred Lunt and Lynn Fontanne in a comedy about an artist's choice between two women. Barry's *PARIS BOUND* (1927) and *HOLIDAY* (1928) presented a charming portrait of the wealthy just before the stock market crash of 1929. His best play, *The PHILADELPHIA STORY* (1939), allowed KATHARINE HEPBURN to dazzle in a light-hearted treatment of life among the wealthy. The best American farce of the 1920s was BEN HECHT and CHARLES MACARTHUR'S *The FRONT PAGE* (1928), a cynical and satirical look at big-city life in Chicago.

Serious drama probed the romantic assumptions underlying American life. War received a realistic and truthful depiction in MAXWELL ANDERSON and Laurence Stalling's *WHAT PRICE GLORY* (1924), which George Jean Nathan thought superior to every other play inspired by WWI. In the same year, O'Neill's *DESIRE UNDER THE ELMS* offered a Freudian interpretation of New England puritanism that relied for much of its power on Robert Edmond Jones's highly symbolic setting. The prolific O'Neill with mixed success examined other aspects of American life in *The Fountain* (1925), *The GREAT GOD BROWN* (1926) and *STRANGE INTERLUDE* (1928), the last a nine-act, five-hour dramatic novel that ran for 432 performances and won a Pulitzer. The same year, Maxwell Anderson and Harold Hickerson's *Gods of the Lightning* brought the Sacco and Vanzetti murder case before a New York audience. SIDNEY HOWARD dissected the American way of life in *THEY KNEW WHAT THEY WANTED* (1924), *Lucky Sam McCarver* (1925), *Ned McCobb's Daughter* (1926), and *The SILVER CORD* (1927), the last about excessive maternal devotion. ROBERT SHERWOOD attracted attention in 1927 with *The ROAD TO ROME,* a bittersweet reenactment of Hannibal's march, starring JANE COWL.

At the end of the decade, radio and motion pictures emerged as rivals for the American theatre audience. Radio had grown from its first regular broadcasts in 1920 to a full-scale entertainment industry by 1930. Motion pictures added sound with *The Jazz Singer* in 1927, which made it possible to film stage plays and show them for a fraction of the cost of a theatre ticket. Between 1920 and 1930 theatres outside New York decreased in number from 1,500 to 500, many converting to film, as the professional theatre in America became almost exclusively located in Manhattan. The Depression was radically to reduce what was left: During the 1927–8 Broadway season, the number of stage productions reached a record of 280; by 1939–40 this had been reduced to 80.

The American theatre in the 1930s directly reflected the nation's political and economic crises. Leftist theatre groups proliferated, including the New Playwrights' Theatre (1926), Workers' Drama League (1929), Workers' Laboratory Theatre (1930), League of Workers' Theatres (1932), and THEATRE UNION (1933), among the most active. They were founded by writers such as Michael Gold and JOHN HOWARD LAWSON, who returned from Russia eager to form a theatre of the Left. CLIFFORD ODETS's inflammatory *WAITING FOR LEFTY* (1935) drew its early sponsorship from the League of Workers' Theatres. The Theatre Union gained an early success with *Peace on Earth* (1933), an antiwar piece, and *STEVEDORE* (1934), a play dealing with the relationship between black and white workers. Left-wing theatre remained a short-lived phenomenon of the 1930s, as its writers and artists were absorbed into the mainstream of American theatre and films. Many were blacklisted during the McCarthy Hearings in the 1950s.

The Harlem Renaissance of the 1920s generated a new interest in black literature, which continued in the 1930s. Plays about blacks by whites – PAUL GREEN's *IN ABRAHAM's BOSOM,* Marc Connelly's *Green Pastures,* and O'Neill's *The Emperor Jones* – had been more successful than those by blacks until W. E. B. Du Bois, LANGSTON HUGHES, and others organized black companies. Hughes's *MULATTO* (1935) was the most successful play by an AFRICAN AMERICAN playwright in the 1930s.

Politically sensitive but more concerned with artistic ideals, the GROUP THEATRE began in 1931 as a palace revolt within the Theatre Guild, led by younger members HAROLD CLURMAN, CHERYL CRAWFORD, and LEE STRASBERG. They were joined by 28 actors, including FRANCHOT TONE, MORRIS CARNOVSKY, Clifford Odets, SANFORD MEISNER, and STELLA ADLER, to set up a summer colony in Connecticut. Under the tutelage of Strasberg, the Group sought an acting technique for realistic plays. After a summer of work and analysis, the Group produced Paul Green's *The HOUSE OF CONNELLY* (1931), followed by John Howard Lawson's *Success Story* (1932) and SIDNEY KINGSLEY's *MEN IN WHITE* (1933). They encouraged Odets as a playwright and produced his *AWAKE AND SING!* and *Waiting for Lefty,* both in 1935. They gave WILLIAM SAROYAN a hearing in 1939 with *MY HEART'S IN THE HIGHLANDS* before running into financial problems in 1941 and disbanding.

In 1935 the FEDERAL THEATRE was organized by the Works Progress Administration to create jobs for out-of-work theatre people. Mrs. HALLIE FLANAGAN of the Vassar Experimental Theatre was appointed first director and charged with locating the unemployed and putting them to work. This, the first subsidized producing agency in U.S. history, was disbanded by the government in 1939 on grounds of leftist infiltration. The Federal Theatre made several distinctive contributions to the American theatre, including the LIVING NEWSPAPER productions. African American units of the Federal Theatre offered new plays by black authors but are remembered mainly for the "voodoo" *Macbeth* (1936), directed by ORSON WELLES, and the *Swing Mikado* (1938).

The CENSORSHIP and closing of the Federal Theatre's production of MARC BLITZSTEIN's *The CRADLE WILL ROCK* (1937) led to the resignations of Welles and JOHN HOUSEMAN, and to their creation of the MERCURY THEATRE. Welles, who had demonstrated a remarkable originality as a director both with Marlowe's *Doctor Faustus* (1937) and the earlier *Macbeth,* directed an impressive modern-dress *Julius Caesar* (1937) with fascist costumes and ABE FEDER's lighting.

The depressed economy sharply reduced the number of Broadway productions, prompting five playwrights – Robert Sherwood, Maxwell Anderson, Sidney Howard, S. N. Behrman, and Elmer Rice – to join together in 1938 to form their own producing organization, the PLAYWRIGHTS' COMPANY. Opening with Sherwood's ABE LINCOLN IN ILLINOIS (1938), they presented Anderson's KNICKERBOCKER HOLIDAY (1938), Rice's *American Landscape* (1938), and Behrman's NO TIME FOR COMEDY (1939), launching an ambitious program that would survive until 1960. Together with the Theatre Guild, they set the standard for Broadway production in the late 1930s.

The successful musicals of the 1930s tended to be both stylish and topical. George S. Kaufman and HOWARD DIETZ's *The Band Wagon* (1931) offered brilliant artistry: directing by HASSARD SHORT and dancing by FRED AND ADELE ASTAIRE. OF THEE I SING (by the Gershwins, George S. Kaufman, and Morrie Ryskind, 1931) satirized the supreme court, president, vice-president, diplomatic corps, and the general humbug of American elections. In 1935, PORGY AND BESS arrived on Broadway, with its serious musical score. In the 1940–1 season, PAL JOEY (by Richard Rodgers and LORENZ HART) and LADY IN THE DARK (by Moss Hart, Ira Gershwin, and KURT WEILL) offered more mature subjects and a worldly tone.

The Depression gripped the nation spiritually as well as economically, and set the tone for serious drama. O'Neill wrote MOURNING BECOMES ELECTRA (1931), a six-hour play based on the *Oresteia;* Philip Moeller directed, Robert Edmond Jones designed, and ALLA NAZIMOVA, ALICE BRADY, and Earle Larimore starred. Two years later TOBACCO ROAD opened for a seven-year run, based on Erskine Caldwell's steamy novel of Georgia backwoods poor white trash, starring Henry Hull as Jeeter Lester. In 1935 *Awake and Sing!,* Sidney Kingsley's DEAD END, and Maxwell Anderson's WINTERSET offered a somber picture of the American dream. LILLIAN HELLMAN's *The CHIL-DREN'S HOUR* (1934) and *The LITTLE FOXES* (1939), JOHN STEIN-BECK's *OF MICE AND MEN* (1937), and THORNTON WILDER's epic *OUR TOWN* (1938) suggested the anxiety underlying American life.

Bad economic times produced some of America's best comic writing. O'Neill penned a domestic comedy in 1933, *AH, WILDERNESS!*, which critics thought sentimental and moralistic but reassuring. SAM AND BELLA SPEWACK's *Boy Meets Girl* (1935) provided a lighthearted spoof of Hollywood. CLARE BOOTHE's *The WOMEN* (1936) was a bitchy satire on idle and wealthy urban women. The Kaufman and Hart collaborations *YOU CAN'T TAKE IT WITH YOU* (1936) and *The MAN WHO CAME TO DINNER* (1939) were the funniest American comedies since *The Front Page,* and have remained classics. RACHEL CROTHERS returned from Hollywood in 1937 to write *SUSAN AND GOD,* a satire on the efforts of a wife to reform her alcoholic husband. *My Heart's in the Highlands* and *The TIME OF YOUR LIFE* (both 1939) established William Saroyan as an important playwright. HOWARD LINDSAY and RUSSEL CROUSE's *LIFE WITH FATHER* (1939), starring Lindsay and DOROTHY STICKNEY, became a smash hit that ran for 3,216 performances, then a record. James Thurber and ELLIOTT NUGENT's *The MALE ANIMAL* appeared the same season and satirized intellectual as well as romantic notions of the nation.

America's favorite acting couple, Alfred Lunt and Lynn Fontanne, remained popular throughout the 1930s, playing comedy with elegance, grace, and perfect teamwork. KATHARINE CORNELL and HELEN HAYES were considered the first ladies of the American stage for their beauty and ability to play classical as well as modern roles. Other important actresses included TALLULAH BANKHEAD, Eva Le Gallienne, RUTH GORDON, and Katharine Hepburn. Except for Alfred Lunt and John Barrymore (before he went to Hollywood), the American stage lacked distinguished males: The better younger players were opting for a career in films.

Broadway prospered during WWII. Irving Berlin's *This Is the Army* (1942), Rodgers and Hammerstein's *OKLAHOMA!* (1943) and *CAROUSEL* (1945), and LEONARD BERNSTEIN's *ON THE TOWN* (1944) set the pace for musical entertainment. Much of America's serious drama depicted the war as simple melodrama, including Moss Hart's *Winged Victory* (1943), Maxwell Anderson's *Storm Operation* (1944), and James Gow and Arnaud D'Usseau's *Tomorrow the World* (1943), which were antifascist. In the spring of 1945, TENNESSEE WILLIAMS's *The GLASS MENAGERIE* opened on Broadway to excellent notices, with fine performances by LAURETTE TAYLOR, EDDIE DOWLING, and JULIE HAYDON. Comedies offered little more than escape, except Thornton Wilder's *SKIN OF OUR TEETH* (1942), which preached survival in a strange theatrical style. More typical were Joseph Kesselring's off-beat farce ARSENIC AND OLD LACE (1941), JOHN VAN DRUTEN's sentimental *I REMEMBER MAMA* (1944), and MARY COYLE CHASE's fantastic HARVEY (1944).

The immediate postwar period saw renewed activity by established writers, including O'Neill's *The ICEMAN COMETH* (1946), Hellman's *Another Part of the Forest* (1946), Maxwell Anderson's *Anne of the Thousand Days* (1948), Clifford Odets's *The COUNTRY GIRL* (1950), and Kingsley's DARKNESS AT NOON (1951), adapted from Arthur Koestler's novel. At the time of O'Neill's death in 1953, his reputation was in decline; a reevaluation of his work began with JOSÉ QUINTERO's 1956 revival of *The Iceman Cometh* at CIRCLE IN THE SQUARE: JASON ROBARDS Jr.'s portrayal of Hickey drew widespread praise and launched his career. Later that year, O'Neill's *LONG DAY'S JOURNEY INTO NIGHT* premiered at the HELEN HAYES THEATRE under Quintero's direction and was hailed as the playwright's greatest work. *A MOON FOR THE MISBEGOTTEN* followed in 1957 and *A TOUCH OF THE POET* in 1958. In 1959, the Coronet Theatre in New York was renamed in O'Neill's honor.

Popular successes at the time reflected the public's continued interest in the war and its own idealism. GARSON KANIN's comedy *BORN YESTERDAY* (1946) made a star of JUDY HOLLIDAY. Other hits included William Wister Haines's melodrama *Command Decision* (1947); NORMAN KRASNA's farce *John Loves Mary* (1947); Thomas Heggen and JOSHUA LOGAN's comedy *MISTER ROBERTS* (1947), starring HENRY FONDA; Donald Bevan and Edmund Trzcinski's thriller *Stalag 17* (1951); and Herman Wouk's courtroom drama *The Caine Mutiny Court Martial* (1954).

After the war, Tennessee Williams, ARTHUR MILLER, and WILLIAM INGE emerged as the major new playwrights. *A STREETCAR NAMED DESIRE* (1947), with stellar performances by MARLON BRANDO, JESSICA TANDY, Karl Malden, and KIM HUNTER, solidified the reputation Williams had established with *The Glass Menagerie* and won both the Pulitzer Prize and the Critics' Circle Award. In 1947, Miller's *ALL MY SONS* drew respectable notices and won the Drama Critics Award; two years later his *DEATH OF A SALESMAN,* under ELIA KAZAN's direction and with a brilliant performance by LEE J. COBB, duplicated Williams's success. Williams and Miller depicted a society that had grown decadent, obsessed with materialism and power. Williams wrote with compassion and poetic insight about people unable to cope who seek escape through booze, drugs, daydreams, and sex. His post-1950 plays include *The Rose Tattoo* (1951), *CAT ON A HOT TIN ROOF* (1955), *Orpheus Descending* (1957), *SWEET BIRD OF YOUTH* (1959), and *The NIGHT OF THE IGUANA* (1961); later his reputation suffered from such lesser pieces as *The Milk Train Doesn't Stop Here Anymore* (1963), *Vieux Carré* (1977), and *Clothes for a Summer Hotel* (1980). Arthur Miller focused more on the larger social and political issues in *The CRUCIBLE* (1953), *A VIEW FROM THE BRIDGE* (1956), and *Incident at Vichy* (1964); his latest plays were not well received in the U.S. Inge's reputation has not worn as well as those of his two colleagues. In 1950 *COME BACK, LITTLE SHEBA* established him as an important playwright and promoted the career of actress SHIRLEY BOOTH. Inge would enjoy meteoric success with hits *PICNIC* (1953), *BUS STOP* (1955), and *The Dark at the Top of the Stairs* (1957) before his star faded in the 1960s; his plays now seem sentimental and contrived, despite a number of recent revivals.

After the war, Rodgers and Hammerstein continued their mastery of the musical with *SOUTH PACIFIC* (1949), *The KING AND I* (1951), and their last major collaboration, *The SOUND OF MUSIC* (1959). This was a golden age of the American musical. Hits by other composers include Berlin's *ANNIE GET YOUR GUN* (1946) and *CALL ME MADAM* (1950); HARBURG and Saidy's *FINIAN'S RAINBOW* (1947); LERNER AND LOEWE'S *BRIGADOON* (1947) and *MY FAIR LADY* (1956); Cole Porter's *KISS ME, KATE* (1948); FRANK LOESSER'S *GUYS AND DOLLS* (1950); Bernstein's *WONDERFUL TOWN* (1953) and *WEST SIDE STORY* (1957); and JULE STYNE'S *GYPSY* (1959). The American musical possessed energy and style and was recognized as the nation's most original contribution to world theatre.

Comedy grew tame and unadventuresome in the 1950s, relying on stock plots and comic devices. Ronald Alexander's domestic comedy *TIME OUT FOR GINGER* was a minor hit the same year (1952) GEORGE AXELROD's sex farce, *The Seven Year Itch,* ran for 1,141 presentations and made a star of Tom Ewell. Another smash hit, JOHN PATRICK's *The Teahouse of the August Moon* (1953), endured for 1,027 performances and won both the Critics' Circle and Pulitzer Prize. SAMUEL TAYLOR's two hits, *Sabrina Fair* (1953) and *Pleasure of His Company* (1958), reminded audiences of Philip Barry and S. N. Behrman. George S. Kaufman and Howard Teichmann cowrote a mild satire about American business methods, *The Solid Gold Cadillac* (1953). Sidney Kingsley's farcical *Lunatics and Lovers* (1954) offered audiences a screwball comedy with Buddy Hackett. Thornton Wilder's *The MATCHMAKER*, which later served as the book for *HELLO, DOLLY!,* opened in 1955; likewise, JEROME LAWRENCE and ROBERT E. LEE's 1956 *AUNTIE MAME* was later transformed into the musical *Mame.* In 1959, PADDY CHAYEFSKY's *The Tenth Man* provided mysticism and love in a plot that threatened to turn serious.

In the work of the ACTORS STUDIO, the postwar American theatre found an acting style in which to interpret the realistic plays of Williams, Miller, and Inge. Elia Kazan, ROBERT

Lewis, and Cheryl Crawford founded the Studio in 1947, joined by Lee Strasberg a year later. Strasberg's system of acting based on Stanislavsky's writings became known as the Method and attracted a generation of actors including Marlon Brando and GERALDINE PAGE. Kazan became the prominent director of his age, mounting important premieres for all three playwrights. As if to underscore the passing of an era, in 1958 Lunt and Fontanne gave their farewell performance in *The Visit*.

In the 1920s, Robert Edmond Jones had set the standard for American stage scenery by evolving a style of simplified sets that suggested rather than reproduced reality. His successor, JO MIELZINER, dominated American stage design from 1930 until his death in 1976. Mielziner used transparent scenery in a cinematic way to complement the poetic quality of plays by Williams and Miller. MING CHO LEE followed Mielziner as the major influence upon more contemporary stage design in a style that features collage, textured surfaces, and scaffolding. Other important scenic artists of the postwar era include BORIS ARONSON, OLIVER SMITH, JEAN ROSENTHAL, SANTO LOQUASTO, and EUGENE LEE.

After WWII, high production costs on Broadway and efforts to establish professional theatre outside of New York resulted in the OFF-BROADWAY and regional theatre movements. Off-Broadway recorded its first major success in 1952 with José Quintero's revival of Williams's *Summer and Smoke* at the CIRCLE IN THE SQUARE. The production reclaimed the play (which had earlier failed on Broadway) and made a star of Geraldine Page. Judith Malina and Julian Beck opened The LIVING THEATRE in 1951; NORRIS HOUGHTON and T. EDWARD HAMBLETON founded the Phoenix in 1953; and JOSEPH PAPP created the most important Off-Broadway theatre, the NEW YORK SHAKESPEARE FESTIVAL, in 1954. Outside New York, in 1947 MARGO JONES founded Theatre '47 in Dallas, and Nina Vance the ALLEY THEATRE in Houston. In 1950 ZELDA FICHANDLER and Edward Mangum created the ARENA STAGE in WASHINGTON, DC. Two years later HERBERT BLAU and Jules Irving established the Actors' Workshop in SAN FRANCISCO. In 1955, the AMERICAN SHAKESPEARE FESTIVAL opened in Stratford, CT, joining the OREGON SHAKESPEARE FESTIVAL (founded in 1935) as a major summer company dedicated to the production of Shakespeare's plays (see SHAKESPEAREAN FESTIVALS). TLM

4. 1960 to the present

From the dawn of Camelot to the age of the Internet – roughly 1960 through 2005 – the American theatre changed profoundly. Most important, it decentralized: For the first time since resident repertory theatre in the late 19th century, theatre people could hope to conduct respectable careers independently of New York, while audiences in other regions gained consistent access to professional theatre. The trend grew, matured, and, some eventually argued, ossified as the first generation of regional theatre artistic and administrative leaders yielded to the second and the third. Still, there was no question that the American theatre, as the century ended, represented more than just the productions on the stages of a tiny speck of midtown Manhattan.

How the American theatre evolved to that state, however, was less about a gold-paved road than one colored crimson. At the start of the 20th century Broadway dominated the American stage; it was the sole locus for generating and casting new works that traveled to other locales – "the road." By the end of the 20th century, that rising cost of production made commercial theatre increasingly unworkable as a forum for artistic experimentation. With ticket prices grossly inflated, Broadway became perceived as a luxury item. Worse, the theatre, which was once the predominant form – arguably the only form – of cultural diversion at the start of the 20th century, faced a growing army of cultural competitors: radio, film, television; the proliferation, presentation, and marketing of professional sports; high-tech video games; the World Wide Web. The theatre still strutted and fretted its hour upon the stage, but as the new millennium dawned, it was but one of many players.

How did this affect "the road"? Whereas 327 companies toured the country in 1900, by the early 2000s the road had been replaced by a network of nonprofit institutional theatres in population centers large and small nationwide. The nonprofits were often linked with, and even founded as, adjuncts to theatre-degree programs at universities and colleges, a practice that has since spread abroad. In major population centers today, there are perhaps one or two commercial houses for touring productions. By contrast, nonprofit theatres, beginning in the 1950s, were cropping up in cities like CHICAGO, WASHINGTON, DC, SAN FRANCISCO, BOSTON, Denver, ATLANTA, and MINNEAPOLIS.

Together with the ALTERNATIVE THEATRES that sprang up Off- and Off-Off Broadway and in metropolitan areas small and large, regional theatres increasingly initiated the creation of most new American plays and a significant percentage of musicals, once Broadway's special preserve, as Broadway proved less and less able financially to support the creation of such work, especially as development methods – workshops, readings, and so on – evolved over the course of the century. As the number of institutional theatres grew, expanding and diversifying their repertoires, the number of Broadway houses and productions in them shrank. In the 1930s, 54 Broadway theatres presented an average of 146 productions per season; only 36 theatres offering 63 shows remained by 1964; by 1991, there were just 28 Broadway openings, and more than half of the houses were shuttered. Things improved in the years leading up to, and past, the new millennium; there were nearly 40 Broadway openings during the 2005–6 season. But what filled Broadway's coffers wasn't so much new product as lowest-common-denominator fare benefiting from the cunning ability of producers to diversify the marketing of commercial theatre – like a centipede, many feet moving in different directions at once. Also reduced was the sample of people prepared to buy expensive tickets for an ever narrower and more conservative range of fare dominated by small-cast comedies, blockbuster musicals, and international imports, especially of British companies and West End hits. Experimentation on Broadway, in essence, was marginalized.

Alterations in the circumstances of production were accompanied by equally extensive ones in other areas of theatre and drama, advanced in the late 1950s and early '60s by a new theatrical generation with priorities at odds with those of the establishment. Socially committed and aesthetically radical, these pioneers were sympathetic to BERTOLT BRECHT's Epic Theatre, Antonin Artaud's Theatre of Cruelty, and the neo-Dada Happenings of the art world. Inspired by director-theoreticians Peter Brook and Jerzy Grotowski – and later successors such as ANNE BOGART and Viewpoints theory – they would try to renew the stage by stripping away accumulated conventions to reach an essence – what Brook and Grotowski called a "holy" core.

In the process, the style, structure, and conventions of new American plays were retooled, as were subject matter and creative methodology. New genres of theatre and interpretive strategies proliferated, among them cross-disciplinary hybrids such as dance-theatre, music-theatre, and PERFORMANCE ART; docudrama, the hyperreal, and simulations; environmental theatre; guerilla theatre; structuralist theatre; poststructuralist or deconstructive theatre; choreodrama; and NEW VAUDEVILLE (and BURLESQUE). With these innovations came altered criteria for actors, directors, and designers. Similarly, orthodox theatre ARCHITECTURE evolved or was abandoned for found environments and other untraditional spaces; arena and thrust stages grew widespread, as did both "black box" and flexible arrangements that combined familiar and novel features. A methodology for site-specific theatre – drama in the found environment – was created.

Meanwhile, the demographics of theatre expanded onstage and in the audience to include members of minority groups along with their cultural priorities, perspectives, and styles. At first heard only on the fringe, the voices of African Americans, Latinos, Asians, gays, and women would soon reach Broadway, where they would win Tony Awards and Pulitzer Prizes, the highest mainstream theatrical honors. This multicultural attitude extended to artistic and intellectual approaches from other countries, particularly Asian ones, to which American theatre became more open than at any previous time in its history.

Government, foundation, corporate, and individual donations joined the box office and private investment in comprising the elements of the industry's ECONOMIC structure. As part of his Great Society program, President Lyndon B. Johnson personally rammed through Congress the 1965 bill creating the NATIONAL ENDOWMENT FOR THE ARTS (NEA). The government was back in show business for the first time since the Great Depression, when the Roosevelt administration's four-year-old FEDERAL THEATRE PROJECT was defunded by Congressional reactionaries. The NEA would fund state arts councils, which in turn spawned municipal counterparts.

This diversification of income sources signaled a growing acceptance of theatre as a cultural resource as worthy of charitable support as museums, symphony orchestras, and libraries. Labor-intensive and handmade in an age of assembly-line technology, theatre was becoming a vulnerable art form, increasingly unable to earn its own way and, therefore, in need of society's commitment to preserve it.

The ideological foundations of many of the transformations combined diluted versions of existentialism and absurdism with the post-Marxian, post-Freudian views of the New Left, plus liberal political theory and smatterings of Zen Buddhism and other Eastern systems of thought. The unconsoling visions of the existential and the absurd captured the temper of an exhausted, postwar Europe better than they did that of the continental U.S., which had escaped invasion and was soon enjoying rapid economic expansion. These philosophies, moreover, ran contrary to a deeply entrenched belief, central to the country's self-image, in the purposeful unfolding of individual and national progress. Turning away from realism and its psychological acting approaches, emerging American playwrights like EDWARD ALBEE, ARTHUR KOPIT, and JOHN GUARE (and in the second generation, CHRISTOPHER DURANG and DAVID LINDSAY-ABAIRE) embraced the absurdist stylistic vocabulary, discarding most of the existentialist content. What remained surfaced through such thinkers as Erich Fromm and Martin Buber as a faith in the redeeming power of interpersonal love.

Purged of Fromm and Buber's theological arguments and eroticized by New Left pundits, love became the buzzword of

1960s idealists. In support of the civil rights movement and in rebellion against the escalating Vietnam War, the children of this generation, armed with flowers, would muster love to challenge the leadership of the nation and the prevailing mores of their society, which they believed hypocritical, soullessly commercial, and militaristic. "All you need is love," sang the Beatles in the era's anthem, a popular-entertainment version of Fromm. In a New Left take on this sentiment, the LIVING THEATRE enacted its signature "love pile" of embracing spectators and performers, and the nude actors of the PERFORMANCE GROUP moved among audience members to caress them.

The chief representatives of the New Left were Herbert Marcuse, Norman O. Brown, and R. D. Laing, who, together with allied social thinkers such as Erving Goffman, Eric Berne, Marshall McLuhan, and Claude Lèvi-Strauss, articulated a rationale for the 1960s social, political, and aesthetic agendas. All took neo-Romantic stances, attacking reason, handmaiden of the science that had promised utopia but delivered the tools for world annihilation; instead they promoted intuition, emotion, and sensuality as antidotes to the pathology of the postindustrial world. Theory and social practice meshed as the youthful counterculture – liberated by relaxed obscenity laws and improved birth-control methods – dropped out of society, turned on to sex and drugs, and tuned in to rock and roll, a phenomenon reflected in plays like Jack Gelber's The CONNECTION (1959), Dale Wasserman's One Flew Over the Cuckoo's Nest (1963), the hippie musical HAIR (1967), the Performance Group's Dionysus in '69 (1968), Michael McClure's The Beard (1968), Lennox Raphael's Che! (1969), Robert Patrick's KENNEDY'S CHILDREN (1970), and MICHAEL WELLER'S MOONCHILDREN (1972).

Recalling a familiar American motif, the free expression of individuality was equated with present satisfaction and a bright future; hostile forces dictating conformity were linked with the past. Taking up this theme, the new generation rejected their parents' material dream along with the competitive instincts and hierarchical structures that accompanied them.

In the theatre, these ideas supported experiments of theatre artists who formed or refocused their companies in the late 1950s and the '60s, among them such diverse talents as Judith Malina and Julian Beck (the Living Theatre), JOSEPH CHAIKIN (the OPEN THEATRE), Peter Schumann (BREAD AND PUPPET THEATRE), RICHARD SCHECHNER, ANDRE GREGORY (the Manhattan Project), and RICHARD FOREMAN. Like the GROUP THEATRE of the 1930s, most would organize their companies communally, a principle they extended to COL-

LECTIVE playwriting and to the stage itself, where the ensemble starred, not individual actors. Often, actors had no formal training, an aspect of the antiprofessional ethos of the outsider-as-art era. Further, these troupes discarded psychological acting for the presentational, realistic and naturalistic dramaturgy for theatricalist idioms, and long-standing conventions of decorum for NUDITY and obscenity. Operating largely outside the commercial system, they reexamined traditional relationships between actor and character, stage and auditorium, theatre and other arts, theatre and life.

"Theatre and life are one," wrote Peter Brook in *The Empty Space* (1968), and in this era they often really were. Political demonstrators co-opted dramatic techniques, producing events with an eye to television, for more than 50 million sets were in American homes by 1960. John Cage used chance procedures and recordings of everyday noise in his musical compositions; choreographers like Merce Cunningham and Ann Halprin created dances from everyday behavior and presented them in everyday locales; and in his Happenings, ALLAN KAPROW blurred the distinction between life and art, artist and audience. Activitist theatre companies such as the Living Theatre, the Bread and Puppet Theatre, EL TEATRO CAMPESINO, and the SAN FRANCISCO MIME TROUPE took to the streets, theatricalizing the environment.

Sociology and psychology, among other disciplines, also cross-pollinated with theatre. Psychoanalysts adapted actor-training techniques to therapy; companies interested in renewing the actor's craft lifted sensitivity-training techniques from psychology. Such groups also explored the games theories of human behavior popularized by Goffman and Berne and adapted for the theatre by Viola Spolin. Her techniques of transformational acting came to both the mainstream and alternative theatres, through not only her influential book, *Improvisation for the Theatre* (1963), but also the work of her son, PAUL SILLS, who in the 1950s practiced his mother's theories at CHICAGO's Compass and SECOND CITY improvisational theatres, then went on in the 1960s to originate another new genre, Story Theatre.

Centered in Manhattan's Greenwich Village, where rents were then low and a bohemian, arts-friendly atmosphere prevailed, the Off-Broadway movement had begun in the 1950s as a low-overhead but still commercial venue for work with scant Broadway potential: classics, revivals of neglected American plays, and American premieres of recent European plays by innovative writers like Genet and Brecht. By 1960, however, the same economic pressures that would cripple Broadway were infecting Off-Broadway, giving rise to the next wave of alternative theatres. By the late 1970s only a few

Off-Broadway producers remained, and, despite a dramatic growth spurt in the early 1990s, there were only a handful of under-299-seat houses still attempting commercial production by 2006. As costs spiraled upward and seating capacity remained stagnant, fare grew less plucky. Revues, improvisational-comedy troupes, and small-scale musicals like The FAN-TASTICKS (which ran nearly 42 years) became staples, while more daring work shifted farther afield.

The collection of cafés and nontraditional or otherwise transformed performance spaces that arose as the 1950s yielded to the '60s eventually became known as OFF-OFF BROADWAY (OOB) – and became known for being what Off-Broadway was not: a forum devoted to new American plays, a laboratory for cutting-edge critical theory, and a home for the artistic expression of heterodox social and political thought. Newcomers, many more interested in process than in creating a lasting work of art, improvised stages in lofts, church basements, galleries, coffeehouses, parks, and garages.

The pioneer Off-Off Broadway venue was the CAFFE CINO (December 1958), which soon began to present plays by writers who went on to subsequent and more mainstream acclaim (MARIA IRENE FORNÉS, TERRENCE MCNALLY, LANFORD WILSON, JEAN-CLAUDE VAN ITALLIE) as well as lesser-known figures whose work was salient to the time (Doric Wilson, H. M. Koutoukas, Robert Heide). In 1961 ELLEN STEWART opened LA MAMA Experimental Theatre Club, then called Café La MaMa, a busy, durable platform for new playwrights and directors such as TOM O'HORGAN, WILFORD LEACH, and ANDREI SERBAN. Other venues followed rapidly: Al Carmines's JUDSON POETS' THEATRE (1961), WYNN HANDMAN'S AMERICAN PLACE THEATRE (1963), Ralph Cook's Theatre Genesis (1964), and JOSEPH PAPP's PUBLIC THEATER (1967), the developmental arm of his NEW YORK SHAKESPEARE FESTIVAL and arguably the most important producing organization of the postwar era. A decade and a half after his death, Papp's big shoes are still daunting to fill. During most of the 1990s and early 2000s they were worn by the multitalented, African American director, playwright, and producer GEORGE C. WOLFE; today, the Public is led by OSKAR EUSTIS, a regional theatre veteran. In circumstances at times adverse and at others favorable, these artistic directors have continued to advance Papp's inclusive, sociopolitical vision.

As the 1970s approached, experimental theatre turned away from the public art of the '60s toward inner visions that were apolitical, antihistorical, and self-reflexive. Individualistic where their predecessors were communitarian, Richard Foreman's Ontological-Hysteric Theatre (1968), ROBERT WILSON's Byrd Hoffman School of Birds (1969), and LEE BREUER with the MABOU MINES (1970) meditated on formalist concerns more closely akin to developments in music, dance, and art than to conventional theatre. Like GERTRUDE STEIN before them, they were fascinated by their own creative processes and the pictures screened in their imaginations. Together with such allied performance artists as PING CHONG, Stuart Sherman, LAURIE ANDERSON, and MEREDITH MONK, this group represents the Theatre of Images, a rubric that reflects the strongly visual, even painterly, qualities of their productions along with a corresponding disruption of language as rational discourse – reversing the time-honored authority of the word over spectacle, mind over sensory perception. Neither are Theatre of Images plays driven by coherent linear plots; rather they operate spatially, with fragments assembled by pastiche – as in another entertainment, the three-ring CIRCUS. Like high-art BARNUMS, imagists overlap motifs, presenting them simultaneously via multiple media and then shifting focus at will. Nor do imagist actors inhabit characters; instead they function performatively, often resembling kinetic sculpture in surreal dreamscapes. Spectators, like visitors to a contemporary art gallery, make what they will of what they individually see.

Wilson's work is mystical and operatic, Foreman's rigorously cerebral, whereas Breuer's juxtaposes icons of popular and elite culture. All, however, exploit postmodern, deconstructive strategies, both for their original work and to reinterpret the classics. These methods have passed to second-generation imagists such as JoANNE AKALAITIS, ELIZABETH LeCOMPTE with the WOOSTER GROUP, MARTHA CLARKE in her dance-theatre, and writer-director JOHN JESURUN, who applies sculptural and cinematic ideas to theatre.

The self-dramatizing impulse of the Theatre of Images is akin to the art-world performances of the 1960s and '70s, in which artists such as California's CHRIS BURDEN exploited their own bodies as a medium. In the name of immediacy, Burden, in a piece called "Shoot," was shot in the arm; in other pieces, he variously crawled on glass and stuck pins in his stomach. The performance artist Ron Athey, a generation later, would explore self-mutilation as a theatrical construct still further. A gentler strain appears in today's numerous autobiographical monologists, among whom SPALDING GRAY was, for a time, king. (His successors include ERIC BOGOSIAN, LISA KRON, Marga Gomez, and TIM MILLER.)

Others showcases for prickly fringe art followed in the 1980s, emerging from the performance clubs of the East Village: PERFORMANCE SPACE 122, DANCE THEATRE WORKSHOP, The KITCHEN, Franklin Furnace; the lucky few played the BROOKLYN ACADEMY OF MUSIC's New Wave Festival and

LINCOLN CENTER's counterpart, Serious Fun. Occasionally like-minded work has even appeared on Broadway, where LILY TOMLIN and WHOOPI GOLDBERG have performed ONE-PERSON shows italicizing race, gender, and self; naturally, though, the commercial theatre's interest in solo perfor-mances reflected fiscal reality. The trend may have crested with *I AM MY OWN WIFE*, Doug Wright's one-person play about a German transvestite, which won the Tony for Best Play in 2004 as well as the Pulitzer Prize for Drama. If this trend reflected the enterprise of actor-writers in a shrinking market, it suggested also the spirit of the narcissistic era that writer Tom Wolfe has called the "Me Generation" and how it morphed in the intervening decades.

Only a decade from its inception, the OOB movement of the 1960s and '70s had grown enough to warrant a collective service organization, the Off-Off Broadway Alliance (OOBA), later succeeded by the ALLIANCE OF RESIDENT THEATRES/ NEW YORK. By 1974–5 OOB included 150 theatres, which had produced 548 plays that season. By 2006 there were more than 200 venues and at least five times that many nonprofit companies producing in them. The economics have never been favorable: After the mid-1970s, the reaction of social and aesthetic forces with erotic energy that had enlivened the 1960s artistic scene slowed at the conclusion of the Viet-nam War in 1973, soon after which inflation rose and the national economy slumped.

The flamboyant sensibilities of Caffe Cino and La MaMa playwrights no longer seemed to capture the post-Vietnam times. During the 1970s and early '80s the Bread and Puppet Theatre retreated to Vermont and the Open Theatre dis-banded, as did the Performance Group, the Manhattan Proj-ect, the Judson Poets' Theatre, Theatre Genesis, and others. In their stead arose not-for-profit theatres with long-term institutional goals and more traditional artistic tastes. The CIRCLE REPERTORY COMPANY (1969), PLAYWRIGHTS HORI-ZONS (1971), ENSEMBLE STUDIO THEATRE (1971), and SECOND STAGE (1979) emphasized American playwrights such as A. R. GURNEY, TINA HOWE, ROMULUS LINNEY, RONALD RIBMAN, or CHRISTOPHER DURANG, whose works had relatively famil-iar dramaturgic genes. Others, such as the CHELSEA THEATRE CENTER (1968), the MANHATTAN THEATRE CLUB (1970), THE-ATRE FOR THE NEW CITY (1971), the ACTING COMPANY (1972), and the DODGER Theatre (1978) mixed new American plays with premieres of foreign plays or freshly interpreted stan-dards. At first outsiders, these groups would become fixtures of the mainstream theatre, burnishing a diminished Broad-way. Since 1970 nonprofits on Broadway – some now defunct – have become common: CIRCLE IN THE SQUARE; ROUND-ABOUT THEATRE COMPANY; the VIVIAN BEAUMONT AND

MITZI E. NEWHOUSE THEATRES of Lincoln Center and MANHATTAN THEATRE CLUB, among them.

Theatre of the 1960s and '70s also embraced racial causes and gender issues, as well as the interests of many other constituencies as diverse as the deaf (NATIONAL THEATRE OF THE DEAF, 1967), former prison inmates (The Family, 1972), and the elderly (Tale Spinners, 1975). Here minority artists found employment, while long-disenfranchised audiences could see plays by one of their own in which the destinies of characters like themselves were central rather than background to the American saga.

AFRICAN AMERICAN THEATRE has won the most prominent place in both nonprofit and commercial arenas. Whereas in 1948 black novelist and playwright JAMES BALDWIN moved to France to escape rascism at home, in 1990 AUGUST WILSON collected his second Pulitzer Prize for Drama. Then as now, Broadway favored musicals and revues by and about African Americans: Some of the hits from 1960–80 were *The Wiz, Ain't Misbehavin'*, and *Sophisticated Ladies;* 1980–2005 saw *Dreamgirls, JELLY'S LAST JAM*, and *The Color Purple*. For a time, commercial productions of legitimate plays had been rare and runs short. Black drama awaited the moral and political momentum of the emerging civil rights movement. The first long-run crossover was LORRAINE HANSBERRY's play *A RAISIN IN THE SUN* (1959), which ran on Broadway for 530 performances and won the New York Drama Critics' Circle Award – a first not only for an African American but also for a woman. It would make both a profit and the careers of the original and later cast members. Its director, LLOYD RICHARDS, went on to open establishment doors for generations of other black artists; he also affected national arts policy as head of the influential NATIONAL PLAYWRIGHTS CONFERENCE and of one of the country's most prestigious theatrical training grounds, the Yale School of Drama, together with its professional arm, the YALE REPERTORY THEATRE.

Although other legitimate hits would follow *Raisin,* the mood of African American drama now turned militant, discouraging commercial producers. The new, increasingly confrontational black drama took its cue more from Malcolm X's black power movement than from Martin Luther King's dream of integration. The fierce, iconoclastic plays of LeRoi Jones (AMIRI BARAKA) and ED BULLINS embraced a view of theatre as the artistic muscle of radical politics and of orthodox dramaturgy as an aspect of white oppression. Writing unsparingly of their dual experiences as women in a man's world and blacks in a white society, award-winning playwrights ADRIENNE KENNEDY and NTOZAKE SHANGE developed unique dramatic forms that owed more to poetry than to theatrical precedent.

At the same time, the Johnson Administration's poverty programs made government funds available to bolster black theatre companies like Baraka's Spirit House in Newark, NJ, support augmented after 1965 by the new NEA. With both public and private monies to encourage their growth, troupes sprang up nationwide, most important among them the FREE SOUTHERN THEATRE (New Orleans), New LAFAYETTE THEATRE (Harlem), NEGRO ENSEMBLE COMPANY (the East Village), Concept East (Detroit), and Black Arts/West (San Francisco). By 1968 there were 40 such groups, and when the first NATIONAL BLACK THEATER FESTIVAL convened in Winston–Salem, NC, in 1989, some 200 theatres were represented.

DOUGLAS TURNER WARD, LONNE ELDER, Joseph A. Walker, Philip Hayes Dean, Sonia Sanchez, Derek Walcott, Leslie Lee, Richard Wesley, and Ron Milner were among the new playwrights. So were ALICE CHILDRESS, the first black woman to have a play professionally produced in America (*Gold Through the Trees,* 1952). CHARLES GORDONE's *NO PLACE TO BE SOMEBODY* (1970) won the first Pulitzer Prize for Drama awarded to an African American dramatist; CHARLES FULLER took the second for *A SOLDIER'S PLAY* in 1981; August Wilson won two, in 1986 and 1990; and SUZAN-LORI PARKS became the first woman so honored in 2002. Among other successful African American writers for the stage, one could also cite REGINA TAYLOR, LYNN NOTTAGE, OYAMO, and the unique ANNA DEAVERE SMITH, who performs solo her multicharacter, multicultural works addressing race and gender issues.

Other racial minorities have also found theatre an effective tool for dealing with discrimination and asserting their place in the national mosaic. HANAY GEIOGAMAH's Native American Theatre Ensemble evolved out of the American Indian Movement of the late 1960s, as did SPIDERWOMAN, a feminist theatre founded by Muriel Miguel and her sisters, Cana/Rappahannock Indians. LUIS VALDÉZ established El Teatro Campesino on a flatbed truck beside the picket lines of California's Chicano and Filipino grape pickers, then embraced the larger dilemma of Chicanos caught between Mexican and American cultures. New York theatres such as INTAR, the REPERTORIO ESPAÑOL, and the PUERTO RICAN TRAVELING THEATRE have expanded the opportunities for Latino actors and directors. Programs for Latino writers at nonprofit theatres have nurtured enough able playwrights – Lynn Alvarez and EDUARDO MACHADO, and NILO CRUZ among them – to fill a recent anthology of contemporary Hispanic American plays. On the fringe, performance artists GUILLERMO GOMEZ-PEÑA, Marga Gomez, and JOHN LEGUIZAMO have explored ethnicity and dramatic form, while in the mainstream GERALD GUTIERREZ became an award-rich director.

Except for such pseudo-Oriental plays by white authors as *Teahouse of the August Moon* or musicals like *The KING AND I* and *Flower Drum Song,* Asians were theatrical shadows until 1965, when the EAST WEST PLAYERS was established in LOS ANGELES, followed by the Asian America Workshop in SAN FRANCISCO and the PAN ASIAN REPERTORY in New York. Today ASIAN AMERICAN playwrights are regularly produced in the subsidized theatre devoted to, and not specifically devoted to, their work: Frank Chin, PHILIP KAN GOTANDA, JESSICA HAGEDORN, and James Yoshimura. The first Broadway recognition went to Chinese American playwright DAVID HENRY HWANG for his *M. BUTTERFLY.* Subsequent writers of note have included Diana Son (*Stop Kiss; Satellites*).

Catalyzed by the efforts of activists to gain social and legal equity for homosexuals, GAY THEATRE troupes surfaced in the 1960s – enough of them by 1973 that TOSOS (The Other Side of Silence) became the first specifically gay-oriented theatre company in the nation, and that, by 1978, a Gay Theatre Alliance was formed. In the vanguard was the Caffe Cino, home of a camp sensibility that was enlarged at Ron Tavel and John Vaccaro's Play-House of the Ridiculous (1965) – see THEATRE OF THE RIDICULOUS – and reached its zenith with CHARLES LUDLAM'S RIDICULOUS THEATRICAL COMPANY (1967). "We have passed beyond the absurd," said Tavel, explaining the psychosocial source of the genre, "our situation is absolutely preposterous." The acceptance of homosexual subjects by mainstream audiences was launched by Mart Crowley's *The BOYS IN THE BAND* (1968), which ran 1,000 performances Off-Broadway. By 1995, Broadway productions of plays and musicals by gay writers and/or featuring gay characters had collectively won many Pulitzers and Tonys.

That is not to say that the focus of the gay artists remained implacable or stagnant. By the mid-1980s, for example, camp had faded, replaced by a sober response to AIDS, for the fatal disorder had devastated the homosexual and arts communities. Playwrights such as William M. Hoffman, Harry Kondoleon, TONY KUSHNER, LARRY KRAMER, PAULA VOGEL, and CHERYL WEST dramatized their grief for the dead and their rage with a sluggish official response to the epidemic, as did gay performance artists, among them David Wojnarowicz, TIM MILLER, and JOHN KELLY. In 1987, Kramer shifted his focus from the stage to the streets, founding the AIDS Coalition to Unleash Power (ACT-UP), which uses theatricalized civil disobedience to prompt political action. For its efforts, ACT-UP has received a Bessie Award, the Tony of performance art.

Drawing strength from the women's liberation movement – itself an offspring of civil rights initiatives – women's and FEMINIST THEATRES were widely established in the 1970s, and women began to enter the professional theatre in unprecedented numbers, not only as actresses, but as everything from artistic directors, to stage managers, to critics. In the 1980s, Pulitzers came to BETH HENLEY, MARSHA NORMAN, and WENDY WASSERSTEIN, raising by fifty percent the total number of the prizes awarded to women playwrights since their inception in 1918; the ranks were increased dramatically in the waning years of the 20th century when Margaret Edson (*WIT*), Paula Vogel, and Suzan-Lori Parks were named winners too. There were other firsts as well. In 1982 ELLEN BURSTYN became the first woman president of the 60-year-old ACTORS' EQUITY ASSOCIATION, followed by COLLEEN DEWHURST in 1984, the same year that HEIDI LANDESMAN won the Tony with her sets for *Big River,* the first such award to a woman designer; JULIE TAYMOR and SUSAN STROMAN became the first women to win Tonys for directing a musical in 1997 and 2000, respectively. The Players, an all-male stronghold for a century, admitted women to CLUB membership in 1989. Another landmark was the inauguration in Buffalo, NY, of an International Women's Playwrights Conference (1988), which drew some 291 women representing 34 nations.

Unlike the Pulitzer winners, playwrights with a feminist vision not only italicized women's lives but often held unorthodox views of dramatic structure, characterization, and other theatrical verities, among them Shange, Fornés, and Kennedy as well as Eve Merriman, MEGAN TERRY, Corinne Jacker, KAREN MALPEDE, ROSALYN DREXLER, and SUSAN YANKOWITZ. Their homes were activist companies of the fringe, which numbered 110 nationwide by 1980. Although performance artists were initially hostile to theatre, by the 1980s the genre had attracted a sizable number of theatre people, particularly feminists. Robbie McCauley and Laurie Carlos, both African Americans, deal with issues of race and gender; RACHEL ROSENTHAL often explores cultural attitudes to the female body, as does KAREN FINLEY; and HOLLY HUGHES looks at lesbian sexuality. All of their work is in part autobiographical, all centered on the performer rather than production values, all both formally and thematically experimental. In tandem with evolving dramatic content and modes of performance, an innovative body of critical discourse has also emerged among feminist literary and theatrical scholars.

Besides ETHNIC and gender diversification, anti-American plays proliferated in the late 1960s as the nation turned against the Vietnam War. The San Francisco Mime Troupe, the Yale Repertory Theatre, and the Living Theatre all performed agit-prop, antiwar material, as would the Bread and Puppet Theatre, the Performance Group, La MaMa ETC, the Open Theatre, and others. Among the antiwar plays were

ROBERT LOWELL's *The Old Glory* (1964), Megan Terry's *Viet Rock* (1966), Joseph Heller's *We Bombed in New Haven* (1968), and DAVID RABE's Vietnam trilogy – *The* BASIC TRAINING OF PAVLO HUMMEL (1968), STICKS AND BONES (1971), and STREAMERS (1976). Most Vietnam plays look at home-front rather than battlefield trauma, with Amlin Gray's *How I Got That Story* (1979) a partial exception. Many also exploit stylistically disruptive tactics that paraphrase the psychosocial consequences of the experience for individuals and the body politic. Likewise, the 1980s witnessed plays in reaction to nuclear proliferation (see below); the '90s, responses to AIDS and the Gulf War; and the early 21st century, reactions to the 9/11 attacks and U.S. involvement in Iraq.

Also arising in the 1970s were docudramas (or DOCUMENTARY THEATRE) inspired by the plays of German writers Rolf Hochhuth and Peter Weiss, who used oral history and the public record to indict corrupt official acts. Daniel Berrigan drew on courtroom transcripts for *The Trial of the Catonsville Nine* (1971), a government prosecution of Berrigan and fellow draft opponents, while ERIC BENTLEY exploited Congressional annals for *Are You Now or Have You Ever Been* (1972), his look at the 1950s McCarthy hearings. Following in this tradition is EMILY MANN's *Execution of Justice* (1982), a montage of perspectives on the murder of a gay San Francisco councilman, Harvey Milk. A related group of protest plays responded to fears of apocalypse in the age of nuclear warfare, among them SAM SHEPARD's *Icarus's Mother* (1965), Edward Albee's *Box* (1968), TENNESSEE WILLIAMS's *The Red Devil Battery Sign* (1975), and the MABOU MINES' DEAD END KIDS: A History of Nuclear Power (1982). In the 1990s the docudrama form was most forcefully represented by the work of the TECTONIC THEATER PROJECT; a powerful example from 2005–6 is *Columbinus,* a dramatic examination of the Columbine school shooting.

Some of the most resonant American drama of the 1970s and '80s came from Off-Broadway's Sam Shepard and Lanford Wilson, together with DAVID MAMET. All focus on values lost in pursuit of the American material dream, but where Wilson is a lyric realist in the tradition of Tennessee Williams, Shepard takes a mythic tone, infused with nostalgia for the Old West. Mamet's signature is a terse and profane urban vernacular that brings to mind the crisp, hard-driving, quick-changing phrases of 1920s Chicago jazz. Mamet's career, in fact, began in Chicago at the St. Nicholas Theatre, which he cofounded in 1974. Anchored by the older GOODMAN THEATRE and the brainy irreverence of Second City – cradle of director MIKE NICHOLS and many familiar actors, comics, and writers – CHICAGO now has a nationally acclaimed alternative enclave of husky Off-Loop companies, the BODY POLITIC,

the ORGANIC THEATRE, VICTORY GARDENS, and STEPPEN-
WOLF among them.

Unlike the pioneer regional theatres of the 1950s, second-
generation companies were designed from the outset as nonprofit organizations and were, therefore, eligible for support
from private foundations and government. Stimulated by
large grants – the first from the Ford Foundation in 1959,
followed by the Rockefeller Foundation, the new NEA, and
others – the movement gained significant momentum by the
mid-1960s. When Ford created the THEATRE COMMUNICA-
TIONS GROUP (TCG) in 1961 to assist the RESIDENT NON-
PROFIT sector, the organization served only 16 theatres; by
1966 TCG had 35 constituents, a number that had grown to a
national network of 238 in 1992 and more than 400 by 2006.

Among important regional companies of the 1960s were
CENTER STAGE of Baltimore, MD, the GUTHRIE THEATER in
Minneapolis, MN, the SEATTLE REPERTORY, WA, and TRINITY
[SQUARE] REPERTORY COMPANY of Providence, RI (1963); the
ACTORS THEATRE OF LOUISVILLE, KY, and HARTFORD STAGE
(1964); and LONG WHARF of New Haven, CT, A CONTEMPO-
RARY THEATRE, Seattle, and the AMERICAN CONSERVATORY
THEATRE in San Francisco, CA (1965). Cultural centers –
including New York's Lincoln Center, the JOHN F. KENNEDY
CENTER in Washington, DC, and the Los Angeles Music
Center – were also built with theatres as part of their complexes. Although many regionals called themselves resident
repertory companies, typically only management was resident, and shows were rarely produced in rotating rep, which
proved prohibitively expensive. Initially, these theatres
favored the conservatively interpreted classics and standards
approved by establishment board members and subscribers,
but by the early 1970s a riskier repertoire, including new
plays, was widely welcomed. Also welcomed was a profession
new to American theatre, the dramaturge or literary manager, who was charged to find promising scripts and help
nurture them.

While the new theatre evolved in downtown New York and
elsewhere, the Broadway of the 1960s and '70s remained
lively, although each year it owed more to properties developed elsewhere. Its leading playwrights were NEIL SIMON
and Edward Albee, who from different angles would both
explore deteriorating family and personal relationships and
the inability of individuals to maintain community. Following twenty overwhelmingly successful years on Broadway,
Simon's comedic oeuvre was finally acknowledged with a
1991 Pulitzer for LOST IN YONKERS. Albee came of age as a
major dramatist with WHO'S AFRAID OF VIRGINIA WOOLF?
(1962), since which his work has earned three Pulitzers, the
first in 1966 for A DELICATE BALANCE, the second for SEASCAPE

in 1976. After an 18-year hiatus, during which his new work languished, he collected the third for *Three Tall Women* – which played not on but Off-Broadway.

Rock music and nudity went mainstream in the 1960s when the counterculture musical HAIR (1967) transferred from the Public Theatre to Broadway, where it remained a cultural as well as an artistic event and spawned a wave of imitations. Although fewer materialized each decade, traditional musicals continued apace, represented by such long-run shows as FIDDLER ON THE ROOF (1964), ANNIE (1977), *Grand Hotel* (1989), and JELLY'S LAST JAM (1992). Since the 1970s, musicals by Britain's ANDREW LLOYD WEBBER have exerted increasing influence, particularly on Broadway economics. From *Jesus Christ Superstar* (1971) to *The Woman in White* (2006), Webber's pop-opera spectacles have whetted audience appetite for elaborate mise-en-scène, in turn boosting production costs and ticket prices industrywide as the competition tried to keep up. If, however, emphasis on settings has encumbered producers, it has liberated America's many world-class designers, some of the most notable of whom are SCENIC DESIGNERS JOHN LEE BEATTY, TONY WALTON, ROBIN WAGNER, SANTO LOQUASTO, and ADRIENNE LOBEL; COSTUME DESIGNERS JANE GREENWOOD, FLORENCE KLOTZ, WILLA KIM, WILLIAM IVEY LONG, MARTIN PAKLEDINAZ, and CATHERINE ZUBER; and PAT COLLINS, BEVERLY EMMONS, JULES FISHER, PEGGY EISENHAUER, KEN BILLINGTON, RICHARD PILBROW, Brian MacDevitt, Andrew Bridge, and JENNIFER TIPTON in STAGE LIGHTING.

Dominating home-grown musical theatre since the mid-1970s is STEPHEN SONDHEIM, today's most original American composer-lyricist. For much of his career he collaborated with director HAROLD PRINCE, himself an important innovator; later on, his collaborations with writer-director JAMES LAPINE and librettist John Weidman were similarly celebrated. Following their lead, American musicals became less dependent on a book than on a concept or theme, a trend that has elevated choreographer-directors to a new position of power. Most celebrated of the new breed were BOB FOSSE and MICHAEL BENNETT, the latter responsible for developing *A CHORUS LINE* (1973), which when it closed had become the longest-running show on Broadway ever.

Along with the British musical invasion beginning in the 1970s, transfers of nonmusical successes from the London stage have often fleshed out Broadway seasons, among them Peter Shaffer's *Equus* and *Amadeus;* David Storey's *The Changing Room* and *Home;* Tom Stoppard's *Travesties, The Real Thing, Hapgood,* and *Arcadia;* Harold Pinter's *The Homecoming* and *Betrayal;* and plays by David Hare, Simon Gray, Caryl Churchill, and others. The Royal Shakespeare Company, which has visited several times, is especially remembered for *The Life and Adventures of Nicholas Nickleby* in 1980, a production whose staging approaches owed something to the theatricalist styles of the American experimental theatre of the 1960s and '70s and subsequently influenced dramaturgy, staging techniques, and box-office prices (with its top $100 ticket, then a new Broadway high). This trend has not abated in the early 2000s, with numerous notable transferrals (often revivals).

As the century's end came into view in 1990, there was no doubt that Broadway was *in extremis*. American originals were the clear commercial exception. As the last decade of the 20th century began, so much about American theatre looked bleak: The demolition in New York of The HELEN HAYES, MOROSCO, and Bijou theatres, and the long-term rental of the MARK HELLINGER, once home to *MY FAIR LADY,* to the Times Square Church, proved that real estate and gentrification will always play Goliath to the theatre's David. Production in the early 1990s hit a nadir from which it would later recover: 29 new musicals opened on Broadway between 1990 and mid-1995 (versus 423 from 1920 to 1930), but between 2000 and mid-2005 there were more than 40. Of course, the definition of the American musical, at least as Broadway defined it, seemed under siege: Must a musical have a book? (*Contact* and *Movin' Out* told stories entirely through dance.) Must an actor sing? (In *The Drowsy Chaperone* the role of Man in Chair requires almost no singing or dancing abilities.) Must a musical be considered "finished" when it opens? (*The Scarlet Pimpernel* had three different openings to showcase revisions in 1997, 1998, and 1999.) Just as formal boundaries between genres seemed increasingly irrelevant elsewhere in the American theatre, the Tony Awards created a Special Theatrical Event category for all it couldn't compartmentalize, be it solo confessional (*ELAINE STRITCH at Liberty*) or spectacle (*Squonk, Blast!*). It became increasingly popular to look to properties that had never been mounted on Broadway in the past but that had titles of a certain coinage, which is how BURIED CHILD and TRUE WEST in 1996 and 2000 marked Sam Shepard's return to Broadway since 1970; and why musicals such as LITTLE SHOP OF HORRORS, which ran Off-Broadway for 2,209 performances, suddenly turned up on Broadway in 2003.

The National Endowment for the Arts, whose founding the federal government had supported, however reluctantly, in the 1960s, was increasingly a political football. Reflecting the national temper, legislators first attempted to censor the NEA, exploiting a rhetoric familiar from the Congressional strike on the Federal Theatre Project fifty years earlier. When rebuffed by the courts on First Amendment grounds, ultra-conservative Republicans, led by a superbly bigoted, unapol-

ogetically homophobic North Carolina senator named Jesse
Helms, pursued de facto CENSORSHIP by enacting punitive
budget cuts aimed at eliminating all Endowment funding.
The federal endorsement had been a seal of approval, a reas-
surance to corporate and foundation contributors, whose
donations began to decline along with those of individuals.
With the NEA under threat and the end of the 1990–1 Gulf
War causing a national recession, funding for the nation's
network of nonprofit regional theatres also became scarcer.
In the end, Helms and his like-minded political brethren
objected publicly and viciously to the ambitious and admittedly button-pushing theatre work of a group of individual
performance artists dubbed the NEA four – Karen Finley, Tim
Miller, John Fleck, and Holly Hughes. In so doing, they succeeded in turning the idea of public funding for the arts from
a noble liberal effort into a reactionary's cause célèbre, a situation that had yet to be fully reversed by 2006, although the
NEA tenure of actress JANE ALEXANDER during the mid-to-
late '90s managed to soothe several conservative nerves. Still,
although an ongoing debate about the role of the arts in a
popular society is a good, since the 1990s it has in practice
fostered a climate of growing racism, misogyny, homophobia, and anti-intellectualism with which a balkanized Left
seems only fitfully able to cope, though doggedly hoping to
do so.

Is there a connection between the political/economic woes
of the American theatre in the early 1990s and the fact that
not a single new American musical qualified for the 1994–5
Tonys, forcing officials to use a revue as widow dressing?
Only in this sense: There was a general malaise in production
levels in the 1990s as Broadway slowly but perceptibly abandoned its commitment to artistic innovation, if not to excellence. Old diehards died hard: When Neil Simon, the quintessential Broadway playwright, defected to Off-Broadway
with his new comedy, *London Suite,* making it ineligible for a
Tony, the move enhanced a general view that commercial
Off-Broadway at last might have economic legs strong enough
to rival Broadway. Near Union Square, the Variety Arts Theatre opened; by 2000, commercial Off-Broadway houses were,
if not thriving, clearly more in evidence. Since 1991 no
winner of the Pulitzer Prize in Drama has *not* played Off-
Broadway, and two plays – Robert Schenkkan's The KENTUCKY
CYCLE and NILO CRUZ's *Anna in the Tropics* – hadn't been produced in New York at the time of their awards. In terms of
developing new work and the artisans who make it, the American theatre now depended less on Broadway than at any time
before. It became a commonplace that works were developed
through nonprofits, in or out of New York, be it Off- or Off-Off
Broadway or Atlanta, Boston, Denver, Houston, Louisville (at

the Actors Theatre of Louisville), New Haven, Minneapolis, San Francisco – even in Los Angeles.

Meanwhile, to describe production costs as astronomical was virtually an act of understatement. Yet increasingly in the new century, it was a matter of perspective: If the musical version of *Lord of the Rings* could be mounted in Toronto for more than $25 million, what's $5 or $8 million in New York? Escapist entertainments, which are not star-reliant and inevitably more minimal in every respect, flourished, from kitschy fare (NUNSENSE, FOREVER PLAID, *Catskills on Broadway*) to spectacle (*De La Guarda, Stomp, Tap Dogs, Blast*) to a flotilla of one-person plays (*Twilight: Los Angeles 1992, Full Gallop*, I AM MY OWN WIFE) and solo performances (*Elaine Stritch at Liberty, Sexaholix*).

Unions grew into bigger thorns in bigger sides as the '90s and the "oughts" evolved: Actors' Equity began battling nonunion tours, and strikes – which Local 802, the Musicians Union, did in 2003 – seemed ever more possible.

High production costs mean high ticket prices – the Broadway top currently wavering between $65 and $100-plus, with corollary inflation in the Off-Broadway and nonprofit worlds. At such levels, most theatregoers are priced out of the market, and those who can afford seats are understandably as reluctant to take risks as are producers. Consequently, audiences are richer, grayer, and whiter than they were even 10 years ago, and less committed to the art form. Except onstage, where nontraditional casting and plays by and about minority groups have gained purchase, the multicultural initiatives of recent decades have stagnated or are in retreat. For instance, only a handful of the 110 women's theatres counted in 1980 are alive today, and a number of esteemed minority showcases, among them the NEGRO ENSEMBLE COMPANY, are now defunct or facing extinction.

Some of this contraction is natural attrition, some assimilation of minority artists and perspectives into the larger culture, and some the fallout of factions competing for a life-sustaining share of the fiscal pie. The pivotal causes, however, were the severe economic recession of the early 1990s and equally severe financial problems that beset the nation following the terrorist attacks of September 11, 2001, and during the nation's subsequent wars in Afghanistan and Iraq. If the generation of the 1960s looked to the future, warning not to trust anyone over 30, the '90s and the 2000s looked to the past, longing for a return to a homogenous, midcentury, golden age that looks and feels much like Thornton Wilder's 1938 *Our Town.*

In competition with mass media and advanced telecommunications, theatre continued to lose ground. Joining the lineup with film and television as the millennium approached were the technological attractions of computer-generated entertainments like virtual reality – an environment that transports users to three-dimensional, artificial locales that exist only electronically – and, of course, the World Wide Web.

Worse, the stage is longer a goal for many, but a stepping-stone to television and film, which have siphoned off its performers with the prospect of national exposure and generous livelihoods unlikely in today's theatre. During the 1990s, it was increasingly common for TV actors in particular to take a role in Broadway show, but typically these were for very short periods of time, when they were not in television production. As such "hiatus" casting was responsible for the success of certain long-running Broadway hits – the 1994 revival of GREASE, the 1996 revival of *Chicago* (more than 4,000 performances at this writing), the 1998 revival of CABARET, Disney's *Aida* in 2000, *Hairspray* in 2002 – TV stars and, later, A-List film stars began seeing Broadway and the theatre as a forum to increase their stature in the industry, a way station on the road to royal Hollywood throne.

Others, of course, begin in the theatre and don't come back. Barbra Streisand, natural heir to MERMAN, hasn't played on Broadway since FUNNY GIRL closed in 1965. AL PACINO, DUSTIN HOFFMAN, and JAMES EARL JONES, as well as successors like MORGAN FREEMAN, BERNADETTE PETERS, MANDY PATINKIN, MERYL STREEP, WILLIAM HURT, KEVIN KLINE, and GLENN CLOSE are sometime visitors, whereas Broadway stalwarts are not household names. Mamet, Shepard, and newcomers KENNETH LONERGAN and NEIL LABUTE and other talented writers now favor film, sometimes over the stage; the grammar of many contemporary plays today have a cinematic breathlessness, a visual edge. Besides the long-familiar use of film clips and projections, post-1970s drama often exploits cinematic techniques like the jump-cut and the cross-fade as well as piecemeal exposition and multiple locales familiar to an impatient and visually literate generation reared on television's short scenic units and the hyperkinetic country of MTV.

Brook and Grotowski long ago predicted that theatre would survive only if it stopped trying to compete with the camera, instead focusing on what sets it apart: the unmediated exchange between actor and spectator and a communal experience. Audiences have in fact begun to seek out immediacy. Witness the popularity of role-playing games and events like Dungeons and Dragons and the Renaissance Fair, as well as PARTICIPATORY THEATRE. A remnant of the environmental stagings of earlier decades, participatory shows range from commerical entertainments such as *Tamara* or *Tony and Tina's Wedding* to New Vaudeville, the performance art of the BLUE MAN GROUP, and the site-specific work of the defunct En

Garde Arts. That film and television have coopted realism may be less a loss to the stage than an opportunity to leave the representational for its age-old strength, the metaphoric – a direction suggested, for instance, by the imagistic theatricalism of JULIE TAYMOR, Basil Twist, and others who use time-honored traditions of PUPPETRY, mask, MIME, and storytelling to create innovative but still widely accessible productions. In particular, puppetry has enjoyed a popular revival, with national festivals cropping up often, and mainstream theatre figuring them prominently in Tony-winning musicals (*AVENUE Q*) as easily as in family drama (VOGEL's *The Long Christmas Ride Home*).

All in all, our theatre is a healthily decentralized, if precarious, national tapestry with porous borders between what is commercial – sometimes even what is *theatre* – and what is not. Amateur, academic, institutional, and experimental stages coexist and interact symbiotically with one another and with for-profit arenas from dinner theatre to SUMMER STOCK to industrial shows to Broadway. Despite tensions between assimilation and difference, the single audience of the past, with its shared expectations, has made room for other constituencies, all served by a medley of theatrical voices and multiple ways and means to underwrite the variety.

There was something of a valedictory air as the 20th century came to a close – it seemed extraordinary that a theatre that had begun so uncertainly, so languidly, yet so giddily should have displayed such astonishing fin de siècle fertility. As the new century began, there was, all adversity aside, a sense that there were still new aesthetics to develop and argue, new paths of dramaturgical exploration yet to take. Money or not, popular or not, at the utter epicenter of American culture or not, the theatre seemed game to get going once again.   CLJ DBW LJ

[*Ed. note:* Various items referred to above are discussed in greater detail in their own (mostly cross-referenced) entries in the text; see also the List of Topical Entries in the front matter.]

A

Aarons, Alexander A. (1891–1943) and **Alfred E. Aarons** (1865–1936) Producers, theatrical managers. Alfred began as a theatrical callboy in Philadelphia, then moved in 1890 to New York, where he managed the Standard Theatre, KOSTER AND BIAL's, the Manhattan Roof Garden, and the BROADHURST THEATRE. He also wrote songs for several undistinguished musicals and produced a number of musicals and plays.

Alexander, Alfred's son, produced several of the GERSHWINS' most successful shows of the 1920s and '30s, including *Lady Be Good* and *Girl Crazy*. With VINTON FREEDLEY he built the ALVIN THEATRE in New York in 1927, but lost it in financial reverses five years later. He worked in Hollywood for several years in a variety of production jobs with MGM and RKO. MK

Abbey, Henry Edwin (1846–96) Impresario known early in his career for presenting costly entertainments to audiences outside major U.S. theatre centers and, from 1880, for his success in booking the best European actors, actresses, and opera singers for U.S. engagements, for which he became known as "The Napoleon of the Managers." The partnership of Abbey, John B. Schoeffel, and MAURICE GRAU managed theatres in New York, BOSTON, and PHILADELPHIA, as well as the tours of domestic and international stars. At the New Park Theatre, New York (1877), he brought together WILLIAM H. CRANE and STUART ROBSON, a starring tandem that flourished until 1889. The partnership took over the Metropolitan Opera House, New York (1883), and until Abbey's death in 1896 the management was distinctive for the great stars they hired. WD

Abbott, George (1887–1995) Director, playwright, and actor who became the most practical showman in Broadway history. As performer, coauthor, play doctor, and director of over 130 productions, Abbott entertained audiences more often and over a longer period of time than anyone else, garnering six Tony Awards and a Pulitzer. He first acted on a Broadway stage in 1913; in the fall of 1989 he directed a workshop produc-

tion of a new musical called *Frankie*, and in 1994 served as consultant for the Broadway revival of DAMN YANKEES. As both director and coauthor his specialities were racy contemporary melodrama (*BROADWAY*, 1926); split-second farce (*THREE MEN ON A HORSE*, 1935); and peppy musicals with vigorous choreography (*ON YOUR TOES*, 1936; *Damn Yankees*, 1955). Gangsters, bookies, gold diggers, politicians, baseball heroes, hoofers, and hookers populated his work, providing colorful slices of Americana. Despite the occasional suggestion of sexual daring (as in *Coquette* [1927] and *New Girl in Town* [1957], his musical version of *ANNA CHRISTIE*) and of political conflict (*The PAJAMA GAME*, 1954; *FIORELLO!* 1959), the typical Abbott show was archly conservative. The famed "Abbott touch" always kept his shows spinning at a brisk clip, but Abbott downplayed his technique, claiming that all he did was make actors "say their final syllables." His autobiography was published in 1963. In 1994 Abbott received the Distinguished Achievement in Musical Theatre Award from the DRAMA LEAGUE. In his honor, the "Mr. Abbott" Award is given annually by the Society of Stage Directors and Choreographers. FH

Abdoh, Reza (1963–95) Iranian-born director who moved from London to Los Angeles at 16 and at 22 staged *King Lear*. During his career, cut short by AIDS, he directed 17 other works, most written or adapted by him, including *The Hip-Hop Waltz of Eurydice* and *Bogeyman* in LA; three final works were produced in New York where he relocated in 1991 (Dar a Luz company). A number of his stagings in NYC were produced by En Garde Arts. By his death Abdoh was considered by many one of the most innovative and original avant-garde directors in the U.S. DBW

Abe Lincoln in Illinois by ROBERT E. SHERWOOD. Biographical play in 12 scenes; winner of the Pulitzer Prize for 1938–9. Sherwood's play featured RAYMOND MASSEY as Lincoln in a loosely constructed work held together only by the presence of the central character in each of its episodes, sketching the life of Lincoln from 22-year-old student of grammar to grim-faced president-elect. The highly praised production was directed by ELMER RICE and was the first project of the newly formed PLAYWRIGHTS' COMPANY; the play opened on 15 October 1938 at the PLYMOUTH THEATRE in New York and ran for 472 performances. A screen version starring Massey was released in 1940. LINCOLN CENTER revived it fall 1993 with SAM WATERSTON.   MF

Abie's Irish Rose   The story of the mixed-up marriage between a Jewish boy and an Irish girl, written and produced by Anne Nichols; opened at the Fulton Theatre on 23 May 1922. Although critics panned it as an ethnic burlesque, audiences loved the heartwarming story, and it made a fortune for its author-producer. Called "the million dollar play," it set a 14-year record of 2,327 consecutive performances (closing in 1927). Its success continued as a play (revived 1937, 1954), a film (1928, 1946), a radio show (1940s), and a TV sitcom ("Bridget Loves Bernie," 1970s). Nichols wrote numerous forgettable plays, vaudeville sketches, and musicals before and after *Abie's Irish Rose*'s phenomenal success.   FB

Abraham, F(ahrid) Murray (1939–) Actor and teacher. Often cast as villains, Abraham is also an accomplished comedian. First appearing on stage in Ray Bradbury's *The Wonderful Ice Cream Suit* (Los Angeles, 1965) and on Broadway in Robert Shaw's *The Man in the Glass Booth* (1969), he is best known for the film *Amadeus* (Academy Award for his Salieri, 1984). A former acting teacher at Brooklyn College, he received an Obie for *Uncle Vanya* (1983) and New York's Mayor's Award of Honor for Art and Culture (1988). Other appearances include *A Midsummer Night's Dream* (NEW YORK SHAKESPEARE FESTIVAL, 1988), *Waiting for Godot* (Lincoln Center, 1988), *King Lear* (AMERICAN REPERTORY, 1991; NYSF, 1996), a revival of MAMET's *A Life in the Theater* (JEWISH REPERTORY THEATRE, 1991), *ANGELS IN AMERICA* (Roy Cohn role, 1994), *A Month in the Country* (1995) with Helen Mirren, the musical *Triumph of Love* (1997) with BETTY BUCKLEY, and as Shylock (2007).   REK

Abuba, Ernest (1947–) Hawaiian-born, FILIPINO playwright, director, and actor, closely associated with the PAN ASIAN REPERTORY. Concerned with social and political themes, his plays include *An American Story* (suicide of a prostitute in an American Filipino ghetto); *The Dowager* (on the Chinese Boxer Rebellion); and *Cambodia Agonistes* (the atrocities suffered by Cambodians since Vietnam); *Empress of China*; and in 2004 *Kwatz! The Tibetan*

Project. *Cambodia Agonistes,* combining dance, music, and drama, was successfully directed at PAR by his then-wife, TISA CHANG, in 1992. A recent acting role was Sakini in the PAR revival of *Teahouse of the August Moon* in 2000; in 2003 he directed *Favorite Colors*.   DBW

Acconci, Vito (1940–) Bronx-born PERFORMANCE ARTIST, poet, sculptor who also works in video and installations. In his 1960s and '70s videotapes and body-art performances (*Following Piece* [1969], *Trademarks* [1970], *Conversions* [1971], and *Seedbed* [1972]), Acconci dramatized visions of failure and aggression, the politics of the body, language, space, and time. Acconci's work is influenced by Catholicism, action painting, minimalism, pop art, psychology, feminism, sociology of language, and the political strategies used during the Vietnam War (self-immolation, surveillance, and boundary protection).   AF

Ackerman, P. Dodd (1876–1963) Designer and scenic artist whose studio provided 78 sets for Broadway in the 1920s and '30s, including *Five Star Final* (1930), a tripartite setting that was one of the first examples of simultaneous settings on Broadway.   AA

Across the Continent; or, Scenes from New York Life and the Pacific Railroad by JAMES J. McCLOSKEY. This sensational melodrama premiered at the Park Theatre, Brooklyn, 28 November 1870. Oliver Doud Byron starred as Joe Ferris, an outcast gambler known as "The Ferret." Byron's wife, Kate Crehan, older sister of ADA REHAN, played a small role. New York's seedy Five Points area provided the primary setting, but the popularity of the last act, set at a western railroad station, inspired a rash of frontier plays: Indians, led by villainous John Adderly, attacked Ferris and his friends, who were saved by the bravery of Ferris, a clever telegraph ploy, and a trainload of Army troops.   RAH

Acting Company JOHN HOUSEMAN and Margot Harley organized the first graduating class of the Drama Division of Juilliard School into a permanent repertory troupe (originally, City Center Acting Company), which began performing at the City Center in New York in 1972. Beginning in 1980 it functioned as the touring arm of the JOHN F. KENNEDY CENTER FOR THE PERFORMING ARTS in Washington, DC, but funding was cut in 1988; headquartered in New York, under the artistic direction of ZELDA FICHANDLER (1991–4) and Hartley (1994–), the latter with the title "producing director," it has continued primarily as a touring company with members selected nationally by auditions and molded into an ensemble. Actors perform a variety of roles, classical and modern. By 2005 the Acting Company had performed over 100 plays in 48 states and 9 foreign countries before 2 million-plus people. Alumni of the company include KEVIN KLINE, PATTI LUPONE, WILLIAM HURT, CHRISTOPHER REEVE, David Schramm, and FRANCES CONROY. In 2003 a Tony was received for excellence.   TLM

Actors' Equity Association Oldest of the major actors' UNIONS, founded by 122 actors in 1913. After years of unscrupulous exploitation, working without a standard agreement or minimum wage, actors by 1895 began to combat these conditions, first with the Actors' Society. After the Society's dissolution in 1912, Actors' Equity, under the leadership of its first president, FRANCIS WILSON, began to fight for support from other labor organizations in order to negotiate successfully a basic contract acceptable to all producers. In 1919, the Association of Actors and Artistes of America, formed and chartered by the American Federation of Labor that year, recognized Equity as the union representing actors in the theatre. A 30-day strike in August 1919 spread to eight cities, closed 37 plays, and prevented the opening of 16 others. Despite efforts by the PRODUCING MANAGERS' ASSOCIATION to negate Equity's effort with their own Actors' Fidelity Association, a five-year contract with Equity was signed by most producers. Over the next decade Equity gained a union-shop agreement (1924), adopted provisions to protect actors in dealing with agents (1929), guaranteed members a minimum wage (1933), and established minimum rehearsal pay (1935). Today Equity has grown into a workforce of over 45,000 actors and stage managers with headquarters in New York City and regional offices in LOS ANGELES, CHICAGO, and SAN FRANCISCO. Though Equity has caused controversy with some rulings, the union has generally fought social injustice, making strong efforts for ethnic minorities, women, and performers with disabilities. A recent concern has been the protest over non-Equity touring companies. In 1991 RON SILVER was elected its president (reelected in 1994), succeeded in 2000 by Patrick Quinn, who died suddenly in 2006 before becoming executive director of Equity.   DBW

Actors' Fund of America Founded in 1882 in response to the needs of aged actors and as a result of a campaign by HARRISON GREY FISKE in

his *NEW YORK DRAMATIC MIRROR,* this charitable organization counted among its incorporators EDWIN BOOTH, JOSEPH JEFFERSON III, LAWRENCE BARRETT, A. M. PALMER, P. T. BARNUM, and EDWARD HARRIGAN, with LESTER WALLACK its first president. Large gifts, beginning with $500 from Edwin Booth, and legacies have ensured the Fund's future, making it, as BROOKS ATKINSON noted, "scrupulous and merciful." The Fund's annual budget is c. $17 million, serving more than 6,000; in 2000, $2.8 million was provided in financial assistance to individuals. The fund offers myriad social services, including retirement communities in Englewood, NJ (established in 1902), New York City, and West Hollywood; comprehensive health insurance programs and initiatives; and AIDS awareness and treatment initiative. Over the years its mission has expanded to provide "for the social welfare of all entertainment professionals" across all mediums. The Fund is the only charitable organization guaranteed by legal contract to receive the net profits from regularly scheduled Broadway benefits. As of 2005, twelve presidents have led the Fund, including theatrical notables such as Palmer, DANIEL FROHMAN, VINTON FREEDLEY, Nedda Harrigan Logan, and BRIAN STOKES MITCHELL, who took office in 2004. In 1994 improved housing for low-income members of the entertainment industry was begun. Through its AIDS Initiative the Fund helps those infected with HIV/AIDS learn to live with and manage the disease.   DBW   LJ

Actors Studio, The Founded in 1947 by GROUP THEATRE alumni ELIA KAZAN, CHERYL CRAWFORD, and ROBERT LEWIS, the Actors Studio is a unique workshop for professional actors. It is not a school; it charges no tuition; and once an actor is accepted (by a rigorous audition process) he or she becomes a member for life, for the Studio's basic assumption is that there is no terminal degree for an actor. Under LEE STRASBERG, who joined the Studio in 1949 and who from 1951 until his death in February 1982 was its strong-willed artistic director, the Studio became renowned as the high temple of the Method. The popular notion of the Studio as a place where the mumble, scratch, and slouch are tokens of integrity derives from films directed by Elia Kazan that feature moody, verbally inarticulate, spectacularly neurotic performances by such Studio members as MARLON BRANDO and James Dean.

Those who admire the Studio's naturalistic style praise it for psychological revelation. Opponents attack the Studio as a place where self-indulgence, mannerism, and inaudibility are encouraged as actors examine their own emotions at the expense of the character or the play. Even Studio detractors, however, admit that the Method is a useful technique for the requirements of realistic film acting. The Studio's achievements continue to be hotly debated, but its influence is undeniable; its Method has come to be identified as the quintessential American style. In 1963, after years of hesitation, the Studio formed its own short-lived theatre on Broadway; but its enduring legacy is the films directed by Kazan and the vibrant film performances of its many illustrious members, from Brando, Dean, and Montgomery Clift to DUSTIN HOFFMAN, ROBERT DE NIRO, AL PACINO, Shelley Winters, GERALDINE PAGE, ARTHUR PENN, and Frank Corsaro. Its current copresidents are ELLEN BURSTYN, Harvey Keitel, and Al Pacino. In a dramatic change from previous policy, in 1994 the Studio initiated with New York's New School a three-year master's program (actors, directors, playwrights), an arrangement discontinued in 2005. The program is now associated with Pace University.   FH

Actors Theatre of Louisville A leading American regional theatre, located in Louisville, KY, noted for encouraging and producing original scripts and attracting an annual attendence of more than 200,000. Richard Block and Ewel Cornett founded the Actors Theatre in 1964. Although successful, Block was replaced at his request in 1969 by JON JORY, who had previously worked at the CLEVELAND PLAY HOUSE and had cofounded New Haven's LONG WHARF THEATRE. Jory left in 2000 (after directing 140 plays and producing 1,300), replaced by Marc Masterson, for 20 years the artistic director of Pittsburgh's City Theatre.

In 1972 the company moved from a converted train station to their present location, the old Bank of Louisville Building. A $1.7 million conversion of the building resulted in the Pamela Brown Theatre (capacity 637) and the Victor Jory Theatre (capacity 159). A new 318-seat venue (Bingham Theatre) opened fall 1994. By 1995 the annual budget for ATL had reached $5.5 million.

In 1976 the Actors Theatre achieved international acclaim by initiating the Humana Festival of New American Plays (by 2005, over 300 plays by more than 200 playwrights had been presented). Scripts such as *The GIN GAME, CRIMES OF THE HEART,* and *DINNER WITH FRIENDS* premiered at the Actors Theatre, moved to New York, and won Pulitzer Prizes for Drama. Other new plays produced included *Extremities, Execution of Justice, Marisol, Slavs!, Keely and Du, Tales of the Lost Formicans,* and *One Flea Spare.* From 1985 to 1997 ATL

presented the Classics in Context Festival, which offered works from world literature supported by films, lectures, and exhibits. Other innovative programs have included Modern Masters (beginning with ANNE BOGART), the Ten-Minute Play Contest, SHORTS Festival (100 new short plays, 1980–5), Flying Solo & Friends, an international touring program (since 1980, 29 cities in 15 foreign countries), and the Bingham Signature Shakespeare project.

Actors Theatre has received numerous awards and prizes as a result of its work. In 1978 they received the MARGO JONES Award for achievement in regional theatres; in 1979 the SHUBERT Foundation's James N. Vaughn Award for encouraging new scripts; and in 1980 they received a special Tony Award as outstanding nonprofit resident theatre.   SMA   DBW

Adams, Edwin (1834–77) Actor. He made his debut in Boston in 1853, and after almost a decade of acting in support of such stars as JOSEPH JEFFERSON III and E. A. SOTHERN, he had his first important New York engagement in 1863 with KATE BATEMAN's company. During the Civil War, he established himself as a traveling star especially distinguished for his playing of romantic or light-comedy characters in such vehicles as *The Lady of Lyons* and *Narcisse.* In 1869, EDWIN BOOTH selected him to play Mercutio opposite his Romeo for the opening of BOOTH'S THEATRE. He was subsequently featured at Booth's Theatre in several roles, including the dual roles of Phidias and Raphael in *The Marble Heart* and most notably the title role in a dramatization of Tennyson's *Enoch Arden,* perhaps his favorite characterization. In 1876, following a starring tour of Australia, Adams returned to the U.S. gravely ill. He made his last appearance at the CALIFORNIA THEATRE in SAN FRANCISCO on 27 May 1876.   DJW

Adams, [Richard] **Lee** (1924–) Lyricist associated with composer CHARLES STROUSE and musicals such as *Bye Bye Birdie* (1960), *Golden Boy* (1964), and *Applause* (1970). A musical version of *Marty* is planned. He was less successful working with composer Mitch Leigh on *Ain't Broadway Grand* (1993).   DBW

Adams [née Kiskadden]**, Maude** (1872–1953) Actress, daughter of Salt Lake City star Annie Adams. At five Maude was starring as Little Schneider in *Fritz, Our Cousin German* in San Francisco. Her adult career began at 16 with a New York debut at the STAR THEATRE in *The Paymaster.* In 1890 she began an association with producer

Maude Adams (and the children) from Act V of James Barrie's *Peter Pan,* first seen in 1905. Photo by Hall. *Courtesy:* Don B. Wilmeth Theatre Collection.

CHARLES FROHMAN that lasted until 1915. A box-office favorite until 1932 (despite an early retirement during 1918–31), she emerged in 1897 as a star, capitalizing on her eternal youthfulness and whimsy, as Lady Babbie in *The Little Minister,* a character rewritten for her by James Barrie. She also starred in U.S. productions of his *Quality Street* (1901), *Peter Pan* (1905), *What Every Woman Knows* (1908), *The Legend of Leonora* (1914), and *A Kiss for Cinderella* (1916). Other parts included Rostand's *L'Aiglon,* the strutting hero in his *Chantecler,* and SHAKESPEARE's Viola, Juliet, and Rosalind. In the 1920s she was a lighting consultant for General Electric. In 1931 she toured with OTIS SKINNER in *The Merchant of Venice.* During 1937–50 she taught theatre at Stephens College, Missouri. Armond Fields's 2004 biography is the most recent.
DBW

Adding Machine, The by ELMER RICE. First directed by PHILIP MOELLER for the THEATRE GUILD, this seminal American expressionistic play opened 19 March 1923 with DUDLEY DIGGES in the leading role. Although not a commercial success, the play influenced an ensuing wave of expressionistic drama. Like the German experiments that inspired it, Rice's play journeys through a series of stylized settings designed imaginatively by LEE SIMONSON; unlike European prototypes, this play has an antihero at its center. Mr. Zero is a bigoted, self-centered, fully Americanized, and stupid man who is nonetheless victimized by advancing technology and the big-business ethic.   RHW

Ade, George (1866–1944) Playwright and librettist. Born and educated in Indiana, Ade made a name for himself as a reporter in Chicago before turning his talents to the theatre. His most popular librettos, *The Sultan of Sulu* (1902) and *The Sho-Gun* (1904), were influenced by GILBERT AND SULLIVAN, but he is best remembered for two dramatic comedies of small-town life, *The COUNTY CHAIRMAN* (1903) and *The College Widow* (1904). The latter introduced the subject of collegiate adventures and the game of college football to the American stage. Because he had an outstanding ear for current slang and a keen eye for characterizing the everyday residents of his native Middle America, his more than a dozen plays and librettos, although seldom revived, illuminate the social record of the turn of the 20th century. Lee Coyle wrote a brief biography in 1964.   LDC

Adler, Celia (1890–1979) Actress-daughter of actors JACOB ADLER and Dina Stettin, raised by

51

stepfather Sigmund Feinman, another actor. She began acting as a child and spent her life in YIDDISH THEATRE in New York and on tour. Associated with intellectually ambitious troupes such as the YIDDISH ART THEATRE, she demonstrated qualities of sensitivity and emotional vulnerability.   NS

Adler, Felix (1895–1960) The American CIRCUS's most famous grotesque white-face clown (in drag), recognized by his oversized red nose (which lit up), his grossly padded rear, exaggerated yellow shoes, minuscule hat, and tiny umbrella. In the tradition of DAN RICE, Adler worked with a piglet that he fed with a bottle. He was also one of the first great producing clowns, developing routines for the entire troupe of RINGLING clowns.   DBW

Adler, Jacob (1855–1926) YIDDISH actor who began his career in theatre as a young man with a small company in Riga, Latvia, and by the 1880s became, in London and then New York, one of its stars. As actor and producer (especially at New York's Grand Theatre), he identified himself with serious emotional roles and with JACOB GORDIN's *The Jewish King Lear* (1892). Also famous for love affairs, for most of his career he was married to Sara Adler and often costarred with her. Of their seven children, six became actors. Especially talented were CELIA, famous on the Yiddish stage, and LUTHER and STELLA, famous on the English-language stage.   NS

Adler, Luther [Lutha] (1903–84) New York–born actor and director whose 1908 Bowery stage debut began a 13-year apprenticeship in his father's YIDDISH THEATRE. Prior to joining the GROUP THEATRE in 1932, he appeared on Broadway in *Humoresque* (1923); *The Monkey Talks* (1925); *Money Business* (1926); *We Americans* (1926); *The Music Master* (1927); *STREET SCENE* (1929); and *Red Dust* (1929), among others. His Group Theatre contributions included Don Fernando in *Night over Taos* (1932); Sol Ginsberg in *Success Story* (1933); Julian Vardaman in *Alien Corn* (1933); Moe Axelrod in *AWAKE AND SING!* (1935); and most notably Joe Bonapart in ODETS's *GOLDEN BOY* (1937). In later years Adler appeared in revivals and replaced stars PAUL MUNI (1946) and ZERO MOSTEL (1965, *FIDDLER ON THE ROOF*). Director of *Angel Street* (1955), *A VIEW FROM THE BRIDGE* (1960), and a national tour of *Jane Eyre* (1943–4), Adler produced *A Flag Is Born* (1966). His last appearances included General St. Pé in *Waltz of the Toreadors* (1969) and Gregory Solomon in *The PRICE* (1970).   GSA

Adler, Richard (1921–), composer; and **Jerry** [Jerold] **Ross** (1926–55), lyricist. Adler attended the University of North Carolina and served in the Navy before turning to composing; Ross appeared in YIDDISH stage productions as a child, then attended New York University. Together, they first contributed songs to the revue *JOHN MURRAY ANDERSON's Almanac* (1953). Their best-known work was for the musicals *The PAJAMA GAME* (1954) and *DAMN YANKEES* (1955). Both shows had contemporary settings and benefited from GEORGE ABBOTT's fast-paced direction and BOB FOSSE's choreography. The Adler–Ross songs were unpretentious, often humorous, pop tunes. After Ross died Adler wrote for television and concert orchestras, also contributing to the musical stage with shows such as *Kwamini* (1961) and *Music Is* (1976). He produced too, notably a 1973 revival of *The Pajama Game* with a multiracial cast, and the musical *Rex* (1976). Adler's memoirs, *You Gotta Have Heart* (with Lee Davis), appeared in 1990.   MK

Adler, Stella (1903–92) Actress and teacher. Daughter of the YIDDISH actor-producer JACOB ADLER, Stella grew up surrounded by great plays and bravura acting. Always interested in the technique of acting, she studied with RICHARD BOLESLAVSKI at the AMERICAN LABORATORY THEATRE in the 1920s even after she had become an established performer. She joined the GROUP THEATRE in 1931 because she believed in its founder, HAROLD CLURMAN, whom she married. A tall, statuesque blonde with imperial carriage and mid-Atlantic diction, Adler ironically had her greatest theatrical success playing downtrodden Depression-era housewives in the Group's productions of CLIFFORD ODETS's *AWAKE AND SING!* (1935) and *PARADISE LOST* (1935). Her last appearance on a New York stage was in 1945 in *He Who Gets Slapped*, but from 1949, when she founded the Stella Adler Conservatory, she served the theatre as a teacher. Reminiscing about her famous acting family and her husband, recalling her experiences studying with Stanislavsky in Paris in 1934, rising from her thronelike chair to demonstrate an action, continuing to flay the memory of her archrival LEE STRASBERG, issuing threats and portents, and regaling students with advice about life as well as art, Adler was a witty, exhilarating teacher. Countering Strasberg's Method with its focus on self, she urged students to transcend their own experiences by developing their imaginations and by investigating the play's circumstances rather than their own, an approach developed in her book *The Technique of Acting* (1988) and in *The Art of Acting* (2000), edited by HOWARD KISSEL.   FH

Adonis, a two-act musical burlesque by William Gill. Opened 4 September 1884 at the Bijou Theatre, New York, running 603 performances. This self-described "respectful perversion" of the Pygmalion myth, which borrowed existing melodies from sources as diverse as Beethoven and David Braham, sees a statue of Adonis (HENRY E. DIXEY) brought to life, pursued by women, reduced to disguises, and finally electing to return to stone. The longest-running hit of its day, it made a matinee idol of Dixey, who revived it throughout his career.   JD

African American theatre   African American theatre had a dual origin. First came the indigenous theatre consisting of folktales, songs, music, dance, and mimicry that blacks performed in cabins, at camp meetings, and in open parks like Congo Square in New Orleans. African in spirit, these expressions were transformed by the American environment (see ETHNIC THEATRE). Then came the AFRICAN THEATRE in imitation of white playhouses and scripted dramas that WILLIAM ALEXANDER BROWN established in 1821. Though Brown began with SHAKESPEARE, he also staged a sketch on slavery and his own play *The Drama of King Shotaway* (1823). His theatre produced two notable Shakespearean actors in JAMES HEWLETT and IRA ALDRIDGE.

The African Theatre had no successors in antebellum America except for two plays written by the ex-slave WILLIAM WELLS BROWN and read by him on abolitionist platforms. One, *The Escape; or, A Leap for Freedom* (1858), survives. Black indigenous expressions, however, were by the 1840s adopted by white comedians and fashioned into blackface minstrelsy that caricatured blacks on southern plantations. Ironically, it was the now-disdained MINSTREL SHOW that opened the professional stage to African Americans. Billed as authentic Negroes, black minstrels inherited the burnt-cork stereotype characters created by whites and gave them validity. At the same time, black performers were polishing acting skills in short farces that were added to their shows. Ernest Hogan, BILLY KERSANDS, and SAM LUCAS were three leading black minstrels, while noteworthy black troupes included Charles B. Hicks's Georgia Minstrels (1865), Callender's Original Georgia Minstrels (1872), and Haverly's Colored Minstrels (1878). Since black playgoers were segregated in an upper gallery section in most theatres, these shows played primarily to white audiences; yet their success ensured perpetuation of the genre into the first decades of the 20th century.

Vying for popularity with the minstrels were ubiquitous "Tom shows" based on the dramatization of UNCLE TOM'S CABIN (1852). Despite the novel's intent to eradicate slavery, stage versions seen throughout the land for 80 years reinforced the theatrical image of blacks as ignorant, submissive, happy-go-lucky creatures. Tom shows also began to employ blacks as slave characters and in plantation choruses, but eventually the play was denounced by black leaders.

Black companies of higher caliber emerged after the Civil War. Anna and Emma Hyers, classically trained prodigies from Sacramento, CA, toured the country in opéra bouffe and original musicals such as *Out of Bondage* (1877). The Astor Place Company of Colored Tragedians under J. A. ARNEAUX came into being in 1884 with a Shakespearean repertoire, and in 1889 Theodore Drury gave the first performance of his Opera Company. Professional concert artists and solo readers like HENRIETTA VINTON DAVIS appeared across the country.

In the popular theatre a shift in the minstrel pattern occurred with white-produced shows. Sam Jack's *Creole Show* (1891–7) introduced women in the lineup and as a dancing chorus. John W. Isham added a story line to olio specialities in *The Octoroons* (1895) and operatic selections for the finale of *Oriental America* (1896). This last production prepared Broadway for the invasion of original black musicals such as *A Trip to Coontown* (1898) by the multitalented BOB COLE and Billy Johnson and *In Dahomey* (1903) by BERT WILLIAMS and George Walker. Teamed with these star performers were the composer Will Marion Cook, who wrote the operetta *Clorindy; or, The Origin of the Cake Walk* (1898), the playwright Jesse Shipp, and the versatile brothers James W. and J. ROSAMOND JOHNSON.

Also prominent at this time were long-lasting road companies in vaudeville, notably Sissieretta Jones's Black Patti Troubadours and Gus Hill's The Smart Set, which was later acquired by brothers Salem Tutt Whitney and J. Homer Tutt.

In straight drama, William Edgar Easton wrote two historical plays on the Haitian revolution, *Dessalines* (1893) and *Christophe* (1911), which were produced by Henrietta Vinton Davis. Scott Joplin composed his opera *Treemonisha* (1911), but it remained unproduced for decades. In 1897 Bob Cole organized a stock company and training school at Worth's Museum in New York. Others followed, urged on by black critics Sylvester Russell of the *Freeman* (Indianapolis) and Lester Walton of the New York *Age,* who felt that resident companies in African American theatres would encourage dramatic plays, provide regular employment to black actors, and permit open seating. In 1906 Robert Motts of Chicago started the Pekin Stock Company, whose success spawned other Pekins in Cincinnati, OH, and Savannah, GA. In New York the Negro Players were formed in 1912, and the LAFAYETTE PLAYERS in 1915. Some of these companies staged original musicals and dramas; others contented themselves with popular Broadway revivals.

Blacks first appeared on Broadway in dramatic roles in *Three Plays for a Negro Theatre* (1917) by the white writer Ridgely Torrence. This auspicious start, cut short by America's imminent entry into WWI, was confirmed by CHARLES GILPIN's stunning performance for the PROVINCETOWN PLAYERS in *The EMPEROR JONES* (1920). However, the commercial success of *SHUFFLE ALONG* (1921) brought a resurgence of black musicals that stirred critics to rail against the pervasive image of black song-and-dance clowns on the professional stage. W. E. B. Du Bois, editor of *The Crisis,* urged formation of a nationwide movement of little theatres presenting plays "about us, by us, for us, and near us." His magazine and *Opportunity* sponsored playwriting competitions and published prizewinning entries. WILLIS RICHARDSON's one-act *The CHIP WOMAN'S FORTUNE* (1923) was the earliest nonmusical black play seen on Broadway. In the years ahead, black college drama professors like RANDOLPH EDMONDS, OWEN DODSON, and Thomas D. Pawley would begin writing and directing original plays with their students.

Three dramas by white playwrights demonstrated the reach of black histrionic talent. PAUL GREEN's *IN ABRAHAM'S BOSOM* (1926) shared Pulitzer Prize honors with an experienced cast including the gifted ROSE MCCLENDON; DOROTHY and DUBOSE HEYWARD's 1927 hit *Porgy* inspired the operatic version by GEORGE GERSHWIN (*PORGY AND BESS*); and MARC CONNELLY's *The GREEN PASTURES* (1930) with De Lawd magnificently played by RICHARD B. HARRISON earned a Pulitzer and a five-year run. The 1930s witnessed an upsurge of socially relevant plays like Hall Johnson's *Run Little Chillun* (1933), LANGSTON HUGHES's *MULATTO* (1935), and *STEVEDORE* (1934) by white authors Paul Peters and George Sklar. The short-lived FEDERAL THEATRE PROJECT, through its Negro Units in 22 cities, sponsored black playwrights and productions including Theodore Browne's *Natural Man* (1937) in Seattle, Theodore Ward's *BIG WHITE FOG* (1938) in Chicago, and ORSON WELLES's production of the "voodoo" *Macbeth* (1936) in Harlem.

In the 1940s the AMERICAN NEGRO THEATRE made steady progress in training and production at its Harlem-based Library Theatre until its successful *ANNA LUCASTA* (1944) transferred to Broadway and caused the breakup of the company. RICHARD WRIGHT's *NATIVE SON* (1941), imaginatively staged by Orson Welles, revealed the driving, versatile talent of CANADA LEE as Bigger Thomas, and Theodore Ward's *Our Lan'* (1946), a moving historical drama about newly freed slaves seeking a homestead, showed well OFF-BROADWAY but lost its appeal when altered for a larger house. PAUL ROBESON's record-breaking *Othello* (1943) belongs to this decade.

After WWII the civil rights movement gained momentum. Plays such as Louis Peterson's *TAKE A GIANT STEP* (1953) on Broadway, William Branch's *In Splendid Error* (1954), ALICE CHILDRESS's *TROUBLE IN MIND* (1955), and LOFTEN MITCHELL's *A Land beyond the River* (1957) at the Greenwich Mews Theatre Off-Broadway dealt unambiguously with the racial problem and used racially mixed casts. The trend toward integration was reflected in LORRAINE HANSBERRY's award-winning drama *A RAISIN IN THE SUN* (1959) and OSSIE DAVIS's satiric comedy *PURLIE VICTORIOUS* (1961). Companies like JOSEPH PAPP's NEW YORK SHAKESPEARE FESTIVAL began to cast black actors in traditionally white roles. Nevertheless, the slow pace of social reform, coupled with a controversial Vietnam War, triggered unrest on college campuses and in black urban communities. African American theatre revealed this frustration in a series of revolutionary dramas led by AMIRI BARAKA's *DUTCHMAN* (1964). As government and foundation funds were hurriedly released to ameliorate conditions in inner cities, black theatres mushroomed nationwide, generating a crop of new playwrights and productions and opening opportunities for directors, designers, and technicians. The search for a black identity led to experimentation with new dramatic forms. In 1969 LONNE ELDER's *CEREMONIES IN DARK OLD MEN* was nominated for and CHARLES GORDONE's *NO PLACE TO BE SOMEBODY* captured the Pulitzer Prize. Other significant playwrights of the period were ED BULLINS, Phillip Hayes Dean, ADRIENNE KENNEDY, RON MILNER, Charlie Russell, Joseph Walker, and Richard Wesley.

Among the few theatre groups to survive when funding was withdrawn were the NEGRO ENSEMBLE COMPANY of New York and the Inner City Cultural Center in LOS ANGELES. African American theatre had gained immeasurably from this period of upheaval but had made little headway in the Broadway commercial theatre, which responded by staging a number of extravagant revivals and adaptations of white musicals with black casts, such as HELLO, DOLLY! (1967), THE WIZ (1975), and *Timbuktu!* (1978). Only THE GREAT WHITE HOPE (1968) by white playwright Howard Sackler, with a bravura performance by JAMES EARL JONES as prizefighter Jack Jefferson (based on Jack Johnson), merits attention. Both Sackler and Jones received top awards for their work. Important black productions of the 1970s and early '80s include NTOZAKE SHANGE'S FOR COLORED GIRLS . . . (1976), VINNETTE CARROLL'S *Your Arm's Too Short to Box with God* (1976), Phillip Hayes Dean's monodrama *Paul Robeson* (1978), and CHARLES FULLER'S Pulitzer Prize–winning A SOLDIER'S PLAY (1981). A young generation of black business majors, acting as producers, created the "Chitlin Circuit," later christened "the Urban Circuit." Their plays, with small casts of gospel singers and perhaps a guest star, moved fron venue to venue for two- or three-night stands. Vy Higginsen and Ken Wydro set the pace with *Mama, I Want to Sing* (1980), which ran for eight years and grossed over $25 million garnered mostly from black church audiences. Shelly Garrett's *Beauty Shop* (1987) followed and grossed $33 million. Near the end of the 1980s, two cities – ATLANTA, GA, and Winston–Salem, NC – launched successful black arts festivals.

The most important voice to emerge in the 1980s was that of AUGUST WILSON, who worked frequently in close collaboration with director LLOYD RICHARDS; Wilson wrote and staged a series of plays chronicling black life in Pittsburgh in each decade of the 20th century. By 2005 every play in the cycle had been produced, with two of them, FENCES (1983) and *The* PIANO LESSON (Broadway, 1990), winning Pulitzer Prizes. In 1998 Wilson initiated the National Black Theatre Summit at Dartmouth College to address major black theatre issues – the first being long-term economic survival. Only a dozen theatre companies had survived for more than a decade, with many defunct or struggling to survive by the early 2000s. The second major issue, "diversity or cross racial casting," became controversial. Did integration of black artists into white companies reduce the number of opportunities for black playwrights to see their plays produced? Wilson's answer was "yes."

In the 1990s a new generation of African American artists had begun to emerge. GEORGE C. WOLFE became artistic director of the PUBLIC THEATRE and set about producing new artists and styles: hip-hop theatre – BRING IN 'DA NOISE, BRING IN 'DA FUNK (1995); GAY AND LESBIAN plays – Brian Freeman's *Civil Sex* (2002); as well as four plays by SUZAN-LORI PARKS, including her Pulitzer Prize winner TOPDOG/UNDERDOG. (Wolfe stepped down from the Public in 2005.) Also emerging during the 1990s were such playwrights and actors as CHERYL L. WEST, ANNA DEAVERE SMITH, Carlyle Brown, Kia Corthron, and Pearl Cleage, as well as directors Tisch Jones, TAZEWELL THOMPSON, and Ricardo Khan. Actors Laurence Fishburne, Samuel L. Jackson, and Denzel Washington have largely moved into films.   EGH   JVH

[*Ed. note:* The original author of this entry, the late Errol Hill, and the author of revisions, James Hatch, have written the first truly definitive history of African American theatre, published in 2003.]

African Grove A pleasure garden (c. 1816–23) situated on Thomas St., lower Broadway. It served the black population of the area with ice cream, tea, ale, wine, and evening entertainment after the fashion of Vauxhall and CHATHAM gardens, which did not admit blacks. Started by WILLIAM ALEXANDER BROWN, who went on to establish the AFRICAN THEATRE (1821) with actors drawn from performers at the garden, this was the first African American theatre company of record.   EGH

African Theatre The first African American company was founded on 21 September 1821 by WILLIAM ALEXANDER BROWN at his AFRICAN GROVE apartments located behind City Hospital, lower Broadway. The company opened with a cut version of *Richard III*. In the succeeding two years it moved to two locations on Mercer St. before being forced to disband by the police. In its repertoire was Brown's *The Drama of King Shotaway,* the earliest known play by a black writer, which dealt with the insurrection of the Caribs of St. Vincent. From this company came the internationally acclaimed actor IRA ALDRIDGE.   EGH

After the Fall by ARTHUR MILLER opened 23 January 1964 at the ANTA–Washington Square Theatre in New York City. Directed by ELIA KAZAN, the LINCOLN CENTER Repertory Company cast included JASON ROBARDS JR. as Quentin, the tortured lawyer who comes to terms with the evil of his own nature during the course of this memory play; Barbara Loden as his second wife Maggie, a character based on Miller's own second wife, Marilyn Monroe; Patricia Roe as Quentin's first wife, Louise; and HAL HOLBROOK, Zohra Lampert, Salome Jens, Paul Mann, Faye Dunaway, Ralph Meeker, David Wayne, and Barry Primus. It ran for 59 performances. A successful revival and its London premiere occurred at Britain's Royal National Theatre in 1990; an unsuccessful revival was seen in NYC in 2004.   BCM

agents The gradual demise late in the 19th century of the STOCK COMPANY resident in its own theatre gave rise not only to the commercialization of American theatrical production in the guise of the "combination system," but also to the emergence of brokers who eventually formed agencies to furnish actors, designers, stagehands, and other necessary personnel to independent managers and producers. Their services frequently included booking touring shows as well as New York productions. Theatre managers from around the country went to them every summer to secure stars and attractions for their seasons.

The first dramatic agency was probably founded in 1859 in New York, but others followed in Chicago and major theatrical centers. The most important agency to emerge was the H. S. Taylor Theatre Booking Agency in New York, which was sold in 1888 to KLAW and ERLANGER and became their base for organizing the Theatrical SYNDICATE eight years later.

Reaction to the Syndicate led to the formation of independent agencies to handle performers and speciality acts; surviving its monopoly, these agencies became and remained a force in the 20th century. The most enduring has been the William Morris Agency, founded by Viennese-born WILLIAM MORRIS, who entered show business as an assistant to a leading agent of foreign vaudeville acts in America. Morris formed his own agency c. 1900, eventually building his roster to include AL JOLSON, EDDIE CANTOR, WILL ROGERS, Charlie Chaplin, and many others, charging 10% of clients' earnings. This agency, still in existence, no longer dominates the field and has competition from several large agencies (notably International Creative Management) and many independents.

Press agents are the descendants of the 19th-century "advance men" of touring "duplicate" companies that emanated mainly from New York. As employees of managers (producers), they arrived in each town on the itinerary usually a day before the show, provided information and lithographs (later, photographs) to local newspapers, posted bills, distributed free tickets for favors given, checked on box-office procedures, and arranged for the company's stay in town. Many came from the ranks of journalists, and a sizable number graduated into the ranks of producers and general managers. One notable 20th-century agent, German-born Helen Merrill, a dis-

coverer of venturesome theatre artists, was a theatrical photographer and art gallery owner before becoming an agent (she opened her own agency in 1973). After several decades of wrangling over working conditions and division of labors, press agents became independent and combined with company and house managers to form the Association of Theatrical Press Agents and Managers (ATPAM) in 1938. Although their function remains historically the same – to create as much (preferably free) publicity for the show for a fee – they no longer handle any business details.   MCH

Ah, Wilderness! EUGENE O'NEILL's lone comedy, which opened on 2 October 1933, proved to be enduring and revivable especially in university and community theatres. PHILIP MOELLER directed and ROBERT EDMOND JONES designed the long-running THEATRE GUILD production, which starred GEORGE M. COHAN (making a rare appearance in another's play) and Elisha Cook in the leading role of young Richard. Celebrating coming to terms with adolescent urges, the comedy is a surprisingly nostalgic and sentimental look at the years of O'Neill's youth. Apparently, the playwright was pining wistfully for the gentle childhood and supportive family life he had never experienced. There have been NYC revivals in 1941, 1975, 1988, and 1998.   RHW

Ahmanson Theatre   see CENTER THEATRE GROUP

Ahrens, Lynn (1948–), and **Stephen Flaherty** (1960–) Musical theatre team whose most popular and arguably most successful work to date is *RAGTIME* (1998), winner of the Tony, Drama Desk, and other awards for score. Ahrens, a New Yorker educated at Syracuse University (journalism), is a lyricist-librettist; Pittsburgh-born Flaherty, who attended the Cincinnati College Conservatory of Music, is a composer. The two met in 1982 at a BMI Musical Theatre Workshop. Other collaborations, beginning with 1988's *Lucky Stiff*, include the Caribbean-flavored *Once on This Island* (1990), *My Favorite Year* (1992), *Seussical* (2000), *A Man of No Importance* (Lincoln Center, 2002), and *Dessa Rose* (Lincoln Center, 2005). Ahrens was lyricist and co-wrote the book with Mike Ockrent for *A Christmas Carol* (1994), the music being by Alan Menken. Flaherty wrote incidental music for NEIL SIMON's *Proposals*; composed the music for Gertrude Stein's *A Long Gay Book* (adapted by FRANK GALATI [for a Chicago production it was renamed *Loving Repeating: A Musical of Gertrude Stein*]); and, for CHITA RIVERA's *A Dancer's Life* (2005), he and Ahrens wrote two new songs. Despite its Broadway failure, *Seussical* ranks as of 2006 among the top three of all shows licensed by MTI [Music Theatre International] (regional/amateur rights). DBW

AIDS in the American theatre An ever-growing menace through the 1980s and into the '90s, the scourge of AIDS (acquired immune deficiency syndrome) had personally affected virtually everyone active in the American theatre by 1990. The deaths of leading artists such as Broadway choreographer MICHAEL BENNETT and writer-director-performer CHARLES LUDLAM alter the course of theatre history; so does the loss of many artists who do not live long enough to attain fame. Producers and playwrights across the country confront fear, rage, and grief – their own and that of their communities – through their work. They are driven to commemorate lost colleagues and take a stand against the homophobia in their society. The result is not only an ever-growing body of "AIDS plays," but also a much wider range of work darkened by the shadow of the disease. In addition, theatre groups made up primarily by those with AIDS, such as AIDS Theater Project (founded 1985) and H.I.V. Ensemble (1993), have appeared, and projects such as Broadway Cares/Equity Fights AIDS (BC/EFA; founded 1988), with its CareBonds (1993) and book *Broadway: Day & Night* (1992), profits of which go to BC/EFA's efforts, have been established. The ACTORS' FUND and Village Care of New York, among other organizations, have also become involved in assisting those with AIDS. The now commonplace symbol of the disease, the red ribbon, was introduced to America at the 1990 Tony Awards ceremony.

AIDS is now woven into the fabric of every kind of theatre, from Broadway comedies (RICHARD GREENBERG's *Eastern Standard*, WENDY WASSERSTEIN's *The Heidi Chronicles*) to the performance art of KAREN FINLEY and TIM MILLER. It is an unspoken presence in CRAIG LUCAS's *Prelude to a Kiss*, the story of a young lover whose beautiful wife comes to inhabit the body of a dying man.

Plays that deal directly with AIDS are almost always personal responses to devastation. *The Normal Heart*, a barely fictionalized account of an activist's struggles, dramatizes the ferocious will of LARRY KRAMER, its author, as does his later *The Destiny of Me*. William M. Hoffman wrote *As Is* – which, like the Kramer play, opened in New York in 1985 – as a way of coping with the death of friends. The late Harry Kondoleon (d. 1994) made public the autobiographical ground of *Zero Positive*, which depicts the moment when the main character learns he carries the virus that causes AIDS.

Noted American playwrights LANFORD WILSON, HARVEY FIERSTEIN, CHRISTOPHER DURANG, TERRENCE MCNALLY, and A. R. GURNEY have also dealt explicitly with the epidemic. By the early to mid-1990s major AIDS plays included CHERYL L. WEST's *Before It Hits Home*, which shows the disease at work in the black community; PAULA VOGEL's poetic tribute to her dead brother, *The Baltimore Waltz*; TONY KUSHNER's epic *Angels in America*; Scott McPherson's metaphorically oriented play *Marvin's Room*, in which illness and dying are dealt with in universal terms, never mentioning AIDS; and Steven Dietz's *Lonely Planet*, which touches on the isolation and panic of the disease; as well as the musicals *Falsettoland* (1990) and *Rent* (1996). Several studies of gay culture and AIDS have now appeared, including notable ones by David Román and Sarah Schulman, both in 1998. MEO DBW

Aiken, George L. (1830–76) Playwright known for one play: *Uncle Tom's Cabin; or, Life among the Lowly*, a dramatization of Mrs. Stowe's novel, presented at Troy, NY, on 27 September 1852, with Aiken in the part of George Harris. In response to audience demand for more episodes from the novel, Aiken prepared a sequel, *The Death of Uncle Tom; or, The Religion of the Lowly*, and in mid-November combined the two plays into one drama of six acts, now the standard version.

G. C. Howard (see HOWARD FAMILY), manager of the company and Aiken's cousin, rewarded the 22-year-old actor-playwright with a bonus of forty dollars and a gold watch for the "week of extra work" required to devise a role (Eva) for his four-year-old daughter Cordelia. RM

Ain't Supposed to Die a Natural Death With book, music, and lyrics by the multitalented Melvin Van Peebles, this two-act 1971 musical, depicting the seamier side of black life in an urban ghetto during the troublesome 1960s, ran for 325 performances on Broadway. It captured several awards, including Drama Desk Awards to the author and to the director, GILBERT MOSES, a Tony Award to actress Minnie Gentry, and a Grammy Award for its recorded music. EGH

airdomes Outdoor performance spaces popular from the turn of the century through 1915; located in large and small communities and consisting of covered stages with seating areas open to the sky. Enclosed by a tall board fence, the airdome offered STOCK, repertory, VAUDEVILLE, and sometimes moving-picture entertainments. Some venues were freestanding structures on the edge

of towns; others occupied vacant lots between buildings in downtown business districts. Opera house owners and promoters developed and controlled airdome circuits, among the most prominent being Kansas City's Bell and Olendorf and the Crawford Circuit. Between 1905 and 1915 there were at least 439 airdomes, the majority in Kansas, Oklahoma, Missouri, Texas, Illinois, Indiana, Ohio, and Pennsylvania. (In their heyday, airdomes were found in 36 states.) By 1915, their alfresco novelty was diminishing and competition from movies and noise from automobile traffic contributed to the airdome's decline. By the 1920s they no longer were a nationwide viable theatrical venue, although a small number still continued to operate. See also TENT SHOW.
RP

Akalaitis, JoAnne (1937–) Actress, director, educator, founding member of the avant-garde group MABOU MINES, and briefly artistic director of the NEW YORK SHAKESPEARE FESTIVAL. As one of the country's most provocative and inventive directors, her experimental works have been performed at major art centers and festivals throughout the U.S. and Europe, including the PUBLIC THEATER (NYC), The KITCHEN (NYC), the Walker Art Center (Minneapolis), the SHAKESPEARE THEATRE (DC), the MARK TAPER (Los Angeles), Théâtre St. Denis (France), Teatro Goldoni (Italy), and the National Galerie (Berlin). During 1983–4 she directed a controversial production of Beckett's *Endgame* with music by her former husband, Philip Glass, at the AMERICAN REPERTORY THEATRE. Productions of *The Screens* (GUTHRIE, 1989), *The Balcony* (ART, 1986), and *Prisoner of Love* (1995, novel coadapted with RUTH MALECZECH) earned her a reputation as a foremost interpreter of Genet. A champion of German writer Franz Xaver Kroetz, she has directed a number of his plays, including productions (1984, 1990) of *Through the Leaves*. Other productions include *Green Card* (Joyce, 1988), *In the Summer House* (LINCOLN CENTER, 1993), *Dance of Death* (ARENA STAGE, 1996), *The Iphigenia Cycle* (THEATER FOR THE NEW CITY, 1999), and *The Birthday Party* (ART, 2004). At the PUBLIC THEATER, she directed *Cymbeline* (1989), *Henry IV, Parts 1 and 2* (1991), *'Tis Pity She's a Whore* (1992), and *Woyzeck* (1992). After being named the artistic director of NYSF in 1991, she was released in spring 1993 in a controversial decision by the company's board. Three months later she received an Obie Award for Sustained Achievement OFF-BROADWAY, and she continues as an active freelance director. Akalaitis teaches at Bard College.   DBW

Akerlind, Christopher (1962–) Lighting and set designer, noted for his close collaboration with innovative directors, who has designed over 400 productions – mostly lighting – at theatre and opera companies around the world, including more than 40 productions for Opera Theater of Saint Louis during a dozen years as resident lighting designer. His Broadway productions include the atmospheric lighting for *The Light in the Piazza* (2005, LINCOLN CENTER), for which he won the Tony, Drama Desk, and Outer Critics Circle awards), *Reckless* (2004), *The TALE OF THE ALLERGIST'S WIFE* (2000), *Seven Guitars* (1996), and *The PIANO LESSON* (1990). Extensive OFF-BROADWAY credits (recently, lighting for ANNE BOGART's *Score;* MARTHA CLARKE's and CHARLES MEE's *Belle Époque;* LISA KRON's *Well;* and lighting and sets for Molière's *Don Juan*) won him an Obie for Sustained Excellence in Lighting Design.   DBW

Akins, Zoë (1886–1958) Prolific playwright, scenarist, and adapter of French and Hungarian plays, began her career with an experimental vers-libre drama, *The Magical City* (1916). Her early sophisticated comedies and wistful tragedies about worldly and slightly jaded women were followed by a rash of typical popular comedies. Her first and best hit was *DÉCLASSÉE* (1919). Others that had either critical or popular success were *Papa* (1919), *Greatness: A Comedy* (1921; also called *The Texas Nightingale*), *Daddy's Gone a-Hunting* (1921), and *The Greeks Had a Word for It* (1929; later filmed as *The Golddiggers*). In 1935, in a controversial decision, Akins received the Pulitzer Prize for her adaptation of Edith Wharton's *The Old Maid*. Her successful screenplays include *Morning Glory* (1932) and *Camille* (1937). A bio by Alan Kreizenbeck was published in 2004.   FB

Alabama Shakespeare Festival, The Founded in 1972 as a summer theatre, the ASF shifted its focus in the 1980s to become a permanent, year-round operation in a $21.5 million state-of-the-art performance complex in Montgomery, AL. The sixth largest Shakespeare festival in the world, ASF produces fourteen shows annually in its two theatres: the Festival Stage (750 seats) and the Octagon (225). Each season three plays by Shakespeare are presented, plus a mix of both new works and classics. In 1991, ASF originated the Southern Writer's Project (directed by artistic director Kent Thompson) to develop and showcase regional themes and the work of southern writers, most recently REGINA TAYLOR. In conjunction with the University of Alabama, ASF offers M.F.A. graduate programs in acting, design, and stage management; there is an extensive educational outreach program. In 2005 Thompson, who left to become the artistic director of the DENVER CENTER THEATRE, was replaced by Geoffrey Sherman, formerly producing artistic director of the BoarsHead Theatre in Michigan.   BF

Albee, Edward (1928–) Playwright who made a spectacular debut with four one-act plays in an absurdist style (*The Zoo Story*, written 1958; *The Death of Bessie Smith*, 1959; *The SANDBOX*, 1959; and *The AMERICAN DREAM*, 1960) and capped his reputation with the Broadway productions of *WHO'S AFRAID OF VIRGINIA WOOLF?* (1962) and an audacious and belligerent metaphysical mystery, *TINY ALICE* (1964). He was greeted as the leader of a new theatrical movement, and his name was linked with those of TENNESSEE WILLIAMS, ARTHUR MILLER, and WILLIAM INGE as a major American playwright. Refusing, however, to capitalize on the qualities that made *Virginia Woolf* so powerful – the lacerating wit and incendiary character conflict – Albee pursued an increasingly rarefied style, one that is emotionally and sexually evasive and that often forsakes dramatic impact for mandarin elegance. Despite a series of critical and commercial defeats, Albee continued to write prolifically in three forms: adaptations (CARSON McCULLERS's *Ballad of the Sad Café*, 1963; James Purdy's *Malcolm*, 1965; Giles Cooper's *Everything in the Garden*, 1967; and Nabokov's *Lolita*, 1980); short chamber plays that are musical in their repetitions and juxtapositions of image and motif (*Box* and *Quotations from Mao-Tse Tung*, 1968; *Listening*, 1975; and *Counting the Ways*, 1976); and full-length plays in which ordered lives are invaded and transformed. His settings may appear realistic, but Albee is at heart a fabulist; like the imaginary child in *Virginia Woolf*, surreal surprises hover over most of his work. In arguably his wisest play, *A DELICATE BALANCE* (awarded the Pulitzer Prize in 1966), Harry and Edna carry a mysterious psychic plague into their best friends' living room. The title character in *The Lady from Dubuque* (1979) is an angel of death. Talking sea creatures emerge from the water to confront sedate picnickers in *Seascape* (which won the Pulitzer Prize in 1975).

Albee's mainstream reputation is now again on the rise, even though his Broadway production (in 1983) of *The Man Who Had Three Arms* was decimated by the critics, and such plays as *Marriage Play* (1987), which did not have a U.S. premiere until 1992 in his own staging (coproduced by the ALLEY and Princeton, NJ's McCARTER THEATRE), and *Fragments* (first seen in Cincinnati, 1993), premiered out of New York, several at the English

Theater in Vienna. However, with *Three Tall Women* (1991), which had its New York viewing in January 1994 and won for Albee the Dramatists Guild Hull–Warriner Award and the Pulitzer Prize, among other recognitions, Albee's reputation has truly had a turnaround, with a critically acclaimed revival of *A Delicate Balance* in 1996 (Tony for Best Revival); *The Play about the Baby* (NYC, 2000, with MARIAN SELDES and BRIAN MURRAY); SECOND STAGE's revival of *Tiny Alice* (2000, with RICHARD THOMAS); his Tony Award–winning (2002) *THE GOAT, OR WHO IS SYLVIA?; Occupant* (2003); a new act added to *THE ZOO STORY* (called "Homelife"), which premiered at the HARTFORD STAGE as *Peter and Jerry* (2004); and the successful 2005 Broadway revivals of *Who's Afraid of Virginia Woolf?* with Kathleen Turner and BILL IRWIN and of *Seascape* with GEORGE GRIZZARD and FRANCES STERNHAGEN. Albee has reclaimed his place as an important stylist, a writer of wit and sensibility, and his impact on American drama is undeniable. In 1993–4 he was playwright-in-residence at New York's Signature Theatre. He received the Kennedy Center Honors (1996), the National Medal of Arts and the Common Wealth Award (both 1997), and, in 2005, a Tony for Lifetime Achievement. His award-winning biography by MEL GUSSOW appeared in 2000.   FH   DBW

Albee, Edward F(ranklin) (1857–1930) VAUDEVILLE producer and executive. The great-grandson of one of the original Colonial Minute Men, Albee, born in Maine, left home in 1876 to join a circus, serving first as common roustabout and later as ticket seller. In 1885 Albee joined B. F. KEITH in BOSTON, where Keith had opened a dime museum in a vacant store in 1883. With business poor, Albee supposedly suggested the exploitation of light opera at variety theatre prices, leading to a pirated, condensed version of GILBERT AND SULLIVAN's *The Mikado* presented five times a day with vaudeville acts between performances. With the slogan "Cleanliness, Courtesy and Comfort," Keith and Albee quickly built a vaudeville empire, with Albee largely responsible for planning the theatre structures that formed the Keith circuit. In 1900 they founded the Vaudeville Managers' Protective Association, followed in 1906 by the UNITED BOOKING OFFICE, both designed virtually to monopolize first-class vaudeville. After Keith's death in 1914 and his son's in 1918, Albee controlled the Keith Circuit, asserting power over his performers with his own in-house union, the National Vaudeville Artists (1916). The Keith circuit, dominating Eastern vaudeville, merged with other circuits in 1927 to form the Keith–Albee

Orpheum Corporation, controlling 700 theatres in the U.S. and Canada and booking some 15,000 performers. Less a showman than a builder, Albee after his partner's death continued the policy of clean, family fare, eschewing coarseness and enforcing his standards with fines and blacklisting. A year before his death, Albee's empire was subsumed by RKO (the Radio–Keith–Orpheum Corporation) led by Joseph P. Kennedy. The most complete telling of Albee's career (with Keith) is Arthur Wertheim's *Vaudeville Wars* (2006).   DBW

Alcazar Theatre Name of four different SAN FRANCISCO playhouses:

1. A distinctive Moorish structure erected in 1885 on O'Farrell St. as a lecture/music hall, but that soon housed a popular resident STOCK COMPANY (including young MAUDE ADAMS) under the able management of Fred BELASCO (brother of David). This theatre perished in the 1906 earthquake.

2. Rebuilt New Alacazar on Sutter St., operating under that name from 1907 to 1911.

3. In 1912 a third was built on O'Farrell, offering a wide range of productions (housed local FEDERAL THEATRE unit in 1936–7). It was known as the Alcazar up to 1939, then again from 1952 until its demolition in 1961.

4. The last Alcazar opened in 1976, in an old Geary St. hotel. Despite community efforts to save it, it was gutted inside in 1982; but it reopened in 1993 after a period of inactivity.   MB

Alda, Alan [né Alphonso D'Abruzzo] (1936–) Actor, son of actor Robert Alda (*GUYS AND DOLLS,* 1950). Though best known for Hawkeye in *M*A*S*H*, which led to a long absence from the stage and ongoing television success (5 Emmys), Alda has thirteen Broadway credits dating from 1959 and including, most notably, *The Owl and the Pussycat* (1964), *The Apple Tree* (1966), *Art* (1998), *QED* (2001), and the acclaimed revival of *GLENGARRY GLEN ROSS* (2005) in the role of Shelley Levene (Tony nomination), one of Alda's recent "snakes and weasels." His autobiography was published in 2005.   DBW

Aldredge, Theoni (1932–) Greek-born American costume designer with more than 200 Broadway credits (at one point, five shows running simultaneously). Aldredge studied and then worked at the GOODMAN THEATRE in Chicago before coming to New York in 1958. From 1962 onward she was a principal designer for the NEW YORK SHAKESPEARE FESTIVAL. From the mid-1970s she was part of the collaborative team – MICHAEL BENNETT, ROBIN WAGNER, and THARON MUSSER – that produced *A CHORUS LINE* and *Dreamgirls,* among others. Aldredge designed landmark productions such as *WHO'S AFRAID OF VIRGINIA WOOLF?* and *HAIR* (prior to Broadway), and also designs for ballet, opera, television, and film, including *Network* and *The Great Gatsby.* She is an excellent collaborative artist, and her designs are integrated with and supportive of the direction and overall visual statement of a production. Costumes for the elegant but troubled and short-lived musical *Nick & Nora* (1991) were designed by her, as were those for *Annie Warbucks* – the 1993 sequel to the 1977 musical *ANNIE,* which she also designed and for which she won one of her three Tony Awards – the 1997 revival of *Annie,* and the 2001 revival of *FOLLIES.* In 2002 she received the IRENE SHARAFF Award for Lifetime Achievement. A recent project, Las Vegas's spectacular *EFX* (at the MGM Grand), involved the design of 500 extraordinary creations.

She is married to the New York veteran character actor **Tom Aldredge**, whose résumé includes more than thirty Broadway credits, ranging from early Ayckbourn comedies in the 1960s to *STICKS AND BONES* (1972) and recently the revivals of *The CRUCIBLE* (2002) and *Twelve Angry Men* (2004).   AA DBW

Aldrich, Louis see *MY PARTNER*

Aldrich, Richard Stoddard (1902–86) Producer. Born in Boston and educated at Harvard (1925), Aldrich learned his trade as business manager of the Jitney Players (1923, 1924, 1927) and general manager of RICHARD BOLESLAVSKI's AMERICAN LABORATORY THEATRE (1926–8) before beginning producing on Broadway (1930). His more than 35 Broadway plays included a revival of Shaw's *Pygmalion* (1945) starring his second wife, GERTRUDE LAWRENCE; *Caesar and Cleopatra* (1949) with Sir Cedric Hardwicke and Lilli Palmer; and *Goodbye, My Fancy* (1948) and *The Moon Is Blue* (1951), which ran for 226 and 924 performances, respectively. Aldrich also presented the Old Vic at the CENTURY THEATRE (1946), the Habimah Players from Tel Aviv, and the Dublin Gate Theatre company (1948). He was a successful SUMMER STOCK theatre producer, operating four theatres and packaging shows for the strawhat circuit.   TLM

Aldridge, Ira (1807–67) African American actor who, starting with the AFRICAN THEATRE in New York, moved to England at the age of 17, and became a touring provincial actor in Britain and Ireland for over 25 years. In 1833 he replaced the mortally ill Edmund Kean as Othello at London's Covent Garden Theatre to a mixed press, and in 1852 began a series of highly successful appearances in Europe and Russia, receiving several decorations from heads of state. His return to London's West End in 1865 was widely praised. Aldridge played more than 40 roles, black and white, many of them Shakespearean. Equally brilliant in tragedy and comedy, he often performed Othello and Mungo (in Bickerstaffe's comic operetta *The Padlock*) on the same bill. He introduced psychological realism in acting in the 1850s well before his European counterparts. He died while on an engagement in Lódz, Poland, in 1867. The standard bio to date (new edition, 1968) is by Herbert Marshall and Mildred Stock.   EGH

Alexander [née Quigley]**, Jane** (1939–) Actress who gained stardom and a Tony Award as the white mistress of the black boxing champion in *The Great White Hope* (1968), a role she first created at the ARENA STAGE in Washington, DC. A New Englander dedicated to regional theatre, she was critically acclaimed as Lavinia in MOURNING BECOMES ELECTRA at the AMERICAN SHAKESPEARE FESTIVAL Theatre in 1971 and at the Eisenhower in Washington, DC, and the Huntington Hartford in Los Angeles in 1972. Three decades later in 2002 she played the conniving, adulterous Christine in the same play at A CONTEMPORARY THEATRE and the LONG WHARF THEATRE. Other New York theatre appearances include *Six Rms Riv Vu* (1972), *First Monday in October* (1978), WILLIAM GIBSON's *Monday after the Miracle* (1982), *Shadowlands* (1990), *The Visit* (1992, directed by her husband, EDWIN SHERIN), *The Sisters Rosensweig* (1992) in an Obie Award–winning, Tony-nominated performance, and *Honour* (1998). In all, she has seven Tony nominations.

Head of the controversial NATIONAL ENDOWMENT FOR THE ARTS (1993–7), Alexander became the first artist to hold the post. It was believed her appointment would make the agency less vulnerable to conservative attacks, though in mid-1995 the future of NEA was in doubt. In 1995 she was honored with the North American Montblanc de la Culture Prize (outstanding arts patronage), the MARGO JONES Award, and the Common Wealth Award (dramatic arts); in 2004 she received the Pell Lifetime Achievement in the Arts award. Since 2003 she has taught acting at Florida State University. Her autobiography *Command Performance* appeared in 2000.   DBW

Alison's House Suggested by the life of Emily Dickinson, SUSAN GLASPELL's three-act realistic

Ira Aldridge as Mungo, the slave of a West Indian planter, in Isaac Bickerstaffe's *The Padlock,* written in 1768 and first performed by Aldridge in the 1820s. *Courtesy:* Don B. Wilmeth Theatre Collection.

drama studies the family of a famous poet 18 years after her death as the survivors wrestle with problems of familial responsibility and an artist's position in society. EVA LE GALLIENNE created the errant niece in the CIVIC REPERTORY THEATRE production, which opened 1 December 1930 and moved uptown to the Ritz (see WALTER KERR THEATRE) in May after winning a Pulitzer Prize. More conventional than Glaspell's earlier work, the play is self-consciously literary, but it achieves an eerie sense of timelessness within its turn-of-the-century setting. In 1999 it was revived by the MINT THEATER.   KF

All God's Chillun Got Wings by EUGENE O'NEILL. In a controversial production directed by JAMES LIGHT for EXPERIMENTAL THEATRE, INC., at the

Provincetown Playhouse, this bitter but sympathetic drama of miscegenation was threatened by the authorities before premiering on 15 May 1924. Centering on the sad marriage of a black man struggling for dignity and a white woman who ultimately falls into madness, this domestic tragedy brought PAUL ROBESON to national attention and featured Mary Blair as the frail wife who cannot cope with ostracism and denigration. Much furor was vented and ink spilt over whether Robeson actually kissed Blair's white hand.   RHW

All My Sons by ARTHUR MILLER opened on 29 January 1947 at the Coronet Theatre in New York, directed by ELIA KAZAN, with a cast including Ed Begley, Beth Merrill, ARTHUR KENNEDY, and Karl Malden, and a set designed by MORDECAI GORELIK. It won the New York Drama Critics' Circle Award, running for 328 performances. In 1987 a Broadway production won the Tony for Best Revival. The tightly structured, Ibsenist play depicts the effects on a Midwestern family of the dawning awareness that the father, Joe Keller, knowingly shipped faulty engine parts that caused the deaths of young pilots during WWII – including, indirectly, that of his son. Miller's play drives inexorably toward Keller's understanding that his moral responsibility reaches beyond providing for his family. It was also revived in 1997 by the Roundable, directed by Barry Edelstein.   BCM

Allen, Fred [né John Florence Sullivan] (1894–1956) Comedian and humorist, remembered for his radio appearances, his stinging observations of American life, and his pronounced nasal intonation. Allen began his career as a comic vaudeville juggler (1911), appearing under several names. After touring Australia/New Zealand, he gained praise as Fred Allen from VARIETY for "probably the brightest talk ever heard on a vaudeville stage," headlining at The PALACE. He chronicled this phase of his career in *Much Ado about Me* (1956). Prior to beginning his radio career (1932), his dour appearance and stand-up patter were featured in musical REVUES including *The Passing Show of 1922, The Greenwich Village Follies,* and *Three's a Crowd* (1930). His memoirs appeared in 1956; Robert Taylor's 1989 biography is noteworthy.   DBW

Allen, Gracie see BURNS, GEORGE

Allen, Viola (1869–1948) Actress who made her stage debut in *Esmeralda* in New York in 1882. In 1884 JOHN MCCULLOUGH engaged her to play his

daughter in *Virginius,* then made her his leading lady. In subsequent seasons she played opposite W. E. Sheridan, the Italian Tommaso Salvini, and JOSEPH JEFFERSON III. For four years she was leading lady in CHARLES FROHMAN's Empire Stock Company. An intelligent and appealing actress, sometimes thought to be overtechnical, she was, until her retirement in 1918, a popular touring star, highly regarded for such portrayals as Viola, the double roles of Hermione and Perdita, and Dolores (*In the Palace of the King*).   FHL

Allen, Woody [né Allen Stewart Konigsberg] (1935–) Actor, playwright-screenwriter, and director who since 1970 has largely devoted his considerable talent to filmwriting and direction. His play *Don't Drink the Water* debuted on Broadway in 1966 at the MOROSCO THEATRE (TV production, 1994,with Allen in cast); it was followed in 1969 by *Play It Again, Sam* (BROADHURST), in which he also played the role of Allan Felix, and in 1981 by *The Floating Light Bulb* (LINCOLN CENTER). His 1994 film *Bullets over Broadway* has a theatrical context, and his 1995 one-act *Central Park West* was staged Off-Broadway as part of a bill titled *Death Defying Acts*. Recent efforts have not been successful (such as *Writer's Block*, written and directed by Allen in 2003; *A Second Hand Memory*, written and directed, 2004). There are noteworthy biographies by Eric Lax (1991; updated 2000) and by John Baxter (1999).   DBW

Alley Theatre, The Established as an amateur organization in Houston, TX, by Mr. and Mrs. Robert Altfeld and Nina Vance, who became artistic head, the theatre began production in November 1947 in a rented 87-seat dance studio, the name inspired by a narrow alleyway that led to the studio. Its second home, an attic-fan manufacturing plant converted to a 231-seat arena theatre, opened on 8 February 1949 with a production of *The CHILDREN'S HOUR* using professional actors. In 1954 the theatre became fully professional. The current building, which opened in November 1968, was named after Nina Vance following her death in 1980. Actress-director Pat Brown, artistic head 1981–8, attempted to fill the two theatres in the complex (one seating 824 and another arena-style holding 296; the latter rebuilt in 2002, and renamed the Neuhaus Stage, along with extensive new production spaces) with more adventurous and experimental fare than its previous conservative offerings. Under Brown, a landmark exchange in June 1983 with the Stephen Joseph Theatre in Scarborough, England, was initiated; in July 1985 they presented Alan Ayckbourn's *Season's Greetings* at New York's Joyce Theatre. After Brown's departure, Gregory Boyd became artistic director in 1989, adding to the theatre's mission "the intent to create for leading theatre artists from around the world a home where they can develop their work." Under Boyd's stewardship several plays and musicals first seen at the Alley have been presented in NYC (dates here are Alley productions), including the musicals *Jekyll and Hyde* (1990) and *The Civil War* (1998), TENNESSEE WILLIAMS's *Not about a Nightingale* (1998), EDWARD ALBEE's *The Play about the Baby* (2000), and RICHARD NELSON's *The General from America* (2002). Its first major musical production was not until 2004 (*A FUNNY THING HAPPENED . . .*). Since 1993 playwright-artist ROBERT WILSON has used the Alley as a U.S. home base, serving as Associate Artist, following productions there in 1991 and 1992; in 1995 he premiered his *HAMLET: a monologue* at the Alley. In 1996 the Alley received – just prior to its 50th anniversary – a special Regional Theatre Tony for excellence.   DBW

Alliance of Resident Theatres/New York (ART/New York) 575 Eighth Ave. 17S, New York, NY 10018. Incorporated in 1972 to promote artistic growth and excellence in the New York City non-profit theatre through professional services and community advocacy, ART/New York grew from more than 100 member theatres in the mid-1990s to over 400 a decade later. As public and private arts funding tightened during this period, the organization found innovative ways to support such growth, from purchasing office buildings in Manhattan and Brooklyn that house scores of groups to partnering with major foundations to support emerging theatres. Virginia I. Louloudes, ART/NY's executive director from 1991, emerged as a credible, powerful voice for the city's non-profit theatre community.   LJ

Alliance Theatre Company The largest resident professional theatre in the Southeast, the Alliance Resident Theatre began in 1968 as a division of the ATLANTA (Georgia) Arts Alliance, an organization that included the Atlanta Opera and the Atlanta Ballet. In 1970 it changed its name to the Alliance Theatre Company, now the Alliance Theatre Company at the Woodruff [Arts Center, 1280 Peachtree St., NE]. During 1990–2001 Kenny Leon served as atistic director, replaced by Susan V. Booth, previously associated with several Chicago theatres, including the GOODMAN. Leon was especially successful in altering the profile of the audience, from less than 5% African American in 1990 to over 25% as of 2005. The Alliance offers ten productions annually with three venues: the 750-seat Alliance Stage; the 200-seat Hertz Stage; and Theatre for Young Audiences offerings in the 14th Street Playhouse (c. 375 seats).   DBW

Alswang, Ralph (1916–79) Set, costume, and lighting designer, director, and producer. Alswang began his career in 1942 with *Comes the Revelation*. After serving in the Air Force he returned to Broadway with *HOME OF THE BRAVE*. Subsequent designs included *The RAINMAKER* (1954), *SUNRISE AT CAMPOBELLO* (1958), and *RAISIN IN THE SUN* (1959). He also served as designer and consultant to several theatres, including the URIS THEATRE in New York and the Garden State Arts Center, NJ.   AA

alternative theatre One of the terms developed to describe theatrical work growing out of the burgeoning cultural movement of the 1960s and '70s, now almost obsolete in use as a meaningful and current descriptor. As the name suggests, alternative theatre defined itself against dominant work – whether in commercial, political, or aesthetic terms – and sought to challenge the status quo as it was represented by mainstream middle-class theatre. Early on, alternative theatres aligned themselves with particular social movements: For instance, the FREE SOUTHERN THEATRE in Louisiana, New Feminist Theater in New York, and EL TEATRO CAMPESINO in California not only responded to but were part of the civil rights, feminist, and farmworkers' movements, respectively. As such, they sought out new audiences, hoping to reflect and represent the experiences of those whose voices were never heard on mainstream stages.

These theatres, and a spate of others like them (there were more than 100 FEMINIST THEATRES in the U.S. in the early 1970s), by definition rejected the values of commercial theatre. More interested in helping to forge political movements than in earning a profit by selling entertainment, they redefined the relationship between spectator and performer, developed new performance styles, and, perhaps most important, attracted a new army of theatre workers – the term itself revealing new attitudes toward the process of theatrical production. Few of those drawn to work in these political theatres were theatre professionals; instead, the theatres were staffed by constituents of the political movements. Thus, alternative theatres often established programs to train people as actors – and for virtually every other theatrical task. More often than not, plays presented by alternative theatres were developed through

63

group improvisation or, at the very least, were written specifically for the group by company members. As part of its alternative impulse, the alternative theatre rejected the mainstream theatre's definition of a script as a commercial property, as well as its rigid divisions of labor. In the alternative theatre, scripts often were not even written down. Meanwhile, company members not only acted but painted scenery, hung lights, played musical instruments, and helped round up an audience.

Although most of the specific issue-related theatres died out by the 1980s, another strand of the alternative theatre movement persisted. While groups like the Free Southern Theatre or the Living Theatre primarily looked outward, concentrating on theatre's role in changing society through its direct engagement of social issues, others looked inward, searching for ways of changing society by offering spectators new ways of seeing and of thinking about themselves and their place in the world. These theatres, often politically radical as well, concentrated more on new aesthetic forms, new styles of creating work, and new approaches to acting.

The Open Theatre, for instance, which began in 1963 (and closed 10 years later), concentrated on developing what director Joseph Chaikin described as the actor's "presence" – that is, the performer, rather than the character, was to be the central focus of his theatre. The realism of the conventional theatre was to be replaced by self-conscious attention to the unique qualities of live performance.

Over the past two decades, techniques pioneered by these early alternative theatres – such as the acting exercises of the Open Theatre or the collective structure of feminist theatres – were adopted and adapted by new alternative theatres. Although these theatres also defined themselves in opposition to the mainstream, that definition tended to become increasingly aesthetic, if only because the social movements of the 1960s and '70s and the counterculture that had grown up with them had themselves faded away. In urban centers like New York, the countercultural life was less possible in the 1980s than in the turbulent decades before: Rents had skyrocketed, making it difficult for alternative theatre artists to support themselves at odd jobs while spending the bulk of their time making theatre; the avant-garde was getting commodified, bringing alternative theatre mainstream media attention and audiences.

Thus, many of the alternative theatres that remained in the 1980s, and those that started up, were more interested in artistic exploration than in political commitment. The formalism of Robert Wilson, for instance, can be counted as part of the alternative theatre in this sense, as can the often autobiographical but still highly formal work of Richard Foreman, the Wooster Group, and Mabou Mines.

Some of these theatres remain active into the 2000s, and a new generation of alternative theatre artists has grown up under their influence. In the absence of a vibrant countercultural movement, however, this new generation more often finds itself working in fragmented ways – experimental directors like JoAnne Akalaitis and Peter Sellars, for example, do not work consistently with the same company. The term "alternative theatre" today rather than connotating a movement or reaction often describes a physical space where alternative works can be booked. (See also collective theatre groups.)
AS

Alvin Theatre see Neil Simon Theatre

AMAS Musical Theatre A multiracial, not-for-profit, Off-Off Broadway company (from summer 2005 located above the Players Theatre in Greenwich Village, its fifth home) specializing in new American musicals for family audiences; founded in 1968 by the late Rosetta Burton LeNoire, Mara Kim, and Gerta Grunen to counter divisive aspects of the civil rights movement. Under LeNoire's artistic direction, AMAS (Latin for "you love") promoted ecumenical understanding by bringing people of different races together for a common artistic goal. In 1999 for her efforts she received the National Medal of Arts. Actors' Equity gives annually in her name an award for commitment to multicultural production and casting. AMAS is rare in its open-submission policy for scripts.   CLJ

Ambassador Theatre 215 West 49th St., NYC [Architect: Herbert J. Krapp]. Built in 1921, when prime sites in the theatre district were being rapidly used up, the Shuberts' architect was forced to design the new 1,100-seat theatre diagonally across the plot to make maximum use of the area. The Ambassador was intended to house operettas, the Shuberts' perennial theatrical product, but it was leased for nonmusicals as well. In 1935, the playhouse was sold, and thereafter it was used for live and film presentations as well as a radio and television studio. In 1956, it was reacquired by the Shuberts, who returned it to legitimate roles.   MCH

Amberg, Gustav (1844–1921) Theatre manager. A native of Prague, Amberg managed German-speaking theatres during the 1870s in Cincinnati and Detroit. In 1879, together with HEINRICH CONRIED and Mathilde Cottrelly, he founded the THALIA THEATER (old Bowery Theatre), which became the preeminent German theatre in New York, engaging German stars Ludwig Barnay (1883–8), Adolf Sonnenthal (1884), and Ernst Possart (1887–8). In 1883 Amberg became sole manager of the Thalia. Disbanding the company in 1888, he opened the Amberg Theatre (later Irving Place) until financial failure in 1891. He worked for the SHUBERT ORGANIZATION in his final years.   RE

Ambrosone, John (1961–) Lighting designer and educator who from 1989 to 2002 was resident lighting designer at the AMERICAN REPERTORY THEATRE (more than 45 productions); is now a freelance designer (theatre, opera, dance) and head of lighting design at Virginia Tech, where in 1986 he received a M.F.A. in lighting design. He has worked with many leading contemporary directors for some 25 regional theatres in addition to theatres in Brazil, France, Germany, Japan, England, Mexico, Russia, Singapore, and Taiwan. He has designed on Broadway (*The Old Neighborhood*), Off-Broadway (*Nocturne*), and for national tours (SERBAN's production of *The King Stag*).   DBW

Amend, Karle Otto (1885–1944) Though primarily known as a scenic artist – his Amend Scenic Studios was one of the major scenic houses in the 1920s and early '30s – Amend was also a designer and created the sets for EARL CARROLL's *Vanities* (1926–32). He began as a performer in his native Ohio and was first identified as a scene painter in 1912. In WWI he was an innovator in camouflage techniques.   AA

America Hurrah by JEAN-CLAUDE VAN ITALLIE. Three short plays made up this evening of theatre that opened at New York's Pocket Theatre on 7 November 1966. (Earlier versions of *Interview* and *Motel* had been previously produced under different titles.) *Interview*, directed by JOSEPH CHAIKIN, satirizes the dehumanizing aspects of job hunting in American business. *TV* and *Motel*, both directed by Jacques Levy, explore other aspects of commercialism and materialism while registering protest against the Vietnam War. The production was hailed for the freshness of its non-realistic devices, especially the actors presented as grotesque puppets in *Motel*, and for the ensemble acting.   FHL

American Academy of Dramatic Arts The first and oldest conservatory of professional acting training in the United States. Located in New York City, the Academy was founded in 1884 as the Lyceum Theatre School of Acting by Franklin Haven Sargent. In 1974 it opened a campus in the Los Angeles area. The Academy's stated purpose is "To provide a broad and practical education to those desiring to make acting their profession." Distinguished alumni include JASON ROBARDS JR., LUCILLE LORTEL, RUTH GORDON, HUME CRONYN, COLLEEN DEWHURST, ANNE BANCROFT, JUDD HIRSCH, and GARSON KANIN. As of 2005, its alums had received 202 Emmys, 57 Tonys, and 72 Oscars.   TLM

American Airlines Theatre Originally the SELWYN, built in 1918 on NYC's 42d St. and billed as the most modern theatre in New York. By the late 1920s it was home to many revues and one hit, *The ROYAL FAMILY*. After Depression-era difficulties, it became a film house in 1934 and remained so until the 1990s when it came under the aegis of the 42d Street Development Project. In 2000 it reopened as home of the ROUNDABOUT THEATRE COMPANY after virtually being rebuilt as a 850-seat venue (originally c. 1,000) and renamed for American Airline in exchange for a promised $8.5 million over ten years toward the projected $21 million cost. The inaugural production, a revival of *The MAN WHO CAME TO DINNER* with NATHAN LANE, was followed by productions of plays by Pinter, MILLER, SHAW, and Coward, among others.   DBW

American Buffalo Winner of a JOSEPH JEFFERSON [III] Award (Chicago), an Obie, and a New York Critics' Circle Award, DAVID MAMET's two-act drama, appearing shortly after SEXUAL PERVERSITY IN CHICAGO, established the writer as a serious new American playwright. In its 1975 CHICAGO premiere as a coproduction of GOODMAN Stage 2 and Mamet's own St. Nicholas company, it was the first of many Mamet plays to be directed by GREGORY MOSHER. Its first Broadway production two years later, directed by ULU GROSBARD and starring Robert Duvall as Teach, ran for 135 performances at the ETHEL BARRYMORE THEATRE. AL PACINO played Teach in a celebrated revival at the LONG WHARF THEATRE (New Haven) in 1980, which moved to OFF-BROADWAY in 1982 and Broadway in 1983, with a stop at the JOHN F. KENNEDY CENTER in between. There was a production at Mamet's ATLANTIC THEATER in 2000, William H. Macy as Teach. A film version with DUSTIN HOFFMAN was released in 1996. On the surface, the drama concerns the bungled heist of an old nickel by three lowlifes based in a Chicago pawnshop. At a deeper level, we are encouraged to view the language of American business and power politics as an insidious force that infiltrates and destroys human relationships.   SF

American Company, The Most prominent theatre company in the American colonies. Founded in 1752 by London theatre manager William HALLAM and his brother Lewis, it was originally known as the London Company of Comedians. Reorganized in 1758 by DAVID DOUGLASS, it assumed the name The American Company of Comedians in 1763, probably to avoid trouble during the anti-importation movement in the post–French and Indian War depression. Touring until 1774, the company went to Jamaica for the duration of the war. Upon their return in 1784, they regained their preeminent position, playing major cities along the eastern seaboard. In 1792 the company was reorganized under Lewis Hallam Jr. and JOHN HENRY, continuing at New York's PARK THEATRE until 1806. (See also INTRODUCTION, §1.)   PAD

American Conservatory Theater (ACT) (previously Theatre) A noncommercial regional repertory company that combines performing with a training school. Founded in 1965 by the late WILLIAM BALL, ACT has made its home in SAN FRANCISCO since 1967. Ball attracted critical notice in 1958 with an OFF-BROADWAY staging of CHEKHOV's *Ivanov*. Subsequent productions throughout the U.S. and Canada made him one of the most promising young directors in America. In 1965 he established ACT at the Pittsburgh Playhouse as an experimental and educational company with a more "dashing style" than he saw elsewhere. Arrangements quickly soured, and Ball took ACT on the road for much of 1966, settling permanently in San Francisco for a January 1967 opening. For much of its history ACT has played in two theatres, the downtown Geary and the Marines Memorial. The late ALLEN FLETCHER joined ACT in 1970 to head the Conservatory training program, today serving 1,900 students annually. The company had a deficit of $900,000 in 1973, which required reductions in the size of the company and its repertoire. Ball was succeeded in 1987 by Edward Hastings, who resigned in 1991, replaced in 1992 by CAREY PERLOFF, formerly artistic director of New York's CLASSIC STAGE COMPANY. As a result of earthquake damage in 1989, various venues were used until the Geary reopened January 1996, after a c. $28.2 mil-

lion restoration, with *The Tempest*. In 1996 ACT received the JUJAMCYN Theaters Award for outstanding contribution to the development of creative talent for the theatre. Over the past three decades ACT has presented more than 300 productions; its outreach programs affect more than 250,000 people.   TLM

American Dream, The One-act play by EDWARD ALBEE produced OFF-BROADWAY in January 1961 (with the unsuccessful one-act opera *Bartleby*, replaced by his *The Death of Bessie Smith*) for 370 performances. Based in part on the earlier *The SANDBOX*, this play featured the same characters, Mommy and Daddy, offering a sketch that shows their vapid lives while caricaturing American values and types. The title character, a muscular and handsome young man, is emasculated by his adopted parents. As C. W. E. Bigsby notes, Albee offers no alternative to the inhumane and venal family, "an icon of the American system." Albee's play proved immediately popular, however, especially with students, and was produced often in university theatres, along with other Albee one-acts (and often in concert with Ionesco short plays).   DBW

American Indians see NATIVE AMERICAN RITUAL/THEATRE; NATIVE AMERICANS PORTRAYED ONSTAGE

American Jewish Theatre Founded in 1974 by Stanley Brechner to produce or coproduce classics, new plays, and musicals that deal with Jewish ideas and culture, the theatre, on West 26 St. in NYC, was essentially defunct by 2005.   DBW

American Laboratory Theatre (ALT) Inspired by the first American visit of the MOSCOW ART THEATRE in January 1923, the ALT (originally termed the Theatre Arts Institute) was founded in New York six months later by a group of wealthy American patrons as a school for training young actors in the Stanislavsky system. Providing a well-rounded three-year program, the school was a significant first step in translating Stanislavsky's ideas about truth in acting into an American idiom. Although courses were offered in mime, ballet, fencing, phonetics, and corrective gymnastics, the school's focus was the classes taught by RICHARD BOLESLAVSKI and MARIA OUSPENSKAYA, two impassioned émigrés from Stanislavsky's company. During 1925–30 the Lab sponsored a theatre, under Boleslavski, modeled on the MAT but billed as America's first native, creative theatre. Most of its productions were of new and revived European plays rather than the American originals its charter promised. The Lab (disbanded in 1933) and its theatre were an important link between the historic appearance of Stanislavsky's company and the establishment in 1931 of America's first truly theatrical collective, the GROUP THEATRE, cofounded by CLURMAN, STRASBERG, and CRAWFORD, who had listened intently to Boleslavski's inspiring lectures.   FH

American Mime Theatre see PAUL J. CURTIS.

American National Theatre and Academy (ANTA) Chartered in 1935 as a tax-exempt, self-supporting "people's" theatre, ANTA languished until after WWII, when a board of directors, infused with theatre personalities and entertainment-industry leaders, raised money to help it acquire the Guild Theater (1950), renamed the ANTA Playhouse, sold in 1981. Noncommercial works, such as *The Tower beyond Tragedy,* ROBINSON JEFFERS's adaptation of Aeschylus' *Oresteia,* and revivals, such as *Twentieth Century* (1932) by BEN HECHT and CHARLES MACARTHUR, were featured. In 1963 ANTA built the Washington Square Theatre, which temporarily housed the Repertory Theatre of LINCOLN CENTER. From 1947 to 1991 ANTA produced nearly 70 productions. Existing still in name, ANTA is essentially dormant (its last produced work was HOROVITZ's *Park Your Car in Harvard Yard*).   WD

American Negro Theatre Founded in Harlem by Abram Hill and FREDERICK O'NEAL in 1940 to provide a permanent company for black theatre artists displaced by the demise of the FEDERAL THEATRE PROJECT. Using the 135th Street Library Theatre, the company enjoyed initial success with Hill's *On Striver's Row* (1940) and Theodore Browne's *Natural Man* (1941), but began to disintegrate after Philip Yordan's ANNA LUCASTA (1944) moved to Broadway, played 957 performances, and became an international hit. The theatre closed in 1950.   EGH

American Place Theatre 111 West 46th St., NYC [Architect: Richard D. Kaplan]. Founded in 1963 as a producing organization dedicated to the presentation of new American plays by living authors (full-scale productions as well as works in progress), the American Place Theatre started at St. Clement's Church on West 46th St. Its founders were WYNN HANDMAN and Rev. Sidney Lanier, the vicar of the church. In 1971, an underground complex of theatres, offices, and workrooms at the rear of the Stevens building on the Ave. of the Americas was presented to the group through changes in the building and zoning laws that permitted the builder of an office skyscraper to add extra stories if a theatre was also added within the structure. The company paid $5 a year (25-year lease) for this space, yet Handman, who continued as artistic director (assisted by Julia Miles, who ran the WOMEN'S PROJECT there [1978–87]), lost control of the space in 2002 to the ROUNDABOUT THEATRE COMPANY. The Roundabout, after renovation, opened the building as the Harold and Miriam Steinberg Center for Theatre, and the theatre space within as the permanent Laura Pels Theatre (opening in 2004 with LYNN NOTTAGE's *Intimate Apparel.*)   MCH   DBW

American Repertory Theatre The first company of this name, founded in 1946 by EVA LE GALLIENNE with MARGARET WEBSTER and CHERYL CRAWFORD, was located in an obsolete theatre on Columbus Circle. Despite a notable company of actors and the objective to become New York's version of Britain's Old Vic or the Comédie-Française, it was defunct by 1948.

The second company of this name (ART) under ROBERT BRUSTEIN began an association in 1980 with Harvard University, using the Loeb Drama Center in Cambridge, MA; former Royal Shakespeare Company director Ron Daniels served as associate artistic director until 1996. Dedicated to neglected works from the past, new American plays ("New Stages"), and innovative classical productions, the theatre has staged controversial productions (such as *Endgame* [1984–5], disclaimed by Beckett), innovative direction, and experimental work, such as the 1985 production of portions of ROBERT WILSON's *the CIVIL WarS,* and Wilson's 1991 staging of Ibsen's *When We Dead Awaken.* It has also mounted inaugural productions, such as MARSHA NORMAN's *'NIGHT, MOTHER* (1982) and the 1985 Tony Award–winning musical *Big River,* later seen in New York. In 1985 ART received the JUJAMCYN Award; in 1986, both a special Regional Theatre Tony and a NATIONAL ENDOWMENT FOR THE ARTS Ongoing Ensemble Award. In 1987 ART began its Institute for Advanced Theatre Training, which began a partnership with the Moscow Art Theatre School in 1997.

Brustein ended his lengthy reign as artistic director in 2002, replaced by frequent ART director ROBERT WOODRUFF, who began his tenure with a season filled with experimental directors including PETER SELLERS, ANNE BOGART, János Szász, and ANDREI SERBAN, and stepped down in 2007. In 2004 a second performance space was introduced, the Theatre at Zero Arrow Street, a flexible, intimate venue. A guide to the Brustein years was compiled by Marilyn J. Plotkins (2005). DBW

American Shakespeare [Festival] Theatre

Founded in Stratford, CT, in 1951 under the guidance of LAWRENCE LANGNER; the word "Festival" was dropped from its name in 1972. The theatre, designed by Edwin Howard as an octagon (ostensibly to suggest the exterior of the original Globe Theatre) with a thrust stage and an auditorium seating about 1,500, opened on 12 July 1955 with *Julius Caesar* as part of an eight-week season. Under a series of artistic directors, roughly 75 productions were staged, including non-Shakespearean works beginning with SHAW's *Caesar and Cleopatra* in 1963. In 1959 special spring performances for students were added. Among the better-known actors to have appeared here were MORRIS CARNOVSKY, JESSICA TANDY, KATHARINE HEPBURN, KATE REID, JAMES EARL JONES, CHRISTOPHER PLUMMER, and ALFRED DRAKE. In 1977 the Connecticut Center for the Performing Arts was established to expand the season to include guest artists and touring companies. The most recent full summer season was 1979, followed by sporadic production and finally virtual inactivity since 1982. In January of that year the theatre filed for bankruptcy with a debt of almost $2 million. A proposed solution to its financial woes has yet to lead to full-time operation, despite the inauguration in 1988 of the Stratford Institution by the University of Connecticut and a brief summer season (as the American Festival Theatre) in 1989 by a company from the AMERICAN CONSERVATORY THEATRE. Periodic reports in the 1990s stated that with state and private funds the decaying structure would be renovated; a 1998 report that Connecticut's Department of Environmental Protection would faciliate matters was followed by a series of benefit readings in the early 2000s by stage luminaries, yet nothing noticeable changed in the delapidated facility's status. In 2005 the town assumed ownership from the state and as of summer 2006 began negotiations with a New York City public affairs/strategic planning firm for a plan and long-term lease to renovate and run the theatre. Stay tuned! DBW

American Theatre

Camp St., New Orleans, LA. English-language theatre was successfully established in New Orleans with the American Theatre, lit with gas and boasting a 38-ft. proscenium opening, which flourished during 1824–40. A substantial brick structure accommodating 1,100 on stuffed seats, the house was built by JAMES H. CALDWELL, who served as its manager for eight years before leasing it to others. Caldwell and his successors assembled competent companies, provided novelties along with the standard repertory, and brought in whatever stars were available each season. After he had launched his larger and more opulent ST. CHARLES, Caldwell disposed of the "pretty little playhouse" on Camp, which was rebuilt as the Camp St. Exchange in 1840. MCH

American Theatre Wing

Founded in January 1940 by RACHEL CROTHERS and six other notable women of the New York theatre, the Wing opened the Stage Door Canteen (216 West 44th St.) in March 1942 to entertain servicemen, and in 1947 created the ANTOINETTE PERRY Award (the Tony). Under the presidency of ISABELLE STEVENSON from 1966 until her death in 2003, the Wing continues as an important theatre-based service organization. DBW

Ames, Winthrop

(1871–1937) Producer and director. Ames, a wealthy Bostonian, was a leader in the art theatre movement. He ran BOSTON's Castle Square Theatre (1904–7), New York's ill-fated NEW THEATRE (1909–11), and finally the two theatres he built: the Little Theatre (1912, West 44th St.) – "a little Pullman car of a place," he called it – and the BOOTH (West 45th St).

Ames was the first American to make a serious study of the European art theatres. In 1907 he visited 64 theatres, saw 53 productions in Paris, London, Berlin, Vienna, and Munich, and kept a detailed notebook including 154 sketches of scenic innovations. In 1912 he introduced the New Stagecraft to New York by bringing over REINHARDT's production of *Sumurun*. He also encouraged NORMAN BEL GEDDES's experiments in stage lighting at his two theatres.

Ames prepared minutely detailed prompt scripts ("mother copies," he called them) for his productions, and the results always reflected his lively imagination and impeccable taste. Most notable: Galsworthy's *The Pigeon* (1912), Schnitzler's *The Affairs of Anatol* (1912, starring John Barrymore [see DREW–BARRYMORE]), SHAW's *The Philanderer* (1913), *Snow White* (1913, Ames's adaptation), Maeterlinck's *The Betrothel* (1918), and KAUFMAN and CONNELLY's *BEGGAR ON HORSEBACK* (1924). RM

Anania, Michael

(1951–) Longtime resident set designer for the PAPER MILL PLAYHOUSE (NJ), where his productions, beginning with *Windy City* (1985), include *SHOW BOAT, The WIZARD OF OZ, FOLLIES*, and *The Chosen*. Distinguished for his opera and musical productions, he has designed several of the Broadway musical revivals at the New York City Opera such as *A LITTLE NIGHT MUSIC* (1990) and *MOST HAPPY FELLA* (1991). In addition he has designed at CENTRAL CITY OPERA HOUSE, the Lake George Opera Festival, and GOODSPEED. Working in these venues he has established a reputation as a creator of large-scale and romantic settings. He has also designed on Broadway (*The Gathering, Run for Your Wife, Canterbury Tales*) and for many regional theatres.   AA

And Miss Reardon Drinks a Little by PAUL ZINDEL opened at the MOROSCO THEATRE 25 February 1971 (108 performances) following his Pulitzer Prize–winning *The EFFECT OF GAMMA RAYS ON MAN-IN-THE-MOON MARIGOLDS* (1971). The play deals with three sisters who are all schoolteachers: one an inebriated realist (ESTELLE PARSONS), another a hardened administrator (Nancy Marchand), and the third a disturbed waif (JULIE HARRIS), who is the catalyst for the play's debate as to whether she should be institutionalized.   KN

Anderson, John (Hargis) (1896–1943) Drama critic who worked as a reporter, feature writer, and a columnist for the *New York Post* (1918–24), serving as drama critic during 1924–8. From 1928 to 1937 he wrote the dramatic column for the *New York Evening Journal,* and for the *Journal-American* from 1937 until his death. Anderson's forte was an astute eye and vivid prose that communicated theatrical excitement to his readers. His books include *Box Office* (1930) and *The American Theatre* (1938).   TLM

Anderson, John Murray (1886–1954) Producer, designer, and director. After beginning his theatrical career as a producer of pageants and civic masques, Anderson applied the New Stagecraft of Gordon Craig and his followers to the American REVUE when he presented the *Greenwich Village Follies* (1919). The show's success, due largely to its simple, imaginative, and beautiful scenery and costumes, launched an annual series of revues that rivaled the ZIEGFELD *Follies* in the taste and artistry of its mise-en-scène. The *Greenwich Village Follies* were also noted for their "ballet ballads," poems and stories set to music and dance. Anderson was soon in demand as a designer, director, and producer. Over the next 30 years he was primarily known as a facile director of musicals, nightclub floor shows, and circuses. Among his musical theatre productions were two editions of the revue *Murray Anderson's Almanac* (1929 and 1953). His autobiography was published in 1954.   MK

Anderson, Judith [née Frances Margaret Anderson-Anderson] (1898–1992) First Australian-born actress appointed DBE (1960), who consistently excelled in powerful, tragic roles. Failing in her planned singing career, she turned to acting and made her debut in Sydney in 1915, followed by a two-year tour with an American stock company. Her first New York appearance was in 1918; her first substantial success was as Elise in *Cobra* (1924), followed by the Unknown One in *As You Desire Me* (1931), and Lavinia in *MOURNING BECOMES ELECTRA* (1932). In 1936 she was Gertrude to John Gielgud's Hamlet in New York; in 1937 she made her London debut (Old Vic) as Lady Macbeth opposite Laurence Olivier (repeated with MAURICE EVANS, New York, 1941). She played the title role in ROBINSON JEFFERS's adaptation of Euripides' *Medea* in 1947 (revived in 1974). At the Old Vic in 1960 she appeared as Irina Arkadina in *The Seagull.* In 1970, with minimal success, she toured as Hamlet. During 1984–7 she appeared regularly as a domineering matriarch on the U.S. television daytime drama *Santa Barbara.* In 1984 a theatre on New York's THEATRE ROW (West 42d St.) was named after her (recently razed).   DBW

Anderson, Laurie (1947–) Chicago-born performance artist, composer, and musician whose work addresses mass audiences and explores popular music idioms. As a child, she studied the violin and took special art classes. She studied art history at Barnard, sculpture at Columbia (M.F.A., 1972), and wrote for major art journals. Her work is influenced by Sol LeWitt, John Cage, Fluxus, Philip Glass, William S. Burroughs, conceptual art, and popular culture. Supported by voice filters, loops, and sequencers that manipulate the pitch and texture of her natural voice, Anderson's media image emphasizes androgyny and explores the ambiguities of language and sound. Her works range from *Automotive* (1972), scored for car horns; to a Fluxus-inspired street performance, *Duets on Ice* (1974), in which she played a prepared violin while standing in blocks of melting ice; to *Empty Places* (1988–90), a concert with media images, projections, songs, storytelling, and stand-up comedy. Her multimedia event *United States* (1978–83) was recorded by Warner Bros., and a section of it, "O Superman" (1980), was a hit in the U.S. and Britain. In 1994–5 she toured her multimedia *The Nerve Bible* (publishing in 1994 *Stories from the Nerve Bible,* a 1972–92 retrospective); 1999 saw her *Songs and Stories from Moby Dick,* a meditation on the power of the sea, at the SPOLETO FESTIVAL. In 2000 an overview of her work by RoseLee Goldberg was published.   AF

Anderson, Mary (1859–1940) Actress. At 16, in 1875, she made her debut as Juliet at MACAULEY'S THEATRE in Louisville, KY, and this quickly led to other engagements. Her major assets were her classical physical beauty and a rich, expressive voice. She made her NYC debut in 1877. W. S. GILBERT wrote a short play, *Comedy and Tragedy,* for her. Americans proudly called her "Our Mary."

During her 14-year career on both sides of the Atlantic, she played 18 leading roles, including such favorites as Rosalind and Galatea in *Pygmalion and Galatea.* She was also the first actress to double the roles of Hermione and Perdita. In 1890 at the height of her career, she retired from the stage, settled in England, and married Antonio de Navarro. She returned to the stage during WWI, however, appearing in various benefit performances. Her memoirs were published as *A Few Memories* (1896) and *A Few More Memories* (1930).   FHL   DJW

Anderson, Maxwell (1888–1959) American playwright and dramatic theorist whose prolific career spanned three decades, although the bulk of his critically acclaimed work came in the 1930s. He won the Pulitzer Prize for BOTH YOUR HOUSES (1933), the Drama Critics' Circle Award for WINTERSET (1935, the first such award ever given), and another for *High Tor* (1937). He gained a reputation as an antiwar dramatist, and WHAT PRICE GLORY (1924), coauthored with Lawrence Stallings, pioneered by bringing onstage the realistic, salty language of men at war. Other Anderson plays with wartime settings or themes include *Valley Forge* (1934), *Key Largo* (1939), *Candle in the Wind* (1941), and *The Eve of St. Mark* (1942).

Anderson turned frequently to the lives of monarchs and other political leaders for the subject matter of his dramas. Important examples include ELIZABETH THE QUEEN (1930), *Mary of Scotland* (1933), KNICKERBOCKER HOLIDAY (1938, a musical written in collaboration with KURT WEILL), JOAN OF LORRAINE (1947), *Anne of the Thousand Days* (1948), and *Barefoot in Athens* (1951). Anderson also successfully adapted others' work for the stage. Examples are LOST IN THE STARS (1949, also in collaboration with Weill) and *The Bad Seed* (1954). Anderson never tired of attempting to justify the use of blank verse in modern drama, and with *The Essence of Tragedy* (1939) became the first American playwright to publish a detailed theory of tragedy. An astute businessman, he was one of the founders of the PLAYWRIGHTS' COMPANY (1938). His biography by Shivers appeared in 1983 and a guide to his work by Barbara Horn in 1996.   LDC

Anderson, Robert W(oodruff) (1917–) New York–born and Harvard-educated playwright Robert Anderson first drew attention by winning the National Theatre Conference prize with *Come Marching Home* (1945). After an eight-year hiatus during which he taught playwriting and adapted 36 plays and several novels for the Theatre Guild of the Air, he burst upon Broadway with the long-running TEA AND SYMPATHY (1953). This sensitive study of a young man's growth from innocence into experience is still considered his outstanding work. He was the only new playwright ever elected to membership (1953) in the PLAYWRIGHTS' COMPANY, which produced three of his plays: *All Summer Long* (1953), *Tea and Sympathy,* and *Silent Night, Lonely Night* (1959). His play *The Days Between* (1965) helped inaugurate the American Playwright's Theatre. He proved that an evening of one-act plays was still viable Broadway fare with *You Know I Can't Hear You When the Water's Running* (1967) and *Solitaire/Double Solitaire* (1970). Anderson adapted several of his plays to film, including the autobiographical *I Never Sang for My Father* (1968), the screenplay for which earned him a 1970 Academy Award nomination.   LDC

André Regarded as one of WILLIAM DUNLAP's best plays; first produced by the Old AMERICAN COMPANY at New York's PARK THEATRE, 30 March 1798. Based on an incident from the American Revolution concerning the capture and execution of a British spy, Dunlap's sympathetic treatment of Major André was a source of criticism at a time when the U.S. was about to pass the infamous Anti-Sedition Act of 1798. It was Dunlap's first attempt at writing native drama and was praised for its structure, though only modestly received. Five years later, Dunlap presented a musical version titled *Glory of Columbia.*   PAD

Andrews, Julie [née Julia Elizabeth Wells] (1935–) Although most of her credits, like MARLON BRANDO's, are in films, this iconic British-born singer-actress has had a major impact on Broadway lore, beginning as Polly in *The Boy Friend* (1954), followed by the creation of Eliza in *My Fair Lady* (1956), Guinevere in CAMELOT (1960), and the title characters in *Victor/Victoria* (1995). Damage to her vocal chords after surgery in 1997 minimized her singing, but in 2005 she turned to directing (*The Boy Friend*, GOODSPEED). Her daughter, by first husband designer-director TONY WALTON, runs the BAY STREET THEATRE in Sag Harbor, NY. Her life was told by Robert Windeler in 1997.   DBW

Angels in America TONY KUSHNER's two-part "A Gay Fantasia on National Themes" (Part One: *The Millennium Approaches;* Part Two: *Perestroika*) is considered by many the major American play of the past 20 years, marking a new direction for Broadway, what the *New York Times* termed a sign of a "youthquake waiting to happen." Part One, which began its development as result of a commission by SAN FRANCISCO's EUREKA THEATRE and OSKAR EUSTIS, in 1987, received all major awards after its 1992 opening in New York (directed by GEORGE C. WOLFE), including the Tony (it garnered the most nominations in history to date), Drama Critics' Circle, and Drama Desk awards for Best Play. Its earlier production in London (at the Royal National Theatre, directed by Declan Donellan), and Los Angeles (the MARK TAPER FORUM, directed by Eustis), where a version of both plays was staged, also received accolades, including the 1992 London Critics' Circle Award as Best Play and, for the L.A. production, the Pulitzer Prize for drama (the first gay-centered play to be so honored). This daring play, focusing on three households in turmoil (e.g., Louis and Prior [JOE MANTELLO, Stephen Spinella]), also deals with the politics of sexuality, and – through the pivotal character of the historical figure lawyer Roy Cohn (in a critically acclaimed, Tony-winning performance by Ron Leibman), who died of AIDS while denying his homosexuality to his deathbed – it is also about power ("power is sex"). Part Two joined the earlier play in repertory on Broadway fall 1993; neither was profitable, albeit the two parts ran for 10 months. Kushner, who would not relinquish rights for a film version, adapted his play as an HBO miniseries in 2003 – directed to acclaim by MIKE NICHOLS and featuring, in an all-star cast, AL PACINO as Cohn and MERYL STREEP in several key roles – which won seven major 2004 Emmys (Outstanding Miniseries; Nichols, Kushner, Pacino, Streep; plus JEFFREY WRIGHT [of the Broadway cast], as Mr. Lies and Belize, and MARY-LOUISE PARKER as the unstable Harper).   DBW

Anglin, Margaret (1876–1958) Actress. Daughter of the Speaker of the Canadian Parliament, she trained at CHARLES FROHMAN's EMPIRE THEATRE School, made her debut in 1893, and toured opposite JAMES O'NEILL and RICHARD MANSFIELD. She became leading lady of the Empire company opposite HENRY MILLER (1899–1905), and under their own management (1905–8), they produced *The GREAT DIVIDE* by WILLIAM VAUGHN MOODY. She then devoted herself to classical plays in productions designed by LIVINGSTON PLATT in the manner of Edward Gordon Craig. Highlights were her summer productions of *Antigone, Electra,* and *Medea* in the Hearst Amphitheatre at the University of California, Berkeley (1910, 1913, and 1915), and her tour in *The Taming of the Shrew, Twelfth Night, As You Like It,* and *Antony and Cleopatra* (1913–14). Except for a few revivals of her Greek productions, she appeared in modern plays from 1915 to 1943. In 1911 she married the actor Howard Hull. A large, commanding woman, she lacked warmth and charm but was unsurpassed at tears and dark interior emotions. A biography by John Le Vay was published in 1989.   DMcD

Animal Crackers A musical farce by GEORGE S. KAUFMAN and MORRIE RYSKIND starring the MARX BROS., with music and lyrics by Bert Kalmar and Harry Ruby, opened on Broadway 23 October 1928 and ran 191 performances. Groucho and Zeppo played an African explorer and his secretary, and Chico and Harpo played musicians, all attending a house party in a Long Island mansion. The character of Chandler was based on OTTO H. KAHN, financier and "angel," and one scene parodied the spoken interior monologues of O'NEILL's *STRANGE INTERLUDE*, which was still running when *Animal Crackers* opened. Paramount released the film version, with screenplay by Ryskind, in 1930.   JDM

animal impersonation This may be the earliest form of acting: Tribal shamans disguised themselves as animal divinities to ensure successful hunts, evoke fertility spirits, or propitiate malign influences. New Mexicans preserved such an aboriginal deer dance to the 20th century. However, the portrayal of animal characters in the theatre was not common until after the French Revolution, when, as a by-blow of Rousseau's ideas, the noble savage was held to exist even under the skin of an ape. The sensitive anthropoid in Gabriel and Rouchefort's pantoMIME *Jocko; or, The Ape of Brazil* (1825) was one of the most successful tearjerkers of all time. Skilled performers like the Englishman Gouffe and the Italo-French Gabriel RAVEL and Joseph Marzetti (d. 1864) popularized Jocko and his epigone Pongo throughout early 19th-century America. Such impersonation remained a speciality of European acrobat families (Martinetti, Lauri), who regularly played comic animals, especially two-man mules and horses, in pantomime and vaudeville.

Perhaps because she changed both species and sex, MAUDE ADAMS failed as the lead in *Chantecler* (1910), Edmond Rostand's metamorphosis of barnyard fowl and forest creatures into alexandrine-spouting humanoids. American realism was chary of the genre and relegated it to CHILDREN'S THEATRE. The most familiar and enduring examples are imports: Nana, the Saint Bernard nursemaid in J. M. Barrie's *Peter Pan* (1904), the anthropomorphized dog and cat in Maeterlinck's *The Blue Bird* (1908), and the grateful lion in SHAW's *Androcles and the Lion* (1913).

Still, a strain of antirealism on the modern American stage has fostered nonillusionistic impersonations, starting with the mammoth and dinosaur in THORNTON WILDER's *The Skin of Our Teeth* (1942), and devolving into the amphibious lizards of ALBEE's *Seascape* (1975) and Mikhail Baryshnikov as the cockroach in Kafka's *Metamorphosis,* adapted by Steven Berkoff. Musical comedy also welcomed it: Caroline the cow in *Gypsy* (1959) is a stallmate of Imogene the cow in *The Wizard of Oz* (1903), whom L. Frank Baum considered a more stageworthy beast than Toto. The bulldog Tige in *Buster Brown* (1905) was well characterized by a human (George Ali), as were Snoopy the beagle in *You're a Good Man, Charlie Brown* (1967), the phallic wolf in *Into the Woods* (1988), and T. S. ELIOT's *Cats.* Horses have been variously portrayed: by characters with hobby-horse suits round their waists in Anouilh's *Becket* (1960) and ARTHUR KOPIT's *Indians* (1969), and by mimes in leotards and cagelike masks in Peter Shaffer's *Equus* (1974). DISNEY's *Beauty and the Beast* (1994) and especially *The Lion King* (1997), with JULIE TAYMOR's imaginative actor–puppet African animal creations, have taken stage animal impersonation to a new zenith.

These functions, however, have been largely assumed by the animated cartoon, for the antics of Felix the Cat, Mickey Mouse, and Bugs Bunny can be more flexible and fantastical than any living embodiment. Only BERT LAHR as the Cowardly Lion in the film of *The Wizard of Oz* (1939) seems to have transcended the limitations of the form.   LS

animals as performers The heyday of the performing animal followed the Age of Enlightenment and the rise of the equestrian CIRCUS: "Animaux savants" were believed to rival the noble savage as an exemplum of natural perfectibility. Hippodrama, in which trained horses took leading roles, became extremely popular. The hit play was H. M. Milner's *Mazeppa; or, The Wild Horse of Tartary* (1831), in which the young prince, stripped down to fleshings, is strapped to a horse set loose on a treadmill and attacked by stuffed vultures. In the U.S., the title role was usually taken by a

woman, most notoriously by ADAH ISAACS MENKEN. Another prime example was BANNISTER's *Putnam, the Iron Son of '76* (1844), with its famous run on horseback down the rocky steps of Horse Neck. Although hippodrama fell into desuetude by midcentury, new technology created concurrent tracks that enabled a horse race to be the climax of Charles Bernard's *The County Fair* (UNION SQUARE THEATRE, New York, 1889) and Lew Wallace's *Ben-Hur* (1899).

Dog drama, a subspecies of melodrama in which a canine saves the victim and identifies the villain, throve in Bowery theatres before the Civil War: One of its principal purveyors was Mary Hewins, who could rewrite any standard play to star a troupe of trained mongrels. VAUDEVILLE became a hospitable milieu for animal acts from Fink's Mules to Swain's Cats and Rats; Consul the chimpanzee (d. 1904) was an international star in his own right. Owing to high costs and danger, horses, elephants, and lions, common in European variety houses, made only rare appearances in American vaudeville. Until Roy Horn was attacked by a white tiger in November 2003, SIEGFRIED AND ROY, German trainers, staged a successful MAGIC show with wild beasts in Las Vegas revues; now only Rick Thomas at the Stardust has a Las Vegas show with white tigers. In today's theatre, live animals are seen, if at all, in musical comedy (e.g., Sandy in *Annie,* 1977): The biggest laugh in BILLY ROSE's *Jumbo* (1935) came when JIMMY DURANTE, with the title character on a lead, walked nonchalantly past a cop; asked where he was taking the elephant, Durante replied, "Elephant? What elephant?"   LS

Anisfeld, Boris Izrailevich (1879–1973) Bessarabian-born painter and designer. As a member of the "World of Art" group he worked with Diaghilev's *Ballets Russes* and the Pavlova Ballet before coming to the United States in 1918. An exhibition of his paintings toured the country that year, and in 1919 he began an extended association with the Metropolitan Opera. Known for his brilliant use of color, he helped introduce unit settings and folk motifs into the vocabulary of the New Stagecraft in America. His production of the world premiere of Prokofiev's *The Love for Three Oranges* (1921) at the Chicago Opera is one of his best known. In 1928 he joined the faculty of the School of the Art Institute of Chicago and taught there for more than 30 years.   AA

Anna Christie In a wonderfully moody production directed by ARTHUR HOPKINS and designed by ROBERT EDMOND JONES, this EUGENE O'NEILL drama was a perfect vehicle for emotional actress PAULINE LORD and character actor George Marion as Anna and Chris, respectively. Originally written and produced as the failed *Chris Christophersen* in 1920, the revision opened a long run at the Vanderbilt Theatre on 2 November 1921. Anna, one of O'Neill's most fully drawn women, is a desperate prostitute who finally finds family and love only to lose them and regain them uneasily and uncertainly in the final scene. Although the play received the Pulitzer Prize, O'Neill eventually denied its importance, claiming that audiences and critics mistakenly took the conclusion for a happy one. Nonetheless, *Anna Christie* was unusually explicit in both language and situation for its time and helped to free the New York stage for yet grittier subject matter as the decade progressed. There have been Broadway revivals in 1952, 1977, and 1993 (Tony for Best Revival), the latter with Liam Neeson and Natasha Richardson. The play was the basis for the BOB MERRILL–GEORGE ABBOTT musical *New Girl in Town* (1973). RHW

Anna Lucasta Three-act drama by Philip Yordan; opened OFF-BROADWAY at the 135th Street Library Theatre in Harlem (16 June 1944) for 19 performances, then moved to Broadway's Mansfield Theatre (30 August 1944) for 957 more, becoming one of the first serious Off-Broadway plays to receive significant critical attention. Abram Hill and Harry Wagstaff Gribble of Harlem's newly founded (1940) AMERICAN NEGRO THEATRE adapted the script, about a Polish American family's struggles in a small Pennsylvania town, to focus on the wayward daughter of a black, working-class family. The production, which featured EARLE HYMAN, CANADA LEE, FREDERICK O'NEAL, and Hilda Simms, served to recognize and validate the AFRICAN AMERICAN voice on Broadway.   EK

Annie Two-act musical comedy, music by CHARLES STROUSE, lyrics by MARTIN CHARNIN, book by Thomas Meehan. Opened 21 April 1977 at New York's ALVIN THEATRE, running 2,377 performances. Based on Harold Gray's classic comic strip, this heartwarming musical of kids, dogs, and Christmas in the 1930s follows Little Orphan Annie's pursuit of her real parents, culminating in adoption by Daddy Warbucks. Pointedly old-fashioned in an age of musicals striving to be sophisticated and up-to-date, its unabashed sentimentality, played without camp, won wide appeal. Initially unable to find a Broadway producer, the show first appeared in 1976 at the

GOODSPEED OPERA HOUSE in East Haddam, CT. There it caught the attention of MIKE NICHOLS, who nurtured it and produced it on Broadway, where it won both the Tony and Drama Critics' Circle awards for Best Musical. *Annie Warbucks,* a sequel, underwent a labyrinthine journey from conception in 1988 to a modest Off-Broadway run in 1993. Charnin in 1977 published a "memoir" of *Annie.* A 20th-anniversary production in 1997 was seen at the Eugene O'Neill Theatre with Nell Carter as Miss Hannigan   JD

Annie Get Your Gun Two-act musical comedy, music and lyrics by IRVING BERLIN, book by Herbert and DOROTHY FIELDS. Opened 16 May 1946 at the IMPERIAL THEATRE, New York, running 1,147 performances. RICHARD RODGERS and OSCAR HAMMERSTEIN II, who produced the show, had originally engaged JEROME KERN to write the score; but after Kern's death in 1945, they'd turned to Irving Berlin. An old-fashioned star vehicle, it tells, amid show-business trappings, the story of the rivalry and romance between ANNIE OAKLEY (ETHEL MERMAN) and Frank Butler (Ray Middleton), competing sharpshooters in "BUFFALO BILL" CODY's WILD WEST EXHIBITION, a setting providing the occasion for lavish production numbers. Of the 14 songs introduced (among them "There's No Business Like Show Business"), 9 featured Merman and 3 of the remaining 5 her leading man. A successful American tour (starring MARY MARTIN) and London production (starring Dolores Gray) followed. For a major 1966 revival at LINCOLN CENTER (again starring Merman), Berlin replaced one of the two songs not sung by Annie or Frank with a new contrapuntal duet for the two of them. A revival in 1999 (1,046 performances plus previews) with other alterations (book by PETER STONE) featured a series of stars in the title role: BERNADETTE PETERS, Susan Lucci, Cheryl Ladd, Reba McEntire, Crystal Bernard). A perennial favorite, *Annie Get Your Gun* was the most successful musical in the long careers of both Berlin and Merman.   JD

ANTA see AMERICAN NATIONAL THEATRE AND ACADEMY

Anthony [né Deuster]**, Joseph** (1912–93) Milwaukee-born actor and director whose acting debut was in a West Coast production of *Mary of Scotland.* Afterward he appeared in New York with the FEDERAL THEATRE in 1937, and later in numerous roles including Casanova in *CAMINO REAL* and Prince Bounine in *Anastasia* (1954). He made his New York directing debut with *Celebration* (1948), and established himself as one of America's premiere directors in film and theatre. His stage credits included *The* RAINMAKER (1954), *The Lark* (1955), *The* MOST HAPPY FELLA (1956), *Winesburg, Ohio* (1958), *The Best Man* (1960), MARY, MARY (1961), *Romulus* (1962), *110 in the Shade* (1963), SLOW DANCE ON THE KILLING GROUND (1964), and *Finishing Touches* (1973).   TLM

Antin, Eleanor (1935–) New York–born Jewish conceptual and PERFORMANCE ARTist, who in southern California also works in photography, video, and film. Antin studied acting at New York's Tamara Daykarhanova School (1955–7). She developed fictional-autobiographical personae, such as a king, a nurse, a black movie star, or a black ballerina. In *My Life with Diaghilev* (1981–5), Antin (who is white) toured as a black Russian dancer, reading from her memoirs. In *The Last Night of Rasputin* (1989), she screened her film about prerevolutionary Russia and reminisced about her fictional life as the black dancer Eleanora Antinova. *Vilna Nights* (1993) gave her view of the Holocaust, and in *The Last Days of Pompeii* (2001) she offered an ironic parable of American culture in the throes of overconsumption.   AF

Antoon, A(lfred) J(oseph) (1944–92) Director who in 1972–3 had two award-winning productions on Broadway – THAT CHAMPIONSHIP SEASON and a *Much Ado about Nothing* set in a turn-of-the-century America – both transfers from the NEW YORK SHAKESPEARE FESTIVAL, for which since 1971 he did much of his finest work. Other productions included GURNEY's *The Art of Dining* (1979) and *Song of Singapore* (1991), his last effort before his death from AIDS.   CLJ

Anything Goes Two-act musical comedy, music and lyrics by COLE PORTER, which opened 21 November 1934 at New York's ALVIN THEATRE, running 420 performances. Conceived as a vehicle to feature stars ETHEL MERMAN, WILLIAM GAXTON, and VICTOR MOORE, the original book by GUY BOLTON and P. G. WODEHOUSE dealt with a group of eccentric characters involved in a shipwreck; but upon the sinking of the *SS Morro Castle*, the book was hastily rewritten by HOWARD LINDSAY and RUSSEL CROUSE (their playwriting debut) to treat romantic complications involving society folk and con men aboard a transatlantic liner. One of the most popular musicals of the 1930s, it introduced many Porter standards – the title song, plus "I Get a Kick Out of You," "All Through the Night," and "You're the Top." The show has proven extremely durable. A version successfully

produced Off-Broadway in 1962, with the book revised by Guy Bolton and songs from other Porter shows interpolated into the score, became a staple of the amateur repertoire. A 1987 Broadway revival starring PATTI LUPONE at Lincoln Center's VIVIAN BEAUMONT THEATRE – with book revised yet again by Timothy Crouse and John Weidman and new interpolations, as well as some restorations to the original score – ran 804 performances, won a Tony Award, and had a successful national tour.   JD

Any Wednesday Two-act comedy by Muriel Resnik; opened on Broadway at the MUSIC BOX THEATRE (18 February 1964) for 982 performances, starring Sandy Dennis (Tony Award) and a young Gene Hackman. Set in New York's Upper East Side, the play addresses personal and business ethics as an arrogant, married business tycoon supports his daffy, innocent, tax-deductible young mistress, losing both wife and mistress in the end. At the time, audiences appreciated the mature subject matter, which acknowledged the many gray areas regarding ethics.   EK

Apollo Theatre Historic showplace of black entertainers at 125th St., Harlem, New York. Originally a burlesque theatre, this two-balconied, 1,463-seat theatre became the mecca of black show business when it was taken over in 1935 by Frank Schiffman and Leo Brecher. Now-famous big bands, instrumentalists, singers, dancers, and stand-up comedians all graced the Apollo stage, some making their first public appearance at the regular Wednesday amateur night show. The theatre was closed in 1977 and later reopened as a television studio for the black cable market. The building was granted landmark status in 1983; in 1991 it was acquired by the State of New York. Its future was unsure for a number of years, but a projected multi-million-dollar renovation, its weekly amateur nights (ongoing since 1934), and the installation in 2002 of the GEORGE C. WOLFE–conceived revue *Harlem Song*, which celebrated the history of Harlem from the 1920s (albeit less successful as a draw than hoped) were signs of an optimistic future. Its $65 million renovation is projected for 2008 completion.   EGH

Arcenas, Loy (1953–) Since the 1990s, one of the busiest scenic designers, especially Off-Broadway, where he has designed more than 45 productions as of May 2005 (1993 Obie for Sustained Excellence of Set Design), and in the regions. Philippines-born Arcenas's style is noted for its leanness and a preference for hand-painted surfaces and selected images, as in his designs for WOLFE's *Spunk* and the musical *Once on This Island* (both 1990). Among his major New York credits are PRE-LUDE TO A KISS (1990), SHEPARD's *Simpatico* and ROUNDABOUT's revival of GLASS MENAGERIE (both 1994), MCNALLY's *Love! Valor! Compassion!* (1995), *A Man of No Importance* (2002), and *Dessa Rose* (2005), the latter two at LINCOLN CENTER. He has worked frequently for the GOODMAN THEATRE and CIRCLE REP, in addition to dozens of other companies nationally. In 1996 he directed *Flip-zoids* for THEATRE FOR THE NEW CITY, and he has served as a resident director for NEW DRAMA-TISTS. He is a frequent designer-director with the FILIPINO AMERICAN troupe the MA-YI THEATRE Company.   DBW

Arch Street Theatre 609–615 Arch St., PHILADEL-PHIA [Architect: William Strickland]. Believing that Philadelphians would support a newer, more elegant playhouse than the CHESTNUT, a group of citizens pledged the money to build the Arch Street Theatre and leased it to WILLIAM B. WOOD, late of the rival theatre. It opened in 1828, but Wood did not last long as manager, and it passed to other hands. Starting in 1861, it enjoyed its most prosperous and famous period when MRS. JOHN DREW became manageress. For nearly a dec-ade, she maintained a peerless company of actors in excellent productions. In 1879, Mrs. Drew was forced to accede to the "combination system," in which each play is individually cast and presented for as long a run as it has the public's interest. After she retired from the theatre's management in 1892, it was often closed. Before it was demol-ished in 1936, the theatre had been used by Ger-man and Yiddish companies.   MCH

architecture, theatre The earliest American the-atres were temporary structures and converted rooms in inns or private homes fitted, at best, with a curtained raised stage and some seats. The first recorded playhouse was built by William Lev-ingston in Williamsburg, VA, between 1716 and 1718; absolutely no evidence survives as to what its interior may have been like. However, from its beginnings the American playhouse was influ-enced by its English counterpart. At first this meant a box, pit, and gallery arrangement for the auditorium, a simple proscenium stage, perhaps with a wing-and-groove scenic system, and, at least in the 18th century, an apron with prosce-nium doors.

There are records of NEW YORK CITY THEATRE spaces in 1732 and 1735. These were followed in 1736 by the DOCK STREET THEATRE in Charles-ton, SC, built to house amateur productions. The first "professional" theatre in colonial America was Plumstead's Warehouse in PHILADELPHIA, made into a performing space by the company of WALTER MURRAY AND THOMAS KEAN in 1749 as they began their American tour. In New York, they performed at the Nassau Street Theatre in 1750. A notice for this theatre in 1751 mentioned 10 boxes – the first record of such a seating arrangement. Also in 1751, a crude playhouse was quickly erected in Williamsburg for the Murray–Kean Company, yet again, little detail is known.

A more professional period began with the arrival in 1752 of LEWIS HALLAM's London Com-pany of Comedians, who bought and renovated Murray and Kean's Williamsburg playhouse, cre-ating a box, pit, and gallery structure with some sort of balcony. As the company toured New York, Philadelphia, and Charleston over the next two years, they converted or reconstructed existing theatres. Notably, in New York, they built a new Nassau Street Theatre on the site of the old one – probably the first American theatre based specif-ically on English theatre architecture. Under DAVID DOUGLASS, who took over the Company of Comedians in 1758, the troupe traveled through the major East Coast theatre centers, building or renovating theatres in the English tradition at each stop. The two most notable were the SOUTH-WARK, built just outside Philadelphia in 1766, and the JOHN STREET in New York, opened in 1767. Both these theatres were relatively well equipped, with a flat-wing and groove system for scenery, a green front-cloth behind the proscenium, oil lamps, and basic audience amenities. Both the-atres no doubt compared favorably with English provincial theatres at the time, if not the better London counterparts.

Plays and other entertainments were banned by the Continental Congress in 1774, temporarily putting an end to most theatre construction. After the Revolution, theatres of varying degrees of sophistication were erected in Richmond, Nor-folk, Alexandria, Annapolis, Boston, Providence, Portland (Maine), Baltimore, Charleston, New Orleans, Newport, New York, and other cities, sev-eral of these under the management of THOMAS WADE WEST; but it was in the last decade of the century that a golden age of theatre architecture began, with architectural style and production facilities equal to those of England. The CHEST-NUT STREET THEATRE, perhaps designed by John Inigo Richards, opened in Philadelphia in 1794 and was, at the time, the most sophisticated the-atre in the country; in 1816 it would become the first theatre in the world illuminated by gaslight (see STAGE LIGHTING). The FEDERAL STREET THE-ATRE in Boston also opened in 1794, and 1798 saw the opening of the PARK THEATRE in New York. These three were similar in all respects to contemporary English playhouses. They were relatively large – the Park seated 2,000 – and contained curved benches in the pit and three tiers of boxes and galleries. The stage machinery, though not elaborate, was up-to-date and allowed for the sort of spectacle that was becoming popular at the turn of the century. The NATIONAL THEATRE opened in Washington, DC, in 1800. Meanwhile, the Olympic Theatre, built to house a CIRCUS, opened in Philadelphia in 1809 but was renovated as a legitimate house in 1811, reopening as the WALNUT STREET THEATRE, which still stands, with a modernized interior. Also in 1811 came the worst theatre disaster to that time: The Richmond Theatre burned, killing 71 spectators including the governor of Virginia (see FIRES).

By 1815 theatre began to follow the general westward expansion of the United States, and makeshift theatres are documented in Ohio, Kentucky, Indiana, and Tennessee. Facilities were primitive. A contemporary account describes a stage 10 ft. wide and 8 ft. deep that became crowded with the introduction of scenery. There was evidence of a theatre in Detroit in 1816, St. Louis records a theatre in 1827, CHICAGO in 1837. (The first Chicago building exclusively for theatre was on Randolph St. in 1847.) New Orleans, too, had become a thriving theatre center with French performances by 1791. The Camp Street or AMERICAN THEATRE (1824) in New Orleans had gaslight two years before any theatre in New York, and the ST. CHARLES THEATRE (1835) was one of the most elegant in the country. A unique development were the floating theatres on the Ohio and Mississippi Rivers. NOAH LUD-LOW may have created the first as early as 1817, but the first SHOWBOAT specifically designed as such was built by William Chapman in 1831 and based in Pittsburgh; it seated about 200 spectators. Spanish-language productions in California were performed in missions, but the first English-language productions and the first theatre structures date from the Mexican–American War. A Monterey lodging house that still stands was converted into a theatre by soldiers in 1848 and is considered California's first theatre. Playhouses appeared in Sacramento in 1849 and SAN FRAN-CISCO in 1850.

After 1800 New York rapidly developed as the nation's largest city and the center of theatrical activity. Through the first half of the 19th century several theatres were built in lower Manhattan, including the second Park (1821); the BOWERY (1826), which was the largest in the country with a 3,500-seat capacity and the first New York theatre with gaslight; the Italian Opera House (1833), which was the first American opera house; and the ASTOR PLACE OPERA HOUSE (1847), site of the infamous anti-Macready riots of 1849. BOSTON, which had been a latecomer to the theatre circuit, added the Washington Street Theatre and the TREMONT THEATRE in 1827 to the existing Federal Street Theatre. Throughout the 19th century almost every city of any size built an "opera house," which was not necessarily intended for opera but was a multiuse performance space that could house a range of traveling entertainments and even nonperformance activities, such as conventions. These spaces were loosely based on European models.

Throughout this period, the theatres were typified by increasing size and elegance and greater refinement in stage machinery. Exteriors were often done in some version of Greek or Roman revival, creating a sense of dignity and sophistication as well as becoming the most imposing edifices in the cities. The frequent FIRES that plagued theatres had the one benefit of allowing a fairly steady renewal and renovation of the structures. The New Park, for example, had a 45-ft. proscenium opening and a 70-ft.-deep stage; it seated 2,500 in an auditorium with a raked pit, three tiers of boxes, and a surrounding gallery. When the Bowery Theatre was rebuilt after the fire of 1845, it had a seating capacity of 4,000 and a stage depth and width of 126 ft., making it one of the largest legitimate theatres in the world. (The Academy of Music, an opera house that opened in New York in 1854, seated 4,500.)

Huge theatres typified by the Bowery were appropriate for large-scale melodrama and spectacle, but as gentlemanly melodrama and realism began to dominate, the trend was reversed. A greater intimacy and a more detailed form of scenery was now required. STEELE MACKAYE's remodeling of the MADISON SQUARE THEATRE is the best documented of the changes these new trends wrought. For greater intimacy MacKaye reduced the theatre to a 700-seat capacity and eliminated the forestage and the orchestra pit – the orchestra was housed above the proscenium arch. Most notably, he installed an elevator stage with two levels, which allowed one scene to be set on the "offstage" level while another was being played; the elevator could be raised or lowered in 40 seconds. Though lacking the technical sophistication, WALLACK'S THEATRE and DALY'S FIFTH AVENUE THEATRE continued this trend as the center of the New York theatre district moved north up Broadway.

American theatre architecture in the second half of the 19th century followed the trend in Europe. The box, pit, and gallery configuration was replaced by a more luxurious orchestra seating area and balconies. Boxes remained as decorative appendages in American theatres into the early 20th century, but the orchestra eventually became the preferred seating area as individual upholstered chairs with armrests became common after the Civil War. The proscenium or picture-frame stage was the norm, and this sort of theatre, often elaborately decorated, continued to be built through the 1920s. Because the theatre builders were more often interested in business than theatre, "nonessential" spaces – lobbies, dressing rooms, and space between rows of seats – were minimal to nonexistent. The 1930s Depression put a virtual end to theatre construction in the U.S. until after WWII.

Richard Wagner's Festspielhaus in Bayreuth, Germany, is often considered the first modern theatre because of its fan-shaped auditorium design and lack of boxes, creating a "democratic" seating arrangement. Though this 1876 theatre would eventually have a profound influence on 20th-century theatre architecture, it had little immediate impact on American playhouse design. Toward the end of the 19th century, however, a conscious rethinking of theatre architecture began to emerge, and many fanciful theatres were proposed, even if virtually none were built. One of the most extravagant was STEELE MAC-KAYE's Spectatorium, designed for the World's Columbian Exposition in Chicago in 1893. It was to hold 10,000 spectators for a pageant chronicling the life of Columbus. The theatre was actually started but never completed because of the financial crisis of 1893.

In terms of innovation and influence, the closest American counterpart to the Bayreuth Festspielhaus was the Chicago AUDITORIUM THEATRE designed by Dankmar Adler and Louis Sullivan in 1889. It was virtually the first theatre in the U.S. to address problems of sightlines and acoustics. The upper and lower balconies could be closed off by means of a hinged ceiling, and the rear of the auditorium closed by a hanging curtain. Thus the seating capacity ranged from 2,500 to 4,000, and all seats had unobstructed views of the stage; side galleries, as at Bayreuth, were abolished. The acoustics achieved a perfection unmatched in previous American theatre architecture. In addition, the theatre contained its own electrical generating plant and air-cooling system. Adler and

Sullivan expressed patriotic and democratic sentiments in their speeches and writings, and saw the Auditorium Theatre as an example of American architecture.

The trends toward intimacy, technical sophistication, and a scientific approach to acoustical and visual design reached a pinnacle with WINTHROP AMES's Little Theatre (1912) in New York. Seating only 299 spectators in a Continental dish-style auditorium, the stage had a revolve and 35 traps. The auditorium ceiling could be lowered to change the angle of lighting. Although a balcony was added in 1919 to enlarge the seating capacity, the theatre was still a financial failure.

The antiquarian movement of the 19th century led to a reexamination of the original staging of classical plays. This, coupled with new movements in European theatre, led to the exploration of new stage spaces and configurations. Drawing on Greek and Elizabethan precedents, the thrust stage emerged as a popular alternative to the proscenium. Some of the first efforts in that direction in the U.S. were the projects for "dome theatres" by NORMAN BEL GEDDES. First described in 1914 and revised in various ways over the years, Bel Geddes's theatres tended to be a variant of a Greek theatre, with a curved stage partially surrounded by curved auditorium seating, all architecturally unified under a single domed structure. A related form of theatre was being used in Germany by MAX REINHARDT. At roughly the same time, several universities began to create makeshift thrust theatres in an attempt to recreate Elizabethan conditions for the staging of Shakespeare. A notable permanent example was the theatre at Sarah Lawrence College, built in 1952 with a trapezoidal apron in front of a picture-frame stage. However, the real triumph of the thrust stage in North America came with TYRONE GUTHRIE's Festival Theatre in Stratford, Ontario (1953–7), designed in collaboration with TANYA MOISEIWITSCH. The general pattern of this theatre was repeated at the GUTHRIE THEATRE (1963) in MINNEAPOLIS and at several theatres around the country built in the 1960s and '70s. It incorporated a stepped thrust stage surrounded on three sides by a curved, stepped auditorium and a balcony. The design could accommodate 1,400 spectators but in a relatively intimate arrangement in which no spectator was more than 80 ft. from the stage.

The theatre-in-the-round or arena stage held a great fascination for theatre architects through the 20th century, but it was rarely a successful venture. One of the earliest examples was a 1914 makeshift arena stage at Teacher's College in New

York. Bel Geddes's Theatre No. 14 (1922), another visionary project never constructed, proposed a method for arena staging. The University of Washington in SEATTLE began experimenting with arena staging in 1932, culminating in the Penthouse Theatre (1940) with a seating capacity of 185. There are several other examples from the 1950s and '60s, the most successful being MARGO JONES's Theatre '47, The ALLEY THEATRE (1949), the Playhouse Theatre in Houston (1950), New York's CIRCLE IN THE SQUARE (1951), and the ARENA STAGE (1961). However, in order to incorporate the scenic demands of the repertoire, these and other arena-type theatres sometimes resort to closing off a section of audience to create a scenic space, thus turning the theatres into a form of thrust stage.

More common since the 1960s is the flexible-space theatre, sometimes known as a "black box." Most often associated with colleges or the studio space for an arts complex, these have no fixed seating and can be reconfigured for each production in virtually any style desired. The trend toward environmental production in the late 1960s and '70s encouraged the development of such spaces, and several were designed by environmental designer Jerry Rojo.

Unlike almost all other periods of theatre history, in which the type of performance and the shape of the theatre evolved simultaneously, the mid-20th century in the U.S. accommodated a conglomeration of styles and shapes. The increasingly popular thrust stage could not work well for opera, for instance, or certain forms of drama. Arena and flexible staging, while successful in some cases, was unacceptable in others. At the same time, civic pride was leading many cities to construct municipal theatres or even more elaborate arts centers. Since few cities could afford to build the complete range of theatres necessary for the different demands of modern performance, compromises were evolved. GEORGE IZENOUR was the champion of the multiuse space, a single auditorium that could be used or mechanically adapted for a wide range of performances. The Loeb Drama Center in Cambridge or the Civic Center in El Paso, TX, are examples. Although a few were successful, most proved less than ideal and often were compromised by acoustical or mechanical difficulties, or proved inadequate for some or all the activities for which they were intended. The VIVIAN BEAUMONT THEATRE (1965) at Lincoln Center (designed by Eero Saarinen and Jo MIELZINER), for example, was an attempt to combine a proscenium and a thrust stage in a flexible format. It was generally considered an unsuccessful compromise and has been plagued by sightline and acoustic problems, though some interior work has improved acoustics.

The most successful theatres of the latter half of the 20th century were modified thrust stages unencumbered by excessive mechanical devices and intended for single-use purposes. Economics has also reduced the construction of completely new theatres since the 1970s, and most new theatres at the end of the past century – coming full circle from colonial times – are renovations of structures intended for other uses, often in fairly simple thrust or end-stage arrangements, such as the MILWAUKEE REPERTORY Theatre created out of an abandoned power station. Also, the frequently good acoustics and intimacy of many older picture-frame theatres have been recognized and restored. As opposed to the postwar years, no one today is advocating any sort of ideal theatre structure.

The end of the 20th century saw increased activity in theatre renovations and new theatre construction. Several regional theatres either planned renovations of existing structures or, like the Guthrie, undertook the building of a major new complex or added new spaces to renovated facilities, as did the Arena Stage. In New York, the migration of most drama away from Broadway to smaller venues triggered a building boom of OFF-BROADWAY theatres. Several existing nontheatre structures, including one cinema multiplex, were converted – most often into unadorned, end-stage spaces. Some new construction took place, including a multiplexlike theatre complex on 42d St. Perhaps most notable were the renovations of older theatres. In New York, several of the early-20th-century theatres of 42d St., including the NEW AMSTERDAM, VICTORY, Selwyn (see AMERICAN AIRLINES THEATRE), Apollo, and Lyric (see HILTON THEATRE) were all transformed, as was the BILTMORE on 47th St. as a new home for the MANHATTAN THEATRE CLUB. In several cities, ornate movies palaces from the 1920s were restored and converted to theatres or performing-arts centers. Most of the latter were not only highly theatrical in their own right, but they generally accommodated audiences of 1,000–2,000 or more and were seen as a response to the success of the megamusicals and spectacle shows of the 1980s and '90s that were touring. The economics of theatre dictated that many of the new theatres, like sports stadia, take on corporate names.

A few small theatres have been designed by internationally known architects: Rem Koolhaas created SECOND STAGE's theatre in New York from an old bank building; Frank Gehry designed a small theatre at Bard College; but their contributions are most evident in the facades and public areas. The demands of the stage and its relation to the auditorium remain largely unchanged. However, while thrust stage and flexible-space theatres continue to be built, much of new building and renovation seems to favor end-stage arrangements.   AA*

Ardrey, Robert (1908–80) Playwright, best known for allegorical plays of the 1930s, especially *Casey Jones* (1938), examining job enslavement, and *Thunder Rock* (1939), which explored Americans' quandary over the war looming in Europe. Although produced by the GROUP THEATRE with direction by ELIA KAZAN, *Thunder Rock* was more popular in Europe.   RHW

Arena Stage   6th St. and Maine Ave., NW, Washington, DC [Architect: Harry Weese]. In 1950, a group of six associated with George Washington University founded a theatrical company, Arena Stage, under the guidance of Prof. Edward Mangum. They opened their first season in a moviehouse, presenting their plays "in the round." When most of the original group drifted away to other pursuits, ZELDA FICHANDLER, one of the founding members, took over the reins of leadership and remained its director until 1991. In 1956, the company moved into an old brewery and gradually built an audience. In 1961, sharing the management with her husband, Thomas, Mrs. Fichandler moved into a new modern theatre with the help of grants from the Ford Foundation and others. In Phase II of its development (1970), a 500-seat, modified-thrust-stage playhouse (the Kreeger) joined the 800-seat mainstage; later, a cabaret theatre (the Old Vat Room) was added. In 1991 Douglas C. Wager, who had been associated with Arena in various capacities since 1974, succeeded Fichandler, resigning in 1996 (but remaining as Resident Director). Molly Smith, founder of Juneau, AL's Perseverance Theatre (and for 19 years its artistic director), succeeded Wager in 1998. The Arena Stage Company supports a full company of actors, directors, and designers and presents new American and European plays along with musicals and classical revivals. In September 2003 it was announced that Canadian architect Bing Thom would "reinvent" its complex (a $100-million project), adding a new 200-seat intimate space (The Cradle) dedicated to the advancement of new American work and decreasing its mainstage to 650 seats. Total square footage is projected to be doubled.   MCH
DBW

Arent, Arthur (1904–72) Playwright remembered for his work with the FEDERAL THEATRE PROJECT. He and a research team created LIVING NEWSPAPERS, volatile, imaginative attempts to confront important social and political issues. His best-known work includes an exposé of utilities, *Power* (1937), which expressed the urgent need for affordable electric power for the ordinary and poor consumers; and *Triple-A Plowed Under* (1936), about the economic vicissitudes of farmers and the agricultural way of life during the Depression. ONE-THIRD OF A NATION (1938), a scathing examination of the plight of the poor and substandard housing (emblemized by a burning tenement designed by HOWARD BAY), was the most dynamic of all Living Newspapers. After the demise of the Federal Theatre Project, Arent moved into film, radio, and television.   RHW

Aria da Capo by EDNA ST. VINCENT MILLAY was first directed by the author and produced by the PROVINCETOWN PLAYERS in New York (5 December 1919). The title of the one-act refers to a song in three parts and reflects the piece's structure: A sequence in which two shepherds play out the consequences of greed and territoriality is framed by ironic displays of trivial interaction using commedia dell'arte characters. Poetic language and stylized props serve as counterpoint to the play's antiwar message, which proved popular after WWI. The piece was subsequently produced by many little theatres across the country.   KF

Arkansas Repertory Theatre   In 1976 Arkansas Rep, the state's major theatre, held its first performances in a former Methodist church, its home for the next 12 years. In 1988 the company moved to new facilities in downtown Little Rock (601 Main St.).   LAB

Arkin, Alan (Wolf) (1934–) Actor and director who began with St. Louis's improvisational Compass Players (1959) and made his New York debut with CHICAGO'S SECOND CITY (1961) and his legitimate debut in Joseph Stein's *Enter Laughing* (Tony, Best Featured Actor, 1963). He appeared in *Luv* (1964) before directing Livings's *Eh?* (CIRCLE IN THE SQUARE, 1966), FEIFFER'S *LITTLE MURDERS* (1969, Drama Desk Award) and *The White House Murder Case* (1970, Drama Desk and Obie awards), Neil Simon's *The SUNSHINE BOYS* (1972, Tony nomination), and Elaine May's *Power Plays* (1998). Arkin's films include *The Russians Are Coming, The Russians Are Coming* (Oscar nomination, 1966), *Wait until Dark* (1967), *Catch-22* (1970), *The In-Laws* (1979), *Noel* (2004), and *Little Miss Sunshine* (Oscar, Best

Supporting Oscar, 2006). *Halfway through the Door,* Arkin's autobiography, appeared in 1979. His sons, Adam (1956–), Matthew (1961–), and Anthony (1967–) are actors. **Adam,** whose Broadway debut was in RUDKIN's *I Hate Hamlet,* is best known for Dr. Aaron Shutt in TV's *Chicago Hope;* his most recent stage appearance was in DONALD MARGULIES's *Brooklyn Boy* (2005).   REK

Arlen, Harold (1905–86) Composer who began in the entertainment field as a nightclub performer and rehearsal pianist. During the early 1930s he wrote songs for Harlem's Cotton Club and for Broadway revues; he also appeared in vaudeville. Starting in the mid-1930s he worked in both theatre and film, contributing songs to the Broadway revue *Life Begins at 8:40* (1934), writing the score for the ED WYNN musical *Hooray for What!* (1937), and composing the music for the film *The WIZARD OF OZ* (1939). While continuing his career in Hollywood, Arlen also wrote the scores for the Broadway musicals *Bloomer Girl* (1944), *St. Louis Woman* (1946), *House of Flowers* (1954), *Jamaica* (1957), and *Saratoga* (1959). Many of Arlen's songs, such as "Stormy Weather," were written in an African American blues style. Edward Jablonski's biographies of Arlen appeared in 1961 and 1996.   MK

Arliss, George [né George Augustus Arliss-Andrews] (1868–1946) British-born character actor and playwright whose greatest successes occurred in the U.S. after 1901. Arliss, immediately recognizable due to his distinctive features (long, narrow face, pointed nose, habitual monocle, and charming voice), spent 40 years perfecting the playing of villains, great historical leaders, and wise old men with an apparent effortlessness that concealed his polished technique. Louis Parker, author of his best-known vehicle, *Disraeli* (1911), said Arliss could "express more with one finger than most actors can express with their entire bodies." His most notable stage roles, in addition to Disraeli, were in *The Second Mrs Tanqueray* (1901) with Mrs. Pat Campbell, *The Darling of the Gods* (1902) with BLANCHE BATES, *Hedda Gabler* (1904) and *Rosmersholm* (1907) with MRS. FISKE, *Paganini* (1915), *The Green Goddess* (1921), *Old English* (1924), and his last formal stage appearance as Shylock (1928). In 1923 he returned to London after a 22-year absence to appear in Archer's *The Green Goddess.* His successful film career began in 1920, and during the 1930s he made more than 20 films, portraying among other characters such historical figures as Voltaire, Rothschild (Meyer and Nathan), Cardinal Richelieu, and Wellington. He wrote or collaborated on six plays and wrote two important autobiographies: *Up the Years from Bloomsbury* (1927) and *My Ten Years in the Studio* (1940).   DBW

Armstrong, Will Steven (1930–69) Set and costume designer. After assisting JO MIELZINER, DONALD OENSLAGER, and BORIS ARONSON, Armstrong began his career at the WILLIAMSTOWN THEATRE FESTIVAL, designing its first 30 productions. His major NY productions included *Ivanov* (1958), for which he won an Obie; *Carnival* (1962) for which he won a Tony; *The Lion in Winter* (1966); and *Forty Carats* (1968). He also designed for the AMERICAN SHAKESPEARE FESTIVAL, PHOENIX THEATRE, and the New York City Opera. Much of his work was typified by an attempt to break through the proscenium.   AA

Arneaux, J. A. (1855–?) African American actor. Born in Georgia of a white French father and a black mother, Arneaux received a good postsecondary education in northern cities and in Paris. A journalist by profession, he took to the stage, first as a song-and-dance artist at TONY PASTOR's Metropolitan Theatre on Broadway, then as a legitimate actor and manager of the Astor Place Company of Colored Tragedians, the leading black dramatic troupe in America in the 1880s. Based in New York, the company also performed to great acclaim in both Philadelphia and Providence, RI. Arneaux's roles included Iago, Macbeth, and Pythias; but his favorite part in which he excelled was Richard III, being ranked with Macready, EDWIN BOOTH, and LAWRENCE BARRETT.   EGH

Arnone, John (1949–) Designer. Intending to be an actor, Arnone was a cofounder of the Lion Theatre Company in New York with director GARLAND WRIGHT. He began to design sets for the company, including the highly successful *Vanities* (1976). Employing styles ranging from elaborate detail, such as the miniature city for *New Jerusalem* (1978), to stark symbolism, Arnone has become associated with directors JOANNE AKALAITIS, DES MCANUFF, and LEN JENKIN. He has also designed for film and television, including *The Days and Nights of Molly Dodd* and *Tales from the Darkside.* Recent credits include *The Who's Tommy* (1993, Tony); the 1995 revival of *HOW TO SUCCEED IN BUSINESS WITHOUT REALLY TRYING;* the revivals of *GORE VIDAL's The Best Man* (2000) and ALBEE's *TINY ALICE* (2001); *The GOAT, OR WHO IS SYLVIA?, Fortune's Fool,* and *The FULL MONTY* (all 2002); and the musical *Lennon* (*2005*). In 1992 he received an Obie for Sustained Excellence of Set Design.   AA

Aronson, Boris (1898–1980) Russian American painter, sculptor, and set designer. Aronson is still considered by many the most respected American designer of the mid-20th century. He was born in Russia and studied with Aleksandra Ekster, a constructivist designer with the Kamerny Theatre. He left Russia for Berlin in 1922, and in 1923 emigrated to the U.S., where his first assignments were for the Unser Theatre and the YIDDISH ART THEATRE. By the 1930s he was designing major shows on Broadway and working with the GROUP THEATRE. His early work reflected the influences not only of Ekster but of Marc Chagall and Nathan Altman, who designed for the Moscow Jewish Theatre. The cubist-fantastic style characteristic of Chagall's paintings can be seen in much of Aronson's early work and even in later works, such as the acclaimed set for *J.B.* (1958).

Despite his enormous output and critical success for plays by WILLIAM SAROYAN, TENNESSEE WILLIAMS, CLIFFORD ODETS, ARTHUR MILLER, WILLIAM INGE, and others, he did not achieve widespread recognition until he teamed up with director HAROLD PRINCE on the 1964 musical *FIDDLER ON THE ROOF*. Six more musicals with Prince followed, including *CABARET* and *A LITTLE NIGHT MUSIC*. This collaboration seemed to bring out Aronson's creativity. His designs ranged from realistic detail for plays like *AWAKE AND SING!* to technological fantasies such as *COMPANY* that used steel, Plexiglas, and projections. Aronson's constructivist influences could be seen throughout his work. His sets always had a strong sense of line and form and a generally subtle but evocative use of color, used symbolically to support the mood of the play. For the 1940 production of Ballet Theatre's *The Great American Goof,* Aronson employed, for the first time, a technique he called "Projected Scenery" – a method of projecting colored slides on neutral, abstract shapes in order to create and change the mood and space of a piece. This technique was displayed in the 1947 exhibition of his work at the Museum of Modern Art, aptly titled "Painting with Light." A major study of his work, coauthored by his wife, Lisa, and FRANK RICH, was published in 1987.   AA

Aronson, Rudolph (1856–1919) Impresario, theatre manager, composer. After studying music in Berlin and Paris, Aronson presented a series of orchestral concerts in New York. In 1882 he opened the CASINO THEATRE, where for 12 seasons he mounted lavish productions of European and British comic operas, most notably *Erminie,* which tallied some 1,200 performances in the decade after its premiere in 1886. Among the many performers who attained stardom at the Casino were LILLIAN RUSSELL, FRANCIS WILSON, DE WOLF HOPPER, and JEFFERSON DE ANGELIS. Aronson also introduced New Yorkers to the pleasures of the roof garden, as he brought his comic operas to the Casino's roof during the summer months. After leaving the Casino, he managed the Bijou Theatre for several years, and was the proprietor of the Metropole Hotel at his death. He also composed more than 150 musical works and left an autobiography, *Theatrical and Musical Memoirs* (1913).   MK

Aronstein, Martin (1936–2002) A prolific lighting designer, Aronstein designed more than 150 Broadway productions. He began his professional career in 1960 with the NEW YORK SHAKESPEARE FESTIVAL and continued his association with it till his death (including the 1972 critically acclaimed *Much Ado about Nothing*). He also designed extensively for regional theatres. Major productions include *TINY ALICE; Play It Again, Sam; AIN'T SUPPOSED TO DIE A NATURAL DEATH; In the Boom Boom Room; Noises Off; Cactus Flower;* and *Promises, Promises.*   AA

Around the World in Eighty Days, Jules Verne's 1873 novel of Phileas Fogg's travels, has served as the basis for several Broadway musicals. An early version by Hungarian brothers Imre, Bolossy, and Arnold KIRALFY, opening 28 August 1875 (the third that year alone), became one of the staples of 19th-century popular musical theatre, revived in New York alone at least six times between 1876 and 1888. The production – with ballets, processions, and song-and-dance acts – consisted of 18 scenes designed to display scenic exoticism and special effects. Fogg's journey had a distinctly Asian feel, and critics singled out the scenes from Borneo, Calcutta, and the Taj Mahal as especially impressive. The sinking of the steamship constituted a particularly special effect. Like *The BLACK CROOK* before it, this extravaganza proved extremely durable.

A freely adapted version with 1,200 performers was staged at New York's *Hippodrome* in the 1911–12 season. Another *Around the World* [sic], with book by ORSON WELLES and songs by COLE PORTER, opened 31 May 1946 at the Adelphi Theatre, New York, under the aegis of the MERCURY THEATRE, and lasted only 75 performances. This extravaganza, with 34 songs and a huge cast, featured Welles as the villain pursuing Fogg in a wide range of disguises and with sufficient outrageous presentational gimmicks that most critics' reviews evoked comparisons to HELLZAPOPPIN.

The Porter score produced no standards, but the show, an extraordinary star turn for Welles, did include a magic show and a train wreck.   JD

Arrow Maker, The, by California native Mary Austin, was the final production of New York's NEW THEATRE (1911). The three-act drama of Native American life was set in the Sierras prior to the white occupation of California. George Foster Platt's direction, which emphasized authentic costumes, folk songs, chants, and dances, failed to mask from critical view the play's turgid language and trite situations. Austin's vituperative criticism of the company's handling of her script further impeded her efforts to get her plays produced on Broadway. The play was later popular with amateur groups and high schools. (See also NATIVE AMERICANS PORTRAYED.)   WD

Arsenic and Old Lace by Joseph Kesselring. A LINDSAY–CROUSE production and Kesselring's only Broadway success, which remains a staple; opened at the Fulton Theatre, 10 January 1941 (1,444 performances). Directed by BRETAIGNE WINDUST, it starred JOSEPHINE HULL and Jean Adair as Aunt Martha and Aunt Abby, two of the nicest maiden ladies who ever invited the minister to tea but who were, in reality, homicidal maniacs poisoning 13 men in "one of the blandest murder games ever played in Brooklyn," wrote BROOKS ATKINSON. Brilliantly revived in 1986 at the 46TH STREET THEATRE, this hilarious murder-farce-comedy starred JEAN STAPLETON and Polly Holliday as the bizarre sisters; Abe Vigoda played the sinister Jonathan (originally Boris Karloff), William Hickey portrayed the strange Dr. Einstein (Edgar Stehli), and TONY ROBERTS assayed the blustering nephew Mortimer Brewster (Allyn Joslyn).   GSA

Artef YIDDISH acronym for Workers' Theater Group; began in New York in 1925 as a dramatic studio/collective under the auspices of the communist daily *Freiheit* (Freedom) (see YIDDISH THEATRE). Several more cohorts of actors entered in successive studios and studied together until assimilated into the performing nucleus. Like other Soviet-influenced groups of the period, Artef's members were committed to spreading radical politics through expressionist, even agit-prop, productions that stressed stylized groupings and mass movement. The press outside the Yiddish community praised its colorful vitality in repertory adapted from the Yiddish canon or translated into Yiddish from contemporaneous American and Soviet plays, some 80 productions

in all. After a last major effort in 1939, Artef performed only sporadically until 1953.   NS

Arthur, Julia [née Ida Lewis] (1869–1950) Canadian-born actress who played the leading feminine roles in about 200 plays, including the first Lady Windermere in America (1893). From her success in 1891 in F. R. Giles's *The Black Masque* at the UNION SQUARE THEATRE until her first retirement in 1899, after her marriage to millionaire Benjamin P. Cheney Jr., Arthur attained acclaim in numerous Shakespearean roles as well as contemporary parts. During 1895–7 she appeared at London's Lyceum with Henry Irving's company. She was most successful in roles featuring unbridled temperament, pathos, and tears. After a 15-year retirement she returned to the stage; her last appearance was on tour in 1924 in *Saint Joan*.   DBW

Asch, Sholom (1880–1957) Polish-born playwright and novelist who wrote in YIDDISH. His plays mainly concern the conflict between Orthodox and emancipated Jew, and he achieved early fame and notoriety with *The God of Vengeance* (1907), the later Broadway production of which was closed down by the police in 1923 for immorality. Other notable plays include *Downstream* (1904), *The Messiah Period* (1906), *Sabatai Zevi* (1908), *Wealthy Reb Shloime* (1913), and *Mottke the Thief* (1917). Several of his novels were dramatized and performed by MAURICE SCHWARTZ.   AB

As Is by William M. Hoffman, the first AIDS play on the commercial stage, directed by MARSHALL MASON, opened at CIRCLE REPERTORY COMPANY on 10 March 1985, moved to Broadway's LYCEUM THEATRE on 1 May, and ran seven months. The play, balancing specific personal issues and broad political concerns, explores the victimization of an AIDS patient who is abandoned by lover and family, before being accepted by his ex-lover "as is." It won both an Obie for Playwriting and a Drama Desk Award for Outstanding New Play.   HFP

As Thousands Cheer, music and lyrics by IRVING BERLIN, sketches by MOSS HART, opened 3 September 1933 at New York's MUSIC BOX THEATRE, running 400 performances. A topical REVUE treating life during the Depression, it took the novel form of a newspaper, with each segment representing a section or column (comics, society pages, lonely-hearts column, etc.). The connection might be far-fetched, as when "weather report" became the excuse for ETHEL WATERS to introduce "Heat Wave," or an occasion for opulence, as in the rotogravure section's "Easter Parade." Most of the skits were lighthearted, although there were some serious overtones: One headline was "Unknown Negro Lynched by Frenzied Mob," which yielded the wrenching "Supper Time." Given a lavish production by SAM H. HARRIS, the show featured, in addition to Miss Waters, MARILYN MILLER, Clifton Webb, and Helen Broderick. A revised and localized version, retitled *Stop Press,* was presented in London in 1935.   JD

Asian American theatre Any attempt to identify such a theatre prior to 1965 is risky. To recollect, reclaim, or reinterpret the theatrical works from early Asian America involves the daunting task of sifting through heterogeneity. Diaspora and immigration are not the only ways to conceive of the passage of Asian bodies, ideas, and identities across the American frontier. In the case of the Filipino theatre, for instance, the migration cannot be understood without considering U.S. policies of Manifest Destiny and benevolent assimilation in the Pacific. When the U.S. government in WWII banished Japanese Americans from all public life and interned them, a variety of Western classics, light comedies, and traditional Kabuki took place within the confines of those camps. Korean American theatre traces its history to the years following the Korean War, when Korean children were brought to the U.S., placed by the tens of thousands throughout the nation, many in the Midwest. In the case of Chinese traditional opera, puppet shows, and acrobatic spectacles imported as early as the 1850s, complicated questions about what counts as "Asian" differ from what may be claimed as "Asian American."

Theatrical activity by Asian Americans is intimately linked to the ethnic consciousness movement of the 1960s and after, which called for political solidarity among ethnic groups of Asian descent; the forging of this collective identity took precedence over internal differences and highly disparate backgrounds. Patterns of legal and institutional exclusion and oppression in U.S. racial history have only served to solidify the symbolic commonality of anti-Asian sentiment. The 1882 Chinese Exclusion Act was but the first of a host of U.S. laws passed by Congress to stem immigration from Asia and to restrict landownership and citizenship. The emphasis on pan-Asian ethnicity has thus resulted in an intensely imagined community with a shared group identity, having had an incalculable influence on the cultural works of playwrights and theatre artists, production logistics, and audience composition,

as well as the politics of reception and the legacy of misrepresentation.

"Asian American" is a demographic shorthand, a monolithic designation of an extremely unhomogenous population that covers Chinese, Filipino, South Asian, Korean, Vietnamese, Laotian, Thai, Cambodian, Singaporean, Indonesia, Pakistani, Pacific Islander, and other similar groups. In part the result of U.S. immigration and antimiscegenation laws, most representations of Asian American theatre history have been skewed toward the experiences of Chinese and Japanese Americans, thus erasing differences of country origin, language, religion, gender, class, education, age, colonial influences, and other factors. On the other hand, the establishment of performance venues in Chinatowns in New York, SEATTLE, Portland, BOSTON, and SAN FRANCISCO cannot be ignored.

One of the immediate manifestations of this pan-Asian coalition is the way it has transformed the meaning of cross-ethnic casting. Scholarly studies on Asian American dramatic literature rarely take into account the abjection of the theatrical body brought about by the disturbing legacy of "Oriental" stereotypes. These stereotypes are perpetuated by the ongoing insistence that shows with Asian themes – from *The First Born* (19th-century melodrama set in San Francisco's Chinatown) and GILBERT AND SULLIVAN's *The Mikado* to post-WWII Broadway hits SOUTH PACIFIC and *The KING AND I* – are "classics." The character of the "Heathen Chinee" in the stage version of Mark Twain and Bret Harte's *Ah Sin* (1877) was praised for "truthfulness to nature and freedom from caricature." Reincarnations of the Butterfly story, from DAVID BELASCO's MADAM BUTTERFLY to Alain Boublil and Claude-Michel Schonberg's *MISS SAIGON* (1989), have haunted Asian American performers, who have been recognized in myriad roles and venues, including traditional Asian theatre and opera, the "Chop Suey" vaudeville circuit, nightclubs such as San Francisco's Forbidden City, as well as Hollywood films and television, where Anna May Wong and Sessue Hayakawa (beginning in silents) and, more recently, George Takei, Pat Morita, and Jackie Chan have achieved professional acclaim. The RODGERS and HAMMERSTEIN musical *Flower Drum Song* (1958), which was not an improvement even though it was based on Chin Yang Lee's novel of the previous year, was for many decades considered the only professional New York production set in a modern Asian American milieu and, therefore, gave employment to numerous stage actors. Given the popular racial sentiment that "all Asians look alike," the actual Asian body is frequently displaced by an exaggerated version – either an Anglo portrayal is made to pass for the real thing, or a Korean or Filipino actor or singer is deemed suitable to portray a Chinese detective or a Vietnamese prostitute. Historically, Asian women have been objectified as evil seductresses, dragon ladies, geishas, frail lotus blossoms, or merely domestic servants.

From the late 1800s to the 1950s, no plays about Asian Americans appeared on the commercial stage. Nor did the FEDERAL THEATRE PROJECT produce any Asian-oriented shows, a stunning omission given its units for African American and Hispanic theatre. After WWII, Broadway did reflect the public curiosity about the Far East with hits such as *The Teahouse of the August Moon*, *The King and I*, and *The World of Suzy Wong* – all of which had sizable Asian characters, nonetheless depicted as foreigners and often played by non-Asian actors.

Born of the identity politics of the late 1960s and '70s, Asian American theatre today flowers with new writers, performers, and theatre companies, both established and emerging. Frustration over the lack of opportunities for nonwhite actors in Hollywood and television led to the establishment in 1965 of the LOS ANGELES-based EAST WEST PLAYERS, the first Asian American theatre company. Other companies followed: Kumu Kahua ("Oriental Stage") in Honolulu in 1971; the Asian American Theatre Company in San Francisco in 1973; the PAN ASIAN REPERTORY in NYC in 1977; and the Northwest Asian Theater Company (formerly the Asian Exclusion Act) in Seattle in 1976.

The 1980s and '90s witnessed new organizations: the Angel Island Theatre Company in CHICAGO; Theater Mu in MINNEAPOLIS–ST. PAUL with its first production, *Mask Dance,* fashioned by playwright R. A. Shiomi in 1993 from recollections of adopted Koreans in the state; Silk Road Theatre Project, created in Chicago to showcase Asian, Middle Eastern, and Mediterranean writers; Pom Siab Hmoob Theatre (formerly the Hmong Theatre Project), founded in 1990 in Minneapolis; the MA-YI THEATRE COMPANY, which built its reputation on Filipino American works; the NATIONAL ASIAN AMERICAN THEATRE COMPANY, which produces classic plays with all-Asian casts in New York; Slant Performance Group, an in-your-face performance group; South Asian League of Artists in America (SALAAM); Yangtze Repertory Theatre, which performs plays in England and Chinese; and Second Generation, founded by Welly Yang, an actor of Hong Kong descent. In total, there

were an estimated 85 Asian American theatre companies across the country, of varying sizes and mission, as of late 2005.

This proliferation is all the more striking considering the dramatic explosion of new works that came about as a result. In the beginning, East West Players had no new play repertoire nor a stable of writers to draw on; like most culturally specific theatres in the growing stages, EWP presented Asian classics in translation or classic works reset in Asia. Later theatres tended to present new plays examining aspects of the immigrant experience, often with elements of traditional dance or drama. This changed in 1972 when controversial and outspoken Frank Chin became the first Asian American dramatist produced Off-Broadway: Not only did his *Chickencoop Chinamen* debut at the AMERICAN PLACE THEATRE, but it was followed in 1974 by the same company's staging of *The Year of the Dragon*.

Suddenly, Asian American theatre became hip, irreverent, and nervy, incisively critiquing the frustrations and paradoxes of the Asian American experience. Eventually these writers became integrated into mainstream institutions. Foremost is DAVID HENRY HWANG, whose early works premiered at New York's PUBLIC THEATER. His *M. BUTTERFLY* won a Tony, and he remains a major Broadway figure, even responsible for a new book for *Flower Drum Song*'s 2002 Broadway revival. Nonprofit theatre such as BERKELEY REPERTORY, EUREKA THEATRE, MANHATTAN THEATRE CLUB, LONG WHARF, PLAYWRIGHTS HORIZONS, SECOND STAGE, NEW YORK THEATRE WORKSHOP, and SEATTLE REP have debuted and mounted plays by Hwang, PHILIP KAN GOTANDA, and CHAY YEW, among others. Yew headed the recently closed Asian Theatre Workshop at the MARK TAPER FORUM.

After two decades, some Asian American themes are unchanged (Japanese WWII internment, generational clashes between Asian-born immigrants and their Americanized children, the persistence of racism), whereas others now include mixed-race families, intermarriages, the struggles of being Asian and gay, and satirical deconstructions of the media. Some playwrights critique the separation of issues of race and ethnicity from those of economics and class, or see ethnic identity as a voluntary choice of lifestyle rather than an impetus for concerted political action. Others span the genres of naturalism, impressionism, ritual drama, postmodern collage, and episodic drama. Until the 1990s Asian American theatre was wary about using traditional Asian forms because of the fear of being Oriental-ized. Ironically, in abjuring a Western, European American style of making theatre, some established Asian American theatres are now tackling plays with traditional Asian subjects and dance forms.

In addition to boosting the careers of many fine Asian American actors, including John Lone, Mako, Nobu McCarthy, Dennis Dun, Joan Chen, Ching Valdez-Aran, and B. D. WONG, Asian American theatre has also fostered several generations of dramatists, many of whom have been categorized into first-, second-, and third-generation Americans with ancestral roots in China, Japan, the Philippines, and so on. In addition to those already mentioned, others include Momoko Iko, Wakako Yamauchi, PING CHONG, Laurence Michael Yep, ERNEST ABUBA, Genny Lim, Jeannie Barroga, Amy Hill, Velina Hasu Houston, JESSICA HAGEDORN, Bina Sharif, Elizabeth Wong, and Victoria Nalani Kneubuhl. And though many of these remain closely allied with Asian American troupes, the ranks have been so integrated into the larger nonprofit realms that a majority of today's youngest generation of Asian American playwrights, such as Julia Cho, Diana Son, Sung Rno, and Naomi Iizuka, have actually grown up or built their careers outside of established Asian American theatre outposts.   MB   RG

Asolo State Theatre Founded in 1960, AST became an official state theatre in 1965 and fully professional in 1966. Besides a full repertory season of classic and original plays, current programs include an acting conservatory associated with Florida State University. In 1989 the company moved to new facilities in the Asolo Center for the Performing Arts (and the 487-seat Mertz Theatre) and in 1994 added a 161-seat space for the conservatory. The original Asolo Theatre – built in Asolo, Italy, in 1798 and brought to Sarasota in 1949 – is today part of the Ringling Museum of Art complex.   LAB

Association of Producing Artists (APA) Founded in 1960 by ELLIS RABB in an attempt to create a collective of theatre artists offering a wide range of material in a repertory structure, APA spent its first four seasons, in addition to touring, with residencies at Princeton, Milwaukee's Fred Miller Theatre, the FOLKSBIENE Theatre in NYC, and at the University of Michigan. In 1964 it joined OFF-BROADWAY's Phoenix Theatre, which had been organized in 1953 by T. EDWARD HAMBLETON and NORRIS HOUGHTON (with STUART VAUGHAN as artistic director, 1958–62) and had presented notable productions of standard plays and new works, including *Once upon a Mattress* (1959) and KOPIT's OH DAD, POOR DAD (1962). For five years the APA at the Phoenix presented a wide range of plays, most notably *Man and Superman* (1964); *YOU CAN'T TAKE IT WITH YOU* (1965); *Right You Are* (1966); *THE SHOW-OFF* (1967); *Pantagleize* (codirected by Rabb and JOHN HOUSEMAN), *The Misanthrope,* and *Exit the King* (1968); and *Cock-a-Doodle Dandy* and *Hamlet* (1969). Several seasons were spent at NYC's LYCEUM THEATRE prior to APA's dissolution in 1970.   DBW

Association of Theatrical Press Agents and Managers (ATPAM) see AGENTS

Astaire [né Austerlitz]**, Fred** (1899–1987) and **Adele** (1898–1981) Dancers, singers, and actors. As children the Astaires spent 10 years in VAUDEVILLE, where they perfected their dancing and teamwork. In 1917 they made their New York MUSICAL THEATRE debut in *Over the Top.* Influenced by the ballroom dancing of Vernon and Irene Castle, the Astaires also studied with Broadway choreographer and director NED WAYBURN. Their dances were fluid, stylish, and often witty, in keeping with the frothy musicals in which they appeared. After featured roles in several shows, the Astaires were the stars of *Lady, Be Good!* (1924), for which GEORGE AND IRA GERSHWIN wrote the score. The successful partnership with the Gershwins was repeated with *Funny Face* (1927). They starred with MARILYN MILLER in *Smiles* (1930), and made their last appearance as a team in the HOWARD DIETZ–ARTHUR SCHWARTZ revue *The Band Wagon* (1931). After Adele's retirement, Fred appeared alone in *The Gay Divorcee* (1932) before leaving for Hollywood and a career in musical films. Critics generally considered Adele to be the stronger dancer and more vivid personality of the partnership. Equally popular in England, the Astaires brought several of their American successes to the London stage during the 1920s. Fred Astaire's autobiography appeared in 1959; biographies were published in 1973, 1985, 1987, and 1997.   MK

Astor Place Opera House Broadway, East 9th St. and Astor Pl., New York City. In their pursuit of operatic pleasure, well-to-do New Yorkers built the Astor Place close to an exclusive enclave on Lafayette St. settled by the Astors and their friends; but opera did not remain long the house's principal fare, and the 1,800-seat theatre was given over to other entertainments. In 1849, during an engagement by the English star William Macready, a riot was triggered from a long-

Astor Place Opera House riot, 1849. *Courtesy:* Don B. Wilmeth Theatre Collection.

smoldering feud between Macready and the American star EDWIN FORREST, which was also fed by anti-English sentiment among the Irish denizens of the Bowery area. The militia was called in to quell the riot, and the order was given to fire at the crowd. When the smoke had cleared, at least 22 (possibly as many as 31) people had died and 150 were wounded. A 1990 play by RICHARD NELSON (*Two Shakespearean Actors*) deals with the Macready–Forrest rivalry. In 1852, the theatre was renamed the New York to rid it of its tainted past, but in 1854 it was sold at auction to the Mercantile Library Association; thereafter it was known as Clinton Hall until it was torn down in 1891. Nigel Cliff in 2007 published the most extensive account of the riot.   MCH

Atkinson, (Justin) Brooks (1894–1984) American drama critic. Educated at Harvard University, where he attended GEORGE PIERCE BAKER'S Workshop 47, Atkinson taught English for a year (1917–18) at Dartmouth College and worked as a reporter on the *Springfield* [MA] *Daily News*. A year later, he began a four-year stint as assistant drama critic to H. T. PARKER on the *Boston Daily Evening Transcript*. In 1922 he became book review editor for the *New York Times,* succeeding STARK YOUNG as the paper's theatre critic in 1926. When war broke out in 1941, he took an overseas assignment, later receiving a Pulitzer Prize (1947) for his reports on the Soviet Union. After the war (1946) he returned to reviewing the Broadway theatre. The most respected critic of his generation, Atkinson offered commonsense opinions in a graceful style, and was known for both his fairness and candor. He thought that the theatre should reach out and relate to the world outside of the art; therefore he did not mingle with theatre people or attend rehearsals, believing that his reviews were for the "average guy who goes to the theatre." At his retirement in 1960, the Mansfield Theatre (built in 1926) was renamed in his honor. His many books include *Broadway Scrapbook* (1948), *Brief Chronicles* (1966), *Broadway* (1970), and *The Lively Years: 1920–1973.*   TLM

Atkinson, Jayne (1959–) Unheralded but solid, statuesque actress, born in England but educated in the U.S. at Northwestern and Yale. Debuted Off-Broadway in 1986 (*Bloody Poetry*) and on Broadway in 1987 in ALL MY SONS. She has been especially effective in roles such as Lizzie in the 1999 revival of *The RAINMAKER,* in 1997 as a replacement Li'l Bit in HOW I LEARNED TO DRIVE, and as Lotty in *Enchanted April* (2003), as well as strong outings at the NEW YORK SHAKESPEARE FESTIVAL in *Henry VIII* (1997) and Caryl Churchill's *Skriker* (1996). In 2005 she began developing a solo performance: *Lionheart: Eleanor of Aquitaine.*   DBW

Atlanta Although this Georgia city has a theatre history that dates back to 1854, when its first theatre, The Athenaeum, opened on the second floor of a brick building on Decatur St. between Peachtree and Prior Sts., it is only in the past two decades that it has started to become a vibrant theatre center, with the ALLIANCE, founded in 1968, still the dominant theatre institution in the Southeast. However, the city that in 1939 saw the world premiere of *Gone with the Wind* in its Loew's Grand Theatre (built in 1893 as DeGive's Grand Theatre; razed 1979) has seen a burst of theatre activity and national recognition in the past 20 years – as host of the Olympic Games, the Super Bowl, and the Democratic National Convention. Though arguably still not a major theatre center, Atlanta has demonstrated a potential comparable to CHICAGO or SEATTLE one to two decades ago. Some early efforts, such as 1969's Atlanta Municipal Theatre (which opened with *Red, White, and Maddox*) have floundered. But since the 1990s, numerous theatres and companies have added to the theatrical landscape, including the Academy (founded in 1956 and the first professional theatre in the South to be integrated); the Actor's Express; Dad's Garage Theatre Company (devoted to comedy and improvisation); the 14th Street Playhouse (at various times housing Theatre Gael, founded in 1984 and the only inter-Celtic theatre in the region; the faith-based group Art Within; and the Atlanta Classical Theatre); Theatrical Outfit (led by Eddie Levi Lee); the New American Shakespeare Tavern, begun in 1990; the Peachtree Playhouse (now at the Ansley Park Playhouse) founded by playwrights John Gibson and Anthony Morris and boasting the longest-running production in Atlanta history (their *Peachtree Battle*); 7 Stages, founded in 1979 to address social, political, and spiritual issues of the day; Georgia Shakespeare, in existence since 1985; and the Jewish Theatre of the South, launched in 1995. Though not all of these have survived, they (among others) have made Atlanta a theatre town that must be noted. In addition to these small to middle-sized operations, Atlanta boasts a number of centers for the performing arts, including major facilities at Georgia State (Rialto), Emory (Schwartz), and the Robert W. Woodruff Arts Center, home of the Alliance.

Prior to these recent developments, Atlanta was an active booking town, with its first opera house in 1866; the Kimball Opera House in 1868 (which served as the state capitol building, 1869–89); the previously mentioned DeGive's Grand Theatre in 1893; the Fox Theatre in 1929 (today a major entertainment center); the Theatre of the Stars founded in 1953 for Broadway road shows; and in 1968 the Memorial Arts Center, now the Woodruff Arts Center. Atlanta is also home of the Center for PUPPETRY Arts, a world-class operation founded in 1978 and, as a result of its 1996 Olympic activities, called by *Newsweek* "one of the most exciting companies in American theater." DBW

Atlantic Theater Company Cofounded in 1983 by playwright DAVID MAMET and actor Willam H. Macy and currently led by Artistic Director Neil Pepe (succeeding Mary McCann, 1985–6), the crit-ically acclaimed company, dedicated to ensemble acting, has produced more than 100 plays in New York (a 182-seat venue on West 20th St.), Chicago, and Vermont, where it began; a second small space on NYC's 8th Ave. was added in 2006. Its productions have included *The Beauty Queen of Leenane,* the New York premiere of *The Cider House Rules,* and an acclaimed revival of AMERICAN BUFFALO (1999, as part of a season dedicated to the plays of Mamet). ATC also maintains an acting school, led by McCann, affiliated with New York University and an ensemble of actors, writers, and directors (including Mamet, Macy, Kristen Johnston, Felicity Huffman [ABC's *Desperate Housewives*], and Camryn Manheim). DBW

Auditorium Theatre [of Roosevelt University] 50 East Congress Parkway, Chicago [Architects: Sullivan and Adler]. Set within a multipurpose building encompassing a hotel, offices, and stores, the Auditorium was intended to be supported by the commercial enterprises in the complex. Designed by the experimental firm of Dankmar and Adler, it introduced no stunningly new concepts architecturally but was provided with near-perfect acoustics and sightlines, a flexible auditorium and stage, and striking interior decoration. It opened in 1889 and was in use as an opera house and theatre until 1942, when it was largely abandoned. Once threatened with destruction, it was restored and reopened in 1967 after a civic campaign was launched to save it, and in 1975 declared a landmark; a $1 million facelift of the lobby/arcade area was completed in 1992 with other major (over $13 million) renovations of the interior (including a new stage) in 2001–2. A protracted legal battle with the Auditorium Theatre Council, founded in 1960, over ownership of the theatre was won in October 2002 when the Supreme Court of Illinois ruled that it was owned by Roosevelt University. Today it is used for Broadway road shows, dance companies, and pop concerts. MCH

Aunt Dan and Lemon by WALLACE SHAWN. Produced in New York (PUBLIC THEATER) in 1985 (and London), this meditation on Nazi atrocities also explores the playwright's relationships with his audience in provocative monologues by Lemon (Leonora), a reclusive young Englishwoman in her 20s, existing on fruit juices and memories of Aunt Dan (Danielle, played by LINDA HUNT), an Oxford don. Before dying, Dan corrupts Lemon's concept of public and private morality with her reminiscences of Mindy, a high-priced prostitute and Dan's lesbian lover who strangled her arms-dealer lover during oral sex. In a thin plot, Dan's verbal tirades corrupt Lemon and lead to her secondhand embrace of Henry Kissinger, the policies of violence that rot our society, and to a defense of Nazi death camps.   GSA

Auntie Mame by Jerome Lawrence and Robert E. Lee, adapted from Patrick Dennis's novel, opened at the Broadhurst Theatre on 31 October 1956 and ran for 639 performances. Seen through the eyes of young Patrick Dennis, the play presents the multiple aspects of his aunt Mame Dennis's character and her ability to convert adversity into success. Mame's flamboyant nature drives the play, which nearly replaces plot with a series of vignettes spanning 1928–46. Rosalind Russell gave her major career performance as Mame in both the play and the 1958 Warner Bros. film, which won Golden Globe Awards for Russell and for Best Comedy. (Peggy Cass won a Best Featured Actress Tony for her Agnes Gooch, a role she repeated in the movie.) *Mame,* the musical adaptation by Lawrence, Lee, and Jerry Herman, opened 24 May 1966 at the Winter Garden, ran for 1,508 performances, and was revived in 1983.   RW

Avenue Q This quirky musical – termed "savvy, sassy and eminently likable" by Ben Brantley – arrived on Broadway (in the small Golden Theatre) unheralded after a lengthy period of workshopping, a staging at Off-Broadway's Vineyard Theatre, and with an unlikely opening date in midsummer 2003. With music and lyrics by Robert Lopez and Jeff Marx, book by Jeff Whitty, and seven largely unknown actors backed by a modest musical ensemble, this very original show – a kind of exploration of the "failure, sex and the general pettiness of life," as Brantley put it, with four live actors (two played four major characters and some bit parts) manipulating and performing alongside Muppet-esque puppets designed by Rick Lyon, as well as three non-puppet-laden actors – was indeed the surprise of the season, beating out *Wicked* for the 2004 Tony for Best Musical, as well as for Best Original Score and Best Book. Though in a seamy Sesame Street–like setting, the lyrics set to simple melodies are very adult, with titles such as "Everyone's a Little Bit Racist," "If You Were Gay," "I'm Not Wearing Underwear Today," and "The Internet Is for Porn." While still running on Broadway, a controversial decision was made to take an abridged version of the show directly to Las Vegas for the new Wynn Hotel in late summer 2005, bypassing the normal national tour. The run there lasted less than a year.   DBW

Avner the Eccentric [né Avner Eisenberg] (1948–) Clown. Unique among American performers, Atlanta-born Avner combines clowning, mime, magic, juggling, rope walking, and an uncanny ability to engage his audience without words (he makes sounds via a kazoo) in creating what John Simon calls "the thinking man's clown." This gentle man sees his role as surrogate for the audience, his one-person show as "clown therapy; comicanalysis." An Irish critic noted that his show "is the play Samuel Beckett would have written for the Marx Bros." Avner, who studied in Paris with Jacques Lecoq and with Mazzone-Clementi in California, was a hit of the 1984–5 New York season, has toured the world with his show. He has appeared as Estragon in *Waiting for Godot,* in the New Vaudeville production of *The Comedy of Errors* seen at Lincoln Center (1987), and on Broadway as the ventriloquist in *Ghetto* (1989), and was unforgettable as The Jewel in the 1985 film *The Jewel of the Nile.* He was a 2002 inductee into the International Clown Hall of Fame.   DBW

Awake and Sing! by Clifford Odets. Along with *Golden Boy,* this play represents Odets at his best and as the voice for his company, the Group Theatre, which first produced it 19 February 1935 under the direction of Harold Clurman. Set in a Bronx apartment designed by Boris Aronson, the naturalistic presentation of this study of a Depression-era Jewish family depicts Bessie, a domineering mother played by Stella Adler, trying to control a family in upheaval, especially restless children: unhappily pregnant Hennie (Phoebe Brand) and starry-eyed Ralph (Jules [John] Garfield), who serves as protagonist of the play and effects the escape of his sister. As her lover, Moe, puts it, "Make a break or spend the rest of your life in a coffin." The children's grandfather, Jacob, who adds a Marxist flavor to the proceedings, sacrifices himself in order to fulfill Ralph's dreams, symbolized by the mail plane periodically flying overhead. A revival by Lincoln Center at the Belasco Theatre in 2006 (Tony for Best Revival of a Play) featured a superb cast including Ben Gazzara (Jacob), Zoë Wanamaker, and Mark Ruffalo (Moe).   RHW

awards, theatrical Various professional theatre and other organizations support excellence with many awards, usually given annually. In recent years the number has constantly grown, so much so that it is suggested that users of this guide seek *Awards, Honors & Prizes,* published frequently in Detroit by Gale Research, for a current list. What follows therefore is a highly selective, alphabetized list of some of the better-known and well-established awards:

The American Academy and Institute of Arts and Letters recognizes a composer, lyricist, or librettist with the MARC BLITZSTEIN Award for Musical Theatre. The RICHARD RODGERS Production Award is given to those who are not already established in the field.

The American Society for Theatre Research gives the Barnard Hewitt Award for the year's best book in "theatre history and cognate disciplines."

The Drama Desk Award honors outstanding achievement in several categories of the Broadway or OFF-BROADWAY scene.

The DRAMA LEAGUE of America annually gives its Distinguished Performance Award.

The DRAMATISTS GUILD annually awards the Elizabeth Hull–Kate Warriner Award to a playwright dealing with a controversial subject in a script produced in New York City.

The GEORGE JEAN NATHAN Award, begun in 1959, honors the author of "the best piece of drama criticism published during the previous year."

The HELEN HAYES Awards, given annually in Washington, DC, recognize all aspects of theatrical production.

The JOHN F. KENNEDY CENTER for the Performing Arts bestows the Kennedy Center Honors, a national tribute to excellence and life achievement in the performing arts.

The JOSEPH JEFFERSON [III] Awards are presented annually in Chicago to promote theatrical excellence.

The Joseph Maharam Foundation, Inc., established the Maharam Theatrical Design Awards in 1965 to honor scenic and costume design in Broadway and OFF-BROADWAY shows.

The JUJAMCYN Theatres Award recognizes regional theatres that have made outstanding contributions.

The LEAGUE OF AMERICAN THEATRES AND PRODUCERS cosponsors with the AMERICAN THEATRE WING the ANTOINETTE PERRY Awards (Tonys), given annually since 1947 for "Distinguished Achievement in the Theatre" – awards being presented for each of several aspects of production on Broadway.

LOS ANGELES Drama Critics' Circle Awards are given annually for outstanding production work in that city.

The MARGO JONES Medals, established 1961, are given annually to "the producing manager of an American or Canadian theatre whose policy of presenting new dramatic works continues most faithfully in the tradition of Margo Jones."

The National Theatre Conference recognizes and encourages excellence in theatre with their PAUL GREEN Foundation Awards. The Conference also gives the Barrie and Bernice Stavis Playwriting Award for emerging writers.

The New York Drama Critics' Circle Awards, established 1936, annually honor outstanding productions.

The Outer Critics Circle Awards, begun 1950, annually honor outstanding achievement in the professional theatre, in addition to granting the JOHN GASSNER Award for an outstanding new playwright.

A Pulitzer Prize for Drama is awarded (almost every year) for a distinguished play written by an American, preferably dealing with American life.

The Society of Stage Directors and Choreographers (SSDC) gives annually the "Mr. ABBOTT" Award for lifetime achievement.

The Theatre Library Association since 1968 has annually recognized a published work in the field of theatre in the U.S. with the George Freedley Memorial Award.

The *VARIETY* New York Drama Critics' Poll, begun in 1939, annually recognizes outstanding achievement in a variety of categories.

The *Village Voice* OFF-BROADWAY Theater Awards (Obies), founded in 1956, recognize theatrical achievement Off-Broadway (i.e., O.B.).

William Shakespeare Awards for Classical Theatre (Wills) are presented by the SHAKESPEARE THEATRE in Washington, DC, to individuals for preservation of the vitality of classical theatre.

Others: the National Medal of Arts; the LUCILLE LORTEL Off-Broadway Awards (Lucys); the CLARENCE DERWENT Awards (presented by ACTORS' EQUITY to promising male and female performers); the Joe A. Callaway and George and Elizabeth Marton Playwriting awards (Foundation of Dramatists Guild); the Callaway Award (Actors' Equity) for classical acting; the THEATRE HALL OF FAME (awarded by American Theater Critics Association); the ELIOT NORTON Awards in Boston; the Design Awards (American Theatre Wing); the ROBERT WHITEHEAD Award (producers); the Edward Kleban Awards (musical theatre); the Rosetta LeNoire Award (artistic contributions to the universality of the human experience in theatre); the Susan Smith Blackburn Award (women playwrights); the KURT WEILL Foundation book prize; and the Kesselring Playwriting Prize (given by National Arts Club)   SMA   DBW

Axelrod, George (1922–2003) New York–born playwright, director, and producer whose reputation rests on two plays: *The Seven Year Itch,* a 1952

three-act comedy that starred Tom Ewell as a Walter Mitty–like imaginative publisher who, while a summer bachelor, dreams of romantic involvement with the girl upstairs (Marilyn Monroe in the film version); and *Will Success Spoil Rock Hunter?* (1955), a Hollywood spoof with Walter Matthau, Orson Bean, and Jayne Mansfield. Axelrod produced GORE VIDAL's *A Visit to a Small Planet* (1957) and directed a number of comedies, including NEIL SIMON's *The Star-Spangled Girl* (1966).
DBW

Ayers, Lemuel (1915–55) American scenic and costume designer. From the late 1930s until his death, Ayers designed some of Broadway's most memorable plays and musicals, including OKLAHOMA! (1943), KISS ME, KATE (also coproduced; 1948), CAMINO REAL (1953), and *The PAJAMA GAME* (1954). Ayers developed a painterly, almost whimsical style, but was also capable of evocative realism, as in *Angel Street* (1941), which had an unusually shallow set painted on black velour.   AA

Azenberg, Emanuel (1934–) Producer (recipient of eight Tonys), called by the *New York Times* one of Broadway's "most successful producers and one of its outspoken critics." Although he had worked closely with the SHUBERT ORGANIZATION, in the mid-1980s he essentially left the Broadway establishment by walking out on the League of American Theatres and Producers. Though he has been producing in New York since 1961 (more than 60 Broadway plays in over 40 years), his greatest successes have been since 1982. His single major client has been NEIL SIMON, all of whose plays since 1972 have been produced by Azenberg. Productions in the 1980s included BILOXI BLUES, a revival of *Joe Egg,* and SONDHEIM's SUNDAY IN THE PARK WITH GEORGE. More recently he has produced Simon's LOST IN YONKERS (1991), *London Suite* (1995; Off-Broadway), *The Dinner Party* (2000), and *The ODD COUPLE* (2005 revival), as well as the Billy Joel–Twyla Tharp musical *Movin' Out* (2002). In 1990 he ventured into film by producing Stoppard's *Rosencrantz and Guildenstern Are Dead.* Since 1985 he has taught at Duke University.   DBW

B

Babes in Arms Two-act musical comedy, music by RICHARD RODGERS, lyrics by LORENZ HART, book by Rodgers and Hart; opened 14 April 1937 at the SAM S. SHUBERT THEATRE, New York, and ran 289 performances. The classic "Hey, kids, let's put on a show" musical, it told of a group of show-business youths, left alone by their touring parents, trying to raise enough money to avoid being sent to a state farm. The low-budget production was appropriately cast with young, generally unknown performers, among them ALFRED DRAKE. The score contributed more Rodgers and Hart standards than any other – including "Where or When," "My Funny Valentine," "Johnny One-Note," and "The Lady Is a Tramp" – and GEORGE BALANCHINE's choreography contributed an early example of the subsequently popular "dream ballet." JD

Babes in Toyland Two-act musical fantasy, music by VICTOR HERBERT, words by Glen MacDonough; opened 13 October 1903 at the old MAJESTIC THEATRE, New York, for a run of 192 performances. Following the earlier 1903 success of their extravagant musical version of The WIZARD OF OZ, producer Fred Hamlin and director JULIAN MITCHELL commissioned this fairy-tale musical, which first appeared in Chicago in June and, after its New York run, toured the country for years. The libretto tells the story of Alan and Jane, who, fleeing their wicked uncle, arrive in Toyland, meet a bevy of Mother Goose characters, and have myriad adventures. The great appeal of the show lay in lavish scenic spectacle (a fearsome spider's forest, the Moth Queen's flowery palace) and Herbert's classic score ("Toyland," "The March of the Toys"). The show was Victor Herbert's first great popular success. JD

Back Stage In 1960, an advertising salesman and an editor – Ira Eaker and Allen Zwerdling – left their positions at the predominant weekly theatrical trade paper in New York City, Show Business, and, putting in $500 apiece, created a rival weekly, Back Stage. In the subsequent decades it has become a recognized resource for the American actor and for the performing arts as a whole, providing casting information for stage and screen in print and online, plus news, features, how-to's, and reviews. In 1993, a Los Angeles edition was created, and in 2005 the two publications and staffs were merged. In 2006 Back Stage received the first Backstage Award from The Players (see CLUBS). LJ

Bacon, Frank (1864–1922) Actor and dramatist. A native of California, Bacon emphasized Yankee character parts in melodramas such as TEN NIGHTS IN A BARROOM and in comedy sketches, mainly in the SAN FRANCISCO area, until the 1906 earthquake, when he departed for New York. There he performed in such plays as Alabama, Pudd'nhead Wilson, and WINCHELL SMITH's The Fortune Hunter. In Lightnin' (1918), written in collaboration with Smith, Bacon achieved his greatest acting success as Lightnin' Bill Jones, a charming rascal and ne'er-do-well who enjoys tall tales and strong drink. Dependent upon Bacon's acting, which he interrupted to participate in the 1919 actors' strike, the plays ran for three years, its 1,291 performances breaking (almost doubling) the old record held by HOYT's A TRIP TO CHINATOWN. WJM

Bagley, Ben [Jamin James] (1933–98) Vermont-born producer who in 1955 presented the first of his many revues, The Shoestring Revue. In 1965 his Decline and Fall of the Entire World as Seen through the Eyes of Cole Porter was a precursor to later revues, such as Ain't Misbehavin' and Sophisticated Ladies, also devoted to a single composer. His recorded "Revisited" series on his own Painted Smiles label (founded 1971) totaled 48 albums and was conceived as revues on record, focusing on musical theatre esoterica. DBW

Bailey, Pearl (Mae) (1918–90) Actress-singer of black and Creek Indian ancestry whose career began in 1933, after winning an amateur contest in Philadelphia, and reached its apogee in 1967 with the title role in an all-black HELLO, DOLLY! featuring Cab Calloway, for which she received a special Tony Award. "Pearlie Mae" considered herself a singer and humorist, not an actress, yet she appeared in four other Broadway musicals besides *Dolly*: *St. Louis Woman* (1946), *Arms and the Girl* (1950), *Bless You All* (1950), and *House of Flowers* (1954). Bailey wrote two volumes of memoirs: *The Raw Pearl* (1968) and *Pearlie Mae: Talking to Myself* (1971).   DBW

Bainter, Fay (1891–1968) Prominent on the New York stage in the 1920s and '30s, Bainter, formerly a child actress in Los Angeles, was notable for wife, understanding mother, or faithful friend roles. After her New York debut in *The Rose of Panama* (1912), she appeared in scores of parts on Broadway, in SUMMER STOCK, and on tour, ranging from Ming Toy in *East Is West* (1918) to Mary Tyrone in a national tour (1957–8) of *LONG DAY'S JOURNEY INTO NIGHT*. She is remembered best for her final film performance as the grim Mrs. Amelia Tilford in *The CHILDREN'S HOUR* (1961).   DBW

Baitz, Jon Robin (1961–) Los Angeles-born playwright who has invited comparison with ARTHUR MILLER for his social and political themes – especially his attacks upon American corporate life for its greed and lack of ethics. His major plays *The Film Society* (1987), *The Substance of Fire* (1991), *The End of the Day* (1993), *Three Hotels* (1993), *A Fair Country* (1996; called by MARGO JEFFERSON the best contemporary American play she had seen at Lincoln Center in some time), *Milansky/Zilinsky, or Schmucks* (1998), and *Chinese Friends* (2004), have premiered OFF-BROADWAY, at such venues as PLAYWRIGHTS HORIZONS and the CIRCLE REPERTORY THEATRE, and regionally, mounted by such companies as STEPPENWOLF. In 2001 his adaptation of *Hedda Gabler* was staged on Broadway. He is author of screen and television scripts including an adaptation of Sinclair Lewis's *Dodsworth,* his own *Three Hotels* (broadcast in 1990; Humanitas Award) and *The Substance of Fire* (1996), and *The People I Know* (2002). Though openly gay (partner from 1990 to 2002 of JOE MANTELLO), Baitz is not considered a gay writer but rather one with gay themes interspersed.   TLM

Baker, Belle [née Bella Becker] (1895–1957) Vaudeville singer who introduced 163 songs, including "Blue Skies" (1926), written for her by IRVING BERLIN. A product of New York's Lower East Side Jewish ghetto, Baker, one of vaudeville's "red-hot mamas" and equally adept at comedy or pathos, earned a 1913 billing at The PALACE. By 1917 her receipts topped all name performers in NYC's KEITH theatres. As late as 1932 she introduced one of her biggest hits, "All of Me."   DBW

Baker, Benjamin A. (1818–90) Playwright. "Uncle Ben Baker" deserted his prompter's post at William MITCHELL'S OLYMPIC Theatre and, for Mitchell's benefit, wrote *A GLANCE AT NEW YORK* in 1848, which opened on 15 February 1848 starring F. S. CHANFRAU as Mose. Encouraged by the "shouts of delight from the Bowery B'hoys in the pit," and a run of 74 performances, Baker created more adventures for Mose: *New York as It Is* (1848), *Mose in California* (1849), and *Mose in China* (1850).   RM

Baker, George Pierce (1866–1935) Educator who, a year after graduating from Harvard University in 1887, returned as an instructor in the English Department. In 1905, he began offering a course in playwriting entitled English 47. Three years later he founded the Harvard Dramatic Club and served as its sponsor. Then in 1912 he established Workshop 47 as a laboratory theatre for plays written in English 47. The program and Baker's growing reputation attracted to Harvard such promising talents as EUGENE O'NEILL, SIDNEY HOWARD, Thomas Wolfe, EDWARD SHELDON, and PHILIP BARRY. He resigned and moved to Yale in 1925 as head of its first Department of Drama, retiring in 1933. Beginning in 1927 he worked to establish the National Theatre Conference, and served as its first president in 1932. He is remembered as a teacher and mentor to the generation of American playwrights who came to the fore in the 1920s. His ideas about the craft of playwriting are set forth in *Dramatic Technique* (1919); his contributions to American theatre are explicated in W. Kinne's 1954 *George Pierce Baker and the American Theatre.*   TLM

Baker, Joséphine [née Josephine Freda McDonald] (1906–75) Entertainer who left her indigent family in St. Louis, MO, at age 16 to play in all-black revues in Philadelphia and New York. Her outrageous comic antics had a succès de scandale in Paris in *La Revue Nègre* (Théâtre des Champs-Elysées, 1925). Some celebrated her as a combination of "boxing kangaroo, sen-sen gum and racing cyclist" (*Candide*), while moralists condemned her as the decline of the West made flesh. "La Baker's" rubber-limbed Charlestons and black bottoms and her cincture of phalliform bananas became fixtures of Parisian night life. Her repertory of American classics ("Always"), French nostalgia ("La Petite Tonkinoise"), and the signature tune "J'ai deux amours" were sung in a thin soprano. After WWII, during which she had worked for the Resistance, she made many "farewell tours" to raise money for the orphans she housed on her estate in Milandes. She returned to the U.S. in

1948 and 1951 and was active for civil rights, though as a performer she never equaled her success abroad. Needy and ailing, she died during the run of a revue at the Paris Bobino. The subject of over a dozen biographies (and author of five autobiographies), her life was recounted in 1993 by her stepson Jean-Claude Baker and Chris Chase.
LS

Baker, Paul (1911–) Educator-director. A Texan who studied with GEORGE PIERCE BAKER at Yale, Baker taught 29 years at Baylor University, staging controversial productions (Hamlet played by three actors) in a venue with three stages surrounding the audience. He resigned in protest when Baylor ordered the closing of his production of LONG DAY'S JOURNEY INTO NIGHT (1963). As first head of the DALLAS THEATER CENTER (1959–82), Baker staged over 60 new scripts and American premieres at the DTC, receiving the first RODGERS and HAMMERSTEIN Award for theatrical contribution in the Southwest (1961). In 1994 he received a Special Merit Award for Service in Arts in Texas (Texas Commission on the Arts). In 2003 a book by Baker, Robert Flynn, and Eugene McKinney surveyed his career.   DBW

Balaban and Katz Theatre Circuit In 1916 A. J. (1889–1962) and Barney (1888–1971) Balaban combined their Chicago movie theatres with those of Sam Katz (1892–1961), presenting thematic musical revues designed by Frank Cambria and staged by VINCENT MINNELLI.   DMcD

Balanchine, George [né Georgi Balanchivadze] (1904–83) Russian-born ballet dancer-choreographer and theatre choreographer. Recognized as one of the leading figures in 20th-century DANCE, Balanchine is credited with establishing the American balletic style. In addition to his work in ballet, Balanchine also contributed to American musical theatrical dance, choreographing such shows as The ZIEGFELD Follies (1935), ON YOUR TOES (1936), BABES IN ARMS (1937), and Song of Norway (1937). Balanchine's theatrical choreography is considered to have been well integrated in the shows, and he never demanded the insertion of a ballet segment. His dances interpreted the essence and feeling of the musical score within the context of the script. He is the subject of numerous biographies, notably by Francis Mason (1991), Robert Gottlieb, and Terry Teachout (both 2004).   LF

Baldwin, James (Arthur) (1924–87) African American novelist, essayist, and playwright. The most widely read black author of the 1950s and '60s, Baldwin wrote two plays. In The Amen Corner (produced at Howard University in 1954 and on Broadway in 1965) a fanatical woman pastor tries unsuccessfully to turn her son against the father whose love she has rejected. Despite a convincing performance by BEAH RICHARDS, the play was coolly received by leading critics. In BLUES FOR MR. CHARLIE (1964) Baldwin examined racial attitudes in the murder of an angry black youth by a white bigot. The writing is often shrill, characters' motivations are questionable, and the author's viewpoint remains ambivalent. David Leeming wrote an extensive biography published in 1994.
EGH

Baldwin Theatre Built as Baldwin's Academy of Music on Market St., this 1,969-seat SAN FRANCISCO theatre opened on 6 March 1876 with Richard III starring Barry Sullivan. Part of the six-story Baldwin Hotel, its elegant accoutrements included red velvet seats, gilt decorations, and crystal chandeliers. It was managed until 1882 by the inveterate THOMAS MAGUIRE, who staged numerous plays by his young assistants, DAVID BELASCO and JAMES HERNE, and maintained a STOCK COMPANY with popular actor JAMES O'NEILL among its leading men. Until it burned in 1895 (see FIRES), the Baldwin hosted many great touring stars and companies of the day and was a favorite of San Francisco's social set.
MB

Ball, William (1931–91) Flamboyant, charismatic American actor-director and founder in 1965 of the AMERICAN CONSERVATORY THEATRE in Pittsburgh. When he brought the company to San Francisco in 1967 Ball almost single-handedly revived legitimate theatre in that city. In 1986 he resigned amid financial and artistic controversy, leaving behind a career record of over 300 productions, 87 of which he directed (including outstanding productions of The Taming of the Shrew [1976] and Cyrano de Bergerac [1974] – both subsequently televised). His book, A Sense of Direction: Some Observations on the Art of Directing, was published in 1984.   DBW

Ballard, Lucinda (1908–93) Costume designer. An assistant to scenic designers NORMAN BEL GEDDES and CLAUDE BRAGDON early in her career, Ballard was an active designer (principally of costumes) for theatre, film, and ballet. She received the first Tony Award for Costume Design for the plays Happy Birthday, STREET SCENE, Another Part of the Forest, John Loves Mary, and The Chocolate Soldier in the 1947 Broadway season. She also won a Tony in 1962 for *The Gay Life* and the 1945 Donaldson Award for I REMEMER MAMA. Her second husband was lyricist HOWARD DIETZ.   BO

Bancroft, Anne [née Anna Maria Luisa Italiano] (1931–2005) Stage and film actress who made her Broadway debut as Gittel Mosca in *Two for the Seesaw* (1958). She secured her stardom with such roles as Annie Sullivan in *The MIRACLE WORKER* (1959) and Mother Courage in *Mother Courage and Her Children* (1963). Other substantial stage roles were in *The Devils* (1965), *The Little Foxes* (1967), *A Cry of Players* (1968), *Golda* (1977), and *Duet for One* (1981). Her awards include Tonys for Gittel Mosca and Annie Sullivan, and the Oscar for Best Actress for *The Miracle Worker* (1962) – although she'll be remembered as Mrs. Robinson in *The Graduate*. Married to film director Mel Brooks, who successfully adapted and produced as a Broadway musical his own *The PRODUCERS* (2001), she appeared in several of his films. An early director, ARTHUR PENN, observed, "More happens in her face in 10 seconds than happens in most women's faces in 10 years." Later, critics spoke glowingly of "her guts and her spirit, the elegance of her style, and the passion of her playing."   SMA

Bandmann, Daniel (1840–1905) German-born actor who first acted in 1857–8 at the Altes Stadt Theatre, NYC, and then in Germany and Central Europe (1859–62). He first acted in English at NIBLO'S GARDEN, New York (15 January 1863), as Shylock. Thereafter he toured the world with a company recruited and rehearsed by costar Louise Beaudet. After settling on his ranch near Missoula, MT (1886), he played only short seasons each fall. He married Mary T. Kelly in 1892 and retired. His most prominent roles were Hamlet, Shylock, Narcisse (in J.-J. Rousseau's play), Richelieu, and Dr. Jekyll (in his own adaptation). He acted in the traditional style, featuring rhetorical declamation and striking poses. In 1885 he published *An Actor's Tour*.   DMcD

Banker's Daughter, The One of BRONSON HOWARD's most popular plays, first produced at the UNION SQUARE THEATRE in 1878 for a run of 137 performances and revived many times over the next four decades. The story of Lilian, who, despite her love of young Routledge, marries an older (and wealthier) man in order to protect her family's failing fortunes, appealed to an audience still recovering from the devastating effects of the financial panic of 1873. The play was also the focus of a lecture Howard delivered in 1886 enti-

tled *An Autobiography of a Play,* in which he details the extraordinary evolution of the work from its original manifestation in 1873 as *Lilian's Last Love* to the 1879 revision, *The Old Love and the New.* The lecture, published in 1914, provides a remarkable insight into Howard's writing process, and helped establish him as America's first true professional playwright.   PAD

Bankhead, Tallulah (1902–68) Stage and film actress noted for her vibrant energy, sultry voice, explosive speech, and impetuous behavior. The daughter of one of the Alabama's most famous political families, she debuted on Broadway in 1919 and achieved fame in 1923 in London in *The Dancers.* She returned to the U.S. in 1923 for film work and reappeared on Broadway in 1933. After a revival of *Rain,* she was widely acclaimed as Regina in *The LITTLE FOXES* (1939) and won the New York Drama Critics' Circle Award for Best Actress as Sabina in *The SKIN OF OUR TEETH.* She published her autobiography, *Tallulah,* in 1952. Her final stage appearance was in *The Milk Train Doesn't Stop Here Anymore* (1964, BROOKS ATKINSON THEATRE). She is the subject of several biographies, most recently one by Joel Lobenthal (2004).   SMA

Bannister, Nathaniel (Harrington) (1813–47) Actor and dramatist who began his career in New York and Philadelphia before going to New Orleans in 1834, where he married the widow of JOHN AUGUSTUS STONE and established his reputation as a playwright. After 1837 the Bannisters performed regularly in New York. The author of at least 40 plays ranging through ancient history (*Gaulantus the Gaul,* 1836), national incidents (*The Maine Question,* 1839), romantic comedy (*The Gentleman of Lyons,* 1838), and moral dilemmas (*The Destruction of Jerusalem,* 1837), Bannister wrote mainly to please the public. His popular spectacle, *Putnam, the Iron Son of '76* (1844), opened with 78 performances and exploited the considerable feats of Black Vulture, a horse (see ANIMALS AS PERFORMERS). The most distinctive actor-dramatist of his time, with six published plays, Bannister was a thoughtful and well-read man, an innovator who enriched theatre managers and died young and a pauper.   WJM

Baraka, Amiri [né Everett LeRoi Jones] (1934–) AFRICAN AMERICAN poet, essayist, and playwright. Assumed his new name and mission in the 1960s when he became leader of the black arts revolutionary movement that viewed theatre as a weapon in the struggle for black liberation.

He has written some 20 plays, many of them one-acts, that powerfully dramatize social and racial problems in expressive forms and with unnerving frankness. Hailed for his "fierce and blazing talent," condemned for his blatant antiwhite posture, Baraka was notwithstanding one of the most prominent American dramatists of the 1960s, with a profound influence on young black playwrights through such plays as the Obie Award–winning DUTCHMAN (1964), *The Slave* (1964), *A Black Mass* (1966), and SLAVE SHIP (1967). He founded the Black Arts Repertory Theatre/School in Harlem (1965–6) and Spirit House in Newark, NJ (1966), where his plays were produced. He later rejected black nationalism for revolutionary socialism, as shown in his play *The Motion of History* (1975). Baraka has also written three jazz operas; his autobiography was published in 1984.   EGH

Baranski, Christine (1952–) Juilliard-trained actress known best as bitter and gin-swilling side-kick Maryann (Emmy Award) to Cybill Shepherd on the sitcom *Cybill* (1995–8), who nonetheless was a comedic mainstay on the New York stage in the 1980s, winning Tonys in *The Real Thing* (1984) and *Rumors* (1988), and also appearing in *A Midsummer Night's Dream* (1982, Obie), HURLYBURLY (1985), *The HOUSE OF BLUE LEAVES* (1986), and the MANHATTAN THEATRE CLUB's *Lips Together, Teeth Apart* (1991) and *The Loman Family Picnic* (revival, 1993). After essaying concert versions of *Sweeney Todd* in Los Angeles and New York, Baranski played Mrs. Lovett to critical acclaim opposite BRIAN STOKES MITCHELL as part of "Sondheim Celebration" at the KENNEDY CENTER in 2002, where in 2006 she also appeared as *Mame*.   DBW

Barbette [né Vander Clyde] (1904–73) Aerialist, born near Austin, TX. He made his circus debut dressed as a girl as one of the Alfaretta Sisters, but soon developed his own single act, under the name Barbette. At the Paris Alhambra (1923) his elegant trapeze artistry became a sensation when he snatched off his blond wig at the end to reveal that the slender aerial queen was male (see FEMALE/MALE IMPERSONATION). He was taken up by Jean Cocteau, who devoted an essay to him and used him dressed in a Chanel evening gown in his film *Blood of a Poet*. After a triumphant career in Europe, Barbette contracted a chill at LOEW's State, a New York movie and VAUDEVILLE theatre (1938); when this developed into a crippling bone disease, he became a popular trainer.   LS

Barefoot in the Park Second Broadway script by NEIL SIMON, opening at the BILTMORE THE-ATRE 23 October 1963 and running 1,530 performances. One of his most successful works (and one of several directed by MIKE NICHOLS), it provided Robert Redford's first major role. Corrie and Paul Bratter's newlywed misadventures show Simon's thematic conviction that harmony demands moderation and compromise rather than change. Using a stairway as a running gag, characters develop more fully than in his first script, *Come Blow Your Horn*. A 2006 Broadway revival directed by SCOTT ELLIOTT was a failure.
RW

Barker, James Nelson (1784–1858) Playwright, poet, and politician. Born into a politically and socially influential American family, Barker combined his love of country with his love of theatre. Among his plays are *America* (1805); *Tears and Smiles* (1807), a patriotic comedy; *The Embargo* (1808), a defense of Jefferson's Embargo Act; *The INDIAN PRINCESS* (1808), the first produced American play about Pocahontas; and *Marmion; or, The Battle of Flodden Field* (1812), in which England's treatment of 16th-century Scotland was transferred to America. Barker's greatest achievements are his 11 essays on drama in the *Democratic Press* (18 December 1816–19 February 1817) and his remarkable tragedy of New England intolerance, *Superstition; or, The Fanatic Father* (1824), in which the villain protagonist, a clergyman, mistakes his own passions for the Word of God. Thereafter, Barker, an avid supporter of Andrew Jackson, absorbed himself in politics, contributing to literature with poetry rather than plays. A biography by Paul Musser was published in 1929.   WJM

Barker, Richard (1834?–1903) British-born director. Originally a performer, Barker joined the staff of London's Savoy Theatre and came to the U.S. as director of the "official" production of GILBERT AND SULLIVAN's *The Mikado* (1885). He went on to direct other works in America, ranging from operetta to extravaganza. A skillful stager of musicals, Barker became, in an age of transatlantic star performers, the first transatlantic director. He frequently returned to the U.S. to direct operetta and comic opera.   JD

Barnabee, Henry Clay (1833–1917) Musical comedy actor. A passionate amateur singer, he worked as a retail clerk in Boston until 1865, when he became a Lyceum (see CHAUTAUQUA AND LYCEUM) entertainer. He made his professional stage debut in Boston the following year and later headed his own concert company. He was a founding member of the BOSTON IDEAL

OPERA COMPANY (1879) and their successors, The Bostonians (1887). A tenor, he specialized in such GILBERT AND SULLIVAN roles as Sir Joseph Porter and Bunthorne, but he was also noted for his Dr. Dulcamera in Donizetti's *The Elixir of Love.* He created the role of the Sheriff of Nottingham in *ROBIN HOOD* by HARRY BACHE SMITH and REGINALD DE KOVEN. In 1913 his autobiography, *My Wanderings,* appeared.   DMcD

Barnes, Clive (Alexander) (1927–) London-born and Oxford-educated dance and drama critic who first established his credentials as a dance critic for *Dance and Dancers* (1950–) and for *The Times* (1961–5). In 1965 he came to the U.S. as dance critic for the *New York Times,* adding the drama post in 1967. A decade later he was replaced as drama critic, and within the year (1977) resigned from the *Times* to become dance/drama critic for the *New York Post.* Noted for his clever style,he has been accused of being pro-British and of supporting the avant-garde more than the Broadway theatre.   TLM

Barnes, Djuna (1892–1982) Avant-garde playwright, primarily a poet, who wrote many short plays (1916–26), some published under the name Lydia Steptoe and several produced by the PROVINCETOWN PLAYERS. A theatre reviewer for *Theatre Guild Magazine* (1929–31), she is best remembered for her blank-verse tragedy *The Antiphon* (publ. 1958), a semiautobiographical work concerning a bitter childhood conveyed in enigmatic, Joycean language. Its only production was in Swedish at Stockholm's Royal Dramaten Theatre (1961). A biography by Philip Herring was published in 1995.   TH-S

Barnes, Gregg (19?–) Costume designer who studied at the University of California, San Diego, and NYU (M.F.A.). He has been resident designer at PAPER MILL PLAYHOUSE and RADIO CITY MUSIC HALL. His designs have been seen at the OLD GLOBE, ARENA STAGE, Glimmerglass Opera, and the Alvin Ailey Company, the Moscow Children's Musical Theatre, among others. *Flower Drum Song* garnered him a Tony nomination (2003) and *The Drowsy Chaperone* a Tony Award (2006).   BO

Barnes, Howard (1904–68) Drama critic. Born in London of American parents, Barnes graduated from Yale in 1925 and studied at Queen's College, Oxford, and the Sorbonne in Paris. He joined the *New York World* as an assistant film critic, switching to the *New York Herald-Tribune* in 1928 as theatrical reporter and dramatic editor under PERCY

HAMMOND, then from 1936 to 1942 as assistant drama critic and film critic under RICHARD WATTS JR. He was chief drama critic from 1942 until his retirement in 1951.   TLM

Barnum, P(hineas) T(aylor) (1810–91) American entrepreneur and showman, a hardheaded businessman of great personal integrity whose modus operandi used deceit and innovative methods of publicity to promote both popular and high culture. Starting as a shopkeeper and editor of a weekly newspaper in Danbury, CT, he moved to New York in 1834 and the next year commenced as a showman by exhibiting an ancient black woman he claimed was 160 years old and George Washington's nurse. In 1841 he purchased a museum (see BARNUM'S AMERICAN MUSEUM), where he mixed freak shows with "moral" drama and brought out the midget Tom Thumb (Charles Stratton), whose European appearances in 1844 made Barnum and the notion of "humbug" notorious. In 1849 the Museum became a STOCK COMPANY, and the next year he organized the American tour of the Swedish soprano Jenny Lind, who received $1,000 a night. Barnum retired in 1855, but soon resumed his business. He did not enter the CIRCUS trade until 1871, merging with James A. Bailey in 1881 to create "The Greatest Show on Earth," a combination of circus, menagerie, and sideshow; the acquisition of the elephant Jumbo was his greatest feat there. Throughout his busy life, Barnum regularly issued versions of his life story and optimistic philosophy, including his *Autobiography* (1854), *The Humbugs of the World* (1865), and *Struggles and Triumphs* (1869 [the best version: ed. G. S. Bryan, 2 vols., 1927]). Important biographies by Neil Harris and A. H. Saxon were published, respectively, in 1973 and 1989.   LS

Barnum's American Museum Broadway and Ann St., NYC. In 1841, P. T. BARNUM, America's greatest showman, bought Scudder's Museum and quickly turned it into a city landmark. As part of the price of admission to see real and fake curiosities and an assortment of human freaks and oddities, Barnum provided concerts and light entertainment in a Lecture Room. In 1849, this was expanded into a full-scale theatre for dramatic performances. In 1850, the seating was increased to 3,000 for the presentation of *The DRUNKARD,* the temperance drama. Thereafter, Barnum presented a series of moral plays in a moral manner with a STOCK COMPANY of actors of unimpeachable morality. In 1865, the museum and theatre burned to the ground. Although he

Barnum's American Museum as it appeared in 1850. *Courtesy:* Historical Collections, Bridgeport Public Library.

moved to 559 Broadway, Barnum's second venture never achieved the success of the first, and after only a few years of operation, it too was destroyed by fire.   MCH

Barr [Baer], **Richard (Alphonse)** (1917–89) American producer-director and the president of the League of American Theatres and Producers for 21 years, best known for bringing early works by EDWARD ALBEE to the American public by coproducing (with CLINTON WILDER) *The ZOO STORY, The AMERICAN DREAM,* and *The Death of Bessie Smith.* These were followed by all of Albee's major plays, including *WHO'S AFRAID OF VIRGINIA WOOLF?,* Albee's first Broadway production, which, due to Barr's initiative, established preview performances in New York (1962). Barr also championed other young playwrights: Both alone and in partnership, he produced early works by LANFORD WILSON, William Hanley, TERRENCE MCNALLY, Jack Richardson, JOHN GUARE, A. R. GURNEY, AMIRI BARAKA (then LeRoi Jones), JEAN-CLAUDE VAN ITALLIE, and PAUL ZINDEL. He also presented American premieres of works by Beckett and Ionesco.   DBW

Barratt, Watson (1884–1962) Scene designer. Barratt became the staff designer for the SHUBERT BROTHERS with *Sinbad* (1918). His work included various Shubert REVUES, including *The Passing Show, Artists and Models,* and *Greenwich Village Follies.* Musicals included *FLORODORA* (1920), *The Last Waltz*

(1921), *BLOSSOM TIME* (1922), and *The STUDENT PRINCE* (1924). In the late 1930s he began to work on more serious productions, including *The TIME OF YOUR LIFE* (1939).   AA

Barreca, Christopher (1957–) Massachusetts-born scene designer educated at the University of Connecticut and Yale (M.F.A.). As a cofounder of the American IBSEN Theatre in Pittsburgh (early 1980s) he worked with directors CHARLES LUDLUM and Travis Preston, among others. His regional theatre credits are extensive, including the MARK TAPER FORUM, the SOUTH COAST REPERTORY, Baltimore's CENTER STAGE, the DALLAS THEATER CENTER, and the AMERICAN CONSERVATORY THEATRE, as well as dance designs for Ballet Hispanico and other companies. He has served as head of production and design at the California Institute of the Arts since 1996.   BO

Barrett, Lawrence (1838–91) Actor and manager who made his debut as Murad in *The French Spy* in Detroit in 1853 and his first important New York appearances in 1857 as a member of WILLIAM E. BURTON's Metropolitan Theatre Company. He subsequently was a member of Boston's HOWARD ATHENAEUM Company (1858–61). Barrett was associated with EDWIN BOOTH throughout his career. In 1863 he acted with Booth at the WINTER GARDEN Theatre, and in 1871–2 at BOOTH'S THEATRE he was the leading supporting actor, appearing most notably as Adrian de Mauprat to Booth's celebrated Richelieu, but also alternating Othello and Iago with him. At Booth's Theatre, Barrett also starred as James Harebell in W. G. Wills's *The Man O'Airlie* (one of his most acclaimed roles), as Leontes in a spectacular production of *The Winter's Tale,* and as Cassius with Booth's Brutus in a lavish revival of *Julius Caesar.* This last production was later toured by Barrett under the management of JARRETT and PALMER. Although a professional disagreement estranged them for the next seven years, Booth and Barrett were reconciled in 1880, and their relationship continued to be close for the rest of their lives. Barrett managed Booth's last starring tours (1886–91), and for the last three seasons they made nationwide "joint starring" tours. Barrett managed the CALIFORNIA THEATRE in SAN FRANCISCO (1866–70, with JOHN McCULLOUGH) and the Variety Theatre in New Orleans (1871–3). In 1884–5 he leased Henry Irving's Lyceum Theatre during the latter's first American tour. Generally, however, Barrett spent most of his career as a touring star, often with his own company. He was also keenly interested in encouraging American drama and dramatists, commissioning numerous original plays and adaptations during his career. He presented W. D. HOWELLS's first full-length play, *Counterfeit Presentment* (1877), and William Young's *Pendragon* (1881) and *Ganelon* (1888), and successfully revived GEORGE HENRY BOKER's *FRANCESCA DA RIMINI* (1883).

Slender, with a sensitive face, deep-set expressive eyes, and an unusual vocal range, Barrett was regarded as a studious, sometimes compelling, but also overly technical actor. His most successful roles after Harebell were Lanciotto in *Francesca da Rimini,* Hernani, Cassius, and (late in his career) Othello. A brief biography of Barrett by Elwyn A. Barron was published in 1889.   DJW

Barrington Stage Company Cofounded in 1995 by Artistic Director Julianne Boyd, this not-for-profit theatre devotes much attention to new plays and musicals, including the 2005 world premiere of *The 25th Annual Putnam County Spelling Bee.* Until 2006, its home was the Consolati Performing Arts Center in Sheffield, MA, where a successful 2005 revival with DONNA McKECHNIE of *Follies* was staged. In 2005 the Berkshire Music Hall, in Pittsfield, MA – built in 1912 and used as the home of a nonprofit repertory theatre during 1983–94 – was purchased as its permanent home. A more extensive year-round operation is thus now envisioned. For its first season, WILLIAM FINN, composer of *Spelling Bee,* curated a season of new musicals.   DBW

Barry, Philip (James Quinn) (1896–1949) A popular dramatist of the 1920s and '30s, Barry got his start with two plays written in GEORGE PIERCE BAKER's Workshop 47 at Harvard: *A Punch for Judy* (1921) and *You and I* (1923), a Broadway success. Focusing on the problems of family relations, romance, sexual intrigue, and professional vocation, he developed a modern comedy of manners: *In a Garden* (1925), *PARIS BOUND* (1927), *HOLIDAY* (1928), *The Animal Kingdom* (1932), and *The PHILADELPHIA STORY* (1939), which starred KATHARINE HEPBURN. These plays regularly feature the "Barry girl," a well-heeled if somewhat spoiled young woman who rejects the smug conventions associated with materialist culture and upper-class society. Barry's protagonists, male and female, struggle to serve the liberal ideals of personal integrity, tolerance, art, and freedom. Less well-received were his quasi-allegorical plays on metaphysical themes: *Hotel Universe* (1930), *The Joyous Season* (1934), *Here Come the Clowns* (1938, perhaps his best serious play), and *Liberty Jones* (1941). Productions in the 1940s were only moderately successful, even though Hepburn acted in *Without Love* (1942), and TALLULAH BANKHEAD starred in *Foolish Notion* (1945). His last play, *Second Threshold* (1951), was finished posthumously by ROBERT E. SHERWOOD. A biography by Joseph P. Roppolo was published in 1965.   TP

Barrymore see DREW–BARRYMORE FAMILY

Barter Theatre Founded in 1933 in Abingdon, VA, when Robert Porterfield and company admitted Depression-strapped patrons to the Opera House for 30¢ or any usable item, especially food. The uniqueness of the company's location and business approach, the quality of its ensemble acting, the generosity of the Abingdon community, and the inspired leadership of Porterfield and his successors, Rex Partington and Pearl Price Hayter, sustained production for more than 50 years. In 1993 Richard Rose was selected as artistic director and producer. In 1996 the season opened after a $1.7 million renovation and addition. Barter Theatre has toured the mid-Atlantic states, and the company has been named the State Theatre of Virginia. A history of the operation by Mark Dawidziak was published in 1982.   WD

Bartlett, Frederick see CONWAY, WILLIAM A.

Barton, James (1890–1962) Comedian, dancer, singer, and character actor. Barton, who began in vaudeville and burlesque, graduated to REVUES and musicals as a top hoofer ("the man with the laughing feet") and in 1934 replaced Henry Hull as the crude, degenerate Jeeter Lester in TOBACCO ROAD, a role he played 1,899 times. Other notable roles included Hickey in *The* ICEMAN COMETH (1946) and the hard-drinking westerner Ben Rumson in PAINT YOUR WAGON (1951).   DBW

Basic Training of Pavlo Hummel, The DAVID RABE's first professionally produced play. Part of his Vietnam trilogy, this Obie winner (for Rabe and for JEFF BLECKNER's direction) premiered at the PUBLIC THEATER on 2 May 1971 and ran for 363 performances with William Atherton as Pavlo. A 1977 revival on Broadway starred AL PACINO. In a blend of fantasy, flashback, and military drills and rituals, Rabe depicts the foolish heroics of Pavlo from boot camp to his meaningless death in a Saigon whorehouse. For Rabe, Pavlo's love of violence is symptomatic of America's Vietnam mentality.   PCK

Bat, The Three-act mystery-drama by AVERY HOPWOOD and MARY ROBERTS RINEHART, based on her novel *The Circular Staircase*. It opened on 23 August 1920 at the MOROSCO THEATRE and continued for 867 performances – at the time the second-longest-running show in Broadway history. A model of its genre, the play starred EFFIE ELLSLER as Cornelia Van Gorder, but May Vokes captured the hearts of the audience as the hysterical maid, Lizzie. It has been revived, filmed, and televised several times.   FB

Bateman family Hezekiah Linthicum Bateman (1812–75), manager, first relied on his child-prodigy daughters before managing London's Lyceum Theatre, where he brought Henry Irving to prominence in *The Bells* (1871) and then in *Hamlet* (1874, for 200 performances).

His wife, **Sidney** (1823–81), wrote SELF (1856), assumed the Lyceum management at her husband's death, and later managed Sadler's Wells (1879).

Daughters **Kate** (1843–1917) and **Ellen** (1844–1936) began performing Shakespeare in New York (1849) when they were six and five; then in London (1851). Kate played Portia, Richmond, and Lady Macbeth, while Ellen played Shylock, Richard III, and Macbeth. Later, Kate played in *Leah, the Forsaken* (1862, New York; 1863, London) and appeared with Irving; Ellen retired.

Daughters **Virginia** (1853–1940) and **Isabel** (1854–1934) made their London debuts in 1865, then joined Irving. Virginia married Edward Compton and was the mother of actress-teacher Fay Compton and novelist Compton McKenzie.

Barter Theater; matinee c. 1937 season. This became the company's rehearsal hall. *Courtesy:* Barter Theatre.

Isabel comanaged Sadler's Wells before becoming Reverend Mother General of the Community of St. Mary the Virgin at Wantage (1898).   RM

Bates, Blanche (1873–1941) Actress. Daughter of Frank Bates, manager of noted STOCK companies in Portland and SAN FRANCISCO, she made her debut in the latter (1893) after an early marriage and a brief career as a schoolteacher. By 1895 she had become a leading lady there. A successful tour opposite JAMES O'NEILL (1899–1900) brought her to New York and the attention of DAVID BELASCO, who starred her as Cho-Cho-San in MADAME BUTTERFLY (1900), Cigarette in *Under Two Flags* (1901), Yo-San in *The Darling of the Gods* (1902), and Minnie in *The* GIRL OF THE GOLDEN WEST (1905). She retired in 1926. Full of power and humor, she portrayed a liberated woman who was always energetic, resourceful, and faithful.   DMcD

Battle, Hinton (1956–) German-born black performer and actor, trained as a dancer (former soloist with the Dance Theatre of Harlem), whose Broadway debut as the Scarecrow in *The* WIZ (1975) was followed by BOB FOSSE's *Dancin'* (1978). Since then he has thrice received the Tony Award for Featured Actor in a Musical (*Sophisticated Ladies* [1981], *The Tap Dance Kid* [1984], and *MISS SAIGON*

Val Diamond in the 2005 version of the San Francisco skyline headdress in *Beach Blanket Babylon.* Photo by David Allen/Larry Merkle. *Courtesy:* Charles Zukow and *Beach Blanket Babylon.*

[1991]). Only in *Chicago* (1998 replacement as Billy Flynn) and in *Miss Saigon* has he not demonstrated his elegant dancing style, instead gaining critical acclaim in the latter for the "grit and passion" of his portrayal as the marine John, the hero's best friend, and for his rousing, revivalist Act II show-stopper "Bui-Doi." DBW

Bay, Howard (1912–86) Stage and film designer whose designs included *The LITTLE FOXES, SHOW BOAT, The MUSIC MAN, FINIAN'S RAINBOW,* and *MAN OF LA MANCHA.* Although he became associated with the sentimental musicals of the 1940s and '50s, which were very painterly in style, he virtually began his career with a superrealistic tenement set for the FEDERAL THEATRE PROJECT's *ONE THIRD OF A NATION.* Bay believed that a designer "must not polish a single style," but rather must be adaptable to any situation; he was thus known as a pragmatist and for his ingenious solutions to design problems. During 1965–82 Bay taught at Brandeis University. He authored the well-respected book *Stage Design* (1974). AA

Bay Street Theatre Located on Long Wharf in Sag Harbor, NY, this not-for-profit 299-seat theatre

was founded in 1991 by Sybil Christopher, first wife of RICHARD BURTON; Stephen Hamilton; and Emma Walton, daughter of JULIE ANDREWS and TONY WALTON. With a season March through December, Bay Street presents new, classic, and contemporary works that challenge as well as entertain in an atmosphere free from commercial pressures. Several productions either developed or premiered there have moved to Broadway or elsewhere, notably *Hedda Gabler* with KATE BURTON, *Full Gallop, Swingtime Canteen,* and *Three Hotels.* Additionally, there is a full range of year-round enrichment programs, especially for young people. DBW

Bayes, Nora [née Eleanor or Leonora Goldberg] (1880–1928) Vaudeville singer-comedienne who, despite an undistinguished voice, was a major star in America and England, praised for her ability to dramatize or "put over" a song. She introduced such standards as "Shine on Harvest Moon," "Has Anybody Here Seen Kelly?," and GEORGE M. COHAN's "Over There" (1917), the most famous song of WWI. Her second husband of five, Jack Norworth, was her stage partner during 1908–13 (the billing was "Nora Bayes, Assisted and Admired by Jack Norworth"). Star of numerous REVUES and musicals, she had a theatre named after her in 1918 (later the 44th Street Theatre, razed in 1945). Although known for her egocentricism and temperament, Bayes nonetheless devoted much time and money to charities, especially those concerned with children (three of whom she adopted), When touring, she earned as much as $5,000 a week. DBW

Beach Blanket Babylon This zany musical spoof of pop culture created by Steve Silver began at the Savoy Tivoli in SAN FRANCISCO's North Beach in 1974. Noted for its wonderfully extravagant costumes and outrageously huge hats (including a 200-pound, 12-ft. headdress of the San Francisco skyline), its popularity soon forced the show to larger quarters at Club Fugazi (400 seats), also in North Beach, which became its permanent home. With more than 30 years of sold-out performances, it claims to be the longest-running musical revue in history. Its content is constantly updated with current parodies of popular icons. A book by Janet Lynn Roseman dedicated to this unique phenomenon was published in 1997. DBW

Beaton, Cecil (1904–80) British-born theatrical set and costume designer, photographer, and writer, knighted in 1972, whose neoromantic style is best known in this country through his costume designs for the Broadway and film versions of *My Fair Lady* (1956, 1964). He won Oscars for that and for *Gigi* (1958), in addition to four Tonys for Best Costume Design. He also created exuberant designs for films and ballet from the 1940s through the '60s. Hugo Vickers's biography of Beaton appeared in 1985.   DBW

Beatty, Clyde (Raymond) (1903–65) Animal trainer, quintessential CIRCUS showman. Beatty was born in the U.S. (unusual for circus animal trainers) and developed the "American style" jungle act (gun and whip in hand, challenging animals to attack). He began as a solo act in 1922 (with polar bears) in the Gollmar Circus; from 1926 until the Depression he was with the Hagenbeck–Wallace show. In 1930 Beatty appeared with 40 jungle-bred big cats in a mixed-animal act (lions and tigers together). In 1936 he founded his own circus (with 500 employees by the 1950s). In all, Beatty trained some 2,000 lions and tigers, as well as bears, leopards, pumas, and jaguars. He wrote or coauthored *The Big Cage* (1933), *Jungle Performers* (1941), and *Facing the Big Cats* (1965).   DBW

Beatty, John Lee (1948–) American designer, educated at Brown and Yale, who approaches scripts much like a director. Active since the early 1970s with the MANHATTAN THEATRE CLUB and CIRCLE REPERTORY COMPANY, among others, by the mid-1980s Beatty had become – and remains – the most prolific designer in New York (with some 80 Broadway credits), having as many as six shows running simultaneously. A master of poetic or lyric realism, he designed the premieres of virtually all the plays of LANFORD WILSON (1980 Tony for *TALLEY'S FOLLY*) and several by BETH HENLEY. His ability to create evocative, often elegant settings through deceptive simplicity has worked well for many new plays at the NEW YORK SHAKESPEARE FESTIVAL (now The PUBLIC) and many regional theatres, as well as for MCNALLY's *Lips Together, Teeth Apart* (1991) and *Ain't Misbehavin'* (1978) and several other musicals (recently *Wonderful Town*, 2003, and *The Color Purple*, 2006). He is also known for playful and theatrical settings, such as the caricature environment for *Song of Singapore* (1991) and the shows by magicians PENN AND TELLER. Credits since 1990 include LINCOLN CENTER revivals of *ABE LINCOLN IN ILLINOIS* (1993), *The Heiress* (1995), *The LITTLE FOXES* (1997), *DINNER AT EIGHT* (2002, Drama Desk Award), and *The Rivals* (2004), as well as SIMON's *London Suite* (1995), the revival of *CHICAGO* (1996), UHRY's *The Last Night of*

Ballyhoo (1997), Auburn's *PROOF* (2000), and SHANLEY's *DOUBT* (2005). Since 1994 he has been scenic consultant for the New York CITY CENTER's *ENCORES!* series. A 1993 Lucille Lortel Award recognized the "body of his work." Recipient of numerous awards, he is in the THEATRE HALL OF FAME (inducted 2003).   AA   DBW

Beaufort, John David (1912–) Journalist and drama critic, noted for balanced criticism. Born in Edmonton, Alberta, Beaufort came to the U.S. in 1922. With the *Christian Science Monitor* he served as film and drama critic (1939–43, 1951–62), drama critic (1971–4), and, afterward, contributing drama critic.   TLM

Beck, Julian see LIVING THEATRE

Bedford, Brian (1935–) Since his 1959 U.S. acting debut in Peter Shaffer's *Five Finger Exercise*, this British-born actor (a naturalized U.S. citizen) has devoted his career to U.S. and Canadian (principally the Stratford Festival) stages, winning NYC awards in *The Knack* (Obie, 1965) and *School for Wives* (Tony, 1971) and five additional Tony nominations. Other New York roles include Alceste in CIRCLE IN THE SQUARE's production of *The Misanthrope* (1983); the British actor W. C. Macready in RICHARD NELSON's *Two Shakespearean Actors* (1992, Drama Desk Award); Timon of Athens for the NATIONAL ACTORS THEATRE (1993); and for ROUNDABOUT, two roles in the *The Molière Comedies* (1995), Sir Harcourt Courtly in *London Assurance* (1997), and Orgon in *Tartuffe* (2003). His Jaques in *As You Like It* (Shakespeare in the Park, 2005) stole the show. In addition to periodic New York engagements, he has been seen (primarily in Shakespeare or Molière) at the JOHN F. KENNEDY CENTER, the OLD GLOBE THEATRE (San Diego), and the SHAKESPEARE THEATRE at the Folger. Since 1975 he has had starring roles in National Tours of *Equus, Deathtrap, Whose Life Is It Anyway?, The Real Thing,* and his own one-man show based on Shakespeare's life and works, *The Lunatic, The Lover & The Poet.* In 2004 he directed and played Sir Peter Teazle in a critically acclaimed production of *The School for Scandal* at Los Angeles' MARK TAPER FORUM.   DBW

Beggar on Horseback by GEORGE S. KAUFMAN and MARC CONNELLY, based on Paul Apel's *Hans Sonnenstössers Höllenfahrt*, opened on Broadway 12 February 1924 and ran 224 performances. Neil McRae (Roland Young) is a penniless composer who must choose between marrying the girl he loves and Gladys Cady, the brassy daughter of a

Sectional drawing of *The Miracle,* staged by Max Reinhardt with designs by Norman Bel Geddes in 1924 at the Century [New] Theatre, which was turned into a cathedral. Original in *Scientific American. Courtesy:* Don B. Wilmeth Theatre Collection.

rich manufacturer whose money could guarantee Neil the artistic freedom he craves. Most of the action involves an extended dream sequence done in an expressionistic style: Neil dreams that he marries Gladys, but after her social calendar and her father's business dehumanize him, he kills her entire family, who refuse to die but return to try him, find him guilty of writing "highbrow" music, and sentence him to labor in the Cady Consolidated Art Factory.   JDM

Behrman, S(amuel) N(athaniel) (1893–1973) Playwright. Although Behrman came from a middle-class family, his plays are typically set in genteel, upper-class drawing rooms. Dramatizing conflicts of conscience and values among wealthy, privileged characters, Behrman produced a steady series of urbane and curiously impersonal high comedies such as *The Second Man* (1927), BIOGRAPHY (1932), *End of Summer* (1936), NO TIME FOR COMEDY (1939), and *But for Whom Charlie* (1964). Two recurrent character types haunt his salons: fashionable, tolerant matrons (often played, charmingly, by INA CLAIRE) and cynically detached self-made artists and sybarites. Not quite problem

plays or plays of ideas in the Shavian mold, Behrman's discussion dramas (notably weak in story and structure) chart the progress of his well-spoken characters toward a position of wordly compromise, a sophisticated via media. The THEATRE GUILD presented most of Behrman's work, and his smart comedies have come to be identified as the Guild's prevailing house style. His autobiography appeared in 1972; his biography by Terry Reed was published in 1975.   FH

Bel Geddes, Norman (1893–1958) American set and industrial designer who pioneered the use of lenses in stage-lighting equipment. Bel Geddes is probably better known for his industrial designs ranging from cars to stoves; he is sometimes called "the father of streamlining." The number of his designs for the theatre was small in comparison to his contemporaries, but they were often visionary and influential. His most ambitious design was for an unrealized project based on *The Divine Comedy.* The set was to include 70-ft. towers and a performance area some 100 ft. wide. His visionary designs are suggestive, emblematic, and possessed of towering grandeur, thus creating a theatrical sense of space. Most of his SCENIC DESIGNS that were executed were detailed and naturalistic, such as DEAD END, because of the demands of the theatre at the time. He is best known for transforming the Century Theatre (the renamed NEW THEATRE) into a cavernous Gothic cathedral for MAX REINHARDT's production of *The Miracle.* Bel Geddes also had projects for innovative theatre spaces that altered the traditional audience–performer relationship. His autobiography, *Miracle in the Evening,* was published in 1960. The Bel Geddes theatre collection is located at the University of Texas. A 2006 book by Christopher Innes pairs Bel Geddes with JOSEPH URBAN, providing bios of both.

His daughter **Barbara** (1922–2005) was an actress who made a dozen Broadway appearances (though she is best known as Miss Ellie Ewing in the TV series *Dallas*), most notably in DEEP ARE THE ROOTS (1945; *Theatre World* Best Debut and Clarence Derwent awards), *The Moon Is Blue* (1951), CAT ON A HOT TIN ROOF (1955, original Maggie), MARY, MARY (1961), and *Finishing Touches* (1973).   AA   DBW

Belasco, David (1853–1931) Director, playwright, and manager. A SAN FRANCISCO native, he made his acting debut there (1872) and toured the West as a supporting player, settling at San Francisco's BALDWIN THEATRE as stage manager and playwright (1878–82). There he collaborated with

JAMES A. HERNE in writing and producing, and first worked with Gustave Frohman, who brought him to New York as stage manager and resident dramatist for the new MADISON SQUARE THEATRE (1882). In 1884 he moved to DANIEL FROHMAN'S LYCEUM THEATRE, performing the same tasks until 1890, when he became an independent producer. His long apprenticeship involved the staging of scores of productions and the writing, alone or in collaboration, of more than three dozen plays. The first play of which he was sole author was *May Blossom* (1884), but his first successes were in collaboration with HENRY C. DeMILLE, beginning with *The Wife* (1887). Until 1902 Belasco produced plays for booking by the Theatrical SYNDICATE. His most notable productions in this period were *MADAM BUTTERFLY* (1900), *Under Two Flags* (1901), *The Auctioneer* (1901), and *DU BARRY* (1901). He broke with the Theatrical Syndicate in a dispute over fees, leased a theatre from OSCAR HAMMERSTEIN, and entered into the richest phase of his career (1902–15). During this period he did 42 original productions and revivals in New York City and on tour. The most famous were *The Darling of the Gods* (1902), *The GIRL OF THE GOLDEN WEST* (1905), *The Rose of the Rancho* (1906), *The EASIEST WAY* (1909), and *The Governor's Lady* (1912). He also built a new theatre (1907) and kept both houses active for the rest of the period. Though he was responsible for another 35 productions between 1915 and his retirement in 1930, his influence had waned, and his work was treated condescendingly.

Even in playwriting his greatest contribution was in creating and managing stage effects. In collaborating with DeMille, Belasco would pace the stage, describing scenes and effects while DeMille took notes. DeMille would then write out the dialogue, which Belasco would polish during rehearsals. As a producer Belasco did nothing that had not been done before, but he did it more elaborately and carefully. Desiring to be realistic without being unpleasant, he combined a scenic realism, which demanded solid, three-dimensional pieces and actual objects whenever possible (see SCENIC DESIGN), with melodramatic action and sentimental idealization of character. Working with the designer Louis Hartman and the technicians John H. and Anton Kliegl, he pioneered the use of electric lights to create mood (see STAGE LIGHTING). He selected talented but relatively unknown performers (BLANCHE BATES, MRS. LESLIE CARTER, FRANCES STARR, and DAVID WARFIELD), whom he cast to type in vehicles created for them. Each piece was rehearsed for 10 weeks (rather than the normal 4), so that as nearly as possible the leading performers were playing carefully derived extensions of their own personalities on stage. Belasco's memoir, *The Theatre through Its Stage Door*, was published in 1919. His most reliable biographies (the first was William Winter's 1918 tome) are those by Craig Timberlake (1954) and Lise-Lone Marker (1975) – the latter more a critical study of productions.   DMcD

Belasco Theatre NYC theatre at 111 West 44th St. Designed by architect George Keister, it opened on 16 October 1907 with a production of *A Grand Army Man*, starring DAVID WARFIELD and directed by the new theatre's owner, producer DAVID BELASCO. (Until 1910 the theatre was called the Stuyvesant, to avoid confusion with another house bearing Belasco's name.) The theatre, which cost $750,000 to erect, was elaborately decorated. The stage and backstage areas were unusually well equipped, and the lighting system – a special interest of Belasco's – was considered to be particularly innovative. In 1909 Belasco added a penthouse, which contained offices and a lavish apartment for himself. Belasco continued to produce at the theatre until his death in 1931. Among his spectacularly conceived productions in the house were *The Return of Peter Grimm* (1911), with David Warfield; *The Governor's Lady* (1912), in which an accurate replica of a Childs Restaurant was built onstage; and a memorable 1922 presentation of *The Merchant of Venice*, with Warfield as Shylock. After Belasco's death the theatre was leased, at various times, to KATHARINE CORNELL, ELMER RICE, the GROUP THEATRE, and the National Broadcasting Company, which used it as a radio playhouse in the early 1950s. It became a legitimate house again in 1953. The Belasco, which seats approximately 1,000 spectators, is currently owned by the SHUBERT ORGANIZATION. Tony Randall's classical repertory company, the NATIONAL ACTORS THEATRE, inaugurated its first season in 1991–2 at the Belasco.   BMCN

Bellamy, Ralph (1904–91) Actor born in Chicago. Working steadily in the 1920s in provincial theatre, directing his own STOCK COMPANY, he debuted in New York in 1929 as Ben Davis in *Town Boy* and made his film debut in *The Secret Six* (1931, with Clark Gable and Jean Harlow). By 1943 he had made 84 pictures and thereafter alternated between film and theatre (*STATE OF THE UNION*, 1945; *DETECTIVE STORY*, 1949), with frequent work in television. In 1958 he won the New York Drama Critics' Award, the Delia Austrian Award, and a Tony for his Franklin Delano Roosevelt in *Sunrise at Campobello*. Between 1952 and 1964 he served four terms as President of Actors' Equity. His reminiscences, *When the Smoke Hit the Fan,* appeared in 1979.   SMA

Bellew, Kyrle (1855–1911) English-born actor, son of a popular preacher and public reader, Bellew served in the British navy and merchant marine. Emigrating to Australia (1870), he abandoned gold mining for the stage (1874). His English debut was in Brighton (30 August 1875). Subsequently, he acted with the Bancrofts and with Henry Irving. He was a fixture in New York at WALLACK'S THEATRE during 1885–7 and from 1902 until his death. Noted for his graceful bearing and beautiful voice, he excelled in polite comedy.   DMcD

Bells Are Ringing Two-act musical, music by JULE STYNE, words by BETTY COMDEN and ADOLPH GREEN; opened 29 November 1956 at the SAM S. SHUBERT THEATRE, New York, and ran 924 performances. Written as a star vehicle for JUDY HOLLIDAY, the libretto, which tells the story of a switchboard operator at an answering service, gave Holliday an opportunity to create a wide range of vocal characterizations as she became involved in the lives of clients, ultimately falling in love with one (Sydney Chaplin, in his debut). One of the few musicals of its day not based on a source from another medium, *Bells Are Ringing* was deftly tailored to the talents of its performers and provided a couple of enduring standards – the ballads "Just in Time" and "The Party's Over." It was revived on Broadway in 2001 with FAITH PRINCE.   JD

Ben-Ami, Jacob (1890–1977) Russian-born actor and director who achieved critical acclaim on both Yiddish- and English-speaking stages. Born in Minsk, he emigrated to New York in 1912 and joined MAURICE SCHWARTZ's Irving Place Theatre in 1918. Dissatisfied with the superficial quality of YIDDISH THEATRE, Ben-Ami sought to modernize the repertoire. Differences with Schwartz in 1919 led him to found his own JEWISH ART THEATRE, where he discarded the old starring system and offered works by Sholom Aleichem, Tolstoy, and Hauptmann. (Schwartz reorganized as the YIDDISH ART THEATRE.) Discovered by ARTHUR HOPKINS, in 1920 he was given his first English-speaking role as Peter Krumback in *Samson and Delilah*. His Broadway acting career extended to 1972 and included Michael Cape in O'NEILL's *Welded* (1924), Arthur Kober in *Evening Song* (1934), and Forman in *The Tenth Man* (1959). He was a member of EVA LE GALLIENNE's CIVIC REPER-

TORY THEATRE (1929–31), portraying a memorable Trigorin in *The Seagull.* He acted and directed for the THEATRE GUILD and toured his Yiddish productions to Africa and South America.   TLM
AB

Ben Greet Players see GREET PLAYERS

Ben-Hur by William Young. This dramatization of Lew Wallace's historical novel opened to wide acclaim on 29 November 1899 at the BROADWAY THEATRE. One of several religious dramas at that time, it represented a pinnacle of spectacular stage realism. It played through the season and in road companies until movie realism displaced it. The play followed Ben-Hur, a Jew, through numerous conflicts with Messala, a Roman. The hero survived an ordeal as galley slave and defeated Messala in a grueling chariot race. He found his mother and sister, whose leprosy was healed by Jesus; was reunited with his lost love, Esther; and became a devout Christian. The lavish spectacle included 120,000 sq. ft. of scenery. The chariot race – the highlight of the presentation – featured treadmills for eight horses and two chariots, a moving wall to convey motion, a fan to simulate wind in the charioteers' faces, and a rolling panorama of spectators. Two major film versions followed (1925, 1959).   RAH

Benchley, Robert (1889–1945) Humorist, actor, drama critic, and professional celebrity. Educated at Harvard University, Benchley wrote for the *New York Tribune* and *Vanity Fair* before becoming dramatic editor of the old *Life* (1920–9) and of the *New Yorker* (1929–40). His short humorous sketches on minor problems of the middle class appeared in *Life, Liberty,* and other popular magazines. Many of these were recycled into vaudeville sketches, and later into short films in which Benchley appeared. In the 1930s, he appeared in numerous feature films. A charter member of the Algonquin Round Table and of the New York Drama Critics' Circle, Benchley was noted for his sophisticated wit and urbanity. Babette Rosman's biography appeared in 1970.   TLM

Bennett [né Di Figlia]**, Michael** (1943–87) Choreographer and director who began his Broadway career as a dancer, creating his first choreography for *A Joyful Noise* (1966). Bennett served as both director and choreographer for *Promises, Promises* (1968) and *Coco* (1969). In the early 1970s he teamed with HAROLD PRINCE and STEPHEN SONDHEIM in the creation of two "concept musicals," COMPANY (1970) and FOLLIES (1971), for which Bennett served as choreographer and codirector. He next directed and choreographed the more traditional *Seesaw* (1973), followed by the critically acclaimed A CHORUS LINE (1975). A concept musical about the lives of Broadway's chorus dancers, *A Chorus Line*'s brilliant DANCE sequences were the most vivid element of the production. Bennett went on to direct and choreograph *Ballroom* (1978) and *Dreamgirls* (1981). Illness forced him to withdraw as director of the London production of *Chess* (1986). As a choreographer, Bennett most often employed a precise, rhythmic, but emotionally expressive style of jazz dance admirably suited to contemporary characters and situations. His biography by Kevin Kelly was published in 1990; Ken Mandelbaum's study of his musicals in 1989.   MK

Bennett, Richard (1873–1944) Actor, born in Deacon's Mills, IN, who first appeared on the stage at the Standard Theatre, CHICAGO, in 1891, and made his NYC debut that year at NIBLO'S GARDEN in *The Limited Mail*. Among his more successful stage roles were He in *He Who Gets Slapped*, Judge Gaunt in WINTERSET, Tony in THEY KNEW WHAT THEY WANTED, and Robert Mayo in BEYOND THE HORIZON. Three of his daughters, Constance, Barbara, and Joan, had successful film careers. A collective biography of the family by Brian Kellow was published in 2004.   SMA

Bennett, Robert Russell (1894–1981) Orchestrator, conductor, and composer, Bennett was the son of musicians. He began as a music copyist and orchestrated COLE PORTER's first hit song, "An Old Fashioned Garden" (1919). Although he set out to be a serious composer, Bennett spent most of his career arranging the scores for some 300 Broadway musicals, including SHOW BOAT, OKLAHOMA!, SOUTH PACIFIC, and MY FAIR LADY. Noted for the speed of his arrangements, he turned out as many as 80 pages of music a day. Bennett also scored more than 30 Hollywood films and served as musical director for NBC television.   MK

Benny, Jack [né Benjamin Kubelsky] (1894–1974) Comedian, born in Chicago to Polish immigrants, who entered variety in 1911 as the violinist half of Salisbury and Benny and first interjected gags in his fiddling while entertaining fellow naval trainees. As a solo act he played VAUDEVILLE, NIGHTCLUBS, and EARL CARROLL's *Vanities*, evolving a persona of prissiness and musical ineptitude. In 1929 he moved permanently to Holly-

wood to make films, and in 1932 initiated his hugely popular radio career, developing the superb comic timing and traits of vanity and avarice that later transferred successfully to television (1950–65). On retiring from TV, he performed ONE-PERSON shows and, at the time of his death, was rehearsing for the film of NEIL SIMON's *The Sunshine Boys*. His autobiography, written with his daughter Joan, was published posthumously in 1990.   LS

Bentley, Eric (Russell) (1916–) English-born (naturalized citizen, 1948) drama critic, translator, editor, playwright, educator, and director. Educated at Oxford and Yale (Ph.D., 1941), Bentley gained recognition in the late 1940s for his translations of BRECHT's plays. He worked in both the U.S. and European theatre, codirecting the German-language premiere of *The* ICEMAN COMETH in Zurich (1950) and directing his translation of *The Good Person of Setzuan* in New York (1956). Drama critic of the *New Republic* during 1952–6, Bentley also held distinguished academic positions as BRANDER MATTHEWS Professor of Dramatic Literature at Columbia University (1952–69), KATHARINE CORNELL Professor of Theatre at SUNY–Buffalo (1977–82), and professor of comparative literature, University of Maryland (1982–9). He is a noted translator of Brecht, Pirandello, and Schnitzler, author of 10 original plays, and author or editor of numerous books, including *The Playwright as Thinker* (1946), *The Life of the Drama* (1964), *The Brecht Commentaries 1943–1980* (1981), and *Thinking about the Playwright* (1987). In 2006 Bentley received a Lifetime Achievement Obie Award.   TLM

Berghof, Herbert (1909–90) Austrian-born actor, director, and teacher who studied with Aleksandër Moisiu (Alexander Moissi), MAX REINHARDT, LEE STRASBERG, and at the ACTORS STUDIO (charter member). He was introduced to the New York theatre world as director of *From Vienna* (1939). He first appeared on Broadway in 1940, codirecting and performing in *Reunion in New York*. He staged the first U.S. production of *Waiting for Godot* (1956). Berghof taught acting at Columbia University, the New School for Social Research, the NEIGHBORHOOD PLAYHOUSE, and the American Theatre Wing. In 1945 he founded the Herbert Berghof Studio, which he directed with his wife, UTA HAGEN. In 1946 he founded the HB Playwrights Foundation, where he gave his last performance in August 1990 in his production of Strindberg's *Easter*.   SMA

Berkeley, (William Enos) Busby (1895–1976) Dance director in theatre and film who claimed that he had no dance or music training, yet became one of the foremost dance directors of his time, particularly in film. *A Connecticut Yankee* (1927) marked Berkeley's debut as a dance director-choreographer. Berkeley set a precedent in *The Street Singer* (1929) by being choreographer, director, and producer (with J. J. SHUBERT). Best remembered for his work in film, Berkeley developed camera techniques that used unique lighting effects and extravagant stage sets as well as animations and his famous "overhead shots." These elements of Berkeley's brilliance and inventiveness were integrated into his DANCE sequences. He supervised the 1971 revival of *No, No, NANETTE,* and authored *The Busby Berkeley Book* (1973). LF

Berkeley Repertory Theatre A popular RESIDENT NONPROFIT company founded (1968) in Berkeley, CA, by actor-director Michael Leibert and known for consistently high production standards. Based first in a tiny College Ave. storefront, it was distinguished by a strong acting ensemble and a repertoire accenting classics and familiar modern works. In 1980 it relocated to a handsome new 400-seat facility downtown. Leibert left in 1983; Sharon Ott (1984–97) did not maintain a permanent company but offered vigorous productions of more daring contemporary plays, plus classics reinterpreted via bold directorial and design concepts; and Tony Taccone (1997–), previously associate artistic director from 1988, witnessed the opening of a new space, the Theatre Next Door, in 2001. In 1986 a "Parallel Season" of new works was instituted, airing scripts by PHILIP KAN GOTANDA, JOSÉ RIVERA, HAN ONG, and other noteworthy American writers. The Tony Award for outstanding regional theatre was received in 1997. MB

Berkshire Theatre Festival Founded in 1928 and located in the historic Stockbridge (MA) Casino (now the Berkshire Playhouse), designed by Stanford White and opened in 1888, this summer theatre served as a showcase for stars (ETHEL BARRYMORE, KATHARINE HEPBURN, JOSE FERRER, etc.) from the 1930s through the '50s, followed by a period of financial difficulty in the '60s and renewed strength since. With two performances spaces, 10–12 productions are staged annually; leadership has included Alexander Kirkland, F. Cowles Strickland, William Miles, ARTHUR PENN, Josephine Abady, Richard Dunlap, Julianne Boyd, Arthur Storch, and currently Kate Maguire (since 1998). DBW

Berlin, Irving [né Israel Baline] (1888–1989) Composer and lyricist. With his family he emigrated to the U.S. from Russia at age 2. He received little formal education and held a variety of jobs before publishing his first song in 1907. Four years later his "Alexander's Ragtime Band" became an international sensation, launching a vogue for popular songs written in a ragtime or pseudo-ragtime rhythm. Berlin wrote his first complete Broadway score for *Watch Your Step* (1914). After contributing songs to other musical comedies and revues, he created the score for an all-soldier show, *Yip, Yip Yaphank* (1918), and in the following year wrote several songs for *The ZIEGFELD Follies.* During 1921–4 Berlin and producer SAM H. HARRIS offered a series of *Music Box Revues,* which introduced many of Berlin's standards, such as "What'll I Do?" and "All Alone." His other shows of the 1920s were *The COCOANUTS* (1925) and *The Ziegfeld Follies* (1927).

In the 1930s Berlin responded to a trend toward treating social and political issues in musicals by creating the score to *Face the Music* (1932), a satire on police corruption. He also included in his score for the revue *AS THOUSANDS CHEER* (1933) the song "Supper Time," a lament about the lynching of a southern black.

After spending several years writing for Hollywood films, Berlin returned to Broadway with the score for *Louisiana Purchase* (1940), and an updated all-soldier show, *This Is the Army* (1942). Four years later Berlin wrote the music for *ANNIE GET YOUR GUN,* proving that he, like RODGERS and HAMMERSTEIN, could write a score in which the song grew naturally out of the dramatic action. In 1950 he wrote the songs for *CALL ME MADAM,* and 12 years later Broadway heard his final score, written for *Mr. President* (1962). However, in 2004 the film of *White Christmas* was adapted for the stage, seen first in San Francisco; in 2005 it was presented in three U.S. cities

One of America's most successful composers of popular music, Berlin's most memorable contributions to the musical stage were individual songs rather than complete scores. Rarely interested in experimentation or innovation, Berlin's strength was his ability to adapt to changing musical styles and to reflect in his music the thoughts, feelings, and aspirations of average Americans. An enormous collection of Berliniana is housed at the Library of Congress. Laurence Bergreen's exhaustive biography was published in 1990. MK

Berlin, Pamela (1952–) Director who, after directing canonical works and operas at regional theatres, served for two years as literary manager of

Ensemble Studio Theatre. She has developed and premiered important new works in New York, notably *To Gillian on Her 37th Birthday* (1983), *Elm Circle* (1984), *Crossing Delancey* (1985), *Steel Magnolias* (1987), Elaine Berman's *Peacetime* (1992), *Snowing at Delphi* (1993), and *Endpapers* (2002). She made her Broadway debut with *The Cemetery Club* (1990). She is a graduate of Radcliffe and Southern Methodist University. Elected president of the Society of Stage Directors and Choreographers in 2001, her current term concludes in 2007.   TH-S

Berlind, Roger S. (1930–) Among the most active individual Broadway producers of the past three decades (especially for musicals), Berlind in 1994 was named Producer of the Year by the National Alliance for Musical Theatre. His productions include *Passion*, the GUYS AND DOLLS revival, CITY OF ANGELS; JEROME ROBBINS' BROADWAY; *Sophisticated Ladies*; *Nine*; *Amadeus*; *The Real Thing*; *Death and the Maiden*; *Lettice and Lovage*; *Passion*; KISS ME, KATE; *Copenhagen*; ANNA IN THE TROPICS; PROOF; *Caroline, or Change*; and DOUBT. Since his producing career began in 1976, his Broadway productions have won (as of 2006) more than 62 Tony Awards, including 13 for best production (6 of these for musicals). A Princeton graduate, in 1998 he donated $3.5 million for a new theatre in the McCARTER THEATRE CENTER FOR THE ARTS.   DBW

Berman, Eugene (1899–1972) Set and costume designer and painter. Born in St. Petersburg, Russia, lived in Paris 1918–39, then the U.S. Berman first visited Italy in 1922, and his studies of Italian landscape and Renaissance and baroque theatrical design influenced him greatly. His wispy, almost surreal sketches are filled with such architectural elements as arches and colonnades and have a strong sense of proportion, all reminiscent of Piranesi. In the 1920s he was classed with a group of artists known as neoromantics. Most of his designs were for ballet and opera, and he frequently worked with GEORGE BALANCHINE. Berman's design for Anthony Tudor's *Romeo and Juliet* with American Ballet Theatre is considered one of his best.   AA

Bernard B. Jacobs Theatre see ROYALE THEATRE

Bernard, John (1756–1828) British actor-manager who had an extensive career in the U.S. Born in Portsmouth, he played provincial theatres before his debut at Covent Garden in *The Beaux' Stratagem* in 1787. WIGNELL brought him to Philadelphia's CHESTNUT STREET THEATRE, where he remained until 1803, thence moving to Boston's FEDERAL STREET THEATRE, which he comanaged during 1806–10. He then toured the U.S. and Canada extensively, returning in 1819 to England, where he died in poverty. He describes his career as a leading low comedian in two books, *Retrospections of America, 1797–1811* (1887) and *Retrospections of the Stage* (1832).   SMA

Bernard [né Barnett]**, Sam** (1863–1927) English-born comedian who as a boy appeared in U.S. variety (1876–84). Later, with a speciality in German dialect (developed at dime museums and pleasure gardens), he appeared with WEBER AND FIELDS, first with their BURLESQUE company and later at their Music Hall (until 1901). A long string of successes followed, most notably Mr. Hoggenheimer in *The Girl from Kay's* (1903), a role reprised in 1927 for his last appearance (*Piggy*).   DBW

Bernard, William Bayle (1807–75) Expatriate American playwright. Born in Boston, son of actor-manager JOHN BERNARD, Bernard moved to England in 1820, became involved in English theatre, and made his reputation as a writer of plays about America and an adaptor of American plays and fiction to English understanding. His adaptation of JAMES KIRK PAULDING's *The LION OF THE WEST* was entitled *The Kentuckian; or, A Trip to New York* (1833). Although several versions of *The Yankee Peddler* existed, Bernard's adaptation for G. H. "YANKEE" HILL – *The Yankee Peddler; or, Old Times in Virginia* – became a popular vehicle. Bernard was also responsible for dozens of incidental farces.   WJM

Bernstein, Aline [née Frankau] (1880–1955) Set and costume designer who became involved in theatre as a founding member of the NEIGHBORHOOD PLAYHOUSE (1915). Her successful designs there, such as *The Little Clay Cart,* led to work with the THEATRE GUILD and on Broadway, and in 1926 actress EVA LE GALLIENNE asked her to design for a newly founded CIVIC REPERTORY THEATRE. Bernstein first worked with producer HERMAN SHUMLIN on *Grand Hotel* and continued her association with him through the 1930s, most notably on the plays of LILLIAN HELLMAN, including *The LITTLE FOXES*. Bernstein's early designs used adaptable unit sets, whereas some of her later work employed mechanical devices for a cinematic change of scenes. Bernstein founded the Costume Museum, which later was absorbed by the Metropolitan Museum of Art. Her autobiography, *An Actor's Daughter* first appeared in 1941. (Her father was Joseph Frankau, who'd appeared with VIOLA ALLEN in STEELE MACKAYE's *Dakolar* in 1885.) Carole Klein's biography was published in 1979.   AA

Bernstein, Leonard (1918–90) Composer. Though his primary career was as a conductor of symphony orchestras, Bernstein wrote the scores for six musicals. In 1944 he composed the music for JEROME ROBBINS's ballet "Fancy Free"; when this was expanded into the full-length musical ON THE TOWN (1944), Bernstein wrote the entire score, and critics complimented him on the fresh, lively sound of his music. Nine years passed before Broadway heard another Bernstein score. WONDERFUL TOWN gave him the opportunity to write a nostalgic score full of pastiches of the "swing" music popular in the 1930s. In 1956 Bernstein wrote the music for CANDIDE, a musical adaptation of the Voltaire novel. Although the show was not a commercial success, Bernstein's score, with its echoes of various classical composers and its dry, satiric sound, was recognized as one of the finest written for the Broadway stage; a 1974 revival proved to be more successful with audiences. Bernstein's most famous score, that for WEST SIDE STORY, premiered in 1957. Critics praised the music for its ability to embody the tensions and passions of the show's teenage characters. Although his contributions to the Broadway stage were relatively few, Bernstein's musically sophisticated and inventive scores earned him a reputation as one of the foremost Broadway composers. His autobiography was published in 1982; two excellent biographies were published in 1994 by Humphrey Burton and Meryle Secrest.   MK

Berry, Gabriel (1950s?–) Costume designer from Omaha, NE, who began her career in 1979 and is known for her collaborations with directors and choreographers, including Yoshiko Chuma, MEREDITH MONK, JOANNE AKALAITIS, ANNE BOGART, PETER SELLARS, Christopher Alden, Mark Wing-Davey, and ANDREI SERBAN. She is the first American to receive an individual medal from the International Design Quadrennial in Prague, where she was awarded a Silver Medal in 1995 for her contributions to experimental theatre. She is resident designer at LA MAMA and has served as an associate at the NEW YORK SHAKESPEARE FESTIVAL and the NEW YORK THEATRE WORKSHOP. She received an Obie for sustained excellence in theatre and a Bessie for her work in dance.   BO

***Best Plays* series** Covering every theatre season from 1919 to the present (with a good deal of focus on New York), this series – whose volume titles vary but always announce the year covered (e.g., 1919–20) – provides the best record available for annual statistics and other data, as well as play summaries (of the 10 chosen each year) or, as has been the case since 2000, commentaries on these selections by critical experts. Since 1919 the editors have been BURNS MANTLE, JOHN CHAPMAN, LOUIS KRONENBERGER, HENRY HEWES, OTIS L. GUERNSEY JR., and, currently, Jeffrey Eric Jenkins. Taking this series as addenda to ODELL's *Annals of the New York Stage* (though there is a gap of some 25 years) provides an extensive coverage of theatre in New York City since its beginning in the 18th century.   DBW

Bettelheim, Edwin Sumner (1865–1938) Theatre journalist and critic who edited the *Albany Mirror* before purchasing the [New York] *Dramatic Times* from LEANDER RICHARDSON in 1888. This he consolidated with the *New York Dramatic News,* which he bought in 1896, to publish and edit the *New York Dramatic News and Dramatic Times* until 1919.   TLM

Beyond the Horizon Although this play opened with poorly staged trial matinees at the MOROSCO THEATRE on 3 February 1920, EUGENE O'NEILL's first Broadway production received the second Pulitzer Prize for Drama. When public and critical interest in the play were aroused, it settled in for a regular run that signaled momentous change in serious American drama. Directed by Homer Saint-Gaudens, assisted by RICHARD BENNETT (who also played the leading role of Robert Mayo), O'Neill's tragic study of two struggling brothers would recur in variations throughout his work for decades. Here the brothers struggled over the love of Ruth (Helen Mackeller) and pitted Robert the artist, trapped on the farm but longing for unseen wonders of the sea, against Andrew (Edward Arnold), the prosaic farming brother who is content with the land but who, after losing Ruth, travels afar without appreciating what he sees at sea or in exotic lands. Robert and Ruth suffer a loveless marriage, and all three major characters are unfulfilled as the play ends with the death of Robert reaching for the rising sun. Like all of O'Neill's work, this play is autobiographical, exploring in part the rivalry, love, and frustration O'Neill experienced with his brother.   RHW

Big Apple Circus This one-ring, thematic CIRCUS ("Grandma Goes West," "Carnevale in Venice," "Clown around Town," "Dreams of a City," etc.) under canvas (1,700 seats) was founded in 1977

by Michael Christensen (the clown Mr. Stubbs and now creative director) and Paul Binder (artistic director and ringmaster) as a nonprofit performing-arts organization. In 2000, for their contributions to New York, they were honored as "Living Landmarks" by the NY Landmarks Conservancy. This show is among the most theatrical of American circuses (in a classic circus format). In addition to a season beginning in October with a 12-week engagement at Lincoln Center and a spring and summer tour of the Northeast and Midwest, the Big Apple includes a number of community initiatives, notably the "Clown Care Unit" and the Circus Arts in Education program. On its 25th anniversary in 2002 bleachers were replaced by individual plastic molded seats. See also BARRY LUBIN. DBW

Big White Fog by Theodore Ward was presented for 10 weeks in 1938 by the Chicago unit of the FEDERAL THEATRE PROJECT. It was the premiere production of the Negro Playwrights Company in New York in 1940, an event notable for its cast (CANADA LEE, Hilda Offley, and Frank Silvera) and the scenic design of Perry Watkins (first black member of the Union of Scenic Artists). The drama spans 10 years (1922–32) and examines the political options available to African Americans. The father in the household is actively involved in Garvey's nationalist movement in opposition to his brother (a capitalist) and, later, his son (a communist). Through the deterioration of the Garvey movement and the Depression, we see the family's cataclysmic struggle to survive. KME

Bikel, Theodore (1924–) Austrian-born actor, folksinger, and past president of ACTORS' EQUITY (1973–82). Bikel apprenticed with the Habimah Theatre in Tel Aviv and appeared in several London stage productions before coming to the U.S. in 1954. A heavy-set character actor, Bikel has played many nationalities, most notably in *The Lark* (1955), FIDDLER ON THE ROOF (over 2,000 times since 1967), SOUND OF MUSIC (1959), *Zorba* (1975), and Arje Shaw's *The Gathering* (1999). He has toured frequently, replaced actors in major roles, and returned to favorite vehicles on many occasions. A popular cabaret performer, described in 1989 as "a good-natured international troubadour," Bikel has also been a political activist for the performing arts, serving as officer of the International Federation of Actors and Associated Actors and Artistes of America (elected 2003 for an eighth two-year term as president). In 1997 he received the first Lifetime Achievement Award in the Arts from the National Foundation for Jewish Culture. His autobiography, *Theo,* appeared in 1994. DBW

Billington, Ken (1946–) Prolific lighting designer and industrial show producer whose lighting credits since his first New York production in 1969 (*Fortune and Men's Eyes*) number over 300 live shows, with more than 80 Broadway productions (since 1972's *Don't Bother Me, I Can't Cope*), including *The Visit,* 1973; SWEENEY TODD, 1979; *Foxfire,* 1982; FIDDLER ON THE ROOF, 1990; *Moon over Buffalo,* 1995; CHICAGO, 1996 [Tony and Drama Desk awards]; *Waiting in the Wings,* 1999; *Drowning Crow,* 2004, *The Drowsy Chaperone,* 2006; *Princesses* 2007. He also has extensive credits Off-Broadway (*Diamonds,* 1984; *Lips Together, Teeth Apart* and *Absent Friends,* 1991; *Sylvia* and *London Suite,* 1995, etc.), in regional theatre (GOODSPEED, LONG WHARF, MARK TAPER, AMERICAN REP, etc.), and for dance (American Ballet Theatre and Pacific Northwest Ballet), opera (esp. New York City and Houston Grand), spectacles (including Las Vegas and, since 1979, RADIO CITY MUSIC HALL), industrials, concerts, and national tours. Television and architectural lighting are also specialties. He has received or been nominated for numerous awards, including four Tony nominations. DBW

Biloxi Blues Second work in NEIL SIMON's "Brighton Beach trilogy"; opened 28 March 1985 at the NEIL SIMON THEATRE, running for 524 performances. Following BRIGHTON BEACH MEMOIRS by several years, the play relates the WWII boot-camp experience of Eugene Jerome (MATTHEW BRODERICK), the semiautobiographical Simon. Through the interaction of six members of Jerome's basic-training unit and their opposition to a sadistic, semipsychotic drill sergeant, Simon continued to illustrate the futility of uncompromising behavior. The actions of a persecuted Arnold Epstein and the indecisive Don Carney introduce the notion that life demands conscious choice, even if drastic consequences result. RW

Biltmore Theatre 261 West 47th St., NYC [Architect: HERBERT J. KRAPP]. Still believing that theatres represented a solid real-estate venture, the Chanin brothers, builders, erected the Biltmore in 1925 with fewer than 1,000 seats for serious plays and comedies. Unfortunately, the Depression robbed them of their theatrical empire. After a year during which it was rented to the FEDERAL THEATRE PROJECT, the playhouse was sold to Warner Bros., who leased it to GEORGE ABBOTT. Over the next 15 years, Abbott presented and often directed about a dozen of his own productions at the theatre. In 1951, the Biltmore was sold and became a CBS-TV studio. In 1961, with another owner, seats were added and it was reclaimed for legitimate production. Dark from 1987 until late 2003, it was sold at auction in 1988, again in 1991, and in the late 1990s was again in demand as a real-estate venture. Finally, due to the Manhattan Theatre Club's efforts (and as part of a new apartment project next door – also named Biltmore), it reopened after a $35 million restoration project (with seating reduced to 650).   MCH

Bingham, Amelia (1869–1927) Actress. While a student at Ohio Wesleyan University, she acted with the traveling company of Lloyd Bingham in the summer of 1890. A year later she married him and toured the Pacific Coast with McKEE RANKIN. Her New York debut was in December 1893. She became a star under CHARLES FROHMAN's management (1897), but was her own producer for CLYDE FITCH's *The Climbers* (15 January 1901), whose Mrs. Sterling was her greatest role. She also played in stock companies and in vaudeville (1905–14). Her last appearance was in *The Pearl of Great Price* (New York, 1927).   DMcD

Biography Comedy by S. N. BEHRMAN produced in 1932 by the THEATRE GUILD and directed by PHILIP MOELLER. Marion Froude, a restless egoist, writes her biography for a magazine edited by Richard Kurt, a fierce young socialist. The politically conservative Leander Nolan, a former lover, fears her revelations will spoil his bid for a seat in the U.S. Senate, and he begs her to quash her story. She destroys her manuscript, then breaks with Kurt, whom she has grown to love. In opting for the middle way between conservatism and radicalism, Marion encapsulates the situation of many mainstream American playwrights of the 1930s.   WD

Birch, Patricia (1930?–) Modern dancer, theatre choreographer-director, and film director who joined the Martha Graham Dance Company in 1950, rising to soloist in 1955. She later danced for AGNES DE MILLE in the New York City Center revivals of *BRIGADOON* (1955), *CAROUSEL* (1954), and *OKLAHOMA!* (1958); and for JEROME ROBBINS, playing the role of "Anybody's" in the national company of *WEST SIDE STORY* (1960). Her first theatrical choreography was *The Carefree Tree* (1956), and she worked only sporadically thereafter. Birch's choreography for *YOU'RE A GOOD MAN, CHARLIE BROWN* (1967) revitalized her career and led to a series of successes, including *The Me Nobody Knows* (1970), *GREASE* (1972), and the reviv-

als of *CANDIDE* (1974 and 1997). Other New York credits include *PACIFIC OVERTURES* (1976), *Parade* (1998), *Band in Berlin* (1999), and *LoveMusik* (2007). It was in the choreography in *A LITTLE NIGHT MUSIC* (1973) that Birch displayed her versatility, breaking from the usual form of flamboyant and spectacular dance numbers by crafting a subtle blend of DANCE and dialogue.   LF

Bird, Robert Montgomery (1806–54) Playwright whose major plays – *The Gladiator* (1831), *Oralloosa* (1832), and *The Broker of Bogota* (1834) – were prizewinners in EDWIN FORREST's playwriting contests and were performed by him. *Gladiator* and *Broker* were retained in Forrest's repertoire, with extraordinary profits for him and only $2,000 for Bird; *Pelopidas* (1830), another winner, was never produced. He wrote two plays in 1827 (*The Cowled Lover* and *Caridorf*), and taught at Pennsylvania Medical College (1841–3), having received a medical degree in 1827. At his death his notebook outlined plans for 11 tragedies, 12 comedies, 33 melodramas, and 25 novels. Curtis Dahl's biography was published in 1963.   RM

Bishop, André (1949–) Producer, known for his skill working with playwrights on new work, who in 1992 succeeded GREGORY MOSHER as artistic director of LINCOLN CENTER Theatre. Just prior to this appointment he had been artistic director of PLAYWRIGHTS HORIZONS (1981–91), producing such successes as *The HEIDI CHRONICLES* (Tony 1989) and working with numerous writers (WASSERSTEIN, CHRISTOPHER DURANG, WILLIAM FINN, etc.) and nurturing productions such as *SUNDAY IN THE PARK WITH GEORGE* and ALFRED UHRY's *DRIVING MISS DAISY*. Bishop's credits with Lincoln Center, where he has worked closely with executive producer Bernard Gersten, comprise more than 50 productions as of early 2007, among them the Tony Award–winners *CAROUSEL* (1994), *The Heiress* (1995), *A DELICATE BALANCE* (1996), *Contact* (2000), and *Henry IV* (2004). In 2005 Bishop produced at Lincoln Center the surprise hit musical *The Light in the Piazza*, and in 2006–7 the Stoppard trilogy *The Coast of Utopia*.   DBW

Black Crook, The Four-act musical extravaganza by Charles M. Barras, music by various composers. Opened 12 September 1866 at NIBLO'S GARDEN, running 475 performances. This first "monster hit" of the American MUSICAL THEATRE was born of disaster: A French ballet troupe – stranded in New York when the theatre they were to perform in burned down – was grafted onto a Gothic Faustian melodrama (by stage-manager-turned-author

Barras) that was scheduled for production at Niblo's. The resultant hybrid was a five-and-a-half-hour amalgam of scenic splendor, earnest melodramatics, and huge ballet interludes, all set to a mélange of pseudoclassical and contemporary popular music. Beyond this range of attractions, the show was vilified in many quarters for the "near-nudity" of dancers in tights, which ensured the show's reputation as a succès de scandale. Grossing over $1 million in its initial engagement, it toured the country and received regular Broadway revivals for the rest of the century.   JD

Black Theatre Network (BTN) An outgrowth of the Afro-Asian Theatre Project (1965) of the American Theatre Association, followed by the African Theatre Project and then the Black Theatre Project. In 1986 BTN was established as a nonprofit organization "to preserve Black Theatre's unique art form and seeks to foster its further development for the enjoyment of generations to come." For its current address, see BTN's Web site.   DBW

blackface minstrelsy see MINSTREL SHOW

Blackstone, Harry [né Henri Bouton] (1885–1965) Though best known for his full-stage illusions, the "Great Blackstone"'s most impressive feats were the vanishing birdcage (complete with bird) and the "Spirit Dancing Handkerchief" (both also performed by HARRY BLACKSTONE JR. [1935–97]). During his long career he appeared in vaudeville, tab shows between movies, and (from 1914) full evenings in legitimate theatres. During WWII he took his show to 165 military posts under USO sponsorship; at the peak of his popularity he starred in his own radio show ("Blackstone – Magic Detective") and was hero of his own comic book. Among his more spectacular stage illusions were "Levitation of Princess Karnac" (which he inherited from KELLAR), the "Vanishing Horse," "Sepoy Mutiny" (a cannon illusion), and sawing a woman in half with a buzz saw (with the victim in full view). His son, who first appeared with his father's show at age 6 months, presented a full-length magic show on Broadway in 1980; it had the longest run of any straight magic show in history (118 performances). A Blackstone biography by Daniel Waldron appeared in 1999.   DBW

Blaine, Vivian (Stapleton) (1923–95) Singer-actress. After attending the AMERICAN ACADEMY OF DRAMATIC ARTS, she appeared in NIGHTCLUBS and SUMMER STOCK before making her Broadway debut as Miss Adelaide in GUYS AND DOLLS (1950); as the forlorn fiancée of gambler Nathan Detroit,

she stopped the show with "Adelaide's Lament." She also succeeded Shelley Winters in A HATFUL OF RAIN (1955) and starred in the musical Say, Darling (1958) and the comedy Enter Laughing (1963).
    MK

Blake, Eubie see SISSLE, NOBLE

Blake, William Rufus (1805–63) Canadian-born actor, playwright, and manager, noted for his portrayal of old men on the American stage. With the possible exception of WILLIAM BURTON, he was without equal in this line. Blake made his New York debut at the CHATHAM GARDEN THEATRE in 1824 and subsequently appeared with great success in the U.S. and Britain. In the 1820s and '30s he managed successively the TREMONT THEATRE, Boston; the WALNUT STREET in Philadelphia; and, with H. E. Willard, the Olympic Theatre, NYC. Later he was principal comedian in the New York STOCK COMPANIES of Burton, LAURA KEENE, and LESTER WALLACK. His final appearance was as Sir Peter Teazle at the BOSTON THEATRE on 21 April 1863; he died suddenly the next day.   DBW

Blanchard, Kitty (1847–1911) Actress whose first professional appearance was at age 10 at the National Theatre in Philadelphia. In the mid-1860s she became a popular comedienne in BOSTON, first with the Continental Theatre company and then with Selwyn's (later the Globe) Theatre company. In 1869 she married the leading man at Selwyn's, ARTHUR MCKEE RANKIN. Together they toured nationwide for almost 20 years, most notably in the melodramas The Two Orphans and The DANITES. In the 1890s, following a separation from her husband, Mrs. Rankin appeared in several CHARLES FROHMAN productions and in support of RICHARD MANSFIELD and E. M. and Joseph HOLLAND.   DJW

Blau, Herbert (1926–) American director and postmodern critic who, in The Impossible Theater: A Manifesto (1964), vowed "to talk up a revolution" and has. Blau's later critical work – Take Up the Bodies: Theater at the Vanishing Point and Blooded Thought: Occasions of Theatre (both 1982), The Eye of Prey: Subversions of the Postmodern (1987), The Audience (1990), To All Appearances (1992), Nothing in Itself (1999), The Dubious Spectacle (2002), and Sails of the Herring Fleet (2003), a collection of essays on Beckett – propounds a Foucauldian "theatrum philosophicum" of the mind. Blau's central themes are "the self-abolishing [and self-observing] thought of theatre," the co-opting of theatrical performance by writing, and the decentering of culture based in logocentric language via the complicating of thought's linguistic expression. Blau and JULES IRVING pioneered stage work on Brecht and Beckett at San Francisco Actors Workshop, which they cofounded (1952), before becoming co–artistic directors of the Repertory Theatre of LINCOLN CENTER (1965). Resigning his position in 1967, following his controversial production of *Danton's Death* (which opened the VIVIAN BEAUMONT THEATRE), Blau cofounded the California Institute of the Arts (1968), where he was in charge of actor training. His later work with KRAKEN (formerly the Oberlin Group) was rigorously physical and group-created. Blau continually promotes modes of seeing – authorship and spectatorship – that address and partially redress the new cultural subjects of division and pastiche. He currently is on the faculty of the University of Washington. SG

Bleckner, Jeff (1943–) Director and television producer. Bleckner has directed for LONG WHARF, ARENA STAGE, La MaMa, MARK TAPER FORUM, and YALE REPERTORY. For the NEW YORK SHAKESPEARE FESTIVAL in 1971 he directed STICKS AND BONES (Drama Desk Award, Outstanding Director) and *The BASIC TRAINING OF PAVLO HUMMEL* (Obie and Drama Desk awards for direction). In 2003 he directed a television version of *The MUSIC MAN* with MATTHEW BRODERICK. REK

Blessing, Lee (1950–) Minneapolis-born playwright, trained at the University of Iowa Graduate Writer's Workshop and author of plays such as *Independence* (1984, ACTORS THEATER), *Eleemosynary* (1988, TheatreWorks), *Cobb* (1989, YALE REP), *Fortinbras* (1991, La JOLLA PLAYHOUSE), *Lake Street Extension* (1992, Ensemble Theater of Cincinnati), *Patient A* (1993, SIGNATURE THEATRE COMPANY), *Down the Road* (1993, ATLANTIC THEATER), *The Rights* (1994, Ensemble Theatre of Cincinnati). He made his Broadway debut with the two-character (a common device for him) *A Walk in the Woods* (1987), in which a Soviet and an American diplomat privately attempt to reach a disarmament agreement. One of his strongest works to date, the play was subsequently produced on PBS's *American Playhouse* (1989) and in London (1988) and Moscow (1989). Blessing spent the 1992–3 season as Playwright-in-Residence at New York's Signature Theatre Company. Other play titles (most premiered in the regions) include *Nice People Dancing to Good Country Music*, *The Authentic Life of Billy the Kid*, *Whores*, *Rewrites*, *Thiefs River*, *Two Rooms*, *A Body of Water* (GUTHRIE, 2005), *The Scottish Play* (La Jolla, 2005), and a notable recent success, *Going to*

St. Ives, seen Off-Broadway in 2005 at 59E59 Theaters. A two-woman play, it deals with the encounter of an eye surgeon and an African woman (the mother of a fictional African dictator), placing them in an intense situation of differing perspectives. CLJ DBW

Blinn, Holbrook (1872–1928) San Francisco–born actor who first appeared onstage locally as a child in *Streets of New York* (1878). After a year at Stanford University (1891–2), he made his New York debut in *The New South* (1893), and his first London appearance in *The Cat and the Cherub* (1897). He began playing leading parts for ARNOLD DALY's Company (1907–8) and afterward for MRS. FISKE (1908–11), portraying Jim Platt in SALVATION NELL (1908) and Karsten Bernick in *Pillars of Society* (1901). In 1911 HARRISON GREY FISKE featured him as Michael Regan in EDWARD SHELDON's *The BOSS*. During the 1913–14 season he produced a series of 30 one-acts at the PRINCESS THEATRE, acting in several. Other starring roles included Lord Illingworth in *A Woman of No Importance* (1916) with MARGARET ANGLIN; Georges Duval in *The Lady of the Camellias* in an all-star revival (1917); and Pancho Lopez in *The Bad Man* (1920), a role that brought him recognition for his comic ability. Blinn was a versatile actor able to play a wide range of roles, from the brutal Jim Platt to the aristocratic Georges Duval. TLM

Blitzstein, Marc (1905–64) Philadelphia-born composer, librettist, and adapter who studied at the Curtis Institute of Music and later trained with Nadia Boulanger in Paris and Arnold Schönberg in Berlin. He is best known as the composer-librettist for *The CRADLE WILL ROCK* (1937), a pro-labor operetta developed within the FEDERAL THEATRE PROJECT. The controversial production, famously recounted in JOHN HOUSEMAN's *Runthrough* (1972), was revived a few months later by ORSON WELLES and Houseman as part of the MERCURY THEATRE's first season. He later translated and adapted BRECHT's *The Threepenny Opera* (1952), an OFF-BROADWAY success (2,611 performances). Other musical works included *Regina* (1949), based on LILLIAN HELLMAN's *The LITTLE FOXES*, and *Juno* (1959), based on Sean O'Casey's *Juno and the Paycock*. At the time of his death, a murder victim in Martinique, he was developing an opera about the Sacco and Vanzetti case. Eric A. Gordon's exhaustive biography was published in 1989. TP

Blondin, Charles [né Jean-François-Émile Gravelet] (1824–97) French wirewalker and son of nomadic performers who studied with the RAVEL family, taking his name from his tutor, Jean Ravel Blondin, and cultivating the bayonet springboard. Fame came in 1859 when, on a U.S. tour with the Ravels, he crossed Niagara Falls on a tightrope; he later repeated this feat blindfolded or pushing a man in a wheelbarrow, or stopping halfway across to cook an omelette. Much imitated, especially by "Female Blondins," he pursued his altitudinous profession until the age of 70.   LS

Bloodgood [née Stevens], **Clara** (1870–1907) Actress. After appearing under CHARLES FROH-MAN's management, beginning with her debut in *The Conquerors* (1898), Bloodgood became a favorite of CLYDE FITCH, appearing first in his *The Climbers* (1901), then in roles written for her – notably Jinny Austin in *The Girl with the Green Eyes* (1902) and Becky Warder, the consummate liar, in *The TRUTH* (1907). She also appeared as Violet Robinson in the American premiere of SHAW's *Man and Superman* (1905). *The Truth,* a hit in London with Marie Tempest, was a disaster in New York but a succcess for Bloodgood on the road. Apparently suffering from depression, the actress shot herself in a Baltimore hotel room shortly before a performance. Fitch denied the suicide had been motivated by a dedication of *The Truth* to Tempest.   DBW

Bloom, Claire (1931–) British-born actress, noted for her intelligence – matched by her beauty – who lives in the U.S. and England. Though best known for her film work, she began a long stage career at 16 with the Oxford Repertory Company, followed by numerous English credits at the Old Vic, in the West End, and recently, three plays at the London Almeida Theatre (1990, 2000, 2004) and *Six Dance Lessons in Six Weeks* at the Theatre Royal, Haymarket (2006–7). She first appeared in the U.S. on tour with the Old Vic in 1956 (Juliet and Queen in *Richard II*). Subsequent U.S. appearances include leading roles in *Rashomon* (1959), *A Doll's House* and *Hedda Gabler* (1971), *Vivat! Vivat Regina!* (1972), *The Innocents* (1976), and since the 1980s her one-woman show, *These Are Women: A Portrait of Shakespeare's Heroines.* A sensitive portrayal of Blanche in *A STREETCAR NAMED DESIRE* in 1974 (London, directed by EDWIN SHERIN) won her three major awards. In 1993 she appeared as Mme. Ranevsky at the AMERICAN REPERTORY THEATRE and in 1996 as Mary in *LONG DAY'S JOURNEY INTO NIGHT.* In 1996 she also appeared in *Women in Mind* at ART and in 1998 *Enter the Actress.* Her autobiographies were published in 1982 and 1996.   DBW

Bloomgarden, Kermit (1904–76) Brooklyn-born producer who made his producing debut in 1940 with Albert Bein's *Heavenly Express,* which promptly closed. In 1945 he sponsored his first hit, *DEEP ARE THE ROOTS,* a drama about racial conflict. This was followed in 1946 by LILLIAN HELLMAN's *Another Part of the Forest,* beginning a long association with the playwright. Success continued with *Command Decision* (1947), *DEATH OF A SALESMAN* (1949), *The CRUCIBLE* (1953), *A VIEW FROM THE BRIDGE* (1955), *The DIARY OF ANNE FRANK* (1955), *The MOST HAPPY FELLA* (1956), *LOOK HOMEWARD, ANGEL* (1957), and *The MUSIC MAN* (1957). He presented Hellman's *TOYS IN THE ATTIC* in 1960, but had few other productions of note until *HOT L BALTIMORE* (1973) and the New York mounting of *Equus* (1974). Bloomgarden believed that producers should interfere as little as possible with artists except to "throw out sparks that will stimulate them to make better use of their own creativity."   TLM

Blossom Time Three-act operetta, music by SIGMUND ROMBERG, words by Dorothy Donnelly; opened 29 September 1921 at the AMBASSADOR THEATRE, New York, running 592 performances. Based on a popular Viennese operetta, this sentimental, highly fictionalized "biography" of Franz Schubert used Schubert's own music as the basis for its songs. Romberg, a house composer for the SHUBERTS who had written scores for 25 shows in seven years, was assigned to revise it for American production, largely on the strength of his successful adaptation of *Maytime* (1917). He and Donnelly drastically revised the original and created a smash success that was the second-longest-running musical of the 1920s (after Romberg's *The STUDENT PRINCE*) and became a staple of road companies for the next 30 years.   JD

Blue Man Group One of the more uniquely innovative and profitable popular entertainments of the late 20th century, a show that evolved in the late 1980s and early '90s on the streets of New York City and in performance art spaces in the East Village, finally settling in at the 298-seat Astor Place Theatre in fall 1991. Subsequent companies have become semipermanent fixtures in Boston (1995), Chicago (1997), Las Vegas (2000; 2005 in their own 1,760-seat theatre at the Venetian Hotel), Berlin (2004), Toronto (2005), and London's West End (2005). Described by critic Vickie Goldberg as a "post-modern romp in a lunatic nursery school," BMG, though creative in a variety of media, is best known for its theatrical performances that feature three identical bullet-headed and shiny cobalt-blue characters who create a multisensory experience combining theatre, percussive music, art, science, and vaudeville into an extraordinarily profitable show.   DBW

Blues for Mr. Charlie by JAMES BALDWIN was produced during the 1963–4 Broadway season and heralded the violence that would erupt as playwrights of the 1960s began to voice the anger of the African American community. A searing analysis of attitudes and emotions based on the factual murder of Emmett Till, the play tells of the black son of a preacher who, returning home to the South, is found dead after an innocent conversation with a white woman. Set simultaneously in Blacktown and Whitetown USA, the play's characters speak to the audience in soliloquy and dialogue during the course of the trial to reveal the fears and hatreds burning in the deep South. The play ends on a somewhat hopeful note.   KME

Bobbie, Walter (1945–) Pennsylvania-born actor, writer, and director known best as the director of the long-running Broadway revival of CHICAGO, for which he received the Tony for Best Director of a Musical (1997) and subsequently directed in London. Before *Chicago* he conceived, authored the book for, and directed RODGERS & HAMMERSTEIN'S *A Grand Night for Singing* (1993) at the ROUNDABOUT, and for several years was artistic director of CITY CENTER'S ENCORES! (directed FIORELLO!; produced CALL ME MADAM, One Touch of Venus, Out of This World, PAL JOEY, DU BARRY WAS A LADY, and *Chicago*); thereafter, as a member of the advisory committee, he has directed *Tenderloin* and GOLDEN BOY. Broadway directorial credits since *Chicago* are *Footloose* (1998), *Twentieth Century* (2004), *SWEET CHARITY* (2005), and the short-lived *High Fidelity* (2006). His first successful Broadway acting assignment was in the original *GREASE* (1980); his most recent acclaim came in mutiple roles in David Ives's *Polish Joke: A Play within a Polka* (MANHATTAN THEATRE CLUB, 2003).   DBW

Bock, Jerry [Jerrold Lewis] (1925–) and **Sheldon** [Mayer] **Harnick** (1924–) Composer and lyricist, each of whom began writing for the Broadway musical stage in the 1950s; however, they did not work as collaborators until *The Body Beautiful* (1958). The following year their show *FIORELLO!* opened, winning the Pulitzer Prize for Drama in 1960. Among their other notable scores were *SHE LOVES ME* (1963; revised to critical acclaim, 1993), *FIDDLER ON THE ROOF* (1964), *The Apple Tree* (1966; revived 2006), and *The Rothschilds* (1970), after which they ended their partnership. Writing in

an era when most musicals had an exotic or period setting, Bock and Harnick were adept at varying their style to match the time and place of each show, while at the same time working within the traditional forms of Broadway show music.   MK

Body Politic Theatre Founded in 1966 by Chicago's Community Arts Foundation under the direction of Jim Shiflett and with help from PAUL SILLS and MIKE NICHOLS, the Body Politic was the seminal theatre in the early development of CHICAGO's Off-Loop theatre renaissance. It folded in 1995 after years of fiscal instability.   SF

Boesing, Martha (1936–) Playwright-director best known as founding manager of At the Foot of the Mountain Theatre (AFOM), 1974–91, a women's COLLECTIVE in MINNEAPOLIS, from which she resigned in 1984. Her early plays with AFOM, dealing largely with women's personal and political issues, include *River Journal* (1975), and *Raped* (1976) and *The Story of a Mother* (1977), created collaboratively with the company. Boesing's nonrealist plays are often participatory ritual dramas.   JDo

Bogart, Anne (1951–) Director whose detailed stagings incorporate music, dance, and large-ensemble performance in original pieces and reinterpreted classics. Influenced by the international avant-garde, during 1980–8 she directed at universities and small theatres in New York and Europe, working with environmental frameworks to investigate political concerns. Most memorable are her *SOUTH PACIFIC* (1984), set in a mental institution; *1951* (with MAC WELLMAN, 1986), on the McCarthy years; *Cinderella/Cendrillon* (1988), reworking Massenet's opera; and her Obie-winning *No Plays, No Poetry* (1988), an original exploration of Brecht. Artistic director of TRINITY REPERTORY COMPANY during 1989–90, she resigned over a budget dispute. After staging *ONCE IN A LIFETIME* (1990) at AMERICAN REPERTORY THEATRE, she returned to New York to freelance and explore vaudeville, resulting in the cowriting (with TINA LANDAU) of *American Vaudeville*, which she directed at the ALLEY in March 1992. She was President of THEATRE COMMUNICATIONS GROUP 1991–3, and in 1992 received an Obie for her direction of PAULA VOGEL's *Baltimore Waltz*. (In 1994 she directed Vogel's *Hot 'n' Throbbing* at ART.) In spring 1994 she conceived and directed *Marathon Dancing* in New York. In 1992 she and Tadashi Suzuki cofounded SITI Company (the Saratoga International Theater Institute).

Projects there have included *The Medium,* based on Marshall McLuhan's work; *Small Lives/Big Dreams,* derived from five Chekhov plays; *Death and the Ploughman; A Midsummer Night's Dream; La Dispute; Score; bobrauschenbergamerica* (collaboration with CHARLES MEE); *Room; War of the Worlds; Cabin Pressure; The Radio Play; Alice's Adventure; Culture of Desire; Bob; Going, Going, Gone;* and plays by Strindberg, Mee, and Coward. She has also directed several operas. Bogart and her work (with stagings of the SITI works and a new production of *The ADDING MACHINE*) were honored in January 1995 when she was the focus of ACTORS THEATRE OF LOUISVILLE's "Modern Masters" (the 10th annual "Classics in Context" Festival). Author of a book on directing, she teaches that subject at Columbia. TH-S DBW

Bogosian, Eric (1953–) Massachusetts-reared, Obie-winning actor, playwright, and monologist, best known for the comedic gallery of profane and power-addicted American males he assembles in ONE-PERSON shows like *Drinking in America* (1986), *Sex, Drugs & Rock and Roll* (1987), *Pounding Nails in the Floor with My Head* (1994), *Wake Up and Smell the Coffee* (1995), and his full-length plays *Talk Radio* (1987; film version, 1988; revised for Broadway, 2007), *subUrbia* (1994, LINCOLN CENTER; revived 2006, SECOND STAGE THEATRE), *Griller* (1998, GOODMAN), *Humpty Dumpty* (2001), and *Red Angel* (WILLIAMSTOWN, 2002). Among fellow monologists, Bogosian's sensibility lies midway between the mainstream focus of LILY TOMLIN and the late Richard Pryor and the experimental perspectives of the late SPALDING GRAY or LAURIE ANDERSON. In recent years he has focused more on acting and writing (novel *Mall,* 2000) and deemphasized solo work. CLJ

Boker, George Henry (1823–90) Playwright and poet. His principal play, *Francesca da Rimini* (1855), first performed by E. L. DAVENPORT (Lanciotto), did not achieve major success until 1882, when LAWRENCE BARRETT appeared as Lanciotto and OTIS SKINNER as Paolo. It was retained in Barrett's repertoire and was revived by Skinner (Lanciotto) in 1901. Boker wrote 10 other plays. The best known: *The World a Mask* (1851) and *The Bankrupt* (1855). Boker once confided to writer BAYARD TAYLOR that he had no ambition to become "a mere playwright" but wanted to be "acknowledged as a poet." He wrote several volumes of poetry: *The Lesson of Life* (1848), *Poems of the War* (1864), and *The Will of the People* (1864). After 1870 he spent time in foreign service. T. M. Kitts's biography appeared in 1994. RM

Boland, Mary (1880–1965) Actress remembered for her fluttery matrons and zany mothers in film. Boland served her apprenticeship in stock and on tour. Her New York debut (1905) was in *Strongheart.* In the teens she was JOHN DREW's leading lady in nine FROHMAN productions. Initially cast in serious roles, her portrayal as the scatterbrained Mrs. Wheeler in *Clarence* (1919) established her as a flexible talent. During the 1920s she was one of America's most popular stage comediennes. Seen onstage infrequently after 1930, her final appearance in 1954 (as the mother in *Lullaby*) provoked one critic to state that she was as "overwrought and mercurial as ever." DBW

Boleslavski (also Boleslavsky), Richard [né Boleslaw Ryszard Srzednicki] (1887–1937) An original member of the MOSCOW ART THEATRE's first Studio, he left Russia in 1920, joined the "Kachalov Group" (an MAT offshoot) in Prague (1921) and settled in the U.S. in 1922. Boleslavski's PRINCESS THEATRE lectures and his article "First Lesson of Acting" (1923) introduced Americans to the Stanislavskian concept of "concentration" in acting and were the basis of his book *Acting: The First Six Lessons* (1933). Boleslavski and former MAT actress MARIA OUSPENSKAYA cofounded the AMERICAN LABORATORY THEATRE (ALT, 1923–30) where a full theatre curriculum was taught. Boleslavski's development of the actor's expressive means and intellectual and cultural awareness linked the MAT tradition to the GROUP THEATRE, though Boleslavski believed one of the founders and former student, LEE STRASBERG, erroneously stressed affective memory over dramatic action in his teaching. Boleslavski had a varied NYC stage directing career (including the ALT subscription series begun in 1925), directed 15 major Hollywood films in the 1930s, and wrote two autobiographical books (published 1932). A biography by J. W. Roberts appeared in 1981. SG

Bolger, Ray[mond Wallace] (1904–87) Dancer and singer. After making his debut with a musical stock company in Boston, Bolger spent a few years in vaudeville before appearing on Broadway in *The Merry World* (1926). His loose-limbed, comic dancing style was featured in several REVUES, including GEORGE WHITE's *Scandals of 1931.* He appeared in *Life Begins at 8:40* (1934) and created the part of Junior Dolan in RODGERS and HART's *ON YOUR TOES* (1936), in which he performed GEORGE BALANCHINE's choreography for the "Slaughter on Tenth Avenue" ballet. During the 1940s Bolger starred in such popular musicals as

Edwin Booth as Hamlet. Photo by Sarony, 1870s. *Courtesy:* Don B. Wilmeth Theatre Collection.

By Jupiter (1942) and *Three to Make Ready* (1946). In *Where's Charley?* (1948; Tony, Best Actor), a musical version of *Charley's Aunt,* Bolger stopped the show with his rendition of "Once in Love with Amy." After a decade away from Broadway, Bolger returned to the musical stage in the 1960s for *All American* (1962) and *Come Summer* (1969), neither of which was a hit. He was of course the Scarecrow in the film *The WIZARD OF OZ* (1939).   MK

Bolton, Guy [Reginald] (1883–1979) Librettist and playwright. He began writing plays in 1911, and soon after turned to writing librettos. In 1915 he joined composer JEROME KERN for the first of the PRINCESS THEATRE musicals, *Nobody Home.* The success of this modest and ingratiating musical comedy was repeated with *VERY GOOD EDDIE* (1915), *Have a Heart* (1917), *Oh, Boy!* (1917), and others. Bolton's Princess Theatre librettos were praised for their unusually coherent plots and well-developed characters. His career as a librettist spanned forty years, encompassing such hits as *SALLY* (1920), *Lady, Be Good* (1924), *Oh, Kay!* (1926), and *ANYTHING GOES* (1934). With lyricist P. G. WODEHOUSE, Bolton coauthored an autobiography, *Bring on the Girls* (1953).   MK

Bonstelle, Jessie [née Laura Justine Bonesteele] (1872?–1932) Director-actress, best known for directing the Detroit Civic Theatre. Born near Greece, NY, by age 9 she could recite 150 selections, mostly Shakespearean. After attending a convent school, Bonstelle entered a road company of *Bertha, the Beautiful Sewing Machine Girl* and later worked for AUGUSTIN DALY and the SHUBERTS. In 1910 she founded a repertory company in Detroit that ran for 14 years. In 1925 she opened the Bonstelle Playhouse and later organized the Detroit Civic Theatre. The Depression threatened the organization, for which she actively campaigned until the time of her death. Among the many stars she developed were KATHARINE CORNELL, MELVYN DOUGLAS, Frank Morgan, and William Powell.   SMA

Booth, Agnes [neé Marion Agnes Land Rookes] (1846–1910) Australian-born actress, made her first American appearances in San Francisco, where she married Harry Perry, a popular actor (1861; d. 1863). After her New York debut in 1865 (Florence Trenchard in *OUR AMERICAN COUSIN*) she supported EDWIN FORREST for a season. From 1866 to 1874 she was with the BOSTON THEATRE Company under the management of JUNIUS BRUTUS BOOTH JR., whom she married in 1867. Following starring tours during 1847–76, she became the leading actress of such New York STOCK COMPANIES as UNION SQUARE, PARK THEATRE, NIBLO'S GARDEN, and, during 1881–91, the MADISON SQUARE company. Her third marriage (1885) was to John B. Schoeffel, a prominent theatre manager. With a singularly rich, distinctive voice and expressive features, Mrs. Booth, a versatile actress, was best playing forceful, spirited women like Cleopatra, Mrs. Ralston in Charles Young's *Jim, the Penman,* and the Duchess of Milford in *The Sporting Duchess.* She appeared last as Rose in an adaptation of *L'Arlesienne* (1897).   DJW

Booth, Edwin Thomas (1833–93) Actor and manager who made his debut in 1849 at the BOSTON MUSEUM as Tressel in support of his father's Richard III. Booth continued to act with his father accompanying him to California in 1852. When the elder Booth left California, Edwin remained, playing in SAN FRANCISCO and Sacramento and touring various small towns and mining camps. During 1854–5, he toured with LAURA KEENE to Melbourne and Sydney, with a brief engagement in Honolulu on the return voyage. In 1856 he returned east, making starring engagements in Baltimore, Richmond, and BOSTON. He made his first major New York appearance at BURTON'S

CHAMBERS STREET THEATRE in May 1857. From this point until his retirement in 1891, his acting career was generally a series of unbroken successes. For 10 years (1864–74), Booth was involved in the management of several theatres, most notably the WINTER GARDEN (1864–7) and his own BOOTH'S THEATRE (1869–74). His management was particularly distinguished by his carefully mounted, visually splendid productions of *Hamlet, Julius Caesar, The Merchant of Venice, Othello,* and *Richelieu.* However, after Booth lost his theatre in 1873 due to poor financial management, he abandoned management and spent the remainder of his career touring.

Early in his career (1861–2) Booth had starred in London (where his only child, Edwina, was born) and in Manchester and Liverpool. In 1881–2, at the height of his powers, he played at London's Princess's Theatre and alternated Othello and Iago with Henry Irving at the Lyceum Theatre. He appeared in London again in 1883 and then toured the provincial circuit. In 1883 he also made a highly successful tour of several German cities. During 1886–91 he completed several extensive national tours in association with his close friend LAWRENCE BARRETT. Booth's last performance was as Hamlet at the BROOKLYN ACADEMY OF MUSIC in 1891.

Darkly handsome and gifted with a slender, graceful figure, a clear, musical voice, and luminous, expressive eyes, he was the finest American tragedian of his time. At his best portraying brooding, melancholy characters like Brutus or Hamlet – his greatest characterization – or capturing darkly sinister personalities like Iago or Bertuccio (*The Fool's Revenge*), Booth was also successful in the playfully comic roles of Benedick and Petruchio, and especially as the wily, histrionic Cardinal Richelieu. Late in his career, his King Lear and Shylock were widely admired

The hallmark of his acting style was a certain vocal, physical, and emotional restraint or "quietude"; this was the chief quality that distinguished his acting from the often violent excesses of the earlier romantic school to which his father, JUNIUS BRUTUS, belonged. Mollie (Mary) Devlin, his first wife, called his style the "conversation, colloquial school." Booth, for example, spoke Shakespeare's verse or the lesser stuff of Edward Bulwer (Lytton) or JOHN HOWARD PAYNE as if it were "natural conversation." An amateur Booth-watcher, Mary Isabella Stone, commented not only on the "naturalness" of Booth's speaking, but also on the richly suggestive, complex "tonalities" of "exquisite sarcasm," or of "sincere, friendly interest and sympathy," or of "mingled grief, astonishment, and anger." Booth's gestures, facial expressions, and movements were also regarded as "natural." He did not strain after effect. Perhaps because of his concentration on feeling, Booth reportedly lost his own personality in a role, creating vivid, completely different, believable characters.

Throughout his career, Booth diligently tried to better not only his art, but also the theatrical profession. He eagerly shared the stage with fellow stars, including not only Irving and Barrett, but also Bogumil Dawison, Tommaso Salvini, HELENA MODJESKA, CHARLOTTE CUSHMAN, and FANNY JANAUSCHEK. In 1888, he established The Players as a social and cultural CLUB for actors and others interested in theatre. (See also INTRODUCTION, §2.) Of the many studies of Booth, those by Eleanor Ruggles (1953), Charles Shattuck (1968), and Daniel J. Watermeier (1971 and 1990), are recommended.   DJW

Booth, John Wilkes (1839–65) Actor, brother of EDWIN. He made his professional debut in 1855 at the Charles Street Theatre in Baltimore as Richmond in *Richard III,* and subsequently played supporting roles for several seasons, principally at the ARCH STREET THEATRE in PHILADELPHIA and the Richmond Theatre. By the early 1860s he was an established popular touring star, playing mainly in the midwestern and southern theatrical circuits. He was undoubtedly a talented, sometimes compelling, but also erratic and undisciplined actor, who was probably at his best playing romantic characters and melodramatic heroes and villains. His first New York appearance was as Richard III at the old WALLACK'S THEATRE (1862); his last stage appearance was as Pescara in *The Apostate* at FORD'S THEATRE on 18 March 1865.

Almost a month later (14 April 1865) in the same theatre, Booth, a southern sympathizer, assassinated Lincoln while the president was watching a performance of Tom Taylor's *OUR AMERICAN COUSIN.* His motive may have been misguided patriotism or a desire for notoriety. Gordon Samples published a biography in 1982; Michael W. Kauffman's 2004 *American Brutus,* however, is particularly good.   DJW   MB

Booth, Junius Brutus (1796–1852) Actor who rose to stardom in London, but who spent the bulk of his career in America. Born in London, Booth tried various occupations before becoming an actor in 1813. After a Continental tour in 1814–15, Booth performed at Brighton and Worthing before starring in 1817 at Covent Garden. Edmund Kean, concerned with a possible new rival, invited Booth to Drury Lane to play Iago to his Othello. After one performance, Booth retreated to Covent Garden, where he starred for a few months, then toured the provinces, playing London only occasionally. In 1821 he deserted his wife and child and emigrated to America with Mary Ann Holmes.

Booth bought a farm in Maryland and toured the U.S. until his death, except for visits to England in 1825–6 and 1836–7. He sired 10 children in Maryland, 6 of whom reached their majority, including JUNIUS JR., EDWIN, and JOHN WILKES BOOTH. His London wife, Adelaide Dellanoy, learned of his American family and in 1851 divorced Booth, who married Holmes a few weeks later.

As an actor, Booth was often compared to Kean, even accused of imitating him. Romantic, passionate, frequently seeming out of control, Booth gained such notoriety in the New World with his often aberrant behavior as to be billed "The Mad Tragedian." Heavy drinking complicated his situation, but Walt Whitman said of him, "The words fire, energy, *abandon,* found in him unprecedented meanings. I never heard a speaker or actor who could give such a string to hauteur or the taunt."

About 1852 Booth began construction on his farm of Tudor Hall, based on an English design – a structure that still stands (although in recent years it has passed through several owners). He played SAN FRANCISCO and Sacramento in 1852, appeared for the last time in New Orleans, and died on a Mississippi River steamboat near Louisville. He is buried in Green Mount Cemetery in Baltimore.   SMA

[*Ed. note:* Stephen Archer's biography (1992) is definitive.]

Booth, Junius Brutus, Jr. (1821–83) Actor and theatre manager, brother of EDWIN and JOHN WILKES, who made his debut in 1834 at the Pittsburgh Theatre as Tressel to his father's Richard III. After over a decade of playing stock at various theatres, including New York's BOWERY and Boston's HOWARD ATHENAEUM, he migrated to California in 1851, where he acted and managed several theatres in SAN FRANCISCO until he returned east in 1864. At various times, he managed for Edwin, the BOSTON THEATRE, the WALNUT STREET THEATRE, the WINTER GARDEN, and, for one season, BOOTH'S THEATRE. He was a competent manager but generally an undistinguished actor, although he was well regarded for his King John and Cassius. He married three women, all actresses: first Clementine DeBar, then Harriet Mace (d. 1859), and finally Agnes Land Perry

(d. 1910), a successful leading actress for many years as AGNES BOOTH. Four of Junius's children pursued stage careers: Blanche DeBar, Marion, Junius Brutus III (d. 1887), and Sydney Barton Booth (1873–1937).   DJW

Booth, Shirley [née Thelma Booth Ford] (1907–92) Actress whose career began in 1919 with the Poli Stock Company. Her first New York appearance was in *Hell's Bells* (1925). She is best known for her haunting portrayal of the anguished and slovenly Lola in INGE'S COME BACK, LITTLE SHEBA (1950), for which she received a Tony Award and, for the film version, an Academy Award. In addition she appeared in such productions as *Goodbye, My Fancy* (1948), *A Tree Grows in Brooklyn* (1951), *The TIME OF THE CUCKOO* (1952), *By the Beautiful Sea* (1954), *The Desk Set* (1955), *Juno* (1959), and *Look to the Lilies* and *Hay Fever* (1970). In 1972 she toured as Mrs. Gibson in *Mourning in a Funny Hat.* During the 1960s she played the comic strip character Hazel on television.   DBW

Booth Theatre 222 West 45th St., NYC [Architect: Henry B. Herts]. Built by the SHUBERT BROTHERS in partnership with producer WINTHROP AMES, the Booth opened in 1913 with its sister house, the SAM S. SHUBERT, and completes the western wall of Shubert Alley, which originated as a fire passage behind the Hotel Astor. A small house, seating about 800, Winthrop Ames envisioned it for his productions of intimate dramas and comedies, which have been its staple ever since. When Ames retired in 1932, the theatre reverted to the Shuberts, in whose possession it still remains. Restored to its original elegance in 1979, its most recent hits were *Dame Edna: The Royal Tour* with Barry Humphries in 1999 and *The Pillowman* in 2005. It has housed four Pulitzer Prize–winning plays: *YOU CAN'T TAKE IT WITH YOU* (1936), *The TIME OF YOUR LIFE* (1939), *THAT CHAMPIONSHIP SEASON* (1972), and the musical *SUNDAY IN THE PARK WITH GEORGE* (1984).   MCH

Boothe (Luce), Clare (1905–87) Playwright, journalist, and national political figure. Although she wrote several plays, none was as successful as *The WOMEN* (1936), which was both praised and condemned for its vitriolic view of society women. A two-term congresswoman and an ambassador to Italy and Brazil, Luce often included current events in her dramas, such as *Kiss the Boys Goodbye* (1938), which she wrote as an allegory about fascism, and *Margin for Error* (1939), a comedy-melodrama that BURNS MANTLE labeled "the first successful anti-Nazi play to reach the stage." Still interested in women, Luce wrote a one-act, contemporary version of *A Doll's House* called *Slam the Door Softly* in 1971. Her most recent biography is by Sylvia Jukes Morris (1997).   FB

Booth's Theatre Built for EDWIN BOOTH at the corner of 6th Ave. and 23d St. in New York, it opened on 3 February 1869 with a production of *Romeo and Juliet*. The theatre was designed by the architectural firm of Renwick and Sands: James Renwick Jr., was a distinguished architect among whose major buildings are St. Patrick's Cathedral, the Smithsonian Institution, and the Main Hall at Vassar College. Booth's Theatre was built of granite in an ornate Second Empire style. The building measured 150 ft. (along 23d St.) by 100 ft. deep and rose to a height of 125 ft. Attached to the west end of the theatre was a five-story wing, the ground floor of which was for commercial shops, with three floors above for artist studios and apartments and the top floor reserved for Booth's private flat. The lavishly decorated and appointed auditorium followed the standard 19th-century horseshoe-shaped configuration, although it had a fairly narrow apron and a sunken orchestra pit similar to that designed for the Bayreuth Festspielhaus some seven years later. There were a number of other mechanical innovations in the design of the theatre, including a forced-air heating and cooling system; a set of hydraulic ramps that raised vertically moving bridges or platforms for changing scenery; a sprinkler system for fire protection (Booth's previous theatre, the WINTER GARDEN, had burned in 1867); and an electrical spark ignition device that for the first time in the U.S. permitted both the auditorium and stage lights to be extinguished during performances. Some of the finest Shakespearean productions of the era were mounted at the theatre during Booth's four-year tenure. After he lost control of it in 1873 – the result of poor financial management – Booth's Theatre was leased and managed by various individuals including JUNIUS BRUTUS BOOTH JR., HENRY C. JARRETT and Henry David Palmer, AUGUSTIN DALY, George Rignold, and DION BOUCICAULT. In 1883, the theatre was rebuilt as a department store, which in turn was razed in the 1960s.   DJW

Born Yesterday Comedy written and directed by GARSON KANIN; opened 4 February 1946 at New York's LYCEUM THEATRE, becoming an instant hit (1,642 performances). Set in Washington, DC, the play follows a boorish businessman intent on buying influence. He hires a *New Republic* writer to educate his wife, a beautiful ex–chorus girl, who lacks the appropriate social graces for the husband's purposes. The cast included Paul Douglas as the boorish husband, Gary Merrill as the writer, and JUDY HOLLIDAY as the wife. Holliday, cast after screen actress Jean Arthur succumbed to stage fright in tryouts, enjoyed rave reviews and is often credited with the play's long success. Fall 2005 saw a revival at the ARENA STAGE.   KN

borscht belt Begun around the turn of the century, this term refers to a chain of some 500 resort hotels, bungalows, and summer camps in the Catskill and Adirondack mountains that catered to a largely New York Jewish clientele. Its name is derived from the popular red beet soup. After VAUDEVILLE's decline, it became an important training ground for comedians (1930s). Dozens of prominent comics (Joey Adams, Danny Kaye, Red Buttons, Milton Berle, Jerry Lewis, etc.) began their careers as "social directors" or *tummlers* (funmakers) in these establishments. A 1991 Broadway show, *Catskills on Broadway*, featuring four comics, did much to capture the ambience of these venues and their humor.   DBW

Bosco, Philip (Michael) (1930–) Practically unknown outside of the New York theatre (despite film and TV appearances), where many would cite him as the classic actor's actor – Bosco has essayed such character roles as the apoplectic opera impresario in KEN LUDWIG's *Lend Me a Tenor* (Tony Award for Best Actor, 1989), Harpagon in CIRCLE IN THE SQUARE's *The Miser* (1990), a comic Italian American gangster in *Breaking Legs* (1991), the fathers in revivals of *An Inspector Calls* (1994) and *The Heiress* (1995), opposite Carol Burnett in Ludwig's *Moon over Buffalo* (1995), Malvolio in *Twelfth Night* (1998), physicist Niels Bohr in *Copenhagen* (2001), Juror #3 in the revival of *Twelve Angry Men* (2004), Grandpa Potts in *Chitty Chitty Bang Bang* (2005), and Shotover in *Heartbreak House* (2006). A tall, heavy-set, rarely unemployed actor since his professional debut in 1954 (in SUMMER STOCK), he is arguably one of our few classically adept actors, having appeared frequently in SHAKESPEARE, IBSEN, and SHAW (including roles in five productions with director STEPHEN PORTER: Undershaft in *Major Barbara*, Boss Mangan in *Heartbreak House*, William in *You Never Can Tell*, Burgoyne in *Devil's Disciple*, and the aforementioned Molière). An actor of rare intelligence, Bosco was a resident actor at ARENA STAGE in Washington, DC (1957–60), the SHAKESPEARE FESTIVAL (Stratford, CT) (1962–4), and LINCOLN CENTER Repertory Theatre (1966–9). Since his Broadway debut in 1960 he has appeared in more than 50 productions on the Main Stem.   DBW

Boss, The, by Edward Sheldon; opened 9 January 1911 in Detroit and 30 January in New York for 88 performances. An effective and violent melodrama that pits a self-made, Irish American, street-dirty labor boss against the WASPish and high-toned capitalist establishment. Caught in the middle are the poor families of the "fourth ward" and the capitalist's daughter, who ministers to the ward. Boss "Shindy Mike" was played by HOLBROOK BLINN, who codirected with producer WILLIAM A. BRADY; EMILY STEVENS was the daughter. On the occasion of a successful revival (CHELSEA THEATRE CENTER, 1976), WALTER KERR noted that the obvious melodrama masked pioneering realistic subtleties.   MR

Boston This major New England city has never accorded theatre courtesies that literature, art, and music have known. The great public library, the symphony, and the art museum satisfied the populace. The legacy of Puritanism and an enduring respect for the Lord's Day were not the only reasons that theatre failed early to be fully accepted here; Boston was a provincial city that held its prejudices dear. The drama was seen as something particularly foreign to the shores of Massachusetts Bay, and narrow-minded patriots kept alive the strictures of their Puritan forebears by opposing any British attempts to circumvent colonial prohibitions on the theatre. Any support of the theatre by Bostonians has been fitful; there was an abundance of theatres in the 19th century, but most genteel patrons would only resort to the theatre that called itself a "museum." After all, this was an era in which Oliver Wendell Holmes would not deign to read a novel on a Sunday, let alone frequent the playhouse. Yet by the 20th century, Bostonians accepted the city's status as a tryout town, were willing to preview New York attractions, and eventually even to support two major regional companies. The first years of the 21st century would see Boston's first new playhouses built in over 80 years and the renovation or restoration of several older theatres.

Theatre began in Boston with several false starts. In 1687 when John Wing tried to set up a theatre in his tavern, he incurred the wrath of Reverend Increase Mather and Judge Samuel Sewall, who stifled his attempt forthwith. Boston's next theatrical venture involved an abortive production of Otway's *The Orphan* (1750) by two English amateurs and sundry locals at The Coffee House on King (now State) St. The performance was broken up by a crush of would-be spectators, and the ensuing melee caused the General Court to proscribe stage plays. This law exacerbated tensions between the colonists and the troops quartered in the city for the next 25 years, since the military, eager for dramatic diversions, claimed that the English Licensing Act of 1737 overruled any provincial provisions. In 1769 even the rumor that the garrison was contemplating a performance caused patriotic unrest. After the revolution broke out, sometime playwright General Burgoyne organized several performances for the benefit of his soldiers' widows and children. One of these, *The Blockade of Boston* (1775) at Faneuil Hall, was terminated by news of the Battle of Bunker Hill. The *New England Chronicle* trumpeted the news of the ill-starred performance by labeling its audience "deluded wretches."

After the war, attempts were made to overturn the theatre ban; and, in 1792, speaking in the legislature, John Gardiner made the first recorded American defense of the theatre. Later that year JOSEPH HARPER's New Exhibition Room was opened on Board Alley (near present-day Hawley St.). Boston's first theatre had a capacity of 500 and was probably little more than a refurbished stable, featuring rope dancing, singing, recitation, and ballet in its opening performances. Plays masquerading as "moral lectures" came afterward; Garrick's *Lethe* and Otway's *Venice Preserv'd* were the first plays presented. Five months after the Room opened, public agitation arose over its allegedly foreign (most of the actors were British) and antidemocratic (most of the characters were lords and ladies) predisposition. Since the theatre ban was still on the books, the sheriff was dispatched to close the Room. His arrival during a performance of *The School for Scandal* caused an uproar: The audience tore down both Governor John Hancock's portrait and the Seal of the Commonwealth from the walls. The performance was stopped, but this law was never enforced again, and was finally repealed in 1797. The Board Alley theatre's brief success encouraged the building of a permanent theatre, and in 1794 the FEDERAL STREET THEATRE was constructed. This was an elegantly appointed house seating approximately 1,000. Two years later the Haymarket opened near the heart of today's theatre district, at the corner of Boylston and Tremont Sts. It was a much larger playhouse – one of the largest structures in the city – and a description exists of its crude technical capabilities.

The Haymarket barely survived the turn of the century, but during the following hundred years a building boom produced 21 theatres. The next significant one was the TREMONT (1827), which hoped to cater to fashionable patrons unsatisfied by the program of only one theatre. Indeed, the growing sophistication of Boston audiences encouraged the proliferation, if not the success, of a variety of theatrical enterprises. The rivalry between the Federal Street and Tremont theatres was so intense that both closed by midcentury.

The city's two most important theatres in the 19th century were the BOSTON MUSEUM and the BOSTON THEATRE. The former housed the best American STOCK COMPANY through the century's middle decade and was the home of WILLIAM WARREN THE YOUNGER, arguably the greatest American comic actor, and the beloved Mrs. J. R. Vincent. The enormous Boston Theatre presented stock, opera, and variety performances as well as touring stars. The city had become a regular stop for English, American, and European tours early in the century – GEORGE FREDERICK COOKE first played Boston in 1811. Edmund Kean, chagrined by a poor turnout for his mistimed second visit (1821), arrogantly refused to go on; Bostonians repaid the insult four years later by running Kean out of town before he could even open. Other performers fared better: Boston was William Charles Macready's favorite American city, and Rachel had one of her most successful American stands there (1855).

Variety acts were popular from the first: A "learned pig" is reported to have entertained Bostonians at Bowen's Columbian Museum in 1798, and 70 years later the ceiling of the HOWARD ATHENAEUM provided the setting for the first human fly act. The "Viennoise Children," the RAVELS, and performers of lesser quality held the stage for so much of the time that William W. Clapp, in his *Record of the Boston Stage* (1853), complained of "Thespis and Melpomene weeping over the tomb of legitimate drama" in Boston. The ascendancy of variety caused him to demand a new theatre that would present drama exclusively. Clapp's call went unheeded until well into the next century. By the time KEITH and ALBEE began their dime "show-store" at the Gaiety Museum (1883), local stock had largely succumbed to the touring combination companies, and variety seemed triumphant. The Boston Theatre was razed in 1928 and replaced with the B. F. Keith Memorial Theatre; intended to be vaudeville's grandest showcase, by 1929 it was a "Big Time" mausoleum, reduced to mixed bills and films. In 1978 Sarah Caldwell's Opera Company of Boston took it over, renaming it The Opera House. Caldwell's managerial irresponsibility led to the theatre's abandonment in the early 1990s.

The Broadway tryout system, pioneered at the Boston Theatre by playwright CHARLES H. HOYT for *A TRIP TO CHINATOWN* (1891), reinvigorated the city's legitimate theatre throughout most of the following century. The SHUBERTS gained a monopoly on the downtown houses by 1934, and anything playing in them was either headed for Broadway or on tour from it. They had to contend with the strictest local CENSORSHIP in the country, which was no longer solely in the hands of the amateur Watch and Ward Society, but was now enforced by an official city censor. In fact if not in name, the bureaucrat's title was "chief of the city's Licensing Division.") "Banned in Boston" became an infamous epithet; it was also, no doubt, attached to barely blue properties by wily press AGENTS. Starting in 1915, every theatrical contract signed by producers and managers had a secret rider appended that prohibited everything from lascivious language to "all forms of muscle dancing by either sex." (This rider was finally overturned by ACLU pressure in 1965.) *STRANGE INTERLUDE*'s consignment to nearby Quincy (1929) was the most notorious banning incident. The system's hypocrisy was transparent: At the "Old" Howard, strippers muscle-danced with impunity.

In the meantime, the Little Theatre movement (see COMMUNITY THEATRE) made its impact on the city. A combination of forces from Mrs. Lyman Gale's Toy Theatre (1912) and the failed Castle Square Theater, which had presented GEORGE PIERCE BAKER's Harvard prize plays (1911–17), were marshaled by Frances and Henry Jewett to form a resident company. The latter managed to construct the Repertory Theatre of Boston (1925), but Henry's death (1930) ended this endeavor.

Through the Depression and WWII, the New England Repertory and the Tributary Theatre of Boston struggled to keep local theatricals alive. A significant black company – the Boston Players, founded in 1930 – was taken over by actor Ralf Coleman later in the decade. After the demise of the local FEDERAL THEATRE PROJECT Negro Unit, he gathered several of its veterans and founded the Boston Negro Theatre, which was active through the 1940s. JEROME KILTY's Brattle Theatre Company briefly vitalized the local scene (1947–52). In 1957 Michael Murray's Charles Playhouse troupe created the first new legitimate performance space in Boston since the Jewetts' when they converted an old church into their own theatre, where they remained for 13 years. The 1960s found Harvard in Cambridge a proving ground for local artistry. Student productions of Thomas Babe and Timothy Mayer set standards that laid the groundwork for the careers of PETER SELLARS,

STOCKARD CHANNING, and many others. Across the river, DAVID WHEELER's Theatre Company of Boston gave the American premiere of Pinter's *The Dwarfs* (1966) and presented AL PACINO in *Richard III* (1973).

The 1970s were a transitional decade; by its end the tryout system was virtually dead. There were still artistically successful small theatres, most notably the Cambridge Ensemble, but many of the efforts of other experimental groups seemed forced. Encouraged by grants from a new state arts council, dozens of fringe companies indulged themselves until the Commonwealth's fiscal collapse in 1989. One small theatre that managed to survive and prosper through these years was the Lyric Stage, which celebrated its 17th season by transferring to a large new theatre (1991). In spite of the economy, there continue to be some 50 companies operating in and around Boston. The climax of the postwar era was the almost simultaneous arrival in town of two resident companies: The AMERICAN REPERTORY COMPANY (ART, 1980) and the HUNTINGTON THEATRE (1982), sponsored by Harvard and Boston University, respectively. The ART is a technically dazzling director's theatre; the Huntington reverences the dramatic text above all else. The creation of the annual ELLIOTT NORTON Award (1982), bestowed by a committee of leading local critics (until the 1990s, including Norton himself), was as much a tribute to the dean of American drama critics as a reflection of Boston's sudden rebirth as a center of regional theatre.

The first years of the 21st century saw the construction of additional playhouses for ART and the Huntington. Another local company, The New Rep, built itself a theatre in a new arts center, after performing in church halls for three decades. Nevertheless, as noncommerical theatre multiplied, Clear Channel Entertainment seemed determined to consolidate its hold on downtown theatrical enterprises. In 2004, after a massive restoration, Clear Channel reopened The Opera House, its fourth Boston acquisition.   TFC*

Boston Ideal Opera Company (The Bostonians) Comic opera company. Founded by Miss E. H. Ober in 1879 in order to present an "ideal" production of *HMS Pinafore,* the company, made up primarily of church choir singers from the Boston area, was noted for its high standards in both the singing and the mounting of comic operas. Although based in Boston, the company toured extensively. Reorganized as the Bostonians in 1887, the company announced its intention of encouraging the development of American comic opera. They launched the career of composer REGINALD DE KOVEN with their production of *Robin Hood* (1891) and performed the same service for VICTOR HERBERT with *Prince Ananias* (1894). After a defection by several members of the troupe in 1898, the company declined, ending its existence in the 1904–5 season.   MK

Boston Museum Tremont St. between Court and School Sts., Boston [Architect: Hammatt Billings, 1846]. In 1841, MOSES KIMBALL opened the Boston Museum and Gallery of Fine Arts at the corner of Tremont and Bromfield Sts. to offer a collection of curiosities to the public at a small admission charge. In combination with the museum was a "concert saloon," which in 1843 was transformed into a regular theatre with a STOCK COMPANY. In 1844, after the phenomenal success of *The DRUNKARD,* which played 100 performances, it provided a steady diet of moral plays, earning it the name of "deacon's theatre." In 1846 the entire enterprise was moved into its new building, and under a succession of astute managers, particularly R. M. Field, it housed the finest dramatic corps in America during the 1860s and '70s. Its most distinguished member, WILLIAM WARREN THE YOUNGER, spent almost his entire career (1847–82) with it. The company was disbanded in 1894, and the theatre fell into the Theatrical SYNDICATE's hands until it was razed in 1903.   MCH

Boston Theatre Designed by architect H. Noury and erected on Washington St. in 1854 through public subscription in response to the closing of the FEDERAL STREET and TREMONT theatres; DION BOUCICAULT called it "the finest theatre in the world." A technical showplace, its seating capacity of 3,140 made it the largest theatre in the country. EDWIN BOOTH made his first starring appearance there (1857), and JOSEPH JEFFERSON III first played RIP VAN WINKLE there (1869). By 1885 the theatre's well-regarded STOCK COMPANY operated independently and spent most of its time touring New England; it dissolved sometime in the late 1890s. B. F. KEITH turned the theatre into a vaudeville and motion picture house after 1909. Sixteen years later it was torn down to make way for the B. F. Keith Memorial Theatre.   TFC

Both Your Houses A political farce by MAXWELL ANDERSON, produced by the THEATRE GUILD on 6 March 1933 and directed by Worthington Miner. The production closed after 72 performances, but reopened on 12 June for 48 performances after its Pulitzer Prize was announced. The action hinges on the passage of an outlandish appropriations bill through Congress that pitted Sheppard Strudwick's idealistic freshman Congressman against the corrupted old guard, an ensemble distinguished by Walter C. Kelly's aging politico. The scenario was a plausible representation of contemporary congressional politics. The dramaturgical machinery is apparent, but the dialogue is sharp and inspiring.   MR

Boucicault, Dion(ysius) (Lardner) (1820–90) Playwright, actor, and manager. Born in Ireland, Boucicault had a substantial reputation in English theatres before coming to America in 1853 as manager of the popular actress AGNES ROBERTSON (1833–1916), his second wife (although he disclaimed the legitimacy of this marriage when he married Louise Thorndyke in 1885). Of the Boucicault children, **Darley George** ("Dot"; 1859–1929) acted in American, Australian, and English theatres, and **Aubrey** (1869–1919) had a minor reputation on the English stage.

A month after landing in New York, this author of at least 22 plays, including *London Assurance* (1841), revealed his great energy by starring Miss Robertson in *The Young Actress,* his version of Edward Lancaster's *The Manager's Daughter.* During that fall season of 1853 New Yorkers saw seven plays by Boucicault. Before returning to England in 1860, Boucicault wrote 30 plays, 7 of which were published. He lectured, although without great success, toured his theatre company frequently, and managed theatres in New Orleans (1855), Washington, DC (1858), and New York (1859). He also expedited the enactment of a U.S. copyright law that gave playwrights "along with the right to present and publish the said composition, the sole right to act, perform or represent the same" (18 April 1856). His major contribution to American drama during these years is shown in two distinctive efforts: *The POOR OF NEW YORK* (1857) and *The OCTOROON* (1859).

During 1860–72 Boucicault lived in England and wrote at least 22 plays, the most important one for Americans being a rewrite of *RIP VAN WINKLE* (1865) for JOSEPH JEFFERSON III. His return to America in 1872 marked the beginning of a period during which he crossed the Atlantic a number of times. From 1877 to 1889 he published 13 essays in the *North American Review;* these explain his dramaturgy and are a major contribution to dramatic theory in America. A master of visual, aural, and theatrical effects, Boucicault pandered to popular tastes for his triumphant success in both England and America during 1855–75. Changes of taste left him confused, and

his popularity declined during the last years of his life. For bios of Boucicault, see R. Hogan (1969) and F. Fawkes (1979).   WJM

Bowery Theatre 46–48 The Bowery, NYC [Architect: Ithiel Town; John Trimble]. When a sprinkling of wealthy and fashionable New York families began to settle near the Bowery, the link to the Boston Post Road, they decided to erect a playhouse more conveniently located for them than the PARK THEATRE. Pledging money and buying land on which Henry Astor's tavern had stood, they erected what came to be known as the Bowery Theatre, although it passed through a succession of names. Superior to the Park in appearance, both inside and out, it presented several seasons of drama, opera and ballet before its audience left it to return to the older house. In 1830, THOMAS S. HAMBLIN secured its lease and, for the next 20 years, dominated its policies. Hamblin's tenure included the high-water years for the playhouse, during which the greatest names of the American theatre (J. B. BOOTH, EDWIN FORREST, the WALLACKS, LOUISA LANE DREW, FRANK CHANFRAU) appeared on its stage. Hamblin eventually bought the theatre, but bad times forced him to lose it. A succession of managers followed, who presented spectacle and melodrama to please the neighborhood.

The district surrounding the theatre became the haven for the newly arriving immigrant groups who poured into New York at midcentury, and the theatre began increasingly to reflect the new populations of the area, becoming the temple of entertainment for New York's Lower East Side. Until 1879 the dramatic fare was in English; thereafter it passed to German acting troupes, who renamed it the THALIA; then to Yiddish performers in 1891; next to Italian vaudevillians; and finally to Chinese vaudeville, which was playing at the time of its fiery demise (1929). It had had a series of fires and been rebuilt several times previously (1828, 1836, 1838, 1845; see FIRES), and each reconstruction had carried it further away from its original neoclassical facade into a strange mixture of architectural styles.   MCH

Boys from Syracuse, The Two-act musical comedy, music by RICHARD RODGERS, lyrics by LORENZ HART, book by GEORGE ABBOTT; opened 23 November 1938 at the ALVIN THEATRE, NYC, running 235 performances. A musical version of *The Comedy of Errors,* this fast-paced, bawdy romp was the first musical-comedy adaptation of SHAKESPEARE. Chosen largely to trade on a striking resemblance between Hart's bother, Teddy, and comedian Jimmy Savo (the two played the twin Dromios), Shakespeare's plot is closely followed, though laced with anachronism, contemporary slang, and such Rodgers and Hart classics as "This Can't Be Love" and "Falling in Love with Love." A 1963 Off-Broadway revival ran for 502 performances, proving the durability of the piece. In 2002 NICKY SILVER was commissioned to update Abbott's book.   JD

Boys in the Band, The, by Mart Crowley was one of the first frank treatments of homosexuality in mainstream theatre (see GAY AND LESBIAN THEATRE). Combining sharp humor with emotional revelation, this portrait of a birthday party turned vicious opened OFF-BROADWAY 14 April 1968 at Theatre Four, after having been produced by the Playwrights Unit, Vandam Theatre, in January 1968. It ran for 1,000 performances, traveled to London, and subsequently received numerous productions throughout the U.S. and Europe. A film version was released in 1970.   KF

Brackenridge, Hugh H(enry) (1748–1815) Author and playwright. Writing for his students at Maryland Academy, he did not consider his plays – *The Battle of Bunker's-Hill* and *The Death of General Montgomery in Storming the City of Quebec* (1777) – finished dramas. Both plays, composed in blank verse, emphasize patriotic virtue and stress the strong emotional qualities that characterized much of Brackenridge's writing. As teacher, judge, legislator, and chaplain in Washington's army, Brackenridge exhibited a belief in persuasive oratory in writing and a sense of mission. A bio by C. Newlin was published in 1932.   WJM

Brady, Alice (1892–1939) Stage and film actress and singer. Making her New York debut as a chorus girl in *The Mikado* at 18, she appeared in major GILBERT AND SULLIVAN roles for the next two years, then as Meg in *Little Women* (1912). After 32 films (1914–23), in 1928 she joined the THEATRE GUILD; her most memorable stage role was as Lavinia in O'NEILL's MOURNING BECOMES ELECTRA.   SMA

Brady, William A(loysius) (1863–1950) American manager and producer. Born in San Francisco, Brady made his first stage appearance in 1882, and his debut as a producer in 1888. He purchased the rights to *After Dark* from DION BOUCICAULT in 1899 and presented it at the BOWERY THEATRE. AUGUSTIN DALY sued him for plagiarizing the locomotive scene from *UNDER THE GASLIGHT;* Brady eventually lost, but attained publicity by

hiring prizefighter James J. Corbett to appear in the cast and later featuring him in several vehicles. In 1896 he leased the Manhattan Theatre, where he enjoyed several successes, including *WAY DOWN EAST* in 1898. A year later he married actress GRACE GEORGE and promoted her career. She opened his Playhouse in 1911 with *Sauce for the Goose,* and later appeared in *The School for Scandal* and SHAW's *Major Barbara.* Brady managed the careers of numerous players, including his wife and his daughter, ALICE. His more than 260 productions included *STREET SCENE* (1929), which ran for 600 performances and won a Pulitzer. Also a sports promoter and film pioneer, Brady was recognized as a "born gambler" with an "uncanny instinct for drama." Brady's memoir, *Showman,* was published in 1937.   TLM

Bragdon, Claude (1866–1946) A self-trained architect, Bragdon did not enter the theatre until 1919 as a designer for WALTER HAMPDEN's productions. Though he worked for no one else, Bragdon's simplified settings and experiments with light were a major influence on the development of the New Stagecraft. Even before entering the theatre Bragdon worked on the development of what he called "color music" – an art form consisting primarily of light and sound. He produced several "Song and Light" shows in the mid-1910s, including one in New York's Central Park that attracted 150,000 spectators over five nights.   AA

Branch, William (1927–) African American writer of protest plays beginning in the early 1950s. In *A Medal for Willie* (1951), a southern black woman rejects the medal posthumously awarded to her soldier son. In *Splendid Error* (1954) abolitionist Frederick Douglass questions his reluctance to support the rebellion when he learns of John Brown's heroic sacrifice at Harper's Ferry. Branch has written other dramas about black leaders for the stage, television, and screen.   EGH

Brando, Marlon (1924–2004) Although his major reputation came from his work as a film actor (*A Streetcar Named Desire, On the Waterfront, The Godfather*), it was as Stanley Kowalski in ELIA KAZAN's stage production of TENNESSEE WILLIAMS's *A STREETCAR NAMED DESIRE* (1947), his final theatre role, that Brando first made his mark as an actor of moody intensity. Among his other limited stage appearances were *I REMEMBER MAMA* (1944), *Truckline Cafe* (1946), and *Candida* (1947). His style is often seen as the most famous product of the ACTORS STUDIO. Brando's autobiography was

Bread and Puppet Theatre in *What You Possess,* 1990. Photo by Tony D'Urso. *Courtesy:* Don B. Wilmeth Theatre Collection.

published in 1994. In the 1990s several biographies appeared, notably by Manso and Schickel; in 2005 Brando's novel *Fan-Tan* was published posthumously.   MBan

Brantley, Ben [Benjamin D.] (1955–) A North Carolina native and Swarthmore graduate, he became chief theatre critic for the *New York Times* in 1996, having been a drama critic there since 1993. Noted for his clear, graceful, witty, and knowledgeable criticism, Brantley succeeded VINCENT CANBY, and had previously been a staff writer for *Vanity Fair* (1987–92) and *The New Yorker* (1992–3) and film critic for *Elle* (1988–93). He edited (2001) *The New York Times Book of Broadway.* In 1997 he shared the GEORGE JEAN NATHAN Award for Dramatic Criticism with Elinor Fuchs and Todd London. There is some belief that, with the advent and growth of the Internet, coupled with the proliferation of marketing platforms for Broadway, there has been a diminution of theatre coverage over the past half-decade in the *Times,* and thus that Brantley's power is now less than that of previous chief critics there.   TLM

Bread and Puppet Theatre Founded in New York in 1961 by Peter Schumann, who had previously organized the New Dance Group in Germany, Bread and Puppet has never been an orthodox group in manning, finance, or artistic policy. Not an ensemble but a loose association of performers under Schumann's firm direction, and supple-

mented as needed by amateurs, the company has so mistrusted the idea of purchasing entertainment that, whenever possible, it offers its services free. This principle is based on its founder's maxim, "theatre is like bread, more like a necessity" – an axiom enacted literally in the course of each performance by the giving of bread to the audience. Deeply involved in the contemporary reaction against what is perceived as the over-intellectualization of Western culture, as epitomized in its powerful tradition of literary theatre, Schumann and his associates work with larger-than-life puppets to create a nonnarrative theatre that addresses contemporary issues – such as the Vietnam War – through disturbing visual images rather than words. In performances such as "The Cry of the People for Meat" and "The Domestic Resurrection Circus" (the latter presented each summer since 1974), religious iconography and political message are combined in an attempt to offer a critique of contemporary society in terms of its own values. After a four-year residence at Goddard College, in 1974 Schumann moved to a farm near Glover, VT, where the company has continued to regroup for summer festivals (in 1993 a new structure was erected for modest winter productions), and for specific tours and commissions, such as the 1975 "Anti-Bicentennial" at the University of California – an angry and moving elegy to the last Indian survivor of white genocide in the state; productions of scripted plays such as Büchner's *Woyzeck* (New York, 1981); and

tours in 1990 of Europe and Russia with *Uprising of the Beast*. In 1994, a production protesting the World Bank, *Mr. Budhoo's Letter of Resignation,* evolved, seen in New York (THEATRE FOR THE NEW CITY) in 1996 in a later form; reappearing there in 2001 with *The Insurrection Mass with Funeral March for a Rotten Idea: A Special Mass for the Aftermath of the Events of Sept. 11.* Stefan Brecht has written a history of the company up to 1988.   AEG
   DBW

Brecht in the American theatre Bertolt Brecht was a preeminent German dramatist, director, and poet whose plays, performance style, and theory of epic theatre have influenced Western theatre, primarily since WWII. In the early 1920s he developed the anti-illusionistic staging techniques evident in his highly successful *Die Dreigroschenoper* (1928, music by KURT WEILL; trans. as *The Threepenny Opera*) in Berlin. Influenced by the work of ERWIN PISCATOR, Brecht's *Verfremdungseffekt* or "alienation effect" in acting and his theory of "non-Aristotelian" drama continue to stimulate intellectual debate. Brecht's concept of epic theatre has had an impact on American left-wing theatre and even in the staging by musical theatre directors such as HAL PRINCE.

The 1933 New York premiere of *Threepenny Opera* at the EMPIRE THEATRE was unsuccessful. Brecht first visited the U.S. during October–December 1935 when his play *Mother* was produced by the New York THEATRE UNION at the CIVIC REPERTORY THEATRE. Fleeing Nazi Germany in 1933, Brecht lived in Denmark, Sweden, Finland, and finally the U.S. Many of his major works were written in exile, including *Mother Courage and Her Children* (1938–9), *The Good Woman of Setzuan* (1938–40), and *The Caucasian Chalk Circle* (1944–5). He arrived in California in July of 1941 and settled in Santa Monica, where he worked on at least 50 film projects, mostly with other German refugees (Fritz Lang, Lion Feuchtwanger, Peter Lorre, Ferdinand Reyher), but received little recognition from Hollywood. *Hangmen Also Die* (1942), written for director Fritz Lang, was his only success. Intended for Broadway, Brecht's *The Caucasian Chalk Circle* remained unproduced during his American years. Unwilling to compromise in his writing to the tastes of Broadway, he was unsuccessful in collaborative efforts in New York, even with Erwin Piscator, who on several occasions expressed interest in producing his works. In 1945 Berthold Viertel directed *The Private Life of the Master Race,* in Brecht's first New York production, at City College's Pauline Edwards Theatre. The production, panned by reviewers, was apparently doomed by barely intelligible German accents, and rehearsals consumed by Brecht elaborating on his acting theories with cast and director. *Galileo* opened in Hollywood in July 1947 with CHARLES LAUGHTON and moved to New York in December. Brecht appeared before the House Un-American Activities Committee one day before leaving the U.S. for Zurich on 31 October 1947. After his return to East Berlin in 1949 and the founding of the Berliner Ensemble at the Theater am Schiffbauerdamm with Helene Weigel, Brecht's "model" productions acquired an international reputation and were produced throughout the world. In 1954 MARC BLITZSTEIN's New York production of *The Threepenny Opera* with LOTTE LENYA popularized Brecht's name in America, but it was primarily through the translation of his major plays and theory by ERIC BENTLEY that Brecht became well known and frequently produced in university and regional theatres in the U.S., especially during the 1960s and '70s. Brecht's major plays continue to be seen; his work with Weill remains popular, including *Threepenny Opera* (most recently an adaptation by WALLACE SHAWN produced by ROUNDABOUT, 2006) and *Happy End.* J. K. Lyon's 1980 book on Brecht in America provides a useful overview.   RE

Breuer, Lee (1937–) Actor, playwright, director, and founding member of the avant-garde theatre company MABOU MINES, for which he has created more than 25 works. Breuer, who calls himself a "reluctant radical," began his career in the early 1960s with the SAN FRANCISCO ACTORS' Workshop, moving to Europe in 1965 to study with the Berliner Ensemble and the Polish Theatre Lab. For Mabou Mines he served as director, author, adapter, producer, and performer. His staging and adaptation of Beckett's work has won him acclaim. His trilogy *Animations* (*The RED HORSE* [1970], *The B. Beaver* [1974] and *The Shaggy Dog* [1978]) was published in 1979, and *Sister Suzie Cinema* (PUBLIC THEATER, 1980) in 1986. In 1988 he wrote and directed a gender-reversed adaptation of *King Lear* with former wife RUTH MALECZECH as Lear. Outside Mabou Mines his most notable effort has been *The Gospel at Colonus* (1983), which he conceived, adapted, and directed for the BROOKLYN ACADEMY OF MUSIC's Next Wave Festival (performed later at Broadway's LUNT–FONTANNE, Washington's ARENA STAGE, in San Francisco, and, for its 1,000th performance in the U.S., at Carnegie Hall in 1996). Also at BAM's Next Wave was *The Warrior Ant* (1988), heard first in concert at LINCOLN CENTER in 1986. In the 1980s, while serving as director of the directing program at the Yale School of Drama, his focus was on creating a new theatre that merges Asian and African arts with American performance techniques. *MahabharANTa* (1992), a satiric look at American cultural conflicts, owed its focus to the influence of Balinese shadow-puppet theatre. Recent work includes his musical, puppet version of *Peter Pan,* called *Peter and Wendy* (adapted by Liza Lorwin; music by Johnny Cunningham), which won two Obie Awards and played successfully at the New Victory Theatre in 1997 (revived 2002); *Animal Magnetisim* (2000), with live events onstage interacting in sync with computer animation; and his 2003 controversial *DollHouse,* a version of IBSEN's *A Doll's House* that, as critic Len Jenkins noted, "requires the audience to filter the dialogue through altered perceptions of power, status and scale" by using actors shorter than four and a half feet in the male roles, whereas the women were exceptionally tall, thus creating a "dizzying visual commentary on sexual politics." First seen at St. Ann's Warehouse in Brooklyn, it won 2 Obies, was part of the 2005 SPOLETO FESTIVAL, USA, and toured widely. In 1997 Breuer received a MacArthur ("genius") Fellowship.   DBW

Brice, Fanny (Fannie) [née Frances Borach] (1891–1951) Comedienne and singer whose gawky walk, repertoire of comic faces, and ability to sing both satiric and serious songs with equal success made her a star of REVUES for over a quarter of a century. After serving an apprenticeship in amateur shows and burlesque, Brice appeared in ZIEGFELD's *Follies of 1910.* She remained with the *Follies* for six more editions through 1923, then switched to IRVING BERLIN's *MUSIC BOX Revue* (1924). An attempt to star in a book musical, *Fioretta* (1929), was a failure. Brice appeared in four more revues: *Sweet and Low* (1930), *Billy Rose's Crazy Quilt* (1931), and two editions of *The Ziegfeld Follies* (1934, 1936) produced by the SHUBERTS after Ziegfeld's death. In most of her songs and sketches Brice affected a Yiddish accent that heightened her satirical treatment of such subjects as the ballet and silent film "vamps." The musical *FUNNY GIRL* is loosely based on portions of Brice's career, recently reexplored by Grossman (1991) and Herbert Goldman (1992).   MK

Brig, The, by Kenneth H. Brown. This LIVING THEATRE production, directed by Judith Malina and designed by Julian Beck, opened 15 May 1963 for 239 performances. The nonplay, with nondialogue and noncharacters, set in a Marine prison in 1957, details the brutal routine of one day. Critics loathed its impersonal violence, based on Brown's own experience, but the play toured Europe, was made into a film, and aired on U.S. and Canadian television.   REK

Brigadoon Two-act musical with book and lyrics by ALAN JAY LERNER and music by FREDERICK LOEWE; opened at Broadway's ZIEGFELD THEATRE (13 March 1947) and ran for 581 performances, winning the Drama Critics' Circle Award for Best Musical. It was revived six times at the New York City Center, and once at the MAJESTIC THEATRE, a 133-performance run beginning 16 October 1980. Originally staged by ROBERT LEWIS and choreographed by AGNES DE MILLE (Tony Award), this romantic, escapist fantasy is set in the 18th-century Scottish village of Brigadoon, which magically remains untouched since it appears only once a century. With its well-integrated lyrical dialogue, songs, instrumentation, and dance, *Brigadoon* charmed postwar audiences and critics. Its songs include "Heather on the Hill" and "Almost Like Being in Love."   EK

Brighton Beach Memoirs by NEIL SIMON opened on 27 March 1983 at the ALVIN THEATRE for 1,530 performances. Simon's return to semiautobiography, this first episode in the "Brighton Beach trilogy" relates the early adolescence of Eugene Morris Jerome (i.e., Simon; played by MATTHEW BRODERICK, Tony Award) as Depression-era stress shifts to that of pre-WWII. The play balances employment ordeals of the father, Jack, and elder brother, Stanley, along with Eugene's adolescent anxieties, against the repressed rivalry of the mother, Kate, and her boarding sister, Blanche. Continuing Simon's theme of moderation, the play suggests the nurturing aspect of a family can stifle if carried to excess.   RW

Bring in 'da Noise, Bring in 'da Funk Conceived by director GEORGE C. WOLFE and tap dancer-choreographer SAVION GLOVER and produced by the NEW YORK SHAKESPEARE FESTIVAL in 1995, the show virtually defied definition – not quite a revue, not a book musical, and not a play, it was described as a "performance piece." In April 1996 it transferred to Broadway's AMBASSADOR THEATRE, where it ran for 1,130 official performances, gave a mainstream audience a history lesson on the African American experience via tap dancing – performed with raw energy – and, as historian Laurence Maslon states, brought "an urban, hip-hop-inflected sound to Broadway," earning Wolfe a Tony for Best Director of a Musical and making Glover (Tony, Best Choreography) a star.   DBW

Brisson, Frederick (1913–84) Producer. Danish-born and English-educated, Brisson worked in Europe before emigrating to the U.S. in the late 1930s. After WWII, he began producing musicals and light comedy on Broadway, either independently or with various partners; these included *The Pajama Game* (1954), *Damn Yankees* (1955), *New Girl in Town* (1957), *The Pleasure of His Company* (1958), *Under the Yum Yum Tree* (1960), *Generation* (1965), *Coco* (1969), and *Twigs* (1971). However, Brisson also challenged Broadway audiences with Peter Shaffer's *Five Finger Exercise* (1959), Harold Pinter's *The Caretaker* (1962), and Tom Stoppard's *Jumpers* (1974).   TLM

Broadhurst, George H(owells) (1866–1952) London-born playwright and theatre manager who emigrated to America in 1886 and managed several regional theatres before gaining some success in New York with farce-comedies – *What Happened to Jones* (1897) and *Why Smith Left Home* (1899). Primarily concerned with commercial theatre, Broadhurst made his best contribution to American drama with *The Man of the Hour* (1906), a melodrama about a young mayor who successfully resists organized political corruption, and *Bought and Paid For* (1911), which exploits the problems of a wealthy, self-made man who counts his wife among his possessions. One of the better writers of social melodrama before WWI, Broadhurst produced a number of successful plays and eventually became known for his light musical comedies. In 1918 a new Broadway venue was named the BROADHURST THEATRE in his honor.   WJM

Broadhurst Theatre 235 West 44th St., NYC [Architect: HERBERT J. KRAPP]. Continuing their custom to name playhouses after prominent theatrical personages, the SHUBERTS opened another of their 1917-built theatres in honor of GEORGE BROADHURST, an English-born playwright, who enjoyed fleeting fame as the author of a string of successful modern melodramas. Broadhurst also often produced his own plays and managed the house in tandem with the Shuberts. Seating about 1,200, its policy has alternated between musicals and dramas. Among its more successful tenants have been *BEGGAR ON HORSEBACK* (1924), *The Green Hat* (with the young KATHARINE CORNELL; 1925), *BROADWAY* (1926), *MEN IN WHITE* (1933), *The PETRIFIED FOREST* (1935), *Victoria Regina* (with HELEN HAYES) (1936), and the musicals *FIORELLO!* (1959), *CABARET* (1967), *Kiss of the Spider Woman* (1993), *Fosse* (1999), and *The History Boys* (2006). It remains a Shubert theatre.   MCH

Broadway by Philip Dunning and GEORGE ABBOTT is a wise-cracking, fast-paced melodrama of nightclub life that opened 9 September 1926 and ran for 601 performances, grossing more than $2 million for its youthful producer, JED HARRIS. The play's volatile combination of both deadly and clownish gangsters, hard-boiled chorus girls, sly cops, contemporary street slang, onstage violence, and the triumph of true love proved a lasting contribution to American popular theatre, setting a pattern repeated by Harris with *The FRONT PAGE* (1928) and by Abbott in *THREE MEN ON A HORSE* (1935). Film versions of *Broadway* were produced in 1929 and 1942.   MF

Broadway, Off- and Off-Off see OFF-BROADWAY and OFF-OFF BROADWAY

Broadway Bound The conclusion of NEIL SIMON's "Brighton Beach trilogy"; opened at the BROADHURST THEATRE on 4 December 1986, running for 756 performances. The semiautobiographical play returns young Eugene Morris Jerome (Simon) to Brighton Beach after WWII. The rising radio-comedy-writing careers of Eugene and his brother, Stanley – a close parallel to Simon's – is balanced against the disintegration of their parents' and grandparents' marriages. The brothers' success lies in the way their strengths complement the other's weaknesses. Each of the marital failures illustrates Simon's thematic involvement with the results of extreme behavior and unwillingness to compromise. A TV version, broadcast in March 1992, included Jonathan Silverman (from the Broadway cast), ANNE BANCROFT, JERRY ORBACH, and HUME CRONYN.   RW

Broadway Theatre Name borne by a succession of New York playhouses (see also DALY'S).

1. 356–8 Broadway, NYC [Architect: John M. Trimble]. The first important New York theatre to bear the name, this Broadway Theatre was modeled on London's Haymarket, and with 4,500 seats was the largest theatre built before 1847, when it opened its doors. Intended to replace the PARK THEATRE in public favor, it never achieved the prominence of the earlier theatre, although many stars appeared on its stage. It was torn down in 1859.

2. Broadway and 41st St., NYC [Architect: J. B. McElfatrick and Co.]. Built in 1888 when 41st St. was still "uptown" for the rest of the city, it was dedicated to musical comedy, operetta, and spectacle. Later, when the new theatre district began to coalesce around 42d St., the theatre was assimilated within its borders. Both EDWIN BOOTH and

Sir Henry Irving made final appearances in New York at the Broadway. Too large for the later dramatic and musical fare, it was used for motion pictures and vaudeville before being torn down in 1929.

3. 1681 Broadway, NYC [Architect: Eugene De Rosa]. Opened as B. S. Moss's Colony Theatre in 1924, the playhouse seesawed between plays and movies for more than 25 years. Renamed the Broadway in 1930, it is a large 1,800-seat house, well suited for musicals. Among its outstanding tenants have been *This Is the Army* (1942), LADY IN THE DARK (1943), GYPSY (1959), EVITA (1979), LES MISÉRABLES (1987), and MISS SAIGON (1991). Since 1943, it has been a SHUBERT theatre.   MCH

Broderick, Matthew (1962–) His onstage alter ego described by Ben Brantley as the "Cinderella schlemiel," this seemingly ageless actor-singer, son of actor James Broderick and writer-producer Patricia Broderick and married since 1997 to actress Sarah Jessica Parker, began to establish his "type" in 1981 as the precocious gay teenager in FIERSTEIN's TORCH SONG TRILOGY. His career accelerated with roles in NEIL SIMON's BRIGHTON BEACH MEMOIRS (1983; Tony, Best Featured Actor) and BILOXI BLUES (1985). His successes continued as J. Pierpont Finch in the 1995 revival of HOW TO SUCCEED IN BUSINESS WITHOUT REALLY TRYING (Tony); the fascinating psychopath in *Night Must Fall* (1999); the proper Brit in SHUE's THE FOREIGNER (2004); and the obsessively tidy Felix Ungar opposite NATHAN LANE's Oscar in the 2005 revival of *The Odd Couple*. His performance as the inhibited accountant Leopold Bloom, also costarring Lane, in THE PRODUCERS (2001) has been his biggest hit to date.   DBW

Brokaw, Mark (1959?–) Emerging during the past decade as a much sought after and effective director, the Yale-trained artist has demonstrated a proclivity for thought-provoking contemporary work and staging technique notable for fluid scene changes and minimal scenery, beginning with the 1991 SECOND STAGE production of Lynda Barry's *The Good Times Are Killing Me*. Since then he has found kindred spirits with such playwrights as Douglas Carter Beane (*As Bees in Honey Drown*) at the DRAMA DEPT., PAULA VOGEL (*How I Learned to Drive, The Long Christmas Ride Home*), CRAIG LUCAS (*The Dying Gaul;* revival of *Reckless*), and KENNETH LONERGAN (*This Is Our Youth*); such New York companies as Second Stage, MANHATTAN THEATRE CLUB, VINEYARD THEATRE, PLAYWRIGHTS HORIZONS, LINCOLN CENTER, and the PUBLIC THEATER; and regional and international theatres ranging from Boston's HUNTINGTON, to Dublin's Gate Theatre, the GUTHRIE, MARK TAPER FORUM, STEPPENWOLF, SEATTLE REP, the LONG WHARF, HARTFORD STAGE, and BERKELEY REP.   DBW

Brooklyn Academy of Music (BAM) Incorporated in 1859, the original 1861 theatre on Montague St. burned down in 1903 (see FIRES). Herts and Tallant's 1908 replacement, a neo-Renaissance building with four auditoriums at 30 Lafayette St., was the first multiple-theatre facility in the U.S. Then as now BAM was a center for all the performing arts. In its heyday, opera singers Nellie Melba and Marian Anderson played there, as did conductor Arturo Toscanini, violinist Jascha Heifetz, dancers Ruth St. Denis and Ted Shawn, and many others.

Under the former direction of Harvey Lichtenstein, BAM became an energetic and resourceful not-for-profit presenting organization and an anchor of urban renewal in downtown Brooklyn. In addition to traditional arts groups such as the Brooklyn Philharmonic and visiting theatre, opera, and dance troupes, Lichtenstein housed three legitimate theatre companies: the Chelsea Theatre (1968–78), the BAM Theatre Company (1977–9 under Frank Dunlop; 1979–81 under David Hugh Jones), and the DODGER Theatre (1978–80). A friend of experimental arts, during the 1970s Lichtenstein began to present ROBERT WILSON, the LIVING THEATRE, and the BREAD AND PUPPET THEATRE, among other theatrical pioneers. Since 1983, BAM's premier program has been its Next Wave Festival, a prestigious, vanguard arts showcase featuring an international roster of progressive dance, music, theatre, and performance artists.

In 1999 Lichtenstein stepped down (becoming chair of the BAM Local Development Corp.) and was replaced by Karen Brooks Hopkins (president) and Joseph V. Melillo (executive producer). In recent years BAM has become the catalyst for other new arts facilities in Brooklyn, including a 299-seat theatre and a 50-seat black box on a lot adjacent to BAM (groundbreaking, 2007), the permanent home of THEATRE FOR A NEW AUDIENCE (founded 1979); the Mark Morris Dance Studio; the BAM Harvey Theater (a remodeled 1904 vaudeville house, the Majestic); and a rehearsal/administrative facility for small theatre companies. Under Melillo, the Next Wave Festival was reinvigorated in 2003 after several years of stagnation.   CLJ

Brooks Atkinson Theatre 256 West 47th St., NYC [Architect: HERBERT J. KRAPP]. When it opened in 1926, the third of the Chanin-built theatres was named after RICHARD MANSFIELD, one of the outstanding actors of a previous generation. After the playhouse reverted to the mortgage company early in the Depression, it was leased to a succession of managements. In 1931, the GROUP THEATRE launched its initial venture, *The HOUSE OF CONNELLY*, from its stage. In 1944, the theatre was sold to Michael Myerberg, who subsequently leased it to CBS-TV during 1950–60. Thereafter, it was returned to legitimate use and renamed the BROOKS ATKINSON after the recently retired and revered *New York Times* drama critic. In 1964, TALLULAH BANKHEAD made her final stage appearance, in *The Milk Train Doesn't Stop Here Anymore,* from its stage. Three years later, the theatre passed to the control of the NEDERLANDER Organization. In 1975, the comedy *Same Time, Next Year* became its longest-running tenant, playing three years. In 1999 the critically acclaimed revival of *The Iceman Cometh* with KEVIN SPACEY (Tony for Best Leading Actor) arrived from London.   MCH

Brougham, John (1810–80) Irish American playwright and actor whose reputation rests principally on his outlandish Indian burlesques: *PO-CA-HON-TAS; OR, THE GENTLE SAVAGE* (1855), "An Original Aboriginal Erratic Operatic Semi-Civilized and Demi-Savage Extravaganza," and *Metamora; or, The Last of the Pollywogs* (1857), in which he poked fun at the stage version of the "noble savage," particularly that of EDWIN FORREST in *METAMORA; OR, THE LAST OF THE WAMPANOAGS.* Brougham had a facile pen – too facile, he once admitted. He wrote 126 wide-ranging pieces – adaptations (*Dombey and Son*, 1848), Gothic melodrama (*The Gunmaker of Moscow,* 1857), tearful melodrama (*Night and Morning,* 1855), sensational melodrama (*The Lottery of Life,* 1868), and social satire (*The Game of Love,* 1856) – but never with any "gall in his ink," according to one critic. As principal actor in most of his pieces, he was praised for his joviality, versatility, topical interpolations, and impromptu "before-the-curtain" speeches.

Born in Dublin, Brougham performed in amateur theatricals at Trinity College, appeared at London's Olympic (1830, with Madame Vestris) and at Covent Garden; leased the Lyceum (1840); came to America (1842), appearing at the PARK and touring the country; became stage manager at BURTON'S CHAMBERS STREET THEATRE (1848); had two flings at management (at Brougham's Broadway Lyceum [1850–2] and the old BOWERY [1856–7]); and was employed as actor-playwright at WALLACK'S for seven seasons – "the brightest part of my artist's life," he reported. He spent the Civil War years in London, returning in 1865 to continue as actor-playwright at the WINTER GARDEN and at DALY'S FIFTH AVENUE THEATRE. William Winter's life of Brougham was published in 1881.   RM

Broun, Heywood (1888–1939) Drama critic and columnist. Born in Brooklyn, Broun attended Harvard before pursuing a career in journalism on the *Morning Telegraph* (1910–11) and the *New York Tribune* (1911–21), including a short stint as drama critic (1915–16). For the *Tribune* he was war correspondent (1917) and literary editor (1918–21) before joining the *New York World* (1921); there he wrote on all subjects, including the theatre, and established his reputation as an important liberal voice. His vigorous defense of Sacco and Vanzetti (1927) cost him his job. Syndicated by Scripps–Howard newspapers during 1928–39, Broun's column remained committed to concerns of the political Left. He was fired in 1939 after successfully establishing the American Newspaper Guild. Broun was a member of the Algonquin Round Table, the author of 13 books, and the father of actor and author Heywood Hale Broun. Broun's biography was written by Richard O'Conner (1975).   TLM

Brown, Arvin (1940–) Artistic director of the LONG WHARF THEATRE during 1967–97. His first production there was LONG DAY'S JOURNEY INTO NIGHT (1966). Among his many Long Wharf productions that have enjoyed transfers to Broadway, *The National Health* (by Peter Nichols, 1974), AMERICAN BUFFALO (1983), and *A VIEW FROM THE BRIDGE* (1983) all received nominations before *A Day in the Death of Joe Egg* (Nichols, 1985) and *ALL MY SONS* (1987) earned their Tony Awards for Best Revival. Brown received the 1992 Stage Directors and Choreographers Foundations's "Mr. ABBOTT" Award, the first recipient to have worked primarily in resident nonprofit theatre. He has directed and lectured around the U.S. and worldwide. Since leaving Long Wharf he has done extensive television directing (*The Gin Game*, PBS, 2003, with Dick Van Dyke and Mary Tyler Moore) and some film. He was married to actress Joyce Ebert, who died in 1997.   MR

Brown, Blair (1946–) Diminutive, auburn-haired actor and director, born in Washington, DC. Although best known as the mid-30s divorced Molly in TV's *The Days and Nights of Molly Dodd* (1987–91), she has had strong stage credits since her Broadway debut in 1976's *Threepenny Opera* (Lucy Brown) at Lincoln Center, including Isobel Glass in *The Secret Rapture* (1989), Hannah Jarvis in

Arcadia (1995), Fraulein Schneider (replacement) in the CABARET revival (1998), Gretta Conroy in *James Joyce's The Dead* (2000), and most notably as Margrethe Bohr in *Copenhagen* (2000, Tony for Best Featured Actress). In 2005 she played Flora Humble in the American premiere of *Humble Boy* (MANHATTAN THEATRE CLUB) and directed Leslie Ayvazian's *Lovely Day* Off-Broadway.   DBW

Brown, Jason Robert (1970–) Composer and lyricist educated at the Eastman School of Music who first gained national recognition as composer and lyricist for *Parade* (1998; Tony), with a book (also Tony) by ALFRED UHRY. Its limited run at the VIVIAN BEAUMONT THEATRE (85 performances), however, was disappointing. Brown's first musical (Off-Broadway) was *Songs for a New World* in 1995, directed by HAL PRINCE's daughter, Daisy. She championed Brown's next work, a critically acclaimed, two-character musical entitled *The Last Five Years* (2001). This was followed in 2003 by *Urban Cowboy* (60 performances), which he wrote with several others; it too failed to provide the major breakthrough desired for Brown's career. He is still, though, a much sought after arranger-conductor and composer of incidental music. DBW

Brown, John Mason (1900–69) Drama critic. Educated at Harvard, Brown began his journalistic career on the *Louisville Courier-Journal* in 1917. During 1923–4 he reported on the European theatre for Boston and Louisville newspapers before becoming associate editor and drama critic for *THEATRE ARTS MONTHLY* (1924–8). In 1929 Brown moved to the *New York Evening Post* and established his column "Two on the Aisle," which remained popular throughout the 1930s. In 1941 Brown accepted a similar position on the *New York World-Telegram,* but the outbreak of the war prompted him to join the Navy in 1942. Two years later he became associate editor and drama critic of *Saturday Review,* where his column "Seeing Things" remained a standard for 10 years. Brown wrote in an easy informal style that JOHN SIMON characterized as "chatty urbanity." His many books include *The Modern Theatre in Revolt* (1929), *Two on the Aisle* (1938), *Seeing Things* (1946), *Dramatis Personae* (1963), and *The Worlds of* ROBERT E. SHERWOOD (1965). TLM

Brown, Lew see DESYLVA, B. G. "BUDDY"

Brown, "Colonel" T(homas) Allston (1836–1918) Dramatic editor, historian, and theatrical AGENT. Brown published *History of the American Stage* (1870) and *A History of the New York Theatre* (3 vols., 1903), and served for seven years as dramatic editor of the *NEW YORK CLIPPER* (1863–70), establishing it as a leading theatrical trade paper with up-to-date information on minstrel shows, circuses, ballet dances, music halls, and burlesques. He also worked as an advance man, business manager, advertising agent, and press agent, parlaying his knowledge of the road into *The Showman's Guide* (1st ed., 1868), containing names of principal halls, lists of distances, best routes, rent per night, seating capacities, and names of bill posters, newspapers, and hotels. Brown established his own dramatic agency in 1870 and continued managing until his retirement in 1906. Although a colorful theatrical personality, "Colonel" Brown was not a first-rate historian, and his books contain numerous errors. TLM

Brown, Tony see MARGOLIS, KARI

Brown, William Alexander (fl. 1820s) African American theatre manager and playwright. An ex–West Indian seaman, Brown became the father of African American theatre when he established the AFRICAN THEATRE in New York in 1821, with a repertoire including condensed versions of plays such as *Richard III, Pizarro, Tom and Jerry,* and *Obi; or, Three-Fingered Jack,* as well as pantomimes. Brown also wrote and produced the first African American play, *The Drama of King Shotaway* (1823), based on personal experience of the 1795 Black Caribs' insurrection on St. Vincent. From his African Theatre emerged JAMES HEWLETT, the first black Shakespearean actor, and IRA ALDRIDGE, a black actor renowned in England and Europe in the 19th century. Brown may also have founded a theatre in Albany, NY, in 1823. EGH

Brown, William Wells (1819–84) An escaped slave, Brown joined the abolitionist movement from his Boston home and wrote two antislavery plays that he read from lecture platforms. The first, *Experience; or, How to Give a Northern Man a Backbone* (1856), satirizes a proslavery northern preacher who recants after being sold into slavery and later released; the second, *The Escape; or, A Leap for Freedom* (1858), describes domestic life on a southern plantation as slaves plot their escape. A biography by W. E. Farrison was published in 1969. EGH

Browne, Roscoe Lee (1925–2007) African American actor of stage, screen, and television. Browne was a world-class track star and college instructor before embarking on a stage career. An actor of controlled power, he was especially comfortable in Shakespeare (he played seven seasons with the NEW YORK SHAKESPEARE FESTIVAL), in such roles as the Fool in *King Lear* in 1962. In 1992 he appeared as Holloway in AUGUST WILSON's *Two Trains Running.* His film credits included the title role in *The Liberation of L. B. Jones* (1970), and he had made numerous appearances on television. Since 1996 he had toured annually with actor Anthony Zerbe in *Behind the Broken Words,* a performative anthology of 20th-century poetry and prose.   EGH

Bruce, Lenny [né Alfred Schneider] (1926–66) Stand-up comic who became a martyr to his cult image. After serving in the Navy during WWII, he studied acting under the GI bill and began as a NIGHTCLUB comedian. Working out of small clubs in Greenwich Village, he first gained notoriety for his liberal use of four-letter words; gradually, he became noted for his savage attacks on establishment hypocrisy. As his act developed into intimate, improvisational harangues of the audience, he shocked the conventional and rejoiced the "hip" with his freewheeling satire of narcotics legislation, organized religion, sexual taboos, and race relations. Frequently arrested for drug abuse and blasphemy (the Home Office refused to let him perform in England), he sank into paranoia and died of an overdose of narcotics. After his death, he became a totem – in KENNETH TYNAN's words, "the man who went down on America's conscience" – and a play, *Lenny,* was devoted to him. In 1998, a documentary on Bruce, directed by Robert B. Weide, was released, and in 2003 Gov. George F. Pataki of New York pardoned Bruce of his 1964 conviction of obscene performances at the Cafe au Go Go in Greenwich Village. Bruce authored *How to Talk Dirty and Influence People* (1965).   LS

Brustein, Robert (1927–) Critic, actor, director, playwright-adapter, and founder of the YALE REPERTORY and AMERICAN REPERTORY theatres. He has served on the faculties of several universities, and was the Dean of the Yale Drama School during 1965–79, years recalled in his book *Making Scenes.* The author of 14 other important books on theatre and society (most notably *The Theatre of Revolt,* 1964; *The Third Theatre,* 1968; *Revolution as Theatre,* 1970; *Who Needs Theatre,* 1986; *Reimagining American Theatre,* 1991; *Dumbocracy in America,* 1994; *Cultural Calisthenics,* 1998; *The Siege of the Arts,* 2001; *Letters to a Young Actor,* 2005), Brustein has been one of the most respected and controversial critics, primarily as drama critic for *The New Repub-*

lic since 1959 (on a regular basis until 1968; he was also sometime critic for the London Sunday *Observer*). He received the GEORGE JEAN NATHAN Award for Dramatic Criticism in 1962 and 1987. In 1979 Brustein was unexpectedly released as Dean at Yale and moved to Harvard, where ART was established, remaining there until his retirement in 2002. At Yale and Harvard, he supervised several hundred professional productions, including of his own plays, *Shlemiel the First, Demons* (a modern Faust play), *Nobody Dies on Friday,* and several other adaptations. He acted in 8 productions and directed 12 at ART. He was the 1995 recipient of the American Academy of Arts and Letters Award for Distinguished Service to the Arts, and in 2002 was inducted into the THEATRE HALL OF FAME.   DBW

Brutus; or, The Fall of Tarquin One of the most popular works by an American in the first half of the 19th century, though written and first performed (3 December 1818) in London, where playwright JOHN HOWARD PAYNE had been working as an actor and writer. Conceived as a vehicle for Edmund Kean's fiery acting style, the play suited many American tragedians over the next 70 years, including EDWIN FORREST and EDWIN BOOTH, who saw the blank-verse tragedy as a great leading role and symbolic of American nationalism. Payne's admitted use of several popular sources to tell the story of Brutus' defeat of Saxton Tarquin caused some to question his originality and validity as a playwright.   PAD

Bryant, Dan [né Daniel Webster O'Brien] (1833–75) Minstrel and manager. After his debut (as dancer) at New York's Vauxhall Garden in 1843, Bryant graduated to blackface minstrelsy (1849) with "Sable Harmonists," and in 1850 joined Charley White at the Bowery's Melodeon Minstrel Hall. In 1857 Dan and his brothers Jerry and Neil founded Bryant's Minstrels – Jerry and Dan the "endmen" and Neil interlocutor. Bryant's became New York's premiere MINSTREL SHOW company. "Dixie," written by troupe member DAN EMMETT, was introduced by them (1859), though Bryant was best known for his "rude and untutored" black character dance, "Essence of Old Virginny." Bryant, also a good Irish-dialect actor, appeared in that guise first in *Handy Andy* (1863). His natural inclination toward blackface comedy brought him back to minstrelsy in 1868.   DBW

Bryggman, Larry (1938–) California-born and -educated actor, a mainstay of daytime television (the villainous Dr. John Dixon, *As the World Turns,*

1969–2004); and yet since his New York debut in 1962 the blond, gaunt actor has been seen frequently onstage, especially OFF-BROADWAY. He has appeared with such major companies as the MANHATTAN THEATRE CLUB, LINCOLN CENTER Theater, SECOND STAGE, and the PUBLIC THEATER. His official Broadway debut was in *Checking Out* (1976) – he was a replacement in *Ulysses in Nighttown* (1974) – and productions there include *The BASIC TRAINING OF PAVLO HUMMEL* (1977), *King Richard III* with AL PACINO (1979), *PRELUDE TO A KISS* (1990), *PICNIC* (1994 revival, as Howard Bevans), *PROOF* (2000, as the mathematician-father, Robert), *Twelve Angry Men* (2004 revival), and *Festen* (2006). Recently he has also appeared with the ATLANTIC THEATER COMPANY (2005 as Gayev in *The Cherry Orchard*).   DBW

Brynner, Yul (1920?–85) Actor and singer whose early life is mired in contradictory accounts. After playing small roles in two Broadway plays, he made his musical theatre debut in *Lute Song* (1946). In 1951 he appeared as the imperious yet likable king in *The KING AND I* (Tony; Oscar, 1957), a role that he played more than 4,500 times and would be identified with him for the rest of his life. He revived the role on Broadway in 1977 and toured with for several seasons, returning it to Broadway in 1985. His biography was written by his son, Rock, in 1989.   MK

Buchanan, McKean (1823–72) Actor. A cotton broker who began playing leading roles with the amateur Histrionic Association (New Orleans, 1848), he appeared in Bristol, England, and New York City the following year. He set off as a traveling star, playing all across the American South and West, the English provinces, and Australia. After 1860 he appeared opposite his daughter, Virginia. A large man (6′ 4″ tall) with a powerful voice, he was frequently compared to EDWIN FORREST and JOHN MCCULLOUGH in style, and he specialized in Shylock, Macbeth, Othello, Richard III, Lear, Richelieu, and Sir Giles Overreach. Critics either praised him or damned him extravagantly, and he was as often noted for his eccentric personal behavior as for his acting.   DMcD

Buckley, Betty (Lynn) (1947–) Texas-born cabaret singer and actress whose Broadway debut in 1969 was in *1776*, though her reputation was established as the original Grizabella (1983 Tony, Best Featured Actress in a Musical) in the New York production of *Cats* (1982), preceded by *Pippin* (1973 replacement). In 1994 she replaced PATTI LUPONE as Norma Desmond in *Sunset Boulevard* in London

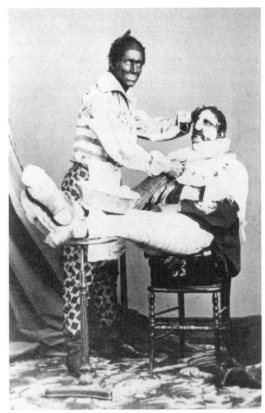

Dan Bryant, a blackface Figaro, shaving Eph Horn (1818–77) in an American minstrel act of the 1860s. Photo by Fredricks, NY. *Courtesy:* Laurence Senelick Collection.

and in 1995 GLENN CLOSE in New York, a choice that catapulted her into cult-star status. Subsequent roles have included Hesione in *Triumph of Love* (ROYALE THEATRE, 1997), Mama Rose in *GYPSY* (PAPER MILL PLAYHOUSE, 1998), and two roles in NICKY SILVER's *The Eros Trilogy* (VINEYARD THEATRE, 1999).   DBW

Bullins, Ed (1935–) African American playwright who began writing fiction but, seeing BARAKA's plays on stage, felt drama was more effective in reaching black audiences. In 1967 he joined the New LAFAYETTE THEATRE as resident playwright, became its associate director, and edited its periodical, *Black Theatre*. Among his best-known plays are *Goin' a Buffalo* (1966), *In the Wine Time* (1968), *The Duplex* (1970), *In New England Winter* (1971), *The Fabulous Miss Marie* (1971), and *The Taking of Miss Janie* (1975). Bullins's experiments in form combine rhythmic, racy dialogue, black ritual, and jazz and blues music as integral elements of his dramaturgy. His work has been recognized with two Obies (1971, 1975) and a 1975 New York Drama Critics' Circle Award. In 1982 Bullins moved to San Francisco, where he had several new plays produced, but then became associated in the early 2000s with the Northeastern University Center for the Arts in Boston. A literary biography by Samuel Hay was published in 1997, the same year the NEGRO ENSEMBLE COMPANY staged his *Boy × Man* in NYC.   EGH

Buloff, Joseph (1899–1985) Gifted YIDDISH THEATRE actor and director first with the Vilna Troupe, then in America, where he acted with MAURICE SCHWARTZ's YIDDISH ART THEATRE and directed for the FOLKSBIENE and others, forming the New York Art Theatre in 1934–5. He eventually moved to English-speaking roles on Broadway (e.g., the salesman Ali Hakim in *OKLAHOMA!*) and was active in Israel during the 1950s and '60s. Posthumous volumes of his memoirs appeared in 1991 and 1993.   AB

Bunker-Hill see BURK, JOHN DALY

Burden, Chris (1946–) Boston-born conceptual and PERFORMANCE ARTist who also works in sculpture, assemblage, installation, video, and language art. He studied architecture and physics at Pomona College and sculpture at the University of California at Irvine. His early 1970s body-art performances, seen in the context of minimalism, conceptual art, and American domestic and foreign politics, included *Five Day Locker Piece* (1971), *Shoot* (1971), and *Trans-fixed* (1974). All of Burden's work, including such installations as *Samson* (1985), *Exposing the Foundations of the Museum* (1987), and more recently *Bridges* (1998–) explore the institutional fantasies of power and technology. After a student in one of his UCLA classes pointed a gun at himself (and in the hall fired a shot) as part of a performance piece (reminiscent of Burden allowing himself to be shot in the arm as part of *Shoot*), Burden and Nancy Rubins, his wife, retired from UCLA in January 2005. AF

Burgess, Neil (1846–1910) Boston-born actor who made his debut with Spalding's Bell Ringers in 1865. He gained attention in a dame role, Mrs. Benjamin Bibbs in *The Quiet Family,* and won stardom in 1879, touring extensively in a dramatization of Alice B. Neal's 1858 novel *The Widow Bedott Papers,* in which he played the garrulous, mala-propistic "widdy-woman" wooed by seedy Deacon Sniffles. He equaled but did not surpass this success as Betsy Puffy in *Vim* (1882) and Aunt Abigail Prue in his own production of Charles Bernard's *The County Fair* (1888). Burgess's comic cross-dressing (see FEMALE/MALE IMPERSONATION) made him one of the richest actors in America, but his fortune evaporated in ill-advised speculations, and, as the stock system declined, he was reduced as of 1899 to playing tabloid versions of his best parts in vaudeville.   LS

Buried Child Three-act drama by SAM SHEPARD, first performed on 27 June 1978 by SAN FRANCISCO's MAGIC THEATRE and produced at New York's THEATER FOR THE NEW CITY on 19 October 1978, later transferring to the Theatre de Lys. Important revivals include those in 1979 at YALE REPERTORY THEATRE and CIRCLE REPERTORY THEATRE; a London production at the Hampstead Theatre Club in 1980; and STEPPENWOLF's revival (directed by GARY SINISE) seen on Broadway in 1996. Shepard has described his Pulitzer Prize–winning play as "a kind of test. I wanted to write a play about a family." MEL GUSSOW's review of the two 1979 productions called it "a dirge for the decline of traditional values, a wake for the American dream, . . . a penetrating excavation into the essence of blood ties." Brantley called the 1996 revival "inspired," "dazzlingly acted" by LOIS SMITH and James Gammon, and a "play for all ages." Using powerful images within a tenuous narrative, the play – set in a shabby Midwestern farmhouse – focuses on a young man's attempt to rediscover his heritage and his identity within a family in the grip of sordid secrets.   FHL

Burk, John Daly (c. 1776–1808) Playwright known for his patriotic spectacle *Bunker-Hill; or, The Death of General Warren* (Boston, February 1797; New York, September 1797) and for his detailed account of the primitive staging: "Our twelve-minute battle . . . Charlestown on fire and Warren animating the Americans amidst the smoak [sic] and confusion produce an effect scarce credible." For 20 years *Bunker-Hill* became the American theatre's standard offering for the Fourth of July and for Evacuation Day (25 November).

Expelled from Dublin's Trinity College, Burk came to Boston in 1796, and in 1808 was killed in a duel. He edited two newspapers, practiced law, and wrote six other plays – *Female Patriotism; or, The Death of Joan of Arc* (1798) the best known – as well as a *History of Virginia* and *History of the Late War in Ireland* (1799).   RM

Poster advertising Mme Rentz's Female Minstrels. London: N. Defries Litho. *Courtesy:* Don B. Wilmeth Theatre Collection.

Burke, Billie (Mary William Ethelbert Appleton Burke) (1886–1970) Actress; quintessential flibbertigibbet on stage and screen. With a cameo-like delicacy of feature and little-bird voice, Billie Burke will always be remembered as Glinda, the Good Witch, in the film *The WIZARD OF OZ* (1939). Daughter of a singing circus clown, Billie spent 1903–7 as a singer in England, returning to New York to star opposite John DREW in *My Wife*. Under CHARLES FROHMAN's management, she became the toast of Broadway. In 1914 she married the showman FLORENZ ZIEGFELD. After his death in 1932, and burdened with his debt-ridden estate, she turned to films as a way to settle her husband's obligations.

Between 1917 and 1944 Burke starred in 12 plays on Broadway. Later she noted that she excelled only in light, gay things. "I often had cute plays but never a fine one." A lover of animals, she once had a menagerie comparable to a fair-sized zoo on her 22-acre New York estate. She wrote (with Cameron Shipp) two autobiographies: *With a Feather on My Nose* (1949) and *With Powder on My Nose* (1959).   DBW

burlesque show A raucous and bawdy style of variety performance, inspired partly by LYDIA THOMPSON and her British blondes, partly by blackface MINSTREL SHOWS and "leg shows" like *The BLACK CROOK*. The manager MICHAEL B. LEAVITT is credited with its invention by his creation of Mme. Rentz's Female Minstrels (Rentz from a popular circus), later the Rentz–Santley troupe (after Mabel Santley, its star). One of its earliest

personalities was May Howard, who ran her own company in the 1880s.

Burlesque rapidly developed a tripartite structure: In Part One, dance and song rendered by a female company was intermingled with low comedy from male comedians; Part Two was an olio of specialities in which the women did not appear; and Part Three comprised a grand finale. "Clean" versions of these preponderantly female productions were widely sponsored by the Miner family. Sam T. Jack, who opened the first exclusively burlesque theatre in Chicago, pioneered "dirty" burlesque or "turkey show," which was especially popular in the Western honky-tonks. The Empire and Mutual Circuits or Wheels reveled in such maculate entertainment, whereas the Columbia Circuit booked only clean shows until 1925, when it too was forced by dwindling receipts to go dirty.

Leading entrepreneurs were the MINSKY brothers: Abe, who brought belly dancers (known as "cootchers") and the illuminated runway from Paris; publicists Billy and Morton; and Herbert, who introduced opera. From the early 1900s to 1935, they molded the image of American burlesque at the Republic Theatre and the National Winter Garden, New York. By present-day standards, the offerings were tame, for the girls never disrobed completely; but the blatant double entendre in the dialogue between straight man and "talking woman," as well as runway interplay between strippers and audience, enraged moralists. The striptease (see also NUDITY), which achieved extraordinary invention and daring, entered burlesque in 1921 with "Curls" Mason,

May Howard (Havill), Canadian-born burlesque performer, who became star of her own company and by 1817 was the first "burlesque queen." This portrait first appeared in the *New York Police Gazette. Courtesy:* Laurence Senelick Collection.

form has inspired ARTHUR HOPKINS's play *Burlesque* (1927), Ralph Allen's musical *Sugar Babies* (1979), and feminist dramas that stress the exploitation of the stripper as commodity. In the early 2000s "New" Burlesque emerged, combining 1980s performance art with anti–political correctness, or as one entrepreneur suggested, revues that reflect a rebellion "against the modern standards of beauty and the obsession with sex our society has." LS

Burn This by LANFORD WILSON opened at the PLYMOUTH THEATRE on 14 October 1987 after performances at the MARK TAPER FORUM, the STEPPENWOLF THEATRE, and the CIRCLE REPERTORY COMPANY; it closed after 437 performances. Structured as a contemporary, conventional romantic comedy, *Burn This* nevertheless is a serious exploration of passionate love and its relationship to death, creativity, and the decline of Western civilization. Directed by MARSHALL W. MASON and featuring JOHN MALKOVICH and Joan Allen as the star-crossed lovers, *Burn This* provoked controversy for its excessive use of profanity, but was widely regarded as Wilson's most forceful play to date. A successful 2002 revival at the UNION SQUARE THEATRE starred Edward Norton and Catherine Keener as the lovers. DJW

and Carrie Finnell performed the first tassel dance, twirling the fringe from her nipples. The most memorable personalities among the strippers were Millie De Leon, the urbane GYPSY ROSE LEE (a protégée of gangster Waxy Gordon), the classy Lili St. Cyr, and the indestructible ANNE CORIO. Among the comedians nurtured by the form were Sliding Billy Watson, BILLY "BEEF TRUST" WATSON, Al Shean (of GALLAGHER AND SHEAN), WILLIE HOWARD, PHIL SILVERS, Abbott and Costello, Jackie Gleason, and JOEY FAYE, while routines like "Floogle Street" became classics.

Changing times brought about an end to classic burlesque. New York courts banned the runway in 1934 and all burlesque in 1942, and the Burlesque Artists Association had its charter revoked in 1957. Go-go dancing, the Las Vegas-style revue, and television siphoned off the remaining talents, and revivals, like Corio's widely toured *This Was Burlesque,* tend to be steeped in nostalgia. The

Burnett, Frances Hodgson (1849–1924) Prolific English-born writer who dramatized and produced 13 of her novels, beginning with *Esmeralda* (1881). *The Real Little Lord Fauntleroy* (1888) was her greatest popular and financial success, both in London and New York. The unauthorized dramatization of this novel caused Burnett to promote the legal right of an author to control such dramatizations and resulted in the 1911 Copyright Act in England. Sentimental and upbeat, many of her books, such as *Fauntleroy, Esmeralda, A Lady of Quality, A Little Princess,* and *The Dawn of Tomorrow* made a successful transition from print to stage to film. *The Secret Garden,* for example, was made into a successful musical in 1991. Her autobiography, *The One I Knew the Best of All,* appeared in 1893. FB

Burns, George [né Nathan Birnbaum] (1896–1996) and **Gracie Allen** [née Grace Ethel Cecile Rosalie Allen] (1895–1964) Burns and Allen were the paradigm of American male–female doubles acts, his wry underplaying setting in relief her staccato dizziness. Burns had been a trick roller skater, dance teacher, and song-and-dance man in vaudeville; Allen had entered show business as a child in an Irish sisters act. They teamed up in

1923 and married in 1926, Burns playing the quizzical straightman to her Dumb Dora. "Lamb Chops," one version of their cross-talk act, was signed to a six-year contract in the KEITH theatres (1926–32). They had their own radio show (1932–49) and moved successfully to television. After Allen's retirement in 1958, Burns, wielding his omnipresent cigar, continued to perform, a high point being his Carnegie Hall recital in 1976. Burns authored autobiographies in 1955 and 1977; the most recent biography was by Martin Gottfried in 1996.   LS

Burnside, R. H. (1870–1952) Producer, writer, composer, and director. Born into a theatrical family in Glasgow, Burnside learned his trade at the Savoy Theatre in London before his arrival in New York (1894) as stage director for LILLIAN RUSSELL. He established his reputation conceiving and staging lavish spectacles at the HIPPODROME (1909–23), and became known as the "man who made the girls disappear into water." He continued in this line until the 1940s, when he staged revivals of GILBERT AND SULLIVAN.   TLM

Burrows, Abe (Abram S.) (1910–85) Playwright, librettist, "play doctor," and director. Born in New York City, Burrows moved to Hollywood in 1939 and divided his time between these two entertainment centers for the rest of his life. Following a successful career in radio (he was the chief writer for "Duffy's Tavern," for example), he first scored as a playwright in 1950 by coauthoring GUYS AND DOLLS with Jo Swerling and FRANK LOESSER. This success (Tony, Drama Critics' Circle Award) propelled him during the next decade into several assignments as lyricist or librettist for musicals, including *Three Wishes for Jamie* (1952), *CAN-CAN* (1953), *Silk Stockings* (1955), *Say, Darling* (1958), *First Impressions* (1959), and *HOW TO SUCCEED IN BUSINESS WITHOUT REALLY TRYING* (1961; seven Tonys, including Best Musical, Best Author of a Musical, and Best Direction [Burrows]; 1962 Pulitzer Prize). He also adapted *Cactus Flower* from a French comedy by Barillet and Gredy for a successful 1965 Broadway production. He made his debut as a director with *Two on the Aisle* (1951), continued with *Can-Can,* and soon became known for his ability to infuse stage comedies with the kind of wit and gentle humor that characterized his personality and allowed him to work harmoniously with testy writers when called upon as an unbilled "doctor" for shows in trouble. In 1991 a theatre at New York University was named after him. His son is the highly successful television director and producer James Burrows.   LDC

Burstyn, Ellen [née Edna Rae Gillooly] (1932–) Actress, past president (first woman) of ACTORS' EQUITY (1982–5), and former artistic director of the ACTORS STUDIO. Once a showgirl on Jackie Gleason's television show and now a champion of women's status in American film and theatre, Burstyn, who has long striven to play roles that intrigued her, irrespective of their size, has played significant parts in plays as disparate as *Same Time, Next Year* (1975, Tony), *84 Charing Cross Road* (1982), *DRIVING MISS DAISY* (1988), *Shirley Valentine* (1989), *Shimada* (1992), *Sacrilege* (1995), and the major failure *Oldest Living Confederate Widow Tells All* (2003). She won an Academy Award for her sensitive portrayal in *Alice Doesn't Live Here Anymore* (1974). Her candid memoir appeared in 2006.   DBW

Burton, Kate (1957–) Swiss-born (British and U.S. citizenships) actor, daughter of RICHARD BURTON and producer Sybil Christopher; wife of stage manager/producer MICHAEL RITCHIE. A major in Russian studies and European history at Brown University, she hesitantly decided to pursue a theatre interest at Yale. Now a versatile leading lady, she nevertheless spent some 20 years in supporting roles, beginning immediately after Yale with GEORGE C. SCOTT in *Present Laughter,* followed by the title role in *Alice in Wonderland* (1983). Off-Broadway productions have numbered *The Playboy of the Western World, Some Americans Abroad, London Suite,* and *Give Me Your Answer, Do!* With leading replacement roles in *The Beauty Queen of Leenane* (1998) and *An American Daughter* (1997), she was more than ready for her critically acclaimed 2001 breakout role as Hedda Gabler (at age 44), then actress Madge Kendal in *The Elephant Man* (2002), and in 2005 Constance Middleton in *The Constant Wife.* Summer 2006 saw her as Helen in THERESA REBECK's *The Water's Edge* (SECOND STAGE) and 2007 as Mme. Ranevskaya in *The Cherry Orchard* at the HUNTINGTON.   DBW

Burton, Lance (1960–) Kentucky-born stage magician with a boyish and affable demeanor. After a five-year run at the Fiesta Theater in Las Vegas's Hacienda Hotel, Burton entered into a contract to star in, produce, and direct a new lavish show in the Monte Carlo Resort & Casino (which venue opened on 21 June 1996). His 13-year agreement was the longest to date for any entertainer in Las Vegas history and also included the custom-constructed $27 million Lance Burton Theatre. Burton presents a classically conceived show of illusions with heavy doses of humor. Patriarch of magic DAI VERNON termed him

"The most brilliant magician of this [20th] century." DBW

Burton [né Jenkins], **Richard** (1924–84) Blessed with a golden voice and a larger-than-life stage presence, this Welsh-born actor never fulfilled his promise, instead turning with reckless abandon to a largely turbulent life of drinking, womanizing, and notoriety, marked by a series of chiefly inferior films. Nevertheless, Burton's mark on American theatre was especially noteworthy. Half of his total stage work, other than seasons with the Old Vic (especially *Hamlet*, 1953) or at Stratford, England, occurred in the U.S.; after 1957 all of his theatre appearances, save one, were there. He first appeared on Broadway in *The Lady's Not for Burning* (1950), followed by *Legend of Lovers* (1951), *Time Remembered* (1957), CAMELOT (1960 and a 1980–1 tour), *Hamlet* (1964, dir. John Gielgud; a record run of 137 performances for the play), *Equus* (1976), and – in an attempt to rekindle some of his old box-office magic – *Private Lives* (1983) with his former wife, Elizabeth Taylor. His daughter, KATE BURTON, is a successful actress. Melvin Bragg's 1988 biography provides a good overview. DBW

Burton, William E(vans) (1804–60) British-born actor and manager who ran one of the best STOCK COMPANIES in the U.S., earning at the same time the reputation, according to critic LAURENCE HUTTON, as the "funniest man who ever lived." Burton's first professional appearance was in 1831 at London's Pavilion Theatre, followed the next year with an engagement opposite Edmund Kean at the Haymarket Theatre. In 1834 he made his American debut at the ARCH STREET THEATRE. In 1841 he entered management in New York at the National Theatre, short-lived due to the destruction by FIRE of the theatre seven weeks later. He also briefly managed the CHESTNUT and Arch Street theatres in Philadelphia, the Washington Theatre [DC], and the Front Street Theatre in Baltimore. In 1848 he leased Palmo's Opera House, renaming it BURTON'S CHAMBERS STREET THEATRE; and in 1856, with increasing competition from J. W. WALLACK, he moved to the Metropolitan Theatre, Broadway, renamed Burton's New Theatre. He withdrew from management in 1858. Burton's Theatres operated successfully during 1848–56 largely without visiting stars, boasting such company members as HENRY PLACIDE, WILLIAM RUFUS BLAKE, GEORGE HOLLAND, CHARLES FISHER, LESTER WALLACK, and JOHN BROUGHAM, who also wrote numerous new pieces for Burton. Audiences, however, came primarily to see Burton perform such roles as Bob Acres, Tony Lumpkin, Bottom, Falstaff, and especially Timothy Toodles in his own *The Toodles,* Aminidab Sleek in Morris Barnett's *The Serious Family,* and Captain Cuttle in Brougham's stage version of Dickens's *Dombey and Son.* His last New York appearance was at NIBLO'S GARDEN in 1859. Burton also wrote plays (nonextant). The most modern of his biographies, by David Rinear, was published in 2004. DBW

Burton's Chambers Street Theatre Chambers St. between Broadway and Centre St., New York. In 1844, well-known Broadway restaurateur Signor Fernando Palmo took the fortune he made from his kitchens and invested it in a small opera house to bring Italian opera to New York. After two disastrous seasons, he returned to the kitchen, losing both his theatre and his money. For several years, Palmo's Opera House housed a variety of entertainments, but it enjoyed its greatest success when actor-manager WILLIAM E. BURTON took it over (1848–56). As Burton's Chambers Street Theatre, it presented farces, burlettas, and light comedy. When Burton joined the uptown exodus, the theatre was taken over by minstrel companies, then rented to the federal government as a courthouse. In 1876, it was demolished. MCH

Bury the Dead by IRWIN SHAW. This antiwar play in one act, produced by the short-lived Actors Repertory Company, was done first at left-wing fund-raisers in March 1936, then opened on Broadway on 18 April 1936, where it ran for 97 performances. The 23-year-old Shaw applied the model of the "strike play" to the circumstances of the war "that is to begin tomorrow night." Despite the pleas of religious leaders, generals, and even their loved ones, six corpses of soldiers refuse to lie down and be buried. Shaw's skillful combination of argumentation, macabre humor, and montage produced an event that – in the words of BROOKS ATKINSON – "burrows under the skin of argument into the raw flesh of sensation." MF

Bus Stop by WILLIAM INGE opened on 2 March 1955 and ran for 478 performances. Directed by HAROLD CLURMAN, the cast was headed by KIM STANLEY as Cherie, a down-on-her-luck nightclub singer who is stranded with fellow travelers at a tiny Kansas restaurant in the dead of night. This collection of misfits, each with a story to tell, created an ensemble production and a mood described as "Chekovian" by LOUIS KRONENBERGER. The play is still frequently staged by amateur and professional groups, including a 1996 production directed by the late Josephine Abady at Circle in the Square with Mary-Louise Parker as Cherie. In making the film version (1956), director Joshua Logan and screenwriter George Axelrod transformed it into a one-woman show that featured Marilyn Monroe in that role.   MR

Busch, Charles (1954–) Stage and film actor and playwright. Born in New York and educated at Northwestern University, Busch has specialized in playing the grande dame in his own drag parodies of Hollywood and Broadway melodramas, such as Fauna Alexander in *Vampire Lesbians of Sodom* and *Sleeping Beauty, or Coma* (double bill in 1984), Irish O'Flanagan in *Times Square Angel* (1985), Chicklet in *Psycho Beach Party* (1987), Gertrude Garnet in *The Lady in Question* (1988), Mary Dale in *Red Scare on Sunset* (1991), a one-person outing in *Flipping My Wig* (1996), Angela A. in *Queen Amarantha* (1997), and Lady Sylvia Allington in *Shanghai Moon* (2003). Other cross-dressing roles include Solange in Jean Genet's *The Maids* at the CSC Repertory playhouse (1993). Busch, who in 1994 appeared out of drag in his *You Should Be So Lucky,* is cofounder of Theatre-in-Limbo and author of *The Tale of the Allergist's Wife* (2000), arguably his greatest success to date, which transferred from the Manhattan Theatre Club to Broadway (777 performances). His most recent play (2006) is *Our Leading Lady* (MTC). A documentary on his life was released in 2006.   TLM

Bush, Anita (1883–1974) African American actress credited with founding the Lafayette Players (1915–32). Bush was a member of the (Bert) Williams and Walker company that toured Britain with their hit musical *In Dahomey* (1903–4). When the company disbanded she ran a dancing chorus for four years. In 1915 she formed the Anita Bush Stock Company to play weekly repertory at Harlem's Lincoln Theatre, transfer-

ring six weeks later to the rival Lafayette Theatre, whose name the players adopted. The company (which Bush left in 1920) produced a galaxy of well-known black actors, but its plays were invariably condensed Broadway material.   EGH

Button, Jeanne (1930–) Costume designer who, after training at the Carnegie Institute of Technology and Yale School of Drama, made her New York debut in 1963 with Langston Hughes's *Tambourines to Glory.* The designer of costumes for *The Robber Bridegroom* (1975), *Wings* (1979), and *The Twilight of the Golds* (1993), among other productions, she received the Hewes Design Award for *MacBird* (1967). Button has designed costumes for many regional theatres, notably the Great Lakes Shakespeare Festival, the Yale Repertory Theatre, and the Tulane Summer Shakespeare Festival, as well as for television. She has extensive Off-Broadway credits, and has taught design at Yale, New York University, and from 1990 until retirement in 2000, Tulane.   BO

Bye Bye Birdie Musical comedy with book by Michael Stewart, music by Charles Strouse, lyrics by Lee Adams; played 607 performances – beginning at the Martin Beck Theatre, where it opened in 1960, and moving twice without missing a beat – winning four Tonys, including Best Musical (1961). Directed by Gower Champion (Tony), it has the distinction of being the first musical to embrace rock 'n' roll, with the title character (played by Dick Gautier) inspired by Elvis Presley's induction into the army. Dick Van Dyke, Chita Rivera, and Paul Lynde were among the stars. Both a film version (1963) and the 1995 television adaptation presaged a 2005 staged concert version in the City Center Encores! series (directed by Jerry Zaks), which had some success, demonstrating undeniably that the squares won the battle. A 1980 sequel – *Bring Back Birdie* – failed.   DBW

C

Cabaret Two-act musical, music and lyrics by JOHN KANDER AND FRED EBB (respectively), book by JOE MASTEROFF; opened 20 November 1966 at the BROADHURST THEATRE, New York, running 1,165 performances. One of the early "concept" musicals in its concern with theme over linear narrative, this metaphor for a world ignoring the coming of Nazism is based on Christopher Isherwood's *Berlin Stories.* The stories of the doomed romances of an American writer and an English cabaret singer and of a German matron and a Jewish fruitseller are told in the context of the cabaret, the world of unreality that opens and closes the show, presided over by its sardonic Master of Ceremonies (JOEL GREY). The numbers in the cabaret serve not to advance the narrative, but to comment on the action and establish the general air of decadence. These Brechtian overtones are enhanced by the WEILL-like music, some of it written to be sung by Weill's widow, LOTTE LENYA, as Fraulein Schneider. *Cabaret* won Tony and Drama Critics' Circle awards as Best Musical, was made into an Oscar-winning film (in revised form) by BOB FOSSE in 1972, was revived in 1987 and in 1998, the latter an enormous success, closing in January 2004 after 2,377 performances. Produced by ROUNDABOUT it won four Tonys, including for Best Revival of a Musical. Seen primarily at Studio 54 on West 54th St., the production, directed by Sam Mendes with choreography by ROB MARSHALL, featured 15 prominent actresses as Sally Bowles (beginning with Natasha Richardson). Alan Cumming won a Tony as the decadent emcee. JD

Cadillac Winter Garden Theatre see WINTER GARDEN THEATRE

Caffe Cino The USA's Ur-theatre of the OFF-OFF BROADWAY movement. Joseph Cino, a former dancer, opened his coffeehouse at 31 Cornelia St. in Greenwich Village in December 1958. Soon local poets were doing readings, and actors were performing scenes. Although the first play presented was a condensed version of Oscar Wilde's *The Importance of Being Earnest,* a new generation of dramatists whose sensibilities were at odds with the commercial mainstream soon made the Cino's 8 × 8-ft. stage their home, paying the expenses of their brief runs by passing the hat. Robert Patrick, Paul Foster, Tom Eyen, LANFORD WILSON, Robert Heide, MARIA IRENE FORNÉS, William M. Hoffman, MEGAN TERRY, Leonard Melfi, Jeff Weiss, JOHN GUARE, and JEAN-CLAUDE VAN ITALLIE were among the regulars whose plays Joe Cino introduced with a whoosh of steam from the espresso machine as he swirled a black thrift-shop cape. Though Cino imposed no artistic criteria, the quintessential Caffe Cino playwright was H. M. Koutoukas, whose plays had a tacky, high-camp glamour suited to an atmosphere that Patrick describes as a cross between "Lourdes and Sodom." The Cino burned down on Ash Wednesday, 1965. Although it did reopen, Joe Cino committed suicide under the influence of drugs in 1967. *Village Voice* critic Michael Smith tried to keep the coffeehouse going for awhile, but the spirit had died with Cino, the first Off-Off Broadway impresario. Wendell C. Stone has recounted Caffe Cino's story (2005). CLJ

Cage Aux Folles, La see LA CAGE AUX FOLLES

Cahill, Marie (1870–1933) Brooklyn-born singer and comedienne who made her Broadway debut in *A Tin Soldier* (1886). After developing her exuberant performing style in featured roles, she scored a triumph with the song "Nancy Brown," which she interpolated into the score of *The Wild Rose* (1902). For the next 15 years she was one of Broadway's biggest attractions, starring and touring in a dozen musicals, including VICTOR HERBERT's *It Happened in Nordland* (1904). Despite objections from Herbert and others, she continued to interpolate vaudeville and specialty numbers into her shows. Her last performance was in *The New Yorkers* (1930). MK

Caius Marius Considered the best of RICHARD PENN SMITH's 20 plays, it was the second script to win EDWIN FORREST's famous playwriting contest. Its theme, of a populist leader fighting the established aristocracy, appealed to the Jacksonian critics. But the five-act, blank-verse tragedy, based on the life of the Roman general Caius Marius, was poorly received by audiences and dropped from Forrest's repertoire shortly after it opened at the ARCH STREET THEATRE on 12 January 1831.   PAD

Caldwell, James H. (1793–1863) British-born actor-manager who pioneered the theatre in the Mississippi Valley. He made his debut in Manchester, England, and came to the U.S. in 1816 to perform in Charleston; but he soon began managing in Kentucky and assembled his own touring company. On New Year's Day, 1824, he opened the Camp Street or AMERICAN THEATRE, the first English-language house in New Orleans and the first U.S. theatre illuminated by gas. Caldwell built theatres for his companies in such cities as Mobile, Nashville, and Cincinnati, thus rising to dominate the Mississippi and Ohio River valleys. His success was such that in 1835 he opened the ST. CHARLES THEATRE with a first-rate company and visiting stars of the highest magnitude. Intense competition with LUDLOW and SOL SMITH fostered excellent theatre in the area, but in 1837 a financial panic ruined Caldwell, the St. Charles Theatre burned down in 1842, and by 1843 he could no longer successfully compete and so retired from the stage. He held several official positions in New Orleans, fled to New York at the beginning of the Civil War, and died there in 1863.   SMA

Caldwell, Zoe (Ada) (1934–) Australian-born actress and director whose professional debut was with the Union Theatre Company, Stratford-upon-Avon, England (1958–9); she made her London debut at the Royal Court in 1960. After seasons in Canada and Australia, her U.S. debut occurred in 1963 at the Tyrone GUTHRIE THEATRE in Minneapolis, followed by her New York debut in 1965 as the Prioress in John Whiting's *The Devils*. While remaining active in regional theatre, she is best remembered for the Tony Award–winning roles in *Slapstick Tragedy* (1966), *The Prime of Miss Jean Brodie* (1968), and *Medea* (1982). Her directing credits include *An Almost Perfect Person* (1977), *Richard II* (1979), *The Taming of the Shrew* and *Hamlet* (1985), and *Park Your Car in Harvard Yard* (1991). In 1988 she assumed the direction of the Glenda Jackson–Christopher Plummer *Macbeth*. After a period teaching in Florida, she returned to the NYC stage in TERRENCE McNALLY's *A Perfect Ganesh* (1993). In 1994 she directed Vanessa REDGRAVE and Eileen Atkins in *Vita & Virginia* (UNION SQUARE) and in

1995 appeared as Maria Callas in McNally's *Master Class* (1996 Tony). A superb technician with great power on stage, she has avoided being typecast, while leaning toward work in the classics. Wife of the late producer ROBERT WHITEHEAD, she was awarded the OBE in 1970 and in 1998 received the Gielgud Award from the Shakespeare Guild of Washington, DC. Her memoir, *I Will Be Cleopatra*, was published in 2001.   DBW

Calhern, Louis [né Carl Henry Vogt] (1895–1956) Actor-director. With his tall, distinguished figure, aristocratic face, and physical grace, Calhern was considered a real "pro," rising from burlesque bit player to elder statesman of films (he made 68). A matinee idol in the 1920s, he afterward made few stage appearances, though he was praised as the Colonel in *Jacobowsky and the Colonel* (1944), Justice Oliver Wendell Holmes in *The Magnificent Yankee* (1946), and *King Lear* (1950).   DBW

California Theatre The most respected SAN FRANCISCO playhouse of its day opened on Bush St. on 18 January 1869 with Bulwer-Lytton's *Money* – an apt choice because Bank of California honcho William C. Ralston bankrolled the luxurious 2,400-seat, $250,000 theatre for actors JOHN McCULLOUGH and LAWRENCE BARRETT. Under McCullough's extended management, a first-rate STOCK COMPANY supported top guest stars (MODJESKA, EDWIN BOOTH, BOUCICAULT) and introduced such innovations to San Francisco as the box set. The theatre's fortunes fell after Ralston's death and McCullough's 1877 departure; it was torn down in 1888. The New California, on the same site, stayed active until the 1906 earthquake, though never recapturing its predecessor's glory.   MB

Call, Edward Payson (1928–) Connecticut-born, University of Maryland–educated director who has worked mainly in regional theatre. He was production manager at CIRCLE IN THE SQUARE (1958–61) before seven years at the GUTHRIE THEATRE (1963–70); the first artistic director of the DENVER CENTER THEATRE COMPANY (1979–83), which he developed on the Guthrie model; and artistic associate at the Arizona Theatre Company (1987–9). Call's freelance credits include the MARK TAPER FORUM, ARENA STAGE, the VIVIAN BEAUMONT, OLD GLOBE, AMERICAN CONSERVATORY THEATRE, Intiman (SEATTLE), and LONG WHARF.   TLM

Call Me Madam Two-act musical comedy, music and lyrics by IRVING BERLIN, book by HOWARD

LINDSAY and RUSSEL CROUSE; opened 12 October 1950 at the IMPERIAL THEATRE, New York, running 644 performances. A straightforward star vehicle, the show follows the adventures of Sally Adams (ETHEL MERMAN), a loud, brassy woman appointed ambassador to "Lichtenburg" as a political plum. Occasioned by President Truman's appointment of socialite hostess Perle Mesta as ambassador to Luxembourg, the show sought to capitalize on the success of the earlier Berlin–Merman effort *ANNIE GET YOUR GUN* (1946); it won both of them Tonys. The role so suited Merman that she made the 1953 film version, her only screen appearance in one of her stage roles.   JD

Camelot Two-act musical, music by FREDERICK LOEWE, words by ALAN JAY LERNER; opened 3 December 1960 at New York's MAJESTIC THEATRE, running 873 performances. Based on T. H. White's *The Once and Future King,* this was Lerner and Loewe's attempt to repeat the success of their *MY FAIR LADY* (1956); it again featured Julie Andrews (Guinevere) playing opposite a nonsinging British actor (Welshman RICHARD BURTON as King Arthur) and the young Robert Goulet as Lancelot. The show was plagued by problems (both Lerner and director MOSS HART were hospitalized during rehearsals, and a newspaper strike shortened its run), but its title song became associated with the new Kennedy administration. It has received frequent professional revivals over the years, featuring the actor playing King Arthur, most frequently Richard Harris. A critically acclaimed revival at New Jersey's PAPER MILL PLAYHOUSE (1991) featured designs by MICHAEL ANANIA and staging by Robert Johanson. Loewe retired after *Camelot,* effectively ending the successful Lerner and Loewe collaboration.   JD

Camino Real by TENNESSEE WILLIAMS opened in New York on 19 March 1953, closing after 60 performances. The cast, directed by ELIA KAZAN, included ELI WALLACH, Jo Van Fleet, Barbara Baxley, and Frank Silvera. In 1957 the play was directed by Peter Hall in London. It was revived at the CIRCLE IN THE SQUARE in 1960, directed by JOSÉ QUINTERO, and at the VIVIAN BEAUMONT in 1970, directed by Milton Katselas with AL PACINO and JESSICA TANDY. The play is an existential fantasy about romantic bohemians who have trouble surviving in a contemporary world pervaded by cynical self-interest, political oppression, and the loss of human feeling.   BCM

Campbell, Bartley (1843–88) American playwright. Born in a suburb in Pittsburgh and pri-

vately educated, he turned to journalism and then to playwriting. The first of his 35 plays was *Through Fire* (1871). During 1872–6 he wrote and staged plays for R. M. Hooley in CHICAGO. From 1876 until his mental breakdown in 1885 he was America's most popular melodramatist. His greatest success was the mining-camp melodrama *MY PARTNER* (1879), which became a starring vehicle for Louis Aldrich as Joe and Charles Parsloe as Wing Lee. Though Parsloe went on to other parts, Aldrich, having purchased the rights to the play for a paltry $10 a performance, played it for the rest of his career. Campbell's other outstanding plays were *The Galley Slave* (1879) and *The WHITE SLAVE* (1881).   DMc

Camp St. Theatre see AMERICAN THEATRE

Canby, Vincent (1924–2000) Theatre critic and playwright. Appointed chief film critic for *The New York Times* in 1968, then Sunday theatre critic in October 1993, and in December 1994 chief theatre critic (replaced DAVID RICHARDS), Canby had previously served as a cultural reporter at the *Times* and a film reporter and critic at *VARIETY* and elsewhere. Author of a 1979 novel, he also wrote three plays, including *End of the War,* produced at NY's Ensemble Studio Theatre in 1978. Canby's position as Sunday *Times* theatre critic was taken briefly by MARGO L. JEFFERSON, a *Times* book critic since July 1993, but he returned to the Sunday slot in 1996.   DBW

Can-Can Two-act musical comedy with book (and direction) by ABE BURROWS and music and lyrics by COLE PORTER; opened at the SAM S. SHUBERT THEATRE (7 May 1953) for 892 performances. Subsequently three revivals were short-lived: August 1959 in Central Park's Theatre-in-the-Park; May 1962 by Broadway's New York City Center Light Opera Company; and April 1981 in the MINSKOFF THEATRE. The 1953 production, hailed for its dancing, garnered two Tony Awards: MICHAEL KIDD (Choreography) and GWEN VERDON (Best Featured Actress). Set in Paris in 1893, *Can-Can* demonstrates the alluring effect of provocative dancing at a shady nightclub on some straitlaced legal investigators. Songs include "C'est Magnifique" and "I Love Paris."   EK

Candide Two-act "comic operetta," music by LEONARD BERNSTEIN, lyrics by RICHARD WILBUR (and others), book by LILLIAN HELLMAN; opened at the MARTIN BECK THEATRE, NYC, 1 December 1956, running 73 performances. The original *Candide,* directed by TYRONE GUTHRIE, is one of the most famous failures in Broadway history. This musical version of Voltaire's novel, an expensive nine-week flop, was recorded by Columbia Records after the show closed. The record, introducing the public to Bernstein's extraordinary score, became an all-time best-seller. The show persisted in concert versions until 1973, when HAROLD PRINCE staged an "environmental" production of a revised version, with a completely new book by Hugh Wheeler, at Brooklyn's CHELSEA THEATRE CENTER. Transferred to Broadway on 10 March 1974, the revision, with the action in and around the audience, played 740 performances and won the Drama Critics' Circle Award for Best Musical. A Prince revival was seen on Broadway in 1997 with JIM DALE, Harolyn Blackwell, and Andrea Martin. The revised version has since entered the repertoire of the New York City Opera and was seen in 1994 at the Lyric Opera of Chicago.   JD

Cantor, Arthur (1920–2001) Producer and press representative. A Boston native, Cantor represented Broadway productions before coproducing CHAYEFSKY's *The Tenth Man* (1959) and Mosel's *All the Way Home* (Drama Critics' Circle Award, 1960). His productions included GARDNER's *A Thousand Clowns* (1962), Bolt's *Vivat! Vivat Regina!* (1972), *Private Lives* (1975), *St. Mark's Gospel* (1978), Thompson's *On Golden Pond* (1979), *Ian McKellen Acting Shakespeare* (1984), *Starlight Express* (1987), and *A Room of One's Own, Caged,* and James Sherman's *Beau Jest* (all OFF-BROADWAY, 1991). Cantor owned the COCONUT GROVE and Tappanzee Playhouses, headed the theatre division of Mercury Records, and was joint managing director of London producers H. M. Tennent, Ltd. He cofounded Washington, DC's HELEN HAYES Awards and is coauthor, with Stuart W. Little, of *The Playmakers* (1970).   REK

Cantor, Eddie (1892–1964) Singer and comedian who, after spending his early years in VAUDEVILLE and English music halls, made his legitimate theatre debut in a London revue. His first American appearance was in *Canary Cottage* (1917). FLORENZ ZIEGFELD hired Cantor for his cabaret show *The Midnight Frolic,* and then featured him in the *Ziegfeld Follies of 1917.* Cantor also appeared in the next two *Follies* (1918, 1919). Like AL JOLSON he often appeared in blackface, a vestige of the American MINSTREL SHOW. During his musical numbers he would skip across the stage and clap his hands while smirking his way through some slightly suggestive lyrics. Cantor also appeared in several *Follies* sketches as a timid but potentially hot-tempered young man. He switched to the SHUBERT

management for a few years, after which Ziegfeld presented him in a book musical, *Kid Boots* (1923). Cantor appeared in two more Ziegfeld shows, the *Follies of 1927* (for which he collaborated on the libretto as well as being the star performer), and *Whoopee!* (1928), a book musical. His final Broadway appearance was in *Banjo Eyes* (1941). In addition to his work in the theatre, Cantor appeared in numerous films and was a star of radio and television. He coauthored two autobiographies: *My Life Is in Your Hands* (1928) and *Take My Life* (1957). Herbert Goldman published a definitive biography in 1997.   MK

Capital Repertory Company A thriving not-for-profit regional theatre in Upstate New York, founded in 1980 by Michael Van Landingham, Oakley Hall III, and Bruce Bouchard, who left as artistic director in 1995 (the current head is Maggie Mancinelli-Cahill). After several seasons in the Catskill community of Lexington, the company relocated to Albany, the state capital. Its eclectic repertoire, which emphasizes 20th-century American drama, balances revivals of recent and older plays with premieres. Its 25th anniversary season opened with the world premiere of *Breaking Up Is Hard to Do: The Neil Sedaka Musical.*   CLJ

caricature/caricaturists The caricature, long established in Europe as a instrument of journalistic ego deflation, appeared in America in the 19th century, practiced by artists for large-circulation weeklies, Thomas Nast of *Harper's Weekly* foremost among them. Best defined as the art of exaggeration with a trace of venom, the caricature could range from gentle to gross distortion for the sake of comment. The comic illustrated magazine, which established the art of caricature in earnest, crossed the ocean with the arrival of Austrian Joseph Keppler and his publication of *Puck* in 1877. The caricature was and continues to be well-suited to the extravagances of the world of the theatre. Hardly one issue of *Puck* went by that did not feature a theatrical caricature; its success inspired imitations, and soon newspapers and established publications began routinely to include caricatures.

American caricaturists borrowed liberally from the styles and techniques of Doré, Daumier, and Hogarth, and from each other. The earliest theatrical caricatures appeared in *The Comic History of the Human Race* (1851), with representations of EDWIN FORREST and P. T. BARNUM among its targets. In 1868, W. J. Gladding drew 12 caricatures of leading players on the American stage, which were assembled and published by the Dunlap

Society in 1897. Thereafter, theatrical caricatures appeared regularly on the pages of most newspapers and periodicals.

Among the best-known artists was James Montgomery Flagg, whose work (on the gentle side of caricature) appeared in almost every popular magazine and newspaper. Ohioan Alfred J. Frueh drew prolifically for the *St. Louis Post-Dispatch* and later for the *New York World* and *New Yorker;* his early caricatures were compiled for a book called *Stage Folk* (1922). William Auerbach-Levy also published his work in a range of New York newspapers and the *New Yorker,* as well as in the book *Is That Me?* (1947). Artist Reginald Marsh augmented his living as a fine artist with a mixture of cartoon and caricature, which he called "cartoonicles," for the *New York News* in the 1920s. Peggy Bacon, frequently called the DOROTHY PARKER of pen and ink, contributed to the *New Yorker,* and Irma Selz provided caricatures for *Vanity Fair, Harper's Bazaar,* and the *New York Post* during her career. Irving Hoffman worked for the *New York Morning Telegraph* and freelanced for such publications as *Theatre Magazine.* Sam Norkin has spent most of his career since 1940 working for the *New York News,* among many publications, and remains active (he has his own Web site). The dean of all theatrical caricaturists was AL HIRSCHFELD, who contributed to the *New York Times* until his death. Hirschfeld regarded Miguel Covarrubias, who died in 1957, as one of the most influential of all theatrical caricaturists, and paid tribute to him for raising the standards of caricature drawing and honing it into an art.

With Hirschfeld's passing, no comparable caricaturist has emerged, although several contemporary poster artists incorporate some caricature traits in their graphic design. Among this number are Paul Davis, prominent in the 1970s and '80s, and James McMullan, for almost 20 years LINCOLN CENTER Theater's principal poster artist. McMullan's work is more abtract than that of Davis, who is remembered for his image of Raul Julia in *Threepenny Opera* (1976), among other actors in PUBLIC THEATER productions from 1975 to 1992. A more recent example of his portrait work is that of CHRISTOPHER PLUMMER in *Barrymore* (1996). Yet neither is a true caricaturist. The one major artist still in the classic tradition today is Robert Risko, whose colorful caricatures of celebrities (not just theatre people) have appeared in periodicals such as *Vanity Fair* and the *New Yorker* since 1974.   MCH

Cariou, Len (1939–) Canadian-born stage and film actor, director, and singer. A classically trained actor whose early career was most closely associated with the Stratford (Ontario) Shakespeare Festival and the Tyrone GUTHRIE THEATRE in Minneapolis, Cariou has received his greatest acclaim as a leading man in Broadway musicals. His first musical comedy appearance was in the role of Bill Sampson in *Applause* (1970). Critics praised his performance as Fredrik Egerman in *A LITTLE NIGHT MUSIC* (1973), complimenting him on his acting ability and fine singing voice. He returned to the musical stage in 1979 to portray the titular, monomaniacal "Demon Barber of Fleet Street" of *SWEENEY TODD.* Cariou's bravura performance in one of the musical theatre's most demanding roles earned him the Tony Award as Best Actor in a Musical. A later musical role, that of Teddy Roosevelt in *Teddy & Alice* (1987), was less successful. In 1991 he appeared on Broadway in STEVE TESICH's *The Speed of Darkness,* in 2000 he was in *The Dinner Party,* and in 2002 as a replacement in *PROOF.* He played Cornelius in *A TOUCH OF THE POET* (1992, LONG WHARF), and spring 1994 he essayed the role of Ernest Hemingway in *Papa* at the COCONUT GROVE PLAYHOUSE, which he repeated OFF-BROADWAY in 1996. Other performances of historical figures have included William O. Douglass in *Mountain* (1990) and Joseph Stalin in *Master Class* (1986), both Off-Broadway. In addition to performing, Cariou has directed several plays, and has served as Artistic Director of the Manitoba Theatre Centre.   MK   DBW

Carle, Richard (1871–1941) Comedian, librettist, and lyricist. Carle made his musical theatre debut in *Niobe* (1891), and soon became a popular comedian and singer in such shows as *A Mad Bargain* (1893), *Excelsior, Jr.* (1895), and *Yankee Doodle Dandy* (1898). Unlike other comic-opera performers, Carle's comic persona was that of a shrewd, worldly prankster rather than a butt or simpleton. Carle also wrote the scripts and lyrics for many of his shows. His last appearance was in *The New Yorkers* (1930). Although reviewers often criticized the double entendres in Carle's material, he toured constantly to appreciative audiences across America.   MK

Carmen Jones by OSCAR HAMMERSTEIN II opened in the BROADWAY THEATRE 2 December 1943 and ran 503 performances. Set during WWII among black workers in a southern parachute factory, it was based on the Meilhac–Halévy adaptation of Prosper Mérimée's *Carmen* but retained Georges Bizet's music almost intact. BILLY ROSE, producer and director, was known for spectacles and is credited for hiring HOWARD BAY (settings), RAOUL PÈNE DU BOIS (costumes), and HASSARD

SHORT (color schemes and lighting). In 1991, Simon Callow directed a critically acclaimed revival at London's Old Vic Theatre.   KN

Carnovsky, Morris (1897–92) Actor who, beginning his long acting career with the THEATRE GUILD in the 1920s, departed in 1931 to join the GROUP THEATRE. Among his many distinguished performances with the Group were those in CLIFFORD ODETS's plays AWAKE AND SING! (1935), PARADISE LOST (1935), GOLDEN BOY (1937), ROCKET TO THE MOON (1938), and Night Music (1940). With his mobile face, leonine profile, and commanding voice, he played characters much older than himself. Like other Group members, Carnovsky developed his own version of the Method; he disagreed with LEE STRASBERG's emphasis on the actor's own emotions but believed that, used properly, the Method could help actors to create classic roles. Beginning in the mid-1950s, in a series of acclaimed Shakespearean interpretations, Carnovsky achieved a fusion of the Method's psychological realism with the demands of poetic style. For the AMERICAN SHAKESPEARE FESTIVAL and various universities he performed Lear, Falstaff, Prospero, and Shylock. Like all the Group alumni he was a lifelong student of the art of acting and continued to be active as both a performer and a teacher. In 1983, with lovely simplicity, he portrayed Firs in Chekov's The Cherry Orchard at New Haven's LONG WHARF THEATRE, and in 1984 he published a book of reflections, The Actor's Eye.   FH

Carousel Considered by many to be RODGERS and HAMMERSTEIN's finest accomplishment; their second collaborative effort. The musical play in a prelude and two acts, based on Ferenc Molnár's _Liliom_ (Broadway, 1921), was presented by the THEATRE GUILD at the MAJESTIC THEATRE on 19 April 1945, running for 890 performances. It is frequently revived and now belongs in the repertoire of several opera companies. Molnár's fantasy was transferred from Budapest to a New England fishing village in the late 1800s, where the leading character, handsome bully Billy Bigelow (JOHN RAITT), an amusement park talker, falls in love with Julie Jordan (Jan Clayton) but proves incapable of providing either her emotional or material needs. When she becomes pregnant, Billy, desperate for money, dies in a robbery attempt. He is allowed to return to Earth to do one good deed, but his daughter, Louise (Bambi Linn), refuses the stolen star he offers her, and he returns to purgatory. As directed by ROUBEN MAMOULIAN and choreographed by AGNES DE MILLE, _Carousel_ climbed new heights of creativity and musical inventiveness, with classics such as "If I Loved You," "June Is Bustin' Out All Over," "Soliloquy," and "You'll Never Walk Alone." A 1956 film starred Gordon MacRae and Shirley Jones, and in 1994 a revival at the VIVIAN BEAUMONT that originated at the Royal National Theatre (UK), directed by Nicholas Hytner, received mostly ecstatic reviews and ran for 10 months.   DBW

Carroll, Earl (1892–1948) Producer, theatre manager, and composer who began his theatrical career as a program seller in Pittsburgh. He tried his hand at songwriting for Broadway (e.g., _Canary Cottage_, 1917) and, after serving as a pilot in WWI, launched into theatrical producing with _The Lady of the Lamp_ (1920). Three years later he inaugurated a REVUE series called the _Earl Carroll Vanities_, which continued annually through 1932, with sporadic editions thereafter. Although featuring established performers such as W. C. FIELDS, JACK BENNY, and Milton Berle, the _Vanities_ were most noted for their daring use of nudity in "living curtain" tableaux, and for Carroll's barrage of outrageous publicity stunts. He opened his own theatre in New York in 1923 but lost it in the Depression. In 1936 he left for Hollywood, where he was an associate producer at 20th Century–Fox. In 1938 he opened the Earl Carroll Theatre and Restaurant in Hollywood. Carroll's life was written by Ken Murray (1976).   MK

Carroll, Vinnette (1922–2002) African American actress, director, and teacher, noted for productions of original musical plays under her direction. Educated at LIU, NYU, and Columbia, Carroll received professional training from ERWIN PISCATOR, LEE STRASBERG, and STELLA ADLER. She taught drama at the High School for the Performing Arts in Manhattan and directed the Ghetto Arts Program in New York before becoming artistic director of the Urban Arts Corps in Greenwich Village, where several of her productions were conceived and staged. Her credits included an Obie for acting in Errol John's _Moon in a Rainbow Shawl_ (1962), the 1972 Los Angeles Drama Critics Circle Award for Best Direction, and several Tony nominations. Memorable among her Broadway productions were _Don't Bother Me, I Can't Cope_ (1972), written by Micki Grant and showing how blacks have used their music to cope with life's problems, and _Your Arm's Too Short to Box with God_ (1976; revived at the Beacon Theatre in 1996), based on stories taken from the Gospel of Matthew. From 1980 to her death Carroll worked in

Fort Lauderdale, FL, where she established her own repertory company.   EGH

Carter, Mrs. Leslie (1862–1937) Actress. Mrs. Carter and DAVID BELASCO, her tutor and director, discovered that striking beauty, emotional pyrotechnics, and a sensational divorce could make a star performer – first in *The Heart of Maryland* (1895, for a three-year run), in which she swung on the clapper of a bell to keep it from ringing, and then in such slightly lurid dramas as *Zaza* (1899), *DU BARRY* (1901), and *Adrea* (1905). According to one critic, Mrs Carter would "weep, vociferate, shriek, rant, become hoarse with passion, and finally flop and beat the floor."

Although after breaking with Belasco (1906) she continued to perform, on the road and sometimes under her own management, in *Camille, The Second Mrs. Tanqueray,* and *The Circle,* she never matched her successes with Belasco.   RM

Casino Theatre Broadway and West 39th St., NYC [Architects: Francis Kimball and Thomas Wisedell]. Designed in a Moorish style complete with turret, the Casino was opened by RUDOLPH ARONSON in 1882. During its long history, it presented musical shows of all varieties: comedies, operettas, comic operas, and REVUES. In 1890, Aronson opened New York's first roof-garden theatre atop the Casino, where light musical fare was served up with light after-theatre refreshments. The house is best remembered for *FLORODORA,* one of the most popular musical comedies of its day. The Casino was torn down in 1930.   MCH

Cassidy, Claudia (1900–96) Drama critic. Born in Illinois, Cassidy spent her girlhood in Chicago and attended the University of Illinois in Urbana. She began her career as a drama and music critic with the *Chicago Journal of Commerce* in 1925, quickly gaining a reputation for being tough but fair. In 1941, she left the *Journal* to organize the music and drama departments of the new *Chicago Daily Sun* (now the *Sun-Times*). Within a year, she was hired by the *Tribune.* Until her retirement in 1965, Cassidy wrote a daily column, "On the Aisle," and contributed to the Sunday edition. She toured Europe during the summers, sending back to the *Tribune* her impressions of "Europe on the Aisle." Considered the most powerful CHICAGO critic, or even the dowager queen of American critics, Cassidy was credited with stopping New York producers from sending weak companies on the road. Her major credo was that the "only way to judge a play is to wait and see if the

theatre brings it to life." A theatre in the Chicago Cultural Center was named for her.   TLM

Cat on a Hot Tin Roof TENNESSEE WILLIAMS's Pulitzer Prize–winning drama, directed by ELIA KAZAN, opened 24 March 1955 at the MOROSCO THEATRE with Barbara BEL GEDDES as Maggie, Ben Gazzara as Brick, Burl Ives as Big Daddy, and MILDRED DUNNOCK as Big Mama. It ran 694 performances. Kazan persuaded the playwright to alter the original ending by bringing Big Daddy back onstage and by making Maggie more sympathetic; thus the play had two different third acts (the reading and stage versions). In 1974 Williams combined the original and the Kazan-inspired revision for the AMERICAN SHAKESPEARE THEATRE production starring Elizabeth Ashley, Keir Dullea, and Fred Gwynne as Big Daddy. A popular revival in 1990 starred Kathleen Turner with CHARLES DURNING (Tony Award) as Big Daddy. The 1958 film version featured Ives's Big Daddy with Elizabeth Taylor and Paul Newman. The play was televised in 1976 with Robert Wagner, Natalie Wood, and Laurence Olivier and in 1984 with Jessica Lange, Tommy Lee Jones, and RIP TORN. A 2003 Broadway revival with Ashley Judd as Maggie and Jason Patric as Brick was most notable for Ned Beatty's Big Daddy. Like other Williams's plays, *Cat* explores levels of love and mendacity – Maggie and Brick; Brick and Big Daddy; and Brick with his college (homosexual?) friend Skipper. The ultimate victor is Maggie who, having finally gotten Brick into bed, hopes the lie about her pregnancy may come true.   PCK

Cats In June 1997, the British musical *Cats* – with music by ANDREW LLOYD WEBBER (and one hit, "Memory"), book based on poems by T. S. ELIOT (*Old Possum's Book of Practical Cats*), direction by Trevor Nunn, choreography by Gillian Lynne, and produced by CAMERON MACKINTOSH – passed the more savvy and sophisticated *A CHORUS LINE* to become the longest-running show in Broadway history up to that time. Credited as the production that initiated the era of the megaspectacle, the Broadway version of the largely plotless musical opened at the WINTER GARDEN THEATRE, completely deconstructed to accommodate the production's unique staging, on 7 October 1982, winning seven Tonys including Best Musical, and closed on 10 September 2000 after 7,485 performances. With its slogan, "Now and Forever," its run became synonymous with longevity, and this mystique helped to account for its long existence (the London run lasted 21 years and almost 9,000 performances) as much as its "purely theatrical magic," in critic Frank Rich's words.   DBW

Cawthorn, Joseph (1868–1949) Comedian. As a child, Cawthorn performed in minstrel shows and in English music halls. Returning to America, he appeared in comic operas as a "Dutch comic," speaking fractured English with a German accent. After early successes in such musicals as *Excelsior, Jr.* (1895) and *Miss Philadelphia* (1897), Cawthorn played leading roles in *The Fortune Teller* (1898), *Mother Goose* (1903), *The Free Lance* (1906), *Little Nemo* (1908), *The Slim Princess* (1911), and many other shows. During WWI he dropped his German accent. His last Broadway appearance was in *Sunny* (1925), which starred MARILYN MILLER.   MK

Cayvan, Georgia (1858–1906) Actress who made her New York debut in 1880 as Dolly Dutton (*HAZEL KIRKE*); however, her forceful portrayal as Jocasta (*Oedipus Tyrannus,* 1881) brought her prominence. Thereafter, as a leading actress of the MADISON SQUARE THEATRE and, during 1887–94, of the LYCEUM THEATRE Company, she acted love-torn heroines in numerous popular comedies and melodramas, such as H. C. DEMILLE and BELASCO's *The Wife,* Buchanan's *Squire Kate,* and Pinero's *The Amazons.* Following a season touring with her own company, she retired in poor health in 1897.   DJW

Cazuran, Augustus R. (1820–89) Playwright, journalist, and drama critic. Arriving in America from Ireland in 1848, Cazuran served as theatre critic for the *New York Herald,* fought for the North in the Civil War, and afterward wrote for the *Washington Chronicle,* in whose pages he reported Lincoln's assassination, having been in the audience at FORD'S THEATRE. Employed at the UNION SQUARE THEATRE as play reader, translator, and adaptor, he was, according to G. C. D. Odell, "ever useful," Although his original plays (such as *The Fatal Letter,* 1884) failed in the theatre, his adaptations were successful, including those of Thomas Hardy's *Far from the Madding Crowd* (1882) and Octave Feuillet's *A Parisian Romance* (1883), which made RICHARD MANSFIELD famous.   WJM

Céleste, Mme Céline (Céleste Keppler) (1811–82) French dancer, the majority of whose unusual career belongs to the English and U.S. theatres. Most works of reference accept her own claim that she was born in 1814, but her marriage in Baltimore in 1828, following her NYC debut in 1827 at the Bowery, as well as the birth of a child in 1829 make that improbable. She had visited the U.S. with a Parisian dance troupe (1827–30), and had already divested herself of husband and child when she made her English debut in 1830. A graceful dancer and mime, she solicited from English playwrights pieces that would either allow her to remain speechless throughout or would accommodate her unrepentant French accent. Céleste became a wealthy woman and had several lucrative and wildly popular American tours as dancer and actress, often playing several roles in the same night (1834–43, 1851, 1865). Her most popular vehicle was *The French Spy.*   PT

censorship (theatre) In the U.S., this most often occurs when a constellation of circumstances converge to challenge the mythologies, laws, and political base of the dominant hegemony. Consequently, theatre has found itself entangled in a succession of snares constructed by churchmen, judges, politicians, and moral crusaders who have sought to halt moral, economic, political, or social change.

The harmful effects of theatre and other para-theatrical amusements were a concern of most English colonial governors and legislatures. The first recorded theatre prosecution was brought against three actors from Virginia, who in 1665 attempted a production of *Ye Bare and Ye Cubb.* However, the vast majority of theatre censorship took place in northern colonies settled by conservative Christian sects. For Quaker settlers of Pennsylvania and Puritan colonists in New England, the stage represented an anarchic site, exempt from the laws of the state and of God. Moreover, theatre was linked to the monarchy from which they had escaped. William Penn prohibited theatre in Pennsylvania in 1682; the colonial assembly outlawed stage plays on three separate occasions only to have its measures vetoed by the crown. Although the London Company of Comedians enjoyed success in PHILADELPHIA from 1753 until the outbreak of the revolution, no theatre was built within the city limits; rather, performances were outside the city and thus beyond the jurisdiction of the city council. Massachusetts had never permitted theatre but officially proscribed it in 1750 with legislation that remained in force until 1793, four years after the Bill of Rights. Wealthy merchants in Newport, RI, welcomed the Comedians, but in Providence in 1762 the assembly voted to forbid theatrical productions in the colony. The Continental Congress (1774) even passed three separate measures prohibiting theatrical enactments during the war.

Early antitheatrical attitudes, fueled by religious objections and a nagging suspicion that theatre was morally subversive, never completely vanished. Yet, during the first half of the 19th century legislators, churchmen, and civic leaders were more concerned with controlling the disruptive behavior of working-class audiences than with blasphemous implications of theatre. During the second half of the century a few complaints about immorality and the stage resurfaced. ADAH ISAACS MENKEN's 1861 appearance in *Mazeppa* strapped to the back of a horse clad only in flesh-colored tights provoked moralists. Later that decade LYDIA THOMPSON's burlesque comedy troupe of "British Blondes" was targeted because their pink tights and brief overgarments suggested nudity. In 1872 Anthony Comstock formed the Committee for the Suppression of Vice, followed in a year by the repressive Comstock Law. These were the first concerted efforts to suppress morally objectional material. Generally, however, American theatre confined itself to innocuous material that supported middle-class virtues (e.g., monogamy, frugality, temperance, modesty). In addition, theatre rarely challenged rigidly defined social conventions that depicted women as asexual beings who possessed little or no political or economic power and whose sole interests were the sanctity of their home and family.

Beginning in 1900 a convergence of social phenomena ended this tranquillity. Educated women entered new fields and proposed that gender differences were socially constructed. Tens of thousands of single men and women migrated to cities in search of jobs, engaging in courtship rituals without supervision of parents, teachers, or ministers. Moreover, a host of playwrights, influenced by European naturalists, began to depict characters driven by sex, power, and greed. Among the first to feel repercussions from those who objected to such a role was Olga Nethersole, producer and star of CLYDE FITCH's *Sapho*, who was hauled into court in February 1900 for endangering public morals. In Fitch's play a reformed courtesan escapes madness and/or death, typical fates for fallen women, and is rewarded at the end of the piece. In February 1905 ARNOLD DALY staged the American premiere of BERNARD SHAW's *Mrs Warren's Profession*, about a successful woman who owns a string of successful European brothels. Chief Magistrate William McAdoo had Daly and his cast arrested and the show closed. Just prior to WWI fear for the welfare of single women intensified as more and more stories of white slavery began to surface. Though the tales of kidnapped white women sold into prostitution were almost entirely fabricated, a spate of plays collectively known as "brothel plays" were produced on the presumption that producers and writers were motivated by a genuine concern for women's welfare. Many district attorneys disagreed, labeling the productions obscene because they often depicted interiors of bordellos, and forced such plays as *The Lure* (1913), *The Fight* (1913), and *The House of Bondage* (1914) to delete such scenes and to alter dialogue or face arrest.

The end of WWI brought a radical transformation of the nation's cultural landscape; mass production and consumption captured the imagination of the populace, who challenged fixed rules regarding sex, religion, sport, music, and attire. This insurgency did not go unchallenged; entrenched business, political, and religious leaders tried to buttress the traditional order. Still, although sexual themes appeared onstage during the teens, producers and audiences now seemed obsessed with nudity, sexual situations, and blunt language. *The Demi-Virgin* (1921) by AVERY HOPWOOD and Al Wood was a frivolous play about an unconsummated marriage between two Hollywood stars, yet the Commissioner of Licenses for Manhattan was not amused, revoking the occupancy license of the Eltinge Theatre housing the production. MAE WEST served ten days in jail for producing, writing, and starring in *Sex* (1926), and was arrested and tried again for *The Pleasure Man* (1928), a tawdry murder tale that contained a scene depicting five transvestites as they dressed for a performance. Partly as a result of *Sex,* New York passed the infamous Wales Padlock Law in 1927, allowing local authorities to arrest actors, lock theatres, and ban productions deemed indecent. Although rarely invoked, it remained on the books for 40 years and led many theatrical producers to modify their work to avoid prosecution.

In truth, authorities were unwilling or unable to discern between frivolous "sexploitation" shows and serious artistic endeavors. The producer and cast of *The God of Vengeance* (1922), the first show on Broadway to deal openly with lesbianism, were arrested and convicted. *The Captive* (1926), which dealt with the same theme, was forced to close. O'NEILL's *ALL GOD'S CHILLUN' GOT WINGS* (1924), a tragedy about a black man married to a white woman, was threatened by the Ku Klux Klan. *WHAT PRICE GLORY* (1924), a WWI drama, was attacked for defaming the military. Perhaps the most sensational censorship case of the decade occurred not in New York but in BOSTON, where Mayor Malcolm Nichols prohibited O'Neill's *STRANGE INTERLUDE* from opening in September 1929.

In the 1930s reformers, fueled by a belief that immorality and profligacy had brought on the Depression, exerted even more pressure on shows that depicted moral or political deviants. Boston's Mayor Frederick Mansfield refused to let Sean O'Casey's *Within the Gates* open in 1935 because it questioned the existence of God. Later that year he threatened *The CHILDREN'S HOUR* because of its treatment of lesbianism. Also in 1935 CHICAGO's Mayor Edward Kelly closed *TOBACCO ROAD* because of its reputedly indecent themes.

Although moral reformers continued their crusades, it was political conservatives who led the majority of antitheatre campaigns until the early 1960s. In May 1938 the House of Representatives established the House Un-American Activities Committee (HUAC). Originally meant to investigate fascist propaganda in the U.S., it almost immediately began to investigate the alleged communist infiltration of the FEDERAL THEATRE PROJECT of the Works Progress Administration. Most of the FTP's productions were noncontroversial, though the LIVING NEWSPAPER in New York mounted several topical presentations that attacked various social and economic stances held by conservative lawmakers. As a result, HUAC reported that communists had invaded the FTP, and Congress voted to eliminate FTP appropriation in 1939. The purges continued until the end of the 1950s, ending the careers of hundreds of film and stage professionals because of accusations of either being communists or associating with them.

During the era of the 1960s – more a state of mind than a specific decade – moral, political, and cultural attitudes underwent another shift. The civil rights movement, multiple political assassinations, urban riots, and the Vietnam War gave rise to a new militant theatre. Many producers, directors, and playwrights vigorously challenged the morally hypocritical, racist, and militaristic practices that they believed dominated national policy, thus marking the beginning of a new chapter in American theatre and censorship. LeRoi Jones (later known as AMIRI BARAKA) openly indicted white America for its racist attitudes in *DUTCHMAN* (1964), *The TOILET* (1964), and *The Slave* (1964). When the latter two opened in LOS ANGELES, police closed them; when they reopened, neither of the two major newspapers would accept advertising. The SAN FRANCISCO MIME TROUPE was denied a permit to perform their radical comedies in city parks. In September 1968 the LIVING THEATRE performed its anarchistic *Paradise Now* at Yale University, where the company's founders and directors, JULIAN BECK and JUDITH

MALINA, were arrested for indecent exposure. Soon after, MIT officials canceled their performances, and arrests and subsequent cancellations occurred in Philadelphia, Madison, WI, and Berkeley. Also in 1968 a college production of Michael McClure's *The Beard* (1967) in California triggered a full-scale legislative inquiry, claiming a direct connection between anti-Vietnam protests and radical theatre. RICHARD SCHECHNER'S The PERFORMANCE GROUP was arrested in Ann Arbor for indecent exposure when they refused to modify the company's well-publicized nude birth scene in *Dionysus in 69*. *HAIR*, arguably the signature production of the 1960s, was put on trial in federal court in both Massachusetts and Arkansas (both exonerated, and decisions rendered helped secure free-speech rights for theatrical productions).

During the late 1980s and '90s transgressive sexuality was again the target the churchmen and public officials who attempted to ban sympathetic depictions of homosexuality and/or AIDS. The furor erupted in 1989 when conservative politicians and fundamentalist Christians tried to eliminate NATIONAL ENDOWMENT FOR THE ARTS funding; the NEA survived but with a severely cut budget. Following Congress's example, county commissions and city councils attempted, by eliminating public funding, to silence theatres whose presentations challenged conservative religious beliefs. Theatre in the Square (Marietta, GA) lost Cobb County funding for support of McNALLY's *Lips Together, Teeth Apart* in 1993. The City Commission of Charlotte, NC, withheld $2.5 million from the Arts and Science Council because Charlotte Rep staged *ANGELS IN AMERICA* and JOHN GUARE's *SIX DEGREES OF SEPARATION*. Similar battles occurred in San Antonio and Anchorage. In 1998 the Catholic League for Religious and Civil Rights mounted in NYC a concerted campaign to prohibit production of McNally's *Corpus Christi*. The tale of a "gay Jesus" was slated to open in September at the MANHATTAN THEATRE CLUB. With support of the *New York Post* and a plethora of phone callers, some threatening to bomb the theatre, MTC first yielded to the pressure and canceled; yet with playwright protest across the country, the play opened amid noisy demonstrations, police, and bomb-sniffing dogs. Ironically, the play and production received tepid critical and popular response.   JHo

Center Stage Founded in Baltimore by committee in 1963 and since designated the State Theatre of Maryland, Center Stage has grown from a theatre dominated by modern classics into one that balances classics with new works. The theatre courted controversy in 1971 with Daniel Berrigan Jr.'s *The Trial of the Catonsville Nine,* based on nearby civil disobedience. Managed for most of its history by Peter Culman, the theatre thrived under the artistic directorship (1977–91) of Stan Wojewodski Jr., replaced by Irene Lewis after his departure to the YALE REP. Premieres include works by ERIC OVERMYER (*ON THE VERGE*), David Feldshuh (*Miss Evers' Boys*), Elizabeth Egloff (*The Lover*), and LYNN NOTTAGE (*Intimate Apparel*). In 1991 the theatre added the flexible Head Theater to its existing 541-seat mainstage, the Pearlstone Theater.   SF

Center Theatre Group (Los Angeles)

A not-for-profit theatre company founded in 1966 to serve as the umbrella organization for activities at both the Ahmanson Theatre and the MARK TAPER FORUM, which, with the Dorothy Chandler Pavilion and the new Walt Disney Concert Hall, form the venues of the Music Center of Los Angeles County. Both the Taper and the Ahmanson were completed in 1967. MICHAEL RITCHIE has been CTG's artistic director since January 2005; GORDON DAVIDSON, who led the company for 38 years, serves as founding artistic director. One of Ritchie's first actions was to cut several minority-based developmental theatre initiatives, a move that has led to controversy not fully resolved as of fall 2005.

At the 1,600–2,400-seat Ahmanson a wide variety of dramas, musicals, comedies, and classic revivals are presented. Seasons have included 13 plays by Neil Simon (6 of them world premieres), as well as plays by other leading American playwrights such as WENDY WASSERSTEIN, AUGUST WILSON, A. R. GURNEY, TERRENCE MCNALLY, JOHN GUARE, and EDWARD ALBEE. Recent highlights include the American premieres of Matthew Bourne's *Swan Lake, Cinderella,* and *The Car Man.*

The 745-seat Taper has presented over 180 mainstage productions, including 55 world premieres and 45 West Coast premieres, from such playwrights as TONY KUSHNER, MCNALLY, LUIS VALDÉZ, JON ROBIN BAITZ, EDWARD MACHADO, ANNA DEAVERE SMITH, LANFORD WILSON, and AUGUST WILSON.

In October 2004 a third theatre opened, the Kirk Douglas Theatre in Culver City. The 317-seat venue, housed within a historically designated moviehouse from the 1940s, is an intimate and adaptable space in which CTG can present new plays and also provide programming specifically for families and young people. The inaugural season included six world-premiere plays by such authors as CHARLES L. MEE and Baitz.

Taper productions have won three Pulitzers and 23 Tonys, and in 1977 the company received the special Tony for regional theatre. Artists have included directors TYRONE GUTHRIE, HAROLD CLURMAN, MARSHALL W. MASON, ATHOL FUGARD, ELLIS RABB, JOSÉ QUINTERO, ROBERT WOODRUFF, JOE MANTELLO, GEORGE C. WOLFE, and Kenneth Branagh; designers MING CHO LEE, PETER WEXLER, THARON MUSSER, and RALPH FUNICELLO; and many well-known film and stage actors.   JDM DBW

Central City Opera House

Built in 1876, during the Colorado gold rush, to take advantage of the continuous stream of talent in transit between San Francisco and the East Coast, the facility fell into disrepair by 1900, with the gold rush over. Willed to the University of Denver in 1931, it was restored in 1932, reopening with LILLIAN GISH in *Camille* and becoming home to an annual summer opera festival hosting world-renowned opera stars. The festival led to a revitalization of the Central City area, which has since become a popular tourist attraction.   PAD

Century Theatre see NEW THEATRE

Ceremonies in Dark Old Men

Domestic tragicomedy by African American playwright LONNE ELDER. Set in a Harlem barbershop that fronts for selling bootleg whiskey, the play exposes the survival strategies of those victimized because of their race. In a 1969 NEGRO ENSEMBLE COMPANY production, the play was mostly praised for its realism and objectivity by New York critics who proposed it as a Tony Award candidate. Dissenting voices thought it overlong, some characters inconsistent, and the ending predictable.   EGH

Cerveris, Michael

(1960–) Actor, singer, and musician, born in Maryland and educated at Yale. Winner of the 2004 Tony for Best Featured Actor in a Musical, the revival of *Assassins* (JOHN WILKES BOOTH), Cerveris also appeared as the tormented Giorgio in *Passion* (Sondheim Celebration, JOHN F. KENNEDY CENTER), in the title role of *SWEENEY TODD* (2005 revival), and as WEILL in *LoveMusik* (2007). Other Broadway roles include Tommy (*The Who's Tommy*), which he originated at the LA JOLLA PLAYHOUSE in 1992, and ship designer Thomas Andrews in *Titanic* (1997); Off-Broadway he excelled as Hedwig in 1998 in *HEDWIG AND THE ANGRY INCH* (described by the *NY Times* as "captivating, mesmerizing and enthralling"). He has also played a wide range of nonsinging roles, including in 2003 that of paraplegic Vietnam vet

Ken Talley in FIFTH OF JULY (SIGNATURE THEATRE). His brother **Todd** is also an actor and playwright (*The Booth Variations*, 2004).   DBW

Chaikin, Joseph (1935–2003) Director, actor, and producer. Born in Brooklyn and educated at Drake University, Chaikin made his New York debut in *Dark of the Moon* (1958). He joined The LIVING THEATRE the following year and appeared in *Many Loves* and *Tonight We Improvise* (1959); *The CONNECTION* and Brecht's *Jungle of Cities* (1961–2); and *Man Is Man* (1962). For the Writers' Stage (1964), he performed in Ionesco's *The New Tenant* and *Victims of Duty*. Chaikin founded The OPEN THEATRE in 1964 as an experimental company to build and perform new scripts. The success of *AMERICA HURRAH* in 1966 (1967 in London) established his reputation. His workshop approach to composition also produced *Terminal* and *The Serpent* in 1970, the latter a series of episodes on the history of murder. Chaikin directed for the NEW YORK SHAKESPEARE FESTIVAL, MANHATTAN THEATRE CLUB, SIGNATURE THEATRE COMPANY, MAGIC THEATRE of SAN FRANCISCO, and MARK TAPER FORUM of LOS ANGELES. An articulate spokesman for the 1960s avant-garde movement, Chaikin won numerous awards, including five Obies. After a stroke in 1984 resulted in aphasia, Chaikin performed in NYC for the first time in 1991 (AMERICAN PLACE) in plays he coauthored with SAM SHEPARD (*The War in Heaven*) and JEAN-CLAUDE VAN ITALLIE (*Struck Dumb*) that reflected that experience. Chaikin, long associated with the plays of Samuel Beckett, directed his *Texts for Nothing* for the NYSF in 1992 and seven years later acted in it. In 1998 he directed Arthur Miller's one-acts *I Can't Remember Anything* and *The Last Yankee* for Signature, and in 2002 directed Beckett's *Happy Days* (Cherry Lane Theatre). At the time of his death he was working energetically on at least three projected productions. In 1984, his career to date was chronicled by Eileen Blumenthal.   TLM

Chalfant, Kathleen (Palmer) (1945–) San Francisco–born actor who, after a solid but largely unheralded 20-year Off-Broadway and regional career, in 1993 won major acclaim in *ANGELS IN AMERICA*, both parts 1 and 2, as Hannah Pitt, Ethel Rosenberg, Rabbi Chemelwitz, and other roles (Tony and Drama Desk nominations) and then Off-Broadway (as well as Los Angeles) in the central role of Professor Vivian Bearing in Margaret Edson's *WIT* in 1998 (Lucille Lortel Award, Drama Desk, Obie for performance). Recent appearances include a once-famous actress in Marguerite Duras's *Savannah Bay* (CLASSIC STAGE COMPANY)

and the monologue *The Last Letter* (THEATER FOR A NEW AUDIENCE), both in 2003. Chalfant, a consummate character actor and social activist, has performed for most major New York companies, and appeared in more than 30 feature films and numerous television series.   DBW

Champion, Gower (1921–80) Dancer, choreographer, and director who appeared as a dancer in *The Streets of Paris* (1939) and several other shows before turning to choreography with *Small Wonder* (1948). After dancing with his wife, Marge, in several Hollywood films, Champion returned to Broadway as the director and choreographer of *Bye Bye Birdie* (1960). The charm and energy of his staging led to further directing and choreography assignments for *Carnival* (1961), *HELLO, DOLLY!* (1964), *I Do! I Do!* (1966), *Irene* (1973), *Mack & Mabel* (1974), and others. Champion died the day that his last show, *42ND STREET*, opened in 1980. His initial directorial work evinced a fresh and inventive approach to staging a musical. *Carnival*, in particular, was praised for its imaginative, stylized production. Champion, along with BOB FOSSE and MICHAEL BENNETT, made the choreographer-director the dominant figure in the musical theatre of the 1970s.   Biographies by David Payne-Carter and John Anthony Gilvey were published in 1999 and 2005, respectively.   MK

Chaney, Stewart (1910–69) Scenic designer of many of the popular Broadway shows of the late 1930 and '40s, including *LIFE WITH FATHER* (1939) and *The Late George Apley* (1944). He became known for clever and stylish interiors, although he was capable of architectural and painterly settings. He wished to strike a balance between three-dimensional realism and artificial theatricality. *The Voice of the Turtle* (1943), simultaneously depicting three rooms of an apartment, including a kitchen sink with running water, was one of his most famous.   AA

Chanfrau, Frank (1824–84) New York–born actor. Inspired to become an actor by a performance of EDWIN FORREST, he gained recognition through his ability to imitate Forrest, starting on a tour of theatres and cities across America that eventually led him to the Olympic Theatre in New York in 1848. As Mose the fire b'hoy in *A GLANCE AT NEW YORK*, written for him by BENJAMIN A. BAKER, Chanfrau became the "lion" of the town. Dressed in the red shirt, plug hat, and turned-up trousers of the New York fireman, Chanfrau was featured in several Mose plays, particularly *The Mysteries and Miseries of New York* by Henry W. Plunkett.

Friends leased the CHATHAM THEATRE for Chanfrau, who renamed it the National and continued to perform the role of Mose for about three and a half years. After this popularity, Chanfrau performed the title role 560 times in KIT, THE ARKANSAS TRAVELLER, and played the lead character in THOMAS deWALDEN's *Sam* 783 times.   WJM

Chang, Tisa (1941–) Chinese American actor, director, and founder–artistic director of PAN ASIAN REPERTORY THEATRE. Born in China, she graduated from Barnard College and studied with UTA HAGEN, performed on Broadway, and first directed at LA MAMA ETC. In 1977 she created Pan Asian Rep with the intention of opening up more opportunities for ASIAN AMERICAN THEATRE artists. The many works she has directed there include new plays by R. A. Shiomi and ERNEST ABUBA (her former husband), cross-cultural versions of classics (a bilingual Mandarin–English *A Midsummer Night's Dream*), ambitious thematic projects (*Ghashiram Kotwal,* an Indian music-drama), Asian-influenced/inspired contemporary plays (*Roshomon* by Fay and Michael Kanin), and plays on Asian pioneers and role models (*China Doll,* celebrating Anna May Wong's 100th birthday in 2005).   MB

Channing, Carol (1921–) Seattle-born and Bennington-educated singer and comedienne who made her New York debut in MARC BLITZSTEIN's *No for an Answer* (1941). Critics praised her work in the revue *Lend an Ear* (1948), and in the following year she became a star with her larger-than-life performance as 1920s vamp Lorelei Lee in the musical version of *Gentlemen Prefer Blondes.* She succeeded Rosalind Russell in WONDERFUL TOWN (1954), appeared in the short-lived musical *The Vamp* (1955) and the revue *Show Girl* (1961), and toured with the Bernard SHAW play *The Million-airess* (1963) before starring in the long-running hit *HELLO, DOLLY!* in 1964 (Tony). As matchmaker Dolly Gallagher Levi, Channing gave a warm, funny, and at times outrageous performance. In subsequent years, she was unable to find vehicles worthy of her unique talents. *Lorelei* (1974) lasted only nine months, and the play *Legends* (1986) with MARY MARTIN closed before reaching Broadway. However, a 30th anniversary tour (1994–5) of *Hello, Dolly!* was a triumph. A special Tony for Lifetime Achievement was presented to her in 1995. Her autobiography was published in 2002.   MK

Channing, Stockard [née Susan Williams Antonio Stockard] (1944–) New York–born and Radcliffe-educated (BA, 1965) actress who began professional stage work in 1967 with the Theatre Company of Boston and, after a stint in California, made her Broadway debut in 1971. Despite some dozen major NYC appearances since, a failed TV series, and poorly received films (excepting *Grease*), it was not until her Tony Award–winning portrayal in *Joe Egg* (1985 Broadway revival) that her extraordinary stage talent began to be recognized. Other notable appearances include NEIL SIMON's *They're Playing Our Song* (1980 replacement), GUARE's *The HOUSE OF BLUE LEAVES* (1986 revival, as Bunny), Ayckbourn's *Woman in Mind* (1988, Drama Desk), GURNEY's *Love Letters* (1989), and especially Guare's SIX DEGREES OF SEPARATION (1990; London, 1992; film, 1993), in which she was critically acclaimed as Ouisa. Other New York appearances include Peter Hall's production of Guare's *Four Baboons Adoring the Sun* (1992) at the VIVIAN BEAUMONT, Stoppard's *Hapgood* (1994) at the Mitzi E. Newhouse, Regina Giddens in the 1997 Lincoln Center revival of *The LITTLE FOXES* ("guile and guts"), and Eleanor opposite Laurence Fishburne's Henry in the 1998 revival of *The Lion in Winter.* Gurney has said that Channing has the ability "to combine a sense of comedy with a sense of pathos to get at the ache underneath." In recent years she has appeared extensively in television.   DBW

Chapman family see SHOWBOATS

Chapman, John Arthur (1900–72) Drama critic. A native of Colorado, Chapman began his career with *The Denver Times* (1917–19) before moving to the *New York Daily News* (1920), where he became dramatic editor (1929) and replaced BURNS MANTLE as drama critic (1943), retiring in 1971. He wrote a popular column, "Mainly about Broadway," in the 1930s, and edited the *Best Plays* series during 1947–53. He was known as "Old Frostface" for his straightforward prose and no-nonsense demeanor.   TLM

Charles II; or, The Merry Monarch Considered by many to be JOHN HOWARD PAYNE's most popular work, this three-act comedy, based on Alexander Duval's *La Jeunesse de Henri V* (1806), was a collaborative effort. Payne, who claimed to have penned the work while in Paris during 1823, was assisted by WASHINGTON IRVING (much of the comic dialogue betrays his style), who had anonymously assisted on five other Payne plays. It opened on 27 May 1824 at London's Covent Garden. Popular on the American stage for much of the 19th century (in the repertoires of JOSEPH

JEFFERSON III and FANNY KEMBLE), it was initially attributed to the English writer Thomas Dibdin and criticized for being a simplistic farce, dwelling on the romantic adventures of Rochester and King Charles II. PAD

Charnin, Martin (1934–) Lyricist, director, and actor. After graduating from Cooper Union, he began to act and to write lyrics, contributing lyrics to the OFF-BROADWAY revue *Kaleidoscope* and playing Big Deal in *WEST SIDE STORY* (both 1957). He wrote lyrics for a number of musicals, notably *Two by Two* (1970), *ANNIE* (1977), *I REMEMBER MAMA* (1979), and *Annie Warbucks* (1994). He also directed several plays and musicals, including *Sid Caesar & Company* (1989), *Carnal Knowledge* (1990), and the 1997 revival of *Annie*. His memoir was published in 1977. MK

Chase, Mary (Ellen) Coyle (1907–81) Playwright and screenwriter. Her first produced play, *Me Third* (1936), was written for the FEDERAL THEATRE PROJECT in Denver. She continued writing plays throughout her career, most of which had limited success, ending with *Cocktails with Mimi* in 1974. In 1952 *Mrs. McThing,* starring HELEN HAYES, was a hit on Broadway; but her most successful drama was *HARVEY,* the name given a giant invisible rabbit, which won the Pulitzer Prize in 1945 and became one of the longest-running plays on Broadway to date. A biography by Westbrook was published in 1965. FB

Chatham Theatre (Chatham Garden Theatre) Park Row between Pearl and Duane Sts., NYC [Architect: George Conklin]. In 1823, Hippolite Barrière, proprietor of the Chatham Gardens, decided to dispense light entertainment along with summer refreshments on the property. He erected a tent theatre, perhaps America's first summer playhouse; the following year, he built a permanent structure and was for several seasons a formidable rival to the PARK THEATRE. After 1827, its vogue passed, it presented everything from SHAKESPEARE to equestrian drama to French opera under a succession of managers that failed to revive its fortunes. In 1832, it was converted to a Presbyterian chapel. MCH

Chautauqua and Lyceum Prominent cultural, educational, and religious organizations of the late 19th–early 20th century, part of a movement initiated by evangelists traveling the "sawdust trail" along the western frontier in gospel tents, beginning in an organized fashion with the Millerites in 1842. Both Chautauqua and Lyceum ultimately offered theatrical or platform entertainment.

Chautauqua, founded by John Heyl Vincent and Lewis Miller, began in New York State during the summer of 1874 as a tent meeting on the shores of Lake Chautauqua. By 1884 Chautauqua had expanded beyond its original intent to offer only religious instruction, and began to include cultural edification of all sorts, including dramatic interpretation and stereoptican views. Experiments with summer Chautauqua circuits began in 1904, first organized by Keith Vawter and Roy J. Ellison; soon there were Chautauqua tents nationwide, carried over established circuits (by 1912 there were over 1,000 independent Chautauquas) in the summer. Very soon, show business became part of the formula of the brown tents (see TENT SHOW) of Chautauqua – brown, in contrast to the white top of the CIRCUS, became a symbol of its quasi-cultural inspiration – and because of the extensive circuits, a good Chautauqua act could survive for years. Typically, a Chautauqua program combined elements of VAUDEVILLE (especially as vaudeville became more "refined") and dramatic sketches, in addition to the usual smattering of lectures and other "cultural" programming. Since early Chautauqua was generally hostile to traditional theatre, preference was given to platform performances, in particular the ONE-PERSON show; as Victorian intolerance for the stage weakened, more actual drama was offered in Chautauqua. As early 1904 the New York Chautauqua offered Ben Jonson's masque *The Sad Shepherd,* and in 1910 Shakespeare plays were presented by the Nicholson Sylvan Players. The ultimate cause (of many) of the Chautauqua circuit's rather abrupt demise in the 1920s was the radio – although there is still an active program at the permanent home in New York. The most recent study of Chautauqua, by Charlotte Canning, was published in 2005.

Quite different from Chautauqua, the Lyceums, active as early as 1826, operated in the winter, in permanent venues and in urban settings, in contrast to tent Chautauqua in rural areas. Although different institutions, both often shared a common pool of talent; but there was less pure entertainment in Lyceum. Still, with skilled promoters – in particular James Redpath in the second half of the 19th century – Lyceum prospered, with a less perceptible collapse than Chautauqua, continuing into the 1940s and gradually having its function usurped by college and university lecture, writer, and performance series. During its heyday, some of the great celebrities of the time appeared as Lyceum presentations, including

Daniel Webster, EDGAR ALLAN POE, FANNY KEM-
BLE, CHARLOTTE CUSHMAN, Charles Dickens, and
Mark Twain.   DBW

Chayefsky, Paddy (1923–81) Playwright. A self-
styled activist social critic, Chayefsky established
himself as a writer during the heyday of live television drama, moved to films with the highly honored *Marty* (1955), succeeded briefly as a Broadway
playwright, and finally abandoned the legitimate
stage to concentrate again on writing for motion
pictures. His Broadway plays were *Middle of the
Night* (1956), *The Tenth Man* (1959; revived 1989, at
VIVIAN BEAUMONT), *Gideon* (1961), and *The Passion
of Josef D* (1964). His last play, *The Latent Heterosexual* (1968), was successfully produced in American
regional professional theatres and at the Bristol
Old Vic in England. The culmination of his filmwriting career came with *Network* (1976). Shaun
Considine published a biography in 1994.   LDC

Chekhov on the American stage The first American translation of a play by Anton Chekhov was
the awkwardly titled *The Cherry Garden* by Max
Mandell (1908). *The Bear* and *The Seagull* received
professional productions from the WASHINGTON
SQUARE PLAYERS (Bandbox Theatre, NYC) in
1915–16, but Chekhov was viewed as alien and
depressing until the MOSCOW ART THEATRE
toured the U.S. in 1923–4. Their productions of
Uncle Vanya, *Three Sisters*, and *Ivanov* impressed the
critics and the profession with their subtle atmosphere and ensemble playing. The GROUP THE-
ATRE was deeply influenced, but their attempt to
produce a *Three Sisters* in 1939 was abortive. Chekhov continued to be seen as a delicate Russian
exotic, which enabled émigrés such as Leo Bulgakov amd Maria Germanova to claim expertise
in staging him in their own nostalgic ways. EVA
LE GALLIENNE's uplifting CIVIC REPERTORY THE-
ATRE adopted Chekhov as a house dramatist, her
productions sedulously imitating the Art Theatre
approach, in the first American *Three Sisters* (1926),
The Cherry Orchard (1928) with ALLA NAZIMOVA as
Ranevskaya, and *The Seagull* (1929), with Yiddish
actor JACOB BEN-AMI as Trigorin. Her theatre
appealed mainly to coterie audiences; the first
commercial titivation of Chekhov was JED HAR-
RIS's *Uncle Vanya* (CORT THEATRE, 1930) with LIL-
LIAN GISH as Yelena and OSGOOD PERKINS as
Astrov, the text revised by Rose Caylor to meet
the romantic expectations of a Broadway public.

The propensity to exploit Chekhov for star vehicles continued with the 1938 *Seagull*, freshly translated by STARK YOUNG, for the LUNTS. GUTHRIE
MCCLINTIC presented *Three Sisters* (ETHEL BARRY-

MORE THEATRE, 1942) as a wartime tearjerker,
showcasing JUDITH ANDERSON, KATHARINE
CORNELL, RUTH GORDON, and Edmund Gwenn.
JOSHUA LOGAN relocated *The Cherry Orchard* to
postbellum Louisiana in *The Wisteria Tree* (MARTIN
BECK THEATRE, 1950) to accommodate the talents of HELEN HAYES. The star-studded approach,
unenlightened by a strong directorial or design
concept, was perpetuated in MIKE NICHOLS's
Uncle Vanya (CIRCLE IN THE SQUARE, 1973), featuring the ill-assorted GEORGE C. SCOTT as Astrov
and Nicol Williamson as Vanya, and his *Seagull*
(Shakespeare in the Park, NYC, 2001) with KEVIN
KLINE as Trigorin, MERYL STREEP as Arkadina,
and PHILIP SEYMOUR HOFFMAN as Konstantin.

By the 1960s Chekhov, now standard fare in
regional repertories, was still becalmed in the
conventions of the Art Theatre. The diminishing
returns of this tradition could be seen in LEE
STRASBERG's *Three Sisters* for the ACTORS STUDIO,
in an adaptation by the poet Randall Jarrell (1964);
the eclectic cast, including KIM STANLEY, GERAL-
DINE PAGE, and SHIRLEY KNIGHT in the title roles,
failed to cohere under Strasberg's rudderless
direction. The only American director to tackle
Chekhov on a regular basis was Nikos Psachara-
poulos, in his red-blooded, energetic interpretations at the WILLIAMSTOWN THEATRE FESTIVAL
(1962–87).

During this period, attempts were made to
update Chekhov, refashioning him either in modern dress (ELLIS RABB's *Seagull*, ASSOCIATION OF
PRODUCING ARTISTS, 1962), or in bland Ameri-
canese (JEAN-CLAUDE VAN ITALLIE's adaptations
for JOSEPH CHAIKIN), or with an all-black cast
(Michael Schultz's *Cherry Orchard*, PUBLIC THE-
ATRE, 1973). ANDRE GREGORY and the MANHAT-
TAN PROJECT offered a largely improved *Seagull*
(Public Theatre, 1974) in which the spectators
moved from act to act as MING CHO LEE's set
changed location. A breakthrough production was
The Cherry Orchard staged by Romanian ANDREI
SERBAN (VIVIAN BEAUMONT THEATRE, NYC,
1977); although derivative of the European work
of Giorgio Strehler and others, its achromatic
scenery by SANTO LOQUASTO, isolated set pieces,
and highly physical acting from IRENE WORTH,
RAUL JULIA, and MERYL STREEP, eliminated the
cluttered box sets and atmospheric maundering
of standard Chekhov. Controversial in the eyes of
conservatives, it effectively generated a spate of
imitative "all-white," schematic designs and a
less reverent attitude to Chekhov. This trend was
abetted by other European newcomers, such as
the Hungarian Squat Theatre (*Three Sisters* played
by three bearded men, NYC, 1980); the Romanian

Lucian Pintilie (*Seagull*, GUTHRIE THEATRE, 1984, which shuffled the scenes; and *Cherry Orchard*, ARENA STAGE, 1987–8, which pushed realism *ad absurdum*), and the Lithuanian Eimuntas Nekrošius (a wilfully antic *Uncle Vanya*, Joyce Theatre, NYC, 1991).

One of the more curious phenomena is the way in which American playwrights, from ARTHUR MILLER to MEGAN TERRY, have confessed a serious debt to Chekhov. TENNESSEE WILLIAMS rewrote *The Seagull* as *The Notebook of Trigorin*, making the title character homosexual in the process. NEIL SIMON concocted a hodgepodge of Chekhov's life and works in the lightweight *The Good Doctor* (1973). *Orchards*, a cluster of one-acts based on Chekhov's short stories, was commissioned from DAVID MAMET, MARIA IRENE FORNÉS, WENDY WASSERSTEIN, JOHN GUARE, and others in 1985. Mamet, LANFORD WILSON, and RICHARD NELSON have felt the need to confect versions of Chekhov's plays in which their lack of Russian was compensated by an inner conviction about the original's intentions. The best known of these adaptations is Mamet's *Uncle Vanya*, originally staged by Andre Gregory as open rehearsals (Victory Theatre, NYC, 1991 [see NEW VICTORY THEATRE]) and then filmed by Louis Malle as *Vanya on 42nd Street* (1994).

As Chekhov has been absorbed into the fabric of American theatre, his characters have been transferred to Hollywood, Jamaica, Chinatown, and Beckettian wastelands, his human comedies skewed to promote environmental and anti-industrial messages. In collaboration with the St. Petersburg Theatre Salon, the Irondale Ensemble of New York created a bilingual work in progress, *The Uncle Vanya Show* (1985–90), with a Michigan radio host deluded into thinking he is Ivan Voinitsky. The WOOSTER GROUP conceived *Three Sisters* as *Brace Up!*, a multimedia deconstruction strongly influenced by Japanese film (1990). Since Chekhov is now accepted as a classic, directors feel free to reorganize this text and restyle his characters, as in *The Seagull 2288*, directed by Russian-Canadian Alexandre Marine (ArcLight Theatre, NYC, 2004). Paradoxically, while the theatrical profession venerates Chekhov and eagerly experiments with his subtle poetry, American theatregoers at large continue to regard him as a bewhiskered purveyor of gloom and doom.   LS

Chekhov, Michael (Mikhail Aleksandrovich)

(1891–1955) Russian stage and film actor, director, and teacher for whom acting represented a "spiritual logic," designed to quell his chaotic soul and to reconcile humanity to inner pain. Chekhov (the playwright's nephew) joined the MOSCOW ART THEATRE's First Studio in 1912, working with Leopold Sulerzhitsky and Evgeny Vakhtangov. Chekhov's theatrical existentialism derived from Eastern and Western philosophy and from Rudolf Steiner's anthroposophy, which Chekhov first encountered in 1922. Steiner's eurythmy, "the science of visible speech" as the soul's "universal language," and Émile Jaques-Dalcroze's eurythmics, or musical kinesis, coalesced in Chekhov's "psychological gesture," the internal, archetypal physicalization of a spiritual-emotional state, from which characterization develops. Attacked for his mysticism and determined to save modern Russian theatrical culture from Soviet censorship, Chekhov emigrated in 1928. He came to New York in 1935 with the Moscow Art Players (formed in Paris, 1934) at Sol Hurok's invitation to perform a program of Russian classics. Chekhov's lectures on the creative process influenced and divided GROUP THEATRE members. The Chekhov Theatre Studio, begun in 1936 at actress Beatrice Straight's family estate in England, relocated to Ridgefield, CT (1939) and NYC (1941), disbanding in 1942. During this period, the Studio Players were critically savaged for a Dostoyevsky mélange entitled *The Possessed* (1939) and toured the U.S. (1940–2), and Chekhov successfully codirected *Twelfth Night* at Broadway's Little Theatre (1941). He later worked in Hollywood (1943–55), instructing many "stars" and appearing in 11 films, including an Academy Award–nominated performance in Hitchcock's *Spellbound* (1945). Chekhov's books include *The Path of the Actor* (autobiography, 1928); *On the Actor's Technique* (in Russian, 1946); *To the Actor* (1953); *Michael Chekhov's To the Director and Playwright* (compiled by Charles Leonard, 1963); and *Michael Chekhov: Lessons for the Professional Actor* (compiled from his class lectures, 1941–2). In 1980, Straight and Robert Cole founded the Michael Chekhov Studio in NYC, where classes were taught by Chekhov's former pupils. An alternative group, the Michael Chekhov Study Center, headed by Eddie Grove, was formed in Los Angeles. His career has been studied in a 1987 book by Lendley Black.   SG

Chelsea Theatre Center see DODGER PRODUCTIONS

Cheney, Sheldon

(1886–1980) Critic and author who championed the modernist movement in the American theatre of the 1910s through his books *The New Movement in Theater* (1914) and *The Art Theater* (1916), and through THEATRE ARTS magazine, of which he was founding editor (1916–21).

Cheney called for a nonnaturalistic aesthetic for the American stage, for a poetic and symbolic treatment of human experience that engaged rather than eliminated the imagination. A graduate of the University of California at Berkeley (1908), Cheney studied with GEORGE PIERCE BAKER at Harvard (1913), and later spent five years in Europe, touring and studying theatres. His 13 books on art history, architecture, and theatre include *The Theatre: 3000 Years of Drama, Acting and Stagecraft* (1929), considered the first comprehensive history of theatre written in this country.
   TLM

Chenoweth, Kristin (1968–) Petite, blonde, Oklahoma native. Trained as a classical singer (Oklahoma City University) with masterful musical phrasing, she emerged in the late 1990s as a versatile comic leading lady with an unusual vocal quality in a wide range of roles, from her Broadway debut as Precious McGuire in *Steel Pier* (1997) to the petulant Sally in the revival of *You're a Good Man, Charlie Brown* (1999; Tony Award for Best Featured Actress in a Musical). She capped her limited Broadway appearances to date – with "undiluted star power," noted BEN BRANTLEY – as Glinda in the musical *Wicked* (2003). Her musical chops, however, were also amply demonstrated in Off-Broadway's *A New Brain*; CITY CENTER'S *ENCORES!* productions of *Strike Up the Band*, *On a Clear Day You Can See Forever,* and *The Apple Tree* (on Broadway in 2006); *Candide* in 2004 with the New York Philharmonic; and in numerous concerts, two solo albums, and her Marian opposite MATTHEW BRODERICK in ABC-TV's version of *The Music Man*. A new opera based on *Alice in Wonderland,* in which she was to star for the Los Angeles Opera, was canceled in 2006.   DBW

Cherry Sisters A VAUDEVILLE sister act from Iowa. Originally there were five sisters – **Jessie** (1871–1903), **Ella** (1854–1934), **Lizzie (Elizabeth)** (1857–1936), **Addie (Addie Rose Alma)** (1859–1942), and **Effie** (1867–1944) – the latter two being the most active, appearing together as late as 1935. As amateurs they confused jeers with adulation, touring the Midwest for three years unofficially as the "world's worst actresses." In 1896 OSCAR HAMMERSTEIN brought four (all but Jessie) to New York's OLYMPIA Theatre, where, billed as the "Charming Cherry Sisters," but better known as the "vegetable sisters" because of the missiles tossed at them – provoked, they were told, by stars jealous of their talent – they began a successful career singing and reciting atrociously but with all seriousness (dancing, they believed,

was immoral). Their peculiar act ("so bad it was great") made them a fortune, though all ended in poverty.   DBW

Chestnut Street Theatre Chestnut near 6th St., Philadelphia [Architect: Inigo Richards?]. Prominent Philadelphians raised the capital to underwrite a theatre to replace the deteriorating SOUTHWARK and locate it in the center of the city. It was leased to THOMAS WIGNELL and Alexander Reinagle, who set about assembling an acting company. Completed in 1793, its opening was delayed for a year because of an outbreak of yellow fever. A handsome, well-appointed house, its exterior continued to be improved upon from plans furnished by Benjamin Latrobe. By 1805, it was considered the finest playhouse with the best acting company in America. In 1816, gaslighting was introduced for the first time in a theatre, but in 1820 the playhouse burned down (see FIRES). It was rebuilt in a version by William Strickland that bore little resemblance to the original. The theatre's most prosperous years occurred under the management of WILLIAM WARREN and WILLIAM WOOD, which ended in 1828. Thereafter, it went steadily downhill as new theatres were built and better acting companies arose to challenge it. In 1855, the theatre was demolished. A new theatre bearing the same name was built six blocks away, but was unlike the original; it, too, was razed in 1917.   MCH

Chicago For much of its colorful history, Chicago theatre was buffeted between fire and New York City, forces that alternately impeded local activity and spurred greater accomplishment. The FIRES of the 19th century, the fire codes of the 20th, and the competition from New York of both centuries provided challenges that ultimately strengthened and defined the character of local stage efforts, leading ultimately to an independent theatre community of considerable verve and originality.

   Like other American cities, Chicago had been a thriving and multifaceted theatrical community in the period prior to the rise of the Theatrical SYNDICATE and the SHUBERTS, and it has been a leader in the movement to decentralize American theatre in the latter half of this century. The period in between the two flourishings was comparatively fallow in terms of local production, thereby making it easy to divide Chicago's theatrical history into three major periods: boom town, road town, and regional center.

   The role of fire in the city's theatrical development also was considerable. The history of theatre in 19th-century Chicago is to a large degree the history of theatres being built, burning down, and being replaced by bigger, fancier structures. Chicago's first theatre was built by J. B. RICE in 1847 and burned down three years later. It was rebuilt, only to be surpassed by more imposing structures – including MCVICKER'S THEATRE, HOOLEY'S THEATRE, The Woods, Crosby's Opera House, Aiken's Theater, and others – most of which were leveled by the Great Chicago Fire of 1871, and many of which were rebuilt with astounding rapidity. A series of fires shortly after the turn of the century were capped by the enormous tragedy of the burning of the Iroquois Theatre on 30 December 1903, killing 600 holiday matinee patrons. That fire led to exceedingly restrictive fire codes that would stay in place for 70 years, severely hampering Chicago's entrance into the regional theatre movement. When *Sun-Times* critic Glenna Syse and others finally succeeded in convincing the Richard J. Daley administration to relax those codes in the early 1970s, there was an immediate emergence of many small storefront theatres of the type that still typifies theatre in that city.

Ironically, the first recorded performance for money in Chicago was an exhibition of fire eating in a private home in 1834, when Chicago was a city of some 4,000 souls. As Chicago grew, one-man exhibitions were joined by CIRCUSES, which in turn were joined by J. B. Rice and the theatres mentioned above. The range of performance during the period bracketing the 1871 fire included so-called legitimate theatre (comedy, satire, melodrama, and tragedy), as well as opera, ballet, pantomime, strolling players, VAUDEVILLE, BURLESQUE, MINSTREL SHOWS, and such singular attractions as Joseph Barton, Mlle. Zoe, BUFFALO BILL CODY, and Texas Jack Omohundro. Leading actors who performed in Chicago in the period included CHARLOTTE CUSHMAN, EDWIN BOOTH, JAMES O'NEILL, and JOSEPH JEFFERSON III. The STOCK COMPANIES of the 1870s gave way to combination companies in subsequent decades.

By the end of the century, waves of immigrants had added foreign-language theatre to the mix of lower-priced entertainment available in the neighborhoods. (IBSEN's *Ghosts* received its world premiere in Chicago in its original Norwegian.) In summer, the shore of Lake Michigan was dotted with musicals. Meanwhile, the Syndicate tightened its grip on commercial production in the big Loop theatres with fare that increasingly relied on star vehicles, machinery, and spectacular scenery.

As a reaction to the glossy values of the commercial stage, Chicago was an active participant in the Little Theatre movement (see COMMUNITY THEATRE). Local leaders included The New Theater (begun in 1906), various companies led by Donald Robertson, Jane Addams's HULL-HOUSE PLAYERS, and the Chicago Little Theatre. Most featured serious European plays ignored by the commercial theatre. The leadership was idealistic, determinedly amateur, and poorly funded. Most of these art theatres did not survive the 1910s.

By 1920, Chicago had made the transition from boom town to road town. One way of plumbing the meaning of that change is to look at the role of the local critics. At the turn of the century, critics like Delancey Halbert, AMY LESLIE, Lyman Glover, BURNS MANTLE, PERCY HAMMOND, W. L. Hubbard, and Barrett Eastman were responsible for shaping a climate of opinion for theatre that was an exuberant mix of high and low culture, locally produced and imported, professional and amateur. By the 1920s, and into the decades that followed, the only significant role left to local critics – led in this period by Leslie, ASHTON STEVENS, and CLAUDIA CASSIDY – was to pass on the merits of shows coming from or heading to New York. The economies of scale enjoyed by touring productions – not to mention radio and movies – virtually eliminated significant local competition. The Hull-House Players continued in various incarnations, as did other small amateur theatres; but the only lasting local theatre of the period was the GOODMAN, which, founded in 1925 with high artistic ambitions, was itself reduced to a purely educational status by the Depression.

The seeds of Chicago's theatrical rebirth can be found in small amateur efforts. Viola Spolin, author of the still popular *Improvisation for the Theater* and other texts, got started as a recreational director inventing games for inner-city children in the 1920s and '30s. Spolin passed her methods for eliciting spontaneous behavior on to her son, PAUL SILLS, who gave them practical use in a series of theatrical enterprises in the 1950s and '60s.

It was David Shepherd, a classmate of Sills at the University of Chicago and a collaborator in the Playwrights Theatre Club, who had the idea for a theatre that would combine commedia dell'arte techniques and German cabaret in a topical format. Following workshops given by Spolin, Sills and Shepherd opened the innovative but short-lived Compass Players in 1955, to be succeeded four years later by the SECOND CITY, a company whose members were greatly to influence the development of comedic theatre across the nation and, especially, on television.

In 1963 the theatre program at the Jane Addams Hull-House was revived by Robert Sickinger. His high artistic ideals, commitment to a community-based ethos, and progressive repertory set a new standard for local production and helped nurture a generation of young artists – including DAVID MAMET – who would build the Chicago theatre in subsequent decades. For the most part, however, 1960s Chicagoan theatre comprised road shows, dinner theatre (which William Pullinsi claimed to have invented with the Candlelight Playhouse in suburban Summit), community and college productions, and a commercial but artistically ambitious effort at the Ivanhoe Theatre. What came to be known as the Off-Loop movement began late in the decade with a pair of theatres on opposite sides of Lincoln Ave. The Kingston Mines hosted a wide variety of work, from the fantastic to musical premieres such as GREASE. Directly across the street, the BODY POLITIC led the way, both with its own productions and by hosting other groups. It was at Body Politic that Paul Sills created Story Theater, and where Stuart Gordon landed with his ORGANIC THEATER after having been closed down when it offered University of Wisconsin students a nude Peter Pan (see NUDITY). The Organic went on to create a string of successful original productions, the most enduring of which was a science-fiction comic-book trilogy called Warp!

The most professional, big-budget resident theatres in the 1970s were the North Shore's Academy Festival Theatre – perhaps most famous for Broadway-bound productions of MOON FOR THE MISBEGOTTEN and MORNING'S AT SEVEN – and the Goodman. The Goodman had turned professional under John Reich in 1969, and gained stability during William Woodman's directorship in the 1970s. With the relaxation of the fire code and the concomitant rise of the Off-Loop scene (Northlight, VICTORY GARDENS, and WISDOM BRIDGE all began in 1974), Woodman brought in young GREGORY MOSHER to start a vigorous Stage 2 series. In the meantime, David Mamet was making a mark by cofounding (also in 1974) the St. Nicholas Theater – the leading Off-Loop theatre in the late 1970s – and writing SEXUAL PERVERSITY IN CHICAGO for the Organic. Mosher and Mamet first joined forces with AMERICAN BUFFALO, a coproduction of Stage 2 and St. Nicholas. They continued to work together throughout Mosher's ascension to leadership positions at the Goodman and New York's LINCOLN CENTER.

A movement toward professionalization went hand in hand with a gradual shift in artistic approach as the 1970s progressed. The stylistic adventurousness of groups like Godzilla Rainbow and Pary Productions gave way to a pronounced naturalism typified by the acting of the STEPPENWOLF THEATRE COMPANY and director ROBERT FALLS's energetic productions at Wisdom Bridge. As Falls replaced Mosher at the Goodman, and Daily News critic RICHARD CHRISTIANSEN – an early supporter of Mamet and Steppenwolf – moved to the powerful Tribune, this highly physical brand of naturalism became entrenched, to the point that it was referred to as "the Chicago style." This term primarily referred to actors, but it also had its exemplars in such playwrights as Mamet, James Yoshimura, Rick Cleveland, Claudia Allen, Dean Corrin, Charles Smith, Steve Carter, Alan Gross, and Jeffrey Sweet (as opposed to the less naturalistic writing of Lonnie Carter, John Logan, Nicholas Patricca, and Darrah Cloud). Writers of all stripes have found support at a variety of theatres specializing in new work, most notably Victory Gardens.

This naturalistic focus led to excellence as well as a certain lack of breadth: By the late 1980s, there was relatively little avant-garde work in Chicago and, with the exception of the Court Theater and The Shakespeare Repertory, few pre-modern productions. In the early 1990s, however, signs of a swing away from naturalism could be seen in the work of small groups like Theater Oobleck, as well as in the increasing success of director FRANK GALATI and MARY ZIMMERMAN, whose productions bridged disparate genres and styles, and the emergence of Michael Maggio (associate artistic director at Goodman) as a director with a national reputation. His death in 2000 robbed Chicago theatre of a major player.

In the late 1980s, membership in the League of Chicago Theatres numbered 150 institutions. Recession reduced the field by 20%, but the volume of continuing activity ensured a degree of creative vitality for some years to come. That vitality encompassed musicals (at Marriott's Lincolnshire Theatre, Candlelight, and the Drury Lane Theatre), ETHNIC THEATRE (at Angel Island, Black Ensemble, Chicago Theatre Company, ETA, Kuumba, and Latino Chicago), numerous improvisational comedy clubs, and the rise of midsized commercial venues (Apollo, Briar Street, Royal George, Wellington) that offered hope of a rising standard of living for local actors. Every other May the International Theatre Festival exposed Chicago to a wide spectrum of performance styles. Theatre programs at Northwestern, DePaul, Columbia, and Loyola – not to mention the state universities – provided a stream of talent for the creation of theatres that began with small budgets and large ambitions: Bailiwick, City Lit, Live Bait, Next, Pegasus, Raven, Remains, Lookingglass, Kingston Mines, Naked Eye, Eclipse, Time-Line, and others.

Some established groups, such as Body Politic and Wisdom Bridge, have struggled to survive yet vanished. Nevertheless, as of fall 2005 there are more than 200 theatre companies in the Chicago area. Furthermore, recent years have seen both new and renovated spaces, such as the new Goodman (2000), Lookingglass's new home in the Water Works (former boiler room) on Michigan Ave. (2003), and a new facility on Navy Pier for the Chicago Shakespeare Company (1999). Chicago wields a major influence in today's theatre, serving as a major tryout center for Broadway-bound productions (e.g., *The Producers*); as a training ground for theatre artists and a major job center in its own right; and as a tightly knit theatre community creating or producing theatre, often with histories outside of Chicago (Mary Zimmerman's *Metamorphosis*, the Goodman's *Death of a Salesman* in 1999, or the tryout at About Face Theatre of Doug Wright's *I Am My Own Wife*, for instance) but equally praised productions seen only there. Chicago theatre is fortunate to have a definitive history by former critic Richard Christiansen (2004).   SF

Chicago   Two-act "musical vaudeville," music by John Kander, lyrics by Fred Ebb, book by Ebb and Bob Fosse; opened at the 46th Street Theatre, NYC, 3 June 1975, running 898 performances. Based on Maurine Dallas Watkins's 1926 play of the same name, *Chicago* treats, in the form of a series of vaudeville acts, the glorification of criminals as celebrities, focusing on two "merry murderesses," Roxie Hart (Gwen Verdon) and Velma Kelly (Chita Rivera). Bob Fosse, following collaborative difficulties on *Pippin* (1972), not only directed and choreographed but took credit for shaping the book, a step toward his eliminating collaborators in *Dancin'* (1978) and *Big Deal* (1986). The vaudeville motif gave Fosse scope to recreate the popular dance forms, classic or sleazy, of the 1920s, while the score makes pointed allusions to memorable melodies from period revues. *Chicago* marked a major achievement in Fosse's record as an auteur director-choreographer of "concept" musicals. A 1996 revival – following a successful City Center's Encores! version – with choreography by Ann Reinking (in the Fosse style) and direction by Walter Bobbie (with James Naughton, Bebe Neuwirth, Marcia Lewis, and Reinking in the cast) won six Tony Awards, including Best Revival of a Musical, and is still playing early in 2007 with more than 4,000 performances, dozens of cast changes (most publicized: Melanie Grif-

fith as Roxie in 2003), and a new reputation as a true American musical gem. Its film version won six Oscars in 2003, including Best Picture – the first for a musical since 1968 (*Oliver!*).   JD

Chicano theatre   Chicano theatre belongs to the larger category of Hispanic theatre in the U.S. Its origins date from the arrival of the Spanish conquerors, including the priests interested in the spiritual conquest, in the 16th century. Dramatic performances were recorded in the Southwest as early as 1598, when Juan de Oñate's band of explorers performed an early religious play near El Paso, TX. Throughout the period of settlement and growth of the following centuries, the dominant Spanish and mestizo culture in the area gave attention to the theatre. During the 19th century, both San Francisco and Los Angeles were major centers of activity that sponsored visits by operatic companies even before the California gold rush. As the railroad linked major cities throughout the Southwest, especially Laredo, San Antonio, and El Paso, the ethnic communities with a strong sense of their heritage and traditions maintained local cultural activities and hosted traveling road companies en route to and from Mexico City.

By the 1920s Chicano theatre flourished from Los Angeles to Chicago. Productions of musical revues and zarzuelas coincided with serious plays that addressed issues particular to Chicano communities. The problems of adapting culturally and linguistically to a predominantly Anglo culture were standard themes. The level of activity subsequently subsided during the Depression and WWII years, although it did not disappear entirely.

The more recent Chicano theatre movement coincided with activism in the U.S. civil rights movement in the 1960s, when activists began to call themselves Chicanos rather than Mexican Americans. In the summer of 1965, Luis Valdéz joined with César Chávez as he was organizing the farmworkers' strike in California, directing the striking farmworkers in collectively created *actos*, as they came to be called: short agitprop pieces that dramatized the need for a union. The new Chicano theatre was, suddenly, a revolutionary theatre committed to social change. From this initial experience, Valdéz established El Teatro Campesino (Farm Workers' Theatre).

This group served as the model for a host of other Chicano theatre groups created throughout the West and Southwest, and extending across the country into Illinois, Indiana, and Wisconsin. Adrian Vargas and Manuel Martinez created

Teatro de la Gente (People's Theatre) in 1970 in San Jose, CA. In 1971 Jorge Huerta developed the Teatro de la Esperanza (Theatre of Hope) in Santa Barbara (moved to San Francisco in 1986), a group whose stability is second only to that of El Teatro Campesino. In 1972 Joe Rosenberg established the Teatro Bilingüe (Bilingual Theatre) in Kingsville, TX. At the peak of the movement, as many as 100 groups were functioning throughout the U.S. Nicolás Kanellos, Rubén Sierra, Daniel Valdéz, and Manuel Pickett are but a few of the other early Chicano directors. A national network called TENAZ (El Teatro Nacional de Aztlán/National Aztlán Theatre) was established in 1971 to maintain linkages among the groups. Between 1971 and 1992 TENAZ sponsored annual and biannual festivals that brought together groups from all over the U.S. as well as from Latin America to learn about their common heritage and share their experiences. The road has not always been smooth: Differences in function and orientation were particularly evident at the fifth festival celebrated in 1974 in Mexico City, where Valdéz was severely criticized by leftists from both sides of the border for his spiritually based *mitos,* or myths. Nevertheless, the festivals provided for a useful interchange and gave opportunity for fresh perspectives on techniques.

The farmworker issue pressed El Teatro Campesino into existence, but the themes captured in its Brechtian-style *actos* were many and varied. *Soldado razo* decried the disproportionate number of deaths of Chicanos in the Vietnam War; *Los vendidos* satirized Chicano stereotypes. Luís Valdéz's Zoot Suit, based on a historical episode of racial violence in East Los Angeles in the summer of 1943, opened in Los Angeles in 1978 as a tremendous critical and popular success – a record that unfortunately did not hold true when it opened months later as the first Chicano show to arrive on Broadway. After a period of reorganization in San Luis Obispo, the company has in more recent years staged Valdéz's *I Don't Have to Show You No Stinking Badges* and *Simply Maria* (1986) by Josefina Lopéz, a young Mexican woman raised in Los Angeles. The latter play builds on Valdéz's sense of the comic while at the same time cutting into the pain and prejudice of cross-cultural living. (Lopéz's 1990 *Real Women Have Curves* has emerged in recent years as the most produced of Latino plays.)

With few trained playwrights to turn to, the initial Chicano theatre groups worked collectively. Teatro de la Esperanza was particularly active in the collective process. Growing out of a student movement at the University of California at Santa Barbara, this Teatro staged its first full-scale production, *Guadalupe* – a play that chronicled the exploitation of Chicanos in a small California community – in 1974. That success led to *La victima* (1976), another DOCUMENTARY drama, which questioned the deportation of Mexican workers alleged to be injurious to the American economy. Later world-premiere plays include *Hijos: Once a Family* (1979), Lalo Cervantes's *Teodolo's Final Spin* (1988), Lopez's *Real Women Have Curves* (1990), Guillermo Reyes's *Deporting the Divas* (coproduced with Theatre Rhinoceros, 1996), and Rodrigo Duarte-Clark's one-woman play *Doña Rosita's Jalapeño Kitchen* (2000).

Since the early 1980s an entire generation of Chicano and Chicana playwrights has emerged. Among the women playwrights the late Estela Portillo Trambley is notable for her *Day of the Swallows* and *Sor Juana,* the latter an impressive and stimulating work that captures both the intellect and the emotion of that 17th-century Mexican nun, herself a brilliant poet and playwright. One of the most important Chicano playwrights is CHERRIE MORAGA, the first Chicana or Chicano to write about homosexuality, in *Giving Up the Ghost* (1986). Her other plays include *Shadow of a Man* (1991), *Heroes and Saints* (1992), and *The Hungry Woman: A Mexican Medea* (2000). Several writers who are not Mexican American are claimed by the movement. One is Milcha Sánchez-Scott, born to a Colombian father and an Indonesian-Chinese-Dutch mother, whose play *Roosters* (1987) deals with family conflicts and Chicano issues around a metaphor of cockfighting. Sánchez-Scott's work in the 1980s was nurtured by a non-Latino company, the LOS ANGELES THEATRE CENTER's Latino Lab, directed by José Luis Valenzuela from 1985 to 1990.

Valenzuela continues as the artistic director of the Latino Theatre Company in LA, an ensemble of professional actors whose productions include *Dementia* (2002), by actor and playwright Evelina Fernandez. (Fernandez adapted *Dementia* for the screen, directed by Valenzuela, in 2005. Lopez's earlier *Real Women Have Curves* was adapted to film with great success in 2002.) Other active Chicano playwrights include Oliver Mayer, Carlos Morton, Octavio Solis, and the nationally recognized comedy trio CULTURE CLASH: Herbert Siguenza, Richard Montoya, and Ric Salinas.

The Chicano theatre is normally written and performed in the peculiar linguistic mixture typical of the Chicano population. Spanish and English words and phrases are constantly interchanged, depending on the context. Most groups perform in the "Spanglish" dialect most comfortable to their situation; some groups prefer to maintain the separation and alternate performances in the two languages. Economic difficulties have dimmed some opportunities for Chicano theatre at the same time that social issues have changed some of the needs. The effort to educate the majority population about Chicano issues while serving the interests of the Chicano population itself presents a major challenge, especially now that not as many groups are functioning as before. Further, most theatre groups are now pan-Latino and can be found in every major center of Hispanic population in the country. The publication of texts continues to be a high priority as a venue for encouraging production. Whereas the Chicano Theatre Movement began as a male-dominated enterprise, there are now Chicana directors such as Juliette Carrillo and Diane Rodriguez as well as artistic directors Elisa Marina González of Teatro Vision in San Jose, CA, and Cora Cardona, of Teatro Dallas (TX). From its humble beginnings the Chicano theatre has achieved an impressive level of accomplishment both on the stage and on the page.   GW   JH

Children of a Lesser God MARK MEDOFF's two-act drama about a relationship between a hearing man and a deaf woman, inspired by Phyllis Frelich, a deaf actress he met in 1977, and developed by Medoff while heading the New Mexico State University Drama Department. GORDON DAVIDSON added the play to the fall 1979 season of Los Angeles's MARK TAPER FORUM; at NYC's LONGACRE THEATRE (opening 30 March 1980) it ran 887 performances, won the Tony for Best Play and the Outer Critics' Circle and Drama Desk awards (as well as Tonys for its two leads; all 1980). The play examines ideas about disabilities as the lead character confronts loving, then marrying, a woman who does not consider deafness an impairment nor speech an attribute.   KN

Children's Hour, The LILLIAN HELLMAN's first and longest-running play "struck Broadway like a thunderbolt" when it opened at MAXINE ELLIOTT's Theatre on 20 November 1934 for a run of 691 performances. Based on a real-life incident in Scotland, the play tells the story of two boarding-school teachers whose lives are ruined by a malicious student who suggests they are lesbians. At the end, Martha (Anne Revere) kills herself when she faces the possibility of the truth of the accusation. Although the play was banned in BOSTON and London, critics compared Hellman to Ibsen and Strindberg and nominated the play for the 1935 Pulitzer Prize; however, the subject matter

Evelina Fernandez's *Dementia,* directed by Jose Luis Valenzuela and produced by the Latino Theater Company at the Los Angeles Theatre Center, 2002. Actors in photo: left background, Tonantzin Esparza; center, Sal Lopez; right background, Danny De La Paz; right foreground, Lucy Rodriguez. Photo by Carol Petersen. *Courtesy:* Evelina Fernandez and Carol Petersen.

was too inflammatory, and the award was instead given to ZOË AKINS's *The* OLD MAID. As a direct result, the New York Drama Critics' Circle Award was established. In 1952 the play had a moderately successful revival, with KIM HUNTER and Patricia Neal, running for 189 performances.   FB

children's theatre In the U.S., children's theatre is considered a 20th-century movement, although dramatic activities for and by children were reported as early as the 18th and 19th centuries. In 1798, minister and schoolmaster Charles Stearns published *Dramatic Dialogues for the Use of the Schools,* which was widely used as a tool in the moral education of young people. On the commercial stage, FRANCES HODGSON BURNETT's *Little Lord Fauntleroy* (1889) marked the beginning of high-profile Broadway productions targeting child audiences, mostly adaptations of popular books and fairy tales. Children were also taken to the 19th-century PANTOMIMES and the popular WILD WEST shows.

Increased industrialization, immigration, and urbanization; the progressive education movement; and the rise of the settlement houses at the turn of the century created a climate that wrested children's theatre from the commercial stage and situated it firmly in the realm of education and social work. In 1903, Alice Minnie Herts, a recreation director at the Educational Alliance, a social settlement on New York's Lower East Side, established the Children's Educational Theatre, a theatre designed specifically for youth. Herts's goals were threefold: to help young people learn the language and customs of their new country; to meet the social needs of the community by providing a place for families to gather; and to help people "create an idea from within rather than to impose one on them from without."

Their first season opened with a highly successful production of *The Tempest,* followed by *Ingomar, As You Like It,* and *The Forest Ring.* The reputation of the Children's Educational Theatre spread rapidly, and within the next few years plays for youth were reported in BOSTON, CHICAGO, SAN FRANCISCO, LOS ANGELES, and other urban centers with large immigrant populations also engaged in children's-theatre activities. Drama classes and clubs were formed for the purpose of providing children with creative outlets: puppetry, acting, and the enjoyment of storytelling. Many of these activities were led by members of the Association of Junior Leagues in America (AJLA), a women's organization dedicated to social service, established by Mary Harriman in 1901. The theatrical endeavors of the Junior League were spearheaded by the Chicago League, which in 1924 made theatre their main focus. The AJLA established a Play Bureau to promote the development of children's theatre, initiated national playwriting competitions, and organized conferences. Several professional theatres of the latter half of the 20th century grew out of the Junior Leagues.

Although Broadway regularly offered productions for children in the first decades of the 20th century, by the 1920s professional children's theatre was primarily limited to revivals of early successes, such as Burnett's *Little Princess* (1903), James M. Barrie's *Peter Pan* (1905; popularized by actress MAUDE ADAMS), and *The Blue Bird* (1910). EVA LE GALLIENNE'S CIVIC REPERTORY THEATRE presented *Alice in Wonderland,* and STOCK companies frequently offered plays suitable for family audiences. CLARE TREE MAJOR, an actress, formed one of the first and longest-lived professional touring companies performing for children and teenagers (1923–54). The children's-theatre productions of the FEDERAL THEATRE PROJECT (1935–9) were the most professional, innovative, and controversial of the first half of the 20th century.

An influential and prolific children's-theatre theorist and practitioner of the early 20th century was CONSTANCE D'ARCY MACKAY. Her book *How to Produce Children's Plays* (1915) was one of the first widely disseminated sources on children's theatre in the U.S. Mackay weaves the history of children's theatre in a narrative of "appropriateness" closely tied to educational values in form and content, and posits it as antidote to the commercial stage. Her ideas were echoed in the works of theorists and practitioners for years to come.

WINIFRED WARD, who taught at Northwestern University, articulated in the late 1920s a distinction between children's theatre (which children enjoy as spectators) and creative drama (in which they participate informally). Ward provided guidance for educators and guidelines for producers. Teaching, writing, lecturing, and organizing leaders in the field, she was instrumental in the formation of a professional organization, now known as the American Alliance for Theatre and Education (AATE). The following decades saw the emergence of educators on all levels and the introduction of university courses designed to prepare teachers, directors, performers, and playwrights in children's theatre and drama. With this leadership came textbooks, scholarly articles, and conferences on regional and national levels. In 1935 Sara Spencer established the first publishing house devoted exclusively to plays for children; in the 1940s CHARLOTTE CHORPENNING, playwright, teacher, and director of children's theatre at the GOODMAN, laid down rules of writing for the child audience, which were widely emulated.

The social upheaval of the 1960s affected children's theatre as it did all of the arts, and challenged the dominance of the "well-made" adaptations and fairy-tale plays. The success of the PAPER BAG PLAYERS, a company founded in 1958, introduced a new and imaginative format that was imitated by a number of groups within the next few years. The "Bags'" scripts comprised short scenes, mime, audience participation, and drawing; set and costumes were constructed of household items. The simplicity of this approach was a first step in the liberation of children's theatre from formal structure and familiar content.

Another long-lasting professional company from the 1960s, focusing primarily on touring productions, is THEATREWORKSUSA founded in 1962.

In the 1970s and '80s subject matter hitherto taboo became acceptable: Plays dealing with death, divorce, prejudice, and unhappy endings were new and controversial choices for the child audience, in part influenced by the emancipatory theatre from Europe. Playwrights like AURAND HARRIS, Suzan Zeder, and, more recently, Laurie Brooks and James Still did much to contest the image of the field as "kids work."

Several professional companies emerged in these years to become leaders in the field. The CHILDREN'S THEATRE COMPANY of Minneapolis (mid-1960s) offered a wide variety of productions for all ages; the SEATTLE CHILDREN'S THEATRE (1975) commissioned, produced, and published new plays; Metro Theatre Company (1973), in St. Louis, MO, created original work. The last decades of the 20th century saw an increased professionalism in all aspects of children's theatre – or Theatre for Young Audiences (TYA), which became the preferred term for professional theatre for children and youth. Practitioners now fell into three categories: community, educational, and professional. While funding remained a major factor in the choices of repertory and production practices, an increased diversity in form, style, and content marked the output of the field. By the new millennium, TYA was recognized as an "exciting" force in the field, with its own professional organization (ASSITEJ/USA), festivals, journal, and specialized degree programs. NMcC MvW

Children's Theatre Company, The MINNEAPOLIS-based children's theatre company; one of the few in the U.S. with its own well-equipped facility (built in 1974). Founded in the mid-1960s by John Clark Donahue (led 1985–97 by Jon Cranny, replaced by Peter C. Brosius), it is dedicated to providing theatre of the highest quality for young people and their families. In addition, classes in the performing arts offer unique opportunities for technical and theatre training. For several years it operated a fully accredited school of the arts. Although most of the productions are adaptations of children's classics, folktales, and fairy tales, many scripts are original. Unlike the majority of theatres for young audiences, performers are young adults. With a staff of about 100 and 23,000 subscribers, in 2003 – the year its production of *A Year with Frog and Toad* enjoyed a brief Broadway run – the company was the first children's theatre to receive the Regional Tony. NMcC DBW

Childress, Alice (1920–94) African American playwright. Born in Charleston, SC, and raised in Harlem, Childress opened the New York stage to black women writers when her play *Gold through the Trees* (1952) was professionally produced OFF-BROADWAY. She had for 12 years been an actress with the AMERICAN NEGRO THEATRE, and her most important play, *TROUBLE IN MIND* (1955), voiced the protest of a veteran black actress against playing a stereotypical "darkie" role in a Broadway-bound production. Other notable plays by Childress that feature strong black women of compassion and dignity are *Wedding Band* (1966) and *Wine in the Wilderness* (1969). Her late works include the screenplay *A Hero Ain't Nothin' but a Sandwich* (1977), on teenage drug addiction, and *Moms* (1987), a play recalling the life of comedienne Jackie "Moms" Mabley. In 1977, the Black Filmmakers Hall of Fame accorded Childress the first Paul Robeson Award for Outstanding Contributions to the Performing Arts. EGH

Chip Woman's Fortune, The One-act folk drama by WILLIS RICHARDSON demonstrating the simple charity of the poor toward the poor in a southern community when the meager savings of a street collector of wood chips are shared to help a friend pay his debt. First produced in 1923 on a triple bill by the Ethiopian Art Players in Chicago, the play was taken to Washington, DC, then to Harlem's LAFAYETTE THEATRE, and finally to Broadway, where it was judged to be "unaffected and wholly convincing." It was the earliest nonmusical black play seen on Broadway. EGH

Chodorov, Jerome (1911–2004) and **Edward** (1904–88) Playwriting brothers who often collaborated, but not with each other. Edward's principal contributions were *Kind Lady* (1935), a GRACE GEORGE mystery, and *Oh, Men! Oh, Women!* (1953), a comedy of the sexes. Jerome was far more successful collaborating with Joseph Fields on many plays, including *MY SISTER EILEEN* (1940), a comedy about neophytes in Greenwich Village, which ran for more than 800 performances. The collaborators in turn adapted the play as the musical *WONDERFUL TOWN* (1953), with music by LEONARD BERNSTEIN. Other Chodorov–Fields successes include the long-running *Junior Miss* (1941), about teenage vicissitudes, and a sentimental Kitty Carlisle vehicle, *Anniversary Waltz* (1954). RHW

Chong, Ping (1946–) Toronto-born (son of Chinese opera performers) but raised in the Chinatown section of New York. Auteur director, choreographer, performer, and filmmaker who also produces videos and site-specific installations. Association with MEREDITH MONK's The House Foundation as a performer/collaborator (1971–8) – culminating in their opera/music theatre piece, *The Games* (1984) – has been an important influence on his avant-garde style. Chong has created more than 50 theatre pieces since 1972 (first with *Lazarus*). He founded the Fiji Theater Company in 1975 (since 1988 known as Ping Chong & Company). Like Monk, Chong employs a multimedia format in which the standard elements of a play are combined with found texts, historical chronology, slide projections, film, dance, sound recording, ritual gestures, miniatures, toys, and puppets. Influence from the cinematic austerity of film producer Robert Bresson results in blending and sifting, rather than mixing or sampling, each constituent medium into a rigorously formal design. Chong's multimedia high-tech and science-fiction theatre pieces have, among other themes, explored the alienation of humanoid and android races (*Angels of Swedenborg*, 1985; *Kind Ness*, 1986; *Elephant Memories*, 1990). In the second half of his oeuvre – since 1992 – his cool, prismatic theatrical journeys shifted from allegory to poetic documentary theatre. The first of these ongoing series, *The Undesirable Elements* (1993), is an assemblage based on the oral histories and personal stories of individuals; the most recent, *Children of War* (2002), draws on interviews with young refugees. The "East–West Quartet," focusing on the shared histories among Asia, the U.S., and Europe, comprises *Deshima* (1990; revised 1993), on Japan and Indonesia; *Chinoiserie* (1995), Chinese immigrants in America; *After Sorrow* (1997), Vietnam; and *Pojagi* (2000), Korean history. A final group of works – *Kwaidan* (1998), *Obon: Tales of Rain & Moonlight* (2000), and *Cathay: Three Tales of China* (1999) in collaboration with China's Shaanxi Folk Art Theatre – represent Chong's forays into puppet theatre.   RG

Chorpenning, Charlotte (1873–1955) One of America's first children's playwrights. A contemporary and associate of WINIFRED WARD at Northwestern University, Chorpenning is best known for her association with the GOODMAN THEATRE of Chicago, where many of her plays were given their first production. In 1931, she was made director of children's plays, a position that enabled her to study audience reactions and put these observations to literary use. In addition to a large body of literature, she set down guidelines for other playwrights. The American Alliance for Theatre and Education awards the Charlotte Chorpenning Cup annually to an outstanding children's dramatist.   NMcC

Chorus Line, A With book by James Kirkwood and Nicholas Dante, music by Marvin Hamlisch (the only surviving member of the team), and lyrics by Edward Kleban, this Pulitzer Prize–winning musical opened at the NEW YORK SHAKESPEARE FESTIVAL's PUBLIC THEATER on 15 April 1975, then moved to the SAM S. SHUBERT THEATRE on 25 July 1975, where it remained for the next 15 years. Its depiction of an audition for Broadway chorus dancers, or "gypsies," was based on 30 hours of taped conversations with 24 dancers, several of whom were also cast in the production. The plot was built on the premise that Zach, a director holding an audition for a Broadway musical, asks the dancers to tell about their own lives so that he can determine if they are suitable for small speaking roles as well as members of the chorus. Director-choreographer MICHAEL BENNETT used dance as the major mode of expression in the show, moving the performers from spoken dialogue into dance sequences molded to the characters' anxieties and hopes as they underwent the painful process of self-revelation. The central character of Cassie, a former gypsy trying to return to the chorus after having moved up to featured roles and some television and film work, was played by Donna McKechnie. Closing in April 1990, the show played 6,137 performances and, as of February 1990, had a profit of $50 million. A 2006 Broadway revival has had some success. (Film, 1985.)   MK

Christiansen, Richard (Dean) (1931–) Widely considered to be the most powerful critic in the modern period of CHICAGO theatre, Christiansen has been a consistent supporter of the Chicago style of naturalistic acting since he began covering amateur theatre for the *Chicago Daily News* in 1963. Noted for his accuracy, fairness, and reportorial style, he was the first major critic to see value in the writing of DAVID MAMET. When the *Daily News* folded in 1978, Christiansen moved to the *Tribune*, where he shared reviewing duties with LINDA WINER until her departure in 1980. From 1983 to his retirement in 2002 he has been both arts and entertainment editor and then chief critic and senior writer at the *Tribune*. His history of Chicago theatre (2004) is an invaluable legacy.   SF

Cincinnati Playhouse in the Park Founded in 1960 in a 166-seat Victorian fieldstone structure,

Climax of the original 1975 production of *A Chorus Line*. Photo by Martha Swope. *Courtesy:* The Public Theater.

once a shelter house, in Eden Park, the Playhouse now serves a three-state region of the Ohio River Valley. The thrust-stage, 626-seat Marx Theatre was built in 1968; a second space located in the original shelter house, the Thompson Shelterhouse Theatre, seats 225. A 1995 capital campaign raised more than $8.1 million making an extensive renovation possible. The Playhouse, which received the 2004 regional theatre Tony Award, casts freelance actors and actresses and employs a resident director and designers in about a dozen professional productions annually. Its broad-spectrum repertory attracts exceptionally strong support from season subscribers. In 1973 HAROLD SCOTT became the first African American artistic director in regional theatre history. In 1992, Edward Stern became its producing artistic director WD DBW

Circle in the Square New York's oldest surviving company, founded in 1951 by JOSÉ QUINTERO, THEODORE MANN, Emilie Stevens, and Jason Wingreen. Starting as the Loft Players in 1949 (originally the Villetta Studio Players in Woodstock, NY) and producing in the round (originally on Sheridan Square, whence its name), the company is "artistically committed to the art of acting." Never avant-garde, the company "hold[s] the classics up to our sunshine in the hope of making them glow." Its 1952 revival of *Summer and Smoke* launched Circle's success, Quintero's and GERALDINE PAGE's careers, and OFF-BROADWAY's heyday. In 1961, Circle opened its school, long associated with New York University. In 1969–70, Circle produced six shows at Washington's FORD'S THEATRE, and in 1972, maintaining its Greenwich Village house, occupied its Broadway theatre. In 1992–3 a fiscal crisis threatened the closing of this venue, though a season was mounted in 1994–5, with a critically acclaimed production of *The Rose Tattoo* in the spring. In September 1994 Josephine Abady joined Mann as co–artistic director, but in 1996 the theatre declared bankruptcy (after Mann had resigned). Abady also resigned and was replaced briefly by GREGORY MOSHER. After shutting down mid-June 1997 the Broadway venue remained closed until 1999, when it became a rental house.

Under Artistic Director Mann, Circle produced many O'NEILL works directed by Quintero, contemporary plays, and classics with such stars as GEORGE C. SCOTT, Cicely Tyson, JASON ROBARDS

Jr., JAMES EARL JONES, Joanne Woodward, PHILIP BOSCO, Vanessa REDGRAVE, and DUSTIN HOFFMAN. Its productions include Capote's *The Grass Harp* (1953), *The ICEMAN COMETH* with Robards (1956), Dylan Thomas's *Under Milk Wood* (1961), FUGARD's *Boesman and Lena* (1970), *Medea* with Irene Papas (1973), a contemporary adaptation of Molière's *The Cheats of Scapino* (*Scapino!*) with JIM DALE (1974), *The GLASS MENAGERIE* (1975), IBSEN's *The Lady from the Sea* with Redgrave (1976), *Macbeth* directed by Nicol Williamson (1982), *Heartbreak House* with REX HARRISON (1983), *Design for Living* directed by Scott (1984), G. B. SHAW's *Arms and the Man* with KEVIN KLINE and RAUL JULIA (1985), TINA HOWE's *Coastal Disturbances* (1987), *Sweeney Todd* (1989), *The Miser* with Bosco (1990), and *Uncle Vanya* with Tom Courtenay (1995). Many later ran on Broadway or television. The Broadway venue – in its latest incarnation – has housed productions of *Not about Nightingales* (1999), *True West* (2000), *The Rocky Horror Show* (2000), and the long-running *Metamorphoses* (2002; 400 performances). Circle in the Square's numerous awards include Tonys, Obies, and Drama Desk awards.   REK

Circle Repertory Company OFF-BROADWAY theatre, founded in 1969 by MARSHALL W. MASON, Robert Thirkield, Tanya Berezin, and LANFORD WILSON, dedicated to rediscovering "lyric realism as the native voice of the American theatre." Formed "for the needs of the artists, based on the relation between the actors and the playwright," the group, at Café LA MAMA and CAFFE CINO since 1965, founded the American Theatre Project in 1968. Devoted to new American writers, CRC operated a Playwrights' Workshop, Projects-in-Progress Series, and Script Evaluation Service, and launched the Young Playwrights Festival. CRC's informal alliance of more than 200 artists was committed "to making the action of the play become the experience of the audience." In 1987, founding Artistic Director Mason turned the company over to Berezin, who, though remaining active at CRC, stepped down herself January 1995, replaced by AUSTIN PENDLETON. The company died in 1996 after a $1 million deficit and poor reviews for recent productions, yet for a company without a commercial instinct its 28-year history and survival were laudable.

Many of Wilson's plays moved to Broadway (*The HOT L BALTIMORE*, 1972; *TALLEY'S FOLLY*, 1979; *FIFTH OF JULY*, 1977; *Angels Fall*, 1983; *BURN THIS*, 1987); other productions include *WHEN YOU COMIN' BACK, RED RYDER?* (1973), *Battle of Angels* (1974), JULES FEIFFER's *Knock Knock* (1976), *GEMINI* (1977), Marty Martin's *Gertrude Stein, Gertrude Stein,*

Gertrude Stein (1979), *BURIED CHILD* (1979), *FOOL FOR LOVE* (1983), *As Is* (1985), *PRELUDE TO A KISS* (1990), and *Three Hotels* (1993). In 1985, CRC became the first American company to tour Japan, presenting *WHO'S AFRAID OF VIRGINIA WOOLF?* and *Fool for Love*. Its many awards include Wilson's Obie for *The Mound Builders* (1975) and a Pulitzer Prize for *Talley's Folly* (1980). CRC received the 1991 Lucille Lortel Award for "Outstanding Body of Work." October 1974 CRC moved from Sheridan Square, where it had been for 17 years, to Circle in the Square Downtown (159 Bleecker), with seating increased from 160 to 199.   REK

circus in America Since its founding in the 18th century by the Englishman Philip Astley, the modern circus has been one of the most international of entertainments. Its performers have freely crossed national boundaries, its programs have rarely been tainted with political or social messages, its appeal (music excepted) has traditionally been to the eye rather than dependent on the intricacies of language. In America itself colonialists occasionally had the opportunity to view performances by itinerant trick equestrians, exotic animals taken around the country either singly or in small groups, and exhibitions by individual acrobats and ropedancers. As early as 1785 the American rider Thomas Pool was employing a clown to amuse spectators between his startling feats of horsemanship; consequently, one can argue for his being the first circus manager in America. Pool's career was relatively brief, however, and this distinction is generally accorded the equestrian John Bill Ricketts, who, in the spring of 1793, assisted by several acrobats and a clown, opened what he was pleased to call a "Circus" in PHILADELPHIA.

Ricketts later erected circus buildings in New York and other cities while touring with this troupe in the U.S. and eastern Canada. The equestrian, dancer, and clown JOHN DURANG worked for him and later set down his recollections of their travels, writing of his manifold duties with the show:

I rode the foxhunter, leaping over the bar with the mounting and dismounting while in full speed, taking a flying leap on horsback [sic] through a paper sun, in character of a drunken man on horsback [sic], tied in a sack standing on two horses while I changed to woman's clothes; rode in full speed standing on two horses, Mr. Ricketts at the same time standing on my shoulders, with master Hutchins at the same time standing in the attitude of Mercury on Mr. Ricketts' shoulders forming a pyramid. I performed the drunken soldier on horsback [*sic*], still vaulted, I dancet [*sic*] on the stage, I was the Harlequin in the pantomimes, occasionelly [*sic*] I sung a comic song. I tumbled on the slack rope and performed on the slack wire. I introduced mechanical exhibitions in machinery and transparencies. I produced exhibitions of fireworks. In short, I was performer, machinist, painter, designer, music compiler, the bill maker, and treasurer!

As is obvious from Durang's account, early circuses, as in Europe, offered stage exhibitions in addition to performances in the ring.

By the time Ricketts left for the West Indies in 1800, several other managers, often of foreign origin, were touring America with small companies of their own. During the first third of the new century a number of Americans took to the road with large menageries, some of which began merging with circus companies as early as 1823. The first American circus star to achieve international fame, the lion "tamer" ISAAC A. VAN AMBURGH, who performed with his big cats at Drury Lane and elsewhere in Europe, began with one such menagerie and eventually ran a large circus of his own. Another important development around this time was the adopting (from menageries) of easily transportable tents, which freed circuses from the necessity of erecting or renting buildings in each locale they visited and allowed them to give single performances in smaller towns.

By the second half of the century some of these "wagon shows" had grown to considerable proportions; gorgeously carved and gilded wagons, initially imported from England, were introduced in what became the traditional street parade; and a few shows were experimenting with new modes of transportation. Beginning in 1852, for example, the circus of Spalding and Rogers plied the Mississippi and Ohio Rivers performing on a huge enclosed barge that seated 3,400 spectators (see SHOWBOATS). The steamboat that towed this *Floating Palace* possessed an auditorium and stage of its own for minstrel and dramatic performances. By the mid-1850s, too, a few managers were taking advantage of the nation's expanding railway system, although the great era of "railroad shows" did not arrive until the 1870s.

The so-called "Golden Age" of the American circus commenced during the decade following the Civil War, by which time managers were almost exclusively American. Various members of the Howes, Nathans, and Sells families; the Chicago-based manager William W. ("Chilly Billy") Cole;

and the Philadelphian ADAM FOREPAUGH all figured prominently in the development of the circus during this gaudy period. But the one showman whose circus was destined to survive and to epitomize the American circus to the present day was none other than P. T. BARNUM, who, in time for the 1871 season, teamed up with the young manager William C. Coup to form "P. T. Barnum's Museum, Menagerie & Circus." A year later, by which time the main tent had added a second ring and could seat up to 12,000 spectators, their huge show took to the rails, crisscrossing the country in leaps of up to 100 miles per night, then giving a spectacular parade the next morning and as many as three performances before moving on to another town in time for the following day.

In 1880 Barnum joined with a new partner, James A. Bailey, to create the great concern that came to be known as "Barnum & Bailey." A third ring was added beginning with the 1881 season, and as platforms for acts requiring firm surfaces were set up between the rings, and all these performance areas were in turn encompassed by a great oval "hippodrome track" on which parades and races were given, spectators were alternately bewildered and delighted by a multiplicity of action. Although Bailey was responsible for daily operations, his veteran partner was indefatigable in thinking up novel ways to publicize the show, and personally negotiated for the acquisition of its most sensational attraction, the mammoth African elephant "Jumbo." The two men ruthlessly set out to crush or absorb all competition, and Barnum himself sometimes dreamed of establishing a monopoly on circus entertainment in America.

Following Barnum's death in 1891, Bailey became sole owner of the "Greatest Show on Earth" and took it to Europe for a five-year tour commencing in 1897. When the show returned to America, it found itself challenged by a powerful new rival, that of the five RINGLING BROTHERS, who had begun their circus careers in 1884 with a small wagon show in the Midwest. After Bailey's death in 1906, the Ringlings purchased his circus and continued running it as an independent show until the end of the 1918 season. They then merged it with their own large establishment to create the famous show that has persisted to the present day, "Ringling Bros. and Barnum & Bailey Circus."

By the 1920s many circuses had become motorized or "truck" shows, and today only Ringling Bros. continues to move by rail. The "Big One," as it is known to fans and performers, remains the largest and best-known circus in America, though at times it has barely escaped extinction. In 1944 its big top caught FIRE during a performance in Hartford, CT, killing 168 persons and injuring hundreds of others. Several of the show's executives were sent to prison, and, for a while, faced with suits for heavy damages, there was talk of liquidation. In 1956, amid difficulties with labor unions, John Ringling North – nephew of and flamboyant successor to the original Ringling Brothers – announced the show would never again play under canvas, but henceforth only in modern, enclosed civic and sports arenas. To many traditionalists this sounded like a death knell, but the move proved brilliantly successful. Besides cutting down considerably on personnel and expenses, the show was now independent of weather conditions and able to extend its season indefinitely. Spectators themselves, their view no longer obstructed by tent poles, now enjoyed the performance in unprecedented, air-conditioned comfort.

In 1967 the "Greatest Show on Earth" entered upon its latest phase when it was sold to a group of businessmen headed by the rock-music promoter Irvin Feld. The next year Feld opened a "Clown College" at the show's Florida winter quarters, and in 1969 he expanded the circus to two independent units – the "Red" and the "Blue" – each of which changes its program in alternate years and makes a two-year swing through cities in the U.S. and Canada. The "Big One" has always attracted the world's greatest circus artists, and from 1969 until his nominal retirement in 1990 (he returned to the show in 1994) the undisputed star of the Red Unit was the sensational German animal trainer Gunther Gebel-Williams (died 2001), whose phenomenal command over tigers, elephants, and horses (with leopards, zebras, and even a giraffe thrown in for good measure) earned him a celebrity usually reserved for rock and movie stars. A number of other three-ring circuses continue to tour under canvas. Of these the principal ones, as of the early 21st century, are the Carson and Barnes, Circus Vargas, and Cole Bros. Circus (until 2004 known as CLYDE BEATTY–Cole Bros.).

Circus programs can range from the tawdry to the magnificent, and size alone has never been a guarantee of excellence. Some of the best continue to be found in one-ring shows, and among these, since 1977, New York's BIG APPLE CIRCUS has undoubtedly been the finest and most elegant. Patterned on the European model, with its colorful, modern tent of Italian manufacture and its musicians perched on a small stage above the ring entrance, this show has consistently engaged superb performers drawn from the world over, including the Mexican trapeze troupe of the Flying Gaonas, the Danish equestrienne Katja Schumann, the French high-wire artist Philippe Petit, and the Big Apple's own truly funny clowns, among them BARRY LUBIN (known to his enthusiastic public as "Grandma"). Although it tours mainly in the East during the summer months, each winter finds the Big Apple back in New York City, where it erects its heated tent next to the Metropolitan Opera House in keeping with another European tradition, the Christmas season. A school of circus arts, whose influence on other American circuses has been considerable, is associated with the show.

In the 1980s a "new wave" type of circus emerged in America, as exemplified by the Pickle Family Circus of San Francisco and above all by the Montréal-based CIRQUE DU SOLEIL (with the addition of its first Las Vegas show in the 1990s). Extravagant claims of "renewing" or "purifying" the circus are made by some of these shows, ticket prices sometimes approach those of a Broadway musical, and fans of more traditional performances have often expressed their outrage at what they see as an attempt to make over the circus into a kind of musical revue. But even the "Big One" is willing to try new wrinkles to keep the circus alive in the U.S. First, in 1999 (for two seasons), the Feld operation toured to urban centers a single-ring tent circus called Barnum's Kaleidoscope; then in 2004 they began Hometown Edition, returning to their more familiar permanent arenas with a much smaller version of their two full-size touring units, one designed for smaller markets. In 2005 they began to rethink their format and physical arrangement, moving more in the direction of other "new wave" circuses and attempting to compete in an electronic age. A new, retooled unit (136th edition) was on the road in 2006 with the first fundamental changes in half a century.

Interestingly, many of the founders of many of these "new" circuses began as street performers, both in American and abroad, and have acknowledged their indebtedness to the Big Apple Circus or the "Cirque à l'Ancienne" of Alexis Gruss in France. The latter, which has revived many elegant equestrian and other acts dating back to the 19th century, has itself been a major influence on the Big Apple Circus, whose director and founder, Paul Binder, once performed as a juggler on the streets of Paris. The schools for circus arts that are often attached to these circuses are also largely inspired by French models. Thus things appear to have come full circle, and in this latest attempt to revitalize the circus in America one sees, again, how truly international the entertainment is – a fact brought vividly home in each issue of the new journal, *Spectacle* (1997). In any case, today the circus in the U.S. seems to be doing well, with sixty circuses operating in 2005. (See also FELIX ADLER, OTTO GRIEBLING, LOU JACOBS, EMMETT KELLY, FRANK OAKLEY.)   AHS

Cirque du Soleil Founded by Guy Laliberté in Quebec City in 1984, with present headquarters in Montréal, this extraordinary operation (though to purists having little to do with the circus) has proven its staying power after 20-plus years and with its five resident shows (as of 2006; six projected) and seven on tour worldwide. Typically, their programs entirely dispense with the use of animals, are given on stages (or as with the phenomenal "O" in a purpose-built theatre that allows much of the action to occur above or in water) rather than in the traditional ring, and emphasize "theatrical" elements: some "story" or plot line that runs throughout the performance; attempts at themes (not always comprehensible) that are social or nobly ecological; dance, mime, and commedia dell'arte; together with (mostly) original music and carefully coordinated costumes, makeup or masks, lighting, and even set design. The story line incorporates and presumably is illustrated by the circus numbers (contortionism, juggling, aerial acts, etc.), and clowns are often the central "characters" in these minidramas. Nothing illustrates Cirque du Soleil's drawing power as do its four resident shows in Las Vegas ("O"; *Mystère*; *ZUMANITY*; *KÀ*); a fifth, *LOVE,* inspired by Beatles music, opened at the Mirage in 2006. By the end of 2004 over 50 million had seen a Cirque production.   AHS   DBW

City, The, by CLYDE FITCH. Subtitled "A Modern Play of American Life in Three Acts," this emotional and violent drama purports to demonstrate how weaker souls can easily be led astray by the temptations and unethical dealings of the big city. Produced posthumously and with great anticipation on 21 December 1909, it created a sensation when Tully Marshall, as the drug-crazed family parasite, uttered, "You're a God damn liar!" – using the phrase "God damn" for the first time on the New York stage. It ran for 190 performances in New York before going on a controversial U.S. tour.   MR

City Center's *Encores!* Founded in 1994 to offer great American musicals in concert and to celebrate rarely heard works by important composers and lyricists. Three scores are heard, and seen in limited staging, each season under the artistic directorship of JACK VIERTEL – and, until 2006, the music direction of Rob Fisher – at New York's City Center on 55th St. JOHN LEE BEATTY has been its scenic consultant, and lighting – a crucial element – has often been designed by KEN BILLINGTON. The series received a Special Tony in 2000 for Excellence in Theatre, among numerous awards for its critically acclaimed concerts. Each offering receives a week's rehearsal and five performances. Musicals to date: 1994 – *FIORELLO!*, *Allegro*, *LADY IN THE DARK*; 1995 – *CALL ME MADAM*, *Out of This World*, *PAL JOEY*; 1996 – *DU BARRY WAS A LADY*, *One Touch of Venus*, *CHICAGO* (became Broadway's longest-running revival); 1997 – *Sweet Adeline*, *Promises, Promises*, *The BOYS FROM SYRACUSE*; 1998 – *STRIKE UP THE BAND*, *Li'l Abner*, *St. Louis Woman*; 1999 – *BABES IN ARMS*, *Ziegfeld Follies of 1936*, *Do Re Mi*; 2000 – *On a Clear Day You Can See Forever*, *Tenderloin*, *WONDERFUL TOWN*; 2001 – *A Connecticut Yankee*, *Bloomer Girl*, *HAIR*; 2002 – *Carnival*, *GOLDEN BOY*, *The PAJAMA GAME*; 2003 – *House of Flowers*, *The NEW MOON*, *No Strings*; 2004 – *CAN-CAN*, *Pardon My English*, *BYE BYE BYE BIRDIE*; 2005 – *A Tree Grows in Brooklyn*, *Purlie*, *The Apple Tree*; 2006 – *KISMET*, *70, Girls, 70*, and *OF THEE I SING*. Similar series exist in Los Angeles, San Francisco, Chicago, and Boston. The 2007 season opened with *FOLLIES*.   DBW

City of Angels Two-act musical comedy, music by CY COLEMAN, lyrics by David Zippel, book by LARRY GELBART; opened 11 December 1989 at the VIRGINIA THEATRE, New York, and closed 19 January 1991 after 912 performances. An original American musical in an age dominated by British imports, *City of Angels* treats the interplay of the travails in Hollywood of Stine (GREGG EDELMAN), a screenwriter, and the film characters he is creating – all of them reflections of people in his own life and played by the same actors, with the exception of his own alter ego, the detective Stone (JAMES NAUGHTON). Gelbart's book cleverly intercuts scenes from the film being written (all in black and white) with scenes from the writer's experience (in color). Coleman's score effectively evokes 1940s popular music, often through the agency of a radio crooner and his backup group. The show won numerous Best Musical awards, including the Tony.   JD

Ciulei, Liviu (1923–) Romanian-born director, scene designer, actor, filmmaker (with a background in architecture), and seminal figure of the Romanian stage. From 1948 until the 1970s he

169

worked at the Lucia Sturza Bulandra Theatre in Bucharest, after which he took assignments as guest director in Germany, France, Canada, Australia, and, finally, the U.S. During 1980–6 he was artistic director at the GUTHRIE THEATER, where his eclectic, idiosyncratic, and cerebral productions included *The Tempest, Eve of Retirement, Peer Gynt, The Threepenny Opera, A Midsummer Night's Dream,* and a stunning *The Bacchae* (1987). Other U.S. credits include *Spring Awakening* and *Hamlet* (1986) at the NEW YORK SHAKESPEARE FESTIVAL (PUBLIC THEATER); *Leonce and Lena* (1974 debut), *Emigrés, Hamlet* (with KEVIN KLINE), *Don Juan, The Lower Depths,* Viktor Slavkin's *Cerceau, The Time of Your Life,* PIRANDELLO's *It's the Truth (If You Think It Is),* and *Hedda Gabler* (1995) and *Ghosts* (1997) at ARENA STAGE; and *Inspector General* at CIRCLE IN THE SQUARE. In recent years he has directed opera worldwide, and was on NYU's graduate acting faculty for a decade, retiring in 2003.   BM DBW

Civic Repertory Theatre   Opened in 1926 by EVA LE GALLIENNE at the FOURTEENTH STREET THEATRE with Benavente's *Saturday Night;* management's progressive ideas for a noncommercial repertory theatre specializing in modern classics and charging low admission was inspired by European subsidized theatres and influenced such American theatres as the THEATRE GUILD and the GROUP THEATRE. CRT boasted an all-female professional staff, promoting, for example, the design talents of ALINE BERNSTEIN and IRENE SHARAFF. Other than modern classics, CRT staged three CHEKHOVS, five IBSENS, and two Rostands; premiered three American plays; and introduced Giraudoux, GOLDONI, and SUSAN GLASPELL's *Alison's House* to New York – for a largely neighborhood audience. Throughout 10 seasons and a 37-play repertory, CRT was beset by financial difficulties, forcing Le Gallienne to bend her repertory rule and in 1933 to move her adaptation of *Alice in Wonderland* uptown for a long run. Nevertheless CRT disbanded in 1935, the result of these fiscal problems.   EH

Claire, Ina [née Inez Fagan] (1892?–1985) Actress noted for her insouciant charm and high comedic sense and style, specializing – from her first appearance in a straight play (1917) to her final one (*The Confidential Clerk,* 1954) – in what *Time Magazine* called "highly varnished comedies of bad manners and good breeding in which the characters misbehave in venomous, perfectly timed epigrams." HAROLD CLURMAN considered her "the most brilliant comedienne of our stage" in

vehicles such as S. N. BEHRMAN's *Biography* and *End of Summer.* She also had an active career in pre-WWI VAUDEVILLE, the ZIEGFELD *Follies,* silent films, and later the talkies.   DBW

Clapp, Henry Austin (1841–1904) American drama critic. Educated at Harvard, Clapp practiced law in Boston, pursuing drama criticism as an avocation. He was music and drama critic of the *Boston Daily Advertiser* from 1868 to 1902, and of the *Boston Herald* during 1902–4. An authority on SHAKESPEARE, Clapp was viewed as an erudite, incorruptible, and fair critic. His *Reminiscences of a Drama Critic* (1902) provides an overview of late 19th-century BOSTON theatrical life.   TLM

Clark, Bobby (1888–1960) and **Paul McCullough** (1883–1936) American comedy team that perfected its raucous, physical style in the circus and vaudeville, Clark and McCullough made the transition to musical theatre in a London REVUE, *Chuckles of 1922.* Their first Broadway show was *The MUSIC BOX REVUE 1922–23,* and after other revue appearances they brought their acrobatic antics to a book musical, *STRIKE UP THE BAND* (1930). Following McCullough's suicide in 1936, Bobby Clark continued alone, appearing in revues such as *The ZIEGFELD Follies of 1936,* musical comedies such as *Mexican Hayride* (1944), revivals of classical comedies such as *Love for Love* (1940) and revivals of operettas such as *Sweethearts* (1947). His last engagement was in the touring company of *DAMN YANKEES* (1956). The crouching, scampering Clark, with his painted-on eyeglasses, ever-present cigar, and stubby cane, was perfectly matched with the tall, giggling McCullough, the straight man of the act.   MK

Clark, Peggy [née Margaret Brownson] (1915–96) A major figure in the establishment of theatrical lighting design as an independent profession, Clark, born in Baltimore, went to Smith College and Yale (M.F.A.). A costume and scenic designer early in her career, she ultimately concentrated on lighting. In addition to more than 150 productions on Broadway, she designed for dance (including for choreographer AGNES DE MILLE) and opera. In 1968 she became the first woman to serve as President of the United Scenic Artists, and in 1978 was named a fellow of the U.S. Institute for Theatre Technology.   BO

Clarke, John Sleeper (1833–99) Actor and theatre manager who made his professional stage debut in 1851 at Boston's Howard Athenaeum as Frank Hardy in *Paul Pry.* A friend of EDWIN BOOTH since childhood, Clarke married Booth's sister Asia in 1859. Clarke was a popular, skillful comedian, highly regarded for his portrayal of eccentric characters like Major Wellington de Boots in Joseph S. Coyne's *A Widow Hunt,* Dr. Pangloss and Zekiel Homespun in Colman the Younger's *The Heir-at-Law,* and Bob Acres in Sheridan's *The Rivals.* In the 1860s Clarke was associated with Booth in the management of several theatres, including Philadelphia's WALNUT STREET THEATRE, the BOSTON THEATRE, and the WINTER GARDEN. In 1867, Clarke emigrated to England, where he remained for the rest of his life, except for occasional starring tours to America. At various times he successfully managed several English theatres, including the Haymarket, the Charing Cross (Toole's) and, for over a decade (1883–9), the Strand. His sons **Creston Clarke** (1865–1910) and **Wilfred Booth Clarke** (1867–1945) also had relatively successful careers in theatre.   DJW

Clarke, Martha (1944–) Baltimore-born experimental theatre and opera director and choreographer. She studied dance as a child and at Juilliard with Louis Horst and choreographers Anthony Tudor and Anna Sokolow, whose company she joined (1965–7). She cofounded Pilobolus (1972–8) and Crowsnest dance companies (1978–). *Nocturne* (1978) and *Portraits* (1979), early sketches, evolved into large-scale productions: *The Garden of Earthly Delights* (1984, inspired by Hieronymus Bosch's painting), *Vienna Lusthaus* (1986, inspired by Egon Schiele's watercolors of women), and *Endangered Species* (1990, based on Henri Toulouse-Lautrec's circus pastels, the American Civil War, and the Holocaust – and something of a critical disaster). In 1993 an 11-minute piece performed to Alban Berg songs, *Dämmerung* (with both the war in Bosnia and AIDS suggested) had a shattering effect, and in 1995 this was expanded into a full-length dance-theatre piece, *An Uncertain Hour.* Clarke explores the grotesque body, archetypical and psychological preoccupations with forbidden pleasures, and the loss of innocence. In 2003 she choreographed LEE BREUER's *DollHouse,* followed in 2004 by a controversial *A Midsummer Night's Dream* at the AMERICAN REPERTORY THEATRE. Influenced by Martha Graham's modern dance style and 1960s theatre of the body (Grotowski, The LIVING THEATER), her work also shares an affinity with Pina Bausch's Tanztheater and ROBERT WILSON's Theatre of Images (see INTRODUCTION, §4).   AF   DBW

Classic Stage Company, The see CSC REPERTORY, LTD.

Classical Theatre of Harlem Not-for-profit company cofounded in 1999 by Alfred Preisser and Christopher McElroen (both white) with $9,000 of their own money at the Harlem School of the Arts on St. Nicholas Ave. Devoted to the Harlem community, this audacious operation – which uses mostly black actors – has presented, among its 25 productions through 2005–6, such plays as *Macbeth* (inaugural production in 2000), *King Lear,* AUGUST WILSON's *MA RAINEY'S BLACK BOTTOM,* Stanisław Witkiewicz's *Crazy Locomotive,* Genet's *The Blacks* (its most acclaimed production to date, with four 2003 Obies), Derek Walcott's *Dream on Monkey Mountain,* Brecht's *Mother Courage,* and KENNEDY's *FUNNYHOUSE OF A NEGRO.* Some believe CTH could be the successor to troupes like the NEGRO ENSEMBLE COMPANY and the New Lafayette Theater.   DBW

Claxton, Kate (1850–1924) Actress, sometimes called "the Sarah Bernhardt of America." Born in Somerville, NJ, she first appeared with LOTTA CRABTREE in 1870, then joined the stock companies of AUGUSTIN DALY and A. M. PALMER. Her most successful roles were in *The Two Orphans, Camille,* and *EAST LYNNE.* After touring *The Two Orphans,* she retired in 1911. She was the heroine of a Brooklyn Theatre FIRE in 1876.   SMA

Clayburgh, James (1949–) Designer who joined the PERFORMANCE GROUP in 1972 after graduating from New York University and designed sets and lights for several of their productions. He was an original member of the WOOSTER GROUP, which emerged from The PERFORMANCE GROUP, and has been their resident designer since its founding in 1980. The Performance Group work was usually environmental, whereas that of the Wooster Group is strongly frontal and often designed in collaboration with director ELIZABETH LeCOMPTE. Typified by simple constructivist components, transformable elements, and unusual spectator–stage spatial relationships, the work contains motifs, patterns, and structures that repeat from one show to the next. Clayburgh has also designed at the PUBLIC THEATER, SECOND STAGE, and elsewhere.   AA

Cleveland Play House East 83–86 Sts. between Euclid and Carnegie Aves., Cleveland [Architects: Philip Small, Charles Rowley, and Francis Draz]. In 1915, Raymond O'Neil, a Cleveland journalist, founded a small amateur theatre group for the production of native plays. Out of it grew the Cleveland Play House, now the oldest producing regional theatre in America. In 1921, Frederic

McConnell took over the amateur company and transformed it into a professional organization. Six years later, the company moved into its complex of two theatres, the 500-seat Drury and the 160-seat Brooks, plus offices and workrooms. When McConnell retired in 1958, he was succeeded by K. Elmo Lowe; then, in 1971, by Richard Oberlin; in 1988 by Josephine R. Abady (whose ouster was a cause célèbre); in 1994 by Peter Hackett; and in 2004 by Michael Bloom. In 1983, the 612-seat Bolton, designed by Philip Johnson, was added to the complex (of five performance spaces). The theatre, despite ups and downs in recent years, maintains its policy of presenting classics, contemporary and new plays, and musicals (in an eight-production season).   MCH

Clifton [née Miller?], **Josephine** (1813–47) Actress, popularly styled "The magnificent Josephine" and at one time regarded as rival to CHARLOTTE CUSHMAN. She debuted at New York's BOWERY THEATRE in 1831 as Belvidera in *Venice Preserv'd,* one critic comparing her figure to that of Sarah Siddons. That same year she was first seen in Philadelphia, where much of her subsequent career was spent. In 1834 she became the first American actress to star in London, a decade before Cushman crossed the Atlantic. On her return, she created *Bianca Visconti,* written for her by NATHANIEL P. WILLIS in 1837. Other roles included Lady Macbeth, Juliet, Mrs. Haller, and Jane Shore. In 1846 she married Robert Place, manager of the AMERICAN THEATRE in New Orleans, and died suddenly the next year. A frequent leading lady to EDWIN FORREST, Clifton, who reputedly had had an affair with the actor, figured prominently in his notorious divorce case of 1851.   DBW

Close, Glenn (1947–) Actress who in only a decade established herself as one of the most respected actresses of her generation. Though best known for films such as *The Big Chill, Fatal Attraction, Hamlet, Paint,* and TV's *The Lion in Winter,* she is a versatile stage performer as well, noted for her "charged stillness." Her Broadway debut – Angelica in a revival of Congreve's *Love for Love* (1974) – was followed by a series of major roles in regional theatres, OFF-BROADWAY appearances (including WENDY WASSERSTEIN's *Uncommon Women and Others* and an Obie-winning performance in Simone Benmussa's *The Singular Life of Albert Nobbs* at the MANHATTAN THEATRE CLUB), and various Broadway appearances, including *The Crucifer of Blood* (1978), the musical *Barnum* (1980), and Annie in the American premiere of Stop-

pard's *The Real Thing* (1984), for which she won the Tony. She was also awarded Tonys in 1992 for her work in MIKE NICHOLS's production of *Death and the Maiden* by Ariel Dorfman, and again in 1994 as Norma Desmond in LLOYD WEBBER's *Sunset Boulevard* (Los Angeles, 1993; New York, 1994), the latter a creation DAVID RICHARDS described as a "legendary performance people will be talking about years from now." In 1995 Close was honored by NEW DRAMATISTS for her artistic contribution to the New York theatre.   DBW

clubs, theatrical By and large a gregarious group, actors in 19th-century America sought to organize themselves into social groups. The first such club was the Actors' Order of Friendship, founded in Philadelphia in 1849. In 1888 a lodge was established in New York City and almost immediately dominated the organization. Primarily designed to supply relief to indigent members, the organization eventually was replaced by the ACTORS' FUND OF AMERICA.

The Benevolent and Protective Order of Elks began as a similar charitable organization in New York in 1868. By the turn of this century, however, the organization had lost its theatrical bent.

The Lambs Club, primarily social in nature, was founded in 1874 and incorporated in 1877. The Lambs became famous for their Gambols, productions in their private theatre, the receipts from which were donated to charity. This convivial club experienced financial trouble in 1974, but still operates on a modest scale.

Of U.S. theatrical clubs, the most distinguished is the Players at 16 Gramercy Park, NYC. Founded in 1888 by EDWIN BOOTH, the club brought together actors and nontheatrical persons; among the charter members were Mark Twain and William Tecumseh Sherman. The clubhouse houses a magnificent collection of theatrical portraits and memorabilia. Booth, who lived in the club for the last five years of his life, donated his personal library to the Players, from which has grown an outstanding American theatre collection. The club for a time gave annual revivals of classic plays, but this practice has been curtailed in recent years. The Players voted in 1988 to accept female members. In 1993 Lynn REDGRAVE became the club's president, the first woman in that position, but she was replaced in 1994 by Michael Allinson (now president emeritus) who was succeeded by Timothy Hutton (reelected in 2004).

In 1904 theatrical press agents formed the Friars and in 1907 incorporated to promote interaction among agents, managers, and other theatrical men. Like the Players, the Friars now accepts women members.

The first actresses' club was the Twelfth Night Club, founded in 1891 in New York to supply aid and social opportunities for actresses. Another organization, the Professional Woman's League, began in 1892 to meet actresses' professional needs.

In 1907 the CHARLOTTE CUSHMAN Club offered lodging for actresses in Philadelphia, a practice discontinued in 1999 with the closing of its theatre district clubhouse. A large collection of Cushman papers and memorabilia were housed in the club, but its holdings were sold in 2000, using the profits for its charitable programs.   SMA

Clurman, Harold (1901–80) Director, critic, author, and teacher who left his mark on the American theatre as founder of the GROUP THEATRE (1931–40). In 25 midnight sessions with New York actors and directors he "talked the Group into existence," becoming its inspirational leader and one of its principal directors. He nurtured the talents of CLIFFORD ODETS and directed five of his plays: *AWAKE AND SING!* (1935), *PARADISE LOST* (1935), *GOLDEN BOY* (1937), *ROCKET TO THE MOON* (1938), and *Night Music* (1940). He also directed IRWIN SHAW's *The Gentle People* (1939) and wrote a history of the Group, *The Fervent Years* (1945).

After the Group's demise Clurman continued directing: *The MEMBER OF THE WEDDING* (1950), *The AUTUMN GARDEN* (1951), *BUS STOP* (1955), *The Waltz of the Toreadors* (1957), *Incident at Vichy* (1965, in Tokyo), *LONG DAY'S JOURNEY INTO NIGHT* (1965), and *The ICEMAN COMETH* (1968).

He was theatre critic for *The New Republic* (1949–52), *The Nation* (1953–80), and the *London Observer* (1955–63). He also assembled three volumes of essays: *Lies Like Truths* (1958), *The Naked Image* (1966) and *The Divine Pastime* (1974), and wrote *On Directing* (1968), *Ibsen* (1977), and *All People Are Famous* (1974), the last in lieu of an autobiography. In addition, he was a professor at Hunter College (1964–80).

Born in New York, he was "reborn in Paris in the 20s" (his words), and became a playreader for the THEATRE GUILD (1929–31). Among his awards – the Donaldson, the GEORGE JEAN NATHAN, and four honorary doctorates – he was proudest of La Croix de Chevalier de la Légion d'Honneur.   RM

Coates, George (1952–) Philadelphia-born experimental theatre director who studied with directors Antoine Bourseiller (1971–2) and GENE FRANKEL (1972–3), performed OFF-OFF BROADWAY and

with the National Shakespeare Company (1973–4), and worked with Blake Street Hawkeyes and other experimental theatre collectives until he formed his company in San Francisco (1977). Collaborating with scientists and artists, Coates's spectacles include live performers and technology-generated sounds and images. Mixing classical stage traditions with popular culture, he explores the relationship between theatre and science. His work is influenced by 1960s and '70s art and technology collaborations, the symbolist stage, Eisenstein's montage films, Mayakovsky's futurist designs, and Marinetti's mechanized performer. Coates's first production, *2019 Blake* (1977–8), was about nonlinear thinking; *The Architecture of Catastrophic Change* (1990) explored the replacement of body parts; *Invisible Site* (1991) simulated virtual reality on stage; and *The Crazy Wisdom Sho* (2001) attempted to upend our understanding of the world using trickster myth, Zen teachings, and a humorous perspective.   AF

Cobb, Lee J. (1911–76) Stage, film, and television actor, best remembered for creating the bewildered, dream-chasing Willy Loman in ARTHUR MILLER's *DEATH OF A SALESMAN*. Born on NYC's Lower East Side, he decided at age 16 to become an actor, ran away from home at 17, and began playing small roles for the PASADENA PLAYHOUSE. In 1934 he joined the GROUP THEATRE. After serving in WWII he returned to Hollywood, but went back to Broadway for *Salesman* (1949). In 1969 he starred in a Broadway production of *King Lear*.   SMA

Coburn, Charles Douville (1877–1961) Actor and manager, remembered for his films, who with his wife, Ivah Wills, founded the Coburn Shakespearean Players (1906), touring major Shakespearean plays and other classics. Additional stage appearances included *The Better 'Ole* (1918), *The YELLOW JACKET* (1916 and 1921), *So This Is London* (1922), *The Farmer's Wife* (1924), *Trelawny of the Wells* (1925, all-star revival), *Diplomacy* (1928), and *Three Wise Fools* (1936). The Coburns helped to found the Mohawk Drama Festival (1934) at Union College, Schenectady, NY, performing there in the summers. He retired from the stage on his wife's death in 1937, returning to play Falstaff in *The Merry Wives of Windsor* for the THEATRE GUILD in 1946, his final appearance on the Broadway stage.   DBW

Cocoanuts, The A musical farce by GEORGE S. KAUFMAN and (uncredited) MORRIE RYSKIND, music and lyrics by IRVING BERLIN; opened on

BUFFALO BILL

Drawing of a young Buffalo Bill Cody. Cover of the Wild West Exhibition program for 1884. *Courtesy:* Don B. Wilmeth Theatre Collection.

Coconut Grove Playhouse The largest regional theatre in Florida opened in 1956 in a lavish old movie palace of the 1920s. Its first production was the American professional premiere of Beckett's *Waiting for Godot.* Over the years the Playhouse has hosted leading writers and directors such as TENNESSEE WILLIAMS, EDWARD ALBEE, ROBERT LEWIS, and GEORGE ABBOTT. The company is committed both to producing plays and musicals of historical significance and to encouraging new works that speak to the multiethnic community it serves. Educational programs such as the In-School Touring program make theatre more accessible to the people of Miami and southern Florida. Under artistic director JOSÉ FERRER (1982–5) and, subsequently, Arnold Mittelman, dozens of major stars have appeared at the Playhouse.   LAB

Cocteau Repertory Theatre see JEAN COCTEAU REPERTORY THEATRE

Cody, William Frederick "Buffalo Bill" (1846–1917) Iowa-born western scout who parlayed his notoriety into success as actor and showman. "Buffalo Bill" Cody personified the excitement of the American frontier in the second half of the 19th century. Publicity gilded his accomplishments, but the stories had some factual basis. His nickname came from a job supplying buffalo meat for railroad workers. Cody gained attention after the Civil War as scout for Generals George Custer and Philip Sheridan. Ned Buntline (E. Z. C. Judson) glamorized his exploits in a serial in December 1869, and in November 1872 John B. Studley enacted him in a play in New York. The immense popularity of plays about Buffalo Bill persuaded Cody to take the stage himself in Buntline's *The Scouts of the Prairie,* 18 December 1872, in Chicago. Audiences tolerated the weak play and Cody's amateurish acting to glimpse the hero with the beard, moustache, and flowing hair. For the next 10 years Cody cultivated a striking stage presence as he played himself in action-filled melodramas.

Between seasons Cody scouted for the Army and arranged hunting parties and entertainments for influential businessmen and European aristocrats. In 1883 he and sharpshooter William F. Carver presented an outdoor WILD WEST EXHIBITION. Problems undermined the partnership, and NATE SALSBURY soon replaced Carver. The Wild West enjoyed phenomenal popularity in America and Europe, but financial setbacks rendered Cody a victim of his success. For 34 years, right up to

Broadway 8 December 1925 and ran 218 performances. In this first of Kaufman's two stage vehicles for the MARX BROS., Chico and Harpo visit Florida, hoping to make a killing in the real-estate boom, and stay in a hotel run by Groucho, who is speculating in a nearby land development. A society matron (Margaret Dumont) presses her daughter to marry a man who is an unscrupulous fortune hunter; the clowns foil both the matron and the evil suitor, the daughter and her true beau happily plan to marry. Groucho and Chico inveigle an exasperated detective into a mock minstrel show, which evolves into a vaudeville routine. Kaufman's script set the pattern for much of the Marx Bros.' subsequent work: a combination of conventional characters (matron, ingenue, juvenile, detective, and villains); an intrigue that threatens a formulaic romance; and a loose situation that gives the clowns the opportunity to wreak mayhem. Paramount released the film version, with Ryskind's screenplay, in 1929. There was an Off-Broadway revival in 1996.   JDM his death, Buffalo Bill rode out to shoot glass balls and entertain audiences, playing successive farewell tours to pay his bills. Though a 20th-century perspective has altered the perception of Cody's border exploits, his stature as the man who brought the frontier to life for generations of Americans is undeniable. Of the numerous biographies of Cody (in addition to his own autobiography), those by Don Russell (1960), Nellie Yost (1979), Robert Carter (2000), and especially Louis S. Warren (2005) are most reliable.   RAH

Coe, Richard Livingston (1916–95) Drama critic. Born in New York and educated at George Washington University, Coe served as assistant drama and film critic for the *Washington Post* during 1938–42. After military service in the Middle East, he returned to the *Post* in 1946 as its principal critic, a position he held until his semiretirement in 1979. Coe was regarded as one of the most perceptive, impartial, and supportive critics of the American stage. He was named Critic of the Year in 1963 by the Directors' Guild of America.   TLM

Coghlan, Charles (1842–99) British-born actor who, after several successes in London, was brought to New York in 1876 by AUGUSTIN DALY. At the FIFTH AVENUE THEATRE he became a favorite in leading roles such as Alfred Evelyn in Bulwer-Lytton's *Money* and Orlando to FANNY DAVENPORT's Rosalind. Subsequent seasons found him at the UNION SQUARE THEATRE, WALLACK'S, and in England again. He joined his sister, ROSE, on several of her tours; together they were outstanding in Sheridan's comedies. Coghlan died in Galveston, TX, on tour in his own play, *The Royal Box.* In 1897 his nephew, **Charles F. Coghlan**, created the part of Alex opposite MRS. FISKE's Tess in *Tess of the d'Urbervilles.*   DBW

Coghlan, Rose (1850/3?–1932) British-born actress whose debut as a child was as one of the witches in a Scottish production of *Macbeth.* Her first New York appearance was in 1872 at WALLACK'S, where she would reign as leading lady during the 1880s. Her Lady Teazle and Rosalind were declared "unsurpassed" on the American stage. During the 1890s and 1900s she appeared principally in London, including starring in the first production of Wilde's *A Woman of No Importance* (1893); after a 1907 U.S. tour in G. B. SHAW's *Mrs Warren's Profession,* she divided her time between New York and London. At her retirement in 1921 she had completed a stage career of more than 52 years.   DBW

Cohan [né Keohane]**, George Michael** (1878–1942) Performer, playwright, director, and producer who was born in Providence, RI, on 3 July (some still believe it was the 4th) while his parents were touring in vaudeville. He first appeared onstage as a child with his family's vaudeville team, the "Four Cohans," and by 15 was writing material for their act. His New York debut came in 1901 with his first full-length play, *The Governor's Son.* In 1904 he formed a producing partnership with SAM H. HARRIS, which lasted until 1920. In 1911 he opened his GEORGE M. COHAN'S THEATRE at 1482 Broadway (razed in 1938). Outstanding among the 50-odd plays and musicals credited to him are *LITTLE JOHNNY JONES* (1904) – featuring the song that most identifies Cohan, "Yankee Doodle Dandy" – *FORTY-FIVE MINUTES FROM BROADWAY* (1905), *The Talk of New York* (1907), *Get-Rich-Quick Wallingford* (1911), *SEVEN KEYS TO BALDPATE* (1913), *The Tavern* (1921), and *The Song and Dance Man* (1923). His most famous song, "Over There" (1917), won him a Congressional Medal. His most notable performances in plays other than his own were as the father in O'NEILL's *AH, WILDERNESS!* (1933) and as the President in KAUFMAN and HART's *I'd Rather Be Right* (1937).

Although Cohan was always the archetype for the glories of turn-of-the-century show business and the representation of a simplistic patriotism to his audience, he was also a complex and lonely man, rarely popular with critics and something of an outcast to his fellow performers when in 1919 he refused to support the establishment of an actors' UNION. His life story was filmed by Warner Bros. in 1942 (*Yankee Doodle Dandy*); a statue of Cohan was erected in 1959 in Duffy Square, NYC; and a musical based on his career, *George M!,* was produced on Broadway in 1968. Cohan's autobiography appeared in 1924; biographies were published in 1943 (Ward Morehouse) and 1973 (John McCabe).   DBW

Cohen, Alexander H. (1920–2000) Producer. Born in New York, educated at NYU and Columbia University, Cohen began producing on Broadway in 1941 with *Ghost for Sale* and *Angel Street.* In 1950 his casting of *King Lear* with blacklisted actors established him as a producer of meritorious if not always commercially successful works. In 1959 he began a series called "Nine O'Clock Theatre" and presented *An Evening with Mike Nichols and Elaine May* (1960), *Beyond the Fringe* (1962), and a revival of John Gielgud in *The Ages of Man* (1963). He presented foreign productions in New York, including the RSC's *The Homecoming* (1967), which won the Tony for Best Play; David Storey's *Home,* starring Gielgud and Richardson (1970); Ben Kingsley as Edmund Kean (1983); Peter Brook's *La Tragédie de Carmen* (1983); and Dario Fo's *Accidental Death of an Anarchist* (1985). Other productions include ANNA CHRISTIE (1977), I REMEMBER MAMA (1979), *A Day in Hollywood/A Night in the Ukraine* (1980), Ronald Harwood's *Taking Sides* (1996), and *The Herbal Bed* (1998). Cohen produced in London and for television, including the Emmy Awards and ANTOINETTE PERRY (Tony) Awards. He was married to producer Hildy Parks. His reminiscences, *Sold Out!,* were published in 1993; he also presented a one-man show, *Star Billing* (1998). TLM

Cole, Bob (1869–1912) and **J. Rosamond Johnson** (1873–1954) African American lyricist and composer. Pioneers in bringing black musicals to the New York stage (see MUSICAL THEATRE), Cole and Johnson were prolific songwriters, librettists, and performers. Cole, in conjunction with Billy Johnson, had written and starred in *A Trip to Coontown* (1898), the first musical entirely created and performed by African Americans. Cole teamed with the classically trained composer J. Rosamond Johnson in 1900. In an era when it was a common practice for songs by several composers to be interpolated into a single musical, Cole and Johnson were in constant demand, providing songs for such shows as *The Belle of Bridgeport* (1900), *Mother Goose* (1903), and *Humpty Dumpty* (1904). Their biggest hit, "Under the Bamboo Tree," was interpolated into *Sally in Our Alley* (1902). Cole and Johnson wrote and appeared in two musicals, *The Shoo Fly Regiment* (1907) and *Mr. Lode of Koal* (1909), but critics of the time were unwilling to accept black performers in musicals that had plots and sympathetic characters. After Cole's death, Johnson continued to write songs and sketches for musicals. Late in his career he appeared in the musicals PORGY AND BESS (1935) and *Cabin in the Sky* (1940). MK

Cole, Jack (1914–74) Choreographer and dancer who received his training in modern dance in the Humphrey–Weidman school and as a member of the Denishawn Company, after which he and his own company of dancers appeared in NIGHTCLUBS. He danced in *Thumbs Up* (1934) and *Keep 'Em Laughing* (1942), and in 1943 was given his first choreographic assignment for *Something for the Boys.* Among the many other shows that he choreographed were *Alive and Kicking* (1950), in which he also appeared; KISMET (1953); *Jamaica* (1957); and MAN OF LA MANCHA (1965). Cole served as both

director and choreographer for the short-lived *Donnybrook!* (1961). A student of the Chinese dancer Mei Lanfang, Cole frequently used "Oriental" movements and gestures in his choreography. He is most noted for creating "jazz dancing," a form characterized by small groupings and angular movements. It became the dominant choreographic style of the 1950s and '60s (see DANCE). His biography by Glenn Loney was published in 1984. MK

Coleman, Cy (1929–2004) Composer. A child prodigy, he attended the New York College of Music before playing in NIGHTCLUBS with a jazz trio. With lyricist Carolyn Leigh he contributed songs to the REVUE *John Murray Anderson's Almanac* (1953), and wrote the scores for the musicals *Wildcat* (1960) and *Little Me* (1962). He then teamed with DOROTHY FIELDS for the score of SWEET CHARITY (1966). Among his more successful scores with other lyricists were those for *I Love My Wife* (1977), *On the Twentieth Century* (1978), *Barnum* (1980), CITY OF ANGELS (1989; 1990 Tony for Best Musical), *The* WILL ROGERS FOLLIES (1991), and *The Life* (1997). Coleman's early interest in modern jazz influenced the upbeat, rhythmic style of his compositions for the musical stage. MK

collective theatre groups During America's burgeoning theatre movement throughout the 1960s, various performance ensembles formed to create an alternative to the prevalent commercial methods of producing. These groups produced such a wide spectrum of work OFF-OFF BROADWAY that, aesthetically speaking, it is difficult to generalize about the nature of their productions; what they have in common, however, is an organizational structure – or sometimes, simply an organizational point of view – that values each participant in a production as a creative collaborator. Collectives tended – sometimes explicitly, sometimes implicitly – to reject both the commercial aims of Broadway and OFF-BROADWAY, as well as their hierarchical and increasingly bureaucratic organization.

Actors especially gravitated to collectives, disenchanted by what they considered the exploitation of their talents in the service of commercial products in the mainstream theatre. Indeed, many collectives, among them the OPEN THEATRE and the Talking Band, developed plays out of actors' improvisational exercises.

In many cases "collective" is a misnomer, since some groups have distinct directors whose own style stamps the group's work and who make the final artistic decisions. This is true, for instance, of some of the theatres that emphasized formal experimentation: the PERFORMANCE GROUP, Manhattan Project (see ANDRE GREGORY), MABOU MINES, and the WOOSTER GROUP. Nevertheless, these ensembles, too, involved actors and other company members in a collaborative process of developing plays, not bound by the short rehearsal periods of Broadway.

Perhaps the prototype of the American collective was the LIVING THEATRE, founded in 1948 by Julian Beck and Judith Malina. In many cases that followed, the plan to work collectively reflected overt political aims, as in the BREAD AND PUPPET THEATRE, started by puppeteer Peter Schumann in the early 1960s; the SAN FRANCISCO MIME TROUPE founded in 1959 by R. G. Davis, which produced open-air political commedialike plays; EL TEATRO CAMPESINO, a group of Chicano farmworkers, founded by LUIS VALDÉZ in response to the 1965 California grape strike; and, an outgrowth of the civil rights movement in the American South, the New Orleans–based FREE SOUTHERN THEATRE.

According to the same principle, in the 1970s the collective became the principal organizational approach for feminist theatres, among them MINNEAPOLIS'S AT THE FOOT OF THE MOUNTAIN and New York's SPIDERWOMAN THEATRE, Women's Experimental Theatre, and SPLIT BRITCHES. The collective ideal, though less prevalent in the 21st century, remains a potent precedent for some theatres being formed to this day. (See also ALTERNATIVE THEATRE.) AS

Collins, Pat (1932–) Lighting designer. Though closely associated with the HARTFORD STAGE, Collins has worked at many regional theatres (CENTER STAGE, LINCOLN CENTER, SIGNATURE, GOODSPEED, OLD GLOBE, etc.) and designed well over 100 productions for the Washington, Boston, Houston, Netherlands, and English National Opera Companies. She has designed several dozen Broadway and OFF-BROADWAY shows, including *The HEIDI CHRONICLES, Ain't Misbehavin', I'm Not Rappaport* (1985, for which she won a Tony), *Conversations with My Father* (1992), *An American Daughter* (1997), and *PROOF* (2000)   AA

Colored Museum, The   Using the musical REVUE form and a group of five actors in multiple roles, author GEORGE C. WOLFE presents a collection of animated museum exhibits that satirize stereotypes and icons from black history and culture. Stingingly lampooned topics range from the harrowing slaveship experience to the prizewinning play *A RAISIN IN THE SUN,* to the show-stopping

entertainer JOSÉPHINE BAKER. Directed by LEE RICHARDSON, the play premiered in 1986 at CROSSROADS THEATRE Company in New Brunswick, NJ, moving to JOSEPH PAPP'S PUBLIC THEATER and then to the Royal Court Theatre in London. It received the Dramatists Guild Award for 1986.   EGH

Comden, Betty (1917–2006) and **Adolph Green** (1914–2002) Librettists, lyricists, screenwriters, and performers. After writing and appearing in a satirical NIGHTCLUB act, Comden and Green made their Broadway debuts as librettists, lyricists, and featured performers in *ON THE TOWN* (1944). Their wry wit appeared to best advantage in the librettos and/or lyrics they created for shows with a satirical tinge, such as *WONDERFUL TOWN* (1953), *BELLS ARE RINGING* (1956), and *Say Darling* (1958). When their fast-paced, wisecracking style of musical comedy declined in popularity in the 1960s, Comden and Green's contributions to the Broadway stage became less frequent. As a taste for satirical books and lyrics returned in the late 1970s and '80s, the partners were again successful with their work for *On the Twentieth Century* (1978) and *Singin' in the Rain* (1985). They began the 1990s with Tony Award–winning lyrics for *The Will Rogers Follies,* music by CY COLEMAN. Comden and Green also wrote the screenplays for several popular musical films of the 1950s. In 1991 they were honored at the Kennedy Center.

Comden's autobiography appeared in 1995. Green was married to actress Phyllis Newman; their daughter, **Amanda** (c. 1963–), is an accomplished songwriter and cabaret performer whose musical *High Fidelity,* written with Tom Kitt and DAVID LINDSAY-ABAIRE, was in 2006 unsuccessful on Broadway.   MK

Come Back, Little Sheba by WILLIAM INGE. Directed for the THEATRE GUILD by DANIEL MANN, Inge's first Broadway production opened to mixed reviews on 15 February 1950. *Sheba* featured bravura Tony Award–winning performances by SHIRLEY BOOTH and Sidney Blackmer, and ran for 190 performances after cast and playwright kept it open by taking pay and royalty reductions. Two years later, Booth received an Academy Award for her performance in the popular film version, adapted for the screen by Ketti Frings.

Adrift in a sterile marriage, the passions of Doc and Lola boil under the surface as the romance of their young boarder is played out on their front porch. Reflecting contemporaneous trends, the two-act play's realistic surface is imbued with Freudian psychology and symbolism. The titular

Sheba was a little puppy, a symbol of happier and livelier times, whose loss is constantly mourned by Lola.   MR

community theatre/Little Theatre movement

Thespian societies and parlor theatricals were common in America long before the advent of the Little Theatres. In 1897 Jane Addams and Mrs. Laura Dainty Pelham organized the HULL-HOUSE Players in CHICAGO because they believed that good plays performed by amateurs could have "a salutary influence on the community." The big movement came a decade later with The Players (1909) in Providence, RI, Thomas H. Dickinson's Wisconsin Dramatic Society in Madison and Milwaukee (1911), Mrs. Lyman Gale's Boston Toy Theatre (1912), Alfred Arvold's Little Country Theatre in Fargo, ND (1912), and Maurice Browne's Chicago Little Theatre (1912). The sudden and simultaneous flowering of Little Theatres can be attributed to the following: the visit of Lady Gregory's Irish Players (1911); PERCY MACKAYE's call for "constructive leisure" in his book The Civic Theatre (1912); the founding of the DRAMA LEAGUE (1909); GEORGE P. BAKER's "Workshop 47" at Harvard (1912); the numerous articles about the European art theatres; dissatisfaction with the offerings of the commercial theatre; and a passionate belief, if sometimes ill-founded, that the arts and crafts of the theatre could be grasped by enthusiastic and ambitious amateurs eager for "self-expression."

The pioneers were quickly joined by Samuel Eliot's Little Theatre in Indianapolis (1915), SAM HUME's Arts and Crafts Theatre in Detroit (1916), Frederick McConnell's CLEVELAND PLAY HOUSE (1916), Gilmore Brown's PASADENA PLAYHOUSE (1918), and Oliver Hinsdell's Dallas Little Theatre (1920). By 1920 there were more than 50 groups scattered across the country who found further support for their endeavors from Gordon Craig's Toward a New Theatre (1913); Hume's exhibition of the New Stagecraft (1914); New York's PROVINCE-TOWN PLAYERS (1914) and WASHINGTON SQUARE PLAYERS (1915); THEATRE ARTS Magazine (1916, later a monthly); and from CONSTANCE D'ARCY MACKAY's The Little Theatre in the United States (1917).

By WWII, the number of groups had grown to more than 100. They performed in improvised venues (family mansions, livery stables, churches, community centers) on temporary platforms framed by proscenium openings of 15 ft. or less and with accommodation for fewer than 100 spectators, most of whom were season subscribers. They specialized in bills of one-act plays, which required minimal scenery and few rehearsals

and offered less demanding roles to more members. The more ambitious attempted the plays of SHAW, IBSEN, and Strindberg, and at one time or another (in the 1920s) most took a turn at laughing at themselves with GEORGE KELLY's The Torchbearers. They also sponsored lectures, play readings, and classes in theatre arts and crafts.

Community theatres (now numbering more than 5,000) have become an integral part of the cultural life of their communities, and many have built their own theatre complexes. A 1984 survey by the American Community Theatre Association found nearly 100 that had been in continuous operation for 50 years or more, including The Footlight Club of Jamaica, MA (1877); the Players of Providence, RI (1909); Indianapolis Civic Theatre (1915); Le PETIT THÉÂTRE DU VIEUX CARRÉ in New Orleans (1919); Theatre Memphis (1920); and the Omaha Community Playhouse (1925). Some have been transformed into regional professional theatres (e.g., Cleveland, Houston, Washington, Dallas), and even those that have maintained their amateur (or semiamateur) status can hardly be called "Little"; they operate on budgets approaching a million dollars and present full seasons of major plays, both old and new.

Numerous attempts to organize such theatres into an association include a Little Theatre Conference at the Pasadena Playhouse (1924), the National Theatre Conference (1920s), and the American Educational Theatre Association (AETA, starting in 1936). In 1958 the National Association of Community Theatres joined members of AETA to form ACTA as a division of the American Theatre Association (formerly AETA). The demise of ATA resulted in a new group, The American Association of Community Theatres (1986), which meets annually and sponsors a play festival (AACTFEST) held every two years with representatives from 10 regions. In 2005 AACT claimed more than 45,000 productions by its contituents.   RM   DBW

Company Two-act musical comedy, music and lyrics by STEPHEN SONDHEIM, book by George Furth; opened 26 April 1970 at the ALVIN THEATRE, New York, running 705 performances. The first of the innovative series of collaborations between Sondheim and director-producer HAROLD PRINCE in the 1970s, *Company* is a "concept" musical dealing with the subject of romantic relationships in a contemporary urban setting. Various couples and single women are tied together by their relationship to Robert (Dean Jones; replaced quickly by Larry Kert, the only replacement ever nominated for a Tony – up to a change in Tony rules in 2005), an unmarried man entering middle age. Rather than advancing the plot, the songs are used (in Sondheim's words) "in a Brechtian way, as comment and counterpoint." Vignettes of Robert and the various characters are used to illustrate various aspects of relationships, and the ending of the show is intentionally vague. The hard-edged urban environment is reflected in Sondheim's relentless music and was visually represented by Boris Aronson's metallic, elevator-dominated set. A notable departure from traditional musical-comedy form, *Company* won the Drama Critics' Circle and Tony awards for Best Musical. There was a 1995 revival by the Round-about Theatre Company; a critically acclaimed revival, seen first in Cincinnati and directed by John Doyle, opened on Broadway in November 2006 (Tony, Best Revival of a Musical, 2007).   JD

Company of Women Founded in 1990 in Massachusetts (various sites; mostly tours to northeastern colleges) by actress and master voice teacher Kristin Linklater and psychologist Carol Gilligan, this unique – albeit short-lived – nonprofit theatre and educational organization believed that "the free voices of women and girls are powerful agents" for social change, and specialized in the performance of Shakespeare's plays (*Henry V, King Lear*) "performed, informed and transformed by multi-cultural, multi-generational, all female casts" while developing original dramatic material and conducting effective workshops ("In Our Own Voices"). In 1996, when the founders moved on to other endeavors (Linklater to Columbia University), the company ceased operation.   DBW

Comstock, F. Ray (1880–1949) Broadway producer renowned for his innovative productions. He managed the Princess Theatre when it housed Holbrook Blinn's experimental drama company (1913–15) and when it was home to a series of pacesetting musical comedies (1915–18) by Jerome Kern, P. G. Wodehouse, and Guy Bolton. With Morris Gest he produced Russian variety artist Nikita F. Balieff and members of a semi-independent branch of the Moscow Art Theatre called "The Bat" in the groundbreaking cabaret *Chauve-Souris;* the 1923–4 MAT tours; and Max Reinhardt's *The Miracle* (1924), a prototype of "environmental" theatre.   WD

Conduct of Life, The Spare play by Maria Irene Fornés that addresses intersections of power and violence at the sites of gender and the state in 19 enigmatic scenes. First performed at Theatre

for the New City on 21 February 1985, with Fornés directing, the play has since received attention from feminist and Hispanic American critics and from alternative theatre producers. Set in an unnamed Latin American country, *Conduct* explores a domestic situation controlled by an army lieutenant who exercises his political and sexual frustrations on his wife and his very young, unwillingly abducted mistress. Its complex description of victimization and resistance and its pessimism about changing power structures has been both praised and abhorred by contemporary critics.   JDo

Congdon, Constance (1944–) Playwright whose *Tales of the Lost Formicans* premiered at River Arts (1988) before playing Off-Broadway (1990). This wry examination of suburban life as seen by aliens won the Oppenheimer Award (1990) and has been performed worldwide. Her other plays include *Gilgamesh* (1976), *Native American* (Portland 1983, London 1988), *No Mercy* (cowinner Great American Play Contest, 1985), *The Gilded Age* (Hartford, 1986), *The Yellow Wallpaper* (libretto, 1989), *Casanova* (New York, 1991), *Dog Opera* (1995), *Lips* (Primary Stages, 1999), *The Automata Pieta* (ACT Young Conservatory, 1999), and several children's plays and adaptations. She has taught playwriting at Amherst College.   TH-S

Conkle, E(llsworth) P(routy) (1899–94) Playwright, theatre educator, and student of George Pierce Baker at Yale (1926–8) who had a half-dozen productions in New York, including the social-protest play *200 Were Chosen* (1936, 35 performances), which dealt with Midwest Depression farmers relocated by the government to Alaska. *Prologue to Glory* (1938, 169 NYC performances), on the topic of the young Abraham Lincoln and his romance with Ann Rutledge, received more than 20 productions across the country by the Federal Theatre Project and was later presented on television (1952). Several collections of plays have been published. During 1939–73 he taught at the Universities of Iowa and Texas.   TP

Conklin, John (1937–) Set and costume designer (and playwright) whose career began in the late 1950s at Yale and the Williamstown Theatre Festival. In the 1960s he began an ongoing association with the Hartford Stage Company. Most of his work through the 1970s was at these and other regional theatres, but he also began to design for opera and teach at New York University (1980). By the 1990s he was designing regularly for the San Francisco, New York City, Metropolitan, and Chicago Lyric Opera Companies as well as at opera houses throughout Europe. He worked extensively with directors ROBERT WILSON, MARK LAMOS, Jonathan Miller, and ROBERT FALLS, among many others, and developed close relationships with such theatres as the AMERICAN REPERTORY THEATRE, the LONG WHARF, and the GOODMAN as well as Hartford, where he has frequently collaborated with lighting designer PAT COLLINS. These associations and his teaching at NYU have made him one of the most influential designers in the U.S. Working in a largely architectural style, Conklin's work is filled with rich detail, texture, and historical reference. His intelligent use of historical art and culture within his settings was a strong influence on postmodernist tendencies in design. He wrote, directed, and designed *The Carving of Mount Rushmore* for ACTORS THEATRE OF Louisville (1992). In the 1990s he accepted staff positions at Glimmerglass Opera and City Opera. In 1994 he received the second Mary L. Murphy Design Award from LONG WHARF THEATRE, where in 27 years he had designed 18 productions.   AA

Connection, The, by Jack Gelber. This play with jazz music by Freddie Redd played 778 times in the LIVING THEATRE's repertory from 15 July 1959 until 1963. Directed by Judith Malina and designed by Julian Beck, it focused on the lives of heroin-addicted musicians listlessly awaiting their "connection," Cowboy. Critics did not know how to respond (London audiences shouted and booed), but it won three Obie Awards (including Best New Play) and has been frequently revived, including a 1980 production at New York's Henry Street Settlement directed by the original cowboy, Carl Lee. The music was recorded in 1960, and a 1962 film of a performance was released despite the New York Board of Regents, which banned it for obscene language.   REK

Connelly, Marc(us Cook) (1890–1980) Playwright, actor, producer, and director who first became known on the Broadway scene as a collaborator of GEORGE S. KAUFMAN on such plays as *DULCY* (1921) and *BEGGAR ON HORSEBACK* (1924), the latter being the most successful of their work together. His greatest contribution as a playwright came with *The GREEN PASTURES* (1930), a Pulitzer Prize–winning adaptation of Roark Bradford's dialect stories. By holding the stage for 640 performances, this funny, touching, and naturally truthful work showed America that a play with an all-black cast could be good box office. Connelly's Broadway acting credits include the Stage

Manager in a 1944 production of *OUR TOWN* and Professor Osman in *Tall Story* (1959), a role he repeated for the motion picture. As a producer-director, his greatest success was *Having Wonderful Time* (1937). His memoirs, *Voices Offstage,* appeared in 1968.   LDC

Conrad, Robert T(aylor) (1810–58) Playwright. Journalist, lawyer, judge, editor, politician, orator, and dilettante in the theatre, Conrad, born to a wealthy Philadelphia family, wrote at least three plays. Neither *Conrad of Naples* (1832), in which JAMES WALLACK acted the lead part, nor *The Heretic* (n.d.) has survived. Conrad's *Jack Cade* (1835) was not successful until he revised it for EDWIN FORREST, who produced it first in 1841 and kept it in his repertoire for years. Sometimes called *Aylmere; or, The Kentish Rebellion* or *Aylmere; or, The Bond Man of Kent, Jack Cade* dramatizes the life of a 15th-century villein (partially freed serf still bound to his lord) who incites an insurrection to abolish the institution of villeinage. Its theme of individual freedom was extremely popular in Jacksonian America. Conrad's later years were spent as a judge and the elected mayor of Philadelphia.   WJM

Conried, Heinrich (1848–1909) Theatre manager. Born in Austria, Conried, Mathilde Cottrelly, and GUSTAV AMBERG organized the highly successful German-speaking THALIA THEATRE Company in New York in 1879 with the objective of establishing a theatre modeled after repertory theatres in Europe. Conried lured many German actors to America, including Marie Geistinger, Josephine Gallmyer, Friedrich Mitterwurzer, and Ludwig Barnay in 1883. He became stage manager for RUDOLPH ARONSON at the CASINO THEATRE in 1883, managed the Irving Place Theatre from 1892, and became managing director of the Metropolitan Opera House in 1903. He was forced to resign in 1908 after controversy over his staging of *Parsifal* and the U.S. premiere of *Salome*. In 1909 he proposed the building of the NEW THEATRE to stage both opera and drama. Montrose Moses wrote a biography in 1916.   RE

Contemporary Theatre, Inc., A Founded in SEATTLE in 1965 by Gregory Arthur Falls, then Director of the University of Washington School of Drama, the company (now known as ACT) – despite a financial crisis in 2003 – has kept to its mission of providing regional audiences with great contemporary stories told through the voices of the uniquely talented Seattle community of theatre artists and artisans. As its budget has risen from the original $35,000 to an excess of $6 million, the company has increased its commitment to playwrights by commissioning new authors of longterm interest – as of the 2005–6 season more than 80 contemporary plays had been staged. Also a major regional influence in young people's theatre, the company's original site, a 449-seat thrust theatre (Queen Anne Hall), was replaced in 1996 with new facilities (two 390-seat theatres) in the Eagles Auditorium, renamed Kreielsheimer Place. Jeff Steitzer served as artistic director in 1988–94, replaced in 1995 by Peggy Shannon (for one season). In 1997 Gordon Edelstein, previously at LONG WHARF, became artistic director, replaced in turn by Kurt Beattie in 2003.   RW

Contrast, The Perhaps the most popular American play of the 18th century, ROYALL TYLER's five-act comedy premiered at the JOHN STREET THEATRE on 16 April 1787. Recognized as the first native comedy to be professionally staged, the work resembles Sheridan's comedies of wit, in particular *The School for Scandal,* which Tyler acknowledged as an inspirational source. The play is notable for its characterization of American types in the wake of the Revolutionary War. Dimple, the snobbish rake who is in line to marry Maria, is exposed as a perfidious fop and hence assumes the vacuous part of the vanquished royalist. Colonel Manly, who eventually wins Maria's hand, embodies the heroic, noble, and victorious American. His servant, Jonathan, the rude country bumpkin (and object of ridicule by Dimple's manservant, Jessamy) is revealed as the folksy and honest YANKEE character, and would be revived in many manifestations throughout the next century as a fundamental American type.   PAD

Conroy, Frances (1953–) Georgia-born actor, educated at Dickinson, Juilliard, and the NEIGHBORHOOD PLAYHOUSE, seen most recently as the quirky mother in HBO's *Six Feet Under,* has had a long and varied legitimate stage career (often playing complex, repressed women) beginning with her Off-Broadway debut with the ACTING COMPANY in 1978. For much of her career the finely nuanced actor has been a utilitarian performer in small film and stage roles (with greater acclaim on Los Angeles and Washington, DC, stages), yet a Tony nomination in 2000 as Theodora in ARTHUR MILLER's *The Ride Down Mt. Morgan,* a role she'd first played in the 1991 London production, firmly established her credentials. Other Miller credits are *The Last Yankee, Broken Glass,* and the 1996 film version of *The CRUCIBLE.* JoANNE AKALAITIS, several times her director,

calls her "a classic actor" and says she is "so sensitive, so detailed, and so serious."   DBW

Conway, H. J. (1800–60) Playwright. Associated with theatres in PHILADELPHIA, BOSTON, and New York, Conway worked as prompter and treasurer and wrote at least 29 plays. Apparently interested in creating a nationalistic drama as well as responding to popular trends, Conway wrote *The Battle of Stillwater* (1840), celebrating the famous Revolutionary War battle of October 1777 with all of the ingredients of successful melodrama, and *Hiram Hireout* (1851), in which he fused patriotism to Yankee humor.   WJM

Conway, Kevin (1942–) New York–born director and actor (UTA HAGEN–trained) with dozens of film (*Gods and Generals*) and television (Mark Twain in Ken Burns's documentary) credits as well as noteworthy stage appearances. Though the stocky, often bearded Conway has rarely been in a major stage hit (although he has won individual awards), from his Off-Broadway debut in *Muzeeka* (1968) and his 1969 Broadway debut in *INDIANS* (Black Hawk) to his most recent appearance as Dan Packard in *DINNER AT EIGHT* (2002) he has amassed a handful of celebrated performances. Foremost among these were his student Mike in *MOONCHILDREN* (1972), mental inmate McMurphy in *One Flew over the Cuckoo's Nest* (replacement, 1973), ominous drifter Teddy in *WHEN YOU COMIN' BACK, RED RYDER* (1973), George in *OF MICE AND MEN* (1974), Jamie in *LONG DAY's JOURNEY INTO NIGHT* (1976, BROOKLYN ACADEMY OF MUSIC), Dr. Frederick Treves in *The ELEPHANT MAN* (1979), and, most memorably, Larry "the Liquidator" Garfinkle in Jerry Sterner's *Other People's Money* (1989). His directing credits include the Chicago production of the Sterner play, a regional production of *The Elephant Man,* and Ted Whitehead's *Mecca* Off-Broadway.   DBW

Conway [né Rugg], **William Augustus** (1789–1828), **Frederick Bartlett** (1819–74), **Sarah Crocker** (1835–75) Anglo–American acting family. William made his London debut 4 October 1813. A leading actor of tragic parts at Covent Garden and Bath, he withdrew because of personal attacks and came to America (1824), where he acted until drowning himself. His son, Frederick, established himself as a leading man in both tragedy and comedy in England before coming to the U.S. (1850). In 1852 he married Sarah Crocker, sister of Mrs. D. P. Bowers, and after starring together they leased the Park Theatre, Brooklyn, which Crocker managed (1864–75).   DMcD

Cook, Barbara (1927–) Singer-actress who possesses one of the finest soprano voices ever heard on the American musical stage. She made her Broadway debut in *Flahooley* (1951), and received critical acclaim for her performance as Cunegonde in *CANDIDE* (1956) and a Tony Award for her Marian Paroo in *The MUSIC MAN* (1957). Cook appeared in *The Gay Life* (1961), *SHE LOVES ME* (1963), and *The Grass Harp* (1971). She also starred in major revivals of *OKLAHOMA!, CAROUSEL, The KING AND I,* and *SHOW BOAT.* In 1965 Cook replaced Sandy Dennis in the comedy *ANY WEDNESDAY,* and thereafter appeared in straight plays as well as musicals. She retired from the stage in the early 1970s and has mostly confined her appearances to concert halls and NIGHTCLUBS, except for limited engagements in her ONE-PERSON shows: *Barbara Cook: A Concert for the Theatre* (1987), *Barbara Cook: Mostly Sondheim* (2002), *Barbara Cook's Broadway* (2004), and *Barbara Cook at The Met (with Special Guests)* (2006). In addition to a singing voice of great range and expressiveness, Cook brought to her roles a winning personality and a deft touch for comedy.   MK

Cook, George Cram (1873–1924) Playwright and director. With his wife, SUSAN GLASPELL, he founded in Massachusetts the PROVINCETOWN PLAYERS (1915), which opened in 1916 in Greenwich Village, where Cook remained inspirational leader until 1922. Although a minor playwright whose best efforts like *SUPPRESSED DESIRES* (1915) and *Tickless Time* (1918) were written in collaboration with Glaspell, he was a mentor to EUGENE O'NEILL, for whom he directed *The EMPEROR JONES* (1920). No art-theatre director was more dedicated to promoting serious American playwriting. Robert Sarlos's biography (with a focus on the Providence Players years) appeared in 1982.   RHW

Cook, Joe [né Joseph Lopez] (1890–1959) Comic. BROOKS ATKINSON called him "the greatest man in the world," yet this zany ("a one-man vaudeville show") is virtually forgotten. With his Rube Goldberg contraptions, his "imitation of four Hawaiians" (a convoluted explanation of how he got rich ends: Why should a wealthy man imitate four Hawaiians?), his landlord gag (attempting to collect rent on a miniature cottage, he finally walks off with it under his arm), and similar absurd novelties, Cook wowed audiences, from his VAUDEVILLE debut in 1907 to his last appearance in an ice show in 1940. In between, other than vaudeville and REVUE appearances, he was most successful in *Rain or Shine* (1928), *Fine and Dandy* (1930), and *Hold Your Horses* (1933).   DBW

Cooke, George Frederick (1756–1812) Dublin-born English romantic actor; the first major foreign star on the American stage. Cooke was a traveling actor in the British provinces from at least 1773 until 1800, essaying some 300 roles. After a successful debut at Covent Garden in 1800, where during 1800–3 he rivaled John Philip Kemble, he restricted himself to a few roles – Shylock, Iago, Macbeth, Sir Giles Overreach, Macklin's Sir Pertinax MacSycophant and Sir Archy MacSarcasm, and especially Richard III – those seen most frequently during his American visit (1810–12), and those most admired for their satanic humor. Although there was a coarseness in his character and acting, Cooke was often noted for his stately carriage, as well as his broad torso and prominent nose. A chronic alcoholic, Cooke was brought to the U.S. by THOMAS A. COOPER and STEPHEN PRICE to appear first at the PARK THEATRE on 11 November. His reputation for drunkenness and debauchery preceded him, but he was on his best behavior (for the most part) during his 160 performances in New York, Boston, Baltimore, Philadelphia, and Providence (where he gave his final performance anywhere on 31 July 1812). Cooke intended to take his U.S.-met last wife (of a possible three to five) back to England, but he died of cirrhosis of the liver in NYC in September. Buried in St. Paul's churchyard, his remains were reinterred in 1821 by his admirer Edmund Kean, who erected a monument over them – still a notable theatre shrine refurbished six times (most recently in 1948). His earliest (and biased) biography was penned by his contemporary William Dunlap (1813); modern biographies were written by Arnold Hare and Don Wilmeth, both dated 1980.   PT   DBW

Cooper, Thomas Abthorpe (1775/6–1849) British-born actor and manager who became the first star of the American stage and initiated the practice of traveling from one company to another performing only prominent roles. While in his teens Cooper performed in Edinburgh and at various provincial theatres; his London debut was as Hamlet in 1795. In 1796, unhappy with his English acceptance, he went to the CHESTNUT STREET THEATRE in Philadelphia. After the settlement of an alleged breach of articles with the Philadelphia management, he joined DUNLAP at the PARK STREET in New York in 1801; during 1806–15 he was in management at the Park. With STEPHEN PRICE as his partner he played the eastern circuit, excelling in heroic characters in poetic drama, such as Pierre in *Venice Preserv'd.* His popularity continued into the 1820s, but by 1830 it was waning, and by 1835 "he had sadly become the seeker instead of the sought after." Two modern biographies exist: by Geddeth Smith (1996) and F. Arant Maginnes (2004).   DBW

Copperfield [né Kotkin]**, David** (Seth) (1956–) One of the world's best-known stage MAGICIANS today, Copperfield has received most attention for spectacular feats designed for television specials – vanishing a Lear jet, the Statue of Liberty, a dining car from the Orient Express. He is best, however, at integrating music, illusion, choreography, and a narrative, so that magical sequences are more like minidramas. His frequent tours (almost 500 performances a year) are extraordinarily successful class acts. He brought *Dreams & Nightmares* to Broadway in 1996 (with more than $6 million in ticket sales in five weeks); his 2003 tour was titled *An Intimate Evening of Grand Illusion*. He is owner of the famous Mulholland Magic Collection (housed in private quarters in Las Vegas) and has added items from others' holdings (including Houdini props).   DBW

Copperhead, The A 1918 melodrama by AUGUSTUS THOMAS that featured a virtuoso performance by Lionel Barrymore (see DREW–BARRYMORE FAMILY) and established him as a major star. The play opened on 18 February 1918 at the SAM S. SHUBERT THEATRE in New York and ran for 120 performances. Adapted from a story by Frederick Landis, Thomas's play about an Illinois farmer who sacrifices his happiness by pretending to be a Confederate sympathizer is split into two "epochs": Acts I and II are set in the 1860s, and Acts III and IV occur 40 years later. Barrymore's triumph was his moving portrayal of Milt Shanks as a young farmer-turned-spy in the first half of the performance and as a dignified, long-suffering old man in the second. Audiences were typically reduced to tears by the play's final scene in which Shanks – his honor at last proven – is restored to the community, proclaiming, "God! It's wonderful . . . to hev friends agin!"   MF

Corbin, John R. (1870–1959) Drama critic. Educated at Harvard and Oxford, Corbin brought a well-trained academic mind to drama criticism at *Harper's Weekly* (1897–1900), the *New York Times* (1902–4; 1917–19; 1922–4), and the *New York Sun* (1904–7). Also he was literary director of the NEW THEATRE (1908–10) and authored 12 books, two on Shakespeare. A conservative critic, Corbin nevertheless supported both realist and American drama but in a style regarded as "learned and plodding."   TLM

Cordelia's Aspirations This late installment in EDWARD HARRIGAN's "Mulligan Guard" series featured the well-known Dan Mulligan (played by Harrigan) forced by his wife, Cordelia (Annie Yeamans), into leaving his beloved home on NYC's Lower East Side for a more respectable address uptown. Tony Hart performed his blackface character, Rebecca Allup, and Yeamans had a famous drunk scene in this treatment of Irish immigrants who aspire beyond their station. David Braham composed music for the comedy, which opened 5 November 1883 at the New Theatre Comique, ran a record-breaking 176 performances, and was frequently revived by Harrigan's company. The *New York Times* called the play (which was never published), "another turn to the kaleidoscope of city life which [Harrigan] has so faithfully constructed."   KF

Corio, Ann [née Anna Coria or Coreo] (1914?–99) With Georgia Sothern and GYPSY ROSE LEE, one of the premiere American stripteasers of the 1930s, although Corio, "probably the prettiest girl in burlesque," took off few clothes. From a member of the chorus in a BURLESQUE SHOW in her hometown of Hartford, CT, Corio rose to soubrette and then headline stripper. Her gimmick became "innocence," dressing as a pretty little girl in a ruffled skirt. "The more innocent I was, the more wicked they [the audience] felt." Under the tutelege of impresario Emmett R. Callahan (who became her first husband), she became the star of *Girls in Blue* and other shows. Probably her most important contribution, however, was the revival of old-time burlesque in her *This Was Burlesque* (also the title of a book she cowrote in 1968), which opened in 1962 (its last performance was 1991 in Florida) and featured some of the great top bananas, including Steve Mills and Conny Ryan.   DBW

Cornell, Katharine (1893–1974) Actress. Called "The First Lady of the Theatre" by ALEXANDER WOOLLCOTT, Cornell, with HELEN HAYES and LYNN FONTANNE, was the reigning actress on the Broadway stage during the second quarter of the 20th century. An accomplished interpreter of romantic and character roles, she brought to her characterizations a resonant voice and a remarkably expressive face that captivated audiences; she could create the illusion that a memorable play was being witnessed when in fact the vehicle was weak. Her New York debut was with the WASHINGTON SQUARE PLAYERS (1916); her London debut was as Jo in *Little Women* (1919). Prominence in the American theatre came with *A Bill of*

Divorcement (1921). She is best remembered as Elizabeth Barrett in *The Barretts of Wimpole Street* (1931) and as SHAW's Candida (1924). Other notable appearances included *Romeo and Juliet* (1934), *The Doctor's Dilemma* (1941), *Antony and Cleopatra* (1947), *The Dark Is Light Enough* (1955), and *Dear Liar* (as Mrs. Patrick Campbell) in 1959. In 1921 she married GUTHRIE MCCLINTIC, who was responsible for most of her productions. On his death in 1961 she retired. Cornell and McClintic wrote autobiographies (1938 and 1955, respectively), and a modern biography by Tad Mosel appeared in 1978. DBW

Cornerstone Theater Company Founded in 1986 as a LOS ANGELES–based touring ensemble, its tours to mostly rural towns with the intent of creating adaptations of classical texts (e.g., a Wild West musical *Hamlet* in Marmarth, ND) lasted until 1991 (12 musicals in 10 states). Since then, the theatre has worked largely with urban centers, creating original productions and adaptations of Western and non-Western texts involving local history and talent in a uniquely community-based theatre. In addition to numerous collaborations in California, Cornerstone has had commissions from other arts organizations, such as ARENA STAGE, Touchstone Theatre in Bethlehem, PA, and LONG WHARF THEATRE. Sonja Kufinec's award-winning study was published in 2003. DBW

Cort Theatre 148 West 48th St., NYC [Architect: Edward B. Corey]. Built and named for John Cort, a West Coast producer (see SEATTLE), the new house was launched in 1912 with a hit production, HARTLEY MANNERS's *PEG O' MY HEART*, which made a star of LAURETTE TAYLOR. With about 1,000 seats, it is best suited for comedies and realistic plays and has housed a series of long-running hits. Two Pulitzer Prize–winning plays premiered at the theatre: *The Shrike* (1951) and *The Diary of Anne Frank* (1955). During 1969–72 it operated as a TV studio, but it reverted to legitimate status thereafter. Since 1927, it has been a SHUBERT theatre. MCH

costume Although costume design came into its own as a major design element in 20th-century American theatre, little research has been done on the development of the profession. In the 19th century, designing new costumes for each production was rarely thought necessary. A company of actors who performed a repertory of plays could maintain a wardrobe and adequately costume their productions. Established companies amassed large wardrobes, and successful costumes were used repeatedly; but because each actor selected his or her wardrobe, productions rarely possessed visual unity. Some attempt might be made to give period plays a historical look, but this was normally a matter of available garments and conventional taste rather than any overriding concern for consistency.

When actors began to work from production to production instead of remaining with one company for several seasons, wardrobes of costumes could no longer be realistically maintained. Instead, company managers selected costumes, often from rental houses with large inventories (see SUPPORT SERVICES), and were more likely to dress a character according to the needs of the role rather than personal preference. If time permitted, a company manager could work toward a unified design of sets, furnishings, and costumes in concert with the intent of the play. Occasionally scenic designers would select or approve costumes, or even design them once the setting was completed. The few individuals who specialized in costumes, including William Henry Matthews, Percy Anderson, and Mrs. John Alexander (who designed for MAUDE ADAMS), seldom received recognition.

During the early decades of the 20th century, as the number of theatres and plays produced in them multiplied, several developments led to the growing recognition of the contribution that a specialist in the costume area might make to a production. For instance, as it became standard practice for a single designer to control all of the visual elements of a production, including scenery, lights, and costumes, assistants began to take responsibility for following the various elements through the construction process. ALINE BERNSTEIN, for example, regularly employed Emeline Clarke Roche as her assistant for scenery and IRENE SHARAFF as her assistant for costumes. Over time designers such as Bernstein, JO MIELZINER, and ROBERT EDMOND JONES admitted the difficulty of maintaining control over this wide range of activities and encouraged their assistants to assume design responsibility. The movement from a single designer for scenery, costumes, and lights to individual ones for each specialty was gradual.

The success of the 1919 actors' strike for better wages and working conditions also aided the trend toward a specialization in costume design. The star system had long been an important aspect of the theatre; performers able to draw large audiences have always had privileged positions – including personal costumes specially designed and constructed by professionals. As a result of this strike, producers were required to provide costumes, wigs, shoes, and stockings for all women in principal roles and in the chorus. Because producers were required to pay for costumes, they increasingly looked to specialists for decisions about costume selections.

Affiliated with the Brotherhood of Painters, Decorators and Paperhangers as Local Union 829 in 1918, the United Scenic Artists Association was known initially as a union for stage painters. In the early 1920s scenic designers began to join, and through UNION activity helped stabilize the role of design in production. By 1936 United Scenic Artists had a special section for costume designers (though not with voting rights until 1966).

In addition, the FEDERAL THEATRE PROJECT influenced the move toward specialization in costume design. Created during the early days of the Depression, the FTP was founded to provide employment for all varieties of theatre professionals. Having many different individuals doing specialized jobs meant that more individuals were paid – however little – for their work. Once the specializations of costume (and lighting) design were developed, there was little possibility of returning to the old format.

Many talented artists became costume designers as a result of these developments. By the 1930s Irene Sharaff, RAOUL PÈNE DU BOIS, Charles LeMaire, and LUCINDA BALLARD all designed costumes regularly, principally for the thriving Broadway theatre. By the 1940s, when designers such as Miles White, Freddy Wittop, and Alvin Colt joined the rapidly emerging profession, almost 50% of the playbills for New York productions credited costume designers, compared with 1% at the turn of the century.

Notable theatre artists, such as Patton Campbell, ANN ROTH, THEONI V. ALDREDGE, and PATRICIA ZIPPRODT, began designing costumes in the 1950s, joined in the '60s by FLORENCE KLOTZ, WILLA KIM, and JANE GREENWOOD, among others. These costume designers continued to work primarily in the theatre but, like most contemporary theatre artists, also design opera, dance, film, television, industrial promotions, and extravaganzas. More recently, GABRIEL BERRY, Judith Dolan, ANN HOULD-WARD, WILLIAM IVEY LONG, Linda Fisher, MARTIN PAKLEDINAZ, GREGG BARNES, and ROBERT PERDZIOLA have become familiar names in the New York theatre. As American theatre has become less centralized, many designers, including Robert Morgan, Steven Rubin, JEANNE BUTTON, SUSAN TSU, William

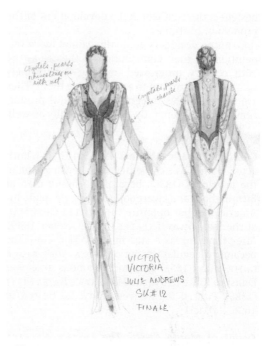

Willa Kim rendering for the final costume worn by Julie Andrews in the 1995 musical *Victor/Victoria. Courtesy:* Willa Kim.

Lane, and Deborah Dryden, have gained recognition for their quality costume design for regional theatres.

The speciality in costume design has not diminished the need for construction specialists. Many regional theatres maintain their own shops for creating costumes, and costume rental houses throughout the U.S. – including Western Costume Company, Norcostco, Inc., TDF Costume Collection, and Stagecraft Studios – are valuable resources.

Today's costumes designers come from various backgrounds. Some began as scenic designers, performers, costume-construction specialists, or as artists in complementary fields such as sculpture, painting, and fiber arts. Others are fashion designers or employees of costume houses. More often, however, many are costume-design specialists trained through an apprenticeship with another designer, in a theatre, or in one of the growing number of graduate programs offering a degree in costume design. Frank Poole Bevan at the Yale School of Drama, Paul Reinhardt and Lucy Barton at the University of Texas, and Barbara and Cletus Anderson at Carnegie–Mellon are among those individuals instrumental in establishing training programs at universities for designers through which the development of the profession continues.

Costume designers gradually gained more recognition for their contribution to theatre as the 20th century progressed, making it extremely rare for programs not to acknowledge them: They are recognized as integral to successful productions not only generally, but individually as well. BO*

Couldock, Charles Walter (1815–98) English-born actor, trained as a carpenter, who began acting in the provinces (1836), becoming leading man at Birmingham and Liverpool (1845–9). He made his American debut opposite CHARLOTTE CUSHMAN at the BROADWAY THEATRE, NYC (October 1849). After traveling as a star in *The Willow Copse,* he became a regular in various New York STOCK COMPANIES (1858). His most famous role was Dunstan Kirke in STEELE MACKAYE's HAZEL KIRKE (1880). Praised for his versatility, he retired in 1896. DMcD

Count of Monte Cristo, The LESTER WALLACK was the first of several U.S. playwrights and actors to adapt Alexandre Dumas's 1844 novel to the stage. CHARLES FECHTER prepared versions in 1868 and 1870 and played the starring role of Edmund Dantès until 1877. JAMES O'NEILL, who first performed Dantès in 1883, bought the rights to Fechter's script in 1885 and toured it until 1916, performing the leading role more than 6,000 times to an estimated 15 million spectators. Although O'Neill made further alterations, Fechter's adaptation had already tightened the action of the sprawling novel to emphasize its melodramatic hightpoints: Dantès's arrest on the eve of his wedding to Mercedes, his daring escape from prison, his discovery of hidden treasures on the Isle of Monte Cristo, his return to French society as the mysterious Count, and his meticulously planned and executed vengeance against the three men who conspired to send him to prison. A pessimistic, postmodern revival of the play, directed by PETER SELLARS at the KENNEDY CENTER (1985), won critical acclaim. BMcC

Country Girl, The A backstage psychological drama by CLIFFORD ODETS about lies, illusions, and the difficulties of love, this play features an alcoholic actor (modeled, Odets noted, on the life of the actress LAURETTE TAYLOR) who struggles successfully to return to the stage; a young director who believes in him yet falls in love with his wife; and the actor's compassionate, maternal wife, who stands by her weak, self-destructive husband, even though he projects his own faults and fears onto her. Lacking a social critique, it still presents Odets's themes of self-deception and the struggle for integrity. He directed the premiere production (1950, 225 performances) starring Paul Kelly, Steven Hill, and UTA HAGEN. Odets sometimes dismissed the well-received play as a commercial piece, but it has proved to be a durable work, revived notably in 1966 and 1972. Also, in Odets's revised form, it was produced in 1968 as *Winter Journey.* TP

County Chairman, The, by GEORGE ADE, opened on Broadway 24 November 1903 and ran 222 performances. In a small town in the Mississippi Valley, a local party boss, Hackler, seeks revenge against an old rival in love, Rigby, a man now wealthy and powerful through sometimes scurrilous means. Hackler backs his young law partner, Wheeler, to oppose Rigby in the election for Prosecuting Attorney, even though Wheeler has been courting Rigby's daughter, who objects to her fiancé defaming her father. After a rough but comic campaign, Wheeler wins the election and marries his beloved. JDM

Cowell, Joe Leathley (Joseph Hawkins Witchett) (1792–1863) English-born actor, manager, and scene painter who, after an abortive career in the navy, became an itinerant actor, establishing a reputation as a low comedian. Emigrating to the U.S. in 1821, he became a well-known figure in the American theatre, both as an actor and a manager of theatres and CIRCUSES. His vivid memoirs appeared in 1844. In 1863 he returned to England. Through marriages he was related to the British Siddons and the BATEMANS. His second son, SAM COWELL, became a music-hall star. His autobiography was published in 1844. DBW

Cowell, Sam(uel) Houghton (1820–64) British actor-vocalist, born in the U.S. Most music-hall stars came either from the working class or from a theatrical background. Cowell, one of the earliest recognized music-hall performers and an early star at the Canterbury, was the son of JOE COWELL, a Drury Lane actor, and began his career in the legitimate theatre, touring the U.S. with his father in the 1830s in Shakespearean productions, billed as "The Young American Roscius." Returning to England at the age of 20, he rapidly converted himself to a comic vocalist – he had already done "coon" songs as entr'actes in America – and burlesque performer. By 1850 he had abandoned the legitimate stage entirely in favor of the song and supper rooms of the West End,

though his early career continued to serve him well in burlesques of Shakespeare. An ugly little man with a lugubrious expression, he specialized in cockney song-and-patter acts, notably "The Rat-catcher's Daughter" and "Vilikins and his Dinah."
    AEG   DBW

Cowl, Jane (1884–1950) Boston-born actress, Jane Cowl made her New York stage debut in 1903 in *Sweet Kitty Bellairs.* Her portrayal of the wronged woman, Mary Turner, in *Within the Law* (1912), established her as a star. Cowl appeared in plays that she wrote or cowrote, including *Lilac Time* (1917); *Daybreak* and *Information Please* (1918); and *Smilin' Through* (1920). In 1923 she offered a "breath-taking" Juliet in a production that ran for 174 consecutive performances. Her successful rendering of Larita in Noël Coward's *Easy Virtue* (1925) was followed by an "appealing" Amytis in *The Road to Rome* (1927) and a "brilliant" Lucy Chase Wayne in *First Lady* (1935). Brooks Atkinson praised her "personal beauty, impeccability of manners, humorous vitality, and simple command of the art of acting." The dark-haired, dark-eyed actress was regarded as a distinguished "lady of the theatre" in London as well as New York.
    TLM

Crabtree, Charlotte (Lotta) (1847–1924) Actress. Born in New York, she and her mother followed her father to the gold mining town of Grass Valley, CA, in 1853. She soon learned to dance and sing, and became a featured performer in mining-camp variety troupes. She conquered San Francisco in 1859 and headed east. Crabtree achieved widespread popularity when she made the transition to legitimate drama in the dual leading roles of *Little Nell and the Marchioness* (1867), dramatized for her from Dickens's *The Old Curiosity Shop* by John Brougham. Though she later had other vehicles, they were only excuses for this tiny, red-haired, black-eyed elf to exhibit her skills at mimicry, banjo picking, and clog dancing. She never married, and retired with comfortable wealth in 1891. Biographies were written by David Dempsey and Raymond Baldwin (1968) and Constance Rourke (1928).   DMcD

Cradle Will Rock, The, by Marc Blitzstein was originally produced by personnel of the Federal Theatre Project but premiered outside of WPA supervision at the Venice Theatre, NYC, on 16 June 1937. In a celebrated bare-stage production directed by Orson Welles and featuring Will Geer and Howard Da Silva, this musical about labor unions in "Steeltown, USA" was performed

Lotta Crabtree in *Little Nell and the Marchioness,* John Brougham's adaptation of *The Old Curiosity Shop,* performed frequently during 1867–91. *Courtesy:* Don B. Wilmeth Theatre Collection.

at the height of battles between "little" steel companies and the CIO and in defiance of a nation-wide WPA postponement order. While much of the musical's notoriety concerned the circumstances of its premiere (and cries of government censorship), *Cradle* remains a compelling proletarian drama with a vital score by one of America's most prominent composers. Welles and John Houseman's newly formed Mercury Theatre produced it in 1938; in 1983 Houseman directed a successful revival with Patti LuPone, Gerald Gutierrez, and the Juilliard Acting Company at the American Place Theatre. Tim Robbins's film, based loosely on the original production, was released in 1999, and the Jean Cocteau Rep staged a revival in 2000.   BBW

Craig's Wife A harshly negative character portrait, this George Kelly three-act drama depicts the machinations of a woman obsessed with maintaining physical perfection in her beautiful home and controlling her husband's life in order to ensure her own security. The revelation of Harriet Craig's selfishness and dishonesty drives her husband away, along with all other members of their household, leaving her completely alone in the play's final moments. Staged by Kelly and featuring Chrystal Herne and Charles Trowbridge as the unhappy couple, the play opened in New York 12 October 1925 at the Morosco Theatre, played for 360 performances, and won the Pulitzer Prize. It was given film and radio treatments before a 1947 Broadway revival, again directed by Kelly, which ran for 69 performances.   KF

Crane, William Henry (1845–1928) Actor who, after a long apprenticeship with a small touring opera company, achieved his first major success in *Evangeline* at Niblo's Garden in 1873. During 1877–89, Crane and Stuart Robson joined to produce a series of very popular American domestic comedies, such as *Our Boarding House, Our Bachelors,* and *The Henrietta.* Crane was also noted for his Dromio, Falstaff, and Sir Toby Belch. In 1890, he began a successful career as a producer-actor in his own vehicle productions when he appeared as Senator Hannibal Rivers in *The Senator,* with which he was to be associated for the rest of his career. In 1896 he toured in Joseph Jefferson's "All Star" production of Sheridan's *The Rivals* as Anthony Absolute. Crane, a thoughtful artist who contributed a number of essays on acting and the theatre to popular journals of the day, published his autobiography *Footprints and Echoes* in 1927.   MR   DJW

Craven, Frank (1875–1945) Actor, playwright, and director, best known for creating the Stage Manager in Thornton Wilder's *Our Town* in 1938. Born in Boston of theatrical parents, Craven was a child actor. At 16 he played in repertory in Philadelphia; his first New York success was in 1911 as James Gilley in *Bought and Paid For.* Craven later wrote several successful scripts for the stage, such as *Too Many Cooks* and *This Way Out.* He played leading roles in several films, adapted some of his scripts to film, and wrote dialogue for Laurel and Hardy. He last appeared on Broadway in 1944. Brooks Atkinson called him "the best pipe and pants-pocket actor in the business."   SMA

Crawford, Cheryl (1902–86) Producer. As executive assistant to Theresa Helburn at the Theatre Guild in the late 1920s, as cofounder with Harold Clurman and Lee Strasberg of the Group Theatre (1931), as creator with Eva Le Gallienne and Margaret Webster of the American Repertory Theatre (1946), and as cofounder with Elia Kazan and Robert Lewis of the Actors Studio (1947), Crawford was at the center of the most vital and idealistic enterprises in the American theatre. A wry, poker-faced midwesterner, she was a remarkably self-effacing impresario. Surrounded by high-strung, visionary colleagues, she always remained level-headed. She kept the peace between Clurman and Strasberg, whom she called Old Testament prophets; she raised money, trimmed budgets, found rehearsal space, arranged theatre rentals, and could always be counted on for a frank opinion of the artistic merit and commercial appeal of both plays and players. For all her commitment to serious theatre, she thought of plays as potential hits or flops, and withdrew from the organizations she helped to foster in order to pursue a career as an independent stage producer with a particular interest in musicals. Her biggest commercial success was *Brigadoon* (1947); other notable Crawford productions include the 1942 revival of *Porgy and Bess; One Touch of Venus* (1943); *Paint Your Wagon* (1951); *Mother Courage* (1963); and four plays by Tennessee Williams – *The Rose Tattoo* (1951), *Camino Real* (1953), *Sweet Bird of Youth* (1959), and *Period of Adjustment* (1960). Her autobiography appeared in 1977.   FH

Crews, Laura Hope (1879–1942) Stage and film actress who toured California as a child performer, became in 1898 the ingenue with San Francisco's Alcazar Stock Company, then joined New York's Henry V. Donnelly Stock Company, reaching Broadway in 1904. Her work with actor-director Henry Miller was especially formative. Notable stage performances included *Much Ado*'s Beatrice opposite John Drew in 1913 and the possessive mother in *The Silver Cord* for the Theatre Guild in 1926 and for the 1933 film. She went to Hollywood as a diction coach, but made a screen career of fluttery character roles like Aunt Pittypat in *Gone with the Wind* (1939).   FHL

Cricket Theatre Having begun producing new American plays in a converted Minneapolis moviehouse under the leadership of William Semans in 1971, the Cricket's continued success prompted Equity professional status in 1975 and the naming of Lou Salerni as artistic director. The Cricket moved to the Hennepin Center for the Arts in 1979 and, after initial growth, became financially overburdened. In 1980, Semans resigned followed by Salerni in 1985 when the board of directors vacated the theatre space and began reorganization. The Cricket reopened in 1987 in another moviehouse with a new artistic director, William Partlan, but moved back to the Hennepin Center in 1994. The theatre, which actively sought out and developed new works by emerging writers, effectively shut down following its 1995–6 season.   KN

Crimes of the Heart by BETH HENLEY. Originally produced by ACTORS THEATRE OF LOUISVILLE, where it was cowinner of the Great American Play Contest (1979), the play premiered in New York at MANHATTAN THEATRE CLUB (1980). It moved to the JOHN GOLDEN THEATRE, opening 4 November 1981 under the direction of Melvin Bernhardt and with a JOHN LEE BEATTY set. Henley's first full-length play, it won a Pulitzer Prize and the New York Drama Critics' Circle Award for Best American Play. Through the reunion of three sisters, this comedy explores female bonding in the face of various repressions. Henley, herself a southerner, presents a gallery of credible, sympathetic southern grotesques: a lonely spinster with deformed ovaries, a rebellious artist, and a suicidal, adulterous lawyer's wife support one another while their domineering grandfather is ill and the adulterer is arraigned for shooting her husband. Although the ending is unresolved, the play celebrates a moment of freedom and rebirth.   TH-S

criticism Critics experienced a difficult time establishing themselves as an important force in the American theatre. Since the theatre itself was considered a dangerous public institution in the late 18th century, the role of the critic was seen more in terms of censorship, guarding against violations of social and moral laws. The earliest extant review of a play appeared anonymously in the *Maryland Gazette* (1760) at a time when papers usually "noticed" a performance with little or no critical evaluation. The subject prompted WILLIAM DUNLAP in his *History of the American Theatre* (1832) to devote a chapter to critics, explaining that in 1796 a group of six "gentlemen" organized themselves into a "band of scalpers and tomahawkers" to write anonymous reviews about New York productions. A few years later, WASHINGTON IRVING wrote the charming and lightly satirical "Letters of Jonathan Oldstyle, Gent." (1802–3), to comment upon the New York stage. Irving also penned reviews for *The Salmagundi* (1807) and *Select Reviews,* later the *Analectic Magazine* (1815). He is regarded as the first American drama critic of importance.

Few daily newspapers published reviews on a regular basis until the 1850s, and even fewer allowed their critics bylines until the end of the century. Theatre notices and criticism became associated more with short-lived dramatic magazines such as *Theatrical Censor* (1806), *Rambler's Magazine and New York Theatrical Register* (1809), *Mirror of Taste and Dramatic Censor* (1810), and the *Broadway Journal and Stranger's Guide* (1847), as well as sporting weeklies such as *Spirit of the Times* (1831), and the NEW YORK CLIPPER (1853). The first important theatrical weekly was the NEW YORK DRAMATIC MIRROR, founded in 1879. Play reviewing, like the theatre itself, was held in low esteem. It was not uncommon for editors to send untrained reporters to "write up" the opening night of a play; nor was it uncommon for critics to review only productions that advertised in their papers. In 1836, EDGAR ALLAN POE called professional reviewers "illiterate mountebanks." WALT WHITMAN, writing in 1847, blamed the vulgarity and coarseness of the theatre upon the "paid puff" system.

The expansion of the newspaper business in the 1850s prompted separate "amusement" departments and separate dramatic columns of news and reviews. Moralists and puffers tended to dominate the profession, although Henry Clapp Jr. returned from France in 1855 or 1856 to set up a coterie of critics at Pfaff's Restaurant to rail against tradition and convention. He advocated that the theatre be judged on aesthetic rather than moral grounds, and wrote bright and witty essays for the *Saturday Press* and other weeklies. The Civil War destroyed the movement, however, and what emerged afterward was a highly moralistic and conservative school headed by WILLIAM WINTER, JOHN RANKEN TOWSE, and HENRY AUSTIN CLAPP. Winter made his reputation on Horace Greeley's *New York Tribune* from 1865 to 1909. Towse headed the dramatic department of the elitist *New York Evening Post* during 1874–1927. Clapp wrote for the *Boston Daily Advertiser* from 1868 to 1902. These "genteel" critics shared the values of the cultured elite and endured until these values changed.

The popular press, however, demanded bright and clever reviews, not moralistic essays, and the innovations introduced by Henry Clapp Jr. were carried on in the aggressive and colorful writing of ANDREW C. WHEELER (alias Nym Crinkle) in the New York Sun, World, and "lesser" dramatic and sporting journals. Alfred J. Cohen (alias ALAN DALE) popularized his "School of the Flippant Remark" from coast to coast for Hearst publications in the late 1890s and early 1900s. Other critics sought reform. STEPHEN RYDER FISKE of *Wilkes' Spirit of the Times* (1879–1902) ridiculed shoddy business practices and productions. He viewed the theatre as a worthwhile place of amusement that should be conducted in a professional manner. EPES W. SARGENT served vaudeville in a similar way, writing for a number of trade papers including VARIETY in 1905. HARRISON GREY FISKE of the *New York Dramatic Mirror* (1880–1911) worked to improve business practices and sought a charity (the ACTORS' FUND) to help the profession. He fought to protect the legal rights of playwrights and to bring an end to the blackmailing efforts of the *New York Dramatic News*. Still other critics worked to improve the American drama. WILLIAM DEAN HOWELLS in the 1880s sought a realistic native drama from his editor's desk at *Atlantic Monthly,* and encouraged JAMES A. HERNE and BRONSON HOWARD. EDWARD DITHMAR of the *New York Times* (1884–1902) encouraged American dramatists and broke with tradition by refusing to judge a play on moral grounds. Academicians such as CLAYTON HAMILTON, WALTER PRICHARD EATON, and BRANDER MATTHEWS wrote books about the history, practice, and theory of the drama, thus educating the public. An important voice for change, JAMES G. HUNEKER, promoted the new European drama of IBSEN and SHAW, and insisted (as had Clapp) that art be judged on aesthetic rather than moral grounds. Huneker influenced a generation of writers, including GEORGE JEAN NATHAN.

As drama critic of *Smart Set* (1909–23), Nathan attacked the shop-worn dramatic devices of BELASCO, the pomposity of the cultured elite, and the ignorance of the masses. He used ridicule, sarcasm, and satire to rid the theatre of stultifying tradition and convention. Like Huneker, he championed Ibsen, Shaw, Strindberg, Maeterlinck, and Hauptmann, and unlike Huneker he found value in the new American drama. He discovered EUGENE O'NEILL and published his early work in *Smart Set.* Although he never wielded the power of his New York peers on the daily press, he commanded the respect of the young intellectuals in the 1910s and '20s. His unwillingness to find value in the political theatre of the 1930s eroded his influence as a vital force in the theatre.

The exuberant ALEXANDER WOOLLCOTT established the power of the *New York Times* in the 1910s with his enthusiastic prose and his battle with the SHUBERTS. PERCY HAMMOND moved from the *Chicago Tribune* (1908–21) to the *New York Tribune* (1921–36) and brought his urbane and satirical style to bear upon that theatre's pretensions. He could dismiss a Shakespearean actor with the flick of his pen by noting: "he wore his tights competently." BURNS MANTLE provided good journalistic prose and sound opinions for the *New York*

Evening Mail (1911–22) and *Daily News* (1922–43). BROOKS ATKINSON served for 34 years as chief critic of the *New York Times* (1926–60), enhancing the paper's reputation and his own for fairness and accuracy. Unlike Nathan, he encouraged the more revolutionary theatre of the 1930s, as did other critics including JOHN ANDERSON (*Post* and *Journal*), GILBERT GABRIEL (*Sun* and *American*), JOHN MASON BROWN (*Post* and *Saturday Review*), and RICHARD WATTS JR. (*Herald–Tribune* and *Post*). In 1950 WALTER KERR began reviewing for *Commonweal,* and a year later for the *Herald–Tribune.* A former drama professor, Kerr brought to his position a historical perspective lacked by most of his colleagues. Upon the retirement of Atkinson in 1960, Kerr was acknowledged as the foremost New York critic, a position he held until his retirement from the *New York Times* in 1983.

Outside New York, the reputation of critics has usually remained local or regional, reflecting the institutions they review. Exceptions include HENRY TAYLOR PARKER of the *Boston Transcript* (1905–35), CLAUDIA CASSIDY of the *Chicago Tribune* (1942–65), ELLIOT NORTON of the *Boston Post* (1934–56) and other papers, and RICHARD COE of the *Washington Post* (1946–79). These critics gained widespread recognition because their writings had an impact upon the national theatre.

As the number of New York newspapers declined after 1920 (15 in 1920; 7 in 1950; 3 in 1970), magazine critics gained in importance. STARK YOUNG appealed to educated tastes in the *New Republic* (1921–47), as did JOSEPH WOOD KRUTCH in the *Nation* (1924–52), and KENNETH MACGOWAN, ROSAMOND GILDER, and EDITH J. R. ISAACS in THEATRE ARTS MONTHLY (1916–64). Discriminating readers also have turned to HAROLD CLURMAN in the *Nation* (1953–80); ERIC BENTLEY (1952–6), STANLEY KAUFFMANN (1969–79), and ROBERT BRUSTEIN (1959–68) in *The New Republic;* HENRY HEWES in *Saturday Review* (1952–77); ROBERT BENCHLEY (1929–40), WOLCOTT GIBBS (1940–58), BRENDAN GILL (1968–87), and EDITH OLIVER (1961–90) in *The New Yorker;* and JOHN SIMON in *New York Magazine* (1969–2005). For years the general public depended upon weekly magazines, with respected critics such as LOUIS KRONENBERGER and T. E. Kalem of *Time* magazine, and Jack Kroll in *Newsweek.* Members of the theatrical profession have relied on *Billboard,* VARIETY*,* and BACK STAGE, while readers wanting to keep abreast of the avant-garde or experimental relied on the *Village Voice* and critics such as Julius Novick, Alisa Solomon, MICHAEL FEINGOLD, and Charles McNulty (now with the *LA Times*). *American Theatre* magazine, an important organ for LORT theatres that is published by the THEATRE COMMUNICA-TIONS GROUP, has included criticism with its regional theatre news. Television critics have long been part of the Broadway scene, but there is no agreement over their role and influence, which is also true of Internet critics, a more recent phenomenon.

What has become apparent in the early years of the 21st century is that theatre criticism now commands less space in the nation's major newspapers, including the *New York Times*. Moreover, weekly magazines such as *Time* and *Newsweek* may notice an important production, but little space is made available for thoughtful criticism. There seems a dearth of drama critics to fill the shoes of Clurman, Bentley, Kauffmann, Hewes, et al., although since 1992 JOHN LAHR of *The New Yorker* has written important criticism that does more than notice a new play. In 2006 the *New York Times* remains the most important and powerful newspaper to review the American theatre and, consequently, their two main critics – BEN BRANTLEY and CHARLES ISHERWOOD – the most powerful individual critical voices. But the nature of the *Times*'s influence has changed since the 1970s. Decentralization of the American theatre and consolidation of newspapers nationwide has resulted in theatre critics in major markets outside of New York gaining influence over the theatre of their areas. For example, DAN SULLIVAN, SYLVIE DRAKE, and as of 2005 Charles McNulty in Los Angeles, RICHARD CHRISTIANSEN and since 2002 Michael Phillips in Chicago, Ed Siegel and the late Kevin Kelly in Boston, and PETER MARKS in Washington, DC, have had real power to make reputations and close shows. Also, with local productions originating with an eye to Broadway, these critics indirectly have gained power over what is seen in New York and elsewhere. The *New York Times*'s critics have immense power in New York and environs but less in the regions, and they are not as important to theatre in Los Angeles, for example, as is McNulty, chief critic for the *LA Times*.   TLM*

Crocker, Sarah see CONWAY, WILLIAM A.

Cronyn, Hume (1911–2003) Actor, director, and writer born in London, ON, Canada. Cronyn studied acting at the New York School of the Theatre and the AMERICAN ACADEMY OF DRAMATIC ART, making his professional debut with Cochran's Stock Company in Washington, DC, in 1931. He also worked for the BARTER THEATRE, during their second season. His Broadway debut was as the Janitor in *Hipper's Holiday* (1934; understudy).

Cronyn soon became a much sought-after character in Hollywood, where he married JESSICA TANDY in 1942. While in Los Angeles, Cronyn directed Tandy as Miss Collins in TENNESSEE WILLIAMS's *Portrait of a Madonna* (1946). This exposure led to Tandy's being cast as Blanche Du Bois in 1947 on Broadway.

Cronyn and Tandy appeared together for the first time in 1951 in *The Fourposter,* in which they were "compared to the LUNTS, in that the team had enough grace, skill, and wit to hold a stage and an audience by themselves." They subsequently costarred in *The Physicists* (1964), ALBEE's *A DELICATE BALANCE* (1966), *Noël Coward in Two Keys* (1974), *The GIN GAME* (1977), and *Foxfire* (1982; coauthored by Cronyn). Between these projects, Cronyn and Tandy played several seasons at the GUTHRIE THEATRE and at the Stratford Festival in Ontario. In 1964 Cronyn played Polonius to RICHARD BURTON's Hamlet, winning a Tony. Cronyn's memoir, *A Terrible Liar,* was published in 1991. The couple in 1994 received the Tony for Lifetime Achievement. Their daughter, **Tandy Cronyn** (1946–), an accomplished actress, was a replacement Sally Bowles in the original *CABARET.*   SMA

Crosman, Henrietta (1861–1944) Stage and film actress. Born in West Virginia, she began acting at 16 with JOHN ELLSLER. She scored her first success as Celia in *As You Like It* under the management of AUGUSTIN DALY. After success in *Gloriana* and *Mistress Nell,* she became the outstanding Rosalind of her time, and also scored a hit in *Sweet Kitty Bellairs.* During 1932–6 she appeared in films, retiring in 1939.   SMA

Crossroads Theatre An active and innovative African American theatre, founded in 1978 and located in New Brunswick, NJ. Under the resourceful artistic leadership of Ricardo Khan, the theatre has attained a distinguished record, presenting an average of six productions each season (including GEORGE C. WOLFE's first success, *The COLORED MUSEUM*), often to critical acclaim. It has supported new playwrights (especially through its GENESIS Festival, founded in 1989), encouraged new forms of staging, presented world premieres, and toured a production annually during Black History Month (February). In 1991 the theatre acquired a new home on Livingston Ave. as part of New Brunswick's Cultural Center complex. and in 1993 it received the fifth annual Rosetta LeNoire Award, given by ACTORS' EQUITY for "outstanding artistic contributions to the universality of the human experience in American theatre."   EGH

Crothers, Rachel (1878–1958) American actress, playwright, and director; the "NEIL SIMON of her day." Crothers' many commercially successful plays chronicled the tension in early 20th-century women between their new economic and sexual freedom and their old traditional values. Her first success, *The Three of Us* (1906), was one of some 30 Broadway plays, most of which she directed and staged herself. Although she wrote some sentimental plays in the teens, her best works were her seriocomic, women-centered plays: *Myself – Bettina* (1908), *A MAN'S WORLD* (1910), *Ourselves* (1913), *Young Wisdom* (1914), *HE AND SHE* (first produced 1911; Broadway 1920), *Expressing Willie* (1924), *Let Us Be Gay* (1929), *As Husbands Go* (1931), *When Ladies Meet* (1932), and *SUSAN AND GOD* (1937).

Besides her undisputed position as the leading commercial woman playwright and director of her time, Crothers was instrumental in the founding of Stage Women's War Relief Fund (1917), United Theatre Relief Committee (1932), and AMERICAN THEATRE WING for War Relief (1940; best known for the Stage Door Canteen). She received the Chi Omega National Achievement Award for 1938. A biography by L. C. Gottlieb was published in 1979.   FB

Crouse, Russel (1893–1966) Playwright, librettist, and producer who began his stage writing career as librettist for *The Gang's All Here* (1931); but it was only after he teamed with HOWARD LINDSAY on *ANYTHING GOES* (1934) that he achieved continued success. Crouse and Lindsay became prolific collaborators. Their first straight play was *LIFE WITH FATHER,* a nostalgic bit of Americana that captured the hearts of the Broadway audience for a contemporary long-run record that held until the 1970s. Working with Lindsay throughout the remainder of his career, Crouse helped write more than 15 plays and librettos, a highly successful example of the latter being *The SOUND OF MUSIC* (1959). They also teamed to produce many plays in New York, including several of their own and the profitable *ARSENIC AND OLD LACE* (1941). Cornelia Otis Skinner wrote a joint biography of Crouse and Lindsay (1976).   LDC

Crucible, The, by ARTHUR MILLER opened in New York on 22 January 1953, running for 197 performances. Directed by JED HARRIS, its cast included ARTHUR KENNEDY as John Proctor, Beatrice Straight as Elizabeth Proctor, Madeleine Sherwood as Abigail Williams, WALTER HAMPDEN as Danforth, and E. G. MARSHALL as the Reverend Hale. Miller's most-produced play, it also ran Off-Broadway for 571 performances in 1958, was first produced in London by Laurence Olivier in 1965 and revived there again in 1990, and served as the inaugural production of Tony Randall's NATIONAL ACTORS THEATRE (1991). A more critically successful Broadway revival (101 performances) was staged in 2002 by Richard Eyre with Liam Neeson, LAURA LINNEY, and BRIAN MURRAY (Danforth). The film version was released in 1996 (starring David Day-Lewis). Although the immediate sociopolitical context of this treatment of the 17th-century Salem witch trials was McCarthyism and the actions of the House Un-American Activities Committee in the 1950s, Miller's larger subject is the effect on a community of an oppressive ideology and the fear and mistrust that it breeds. Miller presents the trials as a result of repressed feelings of guilt, jealousy, revenge, resentment, and sexual attraction among the populace. In the end, John Proctor must decide whether to make a false confession of witchcraft in order to save himself and preserve his farm for his sons or to deny the charge, thus losing his life but maintaining his integrity and his "name" as a legacy of his children.   BCM

Crudup, Billy (né William) (1968–) Stage and film actor, born in Manhasset, NY, raised in Florida and Texas, and educated at U. North Carolina and NYU (M.F.A.). This darkly handsome actor, despite his physical image, has avoided stereotypical leading-man roles, from his Broadway debut as Septimus Hodge in Stoppard's *Arcadia* (1995) to his Bo opposite MARY-LOUISE PARKER in *BUS STOP* (1996), the tile role of Merrick in the 2002 revival of *The Elephant Man*, the central role of the imprisoned and tortured writer in Martin McDonagh's *The Pillowman* (2005) (nominated for Tonys in these latter two), and in 2006 the literary critic Belinsky in *The Coast of Utopia* (Tony, Featured Actor, 2007). His best-known film roles to date were in *Almost Famous* (2001) and the recent *Stage Beauty*.   DBW

Cruz, Nilo (1960–) Cuban-born playwright, educated at Brown (M.F.A.) under PAULA VOGEL, and closely associated with Florida theatre, in particular New Theatre in Coral Gables, where he served as playwright in residence. His 2003 Pulitzer Prize–winning play *Anna in the Tropics* – an unexpected win, based on its script and not a production – premiered there in 2002. Set in 1929 Tampa, this tragicomic story is about a family of Cuban cigar makers and how they are affected by their changing industry and the man hired to entertain the workers (his choice being *Anna Karenina*). After a modest Broadway run directed by EMILY MANN and starring Jimmy Smits, the play was widely produced regionally. (Moreover, *any* Broadway run is a rarity for a Latino-themed drama.) Other Cruz plays include *A Bicycle Country* (1999), *Hortensia and the Museum of Dreams* (2001), *Lorca in a Green Dress* (2003), *Beauty of the Father* (2004), and *A Very Old Man with Enormous Wings* (2005). DBW

Cryer, Gretchen (1935–) Playwright, librettist, actor. With Nancy Ford, Cryer wrote political rock musicals, including *Now Is the Time for All Good Men* (1967), *The Last Sweet Days of Isaac* (1970, Best Musical Obie, etc.), *I'm Getting My Act Together and I'm Taking It on the Road* (1978; three years OFF-BROADWAY), and *Hang On to the Good Times* (1985). TH-S

CSC Repertory, Ltd. (The Classic Stage Company) Founded in 1967 by Christopher Martin as a workshop of New York University students, it was incorporated as the City Stage Company in 1968. Martin, who led the group until 1984, maintained a resident company that presented an international repertoire of old and modern classics plus a smattering of new plays. Artistic director CAREY PERLOFF (who, in 1992, resigned and was replaced by DAVID ESBJORNSON) continued in this tradition, but cast each show individually and favored reinterpretations of neglected works, particularly those that combined theatricality and notable language: Typical of these were productions of Tirso de Molina's *Don Juan of Seville,* Pinter's *The Birthday Party,* Genet's *The Maids,* Molière's *Scapin* (adapt. Shelley Berc and Andrei Belgrader), and Corneille's *The Illusion* (adapt. TONY KUSHNER). Esbjornson was replaced by BARRY EDELSTEIN (1997–2003); he in turn was succeeded by Brian Kulick, who began his tenure (2004) with a bold staging of an adaptation of the medieval *The Mysteries.* New translations, standard classics (*The Winter's Tale,* 2003), and adaptations of foreign-language plays (*The Misanthrope,* adapt. Martin Crimp, 1999; Steve Martin's version of Carl Sternheim's *The Underpants,* 2002) commonly fill a season in its 180-seat venue near Union Square. Having won numerous Obies, for its shows and as a company, in 1999 CSC received the Lucille Lortel Award for Outstanding Body of Work. CLJ

Cuban American theatre The Cuban Revolution of 1959 provides a convenient context to demarcate the phases of Cuban theatre in the U.S., albeit it does not clarify the differences between the dramatic traditions of the homeland versus that of the exile, or between the immigrant experience and a distinctly Cuban American sensibility, where issues of identity are less of a problem.

Daphne Rubin-Vega and Jimmy Smits in the original McCarter Theatre Center production of *Anna in the Tropics* by Nilo Cruz, directed by Emily Mann. Photo by T. Charles Erickson. *Courtesy:* McCarter Theatre Center.

Cuban American theatre lives in a fluid, translational reality; Cuba's proximity to the U.S. intimately links the theatrical currents flowing from both countries.

Prior to 1959 – and reaching back to the final decade of the 19th century – the dramatic output of Cuban authors was largely aimed at a Spanish-speaking immigrant public. Comedies, melodramas, and (often blackface) farces thrived in Ybor City–Tampa, FL, where communities of tobacco workers and their families lived and worked, and later in New York City. In Tampa, several Spanish regional centers or mutual-aid societies offered productions that raised funds to support the war for Cuban independence from Spain, hosted companies on tour from Havana, and supported repertory companies comprised of professional and amateur players. In NYC one such early venue was the Club Lírico Dramático, directed by Luis Baralt, a 30-year veteran of the Havana stage.

Censored by the Spanish authorities for their Cuban nationalist themes, plays by such controversial 19th-century Cuban authors as José Maria Heredia and José Jacinto Milanés were first published in NYC. The first fully professional resident company in New York, where more than half of the Hispanic population was made up of Cubans, was Compañia de Teatro Español, established in 1921. By the 1930s, when the Depression devastated Hispanic theatre in general, Tampa was the only city with a Hispanic company (known as the Cuban Company) supported by the WPA's FEDERAL THEATRE PROJECT. Cuban blackface farces, or *obra bufa cubana,* written or improvised by local playwrights such as Alberto O'Farrill and Juan C. Rivera, as well as the famous Afro-Cuban singer Arquinides Pous and veterans of Havana stages, were ever-present staples.

After 1959, more than a million Cubans – mainly from the upper, middle, and professional classes – left the islands, followed by waves in the late 1960s, '70s, '80s, and in 1994 by members of the working class. This exodus intensified the large-scale theatrical activity in the Cuban communities in Miami and New York, most of which is a theatre of political exile, serious drama, musicals, and satiric entertainments. Cuban dramatists differ in the length of time they spent in Cuba, and, upon reaching the U.S., their immediate environment might be either primarily English or primarily Spanish. Among the most important exiled Cuban playwrights are José Cid Pérez, Leopoldo Hernández, Matías Montes Huidobro, Raül de Cárdenas, Fermín Borges, Réne Ariza, and Julio Matas, all of whom had established careers in Havana. Another set of Cuban playwrights, who dealt with the themes of exile and revolution, began their writing careers in the U.S., where they explored new issues, such as bilingualism, biculturality, the problems of assimilation, and critiques of the American dream; they were also free to tackle thorny topics such as homosexuality and Catholicism, which had been taboo in Cuba. These later playwrights include José Sanchez Boudy, Miguel Gonzáles-Pando, Reinaldo Arenas, Pedro Monge Rafuls, Hector Santiago, Iván Acosta, and Rene R. Alomá.

Naturally, overlaps and exceptions are inevitable. The works of Luis Santeiro, author of *Our Lady of the Tortilla* (1987) and an Emmy-winning writer for *Sesame Street,* extend far beyond the Hispanic community. Playwright Dolores Prida, born in Caribarién on the northern coast of Cuba, has crossed over into New York's commercial stages by writing popular musicals, such as *Four Guys Named José . . . and Una Mujer Named María* (2001). The prolific EDUARDO MACHADO, author of the tetralogy *The Floating Island* (1984–9) and among the most gifted Cuban expatriates, currently heads the graduate playwrighting program at Columbia University.

Towering above them all is the extraordinary dramatist, director, and teacher MARIA IRENE FORNÉS, who arrived in the U.S. in 1945 and in the 1960s became one of the pioneers of the OFF-OFF BROADWAY movement. The author of more than two dozen plays and musicals, including *Promenade* (1965), *Mud* (1983), and *The CONDUCT OF LIFE* (1985), all of which resist classification, Fornés is a pivotal figure in the Hispanic American, feminist, and avant-garde theatre. As director of INTAR's Playwrights-in-Residence, she trained and mentored the likes of Prida, Machado, Manuel Martin, René Aloma, Manual Pereiras Garcia, Charles Gómaz-Sanz, Ana Maria Simo, Caridad Svich, and NILO CRUZ, who is the first Hispanic American playwright to win the Pulitzer Prize.

New York City has been a haven for a number of important Hispanic theatre companies with Cuban or Cuban American leaderships. Gilberto Zaldívar, exiled from Cuba in 1961, founded with René Buch REPERTORIO ESPAÑOL, which presents plays in Spanish and occasionally in English, including Cuban classics by Virgilio Piñera and Carlos Felipe. INTAR, originally founded in 1966 as ADAL by a group of Cubans and Puerto Ricans, has been led by a series of Cuban artistic directors: Max Ferrá, Michael John Garcés, and currently Machado. In the 1970s, Ivan Acosta headed the Centro Cultural Cubano (1972–9), and Francisco Morín founded the group Prometeo (1976–81). In Miami, on the other hand, Maria Teresa Rojas founded in 1972 Teatro Prometeo, which is associated with Miami Dade Community College and remains active. In 1973 actor and producer Mario Ernesto Sanchez founded Teatro Avante, which, since 1986, has presented an International Festival of Hispanic Theatre each June in Florida.

NK   RG

Cullum, John (1930–) Actor-singer. After graduating from the University of Tennessee, he played supporting roles at the NEW YORK SHAKESPEARE FESTIVAL, was featured in *CAMELOT* (1960), was Laertes in the BURTON *Hamlet,* starred in *On a Clear Day You Can See Forever* (1965), and appeared as Edward Rutledge in *1776* (1969, replacement). He won Tony Awards for his portrayals of a stalwart Virginia farmer in *Shenandoah* (1975; he was in the 1989 revival as well) and a frenetic theatre impresario in *On the Twentieth Century* (1978). His most recent musical roles were Captain Andy in *SHOW BOAT* (1994 revival), the lead in a 1996 30th-anniversary production of *MAN OF LA MANCHA* produced by Houston's Theater Under the Stars, the diabolical corporate tycoon in *Urinetown* (2001), and an old man in *Wilder* (2003, PLAY-

WRIGHTS HORIZONS). Equally at home in drama, he replaced the lead in DEATHTRAP (1979), starred as a 50-year-old Tom Sawyer in *The Boys in Autumn* (1986), was Joe Keller in ALL MY SONS (ROUNDABOUT, 1997), played Cardinal Bernard F. Law in *Sin (A Cardinal Deposed)* (2004, NEW GROUP), was Aton Roma opposite ROSEMARY HARRIS (Levana Junk) in Ariel Dorfman's *The Other Side* (2005, MANHATTAN THEATRE CLUB), and during 1990–5 played Hollis on the TV series *Northern Exposure.* MK DBW

Culture Clash Created on 5 May 1984 (Cinco de Mayo), the members of this unique Latino comic performance troupe – Ric Montoya, Richardo Salinas, and Herbert Siguenza – have been called "masters of sketch comedy, political satire and wickedly funny impersonations," constantly breaking down divisions between cultures. With titles such as "Culture Clash in AmeriCCa," "Culture Clash in Bordertown," "A Bowl of Beings," "The Mission," "Carpa Clash," "Radio Mambo: Culture Clash Invades Miami," "Mission Magic Mystery Tour," and "Chavez Ravine," among others, they have appeared at dozens of venues, from the JOHN F. KENNEDY CENTER, LINCOLN CENTER and the MARK TAPER FORUM, to LA JOLLA PLAYHOUSE, INTAR, DALLAS THEATER CENTER, BERKELEY REP, and others, as well as universities, colleges, and comedy clubs nationwide. DBW

Cummings [née Halveerstadt]**, Constance** (1910–2005) American-born actress who, because of her marriage to English playwright Benn W. Levy, spent most of her career in England. Her first London success, *Sour Grapes,* was followed the same year (1934) by her first important New York appearance (*Accent on Youth*). During her long career she appeared in modern and classical plays, including *Madame Bovary* (1937); *Goodbye, Mr. Chips* (1938); *Romeo and Juliet* and *Saint Joan* (both 1939, at the Old Vic); *The* PETRIFIED FOREST (1942); MacLeish's *J.B.* (1961); WHO'S AFRAID OF VIRGINIA WOOLF? (1964, replacing UTA HAGEN as Martha in London); Noël Coward's *Fallen Angels* (1967); and *Hamlet* (Gertrude in Tony Richardson's 1969 production). In 1971 she joined the National Theatre of Great Britain, playing Volumnia in *Coriolanus,* Leda in *Amphitryon 38,* Mary Tyrone in LONG DAY'S JOURNEY INTO NIGHT, Mme. Ranevsky in *The Cherry Orchard,* and Agave in *The Bacchae.* She won a Tony Award in ARTHUR KOPIT's WINGS, first seen in New York (1978) and the following year in London. After that, she appeared in *Hay Fever* and *The Golden Age* in London, *The Chalk Garden* in New York, and *Mrs Warren's Profession* in

Vienna. Her last West End appearance was in *Uncle Vanya* (1999). DBW

Curchack, Fred (1948–) Performance and solo artist, born in New York City but, since 1986, a resident of Texas and professor of art and performance at the University of Texas at Dallas. He has created more than 60 original theatre pieces (21 solo works), which have been seen at dozens of international theatre festivals and throughout the U.S. Frequently honored, he is a 1991 Guggenheim Fellow. His pieces often involve multimedia and are technically sophisticated, such as his 1990 solo *Stuff as Dreams Are Made On* based on *The Tempest,* or 1992's *What Fools These Mortals Be,* adapted from *A Midsummer Night's Dream.* The complexity of his work is mirrored by his studies – Indian Kathakali, Japanese Noh, Balinese Topeng; choreography with Alwyn Nikolais; and acting with Grotowski's Polish Theater Lab. DBW

Curse of the Starving Class by SAM SHEPARD. Although commissioned by JOSEPH PAPP, the play premiered at London's Royal Court Theatre (21 April 1977). Even before the American premiere at NEW YORK SHAKESPEARE FESTIVAL's PUBLIC THEATER (2 March 1978), the play had won an unprecedented and controversial Obie Award on the basis of the published text alone. Important revivals include those of YALE REPERTORY THEATRE (1980) and INTAR (1985). The explosive action focuses on a disintegrating family's craving for food. Father, mother, son, and daughter strain against the blood ties that unite them as the play, according to MEL GUSSOW, "charts the crippling effect of the 'creeping disease' of a consumer society that insists on shortchanging its citizens." FHL

Curtis, Paul J(ames) (1927–) Boston-born director, teacher, performer. A student of ERWIN PISCATOR, in 1952 he founded The American Mime Theatre in New York City, the first MIME company and school in the U.S. in this century. He has created more than 50 mime plays for his company, has taught at major universities, professional performing schools, and art centers, and is the author of *American Mime, The Medium* (1953). In 1972 he founded International Mimes and Pantomimists, which produced a directory and a bibliography. TL

Cushman, Charlotte Saunders (1816–76) The first native-born American actress of the top rank, Cushman, described as commanding rather than handsome, was considered the most powerful

Charlotte and Susan Cushman as Romeo and Juliet.
Courtesy: Harvard Theatre Collection, Houghton Library.

actress on the 19th-century stage. Trained as an opera singer, she misused her voice and was forced to alter her career. Appearing somewhat masculine, with a tall, strong body, unusual voice, and powerful personality, her stage characterizations emerged in heroic outline.

Her acting debut was as Lady Macbeth under the management of JAMES CALDWELL in New Orleans (1836), repeated the same year in New York at the BOWERY. Her first sensational success was as Nancy Sykes in *Oliver Twist* (1839). A failed manager of Philadelphia's WALNUT STREET THEATRE, she appeared opposite W. C. Macready on his American tour in 1843–4 and then went to London, appearing first in 1845 at the Princess's Theatre. After 1844 she performed about 35 roles, with only 10 repeated regularly. By her return to the U.S. in 1849, she was considered by many the greatest living English-speaking actress. During her long career she played more than 200 roles, excelling as Meg Merrilies in *Guy Mannering,* as Romeo opposite the Juliet of her sister Susan, as Lady Macbeth, and as Queen Katharine in *Henry VIII.* During 1852–69 she gave a series of farewell appearances, returning permanently to the stage in 1869 to forget the pain she suffered from cancer.

Cushman's style was marked by sweep, power, and majesty, sometimes overly expressive and extravagant. One critic described her movement as "a galvanized distortion of nature," and said her constant activity conveyed the impression she was "suffering under a violent attack of colic." A biography by Joseph Leach was published in 1970, though it largely sidesteps her sexuality; more candid about her personal life is Lisa Merrill's *When Romeo Was a Woman* (1999).   DBW

Custis, George Washington Parke (1781–1857) Playwright. Born into a distinguished southern family, Custis expressed nationalistic views in his writing. Of his nine plays, *Pocahontas; or, The Settlers of Virginia* (1830) achieved most success in the theatre. *The Eighth of January* (1828) dramatized his enthusiasm for Andrew Jackson; *The Rail Road* (1828) celebrated the opening of the Baltimore & Ohio; and *Northpoint; or, Baltimore Defended* (1833) honored that famous battle from the War of 1812.
    WJM

D

Da Costa [né Tecosky], **Morton** (1914–89) Highly successful Broadway director during the 1950s whose New York directing debut was at the City Center with *She Stoops to Conquer* (1949). His first major success was *Plain and Fancy,* followed by *No Time for Sergeants* (both 1955), Auntie Mame (1956), and *The Music Man* (1957).   SMA

Da Silva [né Silverblatt], **Howard** (1909–86) Actor, director, and producer. Born in Cleveland, OH, Da Silva studied at the Carnegie Institute of Technology and debuted in Eva Le Gallienne's Civic Repertory Company (1929), remaining for five years. His 1935 film debut was in *Once in a Blue Moon.* The same year he directed on radio the Great Classic Series for the Federal Theatre Project. Among his outstanding stage roles were Jud Fry in Oklahoma!, Benjamin Franklin in *1776,* and Ben Marino in Fiorello! (Tony nominee). Da Silva won an Emmy in 1978 for *Verna – USO Girl.*   SMA

Dafoe, Willem (William) (1955–) Wisconsin-born, twice-nominated film (more than 50) and stage actor. Though best known, despite notable screen leading roles, as an eccentric, often dark, heavy, or villainous film actor (Green Goblin in 2002's *Spider-Man*), this trim, angular-featured player with a unique, lanquid voice and a seductive smile was a cofounder of the experimental Wooster Group and has helped create and perform in their work since 1977. He has maintained his theatre credibility in such productions as *LSD, Just the High Points, The Road to Immortality, The Hairy Ape,* and *North Atlantic.* After a 27-year relationship with Wooster cofounder Elizabeth LeCompte, in 2005 he married Italian actress-director Giada Colagrande.   DBW

Dale, Alan [né Alfred J. Cohen] (1861–1928) English-born critic who came to New York in the early 1880s to write for the *Dramatic Times.* In 1887 Joseph Pulitzer employed him as drama critic for the *World.* Dale switched to Hearst's *Morning Journal* in 1897 and *Cosmopolitan* magazine in 1904. Except for the period 1914–17, he remained a Hearst regular until his death. Dale popularized an aggressive and "smart" style of reviewing. *Who's Who in the Theatre* (1914) concluded that his opinions "probably carry more weight than any others in New York."   TLM

Dale, Jim [né James Smith] (1935–) British-born actor/performer whose career has included that of dancer, standup comic, film and TV actor, and Grammy Award winner for his audiobook readings of the *Harry Potter* series. His stage career, first in London with the National Theatre at the Old Vic and with the Young Vic, with whom he came to the U.S. in 1974, has since been primarily on the American stage, including his Tony-winning title performance in *Barnum* (1980), Bri in *Joe Egg* (1985), Bill Snibson in *Me and My Girl* (1987 replacement), Terri in *Privates on Parade* (Roundabout, 1989), various roles in the 1995 *Travels with My Aunt* (Lortel Award), Dr. Pangloss and others in the 1997 revival of *Candide,* the instructor in a revival of Trevor Griffiths's *Comedians* (New Group, 2003), and Peachum (Tony nomination; Drama Desk Award; Richard Seff Award from Equity) in Roundabout's 2006 revival of *The Threepenny Opera.*   DBW

Dallas Theater Center 3636 Turtle Creek Blvd., Dallas, TX [Architect: Frank Lloyd Wright]. Founded in 1959 by Baylor University professor Paul Baker and a group of Dallas citizens, the Dallas Theater Center sprang into being housed in the only theatre designed by Frank Lloyd Wright that he ever lived to see built. The Kalita Humphreys Theatre – a gift of Dallas businessmen and named after a Texas actress killed in a plane crash – consists of a geometric, poured-concrete structure set into a hilly, wooded area a few miles from the center of the city. Its original stage was set at one end of the auditorium and was equipped with a revolve and two side stages. Professor Baker's plan to assemble a permanent acting company to present classics and contemporary plays and to introduce new works in conjunction with a graduate program at Baylor (later at Trinity University, where he transferred his activities) was largely fulfilled, but has been discontinued. To the original 516-seat theatre (now 466) was added the Arts District Theatre in downtown Dallas (500 seats; flexible staging) in 1985 (dismantled in the mid-2000s). At various times an experimental and flexible stage seating 50–100, called In the Basement, and other studio spaces have been used. Under the leadership of ADRIAN HALL (1983–9), DTC became an Equity company. Hall was replaced by 35-year-old Ken Bryant, who died suddenly in October 1990 following an automobile accident. In December 1991 Richard Hamburger, formerly with Maine's Portland Stage, was appointed artistic director, and in 1992 added "The Big D Festival of the Unexpected" to showcase new plays. He stepped down in 2007, replaced by Kevin Moriarty. Anticipated for 2009 is a new home in the projected innovative, 11-story Dallas Center for the Performing Arts (the Dee and Charles Wyly Theatre), which will house five performance venues (for dance, opera, and Broadway tours, in addition to the DTC).   MCH   DBW

Dalrymple, Jean (1902–98) Producer, director, and publicist who began her career as an actress in VAUDEVILLE, then became personal representative with JOHN GOLDEN, and in 1940 formed her own publicity organization. Her initial venture as producer was in 1945 when she presented *Hope for the Best* by William McCleery. Associated with the New York City Center Light Opera Company and the City Center Drama Company from its inception in 1943, in 1953 she became its general director, a position she held for the next 15 years. This experience was recorded in her book *From the Last Row* (1975). During 1968–70 she was executive director of the AMERICAN NATIONAL THEATRE AND ACADEMY, and in 1958 she was coordinator of the performing arts for the U.S. at the Brussels World's Fair.   DBW

Daly, (Peter Christopher) Arnold (1875–1927) Producer and actor. Daly should be remembered as G. B. SHAW's first truly effective champion in the U.S. Even as he was establishing himself as a player of supporting roles in England and America, he pursued his interest in Shaw by directing and acting in a trial matinee of *Candida*, which opened for a regular run in New York in 1903 and then went on tour with *The Man of Destiny*. After visiting Shaw, Daly returned for the 1904–5 season to produce *How She Lied to Her Husband* (written for Daly), *You Never Can Tell*, *John Bull's Other Island*, and *Mrs Warren's Profession*. The first New York performance of this last play was cause for Daly's arrest on moral charges, although he was acquit-

ted. In 1906, Daly added *Arms and the Man* to his repertory and, under the management of the SHUBERTS, conducted a successful national tour. Somewhat dismayed by the vitriolic response of conservative critics, Daly abandoned Shaw for a time to pursue more conventional roles.   MR

Daly, (John) Augustin (1838–99) Dramatist, managing director, and critic who dominated the theatrical scene in the U.S. during the last half of the 19th century. His plays and especially his productions set a new standard for American theatre and exerted a strong influence in England, beginning with a first European tour in 1884 and culminating with the opening of Daly's own theatre in London in 1893. He began his theatre career as a critic, writing for five newspapers during 1859–67. During this period he also wrote or adapted his first plays, most notably *Leah, the Forsaken* (1862) and the melodrama UNDER THE GASLIGHT (1867). From the inception of his writing career he was assisted at every turn by his brother Joseph, though this collaboration was kept secret. Ultimately, the Dalys had over 90 of their plays or adaptations performed. Of this large number few are significant literary accomplishments, though many show Daly to have been an exceptional contriver of effects and theatrical moments and, during the 1870s and '80s, a writer of melodramas and sentimental comedies superior to most of his contemporaries. Among his more successful productions were *A Flash of Lightning* (1868), *Frou-Frou* (1870), HORIZON (1871), DIVORCE (1871), *Article 47* (1872), *Needles and Pins* (1880), *Dollars and Sense* (1883), *Love on Crutches* (1884), and *The Lottery of Love* (1888). He also produced adaptations of English classics and SHAKESPEARE, one of the most successful of which, *The Taming of the Shrew,* was presented at Stratford-upon-Avon in 1888, supposedly the first performance of the play given there.

Many of his more notable productions featured ADA REHAN, JOHN DREW, MRS. G. H. GILBERT, and JAMES LEWIS, known as the "Big Four." Daly was usually adept at discerning and developing talent: More than 75 prominent actors owed their success to his training. Daly also managed and built several important theatres, beginning with the rental in 1869 of the FIFTH AVENUE THEATRE, and took over briefly the Grand Opera House. In 1879, with these theatres behind him, he took over the old Wood's Museum (built in 1867), which he opened as DALY's at 1221 Broadway, remaining there until his death (after which it was run by a succession of managers, including DANIEL FROHMAN and the SHUBERT BROTHERS). Constantly striving for an ensemble effect in his productions, Daly was one of the first directors in the modern sense and the first American régisseur. His brother, Joseph, wrote his biography in 1917; one by Marvin Felheim followed in 1956. (See also INTRODUCTION, §2.)   DBW

Daly's Theatre 1221 Broadway, NYC. Built as a museum in 1867, manager John Banvard used its three-tier, 2,000-seat auditorium for theatrical performances in the afternoons and evenings. A year later, it was taken over by George Wood, who renamed it Wood's Museum and Metropolitan Theatre, in which he presented plays, comic operas, burlesques, and variety for the next few years. In 1876, Banvard reclaimed the lease and renamed it the Broadway Theatre. Its most significant period occurred when AUGUSTIN DALY, responding to the uptown drift of the theatres, took it over in 1879, renovated it extensively, and transformed it into Daly's Theatre. Here, he and his STOCK COMPANY made their last stand against the new system of booking single plays into a theatre to try for a long run. Daly even resorted to leasing the theatre to outside producers and summer rentals to keep it afloat, but when he died in 1899, the house passed to a succession of managers, including DANIEL FROHMAN and the SHUBERT BROTHERS. It met an inglorious end as a BURLESQUE house when the new theatre district was amalgamating around Times Square. In 1920, it was razed and was replaced by a commercial structure.   MCH

Damn Yankees Two-act musical comedy, music and lyrics by RICHARD ADLER and JERRY ROSS, book by GEORGE ABBOTT and Douglass Wallop; opened 5 May 1955 at the 46TH STREET THEATRE, New York, running 1,019 performances. Based on a novel by Wallop, this baseball fantasy treats the struggle of a frustrated baseball fan (Robert Shafer) who sells his soul to the Devil (Ray Walston) and is turned into a star player (Stephen Douglass); trying to abrogate the pact, he must confront the Devil's star seductress, Lola (GWEN VERDON). Mounted by basically the same production team as Adler and Ross's PAJAMA GAME (1954), it was equally successful, contributing two standards ("Heart" and "Whatever Lola Wants, Lola Gets") to popular song literature. After two 1,000-performance successes in two attempts, this was the last Adler–Ross show: Ross died at age 29 six months after it opened. A 1994 (closed summer '95) revival directed by JACK O'BRIEN featured VICTOR GARBER as the Devil, replaced March 1995 by Jerry Lewis in his "legit" Broadway debut.   JD

Gwen Verdon as Lola in *Damn Yankees.* Photo by Fred Fehl. *Courtesy:* Harry Ransom Humanities Research Center, the University of Texas at Austin.

dance in the American theatre Dance and theatre in the U.S., says one myth, had largely been separate until the 1940s paved the way for a change in the genre of musical comedy: Prior to that decade showbiz dance had mainly consisted of divertissements of mixed quality and variable standards, usually characterized by chorus girls executing precision kick lines; this trend reached an apotheosis with the integration of narrative, song, and dance in musical comedy from the '40s on. In this version, the emergence in the 1950s and '60s of the choreographer-director becomes the major defining phenomenon of Broadway's golden age.

The convergence of dance and theatre, albeit rooted in basic fact, is only one part of a larger, complex, discontinuous history, leaning too heavily on a utopian, heroes-only version of dance culture. In many dances, if not most, music and dance are not in unity. There are numerous works in which integration of the two is not the goal. In indigenous dance performances, for example, no clear distinction is made between ritual celebration and social recreation. NATIVE AMERICANS used dance to honor and worship the spirit, to mark rites of passge, to express communal values, or to reflect social relationshps of the people – not to valorize a choreographer's individual vision. All forms of dancing (traditional, modern, theatrical, ritual, social, Western, non-Western) must be taken into account – with a solid formal thrust that interprets and reconstructs the larger significance of dance and other performances to their time, place, and context – in order to construct an accurate dance history in the American theatre.

Because dance has been an irretrievable object of desire, part of the problem is technological. In the 20th century historians had archival records, film reproductions (and videotaping as standard practice in the 1970s), and advanced notational means to document and evaluate its changing developments. Another issue is aesthetic: Showbiz dance is meant largely to entertain. By its very nature, a musical show is produced and created collaboratively, with the profit motive ever in mind; in this context dance is often one integral part of a whole and frequently required to tell or schematize some sort of story line. Yet there is nothing that prevents this dance from also being as personal, serious, and honest an artistic expression as, say, concert dance.

Broadly speaking, American culture had been handicapped by the historical fear or ambivalence of the union of body and soul, which secular dancing represents. In the American South, a 1740 law forbade beating African drums and blowing horns, so black slaves used bone clappers, jawbones, and banja (the original banjo) as musical instruments; their hand clapping and foot stomping served to preserve their African ancestry (and their resistence) in movement and song. In the northern colonies before the American Revolution, the Puritan disapproval of "mixed or promiscuous dancing" was manifested in legal bans against theatrical entertainers – laws that would not be repealed until after the war. Moreover, Europeans in the New World looked down upon the dance dramas of indigenous peoples, regarding Native American dance and movement as forms of devil worship or war preparation or both. Characterized by masquerade, imitation, role reversals, burlesques, and reenactments of myths, Indian dance dramas had intrinsic meanings and symbolic worth of a moral and religious sensibility. Relegated to reservations first in the 1700s, Native Americans developed secular forms in lieu of sacred ones to showcase complicated footwork amid spectacular pageantry and to be performed publicly, shared intertribally, and ultimately to evolve into the modern powwow.

At various times, religious groups have outlawed dancing and expelled church members who dared to flout the rules. Some exceptions were made for English and French performers. New York's JOHN STREET THEATRE (1767) became an outpost for touring engagements from England and France of assorted operas, pantomimes, romance burlettas (musical farces), and other types of show that incorporated dance. From 1791, French dancers and ballet masters became fixtures in stage entertainments from New York to New Orleans. JOHN DURANG became famous in 1784 for his hornpipe in a Philadelphia theatre. Having learned ballet from watching the French, Durang joined the company of LEWIS HALLAM, who had to disguise his popular performances as "lectures." Hallam's company embraced SHAKESPEARE, spectacles, and British pantomimes. By the first quarter of the 19th century Americans enjoyed romantic ballets, shadow plays, circuses, variety shows, masques, and burlesques. In 1853, a Philadelphia-born choreographer, George Washington Smith, staged a corps de ballet of 150 dancers, which toured the U.S. for years.

Versatility was (and still is) a hallmark attribute for performers, who had to sing, dance, act, and be at home in many theatrical formats. Although 19th-century companies did employ dance directors, any dancer could, if the need arose, stage a new number. The standard repertory included hornpipes, clogs, jigs, and traditional ballet numbers based on the gavotte, tyrolienne, bolero, mazurka, polka, fandango, and other popular forms. But the New World also saw the creation of a new type of American dance art that grew directly out of the black experience on the southern plantations. One famous dancer, William Henry Lane ("Master Juba"), was a freeborn black man who toured Europe in the mid-1800s; his eccentric, loose-limbed jigging was quite different from the early minstrel performances of white Irish men in blackface, who embellished their jigs with upper-body movements.

MINSTREL SHOWS swept the nation beginning in 1843. At first, solo dancers impersonated black characters, such as the infamous Jim Crow portrayed by THOMAS RICE. Eventually blackface minstrelsy made a profound impact, offering up burnt-cork imitations and insulting stereotypes of wily, happy-go-lucky, cotton-pickin' blacks. Its most famous dance, the Essence of Old Virginia, was derived from a "Negro shuffle," which was, in turn, a slow-tempo version of a clog, and in time evolved into a smooth soft-shoe, the early stirrings of tap dancing. Minstrelsy was also known for the cakewalk finale, a burlesque of white manners and finery, which became an international fad after its presentation in the 1903 black musical, *In Dahomey*. Other minstrel dances (buck-and-wing, Buzzard Lope, Slow Drag, Pigeon Wing, Snake Hips, Charleston) appeared in VAUDEVILLE and BURLESQUE shows of the later 19th and 20th centuries.

The most influential show in 19th-century America, *The* BLACK CROOK (1866), although tripe and a hybrid, featured lots of long-legged lineups of female dancers, which became a hallmark of the statuesque processionals of the Ziegfeld girls. The show also magnified feelings of foreign supremacy in dance by hiring the best available French ballerinas of the time. This production spurred countless imitations until black performers broke the cycle in the 1900s by singing the blues, developing tap, and evolving their own jazz-dance style. What was absorbed from Europe and Africa was deeply assimilated to the American experience, yet there was no loss of identity in the theatrical outcome.

During the Victorian era, male dancers often faced an indifferent or hostile audience in the ballet and the ballroom. Only the song-and-dance man was able to transcend the stigma attached to male dance expertise. The best known, GEORGE M. COHAN, sometimes called "the father of musical comedy," by 1901 was author, lyricist, composer, director, and star of a series of book musicals. He pranced around in a sort of soft-shoe dance style based on buck-and-wing, counter to the sentimental heroes of the Viennese operetta, becoming a model for the likes of EDDIE CANTOR, Bob Hope, Dan Dailey, Donald O'Connor, Gene Kelly, and TOMMY TUNE.

Meanwhile, the American MUSICAL THEATRE had been developing a synthetic style of its own. Musical REVUES and other crowd-pleasing shows adopted the latest ragtime dances, Latin rhythms, and social dances from the dance halls and supper clubs. Animal dances (Grizzly Bear, Turkey Trot, Bunny Hug, Monkey Glide), black in origin, provided new material for the stage. Vernon and Irene Castle formed a partnership in 1911 and popularized the one-step, hesitation waltz, Castle Walk, and the fox-trot. Eliminating ragtime wiggles and shakes, they brought elegance to the dance floor, appearing in 1914 in IRVING BERLIN's first musical, *Watch Your Step*. Other dance teams followed, notably FRED AND ADELE ASTAIRE, who achieved fame from their successes in musical

shows like *Funny Face* (1927), making their Broadway dance vernacular synonymous with carefree sophistication.

Between 1907 and 1931, Broadway producer FLORENZ ZIEGFELD set a new standard for American musical revues, modeled after the Folies-Bergère. He glorified showgirls, surrounded them with comedians and singers, and created dancing stars out of the Danish ballerina Adeline Genée; the Hungarian American DOLLY SISTERS; MARILYN MILLER; and Ann Pennington, who was known for a form of hootchy-kootchy borrowed from Harlem. Responsible for the format and choreography for the *Follies* – including the Ziegfeld Walk, which allowed showgirls to navigate steep staircases – was dance director NED WAYBURN, whose system of training held sway over Broadway and vaudeville between 1910 and 1930.

Harlem dance directors often traveled downtown to stage numbers for Ziegfeld and others who borrowed from Harlem's black musicals. Yet most black performers remained on the segregated vaudeville circuit until 1921, when SHUFFLE ALONG moved from Harlem to Broadway and introduced jazz styles. FLORENCE MILLS was transformed into a star and JOSÉPHINE BAKER was featured. By 1931 at least 16 all-black shows had appeared in New York, among them *Dixie to Broadway* and *Chocolate Dandies* (both 1924), establishing the new syncopated rhythms of black jazz dancing, which included comic struts, grinds, shuffles, and buck steps. The best in the field, BILL "BOJANGLES" ROBINSON, became the toast of Broadway in *Blackbirds of 1928*, a black revue for white audiences. When the Depression hit and black revues waned in popularity, Robinson went to Hollywood and starred in 14 motion pictures.

Until the arrival of Pavlova in 1910 and Diaghilev's Ballets Russes in 1916, the prevailing view was that American ballet did not improve in quality. Dance had served as diversions in operettas, allowing singers a brief break or costume change. Roles for dancers with specialties were inserted into ballroom scenes or village-square episodes; somtimes choruses of attractive women performed national dances. (One notable exception was in Franz Lehar's *The Merry Widow*, staged in NYC in 1907 with two dancers allowed to express true emotions.) The immigrant spirit ultimately challenged the perception of American dance's inferiority to its European counterparts. In 1933 GEORGE BALANCHINE moved to the U.S. and altered the direction of dance by relying on the beauty of classical ballet technique to create abstract works that did not depend on narrative.

Working with black choreographer Herbie Harper, he melded jazz, tap, and ballet in ON YOUR TOES (1936), in which he created a full-scale ballet parallel to the main plot, his *Slaughter on Tenth Avenue*.

Likewise, as early as 1930 modern-dance choreographers emerged to explore the potential of dance as a serious art form, including Martha Graham, Doris Humphrey, José Limon, Anna Sokolow, and Charles Weidman. The American musical theatre benefited from the techniques of many choreographers of both ballet and modern dance who moved into this area. In the 1930s HELEN TAMIRIS made a name for herself as a modern dancer with the FEDERAL THEATRE PROJECT and later worked in *Up in Central Park* (1945) and ANNIE GET YOUR GUN (1946). In KISS ME, KATE (1948), HANYA HOLM choreographed formal court dances, soft-shoe steps, witty jitterbugs, and dramatic ensemble dancing. In *MY FAIR LADY* (1956) she staged the famous Ascot scene, and in CAMELOT (1960) courtly processionals.

The much-storied synthesis of narrative, song, and dance had strong roots in the powerful dramas of the modern-dance choreographers, but there had been earlier, discrete efforts to bring all the elements together. Between 1915 and 1919, New York's tiny PRINCESS THEATRE featured the intimate "Princess Musicals" by JEROME KERN and GUY BOLTON; the songs in their shows *Nobody Home, Very Good Eddie,* and *Leave It to Jane* were dramatically tied to the plots, and the dances (credited to David Bennett) incorporated Castle Walks, fox-trots, and two-steps. The next musical milestone, SHOWBOAT, and its showbiz setting allowed dance director Sam Lee to break away from conventional chorus-line formulas, to survey the development of dancing styles from the mid-19th century to the 1920s, and to gesture toward racial integration by employing a unit of black performers as part of the chorus. This landmark show led the likes of RICHARD RODGERS and LORENZ HART, Irving Berlin, COLE PORTER, and GEORGE and IRA GERSHWIN and others to embrace coherent books where dance and movement were used to tie all the various elements together. The dance director had become choreographer.

In 1943, modern dancer and ballet choreographer AGNES DE MILLE created a dream-ballet sequence for OKLAHOMA! In this musical she revolutionized the art form by integrating its choreographic numbers with the plot in a way that had not been done before. Her dream ballets, however, were neither a novelty nor an original idea. Balanchine had used dream ballets in ON YOUR TOES, BABES IN ARMS (1937), and *I Married an Angel* (1938). So had Robert Alton in PAL JOEY (1940). Another important choreographer, the Viennese ballerina Albertina Rasch, had expanded the vocabulary by creating three dream ballets in KURT WEILL's LADY IN THE DARK (1941). Still, de Mille's tremendously influential effort was unique in probing deeply into the inner life of the characters and pushing the dramatic action forward. After *Oklahoma!* every musical had to have a ballet number, until eventually the repetition wore out its originality.

Balanchine and de Mille shifted the choreographer's role in the making of musicals. Balanchine took on the choreography for *Cabin in the Sky* (1940), a fable of black life; de Mille choreographed or directed (or both) a dozen or so musicals. Since both Balanchine's and de Mille's dancers came largely from ballet or modern-dance companies, Broadway audiences grew accustomed to a standard of dancing comparable to that on the concert stage; this translated into higher salaries and better working conditions.

Also after *Oklahoma!*, tap dancers fell into disuse, and interest would not return until the mid-1970s, when dance scholars sought out veteran black performers such as Honi Coles and encouraged them to revive their most popular numbers and also to teach a new generation. Meanwhile, American jazz dancing came back into vogue. MICHAEL KIDD staked his jazz claims in GUYS AND DOLLS (1950). A seminal dance figure, JACK COLE, developed jazz idioms from the dances of Harlem, the Caribbean, Latin America, and the Middle East. He virtually invented what we now think of a jazz ballet and created an entirely personal mode of jazz-ethnic-ballet that prevails as the dominant look of and technique for Broadway-style dancing. It was flagrantly sexual, rigorously disciplined, arrogant, and potent; it obliterated nearly all traces of the older, more relaxed, improvisational black-derived jazz traditions of the 1920s. Cole left his mark on GWEN VERDON, BOB FOSSE, Carol Haney, Matt Mattox, Buzz Miller, Rod Alexander, Rob Hamilton, George and Ethel Martin, and Lee (Becker) Theodore, GOWER CHAMPION, PETER GENNARO, MICHAEL BENNETT, Tommy Tune, and GRACIELA DANIELE. Champion's winning choreography for HELLO, DOLLY! (1964) altered the idioms of American jazz to fit the show's period numbers. Also, BOB FOSSE developed a jazz-dance style that insisted on coolly contained minimalism and cynical sexuality. His dance routines for SWEET CHARITY (1966) used distinctive trademarks (bowler hats, fishnet stockings, canes and chairs), which melded hand-ballet swaying and rapid jerks with the vulgar energy of vaudeville and burlesque, particularly in CABARET (1966).

Another dance giant, JEROME ROBBINS, pointed the way for a greater dramatic range. Robbins remains unequaled because his string of Broadway hits came side by side with his successes in the world of ballet. Having shown a flair for comedy, Robbins assimilated and transformed dance material from many styles, periods, and cultures. Robbins set new guidelines for jazz dancing in WEST SIDE STORY (1957, collaborating with Peter Gennaro); he created celebrated dance sequences in The KING AND I (1951); and he directed and choreographed GYPSY (1959), the last great musical in the mode of RODGERS and HAMMERSTEIN, using dances that reflected vaudeville and burlesque. His final musical was FIDDLER ON THE ROOF (1964). Never deserting the ballet, he returned to Broadway in 1989 when he staged JEROME ROBBINS' BROADWAY, a compendium of his work.

Musical-theatre choreography's reliance on a narrative hook, from Balanchine to Robbins, showed that dance could reflect a show's theme and complement its dramatic composition. The dance-drama and psychological ballets, dominant in the 1940s and '50s, yielded plotless works and experiments, a body of repertory modern dances that could be repeated and, if good enough, could be considered classics. After WWII many modern dancers chose not to contribute directly to musical theatre but nonetheless undeniably had an impact, and some became PERFORMANCE ARTists. Among these artists would be Merce Cunningham, Yvonne Rainer, Trisha Brown, Steve Paxton, Lucinda Childs, David Gordon, Valda Setterfield, Paul Taylor, TWYLA THARP (of this group, one of the few to work in ballet and on Broadway), Alvin Ailey, Arthur Mitchell, Robert Joffrey, and Mark Morris, to mention some of the more prominent and best known.

The credo of movement for movement's sake and the direct focus on the body found resonance with young dance makers who favored nonlinear compositions, stream-of-consciousness structures, or adding on other media to convey ideas. Many performers deserted the traditional stage to become closer to the audience. MEREDITH MONK, for example, composes her own music, intersperses live sequences with films, and takes the dance from room to room. She and others moved in individualized directions that ignored prescribed parameters. Vocalizations, pedestrian movement, and other taboos previously considered appropriate only in dramatic theatre became the norm.

Then, suddenly conscious of dance, writers and producers explored the dramatic roles that moving bodies could play on a stage. In A LITTLE NIGHT MUSIC (1973), choreographer PATRICIA BIRCH so cleverly interwove the music and dance into a whole that they were neither distractions nor diversions but rather enhancements of the dramatic action. In 1976, Paula Moss choreographed the actresses in FOR COLORED GIRLS WHO HAVE CONSIDERED SUICIDE WHEN THE RAINBOW WAS ENUF, not to stage spectacular dance sequences but to present the emotions, poetry, and lives of their characters through movement and dance. Noted theatre directors, like ANDREI SERBAN and ELLEN STEWART, began experimenting with dance movement in classic revivals and in new scripts. The real lives of dancers became the subject of A CHORUS LINE (1975), conceived and choreographed by Michael Bennett. STEPHEN SONDHEIM'S SUNDAY IN THE PARK WITH GEORGE (1984), in which characters moved through an impressionistic landscape, credited choreographer Randolyn Zinn with the play's "movement" to reflect the increasing awareness of nonverbal techniques.

The dance boom of the 1960s and '70s derived from a climate of financial giving that permitted the artistic ferment to produce dance of great merit. Serious dance was seen on television; regional ballet companies proliferated; dance festivals encouraged higher-quality dance and choreography; and the study of dance in the academy became more common. Regrettably, a complex of events ended this boom – the passing of first-generation modern-dance pioneers; the death through AIDS-related illness of many theatre and dance artists; and cutbacks in support from the NATIONAL ENDOWMENT FOR THE ARTS in the mid-1990s. A noticeable sea change in the 1980s and '90s led American choreographers to reconsider what had been an emphasis on form. Original multicultural voices emerged, and companies presenting dance from around the world were no longer considered exotic on Western stages. Also, after years of emphasizing concern with pure movement, American dance found itself wrestling with how to express emotion in a nonlinear way. Among those at the forefront of this movement have been artists William Forsythe and ROBERT WILSON, though much of their work has been in Europe. In NYC, dance artists such as MARTHA CLARKE have created dance-theatre works that can not be singularly categorized. Graciela Daniele, from Argentina, heavily accented her dance-drama with Latin passion, machismo, sex, and death. In a more traditional theatre vein, SUSAN STROMAN, the director and choreographer of The PRODUCERS, concocted with playwright John Weidman the dance-play Contact (1999), in which most of the acting was done with swing numbers and without words. And in The LION KING (1997) GARTH FAGAN combined elements of modern dance and ballet with African and Caribbean rhythms and postures.

The new millenium has witnessed a return on the Broadway stage to more traditional dance and choreography, in part because of the revival of musicals from past eras and the creation of new musicals in the mode of earlier musical comedy. A new generation of choreographers has also emerged: Stroman, Daniele, Wayne Cilento, Jeff Calhoun, KATHLEEN MARSHALL, ROB MARSHALL, and JERRY MITCHELL, among others. Still, the changes in American dance over the past century cannot be erased, and past definitions of dance in theatre become largely meaningless today. Each generation of dance artists will bring new methods and approaches to movement that fit the broad range of theatre forms requiring dance as an important component.   LF   RG

Dance Theater Workshop A leading dance and performance-art venue located in the Chelsea district of Manhattan. It was founded in 1965 by a group of neighborhood performers and housed initially in choreographer Jeff Duncan's loft on West 20th St. In addition to dance, music, and alternative-theatrical events, DTW has presented in its Bessie Schönberg Theater early work by talents such as BILL IRWIN, stand-up comic WHOOPI GOLDBERG, and performance artists JOHN KELLY, RACHEL ROSENTHAL, MICHAEL MOSHEN, and Laurie Carlos.   CLJ

Daniele, Graciela (1939–) Argentina-born director and choreographer who came to New York in 1963, where she began her career as a dancer in such productions as Coco, FOLLIES, and CHICAGO. Her first effort as choreographer was DURANG's A History of the American Film (1978), followed by the Pirates of Penzance (dir. WILFORD LEACH), The Rink, The Mystery of Edwin Drood, and Alice in Concert with MERYL STREEP. In 1990 she moved into direction with the Trinidad-inspired folk-fable musical Once on This Island; in 1991 she directed WILLIAM FINN's March of the Falsettos and Falsettoland (together) at the HARTFORD STAGE COMPANY. Subsequent credits include choreography for The Goodbye Girl (1993, Broadway); direction of Herringbone with JOEL GREY (Hartford Stage,1993); direction and choreography, Hello Again (Lincoln Center, 1994); direction of her first nonmusical work, EDWIN

SÁNCHEZ's Clean (Hartford, 1995); cocreation and direction/choreography of Chronicle of a Death Foretold (1995, Broadway); musical staging of RAGTIME (1998); direction/choreography of the ANNIE GET YOUR GUN Broadway revival (1999); Lincoln Center's Marie Christine (1999); CHITA RIVERA: The Dancer's Life (2005); and LaCHIUSA's musical Bernarda Alba at Lincoln Center (2006). In 1998 she received the "Mr. Abbott" award. She is married to lighting designer JULES FISHER.   DBW

Daniels, William (David) (1927–) Actor. For the cultivated, complacent publisher in The ZOO STORY (1960), ACTORS STUDIO member Daniels received CLARENCE DERWENT and Obie awards. A prominent stage actor from 1939 (LIFE WITH FATHER, road) into the 1970s, he appeared in over a dozen New York productions, notably as Albert Amundsen in A Thousand Clowns (1962) and John Adams in 1776 (1969). During 1999–2001 he served as president of SAG.   DBW

Danites; or, The Heart of the Sierras, The, credited to JOAQUIN MILLER; opened at the BROADWAY THEATRE 22 August 1877 and became one of the most popular plays of frontier life. McKEE RANKIN played Sandy McGee, a good-hearted miner who befriended young Billy Piper. Billy, played by KITTY BLANCHARD Rankin, was actually a woman, Nancy Williams, disguised to escape the retribution of the Danites, a band of Mormons sworn to avenge the murder of Joseph Smith. THE DANITES, based on Miller's The First Fam'lies of the Sierras (1876), reflected widespread anti-Mormon sentiment. Although originally credited to Miller, who published a version as The Danites in the Sierras, lawsuits eventually revealed that the script played by Rankin was composed by P. A. Fitzgerald, an obscure Philadelphia writer.   RAH

Danner, Blythe (Katherine) (1944–) Actress, frequently on television (Eccentricities of a Nightingale, 1976; YOU CAN'T TAKE IT WITH YOU, 1979; Back When We Were Grownups, 2004), who emphasizes "the individualization of a dilemma or mood . . . that we all recognize." She debuted OFF-BROADWAY in The Infantry (1966), and on Broadway in Leonard Gershe's Butterflies Are Free (1969; Tony); her recent Broadway appearances include The Deep Blue Sea (1998) and the 2001 revival of FOLLIES. She often appears regionally (for over 25 years at WILLAMSTOWN) and Off-Broadway (e.g., A STREETCAR NAMED DESIRE, CIRCLE IN THE SQUARE, 1988; Much Ado about Nothing, NEW YORK SHAKESPEARE FESTIVAL, 1989; GURNEY's Sylvia, MANHATTAN THEATRE CLUB, 1995). Her roughly 70 films include BRIGH-

TON BEACH MEMOIRS (1986) and *Another Woman* (1988). Danner received a *Theatre World* Award for *The Miser* (1969) and Tony nominations for *Betrayal* (1980), *Streetcar*, and *Follies*. Her husband (d. 2002) was writer-director-producer Bruce Paltrow; her daughter **Gwyneth**, though primarily a film actress (1999 Oscar for *Shakespeare in Love*), occasionally appears onstage, recently as Catherine in the London production of *PROOF*, and subsequently in the 2005 film version. REK

Darkness at Noon Anticommunist melodrama by SIDNEY KINGSLEY. Commissar Rubashov (Claude Rains) is imprisoned, tried, and executed for "political divergences." Winner of the Drama Critics' Circle Award as the Best Play of 1951, this adaptation of Arthur Koestler's 1941 novel focuses on Rubashov's purgative remembrances of his shameful excesses as a party official. At the end he heroically apologizes "to his hundred eighty million fellow prisoners," recants his Marxist commitment to History, and acknowledges the failure of the revolution to consider the human soul. Koestler's attack on Stalinism and the 1937 purges seemed, in the cold-war milieu in which the PLAYWRIGHTS' COMPANY produced the play, a propagandistic repudiation of the Soviet system. WD

Davenport, Edward Loomis (1815–77) Actor, known for his versatility, grace, good taste, musical voice, and gentlemanly manners. ANNA CORA MOWATT said that he simply looked like a leading man. He began his career in Providence, RI (1835), became Mowatt's leading man (1846), went with her to London, remained there for seven years (often playing in support of W. C. Macready), and returned to acclaim for his "intelligent and impressive" conception of Lanciotto in BOKER's *FRANCESCA DA RIMINI* (1855). From then until his final season (1875–6, playing Brutus to LAWRENCE BARRETT's Cassius), he became known for his extraordinary versatility. He was equally effective as Bill Sykes, Hamlet, Sir Lucius O'Trigger, or Othello.

He was the father of the actress FANNY DAVENPORT, and three of his descendants were active in theatre: Anne and WILLIAM SEYMOUR as actors, and May Davenport Seymour as theatre curator at the Museum of the City of New York. A biography edited by E. F. Edgett was published in 1901. RM

Davenport, Fanny (1850–98) English-born actress and daughter of actor E. L. DAVENPORT, "Miss Fanny" had been a popular child actress before her adult debut in 1862 at New York's NIBLO'S GARDEN THEATRE. In 1869 she joined AUGUSTIN DALY'S FIFTH AVENUE THEATRE company and demonstrated remarkable versatility in light comedies, Shakespeare, and finally serious dramatic works like Daly's *Pique* (1876), in which she created Mabel Renfrew, one of her most popular roles, along with Nancy Sykes in *Oliver Twist*. A beautiful, "spirited" actress, she formed her own company and gave the American English-language premieres of four Bernhardt vehicles by Sardou: *Fedora* (1883), *La Tosca* (1888), *Cleopatra* (1890), and *Gismonda* (1894). FHL

Davenport Brothers Ira Erastus Davenport (1839–1911) and **William Henry Harrison Davenport** (1841–77) are credited as the first successful stage mediums. Beginning in their hometown of Buffalo, NY, they first toured the U.S. successfully in the 1860s, producing "inexplicable manifestations" from their mysterious wooden cabinet in which they were securely tied. Denounced as fakes by such prominent British conjurors as John Henry Anderson and John Nevil Maskelyne, they nevertheless toured until William's death, and influenced all subsequent producers of "spirit music." DBW

Davidge, William Pleater (1814–88) English-born actor who made his U.S. debut at the BROADWAY THEATRE in 1850. He reportedly played over 1,100 different roles, but was celebrated for his portrayal of English comic characters like Sir Peter Teazle, Bottom, Toby Belch, and especially Dick Deadeye in *HMS Pinafore*. He was with AUGUSTIN DALY'S company (1869–77) and the MADISON SQUARE company (1885–death). His memoir, *Footlight Flashes* (1863), short on biographical insights, occasionally informs about theatrical organization and business. DJW

Davidson, Gordon (1933–) Director. Educated at Cornell (1956) and at Case Western Reserve (1957), Davidson has directed at the PAPER MILL PLAYHOUSE (NJ), the BARTER THEATRE, and other venues, and stage-managed for Martha Graham. At the AMERICAN SHAKESPEARE FESTIVAL he assisted JOHN HOUSEMAN, who chose him to codirect *King Lear* with the Theatre Group (which brought him to LA) and serve as managing director (1964–6). He was producing director of the Ahmanson (CENTER THEATRE GROUP) during 1989–2005 and artistic director–producer of the MARK TAPER FORUM (1967–2005, his retirement), where he directed nearly 20% of the mainstage productions. In 1995 he received the 11th "Mr. Abbott" Award for Lifetime Achievement. JDM

Davies, Acton (1870–1916) Drama critic. Born and educated in St. Johns, Quebec, Davies came to New York in 1887. He began contributing to newspapers and became a reporter in 1890. In 1893 he succeeded CHARLES B. DILLINGHAM as drama critic for *The Evening Sun,* remaining until 1914. Davies catered to popular taste in a lively, personal style, and acquired a reputation for having an insider's view of the stage. He wrote extensively for popular magazines and was manager for and literary adviser to the SHUBERTS.   TLM

Davis, Henrietta Vinton (1860–1941) AFRICAN AMERICAN actress. For 35 years a preeminent actress and solo elocutionist, Baltimore-born Davis was "a singularly beautiful woman . . . with illustriously expressive eyes [and a] rich, flexible and effective voice." She was universally hailed for her powerful and moving interpretations of a range of dramatic heroines that included Juliet, Portia, Ophelia, Rosalind, Lady Anne, Desdemona, Lady Macbeth, and Cleopatra. Excluded by racial prejudice from the established professional stage, Davis gave concert readings and performed dramatic scenes with other black actors. She produced and played leading roles in three plays by African American dramatists: *Dessalines* (1893) and *Christophe* (1912), both by William Edgar Easton, and *Our Old Kentucky Home* (1898), written for her by the journalist John E. Bruce. During 1919–31 Davis held a major office in the Marcus Garvey movement, working for racial equality and the establishment of a black nation-state in Africa.   EGH

Davis, L. Clarke (1835–1904) Editor, lawyer, and drama critic. Born to pioneering stock in Ohio, Davis grew up in Maryland and was educated at the Episcopal Academy in Philadelphia (1855). An early career in law led to editing a legal newspaper, after which he became managing editor of *The Philadelphia Inquirer* (1870). He wrote drama criticism for the *Inquirer* as well as for *Harper's,* the *Atlantic,* the *Century, Scribners', Lippincott's,* and *Putnam's.* He ended his career as managing editor (1893) and editor-in-chief of the *Philadelphia Public Ledger.* A perceptive critic of acting, Davis noted the essence of JOSEPH JEFFERSON III's *RIP VAN WINKLE* (1867): "the exquisite beauty and excellence of Mr. Jefferson's acting lie mostly in the fact that he has subdued it to the very complexion of nature."   TLM

Davis, Ossie [né Raiford Chatman] (1917–2005) AFRICAN AMERICAN actor and playwright who began acting with the Harlem-based ROSE MC-CLENDON Players and made his Broadway debut in the title role of *Jeb* (1946). Davis joined the national tour of ANNA LUCASTA (1947) and played in various New York productions, including STE-VEDORE (1949), *The* GREEN PASTURES (1951), and *No Time for Sergeants* (1956), before succeeding Sidney Poitier in *A* RAISIN IN THE SUN (1959). In 1961 Davis assumed the lead role opposite his wife RUBY DEE in his hilarious comedy *PURLIE VICTORIOUS,* which pungently ridiculed racial stereotyping. The film version, *Gone Are the Days* (1963), was unimpressive, but success was renewed with the musical *Purlie* (1970). Davis also wrote the plays *Curtain Call, Mr. Aldridge, Sir; Langston;* and *Escape to Freedom* [about Frederick Douglass]. He appeared in numerous films and television shows (a regular on *Evening Shade,* early 1990s), some of which he scripted and directed. Louis D. Mitchell called him "one of the most gifted men in the modern American theatre." Along with his wife Davis supported such regional efforts as CROSSROADS THEATRE where, in 1995, they appeared with their son, Guy, in a new play by Dee. They were honored with numerous lifetime achievement awards, including induction into the THEATRE HALL OF FAME (Dee, 1988; Davis, 1994), and they jointly received the National Medal of Arts (1995) and 2004 KENNEDY CENTER Honors. Their combined autobiography was published in 2000.   EGH

Davis, Owen (1874–1956) The most successful American writing melodrama at the turn of the 20th century. From *Through the Breakers* (1899) to *The Family Cupboard* (1913), Davis wrote 129 melodramas, such as *Nellie, the Beautiful Cloak Model.* Then he stopped, and in "Why I Quit Writing Melodrama" (*American Magazine,* September 1914) explained his art – for example, the importance of the play title and of the stage carpenter in the third act, on which he later elaborated in *I'd Like to Do It Again* (1931). Abandoning his Harvard-trained writing style, he began to write realistic plays, such as *The* DETOUR (1921), in which he depicted a spiritual barrenness. ICEBOUND (1923), concerned with the lost illusions of a New England family, won a Pulitzer Prize. Among later plays, only his adaptation of Edith Wharton's *Ethan Frome* (1936), with his son Donald Davis, was successful. He could not keep pace with the new rank of American dramatists during the 1930s. His total dramatic output numbers 150 to more than 300. His autobiography, *My First Fifty Years in the Theatre,* appeared in 1950.   WJM

Davis, Richard Harding (1864–1916) Playwright, writer, and journalist (probably the best known of his generation). He romped with the glamorous Barrymores (see DREW–BARRYMORE FAMILY), and from the Spanish War in Cuba to WWI reported from the scene. A symbol of the exuberant lifestyle of his age, he wrote too much, too easily – at least 18 plays, dozens of stories, and nonfiction works – and thought too little about his creativity. John Barrymore had a small role in *The Dictator* (1904), a very successful play. Other plays, showing more theatrical than dramatic power, include *The Taming of Helen* (1903), *The Galloper* (1905), and *The Seventh Daughter* (1910). G. Lanfford's biography was published in 1961.   WJM

Davy Crockett; or, Be Sure You're Right, Then Go Ahead by FRANK H. MURDOCH. Although not successful when first introduced at the Rochester Opera House on 23 September 1872, *Davy Crockett* emerged as one of the most beloved plays of the 19th century. FRANK MAYO patiently reworked it and then starred in it for over 20 years. Unlike other frontier plays featuring sensation and gunfire, *Davy Crockett* was romantic and poetic. Davy protected Eleanor Vaughn, his well-educated childhood sweetheart, from a pack of wolves by using his strong right arm to bar the cabin door. Sir Walter Scott's *Lochinvar,* which Davy read aloud, provided the poetic motif as Davy rescued Eleanor from an unwanted marriage and was dramatically transformed from rough-hewn backwoodsman to romantic hero.   RAH

De Angelis, Jefferson (1859–1933) Comediansinger and one of the most beloved stars of comic opera, De Angelis performed in vaudeville as a child, and later on tried his hand at dramatic acting. In 1887 he joined the McCaull Opera Company, appearing as a featured performer in comic operas such as *The Lady or the Tiger?* (1888). For several years he was a regular member of the CASINO THEATRE company, along with LILLIAN RUSSELL and FRANCIS WILSON. His first solo starring part was in *The Caliph* (1896). De Angelis brought to his comic opera roles both an ability to create consistent and individualized characters and the physical skills of an acrobat. His greatest successes were in *The Jolly Musketeer* (1898), *The Emerald Isle* (1902), *Fantana* (1905), and *The Girl and the Governor* (1907). From 1910 until his death, he performed in revivals of comic operas and in straight plays such as *The ROYAL FAMILY* (1927). His autobiography, *A Vagabond Trouper,* was published in 1931.   MK

De Foe, Louis V. (1869–1922) Drama critic. After graduating from the University of Michigan, De Foe pursued a career in journalism, first as Sunday editor then as New York correspondent and theatre critic for the *Chicago Tribune* (1891–9). During 1899–1922 he served as drama critic of the *New York World,* and contributed monthly essays to *Red Book Magazine* (1905–13). Conservative and moralistic, De Foe deplored the IBSEN drama for its lack of imagination, poetry, and romance.   TLM

De Koven, Reginald (1859–1920) Composer. After an extensive musical education in Europe, De Koven, in partnership with librettist HARRY B. SMITH, set out to prove that Americans could write a comic opera in the European style. Their first show, *The Begum* (1887), while not an unqualified success in New York, drew large audiences in CHICAGO, De Koven's hometown. In 1891 De Koven composed the score of *ROBIN HOOD,* the most popular American comic opera of the era. Carefully mounted by the Bostonians (see BOSTON IDEAL), *Robin Hood* was an immediate hit, and the song "O Promise Me" became an enduring American standard. Although he continued to compose comic operas until 1913, De Koven never had another success of this stature. Though his music was largely imitative of European modes, De Koven is remembered for his courage in challenging the supremacy of European comic opera composers on the American stage. His wife published their biographies in 1927.   MK

De Liagre, Alfred, Jr. (1904–87) Yale-educated producer and director who began his professional career in 1930 as stage manager at the Woodstock Playhouse. In 1933 he began producing professionally and worked in both New York and London. De Liagre produced or coproduced more than 30 plays, a number of which he also directed. His more noteworthy credits included *The Voice of the Turtle* (1943), *The Madwoman of Chaillot* (1948), *Second Threshold* (1951), *The Golden Apple* (1954), *The Girls in 509* (1958), *J.B.* (1958; Pulitzer Prize), *Photo Finish* (1963), *Bubbling Brown Sugar* (1976), DEATHTRAP (1978), and *ON YOUR TOES* (revival, 1983).   TLM

de Mille see also DEMILLE; DEMILLE

de Mille, Agnes (1905–93) Choreographer, director, and author, daughter of WILLIAM C. DE MILLE. Trained in the techniques of classical ballet, de Mille appeared as a dancer in the *Greenwich Village Follies* (1928). After choreographing two shows in London, she returned to New York to create the dances for *Hooray for What* (1937) and

Swingin' the Dream (1939). In 1943 RODGERS and HAMMERSTEIN hired her to choreograph OKLAHOMA!, and her use of modern ballet techniques revolutionized musical-comedy DANCE. In particular, the success of *Oklahoma!*'s dream ballet made such sequences a common feature of 1940s MUSICAL THEATRE. She went on to choreograph *One Touch of Venus* (1943), *Bloomer Girl* (1944), *CAROUSEL* (1945), and *BRIGADOON* (1947). Her choreography for *Brigadoon* was acclaimed for its dramatic intensity and its use of traditional Scottish dances. Agnes de Mille served as both choreographer and director for *Allegro* (1947) and *Out of This World* (1950). In the 1950s she created the dances for such shows as *PAINT YOUR WAGON* (1951), *The Girl in Pink Tights* (1954), and *Goldilocks* (1958). Less active in the 1960s, de Mille choreographed *Kwamina* (1961), *110 in the Shade* (1963), and *Come Summer* (1969). Best remembered for her pioneering work in musicals of the 1940s, de Mille is credited with demonstrating dance's potential for furthering a musical's dramatic action. Her dozen books include *Dance to the Piper* (1952), *Speak to Me, Dance with Me* (1973), *Reprieve: A Memoir* (1981), *Portrait Gallery* (1990), and *Martha [Graham]* (1991). A biography by Carol Easton was published in 1996.
MK

de Mille, William C. (1878–1955) Playwright and film director who, following the career of his father, HENRY C. DEMILLE, made his own contributions to American drama. Although plays written with his brother, Hollywood director Cecil B. DeMille, failed (e.g., *The Genius,* 1906), de Mille emphasized powerful confrontations with a socially probing theme in *Strongheart* (1905), an early treatment of love between a white girl and a Native American. *The Warrens of Virginia* (1907) opposed North and South in a Civil War love story; *The Woman* (1911) dramatized political corruption. His daughter is famed choreographer AGNES DE MILLE.   WJM

De Shields, André (1946–) Dynamic, versatile Baltimore-born actor, choreographer, director, composer, and lyricist; graduate of the University of Wisconsin (1970) with advanced work at NYU. Recipient of three Tony nominations – for MARK MEDOFF's *Prymate* (2004), *The FULL MONTY* (2001), and *Play On!* (1997) – he has also appeared on Broadway in *The WIZ* (1975, title role) and *Ain't Misbehavin'* (1978). In 1984 he conceived of, wrote, directed, and chorerographed the musical *Haarlem Nocturne* (in which he also appeared). For the CLASSICAL THEATRE OF HARLEM he excelled in *Dream on Monkey Mountain* (2003), in the title role of

Caligula in 2005 ("passionately rivets our focus"), and as King Lear (2006). His flexibility has been demonstrated vividly outside of New York: Scott Joplin in *Tin Pan Alley Rag* (Coconut Grove Playhouse, 1995); Sheridan Whiteside in *The MAN WHO CAME TO DINNER*, and Willy Loman in *DEATH OF A SALESMAN* (Madison Repertory, WI); Drummond in *INHERIT THE WIND* (Cape Playhouse, 2004); and others.   DBW

Dead End by SIDNEY KINGSLEY was a major success in 1935, running on Broadway for 684 performances at the BELASCO THEATRE. It featured NORMAN BEL GEDDES's realistic set of a New York slum, complete with a practical East River in the orchestra pit. The play focuses on the brutal city life of a gang of teenagers, and popularized Depression-era notions by linking crime with poverty and class conflict with the unequal distribution of wealth. Ironically, after the play was filmed – in 1937 with Humphrey Bogart and six youngsters from the Broadway production – the Dead End "Kids" (Leo Gorcey, Huntz Hall, Gabriel Dell, et al.) went on to considerable material success in a series of films and ultimately pursued Hollywood careers as The Bowery Boys. MICHAEL RITCHIE, a champion of the play, produced revivals at the WILLIAMTOWN THEATRE FESTIVAL (1997) and as his inaugural production as producer at the AHMANSON in LA (2005). The Williamstown production was recreated in 2000 at Boston's HUNTINGTON (2000). All three versions were directed by Nicholas Martin.   BBW

Dead End Kids: A History of Nuclear Power This Obie Award–winning play presented by MABOU MINES on the promise and perils of nuclear power opened at NYC's PUBLIC THEATER on 11 November 1980, conceived and directed by JOANNE AKALAITIS. A collage of text and images, it presents excerpts from U.S. government films on nuclear research, scientific documents, newspaper reports, scientists' diaries, alchemical recipes, and Faust in a variety of theatrical forms – nightclub acts, lecture demonstrations, magic tricks, and stand-up comedy. In short, the play is a kind of avant-garde VAUDEVILLE, one of the first American works to explore overt political content through Theatre of Images (see INTRODUCTION, §4). More than the "History of Nuclear Power" its subtitle promises, *Dead End Kids* is a surreal history of American hopes and nightmares.   AS

Dean, Julia (1830–68) Actress. Her mother, Julia Drake, was the daughter of pioneer Kentucky manager SAMUEL DRAKE; her father, Edwin Dean,

Brian Dennehy as Willie Loman in the 1999 revival of *Death of a Salesman.* Photo by Eric Y. Exit. *Courtesy:* David Richenthal, producer.

was a pioneer manager in Buffalo. Making her debut at the age of 11, she was the leading American tragic actress by 1846. Marriage to Samuel Hayne in 1855 was disastrous, so she went west in 1856 and established herself as a star in California and Utah for the rest of her life. She specialized in suffering heroines, such as SHAKESPEARE's Juliet and Bulwer-Lytton's Pauline, in which her height, blonde good looks, and deep voice were assets. DMcD

Death of a Salesman by ARTHUR MILLER. ELIA KAZAN directed the premiere production (1949, 742 performances), starring LEE J. COBB (Willy Loman), MILDRED DUNNOCK (Linda), ARTHUR KENNEDY (Biff), and Cameron Mitchell (Happy). A masterful blend of realism and expressionism, perfectly captured in JO MIELZINER's evocative design, this award-winning play (Pulitzer, Drama Critics' Circle, Tony) is Miller's masterpiece. The central character, now one of the great roles in modern theatre, is Willy Loman, the self-deceiving but well-intended salesman who dreams of success and fortune for himself and his family but achieves neither. From the point of view of his son Biff, "the man didn't know who he was" – a personal tragedy. But the play also suggests, beyond Biff's summation, that Willy failed to understand the society of success that shaped his dreams; and it is an open question whether Biff, whose role is equally important in the play, achieves sufficient understanding to avoid a similar downward spiral to self-destruction – the tragic pattern (in homecoming drama since the

Oresteia) of possible, if not inevitable, recapitulation. The play centers on a few days, but it gains part of its complexity through the use of memory scenes that extend the action over a number of years. Despite the amazing theatrical success of *Salesman*, critics have argued for decades that the play is possibly flawed because it fails to clarify whether society or the individual is responsible for human suffering. Other debates have focused on Willy's lack of tragic stature, his failure to achieve a recognition. Ever sensitive, Miller himself has entered into the debate, in essays and many interviews, defending his play as a "tragedy of the common man." The play, performed almost every year around the country by a professional company and often around the world (from London to Beijing), was revived in NYC in 1975, with GEORGE C. SCOTT (James Farentino as Biff), again in 1984, starring DUSTIN HOFFMAN (with JOHN MALKOVICH as Biff), and most recently in 1998 (GOODMAN)/1999 (Broadway) with BRIAN DENNEHY (Kevin Anderson as Biff and an outstanding Elizabeth Franz as Linda). TP

Deathtrap Two-act drama by IRA LEVIN; opened 26 February 1978 in Broadway's MUSIC BOX THEATRE and later moved to the BILTMORE THEATRE for a run of 1,809 performances – still the fourth longest-running play on Broadway and the longest-running thriller by an American author. Set in Connecticut, this roller-coaster thriller about playwriting juxtaposes murder plots and subplots in a literate script that is chock-full of surprises and twists. EK

DeBar, Ben (1812–77) English-born actor-manager who came to America as an equestrian performer in 1837, but soon specialized in low comedy. He was also stage manager for NOAH LUDLOW and SOL SMITH at the ST. CHARLES THEATRE, New Orleans; when they retired (1843), he assumed management of their New Orleans and St. Louis theatres. At the outbreak of the Civil War he moved to St. Louis, retaining ownership of the St. Charles until 1876. In St. Louis he moved from the St. Louis Theatre to DeBar's Grand Opera House in 1873. He remained active as a performer, touring the Mississippi River Valley as a star every season, and was the most influential manager in the region.   DMcD

Déclassée Three-act drama by ZOË AKINS. Her first and greatest hit, it opened at the EMPIRE THEATRE on 6 October 1919 for a run of 257 performances. ETHEL BARRYMORE starred as Lady Helen, a woman of somewhat tattered reputation who lives on the fringe of good society. In the midst of a misunderstanding about her future husband, Rudolf Solomon (Claude King), she is killed in a tragic but convenient accident.   FB

Dee, Ruby (1924–) African American actress and playwright. Born Ruby Ann Wallace in Cleveland, OH, Dee first acted with the AMERICAN NEGRO THEATRE, and took over the title role for the tour of ANNA LUCASTA (1944). She appeared in various New York productions, attracting attention as Ruth Younger in A RAISIN IN THE SUN (1959), after which her reputation advanced. She was acclaimed as Lutiebelle, the innocent pawn in her husband OSSIE DAVIS's PURLIE VICTORIOUS (1961), and as the long-suffering Lena in *Boesman and Lena* (1970), for which she won the Obie and Drama Desk awards. Her performance in ALICE CHILDRESS's *WEDDING BAND* (1973) also earned her a Drama Desk Award. In SHAKESPEARE, Dee has played Katharina in *The Taming of the Shrew* (1965), Cordelia to MORRIS CARNOVSKY's King Lear (1965), and Gertrude in *Hamlet* (1975). She coauthored the screenplay *Uptight* (1968), in which she starred, and has written plays including *Twin Bit Gardens* (1976); the musical *Take It from the Top* (1979); the biographical *Zora Is My Name* (1983), about Harlem Renaissance writer and folklorist Zora Neale Hurston; *The Disappearance* (1993), adapted from a Rosa Guy 1979 suspense novel (premiered in 1997 at CROSSROADS); and *Two Hah Hahs and a Homeboy* (1995, compiled from other writings, including her own; premiered at Crossroads). As Amanda she appeared in an all-black *The GLASS MENAGERIE* at Washington, DC's ARENA

STAGE in 1989. Her solo show *My One Good Nerve* had a four-week run in NYC in 1998. In 1988 she was elected to the THEATRE HALL OF FAME. Dee possesses an irresistibly enchanting stage personality and is infectiously funny in comedy. With her late husband she received numerous lifetime achievement awards.   EGH

Deep Are the Roots Melodrama by Arnaud d'Usseau and James Gow, produced in 1945 by KERMIT BLOOMGARDEN and George Heller, directed by ELIA KAZAN. A Negro war hero (Gordon Heath) returns to his small southern hometown only to be falsely accused of stealing, then is beaten and jailed. The play promotes the liberal vision of the deep and tangled roots of white supremacy being eroded by time and the tide of human compassion. Press reports of some audience members' reactionary responses to the romantic tension between the hero and the daughter (Barbara BEL GEDDES) of a racist U.S. Senator (Charles Waldron) made the production a liberal cause célèbre.   WD

Deering, Nathaniel (1791–1881) Playwright, lawyer, journalist, and poet from Maine. Deering claimed several plays, but the names of only three have survived: In *Carabasset; or, The Last of the Norridgewocks* (1830), Deering defended this Maine Indian leader; *The Clairvoyants* (1844) satirized spiritualism; and *Bozzaris* (1851) celebrated the hero of the Greek War of Independence.   WJM

Delicate Balance, A Pulitzer Prize–winning drama by EDWARD ALBEE; opened at the MARTIN BECK THEATRE 22 September 1966, running for 132 performances. ALAN SCHNEIDER directed a cast headed by HUME CRONYN and JESSICA TANDY (with MARIAN SELDES winning a Tony as their daughter). The play is an intriguing evocation of modern malaise among materially comfortable people. Critics acknowledged the probity, wit, and truthfulness of the language, but were nonplussed by what WALTER KERR saw as an attempt to "get hold of hollowness." The Paris production (26 October 1967) was highly successful, as was a 1996 revival (Tony) with GEORGE GRIZZARD, ROSEMARY HARRIS, and an all-star cast. A 1973 American Film Theater version featured KATHARINE HEPBURN, Paul Scofield, Lee Remick, KATE REID, and Joseph Cotten.   FHL

Dell'Arte Players Company A Blue Lake, CA–based professional touring company of performer-creators working in the commedia tradition. Carlo Mazzone-Clementi and Jane Hill cofounded

Dell'Arte, Inc. in Berkeley in 1971, and in 1972 taught their first workshop in Blue Lake, where they took up residency in 1973. Artistic directors Joan Schirle, Michael Fields, and Donald Forrest in 1977 became the Dell'Arte Players Co., which has since created 35 original theatre works. The first year of their training program (Dell'Arte International School of Physical Theatre), founded in 1975, is devoted to physical theatre, the second to ensemble acting, with company members and others as faculty. In 1994 the artistic directors collaborated with the ALLEY on a production of *Tartuffe*. In 2000 Dell'Arte received the Cornerstone Grant from the James Irvine Foundation.   TL

DeMille see also DE MILLE

DeMille, Henry C(hurchill) (1850–93) Playwright, native of North Carolina, who prepared for his career by securing a position as a play reader at the MADISON SQUARE THEATRE in 1882. His first play, *John Delmer's Daughter* (1883), dealing with family problems resulting from social climbing, failed. His next play, a frontier melodrama, *The Main Line* (1886), written with Charles Bernard, succeeded not only in New York but on tour, in later productions, and even as revised with Rosabel Morrison as *The Danger Signal* (1891). DeMille made his reputation, however, collaborating with DAVID BELASCO. *The Wife* (1887), which dramatized a husband's resolve to win the love of his wife, who had married him out of pique, received 239 performances. They wrote *Lord Chumley* (1888) for E. H. SOTHERN, who made the young English nobleman a memorable theatre experience. *The Charity Ball* (1889) contrasts a strong clergyman with his weak brother in a plot revealing seduction and greed resolved by love. Their last collaboration, *MEN AND WOMEN* (1890), builds upon banking, speculation, love, and family. Together they produced four of the most popular plays of that period in America.   WJM

Dennehy, Brian (1938–) Connecticut-born actor easily recognized with his barrel chest, sandy (now graying) hair, and imposing presence. Educated at Columbia and Yale, he has long been a presence onscreen, both in features films and especially television. Yet in the past two decades he has emerged as a major stage actor, winning Tonys for Willy Loman in DEATH OF A SALESMAN (1999) and James Tyrone in LONG DAY'S JOURNEY INTO NIGHT (2003). Dennehy took *Death* to London in May 2005 and won the Laurence Olivier Award for Best Actor in 2006. Both productions began at the GOODMAN THEATRE, where Dennehy fre-

quently collaborates with ROBERT FALLS (also *A TOUCH OF THE POET*, 1996; *The ICEMAN COMETH*, 1992; and *Galileo*, 1986). *Poet* was remounted at Dublin's Abbey in 1992. His Irish ancestry and winning smile worked especially well on Broadway (1995) in Friel's *Translations* and in O'NEILL's *Hughie* (TRINITY REP) in 2004. Other stage productions of note include *Streamers*, Lincoln Center (1976); *Rat in the Skull*, Chicago's WISDOM BRIDGE (1985); Peter Brook's *The Cherry Orchard* (1988); and Brady in a 2007 Broadway revival of *Inherit the Wind*.   DBW

Denver Center Theatre   The $13 million Helen G. Bonfils Theatre Complex opened on New Year's Eve, 1979, as part of the Denver (CO) Center for the Performing Arts. The Bonfils Complex comprises three separate theatres: the 550-seat thrust, the 450-seat environmental, and a 150-seat theatre laboratory/rehearsal hall for new American works. The 195-seat Ricketson proscenium venue is also used. Maintaining a professional resident company, the Denver Center Theatre stages 10–12 productions annually plus a new play festival (U.S. West TheatreFest) each spring. To date, the most acclaimed production has been *Black Elk Speaks*, first presented fall 1993. In August 1993 the Center joined with NYC's Director's Company to form a three-year alliance under the banner of the HAROLD PRINCE Musical Theatre Program to create musical pieces and nurture young directors.   TLM

Derwent, Clarence (1884–1959) English-born actor-director who fled his London home to become a provincial bit player. By 1910 he had appeared back in London; in 1915 he came to the U.S. to appear with GRACE GEORGE in SHAW's *Major Barbara*. He went on to appear in some 500 plays and several movies, and occasionally he directed. In 1945 he founded the Clarence Derwent Awards in London and New York for the best performers in supporting roles. Among his many professional offices were two terms as president of ACTORS' EQUITY and the presidency in 1952 of the AMERICAN NATIONAL THEATRE AND ACADEMY. He also chaired the National Center of the International Theatre Institute and was president of the Dramatic Workshop. His autobiography, *The Derwent Story*, appeared in 1954.   SMA

Desert Song, The   Two-act operetta, music by SIGMUND ROMBERG, words by OTTO HARBACH, OSCAR HAMMERSTEIN II, and Frank Mandel; opened 30 November 1926 at the CASINO THEATRE, NYC, running 471 performances. This sweeping romantic saga in the sands of Morocco sees the Frenchwoman Margot (VIVIENNE SEGAL) carried off by her romantic ideal, the masked leader of the native Riffs (Robert Halliday), only to discover that he is really the shy Frenchman she has disdained. Particularly timely in its day (there really was a Riff rebellion in Morocco, and Valentino's *Sheik* films were all the rage), the operetta has proved extremely durable. Romberg's soaring melodies are timeless, and his "desert music" was so right that it has been imitated in films ever since. *The Desert Song* was equally popular in London, where it has been revived professionally numerous times over the years.   JD

Desire under the Elms Although this EUGENE O'NEILL play, which opened 11 November 1924, was notorious for years and became the object of a strident CENSORSHIP attack by New York's district attorney and moral crusaders, it proved to be O'Neill's most successful play until *STRANGE INTERLUDE*. First produced at the Greenwich Village Theatre by Experimental Theatre, Inc., and designed and directed by ROBERT EDMOND JONES, this tragedy featured simultaneous staging and removable walls for its lonely, 1850 New England farmhouse. The play, freely adapted from the Hippolytus/Phaedra tragedies of antiquity, is a study in family struggles that erupt in physical combat; cravings for possession of the land; near-incestuous adulteries between wife and stepson (renamed Abbie and Eben, portrayed by MARY MORRIS and Charles Ellis); and misguided, lustful obsessions that culminate in the murder of an infant. Its heavy New England dialects and homiletic, biblical tone provide bitter counterpoint for the seething, reckless sexuality that drives so much of the action. Just as important as the sexual struggle is the oppressive conflict of Eben with his father, Ephraim, first played by WALTER HUSTON. The uncompromising patriarch drives his young wife and tormented son to subterfuge and their subsequent crimes of passion. A 1952 Broadway revival starred Karl Malden (Ephraim) and Carol Stone (Abbie).   RHW

Desmond Players Mae Desmond (née Mary Veronica Callahan) (1887–1982) and her husband, Frank Fielder, formed the Mae Desmond Players, a "popular-priced" STOCK COMPANY, in Schenectady, NY, in 1917. After brief stints in Elmira and Schenectady, NY, and Scranton, PA, Desmond and Fielder moved their company to their native PHILADELPHIA, where it flourished until 1929. It reached the height of its popular and financial success while occupying the Desmond Theatre in the working-class neighborhood of Kensington, where the management shaped the troupe's repertory to appeal to German and Irish Roman Catholics in the area. Desmond's manifold appeals as a skilled comedienne, as well as a paragon of Irish beauty, Catholic morality, and fashionable correctness, were keys to the company's success.
    WD

DeSylva, B. G. "Buddy" [né George Gard] (1869–1950), lyricist, librettist; **Lew Brown** [né Louis Brownstein] (1893–1958), librettist, lyricist, director, producer; and **Ray Henderson** [né Raymond Brost] (1896–1970), composer. Although they each worked with others, DeSylva, Brown, and Henderson are best known for the American musicals they created together in the 1920s. DeSylva studied at the University of Southern California before writing songs for AL JOLSON's shows *Sinbad* (1918) and *Bombo* (1921). With GEORGE GERSHWIN he wrote the score of *La, La, Lucille* (1919) and the 1922–4 GEORGE WHITE's Scandals. Born in Russia, Brown wrote popular songs for the publisher Albert von Tilzer and had some of his songs interpolated into Broadway shows. Henderson received musical training at the Chicago Conservatory of Music before becoming a vaudeville accompanist, music arranger, and song plugger. Together, the three wrote the score for the 1926 and 1928 editions of the revue series *George White's Scandals*. In 1927 they created the book and score of *Good News,* a frothy musical with a college setting that ran for 557 performances. Their subsequent shows included *Hold Everything* (1928), *Follow Thru* (1929), and *Flying High* (1930). DeSylva went to Hollywood to become a film producer in the early 1930s, eventually becoming head of Paramount Studios. He continued to write lyrics and librettos, some in partnership with Brown and Henderson, for such shows as *Take a Chance* (1932), *Strike Me Pink* (1933), *DU BARRY WAS A LADY* (1939), *Louisiana Purchase* (1940), and *Panama Hattie* (1940). Brown continued to work on Broadway as a librettist, director, and producer, with shows such as *Calling All Stars* (1934) and *Yokel Boy* (1939); he also produced films in Hollywood. Henderson continued to write music for Broadway shows, such as *Say When* (1934) and the ZIEGFELD *Follies* (1943), as well as for Hollywood films. DeSylva, Brown, and Henderson perfectly captured the lighthearted spirit of the 1920s in songs such as "The Best Things in Life are Free" and "You're the Cream in My Coffee."   MK

Detective Story by SIDNEY KINGSLEY. Presented by CROUSE and LINDSAY, Kingsley directed his play at the Hudson Theatre, with sets by BORIS ARONSON, opening 23 March 1949 (581 performances). Starring RALPH BELLAMY as a fanatical Detective McLeod and Meg Mundy as his wife, with strong assists from Lee Grant as a gabby and moronic shoplifter, Horace MacMahon as a tough detective lieutenant, James Westerfield as a slightly boozy, compassionate detective, JOSEPH WISEMAN and Michael Strong as personifications of evil, and Joan Copeland as a voice for good, it was noted as a rousing, almost-documentary story of good and evil in a New York City police precinct station. Featuring strong characters that could have carried the play in many directions, the ending is powerful, melodramatic, and arbitrary. A credible revival was staged at the Shaw Theatre Festival in Canada in 2002.   GSA

Detour, The Three-act drama by OWEN DAVIS; opened 23 August 1921 at the Astor Theatre in New York and ran a brief 48 performances. Davis, credited with writing some 300 plays, was known for his melodramas; DETOUR departed from this style by telling a more realistic story of a New England family seemingly caught in an unending cycle of farm life from one generation to the next. EFFIE SHANNON played the role of Helen Hardy, a stalwart farm wife who saves her egg money in hopes of enabling her daughter, Kate (played by Angela McCahill) to escape to the city. Augustin Duncan played the husband, Stephen, and directed the play. Davis credits Duncan in his autobiography (*I'd Like to Do It Again,* 1931) as critical to shaping the play.   KN

DeWalden, Thomas Blaydes (1811–73) Playwright and actor, born in London, where he first appeared in the Haymarket in 1834. He came to the U.S. in 1844 and became a productive journeyman playwright whose works occasionally reflected American interests. Of such plays, *The Upper Ten and the Lower Twenty* (1854) ridiculed New York society; *Manifest Destiny* (1855) and *Wall Street* (1855) made fun of America's love of independence and speculation; and *British Neutrality* (1869) suggested the author's view of the Civil War. DeWalden created successful vehicles for F. S. CHANFRAU with *Sam* (1865) – 783 performances – and the pioneer play KIT, THE ARKANSAS TRAVELLER (1870).   WJM

Dewhurst, Colleen (1926–91) Canadian-born actress whose robustness qualified her ideally for certain EUGENE O'NEILL heroines, most notably Josie in *A MOON FOR THE MISBEGOTTEN*, for which she received a Tony in a 1973 revival directed by

JOSÉ QUINTERO. "I love the O'Neill women," she said. "They move from the groin rather than the brain. To play O'Neill . . . you can't sit and play little moments of sadness or sweetness." Ironically, her professional New York career began as one of the Neighbors in *DESIRE UNDER THE ELMS* in 1952 (in 1963 she played Abbie Putnam for CIRCLE IN THE SQUARE). Other O'Neill productions of note included *More Stately Mansions* (1967), a 1972 revival of *MOURNING BECOMES ELECTRA,* and 1988 revivals of *LONG DAY'S JOURNEY INTO NIGHT* and *AH, WILDERNESS!* She also appeared in three EDWARD ALBEE plays, including a 1976 revival of *WHO'S AFRAID OF VIRGINIA WOOLF?* In 1960 she received her first Tony Award for Mary Follet in *All the Way Home.* Dewhurst was also praised for her work in the classics, especially Shakespeare, most notably for JOSEPH PAPP'S NEW YORK SHAKESPEARE FESTIVAL in the late 1950s. In the 1970s she appeared at Papp's PUBLIC THEATER in several productions, including *O'Neill and Carlotta* (1979). In 1985 she was elected president of Actors' Equity, a position she held until shortly before her death. Her final New York stage appearances was in GURNEY'S *Love Letters* (1989); her final film was 1991's *Dying Young* with her son Campbell Scott.   DBW

Dexter, John (1925–90) British director. In addition to successful careers at London's ROYAL COURT THEATRE in the mid- and late 1950s and the NATIONAL THEATRE in the mid-1960s, Dexter was well represented on U.S. stages. His production of Wesker's *Chips with Everything* was seen in 1963, followed by a stunning production of Peter Shaffer's *The Royal Hunt of the Sun* (1965). This effort established a reputation for ingenuity, theatricality, and visual impact, noted in later New York productions of Shaffer's *Equus* (1974) and HWANG's *M. BUTTERFLY* (1988). As the Metropolitan Opera's director of production and later advisor (1974–84), he directed numerous controversial productions, several with David Hockney designs. His final U.S. production was a disastrous revival of *Threepenny Opera* (1989) with Sting. Considered by some "tough, tart, and acerbic" to work for, Dexter, an intuitive rather than intellectual director, also elicited great loyalty from actors willing to adhere to his methodology, a sentiment reflected in the title of his posthumous autobiography, *An Honourable Beast* (1993).   DBW

Diary of Anne Frank, The, opened 5 October 1955 at the CORT THEATRE and ran 717 performances. Adapted by Frances Goodrich (Hackett) and Albert Hackett from *Anne Frank: Diary of a Young Girl,* with Susan Strasberg in the title role, the play dramatizes segments from 13-year-old Anne's diary from July 1942 until her capture in August 1944, and portrays the routine of daily life carried out while the Frank family hid from the Nazis. Anne's persistent attempt to derive joy and a sense of beauty from her rigidly bounded world and the play's poignant optimism are typified in her diary's last line: "In spite of everything I still believe people are really good at heart." The play succeeded internationally, winning the New York Drama Critics' Circle (1955) and Tony (1956) Best Play awards, and the Pulitzer Prize for Drama (1956). A newly revised Broadway version written by Wendy Kesselman and directed by JAMES LAPINE in a less sentimental, more astringent tone was presented in 1997.   RW

Dietz, Howard (1896–1983) Lyricist, librettist, and director. After serving in the Navy during WWI, he began writing song lyrics, at the same time starting a long career as public-relations director for MGM. Teaming with composer ARTHUR SCHWARTZ, he continued to write lyrics for a series of intimate revues, including *The Little Show* (1929), *The Second Little Show* (1930), *Three's a Crowd* (1930), *The Band Wagon* (1931), *Flying Colors* (1932), and *At Home Abroad* (1935). Among later shows were the revue *Inside U.S.A.* (1948) and two book musicals, also with Schwartz: *The Gay Life* (1961) and *Jennie* (1963). His pensive, often ironic lyrics, such as those for "Dancing in the Dark" (also the title of his 1974 autobiography), were a distinguishing feature of the 1930s intimate REVUE.   MK

Digges, Dudley (1879–1947) Actor and director, born in Dublin and a member of the original Abbey Players. He made his New York debut in 1904 with MINNIE MADDERN FISKE. In 1919 he appeared in *Bonds of Interest* for the THEATRE GUILD, for whom he eventually played more than 3,500 times (including the role of James Caesar in *John Ferguson*) and staged four plays. Reviewing his final appearance, as Harry Hope in O'NEILL's *The ICEMAN COMETH*, BROOKS ATKINSON remarked that Digges's "command of the actor's art of expressing character and theme is brilliantly alive; it overflows with comic and philosophical expression." Digges also appeared in more than 50 films and served as vice president of Actors' Equity Association.   SMA

Dillingham, Charles Bancroft (1868–1934) Drama critic for the New York *Evening Post* before becoming a tour manager for JULIA MARLOWE in 1898. He managed several eminent actors and actresses,

including MAXINE ELLIOTT, HENRY MILLER, FRITZI SCHEFF, and Irene Castle, and produced more than 200 plays, musicals, and spectacles. He was most celebrated for lavish, tasteful musicals scored by VICTOR HERBERT or JEROME KERN, and for the elaborate spectacles he produced while managing the HIPPODROME in New York (1914–23). He installed the first moving electric sign in New York for his production of Herbert's *The Red Mill* (1906). He also built the Globe Theatre, near Broadway, and managed it from 1910 until losing it in bankruptcy proceedings in 1933.   WD

Dining Room, The, by A. R. GURNEY JR., opened at the Studio Theatre at PLAYWRIGHTS HORIZONS 24 February 1982, running 511 performances. The play uses attitudes of various generations of several nonspecific families toward a formal dining room to represent the passing of WASP tradition and authority. The attitudes of the characters reveal the type and degree of value each generation places on the room and, by inference, the WASP tradition. By means of overlapping scenes, intermixed chronology, and multiple characterizations, the author focuses attention on the room and the tradition it represents, avoiding the appearance of a dynastic chronicle.   RW

Dinner at Eight by GEORGE S. KAUFMAN and EDNA FERBER, directed by Kaufman, opened on Broadway 22 October 1932 and ran 232 performances. The plot concerns Millicent Jordan's dinner party for Lord and Lady Ferncliffe, as well as the sordid intrigues of the guests' personal lives, which are revealed as the date approaches. Ultimately, although the guests of honor break their engagement, and the hostess's husband develops a fatal heart condition and loses his business to a takeover artist, they proceed heroically with the party. The original cast included Cesar Romero and SAM LEVENE in secondary roles. MGM's film version, released in 1933, starred MARIE DRESSLER, Wallace Beery, Jean Harlow, BILLIE BURKE, and both John and Lionel Barrymore (see DREW–BARRYMORE FAMILY). A 2002 revival at Lincoln Center's VIVAN BEAUMONT THEATRE was directed by GERALD GUTIERREZ.   JDM

Dinner with Friends DONALD MARGULIES's 2000, four-character Pulitzer Prize–winning play that deals with the disintegration of a marriage over a dozen plus years. A suburban couple, Gabe (Matthew Arkin) and Karen (Lisa Emery) bring together Beth (Julie White) and Tom (Kevin Kilner), who marry, bond with their friends, but then separate (due ostensibly to another woman).

Tom confesses that he has never been happy with Beth, thus shattering trust between Gabe and Karen. Opening 4 November 1999 OFF-BROADWAY at the Variety Arts Theater, directed by DANIEL SULLIVAN, the bitter comedy ran 240 performances, after previous productions at ACTORS THEATRE OF LOUISVILLE and SOUTH COAST REPERTORY. DBW

Disney Theatrical Productions Founded in 1994 to exploit properties controlled by Disney for the stage, the company inaugurated its operations with *Beauty and the Beast* (as of May 2007 the sixth-longest-running show in Broadway history, despite tepid critical response). Having paid for the restoration of the NEW AMSTERDAM THEATRE, which reopened in 1997 with Alan Menken and Tim Rice's oratorio *King David,* Disney followed the same year with the megahit *The LION KING* (six Tonys including Best Musical). In June 1999 Disney premiered its first musical outside the U.S. (an adaptation of the film *The Hunchback of Notre Dame* in Berlin), and in March 2000 *Aida* (score by Elton John and Tim Rice) began a 1,852-performance, four-and-a-half-year run at the PALACE THEATRE. A revue/concert, *On the Record,* drawn from Disney's vast catalog of songs, began a national tour November 2004 (foreshortened by critical pans), while *Mary Poppins* (produced with Cameron MacKintosh) was playing in London. (It opened on Broadway in November 2006.) *Tarzan* (music by Phil Collins, book by DAVID HENRY HWANG) opened to tepid reviews in May 2006 and is rumored to have cost $10–15 million. Still in development as of 2006 are stage versions of *The Little Mermaid, Pinocchio,* and a Harlem Globetrotters musical (book and lyrics by SUZAN-LORI PARKS). The corporate giant also develops mini-musicals for its theme parks, such as *Aladdin* at Anaheim's California Adventure (2003). DBW

Dithmar, Edward A. (1854–1917) Drama critic. Born in New York, Dithmar began his career in 1871 with the *New York Evening Post.* He moved to the *New York Times* in 1877, where he became night editor in 1882 and drama critic in 1884, replacing George Edgar Montgomery. After giving way to JOHN CORBIN in 1901, he served as the *Times's* London correspondent (1901–2), editor of its *Saturday Review of Books* (1902–7), and editorial writer (1907–17). He authored *John Drew* (1900) and *Memoirs of Daly's Theatre* (1897), and coedited with AUGUSTIN DALY *A Portfolio of Players.* His business relationship with Daly may have compromised his reputation. Dithmar is best remembered as an outspoken advocate of American drama. TLM

Divorce Five-act drama by AUGUSTIN DALY and, though not the first, the most successful American play of the century on the divorce theme. Opening 5 September 1871, it ran a record 200 continuous performances (236 that season) and had an impressive stage history throughout the 1890s. Daly based the play loosely on Anthony Trollope's novel *He Knew He Was Right,* and added a subplot moving the setting from Europe to the U.S. The threatened divorces of two sisters, Fanny (CLARA MORRIS) and Lu (FANNY DAVENPORT), are complicated by machinations of the shady divorce lawyer Jitt (JAMES LEWIS). DBW

Dixey, Henry E. (1859–1943) Actor. He began acting at age 9 in a Boston production of *UNDER THE GASLIGHT.* Numerous appearances in musicals and straight plays (mostly comedies) during a 58-year career included a season in AUGUSTIN DALY's company and roles in GILBERT AND SULLIVAN. His greatest creation, the title role of *ADONIS* (1884), made him a matinee idol and featured a memorable imitation of Henry Irving. This role was followed in importance by his portrayals of David Garrick in STUART ROBSON's *Oliver Goldsmith* (1899), Lieutenant Robert Warburton in *The Man on the Box* (1905), and Peter Swallow (opposite MRS. FISKE) in *Mrs. Bumpstead-Leigh* (1911). DBW

Dock Street Theatre Charleston, SC, 135 Church St. (formerly Dock). On this site in 1736 was built a theatre claimed by some as the first in the nation. Its fate is unclear – it may have been destroyed in one of numerous "great fires" – but it definitely fades from history after 1738. The Planter's Hotel was built on the lot in 1809, and though it prospered for 50 years, it fell ultimately on hard times. Funds from the WPA in the 1930s led to a restoration of the hotel and the construction within of the present Dock Street Theatre (the stage supposedly on the site of the original theatre). It is owned by the city. DBW

Dockstader, Lew [né George Alfred Clapp] (1856–1925) Comedian who preserved the MINSTREL SHOW's vitality while injecting it with political satire. He had begun in blackface as a teenager and formed his own company with Charles Dockstader in 1876, retaining the name after his partner retired in 1883. His new partnership with George Primrose created the most popular turn-of-the-century minstrel troupe in the U.S. (1898–1913). Dockstader performed in two-foot-long shoes and a coat with a 30-inch tail; his best song was "Everybody Works but Father." Before he became a solo monologuist on the KEITH Circuit, he had given a start to AL JOLSON.   LS

documentary theatre Also called "theatre of fact," "theatre of testimony," "docudrama," or "reality-based theatre." Constructed out of actual dialogue from real people and found texts from historical archives, this form blends advocacy journalism, oral history, and dramatic techniques to create a theatrical representation of societal and political forces using a close reexamination of events, individuals, and situations. Documentary theatre relies on everything from the playwright's selection and treatment of the facts, the director's presentation of the material, and the actors' performances to build its own texture, narrative, and logic. Documentary theatre weaves together fragments of evidence to create a nonfiction script, with the sources of speech often lifted from interviews, court trial transcripts, print media articles, broadcast transcripts, recordings of live speeches, and public hearings. Sometimes the playwright makes his or her presence or position felt within the play so that the spectator can feel oriented with a story that has been subjectively chiseled from rough material.

The history of documentary theatre has been traced as far back as 492 B.C., when Phrynichus wrote *The Capture of Miletus,* about the destruction of the Greek city Miletus during the Persian Wars. Documentary-theatre techniques also arose in the USSR for propaganda purposes after the revolution in 1917; it was likewise present in the epic-theatre tradition initiated by ERWIN PISCATOR and BERTOLT BRECHT in Germany in the 1920s. In the 1960s, post-WWII documentary theatre was associated primarily with Rolf Hochhuth, Peter Weiss, and Heinar Kipphardt, whose political plays presented extracts from recent historical events, especially the official documents and court records detailing the political horrors of the Nazi era and the development of the hydrogen bomb.

The popularity of the American form of documentary theatre largely grew out of The LIVING NEWSPAPER, which was initiated in the U.S. in 1935 as part of the FEDERAL THEATRE PROJECT – although the awareness of the power of the dramatic form could be seen as far back as John Reed's *The Pageant of the Paterson Strike* (1913), which was enacted by more than 1,000 workers in Madison Square Garden, an event supported by the IWW, the Socialist Party, Greenwich Village intellectuals, and a social circle associated with the heiress Mabel Dodge. The Living Newspaper became the most effective and celebrated new theatre form developed by the FTP, until its cancellation in 1939, because it proved to be a valuable instrument of social change, especially in highlighting the statistical and other factual realities of agriculture, housing, and economics.

In the 1960s and '70s, the popular form was used to cut through official versions of recent history; politically committed playwrights exploited the form to fashion dramas about racial prejudice in the United States as well as protests against the war in Vietnam that excerpted materials from the Pentagon Papers or directly culled from the White House tapes of Richard Nixon. Notable works include Martin Duberman's *In White America,* Daniel Berrigan's *Trial of the Catonsville Nine,* and ERIC BENTLEY's *Are You Now or Have You Ever Been?* More distant U.S. history provided the background for HAL HOLBROOK's stage portrayals of Mark Twain (Broadway 1966, 1977, 2005).

Unlike most documentary-theatre productions of the past, in which the larger point concerned the politically effective exploration of social issues as adapted to theatrical presentation, contemporary proponents of the form stress the equal importance of innovative performance techniques and artful presentation, without stinting on or perhaps without giving less emphasis to the necessity of biographical research or of documentation itself. In exploring a diverse array of issues and topics, significant practitioners in the recent wave include EMILY MANN (*Execution of Justice*), Steve Dobbins (*The Dan White Incident*), ANNA DEAVERE SMITH (*Fires in the Mirror: Crown Heights, Brooklyn, and Other Identities* and *Twilight: Los Angeles, 1992*), ROBERT WILSON's *CIVIL WarS,* PING CHONG (*The Undesirable Elements*), SPALDING GRAY (*Swimming to Cambodia*), Marc Wolf (*Another American: Asking and Telling*), Michael Rohd (*Witness Our Schools*), the TECTONIC THEATER PROJECT (*The Laramie Project*), and Doug Wright's Pulitzer Prize–winning *I AM MY OWN WIFE,* among others. In many of these, being faithful to the record is only part of the objective, and sometimes not even the most essential part of the documentary-theatre impulse.   RG

Dodger Productions Founded in 1978, this group also goes by the names Dodger Theatricals, Dodger Stage Holding, Dodger Endemol Theatricals, etc. Its principals include producers Michael David and ROCCO LANDESMAN and director DES MCANUFF. Its roots, however, date back to the Chelsea Theatre Center, founded by director ROBERT KALFIN in 1965, which settled at the BROOKLYN ACADEMY OF MUSIC in 1968 with three Yale School of Drama graduates (Kalfin, artistic direc-

The Dolly Sisters, Rosie and Jenny, during an appearance at B. F. Keith's Alhambra Theatre. *Courtesy:* Laurence Senelick Collection.

tor; David, executive director; Burl Hash, production director) producing sophisticated work and earning commercial transfers – notably the revised, Wheeler–WILBUR–BERNSTEIN musical version of Voltaire's CANDIDE. David and Hash left when Chelsea relocated to Manhattan in 1978; for the next quarter-century Dodger, following a NEW YORK SHAKESPEARE FESTIVAL residency, gradually dominated Broadway producing, from musical revivals (42ND STREET, INTO THE WOODS, The MUSIC MAN, 1776, A FUNNY THING HAPPENED ON THE WAY TO THE FORUM, The KING AND I, GUYS AND DOLLS, HOW TO SUCCEED IN BUSINESS WITHOUT REALLY TRYING), to original musicals (URINETOWN, Titanic, Footloose, The Who's Tommy, JELLY'S LAST JAM, The SECRET GARDEN, Big River). In the 1990s, Dodger's alliance with Stage Holding, a Dutch live-entertainment conglomerate, infused even more cash, permitting it to expand into touring operations, marketing, and management. In 1998, Dodger bought the historic Eaves–Brooks Costume Company (renamed Dodger Costumes) and announced in 2002 it would convert a subterranean multiplex in Midtown Manhattan into five OFF-BROADWAY theatres (Dodger Stages). By 2004, such expensive failures as the jukebox musical *Good Vibrations* soured Stage Holding's ZIEGFELD-esque impresario, Joop van den Ende, on the

alliance. With fiscal ties cut, the costume collection was sold (see SUPPORT SERVICES) and drastic staff reductions ordered. At middecade, it remained unclear if Dodger would remain the producing juggernaut it had been.   LJ

Dodson, Owen (1914–83) Poet, novelist, playwright, director, and teacher. A graduate of Bates College and the Yale School of Drama, Dodson became a prominent figure in African American academic theatre through his many memorable productions, including Shakespeare. He trained a number of successful practitioners, including OSSIE DAVIS, AMIRI BARAKA, and Debbie Allen. Dodson's own plays have been produced in college theatres, including *Divine Comedy*, about the career of the evangelist Father Divine, and *Bayou Legend*, an adaptation of *Peer Gynt* set in Louisiana. James Hatch's biography, *Sorrow Is the Only Faithful One*, was published in 1993.   EGH

Dolly Sisters [née Deutsch] Hungarian-born twins – JENNY (Yansci) (1893–1941) and ROSIE (Roszika) (1893–1970) – who from their vaudeville debut in 1909 became chic VAUDEVILLE and REVUE headliners specializing in unvarying dance routines and attempts at singing. The Gabors of their time, they ultimately made their reputation with their wardrobe and costume changes, especially in numerous appearances at the PALACE, in the ZIEG-FELD *Follies of 1911,* and in myriad musical comedies. In the 1920s, essentially as part of the art deco movement, they were seen frequently in Paris and London music halls. A 1946 film of their lives starred Betty Grable and June Haver.   DBW

Donat, Peter [né Pierre Collingwood Donat] (1929–) Canadian-born actor, nephew of the screen star Robert Donat, who has had success in regional theatre, television, and films. He trained at the Yale Drama School and spent six seasons at the Stratford, ON, Shakespeare Festival before joining SAN FRANCISCO's AMERICAN CONSERVA-TORY THEATER in 1968 with his then-wife, actress Michael Learned. With short breaks for meaty TV and movie character roles, Donat has stayed with ACT to appear in many leading roles, including his poignant Cyrano (filmed for PBS), Dysart in *Equus,* and the betrayed Horace Giddens in *The LITTLE FOXES.*   MB

Donehue, Vincent J. (1915–66) Known as an "unobstrusive though easy and fluent" director, Donehue's Broadway directing debut was FOOTE's *The Trip to Bountiful* (1953). He won a Tony for DORE SCHARY's *Sunrise at Campobello* (1958), and directed *The SOUND OF MUSIC* (1959) and the Mary Martin videotape of *PETER PAN* (1960).   REK

Doubt: A Parable MANHATTAN THEATRE CLUB's production of JOHN PATRICK SHANLEY's critically acclaimed play began its run in November 2004, transferring to Broadway spring 2005. Shanley's first Broadway production – after a lengthy writing career – won a Pulitzer, two Drama Desk Awards (including Best Play), and four Tonys: for Best Play, for CHERRY JONES as Sister Aloysius, for Adriane Lenox (Featured Role, Mrs. Muller), and for DOUG HUGHES as Best Director, among other recognitions. As impeccably directed by Hughes, the four-character play centers on Sister Aloysius, who runs the Saint Nicholas Church School in the Bronx in 1964 (a setting influenced by Shanley's days in a Bronx Catholic school) – although the story also reflects concerns about pederasty in the priesthood in the plot complication (an encounter by the school chaplain, played superbly by Brian F. O'Byrne, with the school's token black student, the unseen Donald Muller), with Sister Aloysius emerging as the heavy (but not a villain). As BEN BRANTLEY noted, the play is "written with an uncanny blend of compassion and detachment" and is far more complex than descriptions suggest.   DBW

Douglas [né Hesselberg]**, Melvyn** (1901–81) Actor, director, and producer who first toured in repertory and STOCK, then spent two years with JESSIE BONSTELLE's company, headed his own company briefly, and debuted on Broadway in 1928. His first hit, *Tonight or Never* (1930), costarred Helen Gahagan, whom he married. From 1931 to 1942 he starred in 45 movies. In 1952 he appeared on Broadway in *TIME OUT FOR GINGER,* and in 1955 replaced PAUL MUNI as Drummond in *INHERIT THE WIND* to critical acclaim. Douglas had begun as a debonair and dapper leading man in romantic comedies, but matured into a forceful character actor of considerable stature. He won a Tony in 1960 for *The Best Man.* An autobiography was published posthumously in 1986.   SMA

Douglass, David (c. 1720–89) British-born actor-manager who became the central figure in the history of the American theatre from his marriage in 1758 to the widow of Lewis HALLAM Sr., in Jamaica, to the American Revolution. Douglass returned to New York in 1758 as head of Hallam's London Company of Comedians (renamed in 1763 The AMERICAN COMPANY of Comedians). For 17 years Douglass's company played up and down the East Coast, erecting temporary theatres in most towns. In 1766 he built the first permanent theatre in the U.S., the SOUTHWARK in Philadelphia, followed in 1767 by the JOHN STREET Theatre in New York. In April 1767 Douglass announced the first professional production of a play by an American-born writer, a comic opera called *The Disappointment;* this was replaced at the last minute by Thomas Godfrey's *The Prince of Parthia,* the first native tragedy to be presented professionally (see INTRODUCTION, §1). Before the outbreak of hostilities, Douglass and his company returned to the West Indies in 1775, where he became a justice, an officer in the militia, and a member of the Council. Douglass was America's first Falstaff and King John; though a poor actor, he was a superb manager.   DBW

Dowling, Eddie [né Joseph Nelson Goucher] (1894–1976) Pulitzer Prize–abetting producer (1940, *The Time of Your Life*), playwright, songwriter, director, and actor who began his career doing a song-and-dance act in his native state of Rhode Island. His Broadway debut was in VICTOR HER-BERT's *The Velvet Lady* in 1919; he appeared in the ZIEGFELD *Follies* of 1919, 1920, and 1921. In 1945, after rejecting a surefire commercial project, he coproduced and codirected (with MARGO JONES) WILLIAMS's *The GLASS MENAGERIE,* in which he also played Tom. The production made theatrical

history and brought Williams out of obscurity. Dowling produced *Richard II* starring MAURICE EVANS in 1937, and during his long career worked with such playwrights as WILLIAM SAROYAN, Paul Vincent Carroll, Sean O'Casey, and PHILIP BARRY.
DBW

Drabinsky, Garth (1950–) Brash, bigger-than-life Canadian producer-impresario (in the tradition of MICHAEL TODD and DAVID MERRICK) who in a decade became a central player in an infiltration of Broadway. His company – founded in the late 1980s as Live Event but changed in 1995 to Livent – was for a time a colossus, both owning theatres (New York, Toronto, Chicago) and developing projects for them – *RAGTIME*, *Kiss of the Spider Woman*, *SHOW BOAT* revival, *CANDIDE* revival, *Barrymore*, *Parade, Fosse*. He was responsible for the miraculous transformation of the old Lyric and Apollo theatres into the FORD CENTER FOR THE PERFORMING ARTS, which opened in 1998; his productions have won four Tonys for Best Musical (one a revival award). Beginning in the late 1990s Drabinsky and his partner, Myron Gottlieb, have been mired in a deluge of litigation (most unresolved as of 2005) – fraud, kickbacks, conspiracy – in the U.S. and Canada, and bankruptcy. In 1997 his company lost $17 million on revenues of $212 million. Nevertheless, Drabinsky, whose autobiography appeared in 1995, continues to operate as an international theatre consultant in Toronto.
DBW

drag shows see FEMALE/MALE IMPERSONATION

Drake, Alfred (1914–92) Singer and actor. One of the most versatile leading men of the American musical stage, Drake began his Broadway career in GILBERT AND SULLIVAN revivals and then the chorus of the original musical *White Horse Inn* (1936). After featured roles in such shows as *BABES IN ARMS* (1937) and *The Straw Hat Revue* (1939), Drake created the role of Curly in RODGERS and HAMMERSTEIN's *OKLAHOMA!* (1943). Five years later, he played Fred Graham in *KISS ME, KATE*. Praised by critics for his romantic, swaggering portrayal of a Shakespearean actor, Drake's comic abilities received a large share of the acclaim. Among his subsequent musical-theatre appearances, only his performance as Hajj in *KISMET* (1953) was notable. Drake's career as an actor included performances as Othello and Benedick at the AMERICAN SHAKESPEARE FESTIVAL THEATRE, and Claudius opposite RICHARD BURTON in *Hamlet* (1964). His last major role was in a 1975 revival of *The SKIN OF OUR TEETH*. MK

Drake, Samuel (1769–1854) Actor-manager who, after managing in the English provinces, brought his family to America in 1810. After a few years in Boston, the Drakes joined JOHN BERNARD's company in Albany, NY (1813), and in 1815, at the invitation of Luke Usher, Drake took his three sons, two daughters, and five assistants as a company to Frankfort, KY. He extended his influence to Louisville, Lexington, and Cincinnati, a circuit he controlled for many years. Although not the leading company in the West at the time, Drake's group improved performance levels in the area and firmly established the FRONTIER THEATRE. Drake was the grandfather of JULIA DEAN.   SMA

Drake, Sylvie (1930–) Drama critic. Born in Alexandria, Egypt, Drake was educated at a British school, where she earned an Oxbridge Higher Certificate with distinctions in French and English literature. She emigrated to the U.S. and entered the PASADENA PLAYHOUSE in 1949, later working as an actress, director, and television writer. Drake began reviewing theatre in 1969 for the weekly *Los Angeles Canyon Crier* and for the *Los Angeles Times* (on assignment) before joining the latter in 1971 as a theatre columnist and critic. In 1991, upon the retirement of DANIEL SULLIVAN, she became the *Times*'s leading critic, the most powerful such position in Los Angeles, prior to her retiring as "Critic Emeritus" in 1993 and becoming an artistic associate (play development) of the DENVER CENTER THEATRE COMPANY.
TLM

Drama Dept. Not-for-profit theatre collective (actors, directors, playwrights, designers) founded in 1994 with playwright Douglas Carter Beane as its main facilitator. Its mission is the development and production of new and neglected works of American theatre (one or two productions a year at various venues, although a new partnership with Zipper Theater began in 2005). A unique partnership of art and commerce, the collective – 102 members in 2005 – has produced 20 works as of 2007, including Beane's *As Bees in Honey Drown*, David and Amy Sedaris's *The Book of Liz*, Isaac Mizrahi's *Les MIZrahi*, CHARLES BUSCH's *Shanghai Moon*, and revivals of works as disparate as the MOSS HART–IRVING BERLIN musical *As THOUSANDS CHEER*, Ring Lardner and GEORGE S. KAUFMAN's *June Moon*, and a controversial version of *UNCLE TOM'S CABIN* in 1997. Its current membership includes Cynthia Nixon, Sarah Jessica Parker, B. D. WONG, BILLY CRUDUP, MARK BROKAW, Stephen Flaherty, RICHARD GREENBERG, and NICKY SILVER, among others.   DBW

Drama League, The, was founded in 1909 by an Evanston, IL, ladies' literary society, the "Riley Circle." Their first national gathering was held in 1910 at a church in Evanston, and at their constitutional convention that year at the Chicago Art Institute, attended by some 200 delegates representing 63 local centers, Mrs. A. Starr Bast was elected president and proclaimed their goals: "to stimulate interest in the best drama"; "to awaken the public to the importance of the theatre as a social force." The organization expanded rapidly from 12,000 members in 25 states in 1911 to 23,000 members, 100,000 affiliated members, and 114 centers throughout the country by the early 1920s. They published a quarterly, *The Drama* (1911), "to cultivate a deeper understanding and appreciation for American drama and theatre"; issued 250 bulletins (1910–16) endorsing current productions; sponsored tours by the HULL-HOUSE Players, the Irish Players, MRS. FISKE, GEORGE ARLISS, and others; published 20 volumes of "good" plays; conducted summer instructional institutes; and held annual conventions in Chicago, New York, St. Louis, Pittsburgh, and Detroit. After the national organization was disbanded (1931), local centers continued to function, in particular the New York Drama League, which celebrated its 75th anniversary in 1992. In addition to a number of major awards this remnant of the League assists young playwrights and oversees the Directors Fellows Program, which provides young directors entry-level intensive professional experience.   RM

dramatic theory
19th century

Without exception, American men and women who wrote plays before the Civil War were either amateurs, journeymen-playwrights who acted or managed theatres, or literary people who decided to write a play or two. They had objectives – vague or particular, commercial or artistic – and some had read traditional dramatic theory, but they did not contribute to it.

This situation did not, of course, eliminate critics of American drama or stridently voiced observations on particular plays or the directions that American drama should take. Such opinions, generally with a religious or national bias, have always been freely expressed. JAMES KIRKE PAULDING made a somewhat desperate plea for "American Drama" in the *American Quarterly Review* of June 1827. Only occasionally did essayists have a theoretical bent. John Neal wrote five essays on "The Drama" for the *Yankee and Boston Literary Gazette* (Aug. 1829), one concerned with "Strictures of Dramatic Writing, Theatrical Representation and the Laws of Drama." Robert Walsh, editor and journalist, included two essays on "The Stage" and "Tragic Acting" in his collected essays, *Didactics: Social, Literary, and Political* (1836). An abundance of essays, mainly critical, sometimes bordering on the theoretical, appeared through the 19th century: W. A. Jones, "Nationality in Literature," *Democratic Review* 20 (1847): 264–72; G. H. Calvert, "A National Drama," *Putnam's Monthly Magazine* 9 (Feb. 1857): 148–51; Mary W. Alexander, "Tragedy and Tragedians," *The Ladies Repository* 25 (Oct. 1865): 615–17; Brander Matthews, "The Dramatic Outlook in America," *Harper's New Monthly Magazine* 78 (May 1889): 924–30.

For late 19th-century playwrights, a single outstanding essay should be noted: "American Playwrights on the American Drama," *Harper's Weekly* 33 (2 Feb. 1889): 97–l00. In brief space, playwrights AUGUSTIN DALY, Edward Harrigan, Bronson Howard, WILLIAM GILLETTE, John Grosvenor Wilson, and STEELE MACKAYE offer some ideas about their dramaturgy. It is an uneven but revealing presentation, capped by WILLIAM WINTER'S summary observation.

Those American playwrights who thought and wrote about their theories of dramaturgy are Dion Boucicault, Bronson Howard, Edward Harrigan, David Belasco, W. D. Howells, and James A. Herne. BOUCICAULT expressed his theories most specifically in 13 essays written for the *North American Review* between 1877 and 1889. For example, in "The Art of Dramatic Composition" (Jan.–Feb. 1878), he defined drama in nearly Aristotelian fashion as "the imitation of a complete action, formed by a sequence of incidents designed to be acted not narrated, by the person or persons whom such incidents befall. Its object is to give pleasure by exciting in the mind of the spectator a sympathy for fellow creatures suffering their fate."

BRONSON HOWARD, a man of definite opinions, presented his theories in a lecture entitled "The Laws of Dramatic Composition" (1886) – published as *The Autobiography of a Play* (1914). This included "Trash on the Stage and the Lost Dramatists of America," in which he emphasized a commonsense approach to character motivations plus those "satisfactory" actions within a well-constructed play that must reach a properly moral and happy conclusion. EDWARD HARRIGAN, as both comedian and playwright, was caught up in a realistic representation of society in New York City. He wanted to present a "series of photographs of life today," he wrote in the *Harper's Weekly* essay, and believed in "Holding the Mirror up to Nature" (*Pearson's Magazine,* Nov. 1903). This was the major thrust of his dramaturgy.

DAVID BELASCO carried his interest in realism to an extreme and constantly wrote about his theories, which he always equated with his life and work: "How I Stage My Plays," *Theater Magazine* 2 (Dec. 1902): 31–2; "Why I Believe in the Little Things," *Ladies Home Journal* 28 (Sept. 1911): 15; "Beauty as I See It," *Arts and Decoration* 19 (July 1923): 9–10; "About Play Production," *Saturday Evening Post* 10 (Jan. 1920): 17; *The Theatre through Its Stage Door,* 1919. WILLIAM DEAN HOWELLS, the father of American realism, looked at drama as a playwright and critic. Most of his theorizing about the drama appears in numerous essays, but *Criticism and Fiction* (1891) contains the essence of his theory of realism as it applied to drama and to fiction. "Prose is now indisputably the dialect of the stage," he stated from "The Easy Chair," in 1902. Dramatists, he noted, are also moralists in both "the larger and lesser sense" – simply propriety or the universal problem of values. Most important, however, the drama must be a truthful and faithful representation of the lives of men and women.

The most significant dramatic theorist of the 19th century was JAMES A. HERNE. A collaborator with Belasco, influenced by Howells as well as Ibsen, Thomas Hardy, and Émile Zola, Herne created his own theory as "Art for Truth's Sake in the Drama" [*Arena* (Feb. 1897): 361–70]. Truthfulness is the "supreme quality" of all drama, which must "interest" and "instruct." Art for Truth's Sake emphasizes "humanity" and "perpetuates the life of its time." WJM

20th century

At the beginning of the 20th century BRANDER MATTHEWS championed drama as an art separate from literature, emphasizing the importance of action, of appeal to the audience, and of understanding a play in light of its original performance conditions. At the same time Joel Elias Spingarn, a Crocean "new critic," condemned Matthews's interest in drama as a special genre and in its historical surroundings, establishing a debate that echoed in America for several generations between the followers of these influential professors.

The great creative surge in turn-of-the-century European theatre reached America during WWI, its critical voice provided by the journal THEATRE ARTS, founded in 1916 by SHELDON CHENEY. Major contemporary European theorists were represented here along with their American disciples, led by KENNETH MACGOWAN, who became

coeditor in 1919, and ROBERT EDMOND JONES, who became editor in 1922. Following theorists like Craig and Symons in England, these called for a reduced emphasis on language in the theatre and a dedication to a total theatre art of light, color, and rhythm. Macgowan and Jones were also codirectors of the PROVINCETOWN PLAYHOUSE, along with EUGENE O'NEILL, whose scattered theoretical comments echo many of their concerns. O'Neill, however, also speculated on the power of tragedy, which he, like many of the German romantics, felt grew out of the very process of human consciousness.

The nature and function of tragedy inspired a major tradition of theoretical writing in America. O'Neill's contemporaries Ludwig Lewisohn, GEORGE JEAN NATHAN, and W. M. Dixon disagreed on the audience and precise social function of tragedy, but all felt it an uplifting and powerful force in the modern world. JOSEPH WOOD KRUTCH sharply disagreed in his influential 1929 essay "The Tragic Fallacy," arguing that modern man's loss of faith in himself had made this genre obsolete.

During the 1930s and '40s a number of theorists rejected Krutch's analysis. Kenneth Burke and Francis Fergusson suggested basic rhythms or structures beneath tragedy that were not seriously affected by changing historical beliefs. MAXWELL ANDERSON insisted that modern consciousness on such matters was no different from that of the Greeks – an assertion pursued, on more philosophic terms, by Una Ellis-Fermor and James Feibleman. ERIC BENTLEY, in his influential *The Playwright as Thinker* (1946), suggested that the serious genre of tragedy in modern times was best combined with a theatre of ideas. Some playwrights also produced theoretical observations on this matter, most notably ARTHUR MILLER, who defended the common man as a suitable hero for modern tragedy.

During the 1930s an important part of the American drama and of its theory was concerned with political questions. *New Theatre* was founded by associates of the GROUP THEATRE in 1933, seeking to express a more political position, and specifically leftist position than the rather aesthetically oriented *Theatre Arts.* In *New Theatre,* and in the closely related Group Theatre, the work and writings of director LEE STRASBERG, designer MORDECAI GORELIK, and playwright JOHN HOWARD LAWSON contributed greatly to developing a consciousness of theatre as a social instrument, and to making Russian theatre in general and Stanislavsky in particular a touchstone of excellence in American theatre.

Socially and politically oriented theory almost disappeared in America during the rather apathetic 1950s. Major theatrical theory concerned itself with more formal and aesthetic matters. Susan Langer, in *Feeling and Form* (1953), called moral and social questions in drama like represented subjects in painting – useful but not indispensable, as was the defining form. Northrop Frye's *Anatomy of Criticism* (1957) interpreted drama and all literary expression through an all-encompassing symbolic system of unconscious archetypes. Tragedy continued to inspire major studies – by Herbert Weisinger, D. D. Raphael, and Murray Kreiger – but a kind of watershed was marked by George Steiner's *The Death of Tragedy* (1961), which followed Krutch in finding the mythologies of modernism inadequate to provide a basis for the tragic vision. Although a number of subsequent theorists, most notably Elder Olson, disagreed with this conclusion, major theoretical work on tragedy became much rarer after 1960, to be replaced by an interest in dark, ironic blendings of comedy and tragedy, attracting such theorists as Cyrus Hoy and Karl Guthke.

During the 1960s the *Tulane Drama Review* became, as *Theatre Arts* had been earlier, a major conduit for new directions and new theoretical speculations. Jerzy Grotowski, whose approach to acting became for many in this generation as central as Stanislavsky's had been in the 1930s, was introduced to American by *TDR*. A special issue in 1965, coedited by RICHARD SCHECHNER and Michael Kirby, featured John Cage and articles on chance theatre and Happenings. Subsequent special issues charted with great accuracy the rapidly changing interests in theory and performance in America in the late 1960s – politically engaged theatre, AFRICAN AMERICAN THEATRE, and the application of anthropological and sociological theory to theatre. Schechner became particularly interested in this last concern, and his subsequent writings and those of anthropologist Victor Turner involved an important convergence of theatrical and anthropological theory in the 1970s, leading in turn to the development of what came to be called the field of performance studies.

Also during the 1970s a strong interest in "structuralist" analysis appeared in America, although this had little relationship to European structuralism of the same period. Such theorists as Jackson Barry, Bernard Beckerman, Paul Levitt, Roger Gross, and Richard Hornby were in fact more directly in the tradition of Aristotle and late 19th-century German analysts in their approach to the dynamics of drama as a functioning system. European structuralism proved much more influential in America through the closely related study of semiotics, which approached the theatre as a system of signs produced and presented to be interpreted by an audience. Most of the semiotic theory appearing in America has been European in origin, but a number of American theorists, such as Jean Alter, Marvin Carlson, Martin Esslin, and Michael Isaacharoff, have pursued variations of this approach.

European poststructuralism, challenging the tendency of structuralism and semiotics to assume stable, authenticated systems, had much influence on literary theory in America during the 1980s but relatively little on specifically theatrical theory. An important exception was HERBERT BLAU, who, in a series of books beginning with *Take Up the Bodies* (1982), explored relationships between performance and consciousness, of perception utilizing theatre as a means of self-reflection. Another important challenge to semiotically oriented theory came from phenomenological theorists, such as RICHARD FOREMAN and Bert States, who emphasized the importance of the physical reality of theatre impacting upon consciousness.

A growing interest in the social positioning of the theatre and of the audience's role marked much American theory of the late 1980s and early '90s. The influence of reception theory, reader-response theory, and the social dynamics of performance are clearly reflected in such semiotic studies as Carlson's *Signs of Life* (1989) or Alter's *A Socio-semiotic Theory of Theatre* (1990). Blau's *The Audience* (1990) positions the concept of the audience at the center not only of theatre and performance but of cultural expression and psychoanalytic understanding. Other, more directly ideological methodologies also appeared during the 1980s; indeed, the new decade was prophetically launched with the publication of Stephen Greenblatt's *Renaissance Self-Fashioning,* a defining work of what its author called new historicism, and with *The Woman's Part,* the first anthology of feminist criticism of Shakespeare.

A common concern with ideology, culture, and the structures of power may suggest a close relationship between the theoretical approaches of new historicism and feminism; however, new historicism has generally differed from feminism in its relative indifference to contemporary sociopolitical concerns. Its focus has been on past practice, especially during the Renaissance, whose theatre is generally seen not as an agent of social change but as a locus of ambiguous flows of energy similar to those that poststructuralist theorists have postulated in the act of performance.

In *The Feminist Spectator as Critic* (1988), Jill Dolan suggested three general orientations in American feminism (see FEMINIST THEATRE): liberal, cultural or radical, and materialist feminisms. Liberal feminism stresses individuality and "universal human" values and standards. Cultural feminists, fearing that this may simply reinscribe women in the male-dominated patterns of the past, have sought a woman's culture, different and separate from the culture of men. This project was strongly influenced by such French poststructuralist psychoanalytic critics as Julia Kristeva and Luce Irigaray.

Materialist feminism has sought to avoid the universalist tendency of liberal feminism and the essentialist of cultural feminism, to study gender not as biological but as culturally constructed and thus related to systems of social relationships and social power formations. Elin Diamond has suggested that Brechtian techniques might be used to reveal this "constructedness," whereas Sue-Ellen Case and others have argued that lesbian performance (see GAY/LESBIAN THEATRE) could offer an alternative representational strategy to disrupt the traditional heterosexual apparatus of drama with the male as the desiring subject.

In the latter part of the 20th century, dramatic theory in America generated for the first time a major part of theatre research, with a rich and diverse field of theoretical approaches being developed. As the 1990s progressed, social and ideological concerns provided the major new directions, but earlier social, psychoanalytical, linguistic, and philosophical approaches remained important both alone and in combination with the newer strategies. The field of performance studies, pioneered by Schechner and Turner in the 1970s, rapidly expanded during the '80s and '90s, as academic programs in performance studies were founded and many books and articles in this area by Schechner and others appeared. Indeed, Jon McKenzie in *Perform or Else* (2001) claimed "performance" as the key theoretical concept of the new century. Among the effects of this new orientation were a growing interests in nonliterary and non-Western performance and increasingly strong ties between such study and the various social sciences.

During the 1990s and early 2000s gay and lesbian studies gave rise to queer studies, represented in theatre by the work of such theorists as Laurence Senelick and Alisa Solomon. Queer theo-rists have emphasized the multiplicity, openness, and contradictory nature of the theatre, particularly with regard to sexual identity. During this same period gender studies grew in magnitude. The writings of Judith Butler, beginning with her *Gender Trouble* (1990), inspired a fruitful convergence of gender theory and performance theory, resulting in such works as Rebecca Schneider's *The Explicit Body in Performance* (1997). A major new interest in psychoanalytic theory was also inspired by this merging of gender studies and performance studies as may be seen in the work of such theorists as Ann Pellegrini, Lynda Hart, and Peggy Phelan.

The other major direction of theoretical work at the turn of the century developed from the materialist concerns with culture and power that emerged in the 1980s. A central example of this new orientation was Joseph Roach's *Cities of the Dead* (1996), combining strategies from cultural analysis, performance, literary and psychoanalytic studies. In its attention to the interplay of circum-Atlantic performance, Roach's book also was an important early example of postcolonial theory, which shares the interest of performance studies in non-European traditions, and the interest of cultural studies in the operations of power between dominant and dominated cultures. Pioneered by such theorists as Gayatri Spivak and Homi Bhaba, postcolonial theory of the drama has been an international project, but has received important American contributions from such theorists as Loren Kruger, Diane Taylor, and Awan Ampka.   MC*

[*Ed. note:* A useful overview of many of the above theories can be found in Carlson's *Theories of the Theatre* (2d ed., 1993).]

Dramatists Guild, Inc., The   Established in 1920 to protect the rights of dramatic authors for U.S. productions of plays and musicals. Services to more than 7,500 members include the use of OFF-BROADWAY, Broadway, and Resident Theatre production contracts that provide "a fair royalty, maintenance of subsidiary rights, artistic control, and ownership of copyright"; subscriptions to the *Dramatists Guild Quarterly* and the *Newsletter;* use of the Guild's headquarters (Sardi Building) for readings and auditions; nationwide symposia by leading professionals; marketing advice; and a member's "Hotline." In spring 2007 the Dramatists Guild president was John Weidman.   TLM

Draper, Ruth (1884–1956) Actress and monologuist who created and performed a repertoire of

MARIE DRESSLER IN TILLIE'S NIGHTMARE

An advertising card for Marie Dressler in *Tillie's Night-mare,* on tour in 1910. *Courtesy:* Laurence Senelick Collection.

Company playing ingenues, but her mastifflike features and stocky build soon relegated her to farcical roles. She entered New York VAUDEVILLE with "coon" songs and impersonations, and had a real success as the music-hall singer Flo Honey-dew in the comic opera *The Lady Slavey* (1896). JOE WEBER invited her to join his company in *Higgledy-Piggledy* (1904). Her most memorable role was the daydreaming boardinghouse drudge Tillie Blobbs in *Tillie's Nightmare* (Herald Square Theatre, 1910), singing "Heaven Will Protect the Working Girl." This led to a film contract with Mack Sennett for *Tillie's Punctured Romance* (1914), in which she was wooed by Charlie Chaplin; but she never flourished in silent pictures. She was prominent in the Liberty Loan drives of 1917–18 and the actors' strike of 1919, but reached such a low ebb in her career by 1927 that she con-templated opening a hotel in Paris. Fortuitously she returned to Hollywood and won a new pub-lic with ANNA CHRISTIE (1930), DINNER AT EIGHT, and *Tugboat Annie* (both 1933). Her autobiogra-phy appeared in 1934. Modern biographiers were written by Betty Lee (1997) and Matthew Kennedy (1999)   LS

Drew–Barrymore family The name Barrymore, with Lionel, Ethel, and John its foremost expo-nents, stands as a synonym for acting. Franklin Delano Roosevelt was called "a newsreel Barry-more"; Mahatma Gandhi was "the Barrymore of the talking newspapers." *Time* magazine coined "Barrymorishly" to describe how Ethel held the stage. Thirty years after she, the last of the trium-virate, died in 1959, the Barrymores remain the undisputed royal family of a kingdom called Broadway.

Their theatrical pedigree is genuine, traceable to 1752 and, according to family tradition, to strolling players in Shakespeare's time. Their maternal grandmother, **Mrs. John Drew** (1820–97), was born Louisa Lane in London to Thomas Fred-erick Lane, an actor of some provincial fame, and Eliza Trenter, a sweet singer of ballads. After her father's early death, the child toured provincial theatres, playing such roles as Prince Agib in *Timour, the Tartar,* before sailing for America with her mother. After playing such roles as the Duke of York to JUNIUS BRUTUS BOOTH's Richard III and Albert to EDWIN FORREST's William Tell (10 years later, she would graduate to Lady Macbeth opposite Forrest's Thane), she made her debut as a child star in 1828, playing Little Pickle in *The Spoiled Child* and five characters in *Twelve Precisely.*

In 1850, after a distinguished adolescent and adult career, she married her third husband, **John**

54 different characters in some 35 sketches. The range of personalities that she assumed was broad, as was the scope of her travels and repu-tation. In addition to accolades for her finely wrought characterizations of women of all ages, types, and cultures were plaudits for her ability to evoke throngs of other "unseen" characters. Prior to her professional debut in 1920, at the Aeolian Hall, London, she had been perfecting her craft before family, friends, and charity audiences. In the three and a half decades that followed, she performed almost nonstop, on every continent, and often at the command of royalty. Her letters, edited by Neilla Warren, were published in 1979.   DBW

Dressler, Marie [née Leila Koerber] (1869–1934) Canadian-born comedienne, daughter of an itin-erant musician. At 14 she joined the Nevada Stock

Drew (1827–62), whose father managed NIBLO'S Theatre in New York. Famous for such popular Irish characters as Dr. O'Toole (*The Irish Tenor*) and Tim O'Brian (*The Irish Immigrant*) and Shakespeare's Andrew Aguecheek and Dromio, Drew briefly managed Philadelphia's National and ARCH STREET theatres. Mrs. Drew undertook the management of the Arch in 1861, one year before her husband's untimely death. During 30 subsequent years at the helm, she essentially contributed to the achievement and acceptance of theatre in America, while continuing to act, by popular demand, in such roles as Mrs. Malaprop and Mistress Quickly. Her autobiography was published in 1899.

Two of her children by Drew began illustrious careers at the Arch. **John Drew [Jr.]** (1853–1927) trained under his mother's stern supervision before joining AUGUSTIN DALY'S FIFTH AVENUE THEATRE company in New York (1875). Among his most popular old and new comedy parts were Orlando, Petruchio, and Charles Surface. By the mid-1800s, he and his fellow Fifth Avenue players, ADA REHAN, JAMES LEWIS, and MRS. G. H. GILBERT, were called "the Big Four." In 1892, Drew agreed to star for manager CHARLES FROHMAN at the unheard-of salary of $500 per week. Following his sensational debut in *The Masked Ball*, his naturalistic acting, elegant bearing, and sartorial correctness won him the uncontested title "First Gentleman of the American Stage" and kept him a reigning star for 35 years. An autobiography appeared in 1922 and a biography by DITHMAR in 1900.

Georgiana Drew (1856–93), after a strict Arch Street apprenticeship, followed her older brother to the Fifth Avenue in 1876. She made an immediate hit with her breezy manner and unique way of tossing lines like nosegays to an audience – a technique that established her as a popular comedienne in such subsequent hits as *The Senator* (1889) with WILLIAM H. CRANE and *Settled Out of Court* (1892) with Frohman's Comedians. Her Fifth Avenue debut, in Daly's popular *Pique*, cast her opposite a young newcomer from England, **Maurice Barrymore** (1847–1905), whom she married in 1876.

The son of a British district commissioner in India, Barrymore left Oxford, became Amateur Middle-Weight Boxing Champion of England, changed his name from Herbert Blyth to spare his proper family, and tried acting. After his 1872 debut at the Theatre Royal, Windsor, he toured the provincial theatres for three years before sailing for America. His early years there were distinguished by successive inclusion in the companies

Photograph of Georgiana Drew and her children: Ethel, Lionel, and John, 1890. *Courtesy:* Michael Morrison.

of America's foremost managers: Augustin Daly, LESTER WALLACK, and A. M. PALMER. His striking beauty, sharp wit, and carefree manner made him a popular matinee idol and a sought-after leading man. His most successful characterizations included Orlando (particularly opposite HELENA MODJESKA), and the title roles in *A Man of the World* (1889) and *Captain Swift* (1888), which reviewers considered his "Monte Cristo" – a role in which he, like JAMES O'NEILL as the count, might have toured profitably for years. But Barrymore's volatile temperament and profligate ways precluded such security. Although three of the eight plays he wrote – *Reckless Temple, Roaring Dick & Co.*, and *Nadjezda* – also were potentially durable vehicles, the author never exploited them. He died of paresis at the age of 58, deranged and unfulfilled, leaving a legacy of three children by Georgie Drew. The definitive biography by James Kotsilibas-Davis was published in 1977.

Ethel Barrymore (1879–1959) became the first of the three siblings to achieve stardom. At the age of 21, after six years of apprenticeship with her grandmother, her uncle John Drew, and Sir Henry Irving in England, her name went above the title during the Broadway run of *Captain Jinks of the*

Horse Marines in 1901. Under the astute management of Charles Frohman, she became a darling of fin de siècle society on two continents. The term "glamour girl" was coined for her, and sons of American millionaires and English peers courted her. Declining Winston Churchill's proposal of marriage, she explained, "I didn't think I could live up to his world. My world was the theatre." Her world remained the theatre as "Ethel Barrymore vehicles," such as *Alice-Sit-By-the-Fire, Cousin Kate, Lady Frederick,* and Déclassé, alternated with the stronger stuff of *A Doll's House, The Second Mrs Tanqueray, The Constant Wife,* Lady Teazle, Camille, Portia, and Juliet. By birth she was queen of the royal family; by achievement, with regal bearing and fluid style, she became the First Lady of the American Theatre – a fact underscored in 1928 when the Shuberts opened the Ethel Barrymore Theatre with Ethel interpreting three ages of woman in *The Kingdom of God.* After the climax of her stage career in *The Corn Is Green* (1940), she opted for lucrative, less taxing movie work until her death in Hollywood two months before her 80th birthday. She published an autobiography in 1955.

Her older brother, **Lionel Barrymore** (1878–1954), began acting at 15 under the tutelage of his grandmother and his uncle **Sidney Drew** (1868–1919); Sidney was Mrs. Drew's illegitimate son – probably by Robert Craig, an actor in her Arch Street company. Sidney became a noted stage and vaudeville comedian, usually opposite his first wife, Gladys Rankin, daughter of actor-manager Arthur McKee Rankin and his actress wife, Kitty Blanchard. Lionel, in support of his uncle John Drew in *The Mummy and the Humming Bird* (1903), excelled in the small role of an Italian organ-grinder without speaking a word of English. His inspired gift for characterization flourished in several subsequent productions – notably as boxer Kid Garvey in *The Other Girl* (1903), written for him by his father's friend Augustus Thomas. But in 1906, Lionel retreated to France with his first wife, Doris Rankin (Gladys's sister), to indulge his first love – painting. Three years later they returned to America and what Lionel called "the family curse" – acting. Interspersed with his pioneer acting in the "flickers" from 1912, his foremost stage vehicles – The Copperhead (1918), *The Claw* (1921), and *Laugh, Clown, Laugh* (1923) – were eclipsed by two costarring ventures with his brother: *Peter Ibbetson* (1917) and *The Jest* (1919). "To the future of such actors," predicted the *New York Times,* "it is impossible to set any limits." But after the failure of his *Macbeth* in 1921 and a series of mediocre plays, Lionel turned irrevocably to Hollywood. The elder Barrymore became acting's unchallenged Grand Old Man after nearly 200 film roles – the last 40 played in excruciating rheumatic pain, but with no less power, on crutches or in a wheelchair until his death at the age of 76. Lionel's autobiography was published in 1951.

His younger brother, **John Barrymore** (1882–1942), was even more resistant to acting. After a brief stint as a newspaper illustrator, he halfheartedly pursued, with the help of family and friends, a career as a stage comedian, while wholeheartedly pursuing debutantes and chorus girls. (Among his conquests in the former category: Katherine Harris, who became his first wife in 1913; in the latter, Evelyn Nesbit and Irene Fenwick, who later became Lionel's second wife.) Then, after a run of light comedy roles like *The Fortune Hunter* (1909), John stunned critics and theatregoers with his expert delineations of tragic roles in *Justice* (1916) and *Redemption* (1918). He followed them with two of the theatre's towering achievements: the Arthur Hopkins–Robert Edmond Jones productions of *Richard III* (1920) and *Hamlet* (1922), illuminated by his poetic beauty, vocal grandeur, and subtle strength. "The new prince was entering his kingdom," observed Hopkins. But at the height of his powers, touted as America's greatest actor, the crown prince of the royal family abdicated. He left the stage for films, returning only once after alcohol and self-indulgence had diminished his talents, playing a parody of himself in a travesty of a play (*My Dear Children,* 1939) three years before his death at 60. Although a biography of sorts appeared in 1926, more complete are biographies by Gene Fowler (1944), John Kobler (1977), and Martin Norden (1995).

Artistry and industry, combined with the color and glamour of their private lives, earned the Barrymores a unique niche in the annals of American theatre. Subsequent Drew–Barrymore generations have pursued theatrical careers with considerably less distinction. Ethel's three children from her marriage to socialite Russell Colt made attempts: two sons, half-heartedly; a daughter, **Ethel Barrymore Colt** (1912–77), with some success, particularly as an opera singer and acting teacher. John's daughter **Diana** (1921–60), by his second wife, socialite-poetess Michael Strange, had a brief, promising acting career curtailed by excesses similar to those of her father. John's only son (by his third wife, actress Dolores Costello), known as John Barrymore Jr. or **John Drew Barry-**

more (1932–2004), also sacrificed a promising screen and stage career to alcohol, drugs, and self-indulgence. But his daughter, named appropriately **Drew Barrymore** (b. 1975), gained stardom, as her great-great-grandmother Mrs. John Drew had, as a child actress – at the age of 7 in the film *E.T.* (1982). Despite a teenage bout with alcohol and drugs, she continues in the 2000s to appear more successfully than ever in films.   JK-D

[*Ed. note*: Of the collective biographies undertaken, those recommended are by Hollis Alpert (1955), Kotsilibas-Davis (1981), Margot Peters (1990), and Carol Stein Hoffman (2001).]

Drexler, Rosalyn (1926–) Playwright whose OFF-OFF BROADWAY avant-garde plays satirize sexual politics, women, violence, and domestic life. Drexler's anarchic humor, often compared to that of the MARX BROS., was evidenced in *Hot Buttered Roll* (1966) and *The Writer's Opera* (1979), but she has also written naturalism (*The Investigation*, 1966); a feminist history of Hatshepsut (*She Who Was He*, 1974); and a poignant study of two lesbian wrestlers (*Delicate Feelings*, 1984). She has won three Obies.   FB

Driving Miss Daisy This 1988 Pulitzer Prize–winning drama in one act by Alfred Uhry opened OFF-BROADWAY at PLAYWRIGHTS HORIZONS (15 April 1987) before transferring to the JOHN HOUSEMAN Theatre, running a total of 1,195 performances. Set in and around Atlanta during 1948–73, the play examines the healing, attitudinal changes regarding racism and old age in the relationship between a difficult southern Jewish widow and her black chauffeur, with extra perspective provided by the widow's son. The show won Obies for actors MORGAN FREEMAN and DANA IVEY; Drama Desk nominations for author Uhry and director Ron Lagomarsino; the Dramatists' Guild's Morton Award; and the Outer Critics' Circle Award. Robert Waldman, Uhry's collaborator on *The Robber Bridegroom*, composed the award-winning incidental music for the production. A film version starred JESSICA TANDY, Morgan Freeman, and Dan Aykroyd.   EK

Drunkard; or, The Fallen Saved, The, by WILLIAM H. SMITH. This allegory of moral reform, first performed in 1844 at the BOSTON MUSEUM, where Smith stage-managed (seen first in New York, 1850), was the most popular and enduring of the many temperance melodramas on midcentury American stages. Tracing the decline into dipsomania of Edward Middleton (first played by Smith), the play climaxed in a delirium tremens scene that required the actor to thrash about in agony on the stage. Domestic bliss and social respectability reward Edward's eventual decision to take The Pledge. Antebellum productions at museum theatres in the Northeast spawned several other temperance plays and helped to convince many working- and middle-class theatregoers to conform to the emerging norms of bourgeois society. Performances mocking the values and conventions of the play have been popular since the 1930s, including a Los Angeles production that ran for 16 years.   BMcC

Du Barry Historical extravaganza written and staged by DAVID BELASCO in 1901. This play on the life of a mistress of Louis XV was typical of Belasco's "historical" mode of scenic naturalism: highly sensational plot, lavish and thoroughly researched costumes and set, actual period furniture imported from France, and a cast of nearly 200. The play, featuring MRS. LESLIE CARTER, opened at the Criterion Theatre on 25 December and had 165 performances.   MF

Du Barry Was a Lady COLE PORTER musical-comedy hit of 1939–40 about a washroom attendant who dreams that he is Louis XV and that the voluptuous singer he desires is Madame du Barry. BERT LAHR and ETHEL MERMAN headed the cast in this energetic romp, first conceived as a film project for MAE WEST, that pressed the limits of sexual and anatomical humor on Broadway. Lahr's madcap performance – along with the release of MGM's *The WIZARD OF OZ* during the run of the show – affirmed his reputation as a master of outrageous comedy. Another box-office draw was Betty Grable in her Broadway debut. The show's book was by Herbert Fields and B. G. "BUDDY" DESYLVA. The musical opened at the 46TH STREET THEATRE on 6 December 1939 and ran for 408 performances.   MF

Du Bois, Raoul Pène (1914–85) Staten Island–born scenic and costume designer who, starting with a single costume design for *The Garrick Gaieties* in 1930, went on to a 50-year career designing creative and colorful costumes, imaginative sets, and occasional lighting designs. In addition to notable Broadway credits, including *DU BARRY WAS A LADY* (1939), *Sugar Babies* (1979), and *No, No, NANETTE* (1971 revival), his costumes and scenery were seen in London and Paris and graced films, ice shows, ballets, NIGHTCLUBS, aquacades, and commercial illustrations. He received Tony

Awards both for costumes (*No, No, Nanette,* 1971) and for scenery (Wonderful Town, 1953).   BO

Duff, Mary Ann (Dyke) (1794–1857) London-born actress, known as "the American Sarah Siddons," after the British actress. She seems to have made her debut in Dublin, but came to America with her husband, John Duff, in 1810 and made her first appearance as Juliet on New Year's Eve that year. Until 1817 she went relatively unnoticed, then suddenly changed her style, showing the "true fire of genius," and emerged as a star. She won fame as a tragic actress in Philadelphia and Boston, rather than New York, noted by critics for her "uniformity of excellence." The death of her husband in 1831 left her with seven children; she then married the actor Charles Young, but the marriage was soon annulled. She married again in 1835 and retired in 1838, but returned to the stage sporadically, appearing as late as 1850 in Toronto. Many of the leading actors of the time considered her the greatest actress in America. A biography by Joseph Ireland was published in 1882.   SMA

Dukakis, Olympia (1931–) Actress, teacher, director, and former artistic director of New Jersey's Whole Theatre Company (1976–90), founded with her brother, Apollo, and husband, Louis Zorich. Best known for *Moonstruck* (Academy Award, 1987), she won Obies for *A Man's a Man* (1963) and *The Marriage of Bette and Boo* (1985). Cofounding Boston's Charles Street Playhouse (1957–60) and the Edgartown (MA) Summer Theatre (1960), she made her Off-Broadway debut in 1960 (Louis Lippa's *The Breaking Wall*) and her Broadway debut in 1962 (*The Aspern Papers,* understudy). She has directed and acted frequently at the Williamstown Theatre Festival; has appeared on TV and in the films *Steel Magnolias, Look Who's Talking,* and *Dad*; guest-starred in Martin Sherman's *Rose* at the Royal National Theatre (1999); taught at New York and Yale Universities; and been a guest artist in the regions (e.g., Amanda in *The Glass Menagerie,* Trinity Rep, 1991; title role in *Hecuba,* adapted by Wertenbaker, American Conservatory Theatre, 1995). In 2004 she essayed Clytemnestra in the Aquila Theater Company's production of *Agamemnon. The Lear Project* – a solo performance, in both its writing and acting – was seen first in 1998. An autobiography was published in 2003.   REK

Duke, Vernon [né Vladimir Dukelsky] (1903–69) Russian-born composer, educated at the Kiev Conservatory, who composed ballet music for the Bal-

lets Russes, and, after an unsuccessful attempt at an American career, wrote the scores for London operettas and musicals. Returning to America in 1929, he contributed songs to several important revues of the 1930s, such as *Three's a Crowd* (1930) and *Americana* (1932). His first complete score, for the revue *Walk a Little Faster* (1932), included one of his best-known songs, "April in Paris." His most successful score was for the *Cabin in the Sky* (1940). In the 1940s and '50s he continued to write musical-comedy scores, as well as ballets, symphonies, and concertos, but although individual songs were sometimes memorable, none of his shows was of lasting importance. His autobiography, *Passport to Paris,* was published in 1955 (Boston).   MK

Dulcy by George S. Kaufman and Marc Connelly, directed by Howard Lindsay, opened on Broadway 13 August 1921 and ran 246 performances. Based on a character created by humor columnist Franklin P. Adams, Dulcy (Lynn Fontanne) is an exaggeration of the "typical" American housewife who invites one of her husband's business associates to a weekend house party, and then sets up the situation to allow her to meddle in everyone else's affairs, happily unaware that anyone might object to the trysts and elopements that she fosters.   JDM

Dunlap, William (1766–1839) Playwright and manager, often termed "the father of American drama." He wrote or translated and adapted more than 50 plays. Half of them were originals; the other half adaptations from the French and German, principally from Kotzebue. He managed the Park Theatre (1798–1805), an undertaking that ended disastrously, as he was apparently too good-natured to be hardheaded about financial matters. Still he persisted, managing the Park again (1806–11) for the actor Thomas A. Cooper. Even if poor at business, he was the first manager to write and present his own plays, the first to champion native subject matter and dramatists, and the first to record his experiences and those of others in his *History of the American Theatre* (1832; repr. with new introduction and index in 2005).

Born in Perth Amboy, NJ, Dunlap began his artistic life as a painter, studied with Benjamin West in England (1784–7). He became fascinated with the theatre when he saw R. B. Sheridan's *The School for Scandal* and *The Critic* with their original casts, and on his return to New York where he saw Royall Tyler's *The Contrast.*

Most notable among his original plays: *Darby's Return* (1789); *The Father* (1799); André (1798), which he later transformed into a patriotic spectacle for holiday performance as *The Glory of Columbia* (1803), with backdrops and transparencies by Charles Ciceri; *Leicester* (1806); and *A Trip to Niagara; or, Travellers in America* (1828), with a diorama of 18 scenes along the Hudson as a steamboat moves up the river from New York to Catskill landing. His most popular adaptations include (from Kotzebue) *The Stranger* (1798), *False Shame* (1799), and *Pizarro in Peru* (1800), as well as (from the French) *The Wife of Two Husbands* (1804, Pixérécourt) and *Thirty Years; or, The Life of a Gamester* (1828, Goubaux and Ducange).

Besides his work in the theatre, he painted a host of miniatures (one of George Washington), and monumental religious canvases such as *Christ Rejected* (12 × 18 ft.). He was director of the American Academy of Fine Arts (1817), a founder of the National Academy of Design (1826), and a professor of historical painting at the National Academy (1830–9). He wrote biographies of the actor GEORGE FREDERICK COOKE (1813) and the novelist Charles Brockden Brown (1815), a *History of the Arts of Design* (1834), *Thirty Years Ago; or, Memoirs of a Water Drinker* (1836), and a *History of New York for Schools* (1837). His revealing diary was published in 1930; biographies in 1917 (Oral Coad) and 1970 (Robert Canary). RM

Dunnock, Mildred (1901–91) Actress and director, remembered by ARTHUR MILLER as "a fiercely dedicated artist." She first appeared in New York in 1932, then she played several seasons of stock. After a number of Broadway appearances, she achieved stardom with such roles as Linda Loman in *DEATH OF A SALESMAN* (1949) and Big Mama in *CAT ON A HOT TIN ROOF* (1955). She played a number of seasons with the AMERICAN SHAKESPEARE FESTIVAL in both classic and modern roles, and in 1965 directed *Graduation* OFF-BROADWAY. She usually appeared in major supporting roles (mothers, spinsters, and eccentric ladies), relying on a birdlike fragile stature and tremendous voice to project an ineffectual gentility. She made her film debut in *The Corn Is Green* (1945), and later appeared in such successful films as *Death of a Salesman* (1951), *Viva Zapata!* (1952), *The Jazz Singer* (1952), *Baby Doll* (1956), and *Sweet Bird of Youth* (1962). She also appeared on many television series and specials. Her daughter Linda McGuire is an actress, as is her granddaughter Patricia McGuire Dunnock. SMA

Durang, Christopher (1949–) Playwright, actor, and cabaret performer, born in Montclair, NJ, and educated at Harvard and Yale. Durang had his first

play produced in 1971, emerging as a new breed of American dramatist in the late 1970s and early '80s. His best-known work includes *A History of the American Film* (1976), *Sister Mary Ignatius Explains It All for You* (1979; Obie, 1980), *The Actor's Nightmare* (1981), *Beyond Therapy* (1981), *Baby with the Bath Water* (1983), *The MARRIAGE OF BETTE AND BOO* (1973; revised 1985, Obie), *Laughing Wild* (1987), a group of short pieces collectively called *Durang Durang* (1994), *Sex and Longing* (1996), *Betty's Summer Vacation* (1999, Obie), *Mrs. Bob Cratchit's Wild Christmas Binge* and *Adrift in Macao* (both 2002), and *Miss Witherspoon* (2005). Durang's style, according to *New York Times* critic Mel Gussow, "has the waggishness of four Marxes and the malice of a Jonathan Swift." His satirical bent – although it has become somewhat more optimistic since the 1980s – has provoked considerable controversy and attempted censorship, especially when he has targeted religion. Since 1994 he has cochaired with MARSHA NORMAN the playwriting program at Juilliard. SMA DBW

Durang, John (1768–1822) Actor, clown, equestrian, puppeteer, scene painter, dancer, pantomimist, and manager. Durang spent most of his life in his native Pennsylvania or used it as home base. As a boy he ran away from home to BOSTON, where he made his debut. In 1785 he joined HALLAM at Philadelphia's SOUTHWARK THEATRE as dancer and pantomimist. With John Bill Ricketts's CIRCUS in the 1790s, he traveled to Canada as the first-known American-born clown. On his return to PHILADELPHIA he worked as a scene painter and dancer, eventually joining THOMAS WIGNELL's company in the winters while traveling with his own companies in summers (1806–10) into Pennsylvania Dutch country, performing scenes from Shakespeare in German. Durang wrote and illustrated his important memoirs (1785–1816), not published until 1966 (ed., Alan S. Downer) by the University of Pittsburgh Press.

All of Durang's children had theatre careers: **Charles** (1796–1870), actor and dancer-choreographer, wrote *The Philadelphia Stages from the Year 1749 to the Year 1855* (published serially by the *Philadelphia Sunday Dispatch*, 1854–60); **Ferdinand** (1798–1831), an actor-dancer, had a short career primarily in New York; **Augustus** (1800–18?) was a child actor; **Charlotte** (1803–24) was a dancer; and **Juliet** (1805–49) worked (as Mrs. Godey) as a provincial actress in leading roles. DBW

Durante, Jimmy [né James Francis] (1893–1980) Comedian, actor, and singer, known affectionately as "Schnozzola" for his prominent nose, the butt of many of his jokes. One of America's most beloved entertainers, Durante began as a saloon pianist on Coney Island and opened his own NIGHTCLUB in 1923 with Eddie Jackson and Lou Clayton. He debuted on Broadway in *Show Girl* in 1929. He later toured England, then appeared on Broadway in such shows as *Jumbo* (1935), *Red, Hot and Blue!* (1936), and *Stars in Your Eyes* (1939). He made his film debut in *Roadhouse Nights* (1930); among his other films were *Palooka* (1934) and *The Man Who Came to Dinner* (1942). He starred on radio's *Rexall Show* (1944–50) and later his own TV show, being voted best television performer in 1951. More a clown than comic, Durante's style eluded analysis, yet his sayings ("Stop the music," "I got a million of 'em," "Everybody wants to get into da act," and "Goodnight Mrs. Calabash, wherever you are") were assimilated into the language, and the presentation of his songs, including his signature "Inka Dinka Doo," prompted FRED ALLEN to characterize his singing as "a dull rasp calling its mate." Biographies have been written by I. Adler (1980), Gene Fowler (1951), and J. Robbins (1991).   SMA   DBW

Durham, Jimmie (1940–) Arkansas-born, Wolf Clan Cherokee Indian PERFORMANCE ARTIST, sculptor, and poet, active in the American Indian Movement (1973–80) and the International Indian Treaty Council (1974–80), and was Representative of the Human Rights Commission to the United Nation (1975). He cofounded Houston's Adept Art Center (1963), and became Executive Director for the New York–based Foundation for the Community of Artists, as well as editor of *Art and Artists* (1982). His first performance, *My Land* (1964), was with boxer Mohammed Ali and Vivian Ayers Allen. In *Thanksgiving* (1982), *Manhattan Giveaway* (1985), and *Savagism & You* (1991), he parodied the "Indian artifact," anthropological constructions of gift-giving ceremonies, and the misinterpretations of indigenous cultures. By representing himself as "savage," and by performing American heroes (George Washington and David Crockett) as his counterpersonas, he challenges the political inscription of his identity (see NATIVE AMERICANS PORTRAYED).   AF

Durning, Charles (1923–) Portly, accomplished, and dependable film and stage character actor born in Highland Falls, NY. A highly decorated WWII vet, educated with the GI Bill at Columbia and NYU, Durning essayed his first New York stage role in 1955, appeared frequently in comic roles with the NEW YORK SHAKESPEARE FESTIVAL during the early 1960s, had his first Broadway role in *Poor Bitos* (1964, understudy), became well known thanks to THAT CHAMPIONSHIP SEASON (1972), and then moved into a prolific career in films and television. With more than 150 major TV and screen roles, it is surprising that he has constantly returned to theatre in central roles on Broadway (and elsewhere) in *The Au Pair Man* (1973), CAT ON A HOT TIN ROOF (1990, Tony, Best Featured Actor), *The* GIN GAME (1997 revival), INHERIT THE WIND (1996 revival), *Gore Vidal's The Best Man* (2000 revival), and WENDY WASSERSTEIN's *Third* (2005; Mitzi E. Newhouse Theatre). His NYC credits alone total over 40.   DBW

Dutchman Long one-act allegorical drama by AMIRI BARAKA (LeRoi Jones) that heralded the era of black revolutionary drama of the 1960s and early '70s. On a subway train, symbolizing the ship *The Flying Dutchman,* a sexy blond woman teases a black intellectual to an angry outburst, then murders him as other white passengers look on unconcerned. First produced by the Playwrights Unit in New York, the play moved to the Cherry Lane Theatre, where it provoked critical controversy, even though it won an Obie Award as the OFF-BROADWAY Best American Play of 1964. It was also produced in Paris, Berlin, and Spoleto, Italy, and was made into a full-length film in 1967.   EGH

E

Eagle Theatre Built on the embarcadero in Sacramento at the height of the gold rush, this was the first theatrical facility in California designed exclusively for that purpose, opening 18 October 1849 with a production of *The Bandit Chief; or, The Spectre of the Forest.* It maintained a season until 4 January 1850 but was destroyed in a flood three days later. PAD

Easiest Way, The The second major success for EUGENE WALTER, it opened at the BELASCO–Stuyvesant Theatre 19 January 1909 and ran for 157 performances, following its Hartford Opera House preview engagement 31 December 1908. This first DAVID BELASCO–Walter collaboration yielded near-naturalism, overturning the assumed happy ending and portraying a theatre life that some found too frank. Called grim and immoral, the play drew considerable public notice and was called the hit of its season. Through a series of nearly melodramatic revelations, actress Laura Murdock, producer Willard Brockton's mistress, fails in her attempt to break the mutually exploitative relationship and marry journalist John Madison. Accepting the inevitable, she shocked audiences with the closing line, "I'm going to Rector's to make a hit, and to hell with the rest." Of further note was the scene for which Belasco purchased the contents of a boardinghouse room, steamed off the wallpaper, and reapplied it to the stage setting. RW

East Lynne Domestic melodrama adapted by several playwrights – including CLIFTON TAYLEURE, Benjamin E. Woolf, McKEE RANKIN, and CLARA MORRIS – from Mrs. Henry Wood's 1861 novel. The play centers on Lady Isabel's conjugal infidelity, her departure from her home, and her later disguised return as a governess to care for her son, who dies. The plot also includes a murder mystery involving Isabel's seducer, and ends with her death. The melodrama evoked tears and self-righteousness from its audience for its scenes of domestic pathos and its lectures on patience and respectability. LUCILLE WESTERN centered her repertory on Lady Isabel, performing Tayleure's 1862 version (premiered: Brooklyn, January 1863) throughout her career. Other actors, including NANCE O'NEIL and BLANCHE BATES, performed the piece, which was occasionally shortened for vaudeville production after 1895. Several films were made of *East Lynne,* and the PROVINCETOWN PLAYERS burlesqued its embrace of Victorian domesticity in 1926. BMcC

East Lynne Theater Company, The Small not-for-profit company founded in 1980 by Warren Kliewer in Jersey City, NJ (currently in Cape May). Led today by Gayle Stahlhuth (since 1999), the ELTC had the distinction when it began of being the only professional company in the U.S. dedicated to an all-American historical repertoire, though other companies have followed ELTC's lead since. Plays by such playwrights as DAVID BELASCO, WASHINGTON IRVING, WILLIAM DEAN HOWELLS, and RACHEL CROTHERS have been staged. Despite its longevity, ELTC has never had a permanent home. DBW

East West Players The first contemporary Asian Pacific American theatre company (see ASIAN AMERICAN THEATRE), founded in LOS ANGELES in 1965 by seven artists of Asian heritage frustrated by their lack of opportunities in mainstream, white-dominated theatre and film. At first EWP presented Asian-cast versions of Goldoni and Brecht, along with plays set in Asia (such as *Rashomon*). In the mid-1970s, under the management of noted actor-director Mako, the focus changed to nurturing and presenting plays by an exciting new crop of dramatists concerned with modern Asian American themes: DAVID HENRY HWANG, Wakako Yamauchi, Valina Houston, and others. Mako left in early 1989; actress Nobu McCarthy became artistic director a year later, replaced in 1993 by Tim Dang, a 13-year veteran with the theatre. This nonprofit company continued to mount seasons of recent Asian American works in a small playhouse on Santa Monica Blvd. (from 1972) until moving in 1998 to a 236-seat house in Little Tokyo. EWP remains the first and largest extant Asian American theatre company. MB

Easton, Richard (1933–) Actor born in Montreal and trained at the Central School of Speech and Drama in London. A citizen of Canada with residence in the U.K. and a U.S. green card; many of his theatre credits are in the U.S. (in the 1960s and '90s to the present). An original company member of the 1953 Stratford Festival in Ontario, his Broadway debut was as Mr. Harcourt in *The Country Wife* (1957). Easton has performed in most of Shakespeare's works; his most recent in NYC was the title role of King Henry IV in LINCOLN CENTER Theater's stellar staging (2003). His most recent roles were Sir Anthony Absolute in Lincoln Center's *The Rivals* (2004) and, not limited to classical roles, Kemp in the revival of Orton's *Entertaining Mr. Sloane* (ROUNDABOUT, 2006). In 2001 he won the Tony for Best Actor in a play for his A. E. Housman at 77 in Stoppard's *The Invention of Love*. Other recent credits include *Waste, Hotel Universe, Noises Off, Every Good Boy Deserves Favor,* and *The Coast of Utopia.* For a decade he taught at the University of San Diego and acted at the OLD GLOBE.   DBW

Eaton, Walter Prichard (1878–1957) Educator and critic. Born in Malden, MA, and educated at Harvard (1900), Eaton wrote for the *Boston Journal* before moving to the *New York Tribune* in 1902 as an assistant to WILLIAM WINTER. In 1907–8 he became drama critic for the *New York Sun,* leaving in 1908 to begin a nine-year association with *American Magazine.* He was associate editor of *The Drama Magazine* and a freelance critic during 1919–31. Following the retirement of GEORGE PIERCE BAKER in 1933, he became Professor of Playwriting at Yale, a post he held until 1947. Author of six books on the theatre, Eaton opposed Broadway's domination of the American stage, and argued that the greatest sufferer from this system is the intelligent playgoer.   TLM

Ebb, Fred see KANDER, JOHN

Ebersole, Christine (1953–) Blue-green-eyed, "bottled blonde," statuesque stage, TV, and film actor-singer, born in Park Forest, IL, and trained at the AMERICAN ACADEMY OF DRAMATIC ARTS after college (McMurray). A modest New York debut in *Angel Street* (1976, replacement) was followed by a number of musical roles, most notably *OKLAHOMA!* (1979) as Ado Annie; Guenevere in *CAMELOT* opposite RICHARD BURTON (1980) and then Richard Harris on tour; Dorothy Brock in *42ND STREET* (2001; Tony, Best Actress in a Musical); and the historical figure "Little" Edie Beale in *Grey Gardens* (2006; Obie and Drama Desk awards), which moved to Broadway (Tony). Her straight

plays in NYC include *The Best Man* (2000), *Dinner at Eight* (2002; her Millicent Jordan a Tony nominee), and *Steel Magnolias* (2005 revival).   DBW

Eckart, Jean (1921–93) and **William Eckart** (1920–2000) This husband-and-wife design team did all their work in collaboration with each other. Trained at Yale, they began their Broadway career in 1951 and for the next 15 years were associated with some of the major musicals of the time, including *The Golden Apple, Once upon a Mattress, FIORELLO!, DAMN YANKEES,* and *Mame.* Their OFF-BROADWAY work includes OH DAD, POOR DAD. . . . They also designed for opera, ballet, television, and industrial shows. As of the 1970s they did less design work. Mr. Eckart taught at Southern Methodist University.   AA

economics The business of American theatre is founded on Puritan principles of commerce and morality dating to the early 18th century. Not only is theatre a vehicle for social intercourse and articulation of moral values, but equally it serves as a traditional commodity, in which its value is only as great as its profit. From the beginning, American theatre has sought to balance these apparently contradictory elements into the Puritans' ideal amalgamation of values: to profit both financially and morally.

The earliest professional players in the New World were mostly English fair performers, seeking new and profitable audiences in a rapidly expanding country. Battling conservative sentiment, hostile merchants, and a deteriorating economy, these performers found security in their traditional touring practices, though they preferred the permanence of a stock company. The first major troupe to arrive was the company of MURRAY AND KEAN. Beginning in 1749, they toured the principal colonies, performing a typical English repertoire with a general operating mode resembling the itinerant English companies of the same period. They were probably organized as a sharing company, with each member assuming a proportionate risk. Numerous benefit performances helped augment individual performers' incomes, but the extent to which these benefits succeeded is difficult to assess. Thus early performers must have found some consistency in following the annual commodity fairs scattered throughout North America and by accepting remuneration in the form of barter, bills of credit, and exchange.

The HALLAMS, successors to Murray and Kean, clearly fared better, although when they arrived in 1752, they too struggled to find a profitable audience. The outbreak of the French and Indian War in 1754 plunged the region into financial chaos, and the company soon left for Jamaica. Upon their return four years later, the reorganized company, under the direction of DAVID DOUGLASS, began one of the most successful eras in theatrical management. For the next 14 years the company regularly toured the colonies and maintained an organization that was financially viable and profitable enough to erect new theatres and replace actors with fresh talent from London. However, rebellious colonists increasingly associated theatre with British goods, and when in 1774 the First Continental Congress passed its anti-importation acts to discourage the use and dissemination of British products, theatre was included. Douglass and his AMERICAN COMPANY, primarily for financial necessity, left for Jamaica, where they remained until war's end.

The professional theatre returned in the early Federalist period to a country ripe for commercial exploitation, though still steeped in the moralist traditions of the past. No longer a threat to mid-level mercantilism nor viewed as a manufacture of British hegemony, theatre prospered in the 1790s after a brief period of difficulty caused by the vestiges of prewar antitheatrical sentiment and a postwar depression. By 1793 BOSTON had suspended enforcement of its 1750 ban on theatrical amusements, and a new playhouse was opened. Elsewhere the formal opposition to theatre faded, and a new confidence, based more on nationalism than on economic stability, was reflected in fundamental changes in company organization. Salaries replaced shares; resident STOCK COMPANIES replaced itinerant troupes. These changes begin in earnest in 1789 with the founding of a constitutional government and a federal presidency. But the biggest boost to theatre was the result of the early attempts at creating a regulated national currency.

The founding of the First Bank of the United States in 1791 provided the nation with a modicum of fiscal stability, necessary for rapid expansion and renewed trade. The regulation of state banks and their notes allowed greater financial consistency internally and abroad. Although great disparity still existed among some state's banks notes, the general climate was conducive to commercial growth and international trade. Confidence in the new currency is evident in the sudden rise in the number of theatres built on funds raised by stock and public subscription between 1789 and 1800 (New York's PARK THEATRE, the FEDERAL STREET THEATRE and Haymarket in Boston, as well as theatres in Providence, Charleston,

and Washington, DC). Among managers to take advantage of the new financial climate was STEPHEN PRICE, who revolutionized the American theatre during 1810–40 by importing major English stars, including GEORGE FREDERICK COOKE, CHARLES MATTHEWS, and Edmund Kean (see INTERNATIONAL STARS). Though this was not a new practice, Price was the first able regularly and successfully to engage individual stars on limited tours, in part because of the relative value and consistency of American currency. As the first American manager who was not also an actor or playwright, he could devote his entire effort to management, leaving the artistry up to his stars. This fundamental shift altered the nature of commercial theatre in America.

Professional managers, stock companies, and the star system expanded during the first half of the 19th century. Most major cities maintained resident stock companies, run by professional managers and supplemented by the occasional star on tour. By 1830 New York had surpassed PHILADELPHIA as the nation's theatrical center, with at least five major companies operating; but the demise of the Second Bank of the United States in 1834 and the subsequent overexpansion of credit led to a period of economic stress that culminated in the Panic of 1837. Within a year, the theatrical industry was in serious decline, especially in New York, which saw only the Park survive intact. Theatrical managers sought new forms of theatrical attraction, relying less on imported actors, reluctant to take American dollars. Among the most successful survivors was WILLIAM MITCHELL, whose MITCHELL'S OLYMPIC Theatre opened in 1839 and continued until 1850. By presenting light comedies (farces, burlesques, and local spectacles) at a reasonable price, Mitchell developed a profitable alternative to the traditional venue, more than covering for the lack of stars. His appeal to the working classes opened up a vast audience base. Along a similar vein, P. T. BARNUM opened his BARNUM'S AMERICAN MUSEUM in 1842, with its freakish displays and a theatre that produced popular melodramas. No longer reliant upon touring stars, popular theatres also found support from the growing immigrant class. By exploiting the superficial qualities of melodrama and recent technical innovations, almost any crowd could be attracted.

By midcentury, the business of American theatre had become a multimillion-dollar industry dominated by independent managers and a few leading actors. Touring was limited to occasional stars and western entrepreneurs. Stock companies, on the other hand, controlled the regular seasons in the larger cities. The Civil War changed all that, though the changes were not entirely the direct result of the conflict. Certainly there were managers in New York and elsewhere who exploited the war to stage timely and spectacular representations of Union victories to theatrical audiences starved for front-line "news"; but the real transformation of the industry came about after the war as a result of the economic collapse of 1873. Stock companies not sufficiently protected failed, and managers once again looked to touring as the safest alternative; however, unlike earlier touring troupes, these new "combinations" were cast, rehearsed, and booked well in advance, and sent out on the newly expanded railroad with a minimum of scenery and a limited repertory. Their purpose was to take advantage of remote towns by arranging brief stops along vast circuits throughout the West, generally untouched by the financial panic. Audiences and money were abundant, and the railroads provided an economical means of transportation. By 1880, most of the major stock companies were gone, replaced by combinations.

Success of the combinations created a new theatrical industry – booking AGENTS. Within a decade, independent booking agents, located mostly in New York and Philadelphia, controlled much of the national market. In 1896 the six most powerful men controlling the three largest agencies joined forces, effectively monopolizing the American theatre industry overnight. The Theatrical SYNDICATE, as it became known, instantly transformed the business of theatre. Its existence removed the manager as the dominate entrepreneur-artist and placed the ultimate control into the hands of a small group of financiers, whose sole objective was to turn a profit. But despite the Syndicate's inviolable monopoly, it soon fell victim to an even greater organization – the SHUBERT BROTHERS. Utilizing management techniques adapted from other big businesses and the change in corporate financing brought about by the Sherman Anti-Trust Act in 1890, the Shuberts created a modern corporation, fully capitalized and able to outmaneuver the cumbersome structure of the Syndicate. In legal action designed to halt the Syndicate's domination, the Shuberts sued under the Sherman Act, hoping to have the pool declared an illegal monopoly; but the Supreme Court ruling of 1907 absolved the Syndicate by declaring theatrical amusements not subject to the Anti-Trust Act since they are not technically manufactured goods. Initially a setback for the Shuberts, this ruling eventually proved to be a boon: After the collapse of the Syndicate in

1916, the Shuberts found themselves protected as a legal monopoly under the ruling. Not until 1956 would the Supreme Court finally declare them in violation of antitrust laws. Nevertheless, the Shubert brothers' operation served as a corporate model in the entertainment industry, especially for the early film companies.

The abuses of big business in the late 19th century contributed to the rise of labor UNIONS. Stagehands organized in 1886, and actors soon followed by forming the Actors' Society of America in 1896, succeeded by ACTORS' EQUITY ASSOCIATION. Other unions included the United Scenic Artists of America (1912) and the DRAMATISTS GUILD (1919). The Actors' Strike of 1919 solidified the labor movement in theatre, leading to a succession of crucial changes in the rights of theatrical employees; but with these changes came added expense and overhead, reflected in the gradual increase in ticket prices. Additionally, decreases in auditorium size, in part the result of stricter fire codes and changes in aesthetic taste, meant less revenue. By the 1930s, the American theatre industry had lost its financial competitiveness and much of its audience to the more economical business of film. Within 20 years, television would surpass them both.

The arrival of the musical in the early 1940s helped slow theatre's decline, but it was not enough to regain the dominance it once held. Investment in professional theatre became a highly speculative business. In the 1950s, formation of limited partnerships, in which several people shared the financial risks and rewards, replaced corporate financing as the preferred method of capitalization, but the risks were often too great for some, who sought other venues for performance. Alternatives to professional theatre are found as early as the late 19th century. Occasional experiments into nonprofit theatre, like the PROVINCETOWN PLAYERS in 1915, paved the way for the explosion in the 1960s as an alternative to the prohibitive costs of commercial theatre. The establishment of the NATIONAL ENDOWMENT FOR THE ARTS in 1966, and changes in the tax law helped expand nonprofit theatre, resulting in the rapid growth of RESIDENT NONPROFIT PROFESSIONAL THEATRE, the 20th-century incarnation of the early 19th-century stock company. However, with the drastic curtailment of NEA appropriation in the mid-1990s, and some politicians pushing for its demise, this theatre sector will likely suffer even more than it has through the difficult economic times of the 1980s and early '90s. (Since 1994 some 23 nonprofit theatres have closed, most due to deficits.)   PAD

Today's theatre is economically bifurcated: the commercial theatre on the one hand, the nonprofit model on the other. Neither is in spectacular fettle, though nonprofits' challenges are well known. The commercial theatre, however, has hurdles of its own. Broadway production costs continue outpacing inflation: Typical capitalizations are $12–14 million for musicals, $2 million for plays, and most costs, tellingly, remain on the side of marketing, advertising, and talent. Spiraling budgets are naturally reflected in ticket prices: Broadway broke the $100-a-ticket barrier in 2001 when The PRODUCERS raised its top price in response to consumer demand. Then came Broadway Inner Circle, a for-profit venture that worked with producers to set aside premium tickets of up to $400 apiece and with 20% service fees; thus came Broadway's first $480 ticket. Critics and arts advocates howled, but producers sold their hottest seats easily to corporate chieftains, who received a variety of conveniences in exhange.

The commercial theatre also became increasingly aware of its impact on New York City's local economy and, more broadly, to the overall fiscal well-being of the American stage. There was a growing sense that just as nonprofits needed to generate new products that might enjoy commercial afterlives, commercial producers needed product or the nation's roadhouses would suffer. As a recession took hold in 2000–1, and in the aftermath of the September 11 terrorist attacks (which knocked Broadway to its knees), economic impact studies became calling cards. The LEAGUE OF AMERICAN THEATRES AND PRODUCERS published 2002 and 2004 studies on Broadway's impact on New York's economy, concluding each time that it added over $4 billion annually to local coffers, generating at least 40,000 jobs. A 2006 study put Broadway's economic impact at $4.8 billion annually and 45,000 jobs. The latter figures included $3.06 billion in "ancillary" tourist spending and $1.72 billion in "spending to produce and run shows." (Broadway's 1994 economic impact was estimated at $2.3 billion.) In 2004, a sweeping Americans for the Arts study made the case national, calculating 548,000 "arts-related businesses, institutions, and organizations" nationwide – 4.3% of all American business – and 2.99 million jobs, representing 2.2% of the population. Armed with data, commercial producers navigated through tough times – which is why, in 2002, New York's mayor, Michael R. Bloomberg, set aside $2.5 million for a ticket-subsidy program tied to consumer spending.

Broadway's ongoing, aggressive branding campaign yielded fruit: In the 2002–3 season, Broadway grossed $721 million on 11.4 million attendance; the 2003–4 and 2004–5 seasons grossed about $770 million apiece on 11.6 million; and the 2005–6 season grossed $861.6 million on 12 plus, a record.   LJ

Edelman, Gregg (1958–) Chicago-born leading man, educated at Northwestern. Outstanding in musicals – beginning with a chorus role in *Evita* (1979) – he has excelled in such Broadway shows as CITY OF ANGELS (1989), *Anna Karenina* (1992), *Passion* (1994), LES MISÉRABLES (1999 replacement as Javert), INTO THE WOODS (2002 revival), and the 2003 revival of WONDERFUL TOWN. His wife is actor Carolee Carmello.   DBW

Edelstein, Barry (1965–) New Jersey native and Tufts- and Oxford-educated (Rhodes Scholar) director who staged the critically acclaimed revival of Miller's ALL MY SONS at the ROUNDABOUT in 1997. From 1997 to 2003 he was artistic director of OFF-BROADWAY's Classic Stage Company (CSC REPERTORY), where he directed successful productions of Marguerite Duras's *Savannah Bay, The Winter's Tale, The Alchemist,* and *The Misanthrope* (with ROGER REES and Uma Thurman), among others. He has been a frequent director of Shakespeare (Gwyneth Paltrow in *As You Like It,* WILLIAMSTOWN) and other classical writers from Aristophanes through the Spanish Golden Age, to G. B. SHAW and other major 20th-century playwrights, as well as contemporary authors. Currently a freelance director, he is on the faculty of the University of Southern California.   DBW

Edmonds, Randolph (1900–83) Considered the dean of African American academic theatre, Edmonds had an illustrious career as student and educator. He established the first theatre department at a black university (Dillard, 1935) and founded the National Association of Dramatic and Speech Arts to support and enhance drama programs at black institutions. He wrote some 50 plays, the most prominent appearing in the collections *Shades and Shadows* (1930), *Six Plays for the Negro Theatre* (1934), and *The Land of Cotton and Other Plays* (1942).   EGH

Edouin, Willie [né William Frederick Bryer] (1845–1908) British-born comedian who began his career in a juvenile company and first appeared in New York in a supporting role in *Ixion* (1870) with LYDIA THOMPSON's troupe. Edouin returned to America in 1877 and remained for several years, appearing in burlesque extravaganzas such as *Hiawatha* (1880). In 1880 he formed his own company, Willie Edouin's Sparks, and offered the popular farce *Dreams; or, Fun in a Photographic Gallery*. He returned to London in 1884, remaining for 16 years before revisiting the U.S. in FLORODORA (1900). As a comedian, Edouin exuded an air of good-tempered perplexity.   MK

Edwards, Ben (1916–99) Designer. Edwards began his career at the BARTER THEATRE in Virginia in 1935 and later achieved acclaim with his sets for JUDITH ANDERSON's *Medea* (1947). From the 1950s on he designed on Broadway regularly, including *The Waltz of the Toreadors* (1957), INGE's *The Dark at the Top of the Stairs* (1957), *Purlie* (1970), and six EUGENE O'NEILL plays with director JOSÉ QUINTERO. He also designed for film and TV and numerous regional theatres. Much of his work since the mid-1960s was in collaboration with his wife, costume designer JANE GREENWOOD. Though Edwards designed in a variety of styles, he acknowledged an influence from ROBERT EDMOND JONES, and his sets were generally suggestive and evocative, such as the 1992 *STREETCAR NAMED DESIRE* revival. In 1998 he received a Tony for Lifetime Achievement.   AA

Effect of Gamma Rays on Man-in-the-Moon Marigolds, The Pulitzer Prize–winning drama in two acts by PAUL ZINDEL opened on 7 April 1970 OFF-BROADWAY at the Mercer–O'Casey Theatre, directed by Melvin Bernhardt and featuring SADA THOMPSON. The play, in the naturalistic tradition, is both comic and serious in tone, dealing with a tyrannical widow and her two daughters. Paralleling the effects of the mother on her offspring, Zindel reveals society's growing concern with exposure to radiation and its possibilities of producing mutations.   ER

Eichelberger, Ethyl [né James Roy Eichelberger] (1945–90) Unique PERFORMANCE ARTIST-writer, a victim of AIDS and suicide. MEL GUSSOW called him "the ultimate autodidact – actor, clown, playwright, singer, director, composer, accordionist, tumbler and fire-eater." After seven years with the TRINITY REPERTORY COMPANY, Eichelberger moved to New York in 1975, began a collaboration with CHARLES LUDLUM and the RIDICULOUS THEATRICAL COMPANY, and established a reputation for outrageous male and female characters (he personally concocted some 32 plays, many challenging sexual barriers), in particular in his deconstructed classics (*Medea, Leer, Ariadne Obnoxious, Hamlette*, and *Jocasta; or, Boy Crazy*). He also appeared at LINCOLN CENTER in *Measure for Measure* and *Comedy of Errors*, and in DEXTER's 1989

Threepenny Opera. (See also FEMALE/MALE IMPERSONATION.) In 2005 PERFORMANCE SPACE 122 inaugurated an annual award in his name; the first recepient was performance artist Taylor Mac.   DBW

Eigsti, Karl (1938–) Designer and educator. For much of his career Eigsti was associated with the ARENA STAGE in Washington as well as other regional theatres, notably the GUTHRIE, AMERICAN SHAKESPEARE FESTIVAL, LONG WHARF, HUNTINGTON, and CINCINNATI PLAYHOUSE. Broadway work has been limited, but he has designed numerous notable shows OFF-BROADWAY, including *The HOUSE OF BLUE LEAVES* (1971). He has two distinct styles: a simplified realism for much of the commercial work, and a bold symbolism often employed for the arena-style productions. He has taught at New York University and heads the design program at Brandeis University.   AA

Eisenberg, Avner see AVNER THE ECCENTRIC

Eisenhauer, Peggy (1962–) Lighting designer, New York City native, and Carnegie Mellon graduate. A partner with JULES FISHER (Third Eye Ltd.), as of early 2007 she had collaborated with him on 29 Broadway designs (beginning with *Tommy Tune Tonight!* in 1992 and including *Caroline, or Change* in 2004 and the 2005 *Chita Rivera: The Dancer's Life*). They share two Tonys (1996 and 2004). She has designed lighting for The Cars, Billy Ocean, Lisa Lisa, and other performers.   BO

El Teatro Campesino (The Farmworkers' Theatre) founded by LUIS VALDÉZ in 1965 to support Filipino and Mexican American strikers against the grape farmers of the San Joaquin Valley in California. Initially an agitprop group tailoring its *actos* (short plays) to the issues and needs of the moment, the company took on a wider political involvement – though still focusing on CHICANO concerns – during the period of maximum opposition to the Vietnam War. In the 1970s the group converted a warehouse into a research-and-development center with a 150-seat theatre in San Juan Bautista, 97 miles south of San Francisco. By the 1980s they began to take productions premiered in the ETC Playhouse to larger venues (plays such as *Corridos!* and *I Don't Have to Show You No Stinking Badges*). Since the 1990s three to six productions have been presented annually; the company also returned in 1992 to the touring practice of the 1970s, when six major tours covered the U.S., Mexico, and Europe. In 1994 ETC

coproduced with the MARK TAPER Valdéz's *Bandido!* In 2000 the troupe remounted *La gran carpa de los Rasquachis* (*The Great Tent of the Underdogs*) and *Zoot Suit* in 2000–3. Today, Anáhuac, Kinán, and Lakín, sons of Luis and Lupe Valdez, are instrumental in running the organization, acting, directing, and producing plays while exploring other media such as film and video. Every Christmas season the company alternates productions of two Spanish religious folk plays in the historic mission at San Juan Bautista: *La pastorela* (*The Shepherd's Play*) and *La Virgen del Tepeyac*, about the appearance of the Virgin of Guadalupe in 1531.
DBW   JH

Elder, Eldon (1921–2000) Designer from Kansas who studied with DONALD OENSLAGER at Yale. Though he has designed over 200 productions for Broadway, OFF-BROADWAY, opera, and regional theatre, his lasting legacy is as designer of the Delacorte Theater, the Central Park home of the NEW YORK SHAKESPEARE FESTIVAL, where he was resident designer during 1958–61. He also designed or consulted on several other theatres, including many regional theatres, with more than 30 productions at the ST. LOUIS MUNICIPAL Opera. Elder taught for many years at Brooklyn College.   AA

Elder, Lonne, III (1931–96) African American playwright and film/TV scriptwriter, highly regarded for his play *CEREMONIES IN DARK OLD MEN* (1969). After the critical acclaim accorded this play, Elder joined the NEGRO ENSEMBLE COMPANY as director of its Playwrights' Unit. He then moved to Hollywood to write scripts for film and television, including the award-winning *Sounder* (1972), which shows the effect of the Depression on a black sharecropping family; its sequel, *Sounder, Part II* (1976); and *Melinda* (1972), about a black disk jockey's entanglement with a crime syndicate. In 1988 Elder's one-person play *Splendid Mummer* opened at AMERICAN PLACE THEATRE: Based on the career of the 19th-century black actor IRA ALDRIDGE and featuring Charles S. Dutton, it failed, however, to win critical approval.
EGH

Eldridge [*née* McKechnie]**, Florence** (1901–88) Actress whose Broadway debut in 1918 was in the chorus of *Rock-a-Bye Baby*. After several appearances on Broadway, she toured with her husband, FREDRIC MARCH, in THEATRE GUILD productions such as *Arms and the Man*, *The SILVER CORD*, and *The Guardsman* in 1927–8. She made her film debut in 1923 in *Six Cylinder Love*, and in 1929 shared the screen with March in *The Studio Murder Mystery*. She frequently appeared onstage with him, as in *The SKIN OF OUR TEETH* (1942) and again in RUTH GORDON's *Years Ago* (1946). One of her greatest successes, again with March, was as Mary Tyrone in *LONG DAY'S JOURNEY INTO NIGHT* (1956), for which she won the VARIETY New York Drama Critics' Poll and was nominated for a Tony.   SMA

Elephant Man, The Play in 21 scenes by New York–born Bernard Pomerance, suggested by the life of Joseph (*not* John) Merrick. This late-19th-century figure suffered from a genetic disorder that made him appear monstrous. Merrick's plight was developed as a play first at London's Hampstead Theatre and then in 73 Off-Broadway performances. The latter, directed by Jack Hofsiss, promptly transferred to Broadway's BOOTH THEATRE, opening 19 April 1979, running 916 performances, and winning many major drama awards. Merrick was played by Philip Anglim, and KEVIN CONWAY portrayed Dr. Frederick Treves, the surgeon who rescued Merrick from ignominy and helped him to achieve some degree of human dignity. Although Merrick can never become the ordinary man of his dreams, his dramatized story is one of human courage and spirit. Pomerance has had several plays produced in England (where he lives), but this is his only U.S. success. A 2002 Broadway revival starred BILLY CRUDUP, KATE BURTON, and Rupert Graves (Treves), but lasted only 57 performances.   DBW

Eliot, T(homas) S(tearns) (1888–1965) Playwright and poet born in St. Louis, Missouri, educated at Harvard, the Sorbonne, and Oxford; settled in England in 1915. Eliot's best-known play, *MURDER IN THE CATHEDRAL*, commissioned for the 1935 Canterbury Festival, was seen in the U.S. at Yale that year and was presented by the FEDERAL THEATRE PROJECT in New York the following year. His other verse plays (*The Family Reunion*, 1939; *The Cocktail Party*, 1949; *The Confidential Clerk*, 1953; and *The Elder Statesman*, 1958) were less successful here. Only *The Cocktail Party*, in the style of drawing-room comedy, was popular as a play, receiving the 1950 New York Drama Critics' Circle Award as Best Foreign Play. In the 1980s and '90s a renewed interest in Eliot resulted from the long-running ANDREW LLOYD WEBBER musical *CATS* – based on Eliot's 1939 poems *Old Possum's Book of Practical Cats* – which opened at NYC's WINTER GARDEN THEATRE in 1982 after its premiere in London.   DBW

Elizabeth the Queen by MAXWELL ANDERSON. A THEATRE GUILD production, this three-act verse play opened 3 November 1930 and ran 147 performances. ALFRED LUNT and LYNN FONTANNE starred as lovers – the young Earl of Essex and the aging Queen Elizabeth. Arrested for treason, Essex refuses to beg for mercy. As he strides toward his execution, she pleads, "Take my kingdom, it is yours!" Percy Waram played Sir Walter Raleigh; Arthur Hughes, Sir Robert Cecil; and MORRIS CARNOVSKY, Francis Bacon. BROOKS ATKINSON described it as magnificent drama, a searching portrayal of character in dialogue of notable beauty. Anderson's earliest historical drama and one of the few blank-verse successes on the American stage, it was revived on tour in 1961 with EVA LE GALLIENNE and in 1966 starring JUDITH ANDERSON.   GSA

Elliott, Gertrude [*née* May Dermot] (1874–1950) Actress; sister to MAXINE ELLIOTT. After making her New York debut in 1894, she acted with Marie Wainwright (1895) and NAT GOODWIN (1897–9), playing Emily in IN MIZZOURA, Lucy in *The Rivals*, and Angelica Knowlton in *Nathan Hale*. She made her London debut in 1899 as Midge in *The Cowboy and the Lady*, and remained in England to play Ophelia to Forbes-Robertson's Hamlet. After the two were married in 1900, she returned to America several times, playing Maisie in *The Light That Failed* (1903), a character in the mold of Hedda Gabler, and creating the role of Cleopatra in G. B. SHAW's *Caesar and Cleopatra* (1906). Critics praised her girlish spirit, playful humor, eloquent speech, and dusky beauty. After her husband retired, she managed London's St. James's Theatre (1918).   TLM

Elliott, Maxine [*née* Jessie Dermot] (1871–1940) Actress and stage beauty; older sister to GERTRUDE ELLIOTT. After making her New York stage debut at PALMER's Theatre in 1890, Maxine Elliott rose rapidly in the theatre, spending a season each with ROSE COGHLAN's and AUGUSTIN DALY's companies (1894, 1895) before her London debut as Sylvia in *Two Gentlemen of Verona* (1895). After touring Australia with NAT GOODWIN (1896), she became his leading lady (1897) and his wife (1898). They costarred in numerous successes, including her first big hit as Alice Adams in *Nathan Hale* (1899). They separated in 1902, after which she established herself as a star with Georgiana Carley in *Her Own Way* (1903) written for her by CLYDE FITCH. Two years later, her Georgiana attracted the attentions of Edward VII in London. She built the Maxine Elliott Theatre in New York (1908) with help from the SHUBERTS, and appeared there in numerous comedies,

including *The Chaperon* and *Trimmed in Scarlet*. In 1911 she retired to England, making only occasional stage appearances thereafter. She was praised as a "rare comedienne of the drawing room" during her 1918–19 American tour of *Lord and Lady Algy*. Although she appeared stiff and mechanical to some critics, all praised her dark and lustrous beauty and her statuesque stage presence. She retired to the Riviera after 1920 to live out her life as a "lady of society." A biography by her niece Diana Forbes-Robertson was published in 1964.   TLM

Elliott, Scott (1963?–) The Long Island native trained as an actor at the Boston Conservatory of Music (later, film at NYU). After a career as a director on the margins (with acclaimed OFF-BROADWAY stagings of Mike Leigh's *Ecstasy* and Stephen Bill's *Curtains*), he emerged by the mid-1990s as an in-demand mainstream director. A Broadway directorial debut in 1996 (Noël Coward's *Present Laughter*) was followed in short order by an unsuccessful CHEKHOV's *Three Sisters* and prestigious jobs at WILLIAMSTOWN. Elliott remains active, including directing annual productions for NEW GROUP (*Hurlyburly* in 2005), an OFF-BROADWAY company he founded in 1991. In 2001 his revival of *The WOMEN* for ROUNDABOUT was a hit; and in 2006 he directed a tepid revival of BAREFOOT IN THE PARK and *The Threepenny Opera* as translated by WALLACE SHAWN and starring Alan Cumming as Macheath.   DBW

Ellis, Scott (1964–) Broadway director who first garnered attention in 1991 with the OFF-BROADWAY revue *And the World Goes Round*, which he conceived and directed. Since then his services have been in constant demand, especially for musical revivals (*She Loves Me, 1776, The Boys from Syracuse*) and often at the ROUNDABOUT (e.g., ARTHUR MILLER's *The Man Who Had All the Luck*, 2002), where since 1998 he has been an associate director. His original musical projects include *Steel Pier* (1997) and the REVUE *The Look of Love* (2003). He has also directed numerous straight plays – and often revivals – such as *A Thousand Clowns, Twelve Angry Men*, and *Entertaining Mr. Sloan*. He has received four Tony nominations as of early 2007.   DBW

Ellsler, Effie (1854–1942) Actress, daughter of JOHN ELLSLER, she first appeared at her father's theatre, where she became the leading lady (1872–6). STEELE MACKAYE brought her to the MADISON SQUARE THEATRE, New York, and wrote the title role of HAZEL KIRKE (1880) for her. Later she starred at the head of her own company. After 1903 she appeared only occasionally, most notably as Cornelia Van Corder in *The BAT* (1920). DMcD

Ellsler, John (1822–1903) Manager. Originally an actor, he assumed management of his own company at Cleveland's Academy of Music in 1855. He opened his lavish Euclid Avenue Opera House in 1875, but the Academy of Music remained his center of operation until 1885. His company toured extensively to surrounding towns in the summers, and between 1871 and 1887 he managed at least one theatre a year in Pittsburgh. His theatre was noted as a nursery of talent: CLARA MORRIS, JAMES O'NEILL, JAMES LEWIS, and MRS. G. H. GILBERT apprenticed there. His daughter, EFFIE ELLSLER, became a leading lady of the next generation. His memoirs were published posthumously in 1950.   DMcD

Elson, Charles (1909–2000) Designer and educator who began his design career in the 1930s. He served as lighting and design assistant to DONALD OENSLAGER on several productions in the 1940s, and did his first Broadway show in 1946. Through the 1970s Elson designed sets and lights at the Metropolitan Opera, AMERICAN SHAKESPEARE FESTIVAL, and Broadway. During 1948–74 he taught at Hunter College.   AA

Eltinge, Julian [*né* William Julian Dalton] (1883–1941) FEMALE IMPERSONATOR, first seen professionally in *Mr. Wix of Wickham*, a musical comedy (1904). His biggest hit was *The Fascinating Widow* (1911 and tours), in which he outshone fashion-plate Valeska Surratt. Its success led grateful producer A. H. WOODS to build the Eltinge Theatre on 42d St., New York. "The ambi-sextrous comedian," as PERCY HAMMOND called him, chose vehicles that enabled him to shift gender by quick change (one act required 11 separate changes). With his company, the Julian Eltinge Players, he played VAUDEVILLE (1906–27) and starred in silent films. A large man with a passable baritone voice, he was a favorite primarily with female audiences, not least for the chic of his wardrobe. One of his last variety appearances – at the White Horse, Los Angeles (1940) – was a fiasco, owing to a police ban on public transvestism; his final appearance was at BILLY ROSE's Diamond Horseshoe, NYC, 1941.   LS

Emery, Gilbert [né Emery Remsley Pottle] (1875–1945) Dramatist who became an actor after serving in WWI and enjoyed a moderate career writing domestic dramas. *The Hero* (1921), his most highly regarded play, dramatized the effect of an apparently dissolute war hero upon the wife of his brother, who stayed home during the war to care for his family. *Tarnish* (1923), concerned with a naive young woman's confrontation with a lover's past, was more successful, but *Episode* (1925), dealing with a husband's acceptance and forgiveness of his wife's infidelities in order to maintain his conventional social life, failed. *Love-in-a-Mist* (1926) was written with Amélie Rives. All reflect American society of a particular period.
   WJM

Emmet, J(oseph) K(lein) "Fritz" (1841–91) Variety performer-actor. St. Louis–born Emmet developed a particular German immigrant character ("not very much like any character ever seen in

Julian Eltinge in drag in *The Crinoline Girl,* Knickerbocker Theatre, New York, 1914. Photo by White, New York. *Courtesy:* Laurence Senelick Collection.

real life"), first on the variety stage and later in a series of "Fritz" plays, beginning with CHARLES GAYLER's *Fritz, Our Cousin German* (1869). His stage actions, including songs ("Emmet's Lullaby") and dances, often seemed unrelated to the plays. In each piece, outfitted in green blouse and cap and wooden shoes, Emmet depicted a slow-witted fellow fond of children. Ultimately, it was his winning personality rather than his talent that pleased the public.   DBW

Emmett, Daniel Decatur (1815–1904) Ohio-born minstrel who traveled with circuses as a musician from 1835. His popular jig songs, including "Root Hog or Die," achieved folkloric status. He teamed his fiddle with William M. Whitlock on banjo, Dick Pelham (Richard Ward Pell), on tambourine, and Francis Marion Brower on bones, all in blackface, to create The Virginia Minstrels (debut, Bowery Amphitheatre, New York, 6 February 1843). This "jazz band of the nineteenth century" set the format for the MINSTREL SHOW first in the U.S., then in England and Ireland in 1844. After the group dissolved, Emmett opened the first minstrel hall in Chicago (1855). With BRYANT's Minstrels, New York, he developed the "walk-around"; an accompanying song, "Dixie's Land" (4 April 1859), became the Confederate anthem. Late in life he toured with Leavitt's Gigantean Minstrels, re-creating his pioneering quartet. His life was recounted by Hans Nathan in 1962.   LS

Emmons, Beverly (1943–) Lighting designer who, after assisting JULES FISHER in the 1960s, became one of the primary lighting designers of the OFF-BROADWAY and OFF-OFF BROADWAY movements. She worked for 13 years on ROBERT WILSON productions, including *Einstein on the Beach* (1976), as well as works by MEREDITH MONK and JOSEPH CHAIKIN. Broadway work includes *The ELEPHANT MAN; Amadeus,* assisting British designer John Bury (who won the lighting Tony); and the SONDHEIM musical *Passion* (1994). In 1995 she received the Maharam (AMERICAN THEATRE WING) Design Award for *The Heiress.* She has also designed extensively for dance, including works by Merce Cunningham, Meredith Monk, Lar Lubovitch, Martha Graham, Trisha Brown, and Lucinda Childs.   AA

Emond, Linda (1959–) New Jersey–born actress, reared in Southern California and educated at the University of Washington. She worked for 11 years in Chicago before moving to NYC, where her debut was OFF-BROADWAY (MANHATTAN THEATRE CLUB) in *Nine Armenians* (1996); her Broad-

way debut was as Abigail Adams in *1776* (1997 revival). Other roles of note have been in KUSHNER's *Homebody/Kabul* (2001; Obie, Lucille Lortel Award) and Inez in Yasmina Reza's *Life (x) 3* (2003). She has appeared in venues such as LINCOLN CENTER, the VINEYARD, SIGNATURE, CSC REPERTORY, and WILLIAMSTOWN, usually playing strong, complex women – though, as with the low-esteemed Reza role, slotting her is not easy.   DBW

Emperor Jones, The, by EUGENE O'NEILL. This historically important and still powerful one-act tragedy of a Pullman porter turned small-time West Indies dictator first opened at the Playwright's Theatre of the PROVINCETOWN PLAYERS in New York on 1 November 1920, under the direction of GEORGE CRAM COOK and with CLEON THROCKMORTON's first theatrical designs. It not only brought popular attention to the Provincetowners, resulting in their first Broadway run, but served as the first important portrayal by a black actor (CHARLES GILPIN as Brutus Jones; later played by PAUL ROBESON) in white-controlled, mainstream American theatre. The semiexpressionistic play explores power hunger and corruption at a crude, visceral level while delving into the mysterious world of voodoo, racial memory, and psychological disintegration. A journey play that carries Jones on a dark pilgrimage from sundown to dawn through his memory, fears, guilt, and cultural heritage, culminates in his destruction by a silver bullet. Interestingly, slowly escalating native drumming underscores nearly all of the play and contributes to, if not causes, the steady breakdown and mounting horror of brutal Brutus Jones.   RHW

Empire Theatre 1430 Broadway, NYC [Architect: J. B. McElfatrick and Co.]. In 1893, when CHARLES FROHMAN built the gemlike Empire some 25 blocks north of the theatre district at Union Square, the spark was ignited to create a new theatre district uptown. This theatre remained the headquarters of Frohman's activities until he died on the *Lusitania* in 1915. During his lifetime, Frohman was Broadway's principal starmaker, a member of the Theatrical SYNDICATE, and the Napoleon of the American theatre. The roster of the stars who appeared at the Empire is etched into a plaque affixed to the wall of the characterless office building that replaced the theatre after it was torn down in 1953. The theatre was managed by Alf Hayman for the Frohman estate on a run-of-the-play basis, and was later leased to producer GILBERT MILLER until 1931. With just over 1,000 seats, it was a compact, well-designed playhouse and a favorite among actors and audiences. It enjoyed a latter-day reputation as a house of hits, crowned by the arrival of LIFE WITH FATHER in 1939, which did not leave its stage for six years. The theatre changed ownership several times before its demise. At the time it closed, it was presenting *The Time of the Cuckoo* with SHIR-LEY BOOTH. MCH

Empty Space Theatre, The Founded in 1970 by M(ilton) Burke Walker, Julian Schembri, James Royce, and Charles Younger as a COLLECTIVE operating in a 65-seat basement in SEATTLE's Pike Place Market. The company concentrated on contemporary American and European works, presenting numerous northwestern and world premieres by major playwrights, including Edward Bond, LEE BREUER, and MARIA IRENE FORNÉS. After formalizing its cooperative structure in 1974, the original 16-member company disbanded in 1976, Walker remaining as artistic director until 1990, when he became head of the University of Washington's directing program. Kurt Beattie followed Walker and in 1993 was replaced by Eddie Levi Lee, who in turn was succeeded in 2001 by Allison Narver. A financial crisis in 2004–5 was averted thanks to a successful emergency fund-raising campaign, and the group moved into Seattle University's new $6.75 million Lee Center for Performing Arts in February 2006 as theatre in residence. However, in October 2006 its closure was announced. Since its founding "The Space" had introduced more than 65 playwrights to Northwest audiences. RW

Encores! see CITY CENTER'S *ENCORES!*

Engel, Lehman (1910–82) Conductor, composer, writer, and educator. He attended music schools in Cincinnati before graduating from Juilliard in 1935. Engel worked as a musical director for the FEDERAL THEATRE PROJECT and then began a 30-year career as a Broadway conductor. He also composed dance music for choreographers such as Martha Graham and Doris Humphrey, and provided background scores for dozens of plays. In 1959 he founded the Lehman Engel Musical Theatre Workshop in conjunction with Broadcast Music, Inc., where he helped to train dozens of young musical-theatre talents. He also wrote several highly regarded books about musical theatre, including *This Bright Day,* his 1974 autobiography. MK

English's Theatre (Indianapolis) Seating nearly 2,000, this theatre opened 27 September 1880

with LAWRENCE BARRETT in *Hamlet.* The newest, most lavish theatre in town, it competed with George Dickson's Grand Opera House until 1886, when it was leased by Dickson's partner, Henry Talbott. Under their management it was a member of an Ohio Valley circuit of theatres that eventually became part of the Theatrical SYNDICATE. DMcD

Ensemble Studio Theatre 549 West 52nd St., NYC. Founded in 1972 by Curt Dempster, its longtime artistic director, this not-for-profit theatre aims to nurture individual artists and to develop new American plays. Its membership now totals some 500 theatre artists. Over 300 projects are presented annually, including one-act plays in its yearly marathon (now almost 30 years old). In 1993–4 it initiated Youngblood in order to introduce works by playwrights between ages 18 and 25. EST has generated more than 3,000 full-length plays which have been produced at over 360 theatres nationally. Dempster died unexpectedly early in 2007. DBW

Enters, Angna (1900?–89) Dancer-MIME, writer, and artist whose international 40-year solo career began in New York in 1924 with her performance of "stage poems without words." She created the costumes, sets, and often the music for 100 dance episodes, ranging from tragedy to parody and portraying mainly women of many periods and countries. At MGM in Hollywood during the 1940s, she contributed a commedia dell'arte sequence for *Scaramouche* and the story line for *Lost Angel.* After her New York art show in 1933, she exhibited annually and also published three books of memoirs, a play, a novel, and *On Mime* (1965) after teaching at Baylor (Texas) and Wesleyan (Connecticut). DM

Epperson, John (1956–) Better known for his alter ego, the lip-synching glamour goddess Lypsinka, termed by MARGO JEFFERSON "one of the most gifted and hard-working women in show business," this unique solo performer, born in rural Mississippi, began his career as a rehearsal pianist at American Ballet Theater and then as composer-lyricist-book writer of two musicals at LA MAMA before graduating to his Lypinska creation. Over the past 20 years, Lypinska cabaret-style shows have included *I Could Go on Lip-Synching!* (his first), *The Fabulous Lypsinka Show, Lypsinka! Now It Can Be Lip-Synched, Lypsinka! A Day in the Life, Lypsinka! As I Lay Lip-Synching, Lypsinka Must Be Destroyed!, The Fabulous Lypsinka Show,* and *Lypsinka! The Boxed Set. Lypsinka Is Harriet Craig!,* in 1998,

241

marked her speaking debut; *Messages for Gary* in 1999 was Epperson's dramatic stage debut (at the New York Fringe Festival). In 2004 Epperson played the stepmother in New York City Opera's revival of the RODGERS and HAMMERSTEIN musical *Cinderella*. His most recent shows are *The Passion of the Crawford* (2005) and *My Deah* (2006), the latter an updated, Lypsinka-less parody of *Medea*. DBW

Epstein, Alvin (1925–) Actor and director who studied acting with SANFORD MEISNER, dancing with Martha Graham, and mime with Étienne Decroux (company member, Paris, 1947–51). Joining the Habima Theatre of Tel Aviv, he acted in European, American, and Yiddish plays (1953–5). He made his Broadway debut with Marcel Marceau (1955) and next year played Lucky in the New York premiere of Beckett's *Waiting for Godot* (JOHN GOLDEN THEATRE). Notable performances include the Fool in ORSON WELLES's *Lear* (1956, City Center), a controversially comic Trotsky in *The Passion of Josef D.* (1964), and an Obie-winning role in *Dynamite Tonite!* (1968). Many of his best roles have been in absurdist or modern plays (*Enrico IV, Endgame, Macbett*). Epstein, a joyous performer who revels in physical theatricality, has worked extensively in musical theatre, with particular success in KURT WEILL vehicles. Cofounder of the BERKSHIRE THEATRE FESTIVAL (1967), associate director of the YALE REPERTORY THEATRE (1973–7), and artistic director of the GUTHRIE THEATRE (1977–9), he has been with the AMERICAN REPERTORY THEATRE since 1980. In 2001 he appeared in *The Madwoman of Chaillot* at the NEIGHBORHOOD PLAYHOUSE; in 2002 in *Tuesdays with Morrie* at Minetta Lane; and in fall 2005 he essayed King Lear with a new Boston company at Boston University and in summer 2006 at LA MAMA. TC

Erlanger, Abraham (Lincoln) (1860–1930) Longtime partner (1887–1919) of MARC ALONZO KLAW who was introduced to theatre management in Cleveland. In New York in 1880, he was an advance AGENT for touring productions, then a tour manager. With Klaw, Erlanger was the organizational genius and chief booking agent for the Theatrical SYNDICATE, a trust formed in 1896 to maximize the trustees' profits. Erlanger purchased most of Klaw's interest in the Klaw and Erlanger Exchange in 1919. In 1921, he sold his extensive theatrical real estate but continued to produce plays until his death. To some, Erlanger epitomized the businessman, devoid of aesthetic taste, propelled by ruthless opportunism to a position of suffocating power over theatre artists.

To others, Erlanger and his partner are notable for developing a centralized booking system that brought order and increasing profitability to all sectors of the theatrical business world. WD

Errico, Melissa (1970–) New York native and Yale graduate whose youthful Broadway debut was in the new musical *Anna Karenina* (1992), followed in quick succession by a series of revivals and concerts – *MY FAIR LADY* (1993) opposite Richard Chamberlain, *CALL ME MADAM* (1995, concert), *One Touch of Venus* (1996, concert), *High Society* (1998), the short-lived Michel Legrand *Amour* (2002), the IRISH REPERTORY's *FINIAN'S RAINBOW* (2004), and *Dracula, the Musical* (2004). Her sense of high style and language has also suited nonmusicals such as *The Importance of Being Earnest* (1996), *Major Barbara* (1997), and *Aunt Dan and Lemon* (2004 revival). DBW

Errol, Leon (1881–1951) Australian actor-director who came to the U.S. only to discover his accent was incomprehensible. He therefore performed as a dancer for two years without speaking, perfecting his pantoMIME. He arrived in New York in 1911, starring in his own show, *The Lillies*. This brought him to the attention of ZIEGFELD, who featured him in the 1911 *Follies*. Errol was considered the best comedian of the *Follies* prior to WWI. He made a considerable success in *SALLY* (1920), later filming the same show. His film roles covered some 20 years, exemplified by Lord Epping in *Mexican Spitfire* (1940). SMA

Esbjornson, David (1953?–) Award-winning director and producer who has worked eclectically throughout the U.S., on Broadway and Off (2004, *Much Ado about Nothing* in Central Park), and in 2005 in London where he directed the U.K. premiere of *A Few Good Men*. From 1992 to 1997 he was artistic director of NYC's Classic Stage Company (see CSC REP), where he broadened the company's notion of what a classic play was, and since 2005 he has served the SEATTLE REPERTORY THEATRE in the same capacity. Although he directed ALBEE's *The GOAT, OR WHO IS SYLVIA?* and MILLER's *The Ride Down Mt. Morgan* on Broadway, he is equally known for premiere productions of KUSHNER's *ANGELS IN AMERICA: Millennium Approaches* (EUREKA THEATRE) and SUZAN-LORI PARKS's *In the Blood* (PUBLIC), among many premieres of plays by cutting-edge, adventurous writers. His work at CSC ended with a LUCILLE LORTEL Award for its Outstanding Body of Work. A native of Minnesota, his undergraduate work was at Gustavus Adolphus College. and his M.F.A. is from NYU. DBW

Esterman, Laura (1950?–) Eclectic actress reared in Lawrence, Long Island, with an English degree from Radcliffe and acting training at LAMDA and, more significant, with UTA HAGEN. Her major impact has been as the leukemia patient Bessie in Scott McPherson's *MARVIN'S ROOM*, first in 1990 at the GOODMAN THEATRE, then two years later in New York (PLAYWRIGHTS HORIZONS and Minetta Lane Theatre), for which she won an Obie. Other roles of note include Teibele in Singer's *Teibele and Her Demon* (1979), Baryshnikov's wretched mother in *Metamorphosis* (1989), Amanda in YALE REP's *The GLASS MENAGERIE* (1999), and Sarah Bernhardt in *Duet* (2003, Greenwich Street Theatre). She has appeared in plays as diverse as CHARLES MEE's *True Love,* MILLER's *The American Clock,* and Shakespeare's *A Midsummer Night's Dream.* DBW

Ethel, Agnes (1852–1903) Actress whose brief career ended when she married in 1873. Ethel studied with MATILDA HERON and made her debut as Camille at the private Jerome Theatre in New York. She then joined AUGUSTIN DALY's company for additional experience. Her greatest successes were as Gilberte in *Frou-Frou* (1870) and the titles roles in *Fernande* (1870) and Sardou's *Agnes* (1872, for A. M. PALMER). OLIVE LOGAN praised her fascinating beauty, starry eyes, and red-gold hair, and for a few years Ethel was among the most popular of American actresses. SMA

Ethel Barrymore Theatre 243 West 47th St., NYC [Architect: Herbert J. Krapp]. ETHEL BARRYMORE, the actress, was lured into the management of the SHUBERTS with the promise of Ethel Barrymore, the theatre. Opening late in 1928, it was one of the last playhouses to be built in the theatre district before the Depression. An intimate, well-designed house, it seats just under 1,100 and is well suited to the realistic play and comedy. Although a number of failures have appeared at the Barrymore, it has also housed a fair share of history-making productions, among which have been *The WOMEN* (1936), *PAL JOEY* (1940), *A STREETCAR NAMED DESIRE* (1947), *LOOK HOMEWARD, ANGEL* (1957), *A RAISIN IN THE SUN* (1959), and *The TALE OF THE ALLERGIST'S WIFE* (2000). It has remained a Shubert house and never altered its name. MCH

ethnic theatre in the United States Ethnic theatre in the U.S. is theatre by and for minority communities whose cultural heritages distinguish them from the Anglo-American mainstream. A pluralistic nation with an indigenous population and immigrants from every corner of the earth, the U.S. has been host to a rich variety of ethnic theatres. These have helped to meet the intellectual and emotional needs of people separated from the mainstream by language, culture, poverty, and discrimination. They have reinforced indigenous or "Old World" languages and traditions, helped immigrants adjust to their new country, provided an arena for talented ethnic actors, directors, and playwrights, and introduced new personalities and techniques to the Anglo-American stage.

Ethnic theatres sprang from a variety of historical conditions. NATIVE AMERICAN THEATRE is rooted in communal celebrations and ancient rituals reflecting the religious outlook and shared values of the indigenous nations that created it. Conquest by whites destroyed entire "Indian" nations, including, of course, their drama. Moreover, the confinement of Native Americans to reservations and the increasing dominance of Western culture often had a negative influence on the drama of nations that did survive.

White Americans were introduced to black performance as early as 1664, when captive Africans were forced to dance and sing for the crew of the English slaveship *Hannibal.* Autonomous AFRICAN AMERICAN THEATRE began in 1821 in lower Manhattan, where the AFRICAN THEATRE, founded by WILLIAM HENRY BROWN, performed Shakespearean drama for audiences of whites and blacks (see SHAKESPEARE ON . . .). In the 19th century whites in "blackface" gave MINSTREL SHOWS, racist parodies of black entertainment; however, independent black theatre persisted, and by the early 20th century, MUSICALS written and performed by blacks were appearing on Broadway and in Harlem.

French theatre entered the country in 1803 when the United States purchased Louisiana from France, and Mexican American (or CHICANO) theatre entered with the conquest of the Southwest from Mexico in 1848. Immigrants from Europe and Asia established theatres soon after their arrival. German theatres appeared in the rural Midwest in the early 1840s and in New York and New Orleans even earlier. Chinese theatre opened in SAN FRANCISCO in 1852, and Japanese troupes entertained in SEATTLE several decades later. Polish, Yiddish, Italian, and other southern/eastern-European theatres were active in urban centers by the turn of the century.

Immigrant theatres faced significant problems, including lack of money, quarrels among the actors, directors, and playwrights, and opposition from inside and outside the community. Scandinavian theatre was opposed by the conservative Lutheran clergy, who associated it with drinking; civil authorities closed Chinese theatres for performing on Sunday (when working-class audiences were free to attend); and German theatre was devastated by boycotts during the WWI.

Nevertheless, as the number of immigrants rose to a million a year in the decade before WWI, immigrant theatres flourished. Actors trained in their homelands pursued careers in the U.S., joined by enthusiastic amateurs who spent long days in the workplace and then rehearsed far into the night. Audiences with sparse resources saved their pennies for tickets. Large communities supported commercial theatres, and virtually every group enjoyed amateur theatre sponsored by lodges, athletic groups, schools, and cultural, nationalist, and socialist societies. Road companies brought theatre to isolated farm and mining communities.

Moved by the same desire for economic opportunity and personal freedom that brought immigrants from foreign countries to the U.S., native-born blacks migrated from the rural South to the industrial and commercial cities of the North in the opening decades of the 20th century. A burst of African American theatrical creativity was part of the cultural and intellectual flowering of the 1920s known as the Harlem Renaissance. While black theatre flourished in many cities, its center was Harlem, where race-conscious plays by, for, and about black America were produced in the 1920s and '30s by companies such as the Krigwa Players (founded by W. E. B. Du Bois), the Harlem Experimental Theatre, the New Negro Theatre, and the Harlem Suitcase Theatre (founded by LANGSTON HUGHES).

An integral part of the life of the immigrant "ghettos" of the early 20th century, ethnic theatres supported the educational, charitable, and political causes important to their communities. Theatre benefits financed Italian parochial schools in St. Louis, social services for Danes and Japanese in Seattle, and orphanages and hospitals in the Ukraine. Their actors having unionized, YIDDISH THEATRES supported the "Uprising of the 20,000," the historic general strike of the largely Jewish shirtwaist makers in New York City in 1909. Thaddeus Dolega-Eminowicz, star and founder of Polish theatres in many American cities, produced and acted in an original play, *With Whom to Side?* in Detroit in 1917 to raise funds for the Polish Legion's participation in WWI.

Immigrant theatres provided a place where the young and old, the educated and the uneducated, the newcomer and the oldtimer, and the poor and the upwardly mobile could gather and share a common experience. To the inhabitants of cramped, dreary tenements, theatres were attractive places to court, gossip, quarrel, eat, joke, and nurture friendships. To actors, directors, and playwrights, the theatre was a self-sufficient social world in which marriages took place and children were reared, sometimes appearing onstage as soon as they could walk and talk. This world was especially important to intellectuals, whose lack of English cut them off from the professions they had pursued in the homeland. It was also important to women, who found in it an alternative to traditional domestic roles and a chance to win money and recognition and adopt unconventional lifestyles with relative impunity. African-born Clara Lemberg made her reputation on the Finnish American stage, Theofilia Samolinska on the Polish, Antonietta Pisanelli Alessandro on the Italian, and Sara Adler on the Yiddish. During the Harlem Renaissance (1918–30) 11 black women published 21 plays.

Ethnic theatre made the history and folklore of the homelands accessible to immigrants, many of whom had been deprived of education in those homelands, and introduced American-born children to the heritage of their parents. Based on the complex novel *Romance of the Three Kingdoms,* Chinese opera transmitted traditional Cantonese values of loyalty, self-reliance, and personal integrity. Yiddish plays depicted episodes from centuries of Jewish history. German theatre dramatized the exploits of Frederick the Great. Polish theatres presented so many plays on historical and national themes that a Polish journalist called them "schools of patriotism."

Immigrant theatres introduced dialect-speaking audiences to the "standard" pronunciation and vocabulary of their native languages and, through the use of English expressions and performance of American plays, to the language and culture of the U.S. Many also introduced the classics of world theatre. Shakespeare was performed in Yiddish, German, Swedish and Italian. Yiddish theatres performed the works of Molière, Schiller, Goethe, Tolstoy, Gorky, Sudermann, Hauptmann, IBSEN, Strindberg, Molnár, and SHAW, as well as those of Jewish playwrights such as JACOB GORDIN, Leon Kobrin, and SHOLOM ASCH.

Theatre groups of politically progressive Germans, Jews, Swedes, Finns, Hungarians, Latvians, Lithuanians, and others used the works of Shaw, Ibsen, and Strindberg as well as original plays to explore temperance, pacifism, and the problems of workers, women, and the aged. Latvian socialist theatres in New York, Chicago, Cleveland, Detroit, San Francisco, and Boston produced dozens of agitprop-type plays, including original political dramas such as Sīmanis Berǵis's *They Will Overcome,* and Dāvids Bundža's *Celebrating May.* Theatres were prominent features in Finnish "Labor Temples" (socialist community centers) across the nation, where plays, both original and imported from Finland, were used for the political education of children and adults. The first Polish play in Chicago was *The Emancipation of Women* (1873), by feminist actress, writer, and community activist Theofilia Samolinska. Translated or adapted versions of Ibsen's controversial drama *A Doll's House* explored the "woman question" in many immigrant theatres.

Despite the importance of educational and ideological plays, most immigrants attended the theatre for entertainment, glamour, diversion, and emotional release. Folk dramas depicting the regional music, dance, and customs of the homeland were popular in German, Swedish, Danish, Hungarian, and Ukrainian theatres, appealing to nostalgia and the desire to escape urban life. A musical folk play, *The People of Varmland* (text by Fredrik August Dahlgren), was the most popular Swedish play, performed at least 62 times in Chicago alone between 1884 and 1921; 90% of all Danish productions were folk plays or operettas.

"Formula" plays in which wily peasants outwitted landlords, true love triumphed, and villains were punished and heroes rewarded were popular among audiences for whom the problems of life were not so easily resolved. Also popular were vaudeville, comedy, and satire. Comic characters such as Olle i Skratthult (Olle from Laughtersville), created by Hjalmar Peterson, and Farfariello, created by EDUARDO MIGLIACCIO, satirized the immigrant community itself, especially "green ones" (new immigrants), using wit and irony to help audiences understand, laugh at, and thus transcend their own often painful adjustment to the U.S.

Plays filled with violence, revenge, suicide, and murder were well received, whether classical tragedies or original melodramas. These plays moved audiences because they dealt with familiar problems, though in exaggerated form; Jacob Gordin's *The Jewish King Lear,* for example, about a pious father abused by heartless daughters, brought tears to the eyes of immigrants less than satisfied with the behavior of American-born children. Tragedy, like comedy, provided emotional release, allowing immigrants to express their grief at the absence of loved ones and the frustrations of American life.

European and Asian immigrant theatres active in the early 20th century declined after 1930, undermined by the immigration restriction laws of 1924, the Americanization and geographic dispersion of audiences, and the rise of movies, radio, and television. Federal assistance through the Works Project Administration helped some immigrant and black theatre to survive during the Great Depression of the 1930s; and a few companies with an interest in artistic experimentation, such as the FOLKSBIENE (Yiddish) theatre in New York City and the Swedish Folk Theatre in Chicago, continued into midcentury. Meanwhile many actors, directors, and writers from ethnic theatres passed into mainstream American entertainment, bringing elements of their traditions with them.

Ethnic theatre revived after WWII, stimulated by the heavy migration of Puerto Ricans to the mainland, and, with liberalized quotas, renewed immigration from Europe, Latin America, and Asia. The black civil rights movement touched off increased political activism and ethnic awareness not only among African Americans but also among Hispanics, Native Americans, and Asian Americans, stimulating new "Third World" theatre activity across the nation. Many older European theatres were rejuvenated in the 1960s and '70s, not only by newcomers but also by the nostalgia of aging immigrants, the desire of acculturated children and grandchildren to explore their roots, and the "new ethnicity," a heightened appreciation of cultural pluralism as an antidote for the anomie and homogenization of modern society.

In the 1960s hundreds of African American theatres performed throughout the nation. In the late 1960s Miriam Colón's PUERTO RICAN TRAVELING THEATRE brought bilingual productions to the Spanish-speaking neighborhoods of New York City (see also NUYORICAN THEATRE), and by the early 1970s provided a laboratory theatre and an actors' training program as well. Original plays about life in contemporary European American ethnic communities as well as productions of Armenian, Latvian, Lithuanian, Polish, and Yiddish classics (often in English) were mounted by ethnic churches and community centers, universities, and professional companies.

By 1980 almost 9 out of 10 new immigrants were from Asia or Latin America rather than Europe, a shift reflected in increased theatre activity in Asian and Latino communities. In the 1980s at least four ASIAN AMERICAN THEATRE companies performed in New York City. The multiethnic EAST WEST PLAYERS of Los Angeles presented original Asian American plays and trained actors of Chinese, Japanese, Filipino, Korean, and

Pacific Island backgrounds. Korean, Thai, and other recent Pacific Rim immigrants introduced traditional forms of cultural expression that integrated theatre, dance, and music. New Central and South American communities, some of which included foreign-trained actors, playwrights, and directors, produced new Spanish-language theatre in New York, Los Angeles, and other urban centers. CUBAN AMERICAN THEATRE emerged in southern Florida.

Overshadowed by the mass media (now often available in ethnic languages), theatre in the post–WWII decades was not as central to ethnic community life as it had been half a century earlier; nevertheless, it continued to educate as well as to entertain. In the 1970s HANAY GEIOGAMAH's Native American Theatre Ensemble used "Western"-style drama to transmit Native American traditions, values, and aesthetics. Byelorussians, Hungarians, Latvians, Ukrainians, Slovaks, and others used theatre in schools, summer camps, and youth groups to teach ethnic language and history to a new generation.

Postwar ethnic theatres informed their communities about social and political issues and were more active than their predecessors in reaching out to inform the mainstream community as well. Dramas from the Baltic nations dealt with political oppression and resistance to tyranny in Eastern Europe and, by implication, everywhere. Similar themes were prominent in the theatres of the new Central and South American communities, including NYC's Teatro Cuarto, which followed the Brechtian tradition of political theatre. The Theatre for Asian American Performing Artists in New York City performed a series of skits about anti-Asian discrimination for the United States Commission on Civil Rights, and produced a satirical review based on those skits at Lincoln Center during the 1976 Bicentennial. LUIS VALDÉZ's EL TEATRO CAMPESINO (Farm Workers' Theatre) developed original *actos* to unionize migrant workers in California, and elaborated them into full-length plays that won national and international acclaim. Adopted by cannery workers in San Jose, tomato pickers in South Jersey, hospital workers in Chicago, and dozens of other groups, Valdéz's "Theatre of the People" became a vehicle for labor protest among Hispanics nationwide.

Ethnic theatre allowed Asian, African, Mexican, and Native American actors, as well as those of other minorities, to move beyond the stereotypical roles usually assigned them in mainstream entertainment. It gave a new generation of playwrights an opportunity to use the language of the ethnic ghetto and to express sensibilities rooted in the unique historic experience of their own communities. "America is illiterate ... deadset against the Chinese American sensibility," wrote the militant Frank Chin, a seventh-generation Chinese American whose award-winning play *The Chickencoop Chinaman* was produced at New York's AMERICAN PLACE THEATRE in 1972; "nothing but racist polemics have been written about us. . . . I don't like that. . . . All my writing is Chinaman backtalk."

Ethnic theatre offered ethnic and mainstream audiences insights into minority experiences that, despite an increase of ethnic material in mainstream theatre, remained unavailable elsewhere. René Marqués's celebrated play *The Oxcart,* which describes a family's disintegration as it moves from rural Puerto Rico to San Juan to New York City, helped Puerto Rican migrants evaluate their gains and losses. The problems of the black family, the impact of the Vietnam War on the Asian American soldier, the destruction of ethnic neighborhoods through "urban renewal," Turkish genocide against Armenians in 1915, the impact of the Holocaust on Jewish survivors, the realities of growing up, getting old, or being a woman in ethnic America, discrimination, assimilation, and the survival of ethnic identities – these and similar themes were explored in post–WWII ethnic theatre.

After the revival and expansion of the post–WWII years, ethnic theatres faced serious problems in the closing decades of the century. In the 1980s political and social support for pluralism eroded. Funding provided in the 1960s and '70s by public and private foundations such as the Rockefeller Foundation, the NATIONAL ENDOWMENT FOR THE ARTS, and stage and local cultural agencies was curtailed due to budget deficits and changing priorities. Many university and neighborhood programs that had trained ethnic playwrights and actors could no longer afford to do so.

Ethnic theatre had internal as well as external problems. New immigrant populations were sometimes so diverse and transient that neighborhood theatres found it difficult to develop a stable base of support. An unprecedented array of foreign-language entertainment – radio, TV, movies, and videos – competed for the immigrant's attention. Well-educated, middle-class immigrants, now a sizable proportion of newcomers, often preferred American theatre or imported classics to the ethnic genres popular with their largely working-class predecessors. The social class and cultural diversity of the new ethnic America was reflected in conflicts about the nature and purpose of ethnic theatre. Should its focus be local or international? Should its methods be traditional or experimental? Should its goal be artistic excellence or social relevance?

Despite the problems, there were reasons for optimism about the future. During the 1980s ethnic theatre gained increased recognition in academic theatre programs, national theatre associations, and scholarly journals, as well as among ethnic and mainstream audiences. Collections of ethnic plays and scholarly works about ethnic theatre were published. Actors, playwrights, and directors experimented with new forms and materials, developed strategies to identify and train new talent, and responded with ingenuity to continuing economic scarcity. In New York City, for example, Italian American playwrights organized the "Forum" for mutual support, and Spanish-language theatres increased audiences and revenues by offering new ethnic plays in English to "general" audiences. In Los Angeles ethnic theatres formed a consortium with other arts groups for more effective fundraising and marketing. The Black Repertory Company of Winston-Salem, NC, drew financial and moral support from an active, dues-paying auxiliary, the North Carolina Black Theater Guild. Politics reinforced artistic and financial creativity: In 1989 a new law increased legal immigration, ensuring the continued growth of the nation's ethnic populations. These developments suggested that ethnic theatre would continue to survive in the U.S., as the 1990s illustrated, not as a curiosity or exercise in nostalgia, but as a living force in American culture.

In the new millenium multiculturalism is almost taken for granted in many communities. The greatest danger to ethnic presence in theatre is this assumption – which, for example, led the Los Angeles CENTER THEATRE GROUP to eliminate its specific ethnic theatre initiatives while promising to develop appropriate plays from various ethnic groups without a set structure to do so. More and more plays that include ethnic minorities appear to deal with racial issues at best incidentally – for some, another concern for the future of ethnic theatre. (See also ethnic-specific entries in the guide, especially for more up-to-date data.)   MS

Ettinger, Heidi (Prentice) (1951–) Born in San Francisco and educated at Occidental College (LA) and the Yale School of Drama, this scenic/costume designer and producer has received two Tonys for scenic design: for *Big River* (1985) and *The Secret Garden* (1991), the latter using the motif of a child's TOY THEATRE. (Both of these were credited to Heidi LANDESMAN, the surname of her former husband, ROCCO.) A boldly theatrical designer who often combines semiabstract elements with realistic detail to create striking, dramatic images, she considers herself a designer who also produces, with credits in the latter category for *Into the Woods* (1987; only producing), *Big River*, and *The Secret Garden*. Other designs: 'NIGHT, MOTHER, *The Red Shoes*, *Smokey Joe's Cafe*, *Moon over Buffalo*, *Triumph of Love*, *Dracula, the Musical*, and, in 2005, *Good Vibrations*.   AA   DBW

Eugene O'Neill Memorial Theater Center In 1964, George C. White, then a 29-year-old TV executive, leased eight and a half acres of the former Hammon Estate – relevant to several plays by EUGENE O'NEILL – from Waterford, CT, White's hometown. Among other goals, White hoped to create a sheltered laboratory for a new generation of American playwrights. Then as now, his vision incorporated three basic elements of professional theatre: playwright, audience, and critics. In 1965, he inaugurated the O'Neill's core program, the NATIONAL PLAYWRIGHTS CONFERENCE, with a five-day retreat. After three volatile shakedown seasons, LLOYD RICHARDS was appointed the NPC's artistic director (1968–99); together with White, Richards established structures and methods of play development that would spread throughout the country and guided the O'Neill to international acclaim – as multiple awards, including a 1979 Special Tony, attest. SIGNATURE THEATRE's James Hougton succeeded Richards until 2003, followed in 2005 by Wendy C. Goldberg. As of 2005 the O'Neill Center had developed 700 plays and musicals.

Subsequent programs included the NATIONAL THEATRE OF THE DEAF (1967); the National Critics Institute (1967); the National Theatre Institute (1970), an academic program; New Drama for Television (1976); the National [Opera] Music Theatre Conference (1978); and a Puppetry Conference. The O'Neill also sponsors Creative Arts in Education, which integrates art into the community, trains teachers, and runs a summer arts camp for teenagers. Media Arts explores the impact of technology on the performing arts, and various international programs encourage cultural exchange and subsidize translations. Monte Cristo Cottage – the O'Neill summer house in adjacent New London, featured in AH, WILDERNESS! and LONG DAY'S JOURNEY INTO NIGHT – houses archives, resident artists, and scholars, and hosts special events. In addition to the Tony, the O'Neill has received the National Opera Award and the JUJAMCYN Award of Theater Excellence.   CLJ

Eugene O'Neill Theatre 230 West 49th St., NYC [Architect: Herbert J. Krapp]. In 1925, the SHU-BERTS opened another theatre and named it the Forrest in honor of America's first star, EDWIN FORREST. They sold it in 1945 to City Playhouses, a real estate holding company, which refurbished it and renamed it the Coronet. It was sold again to Lester Osterman, a Broadway producer, who changed its name again to honor America's greatest playwright, EUGENE O'NEILL. Six years later, it was acquired by NEIL SIMON and David Cogan and served as a showcase for eight of Simon's plays and one of his musicals. As sole owner in 1982, Simon sold it to the JUJAMCYN ORGANIZATION. Its early history was inauspicious and contained a long string of flops, but its later history, particularly the Simon era, has included its share of successes, including the fiftieth-anniversary production of *Death of a Salesman* (1999) and the musical *The Full Monty* (2000).   MCH

Eureka Theatre Company Founded in 1972, this nonprofit theatre has been a vital force in SAN FRANCISCO's prolific fringe-theatre movement and a dynamic producer of politically charged drama (initially under ROBERT WOODRUFF and Chris Silva). From the mid-1970s to the late '80s, a loose COLLECTIVE took over, staging works by Churchill, Dario Fo, EMILY MANN (her *Execution of Justice* was commissioned by them), and other trenchant, topical authors. ETC lost its first church-basement theatre on Market St. to arson in 1981; after several temporary homes, in 1984 it settled into a 250-seat Mission District venue. Regrouping under the new management of Debra Ballinger (1990), ETC offered the premiere of Anthony Clarvoe's computer-industry satire, *Pick Up Axe* (1990), and the debut of TONY KUSHNER's AIDS saga, *ANGELS IN AMERICA* (1991). Artistic directors have included Richard E. T. White, Tony Taccone, and OSKAR EUSTIS. The company was moribund for several seasons after spring 1992, due to financial trouble; it briefly revived in 1996, and since 1998 has operated in a converted cinema in the Jackson Square District, led by former public-relations executive Bill Schwartz.   MB

Eustis, Oskar (1959–) Minnesota-born director and dramaturge, a champion in new play development, community organization, fund-raising, and a strong believer in education (he was instrumental in creating a consortium between TRINITY REP and Brown University). In 1980 he commissioned EMILY MANN's *Execution of Justice* and in 1987 KUSHNER's *ANGELS IN AMERICA*. In addition to Mann and Kushner he has worked closely with playwrights PHILIP KAN GOTANDA, DAVID HENRY HWANG, SUZAN-LORI PARKS, Ellen McLaughlin, and EDUARDO MACHADO, among others. From 1981 to 1986 he was resident director and dramaturge at EUREKA THEATRE, and artistic director until 1989. He spent 11 seasons in the same position at TRINITY REPERTORY THEATRE, and in June 2005 became artistic director at New York's PUBLIC THEATRE.   DBW

Evangeline; or, The Belle of Acadia Three-act musical burlesque/extravaganza, music by Edward E. Rice, words by J. Cheever Goodwin. Opened 27 July 1874 at NIBLO'S GARDEN, running 16 performances. This travesty of Longfellow was, despite its brief initial run, one of the most popular and influential of American musicals throughout the late 19th century. Unlike most burlesques of its day, it had an entirely original score and produced several popular tunes. In other ways, it was quite traditional: Straying wildly from its source for scenic effects, which ranged from Acadia to Africa to Arizona, and loaded with excruciating puns, it featured a woman in tights as the male hero and a man in drag as the heavy, elderly woman (see FEMALE/MALE IMPERSONATION). Its two most famous gimmicks were a grotesque dancing cow (see ANIMAL IMPERSONATION) and the Lone Fisherman, a mysterious silent character who regularly appeared no matter what the change of setting. *Evangeline* established the careers of both Goodwin, who wrote many more librettos, and Rice, who became a major producer.   JD

Evans, Maurice (Herbert) (1901–89) English-born actor-director-producer who became an American citizen in 1941, following a 15-year acting career in England, most notably as Raleigh in *Journey's End* (1929) and with the Old Vic–Sadler's Wells company in 1934 (including a full-length *Hamlet*). In the U.S. he appeared with KATHARINE CORNELL as Romeo (1935) and in 1936 as the Dauphin opposite her Saint Joan. A series of notable Shakespearean performances followed, most directed by MARGARET WEBSTER, including Richard II (1937), gaining him the reputation as the foremost purveyor of SHAKESPEARE ON THE AMERICAN STAGE. During WWII he entertained the troups with his so-called *GI Hamlet*. After the war (between 1947 and 1959) Evans played major roles in four Shavian comedies (see SHAW AND . . .), most notably John Tanner in *Man and Superman*. In 1952 he acted the uncharacteristic role of Tony Wendice in *Dial "M" for Murder,* in 1960 Reverend Brock in the musical *Tenderloin,* and in 1962 the role of H. J.

in *The Aspern Papers*. In the 1950s he presented Shakespeare on television and produced several Broadway shows. In the 1970s and '80s Evans appeared mostly in films and TV, although at the age of 80 he played Norman in *On Golden Pond* in Florida. Shortly before his death he completed his autobiography, *All This . . . and Evans Too!* (Columbia, SC, 1987).   DBW

Experimental Theatre, Inc. Founded in 1940 in New York City to showcase actors and playwrights. Operations halted in 1941, then started again in 1946 with backing from the AMERICAN NATIONAL THEATRE AND ACADEMY (ANTA). Craft unions granted concessions, and subscribers supported a five-show season at the PRINCESS THEATRE. Poor critical response led to reorganization. In 1947–8, the group staged readings of five new plays as well as six productions at MAXINE ELLI-OTT's Theatre. Though two of these had extended runs, the group lost money. Its 1948–9 season of three staged readings was its last.   WD

Eytinge, Rose (1835–1911) Actress, author, teacher. Her professional debut was in 1852 as Melanie in BOUCICAULT's *The Old Guard* in Syracuse, NY. Considered temperamental and often unmanageable, she acted in England and the U.S., specializing in high comedy and tragedy. She worked under the managements of LESTER WALLACK, AUGUSTIN DALY, and A. M. PALMER. Although she excelled in roles such as Cleopatra (1877), she was best known for her Nancy in *Oliver Twist* (1867) opposite E. L. DAVENPORT's Bill Sykes and the younger JAMES WALLACK's Fagin. She dramatized several novels, wrote a play and a novel, and recorded her colorful life in *The Memoirs of Rose Eytinge* (1905).   DBW

F

Fagan, Garth (1940–) Tony-winning choreographer of *The Lion King* (1997). Born in Jamaica, Fagan trained with Ivy Baxter and the Jamaica National Dance Theatre before coming to the U.S., where he attended Wayne State University (1968 graduate) and then studied with Martha Graham, José Limon, Mary Hinkson, and Alvin Ailey before founding his own company in Rochester, NY, in 1970. Fagan's signature style and vocabulary – combining elements of modern dance and ballet with African and Caribbean rhythms and postures – adapted perfectly to the concept of Julie Taymor and her puppet wizardry at the heart of the stage version of the Disney film. (Fagan had previously been to Africa 11 times and had a "real feel for the continent and a deep love for the animals.") DBW

Faith Healer, The Three-act drama by William Vaughn Moody that premiered in St. Louis on 15 March 1909 and in New York at the Savoy on 19 January 1910. The play, though not popular, has remained a critical success to the present day. Focusing on a conflict between science and faith and between love and duty, *The Faith Healer* amply demonstrates the lyrical yet forthright style that is Moody's signature. In refusing to choose among alternatives, proferring instead faith joined to science and love reconciled with responsibility, the play avoids polarizing its characters and their views as good or evil and offers a more liberal view of a classic American subject. RKB

Falls, Robert [Arthur] (1954–) Artistic director of Chicago's Wisdom Bridge Theatre during its most productive period (1977–85), Falls, a graduate of the University of Illinois, directed more than 30 productions there, many marked by energetic staging and ensemble work, most notably an adaptation of Jack Henry Abbott's *In the Belly of the Beast* and premieres of Keith Reddin's *Life and Limb* and John Olive's *Standing on My Knees*. In 1986, he succeeded Gregory Mosher as artistic director of the Goodman Theatre, where his notable productions – a number of which have come to New York – have included *Galileo, The Ice-*

man Cometh, Death of a Salesman, and Long Day's Journey into Night, all starring Brian Dennehy; Cherry Jones in Night of the Iguana (also seen at Roundabout, 1996); *The Young Man from Atlanta;* and *Blue Surge*. In 1994 he directed Bogosian's *SubUrbia* at Lincoln Center and in 1995 a critically acclaimed *Rose Tattoo* at Circle in the Square. During 1989–91 he was president of the board of the Theatre Communications Group. In 2000 he directed the musical *Aida* for Disney, in 2006 Conor McPherson's *Shining City* for the Manhattan Theatre Club, and in 2007 Bogosian's *Talk Radio* on Broadway. SF

Falsettos This 1992 Tony Award–winning musical by William Finn and James Lapine merged two Off-Broadway chamber musicals – Finn's *March of the Falsettos* (1981) and Finn and Lapine's *Falsettoland* (1990) – into a 487-performance success at Broadway's John Golden Theatre. Frank Rich called *Falsettos* "a show in which the boundary separating Off-Broadway and Broadway is obliterated." The musical is about the character Marvin leaving his wife and 12-year-old son for a male lover, breaking up with this lover, and returning to watch him die of AIDS. The story is told mostly through songs (there is little dialogue), with Finn's style inviting comparison with Stephen Sondheim's. Finn's 1979 musical *In Trousers,* at Playwrights Horizons, introduced Marvin's character and is considered the first part of the Off-Broadway "Marvin's Trilogy." *Falsettos* received its first staging in a 1991 Hartford Stage Company production. TLM

Fantasticks, The Two-act musical comedy, music by Harvey Schmidt, words by Tom Jones; opened 3 May 1960 at the Sullivan Street Playhouse, New York, where it closed on 13 January 2002 after some 42 years and 17,162 performances (and more than 12,000 productions countrywide), making it by far the longest-running musical in American theatre history. Initially produced by Lore Noto on a budget of $16,500, this small show (cast of eight, "orchestra" of piano and harp, and a virtually bare stage) relies on telling a simple romantic story with the charm of simplicity and whimsy. Adapted from Edmond Rostand's *Les Romanesques,* it is the tale of young lovers whose naive, youthful view of love must be mellowed by temptations and disappointments, engineered by the omniscient narrator-adventurer El Gallo (JERRY ORBACH), before they are finally ready to enter a mature relationship. The moral suggests that a love without obstacles to overcome is hollow. The score produced a major popular standard, "Try to Remember." A study by Viagas and Farber of the first production was published in 1991. A revival opened August 2006 at the new Snapple Theater Center.   JD

Fashion; or, Life in New York Five-act comedy written by ANNA CORA MOWATT; a successful satire of the nouveaux riches and their pretensions. Mrs. Tiffany, a foolish and extravagant woman, almost ruins her husband with her desire for high society and foreign manners; but all is made right through the good sense of the all-American Adam Trueman and his granddaughter, Gertrude. Mowatt wrote the comedy to earn money when her husband's health failed. It opened at the PARK THEATRE on 24 March 1845 and ran for three weeks – a long run in its day. EDGAR ALLAN POE, writing for the *Broadway Journal,* reviewed the play twice. Mowatt later became a successful actress and performed the part of Gertrude in her own play. It has been revived frequently in this century, with a most successful run in 1924 at the Provincetown Playhouse.   FB

Faversham, William (1868–1940) London-born actor who briefly appeared on the stage there before migrating to America in 1887. He was in the companies of both DANIEL FROHMAN and CHARLES FROHMAN, and played opposite MRS. FISKE and MAUDE ADAMS before becoming a leading man. His physical attractiveness and buoyant personality earned him the label of a "matinee girl's idol." Among his successful Shakespearean roles were Mark Antony in *Julius Caesar* and the title roles in *Romeo and Juliet* and *Othello.* He won his popularity, however, playing vigorous and masculine heroes in such plays as *Lord and Lady Algy, The Squaw Man,* and *The Prince and the Pauper.* His last role came in 1933 when he played Jeeter Lester in TOBACCO ROAD (tour).   RAS

Fay, Frank (Francis Anthony) (1897–1961) Actor-vaudevillian, outstanding as the eccentric alcoholic Elwood P. Dodd in the long-running Broadway hit HARVEY (1944–6), a legitimate-theatre break that came after a long career as headliner in REVUES and VAUDEVILLE (sophisticated satirical humor), and following a series of stage failures written by Fay. Most successful as master of ceremonies at the PALACE (beginning in 1924), by 1926 he had set a record for number of performances. A volume of reminiscences and humorous stories (*How to Be Poor*) was published in 1945. The latter part of his career was devoted to films, nightclubs, and television.   DBW

Faye, Joey [né Joseph Palladino] (1909–97) Last of the great BURLESQUE comics, who, though often returning for burlesque revivals, graduated to theatre (36 Broadway shows), film, and television (famously as a bunch of grapes for a Fruit of the Loom commercial). Second banana for PHIL SILVERS, he appeared in two plays with Silvers, *High Button Shoes* (1947) and *Top Banana* (1951). Faye claimed the creation of two classic burlesque/vaudeville skits, "Slowly I Turn" and "Floogle Street." His final Broadway appearance was in a 1993 revival of THREE MEN ON A HORSE.   DBW

Fechter, Charles Albert (1824–79) Actor, born in London to a German father and English mother; educated in France. He made his Comédie-Française debut in 1844 and became a leading melodramatic actor, particularly at the Porte-Saint-Martin. Fechter moved to London in 1860 and performed in English such roles as Othello and Hamlet (the latter played in a controversial flowing blond wig). G. H. Lewes called him "lymphatic, delicate, handsome"; his iconoclasm was something more than mere display, however. In 1870, he came to the U.S., where he remained, with the exception of a short season in London in 1872, for the rest of his life. He toured for some time, then opened the Globe Theatre in BOSTON as Fechter's Theatre with many innovations, paralleling his earlier managerial experiments at the Lyceum in London, where he had also destroyed many outdated scenic traditions. His managerial ventures in America failed, however, owing to his personal vanity and what his fan and friend Charles Dickens called "a perfect genius for quarreling." He made his final appearances as Monte Cristo, Hamlet, and Ruy Blas at the Broadway Theatre (soon to become DALY'S); then, due to excessive drinking and a bigamous marriage, he was forced into retirement. He died in Quakerstown, PA, where he had tried to set up a farm. His biography by Kate Field appeared in 1882.   SMA

Feder, Abe (1909–97) Designer who virtually invented the field of stage-lighting design. One of his earliest projects was FOUR SAINTS IN THREE ACTS (1934) for director JOHN HOUSEMAN. He went on to do numerous productions with the FEDERAL THEATRE PROJECT, including many of the LIVING NEWSPAPERS and *The CRADLE WILL ROCK* (1938). He designed the first season of Ballet Theatre (1941) and in the following decades designed extensively for the stage, notably lights for *The SKIN OF OUR TEETH* (1942), *MY FAIR LADY* (1956), and *CAMELOT* (1960). As an architectural lighting designer, he designed or consulted on lighting for the 1964 New York World's Fair, exterior lighting for many buildings (including Rockefeller Center and the Pan Am Building), and lighting systems and interior lighting for several theatres, including the JOHN F. KENNEDY CENTER. AA

Federal Street Theatre Federal St. at Franklin Pl., Boston [Architect: Charles Bulfinch]. When the 1750 law prohibiting playacting was overturned, prominent BOSTONIANS pledged money by shares to erect the city's first theatre. In 1794, a handsome brick building by one of America's first architects opened under the management of CHARLES STUART POWELL. The theatre burned in 1798 (see FIRES) and was rebuilt by Bulfinch the following year. After a succession of managers, the theatre, known as "Old Boston," was supplanted by newer theatres and was not used consistently. It closed in 1852 and was replaced by stores. MCH

Federal Theatre Project Established under the Works Progress Administration (WPA) in 1935 by an act of the U.S. Congress, this was the first American example of officially sponsored and financed theatre – and therefore the subject of much political controversy. Under the national direction of the indefatigable and intrepid HALLIE FLANAGAN, head of the experimental theatre at Vassar, the FTP's objectives were to give meaningful employment to theatrical professionals out of work during the Depression and to provide "free, adult, uncensored theatre" to audiences throughout the country. Indeed, 10,000 people were employed at its peak, with theatres in 40 states. During its almost four years of existence, the FTP launched or established the careers of such notable theatre artists as ORSON WELLES, JOHN HOUSEMAN, Joseph Cotten, Arlene Francis, WILL GEER, John Huston, ARTHUR MILLER, Virgil Thomson, HOWARD BAY, PAUL GREEN, MARY CHASE, MARC BLITZSTEIN, CANADA LEE, and ELMER RICE. At low ticket prices, audiences were provided with a large variety of fare, ranging from classics to new plays, CHILDREN'S THEATRE, foreign-language productions, PUPPETRY, religious plays, a Negro theatre, musical theatre, a CIRCUS, and a controversial innovation called the LIVING NEWSPAPER, designed to deal with issues of the day by utilizing documentary sources. In January 1936, with the urging of HELEN TAMIRIS, a separate Federal Dance Project was established, although congressional cutbacks forced a merger with the FTP in October 1937.

The FTP played to millions of people throughout the country; it is estimated that over 12 million attended performances in New York alone. Of the hundreds of productions presented by the FTP, those by its Negro Unit (see AFRICAN AMERICAN THEATRE) were among the most innovative and included the "voodoo" *Macbeth* (1936), *Haiti* (1938), and *The Swing Mikado* (1939). In 1936 Sinclair Lewis's *IT CAN'T HAPPEN HERE,* written for the FTP, was produced simultaneously in at least 20 cities. The U.S. premiere of *MURDER IN THE CATHEDRAL,* which had been rejected by the THEATRE GUILD, was successful in 1936 at popular prices. The 1937 premiere of PAUL GREEN's outdoor historical pageant *The Lost Colony* was in a WPA-built outdoor theatre on Roanoke Island, NC, where it has been seen every summer since. The FTP was endlessly willing to take chances in its selection of plays and was, in HAROLD CLURMAN's words, "The most truly experimental effort ever undertaken in the American theatre."

CENSORSHIP was a problem frequently faced by various units of the FTP; its outspoken criticism, interpreted especially by congressional conservatives as left-wing, ultimately led to a heated debate and the disbanding of the project on 30 June 1939. The epic and convoluted history of the FTP was first recounted by Flanagan in *Arena* (1940). In 1974 the Federal Theatre Project Research Center was established at George Mason University, though original material in the archive was moved to the Library of Congress in late 1994. DBW

Fefu and Her Friends Because of its oblique, poignant discussion of women's oppression, MARIA IRENE FORNÉS's *Fefu* is a classic in the FEMINIST THEATRE canon. First performed on 5 May 1977 by the New York Theatre Strategy (directed by Fornés), it was subsequently produced by the AMERICAN PLACE THEATRE on 8 January 1978. Formally, the play challenges the relationship between spectator and performer. The second of its three parts takes place simultaneously in four different locations around a New England country house; the audience moves in four groups to each location, then reconverges for Part III. In evocative monologues and brief, staccato dialogues between characters in its all-female cast, *Fefu* tentatively describes possibilities for strength in women's community.   JDo

Feiffer, Jules (1929–) Playwright, editorial cartoonist, screenwriter, novelist, and author of children's books. Feiffer studied at NYC's Art Students' League and Pratt Institute. During 1956–97 his cartoons appeared in the *Village Voice* and were widely syndicated. His first play, *The Explainers,* a musical review of his cartoons, was presented at SECOND CITY, Chicago, in 1961. *LITTLE MURDERS,* his first full-length script, won honors in London (1967) and an Obie in New York. Other major plays include *God Bless* (1968), *Feiffer's People* (1968), *The White House Murder Case* (1970, Obie), *Knock Knock* (1976), *Hold Me!* (1977), *Grown Ups* (1981), *Anthony Rose* (1989), *Elliot Loves* (1990), and *A Bad Friend* (2003). His screenplays include *Carnal Knowledge* (1971; staged in play form in 1990), *Little Murders* (1971), *Popeye* (1980), and *I Want to Go Home* (1989), which was directed by Alain Resnais. He received a Pulitzer Prize for Editorial Cartooning in 1986, and was elected to the American Academy of Arts and Letters in 1995.   TLM

Feingold, Michael (1945–) Drama critic, translator, lyricist, and author. Born in Chicago and educated at Columbia and Yale, Feingold has written literate and thought-provoking criticism for the *Village Voice* since 1971, serving as chief critic since 1974. He is a translator of the plays of Brecht, Ibsen, Molière, Wedekind, Diderot, and Schiller. He has been literary manager at YALE REP and the GUTHRIE THEATRE. He received the 1995–6 GEORGE JEAN NATHAN Award for Dramatic Criticism.   TLM

Feist, Gene (1930–) Director-playwright, reared on Coney Island, and cofounder (with his wife, Elizabeth Owen) in 1965 of NYC's ROUNDABOUT THEATRE COMPANY – and its artistic leader until the late 1980s. After graduating from Carnegie Mellon (1951) and New York University (1952), Feist trained at the ACTORS STUDIO and the American Theatre Wing, among other places. At the Roundabout he was producing director of more than 150 productions (including the Tony Award–winning *Joe Egg* revival of 1985. In 1996 he received the Lucille Lortel Foundation's Lifetime Achievement Award.   CLJ

Feldshuh, Tovah [née Terry Sue] (1952?–) Award-winning actress and cabaret performer; a graduate of Sarah Lawrence College, she won an acting scholarship to the University of Minnesota (TYRONE GUTHRIE THEATRE) and subsequently studied with UTA HAGEN and Jacques Lecoq. Although she has appeared in a number of New York productions (*Yentl!, Lend Me a Tenor, AWAKE AND SING!,* etc.), she is known best for cabaret acts (*Tovah: Crossovah! From Broadway to Cabaret* and *Tovah: Out of Her Mind!*) and solo performances/impersonations (as TALLULAH BANKHEAD in *Tallulah's Party* in 1998 and *Tallulah Hallelujah!* in 2000; and as Prime Minister Golda Meir in WILLIAM GIBSON's *Golda's Balcony,* which opened on Broadway October 2003). Other portrayals attempted have included Diana Vreeland, Sarah Bernhardt, STELLA ADLER, SOPHIE TUCKER, and KATHARINE HEPBURN. Her winning Dolly Gallagher Levi in the PAPER MILL's summer 2006 production of *HELLO, DOLLY!* was notable for its prominent Irish brogue.   DBW

female/male impersonation In certain NATIVE AMERICAN tribes, the androgynous *berdache* serves as intermediary with the supernatural – an important function that some scholars think is, in more secular societies, invested in the actor. Europe's saturnalian tradition of men dressing as women on a licensed occasion, to provide a safety valve for gender anxieties, survived in America in several guises: street festivals; all-male college clubs, such as Harvard's Hasty Pudding (founded 1844), Princeton's Triangle Club, and the University of Pennsylvania's Wig & Gown; and small-town "Womanless Weddings" that recruit the whole white male community for its travesties.

Puritans had attacked as "sodomitical" the Elizabethan convention of boys playing girls, and it disappeared with the Restoration; but the accompanying tradition of the "dame" role – an elderly woman impersonated by a male comedian – survived on the American popular stage, carried on by NEIL BURGESS as the Widow Bedotte, George W. Munroe as various Irish biddies, Gilbert Sarony as the Giddy Gusher, and the Russell Brothers as clumsy Irish maids.

In Victorian staging of Shakespeare, women were traditionally cast as boys or sprites, but many actresses took on male leads. CHARLOTTE CUSHMAN played Romeo to her sister's Juliet, and later aspired to Cardinal Wolsey. Other women presented Shylock and Falstaff, but Hamlet proved irresistible: The most memorable was Sarah Bernhardt, who, according to Mounet-Sully, lacked only the buttons on her fly. In our time Dame JUDITH ANDERSON tried the experiment with dismaying results.

The all-male MINSTREL SHOW featured the "wench," a young man sporting a fashionable female wardrobe and "high-yeller" makeup; he often became the star and manager, as did Francis Leon (Patrick Glassey) and Eugene (D'Ameli). It was also common in the CIRCUS for boy athletes to be disguised as girls to make the stunts seem more dangerous, as was the case with equestrian Ella Zoyara (Omar Kingsley). Such performers were said to be in "drag," the train on a gown equated with the drag or brake on a coach. Both the word and a new "drag performer" entered theatrical practice from the homosexual subculture around 1870. Ernest Boulton, who had been unsuccessfully prosecuted in London for solicitation in female garb, introduced to the New York stage (as Ernest Byne) the glamorous impersonator who presented a woman of beauty and chic. At the same time, true male impersonation was introduced by lesbians, the Englishwoman Annie Hindle and her imitator Ella Wesner, in the guise of "fast" young men, swaggering, cigar-smoking, and coarse. These minstrel and music-hall styles lasted longest in African American VAUDEVILLE, where the performers' private lives often nourished their characterizations. Female impersonators included Lawrence A. Chenault, known as "Golden Hair Nell," and Andrew Tribble, who created "Ophelia Snow." The best-known male impersonator in Harlem was Gladys Bentley, alleged to have had an affair with Bessie Smith.

Critics objected when glamour drag successfully entered musical comedy with JULIAN ELTINGE, who put across the images of an elegant young woman and a clean-cut young man. BERT SAVOY popularized an outrageous caricature, garish and brassy, gossiping about her absent girlfriend Margie and launching popular catchphrases. Their best-known successors were Francis Renault (Anthony Auriemma), "The Slave of Fashion," who sang in a clear soprano; and Karyl Norman (George Podezzi), "The Creole Fashion-Plate," who starred in musical comedy.

The popularity of all-male drag revues in the Armed Forces during WWII persisted into the postwar period. The Jewel Box revue, founded in Miami in 1938, enjoyed an eight-year run after the war and launched a number of talents before it folded in 1973. Similar enterprises include Finocchio's (San Francisco), Club 82 (New York), My-Oh-My (New Orleans), and the Ha Club (Hollywood, FL); but the police in Boston, Los Angeles, and other cities often prevented public cross-dressing. The gay liberation movement of the late 1960s encouraged a resurgence of female impersonation, and lip-synching to tapes became ubiq-

uitous in NIGHTCLUBS. Many gay bars provided a token stage, and the female impersonator became almost exclusively what Esther Newton calls "performing homosexuals and homosexual performers." However, a successful means of passing with a mixed audience was to present imitators of female superstars: T. C. Jones, a veteran of the Jewel Box, was introduced to the general public in *New Faces of 1956;* Craig Russell, Charles Pierce, and Lynn Carter were the best-known such "impressionists."

Androgyny had infiltrated the rock music scene with Alice Cooper and David Bowie and reached a logical terminus in the asexual Boy George and Michael Jackson (parodied, in turn, by Madonna). The cult following for the British musical *The Rocky Horror Show,* with its transvestite, transsexual hero, showed that teenagers knew their *psychopathia sexualis.* More anarchic uses of "genderfuck" emerged from the hippie scene on the West Coast: The Cockettes and Angels of Light of San Francisco used campy pastiches of popular culture for radical ends. The Cycle Sluts, hairy bruisers in net stockings, and the street-theatre group The Sisters of Perpetual Indulgence, parodied traditional drag.

Broad dame comedy persisted in clowns like Pudgy Roberts, the all-male Ballets Trockadero de Monte Carlo (founded 1974), the Trockadero Gloxinia Ballet, and their operatic equivalent, the Grand Scena Opera Co. (founded 1982). Drag has also become a fixture in contemporary PERFORMANCE ART, as in JOHN (Lypsinka) EPPERSON's *Ballet of the Dolls* (LA MAMA, 1988), a confrontation of pulp fiction with the clichés of ballet, and *I Could Go on Lip-Synching.* This trend is rooted in the "RIDICULOUS Theatre" movement of 1970s and the Warhol Factory, which fostered Centola, Hot Peaches, and CHARLES LUDLAM: Camp was made the cutting edge of the avant-garde. The 300-lb film star Divine (Glen Milstead) was featured in a number of Off-Broadway plays, most memorably as the prison matron in Tom Eyen's *Women behind Bars.* A leading exponent was ETHYL (Roy) EICHELBERGER, whose one-man *Tempest* and *Jocasta; or, Boy Crazy* are in both the minstrel/vaudeville and avant-garde tradition. Gender confusion is also the main theme of Los Angeles comedian John Fleck and the actor CHARLES BUSCH. Much of this has percolated into the commercial theatre, as testified by the success of the drag-show musical *LA CAGE AUX FOLLES* and DAVID HENRY HWANG's *M. BUTTERFLY.*

With the radical changes in dress and manners that followed WWI, the male impersonator became a relic, revived by contemporary FEMI-

NIST THEATRE groups for political reasons, as in Eve Merriam's *The Club* (1976). Current debates over the nature of gender have inspired much experimental performance. At the "dyke noir" WOW Café in the East Village, New York, the SPLIT BRITCHES COMPANY parodies traditional "femme" and "butch" roles in the double act of Peggy Shaw and Lois Weaver. The lesbian transsexual Kate Bornstein has created shows such as *Hidden: A Gender* (with Noreen Barnes) and *Virtually Yours,* which totally deconstruct traditional gender roles. (See also GAY/LESBIAN THEATRE.)

As the century turned, the acceptance of cross-dressing as a standard theatrical practice was taken for granted. Whether the medium is a rock musical (*HEDWIG AND THE ANGRY INCH* by JOHN CAMERON MITCHELL and Stephen Trask, 1998), a Broadway musical (the dame role Edna Turnblad in *HAIRSPRAY,* 2003), legitimate drama (Doug Wright's 2003 *I AM MY OWN WIFE* (Pulitzer Prize, 2004), or the long-running revue *BEACH BLANKET BABYLON,* gender impersonation is now more a convention than a challenge, with drag queens and kings as licensed clowns.   LS*

feminist theatre This ALTERNATIVE THEATRE movement began and proliferated in the early 1970s. In tandem with the political movement from which they sprang, activist women's theatres with radical techniques and manifestos organized in major urban centers around the country. The groups were innumerable and local, since the theatre they produced spoke directly to its constituents about women's subordinate position in dominant culture and possibilities for change.

The theatrical and political radicalism of feminist theatre grew from the second wave of U.S. feminism, which followed the civil rights movement and the formation of a vocal, active New Left. From within the political upheaval of the late 1960s, activists tried to revise interpersonal relationships and cultural value systems according to more egalitarian ideology. However, within the Left's rhetoric of racial and economic liberation, gender politics remained conservative. The contemporary U.S. women's movement rekindled itself partly out of profound disaffection with the misogyny of the male Left. Through a network of ad hoc consciousness-raising groups, white, middle-class women with some background in radical politics spoke to each other for what seemed like the first time, without mediation. These groups allowed women to exchange previously unheard details of their personal lives. The apparent commonality of their shared experi-

ence provoked a political analysis based on the private sphere their lives seemed to inhabit, and the slogan "the personal is political" gained currency.

What began in the late 1960s as a grass-roots political movement became, through the 1970s, a political and ideological movement with organized impact and increasingly divergent strains. Networks such as the National Organization for Women (NOW), for example, developed strategies for influencing existing social and political systems around women's issues. The liberal feminist movement that was generated works to reform U.S. systems toward women's equality.

Radical feminism, in contrast to the reformism of liberal feminism, theorized women's oppression as systemic and began to analyze how patriarchal domination relegated women to the private sphere and alienated them from the power men wielded in public life. Radical feminism in the late 1960s and early '70s proposed that gender roles were socially constructed and could be changed only after a revolutionary restructuring of cultural power. This position was claimed in the late '80s by materialist feminist ideology.

Early feminist theatre began as a voice of radical feminism and the first manifestations of what eventually came to be celebrated in women's culture. NYC's It's Alright to Be a Woman Theatre, for example, one of the earliest groups, transposed the political movement's consciousness-raising format to performance and used the new public forum to help validate women's personal lives. The troupe used agitprop techniques with a long tradition in political theatre, as well as street theatre and guerilla tactics that they borrowed from the leftist experimental theatres that had multiplied in the U.S. in the late 1960s and early '70s.

Though these experimental theatres addressed in vital ways civil rights issues and the protests against the Vietnam War, they did no more for women than the Left in general. Women such as MEGAN TERRY and Roberta Sklar, who had both worked in the shadow of JOSEPH CHAIKIN's fame at the OPEN THEATRE, left to form specifically women's or feminist theatre groups. At the OMAHA MAGIC THEATRE (OMT) and the Women's Experimental Theatre (WET), respectively, they brought along many of the experimental theatres' innovations with theatre form, including ritual-based theory and borrowings from Brecht, Artaud, and Grotowski.

The LIVING THEATRE, Open Theatre, and the PERFORMANCE GROUP, for example, had broken with the psychological realism that dominated professional U.S. stages. They had formed COLLEC-TIVES that disrupted the politically constricting hierarchy of the playwright–actor–director triumvirate and the separation of spectators and performers formalized by the proscenium arch. The text was no longer sacred; "Happenings" and rituals became the primary base of theatre work; and social issues and politics explicitly informed every performance choice. Feminist theatre, however, set these theatrical techniques in a political arena where the spectators and performers moved along a revised gender axis.

WET, for example, produced a trilogy of plays called *The Daughters' Cycle,* which recuperated the House of Atreus myth from a female perspective, discussing relationships between mothers and daughters elided in male versions of the story. Their later trilogy focused on women's relationship to food. Both the OMT, administered by Terry and Jo Ann Schmidman, and WET, run by Sklar and her collaborator Sondra Segal, no longer produce work.

While such examples of separatist-inclined women's culture thrived through the 1970s, in the '80s liberal feminism continued to gain viability. Although dogged attempts to pass the Equal Rights Amendment failed, consistent lobbying around women's issues instituted a focus on the "gender gap" in U.S. politics. The situation of urban black women and other minorities received little attention on the liberal feminist agenda, but the movement's focus on political and economic equity for white middle-class women became a force with which the dominant culture had to contend.

Mainstream theatre in the 1980s – no doubt as a result of liberal feminism – began to dole out its major awards to women. The visibility of women playwrights, in particular, led to three Pulitzer Prizes for women in that decade: BETH HENLEY for CRIMES OF THE HEART (1981), MARSHA NORMAN for 'NIGHT, MOTHER (1983), and WENDY WASSERSTEIN for *The Heidi Chronicles* (1989). LILY TOMLIN and Jane Wagner's *The Search for Signs of Intelligent Life in the Universe* (1985) proved a major Broadway success. Women's caucuses in professional theatre organizations and the vitality of the WOMEN'S PROJECT (initially at the AMERICAN PLACE THEATRE) helped women playwrights, directors, producers, designers, and actors seem suddenly to appear where they'd never been before in the ranks of Broadway and regional U.S. theatres. Mainstream plays by women, however, conformed to more traditional forms and styles, such as psychological realism and social comedy.

Feminist theatre troupes in the 1970s and '80s continued to search for a "feminine" or "feminist" aesthetic that would give voice to new contents by developing new theatre forms and modes of production. Because of increasing economic burdens and the fractionalization of radical feminism as a concerted political movement, however, the tradition of flourishing, alternative feminist theatres failed to sustain itself.

Of the numerous radical feminist theatre groups that began in the 1970s, only SPIDERWOMAN THEATRE, a collective of NATIVE AMERICAN women operating in New York, and AT THE FOOT OF THE MOUNTAIN THEATRE in Minneapolis continued to produce and tour into the early '90s. When Spiderwoman began in 1975. the group's radical and ethnic focus, along with the lesbian-feminist-oriented performance work of SPLIT BRITCHES, which was formed in the early 1980s in New York's East Village, represented the growing awareness in U.S. feminism of the differences between and among women. Split Britches – Lois Weaver, Peggy Shaw, and DEB MARGOLIN, who now perform mostly solo performance work – appropriated popular cultural forms once anathema to feminist theatre to investigate sexuality as well as gender (see GAY/LESBIAN THEATRE).

A few companies continue to develop "women's" theatre in the 21st century. The Pleiades Theatre Company (est. 1995) in Louisville, KY, presents only plays written and directed by women. New Georges (est. 1992), a downtown New York theatre, produces new plays by women and works to develop women artists. The Magdalena Project (est. 1986), an international women's theatre network spanning 50 countries, made its first appearance in the U.S. in 2005 in Providence, RI, with a festival of performances and workshops by and about women. At That Uppity Theatre Company (est. 1989) in St. Louis, artistic director Joan Lipkin devises topical performances that serve as activist interventions in social issues, including disability and civil rights, as well as gender.

But contemporary feminist theatre is best represented by individual successful playwrights, directors, and performers, rather than by the collectives of the 1970s and '80s. Pulitzer Prize–winning playwrights PAULA VOGEL (HOW I LEARNED TO DRIVE, *The Long Christmas Ride Home*, and *Baltimore Waltz*, among other plays) and SUZAN-LORI PARKS (TOP DOG/UNDERDOG, *Fuckin' A, Death of the Last Black Man in the Whole Entire World, In the Blood*, and others) abandon domestic realism to explore a wider canvas of social issues and concerns in plays with fractured narratives and theatrically imaginative uses of time and metaphor, language, and imagery. Directors ANNE BOGART and TINA LANDAU bring feminist principles to their productions, scrutinizing the relationship between gender and sexuality among bodies represented architecturally in space. Tony Award–winning performer CHERRY JONES has become a role model for feminist actors seeking success of Broadway without compromising their strength and abilities.

While such professionals bring visibility to women's work in the mainstream, committed critics and scholars continue to generate vital feminist performance theory that provokes activist and intellectual work in the theatre profession and in academia. Such work calls attention to the history of feminist theatre in the U.S., while it helps to motivate its varied, eclectic, necessary future. JDo*

Fences Set in a northern city in the 1950s, this is the second of AUGUST WILSON's 20th-century cycle of black experience plays. A 53-year-old garbage hauler and former Negro League baseball star lives with his long-suffering wife and teenage son in a slum neighborhood. Still bitter over his own exclusion from the major leagues, he dissuades his son from accepting a college football scholarship. Unfaithful as a husband, he yet expects his wife to rear the infant child of his latest liaison. The 1983 play, directed by LLOYD RICHARDS and featuring JAMES EARL JONES, enjoyed pre-Broadway runs at the YALE REPERTORY THEATRE, the GOODMAN THEATRE in Chicago, and in SAN FRANCISCO before opening at the 46TH STREET THEATRE in 1987. It established a record for nonmusicals on Broadway by grossing $11 million in its first year, and captured the triple crown: the Pulitzer, the Tony, and the New York Drama Critics' Circle awards. EGH

Fennell, James (1766–1816) A London-born actor who had a substantial career in America. Fennell first studied law, but made his debut in Edinburgh in 1787 as Othello, which became his most successful role, and soon appeared at Covent Garden with minimal success. WIGNELL brought Fennell to Philadelphia in 1792, where he soon became a star. Well over 6 ft. tall with an expressive, handsome face, Fennell brought considerable dignity to such roles as Othello, Lear, and Jaffier in Venice Preserv'd; he was also much admired as Hamlet, Glenalvon in John Home's Douglas, and Iago. Fennell, however, invested his theatrical income in various unsuccessful money-making schemes (including salt manufacture), was arrested for debt, and spent a time in prison. He retired from the stage in 1810, and in 1814 published his memoirs. In 1815 he attempted Lear, but his memory was gone and the exhibition was one of "pitiable imbecility." SMA

Ferber, Edna (1885–1968) A celebrated author of fiction, Ferber began her theatrical career in 1915 with Our Mrs. McChesney, a collaboration with George V. Hobart that starred ETHEL BARRYMORE. In 1920 she wrote the unsuccessful $1200 a Year with Newman Levy and The Eldest, her only solo venture in playwriting, which was composed for the PROVINCETOWN PLAYERS. Minick (1924) began a lucrative partnership with GEORGE S. KAUFMAN, which also yielded The ROYAL FAMILY (1927), depicting chaotic life in a theatrical dynasty; DINNER AT EIGHT (1932), which examined the lives of guests at a fashionable dinner party; and Stage Door (1936), which focused on young actresses in a theatrical boardinghouse. Less successful for Ferber and Kaufman were The Land Is Bright (1941) and Bravo! (1948). Two of Ferber's novels were adapted into the musicals SHOW BOAT (1927) and Saratoga (1959). Her autobiographies, A Peculiar Treasure (1939) and A Kind of Magic (1963), contain valuable impressions of the theatrical writing process. Ferber's biography by Julie Goldsmith Gilbert appeared in 1978. KF

Ferrer, José [né José Vicente Ferrer Otero y Cintron] (1912–92) Puerto Rican–born actor, director, and producer. His professional debut was in a SHOWBOAT melodrama on Long Island Sound in 1934. He made his Broadway debut in 1935, but his first substantial role came in Brother Rat (1936), and he achieved stardom in Charley's Aunt (1940). Ferrer employed his rich and powerful voice in two subsequent revivals, as Iago to PAUL ROBESON's Othello (1943) and in the title role of Cyrano de Bergerac (1946; Tony, 1947). In the latter role, critics praised his "throbbing, vigorous performance." Ferrer directed the New York Theatre Company at the City Center for a time, appearing in several classical revivals.

Two other acting successes were The Silver Whistle (1948) and The Shrike (1952; Tony). Among his directing assignments were Stalag 17 (1951), The Fourposter (1951), The Shrike – he won a Best Director Tony for all three combined – My Three Angels (1953), and The Andersonville Trial (1959). Ferrer appeared often in films, and won an Oscar for his filmed Cyrano; he also appeared in opera and on television. His last stage appearance was in a 1990 musical version of Ionesco's Rhinoceros in England.

Ferrer, ninth president of the Players Club, was the first actor to receive the National Medal of Arts (1985). SMA

Feuer, Cy (1911–2006) and **Ernest H. Martin** (1919–95) Producers. Partners since 1947, Feuer and Martin's Broadway productions included *Where's Charley?* (1948), GUYS AND DOLLS (1950; Drama Critics' and Tony awards), *Can-Can* (1953), *The Boy Friend* (1954), SILK STOCKINGS (1955), *Whoop-up* (1958), HOW TO SUCCEED IN BUSINESS WITHOUT REALLY TRYING (1961; Drama Critics' and Tony awards, Pulitzer Prize), *Little Me* (1962), *Skyscraper* (1965), *Walking Happy* (1966), *The Goodbye People* (1968), and *The Act* (1977). They managed (and later owned) the LUNT–FONTANNE THEATRE (1960–5); served as managing directors of the Los Angeles and San Francisco Civic Light Opera Association (1976–80), succeeding EDWIN LESTER; and produced the motion pictures CABARET (1972), *Piaf* (1974), and *A CHORUS LINE* (1985). Feuer directed or codirected several of their productions, including *Little Me* with BOB FOSSE. In 2003 he received a Special Tony for Lifetime Achievement in the Theatre; the same year his autobiography was published. TLM

Fichandler, Zelda (Diamond) (1924–) Cofounder and from 1951 sole producing director of Washington, DC's ARENA STAGE, the longest artistic tenure in regional-theatre annals. From the beginning she was committed to having a resident acting company present the classics, American drama, and recent plays that had failed on Broadway – an artistic mission that continues to this day. Fichandler, educated at George Washington University and Cornell, spent much of the 1950s articulating the promise of the regional theatre movement, and in 1961 built a permanent home for her company; there she continued to nurture her resident ensemble and began to produce new plays, such as *The GREAT WHITE HOPE* (1967), INDIANS (1969), and MOONCHILDREN (1971). A tour to the Soviet Union in 1973, the first for an American theatre, fed her interest in Soviet and Eastern European drama and led to productions in the 1970s of works by Frisch, Mrozek, Örkény, and others, many of which she directed. In 1976 the theatre's successes culminated in a Regional Theatre Tony Award for Arena – the first such annual award given. Continuing a dedication to the development of young actors, Fichandler became chair of the graduate acting program at New York University's Tisch School of the Arts in 1984, and, in 1991, concluded her visionary tenure at Arena to become artistic director of New York's ACTING

COMPANY. From May 1993 to May 1995 she served as president of the THEATRE COMMUNICATIONS GROUP. In 1997 she received the National Medal of the Arts, one among her many awards (Common Wealth, JOHN HOUSEMAN, MARGO JONES, "Mr. ABBOTT"), and in 1999 she was inducted into the THEATRE HALL OF FAME. LM

Fiddler on the Roof Based on stories by Sholom Aleichem, with book by Joseph Stein, music by JERRY BOCK, lyrics by SHELDON HARNICK; opened at the IMPERIAL THEATRE on 22 September 1964 and ran for 3,242 performances. Set in a shtetl or Jewish village in the czarist Russia of 1905, the musical recounted the struggles of a milkman, Tevye, to survive and keep his family together in the face of government repression and the forces of change that threaten traditional Jewish observance and customs. By turns comic, sentimental, and melodramatic, the plot focused on Tevye's attempts to arrange good marriages for this three oldest daughters, and their insistence on marrying men of their choosing. Warnings that the Jewish settlements are about to be abolished by the government punctuate the plot, until at the end Tevye and the other villagers of Anatevka are forced to gather their possessions and leave on a perilous journey to a new life in America. The score skillfully combined traditional Jewish harmonies with the musical idioms of Broadway. JEROME ROBBINS's direction and choreography added animation and color to such moments as the wedding of Tevye's oldest daughter. As Tevye, ZERO MOSTEL gave an unforgettable performance, whether grappling to comprehend changes taking place in the world or trying to strike a bargain with God in the humorous "If I Were a Rich Man." Maria Karnilova as Tevye's wife, Golde, and Bea Arthur as Yente the Matchmaker provided strong support.

Fiddler has received a number of major revivals. Mostel returned to Tevye for a limited run at the WINTER GARDEN in 1976, Herschel Bernardi essayed the role in 1981, in 1990 Israeli actor Topol appeared in a new staging on Broadway, and in a 2004 Broadway revival ALFRED MOLINA (replaced in 2005 by HARVEY FIERSTEIN) played Tevye. MK

Field, Joseph M. (1810–56) Dublin-born playwright and actor. He debuted in Boston in 1827 and moved west, acting in and out of the SOL SMITH–LUDLOW circuit, finally managing Field's Varieties Theatre in St. Louis (1852–3). Field also acted and wrote for MITCHELL'S OLYMPIC in New York (1842–3). A man of his time, Field wrote *Ore-*

gon; or, *The Disputed Territory* (1846), *The Tourist* (1839), and, more seriously, *Job and His Children* (1852), his only extant work.   WJM

Fields, Dorothy (1905–74) Lyricist-librettist. Daughter of comedian-producer Lew Fields (see WEBER AND FIELDS), she began her career writing songs for shows at the Cotton Club with composer Jimmy McHugh. Together, they wrote songs for *Blackbirds of 1928* and other Broadway REVUES featuring black performers. She spent most of the 1930s in Hollywood, then returned to Broadway with *Stars in Your Eyes* (1939). In the 1940s she wrote the librettos for such shows as *Mexican Hayride* (1944) and ANNIE GET YOUR GUN (1946). She wrote lyrics (and, in some cases, librettos) for *A Tree Grows in Brooklyn* (1951), *By the Beautiful Sea* (1954), *Redhead* (1959), and SWEET CHARITY (1966). Her last show was *Seesaw* (1973), and her songs were featured posthumously in *Ain't Misbehavin'* (1978), *Sugar Babies* (1979), FOSSE (1999), and other revues.   MK

Fields, Lew see WEBER, JOSEPH

Fields, W. C. [né William Claude Dukenfield] (1880–1946) Comedian who ran away from home at the age of 14 and taught himself to juggle. As an eccentric tramp juggler he was the first American headliner at Paris's Folies-Bergère (1902) and a great hit at the London Hippodrome (1904) for his trick pool game and frustrating golf lesson. Taking his cue from Harry Tate's British music-hall persona, the bibulous, bottle-nosed Fields developed the character of a grandiloquent but seedy curmudgeon, muttering indignant asides. He starred in the ZIEGFELD Follies (1915–18, 1920, 1921, 1925), and in *Poppy* (1923) created the type of the moth-eaten but brazen showman he would later repeat on film. His earliest film appearance had been in a short of 1915, and after 1925 he settled in Los Angeles, appearing in a series of comic masterpieces. Of his numerous biographies, the most recent by James Curtis (2003) was acclaimed.
   LS

Fierstein, Harvey (1954–) Playwright, actor, producer, and gay activist. Educated at Pratt Institute, Fierstein made his debut as an actor at LA MAMA in Andy Warhol's *Pork* (1971). He garnered sudden fame in 1981 with the success of his TORCH SONG TRILOGY, a play presenting various views of male homosexuality (see GAY AND LESBIAN THEATRE), and winning him Tonys in 1983 for Best Actor and Best Play. His third Tony came in 1984 for his book for the JERRY HERMAN musical LA

CAGE AUX FOLLES, and its hit status made him the most successful Broadway playwright concerned with gay themes in the 1980s. Efforts from 1983 until 2002 were less successful (e.g., *Safe Sex*, *Spookhouse*, *On Tidy Endings*), devoting more time to television and film roles, but in 2002 he returned to Broadway as Edna Turnblad in HAIRSPRAY (Tony, Best Actor in a Musical) – reprised in a 2006 Las Vegas production – and in 2005 took over Tevye in FIDDLER ON THE ROOF.   TLM

Fifth Avenue Theatre West 24th St. between Broadway and 6th Ave., NYC. Amos Eno, the owner of the Fifth Avenue Hotel, erected a small structure adjoining it for surreptitious and illegal stock-exchange activities, which he was forced to abandon. In 1865, he decided to convert it into a theatre, and for several years it functioned as a minstrel hall. The railroad magnate James Fisk took it over, gutted the interior, and transformed it into a handsome little theatre, which eventually fell into the hands of AUGUSTIN DALY for his introduction into theatrical management. During 1869–73, Daly assembled an attractive company, staged comedies and dramas in perfectly tuned productions, and made this theatre the most fashionable and popular playhouse in New York. When it went up in flames in 1873 (see FIRES), Daly transferred his company to the New Fifth Avenue Theatre at 728 Broadway. In 1879, STEELE MACKAYE rebuilt the old house, renaming it the MADISON SQUARE.   MCH

Fifth of July by LANFORD WILSON was first presented by the CIRCLE REPERTORY COMPANY in NYC on 27 April 1978. Directed by MARSHALL W. MASON, the cast included WILLIAM HURT as Kenneth Talley Jr., a paraplegic Vietnam veteran who has returned to his family home in Missouri to resume his teaching career after eight years; Helen Stenborg as his aunt Sally Friedman; Joyce Reehling as his sister, June, once politically militant; Amy Wright as June's adolescent daughter, Shirley; Nancy Snyder as Gwen Landis, an old friend from Ken's student days at Berkeley who wants to buy the Talley place and turn it into a recording studio; Jonathan Hogan as her husband, John; and Jeff Daniels as Ken's lover, Jed. The play ran for 158 performances. Often compared to Chekhov, Wilson examines the characters' attempts to free themselves from the effect of the past, particularly the Vietnam War and the events surrounding it. In the course of the play, each finds a way to connect with others and create a new future. In a 1980 Broadway version CHRISTOPHER REEVE was Ken; SWOOZIE KURTZ, Gwen. As part of a Wilson season, it was revived in 2002–3 by SIGNATURE THEATRE (ROBERT SEAN LEONARD, Ken; Parker Posey, Gwen).   BCM

Filipino American theatre Because Filipino American dramatic literature is one of the least documented demographic subdivisions in the American theatre, scholarly convention traces its history as a sociopolitical outgrowth of the civil rights era in the 1960s and '70s, or as an ethnic-specific branch of a larger axis known as ASIAN AMERICAN THEATRE. That view, however, presents an incomplete picture. Expediently, it suppresses the almost half-century during which the Philippines was a U.S. territory, from 1898 (when Spain ceded its 300-year colonial rule in exchange for $20 million) until it was granted independence in 1946. Under this direct U.S. rule, the architects of the colonial education system decided that it would be to the advantage of the U.S. to make English the medium of instruction in all Philippine schools. American forms, along with their English and European counterparts, were introduced through the language and media and became assimilated and accepted as models.

American influence on Philippine theatre is found in the songs and dances of what was then called *bodabil* (vaudeville in English; *vodavil* in Spanish), which debuted around 1915 on the American bases. Sometimes called "jamborees" in the provinces, *bodabil* spawned a number of Americanized popular entertainers. The American impact also exerted inself in the Western plays staged in the original English or in English translation, and in the original plays written by Filipinos in English and in Philippine languages and produced by contemporary theatre groups, using such styles as theatre of the absurd, epic theatre, expressionism, and various forms of realism. The first English-language play was *A Modern Filipina* by Jesusa Araullo and Lino Castillejo (1915). With mastery of the language came more playwrights, including Jorge Bocobo, Carlos P. Romulo, and Vidal Tan. By the 1940s and '50s several major Filipino playwrights in English developed: Severino Montano, who studied at Yale; Wilfrido Ma. Guerrero, with over 100 plays to his credit; Alberto S. Florentino, whose collection *The World Is an Apple and Other Prize Plays* (1959) contains his most characteristic work; and Nick Joaquin, whose *A Portrait of the Artist as Filipino* (1951) is generally considered the most important Filipino stage work in English.

In the late 1960s and early '70s – as the nationalist movement brought about the ascendance of theatre in the national language, Filipino, as well as in Tagalog, Cebuano, and other vernaculars – the U.S. saw a new influx of immigrants of Filipino ancestry, many of whom were educated professionals and some political exiles (unlike the students, migrant farmworkers, and cannery laborers before 1965). With the exceptions of rituals, folk dances, and disparate theatrical activities in community events, lounge circuits, literary groups, army bases, and social gatherings, Filipino American theatre artists were largely invisible in the first half ot the 20th century. With the generational shift, the Asian American theatre slowly became the primary artery for plays and musicals about the Asian American history and experience. And while English-language drama moved to a relative standstill in the Philippines, Carlos Bulosan, a Filipino peasant boy who had landed in the U.S. at the start of the Great Depression, taught himself how to write; best known for his 1946 novel *America Is in the Heart,* Bulosan tried his hand at playwriting, notably *The Worldbeaters, The Wall, The Masquerade Ball,* and a verse drama, *Jose Rizal.*

The latter half of the 20th century saw the emergence of new Filipino American playwrights, artists, directors, and theatre companies across the country. One of the first writers, Jeannie Barroga, is a much-anthologized San Francisco-based playwright who has written more than 50 plays, including *Eye of the Coconut* (1987), *Walls* (1989), and *Talk Story* (1991). JESSICA HAGEDORN, considered the doyenne of Filipino American writing, started creating multimedia theatre pieces in experimental performance venues with her *Mango Tango* (1978) and *Tenement Lover: No Palm Trees/In New York City* (1981) and recently adapted for the stage her award-winning novel *Dogeaters* (2000). Other notable playwrights of Filipino descent include ERNEST ABUBA (*The Dowager Empress of China,* 1978); Timoteo Cordova (*Heart of the Son,* 2004); Linda Faigao-Hall (*State without Grace,* 1984); Marina Feleo Gonzales (*A Song for Manong,* 1987); Chris Mellado (*peregriNasyon, or Wandering Nation,* 1998); Randy Gener (*Love Seats for Virginia Woolf,* 2000); Alec Mapa (*I Remember Mapa,* 1997); HAN ONG, who was born Ong Soo-han (*The L.A. Plays,* 1993); Nicky Paraiso (*Asian Boys,* 1994); and Ralph B. Peña (*Flipzoids,* 1996). Moreover, professional Filipino American troupes have been important incubators for veteran actors and directors, such as Ching Valdes-Aran, Mia Katigbak, Jojo Gonzales, Orlando Pabotoy, Sean San Jose, LOY ARCENAS, as well as spoken-word poet Regie Cabico and sound designers Fabian Obispo and Andre Pluess. Katigbak is the artistic director of the NATIONAL ASIAN AMERICAN THEATER COMPANY,

Flipzoids by Ralph B. Peña, produced in 1997 by Ma-Yi Theatre Company and designed by Loy Arcenas. *Courtesy:* Ralph Peña.

which stages all-Asian productions of classics. MA-YI THEATER COMPANY in New York established its reputation through producing Filipino Amerian work. Other important Filipino American ensembles include Teatro NgTanan (loosely, Theatre for Everyone), Bindlestiff Studio, Tongue in a Mood, and Kaliwat Theatre Collective, all in San Francisco; Pintig Cultural Group in Chicago; Sining KilUSAn Performing Arts Ensemble in Seattle; Asian American Writers Workshop, Kinding Sindaw, and DiverseCity Theatre Company in NYC; and QBD Ink of Washington, DC. These Filipino American theatres are dedicated to presenting cutting-edge works by Filipino and Filipino American artists in theatre, comedy, spoken word, music, and dance.   RG

Finian's Rainbow Two-act musical comedy, music by Burton Lane, words by E. Y. HARBURG and Fred Saidy; opened 10 January 1947 at the 46TH STREET THEATRE, running 725 performances. One of the first of a wave of socially conscious postwar musicals, *Finian's Rainbow* tells of an Irishman who, hearing that America's gold is buried in Fort Knox, comes to the southern state of "Missitucky" to "plant" gold he has stolen from a leprechaun. The pursuing leprechaun (David Wayne) creates havoc, notably in turning a racist white politician black, before love turns him human. The show is notable for several reasons beyond its social themes: The central romance ends in separation rather than in union; the cast was thoroughly integrated in an age of mostly all-white or all-black musicals; it marked the Broadway debut as choreographer of MICHAEL KIDD; and it featured a mute character who expressed herself solely through dance. However, it is perhaps best remembered for Harburg's satiric jibes at economic, racial, and social policy – and for Lane's score ("Look to the Rainbow," "Old Devil Moon"). An intimate revival by the IRISH REPERTORY THEATRE was a success in 2004.   JD

Finley, Karen (1956–) Chicago-born visual and performance artist, writer. Though her material is somewhat cliché-ridden and obvious, Finley represents the ever-increasing visibility of performance artists (in 1993 she received a Guggenheim Fellowship), especially since she became the centerpiece in the controversy over the NATIONAL ENDOWMENT FOR THE ARTS funding denial in 1990 (as one of the "NEA four"). She studied PERFORMANCE ART and painting at the Chicago Art Institute (1975–7) and the San Francisco Art Institute (M,F,A., 1981). She collaborated (1981–4) with Brian Rout (aka Harry Kipper, one of Britain's performance art duo, "The Kipper Kids"), to whom she was briefly married. In her theatre piece *The Theory of Total Blame* (1988) and her solo performances (some with minor support), such as *The Constant State of Desire* (1987), *We Keep Our Victims Ready* (1989), *A Certain Level of Denial* (1992), *The American Chestnut* (1997), *The Return of the Chocolate-Smeared Woman* (1998), and *Make Love* (2003), her subject is the dysfunctional nuclear family and victimizing social conditions. Her strategy of overexposing the body is to deeroticize it. One of her recent creations – *George and Martha* (2004) – was based on the idea that George W. Bush and Martha Stewart have had a long secret affair. Her memoirs appeared in 2000.   AF DBW

Finn, William (1952–) Boston-born, Williams College–educated composer-lyricist-teacher whose successes have been modest albeit significant. Foremost among these are *FALSETTOS* (1992) and *The 25th Annual Putnam County Spelling Bee* (2005). The first, a musical play with book by JAMES LAPINE, was based on three earlier Off-Broadway musicals by Finn (*In Trousers*, 1979; *March of the Falsettos*, 1981; *Falsettoland*, 1990). The combined creation, winner of two Tonys in 1992 for Best Book and Best Original Score, centered on a married man leaving his wife for another man, who later dies of AIDS. Despite its then radical topic, it ran for 486 performances at the JOHN GOLDEN THEATRE. The 2005 musical, about six misfits who experience the joys and despair of competition, with final book by Rachel Sheinkin (Tony Award), had a long period of gestation, beginning as an Off-Broadway play in 2002. Its revision was workshopped at the BARRINGTON STAGE COMPANY, then presented by SECOND STAGE, directed by Lapine, and finally moved to Broadway (CIRCLE IN THE SQUARE). In between these hits his work grew grave, notably with *A New Brain* (1998), based on a belief that he was dying of a brain tumor, and *Elegies* (2003), whose subject is death (both at Lincoln Center). Finn teaches music theatre writing at NYU.   DBW

Fiorello! Two-act musical comedy, with music by JERRY BOCK, lyrics by SHELDON HARNICK, book by Jerome Weidman and GEORGE ABBOTT; opened 23 November 1959 at the BROADHURST THEATRE, running 795 performances. This musical depiction of the early career of New York's Mayor Fiorello LaGuardia (Tom Bosley), the first successful Broadway collaboration of Bock and Harnick, won the Pulitzer Prize for Drama, as well as the Drama Critics' Circle and (in a tie) Tony awards for Best Musical. Although other recent musicals had featured nonsingers in the leading male role, *FIORELLO!* was unusual in that it confined his singing entirely to LaGuardia's campaign speeches. With many musical scenes rather than traditional "numbers," the score produced no standard "hits," but rather helped evoke the historical corruption of the era.   JD

fires The U.S. has been plagued with devastating performance-venue fires, beginning with THOMAS WADE WEST's theatre in Richmond, followed by Boston's FEDERAL THEATRE (both in 1798) and continuing unabated until safer materials and strict laws were introduced early in the 20th century. Prior to 1880, mostly small theatres burned (26 in New York, 21 in San Francisco, 17 in Philadelphia, 11 in Boston, 9 in Cincinnati, 8 in New Orleans, 6 in Baltimore). In one two-year period (1865–7), at least five major New York performance spaces burned (BARNUM'S, "444" Broadway, the Academy of Music, the BOWERY, and the WINTER GARDEN). Some theatres suffered fires frequently (the Bowery, for instance, six times). Most fires occurred when venues were dark, but those with the greatest loss of life struck during performances. In 1811 the Richmond (VA) Theatre fire resulted in 71 deaths; the Brooklyn Theatre fire of 1876 accounted for 295 lives lost; the supposedly fireproof Iroquois Theatre in CHICAGO burned in 1903 during a performance of *Mr. Bluebeard* featuring EDDIE FOY, with more than 600 lives claimed; and in 1908 the Rhoads Theatre in Boyertown, PA, burned with 170 lost. Destruction by fire has not been limited to theatres. Three prime examples were the Cocoanut Grove NIGHTCLUB fire in Boston, which in 1942 cost 491 lives; the RINGLING BROS. canvas Big Top conflagration in 1944 (in Hartford, CT), with at least 168 deaths (the worst disaster in CIRCUS history); and the 2003 The Station (West Warwick, RI) nightclub fire, with 100 perishing. In many of these, numerous deaths were not from burns but from asphyxiation or panic-induced crushing and trampling.   DBW

Fisher, Charles (1816–91) English-born actor, son of the theatrical manager Charles Fisher. He came to American in 1852 and for a decade was a member of several New York companies, including W. E. BURTON's and LAURA KEENE's. During 1861–72 he was a principal supporting actor in WALLACK's company and then, until 1890, in AUGUSTIN DALY's. He appeared in a wide range of classical and contemporary roles during his long career, but was celebrated as a light comedian, particularly for his characterizations of Malvolio, Joseph Surface, Anthony Absolute, Falstaff (*The Merry Wives of Windsor*), and Triplet (*Masks and Faces*).   DJW

Fisher, Clara (1811–98) London-born actress who debuted at Drury Lane at age 6, toured England for a decade, and then came to the U.S. in 1827 for a triumphant debut at the PARK. LUDLOW called her "the finest comedy actress in the United States." Among her more noted roles were Viola, Lady Teazle, Lady Gay Spanker, Pauline, and the Fool in *King Lear*. She was first Singing Witch in

Engraving of the burning of Richmond Theatre, 1811. *Courtesy:* Harvard Theatre Collection, Houghton Library.

Macready's *Macbeth* the night of the Astor Place riot. Although she retired in 1884, Fisher would occasionally appear in "old-lady parts," and in 1897 completed her autobiography. SMA

Fisher, Jules (1937–) Lighting designer, theatre consultant, writer, and producer. Fisher had already designed three Off-Broadway shows before graduating from Carnegie Tech in 1960. He has since designed well over 200 productions, including a record eight Tony winners: *Pippin* (1972), *Ulysses in Nighttown* (1973), *Dancin'* (1978), *Grand Hotel* (1990), *The Will Rogers Follies* (1991), *Jelly's Last Jam* (1992), and, with Peggy Eisenhauer, *Bring in 'da Noise, Bring in 'da Funk* (1996) and *Assassins* (2004). As a producer his many works include *Beatlemania*. Because of his work as designer and consultant for several rock tours, notably for the Rolling Stones, KISS, and David Bowie, he has been an innovator in new technology for stage lighting. In professional partnership with Eisenhauer, he is married to director-choreographer Graciela Daniele. AA

Fiske, Harrison Grey (1861–1942) Dramatic editor, critic, producer, manager, and playwright.

Born of wealthy parents, Fiske served an early apprenticeship on the *Jersey City Argus, New York Star,* and *New York Dramatic Mirror*. He left New York University after his sophomore year (1880) to edit the *Dramatic Mirror* when his father bought him a one-third interest in it. He made the paper an important theatrical journal by attacking corruption in the profession and working to raise the tone of the American stage. He led a crusade in 1880 to establish the Actors' Fund. In 1890, he married the actress Marie Augusta Davey (Minnie Maddern Fiske) and managed her career as well as that of a number of leading actors. For her he wrote or adapted numerous plays, including *Hester Crewe* (1893) and *Marie Deloche* (1895). He leased the Manhattan Theatre in 1901 for Mrs. Fiske, and formed the Manhattan Theatre Company to support her. His producing successes included *Kismet* (1911), starring Otis Skinner. Financial problems forced him to sell the *Dramatic Mirror* in 1911, and he declared bankruptcy in 1914, although he was discharged the following year. The death of Mrs. Fiske in 1932 effectively ended his career. Fiske fought commercialism in the theatre, and did much to establish Ibsen on the American stage. TLM

Fiske, Minnie Maddern [née Marie Augusta Davey] (1864–1932) Actress and director. From a theatrical family, she began her career at age 3, remaining in steady demand as a child actress. Her adult New York debut was in Charles Callahan's *Fogg's Ferry* (1882). After a brief first marriage, she wed her second husband, HARRISON GREY FISKE, editor of the NEW YORK DRAMATIC MIRROR, in 1890, retiring for four years after her marriage. During this interlude she wrote several one-act plays and became interested in the realist movement. After 1893 she focused her energies, despite opposition, on plays of this ilk, and worked toward what she called "natural, true acting" in her productions, especially with her MANHATTAN THEATRE COMPANY (1904–8). At the turn of the century she fought the Theatrical SYNDICATE, almost alone, and became a noted humanitarian, fighting against cruelty and abuse to animals. Some of her notable stage appearances were in *Hester Crewe* (1893), *A Doll's House* (1894), Lorimer Stoddard's dramatization of *Tess of the d'Urbervilles* (1897), LANGDON MITCHELL's adaptation of *Vanity Fair*, *Becky Sharp* (1899), *Hedda Gabler* (1903), *Leah Kleschna* (1904), *The NEW YORK IDEA* (1906), *Rosmersholm* (1907), *SALVATION NELL* (1908), *The Pillars of Society* (1910), and *Ghosts* (1927). She is considered today one of the most distinguished actresses ever to have performed on the American stage and its chief promoter of IBSEN. A contemporary critic noted, "She had a peculiar gift of emotion, uniting tears and smiles in the same breath, which was more pathetic than undiluted grief and more diverting than undiluted laughter." Archie Binns's biography of Fiske was published in 1955.   DBW

Fiske, Stephen Ryder (1840–1916) Drama critic. Educated at Rutgers, Fiske learned his trade during the Civil War on the staff of the *New York Herald*. He also contributed to the *Leader* and adapted French plays for local managers. After an eight-year hiatus (1866–74) in London as a journalist and theatre manager, he handled AUGUSTIN DALY's business affairs, comanaged the FIFTH AVENUE THEATRE (1877–9), and cofounded the *NEW YORK [DRAMATIC] MIRROR* (1879). His dramatic column for the *Spirit of the Times* (1879–1902) established his reputation. A pragmatic critic, Fiske offered a commonsense view of theatre – not as an art but as a form of mass entertainment.   TLM

Fitch, Clyde (1865–1909) Playwright. Born in Elmira, NY, he graduated from Amherst (1886), where he had been a leader in the dramatic club and frequently played female roles. Fitch was extraordinarily successful and prolific, writing 60 plays, from *Beau Brummell* (1890, starring RICHARD MANSFIELD) to *The CITY* (1909). In February 1901 four of his plays were running simultaneously in New York: *Lover's Lane, Captain Jinks of the Horse Marines* (with ETHEL BARRYMORE), *The Climbers,* and *Barbara Frietchie*. Best known among his others: *The Moth and the Flame* (1898), *Nathan Hale* (1898), *The Cowboy and the Lady* (1899), *The Girl with the Green Eyes* (1902), *Her Great Match* (1905), and *The TRUTH* (1907). Fitch was a master of sprightly dialogue and documentarylike scenes from contemporary life, and as a director he meticulously controlled every detail of the staging. One critic said that his plays gave a better idea of American life than did newspapers and historical records. He died at Châlons-sur-Marne in France. His letters were published in 1924, and a biography (by A. Bell) appeared in 1909.   RM

Fitzgerald, Geraldine (1914–2005) Actress, writer, and director. Born in Dublin and educated at the Dublin Art School, Fitzgerald made her stage debut at the Gate Theatre in Dublin (1932) and her first appearance in New York as Ellie Dunn in SHAW's *Heartbreak House* (1938). While also working in film, she played onstage in the U.S. an impressive array of classical and modern characters: Jennifer Dubedat, *The Doctor's Dilemma* (1955); Goneril, *King Lear* (1956, with ORSON WELLES); Gertrude, *Hamlet* (1958, AMERICAN SHAKESPEARE FESTIVAL); Queen, *The Cave Dwellers* (1961, solo); Mary Tyrone, *LONG DAY'S JOURNEY INTO NIGHT* (1971, with STACY KEACH); Essie Miller, *AH, WILDERNESS!* (1975, CIRCLE IN THE SQUARE); Felicity, *The Shadow Box* (1977); and Nora Melody, *A TOUCH OF THE POET* (1977, with JASON ROBARDS). She also performed in a ONE-PERSON show on Broadway, *Songs of the Streets* (1976; revamped for ROUNDABOUT, 1979). Fitzgerald made over 40 films, including *Wuthering Heights* (1939), *The Pawnbroker* (1965), and *Arthur* (1981). Later in her career she was as active directing as she was acting, receiving a Tony nomination for *Mass Appeal* in 1982, and in 1993 debuted as a lyricist and book writer with *Sharon*, a musical based on John B. Keane's *Sharon's Grave*, which she also directed. During 1994–5, She is remembered as one of America's most distinguished character actresses. Her son, **Michael Lindsay-Hogg**, succeeded as a film, television, and stage director (*Whose Life Is It Anyway?*, 1980; *Agnes of God*, 1982).   TLM

Flanagan (Davis) [née Ferguson], **Hallie** (1890–1969) Playwright, educator, director, and administrator. Franklin D. Roosevelt called Flanagan the third most powerful woman in America – "after my wife and Frances Perkins" – when she supervised the FEDERAL THEATRE PROJECT. Born in South Dakota, she graduated from Grinnell College in Iowa, studied with GEORGE PIERCE BAKER at Workshop 47, and in 1927 received a Guggenheim Award to study theatre in Europe. On her return she ran a highly successful experimental program at Vassar College. In 1935 Harry Hopkins invited her to administer the new theatre program that had been established under WPA supervision to put qualified people back to work. For the next four years she managed the huge national theatre as it struggled with its double charge of art and relief. In spite of government harassment, crippling bureaucratic regulations, and opposition from the professional theatre, the FTP achieved a remarkable record of accomplishments including LIVING NEWSPAPERS, Negro companies (see AFRICAN AMERICAN THEATRE), CHILDREN'S THEATRES, and distinguished alumni. With the demise of the project in 1939 (after a skirmish with HUAC), Flanagan returned to Vassar. There she wrote a memoir (*Arena*, 1940), then moved to Smith College, where she continued to write and direct. She died in 1969 leaving behind several books and a vision of the theatre as a vibrant social institution that must dare to be dangerous. Joanne Bentley's biography of Flanagan appeared in 1988.   BBW

Flea Theater, The Noninstitutional and "resolutely non-commercial," this complex of two small, state-of-the-art performance spaces (80-seat mainstage and 40-seat Downstairs @ The Flea) sees itself as a throwback to the more experimental days of OFF-OFF BROADWAY. Founded in 1996 by director Jim Simpson (still artistic director), designer Kyle Chepulis, and playwright MAC WELLMAN with the mission to create "a joyful hell in a small space," it presents "edgy and distinctive work (music, dance, and especially theatre) that raises the standards of Off-Off Broadway for artists and audiences alike." *The Guys* – an immediate post-9/11 two-hander about a writer-editor helping a fire captain compose eulogies for his fallen men – ran 13 months and became a feature film. For their adventurous efforts (seen by 17,000 each year), The Flea received in 2004 a Drama Desk Award for Distinguished Achievement. Three major productions are produced annually, with dozens of smaller efforts (as many as four a night) and programs that support not only established names but also emerging and midcareer artists.   DBW

Fletcher, Allen (1922–85) Director and teacher. Born in San Francisco, Fletcher studied at Stanford and Yale Universities, the Bristol Old Vic Theatre School, and LAMDA, on a Fulbright. He made his directing debut in 1948 at the OREGON SHAKESPEARE FESTIVAL and returned there each year through 1956. Other directing credits include the Antioch Shakespeare Festival (1957); the OLD GLOBE in San Diego (1955–66); and the ASSOCIATION OF PRODUCING ARTISTS (1960–1). During 1962–5 he served as principal director and head of the professional training program for the AMERICAN SHAKESPEARE FESTIVAL. In 1966 he took a similar post with the SEATTLE REPERTORY THEATRE, where he modernized the company and ended the rotating repertory. Ousted in 1970, he founded the Actor's Company and became Director of the Conservatory for the AMERICAN CONSERVATORY THEATRE (where he'd guest-directed since 1965). He left ACT in 1984 for a similar post with the DENVER CENTER THEATRE. A premiere classical director, Fletcher is remembered for his 1963 *King Lear* with MORRIS CARNOVSKY.   TLM

Florence, William "Billy" Jermyn (or James) [né Bernard Conlin] (1831–91) Actor whose professional stage debut occurred in 1849 at the Marshall Theatre in Richmond, VA, as Peter in *The Stranger.* In 1853 he married Malvina Pray, the sister of Maria Pray Mestayer Williams, wife of actor BARNEY WILLIAMS. For almost 40 years, the Florences were a successful starring team in both England and America, often in Irish American roles such as *The Irish Boy and the Yankee Girl.* Florence was a skillful comedian noted for his striking, convincingly human characterizations. After his Irish roles, his outstanding performances were as Bob Brierly in Tom Taylor's *The Ticket-of-Leave Man,* Bardwell Slote in Benjamin E. Woolf's *The MIGHTY DOLLAR,* Sir Lucius O'Trigger in *The Rivals,* and Zekiel Homespun in Colman the younger's *The Heir-at-Law.* He also presented the first American production of T. W. ROBERTSON's *Caste* in 1867, only four months after its London premiere.   DJW

Florodora With the exception of GILBERT AND SULLIVAN, this musical (score by Leslie Stuart, lyrics by Stuart, Paul Rubens, and Edward Boyd-Jones) produced at the CASINO THEATRE (opened 12 November 1900) was the most successful British import of its era. With more than 500 performances, the New York production exceeded the 1899 London run, reversing the trend of the day. Frequently revived – and highlighted by its sextette of lovely ladies, with six male partners, and their coquettish number "Tell Me, Pretty Maiden" – the show had its last Broadway revival in 1920. The slight book by Owen Hall concerns an aborted attempt to cheat the heroine out of her inheritance of a famous perfume: Florodora (also the name of the Philippine island where the perfume is manufactured).   DBW

Folger Theatre When the SHAKESPEARE THEATRE left the Folger Shakespeare Library in 1992 for larger facilities in Washington, DC, the Library's public programs division expanded to include theatre peformances in its offerings. After a period of booking attractions, the Folger began producing its own three-play season of Shakespeare and contemporary plays inspired by the Bard in the Folger's 250-seat "Elizabethan" theatre (which claims to be a replica of a generic inn-yard playhouse). Actors seen at the Folger have included Derek Jacobi, Lynn REDGRAVE, Ian McKellen, Diana Rigg, Michael Learned, and numerous local professional actors. Since 1994 Janet Alexander Griffin has served as artistic producer.   DBW

folk and festival performance Like folk painting and music, folk performance is nonacademic art based on traditional techniques and content. Both change constantly, however, as the performance is carried from one community to another. Typically, folk performers have considered themselves less creators of an art than "recreators" of a traditional event of significance. Often that event has its roots in the ETHNIC or immigrant origins of the community – British, Spanish, AFRICAN AMERICAN, NATIVE AMERICAN, or the more recently arrived groups – but adapted to reflect contemporary community needs and interests.

Folk performance is a close cousin to play, games, and sport, on one hand, and to rituals on the other. For example, the line between children's games and fully developed performance is not always clear, but American folk culture contains a rich range of "paraperformance" activities that fall between the two, as in the traditional "play party" activities once common in the rural South.

Performance aspects of a ritual often come to share prominence with its purely functional elements. Examples include the traditional jazz funerals of New Orleans, with their elaborate outdoor processions and marching bands, as well as traditional religious revivals. Many revivalists have become skilled manipulators of the performance element in their religious services, developing complex juxtapositions of song, chant, and exhortation.

Folk plays once existed in abundance throughout the U.S., and may still be found today in some localities. A number originated in mumming or some form of Old World religious drama; many are seasonal and perambulatory in their approach to space, involving movement of performers (and sometimes groups of spectators as well) from one "station" to another, with the presentation of a play at each station. Sometimes these stations are the homes of community members, and the presentations occur during "house visits" in which an ordinary room becomes a temporary performance space. Often improvised outdoor sites are employed.

Between the presentations at various stations there may be a relatively formal procession, as in HISPANIC Good Friday commemorations, or a less controlled general movement, sometimes with tricks, jokes, and horseplay in evidence. Often performers are decked out in fantastic masks and costumes, athough there may be little attempt at impersonation, with marchers clearly identified first and foremost as community members carrying out a traditional performance in disguise or semidisguise.

The traditional Halloween "trick or treat" or "beggars night," Chinese New Years celebrations in New York, and the Purim masking in Jewish communities represent the idea of the perambulatory performance stripped to its most basic elements, with emphasis on masking and unrestricted wandering between visits. Perambulatory performances with elaborately structured recitations or "plays" have been collected among Spanish communities in the Southwest and among Hungarian Americans in Ohio.

Parades and processions, another form of perambulatory performance with little emphasis on the stational, are often presented as part of traditional festivals designed to celebrate, commemorate, reenact, or anticipate events of seasons of significance to the community. New York City's St. Patrick's Day parade and Macy's Thanksgiving parade, which initiates the Christmas-shopping season in the city, are associated with festival days but not with specific festival areas beyond those defined by the parades themselves. Many folk festivals, however, are "environmental," transforming an existing space – a street, square, or park, for example – into a temporary performance site.

Typically, an environmental festival occurs over too large a space and over too long a period of time to be seen as a literal performance by those involved; but, in effect, it becomes both a performance in the broadest sense and the seedbed for a number of smaller, more easily comprehensible performance events of various types, often including processional performance. The Italian American street festivals in New York City and Mardi Gras in New Orleans are examples of environmental performances that temporarily transform existing urban spaces, "festivalizing" them for the duration of the event through an elaborate scenography.

The approaches to organization and "staging" used in the creation of American folk and festival performance are, in effect, little different from those found in many other cultures worldwide. Paraperformance, perambulation, and environmental performance all represent time-honored solutions to the practical problem of presenting issues of significance to the community in an effective and memorable way.   BMcN

Folksbiene (People's Stage) Yiddish Theatre

Beginning in New York City as one of hundreds of Yiddish amateur theatres, it survived to become the longest continuously performing YIDDISH THEATRE in the world (and today the only one in the U.S.), presenting at least one production every winter since 1915. Early on it hired professional directors, such as JOSEPH BULOFF and JACOB BEN-AMI, and eventually began hiring some professional actors as well. Associated with the Workman's Circle, the group is generally committed to presenting Yiddish plays of literary worth, often classics; but in recent years it has also presented lighter entertainments, such as Yiddish translations of popular Israeli comedies. In 1998 it lost its Manhattan home in the Central Synagogue due to a fire. It then moved to Theater 4 on West 55th St., in 2002 to the PCMH Theatre on West 36th, and currently uses a space at the Jewish Community Center in Manhattan. After a bitter struggle, a new generation also took artistic control. In June 2006 it changed its name to the National Yiddish Theatre – Folksbiene.   NS

Follies Intermissionless musical play, music and lyrics by STEPHEN SONDHEIM, book by James Goldman; opened 4 April 1971 at New York's WINTER GARDEN THEATRE, running 522 performances. This extravagant and thought-provoking musical probes the various meanings of "follies." Set amid a reunion of former performers in a ZIEGFELD-like revue the night before their old theatre is torn down, it juxtaposes past and present, memory and reality, dreams and disillusion. Producer-codirector HAROLD PRINCE (who shared a directing Tony with codirector-choreographer

MICHAEL BENNETT) brought back actual celebrities of 50 years before, who performed numbers much like those of yesteryear, but from the perspective of age. He also populated the stage with statuesque showgirls who wandered the stage as ghosts of a bygone splendor, and paired the older actors with younger actors playing their characters' optimistic younger selves. Sondheim's Tony-winning score, combining both a contemporary lyricism and an evocation of older theatre music, has been much admired, and BORIS ARONSON's Tony-winning set created both the derelict theatre and the sumptuous gingerbread of the dreamlike "Loveland" sequence. *Follies* won the Drama Critics' Circle Award for Best Musical, but it has rarely been revived because of both expense and casting difficulties; still, a 2001 revival directed by Matthew Warchus ran for 116 performances. A classic of its kind is Ted Chapin's extraordinary book *Everything Was Possible* (2003), which revisits the creation of the original production.   JD

Fonda [né Jaynes]**, Henry** (1905–82) Nebraska-born actor who made his first stage appearance in 1925 at the Omaha Community Playhouse, and his Broadway debut in 1929. He established himself as a leading actor in *The Farmer Takes a Wife* (1934) before turning almost exclusively to making films. After service in WWII, he played the title role in *MISTER ROBERTS* (1948), which won him a Tony. Working in both Hollywood and New York, Fonda won critical acclaim on Broadway in 1954 with his portrayal of Barney Greenwald in *The Caine Mutiny Court Martial*. He starred with ANN BANCROFT in *Two for the Seesaw* (1958) and with BARBARA BEL GEDDES in *Silent Night, Lonely Night* (1959). Other important stage appearances include the comedy hit *Generation* (1965) and the ONE-PERSON show *Clarence Darrow* (1974). Fonda's screen image as the quiet, unassuming man of integrity and strength dominated his appearances onstage. His autobiography (written with Howard Teichman) appeared in 1981.   TLM

Fontanne, Lynn see LUNT, ALFRED

Fool for Love SAM SHEPARD's 39th play, the first to feature a fully developed female protagonist. The action of the play is both a love story and a power struggle between a half-brother and -sister. Set in a dingy motel room on the edge of the desert, the play allows several interpretations of the interrelationship of the lovers and an Old Man who seems to exist on another plane of reality. Shepard directed Kathy Baker as May and Ed Harris as Eddie in the original production at San

Francisco's MAGIC THEATRE, opening 8 February 1983. That production was brought to New York's CIRCLE REPERTORY THEATRE on 26 May 1983. A 1985 film directed by Robert Altman starred Shepard along with Kim Basinger, Randy Quaid, and Harry Dean Stanton.   FHL

Foote, Horton (1916–) Texas-born playwright and screenwriter whose best-known work, characterized by a "quietly intense dramatic voice," has, until recently, been for film (*To Kill a Mockingbird, Tender Mercies, The Trip to Bountiful*) and television. His nine "Orphans Home Cycle" plays set in and around his real hometown of Wharton (called Harrison in his work) and tracing the travails of Horace Robedaux (based on his father) are important evocations of an era in the American Southwest of 1902–28. His cycle began in 1942 with *Texas Town* and has concluded with *Dividing the Estate* (1989), *Talking Pictures* (1990), and *The Death of Papa* (1997). Many of his screenplays, such as *The Trip to Bountiful,* began as plays (play, 1953; film, 1985). Most of Foote's plays, drawn from stories handed down from his grandparents' days, are written not out of nostalgia but to help him "separate what is permanent from what is not." During the 1994–5 season his work was showcased by the SIGNATURE THEATRE COMPANY, including *Night Seasons, Talking Pictures*, and the world premieres of *The Young Man from Atlanta* (27 January) – recipient of the 1995 Pulitzer Prize – and *Laura Dennis* (10 March). Other awards in 1995 included New York Critics' Circle and Outer Critics Circle citations. Recent plays include *When They Speak of Rita* (2000), *The Last of the Thorntons* (2000), *The Carpetbagger's Children* (2001), and *The Day Emily Married* (written earlier but produced in 2004). A notable revival of *Trip to Bountiful*, beautifully directed by HARRIS YULIN, was produced by SIGNATURE in 2005, with LOIS SMITH as Carrie Watts. Foote's daughter **Hallie Foote** is an actress who has appeared in a number of his plays; his daughter Daisy is a playwright-actress; his son Horton Foote Jr. is an actor; and son Walter Foote is a filmwriter-director. Autobiographies appeared in 1999 and 2001; a literary biography by Charles S. Watson was published in 2003.   DBW

For Colored Girls Who Have Considered Suicide/When the Rainbow Is Enuf This "choreopoem" by NTOZAKE SHANGE, combining dance, poetry, and music, was developed at various venues (including the PUBLIC THEATER) before its Broadway run of 742 performances at the BOOTH THEATRE (1976), directed by Oz Scott. Seven women, identified by the color of their costumes,

explore through passionate, visceral poetry the courageous strength of black women. The play won Obie, Outer Critics Circle, and Audelco awards, as well as a Best Featured Actress Tony for Trazana Beverley. A 20th-anniversary production, staged by the author, was seen at the NEW FEDERAL THEATRE, summer 1995.   TH-S

Forbes, James (1871–1938) Playwright. Beginning with domestic farce in *The Chorus Lady* (1906), which developed from a vaudeville sketch, and plays emphasizing small-town living – *The Travelling Salesman* (1908) and *The Commuters* (1910) – Forbes made his greatest contribution with *The Famous Mrs. Fair* (1919), which explores the problems of a woman, liberated by four years' service in the war, as she returns to a husband and now grown-up family. Consistent with theatre at this time, the traditional domestic pattern is reestablished. Later plays dealt with social situations, such as small-town people trying to gain social status in New York (*The Endless Chain,* 1922) and the problems of youth (*Young Blood,* 1925).   WJM

Forbidden Broadway Long-running REVUE, OFF-BROADWAY, that updates its material each season to parody current Broadway shows and performers. Created by Gerard Alessandrini at the OFF-OFF BROADWAY Palsson's Supper Club, 15 January 1982, the theatre changed its status to Off-Broadway before beginning the 1982–3 season, and moved to a location on East 60th at Theatre East in 1988. When that space was razed, they moved to the 47th Street Theatre in 2005. Alessandrini, born in Boston and a graduate of the Boston Conservatory, set out to create a club act by writing new lyrics to Broadway songs. "Don't Cry for Me, Argentina" became "Don't cry for me, Barbra Streisand/the truth is, I never liked you." The revue has been successful not only in this country but also abroad. In 1992 to celebrate its first decade, Alessandrini presented a retrospective, *Best of Forbidden Broadway.* The show closed briefly in the mid-1990s, but was back in 1996 with *Forbidden Broadway Strikes Back.* In 2005 *Forbidden Broadway: Special Victims Unit* received the Drama Desk Award for Outstanding Revue; it was still running as of March 2007.   TLM

Ford Center for the Performing Arts, The see HILTON THEATRE

Ford, John T. (1829–94) Manager. A bookstore owner in Richmond, VA, he became the agent for a variety troupe, and in 1855–6 leased theatres in Richmond, Baltimore, and Washington, DC. The

Richard Foreman's *Rhoda in Potatoland,* 1974. Photo by Babette Mangolte. *Courtesy:* Richard Foreman.

Richmond theatre closed at the beginning of the Civil War. In Washington he converted the First Baptist Church (1834) into Ford's Atheneum in 1861, and after it burned (see FIRES) in December 1862 he reopened it in August 1863 as FORD'S THEATRE; as a result of Lincoln's assassination, it was closed by the army and purchased for offices and storage by the government. Ford continued to manage one or two theatres in Baltimore, and during 1873–86 he also managed the Grand Opera House in Washington, DC. In the 1880s he became the major producer of combination companies for the entire South.   DMcD

Ford, Ruth (1915–) Mississippi-born actress-playwright who began her career as a photographer's model and then burst upon the New York theatrical scene in 1938 as a member of ORSON WELLES's MERCURY THEATRE Company, appearing in *The Shoemaker's Holiday* and *Danton's Death.* The exotically beautiful actress continued with such diverse plays as *No Exit* and *Requiem for a Nun* (with her husband, actor Zachary Scott). Her most recent roles were in *Harold and Maude* (1980 stage version) and *The Visit* (1982, ALLEY).   DBW

Ford's Theatre Washington, DC. The site of the assassination of President Abraham Lincoln by JOHN WILKES BOOTH, 14 April 1865. The building opened in 1834 as the First Baptist Church; in 1861 JOHN T. FORD converted it into Ford's Atheneum, which burned down (see FIRES) in December 1862. He reopened it on 27 August 1863 and successfully engaged many of America's leading performers, including John Wilkes Booth. After the assassination the government converted the building to an office and storage facility, which collapsed in 1893 during EDWIN BOOTH's funeral in New York. In 1968 the government-restored theatre reopened for public performances, as is detailed in George Olszewski's 1963 book. Ford's Theatre also houses a Lincoln Museum.   SMA

Foreigner, The Following a MILWAUKEE REPERTORY THEATER production (1983), LARRY SHUE's farce opened at New York's Astor Place Theatre on 1 November 1984 and ran 686 performances. It received the Outer Critics Circle Award for Outstanding OFF-BROADWAY Play. Director JERRY ZAKS and actor Anthony Heald (as the mysterious visitor who invents his own language) received Obies. Reflecting the majority of critical views, Gerald Weales noted that it was "designed to make a point about the connection between prejudice and ignorance," and that "its success lies in its nonsense language games, its mechanical tricks, above all its speed and timing."   MR

Foreman, Richard (1937–) Director-designer-playwright, recipient of a 1995 MacArthur Fellowship ("genius" grant), 10 Obies, and a PEN/Laura Pels Master American Dramatist Award, Foreman began the Ontological-Hysteric Theatre company in New York in 1968 as a means to present his own avant-garde works; since 1979 they have been coproduced by the NEW YORK SHAKESPEARE FESTIVAL, the MUSIC THEATRE GROUP/Lenox Art Center, and the WOOSTER GROUP.

Until roughly 1975, Foreman was concerned with "putting [an object] on stage and finding different ways of looking at it." In plays like *Total Recall* (1970), Foreman used untrained performers directed not to show emotion; dialogue was disjointed, often recorded, and spoken without inflection. Furniture and props, which were suspended from the ceiling, were accorded as much focus and expressiveness as actors. Foreman ran the show like a conductor. Perched above the stage, he periodically sounded a loud buzzer that separated phrases of the attenuated action. More recently Foreman has created pieces based directly on the ideas and sketches he collects in notebooks, often featuring a recurring character called Rhoda and played by Kate Manheim. With the stop-and-go action, accelerated parade of images, and often his recorded comments on the performance in plays like *Pandering to the Masses* (1975), *Le Livre de splendeurs* (Paris, 1976), *Penguin Touquet* (1981), *Egyptology* (1983), *Film Is Evil: Radio Is Good* (1987), *Love and Science* (1990), and *Eddie Goes to Poetry City* (1991), Foreman seeks to disrupt the audience's logical and teleological thought processes and "force people to another level of consciousness." Foreman has also directed plays by Büchner, Vaclav Havel, GERTRUDE STEIN, Brecht, and Molière for such theatres as the HARTFORD STAGE COMPANY, the NEW YORK SHAKESPEARE FESTIVAL, and the AMERICAN REPERTORY THEATRE. In late 1991 he assumed control of the upstairs theatre at St. Mark's Church, NYC ("Ontological at Saint Marks") to showcase his work (14 staged there) and that of other companies, including *Samuel's Major Problems* (25th-anniversary production, 1993), an attenuated piece highlighted by a long meditation on death; *I've Got the Shakes* (1995), a quest for enlightenment that turns catastrophe into a moment of revelation; *The Universe, I.E.: How It Works* (1996), the last of a trilogy exploring a quest for knowledge; *Pearls for Pigs* (1997), which premiered in Hartford; *Benita Canova* (1998), featuring a trio of precocious and sexually charged schoolgirls; *Badboy Nietzsche!* (2000), a portrait of the philosopher seen through Foreman's unique prism; and *King Cowboy Rufus Rules the Universe* (2004), a foray into current political reality. With his 2005 offering, *The Gods Are Pounding My Head!* (aka *Lumberjack Messiah*), his typical comment on a society without substance, Foreman stated that his attention would shift to new multimedia projects. And indeed, in his January 2006 production, *Zomboid! (Film/Performance Project No. 1)*, a new hybrid mode was emerging, as it was in the January 2007 *Wake Up Mr. Sleepy! Your Unconscious Mind Is Dead!*

Foreman's plays are collected in six volumes, beginning in 1976 with *Plays and Manifestos*, edited by Kate Davy.   AS

Forepaugh, Adam (1831–90) CIRCUS owner and entrepreneur; a Philadelphia meat and horse dealer who got into the circus when, after selling horses to a circus, he joined the operation to look after his interests. A ruthless businessman, master of deceptive advertising and scams, and a cruel employer, Forepaugh (known everywhere by the symbol "4-Paws") had a circus under his name during 1866–90, ultimately becoming BARNUM and Bailey's major rival. When Barnum bought a gray albino elephant in 1884 (billed as "Scared White"), Forepaugh countered with a whitewashed elephant and the initiation of the famous "White Elephant Wars." Ironically, in 1886, after a falling out with James A. Bailey, Barnum was forced to align with Forepaugh for a presentation at Madison Square Garden of the largest circus seen to date.   DBW

Forest Rose, The Two-act musical drama by SAMUEL WOODWORTH with music by John Davies; premiered at the CHATHAM GARDEN THEATRE on 6 October 1825. Combining the romantic and patriotic elements that characterized American native drama during the early Federalist period, it remained a favorite on American and English stages through the 1850s. Principally remembered for its YANKEE character, Jonathan Ploughboy, it was revived throughout the first half of the 19th century by many of the major Yankee actors, including G. H. HILL and Joshua Silsbee, and was one of the most popular American dramas on the London stage despite its unflattering portrayal of the English.   PAD

Forever Plaid This goofy 1990 revue, conceived, directed, and written by Stuart Ross with music by various 1950s and '60s songwriters, begins immediately after the harmonizing Plaids (Sparky, Smudge, Jinx, and Frankie) have been killed on the way to pick up matching plaid tuxedos in preparation for their first public concert at the Fusil-Lounge at the Airport Hilton. In the afterlife the Plaids are able to perform the hits of their generation (as rock 'n' roll takes dominance in reality) and in a somewhat clichéd theme demonstrate dreams coming true, reaching one's potential, fulfilling one's destiny. The revue illustrates this journey. Surprisingly, after initial engagements at the West Bank Café, the American Stage Company, and Chicago's WISDOM BRIDGE THEATRE, it played more than four years (1,664 performances) at Steve McGraw's cabaret space on NYC's Upper West Side. Within two years there were companies in Boston, St. Louis, Minneapolis, Miami, Los Angeles, South Africa, and elsewhere, some eclipsing the New York run. It has steadily been produced internationally since.   DBW

Fornés, Maria Irene (1930–) CUBAN-born playwright and director who so exemplifies the concerns and style of OFF-BROADWAY theatre that she has won nine Obies since 1965, including one for sustained achievement (1982). Although her plays and musicals deal with serious individual, national, and global problems – *Tango Palace* (1964), *Promenade* (1965), *The Successful Life of Three* (1965), *Dr. Kheal* (1968), *Mud* (1983), *The Danube* (1984), *The CONDUCT OF LIFE* (1985), *Lovers and Keepers* (1986), *Abingdon Square* (1987), *And What of the Night?* (1989), *Terra Incognita* (1992), *Enter the Night* (1993), *The Summer in Gossensass* (1997), *Letters From Cuba* (2000, as part of the SIGNATURE THEATRE season devoted to her work in 1999–2000) – they are most acclaimed for their zany, whimsical humor, and the use of innovative, cinematic techniques. Fornés's greatest critical success, *FEFU AND HER FRIENDS* (1977), is a FEMINIST perspective on female friendship and women's roles in patriarchal society. In recent years her directorial interests have extended beyond her own plays to include standard works (*Hedda Gabler*, *Uncle Vanya*) and Latin American plays. In 2005 she received the TCG Award for extraordinary contributions to the field of theatre.   FB

Forrest, Edwin (1806–72) The first American-born star, who dominated the American stage throughout the mid-19th century as Othello, Lear, Richard III, Coriolanus, Hamlet, Macbeth, Shylock, Richelieu, and in his repertoire of American plays: STONE's *METAMORA*, BIRD's *The Gladiator* and *The Broker of Bogota*, and CONRAD's *Jack Cade,* all of which had been winners in his playwriting contests (1829–47). Lear and Metamora were regarded as his best. Forrest's power derived from his commanding physique, penetrating voice, magnetic presence, and strenuous realism in characters whose driving passions paralleled his own. Although only 5′ 10″ in height, on stage his muscular frame seemed to tower like a giant. He was steady and predictable, in top form at every performance.

Born in Philadelphia, Forrest was stagestruck as a youngster, and at 15 studied the playing of THOMAS A. COOPER, Edmund Kean, and JUNIUS B. BOOTH (Sr.). Six years later, after appearing in Lexington, Louisville, Cincinnati, and New

Edwin Forrest as Richard III ("A horse, a horse, my kingdom for a horse") in an 1858 engraving. *Courtesy:* Don B. Wilmeth Theatre Collection

Orleans, he performed with Kean and Cooper, and the next year alternated with Booth as Iago and Othello. He was quickly recognized as a star in the East and South, along the inland waterways, and later in the far West. He appeared in London in 1836 and again in 1845, when he challenged his British rival, W. C. Macready – a rivalry that precipitated the disastrous ASTOR PLACE OPERA HOUSE riot (1849).

A superpatriot, Forrest was a colorful figure offstage and on. The lurid details of his divorce trial (1850) – *Forrest v. Catherine Sinclair* (she became a theatre manager in San Francisco) – filled the newspapers. He made a fortune, built Fonthill Castle on the Hudson, and had a spacious home in New York and another in Philadelphia (which was to become the Edwin Forrest Home for "decayed" actors, in existence until the late 1980s). He closed his career with Shakespearean readings in Philadelphia, New York, and Boston in 1872. Of four major biographies, the most complete and objective is by Richard Moody (1960).   RM

Forty-five Minutes from Broadway A 1905 melodrama with music by GEORGE M. COHAN, produced by A. L. ERLANGER and MARC KLAW; opened on Broadway 1 January 1906. To accommodate gallery tastes, Cohan made its scenery and costumes calculatedly plain by the era's production standards. Cohan cast vaudevillian VICTOR MOORE as Kid Burns, the slangy, Broadway wise guy who finds the missing will and marries the housemaid who is its beneficiary. As the spunky housemaid from New Rochelle, he chose FAY TEMPLETON, longtime star of WEBER AND FIELDS Music Hall. Critics found the music charming but the melodrama trite and the leading male character distastefully brash and violent. It ran 90 performances, then had a long and profitable touring life.   WD

42nd Street A favorite with theatre parties and out-of-town visitors, this musical, with book by MICHAEL STEWART and Mark Bramble, music by Harry Warren, and lyrics by Al Dubin, opened at the WINTER GARDEN on 25 August 1980 and ran for almost nine years. Based on a 1930s Hollywood film about the auditions, rehearsals, and opening of a Depression-era Broadway musical revue, *42nd Street* made no claims to originality. Its main plot, concerning a chorus girl who becomes an instant star when the leading lady falls ill just before opening night, was familiar to audiences from the original film and many subsequent reworkings; but director-choreographer GOWER CHAMPION (who died on the show's opening night) infused the well-worn materials with lively production numbers based on the breezy 1930s songs of Warren and Dubin, and stars TAMMY GRIMES, JERRY ORBACH, Wanda Richert, and LEE ROY REAMS gave agreeable performances as the leading lady, the perfectionist director, the chorus girl, and the juvenile lead. A revival that opened May 2001 at the then Ford Center (see HILTON THEATRE) ran for 43 months. In May 2004 Shirley Jones and son Patrick Cassidy were replacements.   MK

46th Street Theatre see RICHARD RODGERS THEATRE

Fosse, Bob (1927–87) Choreographer and director. After beginning in vaudeville and burlesque as a teenager, Fosse appeared as a dancer in touring companies of *Call Me Mister* and *Make Mine Manhattan*. He made his Broadway debut in *Dance Me a Song* (1950). Fosse's first choreography, created for *The PAJAMA GAME* (1954), was influenced by JACK COLE's style of jazz dancing (see DANCE). His success with *The Pajama Game* was followed by choreography for *DAMN YANKEES* (1955), *BELLS ARE RINGING* (1956), and *New Girl in Town* (1957). With *Redhead* (1959) Fosse began to direct as well as choreograph. In the 1960s he staged a number of successful musicals, including *SWEET CHARITY* (1966). During the 1970s he created three unusual shows, closer in spirit to the SONDHEIM–PRINCE concept musicals: *Pippin* (1972), *CHICAGO* (1975), and *Dancin'* (1978). Fosse's frequent use of small groups, jerky, rhythmic steps, and sinuous, slow-motion movement, often coupled with derby hats and white gloves, became his choreographic trademark. He also directed a number of films, including *CABARET* and the autobiographical *All That Jazz*. The dance musical *Fosse* (1999) won a Tony for Best Musical. Of several biographies, the most thorough is Martin Gottfried's *All His Jazz* (1990).   MK

Foster, Gloria (1936–2001) African American actress noted for having played strong nonblack characters. For her OFF-BROADWAY debut in the documentary collage *In White America* (1963), Foster won Obie and Vernon Rice awards. Playing the title role in Robinson Jeffers's *Medea* at the Martinique Theatre (1965–6), she gained the *Theatre World* Award for her outstanding performance. She was Yerma in Lorca's play of that name at the VIVIAN BEAUMONT in 1966, and appeared regularly at the PUBLIC THEATER in such roles as Volumnia (*Coriolanus*, 1979), *Mother Courage* (1980), and the mother in *Blood Wedding* (1992). In 1995 she appeared on Broadway as one of the Delany sisters in EMILY MANN's *Having Our Say*. She also appeared in significant film roles and on television.   EGH

Foster, Sutton (1975–) Energetic, youthful looking Georgia-born actress-singer whose career typifies the rags-to-riches story. After a small role on tour in *The WILL ROGERS FOLLIES*, a number of minor parts in *The Scarlet Pimpernel* and *LES MISÉRABLES* (Eponine), and Sandy in *Grease* on Broadway, in 2002, as understudy, she replaced the leading actress in the preliminary production of *Thoroughly Modern Millie* at the LA JOLLA PLAYHOUSE. Opening on Broadway in the title role in April 2002, she received decent notices and won the Tony for Best Actress in a Musical. Foster followed Millie with Jo March in the short-lived musical *Little Women* (2005) and the female lead in *The Drowsy Chaperone* (2006). Her brother, **Hunter**, is also a performer (*URINETOWN*).   DBW

Four Saints in Three Acts Four-act opera, with libretto by GERTRUDE STEIN and music by Virgil Thomson; opened in Hartford and then in New York at the 44th Street Theatre on 20 February 1934. Although the story, which actually dealt with over a dozen saints, was almost impenetrable, the opera won critical acclaim. The production was noted for its all African American cast and its scenery composed entirely of cellophane. Because of her success with this production, Stein became a celebrity and returned to America from France for a lecture tour. Two of Stein's most famous lines occur in the opera: "Pigeons on the grass alas" and "When this you see remember me." FB

Fourteenth Street Theatre 105–109 West 14th St., NYC [Architect: Alexander Saeltzer]. Although it began as the Théâtre Français for the presentation of French-language drama and opera in New York, the house was known as the Fourteenth Street Theatre for most of its existence. After it opened in 1866, it embarked on an exceedingly rocky course as it changed owners, managers, and policy many times. It became, however, the only 19th-century playhouse to enjoy a renaissance late in its history. After being virtually abandoned in 1911, the 1,000-seat house was rediscovered in 1926 by the actress EVA LE GALLIENNE, who installed the CIVIC REPERTORY COMPANY in it, presenting well-cast, well-chosen plays in repertory at affordable prices for five years. After her departure, it was used only sporadically, and then razed in 1948. Its partial history was told by M. B. Steinberg in a 1931 book. MCH

Fox, Frederick (1910–91) Designer. Beginning at the Ivoryton Playhouse in Connecticut in the 1930s, Fox went on to design sets and costumes for over 200 Broadway productions, such as *ANNA LUCASTA* (1944; 1947 revival), *LIGHT UP THE SKY* (1948), and *DARKNESS AT NOON* (1951). and several at the Metropolitan Opera, including their premiere of *Tosca* (1965). Fox was one of the first stage designers to work in live television in the late 1940s and '50s. In the 1960s he began to work as an airport planning consultant. AA

Fox, George Washington Lafayette (1825–77) Comedian who, after years of touring with the Fox–Howard clan (see HOWARD FAMILY), came into his own during his tenure at New York's National Theatre (1850–8), where his uproarious caricatures made him a favorite. He became influential in management by introducing his family's

George L. Fox as Humpty Dumpty. Photo by J. Gurney and Son, New York, 1868. *Courtesy:* Laurence Senelick Collection.

production of *UNCLE TOM'S CABIN,* with Fox in the role of Phineas Fletcher. He temporarily managed the Old BOWERY, the New Bowery, and WALLACK'S FIFTH AVENUE, losing as lessee what he earned as a comic star. Between 1862–7 he staged pantomimes at the Old Bowery, with himself as Clown and his brother Charles Kemble Fox as Pantaloon. More an expressive MIME artist than an acrobat, Fox tempered the stage trickery of the RAVEL FAMILY with his own antic drollery to create a purely American brand of pantomime. This culminated in the immensely successful *Humpty Dumpty* (Olympic Theatre, 1868), which ran for more than 1,200 performances. Fox also made a hit in burlesques of *Faust, Macbeth, Richelieu,* and EDWIN BOOTH's *Hamlet.* After recurring fits of insanity, he was forcibly removed from a performance in 1875 for committal to an asylum. Fox was reputed to be the funniest performer of his

Eddie Foy and the Seven Little Foys making an appearance at the B. F. Keith Theatre, New York. Photo by White, New York. *Courtesy:* Laurence Senelick Collection.

time; he contrived to raise American pantomime to a level of popularity it has never regained. A biography by Senelick was published in 1988. In 2004 actor BILL IRWIN created for the SIGNATURE THEATRE a play based on Fox's career, tied to his own legacy as a clown.   LS

Foy, Eddie (1856–1928) Comedian and singer. Beginning as a child performer in VAUDEVILLE, Foy brought his acrobatic style of comedy and his amusing delivery of comic songs to musicals produced at the Chicago Opera House in 1889–90. His performance in *Bluebeard, Jr.* (1890) received praise in both CHICAGO and New York. After appearing as a featured performer in several other comic operas, Foy was hired as the principal comedian for *The Strollers* (1901). He starred in a number of musicals in the first decade of the 20th century, including *The Wild Rose* (1902), *Mr. Bluebeard* (1903), *Piff! Paff!! Pouf!!!* (1904), *The Earl and the Girl* (1905), *The Orchid* (1907), *Mr. Hamlet of Broadway* (1908), and *Up and Down Broadway* (1910). Always a popular favorite in vaudeville, Foy spent most of his time on the variety stage after 1910, when he began to include his children, billed as "The Seven Little Foys," in his act. The last of the Foy siblings, Irving, died in 2003 at age 94. Eddie Foy published his autobiography, *Clowning through Life,* in 1928; a bio by Armond Fields was published in 1999.   MK

Francesca da Rimini   A five-act romantic tragedy by GEORGE HENRY BOKER, widely considered the best of its type by an American, but very nearly marking the end of the romantic tradition in America. Boker's version stresses the tragedy of a lonely and deformed Lanciotto who experiences love before being plunged into despair. E. L. DAVENPORT starred in the 1855 premieres in New York and Philadelphia, but the production ran only briefly. Twenty-seven years later LAWRENCE BARRETT staged the script after revising it substantially with WILLIAM WINTER; this version won great success in Philadelphia and Chicago before opening on 27 August 1883 in New York, and became a standard for Barrett. In 1901 OTIS SKINNER restaged the script in a production comparable to Barrett's.   SMA

Frankel, Gene (1923–2005) Director and acting teacher. Born in New York and educated at New York University, Frankel made his NYC directing debut in 1949 with *They Shall Not Die,* followed closely in 1950 with *Nat Turner,* both in a reconfigured union hall. He received Obies for his direction of *Volpone* (1957) and *MACHINAL* (1960). Other important New York productions, mostly OFF-BROADWAY, included *The Enemy of the People* (1959), *The Blacks: A Clown Show* (1961), *Brecht on Brecht* (1962), *The Firebugs* (1963), *A Cry of Players* (1968), *To Be Young, Gifted and Black* (1969), and INDIANS (1969). Genet's *The Blacks* ran more than 1,400 performances at St. Mark's Playhouse, and he also directed it at the Akademie der Kunst, Berlin, and at the Teatro la Fenice, Venice (1964). His production of *OH DAD, POOR DAD . . .* was seen at the Atelje 212 in Belgrade (1965). Other notable productions include *Pueblo* at the ARENA STAGE (1971) and a revival of *The DIARY OF ANNE FRANK* at the Hartman Theatre in Stamford, CT (1979). Founder of the Berkshire Theatre, Frankel was also artistic and executive director of the Gene Frankel Theatre Workshop in New York. With his death, classes at the theatre on Bond St., named after him in 1988, ceased.   TLM

Franken, Rose (1895?–1988) Playwright and director whose best plays – *Another Language* (1932), *Claudia* (1941), *The Hallams* (1948) – appear to be domestic dramas aimed for the matinee crowd but are actually cold-eyed looks at the American family and the suffocation caused by love. She also wrote *Outrageous Fortune* (1943), which deals with homosexuality and anti-Semitism; *Doctors Disagree* (1943), examining the double standard; and *Soldier's Wife* (1944), about the problems caused when a husband returns from war. Her autobiography was published in 1963.   FB

Frankie and Johnny in the Clair de Lune by Terrence McNally was first produced by Manhattan Theatre Club Stage II at City Center in New York on 2 June 1987, with Kathy Bates as Frankie and F. Murray Abraham as Johnny, and moved to Stage I in October, with Kenneth Walsh in the latter role. The production was transferred to the Westside Theatre later in the year. A 2002 Broadway revival starred Edie Falco and Stanley Tucci (directed by Joe Mantello). The play depicts the tentative approach to a romantic relationship by two middle-aged people who have often been disappointed in the past: Frankie, a waitress whose humorously tough manner masks her emotional vulnerability, and Johnny, a cook who seems to have won a battle with alcoholism. During a night in a West Side apartment, Johnny, with the help of Debussy and moonlight, tries to persuade Frankie that good sex can still blossom into love. It was less successful as a 1991 film.   BCM

Frazee, Harry Herbert (1880–1929) Beginning as an usher in Peoria, IL, Frazee became a successful producer in the 1910s and '20s. His hits include *Madame Sherry* (1910); *Ready Money* (1912), with companies in London, Chicago, and New York; *A Pair of Sixes* (1914); *Nothing But the Truth* (1916); *Dulcey* (1921), coproduced with George C. Tyler; and *No, No, Nanette* (1925), an international success. *Yes, Yes, Yvette* (1927) failed dismally, ending his career. Frazee also owned theatres in Chicago and New York.   TLM

Free Southern Theatre Inspired by the goals of the civil rights movement, in 1963 John O'Neal, Gilbert Moses, and Doris Derby founded this company, with the support of Richard Schechner, to develop a theatre "as unique to the Negro people as . . . blues and jazz." With a home base in New Orleans, the South's first integrated theatre toured poor rural areas, giving free performances and theatre workshops. Although their aim was to promote black theatre for the African American community, productions of *Waiting for Godot* and *Purlie Victorious* appealed more to white than black audiences. The company disbanded in 1980.   LAB

Freedley, Vinton (1891–1969) Producer who entered into management with Alex A. Aarons in 1923, together building the Alvin Theatre, which they operated until 1932. Their notable productions include the Gershwin musicals *Lady, Be Good* (1924), *Tip-Toes* (1925), *Oh, Kay!* (1926), *Funny Face* (1927), and *Girl Crazy* (1930). Notable

Freedley productions after 1932 include the Cole Porter musicals *Anything Goes* (1934), *Red, Hot and Blue!* (1936), and *Leave It to Me!* (1938), as well as the unconventional *Cabin in the Sky* (1940). Freedley served as president of the Actors' Fund of America, the Episcopal Actors Guild, and the American National Theatre Academy.
MR

Freedman, Gerald (1927–) Director, producer, educator, born in Ohio and educated at Northwestern University. Freedman began his professional career in 1956 as an assistant for *Bells Are Ringing*, and made his New York directing debut in 1959 with the first revival of *On the Town* (Carnegie Hall Playhouse). In 1960 he began a long association with the New York Shakespeare Festival with an Obie-winning *The Taming of the Shrew*, and served as artistic director during 1967– 71. Other notable productions for NYSF include *Hair*, which opened the Public Theater in 1967, and *Hamlet* in 1972, starring Stacy Keach, James Earl Jones, and Colleen Dewhurst. He was coartistic director of the Acting Company during 1974–7, with acclaimed productions of Sheridan's *School for Scandal* (1972), and Waldman and Uhry's *The Robber Bridegroom* (1975), which was transferred to Broadway. In 1978–9 Freedman was artistic director for the American Shakespeare Theatre Festival in Stratford, CT; from 1985 to 1997 he was artistic director of the Great Lakes Theatre Festival (his production there of *King Lear* with Hal Holbrook was at NY's Roundabout in 1990), leaving at the end of the 1996–7 season. He returned to Broadway in 1995, directing *School for Scandal* at the Lyceum Theatre. Since 1991 he has been dean of the North Carolina School of the Arts.   TLM

Freeman, Morgan (1937–) Actor first recognized as the Easy Reader character on public television's *Electric Company* (1971–6). He was the wino Zeke in the short-lived *The Mighty Gents* (1978), earning a Drama Desk Award as Outstanding Featured Actor. He won Obies for his Coriolanus (1979) and Chaplain in *Mother Courage* (1980; with Gloria Foster) at the Public Theater, for the Messenger in *The Gospel at Colonus* (1984, Brooklyn Academy of Music), and for Hoke in the Pulitzer Prize– winning *Driving Miss Daisy* (1987). At the outdoor Delacorte Theater in 1990 he shared honors with Tracey Ullman in A. J. Antoon's Wild West staging of *The Taming of the Shrew*. In 1993 he received the William Shakespeare Award for Classical Theatre from Washington's Shakespeare

THEATRE, and for his 2004 role of ex-boxer Eddie Scrap-Iron in *Million Dollar Baby* he received the Oscar for Best Actor in a Supporting Role.   EGH

Friedman, Bruce Jay (1930–) Playwright. Born in the Bronx, educated at the University of Missouri, and primarily known as a writer of seven novels filled with his own particular brand of black humor, Friedman has rarely ventured into the theatre. His first effort, *Scuba Duba* (1967), a zany, jaundiced look at Jewish intellectual liberalism, has been called by some critics one of the best comedies of the decade. Friedman's other notable play, *Steambath* (1970), is an absurd comedy set in a steam room, later identified as Limbo, featuring God, personified by a Puerto Rican steambath attendant. Friedman was also one of the several contributors of sketches for *OH, CALCUTTA!* (1969) and wrote *Have You Spoken to Any Jews Lately?* (AMERICAN JEWISH THEATRE, 1995).   LDC

Friml, Rudolf (1879–1972) Prague-born composer who studied music under Antonin Dvořák before coming to the U.S. in 1903. His first score for the musical stage was *The Firefly* (1912), which starred opera singer Emma Trentini. Over the next 20 years he composed the scores of numerous operettas and musical comedies, notably *ROSE-MARIE* (1924), *The VAGABOND KING* (1925), and *The Three Musketeers* (1928). Although several of his shows were written in collaboration with lyricist OTTO HARBACH, Friml also worked with many other lyricists, including P. G. WODEHOUSE, OSCAR HAMMERSTEIN II, and Brian Hooker. Throughout his long career as a composer for the American musical stage, Friml never abandoned his musical roots; his scores were heavily indebted to the traditions of European operetta.   MK

Frohman, Charles (1860–1915) Producer and theatrical manager who, after a decade in theatrical business in various capacities, achieved his first major success as a producer with BRONSON HOWARD's *SHENANDOAH* (1889). In 1893 Frohman formed the EMPIRE THEATRE Stock Company, with JOHN DREW as his leading actor. Frohman now began to develop and exploit the "star and combination" system: Members of his company would be made "stars" as quickly as possible and sent, with a supporting cast, on national tours after opening in a Frohman theatre in New York. Frohman successfully employed similar methods in London, principally at the Duke of York Theatre after 1898. Stars who benefited from Frohman's patronage included, among many others, MAUDE ADAMS, WILLIAM GILLETTE, ARNOLD

DALY, ANNIE RUSSELL, MARGARET ANGLIN, JULIA MARLOWE, WILLIAM H. CRANE, OTIS SKINNER, and John Drew and Ethel Barrymore (see DREW–BARRYMORE FAMILY). In 1896, in association with Al Hayman, he joined MARK KLAW and ABE ERLANGER, Fred Zimmerman, and Fred Nixon to organize a monopoly known as the Theatrical SYNDICATE. With the security and efficiency afforded by such control, Frohman produced many contemporary playwrights and helped many aspiring actors to achieve stardom, giving him significant influence in matters of taste and method in the commercial theatre. After 1896 he regularly produced over a dozen shows a year, including Wilde's *The Importance of Being Earnest* (1895), Gillette's *SECRET SERVICE* (1896, NYC; 1897, London; 1900, Paris), Barrie's *The Little Minister* (1896, NYC, with Maude Adams), FITCH's *Barbara Frietchie* (1899, with Julia Marlowe), and Barrie's *Peter Pan* (1899, NYC, with Maude Adams; 1904, London). Frohman died with the sinking of the *Lusitania* in 1915. His brother DANIEL FROHMAN coauthored a 1916 biography.   MR   DJW

Frohman, Daniel (1851–1940) Theatre manager. With his brothers, CHARLES and Gustave, Frohman first came to prominence as business manager in 1880 with STEELE MACKAYE's organization at the MADISON SQUARE THEATRE, where he developed the system of "auxiliary road companies" that toured the country while the original production was playing in New York. Frohman should be noted for his tenure as the producer-manager of the old LYCEUM THEATRE at 4th Ave. and its STOCK COMPANY from 1887 to 1902, and in the new Lyceum on 45th St. from 1902 until his retirement in 1909. Enlisting the talents of a fine acting company, from which E. H. SOTHERN's career was launched and that over the years included HENRY MILLER, WILLIAM FAVERSHAM, EFFIE SHANNON, RICHARD MANSFIELD, MAUDE ADAMS, and JAMES H. HACKETT, Frohman presented a fashionable repertory from contemporary authors including CLYDE FITCH, J. M. Barrie, A. W. Pinero, Henry Arthur Jones, Wilde, and Sardou. Notable productions that featured Sothern included *Lord Chumley* (1888) and *The Charity Ball* (1889), both by BELASCO and DeMILLE, and *The Prisoner of Zenda* (1895). The elaborate new Lyceum opened with Barrie's *The Admirable Crichton* (produced by Charles). In 1899, Frohman began a four-year term as manager and lessee of DALY'S THEATRE, where he imported many musical comedies from London. Frohman served as president of the ACTORS' FUND from 1903 until his death in 1940. Through his association with the Famous Players–

Lasky Film Company after 1912, he brought many theatre stars to the infant film industry. Frohman authored three partial autobiographies in 1911, 1935, and 1937.   MR

From the Mississippi Delta Autobiographical, heartfelt play by Endesha Ida Mae Holland that chronicles her gutsy journey from a tragic childhood (including time as a prostitute), through a personal rebirth shaped by the civil rights movement, to an adulthood of personal and professional triumph. Told by three actresses who create all the characters, the play has been enormously popular throughout the U.S. and England. The play, developed from 1981 (while Holland was a student at the University of Minnesota, where she earned a Ph.D. in American Studies, 1986) to 1990, was presented at GOODMAN, ARENA STAGE, and HARTFORD STAGE before its New York production at CIRCLE IN THE SQUARE in 1991. Holland wrote other plays, but none captured the public imagination as did *Mississippi Delta*.   DBW

Front Page, The, by BEN HECHT and CHARLES MACARTHUR is one of America's most endearing comedies and has been revived in numerous productions since its Broadway premiere in 1928. Both authors had experience in the newspaper business, and this melodrama-farce drew liberally on the shenanigans in a big-city pressroom, where the reporters encounter con men, prostitutes, corrupt politicians, and a runaway convict. Laced with colloquial language and some profanity, the play was lauded for its authenticity in an era in which realism was prominent on the New York stage. The original production was supervised by JED HARRIS and marked the directorial debut of GEORGE S. KAUFMAN, who became one of America's most successful dramatists. Among its featured performers were OSGOOD PERKINS, LEE TRACY, and DOROTHY STICKNEY. It ran for 276 performances at the Times Square Theatre. A wonderful revival featuring Robert Ryan, Bert Convy, HELEN HAYES, Dody Goodman, and Peggy Cass played at the ETHEL BARRYMORE in the 1969–70 season. It was revived at the VIVIAN BEAUMONT in 1986 with RICHARD THOMAS and JOHN LITHGOW, directed by JERRY ZAKS.   BBW

frontier theatre Just as the frontier has been described as the single most distinguishing feature of American history, it also left a distinguishing mark on American theatre history. Theatre in America began in the early settlements on the eastern seaboard, the frontier of the New World; and after PHILADELPHIA, New York, and BOS-TON became theatrical centers, troupes of actors advanced into the western regions quick on the heels of the pioneers.

The following pattern was repeated several times: A principal city developed as the transportation, supply, and finance center for a series of outlying communities in which the region's raw materials were exploited. If these outlying communities were sufficiently remote, intermediate supply towns developed as well. Theatre responded to this pattern: Permanent companies resided in large city theatres, and a dominant manager sent them on tour to the outlying communities. Intermediate towns were served in the same way, but on a more frequent basis.

The first theatre opened in Williamsburg, VA, in 1718; the second, the DOCK STREET in Charleston, SC, in 1736. When in 1752 the Lewis Hallam company arrived from London, they performed in a new Williamsburg theatre. The HALLAMS and other troupes took to the road, found makeshift halls in such settlements as Annapolis, Norfolk, Newport, and Providence, and set the pattern for the western trek that was soon to follow.

Thespian societies were a part of the cultural life of Lexington (1799), Cincinnati (1801), and St. Louis (1815), even before professional troupes arrived. These troupes began their journey from Albany or Philadelphia to Pittsburgh, thence by flatboat down the Ohio River to Cincinnati and Louisville, and, as the frontier expanded, down the Mississippi to St. Louis, Memphis, Nashville, Montgomery, Mobile, and New Orleans.

The James Douglass troupe arrived in Lexington, Louisville, and Frankfort in 1810, and the SAMUEL DRAKE company in 1815. Typical of the accommodation they found was Luke Usher's Lexington theatre, a large room (30 × 60 ft.) on the second floor of his brewery. Two actors in Drake's company, NOAH LUDLOW and SOL SMITH, became the leading managers on the frontier, first as competitors and then as partners. Both wrote detailed firsthand accounts of their adventures.

Cramped and improvised quarters were common: a stage 10 ft. wide and 8 ft. deep, a Memphis theatre where only the women could be seated, and another that had formerly been a livery stable. Even proper theatres like the Columbia Street in Cincinnati (1821), boasting a "spacious gallery," "commodious lobbies," and "two tiers of boxes," squeezed the stage and 800 spectators into a small area (40 × 100 ft.). JAMES H. CALDWELL was the first to provide adequate facilities with his three New Orleans theatres: the 1,100 seat AMERICAN or Camp Street (1824), the St. Charles (1835), and a second St. Charles (1843). The first ST. CHARLES with 4,000 seats was said to be equaled in size and grandeur only by the opera houses in Naples, Milan, and St. Petersburg. When this theatre burned down (1842, a common occurrence; see FIRES), Caldwell built the second St. Charles, less ornate and seating 1,500, and turned the management over to Ludlow and Smith.

Frontier theatres were not all land-based. Showboating on the Ohio and Mississippi began early and continued into the 20th century, first with Ludlow's *Noah's Ark* (1817), then with William Chapman's *Floating Palace* (1831). SHOWBOATS lured audiences with their calliopes and their picturesque names: *French's New Sensation, Snow Queen, Wonderland, Goldenrod, Cotton Blossom,* and *Majestic.*

Theatres appeared almost immediately after a community was settled; for example, CHICAGO (chartered 1837) got JOHN B. RICE's first theatre (1847), his second (1851), and McVICKER'S (1857).

Development of the trans-Mississippi West was similar to that of the East, but more extreme: Distance was greater, population shift more volatile, and wealth more instantaneous and abundant. Although playing conditions were conventional in the cities and towns, they were primitive in the small settlements: Actors arrived by wagon and pack animal, often slept in the open, and performed in stores, houses, and tents. However crude the conditions, though, western audiences were noted for the prodigality of their response.

California was the first region to develop. Its pioneer period began in 1849 and had passed its peak by 1857. The principal city was SAN FRANCISCO, and the outlying communities were the gold-mining camps in the Sierra Nevada; in between were the towns of Marysville, Sacramento, and Stockton. During 1850–84 the "Napoleon" of California managers was TOM MAGUIRE, an illiterate cab driver and saloonkeeper. With only brief exceptions, he managed one or more theatres in the city, and at least one in each intermediate town, thereby ensuring a smooth flow of attractions to the gold mines during the summer and early fall. During 1859–67 the silver mines of Nevada's Washoe Valley became an extension of the California region, and Maguire used Virginia City as an intermediate town for them.

The West's second mining frontier began in 1857 along the eastern slopes of the Rocky Mountains near the South Platte River, and spread north and east with the gold strikes in Montana during the 1860s and in the Dakotas in the '70s. Denver was the region's city, and it was there that its most important manager, John Langrishe, first struck it rich. An actor seasoned by 15 years

of barnstorming in the Mississippi Valley, Langrishe moved with his company in pursuit of bonanza: Denver (1859–67), Helena and Cheyenne (1867–71), and Deadwood (1876–9). The coming of the railroads divided this frontier into separate regions. Denver became the center of the Silver Circuit, which included the mining and resort towns of Colorado and the Mormon communities of Utah; it peaked under the management of Peter McCoart (1885–95). Montana and Wyoming were controlled by John Maguire (no relation to Tom), with its center in Helena (1884–1900), whereas the Dakotas developed their own identity under the management of C. P. "Con" Walker in Fargo after 1892.

Both the Northwest and Southwest waited for eastern rail links in the 1880s. Theatre followed population along the route of the Santa Fe Railroad in the Southwest. LOS ANGELES, where Henry T. Wyatt was the principal manager, became a theatrical center servicing adjacent regions: southern California, the central coast, the central valley, and Arizona–New Mexico. In the Northwest development followed the line of the northern Pacific, which terminated in SEATTLE, where Calvin Heilig and John Cort were the leading managers. A second center was Portland, OR, which was on the way to San Francisco; John Howe was the principal manager there until the coming of the Theatrical SYNDICATE.

Western theatricals had two extensions beyond the continental U.S.: Players had passed through San Francisco to and from the British colonies since 1855, but the management of an American, James Cassius Williamson, in Sydney after 1879 developed the route from Honolulu to Cape Town. The West's final frontier was the Klondike region of Alaska, where there was a gold stampede from 1896 to 1910. Vancouver was the city for this region, and Dawson, Fairbanks, and Nome each had its turn as a principal town.

However unconventional playing conditions and audience behavior in the frontier theatres, productions were otherwise conventional. Each frontier saw the major actors of its day: J. B. BOOTH, EDWIN FORREST, William Macready, EDWIN BOOTH, ANNA CORA MOWATT, JOSEPH JEFFERSON III, LAURA KEENE, TYRONE POWER, LOTTA CRABTREE, ADAH ISAACS MENKEN, JAMES MURDOCH, GEORGE HILL, DAN MARBLE, JOHN McCULLOUGH, and others. These stars played their standard repertory of Shakespeare, old comedy, contemporary farce, and domestic and sensational melodrama in various permutations to suit the ability of the individual performer and the taste of the audience. RM DMcD

Fugard, Athol (1932–) South African playwright, director, and actor who, with the production of *A Lesson from Aloes* at the YALE REPERTORY THEATRE, New Haven (1980), found a gifted and understanding collaborator in LLOYD RICHARDS, then artistic director of the theatre. The production moved to Broadway and was followed by three world premieres at Yale Rep: *Master Harold . . . and the Boys* (1982) also transferred to Broadway and won the Drama Critics' Circle Award (a ROUND-ABOUT revival in 2003 costarred Danny Glover and Michael Boatman); *The Road to Mecca* (1984) reached OFF-BROADWAY in 1988; and *A Place with the Pigs* (1987) was produced in 1988 at London's National Theatre. In addition the Yale Rep staged revivals of Fugard's *Boesman and Lena, Hello and Goodbye,* and *The Blood Knot,* thereby ensuring Fugard an honored place on the contemporary American theatre scene. Fugard has acknowledged Richards's contribution in calling him "my artistic leader." His *Playland* (premiered at Johannesburg's Market Theatre, July 1992) was coproduced by LA JOLLA PLAYHOUSE and Atlanta's ALLIANCE THEATRE summer and fall 1992, and in spring 1993 was seen at the MANHATTAN THEATRE CLUB, which has also presented three other Fugard plays. His *Exits and Entrances* had its world premiere at the small Fountain Theatre in Los Angeles (2004).   EGH

Full Monty, The Based on the 1997 British sleeper hit film – relocated from Sheffield, England, to Buffalo, NY – this musical retained the basic premise of six unemployed working-class men seeking survival (via a strip routine) and became the surprise of the 2000–1 season (though up against *The Producers* it won only the Drama Desk for Outstanding Music for the work of novice composer David Yazbek). Developed at the Old Globe Theatre with direction by JACK O'BRIEN, choreography by JERRY MITCHELL, and book by TERRENCE MCNALLY, on Broadway it had 770 performances, cut short by the 9/11 terrorist attacks. The show was notable for the featured performance (her last) of character actress Kathleen Freeman.   DBW   LJ

Fuller, Charles (1939–) African American playwright. When *A SOLDIER'S PLAY* (1981), dealing with the murder of an unpopular black army sergeant, received the Pulitzer Prize, Fuller was only the second black playwright to be so honored. Philadelphia-born Fuller had several plays produced OFF-BROADWAY, notably by the NEGRO ENSEMBLE COMPANY, which nurtured his talent with productions of *In the Deepest Part of Sleep*

(1974), *The Brownsville Raid* (1976), and the Obie Award–winning *Zooman and the Sign* (1980), as well as *A Soldier's Play,* which was turned into an absorbing film (*A Soldier's Story,* 1984) and revived Off-Broadway in 2005 (SECOND STAGE). Negro Ensemble has also produced other Fuller plays, including *Sally* and *Prince* (1988–9) – the first two in a series of six plays he continued to work on in the 1990s about the post–Civil War quest for black self-determination – but those completed have attracted little serious critical attention. However, his March 1995 Showtime cable film *Zooman,* with Louis Gossett Jr., was well received.   EGH

Funicello, Ralph (1947–) Designer. Though trained at NYU, from the mid-1970s through the '90s he has designed primarily on the West Coast, where he has worked extensively with virtually every major theatre, was director of design at AMERICAN CONSERVATORY THEATRE (1988–90), and holds the Don Powell Chair of Scene Design at San Diego State University. Funicello's work is typified by an understated elegance that he brings to plays of diverse styles and periods. His recent designs in New York for *Henry IV* (2003), *King Lear* (2004), and *Julius Caesar* (2005) are good examples of his unique work.   AA   DBW

Funny Girl Two-act musical with book by Isobel Lennart, music by JULE STYNE and lyrics by BOB MERRILL; opened at the WINTER GARDEN THEATRE (26 March 1964) for 1,348 performances. Set around WWI, the musical tells the story of FANNY BRICE's rise to fame as a ZIEGFELD star and her disastrous marriage to gambler Nick Arnstein. Songs include "People" and "Don't Rain on My Parade." Directed by GARSON KANIN and supervised by JEROME ROBBINS, the show featured Kay Medford, JEAN STAPLETON, and Danny Meehan. Critical acclaim went to Barbra Streisand for her comic performance, in which she sang 11 of the show's 16 songs.   EK

Funny Thing Happened on the Way to the Forum, A Two-act musical comedy, music and lyrics by STEPHEN SONDHEIM, book by Burt Shevelove and LARRY GELBART; opened 8 May 1962 at the ALVIN THEATRE, running 964 performances. This bawdy romp patched together from the plays of Plautus, focusing on the efforts of the slave Pseudolus (ZERO MOSTEL; Tony Award) to win his freedom, marked Sondheim's Broadway debut as composer as well as lyricist. The songs tend to comment on rather than further the story and sometimes seem ironic "serious relief" from the farcical book scenes. The production was directed

Zero Mostel (Pseudolus) and Jack Gilford (Hysterium) in *A Funny Thing Happened on the Way to the Forum,* 1962. Photo by Friedman-Abeles. *Courtesy:* Tony Walton.

by GEORGE ABBOTT, although JEROME ROBBINS (uncredited) was brought in to "doctor" the production, to which he added the opening "Comedy Tonight" sequence. The show, Abbott's last Broadway hit, won the Tony for Best Musical and had a successful London production (1963), a New York revival with PHIL SILVERS (1972, Tony), and another in 1996 with NATHAN LANE.   JD

Funnyhouse of a Negro ADRIENNE KENNEDY's first successful one-act play opened OFF-BROADWAY in 1962 (East End Theatre) and won a 1964 Obie. *Funnyhouse* incorporates autobiographical elements in a surreal, poetic, and mythical work that portrays a disturbed state of mind rather than a lineal progression. The major character, Sarah, hallucinates and transforms into several alter egos, both male and female, black and white. Central to the play is her racial identity and the struggle inherent in being a black woman in a white world. An effective revival was presented in 2006 at the Harlem School of the Arts Theater.
    FB

Fusco, Coco (1960–) Cuban-born, Brown University–educated interdisciplinary performance artist and writer. She is known best for her 1993 documentary account of her caged Amerindian performance with GUILLERMO GÓMEZ-PEÑA, *The Couple in the Cage.* Her 2003 *The Incredible Disappearing Woman,* about art, sex, and death at the U.S.–Mexico border, explores why and how we relate to political violence via technological mediation. Fusco has performed, lectured, exhibited, and curated throughout the world and is the author of several books and many articles/essays. She teaches in the School of the Arts at Columbia University.   DBW

Fyles, Franklin (1847–1911) Drama critic and playwright. Born in Troy, NY, Fyles began as a reporter on the *Troy Budget,* moving in the late 1860s to the *New York Sun,* where he became a star reporter (1875) and drama critic (1885–1903). With an eye toward the popular market, he wrote eight melodramas, four in collaboration with others, including *The Girl I Left behind Me* (1893) with DAVID BELASCO. Fyles also wrote *The Theatre and Its People* (1900).   TLM

G

Gabriel, Gilbert W. (1890–1952) Drama critic. Born in Brooklyn and educated at Williams College, Gabriel began his career with the *New York Evening Sun* in 1912, serving as music critic during 1917–24. He was theatre critic of the *Telegram-Mail* (1924–5); the *Evening Sun* (1925–9); and the *New York American* (1929–37). After WWII, he served as drama critic of THEATRE ARTS and *Cue* (1949–52). Gabriel's lively prose entertained as well as informed readers.   TLM

Gaige, Crosby [né Roscoe Conkling Gaige] (1882–1949) A partner of producers EDGAR AND ARCHIBALD SELWYN, Gaige coordinated financing for new Selwyn and Company theatres in New York and Chicago. He produced or coproduced (with the Selwyns and JED HARRIS) about 150 plays, most notably GEORGE S. KAUFMAN's *The Butter and Egg Man* (1925), Kaufman's only solo full-length play, and the biggest hit of the 1928–9 Broadway season, *Little Accident,* by Floyd Dell and Thomas Mitchell. Gaige retired in 1937, then developed another career in food dehydration and culinary arts. His memoir, *Footlights and Highlights,* was published in 1948.   WD

Gaines, Boyd (1953–) Versatile Atlanta-born stage, film, and television actor-singer-dancer who is the recipient of three Tonys in three categories: Best Featured Actor in a Play for *The HEIDI CHRONICLES* (1989); Best Actor in a Musical for *SHE LOVES ME* (1994, revival); and Best Featured Actor in a Musical for *Contact* (2000). Other notable New York appearances include a COMPANY revival (1995), *Twelve Angry Men* (2004), *Bach at Leipzig* (NEW YORK THEATRE WORKSHOP, 2005), and *Journey's End* (2007). In the 1980s he appeared in the popular films *The Sure Thing, Porky's, Fame,* and on TV's *One Day at a Time.* Gaines has numerous Off-Broadway credits and appearances in regional theatres (in particular, YALE REP, BALTIMORE CENTER STAGE, LONG WHARF, and the GUTHRIE).   DBW

Galati, Frank (1943–) Actor, director, playwright, adapter, and educator who earned his Ph.D. in 1971 at Northwestern, where he serves on the performance-studies faculty. Galati's professional work bridges the worlds of theatre, opera, literature, and film. Schooled in the theories of Chamber Theatre pioneer Robert Breen, he has continued and extended Breen's work through adaptations of texts by GERTRUDE STEIN (in *She Always Said, Pablo*), JOHN STEINBECK (*The GRAPES OF WRATH,* for which he won a Tony), Anne Tyler (filmscript for *The Accidental Tourist*), Alan Paton (*Cry, the Beloved Country,* with music by WEILL and lyrics by MAXWELL ANDERSON from LOST IN THE STARS), and in 1995 William Faulkner (*As I Lay Dying*). Galati began his professional career as a popular Chicago actor (notably in the WISDOM BRIDGE production of Stoppard's *Travesties*), but in the 1980s turned to directing theatre and opera. In 1986 he joined the STEPPENWOLF THEATRE COMPANY and became associate director of the GOODMAN THEATRE. He directed for ROUNDABOUT the 50th-anniversary production of *The GLASS MENAGERIE*, with JULIE HARRIS, in November 1994; the musical RAGTIME in 1997; and the world premiere in 1999 of the opera adaptation of MILLER's *A VIEW FROM THE BRIDGE* for Chicago's Lyric Opera. Since the initial failure of the musical *Seussical*, which he directed in 2000, Galati has focused mostly on Chicago projects, including the musical version of *The Visit* at the Goodman and Alain Boublil and Claude-Michel Schönberg's musical *The Pirate Queen* (opened on Broadway in spring 2007).   SF

Gale, Zona (1874–1938) Playwright and regionalist writer whose dramatization of her novel *MISS LULU BETT* won the Pulitzer Prize in 1921. Gale dramatized her other novels – *Faint Perfume* (1934); *Birth,* produced as *Mr. Pitt* (1924); and *The Neighbors* (1917), a one-act play based on her "Friendship Village" stories – but had no other hits. A biography by H. Simonson was published in 1962.   FB

Gallagher, Helen (1926–) Actress, singer, and dancer. Energetic and versatile, Gallagher began in the chorus and rose to lead actress. She made her Broadway debut in *Seven Lively Arts* (1944), attracted attention in *High Button Shoes* (1947), and received Tonys for PAL JOEY (1952) and *No, No, NANETTE* (1971 revival). She became known for replacing original musical stars, as in SWEET CHARITY (1966), or appearing in revivals. Gallagher developed a cabaret act and performed in straight dramas (*Hothouse,* 1974; *The Gingerbread Lady,* 1977; *Money Talks,* 1990, Promenade Theatre). In the 1970s she joined the television serial "Ryan's Hope" (Emmys – 1976, 1977, 1987). A recent production was *70, Girls, 70* (2000).   REK

Gallagher, Peter (1955–) Dark, heavy-browed actor-singer educated at Tufts and the Actors Studio, who, as a lawyer from the Bronx, found stardom in Fox-TV's 2003 hit *The O.C.* Yet, his career has mainly been onstage in such vehicles (mostly revivals) as *HAIR* (1977), *GREASE* (1978, tour), *LONG DAY'S JOURNEY INTO NIGHT* as Edmund opposite Jack Lemmon and KEVIN SPACEY (1986), Sky Masterson in *GUYS AND DOLLS* (1992), the CITY CENTER ENCORES! concert version of *PAL JOEY* (1995), and as the director, Lloyd Dallas, in *Noises Off* (2001).   DBW

Gallagher and Shean American vaudeville team. Straight man **Ed(ward) Gallagher** (1873?–1929) and comic **Al(bert) Shean** [né Schoenberg] (1868–1949) formed a team in 1910 after years with other partners. For four years they appeared in VAUDEVILLE, BURLESQUE, and REVUES; they then parted, reunited in 1920, and subsequently gained tremendous success, highlighted by 67 weeks in the ZIEGFELD Follies. An entire routine and career was built around one theme song ("Absolutely, Mr. Gallagher?" "Positively, Mr. Shean"). The team dissolved in 1925, though Shean continued as a character actor on stage and in films. Shean's nephews, the MARX BROS., were given much support by their uncle early in their careers.   DBW

Gallo, David (1966–) Scenic designer with numerous New York credits, including *Thoroughly Modern Millie, Gem of the Ocean, The Drowsy Chaperone,* and *Radio Golf* (all Broadway), *Machinal, Bunny Bunny, The Wild Party, BARE: A Pop Opera* (OFF-BROADWAY), and scenic pieces for BLUE MAN GROUP in various locations. Regional designs number Keith Glover's *Thunder Knocking on the Door, Golden Boy, Dark Paradise,* and *Sweeney Todd.* Unique for his striking, original design concepts, Gallo's honors include a 2000 Obie for Sustained Excellence, Drama Desk Awards in 1997 and 2000 (the latter for AUGUST WILSON's *Jitney*), a 2005 Tony nomination for Wilson's *Gem of the Ocean,* and a 2006 Tony for *The Drowsy Chaperone.*   BO

Gallo, Paul (1953–) A versatile lighting designer, Gallo has worked on well over 200 shows – on Broadway (such as *Crazy for You, GUYS AND DOLLS, CITY OF ANGELS, Titanic, The Rocky Horror Show, 42ND STREET, The CRUCIBLE*), OFF-BROADWAY (Obies in 1986 and 1987), and at most major regional theatres. He has done several with director JERRY ZAKS, including revivals of *The HOUSE OF BLUE LEAVES* (1986) and *The FRONT PAGE* (1986), as well as SIX DEGREES OF SEPARATION (1990). He has also collaborated with MARTHA CLARKE on most of her works, most recently *Vienna: Lusthaus (Revisited)* in 2002 (NEW YORK THEATRE WORKSHOP).   AA

Garber, Victor (1949–) Versatile Canadian-born actor on television (2001–6, Jack Bristow in ABC's *Alias*), film (*Titanic, Legally Blonde*), and stage (debut: GODSPELL, Toronto, 1966) who "exudes a kind of unassuming self-assurance that commands rather than demands attention." Garber plays classics (*You Never Can Tell,* 1986; *Ghosts,* 1988, ROUNDABOUT, *Theatre World* Award); contemporary dramas and farces (*DEATHTRAP,* 1978, Tony nomination; SHUE's *Wenceslas Square,* 1988, PUBLIC, Obie; LUDWIG's *Lend Me a Tenor,* 1989, Tony nomination; NELSON's *Two Shakespearean Actors,* as EDWIN FORREST, 1991; Stoppard's *Arcadia,* 1995; Yasmina Reza's *Art,* 1998); and musicals (*SWEENEY TODD,* 1979; *Little Me,* 1982 revival, Tony nomination; *Assassins,* PLAYWRIGHTS HORIZONS, 1990; *DAMN YANKEES,* 1994 revival, Tony nomination). He also appeared in the film of *Godspell* (1973) and in TV specials, including *Valley Forge* (Hallmark Hall of Fame, 1975), *AH, WILDERNESS!* (PBS, 1976), and *Liberace: Behind the Music* (title role, 1988).   REK

Gardenia, Vincent [né Scognamiglio] (1922–92) Italian-born actor who made his professional debut in 1935 and his Broadway debut (*The Visit*) in 1958. Gardenia appeared in MACHINAL (Obie, 1960), *LITTLE MURDERS* (1969; film, 1971), *The PRISONER OF SECOND AVENUE* (Tony, 1971), BENNETT's *Ballroom* (1978), and *Breaking Legs* (1991). He had acted on television since 1955 and film since at least 1958 (*Cop Hater*); other films included *Little Shop of Horrors* (1986) and *Moonstruck* (1987, Oscar nomination).   REK

Gardner, Herb (1934–2003) Brooklyn-born playwright and author of a successful syndicated cartoon (*The Nebbishes*). In 1962 *A Thousand Clowns* ran for 428 performances at the EUGENE O'NEILL THEATRE and was adapted into a successful film (1965), for which Gardner earned an Academy Award nomination. As a New Yorker he considered Broadway his "neighborhood," and his plays are firmly rooted in urban life. *The Goodbye People* (1968) takes place on Coney Island and *I'm Not Rappaport* (1985) in Central Park. The latter, a poignant and comic study of aging in America, was a success on Broadway and in London, winning the 1986 Tony Award for Best Play; it was revived at ROUNDABOUT in 1996 (directed by SCOTT ELLIS) and was filmed in 1996 with Walter Matthau and OSSIE DAVIS. Gardner's final major work, *Conversations with My Father* (1991), an autobiographical study exploring ethnic identity in America, premiered at the SEATTLE REP before moving to New York in 1992 and London in 1995. Both *Rappaport* and *Conversations* were first directed by DANIEL SULLIVAN and starred JUDD HIRSCH.   BBW

Garland, Hamlin (Hannibal) (1860–1940) An early realist in American fiction who, with WILLIAM DEAN HOWELLS, promoted the "radical" IBSEN drama in the 1890s, and defended JAMES A. HERNE's *MARGARET FLEMING* from charges that it was immoral. Neither his realistic plays about contemporary social problems nor his attempt to establish a BOSTON independent theatre movement met with success. He remains known for his short-story collection *Main-Travelled Roads* (1891) and his autobiography, *A Son of the Middle Border* (1917).   TLM

Garrick Theatre 63–67 West 35 St., NYC [Architect: Francis H. Kimball]. In 1890, EDWARD HARRIGAN built his own theatre just above Herald Square and named it after himself. After five years, he relinquished the house to RICHARD MANSFIELD, who changed its name to the Garrick by having his signmaker revise the letters at a minimum cost and effort. In 1896, the Garrick changed hands again and was leased to CHARLES FROHMAN until his death in 1915. When it looked as if the house would be torn down, it was rescued by the millionaire-philanthropist OTTO H. KAHN, who installed Jacques Copeau's Théâtre du Vieux Colombier there in 1917. Two years later, he placed it at the disposal of the infant THEATRE GUILD, in whose hands it remained until it built its own theatre in 1925. Within a few years, it had descended into cheap burlesque and gradual abandonment as a theatre. In 1932, after extensive fire damage, it was razed for safety purposes.   MCH

Gassner, John (Waldhorn) (1903–67) Anthologist, editor, critic, educator. Born in Hungary and educated at Columbia University (1925), Gassner climaxed a distinguished teaching career at Yale

University (1956–67), where he was Sterling Professor of Playwriting and Dramatic Literature; he also served on the Pulitzer Prize drama jury (1957–63). His essays appeared in *New Republic, Atlantic Monthly, THEATRE ARTS,* and other publications; but he established his reputation with more than 20 books, including anthologies of American and world drama, a history of dramatic literature (*Masters of the Drama,* 1940), and works on theory and criticism (*Form and Idea in Modern Theatre,* 1956; *Directions in Modern Theatre and Drama,* 1963).   TLM

Gaxton, William [né Arturo Gaxiola] (1893–1963) Broadway and Hollywood musical star remembered today for his stage roles as President John P. Wintergreen in *OF THEE I SING* (1931) and Billy Crocker in *ANYTHING GOES* (1934). In these and many other musical roles, he was noted for his ability to sell a song. Like VICTOR MOORE, with whom he was frequently teamed, he began his career in vaudeville. Notable film musicals featuring Gaxton include *Fifty Million Frenchmen* (1931, adapted from the stage musical in which he had starred in 1929) and the extravagant *Diamond Horseshoe* (1945).   MR

gay and lesbian theatre An offshoot of the gay liberation movement that must be distinguished from the mere appearance of homosexuals in drama. Before the 1960s, male "deviants" were depicted as flamboyant effeminates (MAE WEST's *The Drag,* 1927; *The Pleasure Man,* 1928), destructive decadents (Mordaunt Shairp's *The Green Bay Tree,* 1933), or curable hypersensitives (ROBERT ANDERSON's *TEA AND SYMPATHY,* 1953). Lesbians were shown as predatory, doomed, or both, as in Édouard Bourdet's *The Captive* (1926) and LILLIAN HELLMAN's *The CHILDREN's HOUR* (1934).

The proliferation of experimental theatre OFF-BROADWAY in the 1950s and the "Sexual Revolution" of the '60s enabled homosexual playwrights, actors, and directors to address their own problems and constituencies, at a time when more conspicuous fellow-travelers like TENNESSEE WILLIAMS, WILLIAM INGE, CARSON MCCULLERS, and EDWARD ALBEE avoided or downplayed these matters. Foremost among venues was the CAFFE CINO in Greenwich Village (1960–7), which nurtured such dramatists as Robert Patrick, William Hoffman, and Doric Wilson.

The watershed play, however, was *The BOYS IN THE BAND* (1968), an Off-Broadway offering by Mart Crowley. Although it perpetuated the idea that the "only happy homosexual is a dead homosexual," it was novel in putting him center stage and uncovering subcultural folkways to the general public. Its success prompted a flood of similar confessional dramas, usually about drag queens. Token swishy types appeared in a number of commercial farces, though gay dramatists attempted to infuse the form with insider knowledge (James Kirkwood's *P.S. Your Cat is Dead,* 1975; Terrence McNally's *The Ritz,* 1975). This trend culminated in *Torch Song Trilogy* (1983) by Harvey Fierstein, a shrewd blend of soap opera, Simonized sitcom, and drag-queen-as-clown variant: These three plays had evolved Off-Off Broadway and then jointly transferred successfully to win a Tony Award for Best Play.

Even before this profusion, the critical animosity of such widely read pundits as Stanley Kauffmann and Howard Taubman had posited a homosexual conspiracy in the theatre that "often poisons what you see and hear." They argued that such playwrights camouflaged their concerns as heterosexual relationships; implicit was a paranoia that show business from costuming to producing was controlled by "perverts." Although LeRoi Jones's (Amiri Baraka's) *The Toilet* (1964) suggested a love-truce between a battered "white" "queer" and a black youth, the black-activist theatre movement of the 1960s was also hostile; typical is the portrayal of the "bull dyke" in Ed Bullins's *Clara's Ole Man* (1965).

The mainstream remained true to form: It welcomed Martin Sherman's *Bent* (1978), a historical play about Nazi persecution, and the glitzy drag musical *La Cage aux Folles* (1983), but had no time for Alan Bowne's *Forty-Deuce* (1981, Off-Off), an unflinching portrayal of teenage hustlers in contemporary Times Square. Still, by the late 1970s, a number of prominent playwrights, themselves gay, could present gay characters as normal features of the American landscape: for example, Robert Patrick in *Kennedy's Children* (1973); Lanford Wilson in *Fifth of July* (1978) and *Burn This* (1987); and Albert Innaurato in *Gemini* (1977).

The first gay revues for general consumption were flashy commercial enterprises like *In Gay Company* (1975); more vital was the explosion of transvestite theatre that emerged from urban subculture. Gender-benders like the Cockettes and the Angels of Light in San Francisco and Centola and Hot Peaches in New York combined shock tactics, high camp, glitter rock, and reverse glamour to achieve their effects (see Female/Male Impersonation). Andy Warhol's Factory nurtured drag actor Jackie Curtis and scenarist Ronald Tavel. An important hothouse was John Vaccaro's Theater of the Ridiculous, which

bred one major talent in the person of Charles Ludlam; his plays are virtual palimpsests, juxtaposing classical allusions and pilferings from pop art. His influence was strong upon such epigones as Charles Busch, whose plays are less literate, less threatening, and more reliant on pop culture than Ludlam's. There was also a short fad for gay musicals: Al Carmines's *The Faggot* (1973) and *Boy Meets Boy* by Bill Solly and Donald Ward (1975).

Gay producing companies – such as TOSOS (The Other Side of the Stage, 1972–7), founded by Doric Wilson; The Stonewall Theatre; The Glines (1976–82), founded by John Glines; and the Meridian Gay Theatre (1982), founded by Terry Miller and Terry Helbing – were dedicated to promoting plays about the gay experience for gay audiences. The proliferation of similar troupes in other cities (Theatre Rhinoceros, San Francisco; Diversity, Houston; Lionheart, Chicago; Triangle, Boston; Alice B., Seattle) led to the 1978 creation of a network, the Gay Theatre Alliance, which held its first festival in 1980.

Feminist theatre groups inspired a score of lesbian ensembles, among them the Lavender Cellar in Minneapolis (founded 1973), the Red Dyke Theatre in Atlanta (1974), and the Lesbian-Feminist Theater Collective of Pittsburg (founded 1977). Although producing plays by Pat Surcicle, Joan Schenkar, and Jane Chambers, whose *Last Summer at Bluefish Cove* (1980) became a repertory staple, they emphasized satiric revue. This was especially so in New York's West Village, where the WOW Café, founded by Peggy Shaw and Lois Weaver in 1982, featured Alice Forrester's subversive parody *Heart of the Scorpion* and Holly Hughes's self-regarding satire *The Well of Horniness* (both 1985). However, the lesbian experience has yet to make a breakthrough in mainstream theatre, although it has been domesticated by cable television's *The L Word.*

The AIDS crisis decimated the performing arts, revealing how dependent they are on homosexual talent. The first wave of AIDS plays were angrily defiant and grieving: Larry Kramer's *The Normal Heart,* William M. Hoffman's *As Is,* Rebecca Ransom's *Warren,* Robert Chesley's *Night Sweat,* Theatre Rhinoceros's *The AIDS Show,* and the five-man political revue *The United Fruit Company* (all 1985). By the 1990s, AIDS was accepted as a fact of life, serving as sardonic background to the musical *Falsettoland* by William Finn and James Lapine (1990), and such comedies as Paul Rudnick's *Jeffrey* (1993) and McNally's *Love! Valour! Compassion!* (1995). The outstanding work of this second phase is Tony Kushner's epic *Angels in America*

(1990–2), in which AIDS becomes a metaphor for both a multiplicity of ills and a state of grace.

The homosexual presence in the American theatre would seem pervasive, with each constituency finding a voice: Pomo Afro Homos, Robert O'Hara, and Shirlene Holmes for African Americans, CHAY YEW for Chinese, Nick Paraiso for FILIPINOS, Luis Alfaro, EDWIN SÁNCHEZ, Guillermo Reyes, and Janis Astor del Valle for Latinos. Every Pulitzer Prize for Drama between 1993 and 1998 was awarded either to a play dealing with homosexual experience (*Angels in America*, *The Young Man from Atlanta*, RENT) or to an openly gay or lesbian playwright (ALBEE, PAULA VOGEL). Recent awards to NILO CRUZ and Doug Wright continue this trend. In addition, a Robert Chesley Award for Lifetime Achievement in Gay Theatre was instituted in 1994. On Broadway, gay male audiences flock to plays that titivate messages of tolerance with full frontal nudity (RICHARD GREENBERG's *TAKE ME OUT*, 2002), while the tired businessman still guffaws at the equally tired stereotypes to be found in *The PRODUCERS* (2003).

Nevertheless, the ban on Chesley's radio play *Jerker, or The Helping Hand* (1986) and the 1990 refusal of the NATIONAL ENDOWMENT FOR THE ARTS to fund the performance artists KAREN FINLEY, TIM MILLER, Holly Hughes, and John Fleck, conspicious for their anarchic irreverence, presaged a hostile cultural climate outside major cities. Plays with homosexual themes were often picketed or banned in regional theatres, and McNally's *Corpus Christi* (1998), which retold Christ's passion as the life of a liberated gay man, was attacked even before it opened (see CENSORSHIP). In response, plays dealing with historic or contemporary homophobia, such as Moisés Kaufman's *Gross Indecency* (1997) and *The LARAMIE PROJECT* (2001), Rudnick's *The Most Fabulous Story Ever Told* (1999), and the opera *Harvey Milk* by Stewart Wallace and Michael Korie (1995) were widely performed. The tension between a gay-friendly theatre and the general public is unlikely to abate in the near future.   LS*

Gayler, Charles (1820–92) Playwright and actor who, after forsaking law to act the title roles of *Hamlet* and *Othello* in Ohio theatres, brought his first play, *The Buckeye Gold Hunters* (1849), to his native New York. Thereafter, he acted, reviewed plays, and wrote, according to contemporary estimates, some 200 tragedies, comedies, melodramas, and operettas. Among his romantic plays are *The Love of a Prince* (1857) and *The Son of Night* (1857). *Bull Run; or, The Sacking of Fairfax Courthouse* was performed in New York on 21 July 1861, less than a month after the event. Further evidence of Gayler's commercial interest in popular subjects is shown in his play titles: *Taking the Chances; or, Our Cousin from the City* (1856); *Our Female American Cousin* (1859); *Fritz, Our Cousin German* (1870); and *Lights and Shadows of New York*.   WJM

Geer [né Ghere], **Will** (1902–78) Actor and director who first acted professionally with SOTHERN and MARLOWE's Shakespearean Repertory Company while a student at the University of Chicago (1924). He was active in left-wing theatre in the 1930s, notably with Theatre of Action and the Actors' Repertory Theatre, and he played "Mister Mister" in *The CRADLE WILL ROCK* (1938). He was also the most enduring Jeeter Lester in Broadway's long-running *TOBACCO ROAD*. Stints with the AMERICAN SHAKESPEARE FESTIVAL (Stratford, CT) and the ASSOCIATION OF PRODUCING ARTISTS punctuated starring and supporting appearances in theatres on both coasts, in motion pictures, and on television. From 1933 he operated the weekends-only Folksay Theater in Los Angeles and taught pre-Shakespearean folklore. In 1951 he was blacklisted from films as a communist. He is best known as Grandpa in the long-running television series *The Waltons*, which allowed him to found the Will Geer Theatricum Botanicum in 1973, a surviving professional theatre and school in Topanga, CA (Geer's home).   WD

Geffen Playhouse Located in the Westwood section of Los Angeles, the original facility, designed by Stiles O. Clement, was built in 1929 as the Masonic Affiliates Club and became the Westwood Playhouse. David Geffen, entertainment mogul and philanthropist, and his foundation made its first donation of $5 million to the theatre in 1995, leading to the theatre's new name. With ongoing support by Geffen, a $25 million capital campaign was initiated in 2002, and in November 2005 the renovated and expanded main auditorium and the new 117-seat Audrey Skirball-Kenis Theater opened at a price tag of $17 million (the balance is part of an endowment). Under the leadership of Gilbert Cates, a leader in television, film, and theatre (and former dean at UCLA), the Geffen offers a hybrid mix of new, risky, or sometimes niche-market fare, and mainstream productions with familiar stars from TV and film playing to more than 130,000 annually.   DBW

Geidt, Jeremy (1933–) British-born actor and teacher, trained at the Old Vic Theatre School with MICHEL SAINT-DENIS and George Devine.

Geidt came to the U.S. in 1962 with the satirical cabaret *The Establishment*, acted on and Off-Broadway and in television prior to joining the YALE REPERTORY as a founding member in 1966, and subsequently appearing in more than 40 of its productions. He moved with ROBERT BRUSTEIN to Harvard in 1980 and helped found the AMERICAN REPERTORY THEATRE where, up to fall 2007, this seasoned character actor has appeared in 93 productions, including recent appearances as Ferapont in *Three Sisters,* Ancient Servant in *Amerika,* Lovewell/Justice of the Peace in *The Provok'd Wife,* Petey in *The Birthday Party,* and Snug in *A Midsummer Night's Dream.* He has lectured and taught extensively and is the recipient of a JASON ROBARDS Award for Dedication to the Theatre and the 1992 ELLIOT NORTON Award for Outstanding Boston Actor.   DBW

Geiogamah, Hanay (1945–) Playwright, director, choreographer, producer. In 1972, Geiogamah founded the first all–NATIVE AMERICAN repertory company – the American Indian (now the Native American) Theatre Ensemble. With ELLEN STEWART's support, this troupe developed traditional myths and contemporary plays for Indian audiences, working to rekindle ethnic pride. Geiogamah's plays include the nightmarish *Body Indian* (1972) and a musical, *49* (1982). In 1987 he became director of the newly founded American Indian Dance Theatre, which performs an intertribal repertory, both authentic and theatrical, and as of 1990 he was a choreographer with the American Dance Theatre in Los Angeles. Currently, he is on the faculty at UCLA.   TH-S

Gelbart, Larry (1928–) Chicago-born playwright who has also written for radio, television, and film. He began with comic sketches while still in his teens, and in 1958 won a television Emmy for an "Art Carney Special." In 1963 he and Burt Shevelove were awarded a Best Author Tony for *A FUNNY THING HAPPENED ON THE WAY TO THE FORUM,* and in 1975 he won the distinguished Peabody Award for the television series *M*A*S*H.* Gelbart is one of America's most respected comic writers; his other theatre credits include *Sly Fox* (1976), *Mastergate: A Play on Words* (1989), *Power Failure* (1991, AMERICAN REPERTORY THEATER), and the book (Tony) for the highly praised musical *CITY OF ANGELS* (1989). Among his film credits are *Oh, God* (1977) and *Tootsie* (1982), both of which earned him Oscar nominations; he also wrote for Bob Hope, Red Buttons, and Sid Caesar. His autobiography, *Laughing Matters,* appeared in 1998.   BBW

Gemini Set in the backyards of adjoining rowhouses in South Philadelphia, this two-act comedy by ALBERT INNAURATO (Obie winner) presents the boisterous Italian Geminiani family and their equally colorful Jewish/Irish neighbors. Francis Geminiani, on vacation from Harvard, experiences conflicting feelings about his working-class background, sexual identity, and life in general when two upper-class WASP friends from school arrive unexpectedly on the eve of his 21st birthday. First performed in a workshop production at PLAYWRIGHTS HORIZONS, *Gemini* was produced at CIRCLE REPERTORY COMPANY (13 March 1977), directed by Peter Mark Schifter. It then moved to Broadway's LITTLE THEATRE (21 May 1977), where it ran until 5 September 1981. It was successfully revived in 1999 at Off-Broadway's SECOND STAGE.   KF

Gennaro, Peter (1924–2000) Choreographer for theatre and television. Gennaro defined his own style of modern jazz. He was featured in the "Steam Heat" dance from *The PAJAMA GAME* (1954), partnering Carol Haney in BOB FOSSE's choreography. Gennaro formed the Peter Gennaro Dancers, who performed on television variety shows, while Gennaro continued to work on Broadway (see DANCE). He assisted JEROME ROBBINS in *WEST SIDE STORY* (1957) and choreographed *The Unsinkable Molly Brown* (1960), the revival of *Irene* (1973), *ANNIE* (1977), and *Annie Warbucks* (1993). Gennaro also worked at RADIO CITY MUSIC HALL as producer and resident choreographer.   LF

George [née Doughtery]**, Grace** (1874?–1961) Actress, manager, director, translator/adapter. This petite comic actress's greatest success was Cyprienne in Sardou's *Divorçons* (1907). In 1911 she opened The PLAYHOUSE, built by her husband, producer WILLIAM A. BRADY. In 1915–16 she managed a repertory season there that included the U.S. premiere of G. B. SHAW's *Major Barbara* (1915, in the title role) and a revival of *Captain Brassbound's Conversion* (1916, as Lady Cicely Waynflete). George sometimes appeared in plays she translated or adapted; in 1929 she demonstrated her skill as director (and star) in *The First Mrs. Fraser,* which ran for 352 performances. Her final performance was with KATHARINE CORNELL in *The Constant Wife* (1951).   DBW

George M. Cohan's Theatre 1482 Broadway, NYC [Architect: George Keister]. Even by Broadway's standards, the active life of George M. Cohan's Theatre was brief. Built in 1911 for the musical-comedy star, then at his peak, it was part of the

Fitzgerald building, which also housed Gray's Drugstore, for years a gathering place for unemployed actors. JOE LEBLANG, who ran a shoeshine stand at the rear of the drugstore, also dealt quite successfully in cut-rate producers' leftover tickets: He bought the drugstore and, eventually, the building and the theatre. During the Depression the theatre was leased for movies; in 1938, the entire building was razed.   MCH

George Street Playhouse Professional, non-profit theatre founded in New Brunswick, NJ, in 1974 by Eric Krebs, who served as producing director for 14 years. In 1998 David Saint, associate artistic director of SEATTLE REP, became artistic director. Serving an audience of c. 140,000 annually and with a staff of 50, the Playhouse produces five mainstage productions and a "Next Stage Festival" of new works in May. Their venue is rented from the New Brunswick Cultural Center. The GSP's best-known production, the musical *The Spitfire Grill,* premiered in 2000 and as of 2005 has been produced at over 100 theatres in the U.S., Canada, and the Caribbean.   DBW

Gerald Schoenfeld Theatre see PLYMOUTH THEATRE

Germania Theatre Company A New York City, German-speaking company organized in 1872 by Adolf Neuendorff with the objective of improving ensemble quality and emphasizing classical repertory. The company, comprising many former STADT THEATER COMPANY actors, occupied Tammany Hall on 14th St. near 3d Ave. until 1881, and the old WALLACK'S THEATRE (Broadway and 13th St.) until 1883. Neuendorff introduced actors from Germany to America, including Magda Irschick (1879), FANNY JANAUSCHEK (1873), Karl Sontag (1881), Friedrich Haase (1882), and HEINRICH CONRIED. Contrary to Neuendorff's intent, the repertory offered primarily comedies, folk plays, and operettas. Competition from Conried's THALIA THEATRE forced Neuendorff to close.   RE

Gershwin, George (1898–1937) and **Ira** (1896–1983) American composer and lyricist. George's first connections with the musical stage were as a song plugger and rehearsal pianist. In 1918 he teamed up with his brother, Ira, who had written prose and verse for various periodicals, to write their first song, "The Real American Folk Song." A year later, George collaborated with lyricist Irving Caesar on one of the most popular songs of the day, "Swanee." For their first ventures in MUSICAL THEATRE, the brothers worked with other collaborators, George contributing songs to *La, La, Lucille* (1919), the REVUE *MORRIS GEST'S MIDNIGHT WHIRL* (1919), and the 1920–4 editions of *GEORGE WHITE'S Scandals,* while Ira wrote lyrics for *Two Little Girls in Blue* (1921). George's early show music was steeped in the idioms of jazz, a form he had learned from listening to black musicians. In 1924 the brothers collaborated on *Lady, Be Good!,* a musical starring FRED AND ADELE ASTAIRE. Encouraged by the show's success, the Gershwins turned out a number of other popular 1920s musicals, including *Oh, Kay!* (1926), *Funny Face* (1927), and *Rosalie* (1928). Their songs of the 1920s were characterized by George's infectious, driving music and Ira's clever, slangy lyrics.

In the early 1930s, the Gershwins created three satirical musicals, STRIKE UP THE BAND (1930), OF THEE I SING (1931), and LET 'EM EAT CAKE (1933). Acclaimed for its trenchant political satire and good-humored score, *Of Thee I Sing* was the first musical to be awarded the Pulitzer Prize for Drama. The brothers did not totally abandon more lighthearted forms of musical comedy, however. *Girl Crazy* (1930) had a frivolous book but contained some of the Gershwins' best songs, such as "I Got Rhythm" and "Embraceable You." In 1992 it served as the inspiration for the Tony Award–winning musical *Crazy for You*, with book by KEN LUDWIG but Gershwin songs.

In 1935 the THEATRE GUILD produced the Gershwins' "American folk opera" PORGY AND BESS. Receiving mixed reviews from both drama and music critics, the original production of *Porgy and Bess* was not a success. Nevertheless, its magnificent score has proven to be the Gershwins' most enduring work.

After George's premature death in 1937, Ira collaborated with other composers. LADY IN THE DARK (1941), which had a score by KURT WEILL, was innovative in confining its musical numbers to a few elaborate dream sequences. *The Firebrand of Florence* (1945), which Weill also composed, and *Park Avenue* (1946), with a score by ARTHUR SCHWARTZ, were failures.

As a composer, George Gershwin helped to popularize jazz on the musical stage in the 1920s. In addition to composing for Broadway, the Gershwins wrote a number of motion picture scores, and George also composed more serious compositions for the concert hall; these prepared him to write *Porgy and Bess,* one of the most ambitious scores ever created for the American musical theatre. Ira's abilities as a lyricist also grew from the facile rhyming of his 1920s songs to the deeper, more eloquent style of his later work. Together, the Gershwins were major forces in raising the level of musical-theatre composition. Of numerous biographies of the Gershwins, the best of George, by William G. Hyland (2003), is the most scholarly and the 1996 study of Ira by Philip Furia the most analytical.   MK

Gershwin Theatre 1633 Broadway, NYC [Architects: Theatre Planning Associates, RALPH ALSWANG]. Originating as the Uris Theatre, this was the first large Broadway playhouse to be built under relaxed zoning constraints in the building code that permitted theatres to be incorporated within commercial structures. Erected by the Uris Corporation, the 1,900-seat theatre is under long-term lease to the Nederlander Organization and Eugene Ostreicher. It opened in 1972 with a spectacular but unsuccessful rock musical; since then, its policy has fluctuated between musical productions and a series of concert appearances of well-known popular performers, dance presentations, and opera productions. In 1979, it received its first critical success with the STEPHEN SONDHEIM musical *Sweeney Todd*. In 1983, it was renamed the Gershwin Theatre in honor of GEORGE AND IRA GERSHWIN. In 1994 it housed the hit revival of *SHOW BOAT*, and since 2003 has held the hit musical *WICKED*. The theatre also encompasses the THEATRE HALL OF FAME within its spacious public areas.   MCH

Gerstein [née Gersten]**, Bertha** (1894–1972) Yiddish actress, born in Kraków and educated in America. She moved when young from vaudeville to drama, playing often with the YIDDISH ART THEATRE, Philadelphia's ARCH STREET THEATRE, and on tour, frequently opposite JACOB BEN-AMI.   NS

Gest, Morris (1881–1942) Russian-born producer who specialized in promoting foreign talent and in producing opulent spectacles at the Manhattan Opera House (1914–20) and CENTURY THEATRE (1917–19). Gest and his partner, F. RAY COMSTOCK, imported the Ballets Russes from Paris, as well as Moscow's *Chauve-Souris* REVUE, featuring Nikita Balieff (or Baliev). They produced the 1923–4 tours of the MOSCOW ART THEATRE, the 1924 production of MAX REINHARDT's *The Miracle,* and the 1925 tour of the Moscow Art Theatre Musical Theatre Studio, under the direction of Vladimir Nemirovitch-Danchenko. After ending his partnership with Comstock in 1928, Gest sponsored the U.S. visit of Aleksandër Moisiu (Alexander Moissi), Reinhardt's leading actor, and he brought the Freiburg Passion Play to the U.S. In addition, Gest was DAVID BELASCO's son-in-law.   WD

Getting Gertie's Garter by AVERY HOPWOOD and Wilson Collison. A typical sex farce so popular in the late teens and early 1920s, this play, produced by A. H. WOODS, opened on 1 August 1921. Although not as long-running as Collison and OTTO HARBACH's *Up in Mabel's Room* (120 vs. 229 performances) its myriad doors, physical vicissitudes, naughty tone, and traditional morals are emblematic of the type. On her wedding night Gertie is confronted by Ken, an old flame, who is adamant about securing the return of a garter bearing his photograph. The incriminating garter remains upon Gertie's person until she loses it, causing endless difficulties as the item passes from one confused character to another. The most suggestive action transpires in the hayloft, where a shrieking wife loses her clothes.   RHW

Getting Out MARSHA NORMAN's first play premiered at ACTORS THEATRE OF LOUISVILLE (1977), where it was cowinner of the Great American Play Contest. Directed by JON JORY and featuring Susan Kingsley, it later opened at NYC's PHOENIX THEATRE (1978) before beginning an eight-month run at Theatre de Lys (1979). The realistic play focuses on the divided character of Arlene (as a child and a young adult). It explores a female criminal's reentry into society, assisted by a former inmate and neighbor, Ruby. Hampered by their "rehabilitation," the two women confront their anger and natural wariness in order to survive their prisonlike existence outside a formal prison. The play won several awards.   TH-S

Geva Theatre Founded in 1972 in Rochester, NY (located in the *Genessee Valley*), this regional non-profit theatre moved into a 500-seat venue in 1985. The modified thrust stage is located in the former Naval Armory in the city's center; there is also a 180-seat Next Stage space for new or small plays.   DBW

Gibbs, Wolcott (1902–58) Drama critic. A native New Yorker, Gibbs joined the *New Yorker* in 1927 as copyreader, and became associate editor (1928) and editorial writer (1937) before succeeding ROBERT BENCHLEY as drama critic (1940–58). Gibbs was often criticized by actors and playwrights for his caustic comments, and gained the reputation of leaving the theatre after the first act of plays he disliked. His comedy *Season in the Sun* (1950) ran on Broadway for 367 performances.   TLM

Gibson, William (1914–) Playwright who first made it to Broadway with *Two for the Seesaw* (1958), a HENRY FONDA–ANNE BANCROFT two-hander, scoring again in 1959 with a stage adaptation of his television play, *The Miracle Worker*. This uncompromising account of Annie Sullivan's struggle to teach the deaf and blind Helen Keller the power of words is now firmly established as a modern American standard. No other Gibson play, including *Miracle Worker*'s sequel, *Monday after the Miracle* (1982), has come close to the success of his first two. He is also the author of *The Seesaw Log: A Chronicle of the Stage Production*, an agonizing account of the compromises necessitated by the collaborative nature of American commercial theatre. Other plays include *A Cry of Players* (1948; 1968 at Vivian Beaumont Theatre), *Dinny and the Witches* (1959), and *Golda* (1977), which he reworked as the solo piece *Golda's Balcony* (2003) for Tovah Feldshuh. LDC

Gilbert, John (Gibbs) (1810–89) American actor famous for comic roles in classic English comedy. Gilbert, born in Boston, made his debut there at the Tremont Theatre as Jaffier in *Venice Preserv'd* in 1828. He played the frontier theatres until 1834 and made his New York debut in 1839. Although he started as a leading tragedian, his greater successes came in comedy, especially as old men. For a time he managed the Chestnut Street Theatre. For 26 years he was with Wallack's company. A very traditional actor, he resisted almost any theatrical change. He died on the road. This life was recounted by William Winter in 1890. SMA

Gilbert, Mrs. George H. [née Anne Hartley] (1821–1904) British-born actress and dancer who married a dancer-manager in 1846 and moved to America in 1849. Gilbert spent most of her career playing "dear old ladies, foolish virgins and peppery viragos." For 30 years (1869–99) she acted in Augustin Daly's company, inevitably playing opposite the comic James Lewis and with Ada Rehan and John Drew (the "Big Four"), as in *Needles and Pins* (1880). Gilbert, a polished technician, was admired for her cooperative spirit and was venerated by the public. After Daly's death she appeared under Charles Frohman's management for the rest of her life. Her memoirs were published in 1901. DBW

Gilbert and Sullivan in America Arthur Sullivan (1842–1900), composer, and William Schwenck Gilbert (1836–1911), librettist and lyricist, created the most popular comic operas in the history of the British theatre, most of them in conjunction with London theatre manager and impresario Richard D'Oyly Carte. An initial American pro-

Mrs. G. H. Gilbert and James Lewis in *7-20-8*. Photo by Sarony, New York. *Courtesy:* Laurence Senelick Collection.

duction of *Trial by Jury* closed soon after its opening in 1875, but the premiere of *HMS Pinafore* in 1878 took the country by storm. The script and music were quickly pirated by managers, who offered all-black *Pinafores*, children's *Pinafores*, and church-choir *Pinafores*. Concerned about the lack of copyright protection, Gilbert and Sullivan opened *The Pirates of Penzance* in New York in 1879, trusting in British copyright law to protect their interests at home. The team's next few musicals received only lukewarm receptions in America, but the 1885 production of *The Mikado* reestablished their preeminence in the field of comic opera.

The phenomenal success of Gilbert and Sullivan's shows helped comic opera displace French *opéra bouffe* as the dominant form on the American musical stage for the rest of the 19th century, contributed to a sharp increase in the number of musicals offered in American theatres, and inspired American-born composers such as John Philip Sousa and Reginald De Koven to adopt the comic-opera form for their work. Even after

American composers had turned to ragtime and jazz for their musical styles in the 1910s and '20s, producers such as WILLIAM A. BRADY and WINTHROP AMES mounted lavish productions of G&S's work. By the 1930s and '40s the musicals were being adapted to contemporary American tastes: *The Swing Mikado* and *The Hot Mikado* competed for audiences in 1939, and in 1945 *Memphis Bound* and *Hollywood Pinafore* both offered modern versions of *HMS Pinafore*.

After WWII, the D'Oyly Carte Company made regular visits to New York, but audiences for the authentic British stagings and orchestrations dwindled – though amateur G&S societies survive to this day (as of 2005 there were seven in Massachusetts alone). While purists grumbled, the NEW YORK SHAKESPEARE FESTIVAL had a big success in 1980 with a version of *The Pirates of Penzance* starring rock vocalists Linda Ronstadt and Rex Smith. The influence of G&S is wide, with song writers as disparate as Tom Lehrer and STEPHEN SONDHEIM acknowledging their debt.   MK

Gilder, (Janet) Rosamond (De Kay) (1891–1986) Dramatic editor and critic. The daughter of Helena Gilder and Richard Watson Gilder, Rosamond established her reputation writing for THEATRE ARTS Magazine in the 1920s, later serving as associate editor, drama critic, and editor (1936–48). She headed the FEDERAL THEATRE's Bureau of Research and Publication (1935), and helped to found the International Theatre Institute (1947), of which she was president for two terms. As director of the U.S. Center of ITI (later ITI of U.S., Inc.), she promoted the international exchange of theatre artists, companies, and information. Her books include *Enter the Actress* (1931), *A Theatre Library* (1932), and *John Gielgud's Hamlet: A Record of Performance* (1937).   TLM

Gilfert, Charles A(ntonio) (1784–1829) Best known as the first manager of the BOWERY THEATRE in New York, from its opening in 1826 through its burning (see FIRES) and reopening in 1828 – until the owners removed him for rent arrears in 1829. Gilfert managed theatres in Charleston, SC, Richmond, VA, and Albany, NY, before securing a theatre lease in his native city, where he was characterized as an able musician but inept businessman and, to some contemporaries, an unprincipled man. Shank suggests Gilfert was an innovative manager, exchanging plays and stars with other theatres; he is credited with introducing press AGENTry, native plays and players, ballets, and operas. He died 30 July, reputedly deranged by the loss of his theatre.   RKB

Gilford, Jack (1907–90) Actor who began his career as a comedian, appearing in nightclubs, revues, and vaudeville. His most successful New York appearances included the roles of Bontche Schweig in *The World of Sholom Aleichem* (1953), Mr. Dussell in *The DIARY OF ANNE FRANK* (1955), King Sextimus in *Once upon a Mattress* (1959), Hysterium in *A FUNNY THING HAPPENED ON THE WAY TO THE FORUM* (1962), and Herr Schultz in *CABARET* (1966). His films included *A Funny Thing . . .* , *Catch-22*, and *Cocoon*. He also starred in televised versions of *Sholom Aleichem* and *Anne Frank*. His last live appearance was in a stand-up comic routine (1988) at New York's The Ballroom, a cabaret. His life is recounted in a dual biography of the Gilfords and Mostels by Kate Mostel and Madeline Gilford (1978).   SMA

Gill, Brendan (1914–97) Theatre, film, and architecture critic, and author. After graduating from Yale (1936), Gill began contributing to the *New Yorker,* serving as film critic (1961–7), theatre critic (1968–87), and architecture critic (1992–7). He authored 15 books, including *The Day the Money Stopped* (1957), adapted into a play with MAXWELL ANDERSON (1958); biographies *Tallulah* [BANKHEAD] (1972) and *Cole* [PORTER], with Robert Kimball (1971); and edited *States of Grace: Eight Plays by PHILIP BARRY* (1975). He is remembered for witty comments such as, "Not a shred of evidence exists in favor of the idea that life is serious."   TLM

Gillette, William (Hooker) (1853–1937) Actor and playwright. Born into a prominent family in Hartford, CT, Gillette left home in 1873 to seek a career on the stage. As an actor he is remembered for his performance in his own SHERLOCK HOLMES (1899), which he played over 1,300 times; his most significant achievement as a playwright was his Civil War spy melodrama SECRET SERVICE (1895), with its fast-moving action, suspense, and the tension between the demands of love and duty. Gillette was the author of numerous adaptations and dramatizations and several original plays in which he frequently appeared himself, in both the U.S. and England. In addition to Holmes, he played Blane in *Held by the Enemy* (1886), Billings in *Too Much Johnson* (1894), and Thorne/Dumont in *Secret Service*. His other notable appearances were in Barrie's *The Admirable Crichton* (1903; title role) and *Dear Brutus* (1918). Other Gillette plays include *The Private Secretary* (1884), *All the Comforts of Home* (1890), *Clarice* (1905), and *Electricity* (1910). In 1913 Gillette delivered his influential and subsequently published lecture *The Illusion of the First Time in Acting,* which explains his cool, understated approach to acting – a contrast to the florid and romantic style that dominated the theatre up to his time. A biography of sorts by Doris Cook appeared in 1970; a long biographical essay appears in *Plays by William Gillette,* edited by R. Cullen and D. Wilmeth (1983).   DBW

Gilman, Rebecca (1964–) Chicago playwright (born in Alabama) whose plays have frequently premiered at the GOODMAN. A writer of social-problem dramas, her plays are frequently disturbing and violent. Her best-known play, *Spinning into Butter* (1999), about racial issues on a college campus, was followed by *The Glory of Living* (1999; nominated finalist for 2002 Pulitzer Prize), a dark and violent play about a Texas teenage murderess who picks up vagrant girls for her boyfriend's sexual games, and *Boy Gets Girl* (2000), which deals with sexual stalking. Other plays include *Blue Surge, The Crime of the Century* (based on Richard Speck's 1966 murders of eight Chicago nurses), and *Bill of (W)rights.* Gilman, recipient of several prizes (including the Goodman's Scott McPherson Award), is a resident playwright of Chicago Dramatists Workshop.   DBW

Gilman, Richard (1925–2006) Drama critic who championed the European avant-garde of the 1960s in *Commonweal* (1961–4) and *Newsweek* (1964–7), and as literary editor of *New Republic* (1968–70). Gilman taught at Yale during 1967–99. His books include *Common and Uncommon Masks* (1971), *The Making of Modern Drama* (1974), *Faith, Sex, Mystery: A Memoir* (1987), *Chekhov's Plays: An Opening into Eternity* (1996), and *The Drama Is Coming Now: The Theater Criticism of Richard Gilman 1961–1991* (2005). He received the GEORGE JEAN NATHAN Award for Dramatic Criticism in 1971.   TLM

Gilpin, Charles Sidney (1878–1930) AFRICAN AMERICAN actor. Introduced at school to amateur theatricals, Gilpin left school at age 14 to become a vagabond vaudevillian, his meager earnings supplemented by sporadic jobs as printer, porter, barber, and elevator boy. In 1907 he joined the all-black Pekin Stock Company of CHICAGO, and later acted at the Lincoln and LAFAYETTE THEATRES in Harlem. His impressive Broadway performance as the slave Custis in John Drinkwater's *Abraham Lincoln* (1919) led to the title role in *The EMPEROR JONES* (1920), in which he scored a resounding triumph. A victim of sudden fame and racial prejudice, Gilpin took to drink, which cut short his career. The black critic THEOPHILUS LEWIS lamented: "He rose from obscurity to the peaks, lived his hour of triumph, and returned again to the shadows."   EGH

Gilroy, Frank D(aniel) (1925–) Playwright and director who gained attention first with his solid drama, *Who'll Save the Plowboy?* (1962), which won the Obie for Best American Play. His next effort was *The SUBJECT WAS ROSES* (1964), a story of the rivalry of a mother and father for the affection of their son who has just returned from the war. Although thinly funded and with a relatively unknown cast for the time, this play became one of the most honored serious dramas of the late 20th century (New York Drama Critics' Circle Award, Best Play Tony, Pulitzer Prize for Drama). Gilroy, also a film director, continues to write plays, but success has eluded his later efforts, including 1993's *Any Given Day.*   LDC

Gin Game, The Two-character drama by Texan D. L. Coburn, which opened on 6 October 1977 for 517 performances. Directed by MIKE NICHOLS, the play explored the relationship of two lonely residents of a home for the aged, played by HUME CRONYN and JESSICA TANDY. Though it won the Pulitzer Prize, critics were divided on its merits: It did bring America's aged population into focus, but some thought it was a static and predictable drama. A 1997 NATIONAL ACTORS THEATER revival with JULIE HARRIS and CHARLES DURNING seemed to reflect this judgment.   MR

Girl of the Golden West, The One of DAVID BELASCO's western plays and probably the most famous, this three-act melodrama about old California opened in New York on 14 November 1905. The naturalistic mise-en-scène, for which Belasco was famous, served this play (with its snowstorm, sunsets, and suspenseful scenes) quite well. Its western dialects and mannerisms drew upon Belasco's familiarity with the region, exemplifying a dramaturgical technique that joined lifelike speech and scenes to exciting, melodramatic actions. Puccini utilized this blend of old and new in his adaptation, probably the first grand opera on an American theme – his *La fanciulla del West,* which premiered at the Metropolitan Opera House 10 December 1910, eclipsing the play in revivals and lasting fame.   RKB

Gish, Lillian (1893–1993) and **Dorothy** (1898–1968) Actresses and sisters who, although they worked together in several films, never considered themselves a team. Dorothy made her stage debut in 1907 on tour in *EAST LYNNE.* In 1912 she made her first film with D. W. Griffith, continuing

Polka dance in Belasco's *The Girl of the Golden West,* 1905. *Courtesy:* Don B. Wilmeth Theatre Collection.

with and without her sister (24 films together) until 1928. Among her films were *Orphans of the Storm, Nell Gwynne,* and *Madame Pompadour.* She then returned to the stage, in plays including Morning's at Seven (1939) and the Chicago company of Life with Father in 1940. She appeared the next year in *The Great Big Doorstep,* followed by *Magnificent Yankee* (1946).

Lillian debuted in *In Convict's Stripes* (1902) and first appeared in New York as Marganie in *A Good Little Devil* (1913). She entered films and appeared in such early works as *The Birth of a Nation, Intolerance, Way Down East,* and *Orphans of the Storm.* She returned to the stage in 1930, starring in such productions as *Camille* (1932), John Gielgud's *Hamlet* (as Ophelia, 1936), *Life with Father* (1940–2), *The Curious Savage* (1950), Horton Foote's *The Trip to Bountiful* (1953), and Robert Anderson's *I Never Sang for My Father.* During 1969–70 she toured worldwide with a one-person concert program. Lillian wrote a memoir of her and her sister in 1973, and in 2001 Charles Affron published a biography of Lillian.   SMA

Glance at New York, A, by Benjamin A. Baker. Baker was prompter at Mitchell's Olympic Theatre when he wrote a sketch for a benefit performance and asked Francis (Frank) Chanfrau to act in it. The first production, 15 February 1848, featured a tough Bowery fireman, Mose the Bowery B'hoy, who generated instantaneous acclaim. Modeled on an actual person, Mose Humphreys, Mose took on epic proportions as a folk hero, a man of the city who could simultaneously fight fires, sing songs, tell jokes, and love women. Chanfrau played the original sketch, rewritten and lengthened, at the Olympic and Chatham Theatre. Over the next five years he acted in a dozen different plays featuring Mose.   RAH

Glaspell, Susan (1876–1948) Perhaps best known as one of the founders of the Provincetown Players (along with her husband, George Cram Cook), Glaspell was also a playwright (contributing 11 plays to the Players), second only to Eugene O'Neill in the founding of a modern American drama that combined contemporary American ideas with European expressionistic techniques. Glaspell's early one-act plays satirized contemporary attitudes and interests, such as pop psychology (Suppressed Desires, 1915) and ultra-idealism (*Tickless Time,* 1918) – both written in collaboration with Cook. However, her Trifles (1916), one of the most frequently anthologized one-act plays, skillfully portrayed hidden, psychological motivation by using realistic settings and dialogue to reveal women's inner conflicts. This play was also her first to use the device of keeping the central female character offstage, a technique she repeated in *Bernice* (1919). In her most controversial play, *The Verge* (1921), she experimented with symbolism and expressionistic settings to reveal the state of mind of a "new" woman who goes mad striving for both abstract idealism and individual fulfillment.

Throughout her career Glaspell never feared to tackle the new and the immediate. In *The Inheritors* (1921) she contrasted post–WWI narrow Americanism with earlier ideals of individual freedom and tolerance, again creating a female character who sacrifices ease and comfort to remain true to her ideals. In a controversial decision, Glaspell won the 1931 Pulitzer Prize for *ALISON'S HOUSE*, loosely based on the life of Emily Dickinson.

Glaspell's contribution to American drama includes her role in the founding of the Little Theatre movement (see COMMUNITY THEATRE), as well as her creation of modern female characters in search of autonomy, portrayed through new and experimental dramatic techniques. During 1936–8 she headed the Midwest Bureau of the FEDERAL THEATRE PROJECT, in Chicago. Linda Ben-Zvi wrote an exhaustive award-winning biography in 2005, preceded in 2000 by Barbara Ozieblo's.   FB

Glass, Montague (1877–1934) Playwright who first dramatized (with CHARLES KLEIN) a number of his stories under the title of *Potash and Perlmutter* (1913). Immediately successful, with 441 performances, the play's Jewish partners – Abe Potash and Mawruss Perlmutter – were transformed into Hebrew comedians, arguing incessantly and wittily, yet sharing joys and sorrows. In America and England the popularity of this play and its sequels – *Abe and Mawruss* (1915, written with ROI COOPER MEGRUE [retitled *Potash and Perlmutter in Society*, 1916]); *Business before Pleasure* (1917), *His Honor, Abe Potash* (1919), and others written with JULES ECKERT GOODMAN – was intense but brief.   WJM

Glass Menagerie, The TENNESSEE WILLIAMS's first major play opened at Chicago's Civic Theatre on 26 December 1944 and revolutionized the American stage with its expressionistic staging and haunting, lyrical dialogue. EDDIE DOWLING (coproducer, codirecter, star as Tom Wingfield) cast the legendary LAURETTE TAYLOR (Amanda), JULIE HAYDON (Laura), and Anthony Ross (Jim).

On 31 March 1945 *Menagerie* moved to New York's PLAYHOUSE THEATRE for 561 performances (Donaldson Award); that Broadway production never used the slide projections found in the reading text. *Menagerie* has had numerous revivals. In New York Amanda was played by HELEN HAYES in 1956 (City Center), MAUREEN STAPLETON in 1965 and 1975, JESSICA TANDY in 1983, and Jessica Lange in 2005. A black cast performed *Menagerie* in 1989 at the CLEVELAND PLAY HOUSE, and a 50th-anniversary production was offered by the ROUNDABOUT in New York with JULIE HARRIS. The KENNEDY CENTER staged the play in 2004 with Sally Field, and in 2006 Berkeley Rep featured RITA MORENO as an Amanda with "sensual vitality."

The Glass Menagerie was the first Williams play turned into a film (in 1950). In 1987 Paul Newman directed another film version with Joanne Woodward as Amanda, JOHN MALKOVICH as Tom, and James Naughton as Jim, the gentleman caller. Televised versions include one on CBS (1966) with SHIRLEY BOOTH, HAL HOLBROOK, and Barbara Loden, and on ABC (1973) with KATHARINE HEPBURN, SAM WATERSTON, and Joanna Miles. A "memory play," *Menagerie* is translucently autobiographical: The narrator-character Tom Wingfield is Tennessee Williams. Like Williams's mother, Edwina, Amanda is a daughter of the Old South. His sister, Rose, like Laura, was sickly and had a glass collection. Laura's only chance for romance is shattered, like the unicorn in her collection, when the gentleman caller announces he is engaged. Though Tom Wingfield tries to escape the domestic and political upheavals of the 1930s, he realizes, as did Williams, that he could never extinguish the light of memory that glows with nostalgia as well as pain.   PCK

Gleason, Joanna [née Joanna Halprin] (1950–) Daughter of game-show host Monty Hall, this Canadian-born actress-singer grew up in California and was educated at UCLA and Occidental College. The high cheek-boned blue-eyed leading lady and director made her Broadway debut in *I Love My Wife* (1977) but emerged as a star in 1985 in *A Day in the Death of Joe Egg* (Clarence Derwent Award), followed by her signature role in 1987 as the Baker's Wife in *INTO THE WOODS* (Tony for Best Actress in a Musical). Other productions of note have included *The Real Thing* (1985, replacement), *Social Security* (1986), *The Normal Heart* (2004, PUBLIC), and *Dirty Rotten Scoundrels* (2005). She met her current husband (since 1994), actor Chris Sarandon, while appearing with him in the ill-fated *Nick & Nora* (1991). Her professional name is that of her second husband, actor Paul Gleason.   DBW

Gleason, John (1941–2003) Lighting designer. A graduate of Hunter College, Gleason designed over 100 Broadway productions and served as resident lighting designer for the Repertory Theatre of LINCOLN CENTER and the MARK TAPER FORUM. During a 30-year career he was known for his innovative use of color on stage. He taught at New York University, 1972–97. AA

Glengarry Glen Ross This Pulitzer Prize–winning drama by DAVID MAMET is perhaps the most successful example of the playwright's exploration of the deceptive uses of language in power relationships – an exploration begun in SEXUAL PERVERSITY IN CHICAGO and AMERICAN BUFFALO and continued in *Speed-the-Plow*. Here we see the battle taken completely out of the personal arena and into the world of fast-talking real-estate salesmen, men who make a pretense of camaraderie as they are stealing each other's clients. The focus in on the brutality of human speech. Jack Kroll wrote of Mamet's dialogue: "His antiphonal exchanges . . . make him the Aristophanes of the inarticulate." The play premiered in 1983 at the National Theatre of Great Britain; the following year GREGORY MOSHER directed a production at Chicago's GOODMAN THEATRE (with JOE MANTEGNA) that transferred to Broadway's JOHN GOLDEN THEATRE, where it ran for 378 performances (winning Mantegna a Tony). A critically acclaimed revival (Tony for Best Revival of a Play) with an all-star cast (including ALAN ALDA and LIEV SCHRIEBER) in 2005 was directed by JOE MANTELLO (137 regular performances). It was also a successful 1992 film with AL PACINO, Jack Lemmon, KEVIN SPACEY, and ALAN ARKIN. SF

Glover, Savion (1973–) Extraordinary dancer and choreographer, born in Newark, NJ, whose Broadway debut was at age 12 in *The Tap Dance Kid*. In the revue *Black and Blue* (1989) he was nominated for a Tony for his performance; and at 18 he portrayed "Young Jelly" in JELLY'S LAST JAM. But it was his choreography and tap dancing in BRING IN 'DA NOISE, BRING IN 'DA FUNK that established him as a unique talent, winning him a Tony for Best Choreographer in 1996 and a nomination for Best Actor in a Musical. GEORGE C. WOLFE, director of *Noise/Funk*, sees in Glover a channeling of tap greats like Buster Brown and Jimmy Slyde. Glover's trademark hoofing style – a physical and furious type of tap – has been used to great effect with his own dance company, NYOTs (Not Your Ordinary Tappers), in concerts and special appearances, including a 35-city tour in 2005 (*Improvography II*). DBW

The Goat, or Who Is Sylvia? EDWARD ALBEE Tony-winning play that opened 10 March 2002 at the GOLDEN THEATRE (309 performances) and remains a regional staple. The play concerns a 50-year-old, globally revered architect and his erudite wife of 22 years, a more benign if still tart-tongued take on Martha from Albee's WHO'S AFRAID OF VIRGINIA WOOLF? When the husband blithely discloses his penchant for the bestial – an affair with a goat named Sylvia – the marriage combusts in a series of devasting confrontations redolent of Albee's earlier masterpiece. A subplot about the couple's gay son, meanwhile, raised questions about Albee's intentions with the play, which became a rare commercial success for him. Directed by DAVID ESBJORNSON, film star Bill Pullman and award-winning MERCEDES RUEHL played the married couple; Jeffrey Carlson played the son and Stephen Rowe the family friend. Following Ruehl's departure, Sally Field stepped in, making her Broadway debut opposite replacement BILL IRWIN. LJ

Gods of the Lightning by MAXWELL ANDERSON and Harold Hickerson. Although a failure when produced 24 October 1928 at the LITTLE THEATRE, this moving play was a strong attack on the xenophobia that characterized the Sacco and Vanzetti trial of 1921. The playwrights sympathetically explored the corruption behind the anarchists' 1927 execution, renaming the victims Macready (a boisterous union organizer) and Capraro (a pacifist rebel). In a travesty of the judicial system, these two are convicted of robbery and murder. "When you take violence into your hands," Capraro observes, "you lower yourself to the level of government, which is the origin of crime and evil." The cast included Leo Bulgakov and Sylvia Sidney. RHW

Godspell: A Musical Based on the Gospel According to St. Matthew was conceived and directed by John-Michael Tebelak (with music and lyrics by STEPHEN SCHWARTZ), who, along with the cast, had recently graduated college. Previously produced at The Café LA MAMA, the play opened at the Cherry Lane Theatre on 17 May 1971 and ran 2,124 performances; transferred to Broadway it ran an additional 527 performances. *Godspell* provided a contemporary view of Christianity during a Broadway season that included two other productions of biblical origin: *Two by Two*, the story of Noah, and *Jesus Christ Superstar*, a rock-and-roll spectacular. It was distinctive for portraying Jesus Christ as a clown, and having "flower children" perform other principal roles; a characteristic that supported the popular-style music, most notably "Day by Day," but trivialized heady philosophical issues with a simplistic view of life and peace.   KN

Gold Diggers, The This popular AVERY HOPWOOD comedy, which inspired three film versions, opened under the aegis of DAVID BELASCO at the LYCEUM THEATRE on 30 September 1919. A supposed look at the bohemian life and catty humor of chorus girls, the play's action all transpires in a New York apartment where theatrical women, who sometimes dream of becoming real actresses, spend most of their time luring stagedoor Johnnies, trying to get from men everything they can while returning as little as possible. The leading character of Jerry Lamar (played by INA CLAIRE) turns out to be genuinely in love, and in a sentimental ending reveals her gold digging as the means to support her mother and the illegitimate child of a dead chorus girl.   RHW

Goldberg, Whoopi [né Caryn Elaine Johnson] (1955–) Winner of the Kennedy Center Mark Twain Prize for American Humor (among dozens of awards), this unique stand-up comic and actor both onstage and in television and feature films (*The Color Purple*) has had a variegated public and private life. One aspect has been her stage career, which began as a child in her native New York City. In 1975 she moved to San Diego and worked with the SAN DIEGO REP (Brecht's *Mother Courage;* NORMAN'S *GETTING OUT*) and honed her comic skills with the improv group "Spontaneous Combustion." In San Francisco she created and performed in *Moms* (Mabley) and *The Spook Show,* the latter seen in NYC by MIKE NICHOLS, who in 1984 directed her solo show *Whoopi Goldberg* on Broadway (and staged the 20th anniversary *Whoopi* in 2004). In 1997 on Broadway she replaced NATHAN LANE as Pseudolus in *A FUNNY THING HAPPENED ON THE WAY TO THE FORUM;* 2003 saw her in an indifferent Broadway revival of *MA RAINEY'S BLACK BOTTOM;* and in 2002 she was a producer of *Harlem Song* at the APOLLO and the Tony-winning musical *Thoroughly Modern Millie.*   DBW

Golden, John (1874–1955) Producer who championed middle-class values through the production of wholesome family plays. He came from Ohio to New York at age 14 to be an actor, but abandoned this effort at age 21 for a profitable 13-year stint selling chemical products. While in this business he continued to write vaudeville sketches, short plays, and lyrics for show songs. Golden turned his full attention to writing and producing in 1918. His production of *Turn to the Right,* by WINCHELL SMITH and John Hazzard – financed by royalties from "Poor Butterfly," written for *The Big Show* (1916) – launched his career as a producer. He produced over 150 plays, more than a dozen of which achieved great popularity. His production of *LIGHTNIN'* (1918), by Smith and FRANK BACON, ran for 1,291 performances, a record that stood for most of the 1920s. He had enduring and productive professional relationships with Smith, actor-author FRANK CRAVEN, and RACHEL CROTHERS. A founder of the American Society of Composers, Authors, and Publishers (ASCAP), he was noted for his gifts of money, personal time, and organizational skill to many civic and cultural groups, including the Stage Relief Fund and the Stage Door Canteen.   WD

Golden Boy by CLIFFORD ODETS. Produced in 1937 by the GROUP THEATRE, directed by HAROLD CLURMAN, designed by MORDECAI GORELIK and starring LUTHER ADLER (as Joe Bonaparte), MORRIS CARNOVSKY (his father), and Frances Farmer (Lorna, his girl). The popular play (250 performances), which financially revived the company, tells the story of a young man's struggle to escape the slums by becoming a fighter instead of a violinist. It presents Odets's abiding conflict – in life and art – between idealism and commercialism, integrity and corruption. Odets wrote the play after leaving the Group for Hollywood. The plot is melodramatic, but effectively so. Revived in 1952, 1975, and by STEPPENWOLF in 1996, the play was also filmed in 1939, starring John Garfield (who played Siggie in the original staging). In 1964 it was transformed by Odets and WILLIAM GIBSON into a musical starring Sammy Davis Jr. (lyrics by Lee Adams, music by CHARLES STROUSE).   TP

Golden Theatre see JOHN GOLDEN THEATRE

Goldfadn [Goldfaden], **Avrom** [né Avraham Goldenfudim] (1840–1908) Playwright and producer, popularly called the "Father of YIDDISH THEATRE." A Russian intellectual who could not make a living, in 1876 he tried writing sketches to be performed in a wine garden in Jassi, Romania, thereby becoming the first professional Yiddish playwright and producer. Typically, he wrote operettas whose form was European but whose substance was Yiddish folk material and life. Many plays were instant successes – for example, *Koldunye; or, The Witch* (1877); *The Fanatic; or, The*

Two Kuni-Lemls (1880?); *Bar-Kokhba; or, The Last Days of Jerusalem* (1883); and *Shulamis; or, The Daughter of Jerusalem* (1883?). Some were also performed in other languages. However, Goldfadn spent much of his life wandering between Europe and America, rarely made a living, and fell from fashion entirely in old age. Nevertheless, about 30,000 mourners followed his funeral procession to Washington Cemetery in Brooklyn, for much of his work had already taken on the status of folk culture: for example, the lullaby "Raisins and Almonds," composed for *Shulamis,* and the clownish character types that he named Kuni-Leml and Shmendrik. His plays, in original form or adaptations, have often been revived.   NS

Goldin, Horace [né Hyman Goldstein] (1873–1939) Polish-born magician who emigrated to the U.S. at the age of 16. He started with a comic magic act, but owing to his heavy accent and stammer, converted it to a rapid-fire silent routine, "45 tricks in 17 minutes," baffling audiences with a quick succession of illusions. He appeared in a musical comedy *The Merry Magician* (Theatre Royal, Brighton, 1911) and was the first conjurer to play the Palace, New York (1913). His most famous illusion was an improvement on P. T. Selbit's 1879 trick, "Sawing a Lady in Half": Goldin eliminated the box and used a buzz saw, as Blackstone did as well.   LS

Gómez-Peña, Guillermo (1955–) Raised in Mexico City, this interdisciplinary artist-performer-writer came to the U.S. in 1978 and now is artistic director of La Pocha Nostra, a collective in San Francisco; from 1984 to 1990 he was a founding member of the Border Arts Workshop/Taller de Arte Fronterizo. He has spent the past three decades exploring through his projects cross-cultural issues, immigration, the politics of language, "extreme culture," and new technologies. Of special interest is U.S.–Mexico relations. His performances, installations, and video work have been presented at more than 700 venues worldwide. Among his better-known performance pieces are *The Loneliness of the Immigrant* (1979), *1991 – A Performance Chronicle, The Couple in the Cage* (1992, with frequent collaborator Coco Fusco), and his most elaborate work, *The Mexterminator* (1998), an interactive installation. Among his numerous recognitions was a 1991 MacArthur Fellowship.   DBW

Goodale, George Pomeroy (1843–1919) Journalist and critic. Born in Orleans, NY, Goodale worked in a printing office and as a newspaper journalist before serving with the Union in the Civil War. He became city and dramatic editor of the *Detroit Free Press* in 1865, and remained at the drama desk until his death. Goodale's criticism was both scholarly and moralistic, not unlike that of his New York compeers William Winter and John Ranken Towse.   TLM

Good Gracious Annabelle! Clare Kummer's first play and one of her most successful. The three-act comedy, produced by Arthur Hopkins at the Republic Theatre, opened on 31 October 1916 and ran for 111 performances. It portrays some agreeably pleasant but insolvent young people who follow the suggestion of Annabelle (played by Lola Fisher) and become servants at a nearby mansion. Annabelle discovers that the wealthy and handsome John Rawson (Walter Hampden), who has rented the mansion, is the mysterious man she married as a teenager and who has supported her for years. In 1924 a Ziegfeld musical version called *Annie Dear*, starring Billie Burke, was a distinct failure.   FB

Goodman, Jules Eckert (1876–1962) Oregon-born playwright, collaborator, and adapter of stories and novels for the stage. Educated at Harvard and Columbia, Goodman followed a short career as a journalist on the New York Dramatic Mirror with some recognition in *Mother* (1910), an original play; *The Silent Voice* (1914), an adaptation of a Gouverneur Morris story; *Treasure Island* (1915), based on the Stevenson novel; and *The Man Who Came Back* (1916), adapted from a John Fleming Wilson novel. A period of successful collaborations followed, including *Business before Pleasure* (1917), *His Honor, Abe Potash* (1919), *Partners Again* (1922), and *Potash and Perimutter, Detectives* (1926), all cowritten with Montague Glass. *Chains* (1923) was a solo effort, followed by a somewhat successful father–son collaboration in *Many Mansions* (1937).   GSA

Goodman Theatre Chicago's Goodman is America's second-oldest regional theatre, founded in 1925, and winner of the 1992 Tony for Outstanding Achievement in Regional Theater. Originally funded as a memorial by the parents of playwright Kenneth Sawyer Goodman, the 683-seat theatre, built alongside the Chicago Art Institute, was to house both a resident professional company and a School of Drama; however, the Depression forced the company to disband, whereas the school continued.

In 1969–70 a professional company returned to the Goodman to varying critical and popular reception. In 1978 its leadership was assumed by

GREGORY MOSHER, who emphasized new works and classic revivals, frequently commissioning scripts from leading American playwrights. In 1985 he became codirector of the theatre wing at LINCOLN CENTER in New York, and was replaced at the Goodman in 1986 by ROBERT FALLS, under whose leadership classical works have been staged with bold imagination and freshness and new works lavished with unusual care. World and American premieres have included MAMET's *Glengarry Glen Ross*, RABE's *Hurlyburly*, Soyinka's *Death and the King's Horseman*, Scott McPherson's *Marvin's Room*, REBECCA GILMAN's *Spinning into Butter*, and AUGUST WILSON's *Seven Guitars*. The Goodman's association with Wilson began in 1986 and was a long and fruitful one. Artistic staff under Falls has included directors Cheryl Lynn Bruce, FRANK GALATI, Henry Godinez, Harry J. Lennix, Michael Maggio, David Petrarca, Chuck Smith, REGINA TAYLOR, and MARY ZIMMERMAN. KEITH REDDIN was appointed resident playwright in 1998.

In 1977 the Goodman Theatre ceased its affiliation with the Chicago Art Institute to become a self-sustaining operation; and in 1978 DePaul University acquired the Goodman School, where it has flourished since. A new $46 million theatre complex [Architect: Kuwabara Payne McKenna Blumberg, Toronto] – on Dearborn between Lake and Randolph – opened in fall 2000 and houses two venues: the 856-seat proscenium Albert Ivar Goodman Theatre and the 325–467-seat flexible Owen Bruner Goodman Theatre. The inaugural production was Alan Ayckbourn's twin plays *House* and *Garden*. SMA DBW

Goodspeed Opera House East Haddam, CT [Architect: Jabez Comstock]. Built in 1876 as an indulgence for his taste for theatre by wealthy entrepreneur William R. Goodspeed, the tiny 400-seat theatre on the Connecticut River was often referred to as "Goodspeed's Folly" by the town's citizens. After his death in 1882, the theatre was largely abandoned, becoming offices and store-rooms by 1920. In 1958, owned by the state, it was slated for the wrecking ball, but a movement spearheaded by a local citizen, Mrs. Alfred Howe Terry, emerged to save it. Restored to its former Victorian elegance in 1963 through local fund-raising and a contribution from the state, it opened as a year-round theatre with the KERN–BOLTON–WODEHOUSE musical, *Oh, Lady! Lady!* Throughout most of its existence, it has been led by Michael P. Price, who established its policy of presenting both old and new musical works; it has sent 17 productions to Broadway, which gar-

nered more than a dozen Tonys. In nearby Chester, CT, the Norma Terris Theatre (formerly a factory built in the early 1900s; renovated as a 200-seat space in 1984) showcases new musicals and emerging artists. The Goodspeed has also set up a library-archive of the American musical in a separate building. Since 2003 there have been preliminary plans to build a new $45 million-plus facility, either in East Haddam or in nearby Middletown. As of early 2007 no final decision seems to have been made. In 1995, Goodspeed received a Tony Award for its Outstanding Achievement in Regional Theater.   MCH

Goodwin, Nat(haniel Carl) (1857–1919) Actor and manager. Born and educated in Boston, Goodwin began his career as a mimic for drawing-room theatricals. In 1874 he made his professional stage debut at Boston's HOWARD ATHENAEUM, and in 1875 his first New York appearance, at TONY PASTOR's Opera House. He enjoyed a major success in 1876 at the New York LYCEUM in *Off the Stage* by giving imitations of popular actors. While Goodwin excelled as a mimic and eccentric comedian, he also was effective in serious parts, such as Jim Rayburn in *In Mizzoura* (1893) and the title role in *Nathan Hale* (1899). Married five times, he gained notoriety for his offstage antics. With his third wife, MAXINE ELLIOTT, he starred in numerous plays including *Nathan Hale* and *When We Were Twenty-One* (1900). He was not, however, successful in Shakespearean roles, including Shylock (1901) and Bottom (1903). In his autobiography, *Nat Goodwin's Book* (1914), he took revenge upon his many enemies.   TLM

Gordin, Jacob (1853–1909) Yiddish playwright, driven from prerevolutionary Russia, because of socialist convictions, to New York's Lower East Side, where he became a journalist of enormous personal authority and influence. Although the intelligentsia scorned YIDDISH THEATRE as parochial and vulgar, in 1891, trying to feed his nine children, Gordin wrote *Siberia*, and thus initiated the close identification of secular Yiddish literary culture with Yiddish theatre. Characteristic of Gordin's many plays was concern for verisimilitude, despite high-flown language and aphoristic tags. They were most often dark and intense, achieving comic relief through colorful minor characters. Gordin wrote to teach: His plays' themes and subjects included socialism, women's rights, and the broader education of the Yiddish masses. Gordin championed pure and literary Yiddish. He attracted the best Yiddish actors of his time – JACOB ADLER, KENI LIPTZIN, DAVID

KESSLER, BERTHA KALISH, Ida Kaminska – and created juicy roles as vehicles for them. His best-known dramas include *God, Man and Devil* (1900), based on *Faust; The Jewish King Lear* (1892; see ETHNIC THEATRE); *Mirele Efros* (1898), sometimes called *The Jewish Queen Lear;* and *The Kreutzer Sonata* (1905). The first three were made into films; all remained staples of finer Yiddish intellectual repertory worldwide and are still considered classics. NS

Gordon, Max [né Mechel Salpeter] (1892–1978) Broadway producer remembered as "a man of wide-ranging tastes, and the possessor of a capacity to gamble." His production of *BORN YESTERDAY* (1946) ran for 1,642 performances. *The WOMEN* (1936), *MY SISTER EILEEN* (1940), *Junior Miss* (1941), and *The Solid Gold Cadillac* (1953) all achieved over 500 performances. His productions of *Roberta, Her Master's Voice, The Shining Hour,* and *Dodsworth* all ran simultaneously in 1934. Gordon came to theatre as a vaudeville advance AGENT. Notable productions presented early in his career in association with SAM HARRIS include *Six-Cylinder Love* (1921) and *The Jazz Singer* (1925). While continuing through the years to work with Harris, he also collaborated on *Missouri Legend* with GUTHRIE MCCLINTIC and *Sing Out the News* with KAUFMAN and HART (both 1938). Gordon also produced the film versions of *ABE LINCOLN IN ILLINOIS* (1940) and RUTH GORDON's *Year's Ago* (retitled *The Actress,* 1953), a play he'd mounted in 1946. He published an autobiography, *Max Gordon Presents,* in 1963. MR

Gordon [née Jones]**, Ruth** (1896–1985) Actress and playwright whose New York debut in *Peter Pan* (1915, with MAUDE ADAMS) was followed by a succession of relatively insignificant roles. It was a revival in 1936 of Wycherley's *The Country Wife,* in which she was the first American cast in an Old Vic (London) production, that changed the direction of her career: Her Mrs. Pinchwife (reprised on Broadway during 1936–7) led to roles that exploited her individualistic technique, whirlwind vivacity, and split-second timing. In 1937 (New York) she played Nora in *A Doll's House,* adapted for her by THORNTON WILDER; in 1942 she was Natasha in *The Three Sisters.* Her most memorable stage creation was Dolly Levi in *The MATCHMAKER* (1954, London; 1955, New York), a role written for her by Wilder. Her last stage role was the lead in *Mrs Warren's Profession* (1976). Gordon was also a successful screen actress, playwright (*Over 21; Years Ago*), and especially screenwriter in collaboration with her second husband,

GARSON KANIN. She was also the author of three lively autobiographies (1971, 1976, 1980).   DBW

Gordone, Charles (1925–95) AFRICAN AMERICAN playwright, actor, director. With his only successful stage play, *NO PLACE TO BE SOMEBODY* (1969), Gordone became the first black playwright to win a Pulitzer Prize. At a time of militancy in black theatre, Gordone dramatized in a number of highly theatrical scenes the murder of an incorrigible black pimp by his closest friend. The NEGRO ENSEMBLE COMPANY rejected the play, which was eventually staged at JOSEPH PAPP's PUBLIC THEATER in New York.   EGH

Gorelik, Mordecai (1899–1990) Russian-born director, stage and film designer. Gorelik studied with ROBERT EDMOND JONES, NORMAN BEL GEDDES, and SERGE SOUDEIKINE and began his career with the PROVINCETOWN PLAYERS in 1920. His 1925 design for *PROCESSIONAL* was a rare example of successful expressionism on the American stage. During the 1930s Gorelik was the primary designer for the GROUP THEATRE's shows, including *MEN IN WHITE* and *GOLDEN BOY.* Early in that decade he was an organizer of a short-lived leftist group, the Theatre Collective. He also designed *ALL MY SONS* and *A HATFUL OF RAIN,* among others on Broadway. Gorelik was a strong advocate of BRECHT's epic theatre, which he emphasizes in his book *New Theatres for Old* (1940). Much of his design (some 40 productions) can be classified as suggestive realism.   AA

Gotanda, Philip Kan (1951–) Leading ASIAN AMERICAN playwright, director, and independent filmmaker, native of Stockton, CA, and third-generation Japanese American. First produced by small Asian American companies, his work has crossed over to such theatres as the MARK TAPER FORUM, the MANHATTAN THEATRE CLUB, and The PUBLIC. Though stylistically diverse, all of his many plays examine the psychosocial dynamics of the Asian American experience. Trained as a musician, Gotanda has written several musicals, including *Bullet Headed Birds* (1981). *The Wash* (1987), about an elderly Japanese American couple in the throes of a wrenching divorce, and *Song for a Nisei Fisherman* (1980), the story of an immigrant doctor, are lyrical, naturalistic in texture. More satiric, *Yankee Dawg You Die* (1987) is a look at Hollywood stereotyping and the generation gap between two Asian American actors, whereas *Fish Head Soup* (1991) is a surreal family drama, and *Day Standing on Its Head* (1993) examines an Asian American professor grappling with middle age.

Ballad of Yachiyo (1995) offers the imagined recollection of a family's life on the leeward side of Kauai early in this century. *Under the Rainbow* (2005) comprises two one-acts: The first, *Natalie Wood Is Dead,* deals with a mother and daughter and their encounter with the Hollywood acting scene; the second, *White Manifesto,* is a monologue by a privileged white male with a penchant for Asian women. His *Yohen,* about a long-term interracial (black–Japanese) marriage, was premiered by PAN ASIAN REPERTORY in 2006. Gotanda's best work conveys the Asian American milieu with a deftness and compassion that renders it universal. In 1995 the University of Washington published four of his plays, followed in 2005 with a second group of four (including *Sister Matsumoto,* about three Japanese American sisters who return to their Stockton, CA, home after time in an internment camp).   MB   DBW

Gottfried, Martin (1933–) Drama critic. Born in New York and educated at Columbia (1955), Gottfried was music critic for the *Village Voice* (1961); drama critic for *Women's Wear Daily* (1962–74); and senior drama critic for the *New York Post* from 1974 until the early '90s. His criticism also appeared in *Saturday Review,* the *New York Times,* and *New York Law Journal.* Among his numerous books are *A Theater Divided* (1967), which won the GEORGE JEAN NATHAN Award for Dramatic Criticism; *Opening Nights* (1969); *Broadway Musicals* (1979); *JED HARRIS: The Curse of Genius* (1984); *All His Jazz: The Life and Death of BOB FOSSE* (1990); *SONDHEIM* (1993); *Nobody's Fool: The Lives of Danny Kaye* (1994); *GEORGE BURNS: The Hundred Year Dash* (1996); *Balancing Act: The Authorized Biography of ANGELA LANSBURY* (1999); and *ARTHUR MILLER: His Life and Work* (2003).   TLM

Gottlieb, Morton (1921–) Producer. An experienced business, company, and general manager when he produced his first ventures (three U.S. tours between 1953 and 1960), Gottlieb's noteworthy productions include *The Killing of Sister George* (1966), *We Bombed in New Haven* (1968), *Sleuth* (1970; Best Play Tony), and *Veronica's Room* (1973). Playwright BERNARD SLADE has benefited from Gottlieb's expertise with productions of *Same Time, Next Year* (1975), *Tribute* (1978, also U.S. tour 1980), *Romantic Comedy* (1979), and *Special Occasions* (1982). Gottlieb also produced the film versions of *Sleuth* (1972), *Same Time, Next Year* (1978), and *Romantic Comedy* (1983). He was recognized in *Barron's* as a frugal producer whose methods have maximized and speeded returns – when there were any – to investors. For instance, to provide a New York tryout with reduced production costs

within Equity regulations, he limited the available seating at the Ritz Theatre (now the WALTER KERR) to 499 for his production of Bill C. Davis's *Dancing in the End Zone* (1985).   MR

Grapes of Wrath, The Adapted and directed by FRANK GALATI for Chicago's STEPPENWOLF THEATRE COMPANY in 1988 and subsequently taken to California and London; won Tony Awards for Best Play and Best Direction when it reached Broadway in 1990. Based on JOHN STEINBECK's 1939 Pulitzer Prize–winning novel about a family of dust-bowl refugees, the production featured GARY SINISE as Tom Joad, LOIS SMITH as Ma, Robert Breuler as Pa, Nathan Davis as Grampa, and Terry Kinney as Rev. Casey. A string band joined a cast of 41 on spare but evocative sets designed and lit by KEVIN RIGDON. The production was created with the permission of Steinbeck's widow, who later praised the company for its faithfulness to her husband's idea of the nobility of the common man.   SF

Grau, Maurice (1849–1907 Austrian-born impresario and author who came to the U.S. at the age of 5. He worked briefly as a lawyer before beginning his theatrical career as manager for the French opera singer Marie Aimée. In 1879 he founded the Maurice Grau French Opera Company, which helped to popularize opéra bouffe in the U.S. In 1883 he began the first of three periods as manager of the Metropolitan Opera House. Grau's productions at the Met were acclaimed for the sumptuousness of the scenery and costumes, and for Grau's innovative use of as many as five stars in a single production. In addition to his operatic activities, Grau managed the American tours of many INTERNATIONAL STARS, including Sarah Bernhardt, Tomasso Salvini, Adelaide Ristori, and Constant Coquelin.   MK

Gray, Spalding (1941–2004) Actor-playwright; product of the avant-garde theatre movement of the 1960s. Gray spent five years as a traditional actor before joining RICHARD SCHECHNER and the PERFORMANCE GROUP in 1970. With the disbanding of that group in 1980, Gray joined his collaborator and director ELIZABETH LeCOMPTE, JAMES CLAYBURGH, WILLEM DAFOE, Libby Howes, and Ron Vawter to form the WOOSTER GROUP. Gray's reputation, however, transcended the Group, because of two bodies of work: initially, *Three Places in Rhode Island* (*Sakonnet Point,* 1975; *Rumstick Road,* 1977; *Nayatt School,* 1978), a trilogy devised by Gray (who said he was extremely "narcissistic and reflective") and LeCompte from

Gray's biography; and later as a result of a series (1979–2000) of 18 monologues ("without peer") drawn from Gray's past, including *Terrors of Pleasure; Sex and Death to the Age of 14; Booze, Cars and College Girls; A Personal History of the American Theatre; India and After; Interviewing the Audience; Swimming to Cambodia; Monster in a Box; Gray's Anatomy; and Skiing to New England* (1995; revised in 1996 as *It's a Slippery Slope*). His final completed work was *Morning, Noon and Night* (1999). Theodore Shank calls Gray's pieces "the most literally autobiographical work that has been presented in the theatre." In 1988 he scored critical success as the stage manager in LINCOLN CENTER's *Our Town,* and in 2000 he played a political candidate in *Gore Vidal's The Best Man.* After struggling mentally (Gray had a history of depression) and physically following a serious car accident in 2001 while in Ireland, it is believed that in January 2004 he jumped to his death from the Staten Island Ferry. (His body was found in the East River in March.) Prior to that event Gray had been developing at PERFORMANCE SPACE 122 *Interrupting Life,* a monologue about the accident and his life since (published in 2005 as *Life Interrupted*). In a 1997 interview, he provided a fitting epitaph: "An American Original: Troubled, Inner-Directed and Cannot Type." Gray also had a successful film career, with some 40 movies, including 4 of his monologues.
DBW

Grease Two-act musical comedy by Jim Jacobs and Warren Casey; opened 14 February 1972 at the OFF-BROADWAY Eden Theatre, eventually running (at several Broadway theatres) 3,388 performances. This "New '50s Rock 'n' Roll Musical," aping the pop-music idiom and manners of the late 1950s, is a nostalgic look at the "greaser" youth of the bygone era of bouffant hairdos and leather jackets, tracing the transformation of a "nice" girl into one of the gang. Originally written for a CHICAGO community theatre, it benefited from the popularity of such contemporary 1950s nostalgia as the film *American Graffiti* and the TV hit *Happy Days.* It had a Broadway revival in 1994, directed and choreographed by Jeff Calhoun; a summer 2007 revival is projected.   JD

Great Divide, The Considered a landmark drama even in its own day, this play by WILLIAM VAUGHN MOODY was inspired by his travels to Arizona and Colorado. It relates the home invasion of three rape-bound men, two of whom are bought off by the third, Stephen Ghent, when he falls for the intended victim, Ruth Jordan. Marriage, business success, remorse, and a child follow the guilt-stricken heroine to Massachusetts, where she is reconciled, across the great divide of conflicting values, with the hero. Its sensational subject matter probably helped the play's triumphal New York opening on 3 October 1906 at the PRINCESS THEATRE (where it ran 238 performances) and the celebrated national and international tours by its stars, HENRY MILLER (who also produced) and MARGARET ANGLIN. Despite continued debate about its premise, the play is still critically praised for its realism, suspense, and study of human psychology. It is often called the first modern American drama.   RKB

Great God Brown, The Perhaps the most mysterious of EUGENE O'NEILL's plays, this drama nonetheless ran successfully for EXPERIMENTAL THEATRE, INC., opening on 23 January 1926 at the Greenwich Village Theatre. In his most sophisticated experiment with masks, O'Neill, with director-designer ROBERT EDMOND JONES, graphically explored the complexity of human masking and unmasking, split character, personality confusion, and even psychological adoption of the personality of another. All was theatricalized by literal masks that were worn, removed, and even borrowed by four major characters: Dion Anthony (played by Robert Keith), an artist torn between Dionysian pleasures and religious asceticism; Billy Brown (William Harrigan), a successful businessman who jealously "becomes" Dion after the artist expires; Cybel (Ann Shoemaker), a seer-prostitute who pronounces the synthesis of Dion and Brown near the play's end; and Margaret (Leona Hogarth), who blindly loves the mask of Dion, be it on the face of either Dion or Brown. Although fascinating in development and spectral in mood, the play is confusing because O'Neill repeatedly alters the mask convention throughout the action.   RHW

Great Lakes Theatre Festival This Cleveland, OH, theatre company began when a peripatetic Shakespeare troupe founded in the early 1950s by Arthur Lithgow (father of JOHN LITHGOW) was persuaded to make the Lakewood Civic Auditorium its home. The Great Lakes Shakespeare Festival began operation in July 1962 with six Shakespeare plays in rotating repertory (today's season includes five full-length productions). Since then there have been six artistic directors – Arthur Lithgow (1962–6), Lawrence Carra (1966–75), Vincent Dowling (1975–85), GERALD FREEDMAN (1985–98), James Bundy, now at Yale (1998–2002), and, since fall 2002, Charles Fee. In 1982 the Festival moved to Playhouse Square (the Ohio Theatre) in downtown Cleveland, changing its name to the Great Lakes Theater Festival to underscore a broader classics-based repertoire.   DBW

Great White Hope, The, by Howard Sackler. Based upon the life of Jack Johnson, this play traces the career of the first black heavyweight boxing champion of the world, whose physical prowess and love affair with a white woman spur a racist society to destroy him. Set in numerous countries, the sprawling three-act drama incorporates direct audience address and dialogue in several foreign languages. EDWIN SHERIN directed the first production, which featured JAMES EARL JONES in "a tidal-wave performance" (WALTER KERR) and JANE ALEXANDER as the ill-fated mistress. Opening at ARENA STAGE in Washington, DC, on 12 December 1967, it moved to Broadway's ALVIN THEATRE on 3 October 1968, where it ran 556 performances and won the Tony and New York Drama Critics' Circle awards for Best Play, as well as the Pulitzer Prize.   KF

Green, Adolph see COMDEN, BETTY

Green, Paul (1894–1981) Playwright and educator. A student of Frederick Koch at the University of North Carolina, Green was taught that he should write about the life he knew – the South, its people, and its religion. In *The Last of the Lowries* (1920) he recreated the rhythmic language of the Negro and simple Southern folk characteristics. His best play, *IN ABRAHAM'S BOSOM* (1926), portrays the tragedy of a Negro idealist, defeated by his own limitations and by the people he wants to help. In both *The Field God* (1927), showing the spiritual disintegration of a man condemned by the religiosity he rejected, and *Shroud My Body Down* (1934, Carolina Playmakers, UNC, Chapel Hill), he dramatized the fascination and violence of religious mania. A liberal and intelligent man of strong opinions, Green broadened his involvement with human protests in *Hymn to the Rising Sun* (1936, FEDERAL THEATRE PROJECT), a condemnation of the chain-gang system, and *JOHNNY JOHNSON* (1936), in which he satirized warmongers through a hero who is confined by society for having "peace monomania." With *The Lost Colony* (1937), a symphonic drama about Sir Walter Raleigh's Roanoke Colony, Green found a new expression. After WWII, he continued to celebrate American history through such pageants as *The Common Glory* (1947), on the efforts of Jefferson during the Revolution; *The Founders* (1957), the story of the Jamestown colony; and *Cross and Sword* (1965). (See also OUTDOOR DRAMA; PAGEANTS/

PAGEANTRY.) A biography by Paul Herbert Roper was published in 2003; Green's letters were edited by L. G. Avery in 1994.   WJM

Green Pastures, The A biblical "fable" by MARC CONNELLY ("inspired by" Roark Bradford's *Ol' Man Adam an' His Chillun*) that was hailed by mainstream critics, awarded the Pulitzer Prize, and counted as one of the most profitable productions of the 1930s. The play opened at the Mansfield Theatre on 26 February 1930 and ran 640 performances. The company then toured continuously for three years, returning to Broadway for 71 more performances in 1935.

Connelly himself directed the large AFRICAN AMERICAN cast in this retelling of Bible stories from the creation of the world to the coming to earth of Jesus Christ as the stories might have been imagined by black children in the rural South. The scenes were augmented by "Negro spirituals" performed by Hall Johnson's gospel choir, and were set within an imaginative, cartoonlike setting designed by ROBERT EDMOND JONES. Despite the general critical reverence (BROOKS ATKINSON called it "the divine comedy of the modern theatre"), *The Green Pastures* was criticized by African American intellectuals such as LANGSTON HUGHES as white America's fantasy of the childlike simplicity of Southern blacks. A controversy arose when the Washington, DC, cast of the play refused to appear before segregated audiences. A film version, codirected by Connelly, was released in 1936; the play was revived briefly on Broadway in 1951.   MF

Green Street Theatre Green St. between Hamilton and Division, Albany, NY. Actor-manager JOHN BERNARD opened the playhouse on 18 January 1813. Sold to the Baptist Society, it became a church from 1819 to 1852, when it was reconverted into a theatre. It was a concert saloon in 1861 and thereafter passed from theatrical annals. Among the theatre's noteworthy events were SOL SMITH's debut at age 14 and ADAH ISAACS MENKEN's appearance for the first time in *Mazeppa*.   MCH

Greenberg, Richard (1958–) Playwright, born on Long Island and educated at Princeton and Yale Drama School, initially produced by the ENSEMBLE STUDIO THEATRE and PLAYWRIGHTS HORIZONS. His output has been steady for almost two decades (28 plays as of spring 2006). *Eastern Standard* premiered at the SEATTLE REP (1988), then transferred to Broadway; *The American Plan* was staged at MANHATTAN THEATRE CLUB (1990);

The Author's Voice (1987, EST) was revived by the DRAMA DEPT. in 1999; *The Extra Man* was first produced at the SOUTH COAST REP (with whom he has a special relationship) in 1991 and then in 1992 at MTC; *Jenny Keeps Talking* was staged at the MTC's Stage II (1993); *Night and Her Stars*, based on the TV quiz scandals of the 1950s, premiered in 1995 at MTC, as did *Three Days of Rain* in 1997; *Hurrah at Last* was presented by ROUNDABOUT in 1999; *Dazzle*, based on the Collyer brothers, whose bodies were found in 1947 in their debris-filled Harlem home, was also presented by Roundabout (2002). Greenberg's first undeniable hit, TAKE ME OUT, transferred in 2003 from The PUBLIC to Broadway, where it ran 355 performances (Tony for Best Play). *The Violet Hour* in November 2003, however, was a troubled production and a disappointment at the newly renovated BILTMORE THEATRE (inaugural production at the new home of the MTC). *A Naked Girl on the Appian Way*, with Jill Clayburgh and RICHARD THOMAS, fared somewhat better as produced in 2005 by Roundabout, and the 2006 revival of *Three Days of Rain*, with Julia Roberts in her Broadway debut, was a modest success, as were *The Well-Appointed Room* (STEPPENWOLF, 2006), *Bal Masque* (DC's Theater J, 2006), and *The House in Town* (2006, Lincoln Center).
BBW   DBW

Greene, Clay Meredith (1850–1933) Successful playwright born and for much of his life based in SAN FRANCISCO. Some of his 80 scripts were written with DAVID BELASCO or others; most are boilerplate melodramas with strong regional flavor. His first success, *M'liss* (1878), was based on a BRET HARTE story about a spunky Sierras orphan; *Sharps and Flats* (1880), coauthored by Slauson Thompson, depicted San Francisco's high-stakes financial world. Other popular dramas include *Chispa, His Japanese Wife*, and *The Red Spider.*   MB

Greenspan, David (1956–) Actor, director, and playwright, characterized by TONY KUSHNER as "probably all-round the most talented theatre artist of my generation." Yet Greenspan, who was educated at University of California–Irvine and moved in 1978 to NYC, is something of a cult figure among the downtown theatre devotees rather than a household name. Initially not finding meaningful theatre jobs, he turned to writing monologues for himself (the 2003 *Myopia* earned him recent recognition), those of the late 1980s and '90s often notable for extreme sexual content. As a director he served from 1990 to 1993 as a resident director at The PUBLIC; as an actor he appeared in LUDLAM's *The MYSTERY OF IRMA VEP* in

Cleveland, BOYS IN THE BAND (1997 NYC revival; Obie), and Broadway's HAIRSPRAY (2002; understudying the elder Turnblads). Of his many plays, recent ones include *Them* (1999) and *She Stoops to Comedy* (2003; Obie). Other notable titles include *Jack, Principia, The Home Show Pieces, 2 Samuel 11, Son of an Engineer*, and *Start from Scratch.*   DBW

Greenwood, Jane (1934–) Costume designer, native of Liverpool, England, who studied at London's Central School of Arts and Crafts and designed for the Oxford Playhouse before emigrating to Canada and subsequently NYC. Her Broadway debut, *The Ballad of the Sad Cafe* (1963), was coproduced by scenic designer BEN EDWARDS, whom she later married. One of New York's busiest costume designers, her credits include *The Circle, I Hate Hamlet, Othello, The Heiress* (1995 Tony nomination), A DELICATE BALANCE, *An American Daughter, Major Barbara*, WHO'S AFRAID OF VIRGINIA WOOLF? (2005 Tony nomination), among many others. She also designs costumes for films, operas, and television, and teaches costume design at the Yale School of Drama. In 1998 she received the IRENE SHARAFF Lifetime Achievement Award and in 2004 was inducted into the THEATRE HALL OF FAME; she has received 15 Tony nominations.   BO

[Ben] Greet Players (also Woodland Players) Originating in England in 1886, the Greet Players toured the U.S. beginning in 1902 and continuing (except for 1919, 1920, and 1922–8) until 1931. Philip Ben Greet introduced U.S. audiences to alfresco performances, using little or no scenery, of medieval and Elizabethan drama, mainly the plays of Shakespeare (see SHAKESPEARE ON . . .). Greet's touring companies also pioneered the "concert booking system," whereby noncommerical producers set admission prices and sold tickets, then kept as profit any receipts above the company fee. Greet's companies were especially popular in Boston and Chicago.   WD

Gregory, Andre (1934–) Director, actor, and producer, identified with the 1960s avant-garde. From producing OFF-BROADWAY (1959), Gregory directed at The Writer's Stage (1962), then founded The Manhattan Project, an environmental theatre group that adapted performance spaces to suit each script. He became famous overnight with the success of the company's *Alice in Wonderland* (1970; Special Obie; Drama Desk Award for Outstanding Director) and *Endgame* (1973). JOSEPH PAPP presented the company at The PUBLIC THEATER in *[The] Seagull* (1975) and

Jinxs Bridge (1976). Always controversial, The Manhattan Project's six actors performed in an eccentric style with words articulated in a strange and often comic manner, and gestures exaggerated as they played the subtext more often than the text. CLIVE BARNES praised Gregory's work, but WALTER KERR dismissed the company as "self-indulgent, slovenly in speech, and childish in antics." His staging of *Uncle Vanya* (in rehearsal over a three-year period) was filmed by Louis Malle as *Vanya on 42nd Street* (1994). Gregory's acting has included *Rumors* on Broadway (1988) and Prospero in *The Tempest* (1989–90) for Shakespeare & Company (Berkshires/Boston). He starred in the film *My Dinner with Andre* (1981) with WALLACE SHAWN, and has appeared subsequently in such offbeat films as *Protocol* (1984), *The Mosquito Coast* (1986), *Street Smart* (1987), *The Last Temptation of Christ* (1988), and *Last Summer in the Hamptons* (1995), in which he appeared with his son Nick. In 1999 he directed the American premiere of Shawn's *The Designated Mourner* in a disused men's club in NYC.
TLM

Greif, Michael (1958–) Obie Award–winning director (*Machinal*, 1990; *Rent,* 1996; *Dogeaters*, 2001) whose professional training was at the University of California, San Diego (M.F.A. 1985). His Broadway debut in 1987 was as assistant director for *Sleight of Hand*; his major credit to date is *Rent,* which he first directed in 1994 for the New York Theatre Workshop (where he has been a regular director). As artistic director of the LA JOLLA PLAYHOUSE (1995–9) he directed a wide range of material, from OUR TOWN and SWEET BIRD OF YOUTH to KUSHNER's *Slavs* and Diana Son's *Boy*. Since returning to New York as a freelance director, he has worked at CSC REP, WILLIAMSTOWN, The PUBLIC, and for ROUNDABOUT, among others. Recent productions include Noah Haidle's *Mr. Marmalade* for Roundabout (2005, Laura Pels Theatre), and, for PLAYWRIGHTS HORIZONS, the thriller *Spatter Pattern* (2004) and the musical *Grey Gardens* (2006), which moved to Broadway at the end of the year.
DBW

Grey [né Katz]**, Joel** (1932–) Cleveland-born actor, singer, and dancer who as a child performed in his father's NIGHTCLUB act. He appeared OFF-BROADWAY in *The Littlest Revue* (1956), and had roles in several Broadway plays and musicals before receiving critical acclaim and a Tony as the decadent Master of Ceremonies in CABARET (1966; film, 1972). Grey's breezy personality and loose-limbed dancing made him a natural choice to portray musical comedy star GEORGE M. COHAN in *George M!* (1968). His other musical roles, in *Goodtime Charley* (1975) and *The Grand Tour* (1979), met with less success. Grey appeared in a revival of CABARET in 1987 and played numerous roles in a one-man musical, *Herringbone* (1982), at HARTFORD STAGE in 1993; in 1996 he played Amos Hart in the hit revival of CHICAGO, and in 2003 created the Wonderful Wizard of Oz in WICKED. His daughter is actress Jennifer Grey.   MK

Griebling, Otto (1896–1972) German-born tramp clown who came to the U.S. in 1910; often compared to and sometimes partnered with EMMETT KELLY. Griebling, as the result of a fall while a bareback rider in 1930, learned to juggle and developed a silent-clown act. Unlike the dour-faced Kelly, he was an affectionate, plump tramp whose best-known routines centered around a persistent attempt to deliver a package to an audience member or to finesse a kiss from an unsuspecting woman in the crowd. These and other routines were perfected over 20 years. In 1951 he joined RINGLING BROS., last appearing with them at Madison Square Gardens in 1970.
DBW

Grimes, Tammy (1934–) Actress and expert comedienne, known for her raspy voice. This Massachusetts native debuted as Cherie in BUS STOP (1955; standby for KIM STANLEY), and established her career with Molly in *The Unsinkable Molly Brown* (1960; Tony Award). She appeared in *Rattle of a Simple Man* (1963) and *High Spirits* (1964) and repeated her earlier awards as Amanda in Coward's *Private Lives* (1969). She starred in New York in *California Suite* (1976), *Tartuffe* (1977), and Simon Gray's *Molly* (1978; 1982, LONG WHARF), and appeared in *Father's Day* (1979, AMERICAN PLACE), *A Month in the Country* (1979, ROUNDABOUT), 42ND STREET (1980), *Over My Dead Body* (1984, Hartman Theater, Stamford, CT), *Paducah* (1985, American Place), and *Orpheus Descending* (1989). She has acted at the Stratford (Ontario) Theatre Festival and appeared in some dozen films, including *High Art* (1998). Her daughter is actress Amanda PLUMMER.
TLM

Grizzard, George (1928–) Actor known for "his ability to become the part." Grizzard made his stage debut in *The Corn Is Green* (1945, in Virginia), then on Broadway in Joseph Hayes's *The Desperate Hours* (1955). He performed for ARENA STAGE, CIRCLE REPERTORY, CIRCLE IN THE SQUARE, OLD GLOBE, PLAYWRIGHTS HORIZONS, HARTFORD STAGE COMPANY, BROOKLYN ACADEMY OF MUSIC, and YALE REPERTORY in comedies, dramas, farces, and melodramas. Disparaging avant-garde theatre, especially Beckett, Grizzard has focused on classics (*Hamlet*, 1963 [the GUTHRIE THEATER's first production]; *Man and Superman*, 1978); American standards (*The GLASS MENAGERIE*, 1965; *The COUNTRY GIRL*, 1972; *The ROYAL FAMILY*, 1975; *A DELICATE BALANCE*, 1996; *Seascape*, 2005); adaptations (*To Kill a Mockingbird*, 1991, PAPER MILL PLAYHOUSE; *Judgment at Nuremberg*, 2001); and premieres (*WHO'S AFRAID OF VIRGINIA WOOLF?*, 1962; LANFORD WILSON's *The Gingham Dog*, 1969; NEIL SIMON's *California Suite*, 1976; PAUL RUDNICK's *Regrets Only*, 2006).   REK

Groener, Harry (1951–) Actor, dancer, and choreographer. Born in Augsburg, Germany, he immigrated to the U.S. as a child, and acquired a degree from the University of Washington. Groener has received three Tony nominations: for a revival of *OKLAHOMA!* (Will Parker) in 1980 (featured role); *CATS* (Munkustrap) in 1983; and, his most successful stage appearance, as Bobby Child in 1992's *Crazy for You*. His film career began in 1985, though he does return to the stage; e.g., in 2002–3 he appeared in Nora Ephron's *Imaginary Friends* in San Diego and then New York; in 2006 he replaced Simon Russell Beale as King Arthur in *Monty Python's Spamalot*.   DBW

Grosbard, Ulu (1929–) Belgium-born director who emigrated to the U.S. in 1948 and attended the University of Chicago, Yale School of Drama, and ACTORS STUDIO. He began his directing career in 1957, making his New York debut in 1962 with *The Days and Nights of Beebee Fenstermaker* at the Sheridan Square Playhouse. His notable productions since include *The SUBJECT WAS ROSES* (1964); *A VIEW FROM THE BRIDGE* (1965, Sheridan Square); *The Investigation* (1966); *The PRICE* (1968); *AMERICAN BUFFALO* (1977); *The Wake of Jamey Foster* (1982); *Weekends Like Other People* (1982, Marymount Manhattan Theatre); and PADDY CHAYEFSKY's *The Tenth Man* (1989 revival, VIVIAN BEAUMONT THEATRE). Since 1961 he has worked mostly in films and television.   TLM

Group Theatre, The Founded in 1931 by HAROLD CLURMAN, LEE STRASBERG, and CHERYL CRAWFORD, the Group was a pioneering attempt to create an American theatre COLLECTIVE, a company of players trained in a unified style and dedicated to presenting new American plays of social significance. With Stanislavsky's MOSCOW ART THEATRE as their model, Group members began a systematic study of an art that had few guidelines and virtually no written record. Prodded by their exacting teacher, Lee Strasberg, and fired by Clurman's messianic fervor, the actors experimented with improvisation, emotional and sensory memories, private moments, and exercises in relaxation and concentration. The inner technique they worked on – which became the basis of the American Method and which Strasberg continued to develop during his 35 years at the ACTORS STUDIO – resulted in acting that was more natural and earthy, more private, more intense, and more psychologically charged than previous styles. Debates over method erupted in the summer of 1934 when Group member STELLA ADLER returned from her studies with Stanislavsky in Paris to announce that the Master had abandoned his earlier emphasis on inner work in favor of a new external technique, the method of physical actions. Adler and Strasberg squared off in a craft war whose wounds have never healed, even after their deaths: Strasberg and his followers have continued to focus on the actor's own emotional resources, whereas Adler and her colleagues have concentrated on the play as opposed to the player.

Among the superb realistic actors the Group helped to develop were John Garfield and FRANCHOT TONE (both of whom defected to movies), Margaret Barker, Ruth Nelson, MORRIS CARNOVSKY, Phoebe Brand, Art Smith, and SANFORD MEISNER. Decades after the Group disbanded in 1941, Strasberg, Adler, Meisner, and Carnovsky continued to be influential teachers, offering their own individual variations of the Method.

Although less successful than its actor-training program, the Group's literary achievement was also substantial. The Group was not a political theatre and, in fact, was strongly criticized by more militant companies; but over a 10-year period it produced 22 new American plays on subjects of contemporary relevance. If only a few of these – JOHN HOWARD LAWSON's *Success Story* (1932) and CLIFFORD ODETS's *AWAKE AND SING!* (1935) and *PARADISE LOST* (1935) – have enduring literary value, all of the Group's plays rose above the level of propaganda, and in Odets the company yielded an American original. The full story of the Group is recounted by Wendy Smith (1990), though Clurman's *The Fervent Years* (1945) remains a classic.   FH

Guare, John (1938–) Playwright whose work is characterized by frank theatricality, lyrical quality, autobiographical base, and satiric vivacity. Some critics have found his plays too cerebral or abstract, lacking focus, but few have failed to praise his use of language. Recognized first for his one-act play *Muzeeka* (1968), he received wide acclaim for his first full-length play, *The HOUSE OF BLUE LEAVES* (1971, OFF-BROADWAY; revived with critical acclaim in 1986, Best Play Tony). Other major plays of the '70s include the adaptation and lyrics for *Two Gentlemen of Verona* (1971, NEW YORK SHAKESPEARE FESTIVAL; revived in Central Park in 2005); *Rich and Famous* (1974) and *The LANDSCAPE OF THE BODY* (1977), both at The PUBLIC; and *Bosoms and Neglect* (1979, GOODMAN, then Broadway). A notable screenplay, *Atlantic City,* written for Louis Malle's 1981 film, was followed by *Lydie Breeze* and *Gardenia* (1982), two parts of a projected tetralogy set in 19th-century New England; a reworking of the two plays received a successful staging in 2000 at the NEW YORK THEATER WORKSHOP. *Women and Water,* chronologically first in this series, was seen in various drafts during 1984–5 in Los Angeles, Chicago, and Washington, DC. *Moon over Miami,* originally meant as screenplay for John Belushi, was staged by Yale Rep in 1989; in a revised version (*Moon under Miami*) it premiered at Chicago's Remains Theatre in 1995. His most successful play to date is *SIX DEGREES OF SEPARATION* (1990), which delves into the vulnerability under New York's brittle surface. Winner of the 1990 Dramatists Guild Hull–Warriner Award (also presented for *Landscape*) and the 1992 Laurence Olivier Award for Best New Play in London, it was a successful film in 1994. *Four Baboons Adoring the Sun* was given a 1992 production directed by Peter Hall at Lincoln Center's VIVIAN BEAUMONT THEATRE. The SIGNATURE THEATRE presented a Guare season in 1998–9, including the world premiere of *Lake Hollywood. Chaucer in Rome* followed in 2001 (also at Lincoln Center). His play *A Few Stout Individuals,* based on U.S. Grant's throat cancer and Samuel Clemens's coaxing that he write his memoirs, was produced by Signature in 2002; also that year *Sweet Smell of Success,* for which he wrote the book, had a brief Broadway run. *His Girl Friday,* an adapted hybrid of *The FRONT PAGE* and the regendered Howard Hawks film, was moderately successful at London's National Theatre in 2003.   DBW

Guernsey, Otis Love, Jr. (1918–2001) Editor and drama critic. Born in New York and educated at Yale (1940), Guernsey wrote for the *New York Herald Tribune* (1941–60), including service as film and theatre critic. He was drama critic and senior editor of *Show Magazine* (1963–4), editor of *Dramatists Guild Quarterly* (1964–94), and editor of the *Best Plays* series (1965–2000), replacing HENRY HEWES. Guernsey was author of *Directory of the American Theatre* (1971); *Playwrights, Lyricists, Composers on*

Theater (1974); *Broadway Song & Story* (1986); and *Curtain Time* (1987). He was a founding member of the American Theatre Critics Association and winner of the MARGO JONES Award.   TLM

Guettel, Adam (1965–) New York native, grandson of RICHARD RODGERS and son of Mary Rodgers, this lyricist, composer, orchestrator, and musical supervisor has thus far created a small but important body of musical-theatre pieces, most notably *Floyd Collins* with writer-director TINA LANDAU (1994; PLAYWRIGHTS HORIZONS, 1996; Obie) and *The Light in the Piazza* (2005, VIVIAN BEAUMONT THEATRE) with CRAIG LUCAS. The former, based on a true story of man trapped in a Kentucky cave in 1925, was the recipient of a Lucille Lortel Award for Outstanding Musical; the latter, based on Elizabeth Spencer's 1960 novella about a middle-class tourist (played with acclaim by Victoria Clark) from North Carolina and her "slow" but beautiful 26-year-old daughter in Florence in 1953, won the Tony for Best Original Score and Drama Desk Award for Outstanding Music, among many recognitions. Guettel has frequently been categorized as one of the "new generation" of musical-theatre composers (with Ricky Ian Gordon, MICHAEL JOHN LaCHIUSA, JEANINE TESORI, JASON ROBERT BROWN) as well as "the next Sondheim" (he is the 1996 recipient of the Sondheim Award), although he claims more affinity with classical composers (Stravinsky, Britten, etc.); his music for *Piazza,* considered by most very romantic, has been compared to Fauré, Debussy, and Ravel.   DBW

Guild Theatre see VIRGINIA THEATRE

Gunn, Moses (1929–93) African American actor. Gunn's first professional engagement was with the remarkably talented OFF-BROADWAY company presenting Genet's *The Blacks* (1962). Thereafter, he performed five Shakespearean roles at the 1964 Antioch, OH, festival and three additional roles with the NEW YORK SHAKESPEARE FESTIVAL, winning acclaim for his portrayal of Aaron the Moor in *Titus Andronicus* (1967). Gunn became a founding member of the NEGRO ENSEMBLE COMPANY and appeared in several of their productions in 1968, for which he won an Obie; a second Obie was forthcoming for his performance with NEC in *The First Breeze of Summer* (1975), which moved to Broadway. His "sensual-melodic" Othello for the AMERICAN SHAKESPEARE THEATRE in 1970, which transferred to the ANTA Playhouse, elicited ecstatic reviews from major New York critics.   EGH

Gunter, Archibald Clavering (1847–1907) Playwright and novelist. Born in England and educated as a mining engineer in San Francisco, where he wrote his first play, *Found the True Vein* (1872), he moved to New York in 1879. During the next decade he wrote a number of moderately successful plays showing a broad western influence upon his creativity: *Courage* (1883), with EFFIE ELLSLER; *Prince Karl* (1886), RICHARD MANSFIELD's first starring role; *Two Nights in Rome* (1886); *The Deacon's Daughter* (1887); and *One against Many* (1887). In 1888 he dramatized his successful novel, *Mr. Barnes of New York* (1887), the adventures of a rich, imprudent American, and thereafter mainly wrote fiction.   WJM

Gurney, A(lbert) R(amsdell) [Pete], Jr. (1930–) Playwright, novelist, and educator, educated at Williams and Yale. The American theatre's John Cheever (in 1994 his *A Cheever Evening* was produced at PLAYWRIGHTS HORIZON, home to several of his earlier plays) and one of America's most prolific and produced playwrights, Gurney writes feelingly about what he fears is an endangered species: well-to-do, or at least well-bred, white Anglo-Saxon Protestants. His wry comedies unfold in a nostalgic haze. Typically, his plays are set in a time and place of poignant transition: at the end of summer, of adolescence, of an era. While his characters reluctantly confront the need for making changes, they also lament the passing of an enclosed and carefully regulated way of life. In one of his best plays, *The* DINING ROOM (1982), place is more important than any of the rotating cast of characters who pass through it; his dining room is a cultural artifact threatened with extinction, a metaphor for genteel traditions. In *The Middle Ages* (1983), the library of an exclusive club serves a similar thematic purpose. Other deft Gurney works include *Children* (1974, London; 1976, NYC), suggested by a Cheever short story, in which a matron chooses duty over pleasure; *What I Did Last Summer* (1983), about a teenager torn between propriety and bohemianism; *The Perfect Party* (1986); *The Cocktail Hour* (1988); *The Snow Ball* (1991, coproduced by HARTFORD STAGE and SAN DIEGO REP); *The Old Boy* (1991); arguably his most successful, *Love Letters* (1989), a two-character play that relates a romance from grade school to middle age and has toured worldwide (1990–3); *The Fourth Wall* (1992, Hasty Pudding Theater); *Later Life* (1993); *Sylvia* (1995); *Overtime* (1995, OLD GLOBE); *Labor Day* (1998); *Far East* (1999); *Ancestral Voices* (1999) and *Human Events* (2001), both at GEORGE STREET PLAYHOUSE; *Big Bill* (2004), about the tennis star Bill Tilden; *Mrs.*

Farnsworth (2004), starring SIGOURNEY WEAVER and JOHN LITHGOW; and *Indian Blood* and *Post Mortem* (both 2006). *O Jerusalem* (2003) moves into new ground for Gurney and wrestles with an international crisis.   FH

Gussow, Mel (1933–2005) Drama critic and author. Born in New York and educated at Middlebury College (1955) and Columbia University (1956), Gussow served as associate editor at *Newsweek* (1959–69), as second-string drama critic for the *New York Times* (1969–93), critic for the *Times*'s radio station, WQXR, and as a writer of in-depth pieces on the theatre scene nationally. With a penchant for the nontraditional and unusual, Gussow drew national attention to the most worthy of OFF-OFF and OFF-BROADWAY talent, including such playwrights as SAM SHEPARD, DAVID MAMET, RICHARD FOREMAN, and JOHN GUARE, and directors ROBERT WILSON and JULIE TAYMOR, among others. Of his eight books, four are conversations with Samuel Beckett, ARTHUR MILLER, Harold Pinter, and Tom Stoppard; three are biographies – of Darryl F. Zanuck (1971), EDWARD ALBEE (1999; winner of Freedley Book Award), and British actor Michael Gambon (2004). He received the GEORGE JEAN NATHAN Award for criticism (1978) and the MARGO JONES Medal in 2002 for his commitment to new work.   TLM

Guthrie Theater 725 Vineland Pl., Minneapolis, MN [Architect: Ralph Rapson]. Conceiving the idea of founding a theatre away from New York, Oliver Rea and PETER ZEISLER searched the country for a hospitable city that would support such an enterprise. Enlisting the aid of the director TYRONE GUTHRIE, they eventually chose MINNEAPOLIS as their site and brought forth the Tyrone Guthrie Theater after much effort in 1963. Part of the Walker Art Center, the original 1,315-seat Guthrie Theater featured a thrust stage, favored by the late director, and in its early seasons presented mainly well-cast productions of classics and significant modern plays.

After Guthrie's departure, his place was taken by his assistant, Douglas Campbell, until 1967, and a few years later by MICHAEL LANGHAM (1971–5). In 1981, after years of diminishing audiences, the direction of the theatre fell to LIVIU CIULEI, the Romanian-born director, who materially changed its policy: The production of new American and European plays, in addition to the classics in a different mode, contributed to a new spirit within the enterprise. In 1986 Ciulei was succeeded by GARLAND WRIGHT, whose work included an innovative 1993 version of the Cly-

Artist's conception of the new (2006) Guthrie Theatre on the Mississippi River. *Courtesy:* Guthrie Theater.

temnestra saga, a triptych based loosely on works by the three great classical writers of tragedy and starring African American actress Isabelle Monk. Renovations in 1992 altered the exterior of the theatre as well as the audience's relationship to the stage. (Instead of wrapping nearly 210 degrees around the stage, the house now did so only 165 degrees.) During 1993–4 additional renovations were executed in the lobby and auditorium, with plans for the expansion of backstage facilities. Wright, who left in November 1995, was replaced by Joe Dowling, former artistic director of Dublin's The Abbey. Under his leadership, the Guthrie resumed national tours, opened a second stage (the Guthrie Lab, seating 300), initiated a B.F.A. program with the University of Minnesota, and launched a new-play program that featured world-premiere productions of ARTHUR MILLER's *Resurrection Blues* (2002), Jane Martin's *Good Boys* (2002), and LEE BLESSING's *A Body of Water* (2005).

In 2006, the Guthrie moved from its original site to a three-theatre complex designed by Jean Nouvel on the Mississippi River. The largest space incorporates a thrust stage similar to the original one, but with 1,100 seats.   MCH   MBD

Guthrie, Tyrone (1900–71) From the 1930s onward, Irish-born Guthrie was an innovative and popular international director, working extensively in Britain, the U.S., and Canada. His Shakespearean work included Laurence Olivier's *Hamlet* and *Henry V,* and a modern-dress *Hamlet* in 1938 with Alec Guinness. He repeated this experiment at the Minneapolis Theatre (later named the GUTHRIE THEATER) in 1963. His other productions included a notable *Peer Gynt* (1944), in which

Ralph Richardson starred. He was director (1953–7) of the Stratford Festival Theatre in Ontario, Canada, and there developed (with TANYA MOISEIWITSCH) his thrust-stage theatre form that was later permanently enshrined both there and in MINNEAPOLIS.

Guthrie's immensely successful operation in Minneapolis, although not the beginning of the regional theatre movement in America, certainly gave it great impetus. Guthrie's successes with classical repertory, and his mastery at directing crowd scenes, garnered immense publicity, thus heightening awareness of theatrical potential in other American cities. Guthrie considered Broadway "a murderous, vulgar jungle," but his productions there included The MATCHMAKER, CHAYEFSKY's *Gideon,* and the original CANDIDE. He also directed several productions at New York's PHOENIX THEATRE, including *Mary Stuart.* Guthrie was knighted in 1961. A biography by James Forsyth was published in 1976.   SMA

Gutierrez, Gerald (1952–2003) Brooklyn-born and Juillard-trained director who established his reputation for clear and deliberate productions, and for a scrupulous sense of reality with enormous flair and style, in the OFF-BROADWAY and regional theatre. After directing for the ACTING COMPANY and McCARTER THEATRE and other companies, Gutierrez began a long association with ANDRÉ BISHOP at PLAYWRIGHTS HORIZONS (*Geniuses,* 1982; *Rise and Rise of Daniel Rocket,* 1983; *Isn't It Romantic,* 1983–4) and later at LINCOLN CENTER, where he won Tony and Drama Desk awards for his direction of *The Heiress* (1995) and *A DELICATE BALANCE* (1996); MANHATTAN THEATRE CLUB

(*Emily* by STEPHEN METCALFE, 1988); The ACTING COMPANY (*Much Ado about Nothing*, 1987); and GOODSPEED (*The MOST HAPPY FELLA*, 1991; Broadway, 1992). Also for Lincoln Center he directed *Ivanov, ABE LINCOLN IN ILLINOIS, Playboy of the Western World, Ring Round the Moon,* and a revival of *DINNER AT EIGHT*. At his death he was preparing *Engaged* for Theatre for a New Audience.   TLM

Guys and Dolls Book by Jo Swerling and ABE BURROWS; music and lyrics by FRANK LOESSER. Based on Damon Runyon's colorful, 1930s short stories of Broadway gamblers and their long-suffering girlfriends, this show opened at the 46TH STREET THEATRE on 24 November 1950 and ran 1,200 performances. It was revived on Broadway in 1965; then in 1976 with an all-black cast; and in April 1992 (1,143 performances), directed by JERRY ZAKS, with FAITH PRINCE (Adelaide), PETER GALLAGHER (Sky Masterson), and NATHAN LANE (Nathan Detroit) critically acclaimed. Original choreographer MICHAEL KIDD and director GEORGE S. KAUFMAN created a fast-moving show about a gambler who loses a bet, and his heart, to an idealistic Salvation Army missionary. The secondary plot, concerning the proprietor of "the oldest established permanent floating crap game in New York" and his cabaret-singer fiancée, allowed Kidd to stage some deliciously second-rate NIGHTCLUB sequences.

Comedy scenes involving formidable gangster Big Jule, who plays craps from memory with blank dice, and a rousing pseudogospel number at the mission, "Sit Down, You're Rocking the Boat" (originally sung by Stubby Kaye), counterpointed the two romantic entanglements. In the 1950 production, Robert Alda and SAM LEVENE starred as the gamblers, with VIVIAN BLAINE as the nightclub singer and Isabel Bigley as the missionary. Its film version was in 1955, with MARLON BRANDO, Frank Sinatra, and Jean Simmons, with Blaine and Kaye reprising their roles.   MK

Gypsy With book by ARTHUR LAURENTS, music by JULE STYNE, and lyrics by STEPHEN SONDHEIM,

Gypsy opened 21 May 1959 at the BROADWAY THEATRE. Based on the memoirs of stripper GYPSY ROSE LEE, the show told the story of a grasping stage mother, Mama Rose, who had channeled her own ambitions into an obsession with the vaudeville careers of her two daughters. After her older daughter elopes and the second daughter, Louise, attains success on her own with a striptease act, Rose ruthlessly examines the price she has paid for her ambition in her bitter and wrenching (and show-stopping) soliloquy "Rose's Turn." The role of Rose proved to be the last major triumph of ETHEL MERMAN's career and enabled ANGELA LANSBURY and Tyne Daly to win Tony Awards for their performances in the 1974 and 1989 Broadway revivals, and BERNADETTE PETERS to be nominated in 2003. Rosalind Russell was Rose in the 1962 film, and Bette Midler took the role in a 1993 television production. Laurents's book captured the tawdry world of small-time VAUDEVILLE and BURLESQUE in the 1920s, and was perfectly complemented by JEROME ROBBINS's evocative choreography (he also directed) and Styne and Sondheim's corny vaudeville numbers, raucous stripteases, and artless ballads.   MK

Gypsy Robe, The A symbol of good luck among Broadway chorus members (called "gypsies" because of the transient nature of their work). The tradition of passing a decorated dressing gown to a selected chorus member with the most Broadway musical credits in the most recent Broadway musical on opening night began in 1950 with dancer Bill Bradley (died in 1997). Bradley was in *Gentleman Prefer Blondes;* he passed the robe to a gypsy in *CALL ME MADAME;* then it went to someone in *GUYS AND DOLLS*. Thus a tradition was born. Made of muslin, the robe bears designs indicative of the musical of each recipient. When a robe is covered, it is retired and a new one created. A version of the robe was donated to the Smithsonian in 2001. Over the years what began as a haphazard ritual has evolved into an organized ceremony with official rules.   DBW

H

Hackett, J(ames) H(enry) (1800–71) Actor, master dialectician, manager, and the first American to appear in London as a star. He first succeeded in New York as Sylvester Daggerwood in *New Hay at the Old Market*. In 1827 he appeared at London's Covent Garden, but failed to win public esteem. Returning to the U.S. he repeated his triumphant Dromio of Ephesus, but audiences preferred his frontier and YANKEE roles, especially Nimrod Wildfire in *The LION OF THE WEST* and *RIP VAN WINKLE*. He secured his reputation as the finest Falstaff of his time, first playing the role in 1828. Hackett periodically essayed management, and was manager of the ASTOR PLACE OPERA HOUSE at the time of the FORREST–Macready riot. His *Notes & Commentaries upon Certain Plays & Actors of Shakespeare, with Criticism & Correspondence* was published in 1863.

His son **James K(eteltas) Hackett** (1869–1926) was a member of FROHMAN's LYCEUM company, starring in such vehicles as *The Prisoner of Zenda*. He married actress Mary Mannering in 1897 and costarred with her in *The Walls of Jericho* (1905). In 1906 he managed Wallack's Theatre in New York (opened 1904 and not to be confused with the theatre associated with the WALLACK family). In 1914 he and JOSEPH URBAN collaborated on a scenically historic production of *Othello*.   SMA

Hagedorn, Jessica (1949–) Playwright/performer, born in the Philippines (see FILIPINO AMERICAN THEATRE) and immigrated to the U.S. at age 13. She began as a poet but soon became interested in the performing arts. In 1974 she was in the original cast of NTOZAKE SHANGE's *FOR COLORED GIRLS WHO HAVE CONSIDERED SUICIDE WHEN THE RAINBOW IS ENUF* in Berkeley. She collaborated and performed with Shange and Thulani Davis in *When the Mississippi Meets the Amazon* at the PUBLIC THEATER in 1977. The Public then produced Hagedorn's first solo playwriting effort, *Mango Tango* (1978). Other works include *Tenement Lover* (1981), *Teenytown* (1988) – in collaboration with Laurie Carlos and Robbie McCauley – and *Airport Music* (1994), with HAN ONG. She adapted her 1990 novel *Dogeaters* into a play in 1998. Her work often deals with intersections of race, gender, and sexuality played out on a larger canvas of history and the legacy of colonialism.   DanB

Hagen, Uta (1919–2004) American actress and teacher who made her debut in 1938 in the LUNTS' production of *The Seagull* and acted only sporadically to her death, though almost always in circumstances as notable: in MAXWELL ANDERSON's *Key Largo* (1939); with PAUL ROBESON and JOSÉ FERRER in *Othello* (1943); opposite Anthony Quinn in *A STREETCAR NAMED DESIRE* (1947–9; replacement and tour); as the lead in ODETS's *COUNTRY GIRL* (1950; Tony); most memorably, as tortured, caustic, vulnerable Martha in EDWARD ALBEE's *WHO'S AFRAID OF VIRGINIA WOOLF?* (1962; Tony); OFF-BROADWAY in the British play *Mrs. Klein* (1995); and as the author, Ruth, in MARGULIES's *Collected Stories* (1998). Her last stage work was in 2001 at the GEFFEN PLAYHOUSE in Los Angeles in Richard Alfieri's *Six Dance Lessons in Six Weeks*.

Known as an actor's actor, Hagen performed in a clean, masterly style; she had an earthy, assertive presence and a deep voice that suggested enormous power in reserve. Although her understatement was ideally suited to film, she chose to appear onscreen only rarely (notably in *The Other* and *The Boys from Brazil*). From 1947 she taught at the HB Studio in New York, begun by her late husband, HERBERT BERGHOF. Famous for the brevity and incisiveness of her comments, she spoke in technical code words – an actor's shorthand – that her students learned to interpret. Like most American teachers she derived her method from Stanislavsky; unlike LEE STRASBERG, another Stanislavsky disciple, she was strongly opposed to the use of emotional memory, which she considered both self-indulgent and self-destructive. She was awarded a LUCILLE LORTEL Award for her Lifetime Achievement in 1995, a Special Lifetime Achievement Tony in 1999, and in 2002 the National Medal of the Arts. She wrote on acting in *Respect for Acting* (1973; a standard reference for both students and professionals) and *A Challenge for the Actor* (1991). Her memoir, *Sources,* appeared in 1983.   FH

Haimes, Todd (1956–) Virtually his entire professional career has been devoted to the not-for-profit Roundabout Theatre Company, where, armed with an MBA from Yale, he began as managing director in 1983 and, after quickly rescuing the company from bankruptcy ($2.5 million deficit), became artistic director in 1990. Briefly in 1998 he added to his responsibilities the position of artistic director at Livent, Garth Drabinsky's failing production company. Under Haimes, Roundabout became the second-largest operating theatre company in America, with an annual budget of more than $30 million and a subscriber base of 40,000-plus. In 2007 this self-proclaimed workaholic, who in 2003 survived sarcoma of the jaw, oversees three active venues and boasts a string of artistic and popular successes.   DBW

Hair Two-act musical, music by Galt MacDermot, words by James Rado and Gerome Ragni; first opened at the Off-Broadway Public Theater (Anspacher), 29 October 1967, running 94 performances; it moved to Broadway's Biltmore Theatre 29 April 1968, running 1,742 performances. This "American Tribal Love-Rock Musical" was a major event in theatre history, as traditional culture met counterculture. *Hair* was a "concept" musical in that it did not attempt to tell a story, but rather sought to explain a way of life: that of the antiwar dropouts of the East Village who had rejected their parents' values for a life of sex, drugs, and freedom. Seemingly unstructured, with an amplified pop/rock score of atmospheric but essentially undramatic music originally played by a small rock band, it was both a plea for understanding from "straight" society and an attempt to shock it. The original production, directed by Gerald Freedman, was the inaugural offering of Joseph Papp's Public Theater. Papp sold the rights to Michael Butler, who produced a far more lavish revised and reorchestrated version, directed by Tom O'Horgan, on Broadway and across the world. Even more popular in London (a less successful London revival was staged at the Old Vic in 1993) than in New York (where a 1977 revival lasted a month), it created a rage for rock music (and its attendant amplification) in the theatre, as well as for other essentially nonnarrative musical depictions of minority segments of society. One of its most publicized controversies was the use of nudity, unique then in a commercial musical production.   JD

Hairspray Musical comedy based on the over-the-top 1988 John Waters movie, with book by Mark O'Donnell and Thomas Meehan and music and lyrics by Scott Wittman and Marc Shaiman. After a tryout in Seattle, the show, directed by Jack O'Brien with choreography by Jerry Mitchell, opened at the Neil Simon Theatre 15 August 2002, ultimately winning all major awards for the season, including the Tony for Best Musical (8 Tonys in all). Set in the early 1960s the musical focuses on Baltimore's Tracy Turnblad (Marissa Jaret Winokur), a big girl with big hair whose one passion is to dance, which she does on a local TV dance show; overnight she is transformed from an overweight outsider to a teen celeb. Harvey Fierstein as Tracy's mother, Edna (played in the film by male performer Divine) almost stole the show (see female/male impersonation). In 2006 a production opened at the Luxor in Las Vegas. Lacking the brazenness of the film – and with little social sensibility – some felt, as did Margo Jefferson, that the musical slights the "sound of race music" and was too "Up With People" ingratiating.   DBW

Hairy Ape, The Eugene O'Neill's final production for the original Provincetown Players opened 9 March 1922 under the direction of James Light, with expressionistic designs by Robert Edmond Jones and Cleon Throckmorton, and was subsequently moved to Broadway by Arthur Hopkins. This journey play functions like a nightmare as it follows the quest of Yank (played by Louis Wolheim), a steamship stoker who searches for a place to belong, only to end up crushed in the arms of a zoo gorilla. The play's language is brutal throughout, and often cast in choric, animallike chants in the stoker and jail scenes. Although subtitled "A Comedy of Ancient and Modern Life," the play is the tragic destruction of the brutish, suffering, barely articulate Yank. The impetus for his quest is his encounter with a society woman who insults Yank through her terror of his very appearance. Among the elite on Fifth Avenue, Yank discovers his physical powers drained as he literally bounces off the strolling masked, mechanical socialites – an arresting scene in the first of six O'Neill plays to be produced using masks.   RHW

Hall, Adrian (1928–) Director-playwright. Artistic director of Providence, RI's Trinity Repertory Company, 1964–89, Texas-born Hall has had a rocky career as a pioneer leader of the resident theatre movement and an artist with a strong belief in a director's theatre. Controversies have often clouded his mission to create a permanent ensemble company producing innovative and daring theatre (often with designer Eugene Lee).

At Trinity his fiercely loyal company presented more than 35 American and world premieres, most directed and many adapted from fiction by Hall and his composer-in-residence, Richard Cumming. From 1983 through the '88–9 season he served as artistic director of both Trinity and the DALLAS THEATER CENTER, a first for an American director. Since then he has freelanced at such theatres as San Diego's OLD GLOBE, the MARK TAPER FORUM (opening the 1990–1 season with *Hope of the Heart*, his adaptation of works by Robert Penn Warren), the YALE REP (premiere of Joshua Sobol's *Underground*), the AMERICAN REPERTORY THEATRE (where he directed F. MURRAY ABRAHAM in *King Lear* [1991], and *Hedda Gabler* [1992]), and the NEW YORK SHAKESPEARE FESTIVAL (*As You Like It*, summer 1992; *Two Gentleman of Verona*, 1994; *King Lear*, 1996). He was the replacement director for the ill-fated *On the Waterfront* (Broadway, 1995). In recent years he has revisited earlier projects from his Trinity days, expanding *All the King's Men* at the University of Delaware in 2003 (where he has taught) and writing a revision of his adaptation of killer Jack Abbott's *In the Belly of the Beast* (29th Street Rep, NYC, 2004). A biography by Jeannie Woods was published in 1993.   DBW

Hallams, The A family of English actors and the first substantially documented company of professional players to appear on the North American continent. Hallams had apparently been in the English theatre from 1707, one being killed by Charles Macklin in a Green Room brawl at Drury Lane in 1735. By 1750 **William Hallam** (d. 1758) had suffered serious financial reverses while managing Goodman's Fields, but creditors allowed him to try to raise his shortages. He therefore sent an advance AGENT, Robert Upton, across the Atlantic with considerable money to investigate theatrical conditions and potentials. Hallam never heard again from Upton, who joined the MURRAY–KEAN company, took charge of the company, headed an engagement in New York in 1751, and then returned to England. The Murray–Kean company soon afterward disappeared.

In the meantime, William Hallam sent his brother, **Lewis Hallam Sr.** (1714–55), Lewis's wife, their three children, and an undistinguished company of 10 to America. (One daughter remained in England, later becoming British actress Mrs. George Mattocks.) After a six-week voyage aboard the *Charming Sally,* the Hallam Company opened in Williamsburg, VA, on 15 September 1752 with *The Merchant of Venice* and *The Anatomist.* They remained in Williamsburg for about 11 months, presenting a repertory comprising SHAKESPEARE,

Rowe, Lillo, Moore, Farquhar, Addison, Cibber, Vanbrugh, Steele, and Gay. They next played New York, opening 17 September 1753 with *The Conscious Lovers.* Although they faced considerable hostility from local Quakers, the company opened a Philadelphia engagement on 15 April 1754 with *The Fair Penitent* and *Miss in Her Teens,* but played only two months. After a three-month engagement in Charleston, the Hallams arrived in Jamaica about January 1755, where they joined forces with a company managed by DAVID DOUGLASS. After the elder Hallam's death, Douglass married **Mrs. Hallam** (?–1773) in 1758, also securing **Lewis Hallam Jr.** (1740–1808) as a leading man.

Mrs. Hallam starred in the AMERICAN COMPANY, as Douglass called his group, being the first actress in New York to play such roles as Juliet, Cordelia, and Jane Shore. Lewis Hallam Jr. remained on the stage for some 50 years, playing almost every significant role in the repertoire of the time. He appeared in Godfrey's *The Prince of Parthia* (1767), the first script by an American to be given a professional production (see INTRODUCTION, §1). After Douglass's death in 1786, the younger Hallam assumed leadership of the American Company with various partners. He retired from management in 1797, but continued to act until his death. His second wife, Miss Tuke, joined the company, but her quarrelsome and intemperate habits caused considerable friction.

Adam Hallam, the younger brother of Lewis Jr., left Jamaica with the company, but his name soon disappeared from the bills. Helen and Nancy Hallam eventually joined the company as well. Important revisions in the lives of the Hallams appear in *Theatre Survey* 41.1 (May 2000).   SMA

Hambleton, T. Edward (1911–2005) Producer, the driving force behind the PHOENIX THEATRE (1953–83); longtime partner to NORRIS HOUGHTON and, for a few seasons, ELLIS RABB (as APA at the Phoenix). During his career he produced or coproduced over 100 productions on and OFF-BROADWAY, including the 1947 American premiere of BRECHT's *Galileo* (directed by the author). Described by those who knew him as patient, serious, passionate, and modest. In 2000 he received a special Tony for Lifetime Achievement.   DBW

Hamblin, Thomas Sowerby (1800–53) Actor-manager who toured the U.S. for five years as an English star before assuming management of New York's BOWERY THEATRE in 1830. He held the lease through the FIRES of 1836, 1838, and 1845, until he died. His controversial private life failed to dim respect for his business ability and charity, and his Bowery in the 1830s and '40s is justly remembered as "the nursery of native talent." Though his own preference was for classics and repertory, they could not survive the popularity of melodrama and stars. His theatre premiered many American character types – stage Negroes, YANKEES, and frontiersmen – and lesser forms of popular entertainment. His patrons were increasingly scorned by the *bon ton* as plebeian, and his active management lessened toward the end of his life as theatrical taste moved literally and figuratively uptown.   RKB

Hammerstein, Arthur (1872–1955) Producer, theatre owner, and lyricist who began as an assistant to his father, OSCAR HAMMERSTEIN I, before producing on his own. Starting with *The Firefly* in 1912, he presented a number of successful operettas, including *High Jinks* (1913), *Wildflower* (1923), *ROSE-MARIE* (1924), *Song of the Flame* (1925), and *Sweet Adeline* (1929). As a producer, he was noted for his lavishness and attention to detail. In 1927 he opened Hammerstein's Theatre, which he was forced to give up after the 1930–1 season. Hammerstein was also a songwriter who contributed lyrics to two songs in *Somebody's Sweetheart* (1918).   MK

Hammerstein, Oscar, I (1847–1919) Impresario, theatre owner, producer. After emigrating to America from Prussia, he worked in a cigar factory. Money from his many patents for improvements in cigar manufacturing enabled him to indulge his passion for opera and theatre. He built a number of playhouses, including the Manhattan Opera House, where his operatic productions were so successful that he was bought out by the Metropolitan Opera, and the OLYMPIA Theatre, whose location north of the established theatre district earned him the nickname "The Father of Times Square." In 1899 Hammerstein opened the Victoria Theatre as a legitimate playhouse, but had to switch to VAUDEVILLE when the Theatrical SYNDICATE lured away legitimate attractions. During 1904–15 Hammerstein's Victoria, under the management of Hammerstein's son Willie (father of Oscar's namesake), was the top vaudeville house in the country. Vincent Sheean wrote a biography of Hammerstein I in 1956.   MK

Hammerstein, Oscar, II (1895–1960) Lyricist and librettist. Born into a theatrical family, Oscar Hammerstein II began his career as a lyricist while a student at Columbia University. In the early 1920s he wrote lyrics for four shows with music by Herbert Stothart and two shows composed by VINCENT YOUMANS. His first big success came with the lyrics for *ROSE-MARIE* (1924), an operetta with music by RUDOLF FRIML. Among other shows of the 1920s for which Hammerstein provided lyrics were *Sunny* (1925) and *The DESERT SONG* (1926). In 1927 Hammerstein wrote both the lyrics and the libretto for the era's most ambitious musical, *SHOW BOAT,* which had a score by JEROME KERN. After writing several other musicals with Kern, Hammerstein teamed up with composer RICHARD RODGERS in 1943 to create one of the most influential of all American musicals, *OKLAHOMA!* This collaboration continued through the 1940s and '50s, resulting in *CAROUSEL* (1945), *SOUTH PACIFIC* (1949), *The KING AND I* (1951), *Flower Drum Song* (1958), and *The SOUND OF MUSIC* (1959).

Although Hammerstein's lyrics have sometimes been criticized for their sentimentality, he is generally credited with making major innovations in the form and subject matter of the American musical through his contributions to *Show Boat* and his later musicals with Richard Rodgers. Hugh Fordin's 1977 biography remains useful.   MK

Hammond, (Hunter) Percy (1873–1936) Drama critic. Born in Cadiz, OH, and educated at Franklin College (1892–6), Hammond began as a reporter and then drama critic for the *Chicago Evening Post* (1898–1908), later serving as theatre critic for the *Chicago Tribune* (1908–21). In 1921 he began a 15-year career as critic for the *New York Tribune*, establishing his reputation as a master of irony and urbane humor. He wrote of the producer AL WOODS: "The anguish which Mr. Woods experiences when he does a thing like *Gertie's Garter* . . . is assuaged by the knowledge that with its stupendous profits he may speculate in the precarious investments of the worthier drama" (1921). Franklin P. Adams and others authored a collection of essays on Hammond in 1936.   TLM

Hampden (Dougherty), Walter (1879–1955) Actor who, though American born, began his career learning the classical repertory and the grand-manner acting style in the British company of F. R. Benson during 1901–4. After playing leading and supporting roles in London and the provinces, he came to the U.S. in 1907 in support of ALLA NAZIMOVA in her repertory of IBSEN and other modern plays. Always more successful in poetic and romantic roles, his desire to act in *Hamlet* and similar plays was not realized until he was able to assume the financial risks for their presentation in 1918. In the 1920s and '30s he brought SHAKESPEARE's plays to appreciative audiences in many American cities. In 1923, he added Rostand's *Cyrano de Bergerac* to his repertory and played the dauntless hero more than 1,000 times in 15 years. From 1925 to 1930 he leased his own theatre, adding the title character from Bulwer-Lytton's *Richelieu* to his repertory in 1929. An active performer for most of his life, Hampden played Cardinal Wolsey in the AMERICAN REPERTORY THEATRE production of *Henry VIII* in 1946 and Danforth in ARTHUR MILLER's *Crucible* in 1953.   MR

Handman, Wynn (1922–) Director and acting teacher, born in New York City and educated at City College, CUNY (B.A., 1942), and Columbia University (M.A., 1949). He served in the Navy in WWII, then, before entering graduate school, studied at the NEIGHBORHOOD PLAYHOUSE under SANFORD MEISNER, who became his mentor. In 1963 he cofounded the not-for-profit AMERICAN PLACE THEATRE, dedicated to new American playwrights, where he remained as artistic director until 2002, when he lost his lease to his long-time space. During his last years there he developed a personal specialty nurturing solo performers and raconteurs. In May 1995 he adapted and directed *Coming Through,* a drama concerned with immigrants arriving on Ellis Island. For achievement in nontraditional casting, Handman and his company received the 1994 Rosetta LeNoire Award from ACTORS' EQUITY.   CLJ

Hanlon-Lees Six English-born brothers (sons of Manchester, England, Theatre Royal manager Tom Hanlon), aerialists, and knockabout comedians who introduced a new style of stage farce. **Thomas** (1833–68), **George** (1835–1926), **William** (1834–1923), **Alfred** (1842–86), **Edward** (1845–1931), and **Frederick** (adopted; 1848–86) took the name of Lees in honor of their trainer, carpet acrobat John Lees (d. 1856). After touring Europe as children, they created a sensation at NIBLO's GARDEN (New York, 1860) with their daring trapeze act, and visited both Americas and Europe (1862–6). Thereafter the troupe split up, forming two troupes, but reconsolidated in 1868. Their *Le Voyage en Suisse* (1879), a farce comedy enlivened with mechanical stunts, played Paris, London, and New York (Park Theatre, 1881). William and Edward settled in Massachusetts, where, in their studio, they developed and promoted the comic extravaganzas *Fantasma* (1884) and *Superba* (1890), briefly reviving U.S. spectacular pantoMIME. A tentative biography of the brothers by John A. McKinven was published in 1998.   LS

Hansberry, Lorraine (1930–65) AFRICAN AMERICAN playwright. Born into a comfortable middle-class home but surrounded by poverty in Chicago's South Side, Hansberry early confronted the plight of black families living in ghetto conditions that formed the background for her landmark drama, *A RAISIN IN THE SUN* (1959). This first play on Broadway by a black woman had a black director, LLOYD RICHARDS, and predominant black financing. It ran for 530 performances and won the New York Drama Critics' Circle Award. Hansberry's next play, *The Sign in Sidney Brustein's Window* (1964), about uncommitted white intellectuals in Greenwich Village, was not successful. After her early death from cancer, her former husband, Robert Nemiroff, completed and produced two plays from her unfinished manuscripts: *To Be Young, Gifted and Black* (1969, OFF-BROADWAY) and *Les Blancs* (1970). In 1997 a useful guide to Hansberry's life and work was written by Richard M. Leeson.   EGH

Hapgood, Norman (1868–1937) Editor and drama critic. Born in Chicago and educated at Harvard, Hapgood learned his trade as a reporter and editorial writer before serving as drama critic of the *New York Commercial Advertiser* and *The Bookman* from 1897 to 1902. He left criticism to become editor of *Collier's Weekly* (1903–12), *Harper's Weekly* (1913–16), and *Hearst's International Magazine* 1923–5) before turning to politics. He is author of *The Stage in America* (1901).   TLM

Harbach [né Hauerbach]**, Otto** (1873–1963) Lyricist-librettist, educated at Knox College; taught English and worked as a reporter and copywriter before beginning his Broadway career with the lyrics for *Three Twins* (1908). Over the next 30 years he was one of the most prolific writers for the musical stage, with books and/or lyrics to more than 40 musicals. He provided lyrics for several shows with composer RUDOLF FRIML, beginning with *The Firefly* (1912); collaborated with OSCAR HAMMERSTEIN II on lyrics and libretti for 10 shows, notably *ROSE-MARIE* (1924) and *Sunny* (1925); and contributed to shows ranging from the operetta *Madame Sherry* (1910) to the bouncy 1920s musical *Mary* (1920) and *No, No, NANETTE* (1925), to the more innovative JEROME KERN musicals *The Cat and the Fiddle* (1931) and *Roberta* (1933).   MK

Harburg, E(dgar) Y. "Yip" [né Isidore Hochberg] (1898–1981) Lyricist, librettist, and composer who attended City College of New York and wrote for newspapers before contributing lyrics to *Earl*

Carroll's Sketchbook (1929). During the 1930s he wrote lyrics with several different composers, including Jay Gorney, VERNON DUKE, and HAROLD ARLEN; their songs were used in REVUES alongside the work of other writers. He also coauthored librettos and worked on Hollywood films. In 1944 he wrote the score for *Bloomer Girl* with Arlen, and three years later had his greatest success with *FINIAN'S RAINBOW*, for which he also collaborated on the libretto. Among his later musicals were *Jamaica* (1957) and *The Happiest Girl in the World* (1961). Harburg's lyrics often reflected his interest in social issues, as in the 1932 song "Brother, Can You Spare a Dime?" A 1993 biography by Harold Meyerson and Ernie Harburg is recommended. MK

Harby, Isaac (1788–1828) Playwright. A South Carolinian, Harby became a Jewish leader, a teacher, an editor, and the author of three plays. His first, *Alexander Severus* (1805), was rejected by the Charleston Theatre. *The Gordian Knot* (1807), set in 16th-century Florence, was not produced until published in 1810. *Alberti* (1819), his best play, followed political intrigues surrounding the Medici. An important early drama critic, Harby wrote a "defense of the drama" that is still worth reading. WJM

Hardwick, Elizabeth (1916–) Literary and drama critic. Born and educated in Kentucky, Hardwick pursued a career in the 1940s as a novelist and literary critic before writing drama criticism, mainly for the *New York Review of Books* (1963–83), of which she was a founder and advisory editor. In 1967 she won the GEORGE JEAN NATHAN Award, the first woman so honored. In 1974, she reappraised IBSEN's major female characters from a feminist perspective. TLM

Harned, Virginia (1868–1946) Actress, once married to E. H. SOTHERN, whom she divorced. She debuted in *Our Boarding House* at age 16; her New York debut was in *A Lost Lane*. She attracted considerable attention as Drusilla Ives in *That Dancing Girl* and later created the role of Trilby in *Svengali* (1895) for a long run. For several years she managed her own company. SMA

Harnick, Sheldon see BOCK, JERRY

Harper, Joseph (fl. 1790–1800) Comedian with the Old AMERICAN COMPANY; first professional theatre manager in BOSTON by opening his New Exhibition Room 10 August 1792, where initially a variety of paratheatrical amusements were presented, followed soon by plays discreetly advertised as "Moral Lectures." After a performance of *The School for Scandal,* his theatre was closed 5 December 1792; he was arrested, tried for violating the antitheatrical act of 1750, and promptly acquitted. The case, however, led to the eventual rescission of Boston's antitheatre laws. Harper joined CHARLES STUART POWELL in the management of the FEDERAL STREET THEATRE in 1801. PAD

Harrigan, Edward (Ned) (1844–1911) playwright-actor, and **Tony Hart** [né Anthony J. Cannon] (1855–91) actor, became the most popular comedy team on the American stage (1871–85). They sang, danced, and played the principal roles (usually Harrigan as the amiable, fun-loving Irish adventurer Dan Mulligan and Hart, in blackface, as the Negro wench Rebecca Allup) in Harrigan's high-spirited "melees": *The Mulligan Guard Picnic* (1878), *The MULLIGAN GUARD BALL* (1879), *The Mulligan Guard Chowder* (1879), *The Mulligan Guard Christmas* (1879), *The Mulligan Guard Nominee* (1880), *The Mulligan Guard Surprise* (1880), *The Mulligan Guard Silver Wedding* (1881), *Old Lavender* (1877), *The Major* (1881), *Squatter Sovereignty* (1882), *CORDELIA'S ASPIRATIONS* (1883), *Dan's Tribulations* (1884), and *Investigation* (1884). Harrigan's farces were not all "knockdown and slambang"; his documentary explorations of New York's Lower East Side and his striking portraits of the Germans, Italians, Negroes, and particularly the Irish in his 40 plays led WILLIAM DEAN HOWELLS to write, "Here is the spring of a true American comedy, the joyous art of the dramatist who loves the life he observes." Another critic called his plays the "Pickwick Papers of a Bowery Dickens."

Harrigan was born on NYC's Lower East Side and appeared first as an Irish comic singer in San Francisco (1867). In 1871 he met Hart, a falsetto-voiced singer from Worcester, MA, and wrote "The Little Fraud," which alerted Boston to their extraordinary talents. They turned out 60 more sketches, most notable of which was "The Mulligan Guard," a satire on New York's pseudomilitary companies (with music by David Braham, Harrigan's future father-in-law and thereafter his musical collaborator). Their antics drew boisterous crowds to the Theatre Comique (514 Broadway) and then to the New Theatre Comique (728 Broadway).

When the second Comique burned down in 1884 (see FIRES), the partners separated. Hart stumbled in and out of three plays, was committed to an asylum, and died at the age of 35. Harrigan continued writing and acting – *The Leather*

Patch (1886), *McNooney's Visit* (1887), and others – and opened a new Harrigan's Theatre on Herald Square with *Reilly and the Four Hundred* (1890).

Three of his children – "Eddie," William, and Nedda (Mrs. JOSHUA LOGAN) – became actors. Biographies of Ned have been written by E. J. Kahn (1955) and Richard Moody (1980).   RM

Harris, Aurand (1915–96) Author of nearly 60 published children's plays, he experimented with content and form in such plays as *The Arkansas Bear,* which tackled the subject of death, and *Androcles and the Lion.* He was first recipient of the NATIONAL ENDOWMENT FOR THE ARTS Creative Writing Fellowship in CHILDREN'S THEATRE and the second American playwright, after ARTHUR MILLER, to be invited to China to stage a play. In 1997 the New England Theatre Conference created a playwriting award in his name to honor his lifetime dedication to all aspects of professional theatre for young audiences.   MVW

Harris, Jed (1900–79) Producer and director. At the height of the 1920s, Harris presented four plays celebrated for their crisp modern style: *BROADWAY* (1926), a raucous backstage melodrama overrun with wisecracking gangsters and gum-chewing chorines; *Coquette* (1927), a tearjerker about the risks of Flaming Youth; *The ROYAL FAMILY* (1927), a satire about a flamboyant theatrical dynasty modeled on the Barrymores (see DREW–BARRYMORE); and *The FRONT PAGE* (1928), a whirlwind comedy-melodrama set in a newspaper office. Quickly growing bored with his success, Harris was content to rest on his laurels; he worked only sporadically thereafter, most notably on *Uncle Vanya* (1930), a response to critics who complained that he wasted his talents on light entertainment; *The Green Bay Tree* (1933), with Laurence Olivier as a kept homosexual; *OUR TOWN* (1938); and *The Heiress* (1947), based on HENRY JAMES's *Washington Square.* After retiring to San Francisco, he broke silence with two books: *Watchman, What of the Night?* (1963), a crusty and self-justifying account of the backstage warfare on *The Heiress,* and *A Dance on the High Wire* (1979), a curiously muted memoir.

There are two enduring legends about Harris: one, obviously untrue, that he had a golden touch that turned every play he handled into a hit; and the other, which has much greater validity, that he was a monster. Harris directed only a few of his plays (including *Uncle Vanya* and *Our Town*), but all of his productions had superb taste and showmanship, achieved at great cost to his collaborators. GEORGE ABBOTT called him "the Little Napo-

leon of Broadway," and stories of Harris's wild mood swings, withering sarcasm, and cruelty are part of theatrical folklore. Martin Gottfried's biography was published in 1984.   FH

Harris, Julie (1925–) Actress whose Broadway debut was as Atlanta in *It's a Gift* (1945). She rose to stardom with such roles as Frankie Addams in *The MEMBER OF THE WEDDING* (1950); Sally Bowles in *I AM A CAMERA* (1951), for which in 1952 she won the first of her five Best Actress Tony Awards (a record); and Joan in *The Lark* (1955; 1956 Tony), performances she later filmed (*Lark* for TV). In 1976 she successfully performed a ONE-PERSON show, WILLIAM LUCE's *The Belle of Amherst* (her fifth Tony), directed by Charles Nelson Reilly, subsequently touring the show and playing a season at the Phoenix, London. Critics have been won over by her air of vulnerability and fragility, coupled with remarkable stage techniques. Her Emily Dickinson in *Belle* – one of numerous women she has portrayed culled from history – was called "astonishing in its sagacity and passion . . . shining." She also received a Tony in 1969 for Jay Presson Allen's *Forty Carats* and in 1972 for *The Last of Mrs. Lincoln.* In 1980 she played the lead in *On Golden Pond* on the West Coast, and in 1989 toured in *DRIVING MISS DAISY* and in 1992–3 in *Lettice & Lovage.* She appeared as Isak Dinesen in the one-woman play *Lucifer's Child* (1991), in Timothy Mason's *The Fiery Furnace* for CIRCLE REP (fall 1993), in a 50th-anniversary production of *The GLASS MENAGERIE* at New York's ROUNDABOUT THEATRE, and a revival of *The GIN GAME* (1997). Harris has also won many awards during her illustrious career in film, stage, and television, including the 1993 Common Wealth Award for the Arts (a Delaware-based prize of $25,000); a special tribute as a leading artist in 1995 from Washington, DC's HELEN HAYES Awards; the 1994 National Medal of Arts; and in 2005 a Career Achievement Award from Drama Desk and a Kennedy Center Honors. She is the author of an acclaimed and partially autobiographical text for beginning performers, *Julie Harris Talks to Young Actors* (1972). Today her home is on Cape Cod and her activities have been curtailed – but certainly not stopped – by illness in recent years.   SMA   DBW

Harris, Rosemary [Ann] (1930–) British-born actress who has appeared in over 150 roles in more than 55 years on the English and American stage, including affiliations with some of the great theatre companies (in England the Bristol Old Vic, Old Vic, the Royal National Theatre, Chichester Festival; in the U.S. the ASSOCIATION OF

Producing Artists, Lincoln Center, Brooklyn Academy of Music, American Shakespeare Theatre, and Williamstown Theatre
Festival). A versatile actress, who once described
herself as "a chameleon on a tartan" and was
described in the *New York Times* as "pure presence,"
she has appeared prominently in *Troilus and Cressida* (Tyrone Guthrie's 1956 production), *Man
and Superman, Much Ado about Nothing, The School for
Scandal, The Seagull, Twelfth Night, The Broken Heart*
(first Chichester season, 1952), *Hamlet* (Ophelia in
National Theatre's inaugural season), *The Lion in
Winter* (1966; Tony, Best Actress in a Play), *Old
Times, Major Barbara, A Streetcar Named Desire*
(1973 revival, Vivian Beaumont), *The Royal Family, All My Sons* (1981 London revival), *Pack of Lies,*
the Broadway revival of *Hay Fever* (1985–6 season),
The Best of Friends (London, 1988; with John Gielgud), *Lost in Yonkers* (grandmother, Broadway
replacement, 1991; London, 1992–3), *An Inspector Calls* (London and New York, 1994), *Women of
Troy* (Hecuba, at RNT, London, 1995), *Waiting in the
Wings* (1999, with Lauren Bacall), Albee's *All Over*
at Roundabout (2002), and, in 2005, a comic turn
in Ariel Dorfman's *The Other Side* (Manhattan
Theatre Club). Her daughter is award-winning
actress **Jennifer Ehle** (Best Actress Tony in 2000
revival of *The Real Thing*).   DBW

Harris, Sam H(enry) (1872–1941) Producer who
began his theatrical career in 1899 as a stagehand. The following year he became a partner in
the firm of Sullivan, Harris and Woods (1900–
4), which produced eight melodramas and burlesques including a hit, *The Fatal Wedding*. He
began a 16-year partnership with George M.
Cohan in 1904, producing more than 50 plays,
including Cohan's own *Little Johnny Jones,
Forty-five Minutes from Broadway,* and *Seven
Keys to Baldpate*. After the partnership was dissolved in 1920, Harris independently produced
Rain (1922), *The Jazz Singer* (1925), *Animal Crackers* (1928), *Dinner at Eight* (1932), *The Man Who
Came to Dinner* (1939), and *Lady in the Dark*
(1941). His productions of *Icebound* (1923), *Of
Thee I Sing* (1932), and *You Can't Take It with
You* (1936) won Pulitzer Prizes; and *Of Mice and
Men* won the 1938 New York Critics' Circle Award.
He preferred comedies and musical comedies to
serious drama, and was noted for paying atten-
tion to the smallest details of a production.   TLM

Harris, William, Sr. (1844–1916), **Henry B.** (1866–
1912), and **William Jr.** (1884–1946) Producers.
William Sr. attained success as a manager and
producer in Boston before joining Marc Klaw,

Abe Erlanger, Charles Frohman, and others
in establishing the Theatrical Syndicate (1895–
6). His older son, Henry, managed the careers of
stars including Amelia Bingham (1902), became
the manager of the Hudson Theatre (1903), and
produced such hits as *Soldiers of Fortune* (1902), *The
Lion and the Mouse* (1905), *The Chorus Lady* (1906),
The Traveling Salesman (1908), and *The Third Degree*
(1909), before going down with the Titanic. His
younger son, William Jr., attended Columbia University, then became a successful producer and
later a director, presenting *Yellow Jacket* (1912),
Twin Beds (1914), *The Thirteenth Chair* (1916), *East Is
West* (1918), *Abraham Lincoln* (1919), *Outward Bound*
(1924), and *The Greeks Had a Word for It* (1930).
TLM

Harrison, Rex [né Reginald Carey] (1908–90) British actor, knighted in 1989, active on both sides
of the Atlantic. Underrated, despite considerable
interpretative skills, he was described by Richard Coe as "Smooth as a pearl, prickly as a por-
cupine." He began his professional career at Liverpool Playhouse in 1924, and arrived in London in
1930, where during a long career he appeared not
only in the comedies of Coward, Rattigan, and
Van Druten, but also in less obvious parts for an
actor of his typecasting: the Uninvited Guest in
Eliot's *The Cocktail Party* (1950), Henry IV in Pirandello's play (1973, NYC; 1974, London), among
others. This debonair star, the quintessential
Henry Higgins in the musical version of Shaw's
Pygmalion, My Fair Lady, his Tony Award–winning
role of 1956 (revived in 1981), appeared frequently
in New York during his 66 years on the stage.
From his Broadway debut in 1936 to his final
role, Lord Porteous in *The Circle* (1989), Harrison
appeared most notably as Henry VIII in *Anne of the
Thousand Days* (1948; Tony), Shepherd Henderson
in *Bell, Book and Candle* (1950), The Man in *The Love
of Four Colonels* (1953), Caesar in Shaw's *Caesar and
Cleopatra* (1977), and Shotover in *Heartbreak House*
(1983). He wrote two autobiographies: *Rex* (1974)
and *A Damned Serious Business: My Life in Comedy*
(1991). A new edition of his biography by Patrick
Garland was published in 2004.   DBW

Harrison, Richard B. (1864–1935) Son of fugitive
slaves, Harrison graduated from the Detroit
School of Art and began to give public readings
throughout the country. He appeared briefly at
the Lafayette Theatre, where he was spotted
for the awesome role of De Lawd in the all-black
production of *The Green Pastures* (1930). Harrison was brilliant, and the production (including
touring) ran for five years. He received many hon-

ors, including the prestigious Spingarn Medal awarded annually by the NAACP. An in-depth study (by W. C. Daniel) of Harrison and his most famous production was published in 1986.   EGH

Hart, Lorenz (1895–1943) Lyricist and librettist. His first theatrical assignment was as a play translator for the Shuberts. In collaboration with Richard Rodgers, who was to be his partner for the rest of his career, Hart contributed four songs to the Broadway musical comedy *Poor Little Ritz Girl* (1920). The first complete scores by Rodgers and Hart were for *The Garrick Gaieties* (1925) and *Dearest Enemy* (1925). In the next 18 years they created an almost uninterrupted string of successful shows, including *The Girl Friend* (1926), *A Connecticut Yankee* (1927; revival 1943), *America's Sweetheart* (1931), *On Your Toes* (1936), *Babes in Arms* (1937), *The Boys from Syracuse* (1938), *I Married an Angel* (1938), *Pal Joey* (1940), and *By Jupiter* (1941). Hart's clever, sometimes sardonic lyrics, often employing complicated internal rhyme schemes, are considered among the finest ever written for the musical stage. His most recent biography was written by Frederick Nolan (1994).   MK

Hart, Moss (1904–61) Playwright, librettist, and director. Although he had written several unsuccessful plays on his own, it was Hart's teaming up with George S. Kaufman during the 1930s that established his career. These two wits delighted American audiences with such hits as *Once in a Lifetime* (1930), *You Can't Take It with You* (1936; Pulitzer Prize), and *The Man Who Came to Dinner* (1939). On his own in the '40s, Hart wrote, among other offerings, the book for the landmark musical about psychoanalysis, *Lady in the Dark* (1941), and the funny theatre in-joke about a play in rehearsal, *Light up the Sky* (1948). Hart devoted much of the latter decade of his career to directing, winning the Tony Award for his work on *My Fair Lady* (1956). His autobiography, *Act One* (1959), is a classic theatrical memoir; recent biographies are those by Steven Bach (2001) and Jared Brown (2006).   LDC

Hart, Tony see Harrigan, Edward

Harte, Bret (Francis Brett Harte) (1836–1902) Writer. Raised in Brooklyn, he moved to California in 1853 and became famous for stories and poems in *The Overland Monthly* (1868–71). His popularity declined as rapidly as it rose, and after 1878 he lived abroad. His best work combines sentiment and low humor in the manner of Charles Dickens. He wrote *Two Men of Sandy Bar* (1875) for Stuart Robson, and collaborated with Mark Twain on *Ah Sin* (1877), a vehicle for Charles Parsloe. Though both failed, they established a genre that Bartley Campbell perfected in *My Partner*. Biographies were written by Pemberton (1903) and Stewart (1931).   DMcD

Hartford Stage Company Since founding director Jacques Cartier opened the not-for-profit company in an abandoned supermarket warehouse in 1964, the Hartford Stage, located in the capital of Connecticut, has developed into a first-rate regional theatre with a playhouse designed by postmodernist architect Robert Venturi. Cartier was succeeded as artistic director first by Paul Weidner in 1968, then by Mark Lamos in 1980. In January 1998 Michael Wilson took the helm.

Initially a traditional company mounting old and modern standards, the Hartford now devotes about half of its season to new or recent American plays and dramatizations of nontheatrical works. Lamos revealed a special gift for large-scale productions of epics, such as Shakespeare's history plays. His costaging with Mary B. Robinson of *The Greeks* (1982), Kenneth Cavender's seven-hour cycle of Greek tragedies, earned the theatre wide acclaim, as did his stagings of *Martin Guerre,* a musical (early 1993) based on the screenplay, and *The Merchant of Venice* (late 1993). Wilson launched the Tennessee Williams Marathon (15 plays to date) and the annual Brand:NEW festival. As of 2005 more than 260 new productions have been seen at HS, including 9 by Albee, 22 by Shakespeare (see Shakespeare on . . .), and 55 world or U.S. premieres. Hartford has received many awards, including the Margo Jones Award and a Tony for Outstanding Regional Theatre.   CLJ DBW

Harvey One of the most successful plays in Broadway history. Written by Mary Coyle Chase, it opened at the 48th Street Theatre on 1 November 1944, ran for 1,775 performances, and won the Pulitzer Prize for 1945. Frank Fay starred as Elwood P. Dowd, an inebriated, sweet-tempered, but dotty soul, who sees and communicates with an over-6´-tall, invisible rabbit named Harvey. In 1950 Universal Studios released a very successful film version starring James Stewart, who had been a replacement Dowd on Broadway. A 1995 London revival with Gorden Kaye and Rue McClanahan was scheduled to transfer to New York but did not.   FB

Harwood, John Edmund (1771–1809) British-born comic actor who was brought to the Chest-

NUT STREET THEATRE by THOMAS WIGNELL in 1793, remaining in Philadelphia until engaged by WILLIAM DUNLAP for the PARK in New York in 1803, where he acted until his death. Among his better roles was Falstaff, which he played first in 1806 opposite the Hotspur of THOMAS A. COOPER. Dunlap, who called him a man of wit and refinement and highly endowed as an actor, but indolent and careless of study, and compared him to the British actor John Bannister. He married a granddaughter of Benjamin Franklin and fathered Admiral Andrew Allen Harwood.   DBW

Hatful of Rain, A Drama by Michael V. Gazzo on the effects of a young man's drug addiction on his lower-middle-class family. The play opened at the LYCEUM THEATRE on 9 November 1955 and ran for 389 performances. Frank Corsaro directed, and the cast featured Ben Gazzara, Shelley Winters, and Anthony Franciosa – all veterans of the ACTORS STUDIO and acting teacher LEE STRASBERG. Steve McQueen, also a Strasberg student, made his Broadway debut when he replaced Gazzara during the run. The anguished, emotional tone of the play epitomized the "kitchen sink" naturalism that was a characteristic element of American theatre of the 1950s.   MF

Haverly, (Christopher) Col. Jack H. (1837–1901) Variety manager. Apprenticed as a shoemaker, he ran away from his home in rural Pennsylvania to Pittsburgh, where he became associated with theatres as doorkeeper, box-office clerk, and treasurer. Organizing his first MINSTREL SHOW company in 1862, he bought his first theatre two years later (Toledo, OH). Part owner and manager of Emerson's Minstrels (1875) and Callender's Colored Minstrels (1878), he was identified with Haverly's Mastodon Minstrels (1878–84). He also leased strategically located theatres in CHICAGO, New York, PHILADELPHIA, and SAN FRANCISCO for his companies to play in. Business speculation bankrupted him in 1898.   DMcD

Havlin, John see STAIR AND HAVLIN

Havoc [née Hovick]**, June** (1914?–) Actor, director, playwright. Havoc's acting career started at age 2 and continued through VAUDEVILLE (with sister GYPSY ROSE LEE), dance marathons, Broadway, Hollywood, major regional theatres, and international tours for over 65 years. Her musical plays are autobiographical: *Marathon 33* (1963), *Love Regatta* (1971), *I Said the Fly* (1973), and *Oh Glorious Tintinnabulation* (1974). In 1995 she starred in Mayo Simon's *The Old Lady's Guide to Survival* at

NYC's Lamb's. She was artistic director of New Repertory Theatre in New Orleans (1969–71) and wrote two autobiographies. In 2003 New York's Abingdon Theatre Company named its new 98-seat theatre (312 West 36th St.) after her.   TH-S

Haydon, Julie [née Donella Lightfoot Donaldson] (1910–94) Actress whose ethereal quality enhanced a handful of outstanding roles: Brigid in *Shadow and Substance* (1938), Kitty Duval in *The TIME OF YOUR LIFE* (1939), and Laura in *The GLASS MENAGERIE* (1944, Chicago; 1945, New York), the latter two roles originated by her. In the 1960s and '70s she performed Amanda in *Glass Menagerie* at various colleges. A champion of her late husband, GEORGE JEAN NATHAN, she presented readings from his works.   DBW

Hayes [née Brown]**, Helen** (1900–93) Actress. Like KATHARINE CORNELL and LYNN FONTANNE, Hayes was often called "the First Lady of the American Theater." Diminutive and homespun, she was distinctly less glamorous than the other Great Ladies; and the qualities of modesty and common sense that she projected helped account for her enduring appeal. A stage star for over 50 years (she retired in 1971), she continued to act occasionally in films and on television, and for a time hosted a radio program addressed to senior citizens.

As a youngster she appeared with JOHN DREW and WILLIAM GILLETTE, and worked for such fabled producers as CHARLES FROHMAN and GEORGE TYLER. Opposite ALFRED LUNT in BOOTH TARKINGTON's *Clarence* (1919), she played a saucy flapper, as she did again in the THEATRE GUILD's *Caesar and Cleopatra* (1925) and *Coquette* (1927). In the 1930s, she had her greatest critical success as the gallant monarchs in *Mary of Scotland* (1933) and *Victoria Regina* (1935). In the 1940s and '50s she starred in showy vehicles like *Harriet* (1943), an episodic biography of Harriet Beecher Stowe; *Happy Birthday* (1946), in which she was a librarian turned siren; and *Mrs. McThing* (1952), in which she was a society matron transformed into a scrubwoman. Her West End debut came in 1948 (Amanda in *The GLASS MENAGERIE*). In her most memorable later work, the PHOENIX THEATRE's 1967 revival of GEORGE KELLY's *The SHOW-OFF*, she played no-nonsense mother-in-law Mrs. Fisher with bracing tartness.

Often criticized for her choice of material and for being cloyingly demure, Hayes was more resourceful, modern, and witty than her reputation generally allowed. She had a remarkably clear, low-pitched, resonant voice, and none of

CLEOPATRA   MARY OF SCOTLAND

Helen Hayes as Cleopatra, Mary of Scotland, and, center, Victoria. *Courtesy:* Don B. Wilmeth Theatre Collection.

the hamminess that flawed the star acting of the tradition she grew up in. She was the author of several memoirs, most notably *My Life in Three Acts* (1990) with Katherine Hatch. Two NYC playhouses have been named the HELEN HAYES THEATRE. The major theatre awards given in Washington, DC, her birthplace, are named after her. Her most recent biography is by Kenneth Barrow (1985), although a bio-bibliography by Murphy and Moore (1993) is useful.   FH

Hays, David (1930–) Set and lighting designer and producer. Hays founded the NATIONAL THEATRE OF THE DEAF and is a cofounder of the EUGENE O'NEILL MEMORIAL THEATRE CENTER. His designs include LONG DAY'S JOURNEY INTO NIGHT (1956), *All the Way Home* (1960), and *No Strings* (1962). Many of his earlier sets show the influence of the poetic realism that dominated the 1950s.   AA

Hayward, Leland (1902–71) Producer responsible for two dozen plays and musicals on Broadway between 1941 and his death, two-thirds of which were unqualified successes both critically and financially. Two of his productions (STATE OF THE UNION, 1945; SOUTH PACIFIC, 1949) won Pulitzer Prizes. Prior to becoming a producer in 1944 with *A Bell for Adano,* Hayward had established a successful talent agency in Hollywood and New York. Other significant plays produced included MISTER ROBERTS (1948), *Anne of the Thousand Days* (1948), CALL ME MADAM (1950), GYPSY (1959), *The SOUND OF MUSIC* (1959), and *The Trial of the Catonsville Nine* (1971). Hayward was also a film and television producer, a pilot and airline executive, and a photographer. In 1936 he married the actress Margaret Sullavan, divorcing in 1948. OLIVER SMITH said that Hayward represented everything that was best in the theatre, being "tenacious and at the same time elegant." A biography by S. Berman appeared in 1995.   DBW

Hazel Kirke This domestic melodrama by STEELE MACKAYE, one of the first of its kind without a villain, enjoyed enormous popularity throughout the country for 30 years after its premiere. Opening at the MADISON SQUARE THEATRE in 1880, the play by 1882 was being presented by 14 road companies. The melodrama traces the breakdown and eventual replacement of patriarchal family relations with Victorian ones, as a stern Scottish father, Dunstan Kirke, learns to accept the love and independence of his daughter Hazel. At the

319

climax of the play, the blinded father is unable to rescue his daughter from an attempted suicide. CHARLES W. COULDOCK and EFFIE ELLSLER played the father and daughter in MacKaye's original production, and both continued these roles on the road, Ellsler later forming her own company and performing Hazel through 1905. GEORGIA CAYVAN, ANNIE RUSSELL, and Phoebe Davis also played Hazel during their careers.   BMcC

He and She First produced in Boston in 1912 under the title *The Herfords,* this play by RACHEL CROTHERS opened on 12 February 1920 at the Little Theatre in New York. Crothers herself played the lead role, Ann Herford, a sculptor who at the end of the play refuses a $100,000 prize she has won in a competition in order to devote herself to her family (since her husband Tom wins second, he will be the winner). Although the play ran for only 28 performances, it was generally praised by critics for dealing forcefully with the issues of a double standard of success and of a woman's role in marriage and in society. ALEXANDER WOOLLCOTT called it a tragedy, "for something fine and strong dies in the last act."   FB

Headley, Heather (1974–) Trinidad-born actress-singer and a graduate of Northwestern University whose Broadway credits include RAGTIME (1996) and *The* LION KING (1997). She was also in CITY CENTER'S ENCORE! staging of *Do Re Mi* (1999). But it was her Tony-winning appearance in Elton John and Tim Rice's *Aida* (2000) that established her reputation for both a striking stage presence and a versatile vocal style.   DBW

Hearn, George (1934–) Actor-singer, equally at home in musicals and classical drama. Hearn attended Southwestern College, then worked for several seasons at the NEW YORK SHAKESPEARE FESTIVAL. He had a featured role in *1776* (1969), and appeared in David Storey's *The Changing Room* and the political comedy *An Almost Perfect Person* (1977) before replacing LEN CARIOU in the title role of SWEENEY TODD (1979). He starred in the musicals I REMEMBER MAMA (1979) and *A Doll's Life* (1982), won a Best Actor Tony for his portrayal of Albin in LA CAGE AUX FOLLES (1983), portrayed the father in *Meet Me in St. Louis* (1989), won a 1995 Tony (Featured Actor) as Norma Desmond's butler and keeper in *Sunset Boulevard* (1994), played Otto Frank in *The* DIARY OF ANNE FRANK (1997 revival), and appeared in the SONDHEIM revue *Putting It Together* (1999). After several years of self-imposed retirement, he returned to Broadway in 2004 as the Wizard in WICKED.   MK

Hecht, Ben (1894–1964) Although a significant figure in American cinema, Hecht is important theatrically for two popular and frequently revived American plays, both collaborations with CHARLES MACARTHUR. Together the playwrights were viewed as bad boys of Broadway. *The* FRONT PAGE, a frenetic, funny, satirical melodrama on the newspaper business (1928), is based on the playwrights' experiences as reporters in Chicago. *Twentieth Century* (1932), an eccentric comedy depicting a desperate producer trying to make a comeback, inspired a John Barrymore (see DREW–BARRYMORE) film and the musical *On the Twentieth Century*. Hecht wrote other plays and musical librettos as early as 1916 and as late as 1953. His autobiography, *A Child of the Century,* appeared in 1954, and a biography by W. MacAdams in 1990.   RHW

Hecht, Jessica (1965–) Born in Princeton, NJ, and trained at NYU (B.F.A., Tisch), this unique actress (described by BRANTLEY as evoking "the professionally neurotic Sandy Dennis crossed with Chelsea Clinton before she acquired poise") has appeared on Broadway as Lala Levy in *Last Night of Ballyhoo* (1997), Louise in AFTER THE FALL (ROUNDABOUT, 2004), and Portia in *Julius Caesar* (2005). Other stage roles include *Plunge* (1997), *Stop Kiss* (1998), and *Lobster Alice* (1999), all OFF-BROADWAY. Though much of her work has been Off-Broadway or in the regions, she is best known as the lesbian lover of the ex-wife of Ross on the sitcom *Friends*.   DBW

Heckart, (Anne) Eileen (1919–2001) Ohio-born stage, film, and television character actress who made her Broadway debut (as understudy) in the long-running *Voice of the Turtle* (1943). She played many important supporting roles before essaying the title role in *Everybody Loves Opal* (1963). Her performance as Mrs. Baker, the overprotective mother, in *Butterflies Are Free* (1969; film, 1972) garnered a Tony nomination and an Oscar for Best Supporting Actress. She played Eleanor Roosevelt on a tour of U.S. cities in *Eleanor* (1976). Regional roles include Mother Courage at the MCCARTER THEATRE (1973), Thelma Cates in 'NIGHT MOTHER at Westport Country Playhouse (1985), and the title character in DRIVING MISS DAISY at the COCONUT GROVE PLAYHOUSE (1991), directed by her son, Luke Yankee (who in 2006 published a memoir of his mother). In 1995 she appeared in the CBS-TV series *The 5 Mrs. Buchanans*. She returned to the stage in fall 1995 in *Northeast Local* (LINCOLN CENTER) followed in 2000 by one of her most acclaimed roles (and her last) in KENNETH LONER-

GAN's *The Waverly Gallery* (Promenade Theatre) as an art-gallery owner stricken with Alzheimer's. That year she received not only Drama Desk, Lucille Lortel, and Obie awards for this role but also a special Tony for career achievement.   MR

Hedgerow Theatre Founded in 1923 in Moylan-Rose Valley, PA, by Jasper Deeter, this theatre was for many years the only true U.S. professional repertory theatre, operating year-round with no stars and frequent changes of bill. Although the repertory scheme was dropped in 1956, by 1985 the theatre had amassed a repertory of over 200 plays. Standard plays, with those of G. B. SHAW most popular, have dominated. Functioning as a cooperative, the theatre operated in a small converted mill with fewer than 170 seats; in late 1985 the playhouse was gutted by a FIRE but was quickly rebuilt, reopening December 1990.   DBW

Hedwig and the Angry Inch Long-running (857 performances) 1998 OFF-BROADWAY (Jane Street Theatre) transsexual rock musical with book by JOHN CAMERON MITCHELL (who played the title role) and music and lyrics by Stephen Trask. This Obie-winning surprise hit is a *Hansel and Gretel* in which a brother and sister are one and the same person – i.e., Hansel is Gretel (or rather Hedwig) and vice versa. Events begin in East Berlin and move to the U.S. after a G.I. urges Hansel to have sex-reassignment surgery, which is botched, leaving the angry inch of mutilated flesh. Ultimately Hedwig forms a rock band called Hedwig and the Angry Inch. In real life, Mitchell and Trask created Hedwig and the band at NYC's gay rock 'n' roll nightclub Squeezebox. Numerous complications explore the fluidity of gender without moralizing or providing easy answers. A 2001 film has achieved cult status, with Mitchell re-creating his stage role, and has inspired numerous productions around the world.   DBW

Heidi Chronicles, The, by WENDY WASSERSTEIN, opened OFF-BROADWAY at PLAYWRIGHTS HORIZONS on 18 November 1988 and transferred to Broadway's PLYMOUTH THEATRE 9 March 1989, closing 1 September 1990. Dramatizing key moments in the life of the title character as she searches for self-actualization from the mid-1960s through the late '80s, it is a satirical yet compassionate portrait of an era and of the dreams, frustrations, failures, and triumphs experienced by many middle-class American women of the time. Reproved by some FEMINIST critics as "antifeminist" in its treatment of women and the feminist cause, it was nevertheless a resounding critical

and popular success, winning numerous awards, including a Pulitzer Prize.   DJW

Heilpern, John (1942?–) British-born, Oxford-educated (law) critic and author. Prior to 1980, when he moved to New York and subsequently became theatre critic for the *New York Observer,* Heilpern was a journalist for *The Observer* in London, where he wrote important profiles of Ralph Richardson, John Gielgud, and Rudolf Nureyev, among others. He worked at the National Theatre as dramaturge on Peter Hall's *Tamburlaine* (1976); that same year his now classic book *Conference of the Birds,* which details the journey of Peter Brook and a group of actors across the desert of Northwest Africa as they developed a theatrical form not dependant on cultural assumptions, was published. His *How Good Is* DAVID MAMET?, a collection of 70 of his theatre essays, appeared in 1999, and his authorized biography of John Osborne in 2007. As a critic he has been a champion of native (i.e., U.S.) theatre work and has proven himself a literate, witty, thoughtful, and sometimes passionate evaluator of American theatre.   DBW

Helburn, Theresa (1887–1959) Director and producer. Born in New York, Helburn received her B.A. from Bryn Mawr in 1908, attended GEORGE PIERCE BAKER's English 47 at Radcliffe, and studied in Paris for a year at the Sorbonne. After a brief career as an actress, she pursued a writing career, becoming drama critic of *The Nation* (1918). Two years later she took over the administration of the struggling THEATRE GUILD with the title of executive director. In 1933 she left for a year in Hollywood but returned as administrative director with LAWRENCE LANGNER. She was responsible for bringing ALFRED LUNT and LYNN FONTANNE together for *The Guardsman* in 1924, which established them as the leading dual acting team in America. With Langner she brought OKLAHOMA! to the stage in 1943, and in the same year *Othello* with PAUL ROBESON. A woman of outstanding executive ability, she was described by Langner as possessing nerves "like whipcord" and willpower "like steel." Her autobiography, *A Wayward Quest,* was published in 1960.   TLM

Held, Anna (1873–1918) Entertainer. Born in Paris of Polish–French parentage, petite Held was discovered in London in 1895 by FLORENZ ZIEGFELD, who married her in 1897 (divorced in 1912) and became her producer-publicist, circulating extravagant stories of bizarre behavior. As star of New York musical shows such as *Papa's Wife, The Little Duchess, Mam'selle Napoleon,* and *The Parisian Model,* the amply endowed Held, with large, expressive brown eyes and red-brown hair, became synonymous with French sauciness and tease, proffering songs such as "Won't You Come and Play Wiz Me?" and "I Just Can't Make My Eyes Behave." Eve Golden's biography of Held was published in 2000.   DBW

Helen Hayes Theatre Name of two different New York playhouses:

1. 210 West 46th St., NYC [Architects: Herts and Tallant]. Originally conceived as a New York counterpart of the Parisian original, the playhouse was opened in 1911 as the Folies-Bergère, a restaurant-theatre, by producers HENRY B. HARRIS and Jesse Lasky. Five months later, recognizing its failure, they rebuilt the interior and, without the restaurant, renamed it the Fulton for the production of legitimate fare. With fewer than 1,000 seats, it became the ideal house for intimate plays. During the Depression decade, it changed owners and policy several times, but in 1941 came back as a legitimate house. In 1955, it was renamed the HELEN HAYES in honor of one of Broadway's first ladies of the stage. Its most famous tenant was the posthumous production of EUGENE O'NEILL's autobiographical play LONG DAY'S JOURNEY INTO NIGHT (1956). In 1982, despite strong protest from the theatrical community, the theatre and four others were torn down to make way for a hotel.

2. 238 West 44th St., NYC [Architects: H. C. Ingalls and F. B. Hoffman Jr.]. In 1912, producer WINTHROP AMES built a 299-seat house named the Little for the production of unusual plays. Five years later, when it became a strain on his finances, he leased it to a succession of producers. To make it a viable Broadway house, a balcony was added and its seating was almost doubled. In 1931, it was sold to the *New York Times* and thereafter used mainly as a concert-lecture hall and a television studio, but was returned to legitimate production in 1974. Extensive restoration of the interior was completed in 1981. In 1983, under different ownership, the theatre was renamed the Helen Hayes during the run of TORCH SONG TRILOGY. Claudia Shear's critically acclaimed *Dirty Blonde* (with Shear as MAE WEST) transferred from Off-Broadway on 1 May 2000 and ran for 352 performances   MCH

Hell-Bent fer Heaven A 1924 melodrama by HATCHER HUGHES about a scheming religious fanatic who nearly causes disaster for two Carolina mountain families. Dependent on amazing coincidences and rendered in quaint dialect ("Are you a-stickin' up fer that reptile?"), the play, by a Columbia drama professor, was a controversial choice for the Pulitzer Prize of 1924: Two Pulitzer jurors resigned when they learned that Professor BRANDER MATTHEWS had intervened with the Columbia panel that awarded the prize on behalf of his younger colleague's play. The jury's choice for the prize had been GEORGE KELLY's comedy *The SHOW-OFF*.   MF

Hellman, Lillian (1906–84) One of America's leading playwrights. Since 1963, when she ceased writing for the theatre, revivals of her plays have been performed regularly throughout the country. She is also known for her controversial memoirs: *An Unfinished Woman* (1969), *Pentimento* (1973), and *Scoundrel Time* (1976). In 1993 a play based on her relationship with Peter Feibleman (*Cakewalk*), starring ELAINE STRITCH, was staged at the AMERICAN REPERTORY THEATRE.

The CHILDREN'S HOUR (1934), based on an episode from William Roughead's *Bad Companions,* shocked and fascinated Broadway with the evil machinations of a child who destroys her teachers by whispering about their "unnatural" relationship. Hellman was labeled a "second IBSEN," "the American Strindberg," and the play ran for 691 performances. Vigorous and unyielding confrontations became her dramaturgical trademark, both in *Children's Hour* and in *The LITTLE FOXES* (1939), *WATCH ON THE RHINE* (1941), *The Searching Wind* (1944), *Another Part of the Forest* (1946), *The Autumn Garden* (1951), *The Lark* (1955, adapted from Anouilh's *L'Alouette*), *CANDIDE* (1956, from Voltaire, with music by LEONARD BERNSTEIN), and *TOYS IN THE ATTIC* (1960). Her plays were always given high-quality productions, first by HERMAN SHUMLIN and then by KERMIT BLOOMGARDEN. Only three plays failed at the box office: *Days to Come* (1936), *Montserrat* (1949, adapted from Emmanuel Roblés's play), and *My Mother, My Father and Me* (1963, adapted from Burt Blechman's novel *How Much?*).

Born in New Orleans, she became an editorial assistant to Horace Liveright in New York, a theatre press AGENT, a playreader, and (in 1931) a script reader in Hollywood, where she met detective-story writer Dashiell Hammett, who was to become her constant companion until his death in 1961. She wrote scripts for such films as *Dark Angel* (1935), *These Three* (1936, based on *The Children's Hour*), *DEAD END* (1937), and *The North Star* (1943). In 1952 she was called before the House Un-American Activities Committee, and her name was automatically added to Hollywood's blacklist. In the 2002 Broadway play *Imaginary Friends* Hellman appears as a character, played by SWOOSIE

KURTZ, opposite Mary McCarthy (CHERRY JONES). Of numerous books on Hellman, those by William Wright (1986), Joan Mellen (1996), and Deborah Martinson (2005) are among the more recent, the latter two especially thorough in their research. RM

Hello, Dolly! Two-act musical comedy, music and lyrics by JERRY HERMAN, book by MICHAEL STEWART; opened 16 January 1964 at the ST. JAMES THEATRE, running 2,844 performances. This musical adaptation of THORNTON WILDER's *The MATCHMAKER* chronicles the exploits of Dolly Levi (CAROL CHANNING) as she settles people's romantic lives, including her own, in the 1890s. The lavish production, brilliantly staged by director-choreographer GOWER CHAMPION in the best tradition of old-fashioned glitz and glitter, won the Drama Critics' Circle and Tony awards for Best Musical (plus 9 other Tonys) and was also a hit in London (with MARY MARTIN). When the New York production began to flag in 1967, producer DAVID MERRICK gave it fresh life with an all-black cast headed by PEARL BAILEY (a 1991 black cast in Long Beach, CA, starred Nell Carter). The show was originally written for ETHEL MERMAN, who declined to create the role of Dolly, but who was the last Dolly when the show closed in 1970. The rousing title song was the score's biggest hit, although Herman (who had uncredited help from others on the score) settled a plagiarism suit over it out of court. A superb national tour in 1994–5 starring Channing with a subsequent New York run brought new life to the musical. JD

Hellzapoppin A VAUDEVILLE REVUE produced by OLSEN AND JOHNSON, with songs by Sammy Fain, Charles Tobias, Earl Robinson, Alfred Hayes, Paul Mann, and Stephen Weiss. Staged by Edward Duryea Dowling, *Hellzapoppin* opened on Broadway 22 September 1938 with songs and dances, low-comedy gags, a fiddler, a unicyclist, much noise from gunshots and firecrackers, and some running gimmicks – such as the woman who wandered the audience searching for "Oscar"; the magician who could not escape from his straitjacket; and a man trying to deliver a potted plant, which seemed to grow larger between appearances. At closing on 17 December 1941, its 1,404 performances made it the third longest-running show on Broadway to date after *TOBACCO ROAD* and *ABIE'S IRISH ROSE.* JDM

Hemsley, Gilbert (1936–83) Lighting designer and production manager who began as JEAN ROSENTHAL's assistant, quickly developing a reputation

not only as a lighting designer but as someone who could brilliantly manage the complex tours and load-ins of opera and ballet companies. He designed more than 35 operas for the New York City Opera Company as well as lighting for Martha Graham, American Ballet Theatre, the Bolshoi Ballet, and inaugural celebrations for Presidents Nixon and Carter. He supervised the premiere of BERNSTEIN's *Mass* at the Kennedy Center (1971) and *Einstein on the Beach* (1976) at the Metropolitan Opera. He also taught at the University of Wisconsin at Madison. His designs, especially at the Met, are still seen more than two decades after his death. AA

Henderson, Mark (1950s–) British theatre, opera, dance, and fashion lighting designer. In the U.S. since 1986 he has designed fifteen productions on Broadway, receiving five Tony nominations and winning in 2006 for *The History Boys*. He has more than 50 credits in London's West End. DBW

Henderson, Ray see DESYLVA, BUDDY

Henley, Beth (1952–) Playwright (and actress) in the Southern Gothic tradition, whose comedies create empathy for bizarre characters who survive their disastrous experiences in outlandish ways. Her first professionally produced play, CRIMES OF THE HEART, won the Pulitzer Prize in 1981, the first play to win it prior to a Broadway opening. A family drama gone awry, *Crimes* portrays with absurdist wit and compassion the rallying of three eccentric Mississippi sisters because one of them has shot her husband. It was revived in 2001 by SECOND STAGE. Henley's other plays (four staged by MANHATTAN THEATRE CLUB) include *The Wake of Jamey Foster* (1982); *Am I Blue?* (1982); *The Miss Firecracker Contest* (1984), another black comedy, about a Mississippi woman's effort to redeem her calamitous life by winning a beauty contest; *The Debutante Ball* (1985); *The Lucky Spot* (1986); *Abundance* (1990), the exploration of a 25-year friendship of mail-order brides in the Old West; *Control Freaks* (1992); *Signature* (1990; lst produced 1995); *L-Play* (written 1995); *Impossible Marriage* (ROUNDABOUT, 1998); *Family Week* (2000); *Ridiculous Fraud* (2006, MCCARTER Berlind Theater). Henley also wrote screenplays for *Crimes* and *Miss Firecracker*. In 1995 she received one of the first of four new play initiative grants from the NEDERLANDER Organization and the Roundabout Theatre. FB

Henning, Doug (1947–2000) Canadian-born magician who arguably was most responsible for the popularity of MAGIC IN THE U.S. during the 1970s

323

and '80s due to his upbeat, boyish demeanor and polished illusions. In 1973, a show that began in Toronto as *Spellbound* was adapted into the musical *The Magic Show* for Broadway, where it ran four and a half years. For several months in 1982 Henning was back on Broadway in *Merlin*. He retired from performing in 1987 and until his death created illusions for others.   DBW

Henrietta, The BRONSON HOWARD's melodramatic portrayal of Wall Street fascinated audiences for over two decades with its technological accuracy and realistic detail. It opened 26 September 1887 at the UNION SQUARE THEATRE. Despite a FIRE that precipitated its premature closing, its depiction of high finance and romantic treachery caused quite a stir. The attempts by young Nicholas Van Alstyne Jr. to manipulate a catastrophic securities collapse for his own gain must have had a chilling effect on a Gilded Age audience swept up in a massive wave of real-life monopolies and robber barons. Although it represented a shift away from his early farces and melodramas into social dramas, Howard's play is remembered as one of his best, ranking among the most important American plays of the 19th century.   PAD

Henry, John (1738–94) Early American actor, born in Ireland and working in London and the West Indies before joining DOUGLASS'S AMERICAN COMPANY. Henry made his first American appearance in Philadelphia on 6 October 1767. The matinee idol of his time, Henry was the first actor in America whose lamentable morals were seized on by opponents of the theatre. A chronic sufferer from gout, Henry was also the first American actor to keep a carriage. He first married a Miss Storer; after her death, lived with her sister, Ann; and finally married a third Storer sister, Maria.

After the Revolutionary War, Henry comanaged the American Company with LEWIS HALLAM JR., and in 1792 he imported JOHN HODGKINSON, who shortly forced Henry into retirement. A tall, handsome Irishman, Henry was most successful in comedy, especially Irish characters. WILLIAM DUNLAP considered him "one of the best performers in the colonies," but Henry's arrogant manner made him many enemies.   SMA

Henry Miller's Theatre 124 West 43rd St., NYC (Architects: Allen, Ingalls & Hoffman). Built by HENRY MILLER in 1918 with only 950 seats and managed by his son GILBERT MILLER after his death in 1926. As the Park–Miller Theatre it became a moviehouse in 1970, and in 1972 as

Avon-at-the-Hudson it featured porn films. In 1978 it became the night club Xenon and in 1998 the Kit Kat Klub, where the revival of CABARET was first presented. In 2001 it returned to its original name, opening with the musical URINETOWN, the theatre's longest-running tenant, evicted in February 2004 to make room for a 57-story skyscraper on the site. The theatre's facade, which has landmark status, remains, and the developer, David Durst, plans a new theatre within the skyscraper.   DBW

Hepburn, Katharine (1907–2003) Stage and film actress, educated at Bryn Mawr, whose professional debut was in *The Czarina* in Baltimore (1928); her New York debut (soon after a bit part in *Night Hostess,* using the name Katharine Burns) was in *These Days* (1928). Of her early roles, Tracy Lord in *The PHILADELPHIA STORY* (1939) was the most memorable. In 1950 she played Rosalind in *As You Like It* at the CORT, then toured. In 1971 she toured in the musical comedy *Coco* after a successful Broadway run (1969–70). Later stage appearances included *A Matter of Gravity* (1976) and *The West Side Waltz* (1981). Her first film role was as Sydney Fairfield in *A Bill of Divorcement* (1932); she won four Oscars as Best Actress. Her autobiography, *Me: Stories of My Life,* was published in 1991. She is the subject of several biographies, most controversial, especially Barbara Leaming's (1995). She has been portrayed by Kate Mulgrew in the one-person show *Tea at Five* (2002, Hartford Stage), and by Cate Blanchett in the film *The Aviator* (2004).   SMA

Herbert, F. Hugh (1897–1958) English-born playwright whose forte was light comedy. *Kiss and Tell* (1943), a play about teenagers, ran for 956 performances, had three road companies, and became a popular radio serial. It was a great escape for a troubled world. In *For Love or Money* (1947) a charming young girl wins the love of an aging leading man. *The Moon Is Blue* (1951), starring Barbara BEL GEDDES, tested moral waters by placing the young heroine in jeopardy. *The Best House in Naples* (1956) was a theatrical failure.   WJM

Herbert, Victor (1859–1924) Irish-born and German-educated composer who came to America at the age of 27 to perform as a cellist with the Metropolitan Opera Orchestra. He became interested in composing for the theatre, and in 1894 his first score, *Prince Ananias*, was heard. The following year, his show *The Wizard of the Nile* had a long run in New York and on tour. After composing the music for several shows for comedian Frank Daniels, Herbert created the score for *The Serenade* (1897), which benefited from an excellent production by the Bostonians (see BOSTON IDEAL). In the last years of the 19th century, Herbert served as musical director of the Pittsburgh Symphony Orchestra. Some of his most enduringly popular songs were written for BABES IN TOYLAND (1903) and *Mlle. Modiste* (1905), the latter created as a vehicle for opera star FRITZI SCHEFF. Herbert's biggest commercial success came with *The Red Mill* (1906), which was also a big hit when revived on Broadway in 1945. Among Herbert's other popular musicals were NAUGHTY MARIETTA (1910), *Sweethearts* (1913), and *Eileen* (1917). He also contributed songs to the 1921 and 1923 ZIEGFELD *Follies.* Herbert was one of the founding members of the American Society of Composers, Authors and Publishers (ASCAP).

Trained in the conventions and traditions of European operetta, Herbert was adept at composing music that appealed to American audiences. Equally at home writing for comic operas, operettas, and musical comedies, he raised the level of American theatre music through the richness and variety of his scores. Edward N. Waters's biography (1955) remains the standard work.   MK

Herman, David (1876–1930) One of the first and most influential of JEWISH ART THEATRE directors, starting with HIRSHBEIN's Troupe in Odessa in 1908, followed by the Arts Corner in Warsaw in 1910, and then the celebrated Vilna Troupe from 1917, where his most memorable of many productions was a stylistic production of *The Dybbuk.* After periods in Warsaw and Vienna, he emigrated to America, exerting a profound influence on the YIDDISH THEATRE scene with his inspired direction of the FOLKSBIENE.   AB

Herman, Jerry (Gerald) (1932–) Composer, lyricist. He attended Miami University, where he wrote and directed a college revue, *I Feel Wonderful,* that impressed audiences and had an OFF-BROADWAY run in 1954. After writing songs for other Off-Broadway REVUES, he contributed his first Broadway score to *Milk and Honey* (1961). His greatest success was the score for HELLO, DOLLY! (1964). Subsequent shows include *Mame* (1966), *Dear World* (1969), *Mack & Mabel* (1974), *The Grand Tour* (1979), and LA CAGE AUX FOLLES (1983). *Jerry's Girls* (1985) was a revue that drew upon Herman's catalog of songs for the stage, as was the 2003 Off-Broadway *Showtune.* Rarely an innovator, Herman is a skillful composer-lyricist of traditional show

tunes. In 1998 he received the coveted RICHARD RODGERS Award from ASCAP. His autobiography (written with Marilyn Stasio) was published in 1996; a biography by Stephen Citron appeared in 2004.   MK

Herne, James A. (1839–1901) Actor, manager, and playwright. Responding to the forces of science and democracy that challenged contemporary society, Herne developed realistic themes and characters in his plays and created a realist creed for drama. Beginning his acting career in 1854, he became a stage manager in SAN FRANCISCO, where he wrote melodramas with DAVID BELASCO (*Within an Inch of His Life,* 1879; *Hearts of Oak,* 1879). Among his own plays, *The Minute Men of 1774–75* (1886) suggested the New England local color later developed in the temperance play *Drifting Apart* (1888), and SHORE ACRES (1892), in which Uncle Nat Berry, with his language and action, personified the Downeaster and made Herne a millionaire.

With the help of WILLIAM DEAN HOWELLS and others who rented Chickering Hall in Boston, Herne staged MARGARET FLEMING (1890–1), his best-known work. This insightful play, about a philandering husband whose illegitimate child is accepted by his morally superior and sensitive wife, revealed Herne's interest in realism and social determinism, as well as his playwriting skills; although revised before its New York production, it was still unsuccessful. *The Reverend Griffith Davenport* (1899), based on a novel by Helen Gardner, dramatized the struggle of a slave owner who opposed slavery during the Civil War.

Relating drama to contemporary literature, Herne wrote "Art for Truth's Sake in the Drama" (*Arena* 17 [Feb. 1897]) to emphasize the "humanity" and "large truth" in the drama that has a "higher purpose" than to amuse. This was a new concept for commercially minded theatre entrepreneurs of this period. Praised by Howells for his "epoch marking" play *Margaret Fleming,* Herne wrote plays that delineated the beginning of modern drama in America. John Perry's biography (1978) is the most thorough.   WJM

Heron, Matilda (1830–77) American actress who made a life's work of *Camille.* Fascinated by Mlle. Doche's playing of Marguerite Gautier in Paris (1854), she made her own adaptation of the play, opening it in New Orleans (1855) and then at WALLACK's (1857). New Yorkers were captivated by Heron's "elemental power," her "animal vivacity," her uninhibited exploitation of a woman's sexual life, and her lifelike naturalness (even turning her back to the audience); and when Camille coughed her way to the grave, tears flowed throughout the house. After an initial run of 100 performances, she toured the play for the next 20 years.

Born in Ireland, Heron had played Juliet to CHARLOTTE CUSHMAN's Romeo (1852), made her New York debut as Lady Macbeth (1852), and appeared at London's Drury Lane (1854) before she discovered Camille.   RM

Herrmann, Alexander (1844–96) German-born MAGICian whose elder brother by 27 years, Carl, was the first Herrmann to achieve international acclaim, including initial appearances in the U.S. in the 1860s. Alexander, who succeeded Carl, was first seen in New York in 1869 and ultimately settled in the U.S., though he continued touring internationally. Although Alexander was HARRY KELLAR's major competition in the 1880s – with illusions such as "Cremation," in which a woman was set on fire and then spectral forms were made to rise from her coffin – Herrmann's widow, Adelaide, and his nephew Leon were unsuccessful in sustaining the popularity of the Herrmann show after his death, and for a time Kellar had little competition. Still, Adelaide performed until 1928, 31 years with her own show, longer than any other Herrmann. Carl and Alexander's lives are recorded by I. G. Edmonds (1979).   DBW

Herrmann, Edward (1943–) Michigan-reared actor who trained at England's LAMDA and made his debut OFF-BROADWAY in *The Basic Training of Pavlo Hummel* (1971) and on Broadway in MOON-CHILDREN (1972). Seen in RICHARD NELSON's "The End of a Sentence" (PBS, *American Playhouse,* 1991) and *Life Sentences* (SECOND STAGE, 1993), he received a Tony for Shaw's *Mrs Warren's Profession* (1976) and a nomination for Hare's *Plenty* (1983). Other notable appearances include *Tom and Viv* (1985), *A Walk in the Woods* (London, with Sir Alec Guinness, 1988), *Psychopathia Sexualis* by SHANLEY (1997), and, on Broadway, *The Deep Blue Sea* in 1998. He appears frequently at the WILLIAMSTOWN THEATRE FESTIVAL and on television (notably as FDR in 1976 and 1977). Herrmann was married to actress-playwright Leigh Curran (now divorced).   REK

Hewes, Henry (1917–) Theatre critic. Born in Boston and educated at Harvard, Carnegie Tech, and Columbia (1948), Hewes worked for the *New York Times* (1949–51) and was a critic at the *Saturday Review* for more than 40 years beginning in 1952. He was editor of *The Best Play Series* (1961–4), shift-ing focus to more national/international coverage. Creator of the Drama Desk Awards (1968) and founder of the American Theatre Critics Association (1974), in 1993 he received the MARGO JONES Medal. The AMERICAN THEATRE WING Design Awards were renamed the Hewes Design Awards in his honor in 1999. He once said in response to an award, "I'm sorry for every nasty thing I wrote. The fact that I was always right is no excuse."   TLM

Hewlett, James (fl. 1821–31) A tailor by trade, Hewlett became principal actor when in 1821 WILLIAM ALEXANDER BROWN formed the AFRICAN THEATRE (NYC). He appeared as Richard III, Othello, and as the Carib chieftain King Shotaway in Mr. Brown's drama on the Carib revolt in St. Vincent. When the company folded, Hewlett began to give ONE-PERSON performances in which he imitated leading actors of the day in their celebrated roles. He performed in New York and Pennsylvania, and may have appeared at the Coburg Theatre in London. He enlivened his program of recitations by singing songs, accompanied by his wife on the piano.   EGH

Heyward, Dorothy (1890–1961) and **(Edwin) DuBose Heyward** (1885–1940) Husband-and-wife playwriting team, in which he primarily supplied stories from his novels, and she, dramatic craftsmanship. Although DuBose wrote one other play and Dorothy had five others produced, their reputation rests on their folk dramas of Negro life – *Porgy* (1927) and *Mamba's Daughters* (1939) – both praised for their realistic depiction of the lives of Southern blacks. *Porgy,* the love story of a crippled black man and an erring woman, became an American legend, particularly after its conversion into a folk opera, *PORGY AND BESS* (1935). by DuBose and the GERSHWINS (a 1976 revival won a Tony Award). The Heywards are credited with providing dramatic opportunities for AFRICAN AMERICAN actors: ETHEL WATERS, in *Mamba's Daughters,* was given her first opportunity to excel in a dramatic role. A 2000 biography of DuBose was written by James M. Hutchisson.   FB

Hickey, William (1928–97) Actor, director, and an acting teacher at New York's HB Studio from 1953 to his death. He specialized in bizarre or eccentric characters in such plays as *Saint Joan* (Broadway debut, 1951), *ON THE TOWN* (1959, Carnegie Hall Playhouse), *Happy Birthday, Wanda June* (1970; film, 1971), *Small Craft Warnings* (1972), MOURNING BECOMES ELECTRA (1972), *Thieves* (1974), and *ARSENIC AND OLD LACE* (1986 revival).   REK

Hiken, Gerald (1927–) Wisconsin-born and -educated character actor-director. After six years in regional theatre, Hiken first appeared in New York in 1955 as Trofimov in *The Cherry Orchard*. Although he has performed in plays by other dramatists (*Good Woman of Setzuan,* 1956; *The Misanthrope,* 1957; *The Iceman Cometh,* 1957; *Gideon,* 1962; *Golda,* 1977; *Strider,* 1979; *Slavs!,* 1994; etc.), he is known as something of a Chekhov specialist: Telegin in *Uncle Vanya* (1956), Medvedenko in *The Seagull* (1956), Andrei Prozorov in *The Three Sisters* (NY, 1959, 1964; London, 1965), and Gaev in *The Cherry Orchard* (1967). During 1966–8 he served as artistic director of the Stanford (CA) Repertory Theatre. In recent years he has performed in his Palto Alto, CA, living room from writings by Proust, W. H. Auden, and Gertrude Stein (he first did this in 1968). DBW

Hilferty, Susan (1953–) Costume designer from Massachusetts; studied at Syracuse, Yale (M.F.A.), and St. Martin's School of Art in London. She designs regularly in regional theatres and in New York; won the Bay Area Theatre Circle Award for the costumes in *Tooth of Crime,* the 2000 Obie for Sustained Excellence in Costume Design, and the 2004 Tony, Drama Desk, and Outer Critics Circle awards for *Wicked*. Since 1997 she has been chair of the Department of Design for Stage/Film at the Tisch School of NYU. She is a frequent collaborator with James Lapine, Robert Woodruff, and Joe Mantello. BO

Hill, Arthur (1922–2006) Canadian-born actor whose major theatrical career was in the U.S. His stage debut was in London as Finch in *Home of the Brave;* his Broadway debut as Cornelius Hackl in *The Matchmaker* in 1955. In 1962 he starred as George in *Who's Afraid of Virginia Woolf?* (1963 Tony Award), repeating the role in London in 1964. He later appeared as Simon Harford in *More Stately Mansions* (1967). After a film and television career he retired in the 1990s. SMA

Hill, George Handel "Yankee" (1809–49) Actor. In the 1830s and '40s Hill was the leading exponent of the "Yankee" roles in William Dunlap's *Trip to Niagara,* Samuel Woodworth's *The Forest Rose,* and J. S. Jones's *The Green Mountain Boy.* Audiences delighted in his plausible cunning, his great industry, and his pliant honesty. One critic said he was "the funniest actor, and cleverest fellow in the Yankee signification of the word – in Christendom." He appeared in London in 1836 and 1838. He first undertook Yankee impersonations with solo recitations of "Jonathan's Visit to Buffalo" and "The Yankee in Trouble; or, Zephaniah in the Pantry." An autobiography appeared posthumously in 1853. RM

Hilton Theatre 213 West 42d St., NYC [Architects: Richard Blinder and Peter Kofman]. Created from elements of two earlier theatres, the Lyric (built by the Shuberts in 1902) and the Apollo (built in 1910 as a vaudeville house named the Bryant) as part of the 42d Street Development Project. The dome of the Lyric was dismantled and reassembled. Originally owned by Canadian entrepreneur Garth Drabinsky's Livent, Inc., which created the new 1,815-seat structure, it was named for the Ford Motor Co. (The Ford Center for the Performing Arts) in 1998 and opened with *Ragtime,* followed by revivals of *Jesus Christ Superstar* (2000) and *42nd Street* (2001). Soon after the opening, Livent declared bankruptcy and the theatre was purchased by a media company, SFX, which was later subsumed by Clear Channel (which joined forces with the Hilton Hotels Corp. and its fiscal support). In 2005 the theatre's name was changed to the Hilton with its first show, a mediocre albeit technically inspiring *Chitty Chitty Bang Bang,* which opened on April 28 but quickly faded. LJ DBW

Hines, Gregory (1946–2003) Consummate actor-singer and dancer who began his diverse career as a child in his native New York City, where he worked in a tap act with both his brother Maurice Jr. (who left the act in 1973) and, later, his father (Hines, Hines, and Dad). The pinnacle of Hines' career was a Tony in 1992 for his portrayal of the egocentric jazz genius Jelly Roll Morton in *Jelly's Last Jam,* a project that took nine years to develop. Although he had a successful film and television career, Hines never forgot his dance origins and remained a tireless advocate for tap in America until his death. DBW

Hingle, (Martin) **Pat**(terson) (1924–) Colorado-born and Texas-educated actor whose professional debut was as Lachie in *Johnny Belinda* in 1950; he made his debut on Broadway as Koble in *End as a Man* in 1953. Among his Broadway hits were the brawling and brusquely considerate Rubin Flood in *The Dark at the Top of the Stairs* (1957) and the Job-like, anguished title role of *J. B.* (1958). Later starring roles include the failed brother in *The Price* (1968), the bewildered Coach in *That Championship Season* (1975, replacement), and Ben Franklin in the 1997 revival of *1776*. He has appeared in more than 110 feature films, as well as numerous television series and programs. Hingle retired to North Carolina. SMA

hippodrama see ANIMALS AS PERFORMERS

Hippodrome Theatre 6th Ave. between 43d and 44th Sts., NYC [Architect: J. H. Morgan]. The Hippodrome was conceived and built in 1905 by Frederic W. Thompson and Elmer S. Dundy, who had created the extravagant Coney Island amusement center, Luna Park. Advertised as the world's largest theatre, its auditorium seated 5,000 and its stage was equipped with every device known to create magnificent spectacles. The costs of production and the maintenance of the house overwhelmed even the canniest of producers, including the SHUBERTS and CHARLES DILLINGHAM. In 1923, it was taken over by the KEITH–ALBEE VAUDEVILLE chain, then leased for popular-priced opera, then as a sports arena. In 1935, BILLY ROSE presented his production of *Jumbo* at the theatre, the last notable event in its history. It was torn down in 1939, but the site was not developed until 1952, when it was covered by a garage and office building.   MCH

Hirsch, Judd (1935–) Actor who in the course of 40 years has established a major reputation as a versatile actor in film, television, and theatre, beginning with his Broadway debut in 1966, replacing Herb Edelman as the Telephone Repairman in BAREFOOT IN THE PARK. Unlike many of his successful contemporaries in film or television, Hirsch returns frequently to the New York stage, as the following partial list of credits illustrates: *The HOT L BALTIMORE* (1973) as Bill, the night manager; FEIFFER's *Knock, Knock* (1976); NEIL SIMON's *Chapter Two* (1977); LANFORD WILSON's *TALLY'S FOLLY* (1979) as Matt Friedman, an immigrant Jewish accountant; CIRCLE REPERTORY COMPANY's *The Seagull* (1983) as Trigorin; HERB GARDNER's *I'm Not Rappaport* (1985) at the AMERICAN PLACE THEATRE, which transferred to Broadway and was revived in 2002 with Ben Vereen; and *Conversations with My Father* (1992), winning Tony Awards in both, a rare feat. He appeared in the latter at London's Old Vic in 1995. Other credits: Lyle Kessler's *Robbers* (1995, LONG WHARF); Richard Dresser's *Below the Belt* (1996); ROUNDABOUT's revival of *A Thousand Clowns* (1996). According to one interviewer, Hirsch has a rugged "street face, a face of interchangeable ethnicities and professions." His career to date supports such a description.   DBW

Hirsch, Louis A. (1881–1924) Originally aspiring to be a concert pianist and serious composer, Hirsch was drawn to songwriting, contributing songs to such shows as *The Gay White Way* (1907) and *The Girl and the Wizard* (1909). His first full

score was for *He Came from Milwaukee* (1910). He continued to write songs for REVUES, including four editions of the ZIEGFELD *Follies* (1915, 1916, 1918, 1922). Among his musical-comedy scores were those for *Going Up* (1917), *The Rainbow Girl* (1918), and *Oh, My Dear!* (1918). His most memorable song, "The Love Nest," was written for *Mary* (1920), produced by GEORGE C. COHAN. Hirsch also wrote the score for Cohan's *The O'Brien Girl* (1921); his last score was for *Betty Lee* (1924). Hirsch was a competent, if not inspired, musical-comedy composer.   MK

Hirschfeld, Al(bert) (1903–2003) Until his passing acknowledged as the dean of American theatrical caricaturists and well known internationally, Al Hirschfeld, a native of St. Louis, studied fine arts in New York and Paris, intending to become a painter or sculptor. Instead, he became fascinated with the manipulation of the thin black line into shapes and attitudes, and hence was drawn into the art of the CARICATURE. His early drawings were submitted to several New York newspapers, but from 1925 to his death he worked almost exclusively for the *New York Times,* flavoring its theatre journalism with drawings of current Broadway personalities and happenings. For many years, Hirschfeld wove the name of his daughter, Nina, into the tapestry of his drawings, slipping a small numeral next to his signature to indicate the exact number of times it appeared. He was the first American artist to be allowed to sign his name on postage-stamp artwork (1991). Among his many books are *The American Theatre as Seen by Hirschfeld* (1961), *The World of Hirschfeld* (1970), *Hirschfeld by Hirschfeld* (1979), *Hirschfeld: Art and Recollections from Eight Decades* (1991), *Hirschfeld: On Line* (2000), and *Hirschfeld's British Aisles* (2005). A documentary about him, *The Line King* (1996), was an Academy Award nominee. He was honored with two Tonys (special award, 1975; BROOKS ATKINSON Award, 1984) and the National Medal of Arts (2002), among other recognitions. Five months after his death, the MARTIN BECK THEATRE was renamed the Al Hirschfeld Theatre (which houses a permanent exhibit of his drawings) – the ultimate Broadway accolade.   MCH

Hirshbein, Peretz (1880–1948) Yiddish playwright who began writing in Hebrew in Russia but in 1906 started writing Yiddish plays, harshly realistic or subtly symbolist. In Odessa he founded the Hirshbein Troupe (1908–10), an acting ensemble dedicated to intellectually ambitious YIDDISH THEATRE. After several years of traveling and writing he settled in New York, where his plays *Green*

Fields, A Secluded Nook, The Blacksmith's Daughters, and *The Idle Inn* (1912–18), all evocative romances of Russian Jewish rural life, won praise. The film version of *Green Fields* is still screened.   NS

Hispanic theatre   Given the substantial and fast-growing Spanish-speaking population within the continental U.S., it is not surprising that a theatre movement reflecting Hispanic language, culture, and values flourishes across the country. This Hispanic population includes immigrants from Spain as well as from every Spanish-speaking country within the Western Hemisphere, but the theatrical impetus derives primarily from three sources: Mexico, Cuba, and Puerto Rico. Although the movement has gained both in strength and popularity within the past 40 years as a result of the widespread civil rights movement, it should be clear that the Spanish-speaking theatre has an extended history in America, even antedating the first English-speaking theatre here. Nicolás Kanellos indicates the first recorded performance took place in a Spanish mission near Miami in 1567, when the Spanish settlers and soldiers utilized the feast day of Saint John the Baptist to present a religious play designed to catechize the local Indian population. In the Southwest, Juan de Oñate's band of colonizers was performing religious plays in and around what is today El Paso, TX, before the end of the 16th century. The orientation of these performances reflected the dual mission of the Hispanic conquest, which was not only military but religious, and therefore served well the objective of instructing native populations about Christianity. Interest in the Magi play (*pastorelas*) and other religious performances can still be found in Hispanic communities throughout the country, especially during Christmas and Easter.

From its earliest beginnings to the present time, Hispanic theatre has had a checkered and often interrupted history. In many cases documentation is scarce because of its depreciated value in traditional circles. Current scholarship divides the movement into three fairly discrete parts: CHICANO THEATRE, primarily in the West and Southwest; CUBAN AMERICAN THEATRE, mostly in New York and Florida; and the New York theatre, sometimes called NUYORICAN, which has a heavily Puerto Rican component. None of these classifications is absolute or unilateral. Manifestations of Chicano theatre can be found across the land, from the Northwest to the East, and as the Spanish-speaking population has become more mixed and more integrated, categorization has become more difficult. The theatre is linguistically structured as well: Chicano theatre still tends to rely heavily on a mixture of both languages, combined into "Spanglish." Cuban American theatre was earlier almost exclusively in Spanish, whereas the younger generation often writes and performs in English. The Nuyorican theatre depends heavily on English, in contrast with the island. The most prominent Hispanic theatres in the country include Bilingual Foundation for the Arts (Los Angeles), Teatro Avante (Coral Gables, FL), and Pregones, PUERTO RICAN TRAVELING THEATRE, REPERTORIO ESPAÑOL (Spanish Repertory), and INTAR of New York City. (See also ETHNIC THEATRE.)   GW   JH

Hitchcock, Raymond (1865–1929) Actor. After a debut in 1890, Hitchcock did not have a starring role until 1903. During a 40-year career he starred in two dozen musical comedies and REVUES, including a series of *Hitchy-Koo* revues (1917–20) – featuring "Hitchy's" whimsicalities and uniquely informal style, and extraordinarily popular until interest suddenly subsided.   DBW

Hoch, Danny (1970–) Actor, solo performer, playwright, and director, called "part sociologist, part moralist, and part super-chameleon." From a graffiti writer, breakdancer, and rapper in the mid-1980s, Hoch in the '90s won acclaim for his re-creations of a variety of characters from the inner-city neighborhood of his youth in ONE-PERSON anthologies titled *Pot Melting, Some People* (Obie), and *Jails, Hospitals, & Hip-Hop.* He has performed these throughout the U.S. and in Latin America. He founded in 2000 The Hip-Hop Theater Festival, which features hip-hop-generation theatrical works from the U.S. and abroad in four cities. A recent play, *Till the Break of Dawn,* about hip-hop politics, Cuba, technology, and what it means to be radical in that generation, was read at the Ojai Playwrights Conference in 2003. He has written extensively on society, race, and class, and received numerous awards for his work, including an NEA Solo Theatre Fellowship and a TENNESSEE WILLIAMS Fellowship.   DBW

Hodgkinson (Meadowcroft), John (1767–1805) British-born actor and manager who, after some provincial experience, accepted an offer in 1792 from JOHN HENRY to join the AMERICAN COMPANY and spent the rest of his career in the U.S. Although his personal reputation has been much maligned, his private life after his arrival in America seems to have been without blemish. He never became a star, but he was a tall, handsome man with an exceptional voice and memory who excelled in high and low comedy, playing at least 379 roles during his 24-year career. During 1794–8 he was joint manager of the JOHN STREET THEATRE. Later he acted in all the principal cities of the Atlantic seaboard until his death from yellow fever.   DBW

Hoffman, Dustin (1937–) Film and stage actor. Hoffman worked at the Theatre Company of Boston with DAVID WHEELER before his 1965 OFF-BROADWAY debut as Immanuel in RONALD RIBMAN's *Harry, Noon, and Night*. The next year he played Zoditch in his *The JOURNEY OF THE FIFTH HORSE*. Also in 1966 he appeared in *Eh?*, winning several awards, as he did on Broadway in 1968 in the title role of *Jimmy Shine*. After an extraordinarily successful stint in films, he starred in a Broadway revival of *DEATH OF A SALESMAN* (1984), praised as a performance of genius and demonic intensity, and in 1989 appeared on Broadway as Shylock in Peter Hall's production of *The Merchant of Venice*. Ronald Bergan wrote a biography published in London in 1991.   SMA

Hoffman, Philip Seymour (1967–) Born in a suburb of Rochester, NY, recipient of a B.F.A. (1989) from NYU's Tisch School of the Arts, this beefy (he prefers "dense"), blond actor has consistently received praise for his stage and film work and, in 2005, universal acclaim – including an Oscar – for the title character in the film *Capote*. Yet before this singular and justly honored portrayal, many considered him the finest character actor – certainly the most versatile – working today. He has earned two Tony nominations – in 2000 in the revival of SHEPARD's *TRUE WEST* (Best Actor) with John C. Reilly and in 2003 for the revival of *LONG DAY'S JOURNEY INTO NIGHT* (featured actor; Jamie) with BRIAN DENNEHY and Vanessa REDGRAVE. Other NYC credits include *The Seagull* (directed by MIKE NICHOLS), *Defying Gravity*, *Shopping and Fucking*, and *The Author's Voice*; he was also in *The Merchant of Venice* at the GOODMAN (1994; directed by PETER SELLARS). As co–artistic director of NYC's LAByrinth Theater Company he has directed Stephen Adly Guirgis's *Our Lady of 121st Street*, *Jesus Hopped the A Train*, and *The Last Days of Judas Iscariot*. For the Manhattan Class Company he directed REBECCA GILMAN's *The Glory of Living*.   DBW

Holbrook, Hal [né Harold Rowe Holbrook] (1925–) Actor and writer who made his debut with a Cleveland STOCK COMPANY in 1942 and spent four seasons in stock. With his first wife he toured for six seasons, presenting famous scenes from the classics, from which developed his immensely successful ONE-PERSON show *Mark Twain Tonight!* He first appeared as Twain in New York in 1955 (at a NIGHTCLUB), and has revived the show periodically (over 2,000 performances), including a 2005 appearance on Broadway to great critical and popular acclaim.

Holbrook spent the 1964 season with the LINCOLN CENTER Repertory, alternating Quentin in *AFTER THE FALL* with JASON ROBARDS JR. and playing Marco Polo in *Marco Millions*. More recently he has turned to classic roles, appearing at Cleveland's Great Lakes Theatre Festival in 1990 as King Lear (later seen at New York's ROUNDABOUT), as Uncle Vanya the following year, and Willy Loman in 1994, as well as Shylock at San Diego's OLD GLOBE THEATRE (summer 1991).   SMA

Holiday A finely crafted PHILIP BARRY comedy of manners (1928, 230 performances), with ARTHUR HOPKINS as producer-director and ROBERT EDMOND JONES as designer. Hope Williams starred as Linda Seton, the rich "Barry girl" who resists the conventional values of her father and sister by falling in love with her sister's fiancé, a carefree, charming lawyer who would rather retire, on extended holiday, than chase after money. The theme is sentimental – love and freedom versus staid upper-class values – but the dialogue is witty and supple, and there's a good character role in the alcoholic brother Nick, originally played by Donald Ogden Stewart. The play was revived on Broadway, less successfully, in 1973 by the New Phoenix Repertory Company, and is also performed occasionally in the regional theatres. The second film version (1938), directed by George Cukor, starred Cary Grant and KATHARINE HEPBURN (who had been Hope Williams's untested understudy in 1928).   TP

Holland, George (1791–1870) British-born actor called a "comedian of peculiar and irrepressible drollery." After seven years on the London stage, he came to the U.S. in 1827, making his debut at the BOWERY THEATRE in *A Day After the Fair*. For 16 years he toured, gaining immense popularity, especially in the South, where he also entered for a time into management with NOAH LUDLOW as well as SOL SMITH. In New Orleans, where he remained from 1835 until 1843, he worked with JAMES H. CALDWELL. For the next six years he played in comedies and burlesques at MITCHELL's OLYMPIC. Beginning in 1855, and for a total of 14 years, he was low comedian with WALLACK's company, leaving in 1869 to join DALY. Of Holland's six children, four became actors, most notably Edmund Milton and Joseph Jefferson Holland.

A biographical sketch of George Holland was published in 1871.   DBW

Holliday, Judy [née Judith Tuvim] (1923–65) Comedienne and singer who appeared, along with BETTY COMDEN and ADOLPH GREEN, in the NIGHTCLUB act "The Revuers" in 1938 and made her New York theatrical debut in *Kiss Them for Me* (1945). Her wide-eyed, baby-voiced portrayal of Billie Dawn in the comedy BORN YESTERDAY (1946) elevated her to stardom. Her first musical role was as meddling telephone operator Ella Peterson in *Bells Are Ringing* (1956), for which she won a Tony Award; she also starred in the short-lived musical *Hot Spot* (1963). Audiences and critics were delighted by her incandescent personality and superb comic timing. Two biographies appeared in 1982 (by G. Carey and W. Holtzman).   MK

Holliday Street Theatre Holliday St. between Fayette and Lexington Sts., Baltimore. Built by THOMAS WIGNELL and Alexander Reinagle, the theatre was opened on 25 September 1794, intended as a satellite of their Philadelphia theatrical operations. Later in its history, it was managed prosperously by JOHN T. FORD. It was pulled down in 1813 and a new theatre built on its site; this the city of Baltimore razed in 1917 to contruct War Memorial Plaza.   MCH

Holm, Celeste (1919–) Film, stage, and television actress whose professional debut was in *The Night of January 16* in a Deer Lake, PA, summer theatre in 1936. Her first New York appearance was as Lady Mary in *Gloriana* in 1938. She created Ado Annie in OKLAHOMA! in 1943 and followed this the next season with Evelina in *Bloomer Girl*. Her first film was *Three Little Girls in Blue* (1946). In 1991 she appeared with Nicol Williamson in PAUL RUDNICK's *I Hate Hamlet*, and in the late 1990s devoted her talent to television (notably *Promised Land*). Her awards include an Oscar for *Gentlemen's Agreement* (1947) and the Sarah Siddons Award – proleptically featured in Holm's 1950 film *All about Eve* – for her performance in the national touring company of *Mame* (1969). In 1979 she was knighted by King Olav of Norway. Her fourth husband was actor Wesley Addy.   SMA

Holm, Hanya [née Johanna Eckert] (c. 1898–1992) Modern dancer-choreographer and theatre choreographer who began her training and performance career in her native Germany before arriving in the U.S. to direct the Wigman School in New York (1931). She opened her own school and embarked on a choreographic career that established her as a leading pioneer in American modern DANCE. Although primarily abstract in form, Holm's choreography was powerful, and critics wrote that she incorporated German constructivism in her work. Not limited to abstract invention, Holm also choreographed using more traditional dance movements for musical-theatre productions. Among her most notable musical theatre credits are *KISS ME, KATE* (1948), *MY FAIR LADY* (1956), and *CAMELOT* (1960). Her professional life was recounted by Walter Sorell (1979).   LF

Home of the Brave by ARTHUR LAURENTS opened 27 December 1945 at the BELASCO THEATRE, running for 69 performances. This wartime drama stood out from its contemporaries through a frank treatment of anti-Semitism and battle trauma. Using hypnotherapy as a flashback device, the play recounted the anxieties leading to the speech loss of the main character, resulting in his third-act cure. The 1949 United Artists screen version modified the script to feature a black protagonist.   RW

Hooks, Robert (Dean) (1937–) AFRICAN AMERICAN actor who, as Bobby Dean Hooks, made his debut in a touring production of *A RAISIN IN THE SUN* (1959), then appeared in several plays on and OFF-BROADWAY, including Genet's *The Blacks* (1962). The role of Clay in DUTCHMAN at the Cherry Lane Theatre (1964) brought him prominence and a name change to Robert Hooks. At the St. Mark's Playhouse he copresented and played in DOUGLAS TURNER WARD's double bill *Happy Ending* and *Day of Absence* (1965); this prepared the way for their founding of the NEGRO ENSEMBLE COMPANY (1967). After appearing in the NEC's early productions, Hooks moved to Washington, DC, where he formed the short-lived D.C. BLACK REPERTORY COMPANY (1972–6). Recently he has appeared primarily on television and in films. He is father of actor-director **Kevin Hooks** (TV's *Lost*).   EGH

Hooley's Theatre, originally called Hooley's Opera House, was perhaps the most successful theatre in 19th-century CHICAGO. R[ichard] M. "Uncle Dick" Hooley moved to Chicago from Brooklyn in 1870 and opened a new theatre in January 1871, only to see it burn nine months later in the great FIRE. His rebuilt theatre, seating 1,412, became the home of a 30-member STOCK COMPANY that included JAMES O'NEILL as its leading man. The theatre's greatest success began in the late 1870s, when Hooley used the combination system to feature traveling stars. Hooley was replaced after his death in 1893 by longtime employee Harry J. Powers, who refurbished the theatre in 1898 and renamed it Powers' New Theatre. SF

Hopkins, Arthur (Melancthon) (1878–1950) Producer and director who began his career as a newspaper reporter, then worked as a VAUDE-VILLE press AGENT, and finally booked attractions himself. His first successful Broadway production (as producer) was *Poor Little Rich Girl* (1913), which ran for 160 performances. Other early successes (produced solo or with others) include *On Trial* (1914), *Good Gracious Annabelle* (1916), *A Successful Calamity* (1917), *Redemption* (1918) with John Barrymore, and *The Jest* (1919) with John and Lionel Barrymore (see DREW–BARRYMORE). He featured ALLA NAZIMOVA in revivals of IBSEN's *Wild Duck, Hedda Gabler,* and *A Doll's House.* In the 1920s, Hopkins produced O'NEILL's ANNA CHRISTIE (1921) and *The* HAIRY APE (1922), and directed and produced Stallings and ANDERSON's WHAT PRICE GLORY (1924) and PHILIP BARRY's *Paris Bound* (1927) and HOLIDAY (1928). His output decreased after 1930, but he staged a successful *The* PETRI-FIED FOREST in 1935 with Leslie Howard and Humphrey Bogart, and *The Magnificent Yankee* in 1946. His notable productions of SHAKESPEARE include John Barrymore in *Richard III* (1920) and in *Hamlet* (1922), and Lionel Barrymore in *Macbeth* (1921). Hopkins discovered PAULINE LORD and KATH-ARINE HEPBURN, and contributed to the success of ROBERT EDMOND JONES. He studied theatrical production in Europe and returned home to develop the revolving stage in America. Hopkins placed artistic above commercial merit. Although many of his directing methods were modern, his reliance upon pictorial effect made his later productions seem old-fashioned. His books included *To a Lonely Boy* (1937) and *Reference Point* (1948), both somewhat autobiographical. TLM

Hopper, De Wolf (1858–1935) Comedian and singer. His abnormally long legs, loose-jointed movements, and strong singing voice made Hopper one of the most beloved performers in comic opera. His debut was in *Our Daughters* (1879), after which he appeared in a number of shows under the aegis of the McCaull Opera Company. Hopper left the McCaull company in 1890 and under a new management was given his first starring role in *Castles in the Air* (1890). His two greatest successes, *Wang* (1891) and *Panjandrum* (1893), followed. After forming the De Wolf Hopper Opera Company, he appeared in *Dr. Syntax* (1894), *El Capitan* (1896), and *The Mystical Miss* (1899). Hopper then joined the WEBER AND FIELDS company for

two shows, then starred in *Mr. Pickwick* (1903), *Happyland* (1905), *The Pied Piper* (1908), and *A Matinee Idol* (1910). In 1911 Hopper made the first of a number of successful forays into the GILBERT AND SULLIVAN repertoire with a revival of *HMS Pinafore.* As the vogue for comic opera waned, Hopper's work was confined to REVUES, such as *The Passing Show of 1917,* and, on occasion, operettas. His last New York appearance in an original work was in *White Lilacs* (1928). Beginning his career at a time when comic opera was at its height, Hopper found ample opportunity to exercise his comic gifts and his forceful singing voice. He was especially noted for his ability to handle long comic speeches and involved patter songs, and for his amusing use of props. His recitation of "Casey at the Bat" is a classic, captured on an early disk. Hopper published his autobiography, *Once a Clown,* in 1927. MK

Hopper, Edna Wallace (1874–1959) Actress and singer who began her stage career at the BOSTON MUSEUM in 1891. As Edna Wallace, she appeared in a number of straight plays produced by CHARLES FROHMAN before making her comic-opera debut as a replacement for Della Fox in *Panjandrum.* Soon after, she married its star, DE WOLF HOPPER, and as Edna Wallace Hopper starred in *Dr. Syntax* (1894), *El Capitan* (1896), *Yankee Doodle Dandy* (1898), and *Chris and the Wonderful Lamp* (1900). She played Lady Holyrood in the American production of FLORODORA (1900). Subsequently, she made the transition from comic opera to musical comedy in such shows as *About Town* (1906), *Fifty Miles from Boston* (1908), and *Jumping Jupiter* (1911). Hopper's popularity in comic opera was generally attributed to her sparkling and vivacious personality rather than to her singing voice, which was too small and delicate. Audiences especially enjoyed her appearances in trousers roles (see FEMALE/MALE IMPERSONATION). MK

Hopwood, Avery (1882–1928) A remarkably successful playwright with 18 "hits" in 15 years – four of them running simultaneously in New York theatres in 1920 – Hopwood understood both popular commercial theatre and the slight and ephemeral nature of his artistry. Most of his best works were written in collaboration with others: *Clothes* (1906), his first play, with CHANNING POL-LOCK; four plays, including *The* BAT (1920), with MARY ROBERTS RINEHART; GETTING GERTIE'S GAR-TER (1921) with Wilson Collison; and *The Best People* (1924) with David Gray. Other play titles suggest the clever, risqué character of his work – *The Gold Diggers* (1919), *Little Miss Bluebeard* (1923),

Naughty Cinderella (1925) – that almost guaranteed success. His biography by Jack F. Sharrar was published in 1989.   WJM

Horizon by AUGUSTIN DALY was initially staged by him at the Olympic Theatre, NYC, in 1871. The production featured AGNES ETHEL as the heroine and GEORGE L. FOX as a comically crooked politician. Influenced by the then-current Indian wars and BRET HARTE's fiction, Daly's mix of sensation and local color paints a more realistic picture of frontier life than had been popular in the theatre. His stage Indian, Wannemucka, for example, is cynical, courageous, and lazy, a more complex portrayal than the conventional noble or murdering savage (see NATIVE AMERICANS PORTRAYED). The plot – which includes Indian attacks, lynching committees, corrupt politics, and a last-minute rescue by the army – centers on a romance between a socially prominent officer and a "white flower of the plains." The self-sacrifice of a gambler finally unites the couple in marriage. The popularity of *Horizon* led to the staging of several other frontier dramas at eastern theatres.   BMcC

Hornblow, Arthur (1865–1942) English-born editor and author who studied in Paris and worked as a correspondent for English and American newspapers before coming to the U.S. in 1889. He pursued a career as a journalist, working first for the *Kansas City Globe* and then the *NEW YORK DRAMATIC MIRROR*. He was foreign editor for the *New York Herald* during 1894–9, and copy-editor for the *New York Times* in 1899. During 1910–26 he served as editor of *Theatre Magazine,* frequently reviewing opening nights. Afterward, for two years, he served as Dean of the JOHN MURRAY ANDERSON–Robert Milton School of Theatre and Dance in New York. Hornblow's greatest financial success came from novelizing popular plays, including *The Lion and the Mouse, The EASIEST WAY,* and *Bought and Paid For.* His two-volume *A History of the Theatre in America* (1919) remains a flawed but standard reference work.   TLM

Horner, Harry (1912–94) Czechoslovakian-born designer, director, and architect who came to the U.S. as an assistant director to MAX REINHARDT on *The Eternal Road* (1936). His greatest acclaim as a designer was for *LADY IN THE DARK* (1941), which employed an elaborate turntable system for scene changes.   AA

Horovitz, Israel (Arthur) (1939–) Massachusetts-born, Harvard-educated playwright-screenwriter-actor spent two years at the London Royal Academy of Dramatic Art (1961–3), a year as resident playwright with the Royal Shakespeare Company (1965), and in 1977 received an M.A. in literature from CUNY. The prolific author of more than 70 plays, he attracted critical attention in 1968 with the New York production one-acts: *It's Called the Sugar Plum, The INDIAN WANTS THE BRONX, Line,* and *Rats* – plays about territoriality and urban violence in America. Also in 1968, his one-act *Morning* appeared on Broadway together with short pieces by TERRENCE MCNALLY and Leonard Melfi. Other early plays include *The Good Parts* (1982) and *The Wakefield Plays* (1974–9), which include *The Alfred Trilogy* and *The Quannatowitt Quartet.* In 1979 Horovitz founded the Gloucester Stage Company in his home state, where most of his plays have since premiered (e.g., *Henry Lumper,* 1985; *The Chopin Playoffs,* 1986; *A Rosen by Any Other Name,* 1987; *Park Your Car in Harvard Yard,* 1991; *Unexpected Tenderness,* 1994; *Lebensraum,* 1996; *My Old Lady,* 1996 [NYC, 2002]; and *Stations of the Cross,* 1998). He retired as its artistic director at the end of 2006. His screenwriting credits include *The Strawberry Statement, Believe In Me, Author! Author!,* and *A Man in Love* (with Diane Kurys). He is the founder of the NY Playwrights Lab and winner of numerous awards.   TLM

Hot l Baltimore LANFORD WILSON's three-act comedy-drama is named for its setting, the lobby of a run-down hotel that has lost an "e" from its marquee. The sweetly eccentric characters who interact there and dream of better times were sensitively portrayed by a fine ensemble directed by MARSHALL W. MASON. The Circle Theatre Company (now CIRCLE REPERTORY) opened the play in an OFF-OFF BROADWAY loft theatre on 27 January 1973. The favorable public and critical response garnered during its 17 performances enabled the production to move OFF-BROADWAY to the CIRCLE IN THE SQUARE, where it opened on 22 March 1973 (1,166 performances). It won the Drama Critics' Circle Award for best play and became the basis for an ABC-TV series in 1975.   FHL

Houdini, Harry [né Erik Weisz] (1874–1926) Magician and escape artist, born the son of a rabbi in Budapest; his stage name was an homage to the 19th-century French conjuror Robert-Houdin. Starting in dime museums and CIRCUSES as the self-styled "King of Cards," he gained prominence in 1895 with his escapes from handcuffs and straitjackets. A genius at self-promotion, he was soon challenging police forces throughout the world to keep him pent up, and once escaped from a chained packing crate at the bottom of a river; these escapes were often engineered by concealed keys, one passed in a kiss from his wife. Other tricks involved making an elephant vanish, and swallowing 70 needles and 20 yards of thread and bringing them up threaded. Houdini was also the first to fly an airplane in Australia (1910), enjoyed a career as a silent-film star, and, after his mother's death in 1913, exposed fraudulent mediums. G. B. SHAW called him one of the three most famous persons in the world (the other two being Jesus Christ and Sherlock Holmes). *Houdini*, a "circus-opera" by Adrian Mitchell and Peter Schat, was performed in Amsterdam in 1977; a musical *Houdini* played at GOODSPEED in 1997. His definitive biography was written by Kenneth Silverman in 1996, complemented by the 2006 study by William Kalush and Larry Sloman.   LS

Houghton, (Charles) Norris (1909–2001) Indiana-born producer, educator, designer, and writer. A 1931 Princeton graduate, he designed eight Broadway productions and directed four between 1932 and 1957. As founder and co–managing director of OFF-BROADWAY's PHOENIX THEATRE, he helped mount almost 75 productions (1953–64). He taught at numerous institutions; his last full-time position was at SUNY–Purchase (1967–80). A frequent writer and editor, Houghton was the author of eight books, including the influential *Moscow Rehearsals* (1936), *Advance from Broadway* (1941), and *Return Engagement* (1962). His superb autobiography, *Entrances and Exits,* was published in 1991. Twice a Guggenheim Fellow, in 1962 he became a Fellow of the American Academy of Arts and Sciences.   DBW

Hould-Ward, Ann (1951–) Montana-born costume designer, educated at Mills College and the University of Virginia. Her career began as an assistant to PATRICIA ZIPPRODT; she received a Tony nomination for her first Broadway production, codesigned with Zipprodt, SUNDAY IN THE PARK WITH GEORGE. Nominated again in 1988 (*Into the Woods*), she won a Tony in 1994 for *Beauty and the Beast*. Her beautiful renderings, often referred to as illustrations, reveal a gift with color and texture that is in demand on and OFF-BROADWAY, in the top regional theatres, and for dance, including American Ballet Theatre's *The Pied Piper*. Her flair for spectacle led to designs for RINGLING BROS. and Barnum & Bailey during 2002–4.   BO

Houseman, John [né Jacques Haussman] (1902–88) Bucharest-born director, producer, and actor. Educated in England, Houseman began producing

in New York in 1934 and was affiliated for a time with the FEDERAL THEATRE PROJECT. Some of his finest work was with ORSON WELLES and the MERCURY THEATRE, which he cofounded in 1937 – notably his production of *Julius Caesar* in modern dress. He served as artistic director for such producing agencies as the AMERICAN SHAKE-SPEARE FESTIVAL (1956–9), the professional Theatre Group of the University of California at Los Angeles (1959–64), and the Drama Division of the Juilliard School of the Performing Arts (1968–76). In 1972 Houseman founded the ACTING COMPANY, originally known as the City Center Acting Company, directing several productions for them.

Houseman won great popular acclaim by playing an acerbic law professor in the television series *Paper Chase* (1978–86). He published three detailed and valuable accounts of his life in the theatre: *Run-Through* (1972), *Front and Center* (1981), and *Final Dress* (1983). The three were conflated into *Unfinished Business* (1989).   SMA

House of Blue Leaves, The, by John Guare was first produced on 10 February 1971 at the Truck and Warehouse Theatre in NYC. Its cast, directed by MEL SHAPIRO, included Harold Gould as Artie Shaughnessy, a middle-aged zoo worker who aspires to be a Hollywood songwriter; Katherine Helmond as his wife, Bananas, who is most comfortable as a dog; Anne Meara as Bunny Flingus, who will have sex with Artie anytime, but refuses to cook for him until after they are married; Frank Converse as Billy Einhorn, Artie's producer friend, who ends up with Bunny; and William Atherton as Artie's son, Ronnie, who blows up Billy's girlfriend with a bomb he had intended for the pope. The play was revived successfully at the VIVIAN BEAUMONT THEATRE at Lincoln Center in 1986 with STOCKARD CHANNING as Bunny, John Mahoney as Artie, and SWOOSIE KURTZ as Bananas. The play, set in Queens during Pope Paul VI's visit to New York in 1965, uses absurdist techniques to critique marriage, the American family, the Catholic Church, and contemporary human relationships generally.   BCM

House of Connelly, The, was written by PAUL GREEN and produced by the newly formed GROUP THEATRE at the MARTIN BECK THEATRE on 28 September 1931. It was directed by LEE STRASBERG and CHERYL CRAWFORD and featured prominent members of the Group, including Art Smith, MORRIS CARNOVSKY, and STELLA ADLER. Set in the American South in 1905, the play dramatized plantation life against a background of family power, class prerogatives, and racial injustice. Widely compared to CHEKHOV and featuring superb ensemble acting, the play received largely positive notices but closed after 72 performances. However, its production was more significant than its dramatic merit: It became the landscape upon which the struggle between the THEATRE GUILD and its "apprentice company" was played out. The Guild had optioned the play to the Group, who had worked on it almost daily in the summer of 1931 in conjunction with their study of the Stanislavsky System. Prior to opening, they squabbled with the Guild Board over the ending, casting, and actor credits. Eventually the Group severed all ties to the Guild and became one of America's most influential companies.   BBW

House of Mirth, The Dramatization with dialogue by Edith Wharton and scenario by CLYDE FITCH of Wharton's popular novel about Lily Bart, whose true love is thwarted by the viciousness of New York society. Starring Fay Davis, the play opened on 22 October 1906 at the Savoy Theatre for a disappointing 14 performances. Following several dramatizations of novels during 1900–6, the play's failure precipitated media discussion of the difficulty of turning a thoughtful psychological novel into a popular Broadway play. An important revival with some textual changes was undertaken in 1998 by the MINT THEATER.   FB

How I Learned to Drive PAULA VOGEL's 1997 Pulitzer Prize–winning play, which opened in March at the Vineyard Theatre then moved to OFF-BROADWAY's Century Theatre, where it ran a year (400 total performances). With MARY-LOUISE PARKER (Li'l Bit) and David Morse (her Uncle Peck) and directed by MARK BROKAW, the play deals with such highly charged issues as incest and pedophilia. Controversial in that the uncle is an engaging pedophile rather than a villain, Vogel's play is typical of her tendency to deal with politically incorrect subjects that seduce the audience with humor and surprising objectivity yet penetrating insight into social or political problems. *Drive* was the most produced play in the U.S. during 1998 (26 regional productions) and continues to be staged frequently.   DBW

How to Succeed in Business without Really Trying Two-act musical comedy, music and lyrics by FRANK LOESSER, book by ABE BURROWS, Jack Weinstein, and Willie Gilbert; opened 14 October 1961 at the 46TH STREET THEATRE, running 1,417 performances. Based on Shepherd Mead's book of the same name, this cynical, cartoonlike satire of American big business traces the rise of its charming cad of a hero (ROBERT MORSE as J. Pierrepont Finch) from window washer to chairman of the board. Overturning many traditional musical-comedy devices, it downplays any romantic element by making its characters strongly unsympathetic; even the primary love ballad is sung by the character to himself in a mirror. The show won the Pulitzer Prize for drama, as well as the Drama Critics' Circle and Tony awards for Best Musical. Morse and Charles Nelson Reilly (as Bud Frump) both won Tonys. Originally staged by Abe Burrows and choreographed by Hugh Lambert, the production was largely reworked by BOB FOSSE, who was called in to doctor it and given credit for "musical staging." A successful revival nurtured at the LA JOLLA PLAYHOUSE was seen on Broadway in 1995 with Matthew Broderick (Tony Award) in the Morse role.   JD

Howard, Bronson (Crocker) (1842–1908) The first professional American playwright; the first to distinguish the American businessman in his plays; and one of the first to define his DRAMATIC THEORY in an essay, "The Laws of Dramatic Composition." Among his businessman plays are *Young Mrs. Winthrop* (1882), a sympathetic treatment of the neglected wife; *The HENRIETTA* (1887), a satire of life on the stock exchange; and *Aristocracy* (1892), which ridiculed new and old American wealth. Howard's awareness of social class stretched from *Saratoga* (1870), adapted to English circumstance as *Brighton* (1874), to *One of Our Girls* (1885), comparing American and French women. *The BANKER'S DAUGHTER* (1878), given notoriety by Howard's lecture "Autobiography of a Play" (1886), and his Civil War melodrama *SHENANDOAH* (1888) epitomized his popular success. Aided by his association with the Theatrical SYNDICATE, Howard raised the status of the American playwright with his plays and as a founder of the American Dramatists' Club in 1891.   WJM

Howard, Sidney (Coe) (1891–1939) Playwright who, in the 1920s, was a crucial figure in lifting American drama from provincial entertainment to an authentic native literature. In a group of provocative plays – THEY KNEW WHAT THEY WANTED (which won the Pulitzer Prize in 1925), *Lucky Sam McCarver* (1925), *Ned McCobb's Daughter* (1926), *The SILVER CORD* (1926), and *Half Gods* (1929) – he looked at such subjects as sex, mother love, psychiatry, and prohibition with a fresh point of view. Like EUGENE O'NEILL, Howard helped to popularize Freudian ideas about family and sexual relationships; but his focus, unlike O'Neill's, was intimate and his tone essentially comic. His best play, *They Knew What They Wanted,* advocates moral and sexual compromise, and in *Ned Mc-Cobb's Daughter* he created one of the era's most appealing New Women, a heroine with more sense than any of the men in her life. Because Howard thought of himself as a skilled craftsman rather than as an artist with a distinctive voice, he was a jack-of-all-trades who wrote in a number of genres: spectacle, romance, the war story, and both urban and rural comedy. He frequently collaborated, and he translated and adapted the work of other writers (*The Late Christopher Bean* [1932] and *Dodsworth* [1934] were both acclaimed). He was also an active screenwriter, winning an Academy Award for *Gone with the Wind* (1939) and nominations for *Arrowsmith* (1931) and *Dodsworth* (1936). His remarkably productive career – at least 27 plays and 13 screenplays – ended suddenly in 1939 when he had a fatal tractor accident on his Massachusetts farm. A dual biography by Arthur Gewirtz of Howard and his actress wife, Clare Eames, was published in 2004. FH

Howard, Willie (1886–1949) and **Eugene** (1880–1965) Comedians. Like many performers of their day, the Howard brothers developed their comic personae in VAUDEVILLE. Their first joint appearance on the legitimate musical stage was in *The Passing Show of 1912.* Eugene served as the straight man for the act, while the sad-faced Willie got most of the laughs. Their talents were best displayed in REVUES: In addition to appearing in six of the *Passing Shows,* they starred in six editions of *GEORGE WHITE's Scandals.* Willie's abilities as a mimic made him especially valuable in revues that emphasized travesties of the latest performers and shows. In addition to their comic talents, both brothers had fine singing voices, which they often displayed in parodies of grand opera. After Eugene's retirement in 1940, Willie continued as a solo performer, but never again had the success that the brothers had achieved as a team. MK

Howard Athenaeum BOSTON theatre; opened in 1845, but burned three months later when a fireball effect during *Pizarro* went awry (see FIRES). The second Howard (1846), the first American theatre to have cushioned seats, offered its 2,000 patrons unobstructed views of the stage. JAMES H. HACKETT was the theatre's first manager, and a STOCK COMPANY was maintained there until the late 1860s. Speciality acts and burlesques were initiated by manager JOHN STETSON in 1871. By 1953 these had degenerated into poorly performed, if fondly remembered, bump-and-grind striptease (see NUDITY), and city authorities closed the the-

atre. The building was razed in 1961 after a serious fire. TC

Howard family Performers. **George Cunnabel Howard** (1820–87), a Canadian-born actor, was engaged at the BOSTON MUSEUM, where he met and married (1844) the actress Caroline Emily Fox (1829–1908). With a STOCK COMPANY that included Caroline's mother and three brothers (see GEORGE L. FOX), they toured New England in abbreviated versions of *The DRUNKARD* and *The Factory Girl* intermingled with an olio of songs and dances. As a respectable family unit they acclimatized theatre in towns that had hitherto condemned all playacting as damnable. The Howards achieved their most durable success with an adaptation of *UNCLE TOM's CABIN* (1852), carpentered by their cousin GEORGE AIKEN and featuring George Howard as St. Clare, Caroline as Topsy, and their daughter Cordelia as Eva; when played in an expanded text at the National Theatre (New York, 1853), it captured the imagination of the times. Cordelia became the star of the family, also creating the title role in *Katy the Hot Corn Girl* and Little Gerty in *The Lamplighter.* LS

Howe, Tina (1937–) Playwright whose plays, characterized by a strong central metaphor and contrapuntal, parallel speeches, present the contrast between polished public behavior and quirky private characters. Heavily influenced by the MARX BROS., her early works – *The Nest* (1969), *Birth and After Birth* (publ. 1973; 2006, ATLANTIC THEATER), *Museum* (1976), and *The Art of Dining* (1979) [both at The PUBLIC] – are farcical criticisms of pretentiousness. Her later plays, most initially directed by Carole Rothman of SECOND STAGE, are realistic plays filled with fantasy. Her first big success was *Painting Churches* (1983, Outer Critics Circle Award), an autobiographical play about a painter making peace with her aging parents. *Coastal Disturbances* (1986), *Approaching Zanzibar* (1989), *One Shoe Off* (1993), *Pride's Crossing* (1997) – the latter made memorable by actress CHERRY JONES – and *Rembrandt's Gift* (2002, Humana Festival) deal with more painful subjects, often in bizarre contexts but still in Howe's unique comedic style, with themes concerning love, loss, and denial of reality. In 1983, Howe won a collective Obie for Distinguished Playwriting. TH-S

Howells, William Dean (1837–1920) Novelist, critic, and playwright. "The Father of Realism" in America, Howells not only praised the work of EDWARD HARRIGAN, JAMES HERNE, and HENRIK IBSEN, but contributed himself to the rise of realism in drama and the development of social comedy. Both *A Counterfeit Presentment* (1877) and *Yorick's Love* (1878) were acted successfully by LAWRENCE BARRETT. The author of some 36 plays, Howells wrote 12 one-act farces featuring social events in the lives of two couples (the Robertses and the Campbells), including *The Garroters* (1885), in which Roberts mistakenly garrotes a friend; *Five O'Clock Tea* (1887), wherein Campbell becomes engaged; and *The Unexpected Guest* (1893), in which Mr. and Mrs. Campbell entertain. A writer of charming dialogue but incapable of producing the melodramatic confrontations demanded by 19th-century audiences, Howells pictured instead such man–woman struggles as broken engagements (*An Indian Giver*, 1897; *Parting Friends*, 1910). Howells was a gentle satirist of Boston manners who became bitter in later plays (*The Impossible*, 1910; *The Night before Christmas*, 1910), and his work appealed more to amateur than professional performers. The most recent biography of Howells – thoroughly researched and documented – is by Susan Goodman and Carl Dawson (2005).   WJM

Hoyle, Geoff (1946–) NEW VAUDEVILLIAN, actor. Born in England and trained in Paris with Étienne Decroux, Hoyle has worked in the U.S. since 1975, when he joined the Pickle Family CIRCUS in San Francisco. Hoyle toured with them until 1982, when he began a career as a solo performer. He has created and performed such shows (largely solo) as *Boomer* (1986), *Feast of Fools* (1988), *Don Quixote de La Jolla* (1990), *The Convict's Return* (1991), *Geni(us)* (1995), and *The First 100 Years* (1999). Hoyle has also appeared with CIRQUE DU SOLEIL and Circus Flora; played Zazu the Hornbill in *The LION KING* (1997) for two years; and often performs at BERKELEY REP and EUREKA THEATRE.   TL

Hoyt, Charles (Hale) (1860–1900) A major writer of farce and satire that, in his best plays, showed social themes and realistic characters. Hoyt, born in Concord, NH, wrote some 20 plays, drawing his material from his own interests and experiences: small-town life (*A Rag Baby*, 1884), his father's early occupation of hotel management (*A Bunch of Keys*, 1882), superstitions (*The Brass Monkey*, 1888), corrupt politics (*A TEXAS STEER*, 1890), Prohibition (*A Temperance Town*, 1893), the hypocrisy of homeguard companies (*A Milk White Flag*, 1894), and baseball (*A Runaway Colt*, 1895). *A TRIP TO CHINATOWN* (1891) – his first at the MADISON SQUARE THEATRE, which he'd taken over and would later rename the Hoyt – had the longest run of any play produced in America to that date (650 performances). Theatre was strictly a business with Hoyt, who revised his work with extreme care and made roughly $485,000 in a good year. There was also stress: Committed to the Retreat for the Insane at Hartford, CT, in 1900, he died that year. Douglas Hunt's biography of Hoyt was published in 1946.   WJM

Hsieh, Tehching (Sam Hsieh) (1950–) Conceptual and PERFORMANCE ARTist, born and raised in rural Noncho, Taiwan; studied painting with Tehgin Shing (1968–9). After being drafted into the Republic of China Army (1970–3), he joined the Merchant Seamen for the Republic of China, jumped ship, and moved to the U.S. (1974). Following his first performance in Taipei (1973), he performed in New York a series of body-art works (1976–7) and a series of one-year-long ordeal performances (1978–86). In his 13-year-long performance (1986–99), he privatized his artwork, neither showing it publicly nor speaking about it. Now retired from performing, his aesthetic was influenced by Asian mysticism and martial arts, the Japanese avant-garde, Christianity, Nietzsche and Kafka, European existentialism, and the *Nouveaux Réalistes*.   AF

Hudson Guild Theatre Founded in 1896 as part of the settlement house movement (see CHILDREN'S THEATRE), the Hudson Guild was established to keep the poor of NYC's Chelsea neighborhood off the streets by involving them in amateur theatricals. The theatre languished after WWII, but it experienced a renaissance in 1975 when it was taken over by David Kerry Heefner and moved into Neighborhood House on West 26th St., amid a multiracial housing project. With professional status, it moved some productions to Broadway. In 1990, the Hudson Guild withdrew its support, and the theatre, newly named the Chelsea Stage Theater, ceased activities.   MCH

Hughes, Barnard (1915–2006) Actor, born in Bedford Hills, NY, and educated at Manhattan College. Hughes made his New York debut in 1934 as the haberdasher in *The Taming of the Shrew*. After minor roles and military service, he developed his range and diversity in major supporting roles on Broadway and Off: *The Teahouse of the August Moon* (1956, City Center), *Enrico IV* (1958, closed out of town), *Advise and Consent* (1960), *A Doll's House* (1963), *Nobody Loves an Albatross* (1963), John Gielgud's *Hamlet* (1964), *Hogan's Goat* (1965), *How Now, Dow Jones* (1967), and *Sheep on the Runway* (1970). One of America's most distinguished character actors, he was acclaimed for his Dogberry in *Much Ado* (1972), Alexander Serebryakov in *Uncle Vanya*

(1973), Falstaff in *The Merry Wives of Windsor* (1974), the title role in *Da* (1978), Father William Doherty in *Angels Fall* (1983), Philip Stone in *End of the World* (1984), Harry Hope in *The Iceman Cometh* (1985), the father in *Prelude to a Kiss* (1990), and Osgood Meeker in Noël Coward's *Waiting in the Wings* (1999). Film credits include *Da* (1988), *The Fantasticks* (1995), and *The Cradle Will Rock* (1999). Hughes was married to actress Helen Stenborg; his son is award-winning director Doug Hughes. TLM

Hughes, Doug(las) (1950?–) During the early 2000s director Hughes's career, though over 30 years in duration, was riding a crest. This native New Yorker, a graduate of Harvard and son of actors (albeit not one himself), won the Tony for his direction of *Doubt,* captured the 2004–5 Joe A. Callaway Award for Excellence in Direction, received numerous nominations for his direction of Bryony Lavery's *Frozen* in 2004, and followed *Doubt* with 2004–5 Roundabout productions of *McKeele, The Paris Letter,* and *A Touch of the Poet.* Other notable NYC productions in recent years include *The Grey Zone* (Obie), *Engaged, Flesh and Blood, The Beard of Avon, A Question of Mercy* (these three for New York Theatre Workshop), and *A Naked Girl on the Appian Way.* His regional successes are equally impressive, with credits for a dozen prestigious companies. From 1997 to 2001 he was artistic director of the Long Wharf (but left with some acrimony); in 1996–7, director of artistic planning at the Guthrie; in 1984–96, associate artistic director of Seattle Repertory and, 1980–3, of the Manhattan Theatre Club. Currently he is resident director at MCC (Manhattan Class Company). Hughes is also a translator-adaptor and is on the faculty of the Yale School of Drama. DBW

Hughes, Hatcher (1883–1945) This southern playwright and teacher, who specialized in folk drama, produced most of his dramatic work in the 1920s and is primarily remembered for one play: the Pulitzer Prize–winning *Hell-Bent for Heaven* (1924). Although many claimed the play won by default when the selection committee's choice of *The Show-Off* was overruled, this rustic melodrama of phony religious zealotry and Carolina mountain feuding, with its heavy dialects, moved numerous audiences and was emblematic of a wave of folk dramas appearing on Broadway in that decade. His other plays of note are *Wake Up, Jonathan* (1921), a comic collaboration with Elmer Rice; *Ruint* (1925), a comedy of enforced marriage, produced at the Provincetown; and a

vehicle for Minnie Maddern Fiske, *It's a Grand Life* (1930). RHW

Hughes, Holly (1955–) Michigan-born poet, playwright, and performance artist who came to New York as a painter and entered the East Village scene of Piezo Electric, Club 57, and the WOW Café. As manager at the WOW Café until 1983, she organized regular "Talking Slide Shows," where artists showed slides and talked about their work. Hughes's first performances were *Shrimp in a Basket* and *The Well of Horniness.* She developed *Dress Suits to Hire* (1987) with Lois Weaver and Peggy Shaw. Her solo performances *The Lady Dick* (1984), *World without End* (1988), and *Dead Meat* (1990) explored the contradictions of multiple pleasures. In late 1993 she began developing *Snatches* (also called *Clit Notes*), a potpourri of narratives dealing with relationships, lesbian desire, gender, and sexual orientation, among other subjects. *Clit Notes: A Sapphic Sampler* was published in 1996. A recent piece, *Preaching to the Perverted* (2000), grew out of her experiences as one of the NEA Four (with Karen Finley, John Fleck, and Tim Miller) who had their grants revoked by the National Endowment for the Arts in 1990. Hughes's autobiographical style is inspired by 1970s feminist insistence on political and sexual autonomy, yet she performs in the stand-up comedic tradition of blasphemy and audience harangues made popular by Lenny Bruce in the 1950s. AF

Hughes, (James Mercer) Langston (1902–67) African American poet, story writer, and playwright. Brought up by his grandmother, whose first husband had died in John Brown's raid at Harper's Ferry, he acquired her racial consciousness and a love of literature. He published his first play, *The Gold Piece,* in 1921, and gained his first Broadway success with *Mulatto* (1935), a melodrama on race relations in a southern town. Hughes achieved substantial New York runs with his folk musical *Simply Heavenly* (1957) and with *Tambourines to Glory* (1963). He received several premieres at the interracial Karamu Theatre in Cleveland, where Hughes attended public school. Among these plays are *Little Ham* (1936; Theatre Row, 2002), *Troubled Island* (1936), *Joy To My Soul* (1937), and *Front Porch* (1938). In addition, Hughes wrote librettos for four produced operas, and the book and lyrics for Kurt Weill's musical version of *Street Scene* (1947). Hughes founded three short-lived theatres: the Harlem Suitcase Theatre, where his polemical *Don't You Want to Be Free?* (1938) ran on weekends for 135 performances;

the New Negro Theatre in Los Angeles (1939); and the Skyloft Players in Chicago (1949). In 1991 his previously unproduced play *Mule Bone* (written with Zora Neale Hurston in 1930) was staged by Lincoln Center at the ETHEL BARRYMORE THEATRE. Hughes's plays are most appealing when his righteous anger is tempered by gentle satire, humor, and lyricism. Definitive is the two-volume biography (1986, 1988) by Arnold Rampersad.
  EGH

Hull, Josephine (1886–1957) Character actress who specialized in eccentric old lady roles. She began by using her maiden name (Sherwood) as she toured, then retired from the stage when she married Shelley Hull in 1910. Upon Hull's death in 1919 she resumed acting. She attracted attention in 1923 in *Neighbors* and increased her stature with CRAIG'S WIFE in 1925. Her style, described as "gasping, fluttery, egregiously middle class," established her stardom in YOU CAN'T TAKE IT WITH YOU (1936), ARSENIC AND OLD LACE (1941), and HARVEY (1944), for the film version of which she won an Oscar. Her last starring role was in *The Solid Gold Cadillac,* during which she collapsed in 1954. William G. B. Carson wrote her biography in 1963.
  SMA

Hull-House Theatre Throughout most of its 90-year history, Chicago's Hull-House offered theatre along with, or as part of, its social-work activity. Founders Jane Addams and Ellen Gates Starr felt from the start (1889) that theatre was an apt tool for social rehabilitation, and the efforts that ensued often exceeded that aim to achieve artistic excellence as well.

The Hull-House Players (1897–1941) were a leader in the Little Theatre movement (see COMMUNITY THEATRE). Edith de Nancrede had long-term (1902–46) success with her CHILDREN'S THEATRE, and Robert Sickinger's revival of the Hull-House theatre program (1963–9) is often credited with having a seminal effect on the reemergence of theatre in CHICAGO.

Two theatre structures outlived the social work: The Jane Addams Theater on Broadway once housed the STEPPENWOLF company (among others), and the Parkway Theater on the South Side housed X-BAG (Experimental Black Actors Guild) during the 1970s and the Chicago Theatre Company (and others) thereafter. SF

Hume, Sam(uel J.) (1885–1962) American set designer and founder of the Detroit Arts and Crafts Theatre. Hume was one of the pioneers of the New Stagecraft (see SCENIC DESIGN) and the Little Theatre movement (see COMMUNITY THEATRE). He studied with Edward Gordon Craig in Florence and subsequently applied Craig's idea of movable screens into "adaptable settings" – unit sets utilizing flats, platforms, draperies, arches, and pylons that could be rearranged, changed, or altered by lighting to fit individual scenes. It was thus a move away from naturalism toward simplification and suggestion, as well as being economical. AA

Huneker, James G(ibbons) (1857–1921) Critic who brought serious public attention to Continental dramatists in the 1890s and early 1900s. Huneker made his debut as a music critic in 1875 for the *Philadelphia Evening Bulletin.* In 1886, after studying piano in Paris, he moved to New York and a position as music critic for the *Musical Courier.* He began writing drama criticism during his tenure with the *New York Recorder* (1891–5). In 1895 he became music and drama critic for the *Morning Advertiser,* and during 1902–4 held the drama post for the *New York Sun.* He also wrote for *Metropolitan Magazine, Puck, Smart Set,* and *New York Times.* His 22 books include *Iconoclasts: A Book of Dramatists* (1905) and his autobiography, *Steeplejack* (1920). Huneker opposed the Genteel Tradition and championed the plays of IBSEN, Strindberg, SHAW, Maeterlinck, and Schnitzler. He brought a lively and impressionistic style to American criticism, and influenced a generation of writers including GEORGE JEAN NATHAN and H. L. Mencken. TLM

Hunt, Linda (1945–) Actress-director, best known as the male Indonesian dwarf in the film *The Year of Living Dangerously* (Academy Award, 1983). Hunt was in MARTHA CLARKE's Obie-winning *A Metamorphosis in Miniature* (1982) and shared an Ensemble Performance Obie for Churchill's *Top Girls* (1983). "Magnetic" and with "a kind of wonderful calm and peaceful wisdom," her size (4′ 9″, 80 lb.) became her signature in KOPIT's *End of the World* (Tony nomination, 1984); *Mother Courage and Her Children* (Boston, 1984); AUNT DAN AND LEMON (The PUBLIC, 1985); EMILY MANN's *Annulla* (New Theatre of Brooklyn, 1988); *The Cherry Orchard* (BROOKLYN ACADEMY OF MUSIC, 1988); and *Three Sisters* (Olga in Mann's MCCARTER THEATRE production, 1992). She has appeared in nearly three dozen feature films. From 1997 to 2002 she was Judge Hiller on television's *The Practice* (24 episodes).
  REK

Hunter, Kim [née Janet Cole] (1922–2002) Stage, film, and television actress whose stage debut was in *Penny Wise* (1939); her Broadway debut was as

Stella in *A Streetcar Named Desire* (1947), a role she re-created on film in 1951, winning an Oscar for Best Actress in a Supporting Role. Hunter, who was blacklisted during the McCarthy era, acted for the Shakespeare Festival Theatre and various stock companies in such roles as Catherine Reardon in *And Miss Reardon Drinks a Little*. After a long stage absence, in 1993 she appeared in Ira Wallach's *The Eye of the Beholder* on Theatre Row and in 1996 succeeded Dulcie Gray as Lady Markby in Peter Hall's production of *An Ideal Husband* on Broadway.   SMA

Huntington Theatre Company, The Founded in 1982 by Boston University, the company, now one of two major non-for-profit theatres in the Boston area (the other, American Repertory Theatre), became a nonprofit corporation in 1986. As of 2007, the Huntington was operating out of three spaces: a 890-seat venue in the heart of the city; the 370-seat Virginia Wimberly Theatre; and the 200-seat Nancy Edward Roberts Studio Theatre, the latter two in the Stanford Calderwood Pavilion at the Boston Center for the Arts. As of 2007 the Huntington had produced nearly 50 New England, American, or world premieres. The current artistic director, Nicholas Martin, succeeded Peter Altman (1982–2000).   DBW

Hurlbut, William J. (1883–1957) Playwright who wrote many Broadway shows between 1908 and 1937, but was most successful with melodramas about women. *The Fighting Hope* (1908), presenting a wife attempting to save her imprisoned husband, and *Lilies of the Field* (1921), in which a divorced woman fights to regain her child, are typical. With *Bride of the Lamb* (1926) he turned to the tragedy of a woman caught up in religious revival and blind love, and produced his most arresting work.   RHW

Hurlyburly David Rabe's play about the coke-snorting Hollywood culture of the 1980s. After premiering at Chicago's Goodman Theatre in April 1984, *Hurlyburly* opened Off-Broadway in June and then transferred to the Ethel Barrymore on Broadway for 343 performances. The original cast, directed by Mike Nichols, included William Hurt (Eddie), Christopher Walken (Mickey [Ron Silver opened on Broadway in this role, but Walken returned]), Sigourney Weaver (Darlene), Judith Ivey (Bonnie; Tony Award), and Jerry Stiller (Artie). Rabe strongly disapproved of Nichols's satiric interpretation and script cuts. A 1986 production at Trinity Rep, directed by David Wheeler, restored Rabe's original script

and intent. In 1988 Rabe directed a production at Los Angeles's Westwood Playhouse; a film version appeared in 1998; and a critically acclaimed Off-Broadway revival in 2005 was directed by Scott Elliott and starred Ethan Hawkes (Eddie), Josh Hamilton (Mickey), Parker Posey (Darlene), and Wallace Shawn (Artie). Focusing on male bonds and identity, *Hurlyburly* is saturated with violence and self-destruction. Hollywood replaces Vietnam as the new battlefield for Rabe. The play's convoluted semantics, laced with nonsense words, mirror the tumultuous discourse of the times. The title – from *Macbeth*, where it signifies confusion – is a fit description of the physical and psychic disorder Rabe dramatizes.   PCK

Hurt [née Supinger]**, Mary Beth** (1946–) Stage and film actress from Iowa, trained at the University of Iowa and NYU, whose "chameleon quality . . . results in a one-woman repertory company," as seen in NYC in DeLillo's *The Day Room* (1987), Hare's *The Secret Rapture* (1989), *Othello* (New York Shakespeare Festival, 1991), Albee's *A Delicate Balance* (1996), and Wasserstein's *Old Money* (2000), as well in as the films *Interiors* (1978), *The World According to Garp* (1982), and *Slaves of New York* (1989). She received the Clarence Derwent Award for *Love for Love* (1974), an Obie for *Crimes of the Heart* (1980), and Tony nominations for *Trelawney of the Wells* (1975), *Crimes* (1981), and *Benefactors* (1985). Divorced from actor William Hurt, she is married to screenwriter-director Paul Schrader.   REK

Hurt, William (1950–) An actor of "distilled and concentrated intensity" whose Off-Broadway debut was in *Henry V* (New York Shakespeare Festival, 1977) and Broadway debut was *Hurlyburly* (1984). Active with the Circle Repertory Company (1977–82), his work since has largely been in films (over 65) – including *Kiss of the Spider Woman* (1985; Academy Award) and *A History of Violence* (2005), for which he won critical acclaim. Hurt won the Obie and *Theatre World* awards for Corinne Jacker's *My Life* (CRC, 1977) and the 1988 Spencer Tracy Award.   REK

Hurwitz, Moishe (1844–1910) and **Jacob Lateiner** (1853–1935) The two main writers of Shund theatre, characterizing the lowest quality of popular American Yiddish theatre (sentimental and melodramatic) during the 1890s. Deliberately writing down to the tastes of the most uneducated and unsophisticated of the "green" immigrants, "Professor" Hurwitz (as he called himself) wrote about 90 plays, and Lateiner more than 150.   AB

Huston, Walter (1884–1950) Canadian-born stage and film actor, noted for his artistic integrity, lack of affectation, and economic style. He began acting in 1902, returned to school, then reentered the theatre in 1909. For almost 18 years he toured the U.S. and Canada. His New York debut was in 1924 in the title role of *Mr. Pitt,* and in the same year he achieved stardom as Ephraim Cabot in DESIRE UNDER THE ELMS. STARK YOUNG called Huston's Ephraim "trenchant, gaunt, fervid, harsh," lauding his "ability to convey the harsh, inarticulate life" of the role. Later BROOKS ATKINSON called Huston "the most honest of actors – plain, simple, lucid, magnetic." He was also acclaimed for his title role in Sinclair Lewis's *Dodsworth* (1934) and for his work in KNICKERBOCKER HOLIDAY (1938), in which he introduced "September Song." In 1948 he won an Academy Award for best supporting actor in *The Treasure of the Sierra Madre,* a film directed by his son, John. His other films included *Dodsworth* and *Duel in the Sun.*   SMA

Hutton, Laurence (1843–1904) Author, critic, and editor. Born in New York and educated at private schools, Hutton worked as a journalist for the *New York Mail* during 1867–75, including two years (1872–4) as drama critic; for *Harper's Magazine* during 1886–98, as literary editor; and for the *Mail and Examiner* in 1903–4. A prolific author, Hutton wrote chatty books about literary landmarks, actors, artists, and famous writers, including *Plays and Players* (1875) and *Curiosities of the American Stage* (1891). He edited the American Actor Series (1881–2) and, with BRANDER MATTHEWS, *Actors and Actresses of Great Britain and the United States* (1886).   TLM

Hwang, David Henry (1957–) Born in Los Angeles to immigrant Chinese parents, and educated at Stanford and Yale, Hwang was the first Asian American playwright to break through to national prominence. He won a Tony (and other prizes) for his 1988 Broadway hit M. BUTTERFLY, a dazzling deconstruction of cross-cultural and sexual delusions. Hwang's career took off in 1980 when *F.O.B,* a sly, enigmatic portrait of a young Chinese immigrant who doubles as a mythic Asian folk god, earned raves at the PUBLIC THEATER. In subsequent works – *The Dance and the Railroad, Family Devotions,* the one-act *The Sound of a Voice* (all at the Public) – Hwang handily mingled history, fantasy, and naturalism to explore a "fluidity of identity" endemic to the multicultural modern age. Though he links himself to the ASIAN AMERICAN THEATRE movement, he refuses to write only about his own ethnic milieu, as witnessed by *Rich Relations* (1986), a satire of upper-middle-class mores, *1,000 Airplanes on the Roof* (1988), a science-fiction collaboration, *Voyage* (1992), an opera, and a 2003 opera version of *Sound of a Voice,* the last three with composer Philip Glass. His *The Dance and the Railroad* and *House of Sleeping Beauties* were presented by EAST WEST PLAYERS in 1993 (directed by P. K. GOTANDA). His comedy about mistaken identity, *Face Value,* closed during previews in New York (1993). *Golden Child,* at The Public in 1996, subsequently moved to Broadway. Hwang was colibrettist for the musical *Aida* (2000), and wrote a new libretto for *Flower Drum Song* (2002) as well as the book for the musical *Tarzan* (2006). For two years he was artist-in-residence at TRINITY REP (1995–7), where he wrote and produced an adapation of Ibsen's *Peer Gynt.*   MB

Hyman, Earle (1926–) AFRICAN AMERICAN actor (born in North Carolina), renowned in classical and contemporary roles. Hyman began with the AMERICAN NEGRO THEATRE and at 17 appeared in ANNA LUCASTA (1944) on Broadway and in London's West End. His earliest Shakespearean role was Hamlet (1951) at Howard University, followed by the first of six Othellos played over a 25-year period in Antioch (OH), New York, Connecticut, Norway, and Sweden. Hyman performed 10 other roles with the AMERICAN SHAKESPEARE THEATRE (1955–60), received rave notices for his Broadway performance in *Mister Johnson* (1956), and the State Award in Oslo, Norway, for his portrayal of the title role in *The* EMPEROR JONES (1965). In 1989 he replaced Morgan Freeman as the chauffeur, Hoke, in DRIVING MISS DAISY, also performing the play in Norway and Denmark (in Norwegian and Danish). In 1991 he essayed the role of Pickering in ROUNDABOUT's nontraditionally cast *Pygmalion,* in 1992 appeared in *The Master Builder* for the NATIONAL ACTORS THEATRE, and starred in 1994 in the PUBLIC THEATER's *East Texas Hot Links* by Eugene Lee. His most recent roles have included Teiresias in *The Oedipal Play* (2001, SHAKESPEARE THEATRE) and Firs in CLASSICAL THEATRE OF HARLEM's *Cherry Orchard* (2004–5). Despite his notable credits Hyman is best known by the public as Bill Cosby's father on the long-running television series *The Cosby Show* (1984–92).   EGH

I

I Am a Camera John Van Druten's three-act drama adapted from Christopher Isherwood's *The Berlin Stories;* opened on Broadway at the Empire Theatre (28 November 1951) for 214 performances, winning the Drama Critics' Circle Award. Directed by the author, the production was praised for Julie Harris's portrayal of Sally Bowles. Set in prewar Berlin in 1930, the action is seen through the eyes of the sensitive young writer Christopher (Isherwood), who is taking mental photographs of the wild characters and liberal, irreverent attitudes surrounding him. The show was revived Off-Broadway in October 1956 at the Actors' Playhouse, Sheridan Square. Cabaret (1966), a musical by Joe Masterhoff and Kander and Ebb, was based on this play.
EK

I Am My Own Wife Doug Wright's Tony- and Pulitzer-winning solo show began Off-Broadway in May 2003 (Playwrights Horizons), moved to Broadway on 3 December, and ran through 31 October 2004 (387 performances). Based on a true story and developed over a decade through interviews, correspondence, and other primary sources by the author with the assistance of the subject of the play, Charlotte von Mahlsdorf (1928–2000), Wright recounts the exotic and inspiring story of the real-life German transvestite who survived both the Nazis and the communists in East Germany. A complex biography is dramatized – with one actor playing von Mahlsdorf and 40 other characters – with sensitivity and effectiveness, despite some structural weaknesses. The production was considerably enhanced by the Tony-winning (Best Actor) Jefferson Mays (in his first Broadway show), whose performance was believable, complex, and remarkable in its detail while navigating a wide range of supporting roles; likewise, Moisés Kaufman's (see Tectonic) direction brought clarity and subtlety to the whole, helping to make this a surprising but well-deserved hit. In London, however, the production, though still with Mays, was considerably less successful, running only a month at the end of 2005, two months fewer than expected. DBW

I Remember Mama by John Van Druten is a two-act drama adapted from Kathryn Forbes's stories, *Mama's Bank Account.* Directed by the author and produced by Rodgers and Hammerstein [II], the production opened at the Music Box Theatre (19 October 1944) for 714 performances, starring Mady Christians and a young Marlon Brando. It was later developed into a film (with Irene Dunne) and a television series (with Peggy Wood). The play depicts struggling Norwegian immigrants in San Francisco in 1910. Warm, sensible, and devoted Mama is the play's pivotal character, who gently and selflessly encourages her family's success. The play served as a nostalgic escape from the war-ridden world of 1944.
EK

Ibsen on the American stage In 1882 a group of amateurs introduced Ibsen to this country when they presented a version of *A Doll's House* in Milwaukee. A year later, Helena Modjeska presented her adaptation of the play in Louisville, KY, but it was withdrawn after one performance. Until the turn of the century Ibsen was considered an iconoclast, and most critics, such as William Winter, were hostile, calling his characters dramatic freaks and attacking the plays as overly pessimistic.

Risking their careers, actresses such as Beatrice Cameron, Blanche Bates, Ethel Barrymore, Nance O'Neil, and Florence Kahn pioneered. Minnie Maddern Fiske revived *A Doll's House* (1894, 1895, 1902) and *Hedda Gabler* (1903), and Mary Shaw presented *Ghosts* (1899, 1903) both in New York and on major national tours. Former generations of actresses had turned to Shakespeare's Juliet to exhibit their virtuosity, but now they turned to Ibsen's heroines.

By 1906 opinion had changed. With the growth of the U.S.'s industrial society and the appearance of emancipated women, major literary critics such as William Dean Howells and James Gibbons Huneker came to Ibsen's defense. Supporting the efforts of Mrs. Fiske were the productions of foreign stars, especially those of the exotic Russian Alla Nazimova, who electrified audiences

Lee Breuer's and Mabou
Mines' *DollHouse,* 2003.
Photo by Richard Termine.
Courtesy: Richard Termine.

with her sensual performances in *Hedda Gabler* (1906), *A Doll's House* (1907), and *The Master Builder* (1907). A few years later she added *Little Eyolf* (1910), and Mrs. Fiske toured *Pillars of Society* (1910).

Oddly, from 1912 to 1922 there were only four New York seasons that included Ibsen productions. No foreign stars toured his plays to the U.S.; no one took his plays on the road. Besides the occasional revival by Mary Shaw or Nazimova, Ibsen's name was kept alive only through silent films based on his plays: *Ghosts* and *Peer Gynt* (1915), *Hedda Gabler* (1917), and *A Doll's House* (1917, 1918, 1922). The neglect was due in part to Ibsen's name being linked with the women's movement: As women slowly gained more rights, his pleas for social reform seemed irrelevant. Another reason was the feverish growth of nationalism after WWI. Americans turned inward and rejected their European heritage, including the plays of Ibsen, which seemed unsuitable and remote.

In the atmosphere of reform that spawned the OFF-BROADWAY movement, however, important critics such as H. L. Mencken, Edmund Wilson, JOSEPH WOOD KRUTCH, and Herman Weigand turned to Ibsen in the early 1920s and proclaimed his genius. Weigand's *The Modern Ibsen* relied heavily on Freudian psychology, which profoundly influenced future productions. In 1923 the THEATRE GUILD starred JOSEPH SCHILDKRAUT in its revival of *Peer Gynt.* That same year Eleanora Duse broke box-office records as she toured America with *The Lady from the Sea* and *Ghosts.* The Actors' Theatre revived *Hedda Gabler* (1924, 1926), *The*

Wild Duck (1925), and *Ghosts* (1926). Other revivals included *Rosmersholm* (1925), *Little Eyolf* (1926), *Ghosts* (1927), and *Enemy of the People* (1927). During the 1928–9 season BLANCHE YURKA offered an Ibsen series that included *The Wild Duck, Hedda Gabler,* and *The Lady from the Sea,* and in 1930 she starred in the American premiere of *The Vikings.* EVA LE GALLIENNE established her CIVIC REPERTORY THEATRE with *The Master Builder* and *John Gabriel Borkman* (1925), and later added *Hedda Gabler* (1928). In 1928 Le Gallienne and Yurka appeared in simultaneous Manhattan productions of *Hedda Gabler;* in 1929 there were six Ibsen productions in New York.

However, with the trauma of the Great Depression, Americans began to reject foreign classics. The temper of the times was introspective, and theatregoers sought American plays that dealt with the nation's contemporary social and economic problems. Eva Le Gallienne persisted in championing Ibsen with her revivals of *The Master Builder* (1934, 1939), *Hedda Gabler* (1934, 1939, 1948), *A Doll's House* (1934), *Rosmersholm* (1935), *John Gabriel Borkman* (1946), and *Ghosts* (1948), but she was attacked for exhibiting sacred relics that belonged in museums. The real center of Ibsen interest was on university and college campuses: In 1956 an Ibsen play either had been or was being planned for production at two-thirds of all American universities.

When John F. Kennedy won the 1960 presidential election, it inaugurated an atmosphere of change and inspired progress and reform in such areas as civil rights and women's liberation. Predictably, this meant renewed interest in Ibsen. James Walter McFarlane's *Discussions of Henrik Ibsen* (1962) set the tone for new interpretations; Rolf Fjelde and Eva Le Gallienne provided new translations. David Ross began a series of revivals at NYC's Fourth Street Theatre: *Hedda Gabler* (1960), *Ghosts* (1961), and *Rosmersholm* (1962). Le Gallienne directed for the National Repertory Theatre a national tour of *Hedda Gabler* that starred Signe Hasso. Between 1965 and 1975 professional productions were presented at most regional theatres around the country, and Ibsen's plays were finally accepted as popular classics. Washington, DC's JOHN F. KENNEDY CENTER FOR THE PERFORMING ARTS opened its new Eisenhower Theatre in 1971 with *A Doll's House*.

A new generation of American actresses began their explorations of his heroines: Jane Fonda, Marsha Mason, CAROLE SHELLEY, JANE ALEXANDER, DIANNE WIEST, KIM HUNTER, IRENE WORTH, and GERALDINE PAGE. European stars imported Ibsen to New York: CLAIRE BLOOM's *A Doll's House* and *Hedda Gabler* (both 1971), Liv Ullmann's *A Doll's House* (1975) and *Ghosts* (1982), Glenda Jackson's RSC *Hedda* (1975, NATIONAL THEATRE; 1976, film), Vanessa REDGRAVE's *Lady from the Sea* (1976), and Susannah York's *Hedda Gabler* (1981, ROUNDABOUT).

The Ibsen Society of America (founded in 1979) inspired the establishment in 1982 of the American Ibsen Theater, which lasted three seasons. Ibsen's plays had finally become so absorbed into the fabric of American culture that BETTY COMDEN AND ADOLPH GREEN wrote a musical sequel to *A Doll's House* called *A Doll's Life* (1982), and a new version of that play by Irish writer Frank McGuinness ran at the BELASCO in 1997 with a Tony Award–winning performance by the statuesque British actress Janet McTeer. In 2003 director LEE BREUER presented a controversial version called *DollHouse*, with actors in the male roles shorter than four and a half feet, while the women were exceptionally tall. In 1984 CHARLES LUDLAM starred in a transgender interpretation of *Hedda Gabler* (Pittsburgh); KATE BURTON, bringing humor to the role, starred on Broadway in JON ROBIN BAITZ's version of the play in 2001; in 2004 Christopher Hampton's translation directed by the Flemish director Ivo van Hove with Elizabeth Marvel as a modern antiheroine was seen at the NEW YORK THEATRE WORKSHOP in a production termed "strange and strangely enthralling"; and in 2006 the Australian actress Cate Blanchett offered a riveting yet emotionally cold Hedda in the Sydney Theatre Company production at the BROOKLYN ACADEMY OF MUSIC.   RAS

Icebound Pulitzer Prize–winning drama by OWEN DAVIS, produced by SAM HARRIS; opened 10 February 1923 at the Sam H. Harris Theatre for 170 performances. Though *Icebound* seemed to confirm Davis's turn from facile melodrama, all of its characters – hardened by greed and a rigorous existence in rural Maine – get their just deserts when the family matriarch dies. The cast featured Robert Ames as the black-sheep son who inherits the estate, and Phyllis Povah as the distant relation.   MR

Iceman Cometh, The Though EUGENE O'NEILL's play premiered 9 October 1946 produced by the THEATRE GUILD at the MARTIN BECK THEATRE, ably directed by EDDIE DOWLING and beautifully designed by ROBERT EDMOND JONES, it was not regarded as of the first rank until its splendid arena revival of 8 May 1956 at CIRCLE IN THE SQUARE, staged by JOSÉ QUINTERO with JASON ROBARDS JR., in the pivotal role of Hickey. A similar success greeted the 1999 Broadway revival with KEVIN SPACEY as Hickey (following a year at the Almeida Theatre in London). This long, "lower depths" play recaptures many of O'Neill's experiences and friends while habituating cheap West Side gin mills and their back rooms, like Harry Hope's saloon, in his alcoholic youth (1912). Into a world of lost dreams and hopeless hopes, where people drink to kill the pain, O'Neill interjects a reformed savior Hickey who attempts to drag his alcoholic friends out of their stupor and pipe dreams to face truth. He convinces some to discard their habitual excuses and actuate their dreams. All fail, of course, and use Hickey's confession of murdering his wife to return to stasis and the oblivion of alcohol. A beautifully written but depressing study of humankind's inability to act, the play marks O'Neill's return, after many years of theatrical experiment, to a realism from which he never again diverged.   RHW

Idiot's Delight by ROBERT E. SHERWOOD. Winner of the 1936 Pulitzer Prize for Drama, this three-act comedy-melodrama with music opened at the SAM S. SHUBERT THEATRE on 24 March 1936 and ran for 299 performances. The elegant THEATRE GUILD production was designed by LEE SIMONSON and featured ALFRED LUNT AND LYNN FONTANNE as an American hoofer and phony Russian countess stranded in a resort in the Italian Alps as world war erupts. The unusual tension of the play between its antiwar theme and romantic-comedy framework effectively captured American anxieties about a coming war in Europe. A film version starring Clark Gable and Norma Shearer was released in 1939, and Sherwood's play served as the basis of an unsuccessful 1983 musical by ALAN JAY LERNER and CHARLES STROUSE called *Dance a Little Closer.*   MF

Imperial Theatre 249 West 45th St., NYC [Architect: HERBERT J. KRAPP]. Built by the SHUBERT BROTHERS to house their special brand of musical theatre, the playhouse opened in 1923, and has since booked fewer than 60 productions, giving it a reputation as a "lucky house." Among its most interesting nonmusical tenants have been Leslie Howard in *Hamlet* (1936), Jean Arthur in *Peter Pan* (1950), and John Osborne's *A Patriot for Me* (1969). Leading the list of its extraordinary musical successes have been *Oh, Kay!* (1926), ON YOUR TOES (1936), ANNIE GET YOUR GUN (1946), FIDDLER ON THE ROOF (1964), *Dreamgirls* (1981), JEROME ROBBINS' BROADWAY (1989, a pastiche of his past hits), and LES MISÉRABLES (which transferred from the Broadway in 1990 and broke house records, closing in May 2003 after 6,680 performances). The 1,500-seat theatre remains a Shubert house, which they refurbished.   MCH

In Abraham's Bosom This Pulitzer Prize–winning play by PAUL GREEN was originally staged by Jasper Deeter for the PROVINCETOWN PLAYERS in 1926, with designs by CLEON THROCKMORTON. It featured Jules Bledsoe and ROSE McCLENDON in leading roles. Though some critics claimed that it was too long and structurally awkward, Green's touching folk play about a Negro man who wants to educate his people eventually won a large following and was transferred uptown to the GARRICK. McClendon went on to a brief but significant career, cofounding and working with the Negro People's Theatre and starring in MULATTO before her untimely death.   BBW

In Mizzoura by AUGUSTUS THOMAS. A star vehicle for NAT C. GOODWIN rather than a high point in Thomas's dramaturgy, this four-act drama opened at New York's FIFTH AVENUE THEATRE on 4 September 1893. Its regional sheriff-hero, train-robbing villain, blacksmith father, and three sets of lovers allowed Thomas to tie his characters to both his native state and early career as a railroad employee, and to display the local-color language and mannerisms at which he excelled. Indeed, the dialect is as timely today as when the play was written, despite the melodrama's now shopworn plot featuring a fair-playing villain, a noble and self-sacrificing hero, a heroine misled by her college education, and a community of poor-but-honest folk of limited social views.   RKB

Indian Princess; or, La Belle Sauvage, The "An Operatic Melo-Drame" by JAMES NELSON BARKER, with music by English actor John Bray. It was first performed at the CHESTNUT STREET THEATRE in Philadelphia on 6 April 1808. The libretto offers the earliest surviving treatment of the Pocahontas legend, but focuses less on her rescue of John Smith than on the five pairs of lovers that comprise most of the cast. Bray's music prefigures, by two generations, Sir Arthur Sullivan. The piece was performed at the PARK THEATRE in New York 14 June 1809 and then adapted for its Drury Lane (London) premiere on 15 December 1820 under the title *Pocahontas; or, the Indian Princess.*   JDM

Indian Wants the Bronx, The A one-act realistic play by ISRAEL HOROVITZ staged by James Hammerstein with Horovitz's *It's Called the Sugar Plum* at the Astor Place Theatre (New York), opening 17 January 1968. In this OFF-BROADWAY production, AL PACINO appeared as "Murphy," one of two sadistic punks who senselessly torment a man from India (John Cazale) that they encounter at a street corner in the Bronx. Unable to speak English and apparently separated from his son, the Hindu is subjected to senseless youth violence in a big city. The play, Pacino, and Cazale all won Obies.   ER

Indiana Repertory Theatre Established in Indianapolis, IN, in 1972 by Benjamin Mordecai, Gregory Poggi, and Edward Stern, this is the only not-for-profit professional resident theatre in the state, with an annual audience of 132,000. The group occupied the Atheneum Theater and produced seasons of up to 10 productions of plays from a broad spectrum of types. In 1980, under the leadership of new artistic director, Tom Haas, it moved to the renovated Indiana Theatre, containing three venues: a thrust-proscenium facility seating 607, a smaller proscenium theater seating 269, and a cabaret seating 150. After Haas's death in 1991, Libby Appel was appointed artistic director (July 1992) but resigned in late 1995, replaced in 1996 by Janet Allen, who had been an associate director since 1986 and with the theatre since 1980. Between 1997 at 2001 its theatres were renovated.   WD

Indians by ARTHUR KOPIT had its U.S. premiere at Washington, DC's ARENA STAGE in May 1969, moving to NYC's BROOKS ATKINSON THEATRE in October for 96 performances. In a cast of more than 50 characters, STACY KEACH starred as "BUFFALO BILL" CODY and Manu Tupou was Sitting Bull. Kopit's epic play, staged on an open apron stage, effectively presented a complex drama concerned with genocide, the myth of the West, and, as Kopit later indicated, an exposure of the madness of our involvement in Vietnam. More obvious is the WILD WEST EXHIBITION as symbol for white man's cruelty to, and subjugation of, the Indians (see NATIVE AMERICANS PORTRAYED). In a larger sense, *Indians* deals with the U.S. need to create myths about unpleasant behavior so as to mask historical fact. In demonstrating this theme, Kopit likewise distorts history, but less blatantly than the 1976 film version, *Buffalo Bill and the Indians,* with screenplay by Robert Altman and Alan Randolph.   DBW

industrial drama movement   From 1900 into the mid-1920s, American industries subsidized dramatic clubs, staged company shows, and financed community plays and pageants to promote their public image, Americanize immigrant labor, and control their workers' leisure time. Fearful of strikes and radical political action, and determined to uphold bourgeois morality, businessmen intended their first company theatricals, such as the "Goodyear Greater Minstrels," to compete with and replace working-class entertainments in dance halls, vaudeville theatres, and saloons. Following WWI, the Playground and Recreation Association of America (founded in 1906), financed by businesses and drawing on its wartime service with the Liberty Theatres, propagated the military-camp theatrical as the model for community drama. By 1921, the association's activities, plus the onset of Prohibition and the "Red Scare," induced companies in all the industrial cities and over 300 towns to sponsor the production of local theatricals by and for workers. These included a pageant at the Ford Motor Company advocating a "melting pot" for immigrant culture, and a Labor Day celebration glorifying hard work. The concern of industrial psychologists to merge the cultures of work and play shaped later productions, such as the "Hawthorne Follies," sponsored by a subsidiary of AT&T. The industrial drama movement died out during the 1930s, but continued to influence the policies of numerous COMMUNITY THEATRES.   BMcC

Inge, William (Motter) (1913–73) Playwright. On the strength of his first play, COME BACK LITTLE SHEBA (1950), the critics touted Inge as having the promise to join ARTHUR MILLER and TENNESSEE WILLIAMS in a triumvirate of outstanding American dramatists. Although he never fulfilled that promise, he made considerable impact on American theatre with PICNIC (1953), BUS STOP (1955), and *The Dark at the Top of the Stairs* (1957). Born in

Independence, KS, and educated at the University of Kansas, he taught at Stephens College in Columbia, MO, and at Washington University in St. Louis, and he toured for a season under canvas with a TOBY show; he was thus a product of mid-America, and his works reflected this background. He seemed to cherish his lonely characters: Even as he laid bare their weaknesses, he surrounded them with love and understanding. Inge also recorded their speech with an accurate, appreciative ear. His later works, such as *A Loss of Roses* (1959), *Natural Affection* (1963), and *Where's Daddy?* (1966), drew neither critical acclaim nor much of an audience. He suffered from depression and alcoholism, and his death was by suicide. Since 1981 there has been an annual Inge Festival at the Independence (Kansas) Community College. Ralph Voss's 1989 biography is serviceable.   LDC

Inherit the Wind by JEROME LAWRENCE AND ROBERT E. LEE. Based on the Scopes "Monkey Trial" of 1925, this three-act play dramatizes the furor that erupts when a Tennessee schoolteacher is prosecuted for introducing evolution into the public classroom. The struggle between legislated creationism and freedom of thought is focused in the clash of two powerful men: the persuasive orator Matthew Harrison Brady (based on William Jennings Bryan and first performed in New York by Ed Begley) and the brilliant attorney Henry Drummond (based on Clarence Darrow and performed by PAUL MUNI). The play premiered at Theatre '55 (Dallas, TX) on 10 January 1955, its local cast directed by MARGO JONES, then opened in New York, directed by HERMAN SHUMLIN, 21 April 1955 at the National Theatre, where it ran for 806 performances. The NATIONAL ACTORS THEATRE – whose founder, Tony Randall, had originated the role of E. K. Hornbeck (based on H. L. Mencken) on Broadway – revived the play in 1996 with GEORGE C. SCOTT (Drummond) and CHARLES DURNING (Brady). A 2007 Broadway revival starred BRIAN DENNEHY (Brady) and CHRISTOPHER PLUMMER (Drummond).   KF

Innaurato, Albert (1948–) Obie-winning playwright educated at Temple University and the Yale School of Drama. Drawing on his south Philadelphia background, Innaurato's most successful play, GEMINI, produced in 1976 (PLAYWRIGHTS HORIZONS), deals with an Italian and Catholic family (with the hero, Francis Geminiani, home from Harvard) in this ethnic neighborhood. Other plays include *The Transfiguration of Benno Blimpie* (1973), *Earth Worms* (1974), and *Ulysses in Traction* (1977, CIRCLE REP). In 1980 a collection of his plays appeared, appropriately titled *Bizarre Behavior*. Efforts since *Gemini* have received scant attention, including *Coming of Age in Soho* (1985, The PUBLIC) and *Dreading Thekla* (1997, WILLIAMSTOWN). DBW

INTAR Hispanic American Arts Center This not-for-profit company's name is an acronym for International Arts Relations, suggesting a portion of its artistic policy. Founded in 1966 by a group including Max Ferra, who remained the artistic director until replaced by EDUARDO MACHADO in 2003, INTAR (previously on THEATRE ROW; now at the Annex at 500 West 52d St.) develops and presents contemporary Latin and Hispanic plays, native and foreign. Its seasons have frequently included at least one musical, a new American play, and a residency by an internationally known artist. INTAR is the oldest Latino theatre company in the U.S., with more than 65 world premieres of plays by U.S. Latino authors. CLJ

Interart Theatre A program of the Women's Interart Center, a not-for-profit, FEMINIST arts complex founded in 1971 by Marjorie De Faxio, Alice Rubenstein, Jane Chambers, and Margot Lewitin, who remains artistic director. In addition to theatre, both experimental and more traditional, the Center develops and presents American dance, music, visual art, and video art by or about women, and encourages events that integrate disciplines. In fall 1996 the Theatre merged administration with the WOMEN'S PROJECT and did a coproduction of FORNÉS's *Terra Incognita*. CLJ

international stars and companies From its inception to the present, the American theatre's artists, institutions, and audiences have been enriched, influenced, stimulated, and entertained by non-U.S.-born talent. As L. W. Conolly suggests, the touring and permanent influences of these important individuals and groups "might well be said to encompass the continent's entire theatrical history." In some areas of popular theatre – the CIRCUS, for example – a majority of the stars have been foreign-born. Many artists who began careers abroad immigrated into the U.S. and established reputations on these shores; others visited often or effectively split their professional lives between this country and their native lands; some came only once or twice. This pattern has changed little up to the present, although the British invasion was been a subject of intense controversy during the 1980s and early '90s, reaching a kind of climax in 1990–1 with ACTORS' EQUITY's hesitancy to allow Jonathan Pryce, the white British star, to play a Eurasian in the original cast of the musical *Miss Saigon*.

Initially, the American theatre was essentially a British institution, so it is not surprising that early stars were British and that acting styles of the 18th and early 19th century reflected the grand style of London's leading actors, the Kembles. Early American stars such as JOHN HENRY, JOHN BERNARD, MRS. ANNE MERRY, and THOMAS A. COOPER influenced the American scene with classical British training. Ironically, however, the first major stars to appear in the U.S. were of a more romantic bent. GEORGE FREDERICK COOKE in 1810 helped to place the wedge in the repertory system that led to the phenomenon of the traveling star, followed by JAMES W. WALLACK in 1818. Edmund Kean, who appeared in 1820–1 and 1825–6, though England's greatest actor at the time, created more controversy over his refusal to act in Boston than he did any lasting influence. Indeed, JUNIUS BRUTUS BOOTH, frequently accused of being a copy of Kean, had a more permanent effect on American acting.

By the 1830s and for the remainder of the 19th century, the touring of foreign stars became commonplace, and the age of the international star was firmly established. A litany of major foreign theatrical names fills the annals of the American stage. For example, from Britain (with year of first and, in notable instances, final U.S. appearance) came CHARLES MATHEWS (1822), William Charles Macready (1826; 1849), Charles Kean (1830), Ellen Tree (1836), Charles Kemble and his daughter FANNY KEMBLE (1832), TYRONE POWER (1833), JOHN M. VANDENHOFF (1837; 1844), Madame Vestris (1838), John Baldwin Buckstone (1840), CHARLES FISHER (1852), EMMA WALLER (1857), LYDIA THOMPSON (1868), Charles Wyndham (1869), CHARLES FECHTER (1869), Adelaide Neilson (1872; 1880), Oscar Wilde (1882, as a lecturer), Lillie Langtry (1882), Henry Irving (1883; 1904), Ellen Terry (1883; 1907), Johnston Forbes-Robertson (1885; 1915), Wilson Barrett (1886), Mr. and Mrs. Kendal (1889), Marie Tempest (1890), Olga Nethersole (1894; 1913), and Herbert Beerbohm Tree (1895; 1916).

No company (or actor) is more important in the U.S. during the 19th century than Henry Irving's Lyceum Theatre company (most often featuring Ellen Terry). Between 1883 and 1905 Irving toured eight times, playing most major U.S. cities (the sixth tour, for example, included 30 cities in six months) for a total of 209 weeks. Irving illustrated the quality of his Lyceum productions to American audiences, demonstrating his careful use of historical accuracy in scenery and costuming, his artistic use of lighting, and his personal control and coordination of all production elements. In turn, Irving learned much about American business ethics from the entrepreneur HENRY EDWIN ABBEY.

Visitors during the 20th century from Britain form a Who's Who of the English stage. Since the improvement of transatlantic travel, British actors have rarely been given international status until an appearance in New York or on tour. Their numbers are legion. [See earlier editions of this *Guide* for specific names and dates; a number of these actors have entries in the present volume.] Of the current mature generation of British actors, significant U.S. appearances have been made by such stars as JIM DALE, Albert Finney, Anthony Hopkins, Alan Howard, Derek Jacobi, CLAIRE BLOOM, Glenda Jackson, Ian McKellen, Jonathan Pryce, Alec McCowen, Vanessa REDGRAVE, Diana Rigg, Maggie Smith, Margaret Tyzack, Paul Rogers, Ian Holm, John Wood, Roy Dotrice, Donald Sinden, Jean Marsh, Tom Courtenay, Tom Conti, Joan Plowright, Jane Lapotaire, ROGER REES, Eileen Atkins, Ben Kingsley, Robert Lindsay, Nicol Williamson, Judi Dench, Michael Gambon, and the late Alan Bates and Dorothy Tutin, among many others.

RICHARD BURTON, though his stage career was disappointing, is typical of British actors who appear in the U.S. as often as they do elsewhere. Of recent British actor-directors, Sir John Gielgud had the longest history in this country, having appeared in 14 productions since his debut and directed half a dozen productions, including in 1964 the Burton *Hamlet.*

Although the British have dominated among foreign stars on U.S. stages, with several notable periods of influx (most recently the musicals of ANDREW LLOYD WEBBER), the last half of the 19th century and the early 20th century nonetheless saw international stars from many countries: some with their own companies, performing in their native language; others in bilingual productions; and a few acting in English. [See earlier editions of this *Guide* for a list, and see specific actor entries herein.]

Notable international companies (especially in the 1920s and '30s) made greater impact than any individual artist, influencing American acting methods, staging techniques, and innovative design concepts (the New Stagecraft). Foremost among these were Israel's Habimah (1926–7 New York season, then headquartered in Moscow); England's D'Oyly Carte (1879, *HMS Pinafore*); the MOSCOW ART THEATRE (1922–3); Dublin's Abbey

Theatre (1911, 1913, and several visits in the 1930s); MAX REINHARDT and company (with the Oriental pantomime *Sumurun* [1912], his re-created production of *The Miracle* [1924], and his German troupe [1927]); the Chauve-Souris company (1922–3, presenting Russian vaudeville under Nikita Balieff); and Jacques Copeau and the Vieux-Colombier (in residence at New York's GARRICK THEATRE, 1917–19).

At midcentury there seemed to have been a slacking off of notable foreign visitors. By the 1960s, however, this began to change with visits from such companies as the Moscow Art Theatre, the Royal Shakespeare Company, the D'Oyly Carte, the Comédie-Française, the Piraikon Theatre of Athens, the Schiller Theatre, the Bavarian State Theatre, the Bunraku Puppet Theatre of Japan, the Grand Kabuki, the Jewish Theatre of Poland (with Ida Kaminska), the Vienna Burgtheater, the Compagnie du Théâtre de la Cité de Villeurbanne, and Jerzy Grotowski's Polish Laboratory Theatre, among others. In the past 40 years there has been an explosion of imported foreign plays (especially British), including the introduction of works by such authors as ATHOL FUGARD (South Africa); Christopher Hampton, David Storey, Simon Gray, Peter Nichols, Caryl Churchill, Alan Ayckbourn, David Rudkin, David Edgar, Hugh Leonard, Brian Friel, Conor McPherson, Martin McDonagh, et al. (British Isles); Dario Fo (Italy); Michel Tremblay (Canada); and Franz Xaver Kroetz (Germany), to mention just a few. The U.S. has also witnessed notable productions by nonnative directors, including JOHN DEXTER, Peter Brook, Vittorio Gassman, Anatoly Efros, Grotowski, Jean-Louis Barrault, Franco Zeffirelli, Josef Szajna (Poland), Harold Pinter, Trevor Nunn, Clifford Williams, Ingmar Bergman, Joe Dowling, Georgio Strehler, Sean Mathias, Stephen Daldry, Nicholas Hytner, Silviu Puracarete (Romania), Patrice Chéreau, Tadeusz Kantor, et al. Foreign companies have continued to travel to the U.S. in sizable numbers, appearing in recent years not only as independent touring companies but as part of major international theatre festivals (e.g., New York International Festival of the Arts, Festival Latino [NEW YORK SHAKESPEARE FESTIVAL], International Theatre Festival at Stony Brook, Chicago International Theatre Festival, and the short-lived Los Angeles Theatre Festival coordinated by PETER SELLARS). Among companies over the past decade have been England's Cheek by Jowl (in an acclaimed *As You Like It*), Brazil's Teatro de Ornitorrinco and Grupo de Teatro Macunaíma, Catalán's Muestra Espanola, the Sovremennik Theater of

Moscow, the State Theatre of Lithuania, the Dublin Gate Theatre, the Royal Dramatic Theatre of Sweden, Yume no Yuminsha from Japan, productions from London's Royal Court Theatre (in exchange with the New York Shakespeare Festival), the Royal Shakespeare Company (notably the 1981–2 production of *The Life and Adventures of Nicholas Nickleby*), the Almeida Theatre Company (*Medea*, 1994, with Diana Rigg [Tony]; *Hamlet*, 1995, with Ralph Fiennes [Tony]; etc.), the Grand Kabuki from Japan, Ariane Mnouchkine's Théâtre de Soleil from France (*Les Atrides*, 1992), Russia's Maly Theatre (*Gaudeamus*, 1994), Czech Republic's National Theatre, Piccolo Teatro di Milano (Pirandello's *The Mountain Giants,* 1995), National Theater of Greece, Equestrian Theatre Zingaro, Comédie-Française, and Tel Aviv's Cameri Theatre.

Since its beginning the American theatre has been, and continues to be, enriched and influenced in every possible way by non-U.S. theatre artists and companies. The 2005–6 Broadway season, one indicator, identified two Anglo-Irish, one British, and only one American effort for a best Tony nomination (the winner, Alan Bennett's *The History Boys*). Four acting awards went to non-U.S. performers. A Canadian-developed musical (*The Drowsy Chaperone*) won five Tonys.

With the emergence of the predominant global marketplace as a new millennium got underway, more stateside presenting organizations, particularly those in large population centers, increasingly noted not just the social but the economic advantages of upping the quantity and variety of international companies performing in the U.S.

At the same time, however, in the aftermath of the terrorist attacks of 11 September 2001, the U.S. Immigration and Naturalization Service began an unprecedented hyperscrutinizing of any individual, artist or otherwise, applying for a visa to enter the country. Over time, the federal government created a remarkable series of roadblocks intended to deter the unwanted from gaining access to our shores. The shockingly byzantine process of gaining approval to bring foreign artists and companies to the U.S. flustered all but the most fiercely dedicated presenters, who have had to face long lead times and far larger fees in order to have a shot at achieving their programming goals.

Even without such formidable obstacles, the importation cost of full companies from abroad remained nearly prohibitive. The recent festival phenomenon remained a hopeful sign that this flow will not abate; yet a steadily growing pile of anecdotal evidence suggested that the trouble involved in bringing foreign artists stateside was taking a toll. (See also ETHNIC THEATRE; also see the numerous entries on specific nonnatives who have made significant contributions to the American stage.)   DBW LJ

Intiman Theatre Founded in 1972 by Margaret Booker in SEATTLE and incorporated as a nonprofit theatre in 1973, the Intiman (Swedish for "intimate") – named after August Strindberg's small 1907 Stockholm theatre – operated in various venues (including, for nine seasons, SECOND STAGE) until 1987, when it moved into the renovated Seattle Center Playhouse (now Intiman Playhouse). That season began with a new artistic director, Elizabeth Huddle, who stayed six years, succeeded by Warner Shook, who established the theatre's national reputation with Robert Schenkkan's *The* KENTUCKY CYCLE (which won the 1992 Pulitzer) and the first regional theatre to produce the two parts of ANGELS IN AMERICA (Part 1, 1994; Part 2, 1995), its most successful production to date. Intiman's current artistic director (since 2000) is Bartlett Sher, responsible for CRAIG LUCAS and ADAM GUETTEL's *The Light in the Piazza* at the GOODMAN and LINCOLN CENTER (2005). The theatre received the 2006 Regional Theatre Tony Award.   DBW

Into the Woods Two-act musical with book by JAMES LAPINE, music and lyrics by STEPHEN SONDHEIM; opened at the MARTIN BECK THEATRE on 5 November 1987 (764 performances); it was a critical success in London in the early 1990s. Using the characters and situations of children's fairy tales (primarily the Brothers Grimm), including the Baker and his Wife, Cinderella, Jack and the Beanstalk, and Little Red Riding Hood, the musical explored the real human consequences of journeying "into the woods" after one's dreams. As the characters encounter magical and often violent obstacles to getting what they want, they develop more mature perceptions of love, responsibility, and guilt. At the end, those who survive begin to form a new community, assuring one another that "No One Is Alone." Lapine's book and Sondheim's score combined the rollicking adventure of the fairy tales with quiet moments of self-discovery. As the Witch who provoked most of the action, BERNADETTE PETERS enchanted the critics, and JOANNA GLEASON received a Tony Award for her performance as the Baker's Wife. The atmosphere of mystery and wonder was enhanced by TONY STRAIGES's settings, RICHARD NELSON's lighting, and Charles Reynolds's special magic effects. A 2002 Broadway revival featured Vanessa Williams and JOHN MCMARTIN.   MK

Irish Repertory Theatre, The Founded in 1988 by Ciarán O'Reilly and Charlotte Moore, who remain producing director and artistic director, respectively, it opened with Sean O'Casey's *The Plough and the Stars.* Its mission then and now is to bring works by Irish and Irish American writers (classics and contemporary) to American audiences while providing a context for understanding the contemporary Irish American experience and encouraging new works that focus on the Irish and Irish American experience (as well as other cultures). Located since 1995 in Chelsea and utilizing two small spaces (Main Stage and W. Scott McLucas Studio), the theatre has received a special Drama Desk Award for its mission and a LUCILLE LORTEL Award for "Outstanding Body of Work." In 2005 works by playwrights Brian Friel, Oliver Goldsmith, Samuel Beckett, Edna O'Brien, Noël Coward, and BERNARD SHAW were presented.   DBW

Irving, Jules (1924–79) New York–born producer and director, educated at New York and Stanford Universities. Together with colleague HERBERT BLAU, he founded the San Francisco Actors Workshop (1952–64), which became known for its experimental productions. In 1965 they became codirectors of the Repertory Theatre of LINCOLN CENTER; after Blau resigned in 1967, Irving continued as director until 1972. During his controversial tenure at Lincoln Center, Irving became known for his carefully crafted productions of the classics and for innovative presentations of plays by BRECHT, Beckett, and Pinter. In 1971 he staged the U.S. premiere of Pinter's *Landscape* and *Silence.* His daughter, **Amy Irving**, acts for films, television, and the theatre (*Broken Glass,* 1994; *The Guys,* 2002, FLEA THEATER; *Ghosts,* 2002, CSC REP; *Celadine,* 2004, GEORGE STREET; *A Safe Harbor for Elizabeth Bishop,* 2006, PRIMARY STAGES; *The Coast of Utopia,* parts 1 and 2, 2006).   TLM

Irving, Washington (1783–1859) First important American man of letters, who enjoyed the theatre and wrote occasionally about it. In 1802–3 he published nine letters in the *Morning Chronicle,* under the name of Jonathan Oldstyle, that commented in a lightly satirical style upon the provincial state of New York theatre. Later he collaborated with JOHN HOWARD PAYNE on *Richelieu; or, The Broken Heart* and *CHARLES II,* which played in London in 1824. Irving remains best known for *The Sketch Book* (1822), which contains the short stories "The Legend of Sleepy Hollow" and "RIP VAN WINKLE,"

the latter adapted into a star vehicle for actor JOSEPH JEFFERSON III and others. C. D. Warner's biography was published in 1981.   TLM

Irwin, Bill (1950–) Actor, entertainer, playwright, director, and choreographer; the best known among disparate practitioners of the so-called NEW VAUDEVILLE. Irwin, born in Santa Monica, CA, has made made innovative use of his clown skills to create exciting visual metaphors for the broader actions and emotions of a play. He moved from conventional theatre training at UCLA to experimental theatre training with HERBERT BLAU at Oberlin College, to the RINGLING BROS. Clown College, the Pickle Family Circus, and the avant-garde Oberlin Dance Collective before evolving what Ron Jenkins, a former circus clown, calls Irwin's "metaphysical slapstick." Irwin's first major New York vehicle was *The Regard of Flight,* played elsewhere before and after its 1982 performance at the AMERICAN PLACE THEATRE. This production effectively and comedically satirized the so-called new, postmodern theatre. It also established his stage persona of the beleaguered but resilient all-American, a character that he uses often. Other appearances include *The Courtroom* (St. Clements, NYC); *Waiting for Godot* (a memorable Lucky at Lincoln Center in 1988; Vladimir 1996 in Seattle); *Accidental Death of an Anarchist;* his Tony-nominated performance as "Post-Modern Hoofer" in his nonverbal *Largely New York* (1989; Drama Desk Award for Unique Theatrical Experience), which he also directed and choreographed; Beckett's *Texts for Nothing* (1992; Obie; revived in 2000); the clown show *Fool Moon* (1993; another Drama Desk – Unique award; revived 1995 and 1998, receiving a special Tony for Live Theatrical Presentation in 1999) with David Shiner, former star of CIRQUE DU SOLEIL; *Scapin,* which he coadapted, directed, and starred in at the SEATTLE REP (spring 1995; revived 1997 at ROUNDABOUT); and *The Tempest* (as Triniculo) in Central Park for the NEW YORK SHAKESPEARE FESTIVAL. For the 2003–4 season Irwin was playwright-in-residence at the SIGNATURE, where he appeared in his *The Harlequin Studies, The Regard Evening,* and *Mr. Fox: A Rumination,* the latter based on the career of GEORGE L. Fox and first created at the Seattle Rep in 1992. Irwin continued to surprise many with his legitimate roles in *THE GOAT, OR WHO IS SYLVIA?* (2002 replacement) and then as George in the 2005 revival of *WHO'S AFRAID OF VIRGINIA WOOLF?,* for which he won the Tony for Best Actor. In 1984 he became the first American performing artist to receive the prestigious MacArthur Foundation Fellowship.   DBW

Irwin, May [née Georgia or Ada Campbell] (1862–1938) Canadian-born actress. Dubbed "Secretary of Laughter" in the teens by Woodrow Wilson, she began her career singing duets with her sister Flo at the Adelphi Theatre, Buffalo, NY (1875). By January 1877 they were STOCK members of TONY PASTOR's Music Hall company, remaining six years. In 1883 May joined AUGUSTIN DALY as a legitimate actress, leaving in 1887 and returning to the legitimate stage only briefly in 1893 under CHARLES FROHMAN's management. The balance of her career was devoted to farce comedies with music. She reached star status in *The Widow Jones* (1895), and offered a series of comedies under her own management in the teens. A plump, jolly blonde, known for her rollicking exuberance, she introduced such popular songs as "A Hot Time in the Old Town" and "I'm Looking for de Bully" (in the style later known as Negro ragtime). She retired in 1922.   DBW

Isaacs, Edith J(uliet) R(ich) (1878–1956) American editor and critic. Born and educated in Milwaukee, Isaacs began her writing career as a reporter and later literary editor for the *Milwaukee Sentinel* before moving to New York in 1904 to marry and begin a family. She was a drama critic for *Ainslee's Magazine* and a freelance writer before joining the editorial board of THEATRE ARTS in 1918. During 1922–46 she served as editor (and majority stockholder), moving the magazine from quarterly to monthly (1924) and featuring prominent new artists each month, such as EUGENE O'NEILL and ROBERT EDMOND JONES. She was actively involved in establishing the National Theatre Conference (1925), the AMERICAN NATIONAL THEATRE AND ACADEMY (1935), and the FEDERAL THEATRE PROJECT (1935–9) because she believed in a national theatre.   TLM

Isherwood, Charles (1964–) Theatre critic, born in California and educated at Stanford. Beginning in 1993 he served as VARIETY critic for West Coast productions, promoted in 1998 to senior editor and chief theatre critic. In 2004 he replaced MARGO JEFFERSON as the second-string critic for the *New York Times*. At the time of his appointment his work was praised for "clarity and directness, precision and gentle wit, and for evident knowledge of the field and the people in it."   TLM

Israel, Robert (1939–) Though a theatre and opera set and costume designer, Israel's background is in fine arts, and his work is more closely related to European theatricalists than to typical American designers. In addition to more than 70 opera and ballet productions, including Philip Glass's *Satyagraha* (1981), *Akhnaten* (1984), and *Orphée* (1993, Loeb Drama Center), and the Seattle Opera's "Ring Cycle" (1985–6), he has worked in collaboration with director MARTHA CLARKE on several creations, including *Vienna: Lusthaus* (1986) and *Vienna: Lusthaus (Revisited)* (2002). His postmodernist work is typified by spare though stunning images and intellectual metaphors.   AA

It Can't Happen Here occupies a unique position in the American theatre because its production – under the supervision of the FEDERAL THEATRE PROJECT – allowed for at least 20 simultaneous openings on the night of 27 October 1936. Adapted by John C. Moffitt and Sinclair Lewis from Lewis's best-selling novel of the same name, the play portrayed the emergence of a fascist dictator in the U.S. and was interpreted by critics as both pro–New Deal and anti-Roosevelt. The circumstances of its production were unusually chaotic because the demand for a nationwide opening raised havoc with individual productions. Rewrites arrived daily in the various theatres; some productions were more advanced than others (but postponements were disallowed); and little provision was made for the variety and richness of individual units (a black company in SEATTLE; a YIDDISH one in New York). Still, the experiment demonstrated the potential for professional theatre outside of NYC and contributed to the political debate that would eventually undermine the WPA theatre.   BBW

Italian Actors Union Also known today as the Guild of Italian American Actors (GIAA), IAU was founded by Antonio Maiori in 1937 as an affiliate of the AFL–CIO. It has grown from 68 active members in 1998 to over 250 today (actors, writers, singers, directors, producers, comics). Its goals are similar to most theatrical unions, with the added dimension of promoting positive images of Italian Americans in the media – while acknowledging that actors must on occasion accept stereotypical roles in order to "earn a living" in a tough industry – and of facilitating job opportunities for Italian American artists, preserving Italian culture and heritage, and encouraging the study of the Italian language, Italian American theatre, and Italian history.   DBW

Ives, David (Johnson) (1950–) Quirky comic playwright born in Chicago and educated at Northwestern and the Yale Drama School (M.F.A.). A master of verbal wit and insight into human foibles, he is rare in that his best works are one-act plays, although one of his recent efforts, *Polish Joke* (2003, MANHATTAN THEATRE CLUB), is a full-length comedy. More typical is his best-known title, *All in the Timing* (1993, PRIMARY STAGES), a group of six short plays which moved to THEATRE Row and ran over 600 performances, as well as *Mere Mortals* (1990) and *Long Ago and Far Away* (1993), both from ENSEMBLE STUDIO THEATRE's one-act Marathons. In 1995–6 *Timing* was the most performed contemporary play in the country. Ives has written more than 30 plays, including *Don Juan in Chicago* (1995) and *Roll Over, Beethoven* (published 2005). In 2002 Ives, who had adapted shows for the CITY CENTER ENCORES! series, moved into full-blown musical theatre, first with the failure *Dance of the Vampires* (credited with the book) and then with the more successful *Wonderful Town* revival in 2003 (credited with script adaptation). He was originally slated to write the book for Disney's staged *The Little Mermaid* (which went to Doug Wright). Ives currently is an adjunct playwriting instructor at Columbia.   DBW

Ivey, Dana (1942–) Extraordinarily versatile Atlanta-born actress and teacher who, after studying at LAMDA on a Fulbright, became a leading actress in Canada before her Broadway debut in *Present Laughter* (CIRCLE IN THE SQUARE, 1982); she returned with *Heartbreak House* (CITS, 1983, Tony nomination; TV, 1984), SUNDAY IN THE PARK WITH GEORGE (1984, Tony nomination; TV, 1985; revival concert, 1994), Whitemore's *Pack of Lies* (1984), DURANG's *Sex and Longing* (1996), UHRY's *The Last Night of Ballyhoo* (1997), G. B. SHAW's *Major Barbara* (2001), and Peter Nichols's *A Day in the Death of Joe Egg* (revival, 2003). OFF-BROADWAY, Ivey did Simon Gray's *Quartermaine's Terms* (LONG WHARF, 1982; NYC, 1983, Drama Desk nomination, Obie [Ensemble]), *DRIVING MISS DAISY* (1987, Obie), *Hamlet* (NEW YORK SHAKESPEARE FESTIVAL, 1990; St. Clair Bayfield Award), *The SUBJECT WAS ROSES* (ROUNDABOUT, 1991), SHANLEY's *Beggars in the House of Plenty* (MANHATTAN THEATRE CLUB, 1991), Diane Samuels's *Kindertransport* (MTC, 1994), Mistress Quickly in *Henry IV* (2003) and Mrs. Malaprop in *The Rivals* (2004), both at the VIVIAN BEAUMONT, and the title role in Shaw's *Mrs Warren's Profession* (2005, IRISH REP). Films include *The Color Purple* (1985), *Dirty Rotten Scoundrels* (1988), and *Two Weeks Notice* (2002). A 1983 Clarence Derwent Award winner, Ivey has taught acting at several schools.   REK

Ivey, Judith (1951–) El Paso-born, actress ("A chameleon onstage" able "to be liked in difficult roles"), educated at Illinois State University, who made her debut in *The Sea* (GOODMAN THEATRE, 1974), then on Broadway in Ayckbourn's *Bedroom Farce* (1979). She has performed with such companies as the Evanston (IL) Theatre Company, ARENA STAGE, NEW YORK SHAKESPEARE FESTIVAL, and MANHATTAN THEATRE CLUB. Stage credits include *Piaf* (1981), Nell Dunn's *Steaming* (1982; Tony, Drama Desk Award), HURLYBURLY (Goodman, 1983; NYC, 1984; Tony, Drama Desk Award), George Furth's *Precious Sons* (1986), *Blithe Spirit* (1987), HOROVITZ's *Park Your Car in Harvard Yard* (1991), BAITZ's *A Fair Country* (1996, LINCOLN CENTER), Martin Sherman's *A Madhouse in Goa* (1997, SECOND STAGE), *Voices in the Dark* (1999), and the 2001 Broadway revival of FOLLIES. Films include *BRIGHTON BEACH MEMOIRS* (1986), *In Country* (1989), and *What Alice Found* (2003). In 1990–1 she starred in television's *Down Home* and in 1992–3 *Designing Women*. In recent years she has essayed solo performances: *Women on Fire* (2003), in which she portrayed 12 disparate women, and *Dirty Tricks* (2004), John Jeter's portrait of the notorious Martha Mitchell, wife of Attorney General John Mitchell of the Watergate era (both Off-Broadway).   REK

Izenour, George C. (1912–2007) Theatre designer, engineering consultant, acoustician, and inventor of the inverse polarized rectifier circuit for dimming and switching in STAGE LIGHTING, the synchronous winch system, and the steel acoustical shell. He was a design and engineering consultant for more than 100 theatres worldwide since the 1950s, and as such was a dominant force in theatre design and technology. Because economics dictates that a single theatre must be employed for many uses (spoken drama, opera, concerts, and so forth), he was an advocate of the multiuse and multiform theatre, in which the size and shape and auditorium can be altered for different needs and acoustical requirements. Recipient of the Distinguished Service Award from the American Theater Association and the 2004 Wally Russell Award for Lifetime Achievement in Lighting, Izenour was the author of three acclaimed books: *Theater Design* (1977; 2d ed. 1997), *Theater Technology* (1988; 2d ed. 1997), and *Roofed Theaters of Classical Antiquity* (1992). His late son, **Steven**, was an architect and coauthor of *Learning from Las Vegas* (rev. ed., 1977).   AA

J

Jackson, Anne see WALLACH, ELI

Jacobs, Lou [né Ludwig] (1904–92) German-born clown and the American CIRCUS's best-known *auguste* (slapstick clown who appears stupid and clumsy, appearing in flamboyant costume and makeup). Jacobs, brought to the U.S. in 1923 as a tumbler, was to many the quintessential image of a circus clown, with his enlarged, cone-shaped head, distinctive white patches around his eyes, fringed red hair, and red-rubber-ball nose. From 1926 until his retirement in 1988, Jacobs, who was generally recognized as the greatest living circus clown, mesmerized audiences for RINGLING BROS. by his presence – in particular, with his midget car routine (seen first in 1946) and later his hunting-dog routine, with his mutt, Knucklehead.   DBW

James, Henry (1843–1916) Expatriate American novelist and critic who found U.S. culture provincial, and its theatre melodramatic and bombastic, lacking subtle character delineation and refinement of style. While spending much of his career in England, he wrote about the theatre in *The Nation, The Atlantic, The Century,* and *The Galaxy* (1875–87), republished in *The Scenic Art* (1948). A failed playwright, James was too dependent on the "well-made" dramas of Scribe and Sardou. Dramatizations of his novels by others have been more successful, including *Berkeley Square* (1929), from *The Sense of the Past; The Heiress* (1947), from *Washington Square;* and *The Innocents* (1950) from *The Turn of the Screw.*   TLM

Jampolis, Neil Peter (1943–) Designed numerous OFF-BROADWAY productions in the 1970s, including *One Flew Over the Cuckoo's Nest* (1971). He won a Tony for lighting design for SHERLOCK HOLMES (1974, revival); other Broadway productions include LILY TOMLIN's *The Search for Signs of Intelligent Life in the Universe* (1985). He designed the long-running *Forever Plaid* (1990) in NYC and elsewhere (including a special holiday edition in 2001 at the PASADENA PLAYHOUSE), as well as the highly successful *Over the River and Through the Woods* (1998) and *I Love You, You're Perfect, Now Change* (1996). Since 1976 Jampolis has designed lights for the Pilobolus Dance Company. He has also designed for the New York City Opera and several international opera productions. He teaches at UCLA.   AA

Janauschek, Francesca [Fanny] (1830–1904) Czech-born actress who made her debut at 16 at the Royal Theatre of Prague and two years later was engaged as leading actress of the State Theatre, Frankfurt, where she remained for 10 years. She was an internationally renowned tragedienne before making her 1867 New York debut, performing Medea in German while the rest of the cast acted in English, as did EDWIN BOOTH opposite her German Lady Macbeth in 1868. After a year devoted to learning English, she launched her English-speaking career in 1870. With her statuesque figure, emotional power, and vibrant but controlled voice, she excelled in heroic roles like Brunhilde, Deborah, Mary Stuart, and later Meg Merrilies (in *Guy Mannering*). She was also popular in the dual roles of the coquettish French maid and the haughty Lady Dedlock in *Chesney Wold* (based on Dickens's *Bleak House*). She was one of the last great actresses in the "grand style," but ended her career (after 1898) playing melodramas.   FHL

Janis [née Bierbower]**, Elsie** (1889–1956) VAUDEVILLE entertainer, one of its greatest stars, and considered by many the queen of the form. The product of one of the archetypical stage mothers, from her debut in 1897 to the end of her career in 1932, Elsie appeared as a headliner in vaudeville, musical comedy, and REVUE. During WWI she frequently entertained the troops. The society darling of two continents, the attractive, slender Janis specialized in impersonations and comic songs, introducing such popular songs as "Fo' de Lawd's Sake, Play a Waltz" and "Florrie Was a Flapper." On her death, lifelong friend Mary Pickford remarked, "This ends the vaudeville era." Her autobiography, *So Far, So Good!* was published in 1932.   DBW

Jarrett, Henry C. (1828–1903) Theatre manager whose career began in 1851 when he purchased the Baltimore Museum. At various times, Jarrett managed several major U.S. theatres, including Washington's NATIONAL THEATRE, the BROOKLYN ACADEMY OF MUSIC, and NIBLO'S GARDEN. When EDWIN BOOTH lost his theatre in 1874, Jarrett joined with Henry David Palmer to manage BOOTH'S THEATRE until 1877. Jarrett and Palmer also produced the popular musical fantasy *The Black Crook* at Niblo's Garden in 1866, and in 1875–6 mounted a spectacular production of *Julius Caesar* at Booth's, with LAWRENCE BARRETT as Cassius and E. L. DAVENPORT as Brutus.   DJW

Jay, Ricky [né Ricky Potash?] (1948?–) Born in Brooklyn and lives in Los Angeles; much about this phenomenal performer, film (many Mamet films) and television actor (*Deadwood*), and scholar of magic and unusual entertainment – arguably the most gifted sleight-of-hand artist today – is secretive, including his age and his surname (he uses his first and middle names). Yet his two stage productions – notable for their urbane, wryly witty, and erudite patter in addition to the magic – directed by DAVID MAMET – *Ricky Jay and His 52 Assistants* (1994) and *Ricky Jay: On the Stem* (2002) – both at NYC's SECOND STAGE – were enormously successful, the former winning an Obie and both playing many other venues. Jay's other unique talent is card throwing (the topic of his first book, *Cards as Weapons*, 1977); and his personal collection on magic and other unique forms of entertainment/exhibition is extraordinary. His other books are *Many Mysteries Unraveled, Learned Pigs & Fireproof Women, Jay's Journal of Anomalies, Dice: Deception, Fate and Rotten Luck,* and the 2005 *Extraordinary Exhibitions: The Wonderful Remains of an Enormous Head, the Whimsiphusicon & Death to the Savage Unitarians.*   DBW

J. B. by ARCHIBALD MACLEISH won the Tony Award for Best Play and the Pulitzer Prize (1959). Based upon the biblical figure Job, it remains one of the few American plays written in verse. Set in a circus environment, it updates the story of his trials. Its New York production (opened 11 December 1958) was directed by ELIA KAZAN and ran 364 performances. Critics were mixed in their reactions.   KN

Jean Cocteau Repertory Theatre Founded in 1971 by Eve Adamson, a pioneer of the OFF-OFF BROADWAY movement, in a storefront on Manhattan's Lower East Side, the company moved in 1974 to the Bouwerie Lane Theatre, where it resides today. Distracting from its mission to produce theatre of classic scope and vision has been upheaval over the past several years, a result of a reduction in its ensemble philosophy and move away from the "classics," according to several longtime actors and board members. Much of the contretemps occurred during the tenure of David Fuller (appointed in 1999) who, in 2005 – after converting the Cocteau into an Equity company in 2002 – turned the artistic directorship over to Ernest Johns and became a resident director. Exacerbating the problem in 2006 were financial problems and a decision to revitalize its productions and attract new audiences by a merger with EgoPo Productions, a New Orleans company displaced by Hurricane Katrina, and the Catskill Mountain Foundation in upstate New York (with the new name – EgoPo/Cocteau). Whatever its future, the Cocteau has long taken a leading role in bringing fresh visions of neglected classics to the American stage. Its 2005–6 season included plays by BRECHT, Euripides, SHAW, Strindberg, and O'NEILL.   DBW

Jeffers, (John) Robinson (1887–1962) A Pulitzer Prize–winning poet, Jeffers wrote a modern version of *Medea* that starred JUDITH ANDERSON on Broadway in 1947. Other plays include *The Tower beyond Tragedy* (1950), from his own poem of Aeschylus' *Oresteia,* and *The Cretan Woman* (1954, ARENA STAGE) from Euripides' *Hippolytus.*   TLM

Jefferson, Margo L. (1947–) Cultural critic and essayist whose writings have explored the postmodern theatre and contemporary American culture at large, with insightful observations on many issues, including race and gender. Born in Chicago, she was educated at Brandeis and Columbia (M.S. in journalism, 1971), after which she worked as a contributing editor at *Newsweek* (1973–8), assistant professor at NYU (1979–83; 1989–93), contributing editor for arts at *Vogue* (1984–9), contributing editor to *7 Days* magazine (1988–9), lecturer in performing-arts criticism, writing, and literature at Columbia (1991–3), and, in 1993, cultural critic at the *New York Times.* In 1995 she was briefly Sunday theatre critic; then in 1996 she became critic-at-large covering theatre and books, and since 2003 she has frequently covered theatre as a second-string critic. She is the author of several books, including a biography of Michael Jackson (2006). In 1995 she received the Pulitzer Prize for Criticism.   TLM

Jeffersons, The A famous Anglo–American acting family, traced back to **Thomas Jefferson** (1732–

1807), an actor with Garrick and an occasional manager of provincial English theatres. One of his children, **Joseph Jefferson I** (1774–1832), came to America in 1795 and remained here. He became a favorite at the JOHN STREET and PARK THEATRES in New York, although somewhat overshadowed by JOHN HODGKINSON. In 1803 he moved to the CHESTNUT STREET THEATRE in Philadelphia, remaining until 1830. Most of his progeny worked in the theatre, including **Joseph Jefferson II** (1804–42), a better scene painter than actor. His marriage to the actress Cornelia Thomas in 1826 made him the step-father of actor Charles Burke.

The greatest of the Jefferson clan, however, was **Joseph Jefferson III** (1829–1905), who first appeared on stage at age 4, in support of T. D. RICE. Jefferson toured with his family, garnering some fame by the midcentury and visiting Europe in 1856. He then joined LAURA KEENE's company, winning approval with such roles as Dr. Pangloss in the younger Colman's *The Heir-at-Law.* He spent some time at the first WINTER GARDEN THEATRE in New York, toured Australia for four years, and in London in 1865 first performed the role for which he was most noted, RIP VAN WINKLE, dramatized for him by DION BOUCICAULT. In this role, Jefferson's dignity and sympathetic personality soon won him popular and critical acclaim. Of him, the critic WILLIAM WINTER said: "The magical charm of his acting was the deep human sympathy and the liveliness and individuality by which it was irradiated – an exquisite blending of humor, pathos, grace and beauty."

Jefferson also triumphed as Bob Acres in Sheridan's *The Rivals,* Caleb Plummer in *Dot,* and Salem Scudder in *The OCTOROON; OR, LIFE IN LOUISIANA.* In 1893 he succeeded EDWIN BOOTH as president of the Players (see CLUBS). His autobiography, a classic theatrical memoir published in 1890, indicates much of Jefferson's warmth and humanity.

Of his children, four went on the stage, the most distinguished being **Charles Burke Jefferson** (1851–1908), who served for a time as his father's manager. The most exhaustive biography of Joe III is by Arthur Bloom (2000); a new one by Benjamin MacArthur is scheduled for 2007.   SMA

Jelly's Last Jam Musical created by GEORGE C. WOLFE (book), Susan Birkenhead (lyrics), and Luther Henderson (music adaptation) to celebrate the music and examine the life of Jazz pioneer Jelly Roll Morton. A controversial figure, Morton was a light-skinned New Orleans Creole who denied his own blackness. After a 1991 production at the MARK TAPER FORUM in Los Angeles, *Jelly's Last Jam* opened 26 April 1992 at the VIRGINIA

THEATRE on Broadway and ran 569 performances. Directed by Wolfe, it starred GREGORY HINES, who won a Tony for his portrayal of Morton.   TLM

Jenkin, Len (1941–) Screenwriter, novelist, director, teacher, and playwright who has been categorized along with MAC WELLMAN and ERIC OVERMYER for his "language" fascination and experimentation with dramatic form. Author of more than 20 stage plays, many produced regionally and OFF-BROADWAY, his work includes *Kitty Hawk* (1972), *Grand American Exhibition* (1973), *The Death and Life of Jesse James* (1974), *Mission* (1975), *Gogol: A Mystery Play* (1976), *Kid Twist* (1977), *Limbo Tales* (1980), *Five of Us* (1981), *Dark Ride* (1981), *My Uncle Sam* (1983), *American Notes* (1986), *Poor Folk's Pleasure* (1987), *Pilgrims of the Night* (1991), *Careless Love* (1993), *Ramona Quimby* (1994), *Like I Say* (2003), and *The Dream Express (Out Takes)* (2004). Until recently he insisted on directing the first production of each of his plays. A 1987 Guggenheim Fellow, he is the recipient of three Obies for directing and playwriting, among numerous other awards.   DBW

Jenkins, George (1908–2007) Designer whose theatre career spanned the 1940s–1970s and included *I REMEMBER MAMA* (1944), *LOST IN THE STARS* (1949), *Two for the Seesaw* (1958), *The MIRACLE WORKER* (1959), *Sly Fox* (1976 and 2004 revival). On the stage and in film Jenkins was admired for precise and detailed settings.   AA

Jerome Robbins' Broadway Two-act musical retrospective that opened 26 February 1989 at the IMPERIAL THEATRE, running 633 performances. Master director-choreographer JEROME ROBBINS's 23-year absence from Broadway ended not with a new show, but with this compendium of production numbers from his Broadway shows from *ON THE TOWN* (1944) to *FIDDLER ON THE ROOF* (1964), featuring 50 dancers and 400 costumes. Robbins took scrupulous care in re-creating the original choreography, and the large company and long rehearsal process led the producers to charge a then-new high standard ticket price of $60 for the best seats. After debate as to its eligibility, the Tony Awards committee declared it a new musical rather than a revival, and it was awarded the Tony as Best Musical.   JD

Jessop, George Henry (d. 1915) Irish-born playwright and novelist who began his playwriting career in New York and later went to SAN FRANCISCO. He returned to Ireland in 1891 when he inherited $100,000. His most popular play, SAM'L OF POSEN (1881), showed a Jewish immigrant store clerk who vowed that he would own the business. With BRANDER MATTHEWS, Jessop wrote *A Gold Mine* (1887) and *On Probation* (1889); with AUGUSTUS PITOU, *The Irish Artist* (1894) and *The Power of the Press* (1891).   WJM

Jesurun, John (1951–) Michigan-born playwright, filmmaker, and experimental theatre director who studied sculpture at Philadelphia College of Art (B.F.A., 1972) and at Yale (M.F.A., 1974). Producer of several films (1977–89), he became aware of the influence of television on daily life while working for CBS (1976–9) as media analyst and with *The Dick Cavett Show* (1980–2). Jesurun's theatre pieces explore cultural stereotypes and the psychological subtexts of social relationships. His cinematic effects mixed with live action deconstruct and suspend the realities of his characters onstage. His influences are Hitchcock, GERTRUDE STEIN, Pirandello, surrealism, Brecht, The WOOSTER GROUP, and RICHARD FOREMAN. His first theatre piece, *Chang in a Void Moon* (1983–present), is a serial of half-hour episodes initially performed weekly at the Pyramid Club in Manhattan, then again in 1996 at The KITCHEN, home to a number of his later offerings. Important works are *White Water* (1986), *Shatterhand Massacree* (1985), *Blue Heat* (1991, INTAR). and *Point of Debarkation* (1993, LA MAMA Annex). In 1986 he won an Obie for his play *Deep Sleep,* and in 1996 he received a coveted MacArthur (genius) Fellowship.   AF

Jewish Art Theatre, The   A company closely modeled on Stanislavsky's MOSCOW ART THEATRE, set up by JACOB BEN-AMI in 1919 at NYC's Garden Theatre (27th at Madison), with Emanuel Reicher, associate of REINHARDT and a founder of the German Freie Bühne, as play director. Rave reviews greeted PERETZ HIRSHBEIN's *The Haunted* [or *Idle*] *Inn* and *Green Fields,* with Ben-Ami scoring a personal triumph in both. In spite of further successes, including DAVID PINSKI's *The Dumb Messiah,* Ossip Dimov's *Bronx Express,* and Tolstoy's *The Power of Darkness,* internal dissension brought the venture – which had reached probably the high point of YIDDISH THEATRE – to a close after two seasons and 14 productions.   AB

Jewish Repertory Theatre   Founded in 1974 by Artistic Director Ran Avni. In addition to revivals such as *AWAKE AND SING!* (most recently in 1995 with TOVAH FELDSHUH) and *Incident at Vichy,* JRT has rediscovered plays such as *Me and Molly, Success Story,* and *Cafe Crown;* has produced such musicals as *Vagabond Stars* (1982), *Kuni-Leml* (1984), which won three Outer Critics Circle Awards, and *Show Me Where the Good Times Are* (1993); and has developed new works in its JRT Writers' Lab. The theatre has also staged Jewish-oriented work by established American writers and reinterprets the work of non-American playwrights (Pinter, Sartre, CHEKHOV, etc.) in the light of Judaism. In 1989 JRT won an Outer Critics Circle Award for Continued Outstanding Productions. However, since 2003 JRT's future has been tenuous, and it has struggled along without a permanent home.   DBW

Joan of Lorraine by MAXWELL ANDERSON, a PLAYWRIGHTS' COMPANY production, opened at the ALVIN THEATRE 18 November 1946. Directed by MARGO JONES with settings, lighting, and costumes by LEE SIMONSON, it starred Ingrid Bergman as Mary Grey (the actress playing Joan), SAM WANAMAKER as the harrassed director, Romney Brent as an amusingly corrupt Dauphin, and Harry Irvine as the cunning Archibishop. This play about a play marked Bergman's successful return to Broadway after her disappointment in *Liliom* (1940). BROOKS ATKINSON described it as "an engrossing play that is variously poignant, rhapsodic, and genial," and RICHARD WATTS JR., the *New York Post* critic, wrote, "*Joan of Lorraine* neither adds to nor decreases the dramatic stature of Maxwell Anderson, but it should make us all appreciate Miss Bergman."   GSA

Joe Turner's Come and Gone   Another in the black-experience, Pittsburgh cycle of plays written by AUGUST WILSON (1984) and directed by LLOYD RICHARDS. It is set in 1911 in a Pittsburgh boardinghouse where the tenants, mostly new arrivals from the South, live aimless lives. They are aroused when Herald Loomis comes in with his young daughter, searching desperately for the wife he left behind when he was impressed for seven years' labor on a plantation owned by Joe Turner, a real-life Mississippi character. Loomis hopes to rebuild his life with his wife and child. Calling this his favorite play, author Wilson claims his work shows how the past must inform the future. The play, like earlier ones, was premiered at the YALE REPERTORY THEATRE and presented at several regional venues prior to opening on Broadway in 1988.   EGH

John F. Kennedy Center for the Performing Arts   1701 Pennsylvania Ave., Washington, DC [Architect: Edward Durrell Stone]. A national cultural center had been created by law in 1958 during the presidency of Dwight D. Eisenhower, but it did not get started until it was deemed a fitting monument to the assassinated President John F. Kennedy. It opened in 1971 on the banks of the Potomac and encompassed three theatres: the Eisenhower with 1,140 seats for dramatic presentations, the Concert Hall with 2,670 seats, and the Opera House with 2,200 seats. The Center was guided by ROGER STEVENS, its president during 1961–88; he was succeeded upon his retirement by Ralph Davidson (1989–90), James Wolfensohn (1990–6), Lawrence J. Wilker (1996–2000), and Michael Kaiser (2001–). In 1978 a fourth theatre was added on the roof-terrace level: the Terrace Theatre, which seats 500 for films, dance concerts, experimental productions, and CHILDREN'S THEATRE. In 2003 $650 million was approved for additions and improvements (a 10-year project). As part of this project the former American Film Institute space was made into the 324-seat Family Theater for children in 2005. Some productions originate at the Center, but many others are booked in.   MCH

John Golden Theatre 252 West 45th St., NYC [Architect: Herbert J. Krapp]. In 1927, as part of their chain, the Chanin construction interests built the Theatre Masque with only 800 seats, intending it for the presentation of intimate or experimental plays that may not have been able to survive on Broadway at the time. Unfortunately, the playhouse was destined to pass from their control in the early 1930s. In 1934, the SHUBERTS bought it and promptly leased it to producer JOHN GOLDEN, who assigned his own name to the theatre. It is considered ideal for ONE-PERSON and small-cast plays, and such performers as Victor Borge, Yves Montand, COMDEN AND GREEN, NICHOLS and MAY, Bob and Ray, CORNELIA OTIS SKINNER, Emlyn Williams, and Jackie Mason have presented shows of their own creation on its stage. In 1956, Samuel Beckett's *Waiting for Godot* appeared at the Golden, marking the first (and only) time a Beckett play has appeared on Broadway. Apart from two years when it was leased as a movie theatre, the playhouse has seldom been closed. It remains a Shubert house.   MCH

John Street Theatre 15–21 John St., NYC. The third and most substantial theatre to be built in New York by DAVID DOUGLASS, the playhouse in John Street served the city until 1798, when it was replaced by a new theatre afterward known as the PARK. There were three periods in the John Street's history. The first, prior to the Revolution,

consisted of two long seasons beginning in 1767; the second commenced in 1777, when the British troops took it over, renamed it the Theatre Royal, and presented plays as an antidote to tedium in their long occupation; and the last and most important period began in the summer of 1785 with the return of LEWIS HALLAM the Younger, who began with "entertainments," which blossomed into full-scale productions. Hallam established a permanent resident company and was joined by actor JOHN HENRY in its management, but both were replaced by JOHN HODGKINSON and WILLIAM DUNLAP in its final years.

No iconography exists of the John Street. William Dunlap described it as "principally of wood, an unsightly object, painted red." It contained two tiers of boxes, a pit, and a gallery, with dressing rooms and a greenroom located in a shed nearby. A description of the interior was included in ROYALL TYLER's *The CONTRAST* (1787), which premiered at the theatre. When it was closed, it was annexed to a feed-and-grain store next door.   MCH

Johnny Johnson by PAUL GREEN, music by KURT WEILL; opened on Broadway 19 November 1936 and ran 68 performances. LEE STRASBERG staged this GROUP THEATRE production, with scenery by DONALD OENSLAGER and a cast that included SANFORD MEISNER, LEE J. COBB, ELIA KAZAN, LUTHER ADLER, and MORRIS CARNOVSKY in supporting roles. Against his pacifist principles, Johnny Johnson (Russell Collins) enlists to fight in WWI in order to "end all wars" and prove himself worthy to marry Minny Belle. Overseas, he tries to arrange a cease-fire, but the general staff insist on an offensive. Minny marries a man who avoided enlistment; Johnny spends 10 years in a mental hospital, then hawks toys on the street while everyone in town assembles to celebrate the beginning of the next war.   JDM

Johnson, Albert R. (1910–67) Designer who landed his first Broadway show, *The Criminal Code* (1929), at the age of 19. The next year he did *Three's a Crowd*, which established his reputation as a designer of large musicals. Working frequently with director HASSARD SHORT, Johnson became known for his innovative and elaborate use of turntables. Productions included *The Band Wagon* (1931), *As THOUSANDS CHEER* (1933), and *The Great Waltz* (1934), which utilized one of the most elaborate sets in Broadway history. He also designed 30 productions for RADIO CITY MUSIC HALL as well as industrials and expositions, including the 1939 New York World's Fair.   AA

Johnson, Gloria Douglas (1886–1966) African American poet and playwright whose Washington, DC, home was for decades a meeting place for black artists, writers, and intellectuals. During the 1920s and '30s, Johnson wrote a number of one-act plays that were published in anthologies and produced by Little Theatre groups (see COMMUNITY THEATRE) such as the Krigwa Players in New York. Two of her plays were cited in the *Opportunity* magazine contest: *Blue Blood*, about a married couple who discover that they have the same white father, received honorable mention in 1926; *White Plumes,* treating the funeral beliefs of poor blacks, won the first prize in 1927. EGH

Johnson, J. Rosamond see COLE, BOB

Jolson, Al (1886–1950) Singer and comedian. After spending his early years in CIRCUSES, MINSTREL SHOWS, and VAUDEVILLE, Jolson made his stage debut in *La Belle Paree* (1911). In *The Whirl of Society* (1912), he first played the blackfaced servant Gus, a character he was to impersonate in a series of loosely plotted musicals, including *Robinson Crusoe, Jr.* (1916), *Bombo* (1921), and *Big Boy* (1925). The use of blackface, a common practice in the minstrel shows where Jolson had received his early training, gave racist overtones to much of the humor in his productions. Most spectators came to Jolson's shows to hear him sing his repertoire of hit songs, and on many occasions he obliged them by stopping the performance, dismissing the other actors, and spending the rest of the evening singing directly to the audience. After his motion picture debut in *The Jazz Singer* (1927), Jolson moved to Hollywood. His only other Broadway appearances were in the revue *The Wonder Bar* (1931) and in the musical comedy *Hold on to Your Hats* (1940). Possessed of a good baritone voice, Jolson was a charismatic performer whose energy, good humor and emotional singing style made him the most popular musical-comedy performer of his day. The most recent (1994) scholarly study of Jolson is by James Fisher. MK

Jones, Cherry (1956–) This Tennessee-born and Carnegie Mellon–trained actress, termed by MEL GUSSOW "a virtuosic theatrical professional," is typical of New York's "overnight" successes, yet since her 1983 OFF-BROADWAY debut in *The Philanthropist*, Jones has steadily built her career, appearing prominently in such productions as *Our Country's Good* (1991; Tony nomination) and *Baltimore Waltz* (Obie), plus dozens of roles at the AMERICAN REPERTORY THEATRE (25 plays in six seasons), WILLIAMSTOWN, and GOODMAN (Jeffer-

son Awards for *THE GOOD PERSON OF SETZUAN*, 1992; *NIGHT OF THE IGUANA*, 1994). In 1995 for her performance in the revival of *The Heiress* she finally gained national recognition and received among many awards a Tony, a Drama Desk, and the Distinguished Performance award from the DRAMA LEAGUE; also in 1995 she received the ELIOT NORTON Prize (Boston) for Sustained Excellence. Since then her career has continued to blossom, with roles such as Hannah in *Iguana* (Broadway, 1996), Mabel in *Pride's Crossing* (Lincoln Center, 1998), Josie in *A Moon for the Misbegotten* (Broadway, 2000), the title role in *Major Barbara* (ROUNDABOUT, 2001), Mary Stassos in *Flesh and Blood* (2003), Sister Aloysius in *DOUBT* (NEW YORK THEATRE WORKSHOP, 2004; Broadway, 2005), and Grace in the revival of *Faith Healer* (2006). For *Doubt* Jones – termed by BEN BRANTLEY one of the chief treasures of the American theatre – received every major actor award, including the Obie and Tony. DBW

Jones, James Earl (1931–) Son of the actor Robert Earl Jones, James Earl trained at the University of Michigan, the AMERICAN THEATRE WING, and with LEE STRASBERG before making his 1958 Broadway debut in *Sunrise at Campobello*. He soon attracted attention, winning several acting awards for performances in NEW YORK SHAKESPEARE FESTIVAL productions (1960–6) as well as in *Moon on a Rainbow Shawl* (1962, Obie), and *Baal* (1965) OFF-BROADWAY. Jones was unforgettable as the despised prizefighter Jack Jefferson in *The GREAT WHITE HOPE* (1968), a role that earned him a Tony Award. An actor of magnetic physical presence and vocal power, he has frequently been cast nontraditionally: He has played King Lear, Macbeth, Coriolanus, Lopahin in *The Cherry Orchard* (1973, Drama Desk Award), Hickey in *The ICEMAN COMETH* (1973), and Lenny in *OF MICE AND MEN* (1974). He gave a memorable performance in the monodrama *Paul ROBESON* (1978), despite controversy surrounding the production, and he won further acclaim for his Othello (his seventh) to CHRISTOPHER PLUMMER's Iago on Broadway in 1982. He has appeared in several of ATHOL FUGARD's South African plays under the direction of LLOYD RICHARDS, and in 1987 won a Tony in AUGUST WILSON's Richards-directed *FENCES*. In the 1990s he devoted himself primarily to film and television, although in 2005 he returned briefly to Broadway in a revival of *On Golden Pond* opposite Leslie Uggams. His autobiography, *Voices and Silences,* written with Penelope Niven, was published in 1993. In 1992 Jones received the National Medal of Arts, and in 1995 he was presented the ACTING

Robert Edmond Jones's design for Anatole France's *The Man Who Married a Dumb Wife,* 1915. *Courtesy:* Don B. Wilmeth Theatre Collection.

COMPANY'S JOHN HOUSEMAN Award for career achievement.   EGH

Jones, Joseph S(tevens) (1809–77) Actor, manager, and playwright. Beginning with *The Liberty Tree* (1832), he may have written as many as 150 plays (he could never remember). In all, however, he infused his heroes with the qualities of individuality, personal conviction, and freedom of spirit that identified Jacksonian America. For his good friend and YANKEE actor GEORGE H. HILL he wrote *The Green Mountain Boy* (1833) and *The People's Lawyer* (1839), a favorite with several Yankee actors. Melodramas such as *The Surgeon of Paris* (1838) and *The Carpenter of Rouen* (1840) provided the spectacles audiences demanded, but his most lasting play was *The Silver Spoon* (1852), in which WILLIAM WARREN acted until 1883. *Zafari the Bohemian* (1856) suggests Jones's greater ambitions as a playwright. Generally associated with Boston, where he managed the TREMONT and National Theatres, Jones was a thoroughly professional man of the theatre who supported copyright protection and adequate recompense for playwrights. A medical doctor (Harvard, 1843), he was advertised in theatres as "the celebrated Dr. Jones."   WJM

Jones, Margo (Margaret Virginia) (1913–55) Director, producer, and pioneer in the regional theatre movement whose major contributions were made in her home state of Texas, where she managed a theatre in Dallas dedicated to the production of new plays. Her New York credits included the codirection, with EDDIE DOWLING, of *The GLASS MENAGERIE* (1945), Maxine Wood's *On Whitman Avenue* (1946), ANDERSON'S *JOAN OF LORRAINE* (1946), *SUMMER AND SMOKE* (1948), and Owen Crump's *Southern Exposure* (1950), the latter two first presented in Dallas. The Dallas theatre opened as Theatre '47 (with yearly name changes until Jones's accidental death, when it became the Margo Jones Theatre). During its 12 seasons, 133 plays were presented, 86 of which were new plays, including INGE's *The Dark at the Top of the Stairs,* WILLIAMS's *Summer and Smoke,* and LAWRENCE AND LEE's *INHERIT THE WIND.* Jones's theatre became the most celebrated home of arena staging in the U.S. and a pioneer in the decentralization of the American theatre; others emulated her example partly as a result of her book, *Theatre-in-the-Round* (1951). Her biography was written by Helen Sheehy in 1989; a television documentary was broadcast in 2006.   DBW

Jones, Robert Edmond (1887–1954) Set and costume designer whose 1915 design for *The Man Who Married a Dumb Wife,* directed by Harley Granville Barker, is generally considered the beginning of the New Stagecraft in America. Rebelling against the romantic realism of DAVID BELASCO and other producers of the late 19th century, Jones evolved a style of simplified sets that were suggestive, rather than a reproduction of the real world. Having traveled in Europe and observed MAX REINHARDT for a year at the Deutsches Theater,

Jones returned to the U.S. with an appreciation for the power of symbolic or emblematic elements. Paraphrasing from *Hamlet,* Jones wrote, "Stage designing should be addressed to [the] eye of the mind." He advocated a style of design that elicited an underlying feeling for the play, not one that eliminated the imagination. For director ARTHUR HOPKINS, Jones designed the sets for several SHAKESPEARE plays in the early 1920s. The designs employed unit sets – then, virtually unknown – and a strong use of light and shadow in the style of Adolphe Appia. For *Macbeth,* the three witches were portrayed by three large masks hanging over the stage. Jones was also an early member of the PROVINCETOWN PLAYERS and designed most of EUGENE O'NEILL's plays, including *ANNA CHRISTIE, THE GREAT GOD BROWN,* and *MOURNING BECOMES ELECTRA.* From 1923 to 1929 Jones served as a producer, with KENNETH MACGOWAN and O'Neill, of the EXPERIMENTAL THEATRE, INC. – the successor to the Provincetown. Perhaps as important as his revolutionary design was his writing – most notably the book *The Dramatic Imagination* (1941) – in which he expressed the visionary ideas that made him an inspiration to theatre artists in the next generation. His designs were published in 1958 and 1970, and a previously unpublished collection of lectures appeared in 1992.   AA

Jones, Simon (1950–) British actor-director, a fixture of the New York stage, whose career is active on both sides of the Atlantic. In the U.S. he is co–artistic director of NYC's The Actors Company Theatre (TACT), dedicated to concert readings. After a successful West End career, he made his Broadway debut in *The Real Thing* (1984, replacement), and since has appeared in eight Broadway productions (as of mid-2007), including *Benefactors* (1985), *The School for Scandal* (1995), *The Herbal Bed* (1998), and *Waiting in the Wings* (1999). Comparable Off-Broadway credits include the world premiere of Noël Coward's *Long Island Sound* (2002, American Theater of Actors). At TACT he has directed Shaw's *Widowers Houses* and Rattigan's *Flare Path.* He also directs and acts in regional theatre. Jones is best known as Arthur Dent in the radio and television miniseries versions of *The Hitchiker's Guide to the Galaxy.* (In the 2005 film, he appeared as the Ghostly Image.)   DBW

Jordan, Julia (1970?–) Playwright-librettist on the rise in the early 2000s. A native of Minnesota, Jordan attended Barnard (English), the NEIGHBORHOOD PLAYHOUSE (acting), and Juilliard (playwrit-

ing under CHRISTOPHER DURANG and MARSHA NORMAN). Most of her plays have dealt with teenagers and siblings, especially awakening sexuality of young girls. Shortly after finishing work at Juilliard (1996) she had a year's residency at the MANHATTAN THEATRE CLUB, and in 1997 her second play, *Tatjana in Color,* was published. Productions came slowly, but then during 2003–4 she had four plays staged Off-Broadway: *St. Scarlet* (at Ontological Theatre); *Summer of the Swans* (Lucille Lortel Theatre); *Tatjana in Color* (The Culture Project); and *Boy* (Primary Stages). *Sarah, Plain and Tall* (book, 2002) and *Walk Two Moons* (2005), like *Swans,* were produced Off-Broadway by THEATREWORKS. In 2004 she received the coveted Kleban Award for excellence in musical-theatre writing (she collaborates with Laurence O'Keefe, composer-librettist of *Bat Boy*) for *Sarah, Plain and Tall.*   DBW

Jory, Jon (1938–) A founder of the LONG WHARF Theatre, he was producing director from 1969 to fall 2000 of the ACTORS THEATRE OF LOUISVILLE, where he directed more than 140 plays and produced over 1,300. He has also directed at other regional theatres, including ARENA STAGE, AMERICAN CONSERVATORY THEATRE, and the McCARTER. Committed to regional repertory, the encouragement of new writers, and the production of new American plays, Jory developed the Humana Festival of New American Plays (1976–), the Shorts Festival (1980–5) for one-act plays, and the Brown–Forman Classics in Context Festival (1985–97), among other innovative programs. A published playwright himself (and suspected to be the playwright JANE MARTIN) as well as the author of *Tips: Ideas for Actors* (2000), *Tips II for Actors* (2005), and *Tips: Ideas for Directors* (2002), he has twice received the MARGO JONES Award for the production of new plays, among other awards. Jory left ATL to join the theatre faculty at the University of Washington, Seattle. He is the son of the late film and stage actor Victor Jory.   DBW

Judah, Samuel Benjamin Helbert (c. 1799–1876) Playwright and lawyer, who, as a young man, had three plays produced at the PARK THEATRE and then disappeared from theatrical circles. His two romantic melodramas with European settings – *The Mountain Torrent* (1820) and *The Rose of Arragon* (1822) – and his nationalistic comedy, *The Battle of Lexington* (1822), depended upon his ability to create spectacular scenes. In addition to two dramatic poems, Judah published a satiric play entitled *Buccaneers, A Romance of Our Own Country* (1827).   WJM

Judson Poets' Theatre (1961–81) A seminal OFF-OFF BROADWAY venue, located at the Judson Memorial Church on Washington Square South in the heart of Manhattan's Greenwich Village. Starting in 1958, the Rev. Howard Moody opened the 1892 church to local musicians, artists, and poets, among them Allen Ginsberg, ALLAN KAPROW, Claus Oldenberg, and Robert Rauschenberg. In 1961 the new assistant minister, Al Carmines, a gifted composer, founded the JPT, a hub for two decades of ALTERNATIVE THEATRE, PERFORMANCE ART, and unfettered social and political dissent. There Nam June Paik sliced his arm with a razor, accompanied by cellist Charlotte Moorman, nude from the waist up; there Carmines and MARIA IRENE FORNÉS collaborated on *Promenade* (1965), the theatre's greatest hit and – like Ron Tavel's camp classic *Gorilla Queen* (1967) with its Carmines score – among the Judson's transfers to commercial runs. CLJ

Jujamcyn Theaters Producing company founded in 1956 by 3M Chairman William L. McKnight and named for his grandchildren, Judy, James, and Cynthia. The third largest New York theatre owner, its Broadway theatres are the ST. JAMES, Hirschfeld (formerly the MARTIN BECK), O'NEILL, VIRGINIA, and WALTER KERR. At one time it also operated BOSTON's Colonial, PHILADELPHIA's Shubert, and CHICAGO's Civic and Royal George Theatres. In 2005 ROCCO LANDESMAN paid less than $30 million for the chain's five NYC theatres. (The company's chairman, James H. Binger – husband of McKnight's daughter, Virginia – had died 3 November 2004.) Landesman's first production as owner was *DOUBT* – a most auspicious beginning.

Because President Landesman, Producing Director Paul Libin, and Creative Director JACK VIERTEL were all associated with resident theatres, Jujamcyn actively develops new works for Broadway. Since 1984 the company has given the Jujamcyn Award to a resident theatre for "contribution to the development of creative talent for the the-ater." In 1986 Jujamcyn helped launch the American Playwrights Project to commission new plays for commercial production, and, with British producers, the International Theater Development Fund. In 1990 Jujamcyn helped start the short-lived New Musicals at SUNY–Purchase for "the revitalization of the American musical theatre," and in 1991 began similar initiatives in association with Albany's CAPITAL REPERTORY COMPANY (including a revision by RICHARD GREENBERG of *PAL JOEY*, staged during HUNTINGTON THEATRE's 1992–3 season).

Jujamcyn productions include Hauptman and Miller's *Big River* (Tony, 1985), INTO THE WOODS, *M. BUTTERFLY*, CITY OF ANGELS, STEPPENWOLF's GRAPES OF WRATH, *The PIANO LESSON*, KUSHNER's ANGELS IN AMERICA, *The Who's Tommy*, JELLY'S LAST JAM, the boffo hit *The PRODUCERS,* and Greenberg's *Take Me Out*. Revivals include GYPSY (1989), GUYS AND DOLLS (1992), and A FUNNY THING HAPPENED ON THE WAY TO THE FORUM (1996). REK

Julia, Raul [né Raúl Rafael Carlos Juliá y Arcelay] (1940–94) Puerto Rican–born film and stage actor whose New York debut was as Astolfo in *Life Is a Dream* in Spanish (1964, OFF-BROADWAY). Principal stage appearances included classical roles at the Delacorte (see NEW YORK SHAKESPEARE FESTIVAL) and the VIVIAN BEAUMONT in New York. In 1982 he starred in *Nine* as Guido Contini, in which critics referred to him as "a standout" and "childishly wise, boyishly insincere, and totally right." For *Nine* he was nominated for a Tony Award, as he had been for *The Threepenny Opera* (1976), *Where's Charley* (1974), and *Two Gentlemen of Verona* (1971). In 1991 he was largely unsuccessful as Macbeth at the NYSF, where he essayed Othello for the second time the following year (the first was in 1979) opposite the Iago of CHRISTOPHER WALKEN. He was seen in 1991 as Don Quixote in a national tour of MAN OF LA MANCHA (on Broadway in 1992). Julia's biggest popular success was in the film version of *The Addams Family* (1991). SMA

K

Kaczorowski, Peter (1956–) Lighting designer with extensive New York, regional theatre, and opera credits in the U.S. and abroad. He began his career as assistant to John Bury, BEVERLY EMMONS, Craig Miller, TOM SKELTON, NEIL PETER JAMPOLIS, and Andy Phillips. He is equally adept with big musicals (*The MUSIC MAN,* 2000; *WONDERFUL TOWN,* 2003; *KISS ME, KATE,* 1999; *Contact,* 2000 (Drama Desk Award); *The PRODUCERS,* 2001 (Tony); *PAJAMA GAME,* 2006) and plays (*WHO'S AFRAID OF VIRGINIA WOOLF?,* 2005; *A Naked Girl on the Appian Way,* 2005). BO

Kahn, Michael (1937–) Brooklyn-born, Columbia-educated director and educator who during his career has staged plays ranging from avant-garde satires to musical comedies and opera, at venues Off-Broadway, on Broadway, and beyond. He is known principally, however, as a talented Shakespearean director and as the artistic director of the AMERICAN SHAKESPEARE THEATRE (1969–74), the MCCARTER THEATRE Company (1974–9), the ACTING COMPANY (1978–88) and, since 1986, the SHAKESPEARE THEATRE (Washington, DC), renamed in 2005 the Shakespeare Theatre Company. Drawing eclectically on both traditional and postmodernist directorial approaches, Kahn's Shakespearean stagings are noted for their vigor, clarity, and originality and have contributed significantly to a revival of public interest in SHAKESPEARE ON THE AMERICAN STAGE in the 1980s and '90s. In the training of actors, he headed The Chautauqua Conservatory for five years and was a master teacher at CIRCLE IN THE SQUARE. He has been especially influential as the RICHARD RODGERS Director of the Drama Division of the Juilliard School (appointed in 1992 after chairing the Acting Department; in 2006 stepped down [replaced by James Houghton], but he continues teaching a third-year acting class). DJW

Kahn, Otto H(ermann) (1867–1934) German-born banker who immigrated to New York in 1893 and became the greatest individual patron of the arts the U.S. has yet known. The close personal friend and financial adviser of railroad titan Edward H.

Harriman, Kahn was regarded in his time as the most liberal and democratic multimillionaire in the country. He was the chief benefactor of the Metropolitan Opera Company and a founder and backer of the NEW THEATRE. His international contacts and his personal wealth facilitated the U.S. tour (1916–17) of Serge Diaghilev's Ballets Russes, a visit that deflected American ballet from an Italian toward a Russian model. He backed the visits of Copeau's Théâtre du Vieux Columbier (1917–19), the MOSCOW ART THEATRE (1922–3), and the Théâtre de l'Odéon (1924–5). He underwrote MAX REINHARDT's 1924 production of *The Miracle* in the amount of $600,000. Kahn also provided critical support for influential art theatres such as the WASHINGTON SQUARE PLAYERS, the PROVINCETOWN PLAYERS, the New Playwright's Theater, the CIVIC REPERTORY THEATRE, and the HEDGEROW THEATRE, as well as numerous individual writers, actors, and artists. The most recent Kahn biography is by Theresa M. Collins (2002). WD

Kalfin, Robert (1933–) Bronx-born director and producer educated at Alfred University (B.A., 1954) and the Yale School of Drama (M.F.A., 1957). He made his directorial debut with H. Leivick's *The Golem* at St. Mark's Playhouse in 1959, then freelanced in regional theatre before founding the influential CHELSEA THEATRE CENTER in 1965. After the Chelsea closed in 1983, Kalfin spent a season as director of the CINCINNATI PLAYHOUSE, and subsequently returned to freelance direction in regional theatre, New York, and abroad. CLJ

Kalish [Kalich]**, Bertha** (1872?–1939) Polish (Lemberg)-born actress who first performed in Polish opera but shifted to YIDDISH THEATRE. In 1896, already successful, she came to America with her husband and children. Her beauty, grace, and dignity won praise as the star of such plays as GOLDFADN's *Shulamis* and GORDIN's *Sappho* and *The Kreutzer Sonata* (which he supposedly wrote to show off her thrilling voice and beautiful thick hair). In 1905 she contracted with the American producer HARRISON FISKE to star in productions such as *Fedora* and *Monna Vanna*, as well as English translations of her Yiddish successes, and for the next 20 years she performed at least as much in English as in Yiddish. However, near the end of her life, completely blind, she returned exclusively to the Yiddish stage.   NS

Kander, John (1927–), composer, and **Fred Ebb** (1927–2004) lyricist. After receiving a Master's degree from Columbia University, Kander worked as a rehearsal pianist, conductor, and arranger. His first Broadway score was for *A Family Affair* (1961). Ebb also received a Master's from Columbia; he wrote plays and song lyrics before joining with Kander to write scores for Broadway, notably *Flora, the Red Menace* (1965), CABARET (1966; Tony, Best Musical), *Zorba* (1968), CHICAGO (1975), *Woman of the Year* (1981; Tony, Best Original Score), *Kiss of the Spider Woman* (1992, Toronto & London; Broadway, 1993; Tony, Best Musical), *Steel Pier* (1997), and *Curtains* (2007). They wrote the songs for two of LIZA MINNELLI's ONE-PERSON shows, and she appeared in their musicals *Chicago* (as a replacement for GWEN VERDON), *The Act* (1977), and *The Rink* (1984). In several of their musicals they proved skillful at duplicating the sounds and idioms of foreign cultures and bygone eras. In 1991 they were inducted into the New York THEATRE HALL OF FAME, and in 1996 they received the "Mr. Abbott" Award for outstanding contribution to the American theatre.   MK

Kanin, Garson (1912–99) Rochester, NY–born actor, director, and author of short stories, novels, documentaries, and stage, screen, and television plays (often with his first wife, RUTH GORDON). Beginning in VAUDEVILLE, he debuted as Tommy Deal in *Little Ol' Boy* (1933), and appeared in *Spring Song* (1934) and *Ladies' Money* (1934), among others. He directed *Hitch Your Wagon* and *Too Many Heroes* (both 1937), and was assistant director to GEORGE ABBOTT (1935–7) before moving to Hollywood to direct feature films. With Carol Reed he received an Oscar for Eisenhower's army documentary *The True Glory* (1945); alone he directed his best-known Broadway work, BORN YESTERDAY (1946; cowrote [uncredited] 1956 film), and his own libretto of *Die Fledermaus* (Metropolitan Opera, 1950). For Broadway, he also directed *The DIARY OF ANNE FRANK* (1955); *Do Re Mi,* for which he also wrote the book (1960); and FUNNY GIRL (1964). In Los Angeles, he directed a revival of *IDIOT'S DELIGHT* (1970). Known as a playwright of strong liberal sentiments, Ganin received the American Academy of Dramatic Arts Award of Achievement (1958) and the "Mr. Abbott" Award

for Lifetime Achievement (1997). His younger brother was playwright-screenwriter Michael Kanin, who collaborated with his wife, Fay Mitchell Kanin. In 1990 Garson married actress MARIAN SELDES.   GSA

Kansas City Repertory Theatre see MISSOURI REPERTORY THEATRE

Kaprow, Allan (1927–2006) New Jersey–born PERFORMANCE ARTIST, art historian, writer. Formerly a painter who had studied with Hans Hoffmann (1947–8) and at New York University (B.A., 1949), Kaprow also studied art history at Columbia University (M.A., 1952) and music composition with John Cage (1957, 1958). He developed "Happenings" (1959) and other models for merging art with life, such as the "Un-artist" (1971–4) (one who deconstructs art) and the notion of "life-like" art (as opposed to "art-like" art) (1983). Influenced by Marcel Duchamp, Jackson Pollock, Cage, the *Nouveau Réalistes,* Japanese Gutai, and Zen Buddhism, Kaprow's aesthetic of everyday life questioned traditional illusionism and theatricality in art. From the late 1970s Kaprow's performances were meditative and private practices, ethnographic studies, and social interventions, such as *Standards* (1979) and *Digging a Hole* (1980). He taught visual art at various institutions, including at the University of California-San Diego (1974–93), his final position. His work has recently been studied by Jeff Kelley (2004).   AF

Karamu House A private metropolitan center for the arts founded in 1915 by Oberlin College graduates Rowena and Russell Jelliffe and located in Cleveland, OH. The original center burned down in 1939, but a new and expanded facility opened 10 years later, after WWII. The adult theatre group, launched in 1921, was initially called the Gilpin Players, after actor CHARLES GILPIN. It was from the start multiracial, but a demographic change has given it a core constituency of inner-city blacks. The center contains a proscenium and an arena theatre, both nonprofit, in which some 11 productions are mounted each season, including musicals and, in the past, operas. Karamu enjoyed a special relationship with playwright LANGSTON HUGHES and premiered six of his plays. In 1981 an attempt was made to establish a black Equity unit, but traditional operating procedures thwarted the move, and Equity personnel returned to New York. Karamu (Swahili for "a place of joyful gathering") considers its theatre to be the oldest continually active AFRICAN AMERICAN THEATRE in America.   EGH

Kauffmann, Stanley (1916–) Drama and film critic; educator, actor, playwright, and novelist. Born in New York and educated at NYU (1935), Kauffmann established his reputation as film (1958–65; 1967–) and theatre (1969–79) critic for *New Republic,* and as theatre critic for the *New York Times* (1966) and *Saturday Review* (1979–85). During 1963–5 he served as drama critic for WNET-TV. He has held academic appointments at Yale (1967–73; 1977–86), CUNY (1973–6; 1976–93), and Adelphi University (1993–6). His 17 books include *Persons of the Drama* (1976), *Theater Criticisms* (1984), *Distinguishing Features* (1994), and his memoirs, *Albums of Early Life* (1980), as well as seven novels. His numerous honors include the GEORGE JEAN NATHAN Award for Dramatic Criticism in 1972–3 and in 1995 the Lifetime Achievement Award in Academic Theatre from the Association for Theatre in Higher Education.   TLM

Kaufman, George S(imon) (1889–1961) Playwright and director. A Founding Father of the American popular theatre, Kaufman enjoyed a long and extraordinarily productive Broadway career. On his own he wrote only one full-length play, a satire of the theatre called *The Butter and Egg Man* (1925); in collaboration he wrote 40 plays, more than half of them certified hits. His partners included MARC CONNELLY (*DULCY,* 1921; *BEGGAR ON HORSEBACK,* 1924); EDNA FERBER (*The ROYAL FAMILY,* 1927; *DINNER AT EIGHT,* 1932; *Stage Door,* 1936); MORRIE RYSKIND (*The COCOANUTS,* 1925; *ANIMAL CRACKERS,* 1928 – two MARX BROS. vehicles – and *OF THEE I SING,* 1931, Pulitzer Prize); and MOSS HART (*ONCE IN A LIFETIME,* 1930; *YOU CAN'T TAKE IT WITH YOU,* 1936, Pulitzer Prize; *The MAN WHO CAME TO DINNER,* 1939). Whereas his partners were stronger on plot contrivance, Kaufman's speciality was dialogue, which he enlivened with witty, sarcastic rejoinders: the fabled Kaufman wisecrack. He was a born satirist whose targets included not only his own beat, the New York theatre world, but also Hollywood, big business, politics, and provincialism (although Kaufman himself was accused of being parochial in his subject matter). His subjects were drawn from life, but his artificial, well-made plots were manufactured for the theatre. Kaufman's dry wit earned him a seat at the Algonquin Round Table, and his instinctive abhorrence of romance, sentiment, and melodrama provided a counterbalance to his less cynical collaborators. Though his tone was captious and ironic, Kaufman was never so abrasive as to offend the large popular audience on which his bread and butter depended; at the finale he tempered his sting with forgiveness.

Kaufman began his directing career in 1928 with a jumpy, frenetic production of *The FRONT PAGE.* Like a terse Kaufman script, a Kaufman-directed show had remarkable precision. Swift timing was his trademark; he had no patience for analysis or introspection, and when a solemn actor once made the mistake of asking about motivation, Kaufman snapped "Your job." The subject of a number of biographies, the most scholarly are by Malcolm Goldstein (1979) and Jeffrey Mason (1988).   FH

Kaufman, Moisés see TECTONIC THEATER PROJECT

Kaye, Judy (1948–) Singer-actress who, after attending UCLA, made her Broadway debut as a replacement in *GREASE* (1977), then succeeded Madeline Kahn as Lily Garland early in the run of *On the Twentieth Century* (1978). After several years working in NIGHTCLUBS, touring shows, and regional theatre, she received critical kudos for her impressive singing and scene-stealing comedy as opera diva Carlotta Guidicelli in the American production of *PHANTOM OF THE OPERA* (1988). She subsequently appeared in a New York City Opera revival of *PAJAMA GAME* (1989), a production of *The MERRY WIDOW* at the New Jersey's PAPER MILL PLAYHOUSE (1991), as Emma Goldman in *RAGTIME* (1998), as Rosie in *Mamma Mia!* (2001), and in the New York City Opera revival of *CANDIDE* (2005). In 2005, after workshop and summer appearances, she repeated on Broadway her cult favorite, Florence Foster Jenkins, a real-life legend for singing badly, in *Souvenir.* She is in frequent demand for concert performances of classic American musicals.   MK

Kazan [né Kazanjoglous], **Elia** (1909–2003) Greek-born American director and actor, GROUP THEATRE member, and cofounder of the ACTORS STUDIO. Kazan was long considered America's leading director of actors for both stage and film. His stage productions of *A STREETCAR NAMED DESIRE* (1947), *DEATH OF A SALESMAN* (1949), *CAT ON A HOT TIN ROOF* (1955), and *SWEET BIRD OF YOUTH* (1959), and his films *Streetcar . . .* (1951), *On the Waterfront* (1954), and *East of Eden* (1955) earned him the reputation of preeminent Method director whose overheated, naturalistic style is synonymous with the work of the Actors Studio. A Kazan-directed performance is excitingly high-strung, notable for its depth and intensity of feeling, its verbal stammers and backtracking, its emotional ambivalences, and its sexual vibrancy. Kazan's method, influenced by the ideas of Stanislavsky and LEE

STRASBERG, depended on personal contact with his actors. A shrewd judge of character, he took actors off to the side, his arm draped casually over their shoulders, to whisper some private confidence or observation. Kazan was castigated in 1952 for cooperating with the House Un-American Activities Committee. Though he rarely directed, in films or theatre, after he resigned in 1964 as codirector of the VIVIAN BEAUMONT THEATRE, he remained a revered figure among New York actors. His controversial autobiography appeared in 1988, and he published four novels (the most recent in 1994). A biography by Richard Schickel was published in 2005. In 1999 Kazan received an Oscar for Lifetime Achievement. FH

Keach, Stacy (1941–) Stage, film, and television actor who gained critical attention in the title role of *MacBird!* OFF-BROADWAY in 1967, as "BUFFALO BILL" CODY in KOPIT's *INDIANS* at the ARENA STAGE and on Broadway in 1969, and as Jamie in *LONG DAY'S JOURNEY INTO NIGHT* (1971 revival, Promenade Theatre). He has thrice played Hamlet, most recently at Los Angeles's MARK TAPER FORUM (1974). In 1990 he appeared as the title character in MICHAEL KAHN's production of *Richard III* at the SHAKESPEARE THEATRE in Washington, DC, as well as Macbeth there in 1995; Broadway appearances in *Solitary Confinement* (1992) and *The Kentucky Cycle* (1993) were short-lived productions; in 1997 he was Birling in *An Inspector Calls* in LA and Seattle; and in 1998 Marc in *Art* (first American cast in the London version). From 2000 until it ended after three seasons he played the hard-living father Ken Titus in the Fox series *Titus*. In 2006 he played King Lear at the GOODMAN. His father, Stacy Sr., was an actor, as is his brother, James. DBW

Keane, Doris (1881–1945) Actress known for her success in a single role. Educated in Europe, she also studied at the AMERICAN ACADEMY OF DRAMATIC ART. Various roles quickly led to her starring engagement as the opera star and ill-fated lover Margherita Cavallini in EDWARD SHELDON's *Romance* (1913), which she also played to an adoring public in London (1915). She continued to play the role in the U.S. and London until just before her retirement (c. 1930). Critics praised her unfathomable beauty, excellent stage technique, and richly nuanced performance. STARK YOUNG attributed her success to a deep spirituality that transcended all of these qualities. MR

Kean, Thomas see MURRAY, WALTER, AND THOMAS KEAN

Keene, Laura [née Mary Frances Moss] (1826?–73) English-born actress and manager. Although facts about her origins, training, and name are disputed, Laura Keene apparently made her London debut in 1851, a year before JAMES W. WALLACK hired her as leading lady for his company in New York. Her grace and charm as well as her comic ability endeared her with New York audiences in her favorite roles of Lady Teazle, Lady Gay Spanker, and Beatrice in *Much Ado*. After a year with Wallack's company, she spent the next two seasons in Baltimore and SAN FRANCISCO before touring Australia with young EDWIN BOOTH. In 1855 she returned to New York and opened her own Laura Keene Varieties Theatre. During 1856–63 she managed and acted in her Laura Keene's Theatre, which became known for its lavishly mounted comedies. She encouraged the production of new American plays and closely supervised an excellent company that included E. A. SOTHERN, JOSEPH JEFFERSON III, Kate Reignolds, W. J. FLORENCE, Agnes Robertson, JOHN T. RAYMOND, and CHARLES W. COULDOCK. She returned to touring in 1863, and was performing in *OUR AMERICAN COUSIN* at FORD's THEATRE in Washington, DC, when President Lincoln was assassinated. During her career, she became closely identified with the emotional drama (e.g., *Camille*). Though flawed, the most recent biographies are by Ben G. Henneke (1990) and Vernanne Bryan (1997). TLM

Keith, B(enjamin) F(ranklin) (1846–1914) Vaudeville entrepreneur and theatre proprietor who, with EDWARD F. ALBEE, created the most extensive vaudeville theatre chain in the U.S. Born in New Hampshire, Keith grew up on a farm, worked as a mess boy on a coastal freighter, and spent the 1870s working and traveling with CIRCUSES, where he most likely first met Albee. In 1880 he made and sold brooms in Providence, RI, but by 1883 had moved into the dime-museum business with the rental of a vacant store in Boston. After Albee joined him in 1885 and continuous performances had been initiated, he became part owner of the Gaiety Musée; in 1886 he added the adjoining Bijou Theatre. Keith is often credited with the first use of the word "vaudeville" in order to circumvent the stigma attached to "variety" and the earlier concert saloon's sleazy reputation. With the formula of continuous, completely respectable vaudeville, the Keith–Albee circuit (nicknamed "the Sunday School Circuit") grew quickly with the construction or acquisition of vaudeville theatres in many cities, including Boston's Colonial Theatre (1894) and New York's The PALACE

Clown Emmett Kelly as Weary Willie. *Courtesy:* Ringling Bros.–Barnum & Bailey Circus.

(built by Martin Beck in 1913 but virtually controlled by Keith–Albee) and The ORPHEUM (built in 1899 by PERCY WILLIAMS but bought by Keith in 1912). Despised by many vaudevillians, Keith–Albee sought to monopolize first-class vaudeville through the Vaudeville Managers' Protective Association (1900) and the UNITED BOOKING OFFICE (1906), headed by Keith and his major competitor, F. F. PROCTOR. After Keith's death, Albee ultimately gained control of the operation. The life and careers of Keith and Albee have recently been chronicled by Arthur F. Wertheim (2006). DBW

Kellar, Harry [né Heinrich Keller] (1849–1922) Magician who acted as assistant to the Fakir of Ava (I. Harris Hughes) and the DAVENPORT BROTHERS before striking out on his own. Kellar tended to appropriate and refashion tricks conceived by others. A master of publicity, he won fame with Buatier de Kolta's "Vanishing Birdcage"; from Maskelyne, he derived the disappearing act "The Witch, the Sailor and the Monkey" as well as his supreme illusion, "The Levitation of the Princess Karnac" (1904). After touring the world in 1880, he resettled in the U.S., where he set a record of 323 consecutive performances at Philadelphia's Egyptian Hall (1884) and 179 at the Comedy The-

atre, New York (1886–7). He retired on a well-invested fortune in 1908, naming HOWARD THURSTON as his successor. His memoirs were published in 1886. LS

Kellogg, Marjorie Bradley (1946–) Set designer. Strongly within the tradition of American selective realism, Kellogg's sets are meticulously researched, yet moody and evocative. She has worked extensively at regional theatres and has done several shows with CIRCLE IN THE SQUARE. Broadway credits include *The Best Little Whorehouse in Texas, Da,* and *Steaming.* Her work was honored by LONG WHARF THEATRE, where she designed frequently, with the 1995 (and third) Mary L. Murphy Award for Excellence in Design. Recent productions include *Everybody's Ruby* (PUBLIC, 1999), LINNEY's *A Lesson before Dying* (2000), and BLESSING's *Thief River* (2001) (both at SIGNATURE). AA

Kelly, Emmett (1898–1979) The prototypical tramp clown (as was OTTO GRIEBLING) and a consummate MIME. Initially a trapeze artist, Kelly was first seen as the clown "Weary Willie" in 1924, a character he originated as a cartoon. The dirty, unshaven tramp's great popularity began in 1933 during the Depression. The silent, unsmiling clown was – according to Kelly's 1954 autobiography, *Clown* – the hobo who learns that the deck is stacked against him but keeps trying because of that one "spark of hope still glimmering in his soul." Kelly's most famous routine involved the sweeping of a circle of light from a spotlight. In the 1940s he was the star of RINGLING BROS. and BARNUM & Bailey Circus. Sedan, KS, is home to a Emmett Kelly Museum. DBW

Kelly, George E(dward) (1887–1974) Playwright. A member of the famed Philadelphia Kellys and uncle of Princess Grace, Kelly had three major Broadway successes in the 1920s: *The Torchbearers* (1922), a satire of Little Theatre (see COMMUNITY THEATRE) enthusiasts; *The SHOW OFF* (1924), a comedy of provincial manners about the battle between a commonsensical mother and braggart son-in-law; and *CRAIG'S WIFE* (1925, Pulitzer Prize), an exposure of an American ice maiden whose immaculate home is more important to her than her husband. Although he was a practical man of the theatre – he began his career in 1912 as an actor on the VAUDEVILLE circuit – Kelly did not want to be labeled as a popular entertainer, and he insisted on directing each of his plays to preserve their distinctive rhythms. In later work such as *The Deep Mrs. Sykes* (1945) and

The Fatal Weakness (1946), he deliberately muted comic elements. Kelly – a well-hidden homosexual – thought of himself as a moralist whose satires were designed to instruct and improve as well as to amuse. His work gains its idiosyncratic stamp from the targets he chose: bossy, smug suburban matrons, untalented would-be actors and playwrights, and freeloaders. Although he worked within a conventional range of modest domestic settings, seemingly dictaphonic dialogue, and characters and situations drawn from middle-class American life, Kelly's writing achieves a unique voice: tart, scolding, droll and delightfully eccentric. Foster Hirsch wrote a study of Kelly in 1975. FH

Kelly, John (1954–) New Jersey–born experimental performance artist, author, visual artist, choreographer, and director (especially opera), who creates both solo and ensemble mutidisciplinary theatre works. According to his wonderfully illustrated autobiography (published 2001), between 1984 and 2000 he created some 20 performance works, including in 2004 *The Skin I'm In*, a quasi-retrospective with performance (six performers), film, and projections. It included sections from earlier works inspired by Egon Schiele, Jean Cocteau, German Expressionist silent films, Greek myths, Maria Callas, and Kelly's own experience surviving a trapeze accident in which he broke his neck. Kelly, who often morphs into exotic alter egos, also channeled Dagmar Onassis (purportedly Maria's illegitimate daughter), the Mona Lisa, Vander BARBETTE (cross-dressing trapeze artist), and Baptiste (mime from the film *The Children of Paradise*). He created the role of Bartell D'Arcy on Broadway in *James Joyce's The Dead* (2000) and in 2005 played Cupid in Marlowe's *Dido, Queen of Carthage* at AMERICAN REPERTORY THEATRE. This multitalented artist has won numerous awards, including Obies, Bessies, and a Guggenheim. In 2004–5 he was a Radcliffe Institute Fellow in Cambridge, MA. DBW

Kelly, Patsy [née Sarah Veronica Rose Kelly] (1910–81) Actress-comedienne who first appeared on the New York stage in *Harry Delmar's Revels* (1927) and was, for the next few years, in the cast of several other REVUES, including *EARL CARROLL'S Vanities* (1930), *The Wonder Bar* (1931), and *Flying Colors* (1932). After a stint in VAUDEVILLE she began a long career in films, usually playing the dumpy, wisecracking maid or friend of the heroine. She returned to Broadway in the acclaimed revival of *No, No, NANETTE* (1971), and received

costar billing with Debbie Reynolds for her performance as Mrs. O'Dare in the revival of *Irene* (1973). MK

Kemble, Fanny (Frances Anne) (1809–93) English actress and author; in 1832 she came with her father, Charles Kemble, for a star tour beginning at New York's PARK THEATRE. Their visit was welcomed by an audience eager to see an element of refinement in the American theatre, though the critic for the *New York Mirror* noted that "many accustomed to a less chaste and more boisterous style" failed to appreciate her. Fanny Kemble pleased her more discerning public with intensely rendered romantic heroines, such as Julia in *The Hunchback* and Shakespeare's Juliet. FRANCIS C. WEMYSS declared that "she revived the prostrate fortunes of the drama in the United States." Fanny retired in 1834 in order to marry Pierce Butler, a South Carolinian. She was a staunch abolitionist, and the marriage foundered on this issue. For 26 years (1845–74) she gave a well-received series of readings from SHAKESPEARE in England and the U.S. Between 1835 and 1890 she published nine volumes of memoirs. J. C. Furnas's 1982 biography is definitive   MR

Kennedy, Adrienne [née Adrienne Lita Hawkins] (1931–) African American playwright who blends symbols, historical figures, racial images, and myths to create surreal, highly personalized one-act plays, all of which she claims are autobiographical. *FUNNYHOUSE OF A NEGRO*, which won an Obie in 1964 (CIRCLE IN THE SQUARE), depicts the final moments before the suicide of Sarah, a mulatto psychically torn by an inability to reconcile herself to her mixed racial heritage. *The Owl Answers* (LORTEL's White Barn Theatre, CT, 1965) portrays another mulatto woman caught in a hallucinatory nightmare of confused racial identity in which biographical and historical characters emerge, dissolve, and metamorphose. Kennedy's other plays include *A Rat's Mass* (Boston, 1966), a fantasy of war and prejudice; *The Lennon Play: In His Own Write* (London, 1967), an adaptation of musician John Lennon's autobiographical writings; *A Movie Star Has to Star in Black and White* (The PUBLIC, 1976, dir. JOSEPH CHAIKIN); *A Lancashire Lad* (1980), a CHILDREN'S THEATRE piece based on the early life of Charlie Chaplin; *Ohio State Murders* (Cleveland, 1992; 1993 Lecomte de Nouy Award). In 1995–6 she was resident playwright for SIGNATURE, where her *The Alexander Plays. . . Suzanne In Stages* had its NYC premiere and *Sleep Deprivation Chamber* (Obie; coauthored by her son Adam) was presented. A memoir was published in 1987; a brief bio and overview of her work by Philip C. Kolin was published in 2005.   FB

Kennedy, Arthur (1914–90) Film, stage, and television actor who began acting with the GROUP THEATRE and made his debut on Broadway as Bushy in *Richard II* (1937). Later successes were Chris in *ALL MY SONS* (1947), Biff in *DEATH OF A SALESMAN* (1949), and John Proctor in *The CRUCIBLE* (1953). Awards included a Tony for Biff (1949), the New York Film Critics' Award for *Bright Victory* (1951), and a Golden Globe Award for *Trial* (1955). After his film debut in 1940, Kennedy appeared in more than 70 films.   SMA

Kennedy Center see JOHN F. KENNEDY CENTER FOR THE PERFORMING ARTS

Kennedy, Charles Rann (1871–1950) Playwright and actor from England who became an American citizen in 1917. An advocate of Christian principles, which he dramatized with more ardor than theatrical effectiveness, Kennedy helped bring the Social Gospel movement to the American stage. In *The Servant in the House* (1908), his best-known play, he presented a Christ figure who reveals the hypocrisy of organized religion. Later plays – many written for his actress wife, Edith Wynne Matthison – include *The Idol Breaker* (1914) and *The Terrible Meek* (1912), a daring antiwar play. Leaving Broadway, the Kennedys became associated with Bennett College, where he continued to write plays and direct Greek plays.   WJM

Kennedy's Children by Robert Patrick, a two-act drama that in its final form opened at Clark Center for the Performing Arts under the auspices of PLAYWRIGHTS HORIZONS on 30 May 1973 and reached Broadway directed by Clive Donner on 3 November 1975 at the Golden Theatre. A series of unrelated monologues in a downtown New York City bar, the play depicts a lost generation of Americans in the aftermath of the Kennedy assassination. Five characters, including a pill-popping Vietnam veteran, a Marilyn Monroe–type blonde, and a young radical, reveal shattered dreams and self-explorations in a painful lament for the 1960s.   ER

Kentucky Cycle, The Nine related one-act plays by Robert Schenkkan about three Appalachian families over seven generations, from 1775 down to 1975. Set in the Cumberland Plateau of Eastern Kentucky, the cycle presents the dark side of the American dream: blood feuds, murder, land grab-

bing, and the destruction of the land. Beginning with two workshop performances at the MARK TAPER FORUM (1988, 1989), the cycle had its world premiere at the INTIMAN THEATRE in SEATTLE (1991); a revised production at the Taper (1992) ran for 10 weeks and won five Los Angeles Drama Critics' Awards. It was also awarded the Pulitzer Prize for Drama in 1992, the first time that a play unproduced in New York had won. After a tryout at the JOHN F. KENNEDY CENTER, the $2.5 million production opened on Broadway at the ROYALE THEATRE, 14 November 1993 (34 performances), where critics thought it old-fashioned, with cliched language and melodramatic plots and characters. Schenkkan had a dry spell after the play's failure in New York until *Handler* in 2000 (Actors Express, ATLANTA) and especially 2005–6: *By the Waters of Babylon* (OREGON SHAKESPEARE FESTIVAL), *The Marriage of Miss Hollywood and King Neptune* (UT Austin; his alma mater), *Lewis and Clark Reach the Euphrates* (Taper) – a critique of the war in Iraq – and *The Devil and Daniel Webster,* a new version for the SEATTLE CHILDREN'S THEATRE.   TLM

Kern, Jerome (1885–1945) Composer who, after studying musical composition, began his theatrical career as a house composer for producer CHARLES FROHMAN in London. Returning to the U.S., he worked as a song plugger and rehearsal pianist. Individual songs by Kern were interpolated into several Broadway musicals before he was given his first opportunity to compose a complete score, *The Red Petticoat* (1912). In 1915 Kern was asked by producers F. RAY COMSTOCK and ELISABETH MARBURY to write the score for a modest musical that would be appropriate to the tiny, 299-seat PRINCESS THEATRE. The result, *Nobody Home,* enchanted critics and audiences with its personable cast, contemporary setting, and lively score. An even greater success was the second Princess Theatre musical, *VERY GOOD EDDIE* (1915). With librettist GUY BOLTON (a previous collaborator) and lyricist P. G. WODEHOUSE, Kern created *Have a Heart* (1917), *Oh, Boy* (1917), *Leave It to Jane* (1917), and *Oh, Lady! Lady!* (1918). By replacing the mythical kingdoms and stilted language of European operetta with recognizable characters, believable dramatic situations, and American musical idioms, these shows strongly influenced the direction in which American musical comedy was to evolve in the 1920s.

After writing a number of successful, if conventional, musicals in the first half of the 1920s, Kern again pioneered a new style of MUSICAL THEATRE with his score for *SHOW BOAT* (1927). Conceived as a musical drama, *Show Boat,* with book and lyrics by OSCAR HAMMERSTEIN II, proved that shows with serious librettos and songs that grew naturally out of the dramatic action could be successful. Kern's shows of the 1930s, although containing many fine songs, were more traditional operettas and musical comedies. His last complete score for Broadway was *Very Warm for May* (1939). He is remembered as an innovator whose scores for the Princess Theatre musicals and *Show Boat* were landmarks in the evolution of modern musical theatre. Gerald Bordman's 1980 biography appeared in a reprint edition in 2005; however, the most recent study of Kern is Stephen Banfield's (2006). MK

Kerr, Jean (1923–2003) Playwright and author who wrote 10 successful plays noted for their lighthearted comedy and witty dialogue, such as *Touch and Go,* with husband WALTER (1949); *King of Hearts,* with Eleanor Brooke (1954; dir. Walter); *Finishing Touches* (1973); and *Lunch Hour* (1980). Her biggest hit was MARY, MARY (1961), with Barbara BEL GEDDES. She was also noted for her humorous writings, particularly *Please Don't Eat the Daisies,* which became both a film and a TV series. FB

Kerr, Walter (Francis) (1913–96) Drama critic, playwright, lecturer, teacher, and director. Kerr, born in Evanston, IL, was educated at Northwestern University before beginning in 1938 an 11-year career as teacher of drama at Catholic University. There he wrote or cowrote and directed a number of new scripts, four of which reached Broadway. With his wife, JEAN, he collaborated on several shows, including the musical comedy *Goldilocks* (1958). In 1950, Kerr began reviewing for *Commonweal.* The following year, he replaced HOWARD BARNES as drama critic for the *New York Herald Tribune,* a post he held until that paper's demise in 1966. The *New York Times* then hired him as chief critic for the Sunday edition, a position he held until his retirement in 1983. Regarded as the most perceptive critic reviewing the Broadway theatre during the 1960s and '70s, Kerr brought intelligence, insight, knowledge, and a graceful style to his work. He believed that a play's truths must be perceived by an audience intuitively rather than intellectually, and that a play must touch a group consciousness so that there is a "single unified response." Author of ten books, his views are most cogently expressed in *How Not to Write a Play* (1955), *The Decline of Pleasure* (1962), *The Theatre in Spite of Itself* (1963), *Tragedy and Comedy* (1967), *The Silent Clowns* (1975), and *Journey to the Center of the Theatre* (1979). He won a Pulitzer Prize for Dramatic Criticism in 1978. In 1990 the restored Ritz Theatre, built in 1921 and renovated in 1983, was renamed the WALTER KERR THEATRE in his honor. His death marked the end of an era in theatre criticism. TLM

Kersands, Billy (c. 1842–1915) African American minstrel entertainer for more than 40 years. Kersands was the leading low comedian of several MINSTREL SHOW companies, including his own. Large of stature, he was nevertheless an excellent dancer, credited with introducing the soft-shoe and buck-and-wing dances. He was also praised for his gymnastic drumming, and his troupe led the Mardi Gras parade in 1886. He caricatured the slow-witted Negro character and used his unusually large mouth to advantage in facial antics. His popularity in the southern states forced theatre owners to suspend segregationist seating to accommodate increased black patronage when he appeared. EGH

Kerz, Leo (1912–76) Berlin-born theatre and film set designer who studied with BERTOLT BRECHT and Laszlo Moholy-Nagy, and from 1927 worked as an assistant designer to ERWIN PISCATOR. These influences remained with him throughout his career, and his sets tended toward sweeping proportions and emblematic scenic elements. Like Piscator, he also incorporated film and projections into many of his designs. He left Berlin soon after Hitler assumed power, and worked in London, Amsterdam, and Prague before founding the Pioneer Theatre in Johannesburg, South Africa. Kerz came to the U.S. in 1942, assisted JO MIELZINER, WATSON BARRETT, and STEWART CHANEY, and resumed his work with Piscator. He made his Broadway debut as a scenic designer in 1947 with *Open House,* followed by the KATHARINE CORNELL production of *Antony and Cleopatra.* He is best known for his opera designs for the Metropolitan and New York City Opera companies, among others, and for his work at the ARENA STAGE during 1969–71. He also designed for television and film. AA

Kessler, David (1860–1920) Moldavian (Kishenev)-born actor who was 17 when the new invention, YIDDISH THEATRE, came to town. Fascinated, he first joined as a stagehand and, by 1886, when he arrived in New York, he had progressed to leading man. Kessler, an emotional actor, was capable both of melodramatic sensationalism, which excited the masses, and sensitive characterizations, which delighted the intelligentsia. His most famous roles were in GORDIN's *God, Man, and Devil*

(1900) and *Shlomke Charlatan,* and PINSKI's *Yankl the Blacksmith* (1906). Much of his career he functioned not only as actor but as star-manager of his own company.   NS

Kidd, Michael [né Milton Gruenwald] (1919–) Ballet dancer and choreographer for theatre and film (see DANCE). Kidd performed with BALANCHINE's American Ballet, Ballet Caravan, and Ballet Theatre before making his impact in American MUSICAL THEATRE. From his choreographic debut in *FINIAN'S RAINBOW* (1947, Tony) to the ever-popular barn-raising dance in the film *Seven Brides for Seven Brothers* (MGM, 1954), Kidd has been lauded for his energetic and spirited successes. He had a series of successes – *GUYS AND DOLLS* (1950), *CAN-CAN* (1953), *Li'l Abner* (1956), and *Destry Rides Again* (1959) – for which he won four successive Tony Awards, becoming the first nominee ever so honored. After a long absence from direction, he replaced GENE SAKS as director of *The Goodbye Girl* in 1993, for which he was nominated for a Tony.   LF

Kiesler, Frederick (1890–1965) Austrian-born architect and designer. Very little of Kiesler's visionary theatre was ever fully realized, yet his plans and projects exerted a strong influence on the development of mid-20th-century theatre architecture and the emergence of environmental theatre. Most of his projects were variations on the so-called Endless Theatre – a futuristic theatre of ramps and spirals within an ellipsoidal shell. His more practical projects included flexible theatres capable of changing size and configuration, and "space stages," which were essentially nonscenic architectural stages. He came to the U.S. in 1926 with the International Theatre Exhibit – the first look many Americans had at new European design – and stayed, but Kiesler never achieved the prominence he had known in Europe. Despite many projects, his only significant theatre fully realized in the U.S. was the Eighth Street Cinema in New York (1930).   AA

Kiley, Richard (1922–99) Chicago-born actor-singer who made his acting debut in local radio and, after serving in the Navy, toured as Stanley in *A STREETCAR NAMED DESIRE.* His Broadway debut was in SHAW's *Misalliance* (1953), and in the same year he played the juvenile lead in *KISMET.* He received a Tony for his performance opposite GWEN VERDON in *Redhead* (1959) and had leading roles in the musicals *No Strings* (1962) and *I Had a Ball* (1964). In 1965 he created the dual role of Cervantes and Don Quixote in the musical *MAN OF LA MANCHA* (Tony), the show with which he is most closely identified. Possessed of a powerful singing voice, Kiley was also a fine actor with many film and television credits.   MK

Kilty, Jerome (Timothy) (1922–) Actor, playwright, director. Brattle Theatre (Cambridge, MA) cofounder-director (1948–52), Kilty's extensive résumé includes Broadway roles and countless resident-theatre assignments (including over two decades at the AMERICAN REPERTORY THEATRE). Author of nine plays, he has directed versions of his best known, *Dear Liar* (1957), in four languages. A sometimes visiting actor-director at the ALLEY, in 1995 he directed *Arms and the Man* there.   DBW

Kim, Willa (1917?–) Costume designer from California. From the 1950s through the '70s Kim designed costumes for many of the major OFF-BROADWAY productions, including *Scuba Duba, Promenade, Operation Sidewinder* (1970, Lincoln Center), *Lydie Breeze,* and Genet's *The Screens,* as well as for *Dynamite Tonight* (1964, ACTORS STUDIO). She later became associated with large-scale glitzy musicals, such as *Sophisticated Ladies* (1981, Tony), *Dancin', Song and Dance, Legs Diamond, The WILL ROGERS FOLLIES* (1991, Tony), and *Victor/Victoria* (1995; see rendering s.v. COSTUME). Plays include *Jumpers* and the 1986 revival of *The FRONT PAGE* at the VIVIAN BEAUMONT. She first designed for ballet in 1962, and since has designed extensively for the Feld Ballet, the Joffrey, and the San Francisco Ballet, as well as for opera. In 1999 she was honored with the IRENE SHARAFF Lifetime Achievement Award.   AA

Kimball, Moses (1810–95) A merchant and entrepreneur, Kimball opened the BOSTON MUSEUM in 1841 and introduced plays in 1843. Withdrawing from active management in the 1860s to concentrate on politics, Kimball maintained (until 1893) probably the longest-lived repertory company in U.S. theatrical history. The successful formula stressed family entertainment, low prices, prizes for moral dramas (*The DRUNKARD* premiered here in 1844), and quality acting.   RKB

King, Bruce (195?–) A member of the Turtle Clan of the Haudenosaunee–Oneida Nation (Wisconsin), he began writing plays after returning from three years' service in the Vietnam War. Since then, his plays have been performed throughout the U.S., largely in reservation and urban Native communities. As a playwright, director, filmmaker, and teacher, King has nurtured the talents of two generations of Native theatre artists. In

Gertrude Lawrence and Yul Brynner in *The King and I*, 1951. *Courtesy:* Belknap Collection for the Performing Arts, University of Florida Libraries.

recent years his new works have oftened premiered with the Thunderbird Theatre at Haskell Indian Nations University (Lawrence, KS). In plays like *Evening at the Warbonnet* (1993) and *Threads* (2001), King deftly merges indigenous cultural values with Western playwriting techniques.   AH

King, Dennis (1897–1971) English-born actor and singer who began his career with the Birmingham Repertory Theatre. After his arrival in New York in the early 1920s, King appeared in the THEATRE GUILD production of SHAW's *Back to Methuselah* and as Mercutio in *Romeo and Juliet*. His fine baritone voice and his training as an actor made King the ideal leading man for operetta. In 1924 he appeared as Jim Kenyon in ROSE-MARIE, and his success in that role was followed by critically acclaimed performances as François Villon in *The VAGABOND KING* (1925) and as D'Artagnan in *The Three Musketeers* (1928). From the 1930s on, King concentrated on acting in straight plays, returning to the musical stage on rare occasions, most notably to create the role of Willie Palaffi in RODGERS and HART's *I Married an Angel* (1938).   MK

King, Woodie, Jr. (1937–) AFRICAN AMERICAN producer and director. King was cofounder and artistic director of Concept East Theatre in Detroit during 1960–3 before moving to New York City. There in 1970 he cofounded and still serves as artistic director of the NEW FEDERAL THEATRE at the Henry Street Settlement, where he has produced and directed more than 180 plays by budding and significant black playwrights, including AMIRI BARAKA, ED BULLINS, and NTOZAKE SHANGE. He was founder of the National Black Touring Circuit in 1974, which he still heads. In 2003 he received the ACTORS' EQUITY Foundation's PAUL ROBESON Award.   EGH

King and I, The   The fifth collaboration between RICHARD RODGERS (music) and OSCAR HAMMERSTEIN II (book and lyrics) opened at the ST. JAMES THEATRE on 29 March 1951 and ran 1,246 performances. Based on Margaret Landon's novel *Anna and the King of Siam*, this musical play recounted the attempts of a widowed Welsh schoolteacher to bring Western values to the court and children of a 19th-century Siamese king. The role of Anna Leonowens capped the musical-comedy career of GERTRUDE LAWRENCE, and the king would ever after be associated with YUL BRYNNER, who created the part. Rodgers's music cleverly evoked Asian rhythms and sounds while staying within the traditions of the Broadway musical score. Hammerstein's book and lyrics explored the clash between two disparate cultures as exemplified by two hard-headed but likable characters who are attracted to each other despite their philosophical differences. A production highlight was JEROME ROBBINS's choreography for a Siamese version of UNCLE TOM'S CABIN called "The Small House of

Uncle Thomas." Using Thai dance forms, costumes, and masks, Robbins successfully combined the exotic and the familiar in a showstopping production number that also crystallized the central conflict of the story. A opulent Broadway revival (Tony) based on a 1991 Australian production was presented with Lou Diamond Phillips (his Broadway debut) and DONNA MURPHY (Tony) in 1996.   MK

Kingsley, Sidney (1906–95) Playwright who made his reputation with realistic social melodramas. DEAD END (1935), concerned with the effect on a group of kids of slum life near New York's East River, is his most memorable success, but MEN IN WHITE (1933), about a young doctor's experiences in a hospital, stabilized the financially troubled GROUP THEATRE and won Kingsley a Pulitzer Prize. His antiwar play, *Ten Million Ghosts* (1936), failed, and *The Patriots* (1943), contrasting the political theories of Thomas Jefferson and Alexander Hamilton, was a weak effort. Forsaking propaganda for realistic and vivid melodrama, Kingsley wrote DETECTIVE STORY (1949), featuring a conscientious police detective whose emotional involvement drives him to sadism, and a dramatization of Arthur Koestler's novel DARKNESS AT NOON (1951). Later plays included a farce entitled *Lunatics and Lovers* (1954) and *Night Life* (1962), a murder melodrama with overtones of labor and politics. A playwright whose career spanned more than half a century, Kingsley remained active in the DRAMATIST GUILD up to his death.   WJM

Kiralfy [né Königsbaum] **family** Jewish Hungarian family of dancers and impresarios. After a distinguished European career popularizing Magyar folk dances, the brother **Imre** (1845–1919), **Arnold** (d. 1908), and **Bolossy** (1848–1932) came to New York with their sisters **Haniola** (1851–89) and **Emilie** (1855–1917) to perform a *csárdás* in G. L. Fox's pantoMIME *Hiccory Diccory Dock* (1869). Imre and Bolossy soon branched out on their own to stage lavish musical spectacles, including a revival of *The* BLACK CROOK (1873), *The Deluge* (1874), and three Jules Verne works: AROUND THE WORLD IN EIGHTY DAYS (1875), *A Trip to the Moon* (1877), and *Michael Strogoff* (1881), all noted for skillful deployment of throngs of chorines and supernumeraries. They built the Alhambra Palace, PHILADELPHIA (1876), and innovated in ventilation and STAGE LIGHTING: For *Excelsior* (NIBLO'S GARDEN, 1883) they commissioned Edison to light the whole stage by electricity. In 1886, Imre and Bolossy split over financial differences. Bolossy concentrated his choreographic skills on a series

of spectacles staged OUTDOORS or in mammoth exhibition halls, including *King Solomon* (1891), *Constantinople* (London Olympia, 1894), *The Orient* (Berlin, 1896), and *A Carnival in Venice* (Portland, OR, 1905). Imre produced *The Fall of Babylon* (1890), an open-air spectacular with 1,000 participants, and, with P. T. BARNUM, *Columbus* (1892). He settled in London, where his projects during 1892–1912 included a reconstruction of the Earl's Court Exhibition Hall, the creation of White City, and a number of grandiose expositions. Useful is Barbara Barker's study of Bolossy (1988).   LS

Kismet Two-act operetta, music and lyrics by George Forrest and Robert Wright, book by Charles Lederer and Luther Davis; opened 3 December 1953 at the ZIEGFELD THEATRE, running 583 performances. Based on an old OTIS SKINNER vehicle by Edward Knoblock (1911), this "Musical Arabian Night" follows the rise of Hajj (ALFRED DRAKE) from beggar to Wazir of Baghdad in a single day. As they had in *The Song of Norway* (1944), Wright and Forrest took their music from the work of a single composer, this time Alexander Borodin; but whereas in *Song of Norway* they had taken Edvard Greig's most familiar melodies and added lyrics written to them, in *Kismet* they adapted and modified Borodin's music into a novel, romantic, evocatively Oriental score, from which "Stranger in Paradise" and "Baubles, Bangles and Beads" proved the most popular standards. A London production (1955) with many of the American leads proved even more successful. In 1978 an all-black variation, *Timbuktu!,* was seen on Broadway; in 1985 *Kismet* joined the repertory of the New York City Opera; and in 2006 it was reprised as part of CITY CENTER'S ENCORES! concert series, with BRIAN STOKES MITCHELL in the Drake role and MARIN MAZZIE as Lalume.   JD

Kissel, Howard William (1942–) Drama critic, born in Milwaukee and educated at Columbia College and in journalism at Northwestern (M.S.). Kissel served as a reporter for *Daily News Record;* feature writer for *Gentleman's Quarterly;* and Arts editor for *Women's Wear Daily,* reviewing films, books, classical music, and the theatre. Since 1986 he has been chief drama critic of the *New York Daily News.* He is author of a biography of producer DAVID MERRICK and compiler-editor of *STELLA ADLER: The Art of Acting* (2000).   TLM

Kiss Me, Kate Two-act musical comedy, music and lyrics by COLE PORTER, book by SAM AND BELLA SPEWACK; opened 30 December 1948 at

Program cover for Imre
Kiralfy's *Fall of Babylon,* 1890.
Courtesy: Don B. Wilmeth
Theatre Collection.

New York's New Century Theatre, running 1,077 performances. Starring ALFRED DRAKE and Patricia Morison, this musical about producing a musical version of Shakespeare's *Taming of the Shrew,* stresses the parallels between the relationship of the actors in the play-within-a-play and the Shakespearean characters they play, with the book cleverly weaving sections of Shakespearean dialogue into its scenes. The score (including "So in Love," "Too Darn Hot," and "Always True to You in My Fashion") is perhaps Porter's most dramatic, as the songs are more tightly integrated with the story than usual, and the show was the biggest hit of Porter's career. Winner of the Tony Award for Best Musical, it is generally listed high among the masterworks of American musical theatre. An outstanding revival (Tony) opened in November 1999, starring BRIAN STOKES MITCHELL and MARIN MAZZIE; its Australian-born director, Michael Blakemore, won the directing Tony and Drama Desk awards for a musical – and a matching pair for directing the play *Copenhagen.* which opened April 2000.   JD

Kit, the Arkansas Traveller by Edward Spencer, THOMAS B. DEWALDEN, and CLIFTON W. TAYLEURE. The original *Kit,* written by Edward Spencer, premiered in Buffalo on 20 April 1869. It was revised by DeWalden and then by Tayleure (or Taylor) before its New York success at NIBLO'S GARDEN in May 1871, which helped to popularize border drama. The play allowed FRANCIS S. CHANFRAU, already famous for his portrayal of Mose, to create another distinctive characterization with the FRONTIER hero, a role he played over 4,300 times in 15 years. Kit Redding was an Arkansas farmer whose wife and daughter were abducted. Kit tracked the scoundrel for 12 years (15 in one version) until he recovered his daughter and dealt revenge to the villain in a much-imitated Bowie knife fight.   RAH

Kitchen, The Founded in June 1971 as an artist COLLECTIVE when video artists Steina and Woody Vasulka opened a performance space in the kitchen of NYC's Mercer Arts Hotel, this organization – now nonprofit and interdisciplinary – has moved from Mercer to Broome and now to 19th Street. Its space provides innovative artists working in the media, literary, and performing arts with exhibition and performances opportunities. An influential venue, The Kitchen has helped to launch the careers of numerous artists who have helped define the American avant-garde, including VITO ACCONCI, Kiki Smith, Lucinda Childs, Bill T. Jones, LAURIE ANDERSON, and MEREDITH MONK, among many others.   DBW

Klauber, Adolph (1879–1933) Producer and critic. Irregular employment forced Klauber from acting into journalism, first for the *New York Commercial Advertiser,* then for the *New York Tribune,* and finally for the *New York Times,* where he became drama critic during 1906–18. He married actress JANE COWL and was associated with her productions of *Lilac Time* (1917) and *Smilin' Through* (1919), as well as with the SELWYNS on *Romeo and Juliet* (1923), *Pelleas and Melisande* (1923), and *Antony and Cleopatra* (1924). Klauber was also coproducer of EUGENE O'NEILL'S *The EMPEROR JONES* and *Diff'rent* in 1920.   TLM

Klaw, Marc (Alonzo) (1858–1936) Newspaperman and lawyer who formed a partnership in 1887 with A. L. ERLANGER. The soft-spoken Klaw was the gently persuasive and gracious member of the partnership. Compelled by their business sense to reform a chaotic tour-scheduling system, the Klaw and Erlanger Exchange negotiated exclusive contracts with tour managers and theatre managers, thereby imposing needed order and greater profitability but also monopolistic control over nearly 200 theatres, mostly in the South. By 1895 theirs was the second largest booking agency in the U.S. In 1896, Klaw and Erlanger joined with five powerful theatrical entrepreneurs to form the Theatrical SYNDICATE, a trust that monopolized legitimate theatre in the U.S. for 15 years. The Syndicate dissolved in 1916, and Klaw continued his partnership with Erlanger until 1920. He built the Klaw Theatre in New York in 1920 and retired to live in England in 1927.   WD

Klein, Charles (1867–1915) Playwright. Emigrating from London at age 16, Klein had a brief career as a juvenile actor. His first play was *By Proxy* (1891), and he wrote another 15 strong domestic melodramas, the best of which was *The Music Master* (1904), produced by DAVID BELASCO and starring DAVID WARFIELD. He then wrote six social plays in the muckraking manner of Ida Tarbell and Upton Sinclair. Typical of these were *The Lion and the Mouse* (1905), which exposed legislative corruption at the hands of big business, and *The Third Degree* (1909), which dramatized police brutality.   DMcD

Kline, Kevin (1947–) St. Louis–born actor and director, educated at Indiana University, trained at Juilliard. A founding member of the ACTING COMPANY, he performed with them from 1972 to 1976. He won recognition (and a Tony) for Bruce Granit in *On the Twentieth Century* (1978) and Paul in *LOOSE ENDS* (1979), followed by critical acclaim (and a second Tony) as the Pirate King in *The Pirates of Penzance* (1980, NEW YORK SHAKESPEARE FESTIVAL; 1981, Broadway), which established him as a star. Other performances with the NYSF include playing Hamlet on two occasions (1986, 1990) and Trigorin in *The Seagull* (Stoppard adaptation, 2001, with MERYL STREEP) in Central Park. His Falstaff in *Henry IV* at the VIVIAN BEAUMONT in 2003 won him critical acclaim and a Tony nomination; and for The PUBLIC in early 2007 he essayed King Lear. Other NYC roles include Bluntschli in SHAW'S *Arms and the Man* (1985, CIRCLE IN THE SQUARE) and the title role in *Ivanov* (David Hare's adaptation, 1997) at Lincoln Center. His film credits include *Sophie's Choice* (1982), *The Big Chill* (1983), *A Fish Called Wanda* (1988; Academy Award), *Dave* (1993), *A Midsummer Night's Dream* (1999), *The Emperor's Club* (2002), and *De-Lovely* (2004). In 1989 he received the second William Shakespeare Award for Classical Theatre from the SHAKESPEARE THEATRE [at the Folger], in 2002 became the first American actor to receive the Sir John

Gielgud Golden Quill Award, and in 2004 was inducted into the THEATRE HALL OF FAME. TLM

Klotz, Florence (c. 1920–2006) Costume designer who, by her own admission, became involved in design almost by accident. Through the 1960s she designed several light contemporary comedies. In 1971 she teamed up with director HAROLD PRINCE to design *Follies,* which had 140 costumes ranging from rags to lavish show costumes spanning half a century and won her a 1972 Tony. She subsequently designed other Prince–STEPHEN SONDHEIM musicals, each with a distinctly different style and period (*A LITTLE NIGHT MUSIC, 1973; PACIFIC OVERTURES, 1976;* Tonys for both). Designs for *Kiss of the Spider Woman* and the Broadway revival of *SHOW BOAT* (more than 500 costumes, for 72 actors), both Prince-directed, won her Tony Awards in 1993 and 1995. Her earlier designs for *Grind* (1985) had also yielded her a Tony. Klotz, whose costumes managed to combine contemporary sensibilities with period style, received the PATRICIA ZIPPRODT AWARD for Innovative Costume Design in 2002. AA

Knickerbocker Holiday (1938) Musical comedy in two acts, book and lyrics by MAXWELL ANDERSON and music by KURT WEILL, produced by the PLAYWRIGHTS' COMPANY on 19 October 1938 (168 performances). Anderson drew upon WASHINGTON IRVING's *History of New York* (1809) in satirizing the complex mixture of socialism and fascism pervading American politics in the late 1930s, and expressing his concern about the dangers of big government. The hero is a tinker afflicted with a peculiar malady: He can't take orders. The lovably authoritarian Governor Pieter Stuyvesant (WALTER HUSTON) sang what became Anderson's most profitable piece, "September Song." Anderson intended his characterization of Stuyvesant to deprecate the incipient despotism of President Franklin D. Roosevelt, but toned down his satire at the urging of associates in the Playwrights' Company. Roosevelt, in a rare visit to the theatre, saw the production in Washington, DC, reportedly enjoyed it, and entertained the cast at the White House. WD

Knight, Shirley (Enola) (1936–) Born in Goessel, KS, educated at Wichita State and the University of California, and trained with ERWIN PISCATOR and LEE STRASBERG, this serious and dedicated actor's career began with Alison Porter in *Look Back in Anger* at the PASADENA PLAYHOUSE in 1958. Known for her in-depth, multifaceted characterizations – in film and television more than on the stage – her theatre career nevertheless includes, among others, *The Three Sisters* (1964 revival), *KENNEDY'S CHILDREN* (1975, Tony), *LANDSCAPE OF THE BODY* (1977, The PUBLIC), *Happy End* (1977, Theatre Four), *COME BACK, LITTLE SHEBA* (1984, ROUNDABOUT), FOOTE's *The Young Man from Atlanta* (1996), and *Cycling Past the Matterhorn* (2005, THEATRE ROW). In 1965 she played Lula in Leroi Jones's (see AMIRI BARAKA) *DUTCHMAN* in Los Angeles, a performance she repeated in its film version (1967). Other notable films are *The Dark at the Top of the Stairs* (1960), *Sweet Bird of Youth* (1962), and *The Rain People* (1969); she garnered Oscar nominations for the first two. For television work she has received two Emmys and a Golden Globe Award. DBW

Komisarjevsky, Theodore [né Fyodor Fyodorovich Komissarzhevsky] (1882–1954) Russian director, designer, teacher, and theorist who, during his international career, searched for an ideal "synthetic theatre" – combining the play's "inner rhythm, spirit and ideology" with the theatre's musical-plastic form – and for the "universal actor" to express it. Despite alienating Stanislavsky by misrepresenting his teachings in a 1916 book, Komisarjevsky became a chief interpreter of Stanislavsky's System in England. His all-star stagings of Chekhov's major plays (1926–7, 1936) fostered a romantic view of the Russian intelligentsia, which suited English classist society. Despite attacking modern-dress Shakespeare in *Myself and the Theatre* (1929), Komisarjevsky's seven productions at Stratford-upon-Avon (1932–9) altered the text, tone, and locales of Shakespeare's plays in light of modern history. He directed two productions for the THEATRE GUILD (1923) and in 1939 emigrated to the U.S., where he established the Komisarjevsky Theatre Studio (NYC); taught at Yale University (1940–2); directed three productions for the New York City Opera Company (1948, 1949, 1952), the last two designed by Mstislav Dobujinsky; and staged a famous *Crime and Punishment* (1947), starring John Gielgud and LILLIAN GISH (with SANFORD MEISNER and MARIAN SELDES). Komisarjevsky also wrote *Theatrical Preludes* (1916), *Costume of the Theatre* (1931), and *The Theatre and a Changing Civilization* (1935). SG

Kopit, Arthur (Lee) (1937–) New York–born and Harvard-educated playwright who has had a distinguished place in the American theatre as a serious and inventive writer for more than 30 years, though he has rarely gained popular acceptance. He first received international attention with *OH DAD, POOR DAD, MAMA'S HUNG YOU IN THE CLOSET*

AND I'M FEELIN' SO SAD (1962, PHOENIX THEATRE), a brilliant parody of the Oedipus complex. Since *Oh Dad* he has written a number of plays that experiment with dramatic form, most notably *The Day the Whores Came Out to Play Tennis* (1965, Players Theatre), a comic portrayal of social-climbing country clubbers; *INDIANS* (1969, ARENA STAGE), a study of genocide of the Indians by white Americans; *WINGS* (1978. YALE REP), a portrait of a stroke victim (the basis of a 1992 musical); *The End of the World* (1984, Broadway), a dark comedy about nuclear proliferation; *The Road to Nirvana* (1991, CIRCLE REP), a scatological comedy about the business of Hollywood; and *Y2K* (1999) at the ACTORS THEATRE OF LOUISVILLE and MANHATTAN THEATRE CLUB. Kopit also wrote the book for the Broadway musicals *Nine* (1982; revived in 2003 starring Antonio Banderas) and *High Society* (1998), and for a popular musical *PHANTOM* with a MAURY YESTON score (1991, Theatre under the Stars, Houston, TX).   DBW

Korder, Howard (1957–) Playwright and screenwriter, born in New York City and educated at SUNY Binghamton. Korder has been called a second-generation DAVID MAMET for his "sharp wit and insiders grasp of contemporary jargon" (GUSSOW). His *Boys' Life,* about the "post adolescent rituals of drinking, puking, courting and infidelity," was presented at LINCOLN CENTER in 1988 (dir. William H. Macy), and nominated for a Pulitzer Prize. *Search and Destroy,* a cynical play about greed and violence, was commissioned by and premiered at the SOUTH COAST REPERTORY in 1990; a production at YALE REP preceded its Broadway opening at CIRCLE IN THE SQUARE and a Royal Court London premiere (both 1992; film, 1995). His other plays include *Night Maneuver* (1982, Floating Rep, NYC); *The Middle Kingdom* and *Lip Service* (1985 one-acts, THEATRE ROW); *Episode 26* (1985); *Fun* and *Nobody* (1987 one-acts, Theatre Row); *The Lights* (1993, Lincoln Center), which won an Obie; and *Sea of Tranquility* (2004, ATLANTIC THEATER). His screen- or television plays include *Stealing Sinatra* (2004), *The Passion of Ayn Rand* (1999), and *Lip Service* (1988 adaptation), which won an ACE Award. Korder is the first Playwright-in-Residence at the OLD GLOBE.   TLM

Koster and Bial's Music Hall 116–117 West 23rd St., NYC. Built in 1869 as the 23rd Street Opera House, it was leased to DAN BRYANT and his MINSTRELS the following year. After Bryant's death in 1875, it passed to other managers and eventually to the partnership of John Koster and Albert Bial in 1879. Replacing the stage with a small plat-

form, enlarging the building, and adding outdoor gardens, the partners transformed it into Koster and Bial's Music Hall, a concert saloon that dispensed alcoholic beverages with variety entertainment – skirting existing laws against serving both in the same establishment by using a giant fan as a curtain, which fell apart to reveal the performers. However, when the laws were tightened, they abandoned this enterprise and fell in with OSCAR HAMMERSTEIN (I) to create Koster and Bial's New Music Hall on West 34th Street. The old theatre struggled along for a few more years and was torn down in 1924, but the newer theatre had an even shorter life and was eventually razed to become part of Macy's Department Store in 1901.   MCH

Krakowski, Jane (1968–) New Jersey–born actress and dancer who bypassed college and went directly into performance, debuting on Broadway in *Starlight Express* in 1987. A regular on television's *Ally McBeal* (1997–2002) as Elaine, she has a handful of Broadway/LA credits, most in musicals: *Grand Hotel* (1989), *COMPANY* (1995 revival), *Once upon a Mattress* (1996 revival), *Mack and Mabel* (2000 concert revival in LA), and most recently a Tony-winning role in the 2003 revival of *Nine* with Antonio Banderas (as his sultry mistress, Carla). In May 2005 she appeared in the West End revival of *GUYS AND DOLLS* (Olivier Award). Beginning in 2006 she was a regular on the NBC sitcom *30 Rock*.   DBW

Kramer, Larry (1935–) Writer, playwright, and AIDS activist. Author of the polemical and strident *The Normal Heart* (1985, The PUBLIC; revived there in 2004), a breakthrough drama in the fight to combat AIDS (with over 600 productions worldwide), and its more substantial and human sequel, *The Destiny of Me* (1992, Theatre de Lys; Obie), Kramer, according to a 1993 BBC documentary, almost single-handedly "turned AIDS into a political issue." In the 1980s he cofounded Gay Men's Health Crisis and ACT UP (AIDS Coalition to Unleash Power). Also a novelist, essayist, and screenwriter, his other plays include *Sissies Scrapbook* (1973; revised as *Four Friends,* 1975, LUCILLE LORTEL) and *Just Say No, a Play about a Farce* (1988, WPA Theatre).   DBW

Krapp, Herbert J. (1886–1973) Virtually forgotten but historically important architect-designer of more than 40 playhouses, many in the Broadway district of Manhattan. His work, renowned for both visual and acoustic excellence, was mostly for the SHUBERTS. Of his New York projects, 15

theatres still stand: the BROADHURST, the PLY-MOUTH, the MAJESTIC, the AMBASSADOR, the ROYALE, the JOHN GOLDEN, the NEIL SIMON (Alvin), the Ed Sullivan (Hammerstein's), the ETHEL BARRYMORE, the WINTER GARDEN, the IMPERIAL, the RICHARD RODGERS (46th Street), the BILTMORE, the EUGENE O'NEILL (Forrest), and the BROOKS ATKINSON (Mansfield).   DBW

Krasna, Norman (1909–84) Long Island–born playwright, screenwriter, and critic whose early Broadway successes *Louder, Please* (1931) and *Small Miracle* (1934) were followed by less successful (or just lesser) works *The Man with Blonde Hair* (also directed, 1941), *Time for Elizabeth* (with Groucho MARX, 1948), *Love in E Flat* (1967), and *We Interrupt This Program* (1975). His longest-running hit, *Dear Ruth* (1944; 680 perfs.), a lightweight sex comedy, his *Who Was That Lady I Saw You With?* (1958; with Ray Walston), and *Sunday in New York* (1961; with Robert Redford) were highlights of a promising Broadway career more attuned to Hollywood. He adapted to film those as well as *Small Miracle, John Loves Mary* (1947; 423 perfs.), and *Kind Sir* (1953; filmed as 1958 *Indiscreet*), and captured screen credits for more than 25 films, including *Princess O'Rourke* (Academy Award, 1943).   GSA

Krass, Michael (1955–) Connecticut-born and William and Mary–educated costume designer whose 1996 Broadway debut (ROUNDABOUT), *The Rehearsal*, received Drama Desk and American Theatre Wing nominations. Since then, his credits, especially regional and OFF-BROADWAY, are extensive, including many seasons at the Hangar Theatre (Ithaca, NY) and numerous collaborations with directors Michael Mayer (e.g., *A VIEW FROM THE BRIDGE*, which moved to the Roundabout), MARK BROKAW, SCOTT ELLIS, and Nicholas Martin (the latter during ten seasons at the WILLIAMS-TOWN THEATRE FESTIVAL with productions such as *CAMINO REAL, The Man Who Had all the Luck*, and *Hedda Gabler,* the latter seen also on Broadway in 2001). A recent design was for Roundabout's stylish 2005 *The Constant Wife*.   BO

Kron, Lisa (1961–) Born in Ann Arbor and educated at Kalamazoo College, this actor-writer-comedian and a founding member (1989) of the award-winning company The Five Lesbian Brothers (seen in *Oedipus at Palm Springs* in 2005 at the NEW YORK THEATRE WORKSHOP), has established her personal reputation largely on the basis of her solo work (beginning in 1984), according to BRANTLEY characterized by "wry, rueful wit and thorny eloquence." Best known are *2.5 Minute Ride*

(developed in 1996–7) and *101 Humiliating Stories* (developed 1993–5). The former is a roller-coaster ride through her family album; the latter, a transforming of painful personal moments into comedy. Both have been presented throughout the U.S. Her play *Well,* not a solo work, was seen at the PUBLIC in 2004 (she played a character named Lisa Kron) and in 2006 on Broadway (Tony nomination), where Brantley declared that Kron "may well be the best stand-up memorist of the American theater."   DBW

Kronenberger, Louis (1904–80) Drama critic. Born and educated in Cincinnati, Kronenberger began his career as an editor for Boni and Liveright (1926), Alfred A. Knopf (1933), and *Fortune Magazine* (1935). He was drama critic for *Time* (1938–61) and *PM* (1940–8), gaining a reputation as a demanding but stylish and elegant writer. VARIETY placed him second in toughness among New York critics in 1942–3. He adapted Jean Anouilh's *Mademoiselle Colombe* for Broadway in 1954; edited the *Best Play* Series during 1952–61; and taught at Brandeis University during 1951–70. His books include *The Thread of Laughter* (1952) and his memoirs, *No Whippings, No Gold Watches* (1970).   TLM

Kruger, Otto (1885–1974) Stage, screen, and television actor who began in VAUDEVILLE and STOCK COMPANIES. Some note his first appearance in 1900, but Kruger's first professional roles were with a Kansas company during 1906–9. His debut as Jack Bowling in *The Natural Law* (1915) extended to 33 Broadway productions and roles in Chicago, San Francisco, Los Angeles, and touring companies. He succeeded Noël Coward in *Private Lives* (1931), GEORGE M. COHAN in *The Meanest Man in the World* (1921), and PAUL MUNI in *Counsellor-at-Law* (1932). Between 1923 and 1959, he made 71 films. His television career, begun in 1934, included several 1950s TV playhouses.   RW

Krutch, Joseph Wood (1893–1970) Drama critic. Born in Knoxville, TN, Krutch was educated at the University of Tennessee and Columbia University (M.A., Ph.D.) before becoming drama critic for *The Nation* (1924–52); also, he held the BRANDER MATTHEWS Chair of Dramatic Literature at Columbia University during 1943–52. A scholarly critic, Krutch wanted size and style in the American drama but found EUGENE O'NEILL "almost alone among modern dramatic writers" possessing such traits. In the early 1950s, poor health forced him to move to Arizona, where he lived in the desert, writing on natural history. His theatre books include *Comedy and Conscience after the Restoration* (1924) and *The American Drama since 1918* (1939, rev. 1957).   TLM

Kulick, Brian (1963–) Considered one of the most original, bright, and innovative (sometimes verging on too clever) directors of the early 21st century, Kulick, who became the fifth artistic director of the CLASSIC STAGE COMPANY in 2003, had previously been an artist-in-residence at the MARK TAPER FORUM, associate artistic director at TRINITY REP (1994–6), and artistic associate at The PUBLIC (1996–2003), directing acclaimed productions for the latter of *Twelfth Night, Winter's Tale,* and *Timon of Athens* at the Delacorte Theatre in Central Park. Since joining CSC he has directed *The Mysteries* (2004), with constant transformation of the stage space using symbolic props, *Death and the Ploughman* (2004), *The False Servant* (2005), and Michael Cumpsty in a modern *Hamlet* (2005) and *Richard II* (2006). Kulick, who has a fondness for the classics, also works with new talent and established contemporary writers.   DBW

Kummer [née Beecher], **Clare (Rodman)** (1873?–1958) A prolific writer who created a Broadway play almost annually, beginning with her greatest hit, GOOD GRACIOUS ANNABELLE! (1916). In addition to several original plays – such as *Be Calm, Camilla* (1918), *A Successful Calamity* (1917, written as a vehicle for WILLIAM GILLETTE), *Rollo's Wild Oat* (1920), *Pomeroy's Past* (1926), and *Her Master's Voice* (1933) – she also successfully adapted foreign plays and wrote a FLORENZ ZIEGFELD adaptation of *Annabelle!* called *Annie, Dear* (1924). Although her plays were criticized for their weak plots and contrived situations, audiences enjoyed her humorous dialogue and her pleasant, rather eccentric characters.   FB

Kurtz, Swoosie (1944–) Nebraska-born, USC-educated actress who made her debut at the CINCINNATI PLAYHOUSE IN THE PARK (1966), then OFF-BROADWAY in The EFFECT OF GAMMA RAYS ON MAN-IN-THE-MOON MARIGOLDS (1970). Portraying "eccentrics with an edge," she received Tony nominations (*Tartuffe*, CIRCLE IN THE SQUARE, 1977); Tonys (FIFTH OF JULY, 1981; *The* HOUSE OF BLUE LEAVES, LINCOLN CENTER [both houses], 1986); Obies (WASSERSTEIN's *Uncommon Women and Others*, PHOENIX THEATRE, 1977; *House of Blue Leaves; The Mineola Twins,* 1999, ROUNDABOUT); and Drama Desk Awards (DURANG's *A History of American Film*, 1978; *Fifth of July*). She was in MCNALLY's *Lips Together, Teeth Apart* (MANHATTAN THEATRE CLUB, 1991); played the dual roles Myrna/ Myra in

VOGEL's *Mineola Twins;* created her take on LILLIAN HELLMAN in *Imaginary Friends* and Joan in The FLEA's *The Guys* (both 2002); and recently received critical acclaim both in Bryony Lavery's *Frozen* (2004; another Tony nomination), opposite Brían F. O'Byrne, as a mother grieving her murdered child beneath a pragmatic exterior, and for her Hesione in Roundabout's *Heartbreak House* (2006). Her films include *The World According to Garp* (1982), *Dangerous Liaisons* (1988), *Cruel Intentions* (1999), and *Bubble Boy* (2001). Kurtz, who played Alexandra in TV's *Sisters* (1991–6), won an Emmy for her role on *Carol & Company* (1990).   REK

Kurz Stadt Theater   Successful German-language theatre, also known as the German Stock Company, organized by Heinrich Kurz in 1868 in Milwaukee. The company offered 22 seasons, totaling 1,800 productions, until Kurz sold the theatre (217 Third St.) to Frederick Pabst in 1890. Kurz's first business manager, Eduard Härting, came from New York's STADT THEATER COMPANY. Kurz engaged such German notables as Ludwig Barnay, Franziska Ellmenreich, Friedrich Mitterwurzer, and Ernst von Possart. The company maintained a balanced repertory of popular comedies and German classics. Supported primarily by its box-office income, deficits were subsidized by Milwaukee's leading German families.   RE

Kushner, Tony (1956–) Although the author of only one truly monumental play ("A Gay Fantasia on National Themes"), the two-part ANGELS IN AMERICA (Part One: *The Millennium Approaches;* Part Two: *Perestroika*), no American playwright of the past 30 years has received as much attention for a work as he has. More significantly, Kushner's work marked a possible new direction for Broadway, what the *New York Times* termed a sign of a "youthquake waiting to happen." Part One (1993, Broadway) received all major awards, and Part Two joined the earlier play in repertory on Broadway six months later. Kushner, a gay, Jewish socialist, raised in Louisiana and a graduate of Columbia with a graduate degree from NYU, is also the author of (among others) *A Bright Room Called Day* (1985, Theatre 22, NYC); *Slavs! Thinking About the Longstanding Problems of Virtue and Happiness* (1993–4, Humana Festival; from material not used in Part Two of *Angels;* also 1995, NEW YORK THEATRE WORKSHOP, Obie); *Hydriotaphia, or The Death of Dr. Browne* (1987, NYC; 1998, ALLEY THEATRE); *Homebody/Kabul* (2001, NYTW; 2004, BROOKLYN ACADEMY OF MUSIC), and *Henry Box Brown, or The Mirror of Slavery* (in progress). His also wrote books for two musical plays, *St. Cecilia, or The Power* *of Music* (music by Bobby McFerrin) and *Caroline, or Change*, the latter produced at The PUBLIC before transferring to Broadway in 2004. *Caroline* won Obies for Kushner, JEANINE TESORI (who wrote the music), and actress TONYA PINKINS. Kushner has adapted Corneille's *L'Illusion comique* (*The Illusion*) (1988, NYTW); Brecht's *Good Person of Setzuan* (1994, La Jolla Playhouse) and *Mother Courage* (seen with Meryl Streep in Central Park, 2006); Ansky's *The Dybbuk* (1997, The PUBLIC); and Goethe's *Stella* (1987, NYTW). He wrote the screenplay for *Angels* (2003; TV miniseries, directed by MIKE NICHOLS) and for Steven Spielberg's 2005 film *Munich*, and wrote an American version of the children's opera *Brundibar*, which had been performed by children in the Terezín concentration camp (published 2003, illustrated by Maurice Sendak; staged 2005, BERKELEY REP, and 2006, NEW VICTORY). Kushner sees his work, especially his plays, as part of a greater political movement, one concerned with moral responsibility during repressive times.

DBW

L

La Cage aux Folles Two-act musical comedy, music and lyrics by JERRY HERMAN, book by HARVEY FIERSTEIN; opened 21 August 1983 at the PALACE THEATRE, directed by ARTHUR LAURENTS, and ran 1,761 performances. A Broadway revival directed by JERRY ZAKS – most notable for its all-male dance ensemble – opened late 2004. Based on a French play by Jean Poiret and the subsequent French movie (1978), this was the first large-budget Broadway musical to treat the subject of homosexuality, as two gay men (GEORGE HEARN, Gene Barry) who own the eponymous transvestite nightclub strive to appear "normal" to impress the family of one of the men's son's fiancée (see GAY/LESBIAN THEATRE). The extravagant production numbers set in the club (including "The Best of Times Is Now") featured a "female" chorus line with two women among the many men in drag (see FEMALE/MALE IMPERSONATION), inviting the audience to try to pick out the real women. The show won six Tony Awards, including for Best Musical. JD

La Jolla Playhouse The La Jolla Playhouse had been a summer theatre for film actors (1947–64), and in 1978 its Board of Trustees contributed $3.25 million to the University of California, San Diego, for the purpose of reviving the company. Under DES MCANUFF (1983–95), the Playhouse prospered and featured such artists as PETER SELLARS, ROBERT WOODRUFF, GEOFF HOYLE, BILL IRWIN, LEE BLESSING, and Lynn REDGRAVE. MICHAEL GREIF replaced McAnuff in 1995 as artistic director, replaced briefly by Anne Hamburger; but in 2000 McAnuff returned, only to announce his departure once again (in April 2007). Located today on the university campus, three venues are used, the most recent – a black box – opened in 2005 (after a $44 million capital campaign led to other additions and renovations). The Playhouse boasts of its 41 world premieres, 24 West Coast premieres, and 7 U.S. premieres (as of 2006). Transfers to Broadway include *Big River* (1985), LEE BLESSING's *A Walk in the Woods* (1988), *The Who's Tommy* (1993), *HOW TO SUCCEED IN BUSINESS WITHOUT REALLY TRYING* (1995), *Thoroughly*

Modern Millie (2002), and the 2006 Tony-winning Best Musical *Jersey Boys* (2005). In 1993 the Playhouse received the special Regional Theatre Tony. JDM   DBW

La MaMa OFF-OFF BROADWAY theatre begun in 1961 by ELLEN STEWART, a self-described Cajun who arrived penniless in New York in 1950 and became a successful fashion designer. With her earnings, she began Café La MaMa in a cramped, decrepit Manhattan basement, and moved several times before settling on 66 East 4th St. in 1969. The Café became La MaMa ETC (Experimental Theatre Club), and Stewart still functions as artistic director, fund-raiser, tour manager, and maternal spiritual guardian. Having produced 2,500 shows (and more than 1,000 original musical scores), La MaMa introduced such American playwrights and directors as ROCHELLE OWENS, MEGAN TERRY, Jeff Weiss, SAM SHEPARD, HARVEY FIERSTEIN, H. M. Koutoukas, LANFORD WILSON, Julie Bovasso, ADRIENNE KENNEDY, and TOM O'HORGAN, also presenting works by avant-garde directors RICHARD FOREMAN, MEREDITH MONK, PING CHONG, and others. In addition, La MaMa has brought to America such artists as Jerzy Grotowski, ANDREI SERBAN, Peter Brook, Eugenio Barba, and Tadeusz Kantor, and has played host to artists from 70 countries. In 1980 La MaMa established the Third World Institute of Theatre Arts and Studies (TWITAS).

La MaMa, honored with more than 30 Obies, among other awards, comprises three theatres – The First Floor Theatre, The Club (cabaret space), and The Annex, the latter its largest space – as well as an art gallery, plus a six-story rehearsal/studio building at 47 Great Jones St. The La MaMa cabaret, despite dire financial problems, still provides a venue for new experimentation in comedy and performance art.   AS

La Turista by SAM SHEPARD. Originally produced by NYC's AMERICAN PLACE THEATRE on 4 March 1967 (29 performances), the play baffled critics and theatregoers alike with its shifting identities and nonlinear structure. Act I is set in a Mexican

hotel room, where witch doctors visit a young couple suffering from "la turista." Act II occurs earlier, in an American hotel room; this time the doctors wear Civil War–era costumes. CHARLES MAROWITZ noted that if one did not already know Shepard's work, "*La Turista* would be a perfect case of the emperor's new clothes. But there is a consistency in Shepard and a richness of texture which encourages one to suspend judgment."
FHL

LaBute, Neil (1963–) Playwright, film and stage director, known for his edgy, politically incorrect, controversial, and frequently dark portrayals of modern relationships and even brutal sexual dynamics. Born in Detroit, raised in Spokane, and educated at Brigham Young (for years he was a Mormon) with graduate work at Kansas (theatre) and NYU (playwriting), LaBute's success has frequently begun in London and often at the Almeida Theatre (including *A Gaggle of Saints*, 2000; *The Shape of Things*, 2001; *The Distance from Here*, 2002). Key productions have also been seen in Ireland (e.g., *Wrecks*, 2005, Cork). His first major play, *In the Company of Men* (1992, Brigham Young University), focuses on two men fed up with how women have taken over American society; *Bash: Latter-Day Plays* (1999, THEATRE ROW) deals with casual atrocity in a set of three short plays; *The Shape of Things* portrays a controlling woman and the destructive results; *The Mercy Seat* (2002, MCC Theater) was a response to 9/11 that confronted an urban legend connected to the tragedy; *Fat Pig* (2004, MCC), a more comedic play, focuses on a romance between an attractive man and an overweight woman but with a serious subtext; and *This Is How It Goes* (2005, The PUBLIC) concerns bigotry and betrayal. His filmography as director includes *In the Company of Men* (1997), *Nurse Betty* (2000), and *The Shape of Things* (2003). Christopher Bigsby has authored a study of LaBute (2007).
DBW

LaChiusa, Michael John (1962–) Composer, lyricist, and librettist born in Chautauqua, NY. Despite some success, with works produced at The PUBLIC, LINCOLN CENTER, and on Broadway – *First Lady Suite* (1993,), *Hello Again* (1993; musical adaptation of *La Ronde*), *The Petrified Prince* (1994), *Marie Christine* (1999; written for AUDRA McDON-ALD, a favorite of his for projects), *The Wild Party* (2000; book with GEORGE C. WOLFE), *See What I Wanna See* (formerly *R Shomon*, 2005), and a musical version of Garcia Lorca's *[The House of] Bernarda Alba* (2006) – this talented artist has yet to gain the stature predicted by critics. Always eager to take on challenging projects in his unique and innovative musical style, LaChiusa – with over 20 musicals or operas to his credit – believes that musicals should entertain but also should be reflectors of current culture and not "nostalgia" boosters. He has refused to compromise, and keeps his standards high. LaChiusa, who has been nominated for five Tonys and six Drama Desk Awards, is an adjunct in the graduate musical writing program at NYU.   DBW

Lackaye, Wilton (1862–1932) Actor who began his professional career in 1883 as Lucentio in LAWRENCE BARRETT's revival of BOKER's *FRAN-CESCA DA RIMINI*. During a very active career he played hundreds of roles for many managements. In 1886 he supported FANNY DAVENPORT at the UNION SQUARE THEATRE. In 1906 he adapted Hugo's *Les Misérables* into the play *Law and the Man*, in which he played Jean Valjean and M. Madeleine. He is remembered, however, as the original Svengali in Du Maurier's *Trilby* (1895), which he revived frequently. A devout Catholic, he founded the Catholic Actors' Guild and assisted with the organization of the ACTORS' EQUITY ASSOCIA-TION.   DBW

Lacy, Suzanne (1945–) California-born PERFOR-MANCE ARTist, writer, educator, and social activist who first studied zoology and psychology, and then social design at California Institute of the Arts (M.F.A., 1972). Lacy's pageantlike performances are influenced by Judy Chicago's Feminist Art Program (1970–1) and ALLAN KAPROW's aesthetic of daily life. Her community-building performance strategies include extensive community dialogues that incorporate women's consciousness raising, media analysis, and practices of resistance. In *Three Weeks in May* (1977) Lacy protested violence against women. In *Black Madonna* (1986), performed primarily by women of color as a *tableau vivant*, she confronted racism. *Whisper, the Waves, the Wind* (1984) addressed aging, and *The Crystal Quilt* (1987) was a dramatic reclamation of social space for women. In the 2000s she conducted community-based art programs in Charleston, SC, and elsewhere. She edited the influential *Mapping the Terrain: New Genre Public Art* (1995).
AF

Lady in the Dark Two-act musical comedy, music by KURT WEILL, lyrics by IRA GERSHWIN, book by MOSS HART; opened 23 January 1941 at the ALVIN THEATRE, running 467 performances (including a return engagement in September). This inventive musical follows the attempts of magazine editor Liza Elliot (GERTRUDE LAW-RENCE) to resolve the romantic and professional complications of her life through psychoanalysis. Basically a straight play with musical interludes, the music is confined almost entirely to the four elaborate dream sequences she relates in her therapy. The sole exception is "My Ship," a melody that draws her into her dreams and (like the "Mysterious Melody" in NAUGHTY MARIETTA) ultimately provides the key to resolution. The score, an effective amalgam of Weill's European and American styles, was the first to which Ira GERSHWIN wrote lyrics since his brother George's death. The show also made a star of Danny Kaye, who introduced the tongue-twisting "Tchaikowsky."

JD

Lafayette Players (1915–32) An AFRICAN AMERICAN STOCK COMPANY organized by actress Anita Bush to provide dramatic entertainment for the Harlem community in place of VAUDEVILLE and MINSTREL SHOWS that often ridiculed blacks. On a weekly schedule the company presented at the LAFAYETTE THEATRE abridged versions of popular Broadway comedies and melodramas, hoping to demonstrate that black actors could play dramatic roles as well as song-and-dance clowns. As these productions gained popular support, the Players formed road companies for touring. In 1928 they moved to LOS ANGELES, where they played successfully to mixed audiences. Overall, they compiled a production record of 250 plays over 17 years before becoming a casualty of the Depression. Among well-recognized former players are CHARLES GILPIN, Clarence Muse, "Dooley" Wilson, Inez Clough, Evelyn Ellis, and Abbie Mitchell.

EGH

Lafayette Theatre Located in Harlem at 132d St. and Seventh Ave., this theatre had been home to the LAFAYETTE PLAYERS for 13 years (1915–28) when they moved to LOS ANGELES. During their Harlem period, the company produced cut versions of standard commercial plays on a weekly basis, sharing the stage with musical REVUES, VAUDEVILLE acts, and feature films. During the era of the FEDERAL THEATRE PROJECT (1935–9), the Lafayette became headquarters for the Negro Theatre Unit in Harlem. It was here that ORSON WELLES produced the well-known "voodoo" *Macbeth* (1936). The theatre's main auditorium was eventually turned into a church. The New Lafayette Theatre established by Robert Macbeth in 1966 used a rehearsal hall in a second-floor wing of the old building; this wing burned down in 1968. EGH

Lahr, Bert [né Irving Lahrheim] (1895–1967) Comic actor. After an apprenticeship in juvenile VAUDEVILLE acts, Lahr broke into BURLESQUE as a Dutch comedian. His first feature part, a punch-drunk fighter in *Hold Everything* (1928), won him critical acclaim and starring roles in musical comedies: *Flying High* (1930), *Hot-Cha!* (1932), and *The Show Is On* (1936). Lahr's stock-in-trade included a grimace like that "of a camel with acute gastric disorder" and a laryngeal bleat "like a lovesick ram." His style was too broad for film, although he is immortalized as the Cowardly Lion in *The WIZARD OF OZ* (1939). He returned to Broadway in *DU BARRY WAS A LADY* (1939). Lahr considered the turning point in his career to be Estragon in *Waiting for Godot* (1956), an association with the avant-garde that brought him roles in Shaw, Molière, and Shakespeare (Bottom). He enlivened five roles in S. J. PERELMAN's *The Beauty Part* (1962). Lahr never retired but died during the shooting of *The Night They Raided MINSKY's*. His son, JOHN, authored a classic biography of the actor (1969).

LS

Lahr, John (1941–) Drama critic and author. Born in Los Angeles, Lahr studied at Yale and Oxford University. He worked as a dramaturge for the GUTHRIE THEATRE (1968) and for the Repertory Theatre of LINCOLN CENTER (1969–71). He has served as contributing editor of *Evergreen Review,* theatre editor of Grove Press, drama critic of the *Village Voice* and, since 1992, *The New Yorker.* Lahr asks that theatre be socially responsible and forge new images to "revitalize the imaginative life of its audience." Such theatre, he feels, must be "shocking, violent, and unpredictable." Lahr, twice winner of the GEORGE JEAN NATHAN Award, is the author or editor of over 50 books, including a masterful biography of his father, comedian BERT LAHR, *Notes on a Cowardly Lion*; a biography of playwright Joe Orton, *Prick Up Your Ears* (1978); a biography of comedian Dame Edna Everage/Barry Humphries (2000); and *Show and Tell* (2002). His stage version of *The Manchurian Candidate* (updated to 1996) premiered at London's Lyric Hammersmith Theatre in 1991 and was staged at Hollywood's West Coast Ensemble in spring 1994. He won a 2002 Drama Desk Award for Outstanding Book of a Musical (with ELAINE STRITCH, for her solo show). TL

Lahti, Christine (1950–) Statuesque stage, screen, and television actress and director, born in Michigan, educated at the University of Michigan and Florida State. Her career in recent years has focused on films and especially TV (*Chicago Hope,*

Jack and Bobby), always with high standards and selectivity. Her first major OFF-BROADWAY role (1978) was Ruth in *The Woods;* her Broadway debut was as a replacement in *Loose Ends* (1979). Subsequent credits of note include *Present Laughter* (1982), *The* HEIDI CHRONICLES (1989, replacement), both Broadway, and *The Exonerated* (2002–4, rotating cast, 45 Bleecker Theater). Her breakthrough film was . . . *And Justice for All* (1979).   DBW

Lamos, Mark (1946–) Director, actor, and artistic director of HARTFORD STAGE COMPANY (1980–98). An innovative director of opera and the classics, Lamos specializes in expansive productions emphasizing the spectacular and the fantastic. While remaining faithful to the texts, Lamos alters periods, settings, and moods. His popular *Twelfth Night* (1985) was staged as a late-night party with COLE PORTER piano background, and his dreamlike *Pericles* (1987) borrowed imagery from both Magritte and the Neo-Expressionists. A commedia-inspired *School for Wives* (1988) featured an Arnolphe in the style of Charlie Chaplin. His visually arresting, two-part *Peer Gynt* (1989) starred RICHARD THOMAS. In 1988 he directed O'NEILL's *DESIRE UNDER THE ELMS* at Moscow's Pushkin Theatre, becoming the first American to direct a Russian company in the Soviet Union. Lamos has also developed new plays, notably the work of ERIC OVERMYER and CONSTANCE CONGDON; his production of Timberlake Wertenbaker's *Our Country's Good* (1990) moved from Hartford Stage to Broadway (1991), receiving six Tony nominations. Recent NYC productions include a stylish *The Rivals* at the VIVIAN BEAUMONT, *As You Like It* (2005) at Central Park's Delacorte, and *Seascape* (2005) at Broadway's BOOTH THEATRE.   HFP

Landau, Tina (195?–) Writer, freelance director, teacher, and since 1997 a member of the STEPPENWOLF THEATER ensemble in Chicago, where she has directed her own play *Space* (in 1999; also at the PUBLIC and the MARK TAPER), as well as *Time to Burn, Berlin Circle, Ballad of Little Jo,* and *Maria Arndt.* Her other original work includes the music-theatre piece *Dream True* (with composer Ricky Ian Gordon), produced at the VINEYARD in 1999 (where in 2005 she directed Kirsten Childs's *Miracle Brothers*), and her well-known musical *Floyd Collins* (with composer ADAM GUETTEL), which played at PLAYWRIGHTS HORIZONS, winning the 1996 LUCILLE LORTEL Award for Outstanding Musical and an Obie. She was responsible for *Stonewall: Night Variations* (1994) for the now defunct En Garde Arts. She wrote (and directed) *Beauty,* a reconfiguring of the Sleeping Beauty

story into a feminist tale in 2003 for the LA JOLLA PLAYHOUSE. As a cutting-edge, adventurous artist, directing BELLS ARE RINGING (2001) for her Broadway debut was a bit of a surprise – and one not since repeated. But Landau, born in NYC and a Yale graduate, is a flexible director, as her 2002 success with *Time of Your Life* at Steppenwolf illustrates. She is coauthor with ANNE BOGART of a book (2005) on viewpoints and composition, an improvisation technique.   DBW

Landesman, Heidi see ETTINGER, HEIDI

Landesman, Rocco (1947–) Producer. A graduate of the Yale School of Drama, where he remained as a faculty member until 1978, Landesman subsequently moved into the stock market and also became the owner of a string of racehorses. Coproducing *Big River* (1985; with then-wife, HEIDI ETTINGER) and subsequently INTO THE WOODS (1987) brought him back into the theatre. In 1987 he became president of JUJAMCYN THEATERS, the third-largest theatre owner on Broadway, for whom he has overseen a series of successes, including CITY OF ANGELS, a GYPSY revival (1989), *The* PIANO LESSON, *Grand Hotel* (1989), DEATH OF A SALESMAN revival (1999), PROOF, *The* FULL MONTY, *The* PRODUCERS, URINETOWN, TAKE ME OUT, DOUBT, and *Jersey Boys* (2005). Named in 1995 Producer of the Year by the National Alliance for Musical Theatre, in 2005 he became owner of the Jujamcyn theatre chain.   DBW

Landscape of the Body by JOHN GUARE premiered on 27 September 1977 at the PUBLIC THEATER in New York. John Pasquin directed a cast including SHIRLEY KNIGHT, F. MURRAY ABRAHAM, Peg Murray, and Paul McCrane. In 1984, GARY SINISE directed a successful revival at the Second Stage in New York, and in 2006 MICHAEL GREIF guided a superb version for SIGNATURE THEATRE. An absurdist study of the nature of innocence and experience, the play depicts the journey of Betty Yearn, who comes to Greenwich Village from Bangor, ME, to save her sister Rosalie from a seedy life as a porn actress. In the course of the play, Rosalie is killed, and Betty inhabits her life. She becomes a suspect in the murder of her 14-year-old son, Bert, who has been luring gay men to their apartment and robbing them. Betty ends up on the Nantucket ferry with the investigating detective, throwing bottles containing her life's confession into the ocean.   BCM

Lane, Burton (1912–97) After writing music for songs incorporated into revues, he wrote the entire score for *Earl Carroll's Vanities of 1931,* followed by songs for *Hold on to Your Hats* (1940), *Laffing Room Only* (1944), and then the score for his crowning glory, *Finian's Rainbow* (1947). He wrote numerous popular songs with such lyricists as E. Y. Harburg, Alan Jay Lerner, Ira Gershwin, Frank Loesser, and Harold Adamson. With Lerner he wrote *On a Clear Day You Can See Forever* (1965). A native New Yorker, Lane was a high-school dropout who began his career as a song plugger in Tin Pan Alley. Although many of his nontheatre songs are memorable ("Everything I Have Is Yours," "Too Late Now"), other than *Finian's Rainbow* his musical theatre contributions were modest.   DBW

Lane, Nathan (1956–) New Jersey–born actor who made his Off-Broadway debut in *A Midsummer Night's Dream* (1978), and has established himself as major star, especially in comedy. Following his Broadway debut in 1982 as Roland Maule in Noël Coward's *Present Laughter,* Nathan developed his career Off-Broadway, as Tony Lumpkin in *She Stoops to Conquer* (1984), Nick Finchling in Simon Gray's *The Common Pursuit* (1986–7), Jonathan Balton in Jon Robin Baitz's *The Film Society* (1988), and as the opera queen, Mendy, in Terrence McNally's *The Lisbon Traviata* (1989), a bravado performance that contributed to his growing fame. Lane enhanced his reputation in McNally plays (*Bad Habits,* 1990; *Lips Together, Teeth Apart,* 1991), both at the Manhattan Theatre Club. His Broadway roles included Mr. Brink in *On Borrowed Time* (1991), Nathan Detroit in *Guys and Dolls* (1992), Max Prince in *Laughter on the 23rd Floor* (1993), Buzz in McNally's *Love! Valour! Compassion!* (1994, MTC; 1995 Broadway), Pseudolus in a revival of *A Funny Thing Happened on the Way to the Forum* (1996, Tony), and Sheridan Whiteside in *The Man Who Came to Dinner* (2000). In 2003 he appeared in *Butley* at the Huntington (Broadway, 2006). His Max Bialystock in the Mel Brooks musical *The Producers* (2001) established him as the foremost musical comedian of his generation, winning him a Tony and critical acclaim. Subsequently he has starred in *The Frogs* at the Vivian Beaumont (2004), Terrence McNally's *Dedication or the Stuff of Dreams* (2005, Primary Stages), and a Broadway revival of *The Odd Couple* (2005) with Matthew Broderick. He reprised his Bialystock role in the moderately successful film of *The Producers* (2005).   TLM

Langella, Frank (1940–) Born in Bayonne, NJ, educated at Syracuse University, this versatile actor-director began his performing career at a young age and has always expressed his preference for the stage. Since the 1960s he has essayed leading roles – classical and contemporary – on New York stages. His New York debut (Off-Broadway) was as Michel in *The Immoralist* (1963). Since then, memorable roles in a wide range have included, among many, Benito Cereno in *The Old Glory* (1964, Obie); the young Shakespeare in *A Cry of Players* (1968); Leslie the lizard in *Seascape* (1975; Tony, Featured Actor); title role in the Edward Gorey–designed *Dracula* (1977) – to some his signature part, re-created on the screen in 1979 – Quentin in *After the Fall* (1984, Playhouse 91); Sherlock Holmes in *Sherlock's Last Case* (1987); Junius in *Booth* (1994, York Theatre Co., NYC); Captain in *The Father* (1996); Garry Essendine in *Present Laughter* (1996); Cyrano in his own version (also directed) of *Cyrano de Bergerac* (1997, Roundabout), the fop Tropatachov opposite Alan Bates in *Fortune's Fool* (2002; Tony, Featured Actor), the aging choreographer-dance teacher Tobi Powell in *Match* (2004), and Richard M. Nixon in *Frost/Nixon* (2007; Tony, Leading Actor). He has also performed in over 50 roles in regional theatres. His unique, almost aloof stage presence works less well in film, though in recent years he has excelled in character parts, often villains.   DBW

Langham, Michael (1919–) English director who in the 1950s became a reputable classical director in England and Scotland, though North American work has comprised most of his career. He was appointed Tyrone Guthrie's successor as artistic director of the Stratford (Ontario) Festival in 1955 and enjoyed great success expanding the festival to include touring, film and television projects, a training program, and school performances. Though critically praised, he was criticized often for employing too many Britons. After departing in 1968, Langham directed in English and American venues until 1971, when he was named artistic director at the Guthrie Theater, Minneapolis. Again following in his mentor's footsteps, Langham used his Stratford techniques to pull the Guthrie from near financial disaster. In 1979 he left to become Director of Drama at the Juilliard School, where he was responsible for all training and theatrical productions until 1992. Free from this responsibility he ventured into more freelance directing, beginning winter 1993 with *Saint Joan* for the National Actors Theatre and *Love's Labour's Lost* for Theatre for a New Audience, and in fall 1993 as artistic advisor of the NAT with *Timon of Athens* and *The Government Inspector.* Early in 1995 he directed Brian Bedford in *The Molière Comedies* (two one-acts) at the ROUNDABOUT. His last Broadway credit was *Waiting in the Wings* in 1999.   KN

Langner, Lawrence (1890–1962) One of the most enlightened producers in American theatre history, Langner grew up in London and studied to be a patent lawyer. In 1911 he emigrated to New York and established himself in that profession, later heading a large international firm. In 1914 he helped organize the WASHINGTON SQUARE PLAYERS and wrote several one-act plays for the group. After it disbanded because of the war (1917), he brought together members of the group in late 1918 to form the THEATRE GUILD. The most important of these was THERESA HELBURN, who, together with Langner, managed the organization throughout much of its active life. They pursued artistic aims and built a subscription audience of 25,000 by 1925. The success of the Guild's second production, *John Ferguson* (1919), established them artistically and commercially. Langner encouraged the production of foreign plays, including works by Toller, Kaiser, Molnár, and Pirandello. He obtained for the Guild SHAW's *Heartbreak House* (1919), *Back to Methuselah* (1922), and *Saint Joan* (1923), and he persuaded the Guild to stage O'NEILL's STRANGE INTERLUDE (1928). With his wife, Armina Marshall, Langner built the Westport County Playhouse in 1931 and formed an acting company. In the early 1950s he founded the AMERICAN SHAKESPEARE FESTIVAL at Stratford, CT. Called by BROOKS ATKINSON "one of the most articulate men alive," Langner, whose memoirs (*The Magic Curtain*) were published in 1951, brought an able business mind to bear upon the American theatre for almost 50 years.   TLM

Langtry, Lillie [née Emily Charlotte le Breton] (1853–1929) English actress and society beauty, born in Jersey, of which her father, the Very Reverend William le Breton, was Dean. She made her London social debut in 1877 and her theatrical debut under the Bancrofts at the Haymarket in 1881. Her notoriety was enhanced by Millais's portrait of her, holding a Jersey lily; and it was as "the Jersey Lily" that she continued to draw audiences in England, South Africa and, most of all, in the U.S. (where she debuted in 1882 and made numerous visits) until her retirement in 1918. At best a competent actress and a shrewd company manager, she was best known in this country in *Gossip* (1895) and Sydney Grundy's *The Degenerates* (1900), the latter scandalizing her public by offering glimpses of autobiographical sin in high society. The author of an evasive autobiography, *The Days I Knew* (1921), she died in her villa in Monte Carlo. There have been several mediocre biographies.   PT   DBW

Lansbury, Angela (Brigid) (1925–) London-born actress and singer who came to the U.S. for a career in films, under contract to MGM (1943–50), for whom she performed mostly supporting roles. In 1957 she made her Broadway debut in *Hotel Paradiso*; subsequently she appeared as the mother in *A Taste of Honey* (1960). Lansbury made her musical debut as the Mayor in the ill-fated *Anyone Can Whistle* (1964) before winning the first of her four Tony Awards as the madcap "Auntie Mame" Dennis in *Mame* (1966). Her other Tonys were for performances as the eccentric Countess Aurelia in *Dear World* (1969), the compulsive Mama Rose in a revival of *Gypsy* (1974), and the maniacal Mrs. Lovett in SWEENEY TODD (1979). She brought a powerful singing voice, a flair for comedy, and a rare depth of characterization to her musical roles. An actress of considerable versatility, she has also appeared with the Royal Shakespeare Company and at the Royal National Theatre of Great Britain. She returned to the NYC stage in 2007 opposite MARIAN SELDES in McNALLY's *Deuce*. During 1984–96 she starred as a quirky and personable writer and crime buff in the popular TV series *Murder, She Wrote*. In 1994 she received a CBE from Queen Elizabeth II. Her authorized biography by MARTIN GOTTFRIED was published in 1999.   MK

Lapine, James Elliott (1949–) Playwright-director. Recognized initially for his OFF-BROADWAY plays (*Table Settings*, 1979; *Twelve Dreams*, 1981, revived 1995), Lapine emerged as a resourceful and imaginative director with his staging of WILLIAM FINN's *March of the Falsettos* (1981). He successfully directed and wrote the books for SONDHEIM's SUNDAY IN THE PARK WITH GEORGE (1984), INTO THE WOODS (1987), and *Passion* (1994). His collaboration with Finn continued in 1990 when he coauthored and directed *Falsettoland*, the third installment of Finn's "Marvin Trilogy" (which had begun in 1979 with *In Trousers*). Much of its success was due to Lapine's sensitive and intimate direction. Lapine directed and received a Tony as coauthor of the 1992 Broadway musical FALSETTOS, based on parts 2 and 3 of the trilogy. In 1998 he collaborated with Finn on *A New Brain*. *Luck, Pluck and Virtue* (based on Nathanael West's *A Cool Million*; book and directed by Lapine) premiered at the LA JOLLA PLAYHOUSE in 1993 and was seen at NYC's ATLANTIC THEATER COMPANY in spring 1995, followed by directing assignments: on Broadway, the 1997 revival of *A DIARY OF ANNE FRANK*, DAVID HENRY

HWANG's *Golden Child* (1998), *Dirty Blonde* (conceived and directed) in 2000, a revival of *Into the Woods* (2002); Off-Broadway the 2004 hit *Modern Orthodox* by Daniel Goldfarb, *The 25th Annual Putnam County Spelling Bee* (2005), and *King Lear* with KEVIN KLINE (2007, The PUBLIC). Other original plays of his, both at PLAYWRIGHTS HORIZONS, are *The Moment When* (2000) and *Fran's Bed,* with Mia Farrow and HARRIS YULIN (2003; also directed), In 1999 he wrote the book for and directed Disney's *The Hunchback of Notre Dame*, which premiered in Berlin and ran for three years. Nominated for 11 Tonys, he has won 3 (books for *Passion, Falsettos,* and *Into the Woods*). He also received the Pulitzer Prize for *Sunday in the Park. . . .* DBW

Laramie Project, The Following the brutal 1998 homicide of Matthew Shepard, a young gay man, in a rural part of Laramie, WY, director Moisés Kaufman and members of his TECTONIC THEATER PROJECT forged this three-act docudrama (see DOCUMENTARY THEATRE) based on more than 200 interviews with local townsfolk, some sympathetic, others not. The piece traces how life in Laramie – population c. 27,000 – changed in the tumultuous year after Shepard's murder, which generated national attention and resulted in a push for national hate-crimes legislation at the federal level and a local staging of TONY KUSHNER's *ANGELS IN AMERICA*. After a wildly successful world premiere in 2000 at the DENVER CENTER for the Performing Arts, *The Laramie Project* moved mid-March to OFF-BROADWAY's UNION SQUARE THEATRE, and a film version was produced by HBO in 2002. Together with its earlier work, *Gross Indecency: The Three Trials of Oscar Wilde,* based on actual transcripts of the Irish scribe's indecency trials, Tectonic aimed to create a new kind of presentational theatre based on Kaufman's belief in exploring "watershed historical moments." LJ

Larkin, Peter (1926–) Designer. Though not as innovative as his more famous contemporaries, Larkin was one of the major Broadway designers of the 1950s and '60s. His productions include *Dial M for Murder* (1952), *The Teahouse of the August Moon* (1953), the MARY MARTIN *Peter Pan* (1954), *INHERIT THE WIND* (1955), and *No Time for Sergeants* (1955). His theatre work continued through the 1980s with such productions as *Dancin'* (1978) and *Doonesbury* (1983), but he became more active in films such as *Tootsie* and also designed for ballet. He has won four Tonys. AA

Last of the Red Hot Lovers by NEIL SIMON; opened 28 December 1969 at the EUGENE O'NEILL

THEATRE for 706 performances. This return to Simon's three discrete one-act play form provides stronger thematic integration through main character Barney Cashman (James Coco). The play examines the futility of the sexually promiscuous lifestyle of the 1960s from Barney's middle-aged viewpoint as he attempts to seduce three separate women in his mother's apartment on three different occasions. More significant, Barney explicitly voices a notion that runs throughout Simon's work with his third-act realization that life's futility can only be endured by providing aid rather than seeking it. RW

Lateiner, Jacob see HURWITZ, MOISHE

Lauder, Harry [né Henry MacLennan Lauder] (1870–1950) Scottish music-hall performer who became the highest paid British performer of his time. His repertory originally contained a whole gallery of Scottish types, but eventually he settled into a cosy, chuckling caricature of the canny Scot, invariably singing "I Love a Lassie" and "Roamin' in the Gloamin'." A fixture on U.S. VAUDEVILLE stages, he made 22 U.S. tours during 1909–32. He authored three autobiographies: *A Minstrel in France* (1918), *Between You and Me* (1919), and *Roamin' in the Gloamin'* (1928). A biography by Gordon Irving was issued in 1968. LS

Laughton, Charles (1899–1962) British-born actor who, with his actress wife, Elsa Lanchester, became an American citizen in 1950. His first professional role, in *The Inspector General* (1926, London), was followed by parts including Hercule Poirot in *Alibi* and William Marble in *Payment Deferred,* the latter also marking his 1931 New York debut. At London's Old Vic (1933–4) he played in seven productions, including leading roles in *The Cherry Orchard, The Tempest,* and *Macbeth.* As the first English actor to perform at the Comédie-Française (1936), he appeared in *Le Médecin malgré lui.* After a decade of film work, he returned to the stage in 1947 with *Galileo,* adapted with BRECHT and first performed in LOS ANGELES (Coronet Theatre). For several years he toured the U.S. reading from Bible, Shakespeare, and modern classics. As both director and the Devil in SHAW's *Don Juan in Hell* (1951), he earned critical acclaim. He played Bottom in *A Midsummer Night's Dream* and King Lear at Stratford-upon-Avon (1959). Simon Callow's 1988 biography is definitive, although Lanchester's of 1983 is enlightening. DBW

Laurents, Arthur (1918–) Screenwriter, director, and dramatist. Although not a great success in the theatre, HOME OF THE BRAVE (1945), concerned with a Jewish soldier's wartime problems, won Laurents the attention of critics and a reputation for insight into human nature and an interest in character development and language. In *The TIME OF THE CUCKOO* (1952; revived at LINCOLN CENTER, 2000), *A Clearing in the Woods* (1957), and *Invitation to a March* (1960), he wrote about women whose psychological problems drive them toward disaster. *The Bird Cage* (1950) builds upon the sexual frustrations of a vicious nightclub owner. Laurents wrote the book for the musicals WEST SIDE STORY (1957; revived 1964, 1980) and GYPSY (1959; revived 1974, 1989, 2003), *Hallelujah, Baby!* (1967), and the ill-fated *Nick and Nora* (1991; also directed). He also wrote the screenplay for ANNA LUCASTA (1949) and *Anastasia* (1956). Laurent's 1970's work – e.g., *The Enclave* (1973) – has been less appreciated. His most recent plays are *Jolson Sings Again* (1995, SEATTLE REPERTORY THEATRE); *The Radical Mystique,* built around a fund-raiser for the Black Panthers in 1969 (1995, MANHATTAN THEATRE CLUB); *My Good Name,* about greed destroying identity (1996, SEATTLE REP); *Claudia Lazlo* and *Attacks on the Heart* (2001 and 2003, respectively, GEORGE STREET PLAYHOUSE, NJ); and *2 Lives* (2003, Lincoln Center). His memoirs appeared in 2000. WJM

Lavin, Linda (1937–) Maine-born actress, educated at William and Mary, who made her NYC debut in 1960 with an OFF-BROADWAY revival of *Oh, Kay!,* establishing her career with such featured roles as Patsy Newquist in LITTLE MURDERS (1969, CIRCLE IN THE SQUARE) and Elaine Navazio in *The LAST OF THE RED HOT LOVERS* (1969; Tony nominee). In the 1970s appearances with the NEW YORK SHAKESPEARE FESTIVAL, YALE REPERTORY, and AMERICAN REPERTORY THEATRE supplemented her work in television, which included Alice Hyatt in the CBS series "Alice" (1976–85). She created the Jewish mother Kate in NEIL SIMON'S *BROADWAY BOUND* (1986), winning a Tony and critical acclaim. In 1990 she replaced Tyne Daly as Rose in GYPSY and in 1993 took over the role of Dr. Gorgeous Teitelbaum in *The Sisters Rosensweig,* both on Broadway. In 1995 she appeared at Variety Arts Theatre in two of three short plays (by ELAINE MAY and WOODY ALLEN) under the umbrella *Death Defying Acts,* receiving an Obie and a LUCILLE LORTEL Award for her performance. The next year, she played LILLIAN HELLMAN in *Cakewalk* at the same venue. In 1998 she was nominated for a Tony for her performance as Mrs. Van Daan in *The DIARY OF ANNE FRANK,* and again in 2000 for Marjorie in *The TALE OF THE ALLERGIST'S WIFE.* In 2002 she portrayed the teenaged Carol

Burnett's grandmother in *Hollywood Arms,* and since 2004 she has performed in her own cabaret show, *Songs to Remember When.* TLM

Lawrence, Gertrude (1898–1952) English singer, dancer, and comedy actress. From infancy "Gertie" toured with her actress mother, making her own debut in 1910 as a dancer in *Babes in the Wood.* Her New York debut in *André Charlot's Revue of 1924* launched a brilliant American stage career in which LADY IN THE DARK (1941) and *The KING AND I* (1951) were high points. Noël Coward wrote *Private Lives* for her (1931; she played Amanda), and they appeared on Broadway together in his *Tonight at 8:30* (1936). During WWII she entertained British and American troops. JOHN MASON BROWN described her as "a musical comedy performer" who "grew into an admirable actress." Vivacity, warmth, and a sense of fun characterized her remarkable stage presence. Her memoirs were published in 1945; a biography by Sheridan Morley in 1981. FHL

Lawrence, Jerome (1915–2004) and **Robert E(dwin) Lee** (1918–94) This pair of Ohio-born dramatists joined in formal partnership in 1942 and subsequently wrote dozens of plays, many produced in New York and most extremely popular with regional and amateur groups. Perhaps their best received effort was INHERIT THE WIND (1955), a faithful, flashy, dramatic retelling of the story of the famous Scopes "monkey trial." Also extremely popular was their adaptation of AUNTIE MAME (1956) and the subsequent musical version, *Mame* (1966), for which they wrote the libretto. Their play *The Night Thoreau Spent in Jail* (1970), a standard for several years with amateur groups, was an early offering of the American Playwrights' Theatre at Ohio State University. Their final collaboration was *Whisper in the Mind* (1994, MISSOURI REP). This versatile and prolific team was also responsible for many one-act operas, screenplays, television plays, and radio programs. In 1961 they founded the Margo Jones Medal (awarded to them posthumously in 2005–6). A research center/archive at OSU is named for them. LDC

Lawson, John Howard (1895–1977) Playwright who, in the theatre of the 1920s, was an anomaly: a dramatist of fiery left-wing convictions. Striking out against the convention-bound commercial theatre on the one hand and the ivory-tower art theatre on the other, he attempted to forge a new theatrical style, which he called "political vaudeville." His most successful experiment was

PROCESSIONAL (1925), a staccato, fragmented series of sketches set in a West Virginia town during a coal strike. In 1926 he was a cofounder of the short-lived, politically radical New Playwrights' Theatre, for which he wrote a strident satire of political campaigning called *Loud Speaker*. Lawson changed his style in the 1930s, replacing extravagance with a richly idiomatic realism that had a strong influence on CLIFFORD ODETS. The eloquently embittered, working-class antiheroes of his *Success Story* (1932) and *Gentlewoman* (1934) speak a racy urban poetry. An active screenwriter (*Blockade, Action in the North Atlantic*) and a president of the Screen Writer's Guild, Lawson was imprisoned in 1948 for defending the Bill of Rights against the inquisition of the House Un-American Activities Committee. In 1936 he published a now standard work, *Theory and Technique of Playwriting*, which became a fundamental resource for radical theatre companies; revised in 1949 to include screenwriting, the title changed to reflect this addition. Jonathan L. Chambers is the author of a recent study of Lawson (2006).   FH

Layton, Joe [né Joseph Lichtman] (1931–94) Theatre and ballet choreographer. As a dancer, Layton made his debut in 1947 in OKLAHOMA! and continued dancing in *High Button Shoes* (1947), *Gentlemen Prefer Blondes* (1949), and WONDERFUL TOWN (1953). His choreographic debut was *Once upon a Mattress* (1959); that same year, he choreographed another enormous success, *The SOUND OF MUSIC*. Layton worked steadily as a choreographer, making the transition to director in *No Strings* (1962), and he also revived GEORGE M. COHAN'S DANCES for the musical *George M!* (1968), winning Tonys for both. Widely recognized for his work with Hollywood stars on their television specials, Layton also ventured into ballet, producing works for the Royal Ballet (London) and the Joffrey Ballet.   LF

Le Gallienne, Eva (1899–1991) Best known as an actress, the London-born Le Gallienne participated in every aspect of American theatre. Her New York debut was in *Mrs. Boltay's Daughter* (1915), but her first big success was as Julie in *Liliom* (1921). For the next 60-plus years Le Gallienne played most of the major female roles in Western drama, receiving critical acclaim for performances in plays by IBSEN, CHEKHOV, and Shakespeare (see SHAKESPEARE ON . . .), as well as for her Queen Elizabeth in both Schiller's *Mary Stuart* (1957, PHOENIX THEATRE, dir. TYRONE GUTHRIE) and MAXWELL ANDERSON'S *ELIZABETH THE QUEEN*. She described her acting technique as "getting rid of 'Me' in order to become the part."

Le Gallienne's contribution to American theatre included more than her considerable acting skill. She introduced audiences throughout the country to Ibsen, Chekhov, and French playwrights through her translations and productions of their plays. A lifelong proponent of repertory theatre, Le Gallienne founded the CIVIC REPERTORY THEATRE (1926–33), where she produced, directed, and starred, offering quality theatre at bargain ticket prices. The Civic presented 1,581 performances of more than 30 plays, including many of the classics, GLASPELL'S *ALISON'S HOUSE, Peter Pan* (in which Le Gallienne was the first actress to "fly" into the audience), and *Alice in Wonderland* (adaptation by Le Gallienne and Florida Friebus). In 1946, Le Gallienne, CHERYL CRAWFORD, and MARGARET WEBSTER founded the AMERICAN REPERTORY COMPANY, which lasted only one season.

Le Gallienne directed and acted for the National Repertory Theatre (1961–6); acted on Broadway in a revival of *The ROYAL FAMILY* (1976), *To Grandmother's House We Go* (1981), and the brief revival of *Alice in Wonderland* (1982; her last stage appearance); and acted in the film *Resurrection* (1980). She also published her translations of Ibsen and Chekhov, a biography of Eleonora Duse, and two autobiographies: *At 33* (1934) and *With a Quiet Heart* (1953). In addition, she garnered most of the major awards in American performing arts, including Woman of the Year (1947), ANTA (1964, 1977), a special Tony (1964), an Emmy (1978), and the National Medal of Arts (1986). Modern biographies were written by Robert Schanke (1992) and Helen Sheehy (1996).   FB

Leach, Wilford (Carson) (1929–88) Director, teacher, playwright, and designer. Born in Virginia, Leach attended William and Mary and the University of Illinois (Ph.D.) and then taught at Sarah Lawrence College. During 1970–7 he was artistic director of LA MAMA ETC. From 1977 he worked mainly for the NEW YORK SHAKESPEARE FESTIVAL, designing as well as directing productions. His major credits included *Mandragola* (1977); *All's Well* and *The Taming of the Shrew* (1978); *Othello* (1979); *Mother Courage* (1980); *The Pirates of Penzance* (1980); *The Human Comedy* (1983); *La Bohème* (1984); and *The Mystery of Edwin Drood* (1985). Leach's highly original style drew on VAUDEVILLE, film, animated cartoon, opera, and PUPPET theatre.   TLM

League of American Theatres and Producers
Founded in 1930 as the League of New York Theatres, the name altered to the League of New York

Theatres and Producers in 1973 and to its present name in 1985, the League negotiates union contracts, administers the ANTOINETTE PERRY (Tony) Awards, and serves as a trade organization representing Broadway theatres. In 1995, longtime executive director of the League and former press agent HARVEY SABINSON, who retired that year and was replaced by Jed Bernstein (through the 2005–6 season), was presented a special Tony for his years of service to the Broadway theatre. Charlotte St. Martin succeeded Bernstein.   DBW

Leavitt, M(ichael) B(ennett) (1843–1935) Polish-born manager-impresario. A blackface minstrel in the 1850s, Leavitt, after establishing several minstrel troupes under his control, created the first fairly reputable early burlesque show in the U.S. Substituting female performers for male actors, he first feminized a MINSTREL SHOW (Mme Rentz's Female Minstrels) in 1870, ultimately merging this show, VAUDEVILLE, and musicalized travesty into what he called BURLESQUE, originally in The RENTZ–SANTLEY Novelty and Burlesque Company (starring Mabel Santley). Leavitt burlesque eschewed the earlier classic, satiric focus for greater suggestiveness and lusty humor. A typical Leavitt afterpiece, Anthony and Cleopatra, with Octobus Sweezur, Cheesi Hankipanki, and Hoctasuper, became a favorite of burlesque comics. Leavitt also operated two chains of legitimate theatres. Retiring in 1912, he published that year a sprawling 700-page memoir, Fifty Years in Theatrical Management.   DBW

Leblang, Joe (1874?–1931) Hungarian-born refugee who, beginning in the 1890s, developed by 1913 a thriving cut-rate ticket brokerage in Gray's Drugstore, where he ran a shoeshine stand. He did so well that, in 1914, he bought the drugstore; eventually, he also bought the building (43d St. and Broadway), which included GEORGE M. COHAN'S THEATRE. By 1930 Leblang's, New York's leading brokerage, was selling over five million tickets annually. After his death, his wife Tillie carried on until shortly after WWII. A book on his ticket empire, by Jerry D. Eisenhour, was published in 2003.   DBW

LeCompte, Elizabeth (Alice) (1944–) Director and playwright and, since 1979, artistic director of the experimental theatre COLLECTIVE known as the WOOSTER GROUP. With SPALDING GRAY and other members of the group, she cowrote and directed Sakonnet Point (1975), Rumstick Road (1977), and Nayatt School (1978), a trilogy called Three Places in Rhode Island; in 1979 LeCompte and the Group created "an epilog" (without dialogue) to this trilogy called Point Judith (1979). She was also instrumental in the creation of Route 1 & 9 (1981) and L.S.D. (. . . Just the High Points . . .) (1984), and participated in the creation of such pieces as Frank Dell's The Temptation of St. Antony (1987) – these three constituting the trilogy The Road to Immortality – and Brace Up! (1991; revived 2003). Her 1997 production of The EMPEROR JONES with Kate Valk, cross-gendered and blackfaced in the title role (and WILLEM DAFOE as Smithers), was revived in 2006 (sans Dafoe). In 1984 she was appointed associate director of the short-lived American National Theatre (under PETER SELLARS) at the JOHN F. KENNEDY CENTER. In the 1980s and '90s she has been a leader in the nourishing of a sometimes radical NYC avant-garde theatre, rewarded in 1995 for her creative efforts with a MacArthur "genius" Fellowship.   DBW

Lederer, George W. (1861–1938) Producer who originated, with The Passing Show (1894), the U.S. version of the musical REVUE. He also pioneered the form and many of the features of American and English musical comedy in producing The Belle of New York (1897), FLORODORA (1899, London; 1900, NYC), and Madame Sherry (1910). Lederer managed VAUDEVILLE companies and New York theatres (CASINO, NEW YORK THEATRE), was the AGENT for LILLIAN RUSSELL and other leading players, and produced motion pictures.   WD

Lee, Canada [né Leonard Canegata] (1907–52) African American actor whose successful boxing career was halted by an eye injury, yet whose fighting spirit was manifested in several memorable roles. He played Blacksnake in the 1934 revival of the antilynching drama STEVEDORE, Banquo in the FEDERAL THEATRE's "voodoo" Macbeth (dir. WELLES, 1936), and the emperor Christophe in Haiti (1938). His finest performance was as Bigger Thomas in RICHARD WRIGHT's NATIVE SON (1941). Lee played Caliban in MARGARET WEBSTER's 1945 production of The Tempest and a whiteface Bosola in The Duchess of Malfi (1946). He was a powerful actor of animallike grace who was committed to a theatre of social relevance. His bio by Mona Z. Smith was published in 2004.   EGH

Lee, Eugene (1939–) Set designer, unique among American designers in both concept and execution. Approaching each production without preconceived ideas, Lee treats the whole space of the theatre – not only the stage – as a place to be designed. From the late 1960s onward (except for 1989–90) he has been resident designer for the

TRINITY REPERTORY COMPANY in Providence, RI, and for seven years was head of design at the DALLAS THEATER CENTER. Together with director ADRIAN HALL he created iconoclastic, often environmental, settings, including the 1992 *As You Like It* in Central Park. He brought environmental design to OFF-BROADWAY with *Slave Ship* and The Manhattan Project's *Alice in Wonderland* (both in 1970), and to Broadway with CANDIDE (1974 revival; Tony). Even with more conventional productions his sets tend to be large and use moving parts and real materials. Lee has worked with Peter Brook in Shiraz and Paris and with HAROLD PRINCE on several shows, including in New York: *Sweeney Todd* (1979; Tony), *Grandchild of Kings* (1992, IRISH REP at THEATER FOR THE NEW CITY) – and in Toronto and New York for *SHOW BOAT* (Drama Desk Award). Recent Broadway credits include *RAGTIME* (1998), the problem-ridden *Seussical* (2000), the highly original *WICKED* (2003; Tony), and the epic *The Pirate Queen* (2007). He has been production designer for television's *Saturday Night Live* from its inception and has designed stage shows for its cast members (Gilda Radner, Colin Quinn), several TV specials, and concert tours for Paul Simon. His first wife, **Franne Lee** (1941–), worked in collaboration with Eugene through the 1970s, receiving costume Tonys for *Candide* and *Sweeney*. Her most recent Broadway project was the 1993 revival of *CAMELOT*. She lives in Nashville, where in 2001 she founded an artists' cooperative. AA DBW

Lee, Gypsy Rose [née Rose Louise Hovick] (1914?–70) BURLESQUE artist and writer. After performing a child act with her sister JUNE (HAVOC) in VAUDEVILLE (1922–8), she starred in MINSKY's Burlesque by the age of 17. Her act comprised more "tease" than "strip," tantalizing with suggestive silk stockings, lace panties, and a rose garter tossed into the audience as a coda. H. L. Mencken coined the term "ecdysiast" to label her speciality, and her sophisticated pose was parodied in the musical PAL JOEY (1940). Seen in the ZIEGFELD *Follies of 1936*, NIGHTCLUBS, fairs, and carnivals, she was the first celebrity stripper (see NUDITY). Her writings include a play, *The Naked Genius* (1943); some murder mysteries; and a memoir, *Gypsy* (published 1957), turned into a popular musical comedy (*GYPSY*, 1959). Her final major creative effort was a one-person show called *A Curious Evening with Gypsy Rose Lee* (1958), though in the 1960s she appeared frequently on television. Her son, Erik Preminger, published a memoir in 1984. LS

Lee, Ming Cho (1930–) Generally considered the current doyen of American set designers, his style and technique have significantly influenced the look of opera and theatre design since the mid-1960s. Lee was born in Shanghai and studied Chinese watercolor before emigrating to the U.S. in 1949. In 1954 he became an assistant to JO MIELZINER, to whose poetic realism Lee's trademark spare, minimalist, emblematic style – best exemplified in the 1964 production of *Electra* at the NEW YORK SHAKESPEARE FESTIVAL – was, in part, a response. Lee is usually associated with pipework scaffolding, textured surfaces, and collage; but since the late 1970s, his work has turned to detail and ultrarealism, as in the production of *K2*, for which he created a mountain on the stage (1983; Tony). He is constantly working with new materials and new approaches. Despite his importance, he has designed little on Broadway (nothing since 1986): Much of his work has been with the NYSF (22 Shakespearean productions in 11 years) and regional theatres, as well for as opera – most notably, the New York City Opera and internationally. Since the mid-1980s Lee, who cochairs the design program at the Yale School of Drama, has devoted more time to teaching (appointed in 1995 to the DONALD OENSLAGER Chair), though his designs for *Annie Warbucks* and *A Perfect Ganesh* were seen in New York (both 1993). In 1994 he was the recipient of the first Mary L. Murphy Award in Design presented by LONG WHARF THEATRE. He received a 2002 National Medal of Arts and has an Obie for Sustained Achievement. AA

Lee, Robert E. see LAWRENCE, JEROME

Leftwich, Alexander (1884–1947) Producer and director. From staging plays for the FROHMANS and SHUBERTS (c. 1915–26), Leftwich became a leading director of musicals, including *Hit the Deck* (1927), *A Connecticut Yankee* (1927), *Rain or Shine* (1928), *STRIKE UP THE BAND* (1930), and *Girl Crazy* (1930). He later acted in films in Hollywood. TLM

Leguizamo, John (1964–) Actor-performer and writer, called by BRANTLEY a "perpetual motion machine," was born in Bogotá, Colombia, son of a Puerto-Rican father and Colombian mother; he came to the U.S. at age 4, settling with his family in Queens. After studying theatre at NYU, he began his career as a stand-up comic but soon got small television and film roles. In 1991 he wrote and performed the Obie-winning ONE-PERSON *Mambo Mouth*, in which he played seven characters. This was followed in 1993 by his *Spic-O-Rama*, winning praise (and a Lucille Lortel Award) for his solo show poking fun at Latino stereotypes in the U.S. His third solo show and his Broadway debut in 1998 was *Freak*, nominated for two Tonys (actor and writing). In 2001 a fourth solo performance, *Sexaholix . . . A Love Story*, was produced. He has worked with director Peter Askin on most of his solo shows. After numerous film roles – running the gamut from Toulouse-Lautrec in *Moulin Rouge!* to a hustler in *Empire*, a gangster in *Carlito's Way*, a drag queen in *To Wong Foo*, and a drug dealer in *Spun* – in 2005 he joined the cast of TV's *ER* as Dr. Victor Clemente. A memoir was published in 2006.   DBW

Leiber, Fritz (1883–1949) Leading actor who began as a member of the Ben GREET PLAYERS in 1902, playing Shakespearean roles and making his New York debut in 1905 as Macduff in *Macbeth*. After several silent films and one year with JULIA MARLOWE, he became a leading actor with ROBERT MANTELL, playing numerous roles in Shakespeare (see SHAKESPEARE ON . . .). In 1920 he married Mantell's leading actress, Virginia Bronson, and formed the Shakespeare Repertory Company, touring extensively until 1929, when he founded the Chicago Civic Shakespeare Society. Lured to Hollywood in the 1930s with the prospect of playing Shakespearean roles on film, he instead played small character roles (e.g., Franz Liszt in the 1943 *Phantom of the Opera*). The Leiber Collection is at the University of Illinois.   RE

Leight, Warren (1957–) Playwright who grew up in NYC and attended Stanford at the age of 16 on scholarship, majoring in journalism. He has written for film, television, and the stage; several of his plays incorporate aspects of his autobiography. *Side Man*, which won the Tony for best play in 1999, is about a group of jazz musicians and is loosely based on his relationship with his musician father. *No Foreigners beyond This Point* (2005) draws on the writer's own experience teaching English in communist China. Other theatre credits include the book for the Broadway musical *Mayor* (1985), with music and lyrics by CHARLES STROUSE, and the play *Glimmer, Glimmer and Shine* (2001, MANHATTAN THEATRE CLUB).   DanB

Lenya, Lotte [née Karoline Blamauer] (1900–81) Vienna-born actress and singer who went to Germany to begin an acting career. In 1928 she appeared in the Berlin premiere of the BRECHT–Weill *Die Dreigroschenoper* (*The Threepenny Opera*).

After immigrating to the U.S. with her husband, composer KURT WEILL, she made her Broadway debut in *The Eternal Road* (1937). She appeared in several plays and musicals, but is remembered for the OFF-BROADWAY *Threepenny Opera* (1954, as Jenny) and REVUE *Brecht on Brecht* (1961), as well as the Broadway musical CABARET (1966). A biography by Donald Spoto was published in 1989, and a wonderful "pictorial autobiography" (ed. David Farneth) appeared in 1998.   MK

Leonard, Robert Sean (1969–) Youthful-looking actor, born in New Jersey, educated at Columbia University, who began his stage career at age 12 and made his OFF-BROADWAY debut in *Sally's Gone, She Left Her Name* (1985) and his Broadway debut as a replacement (Eugene) in *Brighton Beach Memoirs* (1987). But his first true attention came as the would-be actor driven to suicide in the film *Dead Poet's Society* (1989). With several fellow actors in that project (Ethan Hawke, James Waterston) and others he cofounded the short-lived Malaparte Theater Company in the mid-1990s. His most publicized Broadway roles include Christopher in *Breaking the Code* (1987), Marchbanks in *Candida* (1993; Tony nomination), Valentine Coverly in *Arcadia* (1995), young A. E. Houseman in *The Invention of Love* (2001; Tony, Best Featured Actor), and Edmund in the all-star revival of LONG DAY'S JOURNEY INTO NIGHT (2003; Tony nomination). Since 2004 he has been a regular on the TV series *House M.D.*   DBW

Lerner, Alan Jay (1918–86) and **Frederick Loewe** (1904–88) Lyricist and composer. Loewe, a classically trained composer born in Vienna, and Lerner, who had studied at Juilliard and Harvard, collaborated on their first musical score, *What's Up?*, in 1943. Four years later the team had its first major success with BRIGADOON, a fantasy set in a magical Scottish village. Their next show, PAINT YOUR WAGON, achieved a modest run. In 1956, Lerner and Loewe wrote the score for MY FAIR LADY, a musical version of G. B. SHAW's *Pygmalion*. One of the most successful musical comedies ever produced, *My Fair Lady*'s score was a perfect blending of Loewe's operetta music with Lerner's pseudo-Shavian lyrics. Their next show, CAMELOT (1960), was generally conceded to be inferior to its predecessor. Lerner and Loewe collaborated on only one other Broadway musical, a 1973 adaptation of their film *Gigi*. After Loewe's retirement, Lerner worked on a number of shows with other composers: BURTON LANE, André Previn, LEONARD BERNSTEIN, and CHARLES STROUSE.

Loewe's music successfully combined the older operetta tradition with more modern Broadway musical idioms. Lerner's versatility as a lyricist was demonstrated in songs whose styles ranged from the sophisticated verbal trickery of LORENZ HART to the simple treatment of OSCAR HAMMERSTEIN II. A combined biography of the partners by Gene Lees was published in 1990. Lerner's bio was written in 1996 by Edward Jablonski.   MK

Les Misérables Based on Victor Hugo's novel, this immensely successful musical, the third-longest running show in Broadway history, logged 6,680 performances (1987–2003) and was revived in 2006 by producer CAMERON MACKINTOSH. Despite a telescoped story and sentimental score (by Claude-Michel Schönberg and Alain Boublil; English lyrics by Herbert Kretzmer), Trevor Nunn and John Caird's fluid, inventive staging helped forge a global phenomenon, with productions in nearly 40 countries and 31 cast recordings. In New York, it won 8 out of 12 Tonys, including Best Musical, Book, Score, Direction, Featured Actor and Actress (Michael Maguire, Frances Ruffelle), and Scenic and Lighting Design (John Napier, David Hersey). In addition to Irish tenor Colm Wilkinson's Tony-nominated work as Jean Valjean, "Les Miz" offered career-advancing opportunities for scores of stateside actors, such as Judy Kuhn and Terrence Mann (Tony nominations for both), future Tony winners Anthony Crivello, Randy Graff, SUTTON FOSTER, Shuler Hensley, and Rachel York, and pop stars Ricky Martin and Deborah Gibson.   LJ

lesbian theatre see GAY AND LESBIAN THEATRE

Leslie (Brown; Buck), Amy [née Lillie West] (1860–1939) Drama critic of the *Chicago Daily News.* An actress early in life, Leslie wrote reviews and profiles, marked by an effusive, star-struck quality, of nearly every famous player of her day that were. As BEN HECHT recalled in *THEATRE ARTS* magazine (July 1951), "Her prose was ornate and endless. . . . No drama critic I have read since, not even ALEXANDER WOOLLCOTT, could swoon as madly in front of the footlights as our Amy Leslie." She helped make the career of adventurer Frank "Bring 'em Back Alive" Buck, whom she married when she was 35 and he was a 20-year-old bellboy.   SF

Lester, Edwin (1895–1990) Producer. After establishing himself in the Los Angeles music business (1923–33), Lester organized the LOS ANGELES Light Opera Festival (1935). He later founded the

SAN FRANCISCO Civic Light Opera Association (1937) and the Los Angeles Civic Light Opera Association (1938), managing both groups until he retired in 1976. Noted for his opulent style, his most notable productions include world premieres of *Song of Norway* (1944), *KISMET* (1953), and *Gigi* (1973).   TLM

Letts, Tracy (1965–) Playwright, actor, director, born in Tulsa, OK, who began performing with Chicago's STEPPENWOLF THEATRE in 1988 and became an ensemble member of the company in 2002. He is best known for his playwriting work, which frequently depicts the dark underbelly of American life. Major plays include *Killer Joe*, which debuted at the Next Lab in Chicago in 1993 and became a hit OFF-BROADWAY in 1998; *Bug*, which debuted in London at the Gate Theatre in 1996 and had a critically acclaimed Off-Broadway run in 2004; and *Man From Nebraska*, produced at Steppenwolf in 2003 and a finalist for the 2004 Pulitzer Prize for Drama.   DanB

Leve, Samuel (1908/10–99) Russian-born designer who began his career with the FEDERAL THEATRE PROJECT and the MERCURY THEATRE, where his designs included ORSON WELLES's *Julius Caesar* (1937). He then worked for MAURICE SCHWARTZ's YIDDISH ART THEATRE. On Broadway he designed productions for MAURICE EVANS, KATHARINE CORNELL, and JUDITH ANDERSON. As a designer for the Metropolitan Opera he created a notable unit set for *The Flying Dutchman;* in the 1950s he designed extensively for television.   AA

Levene [né Levine], **Sam(uel)** (1905–80) One of the more durable character actors on the New York stage for over 50 years, Levene specialized in roles that capitalized on his dour expression and his prominent New York accent, frequently New York Jewish types. He is best remembered for Patsy in *THREE MEN ON A HORSE* (1935), Gordon Miller in *ROOM SERVICE* (1937), Sidney Black in *LIGHT UP THE SKY* (1948), Nathan Detroit in *GUYS AND DOLLS* (1950), Al Lewis in NEIL SIMON's *The SUNSHINE BOYS* (1972), and Oscar Wolfe in the revival of *The ROYAL FAMILY* (1975), his last major appearance. Adept in vehicles that ranged from popular farce to the more serious, Levene also appeared on Broadway notably in *The Last Analysis, The Devil's Advocate, Heartbreak House, DINNER AT EIGHT,* as well as in the London production of *The MATCHMAKER* with RUTH GORDON.   DBW

Levin, Ira (1929–) New York–born playwright and novelist who, with a Broadway presence of three decades, scored major successes with *No Time for Sergeants* (1955, adapted from Mac Hyman's novel), *Critic's Choice* (1960), and DEATHTRAP (1978), the longest-running Broadway mystery to date (1,793 performances). Dependent on interesting characters caught in comic situations, his works include *Interlock* (1958), *General Seeger* (1962), *Drat! The Cat!* (1965), *Dr. Cook's Garden* (1967), *Veronica's Room* (1973), *Break a Leg* (1979), *Cantorial* (1989, JEWISH REP), *Footsteps* (2003, unstaged but televised). Successful film adaptations were made of several plays and especially his novels (e.g., *Rosemary's Baby*). GSA

Lewis [né Deming], **James** (1837?–96) Actor. After a 15-year career as low comedian in various companies throughout the county, Lewis joined AUGUSTIN DALY in 1869, succeeding notably as Bob Sackett in BRONSON HOWARD's *Saratoga* (1870). In 1880 the short, thin, wiry actor with animated face and eccentric, high voice became part of the "Big Four," performing older, comic foils with MRS. G. H. GILBERT opposite JOHN DREW and ADA REHAN (e.g., in *Needles and Pins*, 1880). DBW

Lewis, Robert (1909–97) Director, producer, and actor, Lewis first appeared with the CIVIC REPERTORY THEATRE during the 1929–30 season. From 1931 to 1941 he worked with the GROUP THEATRE, for whom he directed the road company of *GOLDEN BOY* in 1938 (having appeared in its Broadway run). He made his first appearance in London in the same year. After the war he directed extensively on Broadway; among his hit productions were *BRIGADOON* (1947) and *The Teahouse of the August Moon* (1953). With ELIA KAZAN and CHERYL CRAWFORD, he founded the ACTORS STUDIO in 1947. Lewis has also appeared in many films, taught acting and theatre at Sarah Lawrence College and Yale, and is the author of *Method – or Madness?* (1958), an explication of the Stanislavsky System of acting. In 1984 he published his autobiography, *Slings and Arrows*. Kent State University, which houses Lewis's papers, inititated the "Robert Lewis Medal for Lifetime Achievement in Theater Research" in 1991 but discontinued it after his death. SMA

Lewis, Theophilus (1891–1974) Leading AFRICAN AMERICAN drama critic of the Harlem Renaissance. He wrote for the monthly magazine *The Messenger* during 1923–6, his perceptive notices often censuring the popular VAUDEVILLE REVUES for lack of taste while reserving credit for the talented performer like FLORENCE MILLS. Lewis

believed the serious drama alone could produce a truly racial theatre. He encouraged Little Theatre groups (see COMMUNITY THEATRE) and urged the cultivation of black playwrights and black ownership of theatre buildings. EGH

Lewisohn, Alice (1883–1972) and **Irene** (1892–1944) Performing artists, directors, producers, and patrons. Orphaned in 1902, the sisters each inherited a fortune along with a commitment to philanthropic service. Their volunteer efforts at the Henry Street Settlement on NYC's Lower East Side soon included organizing amateur dance and drama productions, often reflecting the varied ETHNIC heritages of the "Neighborhood Players" and their audiences, as well as the Asian and Middle Eastern fare that interested the world-traveling sisters. The NEIGHBORHOOD PLAYHOUSE, which they built and presented to the settlement, opened in 1915; for 12 years it offered an esoteric repertoire, winning special acclaim for the Hindu *The Little Clay Cart* (1924) and the YIDDISH *Dybbuk* (1925). Although the playhouse closed in 1927, the renowned Neighborhood Playhouse School of the Theatre opened in 1928 with Irene as codirector. Alice married Herbert E. Crowley and in 1959 published a memoir, *The Neighborhood Playhouse*. FHL

Liebler, Theodore A. (1852–1941) Producer of nearly 240 plays in association with GEORGE C. TYLER, beginning with *The Royal Box* (1897). He also produced the riot-plagued U.S. tour (1911) of Ireland's Abbey Theatre. Many of the greatest hits of Liebler and Company, such as *The Christian* (1898), *Alias Jimmy Valentine* (1910), and *The Garden of Allah* (1911), were adapted from popular fiction. Liebler's greatest hit was BOOTH TARKINGTON and HARRY LEON WILSON's chauvinistic *The Man from Home* (1908), which ran 496 performances. He retired when a series of expensive failures after WWI caused the collapse of Liebler and Company. WD

Lie of the Mind, A by SAM SHEPARD, who directed the premiere (New York's Promenade Theatre on 5 December 1985) with a cast featuring GERALDINE PAGE, Amanda PLUMMER, Harvey Keitel, and Aidan Quinn, and music by the Red Clay Ramblers. A London production opened 14 October 1987 at the Royal Court Theatre. Though episodically structured, the play offers one of Shepard's strongest narratives; it was also his last work for the stage until 1991. It brings together many of Shepard's familiar themes and devices: rival brothers, the disintegrating family, the search for identity, a wounded leg, the road, guns, and a culminating fire. The action, shifting between family homes in California and Montana, proceeds from a head injury inflicted by Jake on his wife, Beth. During her slow recovery, she undertakes a bizarre courtship of Jake's brother, Frankie.   FHL

Life with Father by HOWARD LINDSAY and RUS-SEL CROUSE opened on Broadway 8 November 1939. The play was based on the stories of Clarence Day, first published in the *New Yorker, Harper's Magazine,* and the *New Republic* (1920–35), and then collected into novel form (1935). A sentimental and nostalgic domestic comedy set in the late 1880s, the play dramatizes the attempts of Father (Lindsay) to assert his authority and the rather more successful, although affectionate, schemes of his wife (Lindsay's wife, DOROTHY STICKNEY) and their four sons to have their own way in spite of him. At closing on 12 July 1947, it was Broadway's longest-running play, with 3,224 performances.   JDM

Light, James (1894–1964) Actor, designer, and director identified with the experimental work of O'NEILL and the PROVINCETOWN PLAYERS (and successors), with whom he served as a director for 13 years starting in 1917. A design student at the Carnegie Institute, Light codirected O'Neill's *The HAIRY APE* (1922), and directed *ALL GOD'S CHILLUN GOT WINGS* (1924) and the American premiere of Strindberg's *The Dream Play* (1926). Dean of the theatre faculty at the New School for Social Research (1939–42), he was also codirector of the FEDERAL THEATRE PROJECT in New York, then its director in Philadelphia.   TP   DBW

Light Up the Sky Comedy by MOSS HART; opened on Broadway 18 November 1948 under Hart's direction and ran 216 performances. Its story and the actual circumstances of the production were virtually identical: A play opens in BOSTON for an out-of-town tryout, the audience and the critics give it a mixed reception, and the playwright retreats to his room in the Ritz-Carlton to revise his creation.   JDM

Lightnin' by WINCHELL SMITH and FRANK BACON opened 26 August 1918 at the Gaiety Theatre, where the humorous rural melodrama recorded a long-run record 1,291 performances. Bacon, who originally conceived and wrote the play, received praise as the slow-talking, slow-moving "Lightnin'" Bill Jones. A boozy prevaricator who claimed a variety of previous occupations, Jones conveyed

a folk-hero quality, which placed him in the tradition of RIP VAN WINKLE and the stage YANKEE. Smith collaborated on the script, in which Lightnin', who operated a rundown hotel on the California–Nevada border, foiled the machinations of landsharks.   RAH

Lillie, Beatrice Gladys (Lady Robert Peel) (1894–1989) Canadian-born comedienne, billed as "the funniest woman in the world," appeared in variety as a child. Her debuts came in London revues *Not Likely* (1914) and *André Charlot's Revue of 1917;* a 1924 edition of the latter brought her to the U.S. (as it did GERTRUDE LAWRENCE). Her New York successes include *This Year of Grace* (1928) with Noël Coward; G. B. SHAW's *Too True to Be Good* (1932); *The Show Is On* (1936) with BERT LAHR; *Set to Music* (1939), in which she introduced Coward's "I've Been to a Mahhhvelous Party"; and *Inside USA* (1948). Lillie was the consummate REVUE performer, wielding the slapstick with a raised pinky, puncturing her own poses of sophisticated grandeur with lapses into raucous vulgarity. She performed in the ONE-PERSON show *An Evening with Beatrice Lillie* (1952); a 1957 revival of the ZIEGFELD *Follies;* as *AUNTIE MAME* (1958 replacement); and, in her final New York appearance, as the medium Mme Arcati in *High Spirits* (1964). She also wrote an autobiography, *Every Other Inch a Lady* (1972). Her biography by Bruce Laffey was published in 1989.   LS

Lincoln Center for the Performing Arts see VIVIAN BEAUMONT AND MITZI E. NEWHOUSE THEATRES

Lindsay, Howard (1889–1968) Playwright, director, actor, and producer. Born in Waterford, NY, Lindsay attended Harvard University for one year and the AMERICAN ACADEMY OF DRAMATIC ARTS for six months before launching his acting career in 1909. Numerous stage appearances followed in vaudeville and burlesque; on tour with McKEE RANKIN; and as a member of MARGARET ANGLIN's Company (1913–18). After military service in WWI he returned to the stage, and in 1921 directed as well as acted in *DULCY.* In the 1920s Lindsay established himself on Broadway as both a director and actor. He married actress DOROTHY STICKNEY in 1927, and starred with her in *LIFE WITH FATHER* (1939), a play he cowrote with RUSSEL CROUSE. Other collaborations with Crouse included the book for *ANYTHING GOES* (1934); *STATE OF THE UNION* (1945), which won the Pulitzer Prize; the book for *CALL ME MADAM* (1950); *The Great Sebastians,* which featured ALFRED LUNT and

LYNN FONTANNE; and the books for *The SOUND OF MUSIC* (1959) and *Mr. President* (1962). Lindsay's most popular role, Father in *Life with Father*, drew praise from BROOKS ATKINSON for its "rare taste and solid heartiness." He was a craftsman more than an artist, able to "pull together" stageworthy theatrical pieces with his collaborators. CORNELIA OTIS SKINNER wrote a bio of Lindsay and his partner in 1976. TLM

Lindsay-Abaire, David (1969–) Youthful playwright born in Boston in a blue-collar family; one of five children. Educated at Sarah Lawrence and Juilliard, his early career has been championed by the MANHATTAN THEATRE CLUB: *Fuddy Meers* (1999), *Wonders of the World* (2001), *Kimberly Akimbo* (2003), *Rabbit Hole* (2006, Tony nomination, Pulitzer Prize; Best Actress award to Cynthia Nixon), and book for the musical *High Fidelity* (2006). Although not always critically acclaimed, his unique work is a mix of grave reality and upbeat lunacy, described as "whimsical," "wicked," "cleverly odd," and "cock-eyed." DBW

Linney, Laura (1964–) New York-born, Brown- and Juilliard- (1990) educated and trained actress of immense sensitivity and depth. She is especially superb in large, emotional roles, portrayed with effective understatement. To her, the work is foremost – eschewing fame and celebrity – as her choice of roles in all media attests. Honored with numerous nominations and awards, Linney, daughter of playwright ROMULUS LINNEY, plays roles often more complex than they seem on the surface. In film she has excelled in such independent films as *You Can Count on Me* and *The Squid and the Whale;* in television she played Mary Anne Singleton in PBS's *Tales of the City* and its sequels; and on the stage, to which she often returns, Broadway credits have included *Six Degrees of Separation* (1990, her first on the main stem, replacing Tess), *The Seagull, Hedda Gabler* (1994, as Thea; Callaway Award for classical acting), *Holiday, Honour, Uncle Vanya, The Crucible* (2000; Tony nomination for her Elizabeth Proctor), and *Sight Unseen* (2004; Tony nomination for the "charismatically uncertain woman" Patricia; also Theatre World Award). In the latter BEN BRANTLEY described her as a "sorcerer" who, with her "emotional incandescence," made the play her own. DBW

Linney, Romulus (1930–) Director, educator, novelist, and playwright. Trained at the Yale School of Drama, Linney's career has been nurtured primarily by the RESIDENT NONPROFIT PROFESSIONAL THEATRE outside New York and by OFF-BROADWAY, as well as by repertory theatres of Great Britain, Canada, Germany, and Austria. His critically acclaimed plays (numbering more than 40) include *The Sorrows of Frederick* (1967), *The Love Suicide at Schofield Barracks* (1972), *Holy Ghosts* (1976), *Childe Byron* (1978), *Tennessee* (1979; Obie Award, 1980), *Laughing Stock* (1984), *Woman without a Name* (1985), *Pops* (1986), *Three Poets* (1989), *Unchanging Love* (1991), *2: Göring at Nuremberg* (1992; 1995, PRIMARY STAGES), *Oscar Over Here* (1995, Duke U.), *Gint* (1998), *A Lesson before Dying* (2000, adapted from Ernest Gaines's 1993 novel), *Klonsky and Schwartz* (2005, ENSEMBLE STUDIO). Critic MARTIN GOTTFRIED has called Linney "a playwright of true literacy, a writer in the grand tradition," and MEL GUSSOW termed him "poet of America's heartland." In 1984 he received the Award in Literature and in 1999 the Award of Merit Medal for Drama from the American Academy and Institute of Arts and Letters. In 1991 he was appointed the first playwright-in-residence at NYC's SIGNATURE THEATRE, which opened its first full season with *The Sorrows of Frederick,* directed by Linney, and devoted the 1991–2 season to his plays (concluding with a new one, *Ambrosio,* in April). Linney is constantly developing plays, such as the recent *Shotgun* (Humana Festival, 1994), his first major play about contemporary people. He's also written the book for two operas: *The Death of King Philip* (1978) and *Democracy* (2005). He was awarded an Obie in 1992 for Sustained Excellence in Playwriting. His daughter is actress LAURA LINNEY. DBW

Lion King, The Musical play, based on the 1994 DISNEY film, with book by Roger Allers and Irene Mecchi, music by Elton John, and lyrics by Tim Rice. Director-designer JULIE TAYMOR wrote a detailed account of its evolution in 1997. (See the cross-references above, as well as GARTH FAGAN and NEW AMSTERDAM, for more on the production herein.) DBW

Lion of the West, The, by JAMES KIRKE PAULDING opened at the PARK THEATRE on 25 April 1831, after winning a $300 prize offered by JAMES H. HACKETT for a comedy with an American leading character. Paulding's hero was Nimrod Wildfire, a larger-than-life representation, "half horse, half alligator, a touch of the airth-quake," modeled loosely on DAVY CROCKETT and played by Hackett. Hackett's portrayal marked the first appearance of the backwoods character in a drama. Ironically, the play was not set on the frontier but in New York, as Wildfire visited his city relatives. In this satire the city represented greed and corruption while the backwoods stood for strength and honesty. JOHN AUGUSTUS STONE revised Paulding's work, and in 1833 WILLIAM BAYLE BERNARD adapted it for production in London, where it was called *The Kentuckian; or, A Trip to New York.* Hackett continued to play Wildfire for more than 20 years. RAH

Lippa, Andrew (1965?–) One of several promising, respected, but still largely unheralded musical-theatre composers, lyricists, and writers. Lippa is also a singer and producer. A graduate of the University of Michigan, he moved in 1987 to NYC, where in 1995 wrote the music and coauthored the book for *john & jen* (Lambs Theatre), and in 1999 he contributed three new songs to Broadway's *YOU'RE A GOOD MAN, CHARLIE BROWN.* However, his most prominent credit to date is the award-winning 2000 *The Wild Party* (book, music, and lyrics) which premiered at the MANHATTAN THEATRE CLUB. *A Little Princess*, for which he wrote the score, premiered at TheatreWorks in Palo Alto, CA, summer 2004. He often sings in concert and cabaret settings. DBW

Liptzin, Keni (1856–1918) YIDDISH actress. Survivor of a Eastern European childhood so unhappy that it provided the plot for GORDIN's melodrama *Hasye the Little Orphan Girl,* she went on the stage around 1882, performed in London, and arrived in New York in 1887. Although physically tiny, she was known for her commanding presence and intensity. With the help of her husband, Michael Mintz, a Yiddish newspaper man and publisher, she consistently chose to produce and star in plays by Gordin and other dramatists of literary worth rather than lighter entertainments. Her most famous role was as Gordin's *Mirele Efros* (*The Jewish Queen Lear*). NS

Lithgow, John (1945–) Stage, film, and television actor; author of children's books; painter; composer. Son of director and producer Arthur Lithgow. Stage appearances have included *The Changing Room* (1973, Tony), *My Fat Friend* (1974), *Beyond Therapy* (1982), *The Front Page* (1986), *Requiem for a Heavyweight* (1985), *M. BUTTERFLY* (1988), *Sweet Smell of Success* (2002, Tony), *The Retreat from Moscow* (2003), and *Dirty Rotten Scoundrels* (2005). In films Lithgow is best known for bizarre roles, from transsexual football players (*The World According to Garp*) to lunatic scientists (*The Adventures of Buckaroo Banzai . . .*), schizoid murderers (*Ricochet*), good/evil twins (*Raising Cain*). and deranged husbands (*Mesmerized*); but he played a bashful banker in *Terms of Endearment.* Recent films: *Kinsey* and *Life and Death of Peter Sellers* (both 2004). On television

he starred as Dick Solomon in the 1996–2001 NBC series *3rd Rock from the Sun.* In 2006 he was inducted into the THEATRE HALL OF FAME. DBW

Litt, Jacob (1860–1905) Producer who mounted popular melodramas for tours of the midwestern U.S. from his theatres in Milwaukee, WI. He managed midwestern operations for CHARLES FROHMAN and other Broadway producers, and built theatres in St. Paul and MINNEAPOLIS. A production of Charles T. Dazey's *In Old Kentucky* (1893) by Litt's STOCK COMPANY proved an extraordinary success and propelled Litt to the pinnacle of his career as owner and manager of the BROADWAY THEATRE, New York, which he acquired in 1899. Litt also owned MCVICKER'S THEATRE, Chicago, for a time. WD

Little Foxes, The Drawing from stories of her mother's southern family, LILLIAN HELLMAN created a three-act drama that revealed with devastating directness the ruthless greed of the Hubbard family. The play opened at NYC's National Theatre on 15 February 1939, directed by HERMAN SHUMLIN and starring TALLULAH BANKHEAD. It ran for 410 performances, was nominated for the Drama Critics' Circle Award, and was praised by critics for its Chekhovian style. The Hubbard brothers, Ben and Oscar, are so driven by ambition and greed that they sacrifice their morals for profit; but they are bested by their sister, Regina, who has married for money and who furthers her own ambition and eventually gains power over her brothers after she coldly refuses to give her husband his heart medicine and lets him die. The play is a classic of American theatre, performed countless times since its premiere. In 1949 it was the basis for an opera, *Regina*, by MARC BLITZSTEIN. A Broadway revival in 1967 starred ANNE BANCROFT, GEORGE C. SCOTT, and E. G. MARSHALL as the conniving sibs; one in 1981 starred Elizabeth Taylor as Regina; another in 1997, STOCKARD CHANNING. Hellman also wrote the screenplay for the 1941 RKO film, which starred Bette Davis. FB

Little Johnny Jones established GEORGE M. COHAN as playwright and star performer. This, his fifth full-length play, saved him financially, beginning a long-term partnership with producer SAM HARRIS. Supposedly inspired by American jockey Tod Sloan, the play depicts Jones dominating English racing until accused of throwing the Derby, a charge he disproves. Despite melodramatic devices, it was Cohan's most developed plot to date. Critical disfavor contrasted with strong public appeal of the play's chauvinism, typified by the songs "I'm a Yankee Doodle Dandy (The Yankee Doodle Boy)" and "Give My Regards to Broadway." It previewed in Hartford beginning 10 October, played 52 performances from 7 November 1904 at the Liberty Theatre, was revived twice in 1905, and toured successfully. A 1982 revival closed opening night.   RW

Little Mary Sunshine Two-act musical comedy with book, music, and lyrics by Rick Besoyan; opened OFF-BROADWAY at the ORPHEUM THEATRE (18 November 1959) for a run of 1,143 performances. Critics praised Eileen Brennan (Obie for Best Actress) in the first Off-Broadway show to feature an "original cast album." Set in the Rocky Mountains at the turn of the century, the musical depicts the antics of resident Indians, Forest Rangers, and young ladies of Eastchester Finishing School in a spoof of the archaic and sentimental operetta form seen in the RUDOLF FRIML–Herbert Stothart 1924 Broadway hit *ROSE-MARIE* and its screen version (1936) starring Jeanette MacDonald and Nelson Eddy. Despite its success, producers refused to move it to Broadway, thus indirectly encouraging the development of the Off-Broadway musical.   EK

Little Murders by JULES FEIFFER was first presented by the Royal Shakespeare Company at the Aldwych Theatre, London, on 3 July 1967. Christopher Morahan directed a cast including Derek Smith as Carol Newquist, Brenda Bruce as his wife, Marjorie, John Allison as their budding transvestite son, Kenny, Barbara Jefford as their daughter, Patsy (who is killed by a stray gunshot on her wedding day), and Derek Godfrey as Alfred Chamberlain, the man she marries. The play failed on Broadway in 1967, but was revived successfully OFF-BROADWAY in 1969 by ALAN ARKIN with a cast including LINDA LAVIN and VINCENT GARDENIA. Set on New York's Upper West Side during the 1960s, the play uses absurdist techniques to depict the grotesque state of urban life in a city overwhelmed by seemingly pointless crime. Feiffer also uses humor to critique marriage, the family, the moral relativism of the '60s, and the legal and law-enforcement systems.   BCM

Little Night Music, A Two-act musical comedy, music and lyrics by STEPHEN SONDHEIM, book by Hugh Wheeler; opened 25 February 1973 at the SAM S. SHUBERT THEATRE, running 601 performances. This musical adaptation of Ingmar Bergman's film *Smiles of a Summer Night* was the most conventional of the HAROLD PRINCE–Sondheim collaborations of the 1970s and the most widely popular. A bittersweet romance set in turn-of-the-century Sweden, it involves a complex game of interchanging romantic partners, all set to music that is mostly in variations on three-four waltz time. One notable aspect of the show was the onstage Leibesleider quintet, which narrates and comments on the action. The show, which won the Drama Critics' Circle and Tony awards for Best Musical, also introduced Sondheim's only popular "hit" song of the '70s, the ironic ballad "Send in the Clowns."   JD

Little Shop of Horrors, with book, lyrics, and direction by Howard Ashman and music by Alan Menken, was a musical adaptation of the 1960 Roger Corman film. Premiering 6 May 1982 at the WPA Theatre, it moved (still OFF-BROADWAY) and opened 27 July at the ORPHEUM THEATRE, produced by David Geffen and CAMERON MACKINTOSH, two powerful entertainment figures of the 1980s. The story, slight but humorous, concerns Seymour, a retiring flower shop clerk whose life changes when a plant responds to the taste of blood, grows to amazing size, and consumes his rivals. The musical is remembered for its pop score, Ellen Greene as coworker and love interest Audrey, and the amazing PUPPETRY required to make the plant devour people. JERRY ZAKS shepherded a "pleasant" 2003 revival.   KN

Little Theatre movement see COMMUNITY THEATRE/LITTLE THEATRE MOVEMENT

Livent, Inc. see DRABINSKY, GARTH

Living Newspaper Although antecedents can be identified, this term most frequently is associated with the FEDERAL THEATRE PROJECT. A DOCUMENTARY methodology was used, defining a problem and then calling for specific action. Bringing together both unemployed newspaper men and theatre personnel, presentations were written on such varied problems as housing, health care, labor unions, public utilities, cooperatives, natural resources, Negroes, and even the motion pictures. Six examples were produced by the New York unit, although the first – *Ethiopia,* on the war in Abyssinia – was canceled under pressure from the U.S. State Department. The three most successful attempts were by ARTHUR ARENT: *Triple-A Plowed Under,* on the need for farmers and consumers to unite for better incomes and cheaper food, which was a great success in 1936; *Power* (1937), a plea for public ownership of utilities; and

Arthur Arent's *Triple-A Plowed Under,* 1936, a Living Newspaper of the FTP, as produced in Chicago. Photo by Edmund Teske. *Courtesy:* Laurence Senelick Collection.

ONE-THIRD OF A NATION (1938), an exposé of urban housing conditions. Less successful were *1935,* a 1936 satire of the public's indifference to social issues, and *Injunction Granted* (1936), an account of labor's treatment in the courts. Units in other cities developed living newspapers on local problems, though few were produced. The techniques have been applied to more contemporary didactic theatre, such as the so-called Theatre of Fact begun in the 1950s.   DBW

living picture (*tableau vivant*) see NUDITY

Living Theatre (USA) When Julian Beck and his wife, Judith Malina, founded the Living Theatre in 1948, they inaugurated the experimental OFF-OFF BROADWAY movement in NYC. With one of the most influential and long-lasting avant-garde companies in American history, the Becks became the prophets of the burgeoning theatrical experimentation that was to explode during the 1960s.

From the very beginning, the Living Theatre sought the marriage of a political and aesthetic radicalism. "We insisted," Beck said, "on experimentation that was an image for a changing society. If one can experiment in theatre, one can experiment in life." This principle took a variety of shapes as the LT developed, but the Becks' anarchist-pacifist viewpoint remained a constant.

The Theatre began producing plays by Paul Goodman, GERTRUDE STEIN, García Lorca, Piran-

dello, Cocteau, and BRECHT, seeking an antirealism that could match the contemporary fervor in the visual arts and music. The group, which included JOSEPH CHAIKIN, did not find a permanent performance space until 1959 – and they lost it four years later when the Internal Revenue Service evicted them for nonpayment of taxes. Early landmark productions, from before this dispossession, were profoundly influenced by Artaud's *The Theatre and Its Double,* including Jack Gelber's *The CONNECTION* (1959), about heroin addicts awaiting a promised fix; Brecht's *Man Is Man* (1962); and Kenneth Brown's *The Brig* (1963), a detailed documentary of daily brutal routine in a U.S. Marine Corps brig in Japan, which was the company's last NYC production. Having defied IRS orders to leave its building, the LT gave its final performance of *The Brig* in a padlocked theatre; the audience had to enter by climbing in the windows.

From September 1964 to August 1968, the LT performed only in Europe, concentrating on works made up of exercises and improvisations, and created collectively. This experimentation culminated in *Paradise Now* (1968), a "spiritual and political voyage for actors and spectators."

A tour to the U.S. in 1968 helped convince the Becks that they no longer wanted to perform for a middle-class audience, but preferred to work in the streets with the people. After a brief return to Europe, the company went to Brazil in 1970 and stayed 13 months, experimenting with COLLEC-

TIVE creation before returning to the U.S. to work with coal miners and steel-mill workers in Pittsburgh. They then went back to Europe for further exploration of dramatic form and acting.

In 1984 the LT settled once again in New York. Since Julian Beck's death in 1985, the company has continued under the direction of Judith Malina and Hanon Reznikov. After more than 25 years, the LT found a home in Manhattan, a garagelike theatre on East 3rd St. – yet in 1993, after three and a half years, the LT was forced to vacate its East Village home due to occupancy regulations and once more took to the road, dividing its time between creating new works commissioned in Europe and performing them in NYC and on tour. A new home on the Lower East Side (Clinton St.) opened April 2007 with *The Brig*.

The Becks' works and ideas are described in Beck's 1972 book, *The Life of the Theatre,* and in Malina's *Diaries 1947–57* (1984).   AS

Lloyd, Norman (1914–) Actor-director, recognized today chiefly for his role of Dr. Auschlander on the 1980s TV series *St. Elsewhere*. During his long, distinguished theatrical career, Lloyd apprenticed with Eva Le Gallienne's Civic Repertory Theater (1932), played Japhet in *Noah* on Broadway (1935), appeared in three of the Federal Theatre Project's Living Newspapers (1936–7), and became a member of Orson Welles's Mercury Theatre. He played Fool in *King Lear* (1950, opposite Louis Calhern) and Lucio in *Measure for Measure* (1956, American Shakespeare Festival Theatre; 1957, Phoenix Theatre). Though slight in build, Lloyd most often portrayed heavies in his early career, especially onscreen. A stage, TV, and film director and producer, Lloyd staged or produced numerous serious dramatic works in the 1970s, mostly for PBS ("Hollywood Television Theatre"). His autobiography, *Stages,* was published in 1993.   DBW

Lloyd-Webber, Andrew see Webber, Andrew Lloyd

Lobel, Adrianne (1955–) Having trained with Ming Cho Lee, Lobel has become one of the most daring of the postmodern designers and is closely associated with director Peter Sellars. Together they have created controversial productions of *Cosí fan tutte* (1986, set in a roadside diner), *Nixon in China* (1987), *The Marriage of Figaro* (1988, set in Trump Tower), and *The Magic Flute* at Glyndebourne (1990, set in Southern California). Her sets are typified by bold uses of line and color to create dominant images with a humorous or ironic

sensibility. She has also worked extensively in regional theatre. Recent Broadway designs: *The Diary of Anne Frank* (1997), *On the Town* (1998), and *A Year with Frog and Toad* (2003).   AA

Loesser, Frank (1910–69) American composer and lyricist. After contributing songs to *The Illustrators' Show* (1936), Loesser spent 12 years in Hollywood writing the lyrics for numerous motion picture musicals. He returned to Broadway with the score for *Where's Charley?* (1948), a musical version of *Charley's Aunt*. Two years later Loesser wrote his most memorable songs for Guys and Dolls, an oft-revived musical based on Damon Runyan's short stories about tough but softhearted New York gamblers and their girlfriends. He then devoted four years to writing the score for The Most Happy Fella (1956; successfully revived on Broadway in 1992), an ambitious musical whose 30 songs ranged from operatic arias to typical Broadway specialty numbers. After a failure with *Greenwillow* (1960), Loesser wrote his last Broadway score for How to Succeed in Business without Really Trying (1961; Broadway revival, 1995), a satire on corporate politics and chicanery. Loesser also operated a musical publishing house, through which he furthered the careers of several young composers. His daughter Susan Loesser wrote a biography published in 1993.   MK

Loew, Marcus (1870–1927) Theatre owner and impresario, dubbed "the Henry Ford of show biz." Considered an honest and generous showman, Loew joined with David Warfield and, briefly, Adolph Zukor, in the penny-arcade business. In 1904 Loew and Warfield formed their own company, and Loew emerged as a pioneer in the emerging film industry. Subsequently, he added low-price vaudeville between pictures. At his death he controlled 300 entertainment venues, headed Metro–Goldwyn–Mayer Pictures, and was president of numerous vaudeville and booking companies.   DBW

Loewe, Frederick see Lerner, Alan Jay

Logan, Cornelius A(mbrosius) (1806–52) Actor and playwright. A popular comedian, mainly in the West and South, Logan also defended the theatre with a vigor later displayed in the work of his daughter Olive Logan. As a playwright, Logan wrote a few successful Yankee vehicle plays. He wrote *The Wag of Maine* (1834) for James Hackett, revising it as *Yankee Land* (1842) for Dan Marble, who portrayed Deuteronomy Dutiful, a talkative country bumpkin, in Logan's *The Vermont*

José Quintero's 1956 production of *Long Day's Journey into Night* with Florence Eldridge and Fredric March. *Courtesy:* Don B. Wilmeth Theatre Collection.

Wool Dealer (1838). Joshua Silsbee acted Lot Sap Sago in Logan's *The Celestial Empire; or, The Yankee in China* (1846). Logan wrote and acted successfully in *Chloroform* (1849), his last play.   WJM

Logan, Joshua (1908–88) Director, producer, and playwright associated with many of Broadway's most successful plays and musicals as director, coproducer, or coauthor (frequently all three): SOUTH PACIFIC (1949), for which he and coauthor OSCAR HAMMERSTEIN II received the Pulitzer Prize (1950); *The Wisteria Trees* (1950), based on CHEKHOV's *The Cherry Orchard* and written by Logan; *Wish You Were Here* (1952); and *Fanny* (1954). He was director and coproducer of *John Loves Mary* (1947) and PICNIC (1953). MISTER ROBERTS (1948) was directed by him and written with Thomas Heggen. Other plays and musicals exhibited Logan's skill as an inventive director: *On Borrowed Time* (1938), KNICKERBOCKER HOLIDAY (1938), MORN-ING'S AT SEVEN (1939), *Charley's Aunt* (1940 revival), *By Jupiter* (1942), ANNIE GET YOUR GUN (1946), and *Happy Birthday* (1946). He also directed the motion pictures BUS STOP (1956), *South Pacific* (1958), and CAMELOT (1967).

His apprenticeship began with the Triangle Club at Princeton and continued with the University Players. He married Nedda Harrigan (daughter of EDWARD HARRIGAN) and wrote two volumes of autobiography: *Josh* (1976) and *Movie Stars, Real People, and Me* (1978).   RM

Logan, Olive (1839–1909) Actress, lecturer, playwright, and daughter of CORNELIUS LOGAN. Like her sisters Eliza and Celia, Olive won respect as an actress, but she left the stage in 1866 to concentrate on writing. Having lived in England and France during 1857–63, she drew upon her experiences abroad in novels like *Chateau Frissac* (1862), memoirs like *Photographs of Paris* (1866), and in certain topics during her dozen years on the nationwide lecture circuit. AUGUSTIN DALY employed her to translate French plays and produced her *Surf* (1870) and *Newport* (1879). In lectures, articles, and pamphlets she called for equal rights for women while deploring "the leg business," which put scantily clad women on stage. Her major books were *Apropos of Women and Theatre* (1869), *Before the Footlights and Behind the Scenes* (1870), and *The Mimic World* (1871).   FHL

Lonergan, Kenneth (1963–) Manhattan-born playwright, screenwriter, and director, educated at Wesleyan (Connecticut) and NYU. After graduation he became a member of the theatre company Naked Angels, where his first plays were presented. His 2000 film *You Can Count on Me* (which he also directed and appeared in) brought him numerous awards and critical acclaim. Other films include *Analyze This* (1999), *The Gangs of New York* (2002, script doctor), and *Margaret* (2007; also directed). Lonergan moves seamlessly between stage and screen. His stage works have had strong accolades, from the OFF-BROADWAY version of *This Is Our Youth* (1998) to *The Waverly Gallery* (2000, Promenade; Pulitzer Prize runner-up in 2001), a semiautobiographical play with EILEEN HECKART in a role modeled on his grandmother, and *Lobby Hero* (2001) at PLAYWRIGHTS HORIZONS. He wrote and will direct a new work, *The Starry Messenger,* now scheduled for MANHATTAN THEATRE CLUB's 2007–8 season (with MATTHEW BRODERICK). He has also had success in London's West End. Lonergan is married to the exceptional actress J. SMITH-CAMERON.   DBW

Long Day's Journey into Night by EUGENE O'NEILL was first produced at the Royal Theatre, Stockholm. Its American premiere opened 7 November 1956, 16 years after the play's completion. Directed by JOSÉ QUINTERO and starring FREDRIC MARCH as James Tyrone, FLORENCE ELDRIDGE as his wife, Mary, JASON ROBARDS JR. as their son Jamie, and Bradford Dillman as their son Edmund, it ran for 390 performances and won O'Neill his fourth Pulitzer Prize. Actors such as Laurence Olivier, Timothy West, COLLEEN DEWHURST, GERALDINE FITZGERALD, CLAIRE BLOOM, ELLEN BURSTYN, BRIAN MURRAY, FRANCES STERNHAGEN, BRIAN DENNEHY, and Vanessa REDGRAVE have appeared in the play's many revivals since, including a major Broadway production in 2003. Generally considered O'Neill's finest play, it is an autobiographical account of the tragic family life of the four haunted Tyrones and their struggle to escape the effects of lost dreams and illusions through alcohol and morphine. Unable to confront the fact that her son Edmund has consumption, Mary resumes taking morphine after a temporary "cure" when the play begins. The play depicts the harrowing events of the next 16 hours, as each family member simultaneously drifts further into drug-induced oblivion and reveals his personal suffering to the audience.   BCM

Long Wharf Theatre (New Haven, CT) Founded in 1965 by JON JORY (who later left for ACTORS THEATRE of Louisville) and Harlan Kleiman, this RESIDENT NONPROFIT theatre, playing to more than 100,000 patrons annually, was under the leadership of ARVIN BROWN (1967–96) followed by DOUGLAS HUGHES (1997–2002). Today, the artistic director is Gorden Edelstein, who came to Long Wharf from A CONTEMPORARY THEATRE in SEATTLE. Known as an actor's theatre, Long Wharf, with two intimate performance spaces (487- and 199-seat capacities) in the New Haven Meat and Produce Terminal, emphasizes the production of new and established, home-grown and foreign works that explore human relationships. Though transference to New York is not a priority at LWT, more than 20 productions have made the move virtually intact, including *The Shadow Box*, STREAMERS, *The Changing Room*, *Sizwe Banzi Is Dead*, *The GIN GAME*, *Quartermaine's Terms* (Playhouse 91), *Broken Glass*, *Travels with My Aunt* (MINETTA LANE). *Wit* (UNION SQUARE THEATRE). and Broadway revivals of *AH, WILDERNESS!*, *ALL MY SONS*, *A VIEW FROM THE BRIDGE*, *AMERICAN BUFFALO*, and *Hughie*. LWT has won praise and numerous awards, including the MARGO JONES Medal (1966) for the production of new works, a special citation from the Outer Critics' Circle (1974), the JUJAMCYN THEATERS Award (1986), and a special Regional Theatre Tony Award (1978) for the quality of its productions as well as the stability of its organizational structure. In 2004 LWT announced the intent to build, over a five-year period, a new $30 million facility in a downtown location – a goal reiterated in 2007.   DBW

Long, William Ivey (1947–) Pennsylvania-born costume designer, educated at the College of William and Mary, Yale, and the University of North Carolina, known for his wide range of activities – arguably the busiest costume designer on Broadway (in the 2001–2 season he had seven shows running). He received the 1982 Tony, Maharam, and Drama Desk awards for his costume designs for *Nine,* the 1991 Obie for Sustained Excellence, the 1992 Tony for *Crazy for You,* the 2001 Drama Desk and Tony awards for *The PRODUCERS,* and the same awards in 2003 for *Hairspray.* Long's designs are seen in the theatre (SIX DEGREES OF SEPARATION, *Lend Me a Tenor;* Broadway revivals of *The Homecoming, Private Lives,* GUYS AND DOLLS; *TRUE WEST* [The PUBLIC]), opera (LEONARD BERNSTEIN's *A Quiet Place, Trouble in Tahiti*), rock concerts (Patti LaBelle, The Pointer Sisters, The Rolling Stones), and dance (TWYLA THARP, Paul Taylor, Peter Martins, GARTH FAGAN). In 2007 he designed the new KANDER AND EBB musical *Curtains* and is slated to design the new musical *Princesses.*   BO

Longacre Theatre 220 West 48th St., NYC [Architect: Henry B. Herts]. Built in 1913 by H. H. Frazee, a baseball magnate who liked to dabble in play production, the compact Longacre is ideally suited for small musicals and intimate comedies and dramas, which indeed have been its regular fare. Seating just over 1,000, it was leased to the SHUBERTS during the Depression and has since passed to their ownership. During 1944–53 it was used as a radio and television playhouse, but then it returned to play production and has remained a legitimate house since. Among its noteworthy tenants have been *PARADISE LOST* (1935), OSBORN's *On Borrowed Time* (1938), *Rhinoceros* (1961), *Ain't Misbehavin'* (1978; its longest-running tenant), CHILDREN OF A LESSER GOD (1980), and FOOTE's *The Young Man from Atlanta* (1997).   MCH

Look Homeward, Angel by Ketti Frings. Based on the novel by Thomas Wolfe, this emotional family drama set in 1916 focuses on 17-year-old Eugene Gant, whose artistic temperament and thirst for knowledge lead him to break free of the stifling atmosphere of his mother's boardinghouse. For the first production, director George Roy Hill set a style of speaking and movement that was "wild and frenetic without seeming to be uncontrolled" (BROOKS ATKINSON). Anthony PERKINS created the role of Eugene, Jo Van Fleet played his shrewd, domineering mother, ARTHUR HILL his doomed older brother, Ben, and Hugh Griffith his once-titanic father. Designed by JO MIELZINER, the play opened at the ETHEL BARRYMORE THEATRE 28 November 1957, ran for 564 performances, and won the Pulitzer Prize for Drama.   KF

Loos, Anita (1893?–1981) Actress, screenwriter, and playwright noted for her satiric comedies. Loos, who wrote some 200 scripts for both silent and sound movies, created the art of writing film captions, beginning with D. W. Griffith's silent films, such as *Intolerance* (1916). In 1926 she and her husband, John Emerson, dramatized her successful novel *Gentlemen Prefer Blondes.* Noted for Lorelei Lee, the stereotypical "dumb blonde," the play was made into a musical in 1949 by Loos and Joseph Fields. Throughout her career Loos wrote plays (*Happy Birthday,* 1946) and screenplays (*San Francisco,* 1936; *The Women,* 1939, based on CLARE BOOTHE's play); adapted the novels of Colette into American shows (*Gigi,* 1951; *Chéri,* 1959); and wrote witty, gossipy memoirs of her career in Hollywood (*A Girl Like I,* 1966; *Kiss Hollywood Good-bye,* 1974; *Cast of Thousands,* 1977). Gary Carey's biography of Loos appeared in 1988.   FB

Loquasto, Santo (1944–) Scenic and costume designer; master of both realistic detail (*LOST IN YONKERS,* 1991) and conceptual and theatricalist productions. Early Broadway and regional successes, such as THAT CHAMPIONSHIP SEASON and AMERICAN BUFFALO and later work including *Cafe Crown* (1989; Tony, sets) are almost photorealist in their painstaking detail. His work in the 1970s with the NEW YORK SHAKESPEARE FESTIVAL, especially at the outdoor Delacorte Theater, and his extensive work for dance, notably with TWYLA THARP and Mikhail Baryshnikov, emphasized sculptural and emblematic design and frequently included angular, large-scale, constructivistlike designs. Many of these tendencies came together in the Broadway musical *Grand Hotel,* which won him a 1990 Tony (costumes). His costumes possess the same detail, sense of color, and texture as his sets, and for dance he often designs costumes alone. Loquasto has worked frequently on films, notably with Woody Allen.   Recent work includes costumes for *RAGTIME* (1998); sets for *Movin' Out* (2002); and costumes and/or sets for revivals of *LONG DAY'S JOURNEY INTO NIGHT* (2003), *GLENGARRY GLEN ROSS* (2005), and *A TOUCH OF THE POET* (2005). In 2006 he designed the production of RICHARD GREENBERG's *Three Days of Rain* with Julia Roberts. Among his many awards are three Tonys (his first

was for *The Cherry Orchard,* 1977) and five Drama Desk Awards.   AA

Lord, Pauline (1890–1950) Actress who at 13 made her professional debut playing the maid in *Are You a Mason?* at the ALCAZAR THEATRE in San Francisco, her hometown. After years of touring engagements, she achieved New York success in *The Talker* (1912). Among her great roles were the downtrodden Sadie in *The Deluge* (1917), Anna in *ANNA CHRISTIE* (1921), Amy in *THEY KNEW WHAT THEY WANTED* (1924), and Nina in the touring production of *STRANGE INTERLUDE* (1928–9). Often compared to Duse, she conveyed – according to STARK YOUNG – "a subtle variety and gradation and shy power that are indescribable."   FHL

Lortel, Lucille (1900–98) Producer, known as "Queen of Off-Broadway." Born in New York, Lortel attended the American Academy of Dramatic Arts (1920) before studying in Germany with Arnold Korff and MAX REINHARDT. After a year in STOCK (1924), she made her Broadway debut in a minor role. Upon her marriage in 1931, she gave up the stage until 1947, when she offered her Westport, CT, barn for a dramatic reading. After two seasons of readings, she remodeled it into a functioning theatre, the White Barn Theatre, which served as a showcase for new talent and continued summer seasons until 2002 (it is now a museum). Lortel acquired New York's Theatre de Lys in 1955 as a transfer venue for worthy White Barn productions. Her first Theatre de Lys production, *The Threepenny Opera* – with LOTTE LENYA in the opening cast – ran for seven years. In 1956 she began offering a Matinee Series, which continued for 20 years. At both theatres she presented lesser-known plays by BRECHT, Ionesco, Genet, Mario Fratti, and ATHOL FUGARD, among others. The more successful presentations at the Theatre de Lys (rechristened the Lortel in 1981) include *Dames at Sea,* MAMET's *A Life in the Theatre,* BURIED CHILD, GETTING OUT, *Cloud 9, Woza Albert!,* and KRAMER's *The Destiny of Me.* She was a cofounder of the AMERICAN SHAKESPEARE FESTIVAL, and the recipient of the first MARGO JONES Award (1961) for her dedication to new plays as well as of the DRAMA LEAGUE's 1993 Unique Contribution to Theatre Award. She is the subject of a documentary film, *The Queen of Off-Broadway.* The OFF-BROADWAY Lucille Lortel Awards, established in 1986, are given annually in her honor.   In 2006 the foundation in her name made a \$2 million capital grant to the WESTPORT COUNTRY PLAYHOUSE to name the building adjacent to that theatre "The Lucille Lortel White Barn Center." A bio-bibliography was published in 1993 (by S. McCready), and a biography by Alexis Greene in 2004.   TLM

Los Angeles The city's first English-language theatrical performances were given in 1848 by the Seventh New York Volunteers in Don Antonio Coronel's 300-seat, open-air theatre. Stearns' Hall was the area's first commercial theatre (1859), and on 28 October 1860 the Stark Company from SAN FRANCISCO gave the first performance by a professional troupe, appearing in John Temple's remodeled hall in an upper story of the City Market. The three major houses of the late nineteenth century were the Merced Theatre (1870); the 1500-seat Grand Opera House (1884) built by Ozro Childs for over $100,000 (where EDWIN BOOTH grossed $14,046 in five performances during March 1888); and the New Los Angeles Theatre (1888), which served as the city's principal road-house during 1894–1903.

In the early 1890s, David S. Burbank, a dentist, built the Burbank Theatre and established a resident STOCK COMPANY; OLIVER MOROSCO took control (1899) and combined the roles of business manager with producing artistic director, during 1905–22 presenting not only IBSEN but 84 premieres, including PEG O' MY HEART and ABIE'S IRISH ROSE. PAGEANT plays became popular with John Steven McGroarty's *The Mission Play,* produced 1912–29 at the Mission San Gabriel Arcangel. Other pageants included *The Pilgrimage Play* (1920), an "authentic" life of Christ composed of dialogue from the New Testament, and *Ramona* (1923–80s), performed at the foot of the San Jacinto Mountains with a cast of 250.

Theatre prospered in the 1920s and led to the construction of the Biltmore, the El Capitan, the Belasco, the Vine Street Theatre (later renamed the Mirror, then the Huntington Hartford), the Hollywood Playhouse, and the Figueroa Playhouse.

In the 1930s, activity subsided because of the Depression and the advent of talkies, but there were exceptions: The Theatre Mart production of *The DRUNKARD* opened on 6 July 1933 and played 9,477 performances, closing on 17 October 1959; also, MAX REINHARDT's Hollywood Bowl production of *A Midsummer Night's Dream* (1934) [see SHAKESPEARE ON . . .], which included the Los Angeles Philharmonic playing the complete score by Mendelssohn, drew 150,000 people to seven performances.

During the 1940s, the Actors' Lab produced plays in a building behind Schwab's Drugstore before falling victim to the Tenney and House Un-American Activities committees; in 1947, JOHN HOUSEMAN directed CHARLES LAUGHTON in BRECHT's *Galileo* at the new Coronet Theatre. Debuts in the 1960s included Actors Studio West (1965), a branch of New York's ACTORS STUDIO; the EAST WEST PLAYERS (1965), a prominent Asian American troupe; the Globe Playhouse (1967), home of the Shakespeare Society of America; and Ron Sossi's Odyssey Theatre (1968). ACTORS' EQUITY instituted the Workshop Code (no advertising, no charge for admission, at least nine performances), but the actors rebelled, and in 1972 Equity established the Waiver, which allowed theatres seating up to 99 to charge admission for open-ended runs and hire Equity actors on nonunion contracts. This was revised in 1988 as the more heavily regulated "99-seat plan."

The 1970s saw the opening of the 1,824-seat SHUBERT Theatre (1972), a major roadhouse, as well as the creation of Teatro Intimo (1974), a Spanish-language company. Theatre in Los Angeles has for decades lived in the shadow of the film and television industries; commercial producers frequently engage the services of a prominent film star in order to market a production to the Los Angeles audience. Because many actors are reluctant to make long-term stage commitments that would preclude more lucrative work in front of a camera, resident theatres tend to cast each production separately rather than try to maintain a core company for even one season. Offerings in the 1980s and early 1990s included large touring musicals from New York, diverse subscription seasons by the large nonprofit companies, more daring fare from smaller troupes, plays presented by and for the city's larger ethnic minorities (basically HISPANIC, AFRICAN AMERICAN, and various ASIAN AMERICAN groups), and a wide variety of academic and amateur theatre.

Excellence in LA theatre began to be recognized in 1977 with *Drama-Logue* Critics Awards, joining the older LA Drama Critics Circle Awards (from 1969). The early years of the new millennium saw major changes in leadership at the CENTER THEATRE GROUP, founded in 1966 and arguably the best-known LA theatre complex of recent years. The GEFFEN PLAYHOUSE (1995) has become a major venue as well; yet another, and one that remains in limbo in the early 21st century, is the LOS ANGELES THEATER CENTER.   JDM

Los Angeles Theater Center began as the Los Angeles Actors' Theatre (1975) under Ralph Waite and Diane White, modeled after New York's PUBLIC THEATER. Within 10 years, the company presented more than 200 world, American, and West Coast premieres. In 1985 it moved to Spring St. in downtown Los Angeles to take over a remodeled bank building, where it adopted its present name under Artistic Director Bill Bushnell, who ran the group from 1978. Performance spaces included a 99-seat black box, a 296-seat proscenium house, a 323-seat thrust stage, and a 503-seat open stage. The typical season involved 14 plays, over half being world premieres, including works by LUIS VALDÉZ, DAVID HENRY HWANG, and ANNA DEAVERE SMITH. In 1989, the operating budget was $7.4 million. Special projects, which reflected the company's multicultural urban mission, included the Latino Theatre Lab (later Latino Theatre Company), the Black Theatre Artists Workshop, the Asian American Theatre Project, the Women's Project, and the Young Conservatory. In late 1991 its doors closed, denying the area of an important innovative company; its venues are currently rental spaces. As of 2007 the future of the 85,000-square foot building is uncertain, despite a large renovation grant secured by the Latino Theatre Company that is entangled in a legal squabble of gigantic proportions.   JDM

Lost in the Stars by MAXWELL ANDERSON and KURT WEILL; opened 30 October 1949 at the MUSIC BOX THEATRE for 273 performances. This successful adaptation of Alan S. Paton's *Cry, the Beloved Country* achieved operatic unity of action and music in a serious American drama. The play suggests hope amid the tragic irony and despair of apartheid when a black minister and a white landowner are united following the execution of the minister's promising son for killing the liberal son of the landowner. The 39-performance 1972 IMPERIAL THEATRE revival drew Tony nominations for Best Actor and Supporting Actor in a musical.   RW

Lost in Yonkers by NEIL SIMON, his 27th effort, a two-act comedy set in Yonkers in 1942; opened 21 February 1991 at the RICHARD RODGERS THEATRE. Following two failures (*Rumors,* 1988; *Jake's Women,* 1990 San Diego production), *Lost in Yonkers* was not only a critical success, despite a somewhat formulaic Simon ending, but garnered the award that had always eluded the playwright – the Pulitzer Prize (plus the Tony for Best Play and the Drama Desk Award). Unlike Simon's previous autobiographical plays, this darkest and most complex of his comedies pulls "the family itself out of shape" and turns "it into a grotesque version of itself" (in critic DAVID RICHARDS's words). The characters here are deeply disturbed, dominated by a tyranical German-Jewish grandmother (IRENE WORTH) who is given the responsibility of

superintending two grandsons while their father goes South to sell scrap iron. Directed by GENE SAKS (his seventh Simon staging) and designed by SANTO LOQUASTO, the production also starred MERCEDES RUEHL and KEVIN SPACEY as two of the old lady's children. Ruehl won the Tony for leading actress in a play, while Worth and Spacey garnered Tonys for featured roles.   DBW

Lotito, Louis A(nthony) (1900–80) Theatre manager and one of the most powerful theatre executives in New York. Lotito managed the Center Theatre in Rockefeller Center (1934), followed by the MARTIN BECK THEATRE (1938), and during 1943–67 served as President of City Playhouse, Inc., owners of Broadway theatres including the ANTA, HELEN HAYES, MARTIN BECK, and MOROSCO, as well as the NATIONAL THEATRE in Washington, DC. He also served as president of the ACTORS' FUND OF AMERICA (1969–80).   TLM

Loudon, Dorothy (1933–2003) Boston-born actress and singer who performed in VAUDEVILLE at the PALACE (1953), on early television (*The Garry Moore Show,* 1962–4), in NIGHTCLUBS (The Blue Angel and Flamingo Hotel), and in several Broadway plays before her triumph as Miss Hannigan in ANNIE (1977) brought rave reviews and a Tony, among other awards. "As the wicked Miss Hannigan, Dorothy Loudon, eyes bulging with envy, face sagging with hatred, is deliciously and deliriously horrid. She never puts a sneer, a leer or even a scream in the wrong place, and her singing has just the right brassy bounce to it" (CLIVE BARNES). Starring roles as Bea Asher in MICHAEL BENNETT's *Ballroom* (1978), Mrs. Lovett (succeeding ANGELA LANSBURY) in SWEENEY TODD (1980), and Cara Varnum in *The West Side Waltz* (1981), preceeded her triumph as the broken-down television comedian Dottie Otley in *Noises Off* (1983), which drew universal praise. Loudon also starred in *Jerry's Girls* (1985), *The MATCHMAKER* (1991, for ROUNDABOUT), and an early version of *Annie 2: Miss Hannigan's Revenge* (which closed out of New York in 1990). She has also toured widely, most prominently with DRIVING MISS DAISY and *Love Letters.*   TLM

Lowell, Robert [né Traill Spence Jr.] (1917–77) Pulitzer Prize–winning poet and playwright, considered by many the best English-language poet of his generation. He is best known for the trilogy of plays adapted from Nathaniel Hawthorne and Herman Melville, titled *The Old Glory* (*Benito Cereno; My Kinsman, Major Molineux;* and *Endecott and the Red Cross*), the first two parts of which premiered at the AMERICAN PLACE THEATRE in 1964. *Benito Cereno,* the most successful of the trilogy, was seen in 1967 at London's Mermaid. Lowell also adapted Racine's *Phèdre* (published 1960) and Aeschylus' *Prometheus Bound* (1966), the latter seen at the Mermaid in 1971.   DBW

Lubin, Barry (1953–) One of the most identifiable and lovable clowns working in American circuses today, known for his alter ego "Grandma" more than for his true persona (so much so that a protégé, Mark Gindick, is capable of stepping in when necessary). A graduate of the 1974 class of Ringling Bros. and Barnum & Bailey's Clown College, Lubin appeared for five seasons with the Greatest Show on Earth. Since 1982 he has been featured in 14 seasons of the Big Apple Circus, including 2005's "Grandma Goes to Hollywood." He has been director of clowning since 1999. In 2002 he was inducted into the International Clown Hall of Fame. Small in stature, Lubin as Grandma is immediately recognizable in his red dress, curly wig, pearls, and greasepaint with the large white grin.   DBW

Lucas, Craig (1951–) Playwright-screenwriter and actor. Born in Atlanta and educated at Boston University, Lucas, after singing in Broadway musical choruses for seven years, was one of the most produced American dramatists during the 1980s. *Reckless* (1983) and *Blue Window* (1984) both premiered OFF-OFF BROADWAY via The Production Company, and *Three Postcards* (1986) and *PRELUDE TO A KISS* (1987) at the SOUTH COAST REPERTORY in California. Each has had subsequent professional productions, including a Broadway run for *Prelude* in 1990, a 1996 MANHATTAN THEATRE CLUB production for *Blue Window,* a 1994 CIRCLE REP production of *Postcards,* and an MTC revival at the BILTMORE of *Reckless* in 2004. He wrote the words for an opera, *Orpheus in Love* (music by Gerald Busby) seen at CIRCLE IN THE SQUARE in 1992, and the book for the acclaimed *The Light in the Piazza* (2005; Tony nominations, Best Book and Musical; won Best Score). Other plays, all produced OFF-BROADWAY, include *Missing Persons, God's Heart, Stranger, The Dying Gaul, This Thing of Darkness* (with David Schulner), *Small Tragedy* (Obie), and a new translation of Strindberg's *Miss Julie.* Lucas has won numerous prizes, including Guggenheim and Rockefeller grants and the GLAAD Award for his screenplay *Longtime Companion* (1990), the first mainstream American film to deal directly with AIDS. In 2005 he was praised for his screenplay and direction of the film version of *The Dying Gaul.*   BBW

Lucas, Sam (1848–1916) Son of former slaves, Lucas rose from farmhand to become "dean of black theatricals." He came to New York City with the Original Georgia Minstrels in 1874 (see MINSTREL SHOW) and appeared in the Hyers Sisters' musical comedy *Out of Bondage.* He was the first authentic black in the title role of UNCLE TOM'S CABIN (1878) and headed up *The Creole Show* (1890) organized by Sam T. Jack. Lucas appeared in COLE AND JOHNSON's three musical comedies from 1897 to 1909. In the movie version of *Uncle Tom's Cabin* he allegedly was required as Uncle Tom to leap into a partially frozen river to save little Eva, catching the pneumonia that led to his death.   EGH

Luce, Clare Boothe see BOOTHE, CLARE

Luce, William (1941–) Born in Portland, OR, Luce is known for his ability to create dramatic portraits of celebrated figures, in particular Emily Dickinson in the ONE-PERSON play *The Belle of Amherst* (1976), which became the vehicle for JULIE HARRIS's fifth Tony. Harris also appeared in his solo piece *Lucifer's Child* (1991), about Isak Dinesen. *Barrymore* (1997) was a Tony-winning play for CHRISTOPHER PLUMMER. *Lillian* (1986) starred ZOE CALDWELL as LILLIAN HELLMAN. Others in his canon: *The Last Flapper* (1987, ALLEY THEATRE), *Brontë* (1988, San Francisco; with Harris), *Bravo, Caruso!* (1991, CLEVELAND PLAY HOUSE), *Nijinsky* (2000, Tokyo), and *Baptiste: The Life of Molière* (2001, HARTFORD STAGE).   DBW

Ludlam, Charles (1943–87) Actor, director, playwright, and an early member of John Vaccaro's Play-House of the Ridiculous, an OFF-OFF BROADWAY theatre that presented his *Big Hotel* (1967) and *Conquest of the Universe* (1967). Splitting with Vaccaro in 1967, Ludlam started his own theatre, The RIDICULOUS THEATRICAL COMPANY, where his plays included *Bluebeard* (1970), *Camille* (1973; revived 1990), *Stage Blood* (1974), *Professor Bedlam's Educational Punch and Judy Show* (1975), *Der Ring Gott Farblonjet* (1977), *Le Bourgeois Avant-Garde* (1983), and *The Mystery of Irma Vep* (1984). These plays combined popular and high-art forms, mixing colorful staging, scatological humor and FEMALE IMPERSONATION with plots and styles drawn from dramatic and operatic literature. Ludlam's treatments of *Hamlet,* Wagner's *Ring,* and *Camille* went beyond mere spoofing; his depth of involvement, he explained, gave rise to independent works that transcend parody. The Ridiculous Theatrical Company, one of the first New York theatres to deal explicitly with homosexual themes, often

Alfred Lunt and Lynn Fontanne as Petruchio and Kate in *Taming of the Shrew. Courtesy:* Don B. Wilmeth Theatre Collection.

featured Ludlam in female roles – which he didn't necessarily play campily. In 1984 Pittsburgh's American IBSEN Theatre invited Ludlam to play Hedda Gabler. *The Complete Plays of Charles Ludlam* (29 plays in all) was published after his death from AIDS in 1987, and a collection of his essays and opinions in 1992. A superb biography by David Kaufman was published in 2002.   AS

Ludlow, Noah Miller (1795–1886) Actor-manager who, with SOLOMON FRANKLIN SMITH, brought the legitimate theatre to the Ohio and Mississippi Valleys. First employed by SAMUEL DRAKE in 1815 to barnstorm in Kentucky, Ludlow formed his own company, playing New Orleans and remote corners of the South and West. In 1828 he joined T. A. COOPER as manager of the CHATHAM THEATRE in New York, but failed financially. With Smith, Ludlow formed the Ludlow and Smith Company (1835–53), building and operating theatres in Mobile, New Orleans, St. Louis, and other cities, engaging many of the leading stars of the day. The partnership dissolved in hostility: Smith's journals never mention his partner. Ludlow's autobiography, *Dramatic Life as I Found It* (1880), although bitter in condemnation of Smith, offers an unequaled factual account of the FRONTIER THEATRE in America.   SMA

Ludwig, Ken (1950–) Born in York, PA, and educated at Haverford College, Cambridge, and Harvard (law), Ludwig is a specialist in writing traditional, slapstick farces, from the backstage mayhem of *Lend Me a Tenor* (1989, ROYALE THEATRE) to less successful efforts such as *Moon over Buffalo* (1995, MARTIN BECK THEATRE), *Shakespeare in Hollywood* (2003, ARENA STAGE), *Leading Ladies* (2004, CLEVELAND PLAY HOUSE), and *Be My Baby* (2005, ALLEY THEATRE). He also wrote books for the Broadway musicals *Crazy for You* (1992), a hit, and *The Adventures of Tom Sawyer* (2001), a failure. He revised and tightened – and updated six years to 1938 – BEN HECHT and CHARLES MACARTHUR's *Twentieth Century* when it was revived on Broadway in 2004.   DBW

Luker, Rebecca (1961–) Born in Helena, AL, and reared in Birmingham, with a music degree from the University of Montevallo, this blond singer-actress has excelled in a handful of leading-lady roles in prominent musicals: debut in PHANTOM OF THE OPERA (1988; promoted in 1989 to Christine); Lily in *The Secret Garden* (1991); Magnolia in HAL PRINCE's revival of *SHOW BOAT* (1994); Fiona in New York City Opera's *BRIGADOON* (1996); Maria in the revival of *The SOUND OF MUSIC* (1998); Marian in the revival of *The MUSIC MAN* (2000); as a replacement Claudia in *Nine* (2003); and as Winifred Banks in *Mary Poppins* (2006). Appearances in concert, with regional theatres (including Clara in *Passion* for the 2002 KENNEDY CENTER's SONDHEIM Celebration), on television, and in recordings are frequent.   DBW

Lunt, Alfred (1892–1977) and **Lynn Fontanne (Lillie Louise)** (1887–1983) Actors. Alfred Lunt became a star as the oafish lead in BOOTH TARKINGTON's *Clarence* in 1919. Lynn Fontanne's first major role was as the dizzy matron addicted to clichés in KAUFMAN and CONNELLY's 1921 satire *DULCY*. It wasn't until they appeared together, two years after their marriage, in the THEATRE GUILD's sparkling 1924 production of *The Guardsman,* Molnár's droll comedy of sexual intrigue, that their reputations and the future course of their career were ensured. From then on they were known as the Lunts and, until their farewell in *The Visit* in 1958, had what was probably the most successful acting partnership of the 20th century. Audiences, critics, and fellow actors were delighted by the charged intimacy of their dual performances; their good friend Noël Coward quipped that they were really one person. Though every gesture and fraction of a pause was scrupulously intentioned, the Lunts created the illusion of spontaneity. To later generations they came to represent an outmoded stylized tradition, over-deliberate and genteel, but in their heyday they were thought to have introduced a new American style. They broke with old-fashioned Broadway acting techniques by playing comedy in a conversational way, their love scenes were startlingly physical, and their overlapping method of speaking their lines – at times they seemed to be talking simultaneously – surprised audiences of the 1920s.

Individually, each had a few notable achievements in dramas: Fontanne was the original Nina Leeds in STRANGE INTERLUDE (1928), a role she professed not to understand, and Lunt was memorable when cast against type as a tough-talking bootlegger in SIDNEY HOWARD's *Ned McCobb's Daughter* (1926); but it was in a high comedy that they excelled. Their favorite playwrights, ROBERT E. SHERWOOD and S. N. BEHRMAN, provided them with vehicles in which the war between the sexes is a duel of wit and sly, charming manipulation. Highlights of their career include Behrman's *The Second Man* (1927), *Amphitryon 38* (1937), and *I Know My Love* (1949); Sherwood's *Reunion in Vienna* (1931), IDIOT's DELIGHT (1936), and *There Shall Be No Night* (1940); Sil-Vara's *Caprice* (1928); a rollicking *Taming of the Shrew* (1935), noted more for its vaudevillian spirits than for its poetry; *The Seagull* (1938); and Coward's *Design for Living* (1933). They became so closely identified with cosmopolitan comedy that producers as well as audiences were reluctant to let them try anything else; at the end of their career the Lunts expressed regret that they hadn't been asked to do such plays as DEATH OF A SALESMAN and LONG DAY's JOURNEY INTO NIGHT.

The Lunts were renowned among actors for their dedication (holding rehearsals for minor adjustments on the last day of a run) and for their career-long devotion to "the road" (playing more one-night stands in remote towns than any other stars). They were also remarkable for their lack of greed: Unlike other stage stars, they resisted Hollywood except for one unhappy venture in 1931, when they made a film of *The Guardsman*. (Fontanne had played a bit role in *Second Youth*, a 1924 silent starring Lunt – before their joint success.) They could have commanded higher salaries from independent producers, but maintained their loyalty to the Theatre Guild. In 2003 their home in southwestern Wisconsin, "Ten Chimneys," was opened to the public as a museum and arts center. Their lives have been told by Jared Brown (1986) and Margot Peters (2003).   FH

Lunt–Fontanne Theatre 205 West 46th St., NYC [Architects: Carrere and Hastings]. Producer CHARLES DILLINGHAM achieved the hallmark of success when he was able to build a theatre for his own productions in 1910. Originally known as the Globe, the Renaissance-style structure also housed his offices and apartments where he could entertain his stars and backers. In 1931, Dillingham lost his theatre, which was bought by a movie chain. It was reclaimed in 1958 by new owners, who then completely renovated it and renamed it the Lunt–Fontanne for the famous husband-and-wife acting team. The entrance, which was originally on Broadway, was diverted to West 46th St. The first production in the restored house was the American premiere of Friedrich Dürrenmatt's *The Visit*, starring the eponymous LUNTS. The theatre is now owned by the NEDERLANDER Organization, who, in 1999 renovated it once more and set the stage for the continued long run of *Beauty and the Beast*, which transferred from the PALACE there the same year.
MCH

LuPone, Patti (1949–) Actress. Born in Northport, NY, LuPone studied acting at the Juilliard School, graduating in 1972. A founding member of the ACTING COMPANY, she demonstrated her versatility in a variety of roles before her portrayal of the title character in EVITA (1979) won her a Tony Award and established her career. Subsequently, she appeared in *The Woods* (1982, SECOND STAGE), *The CRADLE WILL ROCK* (1983, Acting Company), as Nancy in *Oliver!* (1984), and in *Accidental Death of an Anarchist* (1984) before creating Fantine in LES MISÉRABLES (1985, London), winning an Olivier Award for Best Actress in a Musical. In 1987 (at the VIVIAN BEAUMONT) she played Reno Sweeney in ANYTHING GOES (Drama Desk Award). She then created Norma Desmond in the London *Sunset Boulevard* (1993), won an Outer Critics Circle Award for *Patti LuPone on Broadway* (1995), replaced ZOE CALDWELL in MCNALLY's *Master Class* (1996), appeared as Jolly in MAMET's *The Old Neighborhood* (1997), as Dotty in the 2001 revival of *Noises Off,* and created another concert (*The Lady with the Torch*) in the 2004–5 season. In 2005 she won critical acclaim (and a Tony nomination) as Mrs. Lovett in John Doyle's unique staging of the Broadway revival of SWEENEY TODD. She has also ventured into opera.   TLM

Luv by MURRAY SCHISGAL, starring ANNE JACKSON, ELI WALLACH, and ALAN ARKIN, opened at NYC's BOOTH THEATRE on 11 November 1964

under the direction of MIKE NICHOLS. This two-act comedy combines a number of styles, including farce, comedy of manners, VAUDEVILLE, and low comedy, as it hints at absurdist drama as well. As marriages are made and unmade between two men and a woman, each ends up with greater misunderstandings and problems, and the play ends in an apparent circular pattern just as nonsensical as it had begun. In 1984 it was adapted into the musical *Love*, revived in 1991 as *What about Luv?* at the York Theatre on NYC's Upper East Side.   ER

Lyceum see CHAUTAUQUA

Lyceum Theatre Theatre at 149 West 45th St., NYC; designed by the architectural firm of Herts and Tallant for manager DANIEL FROHMAN. Originally known as the New Lyceum to distinguish it from Frohman's earlier playhouse on 4th Ave. and 23rd St,, the theatre opened on 2 November 1903 with a performance of *The Proud Prince,* starring E. H. SOTHERN. Under Frohman's management, the Lyceum was the home of first-class productions; it suffered a serious decline during the Depression, however, and was in danger of being torn down in 1939 when it was purchased by a group of investors that included playwrights GEORGE S. KAUFMAN and MOSS HART and producer MAX GORDON. In 1945 the investors sold the Lyceum, and it is presently owned by the SHUBERT ORGANIZATION. During the late 1960s it was leased to the APA–Phoenix Repertory Company (see ASSOCIATION OF PRODUCING ARTISTS).

The Lyceum seats approximately 900 and contains the most extensive complex of scene shops of any Broadway theatre, as well as an elaborate penthouse apartment. The penthouse is currently the home of the Shubert Archive, a collection of materials related to the history of the Shubert Organization. The Lyceum, the oldest Broadway theatre still in continuous operation, was declared a landmark in 1975. For much of the 1990s it was home to the NATIONAL ACTORS THEATRE founded by Tony Randall, and in 2003 housed the Pulitzer Prize–winning *I AM MY OWN WIFE.*   BMcN

Lynch, Thomas (1953–) Asheville, NC–born scenic designer who studied at Yale (B.A., M.F.A.) and has been active in major regional theatres, including the GOODMAN and SEATTLE REP, and opera companies including the Metropolitan Opera and the Seattle Opera, where he collaborates frequently with Stephen Wadsworth. He received Tony nominations for *The HEIDI CHRONICLES* (1989) and *The MUSIC MAN* revival (2000). Designs for LEONARD BERNSTEIN's *A Quiet Place*, for the Vienna State Opera, were included in the 1987 Prague Quadrennial Scenography Exhibition. Designer of the OFF-BROADWAY production and national tour of *DRIVING MISS DAISY,* he was named in 2005 the inaugural Floyd and Delores Jones Professor of the Arts at the University of Washington.   BO

M

M. Butterfly The first play by an ASIAN AMERICAN to win a Tony Award, this enigmatic two-act drama by DAVID HENRY HWANG debuted at the EUGENE O'NEILL THEATRE 20 March 1988 and ran 777 performances. JOHN DEXTER directed; JOHN LITHGOW and B. D. WONG starred. It also won the Drama Desk, JOHN GASSNER, and Outer Critics Circle awards, and toured nationally. Set in Beijing from the 1960s to the '80s, and loosely based on a true incident, the plot is a sly reversal of the Madame Butterfly story. It tracks the cross-cultural love affair between René Gallimard, an insecure French diplomat, and Song Liling, a Chinese Opera "actress" – really a Maoist male spy posing as a woman. A series of impressionistic flashbacks reveal how Gallimard is duped by his own chauvinistic assumptions. Asian theatrical sensibilities and Western dramaturgy are fused into an intricate meditation on the tensions between the sexes, East and West, truth and fantasy, art and authenticity. Hwang has called the play "an extreme example of the self-delusion any of us go through when we fall in love."   MB

Ma Rainey's Black Bottom The first (1984) of AUGUST WILSON's 20th-century cycle of plays on the black experience (one for each decade) to reach Broadway. The action takes place in 1927 Chicago, where the relationships between black musicians and white managers in the confined space of a recording studio symbolize the oppressive nature of the larger society outside. Gertrude "Ma" Rainey (Theresa Merritt), reigning queen of the blues, insists on maintaining the integrity of her music while Levee (Charles S. Dutton), an ambitious and volatile trumpeter in her band, turns to violence out of frustration. The play was first produced at the YALE REPERTORY THEATRE by artistic director LLOYD RICHARDS before moving to the CORT THEATRE on Broadway and winning the Drama Critics' Circle Award (and being nominated for a Best Play Tony). The cordial and productive relationship between playwright and director has served Wilson well in his later plays. It was disappointingly revived on Broadway in 2003 with WHOOPI GOLDBERG.   EGH

Mabou Mines A collaborative, experimental theatre company, established formally in 1970 after years of collaborative work among founding members JOANNE AKALAITIS, LEE BREUER, Frederick Neumann, and RUTH MALECZECH in SAN FRANCISCO, and later in Europe with Philip Glass and DAVID WARRILOW. It was named for a community in Nova Scotia near which *The RED HORSE ANIMATION* was created. The company has developed a formal performance style that synthesizes traditional motivational acting, narrative techniques, and mixed media – revealing the influence of the group's regular collaboration with painters, sculptors, video artists, filmmakers, and composers. Though this distinctive acting style is

Theresa Merritt as blues singer Ma Rainey in August Wilson's *Ma Rainey's Black Bottom,* Yale Rep, 1983. Photo by George G. Slade. *Courtesy:* Yale Repertory Theatre.

always evident in Mabou productions, the group's directors leave their own particular stamps. Breuer's *The Red Horse Animation* (1970), *The B. Beaver Animation* (1974), and *The Shaggy Dog Animation* (1978) are theatrically clever and inventive, funny and self-reflexive; as opposed, for instance, to Akalaitis's ironically romping DEAD END KIDS (1980) or her hyperreal production of Kroetz's *Through the Leaves* (1984). In addition to creating original works, Mabou is considered one of the foremost interpreters of Samuel Beckett: Its influential productions of *The Lost Ones, Play, Come and Go, Cascando,* and *Company* combine narration and elaborate visual spectacle. In all, eight pieces by Beckett have been produced, six of them world premieres of text not originally written for the theatre. More recent productions include a gender-reversed *Lear* (1990), Frederick Neumann's *Reel to Real* (1994), *Peter and Wendy* (1996), *Animal Magnetism* (2000), *Ecco Porco* (2001), *Mabou Mines DollHouse* directed by Breuer (2003), *Red Beads* (2005). In residence for three years at LA MAMA, Mabou has performed at the NEW YORK SHAKESPEARE FESTIVAL and elsewhere (The KITCHEN, PERFORMANCE SPACE 122, etc.) since 1975. In 1986 they received an Obie for Sustained Achievement, one of many awards since 1974.   AS

McAnuff, Des (1952–) Artistic director of the LA JOLLA PLAYHOUSE from 1983 until 1994 (replaced by MICHAEL GREIF) who returned to this position in 1999, announcing his departure again for April 2007. (In 2008 he is to become one of three artistic directors of Ontario's Stratford Festival.) He also is a freelance director. A playwright, composer, and director in Toronto in the early 1970s, McAnuff moved to New York (1976) to become associate director and literary manager of the CHELSEA THEATER CENTER. He cofounded DODGER THEATRICALS at the BROOKLYN ACADEMY OF MUSIC (1978) and joined briefly the faculty of the Juilliard School (1979). Artistically, he directed a new version of his own *Leave It to Beaver Is Dead* for the NEW YORK SHAKESPEARE FESTIVAL'S PUBLIC THEATER (179), staged *Henry IV, Part 1* in the Festival's Delacorte Theater in August 1981, and became artist-in-residence at the Festival for the 1981–2 season. McAnuff is best known as the director of musical productions developed at La Jolla and elsewhere and transferred to Broadway, including *The Who's Tommy* (also coadapted; NYC, directing Tony and Drama Desk awards, 1993), the revival of *HOW TO SUCCEED IN BUSINESS WITHOUT REALLY TRYING* (NYC, 1995), *URINETOWN* (2001), and the smash hit *Jersey Boys* (2005). His direction of *Big River* (1985) for Dodger Theatricals won him

a Tony. Dodger's 2004 *Dracula, the Musical* was a rare failure for him.   JDM

MacArthur, Charles (1895–1966) Playwright. A Chicago newspaperman who collaborated with BEN HECHT, another Chicago newspaperman, on their most famous play, *The FRONT PAGE* (1928), a farcical caricature of newspaper life. Before this, he had collaborated with EDWARD SHELDON on *Lulu Belle* (1926), about a black courtesan, and with SIDNEY HOWARD on *Salvation* (1928), about a woman evangelist; both are weak melodramas. The partnership with Hecht also produced *Twentieth Century* (1932), a broad comedy on theatre people; *Jumbo* (1935), a circus musical; *Ladies and Gentlemen* (1939), a murder mystery that served as a vehicle for his wife, HELEN HAYES; and *Swan Song* (1946), a suspense melodrama. Alone, he wrote *Johnny on a Spot* (1942), a political satire. He also did some screenwriting. Hecht published a biography of MacArthur in 1957.   TP

Macauley, Barney (1837–86) Actor and manager. Beginning his career as an actor in Buffalo, NY (1853), he became a leading actor in the Ohio Valley in 1861, and made his NYC debut opposite MATILDA HERON during 1864–5. He entered management in partnership with John Miles of Cincinnati (1868–72), and in 1872 assumed solo management in Louisville, KY, where he had always been popular. He built his MACAULEY'S THEATRE there in 1873; in 1878 he turned the management over to his brother, John, spending the rest of his career as the star of his own combination playing a rural melodrama, *The Messenger from Jarvis Section*.   DMcD

Macauley's Theatre (Louisville) Seating 1,800, it was the leading theatre in town when it opened in 1873. Its STOCK COMPANY was disbanded in 1878, and it became a combination house under BARNEY MACAULEY's brother, John. After 1880 it was part of the circuit organized by George Dickson, though John Macauley bought it from his brother's creditors in 1881. The last live performance staged there was in 1925.   DMcD

MacBird! by Barbara Garson. The Obie-winning (for its title actor) satire opened 22 February 1967 and, despite negative reviews, ran 386 performances at New York's Village Gate, CIRCLE IN THE SQUARE, and Garrick Theatre (Bleecker St.). Directed by Roy Levine, replaced a few weeks before opening by GERALD FREEDMAN, the play uses Shakespeare's *Macbeth* to blame Lyndon Johnson for President Kennedy's death. The cast included STACY KEACH (Macbird), Rue McClanahan (Lady Macbird), William Devane (Robert Ken O'Dunc), and Paul Hecht (John Ken O'Dunc).   REK

McCann, Elizabeth (Ireland) (1931–) and **Nelle Nugent** (1939–) Producers who met while working for JAMES NEDERLANDER. McCann came to Nederlander in 1967 with a law degree and experience with other producers; Nugent came in 1971 after a decade of stage managing. In 1976, they formed McCann & Nugent Productions, one of the most successful firms in New York until its dissolution in 1987. By 1985, when Nugent went to California to produce film and television, the team had earned 58 Tony nominations and 20 awards for their 22 Broadway productions. Their most successful shows included *Dracula* (1977 revival), *The* ELEPHANT MAN (1979), *Amadeus* (1980), MORNING'S AT SEVEN (1980 revival), *Mass Appeal* (1981), *Nicholas Nickleby* (1981), *The Dresser* (1981), CRIMES OF THE HEART (1981), and HOWE's *Painting Churches* (1983, The Lamb's). In 1978, they became general managers of the VIVIAN BEAUMONT THEATRE. Working together harmoniously, McCann handled the overview (contracts, marketing) and Nugent the details (designers, crews). They were closely involved in all their projects, and worked effectively with the feuding Nederlander and SHUBERT ORGANIZATIONS. As women lacking established financial backers, their success was unusual. Nugent is now managing and general partner of Foxboro Entertainment in California, and she coproduced the 2004 Broadway revival of *Sly Fox*. McCann still produces theatre in New York: ALBEE's *Three Tall Women* (1994, Promenade), *The* GOAT, OR WHO IS SYLVIA? (2002), and the 2005 revival of WHO'S AFRAID OF VIRGINIA WOOLF?; *Copenhagen* (2000); LISA KRON's *Well* (2006). The two briefly reunited in 2002 to produce Michele Lowe's *The Smell of the Kill*.   TH-S

McCarter Theatre Center for the Performing Arts Located on the campus of Princeton University (NJ) and built originally in 1929 as home for Princeton's Triangle Club, the theatre, with over 1,000 seats, became a favorite in the 1930s and '40s for pre-Broadway tryouts and post-Broadway tours. (OUR TOWN and BUS STOP premiered there.) In 1973 the Center became a nonprofit corporation with a RESIDENT theatre company presenting a core of five productions annually (with more than 200 presentations at the Center each year). New play development and international exchange have been key ingredients in McCarter programming. Artistic heads began with Milton

Lyon, Arthur Lithgow, and MICHAEL KAHN. In 1990 playwright-director EMILY MANN succeeded Nagle Jackson as artistic director, offering as her inaugural production (January 1991) *The* GLASS MENAGERIE with SHIRLEY KNIGHT. Under Mann the McCarter has gained national recognition; in 1994 it received a Tony for outstanding regional theatre. Recent productions that have gained further recognition include RUBEN SANTIAGO HUDSON's *Lackawanna Blues* (2001), NILO CRUZ's *Anna in the Tropics* (2003), and CHRISTOPHER DURANG's *Miss Witherspoon* (2005). In 2003 the ROGER S. BERLIND Theatre opened, a 350-seat venue designed by Hugh Hardy.   DBW

McCaull, John A. (c. 1845–94) Scottish-born impresario of American comic opera in the 1880s. From soldiering for the South during the Civil War, McCaull turned to theatre as a promoter and producer. FRANCIS WILSON suggests that "he had been trained to the law" and, after "defending some theatrical suit," found a career in the theatre. He established the McCaull Opera Comique Company, with branches in Philadelphia, Washington, DC, and New York. He produced the operettas of American composers, including John Philip Sousa and the team of HARRY B. SMITH and REGINALD DE KOVEN, and presented imported European opéras bouffes. Comic opera stars Marion Manola, Lilly Post, Francis Wilson, and JEFFERSON DE ANGELIS worked with McCaull in their early days.   TLM

McClendon, Rose (1884–1936) African American actress who became totally committed to theatre after winning a scholarship to the AMERICAN ACADEMY OF DRAMATIC ART. Playing her first professional role in Galsworthy's *Justice* (1919), she advanced steadily to the top of the profession, holding lead roles on Broadway in PAUL GREEN's 1926 Pulitzer Prize play IN ABRAHAM'S BOSOM and in DOROTHY AND DUBOSE HEYWARD's melodrama *Porgy* (1929; see PORGY AND BESS), in which she was called "the perfect aristocrat of Catfish Row." Known on Broadway as the "Negro race's first lady," she used her influence with the union to promote the needs of fellow black actors. In 1935 she cofounded the Negro People's Theatre and appeared as Cora in LANGSTON HUGHES's long-running melodrama MULATTO, from which she withdrew in ill health, dying the following year.   EGH

McClintic, Guthrie (1893–1961) Actor, director, and producer. Born in Seattle, McClintic studied acting at the AMERICAN ACADEMY OF DRAMATIC

ARTS before making his first stage appearance in 1913, and his New York debut at the end of that year. During the 1915–16 season, he appeared in numerous roles with GRACE GEORGE's Company at the PLAYHOUSE THEATRE, followed by a 10-year association with producer WINTHROP AMES. McClintic began his career as a director and producer in 1921 by presenting A. A. Milne's *The Dover Road*. In the same year he married actress KATHARINE CORNELL and began a long professional association with her as the director of her major successes. Recognized as one of the most distinguished directors in the American theatre, McClintic staged more than 90 productions, including the Pulitzer Prize–winning *The Old Maid* (1935) and *WINTERSET* (1935), which won the New York Drama Critics' Circle Award. His other major credits include *The Barretts of Wimpole Street* (1931); *Yellow Jack* (1934); *Ethan Frome* and *The Wingless Victory* (1936); *High Tor* and *Candida* (1937); *NO TIME FOR COMEDY* and *Key Largo* (1939); *The Doctor's Dilemma* (1941); *You Touched Me* (1945); *The Playboy of the Western World* (1946); *Antony and Cleopatra* (1947); *Life with Mother* (1948); *Medea* (1948–9, tour); *The Constant Wife* (1951); and *Bernadine* (1952). He was known for casting his shows wisely and knowing how to get the most out of his actors. BROOKS ATKINSON called McClintic "one of our most accomplished directors, especially for plays that depend on taste and elegance."   TLM

McCloskey, James J. (1825–1913) Actor, playwright, manager. For some time the manager of the Park Theatre in Brooklyn, the Canadian-born McCloskey was best known as a playwright. His action-packed melodramas, such as *ACROSS THE CONTINENT* (1870), which starred Oliver Doud Byron, and *Jesse James, The Bandit King* (1881), which he wrote for James H. Wallick, often drew on his California mining experiences. It was said that five of McCloskey's dramas once played in five New York theatres at the same time. In addition to this theatrical activities, McCloskey served for 35 years as clerk of the City Court of New York.   RAH

McCree, Junie [née Gonzalvo Macrillo] (1866–1918) Vaudevillian and writer. As a member of the Bella Union STOCK COMPANY in SAN FRANCISCO, McCree worked out the "dope fiend" character he played with great success on the variety stage in the sketch "Sappho in Chinatown." He was elected Big Chief of the early VAUDEVILLE union The White Rats, directing its strike in 1916. After opening an agency in New York, McCree became the most sought-after writer in vaudeville

and BURLESQUE, supplying sketches and patter for hundreds of acts. His material, including such standards as "Roxie" and "The Traveling Salesman," launched slang and catchphrases (e.g., "coffin nails" for cigarettes) that became part of the American vernacular, but lexicographers have never given him the credit he deserves.   LS

McCullers, (Lula) Carson (1917–67) Novelist, poet, and playwright whose 1950 dramatization of her novel *The MEMBER OF THE WEDDING* was acclaimed, and later successfully filmed and televised. A musical version, *F. Jasmine Addams*, was staged in 1971 (CIRCLE IN THE SQUARE). Although other playwrights dramatized her novels (e.g., ALBEE's *The Ballad of the Sad Cafe*, 1963), McCullers's only other play was *The Square Root of Wonderful* (1957). A biography by Virginia Spencer Carr was published in 1975 (repr. 2003).   FB

McCullough, John (1832–85) Irish-born actor who made his stage debut at the ARCH STREET THEATRE in Philadephia in 1857 in *The Belle's Stratagem*. He subsequently toured with E. L. DAVENPORT (1860–1) and EDWIN FORREST (1861–5). A tall, classically handsome man in the heroic mold, McCullough's volatile, physically robust acting style resembled Forrest's. After the latter's death in 1872, he assumed several of Forrest's major roles, including Spartacus in *The Gladiator*, Virginius, and Jack Cade. He also excelled as Othello, King Lear, Coriolanus, and Mark Antony. During 1866–77 he managed the CALIFORNIA THEATRE in SAN FRANCISCO, for the first four years in association with LAWRENCE BARRETT. A heavy financial loss forced his retirement from management, and he spent the rest of his career as a successful touring star. In 1881 he made a brief starring engagement at London's Drury Lane, appearing as Virginius and Othello. In 1883, his health declined; in the summer of 1885, he was placed in a mental institution.   DJW

McCullough, Paul see CLARK, BOBBY

McDonald, Audra (Ann) (1970–) Within a decade, this extraordinary singer-actor received four Featured Actress Tony awards: for Carrie Pipperidge in the 1994 revival of *CAROUSEL*, for Sharon in *Master Class* (1995; Tony 1996), for *Sarah* in *RAGTIME* (1998), and in 2004 for her Ruth Younger in the revival of *A RAISIN IN THE SUN*. Other notable roles include the title character in the musical *Marie Christine* (1999, Tony nomination), although the show failed; Lady Percy in *Henry IV* (2003, VIVIAN BEAUMONT); and on HBO, Susie Monahan in

Wit (2001; Emmy nomination). She appears frequently in concert and on recordings (three solo albums), including a solo concert in the *Divas at the Donmar* series (London; aired on PBS 2002). Her Carnegie Hall debut was in 1998 with Michael Tilson Thomas and the San Francisco Symphony; another Carnegie appearance in 2006 was critically acclaimed.

Born in Berlin, Germany, McDonald grew up in Fresno, CA, and performed often as a young actress, including regionally as Aldonza in MAN OF LA MANCHA. A 1993 graduate of Juilliard, this mezzo-soprano received her classical vocal training there; ironically, her vocal power makes finding parts for her large talent difficult in today's musical theatre.   DBW

MacDonald, Christie (1875–1962) Singer and actress who began her career in a summer theatre in Boston, and by 1892 was singing supporting roles in the FRANCIS WILSON Opera Company. Her first starring role was in *Princess Chic* (1900), after which she appeared in a succession of comic operas, including *The Toreador* (1902), *The Sho-Gun* (1904), *The Belle of Mayfair* (1906), *Miss Hook of Holland* (1907), and *The Prince of Bohemia* (1910). MacDonald made her greatest success in *The Spring Maid* (1910). In 1913 she starred as Sylvia in the operetta *Sweethearts,* which VICTOR HERBERT had composed with her in mind. She was also seen in a revival of *FLORODORA* (1920). Possessed of a sweet, delicate, slightly weak singing voice of impressive range, MacDonald captivated audiences with her vivacious, unaffected personality and her nimble dancing.   MK

Macgowan, Kenneth (1888–1963) Producer and critic. For years Macgowan wrote reviews chiefly for the *New York Globe* and THEATRE ARTS, sometimes whimsically reviewing plays he produced for EXPERIMENTAL THEATRE, INC., which he cofounded with ROBERT EDMOND JONES and EUGENE O'NEILL (1924). There he produced six of O'Neill's plays, including *ALL GOD'S CHILLUN GOT WINGS* (1924), *DESIRE UNDER THE ELMS* (1924), and *The GREAT GOD BROWN* (1926), as well as the first New York production of Strindberg's *Ghost Sonata* (as *The Spook Sonata,* 1924) and a popular revival of MOWATT's *FASHION* (1924). Although he produced into the 1930s, perhaps his greatest contributions were his books on masks and modern theatrical practice. The most influential of these were *The Theatre of Tomorrow* (1921), *Footlights across America* (1929), *Continental Stagecraft* (1922) with Robert Edmond Jones, and *Masks and Demons* (1923) with HERMAN ROSSE.   RHW

Machado, Eduardo (1953–) CUBAN-born playwright and director who grew up and performed as an actor in California before working with MARIA IRENE FORNÉS in the Padua Hills Playwrights' Festival (1978) and in the first INTAR playwriting workshop in New York. The author of more than 40 plays, Machado has been produced at major theatres in New York, San Francisco, Los Angeles, London, New Haven, and Santa Fe. He has written four plays based on the tribulations of his family in Cuba, including *Broken Eggs,* first produced by New York's ENSEMBLE STUDIO THEATRE in 1984, and *In the Eye of the Hurricane,* produced by the ACTORS THEATRE OF LOUISVILLE Humana Festival (1991). The quartet (under the title *The Floating Island*) was staged in two segments by OSKAR EUSTIS at the MARK TAPER FORUM in 1994. *Crocodile Eyes* was seen in 1999 at THEATER FOR THE NEW CITY. The COCONUT GROVE PLAYHOUSE presented *Once Removed* in 2003; INTAR presented his *The Cook* later that year. His recent (2005) *Kissing Fidel* at INTAR was called by the *New York Times* a "confused and overwrought comedy." In 1995 Machado received one of the first of four new-play initiatives for the NEDERLANDER organization and the ROUNDABOUT THEATRE COMPANY. In 1997 he became head of Columbia University's playwriting program. Since July 2004 he has served as the artistic director of INTAR.   ER

Machinal SOPHIE TREADWELL loosely based her innovative drama on the sensational Ruth Snyder–Judd Gray murder trial. Produced by ARTHUR HOPKINS, with sets by ROBERT EDMOND JONES, it opened on 7 September 1928 at New York's PLYMOUTH THEATRE for 91 performances. Starring Zita Johann as the "young woman" and a little-known actor, Clark Gable, as her lover, the play depicted a woman victimized and dehumanized by all around her. Nine short episodes deal with various stages of her numbed life. Only briefly, with her lover, is she freed from her stupor – enough so that she kills her husband and is sentenced to the electric chair. The play, which JOHN GASSNER called "one of the most unusual plays of the 20s," was praised for its expressionistic style and staccato dialogue, which so aptly matched the theme. In 1933 it was performed successfully in Moscow, and it has had numerous revivals in the U.S., including in NYC a critically acclaimed one by the NEW YORK SHAKESPEARE FESTIVAL (1990), others at the OFF-OFF Ohio Theatre (2001), and at THEATRE FOR THE NEW CITY (2003). In recent years it has been especially popular in academic theatre.   FB

McIntyre, James (1857–1937) and **Thomas Heath** (1852–1938) Two-man blackface act, the longest lasting (1874–1924) of all major MINSTREL–VAUDEVILLE duos. Though born elsewhere, both grew up in the South, where they learned to mimic blacks. McIntyre, a former clog dancer and small-time actor, was the comic; Heath, the straight man, was an ideal feeder for his partner, leading him into preposterous predicaments in sketches such as "The Georgia Minstrels," "The Man from Montana," "Chickens" (with McIntyre in drag), and "The Ham Tree" (the last becoming a full-length piece presented by producers KLAW and ERLANGER, first in 1905). In 1916 the *NEW YORK DRAMATIC MIRROR* carped that 90% of their act was tedium, 10% laughs; yet they persisted for almost a decade longer. Rumor that they did not speak for 25 years was vehemently denied.
DBW

Mack, Charles see MORAN, GEORGE

Mackay, Constance D'Arcy (1887–1966) Pioneer in CHILDREN'S THEATRE, community drama, and PAGEANTRY. A prolific writer, she published her first collection of children's plays in 1909 and her first pageant in 1911; her last play was published in 1952. Her book *The Little Theatre in the United States* (1917) was an early effort to proselytize for COMMUNITY THEATRE. During 1918–19 she was Director of Pageantry and Drama for the War Camp Community Service. Her plays and pageants were imaginative and well crafted, drawn from folk and historical sources. NP

MacKaye, Percy (1875–1956) Playwright whose grand dramatic visions resembled those of his father, STEELE MACKAYE. He wrote *St. Louis Masque* (1914), celebrating the 150th anniversary of the city's founding; *Caliban by the Yellow Sands* (1916, in Central Park), to commemorate the tercentenary of Shakespeare's death; and his tetralogy, *The Mystery of Hamlet* (published 1949), which explored 30 years of the Hamlet saga prior to Shakespeare's play. His best-known plays were *The SCARECROW* (1910, CT; NYC, 1911), adapted from Hawthorne's *Feathertop*, and *Jeanne D'Arc*, which starred JULIA MARLOWE and E. H. SOTHERN (Philadelphia, 1906; NYC, 1907). He crusaded for "a theatre for the people" in *The Playhouse and the Play* (1909), *The Civic Theatre* (1912), and *Community Drama* (1917), wrote 13 other plays and seven masques, six volumes of stories and poems, and an opera, *RIP VAN WINKLE* (1919; music, REGINALD DE KOVEN). (See also PAGEANTS/PAGEANTRY.) RM

MacKaye, (James Morrison) Steele (1842–94) Actor, playwright, teacher, architect, and inventor. The innovations in stage mechanics of this brilliant, if erratic, dreamer, and his crusade for realism in acting and "true-to-life" dialogue marked MacKaye as "the most unsuccessful successful figure in the American theatre." His early dreams of becoming an actor and artist, supported by unrestricted family funds, permitted him to study painting with George Inness and acting with François Delsarte (in Paris, 1869), and to found a "school of expression" in New York (1871) for propagating the Delsartean system. He made his professional debut as actor, playwright, and manager with *Monaldi* (New York, 1872), played Hamlet in London (Crystal Palace, 1873), and then achieved success as a playwright with *Rose Michel* (1875) and *Won at Last* (1877), both in New York. Of his 30 plays, *HAZEL KIRKE* (1880), presented in his MADISON SQUARE THEATRE [at which entry see illustration] was the best: It ran for over a year and was repeatedly revived during the next two decades; but MacKaye had unwittingly contracted to assign the profits to his financial backers, the Mallory brothers.

The Madison Square Theatre, MacKaye's first venture into architecture, had an elevator stage that changed scenes in two minutes, a lighting system devised by Edison, folding seats, and an ingenious ventilating system. His second theatre, to be combined with a hotel, never progressed beyond the blueprint stage. His third, the Lyceum (1885), incorporated new stage machinery, firefighting equipment, an orchestra pit on an elevator, and quarters for America's first dramatic school. His ultimate theatrical dream, a Spectatorium (480 ft. long, 380 ft. wide, and 270 ft. high) for the Chicago World's Fair (1893) to house his chronicle of Columbus's adventures, *The World Finder*, was disrupted by the national financial panic and was reduced to a scaled-down Scenitorium. A detailed account of his life and work was written by his son, playwright PERCY MACKAYE (*Epoch*, 1927). RM

McKechnie, Donna (1940–) Detroit-born performer and choreographer who is remembered for her Cassie in *A CHORUS LINE* (1975), which won her the Tony for Best Actress in a Musical. Prior to this career highpoint she had performed in the chorus of *HOW TO SUCCEED IN BUSINESS WITHOUT REALLY TRYING* (1961) and as Vivien Della Hoya in *Promises, Promises* (1968), Kathy in *COMPANY* (1970), and Ivy Smith in *ON THE TOWN* (1971). In 1976 she married the director MICHAEL BENNETT, though their marriage was short-lived. In 1980 she was diagnosed with arthritis, yet after various healing remedies returned to *Chorus Line* in 1986, and during the balance of the 1980s appeared in touring productions of *Sweet Charity* and *Annie Get Your Gun*, and in the London revival of *Can-Can*. She played Sally in an acclaimed revival of *Follies* at the Paper Mill Playhouse in 1998 and another in 2005 at the Barrington Stage Company. Since 1997 she has toured in solo performances or appeared in cabaret shows: *Inside the Music, My Musical Comedy Life, Gypsy in My Soul*, and *It Started with a Dream.*   DBW

Mackintosh, Cameron (Anthony) (1946–) Though British (and one of the richest men in that country), this powerful producer had an enormous impact on Broadway production in the 1980s and 1990s. His megamusical hits have included *Cats, Les Misérables, The Phantom of the Opera*, and *Miss Saigon*. Sheridan Morley and Ruth Leon have written a book about the producer (1998).   DBW

Mackintosh, Robert (1925–98) Theatre, film, and television (*Garry Moore Show*, 1960–4) costume designer and author who also designed for *Holiday on Ice*. He created costumes for numerous important New York productions, including *Silk Stockings* (1955), *Butterflies are Free* (1969), and *Mame* (1966, 1983), as well as for individual performers (Charles Busch, Ruby Dee, Angela Lansbury). In addition to two novels, he wrote a biography of the late cabaret performer Bobby Short.   BO

MacLeish, Archibald (1892–1982) Poet and playwright whose dramatic reputation rests chiefly on the success of one script, *J.B.* (1958), a 20th-century version of the Book of Job. MacLeish's other verse dramas did not succeed, nor did *Scratch* (1971), based on Stephen Vincent Benét's story "The Devil and Daniel Webster."   SMA

McMartin, John (1932–) Indiana-born actor and singer. McMartin first appeared Off-Broadway in *Little Mary Sunshine* (1959; *Theatre World* Award) and sbsequently, on Broadway, in *Sweet Charity* (1966, Tony nomination; film, 1969), *Follies* (1971), *The Great God Brown* (1972; Drama Desk Award), and *Don Juan* (as Sganarelle, 1972; Tony nomination and Drama Desk Award). He played Julius Caesar at The Public (1988), Donner in Stoppard's *Artist Descending a Staircase* (1989), and earned further Tony nominations as Cap'n Andy in the *Show Boat* revival (1994), Uncle Willie in the short-lived *High Society* (1998), and the Narrator in a revival of *Into the Woods* (2002). His most recent Broadway show is *Grey Gardens*

(2006). His films include *All the President's Men* (1976), *Pennies from Heaven* (1981), *The Dish* (2000), and *Kinsey* (2004), and he often appears on television.   REK

McNally, Terrence (1939–) Texas-born prolific playwright whose first produced script was *And Things That Go Bump in the Night* at the Guthrie Theater in 1964 and on Broadway the following year. *Bad Habits*, a double-bill of *Ravenswood* and *Dunelawn*, was produced Off-Broadway and moved to the Booth Theatre in 1974. Other Broadway productions include *The Ritz* (1975) and his back-to-back Best Play Tony and Drama Desk winners *Love! Valour! Compassion!* (1995) and *Master Class* (1995; awards 1996). Other plays include *Where Has Tommy Flowers Gone?* (1971, NYC's Eastside Playhouse), *It's Only a Play* (1982, Manhattan Punch Line; 1986, Manhattan Theatre Club), *Frankie and Johnny in the Clair de Lune* (1987, MTC; 2002, Broadway), *The Lisbon Traviata* (1985, Theater Off Park; 1989, MTC), *Lips Together, Teeth Apart* (1991, MTC), *A Perfect Ganesh* (1993, MTC), *The Stendhal Syndrome* (2004, Primary Stages), *Some Men* (2007, Second Stage), and *Deuce* (2007, Music Box). His books for the musicals *Kiss of the Spider Woman* (1993) and *Ragtime* (1998) won Tony Awards. He also wrote the books for *The Full Monty* (2000), *A Man of No Importance* (2002, Lincoln Center), and *Chita Rivera: The Dancer's Life* (2005), as well as the libretto for the opera *Dead Man Walking* (2002, City Center Opera). A musical version of Dürrenmatt's *The Visit* awaits major staging.

McNally's initial plays involved the larger concerns of the late 1960s and early '70s – assassination, the Vietnam War, rebellion, and the sexual revolution. Although he began as an angry and outraged playwright, his more recent work is in contrast more lyrical and positive, offering unsentimental hope for intimacy at a time when fear and death rule. His *Love! Valour! Compassion!* concerned the fortunes of seven men, one of whom is dying of AIDS, in an isolated country home. Seen first at MTC in 1994 (directed by Joe Mantello, who shared an Obie with the cast; another went to the playwright), it transferred to Broadway in February 1995 and won the Drama Desk and Tony awards for Best Play. *L'Age d'Or*, a work in progress, deals with Bellini's relationship with rival diva sisters (reflecting McNally's great love of opera, as does *Master Class*). His most controversial play to date was *Corpus Christi* (1998), about 13 gay men who meet to enact the story of Jesus; it was at first canceled by MTC but ultimately seen with only minor demonstrations.   SMA   DBW

415

McNeil, Claudia (1917–93) AFRICAN AMERICAN actress best known for her role as Lena Younger in *A RAISIN IN THE SUN* (1959), which ran on Broadway for more than two years. McNeil was a nightclub singer before her OFF-BROADWAY debut as Mamie in LANGSTON HUGHES's *Simply Heavenly* (1957; moved to Broadway). She was next seen as Tituba in *The CRUCIBLE* (1953, replacement); played a Jewish mother in Carl Reiner's *Something Different* (1967); and was Ftatateeta in *Her First Roman* (1968). Appearing in London as Sister Margaret in JAMES BALDWIN's *The AMEN CORNER* (1965), she was voted best actress of the year by the critics. She had a variety of film (e.g., *The Last Angry Man,* 1959) and television appearances and returned to cabaret in 1978. McNeil was hospitalized for surgery in 1982 and later admitted to The Actors' Fund Nursery Home in New Jersey, where she died. EGH

McRae, Bruce (1867–1927) India-born actor of British parents. As support to such stars as Marie Burroughs, OLGA NETHERSOLE, WILLIAM GILLETTE (the original Watson to his Holmes in 1899), JULIA MARLOWE, ETHEL BARRYMORE (for seven years), and MRS. FISKE (John Rosmer in *Rosmersholm,* 1907), McRae developed into a solid craftsman and leading man but never reached true stardom. DBW

McVicker, James Hubert (1822–96) Actor and theatre manager who first achieved national recognition as an actor of "YANKEE" characters in the 1850s. In 1857 he settled in CHICAGO and built his MCVICKER'S THEATRE, which he managed successfully until his death. Although the theatre was destroyed in the great Chicago FIRE of 1871 and burned again in 1890, it was rebuilt on both occasions in less than a year. McVicker was a highly regarded manager, noted for the quality of his STOCK COMPANY and for his carefully mounted revivals of *The School for Scandal, A Midsummer Night's Dream,* and *The Tempest.* His adopted daughter, Mary Runnion McVicker, married EDWIN BOOTH in 1869, and McVicker managed one of Booth's starring tours, including an engagement at New York's LYCEUM THEATRE in 1876. DJW

McVicker's Theatre Madison St., Chicago [Architect: Otis Wheelock]. Built in 1857 by actor-manager JAMES H. MCVICKER, the theatre was a commodious clapboard version of an Italianate palazzo and the best theatre in the West. Though he maintained a STOCK COMPANY, McVicker presented a succession of stars, from Sarah Bernhardt to EDDIE FOY. At his death in 1896, the house passed to JACOB LITT, who tried to retain first-rate legitimate fare in the face of competition from VAUDEVILLE and the movies; in 1913, the house was surrendered to first one, then the other. During its history, it was rebuilt four times. In 1871, after a remodeling, the theatre was consumed by the Chicago FIRE and was rebuilt. In 1885, McVicker engaged Adler and Sullivan to remodel it and, in 1890, after it burned for a second time, it was again resurrected. In 1922, it was razed and a new house for movies was erected on the site; it, too, was demolished in 1984. MCH

Madame Butterfly Conceived as a curtain-raiser to a full-length farce, this one-act by DAVID BELASCO provided the basis for Giacomo Puccini's famous opera. Belasco adapted the play from a short story by John Luther Long and produced it with BLANCHE BATES at the Herald Square Theatre in 1900. His lighting effects – especially one 14-minute scene of lighting changes without dialogue – plus Bates's innocence and motherly passion helped to ensure the production's success. Billed as a "tragedy of Japanese life," the play represents Cho-Cho-San as an atypical and too trusting Japanese woman who, believing she is married to an American naval officer named Pinkerton, awaits his return with the child of their love. When Pinkerton finally arrives with his American wife, Cho-Cho-San kills herself (Belasco's addition to the story). Belasco's production toured widely in the U.S. and to London, where Puccini saw it in 1900. In his *M. BUTTERFLY* (1988), playwright DAVID HENRY HWANG attacked the gendered ethnocentrism of Puccini's opera and, implicitly, Belasco's play. The opera also served as inspiration for the musical *Miss Saigon.* BMcC

Madison Square Theatre West 24th St., between Broadway and Sixth Ave., NYC. When the FIFTH AVENUE THEATRE burned (see FIRES) and its manager. AUGUSTIN DALY. moved to another theatre, the house was not immediately rebuilt. Four years later, in 1877, it was resurrected to become Minnie Commings's Drawing Room, with an open stage. In 1879, backed by the Mallory brothers, STEELE MACKAYE gutted and redesigned the house, installing his famous double stage, experimenting with atmospheric lighting, relocating the orchestra above the stage, and improving the comfort of his patrons with his invention of the folding chair. The theatre was renamed the Madison Square. In 1880, he had his greatest triumph with *HAZEL KIRKE;* the play brought about a financial falling-out with the Mallorys, and MacKaye left the playhouse. In 1884, A. M. PALMER was

The elevator stage at the Madison Square Theatre. Original in *Scientific American,* 1884. *Courtesy:* Don B. Wilmeth Theatre Collection.

asked to take over, and his businesslike methods and his policy of presenting stars in imported and stageworthy plays brought great prosperity to the house. In 1891, CHARLES H. HOYT secured the lease to showcase his own plays and eventually changed the name to Hoyt's Theatre. On his death, it was rented on a run-of-the-play basis; but in 1908, obsolete and too far downtown, it was razed to make way for an office building.
MCH

magic in the United States Outlawed from performance by strict New England Puritans in the 17th century, by the mid-1700s itinerant conjurers cut a path through burgeoning American communities with their trunks full of wonder.

Performing in taverns and assembly rooms, a handful of performers, skillful and audacious, earned a reputation and a living.

NATIVE AMERICANS created fascinating magic as part Shamanistic rites and ritual performances; but the first American magician to gain fame, Jacob Meyer, born in 1734, was ironically never acknowledged in his homeland. Adopting the name of his native city, JACOB PHILADELPHIA became one of the most famous performers of Europe. His show was a combination of mechanical and sleight-of-hand illusions and ghostly projections of eerie figures produced by a hidden magic lantern, called "Phantasmogoria."

At the beginning of the 19th century RICHARD POTTER became the first indigenous magician to gain prominence in the U.S. Potter, a mulatto, performed successfully, also exhibiting ventriloquism and fire resistance, and was able to retire with a small fortune.

By the middle of the 19th century, magicians were performing in legitimate theatres and presenting full-evening shows. Native-born stars like Jonathan Harrington and John Wyman enjoyed great popularity. Wyman was an early proponent of gift shows, promising the members of his audience prizes of a variety of items, such as glassware, comestibles, and livestock, in a minilottery designed to boost attendance.

The relationship of magic to religion was responsible for a distinctly American branch of performance that began with the birth of spiritualism in 1848. In that year, Margaret and Kate Fox, young daughters of a modest farmer on the outskirts of Rochester, NY, produced strange rapping noises that were interpreted to be communications from the spirit world. Although the Fox sisters later confessed they were able to make these mystical sounds by imperceptibly cracking the knuckles of their toes, millions of people embraced spiritualism, and entertainers began to exploit the phenomenon by staging shows that apparently utilized psychic agency.

A host of performers, like the DAVENPORT BROTHERS from Buffalo, NY, learned methods to extricate themselves from restraints, produce phenomena, and then cleverly rebind themselves. These performers led the way to stage mind readers, another American innovation, which began with the performances of J. Randall Brown and Washington Irving Bishop. Bishop, in a spectacular test, would ask for a pin to be hidden anywhere within a five-mile radius. Blindfolded and placed in a horse-drawn carriage, he madly led his team through the streets of New York; stopping suddenly in front of a particular building, he would rush into the lobby and retrieve the hidden object.

By the 1870s, American magic had its first superstar in ALEXANDER HERRMANN, whose father and elder brother were also conjurers of note. Alexander captured the imagination of the American public with his skill, personality, and appearance (his formally dressed, lean and goateed look set the standard for magicians for decades to come). At his death in 1896 he was one of the country's most beloved theatrical figures, much lauded and lamented. His wife Adelaide, a former trick cyclist and long-time assistant, continued with the show, becoming the country's most famous woman magician during a 40-year career.

HARRY KELLAR, an Ohio-born conjurer, then ascended to the position of America's most prominent and beloved magician. Heavily influenced by England's great magicians, Maskelyn and Devant, Kellar imported mysteries and stamped them as his own. His exquisite levitation of a sleeping lady was a sensation.

In 1907 Kellar toured with HOWARD THURSTON, to whom he awarded his mantle of magic upon retirement. The youngster greatly enlarged the Master's show and presented the biggest illusion spectacle ever seen. Traveling with tons of equipment, Thurston became the premier prestidigitator in America with his massive and intriguing illusions.

Only one performer rivaled him: HARRY HOUDINI, the legendary perplexer whose name came to be synonymous with magic itself. Born in Budapest in 1874, Houdini claimed to have come from Appleton, WI, where his family emigrated. He built his act on a unique principle – the challenge – daring his audience to find a restraint from which he could not escape. He extricated himself from straitjackets, tanks of water, prison cells, giant footballs, and even the belly of a sea serpent. An unrelenting publicist, he continually dreamed up stunts to keep his name in front of the public. Recognizing the importance of the nascent cinema industry, he appeared in films and even started his own movie company. Ironically, he never succeeded with a large-scale magic show.

When Houdini died in 1926 magic was enjoying enormous popularity. The big illusion show of Thurston, as well as those of Carter, Nicola, Raymond, BLACKSTONE, and Dante entertained thousands both in the U.S. and abroad.

Surprisingly, a much more modest show by an American emigrant from Austria-Hungary, Max Malini, generated the headlines the big illusionists greatly coveted. A combination of startling impromptu sleight-of-hand, unlimited chutzpah, and a distinctive personality ensured Malini's success. He pioneered the lucrative field of private entertainments in the homes of America's most prominent and wealthy families, often entertaining presidents and foreign royalty.

The VAUDEVILLE era brought speciality to magic. Houdini with his escapes, "King of Koins" T. Nelson Downs, Nate Leipzig the elegant card worker, and others who performed exclusively with objects such as watches, billiard balls, or silk handkerchiefs outlived vaudeville itself.

The CHAUTAUQUA AND LYCEUM circuits provided a home for magicians specializing in family entertainment. The NIGHTCLUB era introduced great acts like Cardini, with his impeccable production of lit cigarettes, and Channing Pollock, who elegantly produced live doves. These two influential stage magicians spawned more imitators than can be imagined, as a consequence of both live and televised appearances in the 1950s.

American magicians have excelled in the presentation of impromptu or close-up magic using sleight-of-hand. A Canadian performer transplanted to California set the standard for all such artists in the 20th century: DAI VERNON revolutionized this branch of the conjurer's art with his approach to naturalness, his technical innovations, and his dignified presentations.

Television created both opportunities and problems for magicians, who suddenly found a single audience numbering more people than would witness an entire career of live theatrical performances. In spite of the credibility gap created by magic on television, the medium has proven most viable for modern performers. The late DOUG HENNING, SIEGFRIED AND ROY, PENN AND TELLER, LANCE BURTON, DAVID COPPERFIELD and others utilized television appearances to attract large audiences to their live shows, attesting to the continuing popularity of magic as a theatrical entertainment. A few performers – such as Joseph Gabriel, Marc Salem, and RICKY JAY – have staged successful stage shows on and OFF-BROADWAY in recent years.   RJ

Magic Theatre, The Though it has premiered works of numerous modern playwrights (more than 200 as of 2006), this SAN FRANCISCO company is best known for unveiling major plays by SAM SHEPARD: BURIED CHILD (1978), TRUE WEST (1979), and FOOL FOR LOVE (1983). Founded in a Berkeley bar in 1967 by director John Lion, an admirer of European absurdism, the Magic soon turned to new American plays and PERFORMANCE ART, forming alliances with Shepard, Michael McClure (whose The Beard catalyzed a CENSORSHIP battle in 1974), Adele Edling Shank, and others. In 1977 the Magic settled into two small theatres in Fort Mason Center, naming critic-scholar Martin Esslin dramaturge. New, nonnaturalistic plays were emphasized until the late 1980s, when mainstream OFF-BROADWAY hits (and even an O'NEILL drama) crept onto the schedule. In 1990 Lion resigned; in 1994 he became director of the KENNEDY CENTER American College Theatre Festival. He was replaced by Harvey Seifter, then Larry Eilenberg (1992–3) who in turn was succeeded in 1993 by playwright-director Mame Hunt, who left in 1998. Eilenberg returned and was followed in 2003 by Chris Smith. Though more eclectic, the Magic still premieres new plays, for which it received the 1985 MARGO JONES Award.   MB

Maguire, Thomas (Tom) (1820?–96) Dominant gold-rush theatre producer, dubbed the "Napoleon of the San Francisco stage." Born in New York of poor Irish immigrants parents, he worked as a hackney driver and bartender before moving west in 1849. In SAN FRANCISCO he first managed a gambling saloon, then opened three different theatres called the Jenny Lind. (The first two burned down [see FIRES]; the third became the town's first City Hall.) He later operated Maguire's Opera House, Alhambra Theatre, BALDWIN THEATRE, and other key venues. A flamboyant risk-taker with a keen eye for talent, he lured stars like ADA ISAACS MENKEN and CLARA MORRIS to California, formed the San Francisco Minstrels (1853), set up an early western touring circuit, and gave breaks to young DAVID BELASCO and LOTTA CRABTREE. In 1882, after financial ruination at the Baldwin, Maguire returned to New York and died there in obscure poverty.   MB

Maher, Joseph (1933–98) Irish-born actor, director, and playwright. Maher played farce (OFF-BROADWAY in Orton's trio Entertaining Mr. Sloan, 1981; Loot, 1986 [to Broadway]; and What the Butler Saw, 1989), drama (Roose-Evans's 84 Charing Cross Road, 1982–3, Broadway, with ELLEN BURSTYN), and "horrendous villains" (The Evil That Men Do, film, 1984]). He debuted in The Taming of the Shrew (1959. Toronto), Off-Broadway in The Hostage (1962), and on Broadway in Bagnold's The Chinese Prime Minister (1964). Maher won a 1977 Obie for Hampton's Savages (HUDSON GUILD) and Tony nominations for Parker and Kennedy's Spokesong (1979), Stoppard's Night and Day (1980), and Loot. In 1995 he starred as Archie Rice in The Entertainer at the LONG WHARF. Also a playwright-director, he wrote *Dance for Me, Simeon* (GEORGE STREET PLAYHOUSE, 1979). He frequently acted in film and on television.   REK

Majestic Theatre 245 West 44th St., NYC [Architect: Herbert J. Krapp]. The Majestic (1927) was the last of the Chanin-built houses in the theatre district and, like the 46TH STREET THEATRE, it was designed with a rising orchestra floor somewhat like an amphitheatre. Intended for operetta and musical comedy, it had an original seating capacity of 1,700, later increased to make it one of the largest of the Broadway theatres. In 1934, it was taken over by the SHUBERT BROTHERS, and has remained a Shubert house ever since. During most of its early history, it presented a less-than-notable series of musicals and operettas, except for its GILBERT AND SULLIVAN revivals; but during its later history, it could boast of four RODGERS and HAMMERSTEIN musicals, beginning with *CAROUSEL* (1945) and continuing with *Allegro* (1947), *SOUTH PACIFIC* (1949), and *Me and Juliet* (1953). In 1957, *The MUSIC MAN* took its stage, only to give it up to *CAMELOT* in 1960. The long-running *PHANTOM OF THE OPERA* opened there in 1988, becoming the biggest hit in the venue's history (and the longest-running in Broadway's). Because of its large seating capacity, musicals that become hits at other theatres are frequently moved to the Majestic to take advantage of the extra seats. A case in point is the musical *42ND STREET*, which originated at the WINTER GARDEN and continued its run at the Majestic (1981–7).   MCH

Major, Clare Tree (1880–1954) Founder and director of the company that bore her name; an English actress who came to the U.S. in 1916. She was first associated with the WASHINGTON SQUARE PLAYERS, but her interest in entertainment for young people led her to establish a professional company that toured nationally during 1923–54. By 1940 the company had tripled, with a repertory of six plays for sponsors booking a series.

With a school in Pleasantville, NY, she trained her own performers and worked with the New York Board of Education to present plays of literary quality and appropriate content for elementary and high-school students (see CHILDREN'S THEATRE). Mrs. Major stressed the use of international material to promote appreciation of different cultures. Her scripts were generally her own dramatizations of folk and fairy tales and children's classics. Many actors in adult theatre today got their start in Clare Tree Major's Company.   NMcC

Male Animal, The Comedy by James Thurber and ELLIOTT NUGENT, more closely associated with Thurber due to his established reputation as a cartoonist and writer for *New Yorker* magazine. The play follows a professor facing accusations of communist sympathies by college regents while his wife is wooed by a former football star. It is a situational comedy similar to Thurber's stories and cartoons – an ordinary man dealing with extraordinary circumstances – yet offers poignant commentary on pre-WWII ideals regarding personal freedom and gender-related expectations. *Male Animal* opened at the CORT THEATRE 9 January 1940 to run 243 performances. It was produced and staged by HERMAN SHUMLIN and starred the coauthor, Nugent, as Professor Tommy Turner, Ruth Matteson as his wife, and, in a smaller role, Gene Tierney.   KN

Maleczech, Ruth (1939–) Cofounder of MABOU MINES, actor, and director. Maleczech worked with the Actors Workshop and the SAN FRANCISCO MIME TROUPE in the 1960s, then studied in Europe with Grotowski and the Berliner Ensemble before returning to New York in 1970 to form the experimental COLLECTIVE Mabou Mines with (then-husband) LEE BREUER, DAVID WARRILOW, JoANNE AKALAITIS, and Philip Glass. Her acting – direct, distanced, economical – has earned acclaim (and several Obie Awards) in Mabou Mines productions such as *The Shaggy Dog Animation* (1978), *Hajj* (1983), and *Through the Leaves* (1984). In 1990 she played the title role in Mabou's gender-reversed production of *Lear*. As a writer-director, Maleczech has collaborated with INTAR on the music-theatre works *Suenos* (1988), about dictatorship, and with Valeria Vasilevski on *Fire Works* (1987), about censorship. In 1995 she adapted (and performed) with JOANNE AKALAITIS (director) and Chiori Miyagawa Genet's last novel, *Prisoner of Love*. Recent performances number MARTHA CLARKE's and CHARLES L. MEE's *Belle Époque* at Lincoln Center (2004) and for Mabou Mines, playing opposite her daughter, **Clove Galilee**, *Cara Lucia* (2003) and *Red Beads* (2005).   AS

male impersonation see FEMALE/MALE IMPERSONATION

Malina, Judith see LIVING THEATRE

Malkovich, John (Gavin) (1953–) Actor and director, who as a member of Chicago's STEPPENWOLF THEATRE COMPANY since its founding in 1976 became both its most famous actor and the one whose physically engaging approach best typified the company's appeal to audiences locally and abroad. Malkovich's extraordinary ability to generate a menacing physical presence was evident when he played the violent brother in SAM SHEPARD's TRUE WEST – a performance that won him a Joseph Jefferson Award (Chicago, 1982) and Clarence Derwent and Obie awards (1983) – and in the 1993 film In the Line of Fire as a protean villain. At the opposite end of the emotional spectrum, his tearful vulnerability in a flashback scene as Biff (opposite DUSTIN HOFFMAN) in DEATH OF A SALESMAN helped earn him a Drama Desk Award (1984) and an Emmy (1986). Malkovich's work as a director includes dynamic revivals of LANFORD WILSON's Balm in Gilead, for which he won Jefferson (1981), Obie (1985), and Drama Desk (1985) awards. Beginning in the mid-1980s, he appeared in a series of films, including Places in the Heart, Making Mr. Right, Dangerous Liaisons, Being John Malkovich, Riplay's Game, The Libertine, and Klimt. Recent stage appearances include a 1991 London run in Wilson's Burn This and Shepard's States of Shock in NYC (AMERICAN PLACE); directing assignments include a 1994 staging of his adaptation of Don DeLillo's Libra for Steppenwolf. His most recent Steppenwolf appearance was in 2005 in British playwright Stephen Jeffreys's Lost Land.   SF

Malpede, Karen (1945–) Writer and director. Malpede writes theatre history and plays combining myth, movement, and poetry to reexamine history as a FEMINIST and pacifist. Many of her works appeared at New Cycle Theatre (Brooklyn), which she founded with Burl Hash in 1977. Influenced by Malina, Beck (see LIVING THEATRE), and CHAIKIN, she focuses on birth and nonviolent change in Lament for Three Women (1974), Rebeccah (1976, PLAYWRIGHTS HORIZONS), The End of War (1977), Making Peace (1979), A Monster Has Stolen the Sun (1981), Sappho and Aphrodite (1983), and Us (1988). The Beekeeper's Daughter (1997, THEATRE ROW) is about a Bosnia refugee and an eccentric American family. I Will Bear Witness (coauthored with and starring George Bartenieff, 2001, CLASSIC STAGE) is based on Victor Klemperer's diaries.   TH-S

Mamet, David (1947–) One of the most important and highly regarded dramatists to emerge from the 1970s, Mamet, born in a suburb of CHICAGO, first attracted attention with such one-acts as SEXUAL PERVERSITY IN CHICAGO and Duck Variations (1976 Obie for the pair). The 1977 production of AMERICAN BUFFALO, which marked his Broadway debut, offers a minimal plot; subtle character development emerges in its place. A similarly

minimal script, A Life in the Theatre (1977, Theatre De Lys), presents an elderly and a youthful actor, both on- and backstage, contrasting their different attitudes toward their work. Although many traditionalists have been hostile toward or bewildered by Mamet's work, or offended by his liberal use of profanity and sexual language, the 1983 London and 1984 New York productions of GLENGARRY GLEN ROSS led to a Pulitzer Prize for Mamet. It is arguably his most successful play, filmed in 1992 and revived to acclaim on Broadway in 2005. Later successes include the LINCOLN CENTER production (at the ROYALE) of Speed-the-Plow (1988); the provocative Oleanna (1992), a play built on the theme of sexual harrassment and seen first in Boston (then presented in New York and London; film, 1994); The Cryptogram (London and Boston, 1994; NYC, 1995, Obie for Best New Play); An Interview, part of a three-play bill called Death Defying Acts (OFF-BROADWAY, March 1995); The Old Neighborhood, a work inspired by Mamet's Jewish background, which premiered at the AMERICAN REPERTORY THEATRE in the 1996–7 season; and Boston Marriage (ART, 1999; PUBLIC THEATER, 2002), a response to critics who attacked him for not writing good female roles. Much of Mamet's attention as of the late 1980s was devoted to filmwriting (some 25), directing, CHEKHOV adaptations, and nonfiction efforts such as Writing in Restaurants (1986) and True and False (1999) on acting, as well as three novels. His adaptation of Granville Barker's The Voysey Inheritance was praised (ATLANTIC THEATER, 2006). The American Academy of Arts and Letters in 1993 awarded him its Award of Merit Medal for outstanding work over the course of a career, and the DRAMA LEAGUE recognized him in 1995 for unique contribution to the theatre.   SMA   DBW

Mamoulian, Rouben (1897–1987) Russian-born American director. While preparing for a law career at the University of Moscow, Mamoulian attended Vakhtangov's Studio Theatre. After graduation he went to London, and in 1922 successfully staged The Beating on the Door at the St. James's Theatre. In 1923 he was invited to Rochester, NY, by George Eastman, and for the next three years headed the Eastman Theatre. In 1926 he became a teacher at the THEATRE GUILD in New York, and a year later made his Broadway directing debut with Porgy, gaining a reputation for integrating music, drama, and dance into a rhythmic whole. He staged six plays in 1928, including O'NEILL's Marco Millions; two plays in 1929, including Karel Capek's R.U.R.; and four in 1930, including A Month in the Country. Dividing his time between

Hollywood and New York during the 1930s, his theatrical output declined. His other outstanding stage credits include PORGY AND BESS (1935); OKLAHOMA! (1943); CAROUSEL (1945); and LOST IN THE STARS (1949). His 17 (or so) films include *Applause* (1929), *Dr. Jekyll and Mr. Hyde* (1932), GOLDEN BOY (1939), *Blood and Sand* (1941), and SILK STOCKINGS (1957). His career was recounted in a book by Mark J. Spergel (1993).   TLM

Man of La Mancha Intermissionless musical play, music by Mitch Leigh, lyrics by Joe Darion, book by Dale Wasserman; opened at the ANTA–Washington Square Theatre 22 November 1965, running 2,328 performances. This musical version of the Don Quixote story adds the further dimension of Cervantes, arrested for heresy, telling his story in prison as it is acted out by the prisoners. The ultimate lesson of Cervantes/Quixote (RICHARD KILEY) is that it is the dream, not the truth, that keeps humankind going. The show was produced, on Broadway contracts, in a large temporary theatre in Greenwich Village, where the lack of an orchestra pit led to placing the orchestra (featuring acoustic guitars) upstage and split on either side of the action – a practice continued after the show transferred to a traditional Broadway house the (MARTIN BECK). Leigh's score, vaguely reminiscent of Spanish music, produced one huge hit, "The Impossible Dream." The show, first produced at the GOODSPEED OPERA HOUSE before coming to New York, won the Drama Critics' Circle and Tony awards for Best Musical. For its 25th anniversary production (1991–2), RAUL JULIA took the title role in a touring production that opened on Broadway in March 1992; a 2002 Broadway revival starred BRIAN STOKES MITCHELL.   JD

Man of the Hour, The Political melodrama by GEORGE BROADHURST that premiered 4 December 1906 at the Savoy Theater, NYC, and ran 479 performances. Set in "any large city in America," it concerns the efforts of an unscrupulous financier and a corrupt alderman to obtain a perpetual franchise for a streetcar line. Needing the mayor as an ally, they back the wealthy and popular but naive Alwyn Bennett (Frederick Perry) for the office. Alwyn loves the financier's niece, Dallas Wainwright (Lillian Kemble), who stirs Bennett to resist the blandishments and slanderous allegations of the corrupters, although her trust is invested in the streetcar line. A tough, honest alderman sides with him; in addition the financier's secretary (played by Douglas Fairbanks), secretly avenging the financier's ruination of his

father, provides helpful information. Critics approved Broadhurst's adept plotting, natural dialogue, and forceful characterizations.   WD

Man Who Came to Dinner, The by GEORGE S. KAUFMAN and MOSS HART, directed by Kaufman and with scenic design by DONALD OENSLAGER; opened on Broadway 16 October 1939 and ran 739 performances. The authors intended to create a vehicle for their friend ALEXANDER WOOLLCOTT, the theatre critic and raconteur, and so modeled the leading role after him. Other principal roles were travesties of GERTRUDE LAWRENCE, Noël Coward, and Harpo MARX. Woollcott decided against playing himself on Broadway (although he did assay the role in California in 1940), so Monty Woolley created Sheridan Whiteside. The gimmick of the farce is that Whiteside slips on the ice outside the Ohio home he has just visited, is compelled to remain for some weeks while his ostensibly broken hip knits, and takes over the household. Other cast members included Mary Wickes as Miss Preen, the nurse, and Edith Atwater as Maggie Cutler, Whiteside's confidential secretary. Warner Bros. released the film version in 1942, featuring Woolley, Wickes, Bette Davis, and JIMMY DURANTE. It was revived in 2000 with NATHAN LANE in the lead for the opening of ROUNDABOUT's AMERICAN AIRLINES THEATRE.   JDM

Man's World, A One of RACHEL CROTHERS's earliest plays, it remains one of her most provocative as well. In a serious study of the effects of the double standard, Crothers tells the story of Frankie Ware, a successful feminist writer who rejects marriage with the man she loves, Malcolm Gaskell, when she learns he is the father of the waif she has adopted and when he insists that men can live a different kind of morality from women. Called by Arthur Hobson Quinn "one of the most significant dramas of the decade," it opened 8 February 1910 at the Comedy Theatre and ran for 71 performances. The play elicited much debate in the press, as well as a parody a year later by AUGUSTUS THOMAS, called *As a Man Thinks*, which defended the double standard that Crothers attacked.   FB

Manhattan Theatre Club OFF-BROADWAY company founded in 1970 to develop new work. Under artistic director (since 1972) LYNNE MEADOW, MTC's goal is "to present well-crafted, bold, challenging plays by major writers from America and around the world"; but, according to Meadow, "we don't do non-linear plays." MTC's productions have included McNally's *Bad Habits* (1973–4); Jacker's *Bits & Pieces* (1974); Fugard's *The Blood Knot* (1976); David Rudkin's *Ashes* (1976, with New York Shakespeare Festival; Obie); *Ain't Misbehavin'* (1978, Tony); Beckett's *Play, That Time,* and *Footfalls* (1977); Bill C. Davis's *Mass Appeal* (1980); Henley's *Crimes of the Heart* (1981, Pulitzer Prize) and *The Miss Firecracker Contest* (1984); van Itallie's new translations of Chekhov's *The Seagull* (directed by Joseph Chaikin, 1975) and *The Three Sisters* (1982); Orton's *Loot* (1986); *Frankie and Johnny in the Clair de Lune* (1987); *Hunting Cockroaches* (1987); Richard Greenberg's *Eastern Standard* (1988); McNally's *The Lisbon Traviata* (1989–90; Lucille Lortel Award, Director); Friel's *Aristocrats* (1989; Lucille Lortel Award, Play); Wilson's *The Piano Lesson* (1990, with Yale Rep and Center Theatre Group; Pulitzer); Ayckbourn's *A Small Family Business* (1992); Donald Margulies's *Sight Unseen* (1992; revived in 2004); McNally's *A Perfect Ganesh* (1993) and *Love! Valour! Compassion!* (1994; Tony), Gurney's *Sylvia* (1995), Fugard's *Valley Song* (1995), Shelagh Stephenson's *An Experiment with an Air Pump* (1999), Lindsay-Abaire's *Fuddy Meers* (1999), *Proof* (2000; Pulitzer Prize), Busch's *The Tale of the Allergist's Wife* (2000), Charlotte Jones's *Humble Boy* (2003), and the operas *Little Mahagonny* (1973) and *The Breasts of Tiresias* (1974). MTC received a 1977 Obie for Sustained Excellence and a 1989 Drama Desk Award for "setting high standards, encouraging new playwrights and importing unusual plays from abroad." Late in 2003 MTC opened the remodeled Biltmore Theatre as a new home, though its first season was largely disastrous both artistically and publicly. However, the revival late in the season of Margulies's *Sight Unseen* starring Laura Linney marked a turning point, leading to plays the next season by Craig Lucas (*Reckless* revival) and Margulies (*Brooklyn Boy*) and in 2005–6 by Lindsay-Abaire (*Rabbit Hole;* Pulitzer Prize) and Nilo Cruz (*The Beauty of the Father*). The first 25 years of MTC's history is chronicled in John W. Pereira's *Opening Nights* (1996).   REK

Manhattan Theatre Company Harrison Grey Fiske established this company at the Manhattan Theatre (formerly the Standard Theater) in 1901 to produce plays starring his wife, popular actress Minnie Maddern Fiske. H. G. Fiske, editor of the *New York Dramatic Mirror* and arch opponent of the Theatrical Syndicate, employed a small nucleus of continuing performers and many new players for each production. The group produced between two and nine plays each season. From 1906, when Fiske abandoned the Manhattan

Theater, to 1914, the Manhattan Company was on tour in support of Mrs. Fiske. Fiske was noted for his tasteful direction, his exciting crowd scenes, and his attention to detail in acting, scenery, and costumes. He recruited fine performers and molded them into an expressive ensemble.
WD

Mann, Daniel (Chugerman) (1912–91) Director. Starting at the Canadian Drama Festival (Toronto, 1939), Mann made his mark with *Come Back, Little Sheba* on Broadway (1950), followed by the film version (1952). He also directed *The Rose Tattoo* (stage, 1951; film, 1955), *Paint Your Wagon* (1951), and *A Loss of Roses* (1959). His major directing assignments from the late 1950s to 1980 were film and television projects, including *Playing for Time* (TV, 1980; script by Arthur Miller).
REK

Mann, Emily (1952–) Director and playwright. Currently the McCarter Theatre Company's artistic director, Mann has directed at the Guthrie Theater, Brooklyn Academy of Music, American Place Theatre, and Actors Theatre of Louisville. *Execution of Justice* (1986) marked her Broadway directing and playwriting debut. Mann describes her plays – *Execution, Annulla: An Autobiography* (1977; staged 1988, New Theater of Brooklyn, starring Linda Hunt), *Still Life* (1980, Chicago), *Betsey Brown* (1989, Philadelphia; cowritten with Ntozake Shange, on whose story and novel it was based), and the screenplay *Winnie: The Winnie Mandela Story* – as "theatre of testimony" (see documentary theatre).

Productions of *Execution of Justice* won regional awards and a 1986 Drama Desk nomination for Outstanding New Play; *Still Life* won the 1981 Best Production Obie. *Having Our Say,* which she wrote and directed (based on the story of the Delaney sisters), won her 1995 Tony Award nominations in both categories and the Dramatists Guild's Hull–Warringer Award. She directed Anna Deavere Smith in the original production of *Twilight: Los Angeles, 1992* (1993, Mark Taper Forum and McCarter) and Nilo Cruz's Pulitzer-winning *Anna in the Tropics,* first at the McCarter and then on Broadway (both 2003).   REK

Mann [né Goldman]**, Theodore** (1924–) Producer and director. Mann cofounded Circle in the Square Theatre (with José Quintero, 1951), and, as artistic director, directed Circle's Broadway revival of *Mourning Becomes Electra* (1972); other plays include *A Moon for the Misbegotten* (1968), *Ah, Wilderness!* (1969, Ford's Theatre,

Richard Mansfield as the title character in *Beau Brummel,* first performed in 1890. *Courtesy:* Don B. Wilmeth Theatre Collection.

Washington, DC), *The ICEMAN COMETH* (1973), *The GLASS MENAGERIE* (1975), *PAL JOEY* (1976), and *The Boys in Autumn* (1986); he has also directed various operas and teleplays. Mann cofounded Circle's school (1961), and initiated an exchange with Moscow's Maly Theatre (1989). As a producer, he received 1957 Tony and Drama Critics' Circle awards for *A LONG DAY'S JOURNEY INTO NIGHT* and a special 1976 Tony.   REK

Manners, J. Hartley (1870–1928) Playwright and director. Although London-born, his career after 1902 transpired in New York. Many of his plays were written as vehicles for his wife, LAURETTE TAYLOR, especially *PEG O' MY HEART* (1912), a sentimental comedy of the poor outsider who reforms her rich relatives. This play, which ran for over 600 performances, proved one of the most popular comedies of the American theatre. Manners was also successful with *The Harp of Life* (1916) and *Happiness* (1917), both with Taylor.   RHW

Mansfield, Richard (1854–1907) Actor-producer. Hailed by many as America's answer to Henry Irving after the death of EDWIN BOOTH, this strong personality generated critical controversy whenever he performed. He played his first important role of Baron Chevrial in *A Parisian Romance* in 1883 after a series of minor roles in England and the U.S. In 1886 he launched a production with himself as the star in the title role of *Prince Karl;* with this role, he began his successful career as a star and producer. Each year, Mansfield would arrange to occupy theatres in New York and on the road to present a repertory consisting of one or two new characters and revivals of his more successful previous vehicles. A compelling, intense actor and skillful producer, his notable roles and productions included the dual-role *Dr. Jekyll and Mr. Hyde* (1887); *Richard III* and *Henry V;* CLYDE FITCH's *Beau Brummell* (1890); Bluntschli in *Arms and the Man* (1894, the first U.S. production of SHAW); the title role in *Napoleon Bonaparte* (1894); Dick Dudgeon in Shaw's *The Devil's Disciple* (1897); *Cyrano de Bergerac* (1889); BOOTH TARKINGTON's *Beaucaire* (1901); and IBSEN's *Peer Gynt* (1907). Mansfield also produced, but did not play in, *A Doll's House* in London (1888) and in New York (1889), with Beatrice Cameron (whom he was to marry in 1892) as Nora. His productions were characterized by lavish spectacle and a meticulous attention to realistic detail. Mansfield was a forceful transitional figure on the American stage at the turn of the 20th century, representing the waning traditions of the old era and the emerging tendencies of the new century. An exhaustive biography in two volumes was written by William Winter (1910).   MR   DJW

Mantegna, Joe [né Joseph Anthony Mantegna Jr.] (1948–) Chicago-born actor and writer whose work has been closely identified with plays and films of DAVID MAMET, a longtime friend and associate. (Critic Jack Kroll described Mantegna in 1988 as "gloriously Mametic.") He appeared in premieres at the GOODMAN THEATRE of Mamet's *A Life in the Theatre* (1977), *The Disappearance of the Jews* (1983), and *GLENGARRY GLEN ROSS* (the role of Richard Roman), winning a Tony on Broadway for the latter in 1984. He also appeared in Mamet's *Speed-the-Plow* (1988) and his films *House of Games* (1987), *Things Change* (1988), *Homicide* (1991), and *Edmond* (2005), and directed Mamet's screenplay *Lakeboat* in 2000. Active early with CHICAGO's ORGANIC THEATRE COMPANY – where he conceived and helped write the play *Bleacher Bums* (1977), which ran in LA for more than five years – Mantegna in recent years has focused more on films and television (father in *Joan of Arcadia,* 2003–5) than on stage work.   DBW

Mantell, Robert Bruce (1854–1928) Scottish-born actor who trained in England under some of the leading late 19th-century practitioners of "classical" acting, such as Barry Sullivan and Samuel Phelps. He came to America in 1878 as a member of HELENA MODJESKA's touring company. He returned to England, but came back to play in support of FANNY DAVENPORT in *Fedora* in 1883. In 1886 he made his first star appearance in *Tangled Lives,* a modern domestic melodrama. A series of starring tours in modern heroic melodramas outside of New York were only limited successes until he began to incorporate Shakespearean tragedies (see SHAKESPEARE ON . . .) and the "classical" romances of Bulwer-Lytton into his repertory in the 1890s. In 1904 he made a triumphant return to New York and established himself as the last remaining representative of a robust, passionate "old school" of tragic acting in America, generating much discussion over the merits of this system. Among his more celebrated roles were Othello, Shylock, King John, King Lear, Macbeth, Richard III, Richelieu, and Louis XI.   MR   DJW

Mantello, Joe (1962–) Actor turned director, born in Rockford, IL, and educated at North Carolina School of the Arts, whose talent first received major attention as a result of his seamless direction of the ensemble cast in MCNALLY's Tony Award–winning play *Love! Valour! Compassion!* (1994; nominated for a 1995 Tony for direction, winner Best Play). As an actor Mantello had previously gained recognition (after his debut OFF-BROADWAY in *Crackwalker,* 1987) as Louis Ironson in ANGELS IN AMERICA (receiving major awards and nominations for *Millenium Approaches*) and as "The Third Man" and Doctor in *The Baltimore Waltz* (1992, CIRCLE REP). His Broadway directorial credits alone since 1995 are impressive: FRANKIE AND JOHNNY IN THE CLAIR DE LUNE (2002), TAKE ME OUT (2003; directing Tony), WICKED (2003; Drama Desk for direction), *Assassins* (2004; Tony), the revivals of GLENGARRY GLEN ROSS and THE ODD COUPLE (both 2005), and RICHARD GREENBERG's *Three Days of Rain* with Julia Roberts (2006). He is an associate artist at the ROUNDABOUT.   DBW

Mantle, (Robert) Burns (1873–1948) Drama critic and annalist. Trained as a printer, Mantle turned to dramatic criticism in 1898 for the *Denver Times,* moved to the *Denver Republican* in 1901, and during the same year left for Chicago and a six-year stint as critic for the *Inter-Ocean* (1901–7). In 1907 he spent a year as reviewer for the *Chicago Tribune* before becoming that paper's Sunday editor. In 1911 he accepted the dramatic post for the *New York Evening Mail,* and changed jobs one last time in 1922 when he moved to the *Daily News* (1922–43). A strong supporter of the American drama, Mantle wrote in a bright and newsy style. His *Best Play* series, which he edited from 1919 until 1947–8, remains his most enduring contribution to the American stage.   TLM

Marble, Danforth (1810–49) American actor who began a successful career in 1832 telling Yankee stories. In competition with GEORGE H. HILL and JAMES H. HACKETT, Marble developed a distinctive YANKEE character with broad American idiosyncrasies. His vehicles included *The* FOREST ROSE, *The Vermont Wool Dealer, Yankee Land,* and *The Backwoodsman; or, The Gamecock of the Wilderness,* but his particular success was as *Sam Patch; or, The Daring Yankee* (1836). The real Sam Patch made a career of jumping from high places: His last jump was from the top of the Genesee Falls (Rochester, NY) in 1829, a distance of 125 feet. Marble made his jumps in theatres as spectacular as possible. A consummate teller of tales and strikingly costumed, he enjoyed a successful visit to England in 1844, playing before the king and queen; he sponsored a playwriting contest for new material in 1845 and toured America extensively. He died of cholera on the night of his benefit – the play, *A Cure for the Cholera.* A brief biography by Jonathan Kelly appeared in 1851.   WJM

Marbury, Elisabeth (1856–1933) Agent, producer, playwright. First dramatist's AGENT in the U.S., Marbury developed an international clientele of writers and performers, including FRANCES BURNETT, SHAW, Wilde, Barrie, Sardou, Feydeau, FITCH, CROTHERS, the Castles, and Rostand. An astute socialite and businesswoman, she convinced international authors to negotiate royalties rather than one-time fees. She sometimes influenced casting and script development, and lobbied for improved conditions for actors. With John W. Rumsey, she founded the American Play Company in 1914, a worldwide agency. She produced the PRINCESS musicals (beginning 1915), developing the story-focused musical. Decorated for war services, she was politically active. Her memoirs were published in 1924.   TH-S

March, Fredric [né Frederick McIntyre Bickel] (1897–1975) Actor. Educated at the University of Wisconsin, March made his theatrical debut (under his real name) in 1920 in Sacha Guitry's *Deburau*. His first major role, still as Bickel, was in WILLIAM A. BRADY's production of *The Law Breaker* (1922). After an assortment of juvenile leads – and appearing as March in *The Melody Man* (1924) – he performed in Molnár's *The Swan* in Denver with actress FLORENCE ELDRIDGE (1926). They were married a year later and worked together for the rest of their careers. After spending most of the 1930s in Hollywood, March returned to the stage in 1938, costarring with his wife in *Yr. Obedient Husband*. Working in both media, he created for the stage the roles of Mr. Antrobus in *The SKIN OF OUR TEETH* (1942); Major Victor Joppolo in *A Bell for Adano* (1944); Nicholas Denery in *The Autumn Garden* (1951); and James Tyrone in *A LONG DAY'S JOURNEY INTO NIGHT* (1956), which won him his second Tony (first for *Years Ago*, 1946). He appeared in 69 films, including starring roles in *Dr. Jekyll and Mr. Hyde* (1931), which won him an Oscar; *Les Misérables* (1935); *A Star Is Born* (1937); *The Best Years of Our Lives* (1946), which won him an Oscar; *INHERIT THE WIND* (1960); and *The ICEMAN COMETH* (1973). March considered the role of James Tyrone his finest work. BROOKS ATKINSON wrote: "As the aging actor who stands at the head of the family, Fredric March gives a masterly performance that will stand as a milestone in the acting of an O'NEILL play." Deborah C. Peterson's biography appeared in 1996. TLM

Margaret Fleming Domestic drama (1890) in four acts by JAMES A. HERNE. WILLIAM DEAN HOWELLS hailed its production at BOSTON's Chickering Hall on 4 May 1891 as "epoch-making" (or "marking") in the rise of realism in Amer-ican fiction and drama. HAMLIN GARLAND, Herne's friend and promoter among Boston's radical intelligentsia, proclaimed it "one of the most radical plays from a native author ever performed in America." Margaret's husband fathers a child with a mill worker in his hire. Early versions of the play end with Margaret spurning her husband's efforts at reconciliation. In the revised version, Philip is permitted to return, and emphasis shifts to a critique of the double standard of sexual morality: defamation and death for the woman offender; forgiveness and acceptance for the man. Critics who rejected the play were especially offended by the spectacle of Margaret breast-feeding her husband's starving bastard. Nevertheless, Katharine Corcoran Herne, the author's wife and a major collaborator in writing and revising the play, won nearly universal acclaim for her acting in the title role. WD

Margolin, Deb(orah) (1953?–) Playwright, performance artist, and founding member of SPLIT BRITCHES, whose work has influenced feminist theatre since the early 1980s. Author of seven full-length solo performance pieces and recipient of an Obie in 2000 for Sustained Excellence of Performance. She has also written numerous plays, most notably *Three Seconds in the Key* (2001, P.S. 122; 2004. New Georges), about a terminally ill mother and her son who pass time by watching basketball on television. MARGO JEFFERSON reflected that every minute and every move counted; "We glory in the craft and heart that take us beyond the boundaries of everyday time for a short time." For this effort, Margolin received the 2005 Kesselring Prize for Playwriting. DBW

Margolis, Kari (1955–) and **Tony Brown** (1951–) Co–artistic directors of Margolis/Brown Adaptors (now the Margolis Brown Theatre Co.), a multimedia movement theatre founded in 1983; located first in NYC, then from 1993 in MINNEAPOLIS, and as of 2005 in the foothills of the Catskills. Students of Étienne Decroux (see MIME) during 1975–8, they were founding members of Omnibus (Montréal), directed by Jean Asslin and Denise Boulanger, from 1978 to 1982. Group works they have created with students trained in their school are *Autobahn* (1984); *Deco Dance* (1986); *Bed Experiment One* (1987); *Decodanz: The Dilemma of Desmodes and Diphylla* (1991), a duet for Margolis and Brown; *Kopplevision and Other Digital Dieties* (1991), a work for 18 actors; *Vanishing Point* (1995); *Bed Experiment II* (1997); *Vidpires!* (1998); *American Safari* (2001); *Sleepwalkers* (2002). TL

Margulies, Donald (1954–) Born in Brooklyn and grew up in Trump Village, a Coney Island housing project; educated at Pratt Institute and State University of New York. His play *DINNER WITH FRIENDS,* a bittersweet comedy about marriage and divorce commissioned by ACTORS THEATRE OF LOUISVILLE (1998) and produced Off-Broadway in 1999, won the 2000 Pulitzer Prize for Drama. Much of his work (unlike *Friends,* which is essentially realistic) has a slightly fantastic bent, with ghosts and mythic figures: In *The Loman Family Picnic* (1989), for example, characters express hidden thoughts, burst into musical numbers, and have visitations from dead relatives. Author of numerous one-acts, Margulies's major full-length plays include *What's Wrong with This Picture?* (1990, JEWISH REP), *Sight Unseen* (1992, Obie; Pulitzer nominee; revived with acclaim by the MANHATTAN THEATRE CLUB in 2004), *Broken Sleep* (1997, WILLIAMSTOWN THEATRE FESTIVAL), *Collected Sto-*

ries (1996, SOUTH COAST REP; 1997 Pulitzer nominee), and *Brooklyn Boy* (2005, MTC). A 1993 Guggenheim Fellow, he teaches playwriting at the Yale School of Drama.   DBW

Mark Hellinger Theatre 237 West 51st St., NYC [Architect: Thomas W. Lamb]. In the early years of the Depression, many theatres that became unprofitable for their owners were turned into moviehouses; but the Hollywood Theatre, built by Warner Bros. to showcase their most important movies, appeared to have reversed the trend. Opening in 1930, it switched to legitimate fare in 1934, but from then until 1949, when the film company disposed of it, it changed name and policy frequently. Even the entrance was diverted from Broadway to West 51st St. in 1936. In 1949, its name became the Mark Hellinger in honor of the Broadway columnist, and so it remained for the rest of its theatrical life. In 1956, the theatre received its most illustrious tenant in its lackluster history when MY FAIR LADY opened and held its stage until 1962 (replaced by *The SOUND OF MUSIC*). Since then, with the exception of the rock musical *Jesus Christ Superstar* (1971) and *Sugar Babies* (1979), which introduced Mickey Rooney to Broadway, there have been few outstanding productions at the theatre. Until late 1991 part of the NEDERLANDER chain, it was closed in 1989, leased to the Times Square Church for five years, and then sold to them.   MCH

Mark Taper Forum Theatre 135 North Grand Ave., LOS ANGELES [Architect: Welton Beckett]. Rising from the center of a cultural corridor in downtown Los Angeles is the giant, concrete, mushroom-shaped Mark Taper Forum, one of the homes of CENTER THEATRE GROUP, a not-for-profit theatre company that grew out of a professional company attached to the University of California at Los Angeles and is now overseen by MICHAEL RITCHIE. Opening in 1967, the Taper and its sister theatre, the AHMANSON – as well as the new (2004) Kirk Douglas Theatre – have made CTG one of the largest and most active theatre companies in the country. The Taper is named after a Los Angeles financier-philanthropist who was instrumental in planning and building the Los Angeles Music Center, of which the 745-seat Mark Taper Forum is part.   MCH

Marks, Josephine Preston Peabody (1874–1922) Playwright-poet with a dominating interest in historical or literary material. She wrote *Marlowe* (1901), an idealized view of the poet-dramatist as revealed through his "passionate shepherd"

poem, and in *The Wolf of Gubbio* (1913) dramatized the influence of St. Francis of Assisi in a man's struggle between love and greed. *Portrait of Miss W* (1922) was based on the love of Mary Wollstonecraft and William Godwin. None of these plays was produced. Marks's best work, *The Piper* (1910), impressed OTIS SKINNER, won the Stratford-on-Avon Memorial Prize ($1,500), and was staged in NYC at the New Theatre (1911; revived at the Fulton Theatre, 1920). Her piper was a "fanatical idealist" in whom the forces of love, greed, and the supernatural present a universal human struggle as cynical bitterness wars with self-denying love. Marks's plays are more appreciated in the library than in the theatre.   WJM

Marks, Peter J. (1955–) Brooklyn-born theatre critic, educated at Yale (1977). He began his career as a reporter at the *Newark Star-Ledger* (1978–82), *The Bergen Record* (1982–5), and *Newsday* (1985–93). From 1993 to 2002 he served as theatre critic, arts reporter, and political reporter for the *New York Times*. In 2002 he became the chief theatre critic for the *Washington Post*. Since 2004 he also has taught in honors and theatre at George Washington University. He received the Public Humanities Award in 2004 from the Humanities Council of Washington, DC.   TLM

Marlowe, Julia (1866–1950) British-born actress. From 1904, when E. H. SOTHERN and Julia Marlowe first appeared together, until her retirement in 1924, American theatregoers identified Shakespeare with Sothern and Marlowe (see SHAKESPEARE ON . . .). They were an established team even before their marriage in 1911. The roles of Rosalind, Viola, Juliet, Ophelia, and Portia became her property, and she captivated the critics, who praised her feminine loveliness, magnetic warmth, and admirable grace. When the pair appeared in England in 1907, Arthur Symons wrote: "No actors on the British stage could speak English verse so beautifully."

Marlowe had a long and steady apprenticeship. Her family emigrated from England when she was 5 and settled in Cincinnati, where she appeared with a juvenile company and was tutored in the "classic" repertoire by Ada Dow, a retired actress. In 1884 Miss Dow brought her to New York, securing touring engagements for her in roles such as Lady Teazle and Miss Hardcastle, and (in 1886) as Lydia Languish with JOSEPH JEFFERSON's touring company. Her first New York triumph came in 1899 in the title role in CLYDE FITCH's *Barbara Frietchie*. Sothern edited a version of her life, which was published in 1954.   RM

Marowitz, Charles (1934–) Director, translator, playwright, author, and critic. American-born and English-educated, Marowitz remained in England during 1958–81 as director, In-Stage Experimental Theatre (1958); as an associate of Peter Brook's on *King Lear* (1962) and a "Theatre of Cruelty" season (1964), which was reflected in his "collage" versions of *Hamlet* (1966), *Macbeth* (1969), *Othello* (1972), *The Taming of the Shrew* (1974), and *Measure for Measure* (1975); as assistant director, RSC (1963–5); artistic director, Traverse Theatre (1963–4); and founder of the Open Space Company (1968–81), which introduced the American avant-garde to English audiences. Returning to the U.S., Marowitz founded the Open Theatre of Los Angeles (1982) before becoming associate director, Los Angeles Theater Center (1984–9), and, later, founding artistic director for the Malibu Stage Company. He has written for *Encore Magazine, Plays and Players,* the *Village Voice,* the *New York Times,* the *LA Herald Examiner, TheatreWeek,* and *Swans Commentary* (online). His more than two dozen books include *The Method as Means* (1960), *Confessions of a Counterfeit Critic* (1973), *The Marowitz Shakespeare* (1978), *Prospero's Staff* (1986), *Recycling Shakespeare* (1990), his memoirs, *Burnt Bridges* (1990), *Directing the Action* (1991), *Alarums and Excursions* (1996), *The Other Chekhov* (2004), and *The Other Way: An Alternative Approach to Acting and Directing* (2006). His play *Sherlock's Last Case* ran on Broadway in 1987 with Frank Langella. TLM

Marquis Theatre 1535 Broadway, NYC [Architect: John C. Portman Jr., with Roger Morgan] The newest Broadway playhouse and the first theatre built as an integral part of a hotel, the Marriott Marquis, it is under lease to the Nederlander Organization for 35 years. The theatre is on the third floor, with the box office at street level. It boasts many innovations, notably concealed lighting and sound equipment in the ceiling, a steeply raked orchestra floor, and complete accessibility for handicapped persons. With a seating capacity of 1,600, it is best suited for musicals, which have been its fare since opening with *Me and My Girl* in 1986, a show that ran for nearly three and a half years. The revival of *Annie Get Your Gun,* which opened in 1999, amassed 1,046 performances. MCH

Marriage of Bette and Boo, The, by Christopher Durang. After productions of a shorter version at the Yale School of Drama and the Williamstown Theatre, the full play was presented by Joseph Papp's New York Shakespeare Festival on 16 May 1985, directed by Jerry Zaks, with a cast including Christopher Durang as the narrator, Matt, whose memory play this is; Joan Allen as his mother, Bette; Graham Beckel as his father, Boo; and Olympia Dukakis as his grandmother, Soot. Using Thomas Hardy's naturalistic novels as a literary context, Durang's black comedy depicts the effects of alcohol, emotional instability, and the Catholic Church on a contemporary American family's inability to function. Attempting to understand his own life by analyzing it as if it were a literary work, narrator Matt guides the audience through the series of hilariously tragic events that he feels have determined his character and defined his life. BCM

Marshall, E(dda or Everett) G(unnar) (1914–98) Stage, film, and television actor, born in Minnesota. A distinguished veteran performer who took on a wide range of character types, Marshall came to Broadway in the 1930s. Notable early roles included Willie Oban in *The Iceman Cometh* (1946), Rev. John Hale and then John Proctor in *The Crucible* (1953, replacement), and Vladimir in the famous production of Beckett's *Waiting for Godot* with costar Bert Lahr (1956). He also appeared in such revivals as *John Gabriel Borkman* (1980) and an *She Stoops to Conquer* (1984, Roundabout). Four years on the television series *The Defenders* (1961–5) earned him two Emmy Awards (1962, 1963). MR

Marshall, Ethelbert A. (d. 1881) Manager, credited as the first businessman to dominate the American theatre. After an apprenticeship as a printer, Marshall turned to theatrical management about 1838, beginning his empire in 1840 with the Walnut Street Theatre (Philadelphia). By the mid-1840s, with the additional control of theatres in Baltimore and Washington, DC, he turned to starring vehicles with actors such as Forrest, Booth, Wallack, and Cushman. In 1848 he moved into New York, controlling the 4,500-seat Broadway Theatre. By 1850 he was the acknowledged star maker of the American stage. Despite alliances with theatre owners in Cincinatti, Louisville, St. Louis, and New Orleans, by the mid-1850s his operation began to decline. He sold the Broadway in 1858 and spent the balance of his career as manager of the Philadelphia Academy of Music. DBW

Marshall, Kathleen (1963–) Wisconsin-born, Pittsburgh-raised, Smith College–educated choreographer, recipient of the 2004 Tony for her choreography of the revival of *Wonderful Town* in 2003 (also her directorial debut). Sister of Rob

MARSHALL she began her NYC career as assistant to him on *Kiss of the Spider Woman* (1993), then *SHE LOVES ME* (1993) and *DAMN YANKEES* (1994). To date this respected choreographer has handled eight Broadway shows, including *KISS ME, KATE* (1999; London, 2001), *Seussical* (2000), *FOLLIES* (2001), *Little Shop of Horrors* (2003), and *The PAJAMA GAME* (2006, Tony nominations for direction and choreography, winning the latter) as well as three TV musical presentations: *Kiss Me, Kate* (2003), *The MUSIC MAN* (2003), and *Once upon a Mattress* (2005). In 2005 she directed and choreographed the musical revival *Two Gentlemen of Verona* at the Delacorte, and she is slated to do both for a new Broadway revival of *Grease.* For several years she was artistic director for the CITY CENTER ENCORES! series. In 2005 she shared the "Mr. Abbott" Award in direction with her brother.   DBW

Marshall, Rob (1961–) Born in Wisconsin but raised in Pittsburgh, where he attended Carnegie Mellon (1982 graduate), this esteemed chorographer-director began as a dancer in *CATS, Zorba, The Rink,* and *The Mystery of Edwin Drood* but in 1993 moved into choreography as a collaborator on *Kiss of the Spider Woman.* In addition to that show he has been nominated for the Tony for *SHE LOVES ME* (1993; 1994 nom.), *DAMN YANKEES* (1994), *Little Me* (1998; 1999 nom.), and, for Best Direction of a Musical with collaborator Sam Mendes, *CABARET* (1998). Marshall is best known, however, as director of the award-winning film version of *CHICAGO* (2002), for which he received an Academy Award nomination. In 2005 he directed the film *Memoirs of a Geisha.* Marshall's partner is choreographer and director John DeLuca, who in 2005 choreographed JULIE ANDREWS's production (GOODSPEED, tour) of *The Boy Friend.* His sister is KATHLEEN MARSHALL.   DBW

Martin, Ernest H. see FEUER, CY

Martin, Jane (pseud.?) Supposedly a Kentuckian, Martin is called "America's best known, unknown playwright." Since the premiere in 1981 of Martin's *Talking with . . . ,* a group of 11 monologues about obsessive enthusiasms, at ACTORS THEATRE OF LOUISVILLE, her true identity has become one of the American theatre's greatest mysteries. Since that event, virtually all of Martin's plays (her works number over 30, many short) premiered at ACT (including 10 full-length plays between 1982 and 2001), all directed by former artistic director JON JORY, believed by many to be the true author (possibly in collaboration with his wife, Marcia Dixcy). Regardless, the best-known and critically

most successful of the corpus is *Keely and Du* (1993), a finalist for the 1994 Pulitzer in Drama, which tackles the abortion debate. Other recent titles: *Jack and Jill* (1996), *Anton in Show Business* (2000), *Flaming Guns of the Purple Sage* (2001), and *Bill of (W)Rights* (2004, MIXED BLOOD THEATRE).   DBW

Martin, Mary (1913–90) Singer and actress who made her Broadway debut in *Leave It to Me* (1938), in which she stopped the show with her teasing rendition of "My Heart Belongs to Daddy." Her first starring role was as a statue come to life in *One Touch of Venus* (1943). Three years later, she played the faithful wife in *Lute Song,* a musical version of a traditional Chinese play. In 1947 she headed the national company of *ANNIE GET YOUR GUN.* Martin had the greatest success of her career as Nellie Forbush, a Navy nurse from Little Rock, AR, in RODGERS and HAMMERSTEIN's *SOUTH PACIFIC* (1949). Among the songs she introduced in the show were "A Cockeyed Optimist," "I'm Gonna Wash That Man Right Outa My Hair," and "I'm In Love with a Wonderful Guy." The role was ideally suited to her sunny temperament and buoyant singing style, and also gave her an opportunity to demonstrate her skill as an actress during the show's more serious scenes. In 1954 she appeared in a musical version of James M. Barrie's *Peter Pan,* a role she repeated in two television versions of the show. Although rather mature for the part of a young novice, Martin's performance in *The SOUND OF MUSIC* (1959) was a favorite with audiences. Her next show, *Jennie* (1963), was a failure. She starred in the London company of *HELLO, DOLLY!* before appearing with ROBERT PRESTON in *I Do! I Do!* (1966), a two-character musical that followed a couple through 50 years of married life. In most of her musical-theatre roles Martin portrayed a warm-hearted idealist who ultimately triumphs over the problems she faces. Her clear singing voice, winning personality, and high spirits contributed greatly to the success of the shows in which she appeared. Her final stage role was in *Legends* in 1986 with CAROL CHANNING (closed in tryouts). Her autobiography (*My Heart Belongs*) was published in 1976; a collection devoted to her career is in the Doss Heritage and Culture Center in her hometown of Weatherford, TX.   MK

Martin Beck Theatre 302 West 45th St., NYC [Architect: G. Albert Lansburgh]. Built in 1924 as a monument to its owner, the 1,300-seat playhouse was named after Martin Beck, a leading VAUDEVILLE producer of the era. Located west of Eighth Ave. on the edge of the theatre district, the theatre was thought to be too far away to attract productions and audiences, but the skeptics were confounded. Opening with an operetta, it has subsequently housed a mixture of large and small productions, musical (recently *Grand Hotel*) and nonmusical, and did not endure long periods of inactivity. Its most noteworthy tenants have included productions by the THEATRE GUILD, the Irish Abbey Players, and the D'Oyly Carte Company, as well as plays by EUGENE O'NEILL, ROBERT E. SHERWOOD, LILLIAN HELLMAN, MAXWELL ANDERSON, PHILIP BARRY, EDWARD ALBEE, and TENNESSEE WILLIAMS. The theatre was a special favorite of KATHARINE CORNELL and GUTHRIE MCCLINTIC, who booked the house for their repertory. Two Pulitzer Prize winners opened at the Martin Beck: *The Teahouse of the August Moon* (1953) and *A DELICATE BALANCE* (1966). When Martin Beck died in 1940, his widow continued to operate the theatre, but in 1966 she sold it to the JUJAMCYN Organization. In 2003 it became the AL HIRSCHFELD Theatre.   MCH

Marvin's Room Scott McPherson's 1990 play, which, though it deals with lingering and terminal illness, along with other unpleasant topics, was conceived as a VAUDEVILLE-style doctor sketch. Marvin, the title character who has been dying for 20 years, remains a shadow throughout the play. Produced first at the GOODMAN, then HARTFORD STAGE, then in NYC by PLAYWRIGHTS HORIZONS in 1991 prior to transfer to Minetta Lane (for a total of 313 performances). LAURA ESTERMAN, who played Marvin's daughter Bessie, received an Obie for her performance (played in the film by Diane Keaton). McPherson wrote the screenplay but died shortly afterward from AIDS-related complications. The film, directed by JERRY ZAKS, with Keaton, MERYL STREEP, and Leonardo DiCaprio, was released in 1996. This was the author's only notable play/film.   DBW

Marx Bros. (their preferred billing) Comedy team. The first to perform were **Gummo** [Milton] (1897–1977) and **Groucho** [Julius] (1895–1977)], with material written by their uncle, Al Shean of GALLAGHER & SHEAN; **Chico** [Leonard] (1891–1961)] and **Harpo** [Adolph] (1893–1964)] joined later. Shean wrote their act "Fun in Hi Skool" (1912), with Groucho as a Dutch-accented schoolmaster, and "Home Again" (1914), directed by their formidable mother, Minnie Palmer. When Gummo was drafted into war service, ZEPPO [Herbert] (1901–79)] stepped in. By the time they topped the bill at the PALACE in 1920, they were commanding $10,000 a week for their hilarious mayhem.

By then, their distinctive characteristics were in place: Zeppo, the handsome, bemused straight man; Harpo, the uninhibited curly-headed mute, honking his horn, goosing showgirls, and taking every metaphor literally; Chico, the saturnine Neapolitan, interrupting his con games only to crack bad puns and play ragtime piano; and Groucho, with his greasepaint moustache and eyeglasses, stooping lope and unflagging cigar, confuting reason on every plane. They played London in 1922, but tiring of VAUDEVILLE moved to REVUE in *I'll Say She Is* (1924, CASINO), with its famous Napoleon scene in which Groucho ordered the band to strike up "The Mayonnaise." Their next shows, *The COCOANUTS* (1925, Lyric) and *ANIMAL CRACKERS* (1928, 44th St.), were cowritten by GEORGE S. KAUFMAN, who, with S. J. PERELMAN, was largely responsible for perfecting their verbal style. With the filming of these productions, the brothers moved successfully to Hollywood, although they continued to make stage appearances during their MGM period to try out the comic scenes in their screenplays. Not so much satirists as anarchists, they flouted normality whenever they confronted it. Their film career petered out in the 1940s; Groucho became the star of a television quiz show (1950–1) and played a one-person show at Carnegie Hall (1972). The most recent extensive bio of Groucho by Stefan Kanfer appeared in 2000.   LS

Mary, Mary Three-act comedy by JEAN KERR, opened at the HELEN HAYES THEATRE 8 March 1961 for 1,572 performances; then Broadway's ninth longest-run production and fifth longest-run play. Starring Barbara BEL GEDDES (for whom Kerr wrote the role) and Barry Nelson, the play comments on the attractions and distractions of marriage, divorce, and reconciliation. Critics praised Kerr, an established writer with popular books *Please Don't Eat the Daisies* and *The Snake Has All the Lines*, for her charming, articulate script liberally laced with witticisms and wisecracks. A film version starring Debbie Reynolds was made early in the run, but the play outran it by far.   EK

Mason, Marshall W. (1940–) Texas-born director and a cofounder and former artistic director of the CIRCLE REPERTORY COMPANY in NYC. Trained at the ACTORS STUDIO, Mason had specialized in the production of new American plays, especially those of LANFORD WILSON (most notably *The HOT L BALTIMORE*, 1973; *FIFTH OF JULY*, 1978; *TALLEY'S FOLLY*, 1979; *Angels Fall*, 1983; *BURN THIS*, 1987; *Redwood Curtain*, 1993). In 1985 his award-winning Circle Rep production of William M.

Hoffman's *As Is,* one of the first American plays to deal with the disease AIDS, was transferred to Broadway. In 1992 he directed LARRY KRAMER's award-winning AIDS play, *The Destiny of Me* OFF-BROADWAY. He, Wilson, and the company shared a 1983 Obie Award for Sustained Achievement. In 1986 Mason resigned from Circle Rep, replaced in 1987 by Tanya Berezin. In recent years he has worked at such theatres as STEPPENWOLF and SOUTH COAST REPERTORY in California, and for a decade taught at Arizona State Univerity (retired in 2004).   DBW

Massey, Raymond Hart (1896–1983) Canadian-born actor and director who became a U.S. citizen in 1944. From 1922, when he made his debut in London as Jack in O'NEILL's *In the Zone* at the Everyman Theatre, until 1931, when he made his Broadway debut as Hamlet in NORMAN BEL GEDDES's unorthodox production, he acted in England in several dozen plays and directed numerous others. His subsequent career, largely limited to the U.S., ranged from Shakespeare (see SHAKESPEARE ON . . .), Strindberg, SHAW, O'Casey, and O'Neill in the theatre, to a wide range of villains and heroes in films (more than 70), and the role of Dr. Gillespie in the television series *Dr. Kildare.* His most memorable stage role was Lincoln in ROBERT E. SHERWOOD's ABE LINCOLN IN ILLINOIS (1938), which suited his imposing presence, craggy handsomeness, and vibrant voice. Other notable roles included Ethan Frome in an adaptation of the novel (1936), Harry Van in IDIOT'S DELIGHT (1938, London), Sir Colenso Ridgeon in *The Doctor's Dilemma* (1941), James Morell in *Candida* (1942), Higgins in *Pygmalion* (1945), Mr. Zuss in *J.B.* (1958), and Tom Garrison in I NEVER SANG FOR MY FATHER (his return to the London stage in 1970). Massey was the author of two autobiographies, *When I Was Young* (1976) and *A Hundred Different Lives* (1979). His children, Daniel and Anna, born in England, have had successful careers in the theatre. **Daniel** appeared on Broadway four times (last in *Taking Sides,* 1996); **Anna** only once (*The Reluctant Debutante,* 1956).   DBW

Masteroff, Joe (Joseph) (1919–) Philadelphia-born librettist educated at Temple University. His first success came with the libretto for SHE LOVES ME (1963), the musical adaptation of the film *The Shop around the Corner.* In 1966 working in collaboration with producer-director HAROLD PRINCE, he wrote the book for CABARET, a musical based on JOHN VAN DRUTEN's play *I AM A CAMERA* and Christopher Isherwood's *Berlin Stories.* With Prince, he invented the character of the decadent

Master of Ceremonies, whose musical sequences punctuate and comment upon the action. He worked with others on the libretto of *70, Girls, 70* (1971), the ONE-PERSON show *Jane White, Who? . . .* (1980, OFF-BROADWAY), and *Six Wives* (1992). He also wrote the libretto for the opera DESIRE UNDER THE ELMS (1989).   MK

Mastrosimone, William (1947–) New Jersey–born playwright whose controversial *Extremities* (1982), which dealt with an attempted rape and its subsequent violence, won an Outer Critics' Circle Award and was adapted as film with Farrah Fawcett (1986). Like many talented writers of his generation, his work has been produced in the regional theatres rather than on Broadway. *Cat's Paw* (1986) and *The Understanding* (1987) both premiered at the SEATTLE REPERTORY, *Sunshine* (1989) at the CIRCLE REPERTORY, and *The Afghan Women* (2003) in Trenton, NJ. Among his awards are a 1982 LA Critics' "Best" for *The Woolgatherer* (Gallery Theater; premiered 1980, Circle Rep) and a 1984 Warner Communication citation for *Shivaree* (1983, Seattle Rep). His play about the Soviet invasion of Afghanistan, *Nanawatai* (1984, Norway; 1985, LOS ANGELES THEATRE CENTER), became the Columbia Pictures film *The Beast* (1988).   BBW

Matalon, Vivian (1929–) Director who studied at the NEIGHBORHOOD PLAYHOUSE and made his professional debut as Urban in *The Caine Mutiny Court Martial* (1956) in London. He joined the LAMDA staff in 1959 and directed his first professional show, *The Admiration of Life,* in 1960. Later in London he directed *The GLASS MENAGARIE* (1965), ROBERT ANDERSON's *I Never Sang for My Father* (1970), and NEIL SIMON's *The Gingerbread Lady* (1974). On Broadway Matalon has directed *P.S. Your Cat Is Dead* (1975), MORNING'S AT SEVEN (1980; directing Tony), *The Tap Dance Kid* (1983), and *Souvenir* (2005) with JUDY KAYE. During 1970–3 he served as artistic director at London's Hampstead Theatre Club, and in 1979 was appointed artistic director of the Academy Festival Theatre, Lake Forest, IL. Since 1960 he has also directed on television.   SMA

Matchmaker, The THORNTON WILDER play, a revision of his 1938 comedy *The Merchant of Yonkers,* which had been a disappointment in a New York production directed by MAX REINHARDT. Wilder reshaped the comedy by focusing more on the character of Dolly Levi and the talent of RUTH GORDON, who re-created her earlier English tryout performance (1954–5 season), directed

The Mathew-orama for 1824 — or —
"Pretty considerable d—d particular" Tit Bits; from America — bang'ill well at Natchetoches".

English actor-playwright Charles Mathews in an 1824 engraving of the many characters he played in *Trip to America,* an important stimulus for Yankee plays and characters. *Courtesy:* Don B. Wilmeth Theatre Collection.

by TYRONE GUTHRIE. *The Matchmaker* opened at the ROYALE THEATRE in 1955 and was an immediate hit, running for 486 performances. Its cast – which included ARTHUR HILL, ROBERT MORSE, and Eileen Herlie – delighted the critics. The play has had a number of professional and amateur revivals (e.g., ROUNDABOUT THEATRE's 1991 production featuring DOROTHY LOUDON), but it's probably most famous as the inspiration for *HELLO, DOLLY!* (1964).   BBW

Mathews, Charles (1776–1835) English actor who owed most of his contemporary fame to his gift for mimicry and was a major influence in the U.S. During 1813–17, he reshaped an earlier vehicle, *Mail Coach Adventure* (1808), for himself alone. This evolved into a famous series under the title *Mr. Mathews at Home,* an annual feature of his career from 1818 until its end. A combination of mimicry, storytelling, quick-change artistry, comic songs, and improvisation, this series was equally popular in England and the U.S., which Mathews

toured in 1822–3 and 1834. On his first trip he became the first performer to exploit the stage Yankee, and provided a strong influence on the subsequent development of YANKEE THEATRE.

His son, **Charles James Mathews** (1803–78), became an actor after his father's death, touring the U.S. in 1839 (with his wife, the manager-actress Madame Vestris) and in 1857–8, immediately after Vestris's death and a second term of imprisonment for bankruptcy (both the result of theatre mismanagement). His memoirs in four volumes (1857) were edited by his second wife, Anne.   PT   DBW

Mathews, Cornelius (1817–89) Playwright remembered by the *NEW YORK CLIPPER* in its obituary as the "Father of America Drama," and called by historian George Seilhammer "the most promising and successful American dramatist of the last generation" (1881). Mathews's first effort, *The Politicians* (1840), a satire on elections, was not performed. *Witchcraft; or, The Martyrs of Salem* (1846) dramatizes the tragedy of Gideon Bodish, whose mother is accused of witchcraft. A poetic sensitivity and craftsmanship place this work among the first rank of plays written before the Civil War. Mathews also wrote *Jacob Leisler, The Patriot Hero* (1848), *Broadway and the Bowery* (1856), and *False Pretenses* (1858).   WJM

Matthews, (James) Brander (1852–1929) Educator, scholar, critic, and playwright. Born in New Orleans to wealthy parents, Matthews grew up in New York and was educated at Columbia University. He entered law school in 1871, but became more interested in French drama and in writing novels and plays. From 1875 to 1895 he wrote for the *Nation;* in 1878 he penned his first original play, *Margery's Lovers* (MADISON SQUARE THEATRE, 1887), collaborated with both GEORGE H. JESSOP and BRONSON HOWARD, and from 1891 until his retirement in 1924 he taught drama at Columbia. In 1899 he was given the title of Professor of Dramatic Literature, the first such post in American universities. His wide knowledge of French, English, and American theatre is reflected in his 24 books; the best known are *The French Dramatists of the Nineteenth Century* (1882); *Development of the Drama* (1903); and *Principles of Playmaking* (1919). He also wrote two volumes of memoirs: *These Many Years* (1917) and *Rip Van Winkle Goes to the Play* (1926). His position that a play is intended primarily to be performed rather than read brought credibility to theatre as an academic subject.   TLM

May [né Berlin], **Elaine** (1932?–) Performer, playwright, screenwriter, and film director. Born in Philadelphia, daughter of Jack Berlin, an actor, director, and writer for a traveling Jewish theatre company, May appeared onstage as a child in little-boy roles. While attending the University of Chicago she met MIKE NICHOLS; they worked wth the Compass Players and helped to found SECOND CITY. As an improvisational team (1957–61) noted for their dry wit and wry humor they gained great popularity, especially in *An Evening with Mike Nichols and Elaine May* on Broadway, but broke up immediately, not partnering again until the film *The Birdcage* in 1996 (except for a one-night Broadway benefit in 1992). May's successful screenplays include *A New Leaf* (1971; also costar and director) and *Primary Colors* (1998), but her career as a playwright, on Broadway and off, has been indifferent: *Not Enough Rope* (1962), *Adaptation* (1969), *Mr. Gogol and Mr. Preen* (1991), *Taller Than a Dwarf* (2000), *Adult Entertainment* (2002), and *After the Night and the Music* (2005), the latter

two starring her daughter, **Jeannie Berline**, who also appeared in the May-directed film *The Heartbreak Kid* (1972).   DBW

Mayer, Edwin Justus (1896–1960) This playwright's interest in historical events and novels resulted in occasional works for the theatre. Most notably, the popular *The Firebrand* (1924), which followed the comic adventures of Benvenuto Cellini in the Renaissance, was considered risqué at the time. The both cynical and sentimental *Children of Darkness* (1930), based on an 18th-century Fielding novel, was revived very successfully by CIRCLE IN THE SQUARE in 1958 with GEORGE C. SCOTT and COLLEEN DEWHURST.   RHW

Mayer, Michael (1960–) Born and raised in Bethesda, MD, graduated from NYU's Tisch School in 1983 (acting), this actor turned stage and film director (since 2004) directed his first Broadway show in 1997, a disappointing *Triumph of Love*. This was followed, however, with a string of successes: *A VIEW FROM THE BRIDGE* (1997) with Anthony LaPaglia; WARREN LEIGHT's *Side Man* (1998), which, like *Triumph*, began OFF-BROADWAY at CSC REP; *YOU'RE A GOOD MAN, CHARLIE BROWN* (1999); *The Lion in Winter* revival (1999) with Laurence Fishburne and STOCKARD CHANNING; *Thoroughly Modern Millie* (2002; Drama Desk for direction); *After the Fall* revival (2004); and *'night Mother* revival (2004). With over a dozen Off-Broadway credits since 1990 (including *Stupid Kids*, 1998; and the celebrated musical version of *Spring Awakening*, 2006, which moved to Broadway), he was also director of the national tour of KUSHNER's *ANGELS IN AMERICA*.   DBW

Ma-Yi Theatre Company Founded in 1989 in NYC, Ma-Yi is a nonprofit company that takes its name from the precolonial appellation for the Southeast Asian islands that the Spanish dubbed The Philippines. Originally devoted to producing plays by Filipinos and FILIPINO AMERICANS, the company has expanded its mission to includes works by ASIAN AMERICAN playwrights of all ethnicities, as well as plays about the Asian or Asian American experience written by non-Asian playwrights. It was awarded a 2001–2 Obie Grant, and its 2003 production of *The Romance of Magno Rubio* received an Obie for outstanding ensemble. Other notable productions include *Flipzoids* (1997) by the company's artistic director, Ralph B. Peña; *perigriNasyon* (1998) by Chris Millado; *Watcher* (2001) by HAN ONG; *The Square* (2001), a project curated by CHAY YEW involving 16 American playwrights of various ethnicities; *wAve* (2004) by Sung Rno; and

433

No Foreigners Beyond This Point (2005) by WARREN LEIGHT.   DanB

Mayo, Frank (1839–96) Actor and manager. Born and educated in Boston, Mayo made his stage debut in 1856 at the AMERICAN THEATRE in SAN FRANCISCO; served as leading man at MAGUIRE's Opera House during 1863–5; and took a similar position at the BOSTON THEATRE during 1865–6. He was competent in roles such as Hamlet, Iago, Othello, and Jack Cade, but garnered critical and popular acclaim for his Badger in *The Streets of New York*. Making his New York debut in 1869, Mayo remained an outsider, touring as a star in his own company. In 1872 he first acted the frontiersman in the play *DAVY CROCKETT*, a part he would perform over 2,000 times. He wrote several plays in the 1880s, but none was successful. In 1895 he adapted Mark Twain's *Pudd'nhead Wilson* for the stage and played the title role to popular acclaim until his death the following year. In his day he was thought a "natural" actor because he underplayed the emotional scenes. While a versatile actor, Mayo found success only in roles that promoted YANKEE individualism or the myth of the American frontier.   TLM

Mayrhauser, Jennifer von see VONMAYRHAUSER, JENNIFER

Mazzie, Marin (1960–) Statuesque musical-theatre leading lady and much-in-demand Broadway diva, thanks to her extraordinary soprano voice. Born in Rockford, IL, and educated at Western Michigan University, her Broadway debut was as Mary Jane Wilkes (replacement) in *Big River* in 1986, followed by Rapunzel in *Into the Woods* (1989, also replacement), Clara in *Passion* (1994), the Mother in *RAGTIME* (1998), Lilli/Kate in *KISS ME, KATE* (1999), and Aldonza, as replacement, in the revival of *MAN OF LA MANCHA* (2003). For Kate, Mother, and Clara she was nominated for Tonys. She frequently appears in concert, sometimes with her husband, actor-singer Jason Danieley (*CANDIDE*, *The FULL MONTY*), OFF-BROADWAY, and in regional theatres.   DBW

Meadow, Lynne (Carolyn) (1946–) Director who has served as artistic director of the MANHATTAN THEATRE CLUB since 1972, responsible for more than 400 New York and world premieres. Her directorial work includes David Rudkin's *Ashes* (1976, Obie), David Edgar's *The Jail Diary of Albie Sachs* (1979), Simon Gray's *Close of Play* (1981), Ayckbourn's *Woman in Mind* (1988), LEE BLESSING's *Eleemosynary* (1989), Ayckbourn's *A Small Family Business* (1992, MUSIC BOX), DONALD MARGULIES's *The Loman Family Picnic* (1993), Leslie Ayvazian's *Nine Armenians* (1996), and CHARLES BUSCH's *The Tale of the Allergist's Wife* (2000, moved to Broadway). Her style is described as "smooth and unobtrusive," aimed at getting "something reduced to its essence." A Bryn Mawr and Yale School of Drama graduate, Meadow received 1981's MARGO JONES Award, and Torch of Hope Award, 1990's Distinguished Woman's Award from the Northwood Institute, 1992's National Theatre Conference's person of the year, and the 2003 "Mr. Abbott" Award for Lifetime Achievement. She has taught in the CIRCLE IN THE SQUARE Theatre School, Yale and New York universities, and SUNY–Stony Brook.   REK

medicine shows The North American descendants of the mountebanks of Renaissance Europe, these itinerant peddlers of patent medicines, working from caravan wagons, enlivened their sales pitch with variety acts, ranging from simple card tricks and banjo solos to the elaborate powwows and war dances of the turn-of-the-century Kickapoo shows. To meet competition from VAUDEVILLE, the medicine show began to offer an idiosyncratic form of variety only occasionally broken by a commercial message. The performances, often changed nightly, were dominated by a blackface comedian generically called Sambo or Jake, a hybrid of MINSTREL endman and hobo clown. The shows themselves, a mixture of ventriloquism, chalk talks, burlesque comedy, prestidigitation, and banjo picking, usually lasted two hours, the 8 or 10 numbers interrupted by a few lectures with their medicine "pitches." The afterpiece, an audience favorite, was a chaotic farce involving a sheeted ghost. Certain medicine men like Fred Foster Bloodgood and Tommy Scott continued to play their routes well into the late 20th century, and in 1983 *The Vi-Ton-Ka Medicine Show*, a reconstruction with original performers, was staged at the AMERICAN PLACE THEATRE, NYC.   LS

Medina, Louisa (c. 1813–38) Unique in her day as a successful woman dramatist, Medina is credited with 34 plays between 1833 and 1838; however, only 11 have been documented, and only 3 are extant. All of her plays were written for THOMAS S. HAMBLIN, manager of the BOWERY THEATRE and possibly her husband, and probably all were dramatizations of historical and adventure novels. Medina's talent for increasing the dramatic

and spectacular elements of the novels made her plays successful and profitable melodramas, the staple of the Bowery. Her dramatization of Bulwer-Lytton's *Last Days of Pompeii* had 29 performances in 1835 – the longest run on a New York stage to that date; and her dramatization of ROBERT MONTGOMERY BIRD'S *NICK OF THE WOODS* (1838; staged 1839) remained a consistent draw for most of the century. Other successes include *Rienzi, Norman Leslie,* and *Ernest Maltravers.*
FB

Medoff, Mark (1940–) Playwright, director, educator, and actor who has written more than 26 plays and 9 screenplays. Medoff first won success OFF-BROADWAY with *WHEN YOU COMIN' BACK, RED RYDER?* (1973) and *The Wager* (1974). *CHILDREN OF A LESSER GOD* in 1980 won Medoff a Tony Award for Best Play. After *Children* Medoff worked primarily in film and television, but in 1985 the AMERICAN CONSERVATORY THEATRE staged his *The Majestic Kid*; in 1989 a sequel to *Red Ryder, The Heart Outright,* was presented at New York's THEATRE FOR THE NEW CITY; and in 2004 his controversial *Prymate,* with ANDRÉ DE SHIELDS, ran briefly on Broadway. Since 1966 Medoff has taught at New Mexico State University. SMA

Mee, Charles (Chuck) L(ouis) (1938–) Chicago-born and -raised playwright, historian, and editor who graduated from Harvard in 1960 with an interest in playwriting that gave way to work as an editor, political activist, and a career as a historian. He resumed playwriting in the 1980s, leading to associations with such vanguard directors as MARTHA CLARKE, ROBERT WOODRUFF, ANNE BOGART, and TINA LANDAU. Inspired by the aesthetics of collage and based on his conviction that art and culture are a perpetual process of remaking, he wrote a series of radical revisions of Greek tragedies in the 1990s that combine elements of the original with his own writing and texts imported verbatim from a wider range of popular and literary sources. After *Orestes 2.0* (1992, SITI and ART Institute) and *Trojan Women: A Love Story* (1996, En Garde Arts, NYC) came *Big Love* (2000), Mee's take on Aeschylus' *The Suppliants,* which premiered at ACTORS THEATRE OF LOUISVILLE and went on to productions all over the U.S. This play signaled a gradual pivot of his work from dark, apocalyptic smash-ups to idiosyncratic love plays inspired in part by Shakespeare. Beginning with his collaboration with the SITI Company on *bobrauschenbergamerica* (2001), he also wrote a series of plays based on important artists, includ-

ing Toulouse-Lautrec (2004), and Joseph Cornell (2006). SC

Ed. note: A book on Mee and Bogart, written by the author of this entry, was published in 2006.

Megrue, Roi Cooper (1883–1927) Playwright, director, and producer who frequently directed his own scripts. He was associated with ELISABETH MARBURY, and with the SELWYNS, who produced several of his plays. His *Under Cover* (1914), *Under Fire* (1915; codirector), and *Under Sentence* (1916, coauthor-director) are effective thrillers. *It Pays to Advertise* (1914), *Potash and Perlmutter in Society* (aka *Abe and Mawruss;* 1915, coauthor [with MONTAGUE GLASS]-director), *Seven Chances* (1916), and *Tea for Three* (1918, also director) are contemporary farces. He directed and coproduced the Pulitzer Prize–winning *WHY MARRY?* in 1917. His career was cut short by an untimely death due to illness. MR

Meisner, Sanford (1905–97) Actor, teacher, director. As an original member of the GROUP THEATRE, Meisner appeared in most of their productions throughout the 1930s. He codirected, with ODETS, *WAITING FOR LEFTY* (1935), and had roles in all the other Odets plays, from *AWAKE AND SING!* (1935) to *Night Music* (1940). Before joining the Group, he had acted in several productions at the THEATRE GUILD. In 1935 he began teaching the Group's "Method" acting at the NEIGHBORHOOD PLAYHOUSE School of Theatre, and became head of the school the following year. He continued in this position until 1959, then taught in LOS ANGELES for two years at Twentieth Century–Fox before returning to NYC and his headship position in 1964, retiring from teaching in 1994. During the 1940s and '50s he directed several plays, including a revival of *The TIME OF YOUR LIFE* (1955, New York City Center). He continued to act occasionally, his last role being a patient in a 1995 episode of television's *ER.* In 1987 he coauthored a book on his approach to acting. TP

Melmoth (Mrs. Samuel Jackson Pratt), Mrs. (Courtney) Charlotte (1749–1823) British actress who debuted in the U.S. in March 1793 (recitations in NYC), joining the JOHN STREET THEATRE company eight months later, remaining until 1798, then moving to the new PARK. She continued to act in NYC and PHILADELPHIA until 1812. DUNLAP in 1793 claimed she was the "best tragic actress" New York had ever seen. After retirement she taught elocution and did some dairy farming. DBW

Member of the Wedding, The, by Carson Mc-Cullers. Adapted from the author's novel, this sensitive character study focuses upon Frankie, a gangling, imaginative girl on the brink of adolescence, and Berenice, her father's housekeeper and Frankie's only maternal influence. McCullers weaves an impressionistic portrait of life in a small southern town of 1945, touching upon race relations, changing personal relationships, and deep feelings of loss. Directed by Harold Clurman, the play opened in NYC 5 January 1950 at the Empire Theatre and featured Julie Harris and Ethel Waters. Critics doubted that a piece with little overt dramatic action would attract a wide public, but they were impressed by stunning performances. Defying predictions, the play ran for 501 performances, won the New York Drama Critics' Circle Award, and became a successful motion picture in 1952.   KF

Men and Women This fourth collaborative effort by Henry C. DeMille and David Belasco for producer Charles Frohman opened in 1890 with William Morris and Frank Mordaunt in leading roles and Maude Adams in a minor part. The plot hinges on a bank robbery, based on a contemporary scandal, and involves four pairs of lovers. At its climax, William Prescott (Morris) seizes the handcuffs meant for his friend, a clerk accused through circumstantial evidence, and confesses the crime. After running the play for more than 200 performances in New York, Frohman toured it intermittently through 1906, when the William Morris Stock Company bought the rights to the play and continued its touring.   BMcC

Men in White by Sidney Kingsley was the first major success of the Group Theatre, opening 26 September 1933 and running for 351 performances. The cast, directed by Lee Strasberg in a truly ensemble performance, included Luther Adler, J. Edward Bromberg, Alexander Kirkland, Sanford Meisner, Robert Lewis, Morris Carnovsky, Art Smith, and Ruth Nelson, as well as Clifford Odets and Elia Kazan. The production's precision and finish, particularly in the operating room scene, which achieved an almost balletic quality, helped establish the reputation of the Group Theatre and Strasberg's Method. The play, a reverent treatment of the medical profession, depicts the conflicts of a young doctor who wants to dedicate his life to scientific research, but must resist the pressure from his fiancée and her family to pursue a lucrative practice instead.   BCM

Menken, Adah Isaacs [née Ada C. McCord or Adèle Theodore] (1835?–68) Actress and poet, born near New Orleans or in Memphis (her myth-making hopelessly obscures her early years). Legally separated from the musical conductor Alexander Isaacs Menken, she embarked on an acting career, making her debut in Shreveport as Pauline in *The Lady of Lyons* (1857); her dark good looks and splendid figure compensated for her mediocre talent. When a bigamous marriage to the pugilist John Heenan (1859) ended in scandal, she exploited it by appearing in flesh-colored tights bound to a "wild horse of Tartary" in Milner's melodrama *Mazeppa* (Green St. Theatre, Albany, NY, 1861). This role, played throughout the U.S. North and West, brought her notoriety and stardom as the "Naked Lady." Marriage to humorist Orpheus C. Kerr (R. H. Newell) made her popular with the literati of New York and San Francisco. At Astley's Amphitheatre, London (1864), she played Mazeppa and Don Leon in *The Child of the Sun* for £500 a performance, the highest salary yet earned by an actress. After a fourth marriage, the last phase of her career unfolded in Paris, in a silent equestrian role in *The Pirates of the Savannah* (Gaîté, 1867). Her last performance was at Sadler's Wells (1868), before sudden death from peritonitis. A superb book on Menken by Renée Sentilles was published in 2003.   LS

Mercury Theatre, The A repertory company established in NYC in 1937 by Orson Welles and John Houseman. The brief but historically significant two-year history – from the Welles–Houseman withdrawal from the Federal Theatre Project over the denial by Washington bureaucrats to produce Marc Blitzstein's proletarian drama with music *The Cradle Will Rock,* to the final production of *Danton's Death* (1938) – is told vividly in Houseman's *Run-Through* (1972). Other imaginative productions were *The Shoemaker's Holiday, Heartbreak House,* and a modern-dress *Julius Caesar* intended as an anti-Fascist tract – though, in fact, Welles's cutting of the text led to confusion. The ensemble included Norman Lloyd, Joseph Cotten, Martin Gabel, Vincent Price, Ruth Ford, Hiram Sherman, and Geraldine Fitzgerald. The Mercury Theatre of the Air was responsible for the infamous broadcast of "The War of the Worlds" (1938), and many of the company members appeared in Welles's film *Citizen Kane* (1941).   DBW

Meredith, (Oliver) Burgess (1907–97) Actor-director born in a suburb of Cleveland and an Amherst College dropout. Identified today as the crusty trainer in the *Rocky* films, the diminutive man with the crumpled look had established himself by the 1940s as an actor variously described as impressive, brilliant, heartbreaking, sinewy, and sensitive. From his apprenticeship with the CIVIC REPERTORY THEATRE (1929–33) to his outings as an innovative director (*Ulysses in Nighttown*, with ZERO MOSTEL, 1958 [OFF-BROADWAY; 1974, Broadway]; *A Thurber Carnival*, 1960; *BLUES FOR MR. CHARLIE*, 1964, etc.), Meredith appeared in a long series of productions, including *She Loves Me Not* (1933, as Buzz Jones), *WINTERSET* (1935, as Mio, a part written for him), *Liliom* (1940, title role), *Candida* (1942, Marchbanks), *The Remarkable Mr. Pennypacker* (1953, Pa), and *Major Barbara* (1956. Cusins). In the late 1930s he held various offices in ACTORS' EQUITY. His autobiography, *So Far, So Good*, was published in 1994. DBW

Merman [née Zimmerman], **Ethel** (1909–84) Singer and actress who made an auspicious stage debut in *Girl Crazy* (1930), where her renditions of two GERSHWIN songs, "I Got Rhythm" and "Sam and Delilah," stopped the show nightly. She was soon typecast as a brassy, big-hearted nightclub singer, a role she played, with slight variations, in *Take a Chance* (1932), *ANYTHING GOES* (1934), and *Red, Hot and Blue!* (1936). Although she appeared in secondary roles in these shows, Merman was often given the best songs to sing because of her powerful voice and exemplary diction. She received her first solo star billing for *Panama Hattie* (1940), in which she again portrayed a nightclub singer. After a change-of-pace role as a defense worker in *Something for the Boys* (1943), Merman appeared in IRVING BERLIN's *ANNIE GET YOUR GUN* (1946). The part of western sharpshooter ANNIE OAKLEY gave Merman a rare opportunity to portray a character that differed significantly from her own personality. Four years later Merman was back in another Berlin show, *CALL ME MADAM*, in which she portrayed a Washington hostess appointed ambassador to a tiny European kingdom. Her next musical, *Happy Hunting* (1956), gave her a similar role as a Philadelphia socialite seeking a husband for her daughter. In 1959 Merman capped her career with her performance as Rose, the quintessential stage mother, in *GYPSY*. Both her singing and her acting received superlative reviews from the critics. A decade later Merman made her last Broadway appearance when in 1970 she took over the title role in *HELLO, DOLLY!*

Although most of the shows in which she appeared were haphazard assemblages of stale musical-comedy formulas, their major appeal lay in Merman's electrifying interpretations of songs by such important musical-comedy composers as the Gershwins, COLE PORTER, and Irving Berlin. She published autobiographies in 1955 and 1978 (with George Eells). MK

Merrick, David (1912–2000) Producer. Beginning with his first success, *Fanny*, in 1954, Merrick produced or coproduced more than 80 plays, including many imported foreign hits. Some of his more successful ones included *The Entertainer* (1958), *GYPSY* (1959), *Becket* (1960), *Stop the World – I Want to Get Off* (1962), *Luther* and *One Flew Over the Cuckoo's Nest* (1963), *Oh What a Lovely War!* and *HELLO, DOLLY!* (1964), *Marat/Sade* (1965), *I Do! I Do!* (1966), *Rosencrantz and Guildenstern Are Dead* (1967), *Play It Again, Sam* (1969), *Travesties* (1975), and *42ND STREET* (1980).

Merrick's publicity stunts for his shows were legendary on Broadway. To publicize *Fanny*, he commissioned a nude statue of Nejla Ates, the show's belly dancer, and had it placed in Central Park, opposite a bust of Shakespeare; *Life* covered the story, and *Fanny* ran for 888 performances. Of such stunts, Merrick said, "Other things being equal, using promotion stunts would allow me to get ahead of my competitors. I'd say that's been a big factor in my success."

In 1983 Merrick suffered a stroke that rendered him incapable of administering his $50–70 million estate; but in 1985 the New York Supreme Court ruled him sufficiently recovered to manage his affairs. His first production after recovery (his 88th overall) was an unsuccessful all-black revival in 1990 of the musical *Oh, Kay!*, which had originated in 1989 at the GOODSPEED OPERA HOUSE. Finally, in 1996, thanks to a $1 million investment, his name appeared above the title as "David Merrick Presents" *State Fair*, his last Broadway production. A biography by HOWARD KISSEL was published in 1993. SMA

Merrill, Bob [né Henry Robert Merrill Lavan] (1921/23?–98) Composer-lyricist. After serving in WWII, Merrill was an actor, radio writer, casting director, NIGHTCLUB singer, and writer of a number of popular songs (such as "How Much Is That Doggie in the Window?") before turning to Broadway. His first score was *New Girl in Town* (1957), followed by *Take Me Along* (1959) and *Carnival* (1961), and he wrote the lyrics for *FUNNY GIRL* (1964) and *Sugar* (1972). His few attempts at writing scores in the 1970s and '80s were failures. Suffering from depression, he committed suicide. Merrill's most successful scores captured the mood and musical idioms of the first decades of the 20th century. MK

Merry [née Brunton], **Anne** (1769–1808) British-born actress and manager noted for appearances on the American stage, where, according to her biographer Gresdna Doty, she was the artistic pace-setter. Daughter of John Brunton, provincial English actor-manager, she followed her successful debut at Bath in 1785 with an engagement at London's Covent Garden for the next season, remaining there until her retirement in 1792 after her marriage to minor poet Robert Merry. Soon Merry lost his money, and Anne accepted an offer in 1796 from THOMAS WIGNELL to join the CHESTNUT STREET THEATRE company in PHILADELPHIA. Widowed four years, she married Wignell in 1803. When he died seven weeks later, she comanaged the Chestnut Street. In 1806 she married WILLIAM WARREN; two years later she died in childbirth at 39. As an actress she was known for her excellence in tragic roles and especially for the sweetness of her voice, her gentleness, simplicity, and grace on stage. Her brother, John, and sister, Louisa, were also actors. An excellent biography by Gresdna Doty was published in 1971. DBW

Merry Widow, The Two-act operetta, music by Franz Lehár, words by Victor Leon and Leo Stein. First produced in Vienna in 1905, *Die lustige Witwe* was soon seen throughout the German-speaking world. The sentimental yet lighthearted story, set to Lehár's enduring melodies (the most famous: the waltz "I Love You So") tells of a rich eastern European widow in Paris pursued by legions but won by the seemingly indifferent embassy secretary. In 1907, George Edwardes produced a version by Adrian Ross and Edward Morton, which changed place and character names, in London, where it ran 778 performances. This adaptation opened 21 October 1907 at NYC's NEW AMSTERDAM THEATRE, running 416 performances and becoming the rage of its day, generating an entire industry of "Merry Widow" fashions, hairstyles, and even cocktails. It has since never left the international stage and remains a staple of the light-opera repertoire. JD

Metamora; or, The Last of the Wampanoags by JOHN AUGUSTUS STONE, selected by EDWIN FORREST as the first winner of a contest for an aboriginal drama by an American; premiered 15 December 1829 at New York's PARK THEATRE and remained in Forrest's repertoire for 40 years. Based loosely on King Philip's War (1675–6), it gained the greatest popularity of all Indian plays produced during the Jacksonian period, due in part to Forrest's protean performance. The drama illustrated the incompatibility of the two races and suggested the impossibility of reconciliation. The title character incorporates traits of both the noble savage and its antithesis, the red devil, often rising above both stereotypes (see NATIVE AMERICANS PORTRAYED). Metamora justifies his actions with a coherent moral code until he sees no options, becomes single-minded in his attack, and then is considered by his enemies part of a "savage race, hated of all men – unblessed of heaven." Numerous Indian plays followed Stone's, including a JOHN BROUGHAM burlesque treatment of it and Forrest: *Metamora; or, The Last of the Pollywogs,* 1847. The Stone and Brougham plays were published in Wilmeth's *Staging the Nation* in 1998. DBW

Metcalf, James Stetson (1858–1927) Drama critic. Born in Buffalo, NY, and educated at Yale, Metcalf made his reputation writing for *Life* magazine (1888–1920). Afterward he wrote for *Judge* (1920–1) before becoming the first drama critic of the *Wall Street Journal* (1922–7). His satirical style often offended: The Theatrical SYNDICATE barred him from their theatres and accused him of being anti-Semitic. Although conservative and reactionary, he exposed corruption in the commercial theatre. TLM

Metcalfe, Stephen (1953–) Playwright, director, and screenwriter. Produced mainly by the MANHATTAN THEATRE CLUB and at San Diego's OLD GLOBE, he is author of some 10 plays, including *Vikings* (1980), concerning three generations of Danish American men; *Strange Snow* (1982), about Vietnam veterans; *Emily* (1988), about a woman obsessed with material success; *Pilgrims* (1995), about the coming of age of a teenage girl in 1970; and *Loves and Hours* (2003), a romantic comedy about a midlife crisis. TLM

method acting see ACTORS STUDIO

Mexican American theatre see CHICANO THEATRE

Middle Ages, The, by A. R. GURNEY JR., opened at the The Theatre at St. Peter's Church (23 March 1983) for 110 performances; this followed productions at the MARK TAPER FORUM (1977), Hartman Theatre in Connecticut (1978), and a showcase production at New York's Ark Theatre in 1982. Using the trophy room of a men's club as an emblem of the East Coast establishment, Gurney shows protagonist Barney on the day of his father's funeral recalling incidents from the mid-

1940s to the late '70s in which he systematically demolishes every standard of the upper class. Barney's final acceptance by childhood girlfriend Eleanor and ownership of the club both confirm his persistent romanticism and the emergence of a new social order. The New York run came hard upon that of Gurney's *The Dining Room*, producing a double success. **RW**

Mielziner, Jo (1901–76) The most dominant figure in American set and lighting design from the mid-1920s until his death, Mielziner created the sets for virtually every major American drama and musical in the 1930s, '40s and '50s, exerting a great influence not only on the field of design but on the plays themselves. Dramas such as *A Streetcar Named Desire* and *Death of a Salesman* were in part shaped by his designs, and their success was to some degree dependent upon them. His use of scrims and a painterly style created a visual counterpart to the poetic realism of the plays of the period, notably the works of Tennessee Williams. The scrims, together with fragmented scenic units, allowed a cinematic transformation from one scene to the next through the manipulation of light rather than the shifting of scenery; this was in keeping with the trend in playwriting toward a cinematic structure. He was equally capable of realism, as demonstrated by his set for *Street Scene* (1929), in which he re-created the facade of a tenement and a New York City street. His designs for musicals such as *Carousel*, *Annie Get Your Gun*, and *Guys and Dolls* captured the vibrancy of the American musical at its peak. The power of Mielziner's designs is demonstrated by the fact that some of his designs have outlasted the plays or are integrally entwined with them: His design for Maxwell Anderson's *Winterset* [at which entry see photo] – a soaring panorama of the Brooklyn Bridge receding into the fog – is better remembered than the play itself; and designers today trying to re-create *Death of a Salesman* must compete with the ghost of Mielziner's set. Mielziner also lit most of his own plays in order to control light, mood, and color. Working together with Edward F. Kook, he was responsible for many improvements in lighting instruments. Mielziner also worked as a theatre designer and consultant on many theatres, including the somewhat controversial Vivian Beaumont Theatre in New York. Mary Henderson's definitive biography was published in 2001. **AA**

Mighty Dollar, The A four-act comedy by Benjamin E. Woolf produced at the Park Theatre, NYC, 6 September 1875. Billed as "an American comedy," this play is set in a Washington, DC, salon (Grabmoor) where "polished and unpolished scoundrels ... congregate." Starring W. J. Florence as a Congressman, the Hon. Bradwell Slote, and Mrs. Florence as Mrs. General Gilflory, the play lampooned Washington politicians but made little sense to critics. Nevertheless, it ran 104 performances and established Slote as an American type. **TLM**

Migliaccio, Eduardo (Edoardo; Edward) (1882–1946) Actor-impressionist. Born in Cava dei Terreni, near Naples, Migliaccio came to America in 1897. In Little Italy's *caffè-concerto*, restaurants offering entertainments, Migliaccio created *machietti coloniali*, character sketches combining verse, prose, and song, satirizing the immigrant experience. Around 1900, he created Farfariello, the greenhorn who "turned the tables on the ethnic stereotype," as whom he became nationally known. Using dialect and immigrant types, Migliaccio, some of whose songs were recorded by RCA Victor, became one of the most popular figures in Italian American theatre. **REK**

Miles, George H(enry) (1824–71) Playwright and poet. When Edwin Forrest commended Miles's tragedy *Michael DiLando, Gonfalonier of Florence* in 1847, Miles immediately submitted *Mohammed, the Arabian Prophet*, for which Forrest awarded $1,000 as the "best original tragedy," though he never produced it. Miles's *DeSoto* (1852), produced by James Murdoch, was popular for a decade. *Blight and Bloom* (1854), *Mary's Birthday* (1857), and *Senor Valente* (1858) are comedies. Among his other plays are *Oliver Cromwell*, *The Parish Clerk Emily Chester*, and *Thiodolf the Icelander*. **WJM**

Millay, Edna St. Vincent (1892–1950) Actress, poet, playwright, and director. In 1917 Millay began her acting career with the Provincetown Players, where she performed in productions of her own plays, such as *The Princess Marries the Page* (1918) and *Aria da Capo* (1919). She also wrote *The Lamp and the Bell* (1921) and the libretto for Deems Taylor's opera *The Kings' Henchmen* (1927). Nancy Milford's 2001 biography is definitive. **FB**

Miller, Arthur (1915–2005) Playwright and director. Following the death of Tennessee Williams in 1983, Arthur Miller remained relatively unchallenged as America's greatest living playwright. His first produced play, *The Man Who Had All the Luck* (1944), was a consummate failure, but *All My Sons* (1947) proved that Miller could create powerful scenes and believable characters. His next play, DEATH OF A SALESMAN (1949), won him both the Pulitzer Prize for Drama and the Drama Critics' Circle Award. Shifting neatly between realism and expressionism, this piercing study of an aging "drummer" (commercial traveler) elicited highly praised, prizewinning efforts from the entire original production company and has subsequently been performed all over the world. His adaptation of IBSEN's *An Enemy of the People* (1950) was a thematic prelude to *The* CRUCIBLE (1953), a drama of the Salem witchcraft trials written in passionate response to Senator Joseph McCarthy's investigations of accused subversives. This spellbinding drama of real conflict and impassioned action, revived on Broadway in 1991, has outlived the immediacy of its inception and may yet prove to be Miller's finest work. *A* VIEW FROM THE BRIDGE (1955), which played in New York the same year Miller married beautiful film star Marilyn Monroe, continued his exploration of the tragedy of the common man. This time his hero is a hardworking Sicilian longshoreman who is killed because he breaks the community's law of silence about some illegal immigrants. Miller's stage voice was silent for the next eight years, during which time he divorced Monroe (1961) and married photographer Ingeborg Morath (1962). He returned to the stage in 1964 with AFTER THE FALL, apparently a highly personal play based on his life with Monroe. *Incident at Vichy,* an examination of the Nazi–Jewish conflict during WWII, followed in the same year. *The* PRICE (1968), a heartwrenching confrontation between two brothers, became the last Miller play to achieve anything like a popular success. *The Creation of the World and Other Business* (1972) and *The American Clock* (1980) failed and were hastily withdrawn. In the 1980s and early 1990s Miller's plays were given significant revivals or premieres in England, where he seemed more popular than in the U.S. (In 1989 the University of East Anglia opened the Arthur Miller Centre for American Studies; London revivals of *After the Fall* and *The Crucible* occurred in 1990; *View from the Bridge*, 1995.) In 1987 two new one-acts were presented at Lincoln Center as *Danger: Memory!,* though the bill was more successful in London. *The Archbishop's Ceiling* was staged by the Royal Shakespeare Company in 1986. Likewise, his *The Ride Down Mt. Morgan* also opened in London in 1991 prior to any New York production, though in 1993 *The Last Yankee* was seen both in NYC and London and a new work, *Broken Glass* (with RON RIFKIN and Amy IRVING), was staged first at Long Wharf in 1994 and then moved to Broadway; a London production at the National Theatre (transferred to the West End) was more successful, running into 1995 and winning the Olivier Award for Best Play. In the late 1990s and up to his death Miller's work underwent something of a Renaissance in the U.S., in part due to superb revivals. A not-for-TV film version of *The Crucible* was finally made in 1996. In 1997–8 he was SIGNATURE THEATRE's playwright of the season, for which a new play, *Mr. Peters' Connections* with Peter Falk and Anne Jackson (see ELI WALLACH), was staged in 1998. The year marked the beginning of a series of revivals: *All My Sons* and *A View from the Bridge* (both 1997, ROUNDABOUT); although not the first, a revival of *Death of Salesman* with BRIAN DENNEHY was highly praised in 1999; and *The Price* (previously seen at WILLIAMSTOWN) with HARRIS YULIN was revived later that year. *The Ride Down Mt. Morgan* finally had its first Broadway outing, starring Patrick Stewart, in 2000 (seen earlier in 1998 at The PUBLIC). In 2000 and 2002 his first play produced on Broadway, *The Man Who Had All the Luck,* was revived by LOS ANGELES's Antaeus Company and in New York by Roundabout. Also in 2002 the GUTHRIE staged a new play, *Resurrection Blues* (a satirical comedy), but it failed to excite critics or audiences; but a revised version at San Diego's OLD GLOBE in 2004 was more effective. Miller's final play, *Finishing the Picture,* which dealt with the making of his 1961 film, *The Misfits* (and arguably offering an unflattering portrait of LEE STRASBERG), premiered at the GOODMAN in Chicago in 2004.

Throughout his career Miller produced a rich collection of essays about the craft of playwriting, especially the nature of modern tragedy. These pieces, published as *The Theatre Essays of Arthur Miller* (rev. ed., 1996), remain the closest thing to a complete "poetics" yet written by an American playwright. Frequently honored, in 1994 he received the Unique Contribution to Theatre Award from the DRAMA LEAGUE and in 1999 a Tony for Lifetime Achievement. After his death, TONY KUSHNER said Miller had had the "curse of empathy" and thanked him for writing plays that ask, "What is your relevancy to the survival of the race?" *Timebends,* Miller's autobiography, was published in 1987. A biography by MARTIN GOTTFRIED appeared in 2003, and a more perceptive literary bio by Christopher Bigsby in 2005.
LDC   DBW

Miller, Gilbert Heron (1884–1969) Producer, director, theatre manager; son of actor HENRY MILLER and actress Bijou (Heron). Miller produced for half a century. He was known for his elegant staging of high comedy by such writers as PHILIP BARRY, Somerset Maugham, and other masters of literate dialogue. He introduced to the American stage such British actors as CHARLES LAUGHTON, Alec Guinness, and Leslie Howard. From 1918 until its demolition in 1958 he owned the St. James's Theatre, London; from 1929 until his death, the Lyric Theatre, London; and during 1926–68 HENRY MILLER'S THEATRE in New York. His greatest success was *Victoria Regina* (1936) with HELEN HAYES. Other significant productions included Maugham's *The Constant Wife* (1926), Sherriff's *Journey's End* (1929), ELIOT's *The Cocktail Party* (1950), and Thomas's *Under Milk Wood* (1957). DBW

Miller, Henry (1859–1925) London-born actor and manager who emigrated with his parents to Canada, where he made his debut in 1876. He quickly became a juvenile leading man in America opposite a variety of young actresses, including Bijou Heron, whom he married in 1883. In 1893 he became leading man of CHARLES FROHMAN's new EMPIRE THEATRE Stock Company. During 1905–8 he and MARGARET ANGLIN starred under their own management, notably in *The Great Divide* by WILLIAM VAUGHN MOODY. Though he continued to act until after WWI, Miller's principal occupation after 1908 was as a producer for others. He launched the career of ALLA NAZIMOVA, and became manager and producer for WALTER HAMPDEN, LAURA HOPE CREWS, and Ruth Chatterton, among others. As an actor, Miller personified the American ideal of honest, sympathetic, taciturn masculinity. A bio by Frank P. Morse was published in 1938. DMcD

Miller, Joaquin [né Cincinnatus Hiner Miller] (1839–1913) Writer whose early life among the miners and Indians of California and Oregon is confused by his autobiographical embroidery. In 1863 he settled as a newspaper editor in Oregon. When his early poems and stories were favorably received, he moved to San Francisco (1870), but his Byronic appearance, behavior, and writing were most popular in England. His best works were the books *Songs of the Sierras* (1871) and *Life Among the Modocs* (1873). He also wrote four plays, and *The DANITES in the Sierras* was performed in a heavily revised version by McKEE RANKIN (1877–81). DMcD

Miller, Marilyn [Marilynn; née Mary Ellen Reynolds] (1898–1936) Dancer and singer. As a child she appeared in VAUDEVILLE, and was dancing in a London club when she was discovered by Lee SHUBERT. She made her Broadway debut in *The Passing Show of 1914*. Miller was a featured per-

former in two editions of the ZIEGFELD *Follies* (1918, 1919). In *SALLY* (1920), she was given her first starring role, as a poor dishwasher who becomes a star of those same *Follies*. Critics found her performance enchanting, complimenting her on her graceful dancing, her delicate beauty, and her buoyant personality. After a long run and national tour in *Sally,* Miller returned to Broadway in *Sunny* (1925), where her weekly salary was reported to be $3,000, making her the highest-paid musical-comedy performer of the 1920s. Her next shows, *Rosalie* (1928) and *Smiles* (1930), were not as successful as the previous two. In 1933 she made her final Broadway appearance in *As THOUSANDS CHEER,* a REVUE with a score by IRVING BERLIN. Although her singing voice was so weak as to be inaudible at times, Miller's radiant beauty and elegant dancing made her the reigning queen of musical comedy in the 1920s. A biography by Warren Harris appeared in 1985. MK

Miller, May (1899–1995) African American poet and playwright. Active in plays at school and college, Miller trained with Montgomery Gregory at Howard University and Frederick Koch at Columbia University. She entered *Opportunity* magazine playwriting contests, gaining third prize (for *The Bog Guide,* 1925) and a citation, and was a member of the Washington, DC, branch of the Krigwa Players. She wrote some 14 plays, including *Scratches* (1929), *Riding the Goat* (1930), and *Nails and Thorns* (1933), a number of which were published in early anthologies of black plays. EGH

Miller, Tim (1958–) Internationally acclaimed solo performer, teacher, and writer. Hailed for their humor and passion, his performance works have been seen at such prestigious venues as the Yale Repertory Theatre, the London Institute of Contemporary Art, the Walker Art Center, ACTORS THEATRE OF LOUISVILLE, and the BROOKLYN ACADEMY OF MUSIC Next Wave Festival. Miller's creative work explores the artistic, spirtual, and political topography of his identity as a gay man. Miller has delighted and emboldened audiences in such pieces as *Postwar* (1982), *Cost of Living* (1983), *Democracy in America* (1984), *Buddy Systems* (1985), *Some Golden States* (1987), *Stretch Marks* (1989), *Sex/Love/Stories* (1991), *My Queer Body* (1992), *Naked Breath* (1994), *Fruit Cocktail* (1996), *Shirts & Skin* (1997), *Glory Box* (1999), *US* (2003), and *1001 Beds* (2006). The author of four books, Miller teaches frequently, often in conjunction with performance dates. He was a founder of PERFORMANCE SPACE 122 (NYC) and Highways Performance Space (Santa Monica, CA). DBW

Mills, Florence (1895–1927) African American comedienne, singer, and dancer who became the idol of Harlem. At age 5 she appeared in Williams & Walker's musical comedy *Sons of Ham* (see BERT WILLIAMS), and at 15 joined her two sisters in a musical trio, *The Mills Sisters*, that toured the country in VAUDEVILLE shows. Her first major billing came when she replaced Gertrude Sanders as leading lady in the hit musical SHUFFLE ALONG (1921) at NYC's 63rd Street Theatre. The next year Mills was on Broadway in *Plantation Revue*, which extended her fame internationally. Performances followed in Paris and London in *From Dover to Dixie* (1923–4) and as the star of *From Dixie to Broadway* (1924) back in the U.S. In Lew Leslie's *Blackbirds* (1926), written specially for her, she again toured Paris and London, leaving the show because of ill health. She died in 1927. A pixie of a woman, small, delicate and stunningly attractive onstage, she was beloved by the 150,000 people who followed her funeral procession in Harlem.   EGH

Milwaukee Repertory Theater Organized in 1954 as the Fred Miller Theater Company, a professional STOCK COMPANY, in Milwaukee, WI. After seven years in the Miller Theater (a converted moviehouse) and the production of 71 plays with well-known guest stars, the governing board employed a resident ensemble, turning first to the ASSOCIATION OF PRODUCING ARTISTS, then to the AMERICAN CONSERVATORY THEATRE for brief seasons. The organization became the Milwaukee Repertory Theater in 1964, and has since featured its RESIDENT [NONPROFIT] PROFESSIONAL acting company. Four artistic directors have been standouts: Tunc Yalman (1966–71) managed the company's move to the Todd Wehr Theater in Milwaukee's Performing Arts Center and the growth of the group's subscription base to 16,000. Nagle Jackson (1971–7), added productions at the Court Street Theater in 1974 and at the historic Pabst Theater (built in 1895). John Dillon (1977–93) included resident playwrights in the company, conducted international tours with the group, and, in 1987, moved it to a new three-theater facility on the east bank of the Milwaukee River; typical of Dillon's productions was a non-traditionally cast OUR TOWN (1991). Finally, Joseph Hanreddy (1994–present) has continued the rep-company tradition and strong seasons in the Quadracci Powerhouse Theater and the more intimate Stiemke Theater. Musical entertainment is provided in the Stackner Cabaret, and *A Christmas Carol* is presented annually in the Pabst Theatre.   WD

mime and pantomime
Beginnings through the 19th century
Mime and pantomime first came to these shores in the guise of "night scenes," the simplified commedia dell'arte sketches performed by French actors in early 18th-century London. The tricks of Harlequin and Scaramouche were performed at Henry Holt's Long Room in New York in 1738–9. These were supplanted by bipartite English pantomime, with its opening drawn from classical mythology or traditional folktale and its transformation of characters into Harlequin, Pantaloon, and Columbine for the knockabout comedy of the harlequinade. Some were adapted to American material, such as *Harlequin Traveller and the Temple of the Sun* (1800) and *Harlequin Panattahah; or, The Genii of the Algonquins* (1810).

Although the innovations of Regency pantomime and Grimaldi's Clown were brought to New York in 1831 by Charles Parsloe, they did not catch on. The first truly popular exponents of mime were the RAVEL FAMILY, who interspersed the French ballet-pantomime with elaborate acrobatic feats, elegant staging, and magic trickery. The silence and spectacle were more appealing to naive audiences than were the pun-filled scripts of the English panto. The Ravels were imitated "by the great clown GEORGE L. FOX, who featured pantomime at the BOWERY THEATRE in the 1850s, Americanizing the locales and emphasizing violent slapstick comedy at the expense of acrobatics and grace. The longest-running show of its time, Fox's *Humpty Dumpty* (1868), the first American panto in two acts and the first to play Broadway, was widely imitated. The word "pantomime" became generic for any entertainment that mingled variety acts, ballets, and harlequinade characters. Such shows toured the country well into the 1880s, although their popularity was superseded in larger cities by that of the extravaganza and the musical comedy.

Exuberant acrobatic comedy was returned to the form by the HANLON–LEES in *Le Voyage en Suisse* (1881) and The Byrne Brothers in *Eight Bells* (1890); as impresarios the Hanlons also toured the spectacular fairy pantomimes *Fantasma* (1884) and *Superba* (1890), which mingled horseplay with sumptuous scenic effects. However, silent comedy quickly became the province of the cinema, and many of its stage exponents, including the Hanlons and Buster Keaton, gravitated to it.

A more recherché form of pantomime was imported from France in the shape of *L'Enfant prodigue* (1890) by Michel Carré: This delicate divertissement featured a Pierrot (played by an actress) who leaves home for modern urban fleshpots but soon sees the error of his ways. Fashionable among theatrical sophisticates, it promulgated the fin de siècle image of the lovelorn Pierrot, which would crop up in such precious pieces as Edna St. Vincent Millay's ARIA DA CAPO (1919) and the more chichi REVUES of the 1920s.   LS

20th century and the present

Distinguishing a stage tradition as wholly distinct from film and television is impossible in regard to 20th-century America, as most performers worked (and work) wherever they can. However, American VAUDEVILLE performers (and, later, NEW VAUDEVILLIANS and PERFORMANCE ARTISTS) and film (and, later, TV) actors were the natural heritors of the traditions of the Greek mime and the commedia dell'arte.

Historically, mime and pantomime have been silent for few brief periods, and then usually because of governmental restriction. Technological limitation, however, caused the muteness of American silent-film actors of the early years of the 20th century, who in the verve and clarity of their physical acting have influenced generations of performers. The Keystone Cops, Chaplin, and Keaton, the first great American mimes, were influenced by the English music-hall tradition and were a part of American vaudeville. When sound was added successfully to film, the MARX BROS. continued in the line of the commedia dell'arte with brilliantly improvised physical, musical, and verbal comedy.

In 1952 PAUL J. CURTIS founded the American Mime Theatre in NYC, a school and performing organization that continues today; it has defined a form of silent acting outside the charming, whitefaced image popularized in the U.S. as of 1955 by Marcel Marceau through television performances that made his name a household word and ensured months of sold-out performances. In 1957 Étienne Decroux, innovator of corporeal mime or modern mime, began five years of teaching and performing in the U.S.

The SAN FRANCISCO MIME TROUPE, founded in 1959 by R. G. Davis, quickly found its voice and joined the thousand-year-old mainstream of mime performance: mime as an actor's theatre of voice, movement, poetry, and music, a politically engaged commedia dell'arte.

Those who think that mime is a charming interlude performed by lithe whitefaced mutes will find little of it currently in American outside shopping malls. However, the incisive energy, the zany, manic, ribald, ironic, and dangerous wit mime has always manifested as marginalized, unofficial, actor's theatre – these qualities are found among American performance artists who are testing limits politically, socially, and theatrically in lofts and storefront theatres of metropolitan and university centers. Many of them don't know the performance tradition of which they are a part; they think they made it up, and would cringe at the word "mime," yet mimes they are, in the fullest and most historically accurate sense of the word. Others, students of Decroux and Jacques Lecoq who have innovated U.S. postmodern mime, know that speech is as much a part of mime as is movement. Since 1974 (22 volumes) *Mime Journal* has provided coverage contemporary developes in mime and related topics.   TL

Miner, Henry Clay (1842–1900) Theatre businessman. Son of an engineer, he served in the Civil War and attended the American Institute of Physicians and Surgeons; this was the basis on which he entered the drug business, manufacturing and retailing cosmetics, including those for theatrical use. After 1875 he began to build and lease theatres, owning five in the NYC area. He also served as an AGENT for traveling theatrical companies, and published a theatrical directory in 1885. He also served in the Fifty-fourth Congress (1895–7).   DMcD

Minneapolis–St. Paul Also known as the Twin Cities, they rest along the shores of the Mississippi River in east-central Minnesota and have the largest population (2,968,806 as of 2000) of metropolitan areas in the upper Midwest. Since the mid-1970s, the cities have been credited with the greatest number (per capita) of performing-arts groups outside New York, including a multitude of educational, community, and professional profit and nonprofit theatres. As of 2005 there were more than 100 performing companies active in the area. The history of Twin Cities theatre activity began before statehood (1858), and may be generalized into four developmental periods: touring troupes (1850–1900), stock companies and roadhouses (1900–1930), amateur groups and early professional groups (1930–60), and the post-1960s expansion.

The first troupe that visited Minnesota was the New Orleans–based Placide's Varieties, which performed in St. Paul's Mazourka Hall in August 1851. Such touring performances would comprise the majority of theatre activity in St. Paul for 30 years, though there were attempts at establishing resident companies, notably Henry Van Liew's People's Theatre (1857) and various German-language presentations at the Athenaeum Theatre during 1857–86.

After the Civil War, Minneapolis would join St. Paul in hosting touring troupes as theatres were constructed in both cities. In February 1867 the Opera House opened in St. Paul, and in June of the same year the Pence Opera House opened in Minneapolis. Though the permanent theatres fostered competition between these cities for better entertainment, often the same company would perform in both places, such as the A. McFarland Company (1864) or the Mrs. James A. Oates Burlesque Opera Company (1869).

After 1878 STOCK COMPANIES began developing in addition to roadhouses. The Murray–Cartland Company (also known as The Great Metropolitan Theatre Company), formally a touring group, returned to St. Paul's Pence Opera House in September 1878 and began residency there as a stock company.

After 1900 two stock companies, the Ferris Stock Company and the Bainbridge Players, became the models for others to follow. Dick Ferris began his company with his actress wife, Grace Hayward, in 1902 at Minneapolis's Lyceum. Known for producing melodramas, Ferris acted as manager, director, and star in many of the productions, and the company lasted three years. The Bainbridge Players, led by Buzz Bainbridge, was formed in Minneapolis (1911) and developed a credible reputation by performing plays by Shakespeare (see SHAKESPEARE ON . . .), IBSEN, and O'NEILL, as well as more popular fare. Bainbridge was quite popular in Minneapolis and was elected mayor in 1933, two years following the Players' demise.

The development of a road organization with national touring connections can be linked to Louis Napoleon (L. N.) Scott, who began his career as St. Paul's Grand Opera House manager in 1883. He moved to St. Paul's Metropolitan Opera House in 1890 and acquired controlling interest in the Metropolitan, Duluth's Lyceum, the Grand in Superior, WI, and, in 1895, the new Minneapolis Metropolitan Opera House. He initiated contact in 1888 with MARC KLAW and ABE ERLANGER, who subsequently purchased the local Taylor Talent Agency and furthered their development of the Theatrical SYNDICATE.

Another important manager between 1900 and 1930 was Theodore Hayes, who managed the People's Theatre (later the Bijou) in Minneapolis and the JACOB LITT Grand Opera House in St. Paul during 1886–1917. His importance lies less in managing theatre than for organizing the Twin City Scenic Studio in 1895: He employed Peter Gui Clausen, a popular scenic artist, and began to produce scenery for opera houses, theatres, schools,

and Scottish Rite temples throughout the upper Midwest. Twin City Studio cornered this market until the last studio closed in Detroit in 1937.

After the Great Depression, professional theatre productions declined significantly. Many theatres were converted to moviehouses or were simply destroyed. Activity continued during 1930–60 but in other venues, and principally by amateur groups.

St. Paul enjoyed the Edyth Bush Theatre during 1940–65. Started by its namesake, whose husband helped found the Minnesota Mining and Manufacturing Company (3M), Mrs. Bush personally ran the theatre until illness prevented her continuance. Eleven years after the Bush started, the Theatre in the Round Players began performing in Minneapolis (1951). The group offered a diverse playbill from SHAW and Shakespeare to MAMET and SHEPARD, and included original plays.

Educational groups offered plays as well. Principal among these ACADEMIC THEATRES was that of the University of Minnesota, which produced plays from 1930 onward. Under the leadership of Frank M. Whiting during 1943–73, the theatre began offering a recurring CHILDREN'S THEATRE program, produced plays on a converted riverboat, contributed to the formation of the American Educational Theatre Association, was host to Arthur Ballet's Office of Advanced Drama Research, and helped attract the GUTHRIE THEATER to Minneapolis.

Two smaller professional organizations started in this period. Don Stolz opened his Old Log Theatre outside Minneapolis in 1940; it offers a popular bill of comedies and farces. Dudley Riggs, a former circus performer, opened his Brave New Workshop in 1958 and has continually offered topical plays built upon improvisation.

The year 1961 marked the beginning of a great expansion in theatre, as Beth Linnerson started the Moppet Players for children. Three years later John Clark Donahue split from the Players and formed the CHILDREN'S THEATRE COMPANY at the Minneapolis Society of Fine Arts; it quickly became distinguished for dazzling productions of classic and contemporary children's stories. In 1974 the Children's Theatre moved into a newly constructed facility adjacent to the Minneapolis Institute of Arts, and thereafter gained international acclaim for its productions of works by Theodore Geisel ("Dr. Seuss"), Tomie dePaola, and Maurice Sendak, among others. The Children's Theatre received great favor until 1984, when Donahue was convicted of sexual misconduct with adolescents. The Theatre's Board of Directors rallied to save the organization, hired Jon Cranney as artistic director, and entered a successful period of reorganization. Peter Brosius became artistic director in 1997, and new work on multicultural themes became a part of the CTC repertoire. CTC garnered a Regional Theatre Tony in 2003 and expanded its facilities with a new theatre and classrooms designed by Michael Graves in 2005.

In 1960, one year prior to the beginnings of the Children's Theatre, TYRONE GUTHRIE, Oliver Rea, and PETER ZEISLER chose Minneapolis as the home for their new professional theatre operation, the Minnesota Theatre Company (renamed the GUTHRIE THEATER following Guthrie's death in 1971). Three years later, on May 7, 1963, *Hamlet* was offered as its first production in a new Ralph Rapson–designed theatre. Conceived as a professional resident acting company performing classic plays, the Guthrie Theater has been termed the "flagship" of regional professional theatres, distinguishing itself with productions such as *The Caucasian Chalk Circle* (1965), *The House of Atreus* (1967), *Oedipus the King* (1972), *The Tempest* (1981), *Peer Gynt* (1983), *The Misanthrope* (1987), and 1990's repertory *Richard II*, *Henry IV (1 & 2)*, and *Henry V* (1990), with cast members performing continuing roles throughout the cycle. Following Tyrone Guthrie's initial leadership (1963–6), the theatre has been shaped mainly by four artistic directors: MICHAEL LANGHAM (1971–7), LIVIU CIULEI (1981–6), and GARLAND WRIGHT (1986–95), and Joe Dowling (1995–). In 2006 the Guthrie moved into its new $125 million, three-theatre complex.

The success of the Children's Theatre Company and the Guthrie Theatre in particular coincided with growth in the Twin Cities' young, educated, and affluent population and the continued rise in white-collar employment, all enabling great growth in theatre. Between 1971 and 1983 a number of groups began offering specialized repertories: The CRICKET THEATRE (1971) offered new American works; the Playwright's Center (1971) nurtured new playwrights; the Heart of the Beast Theatre (1973) featured PUPPETS of all shapes and sizes to inner-city audiences; the Illusion Theater (1974) pioneered socially conscious productions with its sexual-awareness program; At the Foot of the Mountain (1974–91) was a pioneering theatre for and by women; MIXED BLOOD THEATRE (1976) instituted color-blind casting; PENUMBRA THEATRE (1977) became Minnesota's first AFRICAN AMERICAN professional theatre; Actor's Theatre of St. Paul (1977–90) emphasized intimate actor vehicles; the Great North American History Theatre (1978) produced original plays about Minnesota history; Brass Tacks Theatre (1979–91)

offered new alternative plays; THEATRE DE LA JEUNE LUNE (1979) performed half a year in Minneapolis and half in Paris and received a Regional Theatre Tony in 2005; Red Eye Collaboration (1983) began producing new works, including those of LEE BREUER; Park Square Theater renovated its downtown theatre in St. Paul in 2003; and a citywide theatre award program, the Ivey Awards, was launched in 2004. Touring theatre activity expanded as well at such venues as Northrop Auditorium, the Orpheum Theatre, and the Walker Art Center in Minneapolis, and at Ordway Music Theatre in St. Paul.

Changing social and economic environments have brought about the closing of many theatres, both large and small, in the Twin Cities, but many more sprung up in their places, giving the impression that Minneapolis–St. Paul would remain a vibrant theatre area for some time to come. One sign of its theatrical vitality is the number of ACTORS' EQUITY members in the Twin Cities as of 2005 (compared to 1988) – the number has increased from 289 to 422, more than in SEATTLE (396) or WASHINGTON, DC (375). A history of theatre in Minnesota by Frank Whiting was published in 1988.   KN   MBD

Minnelli, Liza (1946–) Actress-singer, daughter of Hollywood luminaries Judy Garland and VINCENTE MINNELLI. She made her New York debut in an OFF-BROADWAY revival of *Best Foot Forward* (1963). In 1965 her oversized singing voice and gamine personality were applauded on Broadway in *Flora, the Red Menace*, but reservations were expressed about *The Act* (1977), although it won her a Tony, and *The Rink* (1984). She has been more successful with her ONE-PERSON Broadway REVUE *Liza* (1974), and in concerts and film, especially as Sally Bowles in the film version of *CABARET* (1972). In 1997 she replaced JULIE ANDREWS to acclaim in *Victor/Victoria*. Health and personal problems, including a bitter divorce from her fourth husband, have plagued her in recent years. George Mair's biography was published in 1996, one of several in the 1980s and 1990s.   MK

Minnelli, Vincente (1910–86) Director and designer who began his theatrical career at the age of 3 with the family TENT SHOW. In his teens in Chicago he designed sets for the stage shows that accompanied movies. In 1930 he moved to New York to design stage shows at the Paramount Theatre. He subsequently designed for *EARL CARROL's Vanities* (1930–2) and several Broadway musicals, and served as art director at RADIO CITY MUSIC HALL during 1933–5, designing sets and lights for all the weekly shows, as well as directing some. Moving to Hollywood, his film directorial credits include *Cabin in the Sky* (1943), *Meet Me in St. Louis* (1944), *An American in Paris* (1951), and *Gigi* (1958), for which he won an Oscar.   AA

Minskoff Theatre 1515 Broadway, NYC [Architect: Robert Allan Jacobs]. Like the GERSHWIN THEATRE to the north, the Minskoff, named after entrepreneur Jerome Minskoff (1916–94), resides within the lower floors of a commercial office building and is reached by banks of escalators. The building stands on the site where the Hotel Astor formerly stood, and the playhouse is named after its original owners and builders. A large house seating more than 1,600, it is best suited for musicals and opened with a successful revival of *Irene* (1973). Since then, its fare has been a succession of original musicals and revivals, the most notable being the NEW YORK SHAKESPEARE FESTIVAL's adaptation of GILBERT AND SULLIVAN's *The Pirates of Penzance* (1981), a revival of the musical *Sweet Charity* (1986), and ANDREW LLOYD WEBBER's *Sunset Boulevard* (1994) – the latter's 997 performances being the record for the house. The NEDERLANDER Organization shares the management of the theatre with the Minskoff Organization. Since June 2006 *The LION KING* has been its occupant.   MCH

Minsky Brothers Synonymous with post-1920s stock BURLESQUE in New York, in particular the popularization of the striptease (see NUDITY). BILLY (MICHAEL WILLIAM) (1887?–1932), the showman of the family, was soon joined by ABE (ABRAHAM) (1881–1949), HERBERT KAY (1892?–1959), and, by the early 1920s, MORTON (1902–87) in running their father Louis's National Theatre and Winter Garden (1912). The theatre ran the gamut of entertainment ventures until 1923–4, when it emerged as the National Winter Garden, a paradigm for all burlesque theatres in the country, including a dozen subsequent Minsky houses (in particular, The Republic, 1931). Innovations included illuminated runways; slim, attractive and scantily clad Minsky girls, such as GYPSY ROSE LEE and Margie Hart; and good comics (such as Steve Mills and PHIL SILVERS). Some feel the Minskys caused burlesque's downfall, for as they developed dirty, escapist shows that attracted sizable patronage, censors also took notice. Mayor Fiorello LaGuardia helped effect the closing of their operation in 1937, although a legal ban did not exist until 1942. A year prior to his death Morton (with M. Machlin) wrote his memoirs of the brothers' empire.   DBW

minstrel show An American medley of sentimental ballads, comic dialogue, and dance interludes, ostensibly founded on Negro life in the South. Its origin is attributed to T. D. RICE, who copied the eccentric mannerisms of an elderly black in Baltimore or Louisville in 1828 and adopted blackface and banjo to produce the wildly popular "Jim Crow." At first a solo act, minstrelsy grew to four performers of violin, banjo, bones (a rhythm instrument), and tambourine with the Virginia Minstrels, founded by DAN EMMETT (1842–3); despite the burnt cork, their repertoire drew heavily on traditional English choral singing and lugubrious parlor ballads. The same held true of the troupe of E.P. Christy, who invented whitefaced master-of-ceremonies Mr. Interlocutor and the semicircular arrangement of performers; his troupe had 30 members and gave 2,500 performances in New York in a single year. By the early 1850s Christy had evolved what was to be the standard tripartite program: In the first part, the performers would enter in the "walk-round" until told, "Gentlemen, be seated." Vocal numbers, both lively and sentimental would be sung, interspersed with comic chat from the "endmen" (in England, "cornermen"), Mr. Tambo and Mr. Bones. Part Two, the olio, was a fantasia of speciality acts before the drop curtain; these included the stump speech, perfected by James Unsworth, and the wench impersonation, originated by George N. Christy (né Harrington). Part Three comprised a sketch, either a plantation scene with dancing "darkies" or burlesques of Shakespearean plays and melodramas. Originally most of the performers and composers were white northerners who, like Stephen Foster, had little firsthand acquaintance with Southern life; consequently the blacks they portrayed (like Zip Coon, the urban dandy) were extravagant fictions, and blackface comprised a theatrical mask not unlike Harlequin's.

After the Civil War, competition from other popular forms, especially variety and musical comedy, compelled the minstrel show to expand and change its homely character. In 1878 J. H. HAVERLY combined four troupes in his United Mastodon Minstrels with his slogan, "Forty – Count 'Em – Forty." Sumptuous costumes and lavish scenery became the rule. Primrose and West even omitted the blackface and dressed their minstrels in 18th-century court dress. From 1880 the traditionalists complained loudly about such changes.

A more significant factor was the presence in troupes of AFRICAN AMERICANS themselves. As early as the 1850s, black troupes, such as the Luca

Boston Minstrels, illustrating two stereotypes: "dandyism" of the North and "Ethiopians of the South." An Endicott lithograph sheet music cover for "Cudjo's Wild Hunt" by Anthony Winnemore. Six members of the company are shown in both types of role, with Winnemore (playing banjo) second from left in both rows, 1843. *Courtesy:* Brown University Library.

Family, toured the Eastern states, often performing for abolitionist societies. These black-owned companies were popular throughout the Civil War years, but in the 1870s were taken over by white managers. Thus, Callender's Georgia Minstrels, featuring the great comic BILLY KERSANDS, was sold to Haverly, who then claimed falsely to have launched "colored minstrels." A major component of black shows, whatever the race of the management, was female performers: Sam T. Jack's Creoles even had an all-black female first part. By adopting such stereotypes as the loyal uncle, warm-hearted mammy, and shifty lazybones, black performers perpetuated the notion that these caricatures were true to life. Nevertheless, the minstrel show provided a valuable training ground for such talents as SAM LUCAS, Billy McLain, and composer James Bland.

The minstrel show was one of the few truly indigenous American entertainments, and made a profound impression worldwide. Its influence can be traced in much American popular music and theatre, and many outstanding performers, including EDDIE CANTOR, AL JOLSON, and BERT WILLIAMS, owed a great deal to its traditions. Great Britain took rapidly to minstrelsy, sending its own troupes as far afield as India and Australia. Anglo-Saxon blackface artists were well entrenched throughout the British Empire long before the first minstrels arrived in strength in the 1870s; as a result, the ingrained stereotypes were even more remote from African American reality than in the USA.   LS

Mint Theater Company Founded by Kelly Morgan in 1992 to bring "new vitality to worthy but neglected plays," since 1995 this NYC company has been led by Artistic Director Jonathan Bank, a director-dramaturge. A production house more than an ensemble, the Mint has mounted a fleet of aging works from U.S. and U.K. dramatists – Harley Granville Barker (*The Voysey Inheritance*), A. A. Milne (*Mr. Pym Passes By*), JOHN VAN DRUTEN (*The Voice of the Turtle*), S. N. BEHRMAN (*NO TIME FOR COMEDY*), Thomas Wolfe (*Welcome to Our City*), D. H. Lawrence (*The Daughter-in-Law*), and Arthur Schnitzler (*Far and Wide*), among them. The Mint is highly lauded for rediscovering obscure gems, like the CLYDE FITCH–Edith Wharton adaptation of *The House of Mirth* and two Pulitzer Prize winners: ZONA GALE's *MISS LULU BETT* and SUSAN GLASPELL's *ALISON'S HOUSE*. The Mint's honors include a 2002 Special Drama Desk Award and a 2001 Obie. Its success in producing yesteryear's theatre bolstered the creation of three other New York–based groups: Peccadillo Theatre Company, Keen Company, and Metropolitan Playhouse.   LJ

Miracle Worker, The WILLIAM GIBSON's play dramatically condenses the true story of Annie Sullivan's early attempts to teach the deaf and blind Helen Keller. Cutting across time and place, the three-act play suggests strong motivation in Sullivan's wretched childhood, but concentrates more specifically on the struggle of wills between a stubborn young woman and bright but virtually untamed child. The first production, staged by ARTHUR PENN, opened 19 October 1959 at The PLAYHOUSE, NYC, and fascinated audiences with its highly physical confrontations of the principals, ANNE BANCROFT and Patty Duke. Although criticized for its loose construction, the play was praised for the power of its emotional moments, particularly Keller's miraculous awakening to the concept of language. It ran until 1 July 1961.   KF

Miss Lulu Bett ZONA GALE's dramatization of her novel premiered at Sing Sing prison to inaugurate a portable stage given by DAVID BELASCO, but it opened the next night, 27 December 1920, at the Belmont Theatre for a successful run. The play tells the story of a spinster who is economically dependent on her sister's husband, the unctuous Dwight Deacon, and exploited by her relatives to be little better than a servant. It won an even greater following when Gale changed the ending. In the original, Lulu becomes a more liberated woman, but with a tenuous future; in the changed version, she is happily married. The play was awarded the Pulitzer Prize for 1921. The MINT THEATER revived it in 2000.   FB

Miss Saigon One of the more successful megamusicals imported from London (4,095 performances) with music by Claude-Michel Schönberg, book and lyrics by Alain Boublil (adapted by Richard Maltby Jr.), direction by Nicholas Hytner, and spectacular scenery (including the infamous helicopter that descended from the flies). At the time, its $10 million capitalization was a record. This updated version of *Madame Butterfly* was controversial when it opened at the BROADWAY THEATRE in 1991, due to its stereotypical portrayal of Asians and insulting treatment of women, and for Actors' Equity attempt to prevent actor Jonathan Pryce from recreating his London performance as the manipulative Eurasian Engineer – and still is, among critics. It was nominated for 11 Tonys and won 3 – including Best Actor for Pryce!   DBW

Missoula Children's Theatre (MCT) Founded in 1970 by Jim Caron in Montana, this unique operation has evolved into a nationwide touring company, bringing theatre to many small communities. Uniquely, there are local youths (as many as 50 to 70) incorporated into a 70-minute musical with only five days of rehearsal. With 50 full-time employees at its home base in Missoula, there are approximately 32 teams on the road staging shows in more than 900 communities in all 50 states (and some 29 foreign countries).   DBW

Missouri Repertory Theatre Begun in 1964 as a two-play summer repertory theatre, the company had expanded by 1977 to an eight-play, year-round, rotating-repertory season. Founder Patricia McIlrath served as its artistic director until her retirement in 1985, when she was succeeded by George Keathley, who remained until 2000. The current head is Peter Altman, who came from Boston's HUNTINGTON. In 1979 The Rep moved into the 733-seat Helen F. Spencer Theatre (a second space, the Unicorn Theatre, seats 170) and became a nonprofit corporation separate from its host institution, the University of Missouri–Kansas City; however, the university's professional theatre training program ensures an ongoing organic relationship with the company. In 2004, for reasons not altogether clear, the company's name was changed to Kansas City Repertory Theatre.   FHL

Mister Roberts Comedy by Thomas Heggen and JOSHUA LOGAN from Heggen's collection of stories with the same title. Directed by Logan, it opened on 18 February 1948 at the ALVIN THEATRE for 1,157 performances, with HENRY FONDA as the irrepressible Lieutenant and David Wayne as his debonair sidekick, Ensign Pulver. Three separate road companies played between 1949 and 1951; productions in London and Paris were also well received. The film version (1955) was successful and led to a spin-off movie featuring the ensign (1964), and later to a television series (1965–6). A superb ensemble supporting Fonda's stage performance, broad humor, and patriotic sentiment were the key ingredients to the success of this tale about an assortment of sailors sailing around the Pacific on the periphery of WWII. The show won five Tonys, including Best Play. America loved Mister Roberts, a positive vision of the quintessential American who had just won the war: He was fun-loving, humble, heroic, loyal, self-sacrificing, and warm.   MR

Mitchell, Brian Stokes (1958–) Seattle-born charismatic actor-singer termed by the *New York Times* "The Last Leading Man." His acting range, physical grace, and clear baritone voice have made him a perfect fit in a series of musical roles: Coalhouse Walker Jr. in RAGTIME (1998; Tony nomination), Fred Graham/Petruchio in KISS ME, KATE (1999; 2000 Tony for Best Actor in a Musical), and Don Quixote/Cervantes in MAN OF LA MANCHA (2002; Tony nomination). Despite several television roles and unspectacular Broadway parts, he first gained attention when he replaced GREGORY HINES in JELLY'S LAST JAM (1993); in 1995 he stepped into the role of Valentin in *Kiss of the Spider Woman.* He proved his nonsinging acting ability when he played King in AUGUST WILSON's *King Hedley II* in 2001, once more a Tony nominee. In 2005 he made his cabaret debut in *Love/Life*, first at Feinstein's at the Regency and then at the VIVIAN BEAUMONT at Lincoln Center. June 2005 he performed at Carnegie Hall in a concert version of *SOUTH PACIFIC* with Reba McEntire. He is in much demand as a concert soloist with major orchestras and conductors (Michael Tilson Thomas, Leonard Slatkin, Marvin Hamlisch, John Williams, etc.).   DBW

Mitchell, David (1932–) Set designer, recipient of two Tony Awards, whose early work (late 1960s, early '70s) was split among realistically oriented frontal and symmetrical designs for shows like *The BASIC TRAINING OF PAVLO HUMMEL* (1971) and *SHORT EYES* (1974), both at The PUBLIC); a variety

of works for the NEW YORK SHAKESPEARE FESTIVAL, many influenced by MING CHO LEE; and opera. With ANNIE (1977), however, he became associated with large-scale musicals and fluid, cinematic sets, as in *Barnum* (1980), *LA CAGE AUX FOLLES* (1983), and *BRIGHTON BEACH MEMOIRS* (1983), a nonmusical but cinematic play. He has also designed many classical ballets, including the New York City Ballet's *Sleeping Beauty* (1991).   AA

Mitchell, Jerry (1959/60?–) This in-demand choreographer is from Paw Paw, MI. Soon after college he was cast as a dancer by AGNES DE MILLE in a 1980 revival of BRIGADOON. By the late 1980s he had begun the transition from chorus boy to choreographer, serving as assistant to JEROME ROBBINS (*Jerome Robbins' Broadway*) in 1989 and associate choreographer on *Grease* (1994 revival) before his first full credit – the revival of YOU'RE A GOOD MAN, CHARLIE BROWN in 1999. Subsequent Broadway credits include *The FULL MONTY* (2000; Tony nomination), *The Rocky Horror Show* (2000 revival), HAIRSPRAY (2002; Tony nom.), GYPSY (2003 revival), *Never Gonna Dance* (2003, Tony nom.), *LA CAGE AUX FOLLES* (2004 revival), and *Dirty Rotten Scoundrels* (2005) – the latter two both nominated for a 2005 Tony, which he won for the former. Mitchell is fondly known as the creator in 1992 of *Broadway Bares*, a benefit that raises money for Broadway Cares/Equity Fights AIDS, which he choreographs annually. Most recently he directed (for the first time) and choreographed the musical version of *Legally Blonde,* which opened on Broadway in spring 2007.   DBW

Mitchell, John Cameron (1963–) Born in El Paso, TX, son of a retired general and raised largely in Colorado Springs, this extraordinary actor, writer, and director quietly built a reputation as an actor in the role of Trent in SIX DEGREES OF SEPARATION (1990), Dickon in *The Secret Garden* (1991), and as Alexander Weeks in *The Destiny of Me* (1992, Obie) before bursting through with HEDWIG AND THE ANGRY INCH (1998 stage, Obie; 2001 film), which he wrote, directing the film version. The film role of the transsexual rock star Hedwig brought him *People Magazine*'s designation as one of their breakthrough stars of 2001. In the stage role he was termed an "electric sexpot."   DBW

Mitchell, Julian (1854–1926) Director. After an early career as a performer, Mitchell served as assistant director on several of CHARLES HOYT's farce comedies. He directed a number of burlesques for WEBER AND FIELDS, after which he turned to the staging of elaborate comic operas

449

such as *The WIZARD OF OZ* (1903) and *BABES IN TOYLAND* (1903). During 1907–14 he directed the *ZIEGFELD Follies,* and he is credited with creating the chorus of beautiful, lively, and individualized girls that became the hallmark of those shows. He continued to be in demand as a director of musicals up to the time of his death.   MK

Mitchell, Langdon (Elwyn) (1862–1935) Playwright. Son of the eminent physician and novelist Silas Weir Mitchell, he is principally known for one play, *The NEW YORK IDEA* (1906). This witty satire on easy divorce and easy marriage, defined as "three parts love and seven parts forgiveness of sin," prompted critics to call him "the American SHAW." "What I wanted to satirize," Mitchell once wrote, "was the extreme frivolity of our American life." Written for MINNIE MADDERN FISKE, it was revived by GRACE GEORGE (1915), and was produced by MAX REINHARDT in Berlin (1916). Mitchell also wrote *In the Season* (1893); *Becky Sharp* (1899), an adaptation of *Vanity Fair* and a vehicle for Mrs. Fiske; *The Kreutzer Sonata* (1906), an adaptation from the Yiddish of JACOB GORDIN; *The New Marriage* (1911); and *Major Pendennis* (1916), adapted from Thackeray's novel.

He was educated at St. Paul's, studied in Dresden and Paris, attended law school at Harvard and Columbia, was admitted to the New York bar in 1886, and in 1892 married English actress Marion Lea, who appeared in *The New York Idea.*   RM

Mitchell, Loften (1919–2001) AFRICAN AMERICAN playwright, teacher, and theatre historian who studied playwriting with JOHN GASSNER and had three of his early plays produced in Harlem before gaining recognition with *A Land beyond the River* (1957, OFF-BROADWAY), a drama based on the life of the Rev. Dr. Joseph DeLaine, who fought to end discrimination in public schools. Mitchell cowrote the book for *Ballad for Bimshire* (1963) and the freedom pageant *Ballad for the Winter Soldiers* (1964). Alone, he wrote the television documentary *Tell Pharaoh* (1963), dramatized the BERT WILLIAMS story in *Star of the Morning* (published 1971), and also wrote the book and some lyrics for the successful *Bubbling Brown Sugar* (1976). His informal history *Black Drama* (1967) and *Voices of the Black Theatre* (1975) chronicle the experiences of African Americans in the American theatre.   EGH

Mitchell, Margaret (Maggie) (1832–1918) A tiny, boyish ingenue, she followed two half-sisters on the stage, making her debut in June 1851 at BURTON'S THEATRE, NYC. Often playing breeches parts, she achieved her first starring success in

Cleveland (1853). She became identified with the title role of *Fanchon, The Cricket,* which she first played at the ST. CHARLES THEATRE, New Orleans (January 1861). It became her starring vehicle, and into it she interpolated an extensive repertory of songs, dances, and impersonations of other performers. She retired in 1892.   DMcD

Mitchell, William "Billy" (1798–1856) English-born actor, playwright, and theatre manager. A distinguished comedian from London and English provincial theatres since 1831, Mitchell appeared first in the U.S. at New York's National Theatre in 1836. His particular achievement was his management of MITCHELL'S OLYMPIC in New York from 9 December 1839 to 9 March 1850, the year of his retirement. Advertising the production of "Vaudevilles, Burlesques, Extravaganzas, Farces, Etc.," Mitchell made the Olympic a popular success when other theatres were failing. As an actor Mitchell was a favorite as Vincent Crummles in a farce created from Dickens's *Nicholas Nickleby* entitled *The Savage and the Maiden.* A staff of actor-playwrights – Henry Horncastle, CHARLES WALCOT, Alexander Allen, and BENJAMIN A. BAKER – provided him with novelties. *1940; or, Crummles in Search of Novelty* was repeated as *1941; . . .* and *1942; . . . .* Catching the topic of the day was the clue to Mitchell's success. When BOUCICAULT's *London Assurance* came to New York City, Mitchell responded with *Olympic Insurance;* he burlesqued Dickens's visit in *Boz* and the EDWIN FORREST–William Macready feud in three sketches; he wrote and starred in *Billy Taylor,* a local extravaganza. The greatest event at Mitchell's Olympic, however, was Baker's *A GLANCE AT NEW YORK* (1848), with Mose the fire b'hoy. Mitchell's life is recounted in David Rinear's *The Temple of Momus* (1987).   WJM

Mitchell's Olympic 442–4 Broadway, NYC [Architect: Calvin Pollard]. In 1837, Willard and Blake opened the Olympic, patterned after Madame Vestris's famous London Olympic both in physical structure and policy. They presented comedies, farces, vaudevilles, and musical pieces, and, since the city was surfeited with theatres and entertainment, quickly lost their theatre. In 1839, despite hard times, WILLIAM "BILLY" MITCHELL revived the fortunes of the house with a combination of his own talents and managerial prowess. His reduced prices and his diet of light comic entertainment and burlesques made it the most popular theatre in town. When he retired in 1850, the playhouse passed to other managements and was used briefly as a minstrel hall and a German-language theatre. In 1852, it was converted to business uses, and two years later, the structure burned to the ground.   MCH

Mitzi E. Newhouse Theatre see VIVIAN BEAUMONT AND MITZI E. NEWHOUSE THEATRES

Mixed Blood Theatre Company, The   Founded in 1976 to promote successful pluralism and individual equality through artistic excellence, this company is situated in a 200-seat, flexible converted 1887 firehouse in an ever-changing MINNEAPOLIS immigrant neighborhood. Branding itself not a multicultural theatre, but rather culturally specific times 5 or 50 or 500, it embodies a world on its stage where people pay positive attention to their differences. The Equity (since 1977) company produces primarily original American works with multiracial casts. Part of a 1970s new wave of professional theatres in Minneapolis, Mixed Blood, since 1980, has coupled its mainstage productions with annual tours of culturally specific productions throughout the upper Midwest (up to 625 performances on the road yearly). Founder Jack Reuler has remained artistic director since 1976.   MBD

Modjeska [Modrzejewska], **Helena** [née Jadwiga Benda/Jadwiga Opid] (1840–1909) Polish-born actress, daughter of the widowed Madame Benda, she used the name of the family guardian, Michal Opid, until she married Gustave Sinnmayer Modrzejewski in 1856 and made her stage debut as Helena Modrzejewska in 1861. Managed by her second husband, Count Bozenta, she became an INTERNATIONAL STAR before emigrating to the U.S. in 1876. She learned English and made her American debut in 1877 in Scribe's *Adrienne Lecouvreur,* one of her great roles, along with Camille and Shakespeare's Rosalind, Viola, Beatrice, and Portia. The tall, comely actress was noted for her charm, naturalness and, in WILLIAM WINTER's words, "exquisite refinement and grace." Her memoirs were published in 1910. Her biography by Marion Coleman was published in 1969.   FHL

Moeller, Philip (1880–1958) Director, producer, and playwright. Born in New York, Moeller graduated from Columbia University and joined the WASHINGTON SQUARE PLAYERS in the winter of 1914. His one-act plays *Two Blind Beggars and One Less Blind* and *Helena's Husband* were produced by the group and attracted critical attention; but Moeller made his reputation as a director, and was regarded by LAWRENCE LANGNER as one of the most brilliant directors of comedy in this country. A founder and director of the THEATRE GUILD, he staged their first production, *The Bonds of Interest,* in 1919. He was especially adept in directing the plays of EUGENE O'NEILL. His Guild credits include *STRANGE INTERLUDE* (1928), *Dynamo* (1929), *MOURNING BECOMES ELECTRA* (1931), and *AH, WILDERNESS!* (1933). BROOKS ATKINSON called his direction of *Strange Interlude* a "tremendous achievement" because he found a way to distinguish between the speeches and the asides. Atkinson also praised Moeller for finding the "exact tempo and style" in *Mourning Becomes Electra.* Moeller thought of himself as an inspirational director. After directing films for RKO Radio in the early 1930s, he went into virtual retirement.   TLM

Moffat, Donald (1930–) British-born actor and director, trained at RADA, who, after a brief career in England, made his Broadway debut in *Under Milk Wood* (1957), then did *The Bald Soprano* (1958, OFF-BROADWAY), Hailey's *Father's Day* (1970), Howe's *Painting Churches* (1983, SECOND STAGE), *The ICEMAN COMETH* (1985 revival), Jeremy Lawrence's *Uncommon Ground* (1991, Evanston, IL), *The Heiress* (1995 revival), and as U. S. Grant in GUARE's *A Few Stout Individuals* (2002, SIGNATURE). He has acted at the Ohio and Akron Shakespeare Festivals and regional companies like the McCARTER THEATRE, and directed at the Great Lakes Shakespeare Festival, ASSOCIATION OF PRODUCING ARTISTS (APA)–Phoenix, and Los Angeles Actors' Theatre (see LOS ANGELES THEATER CENTER). After Moffat's first film, *Pursuit of the Graf Spee* (1957), he appeared in *Rachel, Rachel* (1968), *The Right Stuff* (1983), *The Unbearable Lightness of Being* (1988), *The Bonfire of the Vanities* (1990), *Clear and Present Danger* (1994), and *Cookie's Fortune* (1999) as well as in a number of TV roles, including *Tartuffe* (1978). Moffat received 1967 Tony nominations for *The Wild Duck* and *Right You Are . . . .*   REK

Mogulesko, Sigmund (1858–1914) Born in Bessarabia (Moldavia), this Yiddish actor and composer began performing in childhood as a choirboy and joined AVROM GOLDFADN, the "Father of YIDDISH THEATRE," in his early efforts. He acted – in women's roles, for there were no Yiddish actresses as yet – and also composed. When he arrived in America in 1886, his fame preceded him, and he continued for the rest of his life to be the public's darling for his mischievous charm, especially in character roles, and his sweet voice. He continued to perform and compose with great success despite a period of difficulties with his voice.   NS

Moiseiwitsch, Tanya (1914–2003) British-born set and costume designer noted for her collaborations with director TYRONE GUTHRIE and the bold thrust stage and innovative auditorium she designed for the Shakespeare Festival Theatre in Stratford, Ontario (1957) and the similar GUTHRIE THEATER in Minneapolis (1963). Moiseiwitsch began her career in London in 1934. The following year she went to the Abbey Theatre in Dublin, where she designed more than 50 productions through 1939. She subsequently designed for the London's Old Vic beginning in 1944 and at the Shakespeare Memorial Theatre in Stratford-upon-Avon from 1949, as well as commercial theatre in London and theatres in Italy, the U.S., and Australia. She is most closely associated with the plays of Shakespeare, but notable productions include *Oedipus Rex* at Ontario (1954; film 1957) and *The House of Atreus* at the Guthrie (1967), both of which contain what is perhaps the most successful use of masks in the 20th century. Beginning with her work at the Abbey, Moiseiwitsch's designs were typified by simple, direct, presentational sets that embodied the visual metaphor of the play. Since she generally designed costumes as well, there was a strong visual unity to her productions. With the polygonal, stepped stages at Ontario and Minneapolis that jutted into the steeply banked auditoriums, Moiseiwitsch was able to eliminate most scenery and provide a space in which her highly textured costumes could be sculpted by light. A major retrospective of her work was seen at Stratford, ON, in 1992.
AA

Molina, Alfred (1953–) British-born (Spanish father and Italian mother) character actor who, after attending the Guildhall School of Music and Drama, began his stage career in the U.K. (at the National: Shannon in WILLIAMS's *The Night of the Iguana* and Fox in MAMET's *Speed-the-Plow*) but since the 1980s has lived and worked largely in the U.S. His major NYC stage roles have been in a 1995 revival of *Molly Sweeney* at the ROUNDABOUT; as Yvan in Yasmina Reza's *Art* with ALAN ALDA and VICTOR GARBER in 1998; as Tevye in *Fiddler on the Roof* (2004); and as a failed showbiz agent in Patrick Marber's *Howard Katz* (2007, Roundabout). For Yvan and Tevye he received Tony nominations. Molina has performed stunning personalities in films, from Satipo in *Raiders of the Lost Ark* (1981) to Kenneth Halliwell in *Prick Up Your Ears* (1987), Rahad Jackson in *Boogie Nights* (1997), Diego Rivera in *Frida* (2002), Dr. Octopus in *Spider-Man 2* (2004), and Bishop Aringarosa in *The Da Vince Code* (2006). DBW

Monk, Meredith (1942–) Choreographer, composer, director, PERFORMANCE ARTIST and leading innovator in the so-called Next Wave since the mid-1960s and her association with the Judson Dance Theatre (NYC). Her dances have evolved into multimedia, nonverbal theatre pieces, such as *Vessel* (1971–2) and *Quarry* (1975–6), both termed "opera epic." In the early and mid-1970s she also created several chamber-theatre works: the "travelogue" series (*Paris, Chacon, Venice/Milan*) in collaboration with PING CHONG, and the "archaeology" pieces (*Small Scroll, Anthology, The Plateau Series, Recent Ruins*). In the late 1970s she began to concentrate on musical composition and performance, having begun to "distrust the theatre a little bit," although by the early 1980s two multimedia theatre pieces had been added to her canon: *Specimen Days* (1981) and *The Games* (1983), the latter commissioned by Peter Stein's Schaubühne repertory theatre in West Berlin, with its U.S. premiere at the BROOKLYN ACADEMY OF MUSIC's Next Wave Festival the following year. In the early 1990s she devoted attention to her unique form of opera, such as *Atlas* (1991), most notably with commissions from the Houston Opera, and additional performances pieces, such as *Facing North* (1991) with Robert Eden; *Volcano Songs* (1994), a solo piece; *The Politics of Quiet* (1996), a blend of vocalization and choreography; and *Impermanence* (2004), a multidisciplinary look at change. In 1995 she received a MacArthur "genius" Fellowship and in 1996 the Samuel H. Scripps / American Dance Festival Award. July 2004 marked the beginning of a celebration of her 40th year as performer (culminating in a four-hour music marathon at New York's Zankel Hall in 2005). Her career has been chronicled by Deborah Jowett (1997). DBW

monodrama see ONE-PERSON PERFORMANCES

Montague [né Mann], **Henry James (or John)** (1843–78) English-born actor whose American debut in 1874 (Tom Gilroy in *Partners for Life*) at WALLACK'S THEATRE followed a successful London career. Handsome and gentlemanly, he became a popular leading man in New York and later on tour in such roles as Captain Molyneux (*The Shaughraun*), Captain D'Alroy (*Caste*), and Tom Dexter (*The Overland Route*). He died suddenly while playing an engagement at San Francisco's CALIFORNIA THEATRE. DJW

Montanaro, Tony (1927–2002) Illusionistic MIME and storyteller, teacher. A student both of Louise Gifford at Columbia University and (to a lesser extent) of Étienne Decroux, Montanaro was most strongly marked by his studies with Marcel Marceau in Paris. Montanaro lived and worked in NYC until the early 1970s, when he founded the Celebration Barn Theater in Maine. An influential teacher, he inspired generations of performers and created a video book entitled *Mime Spoken Here* (1991).   TL

Montano, Linda (1942–) Conceptual and PERFORMANCE ARTIST-writer. A native of Saugerties, NY, Montano attended Catholic schools, joined the missionary order of Maryknoll Sisters (1960–2), studied art at the College of New Rochelle (B.A., 1965) and sculpture at the Villa Schiffanois, Italy (M.A., 1966) and the University of Wisconsin, Madison (M.F.A., 1969). Montano's performances draw on spiritual traditions and practices (Catholicism, Buddhism, Zen, Hinduism) and are based on an aesthetic of everyday life developed by Marcel Duchamp, Claes Oldenburg, John Cage, and ALLAN KAPROW. For her early performances (1969–72), she developed the "Chicken" persona. Other important performances were *Handcuffed to Tom Marioni for Three Days* (1973), *Mitchell's Death* (1978), *Art/Life, One Year Performance* (1983–4) with TEHCHING HSIEH, *Fourteen Years of Living Art* (1984–98), *Attention to the CHAKRAS* (1991–5), and *Blood Family Art* (1997–present). She has published six books on her art.   AF

Montez, Lola [née Maria Dolores Eliza Rosanna Gilbert] (1820–61) Irish-born adventuress, who, when her first marriage failed, went on the stage as a dancer (London, 1843), performing in Europe, America, and Australia. Her beauty and charm compensated for her lack of talent and musical sense. Her liaison with Ludwig I of Bavaria (1847–8) culminated in his forced abdication, and she came to the U.S., making her New York debut (1851) in *Betley the Tyrolean;* a biographical play, *Lola Montes [sic] in Bavaria,* by C. P. T. Ware (1852), capitalized on her sensational past. She toured to the gold-rush country, performing a Spider Dance that shocked San Francisco audiences, and took child actress LOTTA CRABTREE under her tutelage. After 1856, she appeared as a spiritualist and lecturer, speaking on fashion, gallantry, and Roman Catholicism. She underwent a religious conversion and became a recluse after 1859. The most trustworthy biography is by Bruce Seymour (1996).   LS

Montgomery, Dave (David Craig) (1870–1917) and **Fred** [Val] **(Andrew) Stone** (1873–1959) Comedy team (1894–1917) prominent in VAUDEVILLE and musical comedy. Initially a blackface act, they soon became headliners, appearing at London's Palace as early as 1900. Their greatest successes came in The WIZARD OF OZ (1902, CHICAGO; 1903, NYC) and VICTOR HERBERT's *The Red Mill* (1906). In the former Stone played the Scarecrow and Montgomery the Tin Woodsman; in the latter Stone, who began a long association with CHARLES DILLINGHAM, was a hit as Con Kidder. Montgomery and Stone were also two of the seven founders of the White Rats (1900), a fraternal order for vaudevillians. After Montgomery's death, Stone, an unusually versatile performer, appeared in films and onstage, his last major appearance being Grandpa Vanderhof in *You CAN'T TAKE IT WITH You* (City Center, NYC, 1945). Stone's daughters (Paula, Dorothy, and Carol) were in show business. His autobiography, *Rolling Stones,* was published in 1945; Armond Fields's biography in 2002.   DBW

Moody, William Vaughn (1869–1910) Indiana-born dramatist who took a degree in English at Harvard (1893) and taught there and at the University of Chicago (1895–1902). He cowrote a standard history of English literature, and was widely regarded as the best lyric poet of his generation. With Harriet Brainard, whom he married (1909), he was active in Donald Robertson's New Theatre. He experimented with two verse plays, but turned to prose when he dramatized a story about a woman kidnapped by a band of drunken cowboys. *The GREAT DIVIDE* was premiered by MARGARET ANGLIN at a matinee in Chicago (April 1906). It was easily the finest American play of its time, successfully blending realistic motivation with poetic treatment of the national myth. His last play, *The FAITH HEALER* (1909), was a failure in performance, and Moody died of a brain tumor soon after. A biography by Maurice Brown appeared in 1973.   DMcD

Moon for the Misbegotten, A, by EUGENE O'NEILL. Four-act drama written in 1943 that failed to reach New York in its original 1947 THEATRE GUILD production, and ran but 68 performances a decade later on Broadway (2 May 1957) starring Wendy Hiller, FRANCHOT TONE, and Cyril Cusack. The play gained stature with the 1968 revival at the CIRCLE IN THE SQUARE Theatre (THEODORE MANN, director), and was acclaimed a masterpiece with the 1973 revival on Broadway directed by JOSÉ QUINTERO (Tony Award) and starring COLLEEN DEWHURST, Ed Flanders (Tonys for both), and JASON ROBARDS JR. Other notable revivals include the GOODMAN's production in

2000, which transferred to the WALTER KERR THEATRE with Roy Dotrice as Phil Hogan (Tony and other awards), CHERRY JONES as Josie, and Gabriel Byrne as Jamie Tyrone; and the Old Vic production with KEVIN SPACEY in 2007.

The play is autobiographical, an attempt by O'Neill to understand and forgive his brother Jamie's actions before and after the death of their mother in Los Angeles and the subsequent return of her body by train to New York. In terms of the theatre, however, the play concerns the ill-fated mating of the guilt-ridden and alcoholic Jamie with Josie, a large, shy woman who pretends to be a wanton to hide her shyness and real feelings for Jamie. Although O'Neill paints life in harsh colors and depicts his characters as having little control over it, Jamie does find a measure of forgiveness and redemption through Josie's love.   TLM

Moonchildren by MICHAEL WELLER was first produced (as *Cancer*) in London in 1970, directed by Roger Hendricks Simon and Peter Gill. As *Moonchildren*, it was first produced at Washington, DC's ARENA STAGE in 1971, with ALAN SCHNEIDER directing a cast that included James Woods, Jill Eikenberry, ROBERT PROSKY, and Cara Duff-MacCormick. When DAVID MERRICK moved the production to Broadway, 21 February 1972, it closed after 16 performances; but a new production, directed by John Pasquin, ran for a year at the Theatre de Lys (1973–4), and the play has had well over 1,000 productions worldwide. Set in a college apartment shared by five men and two women in the mid-1960s, the play is a microcosm of a college generation whose every action was taken in reference to the Vietnam War. Through a thin layer of dark and evasive humor, Weller depicts the hopelessness of a generation for whom life decisions and permanent commitments are impossible.   BCM

Moore, Victor (1876–1962) Broadway actor who was described in the *New York Times* as "the chubby little comedian with the teetering walk and the quavering voice." His first of many Broadway roles was Kid Burns in *FORTY-FIVE MINUTES FROM BROADWAY* (1906). His best-known roles were those of vice president Alexander Throttlebottom in *OF THEE I SING* (1932) and Reverend Dr. Moon (Public Enemy #13) in *ANYTHING GOES* (1934). He was frequently cast as a foil to WILLIAM GAXTON's leading man. He received the San Francisco Drama Critics Council Citation as Best Actor for Gramps in a Broadway-bound 1952 revival of *On Borrowed Time*. He also appeared in many films, including *The Seven Year Itch* (1955).   MR

Moorehead, Agnes (1906–74) Stage, film, and television actress. She appeared in SUMMER STOCK aged 10 and spent four years with the St. Louis Municipal Opera. Moorehead earned a doctorate in literature at Bradley University, taught dramatics at the Dalton School, and began to appear on Broadway in such shows as *Marco Millions*. During the Depression, she turned to radio, appearing on *The March of Time* and in the suspense classic *Sorry, Wrong Number*. Moorehead was a charter member of the MERCURY THEATRE, and made her movie debut in *Citizen Kane* with ORSON WELLES. In 1951 she first appeared with the highly acclaimed First Drama Quartet in a Broadway reading of *Don Juan in Hell*. She made about 75 films, garnering four Academy Award nominations, yet was best known to modern audiences as Endora in the television situation comedy *Bewitched*. A biography by Charles Tranberg was pubished in 2005.   SMA

Moraga, Cherríe (1952–) California-born poet, playwright, and essayist, Moraga is well known as the coeditor, with the late Gloria Anzaldúa, of the groundbreaking 1981 anthology *This Bridge Called My Back: Writings by Radical Women of Color*. She began her theatrical career with *Giving Up the Ghost*, which premiered at THEATRE RHINOCEROS in 1989. Other plays, many of which have also premiered in SAN FRANCISCO, include *Shadow of a Man* (1990, SF; dir. MARÍA IRENE FORNÉS), *Heroes and Saints* (1992, SF), *Heart of the Earth: A Popul Vuh Story* (1995, INTAR), *Watsonville: Some Place Not Here* (1996, SF), and *The Hungry Woman: A Mexican Media* (2002, LA). She has received numerous awards for her playwriting, including an NEA Theatre Playwrights' Fellowship in 1993. The majority of her work deals with intersections of race, gender, and sexuality, with particular focus on the Latina experience.   DanB

Moran, George (1882–1949) and **Charles Mack** (1888–1934) Blackface comedy team ("The Two Black Crows") in the tradition of MCINTYRE AND HEATH. Never consciously racist in their routine, the team garnered black as well as white fans. Partnered first in the late teens, they became stars in 1927 after recording "The Early Bird Catches the Worm," featuring Mack as a shuffling, lazy black. Though they each began as singles in VAUDEVILLE, as a team they were most successful in 1920s REVUES. When Mack – who wrote most of the material and owned the Moran and Mack name as a trademark – refused Moran equal pay, Moran left the act briefly in 1930 (returning a few months later), and was replaced by Bert Swor (still billed as Moran and Mack).   DBW

Morehouse, Ward (1899–1966) Theatre journalist and critic. A native of Georgia, Morehouse was best known for his "Broadway After Dark" column and for vivid and racy theatrical interviews with stars. His writings appeared in the *New York Sun* (1926–48), the *New York World-Telegram and the Sun* (1950–6), and, from 1956 until his death, with S. I. Newhouse Newspapers. His books include *Forty-Five Minutes Past Eight* (1939), *Matinee Tomorrow* (1949), and GEORGE M. COHAN, *Prince of the American Theatre* (1943). Ward Morehouse III, his son, is a critic and writer. TLM

Moreno, Rita [né Rosita Dolores Alverio] (1931–) Puerto Rican–born American actress who initially worked as a Spanish dancer and NIGHTCLUB entertainer. She appeared in *The* SIGN IN SIDNEY BRUSTEIN'S WINDOW (1964) and several other plays before winning a Tony Award for her supporting role in *The Ritz* (1975). In 1985 she toured in a female version of SIMON's *The* ODD COUPLE. Moreno is one of nine performers to have won an Academy Award, a TV Emmy, a Broadway Tony, and a Grammy (recording). In 1994–5 she appeared on *The Cosby Mysteries* TV series and in 1997–2003 as Sister Peter Marie Reimondo on *Oz* on HBO. MK

Morfogen, George (1933–) A character actor – often in plays by Shakespeare, SHAW, CHEKHOV, ALBEE, WILLIAMS, or IBSEN – who since the 1950s has been a dependable and extensively utilized and flexible performer, termed by one recent critic "always the pro" and another "incapable of giving a static performance." A native New Yorker, Morfogen attended Brown and the Yale School of Drama (M.F.A. in directing); he also studied with EVA LEGALLIENNE. With his bald head and short, stout build, this intelligent actor seems ideal in many roles (since 1997 he has been Robert Rebadow on HBO's *Oz*). Although he has few Broadway credits (notably in 2002 Ivan Kuzmitch Ivanov in *Fortune's Fool*), his OFF-BROADWAY (more than 32 productions) and regional credits – as well as film and television appearances – are extensive and impressive, including 16 seasons at WILLIAMSTOWN and as a board member for the MINT THEATER COMPANY, where, in 1999 and 2000, he excelled as Mr. Voysey Sr. in *The Voysey Inheritance*. In 1995 he appeared in the title role of *Uncle Bob* (revived in 2001) in a play written especially for him by AUSTIN PENDELTON. DBW

Morgan, Roger (1938–) Lighting designer and theatre consultant who designed lights for many of the significant OFF-BROADWAY and OFF-OFF BROADWAY productions in the late 1960s and '70s, as well as productions for the NEW YORK SHAKESPEARE FESTIVAL, AMERICAN PLACE THEATRE, and the CIRCLE IN THE SQUARE. Broadway credits include *Dracula*, *Agnes of God*, *Me and My Girl*, and *The Crucifier of Blood* (1979 Tony for Best Lighting Design). Since the 1980s Morgan (Sachs Morgan Studio) has been active as a consultant to numerous new theatres and renovations, including the MARQUIS THEATRE in NYC, the DENVER CENTER Theatre complex, the Playhouse Square project in Cleveland, Center Stage in Baltimore, Warner Theatre in Washington, DC, and FORD CENTER FOR THE PERFORMING ARTS. Morgan received the Broadway Theater Institute's 1994 Award for Excellence for his restoration work on the WALTER KERR THEATRE. AA

Morning's at Seven by PAUL OSBORN premiered in 1939 at the LONGACRE THEATRE in a production directed by JOSHUA LOGAN and designed by JO MIELZINER. This gentle comedy about the lives of four sisters in a Midwestern community evoked Chekhov and WILDER but generated little enthusiasm and totaled only 44 performances. In 1980, however, a splendid revival directed by VIVIAN MATALON at the LYCEUM featured Nancy Marchand, Teresa Wright, Maureen O'Sullivan, and ELIZABETH WILSON as the Gibbs sisters, with strong supporting work by Gary Merrill and David Rounds. It ran 564 performances and won Tonys for Best Revival, Direction, and Featured Actor (Rounds). A solid revival in 2002 directed by DANIEL SULLIVAN was presented at the Lyceum by LINCOLN CENTER. BBW

Morosco, Oliver (Mitchell) (1876–1945) Utah-born manager and producer who moved to San Francisco at an early age and appeared as an acrobat in the troupe of Walter Morosco. After adopting his mentor's name, he managed several theatres in the Bay area, later acquiring on his own at least six theatres in LOS ANGELES. He began producing in 1909, and later offered in New York *The Bird of Paradise* (1912) and PEG O' MY HEART (1912), both starring LAURETTE TAYLOR; and, in 1915, *The Unchastened Woman* with EMILY STEVENS. The SHUBERTS built the MOROSCO THEATRE for him in New York (1917), which he opened with his own play, *Canary Cottage*. The author of numerous plays, all undistinguished, Morosco went bankrupt in 1926 in a scheme to build a motion-picture settlement in California. Helen Morosco and Leonard Dugger published a biography of him in 1944. MCH TLM

Clara Morris in an unidentified role; most likely in the late 1870s. *Courtesy:* Don B. Wilmeth Theatre Collection.

Morosco Theatre 217 West 45th St., NYC [Architect: Herbert J. Krapp]. The Morosco was the first of many theatres to be designed for the SHUBERTS by Herbert J. Krapp, a talented young architect who had served his apprenticeship with Henry B. Herts, an earlier favored Shubert architect. Built in 1917, it was intended as a showcase for the productions of OLIVER MOROSCO. An intimate, 1,000-seat, one-balcony house, it was well suited to realistic dramas and intimate musicals. On its stage was launched the Broadway career of EUGENE O'NEILL, whose first full-length play, BEYOND THE HORIZON (1920), was presented at matinee performances. The same year the long-running The BAT opened there. In 1936, the Shuberts were forced to relinquish the theatre, which changed hands several times before it was razed in 1982 to make way for a new hotel. In addition to O'Neill, its stage had proved kind to such American playwrights as THORNTON WILDER, TENNESSEE WILLIAMS, ARTHUR MILLER, ROBERT ANDERSON, and ARTHUR KOPIT. MCH

Morris [née Morrison], **Clara** (1846/8–1925) Actress, born in Canada, possibly of a bigamous union, who received her early training in JOHN A. ELLSLER'S STOCK COMPANY in Cleveland (1861–9). For years she sustained a reputation as one of America's greatest emotionalistic actresses, although her career is one of incongruities. In the 1870s she was praised as realistic, though by the '80s she was denounced by many as the queen of spasms and the mistress of the tricks of the acting trade. In 1870 she began her New York career as a member of AUGUSTIN DALY's company, excelling in plays like *Man and Wife*, DIVORCE, and especially Daly's *Article 47*, in which she played Cora the Creole. She left Daly in 1873 and spent most of her remaining career as a traveling star, appearing in popular roles such as Camille and Miss Multon (in a version of *EAST LYNNE*). Although she attempted classical roles, she was always more successful when playing pathetic girls in melodrama, which allowed her to use her "tearful" voice and to loose a veritable flood of emotion on her audience. She appeared in VAUDEVILLE in the 1900s and made her last appearance in Washington, DC, in 1906. She wrote three unreliable autobiographies (1901–6). Her diary (54 volumes), 1867–1924, is housed at Radcliffe College. A biography by Barbara Grossman is projected for 2008.
  DBW

Morris, Mary (1895–1970) Actress. At Radcliffe College Morris performed in GEORGE PIERCE BAKER's Workshop 47, but left to gain practical theatre experience. After a year as an unsalaried prompter, she made her professional debut in *The Clod* with the WASHINGTON SQUARE PLAYERS in 1916. In 1918 she toured *Alexander Hamilton* with GEORGE ARLISS, whom she credited with teaching her the most about acting. For two years (1924–6) she played Abbie in DESIRE UNDER THE ELMS. She appeared with numerous STOCK companies, on Broadway, and in two films. In 1937 she made her London debut. She taught and directed at Carnegie Institute of Technology (1939–60) and at the AMERICAN SHAKESPEARE FESTIVAL and Academy (1961–2). FHL

Morris, William (1873–1932) German immigrant who founded the agency that still bears his name. He went into business in 1898 in NYC as "William Morris, Vaudeville Agent." Becoming the leading independent vaudeville AGENT and booker and ultimately bucking the power of the UNITED BOOKING OFFICE when founded in 1906. Morris incorporated on 31 January 1918, joined by his son, William Jr., and former office boy, Abe Last-fogel. Morris, a true showman and promoter, was a favorite with performers. He was responsible, for instance, for bringing HARRY LAUDER to the U.S. and VAUDEVILLE – and Lauder, in turn, like many clients, remained faithful to Morris. By 1930 Morris passed leadership to his son and Last-fogel. Today, the William Morris Agency is considered the largest diversified talent and literary agency in the world, with offices in New York, Beverly Hills, Nashville, Miami, London, and Shanghai. A biography of Morris by Frank Rose was published in 1995.   DBW

Morse, Robert (1931–) Actor and singer from Newton, MA, first seen on Broadway in *The* MATCH-MAKER (1955); his musical debut was in *Say Darling* (1959). He charmed critics and audiences as the boyish but determined J. Pierpont Finch in *How TO SUCCEED IN BUSINESS WITHOUT REALLY TRYING* (1961; Tony) and starred in the long-running musical *Sugar* (1972) and the less successful *So Long, 174th Street* (1976). After a long absence, he returned to Broadway in a Tony Award–winning performance as Truman Capote in the acclaimed ONE-PERSON show *Tru* (1989). He was Cap'n Andy in the 1993 revival of *SHOW BOAT* in Toronto but did not appear in the New York production.   MK

Mortimer, Lillian (c. 1880–1946) Actor, author, and manager who produced her own and other plays on the STAIR AND HAVLIN 10–20–30 circuit (1903–9). Declining receipts led her to disband her company and headline as a comedienne on the KEITH circuit from 1909 until about 1930, when she retired.   RKB

Morton, Martha (1865?–1925) "The dean of America's women playwrights," Morton, also a director, was the first to crack the gender barrier on Broadway with her many commercial, if not critical, successes. In 1891 she wrote *The Merchant,* followed by *Geoffrey Middleton* (1892), *A Fool of Fortune* (1896), *A Bachelor's Romance* (1897), *The Triumph of Love* (1904), and others. In 1907 she organized the Society of Dramatic Authors because the American Dramatists Club refused to accept women.   FB

Moschen, Michael (1955–) NEW VAUDEVILLE and PERFORMANCE ARTist who is to juggling what FRED ASTAIRE was to tap dancing. He has performed with CIRCUSES (BIG APPLE CIRCUS, Lotte Goslar's Pantomime Circus), BILL IRWIN, and with Fred Garbo and Bob Berky. He created a solo show, *Moschen in Motion* (1988) for the BROOKLYN ACADEMY OF MUSIC's "Next Wave Festival," and in 1991 created and starred in "In Motion with Michael Moshen" on PBS's *Alive from Off-Center.* Sculptor John Kahn has inspired and been a collaborator in much of Moschen's work, which uses beautifully designed objects manipulated daringly and poetically in ways that fully engage the imagination and attention. Moschen has received, among other prestigious awards, a five-year MacArthur Foundation "genius" Fellowship.   TL

Moscow Art Theatre (MAT) MAT's five-nation European and American tours (1922–3) were undertaken for several purposes: to regain internal stability and financial solvency for a company denied government subsidies and attacked for being bourgeois elitist under the new Soviet regime; to demonstrate the new centralized Soviet theatre's good health; and to introduce American audiences to ensemble, as opposed to "star" acting. Producer MORRIS GEST widely and unrealistically promoted MAT as an ideal acting ensemble, prior to the American tour, which originated in NYC (JOLSON's 59th Street Theatre, 8 January–31 March 1923). Stanislavsky was struck by theatre's devaluation in such an advanced society, while the American press accused MAT of being a communist propaganda tool. MAT performed (in Russian and in rep) A. N. Tolstoy's *Tsar Fyodor Ivanovitch,* Gorky's *The Lower Depths,* CHEKHOV's *The Three Sisters, Uncle Vanya,* and *The Cherry Orchard* (despite Stanislavsky's questioning of Chekhov's continued relevance in Soviet society), and Turgenev's *The Lady from the Provinces.* The tour was a popular and artistic success (especially the Chekhov) but a financial failure for the company. Praised for its new style of play, MAT performed only its accessible, realistic repertory staples, not the symbolist and new Soviet plays and stylized stagings of the classics it offered in Russia. MAT's visits inspired the American studio theatre movement's continued growth, the dissemination of early and false versions of the Stanislavsky "system," and Stanislavsky's hasty publication of his autobiography *My Life in Art* – a valuable but patchwork and awkwardly translated reminiscence that the author edited and improved for its Russian publication. To erase a $25,000 debt incurred on a second European tour, MAT again toured the U.S., November 1923–May 1924. The company added IBSEN's *An Enemy of the People,* Goldoni's *The Mistress of the Inn,* Nemirovich-Danchenko's adaptation of *The Brothers Karamazoff,* A. N. Ostrovsky's *Too Clever by Half,* and Chekhov's *Ivanov* to its touring repertory (plus two more on Broadway) and eight cities to its touring circuit. MAT actors MARIA OUSPENSKAYA, Leo and Barbara Bulgakov, Akim Tamiroff, and Vera Soloviova (who arrived in 1935 with a later MAT tour) remained in the U.S. permanently. SG

Moses, Gilbert, III (1942–95) Director. Born in Cleveland and educated at Oberlin College, Sorbonne, and NYU, Moses edited the *Free Press*, Jackson, MS, before cofounding with John O'Neal the Free Southern Theatre (1963) in Jackson and later New Orleans. Important to the Black Theatre movement (see African American theatre), Moses directed LeRoi Jones's (Amiri Baraka's) *Slave Ship* (1969), winning an Obie (1970); Ed Bullins's *The Taking of Miss Janie* (1975), a play that won both Obie and Drama Desk awards; and *Ain't Supposed to Die a Natural Death* (1971), for which he was a Drama Desk winner and Tony nominee (1973). TLM

Moses, Montrose Jonas (1878–1934) Scholar and critic. Born in NYC, Moses began his career with the *Literary Digest* (1900–2), becoming dramatic editor of the *Reader's Magazine* (1903–7) and drama critic of the *Independent* (1908–18), the *Book News Monthly* (1908–18), and the *Bellman* (1910–19). His books include *Famous Actor Families in America* (1906), *Henrik Ibsen, The Man and His Plays* (1908), *The American Dramatist* (1911, 1917), and *The Fabulous Forrest* (1929). His edited collections include *Representative Plays by American Dramatists* (3 vols., 1918), *The American Theatre as Seen by Its Critics, 1752 to 1934* (with John Mason Brown), and four volumes (1915) of Clyde Fitch plays (with Virginia Gerson). TLM

Mosher, Gregory (Dean) (1949–) Best known as the first director of works by David Mamet, Mosher was also the first artistic administrator to have popular success with the theatre program at New York's Lincoln Center. Having studied theatre at Oberlin, Ithaca, and Juilliard, Mosher went to Chicago's Goodman Theatre in 1974 to direct its Stage 2 program. As Goodman artistic director (1978–85), he concentrated on new works by such authors as Mamet, John Guare, David Rabe, Michael Weller, Wole Soyinka, Tennessee Williams, and Edward Albee, a policy that met with some resistance from subscribers. Ironically, Mosher's tenure at Lincoln Center (1985–91) was criticized for being *too* popular, for blurring the line between nonprofit and commercial production (e.g., his 1988 *Our Town*, which received a Tony for Best Revival). Mosher left Lincoln Center in 1991 to pursue independent film and theatre work, including on Broadway a 1992 revival of *Streetcar Named Desire* and the 2000 musical *James Joyce's The Dead*. In 1996 he was briefly asso-

ciated with Circle in the Square. In 2004 he was appointed director of University Arts Initiatives at Columbia University. SF

Most Happy Fella, The Three-act musical comedy by Frank Loesser, opened 3 May 1956 at the Imperial Theatre, running 676 performances. Loesser's masterwork, for which he wrote all the music and words, is almost entirely sung. Based on Sidney Howard's *They Knew What They Wanted*, it tells of a hardbitten waitress (Jo Sullivan) who goes to California's wine country as a mail-order bride and finds herself torn between a younger and an older man. Skillfully through-composed in virtually operatic dimensions, it required far above-average voices, notably Metropolitan Opera baritone Robert Weede, who played the title role. The score's greatest popular hits, however, came from the comic subplot: "Standing on the Corner (Watching All the Girls Go By)" and "Big D." The original production won the Drama Critics' Circle Award for Best Musical, and a production starring Giorgio Tozzi played Broadway in 1979. The show is now in the repertoire of the New York City Opera, and in 1991 was revived by the Goodspeed Opera House, a production successfully brought to Broadway in early 1992. JD

Mostel, Zero (Samuel Joel) (1915–77) Actor. Trained as an artist, Mostel became an immensely talented comic actor, noted for his sagging jowls and large paunch but dancer's grace, acrobat's control, and enormously expressive face. After appearing in sketches at a Greenwich Village nightclub in 1942, he made his official Broadway debut the same year in *Keep 'em Laughing*. Subsequent roles of note included Shu Fu in *The Good Woman of Setzuan* (1956, Phoenix Theatre), Leopold Bloom in *Ulysses in Nighttown* (1958, 1974), Jean in *Rhinoceros* (1961, with Eli Wallach and Anne Jackson; Tony Award), Pseudolus in the musical *A Funny Thing Happened on the Way to the Forum* (1962; Tony), and his greatest popular triumph, Tevye in *Fiddler on the Roof* (1964 [Tony], 1976). His memoirs were published in 1965. Mostel died in Philadelphia rehearsing Shylock in Arnold Wesker's *The Merchant*. His son **Josh** is also an actor (Milo Crawford in *Texas Trilogy*, 1976; Off-Broadway, Norman in *The Boys Next Door*, 1987); in the 1990s he became a familiar face on television. The most recent biography of Zero, by Arthur Sainer, was published in 1998. DBW

Motley Trade name of scenery and costume designers from Britain who, from 1932 to 1976, designed theatre, opera, and ballet in England

Anna Cora Mowatt as Rosalind in *As You Like It. Courtesy:* Don B. Wilmeth Theatre Collection.

and the U.S. The trio consisted of sisters Margaret Harris (1904–2000) and (Audrey) Sophia Harris Devine (1901–66), who worked mainly in the U.K., and Elizabeth Montgomery (1904–93), who worked primarily in the U.S. (beginning in 1940). Among their U.S. productions (usually costumes) were SOUTH PACIFIC (1949), *Peter Pan* (1950), PAINT YOUR WAGON (1951), *The* MOST HAPPY FELLA (1956), LONG DAY'S JOURNEY INTO NIGHT (1956), *The First Gentleman* (1958; Tony), *Becket* (1961; Tony). Montgomery/Motley designed eight productions for the AMERICAN SHAKESPEARE FESTIVAL (1957–67).
    DBW

Mourning Becomes Electra This dark, brooding, majestic adaptation by EUGENE O'NEILL of *The Oresteia* opened 26 October 1931 at the Guild (see VIRGINIA) Theatre. Under the direction of PHILIP MOELLER, and graced by impressive Greek-revival designs by ROBERT EDMOND JONES, the tragic trilogy, like STRANGE INTERLUDE, was produced with a dinner intermission and required over five hours of performance time. Featuring characters with masklike faces, the play capitalizes on formality, frustration, and hidden passion. The House of Atreus at the close of the Trojan War becomes the powerful New England Mannon family at the end of the American Civil War. Clytemnestra is Christine (played with sinister charm by ALLA NAZIMOVA), and Electra becomes calculating Lavinia (played as stoically merciless by ALICE BRADY), who takes the focus Aeschylus awarded Orestes, renamed Orin (played by Earle Larimore). Orin's furies are not personified but haunt the young matricide and drive him to madness and suicide. Lavinia, who experiences incestuous and protective feelings for the men in her family, dominates all but her father, Ezra Mannon, and is the chief instrument for revenging Christine's murder of Ezra before sentencing herself to imprisonment within the unpeopled Mannon mansion, haunted by the ghosts of her family's cruel history.   RHW

Mowatt (Ritchie), Anna Cora Ogden (1819–70) Playwright and actress. Although now best known for *FASHION* (1845), a satire on the nouveaux riches who make themselves ridiculous by aping foreign manners, in her own time she was also known as a public reader and actress. Encouraged by Longfellow, she began her readings in Boston (1841) and the following year in New York. After the success of *Fashion,* she toured for 200 nights as Lady Teazle, Juliet, and Pauline in Bulwer-Lytton's *The Lady of Lyons;* she toured again in 1852, and performed in England (1847, 1851). As an actress she was admired for her grace, radiant smile, and naturalness, which EDGAR ALLAN POE found "so pleasantly removed from the customary rant and cant."

Her second play, *Armand* (1847), was also well received, and she wrote two vivid accounts of theatrical life: *Autobiography of an Actress* (1854) and *Mimic Life; or, Before and Behind the Curtain* (1856). A modern biography was written by Eric W. Barnes (1955).

She had read all of Shakespeare by age 10; at 14 translated, staged, and acted in Voltaire's *Alzire* in the family parlor; wrote her first play, *Pelayo,* when she was 17; and became a regular contributor to *Graham's Magazine* and the *Columbian.* She married James Mowatt when she was 15, and after his death (1851) married William F. Ritchie.   RM

Mulatto Play by LANGSTON HUGHES on miscegenation and filial rejection; intended as a tragedy but altered by producer Martin Jones into a melodrama. However, the 1935 production was saved by scenes of strong racial antagonisms and by the performance of ROSE MCCLENDON as Cora, Colonel Norwood's black mistress and the grieving mother of a rebellious son who was lynched. The production ran for 373 performances on Broadway and then toured the country for eight months. The play is based on Hughes's short story "Father and Son," and was later turned into an opera titled *The Barrier* (1950). The author's original version is published in *Five Plays by Langston Hughes,* 1963.   EGH

Mulligan Guard Ball, The EDWARD HARRIGAN's first highly successful play in his Mulligan series, this was a comic depiction of immigrant life on NYC's Lower East Side. Regarded by contemporaries as a realistic chronicle of the city, the piece focuses on rivalries between various ethnic groups, while the elopement of a young couple furnishes a pretext for the action. It opened 13 January 1879 at the Theatre Comique with Harrigan as Dan Mulligan, ringleader of the Irish; his long-time partner, Tony Hart, as his son, Tommy; and Annie Yeamans as his wife, Cordelia. With

music by David Braham, the popular mixture of song, dance, broad physical action, and scenic display ran 153 performances and then became a staple in the Comique repertory.   KF

Munford, Robert (c. 1737–83) Playwright and politician. An influential member of Virginia's elected representatives, both before and after the Revolution, Munford wrote two plays that are outstanding examples of America's early comic drama and its interest in satire. *The Candidates; or, The Humours of a Virginia Election* (1770) satirizes the methods by which politicians win elections. *The Patriots* (1779) attacks half-hearted and hypocritical patriots as well as Tory and Whig politics. Not interested in a playwriting career, Munford wrote mainly to air his views, showing some skill in contriving plots and creating amusing scenes with stereotypical characters. Both plays were published in 1798. The only biography of Munford is by R. M. Baine (1967).   WJM

Muni, Paul [né Meshilem Meier Weisenfreund] (1895–1967) Actor who emigrated with his parents, trouping Yiddish actors, from Lemberg, Austria, to Cleveland in 1902. By 1913 he was actively touring, often in female or graybeard roles. He became a leading man in the YIDDISH ART THEATRE in 1920 in such plays as Sholom Aleichem's *Hard to Be a Jew.* In 1926 he moved to Broadway, and a year later to Hollywood, where he starred in such films as *Scarface* (1932), *The Life of Emile Zola* (1937), and *The Last Angry Man* (1959). Broadway stardom came with his Jewish lawyer (George Simon) in *Counsellor-at-Law* (1931). His final major stage appearance was as Henry Drummond (Clarence Darrow) in INHERIT THE WIND (1955). Jerome Lawrence wrote a biography in 1974.   NS

Murder in the Cathedral A 1935 Canterbury Festival verse play by T. S. ELIOT about the martyrdom of Archbishop Thomas à Becket in December 1170. Following its American premiere at Yale in 1935 and its successful production by the FEDERAL THEATRE PROJECT, it has become a modern classic. Set as a medieval morality play, with four Tempters personifying Becket's thoughts, and supported by a Greek chorus of Canterbury women who have a premonition of doom, it objectifies the preparation of Becket's soul for the final ordeal: "Unbar the door!" declares a resolved Archbishop, "It is out of time that my decision is taken. . . . To which my whole being gives entire consent." The drunken knights enter and Becket is martyred. The play ends with a chorus of *Te Deum;* the priests celebrate the church's new saint.   GSA

Murdoch, Frank (Hitchcock) (1843–72) Actor and playwright. An actor of comedy roles who borrowed his last name from his uncle, JAMES E. MURDOCH, Murdoch spent his entire career with LOUISA DREW's ARCH STREET THEATRE Company in PHILADELPHIA. Murdoch wrote *DAVY CROCKETT* (1872) for FRANK MAYO, who, after its early discouraging reception, helped create the popular version that emphasized the gentle side of the Westerner in scenes of spectacle and romance. His other plays include *Light House Cliffs* (1870?); *Bohemia; or, The Lottery of Art* (1872), a satire on critics; and *Only a Jew* (1873).   WJM

Murdoch, James Edward (1811–93) Actor whose debut was in 1829 at the ARCH STREET THEATRE in Philadelphia as Frederick in Kotzebue's *Lover's Vows.* In 1833, he supported FANNY KEMBLE during her appearance at the CHESTNUT STREET THEATRE. For the next decade, he appeared in various theatres in New Orleans, Mobile, Pittsburgh, Philadelphia, New York, and Boston. For two years, he retired from the stage and lectured on Shakespearean characters and "The Uses and Abuses of the Stage," as well as gave elocution lessons. He returned to the stage in 1845, and for the next 15 years established a reputation as both a tragedian and a light comedian. In 1856, he appeared at London's Haymarket Theatre for 110 nights and was also engaged briefly in Liverpool. He retired again in 1861 and 1879, but appeared intermittently until 1889. Among his more acclaimed roles were Hamlet, Charles Surface in Sheridan's *The School for Scandal,* Benedick, Orlando, and Mercutio. His reminiscences, *The Stage; or, Recollections of Actors and Acting from an Experience of Fifty Years,* were published in 1880.   DJW

Murphy, Donna (1959–) Stage, film, and TV actress-singer born in Corona, Queens (NYC), and raised on Long Island and in Topsfield, MA. She was educated at NYU (B.F.A.) and studied with STELLA ADLER. A two-time Tony winner – Fosca in SONDHEIM and LAPINE's *Passion* (1994; televised on PBS, 1996) and Anna in the 1996 revival of *The KING AND I* – she possesses a strong stage presence with a superb, versatile mezzo-soprano voice. Murphy made her professional debut as a replacement in *They're Playing Our Song* (1979), followed by, among others, *The Mystery of Edwin Drood* (1986), *Privates on Parade* (1989, ROUNDABOUT), *Song of Singapore* (1991, OFF-BROADWAY), *Miss Julie*

(1993), *Passion,* and *King and I.* She played in *Helen* (based on Euripides) at the PUBLIC in 2002 (Drama League Award, directed by TONY KUSHNER. In the revival of *WONDERFUL TOWN* (2003; Drama Desk, Tony nomination), as Ruth, she demonstrated her comic, playful side. She is married to actor **Shawn Elliott** (*Marie Christine,* CITY OF ANGELS).   DBW

Murray, Brian (1937–) The epitome of the working New York actor (and director), Murray – born in Johannesburg, South Africa, but a New York fixture (and now a U.S. citizen) since the mid-1960s, after three years in London – has appeared in or directed some 20 Broadway shows and almost 30 OFF-BROADWAY. Rarely "at liberty" – thanks to his virtuosity – he has been called an "inexhaustible acting machine," and yet his performances invariably receive positive notices and his award nominations are numerous. (His wins are few; perhaps as one critic suggested, "It is not easy to define a Brian Murray role, which is why he can seem so infinite.") In 1998 he was honored with the LUCILLE LORTEL Special Award for Outstanding Body of Work and the Obie for Sustained Excellence in Performance; in 2004 he was inducted into the THEATRE HALL OF FAME.

Murray's Broadway debut was in *All in Good Time* (1965), but he was established on the American scene with his Rosencrantz in *Rosencrantz and Guildenstern Are Dead* in 1967. His first Off-Broadway role was in *The Knack* (1964). Since then, outstanding Off-Broadway credits include *Hamlet* (Claudius), *The Merry Wives of Windsor* (Falstaff), *Travels with My Aunt,* *The Entertainer* (Archie Rice), *LONG DAY's JOURNEY INTO NIGHT* (James), *The Play about the Baby,* *Much Ado about Nothing* (Dogberry), *Colder Than Here,* *Scattergood,* and *Beckett/Albee;* and his Broadway credits include *Sleuth* (Milo Tindle), *Da* (Charlie Now), *Noises Off* (Lloyd Dallas), *A Small Family Business,* *Racing Demon,* *The LITTLE FOXES* (Benjamin Hubbard), *Twelfth Night* (Sir Toby), *Uncle Vanya* (Serebryakov), *The CRUCIBLE* (Danforth), and *The Rivals* (Sir Lucius). Spring 2005 he played his first Prospero in *The Tempest* at the Pittsburgh Public Theater. The Murray watch continues.   DBW

Murray, Walter, and **Thomas Kean** led one of the first professional groups of touring players in colonial America (1749–52). Often following a crude circuit of commodity and racing fairs, they performed a typical English repertoire. After opening in PHILADELPHIA with a production of *Cato,* the company performed two seasons in New York before moving to Williamsburg (fall 1751). In 1752 they briefly toured Maryland and Virginia,

461

then disappeared. Murray surfaced in 1760 as a member of DAVID DOUGLASS's company performing in Maryland.   PAD

Murray Hill Theatre 162 East 42d St., NYC. The first playhouse to be opened on what was then the Upper East Side, the Murray Hill was built on property owned by the Goelet family and began performances on 19 October 1896, under manager Frank B. Murtha; but it was leased to the Henry V. Donnelly and W. T. Keogh STOCK COMPANIES for the next decade and to VAUDEVILLE thereafter. In 1917, it began to present movies as Loew's 42nd Street. It was demolished in 1951.   MCH

Music Box Theatre 239 West 45th St., NYC [Architect: C. Howard Crane]. The Music Box was named by IRVING BERLIN, one of its three original owners, who also lent the name to a series of REVUES that opened the house in 1921 and continued annually until 1925. With a seating capacity of 1,000, its presentations have alternated between musicals and plays, but more recently it has housed nonmusical productions or intimate, small-cast musicals. Till his death, Berlin was half-owner of the theatre with the SHUBERT ORGANIZATION. During the Depression years, one of its tenants, OF THEE I SING (1931), not only became the first musical to win the Pulitzer Prize but also helped to save the theatre for its owners. During its history, nearly a dozen of the GEORGE S. KAUFMAN collaborations appeared on its stage.   MCH

Music Man, The Two-act musical comedy by MEREDITH WILLSON, opened 19 December 1957 at the MAJESTIC THEATRE, running 1,375 performances. This nostalgic story of con man Harold Hill (ROBERT PRESTON) selling dreams in 1912 Iowa marked the Broadway debut, at age 54, of Willson, a bandleader and occasional pop composer. It became the hit of the season, winning both the Drama Critics' Circle and Tony awards for Best Musical, over *WEST SIDE STORY.* as well as Tonys for Preston and BARBARA COOK (as Marian Paroo). It was revived briefly on Broadway in 1980 with Dick Van Dyke and again in 2000 in a production directed by SUSAN STROMAN for a decent 698 performances.

The show evokes the heartwarming exuberance of period Middle America, and the inventively rhythmic score draws on popular musical forms from barbershop to polka to sentimental ballad ("Till There Was You"). A particularly effective musical device is having the heroine's wistful ballad ("Goodnight, My Someone") and the hero's

central march ("Seventy-Six Trombones") built on the same melody, thus prefiguring their ultimate union.   JD

musical theatre The first musical performances on the American stage occurred during the colonial period, when ballad operas were presented by touring companies of English actors. After the Revolution (1776–83), resident composers and writers created the first American comic operas. Notable among these was *The Archers,* with book and lyrics by WILLIAM DUNLAP and music by Benjamin Carr.

By the 1840s several types of European entertainment were contributing to the growth of American musical theatre. Burlesque reached the U.S. in the 1830s, and by the 1850s there were numerous American burlesques on native subjects, such as JOHN BROUGHAM's *PO-CA-HON-TAS; OR, THE GENTLE SAVAGE* (1855). Another imported form that proved popular with American audiences was the spectacle, which made use of lavish scenery and special effects as well as music and dance to tell its story. Meanwhile, the MINSTREL SHOW brought a uniquely American form of musical entertainment to its audience.

Theatre activity in the U.S. was retarded by the Civil War. After the war, pantoMIME reached the height of its appeal in America with *Humpty Dumpty* (1868) starring GEORGE L. FOX, while BURLESQUE received a boost from periodic visits by the English star LYDIA THOMPSON and her troupe of "British Blondes." Minstrelsy continued to be popular, with several companies establishing permanent theatres in the larger cities in addition to taking advantage of the expanding railroad lines to tour across the country.

Despite the existence of this lively and diverse assortment of musical forms, the event most often singled out as the starting point of American musical theatre is the production of *The BLACK CROOK* in 1866. This show, created when a melodrama on Faustian lines was augmented with dances by a French ballet company stranded in New York, is viewed as a primitive example of musical comedy because of its use of music, dance, and spectacle, as well as scantily clad chorus girls, in the telling of its story. *The Black Crook* was successfully revived a number of times during the 19th century, and spawned a host of imitators. Other spectacles combined elaborate settings with a burlesque of some classical or current literary work in a form called "extravaganza." *EVANGELINE,* the most popular show of this type, opened in 1874 and toured the country in various revivals for the rest of the century.

Opéra bouffe, particularly the works of Jacques Offenbach, had a vogue on the American stage in the 1870s and '80s, when noted French singers were imported to the U.S. by impresario MAURICE GRAU. Also available to audiences were native entertainments such as the MULLIGAN GUARD series of musical plays, created and performed by EDWARD HARRIGAN AND TONY HART, depicting life among New York's Irish, Germans, and blacks.

The triumphant American premiere of GILBERT AND SULLIVAN's HMS Pinafore in 1879 made British comic opera the dominant musical form for the rest of the century. Most distinguished of the American composers of comic opera was REGINALD DE KOVEN, whose ROBIN HOOD (1891) was frequently revived. Since comic-opera plots typically combined high-flown romantic fantasy with comic horseplay, star billing often went to comedians such as JEFFERSON DE ANGELIS, DE WOLF HOPPER, FRANCIS WILSON, and EDDIE FOY.

Most musical-theatre librettos in this period were constructed in such a way as to allow for interpolations of unrelated songs and dances by members of the company. This taste for unrelated specialities – also found in the "olio" portion of the minstrel show and the second act of farce comedies such The Brook (1879) – led to the development of the REVUE, a form of musical theatre in which songs, dances, comedy sketches, and elaborate production numbers were loosely connected by a plot or recurring theme, such as a "review" of the year's events. The first American revue was The Passing Show (1894).

In the last decade of the 19th century, comic opera and opéra bouffe declined, while burlesque was given a temporary reprieve in the shows of WEBER AND FIELDS, many of which featured comic-opera soprano LILLIAN RUSSELL. As the 1890s progressed, signs of change began to appear in the musical stage. In 1894, the Bostonians (see BOSTON IDEAL OPERA) presented the comic opera Prince Ananias, which contained the first full score by VICTOR HERBERT, destined to be one of the most important composers of operettas for the American stage. Also appearing in 1894 was A Gaiety Girl, a British musical that abandoned the exotic locales and stilted language of comic opera in favor of a contemporary setting and more topical humor. In 1898 two musicals written and performed by AFRICAN AMERICANS made their appearance: BOB COLE and Billy Johnson's A Trip to Coontown, and Paul Laurence Dunbar and Will Marion Cook's The Origin of the Cakewalk; or, Clorindy. Despite the warm reception these two shows received, few black artists were seen on the Broadway stage before the 1920s.

Comic opera, operetta, musical comedy, and revue were the dominant forms on the American musical stage at the dawn of the new century. Although New York was now the theatre capital of the country, the vast national system of railroads made possible extensive tours for shows that had been a success on Broadway. The most successful show of the decade was FLORODORA (1900), a British comic opera. Victor Herbert continued to compose operettas such as BABES IN TOYLAND (1903), Mlle. Modiste (1905), The Red Mill (1906), and NAUGHTY MARIETTA (1910). The increasing prestige of American operetta lured European opera stars such as FRITZI SCHEFF onto the musical stage.

With the arrival of Franz Lehár's The MERRY WIDOW in New York in 1907, a vogue for Viennese operetta was launched that lasted until the advent of WWI. In the same year, FLORENZ ZIEGFELD produced the Follies of 1907, the first in a series of annual revues that diverged from the traditional topical humor toward a greater emphasis on elaborate scenery, beautifully costumed chorus girls, and star comedians and singers such as FANNY BRICE, BERT WILLIAMS, and WILL ROGERS. The native comic tradition of Harrigan and Hart was continued by GEORGE M. COHAN in a series of musical comedies, such as LITTLE JOHNNY JONES (1904), that emphasized contemporary characters and settings, wisecracking humor, and a generous dose of patriotic sentiment.

Some significant innovations took place on the American musical stage during WWI. Several of the shows written during that era rejected European styles in favor of American musical idioms, most notably ragtime. Developed by black musicians, ragtime was first heard on the musical stage in the form of individual songs interpolated into shows. In 1914 IRVING BERLIN composed a ragtime score for the revue Watch Your Step. Although it has been argued that many of Berlin's songs were not true ragtime, the success of his work brought ragtime to the forefront of musical styles for the legitimate stage.

Meanwhile, composer JEROME KERN and librettist GUY BOLTON (later joined by lyricist P. G. WODEHOUSE) were experimenting with small casts, simple settings, and recognizable characters and situations in their PRINCESS THEATRE shows, such as VERY GOOD EDDIE (1915) and Oh, Boy! (1917). In the years immediately following the war, such musicals as Irene (1919) and Kern's own SALLY (1920), which starred MARILYN MILLER, demonstrated that contemporary American plots and settings, as well as fresh musical styles, could be effectively employed in more elaborate shows.

Despite the changes being wrought in American musical comedy, the demand for operetta did not abate. A new generation of European-trained composers, most notably RUDOLF FRIML and SIGMUND ROMBERG, joined Victor Herbert in the creation of operetta for the American stage. Friml's scores during the 1920s included ROSE-MARIE (1924), The VAGABOND KING (1925), and The Three Musketeers (1928). Among Romberg's best works were Maytime (1917), The STUDENT PRINCE (1924), The DESERT SONG (1926), and The NEW MOON (1928). American singers such as VIVIENNE SEGAL and Robert Halliday starred in many of these new operettas.

In the early postwar years a number of new revue series appeared, including the Greenwich Village Follies, GEORGE WHITE's Scandals, the Music Box Revues, the Grand Street Follies, and EARL CARROLL's Vanities. The early 1920s also marked the reappearance of the black musical on the American stage: Although there had been a few isolated efforts since the turn of the century, including In Dahomey (1903), Abyssinia (1906), and The Shoo Fly Regiment (1907), African Americans had their greatest impact on the Broadway musical stage in the 1920s. Beginning with SISSLE AND BLAKE's SHUFFLE ALONG (1921), a succession of black book musicals and revues both popularized a form of jazz that replaced ragtime as the dominant musical-comedy style, and also introduced many new dance steps, such as the Charleston, to the musical stage. In addition, a number of black performers, including BILL ROBINSON, Adelaide Hall, and FLORENCE MILLS, were featured in shows created by whites.

During the 1920s a new generation of composers began to make their mark on the Broadway stage. Writing in the jazz-influenced style that had evolved in the years following the Princess Theatre shows, GEORGE AND IRA GERSHWIN had a series of successes with Lady, Be Good! (1924), Tip-Toes (1925), Oh, Kay! (1926), and Funny Face (1927). The Gershwins' tricky rhythms and sophisticated lyrics ideally suited the talents of GERTRUDE LAWRENCE and dancers FRED AND ADELE ASTAIRE. As the 1930s dawned, the Gershwins moved into political satire with STRIKE UP THE BAND (1930) and the Pulitzer Prize–winning OF THEE I SING (1931). Matching the Gershwins in sophistication were the new songwriting team of RICHARD RODGERS and LORENZ HART, whose successes in the 1920s included The Garrick Gaieties (1925), Dearest Enemy (1925), A Connecticut Yankee (1927), and Present Arms (1928). Other composers writing musical comedies in the 1920s included VINCENT YOUMANS and DeSYLVA, BROWN, AND HENDERSON.

Jerome Kern, who had pioneered the style of contemporary musical comedy so popular in the 1920s, took musical theatre in another direction when he composed SHOW BOAT (1927), an operetta that used both traditional and contemporary musical idioms in depicting the lives of a family of showboat performers from the 1880s to the 1920s. With lyrics by OSCAR HAMMERSTEIN II, Show Boat pointed the way to the serious musical plays of the 1940s and '50s.

The 1927–8 season, with some 250 shows, was a quantitative high point in the history of the Broadway stage. Events outside of the theatre, including the advent of sound films and the stock-market crash of 1929, would prevent it from ever again reaching that level of production. By the 1930–1 season there was a marked decline in the number of shows produced on Broadway, and those that did appear were usually presented on a more modest scale. Although Florenz Ziegfeld, George White, and Earl Carroll were able to mount a few more spectacular editions of their trademark shows, most revues now emphasized singing, dancing, and satiric comedy rather than expensive sets and costumes.

The musical theatre was invigorated at the end of the 1920s by the appearance of some new composers and lyricists. COLE PORTER wrote insinuating melodies and clever lyrics for a number of frothy musical comedies, including Fifty Million Frenchmen (1929), The New Yorkers (1930), and ANYTHING GOES (1934), while the songwriting team of ARTHUR SCHWARTZ and HOWARD DIETZ brought a new, more subdued and melodic sound to their scores for the revues The Little Show (1929), Three's a Crowd (1930), and The Band Wagon (1931).

Despite the appearance of these new contributors to the musical theatre, two of the more impressive musicals of the 1930s were created by composers, lyricists, and librettists who had begun their careers in the previous decade: PORGY AND BESS (1935) by the Gershwins (with DUBOSE HEYWARD) and ON YOUR TOES (1936) by Rodgers and Hart (with choreography by GEORGE BALANCHINE).

As the Depression worsened, musicals began to reflect the country's growing unrest. In 1936 the GROUP THEATRE produced JOHNNY JOHNSON, a musical with an antiwar message; the following year the International Ladies' Garment Workers Union presented a "socially significant" revue called PINS AND NEEDLES, with songs by Harold Rome; and in 1938 the MERCURY THEATRE offered MARC BLITZSTEIN's controversial capitalist-vs.-labor parable, The CRADLE WILL ROCK. This interest in the issues of the day was short-lived, however, for with the advent of WWII the musical theatre once again turned its back on political and social commentary in favor of escapist shows with flimsy plots. Nevertheless, a few musicals of the early 1940s demonstrated that the seriousness of the '30s had not entirely dissipated. Rodgers and Hart's PAL JOEY (1940) had an amoral gigolo, played by Gene Kelly, for its hero, while the KURT WEILL–Ira Gershwin musical LADY IN THE DARK (1941) dealt with a mentally disturbed magazine editor (Gertrude Lawrence) whose problems were solved through psychoanalysis.

Musical theatre experienced another change in direction in 1943 as a result of the unprecedented popularity of OKLAHOMA!, the first musical by the new partnership of Richard Rodgers and Oscar Hammerstein II. Oklahoma!'s affirmation of the simple values of an earlier America gave it a broad and lasting appeal. Although it adhered in many ways to the traditions of operetta, its departures from standard musical-theatre practice – such as allowing a killing to take place onstage and using a "dream ballet" to amplify the dramatic action – made Oklahoma! the most influential and widely imitated musical of its day. Among the subsequent "musical plays" created by Rodgers and Hammerstein were CAROUSEL (1945), SOUTH PACIFIC (1949), The KING AND I (1951), Flower Drum Song (1958), and The SOUND OF MUSIC (1959). MARY MARTIN, whose winsome personality and good humor made her an ideal Rodgers and Hammerstein heroine, starred in both South Pacific and The Sound of Music.

Despite the pervasive influence of Rodgers and Hammerstein, the formulaic musical comedy continued to flourish in the 1940s and early '50s. ANNIE GET YOUR GUN, with a score by Irving Berlin and a bravura performance by ETHEL MERMAN as backwoods sharpshooter ANNIE OAKLEY, opened to critical acclaim in 1946. FRANK LOESSER received enthusiastic notices for GUYS AND DOLLS (1950), a musical about Broadway gamblers and their perennial girlfriends. WONDERFUL TOWN (1953), by the team of LEONARD BERNSTEIN and COMDEN AND GREEN, dealt with life in Greenwich Village in the 1930s. PAJAMA GAME, a musical about management–labor strife in a pajama factory, introduced the songwriting team of RICHARD ADLER AND JERRY ROSS to Broadway in 1954. A year later DAMN YANKEES, also by Adler and Ross, combined the Faust legend with baseball, and elevated dancer GWEN VERDON to stardom.

In 1956, ALAN JAY LERNER AND FREDERICK LOEWE adapted Bernard SHAW's comedy Pygmalion into the musical MY FAIR LADY. Like Show Boat and Oklahoma! before it, My Fair Lady changed

the course of musical theatre: Its opulent OLIVER SMITH setting and CECIL BEATON period costumes inspired a vogue for operettas set in bygone eras; the matchless performance of REX HARRISON as Henry Higgins inaugurated a trend toward hiring actors rather than singers for important musical-theatre roles; and the skill with which Lerner converted the Shaw play into a musical led other librettists to concentrate on adapting already successful plays, films, and novels rather than creating original librettos.

Although they had changed greatly in the past two decades, the two basic threads of musical theatre, operetta and musical comedy, continued to flourish from the mid-1950s through the mid-1960s. As usual, the operettas tended to be the more elaborate and ambitious works. Leonard Bernstein, ARTHUR LAURENTS, STEPHEN SONDHEIM, and JEROME ROBBINS based WEST SIDE STORY (1957) on the Romeo and Juliet legend. The songwriting team of JERRY BOCK and SHELDON HARNICK caught the flavor of European operetta with SHE LOVES ME (1963; successfully revived in 1993), and in the following year created one of the most popular of all American musicals, FIDDLER ON THE ROOF. MAN OF LA MANCHA, based on Cervantes's Don Quixote, received excellent reviews when it opened in 1965.

The creators of musical comedy tried to vary the traditional formulas by exploring new settings and subjects. GYPSY (1959) was based on the life of stripper GYPSY ROSE LEE. FIORELLO (1959) followed the career of New York mayor Fiorello La Guardia. HOW TO SUCCEED IN BUSINESS WITHOUT REALLY TRYING (1961) satirized corporate backstabbing and in-fighting. HELLO, DOLLY!, while blazing no new trails in subject matter, made more extensive use of dance than was the custom in musical comedy. CABARET (1966) was set in the decadent Berlin of the 1930s. HAIR (1968) brought a more authentic rock sound and NUDITY to the Broadway musical stage.

Music, particularly rock, was an integral part of many ALTERNATIVE THEATRE pieces of the 1950s and '60s, such as MEGAN TERRY's Viet Rock (1966). Traditional notions of musical theatre were challenged by a number of OFF-BROADWAY and OFF-OFF BROADWAY artists, notably composer-lyricist-librettist Al Carmines, who created several experimental musicals, including Peace (1968) and Promenade (1969), the latter with book and lyrics by MARIA IRENE FORNÉS. Several more traditional shows produced Off-Broadway, such as The FANTASTICKS (1960–2002; revived 2006) and Dames at Sea (1968), demonstrated anew that elaborate spectacle was not a necessary component of the musical stage; and several modest shows produced in NIGHTCLUBS and Off-Broadway theatres by Ben Bagley and Julius Monk continued the revue custom of emphasizing satire and topical humor.

By the beginning of the 1970s, however, it had become clear that the musical theatre was failing to develop new artists and audiences. The Off-Off Broadway revolution was fading away, having contributed relatively few new performers, composers, or choreographers to the mainstream theatre. On Broadway an increasing number of revivals of older shows, coupled with revues created out of the songs of veteran composers, held the stage. The only new composer-lyricist to contribute importantly to the musical theatre in the 1970s was Stephen Sondheim. His brilliant but often controversial shows of the 1970s and '80s included COMPANY (1970), FOLLIES (1971), A LITTLE NIGHT MUSIC (1973), PACIFIC OVERTURES (1976), SWEENEY TODD (1979), Merrily We Roll Along (1981), SUNDAY IN THE PARK WITH GEORGE (1984), and INTO THE WOODS (1987). (His only somewhat successful show since is Passion, 1994.) Aided by orchestrator JONATHAN TUNICK, Sondheim created a unique sound using electronic instruments and tempered rock rhythms. His lyrics were often cerebral, unflinching, and cynical.

The Sondheim shows produced and directed by HAROLD PRINCE popularized the "concept musical," a show in which the director and designers, instead of attempting to translate a preexisting libretto and score into theatrical terms during rehearsals, collaborate with the composer, lyricist, and librettist during the creation of the show, so that every element is conceived in terms of production. Because of the emergence of the concept musical – and because so few new composers, lyricists, and librettists of stature appeared during the period – the musical theatre of the 1970s and '80s was dominated by the choreographer-director. Such shows as BOB FOSSE's Pippin (1972), CHICAGO (1975), and Dancin' (1978), MICHAEL BENNETT's A CHORUS LINE (1975) and Dreamgirls (1981), and TOMMY TUNE's Nine (1982) and The WILL ROGERS FOLLIES (1991) benefited immeasurably from the imaginative and energetic staging that their director-choreographers created for them. The concept musical went out of fashion in the 1980s as its most talented practitioners died or retired; by the end of the decade and into the 1990s only Tommy Tunewas still actively creating shows for the Broadway stage. (MICHAEL KIDD returned to direct 1993's The Goodbye Girl). Producers turned instead to shows with librettos based on vintage Hollywood films, such as Grand Hotel (1989), CITY

OF ANGELS (1989), Nick and Nora (1991; a disappointing $4.3 million failure that had been under development for several years), The Red Shoes (1993, an $8 million loss), and ANDREW LLOYD WEBBER's Sunset Boulevard (New York, 1994), the latter the only new book musical of the 1994–5 season.

The period of the 1970s and '80s was a time of reassessment of the musical theatre in the light of rising production costs and prohibitive ticket prices. Many artists and producers preferred to work in the more relaxed surroundings of Off- or Off-Off Broadway, some of their more successful creations eventually finding their way to the Broadway theatre. Also contributing shows to Broadway were regional theatres, notably the GOODSPEED OPERA HOUSE in East Haddam, CT, where ANNIE premiered, and the SOUTH COAST REPERTORY in California, where the revised version of the rock musical Tommy was developed. Since relatively few American musicals were produced each year, writers, directors, and performers often worked more frequently in film and television than in live theatre. The dearth of American musicals led producers to look to Europe and Great Britain for new shows: LES MISÉRABLES and MISS SAIGON were created by a French songwriting team, and Webber brought New York a number of his London successes such as CATS, PHANTOM OF THE OPERA, and in 1994 Sunset Boulevard. Even the KANDER AND EBB Kiss of the Spider Woman had succeeded in Toronto and London before it opened on Broadway in 1993 (and won the Tony for best musical). In 1996 RENT opened to acclaim with its energy and its youthful focus and music, even transferring to Broadway; yet a trend did not follow, nor did the long-running show revitalize the musical as a whole.

As New York Times critic BEN BRANTLEY observed at the end of the 2005–6 season, for a decade little of true originality or innovation in musical theatre had appeared, despite some successes like Contact, FALSETTOS, RAGTIME, The LION KING, The PRODUCERS, Monty Python's Spamalot, WICKED, HAIRSPRAY, URINETOWN, AVENUE Q, The Light in the Piazza, The Color Purple, The 25th Annual Putnam County Spelling Bee, and The Drowsy Chaperone, with interesting, off-beat efforts such as Caroline, or Change, Floyd Collins, and Grey Gardens. However, the musical "as an artificial aide-mémoire" has dominated, "colorless and thin" – with dozens of retreads/revivals (though some unique exceptions, such as SWEENEY TODD, 2005; PAJAMA GAME, 2006); musicals inspired by movies (Dirty Rotten Scoundrels, Tarzan, The Wedding Singer), pop songbooks (the so-called jukebox musical, best represented by Smokey Joe's Cafe, 1995; Mamma Mia, 2001; Movin' Out,

2002; *Jersey Boys,* 2005; with numerous failures, such as *Lennon, All Shook Up, Good Vibrations, Ring of Fire*); and musicals based on best-selling novels (*Lestat, The Color Purple*). *Jersey Boys* was a major surprise in 2005–6, winning a Best Musical Tony, as well as both male actor Tonys (Christian Hoff, Best Featured; John Lloyd Young, Best Leading).

Sometimes called the only uniquely American contribution to world theatre, the Broadway musical continues to face severe economic (with costs as high as $14 million) and artistic tests in the years to come. Although emerging creative originators are scarce, there is some optimism due to the work of original talents such as WILLIAM FINN, MICHAEL JOHN LACHIUSA, JEANINE TESORI, ADAM GUETTEL, and a few others. The development of new musicals in not-for-profit or regional venues, an ongoing trend, is likewise an encouraging sign.   MK

Music-Theatre Group   Founded in 1971 by director (and former associate of ROGER L. STEVENS) Lyn Austin – who was tragically killed by a taxi in 2000 – this innovative nonprofit organization is dedicated to the development of works in which theatre, music, dance, and the visual arts are combined to create new forms. Originally called the Lenox Arts Center, MTG produces OFF-BROADWAY and on tour (as well as in Stockbridge, MA, summers), utilizing artists as diverse as MARTHA CLARKE, ANNE BOGART, TOMMY TUNE, RICHARD FOREMAN, BILL IRWIN, and ELIZABETH SWADOS. Recipient of a 1984 Obie for Sustained Achievement and a 2003 Opera Fund grant, MTG has developed such productions as *Juan Darien, The Garden of Earthly Delights, Vienna: Lusthaus, The Mother of Us All, Endangered Species, Running Man,* and *Swimming with Watermelons* – many of which garnered their own Obies). The current producing director is Diane Wondisford.   DBW

Musser, Tharon   (1925–) Lighting designer who began her career as designer and stage manager for the José Limon Dance Company and made her Broadway debut with the premiere production of *A LONG DAY'S JOURNEY INTO NIGHT* (1956). By the late 1960s she was probably the dominant lighting designer on Broadway. Her versatility is apparent from her credits, which include several seasons with the AMERICAN SHAKESPEARE FESTIVAL, most of NEIL SIMON's plays since *The PRISONER OF SECOND AVENUE* (1971), and musicals such as *Mame* (1966), FOLLIES (1971; Tony), and *The Secret Garden* (1991). From 1975 she teamed up with designers ROBIN WAGNER and THEONI ALDREDGE and the late director MICHAEL BENNETT to design

Julie Andrews in *My Fair Lady,* 1956. Photo by Fred Fehl. *Courtesy:* Harry Ransom Humanities Research Center, the University of Texas at Austin.

A CHORUS LINE (1975; Tony; 2006 revival), *Dreamgirls* (1981; Tony), and several others. Her style ranges from flashy production numbers to painstakingly researched re-creations of specific light qualities and moods (as in *A LITTLE NIGHT MUSIC,* 1973).   AA

My Fair Lady by ALAN JAY LERNER AND FREDERICK LOEWE (book/lyrics and music, respectively); opened on 15 March 1956, running for a then–record-breaking 2,717 performances. A musical adaptation of Bernard SHAW's comedy *Pygmalion,* directed by MOSS HART, the musical related the transformation of a Cockney flower girl into a stately lady by a phonetics expert who bets that improving the girl's speech will convince everyone she is a duchess. REX HARRISON, a perfect choice for phonetician Henry Higgins, was given a number of witty patter songs that made the most of his limited singing range while remaining faithful to Shaw's irascible character. JULIE ANDREWS brought a freshness and vitality to Eliza Doolittle, the Cockney flower girl. *My Fair Lady* was a fine example of the "integrated musical," in which the songs and dances helped to further the plot rather than existing for their own sake. Thus, in the "Ascot Gavotte" sequence, CECIL

BEATON's black-and-white costumes, Lerner and Loewe's comically understated recitative, and the severely repressed dance movements created by choreographer HANYA HOLM vividly illustrated the world of upper-class decorum that Eliza was about to shatter. Notable revivals were staged in 1964, 1968 (both at City Center, NYC), 1976, 1981 (with Harrison, who also re-created his role in the 1964 film version), and 1993, with Richard Chamberlain. An excellent revival was produced by the National Theatre, London, in 2001, and a concert staging at Lincoln Center in 2007.   MK

My Heart's in the Highlands WILLIAM SAROYAN's play was produced OFF-BROADWAY by the GROUP THEATRE before opening at the GUILD THEATRE on Broadway on 13 April 1939 for 44 performances. ROBERT LEWIS directed this major artistic success for the Group, its cast including Philip Loeb as the penniless poet, Ben Alexander; Sidney Lumet as his young son, Johnny; Art Smith as the old violinist, Jasper MacGregor; and William Hansen as Mr. Kosak, the grocer. The play is a fantasy about the importance of art to ordinary people and the devaluation of artistic creativity by the American socioeconomic system. Although the people of a poor neighborhood welcome the musician and support the poet with gifts of food, neither artist can survive for long.   BCM

My Partner BARTLEY CAMPBELL's play, produced by A. M. PALMER at the UNION SQUARE THEATRE on 16 September 1879, was one of the most successful plays of the 1880s, extending the popularity of FRONTIER drama. The gold-mining partners of the title were the dapper but shallow Ned Singleton and the plain, good-hearted Joe Saunders. Ned's dalliance with Mary Brandon, Joe's secret love, led Josiah Scraggs to kill Ned and frame Joe. To shield Mary from disgrace, Joe claimed to be her husband. Eventually Wing Lee, a Chinese servant, revealed evidence that convicted Scraggs and freed Joe to wed Mary.

My Partner starred Louis Aldrich (Joe) and Charles T. Parsloe (Wing Lee), the latter a special-ist in comic Chinese caricatures (also in Mark Twain's *Ah Sin,* Twain and BRET HARTE's *Two Men of Sandy Bar,* and *The DANITES*). Aldrich gained prominence as the Parson in *The Danites* before starring as the quiet mining hero of *My Partner.* He retired from the stage in the late 1890s to devote full time to the presidency of the ACTORS' FUND OF AMERICA.   RAH

My Sister Eileen Three-act comedy by Joseph Fields and JEROME CHODOROV, adapted from the stories by Ruth McKenney; opened at the BILTMORE THEATRE (26 December 1940) for 864 performances. Directed by GEORGE S. KAUFMAN and featuring SHIRLEY BOOTH, this light-hearted comedy, set in Greenwich Village, relates the wild antics of two sisters who have moved to New York from Columbus, OH, in search of fame and fortune as writer and actress. A film version starring Rosalind Russell appeared in 1942. The authors later collaborated with LEONARD BERNSTEIN and BETTY COMDEN AND ADOLPH GREEN on WONDERFUL TOWN, a 1953 musical adaptation of the play, once again starring Russell.   EK

Mystery of Irma Vep, The Of CHARLES LUDLAM's 29 plays, this one (1984, subtitled *A Penny Dreadful*) was arguably the most acclaimed example of his THEATRE OF THE RIDICULOUS. A mélange of genres and styles that included Victorian melodrama, horror flicks, and Gothic romance, the original production of *Irma Vep* starred Ludlam and his partner, EVERETT QUINTON, and ran nearly a year. Together they played eight roles – primarily Lord Elgar (Ludlam), an Egyptologist lonely for his first wife, Irma, since remarried to Lady Enid (Quinton) – while navigating through an array of speed-of-light costume changes and nutty sound cues. Much humor resulted from Lord Elgar's yearning for Irma, and the plays climaxes with a painting of Irma slowly bleeding. In 1998 a highly successful commercial production ran OFF-BROADWAY, Quinton playing Elgar and directing, with actor Stephen DeRosa as Lady Enid.   LJ

N

Naked Angels Theater Company Founded in 1986 as a theatre collaborative dedicated to a supportive environment, risk taking, and innovation. The name is from John Tytell's book on the Beats, who reflected the collaborative's own mission. The group produces plays for the stage, for radio (NPR's *Naked Radio* program), and indirectly for television (*Naked TV*, one-acts conceived as live pilots, through a partnership with Fox Broadcasting), as well as readings of new screenplays at film festivals. An educational program in acting and writing for the emerging artist was added in 1999. Based in New York, Naked Angels maintains a strong link in Los Angeles, where several plays a season are produced. A founding member, Tim Ransom, was artistic director 2001–5, succeeded by Jenny Gersten. DBW

Nathan, George Jean (1882–1958) Critic. Born of wealthy parents in Fort Wayne, IN, Nathan graduated from Cornell University in 1904 and studied abroad for a year at the University of Bologna (1905). In 1906 he worked as a reporter for the *New York Herald,* after which he reviewed plays for *Outing* and *The Bohemian.* He became drama critic of *Smart Set* in 1909, joining H. L. Mencken, who had been hired in 1908 to review books. The two served as coeditors during 1914–24 and made *Smart Set* a cult publication among young intellectuals. Their irreverence and iconoclasm seemed to epitomize a generation attempting to rid itself of the Genteel Tradition. They founded the *American Mercury* in 1923 but quarreled in 1924, with Nathan continuing only as drama critic until 1932. He founded and edited the *American Spectator* (1932–5), then reviewed for numerous publications, including *Newsweek,* Theatre Arts, *Saturday Review,* and *Esquire.* Influenced by James Huneker and George Bernard Shaw, Nathan wrote in a lively, impressionistic style and fought for a drama of ideas. He became a champion of Eugene O'Neill, publishing his early plays in *Smart Set,* and arranging for professional productions of his work. He reviewed musical revues, noting that "Good drama is anything that interests an intelligently emotional group of persons assembled together in an illuminated hall." His reputation declined after his death in 1958 because his "hot" impressionistic style cooled with age, and many of his opinions after 1930 proved to be erroneous. Nathan reworked his criticism into books, which appeared almost every year during 1915–53. From 1943 to 1951 he published an annual *Theatre Book of the Year.* In 1955 he married actress Julie Haydon, and in his will left a provision for the George Jean Nathan Award for Dramatic Criticism to be given annually. A quasi-biography was compiled in 2000 by Charles Angoff. TLM

National Actors Theatre Founded in 1991, first at the Belasco and then the Lyceum, among other venues, by the indefatigable actor-director Tony Randall in an attempt to create an institution comparable to national theatres in other countries and to present great plays of the world with the best actors available at affordable ticket prices – a grand ambition never quite accomplished. Although officially still in existence, the company has had a turbulent and financially difficult history, managing only 17 productions on Broadway (the first, The Odd Couple; the last, *Judgment at Nuremberg*) prior to having to move to a less costly and gradiose space at Pace University in downtown Manhattan. To its credit, NAT began with a true repertory company (with name stars brought in) but stumbled early and by the mid-1990s, following a good production of Inherit the Wind (1996), became more populist and frugal in its choices. Ironically, the final productions at Pace were more critically successful and artistically daring: Brecht's *The Resistible Rise of Arturo Ui* with Al Pacino, Aeschylus' *The Persians* in a version by Ellen McLaughlin, and in December 2003 Luigi Pirandello's *Right You Are,* with Randall in his last role. DBW

National Alliance of Theatrical and Stage Employees Stagehands began organizing a union locally in the late 1880s, and on 17 July 1893 representatives from New York, Brooklyn, Chicago, Pittsburgh, Cincinnati, St. Louis, Denver, Philadelphia, Syracuse, Buffalo, and Boston agreed to form a national union. In 1898 they became affiliated with their Canadian counterpart, and in 1902 changed their name to the International Alliance (IATSE). DMcD

National Asian-American Theatre Company (NAATCO) Founded in 1989 by Mia Katigbak and Richard Eng, NAATCO's original mission was to provide Asian American actors the opportunity to perform in European and American works that are usually cast with white actors. Their productions have included such disparate fare as EUGENE O'NEILL's *LONG DAY'S JOURNEY INTO NIGHT*, WILLIAM FINN's *Falsettoland*, and Anton CHEKHOV's *Ivanov*. NAATCO recently expanded its mission to include also adaptations of classic texts, penned by Asian American authors. Michael Golamco's *Cowboy v. Samurai* (2005), with actor Joel de la Fuente – a contemporary retelling of Edmond Rostand's *Cyrano de Bergerac,* which substitutes race for an oversized nose as the central issue – marked the first production within the new mission. DanB

National Black Theatre Founded by actress and director Barbara Ann Teer in 1968 as a temple of liberation, this AFRICAN AMERICAN THEATRE group first met in a ramshackle building in central Harlem "to educate and spiritually enlighten the people it serves." Initial performances took the form of rituals based on the black experience and developed in training workshops. By 1978 standard plays such as *Wine in the Wilderness* by ALICE CHILDRESS were being produced. When the building burned in 1983, activities continued in an adjacent space while funds were sought for rebuilding. In 1990 a new $10 million home was opened containing a 288-seat theatre. EGH

National Black Theater Festival Founded in 1989 by Larry Leon Hamlin in Winston–Salem, NC (in conjunction with the North Carolina Black Repertory Company), this annual six-day festival brings together some 20 of the best black theatre companies in the U.S. offering 90 performances for about 40,000 attendees. DBW

National Endowment for the Arts Founded in 1965 as one of Lyndon Johnson's Great Society programs, NEA has proven a boon to individual artists and theatre companies alike, providing much-needed seed money and matching grants. Since its inception, more than 100,000 grants have been given, yet its level of funding per capita has always been below that of most Western European nations. In 1995 the shrinking allotment was $167.4 million (an annual outlay of roughly 65 cents per person). Yet NEA has served as a symbol about what the nation values as much as a funding agency. Nevertheless, as a result of controversial grants (only 40 in 30 years had fallen into this category), attacks on NEA increased, beginning with 1989 grants to artists Robert Mapplethorpe and Andres Serrano and climaxing with the initial rejection of grants to performance artists KAREN FINLEY, TIM MILLER, HOLLY HUGHES, and John Fleck. The 1995 Republican Congress and its "contract with America" threatened to eliminate the Endowment, giving JANE ALEXANDER, head of NEA from 1993 to 1997, the most important challenge in the Endowment's history. Alexander was succeeded by William J. Ivey, a Clinton appointment who inherited the battle (the antisupport position was defeated July 1998), and then in 2003 by poet Dana Gioia (the eighth chair). Support has remained relatively level, in 2005 totaling $131 million, a slight increase over previous recent years. DBW

National Playwrights Conference Established in 1965 by George C. White and directed from 1968 to 1999 by LLOYD RICHARDS, then briefly by James Houghton (SIGNATURE THEATRE) and since 2005 Wendy C. Goldberg (artistic associate, ARENA STAGE), the NPC is the most prestigious program of the EUGENE O'NEILL MEMORIAL THEATRE CENTER in Waterford, CT. The grandaddy of American play-development workshops, the NPC's philosophies and methods dominate developmental perspectives in the U.S. and have spread internationally.

The monthlong summer workshop focuses on up to 15 stage plays each year. Dramaturges, directors, and professional actors concentrate on each play for four or five days, then present two staged readings – a format that tends to favor realistic theatre. Stressing process not results, actors work with book in hand, production is minimal, and reviews and bids from producers are forbidden.

An important crucible of new American plays, NPC's alumni include such well-known playwrights as JOHN GUARE, WENDY WASSERSTEIN, ARTHUR KOPIT, ADAM RAPP, DAVID LINDSAY-ABAIRE, and AUGUST WILSON. CLJ

National Theatre 1321 Pennsylvania Ave. North, Washington, DC [Architect: McElfatrick, 1885]. In 1834, the first National Theatre opened its doors through the financial support of six Washington businessmen, who decided that the city needed a new place of entertainment. FIRES destroyed the house in 1845, 1857, 1873, and 1885, and all but obliterated the early features in the rebuilt versions. In 1885, the theatre was completely redesigned, and is the structure that still stands. The fortunes of the National followed the pattern typical of the 19th-century playhouse, beginning with a resident STOCK COMPANY and ending as a theatre for booked-in performances. During long periods in the 20th century the house was not used. In 1974 it became a not-for-profit organization. Owned and renovated in 1983 (new seats in 2002) by the Pennsylvania Avenue Development Corp., it is leased to the SHUBERT ORGANIZATION, which manages the theatre and books its touring Broadway attractions.   MCH

National Theatre of the Deaf In 1967, Broadway scenic designer DAVID HAYS gathered the nucleus of a company from actors at Gallaudet, the renowned college for deaf students, to found the National Theatre of the Deaf, which remained a project of the EUGENE O'NEILL MEMORIAL THEATRE CENTER until 1983, when it moved to Chester, CT. Under Hays's direction the NTD established a training institute, a core professional troupe, and the Little Theatre of the Deaf, which toured story theatre to young audiences.

NTD has peformed on Broadway, throughout the U.S., and worldwide, appeared in films and on television, and has collaborated with director Peter Brook at his International Center of Theatre Research in Paris. Ten years of acclaim were marked in 1977 with a special Tony Award for Theatrical Excellence. As of 2005 there had been 100 national and 31 international tours and over 10,000 performances.

NTD's repertory ranges from classics such as *Iphigenia in Aulis* or *Volpone* to avant-garde works like STEIN's *FOUR SAINTS IN THREE ACTS* and to group-created collages – all performed in a theatricalized sign language that has helped to remove long-standing prejudice against signing by elevating it to an art. As deaf players pantomime the action, hearing actors in the background speak the lines, a convention familiar in such Japanese theatre forms as Kabuki and Bunraku.

The NTD has inspired the formation of other companies of deaf actors and has helped stimulate signed performances everywhere from classrooms to the Academy Awards broadcasts. In its wake, some commercial roles have opened to deaf actors. NTD's Linda Bove has been a regular as Linda on TV's *Sesame Street,* and in 1980 founding NTD member Phyllis Frelich won a Tony for her performance in MARK MEDOFF's *CHILDREN OF A LESSER GOD.* Averting financial controversy in 1995, NTD sponsored a major international conference in August of that year, funded in part by the U.S. Dept. of Education. In 2000 it moved to Hartford, CT, and then in 2004 to the campus of the American School for the Deaf in West Hartford. A history, titled *Pictures in the Air,* was published in 1993.   CLJ

Native American ritual/theatre Indigenous cultures of the present U.S. have long performance histories. In religious ceremonies and social activities, performance elements such as enactments, dance, and storytelling were and are common. However, U.S. policies made religious celebrations illegal, and because much dance and music has a spiritual basis, indigenous performance in its traditional sense was forced underground. Nevertheless, many dramas, such as the Plains Sun Dances, the Cheyenne Sacred Arrow Ceremony, the Iroquois False Face Drama, and the Navajo chantways, survived and continued their time-honored functions of uniting their communities and reinforcing traditional beliefs. In a parallel history, non-Native authors began to write plays and musicals with so-called Indian characters in them (see NATIVE AMERICANS PORTRAYED), establishing early in the nineteenth century a tradition in American theatre of "Indian types" on the stage. Such stories had little grounding in the realisms of Native life.

Native America was not granted religious freedom by the U.S. government until 1978; some scholars and Native theatre professionals believe this lack of freedom limited the development of uniquely Native American theatre forms. When Native people did begin to write their own stories for the stage, some of them indeed had spiritual significance. The Native American Theatre Ensemble founded by HANAY GEIOGAMAH (Kiowa/Delaware) in 1972 was the first Native company to have lasting success. Among their first productions was an experimental piece entitled *Na Haaz Zaan,* a dramatization of the Diné (Navajo) creation story. The Native American Literary Renaissance (1969 and forward) also gave impetus to a Native American Theatre Movement, as Native people began to write their contemporary stories for the stage. As with any alternative movement in the theatre, the work being produced by Native artists today is wide-ranging in both style and content, from the biting social satire of SPIDERWOMAN THEATRE (Kuna/Rappahannock), founded in 1975, to the realisms of contemporary Native life in the work of WILLIAM S. YELLOW ROBE (Assiniboine) and BRUCE KING (Oneida). (See also FEMALE/MALE IMPERSONATION; JIMMIE DURHAM; ROLLIE LYNN RIGGS.)   MS   AH

Native Americans portrayed onstage One of a number of native types depicted on the American stage, the stage "Indian" – represented in over 600 plays from 1606 to the present (both South and North American aborigines) – has inevitably been stereotyped, ranging from the noble savage to ruthless, varmint redskins or lazy, drunken, dissipated rascals, and from the Indian princess to the squaw on the fringe of white society.

Plays featuring Native Americans can rarely be defined by geography; most have focused on forest, northwestern, or East Coast Indians; surprisingly few take place on the geographical plains, in the Indian Territory, or in the far West. The frontier inhabited by the stage Indian is more commonly a mythic area. The earliest plays with Indians were seen on the London stage; the first seen in North America were French, performed in Nova Scotia (1606) and possibly as early as 1753 in New Orleans. Most early Indian plays – including the influential *Columbus; or, A World Discovered* (1792) by Thomas Morton, the first of many Columbus plays – view the Indian in European terms, in keeping with Rousseau's noble savage.

Indians were promising material for drama from the beginning, combining the strange and the familiar, though the genus never became a major one. The earliest extant plays, however, had little influence (Robert Rogers's *Ponteach*, 1766); Joseph Croswell's *A New World Planted*, 1802; JAMES NELSON BARKER's *The Indian Princess*, 1808, the first Pocahontas play). From the turn of the century to about 1825 (and excluding Peruvian Indian plays), more than 25 such plays were written (most notably Anne Kemble Hatton's *America Discovered; or, Tammany, the Indian Chief*, 1794; MORDECAI NOAH's *She Would Be a Soldier*, 1819; Henry J. Finn's *Montgomery*, 1825; G. W. PARKE CUSTIS's *The Indian Prophecy*, 1827). This spurt of activity parallels a period of great stress and clash between Indians and white settlers. During this influential time, and even later, few real Native Americans participated in theatrical performances; those who did were given minor roles or simply demonstrated theatrical elements of their special culture.

The play that gained the greatest popularity and had the largest impact during this early era was JOHN AUGUSTUS STONE's *METAMORA*, chosen in 1829 as a vehicle for EDWIN FORREST and based in part on King Philip's War. A rush of plays followed *Metamora*'s enormous success, some based on specific Indians (RICHARD PENN SMITH's *William Penn*, 1829; NATHANIEL DEERING's *Carabasset*, 1830; R. M. Bird's *Oralloossa*, 1832; Richard Emmons's *Tecumseh*, 1836; Alexander Macomb's *Pontiac*, 1836; NATHANIEL BANNISTER's *Putnam*, 1844; LOUISA H. MEDINA's *NICK OF THE WOODS*, 1838 [staged 1839]; and three new Pocahontas plays by Custis, Robert Dale Owen, and Charlotte Barnes).

Following the Indian play's apogee in the 1830s – and as the Indian problem became severe in the '60s – the subject's popularity declined, and the Indian figure became a more villainous and dangerous antagonist or a burlesqued figure, as in the plays of JOHN BROUGHAM at midcentury. However, after the Civil War, a desire for western spectacle, customs, and characters led to a new rage for Indian melodramas (JAMES McCLOSKEY's *ACROSS THE CONTINENT*, 1870; AUGUSTIN DALY's *HORIZON*, 1871; and especially melodramas with or about WILLIAM F. CODY [and, in the '80s, his WILD WEST EXHIBITION]). Through the 1890s real Indians were seen in variety and the CIRCUS, and were parodied in MINSTREL SHOWS. Somewhat serious efforts at the turn of the century by such writers as HERNE, BELASCO, WILLIAM C. deMILLE, Edwin Milton Royle, and Mary Austin (*The ARROW MAKER*) did little to change the distorted image of the Native American, though verisimilitude seemed greater. New venues for Indian characters included PAGEANTS, operettas, and operas.

Some interest in Indian plays existed in the 1920s and '30s, paralleling new Indian reform movements, though most Indians (especially of the red-varmint variety) transferred to the movies. Over the past half-century Native American characters have appeared from time to time, most notably in historical outdoor dramas and in plays such as KOPIT's *INDIANS* (1968; U.S., 1969) and the early work of SAM SHEPARD.

Only a few Native American writers, such as ROLLIE LYNN RIGGS, HANAY GEIOGAMAH, WILLIAM S. YELLOW ROBE, Annette Arkeketa, BRUCE KING, Ray Baldwin Louis, Wallace Hampton Tucker, and Pulitzer-winning novelist N. Scott Momaday (*The Indolent Boys*), have written Native American plays; fewer have lived up to their early promise (see NATIVE AMERICAN RITUAL/THEATRE). Most Indian drama has depicted Indians conceived by white writers for predominantly white audiences, contributing little to the understanding of the problems and frustrations of Native Americans – although white writer Christopher Sergel's play *Black Elk Speaks* (1981, OFF-BROADWAY; revised 1993, DENVER CENTER) has reversed that trend somewhat. In 1997 Project HOOP (Honoring Our Origins and Peoples through Native Theater, Education, and Community Development) was founded. This national, multidisciplinary inative to advance Native American theatre and performance is located at UCLA (led by HANAY GEIOGAMAH and Jaye T. Darby). DBW

Native Son by RICHARD WRIGHT and PAUL GREEN. Adapted from Wright's powerful novel depicting the corrosive effects of racism, this drama in 10 scenes follows Bigger Thomas, a young black man whose hatred and fear lead him to murder a young white woman accidentally. ORSON WELLES directed a stunningly theatrical production starring CANADA LEE, which opened 24 March 1941 at NYC's ST. JAMES THEATRE. After playing three months, it toured major U.S. cities and reopened on Broadway in a "popular-priced revival," 23 October 1942 (84 performances). KF

Naughton, James (1945–) Suave, handsome leading man with a strong baritone voice, born in Middletown, CT, and educated at Brown and the Yale Drama School. Winner of two Tonys (Stone in *CITY OF ANGELS*, 1989; Billy Flynn in the 1996 revival of *CHICAGO*). His Broadway debut was as Wally in *I Love My Wife* (1977). In 1971 he received a Theatre World Award for his OFF-BROADWAY role as Edmund in *LONG DAY'S JOURNEY INTO NIGHT* with Robert Ryan and GERALDINE FITZGERALD. In *Democracy* (2004) he played Willy Brandt. His cabaret shows have included *James Naughton: Street of Dreams* (directed by MIKE NICHOLS) and *It's about Time* (also title of a 2002 CD). A respected director, he was responsible for the 1999 revival of *The PRICE* and the 2002 revival of *OUR TOWN* with Paul Newman. As an actor and director he has frequently worked at the WILLIAMSTOWN THEATRE FESTIVAL and the WESTPORT COUNTRY PLAYHOUSE. He has been on the screen since the 1970s (*The Paper Chase, Oxygen, Fascination*). His brother David and his son and daughter, Gregory and Keira, are actors. DBW

Naughty Marietta Two-act operetta, music by VICTOR HERBERT, words by Rida Johnson Young; opened 7 November 1910 at the New York Theatre, running 136 performances. Set in 18th-century New Orleans, this romance tells of a vivacious "casquette girl" or hired bride (Emma Trentini) and the dashing Captain (Orville Harrold) who proves himself her true love when he knows her haunting "mysterious melody" ("Ah, Sweet Mystery of Life"). Commissioned by OSCAR HAMMERSTEIN I for his leading opera singers, this quintessential American operetta gave Herbert scope to write soaring melodies for highly trained voices. Standards from the score include the march "Tramp, Tramp, Tramp" and the coloratura showpiece "The Italian Street Song." JD

Nauman, Bruce (1941–) PERFORMANCE ARTist born in Ft. Wayne, IN, and educated at the Universities of Wisconsin and California (Davis), now living in New Mexico. Nauman works in the media of sculpture, video, film, printmaking, performance, and installation, with an interest in the process of art – his work demonstrating the alternately political, prosaic, spiritual, and even crass methods with which he examines life. His performance – using his own body and exploring video as a theatrical stage – was influenced by the experimental work of Merce Cunningham, MEREDITH MONK, Phillip Glass, and Steve Reich, among others. A useful collection on his work was compiled by Robert C. Morgan (2002). DBW

Nazimova, Alla (1879–1945) Russian-born actress who studied with Vladimir Nemirovich-Danchenko, acted with the MOSCOW ART THEATRE, and became leading lady of a St. Petersburg theatre. She toured Europe and America in 1905. In New York in 1906–7 she presented, in English, matinee performances of IBSEN's *Hedda Gabler, A Doll's House,* and *The Master Builder.* She appeared different from the popular personality actresses of the day, since she could transform herself externally into various characters. She remained in the U.S., but by 1918 her fame had faded, and she was considered another personality actress capitalizing on her sensuous exoticism. After 10 years starring in Hollywood films such as *Camille* and *Salome,* she performed with the CIVIC REPERTORY THEATRE and the THEATRE GUILD (appearing in *MOURNING BECOMES ELECTRA* in 1931). In 1935 she directed and starred in her own version of *Ghosts.* By the end of the decade she returned to filmmaking. Her bio by Gavin Lambert appeared in 1997. RAS

Nederlander, James M. (1922–) Scion of an American family prominent for three generations in producing and the operation of theatres. Born in Detroit, Nederlander – recipient of a 2004 Tony Lifetime Achievement Award – was a member of the Air Force staff, producing *Winged Victory* in New York in 1943. One of the major forces in the Broadway theatre, the Nederlander Producing Company of America (James is currently chairman emeritus) owns or operates nine Broadway theatres and runs a large chain of legitimate theatres (about 30), including some in Detroit, Chicago, San Francisco, San Diego, Los Angeles, and London. Broadway productions have included *Nicholas Nickleby, Whose Life Is It Anyway?, LA CAGE AUX FOLLES, Me and My Girl, Shadowlands, Beauty and the Beast, RENT, The LION KING, WICKED, HAIRSPRAY,*

AVENUE Q, *The Woman in White*, and revivals of *Peter Pan* (twice), SWEET CHARITY, *Orpheus Descending*, HELLO, DOLLY!, PORGY AND BESS, SHE LOVES ME, FIDDLER ON THE ROOF, *The Odd Couple*, and many others. Son **James L. Nederlander** is president of the organization and active as a producer/booker (e.g., 2005 Best Revival Tony for *La Cage aux Folles*).   MCH   DBW

Nederlander Theatre 208 West 41st St., NYC [Architect: William Neil Smith]. Built as the National in 1921 by Walter C. Jordan, a leading theatrical AGENT, it stands today as the only commerical Broadway theatre below 42d St. With about 1,200 seats, it can be used both for musicals and dramas. In 1927, the SHUBERTS added it to their chain, then sold it in 1934, bought it back in 1944, only to be forced to relinquish it again in 1956 to satisfy a court-mandated consent decree. In 1958, it was acquired by BILLY ROSE, who, after extensive renovation, reopened it under his own name the following year. In 1979, it was bought from his estate by the Nederlander Organization, which renamed it briefly the Trafalgar, then the David Nederlander after the founder of the theatrical dynasty, who died in 1967. Among its noteworthy tenants have been ETHEL BARRYMORE in *The Corn Is Green* (1940); KATHARINE CORNELL in *Dear Liar* (1960), which ended her long career; and *Lena Horne: The Lady and Her Music,* her autobiographical recital, in 1981. In 1991 it housed the first critically successful venture of the short-lived Broadway Alliance (Wertenbaker's *Our Country's Good*). RENT, its first hit in decades, has been playing there since 1996.   MCH

Negro Actors Guild An organization formed in 1937 to provide financial assistance and comfort to indigent theatre people and to uphold the highest standards of the stage. An internal struggle for control of the guild led to its demise circa 1982. In 1986 the aborted Afro-American Association of Performing Artists was established in hopes of taking its place.   EGH

Negro Ensemble Company Established in 1967, during racially troubled times, with a generous Ford Foundation grant, the predominantly AFRICAN AMERICAN company inhabited the OFF-BROADWAY St. Mark's Theatre. Under DOUGLAS TURNER WARD's leadership, it began a program of training young theatre aspirants and producing plays relevant to black Americans. The company was initially criticized for locating outside the black community and producing foreign plays, but its successful nurturing of black writers, performers, directors, and technicians, and the sustained excellence of its productions brought it national and international renown. In over 25 successive seasons, through good times and lean, it presented more than 50 major productions of new plays, with twice that number of workshop presentations and staged readings. It has undertaken national tours and performed abroad in London, Rome, Bermuda, Munich, and on tour in Australia. Among its many awards are Tonys in 1969 for Special Achievement and in 1974 for *The River Niger* (Best Play); three Obie Awards for Sustained Excellence or Achievement; and additional Obies garnered by its outstanding new plays (e.g., *The First Breeze of Summer*, 1975), performances (e.g., Best Ensemble for A SOLDIER'S PLAY, which won the 1982 Pulitzer Prize; MOSES GUNN, twice), and productions (e.g., *Song of the Lusitanian Bogey,* 1968; *Dream on Monkey Mountain,* 1971). From 1980 to 1990 the company relocated its offices in NYC's theatre district and its productions to Theatre Four (West 55th St.); but until 1993 it rented various Off-Broadway theatres while searching for a more permanent home. In 1993 the first mainstage production in two years was mounted following a period of financial uncertainty (a frequent problem during the NEC's history). Today, working out of the 45th Street Theatre, the offerings of the NEC are modest, with workshop and lab productions and readings dominating.   EGH

Neighborhood Playhouse, The Like the PROVINCETOWN PLAYERS and WASHINGTON SQUARE PLAYERS, the Neighborhood Playhouse (1915–27) was a pioneering OFF-BROADWAY theatre. Remote both geographically and temperamentally from the commercial theatre, the Playhouse, located on NYC's Lower East Side, was an experimental outpost connected with the Henry Street Settlement House, a social agency for the area's immigrant population. The Playhouse's major interest was in exploring through FOLK drama the theatre's ritual, lyric, mystical roots. Among its celebrated offerings were an ancient Hindu comedy entitled *The Little Clay Cart* (1924), Ansky's *The Dybbuk* (1926), a 14th-century French mystery, a Japanese Noh drama, a dance drama based on Celtic legend, a Norse fairy tale, and a medieval interlude, as well as such more conventional fare as Galsworthy's *The Mob* (1920), O'NEILL's *The First Man* (1922), James Joyce's *Exiles* (1924), and five editions of a musical REVUE called *The Grand Street Follies.*

Organized as an educational and philanthropic enterprise, the Playhouse achieved a renown its amateur patrons, ALICE AND IRENE LEWISOHN, had never envisaged. Ellen Terry, Yvette Guilbert, ETHEL BARRYMORE, and RICHARD BOLESLAVSKI, among others, offered their services. The theatre provided an important impetus to Martha Graham and to scene designers ALINE BERNSTEIN and DONALD OENSLAGER, and generated both the Neighborhood Playhouse School of the Theatre, which began in 1928 and flourished for over 50 years under the direction of SANFORD MEISNER (who headed the acting program; others officially operated as directors of the school), and the Costume Institute of the Metropolitan Museum, founded in 1937. Its auditorium is now the NEW FEDERAL THEATRE. In 1959 Alice Lewisohn Crowley published *The Neighborhood Playhouse: Leaves from a Theater Scrapbook,* a modest and charming memoir.   FH

Neil Simon Theatre 250 West 52d St., NYC [Architect: Herbert J. Krapp]. As the Alvin Theatre, the 1,400-seat playhouse on the outer fringe of the theatre district had enjoyed a spectacularly successful history under the management of its two founders, ALEX AARONS and VINTON FREEDLEY, who combined the first syllables of their names to give it its name. They opened it in 1927 to house the highest forms of musical comedy; and until 1932, when they lost control of the house, they fulfilled their promise by presenting works by the GERSHWINS, RODGERS AND HART, and JEROME KERN. In 1934, a young ETHEL MERMAN debuted there, and in 1964 the veteran BEATRICE LILLIE bade her farewell from its stage. Under a succession of owners, the Alvin presented nonmusical fare as well – *MISTER ROBERTS* (1948), *The GREAT WHITE HOPE* (1968), and *No Time for Sergeants* (1955) – but nothing to equal its musical triumphs, which continued with *LADY IN THE DARK* (1941), *A FUNNY THING HAPPENED ON THE WAY TO THE FORUM* (1962), *COMPANY* (1970), and *ANNIE* (1977). Its current resident, *HAIRSPRAY,* opened there in August 2002. The one musical production presented on its stage that should have been successful but was not at its introduction was *PORGY AND BESS* (1935). In 1983 NEIL SIMON's *BRIGHTON BEACH MEMOIRS* opened to hold its stage for two years; perhaps in gratitude, the NEDERLANDERS renamed the theatre for him the same year.   MCH

Nelson, Richard (1938–96) Lighting designer whose career included modern dance, avant-garde theatre, and Broadway. He stage-managed or designed lights for three early works for ROBERT WILSON, including *The King of Spain* (1969) and *Deafman Glance* (1970). His Broadway credits include *SUNDAY IN THE PARK WITH GEORGE* (for which he won a 1984 Tony), *INTO THE WOODS, The Tap Dance Kid,* and *The Molière Comedies* (ROUNDABOUT).   AA

Nelson, Richard (1950–) American playwright, director, and dramaturge born in Chicago and educated at Hamilton College; America's most prolific dramatist during the decade of the 1980s, with such productions as *Rip Van Winkle, or "The Works"* (1981, YALE REP), *The Return of Pinocchio* (1983, EMPTY SPACE), *Between East and West* (1984, SEATTLE REP) and *Principia Scriptoriae* (1986, MANHATTAN THEATRE CLUB). He won Obies for *The Vienna Notes* (1978, GUTHRIE; 1979, PLAYWRIGHTS HORIZONS) and his "innovative programming" while literary manager at the BROOKLYN ACADEMY OF MUSIC. He has adapted a number of classics, such as *The Suicide* (1980), *The Marriage of Figaro* (1982), *The Three Sisters* (1984), *The Father* (1996), and *The Seagull* (2001); was dramaturge for the Guthrie Theater; and wrote the book for the musical *Chess* (1988).

His plays have had a wide following in England, where he has written radio dramas for the BBC: It has been claimed that over an 11-year period he was the second most produced playwright in the U.K., after Shakespeare; *Some Americans Abroad* (1989) and *Two Shakespearean Actors* (1990) debuted at the Royal Shakespeare Company prior to LINCOLN CENTER productions; and his *Life Sentences* (1993, SECOND STAGE) was staged by British director John Caird. A commissioned play, *Misha's Party,* written in collaboration with Russian dramatist Aleksandr Gelman, also premiered at the RSC (1993) prior to production at the Moscow Art Theatre (fall 1993). *New England* premiered at the RSC in December 1994 and *The General from America* (about Benedict Arnold) in 1996, the same year he was made an honorary associate artist of the RSC, the first American so honored. Most of these plays have subsequently been produced in the U.S., many Off-Broadway or in regional theatres. *Goodnight Children Everywhere,* honored in London with an Olivier Award, was seen in 1999 at Playwrights Horizons, a frequent producer of his work (e.g., *Rodney's Wife* in 2004), and one for which Nelson sometimes has directed his own plays.

His career has recently, to some extent, shifted from the U.K. to the U.S. In 2000 he won a Tony for the book for *James Joyce's The Dead* (for which he also cowrote the lyrics). The ATLANTIC THEATER offered his *Franny's Way* in 2002. In 2003 he wrote the book for (and directed at Playwrights Horizons) the musical *My Life with Albertine* (music by Ricky Ian Gordon). He is chair of the playwriting program at the Yale School of Drama.   BBW

Neuwirth, Bebe [né Beatrice] (1958–) Versatile actor, fair-skinned, long-legged dancer and singer, raised in Princeton, NJ. Neuwirth trained in dance at Juilliard (1976–7) and debuted on Broadway as a replacement (Sheila) in *A Chorus Line* in 1980. Since then she has earned two Tonys, first as Nickie (featured role) in a revival of *Sweet Charity* (1986) and then as Velma Kelly in the 1996 revival of *Chicago* (returning to the show in late 2006 as Roxie Hart). Other Broadway credits include *Dancin', Little Me, Damn Yankees, Fosse,* and *Funny Girl,* all but *Dancin'* and *Fosse* revivals. Despite numerous films, she is likely best known as Lilith on TV's *Cheers* (Emmys in 1990 and '91) and later *Frasier.* In a change of pace, in 2004, she began a series of appearances at the Zipper Theatre (a former zipper factory on NYC's West Side) in *Here Lies Jenny,* a late-night offering dedicated to songs by Kurt Weill (all about women) directed by Roger Rees. In the short-lived 2005 TV series, *Law & Order: Trial by Jury,* she costarred as Assistant DA Tracey Kibre.   DBW

New Amsterdam Theatre 214 West 42d St., NYC [Architects: Herts and Tallant]. When built in 1903 by Klaw and Erlanger, this was intended to be their premier theatre for musical productions and spectacles. Between 1913 and 1937, 12 editions of the *Ziegfeld Follies* were presented on its stage; but in 1937 it was sold to motion-picture interests and became one of the "grind" (continuous-show) moviehouses lining 42d Street. In 1982, as part of the reclamation program of 42nd Street, NYC's Industrial Development Agency took title to the theatre and leased it to the Nederlander Organization to return it to legitimate fare. Work began on the building, but unforeseen structural faults halted the project, and the theatre was boarded up. Extensive renovations had been postponed until the city agencies coordinated efforts for the greater 42d Street Development Project. Almost as famous as the ornate 1,700-seat auditorium is the Roof Garden above the theatre, which dispensed light entertainment and refreshment to after-theatre crowds for many years. In 1937, it was rented first as a radio studio, then as a television studio; more recently, it served as a rehearsal hall but then was closed for a decade. Finally, under lease to the Disney Company, a $50 million-plus renovation under the oversight of architect Hugh Hardy began. On 8 May 1997 the theatre in its original spendor reopened. Its first hit, *The Lion King,* opened on 13 November 1997 with a run that continues.   MCH

[*Ed. note:* The original author of this entry produced a glorious book on the renovation (1997).]

New Dramatists (1949–) Tony-winning (2001) not-for-profit American service organization for playwrights. Founded in NYC by Michaela O'Harra with assistance from Robert Anderson, Richard Rodgers, Howard Lindsay, and others, New Dramatists exists to "encourage and develop playwriting in America." After a screening process, accepted members are provided a cast and director for readings of their plays. A critique session with other playwrights and professionals gives the writer a frank evaluation and suggestions for rewriting. Members also may be assigned to review a Broadway production from beginning rehearsal to opening. New Dramatists informs members about current writing opportunities; provides classes on the craft of writing; solicits tickets to current theatre productions; maintains a library of current periodicals and trade journals; and provides loans for members with plays in production. Since its inception, over 500 writers have been served; 14 members have received Pulitzers. Successful alumni include John Guare, Lanford Wilson, William Inge, Ed Bullins, Megan Terry, Maria Irene Fornés, Paddy Chayefsky, Horton Foote, Eric Overmyer, John Patrick Shanley, Nilo Cruz, Paula Vogel, Donald Margulies, Suzan-Lori Parks, and August Wilson.   TLM

New Federal Theatre Stimulated by a NYSCA initiative in ghetto arts, in 1970 director and producer Woodie King Jr. founded this nonprofit theatre, which he named for the Depression-era Federal Theatre Project. For most of its history NFT has been located at the Henry Street Settlement's Arts for Living Center at 466 Grand St. on Manhattan's Lower East Side. Reflecting the ethnic composition of the district, the theatre has produced new work by minority dramatists, and played a role in bringing minority theatre to national attention, a mission that remains essentially the same. Funded by the philanthropic Lewisohn sisters in 1915, the main auditorium, now renamed the Henry DeJur Playhouse, was originally the Neighborhood Playhouse, a crucible of the Stanislavsky System in America. Through 2005, NFT had staged more than 180 productions.   CLJ

New Group, The Nonprofit Off-Broadway group founded in 1995 by artistic director Scott Elliott, who directed the first production there, Mike Leigh's *Ecstasy,* and has directed over a dozen subsequent ones. Other directors have numbered Jo Bonney, Sean Mathias, Joe Mantello, and Mark Brokaw. Dedicated to the development and production of plays that address complex issues and explore all aspects of human experience, with a focus on "naturalistic" and ensemble acting, recent offerings have included Trevor Griffiths's *Comedians* and *Avenue Q* (2003), Michael Murphy's *Sin* (2004), Leigh's *Abigail's Party* and a revival of *Hurlyburly* (2005), and the world premiere of the "play/opera" *The Music Teacher* with words by WALLACE SHAWN and music by Allen Shawn (2006).   DBW

New Line Theatre   St. Louis theatre – a nonunion professional company – founded in 1991 under the artistic direction of Scott Miller, author of several books on the musical genre, as an alternative musical-theatre operation offering provocative, politically and socially relevant works, usually lesser-known Broadway and OFF-BROADWAY shows, such as *Floyd Collins, A New Brain, Passion, The Robber Bridegroom, The Nervous Set,* and *Bat Boy.* A few more traditional musicals are added to the mix. Located in a downtown black-box theatre, it offers four or five productions a season.   DBW

New Moon, The   Two-act operetta, music by SIGMUND ROMBERG, words by OSCAR HAMMERSTEIN II, Frank Mandel, and Laurence Schwab; opened 19 September 1928 at the IMPERIAL THEATRE, running 509 performances. This soaring romance, set in 18th-century New Orleans, tells of the French bond servant Robert Mission (Robert Halliday) who, with his love, the noble Marianne (Evelyn Herbert), establishes a free government on a Caribbean island. The score is often characteristic of traditional operetta (the march "Stouthearted Men" and several romantic waltzes), but it also shows Romberg's capacity for adapting less traditional forms to operetta, notably the lyric tango "Softly, as in a Morning Sunrise" and the rhythmic ballad "Lover, Come Back to Me." The last of Romberg's great 1920s operettas, it has consistently held the stage and is currently in the New York City Opera's repertoire.   JD

New Theatre   New York's first major art theatre, at Central Park West and 62d St. – a stone's throw from the present Lincoln Center complex – had an auspicious dedication ceremony (6 November 1909) with speeches by J. Pierpont Morgan, Woodrow Wilson, GEORGE PIERCE BAKER, W. D. HOWELLS, Thomas A. Edison, and WILLIAM ARCHER, preceding the performance of *Antony and Cleopatra* with E. H. SOTHERN and JULIA MARLOWE. The idea for the New Theatre originated with HEINRICH CONRIED, director of the Metropolitan Opera. Funds were subscribed by 30 wealthy

opera patrons to build an elegant Italian Renaissance structure with magnificent staircases and lobbies, a roof garden, a spacious orchestra pit, and the latest stage equipment, including the first electrically operated revolving stage. WINTHROP AMES from Boston's Castle Square Theatre was appointed director.

The New got off to a poor start. The production was not ready, the house (seating 2,500) was too large, and the acoustics were abominable. Clearly, the plan to stage operas and plays in the same theatre had been a mistake. In two seasons only GALSWORTHY's *Strife,* EDWARD SHELDON's *The Nigger,* and Mary Austin's *The Arrow Maker* could properly be called "new." The lessons from its brief life (1909–11) were clear: An art theatre could not be bought with dollars. The new theatre movement demanded intimate quarters.

The SHUBERT BROTHERS acquired the building and renamed it. As the Century (1911–30), it housed an assortment of musicals by VICTOR HERBERT, Offenbach, ROMBERG, and Oskar Straus; MORRIS GEST's production of REINHARDT's *The Miracle* (1924), for which NORMAN BEL GEDDES transformed the theatre into a massive Gothic cathedral; and, earlier that same season, Eleonora Duse in 11 matinees of five plays, including *Lady from the Sea* and *Ghosts.* It was demolished in 1930 and replaced with the Century Apartments.   RM

New Vaudeville   Sprawling category of performers (most dislike intensely this moniker) who harness traditional popular entertainment skills and a carnival spirit to a postmodern aesthetic. The versatility of such actor-athletes as clown, MIME, and eccentric dancer BILL IRWIN, dancer and master juggler MICHAEL MOSCHEN, musician and PUPPETEER Bruce D. Schwartz, the late monologist SPALDING GRAY, table-top puppeteer and political satirist Paul Zaloom, is a hallmark. Ensemble groups such as the Pickle Family and BIG APPLE circuses can be considered part of New Vaudeville. Unlike the players of old-time variety shows, New Vaudevillians are mostly college-educated children of the middle class. While acknowledging forebears from commedia dell'arte to the Three Stooges, these are the thinking man's clowns, whose physical talents serve thematic and stylistic agendas with roots in the antiestablishment theatres of the 1960s (themselves in debt to such diverse influence as BRECHT, Meyerhold, Dada, and Bunraku).

While each New Vaudevillian is unique, they share a number of traits. Most reject the conventions of realistic theatre, substituting physical virtuosity and violating the fourth wall with direct address and audience interaction: Slack-wire acrobat and silent clown AVNER "THE ECCENTRIC" EISENBERG brings audience members onstage; crackerjack banjo player and storyteller Stephen Wade pitches ballpoint pens to the house; and during Bill Irwin's *The Regard of Flight*, the quintessential New Vaudeville show, players invade the auditorium, as they do in Irwin's and David Shiner's 1993 show, *Fool Moon* (revived 1995, 1998).

Despite their avant-garde affinities, New Vaudevillians forsake elitist aspects of experimental theatre for populist perspectives, and expose the mysteries of their entertainment specialities. Disillusionistic magicians PENN AND TELLER unmask their own tricks; the Flying Karamazov Brothers, a four-man (originally five) juggling team (Paul David Magid, Michael Preston, Sam Williams, and Howard Jay Patterson; in 2006 Magid and Patterson remain), maintain an ironic, midact commentary on their craft. Together with their self-reliance, such egalitarian attitudes constitute a reaction against the modern, technological world, demonstrating, as Ron Jenkins puts it, "an affirmation of what a human being can accomplish without the aid of machines." In recent years New Vaudevillians have obtained mainstream popularity, suggesting the appeal and staying power of the fresh theatrical visions that they have created using familiar means, and the term has largely vanished in the 2000s.   CLJ

New Victory Theatre   The first theatre to be renovated as part of the revitalization plan for New York's Broadway strip (42d St.) was the Victory, a 1900 theatre designed by J. B. McElfatrick for OSCAR HAMMERSTEIN (as the Theatre Republic). Renamed the BELASCO in 1902. In 1931 burlesque producer Billy MINSKY added his name to the venue and turned into the first BURLESQUE house in the area. In 1942 it was renamed the Victory and became a second-run movie theatre, and then in the 1970s a pornographic moviehouse. It essentially stood empty after 1990. The new space (c. 500 seats), overseen by Hardy Holzman Pfeiffer Associates, was a $11.4 million renovation that turned the venue into the city's first full-time performing arts center for children and families. The exterior now has returned to the Hammerstein look; the interior, the decor of Belasco's.   DBW

New York City theatres   From its inception, New York – or, more specifically, the island of Manhattan – was blessed with an air of cosmopolitanism. Settled by the Dutch at the toe of the island early in the 17th century, its population grew to include English, French, Irish, German, and Jewish inhab-

itants plus Negro slaves. If, when the English took over the settlement later in the century, the Anglican church dominated its religious life, the tone had been set by the fundamentalism of the Dutch Reformed church. The arrival of the Presbyterians and Methodists served to strengthen the conservatism of the early population, which found its entertainment within the family and home and in simple outdoor pursuits and sports.

The creation of a miniature English court at the beginning of the 18th century, plus the growing prosperity of the colonials, brought people out of their homes and into society. Early records suggest amateur theatrical entertainment in and around the colonial court and, perhaps, itinerant performers in the early taverns. Then, in 1732, a newspaper advertisement referred to a theatre owned by "the honourable Rip Van Dam"; later a map (1735) showed a playhouse close to the English fort, the site of the governor's residence. Both theatres were probably rudimentary and makeshift, but they point to a greater interest in theatrical activity among the colonial population.

By the mid-18th century, two theatrical companies visited New York, the second of which comprised professional actors from London. They settled in a theatre on Nassau St., which may well have been the Rip Van Dam warehouse theatre used by the amateurs some 20 years before. Though it still encountered religious opposition, a company assembled by DAVID DOUGLASS in Jamaica, from the remnants of the old HALLAM company, returned to New York in 1758 and was emboldened by a palpable interest in theatrical entertainment to build three theatres in the next nine years. One of them, the Theatre in JOHN STREET built in 1767, was to serve Douglass until his withdrawal from the mainland before the Revolution, and was later used by the occupying English troops during the war. When Lewis Hallam the Younger returned to New York in 1785, he reopened the theatre and used it until 1798.

The first substantial playhouse to be built in New York was subscribed by the city's important and wealthy citizens and located in a site destined to become an early municipal center: at a place where Broadway was to merge with the Bowery, the main road to Boston from the city. Here, in 1798, theatre was established as a necessary concomitant of urban living. Designed by French architect Joseph Mangin, the playhouse, which came to be known as the PARK THEATRE, had an ugly exterior but provided reasonable comfort for its patrons in the auditorium; it represented a distinct improvement over the old, unattractive, and uncomfortable wooden John Street house.

While the Park dominated theatrical activity through the early years of the 18th century, it provided the spur for the building of other theatres in the burgeoning city. To the east and north of it, a more elegant theatre was built on the BOWERY, but quickly fell out of favor with the fashionable class; it survived into the 20th century as a "neighborhood house," catering for the tastes of its shifting and immigrant population. For the sixth and last time, it was destroyed by FIRE in 1929.

By 1825, New York had emerged as the premier theatre city of America. Theatres dotted the urban landscape, but they never strayed too far from Broadway, the principal thoroughfare of the city. Stars from England and Europe generally made New York the first stop on their lucrative tours. When the fortunes of the Park waned, other theatres arose to take its place. Comedian WILLIAM "BILLY" MITCHELL made MITCHELL'S OLYMPIC THEATRE the most popular theatre on Broadway in the late 1830s and early '40s. Another comedian, WILLIAM E. BURTON, turned a little opera house into BURTON'S CHAMBERS STREET THEATRE, dispensing his merry entertainment to enthusiastic audiences. Theatres tended to get bigger and more comfortable, culminating in the 4,500-seat BROADWAY THEATRE, modeled on London's Haymarket.

As the city pushed northward, so did the theatres. By midcentury, Broadway was no longer residential, but mixed factories, office buildings, shops, and department stores together with theatres along its way. Playhouses purveyed everything from MINSTREL SHOWS to opera to urbane English comedy, and became more attractive architecturally as they reflected the trends from Europe. NIBLO'S GARDEN had a grand foyer for its patrons, and most theatres included refreshment stands. Seats were upholstered in the National Theatre (NW corner of Leonard and Church Sts.), and the pit was rendered into the orchestra and made respectable, as the gallery became the family circle to combat the rowdyism of its early denizens. The familiar tiers of boxes atrophied into ceremonial sidewall appendages, as the stage was pulled closer to the curtain line.

In the last decades of the 19th century, following the process of urbanization, a theatre district began to form around Union Square, at the junction of Broadway and Fourth Ave. at 14th St. The Academy of Music, WALLACK'S THEATRE, the UNION SQUARE, and TONY PASTOR'S all offering different entertainment, forming a core around which a small support industry of AGENTS, costumers, photographers, managers, restaurants, theatrical boardinghouses, and hotels sprang up.

More theatres were built above Union Square, reaching to Herald Square and beyond, to satisfy an entertainment-hungry population. In 1869, EDWIN BOOTH built his elegant BOOTH'S THEATRE at the corner of Sixth Ave. and 23rd St. and provided a new look in theatres: Gone was the raked stage and, with it, the wing-and-drop setting; in their place, illusory walls of canvas and lath were fastened to the stage floor to create rooms and scenes of extraordinary realistic detail.

In 1893, CHARLES FROHMAN built his EMPIRE THEATRE on Broadway at 40th St., and OSCAR HAMMERSTEIN I crossed 42d St. to build his OLYMPIA at 44th St. just two years later. Both structures signaled the development of a new theatre district around Longacre (later Times) Square. During 1900–28, an unprecedented boom in theatre building ensued, providing New York's population with more playhouses than it could support. The new theatres reflected the change in theatrical production. The 19th-century STOCK COMPANY resident in its own theatre was supplanted by the "combination system," the assembling of a cast for the presentation of a single play to be produced at a rented theatre. Consisting of a stage, dressing rooms, a box office, an auditorium, and a small lobby, 20th-century playhouses served the new system; with fewer than 2,000 seats, they were well-suited for the plays and musicals presented on their stages.

Some 80 theatres were built during this era and filled Broadway from 39th to 54th St. and its side streets. Some were erected on odd-shaped parcels of land; others had proper facades designed in a variety of styles from Egyptian to Georgian; all were proscenium theatres. They were largely the architectural work of J. B. McElfatrick and Company and Herbert J. Krapp. Beginning with the Depression and extending into the years beyond WWII, more than half of them fell victim to the competitive effects of movies and television and the rise of New York's ALTERNATIVE THEATRE, OFF-BROADWAY, and OFF-OFF BROADWAY. Some were torn down, others were converted to moviehouses (those lining 42d Street), and a few were rebuilt to serve other purposes.

With the recognition that New York's theatres were rapidly becoming an endangered species, a succession of the city's mayors began to take steps to protect the standing playhouses while stimulating the erection of others. Zoning laws were changed to permit the incorporation of theatres within tall office buildings, which resulted in the GERSHWIN (1972) and MINSKOFF (1973) theatres and two smaller playhouses in the early 1970s. Only a few have been protected by the landmark law, and the fate of the others depends heavily on the availability of plays and musicals suitable for production and the willingness of investors to wager ever greater sums of money to mount them. In 1982, an advisory panel was appointed by then–Mayor Edward I. Koch to study the situation and to make recommendations for the preservation of the remaining theatres. The project moved forward in the late 1990s and early 2000s, with major renovations of the Victory Theatre (see NEW VICTORY), the NEW AMSTERDAM, and the Lyric and the Apollo (becoming the HILTON THEATRE), all on 42d Street.

Despite some demolished Off- and Off-Off Broadway theatres (e.g., the Douglas Fairbanks and the John Houseman on THEATRE ROW; 750 Eighth Ave., housing several Off-Off companies; the HENRY MILLER THEATRE) or closures (e.g., the Blue Heron Arts Center on 24th St.) beginning in the late 1990s there was something of a theatre building boom in Manhattan and surrounding environs, one arguably the most active since the teens and twenties. In some cases major renovations were undertaken for companies, including SIGNATURE THEATRE, THEATRE FOR A NEW CITY (Brooklyn), MANHATTAN THEATRE CLUB, SECOND STAGE, ROUNDABOUT (former home of AMERICAN PLACE and the former Studio 54), Pregones Theater (South Bronx), and the Chocolate Factory in Queens. New spaces included several on Theatre Row, the Little Shubert (499-seat space adjacent to Theatre Row), on 59th St. (59E59, three stages and home of PRIMARY STAGES), the Clinton Green Project on the far West Side (housing the Ensemble Studio Theatre and offices for INTAR), the Zipper on West 37th St., and the five-theatre complex first named DODGER Stages Theatre (out of the defunct Worldwide Plaza Cinemas on West 50th) and now New World Stages. Yet in the early 2000s pricey Manhattan real estate had made it difficult for small theatre companies to find or retain adequate spaces. MCH DBW

New York Clipper Founded in 1853 by Frank Queen as a sporting and theatrical paper, the *Clipper* published news about music halls, MINSTREL SHOWS, CIRCUSES, fairs, concerts, plays, and operas under the heading of "Amusements." Dramatic editors T. ALLSTON BROWN (1860s), Henry Ashley (1870s), and J. Austin Fynes (1880s) developed theatrical coverage. With much of the profession "on the road," the *Clipper* provided routes, playing dates, and mail information. It maintained a circulation of around 20,000 until first challenged by (1905) and then incorporated into VARIETY (1924). TLM

New York Idea, The This social satire by LANGDON MITCHELL opened at NYC's Lyric Theatre 19 November 1906, after out-of-town tryouts in Chicago and St. Louis, and ran for 66 performances. The star-studded cast included MINNIE MADDERN FISKE, GEORGE ARLISS, and DUDLEY DIGGES. Long a staple of American STOCK COMPANIES and critically well-regarded for its witty language, the play satirizes ideas about marriage and divorce among the well-to-do, eventuating in the separation of one couple and the reuniting of another. Though its views of marriage now seem dated and the invalid divorce decree a stock device for reuniting a loving couple, the play exemplifies quite well Mitchell's skill as a social analyst of contemporaneous American life. In 1977 British director Frank Dunlop successfully revived the play as high comedy at the BROOKLYN ACADEMY OF MUSIC with a cast headed by BLYTHE DANNER, ROSEMARY HARRIS, and Stephen Collins. RKB

New York International Fringe Festival Billed as "the largest multi-arts festival in North America," planning began in late 1996 for this annual celebration of ALTERNATIVE, occasionally hard-to-classify theatre, and the first festival launched in August 1997 with almost 200 productions, a benchmark that held steady through subsequent years. Founded by four mainstays of NYC's downtown scene – Aaron Beall, John Clancy, Jonathan Harris, and Elena K. Holy – FringeNYC differs from many fringe festivals elsewhere in that works are adjudicated by theatrical professionals and many later enjoy artistic and commercial success. The best example is probably URINETOWN, a postmodern musical that ultimately won three 2002 Tony Awards. Other successful FringeNYC productions are *Matt & Ben,* a gender-reversed satire of actors Matt Damon and Ben Affleck; *21 Dog Years,* a solo play about performer Mike Daisey's stint working for amazon.com; *Debbie Does Dallas,* based on the iconic porn film; *Dog Sees God,* loosely based on Charles Schultz's "Peanuts"; Daniel MacIvor's surreal *Never Swim Alone;* and Arlene Hutton's two-hander *Last Train to Nibroc.* Initially, the 20-odd FringeNYC venues were exclusively on Manhattan's Lower East Side. When property values forced those venues to shutter, FringeNYC spread out, ultimately mounting its 16-day festival each August in scores of venues below 14th St. There are also miniprojects within FringeNYC, including FringeJr (youth theatre), FringeAlFresco (outdoor theatre), FringeU (panels and seminars), and a daily newspaper, *Propaganda.* Officially, FringeNYC is mounted by The Present Company, a nonprofit founded by Clancy and Holy that also develops new works. After Clancy and the other founders moved on, Holy became producing artistic director and was viewed as a powerful spokesperson for adventurous theatre. Rarely fiscally secure, FringeNYC operates with a largely volunteer staff.   LJ

New York [Dramatic] Mirror Founded in 1879 by STEPHEN RYDER FISKE and Ernest Havier to combat the blackmailing practices of the *New York Dramatic News,* the *Mirror* (later, *Dramatic Mirror*) became an important theatrical journal under the editorship of HARRISON GREY FISKE from 1880 to 1911. Fiske worked to eliminate corrupt practices and to raise standards of production, while fighting the Theatrical SYNDICATE and promoting the career of his wife, MINNIE MADDERN FISKE. In decline after his departure, the *Mirror* incorporated *The Theatre World* (1920) and ceased publication in 1922.   TLM

New York Public Theater see PUBLIC THEATER

New York Shakespeare Festival NYC's busiest company, founded in 1954 by JOSEPH PAPP as the Shakespeare Workshop "to encourage and cultivate interest in poetic drama with emphasis on . . . Shakespeare . . . and to establish an annual summer Shakespeare Festival." Every summer, NYSF (now called Shakespeare in the Park) performs free productions in Central Park's Delacorte Theater, built for it in 1957. Bernard Gersten became associate producer in 1960 (until 1978). In 1967, NYSF established the PUBLIC THEATER in the East Village. During 1973–7, Papp directed Lincoln Center's VIVIAN BEAUMONT AND MITZI E. NEWHOUSE theatres. In 1982, NYSF started the Festival Latino de Nueva York, and in 1983 it adopted the Young Playwrights Festival (until 1985) and established an exchange with London's Royal Court Theatre. In 1986, NYSF launched a short-lived project, directed by actress ESTELLE PARSONS, to present SHAKESPEARE ON Broadway for schoolchildren, and in 1987 it inaugurated a six-year plan to produce all of Shakespeare's plays (not completed until 1997). In 1990, JOANNE AKALAITIS was appointed artistic associate and, after Papp's death in October 1991, artistic director, but without Papp's title of "Producer." Fired abruptly in 1993, she was replaced by GEORGE C. WOLFE who did assume this title; actor-director KEVIN KLINE was appointed artistic associate. One of Wolfe's initiatives was "New Work Now!," a reading series begun in 1994. When Wolfe stepped down he was replaced in 2005 by OSKAR EUSTIS in tandem with a new executive director, Mara Manus.

NYSF has not limited itself to classics but, as time passed, has staged more and more new American plays, both Off- and on Broadway, including HAIR (1967), NO PLACE TO BE SOMEBODY (1969), Galt MacDermot and JOHN GUARE's musical *Two Gentlemen of Verona* (1971; Tony), STICKS AND BONES (1971; Tony), THAT CHAMPIONSHIP SEASON (1972; Tony and Pulitzer), A CHORUS LINE (1975; Tony; then Broadway's longest-running show), FOR COLORED GIRLS WHO HAVE CONSIDERED SUICIDE WHEN THE RAINBOW IS ENUF (1976), ELIZABETH SWADOS's The Haggadah (1980), The MARRIAGE OF BETTE AND BOO (1985), LARRY KRAMER's The Normal Heart (1985), Rupert Holmes's The Mystery of Edwin Drood (1985), WALLACE SHAWN's AUNT DAN & LEMON (1985), George C. Wolfe's The COLORED MUSEUM (1986), LARRY SHUE's Wenceslas Square (1987), Harry Kondoleon's Zero Positive (1988), ANNA DEAVERE SMITH's Fires in the Mirror (1992), SAM SHEPARD's Simpatico (1994), ELAINE STRITCH at Liberty (2001), RICHARD GREENBERG's TAKE ME OUT (2003), KUSHNER and Jeanine Tesori's Caroline, or Change (2003), NEIL LABUTE's This Is How It Goes (2005).

NYSF also hosts visiting companies and artists, such as MABOU MINES, MEREDITH MONK, RICHARD FOREMAN, JOSEPH CHAIKIN, and ANDREI SERBAN, and produces American premieres of foreign works, including VÁCLAV HAVEL's The Memorandum (1968) and Largo Desolato (1986), Roberto Athayde's Miss Margarida's Way (1977), David Hare's Plenty (1982), Caryl Churchill's Top Girls (1982), Fen (1983), and Serious Money (1987), Louise Page's Salonika (1985), NYC premiere of Martin McDonagh's The Cripple of Inishmaan (1998).

Over the years NYSF productions have won numerous awards, including (as of the 2005–6 season) 38 Tonys, 135 Obies, 4 Pulitzers, 37 Drama Desks, and 18 Lucille Lortel awards. As of the end of 2005, 49 shows had been transferred to Broadway. During George C. Wolfe's decadelong tenure he directed hit productions of ANGELS IN AMERICA, TOPDOG/UNDERDOG, and BRING IN 'DA NOISE, BRING IN 'DA FUNK. Yet Broadway-transfer failures like On the Town (1997) and Wild Party (1999) – a combined loss of $14 million – put the operation in some financial jeopardy by 2002, a situation largely rectified by 2004. With a number of organizational names attached to this operation since its founding, in 2004 it was finally pared down to The PUBLIC THEATER (now the name of the institution and not the physical spaces), simplifying the nomenclature and complicating the historical record.

REK   DBW

Interior view of Niblo's [Garden] Theatre, New York, during a performance of Auber's opera *Masaniello*. From *Ballou's Pictorial*, 24 Feb. 1855. *Courtesy:* Laurence Senelick Collection.

New York Theatre Workshop Founded in NYC's East Village in 1979 and producing annually six or seven innovative productions and 50–100 readings and workshops in its 188-seat theatre and rehearsal studio. Since 1988 its dynamic leader has been James C. Nicola, who has forged the operation into an essential part of the city's cultural life, producing works as diverse as Caryl Churchill's *Mad Forest* (1991) and *A Number* (2004), Doug Wright's *Quills* (1995), Jonathan Larson's RENT (1996), Claudia Shear's *Dirty Blonde* (2000), CHARLES MEE's *First Love* (2001), KUSHNER's *Homebody/Kabul* (2001), Amy Freed's *The Beard of Avon* (2003), Flemish director Ivo van Hove's controversial *A Streetcar Named Desire* (1999) and *Hedda Gabler* (2004), and Itamar Moses's *Bach at Leipzig* (2005). *Rent* and *Dirty Blonde* became mainstream Broadway hits; but it is service to the theatre artists collectively known as the "Usual Suspects," not commercial success, that defines NYTW's mission.
   DBW

Niblo, William (1789–1878) Victualler and businessman, Niblo opened the Sans Souci Park in 1828, a restaurant garden containing a 1,200-seat concert hall. Under various managers (including CHARLES A. GILFERT, Joseph Sefton, and J. W. WALLACK) it became home to VAUDEVILLE and light entertainment. NIBLO'S GARDEN expanded in 1839 to include a conventional theatre catering to musical events and standard fare. In 1848, after the complex burned (see FIRES), Niblo took the lease of the ASTOR PLACE OPERA HOUSE, which he held during the riot that year. The Garden's theatres reopened in 1849 and continued to feature stars of music, comedy, dance, pantoMIME, and extravaganza. Niblo retired from management in 1861.   RKB   MCH

Niblo's Garden NE corner of Broadway and Prince St., NYC. A tavern keeper, WILLIAM NIBLO, leased the Columbian Gardens from the Van Rennselaer family and turned it into a summer retreat for New Yorkers. In 1828, he converted a stable into a summer theatre named the Sans Souci. He later added a proper theatre as a yearlong enterprise and presented regular dramatic fare. From then on, it simply became known as

"Niblo's Garden." When the complex was leveled by FIRE in 1846, Niblo retreated to his country estate a millionaire; however, he was induced to rebuild it a few years later. The Van Rennselaers built the Metropolitan Hotel on part of the same site, and the theatre was entered through the hotel lobby. During its long history, every kind of entertainment and most of the reigning stars appeared on its stage, but none more popular than the RAVEL family of comedians, who performed here for 30 years, and *The BLACK CROOK,* which opened in 1866 and ran for 16 months. Another fire in 1872 destroyed the theatre, but it was rebuilt and survived until 1892, when both the hotel and the theatre were razed.   MCH

Nichols, Anne see *ABIE'S IRISH ROSE*

Nichols, Mike [né Michael Igor Peschkowsky] (1931–) American actor, director, and producer. Born in Berlin, Nichols fled to New York with his parents to escape the Nazis. He attended the University of Chicago for two years, after which he studied with LEE STRASBERG at the ACTORS STUDIO. He began his professional career in CHICAGO. performing with a comedy group that included ELAINE MAY. In 1957 Nichols and May developed their own act, which comprised regular satirical sketches and improvisations. They gave two New York concerts in 1959, followed by *An Evening with Mike Nichols and Elaine May* on Broadway in 1960, establishing both performers as major stars. Nichols turned to directing in 1963 with NEIL SIMON's *BAREFOOT IN THE PARK,* followed by *The Knack* (1964, OFF-BROADWAY), *Luv* (1964), *The ODD COUPLE* (1965), *The Apple Tree* (1966), *PLAZA SUITE* (1968), and *The PRISONER OF SECOND AVENUE* (1971). His comic inventiveness made him one of the most sought-after directors in New York. Beginning in the 1970s Nichols turned to more serious fare, including *STREAMERS* (1976), *Comedians* (1976), *The GIN GAME* (1977), *The Real Thing* (1984), *HURLYBURLY* (1984), *Waiting for Godot* (1989), *Elliot Loves* (1990, Promenade), and *Death and the Maiden* (1992), demonstrating skill and vitality in shaping complex dramatic works. Richard Schickel (*Time*) praised his "uncanny sense of modern body language" in communicating the shapeless lives in DAVID RABE's *Hurlyburly.* In 2005 he won his seventh Tony, for directing *Spamalot.* His producing credits include the musical ANNIE (1977) and *The Gin Game.* His major films include *WHO'S AFRAID OF VIRGINIA WOOLF?* (1966), *The Graduate* (1967; Academy Award), *Catch-22* (1970), *Carnal Knowledge* (1971), *Postcards from the Edge* (1990), *Wolf* (1994), *WIT* (2001, HBO; Emmy), *ANGELS IN AMERICA*

(2003, HBO miniseries; Emmy), and *Closer* (2004). In 2001 he received the National Medal of Arts and in 2003 the Kennedy Center Honors recognition. Nichols remains one of the most successful American directors of his generation.   TLM

Nick of the Woods Adapted from the 1837 novel of the same title by ROBERT MONTGOMERY BIRD, LOUISA MEDINA's dramatization – one of several by her on a frontier subject – opened 5 February 1839 at the BOWERY THEATRE for a week's uninterrupted run (then quite a success). With its Kentucky setting, fiendish Indians (see NATIVE AMERICANS PORTRAYED), "ring-tailed roarer" brag speech, and the Jibbinainosay (Nick – or Satan – of the Woods), Bird's novel provided ample opportunity for spectacular raging cataracts, canoes of fire precipitated over waterfalls, rescues from bridges dangling over rocky passes, and songs. The melodrama served Joseph Proctor as a starring vehicle for years, remained in the Bowery repertory for decades, and was the abiding dramatization of the novel, still played in 1921.   RKB

Nigger, The EDWARD SHELDON's controversial play was produced by WINTHROP AMES and opened 4 December 1909 as part of the initial season at the NEW THEATRE. The play, which received conflicting critical notices, concerns Philip Morrow, the governor of a Southern state who discovers on the eve of his marriage that his grandmother was a Negro. Rather than allow his enemies to destroy him, he resigns his office and engagement to work for his "new" race. Originally titled *Philip Morrow,* Sheldon changed the name to reflect what he perceived as the attitude of white people toward blacks in the play. Fox Films produced a cinema version in 1915, but it was withdrawn and retitled *The New Governor* after protests in a number of cities.   BBW

'night, Mother by MARSHA NORMAN. This intermissionless, 90-minute, two-act character drama was given a staged reading at CIRCLE REPERTORY THEATRE (November 1981) prior to its January 1983 premiere production at AMERICAN REPERTORY THEATRE, which then moved to Broadway (JOHN GOLDEN THEATRE, 31 March 1983). It won both the Pulitzer and the Susan Smith Blackburn prizes. Kathy Bates played Jessie, an overweight divorcée who can find nothing of value in her very ordinary existence. The uncompromising action – a last evening with her mother before committing suicide – is structured in classic sonata form. Although it "looks like simplicity itself," noted FRANK RICH, it is "a shattering evening." Many regional productions followed, as well as a 1986 film with ANNE BANCROFT and Sissy Spacek and a Broadway revival in 2004 with Edie Falco and Brenda Blethyn.   FHL

Night of the Iguana, The, by TENNESSEE WILLIAMS premiered 28 December 1961, directed by Frank Corsaro at NYC's ROYALE THEATRE, with Patrick O'Neal (Shannon), Bette Davis (Maxine), and Margaret Leighton (Hannah; Tony for Best Actress). Running for 316 performances, it won the New York Drama Critics' Circle Award. A 1976 revival starred Richard Chamberlain, Dorothy McGuire (Hannah), and Sylvia Miles (Maxine). CIRCLE IN THE SQUARE produced it in 1988 with JANE ALEXANDER as Maxine, and ROUNDABOUT in 1996 with CHERRY JONES (Hannah), WILLIAM PETERSEN, and Marsha Mason (Maxine). A 1963 screenplay by Tony Veiller, directed by John Huston, featured RICHARD BURTON, Ava Gardner (Maxine), and Deborah Kerr (Hannah). T. Lawrence Shannon, a defrocked priest turned tour conductor, guides women from a Baptist female college to Hotel Costa Verde in Mexico. Shannon is caught between two women who represent different yet (for Williams) typical poles – Maxine, the sensualist, and Hannah, the spinster/Madonna. Earlier, Williams had combined these types in Blanche Du Bois. The iguana symbolizes animal passion and the characters' common humanity, chained and then liberated in the play.   PCK

nightclubs Venues where the consumption of food and drink is interspersed with entertainment, nightclubs may have originated in concert saloons like the Melodeon (New York, 1859), dance cellars, beer gardens, or Bowery joints like Harry Hill's. The earliest distinct avatars are cabarets, restaurants in New York, Saratoga, BOSTON, and New Orleans that offered variety acts between the courses. With the Folies-Bergère of 1911, rathskellers took on the name "cabaret" to acquire chic, and by WWI had become major tourist attractions. Reisenweber's in Columbus Circle (NYC) was a pioneer in dinner entertainment, popularizing the floor show, a Dixieland Jazz Band, Hawaiian music, and the *thé dansant*. New York roof-garden theatre presentations, such as ZIEGFELD's *Midnight Frolics* on the roof of the NEW AMSTERDAM, and MORRIS GEST's *Midnight Whirl* on the CENTURY roof, offered attractive REVUES in a relaxed atmosphere.

Although hotels benefited from not having to observe a 3 A.M. curfew, wartime censorship caused many cabarets to turn into dance palaces, and Prohibition sounded their deathknell. They were replaced by nightclubs (the first so-called was the Club Deauville, which had no closing time) and speakeasies; there were 5,000 in Manhattan by 1922. Critical to a club's popularity was often the master or mistress of ceremonies: Texas Guinan with her cynical greeting "Hello, Sucker" was the most celebrated. Nightclubs were valuable showcases for such talent as Clayton, Jackson and DURANTE, SOPHIE TUCKER, Helen Morgan, HARRY RICHMAN, and the bands of Rudy Vallee and Paul Whiteman; but the link with bootlegging made for the entrance of organized crime into show biz, particularly in Chicago, where comedian Joe E. Lewis was brutalized for his recalcitrance. Harlem's Cotton Club was also run by the Mob; it and such other uptown New York "niteries" as Connie's Place presented all-black entertainment to all-white thrill seekers. "Clip joints," where the customers were wildly overcharged, became common.

Prohibition's repeal and the New Deal led to a proliferation and aggrandizement of the nightclub: Many of them offered seminude shows (see NUDITY) and did away with the exorbitant cover charge. BILLY ROSE set the pace with the Casino de Paree; other prominent New York nightspots included the glass-walled Rainbow Room, El Morocco, and Leon & Eddie's. The exclusive Stork Club maintained a color bar well in the 1950s. These "supper clubs," often staffed by debutantes, boasted a kind of pseudosophistication, heavy on "French-style" *diseuses* like Hildegarde and intimate songs with suggestive lyrics. During WWII, a federal amusement tax temporarily curbed profits, but by 1945 such clubs as the Copacabana, the Latin Quarter, and the Diamond Horseshoe were high-profit business enterprises.

With the advent of television, Americans, even outside New York, could stay at home and watch the Stork Club on its own program. By the late 1950s, younger audiences were bypassing the old-style metropolitan nitery to attend folk-song clubs and improvisational-comedy REVUES: CHICAGO made the breakthrough with the Gate of Horn and SECOND CITY. However, in resorts like Las Vegas and Miami, the floor show was pumped up into a hyperbolic extravaganza, a backdrop for star singers, comedians, and even animal trainers, playing to what Noël Coward called "Nescafé society." The nightclub's more intimate attractions bifurcated into the piano bar and the comedy club, a forcing house for standup comics, where entertainment and food vie in monotony. Two of the most tragic FIRES in U.S. history were at the nightclubs Cocoanut Grove (1942) and The Station (2003).   LS

Nina Vance Alley Theatre see ALLEY THEATRE

No, No, Nanette Three-act musical comedy with music by VINCENT YOUMANS and words by Irving Caesar, OTTO HARBACH, and Frank Mandel. It opened 11 March 1925 in London, running 665 performances, and 16 September 1925 at New York's Globe Theatre, running 321 performances. The most successful musical comedy of the 1920s, it does not have the longest NYC run; but by its opening it had played a year in CHICAGO and had had numerous American road tours, in addition to beginning its smash-hit London engagement. This youth-oriented flapper comedy, stressing the conflict between open-minded modernity and repressive conservatism, follows the complex romantic misunderstandings surrounding a big-hearted Bible salesman (Charles Winninger) and his flapper ward, Nanette (Louise Groody). Hip, flip, and up-to-the-minute, it introduced two enduring standards: "I Want to Be Happy" and "Tea for Two." A thoroughly revised version, broadly adapted by Burt Shevelove, appeared on Broadway in 1971, running 861 performances and setting off a series of Broadway "revivals" (actually adaptations) of 50-year-old musicals.   JD

No Place to Be Somebody First Pulitzer Prize–winning play (1970) by an AFRICAN AMERICAN writer, CHARLES GORDONE. A bar owned by small-time hustler Johnny is inhabited by a motley group of black and white social outcasts. Johnny's plans to swindle the Mafia come to nought, but the lives of his companions are sympathetically revealed. The play was first presented at the Sheridan Square Playhouse in NYC (1969), and later at the PUBLIC THEATER and Promenade.   EGH

No Time for Comedy Three-act comedy by S. N. BEHRMAN featuring KATHARINE CORNELL and Laurence Olivier; opened at the ETHEL BARRYMORE THEATRE on 17 April 1939 and ran for 185 performances. Chronicling Behrman's own doubts about writing comedy in a time of economic disaster and impending war, the play shows a popular comic playwright who attempts to write a "serious" play to please a pretentious dilettante. Cornell's restrained performance as the witty actress-wife who restores her husband's belief in the value of laughter was a fine match to Behrman's intelligent comedy. A specific and personal response to its cultural moment, the play has seldom been revived.   MF

Noah, Mordecai M(anuel) (1785–1851) Playwright. Noah was an active Zionist who sought his livelihood in politics (surveyor of the Port of New York, judge of the Court of Sessions) and journalism (*New York Enquirer, The Commercial Advertiser, The Times and Messenger*) and his diversion in the theatre. He was an inveterate theatregoer, an intimate of the managers (PRICE, SIMPSON, DUNLAP, and SOL SMITH), and an occasional playwright. His ardent patriotism was reflected in his documentarylike plays: SHE WOULD BE A SOLDIER (1819), based on the Battle of Chippewa (1814) and written for Catherine Leesugg; *The Siege of Tripoli* (1820), the piratical menace with which Noah had had firsthand experience as Consul to Tunis; *Marion; or, The Hero of Lake George* (1821), based on the Battle of Saratoga (1777); *The Grecian Captive* (1822), on the Greek Revolution (which had only just begun the year before); and *The Siege of Yorktown* (1824), set during the Revolutionary War. *She Would Be a Soldier* became a popular patriotic piece for national holidays for more than 40 years. A 1981 biography was written by J. D. Sama.   RM

Noguchi, Isamu (1904–88) Los Angeles–born sculptor and designer who moved to Japan with his Japanese mother at age 2, returning to the U.S. in 1917. Although he designed almost solely for dance, his abstract design, use of objects, and ability to focus the cubic volume of the stage space had a significant effect on mid-20th-century design. In 1926 he designed masks for actress Ito Michio in Yeats's *At the Hawk's Well,* his first theatre work. In 1935 choreographer Martha Graham asked him to design a set for *Frontier;* it was the first set she had ever used, and it began a collaboration that lasted until 1966 and included *Appalachian Spring* (1944) and *Seraphic Dialogue* (1955). Drawing on the tradition of Noh and the vocabulary of his own sculptures, Noguchi's designs were simple distillations of images, creating psychological rather than literal space. He also designed for GEORGE BALANCHINE, Erick Hawkins, Merce Cunningham, and the Royal Shakespeare Company (*King Lear,* 1955).   AA

Noone, James (1961–) Scene designer from upstate New York who began his career at the Lake George Opera Festival as a stagehand at age 12. His extensive credits in regional theatres – GOODSPEED OPERA HOUSE, the WILLIAMSTOWN THEATRE FESTIVAL, Chicago Shakespeare, among others – were amassed during the late 1980s and early 1990s. Since the revival of INHERIT THE WIND in 1996 he has designed extensively in New York, including *Jekyll & Hyde* (1997 Drama Desk Award), *Judgment at Nuremburg* (2001), and *Match* (2004).

Noone is known for a combination of striking originality and naturalistic details.   BO

Norman, Marsha (1947–) Playwright whose realistic characters confront some devastation in their past to determine whether and how to survive. GETTING OUT (1977, Louisville; 1978, NYC) reveals the internal conflict of a woman parolee in her choice for a new beginning – dramatized by two actresses who simultaneously portray her violent, younger self and her present, numbed self. In 1983 Norman won the Pulitzer Prize for 'NIGHT, MOTHER, a wrenching enactment of the last night in the life of a hopeless young woman as she prepares herself and her mother for her suicide, and of the mother's desperate attempts to prevent it. Other works, premiering regionally, include *Third and Oak: The Laundromat [and] The Pool Hall* (1978), *The Holdup* (1983), *Traveler in the Dark* (1984), *Winter Shakers* (1987; a musical, with Norman L. Berman), *Sarah and Abraham* (1988), *Loving Daniel Boone* (1993), several television plays, and the screenplay for *'night, Mother*. An eight-year absence from Broadway ended with *The SECRET GARDEN* (1991), a musical based on FRANCES HODGSON BURNETT's classic novel, with book (Tony Award) and lyrics by Norman (as part of an all-female creative team), followed in 1993 with *The Red Shoes* (lyrics and book; music by JULE STYNE). Other recent work OFF-BROADWAY includes *140* (1998, one-act in multiauthored *Love's Fire*), *Trudy Blue* (1999, NY) and *Last Dance* (2003). In 2005 she wrote the book for Broadway's *The Color Purple*, and she is slated to write one for a musical based on the film *Don Juan DeMarco*. She codirects the Juilliard playwriting program with CHRISTOPHER DURANG.   FB

Norton, (William) Elliot (1903–2003) Boston-born critic who attended Harvard University, where he studied with George Lyman Kittredge and GEORGE PIERCE BAKER. After graduation in 1926, he worked as a reporter for the *Boston Post*, taking over as drama critic when Edward Harold Crosby retired in 1934. With the demise of the *Post* in 1956, he switched to Hearst's *Record American*, retiring in 1982, though he remained visible in Boston theatre circles. The Boston-based award named for him was first granted in 1983. Norton, who reviewed more than 6,000 productions, acquired the reputation of being honest and reliable about new shows that were Broadway-bound. MIKE NICHOLS and JOSHUA LOGAN thought that he had a "smell for the public" and for "what the public is feeling." He was not a great stylist, nor did his reviews break new critical ground; but NYC producers respected his opinion and made changes in their shows based upon his reviews (he often attended more than once). He received the GEORGE JEAN NATHAN Award for Dramatic Criticism in 1964, and a special Tony in 1971.   TLM

Nottage, Lynn (1964–) Playwright, native of Brooklyn and educated at Brown and the Yale School of Drama. Her best-known play to date is *Intimate Apparel*, commissioned by CENTER STAGE and SOUTH COAST REP and which in 2004 opened the ROUNDABOUT's new Harold and Miriam Steinberg Center for Theatre on 46th St. About a successful black seamstress living in a Lower Manhattan boardinghouse who finds love with a Panama Canal worker in 1905, it won numerous awards, including the Steinberg New Play and the Primus awards and the New York Drama Critics' Circle Best Play award. A playwright with many voices, her corpus also includes *Por' Knockers* (1995, VINEYARD), in which four African Americans and a Jewish activist argue the value of violence after blowing up an FBI building; *Las Meninas* (2002, San Jose Rep), about the wife of Louis XIV and her child (an African dwarf) with the court's royal fool; *Fabulation* (2004, PLAYWRIGHTS HORIZONS; Obie), an unpredictable tale of a self-invented public relations diva humbled. Other plays OFF-BROADWAY: *Crumbs from the Table of Joy* (1995), *Mud, River, Stone* (1997), "Ida Mae Cole Takes a Stance" (a monologue in the 1993 musical revue *A . . . My Name Is Still Alice*).   DBW

nudity A loosely interpreted phenomenon in the theatre: Most of what passed for flesh onstage was cunningly dyed fabric; often it was the contour of breast and leg, uncamouflaged by current fashion, that was read as nakedness. The chorines in *The BLACK CROOK* (1866) scandalized with shocking pink tights, and ADAH ISAACS MENKEN won her billing of "The Naked Lady" while wearing fleshings and a gauze drapery.

The display of the relatively undraped human form onstage was chiefly confined to static configurations. *Tableaux vivants* or living pictures were introduced into New York in 1831 by Ada Adams Barrymore illustrating the painting *The Soldier's Widow*. This respectable exercise of *tableaux vivants* – a flesh-and-blood imitation of a famous work of art – was returned to the legitimate stage by LAURA KEENE in 1856, and it has persisted to our day in musical comedy, with the reproduction of Copley's *Signing of the Declaration of Independence* in *1776* (1976) and of Seurat's *Sunday on the Isle of La Grande Jatte* in *SUNDAY IN THE PARK WITH GEORGE* (1983).

Canny entrepreneurs, such as Dr. Collyer with his Living Models (1847), found that by exhibiting facsimiles of classical sculpture they could venture barer skin and sharper outlines than the dramatic stage allowed. The female form was incarnated in artist's models and prostitutes, while prizefighters and strongmen exhibited male musculature. Such *poses plastiques,* despite their alleged biblical or Grecian inspiration, were usually staged in night cellars and dime museums, subject to police raids and harassment by moralists and reformers. This type of exhibition was given a high-culture gloss by the Hungarian Eduard Kilyanyi starting with *1492* (1894); and a relaxation in American mores permitted FLORENZ ZIEGFELD, EARL CARROLL, and GEORGE WHITE in their REVUES to mass bevies of scantily clad beauties in slowly moving pageants.

Stage nudity was pictured in the early 20th century less as the high-minded, undraped DANCE innovations of Isadora Duncan and Ted Shawn than as the BURLESQUE SHOW. The striptease, a ritual wherein various garments are serially discarded, leaving the performer more or less undressed, evolved in France. Legend has it introduced to the U.S. by the trapeze artist Charmian, who accidentally lost her tights during her act; but it more likely made its entrance with Omeena's cooch dance at the St. Louis World's Fair (1896). By 1920 it had become a burlesque attraction offered by Millie de Leon, and was later perfected as a dance number by GYPSY ROSE LEE and ANN CORIO. The pasties that covered the nipples might be flung to the audience, but the *cache-sexe* or G-string usually stayed in place, and a blackout or fall of curtain would supervene. SALLY RAND's fan dance, first seen at the Chicago Exposition in 1933, became a byword for teasing nonrevelation. By the 1960s performers left nothing to the imagination, but a 1991 Supreme Court decision permits communities to ban nude dancing for reasons of "public morality."

The ALTERNATIVE THEATRE of the 1960s utilized nudity as a tactical weapon, a direct assault on middle-class sensibilities and an alignment with "Nature," though it was usually seen in semiprivate Happenings. Its *annus mirabilis* was 1967, when the rock musical *HAIR* displayed its unclad cast frontally; the LIVING THEATRE's players were arrested in San Francisco for disrobing ("We can't take off our clothes in public" became one of their opening plaints), and Sally Kirkland was the first New York actress to appear nude throughout an entire play, TERRENCE MCNALLY's *Sweet Eros.* (In contrast, McNally's *Love! Valour! Compassion!,* 1994, features much male nudity.) The commercial the-

atre was quick to adopt this licence in *OH! CAL-CUTTA!* (1969) whose company, male and female, shed its bathrobes in the first moments. Nudity soon turned into a token of stage realism (David Storey's *The Changing Room,* 1971, London; 1973, NYC) and a touchstone of gender identification (DAVID HENRY HWANG's *M. BUTTERFLY,* 1989). PERFORMANCE ARTISTS like KAREN FINLEY and TIM MILLER exaggerate and sometimes abuse the naked body for shock effect, to make political points about sexual exploitation; but the resurgence of CENSORSHIP and recent court decisions created a chilling climate that compelled actors for a time to put their clothes back on.

Still, full frontal nudity never left the stage during certain gay plays, such as Anthony Bruno's *Soul Survivor* (1987, NYC; 1989, SF), David Dillon's *Party* (1992, Chicago), and James Edwin Parker's *Two Boys in a Bed on a Cold Winter's Night* (1995, NYC), both to titillate and to express comfort with the male body. It also appears episodically in such homosexually themed plays as Neal Weaver's *Strip/Tease* (2002, LA) and RICHARD GREENBERG's *Take Me Out* (2002), and became the central attraction of the plays of Ronnie Larsen, produced to bring the audience in contact with male porn stars. *Naked Boys Singing!* (1998), a musical review devised to save LOS ANGELES's Celebration Theatre, was much revived and copied, most prominently by the annual *Broadway Bares* (begun 1990), in which legitimate chorus boys and girls bare their all to raise funds for Broadway Cares/Equity Fight AIDS. One of the strangest offshoots of this exhibitionism has been *Puppetry of the Penis* (1998, Australia; 2001, NYC), "the ancient Australian art of genital origami." Broadway and Off-Broadway in the past 15 years has seen approximately 25 plays with full frontal nudity, including even mainstream plays such as JON ROBIN BAITZ's *The Paris Letter* (2005) and Margaret Edson's *WIT* (1998) as well as partial nudity in Broadway's *The Blue Room* (1998) and *The Graduate* (2002). LS*

Nugent, Elliott (1896–1980) Playwright, actor, producer, and director. Nugent performed with his parents (J. C. and Grace Nugent) and on the KEITH–Orpheum VAUDEVILLE circuit before making his Broadway debut as Tom Sterrett in *DULCY* (1921). *Kempy* (1922), which he wrote and produced with his father, was his first success as a playwright. He is best remembered for *The MALE ANIMAL* (1940), which he wrote with James Thurber; for acting the role of Bill Page in *The Voice of the Turtle* (1943); for directing *Tomorrow the World* (1943); and for coproducing *The Seven Year Itch* (1952). TLM

Nugent, Nellie see McCann, Elizabeth

Nunsense This intimate over-the-top musical, the premise of which began as a line of greeting cards and then a club act in 1984, with music, lyrics, and book by Michigan native Dan Goggin, debuted Off-Broadway in 1985, winning an Outer Critics' Circle Award for Best Off-Broadway Musical, and another for Book and Music. Five Little Sisters of Hoboken put on a talent show to raise money to bury some members of the community accidentally poisoned by cook Sister Julia (Child of God). Since its premiere, it has been translated into 19 languages, played in more than 26 countries, and involved some 25,000 actresses. The New York production ran 10 years; a Philadelphia company lasted 9 and a Boston 8. Sequels in this industry have included *Nunsense 2: The Second Coming, Nunsense 3: The Jamboree, Nunsense A-Men!* (a drag version), *Nuncrackers: The Nunsense Christmas Musical, Meshuggah-Nuns: The Ecumenical Nunsense*, and the most recent, *Nunsensations: The Nunsense Vegas Revue* in 2005. A 20th century all-star tour in 2003–4 played 20 cities.   DBW

Nuyorican theatre Like Chicano theatre, a neologism referring to the Mexican American theatre in the Southwest and California, Nuyorican refers to the working-class Puerto Rican culture in New York City. It is frequently used by offsprings of Puerto Ricans who migrated to the city in large numbers during and after WWII. Some Puerto Rican artists and critics, however, contend that it is a pejorative term coined by native-born Puerto Ricans, with the implication that New York–born Puerto Rican theatre artists are viewed as Americanos by Puerto Ricans and as Puerto Ricans by white Americans. Since it is meant to denote and affirm an East Coast cultural breed divergent from that of the island of Puerto Rico as well as mainstream America, a less contentious term might be "Puerto Rican American theatre." Regardless, "Nuyorican" or "Neo-Rica" was first applied in 1964 to literature and theatre by Puerto Rican playwright/novelist Jaime Carrero, one of the members of the first group of literary and political rebels and intellectuals who freely and unselfconsciously defined a literary and artistic Puerto Rican flowering in New York brought about by the ethnic revivalism and civil rights movement.

Several important Puerto Rican playwrights lived in New York even before the term "Nuyorican" was created. Gonzalo O'Neill, Franca de Armiño, Manuel Méndez Ballester, Francisco Arrivi, and Rodríguez Suárez (who also founded the Nuevo Circulo Dramatico, which provided a training ground for actors and directors) are key figures in the estabishment of Puerto Rican presence in the New York theatre. Early street-theatre collectives (Teatro Orilla, Nuevo Teatro Pobre de America, Teatro Jurutungo, Teatro Guazabara, Teatro Cuatro) were bilingual, bicultural, and working class in socioeconomic orientation. Luis Rafael Sánchez (a k a Wico), whose greatest play is *La Guaracha del Macho Camacho* (*Macho Camacho's Beat*), is an early pioneer who explored the Americanization of Puerto Rican identity.

René Marqués is considered "the father of Puerto Rican drama" since the birth of Nuyorican theatre dates from 19 December 1966, the Off-Broadway opening of the English-language version of his most influential play, *The Oxcart* (*La caretta*, 1951), starring the acclaimed Mirian Colón opposite Raul Julia. The Spanish version of the play, produced by Puerto Rican playwright and director Roberto Rodríguez in 1954 at the Church of San Sebastian in Manhattan, had motivated Colón, who played Juanita in both productions, and Rodríguez to form the first Hispanic theatre group with its own 60-seat theatre, called El Circulo Dramatico. In 1967, Colón founded Puerto Rican Traveling Theatre, an important NYC nonprofit troupe, performing *The Oxcart* in English and Spanish in parks and playgrounds. A touring unit, playwrights' workshop, and performance space, this bilingual theatre company produced work of such authors as Federico Fraguada, who wrote *Bodega* (1986); Reuben Gonzalez, whose *The Boiler Room* was mounted in 1987; Eduardo Iván Lopéz (*Spanish Eyes*, 1990); and Richard V. Irizarry (*Ariano*, 1990).

Other troupes that stage Puerto Rican works are Shaman Theatre Repertory Company; Duo Theater (Spanish English Ensemble Theater); the Bronx-based Pregones Theater, founded in 1979; Puerto Rican Bilingual Workshop, founded by Carlos Pinza in 1973; the African Caribbean Poetry Theatre, headed since 1983 by the playwright Juan Shamsul Alam and his wife, Sandra Maria Estéves; ROSA (Ricans Organization for Self-Advancement); Teatro Moderno Puertorriqueño; as well as Intar, New Federal Theatre (which produced Ramiro Ramirez's salsa musical *Mondongo*), and Joseph Papp's New York Shakespeare Festival.

The center of Nuyorican theatrical expression remains New York's famed Nuyorican Poets' Café, founded in 1974 by the poet-playwright Miguel Algarin along with a group of artists including

MIGUEL PIÑERO. In exemplifying the experimental Lower East Side spirit of the Nuyorican scene, in conjunction with Joseph Papp and Raymond Barry of the OPEN THEATRE, the Café gave Nuyorican writing a folk-lyricist stamp through a cadre of poet-playwrights, such as the virtuoso bilingual poet Tato Laviera, Pedro Pietri, Lucky Cienfuegos, and Miguel Piñero. Cienfuegos and Piñero were ex-convicts who had begun their writing careers while incarcerated, and they chose to develop their dramatic material from prison, street, and underclass culture. Produced by Papp, Piñero's prison drama SHORT EYES displayed an astonishing brilliance in poeticizing the street language; it won the Obie and New York Drama Critics' Circle awards for Best American Play in 1973–4.

Today a large segment of Nuyorican theatre bears little or no root memories of the island, signaling a break from the mood of diaspora before 1979. The theatre of JOHN JESURUN verges on PERFORMANCE ART. The dramas (and musicals) of JOSÉ RIVERA, Edward Gallardo (*Simpson Street,* 1995, PRTT), Yolanda Rodriguez, Yvette Ramirez, and Migdalia Cruz represent a new generation of Nuyorican lyrical modes and styles, which attest to the continuing relevance and substantial place Puerto Rican drama now holds in the American tradition. Husband-and-wife playwrights Cándido Tirado and Carmen Rivera are cofounders of Latino Experimental Fantastic Theatre (LEFT), which in 1998–9 produced pieces about domestic abuse (*Betty's Garage*) and Latinas living with AIDS (*Positive Women*). NK RG

O

Oakley, Annie [née Phoebe Anne Oakley Mozee] (1860–1926) Sharpshooter, born in Ohio, where she developed her shooting skills hunting game. When almost 16 she competed with vaudevillian Frank Butler, defeating him by one point. Subsequently they married and she became the star of their act; he acted as assistant and business manager. In 1885 Oakley joined BUFFALO BILL CODY'S WILD WEST EXHIBITION, and for 17 years, with one brief interruption, she remained a chief attraction. Despite a paralyzing injury in a 1901 railroad wreck, she performed for two more decades. A legendary shot with shoulder and hand arms, Oakley was dubbed by her friend Sitting Bull "little sureshot." Her career was inspiration for the musical ANNIE GET YOUR GUN. Modern biographies have been written by Shirl Kasper (1992) and Glenda Riley (1994); a documentary was shown on PBS (2006). DBW

Oakley, Frank "Slivers" (?–1915) CIRCUS clown, considered during the first decade of this century the greatest of the solo pantoMIME jesters. For five minutes Oakley held BARNUM & Bailey audiences spellbound with his one-man pantomime baseball game, portraying 18 players, climaxed with a heated argument with an umpire, with Slivers in both roles. In 1905 he compared his circus outing to a "scrimmage against Yale." As circuses became larger and clowning more flamboyant, solo clowns became passé. Oakley's act was cut and his salary reduced from $750 weekly to $50. He quit in disgust and in 1915 committed suicide. DBW

O'Brien, Jack (George) (1939–) Artistic director of the OLD GLOBE THEATRE since 1981; recipient of the 2002 "Mr. Abbott" award for direction. Born in Michigan, educated at the University of Michigan, O'Brien taught at Hunter College before joining the ASSOCIATION OF PRODUCING ARTISTS (APA) as ELLIS RABB's assistant (1964–9). After several years of freelance work, he became associate director of JOHN HOUSEMAN's The ACTING COMPANY at the Juilliard School (1974–5). Directing credits include the Houston Grand Opera production of PORGY AND BESS (1976), *The Magic Flute* for the San Francisco Opera, STREET SCENE for the New York City Opera, *Mary Stuart* and *A Man for All Seasons* at the AHMANSON THEATRE, and several productions at the AMERICAN CONSERVATORY THEATRE. Television directing credits include *The Good Doctor* for PBS and various productions for *American Playhouse* (e.g., *Painting Churches*). O'Brien made his directing debut at the Old Globe with *The Comedy of Errors* (1969), and has directed more than 60 productions since, including a number of world premieres and productions that moved on to Broadway (dates shown), such as DAMN YANKEES (1994 revival), *The FULL MONTY* (2000), Nora Ephron's *Imaginary Friends* (2002), and *Dirty Rotten Scoundrels* (2005). He won major awards for his direction of *The Invention of Love* (Drama Desk, 2001), HAIRSPRAY (Tony and Drama Desk, 2003), and *Henry IV* (2003, LINCOLN CENTER; Tony and Drama Desk, 2004), and recently directed the epic trilogy *Coast of Utopia* (2006–7; Tony). JDM

Octoroon, The; or, Life in Louisiana A sensation melodrama by DION BOUCICAULT first performed at the WINTER GARDEN THEATRE in 1859 as a vehicle for him and his wife, Agnes Robertson. This adaptation of the novel *The Quadroon* centers on the sale of Zoe, a freed, "one-eighth" African American woman, back into slavery to pay the debts of respectable plantation owners in Louisiana. Although noncommittal on the divisive issue of the expansion of slavery, the play confirmed the racism of most of its northern audiences in its assumption that the "taint" of Negro blood rendered Zoe helpless and pitiable. Contributing to the play's success were a bowie-knife fight, the use of a camera onstage, MINSTREL-like scenes involving loyal "darkies," and the explosion of a steamboat, the sensational climax of the play. The initial production also featured JOSEPH JEFFERSON III as a sympathetic YANKEE who unmasks the villain. *The Octoroon* remained popular on northern and western stages into the 1890s. BAMcC

Odd Couple, The, by Neil Simon opened 10 March 1965 at the Plymouth Theatre, running 964 performances. The play followed Barefoot in the Park both chronologically and thematically. Newly separated, obsessively tidy Felix Ungar (Art Carney) and his slovenly poker friend Oscar Madison (Walter Matthau) become roommates and illustrate the impossibility of coexistence without compromise, carrying on Simon's concern for moderation. More significant, Simon attempts to avoid confining the theme to domestic behavior stereotypes by playing the theme out through two male characters. Even so, the characters still embody supposedly gendered traits, rather than a combination; Felix exhibits assumed feminine behavior, while Oscar caricatures the masculine. The characters' incompatibility is intended to be in terms of their inability to modify their habitual behavior, rather than in terms of gender conflict. A 1985 reprise of the play with a female cast (Rita Moreno played Olive Madison) ran 295 performances, suggesting the attempt to transcend gender roles was only partly successful. In 2005 Matthew Broderick (Felix) and Nathan Lane (Oscar) appeared in a revival with a $21 million advance, the largest in history for a straight play, yet Brantley termed the production (249 performances) "bland, mechanical." RW

Odell, George C[linton] **D**[ensmore] (1866–1949) Historian and educator, born in Newburgh, NY, and educated at Columbia where, in 1924, he succeeded Brander Matthews as Professor of Dramatic Literature. Between 1927 and 1949 he published his magisterial and still definitive Annals of the New York State (15 vols.; beginnings to mid-1894). Though less influential, his Shakespeare: From Betterton to Irving (1920, 2 vols.) also remains a standard work. DBW

Odets, Clifford (1906–63) In the entire sweep of American theatre history, Odets is the one true company playwright. In the early days of the Group Theatre, as he listened to Harold Clurman's orations and followed Lee Strasberg's formulations of the basic principles of Method acting, Odets was absorbing the elements of a theatrical style that erupted on 6 January 1935, when the Group presented Waiting for Lefty, his incendiary play about taxi drivers driven to call a strike. In a series of short, jabbing scenes and in language alive with the rhythms and inflections of urban folk idiom, Odets expressed the fury, passion, and sorrow of the dispossessed working class. With this play the Group discovered its voice: Lefty released the full potential of the new realistic acting style that its members had been investigating for four years.

Later in the same year the Group produced two other Odets plays, Awake and Sing! and Paradise Lost, family dramas whose contemporary but archetypal Jewish sufferers speak in a language of their own, a dense idiom of metaphor and incantatory repetition that alternates irony with exultation and brief, stabbing sentences with longer speeches of operatic intensity. When Odets left for Hollywood at the end of his triumphant year, his Group colleagues felt betrayed. As if in compensation, Odets presented them with a new play, Golden Boy (1937). In it, his hero's hard choice between being a violinist and a prizefighter expresses Odets's own conflict about whether to serve art or commerce. Though this central premise is spurious, the play proved to be the Group's biggest moneymaker. Odets's final works for the Group, Rocket to the Moon (1938) and Night Music (1940), are diminished in their thematic scope and vitality. By 1940, when the Group itself had lost its focus, Odets had also apparently reached a creative impasse. Despite their ripe language and strong conflict, Odets's four remaining dramas – Clash by Night (1941), The Big Knife (1949), The Country Girl (1950), and The Flowering Peach (1954) – don't have the same sense of occasion as even the least of the Group efforts. To accomplish his most vibrant work Odets seemed to require a Depression background; he is now regarded as the quintessential 1930s playwright, who transmuted working-class pressures into timeless theatrical eloquence. His life to 1940 was well recounted by Margaret Brenman-Gibson (1981) FH

Oenslager, Donald (1902–75) Set designer and educator. His influences include George Pierce Baker; the work of Appia and Craig, which he saw in Europe in 1921; and Robert Edmond Jones, whom he assisted in the early 1920s. Oenslager designed some 250 productions, including Anything Goes, You Can't Take It with You, and The Man Who Came to Dinner. Though he emphasized the need to find the proper style for each play, his designs were frequently decorative and elegant. His greatest contribution, however, was as a teacher: He was a professor of design at Yale University for nearly 50 years (1925–71), and many of the major figures in American design were trained by him. He is the author of Scenery Then and Now (1936) and Stage Design: Four Centuries of Scenic Invention (1975), the latter illustrated with drawings from his extensive private collection; a collection of his own designs was published in 1978.   AA

Of Mice and Men by JOHN STEINBECK opened 23 November 1937 in New York, running for 207 performances. The cast included Broderick Crawford as Lennie, a mentally retarded man of tremendous physical strength; Wallace Ford as George, who travels with him and looks out for him; Sam Byrd as Curley, the mean-spirited son of the owner (Thomas Findlay) of the ranch where they find work; Claire Luce as Curley's wife, whom Lennie kills in a moment of panic; and WILL GEER, John F. Hamilton, Charles Slattery, Walter Baldwin, and Leigh Whipper as the other cowboys. An adaptation of Steinbeck's novella, the play depicts the relationship between Lennie and George, which is based on a human need for companionship. Their dream of a ranch of their own sustains them until the reality of sex intrudes on their private world in the person of Candy's wife, and Lennie destroys her, leaving George no choice but to destroy Lennie. It is frequently revived, including a 1974 Broadway staging with KEVIN CONWAY and JAMES EARL JONES, STEPPENWOLF'S with GARY SINISE and JOHN MALKOVICH (1981), and a 2003 British production that toured the U.K.   BCM

Of Thee I Sing Musical comedy by GEORGE S. KAUFMAN and MORRIE RYSKIND, with music and lyrics (repectively) by GEORGE AND IRA GERSHWIN; directed by Kaufman, it opened on Broadway 26 December 1931 and ran 441 performances. Awarded the Pulitzer Prize for Drama in 1932 (the first musical so honored), *Of Thee I Sing* was the first American musical to be published (Knopf, 1932). In this political burlesque, John P. Wintergreen (WILLIAM GAXTON) runs for president on a platform of love, first vowing to woo the winner of a beauty contest, but instead falling for Mary, an "ordinary" girl who bakes corn muffins without corn (pun and absurdity intended). The beauty queen, who is of French extraction, enlists the advocacy of the French ambassador, and Wintergreen escapes impeachment only because Mary gives birth to twins. VICTOR MOORE played the vice president, Alexander Throttlebottom, whose presence and name is virtually unknown. It was the final concert production for CITY CENTER'S *ENCORES!* in the 2005–6 season.   JDM

Off-Broadway The term, coined in the 1950s, for both NYC productions and theatres outside the so-called Broadway area surrounding Times Square – including several houses along THEATRE Row – and for an ACTORS' EQUITY ASSOCIATION contract for theatres with 100–299 seats. (Other unions adopted Equity's designation.) Critic Stuart W. Little notes, however, that "Off-Broadway is a state of mind . . . a way of looking at theater at every point at odds with Broadway's patterns."

Off-Broadway began in the early 1900s as the "Little Theatre movement" (see COMMUNITY THEATRE). Offering artistically significant plays in an inexpensive, noncommercial atmosphere, groups such as the WASHINGTON SQUARE PLAYERS and the PROVINCETOWN PLAYERS staged, in small, out-of-the-way theatres, plays Broadway ignored. Other companies included the NEIGHBORHOOD PLAYHOUSE, Cherry Lane Theatre, CIVIC REPERTORY COMPANY, and GROUP THEATRE. Many were not only experimental but amateur as well, lasting only a few years before falling victim to their own success as artists parlayed triumphs into jobs in commercial theatre and, later, Hollywood. After WWII, however, Off-Broadway attracted critical attention. Several successes transferred to Broadway, beginning with New Stages's production of Sartre's *The Respectful Prostitute* (1948).

In the 1950s and early '60s, several companies had an impact on American theatre. With untried, noncommercial, or experimental plays or productions, using then-unknown talent and shoestring budgets, Off-Broadway became an artistic magnet. Serious attention started with the 1952 revival of TENNESSEE WILLIAMS'S *SUMMER AND SMOKE,* launching the careers of JOSÉ QUINTERO and GERALDINE PAGE. Such companies as the LIVING THEATRE, Phoenix Theatre (see ASSOCIATION OF PRODUCING ARTISTS), NEW YORK SHAKESPEARE FESTIVAL, AMERICAN PLACE THEATRE, NEGRO ENSEMBLE COMPANY, ROUNDABOUT THEATRE COMPANY, CHELSEA THEATRE CENTER, CIRCLE REPERTORY, and MANHATTAN THEATRE CLUB presented failed commercial or neglected plays. Over the years, a split developed between commerical Off-Broadway houses such as the Astor Place, LUCILLE LORTEL, ORPHEUM, Westside Arts, Perry Street, Promenade, Minetta Lane, and Criterion Center – represented by the League of Off-Broadway Theatres and Producers – and nonprofit companies such as the WPA, JEWISH REPERTORY, PAN ASIAN REPERTORY THEATRE, BROOKLYN ACADEMY OF MUSIC, RIDICULOUS THEATRICAL COMPANY, Hudson Guild, LINCOLN CENTER THEATRE COMPANY, SECOND STAGE, and NEGRO ENSEMBLE COMPANY that also fostered new works and U.S. productions of European plays. Mostly, however, real experimental and avant-garde theatre has moved from Off- to OFF-OFF BROADWAY.

Off-Broadway theatres have presented such works as Beckett's *Endgame*, ALBEE's *The Zoo Story*, Gelber's *The Connection*, Jones and Schmidt's *The Fantasticks*, Genet's *The Blacks*, Orton's *What the Butler Saw*, Pomerance's *The Elephant Man*, FULLER's *A Soldier's Play*, Churchill's *Cloud 9*, UHRY's *Driving Miss Daisy*, BENNETT's *A Chorus Line*, Brook's *Mahabharata*, FUGARD's *The Road to Mecca*, Harling's *Steel Magnolias*, HENLEY's *Crimes of the Heart*, SHUE's *The Foreigner*, FIERSTEIN's *Torchsong Trilogy*, and Ashman and Menken's *Little Shop of Horrors*, to name a few. Other writers have included KOPIT, SCHISGAL, BARAKA, VAN ITALLIE, LANFORD WILSON, GUARE, BULLINS, Vonnegut, RABE, MAMET, ZINDEL, INNAURATO, BOGOSIAN, DURANG, FORNÉS, GURNEY, HWANG, KRAMER, SHEPARD, WASSERSTEIN, ROBERT WILSON, LaBUTE, Amy Freed, REBECCA GILMAN, GREENSPAN, IVES, LETTS, LINDSAY-ABAIRE, MARGULIES, VOGEL, and NOTTAGE, et al.

The talent in these productions included some of the country's more adventurous directors, such as BOGART, Quintero, SCHNEIDER, Grotowski, O'HORGAN, SERBAN, ZAKS, and GROSBARD. Off-Broadway is frequently a place for established actors to try unfamiliar roles, including that of director. From the 1980s forward, as Broadway productivity has shrunk, Off-Broadway, along with Off-Off Broadway, has produced an ever-increasing number of NYC productions, especially those of a serious or experimental nature. In 1955, the *Village Voice* established the Obie Awards to recognize accomplishments in this arena. The Lucille Lortel Awards are also given for excellence Off-Broadway.   REK

Off-Off Broadway The term coined in the early 1960s to distinguish professional, commercial theatre (Broadway and OFF-BROADWAY) from noncommercial theatre presented in coffeehouses, churches, lofts, and storefronts in New York's Greenwich Village and Lower East Side. Technically, the term also refers to productions that fall under ACTORS' EQUITY Tiered Non-Profit Theatre Code for performances with limited runs that feature unsalaried union actors in noncontractual theatres of not more than 100 seats.

Often perceived as a movement, Off-Off Broadway has encompassed a wide spectrum of theatrical activity so diverse in impulse, conception, method, and intent that no common objective characterizes it. Off-Off Broadway has spawned works of numerous types and terms to go with them: experimental, avant-garde, COLLECTIVE, ALTERNATIVE, environmental, radical, guerilla, and Theatre of Images (see INTRODUCTION, §4).

Off-Off Broadway is usually considered an alternative theatre grounded in exploration and experimentation, and questioning the limits of performance. The initial impulse was to generate new approaches and methods in a climate free from the demands of popular taste that inform commercial theatre artistically and economically. Frequently, though, Off-Off Broadway productions increasingly mirror commercial theatre values and standards.

CAFFE CINO became the first Off-Off Broadway theatre when Joe Cino began to present plays in his one-room coffeehouse in 1959. By 1965 there were several small producing organizations; the major ones include JUDSON POETS' THEATRE, formed in 1961 by Al Carmines; Café LA MAMA, founded by ELLEN STEWART in 1962; and Theatre Genesis, founded in 1964 by Ralph Cook. Devoted primarily to producing work of new American playwrights, these houses mounted plays by writers like JULIE BOVASSO, ED BULLINS, ROSALYN DREXLER, Tom Eyen, MARIA IRENE FORNÉS, Paul Foster, ISRAEL HOROWITZ, ADRIENNE KENNEDY, H. M. Koutoukas, Ruth Krauss, CHARLES LUDLAM, TERRENCE MCNALLY, Leonard Melfi, ROCHELLE OWENS, SAM SHEPARD, Ronald Tavel, MEGAN TERRY, John Vaccaro, JEAN-CLAUDE VAN ITALLIE, Jeff Weiss, and LANFORD WILSON.

The term quickly expanded to include a new breed of theatrical work as Off-Off Broadway spawned a visually oriented, nonlinear, nonnarrative – some might even say, nondramatic – type of performance by such companies as the WOOSTER GROUP, Manhattan Project (see ANDRE GREGORY), MABOU MINES, RIDICULOUS THEATRICAL COMPANY, and SPLIT BRITCHES, and by individual artists who mounted their own productions, like MEREDITH MONK, RICHARD FOREMAN, and ROBERT WILSON.

In the 1980s and '90s, as theatrical techniques once associated with Off-Off became commonplace in commercial Broadway venues (e.g., the autobiographical and spare nature of *A Chorus Line*, the cross-dressing theme in DAVID HENRY HWANG's *M. Butterfly*, or the postmodern mixing of stage and filmic perspectives in the musical *City of Angels*), the boundaries among Broadway, Off-Broadway, and Off-Off Broadway became more and more slippery.

Off-Off still, however, evokes experimental or alternative theatre. That rubric has expanded to include not only the collectives and performance spectacles that developed in the 1970s, but also the explosion in the late '80s of PERFORMANCE ART – small-scale pieces, often combining abstract movement or visual elements with nonlinear, often autobiographical text, usually performed by its author (e.g., SPALDING GRAY, HOLLY HUGHES, ERIC BOGOSIAN, KAREN FINLEY, and Robbie McCauley). In 2004, an excellent account by Stephen Bottoms of the early years of Off-Off Broadway was published.   AS

Oh! Calcutta! A musical REVUE of erotica (skits, song, dance) devised by KENNETH TYNAN, and conceived and directed by Jacques Levy, with contributions by Samuel Beckett, JULES FEIFFER, John Lennon, Leonard Melfi, and SAM SHEPARD, among others. It opened OFF-BROADWAY at the Eden Theatre (17 June 1969), running for 704 performances before transferring to Broadway's BELASCO THEATRE (25 February 1971) for 610 performances. Due to its extensive NUDITY and blatant sexual content, the show achieved notoriety, prompting nationwide debates about the issue of CENSORSHIP. Musical numbers include "Was It Good for You Too?" and "Coming Together, Going Together." Revived on 24 September 1976 at the Edison Theatre for 5,959 performances, *Oh! Calcutta!* closed on 6 August 1989.   EK

Oh Dad, Poor Dad, Mamma's Hung You in the Closet and I'm Feein' So Sad by ARTHUR KOPIT opened at the Phoenix Theatre in New York on 26 February 1962, running for 454 performances. The cast included Jo Van Fleet as Madame Rosepettle, AUSTIN PENDLETON as her son, Jonathan, and Barbara Harris as Rosalie. The play opened on Broadway on 27 August 1963, running for 47 performances. An absurdist treatment of the destructive effect of the castrating woman and domineering mother, the play depicts Madame Rosepettle's bullying of her son, whose dead father she has had stuffed and takes along on her travels.   BCM

O'Horgan, Tom (Thomas Foster) (1926?–) Avant-garde composer and director who describes his work as "theatrical disobedience." O'Horgan is most famous for *HAIR* (Drama Desk Award), a NEW YORK SHAKESPEARE FESTIVAL workshop that moved to Broadway in 1968. He also staged ROCHELLE OWENS's *Futz* (1967–8, Obie; film, 1969; revival, 1991), Paul Foster's *Tom Paine* (1967–8), Julian Barry's *Lenny* (1971; Drama Desk), *Jesus Christ Superstar* (1971), and Arrabal's *The Architect and the Emperor of Assyria* (1976) – the Off-Broadway plays originating at LA MAMA. He directed the film *Rhinoceros* (1974), and "The Eighth Wonder," the Brooklyn Bridge centenary sound-and-light show. His productions favor contact and confrontation with the audience, and "emphasized the physical . . . side of performance."   REK

Oklahoma! The first Broadway collaboration between RICHARD RODGERS (music) and OSCAR HAMMERSTEIN II (book and lyrics), based on LYNN RIGGS's play *Green Grow the Lilacs;* opened 31 March 1943 (2,212 performances). The musical's nostalgic story of farmers and cowmen in the 1907 Oklahoma Territory, acclaimed for its innovations, touched wartime theatregoers. Its main plot – a rather melodramatic love story in which the romance of a cowboy, Curly, and a farm girl, Laurey, is threatened by the machinations of a villainous farmhand, Jud – was brightened by a cast filled with talented, largely unknown performers, such as ALFRED DRAKE (Curly), Joan Roberts (Laurey), and CELESTE HOLM (the man-crazy Ado Annie of the subplot), along with HOWARD DA SILVA (Jud) and JOSEPH BULOFF (Ali Hakim). Rodgers and Hammerstein's rich score was filled with charming love songs and playful comic numbers. *Oklahoma!,* with its onstage death (Curly kills Jud in self-defense), brought a new seriousness to the musical stage, but its major innovation lay in the extent to which dance was employed to advance the plot and express latent emotion. AGNES DE MILLE's choreography – particularly in the "Dream Ballet" in which Laurey's repressed fears of Jud were given colorful and menacing life onstage – established dance, and particularly the idiom of modern dance, as an important feature of musical comedy. A road company toured for over a decade; revivals were staged in 1951, 1969, 1979, and 2002; films were made in 1955 and (for TV) 1999.   MK

Olcott, Chauncey [né Chancellor John] (1860–1932) Singer-actor who, after beginning in MINSTREL SHOWS, appeared in comic operas with LILLIAN RUSSELL. Following the death of W. J. Scanlan, American-born Olcott was the most popular "Irish" tenor on the musical stage. For decades he starred in idealized musicals of Irish life, such as *The Irish Artist* (1894) and *A Romance of Athlone* (1899). Olcott introduced a number of his songs, notably "When Irish Eyes are Smiling." A biography by Rita Olcott was published in 1939.   MK

Old Globe Theatre opened 29 May 1935 in San Diego as a temporary so-called replica of the original Globe and one of the attractions at the 1935–6 California Pacific International Exposition. A group of citizens raised $10,000 to remodel the theatre in order to prevent its postexposition demolition, and the San Diego Community Theatre was chartered 3 February 1937; in 1958, the name was changed to the Old Globe to conform to popular usage. Craig Noel, who had acted and directed with the company since 1937, became artistic director in 1947. The company joined with San Diego State College to present summer productions of Shakespeare (1949–52), then took the name of the San Diego National Shakespeare Festival (1954) and began hiring Equity actors (1959). Noel began producing plays at the Falstaff Tavern (1963), and the space was remodeled to become the 225-seat Cassius Carter Centre Stage (1969). An arsonist's FIRE destroyed the Old Globe on 8 March 1978; the board raised $6.5 million in 20 months to rebuild it. In January 1981, Noel became executive producer; JACK O'BRIEN, who was named artistic director, has since transferred a number of shows to Broadway. The rebuilt 581-seat Old Globe Theatre opened on 14 January 1982, part of a three-theatre complex named the Simon Edison Centre for the Performing Arts. The company received a special Regional Theatre Tony Award (1984). Another arson destroyed the Festival Stage (29 October 1984); in its place the 612-seat outdoor Lowell Davies Festival Theatre opened on 7 June 1985. Today there are three venues offering 14 productions each year and nearly 600 performances. Productions range from Shakespeare to world premieres.   JDM

Old Homestead, The DENMAN THOMPSON's sentimental tribute to rural American values opened 5 April 1886 at the BOSTON MUSEUM. It was the singular creation of Thompson, who conceived, wrote, and acted it. Thompson first performed a shorter version in 1875, which he extended in 1877 and then, with George Ryer, revised again for the 1886 production. He enacted the central role of Yankee farmer Joshua through 1910. With his homespun philosophy and local color jokes, Joshua represented a late 19th-century updating of the traditional YANKEE character. In the play, Joshua journeys to New York to find his son, Reuben, who fled after being accused of a crime. The action provides ample opportunity for humorous comments on New England speech and customs as well as contrasts between city and country living. Swanzey (Center), the New Hampshire town that inspired Thompson's play, has staged it every summer for 66 years (as of 2007).   RAH

Old Maid, The Dramatization by ZOË AKINS of Edith Wharton's novel, opened at the EMPIRE THEATRE on 7 January 1935 for a run of 305 performances. Although critics considered it too sentimental, audiences, particulary the women in the matinee crowd, loved its theme of the maternal instinct. The story tells of the sacrifice made by two cousins for the sake of respectability: Delia

(JUDITH ANDERSON) by marrying a properly rich man, and Charlotte (Helen Menken) by denying her illegitimate daughter and allowing Delia to adopt her. When the play was awarded the 1935 Pulitzer Prize, the critics were so enraged at the exclusion of other superior plays – particularly LILLIAN HELLMAN's The CHILDREN'S HOUR – that they formed their own group to award the Drama Critics' Circle Award.   FB

Oldmixon, Mrs. John [née Georgina George] (?–1835) Recruited by THOMAS WIGNELL in 1793 for Philadelphia's CHESTNUT STREET THEATRE company, this British-born actress-singer made her U.S. debut on 14 May 1794 as Clorinda in Robin Hood. In 1798 she joined DUNLAP's company in New York. She continued to perform intermittently until 1813, giving occasional concerts in PHILADELPHIA after that date. Although never a major star in England, she was considered the most accomplished early vocalist in America, and excelled as a comic actress.   DBW

Oliver, Edith (1913–98) Drama critic who, after attending Smith College (1931–3) and studying acting privately, pursued a career in radio (1937–52), acting on programs like True Detective and Philip Morris Playhouse, and writing and producing quiz shows such as The 64 Dollar Question. In 1948 she joined the staff of the New Yorker and became OFF-BROADWAY reviewer in 1961 and senior critic in 1986, retiring in the early 1990s. Attuned to the American avant-garde, she discovered and introduced important young talent to a national audience. In 1998 the Edith Oliver Award for Sustained Excellence Off-Broadway was established in her honor.   TLM

Olsen, (John Siguard) "Ole" (1892–1963) and **(Harold Ogden) "Chick" Johnson** (1891–1962) Comedy team. Infamous for "gonk" ("hokum with raisins," their unique blend of slapstick), Olsen and Johnson, each with a zany character, played VAUDEVILLE in the U.S., England, and Australia beginning in 1915; by the 1930s they were well known onstage and in forgettable films. In 1938 they brought their mayhem to the critically damned but enormously popular and ultimate-in-comic-vaudeville-style REVUE, HELLZAPOPPIN. The balance of their career was spent trying, with limited success, to recycle this hit in four subsequent revues and a 1941 film version of the first.   DBW

Olympia, The (music hall and theatre) Broadway between 44th and 45th Sts., NYC [Architect: J. B. McElfatrick and Co.]. OSCAR HAMMERSTEIN I officially launched the new theatre district at Longacre (Times) Square with the opening of the Olympia in 1895, an entertainment center that was to include three theatres, a roof garden, billiard rooms, a bowling alley, a turkish bath, and restaurants for one admission. He completed only two theatres, which he lost to creditors within three years. His Music Hall became the New York Theatre for VAUDEVILLE, and CHARLES FROHMAN changed the Lyric to the Criterion for legitimate fare. Under KLAW and ERLANGER, the roof garden eventually became the Jardin de Paris, where the prototype of FLORENZ ZIEGFELD's *Follies* was presented in 1907. The theatres quickly succumbed to films and were razed in 1935.   MCH

Omaha Magic Theatre Founded in 1968 by Jo Ann Schmidman, the OMT has created and presented well over 100 new American music-theatre plays and PERFORMANCE ART events in its storefront theatres in downtown Omaha. Its mission has been to "push the boundaries of what has previously been recognized as theatre to new limits . . . to present the freshest text, directorial performer, and visual art images and clearest musical voice in an integrated performance form." A founding member of JOSEPH CHAIKIN's OPEN THEATRE, MEGAN TERRY, joined OMT as resident playwright in 1974 and, together with Schmidman, brought national recognition and major grants to this Midwest theatre. Although closed in the late 1990s and early 2000s, the OMT in 2005–6 has a company of 25 performers, designers, and musicians focused on "creating contemporary performance art . . . from a fashion, poetry, photography, and visual art base." Works created in the season included *Exposures*, *Video Reaction*, and *Erotic Artshow*.   TLM

On the Town Musical comedy with books and lyrics by BETTY COMDEN AND ADOLPH GREEN, and music by LEONARD BERNSTEIN, based on an idea by JEROME ROBBINS; opened at the Adelphi Theatre on 28 December 1944. Staged by GEORGE ABBOTT with choreography by Robbins, it ran for 463 performances, featuring Sono Osato, both Comden and Green, and Nancy Walker. In two acts and 17 scenes, New York is viewed through three sailors on shore leave. When sailor Gabey (John Battles) sees a picture in the subway of "Miss Turnstiles" (Osato), he falls in love with her. His two buddies help him search for her in Central Park, Carnegie Hall, and Coney Island. *On the Town*'s themes of patriotism and nationalism proved extremely popular on the American stage in the midst of WWII. A film version (1949) starred

Gene Kelly and Frank Sinatra. Comden and Green went on to write many film musicals, including *Singin' in the Rain* (1952 film; 1985 musical). A disappointing revival directed by GEORGE C. WOLFE in 1998 lasted only 69 performances.   ER

On the Verge; or, The Geography of Learning The premiere production of ERIC OVERMYER's play (8 January 1985) at Baltimore's CENTER STAGE was directed by Jackson Phippin, with set design by TONY STRAIGES, costumes by Del Risberg, and music by Paul Sullivan. Stan Wojewodski, former artistic director of Center Stage, chose *Verge* as his opening production as head of the YALE REPERTORY (1991) after stagings in regional theatres throughout the U.S. in the 1980s. In a linguistically rich, magical tour of the comic imagination, three time-traveling Victorian women venture "forward, into the future" – assisted by will, intelligence, passion, confidence, courage, and "plot thickener" – from 1888 to 1955, when they reach the pinnacle of the future, "Paradise 55."   GSA

On Your Toes Two-act musical comedy, music by RICHARD RODGERS, lyrics by LORENZ HART, book by Rodgers, Hart, and GEORGE ABBOTT; opened 11 April 1936 at the IMPERIAL THEATRE, running 315 performances. The chronicle of a former VAUDEVILLE hoofer (RAY BOLGER), now a WPA music teacher, who convinces a Russian ballet company to produce his "jazz ballet," it was a milestone in music-theatre history for its integration of dance into musical comedy. Choreographer GEORGE BALANCHINE, in his first Broadway "book musical," staged two lengthy ballet sequences, both vitally integral to the story. The first-act "Princess Zenobia" was a burlesque of classical ballet, but the jazzy second-act "Slaughter on Tenth Avenue" served as the climactic moment of the plot and has had continued life as a concert piece. The rest of the score provided several standards, notably "There's a Small Hotel." The show has been revived on Broadway twice, most recently in a 1983 production supervised by Abbott and DONALD SADLER, which ran 505 performances and won a Best Revival Tony.   JD

Once in a Lifetime Comedy by MOSS HART and GEORGE S. KAUFMAN; directed by Kaufman, opened on Broadway 24 September 1930 and ran 406 performances. Hart wrote the first version, then Kaufman agreed to collaborate on the revision. The play concerns three young vaudevillians who hear that "talkies" are changing Hollywood and head West in search of fame and fortune.

The only one to succeed is George, an ingenuous innocent whose blunders become master strokes through sheer luck and the inexplicable lunacy of the film industry. Kaufman played the role of Larry Vail, a New York playwright, who comes to Hollywood as a screenwriter, suffers from the studio's neglect, and finally breaks down from underwork; Hart took over the role 4 May 1931.

JDM

O'Neal, Frederick (1905–92) AFRICAN AMERICAN actor and theatre administrator. O'Neal performed in St. Louis and organized the IRA ALDRIDGE Players before moving to NYC, where he attended the New Theatre School in 1936–40. With Abram Hill he founded the AMERICAN NEGRO THEATRE (1940–50), and in 1944 he played Frank (Clarence Derwent Award) in its Broadway production of ANNA LUCASTA. Subsequently he performed a variety of roles on and OFF-BROADWAY (TAKE A GIANT STEP, 1953; LOST IN THE STARS, 1958 revival, City Center), on television, and in films. O'Neal held several important positions, such as president of the Negro Actors Guild (1961–4) and of ACTORS' EQUITY ASSOCIATION (1964–73). His many awards testified to his achievements as actor and leader in the theatrical profession. In 1996 R. A. Simmons published a biography.   EGH

O'Neil, Nance (1874–1965) Actress who joined the ARTHUR MCKEE RANKIN company in San Francisco in 1893. Rankin soon built her into a star, booking her into several national tours, and in 1900 sponsored her world tour of *Magda, Fedora, La Tosca,* and *Camille.* In 1903 she added IBSEN'S *Lady Inger of Ostrat* to her repertoire and played it in San Francisco and Boston. Two years later she began performing *Hedda Gabler* and eventually took it to New York. Billed as the great tragedienne, she was usually considered to stand in the shadow of other great emotional actresses.   RAS

O'Neill, Eugene (Gladstone) (1888–1953) The first American playwright of major talent, the only one ever to win the Nobel Prize for Literature (in 1936), and still universally regarded as one of America's finest. Also, having written his autobiography not only in LONG DAY'S JOURNEY INTO NIGHT but also piecemeal, under less or greater disguise, in most of his works, he is among the most subjective of dramatists. Probably only August Strindberg, whom he called his mentor, was as obsessed with his own life and family history. The son of actor JAMES O'NEILL, Eugene used to deride the sentimental and melodramatic theatre of his father's day, yet he stood on his father's shoulders in attaining his preeminent position. Immersed in a theatrical milieu from birth, he unconsciously absorbed, as though by osmosis, the basics of stagecraft and playwriting. In youth and early manhood, however, there was virtually no indication that he would ever, in any field, amount to much: It appeared, rather, that he, like his self-destructive older brother, Jamie, would become a hard-drinking wastrel.

Perhaps the key to understanding him is that he suffered from lifelong feelings of guilt, born apparently of the fact that his mother, a shy, devout Catholic, innocently became a drug addict as a result of his birth. Recalling how wretched he felt on learning of her morphinism and of his role in her downfall, he says through his counterpart in *Long Day's Journey:* "God, it made everything in life seem rotten!" Turning against his ancestral faith, the apostate began to question all orthodoxies, all authority. Despite his familiarity with the ancient Greeks and Shakespeare, his sense of tragedy grew from his own life, not from the classics. He was an emotional hemophiliac whose family-inflicted wounds never healed. Here, then, we find the original of his sombre outlook on life, the major source of the power and anguish pounding throughout his writings.

After an unimpressive record at Catholic and secular schools, he sought the lower depths, intent on experiencing "real life." He went to sea, drifted on the waterfronts of Buenos Aires and New York, and once became so depressed that he attempted suicide. O'Neill often said that he never thought of being a writer till his health broke down, in his midtwenties, confining him to a TB sanatorium for months. While recuperating, he "really thought" about his life for the first time and resolved to become a playwright. After his recovery in 1913, plays began to pour out of him, most of them tales of the sea and of the underside of life; what, in other words, had seemed misspent years, proved to be a major part of his working capital as a writer.

In a move beneficial to both parties, Eugene in 1916 joined a group of amateur playmakers on Cape Cod, who became known as the PROVINCETOWN PLAYERS on moving to Greenwich Village, with O'Neill as their most imaginative and gifted writer. When he made his Broadway full-length debut in 1920 with BEYOND THE HORIZON (written in 1918), a story of defeat on a farm with the sea beckoning in the background, most of the critics, though faced with something novel in their experience – an American tragedy – were enthusiastic; but several complained that the play was too long, while another criticized its many changes of scene. The harsher critics failed to realize that the author, who eventually would ignore most stage conventions, was determined to hack out his own course. The play enjoyed a good run for so somber a work and won for O'Neill the first of his four Pulitzer Prizes. The others were for ANNA CHRISTIE (1920), STRANGE INTERLUDE (1926–7), and Long Day's Journey into Night (1939–41) [all dates = of writing].

A veritable Proteus of the drama, O'Neill kept changing his style. Starting as a realist, with occasional returns to the genre, he also wrote expressionistic works (The EMPEROR JONES, 1920; The HAIRY APE, 1921), costume drama (The Fountain, 1921–2; Marco Millions, 1923–5), Strindbergian views of marriage (Welded, 1922–3), biblical fables (Lazarus Laughed, 1925–6) and even a comedy (AH, WILDERNESS!, 1932). As though set on avenging his father's bondage to plays pandering to popular taste, he made demands on his audiences with extralong works, namely Strange Interlude, nine acts; MOURNING BECOMES ELECTRA (1929–31), a trilogy in 13 acts; and The ICEMAN COMETH (1939), twice the standard length. He also, testing what the public would accept, writing The GREAT GOD BROWN (1925), a bewildering work in which the characters constantly mask and unmask; ALL GOD'S CHILLUN GOT WINGS (1923), a poignant story ahead of its day about a white girl married to a black; and DESIRE UNDER THE ELMS (1924), a drama of greed, incest, and infanticide. In writing some 30 long works and nearly a score of short ones in so many different styles, O'Neill almost exhausted the stage's nonverbal resources through his use of song, pantoMIME, dance, masks, imaginative scenic devices, and novel sound effects. In the end, though, after all his imaginative flights, realism proved his forte, as was demonstrated by The Iceman Cometh and Long Day's Journey into Night, his masterpieces.

In the 1930s he worked for years on his most ambitious project, a cycle entitled A Tale of Possessors Self-Dispossessed that would span a large part of the American past in dramatizing highlights in the history, generation after generation, of a "far from model" family. In the work, first envisioned as five plays (then 7, next 9, and, for a time, 11), O'Neill aimed to show that materialism and greed had corrupted America. Unfortunately, a number of factors, particularly ill health and his despair as WWII loomed, prevented him from achieving his goal. After he had destroyed most of his cycle writings, all that survived was one finished play, A TOUCH OF THE POET (1935–42), and, by chance, a rough draft of another, More Stately Mansions (1935–40), which was staged posthumously (1967) in truncated form.   LSh

[Ed. note: In 2000 Arthur and Barbara Gelb published a new version of an earlier biography (covering early years); but the late Louis Sheaffer's two-volume life remains standard (1968, 1973).]

O'Neill, James (1846–1920) Irish-born actor. Despite his great popularity in the late 19th century, he is primarily remembered today as the father of EUGENE O'NEILL. For a time, appearing opposite such stars as CHARLOTTE CUSHMAN, ADELAIDE NEILSON, and EDWIN BOOTH, it seemed that he would attain similar stature, that he would become Booth's successor. His promise faded, however, particularly after he had, as his son said, "the good bad luck" to find a gold mine in CHARLES FECHTER's dramatization of Dumas's The COUNT OF MONTE CRISTO. Initially O'Neill, who had suffered a hungry childhood, rejoiced in his prosperity as the Dumas hero, but as the decades piled up and the audiences flocked to see him only when he played Edmond Dantès, the role became a straitjacket that gradually diminished his talent. Fragments of his history are woven into his son's devastating family portrait, LONG DAY'S JOURNEY INTO NIGHT.   LSh

one-person performance Though the phenomenon of one-person telling or acting out a story to a group is obviously spread widely through space and time, and despite the fact that certain 18th-century British satirical performers are immediate predecessors of solo artists in the U.S., the form, with its emphasis on the self-sufficient individual, seems especially suited to the American psyche. One-person performance has flourished in this country since the mid-19th century, and is much in vogue today.

Well into the 20th century much of the popularity of solo performance in American resulted from the theatre's disrepute, grounded in puritan prejudice. Many too proper to attend the theatre turned out for "platform performances" by a renowned actor or writer. Charles Dickens put on the 19th century's most successful one-man shows; those of Mark Twain were also popular throughout the English-speaking world. The appeal of these events derived from the celebrity of the performers, which in turn came from the power of their prose. When in the 1950s the contemporary renaissance of one-person performance was launched by HAL HOLBROOK as Twain and Emlyn Williams as Dickens, the drawing power of this well-loved material was again confirmed.

The tradition of leading actors (John Gielgud, Ian McKellen, BRIAN BEDFORD) performing solo recitals of Shakespeare also shows the pull of great literary content. Biographical shows, rather frequent in the American theatre since the 1950s, are often about writers, whose work as well as lives can be used, and they frequently base their hopes for success on the double celebrity of subject and star performer – JULIE HARRIS as Emily Dickinson and Isak Dinesen, James Whitmore as WILL ROGERS, ZOE CALDWELL as LILLIAN HELLMAN, JOHN CULLUM as Carl Sandberg, IRENE WORTH as Edith Wharton. Nonliterary biographical shows have included HENRY FONDA as Clarence Darrow, JAMES EARL JONES as PAUL ROBESON, and the late Randy Allen as Bette Davis.

Other solo performers create their own material – and their own renown. Among these artists RUTH DRAPER is preeminent, capitvating audiences and fellow actors from early appearances in the 1920s until her death in 1956. Through their platform performances of Shakespeare and other literature, the courageous 19th-century artists ANNA CORA MOWATT, FANNY KEMBLE, and CHARLOTTE CUSHMAN had established the propriety of one-woman shows. Draper composed playlets that featured impersonations of a wide range of characters, making her the godmother of such current performers as LILY TOMLIN and WHOOPI GOLDBERG (who, also heirs of the stand-up comedy tradition, do not necessarily write their own monologues). Men like ERIC BOGOSIAN and JOHN LEGUIZAMO, whose characters are drawn from contemporary urban life, can also be considered Draper descendants. Ron Vawter joined the tradition in 1992 with a solo performance that examined homosexual identity in America (see GAY/LESBIAN THEATRE).

Solo performance is an extreme of theatre, the opposite of epic extravaganza. As such, it has interested any number of playwrights, notably the subversive minimalist Samuel Beckett. Well-known American playwrights LANFORD WILSON, CHRISTOPHER DURANG, EMILY MANN, and DAVID MAMET, among others, have written monologues for actors to perform. This sort of one-person performance is simply a part of contemporary playwriting, a way to test supposed requirements of the art form (*Is* conflict the essence of drama?); and the one-character play is more likely to be produced, in an era when most theatres are short of funds, than a large-scaled experiment.

The 1980s saw the rise of the autobiographical monologue, its leading practitioner the late SPALDING GRAY, the WASP from Rhode Island who portrayed himself as an innocent abroad in a crazy contemporary world. Storytellers who enact their narratives with vigorous physicality include John O'Keefe, who re-creates the hardships of his Iowa childhood and San Francisco young manhood with exuberant intensity, and Kevin Kling, whose depictions of his Minnesota-based life are both comic and touching. Others, like Gray and Mike Feder, who grew up in Queens and began telling his life on New York radio, took pride in their theatrical minimalism, and simply sat and talked. Audiences continue to come to autobiography for direct connection and great stories, both sometimes hard to find in today's theatre.

Heading into the 1990s, women PERFORMANCE ARTISTS came to the fore, their daring and imaginative pieces often semiautobiographical but also given to flights of poetry or political outrage. Two of the best were over 65: Beatrice Roth, who recollected her Jewish upbringing in a mostly Protestant Pennsylvania town, and RACHEL ROSENTHAL, born abroad, whose concerns encompass the earth and its nonhuman inhabitants. HOLLY HUGHES is wittily, outrageously, eloquently lesbian; the shamanistic KAREN FINLEY breaks sexual taboo. ANNA DEAVERE SMITH presents a series of monologues based on personal interviews to explore through impersonation urban racial and class conflict. Laurie Carlos, Robbie McCauley, and JESSICA HAGEDORN, two black women and a FILIPINO, have found individual ways, even when working together, to convey their particular experience of late 20th-century America.

The number of solo performances by the mid-1990s had mushroomed, and by the new millennium, thanks in part to the economy and cost of production, the phenomenon had become commonplace, including pieces by traditional and performance artists such as ELEANOR ANTIN, Eileen Atkins, Rob Becker, Kate Bornstein, Niall Buggy, Dan Butler, David Cale, Michael Chiklis, Michael Isaac Connor, Brian Copeland, Wayne Corbitt, Brian Cox, Tyne Daly, David Drake, Eve Ensler, JOHN EPPERSON, Steven Fales, Emmett Foster, Max Gail, Anne Galjour, Ben Gazzara, Ronnie Gilbert, Sherry Glaser, Judy Gold, Marga Gomez, GUILLERMO GOMEZ-PEÑA, Dan Gordon, Julie Halston, Evan Handler, DANNY HOCH, Jack Holmes, Amy Irving, Eddie Izzard, Sarah Jones (2006 Special Tony for *Bridge & Tunnel*), JOHN KELLY, Josh Kornbluth, LISA KRON, Dan Kwong, SUZANNE LACY, James Lecesne, Bradford Louryk, Laurence Luckinbill, Rita MacKenzie, DEB MARGOLIN, David Margulies, Ann Magnuson, Jude Narita, Jackie Mason, Keith Antar Mason, Jefferson Mays, Art Metrano, Susan Miller, TIM MILLER, ROBERT MORSE, Holly Near, Dael Orlandersmith, ESTELLE PARSONS, Jon Peterson, Owen Rackleff, Heather Raffo, Pamela Ross, RUBEN SANTIAGO-HUDSON,

Fiona Shaw, Peggy Shaw, Claudia Shear, Roger Guenveur Smith, Barnaby Spring, JEAN STAPLETON, Phyllis Yvonne Stickney, Nilaja Sun, Julia Sweeney, REGINA TAYLOR, Karen Trott, Charlie Varon, Shonn Wiley, Marc Wolf, CHARLAYNE WOODARD, Heather Woodbury – and many others. With 671 performances, Rob Becker's *Defending the Cave* became in 1997 the longest-running solo show in Broadway history.   MEO   DBW

One-Third of a Nation A LIVING NEWSPAPER produced by the FEDERAL THEATRE PROJECT in 1938. Although it was performed by 10 other units, the New York production was the most famous and was a highlight of the short-lived WPA theatre. Written by ARTHUR ARENT and his Living Newspaper staff, the play depicted New York City slums and the poverty and greed that created them. Inspired by Roosevelt's Second Inaugural Address, the production provoked a controversy because it quoted actual politicians and congressional bills. It also featured an imposing 70-ft-tall tenement set designed by HOWARD BAY, which added realistic detail to the plight of the poor and was used dramatically in the first scene to suggest a slum fire.   BBW

Ong, Han (1968–) Playwright, ethnically Chinese but born in the Philippines (see FILIPINO AMERICAN THEATRE), who immigrated to the U.S. at the age of 16. A high-school dropout, he was awarded a MacArthur "genius" Grant in 1997, one of the youngest playwrights ever to be accorded such an honor. His works often deal with issues of sexuality, ethnicity, and being an outsider. Plays include *Swoony Planet* (1993), *The Chang Fragments* (1996, The PUBLIC), *Middle Finger* (2000), and *Watcher* (2001); a number were produced by MA-YI and/or directed by LOY ARCENAS. He also wrote and performed the multimedia performance piece *Airport Music* (1994) with fellow playwright/performer JESSICA HAGEDORN. In addition, Ong is a critically acclaimed novelist.   DanB

Opatoshu [né Opatovsky], **David** (1918–96) Actor and writer who made his debut in *GOLDEN BOY* (1938, Newark, NJ) and on Broadway in *Night Music* (1940). Working in YIDDISH THEATRE, Opatoshu also appeared in *SILK STOCKINGS* (1955), *Does a Tiger Wear a Necktie?* (1969), and *The Big Winner* (1974), which he wrote and directed, as well as in regionally and OFF-BROADWAY. He wrote the film *Romance of a Horsethief* (1971), and acted in *The Naked City* (1948), *The Brothers Karamazov* (1958), *Exodus* (1960), *Torn Curtain* (1966), and *Who'll Stop the Rain* (1978), and in many TV shows.   REK

Open Theatre An experimental, influential OFF-OFF BROADWAY acting company during 1963–73. JOSEPH CHAIKIN left the LIVING THEATRE after playing Galy Gay in Brecht's *Man Is Man* to establish a study group for exploring new styles of acting. This collection of actors, writers, and dramaturges came to be known as the Open Theatre. Chaikin believed that the creative intervention of the performer could lead to a new dramatic expression, and he developed a technique based on the ideas of *presence* (focusing on the performer, not the character) and *transformation* (the actor changing from one role to another before the audience's eyes). This approach is described in Chaikin's book *The Presence of the Actor*. Open Theatre workshops combined vigorous physical, vocal, breathing, and improvisational exercises with discussions led by critics GORDON ROGOFF and RICHARD GILMAN. Gradually the group began to work on ensemble creations shaped by a single writer, resulting in *Viet Rock* by MEGAN TERRY (1966), *The Serpent* by JEAN-CLAUDE VAN ITALLIE (1968, Rome; 1970, NYC), and *Terminal* by SUSAN YANKOWITZ (1969). The Open Theatre gave these works full productions and then created some chamber works, including *The Mutation Show* (1971) and *Nightwalk* (1973); but as it edged away from being an acting workshop toward becoming a producing company, it decided to close – in Rogoff's words, it was "doomed to succeed."   AS

Oppenheimer, George (1900–77) Drama critic. After graduating from Williams College (1920), Oppenheimer worked for Alfred A. Knopf (1921), and cofounded Viking Press (1925) before becoming a screenwriter for MGM (1933–49). Beginning in 1955 he wrote the column "Onstage" for *Newsday*, becoming daily critic in 1963 and Sunday critic in 1972. A master of the clever one-liner, Oppenheimer thought much of the 1960s avant-garde theatre formless and obscure. His books include *The Passionate Playgoer* (1958) and his memoirs, *View from the Sixties* (1965).   TLM

Orbach, Jerry (1935–2004) Actor-singer who, after attending the University of Illinois, went to New York to study acting. He appeared in the OFF-BROADWAY revival of *The Threepenny Opera* in 1955 and created the role of the narrator, El Gallo, in *The FANTASTICKS* (1960). A year later he played the embittered puppeteer in *Carnival*. After starring in a number of revivals and straight plays, including the controversial *Scuba Duba* (1967), he returned to the musical stage in *Promises, Promises* (1968), for which he won a Tony. He abandoned his "nice guy" image to star as the shyster lawyer in CHI-CAGO (1975) and as the perfectionist director in 42ND STREET (1980). In 1994 he joined the cast of TV's *Law & Order* and had begun work on a spin-off when he died.   MK

Oregon Shakespeare Festival (1935–) The Festival was founded by Angus L. Bowmer in Ashland, OR, to produce Shakespeare's plays in an Elizabethan-style setting. Beginning on a rough, WPA-era stage, the Festival built the third and present stage in 1959 (seats 1,190). Designed by OSF's principal scenic and theatre designer, Richard L. Hay, who has designed all OSF's spaces, the theatre is patterned on London's 1599 Fortune Theatre (as of 1992 enclosed by the $7.6 million Allen Pavilion). In 1970 the Festival opened the new 600-seat indoor Angus Bowmer Theatre to house non-Shakespeare works; and in 1977, for more experimental productions, the 140-seat Black Swan – replaced in 2001 by the intimate, flexible $21 million New Theatre (270–360 seats). From 1988 to 1994 the Festival operated a resident company in the new Portland Center for the Performing Arts for a five-play, six-month seson. In 1994 this company became the Portland Center Stage. Noted for a house style that emphasizes the clarity and beauty of the text, the Festival has completed the Shakespeare canon three times: for the first time in 1958 with *Troilus and Cressida;* and for the second and third times in 1978 and 1997 with *Timon of Athens.* In the early 21st century, the mission of the Festival is changing, as it has undertaken a coproduction with the BERKELEY REPERTORY THEATRE (2003), and is now commissioning and producing new plays. Attendance continues to rise. Artistic directors have included Angus L. Bowmer (1935–71), Jerry Turner (1971–91), Henry Woronicz (1991–5), Libby Appel (1995–2007), and Bill Rauch (2007–). In 2006 the three Festival theatres were producing 11 plays, in a season from February to the end of October, for more than 400,000 playgoers.   AR TLM

Organic Theater Company Nonprofit operation founded in 1969 by Stuart Gordon and fellow University of Wisconsin students. Not long after the forced closing of its partly nude (see NUDITY) production of *Peter Pan,* the company moved to Chicago in 1972, where it found temporary quarters at the BODY POLITIC before establishing its own spaces on the North Side. Since 2005 performances have been presented at the Kathleen Mullady Memorial Theatre on the campus of Loyola University. Populist, often ribald, comedic fantasy typified much of the company's work under Gor-

don's direction (1969–85). Notable productions include *WARP* (which had a short Broadway run in 1973), DAVID MAMET's SEXUAL PERVERSITY IN CHICAGO (premiere, 1974), Ray Bradbury's *The Wonderful Ice Cream Suit* (1975), and the collaborative *Bleacher Bums* (1977) and *E/R* (1982). As of early 2006 Alexander Gelman is artistic director.   SF

Orpheum Theatre 126 Second Ave., NYC. Opening in 1905 as the Orpheum Concert Gardens, the small theatre quickly switched to movies in 1911 as the Orpheum Moving Pictures Theatre. During the 1920s and '30s, it became renowned for its accompanying YIDDISH variety shows. For many years, it remained a neighborhood moviehouse. In 1958, it was legitimatized into an OFF-BROADWAY theatre and housed several hits under a succession of managements: LITTLE MARY SUNSHINE (1959), a revival of ANYTHING GOES (1962), capped by a 5-year run of LITTLE SHOP OF HORRORS (1982). Then in 1994 *Stomp*, a unique entertainment with eight performers creating rhythms, music, choreography, and comedy with their hands and feet and noisy found objects, began a run that continues into 2007.   MCH

Orpheum theatre circuit Established in 1899 by Morris Meyerfield, owner of SAN FRANCISCO's Orpheum Theatre, and Martin Lehman, owner of a VAUDEVILLE theatre in LOS ANGELES. The pair acquired other theatres in West Coast cities, then established a CHICAGO booking office, with Martin Beck in charge. By 1923 Beck booked a circuit of more than 250 theatres in the West from offices in New York. In 1928, the Orpheum circuit merged with the KEITH–ALBEE vaudeville theatre chain, dominant in the East, and in 1930, as motion pictures displaced vaudeville, the whole merged with the Radio Corporation of America to form RKO.   WD

Osborn, Paul (1901–88) Playwright, educated at the University of Michigan and Yale. Osborn's best-remembered plays are *On Borrowed Time* (1938; revived in 1991 with GEORGE C. SCOTT) and *MORNING'S AT SEVEN* (1939). The former was a touching study of an old man's attempt to cheat death. The latter, although praised by some critics after its brief original production and kept alive in anthologies, had to await a 1980 revival to achieve wide acclaim. It took a nostalgic and sometimes bittersweet look at the life of four sisters in an American small town. Most of Osborn's works to reach Broadway were adaptations of novels, such as *A Bell for Adano* (1944), *Point of No Return* (1951), and *The World of Suzie Wong* (1958). His plays

E. A. Sothern as Lord Dundreary in *Our American Cousin.* Photo by Heath & Bow, London. *Courtesy: Laurence Senelick Collection.*

provide a mélange of characters drawn with skill and affection.   LDC

Ostrow, Stuart (1932–) Producer and writer, born in New York and educated in music at NYU, who began his career with a failure, *We Take the Town,* which closed during its pre-Broadway tryout. He then produced *Here's Love* (1963), which he also directed; *The Apple Tree* (1966); *1776* (1969), which won the Drama Critics' Circle and Tony awards; *Scratch* (1971); *Pippin* (1972); *Stages* (1978), of which he was also author; *Swing* (1980), of which he was also director; *The Moony Shapiro Songbook* (1981); *American Passion* (1983, OFF-BROADWAY); *M. BUT-TERFLY* (1988); and *La Bête* (1991). He established the Stuart Ostrow Foundation for the advancement of musical theatre in 1973. In 1993 Ostrow, who holds a distinguished professorship at the

University of Houston, was chosen producer of the year by the National Alliance for Musical Theatre. An autobiography appeared in 1999; he also wrote *Present at the Creation, Leaping in the Dark,* and *Going against the Grain* (2005).   TLM

Our American Cousin Englishman Tom Taylor wrote this farce in 1851 as a vehicle for Joshua Silsbee, who was then performing in England, but it remained unproduced until 1858, when LAURA KEENE staged it in New York. She cast JOSEPH JEFFERSON III as Asa Trenchard, the aggressive but sympathetic YANKEE hero, and convinced EDWARD A. SOTHERN to perform the minor comic role of Lord Dundreary by telling him to "gag" it as he wished. Sothern's Dundreary became the hit – a lisping, hopping, fatuous English lordling, played in a foppish costume, drooping whiskers, and a monocle. The farce concerns the misadventures of Asa in England, where he has arrived to claim Trenchard Manor as an inheritance. Its slight plot has Asa foil the greed of the family's financial agent and win the heart of a rustic maid. The popular farce gained further notoriety as the play President Lincoln was watching at FORD'S THEATRE when he was assassinated.   BAMcC

Our Town by THORNTON WILDER, produced in 1938 at HENRY MILLER'S THEATRE in New York, is one of the most famous and most produced plays in the history of American drama. Wilder dispensed with realistic stage conventions and created "Grovers Corners, N.H." with some furniture, ladders, and the narration of a Stage Manager (Frank Craven) who addressed the audience directly. The play chronicles the daily lives of the residents of a rural community in the years prior to WWI, and its simplicity created a vivid impression on both audiences and critics. It ran for 336 performances and won the Pulitzer Prize. In 1940 a film version with Martha Scott re-creating her role as Emily (as Craven did his) and music by Aaron Copland further enhanced its popularity. In subsequent years *Our Town* has been revived in thousands of professional and amateur productions. It was performed by American soldiers in Italy during WWII, by countless high schools and COMMUNITY THEATRES, and in a television musical adaptation with Frank Sinatra. Significant NYC revivals (and their Stage Managers) include a 1959 production at CIRCLE IN THE SQUARE directed by JOSÉ QUINTERO, with Art Carney (385 performances); an "all-star" version at ANTA in 1969, with HENRY FONDA; a 1988 LINCOLN CENTER production directed by GREGORY MOSHER, with SPALDING GRAY; and a 2002 Broadway production that began at WESTPORT COUNTRY PLAYHOUSE, directed by JAMES NAUGHTON and starring Paul Newman. BBW

Ouspenskaya, Maria (1876–1949) Russian-born actress and teacher. After working as a touring actor in the Russian provinces, she joined the MOSCOW ART THEATRE, with whom she appeared in New York in 1922. Choosing to remain in the U.S., she first worked as principal acting teacher for RICHARD BOLESLAVSKI's American Laboratory Theatre (teaching her version of the Stanislavsky system). Two of her students were STELLA ADLER and LEE STRASBERG. In 1929 she opened her own School of Dramatic Art. From 1923 to 1936 she was active as a character actor in New York (e.g., CLARE BOOTHE's *Abide with Me,* 1935) and thereafter in film. DBW

outdoor drama This phenomenon could be considered a late phase of the American civic PAGEANTRY movement, gaining impetus in 1937 with PAUL GREEN's *The Lost Colony,* a retelling of the story of the first English colonization effort by Walter Raleigh on Roanoke Island, staged in Manteo, NC. These works, many written by Green, Kermit Hunter, William Hardy, or Allan Eckert, are sometimes called "symphonic dramas" and usually recount some notable historical event of a specific region or locale, combining drama, dance, music, and spectacle. More than half of these productions pay, in full or part, staff and cast members (some with ACTORS' EQUITY contracts). The dramas are staged during the summer months and have annual repeats (often for many years). In recent years as many as 100 outdoor dramas (including religious pageants, outdoor Shakespearean productions, etc.) have been presented, a number celebrating runs of 50 years. Some 43 historical/symphonic dramas were presented in 2005. In addition to *The Lost Colony,* among the most celebrated examples of this type (with the year and location of their inaugural season) are *The Common Glory* (1947, Williamsburg, VA), *Faith of Our Fathers* (1950, Washington, DC), *Unto These Hills* (1950, Cherokee, NC), *Wilderness Road* (1955, Berea, KY), *The Stephen Foster Story* (1959, Bardstown, KY), *Texas* (1966, Canyon, TX), *The Trail of Tears* (1969, Tahlequah, OK), and *Trumpet in the Land* (1970, Dover, OH).

Much of the impetus for the outdoor drama movement came from the Dept. of Dramatic Art at the University of North Carolina, Chapel Hill, where Frederick Koch founded the Carolina Playmakers, originally dedicated to instructing students in the techniques of writing and producing plays focused on regional sections of the South. Green participated in theatre activities under Koch in the 1920s and helped perpetuate the interest in outdoor drama after he became a philosophy professor at North Carolina in the 1930s. In 1963, when it became burdensome for the Dept. of Dramatic Art to serve as a conduit for information on outdoor drama, the Institute for Outdoor Drama was established at UNC. The Institute continues to serve as a source of stimulation, advice, and information. In 2005 a second edition of *Creating Historical Drama* was issued. DBW

Overmyer, Eric (1951–) Colorado-born playwright fascinated with language; a favorite playwright of 1980s regional theatres. His plays, many of which premiered at CENTER STAGE, include *Native Speech* (1983, LA), *On the Verge; or, The Geography of Learning* (1985), *In a Pig's Valise* (1986), *In Perpetuity throughout the Universe* (1988), *Don Quixote de La Jolla* (1990, La Jolla), *The Heliotrope Bouquet by Scott Joplin & Louis Chauvin* (1991), *Dark Rapture* (1992, Seattle), *Figaro/Figaro* (1994, YALE REP; an adapation of Figaro plays by Beaumarchais and von Horváth), and in 1995 a translation of Heinrich von Kleist's *Amphitryon* (CSC REP). For the past decade he has written and produced for television. GSA

Owens, John Edmond (1823–86) Liverpool (England)-born actor and manager who came to Philadelphia in 1828, began there as a supernumerary at BURTON's National Theatre (1841), quickly graduated to speaking roles, and then played in all the principal American cities and in London (1865). He bought and managed the Baltimore Museum (1849–52), made his New York debut (1851) as Uriah Heep in JOHN BROUGHAM's adaptation of *David Copperfield,* and in 1864 appeared as the "YANKEE" Solon Shingle in JOSEPH JONES's *The People's Lawyer* – the role for which he became best known and which prompted the critics to speak of his "merry temperament, his exuberant and incessant glee." His memoirs, edited by his wife, appeared in 1892. RM

Owens, Rochelle (1936–) Playwright, poet, and Obie winner. Her highly controversial play *Futz* (1967, Obie; revived in 1991 at LA MAMA) is a tragicomedy relating the sexual love of a man and his pig and the violent, demented response of his repressed neighbors to his sodomy. TOM O'HORGAN gave the piece an energetic staging and supplied original music. Owens continued to explore the conflict of individual primal impulse with a self-righteous society in such OFF-BROADWAY (and OFF-OFF) plays as *Istanbul* (1965, JUDSON POETS');

Beclch (1968); *Kontraption* (1970); *He Wants Shih* (1975); *Chucky's Hunch* (1981); and two surreal historical biographies – *The Karl Marx Play* (1973, AMERICAN PLACE) and *Emma Instigated Me* (1977). Her papers are housed at Columbia University.
  FB

OyamO [né Charles Gordon] (1943–) Playwright, born in Ohio, son of a steelworker and a housewife, he attended several schools before earning a B.A. in liberal arts from the College of New Rochelle and then a M.F.A. from the Yale School of Drama (1981). Believing his name too similar to writer CHARLES GORDONE's, he chose OyamO as a pen name. He is the author of more than 30 plays, including *The Resurrection of Lady Lester* (1981, YALE REP), *Let Me Live* (1991; 1998, GOODMAN), *I Am A Man* (1992), and *Killa Dilla (An Ogunde Minstrel Show for Jim Crow)* (2006), these last three produced OFF-BROADWAY by Working Theatre. A musical, *Famous Orpheus,* was first staged in 1992. OyamO has been produced throughout the country. He is currently on the theatre faculty at the University of Michigan.   DBW

P

Pacific Overtures Two-act musical play, music and lyrics by STEPHEN SONDHEIM, book by John Weidman; opened 11 January 1976 at the WINTER GARDEN THEATRE, running 193 performances. Perhaps the most daring of the 1970s HAROLD PRINCE–Stephen Sondheim collaborations, *Pacific Overtures* traces the opening of Japan to the West from the Japanese point of view, focusing on the tension between tradition and modernization as represented by Manjiro (Sab Shimono) and Kayama (Isao Sato). Performed by an all-Asian (and, until the final scene, all-male) cast, Prince's production was highly stylized and used a wide range of Japanese staging devices, particularly Kabuki, brilliantly melded in BORIS ARONSON's spectacular scene design (Tony, Drama Desk). Similarly, Sondheim's score drew on a wide range of Japanese theatre-music styles, enhanced by Japanese instruments, which became progressively more "Westernized" at the play progressed. The show, which won the Drama Critics' Circle Award for Best Musical, was revived OFF-BROADWAY in 1984, by the English National Opera in 1988, in a Japanese production at LINCOLN CENTER and the KENNEDY CENTER in 2002, and on Broadway (ROUNDABOUT) with B. D. WONG (and Shimono as Lord Abe) in 2004 – both these last productions directed by Amon Miyamoto. JD

Pacino, Al (1940–) Actor who studied with LEE STRASBERG and is a member of the ACTORS STUDIO. Pacino made a strong impression onstage in the late 1960s playing jittery, violent low-life New Yorkers, OFF-BROADWAY in *The INDIAN WANTS THE BRONX* (1968) and in his Broadway debut as a drug addict in *Does a Tiger Wear a Necktie?* (1969; Tony). His naturalistic style proved ideal for film (*The Godfather, Serpico, Scarface*). In his periodic returns to the stage, Pacino has tried with limited success to overcome the typecasting of his films. His *Richard III* (1973) was brave though unavoidably contemporary. He was more comfortable as TENNESSEE WILLIAMS's Everyman, Killroy, in the 1970 Lincoln Center revival of *CAMINO REAL;* as the nonentity swept up by the Vietnam War in the 1977 revival of RABE's *The BASIC TRAINING OF PAVLO HUMMEL* (Tony); and as a wheezing, shuffling, pinch-voiced crook with a battery of tics in a revival of MAMET's *AMERICAN BUFFALO* (1981, CIRCLE IN THE SQUARE; 1983, Broadway). In summer 1992 he appeared in two plays in repertory at Circle in the Square: Wilde's *Salome* and Ira Lewis's *Chinese Coffee*. He was seen in 1996 in O'NEILL's *Hughie* at the LONG WHARF and Circle in the Square (and again in 1999 at the MARK TAPER). Considered by some his best performance to date, his Arturo Ui, in BRECHT's *The Resistible Rise of Arturo Ui*, was seen in the 2002 NATIONAL ACTORS THEATRE's production. In 2003 he repeated Herod on Broadway in *Salome: The Reading* directed by ESTELLE PARSONS. He received the 1993 Academy Award for Best Actor in *Scent of a Woman*.   FH

Page, Geraldine (1924–87) Missouri-born actress who attended the GOODMAN THEATRE Dramatic School (1942–5) in Chicago before making her NYC debut in the Blackfriar's Guild production of *Seven Mirrors* (1945). JOSÉ QUINTERO cast her as Alma in the OFF-BROADWAY production of *SUMMER AND SMOKE* at the CIRCLE IN THE SQUARE (1952) to rave reviews, establishing her career. Her Broadway debut as Lily in *Mid-Summer* (1953) again received critical acclaim; WOLCOTT GIBBS in the *New Yorker* praised her "charm and pathos and almost matchless technique." Her later work included Lizzie in *The RAINMAKER* (1954); Alexandra del Lago in *SWEET BIRD OF YOUTH* (1959); Olga in *The Three Sisters* (1964); Baroness Lemberg in *White Lies* and Clea in *Black Comedy* (1967); Marion in *Absurd Person Singular* (1974); and Mother Miriam Ruth in *Agnes of God* (1982). From 1983 she was a member of the Mirror Theatre Company. Her husband was actor RIP TORN.

While Page appeared too often in neurotic roles, she was a versatile actress capable of a wide emotional range. Her Alexandra del Lago provoked BROOKS ATKINSON to eloquence: "Loose-jointed, gangling, raucous of voice, crumpled, shrewd, abandoned yet sensitive about some things that live in the heart, Miss Page is at the peak of form in this raffish characterization." Her numerous film appearances included *Summer and*

Smoke (1961) and Woody Allen's *Interiors* (1978). In 1986 she won an Academy Award for her portrayal of Carrie Watts in HORTON FOOTE's *The Trip to Bountiful* (her eighth Oscar nomination).   TLM

pageants/pageantry Refers to a widespread phenomenon from 1908 through the 1920s, with earlier manifestations in 19th-century America and inspiration from British historical pageantry developed as part of the Arts and Crafts movement. In the U.S. these stagings of secular scripted spectacles for seated audiences were more influential and instrumental in the development of regional theatres, university-based performing-arts programs, utilization of American thematic material, and new techniques of creative expression in music, theatre, and dance. Initiated by a community to celebrate an important historical event or person, they differed from conventional plays in comprising three to seven self-contained episodes covering 200–2,000 years. Introduced by a spoken prologue, they concluded with a colorful "march past," integrating vocal and orchestral music, expressive and symbolic movement, group pantoMIME, poetry, and dialogue throughout. Performances usually took place OUTDOORS on a site symbolic of the event or person, though armories and schools were also used. Audiences numbered 2,000–80,000; participants included as many as 5,000 onstage and no fewer than 200 in preparation and production.

Community committees were established for funding, publicity, costuming, stage design, and historical research. The pageant master was hired months in advance. Budgets were in the range of $10,000–100,000; pageant master salaries were $1,000–2,000, dance directors $500, music commission or performance $2,000–6,000. Wealthy community members were asked to guarantee backing if the pageant was not self-sustaining, and sometimes boards of trade or state, city, or local agencies supplied seed funding. Productions were often repeated several times within a period of a few weeks related to specific historic celebrations, but were not designed for commercial gain or further performance. Tickets were usually 25¢–$2, with free tickets often available.

Written and organized by Progressive-era reformers (settlement workers, civic leaders, playground organizers, suffrage activists, and innovators in education and the arts), pageants were designed to entertain and educate, and reflected multiple forces in early 20th-century America, including urbanization, escalated immigration, and corporate control in economic and political spheres. Pageantry's legacy comes to us through the work of several individuals who saw the form in the broad context of society's needs.

GEORGE PIERCE BAKER, Frederick Henry Koch, and Thomas Wood Stevens developed ACADEMIC THEATRE programs at Harvard and Yale (Baker), the Universities of North Dakota and North Carolina (Koch), and Carnegie Institute of Technology (Stevens) while actively writing and directing pageants. They passed on to their students the belief in theatre as a creative and moral force in daily life and the need for American playwrights to develop indigenous thematic material. They also utilized their pageant work to explore the integration of music, poetry, dance, and new lighting and staging techniques. Among their students were EUGENE O'NEILL, SIDNEY HOWARD, Agnes Morgan, PAUL GREEN, Munroe Pevear, THERESA HELBURN, ROBERT EDMOND JONES, John Reed, HEYWOOD BROUN, Thomas Wolfe, HALLIE FLANAGAN, and Frederick McConnell.

PERCY MACKAYE lectured and wrote extensively on pageantry as an essential component of democracy through the educated participation of individuals in the life of the community, creating "art of the people, by the people, for the people." His major ideas are encompassed in three books: *The Playhouse and the Play* (1909), *The Civic Theatre* (1912), and *A Substitute for War* (1915). His sister, Hazel, was active in pageantry and made pageants a powerful took for women's suffrage. William Chauncy Langdon, who published many articles on pageantry in popular magazines during the time he was a professional pageant master, was instrumental in spreading the idea of theatre as an essential component of community life and instrument for social change.

Pageantry was seen as a respectable form of theatre, and women assumed significant roles as writers and directors. Mary Porter Beegle not only created several acclaimed pageants but also was instrumental in making expressive DANCE an integral part of the university curriculum, as part of pageantry courses and as a separate entity. With Jack Randall Crawford she coauthored *Community Drama and Pageantry* (1916), which has extensive pioneering material analyzing dance as a creative form. Other women active as pageant masters were Lotta Clark, Gertude Colby, Margaret McLaren Eager, CONSTANCE D'ARCY MAC-KAY, Mary Wood Hinman, and Virginia Tanner.

The American Pageant Association was created in 1913, and through 1921 issued bulletins and organized meetings focused on various aspects of pageants and masques. By the late 1920s pageants had become standardized and scripts had very little artistic merit; the image of America as land of the free, home of the brave espoused by many of the writers was an image tarnished when juxtaposed with existing conditions.   NP

Paid in Full EUGENE WALTER's first major success opened at the Astor Theatre 25 February 1908 and ran for 167 performances. One of the earliest dramas to tour for revision, the play drew great attention in spite or because of its controversial portrayal of a young wife nearly coerced into prostituting herself to advance her ruthless young husband's business career. Criticized as melodramatic and seamy, the play avoids several melodramatic devices when the wife saves herself from degradation, recognizes her husband's ruthlessness, and chooses to leave him. She then emerges as the strongest character in the work. The play produced a strong effect, though actually antimelodramatic. The impact of the play attracted the attention of DAVID BELASCO, resulting in his later collaboration with Walter on *The EASIEST WAY*.   RW

Paint Your Wagon Two-act musical comedy, words and music by ALAN JAY LERNER AND FREDERICK LOEWE (respectively); opened 12 November 1951 at the SAM S. SHUBERT THEATRE, running 289 performances. Lerner and Loewe's excursion into period Americana tells of a widowed prospector (JAMES BARTON) whose land, when gold is discovered, becomes a boomtown until the gold runs out. The gold-rush setting provides an occasion for hoedown production numbers, and a touching sentimentalism is added by the prospector's habit of talking to his dead wife and by his ultimate death. The score occasionally descends into bathos ("I Still See Elisa"), but also evokes both Western optimism (the rousing title number) and emptiness (the haunting "They Call the Wind Maria").   JD

Pajama Game, The Two-act musical comedy, music and lyrics by RICHARD ADLER AND JERRY ROSS, book by GEORGE ABBOTT and Richard Bissell; opened 13 May 1954 at the ST. JAMES THEATRE, running 1,063 performances. Based on Bissell's novel *7½ Cents,* the story tells of the romance between a management superintendent (JOHN RAITT) and an activist worker (Janis Paige) amid a threatened strike in a pajama factory. Director George Abbott wanted JEROME ROBBINS to choreograph, but Robbins wanted to codirect and assigned the choreography to BOB FOSSE, who made his Broadway choreographic debut on this show (Tony Award). Fosse's most notable contribution was the staging of "Steam Heat," which

became his seminal signature piece. Other notable hits from the show include "Hey, There" and "Hernando's Hideaway." It won the Tony for Best Musical and had a successful London production. A revival at City Center opened six months after the original production closed. The 1957 film version, with many of the stage cast, reproduced much of the original staging. A major acclaimed Broadway production (Tony for Best Revival) was by the ROUNDABOUT in 2006 with Harry Connick Jr. and Kelli O'Hara, directed by KATHLEEN MARSHALL. Other NYC revivals were in 1973 (Broadway) and 1989 (New York City Opera).   JD

Pakledinaz, Martin (1953–) Detroit-born costume designer who studied directing (Wayne State) before turning to costumes (Michigan). He began as an assistant to THEONI V. ALDREDGE and first designed costumes on Broadway in 1981 (*Inacent Black*); his debut at the New York City Opera was 1992 (*Xerxes*). KISS ME, KATE (1999) and *Thoroughly Modern Millie* (2002) won him Tonys, and he received nominations for *The Life* (1997) and *Golden Child* (1998). In 1998 he received the IRENE SHARAFF Young Master Award.   BO

Pal Joey Two-act musical play, music by RICHARD RODGERS, lyrics by LORENZ HART, book by John O'Hara; opened 25 December 1940 at the ETHEL BARRYMORE THEATRE, running 374 performances. A musical of major historical import, *Pal Joey* follows the adventures of Joey Evans (Gene Kelly), an unscrupulous, womanizing nightclub singer in Chicago who dumps his good-hearted girlfriend (Leila Ernst) for Vera (VIVIENNE SEGAL), a wealthy, older, married woman. After she tires of him, the curtain falls on Joey, unrepentant, pursuing another fresh young thing. The show was recognized as an important departure, but its immoral, self-serving central characters were very controversial. Not until a 1952 Broadway revival, which ran 542 performances and won the New York Drama Critics' Circle Award for Best Musical (with Segal reprising her role), was *Pal Joey* fully appreciated. Beyond the many intentionally tacky NIGHTCLUB numbers, the score produced two enduring standards: Joey's insincere song of seduction "I Could Write a Book" and Vera's contemplative "Bewitched, Bothered, and Bewildered." It also included, well before OKLAHOMA!, a dream ballet, choreographed by Robert Alton, at the end of Act I. There have been two revivals at New York's City Center (1961, 1963) and a concert version in 1995 (CITY CENTER'S ENCORES!). CIRCLE IN THE SQUARE staged a revival in 1976.   JD

Palace Theatre The legendary mecca for VAUDE-VILLE performers, this New York theatre was built by Martin Beck, who then had to turn over 75% of the stock to EDWARD F. ALBEE for permission to use KEITH-circuit acts; Albee in turn paid OSCAR HAMMERSTEIN I $225,000 for the rights to offer Keith acts in that neighborhood. Located at Broadway and 47th St., the theatre, which seated 1,800, opened on 25 March 1913, and, after a slow start, gained popularity with the booking of Sarah Bernhardt. "Playing the Palace" was the ambition of every American variety act, although names did not go up in lights until 1928. The record bill was for a nine-week teaming of EDDIE CANTOR and George Jessel in 1931. On 7 May 1932, the Palace became a four-a-day theatre – the live performance mingled with newsreels and cartoons – and on 16 November turned into a five-a-day cinema; this date marks the official death of vaudeville as a dominant entertainment form. After a period as a BURLESQUE house and a brief revival of vaudeville in 1950, the Palace was converted into a theatre for musical comedy in 1965 (*SWEET CHARITY*, 1966); in 1987 it closed for extensive renovations, reopening in April 1991 with the musical *The WILL ROGERS FOLLIES*. During 1994–9 it housed *Beauty and the Beast*. In 2000 Elton John's and Tim Rice's *Aida* moved in. *Lestat*, based on Anne Rice's character creation, with music by John and lyrics by Bernie Taupin, opened March 2006 but closed soon thereafter. The film-adapted musical *Legally Blonde* opened in April 2007.　LS

Palmer, A(lbert) M(arshman) (1838–1905) Theatrical manager who first entered the business in 1872 as comanager of the UNION SQUARE THEATRE with Sheridan Shook. Although trained as a lawyer and without theatrical background or experience, he established a reputation as one of the leading managers of his time, with a keen business sense and cultivated theatrical tastes. During his 10-year tenure at the Union Square, he improved both the quality of the acting company and production standards. He also fostered the production of contemporary (particularly American) drama, often commissioning new plays, translations, and adaptations. In 1883, following a dispute with Shook, he left the Union Square; however, he subsequently managed the MADISON SQUARE THEATRE during 1884–91. In 1888, he secured control of WALLACK'S THEATRE, renaming it Palmer's, and in 1891 he moved his famous Madison Square STOCK COMPANY to this theatre.

Unlike DALY and FROHMAN, Palmer was not a "star maker," but he did promote the careers of numerous actors and actresses, including AGNES

BOOTH, RICHARD MANSFIELD, W. H. CRANE, Maurice Barrymore (see DREW–BARRYMORE), CLARA MORRIS, and JAMES O'NEILL. Among his more notable productions of American plays were BRONSON HOWARD'S *The BANKER'S DAUGHTER* (1878), BARTLEY CAMPBELL'S *MY PARTNER* (1879), CLYDE FITCH'S *Beau Brummel* (1890), JAMES A. HERNE'S *MARGARET FLEMING* (1891), and AUGUSTUS THOMAS'S *Alabama* (1891). He also produced plays by Henry Arthur Jones, Oscar Wilde, W. S. Gilbert (see GILBERT AND SULLIVAN). and a popular dramatization of Du Maurier's *Trilby* (1895). Palmer was also among the first American managers to pay foreign authors royalties for the performance of their plays, and he was a major force in the founding in 1882 of the Actors' Fund of America.　DJW

Palmo's Opera House see BURTON'S CHAMBERS STREET THEATRE

Pan Asian Repertory Theatre Founded in 1977 by artistic director TISA CHANG, this OFF-OFF BROADWAY group is the vital New York link in the ASIAN AMERICAN THEATRE network. Intended as a major showcase for the talents of professional Asian American artists, it is committed to producing contemporary Asian American authors, translated Asian masterworks, and multicultural adaptations of Western classics. This eclectic mandate has yielded such noteworthy productions as *Teahouse,* Lao She's drama about 50 years of modern Chinese history; R. A. Shiomi's *Yellow Fever,* a wry twist on the hard-boiled detective genre; *Shogun Macbeth,* a Japanese reworking of the classic tragedy; as well as works by DAVID HENRY HWANG, Momoko Iko, PHILIP GOTANDA, and a collaboration with experimental director PING CHONG. Though much of the work has had an East Asian slant, in the 1990s it broadened to include plays with South Asian and Southeast Asian themes (*Gandhi* and ERNEST ABUDA'S *Cambodia Agonistes*).　MB

pantomime see MIME AND PANTOMIME

Paper Bag Players, The Founded in 1958 by Judith Martin and based in NYC, this is one of America's best-known and most imaginative CHILDREN'S THEATRE companies, having performed in 37 states and toured internationally. Its format of short skits has influenced other companies to experiment with subject matter, style, and form. The "Bags" deliberately eschewed elaborate costumes and sets in favor of uniform garments, adding accessories as needed. Props are moved on- and offstage by the four actors. The composer-accompanist works with the group to develop original scripts. Recipient of an Obie (1965), they are the only children's theatre to be so honored. NMcC

Paper Mill Playhouse Founded in 1934 in Milburn, NJ, in a derelict paper mill dating from 1795, the 1,200-seat facility is designated as the State Theatre of New Jersey. Noted especially for its musical revivals (*SHOW BOAT, FOLLIES, RAGTIME*, etc.), its productions, many designed by MICHAEL ANANIA, are often sumptious. Stepping down in 2002 were both its longtime president, Angelo Del Rossi (replaced in 2003 by Michael Gennaro, previously at STEPPENWOLF, who left early in 2007 to become executive director at TRINITY REP), and artistic director Robert Johanson. As of April 2007 the theatre faced a fiscal crisis. DBW

Papp [*né* Papirofsky], **Joseph** (1921–91) Director and producer; founder of the NEW YORK SHAKE-SPEARE FESTIVAL in 1954. Starting as a Broadway and CBS-TV stage manager (1952–60), Papp began the Shakespeare Theatre Workshop on NYC's Lower East Side in 1953. After *Cymbeline* (1955) and *The Changeling* (1956), Papp continued to direct occasionally for NYSF: e.g., *Twelfth Night* (1958, 1963, 1969), *Hamlet* (1964, 1967, 1968, 1983), RABE's *In the Boom Boom Room* (1973), Babe's *Buried Inside Extra* (1983), and *Measure for Measure* (1985). He directed the productions of *The Merchant of Venice* (1962), *Antony and Cleopatra* (1963), and *Hamlet* (1964) that were telecast by CBS-TV. During 1973–7, Papp ran Lincoln Center's VIVIAN BEAUMONT AND MITZI E. NEWHOUSE THEATRES. In 1990 he appointed JOANNE AKALAITIS his artistic associate and hired three young staff directors (GEORGE C. WOLFE, MICHAEL GREIF, DAVID GREENSPAN), easing away from the Festival's daily operation. By mid-1991 he had retained the title "producer" but was no longer involved with the actual running of the NYSF, having appointed Akalaitis artistic director several months before his death in October 1991.

In 1958, Papp, "driven . . . to create theater without regard for . . . cost or human interference," received a Tony for Distinguished Service to Theatre. That year, he refused to identify left-wing artists for the House Committee for Un-American Activities; this caused problems when he later proposed taking productions into city schools. Frequently taking chances, Papp advocated creative freedom, saying, "If this theatre isn't being criticized for being too extreme, there's something wrong." In 1990 he rejected $748,000 from the NATIONAL ENDOWMENT FOR THE ARTS because of its restrictive antiobscenity pledge. (For this he was awarded a Special Obie, his second.) In 1988 he became the first recipient of the William Shakespeare Award for Classical Theatre from the SHAKESPEARE THEATRE at the Folger. He also received ACTORS' EQUITY's 1987 PAUL ROBESON Award. REK

Paradise Lost by CLIFFORD ODETS. Produced in 1935 by the GROUP THEATRE, it ran for only 73 performances and disappointed most critics, who compared it unfavorably to *AWAKE AND SING!* HAROLD CLURMAN was director, BORIS ARONSON designer. A rambling story of family life and work in the Depression, it provided a variety of interesting character roles for the company actors, thus illustrating the ensemble approach they were forging together. Though realistic in its social setting and characters, it has qualities that tend toward symbolic typology and rhetorical flourish. That it is occasionally revived by companies around the country (such as Baltimore's CENTER STAGE in 1987–8) reveals that the initial response was perhaps too harsh. TP

Parichy, Dennis (1938–) Lighting designer associated with the new poetic realism of writers like TINA HOWE and LANFORD WILSON, he is considered one of the best creators of mood, time, and place through light in the contemporary theatre. He has designed hundreds of productions with CIRCLE REPERTORY THEATRE (resident lighting designer since 1976), MANHATTAN THEATRE CLUB, NEW YORK SHAKESPEARE FESTIVAL, SIGNATURE THEATRE, as well as for regional theatres and on Broadway. New York productions include *BURN THIS, TALLEY'S FOLLY, CRIMES OF THE HEART, Coastal Disturbances, Redwood Curtain, FIFTH OF JULY, As Is, The Cryptogram, Book of Days*, and *Pudd'nhead Wilson*. He joined the theatre faculty at Brandeis University in 1990 but now teaches at Purchase College. AA

Paris Bound This comedy of manners by PHILIP BARRY captured popular audiences with its glib style and serious subject, marital infidelity. Opening at the MUSIC BOX THEATRE on 27 December 1927, produced and directed by ARTHUR HOPKINS and designed by ROBERT EDMOND JONES, this play presents a wealthy six-year marriage that theoretically claims openness and trust, though an apparent affair nearly wrecks the family. Interestingly, both marriage partners, Mary and Jim Hutton (Madge Kennedy and Donn Cook), suffer at the thought of a spouse involved with another,

Interior of the Second Park Theatre, 1822. *Courtesy:* Harvard Theatre Collection, Houghton Library.

yet both avoid confrontation and all ends happily without the expected showdown. In Barry's greatest success until *HOLIDAY,* he demonstrated some of his most scintillating dialogue, especially among partying supporting characters, which enthralled his critics and audiences.   RHW

Park Theatre 21–25 Park Row, NYC [Architect: Joseph Mangin]. In 1795, tired of the deteriorating and déclassé JOHN STREET THEATRE, a group of prominent New Yorkers subscribed money to erect a new theatre in an area that promised to become the heart of the early 19th-century city. Three years later, it opened as the New Theatre in an unfinished state. The unattractive exterior belied a comfortable and handsome interior, which was designed Continental-style with three tiers of boxes overhanging a U-shaped pit, and a gallery above the highest tier. The first managers were actors JOHN HODGKINSON and LEWIS HALLAM, who moved their John Street company into the new house. WILLIAM DUNLAP was added to the management, and he succeeded them as sole manager for several years until forced into bankruptcy in 1805. The house, by then known as the Park, was bought by John Jacob Astor and John Beekman, who eventually leased it in 1808 to STEPHEN PRICE. Credited with introducing the "star system" to American theatre practice, Price bolstered flagging box-office receipts by importing English stars and managing their tours. In 1810,

he brought over GEORGE FREDERICK COOKE, and in 1820 lured Edmund Kean to America. Because he spent so much time in England, Price left actor EDMUND SIMPSON in charge of the theatre during his absences. In 1820, the Park burned to its exterior walls, but was rebuilt the following year. For more than a decade, the Park established itself as the first theatre in the land with an outstanding resident company. In addition to English stars, it helped to create such American stars as EDWIN FORREST and CHARLOTTE CUSHMAN. In its last decades, the high status of the Park was eclipsed, and Simpson was forced to place meretricious fare on its stage. In 1848, FIRE again consumed the house, and the Astor heirs replaced it with commercial buildings.   MCH

Parker, Dorothy (Rothschild) (1893–1967) Author and critic who, after writing for *Vogue* and *Vanity Fair* in the 1910s, began her long association with Harold Ross's *The New Yorker* in 1925, contributing sharp and witty dramatic reviews for the rest of her career. She founded the Round Table at the Algonquin Hotel, which brought together in the 1920s New York's sharpest wits, including ROBERT BENCHLEY, ROSS, GEORGE S. KAUFMAN, and James Thurber. Though the author of more than 20 screenplays, eight plays or revues, four books of poetry, and three collections of short stories, she is best remembered for her witty one-liners.   TLM

Parker, H(enry) T(aylor) (1867–1934) Drama critic. Born in Boston and educated at Harvard, H. T. (as he was called) served as the New York correspondent for the *Boston Transcript* (1892–8, 1901–3), and later covered London for the *Transcript* and *New York Commercial Advertiser* (1898–1900). He became dramatic and music critic for the *New York Globe* (1903–5) and for the *Transcript* (1905–34), establishing his reputation as one of the most perceptive and influential critics of his generation. Parker had no equal in capturing the essence of a production in a few well-turned phrases. TLM

Parker, Mary-Louise (1964–) Born in South Carolina, trained at the North Carolina School of the Arts, she is arguably the most critically praised actress of the late 1990s/early 2000s, with notable stage roles in Craig Lucas's *Prelude to a Kiss* (1990) as Rita, Inge's *Bus Stop* (1996) as Cherie, Paula Vogel's *How I Learned to Drive* (1997; Obie) as Li'l Bit, and especially as the enigmatic Catherine in David Auburn's *Proof* (2000) for which she won a Tony. Parker, who has had a healthy film career, spent the early 2000s making movies and appearing on television – as Amy Gardner in *The West Wing* (2001–6) and on Showtime's *Weeds* (2005–), playing Nancy Botwin (Golden Globe), a suburban mother who after her husband's death decides to sell marijuana while maintaining her community respectability. In 2003 she portrayed Harper Pitt (Golden Globe, Emmy) in the HBO production of *Angels in America*. She returned to the stage in 2004 to play Rachel in Lucas's *Reckless*. DBW

Parks, Hildy (De Forrest) (1926–2004) Producer, writer, actor. A stage and television actor (1945–58), Parks, with her third husband, Alexander Cohen, resuscitated the Antoinette Perry (Tony) Awards ceremonies by producing them as television extravaganzas (1967–86) written by Parks, with annual themes that sell Broadway – like her "Welcome Home" show (1974) featuring television stars who began on Broadway. They also produced shows in New York and London, including *Baker Street* (1965), an *Anna Christie* revival (1977), and the musical *I Remember Mama* (1979). Parks wrote and produced other celebratory shows for television, and won Emmys for "The 34th Annual Tony Awards" (1980) and "Night of 100 Stars" (1982). TH-S

Parks, Suzan-Lori (1963–) 2002 Pulitzer Prize–winning playwright, educator, songwriter, screenwriter, and novelist. Born in Kentucky and a grad-

Don Cheadle and Jeffrey Wright in Suzan-Lori Parks's *Topdog/Underdog* at the Public Theater in 2001. Photo by Michal Daniel. *Courtesy:* Public Theater.

uate of Mount Holyoke College, where she studied with James Baldwin, Parks was named in 1989 "the year's most promising new playwright" by Mel Gussow in the *New York Times*. She won an Obie for her play *Imperceptible Mutabilities in the Third Kingdom* (1989) – a dreamlike exploration of the black experience – followed in 1990 by *The Death of the Last Black Man in the Whole Entire World* (both at BACA Downtown, Brooklyn), which Parks calls "a requiem mass in the jazz aesthetic." Full-length plays that followed include *The America Play* (a black man's obsession with the life and death of Lincoln) at Yale Rep and Papp's Public Theater in 1994; *Venus*, about the historical figure Saartjie Baartman, a Hottentot woman, which also had its world's premiere at Yale Rep (1996), directed by Richard Foreman, and moved to The Public (Obie); and *In the Blood* (1999, Public; a Pulitzer finalist) and *Fucking A* (2000, Houston, TX; 2003, Public), both her takes on Hawthorne's 1850 novel *The Scarlet Letter*. Her *Topdog/Underdog*, a two-man play rife with cultural allusions, featuring brothers with the adversarial names of Lincoln and Booth, was produced at The Public in 2001. Directed by GEORGE C. WOLFE and starring Don Cheadle (Booth) and JEFFREY WRIGHT (Lincoln), it moved to Broadway in 2002 (with Mos Def as Booth) and won the Pulitzer Prize for Drama. BRANTLEY termed it a "thrilling comic drama" that "vibrates with the clamor of big ideas, audaciously and exuberantly expressed." Her first novel, *Getting Mother's Body*, based on her youth in West Texas, was published in 2003. In 2001 she received a MacArthur "genius" grant. She has taught playwriting at Yale and the California Institute of the Arts.   DBW

Parnell, Peter (1953–) New York City native who attended Dartmouth and began writing plays in high school. As the author of large-scale plays written from a literary sensibility, often examing sexual and artistic passion, his plays are not well known, despite a number of productions at PLAYWRIGHTS HORIZONS, the AMERICAN PLACE THEATRE, and the PUBLIC beginning in the late 1970s. His work includes *Sorrows of Stephen* (1979). *Romance Language* (1984), *Flaubert's Latest* (1992), *Hyde in Hollywood* (1989), *An Imaginary Life* (1993), *Rise and Rise of Daniel Rocket* (1982), and *Scooter Thomas Makes It to the Top of the World* (1977, Waterford, CT). His best-known plays are *The Cider House Rules, Part 1 and Part 2* (1995–6, SEATTLE REP), based on John Irving's 1985 novel, and *QED*, a ONE-PERSON play staged first at the MARK TAPER in 2001 with ALAN ALDA as Nobel-winning physicist Richard Feynman.   DBW

Parsons, Estelle (1927–) Massachusetts-born actress, best known for her brash Oscar-winning performance in *Bonnie and Clyde* (1967) and her more recent TV appearances as the mother of *Roseanne*. Parsons prefers theatre, which she considers an actor's medium, to film, which she feels belongs to directors and editors. With her sharp nasal voice and lived-in face, Parsons sounds and looks refreshingly real; and though she was trained in LEE STRASBERG's method of psychological realism. she has eagerly sought work in other styles, from Shakespeare to musical theatre. Her richest parts on Broadway – often of fanatical or neurotic women – have been as TENNESSEE WILLIAMS's dotty, good-natured stripper in *The Seven Descents of Myrtle* (1968); as the alcoholic title character in *AND MISS REARDON DRINKS A LITTLE* (1971); in the PUBLIC THEATER's *Pirates of Penzance* (1981); as the caustic, deranged, dictatorial schoolteacher in Roberto Athayde's *Miss Margarida's Way* (1977,

revived 1990), a virtuoso ONE-PERSON show in which she fenced improvisationally with the audience; and as Cora Swanson in the 2002 revival of *MORNING'S AT SEVEN*. In 2003 she directed AL PACINO in *Salome: The Reading*. Her experiments OFF-BROADWAY and regionally include BRECHT's *Mahagonny* (1970); JUNE HAVOC's *Oh Glorious Tintinnabulation* at ACTORS STUDIO (1974); Dario Fo's *Orgasmo Adulto Escapes from the Zoo* (1983, solo); Kroetz's *Extended Forecast* (1993) at LA MAMA; Winnie in *Happy Days* at HARTFORD STAGE (1998); and Maude in a musical version of the film *Harold and Maude* at the PAPER MILL PLAYHOUSE (2005). She served as artistic director of the Actors' Studio for five years.   FH

participatory theatre Environmental theatre of the 1960s and early '70s – concerned with social and political issues and sexual repression, often urging audience involvement, and invariably taking itself very seriously – gave way in the 1980s and '90s to a new, less intimidating, escapist form of participatory theatre. From mystery trains in the Midwest and New England, to mystery weekends, Renaissance fairs, and role-playing events such as *Dungeons and Dragons* or *Assassin*, to satiric cabarets in New York and Los Angeles, this phenomenon spread nationwide. Prime examples include *SHEAR MADNESS*, a mystery comedy with audience members as questioners, running in BOSTON for more than 27 years (over 50 productions worldwide); *FORBIDDEN BROADWAY*, in several editions since 1982; *Tony 'n' Tina's Wedding* (1988, NYC; restaged in 100 other cities worldwide), where the audience travels from the marriage ceremony to a restaurant reception; *Tamara*, a Canadian import that led patrons through a villa in dramatizing its story of sex and intrigue (1984, Los Angeles; 1987, NYC); *Song of Singapore* (1991), a lavish entertainment (with slim plot) designed by JOHN LEE BEATTY that evolved over eight years; *FOREVER PLAID* in New York (1990), Boston, and elsewhere; and *Pageant*, a 1991 OFF-BROADWAY offering in which audience members judge six beauty contestants (played by men) in an effective commentary on the packaging of women and co-opting of their images by society.

Others since 1990 have included *Grandma Sylvia's Funeral, Late Nite Catechism, Pomp Duck and Circumstance, Prom Queens Unchained, Game Show, Lifegame, De La Guarda*, and *Aunt Chooch's Birthday*, among others. As dinner theatre, this phenomenon continues. In the New England area *Joey and Maria's Comedy Italian Wedding* gave way to *The Soprano's Last Supper, Maria's Bachelorette Party, Nick and Zita's Fat Funny Greek Wedding*, ad nauseum.

In 2003 a more esoteric form of participation was offered by director Deborah Warner's mystical walking tour of New York, *The Angel Project.* DBW

Pasadena Playhouse Founded in California in 1917 by Gilmor Brown and incorporated in 1918, the Pasadena Playhouse grew into an important theatre institution. Brown depended upon amateur talent and volunteer help. He built a new theatre in 1925, adding a school for training actors in 1928 and an intimate Playbox Theatre in 1929. Premieres of new works, including O'NEILL's *Lazarus Laughed* (1928), and revivals of seldom-produced classics made the Playhouse famous. Beginning in 1935 it offered a series of Midsummer Drama Festivals that attracted wide attention. The theatre gained a reputation as a showcase for aspiring film actors, with Randolph Scott, TYRONE POWER, and Robert Young among the stars discovered. Brown served 31 years as president and retired as director of the Playhouse in 1959. After it closed in 1970, the Playhouse was designated a historical landmark, renovated, and reopened in 1985, with Paul Lazarus III as artistic director from 1990, replaced in 1997 by Sheldon Epps. The facility was heavily damaged by a 1991 earthquake. TLM

Pastor, Tony [Antonio] (1837–1908) Variety performer and manager, called "The Father of Vaudeville." The son of a theatre violinist, he made his professional debut in 1846 as an infant prodigy at BARNUM'S AMERICAN MUSEUM. He later traveled as a CIRCUS clown, MINSTREL, and ballad singer, with a repertory of some 1,500 songs, arranging concerts in small towns. He first booked variety into the rowdy American Theatre, at 444 Broadway, New York (1861), and, determined to attract a respectable audience, took over the Volksgarten at 201 Bowery in 1865. Renaming it the Opera House, Pastor advertised it as "The Great Family Resort" and invited women and children to special matinees; but even door prizes of turkeys, hams, and barrels of flour were insufficient to attract a God-fearing public. The fat man with the waxed moustache and mincing step moved his clean bill of variety to 585 Broadway in 1875, where he introduced the theatre checkroom, and then to 14th St. (between 3d Ave. and Irving Place) in 1881. There he finally succeeded in promoting clean VAUDEVILLE to a family audience, paving the way for KEITH and ALBEE; performers he sponsored include NAT GOODWIN, LILLIAN RUSSELL, and WEBER AND FIELDS. A devout Catholic who kept a shrine backstage, he continued to pay low salaries, lost his stars to sharper managers, and died a relatively poor man. LS

Patel, Neil (1964–) Born in Wales, reared in Wisconsin, this prolific scenic designer studied at Yale (B.A. in architecture), the Accademia di Belle Arti Brera in Milan, and the University of California–San Diego. Since the early 1990s, he has designed steadily in major regional venues, on Broadway and Off-, and abroad. He has received two Obies (1996, for Sustained Excellence; 2001), in 2000 an EDDY award for designs for ANNE BOGART and the SITI Company, and Drama Desk nominations in 1996 for *Quill,* 2000 for DINNER WITH FRIENDS, and 2003 for *Endpapers.* He has worked often with playwright WARREN LEIGHT (*Side Man; Glimmer, Glimmer and Shine*). BO

Patinkin, Mandy (Mandel) (1952–) Actor-singer who attended Juilliard and then spent several years playing supporting roles for the NEW YORK SHAKESPEARE FESTIVAL. Possessed of a fine tenor voice, he received a Tony Award for his performance as Ché Guevara in *EVITA* (1979). He created the role of Georges Seurat in SONDHEIM's musical *SUNDAY IN THE PARK WITH GEORGE* (1984), appeared in the British musical *The Knife* at the PUBLIC THEATER (1987), played Archibald Craven in *The Secret Garden* (1991), and Marvin (replacement) in *FALSETTOS* (1993). Other credits: *The Winter's Tale* (1989, Public), Burrs in *Wild Party* (2000), Dr. Stockman in *Enemy of the People* (2003, WILLIAMSTOWN). He has also appeared on Broadway in ONE-PERSON concerts in 1989, 1997, 1998, and 2001. During 1994–5 he starred in the television series *Chicago Hope,* leaving after one season (though making occasional appearances) and returning in force in 1999; as of 2005 he has starred on TV's *Criminal Minds.* MK

Patrick, John (1905–95) Prolific playwright who has been a favorite among American regional theatres, dinner theatres, and amateur groups. His two best remembered Broadway successes both grew out of WWII: *The Hasty Heart* (1945) told the touching story of an obstreperous Scottish soldier dying in a field hospital filled with a comic group of recuperating soldiers, representing most of the Allied armies, tended by a sympathetic nurse. *The Teahouse of the August Moon* (1953) pictured the foibles of an attempt to Americanize an Okinawan village. Regional and amateur groups also continue to revive *The Curious Savage* (1950) and *Everybody Loves Opal* (1961). Until his death Patrick wrote two or three plays a year for companies seeking light, entertaining comedies. LDC

Paulding, James Kirke (1778–1860) is significant in American theatre for two reasons. First, writing about "American Drama" for the *American Quarterly Review* (1827), he urged a carefully supported "National Drama." Second, his play *The LION OF THE WEST* (1830), won a prize from JAMES H. HACKETT; from its conventional plot involving lost relations and international characters, as revised by JOHN AUGUSTUS STONE, Hackett created a substantial vehicle with Colonel Nimrod Wildfire, a humorous imitation of Davy Crockett. As *A Kentuckian Trip to New York in 1815*, WILLIAM BAYLE BERNARD adapted the play for English audiences in 1833. Paulding also wrote *The Bucktails; or, Americans in England* (publ. 1847).   WJM

Payne, B(en) Iden (1881–1976) British director, educator, and actor. A full career in the British theatre (actor with Frank Benson, director of the Abbey Theatre, Manchester's Gaiety Theatre, the Shakespeare Memorial Theatre, etc.) was balanced with more than 50 years in the U.S. During 1913–34 he directed such prominent actors as JOHN DREW and HELEN HAYES, as well as acted (e.g., Milne's *The Great Broxopp*, 1921). He also began teaching: During 1919–34 he taught at Carnegie Institute, returning there in 1943, after a decade in England, to head Drama and develop his "modified Elizabethan staging"; subsequently he taught at many universities, most notably the University of Texas (1946–73), which named its main theatre after him in 1976. During 1949–61 he directed at the OLD GLOBE (San Diego) and the OREGON SHAKESPEARE FESTIVAL. His autobiography, *A Life in a Wooden O*, was published in 1977.   DBW

Payne, John Howard (1791–1852) American (NYC-born?) actor and playwright. Now remembered for the lyrics to "Home, Sweet Home!" (music by H. R. Bishop) in his *Clari, the Maid of Milan* (London's Covent Garden, 1823), he wrote or translated and adapted from the French some 60 plays. Among the best known are *Brutus; or, The Fall of Tarquin* (starring Edmund Kean, London's Drury Lane, 1818; EDWIN FORREST in New York, 1829); *Thérèse; or, The Orphan of Geneva* (Drury Lane, 1821; Forrest in New York, 1829); *Clari;* and two collaborations with WASHINGTON IRVING – *CHARLES II; OR, THE MERRY MONARCH* (Covent Garden, 1824); and *Richelieu* (Covent Garden, 1826). In spite of close friendships with Irving, Coleridge, Lamb, and (in Paris) Talma, who encouraged him to translate French melodramas – and despite his occasional appearances as an actor and one season as manager of London's Sadler's Wells (1820)

– Payne's years abroad (1813–32) were marked by financial distress: Twice he was confined to debtor's prison.

Payne made his acting debut as Young Norval in Home's *Douglas* (New York's PARK THEATRE, 1809), appeared as Hamlet and Romeo, quickly became known as "Master Payne, the American Roscius," and was favorably compared with "Master Betty." His writing debut had come earlier with little magazines: *The Fly* (coedited with SAMUEL WOODWORTH, 1804); *Thespian Mirror* (1805); and his first play *Julia; or, The Wanderer* (1806).

In 1842 President Tyler appointed Payne Consul at Tunis (a reward for his crusade on behalf of the Cherokee Indians), where he served until 1845 and again from 1851 until his death. Grace Overmyer's biography is the most recent (1957).   RM

Payton, Corse (1866–1934) Actor-manager born (and buried) in Centerville, IA; named by his father after General John M. Corse of the Sixth Iowa Infantry. After a brief stay with a traveling CIRCUS, he returned home to organize a STOCK COMPANY (Corse Payton's Comedy Company). In 1900 after years of trouping the Middle West he moved to Brooklyn, bought a theatre for $5,000, and named it Payton's Lee Avenue. Over a fifteen year period – having originated the "10–20–30 cent" scale of prices – he produced more than 300 plays. His first wife, Etta Reed (d. 1915), was his leading lady in the 1900s. Corse was a respectable character actor even though he became known as "America's Best Bad Actor." Although he lost his theatre in 1915, he later built Keeney's (which became SHUBERT's) in Newark, NJ, and finally returned to stock in Jamaica, NY, leasing his Carlton Theatre there as a motion-picture venue shortly before his death.   DBW

Peabody, Josephine Preston see MARKS, JOSEPHINE PRESTON PEABODY

Pearl Theatre Company, The The only NYC theatre almost exclusively devoted to classical theatre, with a resident acting company of 11 (ages 30–84). Founded in 1984 by artistic director Shepard Sobel in a 72-seat space on West 22d St., the company since 1994 has been housed in the 160-seat Theatre 80 in the East Village. During its history, the Pearl has produced more than 100 "classical masterpieces," including 21 Shakespeares, 9 SHAWS, 7 IBSENS, 5 Sophocles, and 4 each of Molière, CHEKHOV, and Racine. Frequently honored with awards for itself (1993 Obie grant) and its members (Obies, Callaways), the Pearl is the subject of a 1993 book by David Hapgood.   DBW

Peg o' My Heart Tested out of town, J. HARTLEY MANNERS's blockbuster hit for his actress-wife LAURETTE TAYLOR opened at NYC's CORT THEATRE 20 December 1912 and ran for 603 performances. It played for a year in London, had eight companies simultaneously on tour during the 1914–15 season, and logged nearly 6,000 performances by 1918. Taylor's Peg was much celebrated, and she performed it more than 1,000 times, trapped in the role of the Irish waif (she escaped 32 years later with Amanda in GLASS MENAGERIE). Manners is remembered for little else than this sentimental comedy-drama of a half-orphaned heiress who, initially spurned by her aristocratic relations, wins their approval, the hero's heart, and the fortune by play's end.   RKB

Pemberton, Brock (1885–1950) Born and raised in Kansas, Pemberton was first a journalist who gravitated to New York to work as a drama critic, eventually for the *Times* (1911). He resigned in 1917 to assist director ARTHUR HOPKINS, becoming a full-time producer with *Enter, Madame* (1920). He next produced MISS LULU BETT, which won the Pulitzer Prize in 1921. Another major success was Pirandello's *Six Characters in Search of an Author* in 1922. Other shows included Sturges's *Strictly Dishonorable* (1929); CLARE BOOTHE (LUCE)'s *Kiss the Boys Goodbye* (a 1938 hit); and his biggest success, *HARVEY*, which won the Pulitzer Prize in 1945.

In addition to numerous articles, Pemberton wrote summaries of Broadway seasons for the *Times*. President of the League of New York Theatres (among many other leadership positions), he had a generous nature and outspoken manner (he was an early opponent of the FEDERAL THEATRE PROJECT) and won respect in all branches of the profession.   SMA

Pendleton, Austin (1940–) Ohio-born actor, director, playwright, and teacher, educated at Yale University (B.A., 1961), who made his NYC debut as the mother-dominated Jonathan in KOPIT's absurdist farce OH DAD, POOR DAD . . . (1962). His slight build and buck-toothed profile have ensured many related roles on and OFF-BROADWAY: the tailor, Motel, in FIDDLER ON THE ROOF (1964), Irwin in *Hail, Scrawdyke* (1966; CLARENCE DERWENT Award), Leo in *The* LITTLE FOXES (1967), Isaac in *The Last Sweet Days of Issac* (1970; Obie, Drama Desk), and Mr. Dussel in the 1997 revival of DIARY OF ANNE FRANK. Both as an actor and a director, Pendleton also works at prominent regional theatres, such as WILLIAMSTOWN, the LONG WHARF, and the TYRONE GUTHRIE. Among his directorial achievements is his 1974 staging for the MAN-HATTAN THEATRE CLUB of Milan Stitt's *The Runner Stumbles* – which, after a brief run in Stamford, CT, transferred to Broadway (1976) – and his 1997 *Richard III* for the New Perspectives Theater Co. His own plays include *Booth* (seen in New York in 1994), *Uncle Bob* (1995, MINT), and *Orson's Shadow* (2000, STEPPENWOLF). In 1995 he became director of CIRCLE REP, remaining until it closed.   CLJ

Penn, Arthur (1922–) Film and stage director who began his career as an actor, studying with MICHAEL CHEKHOV and debuting in New York in 1940. In 1958 he directed his first Broadway show, WILLIAM GIBSON's *Two for the Seesaw*, which he also directed in London the same year. Among his other directing credits are *The* MIRACLE WORKER (1959), TOYS IN THE ATTIC and Tad Mosel's *All the Way Home* (1960), GOLDEN BOY (1964), *Wait until Dark* (1966), and *Fortune's Fool* (2002). Other credits include *Sly Fox* (1976 and 2004) and *Golda* (1977). Penn has also directed many films, including *The Left-Handed Gun* starring PAUL NEWMAN (1958), *The Miracle Worker* (1962), *Bonnie and Clyde* (1967), and *Little Big Man* starring DUSTIN HOFFMAN (1970). President of the ACTORS STUDIO (1992–2000), he left to serve briefly as executive producer of television's *Law & Order*.   SMA

Penn (Jillette) (1955–) **&** (Raymond) **Teller** (1948–) PERFORMANCE ARTISTS and magicians who first teamed in 1975 as part of an act called "Asparagus Valley Cultural Society," which ran for two and a half years in SAN FRANCISCO. They appeared OFF-BROADWAY in 1985 and in 2000, and received rave reviews on Broadway in 1987. Their 1991 "Refrigerator Tour" culminated in their "Rot in Hell" show at the JOHN HOUSEMAN Theatre. For several years they have performed in a permanent home at Las Vegas's Rio All-Suite Hotel & Casino. Called by one critic "hilarious hustlers," Penn (6′ 6″ and very talkative) and Teller (5′ 9″ and mute) are known for their idiosyncratic approach to magic, replete with plenty of madness, mayhem, and bizarre humor. Their apparent exposure of magical effects has gained resentment from some in the magic community, yet they have enlivened the stage MAGIC show for a new generation.   DBW

Penumbra Theatre Company Founded in 1976 by Artistic Director Lou Bellamy as an outlet for African American voices and perspectives in the MINNEAPOLIS–ST. PAUL theatre community, and Minnesota's only professional black theatre (and one of few in the country). Located in a community center in the Selby–Dale neighborhood of

St. Paul, annually the company performs five productions to some 40,000 people. Penumbra, which in 2000 received the JUJAMCYN Award for development of artistic talent, has helped launch the career of a number of playwright, in particular AUGUST WILSON.   DBW

Perdziola, Robert (1961–) Costume designer. A native of Pittsburgh, he studied at Carnegie Mellon and counts SANTO LOQUASTO, Franco Zeffirelli, Desmond Heeley, and Dante Ferretti among his influences. Theatre credits number many productions at the SHAKESPEARE THEATRE (*The Country Wife*, *King John*, and *A Woman of No Importance*) with directors MICHAEL KAHN and Keith Baxter. Recipient of the 2000 IRENE SHARAFF Young Master Award, he designs opera frequently, including *Così fan tutte* for the Monte-Carlo Opera, which subsequently played at the San Francisco Opera and the Lyric Opera in Chicago, and *Il pirata*, his debut at the Metropolitan Opera in 2002.   BO

Perelman, S(idney) J(oseph) (1904–71) Humorist, occasional playwright, and one of the U.S.'s greatest erudite wits. After two MARX BROS. screenplays (1930–1), he collaborated with Ogden Nash on the book for WEILL's *One Touch of Venus* (1943) and wrote his only well-known Broadway play: *The Beauty Part* (1962), starring BERT LAHR.   DBW

performance art Combines elements from the visual, verbal, and performing arts, popular culture, and daily life, either to introduce the artist's body as a formal art medium, an ideological construction, and a political agent, or to present object art that courts the category of "live." Though performance artists are often trained in one or several artistic traditions, and may use video and slides or film projections, performance art often interrogates the category of art and the limits of tradition. A performance-art work can occur anywhere and be of any duration. It can also be entirely conceptual and exist only in the mind. Central to the history of performance art are the emergence of artistic practices that deconstruct the category of artist-genus and present the artist's body as a political sign and as object. Also central are critical analyses of material culture and art institutions. Wearing the body as a mask, or using it to resist institutional control and market consumption, performance artists become sites for visual self-representation and reflection, conceptual figuration, political agency, and narration.

The inception of American performance art in the 1960s was in part a response to global shifts of power due to U.S. foreign policy, and an outgrowth of public protests surrounding U.S. involvements abroad. It also coincided with a destabilization of prevailing modernist assumptions that had the individual firmly positioned within time and space. Since the 1960s, domestic racial struggles, the rise of the women's movement, gay liberation, and AIDS activism have continued to call these assumptions into question.

Intending social change and attempting to revise 18th-century standards of excellence in art that continued to shape modernist aesthetics, performance artists problematized a Kantian-derived formalism and the modernist primacy of vision. Deploying the theatricality of daily life – resistance, confrontation, and disruption – they challenged their political reality. Sit-ins, peace marches, and riots served as structural and ideological models for the arts activism and interventionist practices of performance artists.

As a revisionary art form and political art movement, performance art can be conceptually and strategically linked to Platonic antitheatrical prejudices against representation and illusion; the history of revolutionary social movements; the subtext of social realism basic to historical avant-garde art movements; and to the modernist fragmentation of the subject. Performance art in the West was also influenced by Japanese Gutai and Butoh. From the 1940s to the '60s, Marcel Duchamp, John Cage, Jackson Pollock, ALLAN KAPROW, and Claes Oldenburg linked the international avant-garde with American idioms, such as abstract expressionism, minimalism, pop art, and conceptual art, finally to create a distinct, yet evolving, American performance-art practice and aesthetic.

Duchamp and Oldenburg represented the commodity value of the body and the art object. Cage's and Kaprow's performances promoted a Zen-inspired art practice of relaxed "attention." These approaches advocated the dissolution of linear time, the rupture of traditional narrative structures, the use of nontraditional theatre and art spaces, the merging of art with life, decentering the position of the artist as director, and dissolving oppositional relations between performers and spectators.

Many women artists in the late 1960s and early '70s confronted issues of sexual discrimination in art and in their lives. To free themselves from oppression and define a place of their own, they used their bodies and the structures of their daily lives as tools with which to politicize and *de*naturalize women's bodies in the private and public spheres.

CAROLEE SCHNEEMANN's early FEMINIST performance *Naked Action Lecture* (1968), where she continuously undressed and dressed while she showed and discussed slides of her visual artwork, reframed the political and art-historical debates about voyeurism and male fantasies raised in *Site* (1964), an early minimalist performance with Robert Morris, in which Schneemann had posed as the artist's model, reclining center stage like Manet's *Olympia,* nude except for a black choker. In *Naked Action Lecture,* Schneemann repositioned herself as active in the scene, much as she had in the 1963 installation *Eye Body*, a groundbreaking intervention in which the artist and object were one.

Performance art is often misconstrued as a strictly solo activity. However, there have been many performance-art collaborations, such as Yoko Ono's and John Lennon's "Bed-Ins" (1969), LINDA MONTANO's *Handcuffed to Tom Marioni for Three Days* (1973), and TEHCHING HSIEH's *Art/Life One Year Performance* with Montano (1983–4). These partnering performances insisted on the political dimension of space and body – the core issue of 1970s and '80s feminist performance art – a dimension that had wide influence in a variety of subsequent political-art arenas. In the late 1990s and early 2000s the group Critical Art Ensemble, like Gran Fury before them, continued to explore space and body, particularly in the intersection of medical practices with biogenetics in work such as *Flesh Machine* (1997).

Ablutions (1972), a collaborative project about rape by Judy Chicago, SUZANNE LACY, Aviva Rahmani, and Sandra Orgel, based on oral histories collected by Lacy and Chicago, represented metaphors of violence against women, aimed so as to effect women's reimpowerment. In this work, cathartic autobiography and self-scrutiny was developed as an important survival tool and community-building strategy.

Ablutions set the stage for later PAGEANTlike women's performances – Chicago's *Dinner Party* (1973–9), Lacy's *Crystal Quilt* (1987) – and anticipated the collaboration of groups such as the Waitresses, the Guerrilla Girls, and the V-Girls. It prefigured such autobiographical performances as Lynn Hershman living as Roberta Breitmore (1973–8); or Robbie McCauley's *Sally's Rape* (1989–90), the story of McCauley's great-great-grandmother's struggle to survive as Thomas Jefferson's slave and mistress; and ADRIAN PIPER's ongoing performance of *My Calling (Card) No. 1: A Reactive Guerrilla Performance for Dinners and Cocktail Parties* (1986–present), which directs a cool but pointed rage against racism.

During the 1970s male artists began to identify with the victimization historically associated with female roles, and produced performances such as CHRIS BURDEN's *Shoot* (1971), VITO ACCONCI's *Conversions* (1971), Tom McCarthy's *Sailor Meat* (1974), and Tehching Hsieh's "Cage" performance (1978–9). Such work foregrounded the artist's often conflicted position toward formations of power, among other issues. While these artists explored the margins of their sexuality, and the relationship between aggression and their fear of death, they also confronted their bodies as objects, and confronted objects as the antitheses of aesthetic distance.

In *Trappings* (1971), Acconci staged an "occasion for self-sufficiency by dividing [himself] in two." He cradled his penis like a baby, spoke to it as a playmate, and covered it with cloth. In *Seedbed* (1972), he hid from spectators and while sexually arousing himself amplified his (orgasmic) voice into the gallery space, forcing spectators to participate vicariously in his autoeroticism. Through an inversion of voyeurism, *Seedbed* addressed processes of seduction, dispersal, the exhaustion of the body, and self-empowerment.

By the 1980s performances like *Naked Action Lecture, Seedbed,* and *Ablutions* had raised issues about the body and representation that would become the focus of major postmodernist theoretical and artistic debates. One of the most prominent participators in this debate, LAURIE ANDERSON, projected her media-consumed body onto the proscenium stage. Speaking at times in a "masculine" and "authoritarian" voice, other times as if a girls choir, Anderson sent her "O Superman" (1980s) voice through electronic filters and loops, and played with a dimpled smile for *and* against technology's seduction: "So hold me mom, in your long arms, in your automatic arms, your electronic arms. . . ."

Unlike 1960s and '70s performances that explored the liminal space between art and life, emerging 1980s CABARET art genres were crossovers from mainstream entertainment. They replaced both art and life with serial and digitized encounters from MTV, phone sex, and the 11 o'clock news. Remakes of popular culture, VAUDEVILLE, B-movies, and soaps were reedited into "queer theater" and "talent shows," or recycled into "living film serials" (e.g., JOHN JESURUN's *Chang in a Void Moon,* 1983–present), or "dyke noir" plays (e.g., HOLLY HUGHES's bawdy solo performances and her scripts for *Well of Horniness* and *Dress Suits for Hire*).

Mixing essentialist identities with difference, urban environments, and border cultures forged styles of "third world" trash and chic. Club performers like Carmelita Tropicana, the Alien Comic, Michael Smith, JOHN KELLY, and ETHYL EICHELBERGER took their cues from film and television stock characters and melodramas. Others, like ERIC BOGOSIAN and John Cale, were indebted to theatrical traditions and to classical NIGHTCLUB entertainers, such as stand-up comics LENNY BRUCE or Karl Valentin.

The success of performances of the early 1980s at NYC's East Village clubs was limited by the required profit margins of club managers, the clipped attention span of audiences raised on 24-hour TV, and white middle-American family values. Appropriating both censorship and apathy through a dialectic of rage and redemption, performance artists, such as KAREN FINLEY (as "Ass Man," 1985) or Martha Wilson (as "Nancy Reagan," 1984–8), parodied the Pollyannish rhetoric of the American Way. Wilson/Reagan, for example, advocated anorexia as a cure for world hunger and blamed "Ronny's" presidential failures on his "bad scripts."

By the end of the 1980s, Reaganomics and gentrification had closed cabaret doors. Performance artists were turning to mainstream stages, or, like Laurie Anderson, being absorbed by popular culture. The California-based performance group Survival Research Lab replaced the human body with a self-destructing, scrap-metal machine. James Luna re-presented his NATIVE AMERICAN body at San Diego's Museum of Man (1986) and at the Studio Museum in Harlem (1990) as an "Artifact" and as a site for political agency.

Art activist performers (e.g., GUILLERMO GÓMEZ-PEÑA and JIMMIE DURHAM), and activist COLLECTIVES (e.g., The Border Arts Workshop, the Los Angeles Poverty Department [LAPD], and AIDS ACT UP survived Reagan's years by holding on to the "body" with a vengeance. Senator Jesse Helms's 1990–1 CENSORSHIP campaign and the performance artists who explicitly address the endless range of human bodies in their work have raised the "body" to national discussion (see NATIONAL ENDOWMENT FOR THE ARTS). By the mid-1990s performance art had become even more autobiographical (see ONE-PERSON PERFORMANCE), and the distinction between performance art and mainstream theatre often blurs. Current trends in American performance art are covered in *The Drama Review* and *High Performance* (a quarterly). AF RS

Performance Group, The One of the most controversial and visible of the environmental theatre groups of the 1960s and '70s; formed in NYC

in 1967 by RICHARD SCHECHNER, critic, director, and editor of *The Drama Review*. Although in practice the work of the Group often seemed amateurish and self-indulgent, Schechner broke through traditional barriers of a text- and stage-bound theatre with productions such as *Dionysus in 69* (1968), *Makbeth* (1969), *Commune* (1970), and Genet's *The Balcony* (1979). Schechner's ideas were codified somewhat in his book on *Environmental Theatre* (1973). Though only partially successful, Schechner's group, performing in the Performing Garage in Wooster Street, was notable for its risk taking, its concern with social issues, and (with some direct influence from Grotowski) its investigation into ritual and the use of other cultures in the development of a new performance art. Schechner left the Garage in 1980; an offshoot, newly named the WOOSTER GROUP, has continued under the nominal leadership of ELIZABETH LECOMPTE. DBW

Performance Space 122 (P.S. 122) Founded in 1979 in an abandoned East Village elementary school by choreographer Charles Moulton, performers Charles Dennis, TIM MILLER, Peter Rose, and various visual artists. The site is now an acclaimed mecca for avant-garde theatre, dance, and music. Mark Russell, executive director from 1983 to 2004, dramatically expanded the building's use, creating theatres, dance spaces, and screening rooms, and offering classes and workshops. In time came commissions to performers, a national touring program, and an ambitious slate of nighly programming that defined postmodern advenurousness in performance. In 2004 Russell, who had shepherded the venue through at least two severe fiscal crunches, was succeeded by Vallejo Gantner, an Australian native who led the Dublin Fringe Festival. His early tenure was marked by efforts to increase international programming. LJ

periodicals/serials Between 700 and 800 periodicals or magazines devoted to the American theatre have come and gone since 1798; a definitive number is difficult to ascertain because many disappeared after a few issues, some after one. General magazines have been part of the French and English worlds of letters since the 17th century, and many contained news of the stage; but the first successful American example did not take hold until Benjamin Franklin's weekly *General Magazine* (founded in 1741), which did *not* report theatrical news.

In 1798, the *Thespian Oracle; or, Monthly Mirror, Consisting of Original Pieces and Selections from Perfor-*

mances of Merit, Relating Chiefly to the Most Admired Dramatic Compositions and Interspersed with Theatrical Anecdotes appeared in PHILADELPHIA, but did not survive its first issue. Theatrical news was reported sparingly in the principal newspapers of BOSTON, New York, and Philadelphia, but lingering prejudices against the theatre and the turbulence of the times politically (both in the late colonial and early republican periods) precluded anything more than announcements of performances, sometimes paid for by the trouping companies themselves.

In 1831, the weekly *Spirit of the Times,* part newspaper and part magazine, was founded in New York, combining theatrical and sporting news; it endured until 1902. In 1853, another weekly, the NEW YORK CLIPPER became the *Spirit*'s principal rival, and it, too, included news of the playing fields. It supplemented its weekly editions with a sporting and theatrical annual, which recorded CHARLOTTE CUSHMAN's stage triumphs with records of aquatic, track and field, and horse-racing feats. In 1924, the *Clipper* was absorbed by VARIETY, sans its sports pages.

The last important 19th-century theatrical weekly was the NEW YORK DRAMATIC MIRROR, which began publication in 1879 and survived until 1922 without the customary sports coverage. In 1880, the *Mirror* was acquired by the 20-year-old theatre-fixated HARRISON GREY FISKE. Under his aegis the magazine found a cause célèbre in the emergence of the Theatrical SYNDICATE, and from 1896 until 1911, when he left the weekly, Fiske crucified the trust and its evil geniuses in every issue.

The *Spirit*, the *Clipper*, and the *Mirror* carried play reviews, commentaries, biographies, personal notices, obituaries, advertisements, feature articles, and editorials on the theatre and performers. They also included illustrations – usually drawings of performers and buildings – and, occasionally, cartoons. Although quartered in New York, they were national publications, which was reflected in their coast-to-coast coverage.

The phenomenon of theatrical publishing remains VARIETY, a weekly that was founded in 1905 by Sime Silverman to report news of the VAUDEVILLE world. Silverman expanded its coverage to include "legit," and his successors have kept the publication alive by focusing on the dominant entertainment medium at any given moment. Silverman created for it a special journalistic argot full of ellipses, abbreviations, and Broadway colloquialisms, which has become its trademark. Although *Variety* devotes a few pages to theatre both in NYC and around the country,

its emphasis today is on movies and television. More theatrical in focus is BACK STAGE (1960–).

Theatre, the magazine of record for the peak years of the American stage, appeared in 1900, and was edited throughout most of its existence by ARTHUR HORNBLOW. Changed to *Theatre Magazine* in 1917, it was a monthly magazine dedicated to the stage and stage folk and profusely illustrated. Chromolithographs of stage stars adorned the covers of its first issues, which were followed later by color photographs once it became possible to transfer them to the printing process. Eventually news of the movie world usurped an increasing number of pages, and when it ceased publication in 1931 it was more a casualty of a diminished theatre, shrinking audiences, and changing tastes than a victim of the Depression.

Two magazines, THEATRE ARTS and *Stage,* grew out of the art-theatre movement. Founded by SHELDON CHENEY, *Theatre Arts* was launched as a quarterly sponsored by the Detroit Society of Arts and Crafts in 1916. It moved to NYC and, under the leadership of EDITH ISAACS, went monthly in 1923, changing its focus in the 1930s to the commercial theatre. In 1923, the still-experimental THEATRE GUILD brought out an occasional publication, *Theatre Guild Bulletin,* which gradually appeared quarterly and then monthly. In 1932, it was enlarged both physically and editorially as *Stage* and was liberally illustrated. In 1939, with both magazines near bankruptcy, they were merged as *Theatre Arts Magazine,* which continued publication until 1964.

Theatre Arts represents the last of the significant broad-based theatre magazines. Current survivors target specific audiences: *Theatre Crafts,* founded in 1967, covers technical aspects of professional and university theatre, as does *Theatre Design & Technology* (1964–); *American Theatre,* a creation of THEATRE COMMUNICATIONS GROUP in 1984, reflects events of regional theatres throughout the country; PLAYBILL *Magazine,* a monthly version of the Broadway theatre program, simply omits show credits; *TheaterWeek,* published from 1987 to 1996 as a tabloid (and replaced briefly by *In-Theatre*), aimed mainly at the New York audience; and a variety of other publications are issued by learned societies or are literary in focus, some without American topics. Among those that do cover American theatre are *Journal of American Drama and Theatre* (1989–), *PAJ: Performing Arts Journal* (1976–), *The Drama Review (TDR)* (1957–), *Theatre History Studies* (1980–), *Theatre Journal* (1949–), *Theatre Research International* (1979–), *Theatre Survey* (1960–), and *Theatre Forum* (1992–).

MCH

Perkins, Osgood (1892–1937) Stage and film actor noted for his versatility and polish. Perkins graduated from Harvard in 1914 after having participated in some of the GEORGE PIERCE BAKER plays. After serving in WWI, he formed the Film Guild, a cinematic production company, and appeared in several of its productions. WINTHROP AMES then cast him as Homer Cady in BEGGAR ON HORSEBACK, his Broadway debut (1924); JED HARRIS next hired him for *Weak Sisters* (1925). Perkins later starred as Walter Burns in *The* FRONT PAGE (1928) and played Astrov in *Uncle Vanya* (1930). He also appeared in such films as *Scarface* and *Madame Du Barry*. He was described as "wiry, nervous, [and] unerring in his attack." Perkins's son, **Anthony (Tony) Perkins** (1932–92), of *Psycho* fame, enjoyed a highly successful stage and film acting career, including stage appearances in TEA AND SYMPATHY (1953), LOOK HOMEWARD, ANGEL (1957), *Greenwillow* (1960), *The Star-Spangled Girl* (1966), *Equus* (1974), and *Romantic Comedy* (1979), SMA

Perloff, Carey (1959–) Director and playwright. Educated in the classics and comparative literature (Stanford and Oxford), Perloff has directed and produced innovative, even controversial, translations of the classics and modern European plays. At the Edinburgh Festival in 1983, she staged the works of Mrożek, David Edgar, and Mayakovsky to critical acclaim. After directorial assignments for a handful of major nonprofit theatres (including AMERICAN PLACE THEATRE, LINCOLN CENTER, NEW YORK SHAKESPEARE FESTIVAL, ROUNDABOUT THEATRE), she became artistic director of two major companies: CSC REP (1986–92), which won a 1988 Obie grant for Artistic Excellence under her leadership, and the AMERICAN CONSERVATORY THEATER (1992–). For CSC she directed the world premiere of Ezra Pound's version of Sophocles' *Elektra* (1987–8); the American Premiere of Tony Harrison's *Phaedra Britannica*, and a new translation of *Don Juan of Seville* (score by ELIZABETH SWADOS) (1988–9); Beckett's *Happy Days* and BRECHT's *The Resistible Rise of Arturo Ui* (1990–1); and Strindberg's *Creditors* and Len Jenkin's *Candide* (1991–2). At ACT, her directing assignments have ranged from Timberlake Wertenbaker's new translation of Euripides' *Hecuba*, starring Olympia Dukakis (1994–5), to the world premiere of COLE PORTER's Broadway-bound *High Society* (1997–8). In 2000 she directed the American premiere of Stoppard's *The Invention of Love,* and in 2002 the world premiere of a commissioned music-theatre work, Lang and WELLMAN's *The Difficulty of Crossing a Field*, based on a short story by Ambrose Bierce and developed in collaboration with the Kronos Quartet. During the 2005–6 season she directed her own version of *A Christmas Carol,* and Brecht's *Happy End* in MICHAEL FEINGOLD's adaptation in June 2006. At ACT Perloff instituted the First Look New Play Festival and symposia with invited scholars and artists to discuss each production. She is noted especially for her strong leadership in erasing a deficit, attracting a new audience, and keeping the company together while the Geary Theatre was remodeled following the earthquake of 1989. Her own plays include *The Colossus of Rhodes* (2001, LORTEL White Barn) and *Luminescence Dating* (2005, ENSEMBLE STUDIO). TLM

Perry, Antoinette (1888–1946) Actress, producer, director, and activist. Following her 1905 Chicago debut, she acted in New York until her 1909 marriage to socially prominent businessman Frank Frueaff. After his death, she returned to the stage in 1924, acting under BROCK PEMBERTON's management, then assisting him, and finally directing such successes as *Strictly Dishonorable* (1929) and *HARVEY* (1944). As chair of the American Theatre Council's Apprentice Theatre (1937–9), she inaugurated and conducted 5,000 auditions to encourage young talent. In 1941 she was president of the Experimental Theatre. She held leadership positions with the Stage Relief Fund, the Actors Thrift Shop, and the AMERICAN THEATRE WING and its Stage Door Canteen. The annual Antoinette Perry (Tony) Awards, named for her, commemorate her extraordinary service to the theatre. FHL

Perseverance Theatre Alaska's largest professional not-for-profit theatre was founded in 1979 in Juneau (located now in Douglas) by former artistic director Molly Smith. It has premiered over 50 new plays by Alaskan and national playwrights. Its mission is to offer these productions – to as many as 20,000 annually – through an Alaskan lens. Smith, who since 1998 has helmed the ARENA STAGE, was succeeded by Peter DuBois (1998–2003) and in 2004 PJ Paparelli. DBW

Peters [née Lazzara]**, Bernadette** (1948–) Singer, dancer, and actress, born in Ozone Park, NY. After singing and dancing for several years in Broadway choruses, beginning with the 1959 revival of *The* MOST HAPPY FELLA, she achieved critical recognition in the OFF-BROADWAY 1930s spoof *Dames at Sea* (1968). She appeared in *George M!* (1968) and the revival of ON THE TOWN (1971), then starred as silent-movie comedienne Mabel Normand in *Mack & Mabel* (1974). She played in SUNDAY IN THE PARK WITH GEORGE (1984), won a Tony Award for her performance in *Song and Dance* (1985), created the role of the witch in INTO THE WOODS (1987), was Paula in *The Goodbye Girl* (1993), played the title role (Tony Award) in the 1999 revival of ANNIE GET YOUR GUN, and appeared as Rose in the 2003 *Gypsy* revival. She frequently gives concerts (including Carnegie Hall), often with symphony orchestras. MK

Peters, (Charles) Rollo (1892–1967) Designer and actor. During the 1920s–1940s Peters was known as a romantic actor, often playing opposite JANE COWL (1922–5). He was also one of the important figures of the New Stagecraft movement and a founder of the THEATRE GUILD. He began acting with the WASHINGTON SQUARE PLAYERS and designed all their early sets. With the Guild he designed and acted in *Bonds of Interest* and *John Ferguson* (1919), among others. One of his most notable settings was for MINNIE MADDERN FISKE's production of *Madame Sand* (1917). AA

Petersen, William (1953–) Star of CBS's *CSI: Crime Scene Investigation* (since 2000), this Evanston, IL–born actor who attended Idaho State on a football scholarship, has a long, respected theatre résumé, including performances with STEPPENWOLF (FOOL FOR LOVE, 1984) and CHICAGO's Remains Theatre Ensemble, which he cofounded. He was Stanley in A STREETCAR NAMED DESIRE in 1984 at Stratford, Ontario; played killer Jack Henry Abbott in *The Belly of the Beast* (1983, WISDOM BRIDGE; 1985, JOHN F. KENNEDY CENTER); and appeared on Broadway opposite CHERRY JONES in *The NIGHT OF THE IGUANA* in 1996. DBW

Peterson, Lisa (1961–) California-born director, graduate of Yale in English and theatre. In the 1990s she was one of the busiest and most versatile talents working OFF-BROADWAY and in the regional theatre, producing new works and reinterpretations of the classics. In 1991 she received an Obie for direction of Caryl Churchill's *Light Shining in Buckinghamshire*. Her credits include *The Waves* at the NEW YORK THEATRE WORKSHOP (1990), TONY KUSHNER's *Slavs!* at NYTW (1994), *The Model Apartment* by DONALD MARGULIES at PRIMARY STAGES (1995),and José Rivera's *Sueño* at MCC Theater (1999), Her work has been seen at the MARK TAPER (where she was a resident director, 1995–2005), SOUTH COAST REP, ACTORS THEATRE OF LOUISVILLE, LA JOLLA PLAYHOUSE (where she served as an associate director), YALE REP, HARTFORD STAGE, PLAYWRIGHTS HORIZONS, the HUNTINGTON, MCCARTER, the ARENA, and other major regional theatres. DBW

Petit Théâtre de Vieux Carré, Le New Orleans's oldest performing-arts organization was founded in 1916 as one of America's earliest "Little Theatres" (see COMMUNITY THEATRE). It soon purchased its present property, a Spanish colonial structure built in 1797 in the French Quarter; later renovations added a 450-seat auditorium and a smaller CHILDREN's THEATRE. The theatre currently produces six mainstage plays and musicals each season, plus two children's series, and is home to the TENNESSEE WILLIAMS/New Orleans Literary Festival. Hurricane Katrina in 2005 did insignificant damage and has not curtailed the theatre's operations. Major renovation began in 2006. LAB

Petrified Forest, The by ROBERT SHERWOOD. In a superb production directed by ARTHUR HOPKINS, this play opened at the BROADHURST THEATRE on 7 January 1935. Capturing the spirit of the 1930s, with arguments over Marxist ideology and the down-and-out, the play combined the excitement of American gunfights with the uplift of newfound purpose – even if that resolve results in assisted suicide to effect the dreams of a young, spirited woman, Gabby (Peggy Conklin). In an isolated gas station/diner in the wilds of Arizona, Alan Squier, a wandering, failed writer (Leslie Howard) finds an unlikely kindred spirit in a fugitive killer, Duke Mantee (Humphrey Bogart). Appropriately, Squier, if killed, requests burial in the Petrified Forest – a symbol both of lost souls like Alan and of the useless wishes of Gabby's father, who perpetuates outworn images of what it means to be American. RHW

Phantom of the Opera, The On 9 January 2006 ANDREW LLOYD WEBBER's musical, which had opened at the MAJESTIC THEATRE 26 January 1988, became the longest-running show in Broadway history, with 7,486 performances (8,029 as of 29 April 2007), surpassing Webber's CATS. Its more than $600 million gross is also a record (worldwide the box office has exceeded $3.2 billion). Up to its record-breaking performance 244 actors had appeared in the NYC production, including 11 Phantoms (the first being Michael Crawford; the most performances by Howard McGillin, almost 1,400). Based on Gaston Leroux's 1911 novel, the book is by Richard Stilgoe and Webber with lyrics by Charles Hart (and Stilgoe); it was directed by HAROLD PRINCE and choreographed by Gillian Lynne, with designs by Maria Björnson. The success of this opulent, romanticized, and sensualized version of the phantom's story – with its falling replica of the Paris Opera

House chandelier and life-size mechanical elephant – virtually defies explanation. A different musical version, called *Phantom* (1991), with book by ARTHUR KOPIT and score by MAURY YESTON, though effective, could not compete.   DBW

Philadelphia Colonial Philadelphia's theatre history was marked by conflict between Quaker-led religious opposition and the more liberal viewpoint represented by the British crown. Strolling players were noted in 1724, and the next year comedians performed at the "new Booth in Society Hill." In 1749 actors led by WALTER MURRAY AND THOMAS KEAN rented a warehouse owned by a former Quaker, William Plumstead. The only play known to have been performed was Addison's *Cato*. The Common Council voted to suppress this "disorder" in January 1750, so Murray and Kean moved on to New York.

LEWIS HALLAM's company arrived in 1754. Despite opposition, Plumstead's building on the waterfront at Pine St. again served as a playhouse. Under special license from the royal governor, the company successfully gave 30 performances before heading for Charleston. DAVID DOUGLASS brought Hallam's company back to Philadelphia in 1759. A new governor gave him a permit to construct a simple theatre on Society Hill, just outside the city's jurisdiction. The company played for six months, beginning with *Tamerlane* on 25 June. This was the longest, most brilliant season thus far in America.

In 1766 Douglass built the SOUTHWARK, at South and Apollo Sts., considered the first permanent theatre in America. Again located just beyond the city limits, it opened 12 November 1766. Here Douglass was successful enough to return nearly every winter until 1773. The first American tragedy, *The Prince of Parthia* (see INTRODUCTION, §1) by Thomas Godfrey was presented at the Southwark on 24 April 1767.

During the Revolution the Continental Congress banned plays and other entertainments; the occupying British Army, however, mounted plays at the Southwark in 1777–8. Restrictions against plays were still in force when Douglass's stepson Lewis HALLAM Jr., came to the theatre in 1784 with lectures, music, and songs. Finally in 1789 prominent citizens successfully petitioned the Pennsylvania Legislature to repeal these laws. Hallam's Old AMERICAN COMPANY responded by offering 15 legal play performances before continuing its tour.

Two years later musician Alexander Reinagle and the American Company's THOMAS WIGNELL began to raise money from the city's leading citizens to build a new theatre in the center of town. The CHESTNUT STREET THEATRE (1794) was considered the most handsome playhouse in the country, with the finest STOCK COMPANY. Recruited mainly in England, the company also toured to Baltimore, Washington, DC, and Alexandria.

On 9 April 1793 equestrian John Bill Ricketts opened America's first CIRCUS, along with a riding academy. The circular wooden building, with its single dirt ring, stood near the State House and across the street from the Chestnut Street Theatre; it burned in 1799. A new circus building was begun in 1808 at 9th and Walnut Sts., opening as the New Circus on 2 February 1809. Variety acts were part of its program, and by 1812 a stage was added for a new acting company. The circus became first the Olympic and finally the WALNUT STREET THEATRE.

The Chestnut Street Theatre, under the able management of WILLIAM WARREN THE ELDER and WILLIAM WOOD, withstood the competition. It burned in 1820 (see FIRES), but was rebuilt and active when the ARCH STREET THEATRE opened in 1828. Rivalry among the three theatres almost proved fatal, but they reorganized and survived. Although subsequent changes in management and policies eventually helped diminish Philadelphia's status as the country's premier theatrical city, the theatres were able to maintain solid stock companies, occasionally augmented by guest stars.

Philadelphia remained a vital theatrical and cultural center. A group of mid-19th century playwrights, known as the "Philadelphia School," included ROBERT MONTGOMERY BIRD and RICHARD PENN SMITH. The following century would bring Pulitzer Prize winners GEORGE KELLY and CHARLES FULLER. America's most important early stage stars built careers in or came from Philadelphia: EDWIN FORREST, CHARLOTTE CUSHMAN, and JOSEPH JEFFERSON III. Among later stars were the DREW–BARRYMORES: not only actor-sibs Lionel, Ethel, and John Barrymore, but their grandmother, Mrs. John Drew, who managed the Arch Street Theatre during 1861–92.

In 1876 Mrs. Drew's theatre was one of the first in the city to drop the stock company in favor of a combination house that booked individual productions. During her era at the Arch, Philadelphia's theatrical scene had expanded and diversified. By 1880 there were nine legitimate theatres, five variety houses, two minstrel halls, and a theatre for German plays.

Philadelphia became a leading MINSTREL center. In 1853 Sam Sanford gave the city its first all-minstrel theatre; but the most important was the 11th Street Opera House, opened by Sanford in 1855. He was succeeded there by the Carncross and Dixey Minstrels, and then by Frank Dumont's Minstrels in 1895. The final show there, 13 May 1911, ended its 56-year record as a minstrel house. Although popular for another decade, minstrels had to compete with VAUDEVILLE, especially the family shows at B. F. KEITH's Theatre (1902).

By the 1920s Philadelphia had become an important tryout town: A convenient 90 miles from Times Square, it had several large downtown playhouses attracting a sophisticated and discriminating audience. The theory was that if a show could survive in Philadelphia, it would have a long run on Broadway. This theory often proved correct, and the city took pride in its favored position.

Over a 50-year period, circumstances of geography and tradition created a dependence on the vitality of the Broadway stage. When times were hard in New York, there were fewer tryouts and road shows coming through Philadelphia. Also, the city was unable to maintain a significant professional showcase for Shakespeare (see SHAKESPEARE ON . . .), the classics, and contemporary drama. These factors contributed to the early rise and continued popularity of Little Theatre (see COMMUNITY THEATRE) groups. Plays and Players (1911) is one of the country's oldest theatre CLUBS and still operates its own playhouse on Delancey St. The Society Hill Playhouse has been producing since 1959. By 1960 there were 100 amateur community and college companies in the city and surrounding area producing over 400 plays a season.

Inspired by Jasper Deeter's HEDGEROW THEATRE, the Theatre of the Living Arts (1965–9) made a noteworthy but short-lived attempt at professional resident repertory. During the 1970s, with dwindling competition from Broadway shows, amateur theatres had the opportunity to develop into professional resident companies. The Philadelphia Drama Guild (1959) turned professional in 1971 but closed in 1995. The Philadelphia Theatre Company (1974) gained full ACTORS' EQUITY status in 1981. The more avant-garde Wilma Theatre (1973) became professional in 1983.

Having survived several restorations, the Walnut Street Theatre was made a National Landmark in 1968 and its interior modernized. It is considered the "oldest theatre in continuous use in the English-speaking world." A resident company was formed there in 1983; with more than 50,000 subscribers in 2006, it had the largest mainstage subscription base of any resident theatre in America. In 1996 and 2001 its mainstage underwent improvements and renovations.

By the early 1990s Philadelphia's thriving theatre scene included some two dozen RESIDENT NONPROFIT PROFESSIONAL THEATRE companies (including the lively People's Light & Theatre Company in nearby Malvern), plus many amateur and youth groups. In addition to the large theatres downtown, The University of Pennsylvania's Annenberg Center (1971) provided space for a variety of performances, including those of the Philadelphia Festival Theatre for New Plays (1981). In early 1994 the University of the Arts's Arts Bank (theatre) opened, joining other performance venues on Broad St., and in September of that year the Barrymore Awards for Excellence in Theatre were announced, the first comprehensive theatre awards ever given in the city.

In the past 10–20 years there has been a growth in midsize companies, and a number of established companies have obtained new homes: The Prince Music Theatre, founded in 1984, moved into a new facility (formerly the Midtown Theater) in 1994; the Philadelphia Theatre Company (with its all-premieres policy), founded in 1974, located a new home on Avenue of the Arts (projected occupancy in 2007); the Arden Theatre, in operation since 1988, bought a space in Olde City in 1995; and The Wilma, founded in 1973 and currently led by Jiri and Blanka Zizka, Czech emigrés, moved into a new 300-seat space on Avenue of the Arts in 1996. In 2001 the Kimmel Center for the Performing Arts (though not a theatre facility per se) opened, adding immeasurably to the artistic life of the city. A number of small companies folded in the 1990s; others, like the Pig Iron Theatre (established in 1995), a "dance-clown-theatre ensemble," have taken up some of the slack. According to the Theatre Alliance of Greater Philadelphia, in 2006 there were roughly 100 producing theatres in the area.   GD   DBW

Philadelphia [*né* Meyer]**, Jacob** (1721–c. 1800) Conjuror, the son of Polish Jews, and the first American-born MAGICIAN to gain international acclaim. He served as a scientific jester for William Augustus, Duke of Cumberland, performing mathematical and physical experiments. After the duke's death in 1765, he went public, traveling through Europe billed as "An Artist of Mathematics." He gained the reputation of a true sorcerer who could pass through doors, grow a second head, and read minds.   LS

Philadelphia Story, The Following seven unsuccessful years, this play confirmed PHILIP BARRY'S reputation as master of polite comedy, lasting 417 performances from its 28 March 1939 opening at the SAM S. SHUBERT THEATRE. The play details the romantic awakening of spoiled, aristocratic Tracy Lord, who achieves emotional security and returns to her former husband following a harmless interlude with a reporter assigned to cover her second wedding. The lack of complication was offset by sophisticated innuendo, such as an implicit nude swim, and, more important, by dialogue that retains its cleverness. By design, the comedy showcased KATHARINE HEPBURN, who shared a 75% investment with Barry and Howard Hughes. The play's complete triumph also resolved one of several financial crises for the THEATRE GUILD, which had supplied the remaining backing. The film version was released in 1940.   RW

Phoenix Theatre see ASSOCIATION OF PRODUCING ARTISTS

photographers Although photography, in the form of daguerreotypy, had been introduced in America shortly after being officially recognized as Louis Daguerre's invention in France in 1839, the value of the photograph to the theatre was not fully comprehended until the arrival of Jenny Lind in America in 1850. Wherever she traveled on her tour, Madame Lind posed for local photographers, and the resulting daguerreotypes were collected avidly by her admirers. By the time the daguerreotype was supplanted by the paper photograph, collecting likenesses became a national mania.

Performers, recognizing the publicity value of portrait photographs, became eager to comply with a request for a picture. Two sizes of photograph were particularly favored: Both the small *carte-de-visite* and the larger cabinet photograph were hawked by street peddlers, stocked in bins at photography shops, inserted as advertisements in candy, cigarette, soap, and corset boxes, and sold through mail-order catalogs.

The first photographer to make a specialty of taking celebrity pictures was Napoleon Sarony. Operating in a 19th-century studio crammed with curios located in his heyday in the Union Square theatrical district, he photographed hundreds of show people, posing them with a special flair against exotic backgrounds. Sarony had imitators in New York and throughout America as the specialty grew. One of his competitors, Benjamin Falk, claimed to have taken the first onstage dramatic scene in America in 1883 at the MADISON SQUARE THEATRE.

After Sarony, photographic studios took over theatrical photography. With improved techniques for indoor photography, the Byron Studio, founded in 1888, began to record productions regularly for producers, who, by this time, knew the value of the scene still. Byron was followed by the White Studio, which, in turn, was succeeded by the Vandamm Studio. The Vandamms held sway over Broadway theatrical photography for more than 30 years. Eventually, the Vandamms' perfectly composed shot was supplanted by the freer candid or instant photography practiced by Eileen Darby and the Friedman–Abeles Studio and by Martha Swope, recently retired (her associates continue to dominate the field). Since the mid-1980s the most prominent new Broadway photographer has been Joan Marcus (over 100 productions). From Sarony to Swope and Marcus, the New York theatre has been blessed with an unparalleled and unbroken iconographic record. Several photographers (e.g., Tom Chargin, T. Charles Erickson, Ken Howard, Craig Schwartz) specialize in regional photography.   MCH

Piano Lesson, The by AUGUST WILSON. Part of Wilson's ten-part cycle on African American history, this Pulitzer Prize–winning drama opened at the WALTER KERR Theatre 16 April 1990 after beginning at YALE REPERTORY THEATRE and touring several regional theatres. Directed by LLOYD RICHARDS and featuring Charles S. Dutton and S. Epatha Merkerson, the play is set in Pittsburgh during the 1930s, and tells the story of a young man's attempt to sell a family piano to buy land on which his ancestors were slaves. The piano has great meaning, however, for his sister, and in the argument that follows, Wilson makes a point about African Americans finding a connection with their past.   TLM

Pickle Family Circus Founded in 1975 in SAN FRANCISCO and singular in the annals of the American CIRCUS for its small size, its close association with SF and environs, and its influence on subsequent circus development, including CIRQUE DU SOLEIL (like Cirque, the Pickle used no animals) and St. Louis's Circus Flora. Unique as a clown-centered, cooperative one-ring circus, it was founded by Peggy Snider, Larry Pisoni, and Cecil MacKinnon. Along with Pisoni, its early clowns included BILL IRWIN and GEOFF HOYLE. Juggling was also intrinsic to the circus's performances. In 1993 the name changed to the New Pickle Circus and it became part of the Circus Center in SF (which includes the SF School of Circus Arts, the New Pickle, and the San Francisco

Circus). The Pickle clowns are analyzed in a 2001 book by Joel Schechter.   DBW

Picnic by WILLIAM INGE opened on 19 February 1953, produced by the THEATRE GUILD and director JOSHUA LOGAN. Inge's second Broadway production, this Pulitzer Prize–winning play solidified his reputation and generated a storm of controversy. Spanning two seasons for 477 performances, it featured a bare-chested Ralph Meeker as the virile Hal Carter – a Midwestern Dionysus – who wanders into the otherwise sterile lives of four women in a sleepy rural town. With a realistic surface, it is a psychological and ritualistic play in which the longings and fears of each of these women are brought to the surface through their contact with Hal. Still frequently staged by amateur and professional groups, including a revival by the ROUNDABOUT in 1994, *Picnic* was also successful as a 1955 film and garnered five Academy Award nominations. Logan directed and William Holden was Hal in this version, adapted by Logan and screenwriter Daniel Taradash. A reworked version of *Picnic*, called *Summer Brave,* was first staged in 1975 (ANTA Playhouse).   MR

Picon, Molly (1898–1992) American entertainer who began performing as a child in Philadelphia, where her mother sewed costumes for Yiddish actresses. After a stint in VAUDEVILLE, she starred internationally in YIDDISH THEATRE, cabaret, and films with husband, Jacob Kalich, as producer, writer, or coperformer. Known for her saucy but innocent gamine charm, through much of her life she has been associated with the roles of very young women and even mischievous schoolboys. She also starred in English-language plays and films, such *Milk and Honey, A Majority of One,* and *Come Blow Your Horn,* and on television and radio. Her autobiography, *So Laugh a Little,* appeared in 1962. Active well into her 80s, in 1979 she wrote and performed in the REVUE *Those Were the Days.*   NS

Pilbrow, Richard (1933–) London-born lighting designer, producer, author, and theatrical consultant, active on both sides of the Atlantic. Having lit the NYC production of *Rosencrantz and Guildenstern Are Dead* (1967), he became the first British national to design an original Broadway musical (*Zorba,* 1968), Pilbrow has added numerous American credits since, including *The Rothschilds* (1970), *Four Baboons Adoring the Sun* (1992), SHOW BOAT (NYC, 1994), *The Life* (1997), and *Our Town* (2002), among many others. As a result of designed projections for Broadway's *A FUNNY THING HAPPENED ON THE WAY TO THE FORUM* and *GOLDEN BOY,* Pilbrow became the first British lighting designer admitted to New York's United Scenic Artists' Union, Local 829 (see UNIONS).   DBW

Pilgrim, James (1825–79) English-born playwright and actor who came to the U.S. in 1849, acted first in his own play, *The Limerick Boy,* in PHILADELPHIA, eventually managed theatres in BOSTON, Philadelphia, and New York, and wrote more than 200 entertainments and plays, some for particular actors – Mr. and Mrs. BARNEY WILLIAMS, MAGGIE MITCHELL, Mary Devlin, and F. S. CHANFRAU. Among his popular plays are *Irish Assurance and Yankee Modesty, Shandy MaGuire,* and *Paddy the Piper.*   WJM

Piñero, Miguel (1947–88) Puerto Rican playwright, author of SHORT EYES (1974) and *The Sun Always Shines for the Cool* (1975), both produced by JOE PAPP, and other published plays (e.g., *Outrageous: One Act Plays,* 1986). A former inmate at Sing-Sing, Piñero was a member of "The Family," a theatrical troupe of former prisoners, as well as a cofounder of the NUYORICAN Poets' Café (1974). He is considered a major influence on young Puerto Rican writers of his generation.   ER

Pinkins, Tonya (1962–) Actress-singer, Chicago native educated at Carnegie Mellon, who won Tony and Drama Desk awards for Best Featured Actress in a Musical for her Sweet Anita, the spitfire chanteuse in JELLY'S LAST JAM (1992). In 2004 she received critical acclaim and the recognition she long deserved for the title role in TONY KUSHNER and JEANINE TESORI's *Caroline, or Change:* Her performance as an African American domestic working for a Jewish Louisiana family in 1963 won her an Obie and LUCILLE LORTEL Award, followed by Tony and Drama Desk nominations. Other credits of note include *Play On!, The Wild Party, Chronicle of a Death Foretold, Merrily We Roll Along* (her Broadway debut in 1981), and, at the PUBLIC, *The Caucasian Chalk Circle* and *The Merry Wives of Windsor.* In 2007 she appeared on Broadway in AUGUST WILSON's *Radio Golf.*   DBW

Pins and Needles Satirical musical REVUE originally produced in 1936 under the auspices of the ILGWU (International Ladies Garment Workers Union) to spoof labor and other "leftish" topics. The first edition at the Labor Stage featured the work of HAROLD ROME and Earl Robinson and was enormously popular. After considerable revision it was produced again in 1937 and was a box-office success. ARTHUR ARENT and MARC BLITZ-

STEIN contributed delightful satire, and Eleanor Roosevelt invited the company to give a "command performance" at the White House. There were several subsequent editions featuring amateur actors from the union and material that satirized BERTOLT BRECHT and HALLIE FLANAGAN, as well as more visible right-wing targets like Father Coughlin. The last edition – *New Pins and Needles* – was produced on 26 November 1939 at the Windsor Theatre, and included a spoof of CLIFFORD ODETS called "Paradise Mislaid." BBW

Pinski, David (1872–1959) YIDDISH playwright who, like many of his contemporaries, began writing in eastern Europe (Warsaw) and died in Israel. In 1899 he arrived in America, where he wrote most of his 38 plays, as well as novels, short stories, and articles. *Isaac Sheftl* (1896) is a naturalistic tragedy. *The Tsvi Family* (1904) and *The Eternal Jew* (1906) are serious symbolic dramatizations of Jewish history, past and contemporaneous. *Yankl the Smith* (1906), eventually filmed, is a domestic drama about love and jealousy. *The Treasure* – staged first in German by REINHARDT in 1910, then in Yiddish, and then in English by the THEATRE GUILD (1920) – is a comedy about poverty and human greed. NS

Pioneer Playhouse of Kentucky Located on 200 acres in Danville, Pioneer Playhouse boasts of being the oldest OUTDOOR repertory theatre in the state. Founded in 1950 by Eben Henson, the Playhouse offers an accredited drama school that has trained more than 3,000 young actors. The grounds include both an outdoor and indoor theatre, a sound stage, campgrounds, and a 19th-century Main Street with train station, general store, and ice cream parlor, used as the setting for several films. Henson also helped start the Kentucky Council of Performing Arts. A documentary about the Playhouse first aired on Kentucky Educational Television in 2002. LAB

Piper, Adrian (Margaret Smith) (1948–) New York–born conceptual and PERFORMANCE ARTIST whose art practices cross many media: visual art, video installation, film, artists' books, and choreography. A student of sculpture at the New York School of Visual Arts, and of philosophy at City College of New York (B.A., 1977) and Harvard University (Ph.D., 1981), her performances are influenced by conceptual art, popular culture, and Kantian and analytic philosophy. In her performances, she identifies racial and gender discrimination embedded in the visual pathology of white America. She began performing with *Meat into*

Meat (1968); this was followed by *Catalysis Series* (1970–1) and *Being Mythic on the Street* (1973), both street performances. *My Calling (Card),* ongoing since 1986, is a "reactive guerrilla performance" against racism. AF

Piscator, Erwin (1893–1966) German director who developed agitprop staging techniques with film, projected scenery, and many ingenious mechanical devices to promote and support the political context of his productions. Dismissed in 1927 for promoting political ideas at the Volksbühne in Berlin, in protest he established his own theatre (Piscator-Bühne) and wrote *The Political Theatre* (1929), which documented his work and ideas. In 1929 he produced MAXWELL ANDERSON and Stallings's antiwar play WHAT PRICE GLORY, adapted by Carl Zuckmayer as *Rivalen,* in Berlin, using elaborate back projections and a treadmill with soldiers marching toward the audience. His DOCUMENTARY approach influenced the LIVING NEWSPAPER of the FEDERAL THEATRE PROJECT and provided a model for BRECHT's ideas on epic theatre. Piscator came to NYC in 1939 and headed the Dramatic Workshop in the New School of Social Research, staging over 100 experimental works, including his adaptation of *War and Peace* (1942). He was also active in the President and Roof-Top theatres. In 1951 he returned to Germany, and in 1962 became director of the new Freie Volksbühne, where he staged Hochhuth's *The Deputy* (1963) and Weiss's *The Investigation* (1965). RE

Pitou, Augustus (1843–1915) Manager and producer. Beginning as a supporting actor in EDWIN BOOTH's company (1867), Pitou turned to management, handling BOOTH'S THEATRE and the FIFTH AVENUE for JOHN STETSON, and later managing the FOURTEENTH STREET THEATRE and the Grand Opera House. He managed the careers of stars including W. J. Scanlan, ROBERT B. MANTELL, CHAUNCEY OLCOTT, and ROSE COGHLAN. Pitou wrote and produced romantic plays about Irish life for Olcott (e.g., *A Romance of Athlone,* 1899) and others, as well as a book of memoirs, *Masters of the Show* (1914). TLM

Pitt, Leonard (1941–) Performer, teacher, and co-artistic director of Life on the Water (1986–93), a SAN FRANCISCO theatre. As author and performer of *2019 Blake, Meantime,* and *Not for Real,* he has drawn upon abilities (developed with Étienne Decroux and in visits to Bali) in MIME and masks. From 1970–88 he ran the Leonard Pitt School of Mime in Berkeley. TL

Pittsburgh Playhouse A COMMUNITY THEATRE established in 1933 that presented its first productions at the Frick Training School for Teachers. It occupied the Hamlet Street Theatre (formerly a speakeasy) in 1935 and attempted professionalization. The community withdrew its support, but returned it under the general management (1937–63) of Frederick Burleigh. The Playhouse acquired the Craft Street Theatre in 1952 and edged again toward greater professionalization. Concerted efforts during 1963–8 to establish a RESIDENT NONPROFIT PROFESSIONAL company brought the organization to the brink of collapse. Point Park College (now University) assumed operational control in 1968, making the Playhouse and its personnel its performing arts department and continuing to offer a professional mainstage season. Since its founding in 1975 the Pittsburgh Public Theater has emerged as a more active nonprofit professional operation serving the diverse Pittsburgh community. Some 18 productions and 235 performances, overseen by producing director Ronald Allan-Lindblom, are experienced by 30,000 patrons annually.   WD

Pixley [née Shea], **Annie** (1855–93) Popular "soubrette" in a string of forgotten comedies (often with songs and dances), although she always longed to perform comic operas. (Her Eastern debut in Philadelphia was as Josephine in *HMS Pinafore*.) Born in Brooklyn but reared in SAN FRANCISCO, where she supported JOSEPH JEFFERSON III (as Gretchen in *RIP VAN WINKLE*) and MCKEE RANKIN (in *The DANITES*) in the late 1870s, she soon came east, where *M'liss, the Child of the Sierras* (1878, NIBLO'S GARDEN) made her a star. Late in her career she was successful in *The Deacon's Daughter* (1887). It was said she combined "a most piquant and agreeable brusquerie" with "all the bewitching softness and charm of an Irish girl." DBW

Placide family A famous family of actors, less known but equal in American theatrical importance to the BOOTHS or JEFFERSONS. The U.S. Placides begin with **Alexander Placide** (?–1812), a French rope dancer and pantomimist (see MIME) of some distinction, who fled from France during the Revolution. He emigrated to the U.S., and first appeared in America at the JOHN STREET THEATRE in 1792. He married a Miss Caroline Wighten, the daughter of a celebrated London actress. For a time, Placide managed theatres in Charleston and Richmond, and was scheduled for a benefit on 26 December 1811, the day of a disastrous Richmond theatre FIRE.

Of Placide's many children, the best known was **Henry Placide** (1799–1870), considered one of the finest character actors of the American stage. After appearing as a child actor by 1814, he made his adult debut in 1823 at the PARK THEATRE in New York, as Zekiel Homespun. He remained at the Park for 20 years, acting more than 500 roles, 200 of which he created. He attempted one London engagement, unsuccessfully. American audiences considered him best in traditional English comedy, Sir Peter Teazle being among his most successful parts.

Henry Placide's older sister, **Caroline** (1789–1881), married WILLIAM RUFUS BLAKE, and his siblings **Eliza** (?–1874) and **Thomas** (1808–77) both had theatrical careers, Thomas managing the Park for some years. **Jane** (1804–35), another sister, made her debut in Norfolk, VA, in 1820, and in 1823 she appeared in New Orleans, playing there almost exclusively for a decade. At that time she appeared as a singer, as well as a dramatic and comic actress. She was said to be the most polished actress in the South in her time, and was referred to as the "Queen of the Drama in New Orleans," her Lady Macbeth and Cordelia being especially admired. She appeared at London's Covent Garden in 1834 and died shortly after her return to the U.S.   SMA

Platt, Livingston (1874–1933/9?) Designer. As artistic director of the Toy Theatre of BOSTON, Platt pioneered the New Stagecraft in America, though his contributions are often overlooked. He went on to a successful Broadway career that included *Rain* (1922), *The First Mrs. Fraser* (1929), and *DINNER AT EIGHT* (1932).   AA

playbill/program By the time professional actors appeared in the American colonies in the mid-18th century, the playbill, handbill, or program, as it has been variously known, was an established institution in English and Continental theatre. The American playbills of this period look very much like provincial English playbills, most giving the name of the play, the cast, time and date, the theatre, and price of admission. The early playbills – usually about 9″ × 7″ in size and printed on the same stock used for newspapers – often doubled as posters, and were frequently hand-distributed by company members to the homes of citizens.

As advancing technology in printing in the 19th century led to the increase in size and variety of typefaces for printed matter, more information could be included in the larger playbill. Managers used it as an advertisement to extol themselves, their stars, the scenery, and costumes, and additionally to provide a brief synopsis of the play along with previews of coming attractions. The introduction of lithography made it possible to print line drawings of the stars or scenes by mid-century.

The customary long, narrow playbills were supplanted by small, folded programs in the late 19th century. By the 1870s, theatres either published their own or were provided with copies of pamphletlike programs that owed their existence to a multitude of large and small advertisements (secured by the publisher as revenue) that effectively smothered the information about the play and cast. When the long-running show became established, managers seized the opportunity for more self-promotion by issuing souvenir programs, often printed on silk or satin, to commemorate landmark performances of 100 or more.

In New York, a young Ohioan, Frank V. Strauss, secured the right in 1884 to gather advertisements for MADISON SQUARE THEATRE programs and later to print programs for it and other theatres. Thus was launched the company that hereafter set the standard for American theatre programs. Strauss standardized playbills by printing them on a better quality of paper, giving them attractive covers, making the size uniform for all theatres, providing feature articles about the theatre, personalities, fashion, local events, and so on, and in other ways transforming them into compact and informative magazines distributed for free. The name *Playbill*® was eventually copyrighted by a subsequent owner, and that publication dominates the field in New York, although facsimiles of its format abound in professional, regional, and amateur theatres across America. Its only true national rival, *Stagebill*, was purchased by *Playbill* in 2002. Today, *Playbill,* distributed in more than 70 NYC theatres, has a daily press run of roughly 80,000. MCH

Playhouse Theatre 137 West 48th St, NYC [Architect: Charles A. Rich]. In 1911, Broadway producer WILLIAM A. BRADY built the small Playhouse for his own productions, which often starred his wife, GRACE GEORGE. With an auditorium seating fewer than 1,000, the theatre also contained his own offices and those of other producers, press AGENTS, and the League of New York Theatres and Producers (see PRODUCING MANAGERS' ASSOCIATION). At the age of 81, Brady sold his theatre, which eventually passed to Rockefeller real-estate interests in 1967; a year later, it was demolished. Its most notable tenants included the first Broadway production of SHAW's *Major Barbara*

(1915), the Pulitzer Prize–winning STREET SCENE, and *The* MIRACLE WORKER (1959). On its stage, LAURETTE TAYLOR played her last and greatest role, Amanda Wingfield, in *The* GLASS MENAGERIE (1945). MCH

Playwrights' (Producing) Company Founded in 1938 by MAXWELL ANDERSON, S. N. BEHRMAN, SIDNEY HOWARD, ELMER RICE, and ROBERT E. SHERWOOD to present their own best efforts, the Playwrights' Company became a major production force in the American theatre for several decades. KURT WEILL and ROBERT ANDERSON were invited to join as partners, as were attorney John Wharton and producer ROGER L. STEVENS. Although dedicated to its own scripts, the Playwrights' Company also coproduced presentations by nonmembers. Their first venture, ABE LINCOLN IN ILLINOIS (1938), was followed by such landmarks as KNICKERBOCKER HOLIDAY (1938), *Key Largo* (1939), *Dream Girl* (1945), the musical STREET SCENE (1947), LOST IN THE STARS (1949), TEA AND SYMPATHY (1953), and CAT ON A HOT TIN ROOF (1955). The death of its key partners forced the dissolution of the company in 1960 after the production of VIDAL's *The Best Man*. MCH

Playwrights Horizons Writer's theatre founded in New York in 1971 at the Clark Center Y by Robert Moss, dedicated to the development of contemporary American playwrights, composers, and lyricists, and the production of their work. In 1976 they moved into two small theatres on THEATRE ROW, and in 2003, after the razing of their old building, opened a new $27 million complex that included two venues: the 198-seat Mainstage Theater and the 96–128-seat Peter Jay Sharp Theater. In its history the organization – through readings, workshops, and full-scale productions – has presented more than 350 writers (up to 2006). Notable works include four Pulitzer-winning plays: WENDY WASSERSTEIN's *The* HEIDI CHRONICLES, ALFRED UHRY's DRIVING MISS DAISY, STEPHEN SONDHEIM and JAMES LAPINE's SUNDAY IN THE PARK WITH GEORGE, and Doug Wright's *I AM My OWN WIFE*. Also important are LYNN NOTTAGE's *Fabulation* (2005 Obie for Best American Play), KENNETH LONERGAN's *Lobby Hero* (2001), Kirsten Childs's *The Bubbly Black Girl Shed Her Chameleon Skin* (2000), Scott McPherson's MARVIN'S ROOM (Drama Desk, 1992), JON ROBIN BAITZ's *The Substance of Fire* (1991), WILLIAM FINN's *March of the Falsettos* (1981), CHRISTOPHER DURANG's *Sister Mary Ignatius Explains It All for You* (1981), *The* DINING ROOM, SUNDAY IN THE PARK WITH GEORGE, DRIVING MISS DAISY, ADAM GUETTEL & TINA LANDAU's

Floyd Collins (1996), and JEANINE TESORI and Brian Crawley's *Violet* (1997), many of which won Obies and/or Lortel Awards. ANDRÉ BISHOP was artistic director during 1981–91, followed by Don Scardino (1992–6) and Tim Sanford (1996–).   TLM

Plaza Suite The first of NEIL SIMON's combinations of three one-act plays opened 14 February 1968 at the PLYMOUTH THEATRE, starring GEORGE C. SCOTT and MAUREEN STAPLETON, and ran for 1,097 performances. Though the plays are apparently linked only by their occurring in Suite 719 of New York's Plaza Hotel, each act suggests thematic connections with the others. The room's occupants for the successive acts are a financially secure middle-aged couple on a doomed second honeymoon, a young Hollywood producer and his former high-school girlfriend in an unsatisfying seduction, and successful middle-class parents on their reluctant daughter's wedding day. As each couple meets its respective crisis, the apparently different circumstances emphasize the similarity of the dissatisfactions they each face. The characters struggle to cope with lives that are lacking fulfillment and essentially empty, despite material stability; the only ones who seem to communicate are the third-act bride and groom, suggesting both the problem and its solution.   RW

Plummer, (Arthur) Christopher (Orme) (1929–) Toronto-born actor who, after playing nearly 100 roles with the Canadian Repertory Theatre, beginning in 1950, made his New York debut in 1954. In the 1950s and '60s his speciality was SHAKESPEARE, appearing at the AMERICAN SHAKESPEARE THEATRE (1955), the Stratford Ontario Shakespeare Festival (1956, 1957, 1960, 1962), and with the ROYAL SHAKESPEARE COMPANY (1961). Roles included Mark Antony, Henry V, Hamlet, Sir Andrew Aguecheek, Benedick, Leontes, Mercutio, and Richard III. In 1981 he returned to the American Shakespeare Theatre as Iago, and in the title role and as Chorus in *Henry V.* He was Nickles in MACLEISH's *J.B.* (1958), Pizarro in *The Royal Hunt of the Sun* (1965), won the Tony Award as Best Actor in a Musical for *Cyrano* (1973), and played Chekhov in NEIL SIMON's *The Good Doctor* (1973). In London he played King Henry in *Becket* (1961) and joined the NATIONAL THEATRE at the New Theatre in 1971. Opposite JASON ROBARDS he appeared at ROUNDABOUT as the glib old poet Spooner in Pinter's *No Man's Land* (1994). In 1996 he received numerous awards (including Tony and Drama Desk) for the title role in WILLIAM LUCE's ONE-PERSON *Barrymore.* After success as King Lear at Stratford, Ontario (2002), in 2004 this

"performance of a lifetime" was seen at Lincoln Center (Tony nomination). A 2007 Broadway revival of *Inherit the Wind* saw the actor as Drummond. In 1990 he received the third William Shakespeare Award for Classical Theatre from the SHAKESPEARE THEATRE at the Folger, in 1998 the coveted Common Wealth Award, and in 2002 the first Jason Robards Award for Excellence in Theatre by ROUNDABOUT. Plummer lives in Connecticut but remains a Canadian citizen.

His daughter, by actress TAMMY GRIMES, is actress **Amanda** (Michael) **Plummer** (1957–) (*Agnes of God,* 1982; Tony), who has appeared on the New York stage some dozen times during 1979–2002, including as Bess Johnson in BETH HENLEY's *Abundance* (1990).   DBW

Plymouth Theatre 236 West 45th St., NYC [Architect: Herbert J. Krapp]. In 1917, backed by the ubiquitous SHUBERTS, producer-director ARTHUR HOPKINS built the Plymouth as the theatrical home for himself and his productions. A man of quiet daring, Hopkins tended to produce the unusual play during his lifetime. At his theatre, he staged *The Jest* (1919, adapted by EDWARD SHELDON) with John and Lionel Barrymore (see DREW–BARRYMORE); the antiwar *WHAT PRICE GLORY* (1924); and SOPHIE TREADWELL's *MACHINAL* (1928). Unfortunately, the Depression years tempered his activities, and he was forced to relinquish his 1,000-seat, one-balcony house to the Shuberts after 1935. In its history, the Plymouth has had many notable tenants, but none more extraordinary than the Royal Shakespeare Company's production of *Nicholas Nickleby* (1981), which ran for eight hours with a dinner intermission and a ticket price of $100. The theatre has remained a Shubert house, and in 2005 it was renamed the Gerald Schoenfeld Theatre (see SHUBERT ORGANIZATION). The first two productions under the new name were *Brooklyn, the Musical* and *Chita Rivera: The Dancer's Life;* a successful revival of *A CHORUS LINE* followed in 2006.   MCH

Po-ca-hon-tas; or, The Gentle Savage A two-act musical burlesque by JOHN BROUGHAM with music adapted by James G. Maeder. Arguably the best of Indian burlesques (see NATIVE AMERICANS PORTRAYED), Brougham's second such effort opened at WALLACK's Lyceum 24 December 1855, and remained a standard burlesque afterpiece until at least 1884. With CHARLES M. WALCOT as Capt. John Smith, Georgina Hodson in the title role, Brougham as her father (King H. J. Pow-ha-tan I), and Charles Peters as a Dutchman (Mynheer Rolff) promised Pocahontas's hand, Brougham turned the popular story inside out (Smith wins Pocahontas via a card game). With corny but clever puns and rhymed-couplet doggerel, it provided music, a libretto, and subjects all relevant to New York life and the country as a whole in the 1850s.   DBW

Poe, Edgar Allan (1809–49) Short-story writer, poet, and critic. The author of "The Raven" and "Annabel Lee" was knowledgeable about the drama, writing occasional essays for *Southern Literary Messenger* (1835–7), *Burton's Gentleman's Magazine* (1839–40), *Graham's Magazine* (1841–2), and the *New York Mirror* (1845). When he became editor of *Broadway Journal* (1845–6), he reviewed live theatre, including Mrs. MOWATT's *FASHION*. Poe advocated a more realistic aesthetic and criticized such conventions as soliloquies, asides, and the reading aloud of private letters. He insisted that American drama must reflect American life, and that native dramatic criticism be rescued from corrupt journalistic practices.   TLM

Polakov, Lester (1916–) Designer and teacher, perhaps best known as the founder (1958) of the Polakov Studio and Forum of Stage Design, the most significant nonuniversity training program in the country until 1988. He began designing in 1940 and designed on Broadway (*Mrs. McThing,* 1952) and Off-, and for opera, film, and industrial shows. In 2006 he received the IRENE SHARAFF Lifetime Achievement Award. His memoirs, *We Live to Paint Again,* were published in 1993. In 2003 an offshoot of his school, the Studio and Forum of Scenic Arts, was initiated by former students.   AA

Pollock, Channing (1880–1946) Playwright and critic who wrote dramatic criticism for the *Washington Post* and *Washington Times* before becoming press representative for WILLIAM A. BRADY (1899–1903) and for the SHUBERTS (1903–6) while establishing himself as a playwright. His more than 30 plays include the potboilers *The Sign on the Door* (1919), *The Fool* (1922), and *The Enemy* (1925). Pollock wrote on theatre for magazines including *Ainslee's, Munsey's,* and *The Smart Set.* He wrote an autobiography in 1943.   TLM

Ponisi, Madame [née Elizabeth Hanson] (1818–99) English-born actress who came to the U.S. in 1848 and established herself as a popular romantic actress in the 1850s, playing opposite EDWIN FORREST in several roles. She created the title role of *FRANCESCA DA RIMINI,* GEORGE HENRY BOKER's poetic tragedy (1855). In the 1870s and '80s,

she played "first old woman" roles in the STOCK COMPANY at WALLACK's THEATRE, and was long remembered for the "vigor and drollery" of those interpretations.   FHL

Poole, John F. (1835–93) Dublin-born playwright and actor who came to America in 1847 and by 1852 was house dramatist at the Old BOWERY THEATRE. Among his numerous plays are *The Massacre of Wyoming* (1859), *Cudjo's Cave* (1864), and *Divorce* (1872). He managed several theatres and owned Poole's Theatre in Astor Place.   WJM

Poor of New York, The DION BOUCICAULT's popular adaptation of *Les Pauvres de Paris* (by Brisebarre and Nus) opened at WALLACK's THEATRE in 1857. This "sensation melodrama" drew praise for its depiction of local New York scenes – including the slums of Five Points and the Academy of Music opera house – and for its thrilling plot. The play begins with a banker stealing money during the Panic of 1837, and then jumps to the Panic of 1857 to examine the consequences of this theft on a business-class family. The "real" poor of New York in the melodrama are the respectable bourgeoisie struggling to hide their poverty – not the unemployed and "the beggar at home whose mattress is lined with gold." Altering the local references to suit the city, Boucicault pieced out new scripts with the same plot entitled *The Streets of Philadelphia* and *The Rich and Poor of Boston.* Later, he adapted his adaptation as *The Poor of Liverpool, The Streets of London,* and even *The Streets of New York,* the title used when the play was further transformed into a melodramatic musical.   BMcC

Porgy and Bess Based on the play *Porgy* by DOROTHY AND DU BOSE HEYWARD (produced by the THEATRE GUILD in 1927), with book by Du Bose Heyward and music and lyrics (respectively) by GEORGE AND IRA GERSHWIN, *Porgy and Bess* opened at the ALVIN THEATRE on 10 October 1935. Billed as "an American folk opera," it is about the black inhabitants of Catfish Row, a slum neighborhood in Charleston, SC. Drawing on black musical idioms, including blues and spirituals, George Gershwin used recitative, arias, and production numbers to tell the story of the crippled Porgy and Bess, the troubled woman he loves. Although its sordid story of gambling, drugs, and violence did little to shatter the stereotypical portrayal of African American characters on the musical stage, it did provide unprecedented opportunities for black singers with trained voices. At its 1935 opening, *Porgy and Bess* received negative reviews from music critics and had a short run. Todd Duncan, who created Porgy, became the first African American singer to join the New York City Opera (1945). A 1942 revival that cut much of the recitative and several of the musical sequences was a greater success. A return to the full score and libretto by the Houston Opera Company in 1976 demonstrated anew the show's power. In 1985 it entered the repertory of the Metropolitan Opera.   MK

pornographic theatre For the Puritans, all theatre was pornographic: It inflamed illicit passions. Even when the offerings were unobjectionable, moralists complained of the playhouse's third tier, where prostitutes congregated and trawled for trade. They, with the lobby bar, were often the real economic pillars of the theatre.

Truly pornographic theatre connotes the graphic enactment of sexual acts intended to bring spectators to a state of sexual arousal. Such spectacles, usually staged in brothels, were rare in the U.S. It was not until the so-called Sexual Revolution of the 1960s that these representations became programmatically exploited, less for erotic effect than as statements of liberation. Michael McClure's play *The Beard* (1967), which climaxes in Billy the Kid performing cunnilingus on Jean Harlow, was merely a tame prelude to Lennox Raphael's *Che!* (1969), featuring a nude Uncle Sam whose participation in oral sex and sodomy caused the cast to be arrested by the New York police. This blatancy was done often in the name of theatrical experimentation and Dadaism, and often as political protest (Tuli Kupferberg's *Fuck Nam*, published 1967), but much was purely commercial. KENNETH TYNAN's revue OH! CALCUTTA! celebrated randiness with full NUDITY and sketches by Samuel Beckett, GORE VIDAL, and JULES FEIFFER; imitations like *Let My People Come* had less pretence to wit.

Throughout the 1980s, actual rather than simulated copulation took place in porno palaces such as Show World in Times Square; the rationale of the mildly comic revue sketches was invariably a sex act. Sadomasochistic demonstrations were offered by The Project and Belle de Jour [sic] at private clubs, which encouraged audience participation. FEMINIST attitudes were split between condemnation of pornography as a degradation of women and promotion of it as a life-enhancing liberation. The latter attitude prevails in the performance art of KAREN FINLEY, Annie Sprinkle, and others who parody standard responses by grotesque caricature. This approach has been widely misconstrued by conservatives who take the parody to be the real thing, and the recent revival of

puritanical CENSORSHIP even proscribes radio simulations of masturbation.   LS

Porter, Cole (1891–1964) Composer and lyricist. Born into a wealthy midwestern family, Porter abandoned his plans for a legal career to study at the Harvard University School of Music. He contributed songs to the Broadway musical *See America First* in 1916. After a stint with the French Foreign Legion, Porter lived in Europe for most of the 1920s. At the end of the decade he wrote songs for two Broadway shows with French settings: *Paris* (1928) and *Fifty Million Frenchmen* (1929). In the 1930s Porter wrote the scores for a series of frothy musical comedies, including *The Gay Divorce* (1932), ANYTHING GOES (1934), *Red, Hot and Blue!* (1936), *Leave It to Me!* (1938), and DU BARRY WAS A LADY (1939). His songs for these shows, generally characterized by ingenious lyrics and unusual rhythms, placed him in the forefront of musical-comedy composers.

After his legs were crushed in a riding accident in 1937, Porter's creativity seemed to wane. His shows of the early 1940s were financially successful but artistically undistinguished. However, in 1948 he created what many consider to be his most theatrically effective and versatile score: KISS ME, KATE (1948), a musical version of Shakespeare's *The Taming of the Shrew*. During the 1950s Porter wrote his final two hit shows: CAN-CAN (1953) and SILK STOCKINGS (1955).

For most of his career Porter was content with providing sophisticated songs for shows with trivial librettos. As a consequence, although his songs still remain popular, few of his shows are revived in their entirety. The most recent biography of note is by William McBrien (1998); a 2004 film, *De-Lovely*, starred KEVIN KLINE.   MK

Potter, Richard (1783–1835) The first successful American conjuror; son of a British tax collector for the port of Boston and a black slave. Potter first joined a British circus and then became assistant to conjuror John Rannie, a Scot who first appeared in the U.S. in 1801 (in Boston). Rannie retired in 1811, leaving the field open to Potter, who toured the U.S. and eastern Canada for 20 years with his "Evening's Brush to Sweep Away Care; or, a Medley to Please." His son, Richard Potter Jr., was also a MAGICIAN and ventriloquist.   DBW

Powell, Charles Stuart (1748–1811) Welsh-born actor-manager who came to America after little success on the London stage, first offering one-man entertainments in BOSTON (1792) before joining JOSEPH HARPER's Boston troupe at the New Exhibition Room and then becoming manager of the FEDERAL STREET THEATRE. Dismissed after its second season (1795), he opened the Haymarket Theatre in December 1796, but was bankrupt by June. After acting in Boston and Hartford for two years, Powell went to Halifax, Nova Scotia, where he ran a theatre for 12 years (with a brief engagement in Boston in 1806–7). Powell's wife, Mary Ann, and two daughters acted, as did his younger brother, Snelling, who had success in the U.S. during 1794–1821.   DBW

Powell, Frederick Eugene (1856–1938) Originally a civil engineering teacher, Philadelphia-born Powell became a master of large illusion shows (see MAGIC) and toured the U.S., West Indies, and South America. Known late in his career as the "Dean of American Magicians," after KELLAR's death, Powell's show – which was twice destroyed (by FIRE in 1915 and flood in 1921) – featured such spectacles as "She," his version of a "Cremation" illusion.   DBW

Power family A family of actors, originally from Ireland, most of whom spent large portions of their careers in the U.S. The first, **Tyrone Power** (1795–1841), successfully played stage Irishmen in London and wrote a number of comedies before coming to the U.S. in 1833. A great success here, he returned often and was drowned at sea on a transatlantic trip. His 1836 *Impressions of America* offers a sympathetic and detailed view of the American theatre at the time. Power's son **Maurice** (?–1849) was also an actor. Another son, Harold, sired **(Frederick) Tyrone (Edmond) Power** (1869–1931), a leading man and member of DALY's company, with whom he appeared in London. Frederick first appeared successfully with Madame JANAUSCHEK, and for a time acted with MINNIE MADDERN FISKE, his Lord Steyne in *Becky Sharp* (1899) being especially well received. In later life, he appeared almost exclusively as major support in Shakespearean revivals.

In turn, his son **Tyrone (Edmund) Power** (1914–58) was for some time on the stage, but won his most substantial reputation as a film actor. He made his debut as Benvolio in KATHARINE CORNELL's production of *Romeo and Juliet*. After his film career began he appeared in *John Brown's Body* (1953) and *The Dark Is Light Enough* (1955), In the 1980s his son, **Tyrone Jr.,** became a film actor, albeit with little notice.   SMA

Powers [né McGovern], **James T.** (1862–1943) Actor who began as a song-and-dance man (1878).

His first musical was a revival of EVANGELINE (1882) with WILLIE EDOUIN; they then starred together in New York and London in CHARLES HOYT's *A Bunch of Keys* (1883). A founding member of the company at New York's CASINO THEATRE (1887), he replaced JAMES LEWIS in AUGUSTIN DALY's company (1893–9). From then until 1915 he toured as a star in a new musical each season. He last appeared in a revival of SEVEN KEYS TO BALDPATE (1935). Short, red-haired, and acrobatic, he was described as having "rubber heels." An autobiography appeared in 1929.   DMcD

Prelude to a Kiss by CRAIG LUCAS premiered at SOUTH COAST REPERTORY THEATRE in January 1988 and was subsequently produced in March 1990 at New York's CIRCLE REP (Obie, Best New American Play). This comic fantasy about the transfer of "souls" between an aging man and a new bride delighted OFF-BROADWAY audiences. In May 1990 it reopened at the HELEN HAYES THEATRE on Broadway, with Timothy Hutton replacing Alec Baldwin as the puzzled bridegroom, and MARY-LOUISE PARKER (winner of a *Theatre World* Award) and BARNARD HUGHES re-creating their roles (and winning applause) as the time travelers. A film version with Baldwin was released in 1992, and a Broadway revival by ROUNDABOUT, starring John Mahoney, opened 8 March 2007.   BBW

Preston (Meservey), Robert (1918–87) Actor and singer, who, after studying at the PASADENA PLAYHOUSE, worked for several years in film and then first appeared on Broadway in 1951 as a replacement for JOSÉ FERRER in *Twentieth Century* (1950 revival). He was in several plays before making a triumphant musical-comedy debut as fast-talking salesman Harold Hill in *The MUSIC MAN* (1957). He played in the all-star revival of SHAW's *Too True to Be Good* (1963) and in *Nobody Loves an Albatross* (1963) before returning to musicals with *Ben Franklin in Paris* (1964). He created the role of Henry II in *The Lion in Winter* (1966) and starred opposite MARY MARTIN in the two-character musical *I Do! I Do!* (1966). He was also seen as silent-movie director Mack Sennett opposite BERNADETTE PETERS in *Mack & Mabel* (1974).   MK

Price, Stephen (1783–1840) The first successful American theatre manager who was neither a playwright nor an actor. Price began gaining control of the PARK THEATRE in New York in 1808, and in 1810 started importing English stars; this practice gradually destroyed the resident repertory tradition in America. Price, with EDMUND SIMPSON, managed to keep the Park open during

the War of 1812, and after the war went frequently to London to recruit new talent. In 1816 he imported Mrs. John Barnes from Drury Lane, beginning an especially prosperous period for the Park. From 1826 to 1830 Price managed the Drury Lane Theatre in London, gaining a monopoly over English stars, forcing other American managers to deal with him for their services. This power caused WASHINGTON IRVING to refer to Price as "King Stephen." Price drained the London stage of its talent to supply visiting stars for the Park; other managers were forced to employ his visiting stars on Price's terms in order to compete. Price was shrewd, even unscrupulous in his dealings, but he read audiences' tastes and preferences accurately on both sides of the Atlantic.
SMA

Price, The, by ARTHUR MILLER opened 7 February 1968 in New York and ran for 429 performances. ULU GROSBARD directed PAT HINGLE as Victor Franz, the middle-aged policeman who gave up his dream of doing scientific research in order to support his father, a businessman who was ruined in the Depression; KATE REID as Esther, Victor's long-suffering wife; ARTHUR KENNEDY as Walter Franz, Victor's brother, who has become a successful surgeon after leaving the family behind to pursue his medical career; and Harold Gary as Gregory Solomon, the octogenarian who wants to revive his used-furniture business by buying the Franz's family furniture – a remnant of the Depression that Victor wants to sell in order to finance his education after his retirement from the police force. The furniture provides the occasion for the brothers to confront their feelings about each other, their father, the family, and their own lives. Through Solomon's agency, Victor and Esther come to an understanding about their personal values and an acceptance of the lives they have chosen. A revival in 1992 at the ROUNDABOUT was directed by JOHN TILLINGER and starred ELI WALLACH; another in 1999 was directed by JAMES NAUGHTON and starred HARRIS YULIN. BCM

Primary Stages Of NYC's major nonprofits, Primary Stages most successfully has resisted choosing seasons by the commercial-transfer potential of the work. Founded in 1984 by Casey Childs, it has instead produced over 80 new plays to "create a library of new works for the American theatre." In a typical season (first in a ramshackle Times Square–area space; later in a sleek glass venue on the dramatically underserved East Side), works by major, emerging, and unknown playwrights were

featured in rough balance. If veteran dramatists were more facile sells – A. R. GURNEY, TERRENCE MCNALLY, HORTON FOOTE, JOHN PATRICK SHANLEY, ROMULUS LINNEY, CHARLES BUSCH – the company's cachet came from its emerging writers: in the 1990s, DAVID IVES (*All in the Timing*), CONSTANCE CONGDON (*Lips*), Jeffrey Hatcher (*Scotland Road*), MAC WELLMAN (*The Hyacinth Macaw*), Conor McPherson (*St. Nicholas*), John Henry Redwood (*The Old Settler*); in the 2000s, JULIA JORDAN (*Boy*), Stephen Belber (the ONE-PERSON *One Million Butterflies*). The company is now led by artistic director Andrew Leynse.   LJ

Prince, Faith (1957–) Actress-singer, born in Augusta, GA, grew up in Virginia, and trained at the University of Cincinnati College Conservatory of Music (1980). This vivacious redhead – often cast in comic roles – had her NYC debut OFF-BROADWAY as a replacement in the revue *Scrambled Feet* (1980), followed by her Broadway debut in *Jerome Robbins' Broadway* (1989). To date her best-known role has been Miss Adelaide in the hit revival of *GUYS AND DOLLS*, for which she won a 1992 Tony. Other Broadways credit are *Nick & Nora* (1991), *The KING AND I* (replacement, 1997), *Little Me* (1998), *James Joyce's The Dead* (replacement, 2000), *BELLS ARE RINGING* (2001), and *Noises Off* (2001). Off-Broadway: *Falsettoland* (1990) and *A Man of No Importance* (2002), among others. In recent years she has starred as Kelly Knipers on Showtime's *Huff.*   DBW

Prince, Hal [né Harold Smith Prince] (1928–) Producer, director, and playwright. Launching his career as a producer in partnership with Robert E. Griffith and FREDERIC BRISSON, Prince had immediate success with *The PAJAMA GAME* (1954) and *DAMN YANKEES* (1955). With Griffith he produced *WEST SIDE STORY* (1957) and *FIORELLO!* (1961), and on his own he produced *FIDDLER ON THE ROOF* (1964). Beginning with *SHE LOVES ME* (1963), he served as both producer and director of a number of successful musicals. Prince's most notable contribution to the musical stage was the series of "concept musicals" he produced and directed in conjunction with composer-lyricist STEPHEN SONDHEIM: *COMPANY* (1970), *FOLLIES* (1971), *A LITTLE NIGHT MUSIC* (1973), *CANDIDE* (1973 and subsequent revivals), *PACIFIC OVERTURES* (1976), *SWEENEY TODD* (1979), and *Merrily We Roll Along* (1981). In recent years he has devoted considerable attention to the direction of opera, both in the U.S. and abroad; his most successful musical-theatre productions of the past few years have been the spectacular ANDREW LLOYD WEBBER

PHANTOM OF THE OPERA (London, 1986; Broadway, 1988), *Kiss of the Spider Woman* (begun 1990; London, 1992; Broadway, 1993), and the award-winning SHOW BOAT revival (Toronto, 1993; Broadway, 1994; Tony for direction). In 1992 he adapted and staged the first two books of O'Casey's six-volume autobiography (*Grandchild of Kings,* IRISH REP); in 1994 he directed LaCHIUSA and Gallardo's *The Petrified Prince* at The PUBLIC; 1998 saw his production of ALFRED UHRY and JASON ROBERT BROWN's *Parade*; and in 2002 he produced and directed *Hollywood Arms*. The next year saw a disappointing production of Sondheim and John Weidman's *Bounce* in Chicago and Washington, DC. In 2007 he directed *LoveMusik* on Broadway.

Winner of eight Tony Awards for Best Direction of a Musical and numerous other awards, in 1991 Prince received the Richard Rodgers Award for Excellence in Musical Theatre (previously given only to MARY MARTIN [1988] and JULIE ANDREWS [1989]); in 1994 he was among the Kennedy Center honorees; in 2000 he received the National Medal of Arts; and in 2006 a Lifetime Achievement Tony (his 21st Tony Award).

Foster Hirsch, author of a 1989 study of Prince (updated/expanded 2005), believes Prince and his collaborators "have altered the popular idea of what a musical can be," and another author, Carol Ilson, concludes that as a risk taker Prince's greatest contribution has been "his unwillingness to repeat himself." His largely autobiographical book, *Contradictions,* was published in 1974. His daughter, **Daisy**, is an actress-director (*Petrified Prince; Merrily . . .*). MK DBW

Prince Karl Comedy by A. C. GUNTER, first performed at the BOSTON MUSEUM 5 April 1886, with RICHARD MANSFIELD in the title role. Its presentation at the MADISON SQUARE THEATRE on 3 May 1886 was the occasion of Mansfield's first starring appearance in New York. Prince Karl von Arnheim, a penniless, young nobleman, escapes an unwanted marriage by feigning suicide. He reappears as a commoner employed in the entourage of his true love. In the end, Karl gains an inheritance, resumes his titled identity, and wins his beloved. Mansfield persistently revised Gunter's play, purging the melodrama and emphasizing the romance and farce. Though it was a staple of Mansfield's repertory until 1899, permitting him to display his manifold talents as a comic actor, pianist, and vocal parodist, he thought it "trash" and "stupid." WD

Princess Theatre 104 West 39th St., NYC [Architect: William A. Swasey]. F. RAY COMSTOCK, who built the tiny playhouse in 1914, was the unwitting godfather of the intimate musical. After trying experimental drama, he hired JEROME KERN, GUY BOLTON, and P. G. WODEHOUSE to construct shows that would be long on imagination but short on cast, scenery, and orchestra. The results were the Princess musicals – notably VERY GOOD EDDIE (1915), *Oh Boy* (1917), and *Oh Lady! Lady!* (1918) – that launched the careers of all three. Except for one period when, as Labor Stage, it housed PINS AND NEEDLES (1937) for 1,108 performances, the theatre showed films as of 1933. It was razed in 1955. MCH

Prisoner of Second Avenue, The NEIL SIMON's comedy opened at the EUGENE O'NEILL THEATRE 11 November 1971 for 780 performances. Main character Mel Edison (Peter Falk) progressively disintegrates under the pressures of the deteriorating society around him. Though a comedy, the play paints a pessimistic picture of the future as Mel suffers a mental breakdown in the face of seeming futility. In the second act, however, Simon returns to his emphasis of individual interdependence. Mel's brother (VINCENT GARDENIA; Tony Award) offers financial help, but is refused. In the final scene, however, Mel he has recovered enough to help his wife, Edna (Lee Grant), whose life is unraveling. Implicit in Mel's seemingly self-generated recovery is Simon's belief in the effectiveness of collaboration as an antidote to life's futility. Here Simon transfers the notion to society's challenges. RW

Processional A "jazz symphony of American life" by JOHN HOWARD LAWSON, first produced by the THEATRE GUILD in 1925 and revived by the FEDERAL THEATRE PROJECT in a revised version of 1937. Lawson's play was groundbreaking as a piece of antirealistic political theatre on a Broadway stage. Conceived as a bitter and ironic vaudeville loosely centered around the events of a West Virginia coal-miners' strike, *Processional* ridiculed racial stereotyping, small-town businessmen, corporate leaders, the government, and the Klan. The work proved to be Lawson's most enduring, far surpassing the dramatic effectiveness of the socialist realism he turned to in the 1930s at the behest of communist cultural theorists. MF

Proctor, F(rederick) F(rancis? Freeman?) (1851–1929) VAUDEVILLE manager ("dean of vaudeville") and theatre owner. Maine-born Proctor began his career touring the U.S. and Europe as Fred Levantine, an equilibrist. In 1886 he bought an interest in an Albany theatre; in 1889 he opened the 23rd

Street Theatre, a legitimate house, in NYC. By the 1890s his focus was clean, continuous vaudeville, first at New York's Proctor Pleasure Palace (1894), then with the first vaudeville circuit and ultimately controlling a group of 25 eastern theatres. Proctor joined his rival B.F. KEITH in 1906 as head of the UNITED BOOKING OFFICE, a virtual monopoly of first-class vaudeville; his theatrical holdings were taken over by the Radio–Keith–Orpheum circuit in 1929.   DBW

Producers, The With a record 12 Tonys (and 15 nominations, also a record, beating out COMPANY with its 14), this old-fashioned farcical musical began as an offbeat film in 1968 created by Mel Brooks. The stage version – directed and choreographed by SUSAN STROMAN, book by Brooks and Thomas Meehan, music and lyrics by Brooks – opened 24 April 2001 at the ST. JAMES THEATRE. With NATHAN LANE as the desperate Broadway producer Max Bialystock and MATTHEW BRODERICK as Leopold Bloom, a repressed public accountant. Their mission is to produce a sure-fire flop, abscond with the backers' investments by raising more than the production requires, and live happily ever after. But alas the show, *Springtime for Hitler,* turns into a hit, and their plan is discovered. For two years this was the hottest ticket on Broadway. The day after opening $3.3 million in tickets were sold, the highest in Broadway history. Yet after the departure of Lane and Broderick in 2002 ticket sales diminished until the two returned in December 2003 for three months, creating such demand that the show beat its own one-day ticket-sale record (c. $3.5 million). In order to capitalize on the presence of the original stars, the producers initiated a $480 ticket for the best rows in the orchestra (100 a performance). With their star power, in early January 2004 the show posted a record one-week gross of $1.6 million (including $600 tickets for New Year's Eve). Its film version in 2005, though with much the same talent, failed to excite audiences. The show closed on 22 April 2007 after 2,502 regular performances.   DBW

Producing Managers' Association (PMA) Apparently the brainchild of producer JOHN GOLDEN (and headed by SAM H. HARRIS), this organization was formed in 1918 as a result of the growing struggle with ACTORS' EQUITY and ultimately as a replacement for the disintegrating United Managers' Protective Association (which included theatre owners and bookers). An unwillingness on the part of PMA to negotiate with Equity precipitated the actors' strike of 1919 and the establishment of PMA's own unsuccessful rival company union, Actors' Fidelity League. Ultimately, PMA was forced to sign the first American labor-management contract. In 1924 a group of disgruntled producers withdrew from PMA and formed the Managers' Protective Association, which evolved in 1930 into the League of New York Theatres and Producers. (Its named was changed in 1985 to LEAGUE OF AMERICAN THEATRES AND PRODUCERS).   DBW

Prolet-Buehne A NYC worker's theatre group formed in 1925 by immigrant German workers. Led by John E. Bonn in 1928–9, the group introduced agitprop techniques into its performances by 1929 to promote socialist and workers' class consciousness and political activism, similiar to groups in Berlin (see PISCATOR) and Moscow. It influenced the performance style of the Workers' Laboratory Theatre, and eventually the LIVING NEWSPAPER. The group disbanded in 1934, and Bonn was later appointed to the German section of the FEDERAL THEATRE PROJECT.   RE

Proof David Auburn's second play to be produced was the surprise critical and popular hit of the 2000–1 season, winning both the Tony for Best Play and the Pulitzer Prize and running for 917 performances at the Walter Kerr Theatre after transferring from Off-Broadway, where it was produced by the MANHATTAN THEATRE CLUB. It closed on 5 January 2003 as the longest-running Broadway play in two decades. The play, directed by DANIEL SULLIVAN (Tony Award) with scenic design by JOHN LEE BEATTY, examines the thin line between genius and madness as well as the traits inherited from forebears – good and bad. Its cast of four was exceptional (all nominated for Tonys): the deceased mathematician, brilliant but mad, was played by LARRY BRYGGMAN; the heart of the play, his daughter, Catherine, an enigmatic young woman who has sacrified her studies to care for her father, was portrayed brilliantly by MARY-LOUISE PARKER (Tony for Best Actress in a Play); the professor's protégé, Hal, who discovers something surprising in the great man's notebooks was Ben Shenkman; and Catherine's older sister, Johanna Day. By early 2004 the play had been performed from Iceland to the Philippines in more than 30 languages. The film version, with Gwyneth Paltrow as Catherine, was released in 2005.   DBW

Prosky [né Porzuczek]**, Robert** (1930–) Philadelphia-born character actor, most closely associated with Washington, DC's ARENA STAGE, where from 1958 he performed more than 150 roles. As

the company's leading actor, he lent his particularly American blend of gravity and warmth to the Stage Manager in its OUR TOWN (1972, 1976, 1990) and played such roles as Mr. Willis in MOON-CHILDREN (1971; Broadway, 1972), Willy Loman in DEATH OF A SALESMAN (1974), Azdak in *The Caucasian Chalk Circle* (1977), and Grandpa in YOU CAN'T TAKE IT WITH YOU (1979, 1998). After leaving Arena in 1982 – but returning periodically, including in 1994 for *The* PRICE, for which he won the HELEN HAYES Award – Prosky appeared on Broadway as Alfieri in *A* VIEW FROM THE BRIDGE (1983), Levine in GLENGARRY GLEN ROSS (1984), Botvinnik in *A Walk in the Woods* (1988 and a subsequent Soviet tour), Herbert Wehner in *Democracy* (2004), and Off-Broadway as Edison in *Camping with Henry & Tom* in 1995 and The Maharal in *The Golem* in 2002. His sons John (Patrick) and Andrew are actors.
LM

Provincetown Players Led by GEORGE CRAM COOK, an enthusiastic visionary from Iowa who revered the ancient Greek drama, a band of amateurs in the summer of 1915 staged several of their own plays in Provincetown, MA. The following year, after EUGENE O'NEILL joined the group and contributed the outstanding work *Bound East for Cardiff,* Cook – backed by O'Neill and journalist John Reed, among others – decided to move their playmaking to Greenwich Village, NYC. Launched in a brownstone at 139 Macdougal St. on 3 November 1916, the Provincetown Players initially featured short works, with O'Neill and SUSAN GLAS-PELL, Cook's wife, as their leading writers. After two years, the Players moved into larger quarters at 133 Macdougal St. Though Cook gave unstintingly of himself for O'Neill's writings, most notably for *The* EMPEROR JONES (1920), he himself had literary ambitions and envied the other's growing fame. In 1922 he and his wife sailed for Greece, where he died two years later. After a hiatus (1922–3), the Players were headed by a triumvirate of O'Neill, KENNETH MACGOWAN, and ROBERT EDMOND JONES, who in turn were succeeded by JAMES LIGHT as director. A casualty of the stock-market crash and the Depression, the Players folded in 1929. LSh

P.S. 122 see PERFORMANCE SPACE 122

Public Theater, The In 1967, JOSEPH PAPP, the founder of the NEW YORK SHAKESPEARE FESTIVAL, opened as its permanent home a large Italianate building he'd acquired at 425 Lafayette St. in New York. The building dates to 1854, when the Astor family dedicated it as a library for New

Yorkers. After two additions, it was completed in 1881, becoming part of the city's public library system until 1911. In 1920, the building was sold to the Hebrew Immigrant Aid Society, which had intended to sell to a developer until the Landmarks Preservation Commission designated it a landmark in 1960. Papp originally assigned Giorgio Cavaglieri and MING CHO LEE to convert it into theatres. Struggling to keep as much of the original building intact, the designers during the next few years created the Newman Theater (proscenium, 299 seats), Martinson Hall (flexible, 190 seats), LuEsther Hall (flexible, 150 seats), Susan Stein Shiva Theater (flexible, 100 seats), and Anspacher Theater (three-quarter arena, 275 seats). Joe's Pub (1998) is the latest space at The Public. In 1992 (on April 23, Shakespeare's birthday), the building's name was officially changed to The Joseph Papp Public Theater in honor of the late producer; as of 2004 it is simply The Public Theater. To celebrate the NYSF's 50th anniversary, the New York Public Library for the Performing Arts mounted a major exhibit in 2005. MCH

Puerto Rican American theatre see NUYORICAN THEATRE

Puerto Rican Traveling Theatre In 1966, stage, film, and television actress Miriam Colón, a student of ERWIN PISCATOR and the first Puerto Rican member of the ACTORS STUDIO, joined a group of bilingual actors to play storefronts, jails, parks, and street corners. Building on this experience, Colón founded the bilingual PRTT. Under her direction, the theatre has become a hospitable venue for contemporary Latino drama, native and foreign, as well as a center for Latino cultural activity in NYC – a role that includes free training units for young people and playwrights. In 1993 Colón received the Obie for Sustained Excellence of Performance. Although the PRTT still travels locally and abroad, its home is now a former firehouse on West 47th St., renovated in 1974 to provide rehearsal and production facilities. A revival in 1994 of *Death and the Maiden* was given in Spanish and English. CLJ

puppetry in the United States A puppet – any object animated by human control – has three requirements: an object to be animated, a person to do the animating, and a method of controlling the object by using all or part of the puppeteer's body (or an extension of it through rods, strings, wires, magnets, poles, cables, or any combination of these). Variations include hand puppets, finger puppets, rod puppets (Sicilian-style rods are operated from above; Asian- and European-style rods are operated from below), shadow puppets, mouth puppets, costume/body puppets, and string puppets (marionettes). In the 1930s "puppet" superseded "marionette" as the generic term for the worldwide family of fantasy figures. Jim Henson coined the term "Muppet" (marionette + puppet) to describe the unique characters he created for television and films, and pioneered in the use of "Waldos" (electronic, remote movement-sensing puppets).

At the beginning of this century, traditional performers were secretive of their work, sometimes masking the back of their setups to keep stagehands from seeing them in action. A new generation turned things around by writing the histories and "how-to's" explaining everything. Performers who published included Tony Sarg, Helen Haiman Joseph, Edith Flack Ackley, Remo Bufano, Paul McPharlin, and Marjorie Batchelder.

Sarg was especially instrumental as a pioneer with marionettes, first performing at his studio (1915–16). His company toured *The Rose and the Ring, Don Quixote, RIP VAN WINKLE,* and others to eager audiences. Tony Sarg and "marionette" became synonymous. An artist-illustrator of note, Sarg also invented the inflatable figures for the Macy's Parade. His advertising shows at the Chicago World's Fair added to his fame and reputation. Other touring companies included Rufus and Margo Rose, Bil Baird, Remo Bufano, Martin & Olga Stevens, The Tatterman Marionettes, Ralph Chessé, Sue Hastings Marionettes, Kingslands Marionettes, the Yale Puppeteers, Leselli Marionettes, Proctor Puppets (on strings), Basil Milovsoroff (rods), and Pauline Benton (shadows). Marionette companies dominated the scene during the pretelevision era.

Touring was a way of life for most puppeteers. Their portable puppet stages were designed to set up easily in any space that could draw an audience. Department stores hired puppeteers for holiday engagements (a practice today of theme and amusement parks for seasonal engagements).

"Permanent" puppet theatres have been difficult to sustain. In 1941 the Yale Puppeteers opened The Turnabout Theatre in LOS ANGELES, and it ran for 13 years. The 1942 Kungsholm Restaurant in CHICAGO offered dinner patrons a lavish opera theatre in miniature. Partially destroyed by FIRE, it was rebuilt and stayed open until 1966. The Bil Baird Theatre on Barry St. (NYC) opened in 1967; productions played there and on tour for 11 years.

The Center for Puppetry Arts in ATLANTA, which in 2005 celebrated its 25th anniversary, has pioneered the concept of a multilayered program of community service beyond performance – maintaining a resident company, a touring company, a puppet museum with an extensive collection on permanent display, and theme exhibits that tour. In addition, various on-site educational programs are offered (for adults and children), plus an experimental project and a summer series featuring the best American companies performing for family audiences.

Broadway beckoned a few in the 1940s and '50s – Bil and Cora Baird played RADIO CITY MUSIC HALL, the ZIEGFELD *Follies of 1943,* and *Flahooley* (1951), a musical about life in a toy factory. The marionettes of Walton and O'Rourke were featured in *Sons o' Fun* (1941), and in 1951 this West Coast team created the memorable hand puppets for MGM's technicolor film *Lili,* starring Leslie Caron. In 1961 DAVID MERRICK produced *Carnival,* a grittier version of the story set to music, with JERRY ORBACH as the puppeteer; Tom Tichenor of Nashville actually designed and performed the puppets. For the OFF-BROADWAY musical LITTLE SHOP OF HORRORS (1982), Martin P. Robinson created Audrey II, a plant that grew to gargantuan proportions by feeding on humans; the 2003 revival used even more sophisticated puppetry (codesigned by the Jim Henson Company).

Such bizarre imagery is the province of puppetry. Puppets and actors who perform together blend the best of both worlds and bridge the distance between the real and the possible. In the 1930s, ventriloquist Edgar Bergen and his sassy sidekick Charlie McCarthy won a national audience on radio: The illusion was so powerful they did not have to be seen to be believed. In 1947 Burr Tillstrom began a daily show on Chicago television called "Kukla, Fran and Ollie" (which continued as a network show until 1957). The Kuklapolitans performed on a puppet stage built to their scale, while Fran Allison, their special friend, stood out front to chat and sing with them. Daily episodes were improvised from a bare outline.

Jim Henson built a global audience for his Muppet characters, but his performances were confined to the camera. A master of camera technique, Henson was an avid experimenter with the technology of computer-generated "images" and remote controls. In a curious reversal, his characters moved off the screen to appear on arena-type stages in touring productions for family audiences. For these "personal appearance" shows ("Sesame Street Live," "The Muppet Show on Tour") the scale was enlarged by using costume/body puppet versions of Kermit, Miss Piggy, and cast. With prerecorded authentic voices, dancers

Basil Twist's puppets (portraying children) in a quasi-Japanese style for Paula Vogel's *The Long Christmas Ride Home.* Photo by T. Charles Erickson. *Courtesy:* Trinity Repertory Theatre.

and skaters in mask/body costumes matched lip sync and movement, creating the pace and energy of a dry ice show. In 1980 The Henson Foundation was established to assist American puppeteers in the creation of new works for adult audiences. Starting in 1992 the Foundation has been a sponsor of an annual international puppet festival.

Modern puppetry is a mix and match of the traditional and the unexpected. The solo performer (long a staple of the field for economic or artistic reasons) is moving toward collaboration with peers. Some puppeteers have moved out from behind the masking to work in the actor's stage space in full view of the audience (Japanese style). The options for variety seem endless because puppet actors can be formed in any size, shape, and substance the designer chooses. Figures can be articulated or rigid, three-dimensional or flat, representational or abstract, smaller-than-human or larger-than-life.

Peter Schumann's BREAD AND PUPPET THEATRE, for example, uses stilt walking and pole puppets for his outdoor Domestic Resurrection Circus in Glover, VT. The heroic scale gives a primitive power to the evocative images he uses to dramatize social and political issues. Paul Zaloom, a solo performer, uses puppets, objects, and wild, satiric humor to alert his audiences to the hazards of our day. JULIE TAYMOR's *Juan Darién: A Carnival Mass* changed image size in a cinematic approach to live performance. Barbara Pollitt designed large puppets for GEORGE C. WOLFE's staging of *Caucasian Chalk Circle* (set in a place like Haiti) in 1991 to provide a portrait of evil, and in

1995, for his *The Tempest* (for the nymphs), puppets attached to dancers' shoulders.

Although the public perception that puppetry is primarily an entertainment for children has been slow to change, today puppeteers like Ralph Lee, Jane Catherine Shaw, Rick Lyon, and the other puppeteers (see below) who speak to adults are developing their own material and their own unique imagery and a new aesthetic in which the humans actors often support the puppets in a symbiotic relationship. The puppet theatre has in recent years, in fact, made a giant surge forward, as was dramatically illustrated in September 1992 with the presentation of the first (and now annual) International Festival of Puppet Theatre, featuring 17 of the world's best and most innovative companies at the PUBLIC THEATER, underscored by the annual National Puppetry Conferences (the first in 1990) held at the EUGENE O'NEILL MEMORIAL THEATER CENTER. But it was the groundbreaking 1997 megahit *The LION KING* and Julie Taymor's creative use of Indonesian shadow puppets, Japanese Bunraku, European miniature, Chinese bird kites, and African masks that made the use of puppets in the theatre fashionable and almost commonplace. In 2003–4, for example, three Broadway shows featured puppets: *Lion King, AVENUE Q,* and the revival of *LITTLE SHOP OF HORRORS.* For Nora Ephron's *Imaginary Friends* in 2002 Michael Levine created life-size rag dolls of LILLIAN HELLMAN and Mary McCarthy. For Off-Broadway during the same few years Basil Twist, whose visibility has grown steadily since 1995 (e.g., his *Symphonie Fantastique*), created puppets crucial to the aesthetics and message of PAULA VOGEL's *The Long Christmas Ride Home*; LEE BREUER continued his longtime use of puppets in his innovative *DollHouse;* in Brooklyn Dan Hurlin staged his *Hiroshima Maiden* in the style of Bunraku in 2004; and at LA MAMA Theodora Skipitares, who has created numerous interpretation of the classics, completed her trilogy on the Trojan War with puppets in 2006 and about the same time in the East Village Qui Nguyen's *Trial by Water* featured puppets by Jane Stein.

Contemporary puppeteers are served by The Puppeteers of American and its publication, *The Puppetry Journal.*   GL

Purdy, Alexander H. (c. 1815–62) Little known except as manager of New York's National Theatre during 1850–9, Purdy here introduced GEORGE L. FOX (1850–8); presented the HOWARD FAMILY in UNCLE TOM'S CABIN for 325 consecutive performances (1852); premiered TEN NIGHTS IN A BAR ROOM (1858); introduced holiday morning and afternoon matinees; created segregated seating for African Americans; and featured such stars as CHANFRAU as Mose, T. D. RICE as Jim Crow, G. E. Locke in YANKEE roles, as well as J. B. BOOTH and the WALLACKS. Repeated remodeling eventually led Purdy to bankruptcy and prefigured the theatre's razing in 1862.   RKB

Purlie Victorious At a time when African Americans were angry at the slow pace of desegregation, OSSIE DAVIS wrote and, with his wife RUBY DEE, starred in this outrageous satire on race relations in the deep South. The play was a relief from serious race drama, treating stereotyped characters, black and white, with equal absurdity. The play ran for 261 performances on Broadway in 1961, enjoyed limited success as the movie *Gone Are the Days* (1963), and in 1970 was converted to the hit musical *Purlie,* which played for 688 performances.   EGH

Q

Quilters by Molly Newman and Barbara Damashek, with music and lyrics by Damashek, is based on *The Quilters: Women and Domestic Art* by Patricia Cooper and Norma Bradley Allen. A celebration of feminine strength and creativity, this episodic piece pulls together both horrifying and joyous stories of pioneer life on the prairie through monologue, song, mime, and multiple role playing. *Quilters*, originally developed and produced at the DENVER CENTER THEATRE, proved popular in regional theatres throughout the country, despite a New York run of only 24 performances in 1984 at the Jack Lawrence Theatre.   KF

Quintero, José (1924–99) Panamanian-born American director, educated at the University of California and the Goodman School of Drama, specializing in the plays of O'NEILL. Having begun directing in 1949, Quintero helped launch CIRCLE IN THE SQUARE in 1951. Attracted by theatre's passion, he firmly believed "the collective product more important than any individual contribution." His O'Neill productions (19 from 1956 to 1996) included the definitive *The* ICEMAN COMETH with JASON ROBARDS JR. (1956; Vernon Rice Award), *LONG DAY'S JOURNEY INTO NIGHT* (1956; Tony), *A MOON FOR THE MISBEGOTTEN* (1973; Tony and Drama Desk awards), *STRANGE INTERLUDE* (1963, produced by ACTORS STUDIO), and *A TOUCH OF THE POET* (1977, Broadway). In 1980 he directed *Ah, Wilderness!* at Mexico's National Theatre, and in 1988 a Broadway revival of *Long Day's Journey* with Robards and COLLEEN DEWHURST. His final O'Neill in 1996 were two one-acts: *The Long Voyage Home* and *Ile* in Provincetown, MA. Awarded the 1981 O'Neill Birthday Medal, Quintero, a member of the THEATRE HALL OF FAME, toured a 1985 revival of *Iceman* with Robards, which won the HELEN HAYES, Los Angeles Drama Critics' Circle, and O'Neill Gold Medal awards.

Other Quintero productions include the revival of TENNESSEE WILLIAMS'S SUMMER AND SMOKE (1952), Behan's *The Quare Fellow* (1958) (both Circle in the Square), JULES FEIFFER's *Knock Knock* (1976, Broadway), and Cocteau's *The Human Voice* (1978,

Melbourne, Australia; 1979, OFF-BROADWAY). After the Broadway failure of Tennessee Williams's *Clothes for a Summer Hotel* (1980), Quintero left New York and worked primarily in Texas and Florida. In 1993 he directed OUR TOWN at Houston's ALLEY, and he also directed at LONG WHARF, the MARK TAPER, and at the Metropolitan Opera (four works). After his death, his Circle in the Square colleague THEODORE MANN declared that Quintero's triumphs of art "were achieved through his fierce poetic vision" and that he directed with "not tricks, just the truth."

Quintero won the 1986–7 Drama League Award for "bringing to renewed life the plays of O'Neill." His autobiography, *If You Don't Dance, They Beat You,* was published in 1974.   REK

Quinton, Everett (1951–) Actor-playwright, partner of the late CHARLES LUDLAM, and for a decade a member of Ludlam's RIDICULOUS THEATRICAL COMPANY, taking on the the job of artistic director and resident grande dame for a decade after Ludlam's death in 1987. In 1989 he wrote and performed *A Tale of Two Cities,* in which a transvestite performs Dickens's novel (and 22 characters), in an effort to stop a baby, left on his doorstep, from crying. During his 21 years with the Ridiculous he performed in more than 70 productions, including *Camille, The* MYSTERY OF IRMA VEP (1984; Drama Desk and Obie awards; commercial revival OFF-BROADWAY in 1998), *The Artificial Jungle* (1986), *Dr. Jekyll and Mr. Hyde* (1989), *Brother Truckers* (1992), and *Call Me Sarah Bernhardt* (1996; also author). A ONE-PERSON show by Quinton was seen in 1994 and another in 2003–4 (the latter *Twisted Olivia,* a free adaptation of Dickens's *Oliver Twist*); in 1994–5 he wrote and produced a camp version of *A Midsummer Night's Dream.* Since the closure of the Ridiculous, Quinton has been a freelance director and actor (onstage and in films), appearing at the SHAKESPEARE THEATRE in *The Merry Wives of Windsor* and touring in the early 2000s in RODGERS and HAMMERSTEIN's *Cinderella* as the Wicked Stepmother with Eartha Kitt (Fairy Godmother) and Deborah Gibson.   DBW

R

Rabb, Ellis (1930–98) Actor, director, and producer, educated at Carnegie Tech; founder (1960) and artistic director of the ASSOCIATION OF PRODUCING ARTISTS (APA), which in 1964 joined with the Phoenix Theatre to become APA at the Phoenix. Until its dissolution in 1970, Rabb directed most of this company's productions and acted in many as well. Of his New York productions, most notable were YOU CAN'T TAKE IT WITH YOU (1965 and 1983), *Twelfth Night* at LINCOLN CENTER (1972), *The* ROYAL FAMILY (1975; Tony, Best Direction), *Caesar and Cleopatra* (1977), and *The Loves of Anatol* at CIRCLE IN THE SQUARE in 1985. A flamboyant and stylish actor and director, Rabb made significant contributions to the American theatre in both areas and was recognized with numerous awards, including the Obie and Vernon Rice awards for his Off-Broadway season with the APA (1961–2) and a Tonys for the APA-Phoenix rep season of 1966–7. To Rabb's credit he worked diligently throughout his career to bring true repertory to the American stage. DBW

Rabe, David (1940–) Iowa-born playwright and screenwriter known for his trilogy of Vietnam War plays. Rabe, a Loras College graduate (1962), also attended Villanova University, where a number of his early plays were performed. Drafted in 1965, he was then sent to Vietnam. Rabe's big break came when, discovered by JOSEPH PAPP, five of his early plays were staged by the NEW YORK SHAKESPEARE FESTIVAL. In 1971 *The* BASIC TRAINING OF PAVLO HUMMEL and STICKS AND BONES ran simultaneously, *Pavlo* at the PUBLIC THEATER and *Sticks* on Broadway (Best Play Tony Award; NY Drama Critics' Circle Special Citation for Rabe). Far less successful were *In the Boom Boom Room* (1973–4), about the victimization of a Philadelphia go-go dancer, and *The Orphan* (1973), Rabe's adaptation of the *Orestia*. STREAMERS, the third play (after *Pavlo* and *Sticks*) in Rabe's Vietnam trilogy, was staged in 1976. Rabe, however, is more than a Vietnam War playwright: *Goose and Tomtom* (1982; 1986 staged reading at Lincoln Center) is an existential comedy about a bizarre robbery; HURLYBURLY (1984; revived 2005, NEW GROUP) is about Hollywood image making and failed dreams. A prequel to *Hurlyburly*, entitled *Those the River Keeps*, premiered in 1991 at the McCARTER (revived disastrously at NYC's Promenade Theatre in 1994). *A Question of Mercy* (1997, NEW YORK THEATRE WORKSHOP), dubbed "an exquisitely controlled work," deals with a doctor who is treating a man terminally ill with AIDS and his struggle with the idea of suicide. An adaptation of Chekhov's story *The Black Monk* premiered at the at YALE REP (2003). Rabe's screenplays include *I'm Dancing as Fast as I Can* (1982) and *Casualties of War* (1989). Rabe's plays, filled with violence, racism, betrayals, foolish heroism, and male tribal customs, combine grotesque comedy, surrealistic fantasy, and bitter satire. Rabe's wife is actress Jill Clayburgh. PCK

Rachel by Angelina Weld Grimké, presented in Washington, DC, 2–4 March 1916, as one of the first productions by the NAACP Drama Committee – with mixed reactions – was an effort to enlighten the American people by using the stage for race propaganda. The play, in three acts, focuses on the effects of race prejudice on a family. The central conflict is borne by Rachel, the daughter, who comes to grips with the struggle between the races. Her brother can find no work because of his color; her father and an older brother were lynched when she was a child. Throughout the play, the audience is made aware of how the innocence of young children will be destroyed by the prejudice and hatred of others. KME

Radio City Music Hall West 50th St. and Ave. of the Americas, NYC [Architects: Feinhard and Hofmeister, Hood and Foulihoux and Corbett, Harison and MacMurray]. Built in 1932 by S. L. "Roxy" Rothafel with Rockefeller money, the 6,200-seat, art-deco theatre – then the world's largest indoor theatre – was originally intended to present popular-priced VAUDEVILLE, but policy and leadership changed quickly: The new formula of showing a movie in combination with a stage show highlighted by the Rockettes, a precision tap-dancing chorus, endured for many years. When the supply of "family-type" films fell off and the attraction of the stage show wore thin, the theatre seemed doomed; but it was declared a landmark in 1979, and was thoroughly renovated to reopen as a showplace for large spectacles and star appearances. It 1985 it earned its first profit since 1955. A recent renovation returned the interior to its original spendor.   MCH

Ragtime Musical play produced by LIVENT, INC., in 1998, based on E. L. Doctorow's 1975 novel, with book (Tony) by TERRENCE MCNALLY, score (Tony) by STEPHEN FLAHERTY (music) and LYNN AHRENS (lyrics), direction by FRANK GALATI, choreography by GRACIELA DANIELE, scenery by EUGENE LEE, and turn-of-the-20th-century costumes by SANTO LOQUASTO. The sweeping story of the intertwining lives of a wealthy family, a poor immigrant and his motherless daughter, and a black man named Coalhouse Walker had a star-studded cast including Mark Jacoby, MARTIN MAZZIE, Peter Friedman, BRIAN STOKES MITCHELL, and AUDRA MCDONALD (Tony). The sumptuous production inaugurated the equally spectacular FORD CENTER on 18 January, after a premiere in Toronto in December 1996 and a LOS ANGELES run in June 1997. Orchestration by William David Brohn also received a Tony. The costly production ($10 million) ran 861 performances and failed to recoup its expenses. A scaled-down staging was produced in London in 2003, seen first in the U.S. at the PAPER MILL PLAYHOUSE (2005).   DBW

Raines, Ron (1949–) Texas City, TX, born actor-singer, trained at Juilliard in opera, who since 1994 has played the villain Alan Spaulding on the soap *The Guiding Light*. His tall, good looks and his strong baritone have also made him a leading musical-theatre performer, seen as Gaylord Ravenal in the 1983 revival of *SHOW BOAT* and as Billy Flynn in *Chicago* in 2002. He also appeared in the brief run of *Teddy & Alice* (1987) and in a number of productions with the New York City Opera. In regional theatres and opera companies he has appeared in *KISS ME, KATE, SOUTH PACIFIC, ANNIE, KISMET, THE KING AND I, NAUGHTY MARIETTA, BRIGADOON, ROSE-MARIE, OKLAHOMA!, CAROUSEL, Side by Side by Sondheim, FOLLIES,* and *MAN OF LA MANCHA*.   DBW

Rainmaker, The This only successful drama by N. Richard Nash premiered at the CORT THEATRE 28 October 1954, running 125 performances. The play focuses on Lizzie Curry (GERALDINE PAGE), a repressed 27-year-old woman whose infatuation

with Bill Starbuck (Darren McGavin), a roguish, wandering rainmaker, gives her the self-esteem necessary to propel her into maturity. By nearly every definition a romance, the play avoids the traditional romantic conclusion by having Lizzie decline to run away with Starbuck, realizing the merit of her own appreciation of herself over the opinions of others. An ill-fated 1999 revival by ROUNDABOUT starred JAYNE ATKINSON and film star Woody Harrelson. Nash wrote the book for the 1963 musical adaptation, *110 in the Shade* (revived by Roundabout, 2007).   RW

Raisin in the Sun, A Warm-spirited drama of black family life by LORRAINE HANSBERRY that opened at the ETHEL BARRYMORE THEATRE on 11 March 1959, won the Drama Critics' Circle Best Play award, and ran 530 performances. Directed by LLOYD RICHARDS, it starred CLAUDIA MCNEIL as the widowed Mama who wants to use her insurance money to move out of the family's poverty-stricken South Side Chicago neighborhood, and Sidney Poitier as her son, Walter, who loses the nest egg in a futile effort to open a liquor store. Also in the superb cast were RUBY DEE, Diana Sands, Louis Gossett, LONNE ELDER II, Ivan Dixon, and DOUGLAS TURNER WARD. The play was hailed for the honesty of its portrayal of a family that struggles to maintain its dignity despite the injustices of the larger world. A musical version, *Raisin,* won accolades in 1973. New York revivals of the original play were presented at the NEW FEDERAL THEATRE in 1979, at the ROUNDABOUT in 1986, and on Broadway in 2004 (with award-winning performances by PHYLICIA RASHAD and AUDRA MCDONALD).   FHL

Raitt, John [Emmet] (1917–2005) Singer-actor who, after starting out in opera, played Curly in the national tour of *OKLAHOMA!* (1944). He created the role of Billy Bigelow in *CAROUSEL* (1945), and starred in *Three Wishes for Jamie* (1952), *Carnival in Flanders* (1953), and *The PAJAMA GAME* (1954). He lent his fine baritone voice to Broadway revivals, SUMMER STOCK, and NIGHTCLUBS from the 1960s to the 1990s. His final Broadway appearance was in *A Musical Jubilee* (1975). Frequently in his last decades he sang with his daughter, Bonnie.   MK

Ramicova, Dunya (1950–) Czechoslovakian-born costume (and sometime lighting) designer who has designed costumes at most regional theatres, working extensively at the HARTFORD STAGE, ARENA THEATRE, GUTHRIE THEATRE, AMERICAN REPERTORY THEATRE, and the YALE REPERTORY THEATRE. She has also designed at European and

American opera houses. Working frequently with directors ANDREI SERBAN, LIVIU CIULEI, and MARK LAMOS, Ramicova is most closely associated with director PETER SELLARS, for whom she has designed *Nixon in China* (1987), the Mozart–Da Ponte cycle at Pepsico Summerfare (1989), and *The Magic Flute* at Glyndebourne, England (1990), among others, as well as the Sellars film *The Cabinet of Dr. Ramirez*. She is equally at home with meticulously researched period pieces and postmodern opera. Since 1988 she has taught in the University of California system.   AA

Ramsay, (Gustavus) Remak (1937–) Princeton-educated actor who often plays stuffy Englishmen and frequently appears Off-Broadway and regionally. His credits include *The Winslow Boy* (1981, ROUNDABOUT THEATRE), Simon Gray's *Quartermaine's Terms* (1982, LONG WHARF; 1983, OFF-BROADWAY, Obie), Ayckbourn's *Woman in Mind* (1988, MANHATTAN THEATRE CLUB), *The Molière Comedies* (1995, Roundabout), *The Heiress* (1995, CORT THEATRE), *Misalliance* (1997, Roundabout), and *She Stoops to Conquer* (2005, IRISH REP). His films include *Heartbreak House* (1986, TV; as Hector Hushabye), *The House on Carroll Street* (1988), and *Fever* (1999).   REK

Rand, Sally [née Helen (Hazel) Gould Beck] (1904–79) Dancer who scandalized America in 1933 by performing a fan dance at the Chicago World's Fair. Born in Hickory County, MO, she worked as an acrobat in CIRCUSES and carnivals, then went to Hollywood in the mid-1920s to appear in such silent films as *The King of Kings* and *GETTING GERTIE'S GARTER* (both 1927). After the Depression she changed her name and began working Chicago speakeasies. She then toured the VAUDEVILLE circuit, headlining at the PALACE in 1928, there reviewed as "indifferently pleasant." After breaking in the fan dance in 1932 in a Chicago NIGHTCLUB, her World's Fair appearance made her a star, and she worked steadily almost till her death. Rand also appeared nude as Lady Godiva – she called it her form of social protest during the Depression – and also developed a bubble dance. Critics called her "saucy, piquant . . . a cute, lithesome charmer . . . radiates personality."   SMA

Rando, John (1961?–) Houston-raised director, educated at the University of Texas with graduate study at UCLA (M.F.A., 1988); worked as an assistant director at the OLD GLOBE and with the ACTING COMPANY, and has established himself as an accomplished comedy and musical specialist, largely on the basis of his directing NEIL SIMON's

The Dinner Party (2000) and *URINETOWN* (2001, OFF-BROADWAY and Broadway; Tony, Best Direction of a Musical). Other notable NYC credits include *Fortune's Fool* (1995; his Off-Broadway debut), *The Wedding Singer* (2006, Broadway; based on 1998 film), and *Pig Farm* by Greg Kotis, also 2006 (ROUNDABOUT). Rando has worked closely with the plays of DAVID IVES, has directed several CITY CENTER ENCORES! musical concerts, and worked for the BERKSHIRE THEATRE FESTIVAL, the GEORGE STREET PLAYHOUSE, the GEFFEN, and other regional theatres.   DBW

Rankin, (Arthur) McKee (1844–1914) A dashing actor-manager, Canadian-born Rankin was a theatrical gambler whose charm usually kept him one step ahead of disaster. Acting with his wife, KITTY BLANCHARD, Rankin achieved his greatest success as the stalwart miner Sandy McGee in *The DANITES* (1877), a tale of Mormon revenge in a gold-mining town. Other roles included another miner, "'49," in a play of that title (1881) and a Canadian hero in *The Canuck* (1891). In 1883–4 Rankin managed the Third Avenue Theatre, and in the 1890s he coached actress NANCE O'NEIL, who would not perform without his assistance. Rankin's legal and marital problems were legend; in 1904 he declared bankruptcy. His oldest daughter, Gladys, married Sidney Drew, and another daughter, Doris, married Lionel Barrymore (see DREW–BARRYMORE). A thorough biography by David Beasley was published in 2002.   RAH

Rapp, Adam (1969?–) Joliet, IL, native who attended Clarke College in Dubuque, IA, and two years in the playwriting program at Juilliard. Since the late 1990s he has emerged as formidable novelist and playwright, with a fistful of awards, fellowships, and other honors; raves for the world premieres of *Nocturne* (2001) and, at the AMERICAN REPERTORY THEATRE, *Animals and Plants* (2001) and *Stone Cold Dead Serious* (2002) escalated his reputation. *Nocturne* was coproduced by the NEW YORK THEATRE WORKSHOP; its West Coast premiere was at BERKELEY REP, fall 2001. As Bruce Miller has noted, there is a "harsh, yet comic grimness and pain that permeates his dramatic work." As another critic noted, there is also a strange tenderness in his writing. He is a writer with a clear, distinctive, personal voice (demonstrated also in his first feature film, *Winter Passing* [2006], and his six published novels). His other plays, several developed at O'Neill Conferences, include *Ghosts in the Cottonwoods* (1996), *Trueblinka* (1997), *Blackbird* (2001, London), *Finer Noble Gases*

(2002, Humana), *Gompers* (2003), *Red Light Winter* (2005, STEPPENWOLF; Pulitzer Prize finalist), and *Essential Self-Defense* (2007, PLAYWRIGHTS HORIZONS). He is slated to direct his *Bingo with the Indians* at the FLEA in fall 2007. His brother **Anthony** is a successful actor (*Rent, Six Degrees of Separation*). DBW

Rasche, David (1944–) Born in St. Louis, grew up in Illinois, attended Elmhurst College, the University of Chicago, and studied with SANFORD MEISNER. This tall, blond, blue-eyed, good-looking stage, film, and television actor possesses a quirky sense of humor that worked well in the 1970s when he was a member of Chicago's SECOND CITY and during 1986–88 when he starred as a violent, chauvinistic cop in the title role of ABC's series *Sledge Hammer!* As a stage actor, he has demonstrated a special affinity for plays by DAVID MAMET, a close friend, including *Sexual Perversity in Chicago* (1974, ORGANIC THEATRE), *Speed-the-Plow* (1988, Broadway replacement), and *Edmond* in the ATLANTIC THEATER COMPANY's revival of 1996 – in which, as Mamet's beleaguered Everyman, he found his ideal role. Other notable OFF-BROADWAY roles were in MARSHA NORMAN's *Last Dance, To Gillian on Her 37th Birthday,* and in 2005 as film director Victor Fleming in *Moonlight and Magnolias* (about the collaboration for the film *Gone with the Wind*) for the MANHATTAN THEATRE CLUB. His own play *Jackie* was produced in both NYC (1993) and LA (1994). DBW

Rashad [née Ayers-Allen], **Phylicia** (1948–) Activist and actress born in Houston, TX, educated at Howard University. As the hardened matriarch in a black family on the brink in 1950s Chicago in the revival of *A RAISIN IN THE SUN*, she became in 2004 the first black woman to win a Tony in the leading-actress category. Although best known as Claire Huxtable on NBC's hit 1980's sitcom *The Cosby Show*, she began her career in 1975 as a singer/actress in *THE WIZ*, followed by *Dreamgirls, INTO THE WOODS, JELLY'S LAST JAM*, and for ROUNDABOUT *Blue* in an unsympathetic role. After *Raisin* she appeared in the east coast premiere of WILSON's *Gem of the Ocean* in Boston and then in New York (2004). Her sister is dancer/choreographer Debbie Allen, who has appeared in six Broadway musicals. DBW

Ravel family French MIMES and dancers, arguably the most popular and influential performers in early 19th-century America. The Ravels included **Gabriel** (1810–82), an excellent pantomimist and acrobat, the troupe's businessman;

Jérôme (1814–90), author of such durable scenarios as *The Green Monster, Pongo the Intelligent Ape,* and *Mazulme; or, The Night Owl;* and **Angélique** (1813–95), **Antoine** (1812–82), and **François** (1823–81). They brought their skillful acrobatics, graceful dance, and advanced trickwork to the PARK THEATRE (1836–7), and then became a fixture at NIBLO'S GARDEN (1842–6, 1849–50, 1857–60), where they were much admired by the boy Henry James and inspired rival clown G. L. FOX. In 1850 the troupe split, with Jérôme and Antoine touring the U.S. and François and Gabriel playing Europe. After the elder Ravels retired to France in 1866, Angélique's children, Marietta and Charles Winter Ravel, perpetuated the family traditions, while the KIRALFY FAMILY revived their pantomimes in spectacular versions. LS

Raymond [né O'Brien], **John T.** (1836–87) A low comedian, Raymond made his debut at Rochester, NY (27 June 1853). After supporting such actresses as JULIA DEAN and ANNA CORA MOWATT, he succeeded JOSEPH JEFFERSON III as Asa Trenchard in *OUR AMERICAN COUSIN* with LAURA KEENE. As a member of the STOCK COMPANY at the CALIFORNIA THEATRE, San Francisco, he created the role of Colonel Mulberry Sellers in an adaptation of Mark Twain's *The Gilded Age* (1873), which sustained the rest of his career. Noted for his extravgant gestures and his poker face, his comic invention often ignored the dramatic situation. DMcD

Reams, Lee Roy (1942–) Performer, director, choreographer, whose stage persona has largely been one that projected, as one critic noted, "indefatigable good cheer." Born in Covington, KY, he graduated from the University of Cincinnati Conservatory of Music. His Broadway debut was in *SWEET CHARITY* (1966), followed by *Applause* as the gay hairdresser (1970), *Lorelei* (1974), *HELLO, DOLLY!* as the Yonkers clerk Cornelius Hackl (1978), and his best-known role as hoofer Billy Lawlor in *42ND STREET* (1980). He has been a replacement in *LA CAGE AUX FOLLES, Beauty and the Beast,* and *The PRODUCERS,* and he directed and choreographed a 1995 revival of *Dolly.* Reams is currently an active cabaret performer; in 1985 he performed successfully a largely autobiographical one. DBW

Rebeck, Theresa (1958?–) Stage, screen, and television writer, born in Ohio and educated at Notre Dame and Brandeis (where she earned three graduate degrees, including a Ph.D. in Victorian literature, with a focus on melodrama). Rebeck has written extensively for *L.A. Law*, *NYPD Blue*, and *Law & Order*, serving for a time as Executive Producer of the latter (*Criminal Intent*). Her theatre work, however, is extensive, including *Omnium Gatherum* (2003, OFF-BROADWAY), coauthored with Alexandra Gersten-Vassilaros (a finalist for the Pulitzer). Other plays, many of which premiered Off-Broadway, include *Spike Heels* (1992), *Loose Knit* (1993), *Sunday on the Rocks* (1994, LONG WHARF), *The Family of Mann* (1994), *View of the Dome* (1996), *Abstract Expression* (1998, Long Wharf), *The Butterfly Collection* (2000), *Dollhouse* (2001, HARTFORD STAGE), and *Bad Dates* (2003). Two recent plays were influenced by her interest in Victorian melodrama: *The Bells* (2005, MCCARTER) – set in Alaska at the tag end of the gold rush – was inspired by Leopold Lewis's 1871 play of the same name; and *The Two Orphans* (2005, Brandeis Theater Company, Waltham, MA) is a musical version of the popular 19th-century melodrama. Her 2006 *The Scene*, a black comedy on middle age set at a Manhattan party, was a hit of the Humana Festival at ACTORS THEATRE OF LOUISVILLE, and was produced in 2007 at SECOND STAGE (which had mounted three of her early plays and, in spring 2006, *The Water's Edge*).   DBW

Reddin, Keith (1956–) Prolific playwright and actor. Educated at Northwestern and the Yale Drama School, Reddin won the Charles McArthur Award after *Life and Limb* premiered 1984 at SOUTH COAST REPERTORY. *Rum and Coke* was produced at YALE REP (1984, Winterfest) and the PUBLIC THEATER (1986), *Big Time* at the AMERICAN REPERTORY THEATRE (1988), *Nebraska* at LA JOLLA PLAYHOUSE (1989), *The Innocents' Crusade* at the LONG WHARF (1991), and three plays at the GOODMAN: *Black Snow*, based on Bulgakov (1993; Joseph Jefferson Award), *Brutality of Fact* (1994, Studio Theatre), and *All the Rage* (1997; Joseph Jefferson Award). *Synergy* premiered at the ALLEY (2001), and *Can't Let Go* and *Almost Blue* (both 2003) OFF-BROADWAY. *Big Time* was filmed by PBS for *American Playhouse*.   BBW

Redgrave family A dynasty of British actors represented on the New York stage by father **Michael** (1908–85) and his three children and granddaughter Natasha. The elder Redgrave, one of Britain's great actors of the post-WWII period, appeared on Broadway six times, first as Macbeth in 1948 and most notably in *Tiger at the Gates* (1955), *The Importance of Being Earnest* (1961), and *The Aspern Papers* (1962). He wrote an autobiography in 1983, athough a recent biography by Alan Strachan (2004) is more candid and thorough.

Michael's offspring (with actress Rachel Kempson) have had a greater impact in the U.S. The eldest, **Vanessa** (1937–), with an extensive career in film and onstage in England, has appeared on Broadway four times: *The Lady from the Sea* (1976), *Orpheus Descending* (1989), and *Long Day's Journey into Night* (2003; Tony for Best Actress), and the ONE-PERSON *The Year of Magical Thinking* (2007). OFF-BROADWAY in 1994 she played Vita Sackville-West opposite Eileen Atkins's Virginia Woolf in *Vita & Virginia* (UNION SQUARE; Obie), and in 1997 Cleopatra for the NEW YORK SHAKESPEARE FESTIVAL in a production that originated at the ALLEY. Vanessa's autobiography was published in 1991. Her daughter, **Natasha Richardson** (1963–), won a Tony for Sally Bowles in the 1998 revival of *CABARET* and had been nominated for the earlier *Anna Christie* (1993) opposite her husband, Liam Neeson. In 1999 she was in *Closer*, and in 2005 she was Blanche in *A STREETCAR NAMED DESIRE*.

Corin (1939–), the middle sibling, like his sister Vanessa, has been active in Trotskyist politics. His Broadway debut was in *Chips with Everything* in 1963. In TENNESSEE WILLIAMS's *Not about Nightingales* (which Vanessa rediscovered) he played Boss Whalen, a prison warden, in 1999. In 2002 he portrayed Benedict Arnold in RICHARD NELSON's *The General from America* Off-Broadway (and earlier in London). Since 2005 he has been severely ill.

The youngest sibling, **Lynn** (1943–) is the Redgrave with the most extensive American stage career, beginning with her Broadway debut in 1967 (*Black Comedy*), five years after her professional debut in London, and including appearances in *My Fat Friend*, *Mrs Warren's Profession* (with RUTH GORDON), *Knock Knock*, *Saint Joan*, *Sister Mary Ignatius Explains It All for You* (Off-Broadway), *A Little Hotel on the Side*, *The Master Builder*, *Shakespeare for My Father* (conceived and written by her), *Moon over Buffalo*, and *The Constant Wife*. Her *Shakespeare* solo performance toured extensively and won numerous honors including the 1993 ELLIOT NORTON Award; in 2002 she was praised (and won a Drama Desk) for her Miss Fozzard in Alan Bennett's *Talking Heads* Off-Broadway, as she was in 2005 for her Mrs. Culver in *Constant Wife*. In 2006 she played Lady Bracknell in Peter Hall's *The Importance of Being Earnest* in LOS ANGELES and at BROOKLYN ACADEMY OF MUSIC. She has lived in the U.S. for over 20 years (a naturalized citizen), dividing her career between the U.S. and U.K. (In 2002 she was invested as an Officer of the Order of British Empire.) In 1993 she was elected the first woman president of the Players (see CLUBS), although she was replaced by actor Michael Allinson a year later.   DBW

Ada Rehan as Lady Teazle in Daly's version of *The School for Scandal.* Photo by Sarony, New York. *Courtesy:* Don B. Wilmeth Theatre Collection.

Red Horse Animation, The   One of three "animations" – along with *The B. Beaver* (1974) and *The Shaggy Dog* (1978) – that LEE BREUER wrote and directed for MABOU MINES, the experimental COLLECTIVE he cofounded. *The Red Horse* (1970) – combining autobiography, a fragmented, nonlinear structure, and an enormous dose of irony – is regarded as one of the prototypical American avant-garde plays of the 1970s. Using a broken, cartoonlike, fabulistic narrative, it examines the flow of consciousness, the process of making art, and what it means to be male. A stage prose poem filled with verbal and visual puns, it is by turns romantic and arch, elegiac, and formalistic. *Red Horse* premiered at NYC's Guggenheim Museum, performed by JOANNE AKALAITIS, RUTH MALECZECH, and DAVID WARRILOW.   AS

Rees, James (1802–85) Playwright and critic, best known as author of *The Dramatic Authors of America*

(1845), a valuable resource for historians; he had only moderate success as a playwright. Like most of the actor-playwrights, Rees adapted popular fiction (J. F. Cooper's *The Headsman,* 1834), wrote many national plays (*Washington at Valley Forge,* 1832; *Lafitte, the Pirate of the Gulf,* 1837; *Mad Anthony Wayne,* 1845), and capitalized on current events (*Patrick Lyons; or, The Locksmith of Philadelphia,* 1843, a man victimized and jailed by bankers). Rees's other plays include *The Miniature* (1834), *The Squatter* (1839), and *Mike Fink, the Last Boatman of the Mississippi* (n.d.).   WJM

Rees, Roger (1944–) Born in Wales, this classically trained actor was originally educated in the visual arts but in the 1960s became an actor, reaching an apogee with the eponymous hero Nicholas Nickleby in London and New York (1981; Tony for Best Actor in a Play) in the Royal Shakespeare Company production (he remains an RSC member). Much of his career since the early 1980s has been in the U.S. (citizenship gained 1989). In 1995 he was nominated for a Tony for Best Actor in a Play in Cocteau's *Indiscretions.* For ROUNDABOUT he acted in *Uncle Vanya* (2000) and *The Rehearsal* (1996), as well as directed *Arms and the Man* (2000). Rees essayed the title role in the critically acclaimed musical *A Man of No Importance* (AHRENS AND FLAHERTY) at LINCOLN CENTER. In 2004 he was appointed artistic director of the WILLIAMSTOWN THEATRE FESTIVAL, where he had both acted and directed. He has acted and directed elsewhere regionally, taught at Florida State University and UCLA, and during 1989–93 was a semiregular on *Cheers* as a feckless British tycoon.   DBW

Reeve, Christopher (1952–2004) Actor, identified with Superman from four films (1978, 1981, 1983, 1987), whose Broadway debut was in Bagnold's *A Matter of Gravity* (1976). Reeve performed for the CIRCLE REPERTORY COMPANY (FIFTH OF JULY, 1980), CIRCLE IN THE SQUARE (*The Marriage of Figaro,* 1985), and NEW YORK SHAKESPEARE FESTIVAL (*The Winter's Tale,* 1989). An equestrian accident left him severely injured in May 1995 and led ultimately to his death, despite a valiant recovery effort.   REK

regional theatre movement see RESIDENT NONPROFIT PROFESSIONAL THEATRE

Rehan, Ada (1860–1916) Actress whose family migrated to Brooklyn from Ireland when she was 5. She made her debut at age 13, and at 15 became a member of Mrs. DREW's ARCH STREET THEATRE company in PHILADELPHIA. In 1877 AUGUSTIN DALY spotted her in Albany and engaged her to appear in New York in his own play *Pique* (1878). He was so impressed with her talents that he persuaded her to join him permanently, and from then until his death (1899) she was his leading lady.

During her 31 years on stage in the U.S. and in England, Rehan played more than 200 roles, ranging from the title role in Daly's *Odette* (1882), to Lady Teazle in *The School for Scandal* (1894), and a host of Shakespearean roles: Katherina, Rosalind, Viola, Beatrice, Miranda, and Portia. She appeared in London at Toole's Theatre (1884), played Katherina at the Shakespeare Memorial Theatre (1888), opened Daly's Theatre (just off Leicester Square) as Viola (1893), made a cross-country tour of the U.S. (1896), and finally after Daly's death toured again with OTIS SKINNER in *The Taming of the Shrew* (1904–5) (see SHAKESPEARE ON . . .).

Critics called her "sweetly reckless," "ardently impetuous," and "piquantly alluring." Ellen Terry described her as "the most lovely, humorous darling I have ever seen on the stage." William Winter published a revised biography in 1898.   RM

Reid, Kate (1930–93) Canadian actress of international stature who was noted for her work in roles demanding intense emotional energy. Her London (U.K.) debut was in the title role of *The Stepmother* (1958). She returned to Canada to appear at the Stratford Festival (1959–62). In 1962 she went to New York to play Martha in the matinee cast of EDWARD ALBEE's *WHO'S AFRAID OF VIRGINIA WOOLF?* (1962), and in 1964 was nominated for a Tony for her performance opposite Sir Alec Guinness in *Dylan*. She costarred in TENNESSEE WILLIAMS's *Slapstick Tragedy* (1966) and spent almost two years in ARTHUR MILLER's *The Price* in New York and London (1968–9). For the AMERICAN SHAKESPEARE FESTIVAL she played Gertrude in *Hamlet* in 1969 and, in 1974, the Nurse in *Romeo and Juliet* and Big Mama in *CAT ON A HOT TIN ROOF*. In 1985 she played opposite DUSTIN HOFFMAN in a major Broadway revival of *DEATH OF A SALESMAN*. She appeared as the Countess in MARK LAMOS's production of *All's Well That Ends Well* at the HARTFORD STAGE COMPANY in 1991. She also had a successful film (*A Delicate Balance*, 1973) and television career.   JA   DBW

Reinhardt, Max (1873–1943) Austrian régisseur who gained a reputation throughout Europe as an innovative director, utilizing new stage and lighting techniques in theatre spaces both large and intimate, but primarily in vast spectacles with huge casts and, later, outdoor stagings. Reinhardt's New York production of *Sumurun* (1912) introduced audiences to the New Stagecraft inspired by Appia and Craig. NORMAN BEL GEDDES's lavish design for Reinhardt's *The Miracle* (1924) transformed NYC's Century Theatre (the renamed NEW THEATRE) into a cathedral. Reinhardt's ensemble toured the U.S. in 1927–8 with *A Midsummer Night's Dream* and *Danton's Death,* among others. He became interested in Hollywood and the prospects of filming Shakespeare, directing his twelfth *Midsummer* in the Hollywood Bowl and the film version in 1935. He staged Franz Werfel's pageant of Jewish history, *The Eternal Road,* in a spectacular production (Bel Geddes design, 1937) at the Manhattan Opera House, and settled permanently in the U.S. in 1938. He popularized THORNTON WILDER's *The Merchant of Yonkers* at the GUILD THEATRE (1938, BORIS ARONSON design). His son Gottfried directed his successful 1929 Berlin version of Strauss's *Die Fledermaus* (retitled *Rosalinda,* 1942) on Broadway. His final production was IRWIN SHAW's *Sons and Soldiers* (1943).   RE

Reinking, Ann (1949–) Choreographer, director, and performer born in Seattle; called by *Time* magazine "Terpsiglorious." Her Broadway debut was in *Coco* in 1969, followed by a series of musicals: *Wild and Wonderful, Pippin, Over Here!, Goodtime Charley, A CHORUS LINE* (1976, replacement, Cassie), *CHICAGO* (1977, replacing GWEN VERDON as Roxie Hart), *Dancin',* and *SWEET CHARITY* (1986, replacement, title role). A gap of almost a decade led to a return in 1996 as both choreographer (in the style of BOB FOSSE, with whom she had had a long personal relationship in the 1970s) and performer in the long-running revival of *Chicago.* A 1997 Tony and Drama Desk honored her choreographic work on that production. In 1999 she codirected and "cochoreographed" *Fosse* (sharing, with the late Bob Fosse, the Olivier Award in 2001 for Best Theatre Choreographer for the London production), and in 2003 she choreographed the short-lived revue *The Look of Love.* In the 1970s and '80s she appeared in a number of musical films, including *ANNIE* and Fosse's autobiographical *All That Jazz.* She is currently artistic director of the Broadway Theater Project in Tampa, FL, a program that connects students and professionals.   DBW

Rent Rock-musical version of *La Bohème* set in Manhattan's East Village. Seven years in the making, its words and music were by the unknown Jonathan Larson, who in late January 1996 died unexpectedly of an aortic aneurysm the night of the show's final dress rehearsal at NEW YORK THEATRE WORKSHOP. *Rent,* directed by MICHAEL GREIF, who had worked early on with Larson on the development of the text (bringing more edge and realism to the mix), was the sleeper hit of the season, transferring to Broadway's NEDERLANDER THEATRE in April where, at this writing, it is still running. It received numerous awards, including the Pulitzer Prize for Drama and the Tony for Best Musical.

During the workshop period a dramaturge, Lynn M. Thomson, had been engaged, and after Larson's death she claimed authorship of nearly half of the musical's book and 9% of its lyrics. A protracted lawsuit ensued, finally settled out of court. Certainly the publicity the show received because of Larson's death and the legal battle had an impact on the public's interest in it, yet the rave reviews it received reflected an excitement in its energy, its uniqueness in adapting an old story to a gritty modern milieu, and the rare successful wedding of rock 'n' roll to musical theatre that transcended these events. The film version was released in 2005 with several of the original cast, including Jesse L. Martin, Adam Pascal, Anthony Rapp, Taye Diggs, and Idina Menzel. DBW

Rentz–Santley Novelty and Burlesque Company

Credited as the first American BURLESQUE SHOW [see poster at that entry], created by MICHAEL B. LEAVITT in 1870. Leavitt first feminized the traditional MINSTREL SHOW (as Mme Rentz's Female Minstrels, a name suggested by a European circus), then added variety acts (the traditional olio) and, as the third act of his show, a musicalized travesty (afterpiece), adapting the tripartite minstrel format. One of the first stars, Mabel Santley, helped establish the model for most reputable burlesque of the 1880s and '90s (editions of the show appeared annually). Rival burlesque companies soon followed, with Sam T. Jack (former Rentz–Santley manager) the most notorious competitor. DBW

Repertorio Español

Award-winning (Obies 1981 and 1996; 1996 Honorary Drama Desk for presentation of quality theatre), nonprofit, Spanish-language repertory company founded in 1968 by Gilberto Zaldívar and René Buch to produce the best of Latin American, Spanish, and HISPANIC American theatre. Headquartered at NYC's Gramercy Arts Theatre (since 1972), the company offers some 300 performances annually of as many as 18 dramatic, musical (especially popular are its Spanish zarzuelas), and dance productions in rotating repertory and on tour. With its infra-red simultaneous translation for English-speaking audiences, the company has served as a catalyst for cultural interaction. DBW

Repertory Theatre of St. Louis

Founded in 1966 as the Repertory Theatre at Loretto–Hilton Center, then operating as the Loretto–Hilton Repertory Theatre during 1973–81, this regional nonprofit theatre was conceived by Marita Woodruff and Wayne Loui on the Webster University campus. The Sisters of Loretto administer the University, and Conrad Hilton, a former student, contributed $1.5 million dollars to the project. The Repertory Theatre presents a substantial series of productions in a mainstage facility (Virginia Jackson Browning Theatre) that can be adjusted to seat 499–1,200 (usually 763) and the Emerson Studio Theatre, seating about 125. A facelift and expansion in 2002 added nearly 20,000 square feet of support spaces. The Center now houses both the Rep and Opera Theatre of Saint Louis. SMA DBW

resident nonprofit professional theatre

As clumsy and unwieldy as this phrase might be, at least it has the value of being descriptive to the point of being comprehensive: It refers to a nationwide movement of diverse, noncommercial, professional theatre companies that had their beginnings in the 1960s, and it encompasses the not-for-profit theatres in New York City. This last point adds a crucial dimension, because this mosaic of regional theatres that spread across the country after WWII has been viewed as an alternative to the commercially oriented and often monopolistic Broadway theatres.

Over the years, a number of simpler, catchier terms – "regional," "repertory," "resident," or "nonprofit" – have been used to encapsulate this decentralized U.S. theatre network. But the term "regional," though still in circulation today, is woefully inadequate because it connotes that these theatres are "provincial." The ideals of developing a "repertory," though invoked in the very names of some institutions, have rarely been fully realized in the almost 50-year history of the movement. (A majority of regional theatres, for instance, do not have permanent acting companies.) Moreover, some nonprofit theatre companies (especially those that work on smaller budgets or have no permanent venues, or rent spaces) cannot always ensure the sort of continuity that would truly signify that they are "resident" in a community.

The nonprofit status, however, is significant. This means that these theatres are eligible for government subsidy; that their ticket prices are substantially lower than in the commercial sector; that productions run for a limited amount of time during a set season; that the main imperative is more the art or process of theatre, rather than the product or the profit-making motive; and that they are concerned with the development of artists, craftsmen, administrators, and even audiences. If a nonprofit company makes more money than anticipated, the excess must go back into the company's operating budget, and not to any staff member or investor. Most resident theatres have a set season with subscribers and are established in their own buildings. Most are dedicated to producing classical works and innovative contemporary drama. Most are engaged in educational programs, community service, and establishing endowments. Not-for-profits are also required to have unpaid boards of directors, drawn from the community, who advise management and participate in fund-raising.

The impetus and inspiration for a "regional theatre" is credited to MARGO JONES, who in the 1940s devised the prototype for this type of theatre with her Theatre '47 in Dallas, TX – both the first modern professional resident theatre and the first professional theatre-in-the-round in this country. In 1951 Jones published a book on arena staging, *Theatre-in-the-Round,* which would become the manifesto for a handful of ambitious, talented theatre people searching for communities to support their work. The thriving movement that Jones helped instigate can point to several other precursors: the proliferation of touring companies that crisscrossed the country in the 19th century; the Little Theatre movement of the 1920s (from which today's COMMUNITY THEATRES have evolved); the proliferation of summer theatres (see SUMMER STOCK) and resident STOCK COMPANIES, also in the 1920s; the GROUP THEATRE of the 1930s and the FEDERAL THEATRE PROJECT of the Depression; and finally the AMERICAN NATIONAL THEATRE AND ACADEMY, which was chartered in 1935 as a nonprofit people's theatre. In the later 20th century, however, it was the mosaic of decentralized, resident, nonprofit, professional, regional theatres that was considered a truly national force. To some scholars, it rivaled Broadway as the American theatre – the nearest thing in the U.S. to a national theatre institution.

The oldest not-for-profit regional theatre is the CLEVELAND PLAY HOUSE, which was founded in 1915 and turned professional in 1921. Following the lead of Margo Jones, Nina Vance founded Houston's ALLEY THEATRE in 1947, and ZELDA FICHANDLER cofounded the ARENA STAGE in an old Washington, DC, moviehouse in 1950. Fichandler has since left Arena, but she is still considered the prime representative of the movement's beginnings and remains a visionary voice for its future. From these beginnings other theatres followed in quick succession: the MILWAUKEE REPERTORY THEATRE and the NEW YORK SHAKESPEARE FESTIVAL (1954), the DALLAS THEATER CENTER (1959), the GUTHRIE THEATER in Minneapolis (1963); in 1964, the ACTORS THEATRE OF LOUISVILLE, NYC's AMERICAN PLACE THEATRE, the HARTFORD STAGE COMPANY and EUGENE O'NEILL MEMORIAL THEATER CENTER (both in CT), SOUTH COAST REPERTORY (Costa Mesa, CA) and TRINITY REP COMPANY (Providence, RI); San Francisco's AMERICAN CONSERVATORY THEATRE and New Haven's LONG WHARF THEATRE (1965); New Haven's YALE REPERTORY THEATRE and the Arizona Theatre Company (1966); Atlanta's ALLIANCE THEATRE (1968); and NYC's CIRCLE REPERTORY COMPANY (1969). The resident theatre movement received a strong shot in the arm early in its history from the Ford Foundation (under the dynamic leadership of W. McNeil Lowry) and Rockefeller Foundation, and later by state arts agencies and the NATIONAL ENDOWMENT FOR THE ARTS – though under recent administrators this latter source of support has failed to increase as it had during the 1960s and '70s.

According to the THEATRE COMMUNICATIONS GROUP, an organization for not-for-profit theatres that annually publishes a report on the fiscal health and attendance statistics, in the U.S. today more than 440 resident nonprofit theatres bring both classics of world drama and daring new plays and musicals to life for audiences as institutionally based and freelance artists nationwide, in 47 states and the District of Columbia. TCG's *Theatre Facts* report on the 2003–4 season (released in 2005) estimates that 1,477 not-for-profit professional theatres in the U.S. offered 169,000 performances of 11,000 different productions in 2004, employing a workforce of 104,000 individuals, 64% of whom are artistic personnel. They raised $715 million in contributions, which constituted 45% of their total income. The balance, $856 million, came from ticket sales and other revenue-generating activities (benefits, auctions, refreshment vending, the sale of gift items, and so forth). Translated into dollars and cents, these 1,477 theatres contributed more than $1.46 billion in direct expenditures to the U.S. economy in 2004.

Surviving on the basis of both public and private subsidies, nonprofit theatres in the U.S. must

549

contend with economic instability not only due to the erratic pattern of contributed support that has failed to close the growing gap between income and expenses. The costs of doing business have grown faster than available income, and long-range planning efforts are increasingly hampered by the shifting philanthropic patterns. Financial reports in the 1990s, for instance, underscore the increasing number of large deficits of major institutions since 1980. The recession of decades, the 2001 downturn following the 9/11 attacks, the onset of the second war in Iraq, as well as the changing consumer entertainment trends (such as the Internet, pay-per-view cable, and DVDs), have each dealt significant blows to these theatres' financial situation.

Nevertheless, the crisis seems to have passed in the last couple of years, according to TCG's Theatre Facts report. Belt-tightening measures, particularly among the more than 80 nonprofit professional theatres represented by the League of Resident Theatres (LORT) – another important organization active in labor relations, as well as the artistic and management needs of its members – have paid off. Despite the sluggish economy, the theatre industry has rebounded with increased productivity in many areas; the huge drop-off in state funding in 2003 has reversed; contributed income as a whole has gone up; the value of theatres' total assets is reported to be at a new high; the number of companies reporting operating deficits is still high, but theatres are, in general, meeting cash-flow pressures. In 2003, more than half of the surveyed theatres ended the year in the red, but the 2004 report turned that statistic on its head. The same proportion – 54% – reported closing their ledgers at break-even or better.

The good news needs to be tempered with several areas of concern. Overall attendance has declined, with ticket sales and subscription renewals (the lifeblood of any theatre) sinking to disturbingly low levels. The aggregate number of performances has dipped, and ticket revenue is down (although single-ticket sales have gone way up). While many theatres are on stable financial footing, others continue to struggle. The hemorrhaging of operating losses has stopped, but this was achieved by cutting back on artistic spending and less ambitious production schedules (fewer guest artists, less ambitious physical productions, smaller casts). Federal, state, and local government funding continues to play a vital but small role in theatres' fiscal ecologies, covering about 6% of budget expenses. As boards carry ever-larger responsibility for the financial bottom line, the leaders of many larger organizations are questioning or reevaluating the dominant model upon which the resident theatre movement was founded – a subscription-based season in which a theatre is run as a partnership between an artistic director and a managing director.

With the nonprofit field now in its fourth decade as a national movement, it is also grappling with issues of isolation, leadership, and succession. The decentralization of the field, one founding precept of the resident theatre movement, means that it has become increasingly difficult for theatre professionals to see enough of each other's work. The decline of intelligent, provocative criticism at newspapers around the country, including the *New York Times,* adds further complications; it affects which new plays will go on to be produced and have future lives on a national scale. Most of the original founders of important regional theatres have left their theatres (either by death, retirement, or resignation), and institutions are now moving into second and third generations of artistic and management leadership. On a national scale, this critical passing of the torch to a younger generation is happening at a time of uncertainty and fieldwide transition. The new group does not feel it has ownership of what has been established.

With the earlier cohesiveness of the movement seeming to dissipate, there has been an ongoing fractionalization of the resident theatre movement into small-, medium-, and large-sized theatres. Smaller organizations generally struggle to become large and more stable, which means they become faced with the constraints of being the "establishment" in a city or community. Funding organizations are providing more support for established companies and less for emerging groups or companies that are smaller by design. Theatres led by people of color are perpetually defined as emerging even when they are 25 or 30 years old, because they have struggled in a system that is institutionally stacked against them, and so are less stable as organizations even though they have consistently made artistically excellent work.

Another founding goal of the resident theatre movement – to provide those companies, including administrative and artistic staff, with a reasonable standard of living – has not been met or sustained. Low salaries, long hours, and chronic organizational understaffing are causing burnout on every level, from support staff to management and artistic leadership. Low compensation is one of the factors causing individual artists and technical and production support staff to find better-paying jobs elsewhere. Low fees and high royalties constitute a double whammy for playwrights. However, not-for-profit theatres can usually offer longer-term commitments than commercial theatres.

Since 2000, there has been an astonishing growth of theatre buildings and performing-arts centers across the U.S. Many established theatre companies have constructed brand-new spaces, renovated existing theatres, or drawn up capital-campaign plans to build black-box venues, mid-sized theatres, and large-scale spaces, frequently designed by name architects (such as Rafael Viñoly, Frank Gehry, or Rem Koolhaas) and often funded by state-sponsored tithing, citywide redevelopment efforts, and some big-name corporate support. The resident theatre movement is vast, and most major American cities, such as CHICAGO, LOS ANGELES, SAN FRANCISCO, and SEATTLE, are mainly epicenters of localized theatre activity. But as new construction continues apace, other cities, such as MINNEAPOLIS and San Diego, and especially those in the Midwest and some parts of the South, are re-creating themselves as cultural destination spots, with theatres and performing-arts institutions associated with specific communities as the key elements in these transformations. Because the work of most nonprofit theatres tends to be eclectic, it becomes difficult to define a house or signature style. Still, it is axiomatic that many companies with a strongly distinct mission statement, cultural demographic, or clear directorial vision are able to distinguish themselves from the huge pack. According to an NEA report on public participation in the arts, theatre is the performing-arts form with the highest level of public participation in the U.S. In every city, stories abound regarding a veritable explosion of theatrical activity – from the emergence of new companies of distinction to increased storefront activity involving formal or informal COLLECTIVES of artists, of emergence of new voices in playwriting.

In fact, the number of playwrights who owe allegiance to the resident theatre is impressive. For example, Chicago's GOODMAN THEATRE (founded in 1925) devoted much of its energy to the development of early plays by DAVID MAMET. The Actors Theatre of Louisville has maintained its mission of giving a national platform for new playwrights with an annual new-play festival. Along with the CAFFE CINO in the 1960s, ELLEN STEWART's still surviving LA MAMA Experimental Theatre Club exemplified the ruggedly individual spirit of OFF-OFF-BROADWAY by producing the early works of SAM SHEPARD, LANFORD WILSON, JEAN-CLAUDE VAN ITALLIE, Paul Foster, and ELIZABETH SWADOS. Nonprofit theatres around the country have nurtured writers as diverse as EDWARD ALBEE, MARSHA NORMAN, CHARLES FULLER, TONY KUSHNER, DONALD MARGULIES, SUZAN-LORI PARKS, PAULA VOGEL, NILO CRUZ, and Doug Wright. Between 1976 and 1984 nine consecutive Pulitzer Prizes premiered in nonprofit theatres before being transferred to commercial theatres on Broadway; and this trend continued between 1992 and 2004, when another 12 consecutive Pulitzer winners also issued from nonprofit theatres. (One of the historical firsts was Arena Stage's 1967 production of Howard Sackler's *The GREAT WHITE HOPE*.) The 10 plays that constitute AUGUST WILSON's 20th-century African American cycle were developed in a series of nonprofit theatres (Yale Rep, the Goodman, HUNTINGTON THEATRE COMPANY, MARK TAPER FORUM, CENTER STAGE) before finding their commercial berth in New York City.

Employing more actors than Broadway and the road combined, nonprofit theatres are the chief originators and producers of significant theatre in America. Even Broadway now looks to the resident theatre for new plays and, occasionally, new musicals. As a result, the nonprofit theatre has been accused of becoming nothing more than a tryout institution for the commercial theatre, a charge that ignores the natural desire to prolong the life of and give greater visibility to significant plays. Since there remains a strong strain of belief in certain quarters that there is no national theatre in the U.S., or at least no single theatre that would embody one, in the minds of many people (particularly in the print and broadcast media), a Broadway mentality dominates. The several dozen houses clustered primarily in Manhattan near the intersection of Broadway and 42d St. are viewed as the endgame. One frequently cited example is the 1975 production of *A CHORUS LINE*, produced by the nonprofit NEW YORK SHAKESPEARE FESTIVAL, which had a significant 15-year Broadway run (it closed in 1990), the considerable profits from which allowed JOSEPH PAPP to produce dozens of less profitable or riskier plays and musicals. However, the NYSF's true assault on Broadway had happened four years earlier, when its 1971 musical version of *Two Gentlemen of Verona*, with a score by *HAIR* composer Galt MacDermot and a book by JOHN GUARE, transferred to the ST. JAMES THEATRE; it was the first instance of a nonprofit company moving a show to Broadway and retaining all its rights.

Unquestionably, in today's nonprofit resident theatre, there is a danger of allowing the artistic product to take second place to an institution's commercial concerns. It is also true that regional audiences are often more conservative and safer than those in New York City, since many companies are less concerned with new plays or traditional classics. Artistic provocation is one of theatre's most essential qualities and one of the most difficult to achieve. The constraints of fiscal responsibility can lead to conservatism in artistic programming. Theatres for young audiences (see CHILDREN'S THEATRE) in particular feel pressure to present the tried-and-true, despite their own desires to engage young people by challenging them. Many theatres do not confront the prevailing – and unspoken – notion of "slots" for plays by artists of color. In 2005, a spate of West Coast institutions that used to develop new ethnically based works (including works by physically disabled artists) had been shut down. Culturally specific theatres are today struggling with the idea of diversity as they face their own audience expectations and seek to define – and continually redefine – their community.

However the new-play development ethos and some avant-garde or true experimentation have definitely taken place in the regions. Examples include the emergence of ensemble-based theatre, DOCUMENTARY THEATRE, community-based drama, high-tech experiments, hip-hop theatre forms, transnational collaborations spearheaded by international directors, new acting theories, and important recent creations from ethnic-based or indigenous theatres. Since the mid-1970s, the lines of commercial and noncommercial theatre have indeed blurred – with Broadway organizations that used to act as merely landlords now employing the resident-theatre model of new-play development (such as JUJAMCYN) or providing grants and seed money to not-for-profit theatres such as the SHUBERT FOUNDATION (whose income is derived from the commercial Broadway theatre). What is frequently less understood is that the American resident theatre system has been the cultural main stem in the U.S., providing the essential platform for new works and classics to be seen audiences nationwide. For good or bad, it has sparked the redefinition of ideas of cultural diversity and plays by artists of color. The resident theatre network is also deeply engaged in realizing the larger important cultural mission of infusing the American repertoire with fresh new creations – often through coproductions, with two or more theatres sharing production costs and extending the life of a production. RG

revue A form of musical entertainment that includes songs, dances, and sketch or stand-up comedy, usually tied together by a theme or narration rather than a story. Among the forerunners of the revue in the American theatre were the olio segments of the MINSTREL SHOW, the literary travesties of JOHN BROUGHAM and others, the topical humor of the comic opera, the variety programs of concert saloons and VAUDEVILLE houses, and the elaborate spectacle of the extravaganza. The French form of the spectacular revue, seen at such theatres as the Folies-Bergère, did not exert a major influence on the American stage until after the turn of the century.

The Passing Show (1894), produced by GEORGE LEDERER, is generally considered the first successful American "review" (the English spelling was employed at first). It combined topical humor, a chorus of beautiful girls posing as "living pictures" (see NUDITY), and an elaborate ballet. Because of its popularity, subsequent revues on the American stage represented variations on its formula: Some were conceived on a modest scale, with sophisticated topical humor and a small but ingratiating cast as their main assets; others emphasized spectacle, ever-growing numbers of scantily clad chorus girls, and the greatest singers, dancers, and comedians of the day.

Producer FLORENZ ZIEGFELD applied his unique brand of showmanship to the revue when he presented the *Follies of 1907,* the first edition of what would be an annual series of "revues" (now using the French spelling) lasting until Ziegfeld's death in 1932. In the early editions, Ziegfeld followed the prevalent revue style by including a good deal of topical humor in his shows. Nevertheless, his revues were most noted for the beauty of the chorus girls, led at first by Ziegfeld's wife, ANNA HELD. By "glorifying the American girl," Ziegfeld found a successful formula that spawned a host of imitators, including the SHUBERT BROTHERS' two series, *The Passing Show* (1912–19, 1921–4) and *Artists and Models* (1923–5, 1927, 1930, 1943); GEORGE WHITE's *Scandals* (1919–31, 1935, 1939); the EARL CARROLL *Vanities* (1923–8, 1930–2, 1940); and many other individual revues.

Topical humor was still the main attraction in three revues put together by GEORGE M. COHAN: *Hello Broadway* (1914) and two editions of *The Cohan Revue* (1916, 1918). Satire on the people and events of the day was also prevalent in several revue series that appeared in the early 1920s: *The Greenwich Village Follies* (1919–25, 1928), the *Grand Street Follies* (1922, 1924–9), and the *Garrick Gaieties* (1925, 1926, 1930). Much of the humor in these shows involved imitations of celebrities and parodies of the season's most notable shows and movies; they thus appealed to a more sophisticated audience than did the "girlie shows." IRVING BERLIN's series of MUSIC BOX Revues (1921–4) benefited from some of his most popular and enduring songs, as well as from a skillful blend of lavish decor and topical humor. In addition to Berlin, many of Broadway's greatest composers and lyricists, including GEORGE AND IRA GERSHWIN, RICHARD RODGERS and LORENZ HART, and the team of DESYLVA, BROWN, AND HENDERSON wrote for the revues of the 1920s. The decade also saw the first all-black revues on Broadway, including The Plantation Revue (1922), Africana (1927), Blackbirds of 1928, and Hot Chocolates (1929) (see AFRICAN AMERICAN THEATRE).

The period 1900–30 saw the production of some 228 revues on Broadway. Although the 1929 stock-market crash and resulting Depression caused a severe curtailment in the number of shows produced on Broadway each season, the revue, with its flexible framework, survived and even flourished in a modest way during the 1930s. A more intimate style of revue – relying on a small, versatile cast, scores by a new generation of composers (including ARTHUR SCHWARTZ and VERNON DUKE), and comedy sketches poking fun at such topics as the Depression and international politics – emerged as the old series of lavish revues died out. Among the most notable of this new style were The Little Show (1929), Three's a Crowd (1930), and The Band Wagon (1931), all by Schwartz and lyricist HOWARD DIETZ. One of the longest-running revues of the 1930s, PINS AND NEEDLES (1937), began as an amateur show put together by the International Ladies Garment Workers Union as an entertainment for the union's members; but it received such critical acclaim that it ran (with changes and updates) for almost three seasons. New Faces, a revue series featuring Broadway newcomers, debuted in 1934 and continued to appear sporadically through 1968.

The revue stagnated in the late 1930s, but producers began offering them in greater numbers with the advent of WWII, since the form's flexibility made it possible to piece together a show out of the talent remaining after the incursions of the draft and the USO. Shows such as Priorities of 1942 and Bright Lights of 1944 (1943) amused war-weary audiences without moving the revue in new artistic directions. Among the most popular revues of the war years were the all-military shows, made up of songs, dance, and comedy by members of the armed services under the guiding hand of professional theatre artists. Thus, Irving Berlin wrote the score for This Is the Army (1942), a revised version of his WWI show, Yip, Yip Yaphank (1918). Also available to audiences were the dance revues of Katherine Dunham, notably Tropical Revue (1943) and Bal Negre (1946), as well as several ice shows.

After the war, topical satire once again flourished in such revues as Call Me Mister (1946), Make Mine Manhattan (1948), and Inside U.S.A. (1948). Ironically, some of the people associated with these revues, including Sid Caesar and Carl Reiner, would contribute indirectly to the demise of the topical revue on Broadway when they brought their satires and imitations to live television, which would achieve a topicality impossible in the Broadway theatre.

Though few revues made it to Broadway in the 1950s, intimate revues became a staple of OFF-BROADWAY and NIGHTCLUBS. Beginning in 1955 Ben Bagley produced a series of Shoestring Revues, while the Phoenix Theatre offered Phoenix '55. Julius Monk produced a sporadic series of revues at his nightclub, Upstairs at the Downstairs. Most of these shows featured young performers and heavy doses of satire.

The 1960s saw a resurgence of topical humor in the revues that opened on Broadway, including A Thurber Carnival (1960) and From the Second City (1961) – and, Off-Broadway, The Mad Show (1965). An even sharper type of satire was seen in two British imports, Beyond the Fringe (1962) and Oh, What a Lovely War! (1964). This vogue for ruthless satire and parody was relatively short-lived, and by the 1970s the revue had taken a turn toward nostalgia, with several shows built around the work of a time or noted composers, such as Bubbling Brown Sugar (1976), about the Harlem Renaissance, and Ain't Misbehavin' (1978), which featured the songs of Fats Waller; the Duke Ellington–inspired Sophisticated Ladies (1981); Eubie! (1978), with 95-year-old Eubie Blake; Beatlemania (1977); and Side by Side by SONDHEIM (1977, Broadway), the first of three Sondheim compilations (also Marry Me a Little, 1980 [OFF-OFF; 1981, Off-], and Putting It Together, 1993 [Off-; 1999, Broadway]). Once again, topical humor moved Off-Broadway, with the opening in 1982 of the satirical revue series FORBIDDEN BROADWAY, built around constantly updated parodies of Broadway shows and performers. Meanwhile, the few revues to be seen on Broadway in the late 1980s and early '90s, such as JEROME ROBBINS' BROADWAY (1989), tended to emphasize spectacle and nostalgia rather than satire and innovation. Ironically, a book musical,

The WILL ROGERS FOLLIES (1991), attained success primarily through director TOMMY TUNE's imaginative re-creations of 1920s *Ziegfeld Follies* production numbers. In 1994–5 one of the two new musicals on Broadway, *Smokey Joe's Cafe,* was actually a revue built around the songs of Jerry Leiber and Mike Stoller (which ran for five years). The end of the decade was punctuated with modest revues such as *The Gershwins' Fascinating Rhythm* (1997, HARTFORD STAGE; 1999, Broadway) and *Swing!* (1999).

In the new millennium interest in revues has increased. With the 1996 *I Love You, You're Perfect, Now Change* leading the way (and still running after more than a decade), the revue form looked profitable; thus the so-called jukebox musical (most modifications of the revue form) exploded with such Broadway shows as *Momma Mia* (2001; based on Abba's songs), the *One Mo' Time* revival (2002; from WILLIAMSTOWN, 2001), *Movin' Out* (2002) with songs of Billy Joel, Boy George's *Taboo* (2003), Elvis Presley's hits in *All Shook Up*, the songs of the Beach Boys in *Good Vibrations*, and *Lennon* (all 2005), and the Dylanesque *The Times They Are a-Changin'* (2006). Few of these truly succeed, often forcing stories unrelated to the songs in order to string them together. A recent exception is *Jersey Boys*, a biographical musical based on the careers of Frankie Valli and the sixties group the Four Seasons (2005).

Although the form as it originally evolved no longer dominates the musical stage, audiences still seem to enjoy the topical humor, captivating stars, and the rarely to be found spectacular chorus numbers that have characterized so many of America's best revues. Most today are miniature versions of the form as it was in its heyday.   MK

Reynolds, James (1891–1957) Designer. Reynolds's *Tents of the Arabs* (1919) was one of the outstanding examples of the New Stagecraft, but he established himself as a designer of lavish and sophisticated REVUES, including several of the ZIEGFELD *Follies* and *Greenwich Village Follies*. Broadway credits include *Fifty Million Frenchmen* (1929) and *Jumbo* (1935).   AA

Ribman, Ronald (1932–) Playwright, born in New York and educated at the University of Pittsburgh, who attracted critical attention with *Harry, Noon and Night* (1965) at the AMERICAN PLACE THEATRE, which produced several of his early works. *The Journey of the Fifth Horse* (1966), loosely adapted from Ivan Turgenev's short story "The Diary of a Superfluous Man," won an Obie. Ribman puts the diary of the gentle Chulkaturin (played by Michael

Tolan) into the hands of an invented character, the mean-spirited Zoditch (DUSTIN HOFFMAN), who cruelly comments on its author. Hoffman displayed the kind of detailed characterization that is now his trademark. An important playwright of the 1960s and '70s, Ribman also wrote *The Ceremony of Innocence* (1965), *Passing through from Exotic Places* (1969), *Fingernails Blue as Flowers* (1971), *A Break in the Skin* (1972, YALE REP), *The Poison Tree* (1973, Philadelphia), *Cold Storage* (1977, moved to Broadway; a Dramatists Guild Award–winning comedy about the function of death), *Buck* (1983), *Sweet Table at the Richelieu, A Serpent's Egg, The Cannibal's Masque* (all 1987, AMERICAN REPERTORY THEATRE), *The Rug Merchants of Chaos* (1991, PASADENA PLAYHOUSE), and *Dream of the Red Spider* (1993, ART). Ribman has also written for television, including *Seize the Day* (1986) and adaptations of his *Journey* and *Ceremony*.   TLM

Rice [né McLaren], **Dan** (1823–1900) Clown and showman, born in Manhattan's notorious Five Points. Starting solo as a strongman, comic singer, and presenter of Sybil, the Learned Pig, he joined his first CIRCUS in 1844 in Pittsburgh. A pugnacious talking clown in whiteface and blackface, when circus was rowdy adult fare in huge tents and urban theatres, he became celebrated offering clever "Shaksperiana," presenting a stair-climbing horse and tightrope-walking elephant, feuding with Horace Greeley, and pitching "aspiration." In stripes and tailcoat, top hat, and famous goatee, Rice embodied Uncle Sam. Leading Dan Rice's Great Show, the Great American Humorist expanded his "hits on the times" into legitimate, Democratic campaigns for office, including a brief 1867 run for president. But changing tastes, equating artistry and decorum, reduced circus to a diversion, clowns to noisy scenery for children, and Rice to drink. In an 1885 comeback lecture tour he peddled fictions of having befriended Abe Lincoln. His commentary suggests WILL ROGERS, but his sharper edge influenced another self-styled "American Humorist," Mark Twain. Sclerotic cultural stratification shoved this American original into obscurity.   DC

[Ed. note: Rice's biography by Carlyon was published in 2001.]

Rice [né Reizenstein], **Elmer** (1892–1967) Playwright whose career started in 1914 with *On Trial,* an experimental play that used flashbacks to reveal aspects of the crime being tried. A New Yorker who graduated from law school before becoming a playwright, Rice used his legal knowledge in several plays, in various disputes with theatres, and in the causes he served – from Marxism in the 1930s to the American Civil Liberties Union. A wise and fearless man, Rice wrote with considerable skill on subjects both popular and unpopular. When his efforts with the FEDERAL THEATRE PROJECT were threatened with government CENSORSHIP, he was outraged and resigned his administrative post. Responding to the high-handed methods of the THEATRE GUILD, he and four other playwrights – ROBERT E. SHERWOOD, S. N. BEHRMAN, SIDNEY HOWARD, and MAXWELL ANDERSON – founded the PLAYWRIGHTS' COMPANY in 1938. He later vigorously opposed Senator Joseph McCarthy's attacks on theatre artists.

Rice's plays reflect his various interest in theatrical experiments, realistic scenes, and protest drama. His best work, The ADDING MACHINE (1923), an expressionistic play about the dehumanization of humankind, was followed by further experiments – The Subway (1929) and Dream Girl (1945). Man's social condition both fascinated and angered Rice, who exclaimed through a character in STREET SCENE (1929): "Everywhere you look, oppression and cruelty!" We, the People (1933), a bitter attack on Depression times, ended in an agitprop call for democratic ideals. In Judgment Day (1934) Rice scourged Nazi fascism, and in Between Two Worlds (1934) he contrasted the political systems of Russia and America. Finally, in American Landscape (1938), Rice maintained his support for American idealism but, disillusioned with both Marxism and American commercial theatre, threatened to stop writing plays. Post-WWII theatre brought him little satisfaction. The Grand Tour, a romance in Europe (1951), The Winner, a crime melodrama (1954), and Cue for Passion, a weak story of a California Hamlet (1958), did little for his reputation. He recounted his experiences in The Living Theatre (1959) and Minority Report (1963), where, always a liberal idealist, he preached individual freedom from all tyranny. A major Rice collection is at the University of Texas. The most recent study of Rice is by Michael Vanden Heuvel (1996). WJM

Rice, J(ohn) B. (1809–74) Actor, manager, theatre owner, and politician. Discovered at 27 singing as he worked in a shoemaking shop in Baltimore, Rice later left the chorus of Philadelphia's WALNUT STREET THEATRE (1837) for a series of theatre-managing jobs in Albany, Buffalo, Milwaukee, and CHICAGO – where, in 1847, he erected that city's first theatre building to coincide with a convention of canal builders. In subsequent years, Rice and his wife performed there, as did such prominent players as EDWIN FORREST, JUNIUS

T. D. Rice as the original Jim Crow. *Courtesy:* Laurence Senelick Collection.

BRUTUS BOOTH, and JAMES H. MCVICKER. The theatre burned in 1850, was rebuilt the following year, and closed in 1861, having been eclipsed in 1857 by the construction of MCVICKER'S THEATRE. Rice, who amassed a small fortune in real estate, subsequently served two terms as a popular Republican mayor of Chicago (1865–9), and was at the end of his first term in Congress when he died. SF

Rice, Thomas D(artmouth) "Daddy" (1806–60) Blackface performer ("Ethiopian delineator") considered the "father of American MINSTRELSY." Between 1828 and 1831 Rice, according to tradition, observed a crippled Negro stableman (possibly in Louisville, KY) sing a refrain and dance with a jerky jump – thus "Jump Jim Crow," after the slave's name. From this single song and dance Rice developed full-length entertainments called "Ethiopian operas." He toured the British Isles in 1836, 1838, and 1843, leaving his stamp on the English stage. In 1858, he played the title role at the BOWERY THEATRE in UNCLE TOM'S CABIN (1850), though generally Rice remained a solo entertainer throughout his career. DBW

Rich, Frank (1949–) Theatre critic and columnist. Born in Washington, DC, and educated at Harvard in American history and literature (1971), Rich was cofounder, reporter, and editor of the *Richmond* [VA] *Mercury* (1972–3); the senior editor and film critic of *New Times Magazine* (NYC, 1973–5); film critic of the *New York Post* (1975–7); film and television critic of *Time* magazine (1977–80); and chief drama critic of the *New York Times* (1980–93). Since late 1993 he has been an opinion-editorial columnist for the *Times,* focusing on the interaction of American politics and popular culture, but he continues to exert influence on theatre. During the 1980s Rich, "The Butcher of Broadway," was arguably the most powerful theatre critic in the U.S. Intelligent, demanding, and generally knowledgeable about theatre and popular culture, Rich wrote for the literate reader with style and authority but – in the estimation of the New York theatre community – little sympathy or affection for the theatre. He is the author of *The Theatre Art of* BORIS ARONSON (cowritten with Lisa Aronson, 1987); *Hot Seat: Theater Criticism for the New York Theater 1980–93* (1998), a selection of his reviews; and *Ghost Light* (2000), his childhood memoir.   TLM

Richard Rodgers Theatre 226 West 46th St., NYC [Architect: Herbert J. Krapp]. Renamed in 1990 in honor of America's foremost theatre music composer, what was formerly known as the 46th St. Theatre was built in 1924 by the Chanin Brothers as part of their chain of Broadway playhouses (cf. ROYALE THEATRE). For several years, it was a theatre in search of a hit; but in 1939, ETHEL MERMAN took its stage as a full-fledged star in *DU BARRY WAS A LADY,* returning the following year in *Panama Hattie.* Thereafter, the theatre housed successful musicals, beginning with *FINIAN'S RAINBOW* (1947), continuing more recently with *HOW TO SUCCEED IN BUSINESS WITHOUT REALLY TRYING* (1961, 1995 revival), and in 2006 the disappointing *Tarzan,* a DISNEY product with music by Phil Collins. Among its more successful nonmusical tenants have been *The Merchant of Venice* (1989) with DUSTIN HOFFMAN and NEIL SIMON's Pulitzer Prize–winning *LOST IN YONKERS* (1991). When the Chanins lost their theatres to creditors in the early Depression, the lease was acquired by the SHUBERTS, who ran it until 1945, when it became part of City Playhouses. It is now part of the NEDERLANDER chain.   MCH

Richards, Beah (1920–2000) AFRICAN AMERICAN actress who trained under RANDOLPH EDMONDS at Dillard University, New Orleans, and at the San Diego Community Theatre. Her principal roles on Broadway were Viney in *The MIRACLE WORKER* (1959), Idella in *PURLIE VICTORIOUS* (1961), and Sister Margaret in *The AMEN CORNER* (1965). For many years she taught acting at the Inner City Cultural Center, Los Angeles, where her play *One Is a Crowd* (1971) and poetic monologue *A Black Woman Speaks* (1974) were produced. Her work in films earned her an Academy Award nomination for Best Supporting Actress in *Guess Who's Coming to Dinner?* and induction into the Black Filmmakers Hall of Fame.   EGH

Richards, David (Bryant) (1942–) Drama critic who established his reputation in Washington, DC, with radio station WGMS (1969–71), the *Star* (1971–81), and the *Post* (1981–90) before becoming chief Sunday critic for the *New York Times* (1990–3). In early 1995 he returned to the *Post* as national cultural affairs correspondent. He is author of *Played Out: The Jean Seberg Story* (1981) and a contributor to the BURNS MANTLE *Best Plays* series.   TLM

Richards, Lloyd (1919–2006) AFRICAN AMERICAN actor, director, and educator (Canadian born), Richards began his professional career as an actor OFF-BROADWAY and as resident director at regional theatres. His major directorial opportunity came with *A RAISIN IN THE SUN* (1959), whose success is legendary. Richards then turned his attention to directing and teaching, accepting assignments at colleges and opening the Lloyd Richards Studio (1962–72). In 1968 he was named artistic director of the NATIONAL PLAYWRIGHTS' CONFERENCE at the EUGENE O'NEILL THEATER CENTER in Waterford, CT, for the development of new plays. Appointed dean of the Yale Drama School and artistic director of the YALE REPERTORY THEATRE in 1979, he used his strategic positions of leadership to promote the work of contemporary playwrights, the most prominent being LEE BLESSING, AUGUST WILSON, and the South African ATHOL FUGARD. He produced seven of Fugard's plays and, while at Yale (his term expired in 1991), directed most of Wilson's, working collaboratively with the author, including six on Broadway (most recently *Seven Guitars,* 1996, the only one after leaving Yale). He won a Tony Award as Best Director for Wilson's *FENCES* (1987). In 1990 Richards was inducted into the THEATRE HALL OF FAME; in 1994 he received the 1993 PAUL ROBESON Award from ACTORS' EQUITY; and he was also the recipient of the National Medal of Arts in 1993 and the "Mr. Abbott" Award for Lifetime Achievement in 1996.   EGH

Richardson, Leander (1856–1918) Theatre journalist whose aggressive and personal style helped establish the tone of theatrical weeklies. Richardson began with the *New York Dramatic News* (1879), which he edited during 1888–96. He wrote for the *Morning Telegraph* (1896–1903) and edited the *New York Enquirer* (1903) before becoming a press AGENT for WILLIAM A. BRADY.   TLM

Richardson, Lee (1926–99) Actor known originally as Lee Richard and considered a leading classical repertory actor. He was in the 1952 CIRCLE IN THE SQUARE revival of *SUMMER AND SMOKE*, making his Broadway debut in *The Legend of Lizzie* (1959). He acted in many classical plays at the NEW YORK SHAKESPEARE FESTIVAL, Hartman Theatre, AMERICAN SHAKESPEARE FESTIVAL, and YALE REPERTORY, and was a founding member of the GUTHRIE THEATER, appearing there during 1963–70. He also performed in such plays as ALBEE's *The Death of Bessie Smith* (1961), Bolt's *Vivat! Vivat Regina!* (1972), *A TEXAS TRILOGY* (1976), HAILEY's *Father's Day* (1979, AMERICAN PLACE), and Gray's *Quartermaine's Terms* (1983), as well as in *Ivanov* (1990, YALE REP) and *Getting Married* (1991). Appearing frequently on television, his film work includes the narrator of *Network* (1976) and roles in *Prizzi's Honor* (1985) and *The Fly II* (1989).   REK

Richardson, Willis (1889–1977) AFRICAN AMERICAN playwright whose one-act play *The CHIP WOMAN'S FORTUNE* (1923), produced by the Ethiopian Art Theatre of Chicago, made history as the first known drama by a black author to be shown on Broadway. A clerk in the U.S. Department of Engraving and Printing, Richardson was inspired to write plays by *Crisis* magazine's contests, of which he was twice winner (1925, 1926). He wrote some 30 one-act and five full-length plays, mostly about rural folk and black historical figures. He is also noted for editing two collections of black plays for adults and a third for children. He was a founder of the Washington, DC, branch of the Krigwa Players. A biography by Christine R. Gray was published in 1999.   EGH

Richman [né Reichman]**, Harry** (1895–1972) Song-and-dance man and composer. Suave, debonair ("Beau Broadway"), and loaded with personality, Richman headlined VAUDEVILLE, *GEORGE WHITE's Scandals* (1926, 1928), and served as master of ceremonies for *The ZIEGFELD Follies of 1931*. With his top hat and tails (or strawhat and blazer) and cane, he established his reputation with such songs as "On the Sunny Side of the Street," "Walking My Baby Back Home" (which he wrote), and

"Puttin' on the Ritz." His Club Richman on Park Avenue was a top NIGHTCLUB in the 1920s. In the 1940s his voice and career deteriorated. His autobiography appeared (written with Richard Gehman) in 1966; titled *A Hell of a Life*, it was a fitting epitaph for his colorful and amorous life.   DBW

Ridiculous Theatrical Company OFF-OFF BROADWAY theatre founded by the late actor, director, and playwright CHARLES LUDLAM after he split off from John Vaccaro's Play-House of the Ridiculous (see THEATRE OF THE RIDICULOUS) in 1967. The Ridiculous was one of the first American theatres to deal explicitly with homosexual themes. Known for their flamboyant style, high camp, and combinations of the lofty and the lowly, plays at the Ridiculous are often based on classical dramatic and operatic texts, which are then both spoofed and celebrated with cross-dressing, scatalogical humor, sight gags, and puns. Ludlam starred in many of his own plays, among them *Bluebeard* (1970), *Camille* (1973; revived 1990), *Der Ring Gott Farblonjet* (1977), and *The Mystery of Irma Vep* (1984). Since Ludlam's death from AIDS in 1987, the Ridiculous has continued under the directorship of Ludlam's life partner EVERETT QUINTON, a longtime actor and designer with the theatre. The company has been reviving Ludlam works as well as developing new pieces, such as Quinton's giddy adaptation of *A Tale of Two Cities* (1988) and his country-western musical, *Linda* (1993), inspired by Trollope's *Linda Tressel* and the Baron Von Sacher-Masoch's *Venus in Furs*; Georg Osterman's *Dr. Jekyll and Mr. Hyde* (1989) and *Brother Truckers* (1992); Quinton's ONE-PERSON show *Movieland* (1994); a camp production of *A Midsummer Night's Dream* (1994–5); and Quinton's version of *Carmen* (1995). After losing its home of 18 years at 1 Sheridan Square, June 1995, the company spent the rest of the year looking for a new venue. In 1996 Quinton appeared in *Call Me Sarah Bernhardt* at P.S. 122. *The MYSTERY OF IRMA VEP* was revived in 1998 at the Westside Theatre, and soon thereafter the operation shut down.   AS

Rifkin, Ron (1939–) NYC–born and educated actor, closely associated in the early 1990s with the plays of JON ROBIN BAITZ (*The Substance of Fire*, 1991; *Three Hotels*, 1993; *The Paris Letter*, 2005). In the first, Baitz created for the actor the role of an autocratic publisher, for which Rifkin won Obie, LUCILLE LORTEL, and Drama Desk awards; he won another Lortel in the second. In the third, Rifkin, in a monologue, took a seemingly harsh man and revealed his vulnerability. Rifkin's Broadway debut was in *Come Blow Your Horn* (1961; replace-

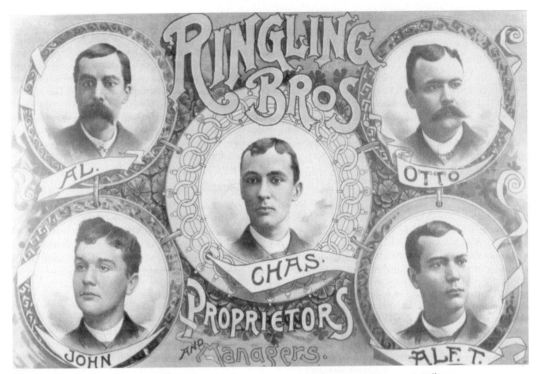

An 1887 poster showing the young Ringling Brothers. *Courtesy:* Ringling Bros.–Barnum & Bailey.

ment), with notable New York appearances following in *The Tenth Man* (1989), *The Art of Dining* (1979, The PUBLIC), ARTHUR MILLER's 1994 *Broken Glass* – in which, according to DAVID RICHARDS, he was "quick, ironic and volatile as a Jew embarrassed by his Jewishness" – and in CABARET as Herr Schultz, for which he won the 1998 Tony for Featured Actor in a Musical. During 2001–6 he played the evil genius in TV's *Alias.*   DBW

Rigdon, Kevin (1956–) Lighting and set designer. Native of Illinois who studied at Drake University and interned at the GUTHRIE, he has been resident scenic and lighting designer for the STEPPENWOLF COMPANY (more than 110 productions), the GOODMAN, the ALLEY, and for Mordine and Company Dance. He has designed for most of the major regional theatres and was nominated for Tonys for both scenery and lighting for the Steppenwolf *The GRAPES OF WRATH* (1990), one of his 12 Broadway credits. He often works with his wife, designer Trish Rigdon.   BO

Riggs, (Rollie) Lynn (1899–1954) Oklahoma-born playwright of Cherokee descent whose only successful play was *Green Grow the Lilacs* (1931), later transformed into the musical OKLAHOMA! Riggs's

central concern was cowboy culture of the Indian Territory, though he also wrote two plays with Native Americans as major characters – *The Cherokee Night* (written 1930) and *The Cream in the Well* (1941). These, along with plays such as *Roadside* (1930) – produced by ARTHUR HOPKINS and considered too obscure or nontraditional – were commercial failures.   DBW

Rinehart, Mary Roberts (1876–1958) Journalist, novelist, and playwright who dramatized her novels, which were a cross between comedies and detective stories. Her best plays were written with AVERY HOPWOOD, the most successful being *The BAT* (1920), an adaptation of her 1908 novel *The Circular Staircase*. Other hits written with Hopwood include *Seven Days* (1909) and *Spanish Love* (1920). She also wrote two less successful plays by herself: *Cheer Up* (1912) and *The Breaking Point* (1923). Her autobiography was published in 1948. A biography by Jan Cohn appeared in 1980.   FB

Ring, Blanche (1876–1961) Boston-born singer-actress, a great VAUDEVILLE star, master of the sing-along (which she probably introduced into vaudeville) and an accomplished monologuist of Irish characters. No single act topped hers for

Scene from Act IV of Jefferson's *Rip Van Winkle*. Rip, after his long sleep and return to his hometown, encounters his wife, Gretchen, and his nemesis, Derrick. Photo by Bachrach, Boston. *Courtesy:* Harvard Theatre Collection, Houghton Library.

more than two decades, beginning 10 years after her debut in a small role opposite RICHARD MANSFIELD in *The Defender* (1902), in which she introduced "In the Good Old Summertime." In 1909 she first sang what became her theme song, "I've Got Rings on My Fingers," in *The Midnight Sons*. When she introduced "Yip-I-Addy-I-Ay" to a vaudeville audience in 1913, she was encouraged to repeat it five times. She debuted her most famous role, *The Yankee Girl,* in 1910 (filmed 1915; she appeared in two additional films [1926, 1940] and made a number of early recordings). Other hit musicals included *The Jersey Lily* (1903), *About Town* (1906), *The Wall Street Girl* (1911), and *The Passing Show of 1919.*   DBW

Ringling [né Rungeling] **Brothers** Baraboo, WI, brothers who entered the American CIRCUS just prior to its golden age and, in the words of John Culhane, "outperformed, outmaneuvered, out-acquired [and] just plain outlasted all their competition." In 1882 brothers **Al[bert]** (1852–1916), **Otto** (1858–1911), **Alf[red] T.** (1861–1919), **Charles** (1863–1926), and **John** (1866–1936) formed a variety show, "Classic Comic and Concert Company."

In 1884, in partnership with ailing circus pioneer Yankee Robinson, who later died that summer, they staged their first circus in Baraboo. Within six years their circus was traveling on rails; by 1895 they opened each spring in CHICAGO. Gaining momentum during a five-year European tour by their major rival, BARNUM & Bailey, they arranged in 1905 to buy a half interest in one of James A. Bailey's properties (FOREPAUGH–Sells Bros. circus); in 1907, after Bailey's death, they purchased all of his interest and the Barnum & Bailey title from his estate. Brother **Henry** (1869–1918) joined the fold, and in 1919 their two properties were combined into Ringling Bros. and Barnum & Bailey. The only member of the family to head Ringling Bros. after the brothers' deaths was their nephew, John Ringling North. In 1967 Ringling Bros. was sold to showmen Irwin and Israel Feld; after Irwin's death in 1984 his son Kenneth assumed control. A new biography by Jerry Apps was published by the Wisconsin Historical Society Press in 2005.   DBW

Rip Van Winkle by JOSEPH JEFFERSON III and DION BOUCICAULT opened at the Adelphi Theatre in London on 5 September 1865 and ran for 170 nights; the next fall it played New York. Thus began for thousands of Americans from coast to coast and for the next 40 years a habit of enjoying Joseph Jefferson as Rip Van Winkle.

Rip Van Winkle as a play, however, did not happen instantaneously. Prior to 1865 there were at least four dramatizations of WASHINGTON IRVING's story: an anonymous adaptation in Albany, NY (1828); a second by John Kerr (1829); a third by Charles Burke, Jefferson's half-brother (1850); followed by a fourth, Thomas Lacy's British version. Jefferson performed his own creation in Washington, DC, in the fall of 1859 and occasionally on a later tour to Australia. Returning to America through London, he commissioned Boucicault to do a rewrite. Though it is impossible to determine the individual work of either author, their intent was to increase the tension and to attract more attention to the title role. As a happy-go-lucky ne'er-do-well, Rip/Jefferson dramatically mingled the comic and the pathetic. Jefferson's sympathetic personality, personal charm, and natural style of acting contributed to the play's tremendous success, but there was also plenty of spectacle and, for many, a delightful wish fulfillment. In 1902 Jefferson published an edition of the play as "Played" by him.   WJM

Ritchard, Cyril (1897–1977) Actor and director, born in Sydney, Australia. He made his debut as a chorus boy in a Sydney musical in 1917 and came to America in 1924 to appear in New York in *Puzzles of 1925*. He is best remembered for Captain Hook in the musical *Peter Pan* (1954) and leading roles in *A Visit to a Small Planet* (1957) and *The Roar of the Greasepaint, the Smell of the Crowd* (1965). Ritchard directed both for the theatre and opera and appeared in films (e.g., Hitchcock's *Blackmail*, 1929). His awards included a Tony and Donaldson Award for Captain Hook. He appeared as Hook on live television in 1954, 1955, and 1960.   SMA

Ritchie, Michael (1957–) Beginning in 1980 and over the next 15 years he stage-managed more than 50 shows on and OFF-BROADWAY, working with many of the outstanding playwrights and directors of the time. The Broadway productions included *OUR TOWN* (with SPALDING GRAY), *Timon of Athens* (with BRIAN BEDFORD), *Heartbreak House* (with ROSEMARY HARRIS and REX HARRISON), and *Arms and the Man* (with KEVIN KLINE and RAUL JULIA). In 1996 he became producer of the WILLIAMSTOWN THEATRE FESTIVAL, a position he held until 2005 when he became artistic director of the CENTER THEATRE GROUP in Los Angeles. The transition from stage manager to artistic director is a rare one in the American theatre. Ritchie's wife is actress KATE BURTON.   DBW

Ritman, William (1928?–1984) Designer who designed many of the Cherry Lane Theatre productions in the early 1960s, including all of EDWARD ALBEE's work – an association that continued to Broadway with *WHO'S AFRAID OF VIRGINIA WOOLF?* (1962), *TINY ALICE* (1964), and many of Albee's subsequent plays. He also designed many of the American productions of the plays of Harold Pinter and Joe Orton, as well as numerous more commercial works, such as *6 Rms Riv Vu* (1972), *Same Time, Next Year* (1975), and *Deathtrap* (1978).   AA

Ritz Theatre see WALTER KERR THEATRE

Rivera, Chita [née Dolores Conchita Figueroa del Rivero] (1933–) Dancer, singer, actress; attended the American School of Ballet before beginning her career as a Broadway dancer in *GUYS AND DOLLS* (1950). Praised by critics for her performance as Anita in *WEST SIDE STORY* (1957), she brought impressive dancing talent and a lively personality to starring roles in such musicals as *Bye Bye Birdie* (1960), *Bajour* (1964), *CHICAGO* (1975), *The Rink* (1984; Tony), *Jerry's Girls* (1985), and *Kiss of the Spider Woman* (1993; Tony). In 2005 she returned to Broadway in *Chita Rivera: The Dancer's Life*.   MK

Rivera, José (1955–) Playwright. Born in Puerto Rico, Rivera's family moved to Long Island (NY) at age 4. Upon graduating from Denison University, he returned to New York, joining Theatre Matrix in the Bronx. In 1983, his *The House of Ramon Iglesias*, selected by ENSEMBLE STUDIO THEATRE as winner of the FDG/CBS New Play Awards, was produced under the direction of Jack Gelber; a teleplay aired nationally in 1986 as part of the *American Playhouse* series. *The Promise* (1988) premiered at the LOS ANGELES THEATRE CENTER, and *Each Day Dies With Sleep* first at BERKELEY REPERTORY THEATRE and then OFF-BROADWAY at CIRCLE REPERTORY THEATRE (both 1990). *Marisol* premiered in 1992 at ACTORS THEATRE OF LOUISVILLE (as did *Cloud Tectonics* in 1995, seen in 1997 at PLAYWRIGHTS HORIZONS, and *Lovers of Red Hair* in 1999); at the PUBLIC, it won a 1993 Obie. *The Street of the Sun* premiered at the MARK TAPER FORUM (1997). *References to Salvador Dali Make Me Hot* premiered at SOUTH COAST REPERTORY (2000) and was later done at the Public (2001; Obie) and in London (2005). *School of the Americas* (about Che Guevara) also was staged at the Public (2006). His screen adaptation of *The Motorcycle Diaries* (2004) was nominated for an Oscar. Rivera's plays often revolve around Puerto Rican traditions and culture (see NUYORICAN THEATRE), with an increasing interest in magical realism.   ER DBW

Road to Rome, The ROBERT SHERWOOD's play was a mild sensation in 1927 because of its sexual innuendos about the Carthaginian conqueror Hannibal and Amytis, wife of the Roman dictator Fabius Maximus. Sherwood, whose conversion from pacificist to "hawk" (*There Shall Be No Night,* 1940) reflected an intense American debate about war, argues in this play that human love can overcome the desire of countries to slaughter one another. WILLIAM A. BRADY produced it at the PLAYHOUSE THEATRE, where it ran for 392 performances and won a "BEST PLAY" accolade. It was designed by LEE SIMONSON; JANE COWL and Philip Merivale were the articulate lovers.   BBW

Robards, Jason (Jr.) (1922–2000) Actor, praised for his rich voice and intense characterizations (and a mentor and inspiration to other actors), who made his debut as Nick in the AMERICAN ACADEMY OF DRAMATIC ART's production of HOLIDAY (1946). After small roles and a stint as a stage manager, he attracted considerable attention as Hickey in a now-legendary production of *The ICE-MAN COMETH* (1956) at the CIRCLE IN THE SQUARE. Robards secured his stardom as James Tyrone Jr. (Jamie) in Broadway's LONG DAY'S JOURNEY INTO NIGHT (1956), in which he was noted as "an actor of tremendous dynamic skill." Another triumph was as Quentin in ARTHUR MILLEr's AFTER THE FALL, for which critics lauded him as "brilliant," "magnificent," and "beyond praise." In 1988 he appeared with COLLEEN DEWHURST in revivals (in repertory) of O'NEILL's *Long Day's Journey* and *AH, WILDERNESS!* Later NYC stage appearances were HOROVITZ's *Park Your Car in Harvard Yard* (1991–2) and the revival of *No Man's Land* in 1994 (opposite CHRISTOPHER PLUMMER) and Brian Friel's *Molly Sweeney* in 1996, both with ROUND-ABOUT, the latter his final New York show. His distinguished film and television career includes *Long Day's Journey* (1962) and *A Thousand Clowns* (1965), as well as film scripts in which he has played various curmudgeons and outcasts. He received eight Tony nominations (won once in 1959 for *The Disenchanted*) and in 1997 received the National Medal of Arts.   SMA

Robbins, Carrie (Fishbein) (1943–) Costume designer who began her professional career in the late 1960s and has become one of the busiest in the theatre. Although she has done contemporary costumes, her best work is in detailed yet theatrical period costumes, such as the 1973 *Beggar's Opera* or the 1992 musical *Anna Karenina,* or lavish operatic ones, such as for the San Francisco Opera's *Samson et Dalila,* which combined a 19th-century sensibility with a biblical epic style. Her work is typified by rich textures and bold lines, and her sketches are detailed and almost frenetic, creating a sense of energy and movement. She has frequently collaborated with set designer DOUG-LAS SCHMIDT, notably on *GREASE* (1972) and *Frankenstein* (1981).   AA

Robbins [né Rabinowitz]**, Jerome** (1918–98) Choreographer and director. Trained in the techniques of classical ballet, Robbins joined the American Ballet Theatre in 1940 and danced in several of its programs. In 1944 he choreographed *Fancy Free,* a ballet with music by LEONARD BERNSTEIN. Later the same year Robbins repeated his role as choreographer when *Fancy Free* was transformed into the Broadway musical ON THE TOWN. For *High Button Shoes* (1947), Robbins created a hilarious Keystone Kops ballet that remains one of the few masterpieces of comic choreography in the American musical theatre. Among his other memorable dances of the period was the "Small House of Uncle Thomas" ballet for *The KING AND I* (1951). For the teenage gang members of WEST SIDE STORY (1957), Robbins created a restless, explosive, yet balletic style of movement. He directed and choreographed two other acclaimed musicals: GYPSY (1959) and FIDDLER ON THE ROOF (1964). In 1989 Robbins re-created his most successful numbers in the retrospective *JEROME ROBBINS' BROADWAY* (Tony for Best Musical). His final choreographic work was "Brandenburg" to the Bach concertos for the New York City Ballet (where he created more than 50 ballets) in 1997. He was given the Common Wealth Award of Distinguished Service in Dramatic Arts in 1990. Recent studies of Robbins were written by Christine Conrad (2000), Jerome Lawrence (2003), and Deborah Jowitt (2004).   MK

Roberts, Tony (David Anthony) (1939–) A New York–born actor and director, son of radio/TV announcer Ken Roberts and cousin of the MERCURY THEATRE's actor Everett Sloane, Roberts has been a comedic leading man since the mid-1960s. His second Broadway role was the young lead Paul

Bratter in BAREFOOT IN THE PARK (a 1965 replacement); his most recent Broadway role, some 40 years later, was as the Bohemian womanizer Victor Velasco in a mundane revival of NEIL SIMON'S play in 2006. In all he has appeared in 21 Broadway productions, in both straight plays (notably *Don't Drink the Water*; *Play It Again, Sam*; *Doubles*; *The Seagull*; *The SISTERS ROSENSWEIG*; *The TALE OF THE ALLERGIST'S WIFE*) and musicals (*How Now, Dow Jones*; *Promises, Promises*; *Sugar*; *Victor/Victoria* [as Toddy, the cabaret entertainer]; and CABARET). He also appeared in SOUTH PACIFIC (1987, as Luther Billis) and BRIGADOON (1991, as Jeff Douglas) at the New York State Theatre, and in 1999 as Scrooge at the theatre in Madison Square Garden. Ultimately he will likely be remembered for six roles in WOODY ALLEN films (e.g., *Annie Hall*, 1977), among more than two dozen films in which he has appeared.   DBW

Robertson, Agnes see BOUCICAULT, DION

Robeson, Paul (Leroy) (1898–1976) AFRICAN AMERICAN actor and singer. A Columbia Law School graduate, Robeson opted for a stage career and gained prominence when he appeared in the PROVINCETOWN PLAYERS' revival of *The EMPEROR JONES* and as Jim Harris, the black lawyer who marries a white in O'NEILL's controversial play ALL GOD'S CHILLUN GOT WINGS (both 1924). Robeson took the lead in *Black Boy* (1926), replaced Jack Carter as Crown in *Porgy* (1928), and was Joe in the London performance of SHOW BOAT (1928; also 1932 Broadway revival and 1936 film), in which he sang "Ol' Man River," a song he refashioned into a lifelong protest against oppression. With a commanding physique, deep, resonant voice, and humane spirit, Robeson was a magnificent Othello, a role he played three times: in London (1930), in New York for a record-breaking run (1943), and at Stratford-upon-Avon (1959). He was also renowned as a concert artist and film actor. Robeson's outspoken opposition to racial discrimination, his embrace of leftist causes worldwide, and his communist sympathies led to professional ostracism at home and the withdrawal of his passport. In failing health, he retired from public life in the 1960s. His life was dramatized in Philip Hayes Dean's 1978 monodrama (see ONE-PERSON) *Paul Robeson*, which starred JAMES EARL JONES. An annual award in his name is given by ACTORS' EQUITY "to those committed to the struggle for justice, equality, and the principles" to which he was devoted. Of many biographies, Martin Duberman's remains definitive (1988).   EGH

Robin Hood Comic opera with libretto by HARRY B. SMITH and music by REGINALD DE KOVEN; opened at NYC's Standard Theatre on 28 September 1891. This production by The Bostonians (see BOSTON IDEAL OPERA COMPANY) featured an excellent ensemble and memorable songs. Challenging the craze for imported light opera, after 40 performances it was moved and played continuously in various theatres. It was successfully revived for almost 50 years. Music-theatre historian Gerald Bordman notes that *Robin Hood* bestowed "a certain theatrical immortality" on Jessie Bartlett Davis who, in the trouser role of Alan-a-Dale, sang "Oh, Promise Me" over 5,000 times in 2,000 performances of the initial production. Bordman notes that this early all-native effort was earthier, plainer, and more realistic than its European counterparts.   MR

Robins, Elizabeth (1862–1952) Kentucky-born actress and author who made her acting debut with the BOSTON MUSEUM Stock Company in 1885 and subsequently toured with EDWIN BOOTH, LAWRENCE BARRETT, and JAMES O'NEILL. She visited London in 1889, remaining there rather than return to New York. Soon she was playing Martha Bernick in *Pillars of Society* (1889); two years later in a revival of *A Doll's House* she played Mrs. Linde. Ultimately, Robins became identified with the introduction of Ibsen to the English stage, appearing as Hedda (1891), Hilda in *The Master Builder* (1893), Rebecca West in *Rosmersholm* (1893), Agnes in *Brand* (1893), Astra in *Little Eyolf* (1896), and Ella in *John Gabriel Borkman* (1897), and holding the stage rights to many of these plays. With the exception of starring in the short-lived U.S. premiere of IBSEN's *Hedda Gabler* (1898), she never performed again in her native land. She retired from the stage in 1902 and devoted herself to writing. Using the nom de plume "C. E. Raemond," she published several novels as well as the suffragist play *Votes for Women* (1907). In later years she wrote *Ibsen and the Actress* (1928), *Theatre and Friendship* (1932), and *Both Sides of the Curtain* (1940). There are biographies by J. E. Gates (1994) and Angela V. John (1995).   RAS

Robins, Laila (1959–) Born in St. Paul, MN, and a graduate of the Yale Drama School, her stage debut was in *Ivanov* at the WILLIAMSTOWN THEATRE FESTIVAL. Her Broadway debut came when she succeeded GLENN CLOSE as Annie in MIKE NICHOL's 1984 production of *The Real Thing*. Other Broadway credits are *The Herbal Bed* as Shakespeare's daughter (1998), and opposite SWOOSIE KURTZ both in *Frozen* (2004), as the unhappy psychiatrist Agnetha, and in *Heartbreak House* (2006), as Ariadne. OFF-BROADWAY she costarred with UTA HAGEN in *Mrs. Klein* (1995) and with RICHARD THOMAS in a revival of *TINY ALICE* (2000). For over a half dozen years she has been a regular with the Shakespeare Theatre of New Jersey (Madison), where she has played a wide range of classic and new roles; in 2004 she excelled as Lady Macbeth. Among other notable non-NYC appearances was Blanche in STEPPENWOLF's 50th-anniversary production of *A STREETCAR NAMED DESIRE* with GARY SINISE. Her talent exudes a well-calibrated intensity. DBW

Robinson, Bill "Bojangles" (1878–1949) AFRICAN AMERICAN dancer and singer who, after many years as a star of VAUDEVILLE, made his musical-theatre debut in *Blackbirds of 1928,* where his seemingly effortless tap dancing helped the show become a hit. Robinson was next seen in *Brown Buddies* (1930), *Blackbirds of 1933,* and *The Hot Mikado* (1939), a jazz version of the GILBERT AND SULLIVAN classic. Unlike the 1920s, when a number of black musicals had been successful on Broadway, the shows of the 1930s were unable to garner long runs, even when featuring popular stars like Bill Robinson. In the 1940s he appeared in two other failures, *All in Fun* (1940) and *Memphis Bound!* (1945), the last a jazz adaptation of Gilbert and Sullivan's *HMS Pinafore.* Although few of Robinson's shows were big successes, his performances were uniformly praised for the matchless ease and grace of his tap dancing. The standard biography remains that by James Haskins and N. R. Mitgang (1988). MK

Robson, Stuart [né Henry Robson Stuart] (1836–1903) Actor who made his stage debut as Horace Courtney in *Uncle Tom's Cabin as It Is,* a dramatic retort to *UNCLE TOM'S CABIN,* at the Baltimore Museum in 1852. Subsequently he appeared with numerous STOCK COMPANIES, including those of LAURA KEENE's Theatre in New York, MRS. JOHN DREW's Theatre in Philadelphia, and the Globe Theatre in Boston. From 1877 to 1889 he teamed with W. H. CRANE, starring in such farces as *Our Bachelors* and *Our Boarding House,* but also in *A Comedy of Errors* as the two Dromios, and *The Merry Wives of Windsor* as Falstaff (Crane) and Slender (Robson). BRONSON HOWARD's *The HENRIETTA* was especially written for them. After 1890, Robson starred on his own, most notably as Tony Lumpkin in *She Stoops to Conquer.* DJW

Rocket to the Moon by CLIFFORD ODETS. Produced by the GROUP THEATRE, this play opened at the BELASCO THEATRE 24 November 1938 (131 performances). Directed by HAROLD CLURMAN and designed by MORDECAI GORELIK, it starred MORRIS CARNOVSKY (dentist Ben Stark), Ruth Nelson (his wife, Belle), LUTHER ADLER (Belle's father), and Eleanor Lynn as Cleo Singer, Ben's secretary and the object of his affections in this triangle play. The Depression is the backdrop for the plot; the focus, however, is not its economic effects but the personal plights of a collection of troubled souls, with the social situation less crucial than in many Odets plays. Mixed reception led to text alterations, but its run remained modest and, despite some brilliant writing and lively characters, it has little stage history. A worthy production, however, was seen in late 2006 at LONG WHARF. DBW

Rockwell, David (1956–) New Jersey–reared and Syracuse University–educated architect and scene designer who founded in 1984 an architectural firm, the Rockwell Group. Among theatre projects are the Kodak (Academy Awards) Theatre, the CIRQUE DU SOLEIL Theatre in Orlando, and the renovation of RADIO CITY MUSIC HALL. But his projects are wide-ranging and have also included Grand Central Terminal's dining concourse, sports stadiums, and restaurants. In 1998 he was named Designer of the Year by *Interiors* magazine. In the 2000s he began designing scenery more frequently, including *The Rocky Horror Show,* HAIRSPRAY (Tony nomination), *All Shook Up,* and *Dirty Rotten Scoundrels.* His most recent Broadway scenic design was for *Legally Blonde* (2007). BO

Rodgers, Richard (1902–79) American composer. After studying music and writing scores for amateur musicals, Rodgers teamed up with lyricist LORENZ HART in 1919. Their songs were heard in *A Lonely Romeo* (1919) and *Poor Little Ritz Girl* (1920). After their first successful score for *The Garrick Gaieties* (1925), they created an almost unbroken string of hit musicals, including *Dearest Enemy* (1925), *The Girl Friend* (1926), *Peggy-Ann* (1926), and *A Connecticut Yankee* (1927). In the early 1930s Rodgers and Hart wrote the songs for several Hollywood musical films, then returned to Broadway to create some of the most popular scores of the late 1930s and early '40s, including *Jumbo* (1935), ON YOUR TOES (1936), BABES IN ARMS (1937), *I'd Rather Be Right* (1937), *I Married an Angel* (1938), *The BOYS FROM SYRACUSE* (1938), *Too Many Girls* (1939), and *By Jupiter* (1942). PAL JOEY (1940), a musical chronicling the adventures of an amoral night-club owner, was initially unpopular with critics and audiences, but more successful in its 1952 revival.

In 1943 Rodgers initiated his partnership with lyricist-librettist OSCAR HAMMERSTEIN II. Their first show was OKLAHOMA! (1951), one of the most popular and influential of all American musicals. The Rodgers and Hammerstein partnership was responsible for some of the longest-running shows of the 1940s and '50s, including CAROUSEL (1945), *Flower Drum Song* (1958), and *The* SOUND OF MUSIC (1959). Their shows were noted for the care with which music and dance were integrated with the libretto.

After Hammerstein's death in 1960, Rodgers served as his own lyricist for *No Strings* (1962), then collaborated with other lyricists on *Do I Hear a Waltz?* (1965), *Two by Two* (1970), *Rex* (1976), and *I Remember Mama* (1979). His autobiography, *Musical Stages,* was published in 1975.

Early in his career Rodgers composed bouncy, jazz-influenced music that complemented the clever lyrics of Lorenz Hart. After demonstrating that he could compose on a grander, more sweeping scale with the "Slaughter on Tenth Avenue" ballet for *On Your Toes,* Rodgers wrote dramatic, emotionally expansive scores for his "musical plays" of the 1940s and '50s. His centenary in 2002 was surrounded with books, recordings, and television specials, including a paperback edition of his autobiography, biographies by William Hyland (1998), Meryle Secrest (2001), and Geoffrey Block (2003), and an *American Masters* documentary on PBS (2001).   MK

Roger Bloomer by JOHN HOWARD LAWSON. This early foray with expressionism was first produced by the Equity Players on 1 March 1923, starring Henry Hull and designed by WOODMAN THOMPSON. The action centers on a confused young loner who flees the Midwest to "chase rainbows" in New York, where he falls into dissipation. Roger is bombarded by commercialism and greed, finally losing his love, Louise, to suicide after stealing money. In jail, suspected of killing Louise, Roger has a long expressionistic nightmare, which seems to exorcise many of the demons of commercialism and sexual confusion that plague Roger throughout the action.   RHW

Rogers, Will (William Penn Adair Rogers) (1879–1935) This warm, gum-chewing American folk hero began in WILD WEST shows, billed as "The Cherokee Kid, the wonderful Lasso-Artist," making $20 a week. At the St. Louis World's Fair in 1904 he dazzled audiences by circling a horse and rider with a lasso in each hand. He made his first appearance in New York in 1905 with a trick roping and riding company (Madison Square Garden) and gradually evolved his technique of commenting drolly on current events in his Oklahoma drawl while playing with his lariat. His stage personality, which used no makeup or comic properties, was basically an extension of his own, winning the audience's trust and affection. Rogers appeared in musicals, the ZIEGFELD *Follies* (1916, 1917, 1918, 1922, 1924, and 1925), on the VAUDEVILLE stage, and in 24 films. In 1934, he played the father in the touring company of O'NEILL'S *AH, WILDERNESS!,* and the next year was lost flying over Alaska with aviator Wiley Post. He has been portrayed by James Whitmore in Paul Shyre's ONE-PERSON show *Will Rogers' USA* (1972), and in 1991 his persona was used as the central character (originated by Keith Carradine) in the musical *The* WILL ROGERS FOLLIES. Ben Yagoda's biography (1993) remains definitive, although as of 2006 five volumes of Rogers documents have been published by the University of Oklahoma; Ray Robinson's 1996 bio is also useful.   LS

Rogoff, Gordon (1931–) Theatre critic, director, and educator. Educated at Yale (1952), Rogoff has had a distinguished academic career, chairing drama departments at SUNY Buffalo and Brooklyn College, serving as associate dean (1966–9) at the Yale Drama School and, beginning in 1987, professor of dramaturgy and dramatic criticism, in addition to initiatives in Ireland and England. Beginning in the 1960s he reviewed for the *Village Voice* and served as dramaturge for the OPEN THEATRE. Reviews and essays have appeared in *American Theatre, Play and Players,* the *Nation,* the *New Republic,* and *Parnassus.* A 1973 Guggenheim Fellow, he received a 1976 Obie for directing, the GEORGE JEAN NATHAN Award for Dramatic Criticism in 1985–6, and the Morton Dauwen Zabel Award (American Academy of Arts and Letters) in 1991. Two books contain many of his reviews: *Theatre Is Not Safe* (1987), criticism 1962–86, and *Vanishing Acts: Theatre since the Sixties* (2000).   TLM

Romberg, Sigmund (1887–1951) Hungarian-born musician who came to the U.S. as a young man and became one of the prolific composers of operetta and musical comedy scores. In 1914 he began a long association with the SHUBERT BROTHERS when he wrote the score for *The Whirl of the World.* As the Shuberts' staff composer, he wrote songs for their REVUE series *The Passing Show,* and also turned out scores for dozens of commonplace musicals. In 1921 he adapted Franz Schubert's melodies for the musical biography BLOSSOM TIME, whose phenomenal success gave him greater freedom in choosing projects. As the 1920s progressed, he wrote the operettas by which he is most remembered: The STUDENT PRINCE (1924), The DESERT SONG (1926), and The NEW MOON (1928). He continued to write operettas and musicals up to his death, though with less success. William Everett's biography is scheduled for publication in mid-2007.   MK

Rome, Harold (1908–93) Composer, lyricist. After receiving a degree in architecture from Yale, Rome studied piano in New York. His first score was for the REVUE PINS AND NEEDLES (1937), sponsored by the International Ladies Garment Workers Union. He contributed songs to other revues, including Sing Out the News (1938), Star and Garter (1942), the ZIEGFELD Follies (1943), and Call Me Mister (1946). In the 1950s he wrote the scores to several successful book musicals, including Wish You Were Here (1952), Fanny (1954), and Destry Rides Again (1959). Barbra Streisand catapulted to fame singing Rome's "Miss Marmelstein" in I Can Get It for You Wholesale (1962). In the early 1970s Rome wrote the score for Scarlett, an ill-fated musical version of Gone with the Wind that played in Tokyo, London, and Los Angeles. Rome was elected to the THEATRE HALL OF FAME in 1991.   MK

Room Service Three-act farce by John Murray and Allen Boretz; opened on Broadway at the CORT THEATRE (19 May 1937) and ran 500 performances. Originally directed and produced by GEORGE ABBOTT, the play has been revived once on Broadway – The PLAYHOUSE, 6 April 1953 for 16 performances, in which Jack Lemmon made his New York debut – and thrice OFF-BROADWAY: Edison Theatre, 12 May 1970 for 71 performances, directed by Harold Stone; ROUNDABOUT THEATRE, 29 January 1986 for 64 performances, directed by ALAN ARKIN; and a successful two-stage run (10 July 2006 at the Bank Street and 28 November 2006 at Soho Playhouse) produced by Peccadillo Theatre Company. Praised for its physical comedy and uninhibited lunacy and gusto in portraying the dodges and makeshifts of show business, the play appealed to the escapist demands of its post-Depression audience. Room Service inspired two film versions, one a 1938 MARX BROS. vehicle.   MK

Rooney, Pat(rick James), Jr. (1880–1962) Performer, songwriter. The diminutive, perennially young song-and-dance man is remembered as master of the waltz clog to the tune of "The Daughter of Rosie O'Grady," the song he introduced at The PALACE in 1919. (In 1925 he starred in a musical built around the song and dance.) The son of performers, Rooney was best known on the VAUDEVILLE stage (1904–32 with his wife, Marion Bent; afterward with Herman Timberg in a Jewish–Irish twosome), although as Arvide Abernathy singing "More I Cannot Wish You" in GUYS AND DOLLS (1950) he created a memorable moment in musical theatre annals. His son, Pat III, was also an entertainer. "As long as I can move my feet, I'm gonna keep working," Rooney once said, which he did right up to his death. In popularity, the Rooneys ranked with the COHANS and the Foys.   DBW

Roosters This two-act drama by Milcha Sánchez-Scott was developed at INTAR's Hispanic Playwrights-in-Residence Laboratory (1984) under the direction of MARIA IRENE FORNÉS, and at Sundance Institute Playwrights Laboratory (1986). Roosters was coproduced by the NEW YORK SHAKESPEARE FESTIVAL, premiering at INTAR in 1987. Set in the Southwest, the play depicts a harsh reality involving a CHICANO family in crisis as a young daughter strives for identity within the family while the father and son compete for dominance. Through numerous plays, Sánchez-Scott is recognized as a spokesperson for HISPANIC American issues.   ER

Rose, Billy [né Samuel Wolf Rosenberg] (1899–1966) Flamboyant showman ("I sell ballyhoo, not genius") and lyricist ("Barney Google," "Without a Song," "Me and My Shadow," etc.). His ventures ranged from NIGHTCLUBS and theatre-restaurants (Back Stage Club, Casino de Paree, the Billy Rose Music Hall in New York during the 1920s and '30s; Casa Mañana in Ft. Worth in the 1930s; New York's Diamond Horseshoe, 1939–52) to epic spectacles such as Jumbo (1935) and the aquacades at the 1939–40 New York World's Fair and the San Francisco Golden Gate Exposition (1940) – as well as to 11 legitimate Broadway productions, CARMEN JONES (1943) and The Immoralist (1954) among them. In the 1950s and '60s he owned two NYC theatres (see NEDERLANDER THEATRE, ZIEGFELD THEATRE). One of Rose's five marriages was to FANNY BRICE (1929). The Billy Rose Theatre Collection of the New York Public Library was funded by his foundation (organized 1958). Stephen Nelson's 1987 study of Rose is recommended.   DBW

Rose, George (Walter) (1920–88) English-born actor. Although to many the archetype of the

British character actor, Rose lived in New York City from 1961, the year he played The Common Man in *A Man for All Seasons,* until his untimely death. His Dogberry in Gielgud's 1959 production of *Much Ado about Nothing* established him as a first-rate Shakespearean clown. After settling in NYC, he appeared prominently in *The Royal Hunt of the Sun* (1965), *MY FAIR LADY* (Doolittle in 1968 [City Center] and 1976 [Broadway] revivals), the musical *Coco* (1969), *My Fat Friend* (1974), *The Kingfisher* (1978), the musical *Peter Pan* (Captain Hook and Mr. Darling, 1979 revival), *The Pirates of Penzance* (Major General Stanley in NEW YORK SHAKESPEARE FESTIVAL's 1980 revival), the 1983 revival of *YOU CAN'T TAKE IT WITH YOU,* and *The Mystery of Edwin Drood* (1985). DBW

Rose-Marie Book and lyrics by OTTO HARBACH and OSCAR HAMMERSTEIN II, music by RUDOLF FRIML, additional songs by Herbert Stothart. One of the great musical hits of the 1920s, it opened at the IMPERIAL THEATRE on 2 September 1924 and ran for 557 performances. Eschewing the European settings of most operettas, Hammerstein and Harbach employed the Canadian Rockies as a backdrop for their tale of singer Rose-Marie LeFlamme (played by opera star Mary Ellis) and her romance with Canadian Mountie Jim Kenyon (played by British singer-actor DENNIS KING). Although the creators of *Rose-Marie* believed the musical sequences were so integral to the plot that they refused to list them separately in the program, the operetta is remembered today for its songs, particularly "Indian Love Call" and the title song, rather than for its story. Long a favorite of warm-weather audiences, *Rose-Marie* has frequently been revived by SUMMER STOCK and tent theatres. MK

Rosenthal, Jean (1912–69) Theatre, architectural, and industrial lighting designer who virtually invented the field of lighting design. When she began working with ORSON WELLES and JOHN HOUSEMAN in the FEDERAL THEATRE PROJECT there were no lighting designers; the job was done by the set designer or electrician. In 1938 she began working for Martha Graham as lighting and production supervisor (and continued until her death). Because dance is so dependent on light, Rosenthal was able to develop the new art of lighting design. A common element in all her designs is an evocative sense of mood. Critics and directors commented on her apparent ability to work magic with her effects. Rosenthal's hundreds of theatre designs include *WEST SIDE STORY* and *The SOUND OF MUSIC.* She also designed the architectural lighting for theatres and projects ranging from airline terminals to hotels. Her ideas and techniques are presented in her book *The Magic of Light* (1972, with Lael Wertenbaker). AA

Rosenthal, Rachel (1926–) PERFORMANCE ARTist. Born in Paris of Russian emigré parents, she studied ballet as a child. Fleeing Nazism, she moved first to Brazil (1940) and then to New York, where she attended school and trained as an actress and visual artist (Jean-Louis Barrault School of Theatre, 1947–8; graphic art with William Hayter and painting with Hans Hoffman, 1946–8; acting with HERBERT BERGHOF, 1954). She assisted ERWIN PISCATOR (1949–50) and set designer Heinz Condell, befriended John Cage, and danced with the Merce Cunningham Dance Company. She later founded Instant Theater (1956–66) and Espace DBD (1980–3), and cofounded and cochaired Womanspace (1971–4) in LOS ANGELES. In the mid-1970s she began working with autobiographical material and social and environmental issues. She incorporates into her performances meditation, martial arts, Asian and Euro-American radical dramatic traditions. She founded the Rachel Rosenthal Company in 1989 in LA. Important performances include *The Death Show* (1978), *Gaia, Mon Amour* (1983), *Pangaean Dreams: A Shamanic Journey* (1990), *Zone* (1994), *Meditation on the Life and Death of Ken Saro-Wiwa* and *Timepiece* (1996), and *The Swans* and *The Unexpurgated Virgin* (1997), among others. Her work is analyzed in a monograph edited by Moira Roth (1997). AF

Ross, Jerry (Jerold) see ADLER, RICHARD

Rosse, Herman (1887–1965) Theatre/film designer and architect. Born in The Hague, Rosse came to the U.S. in 1908, though he returned to the Netherlands for 1933–47. He was head of the School of Design of the Art Institute of Chicago (1919–23). His more than 200 settings for stage and film were typified by a strong modernist style and range from several of the ZIEGFELD Follies to *Ulysses in Nighttown* (1958), including 10 years as resident designer for the Paper Mill Playhouse (1950–60) in New Jersey. His films include *Frankenstein, Murders in the Rue Morgue,* and *The EMPEROR JONES.* Rosse also designed the medallions used for the ANTOINETTE PERRY (Tony) Awards. AA

Roth, Ann (1931–) Since designing costumes for *Maybe Tuesday* on Broadway in 1958, Roth has amassed some 75 credits for Broadway productions, including *Purlie* (1970; 1972 revival), *The ROYAL FAMILY* (1975), *The Crucifer of Blood* (1978),

Death and the Maiden (1992), *The* TALE OF THE ALLERGIST'S WIFE (2000), and *Deuce* (2007). She began her long-term association with MIKE NICHOLS and NEIL SIMON with *The* ODD COUPLE in 1964 (also 2005 revival), and is also known for her collaborations with film director John Schlesinger. Her more than 100 film credits include costumes for *Midnight Cowboy* (1969), *Hair* (1979), *Regarding Henry* (1991), *The English Patient* (1996; Oscar), *The Hours* (2002), and *Cold Mountain* (2003); TV, ANGELS IN AMERICA (2003; Emmy nominee). A major in scene design at Carnegie Institute of Technology (1953), she began her career assisting IRENE SHARAFF on films, including *The* KING AND I (1956), and in 2000 received the Lifetime Achievement Award named for Sharaff.   BO

Roth, Daryl (1946–) Educated at NYU, this respected producer toiled in interior design and on arts nonprofit boards before producing. Her first effort, the musical revue *Closer than Ever* (1987), ran almost nine months OFF-BROADWAY. Known for her warmth, intelligence, and taste – a spiritual successor to ROBERT WHITEHEAD – Roth's producing and coproducing scoreboard increased to include five Pulitzer Prize–winning plays (PROOF, WIT, HOW I LEARNED TO DRIVE, *Three Tall Women*, *Anna in the Tropics*); two Tonys for Best Play (*Proof* and *The* GOAT, OR WHO IS SYLVIA?); original OFF-BROADWAY works (*The Play about the Baby, Old Wicked Songs, Our Lady of 121st Street, The Bombitty of Errors*); major Broadway revivals (WHO'S AFRAID OF VIRGINIA WOOLF? and *Medea*); commercial transfers (*Caroline, or Change; The* TALE OF THE ALLERGIST'S WIFE); and London runs and national tours. In 1996, her purchase of the former Union Square Savings Bank, built in the 1840s, resulted in a spacious theatre (80′ × 45′ with 40′ ceilings) named in her honor, housing the performance piece *De La Guarda* for seven years. An adjacent, more modest space, DR 2, opened in 2002. Roth's son **Jordan** is a noted producer of his own (*The Rocky Horror Show*). She suffered a rare defeat when a musical version of *The Mambo Kings*, produced jointly by mother and son, failed out of town.   LJ

Roth, Wolfgang (1910–88) Designer who joined the Piscator–Bühne in 1928 as assistant to Traugott Müller. Over the next five years he worked with PISCATOR and BRECHT and was an assistant to Caspar Neher on *Die Dreigroschen Oper*. He then worked in Zurich and Vienna before coming to the U.S. in 1938. He designed for Broadway, OFF-BROADWAY, and the Metropolitan and New York City operas as well as for several regional theatres. His designs for the 1952 revival of PORGY AND BESS

(worldwide tour) are considered among his best. He was also an artist with many gallery shows.   AA

Roundabout Theatre Company OFF-BROADWAY theatre founded in 1965 by GENE FEIST and Elizabeth Owens; TODD HAIMES is the current artistic director (since 1990). The Roundabout, one of Manhattan's major not-for-profit organizations, specializes in faithful revivals of modern repertory standards using name performers, a policy that has earned it a large and loyal subscription audience. At the start of the 1991–2 season, the Roundabout moved to a Broadway house, one of many moves in its history, the 499-seat Criterion Center (Stage Right) Theatre at 1530 Broadway. Prior to this move, its Second Stage series addressed smaller-scale or more offbeat plays, a practice reinvigorated with the opening of its Laura Pels Theatre (399 seats) October 1995. Between 1995 and 1999 10 productions – classic and new plays – were staged in this theatre space. In 1998 a critically acclaimed revival of CABARET opened at the HENRY MILLER THEATRE (renamed the Kit Kat Klub) and then transferred to Studio 54, now one of Roundabout's regular spaces. In 2000, after relinquishing its Times Square space, a permanent mainstage home was established in the renovated Selwyn Theatre on 42d Street, renamed the AMERICAN AIRLINES THEATRE and opening with *The* MAN WHO CAME TO DINNER. Between 1999 and 2002 the Laura Pels was temporarily housed in the Gramercy Theatre, moving permanently in 2002 to the former AMERICAN PLACE THEATRE, now known as the Harold and Miriam Steinberg Center for the Theatre (opening in 2004 with LYNN NOTTAGE's *Intimate Apparel*). A fourth space – a black box – will be housed in this facility. As of early 2007, Roundabout's productions have won 22 Tonys, 27 Drama Desk awards, 38 Outer Circle Critics, 27 Theatre World Awards, and 7 Obies, among other recognitions. In 2005–6 its total attendance was 477,048.   CLJ   DBW

Rowson, Susanna Haswell (1762–1824) English-born playwright, actress, and novelist who came to the U.S. for the second time in 1793 as part of THOMAS WIGNELL's company and acted in PHILADELPHIA and BOSTON before retiring in 1796 to open a girl's school. Of her plays, *Slaves in Algiers; or, A Struggle for Freedom* (1794), which savaged tyranny, was her best. Other titles include *The Female Patriot* (1795); *The Volunteers* (1795), her reaction to the Whisky Rebellion; and *Americans in England* (1797). A short study of Rowson by Patricia Parker was published in 1986.   WJM

Royal Family, The This GEORGE S. KAUFMAN and EDNA FERBER romantic comedy, produced by JED HARRIS, opened on Broadway 28 December 1927 and ran 345 performances. The play is about the escapades of an extended family of actors modeled after the DREW–BARRYMORE clan. Paramount released the film version in 1930, starring FREDRIC MARCH. The American Bicentennial Theatre's revival opened on Broadway 30 December 1975 under ELLIS RABB's direction. The cast included EVA LE GALLIENNE as Fanny, SAM LEVENE as Wolfe, ROSEMARY HARRIS as Julie, and GEORGE GRIZZARD as Tony. The play is frequently revived. JDM

Royale Theatre 242 West 46th St., NYC [Architect: Herbert J. Krapp]. Built as one of a chain of six theatres by the Chanin brothers (cf. RICHARD RODGERS THEATRE), the Royale opened early in 1927. The Chanin control did not survive the Depression, and all of their theatres passed to other interests. The SHUBERTS became part owner of the house but did not directly control it until 1940. With 1,100 seats, the playhouse has presented both musical and nonmusical fare. When leased by JOHN GOLDEN (1934–6), it was briefly named after him and served for his own productions. It was also used (1937–40) as a CBS radio studio during this era. It has housed three Pulitzer Prize winners: *BOTH YOUR HOUSES* (1933), *The SUBJECT WAS ROSES* (1964), and *ANNA IN THE TROPICS* (2003). Other memorable productions on its stage have included *Diamond Lil* (1928), *The Boy Friend* (1954), *The MATCHMAKER* (1955), *GREASE* (1972), *A Day in Hollywood/A Night in the Ukraine* (1980), *Art* (1998), *Copenhagen* (2000), a *GLENGARRY GLEN ROSS* revival (2005), and *Frost/Nixon* (2007). In May 2005 it was renamed the Bernard B. Jacobs Theatre, for the late longtime president of the Shubert Organization, and it remains a Shubert theatre. MCH

Rudnick, Paul (1957–) New Jersey–born and Yale-educated (1977) playwright, screenwriter, and novelist who has a true flair for comedy. *Poor Little Lambs* (1982), about a woman joining the all-male Yale Whiffenpoof Singing Group ran for 73 performances OFF-BROADWAY and won an Outer Critics Circle Award. *I Hate Hamlet* (1991), a ghost comedy, played 80 performances at the WALTER KERR THEATRE and attained a certain notoriety because of the onstage antics of British star, Nicol Williamson. His comedy about AIDS, *Jeffrey* (1993), opened OFF-OFF BROADWAY at the WPA Theatre, moved to Off-Broadway (winning an Obie, an Outer Critics Circle Award, and the John Gassner Award for Outstanding New American

Play), and has been filmed. Other plays (most premiering Off-Broadway) include *The Naked Eye* (1996, AMERICAN REPERTORY THEATRE), *The Most Fabulous Story Ever Told* (1998), a gay parody of the creation myth, *Rude Entertainment* (2001), *Valhalla* (2004), and *Regrets Only* (2006). TLM

Ruehl, Mercedes (1948–) Actress, born in Queens of Irish and Cuban extraction; educated at the College of New Rochelle (1969). This statuesque, dynamic talent studied with UTA HAGEN and Tad Danielewski and appeared in regional theatre before her 1985 Broadway debut in *I'm Not Rappaport*. For her portrayal as mentally disabled Bella in the 1991 production of *LOST IN YONKERS* she received a 1992 Best Actress Tony; the same year she won an Oscar for *The Fisher King* (1991). For her OFF-BROADWAY appearance in *The MARRIAGE OF BETTE AND BOO* she shared a 1985 Ensemble Obie, and 20 years later she received a Best Performance Obie for *Woman before a Glass* (2005), in which she became Peggy Guggenheim, the "Mistress of Modern Art," in a ONE-PERSON show by Lanie Robertson. She has received acclaim in *The Shadow Box* (1994), *The Rose Tattoo* (1995), and *THE GOAT, OR WHO IS SYLVIA?* (2002), all on Broadway. DBW

Russell, Annie (1864–1936) English-born actress who, two years after her New York stage debut in 1879, established her career with a brilliant portrayal of the title character in *Esmeralda*. Ill health forced her from the stage for three seasons (1891–4), but she returned to regain her popularity and invite comparison with Eleonora Duse for her simplicity and naturalism. She was effective especially in emotional and comic roles. She created SHAW's heroine in *Major Barbara* (1905, London) and gave memorable performances as Puck in *A Midsummer Night's Dream* (1906), Viola in *Twelfth Night* (1910), Beatrice in *Much Ado* (1912), and Lady Teazle in Sheridan's *The School for Scandal* (1914). Her charming stage presence made her the ideal ingenue. She retired from the stage in 1918 to head the dramatic program at Rollins College, Winter Park, FL. TLM

Russell, Henry (1812–1900) English entertainer and songwriter of Jewish descent; after studying music with Rossini and Bellini, he descended to being an organist and choral director in Rochester, NY. In 1837, he made a debut as a ballad singer at the Brooklyn Lyceum; in a short time he became a hugely popular performer, offering the first solo vocal programs in America, aimed at the common man. He not only sang in a pleasant baritone and accompanied himself on the piano, but composed his entire repertory. This included such warhorses-to-be as "Cheer, Boys, Cheer!," "Woodman! Spare That Tree," "A Life on the Ocean Wave," and "The Old Armchair," as well as temperance, antislavery, and humanitarian ballads. He repeated his triumphs in England, and his entertainment "The Far West; or, The Emigrant's Progress from the Old World to the New" inspired British immigration to the American frontier. He retired about 1865. An autobiography appeared in 1895.   LS

Russell, Lillian [née Helen Louise Leonard] (1861–1922) Singer and actress whose name is synonymous with one of her show titles, *An American Beauty*. Rising from obscurity in Clinton, IA, she became a much sought after star in comic opera, BURLESQUE, VAUDEVILLE, and drama. TONY PASTOR billed her as "The English Ballad Singer" at his Broadway variety theatre in 1880. Cross-country tours and engagements in New York and England followed. She was applauded for her physical and vocal charms in such vehicles as *The Pie Rats of Penn Yan* (Pastor's burlesque of *The Pirates of Penzance*), *The Snake Charmer, The Sorcerer, The Princess of Trebizonde, Iolanthe,* and *The Princess Nicotine*. She enjoyed five seasons (1899–1904) with WEBER AND FIELDS's celebrated troupes. Roles in *Lady Teazle* (1904, musical version of Sheridan's *The School for Scandal*), *The Butterfly* (1906), and *Wildfire* (1908), furthered her already flourishing reputation. She died in Pittsburgh, survived by her fourth husband and a daughter. Armond Fields's 1998 biography is serviceable.   DBW

Russell, Sol Smith (1848–1902) Actor born in Maine and raised in St. Louis, where he became a drummer boy during the Civil War. His first regular engagement was at Deagle's in St. Louis; he later accepted a position with BEN DEBAR'S STOCK COMPANY there. In 1868 he joined the Berger family of bell ringers, giving character impersonations and songs. He first starred in 1880 in *Edgewood Folks,* in which he appeared 1,500 times. Although Russell never succeeded in New York, he was extremely popular in the rest of the nation in such shows as *The Country Editor, Pa, Bewitched,* and especially *The Poor Relation,* his greatest success. His best roles were uncouth country types whose alert minds and large ambitions won the day. Russell left an estate of more than $2 million.   SMA

Ryskind, Morrie (1895–1985) Librettist and lyricist who, after working as a newspaperman and Broadway press AGENT, contributed sketches and lyrics to the KAUFMAN and CONNELLY revue *The '49ers* (1922). He wrote the books for two MARX BROS. shows, *The COCOANUTS* (1925) and *ANIMAL CRACKERS* (1928), then collaborated with GEORGE AND IRA GERSHWIN on three musicals offering trenchant satire of American politics and mores: *STRIKE UP THE BAND* (1930), the Pulitzer Prize–winning *OF THEE I SING* (1931), and *Let 'em Eat Cake* (1933). From the mid-1930s on he spent most of his time working on Hollywood films as writer, producer, and director. Adopting a conservative political stance, in 1960 he became a columnist for the *Los Angeles Times* Syndicate and later for the *Los Angeles Herald Examiner*.   MK

S

Sabinson, Harvey (1929–) Theatre publicist and longtime executive director of the LEAGUE OF AMERICAN THEATRES AND PRODUCERS. Known as "Mr. Broadway," he is a native New Yorker who attended Queens College. As a publicist he was associated with more than 250 Broadway productions, and worked with DAVID MERRICK, CHERYL CRAWFORD, ROGER STEVENS, and ALEXANDER COHEN, among others. He first worked for the League in 1976, and headed the organization 1982–95. In 1995 he received a Lifetime Achievement Tony Award, the same year he was inducted into the THEATRE HALL OF FAME. In 1998 he was invested into the College of Fellows of the American Theatre.   DBW

Saddler, Donald (1920–) Ballet dancer and theatre choreographer who, before joining the company of *High Button Shoes* (1947), was a soloist with Ballet Theatre (1940–3, 1946–7). He was a featured dancer along with BOB FOSSE and Joan McCracken in *Dance Me a Song* (1950). Saddler's choreographic career began with *WONDERFUL TOWN* and *JOHN MURRAY ANDERSON's Almanac* (both 1953). From the unsuccessful *Shangri-La* (1956), Saddler went on to choreograph *Milk and Honey* (1961), *Tricks* (1973), and a 1993 revival of *MY FAIR LADY*. For *NO, NO, NANETTE* (1971 Broadway revival) he received critical and popular acclaim: Capturing the spirit of the show, Saddler had his dancers performing on beach balls (see DANCE). In 2001 he appeared as a performer in a revival of *FOLLIES*. Saddler was also recognized for his work in industrial shows as a producer and choreographer.   LF

Sag Harbor Domestic comedy by JAMES A. HERNE that premiered at the Park Theatre, Boston, 24 October 1899, and ran a record 107 performances. Herne's last play is a revision of his *Hearts of Oak* (1879), written in collaboration with DAVID BELASCO. Kindly and wise Captain Dan Marble (played by Herne himself) teaches a man in love with his brother's wife to accept his situation with equanimity. After an eight-week tour, a brief run in Chicago, and a summer layoff, *Sag Harbor* opened the new Theatre Republic in New York on 27 September 1900. Its reputation is based on its realistically detailed dinner-party scene, its expert character drawing, and the scenic realism of its rustic shipyard setting.   WD

St. Charles Theatre St. Charles St. between Poydras and Gravier, New Orleans [Architect: Antoine Mondelli]. Built by JAMES H. CALDWELL in 1835, the St. Charles, with 4,000 seats, a 55-ft. proscenium opening, and a central chandelier with 23,000 cut-glass drops lit by 250 gas jets, was the largest, handsomest, and probably the most expensive theatre built in America to that date. The original STOCK COMPANY included CHARLOTTE CUSHMAN and JAMES E. MURDOCH. In 1842, it burned to the ground (see FIRES) and was replaced by a lesser structure, which eventually passed to the management of Caldwell's rivals, NOAH LUDLOW and SOL SMITH. During its highwater years, most American and English stars played at the theatre, and the last known performance of J.B. BOOTH occurred on its stage. In 1899, it burned again and was rebuilt in 1901 as a VAUDEVILLE house, which changed to films in the movie era. For a number of years it served as a rehearsal hall for the New Orleans Symphony Orchestra, because of its excellent acoustics, but it was torn down in 1966.   MCH

Saint-Denis, Michel (1897–1971) French director, nephew of Jacques Copeau, whose first directing work was with La Compagnie des Quinze, a group of Copeau's former pupils. In 1935 he left France to direct Gielgud in an English version of the Quinze's success: *Noah* by Obey. He stayed on in London to found the London Theatre Studio, a theatre school modeled on Copeau's ideas, but the venture failed. He helped to revive the Old Vic and establish its theatre school but left in 1951. In 1957 he came to the United States to advise on theatres and theatre training, later becoming codirector of the Juilliard School at LINCOLN CENTER. He also served as artistic adviser to the Royal Shakespeare Company and to the Canadian National Theatre School. In 1960 he published *Theatre: The Rediscovery of Style,* in which methods and approaches derived from Copeau are set out. A study of Saint-Denis by Jane Baldwin was published in 2003.   DB   DBW

St. Emanuel Street Theatre   Theatre in Mobile, AL, associated with NOAH LUDLOW and SOL SMITH during their five-year dominance of the St. Louis and Mobile stages in the 1830s. Ludlow managed Mobile's first theatre (1824–8), then joined with Smith to open the St. Emanuel Street Theatre in 1835. The playhouse's burning in 1838 (see FIRES) ended the Ludlow–Smith domination of Mobile theatre.   DBW

St. James Theatre   246 West 44th St., NYC [Architects: Warren and Wetmore]. Intended to be a personal monument to its builder, ABRAHAM ERLANGER, a partner in the infamous Theatrical SYNDICATE, the theatre was named the Erlanger for the first five years of its existence. Opening in 1927 with a lesser GEORGE M. COHAN musical, the theatre reverted to the Astor estate in the early Depression. It was then leased to a succession of producers until it was bought by the SHU-BERTS, who were later forced to relinquish it to comply with the terms of a consent decree limiting the number of theatres in their control in 1957. It was bought by and has remained a property of the JUJAMCYN ORGANIZATION. Built as a musical house with more than 1,600 seats, Broadway history has been made on its stage. Starting in 1943, the RODGERS and HAMMERSTEIN musical *OKLAHOMA!* held its stage for five years. *The KING AND I,* another Rodgers and Hammerstein production, opened in 1951, and did not close for three years. Their *Flower Drum Song* followed in 1958. Other notable musicals have included *HELLO, DOLLY!* (1964), *Barnum* (1980), *My One and Only* (1983), *The SECRET GARDEN* (1991), *The Who's Tommy* (1993), and *The PRODUCERS* (2001).   MCH

St. Louis Municipal Outdoor Theatre (MUNY)   In 1917 an outdoor theatre with a massive stage and seating 9,500 (now 11,000) opened in St. Louis's Forest Park. After a few seasons of presenting comic opera and operetta with local performers, the MUNY changed to a policy of importing Broadway and Hollywood stars to augment their casts. After the 1950s, full touring productions and concerts by individual performers were being added to the MUNY's nationally acclaimed musical-comedy seasons, which runs June to mid-August (seven productions in 2006).   MK

St. Philip Street Theatre   The second theatre built in New Orleans, this 700-seat auditorium was con-structed in 1808 for the performance of French plays and operas, but soon became the first theatre in the city to house a permanent English-speaking theatrical company. After years of success as home to the companies of NOAH LUDLOW and JAMES H. CALDWELL, the theatre closed in 1832 and soon after was demolished.   LAB

Saint-Subber, Arnold (1918–94) Producer. Born in Washington, DC, and educated at New York University, Saint-Subber served as assistant to JOHN MURRAY ANDERSON for numerous productions, including the *ZIEGFELD Follies of 1943.* His close association with playwright NEIL SIMON established him as an important name on Broadway in the 1960s. Of the more than 25 shows he has produced or coproduced, the more notable are *KISS ME, KATE* (1948; Tony), *The Grass Harp* (1952), *My Three Angels* (1953), *Dark at the Top of the Stairs* (1957), *The Tenth Man* (1959), *BAREFOOT IN THE PARK* (1963), *The ODD COUPLE* (1965), *PLAZA SUITE* (1968), *LAST OF THE RED HOT LOVERS* (1969), *The PRISONER OF SECOND AVENUE* (1971), *Gigi* (1973), and *1600 Pennsylvania Avenue* (197s6).   TLM

Saks, Gene (1921–) Director and actor, born in NYC and educated at Cornell University (1939–43). He studied acting at The ACTORS STUDIO and Dramatic Workshop, and made his New York debut at the Cherry Lane Theatre in 1947 as Joxer in O'Casey's *Juno and the Paycock.* During the next decade he appeared mainly in supporting roles before attracting critical attention in 1962 as Leo Herman in *A Thousand Clowns.* Beginning in 1963 he established himself as one of Broadway's premier directors of comedy, known for his inventiveness and attention to detail. His directing is linked, especially, with the comedies of NEIL SIMON, winning Tonys for *BILOXI BLUES* (1985) and *BRIGHTON BEACH MEMOIRS* (1983), and a Tony nomination for *LOST IN YONKERS* (1991). He also directed Simon's *California Suite* (1976), a revival of *The ODD COUPLE* (1985), *Rumors* (1988), and *Jake's Women* (1992). He also won a Tony for the musical *I Love My Wife* (1977). Other notable directing credits include *Half a Sixpence* (1965), *Mame* (1966), *Same Time, Next Year* (1975) – all bringing him Tony nominations – and *Barrymore* (1997).   TLM

Sally   Musical by GUY BOLTON (book), Clifford Grey (lyrics), with music by JEROME KERN and VICTOR HERBERT; represented prevalent performance styles when it opened 21 December 1920. Like the Tierney–McCarthy *Irene* (1919) and Kern's *Sunny* (1925), *Sally* combined wonderful melodies with Cinderella plots. FLORENZ ZIEGFELD

Production photo of *Salvation Nell* with Minnie Maddern Fiske and Holbrook Blinn pictured at center (setting used in Acts I and II). *Courtesy:* Museum of the City of New York.

produced *Sally* with popular stars – Marilyn Miller, Leon Errol, and Walter Catlett – and lavish sets and costumes by Joseph Urban. *Sally* is a talented dancer who coincidentally meets an exiled European duke and is given a break at stardom when a Russian ballerina fails to make a performance. Such contrivances were willingly accepted in 1920, when the musical ran 570 performances, but dulled the popularity of the play's 1948 revival (which closed after 36 performances). KN

Salsbury, Nathan (Nate) (1846–1902) Actor, playwright, and manager; best known for contributing superb organizational skills to William F. ("Buffalo Bill") Cody's Wild West exhibition, for which he was vice president and general manager from the show's second season in 1883 until his death. Prior to that partnership, Salsbury had organized Salsbury's Troubadours, a popular five-member comic troupe, in 1875. He wrote the group's first plays (loosely knit concoctions of songs, stories, and dances); *The Brook* (1875) influenced early musical comedy by precipitating a fad for spirited, small-scale pieces. In the 1880s the Troubadours adapted a more structured farce format. Although Salsbury left to devote his time to the Wild West, the Troubadours continued under the leadership of comedienne Nellie McHenry. In 1895 Salsbury produced *Black America,* an entertainment with 300 African American performers intended to display black culture, but it lasted only one season. RAH

Salt Lake Acting Company, The A not-for-profit professional founded in 1970 to present innovative and thought-provoking plays for Utah audiences. Its space is a renovated historic building on 500 North St. Dedicated to contemporary American playwrights, SLAC commissions plays and invites submissions. Its 2005–6 season included works by Adam Bock, Tracy Letts, and Julia Jordan, among others. DBW

Salt Lake Theatre This elegant 1,500-seat theatre, modeled after London's Drury Lane, opened 1862 under Brigham Young's ownership to provide entertainment for the Mormon community. In 1865, actors earned $12–65 per week. Through the 1870s, the theatre boasted such actors as J. A. Herne, E. L. Davenport, John McCullough, Dion Boucicault, Tony Pastor, and Harrigan and Hart. Young incurred large debts to the Mormon church, which after his death (1877) took control of the theatre and ran it until it was razed in 1928. JDM

Salvation Nell Local-color melodrama by newcomer Edward Sheldon; opened 17 November 1908 for 71 performances. Yet another serious work produced and directed by Harrison Grey Fiske to showcase the considerable abilities of his wife, MINNIE MADDERN FISKE, as Nell, it marked the appearance of Sheldon, just graduated from GEORGE PIERCE BAKER's Workshop 47 at Harvard, as a promising playwright. *Salvation Nell* depicted the attraction between a God-fearing, selfless Salvation Army officer (Fiske) and a violent, drunken, tough (HOLBROOK BLINN), surrounded by a careful re-creation of the Army's work in the midst of inner-city squalor. A triumph of realistic staging and dialect acting, the vivid depiction of New York's squalid, vulgar, mostly immigrant underclass was a sensation. Mrs. Fiske's portrayal of Nell's unshakable faith and love in the face of such violent conditions generated much pathos, and provided the idealistic ending that made the production palatable.   MR

Sam S. Shubert Theatre 225 West 44th St., NYC [Architect: Henry B. Herts]. In 1913, Lee and J. J. SHUBERT, their position as producers and theatre owners ensured, bought a site that ran through the block from West 44th to West 45th St. behind the Hotel Astor. There they built two theatres, one of which they named after their brother Sam S. Shubert, who had been killed in a railroad accident in 1905. It was to become the flagship of the Shubert enterprises and their headquarters, which it has remained. Ultimately, with the BOOTH THEATRE, it formed the western wall of Shubert Alley. For most of its history, the Shuberts have presented their own brand of musical drama and comedies. In 1975, JOSEPH PAPP moved *A CHORUS LINE* to the Shubert, where it broke all standing records as the longest-running production to date (6,137 performances) on a Broadway stage. In 1996 extensive renovations to the house and stage began. In 1997 the long-running *CHICAGO* revival moved in; since 2005 its tenant has been *Monty Python's Spamalot*.   MCH

Samuel French, Inc. One of the largest, oldest theatrical publishing houses. Samuel French was an American entrepreneur who teamed with Thomas Hailes Lacy, a British actor, playwright, and manager who had moved into bookselling, to publish and license plays on either side of the Atlantic. Though the forerunner of Samuel French was founded in 1830, things were consolidated only in 1873 when Lacy, upon his retirement, sold his share to French, who had taken up permanent residence in London, leaving Thomas Henry French, his son, to run the U.S. arm of the company. Today, headquartered in NYC yet still thriving as a business in London, Samuel French is generally recognized as the premier publisher of plays (mostly acting editions), with a vast backlist

and a dominant position in the areas of amateur and professional rights for plays and musicals new and old.   LJ

Sam'l of Posen A starring vehicle by GEORGE H. JESSOP for M. B. Curtis, this popular farce capitalizes on stereotyped Jewish behavior. Copyrighted by Jessop in 1880, the play was bought by Curtis (little is known of either), and played on regional circuits for years after a successful opening at HAVERLY'S FOURTEENTH STREET THEATRE, NYC, in 1881. With its ethnic types, imperiled hero, loathsome villain, and urban setting, this comedy (of the HARRIGAN variety) may be considered typical of the "play factory" fare of the commerical New York–based touring theatre of the late 19th century.   RKB

San Diego Repertory Theatre Founded in 1976 as an outgrowth of a street-theatre group called Indian Magique, located first in the Sixth Avenue Playhouse and since 1986 in the new Lyceum Theatres in Horton Plaza, the most prominent downtown theatre complex in San Diego. Multicultural and multidisciplinary in intent, its programs have five components: a six-play subscription season; the Calafia Initiative, a binational commissioning and producing project; Kuumba Fest and the Lipinsky Family San Diego Jewish Arts Festival (annual cultural festivals); community partnerships; and education programs. With numerous awards, the Rep in 30 seasons has produced more than 40 world premieres.   DBW

San Francisco From its gold-rush past to its cosmopolitan present, San Francisco has nurtured a freewheeling theatre culture marked by diversity and adventurousness.

Drama took root in the city in 1849, when California's legendary gold rush swelled the remote coastal outpost with fortune seekers from around the world. That year the city saw its first play: Sheridan Knowles's *The Wife*, enacted by members of Sacramento's EAGLE THEATRE at Washington Hall. Soon astute impresarios realized SF's droves of new settlers, most of them male and single, comprised an eager audience for theatre. From 1850 to 1859 more than 50 theatres were built (many soon lost to FIRES), and 1,100 performances of classical dramas, operas, MINSTREL SHOWS, and melodramas given. Though SF was still remote and rustic, artistic standards were surprisingly high; respected acting clans (the Chapmans of SHOWBOAT fame, the Starks) took up residence, and plucky stars (LOLA MONTEZ, Charles Kean) appeared. Top venues included the American

Theatre (erected in 1851), the Metropolitan (managed 1853–9 by Catherine Sinclair, ex-wife of EDWIN FORREST), and Maguire's Opera House (built in 1857 by THOMAS MAGUIRE, SF's leading producer). Chinese opera houses, CIRCUS structures, playhouses for French, Italian, and German drama, and Barbary Coast melodeons (cabarets) added to the entertainment mix. Mark Twain penned an occasional drama review, and young EDWIN BOOTH, LOTTA CRABTREE, and DAVID BELASCO honed their crafts.

The colorful, chaotic pioneer phase of SF theatre ended with the 1869 completion of the transcontinental railroad. More accessible now, SF by the mid-1870s was one of the largest, wealthiest, most culturally sophisticated U.S. cities. A short but lavish California silver boom yielded three important new theatres: the CALIFORNIA (1869), managed by JOHN MCCULLOUGH and LAURENCE BARRETT, with a superior STOCK COMPANY backing guest stars (Salvini, MODJESKA, Booth); the BALDWIN (1876), run by Maguire and Belasco, with JAMES O'NEILL as leading man; and the Grand (originally Wade's) Opera House (1876), soon a major opera/drama touring arena for Sarah Bernhardt, Enrico Caruso, and other titans.

Toward the century's end, stock drama gave way to touring "combinations" and the populist allure of variety and melodrama. The Bush Street Theatre was a linchpin of MICHAEL LEAVITT's early VAUDEVILLE circuit; Gustave Walter's huge Orpheum Theatre became a major vaudeville house in Morris Meyerfield's ORPHEUM THEATRE CIRCUIT. "Sensation" melodrama thrived at the Grand Opera House during Walter Morosco's 1890s reign. By 1900 only one decent stock company was left (the ALCAZAR), and the top drama venue was a SYNDICATE-controlled touring house, the Columbia.

In 1906 a ferocious earthquake destroyed much of the city, including more than a dozen theatres; only one minor facility, the Chutes, survived. Recovery was speedy, however: Within a year several houses had been rebuilt (the Orpheum, the New Columbia) and new ones added (the Colonial, the Davis), with more soon following. After 1910, half the theatres featured vaudeville; but in the next decade many vaudeville palaces would start showing movies, and "legit" drama outlets dwindled to a few – by 1919, principally the Columbia (later renamed the Geary), Cort, Alcazar, and Shubert (later the Curran).

From 1920 to 1950 SF remained a major tour stop for Broadway plays and visiting companies (e.g., the MOSCOW ART THEATRE Players, 1924), and in 1943 the San Francisco Civic Light Opera formed to produce big musicals with star leads; but during this era literary drama was kept alive mainly by the semiprofessional Little Theatres [see COMMUNITY THEATRE]. The Players Club (1912), founded by Reginald Travers, introduced new SHAW and O'NEILL plays to SF. In the 1930s the Theatre Union mounted topical dramas, the Wayfarers did the classics, and FEDERAL THEATRE PROJECT units produced plays, puppet shows (see PUPPETRY), and a hefty research study of SF theatre history. Later, the Interplayers (1946–68) showcased important new plays and classics.

A new dramatic chapter began in 1952 when San Francisco State College professors HERBERT BLAU and JULES IRVING founded the Actor's Workshop. This iconoclastic troupe was the most daring American regional theatre of its era, pursuing vigorous artistic goals in bold versions of innovative European plays. The company worked first in loft spaces and later at the downtown Marines Memorial Theatre; its stagings of *Blood Wedding, Caucasian Chalk Circle,* and *The Balcony* were especially praised. Despite great reviews and foreign touring, not enough subscribers or financial support were generated – due partly to the directors' unwillingness to curry favor with the rich. In 1965 they left to manage a new theatre at LINCOLN CENTER, and the Workshop soon disbanded.

The seeds had been sown for more resident drama, however. In 1959 R. G. Davis started the influential SAN FRANCISCO MIME TROUPE, a radical ensemble employing commedia dell'arte tactics in political satires like *L'Amant Militaire* (1967), which won a Special Obie ("for uniting theatre and revolution and grooving in the park"). Meanwhile, in 1966, flamboyant director WILLIAM BALL and his two-year-old AMERICAN CONSERVATORY THEATRE had relocated from Pittsburgh to SF's Geary Theatre. ACT's splashy stagings of modern masterworks (Pirandello's *Six Characters in Search of an Author*) and classics (Edmond Rostand's *Cyrano de Bergerac*), excellent rep company (PETER DONAT, Marsha Mason), and top-notch acting school attracted the support that eluded the Workshop; it became the city's flagship regional theatre.

From the mid-1960s to the '80s, social-artistic ferment and increased public arts funding catalyzed an explosion of nonprofit drama in SF. Several new resident Equity companies sprang up in satellite cities: the BERKELEY REPERTORY THEATRE (1968), Berkeley (now California) Shakespeare Festival (1974), and San Jose Repertory (1980). In SF a multiethnic plethora of "fringe" groups emerged, among them the Julian Theatre

(1965); the playwright-centered MAGIC (1967), which debuted major works by SAM SHEPARD; the EUREKA (1972; recently revived and refurbished); the Asian American Theatre Workshop (1973); and the gay-oriented THEATRE RHINOCEROS (1977). All began as "Equity Waiver" theatres, allowed to cast union actors without pay in houses with less than 100 seats. (In 1984, the union restricted this practice, resulting in many new Equity minicontracts.) Experimental theatre flourished, spurred on by GEORGE COATES, Chris Hardman, Soon 3, the Blake Street Hawkeyes, and other artists, and innovative venues including Intersection, Life on the Water, and Theatre Artaud.

The early 1980s also brought a resurgence of downtown commercial theatre. Carol Shorenstein Hays and her ex-partner JAMES NEDERLANDER revamped the venerable Orpheum, Golden Gate, and Curran theatres for the "Best of Broadway" series of touring musicals and plays. The Marines Memorial Theatre, Mason Street Playhouse, and Theatre on the Square also became active again.

Although a severe 1989 earthquake damaged ACT's Geary Theatre home and (along with economic recession) hurt other theatres as well, the service organization Theatre Bay Area, founded in 1976, counted over 100 drama groups in the SF region in 1991 and almost 400 by 2006, including numerous new small theatre groups in the past decade. The area claims today the third-largest concentration of Equity members in the country (after NYC and Chicago). Throughout its volatile history the city has displayed a flair for live drama and today continues to attract the creative artists to deliver it. MB

San Francisco Mime Troupe, The, had existed in embryonic form since 1955, but was founded in 1962 by R. G. Davis, who moved to SAN FRANCISCO in 1958 after several years of MIME study in Paris. Over the years it moved from silent mime to avant-garde Happenings to outdoor commedia dell'arte–styled performance and on to radical politics. This theatre COLLECTIVE, an expression of the members' social and political concerns, is based on the highly physical expression of commedia dell'arte and R. G. Davis's dance and mime training. This amplified aesthetic perfectly suits the outdoor venues in which the troupe performs for part of every year. In 1967 Joan Holden became resident playwright and subsequently wrote 30 plays for the company. Davis left the troupe in 1970; in 1975 his book on the first 10 years was published. In recent years the troupe has undertaken extensive touring in the U.S. as well as in Europe and in Central America, including the successful *I Ain't Yo' Uncle,* an African American deconstruction of UNCLE TOM'S CABIN. The year 2006 marked its 35th summer season of free park shows throughout the Bay area; 2004's offering was *Showdown at Crawford Gulch.* As that title suggests, the 21st century and the Bush presidency has led to plays focusing on the corporate takeover of the federal government, unprovoked U.S. military aggression, and terriorism used in a government fear campaign to seize assets for private financial gain. TL

Sánchez, Edwin (1955?–) Puerto Rican–born playwright who moved to NYC in the 1970s. Originally intent on becoming an actor, he switched to playwriting after realizing the limited roles for Latinos. As a member of CIRCLE REP he came to the attention of Milan Stitt, then chair of Yale's graduate playwriting program. Sánchez, without an undergraduate degree, was nonetheless accepted, completing his work in 1994. His first notable OFF-BROADWAY show, *Trafficking in Broken Hearts,* premiered at the ATLANTIC in 1994. Other works include *Clean* (1995, HARTFORD STAGE), *The Road* (1999, CSV Cultural Center, NYC), *Icarus* (2000, Bank Street Theater, NYC), and *Diosa* (2003, Hartford Stage), among others. Sánchez mixes streetwise vernacular with themes of race, class, and sexuality, focusing on such topics as hustling, a romantic relationship between a priest and a young boy, and AIDS. DanB

Sandbox, The, by EDWARD ALBEE was first produced on 15 April 1960 at The Jazz Gallery in NYC. It was revived OFF-BROADWAY at the Cherry Lane in 1962. The play places the image of the sandbox at the center of an absurdist critique of America's treatment of the elderly as well as of the contemporary American family. Two characters called Mommy and Daddy deposit Grandma in a sandbox and wait for her to die. She sits and complains about the treatment she has received from her overbearing daughter, gradually covering herself with sand, until a young man announces that he is the Angel of Death, come to take her. The play ends as Grandma congratulates the young man on his reading of his line. BCM

Sanderson [née Sackett], **Julia** (1887–1975) Actress-singer who made her Broadway chorus debut in 1902 and the next year was promoted from the chorus to the title role in *Winsome Winnie.* She remained a musical-theatre leading lady into the 1920s, after which she became a radio singer. Tiny and wide-eyed, she introduced, with

Donald Brian, JEROME KERN's first hit song, "They Didn't Believe Me," in *The Girl from Utah* (1914). JD

Sandow, Eugen [né Friedrich Wilhelm Müller] (1867–1925) German-born strongman, the first to parlay his physique into a commercial property. Having developed a body-building system based on individual muscle groups, he made his New York debut at the CASINO THEATRE, June 1893. His refusal to meet a challenge from Canadian champion Louis Cyr altered his reputation from strongman to showman of the physique. At the Chicago Columbian Exposition of 1893, FLORENZ ZIEGFELD glorified him with spectacular publicity and abbreviated costumes. Settling in England, Sandow promoted corsets, health oils, and physical-culture magazines until 1907; he died of pneumonia a few weeks after lifting a car out of a ditch. There was a 1994 biography by D. L. Chapman. LS

Santiago-Hudson, Ruben (1956–) Actor and director, he was part of the original cast of JELLY'S LAST JAM (1992) and received a Tony for Best Featured Actor in a Play for his work in AUGUST WILSON's *Seven Guitars.* He was also in the Broadway cast of Wilson's *Gem of the Ocean* (2004). Notable OFF-BROADWAY appearances include *East Texas Hot Links* at the PUBLIC THEATER in 1994, the title role in Shakespeare's *Henry VIII* at Central Park's Delacorte in 1997, and *Deep Down* at INTAR in 1998. Santiago-Hudson won an Obie for his ONE-PERSON play *Lackawanna Blues* (2001), which he later adapted into an award-winning film for HBO in 2005, directed by GEORGE C. WOLFE. DanB

Santley, Mabel see RENTZ–SANTLEY NOVELTY AND BURLESQUE COMPANY

Sargent, Epes (1813–80) Author of four plays who also made an impression as a critic. *The Bride of Genoa* (1837), an imitative verse tragedy, was written for JOSEPHINE CLIFTON. *Velasco,* based on *Le Cid,* was well received in America and later in London, where it opened the 1849–50 season at the Marylebone Theatre. Critics praised Sargent's theatrical effectiveness and his use of poetic language. With *Changes Makes Change* (1845) Sargent attempted to capitalize on the Downeast YANKEE, one Nathaniel Bunker. His five-act, blank-verse version of Bellini's *Norma,* entitled *The Priestess* (1855), was ambitious but not successful onstage. Two "Dramatic Pieces," as he called them – *The Candid Critic* and *The Lampoon* – reveal a dramatist's view of theatre and theatre reviewers. WJM

Sargent, Epes Winthrop (1872–1938) VAUDEVILLE critic. Born in Nassau and educated in Troy, NY, Sargent worked for the *Musical Courier* (1891–4) before joining LEANDER RICHARDSON's *New York Dramatic News* as vaudeville critic (1895–6). He wrote for *Metropolitan Magazine* (1896), switching to the *Morning Telegraph* in 1897 under the pen name Chicot. He changed jobs frequently: Pulitzer's *Evening World* (1903); VARIETY (1905–6); *Chicot's Vaudeville Weekly* (three issues); and the *New York Review* (1909). He spent much of the 1910s and '20s writing movie articles and some 350 screenplays before resuming his Chicot column in *Variety* from 1931 until his death. An astute observer of popular entertainment, Sargent was the first significant critic of vaudeville in America. TLM

Saroyan, William (1908–81) This Californian Armenian made his debut as a playwright with MY HEART'S IN THE HIGHLANDS (1939). Both the GROUP THEATRE and the THEATRE GUILD had a hand in its Broadway production, and although most playgoers were baffled by its loose allegorical form, the play received enough critical acclaim to establish Saroyan as the leading avant-garde playwright of the day. His next play, *The TIME OF YOUR LIFE* (1939), solidified his critical reputation by winning the Pulitzer Prize and the Drama Critics' Circle Award (the first time the two groups ever agreed on a choice). Saroyan rejected the Pulitzer Prize on the grounds that material awards were debilitating to the recipient. Now a modern American classic, *The Time of Your Life,* revived periodically in New York, has appeared on the bill of almost every professional regional theatre, pleasing audiences with its originality, imagination, wit, humanity, and local San Francisco color. Continuing to write for the stage through the late 1950s, Saroyan never again achieved the success of his first two plays, although amateur groups everywhere have produced his uncharacteristically conventional one-act play *Hello Out There* (1942). *The Beautiful People* (1941), directed by the playwright, and *The Cave Dwellers* (1957) found a brief audience and are occasionally revived, but his other works, including *Love's Old Sweet Song* (1940) and *Get Away Old Man* (1943), were quick failures. Much of Saroyan's later years were spent writing novels and autobiographical remembrances. The most recent biography is by John Leggett (2002). LDC

Savoy, Bert [né Everett McKenzie] (c. 1888–1923) FEMALE IMPERSONATOR. "Chair dancer" in a Boston dime museum, chorus boy, and passing as a female singer from Montana to Alaska, Savoy wound up in New York, where he teamed up with Jay Brennan (c. 1913). In their doubles act Brennan played a fey "feed" to Savoy's flamboyant red-haired tart, always talking about her girlfriend Margie. Savoy's brassy style and catchphrases – "You musssst come up," "You slay me," "You haven't heard the half of it, dearier," and "I'm glad you ast me" – may have inspired MAE WEST. The act, an eruption of homosexual subculture into the mainstream, earned $1,500 a week in VAUDEVILLE and REVUE: *The Passing Show of 1915, The* ZIEGFELD *Follies of 1918,* and *The Greenwich Village Follies* (1920–3). After Savoy was killed by a lightning bolt on Long Island beach, Brennan continued the act with other partners.   LS

Satz, Ludwig (1895–1944) Much-loved leading "star" comedian of the American YIDDISH THEATRE from 1918 until his death. Billed as "the man who makes you laugh with tears and cry with a smile," he was a master of characterization, improvisation, and makeup.   AB

Scarecrow; or, The Glass of Truth, The A "tragedy of the ludicrous" by PERCY MACKAYE. Published in 1908, it was first produced in 1910 at the Middlesex Theatre in Connecticut, and then on Broadway at the GARRICK THEATRE in 1911, where it ran for 23 performances. Staged by EDGAR SELWYN, players included Alice Fisher, Edmund Breese, Fola La Follette, Earle Browne, Brigham Royce, and Frank Reicher. It is considered the best of the early plays written by MacKaye. Set in late 17th-century Massachusetts, this symbolic drama in four acts carries the message of love as a redemptive force that triumphs over evil and deception.   NP

scenic design There is almost no documentation regarding the earliest efforts at scenic design in North America. Generally working in makeshift spaces, early theatrical ventures no doubt used some sort of improvised scenery, perhaps pressing easel painters into service to provide a backcloth or a curtain and wings. The few records that make any mention of scenery neither mention artists' names nor describe the decor. The first professional scenery in the colonies arrived with Lewis HALLAM SR.'s London Company of Comedians in Virginia in 1752; though the decor was advertised as newly built, it is generally believed that it came from their defunct London theatre. After a period in Jamaica, the troupe returned to the colonies in 1758 under the management of DAVID DOUGLASS and apparently without its scenic stock. In 1759 they opened the Society Hill

Theatre in PHILADELPHIA with a new stock of scenes created by easel painter William Williams. The next scene painter known by name is Jacob Snyder, who most likely joined Douglass's company in 1762. Descriptions of scenes by these painters mention "views" (most likely painted backdrops) and "transparent scenes." In 1765 and later, Douglass imported new scenery from England, including work by Nicholas Thomas Dall and John Inigo Richards, suggesting that the work of his American painters was inadequate.

Having spent part of the Revolution in Jamaica, Douglass's company, now know as the AMERICAN COMPANY and headed by Lewis Hallam Jr., returned to the States in 1784 with a French scene painter, Charles Busselotte, who was apparently skilled at stage machinery and shadow puppets (see PUPPETRY). Of the artists who came to America after the Revolution the two most notable were Luke Robbins and M. C. Milbourne. The former worked with the Old American Company and later as house artist for the PARK THEATRE in New York. THOMAS WIGNELL imported Milbourne, resident designer for Philadelphia's CHESTNUT STREET THEATRE (1793–6). He introduced topographical scenes to the American theatre and was one of the strongest influences on the development of American scenography. Milbourne, like many of the English emigrés, had worked at Covent Garden. A third major artist of the postcolonial period was the Italian-born Charles Ciceri, who came to the U.S. in 1793 and worked primarily at the Park Theatre. John Joseph Holland, master scene painter at the Chestnut Street Theatre from 1796, developed a major reputation and trained most of the significant American scenic artists of the first half of the 19th century.

The scenery of this period included topographical views, transparent scenes, and spectacular effects as described in a production of *The Tempest* in Richmond in 1791: "a troubled Horizon and Tempestuous Sea where the Usurper's Vessel is tossed a considerable time in sight . . . amidst repeated claps of Thunder, Lighting, Hail, Rain &c and being dashed on a Chain of Rocks. . . ." Stock scenery of this sort continued to travel with companies through the first half of the 19th century. The most significant development, however, was the introduction of gaslight (see STAGE LIGHTING).

First used for auditorium lighting at the Chestnut Street Theatre in 1816, gas lighting became increasingly common onstage in the next decade. Its increased brightness and evenness, as well as the ability to control its intensity, altered the entire approach to scene painting. Colors had to be subdued and the increasingly visible details made more realistic. The first use of overhead border lights may have occurred at the CHATHAM THEATRE in New York in 1827; their introduction allowed the light ladders in the wings to be abolished and opened the wings farther, providing the scenic artist greater possibilities.

Melodrama's popularity early in the 19th century necessitated scenery that would suggest exotic locales and allow for special effects. The increasingly cavernous theatres, especially in New York and Philadelphia, required large and grandiose scenery and depended upon spectacular effects such as fires, waterfalls, and earthquakes. While stock scenery sufficed at first, managers and audiences began to demand new scenery, leading to the emergence of the scenic artist as a dominant figure in American theatre.

Early in the 19th century a few scenic artists began to establish reputations and became attached to specific actor-managers or to specific theatres. Harry Isherwood, for example, worked with the company of JOSEPH JEFFERSON [I] during 1830–45, and Russell Smith was chief scenic artist for the Academy of Music in Philadelphia in midcentury. The most notable 19th-century scenic artist, however, was CHARLES W. WITHAM, who began painting scenes for EDWIN FORREST in BOSTON in 1863 but was soon hired as EDWIN BOOTH's primary painter. He is virtually the only artist of the latter half of the 19th century to receive notice from the critics; the evolution of his art suggests the course of American design of the period. Beginning with architectural settings for Booth, he evolved a more romantic style by the 1880s, and his last work showed the influence of realism.

Although a few dozen scenic artists are known by name, there is little detailed knowledge about their work or lives. In part this is due to the emergence in the last third of the 19th century of scenic studios (see SUPPORT SERVICES); these created scenery and decor for productions, generally without credit to individual artists. Also, it was not unusual for different scenes within a production to be designed by different artists, or for productions to mix stock and newly built decor.

As in Europe, the influence of antiquarianism upon the stage was great, and increasingly realistic and historically accurate details began to appear in the decor. The real impetus for antiquarianism came with the visit of Charles Kean for the 1845–6 season: Although his "illustrated Shakespeare" productions were still several years off, early attempts in that direction were visible here. A new mounting of *Richard III* stunned and delighted audiences with its magnificent scenery.

Kean's crusade was taken up by American actor-manager WILLIAM EVANS BURTON, who began mounting full stagings of Shakespeare in the 1850s (see SHAKESPEARE ON . . .), culminating in a historically accurate production of *A Midsummer Night's Dream* in 1854, for which scholarly citations were published in the program to legitimize his scenic decisions.

With the advent of gentlemanly melodrama, box sets and interiors came to dominate the legitimate stage. The wing and groove system for changing scenes became obsolete. At first, much of the detail for interiors was painted two-dimensionally on flats, but starting in the 1880s, notably in the productions of AUGUSTIN DALY, three-dimensional scenic pieces and architectural elements became more prominent. This trend reached its apex with the work of DAVID BELASCO at the turn of the century. Belasco's attention to the minutiae of decor, insistence on absolute accuracy, and innovations in lighting combined to create the most thorough illusionism seen in America, and possibly the world, to that time. So dominant was his influence that the style became known as "Belasco realism." Belasco, however, was the producer and director (and sometimes writer), not the designer. Although he worked with several artists, his most successful collaborations were with the now virtually forgotten Ernest Gros and electrician Louis Hartmann. Among Belasco's memorable productions were *The Governor's Lady* (1912), in which Childs Restaurant was completely reproduced on the stage, and *The Easiest Way* (1909), for which he purchased the actual furnishings of a cheap boardinghouse. This style of photographic realism could be found throughout the rest of the 20th century in productions such as ELMER RICE's *Street Scene,* designed by JO MIELZINER, or the GROUP THEATRE's production of CLIFFORD ODETS's *Awake and Sing!,* though rarely with Belasco's fervor. There was even a self-consciously ironic resurgence of photorealism in the 1970s, inspired by a movement of the same name in the art world. The PERFORMANCE GROUP's production of *Cops* (1978), designed by JAMES CLAYBURGH, and SANTO LOQUASTO's setting for DAVID MAMET's *American Buffalo* are notable examples.

The reaction to Belasco-style realism was the New Stagecraft, arguably the most significant development in 20th-century American theatre. Inspired principally by the work and writings of Edward Gordon Craig and Adolphe Appia – but also by the work of MAX REINHARDT, Oskar Strnad, and Georg Fuchs in Europe, as well as the work of Viennese emigré JOSEPH URBAN at the

Boston Opera beginning in 1911 – it led American designers to abandon detailed realism for simplified realism, suggestion, and abstraction. Scenery evolved from background and decoration to become an integral part of the production, often encapsulating the themes of the play in a metaphorical image. In addition to Craig's *The Art of the Theatre* (1905) and his monthly journal, *The Mask,* Americans were introduced to the new developments in European staging through Hiram Moderwell's 1914 book, *The Theatre of Today.* That same year, designer SAM HUME put together an exhibition of new designs from Europe that was seen in Cambridge and New York. Furthermore, the work of the Ballets Russes was becoming known, though the troupe would not visit for several more years. The first examples of the New Stagecraft were seen at Boston's Toy Theatre, founded in 1912 as one of the first of the U.S. Little Theatres (see COMMUNITY THEATRE), in the designs of LIVINGSTON PLATT, and at Maurice Browne's Little Theatre founded in CHICAGO in 1912.

However, the production generally acknowledged to mark the arrival of the New Stagecraft in America was *The Man Who Married a Dumb Wife* (1915), directed by British director Harley Granville Barker and designed by ROBERT EDMOND JONES. Unlike the dominant Belasco realism commonly found on Broadway, Jones's set was monochromatic and done in the style of a Japanese woodcut. The medieval costumes were in flat primary and secondary colors. Though this was a radical break with accepted practice, it did not create an immediate revolution in scenography. The true impact of the New Stagecraft began to be felt later that year when Jones teamed up with director ARTHUR HOPKINS on *The Devil's Garden* and the effectiveness of simplified realism became evident. Jones also began to work with the PROVINCETOWN PLAYERS. Related to the idea of simplification was the concept of the unit set, which Jones helped popularize. Jones's association with Hopkins over the succeeding decade, especially on the Shakespeare plays with John Barrymore (see DREW–BARRYMORE), and his designs for most of the major EUGENE O'NEILL plays established an ineluctable connection between the emergent American drama and production and the New Stagecraft. The simplicity of much of this style of stage decor also had economic benefits, and the New Stagecraft flourished in the burgeoning Little Theatre movement.

A second pillar of the New Stagecraft movement was LEE SIMONSON, who began designing with the WASHINGTON SQUARE PLAYERS and then with their successor, the THEATRE GUILD.

As designer of some half the productions of the Guild through the 1920s, Simonson was to be, through sheer volume alone, the most influential of the new designers. He championed the unit set and the "island" stage, in which a scenic unit sat in the midst of the stage surrounded by space; this was often accompanied by projected scenery on a cyclorama. The third pillar of the movement was NORMAN BEL GEDDES, whose collaboration with MAX REINHARDT on *The Miracle* (1924) and his several unrealized projects (for which plans and models were nonetheless constructed and well known) created a bold, theatrical, and uniquely American abstract style. Ironically, Bel Geddes's most successful Broadway design was in a photorealist style for DEAD END. Other significant designers of the New Stagecraft included HERMAN ROSSE, CLAUDE BRAGDON, CLEON THROCKMORTON, ROLLO PETERS, WOODMAN THOMPSON, Irving Pichel, and Robert R. Sharpe. The next generation of American designers began to emerge during the 1920s, including ALINE BERNSTEIN, DONALD OENSLAGER, Jo Mielziner, WATSON BARRATT, and MORDECAI GORELIK.

Though dozens of significant artists can be added to this list, the period of roughly 1920–60 is really dominated by five men: Jones, Simonson, Oenslager, Mielziner, and (from the mid-1940s onward) OLIVER SMITH. BORIS ARONSON is a presence from the late 1920s, but though he was eventually acknowledged as the most significant artist and greatest innovator of the American stage by peers, colleagues, and critics alike, his greatest commercial successes did not come until the 1960s, when he began to collaborate on a series of musicals with HAROLD PRINCE.

While the simplified realism of Jones and Simonson continued through the 1930s, as did naturalism and expressionism and a host of variations on these genres, a more lyrical and elegant style of design began to emerge in the 1930s, largely influenced by Oenslager. The style, best known as poetic or lyric realism, ultimately became associated most closely with Mielziner. Painted scenery resurfaced, often incorporating fanciful and fantastic images, decorative flourishes, and curved lines. In the 1940s, as symbolism and expressionism melded with American psychological realism in the plays of TENNESSEE WILLIAMS and in ARTHUR MILLER'S *DEATH OF A SALESMAN,* Mielziner found the perfect scenic solution to the flow of internal and external reality with the use of the scrim. This device also gave a soft and dreamlike feel to many scenes that emphasized mood over harsh reality. These same characteristics were picked up by Smith, though not always with the use of scrim, in such productions as *My Fair Lady* and *West Side Story*. The painterly, atmospheric setting was the dominant style in the post-WWII era. While the Oenslager–Mielziner approach was largely superseded in the 1960s, its essence reemerged in the 1970s – albeit with a different vocabulary – in the work of JOHN LEE BEATTY.

Although the Berliner Ensemble never visited the U.S., its work and that of several other German designers exerted a profound influence on a new generation of American directors and designers. Most notable among the designers was MING CHO LEE, who shaped a whole generation of American design in theatre and opera: His 1964 *Electra* for the NEW YORK SHAKESPEARE FESTIVAL is generally considered a turning point in postwar American scenography. The shift in design aesthetics was also shaped by the work of ROUBEN TER-ARUTUNIAN and Boris Aronson, who was finally getting his long-deserved recognition. The work of Lee and Ter-Arutunian in particular moved design from a moody, painterly style to a strongly sculptural, textured, and emblematic approach. Largely influenced by Aronson, constructivist elements, the symbolic use of color, and the introduction of new materials and technologies began to dominate the theatre. Through the 1980s, in the designs of Lee and Aronson as well as of Santo Loquasto, DOUGLAS SCHMIDT, MARJORIE KELLOGG, DAVID MITCHELL, ROBIN WAGNER, JOHN CONKLIN, and others, sets were typified by the use of metal and wood scaffolding, wooden-plank flooring, erosion cloth, collage, Mylar mirrors, emblematic scenic pieces, and, above all, a highly sculptural use of space. Significantly, as the quantity and, arguably, the quality, of traditional American playwriting diminished, most of these designers worked in opera and dance as much as in theatre. As a result, American design evolved as a vital force in the theatre of the time.

The renascent avant-garde theatre of the period also inspired design. One popular approach was environmental theatre, which sought to destroy the frontal and separate relationship of performer and spectator. Though with roots going back to the turn of the century, and with precedents in the Middle Ages and various forms of ritual theatre, the modern environment movement in America is associated with director RICHARD SCHECHNER and The Performance Group. His production of *Dionysus in 69* placed the audience on scaffolds shared with the performers, who also involved the audience in parts of the performance. EUGENE LEE's designs with ANDRE GREGORY and later with ADRIAN HALL encompassed the audience in various environments and scattered the performance throughout the auditorium or performance space. The introduction of environmental staging on Broadway in the early 1970s, especially in the Hal Prince production of *CANDIDE*, seemed to signal the end of the proscenium era, but it proved short-lived – though it did reemerge in the 1980s as a popular gimmick for certain instances of PARTICIPATORY THEATRE.

Two avant-garde theatre artists had a profound effect upon many designers: ROBERT WILSON and RICHARD FOREMAN. The former produced "operas" with large-scale and spectacular scenery in a symbolist–surrealist vein. Although Wilson designed most of his early work himself, his more recent work is often done in collaboration with designers like John Conklin and lighting designer JENNIFER TIPTON, thus creating a direct link with much contemporary theatre, opera, and dance production. Foreman too does much of his own design, though he has also worked in collaboration with Nancy Winter. His idiosyncratic work, which consciously refers back to Renaissance design, often manipulates perspective, alters spatial relationships, calls attention to the process of viewing, and juxtaposes objects and images from a wide range of sources simultaneously. This latter characteristic, together with the "ugliness" and homemade quality of much of his work, was a forerunner of postmodernism in American design.

Postmodernism, whose practitioners include ADRIANNE LOBEL, MICHAEL YEARGAN, ROBERT ISRAEL, GEORGE TSYPIN, John Conklin, and the work of the WOOSTER GROUP and James Clayburgh, is typified by a strong frontality, juxtaposition of dissociated images, quotations from historical productions and imagery, a visual irony, and a self-conscious opposition to "prettiness," among other things. While this style has been used in certain dramatic productions, notably at regional theatres such as the HARTFORD STAGE, AMERICAN REPERTORY THEATRE, and the LA JOLLA PLAYHOUSE, it is most common in opera production.

Although certain trends or design styles – whether lyric realism or postmodernism – may become the dominant forces in a particular period, certain tendencies continue. The bulk of mainstream American drama remains realistically based, and the selective realism first seen in the New Stagecraft is still, in one form or another, appropriate today. Moreover, despite a brief trend toward more minimal musicals, audiences still seem enthralled by glamor and spectacle; thus TONY WALTON's version of spectacle, though it may be grounded in a late-20th-century sensibility, is directly connected to the glamor and spectacle of the early part of the century.   AA*

Schary, Dore (1905–80) Playwright and producer. From stage actor to production head at Metro–Goldwyn–Mayer (1948), Schary became one of the most powerful men in Hollywood. After dismissal by MGM in 1956, he wrote and coproduced *Sunrise at Campobello*, which won four Tony Awards for the 1957–8 season. Several other plays by Schary were unsuccessful. He also coproduced and directed *The Unsinkable Molly Brown* (1960).   TLM

Schechner, Richard (1934–) Director, author, and educator who, as editor of *Tulane Drama Review* (now *The Drama Review*) (1962–9) and founder of the PERFORMANCE GROUP (1967–80), established himself as a leader of the new environmental theatre based on the ideas of Artaud and Grotowski. With the Performance Group he explored the nature of COLLECTIVE creation, audience participation, and theatrical language in *Dionysus in 69*, *Makbeth* (1969), and *Commune* (1970). Later he turned to primitive ritual and shamanism. In 1993 he created a new company (East Coast Artists) and first directed his version of Faust for the 1990s (*Faust/gastronome*), followed by *Fragments from Three Sisters* in 1995 (both initially at LA MAMA), *Hamlet* (1999), and *YokastaS Redux* (2005). Internationally renown as the founder of the academic field of performance studies, he has been a Professor of Performance Studies at NYU since 1967. His books include *Public Domain* (1968), *Environmental Theatre* (1973; 1995), *The Future of Ritual* (1993), *Performance Theory* (1985; 2003), *Between Theatre and Anthropology* (1985), and *Performance Studies: An Introduction* (2003). He became editor of *TDR* again in 1985.   TLM

Scheff, Fritzi [née Friedrike Jaeger] (1879–1954) Vienna-born lyric soprano and actress, Scheff made her Metropolitan Opera debut in 1901, where she was known as the "Little Devil of the Opera" because of her diminutive size, red hair, and fiery temper. On Broadway she starred in four VICTOR HERBERT operettas: *Babette* (1903), *Mlle. Modiste* (1905), *The Prima Donna* (1908), and *The Duchess* (1911), as well as several other comic operas and opéras bouffes. She appeared in VAUDEVILLE in the early 1920s, and later in the decade starred in several straight plays. In 1929 she received critical praise in a revival of *Mlle. Modiste*. She had a radio show for several years in the 1930s; her last Broadway appearance was in the benefit REVUE *The ANTA Album* (1950).   MK

Schenck, Joe see VAN, GUS

Schildkraut, Rudolph (1862–1930), and **Joseph Schildkraut** (1896–1964) Father and son actors. Rudolph, born in Constantinople, won fame playing such powerful roles as Lear in German, notably with MAX REINHARDT; he also made German films. While appearing in New York at the then–German-language Irving Place Theatre (1910), he first guest-starred in YIDDISH THEATRE as Shylock. He probably began on the Yiddish stage by speaking his lines in German, but eventually performed altogether in Yiddish, culminating in his best-known Yiddish role, SHOLOM ASCH's *God of Vengeance,* which he later played in English in a controversial Broadway production (1922).

Joseph performed in Yiddish with his father in his youth in New York. He studied theatre in Germany and performed with Reinhardt, but had his first starring role for the THEATRE GUILD. Thereafter he alternated between Broadway (*Liliom,* 1921; *The Firebrand,* 1924; *Uncle Harry,* 1942; *The DIARY OF ANNE FRANK,* 1955) and Hollywood (winning an Academy Award), as well as television. He was also a member of EVA LE GALLIENNE's CIVIC REPERTORY THEATRE in the early 1930s. His autobiography, *My Father and I,* appeared in 1959.   NS

Schisgal, Murray (1926–) This Brooklyn-born playwright had an auspicious start in British theatre – *The Typists, The Postman,* and *A Simple Kind of Love Story* (1960); however, *Luv* failed in London in 1963 before becoming a Broadway hit in 1964. Selected works produced in New York (primarily one-acters with clever dialogue): *Fragments* (1967, OFF-BROADWAY), *Jimmy Shine* (1968, Broadway), *Dr. Fish* (1970, Broadway), *Man Dangling* (1988, OFF-OFF). *Circus Life*, staged by Larry Arrick, was seen on THEATRE ROW in 1995. His awards include the Vernon Rice Award and the Outer Critics Circle Award (both 1963, for *The Typists / The Tiger*). He coauthored the film *Tootsie* (1982).   GSA

Schmidt, Douglas (1942–) American set and costume designer, most closely associated with large-scale, kinetic, multiscene musicals and operas that evoke an almost 19th-century sensibility. Schmidt is also capable of sculptural scenery and realistic detail. After graduating from Boston University he assisted MING CHO LEE and also designed at CINCINNATI PLAYHOUSE IN THE PARK; Lee's influence is very clear in his early work. Schmidt was resident designer for the Repertory Theater of LINCOLN CENTER during 1960–73. He has collaborated frequently with directors RICHARD FOREMAN, DES MCANUFF, Tom Moore, and JACK O'BRIEN. His Broadway productions include GREASE (1972), *Over Here!* (1974, Drama Desk Award, set design), the ill-fated *Nick & Nora* (1991), revivals of *42ND STREET* (2001) and *INTO THE WOODS* (2002, Drama Desk Award, set design), and *Sight Unseen* (2004), and he is projected to design *Princesses* fall 2007. He has also done several productions with the San Francisco Opera and other opera companies (*Porgy and Bess*, New York City Opera, 2000). AA

Schmidt, Paul (1933–99) Translator, playwright, critic, educator, actor, and poet who acted with the WOOSTER GROUP, wrote a stage adaptation of *Alice in Wonderland* directed by ROBERT WILSON with music by Tom Waits, and earned a Ph.D. from Harvard (in Slavic Literature), but is best known for his translations of BRECHT, CHEKHOV, Gogol, Genet, Marivaux, and Khlebnikov for such directors as ELIZABETH LECOMPTE, JOANNE AKALAITIS, Liz Diamond, and PETER SELLARS. The AMERICAN REPERTORY THEATRE staged his translations/adaptations of *Phaedra*, *The Bacchae*, *In the Jungle of Cities*, and *Uncle Vanya*. He wrote *Meyerhold at Work*, among other books, and his translations of Chekhov's plays were published in 1997. DBW

Schneemann, Carolee (1939–) PERFORMANCE ARTIST, painter, filmmaker, writer. A native of rural Pennsylvania and Vermont, Schneemann studied painting and sculpture at Columbia University (1958), the New School for Social Research, Bard College (B.A., 1959), and the University of Illinois (M.F.A., 1961). She cofounded Judson Dance Theatre and participated in Happenings, Fluxus events, and environmental and kinetic theatre pieces. Her work is characterized by research into archaic visual traditions, pleasure wrested from suppressive taboos, and the body of the artist in dynamic relationship with the social body. Her rituallike group performances, such as *Meat Joy* (1964), were influenced by Artaud, the Nouveaux Réalistes, abstract expressionism, Simone de Beauvoir, John Cage, and Wilhelm Reich. Her early, erotic film *Fuses* (1965; part of her "autobiographical trilogy" with *Plumb Line*, 1971, and *Kitch's Last Meal*, 1973–6) and such performances as *Up to and Including Her Limits* (1973–6) and *Interior Scroll* (1975) – including her kinetic sculpture/installation, *Cycladic Imprints* (1990) – are FEMINIST statements against the CENSORSHIP of women's self-representation. She was the recipient of a 1993 Guggenheim Fellowship. AF

Schneider, Alan (Abram Leopoldovich) (1917–84) Russian-born director, known as BECKETT's American interpreter. Schneider worked at Washington's ARENA STAGE (artistic director, 1952–3; acting producer, 1973–4), NYC's NEIGHBORHOOD PLAYHOUSE, and elsewhere across the U.S. Director of the Juilliard Theater Center (1976–9) and, at his death, a co–artistic director of the ACTING COMPANY, Schneider headed the graduate directing program at the University of California at San Diego and was president of the THEATRE COMMUNICATIONS GROUP, which initiated the annual Alan Schneider Director Award in 1986.

Schneider, who believed his main function was "to serve as the intermediary between the playwright and the actual stage production," directed premieres of Beckett's *Waiting for Godot* (1956, COCONUT GROVE), *Endgame* (1958), *Happy Days* (1961), *Play* (1964) (all Cherry Lane Theatre, NYC), and the movie *Film*, starring Buster Keaton (1965). He received a 1963 Obie for his direction of *The Pinter Plays* (*The Collection* and *The Dumbwaiter*), a 1963 Tony for ALBEE's *WHO'S AFRAID OF VIRGINIA WOOLF?*, and a 1977 Drama Desk Award for Preston Jones's *TEXAS TRILOGY*. He was also nominated for Best Director Tonys for three other Albee productions (1964, for *The Ballad of the Sad Café* adaptation; 1965, for *TINY ALICE*; 1967, for *A DELICATE BALANCE*) and in 1968 for ROBERT ANDERSON's *You Know I Can't Hear You When the Water's Running*. Schneider, killed in a traffic accident in London, left an autobiography, *Entrances: An American Director's Journal*, published in 1986. REK

Schreiber, (Isaac) **Liev** (1967–) Actor, born in San Francisco, raised in New York, son of an actor and a painter (who divorced when he was 4 or 5). Briefly a student at Hampshire College, he left to attend RADA in London and ultimately graduated from the Yale Drama School (1992). Winner of a Tony for his featured role of Richard Roma in the 2005 revival of *GLENGARRY GLEN ROSS*, the 6´ 3˝ Schreiber has been termed amazing and brilliant as an actor. BEN BRANTLEY categorized him as "the American theater's finest young interpreter of Shakespeare," always original even in tepid productions, such as the 2003 *Henry V* presented by Shakespeare in the Park at the Delacorte in Central Park. He fared better in PUBLIC THEATER or Delacorte productions as Sebastian in *The Tempest* (1995), Banquo in *Macbeth* (1998), Iachimo in *Cymbeline* (1998, Obie), Hamlet (1999), and especially as Iago in *Othello* (2001), praised as "an immensely complex character who can read others, but not himself." In summer 2006 he played Macbeth in Central Park. Other NYC stage credits include *In the Summer House* (1993), *The Mercy Seat* (2003, OFF-BROADWAY), and *Talk Radio* (2007). His film credits include *The Sum of All Fears* (2002), *The Manchurian Candidate* (2004), murderer Cotton Weary in all three *Scream* films (1996–2000), and the remake of *The Omen* (2006); he appeared as ORSON WELLES in *RKO 281* on HBO (1999). His brother Pablo is a talented actor.   DBW

Schuler, Duane (1950–) Wisconsin-born lighting designer, mentored by GILBERT V. HEMSLEY at the University of Wisconsin–Madison. His work has been seen at major regional theatres and opera companies nationwide. During 1974–8 he was resident lighting designer at the GUTHRIE, then held the same position at the Lyric Opera of Chicago. He is widely known and respected for his opera lighting designs but also designs for theatre, serves as a theatre consultant, and executes architectural lighting designs.   DBW

Schwartz, Arthur (1900–84) Composer, producer, and librettist, trained as a lawyer; his first songs were written for VAUDEVILLE. He contributed songs to several shows before teaming with lyricist HOWARD DIETZ on a series of sophisticated REVUES: *The Little Show* (1929), *The Second Little Show* (1930), *Three's a Crowd* (1930), *The Band Wagon* (1931), *Flying Colors* (1932), *Revenge with Music* (1934), and *At Home Abroad* (1935). Schwartz collaborated with lyricist DOROTHY FIELDS on *Stars in Your Eyes* (1939), *A Tree Grows in Brooklyn* (1951), and *By the Beautiful Sea* (1954), and reunited with Dietz on the revue *Inside U.S.A.* (1948) and the musicals *The Gay Life* (1961) and *Jennie* (1963). During 1939–46 he composed numerous songs for films. Schwartz was particularly adept at writing pensive, pulsating ballads, such as "You and the Night and the Music."   MK

Schwartz, Maurice (1890?–1960) Yiddish actor, producer, and director. At age 1, en route from the Ukraine to America, he was separated from his family and remained in London, where he later supported himself and attended the new YIDDISH THEATRE. In America he became an amateur actor and then a professional, soon making a name for his fire and panache. In 1918–19 in New York he organized the YIDDISH ART THEATRE and managed to keep it going, most seasons, until 1950. Among its most successful productions were *The Brothers Ashkenazi* (1937) and *Yoshe Kalb* (1932; Broadway, 1933), both by I. J. Singer, and *Shylock's Daughter* (1947, by Zahav), as well as Yiddish classics and translations of classics from other cultures. Not only was Schwartz personally famous as an actor – in Sholom Aleichem's *Tevye the Dairyman*, for example, onstage and in film (1939) – he

was also an institution through his Yiddish Art Theatre, which, whether on 2d Ave., on tour, or in temporary disarray, seemed the last bastion of Yiddish theatre's energy, color, and sustained intellectual aspirations. Schwartz was still touring till the year he died.   NS

Schwartz, Stephen (1948–) Composer-lyricist. After studying at Juilliard and Carnegie Institute of Technology, Schwartz wrote the title song for the play *Butterflies Are Free* (1969). While still at Carnegie Tech he had written the score for GODSPELL, a musical based on St. Matthew's Gospel, which opened OFF-BROADWAY in 1971 and ran for five years before moving to Broadway for a sixth. Among Schwartz's other Broadway scores are those for *Pippin* (1972), *The Magic Show* (1974), *Working* (1978), the ill-fated *The Baker's Wife* (1976; reclaimed regionally 2001, 2005), *Rags* (1986; 1991, AMERICAN JEWISH THEATRE), and the hit WICKED (2003). He also wrote the lyrics for LEONARD BERNSTEIN's *Mass* (1971). Schwartz's shows are notable for their unusual subject matter and the contemporary rock style of his scores.   MK

Scott, George C(ampbell) (1927–99) Film and stage actor and director, noted for a strong artistic integrity and intense acting style. His first stage appearance was at the University of Missouri after WWII. After playing some 150 roles in STOCK COMPANIES, Scott made his New York debut as Richard III in the NEW YORK SHAKESPEARE FESTIVAL (1957). He received excellent response to *Children of Darkness* (1958) at CIRCLE IN THE SQUARE Downtown. Alternating stage work with an outstanding film career, he also appeared there as Ephraim Cabot in DESIRE UNDER THE ELMS (1963). A later success on Broadway was *Sly Fox* (1976), based on Ben Jonson's *Volpone*. Although noted for his dramatic intensity, Scott directed and starred in Noël Coward's *Present Laughter* in 1982, directed *Design for Living* in 1984, and directed and starred in OSBORN's *On Borrowed Time* in 1991, all at Circle in the Square. He refused in 1971 to accept the Academy Award for Best Actor in the title role of *Patton* (one of his 50 films). Scott also appeared with the NYSF playing Antony (1959) and Shylock (1962). His last stage play was the NATIONAL ACTORS THEATRE's 1996 revival of *Inherit the Wind* (as Drummond opposite CHARLES DURNING's Brady). **Campbell Scott**, one of his sons with COLLEEN DEWHURST, is also a director and actor (Pericles at the PUBLIC THEATER, 1991).   SMA

Scott, Harold (1935–2006) Actor, producer, educator, and director born in Morristown, NJ, educated at Phillips Exeter Academy and Harvard; recipient in 1995 of the LLOYD RICHARDS Director's Award from the National Black Theatre Festival for his "profound contribution to black theatre." As an actor in the 1960s he was an original company member of the Repertory Theater of LINCOLN CENTER and appeared in *Marco Millions* and *The Changeling* (both 1964). His OFF-BROADWAY debut was in *The Death of Bessie Smith* (1961). However, it is directing that was most prominent in his career, including a stint as artistic director of the CINCINNATI PLAYHOUSE and six years with the EUGENE O'NEILL MEMORIAL THEATER CENTER's National Playwrights' Conference. He directed Avery Brooks on Broadway in *Paul Robeson* (1988 and 1995) and as King Lear at the YALE REP (2004); and Off-Broadway in 1989 he directed Esther Rolle in ROUNDABOUT's 25th-anniversary production of *The Member of the Wedding* (later seen at the JOHN F. KENNEDY CENTER and on PBS). Scott directed for numerous regional theatres as well as for NYC nonprofit venues.   DBW

Seattle Also known as the Emerald City, Seattle lies on the eastern shore of Puget Sound in northwestern Washington State. Settled in 1851, it is part of the region's largest metropolitan area (Seattle–Tacoma–Bellevue, population of 3.2 million in 2005) and claims one of the most active theatre communities west of the Mississippi. Seattle's theatre history can roughly be delineated into four periods: the stock and vaudeville era; an academic and resident-company era of mingled artistic, political, and entertainment impulses; the 1960s renaissance; and a major readjustment phase beginning in the mid-1990s. Affiliation between academic and professional theatre developed during the middle two periods, evolving into a supportive cross-fertilization.

Formal entertainment spaces coincided with Seattle's industrial beginning, when Henry Yesler, later mayor, built Yesler Hall (1861), replacing the makeshift space in his sawmill's dining hall (1852). Official recognition followed in an 1865 ordinance taxing "theatrical exhibitions." Entertainment halls such as Yesler's Pavilion (1865) and Plummer's Hall (1859) multiplied, primarily offering MINSTREL SHOWS, ventriloquists, and "variety acts."

The year 1870 brought traveling companies, the first major group, Fanny Morgan Phelps's troupe, visiting in 1875. "Opera houses," STOCK COMPANY venues, appeared relatively late in Seattle, as in much of the West Coast, but by 1880 Squire's Opera House (1879) and others regularly housed touring shows.

On 6 June 1889, a 25-block FIRE left only the 600-seat Turner Hall (1886), once considered the finest on the West Coast, and Armory Hall (1888), never a full-time theatre. Owners rebuilt within months, the Standard (1888) reopening in November after five months' tent operation.

The 1898 Klondike gold rush and resulting boom prompted a surge in entertainment houses but left theatre behind: During 1899–1901 no stock companies booked into Seattle. In 1902 the Seattle Theatre (1892) and the Third Avenue Theatre (1896), amid 10 VAUDEVILLE houses, began an upswing that peaked in 1909.

Road show and vaudeville energy increased, as syndication made Seattle the base for three national figures. John Cort arrived in 1887 from Illinois and built the first electrically lighted theatre, the second Standard, a year later; this postfire Standard introduced matinees. In 1898 he formed The Fraternal Order of Eagles as an association of theatre managers. By 1890 he held theatre leases in every major town along the Northern Pacific Railroad, effectively shutting out the KLAW–ERLANGER trust. In 1910, he formed the National Theatre Owners' Association with 1,200 theatres and effectively excluded both Klaw–Erlanger and the SHUBERTS from the West Coast.

John Considine came to Seattle from Chicago in 1889 and built People's Theatre (1891). Forming a partnership with Timothy Sullivan in New York, he opened the Coliseum (1907), the largest theatre west of the Mississippi. Seattle quickly became the main office of Sullivan–Considine, the first popularly priced transcontinental vaudeville circuit.

Alexander Pantages arrived from Alaska in 1902 and opened the Crystal (1902), also a vaudeville house. Through keen audience assessment and a strategy that included duplicating his competitors' billings at half admission, Pantages controlled theatres through half the country by 1911 and was able to offer a 50–60-week tour.

La Petite (1902), Seattle's first moviehouse, signaled the end of the era, however. The Odeon chain appeared in 1907, and by 1915 lower overhead and admission had nearly finished the stock and vaudeville houses. By then Considine was ruined. Cort had left for New York, and Pantages operated from Los Angeles.

In 1914, Nellie C(entennial) Cornish founded The Cornish School, the transition from road and vaudeville dominance to the resident companies of the second period. Cornish promoted the arts vigorously and precipitated the enduring connection between academic theatre and professional theatre. With faculty including Martha Graham,

John Cage, Alexander Koiransky, Ellen Van Volkenburg, and Maurice Browne, she attempted to bring an "Eastern" notion of the arts to Seattle, producing such figures as Merce Cunningham and Elena Miramova. The school remains a successful performing-arts conservatory.

In 1922, Cornish hired Florence and Burton James to expand her school's theatre program. The Jameses enhanced its already strong reception, producing both classic and contemporary American and European works. After a 1928 CENSORSHIP dispute, the Jameses resigned to form the Seattle Repertory Playhouse (SRP). On the model of New York's THEATRE GUILD, SRP subsidized its first and later seasons through subscription sales. After renting for two years, they built a 342-seat structure in 1929. For 23 seasons, SRP produced classical and contemporary European plays and American plays from the works of O'NEILL and ODETS to contemporary hits and original scripts. They built the first revolve in the Northwest for IBSEN's *Peer Gynt,* the play's fifth presentation nationally.

In 1935, with FEDERAL THEATRE PROJECT subsidy, SRP sponsored the Negro Repertory Company (NRC), the nation's second most productive black troupe. NRC emphasized script creation and adaptation by its members, resulting in productions of *Lysistrata* and an original REVUE, *Swing, Gates, Swing.*

SRP's success coincided with increased community impact by the University of Washington School of Drama, chaired from 1930 by Glenn Hughes, who featured popular Broadway material. With WPA subsidy, Hughes built the Penthouse Theatre (1940), the nation's first permanent arena theatre. Originally designed by John Ashby Conway and Hughes to be movable, the 172-seat structure was relocated in 1991 after 51 years' continuous use. Although Hughes intended the theatre as a laboratory for film acting, BROOKS ATKINSON called it "the finest arena theatre in America."

Commitment to working-class theatre and productions of Peters and Sklar's *STEVEDORE,* O'Neill's *The HAIRY APE,* and Odets's *WAITING FOR LEFTY* brought SRP conservative attack in 1947. The Jameses' contempt convictions by a state un-American activities committee brought financial collapse in 1951. Hughes immediately acquired SRP's building for his department, and it is presently named for him.

Growing movie popularity during the 1930s completed the 15-year vaudeville and roadhouse decline. The Cornish School, the Seattle Repertory Playhouse, and Hughes's School of Drama, however, sustained and stimulated an active Seattle theatre environment through the Depression.

The 1962 Seattle World's Fair furnished the SEATTLE REPERTORY THEATRE Company (1963; no relation to the SRP) a site and marked Seattle's theatrical rebirth. The Rep's 1990 Tony for Outstanding Regional Theatre acknowledged its aggressive development of new works by major playwrights. The energy of the period persists in such groups as A CONTEMPORARY THEATRE, INC. (1965); The Bathhouse Theatre (1970), an ensemble group; The EMPTY SPACE (1970); Intiman Theatre (1972), a classics-based organization; SEATTLE CHILDREN'S THEATRE (1975), the nation's second-largest CHILDREN'S THEATRE company; and The Annex Theatre (1978), which supports new actors, directors, and playwrights.

Interest-specific companies have also appeared, appealing to audiences restricted or broad-based. Northwest ASIAN AMERICAN Theatre (1972) continues as the nation's second-oldest such company, following its merger with Theatre Off Jackson; On The Boards (1979) supports regional and national PERFORMANCE ART; and New City/Theatre Zero (1982) has presented more than 100 world or regional avant-garde premieres.

Seattle's historic theatre buildings disappeared at an increasing rate as victims of development in the early 1990s. The multimillion-dollar restoration of the 60-year-old Paramount Theatre was a notable exception, reopening in 1995 with the London-company production of *MISS SAIGON.*

The growing software- and technology-based industries provided a middle-class audience willing to support the arts during regional economic reverses in the 1970s, and local economic vitality allowed Seattle's theatre community to ride out the late-1980s recession. The group Patrons of Northwest Civic, Cultural and Charitable Organizations (PONCHO, 1963) has generated millions of dollars, the vast majority supporting performing arts. Other groups supported a corporate 1% arts subsidy that added stability. By 1995 escalated competition decreased the percentage available from state-mandated arts and cultural funds derived from the local hotel and motel tax and from a 1% reserve on public construction budgets, both major innovated funding sources. The downturn of the technology and aerospace industries beginning in the late 1990s forced the theatre community's fourth phase, as several companies disappeared and others struggled through near-insolvency, meeting increasing deficits with staff and season reductions. Despite the 2003 bankruptcy of the Seattle Fringe Festival and the effect of that on participating groups, together with the disappearance of some widely regarded medium-range companies, a community of more than 50 fringe and 29 mainstream professional organizations suggests a positive long-term theatre climate in Seattle, though further attrition remains possible.   RW*

Seattle Children's Theatre Founded in 1975 as the Poncho Theatre; today one of the largest CHILDREN'S THEATRE company in the U.S. Operating from its own facilities under the leadership of Linda Hartzell (since 1985), the theatre produces professional theatre for children of all ages. SCT has an extensive outreach program, including drama workshops, a year-round drama school for students ages 3–19, and a deaf youth drama program. A main contribution of the theatre has been the commission, development, and publication of original scripts. In 2004 SCT and the CHILDREN'S THEATRE COMPANY in Minneapolis formed a partnership to create Plays for Young Audiences (PYA), which provides a centralized clearinghouse for licensing rights of scripts written for children and youth.   MVW

Seattle Repertory Theatre Founded in SEATTLE in 1963 by STUART VAUGHAN in a building erected for the 1962 World's Fair, the company met financial difficulties in its early days; by 1969–70 their deficit was more than a quarter million dollars. W. Duncan Ross was appointed managing director at that time; six years later the company had 22,000 season subscriptions. In 1974 SRT leased a second building, called Stage 2, for an added season of five plays, reduced to three in 1986 following a 10-year period of change. In 1979 Ross left and was replaced by DANIEL SULLIVAN, who, two years later, became artistic director. Sullivan continued previous policy, but added a New Plays workshop (four scripts each spring) and began to employ more local actors.

Since 1985, Benjamin Moore, formerly of the AMERICAN CONSERVATORY THEATER, has held the managing director post, leading the company through its 1990 Tony for Outstanding Regional Theatre. In 2005 DAVID ESBJORNSON joined SRT as artistic director, succeeding Sharon Ott (1997–2005).

In 1983 the company opened the 850-seat Bagley Wright Theatre at the Seattle Center, which also contains the 123-seat PONCHO Forum for new works. The Wright initially presented a six-play season, balancing classics, contemporary works, and premieres of new plays, reduced to five in 1996. In early 1994 the SRT presented the West Coast premiere of MAMET's *Oleanna*. SRT

opened its $8.7 million 286-seat Leo K(reielsheimer) Theatre in 1997), replacing the Forum as its second stage.   SMA   RW*

Second City, The Over the years, the work of this CHICAGO comedy institution has had an incalculable effect on the nature of satire in American theatre, radio, television, and film. At the very least, it has trained dozens of our most successful performers, such as ALAN ALDA, ALAN ARKIN, Ed Asner, Dan Aykroyd, John Belushi, Shelley Berman, Peter Boyle, John Candy, Valerie Harper, Robert Klein, LINDA LAVIN, Shelley Long, ELAINE MAY, Paul Mazursky, Ann Meara, Bill Murray, MIKE NICHOLS, Gilda Radner, Joan Rivers, Paul Sand, Avery Schreiber, Martin Short, David Steinberg, Jerry Stiller, George Wendt, Dan Castellaneta, Amy Sedaris, Tim Meadows, and Fred Willard. More significantly, the company's approach to character, scene, and performance has arguably become the dominant mode of American comic acting.

Ironically, this theatre, known for spontaneity and ensemble, traces its beginnings to the theories of a single person. Viola Spolin, author of the popular *Improvisation for the Theater* (revised 1983) and other texts, got started as a recreational director inventing games for inner-city Chicago children in the 1920s and '30s. Spolin's methods for eliciting spontaneous behavior – based in part on the theories of Stanislavsky – were passed on to her son, PAUL SILLS. The idea for the first improvisational theatre came from David Shepherd, a Sills classmate at the University of Chicago. The two had directed a progressive repertory company called Playwrights Theatre Club, with which Shepherd quickly grew dissatisfied, wanting instead to create a theatre in the spirit of both commedia dell'arte and German cabaret. With a company developed and selected through theatre-game workshops led by Spolin, Sills and Shepherd opened the Compass Players in 1955. Four years later, Sills joined forces with Bernard Sahlins and Howard Alk to found The Second City, which met with immediate success.

In subsequent years, The Second City toured, opened new companies in Toronto (which then launched the popular SCTV series) and other cities, and was copied everywhere (most notably on NBC's *Saturday Night Live*). The basic format has remained the same: Half a dozen actors on a mostly bare stage perform a series of skits satirizing the city's politics and cultural life. A piano player (for many years Fred Kaz) accompanies an occasional comic ditty, and provides mood and interlude music. For the main show, the skits are predominantly set routines, but they are derived from improvisations worked up from audience suggestions at late-night sessions. The program changes two or three times each year. By its 40th anniversary in 1999 there were operations in other cities, touring units, and training centers in New York, LOS ANGELES, and Chicago.

From its beginnings, the question has always been this: Is The Second City successful because of the inborn talent of its improvisers, or are the individuals successful because the system works? Spolin and Sills would explain that the system depends on inborn talent, which the system unlocks. Critic Jeff Sweet adds that The Second City represents one of two major streams in modern American theatre – the other being the "Method" of the ACTORS STUDIO.   SF

Second Stage Theatre New York nonprofit theatre founded by director Carole Rothman and actress (and producer) Robyn Goodman in 1979 to give "second stagings" to contemporary American plays that originally failed to find an audience for some reason (a format followed less frequently in recent years). Beginning as a small operation in a 99-seat house in an Upper West Side hotel, then building in 1984 a permanent home on Broadway at 76th Street (108-seat McGinn–Cazale Theatre, now 2ST's site for its New Plays Uptown series), it has as of 1999 established its "second" home, the 296-seat The Theatre@43rd Street designed by architect Rem Koolhaas (a converted historic bank building). The new space has allowed 2ST to expand its offerings, continuing second stagings and adding more opportunities for emerging playwrights. Its productions to date number over 100. It has also become a home base for midcareer directors such as MARK BROKAW, SCOTT ELLIS, and GRACIELA DANIELLE.   DBW

Secret Garden, The Historically significant 1991 production of a musical play led by a creative team of women. With 706 performances at the ST. JAMES THEATRE, this version of Frances Hodgson Burnett's all-time favorite children's story (1911) recounts how the orphan Mary Lennox (Daisy Eagan, the youngest Tony Award winner) comes to live with her Uncle Archie (MANDY PATINKIN) in Yorkshire, discovers her deceased Aunt Lily's (REBECCA LUKER) abandoned garden, and, by restoring it, brings the family back together. For the first time, a Broadway musical was led by women: HEIDI LANDESMAN, producer and set designer; MARSHA NORMAN, book and lyrics; Lucy Simon, music; Susan H. Schulman, director; THEONI ALDREDGE, costume designer;

William Gillette as Captain Thorne/Lewis Dumont in the famous telegraph scene of *Secret Service,* 1896. *Courtesy:* Laurence Senelick Collection.

and THARON MUSSER, lighting designer. It garnered three Tonys in all, including Best Featured Actress in a Musical, Book (Musical), and Scenic Designer.   DBW

Secret Service A four-act Civil War melodrama by WILLIAM GILLETTE, first seen on 13 May 1895 in PHILADELPHIA with Maurice Barrymore (see DREW–BARRYMORE) in the central role of the Union spy. After radical revision, the play opened in New York on 5 October 1896 with Gillette as Captain Thorne/Lewis Dumont, a part Gillette played 1,791 times. Gillette's best play, it focuses on the rival claims of patriotism and love. The high point is a suspenseful scene in a telegraph office, full of superficial realism, in which the spy is in constant danger of exposure. In 1976 the play was revived by the PHOENIX THEATRE Company in NYC (with JOHN LITHGOW, MERYL STREEP, and MARY BETH HURT) and was later televised.   DBW

Segal, Vivienne (1897–1992) Actress-singer. Originally trained in opera, Segal became, following her Broadway debut in 1915, a leading musical-theatre performer, appearing as the ingenue in such musical comedies as *Oh, Lady! Lady!* (1918) and later as the coloratura heroine of romantic operettas, notably *The Desert Song* (1926). Ten years after that performance, she turned to playing sultry older women, most memorably Vera in *Pal Joey* (1940, 1952) and Morgan Le Fay in the 1943 revival of *A Connecticut Yankee*.   JD

Seldes, Gilbert (1893–1970) Critic of popular culture, Seldes worked as a journalist, editor, and drama critic before writing *The 7 Lively Arts* (1924), a defense of popular over highbrow culture in America. His *The Great Audience* (1950) and *The Public Arts* (1956) discussed the impact of popular culture upon society. Seldes headed television programming for CBS during 1937–45, and was Dean of the University of Pennsylvania's Annenberg School of Communications during 1959–63. Michael Kammen wrote a study of Seldes in 1996.   TLM

Seldes, Marian (1928–) Actress, director, and teacher; daughter of critic Gilbert Seldes; second wife of Garson Kanin (married 1990). One of the great ladies of the stage. A member of the theatre and dance faculties at the Juilliard School during 1967–91, Seldes, an award-winning actress trained in her teens at the Neighborhood Playhouse, appeared in the complete Broadway runs of *Equus* (1974) and *Deathtrap* (1978). Originally a dancer, the tall, regal, articulate Seldes is considered an actor's actor. Noteworthy roles Off-Broadway in Howe's *Painting Churches* (1983–4), Win Wells's *Gertrude Stein and a Companion* (1985–6), and Albee's *Three Tall Women* (1994–5; assumed lead summer 1995), have brought her acclaim. Since 1996, she has added more than a dozen major credits to her résumé, including *Ring Round the Moon, The Butterfly Collection, 45 Seconds from Broadway, The Play about the Baby, Play Yourself, Dinner at Eight,* and *Beckett/Albee* (one-acts with Brian Murray). With Angela Lansbury she appeared in McNally's *Deuce* in 2007 (Music Box). Seldes is the author of an unusual theatre memoir, *The Bright Lights* (1978; revised 1984), a superb analysis of the chemistry of acting, and the novel *Time Together* (1981). She won a Best Featured Actress Tony in 1967 (*A Delicate Balance*), was inducted into the Theatre Hall of Fame in 1996, and received a 2001 Obie for Sustained Achievement.   DBW

Self Satire on New York City society, produced by William Burton at Burton's Chambers Street Theatre; ran for 18 performances, beginning 27 October 1856. Burton also played the part of John Unit, a Yankee character whose homespun good sense rights the wrongs caused by the extravagant Apex family and proves the honesty of his niece, Mary. Owing much to Mowatt's *Fashion, Self* was written by Sidney Frances Cowell Bateman, an actress who married into a theatrical family. She assumed management of the Lyceum Theatre in London when her husband died, and continued as manager of Sadler's Wells until her death in 1881.   FB

Sellars, Peter (1957–) Controversial director who had staged more than 100 productions by the age of 27; as a Harvard undergraduate he directed *The Inspector General* for the American Repertory Theatre (1980–1). After one year as artistic director of the Boston Shakespeare Company (1983–4), Sellars became head of the short-lived American National Theatre (ANT) Company at the John F. Kennedy Center in Washington, DC, a post he left in 1986, becoming head of the Los Angeles Festival and serving as artistic advisor of the Boston Opera Theater, both in 1990. Among Sellars's ambitious and controversial productions have been Handel's *Orlando* (1982); Brecht's *The Visions of Simone Machard* (1983, La Jolla Playhouse); a Gorky–Gershwin melange at the Guthrie called *Hang On to Me* (1984); *The Count of Monte Cristo* (1985) and Sophocles' *Ajax* (1986), both for the ANT (the latter featuring a Rambo-type Vietnam general gone cuckoo); Mozart's *Magic Flute* at Glyndebourne (1990) in a contemporary American setting; Aeschylus' *The Persians* at the Los Angeles Festival (1993) in a new translation by Robert Auletta; an updated and transplanted (to the multicultural world of Venice, CA) *The Merchant of Venice* at Chicago's Goodman Theatre (1994); and in 2003 at ART Euripides' *The Children of Herakles*, in which he gave speaking roles to actual refugee children. After being fired as the original director of Broadway's *My One and Only* in 1983, he received the same week an unsolicited "genius" grant from the MacArthur Foundation. Since the late 1980s he has concentrated on opera, on both sides of the Atlantic, including premiere productions of the contemporary operas by John Adams, *Nixon in China, The Death of Klinghoffer, El Niño,* and *Dr. Atomic;* an iconoclastic 1989 Mozart trilogy (*Don Giovanni* set in a crime-ridden ghetto, *Figaro* in the Trump Tower, and *Così fan tutte* in Despina's Cape Cod diner); a *Tannhäuser* in Chicago staged as the sexual scandal of a television evangelist; the 1995 *I Was Looking at the Ceiling and Then I Saw the Sky* by Adams and poet June Jordan ("opera for the people," "story told in song"); Tang Xianzu's Ming dynasty opera *The Peony Pavilion*. In 1998 he received the Erasmus Prize for his work combining European and American cultural traditions in opera and theatre. In 2001 his unpopular choices led to his resignation as artistic director of the Adelaide (Australia) Festival.   DBW

Selwyn, Archibald (1877?–1959), and **Edgar Selwyn** (1875–1944) Producers. After an early career as actor and playwright (1896–1911), Edgar, with his brother Arch, organized a play brokerage business, which merged with that of ELISABETH MARBURY and John W. Rumsey to form the American Play Company. After successfully producing *Within the Law* (1912), starring JANE COWL, they formed Selwyn and Company (1914) and produced such hits as *Fair and Warmer* (1915), *WHY MARRY?* (1917), *Smilin' Through* (1920), *The Circle* (1921), and *Romeo and Juliet* (1923). They dissolved the company in 1924 but continued to produce independently. Arch brought Noël Coward, GERTRUDE LAWRENCE, Diana Wynyard, BEATRICE LILLIE, and others to Broadway. Edgar was successful with *Gentlemen Prefer Blondes* (1926) and *STRIKE UP THE BAND* (1930). They built three theatres in New York (the Selwyn, the APOLLO, and the Times Square) and two in CHICAGO (the Selwyn and the Harris). In 1916, together with Samuel Goldwyn, they organized Goldwyn Pictures Corporation (later MGM), where Edgar wrote and directed films. The Selwyns – not innovators but astute judges of public taste – gave the public what it wanted.   TLM

Serban, Andrei (1943–) Romanian-born director. Immigrating to the U.S. in 1969, he staged *Arden of Faversham* at LA MAMA ETC (1970) and, after a year with PETER BROOK, *Medea* (1972; Drama Desk Award), *The Trojan Women,* and *Electra* (1974), using music by ELIZABETH SWADOS and obscure languages. He received an Obie for this *Trilogy,* reviving it in Iran (1975), outdoors in France (1976), and again at La MaMa (1978). He soon became one of the prominent figures in contemporary American theatre, with productions of BRECHT's *The Good Woman of Setzuan* (La MaMa, 1975); a controversial comic interpretation of CHEKHOV's *The Cherry Orchard* in an all-white setting (Tonys for costumes and lighting) and *Agamemnon,* both at the VIVIAN BEAUMONT in 1977; *The Ghost Sonata* (at YALE REP, where he worked 1977–8); for NEW YORK SHAKESPEARE FESTIVAL, *Happy Days* and *The Umbrellas of Cherbourg* (1979) and *The Seagull* (1980); *The Marriage of Figaro* (GUTHRIE THEATER, 1982); *Uncle Vanya* (La MaMa, 1983, with JOSEPH CHAIKIN); *Cymbeline* (NYSF at Delacorte, 1998); *The Caucasian Chalk Circle* (LaMaMa, 1998); *Hamlet* (NYSF, 1999). He has worked at the AMERICAN REPERTORY THEATRE for more than

two decades: Gozzi's *The King Stag* and an adaptation of *The Love of Three Oranges* (1984); Philip Glass and Robert Moran's *The Juniper Tree* (1985); RIBMAN's *Sweet Table at the Richelieu* (1987); Gozzi's *The Serpent Woman* (1988); *Twelfth Night* (1989); *Pericles* (2003). He has also staged operas for the Juilliard American Opera Center, the New York City Opera, The Met (debut 2003, Berlioz's *Benvenuto Cellini*), and abroad. His productions are noted for "their minimalism and simplicity of detail" and transform "the spoken word into . . . emotive music," treating "speech as sound rather than as language." While continuing to direct in the West, he became head of Romania's National Theatre (1990–3); in 1992 he was appointed director of the OSCAR HAMMERSTEIN II Center for Theatre Studies at Columbia University and now heads its M.F.A. acting program.   BM   REK

set design see SCENIC DESIGN

Seven Keys to Baldpate A 1913 melodramatic farce in two acts with a prologue and epilogue, adapted from Earl Derr Biggers's novel of the same name, reputedly GEORGE M. COHAN's best play. Billy Magee, a writer of popular mysteries, comes to deserted Baldpate Inn, where he tries, on a bet, to write a novel in just 24 hours. Strangers seeking access to cash in the inn's safe and using six duplicates of Billy's key are actors, parties to a stunt pulled by Billy's betting friend. The epilogue reveals that the play has been an enactment of Billy's novel. Cohan produced and staged this play-within-a-play-within-a-novel, which thrilled Broadway audiences during a yearlong run.   WD

Sexual Perversity in Chicago The first critical and popular success by DAVID MAMET received Chicago's JOSEPH JEFFERSON Award for best new play following its premiere by the ORGANIC THEATER COMPANY in 1974, and an Obie following productions in NYC at St. Clements (1975) and the Cherry Lane Theatre (1976). The comedy consists of 30 short scenes written in the style of SECOND CITY, where Mamet once bused tables. The initially hopeful romance of Danny Shapiro and Deborah Soloman is fatally infected by the sexually hostile language of their best friends, misogynist Bernie Litko and cynic Joan Webber. As in subsequent Mamet works, abusive speech generates, rather than reflects, abusive thought. The film version, *About Last Night,* was released in 1986.   SF

Seymour, William (1855–1933) Actor, director, stage manager. A child actor in New Orleans until 1865, when he went to New York, Seymour served as a callboy at BOOTH'S THEATRE and performed with EDWIN BOOTH, JOSEPH JEFFERSON III, CHARLOTTE CUSHMAN, and EDWIN FORREST. Among Seymour's many management positions were the UNION SQUARE THEATRE, the MADISON SQUARE THEATRE, the Metropolitan Opera House, and CHARLES FROHMAN'S EMPIRE THEATRE, all in New York, and a decade (1879–88) at the BOSTON MUSEUM. In 1882 he married May Davenport, daughter of E. L. DAVENPORT and younger sister of FANNY DAVENPORT. His theatrical memorabilia and personal library form the nucleus of the extensive Princeton University Library theatre collection (integrated, sans curator, into other Princeton holdings in 1992–3). FHL DJW

Shakespeare & Company Cofounded in 1978 by British-born actress-director Tina Packer and voice teacher Kristin Linklater on the grounds of The Mount, Edith Wharton's former estate in Lenox, MA, this year-round operation is a professional, multiracial theatre and training program. In 2001 the operation moved to a new site in Lenox with two theatres: the flexible Founders' Theatre and the more intimate Spring Lawn (101 seats), as well as a tented Rose Footprint (projected as the site of a re-created Rose Playhouse). With more than 300 performances yearly, focusing on Shakespeare, during the summer months a more intensive season is offered. The spoken word and practice of "freeing the natural voice" remain at the center of this company's work. DBW

Shakespeare Behind Bars Founded in 1995 by Curt L. Tofteland, producing director of the Kentucky Shakespeare Festival, SBB was the first North American Shakespeare company within the walls of a medium-security adult male prison (Luther Luckett Correctional Complex) and the prototype of subsequent programs elsewhere. Its objective is to offer this unique population "the opportunity to examine relevant personal and social issues within the structure of an aesthetic experience." Originally 7 inmates participated; today there are 26 active members (a total of 151 have participated). The company has produced scenes from Shakespeare and seven full plays. An award-winning 2005 documentary by Philomath Films followed the nine-month process in 2003 of bringing *The Tempest* to performance. DBW

Shakespeare on the American stage Professionally staged Shakespeare in America can be traced back to at least 1750, when the WALTER MURRAY AND THOMAS KEAN company presented *Richard III* in New York and then toured this and other plays to towns in Maryland and Virginia. Since Murray and Kean seem to have been little more than amateurs, usually the first *professional* production of Shakespeare in America is taken to be *The Merchant of Venice* staged by LEWIS HALLAM's Company of Comedians from London at a theatre in Williamsburg, VA, on 15 September 1752. Until the Continental Congress, preparing for Revolution, prohibited all theatrical activity in 1774, the Hallam company and its successor, the AMERICAN COMPANY, were the principal presenters of Shakespeare in the colonies.

Despite antitheatrical laws and attitudes, economic depression, and outbreaks of yellow fever, theatre in American gradually expanded in the decades after the Peace of 1782. With this expansion, staged Shakespeare increased in quantity and quality, mainly through the presence of British actors recruited by enterprising American managers. Among the more important early actors were ANNE BRUNTON MERRY and THOMAS ABTHORPE COOPER, both of whom were recruited by Philadelphia manager THOMAS WIGNELL in 1796. Merry was America's leading actress for more than a decade, excelling especially as Juliet, and Cooper eventually became America's foremost tragedian, with a repertoire that included most of Shakespeare's major roles. As comanager of the PARK THEATRE, Cooper in 1810 helped recruit London star GEORGE FREDERICK COOKE for an American tour. Cooke excited admiration with his fiery interpretations of Richard III, Shylock, Lear, and Macbeth, and, despite his reputation for drunkenness, remained largely on his best behavior before he died anticipating his return to England. He was but the first of many English Shakespeareans who crossed the Atlantic to enhance their fame and fortune as "visiting stars" (see INTERNATIONAL STARS). The great Edmund Kean, for example, came in 1820 and 1825; William Charles Macready appeared in 1826, 1843, and 1848. Many, like JAMES WILLIAM WALLACK and JUNIUS BRUTUS BOOTH came and stayed, founding dynasties of actors and managers who would significantly influence the development of American Shakespeare throughout the 19th century.

By the 1820s there began to emerge native-born actors whose talents and skills rivaled their British counterparts. JAMES HENRY HACKETT, though renowned mainly for his creation of distinctive "YANKEE" characters, was for many American theatregoers the definitive Falstaff for over 40 years. CHARLOTTE CUSHMAN, generally regarded as the greatest American actress of the 19th century, won plaudits on both sides of the Atlantic for her forceful, domineering Lady Macbeth and, in later years, her majestic Queen Katherine. EDWIN FORREST was acclaimed for his physically compelling portraits of Macbeth, Othello, Coriolanus, and Lear. A belligerent chauvinist opposed especially to visiting British stars, Forrest's bitter quarrel with Macready led to the bloody ASTOR PLACE RIOT of 1849.

Segregated from white mainstream theatre, AFRICAN AMERICANS developed their own theatrical tradition, including productions of Shakespeare. From WILLIAM ALEXANDER BROWN'S AFRICAN THEATRE (1820s) came America's first black Shakespearean actor, JAMES HEWLETT; IRA ALDRIDGE, during a career spent mainly abroad, was celebrated for his naturalistic performances of Othello, Lear, and Aaron the Moor (*Titus Andronicus*).

As American theatre expanded during the 1830s – and despite Forrest's opposition – a new generation of visiting British actors introduced a more refined style of acting to American audiences. In 1832–3, for example, Charles and FANNY KEMBLE (his daughter) charmed the increasingly sophisticated middle-class audiences of New York, Boston, and Philadelphia with their interpretations of Hamlet and Ophelia, Romeo (or sometimes Mercutio) and Juliet, Beatrice and Benedick. Ellen Tree spent three seasons (1836–9) in America, gaining recognition for her decorous, ladylike Rosalind, Viola, and Beatrice. In 1844 she married Charles Kean, and the following year the Keans began a two-season American tour marked especially by their "historically accurate" productions of *Richard III* and *King John*. In so doing, they set a standard for American Shakespearean production throughout the century. In the early 1850s, for example, actor-manager WILLIAM BURTON followed Kean's lead with his own full productions of *The Merry Wives of Windsor, A Midsummer Night's Dream,* and *The Winter's Tale*. A generation later, America's principal régisseur, AUGUSTIN DALY, won praise in both New York and London for his carefully prepared, visually lavish productions of Shakespeare's comedies.

The last third of the 19th century was in many respects a "golden age" for Shakespeare on the American stage. The ties to the British theatre remained close, but American performers and producers achieved an identity of their own. EDWIN BOOTH, a key figure in this period, served his apprenticeship in the frontier theatres of SAN FRANCISCO and Sacramento. Returning to the East Coast in the late 1850s as a touring star, he gradually built a reputation, sustained for over 30 years, as the finest Shakespearean tragedian of his era, acclaimed not only in the U.S., but also in England and Germany – where he toured in the 1880s – for his masterful Iago, Lear, Shylock, and especially Hamlet. Numerous lesser lights illuminated Shakespeare's plays during this period, among them E. L. DAVENPORT, EMMA WALLER, JOHN MCCULLOUGH, and LAWRENCE BARRETT. An expanding rail system brought these traveling stars to the developing towns and cities of America's heartland and far West. In the late 1880s, Booth and Barrett, complete with their own company and stock of "historically accurate" costumes and scenery, embarked on a series of highly successful, nationwide "joint-starring" tours. African American tragedian J. A. ARNEAUX won acclaim for his portrayals of Iago, Macbeth, and Richard III, touring the black communities of New York, Philadelphia, and Providence (RI).

During the "Gilded Age" improved transatlantic travel and a vast theatre market, including many European immigrants, attracted numerous distinguished Shakespeareans from England, Germany, Italy, Poland, and France. Booth's British counterpart, Henry Irving, paid eight visits to the U.S. between 1883 and 1904, bringing his costar, Ellen Terry, and his entire Lyceum Theatre company and mise-en-scènes on each occasion. Tommaso Salvini visited five times between 1873 and 1889, riveting American audiences with his Macbeth, Lear, and especially his passionate, intensely realistic Othello – even though he played exclusively in Italian. In 1886 he played Othello and the Ghost to Booth's Iago and Hamlet. Such polyglot Shakespearean performances became almost commonplace at the time. Booth, for example, at various times in his career teamed with Bogumil Dawison, Adelaide Ristori, HELENA MODJESKA, and Fanny JANAUSCHEK. In 1900, the "divine" Sarah Bernhardt, on one of her numerous American tours, titillated audiences with her Frenchified and feminized portrait of Hamlet. Many of America's new emigrés could also attend performances of Shakespeare completely in their native languages. Antonio Maiori, for example, toured his Italianized adaptations of *Hamlet* and *Othello* to Italian American communities. The well-organized German-language STOCK COMPANIES of New York, Milwaukee, Baltimore, and Chicago regularly mounted high-quality productions of Shakespeare, frequently featuring leading guest artists from Germany or Austria, such as Ludwig Barnay, Adolph Sonnenthal, and Ernst Possart.

At the turn of the 20th century, the American approach to acting and staging Shakespeare established by Booth and Barrett, Daly, and contemporaries, began to wane. It was maintained to some extent by RICHARD MANSFIELD, ROBERT MANTELL, and especially by the team of JULIA MARLOWE and E. H. SOTHERN. By the second decade of the century, however, this old way – and indeed even Shakespeare – was being replaced by a growing taste for modern drama and theatrical entertainment, for movies, and for modern methods of stage production and acting. Certainly one tendency of the modern way with Shakespeare was demonstrated by English director Harley Granville Barker, who brought his original, audacious production of *A Midsummer Night's Dream* to New York in 1916. Influenced by Barker and the New Stagecraft movement, director ARTHUR HOPKINS teamed with designer ROBERT EDMOND JONES and actor John Barrymore (see DREW–BARRYMORE) for striking modernist productions of *Richard III* (1920) and *Hamlet* (1922). Barrymore's Hamlet was widely regarded as the finest since Booth's, but he left the stage for a more lucrative but less significant career in film. It was a route followed by many potentially great American Shakespearean actors in succeeding decades.

In the 1930s and '40s Shakespeare's flame flickered only faintly in the American theatre, though there were several singular productions and performances. In 1936 ORSON WELLES mounted a controversial "voodoo" version of *Macbeth* with an all-black cast, and a year later presented a provocative modern-dress version of *Julius Caesar* that ominously suggested parallels to Fascist Italy. KATHARINE CORNELL and her husband, director GUTHRIE MCCLINTOCK, successfully toured more traditional productions of *Romeo and Juliet* (1933–4) and *Antony and Cleopatra* (1947). In 1937 British-born director MARGARET WEBSTER moved to the U.S. to stage with her former colleague, actor MAURICE EVANS, a series of very successful Shakespearean revivals, including *Richard II* (1937), *Hamlet* (1938), *1 Henry IV* (1939), *Twelfth Night* (1940), and *Macbeth* (1941), with JUDITH ANDERSON as Lady Macbeth. In 1943 Webster staged an outstanding *Othello* on Broadway with actor-singer PAUL ROBESON in the title role, UTA HAGEN as Desdemona, and JOSÉ FERRER as Iago. Robeson's example was followed by several distinguished African American Othello's, including EARLE HYMAN and JAMES EARL JONES. (It also contributed significantly to the integration generally of black actors into mainstream American Shakespearean productions.) After WWII Webster organized the Margaret Webster Shakespeare Company, and for two years toured all over the U.S. and Canada, often to audiences who had little or no exposure to "live" Shakespeare. Indeed, with a decline of interest in classical theatre generally in

the U.S., there were relatively few opportunities even for theatregoers in major cities to see productions of Shakespeare.

In the 1950s, however, this situation changed with the emergence of American SHAKESPEAREAN FESTIVALS. In 1955, for instance, the AMERICAN SHAKESPEARE FESTIVAL opened in Stratford, CT; two years later, the NEW YORK SHAKESPEARE FESTIVAL inaugurated its summer series of free Shakespearean productions in Central Park's outdoor Delacorte Theater. (Though founded in 1935, neither the OREGON SHAKESPEARE FESTIVAL nor the one in San Diego became fully professional until the 1950s.) The success of these pioneering festivals inspired a Shakespeare renaissance in the American theatre.

In the 1970s and '80s numerous festivals were founded all across the U.S. In addition, many of America's regional theatres regularly included a production of Shakespeare in their annual seasons. With increasing frequency, American Shakespearean perspectives also were enriched by visiting productions from various foreign lands, including England, Japan, Sweden, Italy, Romania, Brazil, and Venezuela. By the early 1990s, American theatregoers very likely had greater access to more productions of Shakespeare than any other theatre audience in the world. Some, like a 1998 long-running all-male *Romeo and Juliet* in a small 74-seat Manhattan theatre, received wide attention. A 90-minute version of *Macbeth* in 2003 by the CLASSICAL THEATRE OF HARLEM was praised. Adaptations of Shakespeare remain common: In 1999 *The Donkey Show: A Midsummer Night's Disco* at NYC's Club El Flamingo was a popular hit. And the 2003 *Rose Rage* (the three parts of *Henry VI* "trimmed of fat and put through a meat grinder") proved controversial at the Chicago Shakespeare Theater and the next year in NYC.

In the past 20 years few Shakespeare productions of note have been offered on Broadway. Kelsey Grammer's attempt at Macbeth in 2000 was significant as a great failure, but earlier, in 1995, British actor Ralph Fiennes had received a rare Tony for Hamlet. At Lincoln Center's VIVIAN BEAUMONT THEATRE Helen Hunt was Viola in *Twelfth Night* (1998), KEVIN KLINE essayed Falstaff in an excellent production of *Henry IV* (the two parts combined) in 2003–4, and CHRISTOPHER PLUMMER appeared as a remarkable King Lear (2004) – all three nominated for a Best Revival Tony, which *Henry IV* won. *Julius Caesar* with film star Denzel Washington (2005) was a modest success. Shakespeare in the Park, offered free by the New York Shakespeare Festival/PUBLIC THEATER at the Delacorte, continued unabated into the new millennium. A major innovation began in 2003 when the NATIONAL ENDOWMENT FOR THE ARTS funded *Shakespeare in American Communities*, a touring program that projected 40 companies ultimately on the road.   DJW

Shakespeare Theatre, The   Renamed in 2005 the Shakespeare Theatre Company (opening its new season with Avery Brooks in *Othello*) in anticipation of the opening of a new home, the Harman Center for the Arts.

When the Folger Shakespeare Library building (301 East Capitol St., SE, Washington, DC) was completed in 1932, it included a small auditorium (243 seats) designed to suggest, on a reduced scale, a model Elizabethan theatre. Originally intended for lectures and musical and dramatic recitals, it was converted to theatrical use in 1970 with the founding of the Folger Theatre Group (FTG). In the 1970s the FTG gained national recognition for its fresh, youthful interpretations of Shakespeare and presentations of new, often provocative American and foreign plays. Financial difficulties almost closed the FTG in 1985. With a successful campaign to save the theatre, a new name, and the artistic directorship of MICHAEL KAHN, the Shakespeare Theatre at the Folger rebounded in the late 1980s to become a small but distinguished theatre concentrating on the classics. In early 1992 it dropped "at the Folger" from its name and moved to Washington's 7th Street Arts District (Lansburgh Bldg.) and a 451-seat theatre. (There is also a FOLGER THEATRE today.) In 1991 The Shakespeare Theatre Free For All began at Carter Barron Amphitheatre (more than 500,000 attended during first 14 years). The year 2000 marked the beginning of an M.F.A. program in classical acting in conjunction with The George Washington University.   DJW

Shakespearean festivals   In the U.S., the modern idea of a festival of Shakespearean plays seems to have been initiated by Angus L. Bowmer, who founded the OREGON SHAKESPEARE FESTIVAL in 1935, still the oldest surviving American Shakespearean festival. The San Diego National Shakespeare Festival can also trace its origins back to 1935, although it did not offer a summer festival of plays until 1949. In the 1950s and '60s several other important festivals were founded, including the AMERICAN SHAKESPEARE FESTIVAL (Stratford, CT) in 1951 (its own theatre, 1955), the NEW YORK SHAKESPEARE FESTIVAL (as the Shakespeare Theatre Workshop) in 1954, and the GREAT LAKES Shakespeare Festival in 1961 (operative 1962). Although initially confined to summer seasons,

most of the major festival theatres have gradually extended their seasons and expanded their operations. The Oregon Shakespeare Festival, for example, went from a two-month summer season to a virtually year-round operation. In 1970 the modern, indoor Angus Bowmer Theatre was built adjacent to the outdoor Elizabethan Stage modeled after John Cranford Adams's Globe reconstruction. The present Elizabethan Stage opened in 1959, replacing two earlier outdoor theatres. In the late 1960s and '70s, the San Diego and New York festivals also expanded into additional theatres and longer seasons. In 1984, the ALABAMA SHAKESPEARE FESTIVAL moved into a new two-theatre, multimillion-dollar complex in Montgomery. With such expansion, these major festival theatres have also stretched their repertoires well beyond Shakespeare's works. A typical season will now include not only two or three Shakespearean plays, but also revivals of international classics and productions of contemporary comedies, dramas, and musicals. As an indication of its less restricted repertoire, the Great Lakes festival dropped "Shakespeare" from its name in 1982.

Although Shakespeare's plays present producers with formidable artistic and financial challenges, a Shakespearean festival remains an attractive concept, particularly for theatres operating mainly in the summer. Almost every American region has at least one summer Shakespearean festival; in fact, by the 1990s there were more than 80 Shakespeare festival theatres operating in the USA. Among the principal ones, in addition to those noted above, were California Shakespeare Festival in Orinda, Chicago Shakespeare Theater, Shakespeare at Santa Cruz, FOLGER SHAKESPEARE THEATRE, Houston Shakespeare Festival, the UTAH SHAKESPEARE FESTIVAL, the New Jersey Shakespeare Festival (now Shakespeare Theatre of New Jersey), SHAKESPEARE & COMPANY, the Shakespeare Festival of Dallas, the now defunct Three Rivers Shakespeare Festival in Pittsburgh, the Colorado Shakespeare Festival, and the North Carolina Shakespeare Festival. The quality of presentation of these and later operations vary widely from festival to festival and season to season, but the various festivals do offer thousands of theatregoers the opportunity to experience Shakespeare on the American stage. Moreover, they also provide Shakespearean performance and production opportunities for numerous aspiring and accomplished American actors, directors, and designers.

Many festival productions are usually reviewed on an annual basis in issues of *Shakespeare Quarterly* or *Shakespeare Bulletin.* Glen Loney and Patricia

MacKay's *The Shakespeare Complex* (1975) provides an excellent if somewhat out-of-date overview of both year-round and summer festivals. An international guide to Shakespeare festivals (and companies) edited by R. Engle, F. Londré, and D. J. Watermeier (1995) offers a more comprehensive survey. In 1991, the Shakespeare Theatre Association of American was founded to facilitate communication among the various Shakespearean producing organizations (some 65 members as of 2006) through an annual conference, its newsletter, *quarto*, and its Web site.   DJW

Shange, Ntozake [née Paulette Williams] (1948–) African American playwright and novelist. Born in Trenton, NJ, Barnard College graduate Shange's first play, FOR COLORED GIRLS WHO HAVE CONSIDERED SUICIDE WHEN THE RAINBOW IS ENUF (1976, Broadway), brought immediate acclaim to an exciting and innovative playwright (who has not lived up to expectation). The play called for seven women in individual recitations to recount life experiences. More conventional was *A Photograph: A Study in Cruelty* (1977), followed by *Spell #7* (1979), an extended choreopoem of character revelations using poetry, song, dance, and masks (both at The PUBLIC); *Boogie Woogie Landscapes* (1979, Symphony Space, NYC); a revisionist adaptation of BRECHT's *Mother Courage* (1980); with Emily Mann and Baikida Carroll, a rhythm-and-blues musical, *Betsey Brown* (1989, American Musical Theater Festival), based on her 1985 novel; for CROSSROADS THEATRE COMPANY in 1992, *The Love Space Demands;* and, at STEPPENWOLF, the South African musical *Nomathemba* with Joseph Shabalala and Eric Simonson (1995). Shange's free-form theatre pieces give her a distinctive voice on the contemporary stage. In 1993, to recognize this uniqueness, she received a three-year grant (Lila Wallace–Reader's Digest Writers' Award) for over $100,000 to create a theatre piece with the Freedom Theatre of Philadelphia (*i live in music*, 1995). As of 2007 she had published four novels.   EGH

Shanley, John Patrick (1950–) Playwright, director, and screenwriter. Born in the Bronx, educated at NYU, Shanley won the triple prize in 2005 when his play DOUBT: A PARABLE won the Tony, Drama Desk, and the Pulitzer. Before *Doubt* he was best known for his Oscar-winning screenplay *Moonstruck* (MGM, 1987). The author of 21 plays and 9 screenplays (as of early 2007), he gained recognition in the 1980s and early 1990s (mostly OFF-BROADWAY) with *Danny and the Deep Blue Sea* (1984), *Savage in Limbo* (1985), *Italian-American Reconciliation* (1988), *The Big Funk* (1990), *Beggars in the*

House of Plenty (1991), *Four Dogs and a Bone* (1993), and *Psychopathia Sexualis* (1996, Seattle). Recent plays include *Cellini* (2001), *Dirty Story* (2003), *Sailor's Song* (2004), and *Defiance* (2006), the latter the second play in a projected trilogy that began with *Doubt*.   TLM

Shannon, Effie (1867–1954) Actress who, billed as La Petite Shannon, played Eva in UNCLE TOM'S CABIN in Boston at age 7 and grew up to stardom on Broadway. She joined DAVID BELASCO's Lyceum Stock Company in 1889, and soon married leading man Herbert Kelcey. Outstanding among her hundreds of roles were the leads in *The Moth and the Flame* (1898), *Years of Discretion* (1912), *She Stoops to Conquer* (1924) and plays by Bernard SHAW. Her popularity continued when she moved into character roles, culminating in a two-year stint as Martha Brewster in ARSENIC AND OLD LACE (1942 replacement).   FHL

Shapiro, Mel (1939?–) Director, playwright, and educator who took his M.F.A. at Carnegie Institute of Technology in 1961. He was resident director of ARENA STAGE (1963–5), producing director of the GUTHRIE THEATER (1968–70), and resident director of the NEW YORK SHAKESPEARE FESTIVAL (1971–7). During 1971 he had two plays by JOHN GUARE running simultaneously: the OFF-BROADWAY premiere of *The HOUSE OF BLUE LEAVES* and, at the NYSF's Delacorte, an irreverent musical adaptation of Shakespeare's *Two Gentlemen of Verona* (which he cowrote). The latter transferred to Broadway and London and won Shapiro Obie and Drama Desk awards for direction and a Tony for Best Book (Musical). Shapiro's teaching posts have included NYU, Carnegie Mellon, where he headed the drama department (1980–7), and most recently UCLA. He is author of *The Director's Companion* (1997) and *An Actor Performs* (1996).   CLJ

Sharaff, Irene (1910–93) Theatre and film costume designer who began as an assistant to ALINE BERNSTEIN and by the mid-1930s was designing major Broadway plays and (primarily) musicals such as *As THOUSANDS CHEER* and *ON YOUR TOES*. Through the 1960s she designed many significant musicals, including *The KING AND I* and *WEST SIDE STORY*. Her Hollywood career took off in 1944 with *Meet Me in St. Louis* and later included *An American in Paris, Cleopatra,* and *WHO'S AFRAID OF VIRGINIA WOOLF?* Although this last film demonstrated her ability to create pedestrian costumes, she is best known for stylish design and her use of color. She also had the unusual ability to translate stage productions into film. Her last Broadway show, of 60, was JEROME ROBBINS' BROADWAY in 1989. A book on her work was published in 1976.   AA

Shaw and the American theatre

Success in New York with the lightly cynical *Arms and the Man* (Herald Square Theatre, 1894) and again with the satirical melodrama *The Devil's Disciple* (Fifth Avenue Theatre, 1897) secured for Bernard Shaw a reputation abroad and the financial independence that made possible his relinquishing drama criticism to focus on playwriting. The genie who extracted Shaw's audacious stage genius from the bottle of rejection in England was actor-manager RICHARD MANSFIELD. The Shaw boom continued when a young actor, ARNOLD DALY, secured *Candida,* which had already received two nonprofessional productions (Chicago, 1899; Philadelphia, 1903). Daly managed a New York opening (Princess Theatre, 8 December 1903) and added *The Man of Destiny* and *How He Lied to Her Husband* (11 February 1904, after moving to the Vaudeville), following that with *You Never Can Tell* and *John Bull's Other Island,* both at the GARRICK (1905). He boasted thereafter that he had made Shaw's fortune, and indeed most of his plays thereafter were seen in New York soon after their openings across the Atlantic. *Major Barbara,* the major exception, had to wait 10 years (Playhouse, 1915), until a war made its themes timely.

While Shaw's American theatrical reputation burgeoned, his popular image remained vague until the notorious reception of *Mrs Warren's Profession* in New Haven and then New York (Garrick, 30 October 1905), when, abetted by Anthony Comstock's puritanical Society for the Suppression of Vice (see CENSORSHIP), the press attacked the play as obscene. The cast went briefly to jail, but the play then drew large houses, in 1907 was revived and toured, and Shaw became a household name.

Appropriately, given Shaw's launching as a playwright in America, what may be his greatest dramas received their world premieres in the New World: *Heartbreak House* (1920) and *Saint Joan* (1923), both produced at the Garrick by the fledgling THEATRE GUILD, which would present the American premieres of seven Shaw plays, including the first performance anywhere of *Back to Methuselah* (Garrick, 27 February 1922) and *The Simpleton of the Unexpected Isles* (Guild Theatre, 18 February 1935). *Back to Methuselah,* impracticable when performed over three nights, was expected to lose at least $30,000; when losses proved to be only $20,000, Shaw quipped that the Guild had saved $10,000 because of the clout of his name.

Shaw's impact had long been felt by American playwrights. CLYDE FITCH, in plays like *The Girl with the Green Eyes* (1902) and *The CITY* (1909), already had suggested Shaw, and like LANGDON MITCHELL, whose *NEW YORK IDEA* (1906) resonated with what might be perceived as Shavian satire, Fitch had experienced Shaw plays in their home settings in London. Of the same generation, EDWARD SHELDON, who remained in New York and could not have seen *Major Barbara* before he wrote *SALVATION NELL* (1908), nevertheless may have been inspired by reading Shaw's Salvation Army play. Of Sheldon's time, the most obviously Shavian playwright was RACHEL CROTHERS, whose seriocomic *HE AND SHE* (Boston, 1912; New York, 1920) was seen as influenced by Shaw and "the drama of discussion." Many of her works, whether social satires or ironic feminist dramas, continued to evidence Shavian traits, even as late as her last major play, *SUSAN AND GOD* (1937).

EUGENE O'NEILL claimed Shaw as one of his formative influences, in particular his *The Quintessence of Ibsenism* (1891), which O'Neill read in prep school. Shaw is also in the bookcase in the Tyrones' summer home in LONG DAY'S JOURNEY INTO NIGHT. The elongated, multipart concept of *STRANGE INTERLUDE* may take its inspiration from *Back to Methusalah;* and the broad historical satire of *Marco Millions* may be inspired by Shaw's extravagances in *Caesar and Cleopatra* (U.K., 1899), seen in NYC in 1906 – the year in which *AH, WILDERNESS!* is set – when O'Neill was nearby at school.

The most Shavian of later American dramatists was ROBERT E. SHERWOOD, whose earliest produced play, *The ROAD TO ROME* (1927) – combining elements of *The Man of Destiny* with *Caesar and Cleopatra* – had been rejected by impresario GILBERT MILLER with the sneer, "I don't like even first-rate Shaw!" The play – gibed at as "Shaw in short pants" – established Sherwood in the theatre. His *The PETRIFIED FOREST* (1935) has been called an "Arizona *Heartbreak House*" and *IDIOT'S DELIGHT* (1936) a "cosmopolitan *Heartbreak House*," whereas his last play, *Small War on Murray Hill* (1957), echoes *The Devil's Disciple.*

In the same generation, the social satires of PHILIP BARRY and S. N. BEHRMAN suggest Shaw, Behrman even announcing his admiration in the preface to his *Rain from Heaven* (1934). Behrman not only wrote about Shaw and acknowledged taking Shaw's playwriting advice, but, beginning with *The Second Man* (1927), developed a Shavian drama of ideas adapted to American conventions of high comedy.

With Shaw's reputation in America still strong in the 1930s, the hit FEDERAL THEATRE PROJECT all-black production of *Androcles and the Lion* (1938)

reopened at the 1939 World's Fair in New York. Also in that year, Shaw received Hollywood's Academy Award for Best Screenplay (of 1938) for his adaptation of his own *Pygmalion*. The 1939–45 war, however, would be a watershed, as by its end he was 90, and a new generation of playwrights had begun to displace him.

Although the major American play of the WWII years – THORNTON WILDER's *The Skin of Our Teeth* (1942) – has been linked to James Joyce's *Finnegans Wake* as a burlesque history of humankind, a case can also be made for a Shavian dimension. In Wilder's philosophical farce audiences discovered – as in *Back to Methuselah*, a history of the world from the Garden of Eden to the indefinable future – a Lilith (Sabina in *Skin of Our Teeth*) and a Cain (Henry in Wilder's play) who weave through time, as well as other elements suggesting that the playwright knew his Shaw. The elder dramatist had been attempting to find meaning during one world war; the younger was seeking understanding during the next.

Postwar American dramatists largely turned elsewhere, although TENNESSEE WILLIAMS, at college in the 1930s, had written a term paper on *Candida*. In the early play he wrote with Donald Windham, *You Touched Me!* (1942), he borrowed from *Heartbreak House*. That Williams kept reading Shaw is clear from his afterword to *CAMINO REAL*.

An exception to the decline in Shavian influence was the musical theatre, where *MY FAIR LADY* (1956), a close adaptation of *Pygmalion*, inaugurated a new era in the musical play, in which song and dance and lyrics arose out of situation and character. In *My Fair Lady* many of the lyrics and much of the dialogue came not only directly from *Pygmalion* but also from Shaw's preface.

Among works exhibiting postwar indebtedness was GORE VIDAL's historical satire *Romulus* (1962), with its open thefts from Shaw ("Thank heaven," says one character. "No, don't thank heaven, dear, thank me," quips Romulus, in a steal from Undershaft in *Major Barbara*.) Though EDWARD ALBEE's *WHO'S AFRAID OF VIRGINIA WOOLF?* (1962) has been equated with *Heartbreak House* as an unmasking game, with some lines uncannily parallel, little else in Albee suggests Shaw. Later playwrights too have gone elsewhere for inspiration, although plays in which wit coruscates and paradox abounds are still often labeled Shavian. Today, the major festival devoted to Shaw is in Canada, although for many years (1982–2001) an annual Shaw festival was held at Milwaukee's Chamber Theatre, an annual summer Shaw festival has often taken place at NYC's Westside Repertory Theatre, and a company called ShawChicago

(founded 1994) is dedicated to the work of Shaw. With 2006 marking Shaw's 150th's birthday, a flurry of Shavian productions occurred in New York and elsewhere, ranging from a first-rate *Mrs Warren's Profession* at IRISH REP and a superb *Heartbreak House* by ROUNDABOUT to a Kabuki-inspired *Major Barbara* at LA MAMA and Project Shaw's (NYC) intent to present staged readings of all Shaw's plays.   SW

Shaw, Irwin (1913–84) Writer best known for his popular fiction and short stories, though his career began in the 1930s as a left-wing playwright with his antiwar one-act *BURY THE DEAD* (1936), followed by the more popularly successful melodramatic comedy, *The Gentle People* (1939). His biography, by Michael Shnayerson, appeared in 1989.   DBW

Shaw, Mary (1854–1929) Actress and feminist who debuted with the BOSTON MUSEUM Stock Company in 1878. She championed IBSEN's plays, especially *Ghosts,* which she toured around the country for five months in 1903 and often revived. She played *Hedda Gabler* in Chicago (1904) and starred in the sensational premiere of *Mrs Warren's Profession* (1905) as well as other controversial plays: *Votes for Women* (1909), *Divorce* (1909), and *Polygamy* (1914). She was a charter member of the Professional Women's League, founder of the Gamut Club (West 46th St.), and represented American theatre at the International Congress of Women held in London in 1899.   RAS

Shawn, Wallace (1943–) Actor (study with HERBERT BERGHOF has led to more than 70 stage and film roles, plus numerous TV appearances) and playwright, usually premiered at The PUBLIC: *The Mandrake* (1977), *Marie and Bruce* (1980), *A Thought in Three Parts* (aka *Three Short Plays*, 1976), *Our Late Night* (1975, Obie), *AUNT DAN AND LEMON* (1985; Obie), *The Hotel Play* (1981, LA MAMA), *The Fever* (1990; Obie; revived 2007), *The Designated Mourner* (1996, London; 2000, OFF-OFF). As a screenwriter, he is best known for *My Dinner with Andre* (1981, coauthor, costar). TV appearances include *Taxi, Murphy Brown,* and *Desperate Housewives;* stage, *Aunt Dan and Lemon, The Mandrake, Carmilla* (2003, La MaMa), *The Master and Margarita* (1978, The Public), *The Hotel Play, Chinchilla* (1979, PHOENIX THEATRE), and *A Doll's House* (Portland, OR). In 1994 he appeared as Vanya in the film *Vanya on 42nd Street*. In their treatment of sex, violence, and cruelty, his plays shock, confuse, and sometimes bore audiences. In 2006 a 1983 play/opera of his with music by his brother, Allen, was produced by The

New Group; later that year his translation of *The Threepenny Opera* was presented by ROUNDABOUT. GSA

She Loves Me Cult musical first seen in 1963 (301 performances) but that, after a ROUNDABOUT revival (transferred to Broadway) in 1993, which *Time* magazine called a "comic charmer," has become a popular small musical in professional and amateur venues. Based on the Ernst Lubitsch film *The Shop around the Corner* and the original play by Miklós Lázsló (*Parfumerie*), this delicate, sophisticated musical (one of BARBARA COOK's favorites) boasted a book by JOE MASTEROFF, music by JERRY BOCK, lyrics by SHELDON HAR-NICK, and direction by HAROLD PRINCE. The original production had somehow been drowned out by the likes of *FUNNY GIRL* and *HELLO, DOLLY!* The revival was directed by SCOTT ELLIS, who promoted the new production, and the audience in 1993 found it more enchanting, given events then in Eastern Europe. Set in a middle European city during the mid-1930s, the musical is a love story of employees at a cosmetic shop. They fight at work but after hours carry on a love affair by writing letters to "Dear Friend," completely oblivious to the other's identity until the end of the story.
   KN   DBW

Shean, Al see GALLAGHER AND SHEAN

Shear Madness Comedy whodunit, a prime example of PARTICIPATORY THEATRE, in which the audience solves the crime. The original play, *Scherenschnitt* (written as a serious psychodrama by German writer-psychologist Paul Pörtner in 1963), was discovered by coproducer Bruce Jordan in 1976. With Marilyn Abrams as his partner, the piece evolved into *Shear Madness,* first staged in 1978 in Lake George, NY. In 1980 it opened at the Charles Playhouse (Stage II) in BOSTON (capitalized at $60,000), where as of 31 January 2005 it had been performed 10,475 times; a production at the JOHN F. KENNEDY CENTER's Theatre Lab has had c. 8,500 performances. The Boston version claims to be the longest-running play in the history of American theatre, and the Washington production the second-longest run; Chicago's production, which ran 17 years, claims third place. The play is set in a unisex hairstyling salon or barber shop (in the city in which it plays); the landlady upstairs, Isabel Czerny, is murdered, and each actor has a motivation for doing her in. Although a basic format is followed, each performance is different, with audience questions and solutions, much improvising, and frequent allusions to

media scandals and local news stories. The play has been staged around the world (c. 22 foreign productions) and in some 24 U.S. cities – but not NYC! By 2002 Jordan/Abrams (Cranberry Productions) had grossed $112 million.   DBW

Sheldon, Edward (Brewster) (1886–1946) Playwright. A graduate of GEORGE PIERCE BAKER's Workshop 47 at Harvard College, Sheldon was an early proponent of social realism in America with *SALVATION NELL* (1908), in which a girl avoids a repulsive "profession" by joining the Salvation Army; *The NIGGER* (1909), concerned with the struggle of a Southern governor who discovers that his grandmother was an octoroon slave; and *The Boss* (1911), a drama of labor–management conflicts. However, his romantic conclusions in these plays (with the exception of *The Nigger*) suggest his true interests, as revealed in *The High Road* (1912), a search for beauty, and *Romance* (1913), as an American clergyman explains his love for an Italian diva. When poor health apparently incapacitated Sheldon, he collaborated with such dramatists as SIDNEY HOWARD (*Bewitched*, 1924) and CHARLES MACARTHUR (*Lulu Belle*, 1926). Although none of his later works was outstanding, Sheldon remained a source of inspiration and help on dramaturgical problems for a number of prominent dramatists. His biography by Eric Wollencott Barnes was published in 1956.   WJM

Shelley, Carole (1939–) London-born actress who since her U.S. debut as Gwendolyn Pigeon in *The ODD COUPLE* (1965) has worked steadily in the American theatre, winning a Tony for *The ELEPHANT MAN* (1979) and acclaim for parts in plays by Shaw, Coward, UHRY, and Ayckbourne. Other roles include the mother (replacement) in KRAMER's *The Destiny of Me*, five roles in GURNEY's *Later Life* (both OFF-BROADWAY, 1993), Parthy in *SHOW BOAT* (1994), Fraulein Schneider (replacement, 2002) in the 1998 revival of *CABARET*, and Madame Morrible in *WICKED* (2003).   DBW

Shenandoah One of BRONSON HOWARD's most popular dramas; a romantic and sweeping epic of the Civil War. Opening in Boston, November 1888, the play was declared an immediate failure. After some revision, it reopened the next year at New York's STAR THEATRE, where it ran for 250 performances. Its complex plot, multiple characters, grand spectacle, and patriotic sentiment made it a durable hit and may have presaged the film epic. The theme and action are typical of the age and reflect a long-standing tradition in American playwriting; but it was Howard's attempts to introduce social drama and a modicum of realism to the commercial stage that makes this play an important milestone.   PAD

Shepard, Sam [né Samuel Shepard Rogers] (1943–) Actor and playwright who, though lacking a major commercial Broadway success, is arguably the most critically acclaimed, if the most obscure and undisciplined U.S. dramatist of the past 25 years. *New York Magazine* called him "the most inventive in language and revolutionary in craft," as well as the "writer whose work most accurately maps the interior and exterior landscapes of his society." Uniquely American and contemporary in his subject matter, ranging from myths of the American West, American stereotypes, the death or betrayal of the American dream, the travail of the family, to the search for roots, Shepard defies easy classification. Influenced by rock and roll, the pop and countercultures beginning in the 1950s, the graphic arts and dance, the West of Hollywood, hallucinatory experiences, and a dozen other eclectic forces, his path as a writer is hard to plot. RICHARD GILMAN suggests that it is best to accept the volatility and interdependence of Shepard's plays – "they constitute a series of facets of a single continuing act of imagination." Of his more than 40 plays – beginning with the Theatre Genesis (NYC) productions of *Cowboys* and *The Rock Garden* in 1964 – 11 have received Obie Awards. The following are major works: *La Turista* (1966, AMERICAN PLACE); *The TOOTH OF CRIME* (1972, McCARTER; revived at the LORTEL, 1996), a rock-drama written during a four-year period in London; *CURSE OF THE STARVING CLASS*, written in 1976 and first produced in NYC in 1978 at The PUBLIC THEATER, with a successful NYC revival in 1985; *BURIED CHILD* (1978, Lortel; revived on Broadway by STEPPENWOLF, 1996), for which he won the 1979 Pulitzer; *TRUE WEST* (1980, The Public; Broadway revival by CIRCLE IN THE SQUARE, 2000); *FOOL FOR LOVE*, originally staged in 1983 at San Francisco's MAGIC THEATRE (as was *True West* in July 1980), where Shepard was playwright-in-residence for several years, then moved to NYC; and *A LIE OF THE MIND* (1985, Promenade).

In 1991, *States of Shock,* Shepard's first drama in six years and his ambiguous look at post-Vietnam America, played a brief season at the AMERICAN PLACE THEATRE, and in late 1994 he directed his *Simpatico* at The Public. Shepard has also coauthored three pieces with JOSEPH CHAIKIN – one, *The War in Heaven* (1985, radio), was also revived in 1991 at the American Place; another, *When the World was Green,* premiered at the 1996 Atlanta Olympic Arts Festival and was seen the next year

at the AMERICAN REPERTORY THEATRE. In 1996–7 his work was showcased at SIGNATURE THEATRE, and during Signature's 10th season (2001–2) *The Late Henry Moss* was directed by Chaikin. *Eyes for Consuela* was presented in 1998 at the MANHATTAN THEATER CLUB. *God of Hell* ran briefly OFF-BROADWAY in 2004 (with Randy Quaid and Tim Roth) and then at the Magic Theatre in 2006.

A film actor and screenwriter as well, Shepard has appeared in several successful films, including his own *Fool for Love,* and he wrote the screenplay for *Paris, Texas,* which won the Golden Palm Award at the 1984 Cannes Film Festival. A collection of short stories appeared in 2002. In 2004 he made a rare stage appearance at the NEW YORK THEATRE WORKSHOP as Salter in Churchill's *A Number.* Of the numerous studies/bios of Shepard, Stephen J. Bottoms's (1998) remains definitive.
   DBW

Sherin, Edwin (1930–) Director-actor-producer, more recently executive producer and sometime director of television's *Law & Order.* After a modest acting career in the 1950s, Sherin established a reputation as a director while associate producing director at Washington's ARENA STAGE (1964–8), peaking with his direction of Howard Sackler's *The GREAT WHITE HOPE* (1968), seen that year on Broadway. A handful of Broadway productions followed, including *6 Rms Riv Vu* (1973) and *The Eccentricities of a Nightingale* (1976). As of 2006 he had directed 13 Broadway productions and had over 75 OFF-BROADWAY and regional credits. In London he directed a successful 1974 revival of *A STREETCAR NAMED DESIRE* with CLAIRE BLOOM. During 1980–5 he was director at the Hartman Theatre, Stamford, CT. He is married to actress JANE ALEXANDER, whom he directed in *The Visit* (1992) and five other plays on Broadway. His film credits include *Valdez Is Coming*   DBW

Sherlock Holmes by WILLIAM GILLETTE. Four-act play loosely based on three Conan Doyle stories. After a Buffalo (NY) tryout, it opened at NYC's GARRICK THEATRE on 6 November 1899 with Gillette as Holmes – his greatest histrionic creation – BRUCE McRAE as Dr. Watson, and George Wessells as Holmes's nemesis Professor Moriarty, and ran for an initial 236 performances. Through 1932 Gillette appeared in the role more than 1,300 times in numerous revivals. The play concerned Holmes's efforts to acquire a packet of incriminating letters for a royal client, and, in the process, capture criminal mastermind Moriarty. It succeeded, despite negative criticism, due to Gillette's superb performance, the play's suspenseful action, and Gillette's innovative technical elements. Over the years, Gillette revised it often: As he grew older, for instance, the romantic element was altered for the sake of verisimilitude. Successfully revived by the Royal Shakespeare Company, it played Broadway in 1974.   DBW

Sherwood, Garrison P. (1902–63) Theatre historian, journalist, actor, and director, impetus behind the retrospective volumes of the *Best Plays* series for 1909–19, 1899–1909, and 1894–99 (in that order), thus creating a continuity in coverage from where GEORGE C. D. ODELL's *Annals of the New York Stage* ends. The annual, currently edited by Jeffrey Eric Jenkins, still provides basic data and analysis for each season.   DBW

Sherwood, Robert E(mmet) (1896–1955) Playwright, screenwriter, essayist, historian, and propagandist; a man of strong emotions and good will who preached simplistic solutions to complicated problems. His career started with *The ROAD TO ROME* (1927) and continued with *Waterloo Bridge* (1930) and *Reunion in Vienna* (1931), sentimental and frivolous comedies about emotional problems. With *The PETRIFIED FOREST* (1935), a story of frustrated idealism, *IDIOT'S DELIGHT* (1936), an antiwar play, and *ABE LINCOLN IN ILLINOIS* (1938) Sherwood attained prominence, winning Pulitzer Prizes for the latter two. During the 1930s he also wrote screenplays, served as president of the DRAMATISTS GUILD, and helped found the PLAYWRIGHTS' COMPANY (1938).

With the advent of war in Europe, Sherwood dramatically changed his thinking about conflict and the purpose of drama. Having complained that his plays started with a message and ended only as good entertainment, he wrote *There Shall Be No Night* (1940), a militant condemnation of American isolationism, trumpeted across the land by actors LUNT AND FONTANNE; this play too won a Pulitzer. Having shown his ability to write brilliant propaganda, and his hatred of Hitler, he became a speechwriter for President Roosevelt, who appointed him director of the Overseas Branch of the Office of War Information. Sherwood's postwar plays – *The Rugged Path* (1945) and *Small War on Murray Hill* (1957) – were failures; only in his book *Roosevelt and Hopkins: An Intimate History* (1948) did he again show his considerable writing skills. There are biographies by JOHN MASON BROWN (1965) and Walter Meserve (1970).   WJM

She Would Be a Soldier Best known of M. M. NOAH's seven plays, its comic/romantic portrayal of a young woman who disguises herself to join her fiancé at camp during the Battle of Chippewa remained a favorite on the American stage until the 1840s. The play, written specifically for the leading actress, Catherine Leesugg, was first performed at the PARK THEATRE in 1819. Using a historical event as background, as in all of Noah's works, the play, a blatant appeal to American nationalism, portrayed a magnanimous American army defeating the effete Europeans. The "noble savage" is portrayed by the Indian Chief who ultimately converts to the American side (see NATIVE AMERICANS PORTRAYED).   PAD

Shinn, Christopher (1975–) Youthful playwright-director, born in Hartford, CT, who first received attention in London (including *Four,* Royal Court Theatre, 1998; Soho Theatre, *The Coming World* 2001), and has been produced OFF-BROADWAY at PLAYWRIGHTS HORIZONS, the VINEYARD, and the MANHATTAN THEATRE CLUB, and OFF-OFF at the New York Fringe Festival. When *What Didn't Happen* opened (Playwrights Horizons) in 2002, BRANTLEY noted that the writer "is a welcome paradox among up-and-coming American dramatists: a creator of carefully constructed, dialogue-heavy works that nonetheless resonate with a sense of the unspoken." His other plays (with U.S. production dates) include *Other People* (2000), *Four* (2000, Chicago; 2002, MTC), *Where Do We Live* (2004), *On the Mountain* (2005), and *Dying City* (2007, LINCOLN CENTER).   DBW

Shore Acres A domestic comedy written by JAMES A. HERNE, with the collaboration of Katharine Corcoran Herne, which premiered at McVICKER'S THEATRE, Chicago, 17 May 1892. It dramatizes the near destruction of the harmony of a coastal Maine family by its greedy, domineering father. Uncle Nat, played with great distinction by Herne, helps his niece run away with the man she loves and saves the family farm when his brother mortgages it in a speculative scheme. Its long run contributed to the demise of the BOSTON MUSEUM's STOCK COMPANY in 1893. It ran a full season (1893–4) in New York and on the road for five years, earning Herne more than a million dollars and restoring his fortune, which had been decimated by his efforts to produce MARGARET FLEMING.   WD

Short Eyes A two-act drama by MIGUEL PIÑERO first produced by the Theatre of the Riverside Church. JOSEPH PAPP imported the play to The PUBLIC THEATER (Anspacher), and, after a two-week run at the Zellerbach Theatre in Pennsylvania, to the VIVIAN BEAUMONT at Lincoln Center,

Scene from Hal Prince's 1994 revival of *Show Boat.* Pictured at center: Dorothy Stanley and Joel Blum. Scenic design by Eugene Lee. Photo by Michael Cooper. *Courtesy:* Harold Prince and Live Entertainment.

where it opened as part of the NEW YORK SHAKE-SPEARE FESTIVAL on 9 May 1974. Directed by Marvin Felix Camillo – and acted mostly by former prisoners from Bedford Hills (NY) Correctional Facility, where they'd joined a group called "The Family" – the play was performed internationally, receiving the New York Drama Critics' Circle and Obie awards for Best American Play (plus an Obie for direction). Through vivid character portrayals instead of stereotypes, *Short Eyes* provides a realistic view of prison life both comic and tragic in tone. The title is prison vernacular for men convicted of child-rape; through his play, Piñero reveals a crime that outrages even the most hardened criminals. ER

Short, Hassard (1877–1956) Director. Initially associated with lavish REVUES, Short during the 1920s–1940s became the director to call upon for stylish opulence. He frequently served as codi-

rector, responsible for staging production numbers rather than book scenes. Revues he staged included such landmarks as the MUSIC BOX *Revue*s (1921–3), *The Bandwagon* (1931), and *As* THOUSANDS CHEER (1933); book shows included *Roberta* (1933) and LADY IN THE DARK (1941). A sometime designer as well as a director, he frequently worked for such showy producers as MAX GORDON and MICHAEL TODD. JD

Show Boat Based on EDNA FERBER's novel, with book and lyrics by OSCAR HAMMERSTEIN II, additional lyrics by P. G. WODEHOUSE, and music by JEROME KERN, *Show Boat* opened 27 December 1927, sumptuously produced by FLORENZ ZIEGFELD at his ZIEGFELD THEATRE with scenic design by JOSEPH URBAN. One of the landmarks of the musical stage, it had a complex plot that traced the lives of a family of SHOWBOAT performers over four decades, focusing particularly on the love story of Magnolia Hawks, daughter of a showboat captain, and gambler Gaylord Ravenal. The sprawling plot inspired Kern and Hammerstein to write a brilliant score that employed leitmotifs and reprises (notably the haunting "Ol' Man River") to frame and contextualize the action. Although the musical sequences were not as fully integrated into the plot as in later musicals such as OKLAHOMA!, the combination of serious plot and ambitious score made *Show Boat* far superior to the typical musical fare of the 1920s. Kern and Hammerstein produced a successful Broadway revival in 1946, and it has received a number of other full-scale productions in both theatres and opera houses around the world, as well as three film versions. In 1988 John McGlinn supervised a restored score for EMI Records Limited and, most significant, HAROLD PRINCE "re-created" the musical in 1993 (Toronto) and 1994 (New York; Tony and Drama Desk awards for direction, 1995), the longest-running production of the musical in Broadway history (947 performances). MK

showboats From the early 19th century, flatboats, then steamers and paddlewheelers, plied the Mississippi and Ohio Rivers, offering entertainment to the residents along the banks. Although NOAH LUDLOW, JOSEPH JEFFERSON II, and SOL SMITH dabbled in such amusements, the first intentionally designed showboat was that of William Chapman Sr., launched at Pittsburgh in 1831. The Chapman family in their *Floating Theatre*, a rude shed set on a barge and poled downriver, soon became a familiar sight, making annual tours of the major waterways with a repertory of Kotzebue, SHAKESPEARE, and musical farces. Before Chapman's widow sold out in 1847, they had set the style for similar enterprises, although imitators tended to song-and-dance and lecture entertainments and sometimes lacked the respectable domestic veneer of the Chapmans. The crafts ranged from ramshackle scows to grandiose arks. CIRCUS boats, led by Spalding and Rogers's *Floating Circus Palace* (1851), were capable of seating up to 3,400 spectators and offered MINSTREL SHOWS and a museum of curiosities in addition to sawdust acts.

After the disastrous hiatus of the Civil War, a new period of prosperity came to the showboat. The leading entrepreneur was Augustus Byron French, a riparian BARNUM who operated five boats from 1878 to 1901; he pioneered the use of marching bands on shore to advertise his lavish variety bills, and launched both the apt term and the luxurious vessel the "floating palace." His double-decker *Sensation No. 2* sat 759, but the only full-length drama ever offered was UNCLE TOM'S CABIN. French's main rival was E. A. Price, whose press AGENT Ralph Emerson came up with sensational innovations in publicity, using calliopes, billboards, and postcards to herald the boat's arrival.

The reliance on variety was challenged by the Eisenbarth–Henderson *Temple of Amusement,* which purveyed drama exclusively; these "moral amusements," which included *Faust,* were lit by electricity. As *The Cotton Blossom* under Emerson's management, it featured Broadway hits and spectacular melodramas until 1931. Drama was also the fare provided by Norman Thom, "the John Drew [see DREW–BARRYMORE] of the Rivers," the first actor since Chapman to own a boat; for *The Princess,* he shrewdly chose plays of regional interest. The Bryants specialized in lurid melodrama, offered in direct competition to the rival silent pictures.

During the history of the showboat (as they had come to be known), more than 76 verifiable such craft have existed. There were 26 active in 1910, 14 in 1928, and 5 in 1938. (The last recorded by Philip Graham was *The Goldenrod,* tied up in St. Louis in 1943 [recently refurbished and moved to St. Charles, MO], although the *Majestic,* built in 1923, operates May–September on the Cincinnati city landing.) The decline can be attributed to the closure of the frontier: Unable to compete with the urban entertainments that sprang up in the wake of civilization, the owners suffered greatly from the Depression of 1929. Behind the fashion even in their heyday, the boats became a nostalgic artifact, and imitations were much in use by society promoters in the 1930s. It was JEROME KERN and OSCAR HAMMERSTEIN II's musical SHOW BOAT

(1927), adapted from the novel by EDNA FERBER, that simultaneously immortalized the phenomenon and encased it in an aura of quaintness. Once a unique product of westward expansion, showboats are now adjuncts of tourism and municipal festivals.   LS

Show-Off, The, by GEORGE KELLY is a three-act, realistic comedy set in the living room of a Philadelphia family. The Fishers are dismayed when young Amy is smitten with the vain and boastful Aubrey Piper, whom sister Clara rightly predicts will end up ensconced their house. In Aubrey, Kelly creates an exasperating yet likable antihero, thrown into relief by the sometimes bittersweet lives of the people who surround him. Premiering 4 February 1924 at the PLAYHOUSE THEATRE, NYC, the play ran for 571 performances and was the Pulitzer jury's recommendation – overruled in favor of HELL-BENT FOR HEAVEN – for the Prize for Drama. It was revived in New York in 1932, in 1950 as the first use of arena staging on Broadway, and in 1967 by the ASSOCIATION OF PRODUCING ARTISTS–Phoenix Repertory Company, with HELEN HAYES as the irascible Mrs. Fisher.   KF

Shubert brothers American theatre owners and producers. The family business was founded by three brothers – **Sam S.** (1877?–1905), **Lee** (1875?–1953), and **Jacob J.** (1879?–1963) Shubert – who began their careers in Syracuse, NY, in the late 19th century. The brothers moved to NYC in 1900 and began producing and acquiring theatres, including the Herald Square and the CASINO. Among the stars who worked in Shubert shows during the early years were RICHARD MANSFIELD, Sarah Bernhardt, and LILLIAN RUSSELL. Sam Shubert died in a train crash in 1905, but his brothers continued to operate the business on an increasingly lavish scale, often coming into conflict with the Theatrical SYNDICATE, a rival group of theatre owners and managers that dominated American theatrical activity in the early 20th century. By 1916, however, the Shuberts had broken the Syndicate monopoly and had themselves became the nation's most important and powerful theatre owners and managers. During the 1910s and '20s, the Shubert brothers built many of Broadway's theatres, including the WINTER GARDEN, the SAM S. SHUBERT, and the IMPERIAL. In addition, they came to own or operate more than 100 theatres across the country and to book more than 1,000 others. Among their major stars of the period were AL JOLSON and EDDIE CANTOR, both of whom were great successes at the Winter Garden. The Shuberts were especially well known for their productions of operettas by Sigmund Romberg, among them *Maytime* (1917), *Blossom Time* (1921), and *The Student Prince* (1924). They were also known for their popular annual revues – *The Passing Show,* which appeared regularly during 1912–24, and *Artists and Models,* produced in a number of editions from 1923 to 1943. Although the Shuberts' business was badly hurt by the Depression, they continued to produce throughout the 1930s and '40s, presenting a number of well-known musicals and revues, including the later editions of the Ziegfeld *Follies,* Cole Porter's *You Never Know* (1938), and Olsen and Johnson's *Hellzapoppin* (1938), as well as such popular straight plays as *Ten Little Indians* (1944) and *Dark of the Moon* (1945). During the 1950s the U.S. government brought an antitrust suit against the Shuberts, who were forced to divest themselves of a number of their theatres in 1956. During the 1950s and early '60s the company was run by J. J. Shubert's son **John** (1909–62), and after his death by a great-nephew of the founders, **Lawrence Shubert Lawrence Jr.** (1916–92). The most recent studies of the brothers are by Brooks McNamara (1990) and Foster Hirsch (1996; 1998).   BMCN   DBW

Shubert Organization Theatrical real estate and producing company founded in the late 19th century by the Shubert family. From 1972 to 1996 its chief operating officers were two former Shubert lawyers, Gerald Schoenfeld and Bernard B. Jacobs. Jacobs served as president of the Shubert Organization and Schoenfeld as chairman of the board. In addition, they were respectively president and chairman of the **Shubert Foundation,** a related philanthropic institution that provides support to many nonprofit theatre and dance producing groups. After Jacobs's death in 1996, Schoenfeld continued as head of both the Organization (though later that year Philip J. Smith was appointed president) and the Foundation. The Shubert Organization currently owns and manages 16 of the operating Broadway theatres, including the Ambassador, Ethel Barrymore, Belasco, Booth, Broadhurst, Broadway, Cort, John Golden, Imperial, Longacre, Lyceum, Majestic, Plymouth (renamed the Gerald Schoenfeld in 2005), Royale (renamed the Bernard S. Jacobs in 2005), Sam S. Shubert, and the Winter Garden, plus one Off-Broadway house, The Little Shubert. In addition, the company has a half interest in the Music Box Theatre. Outside NYC, the Organization owns and operates the Shubert in Boston and the Forrest in Philadelphia, and manages the National in Washington, DC. Although the company was not active in theatrical production during the 1950s and '60s, in recent years it has once again become involved in Broadway producing. Some of its representative productions have included *Sly Fox* (1976), Gin Game (1977), *Dancin'* and *Ain't Misbehavin'* (both 1978), *Amadeus* (1980), Children of a Lesser God (1980), *Dream Girls* (1981), *Nicholas Nickleby* (1981), *Cats* (1982), Glengarry Glen Ross (1984), Sunday in the Park with George (1984), *The Heidi Chronicles* (1989), *Dancing at Lughnasa* (1991), *Someone Who'll Watch Over Me* (1992), *Indiscretions* (1995), Bring in 'da Noise, Bring in 'da Funk (1996), *Chicago* (1996), *Art* (1998), *Fosse* (1999), *Copenhagen* (2000), *The Goat, or Who Is Sylvia?* (2002), Avenue Q (2003), *Spamalot* (2005), *The Color Purple* (2005), and *Journey's End* (2007), among many others. The Shubert Organization also produced a highly successful Off-Broadway show, Little Shop of Horrors (1982), which it revived on Broadway in 2003. The company was influential in the revitalization of the Times Square theatrical district, has pioneered a number of innovative theatre business practices – among them the introduction of telephone and charge ticket sales and a computerized ticketing system – and has renovated most of its theatres.   BMcN

Shubert Theatre see Sam S. Shubert Theatre

Shue, Larry (1946–85) Playwright-actor born in New Orleans and educated at Illinois Wesleyan (1968). After graduation he acted in dinner theatres, eventually becoming a member of the Milwaukee Repertory. There his writing flourished with premieres of *The Nerd* (1981) and *The Foreigner* (1982). Both became hits in the regional theatres, and in 1984 *The Nerd* had a successful run in London's West End and *The Foreigner* at the Astor Place Theatre in New York. Shue was writing a screenplay for *The Foreigner* – and had just appeared in *The Mystery of Edwin Drood* at the New York Shakespeare Festival's Delacorte – when he was killed in a plane crash in Virginia.   BBW

Shuffle Along A 1921 black musical comedy that swept New York when it opened at the 63rd Street Music Hall and played for 504 performances. Vaudeville duo Flournoy Miller and Aubrey Lyles teamed with lyricist Noble Sissle and composer Eubie Blake (see Sissle and Blake) to produce what the *New York American* called "an infection of amusement." With a simple story line, catchy lyrics, an unforgettable score, and a talented and energetic cast, the show was irresistible. Two disreputable characters, Sam and Steve, played by Miller and Lyles, contest a mayoralty race in Jimtown on the understanding that the winner will name the other as his chief of police. With the election over, the former buddies quarrel over the spoils of office. Eventually they are run out of town by reform candidate Harry Walton, who wins the next election with his popular song: "I'm Just Wild About Harry." The show's success spawned a rash of new black musicals and established the genre on Broadway.   EGH

Shumlin, Herman (1898–1979) Director and producer who established himself as LILLIAN HELL-MAN's champion with productions of *The CHIL-DREN'S HOUR* (1934), *Days to Come* (1936), *The LITTLE FOXES* (1939), *WATCH ON THE RHINE* (1941), *The Searching Wind* (1944), and a City Center revival of *Regina* (1953). Other noteworthy productions include *The Last Mile* (1930), *The Merchant of Yonkers* (1938), *The MALE ANIMAL* (1940), *The Corn Is Green* (1940), *INHERIT THE WIND* (1955, on which he collaborated with MARGO JONES), and Hochhuth's *The Deputy* (1964). A film director in the 1940s, he made the film version of *Watch on the Rhine* (1943). Producer of serious and worthy drama, called a "crusty perfectionist," his liberal political philosophy was reflected in the plays he chose to present.   MR

Shyre, Paul (1929–89) Playwright, actor, director, and educator who died of septicemia, infections linked to AIDS. He is best known for his adaptations (in which he also performed) – *Pictures in the Hallway* (1956) and *I Knock at the Door* (1957), based on O'Casey's autobiographies, both on Broadway; and *U.S.A.,* based on John Dos Passos's work (OFF-BROADWAY, 1959; his first production, at WEST-PORT COUNTRY PLAYHOUSE, 1953) – and for those of his plays he also directed (mostly Off-Broadway, several ONE-PERSON plays): *Drums under the Windows* (1960), also drawn from O'Casey; *A Whitman Portrait* (1966); *Will Rogers' USA* (1972, Broadway; James Whitmore); *Blasts and Bravos: An Evening with H. L. Mencken* (1975; Shyre as Mencken); and *Paris Was Yesterday* (1980; CELESTE HOLM as Janet Flanner). Shyre was the recipient of a Tony, an Obie, two Drama Desks, and an Emmy award.   DBW

Siedel (or Siedle), **Caroline** (or Carolyne) (1859–1908) Costume designer and maker, native of London, who immigrated to the U.S. after marrying Edward Siedel, property master at the Metropolitan Opera House. Her American debut was *The Princess Nicotine* in 1892. She designed costumes for *The Belle of New York* in 1897 for the CASINO THEATRE, considered to be the first production to originate in New York and then transfer to Lon-

don, complete with original cast, costumes, and scenery. Between 1900 and 1907 she received program credit, unusual for that era, for 42 productions, including *The WIZARD OF OZ* in 1903 (original designs extant in the Billy Rose Theatre Collection, New York Public Library for the Performing Arts, Lincoln Center).   BO

Siegfried (Fischbaker) (1943–) and **Roy (Horn)** (1945–) German-born illusionists who until late 2003 were the masters of the spectacular stage MAGIC show and considered by some the most successful magicians in history – certainly their million-dollar Las Vegas contract made them the best paid. Together since 1960, they had limited their work to Las Vegas and were known primarily for their "Beyond Belief" show at the Frontier Hotel (beginning 1981) and in the 1990s at the Mirage, featuring tigers, elephants, lasers, fire, fog, and slick high-tech illusions. By the unscheduled end of their run in October 2003 – when Roy was mauled by a white tiger during a show – they had appeared in almost 20,000 live shows. As of 2006 he has made remarkable progress toward recovery.   DBW

Sign in Sidney Brustein's Window, The LOR-RAINE HANSBERRY's last work was first presented at NYC's LONGACRE THEATRE 15 October 1964, directed by Peter Kass and featuring Gabriel Dell, RITO MORENO, and Frank Schofield (with a Tony for supporting actress for Alice Ghostley). It ran 101 performances despite lukewarm reviews. This small mixed-cast play, set in Greenwich Village, explores the lives of a group of artists and rebels as they struggle with their disillusionments. It mixes styles as it challenges the apathy of American intellectuals.   KME

Signature Theatre Company Though founded only in 1991 by director James Houghton (as the sole company in the U.S. offering a year's residency for playwrights), Signature has gained critical acclaim, receiving a 1995 special New York Drama Critics' Circle Award for Outstanding Achievement and staging the 1995 Pulitzer Prize for Drama play, Foote's *The Young Man from Atlanta*. Playwrights thus far honored are (in order of residency) as follows: ROMULUS LINNEY, LEE BLESS-ING, EDWARD ALBEE, HORTON FOOTE, ADRIENNE KENNEDY, SAM SHEPARD, ARTHUR MILLER, JOHN GUARE, MARIA IRENE FORNÉS, LANFORD WILSON, BILL IRWIN, and PAULA VOGEL. (Three seasons were devoted to multiple playwrights.) Its 2006–7 season posthumously featured plays by AUGUST WILSON. Located through the 1994–5 season at

NYC's Kampo Cultural & Multimedia Center on Bond St., then at The PUBLIC THEATER for 1995–6, in 1999 Signature moved into a new venue, The Peter Norton Space, on West 42d St. The company now anticipates a future move into a new space in the World Trade Center vicinity.   DBW

Silk Stockings Two-act musical comedy – suggested by the film based on Melchior Lengyel's screen story *Ninotchka* – with music and lyrics by COLE PORTER and book by GEORGE S. KAUFMAN, Leueen MacGrath, and ABE BURROWS; opened on Broadway (24 February 1955) at the IMPERIAL THEATRE for 478 performances. Critics hailed the performances of Don Ameche, Hildegarde Neff, and especially Gretchen Wyler, whose comic timing stole the show. Due to the notorious scare about communism at this time, audiences were interested in a musical comedy about U.S.–Soviet relations. Set in Paris and Moscow, the musical focuses on the budding romance between a Russian commissar and an American agent, with subplots about the film and entertainment industry. Songs include "All of You," "Stereophonic Sound," and "Silk Stockings."   EK

Sills, Douglas (1960–) Detroit-born actor-singer, educated at Michigan and the AMERICAN CONSERVATORY THEATRE, who established himself as a character actor in California theatre and in national tours (*The SECRET GARDEN, INTO THE WOODS*). He created the role of Percy in *The Scarlet Pimpernel* (1997) and contributed palpably to its success after an initial savaging by the critics (in four different versions). For his performance he received a Theatre World Award. In 2002 he played Count Carl-Magnus in the JOHN F. KENNEDY CENTER production of *A LITTLE NIGHT MUSIC* and appeared as Orin (among 10 roles played) in the Broadway revival of *LITTLE SHOP OF HORRORS*. Originally cast as Galahad in *Spamalot*, he withdrew in 2004 before its opening.   DBW

Sills, Paul (1927–) Director. The son of Viola Spolin, author of *Improvisation for the Theater*, Sills has spent most of his life finding practical applications for his mother's theories. He cofounded The Compass Players (1955) and SECOND CITY (1959), helped found the BODY POLITIC THEATRE (1966), developed an audience-participation experiment called Game Theater (1967), and developed an adaptive form called Story Theater, one version of which he took to Broadway in 1970. He currently directs an actor-training school in NYC with MIKE NICHOLS and George Morrison.   SF

Silver Cord, The SIDNEY HOWARD's three-act play, produced by the THEATRE GUILD, opened on Broadway at the JOHN GOLDEN THEATRE 20 December 1926 and ran 112 performances. Mrs. Phelps (LAURA HOPE CREWS) smothers both of her grown sons with love. The elder breaks free and saves his marriage, but the younger is "engulfed," and his fiancée (Margalo Gillmore) breaks their engagement. Critics compared Howard's effort to GEORGE KELLY's earlier *CRAIG'S WIFE*, though the latter was far more popular.   JDM

Silver, Nicky (1960–) Philadelphia-born, NYU-educated playwright of such early zany comedies as *Scopophilia, The Nasty Bits, Fetid Itch,* and *Wanking 'Tards*. He first gained attention with *Pterodactyls* (1993), produced at NYC's VINEYARD THEATRE, an unapologetically biting attack on a dysfunctional family in which a son returns home unexpectedly with the news that he has AIDS. Several wild domestic farces followed, often with neurotic monologues. Some early works – *Fat Men in Skirts* (1988) and *Free Will & Wanton Lust* (1993) (both Vortex Theatre Company, NYC) – serve up shock value and irreverent scenarios. Later plays (most at the Vineyard) – notably *Raised in Captivity* (1995), *The Food Chain* (1994, WOOLLY MAMMOTH), *Fit to Be Tied* (1996, PLAYWRIGHTS HORIZONS), *The Altruists* (2000), *Beautiful Child* (2004), and *The Agony and the Agony* (2006) – though smoother around the edges, still lace seemingly aimless chatter with hilarious non sequiturs and punch lines. As a satirist he tackles serious, dark subjects such as love and hate, loneliness, self-denial, spiritual hunger, and the intimacies (or lack of them) between mothers and sons.   RG

Silver [né Zimelman], **Ron** (1946–) NYC-born actor trained at the ACTORS STUDIO and BERGHOF's HB Studios. He made his stage debut OFF-BROADWAY in *Kaspar* and *Public Insult* (1971). His major appearances have been on Broadway in RABE's *HURLYBURLY*, Andrew Bergman's *Social Security* (both directed by MIKE NICHOLS), and MAMET's *Speed-the-Plow*, the last winning him Tony and Drama Desk awards (1988). He was president of ACTORS' EQUITY (1991–2000) and is an activist for environmentalism and artistic freedom.   DBW

Silvers, Phil [né Philip] (1912–85) Brooklyn-born comic actor who began his career at age 13 as a singer with Gus Edwards's VAUDEVILLE troupe. In 1935 he joined MINSKY's BURLESQUE as a comic, advancing to the Broadway stage by 1939. Though Silvers won Tonys for *Top Banana* (1951) and *A Funny Thing Happened on the Way to the Forum* (1972 revival), the bald, bespectacled funnyman is best remembered for his numerous films and his television creation of the scheming con man Sergeant Ernie Bilko (1955–9).   DBW

Simon, John (1925–) Yugoslavian-born drama and film critic. Educated at Harvard (Ph.D., 1959), Simon has been regarded as a brilliant stylist who demands that the theatre be intelligent and articulate. He wrote about the drama for *Hudson Review* (1960–81); about films and drama for *New York* magazine from 1969 until he was dismissed in 2005; and about films for the *New Leader* since 1962. He now writes theatre criticism for a Web site. He is author of at least a dozen books, including *Singularities: Essays on the Theatre, 1964–73* (1976) and *John Simon on Theatre: Criticism 1974–2003* (2005). Simon believes that the critic is responsible first to himself then to his audience, and that a piece of criticism should be both pleasurable to read and philosophical in nature. A penchant for invective and harsh personal comments, however, has put him at odds with the theatre community and his colleagues.   TLM

Simon, (Marvin) Neil (1927–) Playwright, screenwriter, and producer. Critical acclaim came slowly for Simon whose 28 plays and 5 musicals have included more smash hits than any other American playwright. For most of his career, he has fought a reputation of being a gag writer who catered to the moral hangups and material greed of middle-class America. However, When in 1991 *Lost in Yonkers* won both the Tony and Drama Desk awards for New Play and the Pulitzer Prize for Drama, Simon earned new respect from critics, who began to discuss him as a major American playwright, especially of comedy.

Born in New York, Simon learned his craft by writing comic material for radio and television personalities. With his brother, Danny, he wrote sketches for Broadway shows, *Catch a Star* (1955) and *New Faces of 1956*. His first full-length comedy, *Come Blow Your Horn* (1961), was a hit, followed closely by the musical farce *Little Me* (1962, with Cy Coleman's music and Carolyn Leigh's lyrics). After *Barefoot in the Park* (1963), he penned one of the funniest and wisest plays in 1965, *The Odd Couple* (Tony); and a year later added both *The Star-Spangled Girl* and the musical *Sweet Charity*. With four shows running simultaneously on Broadway, Simon was the most successful play-

wright of the 1960s. He added *Plaza Suite* to his list of smash hits in 1968, together with the musical *Promises, Promises* (Burt Bacharach, music; Hal David, lyrics). After *Last of the Red Hot Lovers* (1969), Simon wrote *The Gingerbread Lady* (1970), which attempted to deal honestly with alcoholism. While audiences rejected it, the playwright seemed more willing to attempt serious themes, and two bittersweet comedies followed: *The Prisoner of Second Avenue* (1971) and *The Sunshine Boys* (1972).

Following the death of his first wife in 1973, Simon reached a low point in his career with two failures: *The Good Doctor* (1973), adapted from short stories by Anton Chekhov; and *God's Favorite* (1976), adapted from the biblical story of Job. However, a move to California resulted in another hit, *California Suite* (1976), a Beverly Hills version of *Plaza Suite*. His marriage to actress Marsha Mason resulted in *Chapter Two* (1977), regarded by some critics as his finest play to that point in his career. (They divorced in 1981.) His fourth musical, *They're Playing Our Song*, proved popular in 1979, but his next three efforts were not successful: *I Ought to Be in Pictures* (1980), *Fools* (1981), and a revised version of *Little Me* (1982). Simon then returned to his own past for a charming *Brighton Beach Memoirs* (1983) and the Tony Award–winning *Biloxi Blues* (1985); and by recasting the two major roles in *The Odd Couple* for women, Simon found himself with three hits in 1985, and new respect from the critics. The following year, *Broadway Bound* proved another popular success, though followed by two failures: *Rumors* (1988), and *Jake's Women* (1990), the latter initially seen only in San Diego but revised for Broadway (1992) with Alan Alda. *Lost in Yonkers* (1991; film, 1993) has proven to be his most critically acclaimed play to date. The musical version of his 1977 film *The Goodbye Girl* had a modest Broadway run in 1993; *Laughter on the 23rd Floor*, which harks back to his days as a young comic writer for TV's *Your Show of Shows*, opened in 1993 on Broadway; and *London Suite*, directed by Daniel Sullivan, premiered at the Seattle Repertory Theatre in 1994 and Off-Broadway (at the Union Square) – a choice that surprised the establishment – in spring 1995.

His recent plays, on Broadway and Off-, include *Proposals* (1997), *The Dinner Party* (2000), *45 Seconds from Broadway* (2001), and *Rose's Dilemma* (2003, Manhattan Theatre Club). Recent Broadway revivals number *Sweet Charity* (2005), *The Odd Couple* (2005) starring Nathan Lane and Matthew Broderick, and *Barefoot in the Park* (2006). He was recognized in 1995 by the Kennedy Center Honors and in 2006 received the Mark Twain Prize for American Humor. Simon is the author of two autobiographies (1996 and 1999)   TLM

Simonson, Lee (1888–1967) Set designer; a founding member and director of the THEATRE GUILD. Simonson studied for three years in Paris and, like ROBERT EDMOND JONES, returned to the U.S. with great excitement about the New Stagecraft. He advocated simplified realism: While creating sets that were based in realism, he stripped away all scenic elements that were unnecessary for mood or information. As resident designer for the Theatre Guild he designed more than half their productions, including *Heartbreak House, Liliom,* and *Green Grow the Lilacs.* His designs for *The ADDING MACHINE* were among the most successful examples of expressionism on the American stage. He authored several important books, including *The Stage Is Set* (1932) and *Part of a Lifetime: Drawings and Designs, 1919–1940* (1943).   AA

Simpson, Edmund Shaw (1784–1848) Manager. From stage manager in 1810 to acting manager in 1821, Simpson became sole lessee of the PARK THEATRE in 1840 upon the death of STEPHEN PRICE. Shrewd manipulators of public taste, Simpson and Price early managed to associate the Park with fashion, despite a commonplace repertory. Extravaganzas and stars like Macready and the KEMBLES, CHARLOTTE CUSHMAN, and WILLIAM WHEATLEY failed to forestall economic reversals or the deterioration of the building. Characterized as industrious but unremarkable as a manager, Simpson sold out to THOMAS S. HAMBLIN in 1848, the year the Park burned [see FIRES].
   RKB

Sinise, Gary (1955–) Born in Blue Island, IL, this stage, film, and television actor-director was a founder in 1974 of the STEPPENWOLF THEATRE COMPANY, where he has acted and directed often: doing both in *TRUE WEST* (1982; also seen OFF-BROADWAY that year), acting in *GRAPES OF WRATH* (1988; Broadway, 1990), for which he was nominated for a Tony as Tom Joad, and playing Stanley Kowalski in *A STREETCAR NAMED DESIRE* (1997). His 1996 direction of *BURIED CHILD* and his 2001 role as Randle McMurphy in *One Flew Over the Cuckoo's Nest* – each originating at Steppenwolf the previous year – were also Tony nominees. His film credits are numerous, including George opposite JOHN MALKOVICH's Lennie in *OF MICE AND MEN* (1992), their earlier onstage roles (Chicago, 1981). Since 2004 he has starred in CBS's *CSI: NY*.   DBW

Sissle, Noble (1889–1975) and **Eubie Blake** (1883–1983) Lyricist and composer. Pianist and composer Eubie Blake met singer-lyricist Noble Sissle in 1915. For several years they performed in VAUDEVILLE in an act featuring their own songs. In 1921 they joined with the vaudeville comedy team of Flournoy Miller and Aubrey Lyles to create the first black musical to play a major Broadway theatre during the regular theatrical season: *SHUFFLE ALONG.* With a book by Miller and Lyles, who also starred in it, *Shuffle Along* was a big hit both in New York and on tour. Critics and audiences delighted in the vitality of the score and the lively dancing of the chorus.

Sissle and Blake went on to write the scores for several other musicals, including *The Chocolate Dandies* (1924) and *Shuffle Along of 1933,* but without the success that had been achieved by *Shuffle Along.* On his own, Blake wrote the music for several other shows. A revival of *Shuffle Along* in 1952 was a failure, but with the rediscovery of ragtime in the 1960s and '70s Sissle and Blake songs were again heard on Broadway in *Doctor Jazz* (1975), *Bubbling Brown Sugar* (1976), and *Eubie!* (1978). Their story is told in a book by Richard Kimball and William Bolcom (1973).   MK

Six Degrees of Separation by JOHN GUARE ran OFF-BROADWAY at the Mitzi E. Newhouse Theatre 19 May–28 October 1990 and was moved to the VIVIAN BEAUMONT THEATRE on 8 November. Directed by JERRY ZAKS, its 17-member cast included STOCKARD CHANNING as Ouisa Kittredge, John Cunningham as her husband, Flan, and James McDaniel as Paul Poitier (Courtney B. Vance at the Beaumont), as well as Sam Stoneburner, Stephen Pearlman, and Kelly Bishop. London's Royal Court staged the play with Channing during the summer of 1992; Channing re-created her role in the 1993 film with Donald Sutherland. The play is based on an incident in 1983, when a young man posing as the son of Sidney Poitier worked his way into the lives of some wealthy New Yorkers and robbed them. Its theme is implied in its title, which refers to a statistical theory that everyone on earth is connected to everyone else by a trail of only six people. Guare uses the incident to satirize liberal guilt, the isolationism of modern urban life, and the generational hostility in the contemporary American family. At the same time he celebrates the creativity of the young con artist who takes advantage of the lack of imagination in his victims.   BCM

Skelton, Thomas (1927–94) One of the more influential of the "second generation" of lighting designers following JEAN ROSENTHAL and ABE FEDER, Skelton designed extensively for DANCE and was closely associated with the Paul Taylor and José Limon companies, the Ballet Folklorico de Mexico, and the Joffrey Ballet, where his work included a startling set and lighting design for the rock ballet *Astarte*. He designed CIRCUS and ice shows as well. Theatre designs included *Purlie, Gigi, OH DAD, POOR DAD . . .*, and *Coco*, as well as several notable revivals.   AA

Skin of Our Teeth, The, by THORNTON WILDER premiered in 1942 in a stormy production featuring FREDRIC MARCH, FLORENCE ELDRIDGE, Montgomery Clift, and TALLULAH BANKHEAD, directed by ELIA KAZAN. Wilder's daring, nonnaturalistic allegory of the human race, which included episodes from the Ice Age to a seven-year war, puzzled many of its cast members, who were already reeling from Tallulah's flamboyant rehearsal behavior. The opening was a success, however, and eventually led to 355 performances and a Pulitzer Prize. Still, controversy stalked the production when two scholars charged in the *Saturday Review* that Wilder had plagiarized some of the play's ideas from Joyce's *Finnegans Wake*. The accusations – and their subsequent discussions – were overblown, but did contribute to a squabble among the critics, who denied the play their prestigious Circle Award. Time and numerous revivals have vindicated Wilder's imaginative vision, and the play has been directed or performed by dozens of theatrical luminaries, including Laurence Olivier, JOHN HOUSEMAN, GEORGE ABBOTT, HELEN HAYES, and Vivien Leigh.   BBW

Skinner, Cornelia Otis (1901–79) Actress, monologuist, humorist, and author; daughter of actor OTIS SKINNER, with whom she made her professional debut in 1921 in *Blood and Sand*. She established her reputation as a fine actress beginning in the 1920s touring the U.S. and Britain in monodramas (see ONE-PERSON PERFORMANCES) she wrote and staged herself. These included *The Wives of Henry VIII* (1931), *The Empress Eugenie* (1932), *The Loves of Charles II* (1933) – all revived in 1937 – and *Paris '90* (1952). In more traditional theatre she appeared in *Candida* (1939, tour), *Theatre* (1941), *Lady Windermere's Fan* (1946), and *The Pleasure of His Company* (1958), the last coauthored with SAMUEL TAYLOR. She also wrote memoirs, light verse, essays, and three critically acclaimed theatrical biographies: *Family Circle* (1948), the story of her famous family; *Madame Sarah*, on Bernhardt (1967); and *Life with LINDSAY and CROUSE* (1976). She is probably most remembered for the

1942 travelogue she cowrote with Emily Kimbrough: *Our Hearts Were Young and Gay*.   DBW

Skinner, Otis (1858–1942) One of America's most versatile actors who, by his own account, played over 140 roles during 1877–9 with the resident companies of the Philadelphia Museum and the WALNUT STREET THEATRE. Between 1879 and 1892, Skinner played in the companies of EDWIN BOOTH, LAWRENCE BARRETT, AUGUSTIN DALY, HELENA MODJESKA, and JOSEPH JEFFERSON III, and occasionally starred as romantic hero, classical tragedian, comedian, and character actor. From 1892, Skinner was a confirmed and popular star who continued to play a varied repertory. In his own time and for later generations, he was best remembered for the role of Hajj, the beggar, in *KISMET*, which he created in 1911, played exclusively for three years, and preserved in two film versions. Skinner, and his actress daughter, CORNELIA OTIS SKINNER, were both prolific writers, the former author of *Footlights and Spotlights* (1924), *The Last Tragedian* (1939, on Edwin Booth), and *One Man in His Time: The Adventures of Harry Watkins, Strolling Player, 1845–1863* (1938, with his wife, Maud).   MR

Slade, Bernard (1930–) Playwright and screenwriter. Born in Toronto and educated in England; a successful television writer before his comedy *Same Time, Next Year* was a Broadway hit in 1975. Working mostly in Hollywood, Slade created eight major television series including *The Flying Nun* and *The Partridge Family*, in addition to his plays *Tribute* (1978, starring Jack Lemmon), *Romantic Comedy* (1979, starring Anthony PERKINS), *Special Occasions* (1982) (all Broadway); *Fatal Attraction* (1984, Toronto), *Return Engagements* (1986, WESTPORT COUNTRY PLAYHOUSE), *Sweet William* (1987, U.K.), *An Act of the Imagination* (1987), and *Same Time, Another Year* (1995), a sequel to his 1975 play. His plays are especially popular in community theatres.   TLM

Slave Ship Historical pageant by LeRoi Jones (AMIRI BARAKA) that traces the journey of African slaves to America and their experiences on arrival. The 1967 play consists of pantomimed actions that portray the revolting conditions below deck accompanied by cries and moans in the Yoruba language; then the slave market, aborted uprisings, and the symbolic destruction of white America. Directed by GILBERT MOSES at the CHELSEA THEATRE in Brooklyn, to music by Archie Shepp, the production was accounted to have been devastating.   EGH

Slow Dance on the Killing Ground Three-act drama by William Hanley; opened on Broadway at the PLYMOUTH THEATRE (30 November 1964) for 88 performances, garnering three Tony nominations. It was revived OFF-BROADWAY at Sheridan Square Playhouse (13 May 1970) for 36 performances. Although realistic, it is laden with symbolism, as three lost souls late one night in a NYC candy store confess their innermost secrets to each other regarding racism, murder, family loyalty, and personal worth.   EK

Smith, Anna Deavere (1950–) Actress, educator, and playwright. Since 1983 Smith has developed a series of unique ONE-PERSON PERFORMANCE pieces collectively called "On the Road: A Search for American Character" (based on interviews about controversial events or subjects; see DOCUMENTARY THEATRE), yet her work was not widely known until 1992 when *Fires in the Mirror: Crown Heights, Brooklyn, and Other Identities* (based on the 1991 stabbing of a Hasidic scholar by a group of young black men in Brooklyn), the 13th in this series, was presented in May 1992 at the [JOSEPH PAPP] PUBLIC THEATER. Her human collage of more than 20 individuals, termed a remarkable theatrical event, won her wide acclaim and multiple honors (including a special Obie, a Drama Desk, and a LUCILLE LORTEL Award), and was a nominated finalist for the Pulitzer Prize for Drama. Her next major work, *Twilight: Los Angeles, 1992* (focused on racial tension in Los Angeles), was first produced at LA's MARK TAPER FORUM (spring 1993), and later Off- and on Broadway in 1994 (Obie, Best Play; Drama Desk, Solo). *House Arrest: First Edition* opened at the ARENA STAGE (1997) and explored the national identity as embodied by the American presidency, present and past; it played at The Public in 2000. A new play, *Let Me Down Easy*, "about how the human body is both resilient and vulnerable to many different forces," is projected for a 2007 completion. She has appeared in several films and as a semi-regular (National Security Advisor) in TV's *The West Wing*. Her book *Letters to a Young Artist* was published in 2006. Smith, who holds an M.F.A. from the AMERICAN CONSERVATORY THEATRE, has taught at Yale, NYU, Carnegie Mellon, USC, and Stanford.   DBW

Smith, Harry B(ache) (1860–1936) Librettist and lyricist. Smith's first connection with the theatre was as a dramatic and musical editor for a Chicago newspaper. For composer REGINALD DE KOVEN he created the libretto and most of the lyrics for the most beloved American comic opera of the late 19th century, *ROBIN HOOD* (1891). Although much of his writing was mediocre by modern standards, Smith's ability to adapt to changing styles and tastes in musical theatre ensured him a long and prolific career, in the course of which he was reported to have written some 300 librettos and 6,000 lyrics. His autobiography appeared in 1931; a biography by John Franceschina was published in 2003.   MK

Smith [né Sultzer], **Joe** (1884–1981) and **Charlie Dale** [né Charles Marks] (1881–1971) Comic VAUDEVILLE team (for 73 years); inspiration for NEIL SIMON's *The SUNSHINE BOYS*. Smith and Dale began in 1898 as a blackface act, singing and dancing in Bowery saloons while working as hash slingers at Childs Restaurant. New names were adopted when calling cards for another team, who chose to change their name (to MORAN AND MACK), were used by a theatre owner to advertise them. In 1901 they joined the Imperial Vaudeville and Comedy Company. When the company folded they stayed with two other members (Will Lester and Jack Coleman) to form the Avon Comedy Four, developing such classic sketches as "Hungarian Rhapsody," "Dr. Kronkhite," "The New School Teacher," and "Venetian Knights." Numerous comics served with the Avon troupe before "Smith and Dale" became headliners in the 1920s, featuring their "Dr. Kronkhite" sketch (Smith the patient, Dale the doctor), thereafter inseparably associated with them. In their sketches Smith, lanky with a pencil mustache, received the punch lines while Dale, smaller and deadpan, was his foil. BROOKS ATKINSON characterized them as "professional performers, acting two low-comedy parts with style, authority and abandon."   DBW

Smith, Lois [née Lois Arlene Humbert] (1930–) Kansas-born actress, whose luminous portrayal of Carrie Watts (Obie and Drama Desk awards) in the 2005 SIGNATURE revival of FOOTE's *The Trip to Bountiful* (directed by HARRIS YULIN) was termed by the *New York Times* "the performance of the decade" and brought her unique talent once more into focus. An enduring talent whose career spans five decades, beginning with her Broadway debut in *Time Out for Ginger* (1952), Smith is able to assume a role in a way that retains an unassailable integrity, be it slovenly Hallie in *Buried Child* (1996) or Ma Joad in *The GRAPES OF WRATH* (1990), both nominated for Tonys. Other notable credits include *The Young and Beautiful* (1955), *Orpheus Descending* (1957), and *BLUES FOR MISTER CHARLIE* (1964). Since 1993 she has been an Ensemble member at STEPPENWOLF. She has extensive film credits (*Five Easy Pieces, East of Eden, Minority Report*), often essaying sensitive, earthy, and even eerie roles. Smith attended the University of Washington and trained with LEE STRASBERG.   DBW

Smith, Oliver (1918–94) Set designer, theatrical producer, and educator who from 1941 designed some 400 theatre, dance, opera, and film productions, and also served as codirector of American Ballet Theatre (1945–81). He began his career designing for dance, notably *Rodeo* and *Fall River Legend* for AGNES DE MILLE, and *Fancy Free* for JEROME ROBBINS. Starting with the 1944 production of ON THE TOWN (which he also coproduced), Smith designed a steady stream of long-running musicals, including MY FAIR LADY, WEST SIDE STORY, and HELLO DOLLY! Smith believed that scenery for musicals should be bright, entertaining, and change quickly and unobtrusively. He talked about scenery in terms of choreography: In *Fall River Legend,* the scenery is, in fact, an integral part of the choreography. In terms of style he frequently mixed painterly backgrounds with sculptural scenic elements. He also had an almost formulaic approach to the arrangement of scenic elements and space, which meshed well with the musicals of the 1940s and '50s and contributed to his prodigious output. Smith also taught design at New York University.   AA

Smith, Richard Penn (1799–1854) One of many American intellectuals who wrote fiction and poetry and edited journals, Smith created some 20 plays, five of them staged in 1829. Of these, *The Eighth of January* celebrated Andrew Jackson's victory, and *William Penn* revealed Smith's talent for comedy. *Caius Marius* (1831), a tragedy based on this Roman's love of country, was selected as a Prize Play by EDWIN FORREST, who performed the title role only a few times. Although Smith enjoyed some success, his interest in the theatre was momentary. Bruce W. McCullough wrote a biography of him in 1917.   WJM

Smith, Solomon Franklin (1801–69) Theatre manager and actor, especially noted for his pioneering work on the FRONTIER. He began his theatrical career in Vincennes, IN, in 1819, and by 1823 had organized his own company, which he managed for four years. He then toured the Mississippi Valley with J. H. CALDWELL, and in 1835 entered into a partnership with NOAH LUDLOW. They dominated the frontier theatre of their time, but ended the partnership in 1853.

In his acting, Smith, affectionately known as "Old Sol," was particularly effective as a low

comedian in such roles as Mawworm in *The Hypocrite.* He eventually went into law and became a Missouri state senator. His three autobiographical volumes, *Theatrical Apprenticeship* (1845), *The Theatrical Journey-work and Anecdotal Recollections of Sol. Smith* (1854), and *Theatrical Management in the West and South for Thirty Years* (1868), are flawed but valuable insights into theatrical conditions of the time.   SMA

Smith, William Henry Sedley (1806–72) Playwright, actor, and stage manager. Born in Wales, Smith began acting with the Theatre Royal, Lancaster (1822), joined Philadelphia's WALNUT STREET company (1827), the TREMONT THEATRE in Boston (1828), and the BOSTON MUSEUM (1843) as stage manager and actor. Smith's *The DRUNKARD; OR, THE FALLEN SAVED* (1844) was the first successful temperance drama and the most enduring. After the initial 100-performance runs in Boston and New York, the play blanketed the country. His later career was spent in San Francisco as manager of the CALIFORNIA THEATRE. RM

Smith, Winchell (1872–1933) Playwright who, starting as an actor, learned how to pick collaborators and to please the public with farce and comic caricature. With Byron Ongley, he wrote *Brewster's Millions* (1906), in which a young man must spend a million dollars. This play marked the first appearance of the theatre's favorite fictional performer, George Spelvin, whom Smith would use many times. *Via Wireless* (1908) written with Paul Armstrong failed, but *The Fortune Hunter* (1909), written solo, proved a successful vehicle for John Barrymore (see DREW–BARRYMORE). *The Boomerang* (1915), with Victor Mapes, was a successful play about a man consumed with jealousy. Equally popular with audiences was *Turn to the Right!* (1916), written with John Hazzard, about two convicts who reform and marry into respectable families. Smith's greatest success came with LIGHTNIN' (1918), written with FRANK BACON, who acted the lovable ne'er-do-well hero. With 1,291 performances, *Lightnin'* broke the old record held by CHARLES HOYT's A TRIP TO CHINATOWN.   WJM

Smith-Cameron, J. [née Jeanie Smith] (c. 1955–) Actress, born in Louisville, KY; raised in South Carolina; educated at Florida State University. Her Broadway debut was as a replacement (the crazy Babe Botrelle) in CRIMES OF THE HEART (1982), her OFF-BROADWAY debut as Sally Middleton in *The Voice of the Turtle* with ROUNDABOUT. Other notable

Broadway credits include *Wild Honey* (1986), *Lend Me a Tenor* (1989, Outer Critics Circle Award for the cast), *Our Country's Good* (1991, Tony nomination), and *Tartuffe* (2003). Off-Broadway she originated in 1994 the role of Sissy Bemis Darnley in RUDNICK's *The Naked Truth* (later retitled *The Naked Eye*); played Libby in LUCAS's *Blue Window* (1996, MANHATTAN THEATRE CLUB); received an Obie for *As Bees in Honey Drown* (1997–8); was Claire in *Fuddy Meers* (MTC); and played Helen in David Marshall Grant's *Pen* (PLAYWRIGHTS HORIZONS). Married to playwright KENNETH LONERGAN, this slender, fine-featured artist is considered an exceptionally diverse stage actor.   DBW

societies and associations, theatrical There are well over 130 theatrical societies and associations in the U.S., far too many to detail here: Listings can be found in *The Encyclopedia of Associations* (Thomson Gale), a frequently updated source. Among the better known are the following: American Association of Community Theatre (AACT, founded 1986); American Society for Theatre Research (ASTR, 1956); American Theatre Critics Association (ATCA, 1974); Association for Theatre in Higher Education (ATHE, 1986); League of Historic American Theatres (LHAT, 1977); League of Resident Theatres (LORT, 1965); Literary Managers and Dramaturgs of America (LMDA, 1985); National Theatre Conference (NTC, 1925); New York Drama Critics' Circle (NYDCC, 1935); THEATRE COMMUNICATIONS GROUP (TCG, 1961); Theatre Historical Society (THS, 1969); Theatre Library Association (TLA, 1937); United States Institute for Theatre Technology (USITT, 1960).

Other theatrically oriented U.S. organizations include (among others) the American Theatre and Drama Society; Association for Asian Performance; College of Fellows of the American Theatre; DRAMATISTS GUILD; Institute of OUTDOOR DRAMA; NATIONAL PLAYWRIGHTS CONFERENCE; NEW DRAMATISTS; ALLIANCE OF RESIDENT THEATRES/NEW YORK; SOCIETY OF STAGE DIRECTORS AND CHOREOGRAPHERS.   SMA

Society of American Dramatists and Composers Playwrights' union founded by BRONSON HOWARD and AUGUSTUS THOMAS (1891). It was absorbed into the DRAMATISTS GUILD of America (1919), which achieved the first standard playwright's contract shortly after the successful strike by ACTORS' EQUITY ASSOCIATION.   DMcD

Society of Stage Directors and Choreographers (SSDC), The Incorporated in 1959, SSDC is a national independent labor union with the pur-

pose of elevating the standards of the art of stage direction and choreography. It represents c. 1,700 members and 300 associates (U.S. and abroad). The first SSDC contract was signed by BOB FOSSE for the Broadway production of *Little Me*. Its president in 2007 is PAMELA BERLIN.   DBW

Soldier's Play, A Pulitzer Prize–winning play written by CHARLES FULLER and staged in 1981 by the NEGRO ENSEMBLE COMPANY. A well-acted revival in 2005 was produced at NYC's SECOND STAGE. The play focuses on the search for the killer of an unpopular black sergeant in a segregated army camp in Louisiana during WWII. Possible suspects include members of the sergeant's own company, a white officer, and rednecks from the nearby town. The investigation, carried out by a black captain from Washington, DC, probes the characters of the men involved. Although the play received fine ensemble acting and a strongly favorable press, black opinion was reserved, holding that the play's resolution was cleverly contrived to appease white sensitivities.   EGH

Sommer, (Maximilian) Josef (1934–) German-born actor who, after debuting at the University of North Carolina at 7, went on to specialize in "hard-boiled, avuncular roles" in "emotionally deep . . . performances." After his New York debut in *Othello* (1970), he appeared with the Repertory Theater of LINCOLN CENTER, AMERICAN SHAKESPEARE FESTIVAL, AMERICAN CONSERVATORY THEATRE, CIRCLE IN THE SQUARE, SEATTLE REPERTORY, HARTFORD STAGE, MARK TAPER FORUM, and LONG WHARF. Sommer's stage performances include *The Trial of the Catonsville Nine* (1971), *The Shadow Box* (1977), *The 1940's Radio Hour* (1979), *Whose Life Is It Anyway?* (1980), all on Broadway; *Lydie Breeze* (1982; Obie), *Largo Desolato* (1986; Obie), *A Walk in the Woods* (1987, YALE REP), *The Visit* (1991, GOODMAN THEATRE); and *Hapgood* (1994) and *Racing Demon* (1995), both at Lincoln Center. His films include *Dirty Harry* (1971), *The Front* (1976), *Reds* (1981), *Silkwood* (1983), *Patch Adams* (1998), *Searching for Paradise* (2002), and *The Elephant King* (2006). Sommer's TV work includes *The Scarlet Letter*, *The Adams Chronicles*, *Law & Order*, and a televised *MOURNING BECOMES ELECTRA*. He was the recipient of a Fulbright Grant to study theatre in Germany.   REK

Sondheim, Stephen (1930–) Lyricist and composer. After an apprenticeship with OSCAR HAMMERSTEIN II, early writing for television, and composing incidental music for straight plays, Sondheim created the lyrics for *WEST SIDE STORY*

(1957) and *GYPSY* (1959). In 1962 he wrote his first complete score (music and lyrics) for *A FUNNY THING HAPPENED ON THE WAY TO THE FORUM.* After a failure with *Anyone Can Whistle* (1964), Sondheim startled the MUSICAL-THEATRE world with scores for a series of highly experimental shows. *COMPANY* (1970) was a collage of musical vignettes about married life in contemporary New York. *FOLLIES* (1971) used a reunion of musical-comedy performers to examine how middle age affects love and marriage. *A LITTLE NIGHT MUSIC* (1973) had a score written entirely in three-four time. *The Frogs* (1974), after Aristophanes, was performed in Yale's Olympic-sized swimming pool. *PACIFIC OVERTURES* (1976) employed Kabuki theatre conventions and an all-Asian cast to dramatize the opening of Japan to the West. *SWEENEY TODD* (1979) adapted Victorian melodrama to modern sensibilities by suggesting the tormented soul behind the "demon barber of Fleet Street." *Merrily We Roll Along* (1981), like the KAUFMAN and HART play that inspired it, debunked the myth of the American success story by tracing backward the lives of its central characters. *SUNDAY IN THE PARK WITH GEORGE* (1984) refracted the artistic process through the work of French pointillist Georges Seurat. *INTO THE WOODS* (1987) unveiled the darker Freudian aspects of fairy tales. *Assassins* (1991, PLAYWRIGHTS HORIZONS) considered the psychologies of those who have attempted to murder U.S. presidents. *Passion* (1994), based on Ettore Scola's film *Passione d'amore* and the 19th-century novel *Fosca,* examined the nature of love and its obsessive tendencies. *Bounce* (2003, GOODMAN), not yet produced in NYC, framed the life of the Mizner brothers against America's rise as a world power. A majority of his musicals were produced by HAROLD PRINCE.

Three compilations of Sondheim songs – *Side by Side by Sondheim* (1976), *Marry Me a Little* (1980), and *Putting It Together* (1993) – have been produced. Sondheim's scores are characterized by brilliant, often cerebral lyrics and driving, unsentimental music; they are usually informed by the work of the book writers with whom he collaborates, such as JAMES LAPINE and John Weidman.

Sondheim has been considered the theatre's most distinguished composer-lyricist since the 1970s and is unquestionably its most lauded. His works are produced regularly worldwide and with rising frequency in NYC, with seven major revivals during 2000–5. A Broadway revival of *Company* opened in November 2006; one of *Sunday in the Park* is slated for 2008. As he approached 75, dozens of recordings appeared, symposia were held, and events were staged, including a 2002

E. H. Sothern and Julia Marlowe in *Romeo and Juliet,* c. 1904. Photo by Hall. *Courtesy:* Don B. Wilmeth Theatre Collection.

all-Sondheim production festival at the JOHN F. KENNEDY CENTER and worldwide celebrations in honor of his 2005 birthday.

Numerous books have been written on Sondheim, including noteworthy efforts by Banfield, Gordon, Gottfried, and Zadan. The most thorough biography to date is by Meryle Secrest (1998).
MK LJ

Sothern, E(dward) A(skew) (1826–81), and **E(dward) H(ugh) Sothern** (1859–1933) Actors. Beginning his career as an eccentric comedian on English stages, the elder Sothern made his American debut as Dr. Pangloss in *The Heir-at-Law* in 1852. He achieved sudden star status with LAURA KEENE's company when he assumed the role of Lord Dundreary in Tom Taylor's *OUR AMERICAN COUSIN* in 1858 for an uninterrupted run of five months. In 1861, after 400 consecutive performances, Londoners indulged in frequent "Dundrearyisms," and his distinctive sidewhiskers, known as "Dundrearies," became popular. Other Sothern roles included Dundreary's Brother Sam in the play of that name by John Oxenford (1862), and the title roles in T. W. Robertson's *David Garrick* (1864) and H. J. Byron's *The Crushed Tragedian* (1878). Excelling in original comic business, the British-born actor remained popular on both sides of the Atlantic and died in London.

In 1879, Sothern provided the opportunity for his American-born son, E. H. Sothern, to make his debut in New York in a small role in *Brother Sam*. Playing in England and America, the younger Sothern gained experience in the companies of JOHN MCCULLOUGH, Helen Dauvray, and others. In 1887 DANIEL FROHMAN engaged E. H. Sothern for the newly formed company at the LYCEUM THEATRE. Sothern quickly established himself as a dashing romantic hero in such roles as Prince Rudolf in *The Prisoner of Zenda* (1895). Still under Frohman's management, Sothern broadened his range to poetic drama in 1900 as the hero in Hauptmann's *The Sunken Bell* and as Hamlet. Under the management of CHARLES FROHMAN, Sothern first appeared with JULIA MARLOWE (whom he married in 1911) in *Romeo and Juliet* in 1904. Together, until Marlowe retired, they reigned for a decade as America's foremost Shakespearean players. Sothern wrote his memoirs in 1916 and retired in 1927. E. A. and E. H. are chronicled by T. E. Pemberton (1908); E. A.'s autobiography appeared in 1916. MR

Soudeikine, Sergei (1882–1946) Russian-born designer and painter who studied art in Moscow and designed in Moscow and St. Petersburg for Meyerhold and Tairov, among others. In 1920 he emigrated to Paris and then to the U.S. in 1922 with Balieff's *Chauve-Souris* cabaret, for which he continued to design over the years. He designed extensively for the Metropolitan Opera as well as at RADIO CITY MUSIC HALL (1934–9). He also designed *PORGY AND BESS* (1935). AA

sound American theatre inherited a tradition of physical or "property" sound effects from European theatre. Using such devices as thunder sheets, wind machines, and other physical devices, the craft of property sound remained vital until the new theatres and changing aesthetics of the 20th century rendered it obsolete.

In response to aesthetics based on cinematic realism, 20th-century American theatre developed a new, visual stagecraft based on novel advances in technology. Prior to 1950, however, neither general understanding of auditory perception nor technical resources in audio electronics were sufficiently mature to permit sound to keep pace with the New Stagecraft.

The seminal figure in the development of sound in American theatre was Harold Burris-Meyer. His work occurred at a time of significant advances in the science of human perception; he applied the gain in scientific knowledge toward the development of an art of sound in theatre. Working in the 1930s with Vincent Mallory, Burris-Meyer devised experiments in acoustical reinforcement and the use of psychoacoustics and built a specialized audio system for theatrical production. Both men were associated with a number of theatre productions in New York, as sound designers as well as consultants. They were directly involved in the FEDERAL THEATRE PROJECT, and designed the first application of acoustical reinforcement to opera at the Metropolitan Opera House. Burris-Meyer's active work in theatre sound ended when he and Mallory were drafted into wartime research.

Although Burris-Meyer initiated an expanded use of audio for theatre, his primary interest was the potential of sound to serve as a controllable psychological tool for the enhancement of dramatic impact. During the period 1940–60, however, most theatre people were simply concerned with understanding and applying the craft of audio. Audio gave promise of enabling a more flexible and extensive use of sound than the property tradition had been able to offer. Midcentury amplifier technology was adequate for almost any theatrical requirement, but early sound capture and storage systems were difficult and inflexible.

The advent of tape recording provided a satisfactory storage and retrieval system, enabling theatre to make adequate use of facsimiles of real sounds instead of simulated effects. Audiotape provided a medium that almost anyone could use, and one that could be edited easily to rearrange the extent and sequence of sounds.

Development of the wireless (radio) microphone encouraged significant use of acoustical reinforcement, especially in musical theatre. Greater audibility implied the possibility of serving larger audiences, and hence larger box-office revenues. Reinforcement techniques for concert performance of popular music were translated to theatre with rock musicals of the 1960s and '70s, particularly the Broadway show *HAIR* and a string of successful productions from composer ANDREW LLOYD WEBBER and lyricist Tim Rice. Modified concert reinforcement methods have now become a permanent part of American musical theatre.

In the years 1980–90, American theatre sound gradually divided into two categories: acoustical reinforcement and "sound scoring." Reinforcement includes the design and implementation of the audio system responsible for capturing the performer's voice and reproducing it throughout the venue. Specialists in this area often overlap with the world of live music, from which most of the equipment and system design is taken. With recent developments of tiny, highly sensitive microphones, the audience may be entirely unaware that a reinforcement device has been placed on a performer. Increased quality of reinforcement systems has both increased vocal clarity for audiences accustomed to film and television as well as reduced the imperative for vocal training among performers. Opinions differ on whether this is a positive trend.

"Sound scoring," a term promulgated by the Sound Design Commission of the U.S. Institute for Theatre Technology, covers the creation of an audio environment, also known as ambiance or "soundscape," to accompany the action of the play. This environment may include music or sound effects, and may be a realistic depiction of an actual location or an abstract amalgam of sounds designed to create a particular emotional response.

Once tape-recorded sound became widely available and easy to control in the 1960s, extended sound scoring began, at first in university and experimental theatres, then, by the early '80s, in regional professional theatre companies. By 1990 the number of sounds artists working in theatre had shown a remarkable increase. Many regional theatre companies now hire a composer as a regular member of the production team, while also retaining an in-house sound designer charged with integrating the music with sound effects.

As modern audiences have become increasingly saturated with film and television media, they have also become more demanding and sophisticated about sounds design. Modern ears are accustomed to realistic audio environments and clear dialogue in the theatre, whether or not the performance is live. Hence, modern sound designers have expanded the complexity of their systems, placing speakers throughout the auditorium and creating more immersive audio environments.

With the advent of digital sampling and digital audio workstations, sound design could take on a level of complexity that was previously impossible. Working in the digital environment, designers can create many more layers of sound, and send them individually to different locations in the theatrical space. Increasingly sophisticated electronics allow designers to "model" different spaces inside the theatre, giving the audience the illusion that they are inhabiting the actual location where the story takes place. With the continued convergence of live theatre and recorded media, the importance of sound design will undoubtedly increase.   JLB   AC

Sound of Music, The The last, and one of the most successful, of the RICHARD RODGERS–OSCAR HAMMERSTEIN II collaborations (with book by HOWARD LINDSAY and RUSSEL CROUSE), it opened at the LUNT–FONTANNE THEATRE on 16 November 1959 and ran 1,443 performances, winning five Tonys (including a shared Best Musical). Based on the life of Maria Von Trapp – a former religious postulant who became governess to the seven children of an Austrian naval captain, married the captain, and fled with him and the children when the Nazis took over Austria – the show gave Rodgers the opportunity to write music ranging from a Gregorian chant to typical Broadway "charm" numbers. Hammerstein's lyrics moved from the unabashed sentiment of "Edelweiss" and the title song to the ironic wit of "No Way to Stop It" and "How Can Love Survive?" MARY MARTIN gave a winning performance as Maria, and THEODORE BIKEL was suitably dignified as the Captain. While some critics were less than enthusiastic about the show's sentiment and idealism, audiences kept it running for more than three years, followed by a successful 1965 film with JULIE ANDREWS and CHRISTOPHER PLUMMER. A 1998 Broadway revival starred REBECCA LUKER.   MK

Source Theatre Company Not-for-profit theatre founded in 1977 in Washington, DC, considered one of the city's oldest small professional venues (located in the 14th St. Arts Corridor). Since the early 1980s its artistic director has been Joe Banno, who promotes the mission to develop and nurture Washington's diverse community with an Equity season of five productions, coproductions, an annual theatre festival (70 new plays developed a year, recently), readings, a Junior Festival, and a 10-minute play competition.   DBW

South Coast Repertory Founded in 1964 as a summer company by David Emmes and Martin Benson, who opened a year-round operation in a rented 60-seat space in Newport Beach, CA, presenting *Tartuffe* on 12 November 1964. Their first permanent home, a marine hardware store that they converted to a 75-seat theatre, opened on 12 March 1965 with *Waiting for Godot*. They moved into a larger space in Costa Mesa (1967), and in 1972 organized their first board of directors as a nonprofit theatre and established both the Summer Conservatory (for aspiring professionals) and the Young Conservatory. They hired their first Equity artist in 1974, and in 1976 initiated a $3.5 million fund-raising campaign to build a 507-seat Main Stage (1978) and 161-seat flexible Second Stage (1979) in a new complex in Costa Mesa. A typical season includes one or two classics but five to eight local or world premieres; the company maintains a separate endowment expressly for the purpose of developing new plays. *Wit* premiered there in 1995; playwrights with premieres number DONALD MARGULIES, Amy Freed, CRAIG LUCAS, KEITH REDDIN, and RICHARD GREENBERG. In spite of this challenging repertory, they have built a large and faithful subscription audience among the highly conservative and conventional Orange County community. A regional Tony was received in 1988, and in 2002 the Rep's success culminated in the opening of the Folino Theatre Center (three venues; two renovated), with the first season in the new 336-seat intimate Julianne Argyros Stage in 2002–3.   JDM

South Pacific Based on James A. Michener's novel *Tales of the South Pacific,* with book by OSCAR HAMMERSTEIN II and JOSHUA LOGAN, music by RICHARD RODGERS, and lyrics by Hammerstein, this Pulitzer Prize–winning musical opened at the MAJESTIC THEATRE on 7 April 1949 and ran 1,925 performances. Set on a small island in the early days of WWII, it tells of two sets of lovers, French exile planter Émile de Becque and Navy nurse Nellie Forbush, and Navy Lieutenant Joe Cable and the Tonkinese girl Liat. Racial prejudice figures in both plots: Nellie is finally able to overcome her aversion to de Becque's two children by a native woman, but Cable cannot bring himself to marry the Asian girl he loves. These two stories unfold against the backdrop of American sailors trying to cope with the exotic island world into which they have been plunged. As Nellie, MARY MARTIN gave a buoyant performance, and Metropolitan Opera star Ezio Pinza brought stature to the role of Émile. Logan, who had served in the Navy, staged the show adeptly, particularly the sailors' chorus number, "There Is Nothing Like a Dame." The musical's first Broadway revival is projected for the LINCOLN CENTER Theater in 2007–8, directed by Bartlett Sher. There was a 1967 staging at the New York State Theatre, a 1987 production by the NY City Opera, and a 2005 concert version at Carnegie Hall (with BRIAN STOKES MITCHELL and Reba McEntire), as well as a national tour with Robert Goulet.   MK

Southwark Theatre South St. between 4th and 5th Sts., PHILADELPHIA. In 1766, DAVID DOU-GLASS erected America's first substantial theatre just outside Philadelphia's city limits to avert official interference; opening 12 November, it was to remain active for 51 years. On its stage, Douglass presented the first play by a American-born playwright, Thomas Godfrey's *The Prince of Parthia* (1767) (see INTRODUCTION, §1). Closed by the Continental Congress in 1774, it was used briefly as a hospital, then reopened by British occupation troops for entertainments to benefit widows and orphans. A drop curtain attributed to Major John André continued to be used until the theatre closed. The playhouse was two and a half stories high, painted red, brick in its lower story, and surmounted by a cupola. In 1784, LEWIS HALLAM JR., reoccupied the theatre, skirting the laws against play-acting by presenting "moral lectures." In 1789, the ban was lifted, and the Southwark was in full operation. Outmoded as newer theatres were built and better companies assembled, the playhouse closed its doors in 1817. When the structure was damaged by FIRE a few years later, a brewery was built on its foundations and survived until 1912.   MCH

Sovey, Raymond (1897–1966) This designer's prodigious output through four decades included such classics as *The FRONT PAGE* (1928), *ANIMAL CRACKERS* (1928), *Green Grow the Lilacs* (1931), *The PETRIFIED FOREST* (1935), *OUR TOWN* (1938), *ARSENIC AND OLD LACE* (1941), and *The Cocktail Party* (1950). He was noted for his ingenious solutions to design problems and his ability to capture the essence of a scene or play with deftly selected images.   AA

Spacey [né Fowler], **Kevin** (1959–) Born in South Orange, NJ, Spacey, who trained for two years at Juilliard, is best known as a two-time Academy Award–winning actor (*The Usual Suspects*, 1995; *American Beauty*, 1999), yet his place in theatre history is equally secure. In 2003 he assumed the artistic direction of London Old Vic, with a first halting season in early 2004 (he sputtered in Dennis McIntyre's *National Anthems,* a play in which he had appeared in the 1980s); gained some momentum as Dexter Haven in *PHILADELPHIA STORY* in May 2005; and received excellent notices for his Richard II (fall 2005). Though 2006 was problematic, *A MOON FOR THE MISBEGOTTEN* received raves and moved to Broadway, opening 9 April 2007. In general, however, London has been good to Spacey, where in 1998 he appeared as Hickey in *The ICEMAN COMETH* at the Almeida Theatre (multiple awards, including the Olivier Theatre Award for Best Actor); the production moved to Broadway in 1999. In 1986 too he had appeared on Broadway in O'Neill – *A Long Day's Journey into Night* with Jack Lemmon. (His Broadway debut had been as Oswald in *Ghosts* in 1982.) Spacey won a Featured Role Tony as Uncle Louie in *Lost in Yonkers* (1991). In 2003 his dream of directing and starring in a biopic about singer Bobby Darin (*Beyond the Sea*) was fulfilled.   DBW

Spewack, Sam (1899–1971) and **Bella (Cohen) Spewack** (1899–1990) One of the most successful husband-and-wife writing teams, the Spewacks collaborated on 12 plays and 20 screenplays. Married in 1922 when both were journalists, they created such classical, madcap comedies and social satires as *Clear All Wires* (1932), *Boy Meets Girl* (1935; Megrue Prize), *Kiss Me, Kate* (1948, Tony and Page One awards; film 1953), and *My Three Angels* (1953). Before their theatre work, Bella wrote primarily fiction; Sam was a foreign correspondent, the basis for the four plays (including *Two Blind Mice*, 1949) and three novels that he authored alone.   TH-S

Spiderwoman Theatre The oldest producing U.S. FEMINIST THEATRE and one of the oldest continually running women's Native theatre company in North America. Located in NYC (though they perform worldwide), the core members of the troupe, founded in 1975, are three Cuna–Rappahannock American Indian sisters – Lisa Mayo and Gloria and Muriel Miguel. They borrow their name from the Hopi goddess of creation, who first created designs and taught her people to weave. Spiderwoman's storyweaving technique – spun with words and movement – result in loosely structured pieces that include *Lysistrata Numbah; Sun, Moon, and Feather; Winnetou's Snake-Oil Show from Wigwam City*; *Power Pipes*; and *Persistence of Memory*. A mix of media and an interweaving of various narrative threads characterizes Spiderwoman's productions, which are aggressively nonlinear and improvisatory. They borrow freely from NATIVE AMERICAN RITUAL traditions and myths and from slapstick comedy.   JDo

Split Britches Feminist and lesbian theatre troupe (see GAY/LESBIAN THEATRE) founded in 1981 by Lois Weaver, Peggy Shaw, and DEBORAH MARGOLIN as an offshoot of SPIDERWOMAN THEATRE. First presented at NYC's WOW (Women's One World) Café, Split Britches' productions – *Split Britches* (1981), *Beauty and the Beast* (1982), *Upwardly Mobile Home* (1984), *Little Women: The Tragedy* (1988), *Belle Reprieve* (1991), *Lesbians Who Kill* (1992), *Salad of the Bad Café* (2000), etc. – include

eclectic combinations of realistic detail with flights of surrealistic fancy. They employ Brechtian techniques and appropriate popular culture genres to critique strict gender roles and compulsory heterosexuality. Their nonlinear political comedies entertain but confront dominant values. In recent years Weaver and Shaw have done more solo work: Weaver (*Faith and Dancing*); Shaw (*Menopausal Gentleman*, *To My Chagrin*). Sue-Ellen Case wrote a book on the troupe (1996).   JDo

Spoleto Festival, USA Founded in 1977 in Charleston, SC, by composer Gian Carlo Menotti as a counterpart to his "The Festival of Two Worlds" (1958, Spoleto, Italy), this annual May–June festival brings together established performers and talented young artists from all over the world to exchange ideas and share their appreciations for the arts. In recent years the theatrical fare has become more experimental, with offerings such as Philip Glass and Allen Ginsberg's *The Hydrogen Jukebox, Pioneer* by the Paul Dresher Ensemble, PING CHONG's *Obon: Tales of Rain and Moonlight,* and several LEE BREUER productions (including *DollHouse,* 2005). As of 2006 100 world premieres and 93 American premieres had been presented. With attendance at all events exceeding 75,000, all available venues are used, including Gaillard Auditorium, the DOCK STREET THEATRE, and the Garden, a converted moviehouse. Running concurrently is Piccolo Spoleto, a fringe festival celebrating local and regional artists. After much acrimony Menotti resigned in October 1993; today the general director is Nigel Redden.   DBW

Spooner Stock Companies Mary Gibbs Spooner (1853–1940) established the first Spooner resident STOCK COMPANY at the Park Theatre, Brooklyn, in 1901 to support her daughters EDNA MAY (1875–1953) and CECIL (1888–1953). The group charged low admission prices to productions of familiar plays and catered to the interests of middle-class women, especially homemakers. It moved to the FIFTH AVENUE THEATRE in Manhattan in 1907. After 1908, Mrs. Spooner and Charles E. Blaney founded companies in several U.S. cities. Cecil headed troupes residing in NYC until 1918.   WD

Stadlen, Lewis J. (1947–) Unassuming comic character actor, born in Brooklyn, trained at the NEIGHBORHOOD PLAYHOUSE and the STELLA ADLER Studio. He first garnered attention as Groucho MARX in *Minnie's Boys* (1970) – and a subsequent solo show as Groucho – and since has excelled in numerous comic turns, most eccentric and broad (Ben Silverman in *The Sunshine Boys*, Voltaire/Pangloss in CANDIDE, Milt in *Laughter on the 23rd Floor*, Senex in *A Funny Thing Happened on the Way to the Forum*, Banjo in *The Man Who Came to Dinner*, and Mickey Fox, the Borscht Belt comic, in NEIL SIMON's *45 Seconds from Broadway* (2001). He was a replacement as Max Bialystock in *The Producers* (2003).   DBW

Stadt Theater Company A German-speaking STOCK COMPANY organized in 1854 by Otto Hoym in New York (old Amphitheatre, 37–39 Bowery). Joined by Eduard Hamann in 1855, the Stadt Theater produced a variety of German comedies, operettas, and classics. In 1864 the company became the Neues Stadt Theater and moved to 45–47 Bowery, where Hoym and Hamann engaged German notables Bogumil Dawison (1866–7) and Friedrich Haase (1868–9). Following Hoym's retirement in 1867, novelty acts and opera became increasingly popular. Hamann went bankrupt in 1872, and many company members joined Adolf Neuendorff's GERMANIA THEATER COMPANY. RE

stage lighting The history of stage lighting, dating back several centuries, forms a continuous path, using candles, oil lamps, and gas as successive form of illumination. Candles were the principal source of illumination until gas illumination, first installed in the CHESTNUT STREET THEATRE in PHILADELPHIA in 1816, enabled control from a single "gas table" and the simultaneous dimming or brightening of large groups of lights. During the last half of the 19th century, use was also made of limelight or calcium light, requiring a mixture of oxygen and hydrogen gases to heat a block of lime to incandescence. Limelight, first used in the theatre in 1837 (and first used extensively in the U.S. for the extravaganza *The Black Crook* in 1866), made possible special lighting effects such as sunlight and moonlight, as well as projections (fire, rainbows, clouds, rain, snow), which depended upon a relatively intense source of light; nearly 20 times brighter than acetylene gas and 750 times brighter than a candle, limelight could be used to advantage. Methods to produce special effects became very highly developed. Hand-painted mica slides were placed within manually operated cam, tilt, and rotating devices designed to create the appropriate motion – altered in our own times mainly by the imposition of photographic methods and electronic controls.

A rapid transition from gas to electric sources in the theatre followed the introduction of Edison carbon filament lamps in 1879, producing three times the light of the acetylene gas jets and considerable improvement in safety. The transformation from gas to electric lamps was almost complete by the turn of the century. In the remodeling of New York's Metropolitan Opera House, following the destruction of its interior by fire in 1892, the new borderlights and footlights combined both traditional gas jets and new electric lamps. (It is not clear whether the gas connections were maintained until the complete renovation of all stage equipment in 1903, but at this time all lighting throughout the building was converted to electric lamps, over 15,000 of them.) As late as 1906, 8 families out of 10 in the U.S. were still using candle and gas-flame sources at home.

Although electric borderlights and footlights, similar strips called winglights (mounted vertically and placed at the sides of the stage), and special-effects machines comprised the main sources of illumination, theatres also used spotlights with simple lenses to concentrate the light ("lens boxes") or as follow spotlights ("chasers"). Open-box floodlights ("Olivettes" and later "bunch lights") could be colored with dyed, translucent silk screens. Carbon-arc light sources (first used in the theatre in 1846), became more prevalent, replacing the limelight source in spotlights and box floodlights. Though safer than calcium lights, carbon-arc sources were sometimes not fully enclosed; sparks from the exposed arc presented a great danger of FIRE, particularly due to close proximity with the cloth and wooden scenery. The Iroquois Theatre fire in CHICAGO in 1903, which originated from a spark from an open-box carbon-arc source falling on the scenery, hastened the adoption of more stringent fire regulations throughout the U.S. Carbon-arc sources could thereafter be used only in enclosed or screened housings, and the theatre became a much safer place for patron and actor alike.

Each successive new development resulted in higher brightness levels; each such increase in brightness revealed, rather disturbingly, the painted nature and cloth construction of the wing and border settings. This potential of higher and higher brightness levels was to continue throughout the 20th century, and ultimately forced a change in the design of the settings themselves. Control over the intensity of stage lights in the gas era had been achieved by means of stopcock valves on the "gas table," whereas the operation of each limelight or carbon-arc source required the presence of a nearby operator. The introduction of the electric lamp and three or four alternating sequential colors of lamps in footlights and borderlights multiplied the need for controlling an increasing number of individual lights and groups of colored lights. In the U.S. early liquid or water-barrel dimmers were soon superseded by variable-resistance wire dimmers, made available in plate form as early as 1892 to allow closer stacking and to regulate voltage going to the lamps and, therefore, their brightness. Over the next three decades a number of mechanical systems were designed to facilitate operation of the increasing number of dimmers. The end of this period saw switchboards, sometimes 30–40 ft. long in larger installations, with dimmers rising upward in three or more tiers, and capable of being locked or unlocked to master color shafts which, in turn, were actuated by a grand master lever or slow-motion wheel.

DAVID BELASCO and his electrician, Louis Hartman, worked together during 1900–30, attempting to make lighting in the theatre more realistic. Belasco's production of MADAME BUTTERFLY (1900) was acclaimed for its subtle naturalistic color effects, in which silk color rolls achieved a slow fade from day to night behind the translucent screens of the setting. Belasco had an affection for the early low-wattage spotlights, and used small "baby lenses" in the production of DU BARRY in 1901 for the specific purpose of throwing a special hue of light on the star, the red-headed MRS. LESLIE CARTER. Only 10,000–15,000 watts of lighting were sufficient for most Belasco productions. In 1915, during the remodeling of the BELASCO THEATRE, Belasco installed permanent "front-lighting" on the audience side of the proscenium arch, utilizing four sections of "X-ray" (silvered-glass) reflectors, each with only four 100-watt lamps. At the same time, footlights were discarded.

The introduction of ductile-tungsten filament lamps in 1910 to replace carbon-filament lamps doubled the efficiency of light sources. Within five years greater efficiency was provided by adding a gas-fill to tungsten lamps (first nitrogen and then, in 1919, argon), enabling lamp efficiency nearly two-thirds of that in today's tungsten lamps. Although these new efficient sources were eagerly adopted by the theatre, soon a reaction set in decrying the new higher brightness levels and "over-illuminating" of the scene.

MAUDE ADAMS, WINTHROP AMES, JOSEPH URBAN, ROBERT EDMOND JONES, and S. L. ("Roxy") Rothafel are among those credited with the early use of spotlights in the period 1915–20. In 1922, LEE SIMONSON used over 60 spotlights for Čapek's The Insect Comedy (on Broadway in 1922 as The World We Live in), and in 1925 he and NORMAN BEL GEDDES installed more than 100 permanent spotlights in the Guild Theatre in New York (now the VIRGINIA). Stage lighting in America had entered the "spotlight era."

The new era was heralded in the early 1920s by "bridge" and "C-clamps," suspension devices that easily repositioned lighting units as appropriate rather than depending on permanent mounts. Monroe Pevear in BOSTON introduced ground-glass slides to soften the hard beam edges of planoconvex lens spotlights; within a few years a spotlight of greater intensity but with the same soft beam edge was produced by the use of square prismatic lenses. By the early 1930s these took the form of the round "Fresnel" lens, still in use today. Simultaneously, studies were undertaken by "lighting consultant" (an early use of the term) Stanley R. McCandless while planning for theatres in Radio City (Rockefeller Center) in New York. McCandless, his associate Edward B. Kirk, and Richard Engelken (then on the staff of Kliegl Bros. Lighting) designed an ellipsoidal reflector unit for general illumination of the auditorium in the RKO Roxy Theatre (1932; later the Center Theatre). This concentrated beam downlight was forerunner to the ellipsoidal-reflector spotlights demonstrated by the Kliegl firm in the spring of 1933.

McCandless, trained as an architect, introduced the first academic stage-lighting coursework in the U.S. at Yale University in 1926; his first "syllabus" was published in 1927, and a definitive work, still popular, A Method of Lighting the Stage, was published in 1932. McCandless students in turn became prominent teachers of stage lighting. Theodore Fuchs, an "illuminating engineer," whose book Stage Lighting was published in 1929, undertook teaching stage lighting at Northwestern University in the early 1930s. Two McCandless students, JEAN ROSENTHAL and PEGGY CLARK, were the first to be titled "lighting designers" in the Broadway theatre, along with ABE FEDER, who was trained at Carnegie Institute of Technology.

By the mid-1930s stage lighting instrumentation now still in use was in place. Skilled specialists, "lighting designers," were being increasingly used to perform work that had been largely performed by stage electricians. The most predominant dimmer in the 1930s was still the resistance plate, largely unchanged in spite of slow improvement over 30 years. The number of stage circuits and instruments continued to escalate, however, rising to 300–400 for the average Broadway production by 1950. The Broadway theatre had traditionally used all portable equipment, bringing in lighting instruments, electric cables, and "road board" dimmer controls anew for each production. A number of non-Broadway theatres and auditoriums, however, were built with permanent equipment. During 1920–30 over two dozen installations were made of reactance dimmers, including the Public Auditorium in Cleveland, the Convention Hall in Atlantic City, the Civic Opera House in Chicago, and the EARL CARROLL and RKO Roxy Theatres in New York. The resistance dimmer rows banked offstage became the "pilot" controls for the reactance dimmers, which controlled the heavy lighting loads. Not much seemed to have changed; but the next step was not long in coming.

Beginning with Severance Hall in Cleveland (1931) and RADIO CITY MUSIC HALL (1932), the Westinghouse Electric Company and the General Electric Company competed with established manufacturers of dimming controls, such as Ward–Leonard and Cutler–Hammer, in developing "remote-control" consoles with miniature "potentiometers" to control remote banks of thyratron tubes, which in turn regulated the reactance dimmers. "Presets" – that is, systems in which a row of potentiometers could be set in advance while an additional row was in actual use – could now be developed. Three-scene preset controls were installed in Radio City Music Hall and the Metropolitan Opera House (1933). The Severance Hall console, designed by McCandless and built by Westinghouse, had a particularly sympathetic layout: By grouping controls it could accommodate eight presets of lighting.

GEORGE C. IZENOUR, who began in 1939 to develop a theatre-lighting control system at Yale, resumed work postwar and in April of 1947 demonstrated a system employing pilot controllers to modulate the output of a pair of back-to-back vacuum tubes, which in turn controlled a pair of back-to-back thyratron tubes. Izenour's design of the main lighting console and an associated preset panel with 10 full presets provided control by only one or, at most, two electricians. Because of its relatively small size it could be placed in the auditorium, where the stage could be seen clearly. The Izenour system, in commercial production by 1951, was eventually installed in hundreds of theatres, along with similar controls developed by others.

In 1959–60 the silicon-controlled rectifier was introduced, soon replacing the thyratron tube as the power element in the control system. This made possible the first major downgrading in size of the dimmer bank, and, since designs could now be made modular, more dimmers would fit into the same allotted space. The mid-1960s witnessed the first electronic computers; developments in stage lighting utilized each new computer device and data-storage system as it was introduced. Punch cards, staple cards, magnetic storage drums, and ferrite-core memories were employed first – more frequently as learning devices for manufacturers than as reliable lighting tools in the theatre. By the early 1970s systems became more reliable. A major breakthrough was accomplished when A CHORUS LINE (1975) used the first lighting "memory" system on Broadway. Large numbers of dimmers and controls through memory computers and miniature consoles were complete by the early 1980s. Lights on the Broadway stage leapt from 300–400 in 1950 to frequently well over 1,000 as the U.S. entered the 1990s.

Advances in the visual style of lighting have often gone hand in hand with technical innovation. One of the most powerful such innovations of the late 20th century came in 1981 when the ShowCo company (later renamed Vari-Lite) partnered with the rock group Genesis and introduced a practical moving light fixture that could not only change color but alter its position and focus automatically. For the first two decades of its existence, this technology was too expensive and unwieldy for live theatre outside of large-scale rock and roll shows, but the standardization of the control technology DMX and other technical improvements has brought it in range for middle-budget regional and academic theatres.

As theatrical spectacles have begun to play to audiences raised on a steady diet of film and television, theatrical designers increasingly have adopted both the style and technology of their media counterparts, igniting a trend toward "convergence," where the worlds of lighting and video projection have blended into one another. This trend follows two major innovations in live video: large, bright projectors and walls of light-emitting diode (LED) panels, both of which provide the design team with a moving image that is sufficiently large and bright to form a major portion of the scenic picture. Simultaneously, innovations in nonlinear editing, three-dimensional modeling, and image processing – now possible on inexpensive personal computers – have put the resources of professional editing suites and animators well within the range of ordinary designers. These technologies have forced directors and designers both to search for a visual style that maintains the immediacy of live performance, yet employs media technology to present themes and story points. Live theatre in nontraditional venues, such as theme parks, has pushed this technological envelope in the popular theatre. Some permanently installed venues, such as *Terminator 2: 3D* at Universal Studios, blur the line between live theatre and media almost into oblivion. Cutting-edge theatrical spectacles, like The BLUE MAN GROUP and the CIRQUE DU SOLEIL, commonly pass media back and forth between the lighting and video systems. Theatrical lighting designers can now use any sort of projected image, from solid color to video image to three-dimensional animation to holographic projection as design elements, whether to bring mood and atmosphere to the theatrical scene, to highlight or unify the actor and the stage environment, to produce effects of sheer spectacle, or to offer what appears to be verisimilitude with the effects of nature. Stage lighting and its converged brethren, video projection, have become more than the revealers of the other design elements. They have now blended with the rest of the design team to create a new technologically charged and coherent style of visual storytelling.   JER AC

Stair and Havlin Theatrical Management Syndicate John H. Havlin (1847?–1924) was business manager for BARNEY MACAULEY and built his own theatre and hotel in Cincinnati (1883). Financing the first Hagenbeck Circus, he later built several theatres in St. Louis. In 1900 he formed a partnership with Edward D. Stair (1859–1951), who owned the *Detroit Free Press* and had acquired Michigan theatres that could not pay their advertising bills in the depression of 1893. Until the dissolution of the firm (1915), Stair and Havlin controlled more than 150 theatres and monopolized the production and booking of popular-priced melodrama.   DMcD

Stanley, Kim [née Patricia Beth Reid] (1925–2001) Actress who studied at the PASADENA PLAYHOUSE (1945–6), performed with STOCK COMPANIES in Louisville and New Jersey, and made her Broadway debut in 1949 as JULIE HARRIS's replacement in *Montserrat*. Further training at The ACTORS STUDIO (under STRASBERG and KAZAN) influenced her psychoanalytic approach to characterization. Her career peaked in the 1950s with such praised performances as Millie in *PICNIC* (1953) and Cherie in *BUS STOP* (1955), and with her acclaimed London debut performance as Maggie in *CAT ON A HOT TIN ROOF* (1958). In the 1960s she turned to

teaching, with occasional stints in film and television. A biography by Jon Krampner was published in 2006.   FHL

Stapleton, Jean (1923–) New York–born and Hunter College–educated actress-singer who began her career with the Robert Shaw Chorale and graduated to STOCK in 1941. She made it to Broadway in the mid-1950s, appearing in such musicals as *DAMN YANKEES* and *BELLS ARE RINGING*. Identified inevitably with Edith Bunker on the 1970s TV series *All in the Family,* Stapleton continues her stage career, most frequently in SUMMER STOCK and national tours (e.g., as Princess Puffer in *Drood!* in 1988). She appeared in *Bon Appétit,* a ONE-PERSON PERFORMANCE (inspired by Julia Child) at CLASSIC STAGE in 1991 and at the AMERICAN CONSERVATORY THEATRE in 1993. Another solo show, *Eleanor: Her Secret Journey* (on Eleanor Roosevelt) has been toured since the late 1990s. In 1996 she played the wife in *The Entertainer* at CSC and Dolly Levi in *The MATCHMAKER* at ACT, and in 2002 the lead in FOOTE's *The Carpetbagger's Children* at Lincoln Center's Mitzi E. Newhouse Theater.   DBW

Stapleton, Maureen (1925–2006) American actress who made her NYC debut as Sara Tansey in *Playboy of the Western World* (1946). Among her outstanding roles were Serafina in WILLIAMS's *The Rose Tattoo* (1951; Tony, Best Featured Actress), Flora in *27 Wagons Full of Cotton* (1955), Lady Torrance in *Orpheus Descending* (1957), and Carrie in *TOYS IN THE ATTIC* (1960; Tony nomination) – a role in which critics described her as "comic, discerning, awkward and pathetic" and "splendid . . . gabby, open-hearted." For Evy, the alcoholic performer in NEIL SIMON's *The Gingerbread Lady* (1970), she won the Tony as Best Actress with a performance described as "remorselessly honest." Stapleton appeared in a number of feature films and many television programs. In 1981 she appeared as Birdie (Tony nomination) in a major revival of *The LITTLE FOXES* with Elizabeth Taylor. In 1981 she was inducted into the THEATRE HALL OF FAME. For her Emma Goldman in *Reds* (1981) she received an Oscar for Best Actress in a Supporting Role. Her autobiography (with Jane Scovell) was published in 1995.   SMA

Star Theatre Corner Broadway and 13th St., NYC. As WALLACK's, the theatre became New York's most celebrated playhouse. Opening in 1861 under the management of JAMES W. WALLACK and later his son, Lester, it was the home of "genteel comedy" gracefully presented by a seasoned company in a comfortable, well-appointed house. When Lester joined the uptown movement in 1881, new managements changed its name to the Star and produced German-language drama and opera followed by a return to English drama. BRONSON HOWARD's SHENANDOAH premiered there in 1889. Eventually, it was leased as a "combination" house before being demolished in 1901.   MCH

Starr [née Grant]**, Frances** (1886–1973) Actress who made her debut in her hometown STOCK COMPANY (Albany, NY, 1901), and for the next four years worked in similar companies in San Francisco, Boston, and NYC. BELASCO hired her as a replacement for the ingenue during the run of *The Music Master,* and then starred her as Juanita in *The Rose of the Rancho* (1906) and as Laura Murdock in EUGENE WALTER's *The EASIEST WAY* (1909). In the latter role she personified the dilemma of the modern woman, morally liberated but economically enslaved. She continued to act until 1940.   DMcD

State of the Union Pulitzer Prize–winning (1946) satire by HOWARD LINDSAY and RUSSEL CROUSE; played 765 performances following its 14 November 1945 Hudson Theatre opening. This three-act play was the ninth in their 12-year (to date) collaboration and their eighth success, following LIFE WITH FATHER. A gibe at politics in general, the comedy recounted fictitious Republican efforts to run a successful presidential candidate, however dishonestly. Using the unexpectedly honest candidate Grant Matthews's disapproval, the playwrights targeted the manipulation of group interests, tempering their caricature with domestic comedy. To maintain timeliness, the authors supplied the touring company with current headlines for use during performances. The role of Matthews's wife, written for HELEN HAYES, marked the Broadway debut of Ruth Hussey after Hayes, KATHARINE HEPBURN, and Margaret Sullavan declined the part.   RW

Stein, Daniel (1952–) Currently school director of the DELL'ARTE International School of Physical Theatre in Blue Lake, CA, he apprenticed with Étienne Decroux and is regarded as the one who changed MIME into movement performance with his solo *Timepiece* (1978). A recent performance is *Measuring Man* (2000), based on events in the life of Leonardo da Vinci.   DBW

Stein, Douglas (1948–) Set designer for theatre, opera, and dance who graduated from Yale and has designed for the major regional theatres, such as the GOODMAN, AMERICAN REPERTORY THEATRE (including a controversial production of Beckett's *Endgame* set in a NYC subway station), LA JOLLA, ARENA STAGE, and a long association at the GUTHRIE. Other designs include the JOANNE AKALAITIS–directed *Through the Leaves,* for which he won an Obie (1984), WILLIAM FINN's *Falsettoland* (1990), the LINCOLN CENTER revival of *OUR TOWN* (1988), Peter Hall's *Troilus and Cressida* (2001), and on Broadway *Dirty Blonde* (2000), *Fool Moon* (1992, 1995, 1998), and JOHN LEGUIZAMO's *Freak* (1998). He has taught at New York and Princeton universities and at the School of Visual Arts. In 2004 he received a Bessie (Dance and Performance award) for his work with choreographer Susan Marshall.   AA   BO

Stein, Gertrude (1874–1946) Playwright, poet, and American icon, Stein wrote more than 75 plays published in three collections: *Geography and Plays* (1922), *Operas and Plays* (1932), and *Last Operas and Plays* (1949). Most were never produced because of the obscurity of the writing, which represented in words the surrealistic techniques of modern art. *Yes Is for a Very Young Man* (1944), *The Mother of Us All* (1945), and *FOUR SAINTS IN THREE ACTS* (1934), the last two with music by Virgil Thomson, are sometimes produced.   FB

Steinbeck, John (Ernest) (1902–68) Nobel Prize–winning (1962) novelist who wrote 24 works of fiction but only three plays, each adapted from a novel. The first, *OF MICE AND MEN* (1937), a tragic fable of the strong and the weak, was dramatized with GEORGE S. KAUFMAN (a musical version was produced in 1958). *The Moon Is Down* (1942), an anti-Nazi play, followed, and *Burning Bright* was adapted in 1950. Others have also adapted Steinbeck's works to the stage: *Tortilla Flat,* about California Mexican American peasants, was dramatized by Jack Kirkland in 1938; in 1955 OSCAR HAMMERSTEIN II adapted Steinbeck's sequel to *Cannery Row,* the novel *Sweet Thursday* (1954), into the musical *Pipe Dream* (music by RICHARD RODGERS); and in 1988 *The GRAPES OF WRATH* was adapted by FRANK GALATI for the STEPPENWOLF THEATRE, whose production, after a season in London, moved to Broadway (1990; Tony for Best Play). In 2003 Steinbeck's widow, Elaine Anderson Steinbeck, one of the first women to become a Broadway stage manager, died. Jay Parini's biography was published in 1995.   DBW

Steinberg, Paul (1946–) Brooklyn-born scene designer who studied environmental design at

Pratt and at the Central School of Art and Design in London. A member of the Tisch School faculty at NYU since 1996, he has designed five baroque operas for David Alden at the Bavarian State Opera in Munich and is a frequent collaborator of JoAnne Akalaitis (*The Birthday Party*, *The Trojan Women*, *The Iphigenia Cycle*). In 1982 he was named a fellow of the American Academy of Rome.   BO

Steppenwolf Theatre Company is the most celebrated group to emerge during Chicago's period of theatrical growth in the 1970s and '80s. Begun in 1974 in the basement of a suburban parochial school, Steppenwolf rapidly became the foremost exemplar of a highly physical, naturalistic approach to acting often referred to as the "Chicago Style." By subordinating repertory to the needs of the actors, this company of recent college graduates (predominantly from Illinois State University) developed both a strong sense of ensemble and a number of powerful individual actors, many of whom found success beyond the company, including John Malkovich, Terry Kinney, Laurie Metcalf, Gary Sinise, Joan Allen, Glenne Headly, and John Mahoney. Since the mid-1980s, Steppenwolf has regularly toured successful productions to Broadway and other venues. Notable productions include *True West*, *Balm in Gilead*, *And a Nightingale Sang*, *Orphans*, *Coyote Ugly*, *Burn This*, company member Frank Galati's adaptation of *The Grapes of Wrath*, *Zulu*, and *One Flew Over the Cuckoo's Nest*. In 1991 it moved into its fourth home, a newly built $8 million facility including 500- and 100-seat houses. Today it has an ensemble of 35 theatre artists.

The history of Chicago theatre is dotted with the corpses of companies that tried to increase revenue by moving into larger venues. As Steppenwolf settled into its new home, it faced both a national recession and the continual struggle of maintaining a cohesive ensemble combining new members with those who have increased commitments to other theatres and media. In 1995, eighth-year artistic director Randall Arney stepped down, with three founders recommitting themselves to work more closely with the theatre, and in August 1995 the appointment of Martha Lavey (ensemble member since 1993) as artistic director. If past success is any indication, Steppenwolf's future continues to look bright. As of 2006 it boasted a subscription base of over 25,000. Among Steppenwolf's many awards are four Tonys, including the 1985 Regional Theatre Award and two for *Grapes*, as well as a Jefferson Award for their Ensemble work (1997) and the National Medal of Arts (1998).   SF

Sternhagen, Frances (Hussey) (1930–) Actress. After a Vassar education and a year of advanced study at Catholic University, she studied acting with Sanford Meisner and made her professional debut in 1948 as Laura in *The Glass Menagerie* and Mrs. Manningham in *Angel Street* at Bryn Mawr Summer Theatre. Her New York debut was at the Cherry Lane Theatre (1955). Obie Awards followed for performances as Lydia Carew in *The Admirable Bashville* (1956) and roles in *The New Pinter Plays* (1965). Her first Tony Award nomination was for Hansberry's *The Sign in Sidney Brustein's Window* (1972 revival), and she received a Featured Actress Tony for her several roles in Neil Simon's *The Good Doctor* (1973). Five other Tony nominations followed, complementing frequent critical recognition of her work, especially in *Equus* (1974; Drama Desk), Thompson's *On Golden Pond* (1979), Terrence McNally's *A Perfect Ganesh* (1993, Manhattan Theatre Club), the 1995 revival of *The Heiress* (Tony for Featured Actress), *Morning's at Seven* (2002), *Steel Magnolias*, and *Seascape* (both 2005). In 2005 she was nominated for a Drama Desk Award for *Echoes of the War* (Mint Theater, 2004), a pair of one-acts including Barrie's *The Old Lady Shows Her Medals*. An actor's actor, Clive Barnes called her one of "the great players of Broadway."   FHL

Stetson, John (1836–96) Financially successful and innovative manager-impresario who managed theatres in Boston and New York. In 1871 at Boston's Howard Athenaeum he presented Harrigan and Hart for the first time, and in 1881 conceived the novel notion of presenting the Italian star Tommaso Salvini in bilingual performances. He also managed tours for Lillie Langtry, Helena Modjeska, and James O'Neill, and presented some of the early imported productions of Gilbert and Sullivan. A Massachusetts native, he began his career as a paid athlete and then publisher of a Boston periodical.   DBW

Stevedore Left-wing melodrama by Paul Peters and George Sklar produced by the Theatre Union at the Civic Repertory Theatre for 174 performances in 1934. This highly effective production (it left Joseph Wood Krutch ready "to crack someone over the head") presented the story of a black dockworker (played by Jack Carter) who succeeds in uniting the black community of New Orleans with sympathetic white union members who rally to fight off a lynch mob. *Stevedore* was the first U.S. commercial production to feature an integrated cast, in which black and white members were treated on equal terms, and to be played before an integrated audience. The play was also successfully staged by the "Negro Unit" of the FEDERAL THEATRE PROJECT of SEATTLE in 1936–7.   MF

Stevens, Ashton (1872–1951) Chicago drama critic. A former banjo teacher who parlayed a chance meeting on a ferry with William Randolph Hearst into a long career on various Hearst papers, Stevens became known as the dean of American theatre critics. Although his reviews were usually quite sunny, the tact of his negative notices earned him a reputation as "the mercy killer."   SF

Stevens, Emily (1882–1928) Actress whose stage debut was with her cousin MINNIE MADDERN FISKE in *Becky Sharp* (1900, tour). Following her vampire role in *The Unchastened Woman* (1915), she built a career playing charming, predatory, and sexually restless women. After two years in films, she returned to Broadway in *The Madonna of the Future* (1918), the THEATRE GUILD's *Fata Morgana* (1924), and the Actors' Theatre *Hedda Gabler* (1926), and replaced LYNN FONTANNE in BEHRMAN's *The Second Man* (1927) before dying from a drug overdose.   RAS

Stevens, Roger L(acey) (1910–98) Detroit-born producer who, after producing *Twelfth Night* on Broadway in 1949, worked steadily with great distinction in the American theatre and was associated with many of the leading theatrical groups of the U.S.: the Producers Theatre, PHOENIX THEATRE, AMERICAN NATIONAL THEATRE AND ACADEMY, Metropolitan Opera Company, ACTORS STUDIO THEATRE, AMERICAN SHAKESPEARE FESTIVAL and Academy, New Dramatists Committee, and the JOHN F. KENNEDY CENTER FOR THE PERFORMING ARTS. While Stevens was a member of the PLAYWRIGHTS' COMPANY (1951–60), that organization produced or coproduced 38 Broadway plays, including *The Fourposter* (1951), TEA AND SYMPATHY (1953), *Ondine* and *The Bad Seed* (1954), and CAT ON A HOT TIN ROOF (1955). Stevens chaired the National Council on the Arts during 1964–9.

As head of the Kennedy Center, Stevens produced more than 30 productions that went on to other theatres. In 1957 he received the Sam S. SHUBERT Foundation Award for the outstanding producer on Broadway; in 1971 was given a special Tony Award; and in 1988 received the Kennedy Center Honor and the President's Medal of Freedom. He was also honored by England (knighted in 1980), Sweden, Italy, Germany, and Austria. His productions won numerous New York Drama Critics', Tony, and Outer Critics Circle awards. In 1988 he retired from the Kennedy Center to pursue his dream of a national theatre, never realized albeit undeterred by the failure of a similar effort in 1984, and to serve as president of ANTA. Stevens was instrumental in the founding of the NATIONAL ENDOWMENT FOR THE ARTS.   SMA

Stevenson [née Lubow]**, Isabelle** (1915–2003) Longtime president of the American Theatre Wing (over three decades) and the embodiment of the annual Tony Awards (receiving in 1999 a special Tony for Lifetime Achievement). Briefly a dancer, she married in 1937 and 20 years later returned to the industry when she joined ATW's board; she became president in 1965, serving until 1998.   DBW

Stewart, Ellen (1919–) Director, manager, and one of the most influential producers in the annals of the contemporary theatre; founder of LA MAMA ETC (Experimental Theatre Club), she is OFF-BROADWAY's first lady. Stewart, noncommittal about her early life, came to New York from her native Louisiana in the early 1950s, worked as an elevator operator, and then became a fashion designer, opening in 1961 a combination boutique and theatre in a tenement basement on NYC's East 9th St. By 1968 La MaMa, as it had become, settled in its fourth and permanent home on East 4th St. Stewart, inspirational leader of La MaMa and a nurturer of a generation of young theatre talent numbering in the hundreds, has always focused on new plays, for which she was awarded the MARGO JONES Award in 1979. An abiding interest in "internationalism" has driven Stewart to take La MaMa to more than 20 countries, exerting considerable influence abroad, and to encourage affiliated groups in a dozen major cities in other countries. She has also brought the very best European and Third World theatre to American audiences at affordable prices and in intimate venues. In 1985 she received a MacArthur "genius" Fellowship; in 1993 she was inducted into the Theatre Hall of Fame; in 1996 she received the Actors' Equity Rosetta LeNoire Award for achievements in nontraditional casting. A study of Stewart and La MaMa by Barbara Horn appeared in 1993.   DBW

Stewart, Michael (1929–87) Librettist who received an M.A. from Yale in 1953, then wrote sketches for REVUES OFF-BROADWAY and for television. He had his first Broadway success with the book for BYE BYE BIRDIE (1960), which won a Best

Musical Tony Award. Notable among his other librettos were *Carnival* (1961), HELLO, DOLLY! (1964; winner of 10 Tonys, including Best Musical), *George M!* (1968), *Seesaw* (1973), *I Love My Wife* (1977), *Barnum* (1980), 42ND STREET (1980; Tony, Best Musical, 1981), *Thoroughly Modern Millie* (2002; Tony, Best Musical). Stewart proved equally adept at writing original scripts and adapting plays and films to the musical stage.   MK

Stewart, Patrick (1940–) British-born actor with a prominent bald head, English accent, and deep baritone voice, whose career has been transatlantic, ranging from Shakespeare to *Star Trek: The Next Generation* (as the skipper, Jean-Luc Picard). Stewart was trained at the Bristol Old Vic Theatre School and made his professional debut in 1959. He joined the Royal Shakespeare Company in 1966 and remained a member for 27 years. He began his U.S. career in earnest in 1987 (though in 1971 he had played Snout in the RSC's *A Midsummer Night's Dream* in NYC). In 1992 he won a Drama Desk Award for his ONE-PERSON version of *A Christmas Carol* on Broadway, which he has revived frequently there. Also on Broadway he has appeared in *The Tempest* (1995), MILLER's *The Ride Down Mt. Morgan* (2000; also 1998 at The PUBLIC), and as Davies in Pinter's *The Caretaker* (2003). At the GUTHRIE he played George in WHO'S AFRAID OF VIRGINIA WOOLF? and at DC's SHAKESPEARE THEATRE, Othello. The Order of the British Empire was bestowed upon him in 2001.   DBW

Stickney, Dorothy (1896–1998) Beloved character actor, wife of playwright HOWARD LINDSAY, in whose coauthored play LIFE WITH FATHER she created the role of the mother, Vinnie (1939), opposite her husband's Clarence Day (for five years). Born in North Dakota, she studied acting in Minneapolis, sang and danced in VAUDEVILLE, acted in STOCK, and made her Broadway debut in a small role in *The Squall* (1926). Soon she was cast in small but wonderfully eccentric roles: Liz, a mad scrubwoman in *Chicago* (1926); suicidal Mollie Molloy in *The* FRONT PAGE (1928); Stella Hallam in *Another Language* (1932; her first important role); and Granny in *On Borrowed Time* (1938). After *Life with Father* she appeared in *Life with Mother* (1948), again as Vinnie. Late in her career (1973) she returned to the stage as Berthe (replacing the late Irene Ryan) in the musical *Pippin*. Her autobiography appeared in 1979.   DBW

Sticks and Bones Second play in DAVID RABE's Vietnam trilogy. Premiered at Villanova University in 1969 (as *Bones*), the play opened at New York's PUBLIC THEATER November 1971, and in March 1972 moved to the JOHN GOLDEN THEATER (Rabe's first Broadway production; Tony for Best Play). The same month CBS canceled a televised version for fear of offending returning Vietnam vets; after lengthy wrangling, the teleplay was aired in August. A pirated version of *Sticks,* denounced by Rabe, was staged in Moscow in 1972 under the title *Brat Bratu* (*As Brother Is to Brother*). A satire of the complacent American family (the Nelsons: Ozzie, Harriet, Ricky) and their crass materialism, *Sticks* dramatizes the homecoming of blind son David, whose lyrical outrage contrasts with the Nelsons' cliched and bigoted thinking. Ironically, he sees moral evils they do not.   PCK

Still Life by EMILY MANN premiered at the GOODMAN Studio Theatre (1980) and opened in New York at the AMERICAN PLACE THEATRE (1981), directed by the author. Despite critical attacks on the play's politics and form, it garnered Obies for Best Production and for all three performers. This DOCUMENTARY drama drawn from interviews with three people in Minnesota – a Vietnam veteran who learned to love killing, his battered, pregnant wife, and his mistress – explores the domestic and international legacy of violence from Vietnam. As the three characters speak directly to the audience and show slides of war and family life, the widespread emotional trauma of Vietnam becomes painfully clear. The play transcends the topic of Vietnam by exploring chains of violence in human relations.   TH-S

stock companies Play production in England and America during the 19th century was typified by the independent stock company of a permanent troupe of actors headed by an actor-manager and performing a number of different works in repertory rotation, either in a permanent house or on tour. Actors were cast according to type or "line," which usually resulted in "stock" characterizations, and productions were mounted from the company's meager collection or "stock" of scenery and props (actors furnished costumes).

Economically undermined by the advent of expensive, visiting INTERNATIONAL STARS (mainly from England), American stock companies were further diminished by the 1880s when rail travel facilitated the growth of "combination companies," which traveled complete with star, full cast, scenery, and costumes. By century's end most professional theatre production was centralized in New York City, and most of the nation's theatres were controlled by the Theatrical SYNDICATE, an

infamous booking outfit. During the first decade of the 20th century, the SHUBERT BROTHERS gained control of legitimate theatre activity, and KEITH–ALBEE monopolized VAUDEVILLE production and booking. Although a few stock companies persisted into the new century, they mostly employed decidedly young and second-rate actors and produced plays with recently completed engagements at first-class theatres. It was during this period that "stock theatre" assumed an inferior connotation (reinforced later by the term "strawhat theatre" to refer to SUMMER STOCK).
SL

Stoddart, James Henry (1827–1907) English-born actor; U.S. debut, WALLACK'S THEATRE (1854) in the small role of Mr. Sowerberry in the farce *A Phenomenon in a Smock Frock*. During his long career, he was associated with most major New York companies, including those managed by LESTER WALLACK, LAURA KEENE, A. M. PALMER, and CHARLES FROHMAN. Although a versatile actor, he was chiefly known for masterly portrayals of eccentric old men, such as Moneypenny (BOUCICAULT's *The Long Strike*), Pierre Michel (DALY's *Rose Michel*), Jacob Fletcher (H. A. Jones's *Saints and Sinners*), and the old trainer in *The Sporting Duchess*. His autobiography, *Recollections of a Player* (1902), is an important theatrical resource.   DJW

Stone, Fred see MONTGOMERY, DAVE

Stone, John Augustus (1800–34) Playwright and actor whose *METAMORA; OR, THE LAST OF WAMPANOAGS* (1829) was the winner over 13 other entries in EDWIN FORREST's first playwriting contest (judged by W. C. Bryant, William Leggett, Prosper Wetmore, and others). The play became Forrest's property and his "warhorse" piece, with over 200 performances. The Stone–Forrest Indian chief epitomized the natural goodness of the "noble savage" (see NATIVE AMERICANS PORTRAYED). Stone's acting debut was as Old Norval in *Douglas* (1820), and through most of his career he played eccentric comics or "rough and bluff" old men. He wrote nine other unsuccessful plays, among them *The Demoniac* (1831), *The Ancient Briton* (1833), and *The Knight of the Golden Fleece* (1834).   RM

Stone, Peter (1930–2003) Los Angeles–born librettist and screenwriter a Yale M.A. (1953), whose first Broadway libretto was for *Kean* (1961), a musical adaptation of a Jean-Paul Sartre play. He wrote the scripts for numerous Hollywood films and television shows and continued his libretto writing with *Skyscraper* (1965), an adaptation of ELMER

RICE's play *Dream Girl*. Stone's most successful libretto was for *1776* (1969; Tony, Best Musical), an original musical about the signing of the Declaration of Independence. Subsequent shows included *Two by Two* (1970), *Sugar* (1972), *Woman of the Year* (1981; Tony, Best Book), *My One and Only* (1983), *The WILL ROGERS FOLLIES* (1991), and *Titanic* (1997; Tony, Best Book). Aside from *1776*, most of Stone's librettos were skillful adaptations of already successful plays and films.   MK

Straiges, Tony (1942–) Set and costume designer best known for his sets for *SUNDAY IN THE PARK WITH GEORGE* (1984; Tony and Outer Critics Circle awards) and for *INTO THE WOODS* (1987). Straiges has designed extensively at the ARENA STAGE, YALE REPERTORY, the ALLEY, HARTFORD STAGE, and several other regional theatres, as well as for OFF-BROADWAY companies (e.g., *Meet Me in St. Louis* for IRISH REP in 2006). His sets often have a sparse elegance or sense of fantasy about them.
AA

Strange Interlude EUGENE O'NEILL's most successful production in his lifetime opened for the THEATRE GUILD on 30 January 1928 at the JOHN GOLDEN THEATRE and subsequently won O'Neill his third Pulitzer Prize. Under PHILIP MOELLER's direction, this nine-act experiment with interior monologue (extended asides) commenced at 5:15 P.M. and took some four and a half hours to perform, interrupted by a dinner break. Although the story of the play is not unusual in its tale of desire, adultery, and power, the production was intriguing as it revealed fully not only the characters' speech but also their thoughts. The audience was able to eavesdrop on the subtext and articulated motivation as the physical action of all but the speaker was arrested for each interior monologue; the subtext proved much more telling than the dialogue. Albeit set realistically by JO MIELZINER, the play seemed mysterious, even eerily otherworldly as Nina Leeds (played by LYNN FONTANNE) cast her erotic, spiritual, and sometimes evil spell over her three men, and ultimately over the audience as well.   RHW

Strasberg, Lee (1901–82) Director and acting teacher who studied at the American Laboratory Theatre, acted with the THEATRE GUILD, and in 1931 helped found and directed for the GROUP THEATRE, espousing the work of the Russian director Konstantin Stanislavsky. Among his directorial successes were *The HOUSE OF CONNELLY*, *Night over Taos* (1932), *MEN IN WHITE*, and *Clash by Night* (1941).

In 1950 Strasberg became a director for the ACTORS STUDIO and emerged as the leading exponent of the Method, based on the Stanislavsky System. In 1965 he directed a highly controversial *The Three Sisters,* with GEORGE C. SCOTT, KIM STANLEY, and LUTHER ADLER, which played at the Aldwych Theatre in London during the World Theatre season. A great many of America's leading film and stage actors studied with Strasberg, either privately or at the Studio, among them MARLON BRANDO, whose internal style as Stanley in *A STREETCAR NAMED DESIRE* became popularly associated with Method acting. Among Strasberg's more famous students were Montgomery Clift, ANN BANCROFT, Shelley Winters, Paul Newman, and Joanne Woodward.

Although his methods and results excited great controversy, little doubt remains that Strasberg had a major effect on modern acting. His thoughts on the Method (*A Dream of Passion*) were published posthumously in 1987.   SMA

Strathairn, David (1949–) After a virtual channeling of Edward R. Murrow in the 2005 film *Good Night, and Good Luck,* this California-born actor, who had trained at Williams College and RINGLING BROS. Clown College (followed by a brief career in a circus), received the recognition he deserved following a quarter of a century of steady work on the stage, in films, and on television. His understated presence and slender, handsome, dark good looks have served him well in supporting roles – many in offbeat vehicles, especially films, beginning with the 1980 *Return of the Secaucus 7,* directed by his college friend John Sayles. His OFF-BROADWAY debut was in 1983's *Blue Plate Special*; his Broadway debut the flop *Einstein and the Polar Bear* (1981). Subsequent plays have included works by Harold Pinter, Vaclav Havel, CHEKHOV, Caryl Churchill, Tom Stoppard, and SAM SHEPARD. His other three Broadway outings have been as Vershinin in *Three Sisters* (1997), Kurt in Strindberg's *Dance of Death* (2001) with Ian McKellen and Helen Mirren, and John the Baptist in ESTELLE PARSON's staged-reading version of *Salome* (2003) with AL PACINO.   DBW

strawhat theatre see SUMMER STOCK

Streamers The last play in DAVID RABE's Vietnam trilogy premiered in January 1976 at the LONG WHARF in New Haven; in April it moved to LINCOLN CENTER and ran for 400 performances. Directed by MIKE NICHOLS and produced by JOSEPH PAPP, it starred Kenneth McMillan as Sgt. Rooney, Dolph Sweet as Sgt. Cokes, and Dorian Harewood as the menacing Carlyle. Robert Altman directed the film version (1983). *Streamers* is about sexual and psychic violence (with an onstage rape and stabbing) in a stateside barracks, where five young soldiers on their way to Vietnam confront the two old sergeants. The title refers to a parachute that fails to open, symbolizing the madness and treachery of Rabe's domestic America.   PCK

Streep, Meryl [née Mary Louise] (1949–) Film and stage actress, trained at the Yale School of Drama. She made her New York debut as Imogen in *Trelawny of the Wells* in 1975; then in 1976, for the PHOENIX, she played Flora in *27 Wagons Full of Cotton* and Patricia in *A Memory of Two Mondays,* as well as appeared in SECRET SERVICE (all Broadway). Over the next two years she played Katharine in *Henry V,* Isabella in *Measure for Measure,* Dunyasha in *The Cherry Orchard,* Katharina in *The Taming of the Shrew* (all NEW YORK SHAKESPEARE FESTIVAL), and Lillian in *Happy End* (Broadway. Soon after, she began a brilliant film career, during which she has won two Academy Awards for *Sophie's Choice* and *Kramer vs. Kramer* (and 12 additional nominations). In 2001, after a 22-year absence from the NYC stage, she appeared with KEVIN KLINE in MIKE NICHOL's production of *The Seagull* at the Delacorte, and played the title role in Brecht's *Mother Courage* in the same venue (summer 2006). April 2005 saw her in a project involving original sound plays, at St. Ann's Warehouse (Brooklyn), called *Theater of the New Ear.* Equally at ease in drama or farce, Streep is noted for meticulous preparation, a wide-ranging intellect, and intense truthfulness in her acting. Since the 1980s she has concentrated on her film career. In 2004 she won an Emmy for her Hannah Pitt (et al.) in the HBO film version of *ANGELS IN AMERICA.* She is considered by many to be one of the greatest living actresses of our time.   SMA   DBW

Street Scene Largely realistic 1929 three-act drama by ELMER RICE depicting the life of some 50 lower-middle-class characters living in a New York brownstone tenement, trapped in a seemingly hopeless environment. Its purpose, writes C. W. E. Bigsby, is "to recreate the social texture of the world of the tenement and partly to suggest the degree to which that variousness was homogenised by context." With two plot lines, one melodramatic and one romantic comedy, Rice illustrates various strains of life intermingled with commonplace incidents, though both the melodrama and romantic intensity are effectively deflated at the ends of Acts I and II.

Marlon Brando and Jessica Tandy in *A Streetcar Named Desire*, 1947. *Courtesy:* Museum of the City of New York.

The play had trouble finding a producer, but eventually received the backing of WILLIAM A. BRADY. Rice directed it himself, with a setting by JO MIELZINER. It opened 10 January and ran 601 performances, garnering considerable critical success, including the Pulitzer Prize for Drama. Adapted into an opera in 1947 with music by KURT WEILL and lyrics by LANGSTON HUGHES, this musical version was revived successfully by New York City Opera in 1959, 1979, and 1990. Since the mid-1930s, Rice's play has often been compared to SIDNEY KINGSLEY'S DEAD END. DBW

Streetcar Named Desire, A TENNESSEE WILLIAMS's masterpiece opened 3 December 1947 on Broadway and ran for 855 performances, winning every major honor, including the Pulitzer Prize, the Donaldson Award, and the New York Drama Critics' Award. Directed by ELIA KAZAN and produced by Irene Selznick, *Streetcar* starred JESSICA TANDY (Blanche), MARLON BRANDO (Stanley), KIM HUNTER (Stella), and Karl Malden (Mitch). UTA HAGEN replaced Tandy, and Anthony Quinn, Brando, at the end of the run. A whirlwind of European premieres followed in 1948–9, including Rome (sets by Franco Zeffirelli), Manchester (Olivier directing Vivien Leigh), and Paris (Jean Cocteau's adaptation with Arletty). Other national premieres include Tokyo (1953), Toruń and Wrocław, Poland (1957), and Tianjin in 1988. The first of many revivals began in 1956 with TALLULAH BANKHEAD (City Center). On its 25th anniversary (1973), *Streetcar* was done at the Ahmanson in Los Angeles (Faye Dunaway and Jon Voight) and at the VIVIAN BEAUMONT in New York (ROSEMARY HARRIS and James Farentino). A 1974 British revival starred CLAIRE BLOOM. Jack Gelber directed the play in 1976 (Academy Festival Theatre, Lake Forest, IL; GERALDINE PAGE and RIP TORN). On Broadway, BLYTHE DANNER and Aidan Quinn starred in 1988; a revival directed by GREGORY MOSHER (with Jessica Lange and Alec Baldwin) opened in April 1992; and a disappointing production with Natasha Richardson (see REDGRAVE FAMILY) and a miscast John C. Reilly was produced by ROUNDABOUT in 2005.

Kazan's acclaimed film version in 1951 featured the original Broadway cast except for Leigh replacing Tandy. In 1952 Valerie Bettis choreographed a ballet *Streetcar* (revitalized by the Harlem Dance Theatre in 1982). In 1984 John Erman directed a graphically sexual television adaptation (Ann-Margret and Treat Williams).

Set in New Orleans, *Streetcar* chronicles Blanche Du Bois's search for protection and her eventual destruction at the hands of her brutish brother-in-law Stanley Kowalski. It is filled with competing mythologies and representations, including two recurring character types – the faded southern belle, both madonna and sensualist, and the seed-bearing male. Blanche's "tender feelings" compete with Stanley's "brutal desire" as these two struggle for control of Stella and Mitch. Written in Williams's lyrically southern idiom, *Streetcar* has made indelible contributions to our national mythology. In 1995 Brenda Murphy published a book on the play in production. PCK

Strike Up the Band Slight musical comedy in three acts written by some of the most influential music and theatre people of the early 20th century: MORRIE RYSKIND and GEORGE S. KAUFMAN (book), and GEORGE AND IRA GERSHWIN (music and lyrics, respectively). Originally produced in 1927, it was recalled for rewrites after tryout performances and opened on Broadway at the Times Square Theatre, 14 January 1930, to run 191 performances. The play satirizes war in a story about a rich chocolate maker who instigates war on Switzerland in order to corner the sweet chocolate market. The production featured two popular comedians, BOBBY CLARK AND PAUL McCUL-LOUGH, and the tunes "Strike Up the Band" and "I've Got a Crush on You."   KN

striptease see BURLESQUE

Stritch, Elaine (1925–) Actress and singer, a member of the THEATRE HALL OF FAME, who studied at the Drama Workshop at the New School for Social Research before making her Broadway debut in *Loco* (1946). She stopped the show with her rendition of "Zip" in the revival of PAL JOEY (1952), appeared in the revival of ON YOUR TOES (1954), and played Grace in BUS STOP (1955). She starred in the musicals *Goldilocks* (1958) and *Sail Away* (1961), and played Martha in matinees of WHO'S AFRAID OF VIRGINIA WOOLF? (as of 1963). Her gravelly voice and acid delivery perfectly suited the role of Joanne in STEPHEN SONDHEIM's musical COMPANY (1970), and she excelled as Parthy in the revival of SHOW BOAT (1994). Summer 1993 she appeared as LILLIAN HELLMAN in Peter Feibleman's *Cakewalk* at the AMERICAN REPERTORY THEATRE; she played Claire in a 1996 revival of *A DELICATE BALANCE;* and in 2002 starred in her Tony-winning solo performance, *Elaine Stritch at Liberty* (written with JOHN LAHR).   MK

Stroman, Susan (1954–) Emerging in the 1990s as the choreographer of her generation, Stroman, before gaining wide attention with her work on *Crazy for You* (1992; Tony), SHOW BOAT (1995; Tony), and *A Christmas Carol* (1995, Madison Square Garden; Outer Critics Circle Award), choreographed productions of *And the World Goes Round* (1991; Outer Critics Circle Award), *A LITTLE NIGHT MUSIC* (New York City Opera, 1990; revived 2003), and a revival of KANDER AND EBB's *Flora, the Red Menace* (1987, VINEYARD), among others – and played Hunyak in the national tour of CHICAGO. In 1996 she shared the Theatre Development Fund's Astaire Award for excellence in dance. Her career has snowballed since then: In 1996 she choreographed the musical version of the film *Big,* followed by *Steel Pier* in 1997. She then both directed and choreographed *Contact* (2000; Drama Desk and Tony awards, Choreography), *The MUSIC MAN* revival (2000), *The PRODUCERS* (2001 Drama Desk and Tony awards for both Direction and Choreography), and the disappointing *Thou Shall Not*, with music by Harry Connick Jr. (2001). For the 2002 revival of OKLAHOMA! she choreographed only (Drama Desk), but in 2004 she was the director-choreographer of the musical version of *The Frogs* at the VIVIAN BEAUMONT (with NATHAN LANE). In 2000, 2001, and 2002 she again won Astaire

Awards, the only four-time winner in the 25-year history of the awards.   DBW

Strouse, Charles (1928–) Composer, lyricist, arranger. After studying at the Eastman School of Music, Strouse worked as a rehearsal pianist. He wrote songs for *The Littlest Revue* (1956, PHOENIX THEATRE), then teamed in 1960 with lyricist Lee Adams on BYE BYE BIRDIE, a show that poked fun at rock singing idols (Tony, Best Musical). With Adams he wrote *All American* (1962), the musical version of GOLDEN BOY (1964), *It's a Bird, It's a Plane, It's Superman* (1966), and *Applause* (1970; Tony, Best Musical). With lyricist MARTIN CHARNIN he wrote the songs for the long-run hit ANNIE (1977; Tony, Best Original Score) and its OFF-BROADWAY sequel, *Annie Warbucks* (1993). His later musicals, such as *Bring Back Birdie* (1981), *Dance a Little Closer* (1983), *Rags* (1986), and *Nick and Nora* (1991) were failures. Others are still in development: *The Night They Raided MINSKY's*, *Marty*, and *You Never Know*. CHITA RIVERA: *The Dancer's Life* (2005) featured songs by Strouse. Strouse's bubbly, vibrant music complemented the contemporary settings of his shows.   MK

Student Prince, The Four-act operetta, music by SIGMUND ROMBERG, words by Dorothy Donnelly; opened 2 December 1924 at JOLSON's 59th Street Theatre, NYC, running 608 performances. Originally produced as *The Student Prince in Heidelberg* and given a sumptuous production by the SHU-BERTS, this was the longest-running musical of the 1920s and is considered by many the masterpiece of American operetta. The story tells of Karl Franz (Howard Marsh), crown prince of Karlsberg, who as a student in Heidelberg falls deeply in love with Kathie (Ilse Marvenga), a waitress at the local tavern. Their dreams are shattered when he is called home to become king, and when he returns to Heidelberg, he finds that the "golden days" of youth cannot be recaptured. Romberg's score, filled with marches and drinking songs as well as such indelible melodies as the "Serenade," is lushly romantic and dramatically served by his skillful use of leitmotifs; a particularly effective device is having each act end with the same song ("Deep in My Heart"), the effect of which alters from romantic hope to heartbreak. Challenging even to highly trained singers, it has remained a staple of the light-opera repertoire, receiving frequent major revivals throughout the world.   JD

Studio Arena Theatre RESIDENT NONPROFIT regional (LORT) theatre, founded in 1965 by Neal DuBrock as a professional extension of the 1927

Studio Theatre School of Buffalo, NY (a city with a rich theatrical past, and presently also home to the African American Cultural Center/PAUL ROBESON Theatre, Alleyway Theatre, Buffalo Ensemble Theatre, and the Theatre of Youth). The Studio Arena operates a 637-seat, thrust-design mainstage and produces 7–10 productions during September–July. Initially, the theatre imported name actors to supplement a resident company, but in recent years it has usually hired pickup casts of local performers for an eclectic, mainstage repertory of old and modern standards plus light, commercial entertainments, and a second-stage program of riskier works. Over the past four decades, Studio Arena has staged more than 298 productions including 44 world or American premieres. In 1991 artistic director David Frank resigned after 11 seasons due to budget cuts; he was replaced by Gavin Cameron-Webb, who left at the end of the 2004–5 season. The new artistic director as of April 2006 has been Kathleen A. Gaffney. CLJ DBW

Styne, Jule [né Julius Kerwin Stein] (1905–94) Composer and producer. Styne attended the Chicago College of Music, then organized a dance band on the West Coast in the 1930s. He wrote his first Broadway scores for *High Button Shoes* (1947) and *Gentlemen Prefer Blondes* (1949). *Two on the Aisle* (1951) marked the beginning of a partnership with librettists-lyricists BETTY COMDEN AND ADOLPH GREEN that included *BELLS ARE RINGING* (1956), *Say, Darling* (1958), *Do Re Mi* (1960), *Subways Are for Sleeping* (1961), and *Hallelujah, Baby!* (1967). Other notable Styne shows were *GYPSY* (1959) with lyricist STEPHEN SONDHEIM, and *FUNNY GIRL* (1964) and *Sugar* (1972) with BOB MERRILL. He also produced several plays and musicals, including *Mr. Wonderful* (1956) and *Will Success Spoil Rock Hunter?* (1955). His last effort was the ill-fated *The Red Shoes* (1993). Styne's music has a traditional Broadway sound but skillfully underscores the show's characters and situations. Theodore Taylor's biography was published in 1979. MK

Subject Was Roses, The Three-character drama by FRANK D. GILROY. Directed by ULU GROSBARD, it opened on 25 May 1964 for 832 performances and received the Pulitzer Prize for Drama and the Drama Critics' Circle and Tony awards for Best Play. JACK ALBERTSON (Tony, Best Featured Actor), Irene Dailey, and Martin Sheen were featured in this delicate and moving tale of a son, newly matured after serving in the armed forces, who returns to his estranged parents. This cast worked with great subtlety to portray the evolving rela-

tionships of this psychological exploration of an American postwar family. Dailey was replaced by Patricia Neal for the 1968 film, which was a critical, but not a popular, success. A 1991 ROUNDABOUT THEATRE revival with John Mahoney, DANA IVEY, and Patrick Dempsey suggested that the play had lost much of its initial impact. MR

Sullivan, Arthur see GILBERT AND SULLIVAN IN AMERICA

Sullivan, Daniel (1935–) Theatre critic and journalist. Born in Worcester, MA, and educated at Holy Cross College (1957), Sullivan served as drama and music critic of the *Minneapolis Tribune* (1962–4), and music writer (1965–6) and assistant drama critic (1966–8) for the *New York Times*, covering OFF-BROADWAY. In 1969 he moved to the *Los Angeles Times*, serving as theatre critic until his retirement in 1991. Since, he has taught journalism at the University of Minnesota and in 1999 became director of the O'Neill National Critics Institute. TLM

Sullivan, Daniel (1940–) Artistic director 1981–97 of the SEATTLE REP, where he directed more than 60 productions, several of which subsequently played Broadway, including *I'm Not Rappaport* (1985, 2002), *The HEIDI CHRONICLES* (1989), *Conversations with My Father* (1992), and *The Sisters Rosensweig* (1993). Other NYC productions OFF-BROADWAY include JON ROBIN BAITZ's *The Substance of Fire* (1991), *The Merry Wives of Windsor* (1994), and NEIL SIMON's *London Suite* (1995). During the early 1970s he was a member of the Repertory Theater of LINCOLN CENTER. Since leaving Seattle he has been a sought-after freelance director, working for various groups on Broadway, in particular the MANHATTAN THEATRE CLUB (*Proof*, 2000 [Tony, Best Direction]; *Sight Unseen*, 2004; *Brooklyn Boy*, 2005; *After the Night and the Music*, 2005; *Rabbit Hole*, 2006), Lincoln Center (*An American Daughter*, 1997; *AH, WILDERNESS!*, 1998; *MORNING'S AT SEVEN*, 2002), ROUNDABOUT (*Major Barbara*, 2001; *PRELUDE TO A KISS*, 2007); as well as for commercial productions of *A MOON FOR THE MISBEGOTTEN* (2000), *The Retreat from Moscow* (2003), and *Julius Caesar* (2005) – and Off-Broadway for The PUBLIC (David Hare's *Stuff Happens*, 2006; Obie and LORTEL awards for Direction). Sullivan has nurtured the careers of several playwrights, notably WENDY WASSERSTEIN, Jon Robin Baitz, and HERB GARDNER, among others. Since 1999 he has been the Swanlund Professor of Theatre at the University of Illinois. DBW

Summer and Smoke Lyrical play by TENNESSEE WILLIAMS, revised as *Eccentricities of a Nightingale*. Premiering in Dallas July 1947, it was directed by MARGO JONES and starred Katherine Balfour (Alma) and Tod Andrews. The play opened at the MUSIC BOX THEATRE 6 October 1948 and ran for 100 performances, again directed by Jones with Andrews as John, but Margaret Phillips as Alma. JOSÉ QUINTERO's OFF-BROADWAY production in 1952 starred GERALDINE PAGE and LEE RICHARDSON. Page re-created Alma in the 1961 film version with Laurence Harvey and RITA MORENO (Rosa). In 1971, *Summer* was made into an opera (music by Lee Hoiby, libretto by LANFORD WILSON; Chicago Opera Theater). Lee Remick starred in a BBC production (aired January 1972). A 1996 Broadway revival was unsuccessful.

Set in Glorious Hill, MS, the plays tells of Miss Alma's love for her childhood sweetheart, Dr. John Buchanan. At first, Alma is all spirit and soul, whereas John is a creature of the flesh and pleasure. At play's end, "the tables have turned with a vengeance." In suffering the "affliction of love," Alma has a spiritual kinship with Blanche Du Bois. The play is almost perfectly balanced between the flesh and the spirit, the worldly and the sensitive that haunted Williams.   PCK

summer stock This term refers to a particular type of summertime entertainment that evolved in the U.S. Northeast during the 1920s and '30s. It is an umbrella term for independent theatres with a resident company presenting a number of different plays in weekly or biweekly repertory, either in a permanent house or on tour, between the months of June and September. The theatres were established in attractive rural environments near the new resorts developed for middle- and working-class clientele who, thanks to advances in corporate management and federal legislation, now enjoyed annual paid vacations. Wherever city dwellers fled to the countryside to escape the heat, chances were a summer-stock theatre would soon appear.

The theatres were built quickly and cheaply, usually by appropriating a nearby barn or other spacious building and converting it into a rustic but workable theatre. They ranged widely in artistic quality and repertoire – although most featured light comedies, mysteries, romances, and thrillers, other specialized in serious drama or in introducing the work of budding playwrights – all fulfilled the dual purpose of providing much-needed work for theatre artists and low-cost entertainment for vacationers. They also brought legitimate theatre to remote areas, thus affording many local residents an opportunity to see professional productions for the first time. Hence, summer stock, as America's first truly REGIONAL THEATRE, had a major effect on the cultural, economic, and sociological development of the U.S.

The first summer-stock theatres – Elitch's Gardens Theatre in Denver (1890) and Lakewood Playhouse five miles north of Showhegan, ME (opened in 1898 but not offering regular summer-stock seasons till 1901) – were actually late 19th-century STOCK theatres that happened to establish themselves as summertime ventures. Summer stock as we know it did not evolve until the 1920s with the establishment of three prominent theatres that are still extant: the Manhattan Theatre Colony, which first opened in 1927 at Mariarden, outside of Peterborough, NH, and then moved to its current home in Ogunquit, ME; the Cape Playhouse, which acquired its permanent home in Dennis, MA, in the middle of Cape Cod in 1927; and the Berkshire Playhouse, now known as the BERKSHIRE THEATRE FESTIVAL, which opened in Stockbridge, MA, in 1928. Although summer stock was not exclusively a New England phenomenon, many of the theatres during its "golden age" from the 1920s through the '60s were located in the six New England states. Notable among these were The Barnstormers in Tamworth, NH (1931); Ivoryton Playhouse in Ivoryton, CT (1931); WESTPORT COUNTRY PLAYHOUSE in Westport, CT (1931); New England Barn Players in New London, NH (1933); and Theatre-by-the-Sea in Matunuck, RI (1931). What became known as the strawhat circuit of summer-stock theatres also extended into New York, New Jersey, Pennsylvania, Maryland, Virginia, Ohio, and the Midwest, and included such prominent venues as Bucks County Playhouse in New Hope, PA (1939); BARTER THEATRE in Abingdon, VA (1933); Peninsula Players in Fishcreek, WI (1935); and the Kenley Players, with companies in Pennsylvania, Ohio, and Michigan (1940s–1980s).

The number of summer-stock theatres grew exponentially between the 1920s and '50s. In the 1920s there were fewer than 30 theatres; by 1936, the first year the ACTORS' EQUITY ASSOCIATION began writing contracts specifically for summer-stock theatres and keeping detailed records, there were 120 companies, about 50 of which were union operations. The number grew steadily each year, although well over 50% of the theatres were dark during WWII, largely because of gas rationing, which prohibited summer travel. Summer stock made a powerful comeback following the war, however. In 1948 there were 130 Equity companies alone; that number grew to 152 by 1950. It is safe to estimate that in addition to the union operations there were at least 100 non-Equity stock theatres. Hence, during the 1950s there were 250–300 stock houses operating principally in the northeastern U.S. each summer.

Sadly, the history of summer-stock paralleled that of its 19th-century precursors all too closely by following the same pattern from resident stock to star system to combination company (known here as "star package" or "package tour") to eventual demise, but within the abbreviated span of a few decades. As early as 1935, JANE COWL was hired by Cape Playhouse business manager RICHARD ALDRICH, soon to be christened the leading summer-stock producer, to appear for $1,000 per week. Soon afterward, other popular stars followed, eager to spend their enforced summer breaks (most theatres were dark between June and August) on lucrative busman's holidays. Eventually, stars of Hollywoods films and, later, television, followed, with weekly salaries at John Kenley's theatres peaking at $30,000 per week. By the time theatres tried to return to resident stock, it was too late – the public's taste for stars was secured. This, along with changes in Americans' vacationing habits and the ever-rising cost of keeping theatres open, spelled the gradual decline of summer stock.

Nevertheless, summer stock was a vital force in the American theatre industry: From the 1930s through the '60s it was the leading employer of theatre professionals in the U.S. More actors, directors, designers, and technicians worked in legitimate theatre during the summer months than at any other time of the year. It also has provided a place for young theatre artists to garner their first professional credentials and to learn their craft. It is still true that most theatre professionals have worked at some time during their careers in summer stock.

Although the golden age of summer-stock theatre is over, there are still, as of early in the 21st century, more than 350 venues offering theatrical entertainments during the summer months. Fewer than 100 offer proper stock sesaons; others host a variety of live entertainments, from legitimate theatre to Renaissance fairs and rock concerts, in locales ranging from old barns seating a few hundred patrons to large arenas holding thousands of theatregoers.   MSL

[*Ed. note:* The definitive history of summer stock, by LoMonaco, was published in 2004.]

Sunday in the Park with George Two-act musical play, music and lyrics by STEPHEN SONDHEIM, book by JAMES LAPINE; opened 2 May 1984 at the BOOTH THEATRE, running 604 performances. This musical, originally developed at OFF-BROADWAY's PLAYWRIGHTS HORIZONS, deals with the nature of artistic creation and revolves around a famous Georges Seurat painting. The first act, set in the 1880s, shows Seurat (MANDY PATINKIN) creating the painting and dealing with his model-mistress Dot (BERNADETTE PETERS). The second act shows their descendants (played by the same actors) dealing with the contemporary art world. Virtually without dance, yet highly inventive visually through Lapine's staging and TONY STRAIGES's scenery, the show won eight Drama Desk Awards (including Outstanding Musical), the Drama Critics' Circle Award (Best Musical), and the Pulitzer Prize for Drama (1985). A Broadway revival is planned by ROUNDABOUT for 2008.   JD

Sunshine Boys, The, opened on 20 December 1972 at the BROADHURST THEATRE and ran for 538 performances, marking NEIL SIMON's return to a nongendered depiction of the destructive effect of extreme behavior. Main characters Willie Clark (JACK ALBERTSON) and Al Lewis (SAM LEVENE) allow Simon to present his theme outside of his customary upper middle-class setting. The two retired VAUDEVILLE performers (based, in part, on SMITH AND DALE) address the relative helplessness of the elderly in society as they continue their long-standing feud over apparent trivialities. Their dialogue sharply outlines the actual basis for the conflict. The ex-partners carry on their battle almost entirely in terms of running gags and one-liners because such choices are as much a part of their lives as their self-destructive behavior; their implicit recognition of both implies that they may be able to work within that which they cannot change. The pair's advancing age underscores Simon's suggestion that a refusal to reconcile differences can result only in isolation. The play was turned into a successful film with Walter Matthau and GEORGE BURNS in 1975. NATIONAL ACTORS THEATRE revived it in 1997 with Jack Klugman (Willie Clark) and Tony Randall (Al Lewis).   RW

Sun-up, written by LULA VOLLMER, opened on 24 May 1923 at the Provincetown Playhouse and was immediately hailed for its portrayal of North Carolina mountain life. The Widow Cagle (Lucille La Verne) struggles against laws she cannot understand that tragically intrude on her simple mountain life. Still suffering from the death of her moonshiner husband, she resists the Great War, which takes her son away from her. The play ran for two years in New York after moving to the

PRINCESS THEATRE, and was also performed in several foreign countries. Vollmer donated all royalties from the play for the education of the mountaineers.   FB

support services, theatrical Developments in the American theatre in the late 19th century hastened the industrialization of production practices. Prior to the Civil War, most theatres carried their own personnel for all backstage work, which embraced building and painting scenery, making stage properties, and sewing costumes. With the expansion of theatrical activity and the building of thousands of theatres after the war, managers resorted to outside sources to obtain scenery and costumes; by the end of the century, and for the first time in history, the theatre building was erected without the customary workrooms and paint frames. When the STOCK COMPANY ceased to be a production entity, specialty houses dealing in scenery, costumes, and (later) lighting equipment sprang up to supply the needs of independent producers and managers. The expansion of the railroad from coast to coast made it possible to ship even bulky pieces great distances via railway express. New York emerged as the center of most of the support services.

Scenery
In 1894, Richard Marston, one of New York's leading and busiest scene painters, decried the "scenery factories" that turned out theatrical settings imitating the work of recognized scene painters but using cheap materials and paints. Although there were indeed scenery studios that fit Marston's descriptions, many produced high-quality work to meet an ever-expanding market. In 1875, Mathias Armbruster, a young German scene painter, settled in Columbus, OH; there he set up the Armbruster Scenic Studios, which became one of the largest manufacturers of stock scenery (see SCENIC DESIGN) in the country. Like other studios, Armbruster could supply Victorian interiors, tropical exteriors, Atlantic City seascapes, Japanese gardens, and deserts in the Holy Land – at a price. By using aniline dyes, backgrounds painted on canvas could be folded or rolled; but pieces painted with distemper had to be shipped flat. Besides specialty scenes, most studios could supply stock interiors and exteriors that would serve for a variety of scenes within most plays.

The studio that advertised itself as the world's largest came into existence in 1891. A young painter, Lee Lash, working on an olio curtain in San Francisco, conceived the idea of incorporating the names of advertisers in natural places within a street scene (rather than the customary practice of painting the names in patchwork style). His idea worked so well that he founded the Lee Lash Studios, which expanded its operations to serve the country. The studio moved to PHILADELPHIA in 1893 and to New York in 1898, selling its scenery to the major producers in New York for the next 30 years and to smaller enterprises throughout the country. Like other studios, it distributed a stock book with illustrations (many in color) of its scenes and curtains. All could be ordered by submitting measurements and diagrams as required.

With the demise of the stock company, the gradual devolution of VAUDEVILLE, and the road to movies and radio after WWI, most of the studios went out of business or reduced their operations to serve their immediate areas. The remaining studios were centered in New York, but no longer producing stock scenes: Each stage set was (and continues to be) customized according to specifications submitted by the designer assigned to the production. In the years immediately after the war, JOSEPH URBAN established a scenic studio that introduced Continental stagecraft techniques to America and later (as Triangle Scenic Studios) became the most active on Broadway. Several studios limited their function either to the building or the painting of scenery, whereas others did both. The lifespan of a studio proved to be short, and Triangle was succeeded by a number of others, the most durable of which is the Nolan Scenery Studios, which was founded at about the same time as Triangle. Although it provided both the building and painting of sets at its inception, it exists today as a painting studio. With ever greater demands imposed by producers for spectacular effects, particularly in musical theatre, small but highly specialized companies, among which is Feller Precision, have arisen to provide the technology for such effects.

Costumes
Until the last half of the 19th century, one of the enduring conventions of theatre in the Western world was the costuming of actors in contemporaneous clothing, with such occasional concessions to period or exotic background or status of the character as turbans for Arabs, feather headdresses for Indians, crowns and ermine for kings, togas over kneebreeches for Greeks, and so on. Although the great patent theatres of England had accumulated extensive wardrobes from which actors could be fitted, the small provincial companies, on which the American system was

patterned, depended on actors to costume themselves, which often resulted in a hodgepodge of styles and periods within one production (see COSTUME).

As the 19th century wore on, however, and the costume practices of William Charles Macready and Charles Kean were introduced in America, managers were disposed to add to theatrical spectacle authentic-looking costumes for period plays. Prosperous American theatres established their own costume collections and installed resident costumers in their own workrooms; small, shoestring companies relied on costume supply houses, which began to spring up at midcentury in most cities with theatres. The earliest was Dazian's, founded in 1842 by Wolf Dazian, a Bavarian immigrant, who started with a dry-goods store in lower Manhattan, supplying such as P. T. BARNUM with stage fabrics. He later expanded into costume making shortly after the invention of the industrial sewing machine at midcentury. Dazian's followed the uptown movement of the theatre district, coming to rest just off Times Square. In 1919, under different management, Dazian's abandoned its costume-making business, and it remains in existence today as a fabric-supply house.

Most costume houses did a thriving rental business, supplying the needs of amateur and collegiate as well as professional theatres. The founders of the Van Horn Costume Company in Philadelphia and the Eaves Costume Company in New York began as actors with a talent for the needle: Albert Van Horn established his business in 1852, and Albert Eaves in 1867; both prospered in the late 19th century. In 1902 Ely Stroock bought out Brooks Costume Company, a small uniform supply house; in 1919 he bought out producer CHARLES FROHMAN's costume warehouses, adding a custom costume shop that dominated Broadway for many years. When Broadway activity diminished, so did the costume business, and in 1981, Eaves, Brooks, and Van Horn merged under Eaves's administrative umbrella (as Eaves–Brooks). In turn they were acquired in 1998 by DODGER THEATRICALS (producing company) and Amsterdam's Stage Holding, but in 2005 were sold to Costume World in Florida, bringing their rental inventory to one million items.

The theatre has also been served by small costume companies, the favorites of leading designers and managers. ROBERT EDMOND JONES patronized Mme. Elise Freisinger's costume house. Helene Pons made the costumes for the Chauve-Souris company during the 1920s and for the PLAYWRIGHTS' COMPANY for many years.

Decreasing production on Broadway has reduced further the number of active costumers, whose existence continues to be precarious. Today, Barbara Matera Ltd. (Matera died in 2001), Parsons–Meares Ltd., and the Grace Costume Company, among a few others, supplement theatrical work with costuming for ballet and opera companies. Specialty costuming and armor by the Martin Izquierdo Studios are fabricated frequently in conjunction with regular costume companies.

As a service for regional and collegiate theatre, the Theatre Development Fund established the Costume Collection, which rents costumes (most donated by producers of Broadway shows) at nominal rates, shipping them throughout the country.

Stage lighting

In the era of gaslight, which embraced most of the 19th century, the equipment necessary to light a production was installed as part of the theatre's permanent equipment (see STAGE LIGHTING). With the introduction of electricity into the theatre building, all that was really necessary was to have a power source to which controls and conducting cables could eventually be attached; the rest of the equipment could be brought into the theatre to serve each production. This concept coincided in time almost exactly with the industrialization of theatrical production at the close of the 19th century, and was responsible for the creation of another support service: the theatrical electrical supply house.

In 1896, two immigrant Austrians founded Kliegl Brothers, a firm that designed and manufactured special housings for incandescent lamps used in theatres throughout the country. They also developed the Klieglight, whose name became eponymous for any intense, bright white spotlight. Other companies followed in its wake, and the principle of renting equipment to independent producers, rather than selling it outright, had become established; this proved to be both lucrative to the lighting-supply companies and a godsend to the producers, who could avoid buying equipment and storing it in a warehouse. One of the most prosperous suppliers, the Century Lighting Company, founded in 1929 by Joseph Levy and Edward Kook, combined rentals and fabrication of specialized lighting instruments, the most successful of which was the Leko-lite, named by assembling the first two letters of their last names; the "Leko," a compact ellipsoidal spotlight equipped with shutters and lenses to direct lighting on specific areas, has become the workhorse of stage lighting. Kliegl and Century, like many of their competitors, leased (and sold) equipment throughout the country and established branch offices outside of New York.

After WWII, other theatrical lighting supply houses arose to challenge the domination of Century and Kliegl, both of which are no longer in business. Leading the field today is Four Star Stage Lighting and, to a lesser degree, Bash Theatrical Lighting Company and Vanco Stage Lighting. Because of the ever-diminishing number of New York productions both on and Off-Broadway and on the road, the solvency of these suppliers depends on their serving regional theatres, industrial shows, college and university theatres, touring companies, popular music concerts, and amusement and theme parks.   MCH

Suppressed Desires Written by Susan Glaspell in collaboration with George Cram Cook, this one-act satire on fashionable psychoanalysis played an important part in the founding of the Little Theatre movement [see community theatre] in the U.S. After being rejected by the Washington Square Players, it was produced on the opening bill of the Provincetown Players, first in the home of two members of the group and later at their Wharf Theatre in the summer of 1915. Glaspell performed the role of Henrietta Brewster, a disciple of Freudian psychology who repudiates its benefits when her husband, Stephen (performed by Cook), and sister, Mabel, are found to have "suppressed desires" that will destroy her marriage. The easy comic treatment of the newly converted has kept the play popular.   KF

Susan and God by Rachel Crothers marked the author's return to the theatre after five years of writing in Hollywood and was her last produced play. Jo Mielziner designed the sets for the first production, directed by Crothers, which opened at the Plymouth Theatre 7 October 1937 and ran for 288 performances. Susan Trexel returns from England with a newfound religious fervor and a desire to reform the lives of her upper-class friends, but finds herself cornered into making a new start with her estranged husband and awkward teenage daughter. Gertrude Lawrence gave a virtuoso performance of the vain yet charismatic Susan (and reprised her role in 1943, at the new City Center). Crothers's sharp dialogue and sensitively drawn characters allow her to explore the theatrics of fashionable conversion and its effects upon delicately balanced relationships. New York's Mint Theater revived the play to end its 2005–6 season.   KF

Swados, Elizabeth (1951–) Composer, writer, and director. After graduating from Bennington College in 1972, Swados became a composer and musical director for renowned director Peter Brook. Beginning in 1977 she was composer-in-residence for several years at La MaMa ETC. For the New York Shakespeare Festival she developed the score of *Runaways* (1978, Broadway), a musical about troubled children. Among her other scores are *Nightclub Cantata* (1977, Top of the Gate), *Dispatches* (1979, The Public), *Alice in Concert* (1980, The Public), *Missionaries* (1997, Brooklyn Academy of Music), and *Jabu* (2005, The Flea). She worked with Gary Trudeau on the Broadway musical *Doonesbury* (1983); composed the score for Ellen Stewart's production of *Mythos Oedipus* (1985) and Andrei Serban's Greek *Trilogy* (1974, 1986); developed *Job: A Circus* (1992, Off-Off) with a group of professional clowns and actors; and wrote, composed, and directed *The New Americans* (1992, Theatre for a New Audience). She also wrote the music for *Rap Master Ronnie* (1984, Top of the Gate). Though only *Runaways* has been popular with general audiences, her compositions for Off-Off Broadway plays and musicals have won her consistent critical praise.   MK

Sweeney Todd, the Demon Barber of Fleet Street Two-act musical play, music and lyrics by Stephen Sondheim, book by Hugh Wheeler; opened 1 March 1979 at the Uris (now Gershwin) Theatre, NYC, running 557 performances. Based on a Victorian thriller, this tale of a demented barber (Len Cariou) slaughtering Londoners as he pursues the judge who ruined his life, and forming a partnership with a woman (Angela Lansbury) who makes meat pies from his victims, was an unlikely basis for a musical. Director Harold Prince turned it into a parable of the dehumanization of the Industrial Revolution, a Grand Guignol in which Dickens met Brecht, with a dissonant chorus wryly narrating the action amid an iron-foundry superstructure so heavy that it necessitated shoring up the theatre's stage. The show is almost entirely sung, and Sondheim's score frequently sets gruesome events and imagery against ironic lyricism, undercut by a dissonant accompaniment. It won New York Drama Critics' Circle, Drama Desk, and Tony awards for Best Musical, and has subsequently entered the opera repertoire and been successfully revived on Broadway (1989) and in London (1985). A unique revival in 2005, starring Patti LuPone and Michael Cerveris and directed and designed by Britisher John Doyle (Tony for direction), featured 10 actors who doubled as musicians, was set in a wooden room (suggesting a mental ward – the story is told by a madman about a world gone mad), and eschewed Victorian spectacle.   JD

Sweet Bird of Youth TENNESSEE WILLIAMS'S play about the "enemy, time, in us all." A one-act work-in-progress version at the Studio M. Playhouse in Miami in 1956 was subsequently revised and expanded to premiere in NYC on 10 March 1959 (383 performances, MARTIN BECK THEATRE). ELIA KAZAN directed GERALDINE PAGE (as aging Hollywood actress Alexandra Del Lago), Paul Newman (as wanderer Chance Wayne), and Sidney Blackmer (as Boss Finley). The 1962 film adaptation by Richard Brooks also starred Newman and Page, but Ed Begley played Boss. A 1975 revival starred IRENE WORTH and CHRISTOPHER WALKEN. A 1989 NBC TV production starred Elizabeth Taylor, Mark Harmon, and RIP TORN. The Princess (Alexandra) and Chance futilely attempt to regain their youth amid drugs, alcohol, physical and sexual violence, and grotesqueries associated with Williams's mythological South.   PCK

Sweet Charity A two-act musical comedy conceived, directed, and choreographed by BOB FOSSE, with book by NEIL SIMON, music by CY COLEMAN, and lyrics by DOROTHY FIELDS. Based on the screenplay *Nights of Cabiria* by Federico Fellini, Tullio Pinelli, and Ennio Flaiano, *Sweet Charity* starred GWEN VERDON and featured the choreography of Fosse (Tony Award) when it opened 29 January 1966, running for 608 performances. A film version starring Shirley MacLaine was released in 1968. The show was revived on Broadway (27 April 1986) starring Debbie Allen and again in 2005 (4 May) with Christina Applegate. Set in NYC, *Sweet Charity* follows the romantic aspirations and desperation of a warm-hearted dancehall hostess. Songs include "If My Friends Could See Me Now" and "Big Spender."   EK

Syndicate, Theatrical The origins of the Syndicate lay in the combination system of producing. The expansion of railroads after the Civil War made it possible to tour a production anywhere in America. This proved more profitable than the previous system of resident companies hosting visiting stars. Consequently, by 1885 nearly all the first-class STOCK COMPANIES had been replaced by combinations from New York City, and both producers and regional theatre owners had opened booking offices there to arrange these tours. In 1896 producer CHARLES FROHMAN joined the booking agency of MARC KLAW and ABRAHAM ERLANGER in a partnership with Alfred Hayman, who leased the most important theatres in the West, and with Fred Nixon and Fred Zimmerman, who controlled PHILADELPHIA and the mid-Atlantic region. This arrangement was called the Theatrical Syndicate, and by 1903 it governed first-class theatrical production in America. The source of its power was its insistence upon exclusive representation: Its clients had to agree to do business only with it, taking the attractions, routes, and dates it specified, and playing the fees it levied.

Its monopoly was broken not by rebellious clients but by even more ruthless monopolists. The SHUBERT BROTHERS, Sam, Lee, and Jacob, were regular clients of the Syndicate, operating some 30 theatres in the Northeast. In 1905, concerned about potential rivalry, the Syndicate ordered them to stop acquiring theatres; instead, the Shuberts secured bank financing and declared war, and by 1913 controlled twice as many theatres as the Syndicate. The last Syndicate agreement expired in 1916; the Shuberts retained a national monopoly on theatres until 1930, and a Broadway one until 1950.

The Syndicate was a means of maximizing profit, not a vehicle for artistic innovation or social welfare; consequently, it was ruthless in its methods and rapacious in its charges. However, monopoly was the accepted way of doing business in the 19th century, and the Syndicate was only doing in theatre what Standard Oil, United States Steel, and American Telephone and Telegraph were doing in their industries. Furthermore, the Syndicate was only one theatrical monopoly: The so-called popular-price theatres were monopolized during 1900–11 by the STAIR AND HAVLIN THEATRICAL MANAGEMENT SYNDICATE. In 1906 B. F. KEITH and EDWARD F. ALBEE organized their UNITED BOOKING OFFICE, which monopolized all of VAUDEVILLE; and Samuel Scribner's Columbia Amusement Exchange virtually monopolized BURLESQUE after 1905.   DMcD

Syracuse Stage Founded in December 1973 by Arthur Storch, its first artistic director, this RESIDENT NONPROFIT PROFESSIONAL THEATRE has produced more than 200 plays in its history (seven productions a year) and is Central New York's premier professional theatre. It does one collaborative show with Syracuse University each season (since 2000), has a Young Playwrights Festival, and a children's touring production. Its total audience exceeds 90,000. Robert Moss, founder of PLAYWRIGHTS HORIZONS, became its third artistic director in 1995, replacing TAZEWELL THOMPSON, who was appointed in 1992.   DBW

T

tableau vivant see NUDITY

Take a Giant Step by Louis Peterson. Opening at New York's LYCEUM THEATRE 24 September 1953, it was directed by John Stix and featured Louis Gossett Jr., Frank Wilson, and FREDERICK O'NEAL. The seventh work by an African American playwright to reach Broadway, the play explores the struggles of a young, middle-class, black youth growing up in a predominantly white neighborhood; it also includes generational and racial conflicts. It was revived OFF-BROADWAY in 1956–7 with a different cast (including BEAH RICHARDS). KME

Take Me Out by RICHARD GREENBERG; originally directed by JOE MANTELLO. As social norms about homosexuality entered the American mainstream, this talky, penetrating drama about a hugely successful professional baseball player who blithely discloses his predilections arrived on the scene. First mounted at London's Donmar Warehouse, the play became a major stateside hit for the prolific writer, opening officially on 5 September 2002 at the PUBLIC THEATER. After revisions and a shift from three to two acts, it moved to Broadway, opening 27 February 2003 for a 355-performance run. In the transfer, the core story remained unchanged: Darren Lemming (Daniel Sunjata), baseball's reigning golden boy, publicly outs himself; it's up to Kippy (Neal Huff), his teammate, and Mason Marzac (Denis O'Hare), his gay, loquacious accountant – and recent convert to America's pastime – to make sense of the fraught, politically charged aftermath. O'Hare won one of the play's three Tonys (Best Featured Actor in a Play; also won Best Play and Direction). Despite long nude shower scenes, by the middle of the decade it became one of the most produced new works. LJ

Tale of the Allergist's Wife, The CHARLES BUSCH comedy first seen at the MANHATTAN THEATRE CLUB 29 February 2000 and then transferred to Broadway's ETHEL BARRYMORE THEATRE (2 November 2000), where it ran 777 performances.

Directed by LYNNE MEADOW with scenery by SANTO LOQUASTO, the play centered on depression and cultural desires of an Upper West Side failed Jewish novelist and arts patron, Marjorie, played by LINDA LAVIN, whose life is impacted by an old friend (Michele Lee) who is the reverse of Marjorie. Involved in the action is Marjorie's allergist husband (TONY ROBERTS) and her potty-mouthed mother (Shirl Bernheim). For Busch this was a definite advancement in his mainstream career. DBW

Talley's Folly A long one-act (90-minute) play by LANFORD WILSON that won him the Pulitzer Prize and Drama Critics' Circle Award in 1980. Directed by MARSHALL MASON, designed by JOHN LEE BEATTY, and starring JUDD HIRSCH and Trish Hawkins, this second of Wilson's trilogy about the Talley family opened OFF-BROADWAY in 1979 at the CIRCLE REPERTORY for a limited run before transferring to Broadway's BROOKS ATKINSON THEATRE (1980) for 277 performances. Set in 1944, the play tells the story of WASPish Sally Talley's wooing by Matt Friedman, a Jewish immigrant accountant, at a decayed boathouse on the Talley farm in Lebanon, MO. *Talley's Folly* drew wide critical praise; WALTER KERR called it "a charmer, filled to the brim with hope, humor and chutzpah." TLM

Tally, Ted (1952–) North Carolina–born playwright, educated at Yale. His first success, *Hooters* (1978, PLAYWRIGHTS HORIZONS), paved the way for that of *Terra Nova* (1977, YALE REP; 1979, MARK TAPER; 1984, GOODMAN and AMERICAN PLACE), a dramatization of the race to reach the South Pole that won two Drama-Logue Awards and was made into a BBC television play in 1984. *Coming Attractions* (1980), produced by Playwrights Horizons, won an Outer Critics' Circle Award. Tally has also written screenplays for *The Father Clements Story* (1987, TV) and *The Silence of the Lambs* (1991, Academy Award). BBW

Tamiment Playhouse, The A resident summer theatre that operated between 1921 and 1960 at

Camp Tamiment, an adult summer camp, in Pennsylvania's Pocono Mountains. Under the directorship of Max Liebman, the playhouse became a workshop for the developing talents of performers and writers including Imogene Coca, Sylvia Fine, Danny Kaye, and JEROME ROBBINS in the 1930s. Liebman's formula for devising an original Broadway-quality REVUE every week evolved in 1950 into television's *Your Show of Shows,* a number of whose personnel, including Coca as well as writers Lucille Kallen and Mel Tolkin, came directly from Tamiment. In the 1950s the Playhouse became a "summer training ground" for grooming such talented writers, composers, and director-choreographers as WOODY ALLEN, JERRY BOCK, FRED EBB, JOE LAYTON, Herbert Ross, Danny and NEIL SIMON, and JONATHAN TUNICK, and performers Carol Burnett, Pat Carroll, BARBARA COOK, Larry Kert, and Dick Shawn.   MSL

Tamiris (Becker), Helen (1905–66) Modern dancer-choreographer and theatre choreographer. After establishing herself in modern dance, primarily as a solo artist, she continued her concert work while choreographing for Broadway musicals. Initially, Tamiris worked with experimental theatre groups, including the PROVINCETOWN PLAYERS and the GROUP THEATRE. Her first musical-theatre productions were *Up in Central Park* (1945), ANNIE GET YOUR GUN, *Park Avenue,* and a revival of *SHOW BOAT* (all 1946). She was associate director for EXPERIMENTAL THEATRE, INC.'s *The Great Campaign* (1947) and choreographed the HAROLD ROME political REVUE *Bless You All* (1950; with Jules Munshin and PEARL BAILEY). Tamiris was highly regarded by her modern-dance contemporaries, many of whom danced in the musicals she choreographed. Using trained dancers raised the standard of dance in musical theatre and made Tamiris's productions tremendously popular.   LF

Tandy, Jessica (1909–94) British-born actress who in 1954 became a naturalized American citizen. Trained in drama school (1924–7), she made her London debut in *The Rumour* (1929) and before she was 25 had become a star. She made her debut on Broadway as Toni Rakonitz in 1930 in *The Matriarch.* Among her later outstanding roles were Ophelia to John Gielgud's *Hamlet* (1934, London) and Blanche Du Bois in *A STREETCAR NAMED DESIRE* (1947; Tony). As Blanche she won rave reviews and achieved Broadway stardom; a critic called the role "deeply moving . . . acted gloriously . . . one of the most arresting and moving performances you are likely to thrill to in many a semester."

Having divorced actor Jack Hawkins in 1940 after eight years of marriage, in 1942 Tandy married actor HUME CRONYN, with whom she subsequently appeared in 11 Broadway productions, including *The Fourposter* (1951), *The Physicists* (1964), *A DELICATE BALANCE* (1966), *Noël Coward in Two Keys* (1974), *The GIN GAME* (1977), and *Foxfire* (1982). She won Tony Awards for the latter two.

Tandy and Cronyn appeared regularly in American regional theatres, chief among them the GUTHRIE THEATRE, which they admired for its adequate rehearsal periods and superior facilities compared to most Broadway theatres. At the Guthrie, Tandy played such roles as Linda in *DEATH OF A SALESMAN,* Gertrude in *Hamlet,* and Madame Ranevskaya in *The Cherry Orchard.*

Tandy, one of the great ladies of the American stage, also acted in numerous British and American television programs, first appearing on British television in 1939. In her final years she devoted more time to film acting, winning an Academy Award for *DRIVING MISS DAISY,* her first major film role, at age 80, and an Oscar nomination for *Fried Green Tomatoes* (1991), completing her film career with a role in *Nobody's Fool* (1994). In July 1994 she and Cronyn were honored with a special Tony for their life's work in the theatre.   SMA

Tanguay, Eva (1878–1947) Canadian-born singer, the "oomph" girl of VAUDEVILLE's heyday, epitomized by her best-known song, "I Don't Care," first sung in *The Chaperons* (1902). Beginning in variety in 1886, she toured for five years with the Redding Company as a child actress, graduating to musical-comedy roles (*My Lady, The Sambo Girl, The Merry World,* and so forth). After *A Good Fellow* (1906), she entered vaudeville, becoming its leading star and leaving it infrequently over the next 25 years. Described by one critic as "not beautiful, witty or graceful," her appeal defies explanation; she claimed it was in the force of her personality. Flamboyant, a bit risqué in costumes (she said her 1908 Salome costume consisted of two pearls) and songs (such as "I Want Someone to Go Wild with Me"), and tempestuous on- and offstage, she seemed to her audiences perennially young. Financial reverses and poor health forced an early retirement.   DBW

Tarkington, Booth (1869–1946) Novelist and playwright. Better known as a novelist, Tarkington was the author of 21 produced plays. Whether taking his theme from history or a contemporary event, Tarkington was a romanticist who enjoyed writing for actors: *Monsieur Beaucaire* (1901) for

RICHARD MANSFIELD, *Master Antonio* (1916) for OTIS SKINNER, *Poldekin* (1920) for GEORGE ARLISS. When the success of *The Man from Home* (1907), written with HARRY LEON WILSON, was followed by failures, Tarkington stopped writing plays for four years. Later, his most successful play, *Clarence* (1919), written for ALFRED LUNT and HELEN HAYES, showed the disruption caused in a normal household by a handsome, bumbling hero. Never feeling that he was taken seriously as a playwright, Tarkington distrusted the theatre as a place for serious art. A collection of his letters was published in 1959.   WJM

Tavern, The Play in two acts by GEORGE M. COHAN that burlesques the conventions of theatrical romanticism, as well as the intellectual pretensions of G. B. SHAW and the sentimental wistfulness of James M. Barrie. All characters were costumed in a pastiche of period styles. In the 1920 premiere ARNOLD DALY played the nameless "Vagabond," seen in 18th-century wig and boots and 19th-century hat, cloak, and coat. It was revived by the ASSOCIATION OF PRODUCING ARTISTS in 1962, with GEORGE GRIZZARD and ROSEMARY HARRIS.   WD

Tayleure, Clifton (1830–91) Playwright. Born in South Carolina and associated with Baltimore theatres, Tayleure combined careers in theatre and journalism. His version of *UNCLE TOM'S CABIN* (1852) reflected Southern political sympathies. Other plays include an adaptation of *Horseshoe Robinson* (1856), *The Man of Destiny* (1856), *The Boy Martyrs of September 12, 1814* (1859). He is best known for his dramatization of *EAST LYNNE* (1863).   WJM

Taylor, Bayard (1825–78) A popular writer of travel literature before the Civil War, Taylor is one of a number of literary-minded people who attempted to write verse drama. Never considered for production, his plays – *The Masque of Gods* (1872), *The Prophet* (1873), *Prince Deukalion* (1878) – explore the human interest in religion.   WJM

Taylor, Charles Western (1785–1874) English-born playwright and actor who in 1819 came to America and became a character actor and journeyman playwright, mainly for New York's National Theatre. Like many others, he dramatized current fiction (J. F. Cooper's *The Water Witch,* 1831; Mrs. Stowe's *Dred,* 1856). He also adapted *UNCLE TOM'S CABIN* (opened 23 August 1852), providing a happy ending with Tom's homecoming; wrote *The Drunkard's Warning* (1856); and always

emphasized spectacle, as in *The Orange Girl in Venice* (1856).   WJM

Taylor, Laurette (Cooney) (1884–1946) Actress who debuted as a child in Gloucester, MA, then went in 1903 to the Boston Athenaeum. She first appeared in New York the same year in *From Rags to Riches.* Her first substantial success came in 1910 in *Alias Jimmy Valentine,* but she achieved stardom in the title role of *PEG O' MY HEART* in 1912, a script by J. HARTLEY MANNERS, who had married Taylor in 1911.

Later roles included Nell Gwynne in *Sweet Nell of Old Drury* (1923) and Rose Trelawny in *Trelawny of the Wells* (1925). After her husband's death in 1928, Taylor retired from the stage, but she returned as Mrs. Midget in the 1938 revival of *Outward Bound.* She costarred in *The GLASS MENAGERIE* (1945), a smash hit that made her once more the toast of Broadway. Her biography by Marguerite Courtney was published in 1955.   SMA

Taylor, Regina (1960–) Actress-playwright-director, born in Dallas, raised in Oklahoma, and educated at Southern Methodist University. In 1986 she was the first black actor to play Shakespeare's Juliet on Broadway, thanks to JOSEPH PAPP's nontraditional casting efforts. In 1989 she won an LA *Drama-Logue* Award for her work in *The Tempest.* As a performer, however, she is best known for her housekeeper Lilly Harper in television's *I'll Fly Away* (1991). Recent efforts have been in writing, most notably her adaptation of *The Seagull, Drowning Crow,* which she presented as an artistic associate at the GOODMAN (2002; 2004, MANHATTAN THEATRE CLUB) and her dramatization of *Crowns: Portraits of Black Women in Church Hats* (simply called *Crowns*), which premiered at the McCARTER in 2002, ran at SECOND STAGE later that year, and subsequently was seen around the country. Other plays include *Oo-Bla-Dee, Watermelon Rinds, A Night in Tunisia, Escape from Paradise, Mudtracks, Between the Lines,* and *Behind Every Good Man.* She conceived and appeared in a 2000 solo performance, *Millennium Mambo.*   DBW

Taylor, Samuel (1912–2000) Chicago-born playwright and librettist who gained his first Broadway experience as a play reader and play doctor. He coauthored *Stop-Over,* which had a brief run in 1938, and then wrote or adapted scripts for *The Happy Time* (1950), *Sabrina Fair* (1953), *The Pleasure of His Company* (1958), *First Love* (1961), and *Avanti!* 1968. The librettist for RICHARD RODGERS's musical *No Strings,* Taylor also wrote extensively for radio and television.   MK

The King Stag as directed at the American Repertory Theatre by Andrei Serban with costumes, masks, and puppets by Julie Taymor. First seen in 1984 and frequently revived. Photo by Richard Feldman. *Courtesy:* ART Public Relations.

Taymor, Julie (1952–) Massachusetts-born director, designer, puppeteer, playwright, and actress; educated at Oberlin College (B.A., 1974). Taymor is one of the foremost contemporary American theatre artists who exploit time-honored strategies of popular entertainment for innovative ends, favoring theatricality over realism, visual imagery over language, and populist perspectives over elitist ones.

Trained with MIME Jacques Lecoq, the BREAD AND PUPPET THEATRE, HERBERT BLAU's experimental COLLECTIVE Kraken, and with Asian dance, PUPPETRY, and wood-carving masters, Taymor evolved an eclectic aesthetic. During a four-year residency in Bali (1974–8), she organized Teatr Loh, a multinational company that cross-pollinated Asian and Western approaches. The 1980–1 New York premieres of their complex, imagistic works, *Way of Snow* and *Tirai*, together with her acclaimed set and puppet designs for ELIZABETH SWADOS's *Haggadah* (PUBLIC THEATER, 1980) launched a career that would bring Taymor an Obie Award for "visual magic" (1985) and a so-called genius award from the McArthur Foundation (1992). Her *Fool's Fire*, based on a POE short story, aired on *American Playhouse* in March 1992, and in 1994 she directed *Titus Andronicus* for New York's THEATRE FOR A NEW AUDIENCE. She frequently directs opera.

Her master works to date include *Juan Darién* (1988, MUSIC-THEATRE GROUP; Obie for Direction [another for Elliot Goldenthal's music]; revived by LINCOLN CENTER Theater, 1996) and *The LION KING* (1997; Tonys for Costume Design and Direction). The former is a dramatization of a Uruguayan short story, adapted by Taymor and composer Goldenthal, her collaborator since 1980. Typically epic in scale and cinematic in structure, this magical carnival mass for people and puppets addresses a favorite Taymor theme: physical and spiritual transformation. The latter, produced at the NEW AMSTERDAM in 1997 for DISNEY, was a Taymor extravaganza: She wrote the lyrics for one new song, designed costumes and with Michael Curry the masks and puppets, and directed. Also noteworthy was her 1996 production of Gozzi's *The Green Bird* at the NEW VICTORY and her innovative staging of the underappreciated films *Titus* (1999) and *Frida* (2002). A recent project was the opera *Grendel* (2006, Los Angeles Opera). Taymor has managed to meet the needs of the commercial NYC theatre while at the same raising the bar. In addition to her MacArthur, she was a 1990 Guggenheim Fellow and in 2004 received the USITT Award, the highest recognition of the U.S. INSTITUTE FOR THEATRE TECHNOLOGY. A book on her career (with Eileen Blumenthal) was reissued in 1999, and one on *The Lion King* was published in 1998. CLJ DBW

Tazewell, Paul (1964–) Baltimore native whose training as a costume designer was at the North

Carolina School of the Arts and NYU (M.F.A. 1989); currently is on the faculty at Carnegie Mellon. His work has been honored with a Tony nomination for BRING IN 'DA NOISE, BRING IN 'DA FUNK (1996), a Michael Merritt Award for Excellence in Design and Collaboration, a HELEN HAYES Award for *The African Company Presents 'Richard III'* (during a stint as resident designer at ARENA STAGE), and the 1997 IRENE SHARAFF Young Master Award. His Broadway credits include *A RAISIN IN THE SUN*, *Carolina, or Change* (both 2004), *The Color Purple* (2005), and *ON THE TOWN* (1998). He also designs for opera. BO

Tea and Sympathy is the drama by ROBERT ANDERSON that catapulted him onto the national theatre scene when it opened at the ETHEL BARRYMORE THEATRE in NYC (30 September 1953) under ELIA KAZAN's direction; it ran 712 performances. Set in a New England boy's school, the play is the story of a sensitive young man subjected to group harassment by the machinations of a homophobic housemaster. The strong cast featured Deborah Kerr as the housemaster's wife, John Kerr (no relation) as the young man, and Leif Erickson as the housemaster. Deborah Kerr's character is remembered for boldly rejecting her husband's behavior and gently introducing the boy to his sexuality. KN

Teal, Ben (1855–1917) California-born director who, other than coauthoring a few plays (notably *The Great Metropolis* with GEORGE H. JESSOP, 1889), devoted a 34-year career to direction, including more than 80 productions in New York alone. Possibly the first successful freelance director in the American theatre, Teal, who began his Broadway career in 1883, peaked as a director (with KLAW and ERLANGER, 1899–1903) of spectacular melodramas with BEN-HUR (1899); subsequently he specialized in staging musical comedy, though after 1900 such directors as DAVID BELASCO, Herbert Gresham, JULIAN MITCHELL, and NED WAYBURN were considered superior to Teal. DBW

Teatro Campesino, El see EL TEATRO CAMPESINO

Tectonic Theater Project This company was founded in 1991, named for the science of structure and dedicated to exploring theatrical language and form. Its prime mover was Moisés Kaufman, born in Venezuela, son of two Holocaust survivors. He grew up Jewish in a primarily Catholic country. At NYU he studied with Stephen Waugh, who helped pioneer a DOCUMENTARY style of theatre with his Boston-based Reality Theatre in the 1970s, a strong influence on Kaufman and Tectonic. Tectonic's first major work was *Gross Indecency: The Three Trials of Oscar Wilde* (1997), which utilized transcripts from Wilde's infamous indecency trials. Following the gay-bashing and death of Matthew Shepard on the outskirts of Laramie, WY, Kaufman and members of Tectonic made six trips to Laramie interviewing townspeople for what would become the company's signature work, *The LARAMIE PROJECT* (2000). Apart from Tectonic, Kaufman directed the Pulitzer Prize–winning play *I AM MY OWN WIFE* (2003). DanB

Templeton, Fay (1865–1939) Favorite actress of the musical-comedy stage at the turn of the 20th century. Born in Little Rock, AR, on Christmas Day, she appeared onstage as a child. She toured extensively with her parents, then joined WEBER AND FIELDS for four seasons, making a hit of the song, "Rosey, You Are My Posey." In 1906 she appeared in COHAN's FORTY-FIVE MINUTES FROM BROADWAY as Mary, singing "Mary Is a Grand Old Name," a huge success. She later appeared in GILBERT AND SULLIVAN, retiring from the stage in 1934 after appearing in *Roberta*. Templeton lived for a time in the ACTORS' FUND Home in Englewood, NJ, and died in San Francisco. SMA

Ten Nights in a Bar-Room Initially produced at New York's National Theatre in 1858, this adaptation by William W. Pratt of T. S. Arthur's 1854 novel became one of the most popular temperance melodramas in the nation. Its allegorical plot traces the drunkenness and sudden reformation of Joe Morgan after his "angel child" daughter sings "Father, dear Father, Come Home with Me Now" (added to the play in 1864) and dies when struck on the head by a rum glass. Morgan's eventual success is contrasted to the drunken decline of Frank Slade, who finally kills his father, a bartender. The play was second only to UNCLE TOM'S CABIN on the country circuits of the late 19th century, and endured frequent burlesque revivals in the 20th. BMcC

Tenney, Jon [né Jonathan F. W. Tenney] (1961–) Handsome leading man born in Princeton, NJ, to professional parents, trained briefly at Juilliard (left for the national tour of *The Real Thing*). He was in *Substance of Fire* in 1991 (PLAYWRIGHTS HORIZONS; LINCOLN CENTER Theater, 1992); in 1995 played opposite CHERRY JONES on Broadway as Morris Townsend in *The Heiress;* and in 1998 was Holly Hunter's husband in BETH HENLEY's *Impossible Marriage* (Roundabout). He is the former husband of *Desperate Housewives'* Teri Hatcher. DBW

tent show An American style of theatrical presentation in which plays or variety shows are trouped from community to community and staged under canvas. One of the earliest entrepreneurs was Fayette Lodowick "Yankee" Robinson, whose touring company performed in the river towns of Iowa and Illinois in 1851; prosperity led him to switch from drama to CIRCUS. By the late 19th century, traveling troupes with repertories extensive enough to provide a week's worth of entertainment had become popular in the summer, when local opera houses were too poorly ventilated to attract the public. The influence of the CHAUTAUQUA circuit, with its portable theatres lit by naphtha lamps, was strong after 1904; its tents were brown to distinguish its educational purpose from the white tops of the circus. In France, Firmin Gémier had commissioned an elaborate canvas structure to house the tours of the Théâtre Antoine in 1911; the average American show tent, however, was limited to a width of 50 or 60 ft., with bare benches or bleachers and a platform stage designed for portability.

The earliest repertories were imitations, often pirated, of standard dramatic fare, primarily melodrama; but as these grew stale and copyright laws stricter, tent showmen composed their own plays, carpentered to a limited company and the familiar themes of rural life. The standbys of this repertory include Charles Harrison's *Saintly Hypocrites and Honest Sinners* (1915) and W. C. Herman's *Call of the Woods,* which pitted homespun virtue against urban corruption. The comic character TOBY, developed c. 1911, became the popular hero of these works, often partnered with the tomboy Susie and the eccentric known as the G-string character, a sage descendant of the stage YANKEE.

After WWI, motor vehicles replaced rail transport, and tent shows proliferated, doubling their rate to $1 admissions. Some 400 shows were traveling through the U.S. by 1927, playing to an estimated audience of 78 million; but the catastrophic effect of the Depression and dust storms on the agricultural population led to a decline in these "rag opries." Price cutting and unionization, the competition from local cinemas, and inability to organize were also contributory factors to the closure of hundreds of long-standing companies in the 1930s. The FEDERAL THEATRE PROJECT absorbed many of these entertainers, and in the 1950s only some dozen troupes survived. In 1976 a revival of the Harley Sadler Show, one of the most prosperous in its time, was staged at Texas Tech University, which houses a Tent Show Collection. Another relevant archive is the Museum of Repertoire Americana in Mount Pleasant, IA.   LS

Ter-Arutunian, Rouben (1920–92) Armenian American set and costume designer; born in (soon Russified) Georgia, educated in Berlin 1927–43, emigrated to the U.S. in 1951. Broadway credits included *New Girl in Town* (1957), *Redhead* (1959; Tony for Best Costumes), *Advise and Consent* (1960), *The Milk Train Doesn't Stop Here Anymore* (1964), *Eh?* (1966, CIRCLE IN THE SQUARE), *Exit the King* (1968), *All Over* (1971), and *The Lady from Dubuque* (1980). In addition to theatre and opera, Ter-Arutunian designed for television in the 1950s (*Twelfth Night,* 1957, Emmy). His work fell primarily into two categories: "decorative" (or painterly), such as his famous *Nutcracker* for the New York City Ballet; and sculptural, such as *Ricercare* for American Ballet Theatre. Ter-Arutunian preferred the latter style, which allowed him to create space around a minimal amount of scenery. He said that he designed "visual counterpart to drama, poetry, music and movement, . . . with simplicity, clarity, and a certain element of mystery."   AA

Terry, Megan (1932–) One of the most important playwrights of the avant-garde, OFF-OFF BROADWAY theatre of the 1960s, Terry wrote plays reflecting important political, social, and sexual issues. In her association with the OPEN THEATRE (1963–8), she helped develop many techniques introduced by that group, such as audience contact, experimental staging, and "transformation," whereby characters, place, time, and action change rapidly and actors switch roles, often regardless of gender. Terry achieved international acclaim with *Viet Rock* (1966), a collaborative effort that was the first rock musical and the first protest play about the Vietnam War. Other plays by Terry (many developed at LA MAMA) include *Calm Down Mother* and *Keep Tightly Closed in a Cool Dry Place* (1965), *The People vs. Ranchman* (1967), *Hothouse* (1974), and *Approaching Simone* (1970) – an Obie-winning chronicle of the brief, heroic life of Simone Weil. Since 1974, Terry has written as playwright-in-residence and literary manager at the OMAHA MAGIC THEATRE. In 1993 she was awarded the first national artist McKnight residency at the Playwrights' Center, MINNEAPOLIS.   FB

Tesich, Steve [né Stoyan] (1942–96) Playwright, born in Yugoslavia. educated at Indiana University and Columbia; was also a successful screenwriter (*Breaking Away,* 1979; *Four Friends,* 1981; *The World According to Garp,* 1982). His play *Baba Goya* (1972, AMERICAN PLACE) won the Drama Desk Award; *Division Street* (1980) played on Broadway with JOHN LITHGOW and CHRISTINE LAHTI; both

Speed of Darkness (1989) and *On the Open Road* (1992) premiered at the GOODMAN THEATRE; *Speed of Darkness* was on Broadway (1991); and his last play, *Arts and Leisure,* was directed by JOANNE AKALAITIS at PLAYWRIGHTS HORIZONS in 1996. His final efforts shifted from his earlier sentimentality and optimism to a kind of helpless outrage over an adopted country that had become selfish and isolationist.   BBW

Tesori, Jeanine (1961–) Theatre composer, arranger, conductor, born in Manhasset, NY, studied music at Barnard, and is considered one of the leading voices in the field today. After arranging dance music for *HOW TO SUCCEED IN BUSINESS WITHOUT REALLY TRYING* (1995), *Dream* (1997), and *The SOUND OF MUSIC* (1998), she received a Drama Desk for her musical score for the 1998 Broadway *Twelfth Night* directed by Nicholas Hytner, followed by arrangements for *Swing!* (1999). Her major credits to date, however, are as composer-arranger in 2002 of *Thoroughly Modern Millie* (which won the 2003 Tony for Best Musical) and for the musical score in 2004 of the Broadway show *Caroline, or Change* (with TONY KUSHNER as librettist), for which she won another Drama Desk. The latter, not a typical musical, falls somewhere between a play, a musical, and an opera. *Violet* (1997), for which she wrote the score (book and lyrics by Brian Crawley), was produced by PLAYWRIGHTS HORIZONS and received numerous honors (Drama Critics' Circle and LORTEL awards for best musical, Obie, and others). She has also written music for several Disney animated features.   DBW

Testa, Mary (1955–) Philadelphia-born, University of Rhode Island–educated character actress-singer, a NYC favorite whose 1979 OFF-BROADWAY debut was in WILLIAM FINN's *In Trousers* and 1980 Broadway debut was in the ensemble of *Barnum*. Since then her Broadway credits include *The Rink* (1984), *A FUNNY THING HAPPENED ON THE WAY TO THE FORUM* (1996), *ON THE TOWN* (1998 Obie when done by The PUBLIC; 1999 Tony nomination as Maude P. Dilly), *Marie Christine* (1999), *42ND STREET* (2001 Tony nomination as Maggie Jones), and the long-running *CHICAGO* revival (as Matron "Mama" Morton in 2005). Off-Broadway credits include some 20 productions, ranging from *Lucky Stiff* (1988) and *Hello Muddah, Hello Faddhu!* (1992) to Finn's *A New Brain* (1998) and MICHAEL JOHN LaCHIUSA's *See What I Wanna See* (2005).   DBW

Texas Steer, A, by CHARLES HALE HOYT, author of plays on contemporaneous subjects. Hoyt's four-act farce premiered 10 November 1890 at the Bijou; he revived it 8 January 1894 at his MADISON SQUARE THEATRE. Focused on American politics, a subject Hoyt observed as a New Hampshire legislator, the play exploits his experience as a western stock raiser to display culture shock, political naïveté, frontier slang, and Texas gaucherie transplanted to Washington, DC, through Congressman Maverick Brander and his family. Discounted as of no literary merit, Hoyt's play stands with HARRIGAN's as topical ethnic and racist urban farces, influencing variety and other forms popular at the turn of the 19th century.   RKB

Texas Trilogy, A, by Preston Jones includes *The Last Meeting of the Knights of the White Magnolia, Lu Ann Hampton Laverty Oberlander,* and *The Oldest Living Graduate*. The three plays were produced in repertory at the DALLAS THEATER CENTER (1973–4) under the direction of PAUL BAKER. The trilogy was presented in repertory at the JOHN F. KENNEDY CENTER FOR THE PERFORMING ARTS for a 10-week season starting on 29 April 1976 under the direction of ALAN SCHNEIDER; it was brought back to the Kennedy Center on 5 August 1976 for a five-week run prior to its NYC opening on 21 September 1976 at the BROADHURST THEATRE. Set in a mythical West Texas town, the play reflected local color and humor, with attitudes and language that significantly defined regional drama on Broadway.   ER

Thalia Theatre 46–48 Bowery, NYC [Architect: Ithiel Town] Built by the city's wealthiest citizens with high hopes of its becoming New York's premier theatre, the New York Theatre (later to be rechristened the BOWERY and, later, the Thalia) opened in 1826 and survived five FIRES (1828, 1836, 1838, 1845, and 1923), but did not survive a final fire in 1929. Considered the handsomest playhouse of its time, it was abandoned by its society patrons as its environs deteriorated. It became a house of melodrama and popular entertainments, reflecting the tastes of its audiences; at its demise, it was presenting Chinese vaudeville.   MCH

Tharp, Twyla (1941–) Dancer-choreographer with a Barnard degree in art history who joined the Paul Taylor Dance Company in 1963 and two years later formed her own, which in 1988 merged with the American Ballet Theatre but in 1991 was reformed as Twyla Tharp Dance. Her theatre work began in 1980 with *When We Were Very Young,* which included text by Thomas Babe. This was followed the next year by *The Catherine Wheel,* in collaboration with David Byrne, *Singin' in the Rain*

641

in 1985, and in 2002 her most successful Broadway musical, *Movin' Out* (1,303 performances) with Billy Joel's music, for which she created a strong American-themed, war-flavored narrative. For the latter show Tharp won Tony and Drama Desk awards for choreography, the 2003 Astaire Award (and awards to lead dancers, the first time in 22 years that one production captured every category), and the Drama League Award for Sustained Achievement in Musical Theatre.   DBW

That Championship Season Two-act drama by Jason Miller that opened to critical acclaim 2 May 1972 in the Estelle Newman Theatre of the New York PUBLIC THEATER. Transferred to Broadway's BOOTH THEATRE (14 September), it ran a total of 844 performances and won the Drama Critics' Circle and Tony awards for Best Play and the Pulitzer Prize for Drama Award (1973). The drama reunites four members of a championship high-school basketball team with their coach; their memories, contrasted with their adult lives, offers insightful commentary on American values. The cast included Walter McGinn, Charles Durning, Paul Sorvino, and Richard Dysart as Coach; the director was A. J. ANTOON (Tony Award). Playwright Miller, who was an outstanding high-school athlete, became a respectable stage and film actor and was nominated for an Oscar in 1974 for his role in *The Exorcist*.   KN

Theater for the New City Not-for-profit OFF-OFF BROADWAY theatre founded (in the spirit of the JUDSON POETS' THEATRE) in 1971 by Lawrence Kornfeld, Theo Barnes, George Bartenieff, and Crystal Field to produce and present untraditional theatre and PERFORMANCE ART. Bartenieff and Field, then married, served as artistic directors for many years; after divorcing, Field led TNC alone. Initially, TNC housed such innovative groups as RICHARD FOREMAN's Ontological-Hysteric Theatre and the MABOU MINES; later, its Resident Theatre Program additionally supported work by leading playwrights such as SAM SHEPARD (including his Pulitzer Prize–winning BURIED CHILD), CHARLES BUSCH, MOISÉS KAUFMAN, MARIA IRENE FORNÉS, and MIGUEL PIÑERO. Devoted to civic activism, TNC has mounted free summer street-theatre tours across NYC for more than 25 years; it created the Village Halloween Costume Ball in 1973 and, in 1996, the Lower East Side Festival of the Arts. In the late 1990s dwindling funding caused TNC to default on its mortgage, forcing it to sell the air rights above its sprawling headquarters in favor of a 17-story condominium.   CLJ   LJ

Theatre Arts Monthly Theatre journal initially established as a quarterly by SHELDON CHENEY in 1916, and published in Detroit by the Arts and Crafts Society. *Theatre Arts* proclaimed its intention to "develop the creative impulse in the American Theatre" and to eliminate the speculator. Cheney moved the magazine to New York in 1917 when a photograph of a German theatre upset war-sensitive Detroit. EDITH J. R. ISAACS, KENNETH MACGOWAN, and Marion Tucker joined Cheney in 1919, with Isaacs assuming the editorship in 1922. As publisher and editor, she expanded *Theatre Arts* into a monthly in 1924, and hired ROSAMOND GILDER as associate editor. Gilder served with distinction until 1948, the last two years as editor. As the magazine became more international in scope, Ashley Dukes became English editor. Essays on Adolphe Appia, Gordon Craig, the FEDERAL THEATRE, EUGENE O'NEILL, and other topics of current interest raised the intellectual tone, especially when compared with the gossipy quality of its competitors. Contributors included ROBERT E. SHERWOOD, Louis Jouvet, HALLIE FLANAGAN, ROBERT EDMOND JONES, RAY BOLGER, THORNTON WILDER, and John Gielgud. Both visionary and practical, *Theatre Arts* transmitted new ideas about theatrical art to a new generation of artists and audience. In 1948 it combined with *The Stage*, ending, for all practical purposes, the original journal. It ceased publication in 1964.   TLM

Theatre Communications Group (TCG) Founded in NYC in 1961, TCG serves as the national organization for RESIDENT NONPROFIT PROFESSIONAL THEATRE, representing more than 440 theatre institutions in 47 states and the District of Columbia, and 17,000 individuals (as of late 2005). As the country's leading independent press specializing in dramatic literature, TCG publishes the monthly magazine *American Theatre*, as well as plays, anthologies, translations, reference books, the annual *Theatre Directory*, *The Dramatist's Sourcebook*, and the jobs bulletin *ArtSEARCH*. TCG offers more than $3 million in grants and fellowships each year. It engages in federal advocacy, management training, surveys, workshops, and research. As the U.S. center of UNESCO's International Theatre Institute (ITI), a global network, TCG is involved in international exchange through travel grants and liaison services for traveling theatre professionals. PETER ZEISLER served as TCG's executive director for 23 years, a role then taken by Ben Cameron, who himself left after eight years in June 2006. He was replaced in 2007 by Teresa Eyring.   RG

Theatre de la Jeune Lune Affectionately known as "the Loonies," this ensemble theatre company was founded in France in 1978 by graduates of the École Jacques Lecoq in Paris, including one Minneapolis native. In 1985 the company permanently settled in MINNEAPOLIS, where it is committed to a permanent ensemble of actors who also create, design, and direct plays. Its unique style comes in part from Lecoq but is also drawn from numerous other techniques, ranging from VAUDEVILLE to CIRCUS and classic farce, as well as psychological theatre. The result is a highly physical, visually exciting, and emotionally involving theatre. The group's name (from a poem by Bertolt Brecht) conveys the search for new ways to explore established works. In 1992 the company moved into a permanent venue (a former cold-storage warehouse), although it tours frequently as well. Its NYC debut was in 2003 at the NEW VICTORY THEATRE with their innovative staging of *Hamlet*. Their work has often been honored, most recently by the 2005 Regional Theatre Tony award. After a five-person co–artistic directorship, 2001–6, Dominique Serrand, a cofounder of the company, became its sole head.   DBW

Theatre Development Fund Begun in 1968, TDF is the largest not-for-profit service organization devoted to the performance arts in the U.S. It is most recognizable for its TKTS® discount ticket booths in Times Square and South Street Seaport, a service started in 1972 and to date responsible for more than 63 million theatre tickets sold. TDF also administers various audience-development and financial-assistance programs that encourage new play and musical production. Its 70,000 individual members receive discounted theatre tickets. Subsidy support has gone to more than 700 plays including 26 Pulitzer Prize honorees; more than $1.1 billion in revenue has been returned to theatre, dance, and music organizations. TDF also presents the TDF/Irene Sharaff Awards in design and the TDF/Astaire Awards in dance/choreography.   DBW

Theatre for a New Audience Founded in 1979 by Jeffrey Horowitz, still artistic director, the OFF-BROADWAY company's mission is "to help develop and vitalize the performance and study of Shakespeare and classic drama." Typical were JULIE TAYMOR's productions of *The Green Bird* (on Broadway in 2000) and *Titus Andronicus* (1994). Its status as an itinerant theatre is scheduled to end with a permanent home planned in the BROOKLYN ACADEMY OF MUSIC Cultural District in Downtown Brooklyn. Its intended 299-seat venue has been designed collaboratively by Frank Gehry and Hugh Hardy.   DBW

Theatre Guild, The In 1915, a group of young actors and writers dissatisfied with the conventions of the commercial theatre organized the WASHINGTON SQUARE PLAYERS. For three seasons they presented a series of one-act plays distinctly modern in both content and form. After the war, in 1919, a patent lawyer and sometime playwright named LAWRENCE LANGNER restructured the Players as the Theatre Guild. Langner and his board – which included PHILIP MOELLER (who was to become the Guild's leading director), THERESA HELBURN (a play reader soon to be made executive director), actress Helen Westley, banker Maurice Wertheim, and scene designer LEE SIMONSON – were determined to shed their amateur downtown status and present challenging full-length plays on Broadway.

In its first few years (almost exclusively at the GARRICK THEATRE until September 1925), the Guild's notable achievements were with European expressionism (Kaiser's *Man and the Masses,* 1924) and with the world premieres of several plays by G. B. SHAW (*Heartbreak House,* 1920; *Back to Methuselah,* 1922; *Saint Joan,* 1923; and, later, *The Simpleton of the Unexpected Isles,* 1935). Although the Guild was criticized for neglecting American writers, two American plays that it presented early in its history – ELMER RICE's *The* ADDING MACHINE (1923) and JOHN HOWARD LAWSON's PROCESSIONAL (1925) – testify to the influence its productions of European plays had on native experiment. Later in the 1920s, and for the following three decades, the Guild produced the work of major American dramatists, including SIDNEY HOWARD (*THEY KNEW WHAT THEY WANTED,* 1924; *The SILVER CORD,* 1926); S. N. BEHRMAN (*The Second Man,* 1927; BIOGRAPHY, 1932); ROBERT E. SHERWOOD (*Reunion in Vienna,* 1931; IDIOT'S DELIGHT, 1936); and MAXWELL ANDERSON (*ELIZABETH THE QUEEN,* 1930; *Mary of Scotland,* 1933). In 1928, with *STRANGE INTERLUDE* and *Marco Millions,* the Guild began regularly to produce the plays of EUGENE O'NEILL.

If in the 1920s the Guild had the luster of an experiment conducted by idealistic upstarts, by the early 1930s it had begun to acquire the reputation of a theatrical dowager. In 1931 some of its younger members defected to form the GROUP THEATRE, whose agenda of knitting systematically trained actors into a true ensemble and encouraging the development of socially relevant plays highlighted two areas where the Guild had failed. Throughout the 1930s and '40s, as it produced popular shows like *The Philadelphia Story* (1939) and musicals like *Oklahoma!* (1943) and *Carousel* (1945) – and depended over and over again on its in-house stars, the Lunts, to rescue it from a financial abyss (thereby violating its original policy of starring the play rather than the player) – the Guild became little different from a commercial producer. Despite its lack of success in maintaining a repertory setup or in developing a company of actors – and despite its concessions to popularity and its literary short-comings (its predilection for airy comedies and stodgy historical romances) – the Guild's record is unique in the history of the American theatre. Through its subscription policy and its extensive national tours the Guild brought more worth-while, well-produced plays to a greater number of people, and over a longer period of time, than any other theatrical organization.   FH

Theatre Hall of Fame Honoring lifetime achieve-ment in the American theatre, the Theatre Hall of Fame was created in 1971 by Earl Blackwell (owner of the Celebrity Register), producers James M. Nederlander and Gerard Oestreicher, and theatrical attorney and photographer L. Arnold Weissberger. Early on, eligibility was limited to theatrical notables – actors, writers, directors, critics, producers, designers – with careers of at least 25 years (and five major credits) on Broad-way. Later requirements were broadened to include non-Broadway personnel. The Hall of Fame is in the upper lobby of the Gershwin The-atre, with more than 500 gold-inscribed names by 2005. New additions are named annually, voted by living members of the Hall of Fame and mem-bers of the American Theatre Critics Association. (This *Guide* has served as a resource to voters.)   LJ

Theatre of the Ridiculous In 1966 the Play-House of the Ridiculous opened Off-Off Broad-way with *The Life of Lady Godiva,* written by Ronald Tavel, directed by John Vaccaro, and featuring Charles Ludlam as actor. Though these three men did not stay together long, independently they continued their "ridiculous" work – a self-consciously wild dramaturgy full of witty word-play, sexual double entendre, theatrical flamboy-ance, sexual ambiguity, and bad taste. Tavel left the Play-House within a year to pursue a writing career, and in 1967 Vaccaro directed two Ludlam works, *Big Hotel* and *Conquest of the Universe,* before Ludlam left to become actor-manager of his own company. Vaccaro toured Europe with the Play-House and then operated it out of La MaMa until 1972, when he closed his theatre. At the Ridic-

ulous Theatrical Company, Ludlam went on to write, direct, and perform in plays such as *Turds in Hell* (1969), *Camille* (1973), and *Der Ring Gott Far-blonjet* (1977).   AS

Theatre Owners' Booking Association A chain of theatres formed to provide year-round work for black entertainers. The principal instigator was S. H. Dudley, a variety showman who had appeared in The Smart Set productions. He began in 1912 with the Dudley Circuit, which rose to 28 black theatres by the end of 1916. In 1919 white-managed theatres were admitted to the circuit, and in 1921 the expanded association came into being. Its abbreviation, TOBA, was often sarcasti-cally interpreted as "tough on black actors (or asses)" because of the allegedly small salaries paid except to headliners; in some circles the TOBA was called the Chitlin Circuit. The association declined and was disbanded during the Depres-sion. (See also African American theatre.)   EGH

Theatre Rhinoceros Founded in San Francisco in 1977 by Allan Estes and others, it is one of the oldest resident theatres specializing in gay and lesbian theatre. Works by noted homosexual authors (Harvey Fierstein, Doric Wilson, Jane Chambers, Robert Chesley, Kate Bornstein, Holly Hughes, etc.) have been produced under an artis-tic policy that embraces sex farces and musical revues as well as serious dramas. One of the most meaningful productions was *The AIDS Show* (1984), an amalgam of comic and tragic skits exploring the AIDS epidemic in its nascent stage. Three of the company's artistic directors, including Estes (in 1984), eventually perished from the disease. Recently the theatre has begun operating under a professional Actors' Equity seasonal agree-ment.   MB

Theatre Row West 42d St. between 9th and 10th Aves., NYC. In 1975, when Playwrights Hori-zons founder Robert Moss needed a theatre, he rented a building on West 42d St. – amid a neigh-borhood of pornographic shops, burlesque houses, and massage parlors – and transformed it quickly and cheaply into a performing space. His success signaled the development of an alterna-tive theatre district on far West 42d St. for Off-and Off-Off Broadway groups. A public–private partnership, the 42d Street Development Project, later bought the block to further the transforma-tion, renting additional spaces to theatre compa-nies that agreed to use them as venues and offices. By 1978, Theatre Row comprised 10 working companies and venues, all nonprofits, all representing diverse artistic goals and ethnicities. Phase II, encompassing the block between Dyer and 10th Avenues, added several additional theatres to the project. By 2000, with efforts to rejuvenate the long-blighted area of West 42d St. between Broadway and 8th Ave. nearing fruition, plans surfaced to demolish Theatre Row, which had physically deteriorated, in favor of a five-theatre state-of-the-art complex. It was completed in 2002, along with a new, expanded home for PLAYWRIGHTS HORIZONS, and the Little Shubert, the first-ever commercial Off-Broadway house built by the SHUBERT ORGANIZATION. All were financed in part by a condominium rising to the sky. Theatre Row and its five venues (the Acorn, Lion, Kirk, Beckett, and the Clurman) serve as rental theatres for itinerant theatre groups as well as a permanent home for several major organizations.   MCH   LJ

Theatre Union, The Though short-lived (1933–7), this was the most professional of the various nonprofit 1930s groups dedicated to the presentation in theatrical terms of problems central to the working class (unemployment, racial discrimination, political corruption, and other social, political, and economic injustices). With a board representing the full spectrum of radical opinion, The Theatre Union offered, at popular prices, eight largely left-wing dramas by writers such as George Sklar and Paul Peters (*STEVEDORE*), Albert Maltz, and JOHN HOWARD LAWSON, author of its last play, *Marching Song*. DBW

TheatreworksUSA Founded in 1961 by Jay Harnick and Charles Hull, both recipients in 2000 of the ACTORS' FUND OF AMERICA Medal of Honor, this organization is the U.S.'s largest and most prolific professional, not-for-profit theatre for young and family audiences. During most of its history it has been a touring theatre, taking 16 shows a year from a repertoire of 117 plays and musicals to venues throughout the U.S. (49 states) and Canada (playing to some 78 million people to date). Since July 2005 Theatreworks has offered a family series at its recent NYC home (LUCILLE LORTEL Theatre). Other programs include special presentations in the categories of MUSICAL THEATRE, PUPPET theatre, storytelling, music and poetry, historical presentations, and MAGIC. Its current artistic director is Barbara Pasternack. Theatreworks has received a Drama Desk and a Lucille Lortel Award (both 1996) and in 2001 was the recipient of the Jonathan Larson Performing Arts Foundation Award. (See also CHILDREN'S THEATRE.) DBW

They Knew What They Wanted by SIDNEY HOWARD earned the Pulitzer Prize in Drama for the 1924–5 season, edging out *WHAT PRICE GLORY* and *DESIRE UNDER THE ELMS*. Featuring strong performances by RICHARD BENNETT and PAULINE LORD – who had played Anna Christie three years earlier – Howard's play was a touching retelling of the Tristram and Yseult [Isolde] story transferred to a contemporary California vineyard. Lord's performance as the waitress who commits adultery but is given a second chance was in keeping with the "new realism" of the period but raised the ire of conventional groups, such as the Play Jury, which found the drama offensive. In 1956 the play became the libretto for FRANK LOESSER's soaring musical *The MOST HAPPY FELLA*. BBW

Thomas, A(lbert) E(llsworth) (1872–1947) The author, alone or with collaborators, of 20 plays, Thomas was not able to achieve distinction in spite of his recognized talent in comedies dealing with marriage problems. His first play, *Her Husband's Wife* (1910), builds upon the idea of a supposedly dying woman attempting to select her husband's next wife. *The Rainbow* (1912) shows the daughter of separated parents stimulating their reunion. His final play, *No More Ladies* (1934), also dealt with marriage. WJM

Thomas, Augustus (1857–1934) Playwright who always dealt with well-documented American scenes in such plays as *Alabama* (1891), *In MIZZOURA* (1893) and *Arizona* (1899, CHICAGO). *The COPPERHEAD* (1918), which made Lionel Barrymore (see DREW–BARRYMORE) a star, details the story of an Illinois farmer who, at the request of President Lincoln, pretends to be a sympathizer with the Confederacy. Many plays explored contemporary issues: capital and labor in *New Blood* (1894); politics in *The Capitol* (1895); hypnotism in *The WITCHING HOUR* (1907); and mental healing in *As a Man Thinks* (1911). Even his farces, *The Earl of Pawtucket* (1903) and *Mrs. Leffingwell's Boots* (1905), had a distinctively American flavor. The prefaces to many of his more than 60 plays provide a lively and intimate account of the dramatist at work. Thomas's autobiography, *The Print of My Remembrance,* was published in 1922. RM

Thomas, Richard (1951–) Actor – born in NYC to two ballet dancers – whose Broadway debut was in *Sunrise at Campobello* (1958) and who as a child performed with such companies as the AMERICAN SHAKESPEARE FESTIVAL THEATRE and NEW YORK SHAKESPEARE FESTIVAL. Other credits include *FIFTH OF JULY* (1981 replacement), *Seagull*

Lydia Thompson as Robinson Crusoe in H. B. Farnie's burlesque of that name, 1877. Photo by Mora, New York. *Courtesy:* Laurence Senelick Collection.

Thomashefsky (Tomashevsky), Boris (1868–1939) Yiddish actor and producer. In 1882, newly arrived from Russia and still only a 13-year-old soprano, he appeared in the first professional YIDDISH THEATRE production in America (GOLD-FADN's *The Witch,* on the Lower East Side). His mellifluous later tenor voice and florid good looks were especially suited to the costume operettas popular through the first half of his career, and his reputation as an irresistible ladies' man enhanced his romantic onstage image. He often produced and costarred with his wife, Bessie, in New York (especially at the National and People's Theatres) or on tour. He also contributed to the writing of some musicals, the best known of which was Moshe Zeifert's *Dos Pintele Yid (The Little Spark of Jewishness,* 1909), and appeared in several Yiddish films. Late in life he ventured, mostly unsuccessfully, onto Broadway (e.g., *The Singing Rabbi,* 1931) and into some nontheatrical enterprises. NS

Thompson, [Henry] **Denman** (1833–1911) New England actor-playwright who became a specialist in ethnic and eccentric comedy. He first played his sketch featuring Uncle Josh Whitcomb in 1875; by 1877 it had become a three-act play, and in 1886, with George Ryer, he completely revised it as *The* OLD HOMESTEAD, which he played until 1910 (some 15,000 times, it is claimed). A derivation of temperance melodrama, *The Old Homestead* was the epitome of sentimental rural Americana. His early biography by J. J. Brady appeared in 1888. DMcD

Thompson, Lydia (1836–1908) British-born actress. Fair-haired and sprightly, she had already made a name for herself as a dancer and comedienne in London, the English provinces, and Germany when she brought her troupe of British Blondes to New York (1868). Heralded by a barrage of publicity, her production of *Ixion; or, The Man at the Wheel,* the first modern burlesque in more than one act, did not so much introduce BURLESQUE to America as combine it with pulchritude in tights to create the "leg show." A strict taskmistress to her underlings and a shrewd businesswoman, Thompson was the first actress to horsewhip a libellous newspaper editor. Teamed with WILLIE EDOUIN for a while, she toured the U.S. several times (1868–71, 1877–8, 1886, 1888–9, 1891), retaining her popularity on both sides of the Atlantic. Her last appearance was with Mrs. Patrick Campbell in *A Queen's Romance* (Imperial Theatre, London, 1904). LS

(1983, CIRCLE REP), *Citizen Tom Paine* (1987, Philadelphia Company and JOHN F. KENNEDY CENTER), *The* FRONT PAGE (1986, VIVIAN BEAUMONT), *Hamlet* (1987, HARTFORD STAGE), GURNEY's *Love Letters* (1989, Promenade and Broadway), TESICH's *Square One* (1990, SECOND STAGE), McNALLY's *The Lisbon Traviata* (1990, MARK TAPER FORUM), *Danton's Death* (1992, ALLEY, directed by ROBERT WILSON), *Richard II* (1993, SHAKESPEARE THEATRE), *Tiny Alice* (2000, Second Stage), *The Stendhal Syndrome* (2004, PRIMARY STAGES), *Democracy* (2004, Broadway), *As You Like It* (2005, NYSF), and *A Naked Girl on the Appian Way* (2005, ROUNDABOUT). After the film *Last Summer* (1969), Thomas became known as John-Boy on television's *The Waltons* (1972–8; Emmy, 1973). Other screen appearances, among dozens, include *Red Sky at Morning* (1971), *Roots: The Next Generations* (TV, 1979), *Andre's Mother* (PBS, 1990), and *The Christmas Secret* (2000). Thomas excelled as Peer Gynt at HARTFORD STAGE (1989) – "a virtuosic accomplishment" – and appeared (2001) as Yvan in the London production of *Art.* He has published three volumes of poetry. REK

Thompson, Sada (1929–) Actress, born in Iowa and trained at the Carnegie Institute of Technology, who made her professional debut in *The Beautiful People* in 1947 and first appeared in New York in a reading of *Under Milkwood* in 1953. Among her best received efforts OFF-BROADWAY have been *The Misanthrope* (1956), Valerie Barton in *The River Line* (1957), and Beatrice in *The EFFECTS OF GAMMA RAYS ON MAN-IN-THE-MOON MARIGOLDS* (1970); on Broadway, Dorine in *Tartuffe* (1965), Ma in *Twigs* (1971), for which she received a Tony, and in *Saturday, Sunday, Monday* directed by Franco Zeffirelli (1974). Of her work in George Furth's *Twigs,* it was said that Thompson "has long since demonstrated a depth of acting technique and a variety of performing outputs while working the range of dramatic literature." Later work has been largely on television (notably as Kate Lawrence on *Family,* 1976–80), although she toured in *On Golden Pond,* in 1987 performed in Chicago the title role in *DRIVING MISS DAISY,* and in November 1993 briefly appeared on Broadway in FRANK GILROY's *Any Given Day.* She is in the THEATRE HALL OF FAME.
    SMA

Thompson, Tazewell (1954–) Theatre and opera director and playwright who in 2006 succeeded Joanne Woodward as artistic director of the WESTPORT COUNTRY PLAYHOUSE. Born and raised in NYC, Thompson has produced and directed more than 60 plays, including 25 world and American premieres, at many regional and New York venues (MANHATTAN THEATRE CLUB, The PUBLIC THEATER, CLASSIC STAGE COMPANY, etc.). He is a former artistic associate of Washington's ARENA STAGE and the ACTING COMPANY and served as artistic director of SYRACUSE STAGE (1992–5). He has also directed at the New York City Opera (*PORGY AND BESS,* 2002, and on PBS; *Patience,* 2005) and at Glimmerglass (*Death in Venice,* 2005). Since the early 2000s his play *Constant Star* on Ida B. Wells, a champion of equality for women and black Americans, has been seen at numerous theatres. He is the recipient of Juilliard's ALAN SCHNEIDER Distinguished Directors Fund Award.
    DBW

Thompson, Woodman (1889–1955) Set and costume designer who taught set and costume design at the newly established program at Carnegie Tech (1915–21) and was probably the first design teacher in the country. He had a notable career in the 1920s and '30s with productions such as *BEGGAR ON HORSEBACK* (1924), *WHAT PRICE GLORY* (1924), and *The COCOANUTS* (1925).   AA

Three Men on a Horse by John Cecil Holm and GEORGE ABBOTT. One of the most popular farces between the wars, this play opened at the PLAYHOUSE in New York under Abbott's direction on 30 January 1935. Capitalizing on Depression economics and popular fascination with gangsters, the playwrights created a host of good-hearted, goofball characters. The most memorable were Erwin, greeting-card poet and theoretical racehorse speculator, played by William Lynn; and an ex-Follies girl, Mabel (SHIRLEY BOOTH), whose fascination with the versifier causes trouble with her gambling boyfriend (SAM LEVENE), who exploits Erwin's uncanny talent for picking winning horses. Through much misunderstanding, Erwin wanders from his tract house in Ozone Heights to a New York gambling den and finds confidence in himself along the way.   RHW

Throckmorton, Cleon (1897–1965) Set designer who began his career with the PROVINCETOWN PLAYERS and designed many of EUGENE O'NEILL's early plays, including *The EMPEROR JONES* and *The HAIRY APE.* In the same way that O'Neill was experimenting with expressionism, Throckmorton employed stylized settings in the manner of various European movements. He designed several plays for the THEATRE GUILD, including *Porgy* (see *PORGY AND BESS*).   AA

Thurston, Howard Franklin (1869–1936) Magician. The son of a carriage maker, he began as a card manipulator, playing at TONY PASTOR's 14th Street Theatre, New York, but developed into a specialist in spectacular illusions. In his acts, he would make vanish an Arabian horse, a girl playing a piano, a Whippet automobile; in "The Triple Mystery" he made a girl materialize in a nested box, suspended her in a mummy case above the stage, and then caused her to appear in a roped trunk above the spectators' heads. He was held over at the London Palace for six months in 1900, purchased HARRY KELLAR's magic show in 1907, and introduced his version of the Indian Rope Trick in 1926. Having lost millions, he toured a ghost play, *The Demon* (1929), finally retiring in 1935. His autobiography, *My Life of Magic,* was published in 1929 (reprinted as *Our Life of Magic* in 1989 with augmentations, including a section by his step-daughter Jane).   LS

Tillinger, John [Joachim] (1939–) English-born, Bristol Old Vic–trained director, actor, and playwright who worked as an actor in London and New York before establishing his reputation as a director at the LONG WHARF THEATRE and OFF-BROADWAY (with transfers to Broadway). In the 1980s and early '90s he seemed especially adept at directing the plays of TERRENCE MCNALLY and A. R. GURNEY, including *The Lisbon Traviata* (1985, 1989), *Sweet Sue* (1986, Broadway), *Perfect Party* (1986), *Another Antigone* (1987, OLD GLOBE), *Love Letters* (1989), *Lips Together, Teeth Apart* (1991), *A Perfect Ganesh* (1993), *Sylvia* (1995), and Gurney's *Buffalo Gal* at WILLIAMSTOWN (2001). He also directed Off-Broadway revivals of Orton's comedies: *Entertaining Mr. Sloan* (1981), *Loot* (1986, moved to Broadway), and *What the Butler Saw* (1989). On Broadway he then directed ARTHUR MILLER's *Broken Glass* in 1994, *Judgment at Nuremberg* with GEORGE GRIZZARD and Maximilian Schell in 2001, and the ONE-PERSON *Say Goodnight, Gracie* in 2002, with Frank Gorshin and (the voice of) Didi Conn; also in 2002 was his staging of *House/Garden* at MANHATTAN THEATRE CLUB. Revivals on Broadway include *Inherit the Wind* (1996) with CHARLES DURNING and GEORGE C. SCOTT (Tony nomination for Best Revival), *The SUNSHINE BOYS* (1997) with Jack Klugman and Tony Randall, and a 2005 *Absurd Person Singular*. FRANK RICH wrote: He "has a keen way with comedies that have a sharp, idiosyncratic edge." TLM

Time of the Cuckoo ARTHUR LAURENTS's greatest commercial success ran 263 performances from its 15 October 1952, EMPIRE THEATRE premiere. The play deals with a vacationing American woman in her thirties (SHIRLEY BOOTH; Tony Award) desperately seeking romance, but finding inhibition and disillusionment in an affair with an Italian businessman. The play revived for 105 performances in 1958, at the Sheridan Square Playhouse. Laurents, RICHARD RODGERS, and STEPHEN SONDHEIM collaborated on its musical adaptation, *Do I Hear a Waltz?*, which opened 18 March 1965 at the 46TH STREET THEATRE for 220 performances – the shortest run for a Rodgers-scored work. The 1955 film version of the play, retitled *Summertime*, starred KATHARINE HEPBURN. RW

Time of Your Life, The by WILLIAM SAROYAN was produced by the THEATRE GUILD, opening in New York on 25 October 1939 and running for 185 performances. Its cast included EDDIE DOWLING as Joe, who is seeking the way to a civilized life; Edward Andrews as Tom, his helper; JULIE HAYDON as Kitty Duval, the prostitute who dreams of a home; Grover Burgess as Blick, the sadistic cop; and a large ensemble cast including Gene Kelly, William Bendix, and CELESTE HOLME. It had a

brief return engagement the next season, and was revived in 1969 and 1975. An example of Saroyan's romance of the commonplace, the play pits the wholesome American values embodied in the mythic figure of Kit Carson against the evil of an oppressive social system embodied in Blick. Good wins out when Kit kills Blick and Tom marries Kitty. BCM

Time Out for Ginger by Ronald Alexander was first produced by the ALLEY THEATRE and opened on Broadway 26 November 1952. Starring MELVYN DOUGLAS as the beleaguered father, this family situation comedy reinforced middle-class values and proved popular enough to run 248 performances. Ginger, the 14-year-old heroine, creates social havoc when she joins the high-school football team, but chooses traditional feminine behavior in the end. Alexander followed this play with three other works for the stage (produced 1955–63) and two screenplays (1961, 1965). His acting credits include five roles on Broadway between 1941 and 1949. KF

Tiny Alice by EDWARD ALBEE. A baffling "allegory about the passion of . . . Christ himself" (Howard Taubman) that opened to mixed reviews on 29 December 1964 at the BILLY ROSE Theatre, directed by ALAN SCHNEIDER, with IRENE WORTH (Tony Award) and John Gielgud in lead roles. BRUSTEIN complained of Albee's "huge joke on the American public"; CLURMAN sniffed, "the play was the sort of thing a highly endowed college student might write"; whereas HENRY HEWES suggested the play "established Albee as the most distinguished American playwright to date." WILLIAM BALL's 1969 AMERICAN CONSERVATORY THEATRE revival at Broadway's ANTA Playhouse drew consistently positive response; an outstanding revival ran 2000–1 at SECOND STAGE. GSA

Tipton, Jennifer (1937–) Columbus, OH–born lighting designer, director, and teacher whose early interest in dance led to an appreciation of the potential of light and its uses and impact on performance. After a degree from Cornell, she studied with lighting designer TOM SKELTON, began her career designing for choreographer Paul Taylor, and since 1965 designed many productions by choreographer TWYLA THARP as well as dance productions for Mikhail Baryshnikov, Robert Joffrey, and JEROME ROBBINS. In theatre she has designed frequently for the NEW YORK SHAKESPEARE FESTIVAL, LINCOLN CENTER (Tony Award for 1977's *The Cherry Orchard*), the GOODMAN THEATRE, and many regional theatres and

OFF-BROADWAY companies. Broadway credits include JEROME ROBBINS' BROADWAY (1989, Tony), *La Bête* (1991), and *James Joyce's The Dead* (2000). Her preference for more "abstract" theatre has led to collaboration with MABOU MINES, ROBERT WILSON, ANDREI SERBAN, and the WOOSTER GROUP (e.g., *The HAIRY APE*, 1996). In 1991 she directed *The Tempest* at the GUTHRIE THEATRE. Tipton's work is typified by a sense of sculptured and textured space. In 1998 she received an Obie for Sustained Achievement and in 2001 the Dorothy and Lillian GISH Prize of $250,000 for work in lighting design.   AA

Tobacco Road   Three-act drama-folkplay by Jack Kirkland, from the novel by Erskine Caldwell; opened at the Theatre Masque 4 December 1933 and ran for 3,182 performances, the longest-running Broadway show at the time. Set on the tenant farm of Jeeter Lester in the back country of Georgia, the play depicts poverty, ignorance, and degradation in the rural South. Its Rabelaisian qualities – obscene language and unconventional sexual behavior – helped give the production "scandal value," which BROOKS ATKINSON credits for its immediate success. Henry Hull created the role of the patriarch Jeeter; Sam Byrd the youngest son, Dude; Ruth Hunter the harelipped Ellie May; Dean Jagger the son-in-law, Lov Bensey; and MARGARET WYCHERLY the mother of the clan, Ada. Few critics liked the play. EDITH ISAACS called it "one of the bitterest plays ever produced in New York, but one of the most compelling."   TLM

Toby   The principal character of the North American TENT SHOW – a redhaired, freckle-faced farmboy. He appears to derive from the rustic low comedians of 18th-century farce; accepted tradition is that Fred Wilson of Horace Murphy's Comedians combined all his "silly kid" roles under the blanket name Toby around 1909. His dramatic function resembles that of the "comic man" in melodrama, providing laughs while contributing to the happy ending. Wilson's Toby was still recognizable as a farmhand in his checked shirt and boots, but the character grew more grotesque. Harley Sadler turned him into a Texas cowpoke in woolly chaps and a phallic pistol, and Neil Schaffner into an awkward dude, whose large freckles and blacked-out front teeth constituted a kind of commedia mask. The female equivalent was Sis Hopkins, created by Rose Melville c. 1898, an "Indiana jay" in pigtails and a pinafore; the type became known as Susie (Schaffner's wife, Caroline, was a famous one). The growing pre-

dominance of Toby and his antics, to the detriment of the dramas in which he appeared, has been cited as a factor in the declining popularity of the tent show.   LS

Todd, Michael [né Avrom Hirsch Goldbogen] (1907–58) A flamboyant producer and showman, Todd believed in giving his customers "high dames and low comedy." His 21 Broadway shows include *The Hot Mikado* (1939), a jazz version of GILBERT AND SULLIVAN, starring BILL ROBINSON; *Star and Garter* (1942); *The Naked Genius* (1943); *Mexican Hayride* (1944); *Up in Central Park* (1945); *As Girls Go* (1948); and *Michael Todd's Peep Show* (1950). His film *AROUND THE WORLD IN 80 DAYS* (1956) won an Oscar for Best Picture. His life was recounted in 1983 by his son, Mike Jr.   TLM

Toilet, The   First produced in 1964 at the St. Mark's Playhouse, in NYC's East Village, this one-act play by Le Roi Jones (AMIRI BARAKA) depicts the severe beating of a "white" youth by a gang of high-school blacks for writing a love letter to their leader. The incident takes place in the school's toilet. The play's indecent language overshadowed its message against stereotyped behavior and prompted a request to the New York District Attorney for obscenity charges to be brought against the work. LOS ANGELES newspapers refused to advertise a local production, bringing protests of prior CENSORSHIP from the Authors' League of America.   EGH

Tomei, Marisa (1964–) Oscar-winning Best Supporting Actress for *My Cousin Vinny* (1992); born and raised in Brooklyn to an Italian American family, she briefly attended Boston University and NYU but acting soon took precedence. Her OFF-BROADWAY debut was in *Daughters* (1986, *Theatre World* Award); her Broadway debut not until 1998 in *Wait Until Dark* as the blind heroine. Despite her successful screen career, Tomei is an accomplished stage actress with notable credits, including the amorous lesbian in *Slavs!* (1994, NEW YORK THEATRE WORKSHOP); Julia, the femme fatale in Overmyer's *Dark Rapture* (1996, SECOND STAGE); and the ESTELLE PARSONS–directed *Salome* (2003, Broadway) with AL PACINO. Onstage she possesses a sensuousness that sometimes belies the depth of her talent. Vincent Canby noted that "she has the mysterious presence that enables her to create her own close-ups in a medium in which close-ups don't exist."   DBW

Tomlin, Lily (Mary Jean) (1939–) Inventive Detroit-born comic performer whose break came in TV's *Laugh-In* (1969), especially with her portrayal of her creation Ernestine, the nasal-voiced, feisty telephone switchboard operator. (She later declined a half-million-dollar phone commercial offer.) Master of the live concert stage, Tomlin received Broadway acclaim for two ONE-PERSON shows developed with longtime partner Jane Wagner: *Appearing Nitely* (1977, special Tony Award) and *The Search for Signs of Intelligent Life in the Universe* (1985, Tony for Best Actress; 398 performances; revived 2000 for another 184). Often compared to RUTH DRAPER, Tomlin created more than a dozen characters of different ages, race, sexes, and classes in her shows.   DBW

Tone, (Stanislas Pascal) **Franchot** (1905–68) Actor. Although an original member of the GROUP THEATRE, he remained in the company only until 1932, when he went to Hollywood and developed a successful film career. Before joining the Group, he had already established himself on Broadway, acting in several THEATRE GUILD productions, including the role of Tom Ames in PHILIP BARRY's *Hotel Universe* (1930) and Curly McClain in LYNN RIGGS's *Green Grow the Lilacs* (1931). Tone returned for a Group Theatre production of IRWIN SHAW's *The Gentle People* (1939), and during the next two decades continued to act in New York, appearing in revivals of works by SAROYAN, CHEKHOV, and O'NEILL. He maintained his career in film and also acted often on television (with over 50 credits).   TP

Tooth of Crime, The The action of this two-act SAM SHEPARD play with music builds to a duel of language and style between two pop stars, Hoss and Crow: Hoss's "true style" loses to the brash newcomer Crow's heartless, manipulative use of shock techniques. The original production, which opened 17 July 1972 at London's Open Space Theatre (directed by CHARLES MAROWITZ) struck British critics as "an intensely American play." The American premiere at the McCARTER THEATRE (NJ) on 11 November 1972 featured Frank Langella as Hoss. A 1973 revival by The PERFORMANCE GROUP (at NYC's Performing Garage), directed by RICHARD SCHECHNER, was filmed for the Whitney Museum. For WALTER KERR, the play evoked "modern man as killer, as faith-merchandiser, as machine." According to CLIVE BARNES, "the language, hip, original, unexpected and rhythmic, flows in and out of the music, which Mr. Shepard himself composed and which is an integral part of the play's design."   FHL

Topdog/Underdog see PARKS, SUZAN-LORI

Torch Song Trilogy by HARVEY FIERSTEIN comprises three one-act plays that opened separately at New York's LA MAMA: *The International Stud* (1978), *Fugue in a Nursery* (1979), and *Widows and Children First!* (1979). As *Torch Song Trilogy,* they opened at the Richard Allen Center (1981); transferred to the OFF-BROADWAY Actors Playhouse (1982); and opened on Broadway 10 June 1982 at the Little Theatre – now the HELEN HAYES – running for 1,222 performances and winning a Tony (1983) for Best Play.

The central character throughout is Arnold Beckoff, a Jewish homosexual drag queen, played originally by Fierstein. In *The International Stud,* Arnold meets the bisexual Ed at a gay bar and, amid 1920s "torchsongs," begins a romance; Ed later rejects Arnold for a heterosexual relationship with Laurel. In the second play, Ed and Laurel invite Arnold and his new love (Alan) to their country house, where Ed is again confused over his sexual preferences. Five years later in *Widows and Children First!,* Ed has left Laurel; Alan is dead from a "fag bash;" and Arnold is planning to adopt David, a gay teenager. In a scene of great hilarity, Arnold's mother arrives to sort things out. Jack Kroll noted *Torch Song Trilogy* Beckoff's "odyssey from self-centered promiscuous drag queen to the oddest solid citizen in the republic." (See GAY/LESBIAN THEATRE.)   TLM

Torn, Rip [né Elmore Rual Torn Jr.] (1931–) Texas-born actor-director, a vivid presence in film since *Baby Doll* (1956) but also a successful actor on Broadway, OFF-BROADWAY, in regional theatre, and on television. A student of SANFORD MEISNER and LEE STRASBERG, Torn assumed the role of Brick in CAT ON A HOT TIN ROOF in 1956 and subsequently appeared in several WILLIAMS plays: *Orpheus Descending* (1958, COCONUT GROVE); *SWEET BIRD OF YOUTH* (1960, Broadway), first as Tom Junior and then as Chance Wayne, succeeding Paul Newman; *The GLASS MENAGERIE* (1975, Broadway); *A STREETCAR NAMED DESIRE* (1976, Academy Festival Theatre, Lake Forest, IL). An Obie winner for his role in Norman Mailer's *The Deer Park* (1967) – as well as for his direction of McClure's *The Beard* (1968) – his other significant acting roles include Eban in DESIRE UNDER THE ELMS (1963, CIRCLE IN THE SQUARE), Bernie Dodd in *The COUNTRY GIRL* (1966, City Center, NYC), Edgar in *The Dance of Death* (1970, ARENA STAGE), Richard Nixon in *Expletive Deleted* (1974, OFF-OFF), Captain in *The Father* (1975, YALE REP), the Howard Hughes role in *Seduced* (1979, AMERICAN PLACE), Chris in the 1992 ROUNDABOUT revival of *ANNA CHRISTIE*, the lead in the Broadway version of HORTON FOOTE's *The Young Man from Atlanta* (1997), and Casanova in *Camino Real* (1999, HARTFORD STAGE). In the 1990s he mastered the role of the producer, Artie, on the HBO series *The Larry Sanders Show*. He was married to actress GERALDINE PAGE. Their daughter, **Angelica Torn**, is an actor (Sylvia Plath in Paul Alexander's *Edge*, 2003).   TP   DBW

Tortesa, the Usurer Five-act romantic comedy written in blank verse; one of N. P. WILLIS's most popular plays. The story concerns a moneylender, Tortesa, who agrees to cover the debts of Count Falcone in exchange for the count's daughter, Isabella. Isabella, of course, loves the young painter Angelo, and, after much romantic maneuvering, all is resolved happily, with the young lovers reunited and Tortesa content with Zippa, the glover's daughter. The play, first performed on 8 April 1839 at New York's National Theatre, starred JAMES WALLACK, for whom the play was written, in the title role. Despite its many faults, the work was sufficiently admired to be revived many times over the next decade.   PAD

Touch of the Poet, A, by EUGENE O'NEILL opened in New York on 2 October 1958, running for 284 performances. HAROLD CLURMAN directed a cast including HELEN HAYES, KIM STANLEY, and Eric Portman. The play was revived on Broadway in 1967, and in 1977 starring JASON ROBARDS and GERALDINE FITZGERALD, directed by JOSÉ QUINTERO. A successful production with Vanessa REDGRAVE and Timothy Dalton was produced by London's Young Vic in 1988; ROUNDABOUT's 2005 staging boasted an extraordinary, almost Lear-like performance by Gabriel Byrne. The only surviving complete play from O'Neill's projected 11-play cycle "A Tale of Possessors Self-Dispossessed," it is set in a Massachusetts tavern in 1828. It centers on Irish American innkeeper Con Melody's pretensions to being an aristocratic Byronic hero and his daughter Sara's desire to marry (the offstage) Simon Harford, the son of a wealthy Yankee family. Both have their pretensions and their pride deflated in the course of the play, as Simon tries to challenge the elder Harford to a duel over an imagined insult but is forcibly ejected from his house and carted off to the police station, and Sara stoops to entrapping Simon through sex. In the end, both accept the social identities that the culture dictates for them.   BCM

Towse, John Ranken (1845–1933) Drama critic. Born in England and educated at Cambridge, Towse came to New York in 1869 as a reporter for the *Evening Post*. In 1874 he was given the drama desk, a position he held until his retirement in 1927. Regarded as a scholarly and trustworthy critic, Towse fought to maintain Victorian tastes in drama and 19th-century standards in the theatre. Like his contemporaries, WILLIAM WINTER and HENRY AUSTIN CLAPP, he could not accept realism, especially the plays of IBSEN. His book *Sixty Years of the Theatre* (1916) provides a detailed account and analysis of 19th-century actors.   TLM

toy theatre/juvenile drama This originated in Regency London as "penny plain, tuppence-coloured" sheets of characters and scenery from popular dramas, to be cut out and staged in miniature playhouses; such sheets were sold from Elton's Theatrical Print Warehouse, NYC, but no American work was reproduced. Scott & Co. issued "Seltz's American Boys' Theatre" (1866–74), renamed versions of plays in *The Boys of England* series, which differed only in the occasional inclusion of an American locale: an Indian encampment or Niagara Falls. From 1894 to c. 1923, many newspaper supplements and magazines included mechanically colored sheets, often of popular fairy tales and generic plays such as *RIP VAN WINKLE* and *UNCLE TOM'S CABIN*. More anachronistically, c. 1950 a pink plastic SHOWBOAT was sold for the staging of *Pinocchio, Heidi,* and *The WIZARD OF OZ.* However, in the U.S. the toy theatre was never used to commemorate contemporary productions.   LS

Toys in the Attic This last major play by LILLIAN HELLMAN opened at Broadway's Hudson Theatre on 25 February 1960 and ran for 556 performances. Hellman focused on a decaying southern culture to show the claustrophobic, almost incestuous relationship of two spinster sisters, Carrie (MAUREEN STAPLETON) and Annie (Anne Revere), and their wastrel brother, Julian (JASON ROBARDS JR.). When Julian marries and brings his wife to live with his sisters, the family is torn apart by jealousy, repressed longings, and the sisters' fear that Julian might break away from his dependence upon them. The play won the New York Drama Critics' Circle Award in 1960.   FB

Tracy, Lee (1898–1968) A commercially successful actor for more than 50 years, Tracy, noted for his exuberance and excitement on stage, is best remembered for his Roy Lane, the hoofer in *BROADWAY* (1926), and Hildy Johnson, the newspaperman, in *The FRONT PAGE* (1928). From his New York debut in *The SHOW-OFF* to his last major role as the ex-president in *The Best Man* (1960), he appeared in a steady stream of forgettable plays – although his London debut as Harry Van in *IDIOT'S DELIGHT* (1938) and his Australian debut as Queeg in *The Caine Mutiny Court Martial* (1955) are noteworthy.   DBW

training, actor Study of theatrical production techniques, as opposed to dramatic literature, did not flourish in colleges and universities until the 20th century, although the beginnings of college dramatics predate the nation's founding. (A survey of academic theatre can be found in earlier editions of the *Guide*.) Till the late 19th century most actors learned their craft as apprentices, usually in resident STOCK COMPANIES; professional theatre schools did not emerge until the late 19th century, when those were replaced by "combination companies." STEELE MACKAYE, an innovator in several areas of the theatre, heavily influenced the beginnings of professional actor training. MacKaye, a student of François Delsarte in Paris, imported the Frenchman's theories to America. Drawing upon his experiences, MacKaye also cofounded with Franklin Sargent the Lyceum Theatre School (later the AMERICAN ACADEMY OF DRAMATIC ART). Although this was the first formal school, others attempted to offer training, including the Lawrence School of Acting in New York, the James E. Frobisher College of Oratory and Acting, and the School of Elocution and Dramatic Art and a Delsarte School of Oratory and Dramatic Art, both in BOSTON.

The success of the Lyceum School, however, stimulated the growth of dramatic schools toward the end of the 19th century. Performers such as ROSE EYTINGE, E. J. Henley, and MCKEE RANKIN lent their names to schools; others sprang up in CHICAGO, PHILADELPHIA, Boston, St. Louis, and Cincinnati. Some schools spent most of their instructional time in rehearsal; others felt the essentials must be taught off the stage.

Several private teachers also began to give lessons. The best known, Alfred Ayres, author of *Actors and Acting and The Essentials of Elocution,* actually castigated dramatic schools, calling half of them confidence schemes. Others felt a year in a dramatic school was the equivalent of 10 years of the slipshod training found in stock companies.

At the turn of the century, the proliferation of schools continued until they appeared in most of the major American cities. The American Academy of Dramatic Art grew in prestige by gathering support from professional leaders, including the FROHMANS, DAVID BELASCO, JOHN DREW, and WILLIAM GILLETTE.

Other notable institutions included the Alvienne Academy in New York, founded by Claude M. Alvienne in 1894; the National Dramatic Conservatory begun by F. F. Mackay in 1898; the Stanhope–Wheatcroft Dramatic School in 1900; and the American School of Playwriting, led by William T. Price. Several schools were operated in conjunction with producing theatre companies, such as the Henry Jewett School of Acting at the Boston Repertory Theatre. A theatrical training school was associated with the Detroit Civic Theatre, managed by JESSE BONSTELLE. Mae DESMOND founded a School of Theatre in Philadelphia; even the WASHINGTON SQUARE PLAYERS and the THEATRE GUILD operated training programs for a time. JAMES E. MURDOCH, who had entertained troops during the Civil War, carried on the scientific methods of James Rush, while others such as S. S. Curry, Charles Wesley Emerson, and Leland Powers offered a more holistic approach to the actor's problems.

An important influence on the evolution of American acting arrived in 1922–3 in the form of the MOSCOW ART THEATRE. By the next year RICHARD BOLESLAVSKI, trained at the MAT, had opened the AMERICAN LABORATORY THEATRE School in New York, using students in productions in their own theatre. Although his work was not yet available in English, Stanislavsky's System indirectly (and sometimes mistakenly) impacted on the work of the GROUP THEATRE and, more specifically, the later ACTORS STUDIO, especially as advocated by LEE STRASBERG.

At present, apprenticeship remains a viable entry to professional acting. Positions are available from LORT (League of Resident Theatres) or from SUMMER STOCK theatres, some associated with URTA (University/Resident Theatre Association), which holds annual auditions for non-[ACTORS'] EQUITY actors. Regional theatre conferences hold auditions as well for summer work.

Commercial or professional training offers another avenue into the profession. Dozens of commercial programs are available, mostly located in New York and LOS ANGELES. Among the most respected in NYC are the NEIGHBORHOOD PLAYHOUSE School of the Theatre, the HB (HERBERT BERGHOF) Studio, the STELLA ADLER Conservatory of Acting, and The Actors Institute; near LA the Actors' Workshop is notable. The Actors Studio conducts classes in both NYC and LA (and for a time had a graduate program with the New School). Many theatre companies have training programs, workshops, or conservatories, such as CIRCLE IN THE SQUARE (NYC), AMERICAN CONSERVATORY THEATER (SF), the DENVER CEN-

TER for the Performing Arts, and DC's SHAKE-SPEARE THEATRE.

The vast majority of American actors, however, receive their first training in colleges and universities. In some cases, apprenticeships and academic credit may be combined. In the past half a century regional theatres and universities have sought to join forces, hoping to offer the student the best of both worlds: The GUTHRIE THEATER in Minneapolis and the University of Minnesota, Florida State University and the ASOLO THEATRE of Sarasota, Harvard University and the AMERICAN REPERTORY THEATRE, the University of San Diego and the OLD GLOBE THEATRE, the University of Utah and Pioneer Theatre Company, Brown University and TRINITY REP, and others have offered joint programs (some ultimately failures). Other outstanding performance-oriented programs can be found at the Yale School of Drama, Rutgers, California Institute of the Arts, NYU's Tisch School of the Arts (which claims to be the largest undergraduate acting program in the world), North Carolina School of the Arts, the Juilliard School, and at other quality institutions.

Some American students seek the more classic training of the Royal Academy of Dramatic Art or the London Academy of Music and Dramatic Art, both of which hold annual U.S. auditions. Although a kind of American realism with a base in emotional training still dominates actor training in the U.S., there are today far more alternative approaches. These range from the use of theatre games and improvisation to the rigorous physical and vocal techniques rooted in Tadashi Suzuki's approach and elaborated in ANNE BOGART's "Viewpoints," among other combinations. SMA DBW

Treadwell, Sophie (1885–1970) Californian-born playwright and journalist (war correspondent, 1916–18). Although other plays of hers were produced – e.g., *Gringo* (1922), *Plumes in the Dust* (1936), and *Hope for a Harvest* (1941) – Treadwell's reputation rests predominantly on her innovative *MACHINAL* (1928). In nine expressionistic scenes, the play perfectly combined form and content, as it told the story of a woman who is robotized by life. A 1960 OFF-BROADWAY revival received two Obies; a 1990 revival won three. FB

Tremont Theatre 76 Tremont St., Boston [Architect: Isiah Rogers]. In 1827, although they were hardly able to support the FEDERAL STREET THEATRE, Bostonians were presented with a second theatre, a handsome and elegant edifice built through the largesse of a group of wealthy and prominent citizens. For the next 16 years, the house struggled to survive as stars were lured to its stage and an excellent STOCK COMPANY was assembled. It was never able to pay for itself, and its managers resorted to a succession of novelties to keep it afloat. In 1835, CHARLOTTE CUSHMAN there made her first appearance onstage, as a singer, in *The Marriage of Figaro*. In 1843, the theatre was sold to the Baptist church and transformed into the Tremont Temple; nine years later, it burned down (see FIRES) and was rebuilt as a church. MCH

Trifles by SUSAN GLASPELL is a tightly constructed, realistic one-act in which the major character never appears. Set in an isolated farmhouse, the play creates suspense and a sense of quiet revelation as two women piece together bits of domestic evidence to prove their absent peer murdered her husband. First produced 8 August 1916 by the PROVINCETOWN PLAYERS at their Wharf Theatre, *Trifles* is generally considered one of the best works to be mounted by this group and was widely translated, studied, and performed. It has more recently been examined as an early treatment of gender issues: The male authority figures, charged with solving the crime, miss essential clues because of their scorn for household matters and their inability to read emotional signs. As the women slowly make discoveries, they increasingly identify with their oppressed counterpart, find justification for her actions, and ultimately decide to conceal their knowledge. KF

Trinity [Square] Repertory Company Founded in 1964 in Providence, RI, by a group of local citizens, this ensemble (and one of the few theatres to maintain a resident acting company) became one of the more adventurous of the regional theatres in the U.S. (with over 50 world premieres in 40 years). During 1965–89 its artistic director was ADRIAN HALL. Before moving in 1973 into their present complex (the Lederer Theatre Center, a converted vaudeville/cinema house), the company performed primarily in a converted church. A federal grant in 1966 (Project Discovery) covered many of the theatre's expenses for three years, allowing it to reach true professional stature. A major grant from the NATIONAL ENDOWMENT FOR THE ARTS allowed financial security for its theatre artists beginning with the 1985–6 season. A varied bill of some 9–12 productions is staged annually in two theatres: the 500-plus Chace Theatre and the 300-seat Dowling Theatre. In 1978 a training program for actors, directors, and playwrights was initiated (originally with Rhode Island College), and in 1986 "Square" was removed from the theatre's original name. ANNE BOGART, known primarily as a freelance avant-garde director, presented a controversial season (1989–90) after Hall's departure; she was succeeded by a longtime company actor-director, Richard Jenkins (1990–4), and then by OSKAR EUSTIS (best known for commissioning KUSHNER'S *ANGELS IN AMERICA*), who left in 2006 to head The PUBLIC in NYC. Under Eustis, a consortium graduate program was begun with Brown University; a branch bank space donated in 2000 has become the Pell Chafee Performance Center, serving as its eductional center. Eustis's replacement is Curt Columbus, previously at STEPPENWOLF. Trinity has won numerous honors including the 1981 Regional Theatre Tony.   DBW

Trip to Chinatown, A, by CHARLES HALE HOYT. Opening at Hoyt's New York MADISON SQUARE THEATRE on 9 November 1891, this "musical trifle" is thought to hold the consecutive long-run record (657 performances) for the 19th century. It also toured every region of the country. Enormously successful at writing comic farces – here in the more modern vein – for which he authored popular songs ("The Bowery," "Reuben, Reuben"), Hoyt would typically revise his plays over months on the road before bringing them to New York. The lively characters (Welland Strong, Rashleigh Gay, Wilder Daly, et al.), songs, dances, breeches and gymsuit soubrette parts, and the stylish settings of *Chinatown* capture Hoyt's typically light and chaste, nationalized social satire, here set against a masquerade ball and a fraudulent trip to San Francisco's Chinatown.   RKB

Trouble in Mind by ALICE CHILDRESS opened at OFF-BROADWAY's Greenwich Mews Theatre 4 November 1955 and ran 91 performances – the first major production for this nascent playwright. (Despite frequent assertions to the contrary, however, it did not win any Obie Award.) The play is an analysis of black and white relations, shown against the backdrop of rehearsals for a mixed-cast play set during slavery to explore the tensions between the races in the 1950s. Its central character is a black actress who must decide whether to continue playing traditional stereotyped roles or to stand up for her beliefs. A revival by the NEGRO ENSEMBLE COMPANY was staged on THEATRE ROW in 1998.   KME

True West This SAM SHEPARD play premiered at SAN FRANCISCO'S MAGIC THEATRE, directed by ROBERT WOODRUFF, with Peter Coyote as Austin (1980). Although credited also as director when the play opened at New York's PUBLIC THEATER on 23 December 1980 for a 24-performance run, Woodruff disowned the production, as did Shepard. FRANK RICH called it "little more than stand-up run-through of a text that remains to be explored." The Cherry Lane Theatre's "act of theatrical restitution and restoration" (MEL GUSSOW) opened 18 October 1982 to the relief and acclaim of critics who had come to expect such theatrical excitement of Shepard. JOHN MALKOVICH and GARY SINISE made their NYC debuts as Lee and Austin, the shiftless drifter and the Hollywood screenwriter whose sibling rivalry carries them into a virtual exchange of identities while evoking the decay of what the West once signified. It remains one of Shepard's most produced plays, successfully revived in 2000 at CIRCLE IN THE SQUARE with PHILIP SEYMOUR HOFFMAN and John C. Reilly alternating Austin and Lee.   FHL

Truth, The Social comedy by CLYDE FITCH that opened 1 January 1907 and ran only 34 performances, though the play was regarded as Fitch's best. CLARA BLOODGOOD starred as Becky Warder, a congenital liar who creates such a web of deceit that she destroys her husband's confidence in her. In many ways, the characters and action of this play parallel those in IBSEN'S *A Doll House,* though the resolution here is a happy one. The failure of the play was devastating to Bloodgood, all the more so because the London production featuring Marie Tempest received unqualified accolades. Feminist scholar Kimberley Marra suggests that Bloodgood's sensational suicide on 5 December 1907 was consequential to a vision of feminine perfection that dominated American culture and that was promulgated in Fitch's plays. In late 2006 it was successfully revived by NYC's Metropolitan Playhouse.   MR

Tsu, Susan (1950–) State College, Pennsylvania, native who studied costume design at Carnegie Mellon. Her design work has included Broadway (the original *GODSPELL;* Paul Foster's *Elizabeth I,* 1972); many major regional theatres, including the OREGON SHAKESPEARE FESTIVAL, HARTFORD STAGE, and the ALLEY THEATRE; also *The Balcony* for the Bolshoi Theatre as part of a U.S.–Soviet Arts Exchange, and *The Joy Luck Club,* a collaboration between The Shanghai People's Art Theatre and the LONG WHARF THEATRE. Her honors include the New York Drama Desk, New York Drama Critics' Circle, and Los Angeles Distinguished Designer Awards. She has taught at Boston University, the University of Texas–Austin, and, since 2003, at Carnegie Mellon.   BO

Tsypin, George (1954–) Soviet-born designer who studied at the Institute of Architecture in Moscow before coming in 1979 to the U.S., where he studied stage design at NYU with JOHN CONKLIN. Tsypin is the foremost practitioner of the postmodern school of design. Working frequently with directors PETER SELLARS, JOANNE AKALAITIS, and recently JULIE TAYMOR, he has designed startling settings for classic and new plays and operas such as *The Death of Klinghoffer* (1991) and, at the Met, *The Magic Flute* (2005). The sets show a strong constructivist influence and often utilize metal, moving parts, and an overlay of projected images; visuals from contemporary culture mingle with references to classical architecture and theatre. In addition to work at the NEW YORK SHAKESPEARE FESTIVAL, GUTHRIE THEATER, GOODMAN THEATRE, and other regional theatres, Tsypin has had a gallery show of his sculptures and did the art direction for Peter Sellars's film *The Cabinet of Dr. Ramirez* (1991). His book *George Tsypin Opera Factory* was published in 2005.   AA

Tucker, Sophie [née Sophia Kalish] (1884–1966) VAUDEVILLE singer, born in Russia; known as "The Last of the Red-Hot Mammas." She made her professional debut at the 116th St. Music Hall, New York, in 1906 in blackface, and won a reputation as a "Coon Shouter," singing ragtime melodies. A brief moment in ZIEGFELD's *Follies of 1909* (from which she was ejected when NORA BAYES found the competition too daunting) was followed by stardom in vaudeville, where she capitalized on her girth and her innuendo in such songs as "He Hasn't Up to Yesterday, but I Guess He Will To-night." In 1911 she introduced "Some of These Days," which became her theme song. She moved easily from ragtime to jazz, made a huge success in England beginning in 1922, appeared in the musicals *Leave It to Me!* (1938) and *High Kickers* (1941), and helped in organizing vaudevillians into the short-lived American Federation of Actors, of which she served as president in 1938. An autobiography appeared in 1945, and a biography by Armond Fields was published in 2003.   LS

Tune, Tommy (Thomas James) (1939–) Dancer, actor, and director-choreographer, educated at the universities of Texas and Houston, who made his Broadway debut in the chorus of *Baker Street* (1965), followed by MICHAEL BENNETT's *A Joyful Noise* (1966). Fabulous tap dancing in the film version of *The Boyfriend* was followed by his Broadway show-stopping clog dance in *Seesaw* (1973), cochoreographed with Bennett: The lanky, 6′ 6″ Texan tap-danced in clogs, traveling down a staircase onto a stage covered with balloons.

Tune's choreography of DANCE sequences has been enormously popular: the locker-room dance in *Best Little Whorehouse in Texas* (1978); the "dance of the feet" in *A Day in Hollywood/A Night in the Ukraine* (1980); the flirtatious water tap dance in *My One and Only* (1983); and Kringelein's ecstatic Charleston in *Grand Hotel: The Musical* (1989). Tune, who has won nine Tonys in all, was the first of only two people to receive Tony Awards in four different categories (the second being HARVEY FIERSTEIN): For Tune these were Featured Actor (Musical), 1974 (*Seesaw*); Choreography, 1980 (*Hollywood/Ukraine*); Direction (Musical), 1982 (*Nine*); and Actor (Musical), *My One and Only* (winning too in Choreography with Thommie Walsh). He is also the first to win Tony Awards for Direction of *and* Choreography of a Musical for two consecutive years, with *Grand Hotel* (1990s Tonys) and the spectacular extravaganza *The WILL ROGERS FOLLIES* (1991). In 1991 he toured in *Bye Bye Birdie,* and in 1994 was associated with the successful revival of *GREASE* and the ill-fated *The Best Little Whorehouse in Texas Goes Public.* Since 1992 he has frequently appeared on tour and in NYC in his own REVUES: *Tommy Tune Tonite, Tommy Tune Moonlighting,* as well as the recent *Tommy Tune: White Tie and Tails* (2002). In 1995 he had been developing and touring a musical called *Busker Alley* with choreographic partner Jeff Calhoun, but a broken bone in his right foot led to the show's cancellation. In 2003 Tune received the National Medal of Arts. His autobiography was published in 1997.   LF   DBW

Tunick, Jonathan (1938–) After receiving a Master's degree from Juilliard in 1960, Tunick began writing songs for REVUES done OFF-BROADWAY. In 1968 he orchestrated the musical *Promises, Promises* using electronic music and a rock beat. With *COMPANY* (1970), Tunick began his long association with composer-lyricist STEPHEN SONDHEIM. In orchestrating for him, Tunick preserved the texture and emotion of the music while allowing the complex lyrics to be heard clearly. In addition to orchestrating many other hit shows from the 1970s to the present, such as *A CHORUS LINE, Nine, Titanic* (1997; Tony), *The Frogs,* and *The Color Purple,* Tunick has arranged and conducted the scores of several films. In 1982 he received a Drama Desk Special Award. He had two openings on Broadway in May 2007: *LoveMusik* and a revival of *110 in the Shade.*   MK

Tyler, George Crouse (1867–1946) Ohio-born manager and producer who managed his first theatre in Chillicothe (the first state capital) at the age of 20. Afterward, he moved to New York and worked as a dramatic reporter, advance AGENT, and producer. In 1897, he joined forces with THEODORE A. LIEBLER to found Liebler and Company, which for the next 17 years produced some 300 plays, brought to America Mrs. Patrick Campbell, Eleonora Duse, Madam Réjane, and the Abbey Theatre, and managed such stars as ARNOLD DALY, JAMES O'NEILL, and GERTRUDE ELLIOTT. After the firm failed in 1915, Tyler was associated with KLAW and ERLANGER until he became an independent producer in 1918. His best-known presentations include BOOTH TARKINGTON's *Clarence* (1919), an early version (1920) of what would become EUGENE O'NEILL's *ANNA CHRISTIE*, KAUFMAN and CONNELLY's *DULCY* (1921), and O'Casey's *The Plough and the Stars* (1927). His revival of *Macbeth* in 1928 was designed by Gordon Craig. Tyler is noted for bringing European talent to the U.S., and for preferring new works to revivals. His memoirs (with J. C. Furnas), *Whatever Goes Up*, were published in 1934.   TLM

Tyler, Royall (1757–1826) American playwright, author of *The CONTRAST* (1787), the first script by an American to receive a successful professional production. Born in Boston and educated at Harvard, Tyler showed some early literary talent and wrote *The Contrast* in three weeks after seeing his first stage production, a New York production (JOHN STREET THEATRE) of Sheridan's *The School for Scandal*. The script contrasts the effete world of fashion and the more manly types of Americans, and introduced the YANKEE character to the American stage. Tyler also wrote a farce, *May Day in Town; or, New-York in an Uproar* (John Street, 1787) and the comedy *A Georgia Spec; or, Land in the Moon* (Boston and NYC, 1797), as well as four other plays, probably never performed. The standard biography is by George T. Tanselle (1967).   SMA

Tynan, Kenneth (Peacock) (1927–80) British drama critic whose acerbic and erudite writings in the London *Observer* (1954–8; 1960–3) and in the *New Yorker* (1958–60; 1976–80) made him influential on both sides of the Atlantic. He championed the new realism of John Osborne and Arnold Wesker, calling Osborne's *Look Back in Anger* (1956) "the best young play of its decade." He promoted BRECHT and other socially conscious playwrights, and was the first literary manager of Britain's National Theatre (1963–9). His "elegant erotica," *OH! CALCUTTA!* (1969), challenged standards of morality. Tynan's most memorable line may be his spooneristic characterization of *Flower Drum Song* (1958) as "the world of woozy song." The most thorough biography is by Dominic Shellard (2003).   TLM

U

Uhry, Alfred (1936–) Born in Atlanta, where he grew up Jewish, and educated at Brown University, where he began his writing career creating college musicals with composer Robert Waldman, subsequently a frequent collaborator (*The Robber Bridegroom*, 1975, among others). His breakthrough play, DRIVING MISS DAISY (1987), ran Off-Broadway for 1,195 performances, earned him the Pulitzer for Drama (1988), and became a successful 1989 film, garnering the Oscar for Best Picture and earning him the Academy Award for screen adaptation. (He had first gained film attention with the screenplay for the 1988 *Mystic Pizza*.) Next came a second comedy located in Atlanta, *The Last Night of Ballyhoo* (1996, ALLIANCE THEATRE), set in 1939 during the premiere of *Gone with the Wind* and concerned with a Jewish family during a key social event (1997 Tony, Best Play). His third Atlanta piece, the musical *Parade* (music and lyrics by JASON ROBERT BROWN), about the 1913 lynching of Jewish factory manager Leo Frank, won him a Tony for Best Book of a Musical. Recent projects include *Without Walls* (WILLIAMSTOWN, 2002; CENTER THEATRE GROUP, LA, 2006) and *Edgardo Mine* (HARTFORD STAGE, 2002; GUTHRIE THEATER, 2006), the latter based on David Kertzer's book *The Kidnapping of Edgardo Mortara* (1997). A Broadway musical, *LoveMusik,* with book by Uhry – and based on the relationship of KURT WEILL (whose music and lyrics are incorporated) and Lotte Lenya – opened May 2007.   DBW

Ulric [née Ulrich]**, Lenore** (1892–1970) Actress who, like BLANCHE BATES, DAVID WARFIELD, and MRS. LESLIE CARTER, was a DAVID BELASCO creation. From her debut in 1916 as an Indian maiden in *The Heart of Wetona* (see NATIVE AMERICANS PORTRAYED), Belasco cast her as a temptress in a series of exotic potboilers. In *The Son-Daughter* (1919) she was a Chinese siren, in *Kiki* (1921) a Parisian chorus girl, in *Lulu Belle* (1926) a Harlem whore, and in *Mima* (1928) a slinky mannequin. Raven-haired, with large dark eyes in an oval face, Ulric made a beguiling 1920s vamp, sultry and sharp-tongued, voluptuous and swivel-hipped. She received good notices even when the primi-

tive, scenically spectacular Belasco vehicles she starred in were critical howlers.   FH

Uncle Tom's Cabin No other American play has had such a remarkable stage history. Mrs. Stowe's novel, published March 1852 (after its serialization), was first dramatized by CLIFTON TAYLEURE and performed in Baltimore (January 1852); a second version, by C. W. TAYLOR, played in New York in August, and a third, by GEORGE L. AIKEN (now the accepted version), with the HOWARD FAMILY in Troy, NY, in September. The Howards made a life's work of "Tomming," as did a host of American actors. In the 1850s productions were seen also in London, Berlin, and Paris.

"Tom" shows were on the road by 1854; by 1893 a national exchange for "Tom" actors opened in Chicago, and in the 1890s some 400 troupes were barnstorming across the country. Every season companies in the major cities called in the hounds to pursue Eliza across the Ohio River, a spectacle not included in the novel. Theatrical novelty became the "Tommer's" stock-in-trade: Bloodhounds, "Jubilee Singers," and dioramas became featured attractions; some troupes carried as few as three actors. In 1901 WILLIAM BRADY's production dwarfed its predecessors with 200 buck-and-wing dancers and singers plus a transformation sequence of 21 scenes. A dozen companies were still on the road in 1927; in 1933 a revival at the Players (see CLUBS) featured OTIS SKINNER and FAY BAINTER.

Thomas Gossett notes how strongly the play has affected American and international thinking on the character of African Americans, the nature of life in the old South, and the struggle between good and evil. Though not essentially antislavery, it served as propaganda for abolition. In the 20th century the popular belief, as expressed by JAMES BALDWIN, was that *UTC* spread the lie that "black equates with evil and white with grace." Few revivals have been seen since the 1930s; however, in 1978 TRINITY REPERTORY COMPANY offered a version with some success. Moreover, as recently as 1990–1 three adaptations were developed: a melodramatic version by the SAN FRANCISCO

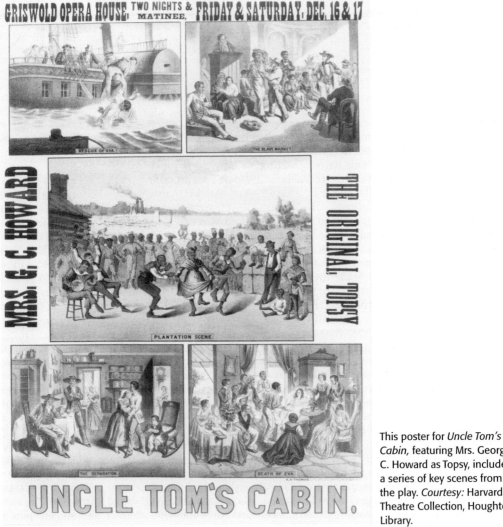

This poster for *Uncle Tom's Cabin,* featuring Mrs. George C. Howard as Topsy, includes a series of key scenes from the play. *Courtesy:* Harvard Theatre Collection, Houghton Library.

MIME TROUPE and the LORRAINE HANSBERRY Theatre; an epic dance-theatre piece by dancer-choreographer Bill T. Jones (*Last Supper at Uncle Tom's Cabin/The Promised Land*); and *Unkle Tomm's Kabin: A Deconstruction of the Novel by Harriet Beecher Stowe* by Seattle's EMPTY SPACE Theatre. Apparently, with racial tensions resurfacing in American society, *UTC* has once more emerged as one vehicle for investigating collective racial images and attitudes, as Misha Berson has suggested in *American Theatre* (May 1991). Typical were productions by NYC's DRAMA DEPT. (1997), a collage of sources and commentary, and the race-reversed, Stowe-narrated version by Virginia's American Century Theater (2002).   RM   DBW

Under the Gaslight; or, Life and Love in These Times by AUGUSTIN DALY. Five-act sensational melodrama produced 12 August 1867 at the New York Theatre, with over 100 performances during the season. Daly's first original play led to his two similarly constructed plays for the next season, *A Flash of Lightning* and *The Red Scarf.* Each had one consummate climactic moment that, though superficially realistic, was sheer spectacle. In *Gaslight* it was a railroad sequence in the final scene of Act IV in which Snorkey (J. K. Mortimer), a thoroughly likable character who suffers without self-pity, is tied to railway tracks. Laura (ROSE EYTINGE), the heroine, is nearby in a shed, locked up intentionally for her safety while she waits for the 10:30 P.M. train. Frantically she attempts to escape in order to free Snorkey while the sounds of the train get progressively closer. Despite its improbable and overly complicated plot, *Gaslight* is one of the best American plays of the 1860s, demonstrating Daly's belief that a new American society should be based on industry rather than inherited wealth and family.   DBW

unions, theatrical Although performers had organized themselves for social and beneficial purposes since the middle of the 19th century, the stagehands were the first to achieve collective bargaining. The NATIONAL ALLIANCE OF THEATRICAL AND STAGE EMPLOYEES was formed in 1893 and became the International Alliance through affiliation with its Canadian counterpart (1898).

Though some performers resisted organization because work was abundant and salaries reasonable, working conditions at the end of the 19th century were intolerable. Actors were required to rehearse without pay for as long as necessary. There was no limit to the number of performances they were required to give during a week, but any cancellation meant a salary reduction. Moreover, actors furnished their own costumes in modern and standard period plays, paid their own way to where a tour started, and paid their own way home; yet they played at the pleasure of the management. Disputes over wages and working conditions were settled by the management, and dismissal required neither notice nor reason.

The first performers to achieve collective bargaining were those in the YIDDISH THEATRE. The Hebrew Actors' Union was founded in 1899 and recognized in 1902. English-language players had formed the Actors' Society in 1896, but it failed to achieve a standard contract. Its last act was to authorize a study group, which then organized itself as ACTORS' EQUITY ASSOCIATION (1913). That group's affiliation with the American Federation of Labor was delayed because the AFL had issued a charter for all performers to The White Rats VAUDEVILLE union in 1910: Formed in 1900, it was crushed in a lockout (1916–17) and surrendered its charter in 1919; with AFL support, Equity then struck in the fall. Ultimately, their membership swelled from 2,700 to 14,000, and the producers capitulated in a month. Subsequently, Equity won a closed shop (1924) and producer contributions to pension and welfare funds (1960).

New unions were created in response to new media. The Screen Actors Guild (SAG) was formed in 1933. The American Federation of Radio Artists was born in 1937, and was expanded to include television (AFTRA) in 1952. The American Guild of Musical Artists was founded in 1936 and the American Guild of Variety Artists (AGVA) in 1939.

Organization of nonperformers also emerged in the 20th century. The DRAMATISTS' GUILD of America became a separate branch of the Authors' League of America (founded in 1912) in 1920. In the same year the Screen Writers Guild was formed. Designers affiliated in the United Scenic Artists (1918), the Association of Theatrical Press Agents and Managers was formed in 1928, and the Society of Stage Directors and Choreographers (SSDC) in 1959.

The most significant development of the past three decades, growing out of concerns following the 9/11 attacks, was the establishment in 2002 of the Coalition of Broadway Unions and Guilds (COBUG), comprising over 75,000 workers from 13 unions and guilds who work on Broadway. Its first test was a musician's strike in 2003 over the minimum size of pit orchestras for musicals and a threat of replacing live musicians with recorded music.   DMcD

Union Square Theatre Union Square South, between Broadway and 4th Ave., NYC. Sheridan Shook, the owner of the Union Place (later the Morton House) Hotel, installed a theatre within the hotel and opened it in 1871 as the Union Square Theatre. A year later, he entrusted it to A. M. PALMER. With no experience in theatrical management but with a passion for the theatre, Palmer succeeded in finding the right actors and in producing a succession of successful romantic melodramas to become a competitor of the nearby WALLACK'S. After he left the theatre in 1883, it passed to the management of J. M. Hill prior to its destruction by FIRE in 1888. Rebuilt, it was taken over by the KEITH–ALBEE chain for continuous VAUDEVILLE in 1893. During 1908–36 it served mainly as a moviehouse. When it was finally closed, the section of the theatre fronting 14th St. was rebuilt into shops; the rear section, however, was walled up and still stands.

A second Union Square on 17th St. (1926) was rescued by the ROUNDABOUT THEATRE COMPANY in the 1980s (before their move to Broadway) and in the 1990s renovated, reopening in 1994 as a 499-seat venue with *Vita & Virginia* (with Vanessa REDGRAVE and Eileen Atkins). Subsequent productions have include *London Suite*, WIT, *The LARAMIE PROJECT*, *Bat Boy the Musical*, and AVENUE Q.   MCH   DBW

United Booking Office With the Vaudeville Managers' Protective Association and the National

Vaudeville Artists, the dominant business force in Big Time VAUDEVILLE. Founded by B. F. KEITH and E. F. ALBEE in 1906 as a kind of clearinghouse that matched managers and performers and ultimately determined what acts could play the major circuits, the UBO created a virtual monopoly of first-class vaudeville. Despite opposition from numerous vaudevillians (and the White Rats, their fraternal organization; see UNIONS), attacks in the press, and even a Federal Trade Commission investigation for blacklisting, the UBO survived until the demise of vaudeville itself. DBW

United States Institute for Theatre Technology (USITT)

A nonprofit corporation founded in 1960 with the mission to promote actively the advancement of the knowledge and skills of its 3,600-plus members (in the U.S., Canada, and 40 other countries). USITT considers itself the association of design, production, and technology professionals in the performing arts and entertainment industry. Among its activities are the publication of *TD&T* (*Theatre Design & Technology*), a major annual conference and stage expo, presentation of awards, and development of industry standards. Its national office is in Syracuse, NY. DBW

Urban, Joseph

(1871–1933) Austrian American set designer. Many of the approaches and techniques adopted by ROBERT EDMOND JONES, LEE SIMONSON, and others were first introduced in America by Urban. In the 1890s in Vienna he designed palaces, exposition pavilions, and a bridge. In 1904 he began to work with the Vienna Burgtheater and spent the next years designing operas throughout Europe. Having come to the U.S. in 1912 to design for the BOSTON Opera, Urban was discovered by showman FLORENZ ZIEGFELD, who persuaded him to design for the *Follies*. His designs were simple in terms of line, but vibrant color created a sense of lushness and complexity. He achieved this by applying pointillist techniques – the juxtaposition of dots of color – to scene painting. This not only added new dimensions to painted scenery, but also allowed parts of the image to appear or disappear under different colored lights. He was also one of the first to use platforms and portals – arched scenic units at the side of the stage, connected at the top. This framed and focused the stage while providing continuous elements for unit sets. A study of his work by Carter and Cole appeared in 1992, and one by C. Innes (pairing him with NORMAN BEL GEDDES) in 2006. AA

Urinetown

Pithy musical with book by Greg Kotis, lyrics by Kotis and Mark Hollman, music by Hollman. Directed by JOHN RANDO; musical staging by John Carrafa. If metatheatrical musicals existed as the millennium began, this was its antecedent. First mounted in the 1999 New York International Fringe Festival, it is a self-styled "melodrama about a city in the midst of a drought so devastating that a malevolent corporation has been able to take control of all the toilet facilities." Amid plenty of "pay-to-pee" jokes, the work's satirical edge had an anodyne quality: the plot was a paean to saccharine American values and invoked BRECHT, celebrated absurdism, traded on irony, and satirized musical theatre, with visual cues from *WEST SIDE STORY*, *HELLO, DOLLY!*, and *LES MISÉRABLES*. With revisions and cast changes, *Urinetown* reopened first at the American Theatre of Actors on 1 April 2001 (with JOHN CULLUM as the robber baron Caldwell B. Cladwell and Spencer Kayden as 12-year-old Little Sally) and then at Broadway's HENRY MILLER'S THEATRE – for 965 performances – on 20 September, the first production to open following the 9/11 terrorist attacks. It won 3 of 10 Tony nominations – Best Direction (Musical), Original Score, and Book. Like the 2005 *The 25th Annual Putnam County Spelling Bee*, *Urinetown* epitomized the wink-at-the-audience musical trend. LJ

Uris Theatre see GERSHWIN THEATRE

Utah Shakespearean Festival

Founded in 1961 by Fred C. Adams (since 2005 executive producer emeritus) in partnership with Southern Utah University in Cedar City, the USF received the 2000 Regional Theatre Tony and a 2001 National Governors Association Award for Distinguished Service in the Arts. Although long a summer destination, USF is now a year-round operation with summer and fall seasons of 9–10 offerings (2006, four Shakespeare plays) in three venues: Adams Shakespearean Theatre dedicated in 1977 (Tudor inspired; open-air; c. 900 capacity); Randall L. Jones Theatre dedicated in 1989 (indoor facility, 769 seats); and The Auditorium Theatre, an older venue renovated in 2004 (853 seats) and used for some matinees and rained out Adams productions. Today, annual audiences total c. 150,000, and USF's budget is more than $6 million. DBW

V

Vagabond King, The Four-act operetta, music by RUDOLPH FRIML, words by Russell Janney and Brian Hooker; opened 21 September 1925 at the CASINO THEATRE, running 511 performances. Set in 15th-century France, this is the tale of vagabond poet François Villon (DENNIS KING), who, made king of France for a day, saves king and country from Burgundy and wins the heart of the noble Katherine (Carolyn Thomson). Second in popularity among Friml's works only to ROSE-MARIE (1924), it is quintessential old-fashioned, romantic operetta, brimming with stirring melodies that include rousing anthems, drinking songs, and waltzes (notably "Only a Rose"). A London production (1927) was equally popular.   JD

Vagina Monologues, The Originally a solo performance written and acted by Eve Ensler. It opened 3 October 1999 at the Westside Theater (after an OFF-OFF BROADWAY run in 1996 and an Obie) and ran for 1,381 performances. In reality this episodic collection of monologues, from serious to comic, poetic, and graphic – ever-evolving and updated – has now been seen in 76 countries and translated in 24 languages, performed yearly on V-Day (Valentine's Day; "Valentine, Vagina and Violence") usually as a benefit for rape crisis centers or other similar resources. Ensler wrote the first version based on 200 interviews with women about their views on sex, relationships, and violence against women; she sees the vagina as a tool of empowerment. Subsequent performances have utilized a varying number of women – from three to an actress for each monologue. Not always embraced, the monologues have been seen by some as antimale and critical of heterosexuality (a number of Catholic colleges have canceled performances). Ensler toured her next effort, *The Good Body* (examining why women worldwide alter themselves physically), during 2005–6.   DBW

Valdéz, Luis (1940–) Chicano director and playwright responsible for the CHICANO THEATRE revolution. University trained and a student activist at San José State in California, he visited Cuba before joining the SAN FRANCISCO MIME TROUPE in 1964. Knowledgeable about commedia dell'arte, Brecht, and pantoMIME, he used bilingual theatre to help César Chávez organize the migrant workers around Delano, CA, in 1965. His efforts led to the *actos,* one-act revolutionary pieces, and the creation of EL TEATRO CAMPESINO (Farmworkers' Theatre), which in turn inspired the formation of other Chicano theatre groups. His early titles include *Las dos caras del patronicito* (*The Boss's Two Faces*), *Quinta temporada* (*Fifth Season*), and *Soldado razo* (*Buck Private*). ZOOT SUIT (1978), based on the Sleepy Lagoon murder trial during WWII, dramatized the stereotypical *pachuco* in a successful run in LOS ANGELES (LA Drama Critics Award), but failed on Broadway. Valdéz's folk musical *Corridos,* based on Mexican folk ballads, opened in SAN FRANCISCO in 1983. His 1981 *Bandido!* (play with music about the notorious bandit/hero Tiburcio Vásquez) was coproduced in 1994 by El Teatro Campesino and the MARK TAPER. In the year 2000 Valdez directed his next play, *Mummified Deer,* about three generations of a Chicano and Yaqui family, produced at the SAN DIEGO REPERTORY THEATER. In 2005 he acted in and cowrote *Corridos Remix* with his son Kinán Valdéz, who directed the production at San Diego Rep. Valdéz also wrote and directed the film of *Zoot Suit* (1981) and *La Bamba* (1987), the story of 1950s Chicano rocker Richie Valens.   GW   JH

Vampire Lesbians of Sodom A campy comedy by CHARLES BUSCH satirizing Hollywood of the 1920s and contemporary Las Vegas, first produced at the Limbo Lounge in the East Village (NYC) before opening OFF-BROADWAY at the Provincetown Playhouse (19 June 1985) as part of a double bill with Busch's *Sleeping Beauty, or Coma*. A female impersonator, Busch appeared in both plays, which ran for a total of 2,024 performances (until 27 May 1990), attracting a cult following and making Busch a star.   TLM

Van Amburgh, Isaac A. (1811–65) "The Lion King" (also "Monarch of the Forest") and, though not the first American CIRCUS performer to enter a cage of big cats, considered the first modern wild

661

animal trainer – and, according to Joys, the first legendary performer in circus history (his name was used as a circus title as late as 1922). Van Amburgh, born in Fishkill, NY, began as an animal caretaker (cage boy), and in 1833 first appeared in a cage with wild animals. To counter religious prejudice against circuses, he quoted the Bible to justify his traveling menagerie. As a trainer, he reportedly combined cruelty with mesmerizing control (his eyes were apparently extraordinary). Between circus seasons he took theatrical roles, such as Constantius the Greek in *The Lion Lord,* and the Arab who rescues a princess thrown to his cats in *The Daughter of the Emir.*   DBW

Van Druten, John (1901–57) Playwright whose dramatic career began in London, though in New York he created his most successful work, which is characterized as witty, domestic comedy that usually reflects contemporary middle-class society. *The Voice of the Turtle* (1943), a romantic three-character, wartime comedy, ran for over 1,500 performances. Nostalgic I Remember Mama (1944) was adapted from a novel; the adaptation *I Am a Camera* (1951), which is more cynical in its portrait of Berlin, inspired the musical Cabaret (1966). *Bell, Book and Candle* (1950) is a clever play about a beautiful witch who must abjure her craft to secure the man she loves. An autobiography was published in 1938.   RHW

Van, Gus [né August Van Glone] (1888–1968) and **Joe (Joseph T.) Schenck** (1892?–1930) Vaudeville singing team; boyhood chums in Brooklyn (where they both worked as trolley car operators) and professional partners ("The Pennant Winning Battery of Songland") from 1910 when they entered vaudeville. Van, a baritone, specialized in dialect songs in Italian or Yiddish; Schenck played the piano and harmonized in his tenor voice. In addition to vaudeville, they appeared in *The Century Girl* (1916), Ziegfeld Follies (1919–21), and nightclubs. Their most famous song, Irving Berlin's "Mandy," was introduced in the 1919 *Follies.* After Schenck's death, Van continued as a successful solo act into the 1940s.   DBW

van Itallie, Jean-Claude (1936–) Playwright, director, producer, and teacher. Born in Brussels, Belgium, van Itallie became a naturalized American citizen in 1952. After studying at Harvard and the Neighborhood Playhouse, van Itallie made his debut as a writer in 1963 with *War* (Playwrights Unit, Vandam Theatre). His *Motel* and *Pavane* were produced at Café La MaMa in 1965, attracting considerable attention to him as a new

talent. In NYC, America Hurrah appeared at the Pocket Theatre in 1966, and *The Serpent* was produced by the Open Theatre in 1969. Other scripts include *The King of the United States* (1972, Theatre for the New City); *Mystery Play* (1973, Cherry Lane); his own versions of Chekhov's *The Seagull* (1973, McCarter), *The Cherry Orchard* (1977, New York Shakespeare Festival at the Vivian Beaumont), and *The Three Sisters* (1979, Rhinebeck, NY); a 1991 play about the effects of aids, *Ancient Boys* (La MaMa), that failed to receive critical acceptance; his dramatization of Bulgakov's novel *Master and Margarita* (1993, TNC); *War, Sex and Dreams* in 1999 (Café at La MaMa); and *Fear Itself: Secrets of the White House*, a cartoonish parody of the George W. Bush administration, staged in 2005 at Theater for the New City.

Van Itallie's affiliation with the Open Theatre and Joseph Chaikin placed him at the forefront of experimental dramaturgy in the 1960s and '70s. Especially with the Open Theatre, van Itallie merged European traditions with a poetic vision of the American experience. Since the 1970s van Itallie has owned a retreat in western Massachusetts (Shantigar), where courses in theatre, meditation, and healing are offered. His archive is at Kent State University.   SMA

Vandenhoff, George (1813–85) British-born actor and lawyer, son of the actor John Vandenhoff. After a debut at Covent Garden in 1839, George began his American career at the Park Theatre in 1842 as Hamlet. As an actor he was noted for his correctness, but he lacked power and apparently never liked the stage. After returning to England in 1853, where he and his new wife acted in the provinces, he retired from the stage in the mid-1850s. Although admitted to the New York Bar in 1858, he spent much of his time teaching elocution and giving public readings. In 1860 he published his reminiscences, *Leaves from an Actor's Notebook.*   DBW

Varieties (Gaiety) Theatre (New Orleans) The first Varieties Theatre, built in 1849 and leased to Thomas Placide, burned in 1854 (see fires). The second structure, built in 1855 on the site of the first, was called the Gaiety. Stock companies managed by Dion Boucicault, William Crisp, Placide (when the building was renamed the Varieties), and John Owens occupied the theatre until the Civil War closed it in 1861. Reopened in 1863, it burned in 1870. The Third Varieties, built in 1871 and renamed the Grand Opera House in 1881, featured touring attractions; it was razed in 1906.   WD

Variety American theatrical trade paper founded by Sime Silverman in 1905 as a weekly to cover all phases of show business. *Variety* has been characterized by its jargon (e.g., show biz, Hollywood pix, Broadway legit) and its financial assessment of the entertainment business. It incorporated *The NEW YORK CLIPPER* (1924), added a daily *Variety* published in Hollywood (1933), expanded international coverage, and in 1998 added a daily New York edition. Reviews, weekly grosses, attendance figures, and end-of-the-year statistics provide an accurate record of legitimate productions.   TLM

vaudeville This essentially American form of variety has nothing to do with the French *vaudeville,* a farce studded with songs set to popular tunes; rather, the term attempted to lend a veneer of elegance to what was originally rough-and-ready entertainment. A so-called vaudeville house had been opened by William Valentine in 1840, and H. J. Sargent's Great Vaudeville Co. was playing in Louisville in 1871, but the term did not catch on till later.

The usual venue for variety performances in the late 1860s was the concert saloon, its "waiter girls" and dancing girls closely allied to the prostitutes who preyed on the all-male audience. MINSTRELS and chorines, unemployed after the decline of the leg show, drifted into these "olio entertainments," as did newly formed doubles acts. Unlike European variety, where song was the standard unit, broad comedy and exuberant dance predominated here. This "honky tonk" style permutated into BURLESQUE, while respectable variety gained greater professionalism and urbanity during 1876–93 to become vaudeville.

TONY PASTOR, hoping to lure a family audience with giveaways and promises of clean amusement, was instrumental in this development, and the traditional, if debatable, date given for the birth of vaudeville is the opening of his 14th Street Theatre, New York, on 24 October 1881. The innovation was enlarged and expanded by BENJAMIN FRANKLIN KEITH and his associate EDWARD F. ALBEE. Keith began with a "store-show," the Gaiety Museum, BOSTON, and had Albee transform it in 1885 into a Japanese tea garden offering a tabloid opera. So great was their success that they soon owned several theatres, and in 1894 opened the first exclusively vaudeville house, B. F. Keith's New Theatre, typical of the opulent palaces designed to lure the middle-class spectator into a fairy-tale world of luxury. Keith and Albee eliminated offensive material, fined offenders, and introduced the continuous show, so that one could enter the theatre at any time between 9:30 A.M. and 10:30 P.M. and see a performance. The invention of "continuous vaudeville," well ensconced by 1896, is also attributed to F. F. PROCTOR, a sometime partner, who claimed "to give the masses what they want," but forbade smoking and drinking in the auditorium.

Competing with these robber barons were Martin Beck, credited with establishing the touring vaudeville company, who backed "class acts" to educate the public; OSCAR HAMMERSTEIN I, who aimed his Roof at an elitist and his Olympic at a more popular public; WILLIAM MORRIS, J. J. Murdoch, and Sylvester Poli. The Keith–Albee circuit dominated the eastern U.S. through its many theatres (over 400 by 1920) and booking offices; Beck's ORPHEUM THEATRE CIRCUIT played the West, though he also built the New York PALACE, which soon was regarded as vaudeville's Valhalla. In addition, there were thousands of small houses scattered throughout the nation, enabling performers to play one-night stands during the season. Vaudevillians became a nomadic race, living much of the year on railway carriages and platforms and in dreary boardinghouses.

By 1900 the typical "polite vaudeville" bill had grown formulaic, and was divided into two parts by an intermission. The first part would open with a "dumb act," animals or acrobats, whose effect would not be damaged by a noisy entering audience. The number three slot was intended to wake up the house, the number four to deliver the first solid punch, and the last before the interval a knockout that would bring them back wanting more. The prime position was "next to closing," where the "headliner" or star of stars appeared. The concluding act was meant as a "chaser," often a cinematic offering, like a newsreel. Turns or "numbers" seldom lasted more than 10–20 minutes, although some popular egoists like the Scot HARRY LAUDER and AL JOLSON might usurp a whole hour. According to GEORGE BURNS, a performer needed only 17 good minutes, which he could play year in, year out across the country, until the act became too pirated or shopworn for use. The diversity of performance was considerable: In addition to the song-and-dance and comedy acts, there were MIMES, ventriloquists, eccentrics, musical virtuosi, acrobats and jugglers, FEMALE AND MALE IMPERSONATORS, miniature musicals, monologuists, trained animals, conjurers, demonstrations of new inventions, and even famous criminals discoursing on their lurid pasts.

Much of the comedy in vaudeville dealt in racial stereotypes, with the Dutch, Irish, Jewish, blackface, Swedish, and Italian comics the most familiar, reflecting the melting-pot nature of urban

American society; by 1910 many of the older types, including the hick and Bowery tough, were passé. Low comedy was categorized as "jazz," a fast routine to speed up an act, or "hokum," crude fun verging on vulgarity. Despite the efforts of the managers, innuendo was often resorted to, particularly in the 1920s, when more sophisticated audiences expected it.

Dance tended to be acrobatic until WWI, when adagio and exhibition ballroom dancing and even imitations of the Ballets Russes arrived. Singers were either sentimental or strenuous, but American audiences – unless exhorted by such devices as "following the bouncing ball" on a projected songsheet – seldom joined in the chorus, another token of the heterogeneity of the public. Among the leading performers spawned by vaudeville or trained in its excellent school were Eva Tanguay, the "I Don't Care" Girl; Elsie Janis; Nora Bayes; W. C. Fields, who moved from juggling to comic skits; Eddie Cantor and Al Jolson, who retained the corked face of minstrelsy, as did black comedian Bert Williams; George M. Cohan, whose family had been variety pioneers; Will Rogers, with his low-keyed commentary; and George Burns and Gracie Allen, whose doubles act refined the Dumb Dora creation of Ryan and Lee. As vaudeville increased in respectability and popularity, stars of the "legit," like Lillie Langtry, Ethel Barrymore (see Drew–Barrymore), and Alla Nazimova, played "tab" (shortened) versions of their dramatic hits on the circuits.

The American language was enriched by vaudeville slang: a success was a "wow," a "panic," or a "riot"; a failure a "flop," "all wet," or "all washed up." Duffey and Sweeney originated the phrase, "We died in . . ." to indicate an utter fiasco. The minstrel Billy Emerson's "hoofer" for dancer became popular, along with the injunction "Strut your stuff" and the exit "Shuffle off to Buffalo." Some terms were too technical to become widespread, such as "grouch bag" for a purse pinned to the underwear for safety's sake, "feeder" for "straight man," "split time" for three days' work in any theatre, or "death trail" for a circuit of small towns; but "coffin nails" for cigarettes, which came from Junie McCree's act, and "belly laughs," coined by Jack Conway, did enter the language.

Vaudeville was the dominant form of American entertainment by 1890, and grew exponentially: In 1896 New York had seven vaudeville theatres; by 1910, 22. It came to be clearly differentiated into the Big Time, with its two-a-day offerings of an eight- or nine-act bill, and the Small Time, with fewer acts and a film played continuously. The empire building of the leading managements created booking agencies that could blacklist performers who did not conform to the rules or who failed to kick back percentages of their salaries (often levies were imposed by the house manager before the salary was paid). Keith–Albee in 1906 created the United Booking Office (UBO), whose impositions were so outrageous that the performers banded into a protest society, the White Rats, which failed to sustain its strike in 1917 (see unions). Astutely, Albee backed a new organization, the National Vaudeville Artists (NVA), in 1916, which ameliorated some of the abuses without seriously harming the managers' interests.

African American performers were exploited by the Theatre Owner's Booking Association or Chitlin Circuit – a busy group of segregated theatres stretching from New York to Florida, Chicago to New Orleans, but primarily centered in the South – that offered black vaudevillians low pay and little future. A re-creation of black vaudeville set in 1931 (Rollin' on the T.O.B.A.) was seen Off-Off Broadway early in 1999.

The decline of vaudeville is attributable to a number of factors. Between 1905 and 1912, the Big Time had grown in sophistication, putting its emphasis on glamour, novelty, and lavish wardrobes; the influence of the musical comedy and revue could be felt. Before 1925, it reached its period of greatest growth, but the cinema proved a powerful rival for lower-class audiences made uncomfortable by vaudeville's aspirations to gentility and its increased admission prices (the Palace went as high as $2). The automobile, put within everyone's financial reach by Henry Ford, enabled city dwellers to escape to the country. During Prohibition, the proliferation of nightclubs offered a sophisticated and alcoholic alternative to those bored by vaudeville's stale material. By the mid-1920s many vaudeville houses were converted to cinemas, and the succumbing of the Palace in 1932, its coup de grâce delivered by the Depression, is considered the symbolic terminus of the form. Some managers like Marcus Loew persisted in alternating films with live performance at their houses, but gradually vaudeville came to be regarded as the seedbed for mass media: Many of the most popular comedians, singers, and dancers in the movies, on the radio and, later, television had honed their skills in vaudeville.   LS

Vaughan, Stuart (John Walker) (1925–) Director, actor, and playwright. Vaughan created lucid productions of the classics in nonprofit regional and New York theatres from the early 1950s until late '80s. He served as artistic director of the NEW YORK SHAKESPEARE FESTIVAL (1956–8), Phoenix Theatre (1958–63) (see ASSOCIATION OF PRODUCING ARTISTS), and SEATTLE REPERTORY THEATRE (1963–6). He was founder and producer-director of the Repertory Theatre of New Orleans (1966–9). His *Two Gentlemen of Verona* for the NYSF (1987–8) was praised for being sexy and funny. In 2000 he directed for the New Jersey Repertory Company. He is the author of *A Possible Theatre* (1969), a record of his regional-theatre experiences.   TLM

Verdon, Gwen (1925–2000) Dancer, singer, and actress. Considered to have been the finest musical-comedy dancer of the 1950s, Verdon studied with choreographer JACK COLE and assisted him with the choreography for *Magdalena* (1948) and *Alive and Kicking* (1950), making her Broadway debut as a dancer in the latter. Given a supporting role in CAN-CAN (1953), Verdon stole the show with her exuberant dancing and her impish clowning. Following her success as the seductive Lola in DAMN YANKEES (1955), Verdon surprised critics and audiences with her poignant acting in *New Girl in Town* (1957), a musical version of O'NEILL's ANNA CHRISTIE. She next appeared in *Redhead*, a vehicle written especially for her. In 1966 she created the role of Charity Hope Valentine in SWEET CHARITY, which was choreographed and directed by her then-husband, BOB FOSSE. Despite reservations about the show's libretto, critics praised Verdon's performance for its innocence and vulnerability. Verdon's only musical of the 1970s was the tawdry, flamboyant CHICAGO (1975, as Roxie Hart), in which she was again directed by Fosse. In all of her musicals, Verdon's sinuous, energetic style of dance ideally suited the jazz choreography created for her by Cole and Fosse. She received the 1993 New Dramatists' Lifetime Achievement Award.   MK

Vermont Stage Company Founded in 1994 by Blake Robison in Burlington, that city's first ACTORS' EQUITY operation in a decade. Beginning as an itinerant company, in 1996 it became the resident theatre company at the University of Vermont, with Mark Nash as artistic director since 2000. Performing in the 150-seat black box FlynnSpace September–May, VSC offers five productions a year, from classics to new work.   DBW

Vernon, Dai [né David Frederick Wingfield Verner] (1894–1992) Termed by conjuror-magic historian and card sleights successor RICKY JAY "the

most influential, compelling, and venerable figure" in the art of sleight-of-hand and a "magician's magican," Canadian-born Vernon, known throughout the world as "The Professor," was arguably the greatest card expert who ever lived, an unrivaled close-up performer (though he began as a stage magician), and the most influential individual in modern MAGIC. His numerous books (several with Lewis Ganson) are among the best in the field, especially for card manipulation. His biography by Karl Johnson was published in 2005.   DBW

Very Good Eddie Two-act musical comedy, music by JEROME KERN, lyrics by Schuyler Green, book by Philip Bartholomae and GUY BOLTON; opened 23 December 1915 at the PRINCESS THEATRE, running 341 performances. The second of the innovative "Princess Musicals" of Kern, Bolton, and (later) P. G. WODEHOUSE, this tale of embarrassingly mismatched couples on a Hudson River cruise was the first big hit of the series. Small in scope, simple in story, and substituting charm for gaudiness, it became a standard for its diminutive successors. A 1975 "revival" at the GOODSPEED OPERA HOUSE – revised, with numerous songs from other early Kern musicals added – moved to Broadway on 21 December 1975, running 304 performances.   JD

Victory Gardens Theater Theatre founded by a group of eight CHICAGO theatre artists in 1974 that has been led by Dennis Zacek and Marcelle McVay for virtually all of its existence. Unlike more famous Chicago theatres, Victory Gardens has not sent many productions on to commercial success. However, it has excelled as a creative center for playwrights and actors of various ethnic backgrounds: The Latino Chicago company began as a Victory Gardens project. In recognition of its contributions it was awarded the 2001 Regional Theatre Tony. Among the playwrights who have worked there are Jeffrey Sweet, Alan Gross, Charles Smith, Rick Cleveland, Claudia Allen, Darrah Cloud, Steve Carter, Dean Corrin, Nicholas Patricca, and Lonnie Carter. There is currently a $9.5 million capital campaign in progress to purchase and renovate the historic Biograph Theatre.   SF

Vidal, Gore (1925–) The prolific author of novels *Myra Breckinridge* (1968), *Burr* (1973), and *Lincoln* (1984) has been successful in the theatre with *Visit to a Small Planet* (1957), a comedy about an invasion from outer space, and *The Best Man* (1960), a drama about political infighting over the nomination for president. The latter was revived in 2000 as *Gore Vidal's The Best Man*. Other plays include *On the March to the Sea* (1961; revised 2005, Theater Previews at Duke), *Weekend* (1968), and *An Evening with Richard Nixon and . . .* (1972).   TLM

Viertel, Jack (1948–) and **Thomas** (1942–). Jack has been creative director of JUJAMCYN THEATERS since 1987, his primary job being to create and identify new projects for the company's five Broadway venues; in that capacity he has worked on such productions as *Grey Gardens, Jersey Boys, The PRODUCERS, The FULL MONTY, PROOF, ANGELS IN AMERICA, JELLY'S LAST JAM,* and the plays of AUGUST WILSON. He also conceived and coproduced the long-running REVUE *Smokey Joe's Café* (1995). In 2001 he was named artistic director of CITY CENTER'S ENCORES!, for whom he has also served as dramaturge. In 2001 he also coauthored the unsuccessful musical *Time and Again* (MANHATTAN THEATRE CLUB). Before moving to NYC, Jack was a dramaturge at the MARK TAPER FORUM for two years and theatre critic for the *Los Angeles Herald Examiner.*

Thomas (Tom), a real-estate executive, has also been a producer for 20 years with the Viertel Baruch Routh Frankel Group. Their coproduced revival of *SWEENEY TODD* did the almost impossible in March 2006 – that is, it recouped its initial $3.5 million investment in 19 weeks. (It is rare for a SONDHEIM show to ever recoup its investment on Broadway.) Considered a tough negotiator with a good business sense, Tom has also been on the Board of Governors of the LEAGUE OF AMERICAN THEATRES AND PRODUCERS and Chairman of the Board of the EUGENE O'NEILL MEMORIAL THEATER CENTER. The brothers both attended Harvard and frequently collaborate in producing. (Tom was a producer of *Smokey Joe's.*)   DBW

View from the Bridge, A by ARTHUR MILLER opened, in its original one-act form, in NYC on 29 September 1955, running for 149 performances. Martin Ritt directed a cast including Van Heflin, J. Carrol Naish, EILEEN HECKART, and Gloria Marlowe. A more successful two-act version opened in London in 1956, and an OFF-BROADWAY revival in 1965 with Robert Duvall ran for 780 performances. Michael Gambon's Eddie won accolades in a 1987 London revival; a 1995 British revival was less successful; and a 1997 ROUNDABOUT revival with Anthony LaPaglia and Allison Janney was acclaimed. Set on the Brooklyn waterfront, the play depicts longshoreman Eddie Carbone's too-intense love for his niece, Catherine, which causes him to violate the code of the Sicilian com-

munity by informing on the illegal immigrant she wants to marry. As narrator Alfieri points out, the play has the primal elements of classical tragedy in the seemingly inevitable course of events that leads to Eddie's destruction.   BCM

Vineyard Theatre Major OFF-BROADWAY non-profit, hard by Union Square, largely devoted to new plays and musicals with a cutting-edge bent. Founded by Barbara Zinn Kreiger in 1981, the Vineyard's main reputation is for being a "chamber company," doggedly championing a small band of selected artists: playwrights (eight NICKY SILVER plays, six directed by David Warren); composers (four Polly Pen musicals, including *Christina Alberta's Father,* 1994, and *Goblin Market,* 1985); and directors (six from MARK BROKAW, including CRAIG LUCAS's *The Dying Gaul* and PAULA VOGEL's *How I Learned to Drive* and *The Long Christmas Ride Home*). The Vineyard also has a reputation for picking works of high artistic integrity, from the musical *AVENUE Q,* which moved to Broadway, to EDWARD ALBEE's Pulitzer Prize–winning *Three Tall Women* (1994) and Becky Mode's *Fully Committed* (1999), all of which enjoyed commercial and popular success. Long led by artistic director (and Hollywood casting director) Douglas Aibel, the Vineyard has a two-venue site, featuring a mainstage and lab space for maximum flexibility.   LJ

Virginia Theatre 245 West 52d St., NYC [Architect: C. Howard Crane]. In 1925, with a good deal of ceremony, the THEATRE GUILD opened its new house, the Guild, which was intended for its own productions. For a number of reasons relating to the design of the theatre and the paucity of seats (fewer than 1,000), it proved to be unpopular with actors and audiences; the Theatre Guild turned to other theatres for its most significant productions while leasing the Guild to other producers. During 1943–50 it was rented as a radio playhouse, then sold to the AMERICAN NATIONAL THEATRE AND ACADEMY to be operated by its board as a not-for-profit "home for the living arts." After extensive renovation, the newly named ANTA Playhouse was only intermittently used for ANTA-sponsored productions and more often leased to commercial producers. In 1981, JUJAMCYN Theaters bought it from the ANTA board, renovated it, increased its seating, and renamed it the Virginia, after the wife of the owner, James Binger. Following a $2.2 million renovation in 1994–5, it reopened spring 1995 with *Smokey Joe's Cafe.* On 16 October 2005, 14 days after the playwright's death, it was renamed the AUGUST WILSON Theatre, with the musical *Jersey Boys* its first occupant under its new name.   MCH

Vivian Beaumont and Mitzi E. Newhouse Theatres Lincoln Center, NYC [Architects: Eero Saarinen with Jo MIELZINER]. Part of the Lincoln Center for the Performing Arts (known collectively as Lincoln Center Theater), this repertory theatre and its experimental appendage began under the aegis of ELIA KAZAN and ROBERT WHITEHEAD, who spent two years planning it. Named after Mrs. Vivian Beaumont Allen, its benefactress, the larger theatre opened in 1965. The playhouse was designed with 11,000 sq. ft. of stage space (compared to the 3,000 of the MARTIN BECK THEATRE on Broadway) and was intended to shift from a proscenium to a thrust stage and to be able to store scenery for the repertory. All of the mechanical and electrical elements are concealed, and the auditorium, designed for a flexible 1,090–1,140 seats (now 1,050), is gently amphitheatrical. The smaller stage (originally called the Forum), with its 299 seats, was designed with all its structural, mechanical, and electrical equipment exposed and was intended for experimental productions. Kazan and Whitehead resigned and were replaced by HERBERT BLAU and Jules Irving in the first year, then by Irving alone in 1967. He was succeeded by JOSEPH PAPP (1973–7), who obtained operating funds from Mrs. Mitzi E. Newhouse, after whom he renamed the Forum. After Papp's departure, for a time the theatres were reopened only intermittently, as the Lincoln Center management struggled to find both a purpose for them and new creative leaders; finally, in 1985, GREGORY MOSHER of Chicago's GOODMAN THEATRE and Bernard Gersten, a Broadway and OFF-BROADWAY producer, began their leadership under the aegis of Lincoln Center for the Performing Arts, Inc. In 1992 Mosher was succeeded by André Bishop, artistic director for a decade of PLAYWRIGHTS HORIZONS, who in turn appointed the late GERALD GUTIERREZ and Nicholas Hytner as associate directors in 1994–5; as of 2005, in addition to Hytner, this group includes GRACIELA DANIELE, SUSAN STROMAN, and DANIEL SULLIVAN. Major renovations were undertaken in 1996; more are expected in the near future, including the addition of a black-box space with fewer than 100 seats. A major coup was the Rodgers and Hammerstein Organization giving Lincoln Center the rights for a Broadway revival of *SOUTH PACIFIC*, projected for the 2007–8 season.   MCH

Vogel, Paula (1951–) Raised in the Washington, DC, area; educated at Catholic University and Cornell. Vogel is the author of *How I LEARNED TO DRIVE,* which premiered in 1997 at the VINEYARD's Century Center (1998 Pulitzer), and of the Obie Award–winning *The Baltimore Waltz* (1992, CIRCLE REP), a play inspired by her brother's death from AIDS (termed Acquired Toilet Disease in this three-person satiric comic drama). A feminist/lesbian writer with a balanced point of view, yet one that incorporates stringent commentary, Vogel has written works that focus on such contemporary topics as the nontraditional family, domestic violence, and gender issues. Among her other produced plays are *Desdemona* (1978, Lexington, NY; 1993, Circle Rep); *The Oldest Profession* (1981, OFF-OFF), *And Baby Makes Seven* (1986, THEATRE RHINOCEROS), *Hot 'n' Throbbing* (1993, AMERICAN REPERTORY), *The Mineola Twins* (1996, PERSEVERANCE), and *The Long Christmas Ride Home*, the latter premiering at TRINITY REP in 2003 before its NYC production at the Vineyard (directed by MARK BROKAW). Recipient of numerous awards and prizes (including a 1995 Guggenheim Fellowship), Vogel directs a graduate playwriting program at Brown (since 1985) where, as of 2002, she has been the inaugural Adele Kellenberg Seaver '49 Professor in Literary Arts. Vogel is an inspired teacher/mentor and is in great demand for master classes and workshops.   DBW

Vollmer, Lula (or Lulu) (1895–1955) Folk dramatist who portrayed strong, righteous North Carolina mountain women. *SUN-UP* (1923) ran for two years and received praise for its presentation of the Widow Cagle, caught between the law and her own beliefs. Vollmer followed *Sun-up* with lesser hits such as *The Shame Woman* (1923) and *The Dunce Boy* (1925).   FB

vonMayrhauser, Jennifer (1948–) Costume designer most closely identified with the CIRCLE REPERTORY COMPANY, where she designed several dozen shows. Broadway credits include *Da* (1978), *TALLEY'S FOLLY, Steaming* (1982), and *The HEIDI CHRONICLES.* She has also designed for television (since 1994 for *Law & Order*). Though associated with modern-dress productions, she is equally adept at period costumes. In 1995 she received an Obie honoring the body of her work. In 2006 she did costumes for LINDSAY-ABAIRE's acclaimed *Rabbit Hole* (MANHATTAN THEATRE CLUB). She teaches at Brandeis University.   AA

W

Wagenhals, Lincoln A. (1869–1931) and **Colin Kemper** (1870–1955) Producers and managers. Beginning their partnership in 1893 as managers of Stone Opera House in Binghamton, NY, Wagenhals and Kemper had arrived on Broadway by 1906, when they leased the new Astor Theatre. They established themselves as producers with the success of EUGENE WALTER's PAID IN FULL (1908). Other hits include MARY ROBERTS RINEHART and AVERY HOPGOOD's Seven Days (1909) and The BAT (1920), the latter running 867 performances. They managed the careers of major stars, including FREDERICK WARDE, MODJESKA, HENRY MILLER, Blanche Walsh, and ANNIE RUSSELL. Their last production was The Joker (1925).   TLM

Wagner, Robin (1933–) Set designer who has been associated with some of the most successful musicals of the post-1960 period, including HAIR (1968, 1977 revival), A CHORUS LINE (1975, 2006 revival), Dreamgirls (1981, 1987 revival), CITY OF ANGELS (1989; Tony), JELLY'S LAST JAM (1992; Tony nomination), and The PRODUCERS (2001; Tony). Wagner began his career in SAN FRANCISCO and worked with the Actor's Workshop, where he was greatly influenced by director HERBERT BLAU and BRECHTian aesthetics. His work at the ARENA STAGE in the mid-1960s led to explorations of stage space and moving scenery. Although he is generally associated with spectacular sets, moving scenery, and stylish decor, his sets by and large are minimal; it is the way in which they move and are integrated into the production that gives the illusion of a great deal of scenery, as in the 1993 ANGELS IN AMERICA. His best-known set was for A Chorus Line: For most of the show it consisted only of a white line on the floor; in the final scene the upstage wall revealed Mylar mirrors. This seemingly simple set was resulted from over a year of stripping away excess and unnecessary scenic elements to arrive at a design that simply and boldly expressed the essence of the play. Wagner has never followed tradition or conventions; he has always explored new ideas, new materials, and new configurations of space. In addition to Broadway he has also designed for opera, dance, and rock concerts. He is on the theatre faculty at Columbia, and was recently inducted into the THEATRE HALL OF FAME.   AA

Wainwright, Marie (1853–1923) Philadelphia-born actress, daughter of a commodore; educated abroad, including three years of dramatic-arts studies in Paris. She made her 1877 debut at BOOTH'S THEATRE as one of five Juliets appearing in a benefit for George Rignold. She was the first American to play Josephine in GILBERT AND SULLIVAN's HMS Pinafore. After touring for five years with LAWRENCE BARRETT, with London performances in 1884, she formed her own company. Other highlights of a career that ranged from VAUDEVILLE to Shakespeare were her 1886 tour as leading lady in the EDWIN BOOTH–Salvini company and performances opposite WILLIAM GILLETTE (e.g., 1910 SHERLOCK HOLMES revival).   FHL

Waiting for Lefty Developed by CLIFFORD ODETS and others in the GROUP THEATRE (yet finished by Odets alone), this one-act play presents, in a series of vignettes, the events leading up to a taxi strike. Codirected by Odets and SANFORD MEISNER, it was first performed at the CIVIC REPERTORY Theatre on 6 January 1935 as part of a Sunday benefit organized by the League of Workers Theatres for the New Theatre Magazine. Immediately it became the historical highlight of the 1930s theatre, the quintessential piece of proletarian drama and agitprop theatre. The audience, in response to calls for action from the stage, erupted with chants of "Strike! Strike!" The Group Theatre soon moved it to Broadway (26 March, LONGACRE), where it ran for almost 200 performances. In that same year, dozens of productions were mounted across the country. The play launched Odets as a playwright and was decisive in convincing the Group Theatre to produce another of Odets's plays, AWAKE AND SING! (which actually had been drafted before Lefty). Though clearly of its era, the play has been revived occasionally, including a ROUNDABOUT THEATRE production in 1967 and a 1996 OFF-BROADWAY staging by Joanne Woodward.   TP

Odet's *Waiting for Lefty,* 1935, with Elia Kazan seen at center, both arms raised. Photo by Vandamm. *Courtesy:* Museum of the City of New York.

Walcot, Charles Melton, Sr. (1815–68) Actor and playwright. Coming to America in 1839, Walcot became associated with William MITCHELL'S OLYMPIC in New York as a superb comic actor and prolific playwright (*Fried Shots*, 1843, a burlesque of Weber's opera *Der Freischütz*; *Brittania and Hibernia*, 1849). In JOHN BROUGHAM'S PO-CA-HON-TAS (1855) – he as Captain John Smith, Brougham as Powhatan – these two "brainy men" brought new heights to burlesque acting. At WALLACK'S THEATRE (1853–61) Walcot also did some of his best writing with *Hiawatha; or, Ardent Spirits and Laughing Water* (1856), a burlesque, loaded with local allusions, that appeared soon after the publication of Longfellow's poem.   WJM

Walken, Christopher (1943–) NYC–born actor who alternates his career among stage, film, and television. Since his Broadway debut at 16 in J.B., he has appeared in more than 100 stage productions (in 1991 as Iago in *Othello* for the NEW YORK SHAKESPEARE FESTIVAL) and more than 90 films (including a 1979 Best Supporting Actor Oscar as a suicidal soldier in *The Deer Hunter*). Known as a sensitive, often understated actor, Walken won an Obie in *Kid Champion* (1975) and a Theatre World Award for his role of Jack Hunter in the City Center revival of *Rose Tattoo* (1966). His play, *HIM*, which he also starred in, received a cool reception at the NYSF winter 1995. Recent stage credits include Sorin in *The Seagull* (2001, NYSF) with MERYL STREEP and KEVIN KLINE, and *James Joyce's The Dead* (1999)   DBW

Walker, George see WILLIAMS, BERT

Wallace, Naomi (1960–) Poet and playwright from Prospect, KY, whose work has often been described as "strong but political" – yet in the 1990s she was especially successful abroad, and in England was praised for her blend of politics and sexuality combined with a lyricism. Her best-known play, *One Flea Spare*, set in 1665 London during the plague, was first seen at London's Bush Theatre in 1995 (1996, Humana Festival; 1997, PUBLIC THEATER, Obie, Best Play). Her adaptation of William Wharton's *Birdy* played the West End in 1997 (2003, WOMEN'S PROJECT). Other plays include *In the Heart of America*, *Slaughter City*, *The Trestle at Pope Lick Creek* (1999, NEW YORK THEATRE WORKSHOP). *The Girl Who Fell through a Hole in Her Jumper* (with Bruce McLeod), *The War Boys*, *The Inland Sea*. Her film writing includes *Lawn Dogs* and a screenplay for *The War Boys* (with McLeod). In 1999 she received a MacArthur "genius" Fellowship.   DBW

Wallach, Eli (1915–) and **Anne Jackson** (1926–) Brooklyn-born Wallach made his NYC debut as the crew chief in *Skydrift* (1945). He won stardom as Alvaro Mangiacavallo, a sexually driven truck driver, in TENNESSEE WILLIAMS's *The Rose Tattoo* (1951). Both Wallach and his wife, Anne Jackson, had substantial successes before their marriage in 1948, but they were acclaimed as an acting duo in *The Typists/The Tiger* OFF-BROADWAY in 1963. Jackson made her professional debut in a touring production of *The Cherry Orchard,* later appearing with EVA LE GALLIENNE's AMERICAN REPERTORY THEATRE in 1946. Jackson and Wallach appeared together on Broadway in *Luv* (1964), a revival of *The Waltz of the Toreadors* (1973), *Twice around the Park* (1982), and a revival of *The Flowering Peach* (1994), among others. Additional Off-Broadway joint appearances include *The Diary of Anne Frank* (1978) and as costars of Anne Meara's *Down the Garden Paths* (2000). Both have appeared in numerous films and television programs, though Wallach has been more prolific as a film actor, beginning with *Baby Doll* in 1956. They have done several films together, such as *Nasty Habits* (1977).

Both members of the team use an internal intensity (they studied at the ACTORS STUDIO) suitable for drama or comedy. Of them in *Luv,* critics said "Miss Jackson can play comedy as straightfaced and doggedly as if she were mining coal, but she turns up diamonds" and "Mr. Wallach has a flair for enduring indignities, whether of poverty or affluence, marriage or divorce." In 1993 they appeared in a compilation of scenes and reminiscences (NJ). Eli's autobiography was published in 2005. SMA

Wallack family A dynasty of actor-managers, of English origin, in the American theatre, inseparably linked with the history of the New York stage for over 50 years. **Henry John Wallack** (1790–1870) – the eldest son of William H. Wallack (1760–1850) and Elizabeth Field (Granger) (d. 1850), popular performers at London's Astley's Amphitheatre and later at the Surrey – came to the U.S. in 1819 with his first wife, dancer Fanny Jones. After lengthy stays in Baltimore, Philadelphia, and Washington, DC, Wallack made his NYC debut at the Anthony Street Theatre in 1821; in 1824 he became leading man at the CHATHAM THEATRE. During 1828–32, 1834–6, and during the summer of 1840 and for some time afterward, he was back in England, acting sporadically. In 1837 he was stage manager, under his brother, at the National Theatre. He gained considerable acclaim for his Sir Peter Teazle in 1847 at New York's BROADWAY THEATRE. One of his last roles was Falstaff in 1858.

Though a versatile and accomplished actor, Henry did not win the fame of other family members in the U.S. Two of his sisters were actors – Mary (Mrs. Stanley) and Elizabeth (Mrs. Pincott), mother of the actress Leonora, later known as Mrs. Alfred Wigan – as was his brother, **James William Wallack** (?1795–1864), known as the Elder to distinguish him from his nephew. This Wallack, also born in England, appeared first in the U.S. at the PARK THEATRE as Macbeth in 1818. For the next 35 years he shuttled between the U.S. and England, though he was best known on the American stage. The most distinguished member of this notable family, he was admired for roles in tragedy and comedy, especially the latter. Though most historians categorize him as a member of the Kemble school, JAMES E. MURDOCH called him "the first romantic actor of America." An exceedingly handsome actor, his Shylock and his Jaques in *As You Like It* were considered innovative. During 1837–9 he managed New York's National Theatre; after its destruction by FIRE, he managed NIBLO's Garden for a time. In 1851 he settled permanently in New York City, assuming control the following year of BROUGHAM's Broadway Lyceum, as WALLACK's; for nine years this theatre prospered. For almost 35 years his company was the leading American ensemble, first under his leadership and later under his son, Lester. In 1861 he built the second Wallack's on Broadway at 13th St.

James's nephew, **James William Wallack Jr.** (1818–73), son of Henry and born in London, became a credible actor in tragedy. More than any other member of the family, he spent most of his career away from New York, spreading the Wallack name to all the major American theatrical centers, and retiring in 1872.

Next to James the Elder, **Lester Wallack** (John Johnstone) (1820–88), his son, made the dynasty's greatest contribution to the American stage. The only major member of the family born in the U.S., he nonetheless served his apprenticeship in England and Ireland, making his American debut in 1847 at the Broadway Theatre as Sir Charles Coldstream in *Used Up.* During his career with the Wallack company he played nearly 300 roles, excelling as Benedick, Charles Surface, Sir Andrew Aguecheek. and Sir Elliott Grey in his own adaptation of *Rosedale* (1863). Lester stage-managed for his father at Wallack's Lyceum, and became the manager of the second Wallack's until 1882, when he opened a third one, where he remained until 1887. Although Lester did little to encourage American works, depending heavily on an English repertoire, he was a highly honored member of the profession until his death. His important memoirs were published posthumously in 1889. A brief biography of James William appeared in 1865. DBW

Wallack's Theatre Broadway and 13th St., NYC [Architect: John M. Trimble]. Although the playhouse on 13th St. was the most famous of the theatres bearing the name of Wallack, there were actually three theatres associated with that family. The first was built by JOHN BROUGHAM in 1850 at 485 Broadway, but passed to JAMES W. WALLACK two years later and was operated by him as Wallack's Lyceum for nine years. In 1861, a new Wallack's went up in the theatre district forming around Union Square and was managed by LESTER WALLACK, who was its principal star for many years. For nearly 20 years, it dispensed impeccably cast English plays with a company of mainly English actors to an elitist audience. Following a trend, Wallack relocated his company to a third theatre at the northeast corner of Broadway and 30th St., but fortune did not follow him. In ill health and faced with an indifferent theatrical public, he retired in 1887. A year later, Wallack died and the house was leased to A. M. PALMER, who changed the name to Palmer's; it reverted to its original name in 1896. All three theatres were torn down: the first in 1869; the second, which was renamed the STAR THEATRE and continued to be leased to producers, in 1901; and the third in 1915. MCH

Waller, Emma (1820–99) British-born actress who married American actor Daniel Wilmarth Waller in 1849 and came with him to the U.S. in 1851. Her earliest known performance was in 1855 on tour in Australia, followed by a London debut in 1856. For her American debut in 1857 at the WALNUT STREET THEATRE in Philadelphia, she appeared on successive nights as Ophelia to Mr. Waller's Hamlet, Pauline in *The Lady of Lyons*, and Lady Macbeth, the latter performed with an "almost painful" intensity of passion. Fullness of characterization and a stately presence were her strengths in roles like Queen Margaret, Queen Katharine, and Meg Merrilies in *Guy Mannering* (1869). She also achieved a succès d'estime as Iago in the 1860s and '70s. She and her husband frequently performed together, from her 1858 New York debut as Marina in *The Duchess of Malfi* (R. H. Horne's adaptation) until her retirement in 1878.
FHL DJW

Walnut Street Theatre 9th and Walnut, PHILADELPHIA. Miraculously eluding the American penchant for tearing down the old and building up the new, the Walnut Street survives today as the oldest functioning playhouse in America. It was opened in 1809 as a domed arena for the Pepin and Breschard CIRCUS, but in 1811 came the first of a string of renovations to transform it into a workable theatre. It was enlarged, fitted with a stage and orchestra pit, and renamed the Olympic. In 1820, the dome was removed and the name changed to the Walnut Street, and it briefly housed a company that rivaled the CHESTNUT STREET. In 1828, John Haviland designed a new Greek-revival facade for it. Eventually, it passed to the ownership of JOHN SLEEPER CLARKE, EDWIN BOOTH's brother-in-law, and remained in his estate until 1919. Intending to raze it and replace it with a new theatre, the new owner discovered that the building code restricted him to a smaller theatre, so he decided to rebuild the old house. In 1968, it was declared a National Landmark, and money was raised to restore it to Haviland's 1828 version, although with a thoroughly modernized interior. MCH

Walter, Eugene (1874–1941) Playwright and film writer. Associated in business management with numerous theatrical enterprises – MINSTREL SHOWS, CIRCUSES, symphony orchestras – Walter contributed most importantly to American theatre with a score of successful, social-realistic melodramas. Essentially, he emphasized the victims of overwhelming social and personal forces: a man caught in the political machine of New York City (*The Undertow*, 1906); a weak husband pushed to immoral limits by the power of business (*Paid in Full*, 1908); a man corrupted by money and brought to ruin and death (*Fine Feathers*, 1913). Walter's best play, *The EASIEST WAY* (1909), remembered for its realistic stage setting by DAVID BELASCO, featured a weak woman who understands and accepts her frailty. Other plays include *The Wolf* (1908), *The Trail of the Lonesome Pine* (1912), and *The Knife* (1917). Walter's skills were easily adapted to films. In 1925 he published a series of lectures entitled *How to Write a Play*. WJM

Walter Kerr Theatre 219 West 48th St., NYC [Architect: Herbert J. Krapp]. Built by the SHUBERTS in 1921 as the Ritz, the theatre was rushed to completion in 66 days. With slightly under 1,000 seats, it was a frequently booked house during the 1920s and '30s and was leased by the FEDERAL THEATRE PROJECT for 1937–9. During 1939–64, it was used as a studio for radio and then television. Thereafter, it entered a rocky period when it served as a theatre, a pornographic moviehouse, and massage parlor, and briefly as the Robert F. Kennedy Children's Theatre. In 1983, after a complete renovation, it returned as a legitimate playhouse owned by JUJAMCYN Theaters. A second renovation and a name change to the WALTER

KERR occurred in 1990. Martin McDonagh's *The Beauty Queen of Leenane* played there in 1998; *PROOF* in 2000; and *Grey Gardens* in 2006.   MCH

Walton, Tony (1934–) British-born set/costume designer for theatre, film, television, opera, and ballet, and stage director. Walton studied at the Slade School of Fine Arts in London and began work at the Wimbledon Theatre; his first New York production was in 1957. He soon became associated in the U.S. with a range of witty and elegant musicals, including A FUNNY THING HAPPENED ON THE WAY TO THE FORUM, *Pippin* (1972; Tony), *Grand Hotel: The Musical* (1989), *The WILL ROGERS FOLLIES,* and the revivals of GUYS AND DOLLS (1992) and SHE LOVES ME (1993). However, like his idol, BORIS ARONSON, his style is mutable, often whimsical, and always inventive. With more than 55 major NYC productions to his credit – including the Lincoln Center revivals of *The HOUSE OF BLUE LEAVES* (1986; Tony), *The FRONT PAGE,* and ANYTHING GOES, plus its SIX DEGREES OF SEPARATION; as well as *The Real Thing,* HURLYBURLY, *Conversations with My Father, Death and the Maiden,* the 1994 *Christmas Carol* (Madison Square Garden), ANNIE GET YOUR GUN, *Steel Pier,* OUR TOWN, and LISA KRON's *Well* – Walton is one of the most active designers in New York theatre today. *Fool's Paradise, The Ginger Man,* MOST HAPPY FELLA, *Caligula,* and *Triple Bill* number among London designs, and his film and television credits include *Mary Poppins, The Wiz, Deathtrap, All That Jazz,* and DUSTIN HOFFMAN's DEATH OF A SALESMAN. For IRISH REP he directed and designed *The Importance of Being Earnest* (1996) and *Major Barbara* (1997). He has received not only three Tonys but also an Oscar, an Emmy, and two American Theatre Wing Awards (among others), and many more nominations. In 1991 he was inducted into the THEATRE HALL OF FAME; he was the inaugural recipient in 2004 of the Robert L. B. Tobin Award for Lifetime Achievement in Theatrical Arts; and in 2005 he received the Hammerstein Award for Lifetime Achievement in Musical Theatre.   AA   DBW

Wanamaker, Sam (1919–93) Born in Chicago, Wanamaker studied for the stage at the GOODMAN THEATRE. He debuted on Broadway in 1942, then made his first London appearance in 1952 in *Winter Journey,* which he also directed. Remaining in England he became artistic director of the New Shakespeare Theatre, Liverpool, in 1957, and joined the Shakespeare Memorial Theatre Company in Stratford in 1959. From 1970 to his death he served as executive director of the Globe Playhouse Trust and World Centre for Shakespeare

Studies, Southwark, London, where he campaigned tirelessly for the erection of a replica Globe Theatre, completed in June 1997, gaining for him an honorary CBE from the Queen in October 1993. His daughter, **Zoë Wanamaker**, was most recently on Broadway as Electra (1998) and in *AWAKE AND SING!* (2006 revival).   SMA

Ward, Douglas Turner (1930–) AFRICAN AMERICAN actor, director, and playwright. Born in Louisiana but educated in the North, Ward trained at the Paul Mann Theatre Workshop in NYC. He acted in OFF-BROADWAY plays before accepting a minor role on Broadway in A RAISIN IN THE SUN (1959). Working with ROBERT HOOKS in 1965, Ward produced his two one-act satiric comedies, *Happy Ending* and *Day of Absence,* for a 14-month Off-Broadway run (Obie and Vernon Rice awards). In 1967 Ward, Hooks, and Gerald Krone founded the NEGRO ENSEMBLE COMPANY, where Ward was artistic director until 2002. He has directed or played leading roles in many of the company's productions, notably CEREMONIES IN DARK OLD MEN (1969; dir. 1985 revival) and *The River Niger* (1972), for which he won an Obie. He directed the 1982 Pulitzer Prize–winning A SOLDIER'S PLAY and has also written *The Reckoning* (1969) and *Brotherhood* (1970).   EGH

Ward, Winifred (1884–1975) Pioneer in child drama (see CHILDREN'S THEATRE). In articulating the principles and demonstrating the effectiveness of creative drama versus formal theatre for children, she changed the direction of drama education in the U.S. She authored four texts: *Creative Dramatics, Playmaking with Children, Stories to Dramatize,* and *Theatre for Children.* Her philosophy, developed during her early years as a classroom teacher, culminated in university courses at Northwestern University and the establishment of the Evanston Children's Theatre. Her most lasting accomplishment was the founding of a professional organization in 1950, now called the American Alliance for Theatre and Education.   NMcC

Warde, Frederick (1851–1935) A successful English provincial actor, he made his American debut (1874) as a supporting player, and found success as a regional star after 1880. Like his contemporaries Thomas Keene, Louis James, Charles Hanford, Joseph Grismer, Phoebe Davis, Kathryn Kidder, and MARIE WAINWRIGHT, who had similar careers, he played an older repertory in an elevated, declamatory style that was innocent of realism. Warde specialized in serious, older men. He continued on the stage and the lecture platform until 1915, and made films of *Richard III* (1912) and *King Lear* (1916). His memoirs, *Fifty Years of Make-Believe* appeared in 1920 (New York).   DMcD

Warfield, David (1866–1951) BELASCO's one great male star was a native of San Francisco who began acting with a traveling STOCK COMPANY in Napa, CA (1888). He played a variety of parts in New York City and on tour until he became a member of the company at the CASINO THEATRE in 1893. He quickly became a specialist in musical parody, which led to an engagement as an eccentric ethnic comic with WEBER AND FIELDS (1899–1901). Belasco coached him in a series of pathetic older parts, in which he was always the gentle, slightly humorous, forgiving victim. His first vehicle was *The Auctioneer* (1901), followed by *The Music Master* (1904), *The Return of Peter Grimm* (1911), and culminating in an unsuccessful production of *The Merchant of Venice* (1922), after which he retired.   DMcD

Warren, Mercy Otis (1728–1814) Colonial Patriot and political satirist, the best representative of "The War of Belles Lettres" during the Revolutionary War. Her propaganda plays – really dialogues without plot, character development, or women – satirized British officials and American Loyalists and were published anonymously in Massachusetts periodicals and as political pamphlets. Several plays have been falsely attributed to Warren; she acknowledged authorship of only *The Group* (1775). Other plays identified as her work include *The Adulateur: A Tragedy: As It Is Now Acted in Upper Servia* (1772), which refers to the Boston Massacre and attacks Governor Thomas Hutchison; *The Defeat* (1773); and two blank-verse historical tragedies, *The Ladies of Castille* and *The Sack of Rome,* both published in *Poems, Dramatic and Miscellaneous* (1790), her first signed work. The most recent study of Warren is by Rosemarie A. Zagari (1995).   FB

Warren, William, the Elder (1767–1832) British-born actor and manager whose 1784 debut was as Young Norval in *Douglas.* When engaged by Tate Wilkinson for his provincial company in 1788, Warren acted in support of Sarah Siddons. In 1796 he joined THOMAS WIGNELL's company. At the CHESTNUT STREET THEATRE he first appeared as Friar Lawrence in *Romeo and Juliet* and Bundle in *The Waterman.* Other than infrequent appearances in New York, the remainder of Warren's career, both as actor and manager, was associated with the theatres in Baltimore and PHILADELPHIA. In 1806 he married the second of his three wives,

actress MRS. ANNE MERRY. In partnership with WILLIAM B. WOOD, Warren's management in Philadelphia and Baltimore prospered until late in his career; in 1829 he retired from management. As an actor, Warren was especially adept at old men in comedy, but he was also capable in tragedy. He was noted especially for his performances as Old Dornton, Sir Robert Bramble, Falstaff, and Sir Toby Belch. He had six children with his third wife, Esther Fortune (sister-in-law of JOSEPH JEFFERSON), all of whom were associated with the stage.   DBW

Warren, William, the Younger (1812–88) The son of WILLIAM WARREN THE ELDER; his acting career is almost totally associated with the BOSTON MUSEUM, the STOCK COMPANY he joined in 1847. During his 50-year career, until his retirement in 1883, he is reported to have given 13,345 performances and to have portrayed 577 characters. No actor of his period was identified so thoroughly with a single theatre, and none received more respect and affection from the public. His versatility in comic roles was practically limitless, although his special talent was with eccentric types. His most famous roles included Dogberry, Polonius, Bob Acres, Sir Peter Teazle, Micawber, Touchstone, and Launcelot Gobbo, although he also appeared in leading roles in numerous forgettable contemporary plays. W. T. Ball wrote a brief bio in 1888.   DBW

Warrilow, David (1934–95) British-born actor and cofounder of MABOU MINES. Warrilow was working as a magazine editor in Paris when JOANNE AKALAITIS, LEE BREUER, RUTH MALECZECH, and Philip Glass invited him to work with them on a production of Samuel Beckett's *Play* (1965, American Cultural Center, Paris). He came to New York with them and helped found the experimental collective Mabou Mines in 1970. Warrilow performed in Breuer's *The RED HORSE ANIMATION* (1970) and *The B. Beaver Animation* (1974), and, to great acclaim, in a 1975 adaptation of Beckett's *The Lost Ones* (1972). Lanky and langorous, and with a deep, sonorous voice, Warrilow has often been called the "consummate" or "quintessential" Beckett actor. Warrilow left Mabou Mines in 1978 and the next year toured in *A Piece of Monologue,* a play Beckett wrote specifically for him; in 1984 he performed in the premieres of Beckett's *Ohio Impromptu, Catastrophe,* and *What Where* (THEATRE Row) directed by ALAN SCHNEIDER.   AS

Washington, DC The League of Washington Theatres, founded in 1982, has (as of 2006), 49 theatre members from the city and its environs. In 2004 DC-area companies presented 383 productions playing to 2,133,731 audience members. These figures certainly support the belief that Washington is one of the most prolific theatre towns in the U.S. To honor resident and nonresident productions in the area the HELEN HAYES Awards, begun in 1974, are given annually. For specifics on the history of theatre in the nation's capital, see the following entries: FORD'S THEATRE, FOLGER THEATRE, JOHN F. KENNEDY CENTER FOR THE PERFORMING ARTS, NATIONAL THEATRE, The SHAKESPEARE THEATRE, SOURCE THEATRE, and WOOLLY MAMMOTH THEATRE. Also consult the League's Web site <www.lowt.org>.   DBW

Washington Square Players A pre-WWI American producing agency, founded in 1915 by amateurs (Edward Goodman, LAWRENCE LANGNER, and others) to improve the level of drama in New York City. Their first three one-acts were produced at a cost of $35 in a theatre seating 40 persons. They received favorable reviews and continued producing one-acts by CHEKHOV, Musset, ZOË AKINS, PHILIP MOELLER, and other then little-known playwrights. After a disastrous production of *The Seagull,* they moved to the Comedy Theatre, just off Broadway, seating 600. There they presented the first Broadway production of EUGENE O'NEILL's *In the Zone.* Several important American actors began or worked with the Washington Square Players: Roland Young, ROLLO PETERS, Frank Conroy, Helen Westley, and KATHARINE CORNELL. In 1918 the group disbanded, but it restructured in 1919 as the THEATRE GUILD, New York's most influential producing organization.   SMA

Wasserstein, Wendy (1950–2006) Playwright, essayist, and novelist who portrayed with wit and understanding the plight of the modern woman caught between feminism and traditionalism. A New York native, she attended Mt. Holyoke, City College, and the Yale School of Drama. Her *Uncommon Women and Others* (1977; Obies for two actors; 1994 revival, SECOND STAGE) depicts the reunion of five women graduates of Mt. Holyoke and their hilarious reflections on their past college days. *Isn't It Romantic* (1983), also OFF-BROADWAY. follows two such women as they confront their parents, their lovers, and their own unclear futures. *The HEIDI CHRONICLES,* which traces the history of the women's movement through the life of one woman and her friends, won a Pulitzer Prize and a Tony Award for Best Play in 1989. *The Sisters Rosensweig* (1992, SEATTLE REP and LINCOLN CEN-

TER; 1994, London), winner of numerous nominations and awards for its actors, author, and director (DANIEL SULLIVAN), explores the relationship of three middle-aged, slightly maladjusted Jewish sisters. *An American Daughter* (1997), inspired by the treatment of women in American politics, ran only 89 performances on Broadway. Lesser-known plays are *When Dinah Shore Ruled the Earth* (1975, Yale Cabaret Theatre; with CHRISTOPHER DURANG), *Montpelier Pizz-zazz* (1976), *Tender Offer* (1983), and the musical *Miami* (1986), all Off-Broadway. Her final two plays – *Old Money* (2000) and *Third* (2005) – were presented at Lincoln Center. In December 2005 it was reported that she had been hospitalized with lymphoma; she died in January.
   FB   DBW

Watch on the Rhine LILLIAN HELLMAN's fourth play contrasted the comfortable life in the U.S. of 1941 with the dangerous world of Europe, where moral choice led inevitably to perilous action. Paul Lukas created the role of the German Kurt Müller, a quietly heroic anti-Fascist, who briefly returns with his American wife to the safety of her upper-class home. Directed by HERMAN SHUMLIN with set design by JO MIELZINER, the first production opened on Broadway 1 April 1941 at the MARTIN BECK THEATRE. Immediately recognized as "a compassionate drama of men, women and children" (BROOKS ATKINSON), the play won the New York Drama Critics' Circle Award and was directed in London the following year by Emlyn Williams.   KF

Waters, Ethel (1896–1977) AFRICAN AMERICAN singer and actress. Born into poverty, Waters started at age 17 as a VAUDEVILLE singer in Baltimore for nine dollars a week. In 1933, she was featured in IRVING BERLIN's REVUE AS THOUSANDS CHEER. Moving from honky-tonks to cellar cafés to New York socialite clubs, Waters attained a glowing reputation as comedienne and singer of such songs as "St. Louis Blues," "Dinah," and "Stormy Weather." Waters emerged as a superb dramatic actress of warmth and sensitivity on the stage or the screen: *Mamba's Daughters* (1939), *Cabin in the Sky* (1940; film 1943), *Pinky* (film 1949), and *The MEMBER OF THE WEDDING* (1950; film 1952). Earl Dancer termed her "the greatest artist of her generation." Her autobiography (with Charles Samuels) appeared in 1951 (*His Eye Is on the Sparrow*); a biography by Twila Knaack, in 1978.   EGH

Waterston, Sam(uel Atkinson) (1940–) Actor, born in Cambridge, MA, and educated at Yale and the Sorbonne, best known for his portrayal of Jack

McCoy on the long-running television series *Law & Order,* beginning in 1994. He made his Broadway debut as Jonathan in OH DAD, POOR DAD . . . in 1963. In the 1960s and '70s he appeared with the NEW YORK SHAKESPEARE FESTIVAL, first as Silvius in *As You Like It* (1963), then Prince Hal in *Henry IV, Parts 1 and 2* (1968), Cloten in *Cymbeline* (1971), Benedick in *Much Ado* (1972, Obie; TV, 1974), Prospero in *The Tempest* (1974), and the title role in *Hamlet* (1975). In the same period he acted on Broadway in *Halfway Up the Tree* (1967), INDIANS (1969), *Hay Fever* (1970), *The Trial of the Catonville Nine* (1971), and *A Doll's House* (1975), and OFF-BROADWAY in *Muzeeka* (1968), *Chez Nous* (1977), *Waiting for Godot* (1978, BROOKLYN ACADEMY OF MUSIC), and *The Three Sisters* (1982). Stage appearances became less frequent as his film/television career accelerated: He appeared as Tom in *A GLASS MENAGERIE* with KATHARINE HEPBURN (TV 1973); as Nick Carraway in *The Great Gatsby* (film 1974); in four Woody Allen films, including *Hannah and Her Sisters* (1986) and *Crimes and Misdemeanors* (1989); and in the Oscar-nominated role of an American journalist in *The Killing Fields* (1984), among others. He returned to the stage in JEAN KERR's *Lunch Hour* (1980), *Benefactors* (1985), *A Walk in the Woods* (1988), as Solness in *The Master Builder* (1991, HARTFORD STAGE), the title role in *Abe Lincoln in Illinois* (1993, VIVIAN BEAUMONT; Drama League's Distinguished Performance Award and Outer Critics Circle Award), James Tyrone Sr. in LONG DAY'S JOURNEY at SYRACUSE STAGE (2000), Leonato in *Much Ado* (NYSF, 2004; with his daughter Elisabeth as Hero), and as Henry Carr in Stoppard's *Travesties* (2005, LONG WHARF). His son James is also an actor.   TLM

Watson, Billy "Beef Trust" [né Isaac Levie] (1866–1945) New York–born "Dutch" comedian-singer and producer, known as "King of Burlesque." His debut, as Billy Buttons, occurred at the Chatham Square Museum (1881). Success as a comedian in VAUDEVILLE and BURLESQUE led to ownership of a Brooklyn theatre, Watson's Cozy Corner (1905). Although Watson first gained prominence in the 1890s as producer-star of *Krausmeyer's Alley* (as a German clarinetist opposite Billy Spencer's Irish sausage maker), with a theme similar to Nichols's ABIE'S IRISH ROSE, he is remembered as the producer of *Watson's Beef Trust* (named after the Chicago stockyard trust), a comic burlesque show, often censured, featuring 190-pound chorus girls made to appear even larger with striped tights. Watson's chorines actually were quite decorous, appearing in one skit as Salvation Army lassies led by Capt. Billy Watson with a big brass drum.

Prior to retirement in 1925, Watson, calling himself "Original," was challenged by comic "Sliding" Billy Watson.   DBW

Watt, Douglas (1914–) Drama critic. Born in New York and educated at Cornell (1934), Watt began his long career with the *New York Daily News* in 1936. He served as dramatic reporter (1940–71), senior drama critic (1971–87), and critic-at-large (1987–early '90s). He has written also for the *New Yorker* since 1946. A simple elegance characterizes his style. As critic emeritus of the *Daily News* he chairs the TDF/Astaire Awards Committee to honor the "Best Dance on Broadway."   TLM

Watts, Richard, Jr. (1898–1981) Drama critic. Born in West Virginia and educated at Columbia University, Watts began his career as a reporter for the old *Brooklyn Times* in 1922. He became film critic for the *New York Herald* in 1924, a position he held until 1936, when he succeeded PERCY HAMMOND as drama critic (1936–42). He spent the war years in the Far East (1942–6) to return as drama critic for the *New York Post* (1946–74). Succeeded by MARTIN GOTTFRIED in 1974, Watts wrote a weekly column until his retirement in 1976. An early champion of Tom Stoppard, Harold Pinter, and EDWARD ALBEE, Watts has been characterized as a gentle, judicious, and civilized critic of taste who loved the theatre.   TLM

Wayburn, Ned [né Edward Claudius Weyburn] (1874–1942) Director and choreographer who, after starting out as a singer and dancer in vaudeville, made his theatrical debut in *The Swell Miss Fitwell* (1897). He served as assistant director of COHAN's *The Governor's Son* (1901), and was soon in demand as a producer, director, and choreographer of musical comedies and REVUES. Among the shows he staged in NYC were two editions of *The Passing Show* (1912, 1913), and six of *The ZIEGFELD Follies* (1916–19, 1922, 1923). In addition to producing and staging hundreds of musicals, Wayburn operated dance studios that trained many of the musical theatre's finest dancers. A study of Wayburn by Barbara Stratyner appeared in 1996.   MK

Way Down East by Lottie Blair Parker (alterations by Joseph R. Grismer) is a four-act "rural" melodrama that opened at the Manhattan Theatre, 7 February 1898, ran for 152 performances, and was revived over the next 20 years. Reminiscent of the popular melodramas *The* OLD HOMESTEAD, SHORE ACRES, and HAZEL KIRKE, the play impressed the *New York Times* reviewer as less crude and uncouth than the usual "rustic" fair, with simple and effective dialogue, acting, and scenery. Lottie Blair Parker also wrote *White Roses* (1897), *Under Southern Skies* (1901), *Lights of Home* (1903), and *The Redemption of David Corson* (1906).   TLM

Weaver, Fritz (1926–) Actor who made his professional debut with Virginia's BARTER THEATRE and his New York debut OFF-BROADWAY as Fainall in *The Way of the World* (1954). After 1955, Weaver appeared frequently with the AMERICAN SHAKE-SPEARE FESTIVAL. He has also appeared in several films and numerous television-network films and series. Among his awards are the CLARENCE DER-WENT Award for Flamineo in *The White Devil* (1955, PHOENIX THEATRE) and a *Theatre World* Award for Maitland in *The Chalk Garden* (1956, Broadway). For *Child's Play* (1970), Weaver received, among other awards, a Best Actor Tony. In 1991 he portrayed King Lear at the SHAKESPEARE THEATRE (then still at the Folger) and appeared with Tony Randall's NATIONAL ACTORS THEATRE in NYC, playing Danforth in its inaugural production of *The Crucible*. Spring 1995 he appeared at CIRCLE REP in Serbian playwright Dušan Kovačević's *The Professional*. For the IRISH REP he played Drumm in Hugh Leonard's *A Life* (2001); in 2004, at the Promenade Theatre, Judge Francis Biddle in *Trying;* and in 2006 Mr. Voysey in *The Voysey Inheritance* at the ATLANTIC THEATER COMPANY.   SMA

Weaver, Sigourney [née Susan Alexandra Weaver] (1949–) Actor and producer, born in NYC, daughter of Sylvester L. "Pat" Weaver Jr. (NBC-TV executive) and Elizabeth Inglis, a British actress. A privileged childhood meant good schools and travel; higher education led to Sarah Lawrence, Stanford, and drama at Yale, although she was generally rejected because of her height (almost 6 ft.). She changed her name in 1963 (after a character in *The Great Gatsby*). After graduation she worked in plays by classmates CHRISTOPER DURANG and ALBERT INNAURATO. Credits in the 1970s included *GEMINI* (PLAYWRIGHTS HORIZONS), *Marco Polo Sings a Solo* (The PUBLIC), *A Flea in Her Ear* (HART-FORD STAGE), and *The Constant Wife* (Broadway, understudy), among others. During 1979–81 she starred OFF-BROADWAY in *Das Lusitania Songspiel,* coauthored with Durang. In 1985 she was nominated for a Best Featured Tony (role of Darlene) in RABE'S *HURLYBURLY*. Her husband since 1984 is Jim Simpson of The FLEA THEATER, where she appeared in *The Guys* (2002). Of her numerous films, she is unforgettable in *Alien* (1979) – and three sequels – and *Ghostbusters* (I and II).   DBW

Webber, Andrew Lloyd (1948–) British composer and producer whose transported musicals have become such Broadway megahits – he has won three Tonys and his producing organization, The Really Useful Company, another three – that his name for a decade or more was to many synonymous with the genre, threatening in the 1980s to engulf the American product. His music has certainly had popular appeal, yet critics term his work derivative or worse. His first show seen in the U.S. was *Jesus Christ Superstar* in 1971 (revived 1977 and 2000), followed in 1979 by *Evita,* both productions preceded by recordings – as was *Joseph and the Amazing Technicolor Dreamcoat* (1982), a work staged 14 years after completion; the lyrics for these three were by Tim Rice. *CATS* followed in 1982; then *Song and Dance* (1985); *Starlight Express* (1987); *PHANTOM OF THE OPERA* (1988), his most successful show to date; *Aspects of Love* (1990); *Sunset Boulevard* (1994), Tony for Best Musical in 1995 (977 performances); and *By Jeeves* (2001), the latter quickly forgotten. Not until 2005 and *The Woman in White,* based on the Victorian thriller by Wilkie Collins, did it seem that Webber might once more match the spectacle and romance associated with his most successful Broadway offerings. The jury is still out, although *Woman* had only a modest run. Although Webber has had few composer followers in this country – FRANK WILDHORN being the one major exception – his impact on musical production and its spectacle was palpable until recently. In 2006 he was named a Kennedy Center honoree.

Invariably, comparison of Webber and the U.S. native STEPHEN SONDHEIM are frequent, usually as opposites. Michael Walsh, author of the best Webber biography to date (1989), has observed in the *New York Times* that they both fit into existing musicohistorical categories: Webber as the Giacomo Meyerbeer of his day and Sondheim as a closer parallel to Schubert or Hugo Wolf. In England, where Webber is a member of the House of Lords (since 1997), he is a major theatre owner (eight in the West End) and producer (Really Useful bringing *Bombay Dreams* to the U.S. in 2004). His biography by John Snelson was published in 2004.   DBW

Weber, Joseph (1867–1942) and **Lew Fields** [né Lewis Maurice Shanfield] (1867–1941) Comedians. After learning their craft as child performers in museums, CIRCUSES, and variety houses, Weber and Fields evolved a knockabout "Dutch comic" act in which the short, rotund, innocent Weber was the foil for the tall, skinny, bullying Fields.

They toured for many years in VAUDEVILLE before playing their first legitimate theatre engagements at the Harlem Opera House and HAMMERSTEIN'S OLYMPIA THEATRE in 1894. Two years later they opened the Weber and Fields Music Hall, where they offered hilarious burlesques of current Broadway successes. The Weber and Fields company, which at various times included such stars as LILLIAN RUSSELL, Peter F. Dailey, SAM BERNARD, DE WOLF HOPPER, DAVID WARFIELD, FAY TEMPLETON, and Bessie McCoy, was also noted for the beauty and animation of its female chorus. Weber and Fields chose many talented writers, designers, and directors to assist them in mounting their shows.

In 1904 the partners separated, with Weber continuing at the Music Hall and Fields producing and starring in musical comedies. In 1912 they reunited for a "jubilee" production at a new Music Hall, after which they toured with the show. Following some vaudeville appearances the partners again split up and concentrated on their producing careers. The rough, acrobatic comic style of Weber and Fields, coupled with the fractured English they spoke in their "Dutch" personas, made them favorites of audiences in NYC and across the country, in both legitimate theatres and vaudeville houses. Armond and L. Marc Fields authored a superb bio of Fields in 1993; the standard bio of both is by Felix Isman (1924).   MK

Webster, Margaret (1905–72) New York–born actress and director. The daughter of Benjamin Webster III and Dame May Whitty, she was the last member of a 150-year-old English theatrical dynasty. Her professional career began in *The Trojan Women* with Sybil Thorndike (1924), followed the next year with a small role in the London company of John Barrymore's (see DREW–BARRYMORE) *Hamlet*. After several years of stock experience she joined the Old Vic in 1929, returning to play Lady Macbeth in 1932–3. In 1934 she began to direct, and this became her chief endeavor, mostly in America. Notable U.S. productions under her direction included *Richard II* (1937) and *Hamlet* (1938), both with MAURICE EVANS, *Twelfth Night* (1940) with HELEN HAYES, *Othello* with PAUL ROBESON, JOSÉ FERRER, and UTA HAGEN (1943), *The Cherry Orchard* (1944), and *The Tempest* with CANADA LEE as Caliban (1945). She founded with EVA LE GALLIENNE and CHERYL CRAWFORD the AMERICAN REPERTORY THEATRE (1946–8). In 1950 she began directing operas, becoming the first woman to direct at the New York Metropolitan Opera. She was the author of important books on

theatre, including *The Same Only Different* (1969) and *Don't Put Your Daughter on the Stage* (1972). Her biography, by Milly Barranger, appeared in 2004.   DBW

Wedding Band by ALICE CHILDRESS. Subtitled "A Love/Hate Story in Black and White," this two-act drama examines the effects of racism through the doomed love affair of a black woman and white man. Julia and Herman are otherwise ordinary working-class people, but their commitment to a 10-year relationship makes them outlaws in the South Carolina of 1918, and Herman's sudden illness brings his scandalized family into direct contact with the multifaceted black community. First produced at the University of Michigan in 1966, *Wedding Band* opened in New York at the PUBLIC THEATER 26 September 1972 directed by Childress and JOSEPH PAPP, with RUBY DEE and James Broderick in the major roles. In 1973 the honest treatment of interracial love still raised controversy when the play was televised nationally by ABC.   KF

Weill, Kurt (1900–50) Composer, born in Dessau, Germany; studied music and directed a small opera company before collaborating with Bertolt BRECHT on such works as *The Threepenny Opera* and *The Rise and Fall of the City of Mahagonny*. With his wife, actress LOTTE LENYA, he came to America in 1935. He composed scores for JOHNNY JOHNSON (1936), KNICKERBOCKER HOLIDAY (1938), LADY IN THE DARK (1941), *One Touch of Venus* (1943), the opera STREET SCENE (1947), and LOST IN THE STARS (1949). His Berlin shows have also been frequently revived in America. Although Weill's compositions for the American stage were more lyrical and optimistic than his Berlin scores, he worked with such noted writers as PAUL GREEN, MAXWELL ANDERSON, and LANGSTON HUGHES in creating shows that tackled serious issues in an uncompromising way. Since 1982 the Kurt Weill Foundation for Music, Inc. (7 East 20th St., NYC 10003) has published a useful newsletter. Jürgen Schebera's illustrated biography was published in 1995 (Yale, trans. Caroline Murphy).   MK

Weissler, Barry (1939–) and **Fran** (1929–) Husband and wife Broadway producing team. He grew up in Jersey City, NJ, and she in a suburb of Boston; they met in 1963, and for 15 years operated the National Shakespeare Company. Their NYC producing debut was *Othello* (1982) with JAMES EARL JONES and CHRISTOPHER PLUMMER. Since then, with Fran in charge of creative decisions and Barry the point person in business, they have been characterized by some as a safe company (National Artists Management) that produces mostly revivals, yet their shows until recently have been quite successful; they are recipients of five Tony Awards. Thus to some, they are simply old-fashioned, frugal, strong-willed producers. Their major credits to date include *Medea* (1982; with Zoe Caldwell), *Zorba* (1983; with Anthony Quinn), Cabaret (1987), Gypsy (1989; with Tyne Daly), Cat on a Hot Tin Roof (1990; with Kathleen Turner), Fiddler on the Roof (1990; with Topol), *My Fair Lady* (1993; with Richard Chamberlain), Grease (1994), Chicago (1996), Annie Get Your Gun (1999; with Bernadette Peters and, later, Reba McEntire), Wonderful Town (2003; with Donna Murphy), and Sweet Charity (2005). A rare original production of theirs was Falsettos (1992), DBW

Welch, Deshler (1854–1920) Editor and author. After writing for Buffalo newspapers (1866–79) and the *New York Tribune* and *Star* (c. 1879–86), Welch became founding editor of *The Theatre* (1886–93), an illustrated weekly magazine on drama, music, and art. He also served as publicity manager for Augustin Daly (1887–91). His books include *Stephen Grover Cleveland: A Sketch of His Life* (1884). TLM

Weller, Michael (1942–) NYC–born playwright (author of some 30 plays), educated at Brandeis and Manchester universities. After productions at the Edinburgh Festival Fringe and at Charles Marowitz's Open Space (London) in 1969, he premiered *Cancer* at the Royal Court in 1970. Retitled Moonchildren, it opened at the Arena Stage in 1971, followed by productions first on (1972) and then Off-Broadway (1973). *Moonchildren* depicts the hangups and idealism of the "children of the sixties," a subject to which Weller returned with *Loose Ends* in 1979. Premiering at the Arena Stage prior to its Broadway debut, *Loose Ends,* directed by Alan Schneider, expresses the disillusionment of the 1970s as young people attempt to reconcile their ideals with the demands of careers, marriages, and families. Weller's *Spoils of War,* which dealt with a boy's attempt to reunite estranged parents, opened at Second Stage in 1988 before moving to Broadway. His other plays include *Fishing* (1975, The Public), *At Home* (1981, London), *Ghost on Fire* (1985, La Jolla Playhouse), *Lake No Bottom* (1990, Second Stage), *¡Help!* (1996, Mixed Blood), *The Heart of Art* (1999, Hypothetical, NYC), *What the Night Is For* (2002, London), and *Approaching Moomtaj: A Fairy Tale for Grownups* (2004, New

Rep, Boston). His screenplays include *Hair* (1979), *Ragtime* (1981), *Lost Angels* (1989), and *Spoils of War* (1994, TV). In 2005 the Broken Watch Theatre Company on West 43d St., NYC, renamed its space the Michael Weller Theatre.   TLM

Welles, (George) Orson (1915–85) Actor, playwright, and director whose place in history is ensured as a result of youthful accomplishments. By 1941 the protean Welles had established himself as a major actor and brilliant theatre director; had directed, cowritten, and starred in *Citizen Kane* (1940), one of the most influential films in cinema history; and had inadvertently created a national panic with his 1938 radio version of H. G. Wells's *The War of the Worlds*. Welles's career began with an appearance at Dublin's Gate Theatre in 1931 as the Duke of Wurtemburg in *Jew Süss*. After touring with Katharine Cornell in 1933–4, he made his New York debut in 1934 in *Romeo and Juliet* (Chorus and Tybalt). In 1936, as director of the classic section of the Federal Theatre Project's Negro Unit, NYC, he staged a controversial "voodoo" version of *Macbeth* with an all-black cast; in 1937, appointed a director of the FTP for NYC, he directed notable productions of *Dr. Faustus* (and acted the title role) and *The Cradle Will Rock*. With John Houseman he cofounded in 1937 the Mercury Theatre, remembered primarily for its modern-dress production of *Julius Caesar*. Although Welles's theatre impact lessened after WWII, he is remembered for his direction of Native Son (1941); his 1946 version of Around the World in Eighty Days; his first appearance in London in 1951 as Othello; his adaptation and direction of *Moby Dick* (London 1955; New York, 1962); his direction and acting in *King Lear* (1956) at New York's City Center; and his direction at London's Royal Court Theatre of Ionesco's *Rhinoceros* (1960). Welles is the subject of two contradictory 1985 biographies by Barbara Leaming and Charles Higham, a 1989 one by Frank Brady, a 1995 biography by Simon Callow (vol. 2 was published in 2006), a David Thomson bio (1996), plus two significant studies of his theatre work by Richard France (1977 and 1990).   DBW

Wellman, Mac (1945–) Cleveland-born playwright (a "language-poet-playwright"), poet, novelist, and editor of two volumes of new American plays. His *Bad Penny* (1989; staged on and around Bow Bridge and Central Park's Lake) and *Crowbar* (1990; staged in the as-yet unrenovated Victory Theatre) shared an Obie Award with his *Terminal Hip* (1990, P.S. 122). Other plays include *Sincerity Forever* (1990, BACA, Brooklyn), a source of controversy ("another NEA outrage"), being an angry work focused on "the eloquent ignoramuses of America"; *7 Blowjobs* (1991, San Diego), companion piece to *Sincerity Forever,* an exploration of the paranoia surrounding seven "obscene" photographs delivered to a U.S. senator's office; and, all in 1994, *Hyacinth Macaw* (PRIMARY STAGES), a dysfunctional family in a bizarre universe, *Swoop* (Soho Rep, NYC), a version of *Dracula,* and *Why the "Y"* (Tampa), a meditation on Tampa's Ybor City. In addition: *The Bad Infinity* (1985, MINNEAPOLIS); *Cellophane* (1988, BACA); *A Murder of Crows* (1991, Dallas); *Strange Feet* (1993, Smithsonian); *Second-Hand Smoke* (1997, Primary Stages), *The Lesser Magoo* (1997, LOS ANGELES); *Hypatia* (2000, Soho Rep); *Jennie Richee* (2001, The KITCHEN); *Anything's Dream* (2003, The FLEA); *Bitter Bierce* (2003, P.S. 122). Wellman, classified as a "downtown" dramatist, in 2003 received an Obie for Lifetime Achievement. He teaches playwriting at Brooklyn College.

BBW

Wemyss, Francis Courtney (1797–1859) English-born actor and manager who, a year after his first London appearance in 1821, made his American debut at the CHESTNUT STREET THEATRE. His forte was comedy and farce, and he excelled in roles such as Vapid in *The Dramatists,* Marplot in *The Busy Body,* and Rover in *Wild Oats.* He later acted in New York with CHARLOTTE CUSHMAN, William Macready, JOSEPH JEFFERSON III, and LAURA KEENE. In 1827 he turned to management, and was widely respected for his taste and integrity. He founded the Theatrical Fund to aid needy actors; edited 16 volumes of plays, published as the *Acting American Theatre;* and wrote an informative autobiography, *Twenty-six Years of the Life of an Actor and Manager* (1847). TLM

West, Cheryl L. (1956?–) AFRICAN AMERICAN playwright whose work – beginning with *Before It Hits Home* (1990 Susan Smith Blackburn Prize; 1991, ARENA STAGE), about AIDS and the initial denial by many blacks – has fared better in regional theatre than in NYC. Subsequent plays include *Jar the Floor* (1991, EMPTY SPACE), *Puddin 'n' Pete* (1993, GOODMAN), *Holiday Heart* (1994, SYRACUSE STAGE, coproduced with CLEVELAND PLAY HOUSE and SEATTLE REP), *Play On!* (1997, book for Broadway musical), and *Birdie Blue* (2005, SECOND STAGE). Championed by director TAZE-WELL THOMPSON, West, trained as a social worker and journalist, combines humor, pathos, and passion in her sometimes brutally honest urban portrayals, criticized by some black critics as negative. DBW

West, Mae (1893–1980) Actress and playwright whose pose of unabashed but self-mocking sensuality made her a cult figure. A VAUDEVILLE headliner by 1911, she achieved notoriety in the lead role of her first play, *Sex* (1926), in which she was arrested (see CENSORSHIP). She continued to defy the censors with *The Drag* (1927, Bridgeport, CT, and Paterson, NJ; banned from Broadway), the first American drama to depict a homosexual party; *Diamond Lil* (1928), a melodramatic comedy about white slavery; and *The Constant Sinner* (1931). Her Hollywood career in the 1930s increased her fame, but the limitations forced on her by production codes brought her back to Broadway in *Catherine Was Great* (1944). West always located her insatiable, man-eating temptresses safely in past eras, and her own attitude was one of worldly bemusement. Her autobiography, *Goodness Had Nothing to Do with It,* was published in 1959. Frequently mimicked, West, in the hands of Claudia Shear in her *Dirty Blonde* (2000), became more a multilayered look at the nature of stardom. Good recent biographies were written by Marybeth Hamilton (1995), Emily Wortis Leider (1997), Jill Watts (2001), and Simon Louvish (2006). LS

West Side Story This updated musical version of *Romeo and Juliet,* with book by ARTHUR LAURENTS, music by LEONARD BERNSTEIN, and lyrics by STEPHEN SONDHEIM, opened at the WINTER GARDEN THEATRE on 26 September 1957. The rival families of Shakespeare's play were transformed by Laurents into gangs of white and Puerto Rican teenagers fighting for supremacy on Manhattan's decaying West Side. JEROME ROBBINS, the director and choreographer, created a series of frenetic dance sequences that stunningly articulated the gangs' restlessness and aggression. For the two young lovers, Tony and Maria (Larry Kert and Carol Lawrence), Bernstein and Sondheim wrote a series of expressive ballads including the soaring "Tonight" and the plaintive "Somewhere." At its opening, some critics complained that its violent story was inappropriate for the musical stage, while others praised it for expanding the boundaries of the musical in both plot and staging. Although its initial run was relatively short (732 performances), the musical returned to the Winter Garden in 1960, and it has gained in stature over the years: The 1961 film version received an Academy Award for Best Picture (and nine other Oscars); a 1980 revival directed by Robbins ran for 333 performances; the score has been played and recorded by philharmonic orchestras; and Bernstein shortly before his death conducted a recorded version featuring operatic voices. MK

West, Thomas Wade (1745–99) An English-born actor who emigrated in 1789, West founded the southern theatrical circuit extending from his theatre in Richmond, VA, to those he built in Norfolk, Alexandria, Fredericksburg, Petersburg, and Charleston. Known alternately as the Virginia Company and the South Carolina Company, West's actors appeared in well-mounted standard fare, for which he gained respect as comic actor, manager, and gentleman until his early death. The circuit continued to operate until the War of 1812.   RKB

Western, (Pauline) Lucille (1843–77) Actress. Born in New Orleans to comedian George Western and an actress later known as Mrs. Jane English, Lucille Western spent her childhood performing with her younger sister, Helen, in a piece designed to show off their dancing and farcical impersonations. As an adult, she excelled in emotional roles such as Lady Isabel in *East Lynne*, Marguerite Gautier in *Camille,* the title roles in *Lucretia Borgia* and *Leah, the Forsaken,* and her most popular role, Nancy in *Oliver Twist* (1869). A dark-eyed beauty, she relied on inspiration more than art and gave the impression of being impulsive and untamed.   TLM

Western theatre see FRONTIER THEATRE

Weston, Jack [né Morris Weinstein] (1924–96) Stage, film, and television actor, accurately described in *The Filmgoer's Companion* as an "American roly-poly character actor" and by FRANK RICH as an "old-school shtick artist." After a six-year stint in New York, which included supporting roles in *South Pacific* (1952 replacement) and *Bells Are Ringing* (1956), Weston pursued a career in film and television. He returned to Broadway to play Gaetano Proclo in *The Ritz* (1975) and re-created this role on film the following year. He received a Tony nomination for his performance as the small-time vaudeville agent involved in a fruitless relationship in *The Floating Light Bulb* (1981). In 1989 he appeared in a revival of *The Tenth Man.* He first wife was actress Marge Redmond, with whom he performed on occasion.   MR

Westport Country Playhouse Founded by LAWRENCE and Armina LANGNER in 1931 in Westport, CT, as a SUMMER-STOCK operation (through transfers to Broadway were not unusual). The playhouse was created by scenic designer CLEON THROCKMORTON out of an old barn. A favorite venue of the acting elite, from 1959 to 2000 the operation was led by James B. McKenzie (419 productions). By the new millennium, however, the Playhouse was in a serious state of disrepair, and saved in large measure by Westport resident Joanne Woodward, who became its artistic head. In 2005, after a major renovation had been undertaken, Woodward stepped down, replaced by TAZEWELL THOMPSON. To mark its imminent 75th anniversary, a book by Richard Somerset-Ward was published in 2005, recording the theatre's rich history and heritage.   DBW

Wetzsteon, Ross (1932–98) Contributing editor at the *Village Voice* for 32 years and a champion of OFF-BROADWAY theatre, promoting the work of many fledging theatre companies and writers, such as SAM SHEPARD, DAVID MAMET, and WALLACE SHAWN. Born in Montana, he attended Cornell and Harvard, beginning at the *Voice* in 1966. For 28 of his years there he chaired its Obie Committee, which administered the Obie Awards that he helped create. A book he completed shortly before his death – *Republic of Dreams: Greenwich Village, The American Bohemia, 1910–1960* – was published in 2002.   DBW

Wexler, Peter (1936–) Set, lighting, and costume designer, as well as theatre consultant, who has designed extensively for the Metropolitan and New York City Operas; his Met debut was with *Les Troyens* (1973). Broadway credits include KANDER AND EBB's *The Happy Time* (1967) and *In the Matter of J. Robert Oppenheimer* (1969); OFF-BROADWAY, *Abe Lincoln in Illinois* (1963). He was the first resident designer for the LOS ANGELES CENTER THEATRE, and created the stage and decor for the New York Philharmonic Promenade Concerts in the 1960s and the stage for White House performances in 1961. In recent years he has been a scenic consultant for the BIG APPLE CIRCUS.   AA

What Price Glory by MAXWELL ANDERSON and Laurence Stallings opened in New York on 3 September 1924, running for 433 performances. The large cast of this iconoclastic treatment of WWI included William Boyd as Sergeant Quirt and Louis Wolheim as Captain Flagg, the hard-boiled professional soldiers whose rivalry over sex, drinking, and fighting provides the main conflict; also Brian Donlevy, Fuller Mellish Jr., and George Tobias as the young soldiers who become hardened and pragmatic under their tutelage. Presented as a realistic deflation of the romantic ideals of honor, bravery, and patriotism that had pervaded America's conception of war prior to the disillusionment of WWI, it replaced these ideals with admiration of the soldier's romantic sense of adventure and blind devotion to duty. It was written originally without the now familiar question mark at the end. BCM

Wheatley, William (1816–76) American theatre manager and actor. Born into a theatrical family, Wheatley made his stage debut at age 10 in 1826 at the PARK THEATRE, New York, as young Albert in William Macready's production of *William Tell.* Following a tour with Macready, Wheatley returned to the Park and played the title role in *Tom Thumb,* establishing himself as a leading juvenile actor. After acting in small roles at the BOWERY THEATRE (1833), he returned to the Park (1834) as a "walking gentleman" to excel as Nicholas Nickleby and as Charles in *London Assurance.* For the 1842–3 season, Wheatley acted with the WALNUT STREET THEATRE company in PHILADELPHIA. After a brief retirement from the stage, he returned to Philadelphia in 1853 to comanage the ARCH STREET THEATRE with JOHN DREW. He was sole manager in 1856, but two years later joined forces with JOHN SLEEPER CLARKE, who ran it with him until the outbreak of the Civil War. In 1862 he returned to New York and leased NIBLO'S GARDEN, where he excelled in producing elaborate romantic dramas including *The Duke's Motto* and *Arrah-na-pogue.* His biggest hit came in 1866, however, when *The BLACK CROOK* began its 475-performance run, creating a vogue for elaborate musical spectacle and making Wheatley a rich man. He retired from the stage in 1868. TLM

Wheeler, Andrew Carpenter (1832–1903) Drama critic also known as Trinculo and Nym Crinkle. Born in New York, Wheeler began his career as a reporter on the *New York Times* in 1857. After traveling in the Midwest, he wrote for the *Milwaukee Daily Sentinel,* reported on the Civil War, and returned to New York to pursue a career in journalism. During 1869–76 he reviewed plays for the *Sunday World;* beginning in 1870 he replaced Henry Clapp Jr. as drama critic of *The Leader;* for 1876–7, he followed Joseph Howard Jr. on the *Sun;* his "Nym Crinkle's Feuilleton" graced the *NEW YORK DRAMATIC MIRROR* during 1886–9; and in 1889 he added a regular column to DESHLER WELCH's *The Theatre.* Wheeler returned to the *World* in 1883 when Joseph Pulitzer purchased the paper. He was known also as a playwright, novelist, and essayist on nature (under the pen-name of J. P. Mowbray). Called by JAMES HUNEKER "more brilliant than reliable," Wheeler popularized an aggressive style marked by devastating sarcasm. He opposed the Genteel Tradition, the aesthete views of WILLIAM WINTER, and the cultural shift of the country away from rugged individualism. TLM

Wheeler, David (1925–) Director. A Harvard graduate who served as JOSÉ QUINTERO's assistant (1958–61), he has been a major force in New England theatre since the early 1960s with well over 200 productions to his credit, including some 80 while artistic director (1963–75) of the Theatre Company of BOSTON, where numerous young actors worked under his tutelage (among them Robert Duvall, AL PACINO, Jon Voight, STOCKARD CHANNING, BLYTHE DANNER, DUSTIN HOFFMAN, and Robert DeNiro). Since 1984 he has been resident director at the AMERICAN REPERTORY THEATRE (*TRUE WEST,* 1982; Don DeLillo's *The Day Room,* world premiere, 1986; *The Homecoming,* 1990; *What the Butler Saw,* 1994; *Waiting for Godot,* 1995; DeLillo's *Valparaiso,* world premiere, 1999; *Othello,* 2001, etc.) and, during the same period, was a frequent director for TRINITY REPERTORY. On Broadway he directed Al Pacino in *The BASIC TRAINING OF PAVLO HUMMEL* (1977) and *Richard III* (1979). In 1997 he directed *The Heiress* for BERKELEY REP. At ART he has often directed the plays of G. B. SHAW (*The Doctor's Dilemma, Man and Superman, Heartbreak House, Misalliance*). DBW

When You Comin' Back, Red Ryder? A suspense drama by MARK MEDOFF, first presented at NYC's CIRCLE REPERTORY THEATRE (November 1973), which provides a glimpse into the Southwest through a diner on a bypassed road in New Mexico. The character of Red Ryder is a pale youth who is among those terrorized and victimized by Teddy (KEVIN CONWAY), a mysterious and ominous figure who comes to the diner with his girlfriend. The portrayal of this demonic character reflects a growing concern about sadistic violence in society, suggesting the menace of Pinter and the surrealism of SAM SHEPARD. Medoff received an Obie Award for distinguished playwriting and the Outer Critics Circle's JOHN GASSNER Playwriting Award. ER

White Barn Theatre see LORTEL, LUCILLE

White, George (1890–1968) Dancer and producer. As a producer of successful musical REVUES in the 1920s, White provided stiff competition for FLORENZ ZIEGFELD. He started out as a dancer in Bowery saloons, gradually working his way up to VAUDEVILLE with a dancing act. Between 1910 and 1918 he appeared as a dancer in a number of musicals, including the *Ziegfeld Follies of 1915.* In

1919 he produced the *Scandals of 1919,* the first in a series of 13 revues bearing the title of *Scandals.* Because of his own background as a dancer, White emphasized dance in his revues, introducing black dance steps such as the Charleston and the black bottom to white audiences. His fast-paced revues were also noted for the jazz music of George Gershwin and DeSylva, Brown, and Henderson. White appeared as a dancer in several of the *Scandals,* and also contributed comedy sketches to several editions.   MK

White, Jane (1922–) African American actress. A Smith College graduate, White came early to Broadway as the female lead in *Strange Fruit* (1945). Thereafter she played mostly in Off-Broadway and regional theatres, taking lead roles in *Blithe Spirit, The Taming of the Shrew,* and *Dark of the Moon* for the Hayloft Theatre in Allentown, PA, in 1948–9. In 1965 she appeared in three productions for the New York Shakespeare Festival – *Love's Labour's Lost, Troilus and Cressida,* and *Coriolanus* – winning an Obie Award for her Volumnia and Princess of France. After engagements in Italy and France, she replaced Irene Pappas as Clytemnestra in the Off-Broadway *Iphigenia in Aulis* (1967). Her Goneril to Morris Carnovsky's King Lear (1975, American Shakespeare Theatre) was hailed for its commanding intelligence, style, and rich contralto voice.   EGH

White, Richard Grant (1822–85) Journalist, philologist, critic, editor, and Shakespeare scholar. A graduate of NYU (1839), White wrote music and dramatic criticism for the *New York Courier and Enquirer,* serving as editor during 1854–9. He contributed essays on the theatre to *Atlantic, Putnam's,* and *Galaxy* magazines. He pursued Shakespeare as an avocation, writing/editing *Shakespeare's Scholar* (1854); the first edition in America of Shakespeare's plays from original sources (1857–63); *Studies in Shakespeare* (1866); and the Riverside edition of Shakespeare (1883). The first American Shakespeare scholar to gain an international reputation, White was the father of Stanford White, the architect.   TLM

White Slave, The A sentimental melodrama by Bartley Campbell that drew heavily on *The Octoroon, Uncle Tom's Cabin,* and *Kit, the Arkansas Traveller.* It opened at New York's Haverly's Theatre 3 April 1882 and ran two months. Although not a critical success, it remained a staple for touring companies until WWI. Judge Hardin hid the illegitimacy of his grandchild Lisa by having her raised by a black servant. After Hardin's death, Lisa was sold as a slave to Lacy, who lusted for her. In the play's most famous moment, Lisa spurned Lacy and defied his threat to make her a field hand, proclaiming: "Rags are royal raiment when worn for virtue's sake, and rather a hoe in my hands than self-contempt in my heart."   RAH

Whitehead, Robert (1916–2002) Producer, born in Montréal and educated at Trinity College School in Canada, who in 1947 began his producing career with *Medea,* starring Judith Anderson. He was managing director for the American National Theatre and Academy (1951), joining Roger Stevens and others in forming the Producers Theatre (1953). He codirected the Repertory Theatre of Lincoln Center with Elia Kazan (1960–4), and maintained a close association with the John F. Kennedy Center. His more than 50 Broadway productions include *The Member of the Wedding* (1950), *Bus Stop* (1955), *The Visit* (1958), *A Touch of the Poet* (1958), *A Man for All Seasons* (1961), *The Price* (1968), *Old Times* (1971), *A Texas Trilogy* (1976), *Betrayal* (1980), another *Medea* (1982, starring his wife, Zoe Caldwell, whom he directed), *Death of a Salesman* (1984 revival), *Lillian* (1986, also directing Caldwell), *A Few Good Men* (1989), *The Speed of Darkness* (1991), Miller's *Broken Glass* (1994), and *Master Class* (1995, Drama Desk and Tony; with Caldwell as Callas). In 1992 an award for promising and innovative emerging producers was established in his name by the Commercial Theatre Institute, presented first in 1993. In 2002 he received a Special Tony for Lifetime Achievement.   TLM

Whitman, Walt (1819–92) Editor, journalist, and poet whose *Leaves of Grass* (1855) remains a major literary achievement of the 19th century. Whitman attended public schools and worked for numerous newspapers, including the *Brooklyn Daily Eagle* (1846–8), for which he contributed dramatic criticism. He faulted the "loud mouthed ranting style" of acting of the Forrest school (1846), and the vulgarity of New York theatres except the Park, which he thought "but a third-rate imitation of the best London theatres" (1847). His standards were high, and his comments are among the most insightful of the age. Jerome Loving's biography was published in 1999.   TLM

Who's Afraid of Virginia Woolf? by Edward Albee opened on Broadway on 13 October 1962, running for 664 performances. Directed by Alan Schneider, its cast included Arthur Hill as George, Uta Hagen as his wife and opponent,

Martha, and GEORGE GRIZZARD and Melinda Dillon as the young couple who stumble into the battle zone of their marriage. Directed by MIKE NICHOLS, the play was made into a prize-winning film (1966) with Elizabeth Taylor, RICHARD BURTON, George Segal, and Sandy Dennis. It has been produced many times with actresses such as Glenda Jackson, KATE REID, COLLEEN DEWHURST, and Kathleen Turner as Martha (the last in 2005 with BILL IRWIN). In three acts entitled "Fun and Games," "Walpurgisnacht," and "Exorcism," the play depicts the series of battle games with escalating stakes upon which George and Martha have built their marriage. When Martha wins at Humiliate the Host, George strikes back with Get the Guests, Martha ups the ante with Hump the Hostess, and George ends the night, and perhaps the games, by killing the fantasy son they have created as a "bean bag" between them. As George and Martha start a new day together without the buffer of games or fantasies, the young couple returns home with a greater understanding of their own marriage. BCM

Why Marry? by JESSE LYNCH WILLIAMS, which would win the first Pulitzer Prize for Drama, premiered 25 December 1917 at the Astor Theatre for a run of 120 performances (and later more than 500 performances in London). The play pits two womanly women against "a sexless freak with a scientific degree" (female), and progressive views of working women, sexual and economic equality, and useful careers, against repressive views of women as chattel and marriage as mercenary, habitual, and loveless. Faced with his own irrefutable arguments against marriage, Williams uses the liberated couple's public vows of love as a plighting of troth and weds them at play's end by default. RKB

Wicked Inspired by Gregory Maguire's novel *Wicked: The Life and Times of the Wicked Witch of the West* (1995), this musical, which opened at the GERSHWIN THEATRE on 30 October 2003 (and is still running spring 2007), featured music and lyrics by STEPHEN SCHWARTZ, book by Winnie Holzman, direction by JOE MANTELLO, musical stagings by Wayne Cilento, and Tony Award–winning scenery and costumes by EUGENE LEE and SUSAN HILFERTY, respectively. This popular spectacle tells the story of Oz from the witches' perspectives. Although failing to win the Tony for Best Musical (which went to *AVENUE Q*), its talented original cast – including KRISTIN CHENOWETH as Glinda, Idina Menzel as Elphaba (Tony Award), her roommate at sorcery school, JOEL GREY as the

Wizard, CAROLE SHELLEY as Madame Morrible, and Norbert Leo Butz as Fiyero – helped to ensure its success along with its mostly positive reviews. *BACK STAGE* described it as "part dark political parable, part mythic psychodrama, and even a meditation on animal rights." DBW

Wiest, Dianne (1948–) Kansas City, MO–born actress and director who made her stage debut in Carol Mack's *Esther* (1977, LORTEL's White Barn) and on Broadway in ROBERT ANDERSON's *Solitaire/Double Solitaire* (1971 replacement). Displaying a "combination of strength and vulnerability," she appeared with ARENA STAGE (1972-7), including *OUR TOWN* and *INHERIT THE WIND* in the USSR (1973), and YALE REPERTORY THEATRE (1980–1); other NYC productions include *Frankenstein* (1981) and *Othello* (1982) on Broadway, *AFTER THE FALL* (1984), TESICH's *Square One* (1990), *In the Summer House* (1993, at the VIVIAN BEAUMONT, directed by AKALAITIS), WALLACE's *One Flea Spare* (1997), Kathleen Tolan's *Memory House* (2005), and WASSERSTEIN's *Third* (2005). Wiest directed *Not About Heroes* OFF-BROADWAY (1985). Among her numerous films are WOODY ALLEN's *The Purple Rose of Cairo* (1985), *Hannah and Her Sisters* (1986, Academy Award, Best Supporting), *Radio Days* (1987), *September* (1987), *Bullets over Broadway* (1994, Academy Award, Best Supporting), and Foster's *Little Man Tate* (1991). She received 1979–80 Theatre World and CLARENCE DERWENT awards as well as two Obies (*The Art of Dining*, 1979; LANFORD WILSON's *Serenading Louie* and Pinter's *A Kind of Alaska*, 1983). During 2000–2 she played D.A. Nora Lewin on television's *Law & Order*. REK

Wignell, Thomas (1753–1803) English-born actor-manager, he joined his cousin LEWIS HALLAM's AMERICAN COMPANY in 1774 and soon became its leading man. Known primarily as a comedian, he played the role of Jonathan in the original production of ROYALL TYLER's *The CONTRAST* and created the prototype of the YANKEE character. In 1791 he left the company and teamed up with Philadelphia musician Alexander Reinagle to form the CHESTNUT STREET THEATRE. When their newly constructed building finally opened three years later it was recognized as one of the finest playhouses in the nation. Wignell recruited many of his players from England, including JAMES FENNELL, MRS. OLDMIXON, WILLIAM WARREN THE ELDER, and THOMAS A. COOPER. For many years the company made PHILADELPHIA the theatrical capital of America and developed a touring circuit encompassing Maryland, northern Virginia, and occasional visits to New York City.

683

When Wignell died, his share in the company passed to his widow. Though she and Reinagle were coowners, management of the company was assumed by actors Warren and WILLIAM B. WOOD. Warren eventually married Mrs. Wignell in 1806, and Wood joined him as owner of the company upon Reinagle's death in 1809. They finally disbanded in 1828.   RAS

Wilbur, Richard Purdy (1921–) Pulitzer Prize–winning poet and translator who has reclaimed the plays of Molière for the English-speaking stage. His translations include *The Misanthrope* (1955), *Tartuffe* (1963), *The School for Wives* (1971), *The Learned Ladies* (1978), *The School for Husbands* (1992), *The Imaginary Cuckold* (1993), and *Amphitryon* (1995), as well as Racine's *Andromache* (1982) and *Phaedra* (1986). Wilbur was a lyricist for the musical CANDIDE (1956).   TLM

Wild West exhibition A re-creation of American frontier life and skills popular in the late 19th century. Occasional exhibits of broncobusting and Indian folkways were staged previously as museum attractions, but P. T. BARNUM billed his Wild West extravaganza *Indian Life; or, A Chance for a Wife* in 1874 as a "thrilling arenic contest." The genre took its definitive shape under the guidance of Col. WILLIAM FREDERICK "BUFFALO BILL" CODY, a former Indian fighter and buffalo hunter, who starred in *Scouts of the Prairie,* a play written by the hack Ned Buntline and seen first in CHICAGO (1872) and in 1873 at New York's NIBLO'S GARDEN. The interest shown in a frontier fair he put on in North Platte, NE, in 1882 led him and crack-shot dentist Dr. W. F. Carver to organize a traveling show, *The Wild West,* which featured a program of shooting, roping, riding, and an attack on the Deadwood stagecoach. In his patent application Cody called it an "equestrian drama," for he disliked the term "show." In 1884 it went on the road under the ownership of Cody, the shrewd theatrical producer NATE SALSBURY, and the sharpshooter A. H. Bogardus, who gave it a coherent dramatic structure, culminating in its absorption into STEELE MACKAYE's *Drama of Civilization* (Madison Square Garden, NYC, 1885). From the first, it presented the white frontiersman as a civilizing factor in overcoming the savage elements of Nature and NATIVE AMERICANS. A European tour in 1887 (and again in 1903–6) made a deep impression, influencing the adventure novels of Karl May and, through him, the young BERTOLT BRECHT.

James A. Bailey took over Cody's Wild West in 1894 and used CIRCUS equipment and methods to enable it to make one-night stands; Cody added a "Congress of Rough Riders of the World," with Cossacks, gauchos, and Arabs bridging the gap between Sioux savagery and Plainsman nobility. The Buffalo Bill enterprise combined with Pawnee Bill's in 1909, but went into bankruptcy in 1913. A rival, the Miller Brothers and Edward Arlington's 101 Ranch Wild West Show – primarily a display of horsemanship minus the frontier-life romanticism – carried on during 1908–16, tried a revival in 1926 to no public interest, and folded in 1931. Motion pictures had taken over and expanded the depiction of cowboys and Indians, while authentic skills were relegated to the rodeo and circus "after-shows."

One of Cody's stars, sharpshooter ANNIE OAKLEY, was to inspire the IRVING BERLIN musical comedy ANNIE GET YOUR GUN (1946). ARTHUR KOPIT's play INDIANS (1969) paints a sardonic picture of the relationship between Cody's exhibitions and the plight of the Native American.   LS

Wilder, Clinton (1920–86) Producer, born in Irvine, PA, and educated at Princeton University; he began his professional career as a stage manager for A STREETCAR NAMED DESIRE in 1947. He turned to producing with *Regina* (1949), *The Tender Trap* (1954), *Six Characters . . .* (1955), and *A Visit to a Small Planet* (1957). He joined with RICHARD BARR to form a production company, Theatre 1960 (later 1961, 1962, etc.), to present noncommercial, avant-garde plays. Their achievements include *The AMERICAN DREAM, The Death of Bessie Smith,* and *Happy Days* (1961, OFF-BROADWAY); in 1962 WHO'S AFRAID OF VIRGINIA WOOLF?* (Broadway) and *Endgame, The SANDBOX, Deathwatch,* and *The ZOO STORY* (Cherry Lane Theatre). Joined by EDWARD ALBEE in 1963, they offered TINY ALICE (Broadway) and DUTCHMAN (Cherry Lane) in 1964; *Malcolm* and *A DELICATE BALANCE* (which won a Pulitzer Prize) on Broadway and *The Long Christmas Dinner* Off (Cherry Lane) in 1966; *Everything in the Garden* (Broadway) and *Rimers of Eldritch* (Cherry Lane) in 1967; and *Seascape* on Broadway in 1975.   TLM

Wilder, Thornton (Niven) (1897–1975) Novelist and playwright. While Wilder may be considered one of America's top playwrights, his reputation rests upon three full-length plays and a half-dozen one-acts, beginning in 1931 with the publication of *The Long Christmas Dinner & Other Plays in One Act.* In 1938 his OUR TOWN, which would win a Pulitzer Prize, opened on Broadway, employing many of the experimental techniques Wilder had used in his one-acts: minimal scenery, narrative descriptions, and the like. *Our Town,* which has been called America's most read and produced play, examines in the first act small-town life in Grover's Corners, NH, for a single day in 1901. Succeeding acts complete the cycle of marriage, birth, and death, ending with Emily Gibbs's conversation with the dead, whom she has just joined.

Wilder's next play, *The Merchant of Yonkers* (1938), closed after only 39 performances, but was revised in 1954 as *The* MATCHMAKER (Broadway, 1955) and became a smash hit in 1964 as the musical HELLO, DOLLY! Of greater impact was *The* SKIN OF OUR TEETH in 1942, a parable of the world's history centered around the Antrobus family. Act One is set in Excelsior, NJ, during the Ice Age; purposeful anachronisms mix with dinosaurs and refugees. Act Two on the boardwalk at Atlantic City closes with Mr. Antrobus loading pairs of animals into his boat to avoid the Great Flood. Act Three finds the Antrobus family coping with the aftereffects of a seven-year war, but finding hope in their very existence. In 2003 a dramatization of Wilder's *Theophilus North* by Matthew Burnett premiered at Rochester's GEVA THEATRE Center. Gilbert A. Harrison's is the most thorough biography (1983).   SMA

Wildhorn, Frank (1958–) Populist composer whose Broadway career began with the contribution of three songs in 1995 to *Victor/Victoria*. A New York native raised in Florida and educated at USC, he began as a pop tunesmith and his show tunes have been castigated by critics as simplistic, repetitive, and lacking connection between song and character, yet many are crowd-pleasers. His formula has been to release albums before productions develop. *Newsday* called the staged versions "galumphing, dunder-headed musicals" that make LLOYD WEBBER's efforts "seem like great art." Wildhorn's first musical, *Jekyll & Hyde* (book and lyrics by Leslie Bricusse), went through three versions (first in 1990 in Houston), opened on Broadway in 1997, and ran for 1,543 performances; *The Scarlet Pimpernel* (1997), with a similar history, book and lyrics by Nan Knighton, lasted 772 performances; *The Civil War* (1999), lyrics by Jack Murphy, only 61; and, although it ran for 157 performances, *Dracula, the Musical* (2004), words by Don Black and Christopher Hampton, was a critical flop, said by BRANTLEY to have "all the animation, suspense and sex appeal of Victorian waxworks in a seaside amusement park." For a time he was married to his leading lady, Linda Eder.   DBW

Wilkins, Edward G. P. (1829–61) A drama critic for the *New York Herald*, Wilkins wrote one of the

"merriest, brightest" and frequently produced contemporary comedies, *My Wife's Mirror* (1856). His *Young New York* (1856), while reflecting local events, satirized society yet retained the positive approach of the heroine, who followed Emerson's preachments.   WJM

Will Rogers Follies, The Musical play with book by PETER STONE, music by CY COLEMAN, and lyrics by COMDEN AND GREEN; opened 1 May 1991 at the refurbished PALACE THEATRE on Broadway, won six Tony Awards (including Best Musical), and settled in for a long run (closed after 983 performances and 34 previews). Directed by TOMMY TUNE and starring Keith Carradine as the cowboy philosopher, this vehicle is a musical biography staged as one of ZIEGFELD'S REVUES. Most critics complained that the format didn't work but praised the showmanship of Carradine, the spectacular staging and choreography of Tune, and the settings of TONY WALTON, costumes of WILLA KIM. and lighting of JULES FISHER. DAVID RICHARDS accurately predicted that the musical's "sumptuous production numbers, exquisite chorus girls, phosphorescent rope tricks in black light, a dog act, songs you actually want to hum, a stairway to paradise (or somewhere thereabouts), close harmony, and shapely legs in kaleidoscopic patterns" would be what audiences wanted to see.   TLM

Williams, Barney [né Bernard O'Flaherty] (1823–76) Irish-born actor whose first appearance on the New York stage was in 1836. In 1850 he married Maria Pray Mestayer (1828–1911), the widow of actor Charles Mestayer. For 20 years, the Williamses achieved considerable success, both in America and Great Britain, as a popular starring team in romantic Irish comedies such as *Born to Good Luck* and Samuel Lover's *Rory O'More*. Williams was regarded as unrivaled as the broadly comic, joking, hard-drinking but appealing stage Irishman. For two seasons (1867–9) he managed the old WALLACK'S THEATRE (by then the Broadway). His last appearance in *The Connie Soogah* and *The Fairy Circle* was at BOOTH'S THEATRE in New York on Christmas night, 1875.   DJW

Williams, Bert [né Egbert Austin Williams] (1874–1922) AFRICAN AMERICAN comedian, born in Nassau, British West Indies, who began in MINSTREL SHOWS, where he had to learn the standard "stage-darky" dialect and affect blackface to conceal his light complexion. From 1893 to 1908, he teamed with George Walker, who played the flashy free-spending urban sport to Williams's

Bert Williams in blackface. Photo by Cavendish Morton, London. *Courtesy:* Laurence Senelick Collection.

melancholy, shuffling fall-guy, both in VAUDE-VILLE and a series of successful all-black musicals, including *Sons of Ham* (1900), *In Dahomey* (1903), and *Bandana Land* (1908). When Walker retired in 1909, the victim of advanced paresis, Williams went solo; already the first black comic to record for Victor (from 1901), he was known nationwide for such lugubrious songs as "I'm a Jonah Man" and "Nobody," and founded the first all-black actors' friendly society in 1906. Over protests from some of the white cast, Williams became the first black performer in The ZIEGFELD *Follies,* in which he played annually during 1910–19 (missing only 1913 and 1918). "The funniest man I ever saw and the saddest man I ever knew," as W. C. FIELDS called him, played in tandem with LEON ERROL and EDDIE CANTOR, and never failed with his one-man poker game. The most recent study of Williams – more than a biography – by Louis Chude-Sokei (*The Last "Darky"*) was published in 2006. LS

Williams, Jesse Lynch (1871–1929) Journalist, writer, and dramatist, remembered primarily as the winner in 1918 of the first Pulitzer Prize for Drama, WHY MARRY? Acted by amateurs and published as *And So They Were Married* (1914), *Why Marry?* first questioned and then carefully defended the institution of marriage as the best that society can offer. *Why Not?* (1922) scrutinized divorce through two mismated couples and arrived at the same conclusion. As other plays reveal (such as *Lovely Lady,* 1925, concerned with parents and children), Williams's comedic solution to society's problems remained conventional. WJM

Williams, John D. (1886?–1941) Producer and director, remembered today as the first producer to put EUGENE O'NEILL on the Broadway stage, having been persuaded by actor RICHARD BENNETT to give BEYOND THE HORIZON a trial matinee (1920). Williams had previously demonstrated that he was willing to produce controversial material with Galsworthy's *Justice* (1916), Maugham's *Our Betters* (1917), and AUGUSTUS THOMAS's *The COPPERHEAD* (1918). He directed the long-running production of *Rain* (1922), adapted from the Maugham short story of a prostitute who resists reformation. He was, for a time, associated with CHARLES FROHMAN, and helped persuade MAUDE ADAMS to return to the stage (1931 tour). MR

Williams, Samm-Art (1946–) AFRICAN AMERICAN actor, producer, screenwriter, and playwright from North Carolina. He joined the NEGRO ENSEMBLE COMPANY in 1973, played a number of prominent roles, and participated in its Playwrights' Workshop. Five of his plays were produced by the company, including *Home* (1979), about a black youth who leaves his southern farm for the urban North: Initially prosperous, he becomes embroiled in illegal dealings, loses everything, and decides to return home and rebuild his life. The play had an extended run at St. Mark's Playhouse and transferred to Broadway (1980) for 279 additional performances, and was revived OFF-BROADWAY by NEC in 1981. It won Williams a 1981 Guggenheim Fellowship in playwriting. Other plays include *Welcome to Black River* (1975, NEC) and *Friends* (1983, Brooklyn). EGH

Williams, Tennessee (1911–83) Playwright. From 1945, with his first success, *The GLASS MENAGERIE,* Tennessee Williams has had a deep impact on the American theatre, bringing to it an original lyric voice and a new level of sexual frankness. The pleasure and the pain of sex was the great, inescapable subject of both his work and his life. In different moods and styles and with varying effectiveness, Williams returned repeatedly to the same neurotic conflicts embedded within the same character types: The spirits of Blanche Du Bois and Stanley Kowalski, the fierce antagonists of his masterpiece, A STREETCAR NAMED DESIRE (1947), haunt practically all of his fables. Blanche is the lady of illusion and artifice, the fluttering southern belle whose veneer of refinement masks emotional starvation and sexual rapacity. Desired and feared by Blanche as well as by Williams, Stanley is the muscled male whose potency contains the promise of both salvation and destruction.

As in *Streetcar,* the battle between repression and release, between the puritan and the cavalier, is at the heart of Williams's most vibrant work: SUMMER AND SMOKE (1948), *The Rose Tattoo* (1951), and *Battle of Angels* (1940, closed in tryouts; rewritten as *Orpheus Descending,* 1957). In some plays (*Battle of Angels; You Touched Me,* 1945; SWEET BIRD OF YOUTH, 1959) lusty men reanimate languishing women; in others (CAT ON A HOT TIN ROOF, 1955; *The Milk Train Doesn't Stop Here Anymore,* 1963) the refusal of desirable males to satisfy deprived women provides the central conflict. Sometimes, as in *Cat on a Hot Tin Roof* and *Suddenly Last Summer* (1958, OFF-BROADWAY), men withhold sex from women because they are homosexual; other times, as in *Milk Train,* because they want to transcend sexual desire. The source of Williams's profound sexual conflicts was the war between his fatally mismatched parents: his mother a rector's prudish daughter, his father a blustery womanizer who called his sensitive son "Miss Nancy." Unable in the American theatre of the 1950s and '60s to write openly about his own homosexual passion, Williams created nominally heterosexual dramas, transmuting tormented autobiography into artistic metaphor.

After *The* NIGHT OF THE IGUANA (1961), an uncharacteristic play of resolution and completion, Williams descended into a critical and commercial decline for the remaining 22 years of his life. Some of his later work, notably *The Gnädiges Fraulein* (1966), *In the Bar of a Tokyo Hotel* (1969, Off-Broadway), and *Out Cry* (1973), chronicles the despair of creators who have lost control of their art. Other plays, such as *Small Craft Warnings* (1972, OFF-OFF BROADWAY) and especially *Vieux Carré* (1977, Broadway), are attempts at self-restoration in which Williams returns to the delicacy of *The Glass Menagerie.* His Rabelaisian middle period is framed, as it were, by the directly autobiographical *Glass Menagerie* and *Vieux Carré,* in both of which Williams displays a healing compassion not only for others but also for himself as a young man. But neither the plays about disintegration nor the ones of partial affirmation have had the impact of his earlier work: Audiences and critics have generally found the dramas too private.

In his later years Williams's personal life seriously deteriorated: He became increasingly dependent on drugs and alcohol and required periods of institutional confinement. Yet he continued to write daily, rigorously devoting himself to his craft. Despite the blurred focus, the occasional self-parody, the lack of control, there remains much of value in these later offerings, passages that testify to Williams's powerful sense of theatre and to his melodic gifts. Even the least of his plays is a vehicle for bravura acting, for in good plays and bad Williams created wonderfully actable neurotics. Twisted by desire, plagued by anxiety, Williams's victims and outsiders speak a poetry of the dispossessed flavored with wit, irony. and gallantry. Posthumously his *Not About Nightingales* (written in 1938) premiered at London's Royal National Theatre in 1998 and then at Houston's ALLEY. Another early play (1937), *Spring Storm* premiered in Texas and California in 1999 and Off-Broadway in 2004. In 1998 the HARTFORD STAGE began a multiyear retrospective of all of Williams's plays; and in 2003–4 a season of Williams's major plays took place at the JOHN F. KENNEDY CENTER, including a critically praised *The Glass Menagerie* with Sally Field (*Cat* and *Streetcar* were the other full-lengths revived).

Williams struggled through a long critical eclipse, but his reputation is now secure. Among American playwrights his achievement is equaled only by that of EUGENE O'NEILL. Recent bios include those by Donald Spoto (1985) and the award-winning *Tom* by Lyle Leverich (1995). FH

Williamstown (MA) Theatre Festival Founded in 1955 by Yale Drama School professor Nikos Psacharopoulos, this festival, held on the Williams College campus, has presented over 330 mainstage productions since its inception. Known for its appeal to established actors, many now primarily in films, as a place where they can return frequently to the stage, Williamstown also uses some of the best directors and designers in the U.S. and presents not only classics but avant-garde risks and unknown new plays. A rotating company of over 400 has been associated with the Festival, including the likes of COLLEEN DEWHURST, FRANK LANGELLA, JAMES NAUGHTON, AUSTIN PENDLETON, CHRISTOPHER REEVE, RICHARD THOMAS, OLYMPIA DUKAKIS, BLYTHE DANNER,

GERALDINE FITZGERALD, BETTY BUCKLEY, LINDA EMOND, MARISA TOMEI, KATE BURTON, Michael York, and Richard Chamberlain. A complex operation producing today 11 plays a season, WTF has gained an international reputation and is considered by many the outstanding summer theatre establishment in the U.S. In 2002 it received the Regional Theatre Tony Award. After Psacharopoulos's death in 1989, Peter Hunt, whose association with Williamstown had begun in 1958, was appointed artistic director, but he was dismissed in 1995. Hunt's successor was former stage manager MICHAEL RITCHIE (1996–2004), who in turn was replaced, after becoming artistic director of the CENTER THEATRE GROUP in LA, by British-born actor ROGER REES. During Ritchie's tenure, nearly two dozen WTF productions transferred to other theatres. With new facilities built for the college (opened 2005), the WTF now has state-of-the-art theatre venues.   DBW

Willis, Nathaniel Parker (1806–67) Playwright and essayist who began an intense but brief association with the theatre in 1837 with *Bianca Visconti,* the winner of actress JOSEPHINE CLIFTON's $1,000 competition, and *The Kentucky Heiress,* also written for Clifton. Both plays failed in production. In 1839 Willis wrote TORTESA THE USURER for JAMES WALLACK, an appealing, well-dramatized story of a rich man who bargains for an aristocratic wife, who unfortunately loves another, but happily accepts an enchanting glover's daughter. Audiences, however, did not appreciate Willis's literary comedy, and starring actors did not want plays with several starring roles. Enjoying a reputation as the foremost essayist in America, Willis stopped writing plays.   WJM

Willson, Meredith [né Robert Meredith Reiniger] (1902–84) Composer, lyricist, and librettist, Willson studied at the New York Institute of Musical Art and played flute in John Philip Sousa's band and in the New York Philharmonic. For many years he worked as conductor and performer on NBC radio. In 1957 he turned his reminiscences of his Iowa boyhood into the hit Broadway musical *The MUSIC MAN,* surrounding the story of a fast-talking traveling salesman with patter songs, barbershop quartets, ragtime dance sequences, and Sousa-like marches. He returned to the same period and some of the same musical styles for *The Unsinkable Molly Brown* (1960). His final musical to reach Broadway, *Here's Love* (1963), was based on the film *Miracle on Thirty-fourth Street.* He wrote three autobiographical memoirs.   MK

Wilson, August [né Frederick August Kittel] (1945–2005) AFRICAN AMERICAN playwright whose position in the theatre rose meteorically in fewer than five years. Winner of the 1987 Pulitzer Prize for Drama for FENCES (set in Chicago, this is the only play of his not in Pittsburgh), and the 1990 Prize for *The PIANO LESSON,* he wrote a series of plays, each set in a different decade (e.g., *Fences,* 1950s; *Piano,* 1930s), that evolved into a cycle of dramas that he termed his "view of the black experience of the 20th century." Wilson focused on what he perceived as the largest idea that confronted blacks in each decade, drawing heavily on his own experience growing up in the Hill district of Pittsburgh, a black slum community. Wilson also was typical of an American playwright whose work was fostered in the regions, with developmental work at the EUGENE O'NEILL MEMORIAL THEATER CENTER's National Playwrights Conference and premieres at the YALE REPERTORY THEATRE under LLOYD RICHARDS's direction and elsewhere, beginning with MA RAINEY'S BLACK BOTTOM (1984; 1920s) and including *Fences, JOE TURNER'S COME AND GONE* (1986; Broadway, 1988; 1910s), *The Piano Lesson* (1987; Broadway, 1990), and *Two Trains Running* (1990; Broadway, 1992; 1960s; with ROSCOE LEE BROWNE). The latter, set in 1968 at a restaurant in Pittsburgh across the street from a funeral home and a meat market, focuses on disenfranchised characters looking back nostalgically and with some confusion at their limited "progress." Other plays in the cycle were *Jitney* (1982, Allegheny Rep, Pittsburgh; 2000, SECOND STAGE; 1970s), *Seven Guitars* (1995, GOODMAN THEATRE; 1940s), *King Hedley II* (2000, Pittsburgh Public; 1980s), *Gem of the Ocean* (2003, Goodman; 1900s), and his final play, *Radio Golf* (2005; 1990s). A solo show written and enacted by Wilson – *How I Learned What I Learned* – was seen in his adopted city of Seattle in 2003 (at SEATTLE REP, which also produced or hosted his full cycle). Up to his death his plays had been seen in more than 2,000 amateur and professional productions.

In addition to the Pulitzer, Wilson won, among many awards, the Drama Desk Award, the New York Drama Critics' Circle Award, and a Tony Award for *Fences,* plus Tony nominations for Best Play for each of his eight other plays produced on Broadway (six directed by Richards). Likened by the Pulitzer board to EUGENE O'NEILL, Wilson emerged as the richest theatrical voice in the U.S. of the past decade and managed to transcend the categorization of "black" playwright to speak through his dissection of black families and communities to a broad-based audience. He died in

2005 of liver cancer. Fourteen days later NYC's VIRGINIA THEATRE was renamed the August Wilson Theatre, becoming the first Broadway house to bear the name of an African American.   DBW

Wilson, Elizabeth (1921–) Actor. Prominent in stage, film, and television, Wilson has worked most often with MIKE NICHOLS, ALAN ARKIN, and JOSEPH PAPP. After 10 years in STOCK theatre, Wilson debuted on Broadway as Christine in PICNIC (1953), the first of some 30 Broadway and OFF-BROADWAY roles. Cast as spinsters, lonely mothers, and eccentrics, Wilson won both Tony and Obie awards for STICKS AND BONES (Harriet, 1971–2), a Drama Desk nomination for Threepenny Opera (Mrs. Peachum, 1976), an Obie for Taken in Marriage (Aunt Helen, 1979), Drama Desk and Outer Critics Circle awards for MORNING'S AT SEVEN (Aaronetta, 1980), and another Obie for Anteroom (Fay, 1985). In the 1990s she played Broadway twice – as Edna in A DELICATE BALANCE (1995) and Bonita Belgrave in Waiting in the Wings (1999) – and also appeared at The PUBLIC as Zofia in Tongue of a Bird (1999). In 2007 she was inducted into the THEATRE HALL OF FAME.   TH-S

Wilson, Francis (1854–1935) Comedian and singer. After an apprenticeship as a utility actor and low comedian with a STOCK COMPANY, Wilson made his musical-theatre debut in Our Goblins (1880). During 1885–9 he appeared in comic operas with the McCaull Opera Company, then established his own company. His greatest role was that of Cadeaux in Erminie (1886), a part he played nearly 1,300 times over 35 years. His other successes included The Merry Monarch (1890), The Lion Tamer (1891), Half a King (1896), and The Toreador (1902). From 1904 on, Wilson confined his efforts to comedy and drama. Because of his training in stock, Wilson brought to his musical roles the skills of a character actor, carefully preparing each move and gesture rather than trusting to improvisation. During 1913–21 he served as the first president of ACTORS' EQUITY. His entertaining autobiography was published in 1924.   MK

Wilson, Harry Leon (1867–1939) Playwright and writer. Wilson had limited success in the theatre. He was a collaborator with BOOTH TARKINGTON on The Man from Home (1907), and although the authors laughed at their hero, audiences laughed with him, and the play ran for five and a half years. However, their nine subsequent plays together – including Foreign Exchange, Your Humble Servant, and Cameo Kirby, all in 1909 – were poorly received.

Wilson also wrote the story from which KAUFMAN and CONNELLY created Merton of the Movies (1922).   WJM

Wilson, John Chapman (1899–1961) Producer and director. Born in New York and educated at Yale (1922), Wilson left a Wall Street career to become business manager for Noël Coward (1925). With Design for Living (1933), he began producing with Coward and LUNT AND FONTANNE, including The Taming of the Shrew (1935), Tonight at 8:30 (1936), IDIOT'S DELIGHT (1936), and Amphitryon 38 (1937). After 1938 he became an independent producer and director, presenting Blithe Spirit (1941), A Connecticut Yankee (1943), Present Laughter (1946), and The Winslow Boy (1947). He also directed KISS ME, KATE (1948), which ran for 1,077 performances on Broadway. He retired in 1958.   TLM

Wilson, Lanford (1937–) Missouri-born playwright who began writing plays at the University of Chicago and then became part of a group of playwrights at the CAFFE CINO in NYC. There his first script was produced, So Long at the Fair, in 1963. Since then his plays have been produced at LA MAMA and elsewhere OFF-OFF BROADWAY in New York, the Mercury Theatre in London, most regional U.S. theatres, and on Broadway.

Among his more successful scripts are The Madness of Lady Bright (1964), Balm in Gilead and This Is the Rill Speaking (1965), Rimers of Eldritch (1966), Lemon Sky (1970), The Great Nebula in Orion (1971, U.K.), The HOT L BALTIMORE (1973), FIFTH OF JULY (1978), TALLEY'S FOLLY (1979), and BURN THIS (1987, MARK TAPER and Broadway; 1991, London). Talley's Folly won Wilson the Pulitzer Prize for Drama and the New York Drama Critics' Circle Award. His 1982 Angels Fall was a critical, but not popular, success.

Wilson was one of the founders of the CIRCLE REPERTORY COMPANY, which staged several of his scripts, many directed by MARSHALL W. MASON. The Hot l Baltimore, involving various social outcasts in a condemned hotel, ran 1,166 performances, then the Off-Broadway record for a non-musical American play. Besides his Pulitzer and Drama Critics' Circle Award, Wilson has won the Drama Desk Vernon Rice Award for The Rimers of Eldritch, and Obies for The Hot l Baltimore, The Mound Builders (1975), and Sympathetic Magic (1997). In recent years Wilson has learned Russian in order to translate CHEKHOV, as for ROUNDABOUT's The Three Sisters (1997). Redwood Curtain (1992, SEATTLE REP) – his most recent original play seen on Broadway (1993), and dominated by JOHN LEE BEATTY's

Robert Wilson's production of Ibsen's *When We Dead Awaken* at the American Repertory Theatre, 1991. Wilson directed, adapted, and codesigned. Pictured is Stephanie Roth. Photo by Dan Nutu. *Courtesy:* American Repertory Theatre.

haunting scenery – was a disappointing yet earnest effort to deal with a combination of fantasy and reality in its treatment of the theme of America's tendency to sublimate its past nightmares, in this case typified by Vietnam. It was more successful in its 1995 ABC-TV version. Two Lanford one-acts (with JUDITH IVEY) under the title *Moonshot and Cosmos* were seen spring 1994 at Circle Rep. *Sympathetic Magic* was directed by Mason at SECOND STAGE in 1997; *Book of Days* premiered at actor Jeff Daniel's Purple Rose Theatre (Michigan) in 1998 (as did *Rain Dance* in 2001); and his version of IBSEN's *Ghosts* in 2002 at CLASSIC STAGE COMPANY. The SIGNATURE THEATRE devoted its 2002–3 season to Wilson: *Burn This, Fifth of July, Book of Days,* and *Rain Dance.* SMA

Wilson, Mary Louise (1932–) Born in New Haven, educated at Northwestern, this redoubtable versatile character actor has given many unforgettable performance since her 1956 NYC debut, from her recent cameo as an outrageous Queen Elizabeth in *The Beard of Avon* (NEW YORK THEATRE WORKSHOP, 2003), to her Obie and Drama Desk–winning portrayal of the high priestess of fashion Diana Vreeland in the ONE-PERSON SHOW *Full Gallop* (1995 and 1996), to Fraulein Schneider in the 1998 revival of CABARET, to her 2006 turn as the eccentric "Big Edie" Beale in PLAYWRIGHTS HORIZONS' *Grey Gardens* (Tony, Best Featured Actress in a Musical). Other credits of note include *The WOMEN* (1973 and 2001), *The ROYAL FAMILY* (1975), *The Importance of Being Earnest* (1977), *The PHILADELPHIA STORY* (1980), and the female *The ODD COUPLE* (1985), all on Broadway. DBW

Wilson, Robert (1941–) Director, designer, artist, and infrequent actor whose training as a painter and architect is evident in his painterly theatre compositions. Wilson's work with brain-damaged children, using physical activity to influence mental activity, also influenced his dreamy pieces, especially their slow pace and repetition of simple movement. Christopher Knowles, an autistic adolescent, became a collaborator with Wilson on pieces like *A Letter to Queen Victoria* (1974, Italy; 1975, ANTA Playhouse) and *Einstein on the Beach* (1976, Metropolitan Opera House), the latter also in collaboration with choreographers Andrew de Groat and Lucinda Childs and composer Philip Glass. Wilson was interested in Knowles's nondiscursive use of language and sought to create onstage his unusual way of structuring perceptions. Operatic in scale, Wilson's streams of visual and aural images lack plots and characters in any conventional sense and often employ massive scenery, animals, and complex lighting effects. Noh-like in tone, they sometimes take place in slow motion, altering the audience's sense of time; a simple action like crossing the stage can take an hour. *Deafman Glance* (1970, Iowa; 1971 BROOKLYN ACADEMY OF MUSIC) lasted eight hours, and *Overture to Ka Mountain,* created for the 1972 Shiraz Festival in Iran, lasted a week. In the 1980s Wilson began centering his work in Europe, where it was easier to find funding. There he created *The Man in the Raincoat* (1981, Cologne), *Great Day in the Morning* (1982, Paris), *The Golden Windows* (1982, Munich), the *CIVIL WarS* (1983, five countries; the German section had its U.S. premiere at the AMERICAN REPERTORY THEATRE, 1985), *The Black Rider: the casting of magic bullets* with music by Tom Waits (1990, Hamburg; U.S. premiere at BAM), the latter more traditionally staged, and *The Days Before: Death, Destruction and Detroit III* (1999, LINCOLN CENTER Festival).

Since the early 1990s, Wilson has been directing operas and plays from the classical repertory, among them *The Magic Flute* (1991, Paris), *Parsifal* (1991, Houston), and Büchner's *Danton's Death* (1992, ALLEY), *FOUR SAINTS IN THREE ACTS* (1996, Lincoln Center Festival); Strindberg's *A Dream Play* (2000, BAM); IBSEN's (adapted) *Peer Gynt* (2006, BAM). A 1995 production of *Alice* (based on *Alice in Wonderland*) with Waits's music was seen at BAM, as was *The Temptation of St. Anthony* (based on Gustave Flaubert's novel) in 2004. In conjunction with his direction of Ibsen's *When We Dead Awaken,* coproduced by ART and the Alley (1991), a major retrospective of his work was mounted at Boston's Museum of Fine Arts (seen later in Houston and San Francisco). *14 Stations,* commissioned by Oberammergau in 2000, was displayed later at MASS MoCA in Western Massachusetts. In 1993 Houston's Alley, with a $100,000 grant from the Pew Charitable Trusts, became an American home base for Wilson, where he evolved, among other productions, his ONE-PERSON deconstructed version of *Hamlet* (HAMLET: *a monologue*), seen in 1995 at the Alley, Lincoln Center (Serious Fun festival), and in Europe and described by the *New York Times* as possibly his "most overtly emotional theater piece" ever. Wilson, a prolific theatre artist with 8–12 new projects each year worldwide,

was the subject in 1998 of a production (*Bob*), conceived by ANNE BOGART (NEW YORK THEATER WORKSHOP). Arthur Holmberg's study of Wilson (1996) provides an excellent introduction. AS

Wiman, Dwight Deere (1894–1951) Producer or coproducer of 56 plays and musicals. A native of Moline, IL, and an officer in the family agricultural implements firm, John Deere and Company, he produced several plays by JOHN VAN DRUTEN and by PAUL OSBORN, and five musicals by RICHARD RODGERS and OSCAR HAMMERSTEIN II, as well as *The Little Show* (1929), its offspring of 1930 and 1931, and *STREET SCENE* (1947). His production of Osborn's *MORNINGS AT SEVEN* (1939) was his proudest achievement. He served as director of entertainment for the American Red Cross in the United Kingdom (1942–6). WD

Winchell, Walter (1897–1972) Broadway columnist and drama critic. A native New Yorker, Winchell began as a reporter for *Vaudeville News* (1922), moving to the *New York Graphic* (1924–9) as drama critic and columnist. He became a national celebrity through his radio programs (1929–56) and the syndication of his columns in Hearst's *New York Mirror* (1929–63). Winchell coined his own expressions ("cupiding" for romance and "mind your Winchell"). His fast-paced and staccato style gave a sense of excitement and importance to everything he covered. In his prime, he could turn a play or movie into a hit with a favorable notice. Neal Gabler's 1994 study is recommended. TLM

Windust, Bretaigne (1906–60) Paris-born director and actor who grew up in New York and attended Princeton University. In 1928 he cofounded the University Players at Falmouth, MA. He began his professional career in 1929 as assistant stage manager with the THEATRE GUILD. In 1932 he staged the London production of *STRANGE INTERLUDE*. He made his NYC acting debut in 1933 and received good notices although the play failed. The LUNTS noticed his work and hired him to play Tranio in *The Taming of the Shrew* (1935). His association with the Lunts continued in 1936 as he directed them in *IDIOT'S DELIGHT* and a year later in *Amphitryon 38.* After staging a successful revival of *The Circle* with TALLULAH BANKHEAD in 1938, Windust was to enjoy a decade of remarkable successes: *LIFE WITH FATHER* (1939), *ARSENIC AND OLD LACE* (1941), *The Hasty Heart* (1945), *The STATE OF THE UNION* (1945), and *FINIAN'S RAINBOW* (1947). Although he turned to films and television after 1947, Windust still enjoyed some success with *The Great Sebastians* (1956) and *The Girls in 509* (1958). His forte was comedy, and his trademark dramatic curtain calls and postcurtain tableaux.   TLM

Winer, Linda (1946–) Critic who immediately after college began her career as theatre, dance, and music reviewer on the *Chicago Tribune* (1969–80). She then joined the entertainment staff of the *New York Daily News* as "cultural affairs specialist" (1982–6), before being named "New York Arts Critic" by the new *USA Today,* reviewing theatre and dance (1982–6). In 1987 she moved to *New York Newsday* as an arts columnist, becoming its chief theatre critic in 1988. In 1979, Winer was the first woman asked to participate for a full week as master critic at the National Critics Institute of the EUGENE O'NEILL MEMORIAL THEATER CENTER. Since 1993 she has been an adjunct associate professor at Columbia University.   JD

Wings by ARTHUR KOPIT was first produced at the YALE REPERTORY THEATRE on 3 March 1978, then at The PUBLIC that June, and was moved to Broadway in 1979. Directed by John Madden, its original cast included CONSTANCE CUMMINGS as Emily Stilson, the stroke victim whose subjective experience the play depicts, and Marianne Owen as Amy, her therapist. Originally written as a radio play, *Wings* uses sound, color, lighting effects, and experiments with dialogue to depict the long process through which Mrs. Stilson's consciousness goes, from the fragmentation caused by the stroke to an integrated perception by means of which she can again recognize herself, her memories, and her experience. In the course of it, she must struggle to maintain her sense of self against both her own confusion and the misunderstanding of others. A musical version was staged in 1992 at the GOODMAN and The Public in 1993 (receiving the LORTEL Award for Best Musical in the 1993–4 OFF-BROADWAY season).   BCM

Winter Garden Theatre NYC theatre at 1634 Broadway, between 50th and 51st Sts. The Winter Garden, an important musical house, was designed for the SHUBERT BROTHERS by architect William Swasey. It opened on 20 March 1911 with a double bill that included a curtain-raiser called *Bow Sing* and *La Belle Paree,* a REVUE. The Winter Garden was less a totally new theatre than an extensive remodeling of an existing building, the American Horse Exchange. The remodeled structure contained a cabaret, as well as a large theatre, which was decorated in a garden motif and contained an unusual feature for the time: a runway extending from the stage into the auditorium. In 1912 the Winter Garden became the home of *The Passing Show* (an annual Shubert revue designed to compete with FLORENZ ZIEGFELD's *Follies*), which continued to be presented regularly through 1924. During the 1910s and early '20s, the theatre was also the home of a number of light musicals conceived as vehicles for Shubert star AL JOLSON. The Winter Garden was extensively remodeled in the 1920s by theatre architect Herbert Krapp. During the 1930s it housed such important musical attractions as the Shubert-produced editions of the *Ziegfeld Follies* and the long-running HELLZAPOPPIN, starring "Ole" Olsen and "Chick" Johnson. From 1928 to 1933, and again during 1945–8, the Winter Garden was used for motion picture showings. Following its second reconversion to live performance, the theatre has been the home of such major musicals as *WEST SIDE STORY* (1957), *GYPSY* (1974 revival), and *CATS* (1982–2000). After *Cats* closed, the theatre shut down briefly but reopened fall 2001 with the musical *Mamma Mia.* It was renamed the Cadillac Winter Garden in 2002 by the SHUBERT ORGANIZATION, which owns the 1,500 seat theatre, but reverted to its original name in early 2007.

An earlier house at 624 Broadway, built as Tripler Hall in 1850, burned down in 1854 (see FIRES), was rebuilt, went through several names and alterations, and finally became the Winter Garden in 1859. EDWIN BOOTH took control in 1864, but it burned down three years later.   BMcN

Winter, William (1836–1917) Drama critic, theatre historian, and biographer. Born in Gloucester, MA, and educated at Harvard University, Winter abandoned a law career for a literary one. Influenced by Henry Wadsworth Longfellow, Winter turned to writing poetry and reviewing books. In 1859 he moved to New York and worked as assistant editor and book reviewer for the *Saturday Press.* In 1860–1 he wrote briefly for *The Leader* before taking charge of the *Albion*'s dramatic department (1861–5), writing under the name of Mercutio. In 1865 he replaced Edward H. House as chief critic for the *New York Tribune,* a position he held until 1909, establishing himself as the foremost drama critic of his generation. The foundation of Winter's critical beliefs was essentially Aristotelian, tempered with 19th-century romantic idealism (later called "the Genteel Tradition"). He considered acting the primary art of theatre and the standard drama preferable to modern plays. He regarded the theatre as a temple of art to elevate and inspire humankind, and rejected the notion that art should depict real life. To Winter, beauty and morality were inseparable in art, and realism had banished both from the stage.

Jo Mielziner's set for *Winterset,* 1935. *Courtesy:* Don B. Wilmeth Theatre Collection.

Thus he saw IBSENism as a "rank, deadly pessimism . . . a disease, injurious alike to the stage and to the public." Winter prepared acting versions of SHAKESPEARE's plays for EDWIN BOOTH and AUGUSTIN DALY. He wrote lengthy biographies on Edwin Booth (1893), ADA REHAN (1898), RICHARD MANSFIELD (1910), JOSEPH JEFFERSON (1913), and TYRONE POWER (1913). His more than 50 books provide a comprehensive record of the late 19th-century American stage.   TLM

Winterset by MAXWELL ANDERSON was one of the author's most celebrated experiments in poetic writing, combining an "elevated language" with realistic, contemporary events. Based on the aftermath of the famous Sacco and Vanzetti trial, *Winterset* was written in blank verse and reflected Anderson's belief that theatre language must be poetic in order to explore universal truths. The play was produced by GUTHRIE McCLINTIC in 1935 and featured a superb performance by BURGESS MEREDITH and a spectacular set design by JO MIELZINER. It received mixed critical notices – although some of the praise was effusive – and ran for 195 performances. Considered by some to be Anderson's masterpiece, this contemporary poetic tragedy lost the Pulitzer Prize to IDIOT'S DELIGHT but was the first play to be voted the prestigious Drama Critics' Circle Award.   BBW

Wisdom Bridge Theatre Founded on the northern edge of CHICAGO by David Beaird in 1974, and flourished under the artistic direction of ROBERT FALLS (1977–85). Its productions were marked by physical energy coupled with creative direction – such as a *Tartuffe* set on a plantation after the Civil War and Kabuki versions of western dramas directed by Shozo Sato. By 1985 Wisdom Bridge had the second-highest budget of a nonprofit Chicago theatre. After several managerial changes staff payroll was suspended in early 1992 and the company's future was in peril, operating in 1994–5 in the Ivanhoe Theatre complex; but in late 1995, having lost its leadership and continuity, it went out of business.   SF

Wiseman, Joseph (1918–) Canadian-born actor who has played a variety of roles from archbishop to rabbi, Nazi officer to Spanish statesman, beggar to lecherous cabbie. He made his stage debut in THREE MEN ON A HORSE (1936, Saugerties, NY) and on Broadway in ABE LINCOLN IN ILLINOIS (1938). Wiseman performed both classical and contemporary roles at the MARK TAPER FORUM, ARENA STAGE, Pittsburgh Public Theater, AMERICAN SHAKESPEARE FESTIVAL, and CIRCLE IN THE SQUARE. Broadway productions include DETECTIVE STORY (1949), GOLDEN BOY (1952), *The Lark* (1955), *Incident at Vichy* (1964), Kipphardt's *In the Matter of J. Robert Oppenheimer* (1968, title role; Drama Desk Award), Wiesel's *Zalmen, or The Madness of God* (1974), and *The Tenth Man* (1989). Other stage: *Unfinished Stories* (1992, MARK TAPER; 1994, NEW YORK THEATRE WORKSHOP), KUSHNER's *Slavs!* (1994, NYTW), and ARTHUR MILLER's *I Can't Remember Anything* (1998, SIGNATURE; Obie). His

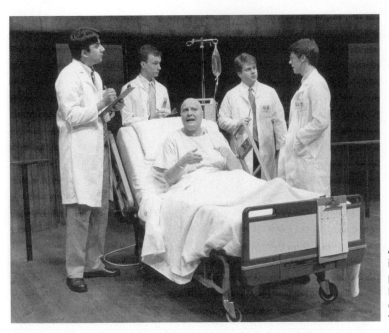

Anne Scurria as Vivian Bearing in Trinity Repertory Theatre's production of *Wit* in 2002. Photo by T. Charles Erickson. *Courtesy:* Trinity Repertory Theatre.

films include *Detective Story* (1951), *Les Misérables* (1952), *Dr. No* (1962), *The Night They Raided* MINSKY's (1968), and *The Apprenticeship of Duddy Kravitz* (1974). At 82 Wiseman returned to Broadway as Dr. Karl Wickert, a legal scholar, in the NATIONAL ACTORS THEATRE production of *Judgment at Nuremberg* (2001).   REK

Wit (alternative title, *W;t*) Play by a former Atlanta kindergarten teacher, Margaret Edson (her only effort), which won the 1999 Pulitzer Prize for Drama and, after a brief run at the MCC Theatre, transferred to the UNION SQUARE THE-ATRE, where it ran for 545 performances. *Wit* was championed by its first director, Derek Anson Jones, who campaigned for its first production in 1997 at the LONG WHARF; it proved Jones's only major success, as he died in 2000 of complications due to AIDS. Despite its theme, the play, about a John Donne scholar who is hospitalized as she is dying from ovarian cancer (but whom we also see in flashbacks), is not somber but uplifting and often humorous. Much of the play's success was due to the sensitive and insightful performance of KATHLEEN CHALFANT (who won an Obie) as Dr. Vivian Bearing, described by JOHN SIMON as a figure "of power and vulnerability, commanding intelligence and compelling irony." A 2001 HBO film, directed by MIKE NICHOLS, starred Emma Thompson.   DBW

Witching Hour, The Though produced by the SHUBERTS, playwright AUGUSTUS THOMAS was able to control many of the arrangements for this production, which opened on 18 November 1907 for 212 performances and was followed by a lengthy tour. It is melodrama in the tradition of those plays that capitalize on subjects and devices of current interest – in this case, mental telepathy and hypnotism. John Mason played the good-hearted gambler who, after he utilizes telepathy to influence a jury and hypnotism to stop an assailant in his tracks, finally understands how he was able to win all those card games.   MR

Witham, Charles W. (1842–1926) was one of the first distinguished scenic artists of the American theatre (see SCENIC DESIGN). He created the settings for all of EDWIN BOOTH's major productions in the late 1860s and '70s. He also was chief artist for AUGUSTIN DALY in the 1870s, and in the '80s he worked for EDWARD HARRIGAN.   AA

Wittstein, Ed (1929–) Set designer for theatre, television, and opera who studied at ERWIN PIS-CATOR's Dramatic Workshop, Parson's School of Design, and NYU. For television he designed the NBC Opera Productions, *Armstrong Circle Theatre,* and the *Steve Allen Show.* He designed several Broadway shows in the 1960s and '70s, including *Enter Laughing* (1963) and *Ulysses in Nighttown* (1974), as well as *The Knack* (1964) OFF-BROADWAY and several seasons at the AMERICAN SHAKESPEARE FESTIVAL. He is best known, though, as the designer of the simple theatrical set for *The FANTASTICKS*, which ran Off-Broadway for 42 years, and was revived in 2006 with his set and costumes.   AA

Wiz, The Musical of L. Frank Baum's novel *The Wonderful WIZARD OF OZ*, with book by William F. Brown; opened 5 January 1975 at the MAJESTIC THEATRE in NYC, running 1,672 performances and winning seven Tonys. Featuring an all-black cast, the familiar Oz story was retold in jive talk, with music and lyrics by Charlie Smalls that included rock, gospel, and soul music. The overall exotic style offered colorful and imaginative sets as the familiar characters appeared with a contemporary black twist, full of humor and satire. High-fashion costumes enhanced the spectacular dance numbers. The production appealed to a wide audience of all ages and ethnic groups.   ER

Wizard of Oz, The, by Paul Tietjens and A. Baldwin Sloane opened in Chicago 16 June 1902 and on Broadway (the Majestic Theatre on Columbus Circle) 20 January 1903. Adapted by L. Frank Baum from his novel *The Wonderful Wizard of Oz* (1900), the libretto transformed Dorothy into a romantic ingenue who traveled through Oz with her pet cow, Imogene (see ANIMAL IMPERSONATION). The production was known for its lavish scenery, including the Kansas Cyclone, the Wizard's Palace, and the Deadly Poppy Field. Vaudevillians MONTGOMERY AND STONE appeared as the Tin Man and the Scarecrow. The show toured the country for eight years, while Baum continued to adapt his Oz stories for the stage and wrote a total of 14 Oz books. He finally settled in Hollywood and founded the Oz Film Manufacturing Company (1914), which made half a dozen silent films during the single year of its existence. Other versions of Oz appeared onstage, in film, and on radio, and in 1939 MGM released the famous movie featuring Judy Garland, RAY BOLGER, Jack Haley, and BERT LAHR.   JDM

Wodehouse, P(elham) G(renville) (1881–1975) A successful London columnist and novelist, his song lyrics, for some of the most successful of English musical comedies of the first quarter of the century, were first heard on the American stage in *Miss Springtime* (1916). He collaborated with librettist GUY BOLTON and composer JEROME KERN on *Have a Heart* and *Leave It to Jane* (both 1917) and contributed lyrics and/or librettos

Fred Stone as the Scarecrow and Dave Montgomery as the Tin Man in the musical comedy *The Wizard of Oz.*
Courtesy: Laurence Senelick Collection.

to numerous other shows in the 1910s and '20s, notably *Oh, My Dear!* (1918), *Oh, Kay!* (1926), *Rosalie* (1928), and *The Three Musketeers* (1928). With George Grossmith and Ian Hay he wrote a series of humorous farces. He was also a drama critic for the magazine *Vanity Fair*. His wry lyrics and witty librettos did much to improve the prestige of Broadway musicals. Other than working in the U.S. frequently, he lived in exile there only in the final three decades of his life. The most recent bio (2004) is by Robert McCrum.   CI   MK

Wolfe, George C. (1954–) Kentucky-born African American playwright and director. Educated at Kentucky State and Pomona College, Wolfe was twice winner at the American College Theatre Festival and spent four years writing and directing in Los Angeles. His first NYC show, the musical *Paradise!* (1985) presented at PLAYWRIGHTS HORIZONS, was unsuccessful, but he followed it with *The Colored Museum* (1986), a hilarious lampoon of black-experience topics. Premiered at the Crossroads Theatre in New Brunswick, NJ, the play later ran for nine months at the Public Theater and moved to London. In 1990 he directed at The Public his play *Spunk*, based on three Zora Neale Hurston short stories (Obie for direction), followed the same year with his Public Theater production of Brecht's *The Caucasian Chalk Circle* set in Haiti and his selection as one of three resident directors at the New York Shakespeare Festival. His musical about Jelly Roll Morton, *Jelly's Last Jam*, premiered in Los Angeles (spring 1991) before opening on Broadway (spring 1992). Shortly prior to his direction of the acclaimed *Angels in America* by Kushner (for which he won the 1993 Tony for direction), Wolfe, termed bold, fearless, and the premier theatre artist of his generation, was appointed in March producer of the NYSF (the Public), an appointment greeted with enthusiasm and one that he held until 2004. Other than *Angels,* projects during that period – those directed by him – include *The Tempest* (1995); *Bring in 'da Noise, Bring in 'da Funk* (1996); *Elaine Stritch at Liberty* (2002); *Topdog/Underdog* (2002); and *Caroline, or Change* (2002). He also directed two failures: *On the Town* (1998 revival) and *The Wild Party* (2000). After leaving the Public Wolfe focused on film, beginning with HBO's *Lackawanna Blues.* EGH DBW

Women, The Biting social satire of Park Avenue elite women. This three-act play written by Clare Boothe Luce was one of the most successful comedies of the 1930s, opening at the Ethel Barrymore Theatre on 26 December 1936 and running for 657 performances. It subsequently was produced in many foreign countries and translated into several languages. No men appear in the play, although the group of indulged and malicious female characters are motivated almost exclusively by their relationships to men. Mary Haines, who is influenced by her catty crowd to divorce her husband because of his affair with a shopgirl, learns from them how to "sharpen her claws" and get him back. In 1939 MGM released an equally successful film version. Broadway revivals were staged in 1973 (Myrna Loy's Broadway debut) and in 2001, the latter directed by Scott Elliott for Roundabout. FB

Women's Project and Productions Producing group. Julia Miles founded The Women's Project in 1978 as part of the American Place Theatre, where she had been associate director since 1967. Initially funded by a Ford Foundation Grant, the Project became independent of American Place in 1987, with support from the Kentucky Foundation for Women. The project's mission is to identify, encourage, develop, and produce women playwrights and to help establish visibility for women directors. Miles frequently stated that her goal would have been met when women playwrights could be known just as playwrights. During 1978–2006 the Project presented more than 125 productions, published nine play anthologies, staged hundreds of rehearsed readings, and supported directors through a Directors Forum. During its history, Project writers have included Constance Congdon, Maria Irene Fornés, Emily Mann, Carey Perloff, Naomi Wallace, Eve Ensler, and Paula Vogel. Miles stepped down in 2003; Loretta Greco is the current producing artistic director. In Miles's honor, the Project's venue (previously Theatre Four) on West 55th St. was renamed the Julia Miles Theater. TH-S

Wonderful Town This musical – which reunited the team of Leonard Bernstein (music), Betty Comden and Adolph Green (lyrics), and director George Abbott, who had created *On the Town* in 1944 – opened at the Winter Garden Theatre on 25 February 1953. It was based on the play *My Sister Eileen* by Joseph Fields and Jerome Chodorov (who also jointly wrote the book for this show) and Ruth McKenney's stories. Set in NYC's Greenwich Village in the 1930s, it told of two sisters, a writer and an actress, who come to New York to pursue their careers. After several adventures the sisters achieve a measure of success, and, in traditional musical-comedy fashion, fall in love. The role of the older sister, Ruth, was played by film star Rosalind Russell, whose stylish humor brightened such songs as "One Hundred Easy Ways to Lose a Man." Edith (Edie) Adams brought a strong singing voice to the part of the younger sister. A breezy, audience-pleasing musical, it broke no new ground in form or content. It was revived in 1994 by the New York City Opera with Tyne Daly and in 2003 with Donna Murphy, who was replaced in late 2004 by Brooke Shields. MK

Wong, B. D. ("Bradd") (1962–) When he auditioned for the 1988 Broadway premiere of David Henry Hwang's *M. Butterfly*, Wong was an obscure actor with few credits since his 1982 debut Off-Broadway (at Town Hall). Cast in the showy role of Song Liling, a Chinese male spy masquerading as a women, he turned the role into a career-launching tour de force, winning all major New York acting honors for 1988, including a Tony for Best Featured Actor. After a gap of good stage roles, in 1999 he played Linus in a revival of YOU'RE A GOOD MAN, CHARLIES BROWN and the Reciter in a revival of PACIFIC OVERTURES in 2004. He has been more active on television as a regular on *Law & Order: Special Victims Unit* and *Oz*.   MB

Wood, Audrey (1905–85) AGENT. A native New Yorker and the daughter of William H. Wood, first manager of the PALACE THEATRE, Wood began her career as reader for the Century Play Company, where she met William Liebling. Together they founded an artists' representative agency, Liebling–Wood, Inc., in 1937, and married in 1938. In 1954, the agency was sold to Music Corporation of America, where she remained until 1962, when she became head of the drama department at International Creative Management. A massive stroke in 1981 closed her successful career. Her most famous clients included TENNESSEE WILLIAMS, ROBERT ANDERSON, WILLIAM INGE, ARTHUR KOPIT, CARSON MCCULLERS, and Truman Capote. A memoir was published in\ 1981.   MCH

Wood, Mrs. John [née Matilda Charlotte Vining] (1831–1915) Liverpool-born actress and manager who acted on provincial English stages for 12 years before marrying actor John Wood and coming to Boston in 1854. After their American debut at the BOSTON THEATRE (September 1854), they appeared in New York at the Academy of Music (1856) before becoming regulars with the Boston Company. Mrs. Wood played a guest engagement at WALLACK'S THEATRE in late 1856, creating the role of Minnehaha in CHARLES WALCOT's *Hiawatha*. At the end of the 1856–7 season, Mrs. Wood and her husband left for SAN FRANCISCO, where she quickly became a star. After the couple separated, Mrs. Wood returned east to play starring engagements for the next four years. In 1863 she began a three-year stint as manager of the Olympic Theatre. She returned to England in 1866 and acted only once more (1872–3) in America. Saucy, impudent, and fun-loving, Mrs. Wood was called by LAURENCE HUTTON "one of the best burlesque actresses our stage has ever known."   TLM

Wood, Peggy [Margaret] (1892–1978) Actress and author who became an established musical and comedy star with the long-running *Maytime* (1917). Though eyebrows were raised when she replaced KATHARINE CORNELL in G. B. SHAW's *Candida* (1925), years later she was remembered in the *New York Times* as a "versatile artist . . . very

much at home with Shakespeare, Bernard Shaw, SIGMUND ROMBERG and Noël Coward." Mama in the popular CBS-TV series *I Remember Mama* (1949–57), she received an Oscar nomination for her Mother Superior in *The SOUND OF MUSIC* (1965). In addition to a remembrance of JOHN DREW (1928), she wrote several volumes of memoirs.   MR

Wood, William Burke (1779–1861) Actor and manager, born of English parents in Montréal, Canada. As a young man he joined THOMAS WIGNELL's Philadelphia company, despite ill-health and lack of theatrical experience. Unsuccessful in tragic roles, Wood proved better suited to genteel comedy and ultimately found his niche in management. After the death of Wignell in 1803, he became assistant to the acting manager of the CHESTNUT STREET THEATRE, WILLIAM WARREN THE ELDER. In 1804 he married Juliana Westray, a good actress who appeared under his management for many years. Warren and Wood shared a prosperous quarter-century together, bringing their Philadelphia, Baltimore, and Washington theatres to international eminence. Wood sold his shares back to Warren before the 1826 season, but remained as a company member. He left in 1828 to manage the new ARCH STREET THEATRE, Philadelphia; and during 1829–46 he was at that city's WALNUT STREET THEATRE. His reminiscences are recorded in *Personal Recollections*, published in 1855.   DBW

Woodard, Charlayne (1955–) Actor and playwright, born in Albany, NY, a graduate of the GOODMAN School of Drama and a member of The ACTORS STUDIO. She is the author of three solo shows – *Pretty Fire*, *Neat*, and *In Real Life* – that have been performed widely (including at MAHATTAN THEATRE CLUB in 1993, 1997, and 2002, respectively). Her most recent play, *Flight* (2006, A CONTEMPORARY THEATRE), deals with an enslaved African community in the American south of the 1850s. Her OFF-BROADWAY acting credits (in addition to her ONE-PERSON performances) include *A . . . My Name Is Alice* (1984), *Hang on to the Good Times* (1985), *Twelfth Night* (Maria, 1989) at the Delacorte, *The Caucasian Chalk Circle* (1990) at The PUBLIC, and FUGARD's *Sorrows and Rejoicings* (2002) at SECOND STAGE. She was in both the original 1978 production of *Ain't Misbehavin'* and its 1988 revival. Her regional theatre and film credits are extensive, including Tituba in the film of *The CRUCIBLE* and Miss Jadie in the 2005 film *Lackawanna Blues*.   DBW

Woodland Players see GREET PLAYERS

Woodruff, Robert (1947–) Freelance director and, from 2001 to 2007, artistic director of the AMERICAN REPERTORY THEATRE. With a graduate degree in theatre from San Francisco State University, Woodruff cofounded the EUREKA THEATRE and created the important Bay Area Playwrights' Festival. He directed the premieres of SAM SHEPARD'S CURSE OF THE STARVING CLASS (1978) for the NEW YORK SHAKESPEARE FESTIVAL and BURIED CHILD and TRUE WEST at the MAGIC THEATRE. He also directed the Flying Karamazov Brothers in A Comedy of Errors at LINCOLN CENTER (1987). Often controversial, Woodruff has been one of our more imaginative avant-garde directors; his adventurous approach continued at ART.   JDM

Woods, A(ladore) H(erman) (1870–1951) Producer; he claimed that *Try and Get It* (1943) was his 409th production in all venues. At the peak of his success in the late 1920s, he had 23 plays running, some on Broadway, most on the road. Born in Budapest, Hungary, Woods grew up on NYC's Lower East Side. The operator of a Bowery nickelodeon, he turned in 1899 to producing low-budget melodramas, such as Theodore Kremer's *Bertha, the Sewing Machine Girl* (1906). In 1912 he built the Eltinge Theatre in honor of JULIAN ELTINGE, renowned female impersonator and star of his 1911 hit *The Fascinating Widow*. Woods's greatest Broadway hit was Bayard Veiller's melodrama *Within the Law* (1912), which ran 512 performances at that theatre. His success was based on the timeless appeal of sex, as in *Up in Mabel's Room* (1919); sentiment, as in *Eyes of Youth* (1917); lurid violence, as in *The Shanghai Gesture* (1926); and ethnic travesty, as in a Jewish-dialect series beginning with *Potash and Perlmutter* (1913).   WD

Woodworth, Samuel (1785–1842) Playwright, best known for his song "The Old Oaken Bucket" and for *The FOREST ROSE* (1825, with music by John Davies), a light-hearted glorification of American farmers that became a vehicle for a host of "YANKEE" actors for 40 years and is often called "the first American musical hit." He wrote seven other plays (including *The Deed of Gift*, 1822; *LaFayette*, 1824; and *The Cannibals*, 1833), a patriotic novel, dedicatory addresses, and sentimental ballads, and edited numerous periodicals and newspapers, notably the *New York Mirror* (1823–42). He received small profit from his literary endeavors and died in poverty.   RM

Woollcott, Alexander (1887–1943) Drama critic who made his debut as a critic for the *New York Times* in 1914, replacing Adolph Klauber. His battles with the SHUBERTS in 1915 made him a celebrity. After military service in Paris (1917–19), he returned to the *Times*, and helped establish that witty "vicious circle" that met for lunch at the "Algonquin Round Table." In 1922 he was hired away by the *Herald*, and later reviewed for the *Sun* (1924–5) and the *World* (1925–8). In 1929 he established his "Shouts and Murmurs" column in the *New Yorker*, began his radio show (later commanding up to $3,500 per program for *The Town Crier*), and collaborated on two plays with GEORGE S. KAUFMAN (*The Channel Road*, 1929; *The Dark Tower*, 1933). He also appeared frequently as an actor, playing, according to BROOKS ATKINSON, "a sort of virtuoso fat man." Woollcott remains best known as the model for Sheridan Whiteside in Kaufman and HART's *The MAN WHO CAME TO DINNER*. Vitality and urbanity were his trademarks. Edwin Hoyt's 1968 bio remains serviceable.   TLM

Woolly Mammoth Theatre Company Nonprofit WASHINGTON, DC, theatre founded in 1980 by actors Howard Shalwitz (current artistic director) and Roger Brady and devoted to new plays. In May 2005 the company moved into its first permanent home, after 13 years in a rented warehouse, a new 265-seat, courtyard-style theatre in downtown DC. The theatre has made a concerted effort to produce works "that explore the edges of theatrical style and human experience" while serving the local community. Its numerous awards includes five Charles MacArthur Awards for Outstanding New Play.   DBW

Wooster Group, The New York ensemble formed in 1975 under the direction of ELIZABETH LECOMPTE, assistant director for RICHARD SCHECHNER's PERFORMANCE GROUP, which it would succeed in Soho's Performing Garage. Wooster Group's other members have included JAMES CLAYBURGH, WILLEM DAFOE, SPALDING GRAY, Peyton Smith, Kate Valk, and Ron Vawter. The Group, recognized as "one of the most radically political, culturally radical theatres in the country, perhaps the world," composes "large ensemble multi-media theatre pieces," which join a repertoire.

The Wooster Group explores frequently unexamined, often suppressed and disturbing elements of society and culture, challenging unquestioned assumptions. Its material is derived from sources whose texts and images are quoted, reworked and juxtaposed with fragments of disparate other elements. It aims "to create a 'theater reality' that incorporates life rather than represents it," habitually restructuring the spectator–performer relationship unconventionally.

Wooster Group pieces have included the trilogies *Three Places in Rhode Island* (1975–8) and *The Road to Immortality* (1981–7), and an epilogue to the latter (*Brace Up!*, 1991, revived 2003; based on CHEKHOV). Another Chekhov-inspired production (a meditation on *Three Sisters*), *Fish Story: A Documentary about Theatre Life in Eight Dances,* begun in 1992, premiered November 1994. Other productions have included The HAIRY APE (1995); *The* EMPEROR JONES (1992; revived 1998, 2006) with Kate Valk as Brutus Jones; *House/Lights* (1998; Obie; revived 2005) inspired by GERTRUDE STEIN; *North Atlantic* (1984, revived 1999); *To You, The Birdie!* (2001; Obie); *Poor Theater* (2003). The Group produces films and videos including Michael Kirby's *White Homeland Commando;* in 1990 they participated in the international Los Angeles Theatre Festival, and in 1991 received an Obie for Sustained Achievement. Since 2002 some performances have been at St. Ann's Warehouse, Brooklyn.   REK

Worth, Irene (1916–2002) American-born actress, a graduate of UCLA, known equally on both sides of the Atlantic. Praised for the musicality of her voice and her commanding stage presence, her talent was held in high esteem by both critics and colleagues. She made her professional debut with a touring company in 1942, then appeared a year later on Broadway with Elisabeth Bergner in *The Two Mrs. Carrolls.* Seeking classical training, she went to London in 1944 to study with Elsie Fogerty. Her first noteworthy appearance in London was as Ilona in Molnár's *The Play's the Thing* (1947). She appeared as Celia in the premiere of *The Cocktail Party* at the Edinburgh Festival (1949). After working with the Old Vic Company (1951–3), she helped found (with TYRONE GUTHRIE and Alec Guinness) the Stratford Festival in 1953. Following a succession of critically acclaimed portrayals in London, New York, and Stratford, Ontario, she joined the Royal Shakespeare Company, appearing as Goneril in Peter Brook's production of *King Lear* (1962). Other notable appearances in the latter part of her career included TINY ALICE (1964, NYC; 1970, RSC), Coward's *Suite in Three Keys* (1966, London), *Heartbreak House* (1967, Chichester), Brook's controversial *Oedipus* (1968, National Theatre), *Hedda Gabler* (1970, Stratford, ON), *The Seagull* (1973, Chichester), *The Cherry Orchard* (1977, NYC), *John Gabriel Borkman* (1980. NYC), a "majestically unruffled" Volumnia in *Coriolanus* at

London's National Theatre (1984), GURNEY's *The Golden Age* (1984, NYC), and Grandma Kurnitz in LOST IN YONKERS (1991, NYC; film version, 1993), for which she won her third Tony (the others being for *Tiny Alice* and a 1975 revival of SWEET BIRD OF YOUTH). A ONE-PERSON show in 1993–4 was based on the works of Edith Wharton; another, which she adapted, directed, and starred in – *The Gypsy and the Yellow Canary* – played at The PUBLIC in 1997; and in late 1998 she briefly appeared at The FLEA as George Sand in *Chère Maître.*   DBW

Wright, Garland (1946–98) Director. Born in Midland, TX, Wright's earliest ambition was to be a painter. His theatre interests developed while he was attending Southern Methodist University, and his professional career began soon after when he joined the AMERICAN SHAKESPEARE FESTIVAL in Connecticut (1970). In 1974 he helped found NYC's Lion Theatre and, coincidentally, began to work OFF-BROADWAY, where he directed *Vanities* (1976). In 1980 he started a three-year stint as GUTHRIE THEATRE's associate director and further molded his craft there with notable productions like *Camille* (1980) and CANDIDE (1982). During 1985–6 he held a similar position at ARENA STAGE; then in 1986 he was named artistic director of the Guthrie Theatre, the youngest in its history. He distinguished himself there with productions of *The Misanthrope* (1987), *Richard III* (1988), *Henry IV (Parts 1 & 2),* and *Henry V* (1990), among others, before his resignation effective at the end of the 1995 season. In November 1995 he became head of the New Directors Program at the Juilliard School. In the late 1990s, prior to his death from cancer, he directed DURANG's *Sex and Longing* at LINCOLN CENTER (1996) and Elizabeth Egloff's *The Devils* at the NEW YORK THEATER WORKSHOP (1997).   KN

Wright, Jeffrey (1965–) Actor, born in Washington, DC, educated at Amherst College, who has proven his versatility and chameleonic ability to inhabit his characters in both film and onstage. His four varied Broadway credits are ANGELS IN AMERICA (parts 1 and 2), for which he won the 1994 Tony for Best Actor in Featured Role (Belize); BRING IN 'DA NOISE, BRING IN 'DA FUNK (1996, as 'da Voice); and Lincoln in TOPDOG/UNDERDOG (2002, Tony nomination). He repeated his Belize in MIKE NICHOLS's film (2003) and gleaned excellent notices as the artist in the film *Basquiat* (1996), Martin Luther King Jr. in HBO's *Boycott* (2001), and as a villain in 2000's *Shaft.*   DBW

Wright, Richard (1908–60) AFRICAN AMERICAN novelist and playwright. Born in Roxie, MS, Wright moved to Chicago at age 19 and taught himself to be a writer. In 1938 he published a book of short stories entitled *Uncle Tom's Children*. The following year the novel NATIVE SON brought him international renown. It was dramatized by Wright and white playwright PAUL GREEN, and directed by ORSON WELLES in 1941, featuring CANADA LEE in the principal role. Wright's comedy *Daddy Goodness* was produced by the NEGRO ENSEMBLE COMPANY in 1968.   EGH

Wycherly, Margaret (DeWolfe) (1881–1956) London-born stage and film actress; student at Boston's Latin School and the AMERICAN ACADEMY OF DRAMATIC ARTS, she made her debut at 17 in *What Dreams May Come* with MME. JANAUSCHEK. She married playwright Bayard Veiller, spent many years performing in STOCK, and toured with RICHARD MANSFIELD. She created the role of Lydia in the stage adaptation of Bernard SHAW's *Cashel Byron's Profession* (1907); played a medium in her husband's *The Thirteenth Chair* (1916); and performed for two years as Ada Lester in *TOBACCO ROAD* (1933). In 1940 she went to Hollywood, where, in addition to *Sergeant York* (1941) and other films, she acted on television in the 1950s.   FHL

Wynn, Ed [né Isaiah Edwin Leopold] (1886–1966) Comedian who began in VAUDEVILLE in 1901, later teaming up with Jack Lewis as two collegians in the act "Rah, Rah, Boys." Starting with *The ZIEGFELD Follies of 1914* and *of 1915,* he found a comfortable solo niche in musical comedy, including *The Perfect Fool* (1921), which became his nickname; *Simple Simon* (1930); *The Laugh Parade* (1931); and *Hooray for What!* (1937). Wynn's stage persona wore horn-rimmed glasses and tiny porkpie hats, spoke with a lisp, giggled, and walked with a mincing gait. Many of Wynn's gags were predicated on an inability to complete an anecdote or a piece of music; his insane inventions included a typewriter carriage for eating corn-on-the-cob and a cigarette lighter that pointed out the nearest matches. During 1932–7 Wynn was "The Fire Chief" on radio; in the 1950s and '60s he played dramatic roles in films and television. Keenan, his son, was a prominent film actor; his memoirs (1959) include a good deal about his father.   LS

Y

Yablokoff, Herman (1904–81) YIDDISH actor. Born near Grodno (Belorussia), he was already a performer when he arrived in the U.S. in 1924. He starred in many musical productions, often directing and producing and even writing them himself. Among his best-known works: *The Clown, The Dishwasher, My White Flower,* and the song "The Cigarette Peddler." He made many recordings and appeared for years on WEVD Yiddish-language radio. After WWII he toured DP camps. Although he rarely performed in the last few decades of his life, he was longtime president of the Hebrew Actors Union and the Yiddish National Theatre.
NS

Yale Repertory Theatre An adjunct to the Yale School of Drama (established as a graduate school in 1955) in New Haven, CT, which in turn grew out of the Drama Department founded in 1925 by GEORGE PIERCE BAKER, this important RESIDENT NONPROFIT PROFESSIONAL THEATRE was founded in 1966 by ROBERT BRUSTEIN, who served as artistic director until 1979. In 1968 it moved into a church converted into a theatre with a thrust stage and seating for 489. Central to each season under LLOYD RICHARDS, who served as artistic director from 1979 to June 1991, were Shakespeare (see SHAKESPEARE ON . . .), ATHOL FUGARD (seven plays in all), and especially AUGUST WILSON, as well as the Winterfest of New Plays. Richards was succeeded by Stan Wojewodski Jr., formerly of Baltimore's CENTER STAGE, who in turn was replaced in 2002 by James Bundy, artistic director of the GREAT LAKES THEATRE FESTIVAL, who has focused on new works and innovative interpretations of the classics that connect to contemporary audiences. As of late 2006, Yale had produced 94 world and American premieres and had sent 10 productions to Broadway. In 1991 the Rep received the Regional Theatre Tony Award.
DBW

Yankee theatre Yankee actors achieved their greatest popularity between 1825 and 1855, though Yankee characters appeared both earlier and later. The first notable "Jonathan" – the most common name (or nickname) – was in ROYALL TYLER's *The* CONTRAST (1787); the last, Joshua Whitcomb in DENMAN THOMPSON's *The OLD HOMESTEAD* (1886). The stage Yankee possessed varying mixtures of the character attributes ascribed to rustic New Englanders ("down-easters"): simple, blundering, sentimental, parsimonious, patriotic, shrewd, critical of city folks, and devoted to tall tales and picturesque speech. This character was a storehouse of riches for eccentric comedians, many of whom began their careers as Yankee storytellers before appearing in plays.

The English comedian CHARLES MATHEWS Sr. was the first to discover the gold mine of good fun to be found in the Yankee in his *Trip to America* (1824) and *Jonathan in England* (1824). Four American actors quickly followed his lead:

1. JAMES H. HACKETT in his own *Sylvester Daggerwood* (1826), as Solomon Swap in *Jonathan in England* (1828), as Major Joe Bunker in *The Militia Muster* (1830), and as Lot Sap Sago in CORNELIUS A. LOGAN's *The Wag of Maine* (1834);

2. GEORGE HANDEL "YANKEE" HILL, often called "the most authentic," as John Bull disguised as Jonathan Doolittle in WILLIAM DUNLAP's *Trip to Niagara* (1828), as Jonathan in SAMUEL WOODWORTH's *The FOREST ROSE* (1832), in *Jonathan in England* (1832), as Jedediah Homebred in J. S. JONES's *The Green Mountain Boy* (1833), as Sy Saco in JOHN AUGUSTUS STONE's *The Knight of the Golden Fleece; or, The Yankee in Spain* (1834), as Hiram Dodge in *The Yankee Pedlar* (Anon., 1835), as Abner Tanner in Jones's *The Adventurer; or, The Yankee in Tripoli* (1835), and as Solon Shingle in Jone's *The People's Lawyer* (1839);

3. DANFORTH MARBLE in E. H. Thompson and Marble's *Sam Patch* (1836), as Deuteronomy Dutiful in Logan's *The Vermont Wool Dealer* (1838), as Jacob Jewsharp in J. P. Addams's *The Maiden's Vow; or, The Yankee in Time* (1838), as Solon Shingle in Jones's *The People's Lawyer* (1839), and as Lot Sap Sago in Logan's *Yankee Land* (1842); and

4. Joshua Silsbee in *The Forest Rose* (1840), *The Yankee Pedlar* (1841), *The Green Mountain Boy* (1853), and *The Vermont Wool Dealer* (1853).

In the 1830s and '40s, the Yankee actors were extremely popular in London, where critics found them not unlike "our own canny Yorkshire lads." RM

Yankowitz, Susan (1941–) Playwright. Using bold visual and verbal imagery, Yankowitz explores racism, sexism, and violence in avant-garde pieces, often created collaboratively. With the OPEN THEATRE, she developed *Terminal* (1969, Drama Desk Award). Other major productions include *The Ha-Ha Play* (1970), *Slaughterhouse Play* (1971, The PUBLIC), *Boxes* (1972), *True Romances* (1978, MARK TAPER Lab), *Night Sky* (1991, WOMEN'S PROJECT), *Under the Skin* (1995), and *Phaedra in Delirium* (1998, Women's Project).   TH-S

Yeargan, Michael (1946–) Scenic and costume designer, a professor of stage design at Yale, where he had previously studied under DONALD OENSLAGER and MING CHO LEE. He has designed extensively at YALE REP, the HARTFORD STAGE COMPANY, AMERICAN REPERTORY THEATRE, the LONG WHARF THEATRE, MCCARTER, GOODMAN, and LINCOLN CENTER Theater as well as on Broadway. His 2005 design for *A Light in the Piazza* won him a Tony. In addition he has designed frequently for opera companies in Europe, the U.S., and Australia. Since a 1977 production of Strindberg's *Ghost Sonata* at Yale Rep, he has worked extensively with director ANDREI SERBAN, including productions of *The Seagull, The Umbrellas of Cherbourg,* and *Lysistrata;* other collaborators have included MARK LAMOS, ARVIN BROWN, and Elijah Moshinsky. His sets are typified by realistically detailed and textured romantic elements, but his theatricality and startling images place him in the postmodern school of design.   AA

Yellow Jacket by George C. Hazelton and J. Harry Benrimo introduced Western audiences to Chinese-style theatre; produced by William Harris Jr. and the SELWYNS for an 80-performance run at the Fulton Theatre, opening 4 November 1912. Frequently revived, the original starred Saxone Morland as Chee Moo, concubine to the Emperor, and George Relph as Wu Hoo Git, her son, both condemned to death because she bore the emperor an ugly baby. The two are spared by a friendly farmer, but Chee Moo soon perishes. Encouraged by a loving Suey Sin Fah (Grace A. Barbour), Wu Hoo defeats his step-brother and earns the right to wear the emperor's yellow jacket. Signor Perugini, functioning as a Greek chorus, narrated the drama, while a stagehand, recalling the visible Chinese property man, arranged settings.   GSA

Yellow Robe, William S., Jr. (1960–) Playwright, actor, director, poet, and educator; enrolled member of the Assiniboine Nation of northeastern Montana. He has written more than 45 plays and a book for a musical, including *The Independence of Eddie Rose, Sneaky, The Star Quilter, The Body Guards, The Council, Better-n-Indins, Falling Distance,* and *The Pendleton Blanket.* His *Grandchildren of the Buffalo Soldiers,* a semiautobiographical drama, was coproduced in 2005 by TRINITY REP (where, on a THEATRE COMMUNICATIONS GROUP grant, he was playwright-in-residence for three years) and PENUMBRA THEATRE. Yellow Robe has taught at Brown University and the universities of Montana and Maine. He often sets his plays in rural or reservation communities, examining complex contemporary Native cultures and issues.   DBW   AH

Yeston, Maury (1945–) An unusually versatile American composer-lyricist who earned a Yale Ph.D., served for eight years as Yale's director of undergraduate studies in music, and won Tonys for the scores to *Nine* (1982, book by ARTHUR KOPIT) and *Titanic* (1997, book by PETER STONE). He also earned a third nomination for his contributed songs to *Grand Hotel* (1990). Yet if Broadway mountings of Yeston musicals are rare, his output is large and his ability to work with librettists of varying sensibilities is widely admired. Other works include *One Two Three Four Five,* about the first five books of the Bible (1987, MANHATTAN THEATRE CLUB; book by LARRY GELBART, later rewritten by David Hahn as *In the Beginning*); *Phantom* (1991, book by Kopit), a version of *Phantom of the Opera* (not the Broadway one) that successfully toured the nation; and *Death Takes a Holiday* (draft completed early 2000s, with book by Peter Stone), based on the classic 1934 film. In 1989 Yeston released a concept album for *Goya . . . A Life in Song,* for which Placido Domingo was to make his Broadway debut. The show floundered, but a single, "Till I Loved You," was a Top-40 hit for Barbra Streisand. Yeston has taught in the BMI LEHMAN ENGEL Musical Theater Workshop for more than 30 years.   LJ

Yew, Chay (1966–) Chinese American playwright-director, raised in Singapore, studied at Pepperdine University at 16. Since 2000 artistic director of SEATTLE's Northwest Asian American Theatre; former director of MARK TAPER FORUM's Asian American Theatre Workshop (1997–2005). While visiting Singapore, Yew had his first play, *As If He Hears* (1989), initially banned because of its sympathetic portrayal of a gay character. Back in the U.S. in 1988 to study film and theatre at Boston

University, Yew wrote a thesis film script, *Porcelain* (a crime of passion in which a Chinese man shoots his white lover in a public East London toilet); as revised for the stage it won the 1992 London Fringe Award for Best Play. Yew's U.S. breakthrough, *A Language of Their Own* (1995), about two Chinese lovers who break up after one is diagnosed with AIDS, starred B. D. WONG (PUBLIC THEATER). Other notable plays include *Red* (1998, INTIMAN; repressive effects of the Cultural Revolution on Beijing opera); *A Beautiful Country* (1998, CORNERSTONE; drag queen Miss Visa Denied recounts history of Asian immigrants in the U.S.); and *The Long Season* (slated for 2007, GEORGE STREET; a musical about Filipino salmon cannery contract workers in Alaska in the 1930s).   RG

Yiddish Art Theatre, The MAURICE SCHWARTZ's company, which opened at NYC's Irving Place Theatre in 1918, moving in 1926 to a new theatre on Second Avenue. Rejecting the popular sentimental and melodramatic improvisations of *shund* (rubbish) theatre in favor of carefully rehearsed plays of quality, ensemble acting, and a high standard of presentation, its first successes came with PERETZ HIRSHBEIN's earthy pastoral play *A Secluded Nook,* followed by the same writer's *The Blacksmith's Daughters,* another delicate, idyllic play of village life. During its second year (its first as the YAT), 15 plays were added to the repertoire, including Sholom Aleichem's *Tevye the Milkman* and four of JACOB GORDIN's plays, including *God, Man and Devil,* based on the Faust legend. Inevitably "stars" were created, like BERTHA GERSTEIN, LUDWIG SATZ, and Muni Weisenfreund (PAUL MUNI). Several productions in English translation transferred to Broadway, including Schwartz's greatest personal triumph: Israel Joshua Singer's *Yoshe Kalb* (1932; Broadway, 1933). The company remained active until the late 1930s.   AB

Yiddish theatre arrived in America early in the period of mass eastern-European immigration with a production of AVROM GOLDFADN's *Koldunye; or, The Witch* (1882) in New York's The Bowery. Because professional secular Yiddish-language theatre was still a new invention, many immigrant artists and audiences first encountered it in the U.S. Because of the relative security and prosperity of America's Jews, the U.S. (especially the Lower East Side of NYC) is where Yiddish theatre flourished earliest, longest, and (at least, in the popular genres) most vigorously.

Yiddish theatres quickly proliferated in New York, Boston, Detroit, Chicago, Baltimore, and elsewhere. By 1914 NYC had some 14 resident companies, as well as individual productions; troupes from there toured throughout the U.S., South America, and the Old Country. Companies developed structures dominated by a star-manager, repertory, or a family nucleus. A cluster of Yiddish theatrical unions organized in NYC (and Buenos Aires), beginning with the Hebrew Actors Union Local One (1887).

Yiddish theatre has always been an important community institution, offering entertainment and escape, reminiscences of home and tradition, portrayals of immigrant life, and political forums. Translations of classics introduced immigrants to world literature; translations of mainstream hits helped them Americanize. Theatregoing was linked with activities of fraternal organizations; streets and cafés in theatre districts were thronged and sociable. In most Yiddish-speaking communities, amateur groups formed for aesthetic, social, and political purposes. Related industries also developed: cabarets, sheet music and recordings of show tunes, radio, and film. The Yiddish press printed related reviews, editorials, and gossip, and play texts were published for reading and amateur productions.

Stars, major community figures, commanded fierce fan (*patriotn*) loyalty. In the early years, the preferred acting style was grand and emotional. Comedy came out of broad character "types," and with music in most plays, all actors sang. Early stage idols included comic SIGMUND MOGULESKO, romantic baritone BORIS THOMASHEFSKY, dramatic actors JACOB ADLER and DAVID KESSLER, and actresses Sara Adler, BERTHA KALISH, KENI LIPTZIN, and Bessie Thomashefsky. Benefit performances honoring a specific star drew many fans, often supplying a major part of the actor's income.

People's tastes in theatre, from highbrow to low *shund,* served to define their positions in many other spheres. Play genres included music hall REVUES, costume operettas, domestic melodramas with music, and intellectual avant-garde. Playwrights included Avrom Goldfadn, "Professor" Moshe Ish HaLevi Hurwitz, Joseph Lateiner, Schomer, and – on a higher literary level – Sholom Aleichem (Sholem Rabinowitz), JACOB GORDIN, and Leon Kobrin. Composers included Alexander Olshanetsky, Sholem Perlmutter, and Joseph Rumshinsky.

Because the more intellectual artists and audiences served as conduit for European (especially Russian) innovations, American Yiddish theatre fostered naturalism and expressionism, "art theatres," and Stanislavskian "method" acting before other U.S. theatres, and the Yiddish avant-garde was often reviewed in the intellectual English-language press. This, along with a vigorous musical tradition, a new benefit system (whereby charitable organizations could raise funds by selling blocks of seats), and a trained community of passionate and committed theatregoers, influenced mainstream American theatre.

After WWI, restricted immigration and demographic movement away from the old neighborhoods began to strangle Yiddish show business. Also, steady assimilation meant loss of Yiddish language and culture. English words crept into dialogue; American fads influenced Yiddish productions. Actually, playgoers were comfortable seeing English-language shows and films, and many of the younger generation preferred them.

Nevertheless, another generation of stars came to prominence: CELIA ADLER, JACOB BEN-AMI, JOSEPH BULOFF, Pesach Burstein, BERTHA GERSTEIN, Samuel Goldenberg, Jennie Goldstein, Jacob Jacobs, Aaron Lebedeff, Michel Michalesko, Moyshe Oysher, MOLLY PICON, LUDWIG SATZ, RUDOLPH SCHILDKRAUT, MAURICE SCHWARTZ, Menashe Skulnik, and HERMAN YABLOKOFF. There were new popular playwrights, such as Z. Libin, H. Kalmanovitch, Max Gabel, William Segal, Anshel Shor, and Isidore Zolotarevsky, and composers such as Sholom Secunda. Little or art theatres – most notably Schwartz's YIDDISH ART THEATRE, Jacob Ben-Ami's JEWISH ART THEATRE (1919–20) and Irving Place Theatre (1926–7), and the ARTEF – performed ambitious repertory by SHOLOM ASCH, Osip Dimov (Joseph Perlman), PERETZ HIRSHBEIN, H. Leivick (Leyvik Halpern), and DAVID PINSKI. Acting styles ranged from broadly popular to abstract left-wing agitprop to Stanislavskian realism, according to the venue. Between 1935 and 1939, the FEDERAL THEATRE PROJECT sponsored several Yiddish troupes, notably in New York and the Boston area.

Hitler and Stalin destroyed the Old World sources of Yiddish culture and Yiddish speakers. Continuing acculturation, movement to the suburbs, ascendence of Hebrew, and the spread of films and television all severely diminished audiences. Ages of performers and spectators rose, making the repertory and performance style seem old-fashioned, while new scripts and performances per season steadily decreased. Limited runs became the norm, with fewer than eight shows per week, including matinees for the convenience of the elderly.

Nevertheless, in the decades since WWII, most New York seasons have offered at least one locally mounted musical comedy; additionally, there has often been a touring company from Israel, Latin America, or Eastern Europe plus revues in various venues. Postwar stars have included Bruce Adler, Mina Bern, Mike Burstyn, Ben Bonus, Reyzl Bozyk, Miriam Kressyn, Shifra Lehrer, Leon Leibgold, Jack Rechseit, Seymour Rexite, Eleanor Reissa, and Mary Soreanu. In NYC, into the 2000s, the Yiddish National Theatre sponsored by the Hebrew Actors Union mounted occasional productions; and the FOLKSBIENE, the world's longest continuously performing Yiddish company (and probably the last surviving one in the U.S.) – yet in recent years struggling for survival – has presented a new production annually (in 2005, *On Second Avenue*). Around the country, scattered amateur groups, many of them affiliated with Jewish community centers or with universities, give readings and performances; Jewish centers also sponsor theatre-related events, such as exhibitions of theatre posters and memorabilia.

After the American Bicentennial in 1976 (coincidentally, also the centenary of professional secular Yiddish theatre), increased interest in ethnic roots briefly fostered various innovative approaches to making Yiddish theatre accessible, including simultaneous-translation devices, English-speaking narrators in the wings, and frequent English interpolations in dialogue and lyrics. Bilingual shows, like *The Golden Land* (1985) and *Songs of Paradise* (1989, The PUBLIC), and English-language shows based on Yiddish theatre material, such as Goldfadn's *Kuni-Leml* (1984, JEWISH REP) attracted non-Yiddish-speaking audiences. For many American Jews – including those who have never seen it – Yiddish theatre retains a romantic resonance and is integrated in their images of their forebears and cultural tradition. Yet, with the death in 2002 of longtime president of the Hebrew Actors Union Seymour Rexite, the Union in 2005 was declared defunct. As of 2006 a great concern is the future of the Union building on East 7th St. and, more critically, the archives and records scattered throughout the structure.

NS

You Can't Take It with You Three-act comedy by MOSS HART and GEORGE S. KAUFMAN; opened at the BOOTH THEATRE, 14 December 1936, and ran for 837 performances. Recipient of the Pulitzer Prize for drama in 1937, the play has been revived regularly since, most notably on Broadway in two productions directed by ELLIS RABB in 1965 and 1983, the latter at the PLYMOUTH THEATRE with a star-studded cast headed by JASON ROBARDS JR., ELIZABETH WILSON, Bill McCutcheon, and COLLEEN DEWHURST.

The play presents lovable nonconformist characters of the Sycamore clan who are surviving the Depression by writing plays, making fireworks, playing the xylophone, and operating an amateur printing press. The most normal member of the family, Alice Sycamore, falls in love with the son of a Wall Street banker, and the play exploits the difference between these two worlds. The theme that money isn't everything was attractive in 1936 and has remained so since.   TLM

Youmans, Vincent (1898–1946) Composer who served in the Navy during WWI, then worked as a song plugger and rehearsal pianist before contributing songs to *Two Little Girls in Blue* (1921) and ultimately writing the scores for two of the most successful musicals of the 1920s: *No, No, Nanette* (1925) and *Hit the Deck* (1927). Songs by Youmans were also heard in *Great Day* (1929), *Nine-Fifteen Revue* (1930), *Smiles* (1930), and *Take a Chance* (1932). Although Youmans's output was relatively small, many of his songs, such as "Tea for Two," "I Want to Be Happy," "Hallelujah," "More Than You Know," and "Time on My Hands," have become classics of the musical stage. Gerald Bordman wrote a biography in 1982.   MK

Young, Stark (1881–1963) Drama critic, translator, playwright, and director. Born in Mississippi, Young earned degrees in English at the University of Mississippi (1901) and at Columbia (1902). After teaching in several universities, he became a contributing editor to *New Republic* in 1921 and an associate editor of *Theatre Arts* magazine (1921–40). Young replaced Francis Hackett as chief drama critic of the *New Republic* in early 1922 and held the position (except for the 1924–5 season, when he reviewed for the *New York Times*) until his retirement in 1947. He was an advocate of the New Stagecraft movement and worked closely with Eugene O'Neill, Kenneth Macgowan, and Robert Edmond Jones at the Provincetown Playhouse. He staged the premiere of O'Neill's *Welded* in 1924. Young wrote several plays, none successful. He is better remembered for his translations of Chekhov's plays, especially of *The Seagull* for the Lunts in 1938. His books include *The Flower in Drama* (1923), *Glamour* (1925), *Theatre Practice* (1926), and *The Theatre* (1927).   TLM

You're a Good Man, Charlie Brown Two-act musical comedy by Clark Gesner, opened 7 March 1967 at the Off-Broadway Theatre 80 St. Marks, running 1,597 performances. Based on Charles Schultz's popular "Peanuts" comic strip, this show began life as a children's record album.

Expanded into a stage musical, its virtually non-narrative book portrays, in a series of scenes much like a series of daily comic strips, a day in the life of Charlie Brown (Gary Burghoff) and the other familiar characters. Much of the charm came from director Joseph Hardy's playfully inventive staging, in which no attempt was made to make the characters resemble the original drawing except in costume (Snoopy was a plainly human actor) and scenes were created by assembling various geometric blocks. The consciously juvenile score contributed one pop hit: "Happiness Is." There was a modestly successful Broadway revival in 1999.   JD

Yulin, Harris (1937–) Actor and director whose stage credits include La MaMa, Hartford Stage, Circle in the Square, Mark Taper Forum, the Guthrie Theater, and Arena Stage. A quiet, thoughtful actor, he has performed classics at New York Shakespeare Festival (*Richard III*, 1966), premieres at Yale Repertory (*A Lesson from Aloes*, 1979), a revival of *The Visit* with Jane Alexander for Roundabout Theatre (1992), and Broadway appearances in *The Diary of Anne Frank* (Mr. Van Dann, 1997), *The Price* (Walter Franz, 1999), and *Hedda Gabler* (Judge Brack, 2001). Yulin directed McNally's *Cuba Si* and Brecht's *The Guns of Carrar* (Theater de Lys, 1968), Molnár's *The Guardsman* (Long Wharf, 1982), Adele Shank's *Winterplay* (Second Stage, 1983), and a critically acclaimed revival at Signature of *A Trip to Bountiful* with Lois Smith (2005). His films include *Another Woman* (1988), *Clear and Present Danger* (1994), *The Cradle Will Rock* (1999), *Training Day* (2001), and *Fur* (2006).   REK

Yurka, Blanche (1893–1974) Czech-born actress, brought to the U.S. as an infant, who began acting in 1907 after training for opera. She applied to David Belasco successfully for work on the legitimate stage, her first leading role being in *Is Matrimony a Failure?* (1909). Over the next decade she shifted to tragedy, playing Gertrude to John Barrymore's (see Drew–Barrymore) Hamlet (1922), Gina in *The Wild Duck* (1925), and later a series of strong-willed female roles, winning praise for her emotional depth and vocal timbre. She was also an active member and organizer of Actors' Equity, being elected to a variety of positions in that organization. In 1955 she retired from the theatre, decrying the poverty of the theatre at that time, but soon returned to both films and Broadway. She often wrote (including an autobiography, *Bohemian Girl*, 1970) and lectured about the theatre.   SMA

Z

Zaks, Jerry (1946–) German-born director. Educated at Dartmouth, Zaks began his theatrical career as an actor (GREASE, FIDDLER ON THE ROOF). His directing credits include *Lend Me a Tenor* (1989), for which he won a Tony. In the same year Zaks was called the outstanding director of comedy in the American theatre, with productions noted for pace, style, wit, and exceptional ensemble acting. He also restaged a successful *ANYTHING GOES* in London after reviving it at the VIVIAN BEAUMONT (1987). During his tenure at Lincoln Center as director-in-residence, he also successfully staged the 1986 revival of GUARE's *HOUSE OF BLUE LEAVES* and his *SIX DEGREES OF SEPARATION* in 1990, winning directing Tonys for both. In 1990 Zaks left Lincoln Center to work for the JUJAMCYN THEATERS, where his first effort was STEPHEN SONDHEIM's musical *Assassins* at PLAYWRIGHTS HORIZONS, followed in 1992 by a critically acclaimed revival of *GUYS AND DOLLS* on Broadway, winning his fourth Tony. Other notable credits include DURANG's *Sister Mary Ignatius Explains It All for You* (1981) and *The MARRIAGE OF BETTE AND BOO* (1985), SHUE's *The FOREIGNER* (1984) (all OFF-BROADWAY), and *Smokey Joe's Cafe* (1995; songs of Jerry Leiber and Mike Stoller), for which he was nominated for a Tony. He was director of Broadway revivals in 1996 of *A FUNNY THING HAPPENED ON THE WAY TO THE FORUM* with NATHAN LANE, in 2000 of *The MAN WHO CAME TO DINNER* (also with Lane), in 2003 of *LITTLE SHOP OF HORRORS*, in 2004 of *LA CAGE AUX FOLLES*, and in 2006 of *The Caine Mutiny Court-Martial* (previously seen in 1954 and 1983). In 1994 he received the 10th annual "Mr. Abbott Award" from the Stage Directors and Choreographers Foundation. SMA DBW

Zeisler, Peter B. (1923–2005) Director from 1972 through 1995 of THEATRE COMMUNICATIONS GROUP, the national organization for RESIDENT NONPROFIT PROFESSIONAL THEATRE. Educated at Columbia University (1947), Zeisler worked as a production stage manager during 1948–59 and helped establish the AMERICAN SHAKESPEARE FESTIVAL. A cofounder of the GUTHRIE THEATRE, he served as its managing director during 1963-7.

He founded the League of Resident Theatres (LORT) in 1967 and became its first president and a major arts advocate. TLM

Ziegfeld, Florenz (1869–1932) Producer. Ziegfeld's first venture into show business was as manager of SANDOW, a VAUDEVILLE strongman. After meeting singer ANNA HELD in Europe, Ziegfeld brought her to New York and presented her in several musicals. (They married in 1897, divorced in 1912.) At her suggestion, he created a Parisian-style REVUE called *Follies of 1907*, the first in a series that he continued to produce for the next quarter of a century. Initially presented on a modest scale, the *Follies* grew increasingly elaborate, eventually moving to the NEW AMSTERDAM THEATRE, where designers such as JOSEPH URBAN were given free reign to create ornate scenery and lavish costumes. In 1911 the show's title was changed to *The Ziegfeld Follies*. The motto "Glorifying the American Girl" underlines the *Follies*'s emphasis on choruses of beautiful women in glittering production numbers. Many of the shows also featured first-rate comedians such as BERT WILLIAMS, FANNY BRICE, W. C. FIELDS, WILL ROGERS, and EDDIE CANTOR, and popular singers and dancers such as NORA BAYES, MARILYN MILLER, and INA CLAIRE.

Besides producing annual editions of the *Follies,* Ziegfeld presented some of the most successful musical comedies and operettas of the 1920s, including *SALLY* (1920), *Kid Boots* (1923), *Rio Rita* (1927), *SHOW BOAT* (1927), *Rosalie* (1928), *The Three Musketeers* (1928), and *Whoopee* (1928; based on OWEN DAVIS's *The Nervous Wreck*). Rarely innovative in his choice of material or his production methods, Ziegfeld built his reputation as a producer on his ability to discover and nurture talented performers, and the care and expense with which he mounted his shows. Of numerous studies of Ziegfeld, the most recent and sumptuous is Richard and Paulette Ziegfeld's 1993 life. MK

Ziegfeld Theatre Corner of 6th Ave. and 54th St., NYC [Architects: Thomas W. Lamb and JOSEPH URBAN] In 1927, FLORENZ ZIEGFELD pushed the outer limits of the theatre district to Sixth Avenue when Hearst and Brisbane built him a theatre to house his productions. Its curved facade, egg-shaped auditorium, and Urban's mural *Lovers through History* were among its unusual features. One year after Ziegfeld's death, it was converted to movies, but in 1944 BILLY ROSE completely renovated it and returned it to legitimate status. During 1955–63 it was an NBC television studio, but from 1963 again a theatre, until it was demolished in 1966.   MCH

Ziemba, Karen (1957–) Elegant dancer, singer, and actor, born in St. Joseph, MI, and raised in Detroit. A Tony winner (as well as Drama Desk and Outer Critics Circle) for her featured role in SUSAN STROMAN's and John Weidman's *Contact* (2000), Ziemba's Broadway debut was a replacement in *A Chorus Line* in the late 1970s, followed by a small role in *42ND STREET,* and finally in the late 1990s as Roxie Hart (replacement) in *CHICAGO,* followed in 1997 by Rita Racine in *Steel Pier* (first Tony nomination). Her third Tony nomination was for *Never Gonna Dance* (2003). Her most recent Broadway appearance is in *Curtains* (2007). For the New York City Opera she has played Lizzie in *110 in the Shade* and Cleo in *The MOST HAPPY FELLA,* and for CITY CENTER ENCORES! has appeared in concert versions of *The PAJAMA GAME, Bye Bye Birdie, Allegro,* and *ZIEGFELD Follies of 1936.*   DBW

Zigler, Scott (1968?–) Director and actor, son of a Yale psychologist and a graduate of NYU's Tisch School of the Arts during which time he studied at the acting school founded by DAVID MAMET and William H. Macy and ultimately became a cofounding member of the ATLANTIC THEATER. His association with Mamet led to small roles in many of the latter's films, the 1991 direction of Mamet's adaptation of CHEKHOV's *The Three Sisters* at the Atlantic (in 2005 he directed a controversial production of a new translation of *Cherry Orchard* there), and the world premiere (AMERICAN REPERTORY THEATRE) of Mamet's *The Old Neighborhood,* as well as its Broadway outing in 1997. Since 1996 Zigler, who retains connection to the Atlantic, has been an associate artistic director and head of the advanced theatre training program at ART. He has also directed for such companies as ACTORS THEATRE OF LOUISVILLE, STEPPENWOLF, the ALLEY, and the MCCARTER.   DBW

Zimmerman, Mary (1960?–) CHICAGO-based director and playwright, a product of the Northwestern University performance-studies program (B.S., M.A., and Ph.D.), where she now teaches. Her training has focused her attention on the adaptation of material from other literary forms, such as her 2002 Tony Award–winning (Best Direction) *Metamorphoses,* based on Ovid and originally staged for Chicago's Lookingglass Theatre Company where she is an ensemble member. A number of her productions have premiered at the GOODMAN THEATRE, where she is an artistic associate (*The Odyssey, The Notebooks of Leonardo da Vinci, Mirror of the Invisible World,* and Philip Glass's opera *Galileo Galilei,* for which she wrote the libretto). Other works include *Journey to the West, The Arabian Nights, Eleven Rooms of Proust, The Secrets in the Wings,* and *Argonautika. Metamorphoses,* a singular success, was staged in and around a 27-foot wide pool that served as a reinforcement in the presentation of a sense of play regardless of the darkness of a tale being dramatized. Indeed, her work, always innovative, in nonetheless accessible and in the best sense very theatrical. In 1998 her creativity earned her a MacArthur "genius" Fellowship. She is also the recipient of eight JOSEPH JEFFERSON Awards for her production efforts in Chicago. Among other directorial assignments have been Shakespeare plays staged in Boston, Chicago, and, in New York (1997), the final play (*Henry VIII*) in the NEW YORK SHAKESPEARE FESTIVAL's Bard marathon begun a decade earlier.   DBW

Zindel, Paul (1936–2003) Playwright. This former high-school chemistry teacher was chiefly known for two plays that provide actresses with exceptionally challenging roles. The first, *The EFFECT OF GAMMA RAYS ON MAN-IN-THE-MOON MARIGOLDS,* was produced at the ALLEY (1964) before moving to New York (1970, OFF-BROADWAY), where it won the Pulitzer Prize and the Drama Critics' Circle Award. The less successful second, *AND MISS REARDON DRINKS A LITTLE* (1971), continued his examination of fragile people who become a part of the madness surrounding them. Minimal theatrical success since *Miss Reardon* (short Broadway runs for *The Secret Affairs of Mildred Wild,* 1972; *Ladies at the Alamo,* 1977) led Zindel to turn to writing television plays and screenplays as well as highly praised novels for young adults.   LDC

Zinn, David (1968–) Set and costume designer active OFF-BROADWAY, in regional theatres, and for opera. An original member of Target Margin Theatre (1991), he received an Obie for a revival of the HEYWARDS' *Mamba's Daughters* in 1998, in collaboration with Artistic Director David Herskovits (and others). He received the 2005 IRENE SHARAFF Young Master Award. His designs have been seen at the GUTHRIE THEATER, OREGON

SHAKESPEARE FESTIVAL, AMERICAN REPERTORY THEATRE, and the LONG WHARF. Collaborators include David Schweizer, Chas Rader-Shieber, and ROBERT WOODRUFF.   BO

Zipprodt, Patricia (1925–99) Costume designer, a graduate of Wellesley, and educator (Brandeis University) who began designing in the mid-1950s and became well known in the 1960s with such productions as FIDDLER ON THE ROOF (1964) and CABARET (1966) (Tonys for both), and the film *The Graduate* (1967). Later, *Pippin* (1972) *and SWEET CHARITY* (1986; Tony) added to her acclaim. She adapted her style to the demands of the script and the director, but if she had a trademark, it was textured clothes. Beginning with *Fiddler,* she developed a technique of creating layers of paint and dye that gave a vibrant or shimmering sense of color to costumes that would otherwise be drab. This approach continued through SUNDAY IN THE PARK WITH GEORGE (1984), in which costumes were heavily textured with dye, paint, brocade, lace, and fabric. In 1992 she was inducted into the THEATRE HALL OF FAME, and in 1997 received the IRENE SHARAFF Award for Lifetime Achievement.   AA

Zoo Story, The, by EDWARD ALBEE premiered OFF-BROADWAY early in 1960 at the Provincetown Playhouse and was a sensational debut for the young writer. On a double bill with Beckett's *Krapp's Last Tape,* Albee's controversial one-act mimicked the "theatre of the absurd" while calling attention to discontent in contemporary American life. Directed by Milton Katselas and featuring George Maharis and WILLIAM DANIELS, the production ran for 582 performances and provoked a variety of articles and critiques about its "meaning." In 1962 it was revived with a production of Albee's The AMERICAN DREAM at the Cherry Lane Theatre, and since has had hundreds of amateur and professional productions. A new act commissioned by the HARTFORD STAGE and added to *Zoo Story* (with the resultant two-act play renamed *Peter and Jerry*) premiered in 2004.   BBW

Zoot Suit A CHICANO drama by LUIS VALDÉZ, with music, was commissioned by GORDON DAVIDSON for the MARK TAPER FORUM and first produced in 1978 by both EL TEATRO CAMPESINO and the LOS ANGELES THEATRE CENTER Group. Considered the first Hispanic American play to reach Broadway, it opened at the WINTER GARDEN THEATRE 25 March 1979 in a revised version. Under the direction of Luis Valdéz, and featuring Edward James Olmos and Daniel Valdéz (music cowritten by the latter), this adaptation of real events that occurred in Los Angeles during WWII combines symbolism with LIVING NEWSPAPER techniques and agitprop theatre. The zoot suit serves as a symbol of protest and dignity with reaction to racial intolerance, injustice, and inequality. The play centers on gang leader Henry Reyna (Daniel Valdéz), who is arrested and convicted in a mass trial for a murder that occurred during a gang fight. The trial in court and through the press was so one-sided that the conviction was later overturned.   ER

Zuber, Catherine (195?–) Costume designer born in England, raised in Queens, NY, and educated at the Museum School of Fine Arts in Boston and the Yale Drama School (M.F.A.). Her numerous awards include Tonys for *The Light in the Piazza* (2005) and *AWAKE AND SING!* (2006), the Henry Hewes in both 2003 and 2004, and an Obie for Sustained Excellence in Costume Design in 1997. In 2006–7 her costumes were seen in the three parts of Stoppard's *The Coast of Utopia* (Tony, Best Costume Design of a Play, 2007). Known for her versatility, she has designed costumes for a wide range of theatres, ranging from the MANHATTAN THEATRE CLUB and LA MAMA to regional theatres including HARTFORD STAGE, GOODMAN THEATRE, LA JOLLA PLAYHOUSE, the GUTHRIE, and the AMERICAN REPERTORY THEATRE. Among her collaborators are Nicholas Hytner, Bob McGrath (Ridge Theatre, NYC), Susan Schulman, and Bartlett Sher.   BO

Bibliography of Select Books since 1995 on the American Theatre

This list of sources is intended as a supplement to sources cited within specific entries (biographies, autobiographies) and as a complement to the list in the 1996 paperback edition. Space limitation necessitates both the exclusion of sources other than published books and those published before earlier editions of this guide, in addition to sources in which theatre is peripheral (with a few notable exceptions). Extensive bibliographies are included in Wilmeth and Bigsby, below. One excellent reference source listed was unavailable during the compilation of this edition: Frank Cullen's two-volume *Vaudeville Old & New*. In consulting this checklist one should be aware that many authoritative efforts are to be found in theses and dissertations as well as in essays in periodicals. The following current serials most often contain research or criticism on American theatre and performance: *Theatre Survey, American Theatre, American Drama, Dramatists Quarterly, The Journal of Arts Management and Law, Journal of American Drama and Theatre, Theatre History Studies, Nineteenth Century Theatre and Film, The Theatre Journal, Performance Arts Resources, TheatreForum, Performing Arts Journal, Theater, The Drama Review, Variety, Back Stage, New York Theatre Critics' Reviews, Playbill, Band-wagon, Spectacle,* and *Performance Art Journal.* Although American theatre is now defined broadly, including many variant forms of performance and venue, this bibliography concentrates on so-called legitimate theatre (though including a few sources on performance art), with a section on popular forms of entertainment and musical theatre. There is a short section of recent reference works and overviews that proved most helpful to the editor. For those interested in more extensive bibliographies on popular entertainments, including the circus, various outdoor amusements, and musical theatre and the revue, three bibliographical essays by Wilmeth in M. Thomas Inge, ed., *Handbook of American Popular Culture,* 2d ed. (Westport, CT: Greenwood, 1989), and his checklists in *Theatre History Studies* (1991 and 1998) might prove helpful. The editor has also consulted hundreds of Web sites, too many to list here. Most require corroboration to verify information. Two, however, have been of constant help and have proven to be extremely trustworthy: IBDB Internet Broadway Database® <www.ibdb.com> and the Internet Off-Broadway Database, or The Lortel Archives <www.IOBDB.com>.   DBW

I. Reference and Overviews

Abbotson, Susan C. W. *Masterpieces of 20th-Century American Drama.* Westport, CT: Greenwood, 2005.

Adler, Steven. *On Broadway: Art and Commerce on the Great White Way.* Carbondale: Southern Illinois UP, 2004.

Ashby, LeRoy. *With Amusement for All: A History of American Popular Culture since 1830.* Lexington: UP of Kentucky, 2006.

The Best Plays of . . . (yearbook series). 1988–96, ed. Otis L. Guernsey, Jr., and Jeffrey Sweet. New York: Applause (1988–92), New York: Limelight (1992–6). 1996–2000, ed. Otis L. Guernsey, Jr. New York: Limelight. 2000– , ed. Jeffrey Eric Jenkins, New York: Limelight.

Bigsby, Christopher. *Contemporary American Playwrights.* Cambridge/New York: Cambridge UP, 1999.

Bloom, Ken. *Broadway: An Encyclopedia.* New York/London: Routledge, 2004.

Bloom, Ken, and Frank Vlastnik. *Broadway Musicals: The 101 Greatest Shows of All Time.* New York: Black Dog & Leventhal, 2004.

Bordman, Gerald. *American Musical Theater: A Chronicle.* 3d ed. New York: Oxford UP, 2001.

Bordman, Gerald, & Thomas S. Hischak, eds. *The Oxford Companion to American Theatre.* 3d ed. New York: Oxford UP, 2004.

Botto, Louis. *At This Theatre: 100 Years of Broadway Shows, Stories and Stars.* Ed. Robert Viagas. New York: Applause & Playbill, 2002.

Bottoms, Stephen J. *Playing Underground: A Critical History of the 1960s Off-Off-Broadway Movement.* Ann Arbor: U. of Michigan, 2004.

Brown, Gene. *Show Time: A Chronology of Broadway and the Theatre from Its Beginnings to the Present.* New York: Macmillan, 1997.

Bryer, Jackson R., and Mary C. Hartig, eds. *Companion to American Drama.* New York: Facts on File, 2004.

Burke, Sally F. *American Feminist Playwrights: A Critical History*. New York: Twayne, 1996.

Butsch, Richard. *The Making of American Audiences: From Stage to Television, 1750–1990*. Cambridge/New York: Cambridge UP, 2000.

Crandell, George. *Tennessee Williams: A Descriptive Bibliography*. Pittsburgh: U. of Pittsburgh, 1996.

Cullen, Frank, Florence Hackman, and Donald McNeilly. *Vaudeville, Old & New: An Encyclopedia of Variety Performers in America*. 2 vols. New York/London: Routledge, 2007.

Dunlap, William. *History of the American Theatre: From Its Origin to 1832*. (1832). Repr. with introduction by Tice L. Miller and index. Urbana: U. of Illinois, 2005.

Gänzl, Kurt. *The Musical: A Concise History*. Boston: Northeastern UP, 1997.

Head, Dominic, ed. *The Cambridge Guide to Literature in English*. 3d ed. Cambridge/New York: Cambridge UP, 2006.

Henderson, Mary C. *Theater in America: 200 Years of Plays, Players, and Productions*. 2d ed. New York: Abrams, 1996.

—. *The City & the Theatre: The History of New York Playhouses; A 250 Year Journey from Bowling Green to Times Square*. New ptg. New York: Back Stage Books, 2004.

Hill, Errol G., and James V. Hatch. *A History of African American Theatre*. Cambridge/New York: Cambridge UP, 2003.

Hischak, Thomas S. *Enter the Players: New York Stage Actors in the Twentieth Century*. Lanham, MD, and Oxford: Scarecrow, 2003.

Hoogstraten, Nicholas Van. *Lost Broadway Theatres*. Updated/expanded ed. New York: Princeton Architectural, 1997.

Izenour, George C. *Theater Design*. 2d ed. New Haven: Yale UP, 1997.

—. *Theater Technology*. 2d ed. New Haven: Yale UP, 1997.

Jackson, Kenneth T., ed. *The Encyclopedia of New York City*. New Haven: Yale, and New York: New-York Historical Society, 1995.

Kantor, Michael, and Laurence Maslon. *Broadway: The American Musical*. New York: Bulfinch, 2004.

Kennedy, Dennis, ed. *The Oxford Encyclopedia of Theatre & Performance*. 3 vols. Oxford/New York: Oxford UP, 2003.

Kolin, Philip C., ed. *The Tennessee Williams Encyclopedia*. Westport, CT: Greenwood, 2004.

Kolin, Philip C., and Colby H. Kullman, eds. *Speaking on Stage: Interviews with Contemporary American Playwrights*. Tuscaloosa: U. of Alabama, 1996.

Krasner, David, ed. *A Companion to Twentieth-Century American Drama*. Malden, MA, and Oxford: Blackwell, 2005.

Lee, Esther Kim. *A History of Asian American Theatre*. Cambridge/New York: Cambridge UP, 2006.

Liu, Miles Xian, ed. *Asian American Playwrights*. Westport, CT: Greenwood, 2002.

Londré, Felicia Hardison, and Daniel J. Watermeier. *The History of North American Theater*. New York: Continuum, 1998.

Nelson, Emmanuel S., ed. *African American Dramatists: An A to Z Guide*. Westport, CT: Greenwood, 2004.

Owen, Bobbi. *The Broadway Design Roster: Designers and Their Credits*. Westport, CT: Greenwood, 2003.

Parkinson, Robert L. *Directory of American Circuses 1793–2000*. Baraboo, WI: Circus World Museum, 2002.

Patterson, Michael. *The Oxford Dictionary of Plays*. Oxford: Oxford UP, 2005.

Peterson, Bernard L., Jr. *Profiles of African American Stage Performers and Theatre People, 1816–1960*. Westport, CT: Greenwood, 2000.

Roudané, Matthew C. *American Drama since 1960: A Critical History*. New York: Twayne, 1996.

Rubin, Don. *The World Encyclopedia of Contemporary Theatre*, vol. 2: *Americas*. London/New York: Routledge, 1996.

Shafer, Yvonne. *American Women Playwrights 1900–1950*. New York: Peter Lang, 1995,

Shank, Theodore. *Beyond the Boundaries: American Alternative Theatre*. Ann Arbor: U. of Michigan, 2002.

Slout, William L. *Olympians of the Sawdust Circle: A Biographical Dictionary of the Nineteenth Century American Circus*. San Bernardino, CA: Borgo, 1998.

Smith, Eric Ledell. *African American Theater Buildings: An Illustrated Historical Directory, 1900–1955*. Jefferson, NC: McFarland, 2003.

Smith-Howard, Alycia, and Greta Heintzelman. *Critical Companion to Tennessee Williams: A Literary Reference to His Life and Work*. New York: Facts on File, 2005.

Suskin, Steven. *Broadway Yearbook 2000–2001*. New York: Oxford UP, 2002.

—. *Broadway Yearbook 2001–2002*. New York: Oxford UP, 2003.

—. *More Opening Nights on Broadway: A Critical Quotebook of the Musical Theatre, 1965–1981*. New York: Schirmer Books, 1997.

Theatre World (yearbook series). 1990– , ed. by John Willis (as of 1999, with Ben Hodges and/or Tom Lynch). New York: Applause.

Whelchel, Harriet, ed. *The Shuberts Present: 100 Years of American Theater*. By the staff of the Shubert Archive (Maryann Chach, Regan Fletcher, Mark E. Swartz, Sylvia Wang). New York: Abrams/Shubert Organization, 2001.

Wilmeth, Don B., and Christopher Bigsby, eds. *The Cambridge History of American Theatre*, vol. I: *Beginnings to 1870*; vol. II: *1870–1945*; vol. III: *Post-World War II*. Cambridge/New York: Cambridge UP, 1998, 1999, 2000. A paperback edition appeared in 2006.

Witham, Barry, ed. *Theatre in the United States: A Documentary History*, vol. I: *1750–1915, Theatre in the Colonies and United States*. Contributors: Martha Mahard, David Rinear, and Don B. Wilmeth. New York/Cambridge: Cambridge UP, 1996.

II. Legitimate Theatre and Performance Art

Ackerman, Alan L., Jr. *The Portable Theater: American Literature & the Nineteenth-Century Stage*. Baltimore: Johns Hopkins UP, 1999.

Ahlquist, Karen. *Democracy at the Opera: Music, Theatre, and Culture in New York City, 1915–60.* Urbana: U. of Illinois, 1997.

Alexander, Doris. *Eugene O'Neill's Last Plays: Separating Art from Autobiography.* Athens: U. of Georgia, 2005.

Allen, Carol. *Peculiar Passages: Black Women Playwrights, 1875–2000.* New York: Lang, 2005.

Alter, Nora M. *Vietnam Protest Theatre: The Television War on Stage.* Bloomington: Indiana UP, 1996.

Andreach, Robert J. *Creating the Self in the Contemporary American Theatre.* Carbondale: Southern Illinois UP, 1998.

Aronson, Arnold. *American Avant-Garde Theatre: A History.* New York/London: Routledge, 2000.

—. *Looking into the Abyss: Essays on Scenography.* Ann Arbor: U. of Michigan, 2005.

Arrizón, Alicia. *Latina Performance: Traversing the Stage.* Bloomington: Indiana UP, 1999.

Banes, Sally. *Subversive Expectations: Performance Art and Paratheater in New York 1976–85.* Ann Arbor: U. of Michigan, 1998.

Bank, Rosemarie K. *Theatre Culture in America, 1825–1860.* New York/Cambridge: Cambridge UP, 1997.

Barnes-McLain, Noreen, ed. *Representations of Gender on the Nineteenth-Century American Stage.* Theatre Symposium, vol. 10. U. of Alabama, 2002.

Bean, Annemarie, ed. *A Sourcebook of African-American Performance: Plays, People, Movement.* New York/London: Routledge, 1999.

Ben-Zvi, Linda, ed. *Susan Glaspell: Essays on Her Theater and Fiction.* Ann Arbor: U. of Michigan, 1995.

Berkowitz, Gerald M. *New Broadways: Theatre Across America: Approaching a New Millennium.* New York: Applause, 1997.

Berkowitz, Joel. *Shakespeare on the American Yiddish State.* Iowa City: U. of Iowa, 2002.

Bial, Henry. *Acting Jewish: Negotiating Ethnicity on the American Stage and Screen.* Ann Arbor: U. of Michigan, 2005.

Bigsby, Christopher, ed. *The Cambridge Companion to Arthur Miller.* Cambridge/New York: Cambridge UP, 1997.

Black, Cheryl. *The Women of Provincetown 1915–1922.* Tuscaloosa: U. of Alabama, 2002.

Black, Stephen A. *Eugene O'Neill: Beyond Mourning and Tragedy.* New Haven: Yale UP, 1999.

Blainey, Ann. *Fanny and Adelaide: The Lives of the Remarkable Kemble Sisters.* Chicago: Ivan R. Dee, 2001.

Bloom, Thomas Alan. *Kenneth Macgowan and the Aesthetic Paradigm for the New Stagecraft in America.* New York: Lang, 1996.

Bogumil, Mary L. *Understanding August Wilson.* Columbia: U of South Carolina, 1999.

Bordman, Gerald. *American Theatre: A Chronicle of Comedy and Drama, 1869–1914.* New York: Oxford UP, 1994.

—. *American Theatre: A Chronicle of Comedy and Drama, 1914–1930.* New York: Oxford UP, 1995.

—. *American Theatre: A Chronicle of Comedy and Drama, 1930–1969.* New York: Oxford UP, 1996.

Bottoms, Stephen J. *Albee: "Who's Afraid of Virginia Woolfe?" Plays in Production.* Cambridge/New York: Cambridge UP, 2000.

—, ed. *The Cambridge Companion to Edward Albee.* Cambridge/New York: Cambridge UP, 2005.

Brantley, Ben, ed. *The New York Times Book of Broadway: On the Aisle for the Unforgettable Plays of the Last Century.* New York: St. Martin's, 2001.

Brater, Enoch, ed. *Arthur Miller's America: Theater & Culture in a Time of Change.* Ann Arbor: U. of Michigan, 2005.

Brewer, Mary F. *Staging Whiteness.* Middletown, CT: Wesleyan UP (Hanover: UP of New England), 2005.

Brown, Dennis. *Actors Talk: Profiles and Stories from the Acting Trade.* New York: Limelight, 1999.

Brown, Linda Ginter, ed. *Marsha Norman: A Casebook.* New York: Garland, 1996.

Bryer, Jackson R. *The Playwright's Art: Conversations with Contemporary American Dramatists.* New Brunswick: Rutgers UP, 1995.

Bryer, Jackson R., and Richard A. Davison, eds. *The Actor's Art: Conversations with Contemporary American Stage Performers.* New Brunswick, NJ: Rutgers UP, 2001.

Buchmuller, Eva, and Anna Koós. *Squat Theatre.* New York: Artists Space, 1996.

Canning, Charlotte. *Feminist Theaters in the U.S.A.* New York/London: Routledge, 1996.

Casto, Marilyn. *Actors, Audiences, & Historic Theaters of Kentucky.* Lexington: UP of Kentucky, 2000.

Chambers, Jonathan L. *Messiah of the New Technique: John Howard Lawson, Communism, and American Theatre, 1923–1937.* Carbondale: Southern Illinois UP, 2006.

Chansky, Dorothy. *Composing Ourselves: The Little Theatre Movement and the American Audience.* Carbondale: Southern Illinois UP, 2004.

Chaudhuri, Una, and Elinor Fuchs, eds. *Land/Scape/Theater.* Ann Arbor: U. of Michigan, 2002.

Cohen, Leah Hager. *The Stuff of Dreams: Behind the Scenes of an American Community Theater.* New York: Viking, 2001.

Cohen-Cruz, Jan. *Local Acts: Community-Based Performance in the United States.* New Brunswick, NJ: Rutgers UP, 2005.

Cohn, Ruby. *Anglo-American Interplay in Recent Drama.* Cambridge/New York: Cambridge UP, 1995.

Cole, Susan Letzler. *Playwrights in Rehearsal: The Seduction of Company.* New York/London: Routledge, 2001.

Connolly, Thomas F. *George Jean Nathan and the Making of Modern American Criticism.* Madison/Teaneck, NJ: Fairleigh Dickinson UP (Cranbury, NJ: Associated UP), 2000.

Corkin, Stanley. *Realism and the Birth of the Modern United States: Cinema, Literature, and Culture.* Athens: U. of Georgia, 1996.

Crandell, George W., ed. *The Critical Response to Tennessee Williams.* Westport, CT: Greenwood, 1996.

Crespy, David A. *Off-Off-Broadway Explosion: How Provocative Playwrights of the 1960s Ignited a New American Theater.* New York: Back Stage Books, 2003.

Cummings, Scott T. *Remaking American Theater: Charles Mee, Anne Bogart and the SITI Company.* Cambridge/New York: Cambridge UP, 2006.

Curry, Jane Kathleen. *John Guare: A Research and Production Sourcebook.* Westport, CT: Greenwood, 2002.

Curtis, Susan. *The First Black Actors on the Great White Way.* Columbia: U. of Missouri, 1998.

Curtiss, Thomas Quinn. *The Smart Set: George Jean Nathan and H. L. Mencken.* New York/London: Applause, 1998.

Dawson, Gary Fisher. *Documentary Theatre in the United States.* Westport, CT: Greenwood, 1999.

Deloria, Philip J. *Playing Indian.* New Haven: Yale UP, 1998.

Demastes, William W. *American Playwrights, 1880–1945: A Research and Production Sourcebook.* Westport, CT: Greenwood, 1995.

—, ed. *Realism and the American Dramatic Tradition.* Tuscaloosa: University of Alabama, 1996.

—, and Iris Fischer, eds. *Interrogating America through Theatre and Performance.* New York: Palgrave Macmillan, 2006.

Dickey, Jerry. *Sophie Treadwell: A Research and Production Sourcebook.* Westport, CT: Greenwood, 1997.

Dixon, Michael Bigelow, and Andrew Carter Crocker, eds. *Humana Festival: 25 Years of New American Plays at Actors Theatre of Louisville.* Louisville: ATL, 2000.

Dixon, Michael Bigelow, and Joel A. Smith. *Anne Bogart: Viewpoints.* Lyme, NH: Smith & Kraus, 1995.

Dolan, Jill. *Utopia in Performance: Finding Hope at the Theater.* Ann Arbor: U. of Michigan, 2005.

Douglas, Ann. *Terrible Honesty: Mongrel Manhattan in the 1920s.* New York: Farrar, Straus, Giroux, 1995.

Duffy, Susan. *American Labor on Stage: Dramatic Interpretations of the Steel and Textile Industries in the 1930s.* Westport, CT: Greenwood, 1996.

Durham, Weldon B. *Liberty Theaters of the United States Army, 1917–1919.* Jefferson, NC: McFarland, 2006.

Elam, Harry J., Jr. *Taking It to the Streets: The Social Protest Theater of Luis Valdez and Amiri Baraka.* Ann Arbor: U. of Michigan, 1997.

—. *The Past as Present in the Drama of August Wilson.* Ann Arbor: U. of Michigan, 2004.

Erdman, Harley. *Staging the Jew: The Performance of an American Ethnicity, 1860–1920.* New Brunswick, NJ: Rutgers, 1997.

Fearnow, Mark. *The American Stage and the Great Depression: A Cultural History of the Grotesque.* New York/Cambridge: Cambridge UP, 1997.

Fesmire, Julia A., ed. *Beth Henley: A Casebook.* New York/London: Routledge, 2002.

Fisher, James. *The Theater of Tony Kushner: Living Past Hope.* New York/London: Routledge, 2001.

Flores, Richard R. *Los Pastores: History and Performance in the Mexican Shepherd's Play of South Texas.* Washington, DC: Smithsonian, 1995.

Frick, John W. *Theatre, Culture and Temperance Reform in Nineteenth-Century America.* Cambridge/New York: Cambridge UP, 2003.

Frome, Shelly. *The Actors Studio: A History.* Jefferson, NC: McFarland, 2001.

Frommer, Myrna Katz, and Harvey Frommer. *It Happened on Broadway: An Oral History of the Great White Way.* New York/San Diego/London: Harcourt Brace, 1998.

Fuchs, Elinor. *The Death of Character: Perspectives on Theater after Modernism.* Bloomington: Indiana UP, 1996.

Fuoss, Kirk W. *Striking Performances/Performing Strikes.* Jackson: UP of Mississippi, 1997.

Gainor, J. Ellen. *Susan Glaspell in Context: American Theater, Culture, and Politics 1915–48.* Ann Arbor: U. of Michigan, 2001.

Geiogamah, Hanay, and Jaye T. Darby, eds. *American Indian Theater in Performance: A Reader.* Los Angeles: UCLA American Indian Studies Center, 2000.

Geis, Deborah R., and Steven F. Kruger, eds. *Approaching the Millennium: Essays on "Angels in America."* Ann Arbor: U. of Michigan, 1998.

Gewirtz, Arthur, and James J. Kolb, eds. *Experimenters, Rebels, and Disparate Voices: The Theatre of the 1920s Celebrates American Diversity.* Westport, CT: Prager, 2003.

—. *Art, Glitter, and Glitz: Mainstream Playwrights and Popular Theatre in 1920s America.* Westport, CT: Praeger, 2004.

Gill, Glenda E. *No Surrender! No Retreat! African American Pioneer Performers of Twentieth-Century American Theater.* New York: St. Martin's, 2000.

Goldberg, RoseLee. *Performance: Live Art since 1960.* New York: Abrams, 1998.

Griffin, Alice. *Understanding Tennessee Williams.* Columbia: U. of South Carolina, 1995.

Gussow, Mel. *Theatre on the Edge: New Visions, New Voices.* New York: Applause, 1997.

—. *Conversations with [Arthur] Miller.* New York: Applause, 2002.

Hall, Roger A. *Performing the American Frontier, 1870–1906.* Cambridge/New York: Cambridge UP, 2001.

Harding, James, and Cindy Rosenthal, eds. *Restaging the Sixties: Radical Theatres and Their Legacies.* Ann Arbor: U. of Michigan, 2006.

Harrington, John P. *The Irish Play on the New York Stage, 1874–1966.* Lexington: UP of Kentucky, 1997.

Harrison, Paul Carter, Victor Leo Walker II, and Gus Edwards, eds. *Black Theatre: Ritual Performance in the African Diaspora.* Philadelphia: Temple UP, 2002.

Hartigan, Karelisa V. *Greek Tragedy on the American Stage: Ancient Drama in the Commerical Theatre, 1882–1994.* Westport, CT: Greenwood, 1995.

Hatch, Anthony P. *Tinder Box: The Iroquois Theatre Disaster 1903.* Chicago: Academy Chicago, 2003.

Henderson, Mary C. *Stars on Stage: Eileen Darby & Broadway's Golden Age (Photographs 1940–1964).* New York: Bulfinch, 2005.

Herrington, Joan, ed. *The Playwright's Muse.* New York/London: Routledge, 2002.

Heuvel, Michael Vanden. *Elmer Rice: A Research and Production Sourcebook.* Westport, CT: Greenwood, 1996.

Hill, Anthony D. *Pages from the Harlem Renaissance: A Chronicle of Performance.* New York: Lang, 1996.

Hischak, Thomas S. *American Theatre: A Chronicle of Comedy and Drama, 1969–2000.* New York: Oxford UP, 2001.

Holmberg, Arthur, ed. *The Lively ART: A Treasury of Criticism, Commentary, Observation, and Insight from Twenty Years of the American Repertory Theatre.* Chicago: Ivan R. Dee, 1999.

Horn, Barbara Lee. *Maxwell Anderson: A Research and Production Sourcebook.* Westport, CT: Greenwood, 1996.

Houchin, John. *Censorship of the American Theatre in the Twentieth Century.* Cambridge/New York: Cambridge UP, 2003.

Huerta, Jorge. *Chicano Drama: Performance, Society and Myth.* Cambridge/New York: Cambridge UP, 2000.

Hyman, Colette A. *Staging Strikes: Workers' Theatre and the American Labor Movement.* Philadelphia: Temple UP, 1997.

Innes, Christopher. *Designing Modern America: Broadway to Main Street* [on Joseph Urban and Norman Bel Geddes]. New Haven: Yale UP, 2005.

Jackson, Shannon. *Lines of Activity: Performance, Historiography, Hull-House Domesticity.* Ann Arbor: U. of Michigan, 2000.

Jenckes, Norma, ed. *New Readings in American Drama: Something's Happening Here.* New York: Peter Lang, 2002.

Johnson, E. Patrick. *Appropriating Blackness: Performance and the Politics of Authenticity.* Durham, NC: Duke UP, 2003.

Johnson, Jeff. *William Inge and the Subversion of Gender.* Jefferson, NC: McFarland, 2005.

Johnson, Odai. *Absence and Memory in Colonial American Theatre: Fiorelli's Plaster.* New York: Palgrave Macmillan, 2006.

Kalb, Jonathan. *Play by Play: Theater Essays & Reviews, 1993–2002.* New York: Limelight, 2003.

Kammen, Michael. *The Lively Arts: Gilbert Seldes and the Transformation of Cultural Criticism in the United States.* New York: Oxford UP, 1996.

Kane, Leslie, ed. *David Mamet's "Glengarry Glen Ross": Text and Performance.* New York: Garland, 1996.

Katvan, Rivka Shifman (photos), Ethan Silverman (intro.), Harold Prince (foreword). *Backstage: Broadway Behind the Curtain.* New York: Abrams, 2001.

Kauffman, Michael W. *American Brutus: John Wilkes Booth and the Lincoln Conspiracies.* New York: Random House, 2004.

King, Donald C. *The Theatres of Boston: A Stage and Screen History.* Jefferson, NC: McFarland, 2005.

King, W. D. *Writing Wrongs: The Work of Wallace Shawn.* Philadelphia: Temple UP, 1997.

Kolin, Philip C. *Williams: "A Streetcar Named Desire."* Plays in Production. Cambridge/New York: Cambridge UP, 2000.

—, ed. *The Undiscovered Country: The Later Plays of Tennessee Williams.* New York: Peter Lang, 2002.

Konas, Gary, ed. *Neil Simon: A Casebook.* Hamden, CT: Garland, 1997.

Koprince, Susan. *Understanding Neil Simon.* Columbia: U. of South Carolina, 2002.

Kritzer, Amelia Howe, ed. *Plays by Early American Women, 1775–1850.* Ann Arbor: U. of Michigan, 1995.

Krasner, David. *Resistance, Parody, and Double Consciousness in African American Theatre, 1895–1910.* New York: St. Martin's, 1997.

—. *A Beautiful Pageant: African American Theatre, Drama and Performance in the Harlem Renaissance 1910–1927.* New York: Palgrave Macmillan, 2002.

Kubiak, Anthony. *Agitated Stages: Performance in the American Theater of Cruelty.* Ann Arbor: U. of Michigan, 2002.

Kuftinec, Sonja. *Staging America: Cornerstone and Community-Based Theater.* Carbondale: Southern Illinois UP, 2003.

Lee, Josephine. *Performing Asian America: Race and Ethnicity on the Contemporary Stage.* Philadelphia: Temple UP, 1997.

Lindroth, Collette, and James Lindroth, eds. *Rachel Crothers: A Research and Production Sourcebook.* Westport, CT: Greenwood, 1995.

Long, Thomas L. *AIDS and American Apocalypticism: The Cultural Semiotics of an Epidemic.* Albany: State U. of New York, 2005.

McAllister, Marvin. *White People Do Not Know How to Behave at Entertainments Designed for Ladies & Gentlemen of Colour: William Brown's African and American Theater.* Chapel Hill: U. of North Carolina, 2003.

McConachie, Bruce A. *American Theater in the Culture of the Cold War: Producing and Contesting Containment, 1947–1962.* Iowa City: U. of Iowa, 2003.

McDonald, Robert L., and Linda Rohrer Paige, eds. *Southern Women Playwrights: New Essays in Literary History and Criticism.* Tuscaloosa: U. of Alabama, 2002.

McDough, Carla J. *Staging Masculinity: Male Identity in Contemporary American Drama.* New York: Garland, 1997.

McLean, Lorraine Arnal. *Dorothy Donnelly: A Life in the Theatre.* Jefferson, NC: McFarland, 1999.

McMullan, James. *The Theater Posters of James McMullan.* New York: Penguin Studio, 1998.

Magnuson, Landis K. *Circle Stock Theater: Touring American Small Towns, 1900–1960.* Jefferson, NC: McFarland, 1995.

Mann, Bruce J., ed. *Edward Albee: A Casebook.* New York: Routledge, 2003.

Marks, Patricia. *Sarah Bernhardt's First American Theatrical Tour.* Jefferson, NC: McFarland, 2003.

Marra, Kim, and Robert A. Schanke, eds. *Staging Desire: Queer Readings of American Theater History.* Ann Arbor: U. of Michigan, 2002.

Marranca, Bonnie, and Gautam Dasgupta, eds. *Conversations on Art and Performance.* Baltimore/London: Johns Hopkins UP, 1999.

Martin, Bradford D. *The Theater Is in the Street: Politics and Public Performance in Sixties America.* Amherst: U. of Massachusetts, 2004.

Mason, Jeffrey D., and J. Ellen Gainor, eds. *Performing America: Cultural Nationalism in American Theater.* Ann Arbor: U. of Michigan, 1999.

Maufort, Marc, ed. *Staging Difference: Cultural Pluralism in American Theatre and Drama.* New York: Peter Lang, 1995.

Merrill, Peter C. *German-American Urban Culture: Writers & Theaters in Early Milwaukee.* Madison, WI: Max Kade Institute, 2000.

Moroff, Diane Lynn. *Fornes: Theater in the Present Tense.* Ann Arbor: U. of Michigan, 1996.

Morrison, Michael A. *John Barrymore, Shakespearean Actor.* Cambridge/New York: Cambridge UP, 1997.

Morrison, William. *Broadway Theatres: History and Architecture.* New York: Dover, 1999.

Mufson, Daniel, ed. *Reza Abdoh.* Baltimore: Johns Hopkins UP, 1999.

Murphy, Brenda. *Miller: Death of a Salesman.* Plays in Production. Cambridge/New York: Cambridge UP, 1995.

—. *Congressional Theatre: Dramatizing McCarthyism on Stage, Film, and Television.* Cambridge/New York: Cambridge UP, 1999.

—. *O'Neill: "Long Day's Journey into Night."* Plays in Production. Cambridge/New York: Cambridge UP, 2001.

—. *The Provincetown Players and the Culture of Modernity.* Cambridge/New York: Cambridge UP, 2005.

—, ed. *The Cambridge Companion to American Women Playwrights.* Cambridge/New York: Cambridge UP, 1999.

Nahshon, Edna. *Yiddish Proletarian Theatre: The Art and Politics of the Artef, 1925–1940.* Westport, CT: Greenwood, 1998.

Nathans, Heather S. *Early American Theatre from the Revolution to Thomas Jefferson: Into the Hands of the People.* Cambridge/New York: Cambridge UP, 2003.

Naylor, David, and Joan Dillon. *American Theaters: Performance Halls of the Nineteenth Century.* New York: John Wiley, 1997.

Paller, Michael. *Gentlemen Callers: Tennessee Williams, Homosexuality, and Mid-Twentieth-Century Drama.* New York: Palgrave Macmillan, 2005.

Peister, Joel. *Staging Depth: Eugene O'Neill & The Politics of Psychological Discourse.* Chapel Hill: U. of North Carolina, 1995.

Pereira, John W. *Opening Nights: 25 Years of the Manhattan Theatre Club.* New York: Peter Lang, 1996.

Pereira, Kim. *August Wilson and the African-American Odyssey.* Urbana: U. of Illinois, 1995.

Plunka, Gene A. *The Black Comedy of John Guare.* Newark: U. of Delaware (Cranbury, NJ: Associated UP), 2002.

—. *The Plays of Beth Henley: A Critical Study.* Jefferson, NC: McFarland, 2005.

Porter, Laurin. *Orphans' Home: The Voice and Vision of Horton Foote.* Baton Rouge: Louisiana State U., 2003.

Rabkin, Gerald, ed. *Richard Foreman.* Baltimore: Johns Hopkins UP, 1999.

Ramírez, Elizabeth. *Chicanas/Latinas in American Theatre: A History of Performance.* Bloomington: Indiana UP, 2000.

Richards, Jeffrey H. *Drama, Theatre, and Identity in the American New Republic.* Cambridge/New York: Cambridge UP, 2005.

Robinson, Marc. *The Theater of Maria Irene Fornes.* Baltimore: Johns Hopkins UP, 1999.

Rogoff, Gordon. *Vanishing Acts: Theater since the Sixties.* New Haven: Yale UP, 2000.

Román, David. *Performance in America: Contemporary U.S. Culture and the Performing Arts.* Durham, NC: Duke UP, 2005.

Rose, Philip. *You Can't Do That on Broadway! "A Raisin in the Sun" and Other Theatrical Improbabilities: A Memoir.* New York: Limelight, 2001.

Roudané, Matthew C., ed. *The Cambridge Companion to Tennessee Williams.* Cambridge/New York: Cambridge UP, 1997.

Sandoval-Sánchez, Alberto. *José, Can You See?: Latinos On and Off Broadway.* Madison: U. of Wisconsin, 1999.

Sandoval-Sánchez, Alberto, and Nancy Saporta Sternbach. *Stage of Life: Transcultural Performance & Identity in U.S. Latina Theater.* Tucson: U. of Arizona, 2001.

Savran, David. *The Playwright's Voice: American Dramatists on Memory, Writing and the Politics of Culture.* New York: Theatre Communications Group, 1999.

—. *A Queer Sort of Materialism: Re-contextualizing American Theater.* Ann Arbor: U. of Michigan, 2003.

Schanke, Robert A., and Kim Marra, eds. *Passing Performances: Queer Readings of Leading Players in American Theater History.* Ann Arbor: U. of Michigan, 1998.

Schanke, Robert A. *"That Furious Lesbian": The Story of Mercedes de Acosta.* Carbondale: Southern Illinois UP, 2003.

Schechner, Richard. *Performance Studies: An Introduction.* 2d ed. London/New York: Routledge, 2006.

Schneemann, Carolee. *Imagining Her Erotics: Essays, Interviews, Projects.* Cambridge, MA: MIT, 2002.

Schroeder, Patricia R. *The Feminist Possibilities of Dramatic Realism.* Rutherford, NJ: Fairleigh Dickinson UP (Cranbury, NJ: Associated UP), 1996.

Schwartz, Bonnie Nelson, ed. *Voices from the Federal Theatre.* Madison, WI: Terrace Books (U. Wisconsin), 2003.

Sell, Mike. *Avant-Garde Performance and the Limits of Criticism: Approaching the Living Theatre, Happenings/Fluxus, and the Black Arts Movement.* Ann Arbor: U. of Michigan, 2005.

Shervey, Beth Conway. *The Little Theatre on the Square: Four Decades of a Small-Town Equity Theatre.* Carbondale: Southern Illinois UP, 2000.

Simonson, Robert. *Role of a Lifetime: Four Professional Actors and How They Built Their Careers.* New York: Back Stage Books, 1999.

Sinfield, Alan. *Out on Stage: Lesbian and Gay Theatre in the Twentieth Century.* New Haven: Yale UP, 1999.

Smith, Susan Harris. *American Drama: The Bastard Art.* New York/Cambridge: Cambridge UP, 1997.

Sponberg, Arvid F., ed. *A. R. Gurney: A Casebook.* New York/London: Routledge, 2004.

Sponsler, Claire. *Ritual Imports: Performing Medieval Drama in America.* Ithaca, NY: Cornell UP, 2004.

Staggs, Sam. *When Blanche Met Brando.* New York: St. Martin's, 2005.

Stone, Wendell C. *Caffe Cino: The Birthplace of Off-Off-Broadway.* Carbondale: Southern Illinois UP, 2005.

Sturman, Janet L. *Zarzuela: Spanish Operetta, American Stage.* Urbana: U of Illinois, 2000.

Taylor, Nancy. *Women Direct Shakespeare in America: Productions from the 1990s.* Madison/Teaneck, NJ: Fairleigh Dickinson UP (Cranbury, NJ: Associated UP), 2005.

Trauth, Suzanne M., & Elizabeth C. Stroppel. *Sonia Moore and American Acting Traning: With a Sliver of Wood in Hand.* Lanham, MD: Scarecrow, 2005.

Vacha, John. *Showtime in Cleveland: The Rise of a Regional Theater Center.* Kent, OH: Kent State UP, 2001.

Vásquez, Eva C. *Pregones Theatre: A Theatre for Social Change in the South Bronx.* New York: Routledge, 2003.

Vorlicky, Robert. *Act Like a Man.* Ann Arbor: U. of Michigan, 1995.

—, ed. *Tony Kushner in Conservation.* Ann Arbor: U. of Michigan, 1998.

Wade, Leslie A. *Sam Shepard and the American Theatre.* Westport, CT: Praeger, 1997.

Wainscott, Ronald H. *The Emergence of the Modern American Theater 1914–1929.* New Haven: Yale UP, 1997.

Walker, Julia A. *Expressionism and Modernism in the American Theatre: Bodies, Voices, Words.* Cambridge/New York: Cambridge UP, 2005.

Watson, Charles S. *The History of Southern Drama.* Lexington: UP of Kentucky, 1997.

Watson, Steven. *Prepare for Saints: Gertrude Stein, Virgil Thomson, and the Mainstreaming of American Modernism.* New York: Random House, 1998.

Weber, Anne Nicholson. *Upstaged: Making Theatre in the Media Age.* London/New York: Routledge, 2005.

Wertheim, Albert. *Staging the War: American Drama and World War II.* Bloomington: Indiana UP, 2004.

Wetzsteon, Ross. *Republic of Dreams: Greenwich Village – The American Bohemia, 1910–1960.* New York: Simon & Schuster, 2002.

Wilmer, S. E. *Theatre, Society and the Nation.* Cambridge/New York: Cambridge UP, 2002.

Wilmeth, Don B., ed. *Staging the Nation: Plays from the American Theatre, 1787–1909.* Boston: Bedford Books, 1998.

Witham, Barry B. *The Federal Theatre Project: A Case Study.* Cambridge/New York: Cambridge UP, 2003.

Wolfe, Peter. *August Wilson.* New York: Twayne, 1999.

Wood, Gerald C. *Horton Foote and the Theater of Intimacy.* Baton Rouge: Louisiana State U., 1999.

Zinman, Toby Silverman. *Terrence McNally: A Casebook.* New York: Garland, 1997.

III. Popular Forms of Entertainment and Musical Theatre

Adams, Bluford. *E Pluribus Barnum: The Great Showman and the Making of U.S. Popular Culture.* Minneapolis: University of Minnesota, 1997.

Adams, Rachel. *Sideshow U.S.A.: Freaks and the American Cultural Imagination.* Chicago: U. of Chicago, 2001.

Albrecht, Ernest J. *The New American Circus.* Gainesville: UP of Florida, 1995.

Anderson, Ann. *Snake Oil, Hustlers and Hambones: The American Medicine Show.* Jefferson, NC: McFarland, 2000.

Anderson, Lisa M. *Mammies No More: The Changing Image of Black Women on Stage and Screen.* Lanham, MD: Rowman & Littlefield, 1997.

Bean, Annemarie, James V. Hatch, Brooks McNamara, eds. *Inside the Minstrel Mask.* Middletown, CT: Wesleyan UP (Hanover, NH: UP of New England), 1996.

Beddow, Margery. *Bob Fosse's Broadway.* Portsmouth, NH: Heinemann, 1996.

Bell, John, ed. *Puppets, Masks, and Performing Objects.* Cambridge, MA: MIT, 2001.

Block, Geoffrey. *Enchanted Evenings: The Broadway Musical from "Show Boat" to Sondheim.* New York: Oxford UP, 1997.

Bridger, Bobby. *Buffalo Bill and Sitting Bull: Inventing the Wild West.* Austin: U. of Texas, 2002.

Brown, Lillian Kiernan. *Banned in Boston: Memoirs of a Stripper.* Bloomington, IN: 1stBooks, 2003.

Brown, Phil. *Catskill Culture: A Mountain Rat's Memories of the Great Jewish Resort Area.* Philadelphia: Temple UP, 1998.

Brown, Rodger Lyle. *Ghost Dancing on the Cracker Circuit: The Culture of Festivals in the American South.* Jackson: UP of Mississippi, 1997.

Bryer, Jackson R., and Richard A. Davison, ed. *The Art of the American Musical: Conversations with the Creators.* New Brunswick, NJ: Rutgers UP, 2005.

Budd, Mike, and Max H. Kirsch, eds. *Rethinking Disney: Private Control, Public Dimensions.* Middletown, CT: Wesleyan UP (Hanover: UP of New England), 2005.

Burana, Lily. *Strip City: A Stripper's Farewell Journey across America.* New York: Hyperion, 2001.

Canning, Charlotte M. *The Most Amerian Thing in America: Circuit Chautauqua as Performance.* Iowa City: U. of Iowa, 2005.

Chapin, Ted. *Everything Was Possible: The Birth of the Musical "Follies."* New York: Knopf, 2003.

Clum, John. *Something for the Boys: Musical Theater and Gay Culture.* New York: St. Martin's, 1999.

Cockrell, Dale. *Demons of Disorder: Early Blackface Minstrels and Their World.* New York/Cambridge: Cambridge UP, 1997.

Comment, Bernard. *The Painted Panorama.* New York: Abrams, 1999.

Condee, William Farley. *Coal and Culture: Opera Houses in Appalachia.* Athens: Ohio UP, 2005.

Connor, Steven. *Dumbstruck: A Cultural History of Ventriloquism.* Oxford: Oxford UP, 2000.

Cook, James W. *The Arts of Deception: Playing with Fraud in the Age of Barnum.* Cambridge: Harvard UP, 2001.

Dahlinger, Fred, Jr. *Trains of the Circus 1872–1956.* Baraboo, WI: Circus World Museum; Hudson, WI: Iconografix, 2000.

Dahlinger, Fred, Jr. and Stuart Thayer. *Badger State Showmen: A History of Wisconsin's Circus Heritage.* Baraboo, WI: Circus World Museum; Madison, WI: Grote Publishing, 1998.

Daniels, Bruce C. *Puritans at Play: Leisure and Recreation in Colonial New England.* New York: St. Martin's, 1996.

Davis, Janet M. *The Circus Age: Culture & Society Under the American Big Top.* Chapel Hill: U. of North Carolina, 2002.

Davis, Lee. *Scandals and Follies: The Rise and Fall of the Great Broadway Revue.* New York: Limelight Editions, 2000.

DeFrantz, Thomas F., ed. *Dancing Many Drums: Excavations in African American Dance.* Madison: U. of Wisconsin, 2002.

Denman, Jeffry. *A Year with "The Producers."* New York: Routledge, 2002.

Dennett, Andrea Stulman. *Weird and Wonderful: The Dime Museum in America.* New York: NYU, 1997.

Desmond, Jane C. *Staging Tourism: Bodies on Display from Waikiki to Sea World.* Chicago: U. of Chicago, 1999.

During, Simon. *Modern Enchantments: The Cultural Power of Secular Magic.* Cambridge: Harvard UP, 2002.

Eaves, Elisabeth. *Bare: On Women, Dancing, Sex, and Power.* New York: Knopf, 2002.

Emerson, Ken. *Doo-dah! Stephen Foster and the Rise of American Popular Culture.* New York: Simon & Schuster, 1997.

Epstein, Lawrence J. *The Haunted Smile: The Story of Jewish Comedians in America.* New York: PublicAffairs, 2001.

—. *Mixed Nuts: America's Love Affair with Comedy Teams from Burns and Allen to Belushi and Aykroyd.* New York: PublicAffairs, 2004.

Erdman, Andrew L. *Blue Vaudeville: Sex, Morals and the Mass Marketing of Amusement, 1895–1915.* Jefferson, NC: McFarland, 2004.

Everett, William A., and Paul R. Laird, eds. *The Cambridge Companion to the Musical.* Cambridge/New York: Cambridge UP, 2002.

Fields, Armond. *Women Vaudeville Stars: Eighty Biographical Profiles.* Jefferson, NC: McFarland, 2006.

Flinn, Denny Martin. *Musical! A Grand Tour.* New York: Schirmer, 1997.

Foley, Brenda. *Undressed for Success: Beauty Contestants and Exotic Dancers as Merchants of Morality.* New York: Palgrave Macmillan, 2005.

Frank, Katherine. *G-Strings and Sympathy: Strip Club Regulars and Male Desire.* Durham, NC: Duke UP, 2002.

Frega, Donnalee. *Women of Illusion: A Circus Family's Story.* New York: Palgrave, 2001.

George-Graves, Nadine. *The Royalty of Negro Vaudeville: The Whitman Sisters and the Negotiation of Race, Gender, and Class in African American Theater, 1900–1940.* New York: St. Martin's, 2000.

Glasscock, Jessica. *Striptease: From Gaslight to Spotlight.* New York: Abrams, 2003.

Glenn, Susan A. *Female Spectacle: The Theatrical Roots of Modern Feminism.* Cambridge: Harvard UP, 2000.

Gordon, Joanne. *Stephen Sondheim: A Casebook.* New York: Garland, 1997.

Gorman, Paul R. *Left Intellectuals & Popular Culture in Twentieth-Century America.* Chapel Hill/London: U. of North Carolina, 1996.

Gottlieb, Robert, and Robert Kimball, eds. *Reading Lyrics.* New York: Pantheon, 2000.

Gottschild, Brenda Dixon. *Waltzing in the Dark: African American Vaudeville and Race Politics in the Swing Era.* New York: St. Martin's, 2000.

—. *The Black Dancing Body: A Geography from Coon to Cool.* New York: Palgrave Macmillan, 2003.

Grant, Mark N. *The Rise and Fall of the Broadway Musical.* Boston: Northeastern UP, 2004.

Grody, Svetlana McLee, and Dorothy Daniels Lister. *Conversations with Choreographers.* Portsmouth, NH: Heinemann, 1996.

Guber, Susan. *Racechanges: White Skin, Black Face in American Culture.* New York: Oxford UP, 1997.

Gustafson, Donna. *Images from the World Between: The Circus in 20th Century American Art.* Cambridge, MA: MIT Press; New York: American Federation of Arts, 2001.

Hamm, Charles. *Irving Berlin: Songs From the Melting Pot: The Formative Years, 1907–1914.* New York: Oxford UP, 1997.

Harding, Les. *Elephant Story: Jumbo and P. T. Barnum under the Big Top.* Jefferson, NC: McFarland, 2000.

Hartzman, Marc. *American Sideshow: An Encyclopedia of History's Most Wondrous and Curiously Strange Performers.* New York: Jeremy P. Tarcher and Penguin, 2005.

Hays, Michael, and Anastasia Nikolopopulou, eds. *Melodrama: The Cultural Emergence of a Genre.* New York: St. Martin's, 1996.

Henderson, Amy, and Dwight Blocker Bowers. *Red, Hot & Blue: A Smithsonian Salute to the American Musical.* Washington, DC: Smithsonian, 1996.

Herman, Jerry, and Ken Bloom. *Jerry Herman – The Lyrics: A Celebration.* New York/London: Routledge, 2003.

Hiaasen, Carl. *Team Rodent: How Disney Devours the World.* New York: Ballantine, 1998.

Hill, Constance Valis. *Brotherhood in Rhythm: The Jazz Tap Dancing of the Nicholas Brothers.* New York: Oxford UP, 2000.

Hirsch, Foster. *Kurt Weill on Stage: From Berlin to Broadway.* New York: Knopf, 2002.

Hischak, Thomas S. *Boy Loses Girl: Broadway's Librettists.* Lanham, MD: Scarecrow, 2002.

Horowitz, Mark Eden. *Sondheim on Music: Minor Details and Major Decisions.* Lanham, MD: Scarecrow (in assoc. with the Library of Congress), 2003.

Ilson, Carol. *Harold Prince: A Director's Journey.* New York: Limelight, 2000.

Jasen, David A., and Gene Jones. *Spreadin' Rhythm Around: Black Popular Songwriters, 1880–1930.* New York: Schirmer Books, 1998.

Jones, Jan. *Billy Rose Presents . . . Casa Mañana.* Ft. Worth: Texas Christian U., 1999.

Jones, John Bush. *Our Musicals, Ourselves: A Social History of the American Musical Theatre.* Waltham, MA: Brandeis UP (Hanover: UP of New England), 2003.

Kander, John, and Fred Ebb, as told to Greg Lawrence. *Colored Lights: Forty Years of Words and Music, Show Biz, Collaboration, and All That Jazz.* New York: Faber & Faber. 2003.

Kasson, John F. *Houdini, Tarzan, and the Perfect Man: The White Male Body and the Challenge of Modernity in America.* New York: Hill & Wang, 2001.

Kasson, Joy S. *Buffalo Bill's Wild West: Celebrity, Memory, and Popular History.* New York: Hill & Wang, 2000.

Kattwinkel, Susan, ed. *Tony Pastor Presents; Afterpieces from the Vaudeville Stage.* Westport, CT: Greenwood, 1998.

Kibler, M. Alison. *Rank Ladies: Gender and Cultural History in American Vaudeville.* Chapel Hill: U. of North Carolina, 1999.

Knoper, Randall. *Acting Naturally: Mark Twain in the Culture of Performance.* Berkeley: U. of California, 1995.

Knopf, Robert. *The Theatre and Cinema of Buster Keaton.* Princeton, NJ: Princeton UP, 1999.

Knowles, Mark. *Tap Roots: The Early History of Tap Dancing.* Jefferson, NC: McFarland, 2002.

Kunhardt, Philip B., Jr., Philip B. Kunhardt III, and Peter W. Kunhardt. *P. T. Barnum: America's Greatest Showman.* New York: Knopf, 1995.

Lamb, Andrew. *150 Years of Popular Musical Theatre.* New Haven: Yale UP, 2000.

Larson, Erik. *The Devil in the White City.* New York: Crown, 2003.

Latham, Angela J. *Posing a Threat: Flappers, Chorus Girls, and Other Brazen Performers of the American 1920s.* Middletown, CT: Wesleyan UP (Hanover, NH: UP of New England), 2000.

Leopold, David. *Irving Berlin's Show Business: Broadway, Hollywood, America.* New York: Abrams, 2005.

Lewis, David H. [David Hammarstrom]. *Broadway Musicals: A Hundred Year History.* Jefferson, NC: McFarland, 2002.

Lewis, Robert M., ed. *From Traveling Show to Vaudeville: Theatrical Spectacle in America, 1830–1901.* Baltimore: Johns Hopkins UP, 2003.

Lhamon, W. T., Jr. *Raising Cain: Blackface Performance from Jim Crow to Hip Hop.* Cambridge: Harvard UP, 1998.

—. *Jump Jim Crow: Lost Plays, Lyrics, and Street Prose of the First Atlantic Popular Culture.* Cambridge: Harvard UP, 2003.

Liepe-Levinson, Katherine. *Strip Show: Performances of Gender and Desire.* London/New York: Routledge, 2002.

Limon, John. *Stand-up Comedy in Theory; or, Abjection in America.* Durham, NC: Duke UP, 2000.

Lowry, Ed, with Charlie Fox. *Joe Frisco: Comic, Jazz Dancer, and Railbird.* Ed. Paul M. Levitt. Carbondale/Edwardswille: Southern Illinois UP, 1999.

Loxton, Howard. *The Golden Age of the Circus.* New York: Smithmark, 1997.

Lust, Annette. *From the Greek Mimes to Marcel Marceau and Beyond.* Lanham, MD: Scarecrow, 2000.

McDonnell, Patricia. *On the Edge of Your Seat: Popular Theatre and Film in Early Twentieth-Century American Art.* New Haven: Yale UP, in assoc. with Frederick R. Weisman Art Museum, U. of Minnesota, 2002.

McKinven, John A. *The Hanlon Brothers: Their Amazing Acrobatics, Pantomimes, and Stage Spectacles.* Glenwood, IL: David Meyer Magic Books, 1998.

McNamara, Brooks. *Day of Jubilee: The Great Age of Public Celebration in New York, 1788–1909.* New Brunswick, NJ: Rutgers UP, 1997.

—. *The New York Concert Saloon: The Devil's Own Nights.* Cambridge/New York: Cambridge UP, 2002.

Maher, William J. *Behind the Burnt Cork Mask: Early Blackface Minstrelsy and the Formation of Antebellum American Popular Culture.* Urbana: U. of Illinois, 1998.

Malone, Jacqui. *Steppin' on the Blues: The Visible Rhythms of African American Dance.* Urbana: U. of Illinois, 1996.

Martell, Joanne. *Millie-Christine: Fearfully and Wonderfully Made.* Winston-Salem, NC: John F. Blair, 2000.

Mazer, Sharon. *Professional Wrestling: Sport and Spectacle.* Jackson: UP of Mississippi, 1998.

Meer, Sarah. *Uncle Tom Mania: Slavery, Minstrelsy & Transatlantic Culture in the 1850s.* Athens: U. of Georgia, 2005.

Miller, Scott. *From "Assassins" to "West Side Story": The Director's Guide to Musical Theatre.* Portsmouth, NH: Heinemann, 1996.

—. *Deconstructing Harold Hill: An Insider's Guide to Musical Theatre.* Portsmouth, NH: Heinemann, 2000.

—. *Rebels with Applause: Broadway's Groundbreaking Musicals.* Portsmouth, NH: Heinemann, 2001.

Mizejewski, Linda. *Ziegfeld Girl: Image and Icon in Culture and Cinema.* Durham, NC/London: Duke U., 1999.

Moore, James Ross. *André Charlot: The Genius of Intimate Musical Revue.* Jefferson, NC: McFarland, 2005.

Mordden, Ethan. *Make Believe: The Broadway Musical in the 1920s.* New York: Oxford UP, 1997.

—. *Coming Up Roses: The Broadway Musical in the 1950s.* New York: Oxford, 1998.

—. *Open a New Window: The Broadway Musical in the 1960s.* New York: St. Martin's, 2002.

—. *One More Kiss: The Broadway Musical in the 1970s.* New York: Palgrave Macmillan, 2003.

—. *The Happiest Corpse I've Ever Seen: The Last 25 Years of the Broadway Musical.* New York: Palgrave Macmillan, 2004.

—. *Sing for Your Supper: The Broadway Musical in the 1930s.* New York: Palgrave Macmillan, 2005.

Moses, L. G. *Wild West Shows and the Images of American Indians, 1883–1933.* Albuquerque: U. of New Mexico, 1996.

Most, Andrea. *Making Americans: Jews and the Broadway Musical.* Cambridge: Harvard UP, 2004.

Mullenix, Elizabeth Reitz. *Wearing the Breeches: Gender on the Antebellum Stage.* New York: St. Martin's, 2000.

Nadis, Fred. *Wonder Shows: Performing Science, Magic, and Religion in America.* New Brunswick, NJ: Rutgers UP, 2005.

Nickell, Joe. *Secrets of the Sideshows.* Lexington: UP of Kentucky, 2005.

Oberdeck, Kathryn J. *The Evangelist and the Impresario: Religion, Entertainment, and Cultural Politics in America, 1884–1914.* Baltimore: Johns Hopkins UP, 1999.

Oettermann, Stephen. *The Panorama: History of a Mass Medium.* Trans. Deborah Lucas Schneider. New York: Zone Books, 1997.

O'Nan, Stewart. *The Circus Fire: A True Story.* New York: Doubleday, 2000.

Orenstein, Claudia. *Festive Revolutions: The Politics of Popular Theater and the San Francisco Mime Troupe.* Jackson: UP of Mississippi, 1998.

Paulson, Don, with Roger Simpson. *An Evening at the Garden of Allah: Gay Cabaret in Seattle.* New York: Columbia UP, 1996.

Peterson, Michael. *Straight White Male: Performance Art Monologues.* Jackson: UP of Mississippi, 1997.

Pullen, Kirsten. *Actresses and Whores: On Stage and in Society.* Cambridge/New York: Cambridge UP, 2005.

Reddin, Paul. *Wild West Shows.* Urbana/Chicago: University of Illinois, 1999.

Register, Woody. *The Kid of Coney Island: Fred Thompson and the Rise of American Amusements.* New York: Oxford UP, 2001.

Reiss, Benjamin. *The Showman and the Slave: Race, Death, and Memory in Barnum's America.* Cambridge: Harvard UP, 2001.

Roach, Joseph. *Cities of the Dead: Circum-Atlantic Performance.* New York: Columbia UP, 1996.

Robinson, David. *From Peep Show to Palace: The Birth of American Film.* New York: Columbia UP, 1996.

Roseman, Janet Lynn. *"Beach Blanket Babylon": A Hats-Off Tribute to San Francisco's Most Extraordinary Musical Revue.* San Francisco: Chronicle Books, 1997.

Rothe, Len. *The Bare Truth . . . Stars of Burlesque from the 40s & 50s.* Atglen, PA: Schiffer Publishing, 1998.

Rydell, Robert W., John E. Findling, and Kimberly D. Pelle. *Fair America: World's Fairs in the United States.* Washington, DC: Smithsonian Institution, 2000.

Rydell, Robert W., and Rob Kroes. *Buffalo Bill in Bologna: The Americanization of the World, 1869–1922.* Chicago: U. of Chicago, 2005.

Sahlins, Bernard. *Days and Nights at the Second City: A Memoir, with Notes on Staging Review Theatre.* Chicago: Ivan R. Dee, 2001.

Sammond, Nicholas. *Steel Chair to the Head: The Pleasure and Pain of Professional Wrestling.* Durham, NC: Duke UP, 2005.

Schechter, Joel. *The Pickle Clowns: New American Circus Comedy.* Carbondale: Southern Illinois UP, 2001.

Schultz, James R. *The Romance of Small-Town Chautauquas.* Columbia: U. of Missouri, 2002.

Scott, David A. *Behind the G-String: An Exploration of the Stripper's Image, Her Person and Her Meaning.* Jefferson, NC: McFarland, 1996.

Seham, Amy E. *Whose Improv Is It Anyway?: Beyond Second City.* Jackson: UP of Mississippi, 2001.

Senelick, Laurence. *The Changing Room: Sex, Drag and Theatre.* London and New York: Routledge, 2000.

Shteir, Rachel. *Striptease: The Untold History of the Girlie Show.* New York: Oxford UP, 2004.

Slout, William L. *Clowns and Cannons: The American Circus during the Civil War.* San Bernadino, CA: Borgo, 1997.

—. *A Royal Coupling: The Historic Marriage of Barnum and Bailey.* San Bernadino, CA: Emeritus Enterprise, 2000.

—. *Chilly Billy: The Evolution of a Circus Millionaire.* San Bernadino: Emeritus Enterprise, 2002.

—, ed. *Life upon the Wicked Stage.* San Bernadino, CA: Borgo, 1996.

Stafford, Barbara Maria, and Frances Terpak. *Devices of Wonder: From the World in a Box to Images on a Screen* [optical entertainments]. Los Angeles: Getty Research Institute, 2001.

Stein, Harvey. *Coney Island.* New York: W. W. Norton, 1998.

Steinmeyer, Jim. *Hiding the Elephant: How Magicians Invented the Impossible and Learned to Disappear.* New York: Carroll & Graf, 2003.

Stencell, A. W. *Girl Show: Into the Canvas World of Bump and Grind.* Toronto: ECW, 1999.

—. *Seeing Is Believing: America's Sideshows.* Toronto: ECW, 2002.

Steyn, Mark. *Broadway Babies Say Goodnight: Musical Then & Now.* New York/London: Routledge, 1999.

Stoddart, Helen. *Rings of Desire: Circus History and Representation.* Manchester: Manchester UP, 2000.

Stone, Laurie. *Laughing in the Dark: A Decade of Subversive Comedy.* Hopewell, NJ: Ecco, 1997.

Swartz, Mark Evan. *Oz before the Rainbow: L. Frank Baum's "The Wonderful Wizard of Oz" on Stage and Screen to 1939.* Baltimore: Johns Hopkins UP, 2000.

Swayne, Steve. *How Sondheim Found His Sound.* Ann Arbor: U. of Michigan, 2005.

Tait, Peta. *Circus Bodies: Cultural Identity in Aerial Performance.* London: Routledge, 2005.

Thayer, Stuart. *Traveling Showmen.* Detroit: Astley & Ricketts, 1997.

—. *The Performers: The History of Circus Acts.* Seattle: Dauven & Thayer, 2005.

Thayer, Stuart, and William L. Slout. *Grand Entrée: The Birth of the Greatest Show on Earth 1870–1875.* San Bernardino, CA: Borgo, 1998.

Thelen, Lawrence. *The Show Makers: Great Directors of the American Musical Theatre.* New York/London: Routledge, 1999.

Thomson, Rosemarie Garland, ed. *Freakery: Cultural Spectacles of the Extraordinary Body.* New York: NYU, 1996.

Traub, James. *The Devil's Play Ground: A Century of Pleasure and Profit in Times Square.* New York: Random House, 2004.

Trav S. D. [Travis Stewart]. *No Applause – Just Throw Money: The Book That Made Vaudeville Famous.* New York: Faber & Faber, 2005.

Waggoner, Susan. *Nightclub Nights: Art, Legend, and Style 1920–1960.* New York: Rizzoli, 2001.

Wallis, Michael. *The Real Wild West: The 101 Ranch and the Creation of the American West.* New York: St. Martin's, 1999.

Watkins, Clifford Edward. *Showman: The Life and Music of Perry George Lowery.* Jackson: UP of Mississippi, 2003.

Watts, Steven. *The Magic Kingdom: Walt Disney and the American Way of Life.* Boston: Houghton Mifflin, 1997.

Wertheim, Arthur Frank. *Vaudeville Wars: How the Keith–Albee and Orpheum Circuits Controlled the Big-Time and Its Performers.* New York: Palgrave Macmillan, 2006.

Whisenhunt, Donald W. *Tent Show: Arthur Names and His "Famous" Players.* College Station: Texas A&M UP, 2000.

Wilk, Max. *Overture and Finale: Rodgers & Hammerstein and the Creation of Their Two Greatest Hits [Oklahoma! and The Sound of Music].* New York: Back Stage Books, 1999.

Wilson, R. L. *Buffalo Bill's Wild West: An American Legend.* New York: Random House, 1998.

Wolf, Stacy. *A Problem Like Maria: Gender and Sexuality in the American Musical.* Ann Arbor: U. of Michigan, 2002.

Wyatt, Robert Lee, III. *The History of the Haverstock Tent Show: "The Show with a Million Friends."* Carbondale: Southern Illinois UP, 1997.

Young, Kay. *Ordinary Pleasures: Couples, Conversation, and Comedy.* Columbus: Ohio State UP, 2001.

Biographical Index

The following is an index of individuals mentioned in various entries who do not have entries of their own in this volume. Great effort has been made to locate correct dates; however, the editor welcomes corrections of errors or missing data. Abbreviations are used to identify many nationalities and fields of endeavor; these are followed by the titles (often shortened) of any entries where the individual is cited. The book's Introduction is referenced by section number – e.g., Intro(§1) – and listed first. For the alphabetization scheme employed, see the Note to the Reader in the front matter.   DBW

Abbreviations

a	actor	Dan	Danish	ltg	lighting	s	singer
adm	administrator	de	designer	m	manager	SAf	South African
ag	agent	drm	dramaturge	ma	Magician	Sc	Scottish
Alb	Albanian	Dut	Dutch	Mex	Mexican	sch	scholar
Am	American	e	entertainer	mi	mime	scpt	scene painter
arc	architect	ed	editor	mm	medicine man	scr	screenwriter
art	artist (graphic)	edu	educator	mu	musician	sh	showman
Astl	Australian	en	entrepreneur	Nor	Norwegian	Sov	Soviet
Aus	Austrian	eq	equestrian	o	opera	Sp	Spanish
ba	banker	f	film	p	producer	sr	social reformer
Bel	Belgian	Fr	French	perf	performance artist	sto	storyteller
Brit	British	Ger	German	ph	photographer	Swe	Swedish
Brz	Brazilian	Gk	Greek	Phi	Philippine	Swi	Swiss
c	critic	Hun	Hungarian	phil	philosopher	t	theatre owner
Can	Canadian	Im	impresario	pi	pioneer	tb	theatre builder
ch	choreographer	Ir	Irish	pl	playwright	te	teacher
Chil	Chilean	Isr	Israeli	po	poet	tech	technician
Chn	Chinese	It	Italian	Pol	Polish	th	theorist
co	composer	Jp	Japanese	pub	publisher	tr	translator
com	comic	j	journalist	Pue	Puerto Rican	v	ventriloquist
cos	costumer	l	lyricist	pug	pugilist	w	writer
Cub	Cuban	Latv	Latvian	pup	puppeteer	We	Welsh
Cz	Czechoslovakian	law	lawyer	R	Russian	WI	West Indian
d	director	lib	librettist	rel	religious leader	Y	Yiddish
da	dancer	Lith	Lithuanian	Ro	Romanian		

Abady, Josephine (1950–2002) d; Berkshire Theatre Festival; *Bus Stop;* Circle in the Square; Cleveland Play House; Spoleto

Abbott, Bud (William) (1895–1974) e; burlesque

Abeles, Joseph (1911–91) ph; photographers

Acosta, Iván (1943/8?–) pl; Cuban American

Adair, Jean (1873–1953) a; *Arsenic . . .*

Adams, Annie (1847–1916) a; Adams (M.)

Adams, Edith (Edie) (1929–) a, s; *Wonderful Town*

Adams, Franklin P. (1881–1960) en, w; *Dulcy*

Adams [né Abramowitz], Joey (1911–99) e; borscht belt

Adams, John (1947–) co; Sellars

Adamson, Eve (1937–2006) d; Jean Cocteau

Adamson, Harold (1906–80) l; Lane (B.)

Addams, Augustus A. (?–1851) a; Intro(§1)

Addams, Jane (1860–1935) sr; community; Hull-House

Addams, John P. "Yankee" (1815–85) a, pl; Yankee

Addison, Joseph (1672–1719) Brit, pl; Intro(§1); Hallams; Philadelphia

Addy, Wesley (1913–96) a; Holm (C.)

Adler, Bruce (1944–) a, e; Yiddish

Adler, Dankmar (1844–1900) arc; architecture; McVicker's

Adler, Sara or Sarah (1865–1953) a; Adler (J.); ethnic; Yiddish

Aeschylus (525/4–456/5 B,C.) Gk, pl; Jeffers; Lowell; *Mourning . . . ;* National Actors Theatre

Affleck, Ben (1972–) a, w; NY International

Aibel, Douglas (19??–) d, p; Vineyard

Ailey, Alvin (1931–89) co; dance; Fagan; Nelson

Alam, Juan Shamsul (1946–) pl; Nuyorican

Albertson, Jack (1910–81) a; *Subject Was Roses*

Alda, Robert (1914–86) a; Alda; *Guys and Dolls*

Alden, Christopher (19??–) co, d; Berry

Alden, David (1949–) d; Steinberg

Aldredge, Tom (1928–) a; Aldredge

Aldrich, Louis (Louis Lyon) (1843–1901) a; Campbell; *My Partner*

Aleichem, Sholom, *see* Rabinowitz, Sholem

Alessandrini, Gerard (1953–) l, p; *Forbidden Broadway*

Alessandro, Antonietta Pisanelli (1869–c. 1940) a; ethnic

Alexander, Mrs. John (Elizabeth) (1867–1947) de; costume

Alexander, Rod (1922–) da; dance

Alexander, Ronald (1917–95) pl; Intro(§3); *Time Out for Ginger*

Alfieri, Richard (1952–) pl; Hagen

Algarín, Miguel (1941–) pl; Nuyorican

Ali, George (1866–1947) a; animal impersonation

Ali, Mohammed (Cassius Clay) (1942–) pug; Durham

Alk, Howard (19??–) a, d; Second City

Allen, Alexander (fl. mid-19th C.) pl; Mitchell (W.)

Allen, Debbie (1950–) a, ch, d, da; Rashad; Reinking; *Sweet Charity*

Allen, Janet (196?–) d; Indiana Rep

Allen, Jay Presson (1922–2006) pl; Harris (J.)

Allen, Joan (1956–) a; *Burn This;* Steppenwolf

Allen, Ralph G. (1934–2004) edu, pl; burlesque

Allen, Randy (1957–95) a; one-person

Allers, Roger (19??–) f d, scr, pl; *Lion King*

Allinson, Michael (1920–) Brit a; clubs; Redgrave

Allison, Fran (1907–89) a, s; puppetry

Allison, John (1942–85) We, a; *Little Murders*

Aloma, René R. (1947–86) Cub, d, pl; Cuban American

Alter, Jean (1925–) th; dramatic theory

Altman, Nathan (fl. 1930s) R, de; Aronson (B.)

Altman, Peter (1943–) d; Huntington; Missouri

Altman, Robert (1925–2006) f d, w; *Fool for Love; Indians; Streamers*

Alton, Robert (1902–57) ch, d; dance; *Pal Joey*

Alvarez, Lynne (1947?–) pl; Intro(§4)

Ameche, Don (1908–93) a; *Silk Stockings*

Ames, Robert (1889–1931) a; *Icebound*

Anderson, Barbara (1935–) de, edu; costume

Anderson, Cletus (1938–) de, edu; costume

Anderson, John Henry (1814/15–74) Sc, ma; Davenport Brothers

Anderson, Kevin (1960–) a; *Death of a Salesman*

Anderson, Marian (1897/1902–93) s; Brooklyn Academy

Anderson, Percy (1851–1929) de; costume

André, Major John (1751–80) Brit, de, spy; Southwark Theatre

Andrews, Edward (1914–85) a; *Time of Your Life*

Andrews, Tod (1920–72) a; *Summer and Smoke*

Anglim, Philip (1953–) a; *Elephant Man*

Ann-Margret (1941–) a; *Streetcar . . .*

Anouilh, Jean (1910–87) Fr, pl; animal impersonation; Hellman; Kronenberger

Ansky, S. (1863–1920) R, pl; Kushner

Anthony, Vincent (1943–) pup; puppetry

Ansaldúa, Gloria Evangelina (1942–2004) w; Moraga

Apel, Paul (1872–1946) Ger, pl; *Beggar on Horseback*

Appel, Libby (1937–) d; Indiana Rep; Oregon

Appia, Adolphe (1862–1928) Swi, de, th; Jones (R. E.); Kiesler; Oenslager; Reinhardt; scenic design; *Theatre Arts Monthly*

Applegate, Christine (1971–) a; *Sweet Charity*

Archer, William (1856–1924) Sc, c; Arliss; New Theatre

Arenas, Reinaldo (1943–90) Cub, pl; Cuban American

Ariza, René (1940–) pl; Cuban American

Arkin, Adam (1956–) a; Arkin

Arkin, Matthew (1961–) a; Arkin; *Dinner with Friends*

Arletty (1898–1992) a; *Streetcar . . .*

Armbruster, Mathias (fl. 1855–1900) de; support services

Armstrong, Paul (1869–1915) pl; Smith (Winchell)

Arnold, Edward (1890–1956) a; *Beyond the Horizon*

Arrabal, Fernando (1932–) Fr/Sp, pl; Feist; O'Horgan

Arrick, Larry (1928–) d; Schisgal

Arrivi, Francisco (1941–) Pue, pl; Nuyorican

Artaud, Antonin (1896–1949) Fr, a, d, th; feminist; Intro(§4); Living Theatre; Schechner; Schneemann

Arthur, Beatrice (1926–) a; *Fiddler . . . ;* Saks

Arthur, Jean (née Gladys Green) (1905–91) a; *Born Yesterday;* Imperial Theatre

Arvold, Arnold G. (1882–1957) d, edu; community

Ashley, Elizabeth (1939–) a; *Cat on a Hot Tin Roof*

Ashman, Howard (1950–91) d, l, w; *Little Shop . . . ;* Off-Broadway

Askin, Peter (1940–) d; Leguizamo

Asner, Ed (1929–) a; Second City

Asslin, Jean (1948–) Can, mi; Margolis

Astley, Philip (1742–1814) Brit, eq; circus

Aston, Anthony (Tony) (c. 1682–c. 1753) a; Intro(§1)

Athayde, Roberto (1949–) Brz, pl; NY Shakespeare Festival; Parsons

Atherton, William (1947–) a; *Basic Training . . . ; House of Blue Leaves*

Athey, Ron (1961–) perf; Intro(§4)

Atkins, Eileen (1934–) Brit, a; Caldwell; international; Union Square; one-person

Atwater, Edith (1911–86) a; *Man Who Came to Dinner*

Auburn, David (1969–) pl; Beatty, J. L.; Parker (M-L); *Proof*

Auden, W. H. (1907–73) Brit, po; Hiken

Auerbach-Levy, William (1889–1964) art; caricature

Austin, Lyn (1922–2000) e, p; Music-Theatre Group

Austin (née Hunter), Mary (1868–1934) pl; *Arrow Maker;* Native Americans portrayed; New Theatre

Avni, Ran (1941–) d; Jewish Rep

Ayckbourn, Alan (1939–) Brit, d, pl; Aldredge; Alley Theatre; Channing (S.); Goodman; international; Ivey (J.); Manhattan Theatre Club; Meadow; Ramsay; Shelley

Aykroyd, Dan (1954–) *Driving Miss Daisy;* Second City

Ayres, Alfred (né Thomas E. Osmun) (1834–1902) a, pl; training

Ayvazian, Leslie (1950?–) a, pl; Brown (B.), Meadows

Babe, Thomas (1941–) d, pl; Boston; Papp; Tharp

Bacall, Lauren (1924–) Harris (R.)

Bacharach, Burt (1929–) co; Simon (N.)

Bacon, Peggy (1895–1987) art; caricature

Bagley, Ben (1933–98) p; musical; revue

Bagnold, Enid (1889–1981) Brit, pl; Maher; Reeve

Bailey, James Anthony (1847–1906) en, sh; Barnum; circus; Forepaugh; Ringling Bros.; Wild West

Bainbridge, Alexander Gilbert "Buzz" (1885–1936) m; Minneapolis

Baird, Bil (1904–87) pup, w; puppetry

Baird, Cora (1912–67) pup; puppetry

Baker, Kathy (1950–) a; *Fool for Love*

Baldwin, Alec (1958–) a; *Prelude to a Kiss; Streetcar . . .*

Baldwin, Walter (1889–1977) a; *Of Mice and Men*

Balfour, Katherine (1921–90) a; *Summer and Smoke*

Balieff (or Baliev), Nikita (1877–1936) R, d, e; Comstock; Gest; international; Soudeikine

Ballester, Manuel Méndez (1909–2002) Pue; Nuyorican

Ballet, Arthur H. (1924–) edu; Minneapolis

Bancroft, Marie Wilton (1839–1921) a, m; Bellew

Bancroft, Squire (1841–1926) Brit, a, m; Bellew

Banderas, Antonio (1960–) Sp, a; Kopit; Krakowski

Bank, Jonathan (1960–) d; Mint

Bannister, John (1760–1836) Brit, a; Harwood

Banvard, John (1815–91) art, museum exhibitor; Daly's Theatre

Baralt, Luis (1892–1969) d; Cuban American

Barba, Eugenio (1936–) It, d; La MaMa

Barber, Philip (1903–81) d, pl; Manhattan Theatre Club

Barbour, Grace A. (fl. 1900s) a; *Yellow Jacket*

Barker, Margaret (1908–92) a; Group Theatre

Barnay, Ludwig (1842–1924) Ger, a; Amberg; Conried; Kurz Stadt; Shakespeare on . . .

Barnes, Charlotte [Conner] (1818–63) pl; Native Americans portrayed

Barnes, Mrs. John (?–1841) a; Price

Barnes, Noreen (1955–) d; gay/lesbian

Barnett, Morris (1800–56) a, pl; Burton (W. E.)

Barras, Charles M. (1826–73) pl; *Black Crook*

Barrault, Jean-Louis (1910–94) Fr, a, d; international; Rosenthal

Barrett, Wilson (1846–1904) Brit, a, m; international

Barrie, James (1860–1937) Sc, pl; Adams (M.); animal impersonation, children's theatre; Frohman (C. & D.); Intro(§2); Gillette; Marbury; Martin; Sternhagen; *Tavern*

Barrière, Hippolite (fl. 1823–4) t; Chatham Theatre

Barroga, Jeannie (1949–) pl; Asian American; Filipino American

Barry, Gene (1921–) a; *La Cage . . .*

Barry, Jackson (1926–) th; dramatic theory

Barry, Raymond (1939–) a, pl; Nuyorican

Barrymore, Ada Adams (?–1862) a; nudity

Bartenieff, George (1933–) Ger-born, a, d; Malpede; Theater for the New City

Barton, Lucy (1891–1971) cos, edu; costume

Barysyhnikov, Mikhail (1948–) R-born, a, da; animal impersonation; dance; Esterman; Nelson; Tipton

Basinger, Kim (1954–) a; *Fool for Love*

Batchelder, Marjorie (McPharlin) (1903–97) pup, w; puppetry

Bateman, Sidney (1823–81) pl; Bateman family

Bates, Alan (1934–2003) Brit, a; international; Langella

Bates, Frank (1842–1879) a, m; Bates (B.)

Bates, Kathy (1948–) a; *Frankie and Johnny; 'night, Mother*

Baum, L. Frank (1856–1919) w; animal impersonation; *Wiz; Wizard of Oz*

Bausch, Pina (1940–) co, d; Clarke (M.)

Baxley, Barbara (1925– 90) a; *Camino Real*

Baxter, Keith (1933–)We, a, d; Perdziola

Beaird, David (1952–) d; Wisdom Bridge Theatre

Beale, Simon Russell (1961–) Brit, a; Groener

Beall, Aaron (1964–) d; NY International

Bean, Orson (1928–) a; Axelrod

Beane, Douglas Carter (1959–) pl; Brokaw; Drama Dept.

Beatty, Ned (1937–) a; *Cat on a Hot Tin Roof*

Beaudet, Louise (1861?–1948) a, m; Bandmann

Beaumarchais, Pierre-Augustin Caron de (1732–99) Fr pl; Overmyer

Beck, Julian (1925–85) a, d, pl; Intro(§§3,4); *Brig;* collective; *Connection;* Living Theatre; Malpede

Beck, Martin (1867–1940) m; Keith; Martin Beck Theatre; Orpheum Theatre circuit; Palace; vaudeville

Beckel, Graham (1955–) a; *Marriage of Bette and Boo*

Beckerman, Bernard (1921–85) c, edu, th; dramatic theory

Beckett, Samuel (1906–89) Ir/Fr, pl; Akalaitis; American Rep; Barr; Blau; Breuer; censorship; Chaikin; Coconut Grove; Epstein; Front St. Theatre; Grizzard; Irish Rep; Irving (J.); John Golden Theatre; Mabou Mines; Manhattan Theatre Club; Marshall (E. G.); Off-Broadway; *Oh! Calcutta!;* one-person; Perloff; pornographic; Schneider; Stein (Douglas); Warrilow; *Zoo Story*

Beckett, Welton (1902–69) arc; Mark Taper Forum

Beegle, Mary Porter (1881–?) ch, d, pl; pageants

Beery, Wallace (1885–1949) a; *Dinner at Eight*

Begley, Ed (1901–70) a; *All My Sons; Inherit the Wind; Sweet Bird* . . .

Behan, Brendan (1923–64) Ir, pl; Quintero

Bein, Albert (1902–90) pl; Bloomgarden

Belasco, Fred (1862–1920) m; Alcazar

Belber, Stephen (1964–) pl; Primary Stages

Belgrader, Andrei (1946–) Ro d; CSC Rep

Bellamy, Lou (195?–) d, edu; Penumbra

Bellini, Vincenzio (1801–35) It, co; Russell (H.); Sargent (Epes)

Belushi, John (1949–1982) a, e; Guare; Second City

Benavente, Jacinto (1866–1954) Sp, pl; Civic Rep

Bendix, William (1906–64) a; *Time of Your Life*

Benét, Stephen Vincent (1898–1943) w; MacLeish

Benmussa, Simone (1932–2001) Fr-born, pl; Close

Bennett, Alan (1934–) Brit, pl; international

Bennett, Barbara (1906–58) a; Bennett (Richard)

Bennett, Constance (1905–65) a; Bennett (Richard)

Bennett, David (fl. 1930s) ch, d; dance

Bennett, Joan (1910–90) a; Bennett (Richard)

Benrimo, J. Harry (1871/4–1942) pl; *Yellow Jacket*

Benson, Frank R. (1858–1939) Brit, a, m; Hampden; Payne (B. I.)

Benson, Martin (1937–) d; South Coast Rep

Bent, Marion (1879–1940) e; Rooney

Bentley, Gladys (1907–60) a, e; female/male

Berezin, Tanya [Harriet] (1941–) d; Circle Rep; Mason

Bergen, Edgar (1903–78) v, en; puppetry

Bergis, Simanis (1887–1957) Latv, pl; ethnic

Bergman, Andrew (1945–) pl; Silver

Bergman, Ingmar (1918–) Swe, d, f d; international; *Little Night Music*

Bergman, Ingrid (1915–82) Swe, a; *Joan of Lorraine*

Bergner, Elisabeth (1900–86) Aus, a; Worth

Berkoff, Steven (1937–) Brit, a, pl; animal impersonation; dance

Berky, Bob (1948–) e; Moschen

Berle (né Berlinger), Milton (1908–2002) a, e, p; Albertson; borscht belt; Carroll (E.)

Berlin, Jeannie (1949–) a; May (E.)

Berman, Norman L. (1949–) co; Norman

Berman, Shelley (1924–) a, e; Second City

Bern, Mina (1920–) Pol-born, a, e; Yiddish

Bernard, Charles (?–1895) p; animals as perfomers; Burgess; DeMille (H.)

Bernard, Crystal (1964–) a; *Annie Get Your Gun*

Bernardi, Herschel (1923–86) a; *Fiddler* . . .

Bernhard, Thomas (1931–89) Aus, pl; Feingold

Bernhardt, Melvin (1931–) d; *Crimes of the Heart; Effect of Gamma Rays* . . .

Bernhardt, Sarah (1844–1923) a; Claxton; Davenport (F.); Feldshuh; female/male; Grau; McVicker's; Palace; San Francisco; Shakespeare on . . . ; Shubert brothers

Bernheim, Shirl (1921–) a; *Tale of the Allergist's Wife*

Bernstein, Jed (1955–) adm, p; League of American . . .

Berrigan, Daniel, Jr. (1921–) pl, w; Intro(§4); Center Stage; documentary

Besoyan, Frank R. (1924–70) pl, l, lib, co; *Little Mary Sunshine*

Bettis, Valerie (1919–82) ch, da; *Streetcar* . . .

Betty, William Henry West (1791–1874) Brit, a; Payne

Bevan, Donald (1920–) pl; Intro(§3)

Bevan, Frank Poole (1903–76) d, edu; costume

Beverley, Trazana (1945–) a; *For Colored Girls* . . .

Bial, Albert (1842–97) t; Koster and Bial's

Bierce, Ambrose (1842–1914) w; Perloff

Biggers, Earl Derr (1884–1933) w; *Seven Keys* . . .

Bigley, Isabel (1926–2006) a; *Guys and Dolls*

Bigsby, Christopher (1961–) Brit c, sch; LaBute; Miller (A.)

Bill, Stephen (1948–) Brit, pl; Elliott (S.)

Billings, Hammatt (1818–74) arc; Boston Museum

Binder, Paul (1942–) en, sh; Big Apple Circus; circus

Bingham, Lloyd (c.1865–1915) a, m; Bingham

Bishop, H[enry] R[owley] (1786–1855) Brit, co; Payne

Bishop, Kelly (Carole) (1944–) a; *Six Degrees* . . .

Bishop, Washington Irving (1856–1889) ma; magic

Bissell, Richard (1913–77) pl, w; *Pajama Game*

Bizet, Georges (1838–75) Fr, co; *Carmen Jones*

Björnson, Maria (1949–) Fr-born, de; *Phantom* . . .

Black, Don (1936–) Brit, co, w; Wildhorn

Blackmer, Sidney (1895–1973) a; *Come Back, Little Sheba; Sweet Bird* . . .

Blackwell, Earl (1913–95) im, pub, w; Theatre Hall of Fame

Blackwell, Harolyn (1955–) a, opera s; *Candide*

Blair, Mary (c. 1895–1947) a; *All God's Chillun*

Blakemore, Michael (1928–) Astl-born, d; *Kiss Me, Kate*

Blanchett, Cate (1969–) Astl, a; Hepburn; Ibsen

Bland, James (1854–1911) co; minstrel show

Blaney, Charles E. (1866/8–1944) m, pl; Spooner Stock

Blechman, Burt (1927–98) w; Hellman

Bledsoe, Jules (1898–1943) a; *In Abraham's Bosom*

Blethyn, Brenda (1946–)Brit, a; *'night, Mother*

Bloodgood, Fred Foster (1910–c. 2004) e, mm; medicine shows

Bloom, Michael (194?–) d; Cleveland Play House

Bock, Adam (196?–) Can, pl; Salt Lake Acting

Bogardus, A. H. (1833–1913) e; Wild West

Bogart, Humphrey (né DeForest) (1899–1957) a; *Dead End; Hopkins; Petrified Forest*

Bolt, Robert (1924–95) Brit, pl; Richardson (L.)

Bond, Edward (1934–) Brit, pl; Empty Space; Yale Rep

Bonn, John E. (fl. 1920s–30s) d; Prolet-Buehne

Bonus, Ben (1920–1948) Y, a; Yiddish

Booker, Margaret (194?–) d; Intiman

Booth, Susan V. (1964–) adm, d; Alliance Theatre

Boretz, Allen (1900–86) pl; *Room Service*

Borge, Victor (1909–2000) Dan-born, e; John Golden Theatre

Borges, Fermín (1931–87) pl; Cuban American

Bornstein, Kate (Alan Herman) (1948–) a, pl; female/male; one-person; Theatre Rhinoceros

Borodin, Alexander (1833–87) co; *Kismet*

Boruzescu, Radu (1944–) Ro, de; Chekhov on . . .

Bosley, Tom (1927–) a; *Fiorello!*

Boublil, Alain (1941–) Fr (Tunisia), co, l, w; Asian American; Galati; *Les Misérables; Miss Saigon*

Boucicault, Aubrey B. (1869–1913) pl; Boucicault

Boucicault, Nina (1867–1950) Brit, a; Boucicault

Boudy, José Sánchez (1927–) pl; Cuban American

Boulanger, Denise (1955–) Can, mi; Margolis

Boulanger, Nadia (1887–1979) co, edu; Blitzstein

Bourdet, Edward (Edouard) (1877–1945) Fr, pl; gay/lesbian

Bourne, Matthew (1960–) Brit, ch, d; Center Theatre Group

Bourseiller, Antoine (1930–) Fr, a, d; Coates

Bove, Linda (c. 1945–) a; National Theatre of the Deaf

Bowers, Mrs. D. P. (Elizabeth Crocker) (1830–95) a; Conway

Bowie, David (1947–) Brit, e, s; female/male

Bowmer, Angus L. (1904–79) d, p; Oregon Shakespeare Festival; Shakespearean festivals

Bowne, Alan (1945–89) pl; gay/lesbian

Boy George (né George Alan O'Dowd) (1961–) e, s; female/male

Boyd, Gregory (1951–) d; Alley Theatre

Boyd, Julianne (19??–) d; Barrington Stage Co.; Berkshire Theatre

Boyd, William (1895–1972) a; *What Price Glory*

Boyd-Jones, Edward (fl. 1900) Brit. l; *Florodora*

Boyle, Peter (1935–2006) a; Second City

Bozyk, Reyzl (1914?–1993) Pol-born, Y, a; Yiddish

Bradbury, Ray (1920–) w; Abraham

Bradford, Roark (1896–1948) pl, w; Connelly; *Green Pastures*

Bragg, Bernard (1928–) a; National Theatre of the Deaf

Braham, David (1838–1905) co; Adonis; *Cordelia's Aspirations;* Harrigan; *Mulligan Guard*

Brainard, Harriet T. (18??–1932) a; Moody

Bramble, Mark (c. 1951–) pl; *42nd Street*

Branagh, Kenneth (1960–) Brit, a, d, f d; Center Theatre Group

Branch, William (1927–) pl; African American

Brand, Phoebe (1907–2004) a; *Awake and Sing!;* Group Theatre

Bray, John (1782–1822) co; *Indian Princess*

Brecher, Leo (1890–1980) p, t; Apollo

Brechner, Stanley (1944–) d; American Jewish Theatre

Brecht, Bertolt (né Eugen Berthold Friedrich) (1898–1956) Ger, d, pl; Intro(§4); Bentley; Blau; Blizstein; Bogart; *Cabaret;* Chaikin; Chicano; Chong; Classical Theatre of Harlem; *Company;* East West; ethnic; Feingold; feminist; Gorelik; Irving (J.); Jean Cocteau; Jesurun; Kerz; Kushner; Laughton; Living Theatre; Los Angeles; Mabou Mines; National Actors Theatre; New Vaudeville; Open Theatre; Perloff; Piscator; *Pins and Needles;* Roth; Schmidt (P.); Sellars; Serban; Shange; Split Britches; *Sweeney Todd;* Théâtre de la Jeune Lune; Tynan; Valdéz; Wagner; Weill; Wild West; Wolfe; Yulin

Breen, Robert (1909–91) d, edu; Galati

Breese, Edmund (1871–1936) a, pl; *Scarecrow*

Brennan, Eileen (1932–) a, s; *Little Mary Sunshine*

Brennan, Jay (1883–1961) a, e; Savoy

Brent, Romney (1902–76) Mex, a; *Joan of Lorraine*

Bresson, Robert (1901–99) f p; Chong

Breuler, Robert (19??–) a; *Grapes of Wrath*

Brian, Donald (1877–1948) a, s; Sanderson

Bricusse, Leslie (1931–) Brit, l, pl; Wildhorn

Broderick, Helen (1891–1959) a; *As Thousands Cheer*

Broderick, James (1927–82) a; Broderick; *Wedding Band*

Broderick, Patricia (1925–2003) p, w; Broderick

Brohn, William David (193?–) orchestrator; *Ragtime*

Bromberg, J. Edward (1903–51) a; *Men in White*

Bronca, Armando (19??–) pl; Cuban American

Bronson, Virginia (fl. 1900–1930s) a; Leiber (Fritz)

Brook, Peter (1925–) Brit, d, f d; Intro(§4); Cohen; Dennehy; international; La MaMa; Lee (E.); Marowitz; National Theatre of the Deaf; Serban; Swados; Worth

Brooke, Eleanor (1905?–87) pl; Kerr (J.)

Brooks, Avery (1948–) a; Scott (H.), Shakespeare Theatre

Brooks, Laurie (1948–) pl; children's

Brooks, Mel (1927–) a, w; Bancroft; Lane (N.); *Producers*

Brooks, Richard (1912–92) d; *Sweet Bird . . .*

Brosius, Peter (1952–) d; children's

Broun, Heywood Hale (1918–2001) a, w; Broun

Brower, Francis Marion (1823–74) e; Emmett

Brown, (James) "Buster" (1913–2002) da; Glover

Brown, Carlyle (19??–) pl; African American

Brown, Charles Brockden (1771–1810) w; Dunlap

Brown, Gilmor (1887–1960) a, d; community; Pasadena Playhouse

Brown, J. Randall (1851–1926) ma; magic

Brown, Kenneth (1936–) pl; *Brig;* Living Theatre

Brown, Pamela (1917–75) Brit a; Actors Theatre of Louisville

Brown, Pat (1929–2003) d, a; Alley Theatre

Brown, Trisha (1936–) co; dance; Emmons

Brown, William F. (1928–) pl, lib; *Wiz*

Browne, Maurice (1881–1955) Brit-born d, p; Intro(§2); community; Seattle; scenic design

Browne, Theodore (1910?–79) pl; African American; American Negro Theatre

Bruce, Brenda (1918–96) Brit, a; *Little Murders*

Bruce, Cheryl Lynn (195?–) a, d; Goodman

Bruce, John E. (1856–1924) j, pl; Davis (H. V.)

Brunton, John, Jr. (1775–1849) a; Merry

Brunton, John, Sr. (1741–1822) a, m; Merry

Brunton, Louisa (1785–1860) a; Merry

Bryant, Billy (1885–1968) en, d; showboats

Bryant, Jerry (1828–61) e; Bryant

Bryant, Ken (1955–90) d; Dallas Theater Center

Bryant, Neil (Cornelius A.) (1835–1902) e; Bryant

Buatier, Joseph (1847–1903) Fr, ma; Kellar

Buch, René (1926–) d; Repertorio Español

Buchanan, Virginia (1846–1931) a; Buchanan

Büchner, Georg (1813–37) Ger, pl; Foreman

Buck, Frank (1884–1950) adventurer; Leslie

Buckstone, John Baldwin (1802–79) Brit, a, m, pl; international

Bulfinch, Charles (1763–1844) arc; Federal St. Theatre

Bulgakov, Leo (1889–1948) Sov, a, d; Chekhov on . . . ; *Gods of the Lightning;* Moscow Art Theatre; van Itallie

Bulgakov, Mikhail Afanasievich (1891–1940) R, pl; Serban

Bulwer-Lytton, Edward (1803–73) Brit, pl; Intro(§2); Booth (E. T.); California Theatre; Coghlan (C.); Dean; Hampden; Mantell; Medina; Mowatt

Bundy, James (1960?–) d; Great Lakes; Yale Rep

Bundza, David (1873–1901) Latv, pl; ethnic

Buntline, Ned (né Edward Zane Carroll Judson) (1823–86) w; Cody; Wild West

Burbank, David S. (fl. 1890s) m; Los Angeles

Burgess, Grover (c. 1892–1948) a; *Time of Your Life*

Burghoff, Gary (1943–) a; *You're a Good Man . . .*

Burgoyne, John (1722–82) Brit, pl; Intro(§1); Boston

Burke, Charles (1822–54) a; Jeffersons

Burke, Kenneth (1897–1993) th; dramatic theory

Burleigh, Frederick (1906–77) d, m; Pittsburgh Playhouse

Burnett, Carol (1933–) a, e; Bosco; Lavin; Tamiment

Burns, Ken (1953–) f d; Conway (K.)

Burris-Meyer, Harold (1902–84) sound pio; sound

Burroughs, Marie (1866–1926) a; McRae

Burroughs, William S. (1914–97) w; Anderson (L.)

Burrows, James (1940–) d, p; Burrows

Burstein, Pesach (d. 1986) Y, a; Yiddish

Burstyn, Mike (1945–) a, e, s; Yiddish

Bury, John (1925–2000) Brit, de; Emmons; Kaczorowski

Bush, Edyth (1879–1972) en, m; Minneapolis

Bushnell, Bill (1937–) d; Los Angeles Theatre Center

Butler, Michael (1927–) p; *Hair*

Buttons, Red (1919–2006) a, e; borscht belt; Gelbart

Butz, Norbert Leo (1967–) a; *Wicked*

Byne (Boulton), Ernest (b. 1848) Brit, e; female/male

Byrd, Sam (1908–55) a, p; *Of Mice and Men; Tobacco Road*

Byrne, David (1952–) Sc mu; Tharp

Byrne, Gabriel (1950–) Ir a; *Moon for the Misbegotten; Touch of the Poet*

Byron, H. J. (1834–84) Brit, pl; Sothern

Byron, Joseph (1846–1923) ph; photographers

Byron, Oliver Doud (1842–1920) a; *Across the Continent;* McCloskey

Byron, Percy C. (1879–1959) ph; photographers

Caesar, Adolphe (1934–86) a; Off-Broadway

Caesar, Irving (1895–1996) l; *No, No, Nanette*

Caesar, Sid (1922–) a, e; Charnin; Gelbart; revue

Cage, John (1912–92) co; Intro(§4); Anderson (L.); dramatic theory; Kaprow; Montano; performance art; Rosenthal; Schneemann; Seattle

Caird, John (1948–) Brit, d, pl; *Les Misérables;* Nelson (R., pl)

Caldwell, Erskine (1903–87) w; Intro(§3); *Tobacco Road*

Caldwell, Sarah (1924–2006) opera d; Boston

Cale, David (1958–) Brit perf; one-person; performance art

Calhoun, Jeff (1960–) ch, d; dance; *Grease;* Tune

Callahan, Charles (1843–1917) pl; Fiske (M. M.)

Callahan, Emmett (1893?–1965) e, en; Corio

Callas, Maria (1923–77) a,s; Caldwell; Kelly (J.)

Callow, Simon (1949–) Brit, a, d; *Carmen Jones*

Calloway, Cab (1908–94) a, s; Bailey

Cambria, Frank (1883?–1966) de; Balaban and Katz

Cameron, Beatrice (1868–1940) a; Ibsen; Mansfield

Cameron, Ben (195?–) adm; Theatre Communications

Camillo, Marvin Felix (1937–88) d; Hispanic

Campbell, Douglas (1922–) Can, a, d; Guthrie Theater

Campbell, Mrs. Patrick (Beatrice Stella Tanner) (1865–1940) Brit, a; Arliss; Cornell; Thompson (L.); Tyler (G. C.)

Campbell, Patton (1926–2006) de; costume

Candy, John (1950–94) a, e; Second City

Canfield, F. Curtis (1903–86) edu; J.B.

Čapek, Karel (1890–1938) Cz, pl; Mamoulion; stage lighting

Capote, Truman (1924–84) pl, w; Circle in the Square; Hoffman (P.); Morse; Wood (A.)

Cárdenas, Raul de (1938–) Cub pl; Cuban American

Cardini (né Richard Valentine Pitchford) (1895–1973) We-born, ma; magic

Cardona, Cora (1949–) d; Chicano

Carlisle [Hart], Kitty (1910–2007) a, s; Chodorov

Carlos, Laurie (1949–) a, pl; Intro(§4); Dance Theater Workshop; Hagedorn; one-person

Carlson, Jeffrey (1975–) a; *Goat, or . . .*

Carlson, Marvin (1935–) edu, th; dramatic theory

Carmello, Carolee (196?–) a; Edelman

Carmines, Al (1936–2005) a, d, co, l; Intro(§4); Drexler; gay/lesbian; Judson Poets'; musical; Off-Broadway

Carney, Art (1918–2003) a; Gelbart; *Odd Couple; Our Town*

Carr, Benjamin (1768?–1836) co, s; musical

Carra, Lawrence (1909–2006), d; Great Lakes

Carradine, Keith (1950–) a; Rogers; *Will Rogers Follies*

Carrère (John Merven) (1858–1911) and (Thomas) Hastings (1860–1929), arc; Lunt-Fontanne Theatre

Carrero, Jaime (1931–) pl; Nuyorican

Carrillo, Juliette (1963–) d; Chicano

Carroll, Pat (1927–) a; Tamiment

Carroll, Paul Vincent (1900–68) Ir, pl; Dowling

Carte, Richard D'Oyly (1844–1901) Brit, en, p; Gilbert and Sullivan

Carter, Charles (1874–1936) ma; magic

Carter, Dixie (1939–) a, s; Holbrook

Carter, Jack (c.1902–67) a; Robeson; *Stevedore*

Carter, Lonnie (1942–) pl; Chicago

Carter, Lynn (1925–85) a, e; female/male

Carter, Nell (1948–2003) a, s; *Annie; Hello, Dolly!*

Carter, Steve (1926–) pl; Chicago

Cartier, Jacques (19??–) d; Hartford Stage

Caruso, Enrico (1873–1921) It-born, s; Burke; San Francisco

Carver, William F. (1840–1927) e; Cody; Wild West

Case, Sue-Ellen (1942–) edu, th; dramatic theory; feminist

Casey, Warren (1935–88) co; *Grease*

Cassidy, Jack (1927–76) a; *She Loves Me*

Cassidy, Patrick (1956–) a, s; *42nd Street*

Castellaneta, Dan (1957–) a; Second City

Castle, Irene (née Foot) (1893–1969) da; Astaire; Dillingham; Marbury

Castle, Vernon (né Blythe) (1887–1918) a, da; Astaire; Marbury

Cates, Gilbert (1934–), d, ed; Geffen

Catlett, Walter (1889–1960) a; *Sally*

Cavaglieri, Giorgio (1911–) arc; Public Theater

Caylor, Rose (fl. 1930s-40s) tr; Chekhov on . . .

Cellini, Benvenuto (1500–71) It, art; Mayer (E. J.)

Cervantes, Miguel de (1547–1616) Sp, w; *Man of La Mancha*

Cerveris, Todd (1971–) a, pl; Cerveris

Cesario, Michael J. (1948–) de; costume

Chadman, Christopher (1948–95) ch; dance

Chagall, Marc (1887–1985) R, art; Aronson (B.)

Chamberlain, Marisha (1955?–) pl; Cricket Theatre

Chamberlain, Richard (1935–) a; Errico; *My Fair Lady; Night of the Iguana;* Weissler; Williamstown

Chambers, Jane (1937–83) pl; gay/lesbian; Interart Theatre; Theatre Rhinoceros

Champion, Marge (née Marjorie Celeste Belcher) (1919–) da, ch; Champion

Chan, Jackie (1954–) a; Asian American

Chanin, Henry (1894–1973) tb; Biltmore; Brooks Atkinson Theatre; John Golden Theatre; Majestic; Richard Rodgers Theatre; Royale

Chanin, Irwin S. (1891–1988) tb; Biltmore; Brooks Atkinson Theatre; John Golden Theatre; Majestic; Richard Rodgers Theatre; Royale

Chaplin, Charles Spencer (1889–1977) a, e; agents; Dressler; Lamos

Chaplin, Sidney (1926–) a; *Bells Are Ringing*

Chapman, William S., Sr. (1764–1839) a, m; showboats

Chatterton, Ruth (1893–1961) a; Miller (H.)

Cheadle, Don (1964–) a; Parks (S-L.)

Chekhov, Anton (1860–1904) R, pl; Intro(§3); Ark Theatre; *Bus Stop;* Carnovsky; Chekhov on . . . ; Civic Rep; dance; Elliott (S.); *Fifth of July;* Hiken; *House of Blue Leaves;* Jewish Rep;

Komisarjevsky; Le Gallienne; *Little Foxes;* Logan (J.); Manhattan Theatre Club; *Morning's at Seven;* Moscow Art Theatre; National Asian-American; Perloff; Plummer; Rabe; Schmidt (P.); Serban; Strathairn; von Itallie; *Washington Square;* Worth

Chen, Joan (1961–) Chn-born, a; Asian American

Chenault, Lawrence A. (1877–?) a, e; female/male

Cheong-Leen, Reggie (195?–) pl; Asian American

Chepulis, Kyle (19??–) de; Flea

Chesley, Robert (1943–90) pl; gay/lesbian; Theatre Rhinoceros

Chicago, Judy (1939–) perf; Lacy; performance art

Childs, Carey (1954–) d, p; Primary Stages

Childs, Kirsten (195?–) pl; Playwrights Horizons

Childs, Lucinda (1940?–) ch; dance; Emmons; Kitchen; Wilson (R.)

Childs, Ozro (fl. 1880s) m; Los Angeles

Chin, Frank (1940–) pl; Intro(§4); Asian American; ethnic

Cho, Julia (1970s?–) pl; Asian American

Christensen, Michael (1947–) e, d; Big Apple Circus

Christians, Mady (1900–51) a; *I Remember Mama*

Christopher, Sybil (c. 1925–) Brit, d, adm; Bay Street

Christy (Harington), George N. (1827–68) e, en; minstrel show

Christy, Edwin P. (1815–62) e, en; minstrel show

Church, Tony (1930–) Brit, a, d; Denver

Churchill, Caryl (1938–) Brit, pl; Intro(§4); Atkinson; dance; Eureka; Hunt; international; NY Shakespeare Festival; NY Theatre Workshop; Off-Broadway; Strathairn

Cibber, Colley (1671–1757) Brit, a, m, pl; Hallams

Ciceri, Charles (fl. late 18th C.) It-born, de; Dunlap

Cid Pérez, José (1906–) pl; Cuban American

Cienfuegos, Lucky (1944–88) pl; Nuyorican

Cilento, Wayne (1949–) ch; dance; *Wicked*

Cino, Joseph (1931–67) da, en; Caffe Cino; Off-Off Broadway

Clancy, John (196?–) pl; NY International

Clapp, Henry, Jr. (1814–75) c, w; criticism; Wheeler (A. C.)

Clark, Lotta (fl. 1908–16) e, d, pl; pageants

Clark, Victoria (1961?–) a; Guettel

Clarke, Creston (1865–1910) a; Clarke (J. S.)

Clarke, Wilfred Booth (1867–1945) a; Clarke (J. S.)

Clarvoe, Anthony (1960–) pl; Eureka

Clausen, Peter Gui (1830–1924) de; Minneapolis

Clayburgh, Jill (1944–) a; Greenberg; Rabe

Clayton, Jan (1917–83) a, s; *Carousel*

Clayton, Jill (1944–) a; Greenberg; Rabe

Clayton, Lou (1887–1950) en; Durante

Cleage, Pearl (1948–) pl; African American

Clemens, Samuel, *see* Twain, Mark

Clements, Stiles O. (fl. 1920s) arc; Geffen

Clift, Montgomery (1920–66) a; Actors Studio; *Skin of Our Teeth;* Strasberg

Cloud, Darrah (1955–) pl; Chicago

Clough, Inez (fl. 1906–17) a; Lafayette Players

Coburn, D. L. (1938–) pl; *Gin Game*

Coca, Imogene (1908–2001) com; Tamiment

Coco, James (1930–87) a; *Last of the Red Hot Lovers*

Cocteau, Jean (1889–1963) Fr, pl; Barbette; Kelly (J.); Living Theatre; Quintero; *Streetcar . . .*

Cogan, David J. (1923–2002) p, t; Eugene O'Neill Theatre

Colagrande, Giade (1976–) It a, d; Dafoe

Colby, Gertrude (1875–1960) d, p; pageants

Cole, William Washington (1847–1915) en, sh; circus

Coleman, Jack (fl. 1900s) e; Smith and Dale

Coleman, Ralf (fl. 1930s and '40s) a; Boston

Coleridge, Samuel T. (1772–1834) Brit, c, w; Payne

Coles, Charles "Honi" (1911–92) da; dance

Collins, Phil (1951–) co; Disney; Richard Rodgers Theatre

Collins, Russell (1897–1965) a; *Johnny Johnson*

Collins, Stephen (1947–) a; *New York Idea*

Collison, Wilson (1892/3–1941) pl; *Getting Gertie's Garter;* Hopwood

Collyer, [Dr.] (fl. 1840s) en; nudity

Colman, George, the Younger (1762–1836) Brit, pl, m; Clarke (J. S.); Florence; Jeffersons

Colón (Valle), Miriam (1935–) a, d; ethnic, Nuyorican; Puerto Rican Traveling Theatre

Colt, Alvin (1915–) de; costume

Columbus, Curt (1965–) d; Trinity Rep

Compton, Edward (1854–1918) Brit, a; Bateman family

Compton, Fay (1894–1978) Brit, a, s; Bateman family

Comstock, Jabez (fl. 1870s) arc; Goodspeed

Conklin, George (fl. 1820s) arc; Chatham Theatre

Conklin, Peggy (1907–2003) a; *Petrified Forest*

Conn [née Bernstein], Didi (1951–) a; Tillinger

Connick, Harry, Jr. (1967–) a, mu, s; *Pajama Game;* Stroman

Conroy, Frank (1890–1964) a, m; *Washington Square*

Considine, John (1862–1943) t; Seattle

Conti, Tom (1941–) Sc-born, a; international

Converse, Frank (1938–) a; *House of Blue Leaves*

Convy, Bert (1934–91) a; *Front Page*

Conway, Jack (1866–1918) e; vaudeville

Conway, John Ashby (1905–87) a, de, edu; Seattle

Cook, Donn (Donald) (1906–61) a; *Paris Bound*

Cook, Elisha (1902–95) a; *Ah, Wilderness!*

Cook, George Cram (1873–1924) p, pl; Provincetown Players

Cook, Ralph (fl. 1960s) d; Intro(§4); Off-Off Broadway

Cook, Will Marion (1869–1944) co; African American; musical

Cooper, Alice (1948–) mu, s; female/male

Cooper, Giles (1918–66) Brit, pl; Albee (E.)

Cooper, James Fenimore (1789–1851) w; Rees; Taylor (C. W.)

Copeau, Jacques (1879–1949) Fr, a, c, d, pl; Intro(§2); Garrick Theatre; international; Kahn (O.); Saint-Denis

Copeland, Joan (1922–) a; *Detective Story*

Copland, Aaron (1900–91) co; *Our Town*

Coquelin, Constant-Benoît (1841–1909) Fr, a; Grau

Corbett, James J. (1866–1933) a, pug; Brady (W. A.)

Corey, Edward B. (fl. 1900s) arc; Cort Theatre

Corman, Roger (1926–) f d; *Little Shop . . .*

Corneille, Pierre (1606–84) Fr pl; CSC Rep; Kushner

Cornish, Nellie C[entennial] (1876–1956) edu, m; Seattle

Coronel, Don Antonio (fl. 1840s) p; Los Angeles

Corrales, José (1937–) pl; Cuban American

Corsaro, Frank (1924–) d; Actors Studio; *Hatful of Rain; Night of the Iguana*

Cort, John (1859–1929) m; Cort Theatre; frontier; Seattle

Corthron, Kia (1961?–) pl; African American

Costello, Lou (Louis Francis Cristillo) (1906–59) e; burlesque

Cotten, Joseph (1905–94) a; *Delicate Balance;* Federal Theatre Project; Mercury Theatre

Cottrelly, Mathilde (1851–1933) s, a; Amberg; Conried

Coup, William C. (1837–95) en; circus

Courtenay, Tom (1937–) Brit, a; Circle in the Square; international

Covarrubias, Miguel (1904–57) art; caricature

Coward, Noël (1899–1973) Brit, a, d, pl; American Airlines; Circle in the Square; Cowl; Cummings; Elliott (S.); Grimes; Hughes (B.); Irish Rep; Jones (S.); Kruger; Lane; Lawrence (G.); Lillie; Lunt and Fontanne; *Man Who Came to Dinner;* Scott; Selwyn; Shelley; Wilson (J. C.); Wood (P.); Worth

Coyne, Joseph S. (1803–68) Brit, pl; Clarke (J. S.)

Coyote, Peter (1942 –) a; *True West*

Craig, Edward Gordon (1872–1966) Brit, d, de, th; Anderson (J. M.); Anglin; community; Hume; dramatic theory; Oenslager; Reinhardt; scenic design; *Theatre Arts Monthly;* Tyler (George C.)

Crane, C. Howard (c. 1885–1952) arc; Music Box Theatre; Virginia Theatre

Cranney, Jon (1943?–) d; Minneapolis

Craven, Frank (1875–1945), a, d, pl; *Our Town*

Crawford, Broderick (1911–86) a; *Of Mice and Men*

Crawford, Michael (1942–) Brit, a; *Phantom . . .*

Crawley, Brian (19??–) l, pl; Playwrights Horizons; Tesori

Crehan, Kate (1846–1920) Ir, a; *Across the Continent*

Crisp, William (1820–74) m; Varieties (Gaiety) Theatre

Cristofer, Michael (1946–) a, pl; resident nonprofit

Crivello, Anthony (1955–) a, s; *Les Misérables*

Crosby, Edward Harold (1859–1934) c, pl; Norton

Croswell, Joseph (1786–1857) pl; Native Americans portrayed

Crouse, Lindsay (1948–) a; Intro(§4)

Crouse, Timothy (1947–) pl; *Anything Goes*

Crowley, Mart (1935–) pl; Intro(§4); *Boys in the Band;* gay/lesbian

Crump, Owen (1903–98) pl; Jones (M.)

Cruz, Migdalia (1958–) pl; Nuyorican

Cukor, George (1899–1983) d, f d; *Holiday*

Cullman, Peter W. (1938–) m; Center Stage

Cumming, Alan (1965–) Brit, a; *Cabaret;* Elliott

Cumpsty, Michael (1958–) Brit-born, a; Kulick

Cunningham, John (1932–) a; *Six Degrees . . .*

Cunningham, Merce (1919–) ch, da; Intro(§4); dance; Emmons; Nauman; Nelson; Noguchi; Rosenthal

Curran, Leigh (1943–) a, pl; Herrmann (E.)

Curry, Michael (19??–) production de, pup; Taymor

Curry, Samuel Silas (1847–1921) te, w; training

Curtis, Jackie (1947–85) a; gay/lesbian

Curtis, M. B. (1851–1920) a; *Sam'l of Posen*

Cusack, Cyril (1910–93) Ir, a; *Moon for the Misbegotten*

Cushman, Susan (1822–59) a; Cushman; female/male

Cyr, Louis (1863–1912) Brit, strongman; Sandow

Dahlgren, Frederick August (1816–95) Swe, pl; ethnic

Dailey, Dan (1913–78) da; dance

Dailey, Irene (1920–) a; *Subject Was Roses*

Dailey, Peter F. (1868–1908) a; Weber and Fields

Daisy, Mike (1973–) a, pl; NY International

Dalcroze, Emile-Jaques, *see* Jaques-Dalcroze

Dall, Nicholas Thomas (fl. 1765–76) Dut, scpt; scenic design

Dalton, Timothy (1944–) Brit, a; *Touch of the Poet*

Daltry, Stephen (19??–) Brit d; international

Daly, Joseph (1840–1916) judge, pl; Daly (Augustin)

Daly, Tyne (1945–) a; *Gypsy; Lavin; Wonderful Town;* Weissler

Damashek, Barbara (19??–) co, l; *Quilters*

Damon, Matt (1970–) a, w; NY International

Dang, Tim (1958–) d; East West

Danieley, Jason (196?–) a, s; *Mazzie*

Daniels, Frank Albert (1856/60–1935) a, e; Herbert

Daniels, Jeff (1955–) a, d, p; *Fifth of July;* Wilson (L.)

Daniels, Ron (1942–) Brit d; American Rep

Dante (né Harry Jansen) (1883–1955) ma; magic

Dante, Nicholas (1942–91) pl; *Chorus Line*

Darby, Eileen (1916–2004) ph; photographers

Darin, Bobby (1936–73) a, s; Spacey

Darion, Joe (1917–2001) l; *Man of La Mancha*

Dauvray, Helen (née Nellie Williams) (1858–1923) a, s; Sothern

Davenport, Ira Erastus (1838–1911) Brit, ma; Kellar

Davenport, May, *see* Seymour, May Davenport

Davenport, William Henry (1841–77) Brit, ma; Kellar

David, Hal (1921–) l; Simon (N.)

David, Lindsay (1953–) de; costume

David, Michael (1937–) a, d, p; Dodger

Davies, John (fl. 1825) co; *Forest Rose;* Woodworth

Davis, Bette (1908–89) a; *Little Foxes; Man Who Came to Dinner; Night of the Iguana;* Davis, Bill C. (1951–) pl; Gottlieb; Manhattan Theatre Club

Davis, Donald (1910–92) pl; Davis (Owen)

Davis, Fay (1872–1945) a; *House of Mirth*

Davis, Jessie Bartlett (1861–1905) a, s; *Robin Hood*

Davis, Luther (1916–) pl; *Kismet*

Davis, Paul (1946–) art; caricature

Davis, Phoebe (1865–?) a; *Hazel Kirke;* Warde

Davis, R. G. (1933–) a, d, pl; collective; mime/pantomime; San Francisco Mime Troupe

Davis, Sammy, Jr. (1925–90) a, s; *Golden Boy*

Dawison, Bogumil (1818–72) Pol, a; Booth (E. T.); Shakespeare on . . . ; Stadt Theater

Day, Clarence (1874–1935) w; *Life with Father*

Day-Lewis, Daniel (1957–) Brit a; *Crucible*

Dazey, Charles T. (1853–1938) pl; Litt

de Groat, Andrew (c. 1948–) ch; Wilson (R.)

de Kolta, Buatier, *see* Buatier, Joseph

de la Fuente, Joel (c. 1970–) a; National Asian Theatre

De Leon, Millie (1870–1922) e; burlesque; nudity

de Nacrede, Edith (fl. 1902–46) d, p; Hull-House

De Niro, Robert (1943–) a; Off-Broadway; Wheeler (D.)

De Rosa, Eugene (fl. 1920s) arc; Broadway Theatre

De Rosa, Stephen (1969–) a; *Mystery of Irma Vep*

de Sica, Vittorio (1902–74) It, d, f d; Montresor

Dean, Edwin (1804–76) a; Dean

Dean, James (1931–55) a; Actors Studio

Dean, Laura (1945–) co, da; Nelson

Dean, Philip Hayes (c. 1939–) pl; Intro(§4); African American; Robeson

DeBar, Clementine (1810–74) a; Booth (J. B., Jr.)

Decroux, Étienne-Marcel (1898–91) Fr, mi, te; Epstein; Hoyle; Margolis; mime/pantomime; Montanaro; Pitt; Stein

Deeter, Jasper (1893–1972) a, d; Hedgerow Theatre; *In Abraham's Bosom;* Philadelphia

Def, Mos [né Dante Terrell Smith] (1973–) a, hip hop art; Parks (S-L.)

Del Rossi, Angelo (19??–) adm, p; Paper Mill

del Valle, Janis Astor (19??–) Pue-born, a, d, pl; gay/lesbian

DeLillo, Don (1936–) pl, w; Hurt (M. B.); Malkovich; Wheeler (D.)

Dell, Floyd (1887–1969) pl; Gaige

Dell, Gabriel (1919/20–88) a, pl; *Dead End; Sign in Sidney Brustein's . . .*

Delsarte, François (1811–71) Fr, a, edu; Intro(§2); MacKaye (Steele); training

DeMille, Cecil B. (1881–1959) a, d, f d; de Mille (W. C.)

Dempsey, Patrick (1966–) a; *Subject Was Roses*

Dempster, Curt (1935–2007) a, d; Ensemble Studio

Dench, Judi (1934–) Brit, a; international

Dennis, Charles (1946–) Can a; Performance Space 122

Dennis, Patrick (Edward Everett Tanner III) (1921–76) w; *Auntie Mame*

Dennis, Sandy (1937–92) a; *Any Wednesday;* Cook (Barbara); Hecht; *Who's Afraid . . .*

Denslow, William Wallace (1856–1915) art; *Wizard of Oz*

Derby, Doris (19??–) en; Free Southern Theatre

Devane, William (1939–) a; *MacBird!*

Devant, David (1868–1941) Brit, ma; magic

Divine, George (1910–65) Brit a, d; Geidt

Devlin, Mary (1840–63) a; Booth (Edwin); Pilgrim

Diaghilev, Sergei Pavlovich (1872–1929) R, impresario; Anisfeld; dance; Kahn (Otto)

Diamond, Elin (1940s?–) edu, th; dramatic theory

Diamond, Liz (196?–) d; Schmidt (P.)

Dibdin, Thomas (1771–1841) Brit, a, m, pl; Charles II

DiCaprio, Leonardo (1974–) a; *Marvin's Room*

Dickens, Charles (1812–70) Brit, w; Chautauqua; Crabtree; Fechter; Harrigan; Harte; Janauschek; Menken; Mitchell

(W.); one-person; Quinton; *Sweeney Todd*

Dickinson, Emily (1830–86) w; *Alison's House;* Harris (Julie)

Dickinson, Thomas (1877–1961) c; community

Dickson, George A. (1853–1903) t, en; English's Theatre; Macauley's Theatre

Diggs, Taye (1972–) a; *Rent*

Dillman, Bradford (1930–) a; *Long Day's Journey . . .*

Dillon, John (1946–) d; Milwaukee Rep

Dillon, Melinda (1939–) a; *Who's Afraid . . .*

Dimov, Osip or Ossip (1878–1959) pl; Jewish Art Theatre; Yiddish

Dinesen, Isak [née Karen von Bixen-Finecke] (1885–1962) Dan w; Luce (W.)

Divine (Harris Glenn Milstead) (1946–88) a, e; female/male; *Hairspray*

Dixcy, Marcia (194?–) costume d, pl; Martin (J.)

Dixon, Ivan (1931–) a; *Raisin in the Sun*

Dixon, W. H. (1866–1946) c; dramatic theory

Dobbins, Steve (19?? –) pl; documentary

Dobujinsky, Mistislav (1875–1957) R, de; Komisarjevsky

Doctorow, E. L. (1931–) w; *Ragtime*

Dolan, Jill (1957–) edu, th; dramatic theory; feminist

Dolan, Judith (1948–) de; costume

Dolega-Eminowicz, Thaddeus (1882–1917) a, pl; ethnic

Domingo, Placido (1941–)Sp s; Yeston

Donahue, John Clark (1938–) d; Children's Theatre Co.; Minneapolis

Donellan, Declan (1953–)Ir d; Kushner

Donizetti, Gaetano (1797–1848) It, co; Barnabee

Donlevy, Brian (1889–1972) a; *What Price Glory*

Donnelly, Dorothy (1880–1928) a, l, pl; *Blossom Time; Student Prince*

Donnelly, Henry V. (c. 1861–1910) a, m, p; Crews; Murray Hill

Dorfman, Ariel (1942–) Chil-Am pl; Close; Harris (R.)

Dos Possos, John (1896–1970) w; gay/lesbian; Shyre

Dostoevsky, F. M. (1821–81) R, w; Chekhov (M.)

Dotrice, Roy (1923–) Brit, a; international; *Moon for the Misbegotten*

Douglas, Paul (1907–59) a; *Born Yesterday*

Douglass, Frederick (1818–95) ed, w; Davis, O.

Douglass, James (fl. 1800s) a, m; frontier

Douglass, Stephen (1921–) a; *Damn Yankees*

Dow, Ada (1847?–1926) a; Marlowe

Dowling, Edward Duryea (1904–67) d, p; *Hellzapoppin*

Dowling, Joe (1948–) Ir, d; Guthrie Theater; international

Dowling,Vincent (1929–) Ir a, d; Great Lakes

Downer, Alan S. (1912–70) edu, sch; Durang

Downs, T. Nelson (1867–1938) ma; magic

Dowse, Sean (1949–) d; Cricket Theatre

Doyle, John (1953–) a, d, de; *Company; Sweeney Todd*

Drake, David (19??–) a, pl; one-person

Drake, Julia (1800–32) a; Dean

Draz, Francis (?–1974) arc; Cleveland Play House

Dresher, Paul (1951–) d, mu; Spoleto

Dresser, Richard (193?–) pl; Hirsch (J.)

Drinkwater, John (1882–1937) Brit pl; Gilpin

Dryden, Deborah (1947–) de; costume

Duarte-Clark, Rodrigo (1949–) pl; Chicano

Du Bois, W. E. B. (1868–1963) w; Intro(§3); African American; ethnic

Du Maurier, Gerald (1873–1934) Brit a, m; Lackaye; Palmer

Duberman, Martin (1930–) pl, edu, w; documentary

Dubin, Al (1891–1945) l; Fields (D.); *42nd Street*

DuBois, Peter (1970–) d; Perseverance

DuBrock, Neal (19??–) d; Studio Arena Theatre

Duchamp, Marcel (1887–1968) Fr, art; Kaprow; Montano; performance art

Duchange, Victor (1783–1833) Fr, pl; Dunlap

Dudley, S. H. (1872–1940) e, en; Theatre Owners' Booking Assoc.

Duff, John (1787–1831) Brit-born, a; Duff

Duff-MacCormick, Cara (195?–) Can-born, a; *Moonchildren*

Dukakis, Apollo (19??–) a, d; Dukakis

Duke, Patty (1946–) a; *Miracle Worker*

Dukes, Ashley (1885–1959) Brit, c, m, pl; *Theatre Arts Monthly*

Dullea, Keir (1936–) a; *Cat on a Hot Tin Roof*

Dumas, Alexandre (père) (1802–70) Fr, pl, w; O'Neill (J.); Perloff

Dumas, Alexandre (fils) (1824–95) Fr, pl, w; Intro(§2)

Dumont, Frank (1848/9–1919) en (minstrel); Philadelphia

Dumont, Margaret (1889–1965) a; *Cocoanuts*

Dun, Dennis (1952–) a; Asian American

Dunaway, Faye (1937–) a; *After the Fall; Streetcar . . .*

Dunbar, Paul Laurence (1872–1906) co; musical

Duncan, Augustin (1873–1954) a, d; *Detour*

Duncan, Isadora (1878–1927) co, da; nudity

Duncan, Jeff (1930–) co; Dance Theatre Workshop

Duncan, Todd (1903–98) a, s; *Porgy and Bess*

Dundy, Elmer S. (1862–1907) en, m; Hippodrome

Dunham, Katherine (1910–2006) ch; revue

Dunlap, Richard (1923–) d; Berkshire Theatre Festival

Dunlop, Frank (1927–) Brit, d; Brooklyn Academy; *New York Idea*

Dunn, Irene (1898–1990) a; *I Remember Mama*

Dunn, Nell (1936–) pl; Ivey (J.)

Dunning, Philip (1891–1957) pl; *Broadway*

Dürrenmatt, Friedrich (1921–90) Swi, pl; Lunt–Fontanne Theatre; McNally

Duse, Eleonora (1858–1924) It, a; Intro(§2); Ibsen; Le Gallienne; Lord; New Theatre; Russell (A.); Tyler (G. C.)

d'Usseau, Arnaud (1916–90) pl; Intro(§3); *Deep Are the Roots*

Dutton, Charles S. (1951–) a; Elder; *Ma Rainey's . . . ; Piano Lesson*

Duvall, Robert (1931–) a; *American Buffalo; View from the Bridge;* Wheeler

Dvořák, Antonin (1841–1904) Cz, co; Friml

Dysart, Richard (1929–) a; *That Championship Season*

Eagan, Daisy (1979–) a, s; *Secret Garden*

Eager, Margaret McLaren (c. 1850s–1919) d; pageants

Eaker, Ira (1922–2002) ed, pub; *Back Stage*

Eames, Clare (1896–1930) a; Howard (S.)

Eastman, Barrett (1869–1910) c; Chicago

Easton, William Edgar (1861–1941) pl; African American; Davis (Henrietta)

Ebert, Joyce (1933–97) a; Brown (Arvin)

Eckert, Allan W. (1931–) pl; outdoor

Eddy, Nelson (1901–67) a, s; *Little Mary Sunshine*

Eder, Linda (1961–) a, s; Wildhorn

Edgar, David (1948–) Brit, pl; international; Meadow; Perloff

Edouin, Willie (William Frederick Bryer) (1841–1908) e; Thompson (L.)

Edson, Margaret (1961–) pl; Chalfant; *Wit*

Edwardes, George (1852–1915) Ir-born, m, p; *Merry Widow*

Efros, Anatoly (1925–87) Sov, d; international

Egloff, Elizabeth (195?–) pl; Center Stage; Wright (G.)

Ehle, Jennifer (1969–) a; Harris (R.)

Eikenberry, Jill (1947–) a; *Moonchildren*

Eisenbarth (Eisanbarth), Eugene E. (1864–1925) d, en; showboats

Eisenstein, Sergei (1898–1948) f d; Coates

Ekster, Aleksandra (1884–1949) R, de; Aronson (B.)

Eliot, Samuel (1821–98) d, edu; community

Ellington, Duke (1899–1974) mu, co; revue

Elliott, Bob (Robert B.) (1923–) a, e; John Golden Theatre

Elliott, Shawn (19??–) a; Murphy

Ellis, Charles (fl. 1920s) a; *Desire under the Elms*

Ellis, Evelyn (1894–1958) a; Lafayette Players

Ellis, Mary (1897–2003) a, s; *Rose-Marie*

Ellis-Fermor, Una (1894–1958) c; dramatic theory

Ellison, Ray J. (fl. 1900s) edu; Chautauqua

Emerson (Redmond), Billy (William) (1846–1902) e, en, co; vaudeville

Emerson, Charles Wesley (1837–1908) te, w; training

Emerson, John (1878–1946) pl; Loos

Emerson, Ralph Waldo (1803–82) essayist, po; Wilkins

Emerson (Gaches), Ralph Waldo (1878–1948) press ag; showboats

Emery, Lisa (19??–) a; *Dinner with Friends*

Emmes, David (1940–) d; South Coast Rep

Emmons, Richard (1788–1837?) pl; Native Americans portrayed

English, Jane (1820–98) a, m; Western

Ensler, Eve (1953–) a, pl; *Vagina;* Women's Project

Ephron, Nora (1941–) pl, scr, w; Groener

Epps, Sheldon (19??–) d; Pasadena Playhouse

Erickson, Leif (1911–86) a; *Tea and Sympathy*

Erman, John (1935–) d; *Streetcar . . .*

Ernst, Leila (1922–) a; *Pal Joey*

Esslin, Martin (1918–2002) Brit, c, edu, th; dramatic theory; Magic Theatre

Estes, Allan B., Jr. (d. 1984) d, w; Theatre Rhinoceros

Eugene (D'Ameli) (1836–70) a, e; female/male

Euripides (485/4?–407/6? B.C.) Gk, pl; Jean Cocteau; Jeffers; Perloff; Sellars

Ewell, Tom (1909–94) a; Intro(§3); Axelrod

Eyen, Tom (1941–91) pl; Caffe Cino; female/male; Off-Off Broadway

Eyre, Richard (1943–) Brit d; *Crucible*

Fain, Sammy (1902–89) co, l; *Hellzapoppin*

Fairbanks, Douglas, Sr. (1883–1939) a; *Man of the Hour*

Fakir of Ava (I. Harris Hughes) (1813–91) ma; Kellar

Falco, Edie (1963–) a; Frankie; *'night, Mother*

Falco, Louis (1942–) co; Nelson

Falk, Benjamin (1853–1925) ph; photographers

Falk, Peter (1927–) a; *Prisoner of Second Avenue*

Falls, Gregory A. (1922–97) d, edu; Contemporary Theatre

Farentino, James (1938–) a; *Death of a Salesman; Streetcar . . .*

Farfariello, character; Migliaccio

Farmer, Frances (1914–70) a; *Golden Boy*

Farquhar, George (1677–1707) Ir, pl; Hallams

Farrow, Mia (1945–) a; Lapine

Feder, Mike (1945–) sto; one-person

Fee, Charles (19??–) adm, d; Great Lakes

Feibleman, James (1904–) c; dramatic theory

Feinman, Sigmund (1862–1909) Y, a, d; Adler (C.)

Feld, Irwin (1918–84) circus owner; circus; Ringling Bros.

Feld, Israel (1910–72) circus owner; Ringling Bros.

Feld, Kenneth (1949–) circus owner; Ringling Bros.

Feldshuh, David (1944–) pl; Center Stage

Felipe, Carlos (1914–76) Cub pl; Cuban American

Fellini, Federico (1920–93) It, d, f d, scr; Montresor; *Sweet Charity*

Fergusson, Francis (1904–86) c, th; dramatic theory

Fernandez, Evelina (1954–) a, pl; Chicano

Ferretti, Dante (1943–) It de; Perdziola

Ferris, Dick (1867–1933) m; Minneapolis

Feuchtwanger, Lion (1884–1958) pl; Brecht

Feuillet, Octave (1821–90) Fr, pl; Cazuran

Feydeau, Georges (1862–1921) Fr, pl; Marbury

Feynman, Richard (1918–88) physicist; Parnell

Fichandler, Thomas (1905–97) d; Arena Stage

Field, Crystal (1940–) a, d; Theater for the New City

Field, Robert Montgomery (1834–1902) m; Boston Museum

Field, Sally (1946–) a; *Glass Menagerie; Goat, or . . .; Williams (T.)*

Fields, Herbert (1897–1958) pl; *Annie Get Your Gun; Du Barry . . .*

Fields, Joe (1943–) a; *Basic Training . . .*

Fields, Joseph (1895–1966) pl; Chodorov; Loos; *My Sister Eileen; Wonderful Town*

Fields, Michael (1954–) d; Dell'Arte

Fiennes, Ralph (1962–) Brit a; international; Shakespeare on . . .

Findlay, Thomas (1873–1941) Can a; *Of Mice and Men*

Fine (Kaye), Sylvia (1913–91) w; Tamiment

Finn, Henry J. (1782–1840) pl; Native Americans portrayed

Finnell, Carrie (1893–1963) e; burlesque

Finney, Albert (1936–) Brit, a; international

Fishburne, Laurence (1961–) a, pl; African American; Channing (S.); Mayer (M.)

Fisher, Charles (1795–1871) m; Fisher (Charles)

Fisher, Linda (1943–) de; costume

Fisher, Lola (1896–1926) a; *Good Gracious Annabelle!*

Fisher, Rob (c.1960s-) musical d; City Center

Flagg, James Montgomery (1877–1960) art; caricature

Flaiano, Ennio (1910–72) It, scr; *Sweet Charity*

Flanders, Ed (1934–95) a; *Moon for the Misbegotten*

Fleck, John (1953–) e; female/male; gay/lesbian

Flying Karamazov Brothers (fl. 1980s-) e; New Vaudeville

Fo, Dario (1926–) It, a, d, pl; Cohen; Eureka Theatre; international; New Vaudeville

Fogerty, Elsie (1866–1945) a, edu; Worth

Fonda, Jane (1937–) a; Ibsen

Fontaine, Joan (1917–) a; Coe

Foote, Daisy (1964–) a, pl; Foote

Foote, Hallie (1953–) a; Foote

Foote, Horton, Jr. (1954–) d; Foote

Foote, Walter (c. 1957–) f d, scr; Foote

Forbes-Robertson, Johnston (1853–1937) Brit, a; Elliott (G.); international

Forbes, Kathryn (Kathryn Anderson McLean) (1909–66) w; *I Remember Mama*

Ford, Nancy (1935–) co; Cryer

Ford, Wallace (1898–1966) a; *Of Mice and Men*

Forepaugh, Adam (1831–90) en, m; circus

Forrest, Donald (1950–) d; Dell'Arte

Forrest, George (1915–99) co; *Kismet*

Forrest, Thomas (1747–1825) pl; Intro(§1)

Forsythe, William (1949–) art, ch; dance

Foster, Hunter (1969–) a; Foster (S.)

Foster, Paul (1931–) pl; Caffe Cino; Off-Off Broadway; O'Horgan; resident nonprofit; Tsu

Foster, Stephen Collins (1826–64) co; minstrel show

Fox, Charles Kemble (1833–75) a; Fox (G. W. L.)

Fox, Della (1871/2–1913) a, s; Hopper (E. W.)

Fox, Margaret (1840–95) spiritualist; magic

Fraguada, Frederico (1932–) pl; Nuyorican

Franciosa, Anthony (1928–2006) a; *Hatful of Rain*

Francis, Arlene (1908–2001) a; Federal Theatre Project

Frank, Leo (1884–1915) factory manager; Uhry

Frankau, Joseph (d. 1898) a; Bernstein

Franz, Elizabeth (1941–) a; *Death of a Salesman*

Fratti, Mario (1927–) It-born pl; Lortel

Frazee, Harry Herbert (1880–1929) en; Long Acre

Freed, Amy (1958–) pl; NY Theatre Workshop; Off-Broadway; South Coast Rep

Freedley, George (1904–67) c, librarian, w; awards

Freeman, Brian (1955–) a, d, pl; African American

Freeman, Kathleen (1919–2001), a; *Full Monty*

Freisinger, Madame Elise (fl. 1900–40) de; support services

Frelich, Phyllis (1944–) a; *Children of a Lesser God;* National Theatre of the Deaf

French (Dolen), Augustus Byron (1832–1902) en; showboats

French, Thomas Henry (d. 1902) pub; Samuel French

Friebus, Florida (1909–88) pl; Le Gallienne

Friedman, Peter (1949–) a; *Ragtime*

Friel, Brian (1929–) Ir, pl; Dennehy; international; Irish Rep; Manhattan Theatre Club

Frings, Ketti (1915–81) pl, w; *Come Back, Little Sheba; Look Homeward . . .*

Frisch, Max (1911–91) Swi, pl;
Fichandler

Frohman, Gustave (1855–1930)
m; Belasco; Frohman (D.)

Frueh, Alfred J. (1880–1968) art;
caricature

Frye, Northrop (1912–91) c;
dramatic theory

Fuchs, Georg (1868–1949) Ger, d;
scenic design

Fuchs, Theodore (1904–1995) ltg
(illumination) engineer, edu;
stage lighting

Fuller, David (197?–) d; Jean
Cocteau

Funicello, Ralph (194?–) de;
Center Theatre Group

Furth, George (1932–) a, pl;
Company; Ivey (J.); Thompson
(S.)

Gabel, Martin (1912–86) a;
Mercury Theatre

Gabel, Max (fl. 1910s-30s) Y, p, pl;
Yiddish

Gable, Clark (1901–60) a; Bellamy;
Idiot's Delight; Machinal

Gabriel [né Wierzbicki], Joseph
(1958–) ma; magic

Gahagen, Helen (1900–80) a;
Douglas

Gaines, Ernest (1933–) w; Linney
(R.)

Gale, Mrs. Lyman (fl. 1900s) d, p;
Boston; community

Galilee [Breuer], Clove (c. 1970–)
a, da; Maleczech

Gallardo, Edward (1949–) pl;
Nuyorican; Prince (Harold)

Gallmeyer, Josephine (1838–84)
Ger, a; Conried

Galsworthy, John (1867–1933)
Brit, pl, w; Ames; McClendon;
Neighborhood Playhouse; New
Theatre; Williams (J. D.)

Gambon, Michael (1940–) Brit, a;
Gussow; *View from the Bridge*

Gammon, James (1940–) a; *Buried
Child*

Gantner, Vallejo (1974–) Astl d;
Performance Space 122

Garbo, Fred (1954–) e; Moschen

Garcés, John (1967–) Cub d;
Cuban American

Garcia, Manual Pereiras (1950–)
Cub pl; Cuban American

Gardner, Ava (1922–90) a; *Night of
the Iguana*

Gardner, Helen (?–1946) w; Herne

Garfield, John (né Julius
Garfinkle) (1913–52) a; *Awake
and Sing!; Golden Boy;* Group
Theatre

Garland, Judy (née Gumm) (1922–
69) a, s; Minnelli; *Wizard of
Oz*

Garrett, Shelly (19??–) p, pl;
African American

Garrick, David (1717–79) Brit, a,
m, pl; Boston; Garrick Theatre;
Jeffersons

Garson, Barbara (1941–) pl;
MacBird!

Gary, Harold (1906–84) a; *Price*

Gassman, Vittorio (1922–2000) It,
a, d; international

Gautier, Dick (1931–) a; *Bye Bye
Birdie*

Gay, John (1685–1732) Brit, pl;
Hallams

Gazzara, Ben (1930–) a; *Awake
and Sing!; Cat on a Hot Tin Roof;
Hatful of Rain;* one-person

Gazzo, Michael V. (1923–95) pl;
Hatful of Rain

Gebel-Williams, Gunther (1934–
2001) Ger-born, animal trainer;
circus

Geffen, David (1943–) p; Geffen;
Little Shop . . .

Gehry, Frank (1929–) arc;
resident nonprofit; Theatre for
a New Audience

Geisel, Theodor(e) [Dr. Seuss]
(1904–91) art, w; Minneapolis

Geistinger, Marie (Maria) (1883–
1903) Ger, a; Conried

Gelber, Jack (1932–2003) pl;
Intro(§4); *Connection;* Living
Theatre; Off-Broadway; Rivera;
Streetcar . . .

Gémier, Fermin (1869–1933) Fr,
a, d; tent show

Genée, Adeline (1878–1970) Dan,
da; dance

Genet, Jean (1910–86) Fr, pl;
Intro(§4); CSC Rep; Classical
Theatre of Harlem; Frankel;
Gunn; Hooks; Kim; Lortel; Off-
Broadway; Performance Group;
Schmidt (P.)

Gennaro, Michael (1950?–) adm,
p; Paper Mill

Gentry, Minnie (1915–93) a; *Ain't
Supposed . . .*

George II, *see* Meiningen, George
II, Duke of

Germanova, Maria (1884–1940)
R-born, a, d; Chekhov on . . .

Gershe, Leonard (1922–2002) pl;
Danner

Gersten, Bernard (1923–) d, p;
Bishop; NY Shakespeare
Festival; Vivian Beaumont

Gersten, Jenny (196?–) d; Naked
Angels

Gersten-Vassilaros, Alexandra (c.
1960–) pl; Rebeck

Gesner, Clark (1938–2002) co, pl;
You're a Good Man . . .

Geva, Tamara (1907–97) R, da;
dance

Ghostley, Alice (1926–) a; *Sign in
Sidney Brustein's . . .*

Gibson, Deborah (1970–) a, s; *Les
Misérables;* Quinton

Gielgud, John (1904–2000) Brit, a,
d; Anderson (Judith); Burton
(R.); Cohen; Gilder; Gish;
Heilpern; Hughes (B.);
Komisarjevsky; Rose; Saint-
Denis; Tandy; *Theatre Arts
Monthly; Tiny Alice*

Gifford, Louise (fl. 1928–60) te;
Montanaro

Gilbert, Willie (1916–80) pl; *How
to Succeed . . .*

Gilder, Helena (née de Kay) (fl.
late 19th C.) art; Gilder

Gilder, Richard Watson (1844–
1909) ed, po; Gilder

Giles, F. R. (fl. 1890s) pl; Arthur

Gill, Peter (1939–) Brit, d;
Moonchildren

Gill, William B. (1842–1919) co;
Adonis

Gillmore, Margalo (1897–1986) a;
Silver Cord

Ginsberg, Allen (1926–97) pl, po;
Judson Poets'; Spoleto

Gioia, (Michael) Dana (1950–)
adm, po; National
Endowment

Giraudoux, Jean (1882–1944) Fr,
pl; Civic Rep

Girón, Arthur (1937–)
Guatemalan-born pl; Chicano

Gladding, W. J. (fl. mid-19th C.)
art; caricature

Glass, Philip (1937–) co; Akalaitis;
Anderson (L.); Hwang; Israel;
Mabou Mines; Maleczech;
Nauman; Serban; Spoleto;
Warrilow; Wilson (R.);
Zimmerman

Glazer, Sherry (1961–) a, pl; one-
person

Gleason, Jackie (1916–87) e;
burlesque; Burstyn

Gleason, Paul (1944–) a; Gleason
(J.)

Glines, John (1933–) d, p, pl; gay/
lesbian

Glover, Danny (1947–) a;
Fugard

Glover, Lyman Beecher (1846–
1915) c, m; Chicago

Godfrey, Derek (1924–83) Brit, a;
Little Murders

Godfrey, Thomas (1736–63) pl; Intro(§1); Douglass; Hallams; Southwark Theatre

Godinez, Henry (195?–) Cub-born, a, d, edu; Goodman

Goethe, Johann Wolfgang von (1749–1832) Ger, pl, d; ethnic

Gogol, Nikolai (Vasilievich) (1809–52) R, pl; Schmidt (P.)

Golamco, Michael (197?–) pl, scr; National Asian-American

Gold, Michael (1894–1967) pl, w; Intro(§3)

Goldenberg, Samuel (1885–1945) Y, a; Yiddish

Goldenthal, Elliot (1954–) co; Taymor

Goldman, James (1927–98) l, pl; *Follies*

Goldoni, Carlo (1707–98) It, pl; Intro(§2); Civic Rep; East West

Goldsmith, Oliver (c. 1730–74) Ir pl; Irish Rep

Goldstein, Jennie (1895–1960) Y, a; Yiddish

Gomez, Marga (196?–) perf; Intro(§4)

Gómez-Sanz, Charles (1954–) Cub pl; Cuban American

Gonzáles, Celedonio (1923–) pl; Hispanic

Gonzáles-Pando, Miguel (1941–) Cub pl; Cuban American

González, Elisa Marina (195?–) a, d; Chicano

Gonzalez, Reuben (19??–) pl; Nuyorican

Goodman, Dody (1915–) a; *Front Page*

Goodman, Edward (1888?–1962) d, p, pl; Intro(§2); *Washington Square*

Goodman, Paul (1911–72) pl; Living Theatre

Goodman, Robyn (c. 1950–) a, p; Second Stage

Goodrich, Frances (1891–1984) pl; *Diary of Anne Frank*

Goodwin, J. Cheever (1850–1912) l, pl; Intro(§2); *Evangeline*

Gorcey, Leo (1915–69) a; *Dead End*

Gordon, David (1936–) ch, da; dance

Gordon, Ricky Ian (1956–) co; Guettel; Landau; Nelson (R., pl)

Gordon, Stuart (1947–) d; Chicago

Gorey, Edward (1925–2000) art, de; Langella

Gorky, Maksim (1868–1936) Sov, pl; ethnic; Moscow Art Theatre; Sellars

Gorney, Jay (1898–1990) co; Harburg

Gorshin, Frank (1933–2005) a. e; Tillinger

Gossett, Louis, Jr. (1936–) a; Intro(§4); Fuller; *Raisin in the Sun; Take a Giant Step*

Gouffe (fl. 1831) Brit, a; animal impersonation

Gould, Harold (1923–) a; *House of Blue Leaves*

Goulding, Ray[mond] (1922–90) a, e; John Golden Theatre

Goulet, Robert (1933–) Can a, s; *Camelot; South Pacific*

Gow, James (1907–52) pl; Intro(§3); *Deep Are the Roots*

Gozzi, Carlo (1720–1806) It, pl; Serban

Grable, Betty (1916–73) a, e; *Dolly Sisters; Du Barry . . .*

Graf, Randy (1955–) a, s; *Les Misérables*

Graham, Martha (1894–1991) ch, d; Birch; Clarke (M.); dance; Davidson; Engel; Epstein; Fagan; Hemsley; Neighborhood Playhouse; Noguchi; Rosenthal

Graham, Philip (1894–1967) edu, sch; showboats

Granger, Maude (1841/6–1928) a; *My Partner*

Grant, Cary (né Archibald Alexander Leach) (1904–86) a; *Holiday*

Grant, Lee (1929–) a, d; *Detective Story; Prisoner of Second Avenue*

Grant, Micki (1941–) pl; Carroll

Granville Barker, Harley (1877–1946) Brit, a, c, pl, d; Intro(§2); Jones (R. E.); Mamet; Mint; scenic design; Shakespeare on . . .

Graves, Rupert (1963–) Brit, a; *Elephant Man*

Gray, Amlin (1946–) pl; Intro(§4)

Gray, David (1870–1968) pl; Hopwood

Gray, Dolores (1924–2002) a; *Annie Get Your Gun*

Gray, Dulcie (1919–) Brit a; Hunter (K.)

Gray, Simon (1936–) Brit, pl; Intro(§4); Grimes; Ivey (J.); international; Lane (N.); Meadow; Ramsay; Richardson

Green, Schuyler (1880–1927) l; *Very Good Eddie*

Greene, Ellen (1951–), a, s; *Little Shop . . .*

Greet, Ben (1857–1936) Brit a, m; Greet Players

Gregory, Lady Augusta Isabella (1852–1932) Brit, en, pl; community

Gregory, Montgomery (1887–c. 1940s) edu; Miller (May)

Gresham, Herbert (1853?–1921) Brit-born, d; Teal

Grey, Clifford (1887–1941) l; *Sally*

Grey, Jennifer (1960–) a; Grey

Gribble, Harry Wagstaff[e] (1896–1981) Brit, a, p, pl; *Anna Lucasta*

Grieg, Edvard (1843–1907) Nor, co; *Kismet*

Griffith, D. W. (1874/75–1948) a, d, f d; Loos

Griffith, Hugh (1912–80) Brit, a; *Look Homeward . . .*

Griffith, Melanie (1957–) a; *Chicago*

Griffith, Robert E. (1907–61) p; Prince

Grimaldi, Joseph (1778–1837) Brit, e; mime/pantomime

Grimké, Angelina Weld (1880–1958) pl; *Rachel*

Grimsley, Jim (1955–) pl; gay/lesbian

Grismer, Joseph (1849–1922) a; Warde

Groody, Louise (1897–1961) a, s; *No, No, Nanette*

Gros, Ernest (fl. 1900s) de; scenic design

Gross, Roger (1931–) edu, th; dramatic theory

Grossmith, George (1874–1935) Brit a, pl; Wodehouse

Grotowski, Jerzy (1933–99) Pol, d; Clarke (M.); Intro(§4); dramatic theory; feminist; international; La MaMa; Maleczech; Off-Broadway; Performance Group; Schechner

Grundy, Sidney (1848–1914) Brit, pl; Langtry

Guggenheim, Peggy [née Marguerite] (1898–1979) art collector; Ruehl

Guilbert, Yvette (1865–1944) Fr, e; Neighborhood Playhouse

Guinan, Texas (1884–1933) a, en; nightclubs

Guinness, Alec (1914–2000) Brit, a; Guthrie; Miller (G. H.); Reid; Worth

Guirgis, Stephen Adly (1970?–) pl; Hoffman (P.S.)

Guitry, Sacha (1885–1957) Fr, a, pl; March

Guthke, Karl (1933–) th; dramatic theory

Gwenn, Edmund (1875–1959) We-born, a; Chekhov on . . .

Gwynne, Fred (1926–93) a; *Cat on a Hot Tin Roof*

Haas, Tom (1938–91) d; Indiana Rep

Haase, Friedrich (1811–86) Ger, a; Germania; Stadt Theater

Hackett, Albert (1900–95) pl; *Diary of Anne Frank*

Hackett, Buddy (1924–2003) e; Intro(§3)

Hackett, Francis (1883–1962) c; Young

Hackett, Timothy P. (1953–) d; Cleveland Play House

Hackman, Gene (1930–) a; *Any Wednesday*

Haidle, Noah (1980?–) pl; Greif

Hailey, Oliver (1932–93) pl; Moffat; Richardson

Haines, William Wister (1908–89) pl; Intro(§3)

Halbert, Delancey (1874–1904) c; Chicago

Halévy, Ludovic (1834–1908) Fr, pl; *Carmen Jones*

Haley, Jack (1899–1979) a; *Wizard of Oz*

Hall, Adelaide (1909/10–93) a, s; musical

Hall, Albert (1937–) a; *Basic Training . . .*

Hall, Huntz (1920–99) a; *Dead End*

Hall, Monty [né Maurice Halperin] (1921–) Can-born, e; Gleason (J.)

Hall, Peter (1930–) Brit, d, m; *Camino Real;* Channing (S.); Guare; Heilpern; Hoffman; Hunter (K.); Redgrave; Stein (D.)

Hallam, Adam (d. 1769) a; Hallam

Hallam, Mrs. Lewis (II) (née Eliza Tuke) (fl. 1785) a; Hallam

Hallam, Nancy (fl. 1759–61) a; Hallam

Halliday, Robert (1891–1975) Sc-born, a, s; *Desert Song;* musical; *New Moon*

Halprin, Ann (1920–) ch, da; Intro(§4)

Halston, Julie (1954–) a, pl; one-person

Hamburger, Anne (1954?–) d; La Jolla

Hamburger, Richard (1951–) d, pl; Dallas Theater Center

Hamilton, John F. (1893–1967) a; *Of Mice and Men*

Hamilton, Josh (1969–) a; *Hurlyburly*

Hamlin, Fred (c. 1863–1904) p; *Babes in Toyland*

Hamlin, Larry Leon (1948–2007) a, d, p, pl; National Black Theater Festival

Hamlisch, Marvin (1944–) co; *Chorus Line;* Mitchell (B. S.)

Hammerstein, James (1931–99) d; *Indian Wants the Bronx*

Hampton, Christopher (1946–) Brit, pl; Ibsen; international; Maher; Wildhorn

Handler, Evan (19??–) a, pl; one-person

Haney, Carol (1924–64) a, da; dance; Gennaro

Hanford, Charles Barnum (1859–1926) a; Warde

Hanley, William (1931–) pl; Barr; *Slow Dance . . .*

Hanreddy, Joseph (1948?–) d; Milwaukee Rep

Hansen, William (1911–75) a; *My Heart's . . .*

Hardwicke, Cedric (1893–1964) Brit, a; Aldrich

Hardy, Hugh (1932–) arc; McCarter; New Amsterdam; Theatre for a New Audience

Hardy, Joseph (1929–) d; *You're a Good Man . . .*

Hardy, Thomas (1840–1928) pl, w; Cazuran; dramatic theory; *Marriage of Bette and Boo*

Hardy, William (1922–) pl; outdoor

Hare, David (1947–) Brit, pl; Intro(§4); Herrmann (E.); Hurt (M. B.); NY Shakespeare Festival

Harewood, Dorian (1951–) a; *Streamers*

Harley, Margot (1935–) adm, p; Acting Company

Harling, Robert (1951–) a, pl; Off-Broadway

Harlow, Jean (1911–37) a; Bellamy; *Dinner at Eight*

Harmon, Mark (1951–) a; *Sweet Bird . . .*

Harnick, Jay (1928–2007) d; Theatreworks

Harper, Herbie (fl. 1930s) ch, da; dance

Harper, Valerie (1940–) a; Second City

Harrelson, Woody (1961–) a; *Rainmaker*

Harrigan, William (1894–1966) a; *Great God Brown;* Harrigan

Harriman, Mary (1851–1932) philanthropist; children's

Harrington, Jonathan (1809–81) ma; magic

Harris, Barbara (1935/7–) a; Off-Broadway; *Oh Dad, Poor Dad . . .*

Harris, Ed (1950–) a; *Fool for Love*

Harris, Henry B. (1866–1912) p; Helen Hayes Theatre

Harris, Richard (1933–2002) Ir, a; *Camelot;* Ebersole

Harrison, Charles (1883–1955) pl; tent show

Harrold, Orville (1878–1933) a, s; *Naughty Marietta*

Hart, Charles (1962–) Brit l; *Phantom . . .*

Hart, Margie (1916–) e; Minsky

Hart, Roxanne (1952–) a; Weller

Hart, Teddy (1897–1971) a; *Boys from Syracuse*

Hartman, Louis (1907–41) de; Belasco; scenic design; stage lighting

Hartzell, Linda (1948–) adm, d; Seattle Children's

Harvey, Laurence (1928–73) a; *Summer and Smoke*

Harwood, Ronald (1934–) SAf pl; Cohen

Hash, Burl (19??–) d; Dodger; Malpede

Hasso, Signe (1910–2002) Swe, a; Ibsen

Hastings, Edward (1931–) d; American Conservatory

Hastings, Thomas, *see* Carrère and Hastings

Hatcher, Jeffrey (19??–) pl; Primary Stages

Hatcher, Teri (1964–) a; Tenney

Hatton, Anne Kemble (fl. 1790s) Brit, pl; Native Americans portrayed

Hauptman, William (1942–) pl; Jujamcyn

Hauptmann, Gerhart (1862–1946) Ger, pl; Ben-Ami; criticism; ethnic; Sothern

Havel, Václav (1936–) Cz, pl; Foreman; NY Shakespeare Festival; Strathairn

Haver, June (1926–) a, s; Dolly Sisters

Haverly, Jack H. (1837–1901) en, m; African American; minstrel show

Haviland, John (fl. 1820s) arc; Walnut St. Theatre

Havlin, John H. (1847?–1924) en, t; Stair and Havlin

Hawkes, Ethan (1970–) a; *Hurlyburly;* Leonard

Hawkins, Erick (1909–) ch; Noguchi

Hawkins, Jack (1910–73) Brit, a; Tandy

Hawkins, Trish (1945–) a; *Talley's Folly*

Hawthorne, Nathaniel (1804–64) w; Lowell; MacKaye (P.); Parks (S-L.)

Hayakawa, Sessue (1890–1973) Jp-born a; Asian American

Hayes, Alfred (1911–85) co; *Hellzapoppin*

Hayes, Joseph (1918–2006) pl; Grizzard

Hayes, Theodore (1867–1945) m; Minneapolis

Hayman, Alfred (1851–1917) m; Intro(§2); Empire Theatre; Syndicate

Hays, Carol Sorenstein (c. 1948–) p; San Francisco

Hayter, Pearl Price (1936–) d; Barter Theatre

Hazelton, George Cochrane (1868–1921) pl; *Yellow Jacket*

Hazzard, John (1881–1935) a, pl; Golden; Smith, W.

Headly, Glenne (1959–) a; Steppenwolf

Heald, Anthony (1944–) a; *Foreigner*

Heath, Gordon (1918–) a; *Deep Are the Roots*

Hecht, Paul (1941–) a; *MacBird!*; Off-Broadway

Heefner, David Kerry (1945–) en, pl; Hudson Guild Theatre

Heeley, Desmond (1931–) Brit de; Perdziola

Heflin, Van (1910–71) a; *View from the Bridge*

Heggen, Thomas (1919–49) pl; Intro(§3); Logan; *Mister Roberts*

Heide, Robert (1939–) pl; Intro(§4); Caffe Cino

Heifetz, Jascha (1901–87) mu (violinist); Brooklyn Academy

Heilbing, Terry (1951–94) a, pl; gay/lesbian

Heilig, Calvin (?–1941) m; frontier

Heller, George (1906–55) p; *Deep Are the Roots*

Heller, Joseph (1923–99) pl; Intro(§4)

Hellinger, Mark (1903/4–47) w; Mark Hellinger Theatre

Helmond, Katherine (1928–) a; *House of Blue Leaves*

Hemingway, Ernest (1899–1961) w; Cariou

Henley, Edward J. (1861–98) Brit, a; training

Hensley, Shuler (1967–) a, s; *Les Misérables*

Henson, Eben (1929–) d; Pioneer Playhouse

Henson, Jim (1936–90) pup; puppetry

Herbert, Evelyn (1898–?) a, s; *New Moon*

Herbert, John (1926–2001) pl; Marowitz

Heredia, José Maria (1803–39) Cub w; Cuban American

Herlie, Eileen (1920–) a; *Matchmaker*

Herman, W. C. (1913–87) pl; tent show

Hernández, Leopoldo (1921–) pl; Cuban American

Herne, Chrystal (1882/83–1950) a; *Craig's Wife*

Herne, Katharine Cocoran (1839–1901) a, pl; *Margaret Fleming*; *Shore Acres*

Heron, Bijou (1863–1937) a; Miller (G. H.); Miller (H.)

Herrmann, Adelaide (1854–1932) ma; Herrmann (A.); magic

Herrmann, Carl (1816–87) ma; Herrmann (A.); magic

Herrmann, Leon (1867–1909) ma; Herrmann (A.)

Hersey, David [Kenneth] (1939–) ltg de; *Les Misérables*

Hershman, Lynn (1941–) perf; performance art

Herskovits, David (19??–) d; Zinn

Herts (Harry [Henry] B.) (1871–1933) and (Hugh) Tallant (1869–1952) arc; Booth Theatre; Brooklyn Academy; Helen Hayes Theatre; Longacre; Lyceum; Morosco; New Amsterdam; Sam S. Shubert Theatre

Herts, Alice Minnie (Heniger) (1870?–1933) d; children's

Hewins, Mary (1842–89) pl; animals as performers

Hewitt, Barnard (1906–87) edu, w; awards

Heyward, Grace (c. 1860–1930) a; Minneapolis

Hickey, William (1928–97) a; *Arsenic . . .*

Higginsen, Vy (19??–) p, pl, w; African American

Hildegarde (1906–2002) e; nightclubs

Hill, Abram (1910–86) pl; American Negro Theatre; *Anna Lucasta*; O'Neal

Hill, Amy (1953–) pl; Asian American

Hill, George Roy (1921–2002) d; *Look Homeward . . .*

Hill, Gus (1860–1940) a, m, pl; African American

Hill, J. M. (d. 1912) m; Union Square

Hill, Jane (1939–) a, mi; Dell'Arte

Hill, Steven (né Solomon Berg) (1922–) a; *Country Girl*

Hiller, Wendy (1912–2003) Brit, a; *Moon for the Misbegotten*

Hindle, Annie (c. 1847–?) Brit, a, e; female/male

Hines, Maurice (1943–), a, ch, da; Hines

Hinman, Mary Wood (1878–1952) d; pageants

Hinsdell, Oliver (fl. 1920s) d; community

Hirschl, Barbara (1916–) art dealer; Manhattan Theatre Club

Hitchcock, Alfred (1899–1980) Brit-born, f d; Chekhov (M.); Jesurun; Ritchard

Hobart, George V. (1867–1926) pl; Ferber

Hochhuth, Rolf (1931–) Ger, pl; Intro(§4); documentary; Piscator; Shumlin

Hockney, David (1937–) Brit-born, de; Dexter

Hodson, Georgina Rosa (1830–?) Ir-born, a; *Po-ca-hon-tas*

Hoff, Christian (1968–) a, s; musical

Hoffman, F. B., Jr. (fl. 1900s) arc; Helen Hayes Theatre

Hoffman, Irving (1909–68) art; caricature

Hoffman, William M. (1939–) a, d, pl; Intro(§4); AIDS; *As Is*; Caffe Cino; gay/lesbian; Mason

Hoffmann, Hans (1902–49) art; Kaprow

Hofsiss, Jack (1950–) d; *Elephant Man*

Hogan, Ernest (c. 1859–1909) e, pl; African American

Hogan, Jonathan (1951–) a; *Fifth of July*

Hogarth, Leona (fl. 1920s) a; *Great God Brown*

Hoiby, Lee (1926–) co; *Summer and Smoke*

Holden, Joan (1939–) pl; San Francisco Mime

Holden, William (1918–81) a; *Picnic*

Holland, Edmund Milton (1848–1913) a; Blanchard; Holland

Holland, Endesha Ida Mae (1944–2006) pl; *From the Mississippi Delta*

Holland, Joseph Jefferson (1860–1926) a; Blanchard; Holland

Holliday, Polly (1937–) a; *Arsenic . . .*

Hollman, Mark (1964?–) co, l; *Urinetown*

Holm, Ian (1931–) Brit, a; international

Holm, John Cecil (1904–81) pl; *Three Men on a Horse*

Holmes, Rupert (1947–) Brit-born, co, l, pl; NY Shakespeare Festival

Holmes, Shirlene (19??–) pl; gay/lesbian

Holy, Elena K. (19??–) adm, d; NY International

Holzman, Winnie (c. 1954–) pl, w; *Wicked*

Home, John (1722–1808) Sc, pl; Fennell; Payne

Hooker, Brian (1880–1946) a, pl; Friml; *Vagabond King*

Hooks, Kevin (1958–) a, d; Hooks

Hooley, Richard M. (1822–93) Ir-born, m; Campbell; Hooley's Theatre

Hope, Bob [né Leslie Townes Hope] (1903–2003) e; dance; Gelbart

Hopkins, Anthony (1937–) We, a; international

Hornby, Richard (1938–) edu, th; dramatic theory

Horncastle, Henry (1801–69) Brit, a, pl; Mitchell (W.)

Horne, Lena (1917–) a, s; Nederlander Theatre

Horowitz, Jeffrey (1949–) a, d; Theatre for a New Audience

Horst, Louis (1884–1964) da, edu; Clarke (M.)

Horváth, Ödön von (1901–38) pl; Overmyer

Houghton, James (1959–) adm, d; Kahn (M.); Signature

House, Edward H. (1836–1901) c, pl; Winter

Housman, A. E. (1859–1936) po; Easton; Leonard

Houston, Velina Hasu (1957–) pl; Asian American

Howard, Alan (1937–) Brit, a; international

Howard, Cordelia (1848–1911) a; Howard family

Howard, Edwin (1896–?) arc; American Shakespeare Theatre

Howard, Joseph, Jr. (fl. 1860s–70s) c; Wheeler (A. C.)

Howard, Leslie (1893–1943) Brit, a; Hopkins; Imperial Theatre; Miller (G. H.); *Petrified Forest*

Howard, May (Havill) (1845–1913?) Can-born, e; burlesque

Howe, John (?–1910) m; frontier

Howes, Libby (195?–) a; Gray

Hoy, Cyrus (1926–) th; dramatic theory

Hubbard, W[illiam] L[ines] (1867–?) c; Chicago

Huerta, Jorge (1942–) d, pl; Chicano

Huff, Neal (c. 1970–) a; *Take Me Out*

Huffman, Felicity (1962–) a; Atlantic Theater

Hughes, Arthur (1894–1983) a; *Detective Story*

Hughes, Glenn (1894–1964) d, edu, sch; Seattle

Hughes, Howard (1905–76) f d, p; *Philadelphia Story*

Hughes, I. Harris, *see* Fakir of Ava

Hugo, Victor (1802–85) Fr, pl, w; Lackaye; *Les Misérables*

Huidobro, Matías Montes (1930/1–) Cub-Amer pl; Cuban American

Hull, Henry (1890–1977) a, pl; Intro(§3); Barton; *Roger Bloomer; Tobacco Road*

Hull, Howard (?–1937) a; Anglin

Hull, Shelley (1885–1919) d; Hull

Humphrey, Doris (1895–1958) ch, d; Cole (J.); dance; Engel

Hunt, Mame (1952–) d; magic

Hunt, Peter (1939–) d, de; Williamstown

Hunter, Kermit (1910–2001) pl; outdoor

Hunter, Robert (d. 1734) pl; Intro(§1)

Hunter, Ruth (1902–76) a; *Tobacco Road*

Hurlin, Dan (1955–) d; puppetry

Hurok, Sol (1888–1974) en; Chekhov (M.)

Hurston, Zora Neale (1903–60) w; Dee; Hughes (L.)

Hurwitz, "Professor" Moshe Ish-HaLevi (1844–1959) Y, pl; Yiddish

Hussey, Ruth (1911–2005) a; *State of the Union*

Huston, John (1906–87) a, d, f d, scr; Federal Theatre Project; Huston; *Night of the Iguana*

Hutton, Arlene [née Beth Lincks] (19??–) a, d, pl; NY International

Hutton, Timothy (1960–) a; clubs; *Prelude to a Kiss*

Hyers, Anna (fl. 1870s) a, s; African American; Lucas (S.)

Hyers, Emma (fl. 1870s) a, s African American; Lucas (S.)

Hyman, Mac (19??–) w; Levin

Hytner, Nicholas (1956–) Brit d; *Carousel;* international; *Miss*

Saigon; Tesori; Vivian Beaumont; Zuber

Ibsen, Henrik (1828–1906) pl; Intro(§§2,3); *All My Sons;* Bosco; Brisson; Chicago; *Children's Hour;* Circle in the Square; Civic Rep; community; criticism; dramatic theory; ethnic; Feingold; Fiske (M. M.); Garland; Hampden; Hardwick; Hellman; Hopkins; Howells; Ibsen on . . . ; Le Gallienne; Los Angeles; Ludlam; Miller (G. H.); Minneapolis; Moses; Nazimova; O'Neil; Robins; Seattle; Shaw (M.); Towse; *Truth;* Wilson (L.); Winter

Iizuka, Naomi (1965–) pl; Asian American

Iko, Momoko (1940–) pl; Asian American; Pan Asian

Ingalls, Harry C. (1876–1936) arc; Helen Hayes Theatre

Inness, George (1825–94) art; MacKaye (S.)

Ionesco, Eugène (1912–94) Ro-born Fr, pl, w; *American Dream;* Barr; Chaikin; Ferrer; Lortel; Welles

Irigaray, Luce (1939–) Fr, th; dramatic theory

Irizzary, Richard Vincent (1956–94) pl; Nuyorican

Irschick, Magda (fl. 1866) Ger, a; Germania

Irvine, Harry (1874–1951) Brit, a; *Joan of Lorraine*

Irving, Amy (1953–) a; Irving (J.); Miller (A.)

Irving, Henry (né John Henry Brodribb) (1838–1905) Brit, a, m; Intro(§2); Arthur; Barrett; Bateman family; Bellew; Booth (E. T.); Broadway Theatre; Dixey; Drew-Barrymore; international; Mansfield; Shakespeare on . . .

Irwin, Flo (c. 1859–1930) e; Irwin (M.)

Isham, John W. (fl. 1890s) a, d, p; African American

Isherwood, Christopher (1904–86) Brit-born, w; *Cabaret; I Am a Camera;* Masteroff

Isherwood, Harry (fl. 1830–40s) scpt; scenic design

Ives, Burl (1909–95) a, s; *Cat on a Hot Tin Roof*

Ivey, William J. (1944–) mu, sch; National Endowment

Izenour, Steven (1940–2001) arc, w; Izenour

Jack, Sam T. (1853–99) e, pl; African American; burlesque; Lucas (S.); minstrel show; Rentz–Santley

Jacker (née Litvin), Corinne (1933–) pl; Intro(§4); Hurt (William)

Jackson, Eddie (1896–1980) en; Durante

Jackson, Glenda (1936–) Brit, a; Caldwell (Z.); Ibsen; *Who's Afraid . . .*

Jackson, Michael (1958–) e, s; female/male; Jefferson (M.)

Jackson, Nagle (1936–) d; McCarter; Milwaukee Rep

Jackson, Samuel L. (1949–) a; African American

Jacobi, Derek (1938–) Brit, a; Folger; international

Jacobs, Bernard B. (1916–96) en, law, p; Royale; Shubert Organization

Jacobs, Jim (1942–) a, l; *Grease*

Jacobs, Robert Allan (1905–?) arc; Minskoff Theatre

Jacoby, Mark (1947–) a, s; *Ragtime*

Jagger, Dean (1903–91) a; *Tobacco Road*

James (Bean), (Mary) Florence (1892–1988) d, edu, m; Seattle

James, Burton Wakely (1889–1951) d, edu, m; Seattle

James, Louis (1842–1910) a; Warde

Janney, Allison (1959–) a; *View from the Bridge*

Janney, Russell (1884–1963) pl, m; *Vagabond King*

Jaques-Dalcroze, Émile (1865–1950) Swi, co; Chekhov (M.)

Jarrell, Randell (1914–65) c, w; Chekhov on . . .

Jeffcoat, A. E. (1924–2002) en; Manhattan Theatre Club

Jefford, Barbara (1931–) Brit, a; *Little Murders*

Jeffreys, Stephen (1950–) Brit pl; Malkovich

Jelliffe, Rowena (1892–) d, en; Karamu House

Jelliffe, Russell (1892?–1980) d, en; Karamu House

Jenkins, Florence Foster (1868–1944) s; Kaye (J.)

Jenkins, Jeffrey Eric (195?–) c, ed, w; Sherwood (G.)

Jenkins, Richard (1947–) a, d; Trinity Rep

Jens, Salome (1935–) a; *After the Fall*

Jessel, George (1898–1981) a, e; Palace

Jeter, John (1960?–) pl; Ivey (J.)

Jewett, Henry (1862?–1930) Astl-born a, m; Boston; training

Joel, Billy (1949–) co, s; revues; Tharp

Joffrey, Robert (1930?–88) ch; dance; Skelton; Tipton

Johann, Zita (fl.1920s) a; *Machinal*

Johanson, Robert (1951–) a, d; *Camelot;* Paper Mill

John, Elton (1947–) Brit co, s; Disney; Headley (H.); *Lion King;* Palace

John, Errol (1924–88) West Indian, pl; Carroll (V.)

Johns, Ernest (197?–) d; Jean Cocteau

Johnson, Billy (1858–1916) a, co, e, l, lib, musical creator; African American; Cole (Bob); musical

Johnson, Hall (1888–1970) co, pl; African American; *Green Pastures*

Johnson, James Weldon (1871–1938) l, pl; African American

Johnson, Philip (1906–2005) arc; Cleveland Play House

Jones, Bill T. (1952–) co, da; Kitchen; *Uncle Tom's Cabin*

Jones, Charlotte (1968–), Brit pl; Manhattan Theatre Club

Jones, David Hugh (1932?–) d; Brooklyn Academy

Jones, Dean (1931–) a; *Company*

Jones, Derek Anson (1961–2000) d; *Wit*

Jones, Fanny (d. 1878?) da; Wallack family

Jones, Henry Arthur (1851–1929) Brit, pl; Intro(§2); Frohman (D.); Palmer

Jones, Preston (1936–79) pl; *Texas Trilogy*

Jones, Robert Earl (1910–2006) a; Jones (J. E.)

Jones, Shirley (1934–) a, s; *Carousel; 42nd Street*

Jones, Sissieretta (1869–1933) s, p; African American

Jones, T. C. (1920–71) a, e; female/male

Jones, Tisch (1948–) d; African American

Jones, Tom (1928–) l, pl; *Fantasticks;* Off-Broadway

Jones, Tommy Lee (1946–) a; *Cat on a Hot Tin Roof*

Jonson, Ben (1572–1637) Brit, pl; Chautauqua; Scott

Joplin, Scott (1868–1919) co; African American; De Shields

Jordan, Bruce (1945?–) d, p, w; *Shear Madness*

Jordan, June (1936–) po; Sellars

Jordan, Walter C. (1877?–1951) ag, p; Nederlander Theatre

Jory, Victor (1902–82) a, d; Actors Theatre of Louisville; Jory

Joseph, Helen Haiman (d. 1983) pup; puppetry

Joseph, Stephen (1927–67) Brit, d; Alley Theatre

Joslyn, Allyn (1905–81) a; *Arsenic . . .*

Jouvet, Louis (1887–1951) Fr, a, d; *Theatre Arts Monthly*

Joyce, James (1882–1941) Ir, w; Barnes; Neighborhood Playhouse; Shaw and . . . ; *Skin of Our Teeth*

Judd, Ashley (1968–) a; *Cat on a Hot Tin Roof*

Jumbo (d. 1885) elephant; Barnum; circus

Kafka, Franz (1883–1924) Cz-born Ger, w; animal impersonation; Chong; dance

Kahn, Florence (1877/8–1951) a; Ibsen

Kahn, John (1956–) art (sculptor); Moschen

Kahn, Madeline (1942–99) a; Kaye (J.)

Kaiser, Georg (1878–1945) Ger, pl; Langner; Theatre Guild

Kalem, T. E. (Theodore Eustace) (1919–85) c; criticism

Kalich, Jacob (1891–1975) e, p, w; Picon

Kalmar, Bert (1884–1947) co, l; *Animal Crackers*

Kallen, Lucille (1922–99) w; Tamiment

Kaminska, Ida (1899–1980) Pol, a, d, p; Gordin; international

Kanin, Fay Mitchell (1917–) pl; Chang; Kanin (G.)

Kanin, Michael (1910–93) pl; Chang; Kanin (G.)

Kantor, Tadeusz (1915–90) Pol, d, de; La MaMa

Kaplan, Richard D. (19??–) arc; American Place

Karloff, Boris (né William Henry Pratt) Brit, a; (1887–1969) *Arsenic . . .*

Karnilova, Maria (1920–2001) a, da; *Fiddler . . .*

Katigbak, Mia (195?–) Phi-born a, d, p; Filipino American; National Asian-American

Katselas, Milton (1933–) d; *Camino Real; Zoo Story*

Katz, Sam (1892–1961) t, en; Balaban and Katz

Kaufman, Moisés (c.1964–) Venezuela-born d, pl; *I Am My Own Wife; Laramie Project;* Tectonic

Kayden, Spencer (1971–) a; *Urinetown*

Kaye, Danny (1913–87) a, e; Intro(§3); borscht belt; Gottfried; *Lady in the Dark;* Tamiment

Kaye, Stubby (1918–97) a, s; *Guys and Dolls*

Keach, James (1947–) a, d; Keach

Keach, Stacy, Sr. (1915–2003) a; Keach

Kean, Charles (1811–68) Brit, a, m; Intro(§1); international; San Francisco; scenic design; Shakespeare on . . . ; support services

Kean, Edmund (1789?–1833) Brit, a; Intro(§1); Aldridge; Booth (J. B.); Boston; Brutus; Burton (W. E.); Cohen; Cooke; economics; Forrest; international; Park Theatre; Payne; Shakespeare on . . .

Keane, John B. (1928–2002) Ir, pl; Fitzgerald

Keathley, George (1925–) d; Missouri Rep

Keaton, Buster (1895–1966) a, e; mime/pantomime; Schneider

Keaton, Diane (1946–) a; *Marvin's Room*

Keene, Thomas Wallace (né Thomas Wallace Eagleson) (1840–98) a; Warde

Keener, Catherine (1960–) a; *Burn This*

Keister, George (fl. 1900s) arc; Belasco Theatre; George M. Cohan's Theatre

Keitel, Harvey (1947–) a; Actors Studio; *Lie of the Mind*

Keith, Robert (1898–1966) a, d, p, pl; *Great God Brown*

Kelcey, Herbert (1855?–1917) a; Intro(§2); Shannon

Kelly, Gene (1912–96) a, ch, da; Intro(§3); dance; musical; *On the Town; Pal Joey; Time of Your Life*

Kelly, Grace (1929–82) a; Kelly (George)

Kelly, Kevin (1930–94) c; criticism

Kelly, Paul (1896–1956) a; *Country Girl*

Kelly, Walter C. (1873–1939) a; *Both Your Houses*

Kemble, Charles (1775–1854) Brit, a; international; Kemble; Shakespeare on . . .

Kemble, John Philip (1757–1823) Brit, a, m; Wallack family

Kemble, Lillian (fl. 1900–22) a; *Man of the Hour*

Kempson, Rachel (1910–2003) Brit a; Redgrave

Kendal, Margaret (Madge) (1848–1935) Brit, a, m; international

Kendal, W. H. (1843–1917) Brit, a, m; international

Kenley, John (1906–) en; summer stock

Kennedy, Jimmy (1903?–84) pl; Maher

Kennedy, Madge (1890–1987) a; *Paris Bound*

Kennedy, Margaret (1932–) en, w; Manhattan Theatre Club

Keogh, W. T. (1860?–1947) m; Murray Hill

Keppler, Joseph (1838–94) Aus, c; caricature

Kerr, Deborah (1921–) a; *Night of the Iguana; Tea and Sympathy*

Kerr, John (1931–94) a; *Tea and Sympathy*

Kert, Larry (1930–91) a, s; *Company;* Tamiment; *West Side Story*

Kesselman, Wendy (1940–) pl; *Diary of Anne Frank*

Kesselring, Joseph D. (1902–67) pl; Intro(§3); *Arsenic . . . ;* awards

Kessler, Lyle (196?–) pl, scr; Hirsch (J.)

Khan, Rick [Richardo] (1951–) d; African American; Crossroads; Theatre Communications

Kidder, Kathryn (1867–1923) a; Warde

Kilner, Kevin (1958–) a; *Dinner with Friends*

Kilyanyi, Eduard or Edward (c. 1852–95) Hun, d, p; nudity

Kimball, Francis Hatch (1845–1919) arc; Casino Theatre; Garrick Theatre

Kimbrough, Emily (1899–1989) w; Skinner (C. O.)

King, Claude (1876–1941) Brit, a; *Déclassée*

Kingsley, Ben (1943–) Brit, a; Cohen; international

Kingsley, Omar, *see* Zoyara, Ella

Kingsley, Susan (1946–) a; *Getting Out*

Kinney, Terry (1954–) a, d; *Grapes of Wrath;* Steppenwolf

Kipphardt, Heinar (1922–) Ger, pl; documentary; Wiseman

Kirby, J. Hudson (1819–48) a; Intro(§1)

Kirby, Michael (1931–97) ed, edu, pl, w; dramatic theory; Wooster Group

Kirkland, Alexander (1908–) a, d, pl; Berkshire; *Men in White*

Kirkland, Jack (1902–69) pl; Steinbeck; *Tobacco Road*

Kirkland, Sally (1944–) a; nudity

Kirkwood, James (1925–89) a, pl; *Chorus Line;* gay/lesbian

Kitt, Eartha (1927–) a, s; Quinton

Kitt, Tom (Thomas Robert) (1974–) co; Comden

Kittredge, George Lyman (1860–1941) edu; Norton

Kleban, Edward (1939–87) l, pl; *Chorus Line*

Kleiman, Harlan (1940–) en; Long Wharf

Klein, Robert (1942–) a, e; Second City

Kleist, Heinrich von (1777–1811) Ger, pl; Overmyer

Kliegl, Anton (1872–1927) ltg tech; Belasco; stage lighting; support services

Kliegl, John H. (1870?–1959) ltg tech; Belasco; stage lighting; support services

Kliewer, Warren (1931–98) d; East Lynne Theater Co.

Kling, Kevin (1957–) sto; one-person

Klugman, Jack (1922–) a; *Sunshine Boys;* Tillinger

Kneubuhl, Victoria Nalani (1949–) pl; Asian American

Knighton, Nan (19??–) l, w; Wildhorn

Knoblock, Edward (1874–1945) pl; *Kismet*

Knowles, James Sheridan (1784–1862) Brit–Ir, pl; Intro(§2); San Francisco

Kobrin, Leon (1873–1946) Y, pl; ethnic; Yiddish

Koch, Frederick Henry (1877–1944) edu; Green (P.); Miller (May); outdoor; pageants

Koestler, Arthur (1905–83) w; Intro(§3); *Darkness at Noon;* Kingsley

Koiransky, Alexander (1876–1956) da, edu; Seattle

Kondoleon, Harry (1955–94) pl; Intro(§4); AIDS; NY Shakespeare Festival

Kook, Edward F. (1903–90) ltg equipment de; Mielziner; support services

Koolhaas, Rem (1944–) Dut arc; architecture; resident non-profit; Second Stage

Korbrin, Leon (1872–1946) pl; ethnic

Korff, Arnold (1870–1944) Aus, a; Lortel

Korie, Michael (19??–) l, lib; gay/lesbian

Kornfeld, Lawrence (193?–) d; Theater for the New City

Koster, John (1844–95) t; Koster and Bial's

Kotis, Greg (1966?–) l, pl; Urinetown

Kotzebue, August Friedrich Ferdinand von (1761–1819) Ger, pl; Dunlap; Murdoch (J. E.); showboats

Koutoukas, H. M. (1947–) a, d, pl; Intro(§4); Caffe Cino; La MaMa; Off-Off Broadway

Kovačević, Dušan (1948–) Serbian pl; Weaver

Krapp, Herbert J. (1887–1973) arc; Ambassador; Biltmore; Broadhurst Theatre; Brooks Atkinson Theatre; Empire; Ethel Barrymore Theatre; Eugene O'Neill Theatre; Imperial; John Golden Theatre; Majestic; Morosco; Neil Simon Theatre; New York City theatres; Plymouth; Richard Rodgers Theatre; Ritz; Royale; Walter Kerr Theatre; Winter Garden

Krauss, Ruth (1911–) pl; Off-Off Broadway

Krebs, Eric (19??–) d, p; George Street

Kreiger, Murray (1923–) c; dramatic theory

Kremer, Theodore (1871–1923) Ger, pl; Woods

Kressyn, Miriam (1910–96) Pol-born, Y, a; Yiddish

Kretzmer, Herbert (1925–) SAf-born, ly; Les Misérables

Kristeva, Julia (1941–) Fr, th; dramatic theory

Kroetz, Franz Xaver (1946–) Ger, pl; Akalaitis; Interart Theatre; international; Mabou Mines; Parsons

Kroll, Jack (1926–2000) c; criticism; Glengarry

Krone, Gerald (1933–) a, d, p; Ward (D. T.)

Kuhn, Judy (1958–) a, s; Les Misérables

Kurz, Heinrich (c. 1827–1906) m, t; Kurz Stadt Theater

La Follette, Fola (1882–1970) a; Scarecrow

La Verne, Lucille (1872–1945) a; Sun-up

Lacy, Thomas Hailes (1809–73) Brit a, pl, m, pub; Samuel French

Ladd, Cheryl (1951–) a; Annie Get Your Gun

Lagomarsino, Ron (19??–) d; Driving Miss Daisy

Laliberté, Guy (1959–) Can, en, p; Cirque du Soleil

Lamb, Charles (1775–1834) Brit, w; Payne

Lamb, Thomas White (1871–1942) arc; Mark Hellinger Theatre; Ziegfeld Theatre

Lambert, Hugh (1930–55) ch; How to Succeed . . .

Lampert, Zohra (1936–) a; After the Fall

Lancaster, Edward (18??–?) pl; Boucicault

Lanchester, Elsa (1902–86) Brit-born, a; Laughton

Landis, Frederick (1872–1934) w; Copperhead

Lane, Thomas Frederick (fl. 1820s) Brit, a; Drew–Barrymore

Lane, William Henry (Master Juba) (1825–52?) da; dance

Lang, Fritz (1890–1976) f d; Brecht

Langdon, William Chauncy (1872–1947) d, p, pl; pageants

Lange, Jessica (1949–) a; Cat on a Hot Tin Roof; Glass Menagerie; Streetcar . . .

Langer, Susan (1895–1985) c, th; dramatic theory

Langrishe, John S. (1830–95) a, m; frontier

Lanier, Sidney, Rev. (1923–) d, edu, p; American Place

Lansburgh, G. Albert (1876–1969) arc; Martin Beck Theatre

LaPaglia, Anthony (1959–) Astl a; Mayer; View from the Bridge

Lapotaire, Jane (1944–) Brit, a; international

Lardner, Ring (1885–1933) pl; Drama Dept.

Larimore, Earle (1899–1947) a; Intro(§3); Mourning Becomes Electra

Larson, Jonathan (1960–96) co, l; NY Theatre Workshop; Rent

Lash, Lee (fl. 1890s–1930) scpt; supply services

Lasky, Jesse L. (1880–1958) m, p; Helen Hayes Theatre

Lázsló, Miklós (1904–73) Hun, pl; She Loves Me

Lateiner, Joseph (1853–1935) Y, pl; Yiddish

Latrobe, Benjamin (1764–1820) arc; Chestnut St. Theatre

Lauri family (fl. 1869) e; animal impersonation

Lavery, Bryony (1947–) Brit pl; Hughes (D.); Kurtz

Lavey, Martha (1957–) d; Steppenwolf

Laviera, Tato (1950–) pl; Nuyorican

Lawrence, Carol (1935–) a, s; West Side Story

Lawrence, D. H. (1885–1930) Brit w; Mint

Lawrence, Jeremy (19??–) a, pl; Moffat

Lazarus, Paul (1954–) d; Pasadena Playhouse

Le Maire, Charles (1897–1985) de; costume

Le Noire, Rosetta Burton (1911–2002) d; AMAS; awards; Handman

Lea, Marion (1864–1944) a; Mitchell (L. E.)

Learned, Michael (1939–) a; Donat; Folger

Lebedeff (Lebedev), Aaron (18??–1960) Y, c; Yiddish

Lebow, Barbara (19??–) pl; Kalfin

Lecoq, Jacques (1921–99) Fr a, mi; Avner the Eccentric; Feldshuh; mime/pantomime; Taymor; Théâtre de la Jeune Lune

Lederer, Charles (1910–76) pl; Kismet

Lee, Carl (1933–86) a, d; Connection

Lee, Eddie Levi (194?–) d, pl; Atlanta; Empty Stage

Lee, Franne (1941–) costume de; Lee (E.)

Lee, Leslie (1935?–) pl; Intro(§4)

Lee, Michele (1942–) a; Tale of the Allergist's Wife

Lee, Ralph (1935–) pup; puppetry

Leesugg, Catherine (fl. 1800s) a; Noah; She Would Be a Soldier

Legrand, Michel (1932–) Fr, co; Errico

Lehár, Franz (1870–1948) Cz-born Hun, co; Intro(§2); dance; Merry Widow; musical

Lehman, Martin (1867–1917) t; Orpheum Circuit

Lehrer, Tom (Thomas Andrew) (1928–) e, song w; Gilbert and Sullivan

Leibert, Michael (1940–) a, d; Berkeley Rep

Leibgold, Leon (fl. 1930s) Y, a; Yiddish

Leibman, Ron (1937–) a; Angels in America

Leigh, Carolyn (1926–) l;
Coleman; Simon (N.)

Leigh, Mike (1943–) a, d, pl;
Elliott (S.)

Leigh, Mitch (1928–) co; Adams
(L.); Coleman; *Man of La Mancha*

Leigh, Vivien (Vivian Mary
Hartley) (1913–67) Brit, a; *Skin
of Our Teeth; Streetcar . . .*

Leighton, Margaret (1922–76)
Brit, a; *Night of the Iguana*

Leipzig, Nate (1873–1939) Swe-
born, ma; magic

Leivick, Halpern (1888–1962) pl;
Kalfin; Yiddish

Lemberg, Clara (?) a; ethnic

Lemmon, Jack (1925–2001) a;
Gallagher (P.); *Glengarry; Room
Service;* Slade; Spacey

Lengyel, Melchior (1880–1974)
Hun-born scr; *Silk Stockings*

Lennart, Isobel (1915–71) pl;
Funny Girl

Lennix, Harry J. (1964–) a, d;
Goodman

Lennon, John (1940–80) Brit, co,
l, pl, s; *Oh! Calcutta!;*
performance art

Lenox, Adriane (1965–) a; *Doubt*

Leon, Francis (b. 1840s) a, e;
female/male

Leon, Kenny (1956–) d; Alliance
Theatre Co.

Leon, Victor (1860–1940) l; *Merry
Widow*

Leonard, Hugh (1926–) Ir, pl;
international; Weaver

Leslie, Lew (1886–1963) co, p;
Mills

Lester, Will (fl. 1900s) e; Smith
and Dale

Levine, Roy (fl. 1960s) d; *MacBird!*

Levingston, William (fl. 1770s) t,
m; architecture; Intro(§1)

Levitt, Paul (1935–) th; dramatic
theory

Levy, Benn W. (1900–73) pl;
Cummings

Levy, Jacques (1935–2004) d;
America Hurrah; Oh! Calcutta!

Lewes, George Henry (1817–78)
Brit, cr, pl; Fechter

Lewis, Irene (1942–) d; Center
Stage

Lewis, Jerry (1926–) a, e, f d;
borscht belt; *Damn Yankees*

Lewis, Joe E. (1902–71) a, e;
nightclubs

Lewis, Marcia (1938–) a; *Chicago*

Lewis, Sinclair (1885–1951) w;
Baitz; *It Can't Happen Here*

Lewisohn, Alice (1883–1972) ch,
d, de; Neighborhood Playhouse

Lewisohn, Irene (1892–1944) ch,
d, de; Neighborhood Playhouse

Lewisohn, Ludwig (1882–1955) c;
Intro(§3); dramatic theory

Lewitin, Margo (1938–) d;
Interart Theatre

Leynse, Andrew (1969–) d;
Primary Stages

Libin, Paul (1930–) p; Jujamcyn
Theaters

Libin, Z. (1872–1955) Y, pl;
Yiddish

Lichtenstein, Harvey (1929–) d,
en; Brooklyn Academy

Liebling, William (1895–1969) ag;
Wood (A.)

Liebman, Max (1902–81) d;
Tamiment

Liebman, Ron (1937–) a; Kushner

Lillo, George (1691?–1739) Brit,
pl; Hallams

Lim, Genny (1946–) pl; Asian
American

Limon, José (1908–72) ch, d;
dance; Fagan; Musser;
Skelton

Lind, Jenny (Johanna) (1820–87)
Swe, s; Barnum; Maguire;
photographers

Lindsay, Robert (1949–) Brit, a, s;
international

Lindsay-Hogg, Michael (1940–) d;
Fitzgerald

Linklater, Kristen (1936–) d, te;
Company of Women;
Shakespeare & Co.

Linn, Bambi (1926–) a, da;
Carousel

Linnerson, Beth (1939?–) d;
Minneapolis

Lion, John (1944–99) d; Magic
Theatre

Lipkin, Joan (1954–) d, pl;
feminist

Lippa, Louis A. (c. 1933–) pl;
Dukakis

Lithgow, Arthur (1915–2004) a, d;
Great Lakes; Lithgow; McCarter

Little, Stuart W. (1921–) c, w;
Cantor; Off-Broadway

Livings, Henry (1929–) Brit, pl;
Arkin

Loden, Barbara (1936–80) a; *After
the Fall; Glass Menagerie*

Loeb, Philip (1894–1955) a; *My
Heart's . . .*

Logan, Celia (1834–1904) a; Logan
(O.)

Logan, Eliza (1829–72) a; Logan
(O.)

Logan, Nedda Harrigan (1900–89)
a; Actors' Fund; Harrigan;
Logan (J.)

Lone, John (1952–) a; Asian
American

Long, John Luther (1861–1927)
pl, w; *Madame Butterfly*

Long, Shelley (1949–) a; Second
City

Longfellow, Henry Wadsworth
(1807–82) w; *Evangeline;*
Mowatt; Walcot; Winter

Lopez, Eduardo Iván (1945?–)
Pue–born pl; Nuyorican

López, Josefina (1969–) Mex-born,
pl; Chicano

Lopez, Robert (1975–) co, l;
Avenue Q

Lorca, García (1898–1936) Sp, pl;
LaChiusa; Living Theatre

Lorre, Peter (1904–64) Hun-born,
a; Brecht

Louloudes, Virginia I. (1956–)
adm; Alliance of Resident

Lover, Samuel (1797–1868) Ir, a,
pl; Williams (Barney)

Lowe, K. Elmo (1899–1971) a, d;
Cleveland Play House

Lowry, W. McNeil (1913–93)
patron; resident nonprofit

Lubovitch, Lar (1943–) co;
Emmons

Lucci, Susan (1948–) a; *Annie Get
Your Gun*

Luce, Claire (1901/3–89) a; *Of Mice
and Men*

Luckinbill, Laurence (1938–) a;
one-person

Lukas, Paul (1891/5–1971) Hun, a;
Watch on the Rhine

Lumet, Sidney (1924–) a, d, f d;
My Heart's . . .

Luna, James (1950–) perf;
performance art

Lyles, Aubrey (1884?–1932) e, pl;
Shuffle Along; Sissle and Blake

Lynde, Paul (1926–82) a; *Bye Bye
Birdie*

Lynn, Eleanor (fl. 1930s) a; Group
Theatre; *Rocket to the Moon*

Lynn, William (1889?–1952) a;
Three Men on a Horse

Lynne, Gillian (1926–) Brit ch;
Cats; Phantom . . .

Lyon, Milton (c. 1930?–) d, p;
McCarter

Lyon, Rick (c. 195?–) a, pup;
Avenue Q

Mabley, Jackie "Moms" (1900–75)
en; Childress; Goldberg

Mac [Bowyer], Taylor (197?–) a,
perf, pl; Eichelberger

Macaulay, John T. (1846–1915)
m; Macauley; Macauley's
Theatre

Macbeth, Robert (1934–) d; Lafayette Theatre

McCahill, Angela (1875–1965) a; *Detour*

McCandless, Stanley R. (1897–1967) ltg consultant, edu; stage lighting

McCarthy, Joseph (1885–1943) l; *Sally*

McCarthy, Mary (1912–89) c,w; Hellman

McCarthy, Nobu (1934–2002) a, d; Asian American, East West

McCarthy, Paul (1945–) perf; performance art

McCauley, Robbie (1942–) a, e, pl; Intro(§4); Hagedorn; Off-Off Broadway; one-person; performance art

McClanahan, Rue (1934–) a; *Harvey; MacBird!*

McCleery, William (1911–2000) pl; Dalrymple

McClure, Michael (1932–) pl; Intro(§4); censorship; Magic Theatre; pornographic; Torn

McCoart, Peter (1856–1929) m; frontier

McConnell, Frederic (1891?–1968) d, p; Cleveland Play House; community; pageants

McCowen, Alec (1925–) Brit, a; international

McCoy, Bessie (1888–1931) a; Weber and Fields

McCracken, Joan (1923–61) a, da; Saddler

McCrane, Paul (1961–) a; *Landscape*

McCutcheon, Bill (1924–2002) a; *You Can't Take It with You*

McDaniel, James (1958–) a; *Six Degrees . . .*

MacDermot, Galt (1928–) co, l; *Hair;* NY Shakespeare Festival; resident nonprofit

McDonagh, Martin (1970–) Brit, pl; Crudup; Walter Kerr Theatre

MacDonald, Jeannette (1903–65) a, s; *Little Mary Sunshine*

MacDonough, Glen (1867?–1924) pl; *Babes in Toyland*

Mace, Harriet (?–1859) a; Booth (J. B., Jr.)

McElfatrick, J. B. (1828–1906) arc; Broadway Theatre; Empire Theatre; National Theatre; New Victory; New York City theatres; Olympia

McEntire, Reba (1955–) a, s; *Annie Get Your Gun;* Mitchell (B. S.); *South Pacific;* Weissler

McGavin, Darren (1922–2006) a; *Rainmaker*

McGillin, Howard (1953–) a, s; *Phantom . . .*

McGinn, Walter (1936–77) a; *That Championship Season*

McGlinn, John (19??–) mu, p; *Show Boat*

McGrath, Bob (1958?–) d; Zuber

MacGrath, Leueen (1915–92) a, pl; *Silk Stockings*

McGroarty, John Steven (1862–1944) pl; Los Angeles

McGuinness, Frank (1953–) Ir, pl; Ibsen

McGuire, Dorothy (1919–2001) a; *Night of the Iguana*

McHenry, Nellie (c. 1853–1935) a, m; Salsbury

McHugh, Jimmy (1896–1967) co; Fields (D.)

McIlrath, Patricia (1917–99) d, edu; Missouri Rep

McIntyre, Dennis (1942–90) pl; Spacey

MacIvor, Daniel (1962–) Can, a, pl; NY International

Mack, Carol K. (1941–) pl; Wiest

Mackay, Frank Finley (1832–1923) a, d, pl; training

Mackaye, Hazel (1888–1944) d, w; pageants

McKellen, Ian (1939–) Brit, a; Cantor (A.); Folger; international; Strathairn

Mackeller, Helen (1895–1966) a; *Beyond the Horizon*

McKenney, Ruth (1911–72) w; *My Sister Eileen; Wonderful Town*

McKenzie, Compton (1883–1972) Brit, pl; Bateman family

McKenzie, James B. (1927–2002), p; Westport

Macklin, Charles (1699–1797) Ir, a, m, pl; Hallams

McKnight, William L. (1887–1978) industrialist; Jujamcyn Theaters

McLain, Billy (1866–1949) e; minstrel show

MacLaine, Shirley (1934–) a, da; *Sweet Charity*

McLaughlin, Ellen (1957–) a, pl; Eustis; National Actors Theatre

MacMahon, Horace (1907–71) a; *Detective Story*

McMillan, Kenneth (1934–) a; *Streamers*

McMullan, James (1934–) art; caricature

Macomb, General Alexander (1782–1841) pl; Native Americans portrayed

McPharlin, Paul (1903–48) pup, w; puppetry

McPherson, Conor (1971–) Ir, pl; Falls; Primary Stages

McPherson, Scott (1959–92) pl; Intro(§4); AIDS; Esterman; Gilman (Rebecca); Goodman; Playwrights Horizons; *Marvin's Room*

McQueen, Steve (1930–80) a; *Hatful of Rain*

MacRae, Gordon (1921–86) a, s; *Carousel*

Macready, William Charles (1793–1873) Brit, a; architecture; Arneaux; Astor Place; Bedford; Boston; Cushman; Davenport (E. L.); Fisher (Clara); Forrest; frontier; Hackett; international; Mitchell (William); Shakespeare on . . . ; Simpson; support services; Wemyss; Wheatley

McTeer, Janet (1961–) Brit, a; Ibsen

McVay [Zacek], Marcelle (195?–) adm; Victory Gardens

McVicker, Mary (1848–81) a; McVicker

Macy, William H. (1950–) a, d; *American Buffalo;* Atlantic Theater; Ziemba

Madden, John (1949–) Brit, d; *Wings*

Madonna (Ciccone) (1958–) e, s; female/male

Maeder, James Gaspard (1809?–76) co; *Po-ca-hon-tas*

Maeterlinck, Maurice (1862–1949) Bel, pl; Ames; animal impersonation; criticism; Hunneker

Maggio, Michael (1951?–2000) d; Chicago; Goodman

Magritte, René (1898–1967) Bel, art; Lamos

Maguire, Gregory (1954–) w; *Wicked*

Maguire, John (1840–1907) m; frontier

Maguire, Michael (1955–) a; *Les Misérables*

Maharis, George (1928–) a; *Zoo Story*

Mahoney, John (1940–) a; *House of Blue Leaves; Prelude to a Kiss;* Steppenwolf; *Subject Was Roses*

Maiori, Antonio (1868–1938) It, a, d; Shakespeare on . . .

Mako (1933–2000) Jp-born a, d; Asian American; East West

Malden, Karl (1913–) a; Intro(§3); *All My Sons; Desire under the Elms*

Malina, Judith (1926–) a, d; Intro(§§3,4); *Brig;* collective; Living Theatre; Malpede

Malini (né Breit), Max (1873–1942) Pol-born, ma; magic

Malle, Louis (1932–95) Fr, f d; Chekhov on . . . ; Gregory; Guare

Maltby, Richard, Jr. (1937–) d, w; *Miss Saigon*

Maltz, Albert (1908–85) pl; Theatre Union

Mandel, Frank (1884–1958) l; *Desert Song; New Moon; No, No, Nanette*

Mandell, Max (fl. 1910s) tr; Chekhov on . . .

Mangin, Joseph (fl. 1790s) arc; New York City theatres; Park Theatre

Mangum, Edward (1913–2001) d, edu; Intro(§3); Arena Stage

Manheim, Camryn (1961–) a; Atlantic Theater

Manheim, Kate (1945–) a; Foreman

Mann, Paul (1908–85) a; *After the Fall*

Mann, Paul (1910–83) co; *Hellzapoppin*

Mann, Terrence [Vaughn] (1951–) a, s; *Les Misérables*

Mannering, Mary (1876–1953) a; Intro(§2)

Manola, Marion (1866–1914) a, s; McCaull

Mansfield, Jayne (1933–67) f a; Axelrod

Mapes, Victor (1870–1943) d, m; Smith (Winchell)

Marber, Patrick (1964–) Brit pl; Molina

Marceau, Marcel (1923–) Fr, mi; Epstein; mime/pantomime; Montanaro

Marchand, Nancy (1928–2000) *And Miss Reardon . . . ; Morning's at Seven*

Marcus, Donald (1946–) d; Ark Theatre

Marcus, Joan (195?–) ph; photographers

Marine, Alexandre (1950–) R-Can; d, pl; Chekhov on . . .

Marion, George (1860–1945) a, p; *Anna Christie*

Marivaux, Pierre Carlet de Chamblain de (1688–1763) Fr, pl; Schmidt (P.)

Mark, Jeff (1970–) co, l; *Avenue Q*

Marley, Donovan (19??–) d; Denver

Marlowe, Christopher (1564–93) Brit, pl; Intro(§3)

Marlowe, Gloria (fl. 1950s) a; *View from the Bridge*

Marqués, René (1919–79) pl; ethnic

Marsh, Howard (?–1969) a; *Student Prince*

Marsh, Jean (1934–) Brit, a; international

Marsh, Reginald (1898–1954) art; caricature

Marshall, Armina (1895–1991) a, p, pl; Langner

Marshall, Susan (1958–) ch; Stein (D.)

Marshall, Tully (1864–1943) a; *City*

Marston, Richard (1842?–1917) de; support services

Martin, Andrea (1947–) a; *Candide*

Martin, Christopher (1942–) d; CSC Rep

Martin, George and Ethel (fl. 1940s–90s) ch, da; dance

Martin, Jane (pseudonym) pl; Jory

Martin, Jesse L. (1969–) a; *Rent*

Martin, Judy (1918–) a, d, de; Paper Bag

Martín, Manuel (1934–2000) pl; Cuban American

Martin, Marty (c. 1954–) pl; Circle Rep

Martin, Nicholas (c. 1930s?–) d; *Dead End;* Huntington; Krass

Martin, Ricky (1971–)Pue-born a, s; *Les Misérables*

Martinetti, Paul (1851–1924) It, a, en; animal impersonation

Martins, Peter (1946–) Dan, ch; Long

Marvel, Elizabeth (1970?–) a; Ibsen

Marvenga, Ilse (fl. 1920s) Ger, a, s; *Student Prince*

Marx, Minnie Palmer (1864–1929) en; Marx Bros.

Marzetti, Joseph (?–1864) e; animal impersonation

Maskelyne, John Nevil (1839–1917) Brit, ma; Davenport Brothers; Kellar; magic

Mason, "Curls" (fl. 1920s) e; burlesque

Mason, Jackie (1934–) perf; John Golden

Mason, John B. (1857–1919) a; *Witching Hour*

Mason, Marsha (1942–) a; Ibsen; *Night of the Iguana;* San Francisco; Simon (N.)

Massey, Anna (1937–) Brit, a; Massey

Massey, Daniel Raymond (1933–98) Brit, a; Massey

Masterson, Marc (1955–) d; Actors Theatre of Louisville

Matas, Julio (1931–) Cub pl; Cuban American

Mathias, Sean (1956–) Brit, d; international

Matteson, Ruth (1909–75) a; *Male Animal*

Matthau, Walter (1920–2000) a; Axelrod; Gardner; *Odd Couple*

Matthews, William Henry (fl. 1915–31) de; costume

Matthison, Edith Wynne (1875–1955) a; Kennedy (C. R.)

Mattox, Matt (1921–) da; dance

Maugham, William Somerset (1874–1965) Fr/Brit, pl; Burke; Miller (G. H.); Williams (John D.)

May, Karl (1848–1912) w; Wild West

Mayakovsky, Vladimir V. (1893–1930) Sov, pl; Coates; Perloff

Mayer, Michael (1960–) d; Krass

Mayer, Oliver (1965–) pl; Chicano

Mayo, Lisa (1924–) pl; Spiderwoman

Mays, Jefferson (1965/6–) a; *I Am My Own Wife*

Mazursky, Paul (1930–) a, f d, scr; Second City

Mazzone-Clementi, Carlo (1920–2000) a, mi; Avner the Eccentric; Dell'Arte

Mead, [Edward] Shepherd (1914–94) w; *How to Succeed . . .*

Meadows, Tim (1961–) a, e, w; Second City

Meara, Anne (1929–) a; *House of Blue Leaves . . . ;* Second City; Wallach and Jackson

Mecchi, Irene (19??–) w; *Lion King*

Medford, Kay (née Regan) (1920–80) a, s; *Funny Girl*

Meehan, Danny (1933–78) a, s; *Funny Girl*

Meehan, Thomas (1929–) pl; *Annie; Hairspray; Producers*

Meeker, Ralph (1920–88) a; *After the Fall; Picnic*

Meilhac, Henri (1831–97) Fr, pl; *Carmen Jones*

Meiningen, George II, Duke of (Saxe-) (1826–1914) d, p, de; Intro(§2)

Meir, Golda (1898–1978) Isr prime minister; Feldshuh

Melba, Nellie (1859/66–1931) Astl, s; Brooklyn Academy

Melfi, Leonard (1935–2001) pl; Caffe Cino; Horovitz; Off-Off Broadway; *Oh! Calcutta!*

Melillo, Joseph V [Vincent] (196?–) adm, p; Brooklyn Academy

Mellish, Fuller, Jr. (1895–1930) a; *What Price Glory*

Melville, Herman (1819–91) w; Lowell

Melville, Rose (1873–1946) a; Toby

Mencken, Henry Louis (1880–1956) c, pl; Huneker; Ibsen; Lee (G. R.); Nathan; Shyre

Mendelssohn, Felix (1809–47) Ger, co; Los Angeles

Mendes, Sam (1965–) Brit, d; *Cabaret;* Marshall (R.)

Menken, Alan (1949–) co; Ahrens and Flaherty; Disney; *Little Shop . . . ;* Off-Broadway

Menken, Helen (1901–66) a, p; *Old Maid*

Menotti, Gian Carlo (1911–2007) It-born, c; Spoleto

Menzel, Idina (1971–) a, s; *Rent; Wicked*

Mérimée, Prosper (1803–70) Fr, w; *Carmen Jones*

Merivale, Philip (1886–1946) a; *Road to Rome*

Merkerson, S. Epatha (1952–) a; *Piano Lesson*

Merriam, Eve (1916–92) pl; Intro (§4); female/male; gay/lesbian

Merrill, Beth (1893–1986) a; *All My Sons*

Merrill, Gary (1915–90) a; *Born Yesterday; Morning's at Seven*

Merrill, Helen (1918–97) ag; agents

Merritt, Theresa (1924–98) a; *Ma Rainey's . . .*

Mestayer, Charles (c. 1820–49) a; Williams (Barney)

Mestayer, Maria Pray (1828–1911) a; Williams (Barney)

Metcalf, Laurie (1955–) a; Steppenwolf

Meyerbeer, Giacomo (1791–1864) Ger co; Webber

Meyerfield, Morris (fl. 1890–1910) m; Orpheum Circuit; San Francisco

Meyerhold, Vsevolod Emilievich (1874–1940) R, d; Chong; New Vaudeville; Soudeikine

Michalesko, Michel (fl.1930s–40s) Y, a; Yiddish

Michener, James A. (1907–97) w; *South Pacific*

Middleton, Ray (1907–84) a; *Annie Get Your Gun*

Midler, Bette (1945–) a, s; *Gypsy*

Miguel, Gloria (1926–) pl; Spiderwoman

Miguel, Muriel (1937–) pl; Intro(§4); Spiderwoman

Milanés, José Jacinto (1814–63) Cub, a; Cuban American

Milbourne, M. C. (fl. 1780s–90s) Brit, scpt; scenic design

Miles, Joanna (1940–) a; *Glass Menagerie*

Miles, John (fl. 1860s–70s) m; Macauley

Miles, Julia (1930?–) d, p; American Place; feminist; Women's Project

Miles, R. E. J. (1834–94) m; Macauley

Miles, Sylvia (1926–) a; *Night of the Iguana*

Miles, William (19??–) d; Berkshire

Miller, Buzz [Vernal Miller] (1923–99) ch, da; dance

Miller, Craig (1950–94) costume de; Kaczorowski

Miller, Flournoy (1887–1971) e, p; *Shuffle Along;* Sissle and Blake

Miller, Jason (1939–2001) a, pl; NY Shakespeare Festival; *That Championship Season*

Miller, Jonathan (1934–) Brit, a, d; Conklin

Miller, Lewis (1829–99) edu; Chautauqua

Miller, Roger (1936–92) co, e; Jujamcyn

Miller, Terry (1947–) a, d, p; gay/lesbian

Milligan, Lisa (1893–1986) d; Ark Theatre

Mills, Steve (1895–1988) e; Corio; Minsky Brothers

Milne, A. A. (1882–1956) Brit, pl; McClintic; Mint

Milner, Henry M. (fl. 1850s) pl; animals as performers; Menken

Milner, Ron (1938–2004) pl; Intro(§4)

Milstead, (Harris) Glen (1945–88) a; female/male

Miner, Worthington (1900–82) d, p; *Both Your Houses*

Miramova, Elena (1906–) ch, da; Seattle

Mirren, Helen (1946–) a; Abraham; Strathairn

Mitchell, Abbie (1884–1960) a; Lafayette Players

Mitchell, Adrian (1932–) pl; Houdini

Mitchell, Arthur (1934–) ch, da; dance

Mitchell, Cameron (1918–94) a; *Death of a Salesman*

Mitchell, Silas Weir (1829–1914) w; Mitchell (L. E.)

Mitchell, Thomas (1895–1962) a, pl; Gaige

Mitterwurzer, Friedrich (1842–97) Ger, a; Conried; Kurz Stadt

Miyamoto, Amon (1958–) Jp, d; *Pacific Overtures*

Mode, Becky (19??–) pl; Vineyard

Moffit, John C. (fl. 1930s) pl, scr; *It Can't Happen Here*

Moholy-Nagy, Lazlo (1895–1946) Hun, de; Kerz

Moisiu, Aleksandër (1879–1935) Alb, a; Berghof; Gest

Molière (1622–73) Fr, pl, a, m; Bosco; Circle in the Square; CSC Rep; ethnic; Feingold; Foreman; Lahr (B.); Wilbur

Molina, Tirsa de (1580–1648) Sp, pl; CSC Rep

Molnár, Ferenc (1878–1952) Hun, pl; *Carousel;* ethnic; Langner; Lunt and Fontanne; March; Worth; Yulin

Momaday, N. Scott (1934–) pl, w; Native Americans portrayed

Mondelli, Antoine (fl. 1830s) arc; St. Charles Theatre

Monk, Isabelle (19??–) a; Guthrie

Monk, Julius (1912–95) p; musical; revue

Monroe, George W. (c. 1857–1932) a; female/male

Monroe, Marilyn (1926–62) a; *After the Fall;* Axelrod; *Bus Stop;* Miller (A.)

Montagu, Ashley (1905–99) Brit-born, w; *Elephant Man*

Montand, Yves (1921–91) Fr, a; John Golden Theatre

Montgomery, George Edward (c. 1858–98) c; Dithmar

Montoya, Richard (1959–) a, pl; Chicano; Culture Clash

Moody, Richard (1911–96) edu, sch; Harrigan; *Metamora*

Moore, Charlotte (1935?–) a, d; Irish Rep

Moore, Demi (1962–) a; Off-Broadway

Moore, Douglas (1893–1969) co; Boleslavski

Moore, Edward (1712–57) Brit, pl; Hallams

Moore, Tom (1943–) d; Schmidt

Morahan, Christopher (1929–) Brit, d; *Little Murders*

Moran, Robert (1937–) pl; Serban

Morath, Ingeborg (1923–2002) Aus-born ph; Miller (A.)

Mordaunt, Frank (1841–1906) a; *Men and Women; My Partner*

Mordecai, Benjamin (1944–2005) en, p; Indiana Rep

Mordkin, Mikhail (1881–1944) R-born, da; Boleslavsky

Morehouse, Ward III (1967–) c; Morehouse

Morgan, Agnes (fl. 1920–30s) a, d, m; pageants

Morgan, Frank (né Francis Philip Wupperman) (1890–1949) a; Bonstelle

Morgan, Helen (1900–41) a, s; nightclubs

Morgan, J. H. (fl. 1900s) arc; Hippodrome

Morgan, Robert (1944–) de; costume

Morison, Patricia (1915–) a, s; Kiss Me, Kate

Morita, Pat (1932–2005) a; Asian American

Morland, Saxone (fl. 1900s–10s) a; Yellow Jacket

Morosco, Walter (c. 1846–1901) en, m; Morosco; San Francisco

Morris, Gouverneur (1752–1816) statesman; Goodman

Morris, Mark (1956–) ch, da; dance

Morris, Robert (1931–) perf; performance art

Morris, William (1861–1936) a; Men and Women

Morrison, George (1928–) a, edu; Sills

Morrison, Rosabel (1869–1911) a, pl; DeMille (H. C.)

Morse, David (1953–) a; How I Learned . . .

Mortimer, John K. (1830–78) a; Under the Gaslight

Morton, Carlos (1947–) pl; Chicano

Morton, Edward (d. 1922) Brit, pl; Merry Widow

Morton, Ferdinand Joseph (Jelly Roll) (1890–1941) mu, co; Jelly's Last Jam

Morton, Thomas (c. 1764–1838) Brit, pl; Native Americans portrayed

Mosel, Tad (1922–) pl; Penn

Moses, Itamar (1976?–) pl; NY Theatre Workshop

Moshinsky, Elijah (1946–) d; Yeargan

Moss, Paula (1950s–) ch; dance

Moss, Robert (1934–) d; Playwrights Horizons; Theatre Row

Mostel, Joshua (1946–) a; Mostel

Motts, Robert (1861–1912) d, m; African American

Moulton, Charles (1954–) ch; Performance Space 122

Mounet-Sully, Jean (1841–1916) Fr, a; female/male

Mrożek, Slawomir (1932–) Pol, pl; Fichandler; Perloff

Müller, Traugott (1895–1944) Ger, de; Roth

Mundy, Meg (c. 1923?–) a; Detective Story

Mulgrew, Kate (1955–), a; Hepburn

Munshin, Jules (1915–70) a; Tamiris

Murdock, John (1749–95) pl; Intro(§1)

Murray, Bill (1950–) a, e; Second City

Murray, John (1906–84) co, pl, l; Room Service

Murray, Michael (1932–) d; Boston

Murray, Peg (1925–) a; Landscape

Murrow, Edward R. (1908–65) j; Strathairn

Murtha, Frank B. (1840?–1903) m; Murray Hill

Muse, Clarence (1889–1979) a; Lafayette Players

Musset, Alfred de (1810–57) Fr, pl; Washington Square

Myerberg, Michael (1906–74) ag, p; Brooks Atkinson Theatre

Nabokov, Vladimir Vladimirovich (1899–1977) R-born, w, tr; Albee (E.)

Naish, J. Carrol (1900–73) a; View from the Bridge

Napier, John (1944–) Brit, de; Les Misérables

Nash (né Nusbaum), N. Richard (1913–2000) pl; Rainmaker

Nash, Ogden (1902–71) pl, po; Perelman

Nast, Thomas (1840–1902) art; caricature

Neal, John (1793–1876) c; dramatic theory

Neal, Patricia (1926–) a; Children's Hour; Subject Was Roses

Neeson, Liam (1952–) Ir, a; Anna Christie; Crucible; Redgrave

Neff, Hildegarde (1925–) a, s; Silk Stockings

Neher, Caspar (1897–1962) Ger, d; Roth

Neilson, Adelaide (1848–80) Brit, a; Intro(§2); international; O'Neill (James)

Nekrosius, Eimuntas (1952–) Lith, d; Chekhov on . . .

Nelson, Barry (1920–2007) a; Mary, Mary

Nelson, Ruth (1905–92) a; Men in White; Rocket to the Moon

Nemiroff, Robert (1921–91), pl; Hansberry

Nemirovich-Danchenko, Vladimir (1858–1943) R, pl, edu, d; Gest; Nazimova

Nesbit, Evelyn (1885–1967) e; Drew–Barrymore

Nethersole, Olga (1870–51) Brit, a; censorship; international

Neuendorff, Adolf (1843–97) Ger, a; Germania; Stadt Theater

Neumann, Frederick (19??–) a; Mabou Mines

Newman, Molly (19??–) w; Quilters

Newman, Paul (1925–) a, f d; Cat on a Hot Tin Roof; Glass Menagerie; Naughton; Our Town; Strasberg; Sweet Bird . . . ; Torn

Newman, Phyllis (1933–) a; Comden and Green

Ngema, Mbongeni (1955–) SAf, a, d, pl; Off-Broadway

Nichols, Anne (c. 1891–1966) pl, p; Abie's Irish Rose

Nichols, Peter (1927–) Brit, pl; Brown (A.); international

Nicola (né William Nicol) (1882–1945) ma; magic

Nicola, James C. (1950–) d, p; NY Theater Workshop

Nicolais, Alwin (1910–93) ch; Curchack

Nixon, Cynthia (1966–) a; Drama Dept.; Lindsay-Abaire

Nixon, Fred G. (né Frederick G. Nirdlinger) (1877–1931) m; Intro(§2); Syndicate

Noel, Craig (1915–) d; Old Globe Theatre

Norkin, Sam (1917–) art; caricature

Norman, Karyl (1897–1947) a, s; female/male

North, John Ringling (1903–85) en; circus; Ringling Bros.

Norton, Edward (1969–) a; Burn This

Norworth, Jack (1879–1959) s, e; Bayes

Noto, Lore (1923–2002) p; Fantasticks

Noury, H. (fl. mid-19th C.) arc; Boston Theatre

Nouvel, Jean (1945–) Fr arc; Guthrie Theater

Novick, Julius (1939–) c; Waterston

Nugent, Grace (?–1930) a; Nugent

Nugent, J. C. (1868–1947) a, d, pl; Nugent

Nunn, Trevor (1940–) Brit, d; international; *Les Misérables*

Nureyev, Rudolf (1938–93) da; Heilpern

Oates, Mrs. James A. (c. 1820–90) m; Minneapolis

Oberlin, Richard (1928–) d; Cleveland Play House

O'Brien, Edna (1936–) Ir, pl, w; Irish Rep

O'Byrne, Brían F. (1968?–) Ir, a; *Doubt*; Kurtz

O'Casey, Sean (1880–1964) Ir, pl; Blitzstein; censorship; Dowling; Irish Rep; Massey; Prince; Saks; Shyre; Tyler (G. C.)

Ockrent, Mike (1946–99) Brit, d, pl; Ahrens and Flaherty

O'Connor, Donald (1925–2003) da; dance

Oditz, Carol (1946–) de; costume

O'Donnell, Mark (19??–) pl; *Hairspray*

O'Dowd, George, *see* Boy George

Oestreicher, Gerard (1917–87) p; Theatre Hall of Fame

O'Farrill, Alberto (1899–?) pl; Cuban American

Offenbach, Jacques (1819–80) Fr, c; Intro(§2); musical; New Theatre

Offley, Hilda (1894–1968) a; *Big White Fog*

O'Hara, John (1905–70) w; *Pal Joey*

O'Hara, Kelli (1977–) a; *Pajama Game*

O'Hare, Denis (1962–) a; *Take Me Out*

O'Harra, Michaela (1913–) adm, pl; New Dramatists

O'Keefe, John (1940–) sto; one-person

O'Keefe, Laurence (197?–) co, l; Jordan

Oldenburg, Claes (1929–) art; Judson Poets'; Montano; performance art

Olive, John (1949–) pl; Chicago; Falls

Olivier, Laurence (1907–89) Brit, a, d, f d, m; Anderson (Judith); *Cat on a Hot Tin Roof; Crucible;* Guthrie; Harris (Jed); *Long Day's Journey . . . ; No Time for Comedy; Skin of Our Teeth; Streetcar . . .*

Olmos, Edward James (1947–) a; *Zoot Suit*

Olshanetsky, Alexander (1892–1946) Y, co; Yiddish

Olson, Elder (1909–92) c, th; dramatic theory

Omohundro, John Baker "Texas Jack" (1846–80) e; Chicago

O'Neal, John (1940–) d; Free Southern Theatre; Moses (G.)

O'Neal, Patrick (1927–94) a; *Night of the Iguana*

O'Neill, Gonzalo (1867–1942), Pue, pl; Nuyorican

O'Neill, James, Jr. (1878–1923) a; O'Neill (E.)

Ongley, Byron (d. 1915) pl; Smith (Winchell)

Orgel, Sandra (1945–) perf; performance art

O'Reilly, Ciarán (19??–) a, d; Irish Rep

Örkény, István (1912–79) Hun, pl; Fichandler

Orton, Joe (1933–67) Brit, pl; Easton; Maher; Lahr (J.); Off-Broadway; Ritman; Tillinger

Osato, Sono (1919–) a, da; *On the Town*

Osborne, John (1929–94) Brit, pl; Heilpern; Imperial Theatre; Tynan

Osterman, Georg (1953–95) pl; Ridiculous

Osterman, Lester (1914–2003) m; Eugene O'Neill Theatre

Ostrovsky, A. N. (1823–86) R, pl; Moscow Art Theatre

O'Sullivan, Maureen (1911–98) a; *Morning's at Seven*

Ott, Sharon (1950–) d; Berkeley Rep; Seattle Rep

Otway, Thomas (1652–85) Brit, pl; Boston

Owen, Marianne (19??–) a; *Wings*

Owen, Robert Dale (1801–77) pl; Native Americans portrayed

Oxenford, John (1812–77) Brit, c, pl, tr; Sothern

Oysher, Moyshe (1907–58) R-born, Y, a; Yiddish

Packer, Tina (1938–) Brit a, d; Shakespeare & Co.

Page, Anthony (1935–) Brit, d; Ibsen

Page, Louise (1955–) Brit, pl; NY Shakespeare Festival

Paige, Janis (née Donna Mae Jaden) (1922–) a, s; *Pajama Game*

Paik, Nam June (1932–2006) co; Judson Poets'

Palmer, Henry David (1832–79) m; Booth's Theatre; Jarrett

Palmer, Lilli (1914–86) Brit, a, w; Aldrich

Palmer, Minnie (1860–1936) a; *My Partner*

Palmo, Signor Fernando (Ferdinand) (1785–1869) en, t; Burton's Chambers St.

Paltrow, Bruce (1943–2002) d, p, w; Danner

Paltrow, Gwyneth (1973–) a; Danner; Edelstein

Pantages, (Pericles) Alexander (1871–1936) en, m, t; Seattle

Paparelli, PJ (19??–) d; Perseverance

Papas, Irene (1926–) Gk, a; Circle in the Square; White (J.)

Parker, Lottie Blair (1898?–1937) pl; *Way Down East*

Parker, Louis (1852–1944) Brit, pl; Arliss

Parker, Sarah Jessica (1965–) a; Broderick; Drama Dept.

Parker, Stewart (1941–) pl; Maher

Parks, Hildy (1926–2004) p; Cohen

Parsloe, Charles Thomas, Jr. (1836–98) a; Campbell; Harte; mime/pantomime; *My Partner*

Partington, Rex (1924–2006) d; Barter Theatre

Partlan, William (1951–) d; Cricket Theatre

Pascal, Adam (1970–) a; *Rent*

Pasquin, John (1945–) d; *Landscape; Moonchildren*

Paton, Alan S. (1903–88) w; *Lost in the Stars*

Patric, Jason (1966–) a; *Cat on a Hot Tin Roof*

Patrick, Robert (1937–) pl; Intro(§4); Caffe Cino; gay/lesbian; *Kennedy's Children*

Pawley, Thomas D., III (1917–) edu, d, pl; African American

Pawnee Bill (Gordon W. Lillie) (1866–1942) e; Wild West

Paxton, Steve (1939–) ch, da; dance

Pearlman, Stephen (1935–98) a; *Six Degrees . . .*

Pelham, Dick (1815–76) e; Emmett

Pelham, Laura Dainty (1849–1924) sr; community

Pen, Polly (1953–) a, l, pl, co; Vineyard

Peña, Mario (1955–) pl; Cuban American

Peña, Ralph B. (1962–) pl; Filipino American; Ma-Yi

Pennington, Ann (1893–1971) da; dance

Pepe, Neil (1963–) a, d; Atlantic Theater

Pepin and Breschard (fl. 1800s), circus en; Walnut St. Theatre

Perkins, Anthony (Tony) (1932–92) a, f d; *Look Homeward . . . ;* Perkins

Perlmutter, Sholem (1884–1954) Y, co; Yiddish

Perry, Agnes Land, *same as* Booth (A.)

Perry, Frederick (1844–1921) a; *Man of the Hour*

Perry, Harry (?–1863) a; Booth (A.)

Perugini, Signor (John Chatterton) (1855–1914) Brit, a; *Yellow Jacket*

Peters, Charles (1825–70) Brit-born, a; *Po-ca-hon-tas*

Peters, Paul (né Harbor Allen) (fl. 1930s) pl; African American; Seattle; *Stevedore;* Theatre Union

Peterson, Hjalmar (Olle i Skratthult) (1886–1960) a; ethnic

Peterson, Louis (1922–98) pl; African American; *Take a Giant Step*

Petrarca, David (1962–) d; Goodman

Phelps, Fanny Morgan (fl. 1854–67) Ir, a; Seattle

Phelps, Samuel (1804–78) Brit, a; Mantell

Phillips, Andy (1941–2004) Brit, ltg de; Kaczorowski

Phillips, Lou Diamond (1962–) a; *King and I*

Phillips, Margaret (1923–84) a; *Summer and Smoke*

Pichel, Irving (1891–1954) a, d; scenic design

Pickford, Mary (née Gladys Mary Smith) (1893–1979) Can-born, a; Burke

Pietri, Pedro (1944–2004) pl; Nuyorican

Pinelli, Tullio (1908–) It, scr; *Sweet Charity*

Piñero, Virgilio (1912–79) Cub, pl; Cuban American

Pinero, Arthur Wing (1855–1934) Brit, pl; Intro(§2); Cayvan; Frohman (D.)

Pintauro, Joseph T. (1930–) pl; Hurt (W.)

Pinter, Harold (1930–) Brit, d, f d, pl; Intro(§4); American Airlines; Boston; Brisson; CSC Rep; international; Irving (J.); Jewish Rep; Perloff; Plummer; Ritman; Roundabout; Schneider; Strathairn; Watts (R., Jr.), *When You Comin' Back . . . ?;* Wiest

Pintilie, Lucian (1933–) Ro, d; Chekhov on . . .

Pinza, Ezio (1892–1957) a, s; *South Pacific*

Pirandello, Luigi (1867–1936) It, d, pl; Bentley; Jesurun; Langner; Living Theatre; National Actors Theatre; Pemberton; San Francisco

Pisanelli, Antonietta, *see* Alessandro, Antonietta Pisanelli

Pixérécourt, René Charles Guilbert de (1773–1844) Fr, pl; Dunlap

Place, Robert (fl. mid-19th C.) m; Clifton

Placide, Mrs. Alexandre (née Wighten) (?–1823) Brit-born, a; Placide family

Platt, George Foster (fl. 1900–20) d; *Arrow Maker*

Plautus (?–c. 184 B.C.) Roman, pl; *Funny Thing . . .*

Plowright, Joan (1929–) Brit, a; international

Plummer, Amanda (1957–) a; Grimes; *Lie of the Mind;* Plummer

Plunkett, Henry W. (H. P. Grattan) (1808–89) Ir, pl; Chanfrau

Poggi, Gregory (1946–) en; Indiana Rep

Poiret, Jean (1926–92) Fr, pl; *La Cage . . .*

Poitier, Sidney (1924–) a, f d; Davis (Ossie); *Raisin in the Sun; Six Degrees . . .*

Poli, S. Z. (né Zeferino Sylvestro Poli) (1860–1937) It-born, en, p; Booth (S.); vaudeville

Pollard, Calvin (fl. mid-19th C.) arc; Mitchell's Olympic

Pollock, Channing (1926–2006) ma; magic

Pollock, Jackson (1912–56) art; Kaprow; performance art

Pomerance, Bernard (1940–) pl; *Elephant Man;* Off-Broadway

Pons, Helene (1898–1990) R, de; support services

Pool, Thomas (fl. late 18th C.) eq; circus

Porterfield, Robert (1905–71) d; Barter Theatre

Portillo Trambley, Estela (1936–) pl; Chicano

Portman, Eric (1903–69) Brit, a; *Touch of the Poet*

Portman, John C., Jr. (1924–) arc; Marquis

Posey, Parker (1968–) a; *Fifth of July; Hurlyburly*

Possart, Ernest Ritter von (1841–1921) a, m; Amberg; Kurz Stadt; Shakespeare on . . .

Post, Lilly (c. 1859–99) a, s; McCaull

Post, Wiley (1900–35) pilot; Rogers

Pound, Ezra (1885–1972) po; Perloff

Pous, Arquímides (1891–1926) Cub, a, pl; Cuban American

Povah, Phyllis (1893–1975) a; *Icebound*

Powell, Mary Ann (1756?–1824) Brit-born, a; Powell (C. S.)

Powell, Snelling (1758–1821) Brit-born, a; Powell (C. S.)

Powell, William (1892–1984) a; Bonstelle

Powers, Harry J. (1859–1941) m; Hooley's Theatre

Powers, Leland (1857–?) te, w; training

Pratt, William W. (1821–64) a, m, pl; *Ten Nights . . .*

Pray, Malvina (1831–1906) a, da, m; Florence

Preisser, Alfred (1963?–) d, pl; Classical Theatre of Harlem

Presley, Elvis (1935–77) s; revue

Previn, André (1929–) co; Lerner and Loewe

Price, Edwin A. (c 1847–1931) en; showboats

Price, Michael P. (c. 1938–) en, p; Goodspeed

Price, Vincent (1911–93) a; Mercury Theatre

Price, William T. (1846–1920) c, pl; training

Prida, Dolores (1943–) pl; Cuban American

Primrose, George H. (1852–1919) e; Dockstader; minstrel show

Primus, Barry (1938–) a; *After the Fall*

Prince, Daisy (1965?–) d; Brown (J.); Prince

Proctor, Joseph (1816–97) a, m; *Nick of the Woods*

Prokofiev, Sergei (1891–1953) R, co; Anisfeld

Proust, Marcel (1871–1922) Fr, w; Hiken

Pryce, Jonathan (1947–) Brit, a; international; *Miss Saigon*

Pryor, Richard (1940–2005) a, en; Bogosian

Psacharopoulos, Nikos (1928–89) edu, d; Chekhov on . . . ; Williamstown

Puccini, Giacomo (1858–1924) It, co; *Girl of the Golden West*

Pulitzer, Joseph (1847–1911) Hun-born, j, pub; Wheeler (A. C.)

Pullinsi, William (194?–) d; Chicago

Pullman, Bill (1953–) a; *Goat, or . . .*

Purdy, James (1923–) pl; Albee (E.)

Quaid, Randy (1953–) a; *Fool for Love;* Shepard

Quinn, Aidan (1959–) a; *Lie of the Mind; Streetcar . . .*

Quinn, Anthony (1915–2001) a; Hagen; *Streetcar . . . ;* Weissler

Quinn, Arthur Hobson (1875–1960) edu, sch; Hagen; *Man's World*

Quinn, Patrick (1950–2006) a; Actors' Equity

Rabinowitz, Aleichem (Sholom Aleichem) (1859–1916) Y, w; *Fiddler . . . ;* Muni; Schwartz (M.); Yiddish

Rachel (1820–58) Fr, a; Boston

Racine, Jean (1639–99) Fr, pl; Lowell; Wilbur

Rader-Shieber, Chas (1962?–) d; Zinn

Radner, Gilda (1946–89) a, e; Second City

Rado, James (1932–) l; *Hair*

Rafuls, Pedro Monge (1943–) Cub, pl; Cuban American

Ragni, Gerome (1942–91) l, pl; *Hair*

Rahmani, Aviva (1945–) perf; performance art

Rainer, Yvonne (1934–) ch, f d; dance

Rains, Claude (1889–1967) Brit, a; *Darkness at Noon*

Raitt, Bonnie (1949–) s; Raitt

Ramirez, Ramon (19??–) pl; Nuyorican

Ramírez, Yvette (1949–) pl; Nuyorican

Randall, Tony (1920–2004) a, d; Intro(§4); *Crucible;* Lyceum Theatre; National Actors Theatre; Nelson; Tillinger; *Sunshine Boys;* Weaver

Rankin, Doris (c. 1880–1946) a; Drew–Barrymore; Rankin

Rankin, Gladys (1874?–1914) a; Drew–Barrymore; Rankin

Ransom, Tim (1963–) a, d; Naked Angels

Ranson, Rebecca (1943–) pl; gay/lesbian

Raphael, D. D. (aka David Daiches) (1912–2005) c; dramatic theory

Raphael, Lennox (1938–) pl; Intro(§4); pornographic

Rapp, Anthony (1971–) a; Rapp; *Rent*

Rapson, Ralph (1914–) arc; Guthrie Theater; Minneapolis

Rasch, Albertina (1896–1967) Aus, ch, da; dance

Rattigan, Terence (1911–77) Brit, pl; Jones (S.)

Rauschenberg, Robert (1925–) art; Judson Poets'

Raymond, Maurice (1878–1948) ma; magic

Rea, Oliver (1923–95) p; Guthrie Theater; Minneapolis; resident nonprofit

Redd, Freddie (1928–) co; *Connection*

Redford, Robert (1937–) a, f d; *Barefoot*

Redmond, Marge (1930–) a; Weston

Redpath, James (1833–91) Scot-born, en; Chautauqua

Redwood, John Henry (1942–2003) pl; Primary Stages

Reed, Carol (1906–70) Brit, a, d, f d; Kanin (G.)

Reed, John (1887–1920) w; documentary; pageants; Provincetown Players

Reehling, Joyce (1949–) a; *Fifth of July*

Reich, Stephen Michael (1936–) co; Nauman

Reicher, Emanuel (1849–1924) Ger, a; Jewish Art Theatre

Reicher, Frank (1875–1965) a; *Scarecrow*

Reignolds, Kate (1836?–1911) a; Keene (L.)

Reilly, Charles Nelson (1931–2007) a, d; Harris (Julie); *How to Succeed . . .*

Reilly, John C. (1965–) a; Hoffman (P. S.); *Streetcar . . . ; True West*

Reinagle, Alexander (1756–1809) en, mu; Intro(§1); Chestnut St. Theatre; Holliday St. Theatre; Philadelphia; Wignell

Reiner, Carl (1922–) a, e, d, f d, pl; McNeil; revue

Reinhardt, Gottfried (1913–94) d, p, w; Reinhardt

Reinhardt, Paul (1929–) de, edu; costume

Reissa, Eleanor (19??–) a, d; Yiddish

Réjane, Mme Gabrielle (1856–1920) Fr, a; Tyler (G. C.)

Relph, George (1888–1960) Brit, a; *Yellow Jacket*

Remick, Lee (1935–91) a; *Delicate Balance; Summer and Smoke*

Renault, Francis (?–1956) e, s; female/male

Renwick, James, Jr. (1818–95) arc; Booth's Theatre

Resnais, Alain (1922–) Fr, f d; Feiffer

Resnik, Muriel (c. 1922–95) pl; *Any Wednesday*

Reuler, Jack (1953–) d; Mixed Blood

Revere, Anne (1906–90) a; *Children's Hour; Toys in the Attic*

Rexite, Seymour (1911–2002) Y, e, s; Yiddish

Reyes, Guillermo (1962–) pl; Chicano; gay/lesbian

Reynolds, Charles (fl. 1960–) ma; *Into the Woods*

Reynolds, Debbie (1932–) a, da, s; Kelly (P.); *Mary, Mary*

Reza, Yasmina (1959–) Fr, pl; Garber; Molina

Reznikov, Hanon (1950–) d; Living Theatre

Rice, Anne (1941–) w; Palace

Rice, Edward E. (1848–1924) co; Intro(§2); *Evangeline*

Rice, Tim (1944–) l; Disney; Headley; *Lion King;* Palace; sound; Webber

Rich, Charles A. (1855–1943) arc; Playhouse Theatre

Richards, John Inigo (fl. 1780s–1810) arc, de; architecture; Chestnut St. Theatre; scenic design

Richardson, Jack (1935–) c, pl; Barr

Richardson, Natasha (1963–) a; *Anna Christie; Cabaret; Streetcar . . .*

Richardson, Ralph (1902–83) Brit, a; Cohen; Guthrie; Heilpern

Richert, Wanda (1958–) a, s; *42nd Street*

Ricketts, John Bill (1760–99) e, m; circus; Durang

Rigg, Diana (1938–) Brit, a; Folger; international

Riggs, Dudley (1934–) d; Minneapolis

Rignold, George (1839–1912) a, m; Booth's Theatre; Wainwright

Ringwald, Molly (1968–) a; Off-Broadway

Risko, Robert (1956–) art; caricatures

Ristori, Adelaide (1822–1906) It, a; Intro(§2); Grau; Shakespeare on . . .

Ritt, Martin (1920–90) a, d; *View from the Bridge*

Rivera, Juan C. (19??–) pl; Cuban American

Rivers, Joan (1933–) e; Second City

Rives, Amélie (1863–1945) pl; Emery

Rno, Sung (1967–) pl; Asian American; Ma-Yi

Robbins, Luke (fl. 1780s) Brit, scpt; scenic design

Robbins, Tim (1958–) a, d, pl; *Cradle . . .*

Robert-Houdin (Jean-Eugène Robert) (1805–71) Fr, ma; Houdini

Roberts, Joan (1918–) a, s; *Oklahoma!*

Roberts, Julia (1967–) a; Greenberg; Loquasto

Robertson, Agnes (1833–1916) a; Boucicault; Keene; *Octoroon*

Robertson, Donald (1860–1926) a, m; Chicago; Moody

Robertson, Lanie (c.1950s?–) pl; Ruehl

Robertson, Thomas W. (1829–71) Brit, pl; Florence; Sothern

Robinson, Earl (1910–91) co; *Hellzapoppin; Pins and Needles*

Robinson, Fayette Lodowick "Yankee" (1818–84) en; Ringling Bros.; tent show

Robinson, Mary B. (19??–) d; Hartford

Robison, Blake (1967–) d; Vermont

Roblés, Emmanuel (1914–95) pl; Hellman

Roche, Emeline Clarke (fl. 1940–52) de; costume

Rodgers, Mary (1931–) co; Guettel

Rodriguez, Diane (1951–) d; Chicano

Rodríguez, Roberto (19??–) d, pl; Nuyorican

Rodriguez, Yolanda (19??–) a, pl; Nuyorican

Roe, Patricia (1932–) a; *After the Fall*

Rogers, Charles J. (1817–95) e, en, m; showboats

Rogers, Isiah (fl. 1820s) arc; Tremont Theatre

Rogers, Robert (1731?–95) pl; Intro(§1); Native Americans portrayed

Rojo, Jerry (1935–) de; architecture

Rolle, Esther (1920?–98) a; Scott (H.)

Romero, Cesar (1907–94) a; *Dinner at Eight*

Ronstadt, Linda (1946–) s; Gilbert and Sullivan; Off-Broadway

Rooney, Mickey (né Joe Yule) (1920–) a; Mark Hellinger Theatre

Rooney, Pat, III (1909–79) e; Rooney

Roose-Evans, James (1927–) Brit, d, pl; Maher

Rose, Edward (1849–1904) Brit, pl; Intro(§2)

Rose, Peter (1955–) a; Performance Space 122

Rosenberg, Joe (19??–) d; Chicano

Rosenblum, M. Edgar (1932–) m, p; Long Wharf

Ross, Adrian (1859–1933) Brit, l, pl; *Merry Widow*

Ross, Anthony (1906–55) a; *Glass Menagerie*

Ross, David (1922/4–66) c, d, p; Ibsen

Ross, Harold Wallace (1892–1951) j; Parker (D.)

Ross, Herbert David (1927–2001) ch, d; Tamiment

Ross, W. Duncan (1918–87) d; Seattle Rep

Rosselini, Roberto (1906–77) It, f d; Montresor

Rossini, Gioacchino (1792–1868) It, co; Russell (H.)

Rostand, Edmond (1868–1918) Fr, pl; Intro(§3); Adams (M.); animal impersonation; Civic Rep; *Fantasticks;* Hampden; Langella; Marbury; National Asian American Theatre; San Francisco

Roth, Beatrice (1919–) perf; one-person

Roth, Jordan (c.1976–) p; Roth (D.)

Roth, Tim (Timothy Simon Smith) Brit, a; Shepard

Rothafel, Samuel Lionel "Roxy" (1881–1936) en, p; Radio City; stage lighting

Rothman, Carole (19??–) d; Howe; Second Stage

Roughead, William (1870–1952) w; Hellman

Rounds, David (1930–83) a; *Morning's at Seven*

Rousseau, Jean-Jacques (1712–78), Swi, phil, w; Bandmann

Rowe, Nicholas (1674–1718) Brit, a, pl; Hallams

Rowe, Stephen (196?–) a; *Goat, or . . .*

Rowley, Charles (fl. 1920s) arc; Cleveland Play House

Royce, James (1914–) a, d; Empty Space

Royle, Edwin Milton (1862–1942) a, pl; Native Americans portrayed

Rubens, Paul Alfred (1875–1917) Brit. l; *Florodora*

Rubin, Steven (1942–) de; costume

Ruby [Rubinstein], Harry (1895–1974) co, l; *Animal Crackers*

Rudkin, David (1936–) Brit, pl; Arkin; international; Manhattan Theatre Club; Meadow

Rudolph, Alan (1943–) w; *Indians*

Ruffalo, Mark (1967–) a; *Awake and Sing!*

Ruffelle, Frances (1965–) a, s; *Les Misérables*

Rukeyser, Muriel (1913–80) w; Music-Theatre Group

Rumshinsky, Joseph (1881–1956) Y, co; Yiddish

Rumsey, John W. (c. 1878–1960) ag; Marbury; Selwyn

Runyon, Damon (1884–1946) c, w; *Guys and Dolls*

Russell, Charlie (1932–) pl; African American

Russell, Craig (1948–91) a, e; female/male

Russell, Mark (19??–) p; Performance Space 122

Russell, Rosalind (1908–76) a; *Auntie Mame;* Channing; *Gypsy; My Sister Eileen; Wonderful Town*

Russell, Sylvester (186?–1930) c; African American

Ryan, Conny (1901?–63) e; Corio

Ryan, Irene (1903–73) a; Awards

Ryan, Robert (1909–73) a; *Front Page;* Naughton

Ryer, George W. (1845–1902) a, pl; Old Homestead; Thompson (D.)

Saarinen, Eero (1910–61) arc; architecture; Vivian Beaumont

Sabinson, Harvey (1924–) gen m, ag; League of American Theatres

Sackler, Howard (1929–82) pl, d; African American; *Great White Hope;* resident nonprofit; Sherin

Sackville-West, Vita (Victoria) (1892–1962) w; Redgrave

Sadler, Harley (1892–1954) a, m; tent show; Toby

Saeltzer, Alexander (fl. mid-19th C.) arc; Fourteenth St. Theatre

Sahlins, Bernard (1921?–) d; Second City

Saidy, Fred (1907–82) d, l, pl; Intro(§3); *Finian's Rainbow*

St. Cyr, Lili [née William Marie Van Schaak] (1918–99) da; burlesque

St. Denis, Ruth (1877–1968) da; Brooklyn Academy; Cole (J.)

Saint-Gaudens, Homer (1880–1958) d; *Beyond the Horizon*

Salem, Marc (1954–) mentalist; magic

Salerni, Lou (1943–) d; Cricket Theatre

Salinas, Ric (1960–) a, pl; Chicano; Culture Clash

Salvini, Tommaso (1829–1915) It, a, m; Intro(§2); Allen (V.); Booth (E. T.); Grau; San Francisco; Shakespeare on . . . ; Stetson; Wainwright

Samolinska, Theofilia (1848–1913) a; ethnic

Sánchez, Luis Rafael (1936–) pl; Nuyorican

Sanchez, Sonya (1934–) pl; Intro(§4)

Sánchez-Scott, Milcha (1955–) pl; Chicano; *Roosters*

Sand, Paul (1935–) a; Second City

Sanders, Gertrude (fl. 1910–20s) a, s; Mills

Sands, Diana (1934–73) a; *Raisin in the Sun*

Sanford, Samuel S. (1821–1905) en, s, clown; Philadelphia

Sanford, Tim (c. 1955?–) adm, d; Playwrights Horizons

Santiago, Hector (1944–) Cub pl; Cuban American

Santley, Mabel (fl. 1870s) e; burlesque; Leavitt; Rentz–Santley

Sarandon, Chris (1942–) a; Gleason (J.)

Sardou, Victorien (1831–1908) Fr, pl; Ethel; George; Frohman (D.); James; Marbury

Sarg, Tony (1880–1942) pup; puppetry

Sargent, Franklin H. (1856–1923) d, edu; American Academy of Dramatic Arts; training

Sargent, H. J. (1843–96) en, m; vaudeville

Sarony, Gilbert (d. 1910) a, e; female/male

Sarony, Napoleon (1821–96) ph; photographers

Sartre, Jean-Paul (1905–80) Fr, pl; Jewish Rep; Off-Broadway; Stone (P.)

Sato, Isao (1950–90) a; *Pacific Overtures*

Sato, Shozo (1933–) d; Wisdom Bridge

Savo, Jimmy (1895–1960) a; *Boys from Syracuse*

Saxe-Meiningen, *see* Meiningen, George II, Duke of

Sayles, John (1950–) a, f d, w; Strathairn

Scanlan, W. J. (1856–98) a; Olcott; Pitou

Scarborough, George (1875–1951) pl; censorship

Scardino, Don (1948–) Can-born, a, d; Playwrights Horizons

Schaffner, Caroline (1901–98) a; Toby

Schaffner, Neil (1892–1969) a; Toby

Schat, Peter (1935–) co; Houdini

Schell, Maximilian (1930–) Aus, a; Tillinger

Schenkar, Joan (1948–) pl; feminist; gay/lesbian

Schenkkan, Robert (1953–) pl; Intiman; *Kentucky Cycle*

Schiele, Egon (1890–1918) art; Kelly (J.)

Schiffman, Frank (1894?–1974) p, t; Apollo

Schifter, Peter Mark (1950?–93) d; Gemini

Schiller, Friedrich (1759–1805) Ger, pl; ethnic; Le Gallienne

Schirle, Joan (1944–) d; Dell'Arte

Schlesinger, John (1926–2003) Brit, d; Roth (A.)

Schmidman, Jo Ann (1948–) d; feminist; Omaha Magic Theatre

Schmidt, Harvey (1929–) co; *Fantasticks;* Off-Broadway

Schnitzler, Arthur (1862–1931) Aus, pl; Ames; Bentley; Huneker; Mint

Schoeffel, John B. (d. 1918) en, m; Abbey; Booth (A.)

Schoenfeld, Gerald (1924–) en, law, p; Plymouth Theatre; Shubert Organization

Schomer (-Schaikevitch) (Nahum Meyer Schaikevitch) (1847?–1905) Y, pl; Yiddish

Schönberg, Arnold (1874–1951) co; Blitzstein

Schönberg, Claude-Michel (1944–) Fr, co, pl; Galati; *Les Misérables; Miss Saigon*

Schrader, Paul (1946–) f d, scr; Hurt (M. B.)

Schramm, David (1946–) a; Acting Company

Schreiber, Avery (1935–2002) a, w; Second City

Schreiber, Pablo (1978–) a; Schreiber (L.)

Schubert, Franz (1797–1828) co; *Blossom Time;* Romberg; Webber

Schulman, Susan H. (1944?–) d; *Secret Garden;* Zuber

Schultz, Michael (1938–) d; Chekhov on . . .

Schulz, Charles (1922–2000) cartoonist; NY International

Schumann, Peter (1934–) d; Intro(§4); Bread and Puppet; puppetry

Schwab, Laurence (1893–1951) l, pl, m; *New Moon*

Schwartz, Bruce D. (c.1958–) e; New Vaudeville

Schweizer, David (195?–) d; Zinn

Scofield, Paul (1922–) Brit, a; *Delicate Balance*

Scola, Ettore (1931–) It, f d; Sondheim

Scott, Campbell (1961–) a; Dewhurst; Scott

Scott, John R. (1808–56) a; Intro(§1)

Scott, Louis Napoleon (1859–1929) m; Minneapolis

Scott, Martha (1914–2003) a; *Our Town*

Scott, Oz (1949–) d; *For Colored Girls . . .*

Scott, Randolph (1903–87) a; Pasadena Playhouse

Scott, Tommy (fl. 1950s) e; medicine shows

Scott, Walter (1771–1832) Sc, w; *Davy Crockett*

Scott, Zachary (1914–65) a; Ford (R.)

Scribe, Augustin Eugène (1791–1861) Fr, pl; James; Modjeska

Scribner, Samuel A. (1859–1941) m; Syndicate

Secunda, Sholom (1895–1974) Y, co; Yiddish

Sedaris, Amy (1961–) a, e, w; Drama Dept.; Second City

Sedaka, Neil (1939–) co, s; Capital Rep

Sefton, Joseph (c. 1811–81) a, m; Niblo

Segal, George (1934–) a; *Who's Afraid . . .*

Selbit, P. T. (1881–1938) Brit, ma; Goldin

Selz, Irma (1908–75) art; caricature

Selznick, Irene (1907–90) p; *Streetcar . . .*

Semans, William (1924–) d; Cricket Theatre

Sendak, Maurice (1928–) pl, w; children's; Kushner; Minneapolis

Sennett, Mack (1880–1960) f pio; Dressler

Serrand, Dominique (194?–) d; Théâtre de la Jeune Lune

Setterfield, Valda (1934–) Brit-born, a, da; dance

Seurat, Georges (1859–91) Fr, art; Patinkin; *Sunday in the Park*

Seuss, [Dr.], *see* Geisel, Theodore

Seymour, Anne (1909–88) a; Davenport (E. L.)

Seymour, May Davenport (1883–1967) a, archivist; Davenport (E. L.); Seymour

Shafer, Robert (?–1956) a; *Damn Yankees*

Shaffer, Peter Levin (1926–) Brit, pl; Intro(§4); animal impersonation; Bedford; Brisson; Dexter; Gill; Rich

Shaiman, Marc (1959–) co, l; *Hairspray*

Sharif, Bina (19??–) Pakistani-born pl; Asian American

Shairp, Alexander Mordaunt (1887–1939) Brit, pl; gay/lesbian

Shalwitz, Howard (19??–) a, d; Woolly Mammoth

Shank, Adele Ealing (1940–) edu, pl; Los Angeles; Magic Theatre; Yulin

Shapiro, Mel (1935–) d; *House of Blue Leaves*

Sharpe, Robert R. (fl. 1920s–30s) de; scenic design

Shaw, [George] Bernard (1856–1950) Ir, c, pl; Intro(§§2,3); Aldrich; American Shakespeare Theatre; Ames; animal imper-sonation; Behrman; Bloodgood; Bosco; Brady (W. A.); Channing; community; Cornell; Coghlan (R.); criticism; Daly (Arnold); Derwent; Elliott (G.); ethnic; Fitzgerald; George; Harrison; Hedgerow; Herrmann (E.); Houdini; Huneker; Ivey (D.); Jean Cocteau; Jones (S.); King (D.); Lahr (B.); Laughton; Lerner and Loewe; Lillie; Mansfield; Marbury; Massey; Mitchell (L. E.); musical; *My Fair Lady*; Nathan; Playhouse Theatre; Preston; Russell (A.); San Fran-cisco; Shannon; Shaw and . . . ; Shelley; *Tavern*; Theatre Guild; Wheeler; Wood (P.); Wycherly

Shaw, Jane Catherine (1958–) pup; puppetry

Shaw, Peggy (1944–) a, d; female/male; feminist; gay/lesbian; Hughes; Split Britches

Shaw, Robert (1927–78) Brit, a, pl; Abraham

Shawn, Dick (1923–87) a, e; Tamiment

Shawn, Ted (1891–1972) ch, da; Brooklyn Academy; Cole (J.); nudity

She, Lao (1899–1966) Chn pl; Pan Asian

Shean, Al (1868–1949) e; burlesque; Marx Bros.

Shear, Claudia (c. 1962–) a, pl; NY Theatre Workshop; West (M.)

Shearer, Norma (1900–83) a; *Idiot's Delight*

Sheen, Martin (Ramon Estevez) (1940–) a, d, p; *Subject Was Roses*

Sheinkin, Rachel (197?–) l, pl; Finn

Shenkman, Ben (1968–) a; *Proof*

Sheperd, David (1926–) d; Chicago; Second City

Shepp, Archie (1937–) co; *Slave Ship*

Sher, Bartlett (1958?–) d; Intiman; *South Pacific*; Zuber

Sheridan, Richard Brinsley (1751–1816) Ir, m, pl; Clarke; Coghlan (C.); Crane; Dunlap; Freedman; Jeffersons; Murdoch (J. E.); Rus-sell (A.); Russell (L.); Tyler (R.)

Sheridan, W(illiam) E(dward) (1839–87) a; Allen (V.)

Sherman, Geoffrey (1948–) d, p; Alabama Shakespeare

Sherman, Hiram (1908–89) a; Mercury Theatre

Sherman, James (1939–) pl; Cantor

Sherman, Martin (1938–) pl; gay/lesbian; Ivey (J.)

Sherman, Stuart (1945–2001) d, e, pl; intro(§4); Off-Off Broadway

Sherriff, R. C. (1896–1975) Brit, pl; Miller (G. H.)

Sherwood, Madeleine (1922–) a; *Crucible*

Shevelove, Burt (1915–82) d, pl; *Funny Thing . . .*: Gelbart; *No, No, Nanette*

Shields, Brooke (1965–) a; *Wonderful Town*

Shiflett, Jim (194?–) d; Body Politic

Shimono, Sab (c. 1942–) a; *Pacific Overtures*

Shiner, David (1954–) en; Irwin

Shiomi, R. A. (1947–) pl; Chang; Pan Asian

Shipp, Cameron (1904?–61) w; Burke

Shipp, Jesse (fl. 1890s–1900s) pl; African American

Shoemaker, Ann (1891–1975) a; *Great God Brown*

Shook, Sheridan (fl. 1870s) m; Palmer

Shor, Anshel (fl. 1930s-40s) Y, pl; Yiddish

Short, Bobby (1924–2005) e, mu; Mackintosh (R.)

Short, Martin (1951–) Can, a, e; Second City

Shue, Larry (1946–85) pl; *Foreigner*

Sickinger, Robert (fl. 1960s) d; Chicago; Hull-House

Siddons, Sarah (1755–1831) Brit, a; Clifton; Cowell (Joe); Duff (Mary Ann); Holm; Warren (W., the elder)

Sidney, Sylvia [née Sophia Kosow] (1910–99) a; *Gods of the Lightning*

Sierra, Rubén (1946–98) pl; Chicano

Siguenza, Herbert (1959–) a, pl; Chicano, Culture Clash

Silsbee, Joshua (1813–55) a; Intro(§1); *Forest Rose*; Logan (C. A.); *Our American Cousin*; Yankee

Sil-Vara, G. (1876–1938) pl; Lunt and Fontanne

Silver, Steve (1944–95) p; *Beach Blanket Babylon*

Silvera, Frank (1914–70) a; *Big White Fog*; *Camino Real*

Silverman, Jonathan (1966–) a; *Broadway Bound*

Silverman, Sime (1873–1933) ed, w; periodicals; *Variety*

Simmons, Jean (1929–) a; *Guys and Dolls*

Simms, Hilda (1920–94) a; *Anna Lucasta*

Simon, Danny (1918–2005) w; Simon (N.); Tamiment

Simon, Lucy (1940–) co; *Secret Garden*

Simon, Paul (1941–) co, s; Lee (E.)

Simon, Roger Hendricks (1942–) Brit, d; *Moonchildren*

Simpson, Jim (1956–) d; Flea; Weaver

Sinatra, Frank (1915–98) a, s; *On the Town*; *Our Town*

Sinclair, Catherine Norton (fl. 1837–59) a, m; Forrest; San Francisco

Sinclair, Upton (1878–1968) w; Klein

Sinden, Donald (1923–) Brit, a; international

Singer, Isaac Bashevis (1904–91) pl, w; Esterman

Singer, Israel J. (1893–1944) pl; Yiddish Art Theatre

Skipitares, Theodora (1946–) pup; puppetry

Sklar, George (1908–88) pl; African American; Seattle; *Stevedore;* Theatre Union

Sklar, Roberta (1940–) d, pl; feminist

Skulnik, Menashe (1892–1970) Y, a; Yiddish

Slatkin, Leonard (1944–) co, conductor; Mitchell (B. S.)

Slattery, Charles (fl. 1930s) a; *Of Mice and Men*

Sloane, A. Baldwin (1872–1925) co; *Wizard of Oz*

Sloane, Everett (1909–65) a; Roberts (T.)

Slyde, Jimmy [né James T. Godbolt] (1927–) da; Glover

Small, Philip (fl. 1920s) arc; Cleveland Play House

Smalls, Charlie (1943–87) co, l; *Wiz*

Smith, Art (1900–73) a; Group Theatre; *House of Connelly; Men in White; My Heart's . . .*

Smith, Bessie (1894–1937) e, s; Albee (E.); female/male

Smith, Chris (1963–) adm, d; Magic Theatre

Smith, Chuck (1939–) d; Goodman

Smith, Derek (1927?–) Brit, a; *Little Murders*

Smith, Evan (1967–) pl; gay/lesbian

Smith, George Washington (fl. 1850s-60s) ch; dance

Smith, Jack (1932–89) a, d, pl; gay/lesbian

Smith, Joseph (1805–44) rel; Rice (D.)

Smith, Kirk (1954–) Ger-born art; Kitchen

Smith, Maggie (1934–) Brit, a; international

Smith, Michael (1935–) c; Caffe Cino

Smith, Michael (1951–) perf; performance art

Smith, Molly D. (1950?–) d; Arena; Perseverance

Smith, Peyton (1948–) a; Wooster Group

Smith, Rex (1956–) a, s; Gilbert and Sullivan; Off-Broadway

Smith, Roger Guenveur (1959–) a, d; one-person

Smith, Russell (1812–96) scpt; scenic design

Smith, William Neil (fl. 1920s–) arc; Nederlander Theatre

Smits, Jimmy (1955–) a; Cruz

Snyder, Jacob (fl. mid-18th C.) scpt; scenic design

Snyder, Nancy (1949–) a; *Fifth of July*

Sobel, Shepard M. (194?–) d; Pearl Theatre

Sokolow, Anna (1910–2000) co; Clarke (M.); dance

Solis, Octavio (1958–) pl; Chicano

Solly, Bill (1931–) pl; gay/lesbian

Son, Diana (1965–) pl; Intro(§4); Asian American; Greif

Sonnenthal, Adolf Ritter von (1834–1909) Ger, a, m; Amberg; Shakespeare on . . .

Sontag, Karl (fl. mid-19th C.) Ger, a; Germania

Sophocles (c. 496–406/5 B.C.) Gk, pl; Perloff; Sellars

Sorvino, Paul (1939–) a; *That Championship Season*

Sossi, Ron (1939–) d, m; Los Angeles

Sothern, Georgia (1917?–1981) e; Corio

Sousa, John Philip (1854–1932) co, conducter; Gilbert and Sullivan; McCaull; Willson

Soyinka, Wole (1934–) Nigerian, p; Goodman; Mosher

Spacek, Sissy (1949–) a; *'night, Mother*

Spalding, Gilbert (1812–80) e, en, m; showboats

Spencer, Edward (fl. 1860s) pl; *Kit . . .*

Spencer, Girard L. (1899–1974) ba; Manhattan Theatre Club

Spielberg, Steven (1946–) f d; Kushner

Spinella, Stephen (1956–), a; *Angels in America*

Spingarn, Joel Elias (1875–1939) c, th; dramatic theory

Spolin, Viola (1906–94) d, edu, th; Intro(§4); Chicago; Second City; Sills

Sprinkle, Annie [née Ellen Steinberg] (1954–) e; pornographic

Stair, Edward D. (1859–1951) m; Stair and Havlin Circuit; Syndicate

Stahlhuth, Gayle (1950–) a, d, w; East Lynne Theater Co.

Stallings, Laurence Taylor (1894–1968) pl; Anderson (Maxwell); censorship; *What Price Glory*

Stanislavsky, Konstanin (1863–1938) Sov-R, a, d; Group Theatre; Hagen; *House of Connelly;* Moscow Art Theatre; Strasberg

Stanton, Harry Dean (1926–) a; *Fool for Love*

Stark, James (1818–75) a; Los Angeles; San Francisco

States, Bert O. (1929–2003) edu, th; dramatic theory

Steele, Richard (1672–1729) Ir, pl; Hallams

Stehli, Edgar (1884–1973) a; *Arsenic . . .*

Stein, Joseph (1912–) pl; Arkin

Stein, Leo (fl. 1900s) Ger, l, pl; *Merry Widow*

Stein, Peter (1937–) Ger, d; Monk

Steinberg, David (1942–) Can, a, e, f d; Second City

Steiner, George (1929–) c, th; dramatic theory

Steiner, Rudolf (1861–1925) Ger, mu, co; Chekhov (M.)

Stenborg, Helen (1925–) a; *Fifth of July;* Hughes (B.)

Stephenson, Shelagh (1955–), Brit pl, Manhattan Theatre Club

Stern, Edward (1946–) en; Cincinnati Playhouse; Indiana Rep

Sterner, Jerry (1938–2001) pl; Conway (K.)

Stevens, Emilie (c. 1925–) Mex-born a, en; Circle in the Square

Stevenson, Robert Louis (1850–94) Sc, w; Goodman

Stewart, Donald Ogden (1894–1980) a, humorist; *Holiday*

Stewart, James (1908–97) a; *Harvey;* summer stock

Stilgoe, Richard (1943–) Brit pl; *Phantom . . .*

Still, James (1959–) pl; children's

Stiller, Jerry (1929–) e, a; *Hurlyburly;* Second City

Sting (né Gordon Sumner) (1952–) Brit, s; Dexter

Stitt, Milan (1941–) pl; Pendleton; Sánchez

Stix, John (1920–2004) a; *Take a Giant Step*

Stoddard, Lorimer (c. 1864–1901) a, pl; Fiske (M. M.)

Stolz, Don (1919–) d; Minneapolis

Stone, Carol (1915–) a, d; *Desire under the Elms;* Montgomery and Stone

Stone, Dorothy (1905–74) a, s; Montgomery and Stone

Stone, Edward Durrell (1902–78) arc; John F. Kennedy Center

Stone, Harold J. (1913–2005) a, d; *Room Service*

Stone, Paula (1912–97) p, a; Montgomery and Stone

Stoneburner, Sam (1934–) a; *Six Degrees . . .*

Stoppard, Tom (1937–) Cz-born Brit, f d, pl; Intro(§4); Bishop, Brisson; Channing (Stockard); Crudup; Easton; Galati; Garber; Maher; O'Brien; Perloff; Straithairn; Waterston; Watts (R., Jr.); Zuber

Storch, Arthur (1925–) d, edu; Berkshire

Storer, Maria (1750?–95) a; Henry

Storey, David (1933–) Brit, pl; Intro(§4); Cohen; Hearn; international

Stothart, Herbert (1885–1949) co, l; Hammerstein II; *Little Mary Sunshine; Rose-Marie*

Stowe, Harriet Beecher (1811–96) w; Aiken; Taylor (C. W.); *Uncle Tom's Cabin*

Straight, Beatrice (1914–2001) a; Chekhov (M.); *Crucible*

Strasberg, Susan (1938–99) a; *Diary of Anne Frank*

Stratton, Charles Sherwood (1832–83) e; Barnum

Straus, Oskar (1870–1954) Aus, co; New Theatre

Strauss (Storrs), Frank V. (1873–1939) publ; playbill

Strauss, Richard (1864–1949) Ger, co; Reinhardt

Strehler, Giorgia (1921–97) It, d; Chekhov on . . . ; international

Streisand, Barbra (1942–) a, f d, s; *Funny Girl;* Rome; Yeston

Strickland, F. Cowles (1903–71) d, edu, w; Berkshire

Strickland, William (1788–1854) arc; Chestnut St. Theatre

Strindberg, August (1849–1912) Swe, pl; *Children's Hour;* community; criticism; ethnic; Hellman; Huneker; Jean Cocteau; Light; Macgowan; Massey; O'Neill (E.); Perloff; Strathairn; Yeargan

Strnad, Oskar (1879–1935) Aus, de; scenic design

Strong, Michael (1918/24–80) a; *Detective Story*

Stroock, (James) Ely (1891–1965) cos; support services

Strudwick, Sheppard (1907–83) a; *Both Your Houses*

Stuart, Leslie (1864–1928) Brit co; *Florodora*

Studley, John B. (1831–1910) a; Cody

Sturges, Preston (né Edmond P. Biden) (1898–1959) f d, pl, scr; Pemberton

Sudermann, Hermann (1857–1928) Ger, pl; ethnic

Sulerzhitsky, Leopold (1872–1916) R, a, d, edu; Chekhov (M.)

Sullavan, Margaret (1911–60) a; Hayward; *State of the Union*

Sullivan, Arthur (1842–1900) co; *Indian Princess*

Sullivan, Barry (1821?–91) Ir, a; Baldwin Theatre; Mantell

Sullivan, Jo (c. 1927–) a, s; *Most Happy Fella*

Sullivan, Louis (1856–1924) arc; architecture; McVicker's

Sunjata, Daniel (1971–) a; *Take Me Out*

Sutherland, Donald (1934–) Can, a; *Six Degrees . . .*

Suzuki, Tadashi (1939–) Jp, a, d; Bogart; training

Svich, Caridad (1963–) Cub pl; Cuban American

Swasey, William A. (fl. 1910s) arc; Princess Theatre; Winter Garden

Sweet, Dolph (1920–85) a; *Streamers*

Sweet, Jeff (Jeffrey) (1950–) c, pl, w; Second City

Swerling, Jo (1897–1964) pl; Burrows; *Guys and Dolls*

Swope, Martha (1933?–) ph; photographers

Swor, Bert (1883–1943) e; Moran and Mack

Symons, Arthur (1865–1945) Brit, c; dramatic theory; Marlowe

Syse, Glenna (1927–2001) c; Chicago

Szajna, Josef (1922–) Pol, d, de; international

Szász, János (1958–) Hun, d; American Rep

Tabori, George (1914–) pl; Manhattan Theatre Club

Taccone, Tony (1952–) d; Berkeley Rep; Eureka

Tairov, A. Y. (1885–1950) Sov-R, d; Soudeikine

Takai, George (1937–) a; Asian American

Talma, François Joseph (1763–1826) Fr, a; Payne

Tallant, Hugh, *see* Herts and Tallant

Tamiroff, Akim (1901–72) R-born, a; Moscow Art Theatre

Tandet, Joseph (1932–) en, p; Manhattan Theatre Club

Tanner, Virginia (1881–1950) d; pageants

Taper, S. Mark (1902–94) financier; Mark Taper Forum

Taradash, Daniel (1913–2003) scr; *Picnic*

Tarbell, Ida (1857–1944) w; Klein

Tate, Harry (1872–1940) Sc, e; Fields (W. C.)

Taubman, Howard (1907–96) c; gay/lesbian

Taupin, Bernie (1950–) Brit, ly; Palace

Tavel, Ronald (1941–) pl; Intro(§4); gay/lesbian; Judson Poets; Off-Off Broadway; Theatre of the Ridiculous

Taylor, Deems (1885–1966) co; Millay

Taylor, Elizabeth (1932–) a; Burton (R.); *Cat on a Hot Tin Roof; Little Foxes;* Stapleton; *Sweet Bird . . . ; Who's Afraid . . .*

Taylor, H. S. (?–1844) ag; agents

Taylor, Paul (1930–) ch, d; Long; Skelton; Tharp; Tipton

Taylor, Tom (1817–80) Brit, pl; Intro(§2); Florence; *Our American Cousin;* Sothern

Tebelak, John-Michael (1949–85) l, pl; Godspell

Teer, Barbara Ann (1937–) a, d, p; National Black Theatre

Teichmann, Howard (1916–87) pl, w; Intro(§3)

Tempest, Marie Susan (Mrs. C. Cosmo Gordon-Lennox) (1864–1942) Brit, a, s; Bloodgood; international; *Truth*

Temple, John (fl. mid-19th C.) m; Los Angeles

Terry, Ellen (1847–1928) Brit, a; Intro(§2); international; Neighborhood Playhouse; Rehan; Shakespeare on . . .

Thackeray, William Makepeace (1811–63) Brit, w; Mitchell (L. E.)

Theodore, Lee (Becker) ch, co (d. 1987); dance

Thirkield, Robert (1936–86) a, d, p, de; Circle Rep

Thom, Norman (1883–1939?) a; showboats

Thomas, Cornelia (1796–1850) a, s; Jeffersons

Thomas, Dylan (1914–53) We, pl; Circle in the Square; Miller (G. H.)

Thomas, Michael Tilson (1944–) conductor; McDonald (A.); Mitchell (B. S.)

Thomas, Piri (1928–) pl; Nuyorican

Thomashefsky, Bessie (1874–1962) Y, a; Thomashefsky; Yiddish

Thompson, Emma (1959–) Brit, a; *Wit*

Thompson, [Richard] Ernest (1949–) pl; Cantor; Sternhagen

Thompson, Frederic W. (1872–1919) m, en; Hippodrome

Thompson, Kent (1954–) d, p; Alabama Shakespeare; Denver Center

Thomson, Carolyn (fl. 1917–26) a, s; *Vagabond King*

Thomson, Virgil (1896–1989) co; Federal Theatre Project; *Four Saints . . . ;* Stein (G.)

Thorndike, Sybil (1882–1976) Brit, a; Webster

Thorndyke, Louise (c. 1864–1956) a; Boucicault

Thorne, Charles R., Jr. (1840–83) a; Intro(§2)

Thumb, Tom, *see* Stratton, Charles Sherwood

Thurber, James (1894–1961) w; Intro(§3); Nugent; Parker (D.); revue

Thurman, Uma (1970–) a; Edelstein

Tierney, Gene (1920–91) a; *Male Animal*

Tierney, Harry (c. 1891–1965) co; *Sally*

Tietjens, Paul (1877–1943) co; *Wizard of Oz*

Tillstrom, Burr (1917–85) pup; puppetry

Tirado, Cándido (1955–) pl; Nuyorican

Tobias, Charles (1898–1970) co, l; *Hellzapoppin*

Tobias, George (1901–80) a; *What Price Glory*

Tofteland, Curt L. (1952–) d; Shakespeare Behind Bars

Tolan, Kathleen (1951?–) pl; Wiest

Tolan, Michael (1925–) a, d; Ribman

Tolkin, Mel (c. 1915–) w; Tamiment

Toller, Ernst (1893–1939) Ger, pl; Langner

Tolstoi, A. N. (1883–1945) Sov, pl, w; Moscow Art Theatre

Tolstoi, Lev (1828–1910) R, pl; Ben-Ami; ethnic; Jewish Art Theatre

Topol, Chaim (1935–) Isr, a; *Fiddler . . . ;* Weissler

Torrence, Fredrick Ridgely (1874–1950) pl; African American

Toscanini, Arturo (1867–1957) It, conductor; Brooklyn Academy

Touliatos, George (1929–) d; Front St. Theatre

Town, Ithiel (1784–1844) arc; Bowery Theatre; Thalia Theatre

Tozzi, Giorgio (1923–) a, s; *Most Happy Fella*

Trambley, Estela Portillo (1936–99) pl; Chicano

Trapp, Maria von (1905–87) s; *Sound of Music*

Trask, Stephen (1967?–) co, l; *Hedwig*

Tree, Ellen (1806–80) Brit, a; international; Shakespeare on . . .

Tree, Herbert Beerbohm (1853–1917) Brit, a, m; international

Tremblay, Michel (1942–) Can, pl; international

Trenter, Eliza (fl. 1840s) Brit, s; Drew–Barrymore

Trentini, Emma (1885?–1959) It, a, s; Friml; *Naughty Marietta*

Tribble, Andrew (?–1935) a, e; female/male

Trimble, John M. (c. 1815–67) arc; Bowery Theatre; Broadway Theatre; Wallack's Theatre

Trollope, Anthony (1815–82) Brit, w; *Divorce*

Trowbridge, Charles (1882–1967) a; *Craig's Wife*

Trudeau, Garry (1948–) cartoonist, pl; Swados

Trzcinski, Edmund (1921–96) a, d, pl; Intro(§3)

Tucci, Stanley (1960–) a; *Frankie and Johnny*

Tucker, Marion (fl. 1900s) w; *Theatre Arts Monthly*

Tudor, Anthony (1909–87) Brit-born, ch, d; Berman; Clarke (Martha)

Tuke, Eliza, *see* Hallam, Mrs. Lewis

Tupou, Manu (1935–2004) a; *Indians*

Turgenev, Ivan (1818–83) R, pl, w; Moscow Art Theatre

Turner, Jerry (1927–2004) d, p; Oregon Shakespeare Festival

Turner, Kathleen (1954–) a; Albee (E.); *Cat on a Hot Tin Roof;* Weissler; *Who's Afraid . . .*

Turner, Victor (1920–83) th; dramatic theory

Tutin, Dorothy (1931–2001) Brit, a; international

Tutt, J. Homer (fl. 1900s) m, p; African American

Twain, Mark (Samuel Langhorne Clemens) (1835–1910) pl; Burke; Chautauqua; clubs; Conway (K.); Harte; Mayo;

one-person; Raymond; Rice (D.); San Francisco

Twist, Basil (1969–) pup; Intro(§4); puppetry

Tyler, Anne (1941–) w; Galati

Tyson, Cicely (1933–) a; Circle in the Square

Tyzack, Margaret (1933–) Brit, a; international

Uggams, Leslie (1943–) a, s; Jones (J. E.)

Ullman, Tracey (1959–) Brit, a; Freeman

Ullmann, Liv (1939–) Nor, a; Ibsen

Unsworth, James (1835–75), e; minstrel show

Upton, Robert (fl. mid-18th C.) Brit, a, m; Hallams

Usher, Luke (fl. early-19th C.) m; Drake (Samuel); frontier

Vaccaro, John (193?–) a, d; gay/lesbian; Ludlam; Off-Off Broadway; Ridiculous Theatrical Co.; Theatre of the Ridiculous

Vakhtangov, Evgeny (1882–1923) R, a, d, edu; Chekhov (M.); Mamoulian

Valdéz, Daniel (194?–) a; *Zoot Suit*

Valdez-Aran, Ching (19??–) a, d; Asian American; Filipino American

Valentine, William (?–1866) en; vaudeville

Valentino, Rudolph (1895–1926) a; *Desert Song*

Valenzuela, José Luis (1951–) d; Chicano

Valk, Kate (1956–) a; LeCompte; Wooster Group

Vallee, Rudy (1901–86) a, s; nightclubs

Valli, Frankie (1937–) s; revue

Van Dyke, Dick (1925–) a; *Bye Bye Birdie*

Van Fleet, Jo (1915–1996) a; *Camino Real; Look Homeward . . . ; Oh Dad, Poor Dad . . .*

Van Hove, Ivo (1958–) Bel, d; Ibsen; NY Theatre Workshop

Van Liew, Henry (c. 1820–90) m; Minneapolis

Van Peebles, Melvin (1932–) d, f d, co, pl; *Ain't Supposed . . .*

Van Volkenburg, Ellen (fl. 1900–20s) a, p; Seattle

Vanbrugh, John (1664–1726) Brit, pl, arc; Hallams

Vance, Courtney B. (1960–), a; *Six Degrees . . .*

Vance, Danitra (c. 1959–94) a, en; Off-Broadway

Vance, Nina (1915–80) d, p; Alley Theatre; resident nonprofit

Vandenhoff, John (1790–1861) Brit, a; international; Vandenhoff

Vargas, Adrian (fl. 1960s) d; Chicano

Varon, Charlie (1959–) a, pl; one-person

Vasulka [née Steinunn Briem Bjarnadottir], Steina (1940–) mu; Kitchen

Vasulka, Woody [né Bohuslav Peter] (1937–) art; Kitchen

Vawter, Keith (?–1937) edu; Chautauqua

Vawter, Ron (1948–94) a; Gray; one-person; Wooster Group

Veiller, Bayard (1869/71–1943) pl; Woods; Wycherly

Venturi, Robert (1925–) arc; Hartford Stage

Vereen, Ben (1946–) a, da; Hirsch (J.)

Verne, Jules (1828–1905) Fr, w; Around the World . . . ; Kiralfy

Vesak, Norbert (1936–) ch; dance

Vestris, Madame (1797–1856) a, m; international; Mathews (Charles, Jr.); Mitchell's Olympic

Viertel, Berthold (1885–1955) Aus, d; Brecht

Vigoda, Abe (1921–) a; Arsenic . . .

Vincent, John Heyl (1832–1920) edu; Chautauqua

Vincent, Mrs. J. R. (1818–87) Brit-born, a; Boston

Viñoly, Rafael (1944–) arc; resident nonprofit

Voight, Jon (1938–) a; Streetcar . . . ; Wheeler

Vokes, May (1885?–1957) a; Bat

Voltaire (1694–1778) Fr, pl, w; Candide; Hellman; Mowatt

Vonnegut, Kurt, Jr. (1922–2007) pl; Off-Broadway

Vreeland, Diana (1906–89) ed, w; Feldshuh; Wilson (M. L.)

Wade, Stephen (1953–) e; New Vaudeville

Wadsworth, Stephen (19??–) d; Lynch (T.)

Wager, Douglas (1949–) d; Arena Stage

Wagner, Jane (1935–) a, pl; female/male; Tomlin

Wagner, Richard (1813–83) Ger, co, pl; architecture; Ludlam

Wagner, Robert (1930–) a; Cat on a Hot Tin Roof

Waite, Ralph (1928–) a, d; Los Angeles Theatre Center

Waits, Tom (1949–) co, mu; Schmidt (P.); Wilson (Robert)

Walcott, Derek (1930–) WI, pl; Intro(§4); Classical Theatre of Harlem

Waldman, Robert H. (1936–) co; Driving Miss Daisy; Freedman; Uhry

Waldron, Charles (1874–1946) a; Deep Are the Roots

Walker, C. P. (fl. 1890s–1900s) m; frontier

Walker, George (1873–1911) e; African American, Williams (Barney), Williams (Bert)

Walker, Jewel (1927?–) te; Stein

Walker, Joseph A. (1935–) pl; Intro(§4); African American

Walker, M[ilton] Burke (1943–) a, d; Empty Space

Walker, Nancy (1922–92) a; On the Town

Wallace, Lew (1827–1905) w; animals as performers; Ben-Hur

Wallace, Stewart (1960–) co; gay/lesbian

Wallach, Ira (1913–95) pl; Hunter

Waller, Daniel Wilmarth (c. 1824–82) a, m; Waller

Waller, Thomas W. "Fats" (1904–43) co, s; revue

Wallett, William (1806/8–92) e; Rice (D.)

Wallick, James H. (née Wallaich) (1844–1908) a; McCloskey

Wallop, Douglas (1920–) pl, w; Damn Yankees

Walsh, Blanche (1873–1915) a; Wagenhals and Kemper

Walsh, Robert (1784–1859) w; dramatic theory

Walsh, Thommie (1950–2007) ch; Tune

Walston, Ray (1916–2001) a; Damn Yankees

Walters, Les (fl. 1980s) d; dance

Walton, Emma (1962–) d; Andrews; Bay Street

Walton, Lester (1882–1965) c; African American

Walton, Paul E. (fl. 1930s and '40s), pup; puppetry

Wanamaker, Zoë (1949–) a; Awake and Sing!; Wanamaker

Waram, Percy (1881–1961) Brit, a; Elizabeth the Queen

Warchus, Matthew (1966–) Brit, d; Follies

Ward, Theodore [James] (1902–83) pl; African American; Big White Fog

Ware, C. P. T. (fl. 1850s) pl; Montez

Warhol, Andy (1926?–87) art, pl; gay/lesbian

Warner, Deborah (1959–) Brit, d; participatory

Warner, Malcolm-Jamal (1970–) a; Off-Broadway

Warren, David (1961?–) d; Vineyard

Warren, Harry (1893–1981) co; 42nd Street

Warren, Whitney (1864–1943), and Charles D. Wetmore (1867–1941) arc; St. James Theatre

Washington, Denzel (1954–) a; African American; Shakespeare on . . .

Wasserman, Dale (1917–) pl; Intro(§4); Man of La Mancha

Waters, John (1946–) f d, p, scr; Hairspray

Waterston, Elisabeth (196?–) a; Waterston

Waterston, James (1969–) a; Leonard; Waterston

Watkins, Maurine Dallas (1901–69) pl; Chicago

Watkins, Perry (1907–67) ch, d, de, p; Big White Fog

Watson, "Sliding" Billy (d. 1939) e, burlesque; Watson

Wayne, David (1914–95) a; After the Fall; Finian's Rainbow; Mister Roberts

Weales, Gerald (1925–) c, edu; Foreigner

Weaver, Lois (1950–) d; female/male; feminist; gay/lesbian; Hughes; Split Britches

Webb, Clifton (1889/93?–1966) a; As Thousands Cheer

Webster, Benjamin (1864–1947) a; Webster

Webster, Daniel (1782–1852) orator; Chautauqua

Wedekind, Frank (1864–1918) Ger, pl; Feingold

Weede, Robert (1903–72) a, s; Most Happy Fella

Weese, Harry Mohr (1915–98) arc; Arena Stage

Weidman, Charles (1901–75) ch, da; Cole (J.)

Weidman, Jerome (1913–98) l, pl; Fiorello!

Weidman, John (1946–) pl; Anything Goes; dance; Dramatists Guild; Intro(§4); Pacific Overtures; Sondheim; Ziemba

Weidner, Paul (1934–) d; Hartford Stage

Weigel, Helene (1900–71) Ger, a; Brecht

Weil, Simone (1909–43) Fr, phil/ mystic; Terry

Weinstein, Jack (19??–) pl; *How to Succeed . . .*

Weisinger, Herbert (1913–) c; dramatic theory

Weisman, Jael (1942–) d; Dell'Arte

Weiss, Jeff (fl. 1960s) pl; Caffe Cino; La MaMa; Off-Off Broadway

Weiss, Peter (1916–82) Ger-Swi, pl; Intro(§4); documentary; Piscator

Weiss, Stephen (1899–1984) co; *Hellzapoppin*

Weissberger, L. Arnold (1907–81) law, ph; Theatre Hall of Fame

Wells, H. G. (Herbert George) (1866–1946) Brit, w; Welles

Wells, Ida B. (1862–1931) ed, j; Thompson (T.)

Wells, Win (1935–83) pl, po, scr; Seldes

Wendt, George (1948–) a; Second City

Wertenbaker, Timberlake (c. 1945–) pl; Dukakis; Lamos; Nederlander Theatre; Perloff

Wertheim, Maurice (d. 1950) ba, en; Theatre Guild

Wesker, Arnold (1932–) Brit, pl; Dexter; Mostel; Tynan

Wesley, Richard (1945–) pl; Intro(§4); African American

Wesner, Ella (1841–1917) a, e; female/male

Wessells, George (fl. 1890s) a; *Sherlock Holmes*

West, Timothy (1934–) Brit, a; *Long Day's Journey . . .*

Westerfield, James (1916–71) a; *Detective Story*

Western, George (d. 1857) en; Western

Western, Helen (1844–68) a; Western

Westley, Helen (1879–1942) a; Intro(§3); Theatre Guild; *Washington Square*

Westray, Juliana (?–1836) a; Wood (Mrs. J.)

Wharton, Edith (1862–1937) w; Akins; Davis (Owen); *House of Mirth;* Mint; *Old Maid;* Shakespeare & Co.; Worth

Wharton, John (1894–1977) law; Playwrights' Company

Wheeler, Hugh (1912–87) pl; *Candide; Little Night Music; Sweeney Todd*

Wheelock, Otis Leonard (1816– c. 1886) arc; McVicker's

Whipper, Leigh (1877–1975) a; *Of Mice and Men*

White, Charles (Charley) (1821– 91) e, m; Bryant

White, George C. (1935–) d, adm; Eugene O'Neill Memorial; National Playwrights Conference

White, Julie (1961–) a; *Dinner with Friends*

White, Miles (1920–2000) de; costume

White, Stanford (1853–1906) arc; White (R. G.)

White, T[erence] H[anbury] (1906–64) Brit, w; *Camelot*

Whitehead, Paxton (1937–) Brit, a; Giovanni

Whitehead, Ted (1933–) Brit, pl; Conway (K.)

Whiteman, Paul (1892–1968) mu; nightclubs

Whitemore, Hugh (1936–) Brit, pl; Ivey (D.)

Whiting, Frank M. (1907–96) edu; Minneapolis

Whitlock, William M. (1813–78) e; Emmett

Whitmore, James (1921–) a; one-person; Shyre; *Will Rogers Follies*

Whitney, Salem Tutt (fl. 1900s) m, p; African American

Whittlesey, Peregrine (1944–) a, drm, en; Manhattan Theatre Club

Whitty, Dame May (1865–1948) Brit, a; Webster

Whitty, Jeff (1971–) pl; *Avenue Q*

Wickes, Mary (1916–95) a; *Man Who Came to Dinner*

Wiesel, Elie (1928–) w; Wiseman

Wigan, Leonora (1805–84) a; Wallack family

Wilde, Oscar (1854–1900) Ir-born, pl; Caffe Cino; feminist; Frohman (Ch. & Daniel); international; Marbury; Pacino; Palmer

Wilkinson, Colm (1944–) Ir, a, s; *Les Misérables*

Wilkinson, Tate (1739–1803) Brit, a, m; Warren (W., the elder)

Willard, Fred (1939–) a, e; Second City

Willard, Henry E. (1802–78) m; Blake (W. R.)

Williams, Clifford (1926–2005) Brit, d; international

Williams, Emlyn (1905–87) We, a, pl; John Golden Theatre; one-person; *Watch on the Rhine*

Williams, Hope (1901–?) a; *Holiday*

Williams, John (1932–) co, conductor; Mitchell (B. S.)

Williams, Treat (1951–) a; *Streetcar . . .*

Williams, Vanessa (1963–) a, s; *Into the Woods*

Williams, William (fl. mid-18th C.) art; scenic design

Williamson, James Cassius (1845–1913) a, m; frontier

Williamson, Nicol (1938–) Brit, a; Chekhov on . . . ; Circle in the Square; Holm; international; Rudnick

Wills, Ivah (1882–1937) a; Coburn

Wilson, "Dooley" (1886–1953) a; Lafayette Players

Wilson, Doric (1939–) a, d, p; Intro(§4); gay/lesbian; Theatre Rhinoceros

Wilson, Edmund (1895–1972) c; Ibsen

Wilson, Frank (1891–1956) a; *Take a Giant Step*

Wilson, Fred (fl. 1900–15) a; Toby

Wilson, John Fleming (1877– 1922) w; Goodman

Wilson, John Grosvenor (fl. late 19th C.) pl; dramatic theory

Wilson, Martha (1947–) perf; performance art

Wilson, Michael (1964–) d; Hartford

Wing-Davey, Mark (1948–) Brit, d; Berry

Wingreen, Jason (1920–) a, p; Circle in the Square

Winninger, Charles (1884–1958) a, s; *No, No, Nanette*

Winokur, Marissa Jaret (1973–) a, s; *Hairspray*

Winters, Shelley (née Shirley Schrift) (1922–2006) a; Actors Studio; Blaine; *Hatful of Rain;* Strasberg

Wisedell, Thomas (d. 1884) arc; Casino Theatre

Witkiewicz, Stanisław Ignacy (1885–1939) Pol, pl; Classical Theatre of Harlem

Wittop, Freddy (1912–2001) de; costume

Wojewodski, Stan, Jr. (1948–) d; Center Stage; Yale Rep

Wolf, Hugh [né Slovenj Gradec] (1860–1903) Aus, co; Webber

Wolf, Marc (197?–) a; documentary

Wolfe, Benjamin E. (?–1901) pl; *Mighty Dollar*

Wolfe, Thomas (1900–38) pl, w; Baker (G. P.); *Look Homeward . . . ;* Mint

Wolfe [née Stephen], Virginia (1882–1941) w; Redgrave

Wolheim, Louis (1880–1931) a; *Hairy Ape; What Price Glory*

Wollstonecraft, Mary (1759–97) w; Marks

Wondisford, Diane (195?–) d, p; Music-Theatre Group

Wong, Anna May (1905–61) a; Asian American; Chang

Wong, Elizabeth (1958–) pl; Asian American

Wood, George (c. 1823–86) m; Daly's Theatre

Wood, John (?–1863) a, m; Wood (Mrs. J.)

Wood, John (1930–) Brit, a; international

Wood, Maxine (1906–93) pl; Jones (M.)

Wood, Natalie (1938–81) a; *Cat on a Hot Tin Roof*

Wood, William H. (?–1926) m; Wood (A.)

Woods, James (1947–) a; *Moonchildren*

Woodward, Joanne (1930–) a; Circle in the Square; *Glass Menagerie;* Strasberg; Thompson (T.); *Waiting for Lefty;* Westport

Woolf, Benjamin (d. 1901) pl; *East Lynne;* Florence

Woolley, Monty (Edgar Montillion Woolley) (1888–1963) a; *Man Who Came to Dinner*

Woronicz, Henry (1954–) d; Oregon Shakespeare Festival

Wouk, Herman (1915–) pl, w; Intro(§3)

Wright, Amy (1950–) a; *Fifth of July*

Wright, Doug (1963?–) pl; Intro(§4); documentary; female/male; gay/lesbian; *I Am My Own Wife;* Ives; NY Theatre Workshop; resident nonprofit

Wright, Frank Lloyd (1869–1959) arc; Dallas Theater Center

Wright, Robert (1914–2005) l, co; *Kismet*

Wright, Teresa (1918–2005) a; *Morning's at Seven*

Wyatt, Henry T. (fl. 1880s) m; frontier

Wycherley, William (1641–1715) Brit, p; Gordon

Wydro, Ken (194?–) p, pl; African American

Wyler, Gretchen (1932–2007) da, a, s; *Silk Stockings*

Wyman, John (1816–81) ma; magic

Wyndham, Charles (1837–1919) Brit, a, m; international

Wynn, Keenan (1916–86) a; Wynn

Wynyard, Diana (1906–64) Brit, a; Selwyn

Yalman, Tunc (1925–) d; Milwaukee Rep

Yamauchi, Wakako (1924–) pl; Asian American; East West

Yang, Welly (c. 1973–) a; Asian American

Yankee, Luke (194?–) a, d, pl; Heckart

Yazbek, David (1961–) co, l; *Full Monty*

Yeamans, Annie (1835–1912) a; *Cordelia's Aspirations; Mulligan Guard*

Yeats, William Butler (1865–1939) Ir, pl; Noguchi

Yellen, Sherman (1934–) pl; American Jewish Theatre

Yep, Laurence (1948–) pl; Asian American

Yesler, Henry (Leiter) (1810–92) t; Seattle

Yordan, Philip (c. 1914–2003) pl; American Negro Theatre; *Anna Lucasta*

York, Michael (1942–) Brit, a; Williamstown

York [Lemanski], Rachel (1971–) a, s; *Les Misérables*

York, Susannah (1941–) Brit, a; Ibsen

Yoshimura, James (19??–) pl; Intro(§4); Chicago

Young, Brigham (1801–77) rel; Salt Lake Theater

Young, Charles (1839–87) Brit, pl; Booth (A.)

Young, Charles (d. 1874) a; Duff

Young, John Lloyd (c. 1975–) a, s; musical

Young, Rida Johnson (1875–1926) l; *Naughty Marietta*

Young, Robert (1907–98) a; Pasadena Playhouse

Young, Roland (1887–1953) a; *Beggar on Horseback; Washington Square*

Young, William (1847–1920) pl; *Ben-Hur*

Zacek, Dennis (194?–) d; Victory Gardens

Zaldívar, Gilberto (1934–) p; Cuban American; Repertorio Español

Zaloom, Paul (1951–) e; New Vaudeville; puppetry

Zeder, Suzan (1948–) pl; children's

Zeffirelli, Franco (1923–) It, d, de, f d; international; Perdziola; *Streetcar . . . ;* Thompson (Sada)

Zerbe, Anthony (1936–) a; Browne (R. L.)

Zimmerman, J. Fred (1841?–1925) m; Intro(§2); Syndicate

Zippel, David (c. 1952–) l; *City of Angels*

Zoe, Mlle Marie (fl. 1860s) Fr, a; Chicago

Zola, Émile (1840–1902) Fr, w, c; dramatic theory

Zorich, Louis (1924–) a; Dukakis

Zoyara, Ella (Omar Kingsley) (1830–70) e; female/male

Zuckmayer, Carl (1896–1977) Ger, pl; Piscator

Zukor, Adolph (1873–1976) Hun-born, en; Loew